KU-746-733

Capital cities have red infills

The time at this longitude when it is 12.00 (noon) at Greenwich

East from Greenwich

DELHI
28° 39'N 77° 13'E

TOKYO
35° 33'N 139° 46'E

PEARS

CYCLOPÆDIA

2017–2018

A BOOK OF REFERENCE AND BACKGROUND
INFORMATION FOR ALL THE FAMILY

EDITED BY

CHRISTOPHER COOK

M.A. Cantab., D.Phil. Oxon., F.R. Hist. S.

One Hundred and Twenty Sixth Edition

NOTE TO READERS

For what is sadly the final edition of *Pears Cyclopaedia* the Publishers would like to thank all those who have helped over the years to make this familiar reference work one of the longest success stories in publishing. A particular thank you is due to Dr Chris Cook, the editor for the last 40 years. It is perhaps fitting that *Pears*, which began in 1897 in the year of Queen Victoria's Diamond Jubilee should cease publication in the year of Queen Elizabeth's Sapphire Jubilee. There is a note on the history of *Pears* at the end of this volume.

PENGUIN BOOKS

UK | USA | Canada | Ireland | Australia
India | New Zealand | South Africa

Penguin Books is part of the Penguin Random House group of companies whose addresses can be found at global.penguinrandomhouse.com.

Penguin Random House UK

First published 1897
126th edition published 2017
Copyright © Penguin Books Ltd, 2017
Visit our website at www.penguin.com

Pears is a trademark of Penguin Books Ltd

Typeset by Jouve (UK), Milton Keynes
Printed in England by Clays Ltd, St Ives plc

A CIP catalogue record for this book is available from the British Library

ISBN: 978-0-141-985541

www.greenpenguin.co.uk

MIX
Paper from
responsible sources
FSC® C018179

Penguin Random House is committed to a sustainable future for our business, our readers and our planet. This book is made from Forest Stewardship Council® certified paper.

CONTENTS

CHRONICLE
OF EVENTS

Historical events from the earliest times to the present day. For the more recent decades, the section provides a detailed chronicle of our ever-changing world. For entries on other historical topics, readers may wish to refer to Section E, The Historical World. For the story of human evolution, see Section T. Background chronologies of events in major countries in the world can be found in Section C.

CHRONICLE OF EVENTS

B.C. **PREHISTORY**

Note to Readers

Although the broad pattern of human evolution is the subject of agreement amongst scientists, almost all the details are contentious. The exact relationship to one another of successive species, for example, is very uncertain and the family tree of modern humans is constantly being revised as new evidence becomes available (*see* **T48–55**).

THE ICE AGES

40,000 First cold phase ends. Neanderthal race becoming extinct. Second cold phase. *Homo sapiens* (modern man). Implements show significant advances: small knife-blades, engraving tools. Paintings and sculpture; magic rites and ceremonies. Cro-Magnons with Aurignacian culture.

18,000 Final culmination of last ice age.
Aurignacian culture dying out to be replaced by Solutrean and then by the Magdalenian cultures. Great flowering of Palaeolithic art.

15,000 First immigrants from Asia to cross Bering Straits?

15,000 Last glaciers in Britain disappeared. Proto-Neolithic in Middle East. Settled way of life leading to such skills as weaving, metallurgy; inventions such as ox-drawn plough, wheeled cart.

THE FIRST CIVILISATIONS

9,500 Ruins of megalithic sites at Göbekli Tepe in Turkey. Evidence of advanced architecture and art.

8,000 Jericho begins continuous existence as occupied town.

4800–3750 Formation of urban settlements in S. Mesopotamia during the Uruk Period. Cuneiform writing developed.

4500 Irrigation used in Indus Valley. Later emergence of Harappan civilisation.

3150–3100 First Egyptian Dynasty; capital at Memphis. Narmer first pharoah. Hieratic writing already perfected.
Early Minoan Age (Crete). Pictorial writing, copper, silver, gold in use. Early Mycenaean civilisation begins.

2900–2334 Early Dynastic Mesopotamia (Sumer & Akkad). Sumerian dominance; Royal Cemetery of Ur.

2870 First settlements at Troy.

2850 Golden Age of China begins (legendary).

2700–2200 The era of the Old Kingdom (Pyramid Age) in Egypt. First Chinese bronze artefacts.

2400 Aryan migrations.

2334–2279 Sargon of Agade; his Akkadian empire collapses soon after the death of his grandson Naram-Sin in 2218.

2205 Hsia Dynasty begins in China (legendary).

2200 Middle Minoan Age: pottery, linear writing in pen and ink.

1800–1400 Stonehenge built and rebuilt.

1792–1750 Hammurabi king of Babylon; famous law code.

1766–1122 Shang Dynasty in China.

1720–1550 Hyksos in Egypt. First war chariots. Hebrews entered Egypt (Joseph) *c.* 1600.

1600 Explosion of Thera (now Santorini) ends Minoan civilisation on Crete.

NEW KINGDOM IN EGYPT

1552–1069 Egyptian New Kingdom: at zenith under XVIIIth Dynasty. Chronology more certain: Late Minoan Age; Linear B script.

1500 Powerful Mitanni (Aryan) kingdom in Asia Minor. Phoenicia thriving—trade with Egypt and Babylonia. Vedic literature in India.

1450 Zenith of Minoan civilisation.

1400 Ugarit (N. Syria) culture at its zenith. Cretan civilisation ends: Knossos burnt. Temple at Luxor built.

1352–1338 Amenhotep IV (Akhenaten), the "heretic" Pharaoh. Diplomatic archive of Tell el-Amarna.

1350 Zenith of Hittite civilisation.

1275 Israelite oppression (Rameses II); Exodus from Egypt (Moses). Phoenician settlements—Hellas and Spain (Cadiz). Tyre flourishing.

1274 Battle of Kadesh.

1250 Israelites invade Palestine (Joshua).

1200 Downfall of Hittite kingdom. Siege of Troy (Homeric). Beginning of sea-power of independent Phoenician cities.

1177 Attacks on Egypt by "Peoples of the Sea".

1122–256 Chou (Zhou) Dynasty in China.

1115 Magnetic needle reputed in China.

1005–925 Kingdom of David and Solomon: Jerusalem as Sanctuary.

1000 *Rig Veda* (India).

925–722 Israel and Judah divided.

893 Assyrian chronological records begin.

850 Foundation of Carthage (traditional).

781 Chinese record of an eclipse.

776 First Olympiad to be used for chronological purposes.

753 Foundation of Rome (traditional).

750 Greek colonists first begin settling in Southern Italy.

ASSYRIA

745 Accession of Tiglath-Pileser III; Assyrian Power at its height.

722 Capture of Samaria by Sargon II: Israel deported to Nineveh.

709 World's first record of a solar eclipse made in China.

700 Homer's poems probably written before this date. Spread of the iron-using Celtic Hallstatt culture about this time.

689 Babylon conquered by Sennacherib.

625 Neo-Babylonian (Chaldean) Empire (Nineveh destroyed 612).

621 Publication of Athenian laws by Draco.

610 Spartan constitution, made rigid after Messenian Wars: later attributed to Lycurgus.

594 Athenian constitution reformed by Solon.

586 Capture of Jerusalem: Judah deported to Babylon (partial return 538).

B.C.

561 Pisistratus tyrant of Athens.

560 Accession of Croesus—prosperity of Lydia.

538 Babylon taken by Persians: Empire founded by Cyrus, soon covers almost all of civilised Middle East.

509 Roman Republic founded (traditional).

508 Democratic constitution in Athens.

500 Etruscans at height of their power in Northern Italy.

GREAT AGE OF GREECE

499 Revolt of Ionian Greek cities against Persian king Darius.

494 Secession of Plebeians from Rome. Tribunes established.

490 Battle of Marathon: Athenian repulse of Persian attack.

480 Death of Buddha. Battle of Thermopylae: Spartans under Leonidas wiped out by Persians. Battle of Salamis: Persian fleet defeated by Athenians under Themistocles; Persian invasion of Greece halted.

479 Battles of Plataea and Mycale: Greek victories by land and sea respectively destroy Persian invasion force. Death of Confucius.

477 League of Delos founded by Athens for defence against Persia; soon becomes Athenian Empire. (467 Naxos kept in by force.)

461 Pericles comes to power in Athens.

458 Cincinnatus saves Rome (traditional).

456 Death of Aeschylus.

447 Building of Parthenon begun.

431 Death of Phidias. Outbreak of Great Peloponnesian War between Athens and Sparta. Pericles "Funeral Oration" (according to Thucydides).

425 Death of Herodotus.

416 Massacre of Melos by Athenians.

415 Sicilian Expedition: flight of Alcibiades from Athens to Sparta.

413 Loss of entire Athenian expeditionary force at Syracuse.

406 Death of Euripides and Sophocles.

405 Battle of Aegospotami: Athenian navy destroyed by Sparta.

404 Athenian surrender to Sparta: beginning of Spartan hegemony in Greece.

403 Beginning of epoch of Warring States in China.

400 Death of Thucydides, Greek historian (?).

399 Death of Socrates.

390 Occupation of Rome by Gauls under Brennus.

371 Battle of Leuctra: Spartans defeated by Thebans: beginning of Theban hegemony in Greece.

370 Death of Hippocrates of Cos (?).

347 Death of Plato.

PERSIAN CONQUEST OF EGYPT

343 Last native Egyptian Dynasty ends; Persians reconquer Egypt.

338 Battle of Chaeronea: Greek city-states defeated by Philip II of Macedon, who becomes supreme in Greece.

336 Assassination of Philip of Macedon: accession of Alexander.

334 Alexander's invasion of Persian Empire. Battle of Granicus River, first victory.

333 Battle of Issus: Alexander defeats Darius of Persia.

332 Alexander's siege and capture of Tyre, occupation of Egypt.

B.C.

331 Battle of Arbela (Gaugamela)—final defeat of Darius.

330 Death of Darius and end of Persian Empire. Alexander heir to civilisations of Middle East.

326 Battle of Hydaspes: Alexander conquers the Punjab.

323 Death of Alexander at Babylon. Beginning of Hellenistic Age in Middle East and Eastern Mediterranean. Ptolemy I founds dynasty in Egypt. Alexandria becomes intellectual centre of Hellenic world.

322 Death of Demosthenes and Aristotle.

321 Maurya dynasty unites N. India.

312 Seleucus I founds dynasty in Asia.

300 Zeno the Stoic, Epicurus and Euclid flourishing.

THE RISE OF ROME

290 End of Third Samnite War. Rome dominates Central Italy.

280 Translation of Pentateuch into Greek.

275 Battle of Beneventum: Rome finally defeats Pyrrhus and the Greek cities of Southern Italy. Rome dominates all Italy.

274 Asoka becomes ruler of two-thirds of Indian sub-continent.

264 Beginning of First Punic War (Rome v. Carthage).

260 Battle of Mylae: first great Roman naval victory.

255 Defeat and capture of Regulus by Carthaginians.

250 Incursion of "La Tène" Iron Age people into Britain.

241 End of First Punic War. Sicily becomes first Province of Rome.

221 Kingdom of Ch'in (Qin) completes conquest of all Chinese states under Shih Huang-ti.

218 Outbreak of Second Punic War: Hannibal crosses Alps.

216 Battle of Cannae: Hannibal wipes out great Roman army.

214 Great Wall of China constructed (by linking existing walls).

213 Burning of Chinese classics.

212 Capture of Syracuse by Romans and death of Archimedes.

207 Battle of Metaurus: defeat and death of Hasdrubal. End of Hannibal's hopes of overcoming Rome.

205 Roman provinces organised in Spain.

202 Battle of Zama: Hannibal defeated by Scipio Africanus, 202–A.D. 220 Han Dynasty in China.

201 End of Second Punic War. Rome dominates Western Mediterranean.

196 After defeating Macedon, Rome proclaims independence of Greek city-states. Death of Eratosthenes the geographer (?).

160 Death in battle of Judas Maccabaeus: Jewish revolt against Seleucids continues successfully.

149 Outbreak of Third Punic War.

146 Carthage destroyed. Roman province of Africa formed. Roman provinces of Macedonia and Achaea formed, and most of remainder of Greece reduced to vassal status.

134 First Servile War; Revolt of slaves in Sicily under Eunus. Suppressed 132.

133 Siege and destruction of Numantia by Romans. Tiberius Gracchus Tribune. Attempted land reforms. Murdered 132.

129 Roman province of Asia formed from lands bequeathed by Attalus of Pergamum.

124 Chinese Grand College to train Civil Service officials.

123 Caius Gracchus Tribune. Attempted land reforms. Murdered 121.

110 Roman expansion to include most of south-east of modern China, under Emperor Wu Ti. Commercial activity in Indian Ocean.

B.C.

106 Jugurtha captured by Marius and Sulla.

104 Second Servile War: revolt of slaves in Sicily under Tryphon and Athenion. Suppressed 101.

102 Chinese expedition to Ferghana and possible knowledge of West.

101 Battle of Vercellae: Marius ends threat of Cimbri to Rome.

91 Social War: revolt of Italian cities against Rome. Suppressed 88. Roman franchise granted to most Italians.

88 Civil Wars of Marius and Sulla begin.

87 Massacre in Rome by Marius.

82 Proscriptions in Rome by Sulla.

75 Belgic invasion of south-eastern Britain.

73 Third Servile War: revolt of slaves in southern Italy under Spartacus the gladiator. Suppressed 71.

63 Conspiracy of Catiline exposed by Cicero.

60 First Triumvirate: Pompey, Caesar, Crassus.

58 Beginning of Caesar's conquest of Gaul.

55 Caesar's first British expedition: second, 54.

53 Battle of Carrhae: destruction of Roman army under Crassus by Persians.

52 Revolt of Gallic Vercingetorix against Caesar. Defeated in ferocious battle of Alesia.

50 Migration to Britain of Commius and his followers.

49 Caesar crosses the Rubicon. Beginning of war against Pompey and the Senate.

48 Battle of Pharsalus: defeat of Pompey by Caesar.

46 Caesar's calendar reforms.

44 Murder of Caesar.

43 Second Triumvirate: Antony, Octavian, Lepidus.

42 Battle of Philippi: defeat and death of Brutus and his associates.

31 Battle of Actium: naval victory of Octavian over Antony and Cleopatra. Octavian unchallenged master of the Roman world.

THE ROMAN EMPIRE

27 Octavian given title of Augustus by Senate.

19 Death of Virgil.

8 Death of Horace.

4 Birth of Jesus (date not certain).

A.D.

6 Civil Service Examination system in China.

9 Radical reforms by Wang Mang (short Hsin dynasty 9–23). Annihilation of Roman army under Varus by Teutonic tribesmen under Arminius.

10 Cunobelinus reigning over much of south-east Britain from Colchester.

14 Death of Augustus.

17 Death of Livy.

18 Death of Ovid.

30 Crucifixion of Jesus (date not certain).

43 Roman invasion of Britain (at Richborough in Kent) under Aulus Plautius. Defeat of huge army led by Celtic chieftains Togodumnus and Caratacus.

51 Caractacus taken to Rome as prisoner.

60 Revolt of Boudicca: defeated at Battle of Watling Street.

63 Great Fire of Rome.

64 Death of St. Paul (date not certain).

65 Death of Seneca.

66 Jews of Palestine rebel against Roman rule.

68 Death of Nero—end of Julio-Claudian line of Roman Emperors.

70 Jerusalem taken and Jewish revolt suppressed by Titus.

A.D.

79 Destruction of Pompeii and Herculaneum by eruption of Vesuvius.

80 Completion of Colosseum (Flavian Amphitheatre).

83 Battle of Mons Graupius: Agricola crushes Caledonians.

96 Accession of Nerva: first of the "Five Good Emperors."

97 Chinese expedition under Kang Yin (lieutenant of Pan Ch'ao) reaches Persian Gulf.

117 Death of Trajan, accession of Hadrian. Roman Empire at its greatest extent.

122 Beginning of Hadrian's Wall (Tyne–Solway) by Aulus Platorius Nepos.

135 Suppression of Bar-Cochba's revolt and Dispersion of Jews.

142 Construction of Antonine Wall (Forth–Clyde) by Quintus Lollius Urbicus.

165 Outbreak of Antonine plague.

180 Death of Marcus Aurelius, last of the "Five Good Emperors." Beginning of the "Decline" of the Roman Empire (Gibbon).

193 Praetorian guards murder Emperor Pertinax, sell Empire to highest bidder (Didius Julianus).

196 Clodius Albinus, governor, withdraws forces from Britain in attempt to become Emperor. Northern Britain overrun by barbarians.

208 Septimius Severus visits Britain to punish Caledonians (death at York 211).

212 Edict of Caracalla. Roman citizenship conferred on all free inhabitants of Empire.

220 End of Han Dynasty: China divided and frequently invaded for next three centuries.

227 Sassanid Empire in Persia.

230 Emperor Sulin—Japanese history emerging from legendary stage.

251 Goths defeat and kill Emperor Decius.

259 Break-away "Gallic Empire" set up: (to 273).

273 Defeat of Zenobia and destruction of Palmyra by Emperor Aurelian.

284 Accession of Diocletian, who reorganises Roman Empire (293) with rigid social laws and heavy taxation.

287 Carausius attempts to found independent "Empire of Britain": suppressed 297.

306 Constantine proclaimed Emperor at York.

313 Edict of Milan. Christianity tolerated in Roman Empire.

320 Gupta dynasty reunites India.

325 Council of Nicaea: first general Council of the Church.

367 Successful attack on Britain by Picts, Scots, Saxons.

369 Restoration of Roman authority in Britain by Theodosius.

378 Battle of Adrianople: Goths defeat and kill Eastern Roman Emperor Valens.

383 Magnus Maximus withdraws forces from Britain to support his attempt to conquer north-western part of Empire.

388 Magnus Maximus defeated and killed in Italy.

395 Death of Emperor Theodosius the Great: the division of the Empire into East and West at his death proves to be the final one.

406 Usurper Constantine III withdraws forces from Britain to support his claims: probable end of Roman military occupation of Britain.

410 Sack of Rome by Alaric the Goth. Emperor Honorius tells Britons to arrange for their own defence.

THE BARBARIAN INVASIONS

415 Visigoths begin conquest of Spain.

419 Visigothic kingdom of Toulouse recognised by Roman government.

429 Vandals begin conquest of North Africa.

432 St. Patrick begins mission in Ireland.

A.D.

446 "Groans of the Britons"—last appeal to Rome (traditional).

451 Châlons: Attila the Hun repelled from Gaul by mixed Roman–Barbarian forces.

452 Attila's raid into Italy: destruction of Aquilea and foundation of Venice by refugees.

455 Rome pillaged by Vandals.

476 Romulus Augustulus, last Western Roman Emperor, deposed by Odovacar: conventionally the end of the Western Roman Empire.

481 Clovis becomes King of the Franks, who eventually conquer Gaul (d. 511).

493 Theodoric founds Ostrogothic Kingdom in Italy (d. 526).

515 Battle of Mount Badon: West Saxon advance halted by Britons, perhaps led by Arthur (?).

BYZANTIUM AND ISLAM

527 Accession of Justinian I (d. 565).

529 Code of Civil Law published by Justinian. Rule of St. Benedict put into practice at Monte Cassino (traditional).

534 Byzantines under Belisarius reconquer North Africa from Vandals.

552 Byzantine reconquest of Italy complete.

563 St. Columba founds mission in Iona.

568 Lombard Kingdom founded in Italy.

570 Birth of Mohammed.

577 Battle of Deorham: West Saxon advance resumed.

581–618 Sui Dynasty in China.

590 Gregory the Great becomes Pope.

597 St. Augustine lands at Ebbsfleet in Kent.

605 Grand Canal of China constructed.

618–907 T'ang Dynasty in China: their administrative system lasts in essentials for 1,300 years.

622 Hejira or flight from Mecca to Medina of Mohammed: beginning of Mohammedan era.

627 Battle of Nineveh: Persians crushed by Byzantines under Heraclius.

632 Death of Mohammed: all Arabia now Muslim. Accession of Abu Bakr, the first Caliph.

634 Battle of Heavenfield: Oswald becomes king of Northumbria, brings in Celtic Christianity.

638 Jerusalem captured by Muslims.

641 Battle of Mehawand: Persia conquered by Muslims.

643 Alexandria taken by Muslims.

645 Downfall of Soga clan in Japan, after establishing Buddhism: beginning of period of imitation of Chinese culture.

650 Slav occupation of Balkans now complete.

663 Synod of Whitby: Roman Christianity triumphs over Celtic Christianity in England.

685 Nectansmere: end of Northumbrian dominance in England.

698 Carthage taken by Muslims.

711 Tarik leads successful Muslim invasion of Spain.

718 Failure of second and greatest Muslim attack on Constantinople. Pelayo founds Christian kingdom of Asturias in Northern Spain.

726 Byzantine Emperor Leo III begins Iconoclast movement: opposed by Pope Gregory II, and an important cause of difference between Roman and Byzantine churches.

THE HOLY ROMAN EMPIRE

732 Poitiers: Muslim western advance halted by Charles Martel.

735 Death of Bede.

750 Beginning of Abbasid Caliphate (replacing Omayyads)

A.D.

751 Pepin King of the Franks: founds Carolingian dynasty. Ravenna taken by Lombards: end of Byzantine power in the West.

754 Pepin promises central Italy to Pope: beginning of temporal power of the Papacy.

778 Roncesvalles: defeat and death of Roland.

786 Accession of Haroun-al-Rashid in Baghdad.

793 Sack of Lindisfarne: Viking attacks on Britain begin.

795 Death of Offa: end of Mercian dominance in England.

800 Coronation of Charlemagne as Emperor by Pope Leo III in Rome.

814 Death of Charlemagne: division of empire.

825 Ellandun: Egbert defeats Mercians and Wessex becomes leading kingdom in England.

827 Muslim invasion of Sicily.

840 Muslims capture Bari and occupy much of Southern Italy.

843 Treaty of Verdun: final division of Carolingian Empire, and beginning of France and Germany as separate states.

844 Kenneth MacAlpin becomes king of Picts as well as Scots: the kingdom of Alban.

862 Rurik founds Viking state in Russia: first at Novgorod, later at Kiev.

866 Fujiwara period begins in Japan. Viking "Great Army" in England: Northumbria, East Anglia and Mercia subsequently overwhelmed.

868 Earliest dated printed book in China.

872 Harold Fairhair King of Norway.

874 Iceland settled by Norsemen.

885–6 Viking attack on Paris.

893 Simeon founds first Bulgar Empire in Balkans.

896 Arpad and the Magyars in Hungary.

899 Death of Alfred the Great.

900 Ghana at the height of its power in North West Africa.

907–960 Five Dynasties in China: partition.

910 Abbey of Cluny founded: monastic reforms spread from here.

911 Rolf (or Rollo) becomes ruler of Normandy.

912 Accession of Abderrahman III: the most splendid period of the Omayyad Caliphate of Cordova (d. 961).

928 Brandenburg taken from the Slavs by Henry the Fowler, King of Germany.

929 Death of Wenceslas, Christian King of Bohemia.

937 Battle of Brunanburh: crowning victory of Athelstan. West Saxon kings now masters of England.

955 Battle of Lechfeld: Magyars finally defeated by Otto the Great and settle in Hungary.

960–1279 Sung (Song) Dynasty in China.

965 Harold Bluetooth king of Denmark, accepts Christianity.

966 Mieszko I king of Poland, accepts Christianity.

968 Fatimids begin their rule in Egypt.

982 Discovery of Greenland by Norsemen.

987 Hugh Capet king of France: founder of Capetian dynasty.

988 Vladimir of Kiev accepts Christianity.

991 Battle of Maldon: defeat of Byrhtnoth of Essex by Vikings—renewed Viking raids on England.

993 Olof Skutkonung, king of Sweden, accepts Christianity.

1000 Leif Ericsson discovers North America.

1001 Coronation of St. Stephen of Hungary with crown sent by the Pope.

1002 Massacre of St. Brice's Day: attempt by Ethelred to exterminate Danes in England.

A.D.

1014 Battle of Clontarf: victory of Irish under Brian Boru over Vikings.

1016 Canute becomes king of England; builds short-lived Danish "empire."

1018 Byzantines under Basil 11 complete subjection of Bulgars.

1040 Attempts to implement Truce of God.

1046 Normans under Robert Guiscard in southern Italy.

1054 Beginning of Almoravid (Muslim) conquests in West Africa.

1060 Normans invade Sicily.

1066 Norman conquest of England under William I after Battle of Hastings.

1069 Reforms of Wang An-Shih in China.

THE ERA OF THE CRUSADES

1071 Manzikert: Seljuk Turks destroy Byzantine army and overrun Anatolia.

1073 Hildebrand (Gregory VII) becomes Pope. Church discipline and Papal authority enforced.

1075 Seljuk Turks capture Jerusalem.

1076 Kumbi, capital of Ghana, sacked by Almoravids: subsequent break-up of Ghana Empire.

1084 Carthusians founded by St. Bruno at Chartreuse.

1086 Compilation of Domesday Book.

1094 El Cid takes Valencia.

1095 Council of Clermont: Urban II preaches First Crusade.

1098 Cistercians founded by St. Robert at Citeaux.

1099 First Crusade under Godfrey of Bouillon takes Jerusalem.

1100 Death of William Rufus in the New Forest. Baldwin I: Latin Kingdom of Jerusalem founded.

1106 Tinchebrai: Henry I of England acquires Normandy, captures his brother Robert.

1115 Abelard teaching at Paris. St. Bernard founds monastery at Clairvaux.

1119 Order of Knights Templars founded.

1120 Loss of the White Ship and heir to English throne.

1122 Concordat of Worms: Pope and Emperor compromise on the Investiture Controversy, but continue to quarrel over other matters (Guelfs and Ghibellines).

1135 Stephen takes English crown: civil wars with Matilda and anarchy ensue.

1143 Alfonso Henriques proclaimed first king of Portugal.

1144 Muslims take Edessa (Christian stronghold).

1148 Second Crusade fails to capture Damascus.

1150 Carmelites founded about this time by Berthold.

1152 Accession of Emperor Frederick Barbarossa.

1154 Henry of Anjou succeeds Stephen: first of Plantagenet kings of England. Adrian IV (first English pope, Nicholas Breakspear).

1161 Explosives used in warfare in China.

1169 Strongbow invades Ireland: beginning of Anglo-Norman rule. Saladin ruling in Egypt.

1170 Murder of Thomas Becket in Canterbury cathedral.

1171 Spanish knightly Order of Santiago founded.

1176 Battle of Legnano: Frederick Barbarossa defeated by the Lombard League. Italian autonomy established.

1185 Kamakura Period in Japan: epoch of feudalism: until 1333.

1187 Hattin: destruction of Latin kingdom of Jerusalem by Saladin.

1189 Third Crusade launched: leaders—Frede-

A.D.

rick Barbarossa, Philip Augustus of France, Richard Lionheart of England.

1191 Capture of Acre by Crusaders.

1192 End of Third Crusade without regaining Jerusalem. Richard I seized and held to ransom in Austria on return journey.

1198 Innocent III becomes Pope.

1202 Fourth Crusade, diverted by Venetians takes Zara from Byzantines.

1204 Fourth Crusade captures Constantinople, founds Latin Empire. King John of England loses Normandy to France.

1206 Temujin proclaimed Genghiz Khan (Very Mighty King) of all the Mongols: soon controls all of Central Asia.

1208 Albigensian Crusade launched: the first against Christians.

1212 Battle of Las Navas de Tolosa: decisive victory of Spaniards over Moors. The Children's Crusade.

THE CULMINATION OF THE MIDDLE AGES

1215 Fourth Lateran Council: the authority of the mediaeval Church and Papacy at its zenith. Dominicans recognised by the Pope. Magna Carta extorted by barons from John.

1223 Franciscans recognised by the Pope.

1229 Emperor Frederick II, through diplomacy, recognised by Muslims as King of Jerusalem.

1230 Teutonic Knights established in Prussia.

1237 Golden Horde (Mongols) begin subjugation of Russia.

1241 Mongol incursions into Central Europe.

1250 St. Louis of France captured on his Crusade in Egypt. Mamelukes become rulers of Egypt. Mandingo king declares his independence of Ghana and embraces Islam.

1256 Conference of Baltic ports; the first form of the Hanseatic League.

1258 Provisions of Oxford: barons under Simon de Montfort force reforms on Henry III of England. Baghdad destroyed by Mongols.

1264 Battle of Lewes: Montfort's party become rulers of England.

1265 Simon de Montfort's Parliament, Battle of Evesham: defeat and death of de Montfort.

1274 Death of Thomas Aquinas.

1279–1368 Mongol (Yuan) Dynasty in China (Kublai Khan).

1231 Repulse of Mongol attack on Japan.

1282 Sicilian Vespers: rising of Sicilians against French ruler.

1284 Completion of Edward I of England's conquest of Wales.

1290 Expulsion of Jews from England. Death of Maid of Norway: Edward I begins attempts to rule Scotland.

1291 Fall of Acre: end of Crusading in Holy Land. Everlasting League of Uri: beginnings of Swiss Confederation.

1294 Death of Roger Bacon (see **B5**).

1295 "Model Parliament" of Edward I (anticipated in 1275).

1308 Death of Duns Scotus.

THE DECLINE OF THE MIDDLE AGES

1309 Papacy moves to Avignon: beginning of the Babylonish Captivity.

1312 Suppression of Templars by king of France and Pope.

1314 Battle of Bannockburn: victory of Robert Bruce secures Scottish independence.

1320 Declaration of Arbroath.

1321 Death of Dante.

1325 Zenith of Mandingo Empire of Mali (North West Africa) under Mansa Musa; superseded at end of 15th century by Songhai empire.

1327 Deposition of Edward II; subsequently murdered.

A.D.

1336 Ashikaga Period in Japan: great feudal lords semi-independent of authority of Shogun.

1337 Death of Giotto.

1338 Beginning of Hundred Years' War between England and France.

1340 Battle of Sluys: English capture French fleet.

1344 Swabian League: weakness of Imperial authority in Germany obliges towns to form leagues for mutual protection.

1346 Battles of Crecy and Neville's Cross: spectacular English victories over French and Scots.

1347 Calais taken by Edward III of England. Cola di Rienzi attempts to reform government of Rome: killed 1354.

1348 Black Death reaches Europe (England 1349, Scotland 1350).

1351 Statute of Labourers: attempt by English Parliament to freeze wages.

1353 Statute of Praemunire: restraints placed on Papal intervention in England.

1354 Ottoman Turks make first settlement in Europe, at Gallipoli.

1355 Death of Stephen Dushan: collapse of Serbian Empire which he had built.

1356 Battle of Poitiers: capture of King John of France by Black Prince. "Golden Bull" regulates Imperial elections in such a way as to place power in the hands of the German princes: valid until 1806.

1358 The Jacquerie: rising of French peasants.

1360 Peace of Bretigny: Edward III makes great territorial gains in France.

1362 English becomes the official language in Parliament and the Law Courts.

1363 Timur (Tamerlane) begins his career of conquest in Asia.

1368–1644 Ming Dynasty in China.

1370 Bertrand du Guesclin Constable of France: regains much territory from the English. Peace of Stralsund: Hansa in complete control of Baltic Sea.

1377 Pope returns to Rome: End of Babylonish Captivity.

1378 Disputed Papal Election: Beginning of Western Schism.

1380 Battle of Chioggia: decisive victory of Venice over Genoa. Battle of Kulikovo: Dmitri Donskoi of Moscow wins first major Russian victory over Golden Horde.

1381 Peasants' Revolt in England under Wat Tyler.

1384 Death of John Wyclif.

1385 Battle of Aljubarotta: Portugal safeguards independence from Castile.

1386 Battle of Sempach: Swiss safeguard independence from Habsburgs. Jagiello (Vladislav V) unites Lithuania and Poland.

1389 Battle of Kosovo: crushing defeat of Serbs and neighbouring nations by Turks.

1396 Battle of Nicopolis: "the last crusade" annihilated by Turks.

1397 Union of Kalmar: Denmark, Norway and Sweden united under one crown: dissolved 1448.

1398 Timur invades and pillages Northern India.

1399 Richard II deposed by Henry IV: first of the Lancastrian kings of England.

1400 Owen Glendower revolts in Wales. Death of Chaucer.

1401 *De Haeretico Comburendo*: the burning of heretics made legal in England.

1410 Battle of Tannenberg: Poles and Lithuanians break power of Teutonic Knights.

1415 Battle of Agincourt: great success of Henry V of England in France. Council of Constance ends Western Schism, burns John Hus.

1420 Treaty of Troyes: English claims to French throne recognised. Hussite Wars begin: Bohemian heretics defend themselves successfully.

A.D.

1429 Relief of Orleans by Joan of Arc.

1431 Burning of Joan of Arc.

1433 Rounding of Cape Bojador: first great achievement in exploration ordered by Henry the Navigator.

1434 Cosimo die Medici begins his family's control of Florence.

1435 Congress of Arras: Burgundians withdraw support from England, in favour of France.

1438 Albert II became German king and began Hapsburg rule over Holy Roman Empire, 1438–1806.

1440 Death of Jan van Eyck.

1450 Rebellion of Jack Cade against government of Henry VI of England.

1453 Battle of Castillon: final English defeat and end of Hundred Years' War. Constantinople taken by Ottoman Turks: end of Byzantine or Eastern Roman Empire.

RENAISSANCE, DISCOVERIES, "NEW MONARCHIES"

1454 First dated printing from movable types in Europe: Papal indulgence printed at Mainz.

1455 First battle of St. Albans: beginning of Wars of the Roses.

1458 Mathias Corvinus becomes king of Hungary. George of Podiebrad becomes king of Bohemia.

1461 Battle of Towton: Yorkist victory in a particularly bloody battle. Louis XI becomes king of France.

1467 Charles the Bold becomes Duke of Burgundy.

1469 Marriage of Ferdinand of Aragon with Isabella of Castile: union of the main kingdoms of Spain (1474). Lorenzo the Magnificent becomes ruler of Florence.

1470 Warwick ("The Kingmaker") turns Lancastrian, dethrones Edward IV.

1471 Return of Edward IV: Lancastrians crushed at Barnet and Tewkesbury. Ivan III of Moscow takes Novgorod: Muscovy rising to supremacy in Russia.

1476 Caxton sets up his press at Westminster.

1477 Battle of Nancy: defeat and death of Charles the Bold: end of the greatness of Burgundy.

1479 Pazzi conspiracy against the Medici in Florence.

1481 Inquisition becomes active in Castile (1484 in Aragon).

1485 Battle of Bosworth Field: beginning of Tudor period in England.

1487 Lambert Simnel's rising fails.

1488 Bartholomew Diaz rounds Cape of Good Hope.

1491 Brittany acquired by King of France (by marriage).

1492 Rodrigo Borgia becomes Pope Alexander VI. Granada, last Moorish foothold in Western Europe, conquered by Spain. Christopher Columbus discovers the West Indies.

1493 Sonni Ali brings Songhai Empire to height of its prestige: Timbuktu renowned centre of literary culture.

1494 Italy invaded by French led by Charles VIII: beginning of Italian Wars and "modern" European diplomacy and international relations. Treaty of Tordesillas: Spain and Portugal agree to divide unexplored part of world; subsequently approved by Pope.

1496 Habsburg–Spanish marriages: foundation of later empires.

1497 Perkin Warbeck captured by Henry VII (hanged 1499). John Cabot discovers Newfoundland.

1498 Savonarola burned. Vasco da Gama at Calicut: the sea route to India found.

1499 Amerigo Vespucci charts part of the South American coast.

A.D.
1500 Brazil discovered by Pedro Cabral.

1503 Casa de Contratación established at Seville; beginnings of Spanish colonial government. Fall of Caesar Borgia.

1507 Alfonso de Albuquerque becomes Viceroy of Portuguese Empire in the East.

1513 Accession of Pope Leo X, zenith of Renaissance Papacy. Machiavelli writes *The Prince*. Balboa discovers the Pacific (South Sea). Battle of Flodden: James IV of Scotland defeated and killed by English.

1514 Battle of Chaldiran: Ottoman victory begins long series of wars with Persian Empire.

REFORMATION, HABSBURG–VALOIS WARS

1515 Francis I becomes king of France: victory of Marignano ends legend of Swiss invincibility. Thomas Wolsey becomes Lord Chancellor of England and Cardinal.

1516 Algiers taken by Barbarossa; beginning of the Corsairs.

1517 Martin Luther nails up his Ninety-five Theses: beginning of the Reformation. Turks conquer Egypt.

1519 Charles V inherits Habsburg lands and elected emperor. Magellan begins first circumnavigation of the world. Death of Leonardo da Vinci.

1520 Suleiman the Magnificent becomes Sultan; Turkish power at its height. Field of Cloth of Gold; celebrated diplomatic meeting, spectacular but with no results.

1521 Mexico conquered by Hernando Cortes. Belgrade taken by the Turks. Diet of Worms; Luther commits himself irrevocably. Charles V divides his dominions: Austrian and Spanish Habsburgs.

1522 Rhodes taken by the Turks; Knights of St. John move to Malta. Election of Adrian VI, first non-Italian Pope since 1378.

1523 Swedes expel Danish overlords, elect Gustavus Vasa King.

1524 Peasants' War in Germany (suppressed 1525).

1525 Battle of Pavia: defeat and capture of Francis I by Imperialists.

1526 Battle of Mohács: Turkish victory ends Hungarian independence. Foundation of Danubian Habsburg Monarchy (Hungarian and Bohemian crowns united with Austrian patrimony of Habsburgs): Holy Roman Empire prolonged for 300 years. Battle of Panipat: Babar begins Muslim conquest of India, founds Mogul Empire.

1527 Sack of Rome by Imperialists. Italy under control of Charles V.

1529 Siege of Vienna by the Turks. Peace of Cambrai; pause in Habsburg–Valois struggle, end of serious French intervention in Italy. Diet of Speyer: origin of the name Protestant.

1532 Peru conquered by Francisco Pizarro.

1533 Ivan IV (the Terrible) becomes Tsar. Marriage of Henry VIII and Catherine of Aragon declared null.

1534 Act of Supremacy: Henry VIII asserts control over English Church.

1535 Coverdale's English Bible printed. Execution of Thomas More and John Fisher.

1536 Execution of Anne Boleyn. Dissolution of smaller Monasteries by Henry VIII and Thomas Cromwell (remainder dissolved 1539). Pilgrimage of Grace: Northern rising because of religious grievances. Act of Union of Wales with England.

1538 Chibchas of Bogota conquered by Gonzalo de Quesada.

1540 Francisco de Coronado begins explorations in North America. Society of Jesus recognised by Pope.

1541 John Calvin regains authority in Geneva.

1542 First Portuguese reach Japan. New Laws of the Indies: first attempt to legislate for welfare of colonial natives, by Spanish government.

1543 Death of Copernicus.

1545 Opening of Council of Trent: the Counter Reformation.

A.D.
1547 Death of Henry VIII: Somerset Protector in the name of the boy king, Edward VI.

1549 First English Book of Common Prayer. Kett's Rebellion in Norfolk, because of economic grievances.

1550 Deposition of Protector Somerset: Northumberland rules England.

1553 Lady Jane Grey proclaimed Queen by Northumberland on death of Edward VI: Mary I succeeds. Servetus burned by Calvin.

1555 Latimer and Ridley burned by Mary. Religious Peace of Augsburg: policy of *cuius regio, eius religio* accepted in Germany.

1556 Charles V abdicated imperial powers in favour of brother Ferdinand. Cranmer burned. Akbar becomes Mogul Emperor (d. 1605).

1557 Macao becomes permanent Portuguese port in China.

1558 Calais lost by English to French. Elizabeth I becomes Queen of England.

1559 Peace of Cateau-Cambrésis: end of Hapsburg–Valois duel.

RELIGIOUS WARS

1561 Mary, Queen of Scots, returns to Scotland.

1562 First War of Religion in France: wars continue intermittently until 1598.

1563 Thirty-nine Articles define Elizabethan Church settlement.

1564 Birth of Shakespeare; death of Michelangelo.

1565 Malta beats off Ottoman threat.

1567 Deposition of Mary, Queen of Scots. Alva in the Netherlands: severe rule.

1568 Flight of Mary, Queen of Scots, to England: imprisonment. San Juan de Ulua: defeat of Hawkins, and end of his slave-trading voyages. Beginning of Anglo-Spanish maritime feud. Revolt of Moriscos of Granada (ended 1570).

1569 Rebellion of Northern Earls (Catholic) in England.

1570 Elizabeth I anathematised by Pope.

1571 Battle of Lepanto: spectacular defeat of Turkish sea-power by Don John of Austria. Bornu (or Kanem) in Central Sudan at its zenith under Idris III.

1572 Dutch "Sea Beggars" take Brill. Massacre of St. Bartholomew in France. Polish Crown elective again, on death of Sigismund II.

1576 Catholic League formed in France, led by Guise family.

1577 Drake begins voyage round world (returns 1580).

1578 Battle of Alcazar-Quivir: death of King Sebastian of Portugal. Parma re-establishes Spanish rule in Southern Netherlands.

1579 Union of Utrecht: seven northern provinces of Netherlands form what becomes Dutch Republic. Death of Grand Vizier Sokolli: decline of Turkish power begins.

1580 Philip II of Spain becomes king of Portugal.

1582 Gregorian Calendar (or New Style) introduced by Pope Gregory XIII.

1584 Assassination of William the Silent.

1585 Hidéyoshi Dictator of Japan: unification of the country. English intervention in Spanish–Dutch War.

1587 Execution of Mary, Queen of Scots. Drake "singes King of Spain's beard." Shah Abbas I (the Great) becomes ruler of Persia (d. 1629).

1588 Spanish Armada defeated. First complete translation of Bible into Welsh.

1589 Death of Catherine de' Medici, Queen-Mother of France.

1592 Moorish conquest of African Songhai Empire.

1593 Henry IV of France becomes Catholic.

1598 Edict of Nantes: French Protestants guaranteed liberty of worship. End of French Wars of Religion.

1600 English East India Company founded. Tokugawa Period begins in Japan (Ieyasu takes title of Shogun, 1603): lasts until 1868.

A.D.

1601 Rebellion and execution of Earl of Essex, Elizabethan Poor Law.

1602 Dutch East India Company founded.

1603 Irish revolts finally suppressed by Mountjoy. Accession of James VI of Scotland as James I of England: Union of English and Scottish Crowns.

1604 Hampton Court Conference: James I disappoints Puritans.

1605 Gunpowder Plot.

1607 Virginia colonised by London company: Jamestown founded. Massive Bristol Channel floods.

1608 Quebec founded by Champlain.

1609 Twelve Years' Truce between Spain and United Provinces: Dutch independence in fact secured. Expulsion of Moriscos from Spain.

1610 Assassination of Henry IV of France.

1611 Plantation of Ulster with English and Scottish colonists. Authorised Version of the Bible in England.

1613 Michael Romanov becomes Tsar: the first of the dynasty.

1614 Napier publishes his explanation of logarithms.

1616 Death of Shakespeare and Cervantes. Edict of Inquisition against Galileo's astronomy.

1618 "Defenestration of Prague": Bohemian assertion of independence begins Thirty Years' War.

1620 Pilgrim Fathers settle in New England.

1624 "Massacre of Amboina": English driven out of spice islands by Dutch. Richelieu becomes Chief Minister in France.

1628 Murder of Duke of Buckingham. Petition of Right by Commons to Charles I. Fall of La Rochelle: French Protestants lose political power. Harvey publishes his work on the circulation of blood.

1629 Charles I begins Personal Rule.

1630 Gustavus Adolphus of Sweden enters Thirty Years' War, turns tide against Imperialists.

1631 Sack of Magdeburg, one of the worst incidents of the Thirty Years' War.

1632 Battle of Lützen: death of Gustavus Adolphus.

1633 William Laud appointed Archbishop of Canterbury. Thomas Wentworth takes up his post as Lord Deputy of Ireland.

1634 Dismissal and murder of Imperialist general Wallenstein.

1635 John Hampden refuses to pay Ship Money.

1636 Japanese forbidden to go abroad.

1637 Russian pioneers reach shores of Pacific.

1638 Covenant widely signed in Scotland.

1639 First Bishops' War: Charles I comes to terms with Scots.

1640 Second Bishops' War: Charles I defeated by Scots. Long Parliament begins: abolition of Royal prerogatives. Great Elector (Frederick William) becomes ruler of Brandenburg. Revolt of Catalonia (finally suppressed 1659). Revolt of Portugal: Duke of Braganza proclaimed king.

1641 Japanese exclude all foreigners (except for small Dutch trading fleet). Massacre of Protestants in Ireland. Wentworth (Earl of Strafford) executed. Grand Remonstrance of Commons to Charles I.

1642 Charles I attempts to arrest the Five Members. Outbreak of English Civil War: first general engagement, Edgehill. Death of Richelieu.

1643 Mazarin becomes Chief Minister of France. Battle of Rocroi: French victory, end of Spanish reputation for invincibility. English Parliament agrees to Solemn League and Covenant, secures services of Scots army.

1644 Marston Moor: decisive battle of English Civil War. North lost to Charles I. Tippemuir: Montrose begins victorious Royalist

A.D.

campaign in Scotland. 1644–1911 Manchu (Qing) dynasty in China.

1645 Formation of New Model Army. Naseby: main Royalist army crushed. Battle of Philiphaugh: Montrose's army destroyed.

1646 Charles I surrenders to Scots. Start of 'grand solar minimum' heralds brutally cold winters.

1647 Charles I handed over to Parliament. Charles I seized by Army. Charles I flees to Carisbrooke Castle.

1648 Second Civil War: New Model Army defeats Scots and Royalists. "Pride's Purge": Parliament refashioned by Army. Peace of Westphalia ends Thirty Years' War.

ASCENDANCY OF FRANCE

1649 Charles I executed. England governed as Commonwealth. Cromwell in Ireland. New Code of Laws in Russia completes establishment of serfdom.

1651 Battle of Worcester: Cromwell's final victory, now master of all Britain. First English Navigation Act. Hobbes' *Leviathan* published.

1652 Foundation of Cape Colony by Dutch under Van Riebeek. First Anglo-Dutch War begins (ends 1654).

1653 Cromwell dissolves Rump, becomes Protector.

1655 Major-Generals appointed to supervise districts of England. Jamaica seized by English.

1656 Grand Vizier Kiuprili: revival of Turkish government.

1658 Death of Cromwell.

1659 Peace of the Pyrenees: France replaces Spain as greatest power in Western Europe.

1660 Restoration of monarch in Britain: Charles II. Royal Society founded.

1661 Death of Mazarin: Louis XIV now rules in person. "Clarendon Code"; beginning of persecution of Non-conformists in England.

1664 New York taken by English: Second Anglo-Dutch War ensues (ends 1667).

1665 Great Plague of London.

1666 Great Fire of London. Newton's discovery of law of gravitation.

1667 Dutch fleet in the Medway. War of Devolution begins: first of Louis XIV's aggressions.

1668 Portuguese Independence recognised by Spain.

1669 Death of Rembrandt.

1670 Secret Treaty of Dover between Charles II and Louis XIV. Revolt of peasants and Don Cossacks under Stenka Razin (suppressed 1671).

1672 Third Anglo-Dutch War begins (ends 1674). Murder of De Witt brothers: William of Orange leads Dutch against French invasion.

1673 Test Act deprives English Catholics and Non-conformists of public offices. Death of Molière.

1675 Battle of Fehrbellin: Swedes defeated by Great Elector; rise of Prussian military power. Greenwich Royal Observatory founded.

1678 "Popish Plot" of Titus Oates utilised by Shaftesbury and the Whigs to bring pressure on Charles II.

1679 Bothwell Brig: suppression of Scottish Covenanters. Habeas Corpus Act passed.

1680 Chambers of Reunion: Louis XIV uses legal arguments to complete annexation of Alsace.

1681 Oxford Parliament: Charles II overcomes his opponents, begins to rule without Parliament.

1683 Rye House Plot. Siege of Vienna by the Turks: last major Turkish attack on Europe.

1685 Sedgemoor: Monmouth's rebellion crushed by James II. Revocation of Edict of Nantes: persecution of French Protestants by Louis XIV.

A.D.

1688 Seven Bishops protest against James II's policy of toleration, and are acquitted. William of Orange lands in England: flight of James II. "The Glorious Revolution."

1689 Derry relieved: failure of James II to subdue Irish Protestants. Killiecrankie: death of Dundee and collapse of Highland rising. Bill of Rights defines liberties established by "Glorious Revolution."

1690 Locke's *Two Treatises on Government* published. Beachy Head: French victory over Anglo-Dutch fleet. Boyne: defeat of James II by William III.

1691 Capitulation of Limerick: surrender of Irish supporters of James II on conditions which are not fulfilled.

1692 Massacre of Glencoe. Government's "lesson" to Highlanders. La Hogue: Anglo-Dutch fleet regains command of the sea.

1693 National Debt of England begun.

1694 Bank of England founded.

1695 Press licensing abandoned: freedom of the press in England.

1696 Peter the Great sole Czar.

1697 Peace of Ryswyck between Louis XIV and William III. Peter journeys "incognito" to the West.

1699 Treaty of Karlowitz: great Turkish concessions to Austrians. Death of Racine.

1700 Great Northern War, involving all Baltic powers, begins (ends 1721). Battle of Narva: Russians defeated by Charles XII of Sweden. Death of Charles II of Spain: under French influence Louis XIV's grandson Philip of Anjou named successor.

1701 War of the Spanish Succession begins. Hungarian revolt led by Francis Rakoczi against Austrians. Elector of Brandenburg receives title of King of Prussia. Act of Settlement establishes Protestant Hanoverian Succession in England.

1703 Methuen Treaty between England and Portugal. St. Petersburg founded. The 'Great Storm' hits Britain; 8,000 lives lost and ships blown as far away as Norway.

1704 Gibraltar taken by Rooke. Blenheim: Marlborough stops France from winning war.

1706 Ramillies: Marlborough's second great victory. Turin: Eugene defeats French in Italy.

1707 Almanza: Anglo-Austrian forces in Spain defeated by French under Berwick. Act of Union: English and Scottish Parliaments united. Death of Aurungzib, last strong Mogul.

1708 Oudenarde: Marlborough's third great victory.

1709 Pultava: Charles XII's invasion of Russia smashed by Peter the Great. Malplaquet: Marlborough's fourth great victory—at great cost in lives.

1710 Tory government in England.

1711 Dismissal of Marlborough.

1713 Peace of Utrecht: England makes advantageous peace with Louis XIV. Bourbon king of Spain grants Asiento (monopoly of Spanish American slave trade) to England.

1714 Peace of Rastatt between France and Austria. Death of Queen Anne: accession of George I. Beginning of Hanoverian Dynasty in Britain. Whig oligarchy rules.

1715 Jacobite Rising defeated at Preston and Sheriffmuir. Death of Louis XIV. France under Regent Orleans.

FIRST BRITISH EMPIRE

1716 Septennial Act: English Parliament prolongs its life from three to seven years. Prince Eugène of Savoy defeated Turks at Petrovaradin.

1720 Collapse of Law's system of banking ("Mississippi Bubble") in France. "South Sea Bubble" in England.

A.D.

1721 Robert Walpole becomes first Prime Minister. Peace of Nystad: Sweden no longer a major power at end of Great Northern War. Russian gains.

1723 Death of Christopher Wren.

1727 First Indemnity Act for Non-conformists.

1729 Methodists begin at Oxford.

1730 Resignation from government of Townshend, who becomes agricultural pioneer.

1733 First Family Compact between Bourbon kings of France and Spain. Withdrawal of Walpole's Excise Bill. John Kay invents flying shuttle, first of the great textile inventions. Jethro Tull publishes *The Horse-Hoeing Husbandry*, advocating new agricultural methods.

1738 Lorraine ceded to France.

1739 Nadir Shah with Persian army sacks Delhi, ruins Mogul power. War of Jenkins' Ear begins between Spain and Britain.

1740 Frederick II (the Great) becomes king of Prussia. Maria Theresa succeeds to Austrian dominions. Frederick seizes Silesia, begins War of the Austrian Succession.

1742 Fall of Walpole.

1743 Dettingen: George II, last British king to command his army in the field, defeats French.

1745 Fontenoy: Duke of Cumberland defeated by Marshal Saxe. Jacobite Rebellion under Prince Charles Edward: initial success, victory of Prestonpans, march to Derby.

1746 Culloden: Jacobites destroyed by Cumberland.

1748 Treaty of Aix-la-Chapelle: Frederick retains Silesia, elsewhere status quo.

1750 Death of J. S. Bach.

1751 First volume of the *Encyclopédie* published in France. Clive takes and holds Arcot: checks plans of Dupleix in Southern India. Chinese conquest of Tibet.

1752 Britain adopts New Style calendar.

1753 British Museum begun by government purchase of Sloane's collection.

1755 Lisbon earthquake. Braddock's defeat and death at the hands of French and Indians.

1756 Diplomatic Revolution (alliance of Austria with France) achieved by Kaunitz; Britain and Prussia perforce became allies. Seven Years' War begins. Minorca taken from British by French (Byng executed 1757). Black Hole of Calcutta: suffocation of many British prisoners.

1757 Pitt Secretary of State, main influence in British government. Rossbach: one of Frederick II's numerous victories against heavy odds. Plassey: Clive conquers Bengal.

1759 "Year of Victories" for Britain: Quebec, Minden, Lagos, Quiberon Bay. James Brindley designs Worsley-Manchester Canal: the beginning of this form of transport in Britain. Voltaire publishes *Candide*. Death of Handel.

1760 Wandewash: decisive defeat of French in India, by Coote.

1761 Panipat: Mahrattas heavily defeated by Afghans. Fall of Pitt.

1762 Catherine II (the Great) becomes Czarina. Rousseau's *Social Contract* and *Emile* published.

1763 Peace of Paris: British colonial gains, First British Empire at its height. Peace of Hubertusburg: Frederick II retains his gains. Pontiac's Conspiracy: failure of Red Indian attempt to destroy British power.

1764 John Wilkes expelled from Commons. James Hargreaves invents spinning jenny.

1766 Henry Cavendish proves hydrogen to be an element.

1768 Royal Academy of Arts founded.

1769 Richard Arkwright erects spinning mill (invention of water frame).

1770 Struensee comes to power in Denmark (executed 1772). "Boston Massacre." James Cook discovers New South Wales.

1772 First Partition of Poland between Russia, Prussia and Austria.

A.D.

1773 Society of Jesus suppressed by the Pope (restored 1814). Revolt led by Pugachov in Russia (suppressed 1775). "Boston Tea Party."

1774 Warren Hastings appointed first Governor-General of India. Treaty of Kutchuk Kainarji; great Turkish concessions to Russia. Karl Scheele discovers chlorine. Joseph Priestley's discovery of oxygen.

1775 Watt and Boulton in partnership at Soho Engineering Works, Birmingham. Lexington: first action in American War of Independence.

1776 American Declaration of Independence. Adam Smith's *Wealth of Nations* published.

1777 Saratoga: surrender of British army under Burgoyne to Americans.

1779 Beginning of great Franco-Spanish siege of Gibraltar (raised finally, 1783). Samuel Crompton invents spinning mule. First Luddite riots against the introduction of machinery for spinning cotton.

1780 Joseph II assumes sole power in Austria. Armed neutrality of maritime nations to restrain British interference with shipping.

1781 Joseph II introduces religious toleration, abolishes serfdom in Austria. Yorktown: surrender of British under Cornwallis.

1782 Battle of the Saints: Rodney's victory save British West Indies.

1783 Treaty of Versailles: American independence recognised. Pitt the Younger becomes Prime Minister of Britain. First flights in hot air (Montgolfier) and hydrogen (Charles) balloons.

1784 Death of Dr. Samuel Johnson.

1785 Edmund Cartwright invents power loom.

1787 American Constitution drafted.

1788 Impeachment of Warren Hastings begins (ends 1795): English fleet commanded by Captain Arthur Phillip landed in Australia.

FRENCH REVOLUTION AND NAPOLEON

1789 Washington the first President of USA. French Revolution begins. Storming of the Bastille (July 14).

1790 Civil constitution of the Clergy is adopted in France.

1791 Flight of Louis XVI and Marie Antoinette to Varennes.

1792 Battle of Valmy: French Revolution saved from intervention of European kings. Denmark becomes first country to prohibit slave trade. France becomes a Republic.

1793 Louis XVI beheaded. Second partition of Poland.

1794 "Glorious First of June." Fall of Robespierre and end of Jacobin Republic. Negro revolt in Haiti led by Toussaint L'Ouverture.

1795 The Directory established. "Whiff of Grapeshot": Napoleon Bonaparte disperses Paris mob, Oct. 5. Batavian Republic set up by France.

1796 First Italian campaign of Bonaparte: victories of Lodi, Arcola.

1797 Treaty of Campo Formio: Bonaparte compels Austria to make peace. Britain left to fight France alone.

1798 Bonaparte goes to Egypt. Battle of the Nile. Vinegar Hill rebellion in Ireland suppressed.

1799 New coalition against France: Suvorov and Russians victorious in Italy. Bonaparte returns to France. *Coup d'état* of Brumaire, Nov. 9. Consulate set up.

1800 Parliamentary Union of Great Britain and Ireland.

1801 Treaty of Lunéville: Austria makes peace; great French gains in Germany.

1802 Peace of Amiens between Britain and France. *Charlotte Dundas*, first practical steamship, on Clyde.

1803 Insurrection in Ireland under Robert Emmet. Britain again at war with France.

A.D.

1804 Bonaparte becomes Emperor. Spain declares war against Great Britain. Serbian revolt against Turks under Kara George.

1805 Battle of Trafalgar, Nelson's great victory and death, Oct. 21. Battle of Austerlitz, Dec. 2.

1806 Death of Pitt, Jan. 23. Confederation of the Rhine: Napoleon's reorganisation of Germany, July 12. End of Holy Roman Empire, Aug. 6. Prussia overthrown at Jena. Napoleon declares Great Britain in a state of blockade—"Continental System."

1807 Slave trade abolished in British Empire. Treaty of Tilsit: with Alexander of Russia his friend, Napoleon controls all of Europe. Occupation of Portugal by French, to enforce Continental Blockade.

1808 Occupation of Spain by French. Spanish rising: guerilla warfare. Peninsular War begins. Battle of Vimeiro (defeat of French by Wellington), Aug. 21.

1809 Battle of Corunna and death of Sir John Moore, Jan. 16. Attempted risings in Germany against Napoleon: Austria renews war. Treaty of Schönbrunn, Oct. 14.

1810 Self-government established in Argentina: first South American state to become independent of Spain.

1811 Massacre of Mamelukes at Cairo. Luddite riots.

1812 Retreat from Moscow: destruction of Napoleon's Grand Army.

1813 War of Liberation starts in Germany. Defeat of French by Wellington at Vitoria, June 21

1814 Soult defeated by Wellington at Toulouse, April 10. Abdication of Napoleon, April 11; Louis XVIII king of France. Congress of Vienna (concluded June 1815) under guidance of Metternich. Resettlement of Europe, usually by restoration of kings. Germanic Confederation under Austrian supervision. Poland ruled by Tsar. Kingdom of Netherlands to include Belgium.

THE OLD ORDER RESTORED

1815 Escape of Napoleon from Elba. Battle of Waterloo, June 18. Corn Law in Britain to safeguard agricultural interests by keeping up prices. Quadruple Alliance (Austria, Russia, Prussia, Britain) to maintain Vienna settlement and hold regular meetings ("Congress System") —frequently confused with Holy Alliance, which was simply a declaration of Christian principles. Napoleon sent to St. Helena, Oct. 16. Massive eruption of Mt. Tambora in Indonesia.

1818 Bernadotte made king of Sweden (Charles XIV), Feb. 6.

1819 Singapore founded by Stamford Raffles. Beginning of Zollverein (Customs Union) in Germany under Prussian influence. Parliamentary reform meeting at Manchester dispersed by military ("Peterloo"), Aug. 16.

1820 Death of George III, Jan. 29.

1821 Death of Napoleon at St. Helena, May 5.

1822 Congress of Verona: congress system breaks down with refusal of Britain (Canning) to intervene against revolutions.

1823 "Monroe Doctrine" announced by USA. President. Dec. 2.

1824 Repeal of Combination Acts in Britain which had forbidden Trades Unions. Charles X king of France.

1825 Independence of all Spanish American mainland now achieved. Nicholas I Czar of Russia. First railway, Stockton to Darlington, opened.

1826 First crossing of Atlantic under steam by Dutch ship *Curaçao*. Menai suspension bridge opened. First known photograph taken.

1827 Battle of Navarino, Turkish and Egyptian fleet destroyed. Death of Beethoven.

1828 Death of Chaka, great Zulu conqueror.

1829 Greece independent. Catholic Emancipation Act in Britain. Metropolitan Police founded.

A.D.

1830 Death of George IV, June 26. Louis Philippe ousts Charles X. Belgium breaks away from Holland. Russian Poland revolts.

1831 First Reform Bill introduced by Lord John Russell. Leopold of Saxe-Coburg becomes king of independent Belgium. British Association founded. Faraday discovers electromagnetic induction.

1832 Reform Bill passed, June 7. Walter Scott, Jeremy Bentham, and Goethe die. Electric telegraph invented by Morse.

1833 Beginning of "Oxford Movement" in English Church. First government grant made to English schools. First British Factory Act.

1834 Poor Law Amendment Act: tightening up of relief in Britain. "Tolpuddle Martyrs" victimised to discourage British working-class movement. Carlist wars begin in Spain.

1835 Municipal Reform Act revises British local government. The word "socialism" first used. "Tamworth Manifesto" of Peel defines aims of Conservative Party.

1836 People's Charter states programme of Chartists. Great Trek of Boers from British South African territory. Texas achieves independence of Mexico.

1837 Queen Victoria succeeds to the throne.

1838 National Gallery (opened in 1824) moved to its Trafalgar Square site.

1839 First Afghan war begins. Chartist riots at Birmingham and Newport. Anti-Corn Law League founded. Aden annexed by Britain.

1840 Penny postage instituted. Queen Victoria marries Prince Albert of Saxe-Coburg-Gotha. "Opium War" with China begins. Union Act gives Canada responsible government. Last convicts landed in New South Wales.

1841 Hong Kong acquired by Britain.

1842 Chartists present second national petition and put themselves at the head of strikes. Great potato famine in Ireland begins.

1846 Repeal of the Corn Laws. Peel resigns.

1847 British Museum opened.

REVOLUTION AND NATIONALISM

1848 Monster meeting of Chartists on Kennington Common, procession abandoned, Apr. 10. General revolutionary movement throughout the Continent. Louis Philippe abdicates; French Republic proclaimed. Swiss Federal Constitution established after defeat of Sonderbund (Catholic succession movement). Rising in Vienna: flight of Metternich, accession of Francis Joseph. Nationalist risings in Bohemia and Hungary. Frankfurt Parliament: attempt to unite Germany on liberal principles. Communist Manifesto produced by Marx and Engels. Gold discovered in California.

1849 Collapse of revolutionary movements. Rome republic besieged by French (June 3), defended by Garibaldi, holds out until July 2. Austrians take Venice, Aug. 22. Repeal of old Navigation Laws. Punjab annexed by Britain.

1850 Cavour becomes Prime Minister of Sardinia. Don Pacifico affair: privileges of British citizenship at their highest defended by Palmerston.

1851 Great Exhibition in Hyde Park. First satisfactory submarine telegraph cable between Dover and Calais laid. Gold in Australia.

1852 Independence of Transvaal recognised by Britain. Napoleon III Emperor of the French.

1853 U.S. Commodore Perry lands in Japan: beginning of Western influence. Russia and Turkey at war.

1854 War declared against Russia by France and Britain. Allied armies land in Crimea, Sept. 14 (Alma, Siege of Sevastopol, Balaklava, Inkerman). Orange Free State set up.

1855 Sardinia joins Britain and France against Russia. Fall of Sevastopol and end of Crimean War. Alexander II Czar of Russia.

A.D.

1856 Peace Treaty signed at Paris. Bessemer invents process for large-scale production of steel. Livingstone completes journey across Africa.

1857 Indian Mutiny. Relief of Lucknow. Canton captured by English and French.

1858 *Great Eastern* launched. Crown assumes government of India. Treaty of Aigun, by which China cedes Amur region to Russia.

1859 Darwin publishes *Origin of Species*. French support for Piedmont in war with Austria (Magenta, Solferino). Piedmont receives Lombardy. Harper's Ferry raid: John Brown hanged, Dec. 2.

1860 Garibaldi and the Thousand Redshirts in Sicily and Naples: most of Italy united to Piedmont. Vladivostok founded; Russia strongly established on N.W. Pacific.

1861 Abraham Lincoln takes office as Pres. of USA. American Civil War commences with 11 states breaking away to form Southern Confederacy. Bull Run (July 21) Confederate success ends Federal hopes of easy victory. Victor Emmanuel proclaimed by first Italian Parliament as king of Italy. Emancipation of Serfs in Russia. Death of Prince Albert, Dec. 14.

1862 Bismarck becomes leading minister in Prussia. Garibaldi attempts to seize Rome but wounded at Aspromonte. Aug. 29. Cotton famine in Lancashire.

1863 Polish rising against Russia (suppressed 1864). French in Mexico. Battle of Gettysburg, July 1–3. Maximilian of Austria made emperor of Mexico.

1864 Cession of Schleswig-Holstein to Prussia and Austria. First Socialist International formed. Taiping rebellion in China ended. Federal army enters Atlanta, Sept. 2: General Sherman captures Savannah ("From Atlanta to the sea"). Dec. 22. Geneva Convention originated.

1865 Death of Cobden, Apr. 2. General Lee surrenders to Grant, Apr. 9. Lincoln assassinated, Apr. 14. Thirteenth Amendment to Constitution: slavery abolished in USA. Death of Palmerston, Oct. 18. Lister introduces antiseptic surgery in Glasgow. Tashkent becomes centre of Russian expansion in Central Asia. Mendel experiments on heredity. William Booth founds Salvation Army.

1866 Austro-Prussian War over Schleswig-Holstein ("Seven Weeks War"). Prussian victory at Sadowa (July 3). Venice secured for Italy, who had, however, been defeated by Austrians at Custozza (June 24) and Lissa (July 20). Treaty of Prague, Aug. 23.

1867 North German Confederation founded. Emperor Maximilian of Mexico shot. Dominion of Canada established. Russia sells Alaska to America for $7 million. Garibaldi makes second attempt to seize Rome, but defeated by Pope with French support at Mentana, Nov. 3. Second Parliamentary Reform Bill passed (Disraeli "dished the Whigs").

1868 Shogunate abolished in Japan: Meiji period of rapid Westernisation under Imperial leadership begins. Ten Years' War (1868–78); struggle for Cuban independence from Spain. Impeachment of President Johnson (USA). Disraeli succeeds Derby as Prime Minister but defeated in general election by Gladstone, Nov.

1869 General Grant, Pres. of USA. Irish Church disestablished. Suez Canal formally opened.

1870 Napoleon III declares war against Prussia. French defeated at Woerth, Gravelotte, and Sedan. Paris besieged. Rome and Papal states annexed to kingdom of Italy. Irish Land Act passed. Forster's Education Act puts elementary education within reach of all children. Papal Infallibility announced.

1871 William I of Prussia proclaimed German emperor at Versailles, Jan. 18. Paris capitulates, Jan. 28. Commune of Paris proclaimed, Mar. 28. Peace signed at Frankfurt-on-Main, May 10. Government troops enter Paris and

A.D.
crush Communards, May 28. Thiers President of the Republic, Aug. 31. Mont Cenis tunnel opened. Trade Unions in Britain legalised.

RIVAL IMPERIAL POWERS

1872 Secret ballot introduced in Britain. Death of Mazzini, Mar. 10.

1873 Death of Livingstone, May 4. Ashanti war.

1874 Disraeli succeeds Gladstone as Prime Minister.

1875 England purchases the Khedive's shares in Suez Canal, Nov.

1876 Bulgarian massacres. Serbo-Turkish war. Bell invents the telephone. Custer defeated and killed in last large-scale Red Indian success. Porfirio Diaz in power in Mexico (until 1911). Victoria declared Empress of India.

1877 Transvaal annexed to British Empire. War between Russia and Turkey. Satsuma rebellion in Japan.

1878 Congress of Berlin: general Balkan settlement. Cyprus leased to Britain (annexed 1914). Second war with Afghanistan (ended 1880). Edison and Swan produce first successful incandescent electric light.

1879 Dual control (Britain and France) in Egypt. Zulu War. Gladstone's Midlothian Campaign. Tay Bridge destroyed, Dec. 28.

1880 Beaconsfield ministry succeeded by second Gladstone ministry. Transvaal declared a republic.

1881 British defeat at Majuba: independence of Transvaal recognised. France occupies Tunis. Gambetta becomes Prime Minister of France. Revolt of the Mahdi in the Sudan. Pasteur's famous immunisation experiment to show that inoculated animals can survive anthrax.

1882 Lord Frederick Cavendish, Irish Secretary, assassinated in Phoenix Park, Dublin, May 6. Triple Alliance (Germany, Austria, Italy) first formed. Alexandria bombarded, July 11. Cairo occupied by British troops, Sept. 14.

1883 National Insurance begun in Germany. Death of Wagner.

1884 Wolseley heads expedition to Khartoum to rescue Gordon. French establish complete protectorate in Indo-China. Evelyn Baring takes over administration of Egypt. Russians capture Merv. Berlin Conference defines rights of European Powers in Africa. Third Parliamentary Reform Bill. Parsons invents his turbine. Greenwich meridian internationally recognised as prime meridian. Fabian Society founded.

1885 Khartoum captured; Gordon slain, Jan. 26.

1886 Upper Burma annexed by Britain. Home Rule Bill defeated in Commons. All Indians in USA now in Reservations. Daimler produces his first motor car. Completion of Canadian Pacific Railway. Gold discovered in the Transvaal.

1887 Queen Victoria's Golden Jubilee, June 21.

1888 William II German Emperor. County Councils set up in Britain.

1889 Mayerling: tragic death of Prince Rudolf of Austria, Jan. 30. Flight of General Boulanger, after attempting to become master of France. Second Socialist International set up. Great London dock strike, Aug. 15–Sept. 16.

1890 Parnell ruined by divorce case: Irish politicians split. Sherman Anti-Trust Law: first attempt in USA to break cartels. Opening of Forth Bridge, Mar. 4. Bismarck resigns, Mar. 17. Caprivi succeeds. Heligoland ceded to Germany.

1891 The United States of Brazil formed.

1892 Panama Canal financial scandals in France.

1893 Home Rule Bill passes third reading in Commons, Sept. 1: Lords reject Bill, Sept. 8.

1894 Opening of Manchester Ship Canal, Jan. 1. Gladstone resigns, Mar. 3, Lord Rosebery succeeds. Armenian massacres by Turks: repeated at intervals for next quarter of century.

A.D.
Japan declares war against China. Dreyfus convicted of treason.

1895 Opening of Kiel canal, June 21. Rosebery resigns, June 22; Salisbury Ministry succeeds. Treaty of Shimonoseki: Japan gets Formosa, free hand in Korea. New Cuban revolution breaks out against Spanish. Marconi sends message over a mile by wireless. Röntgen discovers X-rays. Freud publishes his first work on psycho-analysis. Jameson Raid, Dec. 29.

1896 Jameson raiders defeated by Boers, Jan. 1. Adowa: Italian disaster at hands of Abyssinians, the first major defeat of a white colonising power by indigenous people. Gold discovered in the Klondike.

1897 Cretan revolt leads to Greek–Turkish War. Hawaii annexed by USA. Queen Victoria's Diamond Jubilee, June 22. Great Gold Rush began.

1898 Port Arthur ceded to Russia. Spanish–American War. *Maine*, U.S. warship blown up in Havana harbour. Treaty of Paris, Dec. 10: Cuba freed, Puerto Rico and Guam ceded to USA, Phillippines surrendered for £20 million. Death of Gladstone, May 19. Battle of Omdurman, decisive defeat of Mahdists, Sept. 2. Empress of Austria assassinated, Sept. 10. The Curies discovered Radium.

THE BOER WAR

1899 Boer War begins, Oct. 10.

1900 Boers attack Ladysmith, Jan. 6. Battle of Spion Kop, Buller repulsed with severe losses, Jan. 14. Relief of Kimberley, Feb. 15. Ladysmith relieved, Feb. 28. Mafeking relieved, May 17. Boxer outbreak in China, May. Annexation of Orange Free State, May 26. Roberts occupies Johannesburg, May 31. "Khaki Election." Annexation of the Transvaal, Oct. 25. Australian Commonwealth proclaimed, Dec. 30.

1901 Queen Victoria dies, Jan. 22. Trans-Siberian Railway opened for single-track traffic.

1902 Anglo-Japanese Alliance, Jan. 30. Death of Cecil Rhodes, Mar. 26. Treaty of Vereeniging ends Boer War, May 31.

1903 Congo scandal: celebrated case of misrule and exploitation. Royal family of Serbia assassinated, May 29. First controlled flight in heavier-than-air machine—Orville and Wilbur Wright at Kitty Hawk, USA, Dec. 17.

1904 Russo-Japanese War begins, Feb. 8. Japanese victory at Yalu River, May 1. British forces under Younghusband reach Lhasa, Aug. 3. Treaty with Tibet signed at Lhasa, Sept. 7.

1905 Port Arthur falls to Japanese, Jan. 3. "Bloody Sunday" massacre at St. Petersburg, Jan. 22. Destruction of Russian fleet under Rozhdestvenski at Tsushima by Admiral Togo (May). Treaty of Portsmouth (USA) ends Russo-Japanese war. Separation of Church and State in France. Norway separates from Sweden.

1906 General strike in Russia. San Francisco destroyed by earthquake and fire, Apr. 18. Simplon tunnel opened for railway traffic, June 1. First Duma (Parliament with limited powers) in Russia. Liberal "landslide" majority in Britain: Labour MPs appear. Movement for Women's Suffrage becomes active in Britain. Algeciras Conference: Franco-German crises resolved in favour of France. Death of Ibsen. Vitamins discovered by F. G. Hopkins.

1907 New Zealand becomes a dominion.

1908 Annexation of Congo by Belgium. Young Turk revolution. Annexation of Bosnia and Herzegovina by Austria: severe rebuff for Russia. Asquith becomes Prime Minister of Britain.

1909 Old Age Pensions in Britain. Peary reaches North Pole. Blériot makes first cross-Channel flight. House of Lords rejects Lloyd George's budget. Union of South Africa formed. Henry Ford concentrates on producing Model T chassis: beginnings of cheap motors.

A.D.

1910 Accession of George V on death of Edward VII, May 6. Liberals win two General Elections. Labour Exchanges established in Britain. Death of Tolstoy and Florence Nightingale.

1911 Parliament Act: power of Lords decisively reduced. British MPs paid for first time. National Insurance in Britain. Tripoli taken from Turkey by Italy. Chinese Revolution. Amundsen reaches South Pole, Dec. 14.

1912 China becomes a Republic under Sun Yat Sen. *Titanic* disaster off Cape Race, Apr. 14-15. Great British coal strike. Scott's last expedition. Outbreak of Balkan Wars.

1913 Treaty of Bucharest: most of Turkey-in-Europe divided among Balkan states.

FIRST WORLD WAR

1914 Archduke Francis Ferdinand, heir to the Hapsburg thrones, assassinated at Sarajevo, June 28. Austria–Hungary declares war against Serbia, July 28. Germany declares war against Russia, Aug. 1. Germany declares war against France, Aug. 3. German invasion of Belgium: Great Britain declares war against Germany, Aug. 4. Great Britain declares war on Austria–Hungary, Aug. 12. British Expeditionary Force concentrated before Mauberge, Aug. 20. Battle of Mons; Japan declared war on Germany, Aug. 23. Battle of the Marne, Sept. 5-9. Trench warfare began on Aisne salient, Sept. 16. Three British cruisers (*Aboukir*, *Hogue*, and *Cressy*) sunk by one U-boat, Sept. 22. First Battle of Ypres, Oct. 12-Nov. 11. Raiding of German cruiser *Emden* until destroyed, Nov. 9. Battle of Coronel: German cruisers *Scharnhorst* and *Gneisenau* sink British cruisers *Good Hope* and *Monmouth*, Nov. 1. Great Britain declares war against Turkey, Nov. 5. Destruction of German squadron off Falkland Is., Dec. 8. British protectorate over Egypt proclaimed, Dec. 17. First Zeppelin appeared over British coast, Dec. 20.

1915 Turkish army defeated in Caucasus, Jan 5. Great Britain declared blockade of Germany, Mar. 1. Battle of Neuve Chapelle, Mar. 10-13. Naval attack on Dardanelles called off, Mar. 22. First landing of British, Australian, New Zealand troops on Gallipoli Peninsula, Apr. 25. Second Battle of Ypres, Apr. 22-May 25: Germans first used gas. Sinking of *Lusitania*, May 7. Battle of Aubers Ridge, May 9-25. Italy declares war on Austria, May 22. British Coalition Government formed, May 26. Italian army crosses Isonzo, June 2. Zeppelin destroyed by R. A. J. Warneford, June 7. Second landing of Allied troops at Suvla Bay. Italy declares war on Turkey, Aug. 20. Turks defeated at Kut-el-Amara, Sept 28. Serbia conquered by Austria and Bulgaria, Nov. 28. French and British troops occupy Salonika, Dec. 13. British troops withdraw from Anzac and Suvla, Dec. 20.

1916 Evacuation of Gallipoli completed, Jan 8. Opening of Battle of Verdun, Feb. 21. Republican rising in Ireland, Apr. 24. First Daylight Saving Bill passed. Fall of Kut, Apr. 29. Battle of Jutland, May 31. Brusilov's offensive in Galicia begins, June 4. Kitchener drowned when *Hampshire* struck mine, June 5. Battle of the Somme, July 1-Nov. 13: British losses: 420,000. Italians capture Gorizia, Aug. 10. Hindenburg and Ludendorff chiefs of German staff, Aug. 27. Rumania declares war against Austria and Germany. Aug. 27. Tanks first used by British, Sept. 15. Death of Francis Joseph of Austria, Nov. 21. Lloyd George forms War Cabinet, Dec. 6. Joffre replaced by Nivelle, early Dec.

1917 Unrestricted submarine warfare begins, Feb. 1. British troops occupy Baghdad, Mar. 11. Revolution in Russia, Mar. 12. USA declares war on Germany, April 6. Battle of Arras, Apr. 9-14: Vimy Ridge taken by Canadians, Apr. 10. Pétain replaced Nivelle, May 15. Messines Ridge taken by British, June 7. First American contingents arrive in France, June 26. Allenby assumes Palestine command, June 29. Third Battle of Ypres

A.D.

opened, July 31. Russia proclaimed a Republic, Sept. 15. British victory on Passchendaele Ridge, Oct. 4. French victory on the Aisne, Oct. 23. Caporetto: Italians severely defeated by Austrians. Oct. 24. Bolshevik Revolution, Nov. 7 (Oct. 25 O.S.). Passchendaele captured by British, Nov. 6. Balfour declaration recognised Palestine as "a national home" for the Jews, Nov. 8. Hindenburg Lines smashed on 10-mile front, Nov. 20. Fall of Jerusalem, Dec. 9. Russo-German armistice signed, Dec. 15.

1918 Treaty of Brest-Litovsk, Mar. 3. German offensive against British opened on Somme, Mar. 21. Battle of Arras, Mar. 21-Apr. 4. Second German offensive against British, Apr. 9-25. British naval raid on Zeebrugge and Ostend, Apr. 23. Foch appointed C.-in-C. Allied armies, Apr. 14. Peace signed between Rumania and Central Powers, May 7. *Vindictive* sunk in Ostend harbour, May 9. Last German offensive against French, July 15. British, Canadians, and Australians attack in front of Amiens, Aug. 8. Allenby destroyed last Turkish army at Megiddo, Sept. 19. Bulgarians signed armistice, Sept. 29. General Allied offensive in West began, Sept. 26. Germans accepted Wilson's Fourteen Points, Oct. 23. Great Italian advance, Oct. 24. Turkey surrenders, Oct 30. Austria accepts imposed terms, Nov. 3. Popular government in Poland (Lublin), Nov. 7. Revolutionary movement begins in Germany, Nov. 8. Kaiser abdicates and escapes to Holland, Nov. 9. Armistice signed by Germans, Nov. 11. Proclamation of Kingdom of Serbs, Croats and Slovenes in Belgrade, Dec. 1.

THE INTERWAR YEARS: FASCISM AND NAZISM

1919 Peace Conference in Paris, Jan. 18. Einstein's theory of Relativity confirmed experimentally during solar eclipse, March 29. First direct flight across Atlantic by Sir J. Alcock and Sir A. W. Brown, June 15. Interned German fleet scuttled at Scapa Flow, June 19. Treaty of Peace with Germany signed at Versailles, June 28. Treaty of St. Germain: break-up of Austrian Empire, Sept. 10.

1920 Peace Treaty ratified in Paris. First meeting of League of Nations, from which Germany, Austria, Russia, and Turkey are excluded, and at which the USA is not represented. Prohibition in USA. Peace Treaty with Turkey signed at Sèvres: Ottoman Empire broken up Aug. 10. Degrees first open to women at Oxford Univ., Oct. 14.

1921 Riots in Egypt, May 23. In complete disregard of the League of Nations, Greece makes war on Turkey. Heligoland fortresses demolished, Oct. 14. Irish Free State set up by Peace Treaty with Britain, Dec. 6.

1922 Four-Power Pacific Treaty ratified by U.S. Senate, Mar. 24. Heavy fighting in Dublin, the Four Courts blown up, July 2. Defeat of Greek armies by the Turks, Aug.-Sept. Mussolini's Fascist "March on Rome," Oct. 28.

1923 French troops despatched to Ruhr, Jan. 11. Treaty of Lausanne, July 24. Earthquake in Japan, Tokyo and Yokohama in ruins, Sept. 1. Rhine Republic proclaimed, Bavaria defies the Reich, Oct. 20. Turkish Republic proclaimed; Kemal Pasha, first President, Oct. 29.

1924 Lenin dies, Jan. 21. First Labour Ministry in Britain under MacDonald, Jan. 22; lasts 9 months. George II of Greece deposed and a Republic declared, Mar. 25. Dawes Plan accepted by London conference; Ruhr evacuation agreed to, Aug. 16.

1925 Hindenburg elected German President, Mar. 26. Treaty of Locarno signed in London, Dec. 1. Summer Time Act made permanent.

1926 Ibn Saud proclaimed king of the Hedjaz in Jeddah, Jan. 11. Evacuation of Cologne by British forces, Jan. 31. General strike in Britain.

1927 Lindbergh flies Atlantic alone, May 21.

1928 Earthquake in Greece, Corinth destroyed. Apr. 23. Capt. Kingsford-Smith flies the

A.D.
Pacific, June 9. General Nobile rescued by aeroplane from Arctic one month after disaster, June 24. Kellogg Pact accepted by Gt. Britain, July 18. German airship with 60 persons crosses Atlantic, Oct. 15. Women in Britain enfranchised on same basis as men.

1929 Second Labour Ministry under MacDonald. Graf Zeppelin makes numerous successful intercontinental flights. Commander Byrd flies over South Pole, Nov. 30. American slump and Wall Street crash.

1930 *R.101* destroyed in France on first flight to India, 48 lives lost, Oct. 5—end of British interest in airships.

1931 Great floods in China. Resignation of Labour Government and formation of Coalition under MacDonald. Invergordon naval mutiny.

1932 Manchuria erected into Japanese puppet state of Manchukuo, Feb. 18. Sydney Harbour Bridge opened, Mar. 19. Ottawa Imperial Conference.

1933 Hitler appointed Chancellor by Hindenburg, Jan. 30, and step by step gains supreme control. German Reichstag set on fire, Feb. 27.

1934 Dollfuss, Austrian Chancellor, murdered by Austrian Nazis, July 25. Death of Hindenburg, Aug. 2. Hitler becomes Dictator. Alexander of Yugoslavia assassinated in Marseilles, Oct. 9.

1935 Saar plebiscite for return to Germany, Jan. 13. Baldwin succeeds MacDonald as Prime Minister, June 7. War begins between Italy and Abyssinia, Oct. 3. Ineffectual economic "sanctions" by League of Nations against Italy, Nov. 18.

1936 Accession of King Edward VIII, Jan. 20. Repudiation of Locarno Treaty by Germany, Mar. 7. Remilitarisation of Rhineland, Mar. 8. Italian troops occupy Addis Ababa, May 5. Civil War breaks out in Spain, July 18. Inauguration of BBC high definition TV, Nov. 2. King Edward VIII abdicates after a reign of 325 days, Dec. 10. The Duke of York succeeds his brother as King George VI, Dec. 12.

1937 Coalition Ministry under Chamberlain, May 28. Japanese begin attempted conquest of China—"China incident," July 7.

1938 Austria annexed by Germany, Mar. 13. British navy mobilised, Sept. 28. Munich Agreement between Chamberlain, Daladier, Hitler, and Mussolini, Sept. 29.

1939

February 27 Great Britain recognises General Franco's Government.

March 16 Bohemia and Moravia annexed by Hitler and proclaimed a German Protectorate. **22** Memel ceded to Germany by Lithuania. **28** Anti-Polish press campaign begun by Germany.

April 1 Spanish War ends. **7** Italy seizes Albania. **14** First British talks with Russia. **27** Conscription introduced in Great Britain. **28** Hitler denounces Anglo-German Naval agreement and the Polish Non-Aggression Treaty.

May 12 Great Britain signs defensive agreement with Turkey. **22** Italy and Germany sign pact. **23** France and Turkey sign defensive agreement. **25** Anglo-Polish treaty signed in London.

July 10 Chamberlain re-affirms British pledge to Poland.

August 23 German-Soviet Pact signed by von Ribbentrop. **25** Japan breaks away from the Anti-Comintern Pact. **28** Holland mobilises. **31** British fleet mobilised.

SECOND WORLD WAR

September 1 Poland invaded by German forces. Great Britain and France mobilise. **1–4** Evacuation schemes put in motion in England and Wales: 1,200,000 persons moved. **2** Compulsory military service for all men in Britain aged 20 to 41. **3** War declared (11 a.m.) between Britain and Germany as from 5 p.m. **4** British liner *Athenia* sunk by submarine. RAF raid the Kiel Canal entrance and bomb German warships. **6** First enemy air raid on Britain. **8** Russia mobilises. Russian troops on Polish border. **11** British troops on French soil. **17**

A.D.
Russian troops cross the Polish frontier along its entire length. Russian and German troops meet near Brest Litovsk: loss of *Courageous*. **27** Capitulation of Warsaw. **29** Nazi-Soviet pact signed in Moscow approving partition of Poland: Introduction of petrol rationing in Britain.

October 14 *Royal Oak* sunk in Scapa Flow with a loss of 810 lives.

November 8 Bomb explosion in the Bürgerbräukeller at Munich after Hitler's speech. Germans using magnetic mines. **29** Diplomatic relations between Russia and Finland severed. **30** Finland attacked by Russia.

December 11 Italy leaves the League of Nations. **13** Battle of the River Plate: engagement of German warship *Admiral Graf Spee* by the cruisers *Exeter, Ajax,* and *Achilles*. **14** Rejection by Russia of the League of Nations' offer of mediation in the Russo-Finnish war. Russia expelled from the League of Nations. **17** *Admiral Graf Spee* scuttles herself in the entrance of Montevideo harbour.

1940

February 14 Finnish advanced posts captured by Russians. **16** 299 British prisoners taken off the German Naval Auxiliary *Altmark* in Norwegian waters. **26** Finns lose the island fortress of Kolvisto. Finns retreat from Petsamo.

March 12 British ships to be fitted with a protective device against magnetic mines. Finland concludes a peace treaty whereby she cedes to Russia the Karelian Isthmus, the town of Vipuri and a military base on Hango Peninsula.

April 9 Invasion of Denmark and Norway by Germany. **15** British troops arrive in Norway. **19** British soldiers land in the Faroes.

May 2 British troops withdrawn from Norway. **10** Holland, Belgium and Luxembourg invaded by German forces. Parachute troops landed near Rotterdam. British troops cross the Belgian border. British troops land in Iceland. Rotterdam bombed. **11** National Government formed under Churchill. **13** Queen Wilhelmina arrives in London. **14** Rotterdam captured. Holland ceases fighting. Allied troops land near Narvik. **17** Belgian Government moves to Ostend. **24** German forces enter Boulogne. **27** Belgian army capitulates on the order of King Leopold. British forces to be withdrawn from Flanders. Narvik captured by Allied forces. **29** Ostend, Ypres, Lille and other Belgian and French towns lost to the Germans.

June Evacuation of British army from Dunkirk (May 27–June 4): 299 British warships and 420 other vessels under constant attack evacuate 335,490 officers and men. **5** Hitler proclaims a war of total annihilation against his enemies. **8** German armoured forces penetrate French defences in the West near Rouen. **10** Italy declares war on Great Britain and France. **14** Paris captured by German forces. **15** Soviet troops occupy Lithuania, Latvia and Estonia. **22** French delegates accept terms for an Armistice. **25** Hostilities in France cease at 12.35 a.m.

July 1 Channel Islands occupied by Germany. **3** French naval squadron at Oran immobilised. **10** Battle of Britain began.

August 19 British withdrew from Somaliland. **25** British began night bombing of Germany.

September 6 King Carol of Rumania abdicates in favour of his son Michael. **7** London sustains severe damage in the largest aerial attack since war commenced. **15** Battle of Britain ends with British victory: German aeroplanes destroyed, 1,733; RAF losses, 915. **23** Japanese troops enter Indo-China.

October 7 German troops enter Rumania. **28** Greece rejects an Italian ultimatum.

November 1 Greeks repel Italian attacks, **5** HMS *Jervis Bay* lost defending Atlantic convoy from German warship *Admiral Scheer*. **11** Italian fleet at Taranto crippled by Fleet Air Arm. **14** Coventry heavily attacked, the Cathedral destroyed. **22** Albanian town of Koritza captured by the Greeks.

December 2 Bristol heavily bombed. **11** Sidi Barrani captured by British forces: beginning

A.D.
of Wavell's destruction of Italian forces in Cyrenaica. **29** City of London severely burned by incendiary bombs: Guildhall and eight Wren Churches destroyed.

1941

January 5 Bardia captured. **22** Tobruk captured by Australian troops.
February 7 Benghazi captured. **26** Mogadishu, capital of Italian Somaliland, occupied by Imperial troops. German mechanised troops in Libya.
March 4 British raid Lofoten Islands. **11** U.S. Lease and Lend Bill signed by Roosevelt. **27** Keren—main battle in British conquest of Abyssinia and Somaliland. **28** Cape Matapan: Italian fleet routed by British. **30** Rommel opens attack in N. Africa.
April 4 Addis Ababa entered by Imperial forces. **6** Greece and Yugoslavia invaded by German troops. **8** Massawa capitulates. **11** Belgrade occupied by German forces. **13** Bardia given up by British. Tobruk holds out. **24** Empire forces withdrawing from Greece. **27** Athens captured by the Germans.
May 2 Evacuation from Greece completed. **10** Rudolf Hess descends by parachute in Scotland. **20** Crete invaded by German air-borne troops. **24** HMS *Hood* sunk. **27** German battleship. *Bismark* sunk; British forces withdrawn from Crete.
June 2 Clothes rationing commences. **4** William II (ex-Kaiser of Germany) dies. **18** Treaty of friendship between Turkey and Germany signed. **22** Germany attacks Russia. **24** Russia loses Brest Litovsk.
July 3 Palmyra (Syria) surrenders to Allied forces. **7** U.S. forces arrive in Iceland. **9** General Dentz, the French High Commissioner in Syria, asks for Armistice terms. **25** Fighting round Smolensk.
August 25 British and Russian troops enter Persia. **27** The Dnepropetrovsk dam blown up by the Russians.
September 18 Crimea cut off from mainland. **19** Kiev entered by Germans.
October 6 German attack on Moscow. **16** Soviet Government leaves Moscow. Odessa occupied by German and Rumanian troops. **19** Taganrog on Sea of Azov captured by Germans. **26** Kharkov captured by the Germans.
November 14 *Ark Royal* sunk. **18** Libyan battle opens: Eighth Army's first offensive. **23** Bardia and Fort Capuzzo captured by British. **24** HMS *Dunedin* torpedoed. **25** HMS *Barham* sunk. **30** Russians re-take Rostov.
December 1 Points rationing scheme in force in Britain. **4** German attack on Moscow halted. **7** Japanese attack on Pearl Harbor. **8** Japanese forces land in Malaya. **9** British forces in Tobruk relieved. **10** HMS *Repulse* and *Prince of Wales* sunk off Malaya by Japanese. Phillippines invaded by Japanese. **25** Hongkong surrenders to Japanese.

1942

January 2 Manila and Cavite taken by Japanese. **23** Japanese forces land in New Guinea and the Solomon Islands.
February 9 Soap rationed. **12** Escape through English Channel of German ships *Scharnhorst, Gneisenau*, and *Prinz Eugen*. **15** Singapore surrenders to Japanese. **27** Battle of Java Sea.
March 9 Surrender of Java to Japanese.
April 15 George Cross awarded to the island of Malta.
May 4–8 Battle of Coral Sea. **7** Madagascar invaded by British forces. **7** U.S. forces sink 11 Japanese warships off the Solomon islands. **30** Over 1,000 bombers raid Cologne. Canterbury bombed.
June 3–7 Midway Island: U.S. naval victory turns tide in Pacific. **20** Tobruk captured by the Germans.
July 16 RAF make first daylight raid on the Ruhr.
August 6 Germans advancing towards the Caucasus. **10** American forces land in the Solomon

A.D.
Islands. **11** Malta convoy action (loss of HMS *Eagle, Manchester, Cairo*, and one destroyer). **19** Raid on Dieppe. **23–25** Battle of Solomons.
September 6 Germans halted at Stalingrad.
October 23 El Alamein: Allied offensive opens in Egypt.
November 4 Rommel's army in full retreat. **5** Red Army holding firm at Stalingrad. **7** Allied invasion of N. Africa. **27** German forces enter Toulon. French Fleet scuttled.
December 2 First self-sustained, controlled nuclear chain reaction in uranium achieved by group working under Enrico Fermi at Chicago. **24** Admiral Darlan assassinated.

1943

January 6 German armies in the Caucasus and the Don elbow in retreat. **18** Leningrad 16-month siege ended. **23** Tripoli occupied by the Eighth Army. **27** American bombers make their first attack on Germany. **31** Remnants of the German army outside Stalingrad surrender.
February 9 Guadalcanal Island cleared of Japanese troops. **16** Kharkov retaken by the Russians.
March 1–3 Battle of Bismarck Sea. **23** 8th Army penetrates the Mareth Line.
May 7 Tunis and Bizerta captured by Allies. **12** All organised German resistance in Tunisia ceases. **16** Dams in the Ruhr breached by the RAF. **22** Moscow dissolves the Comintern.
June 3 French Committee for National Liberation formed in Algiers.
July 5 Battle of Kursk begins; largest tank battle in history ends in Russian victory; **10** Allied invasion of Sicily. **25** Mussolini overthrown. **28** Fascist Party in Italy dissolved.
August 17 Sicily in Allied hands.
September 3 Italian mainland invaded. **8** Italy surrenders. **9** British and American troops land near Naples. **10** Rome seized by the Germans. **14** Salamaua captured from the Japanese. **23** *Tirpitz* severely damaged (sunk Nov. 12, 1944). **25** Smolensk taken by the Russians.
October 1 Naples taken. **25** Russians capture Dnepropetrovsk and Dneprodzerzhinck.
November 6 Kiev taken by the Russians. **26** Second Battle of Solomons. **28** Churchill, Roosevelt, and Stalin meet in Teheran.
December 2 Men between 18 and 25 to be directed to the mining industry by ballot in Britain. **26** Sinking of German battleship *Scharnhorst*.

1944

January 22 Allied landings at Anzio. **28** Argentina breaks with the Axis Powers.
February 1 American forces land on the Marshall Islands. **2** Russians penetrate Estonia.
March 15 Cassino (Italy) destroyed by US bombers.
May 9 Sevastopol captured by Russians. **18** Capture of Cassino and Abbey by Allies. **19** 50 Allied officers shot after escaping from a German prison camp. **30** Battle for Rome commences.
June 4 Allied forces enter Rome. King of Italy signs decree transferring his powers to Prince Umberto, his son. **6** *D-Day:* invasion of Europe (over 4,000 ships in invasion fleet). **7** Defeat of Japanese thrust at India, outside Imphal. **9** Heavy fighting near Caen. **12** First V-1 falls on England. **18** Cherbourg peninsula cut by the Americans. Russians break through the Mannerheim Line.
July 3 Minsk captured by Russians. **9** Caen captured by Allies. **20** "Bomb plot" on Hitler's life. **21** Guam captured by Americans.
August 1 Uprising in Warsaw. **4** Myitkyina falls to Allied forces. **15** Allied forces land in southern France. Marseilles taken. Rumania surrenders. **25** Paris liberated. Rumania declares war on Germany.
September 3 Allies in Belgium. **4** Antwerp and Brussels taken by Allies. Holland entered. Finland "ceases fire." **6** Bulgaria asks for an armistice. **7** Boulogne entered by Allies. Bulgaria declares war on Germany. **8** First V-2 falls on England. **11** Allied forces fighting on

A.D.
Reich territory. **17** Allied airborne troops landed at Arnhem. **22** 1st Battle of Philippines.
October 3 Warsaw rising crushed by Germany. **14** Allies occupied Athens. **15** Hungary requested armistice. **20** US troops took Aachen. **25** Battle of Leyte Gulf: Japan's sea-power broken.
December 6 Civil war in Athens. **16** German counter-attack in Ardennes.

1945

January 5 Athens fighting ended. **9** US troops landed on Luzon. **13** Red Army occupied Budapest. **17** Red Army occupied Warsaw. **27** Red Army entered Auschwitz. **28** Burma Rd to China reopened.
February 4 Yalta Conference. **14** Dresden bombed. **19** US troops landed on Iwo Jima.
March 6 Allies took Cologne.
April 1 US invaded Okinawa. **11** Red Army entered Vienna. **12** Pres Roosevelt died. **27** Russian–US link-up in Germany. **28** Mussolini killed by Italian partisans. **29** German and Italian armies in Italy surrendered. **30** Suicide of Hitler.
May 2 Russians took Berlin. **3** British took Rangoon. **4** German forces in NW Germany, Holland and Denmark surrendered. **8** World War II ended; VE Day. **28** Air attacks on Japan.
June 26 World Security Charter to establish UN signed in San Francisco.
July 5 Allies recognised Polish government. **26** Labour won General Election: new PM Clement Attlee. **31** Potsdam Conference.
August 6 Atomic bomb destroyed Hiroshima. **9** Nagasaki atom bomb. **14** Unconditional surrender of Japan. **15** VJ Day.
September 5 Allies reoccupied Singapore.

"COLD WAR": AFRO-ASIAN INDEPENDENCE

October 15 Laval executed. **24** Quisling executed.
November 16 UNESCO founded in Paris. **20** Nuremberg trial opened.
December 27 IMF and World Bank established.

1946

February 1 Trygve Lie 1st UN Secretary-General.
March 5 Churchill's "Iron Curtain" speech.
April 18 League of Nations wound up.
May 25 Jordan independent.
June 30 US atom bomb test at Bikini.
July 13 £937m US loan to Britain. **22** King David Hotel, British HQ in Jerusalem, blown up.
August 1 Paris Peace Conference.
October 16 Nuremberg sentences carried out: Goering's suicide. **23** General Assembly of UN opened in New York.

1947

January 1 Coal nationalised. **14** Vincent Auriol 1st Pres of French IVth Republic.
February 20 Lord Mountbatten last Viceroy of India.
June 5 "Marshall Plan" inaugurated.
August 3 UN mediation ended Indonesia fighting. **15** India and Pakistan independent after partition.
October 6 International organisation of Communist Parties (Cominform) set up. **14** Sound barrier broken.
November 20 Princess Elizabeth married.
December 15 "Big 4" talks on Germany broke down.

1948

January 1 Railways nationalised. **4** Burma independent. **30** Gandhi assassinated.
February 1 Malayan federal constitution came into force. **27** Communists seized power in Czechoslovakia.
March 10 Czech Foreign Minister Jan Masaryk found dead.
April 1 Electricity nationalised. **16** OEEC set up.
May 14 British Mandate in Palestine ended: new State of Israel proclaimed.

A.D.
June 16 State of Emergency declared in Malaya. **28** Cominform expelled Yugoslavia.
July 1 Berlin airlift. **5** NHS inaugurated.
August 1 Economic union of French, US and British zones in Germany.
September 4 Queen Wilhelmina of Netherlands abdicated. **9** N Korea independent, following US Korea. **17** UN mediator in Palestine assassinated.
November 3 Harry Truman elected US Pres. **14** Prince Charles born.
December 10 UN adopted Declaration of Human Rights.

1949

January 22 Chinese Communists took Peking.
April 1 Newfoundland became province of Canada. **4** 12 nations signed N Atlantic Treaty. **18** Republic of Ireland proclaimed.
May 1 Gas nationalised. **12** Berlin blockade lifted. **23** Federal Republic of Germany proclaimed.
August 8 1st meeting of Council of Europe.
September 14 Dr Adenauer 1st Chancellor of FDR. **21** Soviet atom bomb test.
October 1 People's Republic of China proclaimed under Chairman Mao Tse-tung. **12** German Democratic Republic proclaimed in Soviet sector.
December 8 Chinese Nationalist government set up Formosa HQ. **27** Indonesia independent.

1950

January 26 Indian republic proclaimed under Pres Rajendra Prasad.
February 14 USSR–China alliance signed. **23** Labour won General Election.
June 25 N Korea invaded S Korea. **27** US air, naval, and later ground forces supported S Korea.
July 8 Gen MacArthur C-in-C of UN forces in Korea.
August 1 Chinese membership rejected by UN. **7** US offensive in Korea.
September 6 British troops in action in Korea.
October 19 UN forces took Pyongyang. **21** China invaded Tibet. **26** New Chamber of House of Commons opened.
November 26 Chinese offensive into N Korea.
December 4 Chinese took Pyongyang. **19** Gen Eisenhower appointed head of NATO forces.

1951

January 4 N Korean and Chinese troops captured Seoul. **17** French held back Viet Minh offensive in Tonkin.
March 19 Treaty of Paris signed to create European Coal & Steel Community.
April 11 Gen MacArthur replaced by Lt-Gen Ridgway.
May 2 Persian oil industry nationalised. **3** Festival of Britain opened.
June 7 British diplomats Burgess and Maclean vanished.
July 8 Korean ceasefire talks. **16** King Leopold of Belgians abdicated. **20** King Abdullah of Jordan assassinated.
September 1 Tripartite Security Treaty between US, Australia and New Zealand. **8** Japanese peace treaty.
October 16 Pakistan's PM Ali Khan assassinated. **19** British troops seized Suez Canal Zone. **25** Conservatives won General Election: Churchill PM.
December 24 Libya independent.

1952

February 6 George VI died: Accession of Queen Elizabeth II.
March 21 Kwame Nkrumah Gold Coast's 1st PM.
April 23 Japan regained sovereign and independent status.
May 27 European Defence Community Treaty signed.
June 23 US air attack on N Korea hydro-electric plants.
July 23 Military coup in Egypt: later King Faroukh abdicated. **26** Eva Peron died.

A.D.

August 1 Parliament ratified Bonn Agreement: W Germany again independent. **16** Lynmouth floods. **26** S African protests against racial laws.

September 8 Gen Neguib military Gov-Gen of Egypt.

October 3 Britain's 1st atomic bomb test in Monte Bello Is. **20** State of Emergency in Kenya over Mau Mau atrocities.

November 4 Republican Gen Eisenhower won US Presidental Election. **30** US hydrogen bomb test reported.

1953

February 3 E coast floods.

March 5 Stalin died. **14** Krushchev emerged as USSR leader. **24** Queen Mary died. **25** Polio vaccine announced **31** New UN Sec-Gen Dag Hammarskjöld.

April 8 Mau Mau leader Jomo Kenyatta jailed.

May 29 Hillary and Tensing climbed Everest.

June 2 Elizabeth II crowned: ceremony televised. **17** E Berlin anti-Soviet riots. **18** Egyptian republic proclaimed.

July 27 Korean armistice signed.

August 14 Soviet hydrogen bomb test.

November 21 Piltdown skull exposed as hoax. **29** French took Dien Bien Phu.

December 23 Former KGB chief Beria executed.

1954

February 3 1st Central African Federation parliament opened.

March 22 London gold market reopened.

April 18 Nasser took power as Egypt's PM. **21** USSR joined UNESCO.

May 4 Roger Bannister's 4-min mile. **8** Dien Bien Phu fell to Viet Minh. **17** Racial segregation banned in US state schools.

June 2 New Irish PM John Costello. **17** New French PM Pierre Mendès-France.

July 3 Food rationing ended. **21** Sino-French pact to end Indo-China war.

August 5 Persian oil dispute settled.

October 19 Anglo-Egyptian Suez Canal Agreement.

November 1 Algerian nationalist riots.

December 2 Senator McCarthy censured by Congress. **18** Cyprus riots for union with Greece.

1955

February 8 Marshall Bulganin Soviet PM and 1st Sec of Communist Party. **23** New French PM Edgar Fauré. **25** 1st meeting of SEATO.

April 5 Sir Winston Churchill resigned: new PM Sir Anthony Eden. **18** Hungarian PM Imre Nagy dismissed. **24** Afro-Asian Conference of 29 non-aligned nations. **29** Vietnam civil war.

May 5 W Germany attained full sovereignty; Western European Union established. **26** Conservatives won General Election.

June 2 Soviet-Yugoslav relations normalised. **15** UK–US nuclear cooperation agreed.

July 18 "Big 4" Geneva conference.

August 20 Riots in Algeria and Morocco.

September 15 EOKA guerrillas outlawed: British troops in Cyprus. **19** Gen Peron ousted. **22** ITV 1st broadcast.

October 6 New Greek PM Constantine Karamanlis. **20** Syria-Egypt mutual defence treaty. **26** S Vietnam declared independent republic.

November 2 New Israeli PM David Ben-Gurion.

December 7 Clement Attlee resigned. **14** New Labour Party leader Hugh Gaitskell.

1956

January 1 Sudan proclaimed independent republic.

February 25 Khrushchev denounced Stalin. **29** Alabama race riots.

March 2 King Hussein of Jordan dismissed Lt-Gen Glubb, Commander of Arab Legion. **9** Archbishop Makarios deported to Seychelles. **23** Pakistan Islamic Republic within Commonwealth.

April 18 Khrushchev and Bulganin in London.

June 13 British troops left Canal Zone. **23** Nasser elected Pres of Egypt unopposed. **29** Polish anti-Soviet riots.

July 26 Egypt seized Canal Zone.

October 23 Hungarian uprising against Soviet domination. **25** Anti-Soviet Polish unrest. **29**

A.D.

Israel invaded Egypt seizing Sinai peninsula. **31** Anglo-French forces bombed Egyptian targets.

November 1 Premium bonds launched. **4** Soviet tanks crushed Hungarian revolt. **5** Anglo-French troops seized Canal Zone. **6** Pres Eisenhower re-elected. **8** UN Canal Zone ceasefire. **16** Canal blocked. **21** UN troops controlled Canal Zone. **30** Flood of Hungarian refugees.

December 5 140 arrests in S Africa for alleged treason. **7** Anglo-French troops left Port Said.

1957

January 1 Egypt abrogated 1954 Anglo-Egyptian Treaty; Saarland returned to W Germany. **9** Sir Anthony Eden resigned: new PM Harold Macmillan.

February 15 New Soviet Foreign Minister Andrei Gromyko.

March 6 Ghana independent; De Valera won Irish General Election. **25** Treaty of Rome setting up EEC and EAEC (Euratom) signed by Benelux, France, Germany and Italy.

April 8 Suez Canal reopened. **17** Archbishop Makarios in Athens.

May 15 UK's 1st hydrogen bomb test.

June 11 Canada's new Convervative government under John Diefenbaker.

July 8 State of Emergency against IRA proclaimed in Republic of Ireland. **25** Tunisia became republic under Pres Bourguiba.

August 8 Myxomatosis rife. **30** Malaya independent.

September 4 Wolfenden Report published. **15** Chancellor Adenauer re-elected. **23** Asian flu epidemic. **25** National Guard sent in to enforce desegregation in Little Rock, Arkansas.

October 4 Soviet satellite launched. **11** Jodrell Bank radio telescope inaugurated.

November 3 Soviet satellite carrying dog in orbit.

December 19 NATO conference agreed US nuclear bases in Europe.

EUROPEAN INTEGRATION

1958

January 1 Treaty of Rome came into force. **3** British W Indies Federation inaugurated. **28** Turkish Cypriot riots. **31** US satellite launched.

February 1 Syria and Egypt proclaimed United Arab Republic. **6** Munich plane crash: Manchester Utd lost 8 players. **14** Short-lived Jordan–Iraq union. **17** CND founded.

March 2 Dr Vivian Fuchs completed 1st crossing of Antarctica. **8** Yemen entered federation with UAR. **27** Bulganin ousted.

April 4 1st Aldermaston march. **17** Nationalists won S African General Election. **21** Maltese PM Dom Mintoff resigned.

May 13 Algerian French nationalists rebelled. **23** Hovercraft unveiled. **29** Gen de Gaulle returned to power.

June 9 Gatwick airport opened. **20** Greek Cypriots rejected British peace plan.

July 14 King Faisal of Iraq assassinated: republic established. **15** US marines in Lebanon. **17** British troops in Jordan. **24** First life peers announced.

August 5 US nuclear submarine passed under N Pole.

September 2 New S African PM Dr Verwoerd. **9** Notting Hill race riots. **28** French referendum approved Vth Republic.

October 2 EOKA campaign renewed. **9** Pope Pius XII died. **28** Angelo Roncalli elected Pope as John XXIII. **31** 1st heart pacemaker implanted.

December 8 Draft agreement at 3-power Geneva test ban talks. **21** De Gaulle 1st Pres of Vth Republic. **27** Soviet cooperation agreed with Egypt on Aswan dam project. **31** Thalidomide implicated in birth defects.

1959

January 1 Cuba's Batista regime overthrown by Fidel Castro. **12** USSR *Lunik I* satellite 1st to escape Earth's gravity.

February 2 Indira Gandhi leader of India's Congress Party. **23** Archbishop Makarios returned to

A.D.
Cyprus. **26** State of Emergency in S Rhodesia: black nationalist parties dissolved.

March 4 Anti-British riots in Nyasaland: Hastings Banda arrested. **17** Lhasa uprising against Chinese rule: Dalai Lama fled.

May 6 "Cod war" with Iceland. **15** Jodrell Bank transmitted radio message to USA via moon.

June 17 Eamon de Valera voted Ireland's Pres. **26** St Lawrence Seaway opened.

July 5 3 animals recovered safely after Soviet space flight. **18** Castro assumed Cuba's Presidency.

August 18 BMC launched Mini.

September 14 Soviet *Lunik II* landed on moon. **27** Ceylon's PM Bandaranaike assassinated.

October 8 Conservatives won General Election. **26** *Lunik III* sent back photos of dark side of moon.

November 1 Nationalist riots in Belgian Congo. **2** M1 motorway opened. **20** EFTA agreement signed.

December 1 12 nations signed Antarctic Treaty. **3** Fréjus dam disaster. **14** Archbishop Makarios 1st Pres of Cyprus.

1960

January 1 French "new franc" introduced. **29** French settlers' revolt in Algeria.

February 2 De Gaulle granted emergency powers. **3** Harold Macmillan's "Wind of change" speech in Cape Town. **13** French atomic test in Sahara. **29** Agadir earthquake.

March 21 Sharpeville massacre in S Africa: 67 dead.

April 1 Hastings Banda freed. **9** Murder attempt on Dr Verwoerd. **19** Flood of E German refugees. **27** S Korean Pres Synghman Rhee resigned.

May 1 US U-2 military reconnaissance aircraft shot down over USSR. **7** Leonid Brezhnev new Soviet PM. **17** Paris "Big 4" Summit failed; Kariba Dam inaugurated.

June 22 Khrushchev attacked Mao and Chinese policies. **30** Belgian Congo became independent republic of Congo under PM Patrice Lumumba.

July 1 Ghana and Somalia became republics. **6** Congolese army mutiny: whites fled Leopoldville. **11** Katanga declared independence from Congo under Moise Tshombe. **21** Mrs Bandaranaike world's 1st woman PM. **31** Emergency in Malaya officially ended.

August 8 Coup in Laos: new PM Prince Souvanna Phouma. **16** Cyprus declared republic.

September 14 Congolese army took power under Col Mobutu.

October 2 Talks to end "Cod war". **12** Disruptive behaviour from Khrushchev at UN General Assembly. **20** *Lady Chatterley's Lover* trial.

November 9 Democrat John Kennedy elected US Pres. **21** Fighting between Congolese army and UN troops.

December 2 Lumumba arrested; Archbishop of Canterbury met Pope. **31** National Service ended; Farthing abolished.

1961

January 8 Referendum in France and Algeria backed de Gaulle; Portland spy ring arrests.

February 13 Lumumba dead.

March 21 US military aid to Laos. **26** French army rising in Algiers collapsed after 4 days.

April 12 Yuri Gagarin in 1st manned space flight. **19** Cuban exiles in Bay of Pigs invasion. **20** Angolan revolt.

May 1 1st betting shops opened. **5** Alan Shephard made 1st US manned space flight. **17** S Korean military coup. **31** S Africa independent and left Commonwealth.

June 3 Kennedy-Khrushchev Vienna talks. **27** Michael Ramsay enthroned as 100th Archbishop of Canterbury.

August 10 Britain formally applied to join EEC. **13** E Berlin border sealed: later Berlin Wall erected. **14** Kenyatta freed.

September 18 Dag Hammarskjöld killed in Congo plane crash. **30** Syria seceded from UAR.

October 10 Volcanic eruption on Tristan da Cunha: entire population evacuated. **23** 30 megaton Soviet atomic test. **24** Malta independent. **30** Stalin's body moved from Red Sq.

November 7 Adenauer elected Chancellor for 4th term. **28** UN condemned S African apartheid policy.

December 15 Eichmann sentenced to death for

A.D.
crimes against Jewish people. **17** Indian troops invaded Goa and other Portuguese colonies in India.

1962

January 4 More US military aid for S Vietnam. **14** UK smallpox outbreak.

February 8 OAS bomb campaign in France and Algeria.

March 2 Nehru's Congress Party won Indian General Election. **14** Geneva disarmament talks reopened. **15** Liberals won Orpington by-election.

April 8 Algerian peace accord. **13** International agreement on marine pollution. **26** 1st UK satellite *Ariel* launched.

May 10 US troops in Laos. **13** New Indian Pres Dr Radhakrishnan. **25** Coventry cathedral consecrated.

July 1 Commonwealth Immigrants Act came into force. **3** Algeria independent. **10** 1st live tv US-Europe link-up via *Telstar*.

August 22 De Gaulle escaped 4th assassination attempt.

September 3 Trans-Canada highway opened. **27** Yemen proclaimed republic.

October 22 Cuban missile crisis. **28** Soviet missile sites in Cuba to be dismantled. **26** Fighting on China–India border.

November 7 Nelson Mandela jailed for incitement. **20** US Cuban blockade lifted. **21** Ceasefire in China–India border dispute. **26** US Turkish bases to be removed. **29** Anglo-French agreement on Concorde. **30** New UN Sec-Gen U Thant.

December 8 British troops clashed with Brunei rebels opposing Malaysian Federation. **9** Dr Julius Nyrere 1st Pres of Tanganyika. **15** Rightwing victory in S Rhodesian General Election.

1963

January 15 Moise Tshombe finally ended Katanga secession. **18** Hugh Gaitskell died. **22** Franco-German Treaty on political and military cooperation. **29** Britain refused EEC membership; "Kim" Philby disappeared from Beirut.

February 1 Nyasaland self-governing under PM Hastings Banda. **8** Military coup in Iraq: PM Kassim executed. **9** Joshua Nkomo jailed in S Rhodesia. **14** Harold Wilson new Labour leader; 1st successful kidney transplant.

March 8 Military coup in Syria. **27** Beeching Report axed railways. **29** Central African Federation collapsed.

April 6 US–UK Polaris agreement. **8** Liberals won Canadian General Election. **23** New German Chancellor Ludwig Erhart.

May 11 Greville Wynne in Moscow spy trial. **18** Federal troops sent to quell Alabama race riots. **20** Sukarno Life Pres of Indonesia. **25** OAU founded. **27** Kenyatta elected PM in Kenya's 1st General Election.

June 3 John XXIII died. **5** John Profumo, Secretary of State for War, resigned. **6** Martial law in Teheran after Ayatollah Khomeini arrested. **13** Buddhist riots in Saigon. **16** Valentina Tereshkova 1st woman in space. **21** Giovanni Battista Montini elected Pope as Paul VI. **26** Pres Kennedy in W Berlin.

July 22 Stephen Ward on trial in "Profumo affair" aftermath. **26** Skopje earthquake.

August 8 "Great Train Robbery": £2·6m. mailbags stolen. **8** US–UK–USSR test ban treaty. **28** Dr Martin Luther King's "Freedom March" on Washington. **30** Moscow–Washington "hot line" inaugurated.

September 16 Federation of Malaysia created: anti-British riots. **17** Fylingdales early warning missile system operational.

October 1 Nigeria declared republic within Commonwealth. **18** Harold Macmillan resigned: new PM Earl of Home, later Sir Alec Douglas-Home.

November 1 Military coup in S Vietnam. **22** Pres Kennedy assassinated: Vice-Pres Lyndon Johnson sworn in.

December 12 Kenya independent.

1964

January 4 Pope visited Holy Land. **29** Further S Vietnam military coup.

February 11 Turkish–Greek Cypriot fighting.

A.D.
March 19 UN peacekeeping troops in Cyprus.
April 9 Labour won 1st GLC elections. **13** New S Rhodesian PM Ian Smith. **21** BBC-2 on air. **22** Tanganyika and Zanzibar united as Tanzania.
May 27 Nehru died.
June 2 New Indian PM Lal Shastri; PLO founded. **4** Britain's *Blue Streak* rocket launched. **12** Life sentence on Nelson Mandela for treason. **14** Francois Duvallier Haitian Pres-for-Life.
July 2 US Civil Rights Act. **6** Nyasaland independent as Malawi. **10** Congo's new PM Moise Tshombe.
August 2 US destroyer attacked by N Vietnam in Gulf of Tonkin: US air raids in reprisal.
September 2 Indonesian troops landed in Malaysia. **21** Malta independent within Commonwealth.
October 15 Khrushchev deposed: new Communist Party leader Leonid Brezhnev, new PM Kosygin; Labour won General Election: new PM Harold Wilson. **16** Chinese atomic test. **24** N Rhodesia independent as Zambia under Pres Kaunda.
November 1 Vietcong guerrillas attacked US S Vietnamese base. **2** King Saud of Saudi Arabia deposed by brother Faisal. **3** Pres Johnson won US Presidential Election. **17** Arms embargo on S Africa. **26** Belgian paratroopers rescued hostages from Congo rebels.
December 12 Kenya proclaimed republic under Pres Kenyatta.

1965

January 12 Indonesia left UN. **24** Churchill died.
February 7 US air raid on N Vietnam. **24** US bombed Vietcong in S Vietnam.
March 7 US marines in S Vietnam. **18** Soviet cosmonaut made 1st spacewalk. **25** Ceylon's new PM Senanayaka. **28** Alabama civil rights protest. **30** US Saigon embassy bombed.
April 30 US marines in Dominica after military coup.
May 7 Rhodesia Front won Rhodesian General Election. **11** E Pakistan cyclone: 16,000 dead.
June 19 Algerian Pres Ben Bella ousted by Col Boumedienne. **29** US offensive against Vietcong.
July 29 Edward Heath new Conservative leader.
August 9 Singapore seceded from Malaysia. **11** Riots in Watts, Los Angeles.
September 8 India invaded Pakistan after Kashmir fighting: Pakistan air raids on New Delhi and later Bombay. **12** 50,000 more US troops in S Vietnam. **30** UK's 1st woman High Court judge.
October 7 Post Office Tower opened. **17** US and UK anti-Vietnam war protests. **22** India and Pakistan accepted UN ceasefire. **29** Rhodesia conciliation talks failed.
November 11 Rhodesian UDI: Britain declared regime illegal: sanctions imposed. **25** Gen Mobutu deposed Congo's Pres Kasavubu.
December 8 Vatican Council II closed. **17** Rhodesian oil embargo. **19** Pres de Gaulle re-elected.

1966

January 11 Indian PM Shastri died: new PM Indira Gandhi. **15** Army coup in Nigeria. **31** US bombing of N Vietnam resumed: UK Rhodesia trade ban.
February 24 Army coup in Ghana while Pres Nkrumah abroad.
March 31 Labour won General Election.
April 19 Australian troops in Vietnam.
June 30 France left NATO; US bombed Hanoi.
July 20 6-month pay and prize freeze. **30** US bombed Vietnam demilitarised zone; England won World Cup. **31** US urban race riots.
August 11 Indonesia–Malaysia peace agreement. **13** Chinese cultural revolution began.
September 6 Dr Verwoerd assassinated: new S African PM John Vorster. **30** Bechuanaland became independent republic of Botswana; Ancient statues saved from waters of Aswan Dam.
October 4 Basutoland independent as Lesotho; Nigerian tribal fighting. **21** Aberfan coal tip disaster.
November 1 Vietcong shelled Saigon. **9** Florence floods; new Irish PM Jack Lynch.
December 1 Dr Kiesinger new W German Chancellor. **2** Harold Wilson and Ian Smith in inconclusive talks on HMS *Tiger*. **16** UN mandatory oil

A.D.
sanctions against Rhodesia. **22** Rhodesia left Commonwealth.

1967

January 18 New Liberal leader Jeremy Thorpe. **27** Flash fire killed 3 US astronauts during ground test.
February 22 Gen Suharto in power in Indonesia. **26** Major US offensive against Vietcong.
March 9 Stalin's daughter defected to West. **18** *Torrey Canyon* wrecked off Land's End: major pollution. **24** Army coup in Sierra Leone.
April 1 UK's 1st Ombudsman. **14** Conservatives won GLC elections. **21** Greek colonels seized power.
May 11 Britain applied to join EEC. **30** Biafra seceded from Nigeria.
June 5 6 Day War: Israel seized territory from Egypt, Jordan and Syria. **17** 1st Chinese H-bomb test.
July 1 Moise Tshombe arrested when plane hijacked to Algiers; BBC-2 began colour broadcasts. **7** Nigerian troops invaded Biafra. **15** De Gaulle in Quebec. **27** US urban race riots.
August 9 Biafran troops in Nigeria.
September 1 Majority verdicts allowed in UK criminal courts. **3** Swedish traffic switched to right. **20** *QEII* launched.
October 9 Che Guevara killed; New drink-driving laws. **22** Anti-Vietnam war demonstrations in US, UK and W Europe. **25** Abortion Bill passed. **31** Foot-and-mouth disease epidemic.
November 19 £ devalued. **29** Aden independent republic as S Yemen.
December 3 1st successful human heart transplant. **17** Australian PM Harold Holt drowned.

1968

January 5 Alexander Dubcek new moderate Czechoslovak PM. **9** New Australian PM John Gorton. **23** Intelligence ship *USS Pueblo* seized by N Korea. **31** Vietcong Tet offensive against S Vietnam cities: raid on US Saigon embassy.
February 24 US and S Vietnam troops recaptured Hue.
March 6 Black Rhodesians hanged in defiance of Queen's reprieve. **15** Foreign Secretary George Brown resigned. **17** Grosvenor Sq anti-Vietnam war demonstration.
April 4 Martin Luther King assassinated: riots throughout USA. **6** New Canadian Liberal PM Pierre Trudeau. **12** Student riots throughout Europe after shooting of W German student leader Rudi Dutschke. **21** Enoch Powell's immigration speech.
May 5 Student riots in Paris began. **9** Soviet troops on Czech border. **16** Ronan Point tower block collapsed. **19** French General Strike. **30** De Gaulle dissolved National Assembly and called General Election.
June 5 Robert Kennedy assassinated. **30** De Gaulle won landslide victory in French General Election.
July 1 Last EEC customs barriers removed; 36 nations signed Nuclear Non-Proliferation Treaty. **10** Couve de Murville succeeded Pompidou as French PM. **29** Papal encyclical against artificial contraception.
August 22 Warsaw Pact troops invaded Czechoslovakia.
September 11 Soviet tanks left Prague. **16** UK 2-tier postal system. **26** Theatre censorship abolished. **27** France vetoed UK EEC membership.
October 4 Warsaw Pact troops to remain in Czechoslovakia. **6** Londonderry riots against sectarian discrimination. **9** HMS *Fearless* Rhodesia talks failed.
November 1 US halted bombing of N Vietnam. **5** Republican Richard Nixon won US Presidential Election. **7** Prague anti-Soviet demonstrations.
December 27 3 US astronauts completed 10 orbits of moon.

1969

January 3 N Ireland sectarian violence. **19** Student Jan Palach set himself on fire in Wenceslas Sq in anti-Soviet protest.
February 2 Yasser Arafat PLO leader.
March 2 Soviet–China border clashes. **17** New Israeli PM Golda Meir. **19** British troops in

A.D.

Anguilla. **25** Pres Ayub Khan ousted by army coup under Gen Yahya Khan.

April 17 More troops sent to N Ireland; Dubcek replaced as Czech Communist Party leader by Gustav Husak. **18** Bernadette Devlin, civil rights worker, elected in Mid-Ulster by-election, UK's youngest MP. **23** Nigerian troops took Umuahia. **28** De Gaulle resigned after referendum defeat. **29** N Ireland PM Terence O'Neill resigned.

May 1 New N Ireland PM Maj James Chichester-Clark.

June 8 Spain closed Gibraltar border. **15** New French Pres Georges Pompidou: PM Jacques Chaban-Delmas.

July 1 Prince of Wales invested at Caernarvon. **21** Neil Armstrong and "Buzz" Aldrin 1st men on moon; Sen Edward Kennedy in court over Chappaquiddick drowning. **22** Gen Franco named Prince Juan Carlos as future Spanish King.

August 12 3 days of riots in Londonderry after Apprentice Boys' March. **15** British troops took over N Ireland security.

September 1 King Idris of Libya deposed by army revolutionaries under Muammar Gaddafi: republic proclaimed. **3** Ho Chi Minh died. **10** 7,000 troops in N Ireland. **24** Ton Duc Thang new N Vietnamese Pres. **28** Army erected Belfast "peace line": barricades dismantled: traffic curfew.

October 1 Olaf Palme Swedish PM. **10** N Ireland "B Specials" disbanded. **12** Troops used tear gas in N Ireland. **14** 50p coin issued. **15** "Vietnam moratorium" in USA. **21** New W German Chancellor Willi Brandt.

November 2 Starvation in Biafran refugee camps: Nigeria banned Red Cross aid.

December 18 UK death penalty permanently abolished.

1970

January 1 UK age of majority 18. **12** Biafra capitulated. **16** New Libyan PM Gaddafi; UK Hong Kong flu epidemic.

February 9 Equal Pay Bill passed in Commons. **11** Decentralisation of NHS announced.

March 1 US planes bombed "Ho Chi Minh trail" in E Laos. **2** Rhodesia declared republic. **18** Cambodia's Prince Sihanouk ousted. **19** 1st meeting between E and W German leaders.

April 2 Battle between Israeli and Syrian troops. **8** Israeli air raid on Nile delta village. **16** Clifford Dupont 1st Pres of Rhodesia. **17** *Apollo 13* crew rescued. **30** US troops in Cambodia.

May 4 4 student anti-war protesters shot dead at Kent State University, Ohio.

June 7 Jordan troops attempted to expell Palestinian guerrillas. **19** Conservatives won General Election: new PM Edward Heath. **26** Dubcek expelled from Communist Party. **30** UK, Denmark, Ireland and Norway opened talks on EEC entry.

August 2 1st use of rubber bullets in N Ireland. **30** Malayan PM Tengku Abdul Rahman resigned.

September 4 New Chilean Pres Socialist Salvador Allende. **12** Palestinian terrorists blew up 3 hijacked airliners in Jordan desert: 56 hostages held. **14** Palestinian guerrillas in control of N Jordan and Jordan's 2nd city Irbid. **22** New Malayan PM Abdul Razak. **27** Jordan–PLO truce signed in Cairo: PLO expelled from Jordan. **28** Nasser died. **30** All Western hostages freed in exchange for terrorists held by UK, W Germany and Switzerland.

October 5 New Egyptian Pres Anwar Sadat; Quebec separatists kidnapped British diplomat. **10** Quebec Minister Pierre Laporte kidnapped. **16** Trudeau outlawed FLQ and invoked emergency powers. **18** Laporte found dead. **19** Major oil find in N Sea by BP.

November 9 De Gaulle died. **13** Defence Minister Gen Assad seized power in Syria. **20** E Pakistan tidal wave: 150,000 dead.

December 3 Kidnapped British diplomat freed. **7** Pakistan's 1st free elections: Zulfikar Ali Bhutto victorious in W, Sheikh Mujibur Rahman in E.

December 14 Anti-government riots in Poland's Baltic ports: Communist Party leader Gomulka replaced by Gierek.

1971

January 1 Divorce Reform Act in force. **2** Ibrox Park football disaster. **3** Open University inaugu-

A.D.

rated. **8** British ambassador to Uruguay kidnapped by Tupamaros guerrillas. **15** Aswan High Dam inaugurated. **25** Ugandan Pres Obote ousted by army coup under Idi Amin.

February 4 Rolls-Royce bankrupt; Swiss women given vote in national elections. **9** 1st British soldier killed in N Ireland. **15** UK decimal day. **20** Idi Amin Uganda's self-appointed Pres.

March 23 New N Ireland PM Brian Faulkner. **26** Sheikh Mujibur Rahman declared E Pakistan independent as Bangladesh: civil war erupted: Rahman jailed. **29** Lt Calley found guilty of My Lai massacre.

April 5 Thousands dead in E Pakistan fighting. **10** Split between "official" and "provisional" IRA. **18** UAR, Syria and Libya formed Federation of Arab Republics. **22** Jean Claude Duvallier succeeded as Haitian Pres.

May 3 Erich Honeker Gen Sec of E German Communist Party. **13** Labour took over GLC. **14** 2m E Pakistan refugees in India. **28** Egypt–USSR friendship treaty.

June 6 Cholera epidemic in W Bengal: border with Bangladesh sealed. **15** Education Sec Mrs Thatcher announced end of free school milk. **30** 3 Soviet cosmonauts dead at end of space flight.

July 20 Anglo-Maltese defence talks collapsed.

August 10 Internment without trial in N Ireland: riots and firebomb attacks. **22** Right-wing coup in Bolivia.

September 9 British ambassador freed in Uruguay. **24** 90 Soviet diplomats expelled as spies. **27** Chequers talks on N Ireland between 3 PMs.

October 25 China admitted to UN. **27** Congo changed name to Zaire. **28** Parliament voted to join EEC. **31** IRA bomb at PO Tower.

November 23 India–Pakistan border fighting. **24** Rhodesia agreement signed.

December 3 Pakistan declared war on India. **6** India recognised Bangladesh. **7** Libya nationalised £80m BP assets. **17** Pakistan agreed ceasefire. **20** New Pakistan PM Zulfikar Ali Bhutto. **21** New UN Sec-Gen Kurt Waldheim. **26** US resumed N Vietnam bombing.

1972

January 9 Miners' strike. **12** Sheikh Mujibur Rhaman PM of Bangladesh. **13** Ghana coup led by Col Acheampong. **20** UK unemployment passed 1m. **22** Treaty of Brussels signed to admit UK, Denmark, Ireland and Norway to EEC. **30** "Bloody Sunday": army shot 13 Derry marchers dead; Pakistan left Commonwealth.

February 2 British embassy in Dublin burned down. **16** Widespread prolonged power cuts as miners' crisis deepened: State of Emergency declared. **22** IRA Aldershot bomb: 7 dead. **25** Miners ended strike.

March 4 2 killed, 146 injured by Belfast restaurant bomb. **21** 6 died in Belfast shops bombing. **30** Direct rule imposed in N Ireland; N Vietnamese offensive.

April 10 46 nations signed convention to ban biological warfare. **14** US retaliatory bombing of Hanoi and Haiphong. **18** Bangladesh joined Commonwealth.

May 3 Hue evacuated. **9** Israeli troops freed 92 hostages and killed Black September guerrillas at Lydda airport. **16** Segregationist Gov Wallace of Alabama crippled by gunman. **22** Ceylon became republic of Sri Lanka. **28** Duke of Windsor died. **30** Brezhnev–Nixon talks. **30** Tel Aviv airport massacre by PFLP; Official IRA agreed ceasefire.

June 16 5 burglars caught in Watergate building, Democrat campaign HQ; W German Red Army Faction guerrillas captured. **22** Provisional IRA ceasefire. **23** £ floated.

July 1 Pres Nixon's campaign manager resigned. **14** N Ireland ceasefire failed. **31** "Operation Motorman": army dismantled N Ireland barricades.

August 6 50,000 Ugandan Asians expelled to UK. **11** Last ground troops left Vietnam. **20** S Vietnamese troops retreated.

September 1 New Icelandic fishing limit 50 miles. **5** Black September guerrillas killed Israeli athletes at Munich Olympics, kidnapped others: hostages, 5 guerrillas and policeman killed in airport gun battle. **12** Icelandic gunboat sank 2 British trawlers.

October 5 United Reformed Church formed. **13** Bank rate abolished (new term MLR).

A.D.

November 6 Government froze prices, pay, rent and dividend increases for 90 days. **7** Pres Nixon re-elected. **19** Chancellor Brandt re-elected. **20** Silver Wedding of Queen and Prince Philip.

December 2 Gough Whitlam 1st Australian Labor PM since 1946. **18** US resumed bombing of N Vietnam. **21** Treaty between W and E Germany. **23** Nicaraguan earthquake devastated Managua.

1973

January 1 UK, Ireland and Denmark joined EEC. **27** Vietnam ceasefire signed.

February 1 EEC Common Agricultural Policy came into effect. **5** 1st Loyalists detained without trial in N Ireland. **12** 1st US prisoners released by N Vietnam. **21** Israeli fighters brought down Libyan Boeing 727: 104 dead.

March 1 Fine Gael and Labour coalition won Irish General Election: new PM Liam Cosgrave. **8** 2 bombs in central London. **9** N Ireland referendum: 591,820 in favour of retaining UK links. **11** French General Election: Gaullists and allies won absolute majority.

April 1 VAT introduced in UK.

May 7 Pres Nixon denied all knowledge of Watergate. **10** Elections for 36 new metropolitan district councils. **18** Royal Navy frigates sent to protect British trawlers in disputed 50-mile limit off Iceland. **31** Erskine Childers succeeded Pres de Valera of Eire.

June 1 Greece declared republic. **7** Skylab astronauts freed solar panels saving mission. **21** Mr Brezhnev and Pres Nixon signed arms limitation agreement.

July 31 1st sitting of N Ireland Assembly ended in chaos.

August 2 Summerland fire at Douglas, IOM. **19** George Papadopoulos 1st Pres of Greece.

September 3 Dr Henry Kissinger new US Secretary of State. **7** Len Murray new TUC General Secretary. **11** Allende government overthrown in Chile. **14** King Gustav of Sweden died. **20** Chelsea barracks bombed.

October 6 Arab–Israeli war began. **8** UK's 1st commercial radio station opened. **10** US Vice Pres Spiro Agnew resigned. **12** Gen Peron new Pres of Argentina with his wife as Vice Pres **16** Government embargo on arms sales to Middle East. **17** Arab oil producers cut supplies until Israel withdrew from occupied territories. **22** UN ceasefire agreed by Israel, Egypt and Jordan. **31** 3 Provisional IRA leaders freed from Mountjoy prison by hijacked helicopter.

November 8 UK–Iceland "cod war" ended. **12** Miners began overtime ban and ambulance drivers selective strikes. **14** Wedding of Princess Anne and Capt Mark Phillips. **25** Army coup in Greece.

December 5 50 mph speed limit imposed to conserve fuel. **6** Gerald Ford new US Vice Pres. **12** Rail drivers union ASLEF began overtime ban. **20** Spain's PM Admiral Carrero Blanco assassinated. **31** 3-day week imposed.

1974

January 1 Direct rule in N Ireland ended: new N Ireland Executive took office; Golda Meir won Israeli General Elections. **8** Lord Carrington Energy Secretary at head of new department. **9** Commons debate on energy crisis. **18** Israel and Egypt agreed withdrawal of forces. **22** Loyalists expelled from N Ireland Assembly.

February 10 Miners strike began. **28** UK General Election: no clear majority.

March 4 Edward Heath resigned: new minority Labour government. **9** UK resumed 5-day week. **11** Miners returned to work.

A.D.

April 10 Golda Meir and Cabinet resigned. **14** Fighting on Golan Heights and Mt Hermon. **24** S African General Election: Nationalist party won. **25** Army uprising in Portugal: regime in power since 1926 overthrown.

May 6 Chancellor Brandt resigned on discovery of E German spy in Chancellery. **15** Gen Spinola new Pres of Portugal; Israeli troops stormed village school in Ma'alot where children held hostage by Arab terrorists. **16** Herr Schmidt new W German Chancellor. **19** Giscard d'Estaing won French General Election. **28** N Ireland Executive collapsed: direct rule from Westminster resumed.

June 1 Flixborough chemical works explosion. **3** New Israeli PM Mr Rabin.

July 1 Death of General Peron. **9** Pierre Trudeau won Canadian General Election. **13** Senate Watergate Committee Report. **15** Pres Makarios overthrown in Cyprus coup. **17** Bomb at Tower of London. **18** Statutory incomes policy ended. **20** Turkish invasion of Cyprus. **24** Supreme Court ordered surrender of 64 White House tape recordings. **26** Greek junta collapsed: Mr Karamanlis returned to power. **27** 3 articles of impeachment adopted by Judiciary Committee of House of Representatives against Pres Nixon.

August 6 Pres Nixon resigned. **9** Gerald Ford sworn in as US Pres.

September 8 Emperor Haile Selassie deposed. **30** New Portuguese Pres Gen da Costa Gomes.

October 5 Guildford pub bombings: 2 dead, 70 hurt. **10** Labour won UK General Election: overall majority of 3. **15** Riots at Maze prison.

November 2 Vladivostock Summit between Pres Ford and Mr Brezhnev. **7** Woolwich pub bombings: 2 dead. **17** Mr Karamanlis won 1st Greek General Election since 1967. **21** Birmingham pub bombings: 21 dead, 120 hurt. **29** Anti-Terrorism Act proscribing IRA.

December 3 Defence cuts announced. **7** Archbishop Makarios returned to Cyprus. **18** Wave of bombs in London. **25** Cyclone devastated Darwin.

1975

January 1 Watergate defendants found guilty. **24** Dr Coggan enthroned 101st Archbishop of Canterbury. **25** Shaikh Mujibur Rahman new Pres of single party state in Bangladesh.

February 11 Mrs Thatcher elected leader of Conservative Party. **13** Turkish Cypriots declared separate state.

March 13 Portugal's new Supreme Revolutionary Council took power. **25** King Faisal of Saudi Arabia assassinated. **26** S Vietnamese troops evacuated Hué and Da Nang.

April 17 Phnom Penh government surrendered to Khmer Rouge. **21** Pres Thieu resigned as N Vietnamese troops encircled Saigon. **25** 1st elections in Portugal for 50 years. **30** Vietnam War ended.

June 5 Referendum on membership of European Community: UK in favour by 2:1 majority. **5** Suez Canal reopened. **12** Mrs Gandhi convicted of illegal use of government officials in 1971 campaign.

July 1 S S Ramphal the new Commonwealth Secretary-General. **29** Military coup in Nigeria: new Head of State Brig Murtala Mohammed.

August 7 Hottest-ever August day in London. **15** Pres Rahman of Bangladesh assassinated. **27** Bombings in Caterham and London.

September 9 Prince Sihanouk returned to Cambodia. **24** Government steps to check unemployment.

October 3 Dutch industrialist kidnapped in Limerick. **15** Iceland extended fishing rights to 200

A.D.
miles. **21** UK unemployment over 1m. **26** Battles in Beirut between Christian Phalangists and left-wing Muslims.

November 3 Queen formally inaugurated North Sea oil. **11** Angolan independence; Australian Governor-General dismissed Labor government. **22** Prince Juan Carlos crowned King of Spain.

December 4 Detention without trial ended in N Ireland. **10** "Cod war" began. **11** IRA Balcombe St siege in London. **14** Liberal Country Party won Australian General Election. **18** Education Bill compelling comprehensive education published. **29** Sex Discrimination and Equal Pay Acts came into force.

1976

January 19 Commons Devolution debate.

February 11 MPLA recognised as Angola's legal government by OAU. **13** Nigerian Pres Murtala Mohammed assassinated.

March 5 Ulster Convention dissolved: direct rule continued. **16** Harold Wilson resigned. **24** Senora Peron of Argentina deposed. **25** Basil Hume enthroned as Archbishop of Westminster.

April 5 New PM James Callaghan.

May 10 Jeremy Thorpe resigned Liberal leadership. **28** Soviet–US treaty on underground nuclear explosions.

June 1 "Cod war" ended. **16** Riots in African township Soweto near Johannesburg. **24** Vietnam reunified.

July 2 Government emergency powers to control water shortage. **4** Israeli raid on Entebbe airport to free 100 hostages. **7** David Steel new Liberal leader. **10** Explosion at Hoffman-La Roche plant at Seveso: contamination over 7km radius. **14** Official handing-over to Tanzania and Zambia of Chinese-built Tanzam railway. **21** UK ambassador to Ireland assassinated. **28** Earthquake destroyed Tangshan, China.

August 25 PM Chirac of France resigned.

September 2 European Commission on Human Rights found Britain guilty of torture in N Ireland. **10** Zagreb air collision. **20** Sweden's Social Democratic Party ousted after 20 years. **24** Ian Smith accepted UK and US proposals for Rhodesian majority rule.

October 3 Bishop Muzorewa returned to Rhodesia from exile. **4** British Rail high-speed train entered service. **6** Military coup in Thailand. **25** National Theatre officially opened. **28** Geneva conference on Rhodesia's future.

November 1 Jimmy Carter elected Pres of USA. **15** Formal end of Lebanon's civil war: Syrian peacekeeping troops in Beirut.

December 16 Michael Manley won Jamaican General Election. **17** Vladimir Bukovsky, Soviet dissident, and Senor Corvalán, Chilean Communist veteran, exchanged.

1977

January 1 EEC extended fishing limits to 200 miles. **24** Rhodesia talks collapsed.

February 15 1976 deaths exceeded live births for 1st time. **17** Uganda's archbishop and 2 Cabinet ministers killed in mysterious circumstances.

March 1 James Callaghan's government went into minority. **7** Zulfikar Ali Bhutto won Pakistan election. **22** Mrs Gandhi resigned after election defeat. **23** Lib-Lab pact: no-confidence vote defeated. **24** New Indian PM Moraji Desai and Janata Party government sworn in. **27** Tenerife airport disaster.

April 21 Martial law in Pakistan. **22** Ekofisk Bravo oilfield disaster.

A.D.
May 13 N Ireland 11-day strike collapsed. **17** Menachem Begin's Likud Party won Israel election. **18** International Commission of Jurists reported Ugandan atrocities.

June 1 New UK road speed limits. **7** Silver Jubilee celebrations in London. **11** 11-day S Moluccan sieges ended in Holland. **15** 1st Spanish elections since 1936, won by PM Suarez's Union of Democratic Centre. **16** Fianna Fail won Irish General Election.

July 5 Pakistan army deposed PM Bhutto. **21** Mrs Bandaranaika's Sri Lanka Freedom Party defeated.

August 10 Panama Canal Agreement concluded. **13** Violence at Lewisham National Front march. **25** Scarman Report on Grunwick dispute.

October 31 Effective revaluation of £.

November 4 Mandatory UN arms embargo on S Africa. **14** Firemen's strike. **15** Son for Princess Anne. **19** Egyptian Pres Sadat and Israeli PM Begin met in Israel; Bay of Bengal cyclone killed 25,000. **30** National Party won S African General Election.

December 10 Malcolm Fraser's Conservative coalition won Australian General Election: Labor leader Gough Whitlam resigned. **21** OPEC froze oil prices.

1978

January 1 Air India plane crash off Bombay. **4** PLO London representative shot dead. **25** Government defeat on Scottish devolution. **29** Rhodesia talks in Malta with Joshua Nkomo and Robert Mugabe.

February 4 Ethiopian Ogaden offensive. **19** Egyptian commandos stormed hijacked plane at Larnaca.

March 3 Internal settlement agreed in Rhodesia between Ian Smith and 3 black Nationalist leaders. **8** New Italian PM Giulio Andreotti. **15** Israeli thrust into S Lebanon. **16** Aldo Moro, 5 times Italy's PM, kidnapped and murdered; *Amoco Cadiz* aground off Brittany: massive pollution.

April 3 1st regular radio broadcasts from Parliament. **10** Transkei, 1st tribal homeland to gain independence, cut diplomatic links with S Africa. **17.** No cases of smallpox anywhere during previous year. **26** Arab terrorist attack on bus on West Bank. **27** Afghanistan's Pres Daoud deposed in pro-Soviet coup.

May 1 1st UK May Day Bank Holiday. **24** Princess Margaret and Lord Snowdon divorced.

June 3 New Bangladeshi Pres Gen Zia ur-Rahman. **12** Provisional IRA leader Seamus Twomey sentenced in Dublin.

July 5 Ghanaian Pres Acheampong resigned. **9** Former Iraqi PM Gen Razzale al-Naif shot in London. **25** World's 1st "test tube" baby born. **31** Lib-Lab pact ended.

August 6 Pope Paul VI died. **13** Beirut PLO HQ bombed. **22** Gunmen held hundreds hostage in Nicaraguan parliament. **26** Cardinal Albino Luciani of Venice elected as Pope John Paul I.

September 8 Martial law in Tehran. **11** Martial law in Nicaragua. **16** Earthquake in Iran killed 11,000. **17** Camp David talks between Pres Sadat and PM Begin concluded framework for Middle East peace treaty. **28** Pope John Paul I died; New S African PM Pieter Botha.

October 10 New Kenyan Pres Daniel arap Moi. **15** Cardinal Karol Wojtyla of Cracow 1st non-Italian Pope for 450 years as John Paul II. **20** 4-week siege of Beirut lifted.

November 25 National Party won New Zealand

A.D.
General Election. **26** Clashes in Iran during 24-hour general strike. **27** Japanese PM Fukuda resigned. **30** Publication of *The Times* suspended until 13 Nov 1979.

December 17 OPEC announced oil price rise. **20** Israeli attack on Lebanese terrorist bases.

1979

January 1 New Iranian PM Dr. Bakhtiar. **4** Guadeloupe Summit between UK, US, W Germany and France. **7** Phnom Penh captured by Vietnamese and rebel troops. **15** Road haulage strike. **16** Shah left Iran. **17** UK admitted Vietnamese refugees. **30** Rhodesian whites-only referendum: 6:1 in favour of transfer to majority rule.

February 1 Ayatollah Khomeini returned to Iran from exile in Paris. **5** New Iranian PM Dr Bazargan. **14** "Concordat" between government and TUC. **15** Army take-over in Chad. **28** Final meeting of white Rhodesian House of Assembly.

March 1 Scots voting in favour of devolution failed to reach 40 % requirement: Welsh voted overwhelmingly against devolution. **13** Government of Grenada overthrown. **26** Israel–Egypt peace treaty signed. **28** Radiation leak at Three Mile Island nuclear plant, Pennsylvania. **30** Shadow N Ireland Secretary Airey Neave assassinated. **31** Final withdrawal of British navy from Malta.

April 1 Islamic Republic in Iran. **2** 1st visit of)Israeli PM to Egypt. **4** Former Pakistani PM Bhutto executed. **11** Kampala captured by Tanzanian troops and Ugandan exiles: new Ugandan leader Prof Yusofo Lule. **23** 1 died, 300 arrested in clashes at Southall National Front march.

May 3 UK General Election: Margaret Thatcher 1st woman PM: Conservative overall majority 43. **16** Government removed legal obligation towards comprehensive education. **22** Joe Clark's Progressive Conservatives formed minority Canadian government. **29** Bishop Muzorewa Zimbabwe Rhodesia's 1st black MP.

June 4 S African Pres Vorster resigned after "Muldergate" scandal. **11** Conservatives won UK European elections. **18** Pres Carter and Pres Brezhnev signed SALT II treaty. **20** Ugandan Pres Lule deposed. **22** Jeremy Thorpe acquitted in Old Bailey conspiracy trial.

July 13 Abortion Law tightened. **17** Pres Somoza fled Nicaragua.

August 18 Heart transplant carried out at Papworth Hospital near Cambridge. **19** Former Cambodian leader Pol Pot convicted in his absence of murder of 3m people. **27** Earl Mountbatten killed by bomb on boat in Sligo.

September 10 London talks on Zimbabwe Rhodesia constitution. **19** 3-party non-Socialist coalition won Swedish elections. **20** Emperor Bokassa of Central Africa Empire ousted. **26** UK compulsory metrication abandoned. **29** 1st-ever Papal visit to Eire.

October 1 Civilian rule restored in Nigeria. **17** El Salvador colonels imposed martial law. **19** ITV strike ended. **23** Foreign exchange controls removed.

November 1 Military coup in Bolivia. **4** Iranian students occupied US embassy in Tehran. **9** US computer fault led to full-scale nuclear alert. **14** Iranian assets in US frozen.

December 5 Dutch Parliament rejected NATO's Cruise missile plan. **11** New Irish PM Charles Haughey. **12** NATO approved stationing of US missiles in Europe. **21** Rhodesian treaty signed. **27** Afghanistan's Pres Amin ousted in Soviet-backed coup.

1980

January 7 Mrs Gandhi's Congress Party won

A.D.
Indian General Election. **22** Dr Andrei Sakharov, winner of 1975 Nobel peace prize, sent into USSR internal exile. **27** Israel–Egypt border reopened.

February 12 Publication of Brandt Report "North South". **18** Pierre Trudeau won Canadian General Election.

March 4 Robert Mugabe's ZANU(PF) party formed government with absolute majority in Zimbabwe Rhodesia. **24** Archbishop Romero shot dead at altar in San Salvador. **25** Robert Runcie enthroned as Archbishop of Canterbury. **27** Oil accommodation rig overturned in North Sea.

April 2 Riots in St Pauls area of Bristol. **3** 13-week steel strike ended. **9** Israeli troops moved into Lebanon. **13** US Olympic Committee voted to boycott Moscow Games. **18** Rhodesia became independent as Zimbabwe. **25** Unsuccessful attempt to free US hostages in Iran. **30** Queen Beatrix of the Netherlands invested.

May 5 SAS stormed besieged Iranian embassy in London. **18** Mount St Helens erupted.

June 22 Liberals won Japanese General Election. **23** Sanjay Gandhi, son of Indian PM, died in plane crash.

July 17 Military coup in Bolivia. **19** Moscow Olympics opened.

August 13 French fishermen blockaded Channel ports.

September 7 Hua Guofeng resigned as Chinese leader: replaced by Zhao Ziyang. **10** Libya and Syria to merge as unitary Arab state. **22** Outbreak of Iran–Iraq War.

October 5 Helmut Schmidt re-elected W German Chancellor. **10** Algerian earthquake: 4,000 dead. **15** James Callaghan resigned as Labour leader. **18** Liberal and Country coalition won Australian General Election. **23** Soviet PM Kosygin resigned. **24** Polish independent trade union Solidarity recognised by Polish authorities. **27** Hunger strike at Maze prison.

November 4 Ronald Reagan elected Pres of USA. **10** New Labour leader Michael Foot. **23** Earthquake in S Italy.

December 8 Dublin Summit between Mrs Thatcher and Charles Haughey; John Lennon shot dead in New York. **15** Dr Milton Obote sworn in as Ugandan Pres. **17** Prof Alan Walters appointed PM's personal economic adviser.

1981

January 1 Greece joined EEC. **20** US hostages left Iran. **21** Sir Norman Stronge and his son, former Stormont MPs, killed by IRA. **25** Roy Jenkins, Shirley Williams, William Rodgers and David Owen launched Council for Social Democracy; Mao's widow Jiang Qing convicted. **27** Joshua Nkomo appointed Minister without Portfolio in attempt to prevent Zimbabwe confrontation.

February 3 Norway's first woman PM Dr Gro Harlem Brundtland. **12** Rupert Murdoch bought *The Times*. **23** Failed military coup in Spain.

March 26 Social Democratic Party born. **30** Pres Reagan shot outside Hilton Hotel in Washington.

April 5 Pres Brezhnev in Czechoslovakia talks on Polish crisis. **11** Brixton riots.

May 9 Bomb exploded at Sullum Voe during Royal inauguration. **10** François Mitterrand won French Presidential Election. **13** Pope shot by Turkish gunman. **22** Peter Sutcliffe convicted of Yorkshire Ripper murders. **30** Bangladeshi Pres Zia ur-Rahman assassinated.

June 8 Israeli planes destroyed Iraqi nuclear reactor. **10** 8 IRA prisoners escaped from Crumlin Rd jail. **13** Blanks fired at Queen during

A.D.
Trooping of Colour. **16** Liberal-SDP alliance announced. **21** Socialists won French General Election. **22** Ayatollah Khomeini dismissed Iran's Pres Bani-Sadr. **30** PM Begin secured continuation of Israeli coalition government; New Irish PM Dr Garret FitzGerald.

July 3 Southall race riots. **4** Toxteth riots. **15** Red Cross to mediate at Maze prison. **29** Wedding of Prince Charles and Lady Diana Spencer.

August 20 MLR suspended. **25** S African troops crossed into Angola. **30** Iran's Pres and PM killed by bomb.

September 1 Army take-over in Central African Republic. **18** France abolished capital punishment.

October 4 Maze hunger strike ended. **6** Pres Sadat assassinated. **10** IRA bomb in Chelsea: 2 dead. **14** New Egyptian Pres Hosni Mubarak. **18** Gen Jaruzelski new leader of Polish Communist Party. **26** Oxford St IRA bomb killed disposal expert.

November 6 Anglo-Irish Intergovernmental Council agreed. **14** Unionist MP Rev Robert Bradford shot dead.

December 8 Arthur Scargill new leader of National Union of Mineworkers. **11** Javier Perez de Cuellar new UN Secretary-General. **13** Martial law in Poland. **14** Israel annexed Golan Heights. **19** Penlee lifeboat lost during rescue attempt.

1982

January 4 EEC rejected USSR and Poland sanctions. **26** UK unemployment reached 3m.

February 5 Laker Airways collapsed. **19** De Lorean car company failed.

March 9 Charles Haughey new Irish PM. **16** Pres Brezhnev froze deployment of Soviet missiles in Europe. **18** Argentinians in S Georgia to dismantle whaling station raised Argentinian flag. **19** 3-year ban on England cricketers in unofficial S African tour. **24** Martial law in Bangladesh after coup.

April 2 Argentina invaded Falkland Is. **5** Lord Carrington and 2 Foreign Office ministers resigned: new Foreign Secretary Francis Pym. **25** British troops recaptured S Georgia; Israel handed over Sinai to Egypt.

May 2 Argentine cruiser *General Belgrano* sunk in British attack. **4** British destroyer HMS *Sheffield* hit by Exocet missile. **7** Britain extended total exclusion zone to within 12 miles of Argentine coast. **15** British commando raid on Argentine airstrip at Pebble I. **21** British troops established bridgehead at San Carlos. **28** Paratroops captured Goose Green and Darwin; Papal visit to UK.

June 3 Israeli ambassador shot in London. **4** Israel bombed Beirut's Palestinian quarter. **6** British took Bluff Cove and Fitzroy. **7** Argentine raid on *Sir Tristram* and *Sir Galahad* off Bluff Cove. **14** Falklands ceasefire. **17** Argentinan Pres Gen Galtieri ousted. **21** Prince William of Wales born. **23** Labour National Executive acted against Militant Tendency. **25** New US Secretary of State George Shultz.

July 1 New Argentinian Pres Gen Bignone. **2** Roy Jenkins new SDP leader. **20** IRA bombs in Hyde Park and Regent's Park.

August 4 Israeli tanks invaded W Beirut. **12** Ceasefire in Lebanon. **17** China and US agreed Taiwan policy. **21** PLO guerrillas left Beirut.

September 14 Princess Grace of Monaco died; Lebanese leader Bashire Gemayal killed by bomb. **17** Palestinian refugees killed in W Beirut camps. **19** Swedish Social Democrats won General Election.

October 1 New W German Chancellor Christian Democrat leader Helmut Kohl. **8** Polish govern-

A.D.
ment dissolved Solidarity. **11** Tudor warship *Mary Rose* raised. **21** SDLP and Sinn Fein refused to take seats won in Ulster Assembly election. **28** Socialists elected in Spain. **31** Thames barrier inaugurated.

November 1 Channel 4 TV opened. **10** Soviet leader Leonid Brezhnev died: new leader Yuri Andropov. **24** El Al went into liquidation. **25** Ireland's new government formed by Fine Gael and Labour coalition.

December 6 Bomb at bar in Ballykelly killed 16. **12** 30,000 women ringed Greenham Common missile base in protest.

1983

January 25 EEC agreed common fishing policy. **31** New UK seat belt law.

February 9 Derby winner Shergar stolen in Co Kildare.

March 5 Labor Party won Australian General Election. **6** Christian Democrats won W German General Election. **22** New Israeli Pres Chaim Herzog.

April 18 US embassy in W Beirut bombed: many dead. **21** New UK £1 coin. **24** Austrian Chancellor Dr Bruno Kreisky resigned. **26** 8 famine relief workers kidnapped in Ethiopia by Tigré People's Liberation Front.

May 1 Demonstrations in 20 Polish cities. **16** 1st use of wheel clamps by London police. **17** Israel-Lebanon agreement on troop withdrawal. **18** State of Emergency in Sri Lanka. **23** S African raids on Maputo.

June 9 Conservative majority of 144 in UK General Election. **13** New SDP leader David Owen. **14** All-party Commons defence committee endorsed "Fortress Falklands" policy. **15** New Speaker of Commons Bernard Weatherill. **16** Mr Andropov elected Soviet Pres. **24** Syria expelled PLO leader Yasser Arafat.

July 3 Home of former Ulster MP Gerry Fitt burnt out by IRA. **15** 6 killed by bomb at Orly airport. **16** 20 killed in helicopter crash near Scilly Is.

August 4 Italy's 1st Socialist PM since 1946 Bettino Craxi. **5** Lebanese mosque explosion: 19 dead. **11** Chad town Faya-Largeau fell to Libyan troops. **14** French troops in NE Chad. **21** Philippine opposition leader shot dead at Manila airport. **31** S Korean airliner disappeared near Japan: USSR later admitted shooting it down.

September 4 Israeli army withdrew from Chouf mountains above Beirut. **15** Israeli PM Begin resigned. **23** Abu Dhabi air crash: 112 dead. **25** 38 IRA prisoners escaped from Maze prison: prison officer stabbed to death. **26** *Australia II* won America's Cup.

October 2 New Labour leader Neil Kinnock. **10** New Israeli government led by Yitzhak Shamir. **14** Cecil Parkinson resigned. **19** Grenada's PM Maurice Bishop shot by troops: Gen Hudson Austin in control. **23** Suicide bombers killed 229 US marines and 58 French paratroops in Beirut. **25** Troops from US and 6 Caribbean states invaded Grenada. **30** Radical Party leader Raul Alfonsin won Argentine General Election.

November 3 S African white minority voted to give limited representation to Asians and Coloureds. **12** New leader of Irish Republican movement Gerry Adams. **14** 1st Cruise missiles at Greenham Common. **15** Turkish Cypriot UDI under Rauf Denktash. **16** Yasser Arafat retreated to Tripoli. **21** Unionist Party withdrew from N Ireland Assembly in protest at Darkley Gospel Hall killings. **23** USSR quit Geneva disarmament talks. **26** £26m Heathrow bullion robbery. **27** Air crash near Madrid: 181 dead. **28** European space lab launched at Cape Canaveral.

December 6 1st UK heart–lung transplant. **7** Official Unionist Edgar Graham shot dead at

A.D.
Queen's University Belfast. **10** Bomb at Woolwich barracks. **15** NGA industrial action ended. **17** Harrods bomb: 6 dead, many injured. **31** Military coup in Nigeria: new leader Maj-Gen Mohammed Buhari.

1984

January 9 Share prices exceeded 800 on FT index. **20** £1m Christie's diamond robbery. **25** Government ban on union membership at GCHQ.

February 5 Lebanese Cabinet resigned. **8** British peacekeeping troops left Lebanon followed by French, Italians and US. **9** Soviet Pres Andropov died: succeeded by Konstantin Chernenko. **15** Druze and Shi'ite militiamen drove Lebanese army from S Beirut. **29** Canadian PM Pierre Trudeau resigned.

March 12 Miners strike against pit closures. **15** £5m Woburn Abbey silver robbery. **20** UK blamed for collapse of EEC Summit. **23** Foreign Office clerk jailed for leaking documents to *The Guardian*.

April 3 Coup in Guinea after death of Pres Sekou Touré. **17** WPC Yvonne Fletcher shot dead outside Libyan embassy: 10-day siege.

May 7 Christian Democrat Napoleon Duarté won Salvadorean Presidential election. **8** USSR and Warsaw Pact countries boycotted Olympics. **13** Angolan rebels freed 16 hostages. **18** IRA killed 4 members of security forces. **23** Lancs underground pumping station explosion: 15 dead.

June 1 Pres Reagan visited Ireland; Mrs Thatcher and PM Botha in Chequers talks. **5** US increased military role in Gulf. **6** Sikh fanatics in Golden Temple of Amritsar surrendered to Indian army: leader died. **14** UK European elections: Conservatives kept majority. **16** New Canadian Liberal Party leader and PM John Turner. **20** Education Secretary announced new GCSE examinations.

July 9 York Minster fire. **12** Robert Maxwell acquired Mirror Group newspapers. **13** Labour Party won New Zealand General Election. **17** French government resigned. **25** Soviet cosmonaut 1st woman to walk in space. **29** Los Angeles Olympics opened.

August 21 S African Coloured elections won by Labour Party: many arrests. **26** Wakefield salmonella outbreak. **31** TUC backed pit strike.

September 3 Riots in Transvaal townships. **4** Conservatives won Canadian General Election: new PM Brian Mulroney. **5** New Israeli government of national unity; TUC rejoined Neddy. **20** US Beirut embassy bombed. **26** Sino-British declaration on Hong Kong's future.

October 12 IRA bomb at Grand Hotel, Brighton. **23** Violence in S African townships. **30** Kidnapped Polish priest Fr Popieluszko found dead; Famine in Ethiopia. **31** Indian PM Mrs Gandhi assassinated by Sikh bodyguard: new PM her son Rajiv.

November 6 New Nicaraguan Pres Daniel Ortega. **6** Pres Reagan re-elected. **19** Mexico City gas explosion: 600 dead.

December 1 Labor Party won Australian General Election. **3** Leak of poison gas from pesticide factory in Bhopal, India: 2,500 dead, thousands blinded; Massive gains in 1st day's trading in British Telecom shares. **18** Local authorities told to cut capital spending by £1bn in 1985. **28** Rajiv Gandhi won Indian General Election

THE END OF THE COLD WAR

1985

January 3 12,000 Ethiopian Jews airlifted to Israel. **15** Civilian Pres for Brazil. **20** Tamil bomb on Sri Lankan train: 36 dead. **23** 1st House of Lords debate televised. **29** Oxford University refused PM honorary degree.

A.D.
February 4 Spain–Gibraltar border reopened. **18** Riots at Crossroads shanty town, S Africa. **19** S African anti-apartheid leaders arrested. **20** PM addressed joint session of US Congress. **25** £ at record low against $. **28** IRA bombed Newry police station.

March 3 Miners' strike ended. **4** New Zealand PM reaffirmed ban on nuclear weapons. **8** Beirut car bomb: 80 dead. **10** Pres Chernenko died: succeeded by Mikhail Gorbachev. **12** Geneva arms control talks. **15** Belgian government agreed to deploy Cruise missiles. **21** 19 blacks shot dead in Uitenhage on Sharpeville anniversary.

April 6 Sudanese Pres Numeiri deposed by army. **11** Tamil bomb killed 24 in Colombo just prior to Mrs Thatcher's arrival.

May 1 US trade ban on Nicaragua; Ethiopia's largest famine relief camp cleared by troops. **10** Pres Reagan froze defence spending. **11** Bradford City FC fire: 55 dead. **15** Sri Lankan Tamil terrorists killed 146. **22** Fighting in Beirut. **24** Tidal wave swamped Bangladesh islands: thousands dead. **29** 38 killed when wall collapsed at Heysel stadium, Brussels, before Liverpool v Juventus match.

June 10 Israel completed withdrawal from Lebanon. **12** Shi'ite gunmen blew up Jordanian aircraft after releasing hijack hostages.

July 2 New USSR Foreign Minister Eduard Schevardnadze. **3** Robert Mugabe won Zimbabwe General Election. **10** Greenpeace ship *Rainbow Warrior* sunk in Auckland, NZ. **13** Live Aid concert for African famine relief. **19** Dam collapse at Stava, Italy: 260 dead. **21** S African State of Emergency. **27** Ugandan Pres Obote ousted.

August 12 Japanese Boeing 747 crashed near Tokyo: 524 dead. **17** E Beirut car bomb killed 54. **22** Manchester airport disaster: 54 dead. **27** Nigerian government ousted.

September 9 Riots in Handsworth, Birmingham. **11** S African citizenship restored to 8m blacks in tribal homelands. **17** Chancellor Kohl's secretary defected to E Berlin. **28** Brixton riots.

October 1 Israeli air raid on PLO's Tunisian HQ. **6** Policeman killed in riots on Broadwater Farm estate, Tottenham. **7** Italian cruise ship *Achille Lauro* hijacked by PLO. **20** Commonwealth leaders agreed measures against S Africa.

November 2 S African government controls on media riot coverage. **14** W Colombian volcano erupted: 20,000 dead. **15** N Ireland agreement signed by Mrs Thatcher and Dr Garret FitzGerald. **21** Reagan–Gorbachev Summit. **24** Egyptian commandos stormed hijacked Boeing in Malta.

December 5 UK to withdraw from UNESCO. **6** UK to participate in US Strategic Defence Initiative (SDI). **13** Westland helicopters in deal with US and Italian consortium. **27** Terrorist attacks on Israeli check-in desks at Rome and Vienna airports.

1986

January 7 Pres Reagan cut economic links with Libya. **9** Michael Heseltine and later Leon Brittan resigned over Westland affair: George Younger new Defence Secretary. **20** Anglo-French twin tunnel Channel rail link agreed. **24** N Ireland by-elections due to mass resignation of MPs. **26** *Sunday Times* and *News of the World* printed at Wapping despite print union action. **28** *Challenger* shuttle crashed on take-off.

February 7 Jean-Claude Duvalier left Haiti. **16** Mario Suares won Portuguese Presidential Election. **25** Mrs Corazon Aquino took power in Philippines. **28** Swedish PM Olof Palme assassinated.

March 2 Legal independence for Australia. **12** New Swedish PM Ingvar Carlsson. **16** New French PM

A.D.
Jacques Chirac. **24** US navy destroyed missile battery on Gulf of Sidra. **31** GLC and 6 Metropolitan councils abolished.

April 15 US bombed Benghazi and Tripoli in retaliation for Libyan terrorism. **17** 2 UK hostages killed in Lebanon. **26** Major accident at Chernobyl nuclear power plant, USSR: 19 deaths, radioactive cloud over Scandanavia. **30** Police invaded Golden Temple at Amritsar.

May 19 S African commando attacks on Zimbabwe, Zambia and Botswana.

June 6 Chief Constable of W Yorks to replace John Stalker in N Ireland "shoot-to-kill" inquiry. **8** New Austrian Pres Dr Kurt Waldheim. **12** Renewed State of Emergency in S Africa. **20** S Africa legalised 180-day detention without trial; Ban on sheep movement in Cumbria and N Wales due to radiation. **27** EEC Summit called for release of Mandela and recognition of ANC; International Court of Justice ruled US support for Nicaraguan Contras illegal.

July 6 Liberal Democratic Party won Japanese General Election. **22** Commons voted to ban corporal punishment in schools. **23** Prince Andrew named Duke of York on marriage to Sarah Ferguson. **25** Appeal Court banned publications by former MI5 officer Peter Wright.

August 5 Commonwealth sanctions against S Africa. **7** Ulster loyalist mob crossed border into Eire. **18** Mr Gorbachev announced unilateral freeze on nuclear testing. **25** Gas escape from volcanic crater in Cameroon: 1,500 dead.

September 1 Soviet cruise liner sank after collision: 400 dead. **5** Commandos stormed hijacked PanAm jet at Karachi. **16** Kinross goldmine fire in Transvaal: 177 dead.

October 2 US sanctions against S Africa. **7** *The Independent* newspaper launched; New state-funded city technology colleges announced. **12** Reagan–Gorbachev Summit collapsed over Star Wars programme; Queen visited China. **19** Pres Samora Michel of Mozambique killed in S Africa plane crash: new Pres Joaquim Chissano. **20** New Israeli PM Likud leader Yitzhak Shamir. **21** Conservative Party deputy chairman Jeffrey Archer resigned. **27** "Big Bang" day in City: computer failed. **29** Final section of M25 opened.

November 10 EEC (except Greece) backed sanctions against Syria. **13** Pres Reagan admitted arms sales to Iran. **24** Barclays Bank pulled out of S Africa. **25** John Poindexter and Col Oliver North dismissed over sale of arms to Contras.

December 1 DTI investigation into Guinness affair. **23** Dr Andrei Sakharov returned to Moscow.

1987

January 12 Rate Support Grant settlement: cuts of up to 30% imposed on 20 local authorities. **16** General Secretary of Chinese Communist Party Hu Yaobang resigned. **20** Archbishop of Canterbury's special envoy Terry Waite kidnapped in Beirut. **25** Chancellor Kohl's centre-right coalition won German election. **27** Mr Gorbachev offered Soviet people choice of election candidates: criticism of Brezhnev era.

February 10 140 political prisoners released in USSR. **12** Peaceful Moscow human rights demonstration dispersed violently. **22** 4,000 Syrian troops in W Beirut to enforce peace.

March 6 Zeebrugge ferry disaster: 193 dead. **10** Ireland's new PM Charles Haughey.

April 13 9 trains set alight in Soweto. **25** Lord Justice Gibson and Lady Gibson killed by N Ireland car bomb.

May 1 Government abandoned plan to dump nuclear waste. **5** Congressional hearing into Irangate affair. **6** National Party won S African whites-only election: 1m blacks on protest strike.

A.D.
14 Coup led by Lt-Col Sitiveni Rabuka in Fiji. **17** USS *Stark* hit by Iraqi Exocet: 37 dead. **26** US authorised Kuwaiti tankers in Gulf to fly US flag; Sri Lankan government offensive to recapture Jaffna Peninsula. **29** German Matthius Rust landed in Red Sq; S African commandos attacked Maputo targets.

June 1 Lebanese PM Rashid Karami murdered. **11** UK General Election: Conservatives won 3rd term with 101 majority. **12** Princess Anne created Princess Royal. **15** Christian Democrats won Italian General Election.

July 3 Former Gestapo chief Klaus Barbie found guilty of crimes against humanity. **13** Labor Party won Australian General Election. **17** France and Iran cut diplomatic relations. **20** Social Democrats won Portuguese General Election. **29** Indo–Sri Lankan peace accord signed: Colombo riots.

August 6 David Owen resigned as SDP leader after party voted to open merger talks with Liberals. **12** Pres Reagan accepted responsibility for Iran-Contra affair: no knowledge of diversion of funds. **17** Suicide of Rudolf Hess. **19** Hungerford massacre: 16 dead. **27** Pres Aquino crushed 5th coup in 18 months. **29** New SDP leader Robert Maclennan.

September 3 Bangladesh monsoon: 24m homeless. **4** UN Security Council endorsed Iran–Iraq peace plan. **5** Israeli air raid on Palestinian refugee camp: 40 dead. **7** Lebanese kidnappers released W German hostage. **9** Iraqi air raids on Iran. **23** Home Secretary ended sale of arms to Iran.

October 1 Los Angeles earthquake: 7 dead; 5 foreign tankers attacked in Gulf. **6** Fiji declared a republic. **15** Coup in Burkina Faso; US-protected supertanker hit by Iranian Silkworm missile. **16** Hurricane in S England: 19 dead. **17** Indian army crushed Jaffna rebels. **19** "Black Monday": London and NY shares crashed. **22** Iran attacked Kuwait oil loading terminal. **26** Lord Mackay succeeded Lord Havers as Lord Chancellor.

November 1 Deng Xiaoping resigned from Chinese Politburo: replaced by Zhao Ziyang. **5** Former ANC chairman Govan Mbeki released after 23 years. **8** Enniskillen Remembrance Day bomb: 11 dead. **11** Moscow reformist leader Boris Yeltsin dismissed; Arab Summit declared support for Iraq. **18** King's Cross fire: 31 dead. **24** US and USSR agreed to scrap intermediate range nuclear weapons.

December 8 Pres Reagan and Mr Gorbachev signed INF agreement. **16** Roh Tae Woo won allegedly rigged S Korean Presidential Election. **17** Milos Jakes succeeded Czechoslovakian Pres Husak. **20** Manila ferry disaster: 2,000 drowned. **29** Space record of 11 months by Soviet cosmonaut. **31** Robert Mugabe executive Pres of Zimbabwe: Joshua Nkomo 1 of 2 Vice Pres.

1988

January 3 Mrs Thatcher longest-serving 20th century UK PM. **4** Purchases by W German and Japanese banks halted US $ slide. **8** Further Wall St crash. **11** Secret Belfast talks between SDLP and Sinn Fein. **17** Leslie Manigat won Haitian General Election amid protests.

February 2 3 women abseiled into Lords in Clause 28 protest. **5** 2 UN relief workers kidnapped in Lebanon. **7** W Bank and Gaza strip violence. **14** PLO officials killed by bomb in Limassol. **16** Prevention of Terrorism Act made permanent. **17** US Lt-Col William Higgins kidnapped in S Lebanon. **21** New Cyprus Pres George Vassiliou.

March 1 31 dead in riots in Azerbaijan city Sumga'it: Soviet tanks moved in. **3** Liberals and SDP formed Social & Liberal Democrats. **6** 3 IRA members shot dead in Gibraltar after bomb plan uncovered. **10** Prince Charles' friend Hugh Lindsay killed by avalanche: Prince escaped. **14** Gulf War flared; Israel imposed curfew in Gaza and W Bank. **16** Loyalist gunman killed 3 at IRA

A.D.
funeral. **17** US troops in Honduras. **18** State of Emergency in Panama. **19** 2 British soldiers lynched in vicinity of Republican funeral. **25** Government review of justice in N Ireland. **28** S African commandos killed 4 in Botswana.

April 4 3,000 Indian troops moved to Pakistan border. **5** Kuwait Airways 747 hijacked to Mashad, Larnaca, then Algiers. **7** ANC lawyer Albie Sachs injured by car bomb in Mozambique. **10** 80 killed in Islamabad and Rawalpindi arsenal fire. **14** Geneva accord on withdrawal from Afghanistan. **15** PLO military commander Abu Jihad murdered. **17** Iraq recaptured Faw peninsula. **18** John Demjanjuk found guilty on Treblinka charges. **22** Kanak militants rioted in New Caledonia.

May 1 IRA killed 3 British servicemen in Holland. **2** Israeli elections in Lebanon rounded up Palestinian guerrillas. **8** Pres Mitterrand re-elected: new French PM Michel Rocard. **10** Coalition re-elected in Denmark. **17** Commandos stormed Golden Temple. **22** Hungarian Communist Party leader ousted. **27** Syrian troops moved into Shi'ite S Beirut. **29** Moscow Summit: Pres Reagan and Mr Gorbachev signed INF treaty.

June 2 Mine disaster in Borken, W Germany. **10** Millenium of Christianity celebrated in USSR; S Africa extended press curbs. **15** IRA bomb killed 6 soldiers at Lisburn fun-run. **19** Haitian coup: civilian leader fled. **21** Toronto Economic Summit. **23** IRA shot down army helicopter at Crossmaglen; EEC agreed farm price freeze. **26** A320 airbus crash at French air show. **27** 57 dead in Gare de Lyon train crash.

July 1 Communist Party conference approved Gorbachev's democratising proposals. **3** USS Vincennes shot down Iranian airbus "by mistake": 200 dead. **5** Former priest held in Brussels over IRA arms procurement. **6** Explosion on North Sea oil rig Piper Alpha: 170 dead. **12** Nagorno-Karabakh's Armenian majority voted to leave Azerbaijan. **19** Soviet team at Greenham Common for missile check. **22** New EEC Commissioner Leon Brittan. **23** 3 killed by IRA landmine intended for Justice Higgins. **25** Ne Win retired as leader of Burma's ruling Socialist Party after 26 years; UN Gulf peace talks. **28** New SLD leader Paddy Ashdown.

August 1 Bomb at N London barracks killed soldier. **6** Train crash at Gare de l'Est: SNCF Chairman resigned. **8** Iran-Iraq ceasefire; Soviet troops withdrew from Kabul. **11** 6,000 North Sea seals died from canine distemper. **12** Burmese leader Sein Lwin resigned after week of violence: 1,000 dead. **17** Pakistan's Pres Zia killed in plane explosion. **21** 24,000 massacred in Burundi. **22** Allday opening in English and Welsh pubs. **25** Heart of Lisbon gutted by fire. **28** Ramstein air disaster. **31** Nelson Mandela suffering from TB.

September 3 Lee Kuan Yew won Singapore's General Election. **6** Kurdish leader's appeal to UN to intervene against genocide. **7** 2 stranded cosmonauts landed successfully. **12** W German hostage freed in Beirut. **14** Papal Mass pilgrims held hostage in Maseru: S African troops stormed bus. **17** Seoul Olympics opened. **18** Further coup in Burma. **19** Polish PM resigned. **20** New Pres of UN General Assembly Argentina's Dante Caputo. **22** Lebanon's Pres Gemayal appointed Christian PM. **31** Mr Gorbachev new Soviet Pres.

October 2 Estonian Popular Front founded. **6** State of Emergency in Algiers. **9** Serb protests in Yugoslavia. **10** Czechoslovakian PM resigned. **19** Ban on broadcast interviews with pro-violence groups in N Ireland. **20** Criminals' right to silence abolished in N Ireland. **28** Police crushed Prague rally.

November 8 George Bush won US Presidential Election. **10** Hungary legalised political opposition parties. **14** Agreement to end Sudan civil war. **21** Brian Mulroney won Canadian General Election. **22** State of Emergency in Azerbaijan. **23** "Sharpeville 6" reprieved. **24** Police clashed with students in Westminster student loans

A.D.
protest. **27** US banned PLO leader. **30** New Pakistani PM Benazir Bhutto.

December 4 Edwina Currie, junior Health Minister, in "salmonella in eggs" row. **7** Yasser Arafat voiced Palestinian recognition of Israel's existence; Disastrous Armenian earthquake: Pres Gorbachev abandoned US trip. **12** Clapham rail crash. **21** PanAm jumbo jet crashed on Lockerbie: 281 killed: caused by terrorist bomb. **22** Namibian independence accord signed by S Africa, Cuba and Angola. **29** Rajiv Gandhi on 1st working visit to Pakistan by Indian PM for 28 years.

1989

January 4 US jets shot down 2 Libyan MiGs. **7** Emperor Hirohito of Japan died. **8** Boeing 737 crashed on M1 embankment near Kegworth, Leics. **18** 1st steps towards legalisation of Solidarity. **20** Nagorno-Karabakh under Moscow's direct control. **31** White Paper proposed market-orientated NHS.

February 3 Alfredo Stroessner ousted in Paraguay after 35 years: replaced by Gen Rodriguez; Michael Manley won Jamaican General Election. **14** Ayatollah Khomeini ordered execution for blasphemy of Salman Rushdie, author of The Satanic Verses. **21** Leading Czech playwright Vaclav Havel jailed; 2 of Winnie Mandela's bodyguards charged with murder of young activist.

March 2 EC agreed to ban CFCs by 2000. **7** China imposed martial law in Lhasa. **24** Exxon Valdez aground off Alaska: 12m gallons oil spilt. **26** Soviet General Election: many senior officials defeated: Moscow victory for Boris Yeltsin.

April 14 Georgia's Communist leader, Pres and PM resigned. **15** 95 Liverpool supporters crushed to death in Hillsborough disaster; Death of Hu Yaobang sparked Beijing student riots.

May 13 Briton Jackie Mann kidnapped in Beirut. **14** Peronist Carlos Menem won Argentine General Election.

June 2 Tiananmen Sq massacre. **3** Ayatollah Khomeini died. **4** Solidarity won Polish elections. **15** Labour won UK European elections.

July 5 Pres Botha met Nelson Mandela. **19** Gen Jaruzelski executive Pres of Poland. **21** Burmese opposition leader Aung San Suu Kyi under house arrest. **24** Cabinet re-shuffle: Geoffrey Howe deputy PM and Leader of Commons, John Major Foreign Secretary.

August 1 1st Cruise missiles left Greenham Common. **14** Pres Botha resigned: acting S African Pres F W de Klerk. **23** Independence demonstration in Baltic states. **24** 1st non-communist Polish PM for 45 years.

September 6 Pres de Klerk's National Party won S African General Election. **11** Hungary opened border allowing E German refugees to escape. **13** Huge peaceful anti-apartheid protest in Cape Town. **18** Hungary announced transition to democracy. **19** Vietnamese army left Cambodia.

October 1 Thousands of E German refugees escaped through Warsaw and Prague embassies. **2** E Germany closed borders after demonstrations for reform. **4** Soviet workers given right to strike. **13** ANC's Walter Sisulu released after 25 years. **16** CITES banned ivory trade to save African elephant. **17** San Francisco earthquake. **18** E German leader Erich Honecker resigned: succeeded by Egon Krenz. **19** "Guildford 4" released. **26** Chancellor of Exchequer Nigel Lawson resigned: new Chancellor John Major, Douglas Hurd Foreign Secretary.

November 8 E German cabinet and politburo resigned. **9** E Germany opened borders to West: demolition of Berlin Wall began. **10** Bulgarian Communist leader Zhivkov ousted. **12** SWAPO won Namibian General Election. **17** Violent anti-government demonstration in Prague. **23** S African troops withdrew from Namibia after 74 years.

A.D.
24 Communist leader Milos Jakes and Czechoslovak politburo resigned. **28** Soviet parliament restored Azerbaijan's powers over Nagorno-Karabakh. **29** Indian PM Rajiv Gandhi resigned.

December 1 Czechoslovakia began demolition of Iron Curtain along Austrian border; E German Communist Party voted away monopoly of power. **3** Malta Summit: Pres Bush and Pres Gorbachev declared end of Cold War. **6** Egon Krenz resigned. **7** Lithuanian parliament abolished guarantee of Communist supremacy. **10** Czechoslovak Pres Husak resigned. **14** E German Stasi disbanded. **16** Huge violent demonstration against Romanian Pres Ceausescu in Timisoara. **20** US troops invaded Panama. **23** Fighting in Romania. **25** Ceausescus executed. **26** Ion Iliescu Pres of National Salvation Front government and Romania's provisional leader. **28** Alexander Dubcek Chairman of Czechoslovak Federal Assembly: Vaclav Havel, playwright and human rights activist, Pres until elections; Bulgarian demonstration for democracy; Lithuania launched USSR's 1st multiparty system; Latvia abolished Communist power monopoly.

THE CHANGING WORLD ORDER
AFTER COMMUNISM

1990

January 3 Manuel Noriega surrendered to US troops. **11** Independence rally in Vilnius; Armenian parliament voted itself the right to veto Soviet laws. **15** Bulgaria abolished Communist monopoly rule. **22** Yugoslavia's Communist Party voted to abolish Party's monopoly of power. **25** Hurricaneforce winds battered S of England: 46 died.

February 1 New coalition government in Bulgaria **2** 30-year ban on ANC lifted. **5** Temporary Government of National Responsibility in E Germany. **7** Soviet Communist Party abolished monopoly rule. **11** Nelson Mandela freed after 25 years. **13** Conference of World War II allies and E and W Germany ("4 + 2") agreed German reunification formula.

March 6 Soviet parliament passed law sanctioning private property. **11** Lithuania's Supreme Council proclaimed independence. **18** Right-wing Alliance for Germany won E German General Election. **21** Namibian Independence celebrated. **23** Mongolia abolished Communist monopoly of power. **30** Estonian parliament proclaimed start of transition to independence. **31** Violence at massive anti-Community Charge demonstration in London.

April 11 Teesside Customs & Excise officers detained steel cylinders ("supergun") bound for Iraq. **15** Right-wing coalition formed Slovenian government. **19** Pres de Klerk rescinded 2 laws central to apartheid.

May 4 Latvia declared independence. **13** Baltic States Summit requested independence talks with Pres Gorbachev. **20** Romanian elections: NSF won huge victory. **27** First free elections in Poland for 50 years. **29** Boris Yeltsin elected Pres of Russian republic; Opposition League for Democracy, led by Aung San Suu Kyi, won Burmese elections.

June 1 Pres Bush and Pres Gorbachev signed accord on reduction of nuclear missiles. **7** Warsaw Pact Summit pledged radical transformation. **8** First free Czechoslovakian elections for 44 years: Russian parliament voted its laws to take precedence over those of USSR. **12** Russian Federation formally proclaimed sovereignty. **20** Chancellor of Exchequer John Major proposed new currency unit, the Ecu, backed by EMF. **22** Checkpoint Charlie in Berlin Wall removed.

July 6 NATO Summit agreed joint peace declaration with Warsaw Pact countries. **10** Pres Gorbachev re-elected Leader of Soviet Communist Party. **12** Boris Yeltsin resigned from Soviet Communist Party. **16** Ukraine issued declaration of sovereignty. **20** IRA bomb at Stock Exchange. **27** Belorussia declared itself a sovereign state within

A.D.
USSR. **30** Ian Gow MP killed by IRA bomb. **31** Estonia seceded from USSR.

August 2 Iraqi forces invaded Kuwait. **6** Pretoria Minute: political prisoners freed, ANC hostilities suspended. **7** US ships, planes and troops in Gulf as part of multi-national defence force. **8** Iraq annexed Kuwait; Leader of Winnie Mandela's bodyguard sentenced to death for murder of teenage activist. **20** Western hostages in Kuwait held at military bases and potential targets. **24** Irish hostage Brian Keenan released. **31** E and W Germany signed unification treaty.

September 1 Boris Yeltsin demanded resignation of Soviet government. **4** Prime Ministers of N and S Korea met for the first time. **10** All Cambodian factions accepted peace formula to end civil war. **12** 4 Allied Powers of World War II signed Treaty handing back full sovereignty to single united German state. **26** Soviet parliament agreed bill on freedom of conscience and religious practice.

October 3 Germany celebrated reunification. **8** UK joined ERM. **24** Pakistan General Elections: Benazir Bhutto's PPP defeated. **25** Crash of Polly Peck International. **28** EC agreed 2nd stage of economic and monetary union: Britain alone in dissent.

November 1 Sir Geoffrey Howe resigned from Cabinet; Communist Party swept from power in Soviet Georgia. **9** Mary Robinson Ireland's first woman and youngest-ever President. **17** Pres Gorbachev presented constitutional reforms giving him increased powers and reinforcing Federal Council. **21** CSCE conference closed with signing of Charter of Paris for a New Europe. **22** Mrs Thatcher resigned. **25** Nationalist parties in Bosnia-Herzegovina won first free elections for 52 years. **27** John Major won Conservative leadership. **28** New Cabinet included Norman Lamont as Chancellor of Exchequer, Michael Heseltine Environment Secretary. **29** UN resolution to use force against Iraq.

December 2 Chancellor Köhl won German elections. **6** Saddam Hussein announced immediate release of all foreign hostages. **9** Lech Walesa won Polish Presidential election. **13** Oliver Tambo, ANC President, in S Africa after 30-year exile. **20** Soviet Foreign Minister Eduard Shevardnadze resigned.

1991

January 1 Fierce fighting in Mogadishu. **7** Soviet paratroopers in Baltic states. **8** Lithuanian PM Kasimiera Prunskiene resigned. **13** Soviet troops seized TV centre in Vilnius: 14 dead, thousands defended Parliament buildings: Boris Yeltsin and Baltic Presidents in UN appeal. **17** Huge air and missile attack on Iraq by US, British and Saudis, to liberate Kuwait in Operation Desert Storm. **18** Scud missile attacks on Israel. **19** Key Baghdad buildings damaged by missiles. **25** Iraq released millions of gallons of Kuwait oil into Gulf. **29** Nelson Mandela and Chief Buthelezi made peace.

February 1 Repeal of remaining S African apartheid laws. **7** IRA attack on Downing St. **10** Lithuanian referendum in favour of independence. **13** US missiles destroyed Baghdad bunker: 300 civilians killed. **20** Statue of Enver Hoxha toppled in Tirana: Pres Alia announced new government. **22** Iraqis set fire to Kuwait's oil installations. **24** Ground war for liberation of Kuwait began. **26** Kuwait City liberated. **27** Allied ceasefire in Gulf War.

March 3 Peace agreement between Allies and Iraq; Estonian and Latvian referendum in favour of independence. **4** S Iraq towns occupied by Shia Muslim resistance. **14** "Birmingham 6" released. **15** Kurdish guerrillas claimed control of Kurdistan. **17** Referendum on future of united USSR: minimal victory for Pres Gorbachev.

April 9 Soviet Georgia declared independence. **15** European Bank for Reconstruction & Development launched. **23** New Council Tax unveiled to replace Poll Tax.

A.D.

May 5 Virtual civil war between Serbs and Croats. **13** Winnie Mandela found guilty on kidnap and assault charges. **19** Croatian referendum in favour of independence. **21** Rajiv Gandhi assassinated; Pres Mengistu of Ethiopia fled. **26** First-ever Presidential elections in USSR held in Georgia. **29** Ethiopian People's Revolutionary Democratic Front in control in Addis Ababa.

June 5 Pres Bendjedid of Algeria postponed elections, and dismissed government. **9** Mt Pinatubo in Philippines erupted. **13** Boris Yeltsin elected Russian Pres. **17** Congress (I) Party won Indian General Election; S Africa formally abolished apartheid. **25** Slovenia and Croatia declared independence. **26** "Maguire 7" convictions overturned.

July 1 Warsaw Pact disbanded. **4** UK–China agreement on new Hong Kong airport. **5** Bank of Commerce & Credit International (BCCI) collapsed. **6** ANC's first National Congress ended with Nelson Mandela as new Pres and democratically-elected National Executive. **20** Boris Yeltsin banned Communist Party in factories, offices and local government. **22** John Major launched Citizens' Charter.

August 8 British hostage John McCarthy released. **19** Pres Gorbachev deposed in dawn coup: Emergency Committee of 8 hardliners in control: Yeltsin denounced coup. **21** Estonia and Latvia declared independence: 3 killed outside Russian parliament: coup collapsed. Yeltsin assumed control of Soviet troops: Pres Gorbachev reinstated: Soviet troops withdrew from Lithuania. **24** Pres Gorbachev resigned as Communist Party leader, and dissolved Party organisation: Ukraine declared independence. **25** Armenia, Georgia and Belorussia declared independence. **26** Vukovar in E Croatia besieged by Serbs and Yugoslav troops. **28** Central Committee of KGB dissolved. **29** Soviet Parliament voted to curtail Pres Gorbachev's power. **30** Azerbaijan, Kirghizia and Uzbekistan declared independence.

September 3 Nagorno-Karabakh declared independence from Armenia. **5** Pres Gorbachev made sweeping constitutional changes. **9** Leningrad formally reverted to former name, St Petersburg; Macedonian citizens voted for independence. **15** Pro-democracy party won Hong Kong's first election. **24** British hostage Jackie Mann released. **26** Romanian government resigned. **30** Military coup in Haiti: Pres Aristide fled.

October 2 Dubrovnik besieged. **13** Communists ousted in Bulgarian multi-party elections. **30** Middle East peace conference in Madrid. **31** Pres Kaunda defeated in Zambia's 1st multi-party presidential election by Victor Chiluba.

November 5 Body of Robert Maxwell found in sea off Canary Is. **8** EC sanctions on Yugoslavia; Forcible repatriation of Vietnamese boat people. **18** Hostage Terry Waite released; Gen Aideed took control in Mogadishu. **25** "Tottenham 3" freed; Poland's 1st democratic Sejm for 50 years.

December 1 Ukrainian referendum in favour of independence. **4** Hostage Terry Anderson released; £600m missing from Mirror Group pension fund. **8** Leaders of Russia, Ukraine and Belorussia agreed new Commonwealth of Independent States, and declared USSR defunct. **10** Maastricht Summit agreed Treaty of European Union: Britain obtained exclusive opt- out clauses on single currency and social charter. **19** Australian Labor Party voted to replace PM Bob Hawke with Paul Keating, former Treasurer. **20** Opening of Convention for a Democratic S Africa (CODESA). **21** 8 former Soviet republics joined CIS. **25** Pres Gorbachev resigned as Pres of USSR. **26** Soviet parliament met for last time.

1992

January 1 New UN Secretary-General Boutros Boutros Ghali. **12** Algerian Higher Security Council cancelled elections and introduced martial law. **16** Mohammed Boudiaf returned to

A.D.

Algiers as Leader of Council of State. **27** Maxwell pension funds wound up with loss of millions of pounds. **30** Taoiseach Charles Haughey resigned.

February 6 Croatian Pres Tudjman accepted plan for UN peacekeeping force. **11** Albert Reynolds new Taoiseach. **19** N and S Korea declared end to 40-year confrontation. **29** Bosnia-Herzegovina referendum in favour of independence.

March 4 Algeria banned Islamic Salvation Front. **5** CODESA agreed outline of power-sharing interim government. **10** Eduard Shevardnadze Pres of Interim State Council to rule Georgia. **17** S African referendum in favour of Pres de Klerk's moves to end apartheid; UN peacekeeping troops in Croatia. **31** UN arms embargo on Libya.

April 3 Pres Alia of Albania resigned. **6** Fierce fighting in and around Sarajevo between Muslims and Serbs; EC recognised Bosnia. **9** General Election: Conservative majority of 21 and record-breaking 4th term of office. **10** IRA bombs in London: 3 dead. **11** Cabinet re-shuffle: Kenneth Clarke Home Secretary, Michael Heseltine Trade & Industry Sec, Malcolm Rifkind Defence Sec. **13** Neil Kinnock resigned Labour leadership. **27** Betty Boothroyd 1st-ever woman Speaker of Commons. **29** Los Angeles riots: 44 dead.

May 5 EC monitors withdrew from Sarajevo. **19** Serbian troops held 3,500 women and children hostage in Bosnia. **27** Mortar bombs in Sarajevo marketplace: 16 dead.

June 18 Kevin and Ian Maxwell charged with conspiracy to defraud. **20** Czech and Slovak political parties agreed to split Czechoslovakia into 2 separate states. **23** Yitzhak Rabin's Labour Party won Israeli General Election. **29** Pres Boudiaf of Algeria assassinated. **30** N Ireland Protestant leaders and Irish government met in 1st talks for 70 years.

July 9 Chris Patten sworn in as Governor of Hong Kong. **18** John Smith new Labour Party Leader. **20** Czechoslovak Pres Vaclav Havel resigned. **30** UN forces sent to Somalia.

August 3 Confirmation of Serbian detention camps where torture and killings had occurred. **10** Ban on Protestant Ulster Defence Association. **18** British troops in Iraq and Bosnia to protect UN aid convoys. **25** Serb bombardment destroyed National Library in Sarajevo: 90 dead. **27** Iraq accepted exclusion zone; Lord Owen new EC peace negotiator. **28** 3,000th sectarian death in N Ireland.

September 3 New Slovak constitution signed in Bratislava. **7** 28 ANC supporters shot dead by Ciskei troops as protest march crossed border. **9** Georgian forces and Abkhazia rebels agreed ceasefire. **11** £ close to ERM floor. **16** "Black Wednesday": £ withdrawn from ERM in *de facto* devaluation. **20** French referendum on Maastricht Treaty: narrow majority in favour. **21** EC Foreign Ministers agreed ratification of Maastricht Treaty. **24** National Heritage Minister David Mellor resigned.

October 5 £ at record low. **7** Sweeping plans for Hong Kong democracy. **13** Government and British Coal announced closure of 31 collieries. **15** 1st British troops in Croatia to support UN. **16** Pres Babangida declared Nigerian primary Presidential election void. **26** Last Russian troops left Poland. **30** IRA bomb in Whitehall.

November 3 Democrat Bill Clinton elected Pres of USA; GATT talks collapsed. **4** Government 3-vote majority in Maastricht debate. **11** Church of England General Synod voted narrowly in favour of ordination of women. **20** Windsor Castle fire.

December 2 German parliament won veto on EMU in Maastricht debate. **4** US troops in Somalia on food aid mission. **6** Swiss referendum against joining European Economic Area. **9** Prince and Princess of Wales separated. **12** EC Edinburgh Summit: deal saving Maastricht Treaty.

A.D.
1993

January 1 Inauguration of single European market; 2 new states, Czech Republic and Slovakia, came into being. **5** EC report confirmed rape of 20,000 Bosnian Muslim women by Serb forces. **13** Allied aircraft bombed air defence centres in S Iraq. **19** Iraq declared unilateral ceasefire: UN nuclear inspectors given clearance. **24** Croat troops seized Maslenica bridge connecting N Croatia with Adriatic. **26** Vaclav Havel 1st President of new Czech state.

February 12 S African government and ANC agreed plans for elected black and white interim government. **26** Terrorist bomb under World Trade Center, Manhattan.

March 8 Government defeated in Commons Maastricht debate. **13** Labor won record 5th term in Australian General Election. **16** VAT on domestic fuel in 2-stage plan announced in Budget. **20** IRA bombs in Warrington: 2 children dead. **25** Muslims and Croats signed full UN peace plan in New York. **26** UN Security Council voted to take over Somalia peacekeeping. **27** New Chinese Pres Jiang Zemin. **28** Right-wing landslide in French General Election.

April 2 State of Emergency in Azerbaijan. **4** Vancouver Summit: $1·6bn aid package to Russia. **8** UN admitted former Yugoslav republic Macedonia. **10** Chris Hani, Gen Sec of S African Communist Party and ANC leader, shot dead. **12** NATO enforced Bosnian "no fly" zone. **19** Waco siege ended: many dead. **24** IRA bomb in Bishopsgate. **25** Russian referendum: 58 % backed Pres Yeltsin.

May 1 Sri Lankan Pres Premadasa assassinated. **4** Asil Nadir, former Chairman of Polly Peck, fled to N Cyprus. **18** Danish Maastricht Referendum: 56·8 % in favour. **24** Eritrean independence. **27** Florence terrorist bomb: 6 dead, Uffizi museum damaged: Norman Lamont dismissed in Cabinet reshuffle: new Chancellor Kenneth Clarke.

June 6 1st democratic Latvian elections since 1931 won by centre-right alliance. **7** Russian government accepted "safe haven" plan. **11** US air strike against HQ of Gen Aideed. **13** 52 Bosnian Muslims killed in Serb rocket attack on Gorazde hospital.

July 3 Pres Clinton announced 1-year suspension of nuclear testing. **12** 16 Somalis killed in US helicopter attack on Gen Aideed's control centre. **22** Government defeated in Maastricht vote.

August 2 Emergency meeting of EC Finance Ministers: *de facto* suspension of ERM. **4** Serb troops captured Mt Igman overlooking Sarajevo. **7** Buckingham Palace opened to public. **14** Serbs withdrew from Mt Igman. **18** Muslims, Serbs and Croats agreed to place Sarajevo under UN rule for 2 years, after 3-way division of Bosnia decided. **27** Muslims held UN convoy "hostage" in Mostar as protection against Croats. **29** Yasser Arafat won PLO executive committee support for peace plan giving Palestinians control of Gaza strip and Jericho.

September 9 PLO Chairman Yasser Arafat signed mutual recognition agreement with Israel. **13** Israel–PLO agreement signed at White House. **14** Jordan and Israel signed agreement. **21** Pres Yeltsin dissolved Russian parliament, and announced rule by decree: parliament swore in Speaker Alexander Rutskoi as Pres. **22** Pres Yeltsin supported by army, security forces, ministers, central bank and many world leaders. **24** US and Commonwealth lifted S African trade sanctions. **25** Russian Parliament (White House) telephones, power and hot water cut off. **29** Labour Party Conference passed John Smith's "One man one vote" motion.

October 4 Russian troops stormed White House: Alexander Rutskoi and other leaders surrendered: 170 dead. **12** Germany's highest court approved Maastricht Treaty. **19** Benazir Bhutto Pakistan's new PM. **25** Sinn Fein leader Gerry Adams

A.D.
banned from mainland Britain; Canadian General Election: landslide victory for Liberals.

November 1 European Union established as Maastricht Treaty came into force. **9** Stari Most, Mostar's celebrated 16th century bridge, destroyed by Croats. **17** Pres de Klerk and Nelson Mandela ratified S Africa's 1st democratic constitution; US Congress endorsed N American Free Trade Agreement (NAFTA).

December 7 Transitional Executive Council (TEC) inaugurated in Cape Town. **12** Vladimir Zhirinovsky's ultra-nationalist Liberal Democratic Party won most seats in Russian Election. **15** Downing St Declaration by John Major and Taoiseach Albert Reynolds on future of N Ireland; GATT talks agreement. **19** Ruling Socialist Party won Serbian General Election.

1994

January 5 Inkatha boycott of S African General Election. **9** Bosnia peace talks reopened with redrawn map. **13** District Auditor's inquiry charged Westminster City Council with gerrymandering. **17** Los Angeles earthquake; John Major revealed to have approved £234m aid to Malaysia for Pergau dam, linked to arms deal. **19** Serb-Croat pact to normalise relations. **30** US granted Gerry Adams visa for 2-day visit.

February 5 Mortar attack on Sarajevo market: 68 dead. **7** Parliamentary Private Secretary Stephen Milligan found dead. **10** NATO 10-day deadline to Bosnian Serbs to withdraw weapons from Sarajevo area or risk air strikes. **25** Jewish extremist settler shot dead 40 Arabs in Hebron mosque. **28** US jets shot down 4 Bosnian Serb aircraft, NATO's first-ever aggressive intervention.

March 1 Bosnian Muslims and Croats signed US-brokered peace agreement. **9** IRA mortar attack on Heathrow airport. **22** PLO– Israel draft accord on armed presence to protect W Bank and Gaza Palestinians. **25** US troops left Somalia. **27** Italian General Election won by Silvio Berlusconi. **28** ANC security guards attacked Inkatha marchers carrying Zulu weapons: 30 dead. **31** State of Emergency in Natal and KwaZulu.

April 6 Presidents of Rwanda and Burundi died in rocket attack on plane. **7** Civil war in Rwanda: thousands dead, including PM. **10** NATO air strike on Serbian troops advancing on Gorazde. **11** 2nd NATO air strike on Bosnian Serb troops. **12** RPF (Rwandan Patriotic Front) Tutsi rebels captured Kigali: government fled. **17** Bosnian army's defence of Gorazde failed: UN-Serb agreement to restore peace. **19** Agreement brought Inkatha Freedom Party into S African Elections. **23** Western allies' troops began Berlin withdrawal. **24** Bosnian Serbs withdrew from Gorazde after NATO ultimatum. **26** New S African constitution came into force: long queues to vote in Elections.

May 2 Pres de Klerk conceded Election victory to Nelson Mandela: ANC won 63 % vote. **3** 200,000 dead as Rwanda genocide continued. **4** Israel and PLO signed agreement to end 27-year occupation of Gaza and W Bank, initiating Palestinian self-rule. **6** Channel Tunnel officially opened. **9** Nelson Mandela elected Pres of S Africa. **12** Labour leader John Smith died. **13** Jericho under Palestinian control. **19** 1st Channel Tunnel freight service. **23** S Yemen declared independence. **27** Alexander Solzhenitsyn returned to Russia.

June 5 S Africa rejoined Commonwealth. **2** Helicopter crash on Mull of Kintyre killed 29 anti- terrorism experts. **12** European Election: Labour won 62 seats with 44 % vote; Austrian referendum in favour of EU membership.

July 5 Yasser Arafat in Jericho: Palestine National Authority (PNA) sworn in; US, Russian and EU Foreign Ministers unveiled Bosnian peace plan in Geneva. **9** N Korean Pres Kim Il Sung died; G7 Naples Summit admitted Russia, effectively creating G8. **12** Commons inquiry into "cash for questions" and MPs' fees; Kim Jong Il to succeed

A.D.

father as N Korean Pres. **15** Emergency EU Summit endorsed Luxembourg PM Jacques Santer as new EC Pres. **16** 1st of 21 fragments of Comet Shoemaker-Levy 9 collided with Jupiter. **18** Hizbollah car bomb outside Jewish Centre in Buenos Aires: 100 dead; Israel-Jordan peace talks opened; EU brokered UK beef compromise with Germany. **20** Cabinet reshuffle: Michael Portillo Employment Sec, Jeremy Hanley Chairman of Conservative Party. **21** Tony Blair new Labour leader with 57% vote: John Prescott deputy leader. **25** King Hussein of Jordan and Israeli PM Rabin signed declaration ending 46-year conflict.

August 8 New Israel-Jordan border crossing near Eilat inaugurated: Yitzhak Rabin 1st Israeli PM to visit Jordan. **12** "Cradle to grave" NHS ended with abandonment of guaranteed care of elderly. **15** Venezuelan terrorist Carlos "the Jackal" arrested. **16** Republican Senators' delay tactics effectively killed US Health Bill. **26** 1st British patient received mechanical heart. **28** Sunday Trading Act came into force. **31** IRA declared ceasefire: UK government demanded evidence of permanence. Russian army left Latvia and Estonia.

September 12 Suicide pilot crashed light aircraft on White House lawn; Separatist PQ won control of Quebec provincial government. **16** Broadcasting ban on N Ireland extremists lifted. **28** 910 drowned in Baltic ferry disaster.

October 3 Channel Tunnel car service began. **4** At Labour Party conference Tony Blair announced replacement of Clause IV: "common ownership of means of production". **6** Labour Party conference narrowly reasserted backing for Clause IV. **13** N Ireland Loyalist paramilitary groups announced ceasefire. **16** Chancellor Kohl narrowly won 4th term. **19** Tim Smith N Ireland Minister, and later Neil Hamilton Minister at DTI, resigned over "cash for questions" affair. **21** John Major opened way to talks with Sinn Fein: bans on leaders lifted, border roads opened. **25** New body established under Lord Nolan to oversee standards in public life. **26** Israel-Jordan peace treaty signed.

November 8 Republican landslide victory in US midterm elections. **10** High Court ruled UK Pergau dam aid illegal; Saddam Hussein recognised Kuwait. **11** US abandoned Bosnia arms embargo. **14** UK National Lottery inaugurated. **17** Albert Reynolds resigned as Taoiseach. **18** Serb jets attacked UN "safe area" Bihac. **19** Bertie Aherne new Fianna Fail leader. **28** Government won Commons vote on European Finance Bill: Whip withdrawn from 8 Conservative abstainers; Serbs took Bihac; Norwegian referendum against EU membership. **29** Budget day: public spending cuts: VAT on fuel at 17·5% from April.

December 6 Government defeat on planned VAT increase on fuel; CSCE retitled Organisation for Security and Cooperation in Europe. **8** Chancellor of Exchequer's mini-budget to recoup £1bn lost by "VAT on fuel" defeat. **11** Russia invaded Chechnya. **18** Russian troops attacked Grozny.

1995

January 1 Austria, Finland and Sweden joined EU. **8** Sri Lankan government truce with Tamil guerrillas. **11** Pres Yeltsin assumed direct control of Russian armed forces. **12** Army to end Belfast daytime patrols. **17** Over 6,000 dead in Kobe earthquake. **18** Spanish Fishing Rights Bill narrowly passed after UK compensation doubled to £53m.

February 6 US space shuttle Discovery and Russia's Mir space station rendezvous. **10** £267m compensation agreement for Maxwell pension funds. **22** Joint Anglo-Irish document on N Ireland's future published. **26** 233-year-old Barings merchant bank collapsed.

March 2 Nick Leeson, Barings Bank financial trader involved in collapse, arrested in Frankfurt. **6** Spanish peseta and Portuguese escudo devalued after emergency meeting to realign ERM. **7** Dutch bank ING bought Barings in £1·6bn deal. **13** Tony

A.D.

Blair secured overwhelming National Executive support for new Clause IV. **20** Sarin nerve gas attack on Tokyo subway.

April 6 Scottish local elections result in the Conservatives failing to win control of any of the 29 new unitary authorities. **9** ZANU-PF win Zimbabwe general election. **19** Bomb outside a federal building in Oklahoma, USA kills 168; Gas attack in underground station in Yokohama, Japan. **21** FBI arrests Timothy McVeigh for the Oklahoma bombing.

May 7 Chirac defeats Jospin in second round of French Presidential election. **11** Nolan Committee on Standards in Public Life publishes its first report. **13** Alison Hargreaves becomes the first woman to climb Mt Everest alone and without oxygen. **17** Chirac succeeds François Mitterrand as President of France; Alain Juppé new Prime Minister. **24** Death of Lord Wilson of Rievaulx.

June 2 Bosnian Serbs released UN hostages including 11 British soldiers. **14** Chechen rebels seize hundreds of hostages in a hospital in Budyonnovsk in southern Russia. **17** Russian forces attack the hospital freeing 200 hostages. **19** Last Russian hostages released by Chechens; EU Finance ministers set 1 Jan 1999 as date for single currency. **22** John Major resigns as leader of the Conservative Party.

July 4 John Major wins the leadership contest. **5** Cabinet reshuffle: Michael Heseltine the new Deputy Prime Minister. **10** Opposition leader Aung San Suu Kyi released after 6 years house arrest in Myanmar (Burma). **11** Bosnian Serbs capture Srebenica; USA restores full diplomatic relations with Vietnam. **13** All Muslims in Srebenica deported by Bosnian Serbs.

August 4 Croatian offensive into Serb-held Krajina. 100,000 troops advance on 3 fronts. **7** 150,000 Serb refugees flee Krajina after Croat victory. **11** President Clinton vetoes legislation to lift unilaterally the Bosnian arms embargo. **17** Alison Hargreaves, 1st woman to climb Everest alone, dies in an avalanche on K2. **18** Driest summer since 1659. **27** Rugby Union turns professional. **28** Bosnian Serb shelling of Sarajevo kills 35 in city centre; James Molyneaux resigns as UUP leader.

September 5 French nuclear test at Mururoa atoll. **6** Riots in Tahiti, after nuclear test. **8** David Trimble elected new leader of UUP. **10** NATO uses cruise missiles against the Bosnian Serbs. **24** Israel and PLO agree to extend self-rule to most of West Bank. **27** European Court of Human Rights condemned killing of 3 IRA terrorists by SAS in Gibraltar in 1988. **28** Publishers' Association ends Net Book Agreement (NBA).

October 1 Metrication Day; All pre-packed food to be sold in metric units. **2** 2nd French nuclear test in Pacific. **3** OJ Simpson released after a unanimous not guilty verdict. **5** 60-day cease-fire in Bosnia agreed in US-brokered deal. **7** Alan Howarth, Tory MP for Stratford-on-Avon, defects to Labour. **30** Quebec independence referendum results in a No vote; Quebec Premier Jacques Parizeau steps down.

November 4 Israeli PM Yitzhak Rabin assassinated in Tel Aviv. **10** Ken Saro-Wiwa and 8 other human rights activists executed in Nigeria. **11** Nigeria suspended from the Commonwealth. **19** Lech Walesa defeated in Polish Presidential elections. **21** Bosnian peace deal agreed in Dayton, Ohio.

December 1 Nick Leeson sentenced to 6½ years in prison in Singapore. **14** Bosnian peace agreement formally signed in Paris. **15** EU leaders agree to call the new single currency the Euro. **17** Communists come first in Russian parliamentary elections, winning 155 out of 450 seats. **19** Government loses the Fisheries vote in the House of Commons by 2 votes.

1996

January 8 François Mitterrand dies of cancer aged

A.D.
79. **21** Yasser Arafat elected as President of Palestine Authority.

February 9 IRA cease-fire expires as massive bomb explodes in South Quays, east London: 2 killed. **15** Scott Report on the Arms-to-Iraq Affair is published. **18** IRA bus bomb in Aldwych. **26** Government wins House of Commons' vote on the Scott Report by one vote. **28** Princess Diana formally agrees to a divorce.

March 2 John Howard becomes the new Australian PM as the Liberal-National Coalition wins a landslide victory in the general election. **3** José Maria Aznar wins the Spanish general election. **4** Northern Ireland proximity talks start at Stormont without Sinn Fein or the main Unionist parties. **13** Tom Hamilton kills 16 primary school children and their teacher in Dunblane, Scotland, before shooting himself. **19** President Nelson Mandela granted a divorce from Winnie; Bob Dole secures the Republican nomination. **20** The Government admits the possibility of a link between BSE in cows and CJD in humans.

April 18 Israeli bombing of UN refugee centre in south Lebanon kills 101; Islamic fundamentalists shoot 18 tourists dead in Cairo. **22** Italian general election won by Olive Tree alliance: new PM Romano Prodi. **28** Gunman Martin Bryant killed 35 tourists in Port Arthur, Australia.

May 2 Conservatives suffered heavy losses in local council elections. **9** Dame Shirley Porter ordered to pay £31 million surcharge for gerrymandering; National Party withdrew from the Government of National Unity in South Africa. **10** Congress (I) party lost the Indian general election. **31** Likud narrowly won the Israeli general election; Netanyahu new PM.

June 5 European Commission authorised partial lifting of ban on British beef. **10** All-party talks began at Stormont Castle, but Sinn Fein excluded. **14** Irish peace forum opened in Belfast. **15** IRA bomb caused extensive damage and 200 injuries in central Manchester.

July 3 Yeltsin won the Russian Presidential election. **15** Decree nisi granted to Prince and Princess of Wales. **18** 228 killed as TWA jet exploded off Long Island, New York. **20** Centennial Olympic Games opened in Atlanta, Georgia. **27** Nail bomb in Centennial Park, Atlanta, killed 2, injured over 100.

August 1 Somali warlord General Aideed died. **21** The Globe Theatre reopened with the first production of Shakespeare there since 1642.

September 3 27 US cruise missiles fired on southern Iraq in Operation Desert Strike. **9** Pro-Iraqi KDP forces captured PUK stronghold of Sulaimaniya. **19** Kevin Maxwell freed after judge blocked a second trial. **27** Taliban forces capture Kabul: ex-President Najibullah executed.

October 1 Israeli PM Netanyahu and Palestinian leader Arafat met in Washington DC; MP Neil Hamilton admitted taking cash for questions. **4** Ministry of Defence admitted Gulf War troops were exposed to harmful chemicals. **16** Cullen report on Dunblane published: all handguns except smallest calibre (.22) pistols to be banned. **17** Yeltsin sacked National Security Adviser General Lebed.

November 5 President Clinton re-elected: Republicans retained both Houses of Congress; Benazir Bhutto dismissed as Pakistani PM. **17** President Milosevic annulled opposition victories in municipal elections: anti-government protests in Belgrade.

December 10 Government announced official inquiry into Gulf War syndrome; new coalition government in New Zealand: Jim Bolger remains PM. **11** Paymaster-General David Willetts resigned over cash for questions. **12** Labour win Barnsley East by-election: Government now in minority. **17** Tupac Amaru terrorists seized 430 hostages at Japanese embassy in Peru.

A.D.
1997
January 3 President Milosevic admitted defeat in Serbian municipal elections. **26** Violent protests in Albania after the collapse of a pyramid investment scheme.

February 3 Benazir Bhutto and Imran Khan defeated in Pakistani general election: Nawaz Sharif new PM. **5** O.J. Simpson found guilty in civil court case. **10** O.J. Simpson ordered to pay £15 million punitive damages. **19** Chinese Premier Deng Xiaoping died aged 92; 1st National Lottery draw on Wednesday. **21** Bridgewater Three freed after 18 years in jail. **22** Adult sheep (Dolly) successfully cloned by scientists.

March 2 Fighting in Vlore killed 12: state of emergency declared in Albania. **17** John Major called general election for 1 May. **19** Political row erupted over publication of the Downey Report into cash-for-questions.

April 6 BBC correspondent Martin Bell decided to stand on an anti-corruption ticket against Neil Hamilton in Tatton.

May 1 General election held in United Kingdom. Labour won landslide victory under Tony Blair. **2** Gordon Brown became Chancellor of the Exchequer; Robin Cook new Foreign Secretary; John Prescott is Deputy Prime Minister. John Major resigned as leader of the Conservative Party. **4** New Labour Government announces its intention of joining EU Social Chapter. **6** Bank of England given control of interest rates. **12** Russia and Chechnya signed peace treaty. **14** Author Laurie Lee died aged 82. **15** Trade union ban at GCHQ lifted. **16** President Mobutu fled Zaïre. **17** Rebels entered Kinshasa: Zaïre renamed Democratic Republic of Congo by new President, Laurent Kabila. **26** French PM Juppé resigned. **27** NATO-Russian co-operation charter signed in Paris.

June 1 Socialists won the French general election: Lionel Jospin new PM. **2** Liberal Party won Canadian general election; Timothy McVeigh found guilty of Oklahoma bombing. **10** Kenneth Clarke won first round of Tory leadership contest with 49 votes, Hague second with 41, Redwood third with 27: Lilley (24 votes) and Howard (23) withdrew. **11** MPs voted to ban all remaining handguns. **17** In second round, Clarke won 64 votes, Hague 62, Redwood 38: Redwood eliminated. **18** Amsterdam Treaty signed by EU leaders. **19** Hague won final round (92 votes to 70) to become youngest Tory leader since 1783.

July 1 Hong Kong handed over to Chinese rule; UK rejoined UNESCO; actor Robert Mitchum died aged 79. **2** Labour's first Budget; actor James Stewart died aged 89. **3** Downey report into cash-for-questions published: 5 former Tory MPs, including Neil Hamilton, criticised. **6** Orangemen parade in Drumcree led to rioting across N. Ireland. **15** Slobodan Milosevic elected as Yugoslavian President.

August 2 Author William Burroughs died aged 83. **25** Former E. German leader Egon Krenz jailed for Berlin Wall deaths. **26** South African Vice-President F.W. de Klerk retired. **31** Diana, Princess of Wales killed in car crash in Paris: her companion Dodi Fayed and driver Henri Paul also died.

September 5 Mother Teresa died aged 87. **11** Scotland voted Yes-Yes in dual referendum on a Scottish Parliament and its tax-raising powers. **16** Forest fires in Indonesia caused extensive smog across south-east Asia. **18** Referendum in Wales produced narrow vote (50·3 % to 49·7 %) in favour of Welsh Assembly; 7 tourists killed in bus bomb in Cairo. **19** 6 killed in Southall rail crash. **26** Earthquakes in Italy damaged St Francis's Basilica, Assisi.

October 1 Fiji readmitted to the Commonwealth. **9** Romani Prodi resigned as Italian PM; 250 killed as Hurricane Pauline hit Acapulco. **13** Singer John Denver died in plane crash. **14** Piers Merchant resigned as Tory MP for Beckenham. **15**

A.D.
Thrust broke the sound barrier on land (766-109 mph); author Harold Robbins died. **27** Dow Jones index fell 554 points; Chancellor committed UK to EMU after next election.

November 2 Iraq turned back UN nuclear weapons inspectors. **3** Jenny Shipley new PM in New Zealand. **4** Government decided to exempt Formula 1 from ban on tobacco sponsorship. **5** Republicans won decisive victory in mid-term Congressional elections. **8** Controversy over donation to Labour by Formula 1 lobbyist Bernie Ecclestone. **9** BBC launched 24-hour news channel. **13** Iraq expelled 6 US weapons inspectors: UN pulls out inspection teams. **17** 58 tourists killed in massacre at Luxor temple; Windsor Castle reopened. **26** Hastings Banda of Malawi died aged 99.

December 9 Internal market scrapped in NHS reforms. **11** Gerry Adams at Downing St. for talks; *Britannia* decommissioned. **16** Beef-on-the-bone ban implemented. **18** Bill to create Scottish Parliament launched; Opposition leader Kim Dae-Jung won S. Korean presidential election.

1998

January 8 Currency crisis in Indonesia. **9** Mo Mowlam met with Loyalist leaders in Maze prison. **11** Ice storms in Canada left 3 million without power. **12** New British-Irish proposals for N. Ireland peace: cross-border council planned. **21** Sex scandal erupted after allegations of Clinton's affair with Monica Lewinsky.

February 8 Enoch Powell died aged 85. **13** Warmest February day on record (19·6C at Worcester). **16** Iraqi inspections crisis intensified. **19** UN Secretary-General Kofi Annan left on peace mission to Baghdad. **20** Sinn Fein suspended from N. Ireland peace talks: bomb blast in Moira.

March 1 Countryside March in London attracted 250,000 demonstrators. **5** Water discovered on the moon. **13** Private member's bill to ban hunting failed to get Government time in the Commons. **16** Dr Benjamin Spock died aged 94. **23** Pres Yeltsin sacked PM and cabinet.

April 1 Paula Jones sex case against Pres. Clinton dismissed by federal judge. **6** Mitchell draft settlement on N. Ireland published; UK and France ratified Nuclear Test Ban Treaty. **7** Unionists rejected Mitchell blueprint: Blair flew to Belfast for crisis talks. **8** Australian Senate rejected government's land rights' bill. **10** Peace agreement sealed in N. Ireland: new directly-elected assembly to be created. **15** Death of Pol Pot, Cambodian dictator. **17** Death of Linda McCartney (wife of Sir Paul McCartney).

May 2 Official birth of the 'Euro' at Brussels Summit; **11** EU countries have membership confirmed; Wim Duisenberg to take charge of European Central Bank. **7** Local elections in England; referendum in London approved creation of Mayor. **10** IRA prisoners temporarily released to attend Sinn Fein conference which voted for the Belfast Agreement. **11** India conducted three nuclear tests. **13** Frank Sinatra died aged 82. **15** LVF declared ceasefire. **21** President Suharto of Indonesia resigned. **22** Referenda on the Belfast Agreement in both parts of Ireland: 71% in Northern Ireland and 94% in the Republic in favour. **24** Pro-democracy parties won Hong Kong legislative elections; fighting in Kosovo escalated. **28** Pakistan conducted five nuclear tests.

June 2 Reports of Serbian massacres in Kosovo villages. **8** Nigerian President Abacha died. **18** Government announced introduction of minimum wage (£3·60ph) in April 1999. **22** House of Commons voted for equal age of consent for gay men. **25** Northern Ireland assembly elections held under PR.

July 1 David Trimble elected First Minister of Northern Ireland, Seamus Mallon as Deputy. **5** Stand-off between Orange marchers and police at Drumcree began. **7** Nigerian pro-democracy leader

A.D.
Chief Abiola died in jail. **8** Heavy rioting in Nigeria; Australian Senate finally passed government's land rights' bill. **22** House of Lords rejected gay age of consent clause: Government dropped it from bill. **26** President Clinton subpoenaed to appear before grand jury. **27** Cabinet reshuffle: Peter Mandelson and Alistair Darling promoted; former Pakistani PM Benazir Bhutto on trial for corruption. **28** Monica Lewinsky granted immunity from prosecution in return for testifying. **30** Court of Appeal overturned conviction of Derek Bentley, hanged in 1953. **31** UK ban on use of anti-personnel mines.

August 7 Bomb attacks on US embassies in Nairobi and Dar-es-Salaam: 240 dead. **8** Animal rights activists released 6,000 mink in Hampshire. **15** Massive bomb in Omagh, Tyrone, killed 28. **17** President Clinton testified to grand jury; in live television address he admitted to an 'inappropriate relationship' with Ms Lewinsky. **18** Splinter group the Real IRA admitted responsibility for Omagh bomb. **20** US missile attacks on Afghanistan and Sudan. **22** INLA announced ceasefire. **23** President Yeltsin sacked Russian cabinet: Chernomyrdin new PM.

September 3 Swissair plane crashed into sea off Halifax, Nova Scotia; 229 killed. **7** 'Real IRA' declares total cease-fire; William Hague calls ballot of party members over EU single currency question. **10** Historic meeting of David Trimble and Gerry Adams; preliminary details of Starr Report on President Clinton leaked to media. **11** Starr Report released on Internet: Yevgeni Primakov chosen as new Russian Prime Minister. **16** Microsoft becomes largest company in United States. **18** US Congressional Committee sanctions release of the 'Clinton Tapes'. **24** Britain to resume diplomatic relations with Iran. **25** Frenchman Benoit Lecomte became first person to swim the Atlantic (coming ashore at Quiberon in Brittany). **27** German elections: Chancellor Kohl defeated by Social Democrats under Schröder. **28** MCC voted to admit women members.

October 4 Kidnapping of 3 British workers and a New Zealander in Chechnya. **5** Result of Conservative Party ballot on Europe confirmed William Hague's position on single currency. **7** Official visit to China by Tony Blair. **8** House of Representatives voted 258–176 to institute impeachment proceedings against President Clinton. **13** Neill Report revolutionises funding of political parties in the United Kingdom. **15** Channel 4 acquires rights to show Test Match cricket. **16** Nobel Peace Prize awarded jointly to John Hume and David Trimble. **17** Arrest of former dictator of Chile, General Pinochet, at a private London hospital. **19** Terrorist bomb in Beersheba injured over 60; Middle East peace summit threatened. **23** Agreement reached at Maryland peace talks. **27** Arrival of President Menem of Argentina on official visit; abrupt resignation of Ron Davies, the Secretary of State for Wales, after 'lapse of judgement' on Clapham Common. **28** Arrest of General Pinochet overturned in the High Court. **29** Publication of report of Jenkins Commission on electoral reform.

November 4 Massive destruction by Hurricane Mitch in Central America. **8** Death of Lord Hunt (leader of 1953 Everest expedition). **13** Final warnings sent to Saddam Hussein in renewed Gulf Crisis. **14** Iraq complies with Western demands for inspection of sites. **23** EU ban on exports of British beef lifted.

December 8 Four Western hostages beheaded in Chechnya. **9** Home Secretary authorised Pinochet's extradition: Chile withdrew ambassador from UK. **11** House of Representatives passed two articles of impeachment against Clinton; Pinochet extradition hearing started. **12** Two more impeachment articles passed by Congress. **13** Lord Grade died aged 91. **15** House of Lords defeated European elections bill for 6th time: Parliament Act invoked; FA chief Graham Kelly resigned; pensions reforms unveiled. **17** Impeachment vote in Congress postponed; renewed bombing of Baghdad; Law Lords extradition ruling on Pinochet set aside. **19** Clinton

A.D.
impeached by House of Representatives on 2 counts: Speaker-elect Bob Livingstone resigned; bombing of Iraq halted. **23** Mandelson and Robinson both resigned from the Cabinet.

1999

January 3 Heavy snowfalls paralysed eastern USA. **4** Charlie Whelan, Gordon Brown's Press Secretary, resigned. **5** Flu epidemic caused NHS crisis. **7** US Senate sworn in for impeachment trial. **13** Global shares downturn sparked by Brazilian devaluation. **14** Impeachment prosecution case started; MEPs voted not to sack the European Commission. **16** Serb massacre of ethnic Albanians in Kosovo: 45 dead. **19** President Clinton's defence began; Jonathan Aitken pleaded guilty to perjury. **20** Paddy Ashdown announced resignation as Liberal Democrat leader; Lords reform unveiled. **22** International Olympic Committee shamed by bribes scandal. **25** Commons voted for equal age of consent for gay men.

February 1 Monica Lewinsky testified. **7** King Hussein of Jordan died, aged 63. **8** Dame Iris Murdoch died, aged 79. **10** Heaviest snowfalls in 50 years across the Alps: avalanche in Chamonix killed 12. **12** Clinton acquitted by Senate on both charges: 55–45 against perjury, 50–50 on obstruction of justice. **16** Kurdish leader Abdullah Ocalan abducted by Turkish agents in Kenya: worldwide Kurdish protests, Greek embassy in London occupied. **24** Lawrence Report published: Metropolitan Police criticised. **27** General Obasanjo won Nigerian presidential election.

March 5 Lord Denning died, aged 100; last *News at Ten* broadcast. **7** Stanley Kubrick died, aged 70. **9** Budget Day: basic rate of income tax down to 22p, starting rate of 10p introduced. **10** Prince of Wales visited Argentina. **11** Oskar Lafontaine resigned as German Finance Minister; Private Lee Clegg acquitted of murder. **12** Poland, Hungary and the Czech Republic joined NATO; Yehudi Menuhin died, aged 82. **13** Renewed Serb attacks in Kosovo; bombs killed 13 in Istanbul. **15** Report on corruption in the EU Commission released; Kosovo peace talks reopened. **16** EU Commission resigned en masse. **17** 6 IOC members expelled. **20** Over 100 killed in ethnic clashes in Borneo. **24** NATO forces attacked Serbia; fire in Mont Blanc tunnel killed 40; Romani Prodi named EU President.

April 1 3 US soldiers captured by Serbs. **3** NATO attacks on Belgrade. **5** NATO created refugee sanctuaries in Macedonia; Lockerbie suspects flown to Holland. **6** NATO rejected Serb ceasefire offer; bombing continued; Lockerbie suspects charged. **7** Refugee camps in Kosovo cleared by Serb forces. **8** NATO sent 8,000 troops to Albania. **10** Renewed violence in E Timor. **13** Serb attacks across Albanian border; Lords rejected equal age of consent for gays. **14** 64 killed in NATO bombing of refugee convoy. **15** Home Secretary authorised extradition of Gen Pinochet; Benazir Bhutto convicted of corruption. **17** Nail bomb in Brixton injured 50. **19** German Reichstag reopened; Turkish PM Ecevit resigned. **20** 15 killed in High School massacre in Littleton, Colorado. **22** Russia backed Serbian peace offer. **24** Nail bomb in Brick Lane injured 6. **25** First Kosovar refugees arrived in UK. **26** TV presenter Jill Dando murdered. **28** Serbian deputy PM Vuk Draskovic sacked; Sir Alf Ramsey died, aged 79. **30** Nail bomb at gay pub in Soho: 3 killed.

May 6 Voting for first Scottish Parliament since 1707 and new Welsh Assembly leaves Labour short of an overall majority in both polls. **7** Accidental bombing by NATO of Chinese embassy in Belgrade during Balkan conflict. **8** Death of actor, Dirk Bogarde. **11** House of Lords agrees to amendment providing for temporary reprieve of 92 hereditary peers until second stage of reform. **12** Lord Steel elected Presiding Officer of new Scottish Assembly; Alun Michael elected First Minister of Welsh Assembly; Russian Prime Minister, Yevgeny Primakov and his government dismissed by President Yeltsin. **13** Donald Dewar elected First Minister of Scottish Parliament, heading a Labour-Liberal Democrat coalition. **17** Ehud Barak

A.D.
became Prime Minister of Israel. **20** Rebellion of 67 Labour MPs in Commons' vote on welfare reform. **29** Democratically-elected President inaugurated in Nigeria; Nigeria rejoins the Commonwealth.

June 3 ANC returned to power in South African general election; Serbia accepts NATO peace plan. **5** Visit of Pope to Poland. **7** First democratic elections in Indonesia for over 40 years. **9** Serb generals sign peace deal with NATO commander, Sir Michael Jackson. **10** Elections to European Parliament marked by low turnout, Labour losses and increased representation for smaller parties. **12** British troops enter Kosovo, forming part of NATO peacekeeping force. **17** Death of Cardinal Hume. **18** Violence at anti-capitalist demonstration in City of London.

July 1 Formal opening of Scottish Parliament by the Queen; death of Joshua Nkomo, founder of the Zimbabwean African People's Union (ZAPU). **7** Resumption of full British diplomatic relations with Libya. Fighting in Russia on borders of Chechnya and Dagestan. **8** Proposals published to convert Post Office into a public limited company. **12** Dutch government voted to decriminalise euthanasia. **23** Death of King Hassan II of Morocco. **30** Referendum in East Timor votes for independence.

August 1 Ban on export of British beef lifted by European Union. **4** George Robertson, the Defence Secretary, appointed next Secretary-General of NATO. **9** Charles Kennedy elected leader of the Liberal Democrats. **16** Russian Duma approved Vladimir Putin as Prime Minister. **17** Devastating earthquake hits Turkey.

September 3 Forest fires rage in Brazil. **4** Israel and PLO sign new agreement; further withdrawal of Israel from West Bank. **7** Athens rocked by earthquake; over 30 people killed. **9** Publication of Patten Report on future of policing in Northern Ireland. **14** Extensive damage in Caribbean and United States caused by Hurricane Floyd. **20** Taiwan hit by devastating earthquake, leaving over 2,000 people dead; first UN peace-keeping troops arrived in East Timor, following massacres by pro-Indonesian militias. **27** 26 British tourists die in coach crash in South Africa; European Court of Human Rights rules that discrimination against gays in the UK armed forces is unlawful.

October 5 Horrific train crash at Ladbroke Grove, outside Paddington, results in 31 deaths. **11** Return of Peter Mandelson to Cabinet, as Northern Ireland Secretary, in further reshuffle. **12** Military coup in Pakistan ousts discredited civilian government. **18** Pakistan suspended from Commonwealth following military coup. Arrival of President Jiang Zemin for state visit to Britain by leader of communist China. **20** Indonesian parliament selects Abdurrakman Wahid as president after resignation of Habibie. **31** The 217 passengers and crew on an EgyptAir Boeing 767 feared dead after crashing into Atlantic on flight from New York to Cairo.

November 3 Revolt of 54 backbench Labour MPs over welfare reform proposals. **6** Referendum in Australia results in victory for monarchists; Rugby World Cup won by Australia, who defeat France. **12** Second major earthquake in Turkey; pop star Gary Glitter jailed after conviction over child sex pornography. **13** Lennox Lewis defeats Evander Holyfield to become part of heavyweight boxing legend. **25** Michael Portillo returned to Westminster in Kensington by-election. **26** General election in New Zealand won by Labour. **29** Historic steps towards power-sharing in Northern Ireland as new Executive is formed. **30** Riots in Seattle (and on a lesser scale in London) as World Trade Organisation gathering opens; Parliament confirms devolution of power to Northern Ireland (as of midnight on 1 December).

December 11 Death of the authoritarian Franjo Tudjman, President of Croatia, aged 77. **14** Panama Canal returned to Panama by USA, finally giving sovereignty to Panama. **17** Inaugural meeting of British-Irish Council. **19** Return of enclave of Macao to China marks final end of Portuguese empire in Asia; elections to

A.D.
Russian parliament show strong support for pro-government parties and disappointment for Communists. **20** Death toll in floods and landslides in Venezuela passes 5,000 (with thousands more missing). **25** Russian forces launch major assault on Grozny, the capital of Chechnya. **30** Knifeman stabs ex-Beatle George Harrison. **31** Resignation of Boris Yeltsin as President of Russia; Vladimir Putin became Acting President; global celebrations mark advent of the new millennium.

THE NEW MILLENNIUM

2000

January 1 Greenwich Electronic Time launched (new time standard for the Internet). **4** Alan Greenspan nominated to serve fourth 4-year term as head of the US Federal Reserve System. **12** Ban on gay men and women in UK armed forces ended. **21** Military coup in Ecuador. **26** Hans Blix appointed to supervise Iraqi weapons disarmament.

February 4 Lord Archer expelled from Conservative Party. **6** Russian troops take Grozny (capital of Chechnya). **9** Resignation of Alun Michael, First Secretary, Welsh Assembly. **11** Suspension of devolved government in Northern Ireland. **17** Tuvalu to become 189th UN member state.

March 2 UK drops extradition proceedings against former Chilean dictator Pinochet. **7** 'Super Tuesday' primaries confirm Al Gore and George Bush Jnr. as rival leading candidates. **18** Opposition wins presidency in Taiwan (after 50 years of Kuomintang rule). **26** Vladimir Putin elected President of Russia.

April 5 Yoshiro Mori elected Japanese PM. **6** Former Pakistani prime minister Nawaz Sharif sentenced to life imprisonment. **11** Right-wing historian David Irving loses libel lawsuit. **17** Israel announces withdrawal from Lebanon (effective from July).

May 4 Ken Livingstone wins first direct election for Mayor of London. **11** Opening of Tate Modern (art museum) in London. **18** Massive street protests in Belgrade. **24** Last Israeli forces withdrawn early from Lebanon. **29** Former Indonesian President Suharto put under house arrest.

June 5 Bill Clinton first US President to address Russian parliament. **10** Death of President Assad of Syria; Millennium Bridge opens in London (only to be closed a week later for repairs). **13** First-ever visit of a South Korean President to North Korea. **23** Cotonou Agreement between EU and developing countries.

July 17 Germany to pay compensation to those forced into slave labour under the Nazis. **19** 100th birthday celebrations of the Queen Mother. **25** Crash of Concorde on take-off from Paris.

August 3 Suharto formally charged with corruption. **12** Sinking of Russian nuclear submarine *Kursk* in Barents Sea.

September 10 Second elections in Hong Kong under Chinese rule. **15** Olympic Games open in Sydney. **24** Referendum in France votes to shorten presidential term to 5 years. **25** Disputed presidential election in Yugoslavia precipitates crisis; Milosevic refuses to accept Kostunica as victor. **28** Denmark votes to reject euro.

October 5 Popular uprising in Belgrade; revolution sweeps away Milosevic. **12** Terrorist attack on *USS Cole* in Aden, Yemen. **27** First performance of Wagner's music in Israel.

November 1 Yugoslavia re-admitted, as a new state, to UN. **7** Presidential election in USA results in prolonged deadlock (not resolved until Florida awarded to George Bush on 26 November). **27** Victory in Canadian general election for Jean Chrétien's Liberal Party.

December 6 Formal re-opening of the Great Court, British Museum. **9** Israeli PM Ehud Barak

A.D.
announces resignation. **16** Colin Powell nominated as next Secretary of State; 20,000th performance of *The Mousetrap*. **22** World Bank and IMF waive debts of 22 impoverished nations.

2001

January 1 Greece adopts Euro (12th EU member to do so). **23** Assassination of President Laurent Kabila of the Congo; resignation of Northern Ireland Secretary Peter Mandelson. **26** Devastating earthquake in Gujarat, India. **31** One of two Libyans on trial for Lockerbie bombing found guilty.

February 6 Israeli elections won by right-wing Likud under Ariel Sharon. **21** Foot and mouth outbreak discovered at Essex abattoir (start of devastating epidemic).

March 1 Foot and mouth outbreak spreads to Scotland and Ireland. **4** Switzerland referendum rejects talks to join EU. **8** Recovery of *Bluebird* (Donald Campbell's boat) from Coniston Water; Ariel Sharon, Israeli PM, announces 8-party coalition. **21** General election (and local elections) in Britain postponed because of foot and mouth outbreak.

April 10 Euthanasia legalised by Upper House of Dutch parliament. **26** First 15 'People's Peers' created by the Government.

May 1 Anti-capitalist protests by May Day demonstrators in London. **26** Race riots in Oldham between whites and Asians. **30** Afghanistan refuses to extradite Osama Bin Laden, wanted for 1998 bombings of US embassies in Kenya and Tanzania.

June 7 General election returns Labour to power; Labour win 413 seats, Conservatives 166, Liberal Democrats 52. **8** Resignation of William Hague as Conservative leader. **11** Execution of Timothy McVeigh in Indiana for Oklahoma bombing.

July 1 Resignation of David Trimble as First Minister in Northern Ireland. **8** Race riots in Bradford. **13** Beijing selected to host 2008 Olympics. **16** Russia and China sign treaty of friendship. **20** Anti-globalisation protests at G8 meeting in Genoa. **23** President Abdurrahman Wahid ousted in Indonesia; replaced by Megawati Sukarnoputri.

August 11 Devolved government restored in Northern Ireland. **13** Peace agreement signed in Macedonia. **23** USA announces withdrawal from ABM Treaty.

September 9 Assassination of Ahmad Shah Masoud, anti-Taleban leader in Afghanistan. **11** USA attacked in co-ordinated operation when two hijacked aircraft destroy the twin towers of the World Trade Centre; a third hits the Pentagon and a fourth crashes in Pennsylvania. Death toll of over 2,500 estimated. **23** Voters in Poland reject Solidarity; success for former communists (now Democratic Left Alliance).

October 1 Swissair files for bankruptcy protection. **3** President Bush announces support for creation of a Palestinian state. **7** American and British planes attack Taleban positions in Afghanistan; bankrupt Railtrack re-organised. **19** US ground troops in combat in Afghanistan.

November 3 Ruling party wins 9th consecutive election victory in Singapore. **4** Film version of *Harry Potter and the Philosopher's Stone* opens in UK. **6** David Trimble again heads power-sharing government in Ulster; Belgian airline Sabena goes bankrupt. **8** Resignation of Henry McLeish as First Minister in Scotland. **13** Anti-Taleban forces take control of Kabul. **15** US Congress passes Aviation Security Bill. **17** First democratic legislative elections held in Kosovo are won by Albanian nationalists. **29** Death of former Beatle, George Harrison.

December 2 Largest corporate bankruptcy in US history as Enron collapses. **7** Kandahar abandoned by Taleban. **13** Terrorist attack on Parliament House in New Delhi, India; formal US withdrawal

A.D.

from Anti-Ballistic Missile Treaty. **22** Hamid Karzai heads interim Afghan government.

2002

January 1 Euro becomes official currency of 12 EU member states. **11** First prisoners from Afghan war arrive in Guantanamo naval base in Cuba. **14** UK declared free of foot and mouth disease. **18** Israeli tanks surround Yasser Arafat's HQ in Ramallah. **28** Beginning of Doha Round of WTO talks. **29** 'Axis of evil' speech by President Bush identifies Iran, Iraq and North Korea.

February 9 Death of Princess Margaret. **13** Scottish Parliament outlaws foxhunting. **22** UNITA leader Jonas Savimbi killed in Angola. Cease-fire signed in Angola. **27** Muslims set fire to train carrying Hindus in Gujarat; 58 killed.

March 3 Swiss referendum gives approval for UN membership. **13** Re-election of President Mugabe in Zimbabwe widely condemned as blatant fraud. **14** Creation of five new cities in the UK: Preston, Newport, Newry, Lisburn and Stirling. **19** Zimbabwe suspended for one year from Commonwealth. **24** Israeli forces storm Yasser Arafat's compound in Ramallah; Arafat effectively imprisoned. **30** Death announced of the Queen Mother, aged 101.

April 4 Israeli army completes re-occupation of West Bank. **11** Treaty signed creating permanent International War Criminals' Court at The Hague. US boycotts ceremony. **17** Budget promises to double UK health spending over 10 years. **21** First round of presidential elections in France; National Front candidate, Jean-Marie Le Pen, secures second place.

May 1 Massive protests in Paris to denounce National Front leader, Le Pen. **5** Victory for President Chirac in second-round of presidential contest. **6** Assassination of right-wing Dutch politician Pim Fortuyn. **10** Seven killed in Potters Bar rail crash. **17** Re-election of Bertie Ahern as Irish Prime Minister. **29** In Cabinet re-shuffle, Paul Boateng first black Cabinet member.

June 13 Hamid Karzai becomes Afghan leader. **14** Knighthood conferred on rock legend Mick Jagger. **24** New Middle East peace plan proposed by US President Bush.

July 3 First solo balloon flight around the world completed by Steve Fossett when he lands in Australian outback. **6** Assassination of Afghan Vice-President Haji Abdul Qadir. **8** Winnie Mandela in court in South Africa on fraud charges. **9** Ban on marrying of divorcees lifted by Church of England. **19** Enquiry concludes 215 patients killed by jailed doctor Harold Shipman. **25** New Indian President, A P J Abdul Kalam. **30** Peace deal brokered by South Africa to end Congo civil war.

August 3 Outbreak of Legionnaire's disease at Barrow-in-Furness, Cumbria; 39 cases confirmed. **21** Bodies of missing schoolgirls Holly Wells and Jessica Chapman identified. **26** Earth Summit opened in Johannesburg.

September 24 6-year low for shares in UK. **27** Revelation by Edwina Currie of her affair with former PM John Major.

October 12 Terrorist attack on nightclub in Indonesian island of Bali leaves over 200 dead (89 of them Australian). **26** Violent end to theatre siege in Moscow.

November 1 Intervention by the Queen halts trial of royal butler, Paul Burrell. **8** UN Resolution 1441 gives Iraq 'final chance' to disarm. **13** Resolution 1441 accepted by Iraq. **15** Death of Myra Hindley, the Moors murderer. **18** UN Inspectors arrive to resume work in Iraq. **17** North Korea claims it has developed nuclear weapons.

December 5 Negotiations near agreement for peace deal in Sri Lanka. **7** 12,000 page Iraq dossier on arms denies it has any banned arms or weapons

A.D.

of mass destruction. **11** Peace deal brokered in Aceh.

2003

January 8 Blizzards sweep across UK; road and rail transport chaos. **10** North Korea withdraws from nuclear weapons treaty. **22** Controversial white paper on Higher Education proposes 'top-up' fees. **30** Further severe blizzards paralyse UK transport system.

February 1 Disintegration of US space shuttle on re-entry into earth's atmosphere. **11** Outbreak of SARS disease in China. **13** Ban on cigarette advertising comes into force. **15** Massive anti-war protest sees London's biggest-ever demonstration.

March 16 Azores summit of USA, UK and Spain issues ultimatum. **19** UN Inspectors leave Iraq. **20** Second Gulf War begins with air strikes on Baghdad. **22** US forces cross two key points on Euphrates River. **27** US orders 100,000 more troops to the Gulf. **29** First food aid arrives; Robin Cook condemns war as 'bloody and unnecessary'.

April 2 US forces take control of Karbala; advance troops storm 'red zone' around Baghdad. **4** Saddam International Airport near Baghdad seized by US 3rd Infantry Division. **6** Baath HQ destroyed as Royal Marines enter Basra. **14** Capture of Tikrit, Saddam Hussein's home town, marks end of Iraqi resistance. **29** First Palestinian PM, Mahmoud Abbas, sworn in. **30** US-backed 'road map' for peace in the Middle East published.

June 2 50th anniversary of the coronation of HM Queen Elizabeth II. **9** Gordon Brown announces that conditions have not been met for Britain to adopt the Euro. **24** President Putin arrives in London on first state visit by a Russian leader since 1874.

July 17 Tony Blair addresses joint session of US Congress. **18** Body of government weapons expert, Dr David Kelly, found in woods after apparent suicide. **27** Comedian Bob Hope dies aged 100.

August 15 Libya accepts blame for Lockerbie bombing in 1988 and agrees to compensate victims' families. **19** Truck bomb destroys UN headquarters in Baghdad killing 23, including UN special representative, Sergio Vieira de Mello.

September 6 Palestinian PM, Mahmoud Abbas, resigns; Yasser Arafat nominates Ahmed Qurei. **11** Swedish Foreign Minister, Anna Lindh, is stabbed to death whilst shopping.

October 7 Arnold Schwarzenegger elected Governor of California. **15** China launches its first manned space flight. **19** Tony Blair admitted to Hammersmith Hospital with irregular heartbeat. **24** British Airways Concorde makes its last passenger flight. **29** Iain Duncan Smith resigns as Conservative Party leader after losing a vote of confidence.

November 5 Michael Howard becomes Conservative Party leader. **20** Two truck bombs hit British targets in Istanbul; Roger Short, UK consul-general, is amongst the dead. **22** England beat Australia 20–17 in the Rugby World Cup final in Sydney. **23** President Shevardnadze of Georgia resigns after three weeks of protests over claims of election-rigging. **26** Elections for Northern Ireland's National Assembly result in Dr Paisley's Democratic Unionists forming the largest party.

December 8 Commonwealth heads of government meeting in Nigeria agree to continue suspension of Zimbabwe; President Mugabe announces withdrawal from Commonwealth. **9** Britain's first toll motorway opens round Birmingham. **12** Paul Martin succeeds Jean Chretien as Canadian PM. **12** Saddam Hussein captured by US troops. **17** Ian Huntley convicted of the murder of Soham schoolgirls, Holly Wells and Jessica Chapman. **19** Announcement made that Libya is giving up weapons of mass destruction programmes.

A.D.

2004

January 13 Serial killer Harold Shipman hangs himself in his cell at Wakefield prison. **28** Lord Hutton's report into the death of Dr David Kelly published; Gavyn Davies resigns as BBC chairman. **29** Greg Dyke resigns as BBC director-general. Cannabis downgraded from a class B to a class C (least harmful) banned substance.

February 3 Inquiry set up under Lord Butler into intelligence on Iraq and weapons of mass destruction. **5** Twenty-one Chinese migrant workers drown in Morecambe Bay.

March 11 Ten bomb blasts on Madrid commuter trains kill 191 people. **14** Socialists defeat the Popular Party in Spanish general election. **25** Tony Blair meets President Qaddafi in Tripoli. **29** NATO admits Bulgaria, Romania, Slovakia, Slovenia, Estonia, Latvia and Lithuania.

April 2 Michael Grade appointed chairman of the BBC. **5** Thames Trains fined a record £2 million for their part in the Paddington rail disaster in 1999. **20** Tony Blair announces that there will be a referendum on the EU constitutional treaty.

May 1 Estonia, Latvia, Lithuania, Czech Republic, Hungary, Poland, Slovakia, Slovenia, Malta and Cyprus become members of the EU. **19** Tony Blair hit by condoms containing purple flower thrown by protesters in the House of Commons.

June 10 Ken Livingstone re-elected as Mayor of London. **18** Agreement announced at Brussels Summit on a draft EU constitutional treaty.

July 14 Lord Butler's report into intelligence and Iraqi WMDs is published. **26** Democratic Convention opens in Boston; John Kerry and John Edwards nominated to run for president and vice-president.

August 13 The XXVIII Olympic Games open in Athens. **16** Boscastle in Cornwall is devastated by a flash flood following torrential rain. **30** Republican Convention opens in New York; George Bush and Dick Cheney nominated to run for president and vice-president.

September 1 Terrorists seize control of a school in Beslan, North Ossetia; over 300 hostages killed when siege ends on 3 September. **30** Tony Blair announces he will serve a full third term if Labour wins the next election.

October 8 British hostage Kenneth Bigley murdered in Iraq. **9** In Australian general election PM John Howard's coalition government defeats Labour's Mark Latham. The Queen opens the controversial Scottish parliament building in Edinburgh. In Afghanistan presidential election results in victory for Hamid Karzai. **26** Israeli parliament approves Ariel Sharon's plan for withdrawal of soldiers and settlers from Gaza Strip and parts of the West Bank. **29** At Rome Summit, EU member states sign a treaty providing for the introduction of the EU constitution when all 25 members have ratified it.

November 2 In elections in USA President Bush defeats the Democrat challenger John Kerry. **8** In Iraq US-led forces launch major operation to take rebel-held Falluja. **11** Presidential election in Ukraine results in victory for PM Viktor Yanukovich, but is later declared fraudulent.

December 15 David Blunkett resigns as Home Secretary; Charles Clarke appointed. **20** £26·5m stolen in armed robbery at the Northern Bank in Belfast: IRA accused. **26** Earthquake off the island of Sumatra creates tsunamis that kill over 225,000 along the Asian and East African coasts. In re-run of Ukrainian elections Viktor Yuschenko defeats Viktor Yanukovich.

2005

January 1 Freedom of Information Act comes into force. **9** Mahmoud Abbas elected President of the

A.D.

Palestinian Authority. In Sudan, peace agreement signed between the government and rebel forces led by John Garang. **30** In Iraq, elections held for National Assembly and provincial assemblies amidst intensified violence.

February 10 North Korea admits to having nuclear weapons. **16** Kyoto Protocol on climate change comes into force. **18** Act to ban hunting with dogs in England and Wales comes into force. **20** Spain becomes the first country to endorse the proposed EU constitution in a referendum.

March 11 Controversial Prevention of Terrorism Bill becomes law. **31** Robert Mugabe's ZANU-PF Party wins elections in Zimbabwe.

April 2 Pope John Paul II dies. **9** Prince Charles marries Camilla Parker Bowles. **15** Collapse of UK-owned car manufacturer MG Rover. **19** Cardinal Joseph Ratzinger of Germany elected to be the new Pope as Benedict XVI.

May 5 General Election returns Labour Party under Tony Blair for a third term. **29** In a referendum France rejects the proposed EU constitution. **31** French PM Jean-Pierre Raffarin resigns and Dominique de Villepin succeeds him.

June 1 Dutch reject the proposed EU constitution. **6** Government announces it will not proceed with bill for a UK referendum on EU constitution. **13** In California Michael Jackson is acquitted of child abuse. **19** Ugandan-born John Sentamu, Bishop of Birmingham, is appointed Archbishop of York, the first black holder of the post. **24** In Iran the ultra-conservative mayor of Tehran, Mahdi Ahmadinejad, is elected president.

July 6 London chosen to host the 2012 Olympic Games. **7** Suicide bombers explode three bombs on the London Underground and one on a bus; 56 dead. **8** G8 (Group of Eight) nations end their Summit in Scotland with pledge of action over African poverty and debt. **21** Second attempt by terrorists to bomb London's transport system fails when devices do not explode. **22** Brazilian electrician, John Charles de Menezes, is mistaken for a terrorist and shot dead in London. **28** IRA announces an end to its armed campaign to achieve a united Ireland.

August 15 Israeli troops begin removing settlers from Gaza Strip and West Bank. **29** Hurricane Katrina strikes New Orleans, causing catastrophic flooding.

September 7 Hosni Mubarrak re-elected as President of Egypt. **12** Israel completes evacuation of settlers and soldiers from the Gaza Strip. England draw fifth test match against Australia and regain the Ashes. **26** In Northern Ireland decommissioning of IRA weapons declared complete.

October 8 Massive earthquake in Kashmir leaves over 87,000 dead and three million homeless. **15** Referendum in Iraq ratifies new constitution. **19** Trial of former president Saddam Hussein opens in Baghdad. **28** Rioting mainly by ethnic minorities in Paris suburbs followed by weeks of disturbances in cities across France.

November 2 David Blunkett resigns as Secretary of State for Work and Pensions over breaches in the ministerial code of conduct. **22** Angela Merkel formally elected by the Bundestag as first woman Chancellor of Germany. **24** New licensing laws come into force relaxing restrictions on licensing hours.

December 5 Civil Partnership Act providing for registered unions between same-sex couples comes into force. **6** David Cameron defeats David Davis to become Conservative Party leader at the age of 39. **11** Explosions at oil depot at Buncefield, Hemel Hempstead, result in largest fire in peacetime Europe.

2006

January 4 Israeli PM Ariel Sharon incapacitated by a stroke. **7** Charles Kennedy resigns as leader of

A.D.

the Liberal Democrats. **25** In elections for Palestinian parliament militant Islamist group Hamas defeats Fatah party. **31** 100th member of the British forces to die in Iraq since the invasion is killed by a bomb.

February 4 International Atomic Energy Agency votes to report Iran's nuclear programme to the UN Security Council; Iran announces intention to resume uranium enrichment. **7** Muslim cleric Abu Hamza jailed for seven years at the Old Bailey for inciting murder and racial hatred. **22** In Britain's biggest robbery, £53 million stolen from Securitas depot at Tonbridge in Kent.

March 2 Sir Menzies Campbell elected leader of the Liberal Democrats. **11** Former Serbian president Slobodan Milosevic, on trial for war crimes since 2002, found dead in his cell at The Hague. **28** In Israeli general election centrist Kadima Party led by Ehud Olmert emerges as the largest party. **29** The five permanent members of the UN Security Council, plus Germany, call on Iran to suspend its nuclear research within thirty days.

April 10 In Italian elections the centre-left led by Romano Prodi narrowly defeats Silvio Berlusconi's centre-right coalition. **11** Iran announces that it has successfully enriched uranium. **22** Jawad al-Maliki becomes Prime Minister of Iraq. **25** Revelation that over 1,000 foreign nationals have been released from British gaols without being considered for deportation.

May 4 Labour Party loses more than 300 councillors in local elections. **5** Mr Blair carries out major cabinet re-shuffle: John Reid succeeds Charles Clarke as Home Secretary and Margaret Beckett takes over from Jack Straw as Foreign Secretary. **6** Flight-Lieutenant Sarah Mulvihill becomes the first British service woman to die in Iraq as a result of enemy action. **8** Mr Blair says he will give his successor 'ample time' to settle in before the next general election. **20** Formation of new government of national unity in Iraq.

June 2 Police raid on a suspected chemical bomb factory in Forest Gate, East London, in which one man is accidentally shot, proves to be based on false intelligence. **3** Montenegro declares independence from Serbia following a referendum. **7** Head of al-Qaeda terrorists in Iraq, Abu Musab al-Zarqawi, is killed in a US air strike on his hiding place. **25** The kidnapping by Palestinian raiders of an Israeli soldier, Corporal Gilad Shalit, from a military post near the Gaza border leads to Israeli military reprisals.

July 5 Baroness Hayman elected by the House of Lords as its first Lord Speaker. **11** Seven bombs on commuter trains in Mumbai, India result in over 200 dead and 700 injured. **12** Lord Levy, Mr Blair's fundraising chief, is arrested and questioned in the 'cash for peerages' enquiry. Hezbollah fighters cross Lebanon-Israel border and seize two Israeli soldiers: Israel responds with air strikes and cross-border attacks. **30** Final edition broadcast of BBC's *Top of the Pops*, first shown in 1964. **31** In Cuba Fidel Castro relinquishes power to his brother Raul while he undergoes surgery. UN Security Council calls on Iran to halt uranium enrichment by the end of August.

August 9 Israel launches new offensive into Lebanon. **10** Emergency security measures cause chaos at British airports as terrorist suspects arrested over alleged plot to detonate liquid explosives on board planes bound for the USA. **14** UN plan for a cease-fire between Israel and Lebanon comes into effect. **23** In Austria Natascha Kampusch escapes from the home of Wolfgang Priklopil after being held prisoner for eight years.

September 2 Fourteen British servicemen are killed when their Nimrod aircraft crashes in Afghanistan. **7** Following internal Labour Party unrest, Mr Blair announces that the coming party conference will be his last as Prime Minister. **19** In Thailand Prime Minister Thaksin Shinawatra is deposed in a bloodless military coup. **26** Mr Blair

A.D.

makes his final speech as Prime Minister at the Labour Party conference.

October 1 Age Discrimination Act comes into force. **2** In the USA five girls are killed by a gunman at the schoolhouse of an Amish community in Pennsylvania. **9** North Korea claims to have tested its first nuclear weapon. **13** Christmas hamper savings company Farepak goes into administration. **30** 700-page report by Sir Nicholas Stern warns of the economic consequences of global warming.

November 5 In Iraq Saddam Hussein is sentenced to death by hanging for crimes against humanity over the killing of 148 inhabitants of Dujail after an assassination attempt there in 1982. **7** In US mid-term elections the Democrats take control of the House of Representatives and the Senate. In London British al-Qaeda terrorist, Dhiren Barot, pleads guilty to planning attacks in Britain and the USA and is sentenced to life imprisonment with a minimum term of 40 years. **8** Donald Rumsfeld resigns as US Secretary of Defense. **23** Former KGB agent, Alexander Litvinenko, dies in London three weeks after being poisoned with radioactive polonium-210. **26** Palestinian militants and Israel agree a truce in the Gaza Strip.

December 4 Mr Blair announces his government's intention to maintain Britain's independent deterrent by ordering a new generation of nuclear submarines. **14** Lord Stevens' report on the Metropolitan Police's enquiry into the deaths of Princess Diana and Dodi Fayed is published. Mr Blair is questioned by police conducting the cash for peerages enquiry. The Serious Fraud Office bribery enquiry into BAE Systems' arms deal with Saudi Arabia is discontinued 'in the public interest'. Mr Ban Ki Moon of South Korea is sworn in as the new UN Secretary-General. **23** UN Security Council votes unanimously to impose sanctions on Iran for pursuing its nuclear programme. **30** Saddam Hussein is hanged in Baghdad.

WORLD FINANCIAL CRISIS

2007

January 1 Romania and Bulgaria join the European Union. **5** Australian cricketers beat England by 10 wickets in the final test match, regaining the Ashes in a 5–0 series whitewash. **10** President Bush announces that a 'surge' of 21,500 extra American troops are to be sent to Iraq. **27** Final edition of BBC's *Grandstand*, first broadcast in 1958. **28** At a special conference in Dublin Gerry Adams directs Sinn Fein to support the law and order agencies in Northern Ireland. **31** Nine people arrested in Birmingham on suspicion of planning to kidnap and execute a British Muslim soldier.

February 1 Mr Blair questioned by police a second time in the cash for peerages enquiry. **3** An outbreak of the H5N1 strain of bird flu is confirmed at Bernard Matthews' turkey farm in Suffolk and 160,000 turkeys are culled. **5** In Iraq the 100th British military victim of enemy action is killed by a roadside bomb. **13** North Korea agrees to curb its nuclear programmes in return for aid during talks with China, South Korea, Japan, USA and Russia in Beijing. **21** Mr Blair announces a gradual reduction in the British forces in Iraq, beginning with the withdrawal of some 1,500 before the summer. International Atomic Energy Agency reports that Iran has not complied with the UN's demands of 23 December.

March 7 Northern Ireland Assembly elections result in gains for the Democratic Unionist Party and Sinn Fein. House of Commons votes in favour of a fully elected House of Lords. **11** In Zimbabwe opposition leader Morgan Tsvangirai and his supporters are beaten by police after their arrest at a public meeting. **14** Government wins vote in favour of an immediate decision to renew Britain's Trident nuclear weapons system despite Labour Party backbench revolt. **17** Palestinian legislative council endorses a Hamas-Fatah unity cabinet. **18**

A.D.

Pakistan's cricket coach Bob Woolmer is found dead in his hotel room in Kingston, Jamaica during the 2007 Cricket World Cup. **21** Gordon Brown presents his final budget as Chancellor of the Exchequer. **23** Fifteen Royal Navy personnel are detained by Iranian forces while on patrol in the Gulf. **26** Meeting between Rev Ian Paisley and Gerry Adams to agree on power-sharing in Northern Ireland.

April 4 President Ahmadinejad of Iran announces the release of the British naval personnel. **9** Ministry of Defence reverses decision to allow naval personnel held captive by Iran to sell their stories to the media. **12** In Baghdad a suicide bomber penetrates the heavily guarded 'green zone' and blows himself up inside Iraq's parliament building. **16** In the USA a student shoots dead 32 people on the campus of Virginia Tech in Blacksburg, Virginia. **20** Police hand over the results of cash for peerages enquiry to the Crown Prosecution Service.

May 2 Resignation of Lord Browne as Chief Executive of BP. **3** Three-year old Madeleine McCann goes missing from the resort of Praia da Luz, Portugal. Elections for Welsh Assembly, Scottish Parliament and also nationwide local elections: SNP triumph in Scotland, serious reverses for Labour and Liberal Democrats in many areas in England. **6** Nicolas Sarkozy elected in French presidential election. **8** Power-sharing restored in Northern Ireland with Ian Paisley as First Minister and Martin McGuinness as Deputy First Minister. **9** The Home Office is restructured: a separate Ministry of Justice is formed. **10** Mr Blair announces that he will leave Downing Street on 27 June. **16** Gordon Brown is nominated by sufficient MPs to ensure he will become Labour leader and Prime Minister without a contest. Ministry of Defence announces that Prince Harry will not be deployed to Iraq. **21** The historic tea clipper *Cutty Sark* is badly damaged by fire.

June 23 At a summit in Brussels the 27 members of the EU agree on guidelines for a new treaty. **24** Gordon Brown becomes leader of the Labour Party unopposed; Harriet Harman is elected deputy leader. **25** Torrential rain causes extensive flooding in the Midlands and northern England. **27** Tony Blair stands down as Prime Minister and as an MP; Gordon Brown accepts the Queen's invitation to form a government. **29** Two car bombs planted in central London fail to explode. **30** In a terrorist attack at Glasgow International Airport a burning vehicle is crashed into the main terminal building.

July 1 Ban on smoking in enclosed public places comes into force. **9** Four men are convicted of taking part in the failed bomb attacks on London's transport system on 21 July 2005 and jailed for life. **13** In Chicago former media tycoon, Canadian-born Conrad Black, is found guilty on charges of fraud and obstruction of justice and later sentenced to 6½ years in prison. **16** Britain expels four Russian diplomats over Russia's refusal to extradite Andrei Lugovoy, chief suspect in the Alexander Litvinenko murder case. **20** Heavy rain leads to widespread flooding in central England. Crown Prosecution Service announces that there will be no prosecutions as a result of the cash for peerages enquiry. **21** *Harry Potter and The Deathly Hallows*, the seventh and final Harry Potter novel by J K Rowling, is published worldwide. **31** Deployment of British troops in support of the civil power in Northern Ireland officially ends after 38 years.

August 3 Outbreak of foot-and-mouth disease on a farm in Surrey is linked to a nearby animal health research complex. **26** In Greece forest fires threaten the site of ancient Olympia, home of the original games, and cause many deaths.

September 2 Last British troops withdraw from former palace of Saddam Hussein in Basra City to Basra airport. **14** Savers queue to withdraw their money from the Northern Rock bank, the UK's fifth biggest mortgage lender, after the Bank of England is asked for emergency funding. **18** Buddhist monks lead anti-government protests in

A.D.

Rangoon, Burma. **22** The UK's first case of the animal disease 'bluetongue' is discovered on a farm in Suffolk. **26** Ofcom fines GMTV a record £2 million over phone-in competition irregularities. **27** Burmese troops open fire on demonstrators in Rangoon: the dead include a Japanese journalist.

October 2 Gordon Brown makes his first visit to Iraq as Prime Minister. **5** Peter Fincham, Controller of BBC One, resigns following critical report into misrepresentation of the Queen in a documentary trailer. **6** Gordon Brown ends speculation by ruling out an early election. **9** Alistair Darling presents his first Autumn Budget as Chancellor. **15** Sir Menzies Campbell resigns as leader of the Liberal Democrats. **18** Benazir Bhutto returns to Pakistan after eight years in exile: two bombs explode near her vehicle in Karachi, killing 138 people. **19** EU leaders agree on the text of new reform treaty. **20** South Africa defeats England 15–6 to win the 2007 Rugby World Cup. **21** Extensive wildfires in California lead to a state of emergency in seven counties.

November 1 Metropolitan Police fined £175,000 after being convicted of breaching Health and Safety laws over the shooting of Jean Charles de Menezes in 2005. **2** Four fire-fighters are killed tackling a blaze in a vegetable packing warehouse in Warwickshire. **3** President Musharraf declares a state of emergency in Pakistan. **6** The Queen opens the restored St Pancras station as the London terminus for Eurostar trains. **8** The Independent Police Complaints Commission publishes its report into the shooting of Jean Charles de Menezes. **20** HM Revenue and Customs admits it has lost two computer discs containing child benefit data for 7·25 million families. **21** England fail to qualify for Euro 2008 after losing to Croatia; head coach, Steve McClaren, is sacked next day. **22** Pakistan is suspended from the Commonwealth over imposition of state of emergency. **24** Australian Labor Party wins federal elections: Kevin Rudd succeeds John Howard as Prime Minister. **25** Peter Watt, General Secretary of the Labour Party, resigns over the failure to declare the real source of proxy donations made by wealthy businessman, David Abrahams.

December 2 In Russia President Putin's United Russia Party wins a landslide victory in the parliamentary elections. **13** EU leaders sign the Treaty of Lisbon. **14** Fabio Capello is appointed head coach of England's football team. **15** President Musharraf lifts the state of emergency in Pakistan. UN Climate Change Conference on Bali reaches agreement on a two-year process to negotiate a new treaty on climate change. **16** Britain hands control of Basra back to the Iraqis. **18** In South Africa Jacob Zuma defeats Thabo Mbeki for the post of president of the ruling ANC party. Nick Clegg narrowly defeats Chris Huhne to become the leader of the Liberal Democrats. **20** Queen Elizabeth II outlives Queen Victoria to become the oldest British monarch. **27** Benazir Bhutto is assassinated at an election rally in Rawalpindi, Pakistan. Kenya's presidential election leads to violence following accusations that President Kibaki's victory over opposition leader Raila Odinga is rigged.

2008

January 11 Sir Edmund Hillary, the first man to reach the summit of Mount Everest, dies aged 88. **17** A British Airways Boeing 777 crash lands short of the runway at Heathrow airport, but all passengers and crew survive. **21** Stock markets around the world plunge amid fears of a US recession. **24** Italian Prime Minister Romano Prodi resigns after losing a vote of confidence in the Senate. Peter Hain resigns as Work and Pensions Secretary and Welsh Secretary when the Electoral Commission asks the police to investigate undeclared donations to his Labour Party deputy leadership campaign.

February 5 On 'Super Tuesday' 24 American states hold caucuses or primary elections: in the Democratic Party Barack Obama wins an estimated 847 delegates to Hillary Clinton's 834. **17** Chancellor Alistair Darling announces that the

A.D.

Northern Rock bank is to be nationalised. The parliament of Kosovo declares independence from Serbia. **18** Parliamentary elections in Pakistan are won by President Musharraf's opponents. **19** Fidel Castro announces that he is standing down after 49 years as President of Cuba. **28** An American website reveals that Prince Harry has been serving with the army in Afghanistan for the past ten weeks.

March 2 Dmitri Medvedev wins the presidential election in Russia. **4** In Northern Ireland Ian Paisley announces his intention to stand down as First Minister and leader of the DUP. In the US primaries Senator John McCain from Arizona secures enough delegates to win the Republican Party nomination. **10** Buddhist monks in Lhasa begin demonstrations against Chinese rule in Tibet. **18** Details published of the divorce settlement between Sir Paul McCartney and Heather Mills. **19** Sir Arthur C Clarke, science fiction writer, dies aged 90. **27** Chaos on the first day of operation of Terminal 5 at Heathrow airport. **29** People of Zimbabwe vote in presidential and parliamentary elections.

April 5 Charlton Heston, actor and film star, dies aged 83. **6** Anti-Chinese protesters disrupt the Olympic torch relay through London. **7** The jury at the inquest in the deaths of Princess Diana and Dodi Fayed return a verdict of unlawful killing, blaming the gross negligence of their chauffeur and the paparazzi. **14** In Italy Silvio Berlusconi is elected Prime Minister for a third time. **17** In Kenya a unity government is sworn in, with Mwai Kibaki remaining President and Raila Odinga becoming Prime Minister. **23** Prime Minister Gordon Brown makes concessions to avoid a back-bench revolt over the abolition of the 10p rate of income tax.

May 1 In elections for over 4,000 seats in 159 councils in England and Wales, Labour suffers its worse humiliation since the 1960s. In London, Labour's Ken Livingstone is ousted as Mayor by Boris Johnson, the Conservative candidate. **2** Cyclone Nargis kills over 150,000 in Burma. **6** Bertie Ahern resigns as Taoiseach of the Republic of Ireland. **7** Dmitri Medvedev is sworn in as President of Russia and appoints Mr Putin as Prime Minister the following day. **12** Earthquake in Sichuan province of China kills over 80,000. **22** Conservatives win Crewe and Nantwich by-election with a 17·6 % swing from Labour. Nicky Reilly, a recent convert to Islam, is arrested after a failed attempt to bomb an Exeter restaurant. **26** Heavy rain leads to extensive flooding in southern China.

June 2 UN Security Council votes unanimously to allow countries to send warships into Somalia's territorial waters to deal with pirates. **7** In the USA Hillary Clinton officially concedes defeat to Barack Obama and gives him her support as Democratic Party presidential candidate. **11** Gordon Brown has a majority of nine in controversial Commons vote on 42-day detention without charge for terrorist suspects. **12** David Davis, Tory Shadow Home Secretary, resigns his parliamentary seat to fight a by-election on the issue of civil liberties. In a referendum a majority of Irish voters reject ratification of EU Lisbon Treaty. **17** Corporal Sarah Bryant of the Intelligence Corps becomes the first British servicewoman to be killed in Afghanistan. **18** House of Lords votes in favour of ratification of EU Lisbon Treaty; it receives the royal assent the following day. **27** In Zimbabwe Robert Mugabe wins run-off presidential election after violence forces opposition leader, Morgan Tsvangirai, to withdraw.

July 7 The Church of England's General Synod votes to consecrate women bishops. **10** David Davis is re-elected in by-election for Haltemprice and Howden constituency. **16** Israel exchanges Hezbollah prisoners for the bodies of two Israeli soldiers whose kidnapping sparked off the 2006 Lebanon war. **18** Dr Radovan Karadzic, former Bosnian Serb leader, is discovered in disguise in Belgrade and arrested for war crimes. **21** Robert Mugabe and Morgan Tsvangirai sign an agreement to start talks on power sharing in Zimbabwe. **24**

A.D.

In by-election Scottish National Party gains Glasgow East from Labour. Max Mosley, FIA President, wins High Court action against *News of the World* for invasion of privacy in reporting his sadomasochistic activities. **25** Qantas Boeing 707 makes emergency landing at Manila after hole is blown in its fuselage, thought to be caused by an exploding oxygen bottle.

August 3 Russian writer Alexander Solzhenitsyn dies aged 89. **7** After armed clashes Georgia sends troops into the breakaway region of South Ossetia. **8** Summer Olympic Games open in Beijing. **10** Georgia withdraws from South Ossetia in the face of intervention by Russian armed forces. **12** Georgia and Russia reach preliminary agreement on a cease-fire plan brokered by France. **15** ETS Europe's contract is terminated after problems over marking 2008 national curriculum tests. **22** Russia begins to withdraw its armed forces from Georgian territory. **23** Barack Obama picks Senator Joe Biden as his vice-presidential running mate. **24** Britain comes away with 19 gold medals as the Olympic Games close. **26** Russia recognises South Ossetia and Abkhazia as independent states. **29** John McCain picks Governor of Alaska Sarah Palin as his vice-presidential running mate. **31** New Orleans is evacuated but Hurricane Gustav weakens before striking Louisiana next day, so the anticipated loss of life and property is reduced.

September 7 US government takes control of mortgage finance companies Fannie May and Freddie Mac. **8** In London three men are found guilty of a terrorist conspiracy involving homemade liquid bombs. **10** The Large Hadron Collider, the world's biggest particle accelerator, is activated at the CERN (European Organisation for Nuclear Research) facility near Geneva, but develops a fault shortly afterwards. **12** XL Leisure Group, the UK's third largest package holiday firm, collapses. **15** US investment bank Lehman Brothers files for bankruptcy. In Zimbabwe a power-sharing agreement is signed and Morgan Tsvangirai named as prime minister. **17** Lloyds TSB finalises deal to take over ailing rival HBOS. **20** Over 50 people are killed when a suicide truck bomber devastates the Marriott Hotel in Islamabad, Pakistan. **21** In South Africa President Mbeki announces his resignation at the request of his own party. **26** Actor Paul Newman dies aged 83.

October 2 Sir Ian Blair announces his resignation as Metropolitan Police Commissioner. **3** In Cabinet reshuffle Peter Mandelson is appointed Business Secretary. American football star O J Simpson is convicted of armed robbery and kidnapping in Las Vegas. **7** British savers with online Icesave bank have their accounts frozen when its Icelandic parent Landsbanki Bank goes into receivership. **8** Chancellor Alistair Darling announces a rescue package for the British banking system. **10** Russian troops meet deadline for withdrawal from Georgian territory but remain in South Ossetia and Abkhazia. **13** House of Lords rejects Counter-Terrorism Bill, including 42-day detention without charge, by 309 votes to 118. Government announces massive injection of taxpayers' money into major UK banks. **29** BBC suspends Russell Brand and Jonathan Ross for making insulting phone call to actor Andrew Sachs on Brand's Radio 2 show; Brand resigns.

November 2 Britain's Lewis Hamilton becomes the youngest ever Formula One World Champion at the age of 23. **4** In the US presidential election Barack Obama defeats John McCain to become the first African-American to be elected president. **6** In the Glenrothes by-election Labour fights off challenge from the Scottish National Party to retain seat. The Bank of England cuts interest rates from 4·5 to 3 per cent. **11** Following the court case over the death of 'Baby P' there is renewed scrutiny of child protection in the UK. **13** Controversial Human Fertility and Embryology Act 2008 receives the royal assent. **15** Saudiowned oil tanker *Sirius Star* is seized by Somali pirates. **24** Chancellor Alistair Darling presents his Pre-Budget Report, including temporary cut in VAT from 17·5 to 15 per cent. **26** Terrorists kill

A.D.

172 people in co-ordinated attacks on hotels, railway station and other locations in Mumbai, India. Woolworths and MFI go into administration. **27** Shadow Immigration Minister Damian Green is arrested and his home, and his constituency and Commons offices are searched by police in a leaked documents enquiry. Death of two Royal Marines brings to 101 the number of British service personnel killed by enemy action in Afghanistan.

December 1 Barack Obama nominates Hillary Clinton as his Secretary of State. **4** Zimbabwe declares a national emergency over cholera epidemic. Karen Matthews is found guilty of kidnapping her own daughter Shannon in the hope of claiming reward money. Bank of England cuts interest rates to 2 per cent, the lowest since 1951. **7** In Greece the shooting dead of a teenager by a policeman sparks off anti-government rioting in Athens and other cities. **12** Jury returns an open verdict at the inquest into the death of Jean Charles de Menezes. **17** On a visit to Baghdad Gordon Brown announces that British troops will be withdrawn from Iraq by mid-2009. UN Security Council approves land and air attacks on pirate bases in Somalia. **24** Playwright Harold Pinter dies aged 78. **27** Israel launches air strikes against Hamas in the Gaza Strip in response to rocket attacks on Israeli settlements.

2009

January 3 Israeli ground forces cross into the Gaza Strip. **8** The Bank of England reduces interest rates to 1·5 per cent. **9** Somali pirates release oil tanker *Sirius Star* after a ransom is paid. **15** US Airways Airbus A320 makes a successful emergency landing in New York City's Hudson River after a bird strike disables both engines. **18** Israel's unilateral cease-fire in its conflict with Hamas comes into effect. **20** In USA Barack Obama is inaugurated as the 44th and first African-American president. **28** Sir Paul Stephenson succeeds Sir Ian Blair as the Commissioner of the Metropolitan Police.

February 3 Heaviest snow for 18 years causes a week of disruption in UK. **5** The Bank of England reduces interest rates to 1 per cent. **7** Bushfires begin in Australia resulting in 170 deaths. **11** Morgan Tsvangirai is sworn in as prime minister of Zimbabwe. **13** US Congress approves the American Recovery and Reinvestment Act of 2009; it is signed into law by President Obama on 17 February. **23** British film *Slumdog Millionaire* wins eight Oscars at the Academy Awards, including Best Picture. **27** President Obama announces the withdrawal of all US combat forces from Iraq by the end of August 2010.

March 3 Gordon Brown meets President Obama at the White House. In Lahore, Pakistan, terrorists open fire on vehicle convoy carrying the Sri Lankan cricket team. **5** The Bank of England reduces interest rates to 0·5 per cent. **6** In Zimbabwe Morgan Tsvangirai is injured and his wife killed in a road accident south of Harare. **7** Two British soldiers are shot dead by dissident republican gunmen at the gates of Massereene Barracks, Co Antrim. **9** PC Stephen Carroll is murdered in Craigavon, Co Armagh. **19** Josef Fritzl is jailed for life in Austria. **22** Reality-TV star Jade Goody dies aged 27. **24** Mervyn King, Governor of the Bank of England, warns that Britain cannot afford a further fiscal stimulus. **30** The Nationwide Building Society takes over the failed Dunfermline Building Society, minus its 'toxic assets'. In Lahore, Pakistan, terrorists mount a commando-style attack on the police academy.

April 1 During demonstrations relating to the G20 summit in London, newspaper seller Ian Tomlinson is knocked to the ground by a policeman and later dies. **2** World leaders at the G20 summit meeting in London agree on a response to the global financial crisis. **6** A 6·3 magnitude earthquake kills some 300 people around the city of L'Aquila in Italy. **8** Police bring forward the timing of raids on suspected terrorists, including in Manchester and Liverpool, after secret briefing

A.D.

notes carried by Assistant Commissioner Bob Quick are photographed when he arrives in Downing Street; Quick resigns next day. **11** Damian McBride, head of strategy and planning at 10 Downing Street, resigns when his emails suggesting material for a smear campaign against senior Tories are leaked. **12** Captain Richard Phillips of the US container ship *Maersk Alabama* is rescued by the US navy from Somali pirates holding him hostage. **13** US music producer Phil Spector is found guilty of the second degree murder of Lana Clarkson at his home in 2003. **16** The Director of Public Prosecutions announces that there will be no charges against MP Damian Green or the civil servant who leaked Home Office documents to him. **19** President Obama announces that CIA operatives who used harsh interrogation techniques approved by legal advisers will not be prosecuted. **22** Elections in South Africa result in victory for the ANC, whose leader, Jacob Zuma, becomes president. Chancellor of the Exchequer, Alistair Darling, presents his 2009 budget (*see* Table on **A43** for key points). **27** Scottish couple who had been on holiday in Mexico are confirmed as the first cases of swine flu in the UK. **29** Government defeated in Commons' vote over restricting rights of former Gurkha soldiers to settle in Britain. **30** British forces in Basra hand over control of southern Iraq to the US army.

May 1 Carol Ann Duffy becomes the first female poet laureate. **8** *Daily Telegraph* begins to publish leaked details of MPs' expenses claims causing a major political scandal. **19** President of Sri Lanka announces victory over the Tamil Tigers and an end to the 26-year civil war. Michael Martin, Speaker of the House of Commons, is forced to resign over his handling of the MPs' expenses scandal. **21** Following a campaign led by actress Joanna Lumley, the Government announces that Gurkhas who served prior to 1997 will have the same rights of settlement in the UK as those who have served since that date. **25** North Korea carries out an underground nuclear test and fires three short-range missiles. **31** Death of flamboyant drag entertainer Danny La Rue, aged 81.

June 1 GM (General Motors) files for Chapter 11 bankruptcy protection as crisis in car industry intensifies. Air France Airbus A330, carrying 228 people, lost in the Atlantic on flight from Rio de Janeiro to Paris. **2** Revelation that Home Secretary Jacqui Smith, hurt by expenses scandal, is to leave the Cabinet. **3** Hazel Blears, Communities and Local Government Minister, resigns from Cabinet amidst political turmoil at Westminster. **4** Voting in European and Council elections (*see below*). Resignation of James Purnell, Work and Pensions Secretary, as polls close. **5** Cabinet reshuffle: Alistair Darling remains as Chancellor, David Miliband as Foreign Secretary. Alan Johnson promoted to Home Secretary, Bob Ainsworth to Defence, Yvette Cooper to Work and Pensions. Geoff Hoon and John Hutton among ministers to leave Government. **12** Presidential poll takes place in Iran; weeks of unrest follow the disputed re-election of President Ahmadinejad. **14** First swine flu death in the UK occurs in Scotland. **18** MPs' expenses claims since 2004 are officially published but with many details blacked out. **19** British forces launch Operation Panther's Claw in Afghanistan's Helmand Province. **22** Conservative MP John Bercow is elected Speaker of the House of Commons. **25** Pop superstar Michael Jackson dies aged 50. **29** In the USA Bernard Madoff is sentenced to 150 years in prison for investment fraud. **30** In Iraq US forces withdraw from Baghdad and other major cities.

July 10 Eight British soldiers die in Afghanistan in a 24-hour period. **18** First World War veteran Henry Allingham dies aged 113. **23** The National Pandemic Flu Service is launched to provide online and telephone advice about swine flu. Chloe Smith wins the Norwich North by-election for the Conservatives, becoming the youngest MP at the age of 27. **21** In response to the MPs' expenses scandal the Parliamentary Standards Act comes into force, setting up the Parliamentary Standards Authority. **25** The last surviving British Tommy of the First World War, Harry Patch, dies aged 111. **26** Sarah Palin steps

A.D.
down as Governor of Alaska. **30** The House of Lords allows an appeal by multiple sclerosis sufferer, Debbie Purdy, and as a result the Director of Public Prosecutions issues a clarification of the law on assisted suicide on 23 September.

August 5 In Iran President Ahmadinejad is sworn in for a second term despite continuing street protests over the election. **7** Great train robber Ronnie Biggs is released from prison on medical grounds. **20** Convicted Lockerbie bomber, Abdul Baset Ali al-Megrahi, is released by the Scottish government on compassionate grounds and flown to Libya. In Afghanistan voting takes place in the presidential election. **23** England's cricket team defeats the Australians at the Oval to regain the Ashes with a 2-1 series win. **26** US Senator Edward Kennedy dies aged 77.

September 7 At the end of a retrial three British Muslims are convicted in London of plotting to use liquid explosives to blow up at least seven transatlantic airliners in mid-air in 2006. **8** In Afghanistan, following claims of widespread vote-rigging in August's presidential election, the UN-sponsored Electoral Complaints Commission demands that there should be a partial recount. **14** Celebrity TV chef Keith Floyd dies aged 65. **16** With all the votes counted, Afghanistan's Independent Election Commission says that President Karzai has won outright without the need for a run-off. **24** It is announced that a valuable hoard of Anglo-Saxon gold and silver artefacts has been found by a metal detectorist in a field in Staffordshire. **30** *The Sun* declares its support for the Conservatives at the next General Election.

October 1 The UK Supreme Court begins work, replacing the House of Lords as the highest court in the land. **2** In a second referendum in the Republic of Ireland, 67 per cent of those who voted agree to the ratification of the EU Lisbon Treaty. **9** President Obama is awarded the Nobel Peace Prize. **10** President Kaczynski of Poland signs the EU Lisbon Treaty. **12** Sir Thomas Legg informs individual MPs by letter of the results of his inquiry into their second homes expenses claims. **18** British racing driver Jenson Button wins the 2009 Formula One World Championship after finishing fifth in the Brazilian Grand Prix. **19** In Afghanistan the UN-sponsored Electoral Complaints Commission rejects a third of President Karzai's votes so that his share falls below 50 per cent; a run-off against his main rival, Dr Abdullah, becomes necessary. **20** Afghanistan's Independent Election Commission orders that the election run-off take place on 7 November. **22** British National Party leader Nick Griffin appears for the first time on BBC TV's *Question Time*. **29** Norman Painting, who played the part of Phil Archer in *The Archers* for more than fifty years, dies aged 85. **30** Professor David Nutt, chairman of the Advisory Council on the Misuse of Drugs, is sacked by the Home Secretary after criticising government drugs policy.

November 1 In Afghanistan Dr Abdullah pulls out of the run-off election; it is cancelled and President Karzai is declared the winner. **3** The President of the Czech Republic, Vaclav Klaus, signs the Lisbon Treaty, the final EU head of state to do so. In Afghanistan five British soldiers are shot and killed inside their base by an Afghan policeman. **4** Sir Christopher Kelly's Committee on Standards in Public Life publishes its proposals on the reform of MPs' allowances. **5** At Fort Hood, Texas, a Muslim US army major shoots thirteen dead. **7** US House of Representatives backs a healthcare reform bill by 220 votes to 215. **19** Herman Van Rompuy, the Belgian Prime Minister, is chosen as the first permanent President of the European Council; Labour peer Baroness Ashton will be the EU's first foreign minister. **20** Heavy rain causes extensive flooding in Cumbria; PC Barker dies when a bridge is swept away at Workington. **24** The inquiry into the Iraq War chaired by Sir John Chilcot opens in London. **27** The Nevsky Express train travelling from Moscow to St Petersburg is derailed by a bomb, killing 26 people. Top US golfer Tiger Woods sustains minor injuries when he crashes his car as he leaves his house in the early hours of the morning; revelations

A.D.
about his private life leads Woods to announce that he is taking indefinite leave from golf in order to concentrate on his family.

December 1 President Obama orders 30,000 extra US troops to be sent to Afghanistan within the next six months. EU Lisbon Treaty comes into force. **7** The number of British service personnel to die in Afghanistan in 2009 reaches 100. UN Climate Change Conference opens in Copenhagen; draft of Copenhagen Accord on climate change measures is 'noted' by delegates as conference ends on 19 December. **9** Chancellor Alistair Darling delivers his Pre-Budget Report. **19** 2,000 passengers are stranded when five Eurostar trains break down in the Channel Tunnel due to freezing weather conditions in Northern France. **24** US Senate passes healthcare reform bill. **25** A Nigerian Muslim, Umar Abdulmutallab, fails to detonate explosives concealed in his underwear near the end of a transatlantic flight from Amsterdam to Detroit. **30** In Iraq British IT consultant Peter Moore is freed after being held hostage for 2½ years.

2010

January 5 Britain experiences its heaviest snowfall for decades. **8** In the Cabinda province of Angola separatist gunmen attack a bus carrying the Togo national football team taking part in the Africa Cup of Nations. **12** A 7·0 magnitude earthquake devastates the capital of Haiti, Port-au-Prince. **19** Announcement that Cadbury is to be taken over by the US food group Kraft. **25** In Iraq former government minister and cousin of Saddam Hussein, Ali Hassan al-Majid ('Chemical Ali'), is executed. **27** American writer and recluse J D Salinger dies aged 91. **29** Former Prime Minister Tony Blair gives evidence to the Chilcot inquiry into the Iraq War.

February 4 Sir Thomas Legg's report on MPs' expenses is published. **5** In Northern Ireland the Democratic Unionist Party and Sinn Fein reach agreement on the devolution of policing and justice powers. **15** Two trains collide near Halle in Belgium killing eighteen people. **19** Senior Hamas military commander, Mahmoud al-Mabhouh, is murdered in Dubai by assassins using, amongst others, forged British passports. **20** At least 42 die as flash floods and mudslides hit Madeira. **21** Allegations of bullying against Prime Minister Gordon Brown hit the headlines when a new book is serialised in a Sunday newspaper. **25** Director of Public Prosecutions announces new guidelines on assisted suicide cases. **27** An 8·8 magnitude earthquake occurs off the coast of Chile.

March 1 In a statement Lord Ashcroft, Conservative Party deputy chairman and donor, reveals that he is a 'non-dom' for UK tax purposes. **3** Former Labour Party leader Michael Foot dies aged 96. **5** Prime Minister Gordon Brown appears before the Chilcot inquiry. **9** Israel announces construction of 1,600 new homes in East Jerusalem during the visit of US Vice-President Joe Biden, damaging relations between the two countries. **11** Three MPs and a peer appear in court over criminal charges connected with their expenses claims. **21** Pastoral letter from Pope Benedict XVI to Irish Catholics apologising for child sex abuse scandals is read out at Sunday mass in Ireland. **23** Britain expels an Israeli diplomat after evidence points to Israel's involvement in cloning of British passports used in assassination of Hamas commander. President Obama signs his healthcare reform bill into law. **24** Chancellor Alistair Darling presents his Budget in the Commons. **29** Two women suicide bombers blow themselves up on Metro trains in Moscow, killing 39 people. **31** Four men are convicted of armed robbery at the Old Bailey in the first trial to be held without a jury as a result of fears of jury tampering.

April 6 General election campaign begins when Gordon Brown asks the Queen to dissolve parliament and names 6 May as polling day. **8** Presidents Obama and Medvedev sign a new US-Russian Strategic Arms Reduction Treaty in Prague. **10** Polish President Lech Kaczynski, his wife and many senior Polish figures, en route to commemorate the 70th anniversary of the Katyn massacre, are killed when their aircraft crashes as it tries to land in fog at Smolensk. **14** A 6·9 magnitude earthquake strikes Yushu county, Qinghai, China, killing over 2,000 people. **15** The danger to aircraft engines posed by ash from Iceland's erupting Eyjafjallajökull volcano results in the closure of airspace over Britain for six days and massive disruption to travel. Party leaders, Gordon Brown, David Cameron and Nick Clegg, take part in the first-ever television debate in British electoral history. **20** Oil drilling rig *Deepwater Horizon* explodes and sinks off the coast of Louisiana in the Gulf of Mexico, killing eleven; oil flowing from the damaged well results in massive pollution. **22** Catholic bishops in England and Wales publish a 'heartfelt apology' for clerical child abuse scandals. **28** In Rochdale Prime Minister Gordon Brown is overheard describing a Labour voter whom he had just talked to in the street as a 'bigoted woman'.

May 2 European Union and the International Monetary Fund agree austerity measures with the Greek government, clearing the way for a bailout package. **5** Three people die in Athens when rioters protesting against the Greek government's austerity measures set fire to a bank. **6** UK General Election results in a hung parliament: the Conservatives are the largest party but without an overall majority. **8** Mohamed Al-Fayed sells Harrods to the government of Qatar. **9** Europe's finance ministers approve a bailout fund worth 750 billion euros designed to ensure financial stability in Europe. **11** Prime Minister Gordon Brown resigns when the Conservatives and Liberal Democrats agree to form a coalition government: David Cameron becomes Prime Minister with Nick Clegg as his Deputy. **24** Chancellor George Osborne and Chief Secretary to the Treasury David Laws set out spending cuts worth £6·2 billion. **25** In the Queen's Speech the coalition government sets out its first legislative programme. **29** David Laws resigns as Chief Secretary to the Treasury when it is revealed that he had claimed for rent paid to his partner. **31** Nine pro-Palestinian activists are killed when commandos storm their vessel as Israeli forces intercept a flotilla of ships carrying aid to the Gaza Strip.

June 2 In Cumbria taxi driver Derrick Bird shoots 12 people dead before committing suicide. **4** Naoto Kan becomes Prime Minister of Japan. **15** The Saville Inquiry, set up in 1998, publishes its report into the events of Bloody Sunday in Northern Ireland; David Cameron issues an apology. **22** George Osborne presents his emergency budget statement. **23** President Obama relieves General Stanley A McChrystal of his post as US Commander in Afghanistan after his derogatory remarks about members of the administration are published; he is replaced by General David Petraeus. **24** Julia Gillard becomes Australia's first woman Prime Minister when she ousts Kevin Rudd as leader of the Labor Party. **27** England are knocked out of the FIFA World Cup in South Africa, losing 4–1 to Germany.

July 9 Ten Russian agents are expelled from the USA in exchange for four Russians jailed for spying for the West. **11** Spain beats the Netherlands 1-0 in extra time in the FIFA World Cup Final in South Africa. **12** General Synod of the Church of England approves legislation to consecrate women bishops. **15** BP announces that it has finally halted the flow of oil from the *Deepwater Horizon*. **26** Some 92,000 classified intelligence documents relating to the war in Afghanistan are released on the WikiLeaks website, founded by Julian Assange. **27** BP announces that Tony Hayward will be replaced as Chief Executive by Bob Dudley on 1 October. **29** In Russia a heatwave and drought lead to extensive outbreaks of wildfires. In Pakistan monsoon rains begin to cause severe flooding, which affects more than 20 million people during August.

August 5 A cave-in at a copper and gold mine near Copiapo in northern Chile traps 33 miners under ground. In Afghanistan ten aid workers are killed in an ambush, including a British doctor Karen Woo. **21** General Election in Australia results in a hung parliament; Julia Gillard forms a Labor

minority government. **29** Three members of the Pakistani cricket team are alleged to have taken part in a spot-fixing betting scam during the test match at Lord's. **31** President Obama declares the end of US combat operations in Iraq.

September 1 Tony Blair's memoir, *A Journey*, is published. **5** Basque separatist group ETA announces a ceasefire. **16** Pope Benedict XVI begins a state visit to the UK. **18** Parliamentary elections take place in Afghanistan. **25** Result of the Labour Party leadership election is announced after the annual party conference: Ed Miliband defeats his older brother David by 50·65 to 49·35 per cent of the votes.

October 3 Commonwealth Games open in Delhi, India. **8** Kidnapped British aid worker, Dr Linda Nordgrove, is accidentally killed during a US rescue attempt in Afghanistan. **11** Lady Justice Hallett opens the inquests into the victims of the 7 July 2005 London Bombings. **13** The rescue is completed of the 33 Chilean miners trapped underground since 5 August. **19** David Cameron announces the results of the coalition government's Strategic Defence and Security Review. **20** Chancellor George Osborne announces a package of £81 billion public spending cuts in his Comprehensive Spending Review. **21** Outbreak of sickness in Haiti is diagnosed as cholera. **22** Some 400,000 classified US military documents on the war in Iraq are published on the WikiLeaks website. **27** The French National Assembly votes to increase the pension age from 60 to 62 despite weeks of strikes and demonstrations against President Sarkozy's proposals. **29** Al-Qaeda cargo plane bomb plot originating in Yemen is foiled.

November 2 Republicans win control of the House of Representatives in the US midterm elections. **5** A special election court strips Labour MP Phil Woolas of his seat for lying during the General Election campaign and triggers a by-election in his Oldham East and Saddleworth constituency. **10** A student demonstration against increasing tuition fees turns violent at the Tory Millbank headquarters in London. **13** In Burma opposition leader Aung San Suu Kyi is released after seven years under house arrest. **14** British sailors Paul and Rachel Chandler are freed by Somali pirates more than twelve months after they were seized off the Seychelles. **16** The engagement is announced between Prince William and Kate Middleton. **21** Ireland is forced to apply to the EU and the IMF for an international bailout to deal with its financial crisis. **23** North Korea shells Yeonpyeong Island, killing four South Koreans. **28** WikiLeaks website publishes 250,000 diplomatic cables sent by US embassies.

December 2 The 2018 FIFA World Cup is awarded to Russia; England's bid comes last with only two votes. **7** WikiLeak's founder Julian Assange is arrested and remanded in custody in London over alleged sexual assaults in Sweden; he is released on bail on 16 December. **9** A car taking Prince Charles and the Duchess of Cornwall to the Palladium is attacked in central London by student demonstrators; earlier in the day MPs had voted to increase university tuition fees. **10** Chinese dissident Liu Xiabo, who is serving an 11-year jail term for subversion, is awarded the Nobel Peace Prize in Oslo; at the ceremony he is represented by an empty chair. **18** Winter weather in the UK disrupts pre-Christmas travel by air, road and rail.

EUROPE IN CRISIS

2011

January 4 VAT is increased to 20 per cent in the UK. **5** In Tunisia demonstrations continue as the unemployed man who set himself alight in December dies; during January anti-government protests spread to many countries across North Africa and the Middle East. **7** England's cricketers retain the Ashes in Australia. **9** In southern Sudan voting begins in a referendum on independence; 99 per cent vote in favour. **12** Severe flooding in Queensland, Australia reaches the state capital Brisbane. **14** President Zine El Abidine Ben Ali flees Tunisia when a general strike leads to violent clashes. **17** In Egypt demonstrations begin after a protester sets himself alight outside the parliament building in Cairo. **20** Labour Shadow Chancellor Alan Johnson resigns for personal reasons and is replaced by Ed Balls. **24** A suicide bomber kills 35 people at Moscow's Domodedovo airport. **25** Thousands of Egyptians take to the streets in a national 'day of rage' against President Mubarak's government. **31** Egyptian army states that it will not use force against protesters.

February 1 Hosni Mubarak's announcement that he will not stand for another term as president in September fails to satisfy demonstrators. **10** In an address to the nation President Mubarak refuses to resign, to the fury of protesters gathered in Tahrir Square, Cairo. **11** It is announced that President Mubarak has resigned. **17** Coalition Government announces that it is scrapping plans to sell off state-owned woodland. In Libya protesters take to the streets in a 'day of rage' against Colonel Gaddafi's rule. **22** A 6·3 magnitude earthquake hits Christchurch, New Zealand; some 180 people are killed. **25** Irish General Election results in a heavy defeat for governing party Fianna Fail; Enda Kenny becomes Taoiseach at the head of a Fine Gael-Labour coalition. **27** The film *The King's Speech* wins four Oscars, including Academy Award for Best Picture. In Libya a National Transitional Council is formed in the rebel-held city of Benghazi.

March 3 A referendum in Wales approves additional law-making powers for the Welsh National Assembly. **11** A 9·0 magnitude undersea earthquake creates a tsunami that devastates the north-east coast of Japan. **12** There is an explosion at Japan's Fukushima nuclear power plant, damaged in the earthquake and tsunami; there are ongoing fears of radiation leaks. **14** At the request of Bahrain, the Gulf Cooperation Council sends forces into the country, led by Saudi Arabian troops, to quell anti-government protests. **17** UN Security Council adopts Resolution 1973 permitting all necessary measures to protect Libyan civilians under threat of attack. **19** Acting under the UN mandate, the coalition begins military action to establish a no-fly zone over Libya and halt the advance of forces loyal to Colonel Gaddafi. **23** Chancellor George Osborne presents his budget to parliament. Actress Elizabeth Taylor dies aged 79. **26** Up to half a million people take part in a rally in London organised by the TUC against the Coalition Government's cuts in public expenditure.

April 4 Health Secretary Andrew Lansley announces a delay to NHS reform legislation to allow time for more consultation. **8** News International admits liability, apologises and offers compensation in a number of cases brought against it for alleged phone hacking by the *News of the World*. **11** After weeks of fighting in Ivory Coast former president Laurent Gbagbo, who refused to step down after losing the presidential election in November 2010, is finally taken prisoner by supporters of the new president Alassane Ouattara. **21** In Syria, President Assad lifts the state of emergency but unrest continues and many protesters are killed by the security forces. **29** Prince William marries Kate Middleton at Westminster Abbey.

May 1 President Obama announces that Al-Qaeda leader Osama Bin Laden has been killed by US ground forces at Abbottabad near Islamabad, Pakistan. **5** Elections are held for local councils in England and for the Welsh National Assembly, Scottish Parliament and Northern Ireland Assembly; in a referendum the alternative vote system for elections to the House of Commons is rejected by 67·9% to 32·1%. **14** Dominique Strauss-Kahn, head of the IMF and possible Socialist candidate for the French Presidency, is arrested at John F Kennedy Airport, New York City, for an alleged sexual assault on a hotel maid. **17** The Queen begins the first state visit by a British monarch to the Republic of Ireland since it became independent in 1921. **22** UK military operations in Iraq – Operation Telic – officially end.

24 President Obama begins a state visit to Britain.

June 1 The controversial president of FIFA, Sepp Blatter, is re-elected unopposed for a fourth term. **3** President Saleh of the Republic of Yemen is seriously injured in a rebel attack on his palace. **7** David Cameron announces changes to NHS reforms following the end of the 'listening exercise'. **21** Government confirms that proposals by Justice Secretary Kenneth Clarke to increase sentence discount to 50% for early guilty pleas have been shelved. **29** Greek Parliament passes a package of austerity measures, allowing the government to claim the latest tranche of the bailout package.

July 7 News International announces that it is closing the *News of the World* following the revelation that a private detective hacked into the mobile phone of murdered schoolgirl, Milly Dowler. **8** Former editor of the *News of the World*, Andy Coulson, is arrested for questioning over phone hacking. **9** South Sudan becomes an independent state. **13** News Corporation withdraws its bid to take full control of BSkyB after it is referred to the Competition Commission. Three terrorist explosions in Mumbai, India, kill 22 and injure more than 100. **15** Rebekah Brooks resigns as chief executive of News International; she is arrested for questioning over phone hacking on 17 July. **17** Metropolitan Police Commissioner Sir Paul Stephenson resigns over links with a former *News of the World* deputy editor. **19** Rupert and James Murdoch and Rebekah Brooks appear before the Commons Culture, Media and Sport Select Committee to answer questions concerning the phone hacking scandal. **21** Eurozone leaders agree a new plan to bail out Greece. **22** In Norway a right-wing extremist, Anders Behring Breivik, bombs government buildings in Oslo, then shoots dead 69 people at a Labour Party summer camp on the island of Utoeya. **27** The British government recognises the Libyan National Transitional Council.

August 2 In return for a package of spending cuts, the US Congress passes legislation to raise the debt ceiling in order to avoid a default on the national debt; President Obama signs the Budget Control Act of 2011 into law. **3** Trial begins in Cairo of former Egyptian president Hosni Mubarak on charges of killing protesters and abuse of power. **6** A protest march over the fatal shooting by police of a suspect, Mark Duggan, two days earlier, is followed by an outbreak of rioting, arson and looting in the Tottenham area of London. **7** There is widespread disorder in many parts of London. **8** Rioting spreads to other parts of Britain, including the West Midlands, Liverpool, Leeds and Bristol. **9** The presence of 16,000 police officers on the streets of London brings the situation in the capital under control. **10** Three men protecting their neighbourhood are killed in a hit-and-run incident in Birmingham, bringing the death toll during the riots to five. **23** In Libya rebels overrun Colonel Gaddafi's compound as they take control of Tripoli. In New York City a judge dismisses sexual assault charges against Dominique Strauss-Kahn.

September 15 In Libya rebel fighters begin seesaw battle for Colonel Gaddafi's birthplace, Sirte. **20** In Afghanistan former President Rabbani is killed at his home in Kabul when a member of a Taliban delegation detonates a bomb hidden in his turban. **23** Palestinian President Mahmoud Abbas submits a request to the UN Secretary-General to join the UN as a full member state, based on pre-1967 borders.

October 5 Steve Jobs, co-founder of the Apple computer company, dies of cancer aged 56. **14** Defence Secretary Dr Liam Fox resigns over the activities of his friend and self-styled adviser, Adam Werritty. **18** Israel releases 1,027 Palestinians held in Israeli prisons in exchange for Sergeant Major Gilad Shalit, abducted by Hamas in 2006. **20** Colonel Gaddafi and his son Mutassim are captured and killed as they attempt to escape from Sirte. **21** St Paul's Cathedral closes for a week for health and safety reasons after anti-capitalist protesters set up camp on the forecourt; the Canon Chancellor, Dr Giles Fraser, and the Dean, Rt Rev Graeme Knowles, later resign. **23** A major

7·2 magnitude earthquake occurs near the city of Van in eastern Turkey, killing over 600 people. **24** The House of Commons votes to reject a referendum on EU membership by 483 to 111. **27** Michael D Higgins is elected President of the Republic of Ireland. **28** At the Commonwealth heads of Government meeting in Australia it is agreed that daughters of future monarchs will have the same succession rights as sons and that the heir to the throne can marry a Roman Catholic. **27** At a summit meeting in Brussels eurozone leaders agree a package of measures to deal with the European debt crisis. **31** Prime Minister George Papandreou proposes to hold a referendum in Greece on the emergency bailout package; he withdraws the proposal on 3 November under pressure from France and Germany. The UN Population Division estimates that the world's population has reached seven billion.

November 1 Three Pakistani cricketers are convicted of fixing play during the Lord's test match in 2010 and jailed. **4** Seven people are killed in a multiple vehicle crash on the M5 near Taunton. **7** In Los Angeles Dr Conrad Murray is convicted of the involuntary manslaughter of Michael Jackson. **8** Brodie Clark, director of the UK Border Force, resigns after Home Secretary Theresa May says he relaxed border controls without authority. **10** In a second appearance before the Culture, Media and Sport Select Committee, James Murdoch insists he was unaware of the extent of phone hacking at the *News of the World*. **11** In Greece, following the resignation of Mr Papandreou, Lucas Papademos is sworn in as Prime Minister of an interim national unity government. **12** The Arab League votes to suspend Syria over the violent suppression of dissidents. Silvio Berlusconi tenders his resignation as Prime Minister of Italy. **14** Inquiry led by Lord Justice Leveson into the culture, practices and ethics of the British press opens. **17** The government announces that it is selling Northern Rock, nationalised in 2008, to Sir Richard Branson's Virgin Money for £747 million. **19** In Libya Colonel Gaddafi's son, Saif al-Islam, is captured. In Egypt mass protests begin in Cairo's Tahrir Square and elsewhere against the ruling Supreme Council of the Armed Forces. **23** Yemen's President Saleh signs an agreement in Saudi Arabia to leave office. **26** A NATO air strike on a Pakistani border checkpoint kills 24 soldiers. **27** Arab League ministers meeting in Cairo approve economic sanctions against Syria. **28** Egyptians begin voting in the first parliamentary elections since the overthrow of President Mubarak. **29** Chancellor George Osborne announces further austerity measures in his Autumn Statement. **30** Public sector workers across Britain strike over changes to their pensions.

December 4 In Russia voting for the State Duma sees a reduction in support for Mr Putin's United Russia party; there are protests over alleged election fraud. **9** At EU talks in Brussels David Cameron refuses to accept changes to the Lisbon Treaty as part of the eurozone financial rescue plan. **17** North Korea's Supreme Leader Kim Jong-il dies aged 69. **18** The last American troops leave Iraq as the war formally ends. **19** Syria agrees to allow Arab League observers to enter the country to monitor compliance with measures to halt violence against anti-government protesters. **22** More than 70 people are killed in a series of bomb attacks in the Iraqi capital, Baghdad. **23** In Syria 44 people are killed by two car bombs in Damascus as Arab League monitors arrive in the country.

2012

January 3 Two men are convicted of murdering Stephen Lawrence who was stabbed to death by a racist gang in south London in 1993. **13** Cruise ship *Costa Concordia* hits rocks off the Italian island of Giglio and capsizes, resulting in 32 deaths. Standard and Poor's rating agency downgrades the credit rating of France and other eurozone countries. **28** Arab League suspends its observer mission to Syria as violence continues. **31** Sir Fred Goodwin, former Chief Executive of the Royal Bank of Scotland, is stripped of his knighthood.

February 4 Russia and China veto a draft UN Security

Council resolution on Syria. **6** Sixtieth anniversary of Queen Elizabeth II's succession to the throne. **8** Fabio Capello resigns as England football manager after a dispute with the FA. **12** In Greece MPs vote to approve austerity measures in return for a new eurozone bailout. **23** Kofi Annan is appointed UN/Arab League special envoy to Syria. **26** The film *The Artist* wins five Oscars, including best picture, best director and best actor.

March 4 Vladimir Putin is elected for a third term as President of Russia. **11** In Afghanistan a US army staff sergeant shoots dead 16 civilians in Kandahar. **14** The towns of Chelmsford, St Asaph and Perth are awarded city status to mark the Queen's Diamond Jubilee. **16** Kofi Annan submits a six-point peace plan for Syria to the UN; the Security Council adopts a statement backing it on 21 March. **21** Chancellor George Osborne delivers his 2012 budget, which includes a cut in the top rate of income tax from 50p to 45p. **27** The Coalition's Health and Social Care Bill receives the royal assent.

April 1 In by-elections in Burma pro-democracy leader Aung San Suu Kyi and her party win seats in parliament. **3** James Murdoch steps down as chairman of BSkyB. **7** The Oxford and Cambridge Boat Race is disrupted by a swimmer protesting against elitism. **10** The Chinese Communist Party suspends Bo Xilai from the Politburo and the Central Committee; his wife is suspected of involvement in the death of a British businessman, Neil Heywood. **12** A UN-backed ceasefire in Syria comes into effect but fails to bring about a halt to the violence. **16** The trial of Anders Breivik for killing a total of 77 people begins in Oslo, Norway. **22** The controversial Formula One 2012 Bahrein Grand Prix goes ahead. **24** James Murdoch gives evidence to the Leveson Inquiry, followed by his father Rupert on the two succeeding days. **25** UK economy returns to recession after shrinking by 0·2% in first three months of year. **30** Met Office says April the UK's wettest month since records began.

May 1 Presidents Obama and Karzai sign 10-year agreement on US development aid to Afghanistan following withdrawal; House of Commons committee declares Rupert Murdoch unfit to run an international company. **2** Aung San Suu Kyi sworn in as member of Burmese parliament. **3** Labour gains in English and Welsh local elections; in Scotland Labour hold Glasgow but SNP take most seats; Boris Johnson re-elected London mayor. **4** Iranian President Ahmadinejad faces setback as conservative rivals consolidate position in the legislature, the Majlis. **5** Japan shuts down last operational nuclear reactor; Chelsea beat Liverpool 2-1 to take FA Cup. **6** François Hollande defeats Nicolas Sarkozy in French presidential election, with 51·6% of vote to 48·4%; Putin sworn in as President of Russia for third time; Greek election successes for parties opposing EU/IMF bailout terms. **8** Israeli prime minister Netanyahu forms coalition with opposition Kadima. **9** President Obama declares support for gay marriage. **10** Ruling FLN/RND coalition retain power in Algerian legislative elections; UK police mount protest against reforms. **13** Manchester City take Premier League title on beating Manchester United on goal difference. **15** Jean-Marc Ayrault appointed French prime minister. **16** New elections called in Greece after failure to form coalition government. **18** Olympic Flame arrives in Cornwall from Athens in preparation for 2012 Summer Olympics; German singer Dietrich Fischer-Dieskau dies (86). **19** Chelsea beat Bayern Munich to take European Cup. **20** Tomislav Nikolic elected president of Serbia; convicted 1988 Lockerbie bomber Abdelbaset al-Megrahi dies (60); Robin Gibb of The Bee Gees dies (62). **22** Lt.-Commander Sarah West becomes Royal Navy's first female warship commander; Norwegian parliament ends state involvement in religion by abolishing Church of Norway. **23-4** Initial stage of Egypt's first free presidential election. **25** Syrian troops massacre of over 100 civilians in Houla provokes international condemnation; First Minister Alex Salmond launches 'Yes' campaign for Scottish independence. **30** Former Liberian president Charles Taylor sentenced to 50 years for war crimes at The Hague; Irish referendum accepts European Fiscal Compact by 60·3% to 39·7%; WikiLeaks founder Julian Assange loses appeal against extradition from UK to Sweden. **31** Egypt's notorious state of emergency law ends after 31 years in operation.

June 1 UN Human Rights Council condemns 25 May Houla massacre by Syrian forces, Russia, China and Cuba voting against. **2** Former Egyptian President Hosni Mubarak sentenced to life imprisonment for role in death of unarmed demonstrators in January 2011; **2-5** Four-day bank holiday weekend celebrating Queen Elizabeth II's Diamond Jubilee. **4** Over 20 killed in car bomb explosion at Iraq government offices. **5** Science fiction writer Ray Bradbury dies (91). **6** Opposition accuses Syrian government militia of massacre of over 70 civilians in Hama. **7** Former UN secretary general Kofi Annan says Syria faces civil war after failure of peace efforts. **8** International Atomic Energy Agency ends talks with Iran saying there has been no progress; UK Home Secretary announces plans to imprison parents who force arranged marriages on children. **9-10** Flooding in Wales after heavy rains. **10** State of emergency in Burma following Buddhist-Muslim clashes. **11** Russian police raid homes of opposition activists on eve of demonstration. **14** Egyptian Supreme Court declares 2011 elections to legislative lower house unconstitutional. **16** UN suspends peacekeeping mission in Syria. **17** Centre right New Democracy wins 29·7% of vote and far-left Syriza 26·9% in election in Greece. **18** Prince Salman bin Abdulaziz nominated heir apparent to Saudi Arabian throne. **19** WikiLeaks founder Assange seeks asylum in Ecuador's UK embassy. **20** Antonis Samaras becomes Greek prime minister as New Democracy forms coalition with Pasok and the Democratic Left. **22** Paraguay's President Fernando Lugo ousted in 'constitutional coup' and succeeded by Federico Franco. **24** Muslim Brotherhood's Freedom and Justice party candidate Mohammed Morsi declared Egyptian president with 51·7% of vote. **25** Over 30 senior Syrian army officers defect to Turkey. **27** President Bashar al-Assad declares Syria is in a state of war; Barclays Bank fined £290 million for attempted manipulation of interbank interest rates; former Provisional IRA commander Martin McGuinness, Northern Ireland deputy first minister, shakes Queen's hand in historic Belfast meeting. **29** Mercosur suspends Paraguay's membership following ousting of President Lugo. **30** UK government announces independent review of interbank lending following scandal; Israeli former prime minister Yitzhak Shamir dies (96).

July 1 Syrian opposition rejects UN peace plan; Enrique Peña Nieto elected Mexican president. **3** Barclays chief executive Bob Diamond resigns following interbank lending rate scandal. **4** George Entwistle named as next BBC director-general; physicists at CERN, Switzerland, announce discovery of the 'Higgs boson' particle. **5** The Shard, Europe's highest habitable structure, opens in London. **7** Elections held to Libyan General National Congress; Serena Williams (US) beats Agnieszka Radwanska (Poland) in Wimbledon women's singles final. **8** Andy Murray, the first Briton in 74 years to reach Wimbledon men's singles final defeated by Roger Federer (Switz.) **10** UK coalition drops plans for House of Lords reform as substantial number of Tory MPs oppose; Frances O'Grady appointed first TUC female general secretary. **11** Syrian ambassador to Iraq defects; clashes in Madrid as Spanish government introduces further austerity measures. **15** The International Red Cross declares Syria in state of civil war and that Geneva Conventions apply; Nkosazana Dlamini-Zuma of South Africa elected first female chair of African Union Commission. **17** Mahmoud Jibril's National Forces Alliance emerges as largest single party in Libyan elections. **18** Suicide bomber kills Syrian defence minister and other senior officials in attack in capital Damascus; Hezbollah accused of suicide bomb attack on Israeli tourists in Bulgaria. **19** Russia and China veto UN Security Council sanctions on Syrian government; British prime minister Cameron says public sending cuts will continue till end of decade. **22** Arab League calls on Syrian President Assad to resign to end

further bloodshed; Bradley Wiggins becomes first British cyclist to win Tour de France. **23** Syrian government says prepared to use chemical and biological weapons against foreign attack. **24** John Dramani Mahama becomes President of Ghana on death of John Atta Mills (68); Hisham Qandi appointed Egyptian prime minister; UK Crown Prosecution Service confirms Andy Coulson and Rebekah Brooks will face charges related to News International phone hacking. **25** North Korean leader Kim Jong-un's marriage announced; Ivica Dačić becomes Serb prime minister; Scottish Government proposes to legalise same-sex marriage. **27** 2012 Summer Olympic Games open in London. **30** Power failure in 22 of India's 28 states cuts power to 700 million people; 200,000 people flee fighting in Syrian city of Aleppo; Irish writer Maeve Binchy dies (72). **31** American writer Gore Vidal dies (86).

August 2 Former UN Secretary General Kofi Annan resigns as special envoy to Syria as peace plan fails. **5** US rover 'Curiosity' lands on Mars to investigate possibilities of life. **6** Syrian prime minister defects to Jordan, declaring support for opposition. **9** Interim National Transitional Council in Libya passes authority to elected assembly. **12** Egyptian President Morsi asserts civilian control by retiring senior military officers; London Summer Olympics end. **16** South African police kill over 30 strikers at British-owned platinum mine; UN terminates observer mission in Syria as violence heightens; Ecuador grants asylum to Wikileaks founder Julian Assange. **17** Three 'Pussy Riot' punk band members convicted of hooliganism in Moscow for anti-Putin protest and imprisoned. **20** Ethiopian prime minister Meles Zenawi dies (57); President Obama threatens military action if Syria deploys chemical or biological weapons. **21** Total of US military deaths in Afghanistan reaches 2,000. **22** Russia joins World Trade Organisation. **25** Neil Armstrong, first person to land on the Moon, dies (82). **27** President Thein Sein of Burma (Myanmar) promotes economic reformers in cabinet changes. **29** Ukrainian high court rejects former prime minister Yulia Tymoshenko's appeal against conviction for abuse of office; London Paralympic Games open.

September 1 Ruling MPLA wins Angola elections. **2** Unification Church founder Sun Myung Moon dies (92). **4** UK prime minister Cameron's first major cabinet changes since 2010. **6** European Central Bank announces bond buying plan to ease debt crisis. **9** London Paralympic Games end. **10** Somali parliament elects Hassan Sheikh Mohamoud country's president. **11** Militia kill ambassador and three others in attack on US embassy in Libya; Barcelona demonstration demands Catalan independence. **12** Over 300 die in factory fires in Pakistan cities of Karachi and Lahore; liberal VVD and centre-left Labour successes in Netherlands elections. **13** Mustafa Abushagur becomes Libyan prime minister. **14** Duke and Duchess of Cambridge take legal action over topless photographs of Duchess in French magazine. **17** UK government announces sweeping reform of secondary school examinations in England. **18** Two police officers killed in Greater Manchester. **20** Bahrain government promises to adopt UN human rights report recommendations. **23** Libyan government dissolves unofficial armed groups following anti-militia demonstrations; Portuguese government withdraws social security tax rises following street protests. **25** China brings first aircraft carrier into service as dispute with Japan over Senkaku Islands intensifies. **27** Catalan Parliament votes to hold referendum on regional self-determination.

October 1 British historian Eric Hobsbawm dies (95). **2** Ruling United National Movement defeated by Georgian Dream in Georgia elections. **7** Venezuelan President Chavez wins fourth term. **8** €500 billion European Stability Mechanism rescue fund established. **12** EU awarded Nobel Peace Prize. **14** Ali Zidan replaces Mustafa Abushagur as Libyan prime minister. **15** Former King Norodom Sihanouk of Cambodia dies (89); Edinburgh Agreement sets out terms of 2014 Scottish independence referendum. **16** Cuban government eases restrictions on overseas travel. **19** Police begin investigation of DJ Jimmy Savile's alleged sex abuse. **20** TUC mounts anti-austerity protests in London, Glasgow and Belfast. **21** Pope Benedict XVI names seven new saints; 1972 US Democrat presidential candidate George McGovern dies (90). **24** Over 50 die as Hurricane Sandy strikes Caribbean. **25** Double-dip recession officially over in UK; Israeli parties Likud and Yisrael Beiteinu merge. **26** Former Italian prime minister Berlusconi receives prison sentence for fraud. **28** Party of the Regions wins widely criticised Ukraine elections; opposition Social Democrats defeat Homeland Union in Lithuanian elections. **30** Over 90 die as Hurricane Sandy hits northeast United States. **31** UK government defeated in Commons vote on EU budget.

November 6 US President Obama wins second term; Spanish government condemns Catalan independence calls. **9** CIA director David Petraeus resigns over extra-marital affair; Justin Welby named next Archbishop of Canterbury. **10** BBC director general resigns as Savile sex abuse crisis intensifies. **11** Syrian opposition groups sign coalition pact. **14** Israeli forces kill Hamas military chief in Gaza, triggering cross-border clashes; anti-austerity protests in Spain, Portugal, Greece, Italy and Belgium. **15** Xi Jinping succeeds Hu Jintao as Chinese Communist Party secretary general; low turnout in England and Wales Police & Crime Commissioner elections; Labour gains Tory seat in three by-election wins. **19** EU recognises National Coalition for Syrian Revolutionary & Opposition Forces. **20** Church of England general synod rejects appointment of women bishops. **21** Ceasefire between Israel and Gaza Palestinians. **22** Tony Hall appointed BBC director general. **24** Protests against Egyptian President Morsi's decree extending his powers; Northern Ireland First Minister rejects Sinn Fein call for independence referendum. **25** Successes for pro-independence parties in Catalan elections. **26** Mark Carney named next Bank of England governor. **29** Leveson Enquiry into British media recommends new regulatory body; UN general assembly recognises Palestine as a state; Labour retains seats in three by-elections.

December 1 Enrique Peña Nieto sworn in as Mexican President. **2** Borut Pahor elected President of Slovenia. **4** Commonwealth agrees to change rules on monarchy to allow firstborn female succession; NATO agrees Turkish request to deploy Patriot missiles on border with Syria; UK Chancellor says austerity will continue till 2018. **6** Protests in Dublin over austerity budget. **8** John Mahama re-elected President of Ghana. **9** Social Liberal Union coalition victory in Romanian elections. **12** UN condemns North Korean space satellite launch; report reveals 'state collusion' in 1989 murder of Northern Ireland solicitor Pat Finucane. **13** EU finance ministers extend powers of European Central Bank. **14** 28 killed, including 2 children, at school shooting in Newton, Connecticut. **16** Shinzo Abe becomes Japan's prime minister after Liberal Democratic Party's landslide victory; Socialist Party successes in Venezuela gubernatorial elections. **19** Park Geun-hye elected South Korea's first female President. **21** President Obama urges stricter gun control. **23** New Egyptian constitution approved by 63·7 % of voters in low turnout as opposition alleges fraud. **27** Central African Republic appeals for international assistance against rebel attacks. **29** French court declares 75 % tax on country's wealthy unconstitutional. **31** German Chancellor Merkel warns of tougher economic situation in 2013.

2013

January 1 US Congress approves measures to avert 'fiscal cliff' of spending cuts and tax rises. **4** Hamas and Fatah unity rally in Gaza. **6** Syrian President Assad accuses rebels of being Western puppets. **11** French troops aid Mali government against Islamist rebels; Central African Republic government ceasefire with rebels. **14** Major British music retailer HMV goes into liquidation. **15** Horsemeat contamination scandal as horse DNA found in food in UK and Irish supermarkets. **17** Hostage crisis in Algeria as Islamist militants seize workers at natural gas plant. **20** President Obama inaugurated for second term; Austrian referendum vote to retain military conscription. **22** Israeli prime

minister Netanyahu's Likud Yisrael Beiteinu alliance wins majority in elections. **23** UK prime minister Cameron promises EU referendum after renegotiating membership terms; opposition boycotts Jordanian parliamentary elections; US armed forces end ban on women serving in combat. **25** Anti-government protests on second anniversary of Egyptian revolution. **26** Milos Zeman elected Czech Republic president. **28** Queen Beatrix of Netherlands announces intention to abdicate in favour of son Willem-Alexander. **29** UK government Commons defeat on proposals to redraw constituency boundaries. **31** UN report calls for immediate Israeli withdrawal from all settlements in occupied territories.

February 1 John Kerry succeeds Hillary Clinton as US Secretary of State. **2** Japanese prime minister says Japan will defend disputed Senkaku Islands. **4** Exhumed skeleton in Leicester declared that of English King Richard III; former minister Chris Huhne resigns as Lib Dem MP after admitting perverting course of justice. **6** Assassination of Tunisian opposition leader Chokri Belaid heightens instability. **8** EU leaders agree seven-year €34·4bn (£29bn) budget cut. **11** Pope Benedict XVI announces resignation. **12** North Korea conducts third nuclear weapon test; UK Court of Appeal rules compulsory work schemes for unemployed legally flawed. **15** Over 1,000 injured as meteor breaks up near Russian city of Chelyabinsk. **19** Australian Greens withdraw support from minority Labor government. **20** UK prime minister Cameron expresses remorse for 1919 massacre in Indian city of Amritsar; Bulgarian cabinet resigns following anti-government protests. **22** Britain stripped of AAA-rated debt status. **24** Anti-austerity parties make gains in Italian elections; Miguel Diaz-Canel's appointment as Cuban vice present signals eventual succession to the Castros. **25** Cardinal Keith O'Brien resigns as Archbishop of St Andrews and Edinburgh following sexual impropriety allegations. **28** Slovenian prime minister Janša ousted following corruption allegations.

March 5 President Chavez of Venezuela dies aged of 58. **7** Vicky Pryce, ex-wife of former minister Chris Huhne, guilty of perverting course of justice; both jailed. **8** UN Security Council imposes further sanctions on North Korea after nuclear test. **11** North Korea withdraws from 60-year armistice with South. **13** Argentine Cardinal Bergoglio elected Pope, taking name Francis; **15** High Court judgment gives go ahead to HS2 high-speed rail. **24** Central African Republic President Bozizé flees as rebels seize capital. **25** EU agrees €10 billion Cyprus bailout.

April 1 UK government introduces 'bedroom tax' housing benefit penalty on 'under-occupied' rooms. **2** UN General Assembly adopts treaty regulating conventional arms trade. **8** Former prime minister Thatcher dies aged 87. **14** Maduro elected Venezuelan president. **15** Terrorist bomb at Boston marathon kills five. **20** President Napolitano of Italy re-elected. **24** Over 1,000 die in Bangladesh factory collapse. **30** King Willem-Alexander succeeds Beatrix on Netherlands throne.

May 2 Ukip local election successes. **22** Fusilier Lee Rigby killed in London terror attack. **23** Riots in Stockholm cause widespread damage. **26** Anti-same-sex marriage demonstrations in Paris. **31** Tory MP Patrick Mercer resigns from party in 'cash for questions' scandal; eight killed in Istanbul anti-government protests.

June 6 Leaks reveal widespread internet surveillance by US National Security Agency (NSA). **7** US drone attack kills civilians in Pakistan's North Waziristan area. **9** Edward Snowden admits leaking NSA surveillance details, flees to Russia. **17–18** UK hosts G8 summit in Northern Ireland. **26** Australian prime minister Gillard resigns after defeat by Kevin Rudd in Labor leadership contest. **30** Protesters demand Egyptian President Morsi's resignation.

July 1 Mark Carney becomes Bank of England governor; Croatia 28th EU member. **3** Egyptian President Morsi deposed by military. **4** Metropolitan Police claim new evidence in missing Madeleine McCann case. **7** Andy Murray first Briton to win Wimbledon men's singles since 1936. **17** Same-sex marriage legalised in England and Wales from March 2014. **21** King Albert II of Belgium abdicates in favour of son Philippe. **22** Duke and Duchess of Cambridge have son, George, third in line to throne. **30** Irish legislation permitting limited abortion rights signed.

August 14 Many dead as Egyptian security forces attack former President Morsi's supporters; Israel-Palestine talks begin in Jerusalem. **21** Chelsea (formerly Bradley) Manning 35-year sentence for passing information to Wikileaks; Syrian leader accused of chemical attack in which over 1,400 die. **27** Controversial badger cull to combat bovine TB begins in Somerset and Gloucestershire. **29** House of Commons rejects Syrian military intervention by 285 votes to 272.

September 9 Russia proposes Syria gives up chemical arsenal; subsequently accepted. **19** Russia arrests Greenpeace activists protesting against Barents Sea oil drilling. **21** Al-Shabaab Islamists kill over 60 in Nairobi, Kenya, terrorist attack. **25** Labour leader Miliband promises energy price freeze if party elected. **27** UN Inter-Governmental Panel on Climate Change declares man-made global warming theory 95% accurate.

October 3 Over 350 die as migrant ship from Libya sinks off Lampedusa. **10** Peter Higgs and François Englert jointly awarded Nobel Physics Prize for discovery of Higgs boson 'God Particle'. **15** Trading begins in heavily oversubscribed Royal Mail shares. **17** UK announces new nuclear plant at Hinkley C site in Somerset, with Chinese and French involvement. **18** Saudi Arabia rejects offer of seat on UN Security Council. **28** *News of the World* phone hacking trial opens at the Old Bailey.

November 6 Typhoon Haiyan kills 6,000 in Philippines. **21** Ukraine protest demonstrations as government rejects EU association agreement. **24** International sanctions eased as Iran agrees to limit nuclear programme. **25** Anti-government protests begin in Thailand. **26** Scottish government publishes White Paper on independence. **27** Italian parliament votes to expel convicted former prime minister Berlusconi. **29** Ten die in police helicopter crash on Glasgow bar.

December 5 Former South African President Mandela dies aged 95. **6** French troops in Central African Republic as UN peacekeepers. **9** North Korean Jang Song-Thaek, Kim Jong-un's uncle, executed. **14** China lands spacecraft on Moon with Jade Rabbit robot. **15** Ethnic clashes in South Sudan following coup attempt. **18** Great Train Robber Ronnie Biggs dies aged 84. **19** Fusilier Rigby's two killers convicted. **29–30** Over 30 die in suicide bombings in Russian city of Volgograd.

2014

January 1 Latvia becomes 18th EU state to adopt Euro. **5** Awami League wins Bangladesh elections; Portuguese footballer Eusébio dies aged 71. **11** Former Israeli prime minister Sharon dies aged 85. **16** Referendum approves new Egyptian constitution. **17** President Obama announces NSA surveillance reforms. **22** UK unemployment falls to 7·1%. **23** UN-led negotiations on Syrian war in Geneva. **28** Ukrainian prime minister Azarov submits resignation to President Yanukovych.

February 4 Labour moves to loosen links with unions. **5** Rail link to Cornwall and west Devon cut by storms; UN committee criticises Vatican over child sex abuse. **6** Pakistan government begins peace talks with Taliban. **11** Troops deployed as UK flood crisis worsens. **13** Labour hold Wythenshawe & Sale East, Ukip pushes Tories into third place; Belgium removes age limit from euthanasia. **14** Italian prime minister Letta resigns. **15** New Lebanon government under Tammam Salam. **18** UK inflation below 2% for first time in four years. **21** President Yanukovych flees Ukraine; Oleksandr Turchynov interim president. **24** Ugandan President Museveni signs anti-gay law. **25** Boko Haram terrorists kill 59 in Nigeria attack.

March 1 Russia deploys troops in Crimea. **6** US imposes sanctions on Russians involved in Crimea crisis. **8** Malaysian Airlines Flight 370 mysteriously vanishes en route to Beijing. **11** Libyan prime minister Ali Zeidan dismissed. **12** Israel ends military service exemption for ultra-Orthodox Jews. **16** Crimea referendum supports joining Russia. **18** Putin signs Crimea annexation decree. **24** Death sentence on 582 former supporters of Egyptian President Morsi. **27** UN General Assembly declares Crimea annexation illegal. **29** Andrej Kiska elected Slovak President; first same-sex marriage in England. **31** Former Pakistan President Musharraf charged with high treason; Socialists defeated in French municipal elections, Manuel Valis becomes prime minister.

April 5 Afghanistan presidential election. **6** Fidesz and Christian Democrats re-elected in Hungary. **9** Culture Secretary Maria Miller resigns in expenses scandal. **16** South Korean ferry disaster. **17** Algerian President Bouteflika re-elected for fourth term. **22** Ukraine launches operations against pro-Russian forces in east. **24** Israel suspends peace talks after Fatah and Hamas declare reconciliation. **27** Popes John XXIII and John Paul II declared saints. **30** Nigerian 'Million woman march' protest against Boko Haram kidnappings.

May 5 World Health Organisation declares polio spread an international emergency. **7** ANC returns with reduced majority in South African elections. **11** Pro-Russian Ukrainian separatists declare independence. **13** Former Israeli prime minister Olmert sentenced to six years for bribery. **17** Benin, Cameroon, Chad, Niger and Nigeria ally against Islamic terrorist Boko Haram. **21** José Mario Vaz elected Guinea-Bissau President. **22** Army coup in Thailand. **24** South African President Zuma sworn in for second term. **25** Petro Poroshenko elected Ukraine President; former Polish Communist leader Wojciech Jaruzelski dies aged 90. **29** Russia, Belarus and Kazakhstan formed Eurasian Economic Union; Peter Mutharika wins disputed Malawi presidential election.

June 2 Palestinian President Abbas appoints Fatah-Hamas unity cabinet; Spanish King Juan Carlos abdicates, succeeded by Felipe. **3** Abdel Fatah al-Sis victory in Egyptian presidential election. **4** Syrian President Assad takes 89% of vote in opposition-boycotted election. **5** European Central Bank cuts interest rates to revive Eurozone economy. **9** Russia warns Finland against joining NATO. **10** Reuven Rivlin chosen as Israeli president. **15** Juan Manuel Santos re-elected Colombian President. **24** Former News International editor Coulson guilty of phone hacking conspiracy. **27** Ukraine, Georgia and Moldova sign EU association agreement.

July 1 Japan ends ban on Self-Defence Forces fighting overseas. **2** Former French President Sarkozy faces corruption charge; mass arrests of Hong Kong pro-democracy protestors. **3** German Bundestag introduces minimum wage from 2015. **8** Israel launches Operation Protective Edge attack on Gaza following death of three youths; Australia and Japan sign free trade agreement. **10** UK civil servants strike over cuts and pay freeze. **16** European Parliament elects Jean-Claude Juncker European Commission President. **17** Malaysian Airlines Flight 17 shot down over Ukraine. **19** Joko Widodo elected Indonesian President. **20** Red Cross formally declares Ukraine fighting as a civil war. **24** Fuad Masum elected Iraqi President. **29** EU and US intensify sanctions on Russia over Ukraine crisis.

August 7 Two former Khmer Rouge leaders sentenced for part in 1970s Cambodia genocide. **8** World Health Organisation declares West Africa Ebola outbreak an international emergency. **9** Egyptian court dissolves Muslim Brotherhood political wing, the Freedom & Justice Party. **15** 100th anniversary of Panama Canal opening celebrated. **21** Thailand army coup leader Prayuth Chan-ocha becomes prime minister. **26** French President Hollande dismisses ministers opposing spending cuts. **28** Ceasefire ends Israeli attack on Gaza.

September 5 Ukraine and pro-Russian forces agree ceasefire. **6** US denies working with Iran against Islamic State of Iraq & Syria (ISIS). **10** President

Obama increased military aid to Iraq and expands US operations in Syria. **12** Former Northern Ireland First Minister Ian Paisley dies aged 88. **14** Swedish election returns minority Social Democrat-Green coalition. **15** Ewa Kopacz becomes Polish prime minister. **18** Scotland votes 55%-45% against independence. **20** New Zealand National Party forms minority government following general election. **21** Ashraf Ghani becomes Afghan President and Abdullah Abdullah chief executive in post-election unity government. **26** UK Parliament votes 524-43 for air strikes against ISIS in Iraq.

October 5 GERB-led coalition under Boyko Borisov after Bulgarian elections. **6** India and Pakistan troops clash on Kashmir frontier. **7** Burma amnesties prisoners, including dissidents. **9** Estonia first former Soviet republic to legalise gay partnerships. **12** Bolivian President Morales re-elected. **24** EU pledges 40% emissions cut by 2030. **26** Final British and American bases passed to Afghan forces; secular Nidaa Tounes party wins majority in Tunisian elections; Brazilian President Rousseff re-elected; West-friendly parties win Ukraine elections. **28** Zambian President Sata dies; Guy Scott interim leader. **31** Russia restores gas supply to Ukraine.

November 4 Republicans control Senate and House of Representatives following elections. **16** Klaus Iohannis elected Romanian President. **23** Cabinet declare Israel the Jewish nation state. **28** Finland legalises same-sex marriage. **28** Hage Geingob elected Namibian President. **29** Former Egyptian President Mubarak cleared on murder charge; former French President Sarkozy elected UMP leader. **30** President Vazquez of Uruguay re-elected.

December 9 US Senate Intelligence Committee report criticises CIA 'war on terror' interrogation methods. **12** Italian general strike against new labour laws. **14** Liberal Democratic Party-led coalition returns in Japan general election; Hong Kong democracy protests end; first Church of England female bishop. **16** Bank of Russia raises interest rate to protect collapsing rouble. **17** US and Cuba agree to renew diplomatic relations after 55 years. **21** Beji Caid Essebsi elected Tunisian president.

2015

January 1 Lithuania becomes 19th EU state to adopt Euro. **7-9** 17 die in Paris Islamist terrorist attacks. **13** Chancellor Merkel condemns anti-Muslim movement in Germany. **16** Ethel Lang, last surviving Briton born in Victoria's reign, dies aged 114. **20** Pope Francis reiterates Catholic ban on artificial contraception. **22** European Central Bank announces €1·1 trillion Eurozone stimulus. **25** Greek anti-austerity Syriza party wins election, heads coalition government.

February 3 Former British colony of Fiji to remove Union Jack from flag. **12** US Senate confirms Ashton Carter as Defence Secretary. **14** Pope Francis appoints 20 new Cardinals. **15** Fragile Ukraine ceasefire begins. **18** Conservative Prokopis Pavlopoulos elected Greek President. **22** Russian President Putin says war with Ukraine unlikely; ISIS destroys rare books and manuscripts in Mosul, Iraq. **24** British military advisers deployed in Ukraine. **25** Austrian government bans foreign funding of mosques and imams. **27** Russian opposition politician Boris Nemtsov assassinated.

March 3 Slovenia first former Communist state to legalise same-sex marriage. **6** US Central Intelligence Agency restructuring to counter digital espionage. **9** President Obama signs executive order declaring Venezuela a national security threat. **12** Iceland withdraws European Union membership candidacy. **17** Likud wins most seats in Israeli Knesset, giving Netanyahu a fourth term. **19** Greece warned to continue reforms or be forced from Euro. **22** Heavy Socialist losses in French local elections. **23** Former Singapore prime minister Lee Kuan Yew dies aged 91. **25** Germanwings Flight 9525 crashes in French Alps killing 150. **26** King Richard III's remains reburied in Leicester; Saudi Arabian-led coalition airstrikes on Houthi targets in Yemen. **28** Nigerian President Jonathan loses election to former military ruler Muhammadu Buhari.

April 1 Thailand military government ends martial law. **2** Over 140 killed in Kenya college terrorist attack. **11** US and Cuban Presidents meet for first time. **13** Novelist Günter Grass dies aged 87. **19** Centre Party leader Juha Sipilä becomes Finnish prime minister. **23** Loretta Lynch first African-American US Attorney General. **24** Turkey withdraws Vatican ambassador following Pope Francis remarks on 1915 Armenian massacre. **25** President Faure Gnassingbé of Togo wins third term; over 7,000 die in Nepal earthquake. **26** Kazakhstan President Nazarbayev re-elected with 97·7% of vote. **30** Singer Ben E. King dies aged 76.

May 2 Congo Republic bans full-face veils; Duchess of Cambridge gives birth to daughter. **7** Conservatives win UK general election. **11** David Granger wins Guyana presidential election; Picasso's *Women of Algiers* becomes most expensive painting at US$179,365,000. **13** Vatican recognises Palestinian state; abortive military coup in Burundi. **14** Prince Charles' 'black spider memos' to ministers published. **20** Barclays, RBS, Citi, JP Morgan and UBS banks fined $5·7 billion in foreign exchange trading scandal. **27** Football corruption scandal deepens with arrests of FIFA officials in Switzerland.

June 1 Former Liberal Democrat leader Charles Kennedy dies aged 55. **4** St Benet's Hall last Oxford college to admit women. **7** Institutional Revolutionary Party holds power in Mexico elections. **11** Spanish Princess Cristina stripped of titles over tax evasion charge. **12** Moldova prime minister Chiril Gaburici resigns over false education qualifications. **15** Worldwide celebrations of 800th anniversary of Magna Carta. **18** Centre-right opposition Venstre bloc wins Danish general election. **26** US Supreme Court declares state bans on same-sex marriage unconstitutional. **29** Burundi President Nkurunziza claims victory in elections boycotted by opposition.

July 1 Greece becomes first major economy to miss payment to International Monetary Fund. **2** BP agrees to pay $US18·7 compensation for 2010 Gulf of Mexico oil spill. **4** Tupou VI crowned King of Tonga. **5** Greek referendum rejects EU-IMF-European Central Bank austerity plan. **11** Greek parliament passes economic reform package. **12** Report reveals American Psychological Association complicity in Afghanistan and Iraq prisoner torture. **16** Tim Farron elected Lib Dem leader. **28** Obama first US President to address African Union.

August 1 British singer Cilla Black dies aged 72. **5** Kids' Company charity collapse scandal. **8** England cricket team regain the Ashes. **11-13** People's Bank of China devalues currency on three successive days to boost economy. **14** Greek parliament accepts bailout plan rejected in referendum; US reopens embassy in Cuba. **20** Macedonia declares state of emergency over refugee crisis; Greek prime minister Tsipras resigns. **23** Britain and Iran reopen embassies. **29** Protestors in Malaysia demand prime minister Najib Razak's resignation over corruption allegations.

September 1 UN confirms Islamic State of Iraq & Syria (ISIS) has destroyed Syrian Temple of Bel in Palmyra. **6** Pope Francis calls on European Catholics to take in refugees. **7** People's National Movement retains power in Trinidad & Tobago. **9** Elizabeth II Britain's longest-reigning monarch at 63 years and 216 days. **11** Governing People's Action Party Singapore landslide. **12** Jeremy Corbyn elected Labour leader. **20** Tsipras returns in Greek election; Nepal a secular state under new constitution. **23** Volkswagen CEO resigns over emissions scandal. **24** Over 1,600 die in Mecca stampede during Hajj pilgrimage. **28** Catalan nationalist parties win majority in regional elections.

October 3 Labour politician Denis Healey dies aged 98. **4** Centre-right government loses Portuguese elections. **9** Conservative politician Geoffrey Howe dies aged 88; Gaza Hamas leader Ismail Haniyeh declares West Bank 'intifada'. **10** Former German Chancellor Helmut Schmidt dies aged 96. **13** Jamaican writer Marlon James wins 2015 Man Booker Prize for novel *A Brief History* *of Seven Killings.* **20** Over 100 killed in Ankara peace rally bombing. **25** Ivory Coast President Ouattara wins second term; ruling Chama Cha Mapinduzi wins Tanzanian elections. **28** Bidhya Devi Bhandari Nepal's first female president. **30** Last British prisoner in Guantanamo Bay, Shaker Aamer, released. **31** Russian Flight 9268 blown up over Sinai, 224 die.

November 2 Australian prime minister Turnbull declares end to knights and dames in honours. **4** Mexican Supreme Court declares marijuana cultivation for personal use legal. **7** Chinese and Taiwanese presidents' first meeting since 1949 Communist takeover. **13** 130 die in ISIS attacks in Paris; Russian athletes barred from international competition. **19** Peter Robinson resigns as Northern Ireland First Minister and DUP leader. **24** Russian military jet shot down over Turkey; Portuguese Socialist Party leader António Costa prime minister. **25** The Gambia outlaws female genital mutilation.

December 2 House of Commons approves Syria bombing. **3** US defence secretary opens combat roles to women. **5** Storm Desmond opens period of flooding in UK. **12** 195 countries at UN Climate Change Conference agree greenhouse gas emissions reduction. **14** Oil price at lowest level since 2008. **15** Revelation that Prince Charles has received confidential cabinet papers for decades. **16** US Federal Reserve makes first interest rise since 2006. **20** Slovenia referendum rejects same-sex marriage. **28** Japan and South Korea reach compensation agreement for Korean women forced into World War Two sex slavery. **31** Asylum seekers accused of New Year's Eve sex attacks in Cologne and Vienna.

2016

January 4 Four new elements in periodic table: ununtrium, ununpentium, ununseptium and ununoctium; **8** Copies of Hitler's *Mein Kampf* on sale in Germany for first time in 70 years. **10** Musician David Bowie dies aged 69. **12** Junior doctors in England strike over contractual changes. **14** Church of England avoids schism by reaffirming 'traditional doctrine' that only heterosexual marriage is valid. **15** Al Qaida kill over 25 in Burkina Faso terrorist attack. **16** Taiwan elects Tsai Ingwen of Democratic Progressive party first woman president. **22** Former Tory politician and Thatcher confidant Cecil Parkinson dies aged 84. **24** Marcelo Rebelo de Sousa elected Portuguese president. **29** Bank of Japan adopts negative interest rate.

February 1 High Court declares Lord Lucan, missing since 1974, dead. **5** State of disaster proclaimed in Zimbabwe over prolonged drought. **11** Physicists announce discovery of gravitational waves forecast by Einstein. **12** Pope Francis and Patriarch Kirill hold first Catholic-Orthodox church heads meeting since 1054. **19** EU leaders agree on reforms to persuade UK to remain. **19** Ugandan President Museveni declared winner in criticised election. **25** Dame Janet Smith describes BBC 'culture of fear' in report on Savile affair; People's National Party ousted by Labour in Jamaican elections. **26** Fragile Syrian ceasefire in effect; reformers' successes in Iran elections; inconclusive Irish elections.

March 2 Inconclusive Spanish elections. **5** Ruling Smer party loses majority in Slovak elections. **9** Former Brazilian President Lula da Silva faces money laundering charge. **11** New Zealand bans zero-hours employment contracts. **13** Anti-refugee Alternative für Deutschland success in German regional elections. **14** Russia announces Syria troop withdrawals. **15** Htin Kyaw first Burma (Myanmar) civilian president for 53 years. **18** EU-Turkey agreement to alleviate migrant crisis. **20** US President Obama visits Cuba; ruling party wins Kazakhstan elections. **22** Over 30 die in Brussels terrorist attacks. **23** New Zealand referendum rejects new flag. **26** Last print edition of *Independent* newspaper. **27** Suicide bomb in Lahore, Pakistan kills over 70; Syrian troops drive ISIS from Palmyra. **29** UN commission says Falklands (Malvinas) in Argentine territorial waters.

April 2 Tran Dai Quang sworn in as Vietnam President. **3** 'Panama Papers' reveal former and current world

leaders' tax avoidance. **12** British playwright Arnold Wesker dies aged 83. **16** US Army appoints first female combat officers. **20** Former slave Harriet Tubman to replace Andrew Jackson on US $20 note. **21** US singer/songwriter Prince dies age 57. **24** Incumbent Serbian Progressive-led coalition wins elections. **25** British Home Stores goes into administration. **26** 1989 Hillsborough disaster inquest says 96 football fans were illegally killed. **28** Finnish parliament debates abandoning Euro.

May 5 Labour's Sadiq Khan elected first Muslim London Mayor. **11** Rodrigo Duterte wins Philippines presidential election; Italian parliament legalises same-sex unions. **13** Former Argentine President Fernandez indicted for fraud. **14** Ukraine wins Eurovision Song Contest. **19** Montenegro signs agreement on NATO entry. **20** Tsai Ing-wen inaugurated as Taiwan's first female President. **26** 2,400 year-old tomb of Aristotle found in Stagira, Greece. **28** Anti-government riots in Papua New Guinea.

June 1 World's longest and deepest tunnel, Gotthard Base, opens in Switzerland. **3** US boxer Muhammad Ali dies aged 74. **5** Swiss voters reject 'basic income' plan in referendum. **12** 49 killed in mass shooting at Florida gay nightclub. **15** Swiss Federal Assembly votes to withdraw EU membership application. **16** Labour MP Jo Cox murdered. **20** First women mayors, Virginia Raggi and Chiara Appendino, elected in Rome and Turin. **23** UK votes 51·9 % to 48·1 % to leave EU. **26** Inconclusive Spanish elections; enlarged Panama Canal re-opens. **28** Bolivia, Ethiopia, Kazakhstan and Sweden elected non-permanent UN Security Council members.

July 1 Latvia 35th member of Organisation for Economic Co-operation & Development. **2** Holocaust survivor and Nobel laureate Elie Wiesel dies aged 87. **6** Chilcot Report on UK involvement in Iraq War published. **9** NATO agrees to prolong engagement in Afghanistan. **13** Cameron resigns as UK prime minister, succeeded by Theresa May. **14** 85 killed in Nice terrorist attack. **18** Morocco announces intention to rejoin the African Union. **26** Palestinian National Authority to sue UK over the 1917 Balfour Declaration guaranteeing a Jewish homeland.

August 4 Bank of England cuts interest rate to 0·25 %. **5** Summer Olympic Games open in Rio de Janeiro (end 21); **7** Thai referendum approves military-based constitution. **24** Over 500 die in earthquake near Perugia, Italy. **26** Colombia government and FARC guerrillas announce peace agreement; world's largest suspension bridge opens across Bosphorus. **30** EU orders Apple to pay €13 billion back taxes to Ireland. **31** First commercial flight from US to Cuba since 1961.

September 2 Uzbekistan President Islam Karimov dies aged 78. **4** Pope Francis canonises Mother Teresa; Hong Kong legislative council elections. **12** Cameron resigns as MP for Witney. **13** Bank of England issues new polymer £5 note. **15** Japan's Democrat Party elects Sha Renho first female leader. **24** Corbyn re-elected Labour leader with 61·8 % of vote. **28** Former Israeli leader Shimon Peres dies aged 93.

October 1 Transgender individuals eligible for enlistment in US forces. **2** Colombia referendum rejects peace deal with FARC. **9** Peasant & Greens Union form coalition with Social Democrats following Lithuanian elections. **13** US singer-songwriter Bob Dylan awarded Nobel Prize for Literature; Thai King Bhumibol Adulyadej dies aged 88; Maldives leaves the Commonwealth; António Guterres elected next UN Secretary General. **20** UK pardons 65,000 gay and bisexual men once charged with now abolished sexual offences. **24** France officially closes 'The Jungle' migrant camp in Calais. **26** Gambia intends to join South Africa and Burundi in withdrawing from the International Criminal Court for ignoring Western war crimes.

November 2 US bans arms sales to the Philippines over human rights concerns. **6** President Ortega of Nicaragua wins third term in criticised election. **7** Canadian singer-songwriter Leonard Cohen dies aged 82. **8** Indian abolishes large denomination notes to encourage its cashless economy. **12** Colombian government and FARC rebels declare new peace deal. **5** Former Cuban dictator Castro dies aged 90. **18** World Health Organisation declares end to Zika virus global crisis. **21** Irish writer William Trevor dies aged 88. **27** Swiss referendum rejects proposal to end commercial nuclear power. **30** OPEC states agree to cut oil production.

December 1 Crown Prince Maha Vaijralongkom becomes Thai king. **7** Pharmaceutical company Pfizer fined £84·2 million in UK for excessive drug price rise. **8** US astronaut John Glenn dies age 95. **9** EU grants visa free travel to Georgia and Ukraine; South Korean President Park Geun-hye impeached. **16** Riot at HM Prison Birmingham. **18** Actress Zsa Zsa Gabor dies age 99. **19** Terrorist attack in Berlin; Russian ambassador killed in Istanbul; IMF head Christine Lagarde guilty of negligence. **23** UN Security Council tells Israel to end further settlement in occupied territories. **25** Russian military aircraft crashes into Black Sea, 92 die; UK singer George Michael dies age 53. **29** US expels 35 Russian diplomats.

2017

January 1 ISIS gun attack on Istanbul nightclub kills 39; Finland begins 'basic income' pilot scheme. **2** UK rail fares rise an average 2·3%. **3** China issues first ever nationwide smog red alert. **7** Cyprus reunification talks resume in Geneva; Portuguese politician Mário Soares dies age 92. **8** Former Iranian President Akbar Rafsanjani dies age 82. **12** US deploys troops on Poland's Russian border; UK government review backs Swansea Bay tidal lagoon plan. **16** Rolls Royce to pay £671 million in penalties for bribery. **17** Underwater search for Malaysian Airlines Flight MH370 (crashed in 2014) called off. **21** World-wide demonstrations against President Trump's inauguration. **25** British actor Sir John Hurt dies, age 77. **27** US President Trump executive order bars entry from some – predominantly Muslim – states.

Note: For more recent events in world affairs, *see* **Section** C (under individual countries) and **Section** D (for the general election in the United Kingdom). Recent Sporting Winners can be found in **Section** S and the main 2017/18 tax rates in **Section** G.

PROMINENT
PEOPLE

Glimpses of some of the famous people in the history of the world. See also Section D for leading British politicians; Section P for musicians; Section M for many leading literary figures; Section N for key figures in architecture and Section H for biblical characters.

PROMINENT PEOPLE

A

Aalto, Alvar (1898–1976). Finnish architect. Designer of modern public buildings.

Abel, Sir Frederick (1826–1902). English military chemist, an authority on explosives. He and his friend James Dewar patented the propellant cordite (*see* Section L).

Abelard, Peter (1079–1142), one of the founders of scholastic moral theology, b. at Pallet (Palais) near Nantes. He lectured in Paris, where he was sought by students, though persecuted for alleged heresy. His main achievement was to discuss where others asserted. His love for Héloïse, a woman of learning, ended in tragic separation and in a famous correspondence.

Abercrombie, Sir Patrick (1879–1957), architect and town-planner. He was consulted on the re-planning of Plymouth, Hull, Bath *etc.* and pro-duced a plan for Greater London, 1943.

Achebe, Chinua (1930–2013), Nigerian writer. Best-known for his novel *Things Fall Apart*. The "founding father of modern African Literature".

Acton, 1st Baron (John Emerich Edward Dalberg Acton) (1834–1902), English historian. He planned the *Cambridge Modern History*.

Adam, Robert (1728–92), architect, one of four Scottish brothers. He developed a character-istic style in planning and decoration and his achievements in interior design include Hare-wood House, Yorks.; Osterley Park and Syon House, Middlesex; Kedleston Hall, Derbyshire; Luton Hoo, Bedfordshire; and Kenwood.

Adams, John (1735–1826), succeeded Washington as president of the USA. He was the first of the republic's ambassadors to England.

Adams, John Couch (1819–92), English mathematician and astronomer. He shared credit for the discov-ery of the planet Neptune (1846) with the French astronomer Leverrier, working independently.

Adams, John Quincy (1767–1848), 6th President of the USA, 1825–29; son of the 2nd President, John Adams. He had negotiated the peace treaty with Britain after the 1812 War.

Adams, Samuel (1722–1803), American revolution-ary statesman, b. Boston. He advocated "no taxation without representation" as early as 1765; promoted the "Boston tea-party"; in 1776 signed the Declaration of Independence.

Adams, William (*c.* 1564–1620), navigator, b. Gillingham, Kent; the first Englishman to visit Japan. He found favour with the shogun Ieyasu, and an English and Dutch trading settlement was established till 1616.

Addams, Jane (1860–1935), American sociologist who founded Hull House, Chicago, in 1889.

Addison, Joseph (1672–1719), writer and Whig politician. He contributed to the *Tatler*, and was co-founder with Steele of the *Spectator*.

Adelard of Bath (*c.* 1090–*c.* 1150), English mathe-matician who translated into Latin the *Arith-metic* of Al-Kwarizmi and so introduced the Arabic numerals to the West.

Adenauer, Konrad (1876–1967), chancellor of the West German Federal Republic, 1949–63; founder of the Christian Democratic Party, 1945–66. To a defeated Germany he gave stable government and a place in the Western alliance. He promoted reconciliation with France.

Adler, Alfred (1870–1937), Austrian psychiatrist, founder of the school of individual psychology. An earlier pupil of Freud, he broke away in 1911, rejecting the emphasis on sex, regarding man's main problem as a struggle for power to com-pensate for feelings of inferiority. *See* Section J.

Adrian, 1st Baron (Edgar Douglas Adrian) (1889–1977), English physiologist. He shared with Sherrington the 1932 Nobel Prize for medicine for work on the electrical nature of the nerve impulse. O.M. 1942.

Adrian IV (Nicholas Breakspear) (d. 1159), pope 1154–59, the only English pope, b. near St. Albans. He crowned Frederick Barbarossa Holy Roman Emperor. Granted overlordship of Ireland to Henry II.

Aeschylus (524–456 B.C.), founder of Greek tragic drama. Of the many plays he wrote, only seven have come down to us, including *The Seven against Thebes*, *Prometheus Bound*, and a trilogy on Orestes.

Aesop (? 6th cent. B.C.), semi-legendary fabulist, originally a slave. The fables attributed to him probably have many origins.

Agassiz, Louis (1807–73), Swiss-American em-bryologist, author of *Lectures on Comparative Embryology*, intended for laymen, *Researches on Fossil Fishes*, and *Studies on Glaciers*. He was an opponent of Darwinian evolution.

Agricola, Gnaeus Julius (37–93), Roman governor of Britain, who subdued the country except for the Scottish highlands. Tacitus wrote his life.

Agrippa, Marcus Vipsanius (63–12 B.C.). Famous Roman general.

Ahmad Khan, Sir Syed (1817–98), Indian educa-tionist and social reformer who founded what is now the Aligarh Muslim University.

Airy, Sir George Biddell (1801–92), English mathe-matician who was astronomer royal for over 40 years, 1835–81. He set up a magnetic observatory at Greenwich.

Akbar, Jalal-ud-din Mohammed (1542–1605), Mogul emperor of India, son of Humayun. He extended the imperial power over much of India, stabilised the administration, promoted commerce and learning; and, though a Muslim, respected Hindu culture and tolerated Christian missions. His reign saw a flowering of culture.

Akhenaten, the name adopted by the heretic pharaoh **Amenhotep IV** (d. 1338 B.C.), who in-troduced a short-lived but influential religious and artistic reformation. He sought to convert his people from their polytheistic beliefs to a more compassionate religion based on the one supreme sun-god Aten (hence his name). His pacifism caused the temporary loss of most of Egypt's overseas territories. His wife was Nefertiti. He was succeeded by Tutankha-men, who gave in to the conservative priesthood.

Akihito (b. 1933), Emperor of Japan since 1989. Son of Hirohito (*q.v.*). Announced intention to abdi-cate, 2016.

Alanbrooke, 1st Viscount (Alan Francis Brooke) (1883–1963), British field-marshal; chief of the imperial general staff 1941–46.

Alarcón, Pedro Antonio de (1833–91), Spanish novelist. His short story, *El Sombrero de tres picos* (The Three-Cornered Hat) became the subject of Falla's ballet and of Hugo Wolf's opera *Der Corregidor*.

Alaric I (376–410), Visigothic chief who, as first auxiliary to the Roman emperor Theodosius, later attacked the empire, sacking Rome in 410.

Alban, St. (d. *c.* 303), proto-martyr of Britain, con-verted by a priest to whom he had given shelter. He suffered under Diocletian at Verulam (now St. Albans), where in the 8th cent. King Offa of Mercia founded the abbey of that name.

Albee, Edward (1928–2016), one of the great American playwrights whose works include *Who's Afraid of Virginia Woolf?*

Albert, Prince Consort (1819–61), son of the Duke of Saxe-Coburg-Gotha, married Queen Victoria in 1840. He projected the international exhibition of 1851, and in 1861 in a dispute with the United States advised a conciliatory attitude which averted war. He died of typhoid fever and is commemorated by the Albert Memorial in Kensington Gardens.

Albertus Magnus (Albert the Great) (1206–80), Dominican scholastic philosopher, b. Swabia. His interest in nature as an independent obser-ver marked the awakening of the scientific spirit. Among his pupils was Thomas Aquinas.

Albright, Madeleine (b. 1937) American diplomat. First woman Secretary of State, 1997–2001.

Alcibiades (*c.* 450–404 B.C.), Athenian general and statesman. Pupil and friend of Socrates, he was an egoist whose career brought Athens disaster. He was murdered in Phrygia.

Alcott, Louisa May (1832–88), American author of books for girls, notably *Little Women*.

Alcuin (735–804), English scholar, who settled on the Continent and helped Charlemagne with the promotion of education.

Aldred (d. 1069), Saxon archbishop of York who crowned William the Conqueror.

Aldrich, Henry (1647–1710), English composer of church music, theologian and architect. He designed Peckwater quadrangle at Christ Church, the chapel of Trinity College, and All Saints' Church, Oxford, and wrote the "Bonny Christ Church bells."

Alekhine, Alexander (1892–1946), world chess champion, 1927–35, 1937–46. He was born in Moscow but later became a French citizen.

Alembert, Jean le Rond d' (1717–83), French mathematician, philosopher and encyclopaedist.

Alexander of Tunis, Earl (Harold Leofric George Alexander) (1891–1969), British field-marshal. Directed retreat at Dunkirk 1940, and Burma 1942; C.-in-C. Allied Armies in Italy 1943–4, Governor-general of Canada 1946–52.

Alexander II (1818–81), reforming Tsar of Russia, succeeded his father Nicholas in 1855. In 1861 he emancipated the serfs and in 1865 established provincial elective assemblies. Later his government became reactionary; he was assassinated by Nihilists; the pogroms followed.

Alexander the Great (356–323 B.C.), Greek conqueror. Educated by Aristotle, he succeeded his father Philip as king of Macedon in 336 B.C. He led the Greek states against Persia; and, crossing the Hellespont, he defeated Darius and sacked Persepolis. He captured Egypt and founded Alexandria. He penetrated to India. He died suddenly, after a drinking bout and feasting, at Babylon. His father, Philip II, was perhaps the greater ruler and Olympias, his mother, was extraordinarily powerful.

Alexandra, Queen (1844–1925), daughter of Christian IX of Denmark, married the Prince of Wales (afterwards Edward VII) 1863.

Alfieri, Vittorio, Count (1749–1803), Italian poet and dramatist.

Alfonso the Wise (1221–84), king of León and Castile, known for his code of laws and his planetary tables. He caused the first general history of Spain to be written. Dethroned 1282.

Alfred the Great (849–99), king of Wessex who became a national figure. From the outset he had to repel Danish invaders. After years of effort he won the battle of Ethandun (Edington), in 878 and later, probably in 886, made peace with Guthrum, leaving to the Danes the north and east. He was an able administrator, and promoted education, his own translations from the Latin being part of the earliest English literature. The only English king to be styled 'the Great'.

Ali, Muhammad (1942–2016), one of the greatest heavyweight boxers. Born Cassius Clay. Adopted his new name on joining the Black Muslim Movement.

Al-Kwarizimi (fl. c. 830), Persian mathematician said to have given algebra its name.

Allenby, 1st Viscount (Edmund Henry Hynman Allenby) (1861–1936), British general. Commanded in Palestine 1917–18, capturing Jerusalem on 9 December 1917.

Allende, Salvador (1908–73), Chilean radical leader, a Marxist democrat, who won the presidency 1970. He tried to bring social reform by democratic means but died in the 1973 coup.

Alleyn, Edward (1566–1626), great early actor and founder of Dulwich College and Alleyn's School.

Al-Mamun (813–33), caliph of Baghdad, son of Harun-al-Rashid. (*See* **B30**). He built an observatory at Baghdad.

Ambedkar, Bhimrao Ramji (1893–1956), Indian leader of the Untouchables (and champion of the poor).

Amin (Dada), Idi (1925–2003), Ugandan dictator from 1971–79. His brutal dictatorship saw the expulsion of the Uganda Asians and the murder of countless thousands of fellow Ugandans.

Amis, Sir Kingsley (1922–95), novelist, poet and critic, whose first novel, *Lucky Jim* (1954), is a classic of English comic fiction. He won the Booker Prize for *The Old Devils* (1986). *See* **Section M**.

Ampère, André Marie (1775–1836), French physicist who propounded the theory that magnetism is the result of molecular electric currents. The unit of electric current is named after him.

Amundsen, Roald (1872–1928), Norwegian explorer, the first to navigate the north-west passage and to reach the south pole. Sailing in the fishing smack *Gjoa*, he made the north-west passage in 3 years, 1903–6, and in 1911 sailed to the Antarctic in the *Fram*, reaching the pole on 14 December 1911, a month before his English rival Scott. His attempt to rescue Nobile after his crash in the airship *Italia* cost him his life.

Anacreon (c. 569–475 B.C.), Greek lyric poet.

Anand, Mulk Raj (1905–2004), the father of Indian literature in English. His classic novel, *Untouchable*, was inspired by Gandhi. The "Indian Dickens".

Anaxagoras (488–428 B.C.), Ionian philosopher who came to Athens 464 B.C. and inspired Pericles and the poet Euripides with his love of science. His rational theories outraged religious opinion.

Anaximander (611–547 B.C.), Miletan philosopher, pupil of Thales, the first among the Greeks to make geographical maps, and to speculate on the origin of the heavenly bodies. He introduced the sundial from Babylon or Egypt.

Anaximenes (b. c. 570 B.C.), the last of the Miletan school founded by Thales. For him the primal substance was air. He was the first to see the differences between substances in quantitative terms.

Andersen, Hans Christian (1805–75), Danish writer, especially of fairy tales such as *The Little Mermaid* and *The Ugly Duckling*. Also a performer, artist and considerable man of letters.

Anderson, Elizabeth Garrett (1836–1917), one of the first English women to enter the medical profession. She practised in London for many years. Sister of **Millicent Garrett Fawcett**.

Andrea del Sarto (1487–1531), Italian painter, b. Florence, the son of a tailor. Known as the "faultless painter," his chief works are the frescoes of the Annunziata at Florence and his Holy Families. He died of the plague.

Andrée, Salomon August (1854–97), Swedish explorer who attempted in 1897 to reach the north pole by balloon. In 1930 a Norwegian scientific expedition discovered the remains of the Andrée expedition on White Island.

Andrewes, Sir Christopher (1896–1988), British medical researcher. Prominent virologist. Helped discover the common cold virus.

Andropov, Yuri Vladimirovich (1914–84), Russian statesman. State President, 1983–84.

Angelico, Fra (1387–1455), Italian painter. An exquisite colourist, Fra Giovanni (his Dominican name) painted especially religious frescoes, mainly at Florence and Rome.

Ångström, Anders Jöns (1814–74), Swedish physicist who studied heat, magnetism, and spectroscopy; hence the ångström unit used for measuring the wavelength of light.

Annan, Kofi (b. 1938) Ghanaian international civil servant. UN Secretary General, 1997–2006. Shared Nobel Peace Prize, 2001.

Anne, Queen (1665–1714), Queen of Gt. Britain and Ireland. A daughter of James II, she succeeded William III in 1702. The act of union with Scotland was passed in 1707. A well-intentioned woman without marked ability, she was influenced by favourites, at first by the Duchess of Marlborough, but in the main she was guided by Tory and high church principles (she established Queen Anne's Bounty to improve church finances). Her reign was notable for literary output and developments in science (Newton) and architecture (Wren, Vanbrugh).

Anning, Mary (1799–1847), pioneering palaeontologist who discovered early dinosaur fossils.

Anouilh, Jean (1910–87), French dramatist, whose plays include *Eurydice*, *Antigone*, *The Lark*, *Becket* and *The Fighting Cock*.

Anselm, St. (1033–1109), Italian scholar who succeeded Lanfranc as archbishop of Canterbury.

Anson, 1st Baron (George Anson) (1697–1762), English admiral who sailed round the world 1740–44, his squadron being reduced during the voyage from seven ships to one.

Antoninus Pius (86–161), Roman emperor, successor of Hadrian. In his reign, which was peaceful, the Antonine wall between the Forth and the Clyde was built to help protect Britain from attack.

Antonius Marcus (Mark Antony) (c. 83–30 B.C.), Roman triumvir. He supported Caesar, and after the latter's death was opposed by Brutus and Cassius, and defeated by Octavian; committed suicide. His association with the Egyptian queen Cleopatra is the subject of Shakespeare's play.

Antony, St. (c. 251–356), early promoter of the monastic life. B. in Upper Egypt, he retired into the desert, where he was tempted He founded a monastery. Took part in the Council of Nicaea 325.

Apelles, 4th cent. B.C., Greek painter whose chief paintings, which have not survived, were of Alexander the Great holding a thunderbolt and of Aphrodite rising from the sea.

Apollinaire, Guillaume (Wilhelm Apollinaris Kostrowitzi) (1880–1918), French poet who invented the term *surrealism*.

Apollonius of Perga (fl. 220 B.C.), Greek mathematician of the Alexandrian school, remembered for his conic sections; introduced the terms *ellipse, parabola,* and *hyperbola.*

Apollonius Rhodius (fl. 250 B.C.), scholar and poet of Alexandria and Rhodes, librarian at Alexandria. His epic *Argonautica* is about the Argonauts.

Appert, Nicholas (1752–1841), sometimes known as François Appert, invented the method of preserving animal and vegetable foods by means of hermetically sealed cans or tins.

Appleton, Sir Edward Victor (1892–1965), English physicist, best known as the discoverer of the ionised region of the upper atmosphere (the Appleton layer). His researches led to the development of radar. Nobel prizewinner 1947.

Aquinas, Thomas, St. (c. 1225–74), scholastic philosopher and Dominican friar of Italian birth, whose philosophico-theological system (called Thomism) is still accepted by Catholic ecclesiastics. He understood Aristotle well and interpreted his thought in accord with Christian teaching. His most important works are *Summa contra Gentiles* and *Summa theologica.*

Arafat, Yasser (1929–2004). The leader of the PLO (Palestine Liberation Organization). Shared Nobel Peace Prize for his efforts to secure agreement with Israel. Elected President, Palestine National Council, January 1996. A potent symbol of the Palestinian struggle for statehood.

Arago, Dominique François Jean (1786–1853), French astronomer and physicist, remembered for discoveries in electromagnetism and optics.

Archimedes (287–212 B.C.), Greek mathematician, b. Syracuse, son of an astronomer; remembered for his contributions to pure mathematics, mechanics, and hydrostatics, notably the Archimedean screw for raising water, the conception of specific gravity, the doctrine of levers, and the measurement of curved areas. He was killed by the Romans in the siege of Syracuse.

Argand, Aimé (1755–1803), Swiss physician, inventor of the lamp bearing his name, which was the first to admit a current of air to increase the power of the flame.

Ariosto, Ludovico (1474–1533), Italian poet, author of *Orlando Furioso.*

Aristides (d. c. 468 B.C.), Athenian general and statesman, called "the just"; fought at Marathon.

Aristippus (c. 435–356 B.C.), founder of the Cyrenaic school of philosophy. He taught that man should aim at pleasure, but held that the pleasant was identical with the good.

Aristophanes (c. 444–c. 385 B.C.), Greek dramatist and comic poet, who satirised Athenian life. Among his plays are *The Clouds* and *The Birds.*

Aristotle (384–322 B.C.), Greek philosopher, pupil of Plato, after whose death in 347 he left Athens to become tutor to the young prince Alexander of Macedon. Subsequently at Athens he established his famous school in the garden known as the *Lyceum,* where he lectured in the *peripatos* (cloister) which gave his school of philosophy its name *Peripatetic.* He took the whole field of knowledge as his subject, giving it unity, and providing a philosophy which long held its own. He is the first person known to have considered the issue of infinity.

Arkwright, Sir Richard (1732–92), English inventor. His "water frame" (run by water power), patented in 1769, was an early step in the industrial revolution. In 1790 he made use of Boulton and Watt's steam-engine.

Armstrong, Louis (c. 1898–1971), one of the greatest jazz trumpeters and singers. Nicknamed **Satchmo.**

Armstrong, Neil (1930–2012), US astronaut, the first man to set foot on the moon, 21 July 1969.

Arne, Thomas Augustine (1710–78), English composer, remembered for *Rule, Britannia!* (from a masque called *Alfred*), and for Shakespearean songs such as *Where the Bee Sucks.* He also wrote operas (women singers appeared in *Judith* in 1761) and oratorios.

Arnold, Sir Malcolm (1921–2006), the most recorded British composer of all time and the first to win

an Oscar (for his score on *The Bridge on the River Kwai*) in 1957.

Arnold, Thomas (1795–1842), English headmaster, whose influence at Rugby (1828–42) gave it a high position among public schools. His son, **Matthew** (1822–88) was a poet, literary and social critic, and schools inspector. One of his famous poems is "Dover Beach," and his influential books include *Culture and Anarchy* (1869).

Arp, Hans (1887–1966). Poet and sculptor. Leading poet of Dadaism.

Arrhenius, Svante August (1859–1927), Swedish chemist, a founder of modern physical chemistry. Received 1903 Nobel prize for the theory of electrolytic dissociation (ionisation).

Artaxerxes, the name borne by several ancient Persian kings. The first Artaxerxes, son of Xerxes, reigned 464–424 B.C.; he was succeeded by Darius II 424–404 B.C., who was followed by Artaxerxes II, who reigned until 358 B.C. Artaxerxes III, the last to bear the name, was a treacherous man and was poisoned in 338 B.C.

Arthur (c. 500), fabled Celtic warrior, whose feats were first narrated in Geoffrey of Monmouth's *Historia* (c. 1135). In mediaeval times his legend developed an extensive literature, woven together by Sir Thomas Malory in his *Morte d'Arthur.*

Arthur, Chester (1829–86), 21st President of the United States (1881–85). Formerly Vice-President to his Republican predecessor James Garfield.

Arundel, Thomas (1353–1414), archbishop of Canterbury 1396, and for a time lord chancellor. An enemy of heresy, he persecuted the Lollards.

Ashdown, Lord ((Sir Paddy Ashdown) (b. 1941). Leader of the Liberal Democrats, 1988–99. MP, Yeovil, 1983–2001. High Representative, Bosnia, 2002–06.

Ashe, Arthur (1943–93), Afro-American tennis ace and one-time Wimbledon champion.

Asimov, Isaac (1920–92), Russian-born American scientist and author, whose works include *The Intelligent Man's Guide to Science,* 1960; *Asimov's Guide to the Bible,* 1969–70.

Aske, Robert, (c. 1500–37), leader of the Pilgrimage of Grace 1536, directed against the Henrician Reformation; executed 1537.

Asoka (c. 269–232 B.C.), Indian emperor and upholder of Buddhism. At first he expanded his empire by conquest, but on being converted to Buddhism rejected war and aimed at the good of his people. He sent Buddhist missionaries as far as Sri Lanka and Syria. Art flourished.

Asquith, Herbert Henry, 1st Earl of Oxford and Asquith (1852–1928), Liberal prime minister 1908–16. His government enacted social reforms including old-age pensions (1908) and unemployment insurance (1911), but as a war minister he had to give way to Lloyd George. He resigned leadership of his party in 1926.

Assad, Hafez al- (1930–2000), Syrian dictator. President of Syria after 1971. Succeeded by his son **Bashar al-Assad** in 2000 whose regime brought Civil War to Syria. *See* **E25.**

Asser, a Welsh monk of the 9th cent., traditionally author of a life of King Alfred.

Astor, John Jacob (1763–1848), founder of the millionaire family. A native of Heidelberg, went to America, making a fortune in fur.

Astor, Viscountess (Nancy Witcher Astor, *née* Langhorne) (1879–1964), the first woman MP to take her seat in the Commons. An American by birth, wife of the 2nd Viscount Astor.

Atatürk, Kemal (1881–1938), builder of modern Turkey. A fine soldier, he defended the Dardanelles against the British in 1915 and drove the Greeks out of Turkey in 1922. President of the Turkish Republic, and virtually dictator, 1923–38.

Athanasius, St. (296–373), upholder of the doctrine of the Trinity against Arius, who denied the divinity of Christ. He was bishop of Alexandria. He is not now thought the author of the creed which bears his name.

Athelstan (895–940), grandson of Alfred the Great, was crowned king of England in 925, and was the first ruler of all England.

Attenborough, Sir David (b. 1926), British traveller and zoologist. Commentator in TV series *Life on Earth* (1979) and *The Living Planet* (1983). His recent TV series, *Great Barrier Reef* (2015), received great acclaim. Created Companion of Honour (1996). Order of Merit (2005). His younger brother **Lord Richard Attenborough** (1923–2014) was a famous actor, film producer and director.

Attila (406–53), invading king of the Huns from Asia. He defeated the Roman Emperor Theodosius, and entered Gaul, but was defeated in 451 near Châlons-sur-Marne.

Attlee, 1st Earl (Clement Richard Attlee) (1883–1967), Labour prime minister 1945–51, having served as deputy to Churchill 1942–5. Called to the Bar in 1905. Lectured at the LSE, 1913–23. Parliamentary leader of his party 1935–55. His government helped to create a welfare society and granted independence to India.

Auchinleck, Sir Claude John Eyre (1884–1981), British field-marshal; G.O.C. North Norway 1940; C.-in-C. India 1941, 1943–7; Middle East 1941–2.

Auden, Wystan Hugh (1907–73), poet, b. in England. Naturalised an American. Succeeded C. Day Lewis as professor of poetry at Oxford 1956–61.

Auer, Leopold (1845–1930), Hungarian violinist who taught Mischa Elman and Jascha Heifetz.

Augustine of Canterbury, St. (d. c. 605), first archbishop of Canterbury. Sent from Rome in 597 by Gregory the Great to convert the English.

Augustine of Hippo, St. (354–430), one of the great Latin Fathers of the Church. Bishop of Hippo (in north Africa). Author of *Confessions* (400) and *The City of God* (412–27).

Augustus, Caius Octavianus (63 B.C.–A.D. 14), first Roman emperor. Great-nephew of Julius Caesar, he was for 12 years triumvir with Mark Antony and Lepidus; then reigned alone. His reign was notable for peace, and for writers like Horace and Virgil; hence Augustan age for a great period in literature (the title Augustus was given him by the Senate).

Aurangzeb (1618–1707), Mogul emperor of India. Son of Shah Jehan, he obtained power by acting against his father and brothers. In his long reign the Mogul empire reached its fullest extent; but he estranged Hindus and Sikhs; and when he died his authority was in dispute and the Mogul empire broke up.

Aurelius, Marcus Antonius. *See* **Marcus Aurelius Antoninus.**

Auriol, Vincent (1884–1966), French politician. President of the Fourth Republic 1947–54.

Austen, Jane (1775–1817), author of *Emma*, *Mansfield Park*, *Northanger Abbey*, *Persuasion*, *Pride and Prejudice*, and *Sense and Sensibility*. Though confining herself to the personal relations of the English middle classes, she combined artistry, accuracy, imaginative power, satiric humour, sense, and genuine feeling with the ability to create a range of living characters. She spent the first 25 years of her life at her father's Hampshire rectory. She was unmarried. Her picture is to go on the new £10 banknotes.

Austin, 1st Baron (Herbert Austin) (1886–1941), English motor manufacturer, pioneer of the small car—the 7-horsepower car—which he put on the market in 1921.

Avenzoar (Ibn Zuhr) (c. 1090–1162), Arab physician, b. Seville. His chief work was the *Tasir*.

Averroës (Ibn Rushd) (1126–98), Arab philosopher, b. Córdova. He believed in the eternity of the world (not as a single act of creation as demanded by the current theology of Islam, Christianity and Judaism, but as a continuous process) and in the eternity of a universal intelligence, indivisible but shared in by all. He expounded Aristotle to his countrymen, but his teaching was modified by Neoplatonism.

Avicenna (Ali ibn-Sina) (980–1037), Arab philosopher and physician, of Bukhara. His *Canon of Medicine* attempted to systematise all medical knowledge up to his time.

Avogadro, Amedeo (1776–1856), Italian physicist, remembered for his hypothesis, since known as Avogadro's Hypothesis (*see* **Section L**).

Avon, Earl of. *See* **Eden, Anthony.**

Awdry, Reverend Wilbert Vere (1911–97), Anglican clergyman who created *Thomas the Tank Engine*.

Ayckbourn, Sir Alan (b. 1939), the most prolific and most-performed living British playwright. His first West-End success (1967) was *Relatively Speaking*. A master of farce (*e.g. Absurd Person Singular* (1973) and *Joking Apart* (1979).

Ayrton, William Edward (1847–1908), English electrical engineer, inventor of a number of electrical measuring instruments. His first wife, Matilda Chaplin Ayrton (1846–83), was one of the first woman doctors, and his second wife, **Hertha Ayrton** (1854–1923), became known for her scientific work on the electric arc and sand ripples and for her work for woman suffrage.

Ayer, A. J. (Alfred Jules Ayer) (1910–89), English philosopher, exponent of logical positivism. His books include *Language, Truth and Logic* (1936).

Ayub Khan, Mohammed (1907–74), Pakistani military leader; president of Pakistan, 1958–69.

B

Babbage, Charles (1801–71), British mathematician. He designed an analytical engine, the forerunner of the modern digital computer.

Baber, Babar or Babur (Zahir ud-din Mohammed) (1483–1530), founder of the Mogul dynasty which ruled northern India for nearly three centuries; a descendant of Tamerlane. A liberal and progressive ruler.

Babeuf, François (1760–97), early French socialist.

Bach, Johann Sebastian (1685–1750), composer. B. at Eisenach, Germany, he was successively violinist, church organist, and chief court musician. It was as organist at the Thomas-kirche, Leipzig, that he composed the St. Matthew and the St. John Passion and the B minor Mass. His work was in the school of the contrapuntal style (especially the fugue and the chorale); after his day it lost favour, but has now gained in popularity. *See* **Section P.**

Bach, Carl Philipp Emanuel (1714–88), 3rd son of the above, and one of the first experimenters in the symphonic and sonata forms.

Backhaus, Wilhelm (1884–1969), German pianist, who interpreted classical and romantic concertos.

Bacon, Francis, Lord Verulam (1561–1626), English philosopher. He threw over Aristotelian deductive logic for the inductive method (*see* **Baconian method, Section J**); remembered for the impulse his writings gave to the foundation of the Royal Society (c. 1662). His chief work is the *Novum Organum*. His career as statesman under Elizabeth and James I was brought to an end by charges of corruption.

Bacon, Francis (1909–92), Dublin-born artist. A realist who depicted the complexity of human emotions (*e.g.* his *Study after Velazquez* of 1953).

Bacon, Roger (c. 1219/20–94), founder of English philosophy, advocate of the value of observation and experiment in science. He first studied arts at Oxford but when he returned from lecturing in Paris he devoted himself to experimental science, especially alchemy and optics. He became a Franciscan friar in 1257.

Baden-Powell, 1st Baron (Robert Stephenson Smyth Baden-Powell) (1857–1941), founder of Boy Scouts (1908) and Girl Guides (1910). Chief Scout of the World 1921–41. As a young cavalry officer in the South African war he defended Mafeking.

Baer, Karl Ernst von (1792–1876), German naturalist, b. Estonia, founder of the science of embryology. He discovered the mammalian ovum (1827). An opponent of Darwin's theory.

Baffin, William (1584–1622), British navigator and explorer who in 1616 discovered Baffin Bay.

Bagehot, Walter (1826–77), English economist and journalist, editor of *The Economist*. Among his works are *The English Constitution*.

Bailey, Sir Donald (1901–85), inventor of the Bailey bridge; b. Rotherham.

Baird, John Logie (1888–1946), Scottish TV pioneer, inventor of the televisor and the noctovisor.

Baker, Sir Benjamin (1840–1907), English civil engineer. With Sir John Fowler he built the Forth bridge and the London Metropolitan railway. He designed the vessel which brought Cleopatra's Needle to London. In Egypt he was consulting engineer for the Aswan dam.

Baker, Sir Herbert (1862–1946), English architect. Designed the Bank of England, Rhodes House, Oxford, and, with Sir E. Lutyens, New Delhi.

Baker, Josephine (1906–75), black American revue artiste who galvanised Paris in the 1920s.

Bakst, Léon (1868–1924), Russian painter who designed scenery *etc.* for Diaghilev's ballets.

Baldwin of Bewdley, 1st Earl (Stanley Baldwin) (1867–1947), Conservative prime minister, 1923–4, 1924–9, and 1935–7. He handled the crisis over Edward VIII's proposed marriage.

Balfour, 1st Earl (Arthur James Balfour) (1848–1930), statesman and writer. He was Conservative prime minister 1902–5. He was responsible for a declaration on Palestine.

Ball, John (d. 1381), English priest and a leader of the Peasants' Revolt, after which he was executed. The couplet *When Adam delved, and Eve span, Who was then the gentleman?* is attributed to him.

Balliol, John de (d. 1269), the founder of Balliol College, Oxford; a regent for Scotland; sided with Henry III against his barons.

Balliol, John de (1249–1315), king of Scotland. Son of the above, he claimed the throne against Robert Bruce and was chosen by the arbitrator, Edward I of England, whose overlordship he acknowledged. Later, on renouncing homage, he was taken captive and d. in retirement. His son **Edward Balliol** (d. 1363) obtained the kingdom for a time, acknowledging Edward III of England and surrendering Lothian; but retired on an annuity, 1356.

Balzac, Honoré de (1799–1850), French novelist of wide influence, and author of over eighty novels to which he gave the covering title of *La Comédie Humaine*, depicting the appetites and passions of the new social class born of the revolution and Napoleon.

Bancroft, Sir Squire (1841–1926), Victorian actor-manager.

Banda, Hastings (1898–1997), brutal dictator of Malawi who steered his country to independence.

Bandaranaike, Solomon West Ridgway Dias (1899–1959), socialist prime minister of Ceylon from 1956 until his assassination. His widow, **Mrs Sirimavo Bandaranaike** (1916–2000), became the world's first woman premier in 1960.

Banks, Sir Joseph (1743–1820), an amateur scientist of wealth who accompanied Captain Cook on his expedition to the Pacific 1768–71.

Bannister, Sir Roger (b. 1929), athlete who first ran a mile in under 4 minutes in 1954 (3 mins. 59·4 seconds). C. H. (2017).

Banting, Sir Frederick Grant (1891–1941), Canadian physician who with C. H. Best discovered insulin.

Bantock, Sir Granville (1868–1946), composer of songs, orchestral and choral music.

Barbarossa (Ital. = red beard), surname of two brothers who were Barbary pirates: **Uruz** (c. 1474–1518), was killed by Spaniards, and **Khaireddin** (c. 1483–1546) conquered Tunis for the Turks and died in Constantinople.

Barbirolli, Sir John (1899–1970), conductor of the Hallé Orchestra 1943–70; succeeded Toscanini as conductor of the New York Philharmonic Symphony Orchestra 1937–42.

Barbusse, Henri (1874–1935), French writer, author of the war novel *Le Feu*, which portrays the experience of the common soldier.

Barham, Richard Harris (1788–1845), English humorist, author of *The Ingoldsby Legends*, (under his pen-name of Thomas Ingoldsby). His best-known poem is *The Jackdaw of Rheims*.

Barker, Ronnie (1929–2005), famous comic actor. Star of *The Two Ronnies*, *Porridge* and *Open All Hours*.

Barnard, Christiaan Neethling (1922–2001), South African surgeon who first pioneered heart transplant surgery. His first was carried out at Groote Schuur Hospital, Cape Town, in 1967.

Barnardo, Thomas John (1845–1905), founder of homes for orphan-waifs; devoted himself to the protection and care of destitute children.

Barrie, Sir James Matthew (1860–1937), Scottish author and dramatist. His novels include *A Window in Thrums*. Among his plays are *Dear Brutus*, *The Admirable Crichton*, and *Peter Pan* which gained great popularity with children.

Barrow, Isaac (1630–77), divine and mathematician, tutor of Sir Isaac Newton.

Barry, Sir Charles (1795–1860), architect of the houses of parliament at Westminster. Details were contributed by his assistant A. W. Pugin. *See* **N19**(1).

Barth, Karl (1886–1968), Swiss theologian, seen as a Protestant St. Thomas Aquinas.

Bartók, Bela (1881–1945), Hungarian composer. From an early age he was deeply interested in folk-song which inspired his researches into Hungarian and Romanian peasant music. He left for America in 1940, where he lived precariously and apparently unhappily until the end of the war made a return possible, regrettably too late. *See* **Section P.**

Bartolommeo, Fra (di Paolo) (1475–1517), Italian painter. At first influenced by Savonarola. Some of his best work is at Lucca.

Bartolozzi, Francesco (1725–1815), Italian engraver, who settled in England and became a founder-member of the Royal Academy; noted for his stipple engravings.

Bashkirtseva, Maria Konstantinovna (1859–84), a Russian girl, achieved eminence as a painter in Paris, author of a famous diary.

Bassi, Agostino (1773–1856), Italian amateur microscopist who first suggested that infectious diseases might be caused by micro-organisms.

Bates, Sir Alan (1934–2003), actor whose career ranged from the "kitchen sink" theatre of the 1960s to portrayals from Chekhov and Hardy.

Batten, Jean Gardiner (1909–82), New Zealand airwoman who flew solo from England to Australia in 1934.

Baudelaire, Charles Pierre (1821–67), French poet of originality and sensitivity, best known for his *Les Fleurs du Mal*. His life was darkened by poverty and ill-health. A talented draughtsman.

Bax, Sir Arnold (1883–1953), composer and Master of the King's Musick 1942–52. One of his best-known works is the poem, *Tintagel* (1917).

Baxter, Richard (1615–91), noncomformist divine, b. Shropshire; author of many books on theology; imprisoned after the Restoration by Judge Jeffreys.

Bayard, Pierre de Terrail, Seigneur de (c. 1474–1524), French knight, known as the "chevalier sans peur et sans reproche." He fought in campaigns against Italy and fell at the battle of Romagnano.

Bayle, Pierre (1647–1706), French philosopher, author of the *Dictionnaire historique et critique* (1697). His sceptical views influenced Voltaire and the encyclopedists of the 18th cent.

Baylis, Lilian Mary (1874–1937), manager of the Old Vic from 1898 and of Sadler's Wells from 1931.

Bazalgette, Sir Joseph (1819–91), Victorian engineer, famous for building London's sewers.

Beardsley, Aubrey Vincent (1872–98), black-and-white artist, who published much work, some of it controversial (as in the *Yellow Book*).

Beatles, The (Sir Paul McCartney (b. 1942), John Lennon (1940–80), George Harrison (1943–2001), Ringo Starr (b. 1940)), a Liverpool pop group whose highly original and melodic songs held the attention of youth all over the world, especially during the period 1963–5. They parted in 1971. Lennon was shot dead in New York in 1980.

Beatty, 1st Earl (David Beatty) (1871–1936), British admiral; succeeded Jellicoe as commander of the Grand Fleet 1916–19. He fought the German fleet on 28 August 1914 in the Heligoland Bight, and on 31 May 1916 off Jutland.

Beaufort, Sir Francis (1774–1857), hydrographer of the navy, who introduced the wind scale (1805) which bears his name.

Beaumont, Francis (1584–1616), and **Fletcher, John** (1579–1625), joint authors of many plays, including *The Maid's Tragedy* and *Philaster*.

Beaverbrook, 1st Baron (William Maxwell Aitken) (1879–1964), British newspaper owner and politician, a Canadian by birth. He gave energetic service as minister of aircraft production 1940–1. He controlled the *Daily Express*, *Sunday Express*, and *Evening Standard*.

Becket, Thomas (1118?–70), saint and martyr. An able chancellor, 1155–62, on becoming archbishop of Canterbury he made the position of the church his first care; and, coming into conflict with Henry. Murdered in Canterbury cathedral. His shrine became famous.

Beckett, Samuel (1906–89), Anglo-Irish dramatist and novelist, b. Dublin. Plays include *Waiting for Godot*, *Endgame*, *Krapp's Last Tape*, *Happy Days*, *Not I*; novels include *The Nouvelles* (3 stories), the trilogy: *Molloy*, *Malone Dies*, *The Unnamable*, and *How It Is*. His work expresses man's isolation, bewilderment and suffering. Nobel Prize for Literature, 1969.

Becquerel, Antoine Henri (1852–1908), French physicist who in 1896 discovered radioactivity in uranium. Shared with the Curies the 1903 Nobel prize in physics.

Bede, the Venerable (673–735), English historian and scholar; lived at Jarrow. His chief work is his *Ecclesiastical History* to 731. Regarded as the greatest of Anglo-Saxon scholars.

Bedser, Sir Alec (1918–2010), legendary Surrey and England cricketer. A renowned fast bowler.

Beebe, (Charles) William (1877–1962), pioneer oceanographer. Co-inventor of the bathysphere.

Beecham, Sir Thomas (1879–1961), English conductor and impresario. Founded the London Philharmonic Orchestra in 1931; introduced into England the operas of Richard Strauss, Russian operas, and the Diaghilev ballet.

Beecher, Henry Ward (1813–87), American preacher whose church was at Brooklyn.

Beerbohm, Sir Max (1872–1956), critic and caricaturist, master of irony and satire. His works include *Zuleika Dobson* and *A Christmas Garland*.

Beethoven, Ludwig van (1770–1827), composer. B. at Bonn (his father being a tenor singer at the Elector's court), at 17 he went to Vienna, was recognised by Mozart, and eventually settled there; he never married; gradually he became deaf. In the development from simplicity to complexity of musical treatment, he stands midway between Mozart and Wagner; but in him were uniquely combined the power to feel and the mastery of musical resources necessary to express his feelings. Between the years 1805 and 1808 he composed some of his greatest works: the oratorio *Mount of Olives*, the opera *Fidelio*, and the *Pastoral* and *Eroica* symphonies besides a number of concertos, sonatas, and songs. The symphonies, nine in number, rank as the greatest ever written. See **Section P.**

Begin, Menachem (1913–92), b. Brest-Litovsk; leader of Israeli *Likud* party; prime minister 1977–83. Made peace with Egypt (1979) but failed to solve Palestinian problem; took Israel into war in Lebanon (1982), ending his premiership.

Behbahani, Simin (1927–2014), a towering figure in Persian literature. "The Lioness of Iran".

Behring, Emil von (1854–1917), German bacteriologist, founder of the science of immunology. Nobel prizewinner 1901.

Behring, Vitus (1680–1741), Danish navigator who in 1728 discovered the strait which bears his name.

Belisarius (505–65), Roman general under Justinian who fought against the Vandals.

Bell, Alexander Graham (1847–1922), inventor, b. Edinburgh, emigrated to Canada in 1870, later becoming an American citizen. In 1876 he exhibited an invention which was developed into the telephone (though credit should more properly go to Antonio Meucci). He devoted attention to the education of the deaf.

Bell, Gertrude Margaret Lowthian (1868–1926), the "uncrowned queen of Arabia," was a pioneer traveller in the Middle East.

Bellini, family of Venetian painters: **Jacopo** (c. 1400–70) and his two sons, **Gentile** (1429–1507), whose works include the *Adoration of the Magi* (National Gallery); and **Giovanni** (c. 1429–1516), brother-in-law of Mantegna, and teacher of Giorgione and Titian.

Belloc, Hilaire (1870–1953), versatile writer whose works include *The Bad Child's Book of Beasts, The Path to Rome, Hills and the Sea, Cautionary Tales,* and historical studies of Danton, Robespierre, and Richelieu. B. in France, he became a British subject in 1902.

Bellow, Saul (1915–2005), American novelist and short- story writer, author of *Adventures of Augie March, Henderson the Rain King, Mr. Sammler's Planet, Humboldt's Gift etc.* Nobel prize 1976.

Belzoni, Giovanni Battista (1778–1823), Egyptologist. B. at Padua, he settled in England in 1803. His first interest was in hydraulics, and for this purpose he went to Egypt to Mehemet Ali. There he explored Thebes, Abu Simbel, and one of the pyramids.

Benavente y Martínez, Jacinto (1866–1954), Spanish dramatist. Plays include *Los Intereses Creados* (Bonds of Interest). Nobel prizewinner 1922.

Benedict, St. (c. 480–c. 550), patriarch of western monasticism. B. at Nursia, and at first a hermit at Subiaco, he attracted numerous followers and grouped them in twelve monasteries. Later he went to Monte Cassino, where he formulated the widely-adopted Benedictine rule.

Benedict XVI (b. 1927), succeeded Pope John Paul II in 2005. Formerly Cardinal Ratzinger. At 78, the oldest pontiff to be elected since 1730. Seen as doctrinally conservative. Resigned (February 2013), the first Pope in modern history to do so.

Benenson, Peter (1921–2005), human rights campaigner, founded Amnesty International (*see* **L6**).

Benes, Eduard (1884–1948), Czechoslovak statesman; co-founder with Thomas Masaryk of the Czech Republic after the First World War.

Ben Gurion, David (1886–1973), Zionist leader. He helped organise the Jewish Legion in 1918, and became Prime Minister of Israel 1948–63.

Benn, Tony (1924–2014). British Labour politician and Cabinet Minister. An icon of the Left.

Bennett, Alan (b. 1934), much-loved playwright.

Born at Armley, Leeds, a butcher's son. His career highs include *An Englishman Abroad*, the *Talking Heads* series and *The History Boys*. His *Keeping On Keeping On* came out in 2016.

Bennett, (Enoch) Arnold (1867–1931), English author, who wrote of the pottery towns where he was brought up. His novels include *The Old Wives' Tale* and *Clayhanger*.

Bennett, James Gordon (1841–1918), proprietor of the *New York Herald*. He sent out Stanley on an expedition to find Livingstone.

Bennett, Sir William Sterndale (1816–75), English composer, pianist and teacher, best known for his oratorio *The Woman of Samaria*, songs and piano pieces. Founded the Bach Society.

Bentham, George (1800–84), British botanist. The 'quiet giant' of botany and horticulture who compiled many important works. Secretary of the Horticultural Society, 1829–40.

Bentham, Jeremy (1748–1832), utilitarian philosopher and writer whose main works are *Government* and *Principles of Morals and Legislation*. Honorary Citizen of the French Republic, 1792.

Bentley, Richard (1662–1742), classical scholar who did pioneer work in textual criticism.

Benz, Karl (1844–1929), German engineer whose motor car produced in 1885 was one of the first to be driven by an internal combustion engine.

Beresford, 1st Viscount (William Carr Beresford) (1768–1854), British general. He fought under Wellington in the Peninsular War and reorganised the Portuguese army.

Berg, Alban (1885–1935), Austrian composer whose best-known work is the three-act opera *Wozzeck*, based upon a drama by Büchner.

Bergson, Henri Louis (1859–1941). French philosopher, exponent of the theory of creative evolution and the life force. Nobel prizewinner 1927. See **Vitalism, Section J.**

Bériot, Charles Auguste de (1802–70), Belgian violinist, whose wife was the operatic contralto Malibran. His son, **Charles Wilfrid de Bériot** (1833–1914) was a pianist who taught Ravel.

Berkeley, George (1685–1753), idealist philosopher and critic of Locke. His spiritual outlook led him to believe that reality exists only in the eye of God, that it is undiscoverable by science, though it can be revealed by religion. His chief works are *A New Theory of Vision* (1709) and *Principles of Human Knowledge* (1710). Of Irish birth, he became bishop of Cloyne.

Berlin, Irving (1888–1989), American song composer; b. Mahilov (then in Russia, now Belarus).

Berlin, Sir Isaiah (1909–97), British philosopher, b. Riga; Chichele Prof. of Social and Political Theory at Oxford 1957–67. His works include *Karl Marx, The Hedgehog and the Fox,* and *The Age of Enlightenment*. O.M. (1971). One of the foremost modern liberal thinkers.

Berlioz, Hector (1803–69), composer. B. near Grenoble, the son of a doctor, his romantic sensibility, taste for the grand (as in his *Requiem*), and response to literary influence made him a prime figure in the French romantic movement. See **Section P.**

Bernadotte, Count Folke (1895–1948), nephew of King Gustav of Sweden. U.N. mediator for Palestine 1947. Assassinated by Jewish terrorists.

Bernadotte, Jean Baptiste (1764–1844), a French commander who served under Napoleon, and in 1810 was chosen heir to the throne of Sweden. In 1818 he succeeded as Charles XIV.

Bernal, John Desmond (1901–71), physicist, b. Ireland. Prof. of Physics, Birkbeck College, Univ. of London, 1937–63, Prof of Crystallography, 1963–8. Author of *The Social Functions of Science, Science in History, The Origin of Life*.

Bernard, Claude (1813–78), French physiologist whose discoveries eventually paved the way for the work of Pavlov and Hopkins.

Bernard of Menthon (923–1008), patron saint of mountaineers. He founded Alpine hospices in the passes that bear his name.

Bernard, St. (1090–1153), abbot of Clairvaux, which became a chief centre of the Cistercian order. His writings had wide influence in Europe.

Berners-Lee, Sir Timothy. (b. 1955), computer pioneer, founded World Wide Web. O.M. (2007).

Bernhardt, Sarah (1844–1923), French tragedienne, b. Paris, daughter of Dutch jewess. She became a member of the Comédie Française after the siege of Paris. Her first performance in London was in 1879. Her successes included *Phèdre, La Dame aux Camélias, Fédora, Théodora,* and *La Tosca*.

Bernini, Gian Lorenzo (1598–1680), Italian baroque sculptor. Born Naples. Did much work in Rome, designing the piazza for St. Peter's. His masterpiece is the *Ecstasy of St Theresa*.

Bernstein, Leonard (1918–90), Popular American composer, conductor and pianist. His scores included *Candide* (1956) and *West Side Story* (1957).

Berthelot, Marcellin Pierre Eugène (1827–1907), French chemist and politician. The first to produce organic compounds synthetically.

Berzelius, Jöns Jakob (1779–1848), Swedish chemist, founder of electrochemical theory. His work was concerned with the exact determination of atomic and molecular weights and he devised the present system of chemical symbols.

Bessemer, Sir Henry (1813–98), inventor of the process of converting cast-iron direct into steel. This revolutionised steel manufacture, reducing the cost of production and extending its use.

Best, Charles Herbert (1899–1978), Canadian physiologist, who with F. G. Banting discovered the use of insulin in the treatment of diabetes.

Best, George (1946–2005), footballing legend of the great Manchester United team of the 1960s (he appeared 464 times scoring 178 goals).

Betjeman, Sir John (1906–84), English poet, author and broadcaster; Poet Laureate, 1972–84.

Bevan, Aneurin (1897–1960), British socialist politician, architect of the National Health Service which came into operation in 1948.

Beveridge, 1st Baron (William Henry Beveridge) (1879–1963), British economist who drew up the Beveridge Plan (1942), which formed the basis of later social security services.

Bevin, Ernest (1881–1951), British trade union leader; famous general secretary of the Transport and General Workers Union; Minister of Labour 1940–5, and Foreign Secretary 1945–51.

Beyle, Marie Henri. *See* Stendhal.

Bhave, Vinova (1895–1982), Indian reformer, leader of the Sarvodaya movement. A follower of Gandhi, in 1951 he began a walking mission to persuade landlords to help landless peasants.

Bhutto, Benazir (1953–2007), Pakistani Prime Minister, 1988–90, 1993–96. A courageous reformer who was assassinated in December 2007. Daughter of **Zulfikar Ali Bhutto** (1928–79), founder of the Pakistan Peoples Party, President of Pakistan, 1971–73 and Prime Minister, 1973–77. He was executed in 1979.

Bichat, Marie François Xavier (1771–1802), French physiologist whose study of tissues founded modern histology. His theory was that life is "the sum of the forces that restrict death."

Biddle, John (1615–62), unitarian. He taught in Gloucester; was several times imprisoned for his controversial writings. He died of fever.

Biden, Joseph (b. 1942), US Senator from Delaware after 1972. Vice-President under Obama, 2009–17.

Bin Laden, Osama (1957–2011), the ruthless terrorist head of *Al-Qaeda*. Planned 2001 US attack. Killed by US forces in Pakistan, 1 May 2011.

Binyon, Laurence (1869–1943), poet, art critic, and orientalist, who worked at the British Museum 1893–1933.

Birch, Samuel John Lamorna (1869–1955), English landscape painter in watercolour, known for his Cornish and Australian studies.

Birkbeck, George (1776–1841), founder of mechanics' institutes, first at Glasgow, later in London (the Birkbeck Institution developed into Birkbeck College, London University).

Birkenhead, 1st Earl of (Frederick Edwin Smith) (1872–1930), lawyer and politician; lord chancellor 1919–22; secretary for India 1924–8.

Biró, Laszlo (1899–1985), Hungarian inventor who devised the ballpoint pen (the biro).

Bishop, Sir Henry Rowley (1786–1855), English composer who wrote *Home, sweet Home.*

Bismarck, Otto Eduard Leopold von, Prince Bismarck, Duke of Lauenburg (1815–98), Prusso-German diplomat and statesman, chief architect of the German empire. He was of Junker family. Prussian ambassador at St. Petersburg (1859–62) and at Paris (1862). He was recalled to Berlin by the king to become chief Prussian minister. He used a dispute over Schleswig-Holstein to bring about the defeat of Austria at Königgratz in 1866; and he provoked the Franco-Prussian war of 1870–1 when France was defeated at Sedan. Germany then became united under the military leadership of Prussia, with the king as emperor. He presided over the Berlin Congress of European

powers in 1878. In 1884 he began a colonial empire. William II, who succeeded as emperor in 1888, dismissed the "iron chancellor" in 1890.

Bizet, Georges (1838–75), properly **Alexandre César Léopold**, French composer, chiefly remembered for his opera *Carmen.*

Björnson, Björnstjerne (1832–1910), Norwegian poet, dramatist and novelist. His work provides an image of Norwegian life from the period of the sagas (*Kong Sverre*) to contemporary problems (*Over Aevne*).

Black, Sir James (1924–2010). Eminent Scottish scientist. Discovered life-saving drug used to prevent heart attacks. Nobel Prize for Medicine, 1988.

Black, Joseph (1728–90), Scottish chemist. A professor first at Glasgow, later at Edinburgh, he was the first to undertake a detailed study of a chemical reaction. He laid the foundation of the quantitative science of heat and his discovery of latent heat was applied by Watt in improving his steam-engine.

Blackett of Chelsea, Baron (Patrick Maynard Stuart Blackett) (1897–1974), British nuclear physicist who won a Nobel prize in 1948. O.M. 1967.

Blackmore, Richard Doddridge (1825–1900), English novelist and author of *Lorna Doone.*

Blackstone, Sir William (1723–80), English judge. His *Commentaries on the Laws of England* is a classic.

Blackwood, Algernon (1869–1951), English novelist and writer of short stories.

Blackwood, William (1776–1834), originator of *Blackwood's Magazine.*

Blair, Anthony Charles Lynton (b. 1953), Prime Minister, 1997–2007. Leader of the Labour Party, 1994–2007. MP for Sedgefield, 1983–2007. His "New Labour" won a landslide victory in the 1997 general election. He became the youngest Prime Minister since 1812. Became the longest-serving Labour Prime Minister in February 2005. His 2001 election victory was followed by the invasion of Iraq which divided his party. Won historic third election victory, May 2005. Resigned, 2007. He was heavily criticised by the Chilcott Report.

Blair, Robert (1699–1746), Scottish poet, author of *The Grave.*

Blake, Robert (1599–1657), Parliamentary general and an admiral in the Cromwellian navy in the Dutch and Spanish wars.

Blake, William (1757–1827), English poet, mystic, and artist, son of a hosier in Carnaby market, Soho. A solitary and deeply religious man, he had a hatred of materialism. He produced his own books, engraving on copper plates both the text of his poems and the illustrations. His *Book of Job* is a masterpiece in line-engraving in metal, his poems range from the mystical and almost incomprehensible to the delightfully simple *Songs of Innocence.* He has been called "the great teacher of the modern western world." He was widely derided in his own lifetime.

Blankers-Koen, Fanny (1918–2004). The foremost woman athlete of the 20th cent. The most memorable champion of the 1948 Olympics.

Blanqui, Louis Auguste (1805–81), French revolutionary leader, master of insurrection. He invented the term "dictatorship of the proletariat," and his theories influenced Marx.

Blériot, Louis (1872–1936), French airman; the first to fly the English Channel from Calais to Dover, on 25 July 1909.

Bligh, William (1754–1817), sailor, b. Plymouth. He accompanied Cook 1772–4, and discovered breadfruit; but was in 1789 cast adrift from *HMS Bounty* by his mutinous crew. As governor of New South Wales (1806) he fought to suppress the rum traffic.

Blind, Karl (1826–1907), German agitator, b. Mannheim. Active in the risings of 1848, and imprisoned; but escaped and settled in England.

Bliss, Sir Arthur (1891–1975), English composer; Master of the Queen's Musick from 1953.

Bloch, Ernest (1880–1959), composer, whose music is characterised by Jewish and oriental themes.

Blondin, Charles (1824–97), French rope performer, who crossed the Niagara Falls on a tight-rope.

Blücher, Gebhard Leberecht von (1742–1819), Prussian general. He fought against Napoleon, especially at Lützen and Leipzig; and he completed Wellington's victory at Waterloo by his timely arrival.

Blum, Léon (1872–1950), French statesman, leader of the French Socialist Party. His efforts strengthened the growth of the Popular Front and the campaign against appeasement of Hitler. He held office only briefly and was interned in Germany 1940–5.

Blumlein, Alan Dower (1903–42), British electronics engineer and inventor, chiefly remembered for his fundamental work on stereophony.

Blunden, Edmund Charles (1896–1974), poet and critic; professor of poetry at Oxford 1966–8.

Blunt, Wilfrid Scawen (1840–1922), English poet and political writer who championed Egyptian, Indian, and Irish independence; imprisoned in 1888 for activities in the Irish Land League.

Blyton, Enid (1897–1968), enduringly popular writer of more than 700 children's books. A teacher in South London, she is perhaps best remembered for the 'Famous Five' books, the 'Secret Seven' adventures and, of course, Noddy.

Boadicea (Boudicca), queen of the Iceni in eastern Britain, who fought against the Roman invaders, but was defeated in A.D. 61 and killed herself. Archaeologists tentatively identified her palace at Gallows Hill, Thetford, Norfolk.

Boccaccio, Giovanni (1313–75), Italian author, father of the novel. He is chiefly known for his *Decameron* (set in the neighbourhood of Florence during the plague), and for his life of Dante.

Boccherini, Luigi (1743–1805), Italian cellist and composer of chamber music.

Bode, Johann Ehlert (1747–1826), German astronomer remembered for his theoretical calculation (known as Bode's law) of the proportionate distances of the planets from the sun.

Boethius (480–524), Roman scientific writer who translated the logical works of Aristotle and provided the dark ages with some elementary mathematical treatises.

Bohr, Niels Henrik David (1885–1962), Danish nuclear physicist whose researches into the structure of the atom gave him great authority. With Rutherford he applied the quantum theory to study atomic processes. Nobel prize 1922.

Boieldieu, François Adrien (1775–1834), French composer especially of operas, including *La Dame blanche*.

Boileau-Despréaux, Nicolas (1636–1711), French literary critic and poet, best known for his *Satires*.

Boito, Arrigo (1842–1918), Italian poet and composer; he wrote the libretti of *Otello* and *Falstaff* for Verdi.

Boleyn, Anne (1507–36), queen of Henry VIII and mother of Queen Elizabeth. She was maid-in-waiting to Catherine of Aragon and her successor when Catherine's marriage was annulled. She failed to produce a male heir and was beheaded on a charge of adultery.

Bolivar, Simón (1783–1830), South American revolutionary, called the Liberator, b. Carácas. He led independence movements in the north-west of South America against Spanish rule. He founded Grand Colombia (now Venezuela, Colombia, Panama, Ecuador). A Latin American hero.

Bolt, Usain (b. 1986). The world's fastest athlete. Holder of the world record for 100 metres and 200 metres.

Bonaventura, St. (1221–74), Franciscan theologian, b. Orvieto. His mystical theory of knowledge was in the Augustinian tradition.

Bondfield, Margaret Grace (1873–1953), as minister of Labour, 1929–31, she was the first woman to enter the cabinet and become a privy councillor.

Bondi, Sir Hermann (1919–2005), British mathematician, physicist and astronomer, b. Vienna: chief scientist to Min. of Defence, 1971–7.

Bone, Sir Muirhead (1876–1953), architectural draughtsman and etcher, b. Glasgow; excelled in dry-point and drawings of intricate scaffolding; official war artist in both world wars.

Bonhoeffer, Dietrich (1906–45), German Lutheran theologian who opposed Hitler. Executed by Nazis, 1945. He wrote *The Cost of Discipleship*.

Boniface, St. (680–754), apostle of Germany. B. at Crediton, Devon, his name being Wynfrith, he became a Benedictine monk, and went as missionary to Friesland, securing papal approval. He founded Fulda Abbey and became archbishop of Mainz, but was martyred.

Bonnard, Pierre (1867–1947), French painter of landscapes, still life, and nudes.

Boole, George (1815–64). Born in Lincoln. First professor of mathematics at the university in Cork. Seen as the founder of pure mathematics and a father of computer science.

Booth, Edwin Thomas (1833–93), American

Shakespearean actor, brother of John Wilkes Booth who assassinated President Lincoln.

Booth, William (1829–1912), founder and first general of the Salvation Army, b. Nottingham. In 1865, with the help of his wife, Catherine Booth, he began mission work in the East End of London, which led to the creation in 1878 of the Salvation Army (*q.v.*) on military lines. His son **Bramwell** (d. 1929) and his daughter **Evangeline** were among his successors.

Boothroyd, Betty. *See* **D16.**

Borges, Jorge Luis (1899–1986), Argentine poet, critic, and short story writer. Some of his work has been translated into English, including *A Personal Anthology* and *Labyrinths*.

Borgia, Caesar (1476–1507), Italian general. The son of Pope Alexander VI, at 17 he was suspected of murdering his brother. He became captain-general of the church, and made himself master of Romagna, the Marches, and Umbria. Banished by Pope Julius II he met his death fighting in Spain.

Borlaug, Norman Ernest (1914–2009), American wheat scientist, grandfather of the "green revolution" which transformed agriculture in less-developed countries. Nobel Peace Prize, 1970.

Borodin, Alexander Porfyrievich (1833–87), Russian composer who taught chemistry and founded a school of medicine for women. He wrote two symphonies, two string quartets, the symphonic sketch *In the Steppes of Central Asia* and the opera *Prince Igor. See* **Section P.**

Borrow, George Henry (1803–81), English author, for many years agent for the British and Foreign Bible Society; he studied gypsy life and wrote of his experiences in *Lavengro, Romany Rye, Bible in Spain.*

Bosch, Hieronymus (*c.* 1450–1516). Dutch painter, (*e.g. The Garden of Earthly Delights*). Major influence on the surrealists.

Bose, Satyendra Nath (1894–1974), Indian physicist after whom the subatomic boson particle was named.

Bose, Subhas Chandra (1897–1945), Indian nationalist leader; organised anti-British Indian National Army; killed in a plane crash.

Boswell, James (1740–95), Scottish author of *The Life of Dr. Johnson*, with whom he spent some years. His own published journals and letters form an extensive literary collection.

Botha, Louis (1862–1919), South African soldier and statesman. In command of Transvaal forces 1899–1902 in the Boer war. Prime minister of the Transvaal in 1907, and first premier of the Union of South Africa in 1910.

Botham, Sir Ian (b. 1955), English cricketer. Wonderful all-rounder. He played in 102 tests, 12 as captain (1980–81).

Botticelli, Sandro (*c.* 1445–1510), Italian painter. He worked under Fra Lippo Lippi, and was influenced by Savonarola. His art is delicate and poetic. His *Birth of Venus* is in the Uffizi Gallery, Florence, and his *Mars and Venus* in the National Gallery. Illustrated Dante's *Inferno.*

Bottomley, Horatio (1860–1933), English politician, journalist, and notorious fraudster.

Botvinnik, Mikhail (1911–95), Russian chess champion.

Boudicca. *See* **Boadicea.**

Boughton, Rutland (1878–1960), English composer of the opera *The Immortal Hour*, and writer on the history and philosophy of music.

Boult, Sir Adrian (1889–1983), famous conductor of the London Philharmonic Orchestra 1950–7, and of the BBC Symphony Orchestra 1930–50. Musical Director BBC 1930–42.

Boulton, Matthew (1728–1809), engineer who in partnership with James Watt manufactured steam-engines at his Soho works near Birmingham. He also minted a new copper coinage.

Bourgeois, Louise (1911–2010), one of the last great surrealists.

Bowdler, Thomas (1754–1825), issued for family reading expurgated editions of Shakespeare and Gibbon, hence the term "bowdlerise."

Bowie, David (1947–2016). Rock superstar, famous for *Space Oddity* (1969), *Ziggy Stardust etc.*

Boyd Orr, 1st Baron (John Boyd Orr) (1880–1971), British physiologist and nutritional expert. Director-general, FAO, 1945–8. Nobel prize 1949.

Boyle, Robert (1627–91), English scientist who with Robert Hooke laid the foundations of the modern sciences of chemistry and physics. He established the law which states that the volume of a gas varies inversely as the pressure upon it, provided temperature is constant. His chief work is the *Sceptical Chymist* (1661).

Bradley, Omar Nelson (1893–1981), American general. In the second world war he commanded in Tunis, Sicily, and Normandy.

Bradman, Sir Donald George (1908–2001), Australian cricketer who captained Australia in test matches against England 1936–48. One of the greatest batsmen of all time.

Bragg, Sir William Henry (1862–1942), English physicist. Professor of chemistry at the Royal Institution 1923–42. Pres. Royal Society 1935–40.

Bragg, Sir William Lawrence (1890–1971), son of the above. He succeeded Rutherford at the Cavendish laboratory, Cambridge, 1938–53. Dir. Royal Institution 1954–66. Shared with his father the 1915 Nobel prize for their fundamental work on X-rays and crystal structure.

Brahe, Tycho (1546–1601), Danish astronomer. At his island observatory at Uraniborg, provided by his sovereign, he carried out systematic observations which enabled Kepler to work out his planetary laws.

Brahms, Johannes (1833–97), composer. B. in Hamburg (son of a double-bass player). He was a friend of the Schumanns. *See* **Section P.**

Braille, Louis (1809–52), French educationist, who, as teacher of the blind, perfected his system of reading and writing for the blind. As the result of an accident when he was three years old he was himself blind.

Bramah, Joseph (1749–1814), English inventor of the safety-lock and hydraulic press which bear his name. He also invented the modern water-closet (1778) and a machine for printing the serial numbers on bank-notes.

Brancusi, Constantin (1876–1957). Romanian sculptor whose pure abstract forms and refined models changed the face of 20th century sculpture.

Brandes, Georg Morris Cohen (1842–1927), Danish literary critic who exerted a vitalising influence on literature and art.

Brandt, Willy (1913–92), first social democratic chancellor of the Federal Republic of Germany, 1969–74. His main achievements were the Moscow and Warsaw treaties (1972) the treaty between E. and W. Germany (1973) and the Brandt Report setting out a world development programme. Resigned party leadership, 1987.

Brangwyn, Sir Frank (1867–1956), artist of Welsh extraction, b. Bruges; first worked for William Morris making cartoons for textiles; he excelled in murals and in etching.

Breakspear, Nicholas. *See* **Adrian IV.**

Brecht, Bertolt (1898–1956), German dramatist and poet, b. Augsburg, whose brilliant experimental theatre was characteristic of the period in Germany between the two world wars. A Marxist, he left Nazi Germany in 1933 and returned after the war to direct the Berliner Ensemble in E. Berlin. His plays include *The Threepenny Opera* (with music by Kurt Weill), *Mother Courage* and *The Caucasian Chalk Circle.* He may be regarded as the most original dramatist of his time.

Brennan, Louis (1853–1932), inventor, b. Ireland. His inventions include a gyro-directed torpedo and a mono-rail locomotive.

Breton, André (1896–1966), French poet, founder of the surrealist literary movement in France.

Brewster, Sir David (1781–1868), Scottish physicist, noted for his research into the polarisation of light; invented the kaleidoscope. He helped to found the British Association for the Advancement of Science.

Brezhnev, Leonid Ilyich (1906–82). Russian leader who succeeded Khrushchev in 1964.

Bridges, Robert (1844–1930), poet laureate 1913–30. He wrote *Testament of Beauty* (1929).

Bridgewater, 3rd Duke of (Francis Egerton) (1736–1803), founder of British inland navigation by his canal, to the design of James Brindley (*q.v.*) from Manchester to his coal mines at Worsley, later extended to join the Mersey at Runcorn.

Bridie, James (pseudonym of Osborne Henry Mavor) (1888–1951), Scottish author and dramatist. The first of his many successful plays was *The Anatomist*, produced in 1931. Other plays include *Tobias and the Angel, Jonah and the Whale, Mr. Bolfrey, Dr. Angelus.*

Bright, Sir Charles Tilston (1832–88), English telegraph engineer who supervised the laying of the British telegraph network and the Atlantic cables (1856–8).

Bright, John (1811–89), radical Quaker statesman and orator, b. Rochdale; friend of Cobden, with whom he promoted the movement for free trade.

Brindley, James (1716–72), English canal builder, b. Derbyshire, of poor parents, apprenticed as a millwright. He was employed by the Duke of Bridgewater (*q.v.*) and designed and constructed the Bridgewater canal, carrying it over the R. Irwell by an aqueduct, the first of its kind. He also built the Grand Trunk canal linking the Mersey with the Trent.

Britten, Baron (Edward Benjamin Britten) (1913–76), English composer, closely associated with the Aldeburgh festival. O.M. 1965. *See* **Section P.**

Broca, Paul (1824–80), French pathologist, anthropologist and pioneer in neuro-surgery. He localised the seat of speech in the brain.

Broch, Hermann (1886–1951), Austrian novelist, author of the trilogy *The Sleepwalkers.*

Broglie, prominent family of Piedmontese origin; Victor Maurice (1647–1727), and **François Marie** (1671–1745) were marshals of France; **Louis Victor, Prince de Broglie** (1892–1987) received the Nobel prize for his work on quantum mechanics, and his brother **Maurice, Duc de Broglie** (1875–1960), also a physicist, is noted for his work on the ionisation of gases, radioactivity, and X-rays.

Brontë, Charlotte (1816–55), forceful novelist, daughter of an Anglican clergyman of Irish descent, incumbent of Haworth, Yorkshire. She published under a pseudonym *Jane Eyre*, which was at once successful and was followed by *Shirley* and *Villette.* Her sister **Emily** (1818–48) wrote poetry and also *Wuthering Heights*; and **Anne** (1820–49) wrote *Agnes Grey.*

Brooke, Rupert (1887–1915), English poet who died during the first world war, whose works, though few, showed promise and include the poems *Grantchester* and *The Soldier.*

Brougham and Vaux, 1st Baron (Henry Peter Brougham) (1778–1868), English legal reformer; advocate of Queen Caroline against George IV; helped to found London university.

Brown, Sir Arthur Whitten (1886–1948), together with Sir John Alcock (d. 1919) in 1919 made the first transatlantic flight, crossing from Newfoundland to Ireland in 16 hr. 12 min.

Brown, Gordon (b. 1951). Labour politician. Chancellor of the Exchequer, 1997–2007 (the longest-serving of modern times). Succeeded Blair as Prime Minister, 2007–10. Son of a Presbyterian minister. Resigned, 11 May 2010. Retired as MP, 2015.

Brown, James (1928–2006), the 'Godfather of Soul' whose career inspired funk, disco and rap. Black music's most influential artist.

Brown, John (1800–59), American abolitionist. His action in inciting black slaves to rebel in 1859 led to the civil war. He was hanged after failing to hold the captured US arsenal at Harper's Ferry. Known as "Old Brown of Osawatomie".

Brown, Lancelot "Capability" (1716–83), one of Britain's most famous garden designers. Among his masterpieces are Blenheim Palace in Oxfordshire and Chatsworth House in Derbyshire.

Browne, Charles Farrer (1834–67), American humorist (used pseudonym Artemus Ward).

Browne, Hablot Knight (1815–82), English artist, the "Phiz" of many book illustrations, including many of Dickens's novels.

Browne, Sir Thomas (1605–82), author of *Religio Medici* and *Urne-Buriall*, was born in London and practised in Norwich as a physician.

Browning, Elizabeth Barrett (1806–61), English poet. Owing to an injury in childhood, she spent her youth lying on her back, but her meeting with Robert Browning, whom she married, brought a remarkable recovery. In her lifetime her works were more read than those of her husband. They include *Cry of the Children, Sonnets from the Portuguese*, and *Aurora Leigh.*

Browning, Robert (1812–89), English poet. Because of his involved style his reputation grew only slowly. In *Strafford* and *The Blot on the 'Scutcheon* he attempted drama also. He married Elizabeth Barrett and lived mainly abroad. His works include *Dramatis Personae* and *The Ring and The Book.*

Bruce, Robert (1274–1329), Scottish national leader against Edward I and Edward II of England. Crowned king in 1306. He defeated Edward II at Bannockburn in 1314.

Bruce, William Spiers (1867–1921), Scottish polar explorer who led the Scottish national antarctic expedition in the *Scotia* 1902–4 and set up a meteorological station on the South Orkneys. He redrew the map of Antarctica.

Bruch, Max (1838–1920), German musician, best known for his G minor violin concerto.

Bruckner, Anton (1824–96). *See* Section P.

Brueghel, Pieter (*c.* 1520–69), one of the greatest Flemish painters. His great originality and his pictures of peasant life can be seen in The Blind Leading the Blind (1568).

Brummell, George Bryan (1778–1840), "Beau Brummell," fashion leader and friend of the Prince Regent (George IV).

Brunel, Isambard Kingdom (1806–59), English civil engineer, son of **Sir Marc Isambard Brunel** (1769–1849), whom he assisted in building the Thames (Rotherhithe) tunnel. He was engineer of the Great Western Railway and built the ocean liners, the *Great Western*, the *Great Britain* (brought back from the Falkland Is. to Bristol in 1970), and the *Great Eastern*. His other works include the Clifton suspension bridge over the R. Avon at Bristol and the Royal Albert bridge over the R. Tamar at Saltash.

Brunelleschi, Filippo (1377–1446), Italian architect, b. Florence; he adapted the ideals of the Roman period. His work in Florence includes the Pitti Palace, the churches of San Lorenzo and San Spirito, and the cathedral dome.

Bruno, Giordano (1548–1600), Italian philosopher. A Dominican friar, he came to favour the astronomical views of Copernicus and was burnt at the stake.

Bruno, St. (*c.* 1032–1101), German monk, founder in 1084 of the Carthusian order at La Grande Chartreuse in the French Alps.

Brutus, Marcus Junius (85–42 B.C.), conspirator against Julius Caesar; later committed suicide.

Buchanan, George (1506–82), Scottish humanist who spent most of his life in France lecturing and writing Latin poems, plays, and treatises.

Büchner, Eduard (1860–1917), German chemist, remembered for his work on the chemistry of fermentation. Nobel prizewinner 1907.

Büchner, Georg (1813–37), German dramatist. Dying at 24, his limited output (principally *Dantons Tod* and the fragment *Wozzeck*) is marked by power and maturity.

Buddha. *See* **Gautama, Siddhartha.**

Budge, Sir Ernest Alfred Wallis (1857–1934), archaeologist who conducted excavations in Mesopotamia and Egypt.

Buffon, Georges-Louis Leclerc, Comte de (1707–88), French naturalist, author of the *Histoire naturelle* (44 vols., 1749–1804).

Bulganin, Nikolai Alexandrovich (1895–1975), Soviet leader 1955–8; defence minister 1947–9, 1953–5.

Bull, John (*c.* 1562–1628), English composer; possibly the composer of *God save the Queen.*

Bülow, Hans Guido von (1830–94), German pianist and conductor. He married Liszt's daughter Cosima, who later left him to marry Wagner.

Bunsen, Robert Wilhelm (1811–99), German chemist, discoverer of the metals caesium and rubidium, and inventor of the Bunsen burner, battery, and pump. Made important observations in spectrum analysis.

Bunyan, John (1628–88), was originally a travelling tinker and is believed to have served in the Parliamentary army. He joined an Independent church in Bedford in 1655 and became a popular preacher. After the Restoration he was thrown into prison, and there wrote *The Pilgrim's Progress.* Of his 60 works, the best known after *Pilgrim's Progress* are *The Holy War, Grace Abounding* and *Mr. Badman. See* **M10.**

Burckhardt, Jacob Christoph (1818–97), Swiss historian, author of *The Civilisation of the Renaissance in Italy.*

Burghley, 1st Baron (William Cecil) (1520–98), English statesman. He was Queen Elizabeth I's Secretary of State, 1558–72, and Lord High Treasurer, 1572–98.

Burke, Edmund (1729–97), Whig writer and political philosopher. B. in Dublin, he became secretary to Lord Rockingham and entered parliament in 1765. He advocated the emancipation (though not the independence) of the American colonies; and better administration in India; but was against the French revolution.

Burnett, Gilbert (1643–1715) bishop of Salisbury, b.

Edinburgh. He wrote a *History of his Own Times.*

Burnet, Sir John James (1859–1938), architect, b. Glasgow. The north front of the British Museum (King Edward's galleries) is his work.

Burney, Fanny (Madame D'Arblay) (1752–1840), originator of the simple novel of home life. Daughter of the organist, Dr. Burney, she published *Evelina* in 1778, and this brought her into court and literary society. She also wrote *Cecilia* and *Camilla.*

Burns, Robert (1759–96), The bard of Scotland. The son of a cottar, his first poems published in 1786 were at once successful, and he bought a farm. The farm failed, but he had a post as exciseman, and continued to write simply with tenderness and humour. Among his best-known songs are *Auld Lang Syne, Scots wa hae, Comin' through the rye,* and *The Banks of Doon. Auld Lang Syne* is sung all over the world at countless functions. The "ploughman poet". His Birthplace Museum is on Murdoch's Lone in Alloway, Ayr.

Burroughs, William (1914–97), novelist whose controversial work made him a cult figure.

Burton, Sir Richard Francis (1821–90), British explorer and orientalist, who made a pilgrimage to Mecca and Medina in 1853 disguised as a Moslem. He explored Central Africa and translated the *Arabian Nights* (16 vols.).

Burton, Robert (1577–1640), English cleric and scholar, author of *The Anatomy of Melancholy.*

Busby, Sir Matt (1909–94), legendary football manager of Manchester United.

Bush, George Herbert Walker (b. 1924). American politician. Vice-President of America, 1981–89. Elected 41st President, November 1988. Inaugurated, January 1989. First Vice-President to be elected President since Martin van Buren in 1836. His popularity soared in 1991 after the Gulf War, but quickly fell over domestic economic problems.

Bush, George W. (b. 1946). President of the USA from 2001 to 2009. Son of **George Bush** (*see above*). Republican politician. Governor of Texas after 1995. His presidency saw the war on terrorism and the 2003 invasion of Iraq. In November 2004 he was re-elected in a controversial victory for the Republicans. His brother, **Jeb Bush** (b. 1953) was briefly a 2016 Presidential hopeful. A former Governor of Florida.

Busoni, Ferruccio Benvenuto (1866–1920), pianist and composer of three operas (the last *Dr. Faust,* unfinished at his death), much orchestral and chamber music, and works for the piano. *See* Section P.

Butler, Joseph (1692–1752), English bishop, remembered for his *Analogy of Religion,* published in 1736 in reply to deistic attacks.

Butler, Nicholas Murray (1862–1947), American educationist who shared with the sociologist Jane Addams the 1931 Nobel peace prize.

Butler, Baron (Richard Austen Butler) (1902–82), Conservative MP for Saffron Walden 1929–65. Brought in Education Act 1944; helped secure Conservative acceptance of the welfare state; held high office 1951–64. Life peerage 1965.

Butler, Samuel (1612–80), English verse-satirist, author of the poem *Hudibras* against the Puritans.

Butler, Samuel (1835–1902), English novelist and satirist, author of *Erewhon* and its sequel *Erewhon Revisited.* Other works include *The Fair Haven, Life and Habit,* and *Evolution Old and New,* in which he attacked Darwinism. His autobiographical novel *The Way of All Flesh* and his *Notebooks* were published after his death.

Butt, Clara (1872–1936), English contralto; made her début in London in 1892.

Butlin, Sir Billy (1899–1980), famous for promoting holiday camps (the first of which opened in Skegness in 1936).

Buxton, Sir Thomas Fowell (1786–1845), English social reformer; succeeded Wilberforce as leader of the anti-slavery group in parliament.

Buys Ballot, Christoph Henrich Diedrich (1817–90), Dutch meteorologist who formulated the law which bears his name (an observer with back to wind in northern hemisphere has lower pressure to left; in southern hemisphere has right).

Byrd, Richard Evelyn (1888–1957), American rear-admiral, explorer and aviator. He flew over the north pole, 1926; and in 1929 made the first flight over the south pole. He made other expeditions in 1925, 1933–5, 1939 and 1946.

Byrd, William (1543–1623), English composer of

church music, sacred choral music, string music, vocal and instrumental music; and a founder of the school of English madrigalists. He was organist of Lincoln cathedral at 20 and later of Queen Elizabeth's chapel royal. See Section P.

Byron, 6th Baron (George Gordon Byron) (1788–1824), English romantic poet who influenced European literature and thought. At 20 he published Hours of Idleness, which was violently attacked by the Edinburgh Review. This provoked his sensational English Bards and Scotch Reviewers. His Childe Harold's Pilgrimage appeared in 1812. His married life was unhappy. He went to help the Greeks in their struggle for independence and died at Missolonghi.

C

Cable, George Washington (1844–1925), American author and social critic, b. New Oreleans, whose writings reflect the racial problems of his day: Ole Creol Days, The Silent South.

Cabot, John (**Giovanni Caboto**) (1425–c. 1500), famous Genoese explorer who settled in Bristol and sailed westwards under letters-patent from Henry VII of England in 1497. Discovered Newfoundland and Nova Scotia, believing them to be part of Asia, and may have reached the mainland of America before Columbus did. His son:

Cabot, Sebastian (1474–1557), was born in Venice, and in 1509 in search of a north-west passage to Asia sailed as far as Hudson Bay. Entered Spanish service in 1512, and spent several years exploring the Plate and Paraná rivers. Re-entered English service in 1548 and organised expedition to seek a north-east passage to India, which resulted in trade with Russia. English claim to North America is founded on the voyages of the Cabots.

Cabral, Pedro Alvarez (c. 1467–c. 1520), Portuguese navigator who discovered Brazil.

Cadbury, George (1839–1922), liberal Quaker philanthropist of Cadbury Bros., mainly responsible for the pioneer garden city of Bournville.

Cadogan, Sir Alexander (1884–1968), English diplomat who helped to draft the UN charter.

Caedmon, the first English Christian poet, lived in the 7th cent. and, according to Bede, was first a cowherd and later a monk at Whitby.

Caesar, Caius Julius (c. 101–44 B.C.), Roman general and writer. Under the declining republic, he was assigned in 61 the province of Gaul; in the course of pacifying it he invaded Britain (55 B.C.). Opposition in Rome to his career, mainly from Pompey, provoked him in 49 to the defiance of crossing the Rubicon with his army. He defeated Pompey, whom he pursued to Egypt, where he established Cleopatra as queen. At Rome he became dictator. He was murdered in 44. His career paved the way for Rome becoming an empire under his nephew Octavian.

Calderón de la Barca, Pedro (1600–81), Spanish dramatist who also wrote court spectacles for Philip IV. Among his best-known works are La Vida es Suenl〔〕o and El divino Orfeo.

Callaghan, Lord (Sir James Callaghan) (1912–2005), Labour's fourth prime minister, 1976–9; MP for South Cardiff 1950–87; served as Chancellor of the Exchequer, Home Secretary, and Foreign Secretary in the Labour administrations, 1964–70, 1974–76. Succeeded by Foot as leader, 1980. Order of the Garter, 1987. The longest-lived of any former Prime Minister.

Callas, Maria (1923–77). Born New York as Maria Kalogéropoulos. A great operatic soprano.

Calvin, John (1509–64), French Protestant reformer and theologian. B. in Picardy, he broke with the Roman Catholic church about 1533, and subsequently settled in Geneva, where from 1541 he established a theocratic regime of strict morality. His theology was published in his Institutes; See Section J.

Cambridge, Duke of. See under Charles.

Camden, William (1551–1623), English antiquary and historian. His Britannia appeared in 1586.

Cameron, Sir David Young (1865–1945), Scottish etcher and landscape painter.

Cameron, David (b. 1969). Leader of the Conservative Party, 2005–16. MP for Witney 2001–16. He became Prime Minister on 11 May 2010, heading a Conservative-Liberal Democrat Coalition,

the youngest Prime Minister since 1812. After May 2015 he was Prime Minister of a Conservative Government. He called the EU referendum for 23 June 2016. He resigned after losing the vote, becoming the youngest Prime Minister to leave office since 1895.

Cameron, Julia Margaret (1815–79), a pioneer photographer of genius whose work still amazes.

Cameron, Richard (1648–80), Scottish preacher who revolted in defence of the Solemn League and Covenant. Killed at Airds Moss (Ayrshire).

Cameron, Verney Lovett (1844–94), English explorer, the first to cross the African continent from east to west. He surveyed Lake Tanganyika. In 1872 went out to find Livingstone.

Camillus, Marcus Furius (4th cent. B.C.), Roman general. When the Gauls attacked in 387 B.C., he was made dictator and defeated them.

Camoltes, Luis Vaz de (1524–80), Portuguese poet, author of the epic Os Lusiadas.

Campbell, Colin, 1st Baron Clyde (1792–1863), Scottish general who was commander-in-chief in India during the Mutiny.

Campbell, Sir Malcolm (1885–1948), racing driver who held the land-speed record of 301 mile/h (1935) and water-speed record of 141·7 mile/h (1939). His son **Donald** held the water-speed record of 276·33 mile/h (1964); killed in 1967 at Coniston.

Campbell, Mrs. Patrick (Beatrice Stella Tanner) (1865–1940), English actress of beauty and wit.

Campbell, Thomas (1777–1844), Scottish poet, who at 22 published The Pleasures of Hope. His war poems include Ye Mariners of England and The Battle of the Baltic. He was one of the founders of University College, London.

Campbell-Bannerman, Sir Henry (1836–1908), Liberal statesman, prime minister 1905–8.

Camus, Albert (1913–60), French existentialist philosopher and writer, native of Algeria. Preoccupied with the themes of the Stranger and the Absurd. Author of the philosophical essay Le Mythe de Sisyphe, the plays Caligula and The Price of Justice, and the novel L'Etranger. Nobel prize 1957. Killed in car crash.

Canaletto (**Antonio Canal**) (1697–1768), Italian artist. B. at Venice, he painted views of his city. From 1746 to 1756 he worked mainly in London. Some of his work is in the National Gallery, and there is a collection at Windsor.

Canning, George (1770–1827), English statesman. He was an advocate of Catholic emancipation, and was the first to recognise the free states of South America.

Cannizzaro, Stanislao (1826–1910), Italian chemist who followed the work of Avogadro in distinguishing between molecular and atomic weights.

Canova, Antonio (1757–1822), Italian sculptor. He infused grace into the classical style.

Canton, John (1718–72), English physicist and schoolmaster, the first to verify in England Franklin's experiments on the identity of lightning with electricity. He was the first to demonstrate that water is compressible and produced a new phosphorescent body (Canton's phosphorus) by calcining oyster shells with sulphur.

Canute (**Cnut**) (c. 994–1035), king of the English, Danes and Norwegians. The son of a Danish king, after some years of fighting he established himself as king of England and ruled with wisdom.

Capablanca, José Raoul (1888–1942), Cuban chess player, world champion from 1921 to 1927.

Caractacus or **Caradoc**, a king in west Britain, who resisted the Romans in the first century. Captured, but freed by the emperor Claudius.

Caravaggio (**Michelangelo Merisi da Caravaggio**) (1573–1610), Italian painter of immense influence. He used the effects of light and shadow.

Carey, Lord (George Leonard Carey) (b. 1935), 103rd Archbishop of Canterbury, 1991–2002.

Carey, William (1761–1834), first Baptist missionary to India. Helped found Baptist Missionary Society (1792). He published 24 translations of the scriptures as well as compiling Indian dictionaries.

Carissimi, Giacomo (1604–74), Italian composer, b. near Rome. He introduced more instrumental variety into the cantata and oratorio, and brought the recitative to perfection. His Jephtha is still in print, and there are collections of his works at Paris and Oxford. See Section P.

Carlyle, Thomas (1795–1881), Scottish author. Of peasant stock, he went to Edinburgh university, but later lived mainly in England where he lectured. He married Jane Welsh. His individual views pervade his historical writing. His best-known works include *Sartor Resartus, Heroes and Hero Worship, Cromwell's Letters and Speeches,* and the *French Revolution.*

Carnegie, Andrew (1835–1919), philanthropist b. Dunfermline; emigrated to America 1848; after early struggles established the Carnegie iron works. He made munificent gifts to Free Libraries and other educational work.

Carnot, Lazare Nicolas Marguerite (1753–1823), French military engineer, prominent in the French revolutionary wars, 1792–1802. His son, **Sadi Carnot** (1796–1832), was a physicist and engineer who worked on the motive power of heat, establishing the principle that heat and work are reversible conditions.

Caro, Sir Anthony (1924–2013), Britain's greatest sculptor since Henry Moore. His work was ground-breaking and monumental. O.M.

Caroline, Queen (1768–1821), was married to George IV when he was Prince of Wales. They soon separated, but when he became king in 1820, she tried to assert her position. The question came before parliament. In spite of some public sympathy she was unsuccessful.

Carrel, Alexis (1873–1944), American surgeon who won the Nobel prize in 1912 for his success in suturing blood vessels in transfusion and in transplantation of organs. A Frenchman by birth, he returned to France in 1939.

Carroll, Lewis. *See* Dodgson, Charles Lutwidge.

Carson, Baron (Edward Henry Carson) (1854–1935), Irish barrister, solicitor-general for Ireland 1892; attorney general 1915; first lord of the admiralty 1916–17; member of the war cabinet 1917–18. He led a semi-militant organisation against Home Rule.

Carson, Rachel (1907–64), American biologist, remembered for *The Silent Spring.*

Carter, Howard (1873–1939), Egyptologist who was associated with Lord Carnarvon in discovering in 1922 the Tomb of Tutankhamen.

Carter, James Earl (b. 1924), American Democratic President 1977–81; former Governor of Georgia. His main achievements were the treaty between Israel and Egypt, the Panama Canal treaty, SALT II (though not ratified) and the settling of the release of American hostages held captive in Iran. Won 2002 Nobel Peace Prize.

Cartier, Jacques (1494–1557), French navigator, b. St. Malo, who explored Canada, especially the gulf and river of St. Lawrence.

Cartier-Bresson, Henri (1908–2004), French photographer. He evolved concept of "the decisive moment".

Cartland, Dame Barbara (1901–2000), prolific authoress of 723 romantic novels.

Cartwright, Edmund (1743–1823), English inventor of the power-loom, and also of a wool-combing machine, important steps in the weaving side of the textile revolution.

Cartwright, John (1740–1824), brother of the above; reformer and agitator against slavery.

Caruso, Enrico (1873–1921), Italian tenor, b. Naples.

Carver, George Washington (1864–1943), Black American agricultural chemist of world repute.

Casabianca, Louis de (c. 1752–98), captain of the French flagship *L'Orient* at the Battle of the Nile. He and his ten-year-old-son died together in the burning ship.

Casals, Pablo (1876–1973), Spanish cellist and conductor, son of an organist, b. Vendrell, Tarragona. He exiled himself from Spain in 1938. Widely regarded as greatest-ever cellist.

Casanova de Seinfalt, Giacomo (1725–98), Italian scholar, diplomat and religious thinker whose reputation as a lover is much exaggerated.

Casement, Roger David (1864–1916), Irish nationalist. While in British consular service exposed abuses in Belgian Congo. Knighted 1911 (degraded 1916). Hanged after 1916 Easter Rising. His remains are in Glasnevin cemetary, Dublin.

Cash, Johnny (1932–2003), legendary country music singer, 'The Man in Black' whose rugged style spoke of man's dignity under pressure.

Cassin, René (1887–1970), French jurist. Principal author, UN Declaration of Rights of Man. Nobel Peace Prize, 1968.

Cassini, French family of Italian origin, distinguished for work in astronomy and geography. Through four generations (1671–1793) they were heads of the Paris Observatory.

Cassius, Caius Longinus, Roman general who opposed the dictatorship of Julius Caesar, and took part in his murder. He died in 42 B.C. after being defeated by Mark Antony.

Casson, Sir Hugh (1910–99), famous architect who opened the Royal Academy to a wider audience. Architect of the Festival of Britain.

Castle, Baroness (Barbara Anne Castle) (1910–2002), Socialist politician who as Transport Secretary (1965–68) introduced the breath test. Later attempted to reform the trade unions with *In Place of Strife.* Campaigner for social justice.

Castlereagh, Viscount (Robert Stewart Castlereagh) (1769–1822), British minister of war and foreign secretary, who took a leading part in the Napoleonic wars. Committed suicide.

Castro, Fidel (1927–2016), Cuban revolutionary. After two earlier attempts he succeeded in 1959 in overthrowing a police-state. He initiated reforms in agriculture, industry, and education. His acceptance of Russian support led to the "missiles crisis" of 1962. The fall of Soviet communism has left his regime isolated. He resigned as President in February 2008.

Catherine, St. (4th cent.). Traditionally a virgin martyr in Alexandria. Legend represents her as tied to a wheel.

Catherine de' Medici (1519–89), Italian-born wife of Henry II and mother of three French kings (she was regent for Charles IX). Her antagonism to the Protestants may have led to the massacre of St. Bartholomew's day. She was able, and appreciated art and literature, but was unscrupulous and cruel.

Catherine of Aragon (1485–1536), first wife of Henry VIII of England, was daughter of Ferdinand and Isabella of Spain, and mother of Mary Tudor. After the Pope had refused to release Henry VIII from the marriage an English declaration of nullity was obtained (thus precipitating a movement towards the Reformation).

Catherine the Great (1729–96), Empress Catherine II of Russia. Daughter of a German prince, she married in 1745 the future Peter III. Intelligent, cultivated, autocratic, she proved a capable ruler. Her reign was marked by imperialist expansion and extension of serfdom.

Cato, Marcus Porcius (234–149 B.C.), Roman statesman and writer. His tenure of office as censor was characterised by austerity and conservatism. Advocated opposition to Carthage.

Catullus, Caius Valerius (c. 84–54 B.C.), Roman poet who wrote lyrics to Lesbia. His poems show sincere feeling and also Greek influence.

Cavell, Edith Louisa (1865–1915), English nurse in Brussels in 1914–15, who was executed by the Germans for helping Allied fugitives to escape.

Cavendish, Henry (1731–1810), English scientist, remembered for his investigations into the nature of gases. He discovered hydrogen and the chemical composition of water. The Cavendish Laboratory is named after him.

Cavour, Camilo Benso di (1810–61), Italian statesman, who, as premier of Sardinia, helped to bring about the unification of Italy.

Caxton, William (1422–91), the first English printer and publisher, a man of wide-ranging abilities. He probably learnt the art of printing at Cologne (1471–2), setting up his own printing press at Westminster (1476). He printed Chaucer's *Canterbury Tales,* Malory's *Le Morte d'Arthur* and Aesop's *Fables.*

Ceauçescu, Nicolae (1918–89), Romanian communist leader. His dictatorship was ended by the 1989 revolution. Executed 25 December 1989.

Cecil of Chelwood, 1st Viscount (Robert Cecil) (1864–1958), English politician who helped draft the Charter of the League of Nations. Nobel prize for peace 1937.

Cecilia, St. (2nd or 3rd century), patron saint of music, often represented playing the organ.

Cellini, Benvenuto (1500–71), Italian sculptor and goldsmith. B. at Florence, he worked for some years in Rome. His bronze statue *Perseus with the head of Medusa* is at Florence.

Celsius, Anders (1701–44), Swedish physicist and astronomer. Invented centigrade thermometer.

Ceresole, Pierre (1879–1945), Swiss founder of International Voluntary Service. Became a Quaker.

Cervantes, Saavedra Miguel de (1547–1616), Spanish novelist and dramatist, b. at Alcalá de Henares. He was injured at the battle of Lepanto, and thereafter struggled to earn a

B14

livelihood from literature. His *Don Quixote* describes the adventures of a poor gentleman, confused in mind, who on his horse Rosinante with his squire Sancho Panza seeks adventures; it satirised chivalry, but is also a permanent criticism of life. Of his plays only two survive. His remains were rediscovered in a Madrid church in 2015.

Cézanne, Paul (1839–1906), French painter, b. in Aix-en-Provence, the son of a wealthy banker and tradesman. He developed a highly original style, using colour and tone in such a way as to increase the impression of depth. He said that he wanted "to make of Impressionism something solid and durable, like the art of the Museums." He, more than any other artist, determined the course European painting was to take. *La Veille au Chapelet* and *Les Grandes Baigneuses* are in the National Gallery. A friend of Zola.

Chadwick, Sir Edwin (1800–90), English social reformer. Secretary of the Poor Law Board.

Chadwick, Sir James (1891–1974), English physicist, one of Rutherford's collaborators in the field of atomic research. Discovered the neutron in 1932, one of the main steps in the discovery of the fission process (and hence the atom bomb).

Chagall, Marc (1887–1985), Russian-born painter, b. at Vitebsk (now Belarus); the forerunner of surrealism.

Chamberlain, Joseph (1836–1914), English statesman. He began with municipal work in Birmingham. At first a Liberal under Gladstone, he became Conservative. He opposed Home Rule for Ireland, and was the first advocate of a partial return to protection.

Chamberlain, Neville (1869–1940), son of Joseph. He was prime minister 1937–40, when he appeased Hitler by the Munich agreement, 1938.

Chambers, Sir William (1726–96), British architect, b. Stockholm. He rebuilt Somerset House and designed the pagoda in Kew Gardens.

Champlain, Samuel de (1567–1635), French navigator who founded Quebec (1608), and discovered the lake known by his name.

Champollion, Jean François (1790–1832), French egyptologist, who found the key to the decipherment of hieroglyphics in the Rosetta stone.

Chantrey, Sir Francis Legatt (1781–1841), English sculptor who left a fortune to the Royal Academy.

Chaplin, Sir Charles Spencer (1889–1977), first international screen star. *See* **Q19**.

Chapman, George (1559–1634), Elizabethan poet, dramatist, and translator of the *Iliad* and *Odyssey*. His best-known play is *Bussy d'Ambois*.

Chapman, Sydney (1888–1970), English mathematician and geophysicist, who worked on the kinetic theory of gases, geomagnetism, and solar and ionospheric physics. An upper layer of the atmosphere and a crater on the moon are named after him.

Charcot, Jean Baptiste (1867–1936), French explorer, who in 1903–5 and 1908–10 commanded expeditions to the south polar regions. Charcot Island in the Antarctic is named after him.

Chardin, Jean Baptiste Siméon (1699–1779), French painter of still life and domestic scenes.

Chares (c. 300 B.C.), Greek worker in bronze from Rhodes, sculptor of the Colossus of Rhodes.

Charlemagne (742–814), Charles the Great. From being King of the Franks, he came to govern an empire comprising Gaul, Italy, and large parts of Spain and Germany, and was crowned Emperor by the Pope in Rome on Christmas Day, A.D. 800. His revival of the Western Empire was the foundation of the Holy Roman Empire (*q.v.*). His father was Pepin the Short.

Charles, Jacques Alexandre César (1746–1823), French physicist, the first to use hydrogen gas in balloons and who anticipated Gay-Lussac's law on the expansion of gases.

Charles Edward (Stuart) (1720–88), the Young Pretender, grandson of James II, led an unsuccessful rising in 1745 and died in exile.

Charles (Philip Arthur George) (b. 1948), Prince of Wales, Duke of Cornwall and Rothesay, eldest son of Queen Elizabeth II; married Lady Diana Spencer, daughter of 8th Earl Spencer, 1981. A decree nisi ending the marriage was granted in 1996. Their eldest son is Prince William (b. 1982). In April 2005 Charles married Camilla Parker Bowles (who took the title Duchess of Cornwall). In 2013 Prince Charles became the oldest-ever male Heir Apparent. In April 2011 Prince William married Catherine Middleton. They are now styled Duke and Duchess of Cambridge. Their children are Prince George of Cambridge (b. 2013) and Princess

Charlotte (b. 2015).

Charles I (1600–49), King of England, Scotland, and Ireland, succeeded his father James I in 1625. Personally sincere, and having an appreciation of art, he was yet ill-fitted to cope with the political problems of his time. His marriage with the French princess Henrietta Maria was unpopular. He supported Arch-bishop Laud's strict Anglicanism, and he also attempted to rule without parliament. Defeated in the Civil War which broke out in 1642, he was beheaded in 1649.

Charles II (1630–85), King of England, Scotland, and Ireland, son of Charles I; after the Civil War escaped to France, and returned in 1660 when the monarchy was restored. His religious sympathies were Roman Catholic and his personal life was amorous; but in political matters he was shrewd and realistic, and contrived not to "go on his travels" again. He promoted the development of the navy, but had to accept the laws enforcing religious conformity imposed by parliament.

Charles V (1500–58), Hapsburg ruler, succeeded his grandfather, Maximilian I, as emperor of the Holy Roman Empire, and as heir to Ferdinand and Isabella succeeded to the Spanish crown. His rivalry with Francis I of France led to prolonged war. He crushed a revolt of peasants in 1525. He presided in 1521 at the Diet before which Luther appeared, after which religious struggle continued in Germany till the Augsburg settlement of 1555. In that year he retired to a monastery in Spain.

Charles XII of Sweden (1682–1718), a brave but rash and ambitious general. He repelled Russian attacks at Narva in 1700, but was subsequently defeated by Peter the Great at Poltava in 1709; and on invading Norway was killed.

Chateaubriand, François René, Vicomte de (1768–1848), French writer and diplomat. In a varied career he was at first an emigré, and later served as diplomat under both Napoleon and Louis XVIII. He was a friend of Mme. Recamier.

Chatham, 1st Earl of (William Pitt) (1708–78), English statesman and orator. His energetic conduct of the Seven Years War was an important contribution to English victory and to acquisitions in Canada and India at the peace (1763), though by then he was out of office. In the dispute with the American colonies he upheld their right to resist imposed taxation, and collapsed while making a last speech on this dispute.

Chatterton, Thomas (1752–70), English poet who tried to pass off his writings as newly discovered ancient manuscripts. Killed himself at the age of 17.

Chaucer, Geoffrey (1340?–1400), English poet. His main work is *The Canterbury Tales. See also* **M5**.

Chaudhuri, Nirad Chandra (1897–1999), Indian author and broadcaster, who was resident in England after 1970. His best-known book is *Autobiography of an Unknown Indian* (1951). His other works include *A Passage to England* (1959).

Chavez, Cesar (1927–93), Mexican-American (Chicano) trade union leader. Founded the National Farm Workers Association (later the United Farm Workers) in 1962 in California.

Chávez, Hugo (1954–2013). President of Venezuela after 1999. An icon of Latin American socialism.

Chekhov, Anton (1860–1904), Russian dramatist and short-story writer, whose plays include *The Cherry Orchard*, *Uncle Vanya*, and *The Three Sisters*. His stories include *The Steppe*, *The Sleepyhead*, *The Post*, *The Student*, and *The Bishop*. A doctor, he was of humble origins.

Cheney, Richard (Dick) (b. 1941), US Republican Vice-President, 2001–09. Defence Sec., 1989–93.

Chernenko, Konstantin Ustinovich (1911–85) Soviet politician. Succeeded Andropov (*q.v.*) as General Secretary of the Communist Party, 1984–85.

Cherubini, Luigi (1760–1842), Italian-born musician, director of the Paris Conservatoire.

Cheshire, Lord (Group Captain Leonard Cheshire) (1917–92) War hero (most decorated World War II pilot) who founded the world-wide homes for the disabled. He married Sue Ryder (1923–2000).

Chesterfield, 4th Earl of (Philip Dormer Stanhope) (1694–1773), English statesman, whose *Letters* to his natural son, Philip Stanhope, are full of grace, wit, and worldly wisdom.

Chesterton, Gilbert Keith (1874–1936), English essayist, novelist and poet, who also wrote studies of Charles Dickens and Robert Browning. His works include *The Napoleon of Notting Hill*.

Chevalier, Albert (1861–1923), English music-hall comedian known for his coster sketches.

Chiang Kai-shek (1887–1975), Chinese general. He at first fought for Sun Yat-sen. After the latter's death (1925), as commander of the Kuomintang army, he attempted to unite China; but he was more anxious to defeat the Communists than to repel the Japanese in Manchuria in 1931. In 1949 retreated to Taiwan (Formosa).

Chichester, Sir Francis (1902–72), English seaman, who sailed his *Gipsy Moth IV* into Sydney harbour in 1966 after a 107-day voyage from Plymouth, and back again round the Horn.

Chingis Khan. *See* Genghis Khan.

Chippendale, Thomas (1718–79), designer of furniture, b. Otley, Yorks, son of a joiner. His designs are shown in *The Gentleman and Cabinet Maker's Director*, 1754.

Chirac, Jacques (b. 1932), French Gaullist politician. President of France, 1995–2007 (re-elected in 2002). Prime Minister, 1974–76 and 1986–88.

Chirico, Giorgio de (1888–1978), painter associated with the surrealist school, born in Greece of Italian parents.

Chomsky, Noam (b. 1928), American activist, philosopher and theoretical linguist whose *Syntactic Structures* revolutionised the field of linguistics.

Chopin, Frédéric François (1810–49), Polish pianist and composer, son of a French father and Polish mother. He has been called "the poet of the piano" because of the originality and delicacy of his playing. *See* Section P.

Chou En-lai (1898–1976), Chinese revolutionary. He organised revolt in Shanghai 1927, later formed close partnership with Mao Tse-tung, took part in the "long march" 1934–5, becoming prime minister of the new China in 1949.

Chrétien (Joseph Jack) Jean (b. 1934), Canadian Liberal politician Prime Minister 1993–2003.

Christie, Dame Agatha (1890–1976), one of the greatest writers of detective novels. She created the Belgian detective Hercule Poirot and also Miss Marple. Her books have sold over 2 billion copies. Her first detective story was *The Mysterious Affair* at Styles (1916), which introduced Hercule Poirot.

Chrysostom, St. John (c. 347–407), famous preacher. Chrysostom means golden-mouthed. First at Antioch, and later as patriarch of Constantinople, he was an eloquent teacher; but by outspokenness he lost the Empress Eudoxia's favour and died from ill-treatment.

Churchill, Lord Randolph Henry Spencer (1849–95), Conservative politician, who briefly held high office (as Leader of the House and Chancellor of the Exchequer). Father of Winston Churchill.

Churchill, Sir Winston Leonard Spencer (1874–1965), British statesman and author, son of the above. He first entered parliament in 1900. He served as a junior officer with the British forces abroad; and during the Boer War he acted as war correspondent. Ministerial posts included: President of the Board of Trade 1908–10; Home Secretary 1910–11; First Lord of the Admiralty 1911–15; Chancellor of the Duchy of Lancaster 1915; Minister of Munitions 1917; Minister of War 1918–21; Minister of Air 1919–21; Secretary of State for the Colonies 1921–2; Chancellor of the Exchequer 1924–9; First Lord of the Admiralty (again) 1939–40; Prime Minister and Minister of Defence 1940–5; Prime Minister 1951–5. His great achievement was as leader in World War II.

Cibber, Colley (1671–1757), a London actor and dramatist. His best comedies are *The Careless Husband* and *Love's Last Shift*.

Cicero, Marcus Tullius (106–43 B.C.), Roman orator and philosopher, many of whose letters and speeches survive. He held political office but was killed by the troops of the triumvirate.

Cid (El Campeador) (c. 1035–99), name given to the Spanish knight Rodrigo Diaz, a soldier of fortune who never lost a battle. He was later re-invented as a national hero.

Cierva, Juan de la (1895–1936), Spanish engineer who invented the autogiro.

Cimabue, Giovanni (Cenni di Pepo) (1240–1302), Florentine painter of the St. John in Pisa cathedral.

Cimarosa, Domenico (1749–1801), Italian composer. His best-known opera is *Il Matrimonio Segreto*. He held revolutionary views.

Cimon (c. 512–449 B.C.), Athenian statesman and general, son of Miltiades. He defeated the Persian fleet in 468. He worked for cooperation with other states, including Sparta.

Cipriani, Giambattista (1727–85), Italian painter of

historical subjects who worked in London; a founder member of the Royal Academy.

Clare, John (1793–1864), a humble Northamptonshire labourer who became a poet. *Poems Descriptive of Rural Life and Scenery*, and *The Village Minstrel* were among his publications. He died in the county lunatic asylum, but was a visionary poet. He was the poet of birds.

Clarendon, 1st Earl of (Edward Hyde) (1609–74), English statesman and historian. He was chancellor to Charles II, and his daughter married the future James II, but he fell and died in exile. He wrote a *History of the Rebellion*.

Clark, Baron (Kenneth McKenzie Clark) (1903–83), English art historian. He was director of the National Gallery 1934–45, Slade professor of fine arts at Oxford 1946–50, and chairman of the Arts Council 1953–60. O.M. 1976.

Clarke, Sir Arthur C. (1917–2008), science fiction writer, author of *2001: A Space Odyssey* (1968).

Clarkson, Thomas (1760–1846) devoted his life to the abolition of slavery and shares with Wilberforce credit for the passing of the Act of 1807 abolishing the British slave trade.

Claude Lorrain (Gelée) (1600–82), French landscape painter. B. near Nancy, he settled in Rome. He excelled in depicting sunrise or sunset.

Claudius (10 B.C.–A.D. 54), Roman emperor. After the murder of Caligula, he was proclaimed emperor almost accidentally by the Praetorian Guard. He was a sensible administrator. In his time the empire was extended to include Britain, Thrace, and Mauretania. He was probably poisoned by his wife Agrippina.

Clausewitz, Karl von (1780–1831), German military expert whose *Vom Kriege*, expounding his theories on war, dominated Prussia in the 19th cent.

Clayton, Rev. Philip (Tubby) (1885–1972), Australian-born founder of Toc H.

Cleisthenes (570–c.505 B.C.), Athenian constitutional reformer. Charged with redrawing the constitution of Athens after her occupation by Sparta in 510 B.C., he extended the work of Solon (q.v.). Henceforth all Athenians had equality of rights in the election of officials, regardless of wealth.

Clemenceau, Georges (1841–1929), French statesman of radical views; twice premier, 1906–9, 1917–20. He was a defender of Dreyfus.

Cleon (c. 495–429 B.C.) Athenian politician and demagogue, infamous for his extreme anti-Spartan position during the Peloponnesian War and his opposition to Pericles (q.v.).

Cleopatra (69–30 B.C.), daughter of Ptolemy XII, the seventh queen of Egypt by that name, a brilliant, ambitious woman. In 51 she became joint sovereign with her younger brother Ptolemy XIII. She was banished to Syria, but, obtaining the help of Caesar, regained the kingdom. She and Caesar became lovers, and in 47 she bore him a son Caesarion (later Ptolemy XV). After Caesar's murder she returned to Egypt. She met the triumvir Mark Antony and bore him twins; he deserted his wife and broke with his brother-in-law Octavian (later Augustus). But Antony and Cleopatra were defeated in 31 B.C.; Antony fell upon his sword, and Cleopatra killed herself with an asp bite. The last Queen of Egypt, her final resting place is not known.

Clinton, Bill (William Jefferson) (b. 1946), 42nd President of the United States, defeating George Bush in November 1992. President from 1993 to 2001. Born in Hope, Arkansas. A Rhodes Scholar at Oxford. Former Democrat governor of Arkansas. Became first Democrat since Roosevelt in 1936 to win reelection, but his second term was beset by scandal allegations, leading to impeachment (which he survived). His wife, **Hillary Rodham Clinton**, (b. 1947), became the first former First Lady to be elected to the Senate (in 2000). She failed to secure the Democratic nomination for the 2008 election. Secretary of State, 2009–13. Won 2016 Democratic nomination, the first woman to do so. Defeated by Donald Trump.

Clive, 1st Baron (Robert Clive) (1725–74), English general who helped to lay the foundations of English power in India. B. near Market Drayton, he entered the service of the East India Company. He contemplated suicide, but Anglo-French rivalry, culminating in the Seven Years War, gave scope for his military powers in the siege of Arcot and the battle of Plassey. As a governor he showed administrative capacity.

Clovis (c. 465–511), Merovingian king of the Franks

and a convert to Christianity. He defeated the Burgundians and West Goths, and fixed his court at Paris.

Clyde, Lord. See Campbell, Colin.

Cnut. See Canute.

Cobbett, William (1763–1835), one of the greatest political writers. He is known for his *Rural Rides*. Also published a weekly *Political Register* from 1802. A tireless defender of the poor.

Cobden, Richard (1804–65), English advocate of free trade. The son of a Sussex farmer, he led agitation against the laws restricting import of corn, and they were repealed in 1846. He was impoverished by his public work and was helped by subscription.

Cochrane, Thomas, 10th Earl of Dundonald (1775–1860), British seaman, who crippled a French fleet in Biscay (1809), aided the liberation of Chile and Peru from Spanish rule (1819–22), of Brazil from Portuguese rule (1823–5), and assisted the Greeks in their independence struggle.

Cockcroft, Sir John Douglas (1897–1967), Cambridge nuclear physicist who shared with E. T. S. Walton the 1951 Nobel prize. They had worked together at Cambridge in the historic "atom-splitting" experiments beginning with the transmutation of lithium into boron. He helped develop British nuclear power.

Cockerell, Sir Christopher (1910–99), English inventor of the hovercraft. See Hovercraft, Section L.

Cocteau, Jean (1891–1963), French writer and artist in widely varied forms of art.

Cody, Samuel Franklin (1861–1913), American aviator, the first man to fly in Britain (1,390 ft. on 16 Oct. 1908). He became a British subject in 1909. Killed while flying.

Cody, William Frederick (1846–1917), American showman, known as "Buffalo Bill," whose Wild West Show toured America and Europe.

Coetzee, John M. (b. 1940) South African writer. Twice-winner of Booker Prize (*Life and Times of Michael K*, 1983; *Disgrace*, 1999). Nobel Prize for Literature, 2003. A later novel is *Slow Man* (2005).

Cohn, Ferdinand Julius (1828–98), German botanist, founder of the science of bacteriology.

Coke, Sir Edward (1552–1634), English legal author, judge, and rival of Francis Bacon. His legal works are his *Reports* and *Institutes*.

Colbert, Jean Baptiste (1619–83), French statesman under Louis XIV, who fostered new industries, encouraged commerce, reformed the finances and established the navy on a sound basis. A patron of literature, science, and art.

Cole, George Douglas Howard (1889–1959), English economist and political journalist, professor of social and political theory at Oxford, 1944–57. Among his writings are *The Intelligent Man's Guide through World Chaos*.

Coleridge, Samuel Taylor (1772–1834), English poet, critic, and friend of Wordsworth, with whom he published *Lyrical Ballads*. His poems include *The Ancient Mariner, Christabel*, and *Kubla Khan*.

Coleridge-Taylor, Samuel (1875–1912), English composer, the son of a West African doctor practising in London and an Englishwoman. He is best known for his Hiawatha trilogy.

Colet, John (c. 1467–1519), English humanist and divine, founded St. Paul's School (1512). As scholar and friend of Erasmus he helped to bring the new learning to England.

Colette (Sidonie Gabrielle Claudine Colette) (1873–1954), French author of the *Claudine* stories, *Chéri* and *La Fin de Chéri*.

Collier, John (1850–1934), English painter noted for his "problem" pictures.

Collingwood, 1st Baron (Cuthbert Collingwood) (1750–1810), British admiral whose ship, the *Royal Sovereign*, led the fleet to battle at Trafalgar. On Nelson's death assumed command.

Collingwood, Robin George (1889–1943), English philosopher, historian, and archaeologist. His philosophical thought is best studied in *Speculum Mentis, Essay on Philosophical Method, Idea of Nature*, and *Idea of History*.

Collins, Michael (1890–1922), Irish politician and Sinn Fein leader. He successfully organised guerrilla warfare, and mainly negotiated the treaty with Britain in 1921, but was killed in a Republican ambush in the subsequent civil war.

Collins, William (1788–1847), English landscape and figure painter.

Collins, William Wilkie (1824–89), son of the above; one of the first English novelists to

deal with the detection of crime. He wrote *The Woman in White* and *The Moonstone*.

Colt, Samuel (1814–62), of Hartford, Connecticut, invented the revolver in 1835. It was used in the war with Mexico.

Columba, St. (521–97), founder of the monastery of Iona, b. Ireland. From the island shrine he made missionary journeys to the Highlands of Scotland. The founder of Christianity in Scotland.

Columbanus, St. (c. 540–615), Irish abbot who founded a number of monasteries in Europe.

Columbus, Christopher (c. 1451–1506), Italian navigator, b. Genoa, who, prevailing upon Ferdinand and Isabella of Spain to bear the expense of an expedition, in 1492 discovered the Bahamas, Cuba, and other West Indian islands. In 1498 he landed on the lowlands of S. America.

Comenius, John Amos (1592–1670), Czech educationist and pastor, advocate of the "direct" method of teaching languages, of the use of pictures in education, and of equality of educational opportunity for girls.

Comfort, Alex (1920–2000), British sexologist whose books included *Sex and Society* (1963) and the best-selling *The Joy of Sex* (1972).

Compton, Arthur Holly (1892–1962), American physicist whose work on X-rays established what is known as the Compton effect (1923). While professor of physics at the university of Chicago (1923–45) he helped to develop the atomic bomb. Nobel prizewinner 1927.

Compton, Denis (1918–97), English cricketer. A postwar sporting idol and a most elegant batsman.

Compton-Burnett, Dame Ivy (1884–1969), English novelist whose books include *Pastors and Masters, Men and Wives, A House and Its Head, etc.*

Comte, August (1798–1857), French philosopher, founder of positivism (q.v.).

Condé, Louis, Prince de (1621–86), French general who defeated Spain at Rocroi in 1643.

Confucius or K'ung Fu-tse (c. 551–478 B.C.), Chinese philosopher, founder of Confucianism (q.v.).

Congreve, William (1670–1729). Restoration dramatist, whose witty plays include *The Way of the World* and *Love for Love.*

Conrad, Joseph (1857–1924), English novelist of Polish birth, whose parents were exiled to Russia for political reasons. He became master mariner in the British merchant service, and began to write novels after 1884. His novels include *Almayer's Folly, Lord Jim, Nostromo.*

Conscience, Hendrik Henri (1812–83), Flemish novelist who wrote *The Lion of Flanders.*

Constable, John (1776–1837), English landscape painter, b. East Bergholt, Suffolk. Unlike his contemporary Turner, who journeyed over the Continent with his sketchbook, he found his scenes within a few miles of his home. His work was more popular in France than in England at the time and affected the Barbizon school and Delacroix. Examples of his work are in the National Gallery (*The Hay Wain, Flatford Mill*, and *The Cornfield*), the Victoria and Albert, and the Tate (*The Valley Farm*).

Constant, Jean Joseph Benjamin (1845–1902), painter of portraits and Oriental subjects.

Constantine (274–338), called "the Great," the first Christian Roman emperor. He was proclaimed at York by the army in 306. He stabilised the empire after a period of decline, and founded a new capital at Constantinople. A Christian council was held under his auspices at Nicaea in 325. Baptised on his death-bed. His father was Constantinus.

Cook, Beryl (1926–2008), artist famous for her comical representations of fat people.

Cook, James (1728–79), English navigator, son of an agricultural labourer. He entered the Royal Navy and gained a high reputation for his scientific skill. He made voyages of discovery to New Zealand and Australia in the ships under his command, *Endeavour, Resolution*, and *Adventure*. He anchored at Botany Bay in 1770 on his first voyage and gave it that name because of the interesting plants found on its shores. He also surveyed the Newfoundland coast. He was murdered at Hawaii.

Cook, Thomas (1808–92), pioneer of railway excursions and tourism. His first organised trip was from Leicester to Loughborough on 5 July 1841.

Cookson, Dame Catherine (1906–98), prolific authoress whose novels sold over 100 million copies. The illegitimate daughter of an alcoholic mother.

Cooper, Sir Henry (1934–2011), the most popular

British boxer of his time. He floored Muhammad Ali.

Cooper, James Fenimore (1789–1851), American novelist, who produced stirring stories of adventure, among them *The Spy*, *The Last of the Mohicans*, *The Pathfinder*, and *The Deerslayer*.

Cooper, Samuel (1609–72), English miniaturist, represented with his brother Alexander (d. 1660) in the Victoria and Albert Museum.

Copernicus, Nicolas (1478–1543), founder of modern astronomy, b. at Torun in Poland. He studied at Cracow and at a number of Italian universities before settling at Frauenburg in 1512 where he became canon of the cathedral. More of a student than a practical astronomer, he spent most of his private life seeking a new theory of the heavenly bodies. In his *On the Revolution of the Celestial Orbs*, he put forward the novel theory that the planets, including the earth, revolve round the sun.

Coppée, François Joachim (1842–1908), French poet, novelist and dramatist.

Coquelin, Benoit Constant (1841–1909), and **Coquelin, Ernest** (1848–1909), (Coquelin aîné et cadet), brothers, were leading lights of the French theatre.

Corbyn, Jeremy. *See* D16.

Corelli, Arcangelo (1653–1713), Italian composer and violinist, who established the form of the concerto grosso. *See* **Section P.**

Corneille, Pierre (1606–84), French dramatist, who ranks with Racine as a master of classical tragedy. *Le Cid*, *Polyeucte*, and *Le Menteur* marked a new era in French dramatic production.

Cornwallis, 1st Marquess (Charles Cornwallis) (1738–1805), British general who commanded the British forces which surrendered to the Americans at Yorktown in 1781, thus ending the war of independence. He was twice governor-general of India.

Corot, Jean Baptiste (1796–1875), French landscape painter.

Correggio, Antonio Allegri da (1494–1534), Italian painter, b. Correggio. His style anticipates the baroque. His *Ecce Homo* is in the National Gallery.

Cortés, Hernando (1488–1547), Spanish adventurer, b. Medellín, Estremadura, who captured Mexico for Spain, crushing an ancient civilisation.

Coulton, George Gordon (1858–1947), scholar and historian of monasticism in the Middle Ages.

Couperin, a family of French musicians who were organists at St. Gervais, Paris, from about 1650 till 1826. **François Couperin** (1668–1783), called "Couperin the Great," is the best known today for his harpsichord music.

Cousin, Victor (1792–1867), French educationist and philosopher, founder of the eclectic school.

Cousins, Samuel (1801–87), English mezzotint engraver of plates after Reynolds, Millais, Landseer, and Hogarth.

Cousteau, Jacques-Yves (1910–97), French underwater explorer, pioneer of aqualung diving. He opened up the oceans to exploration.

Couve de Murville, Maurice (1907–99), French diplomat; de Gaulle's foreign minister 1958–68.

Coverdale, Miles (1488–1568), one of the early English reformers, b. Yorkshire, later to become bishop of Exeter. He assisted Tyndale in translating the Pentateuch and completed his own translation of the Bible in 1535. The Psalms still used in the Prayer Book and many of the phrases in the authorised version of 1611 are from his translation.

Coward, Sir Noël (1899–1973), British playwright, actor, director and composer. His first success (*The Young Idea*, 1923) was followed by a succession of witty plays and comedies. His popular songs included 'Mad Dogs and Englishmen'.

Cowdrey, Lord (Sir Colin Cowdrey) (1932–2000), English cricketer. Scored 42,719 runs in first-class cricket (and 107 centuries). First captained England, 1959. President of MCC, 1986–7.

Cowper, William (1731–1800), English religious poet. His work is characterised by simplicity and tenderness. His best-known poems are *John Gilpin* and *The Task*.

Cox, David (1783–1859), English landscape painter. A collection of his works is in the Birmingham Gallery and the Tate Gallery.

Crabbe, George (1754–1832), English poet of grim humour; author of *The Village* and *The Borough*.

Craig, Edward Gordon (1872–1966), son of Ellen Terry, producer and author of books on stagecraft.

Cranmer, Thomas (1489–1556), archbishop of Canterbury under Henry VIII, and Edward VI; an ardent promoter of the Reformation. On Mary's accession he at first consented to return to Catholicism, but when called upon to make public avowal of his recantation, refused, and was burnt at the stake.

Crichton, James (1560–82), Scottish adventurer who for his scholarly accomplishments was called "the admirable Crichton." Killed in a brawl.

Crick, Francis Harry Compton (1916–2004), English molecular biologist. With James D. Watson discovered the structure of DNA (1953). Jointly (with Watson and Maurice H. Wilkins) awarded 1962 Nobel Prize for Medicine and Physiology. Author of *The Astonishing Hypothesis: the Scientific Search for the Soul* (1994). Perhaps the greatest British scientist of the last century.

Cripps, Sir Stafford (1889–1952), British Labour statesman. As chancellor of the exchequer in postwar Britain, his programme was one of austerity.

Crispi, Francesco (1819–1901), Italian statesman, who aided Garibaldi and was later premier.

Crispin, St. (*c.* 285), martyr with his brother. By tradition they were Roman and became shoemakers, hence patron saints of shoemaking.

Croce, Benedetto (1886–1952), Italian philosopher and critic. His philosophy is expounded in the four volumes of *Filosofia dello Spirito* (which has been translated into English). He founded and edited *La Critica* in 1908. He was strongly opposed to fascism.

Croesus (d. *c.* 546 B.C.), last king of Lydia, reputed to be of immense wealth. Conquered and condemned to death by Cyrus, he was reprieved when Cyrus heard him recall Solon's saying "Call no man happy till he is dead."

Crome, John (1769–1821), English landscape painter, b. Norwich.

Cromer, 1st Earl of (Evelyn Baring) (1841–1917), British diplomat who, as British comptroller-general in Egypt from 1883 to 1907, did much to maintain order, improve the finances and promote development.

Crompton, Samuel (1753–1827), English inventor of the spinning-mule (1779), which substituted machinery for hand work. He was b. near Bolton, a farmer's son, and benefited little by his invention.

Cromwell, Oliver (1599–1658), Protector of the commonwealth of England, Scotland, and Ireland. B. at Huntingdon, he represented Huntingdon in parliament. When civil war broke out, he served under the Earl of Essex; and then reorganised the parliamentary army, winning victories at Marston Moor and Naseby. Tortuous negotiations with Charles I could not be brought to an end, and he promoted the king's trial and execution in 1649. He defeated the Scots at Dunbar. When continued difficulties beset government he became Protector in 1653, but was soon obliged to govern by major-generals. His handling of Ireland enhanced the difficulties of that country. An able general and a strong character, he was personally tolerant (an Independent), sincere and devout.

Cromwell, Richard (1626–1712), son of the above, and his successor in the protectorate.

Cromwell, Thomas (1485–1540), English statesman, who succeeded Wolsey in the service of Henry VIII, and carried out the dissolution of the monasteries. Fell from favour and was executed.

Crookes, Sir William (1832–1919), English physicist who discovered the element thallium (1861) and invented the Crookes tube (1874) which was used by J. J. Thomson and others in their researches into the conduction of electricity in gases. He was also an authority on sanitation.

Crosland, Anthony (1918–77), Labour Cabinet Minister. Author of *The Future of Socialism* (1956).

Cruikshank, George (1792–1878), caricaturist and book illustrator, whose work includes illustrations to *Grimm's Fairy Tales*, and *Oliver Twist*.

Cuéllar, Javier Pérez de (b. 1920), Peruvian diplomat. UN Secretary-General, 1982–end of 1991. Succeeded in negotiating Iran-Iraq ceasefire (1988) but failed to prevent Gulf War (1991).

Cummings, Bruce Frederick (1889–1919), English zoologist, better known however as the author of *Diary of a Disappointed Man* (1919) written under the pseudonym W. N. P. Barbellion.

Cunard, Sir Samuel (1787–1865), founder of the Cunard line of steam ships. He was born in

Nova Scotia, of a Welsh family of Quakers.

Cunningham of Hyndhope, 1st Viscount (Andrew Browne Cunningham) (1883–1963). British admiral in two world wars.

Curie, Marie Sklodowska (1867–1934), first great woman scientist, b. Poland. Her father was a professor of physics at Warsaw. She came to Paris to study at the Sorbonne and married **Pierre Curie** (1859–1906), professor of physics. Thus began a fruitful collaborative career that led to the discovery of radium for which they shared the 1903 Nobel prize for physics. In 1911 Mme. Curie received the Nobel prize for chemistry(the first person to be awarded the Nobel prize in different fields). Pierre Curie was killed in an accident. *See also* **Joliot-Curie.**

Curzon of Kedleston, 1st Marquess (George Nathaniel Curzon) (1859–1925), statesman and administrator; viceroy of India 1898–1905; member of Lloyd George's war cabinet 1916–18; foreign secretary 1919–24.

Cuthbert, St. (*c.* 635–87), Celtic monk who became prior of Old Melrose (on the Tweed) and later of Lindisfarne. For a time he lived in seclusion on the Farne islands. Bede wrote his life.

Cuvier, Georges (1769–1832), French naturalist, noted for his system of classification of animals and his studies in comparative anatomy. His *La Règne Animal* (1819) became a standard work.

Cuyp, Albert (**Aelbert**) (1620–91), important Dutch landscape painter of sea and river views.

Cyprian, St. (d. 258), bishop of Carthage, and early Christian writer who was martyred.

Cyrano de Bergerac (**Savinien de Cyrano**) (1619–55), talented and original French satirist and writer. A colourful, almost mythical figure, who fought numerous duels. Forever identified by his large nose.

Cyrus (559–529 B.C.), Persian emperor. He founded the Achaemenid line, having defeated the Medes. By conquering Lydia and Babylonia, he controlled Asia Minor. He was a wise ruler, allowing the Jews to rebuild their temple.

D

Dafydd ap Gwilym (*fl.* 1320–70), one of the greatest figures in Welsh literary history. His main theme was love.

Daguerre, Louis Jacques Mandé (1789–1851), French photographic pioneer, who invented the daguerrotype process. *See* **Section L.**

Dahl, Roald (1916–90), British author of Norwegian parentage. He wrote macabre, ingenious stories, including those in *Kiss, Kiss* (1960), and popular books for children, such as *Charlie and the Chocolate Factory* (1964). Some of his stories were dramatised for the TV series, *Tales of the Unexpected.*

Daimler, Gottlieb (1834–1900), German inventor, with N. A. Otto of Cologne, of the Otto gas engine. The Mercédès car, exhibited at Paris in 1900, was named after the daughter of Emile Jellinek, Austrian banker and car enthusiast.

Dalai Lama. *See* **Section L.**

Dale, Sir Henry Hallett (1875–1968), English physiologist. He shared the 1936 Nobel prize for medicine for his work on the chemical transmission of nerve impulses.

Dalhousie, 1st Marquess of (James Andrew Broun Ramsay) (1812–60), governor-general of India. He annexed the Punjab, opened the civil service to Indians and acted against suttee.

Dalton, John (1766–1844), English chemist and mathematician, a Quaker teacher of Manchester. In 1808 in the first number of his *New System of Chemical Philosophy* (1808–27) the modern chemical atomic theory was first propounded (*i.e.* that the atoms of the chemical elements are qualitatively different from one another).

Damien, Father (1840–89), Belgian missionary priest, originally named Joseph de Veuster, who led a fight to help lepers in Hawaii.

Damocles, 5th cent. B.C., Syracusan flatterer who pronounced the tyrant Dionysius the happiest of men. To illustrate the uncertainty of life, Dionysius invited him to a banquet, where a naked sword hung over his head by a hair. Hence the expression "Sword of Damocles" to mean impending danger or threat.

Damrosch, Walter Johannes (1862–1950), American conductor and composer, b. Breslau, Prussia. He promoted musical development

in the USA, when conductor of the New York Symphony Society which his father, Leopold Damrosch (1832–1885) had founded in 1878.

Dankworth, Sir John (1927–2010), jazz saxophonist and composer. The first British 'knight of jazz'. He was married to Dame Cleo Laine.

D'Annunzio, Gabriele (1863–1938), Italian poet, dramatist and nationalist. In 1919 he led a raid on Fiume and seized it, but was eventually forced to surrender. His bodyguard wore the black shirt, later the uniform of the Fascists.

Dante Alighieri (1265–1321), Italian poet, a figure of world literature. He was b. at Florence in a troubled period. Though he saw her but once or twice, he loved a lady whom he called Beatrice, who is believed to have been Bice Portinari who married Simone di Bardi; she died in 1290, after which Dante wrote his *Vita Nuova*. His next work *Convivio* was philosophical. He joined the party of the Bianchi, attained municipal office, but was imprisoned and in 1301 fled. His *Divina Commedia* is a work of moral edification, replete with symbolism. He died at Ravenna.

Danton, Georges Jacques (1759–94), French revolutionary. To his eloquent lead in 1792 was largely due the defeat of the foreign forces attempting to quell the revolution. He was a member of the Committee of Public Safety, and sought to moderate the extremists, but was displaced by Robespierre and was executed.

D'Arblay. *See* **Burney.**

Darby, Abraham (1677–1717), member of the Quaker family of ironmasters of Coalbrookdale, Shropshire, who paved the way for the industrial revolution by developing iron metallurgy. His grandson **Abraham** (1750–91) built the first cast-iron bridge (1779) over the Severn at Coalbrookdale.

Darius I (548–486 B.C.), Persian king and founder of Persepolis. He extended the borders of the Persian empire beyond the Indus, and reorganised it into satrapies. He declared "God's plan for the earth is not turmoil but peace, prosperity and good government." On clashing with the Greeks, however, he was defeated at Marathon. **Darius II** was a natural son of Artaxerxes I and d. 405 B.C. **Darius III** (d. 331 B.C.) was the last of the Persian kings, and was defeated by Alexander and assassinated.

Darling, Grace Horsley (1815–42), English heroine who by putting off in a small boat from the lighthouse on one of the Farne islands, of which her father was keeper, saved the shipwrecked crew of the *Forfarshire.*

Darnley, Henry Stewart, Lord (1545–67), second husband of Mary, Queen of Scots (1565). He plotted the murder of her secretary Rizzio, and was subsequently himself murdered.

Darwin, Charles Robert (1809–82), English naturalist, b. Shrewsbury, one of the pioneers of experimental biology. After returning from his formative voyage round the world as naturalist on the *Beagle* (1831–6), he spent nearly twenty years building up evidence for his theory of evolution before publishing it in *The Origin of Species* (1859). In it he argued that the evolution of present-day morphology had been built up by the gradual and opportunistic mechanism of natural selection. *See also* **Section T.**

Daudet, Alphonse (1840–97), French writer whose works include *Lettres de mon Moulin, Robert Helmont,* and *Tartarin de Tarascon.*

Daumier, Honoré (1808–79) French artist, the most gifted political satirist of his age.

David I (1084–1153), King of Scotland. As uncle of Matilda, daughter of Henry I of England, he supported her claim to the English crown, but was defeated. In Scotland he promoted unity.

David II (1324–71), King of Scotland. He was son of Robert Bruce. In invading England he was captured at Neville's Cross, 1346.

David, Sir Edgeworth (1848–1934), Australian geologist who accompanied Shackleton's antarctic expedition, 1907–9, leading the party that reached the south magnetic pole.

David, Jacques Louis (1748–1825), French painter of classical subjects and an ardent republican.

David, St., 6th-century patron saint of Wales.

Davies, Sir Peter Maxwell. *See* **P22.**

Davies, Sir Walford (1869–1941), English organist, composer, and broadcaster on music.

Davies, William Henry (1871–1940), Welsh poet. He spent some years tramping in both England and America, and his work shows knowledge of and love for nature. He wrote *Autobiography of a Super-tramp.*

Davies, William Robertson (1913–95), Canadian writer whose works included *Rebel Angels* (1981) and *What's Bred in the Bone* (1985).

Da Vinci. *See* Leonardo.

Davis, Jefferson (1808–89), American civil war leader. B. in Kentucky, he was made president of the Confederate States when the civil war broke out. After the war he was tried for treason, but discharged. He wrote *The Rise and Fall of the Confederate Government.*

Davis, John (c. 1550–1605), Elizabethan explorer and discoverer of Davis's Strait, the channel between the Atlantic and Arctic oceans. Invented the backstaff, or Davis's quadrant.

Davitt, Michael (1846–1906), Irish nationalist. The son of a peasant who later came to England, he joined the Fenians, and in 1870 was sentenced to penal servitude. On his release he helped to found the Land League in 1879; was again imprisoned; and wrote *Leaves from a Prison Diary.* He was subsequently returned to parliament.

Davy, Sir Humphry (1778–1829), English chemist, b. Penzance. Much of his work found practical application, *e.g.*, the miner's safety lamp which still bears his name. His *Elements of Agricultural Chemistry* (1813) contains the first use in English of the word "element." Michael Faraday was his assistant at the Royal Institution.

Dawkins, (Clinton) Richard (b. 1941), Oxford biologist. Author of *The Selfish Gene* (1976), *The Blind Watchmaker* (1986), *Climbing Mount Improbable* (1996), *Unweaving the Rainbow* (1998), *The Ancestor's Tale* (2004), *The God Delusion* (2006) etc. His memoir, *An Appetite for Wonder*, appeared in 2013.

Day-Lewis, Cecil (1904–72), poet and critic; professor of poetry at Oxford from 1951–6. He succeeded Masefield as poet laureate in 1968. He wrote crime fiction under the pseudonym Nicholas Blake. His actor son **Sir Daniel** (b. 1957) has won a record three Best Actor Oscars.

De Beauvoir, Simone (1908–86), feminist writer whose work *The Second Sex* is now the icon of feminism.

Debussy, Claude Achille (1862–1918), composer and leader of the French Impressionist school in music. Among his works are *Suite bergamasque*, containing the popular *Clair de lune*; *L'après-midi d'un Faune*, inspired by the poem of Mallarmé, and *La Mer*. He also wrote an opera *Pelléas et Mélisande*. Often described as 'the most French of all musicians'.

Defoe, Daniel (1660–1731), English political writer; also author of *Robinson Crusoe*, *Moll Flanders*, and a *Tour of Gt. Britain*. His *Shortest Way with Dissenters* brought him imprisonment.

De Forest, Lee (1873–1961), American inventor who was the first to use alternating-current transmission, and improved the thermionic valve detector by which wireless and sound films were made possible.

Degas, Edgar (1834–1917), French impressionist painter and sculptor. He painted subjects from everyday life—dancers, café life, the racecourse.

De Gasperi, Alcide (1881–1954), Italian politician who founded the Christian Democrat Party.

de Gaulle. *See* Gaulle, Charles de.

De Havilland, Sir Geoffrey (1882–1965), pioneer of civil and military aviation in Britain; designer of the famous Moth machines.

De Klerk, Frederik Willem (b. 1936), South African State President from 1989 to 1994. He launched a far-reaching reform process in South Africa. Shared Nobel Peace Prize, 1993, with Nelson Mandela. He retired from politics in 1997.

De Kooning, Willem (1904–97), one of the founding fathers of abstract expressionism in modern art.

Delacroix, Ferdinand Victor Eugène (1798–1863), French painter of the Romantic school. Rejected in his own lifetime, he was to inspire Renoir, Matisse and Gauguin.

De la Mare, Walter John (1873–1956), English poet and novelist whose work has a characteristic charm. Much of it was written for children.

Delane, John Thadeus (1817–79), editor of *The Times*, 1841–77, who established its reputation.

Delaroche, Paul (1797–1856), French historical painter.

Delibes, Clément Philibert Léo (1836–91), French composer of much graceful music, including operas, of which *Lakmé* is the best known, and ballets, among them *Coppélia*.

Delius, Frederick (1862–1934), English composer of German parentage. His music, highly

idiosyncratic in idiom, was more readily received in Germany than in England until promoted by Sir Thomas Beecham. *See* **Section P.**

Delors, Jacques, (b. 1925), French socialist politician. President, European Commission, 1985–95.

Deleuze, Gilles (1925–95), a key figure in post-structuralism. Author of *The Logic of Sense.*

Democritus (c. 470–c. 400 B.C.), one of the first scientific thinkers, pupil of Leucippus (fl. c. 440 B.C.). He took an atomic view of matter, denied the existence of mind as a separate entity, and counted happiness and inner tranquility as important moral principles. His attitude was not shared by his contemporary, Socrates, nor by Plato and Aristotle, but was accepted by Epicurus. The atomic theory thus passed into the background for many centuries.

Demosthenes (384–322 B.C.), Greek orator who, by his *Philippics*, roused the Athenians to resist the growing power of Philip of Macedon.

Dench, Dame Judi (b. 1934), outstanding and versatile actress of enduring popularity. C.H. (2005).

Deng Xiaoping (1904–97), Chinese politician, b. Szechwan; rehabilitated at Eleventh Party Congress (1977); effective leader of China in 1980s, target of May 1989 student revolt. Architect of the economic transformation of modern China. His career began with the Long March.

Denning, Lord (Alfred Denning) (1899–1999), English judge. Master of the Rolls, 1962–82. Conducted Profumo affair enquiry, 1963. Outspoken defender of individual liberties. O.M. (1997).

De Quincey, Thomas (1785–1859), English essayist and critic; friend of Wordsworth and Southey. He wrote *Confessions of an English Opium-eater.*

Derain, André (1880–1954), French artist, acclaimed for his Fauve pictures. Influenced by Cézanne.

De Reszke, Jean (1853–1925) and **De Reszke, Edouard** (1856–1917), Polish operatic singers, the first a tenor, the second a baritone.

Derrida, Jacques (1930–2004), French philosopher who founded the philosophical school of "deconstruction". A major influence on literary theory.

Derwentwater, 3rd Earl of (James Radcliffe) (1689–1716), leader of the English Jacobite movement. Defeated at Preston in 1715 and beheaded.

Descartes, René (1596–1650), French mathematician, pioneer of modern philosophy. Unconvinced by scholastic tradition and theological dogma, he sought to get back to why anything can be said to be true. The basis of his Cartesian philosophy is summed up in his own words, *Cogito, ergo sum* (I think, therefore I am).

Desmoulins, Camille (1760–94), French revolutionary. He represented Paris in the National Convention, and wrote witty and sarcastic pamphlets and periodicals. An ally of Danton and was executed with him.

Deutscher, Isaac (1907–67), Marxist historian, biographer of Stalin and Trotsky.

De Valéra, Eamon (1882–1975), Irish statesman, b. New York, son of a Spanish father and an Irish mother. He was imprisoned for his part in the Easter rising of 1916. He opposed the treaty of 1921; and in 1926, when the republican Fianna Fáil was founded, he became its president. Prime minister, 1937–48, 1951–4, 1957–9; president of the republic, 1959–73.

De Valois, Dame Ninette (1898–2001), Irish-born ballet dancer and choreographer. She founded what is now the Royal Ballet in 1931, thus establishing professional classical ballet in England. O.M.

Dewar, Sir James (1842–1923), chemist and physicist, a native of Kincardine. He succeeded in liquefying hydrogen, and invented the vacuum flask. The explosive cordite was the joint invention of himself and Sir Frederick Abel.

Dewey, John (1859–1952), American philosopher, psychologist, and educationist. A follower of William James and an exponent of pragmatism.

De Witt, Jan (1625–72), Dutch republican statesman, who carried on war with England and later negotiated the Triple Alliance, but was overthrown by the Orange Party and murdered.

Diaghilev, Sergei Pavlovich (1872–1929), ballet impresario and founder of *Ballets Russes.*

Diana, Princess of Wales (1961–97), born Diana Frances Spencer. Married Charles, Prince of Wales (*q.v.*) in 1981. Divorced 1996. Tragic death in car crash, 31 August 1997. A popular icon.

Dickens, Charles (1812–70), the great English novelist of the 19th cent., with enormous output and capacity for vivid story-telling. Of humble origin, he was extremely successful. His best-known works are *Pickwick Papers*, *Oliver Twist*, *A Christmas Carol*, *Dombey and Son*, *David Copperfield*, *Little Dorrit*, and *Great Expectations*. His great-granddaughter was **Monica Dickens** (1915–92). See **M20**.

Dickinson, Emily (1830–86), reclusive American poet whose writing has a mystic quality.

Dickinson, Goldsworthy Lowes (1863–1932), English author, an interpreter and upholder of the Greek view of life.

Diderot, Denis (1713–84), French man of letters, critic of art and literature, and editor of the *Encyclopédie* (1713–84).

Diemen, Anthony van (1593–1645), Dutch promoter of exploration. As governor-general in the Far East, he promoted Dutch trade and influence; and despatched Abel Tasman, who in 1642 discovered New Zealand and Van Diemen's Land (now Tasmania).

Diesel, Rudolf (1858–1913), German engineer, inventor of an internal combustion engine which he patented in 1893. See also **Section L**.

DiMaggio, Joe (1914–99), US baseball legend known as Joltin' Joe and The Yankee Clipper.

Diocletian (245–313), Roman emperor and persecutor of Christianity. He divided the empire under a system of joint rule; later abdicated.

Diogenes (412–322 B.C.), Greek cynic philosopher who lived in a tub and told Alexander to get out of his sunshine. He sought virtue and moral freedom in liberation from desire.

Dionysius the elder and younger, tyrants of Syracuse in the 4th cent. B.C.

Dionysius Exiguus (*fl.* 6th cent), famous inventor of the Christian calendar. Known in English as Denis the Little.

Dirac, Paul Adrien Maurice (1902–84), English physicist who shared with Erwin Schrödinger the 1933 Nobel prize for their work on Heisenberg's theory of quantum mechanics. O.M. (1973).

Disney, Walter Elias (1901–66), American film cartoonist, creator of Mickey Mouse. He is known for his *Silly Symphonies*, *Snow White and the Seven Dwarfs*, and *Pinocchio*.

Disraeli, Benjamin, Earl of Beaconsfield (1804–81), British statesman and novelist who helped to form modern Conservatism in England. The son of Isaac (*q.v.*), he published his first novel at 21, and later *Coningsby* and *Sibyl*, which helped to rouse the social conscience. He entered parliament in 1837 and was prime minister 1868 and 1874–80, when he arranged the purchase of shares in the Suez canal. He was rival of Gladstone and friend of Queen Victoria.

D'Israeli, Isaac (1766–1848), father of Benjamin (*q.v.*) and author of *Curiosities of Literature*.

Dix, Otto (1891–1969), German Realist painter, the 'wild man' of German art.

Djerassi, Carl (1923–2015), Austrian-born chemist who played a key role in development of contraceptive pills when he synthesised norethisterone.

Dobson, Austin (1840–1921), English writer of light verse and of 18th century biography.

Dodgson, Charles Lutwidge (1832–98), English writer. Under the pseudonym Lewis Carroll, he wrote poems and books for children, including *Alice's Adventures in Wonderland*. In private life he was a lecturer in mathematics at Oxford.

Dolci, Carlo (1616–86), one of the last Florentine painters.

Doll, Sir Richard (1912–2005), epidemiologist who showed the link between smoking and lung cancer.

Dollfuss, Engelbert (1892–1934). Chancellor of Austria, 1932–34. Murdered in attempted Nazi coup.

Dominic, St. (1170–1221), founder of the Friars Preachers or Black Friars. B. in Castile, he and his followers sought to teach the ignorant. In 1216 they were formed into an order and vowed to poverty. The order spread widely.

Domitian (Titus Flavius Domitianus) (A.D. 51–96), Roman emperor, son of Vespasian. Emperor from A.D. 81. He ruled despotically, aroused the hatred of the senate, and was assassinated as a result of a palace conspiracy.

Donatello (Donato di Niccolò) (*c.* 1386–1466), Italian sculptor, b. Florence, son of Niccolò di Betto di Bardo. He was the founder of modern sculpture, producing statues independent of a background, designed to stand in the open to be viewed from all angles. Among his masterpieces are the statues of *St. George* and *David* (in the Bargello, Florence) and his equestrian *Gattamelata* in Padua, the first

bronze horse to be cast in the Renaissance.

Donizetti, Gaetano (1797–1848), Italian composer. The best known of his sixty operas are *Lucia di Lammermoor*, *La Fille du Régiment*, and *Don Pasquale*. See **Section P**.

Donne, John (1572–1631), English metaphysical poet and preacher (dean of St. Paul's). His poems and sermons marked by passion, wit, and profundity of thought only received full publicity in the 20th century. His writings include *Elegies*, *Satires*, *Songs and Sonnets*, *Problems and Paradoxes* and the *Holy Sonnets*. See **M9**.

Doré, Gustave (1833–83), French artist who painted scriptural subjects and illustrated Dante, Milton, and Tennyson.

Dostoyevsky, Feodor Mikhailovich (1821–81), Russian novelist, b. Moscow. As a result of his revolutionary activity he was sent to hard labour in Siberia. In his books, which include *Crime and Punishment*, *The Brothers Karamazov*, *The Idiot*, and *The Possessed*, he explored the dark places of the human spirit.

Douglas of Kirtleside, 1st Baron (William Sholto Douglas) (1893–1969), British airman; commanded Fighter command, 1940–2, Coastal command, 1944–5. A Labour peer.

Douglas, Norman (1868–1952), novelist and travel writer. A Scot, born in Austria, he settled on the Mediterranean. His works include *South Wind*.

Douglass, Frederick (*c.* 1817–95), prominent US abolitionist and statesman. Born a slave, he became a major force in the crusade against slavery. Later US minister to Haiti.

Doulton, Sir Henry (1820–97), English potter and the inventor of Doulton ware.

Dowden, Edward (1843–1913), English literary critic and Shakespearean scholar.

Dowding, 1st Baron (Hugh Caswell Tremenheere Dowding) (1882–1970), British airman; commanded Fighter Command in Battle of Britain.

Dowland, John (*c.* 1563–1626), English composer of songs with lute accompaniment. His son Robert was later Court lutenist to Charles I.

Doyle, Sir Arthur Conan (1859–1930), British writer, b. Edinburgh, creator of the detective Sherlock Holmes and his friend and foil, Dr. Watson. He was trained as a doctor but after 1890 devoted himself to writing. His previously unpublished first novel, *The Narrative of John Smith* was finally released in 2011.

D'Oyly Carte, Richard (1844–1901), noted English theatrical manager, who built the Savoy theatre and there produced Gilbert and Sullivan operas.

Draco (7th cent. B.C.), Athenian lawmaker who redrew the constitution of Athens in 621 B.C. and substantially increased the penalties for debt, thus giving his name to very severe laws.

Drake, Sir Francis (*c.* 1540–96), English seaman. In 1577–80 he sailed round the world in the *Golden Hind*. In 1587 he destroyed a number of Spanish ships in Cadiz harbour; under Lord Howard he helped to defeat the Armada.

Draper, John William (1811–82), American chemist, b. near Liverpool. He was the first, using Daguerre's process, to take a successful photograph of the human face (1840), and the moon.

Dreiser, Theodore (1871–1935). American novelist of austere realism. Author of *An American Tragedy*.

Dreyfus, Alfred (1859–1935), French victim of injustice. Of Jewish parentage, in 1894 he was accused of divulging secrets to a foreign power, and was sentenced by a military secret tribunal to imprisonment for life on Devil's Island in French Guiana. At a new trial in 1899 he was again found guilty. In 1906 he was entirely exonerated, restored to his rank in the army, and made a Chevalier of the Legion of Honour.

Drinkwater, John (1882–1937), English poet and playwright. His plays include *Abraham Lincoln*, and *Oliver Cromwell*.

Drummond, William (1585–1649), Scottish poet and Royalist pamphleteer. Laird of Hawthornden.

Drury, Alfred (1857–1944), English sculptor, especially of statues of Queen Victoria.

Dryden, John (1631–1700), prolific English poet and dramatist, who also wrote political satire (*Absalom and Achitophel*). Hostile to the revolution of 1688. See **M11**.

Du Barry, Marie Jean Bécu, Comtesse (1746–93), mistress of Louis XV of France and guillotined by the revolutionary tribunal.

Dubček, Alexander (1921–92), Czech political leader. First Secretary, Communist Party, 1968-69.

His reform programme (the 'Prague Spring') prompted the Russian invasion of August 1968. Restored to public life, 1989.

Du Chaillu, Paul Belloni (1835–1903), traveller in Africa, who in 1861 and 1867 published accounts of his explorations. A French-American.

Dufferin and Ava, 1st Marquess of (Frederick Temple Hamilton-Temple Blackwood) (1826–1902), British diplomat, writer, and governor-general of Canada and viceroy of India.

Duffy, Carol Ann (b. 1955). Poet and writer. Appointed Poet Laureate, 2009. The first woman (and the first Scot) to hold the post.

Dulles, John Foster (1888–1959), U.S. Secretary of State, 1953–9. A staunch Cold War warrior.

Dumas, Alexandre (1802–70), French romantic novelist, among whose major works are *The Three Musketeers*, *The Count of Monte Cristo*, and *The Black Tulip*. His remains were interred in the Pantheon in 2002. His lost final epic, *The Last Cavalier*, has now finally been published.

Dumas, Alexandre (1824–95), French dramatist, son of above; author, *La Dame aux Camélias*.

Du Maurier, George (1834–96), contributor to *Punch* and author of *Trilby*.

Dummett, Sir Michael (1925–2011), hugely influential philosopher and social activist.

Dunant, Jean Henri (1828–1910). Swiss businessman whose horror at the suffering of war led to the Geneva Convention and the Red Cross.

Dundee, 1st Viscount (John Graham of Claverhouse), (1648–89), Scottish soldier ("Bonnie Dundee"). Employed to suppress the covenanters, he was defeated at Drumclog, but victorious at Bothwell Brig. At the revolution of 1688 he supported James II, and was killed in the (victorious) battle of Killiecrankie.

Dundonald, Earl of. *See* **Cochrane, Thomas.**

Duns Scotus, John (*c.* 1265–1308), Scottish scholastic philosopher, b. at Maxton near Roxburgh, opponent of Thomas Aquinas. He joined the Franciscans, studied and taught at Oxford and Paris, and probably d. at Cologne. He challenged the harmony of faith and reason.

Dunstable, John (*c.* 1380–1453), the earliest English composer known by name. *See* **Section P.**

Dunstan, St. (908–88), reforming archbishop of Canterbury. He lived through seven reigns from Athelstan to Ethelred, and was adviser especially to Edgar. Under him Glastonbury Abbey became a centre of religious teaching.

Dupleix, Joseph François (1697–1763), French governor in India. He extended French influence and power in the Carnatic, but his plans were frustrated by his English opponent, Clive. He was recalled in 1754 and died in poverty.

Dürer, Albrecht (1471–1528), German painter and engraver. B. at Nuremberg, he was a man of intellectual curiosity and precocious talent. His best work is in his copper engravings, woodcuts, and drawings; the former include *The Knight*, *Melancholia*, and *St. Jerome in his Study*. He was the friend of Luther and Melanchthon.

Durham, Earl of (John George Lambton) (1792–1840), governor-general of Canada after the disturbances of 1837, and in 1839 presented to parliament the *Durham Report*, which laid down the principle of colonial self-government.

Durrell, Gerald (1925–95). Zoo pioneer, conservationist and popular and gifted writer on animals. Author of *My Family and Other Animals*.

Duruflé, Maurice (1902–86), French organist and composer (*e.g. Three Dances for Orchestra*, 1939).

Duval, Claude (1643–70), notorious highwayman who came to England from Normandy and was eventually hanged at Tyburn.

Dvořák, Antonin (1841–1904), Czech composer whose music is rich in folk-song melodies of his native Bohemia. In 1884 he conducted his *Stabat Mater* in London. His *New World* symphony was composed in New York, where he was head of the National Conservatoire (1892–5). *See* **Section P.**

Dworkin, Angela, (1946–2005), US feminist writer and activist who promoted radical lesbianism.

Dylan, Bob (Robert Allen Zimmermann) (b. 1941). Performer and songwriter. One of the most influential and creative musicians in rock music. The first songwriter to be awarded the Nobel Prize for Literature (2016).

Dyson, Sir Frank Watson (1868–1939), English astronomer who was astronomer royal 1910–33, and astronomer royal for Scotland 1905–10.

Dyson, Sir George (1883–1964), English composer and writer. In *The New Music* he analysed the technique of modern schools of composition.

E

Earhart, Amelia (1898–1937), American air pioneer. First woman to fly the Atlantic alone. Disappeared in 1937 during a Pacific flight. She probably died a castaway on a remote South Pacific atoll.

Eastlake, Sir Charles Lock (1793–1865), English painter of historical and religious works.

Eastman, George (1854–1932), American inventor of the roll photographic film and Kodak camera.

Easton, Florence (Gertrude) (1882–1955), English operatic soprano of great versatility. Repertoire of 88 roles. Last woman to sing with Caruso in 1920.

Ebert, Friedrich (1871–1925). German social democrat. First President of the Weimar Republic. His attempts at a moderate policy alienated both extreme left and right.

Eck, Johann von (1486–1543), German Catholic theologian and opponent of Luther.

Eco, Umberto (1932–2016). Italian philosopher and academic. His medieval mystery novel, *The Name of the Rose* was a bestseller.

Eddington, Sir Arthur Stanley (1882–1944), English astronomer (Greenwich observatory 1906–13; Cambridge observatory 1914–44). His works include *The Nature of the Physical World*.

Eddy, Mrs Mary Baker (1821–1910), American founder of the Church of Christ Scientist. Her *Science and Health with Key to the Scriptures* was published in 1875. *See* **Christian Science, J9.**

Edelinck, Gerard (1640–1707), Flemish engraver, b. Antwerp, the first to reproduce in print the colour, as well as the form, of a picture.

Eden, Robert Anthony, 1st Earl of Avon (1897–1977), British statesman. He entered parliament in 1923; became foreign secretary in 1935 (resigning in 1938 over Chamberlain's negotiation with Mussolini) and rebuff to President Roosevelt); deputy prime minister in 1951; succeeded Sir Winston Churchill in 1955. His Suez policy divided the country. He resigned for health reasons in 1957. Earldom 1961.

Edgar (943–75), King of England 959–75. He was advised by Archbishop Dunstan.

Edgar Atheling (*c.* 1060–*c.* 1130), was the lawful heir of Edward the Confessor, but in the Norman invasion could not maintain his claim.

Edgeworth, Maria (1767–1849), Irish novelist, whose stories include *Castle Rackrent*, *The Absentee*, and *Belinda*.

Edinburgh, Duke of (Philip Mountbatten) (b. 1921), consort of Queen Elizabeth II. He relinquished his right of accession to the thrones of Greece and Denmark on his naturalisation in 1947 when he took the name of Mountbatten. The great-great-grandson of Queen Victoria. On 18 April 2009 he became the longest-serving royal consort in British history. He is the oldest-ever male member of the royal family.

Edison, Thomas Alva (1847–1931), American inventor of the transmitter and receiver for the automatic telegraph; the phonograph; the incandescent lamp (shared with the British inventor Swan); and many devices for the electrical distribution of light and power. From being a newsboy on the railway and later a telegraph clerk, he became a master at applying scientific principles to practical ends. He set up a laboratory at Menlo Park, New Jersey.

Edmund II (Ironside) (*c* 990–1016), son of Ethelred, king of the English, made a compact with Canute to divide England, but soon after died.

Edward the Confessor (*c.* 1004–1066), English king before the Norman Conquest and founded Westminster Abbey. Canonised in 1161.

Edward the Elder (*c.* 870–*c.* 924), son of Alfred, succeeded him as king of the West Saxons in 899. He overcame the Danes and reoccupied the northern counties.

Edward I (1239–1307), King of England, succeeded his father Henry in 1272. Able and energetic, his legislation influenced the development of the land law, and he summoned parliamentary assemblies. A soldier, he conquered Wales, building castles, but could not maintain his hold on Scotland.

Edward II (1284–1327), succeeded his father Edward I as king of England in 1307 and was defeated by the Scots at Bannockburn. Weak and inept, he was murdered in 1327.

Edward III (1312–77), succeeded his father Edward II as king of England in 1327. Popular and ambitious he began the Hundred Years War with France. He fostered the woollen industry. Latterly he became senile.

Edward IV (1442–83), able but dissolute Yorkist leader whose reign (1461–70, 1471–83) brought about a revival in the power of the monarchy, in English sea power, and in foreign trade (in which he himself took part). Spent 1470–71, in exile. Began rebuilding of St. George's Chapel, Windsor. Patron of Caxton.

Edward V (1470–83), succeeded his father Edward IV at the age of 12 and was a pawn in the quarrels of baronial relatives. He and his brother were shut up in the Tower by his uncle, Richard, Duke of Gloucester, and there probably murdered, though proof has not been established.

Edward VI (1537–53), succeeded his father, Henry VIII, as king of England when in his tenth year. He was delicate and studious, and his government was carried on successively by the Dukes of Somerset and Northumberland; while under Archbishop Cranmer the prayer book was issued. Named Lady Jane Grey his successor.

Edward VII (1841–1910), King of Great Britain and Ireland. The son of Queen Victoria, he married Princess Alexandra of Denmark in 1863, and succeeded his mother in 1901. Interested mainly in social life and in international contacts. He visited India in 1875.

Edward VIII (1894–1972), King of Great Britain, succeeded his father George V in 1936, and abdicated later that year because of disagreement over his proposed marriage. Created Duke of Windsor. The Duchess of Windsor died in 1986.

Edward, Sir Robert (1925–2013), pioneer of IVF. Nobel Prize for Physiology, 2010.

Ehrlich, Paul (1854–1915), German bacteriologist, who at Frankfurt-on-Main carried out work in immunology. He discovered salvarsan for the treatment of syphilis. Nobel prizewinner 1908.

Eiffel, Alexandre Gustave (1832–1923), French engineer, one of the first to employ compressed air caissons in bridge building. Among his works are the Eiffel Tower (1887–9) and the Panama Canal locks.

Einstein, Albert (1879–1955), mathematical physicist whose theory of relativity superseded Newton's theory of gravitation. He was born in Ulm of Jewish parents, lived for many years in Switzerland, and held a succession of professorial chairs at Zurich, Prague, and Berlin. In 1921 he was awarded the Nobel prize for his work in quantum theory. He was driven by the Nazis to seek asylum in America and became professor at the Institute of Advanced Study at Princeton 1933–45. In August 1939 at the request of a group of scientists he wrote to President Roosevelt warning of the danger of uranium research in Germany and stressing the urgency of investigating the possible use of atomic energy in bombs. *See* Relativity, Section T, Part II.

Eisenhower, Dwight David (1890–1969), American general and statesman. He was C.-in-C. Allied Forces, North Africa, 1942–3; and in Europe 1943–5; and was Republican President, 1953–61.

Eleanor (1246–90), Queen of Edward I. After her death in 1290 the king had memorial crosses erected at the twelve places where her body rested on its way from Grantham to Westminster.

Elgar, Sir Edward (1857–1934), English composer, specially of choral-orchestral works for festivals. His oratorios include *The Kingdom, The Apostles*, and *The Dream of Gerontius*; he also wrote the *Enigma Variations*, and the tone-poem *Falstaff*. He also composed symphonies and concertos.

Elgin, 7th Earl of (Thomas Bruce) (1766–1841), British diplomat who, with the object of saving them, conveyed some sculptures from the Parthenon in Athens to the British Museum.

Eliot, George (1819–80), pen-name of Mary Anne (later Marion) Evans, b. Warwickshire. Her novels include *Adam Bede, The Mill on the Floss, Silas Marner, Middlemarch*, and *Daniel Deronda*. Her works show deep insight. She lived with the writer George Lewes from 1854 until his death 25 years later. (Although Lewes had been deserted by his wife it was not then possible to obtain a divorce.) She brought up his three children.

Eliot, Thomas Stearns (1888–1965), poet and critic.

He was born in St. Louis, Missouri, and became a British subject in 1927. His poems include *Prufrock and Other Observations, The Waste Land, The Hollow Men, Ash Wednesday, Four Quartets*; his verse dramas *Murder in the Cathedral* and *The Family Reunion*. He described himself as "classical in literature, royalist in politics, and Anglo-Catholic in religion". Nobel prizewinner 1948.

Elizabeth (1900–2002), Queen Consort of George VI. Before her marriage in 1923 she was Lady Elizabeth Angela Marguerite Bowes-Lyon.

Elizabeth I (1533–1603), Queen of England, daughter of Henry VIII, succeeded her sister Mary in 1558. Politically and intellectually able and firm, though personally vain and capricious, she chose to serve her able men such as William Cecil; and her long reign was one of stability, victory over the Spanish, and adventure in the New World; while the Church of England was established. It was marred by the execution of Mary, Queen of Scots.

Elizabeth II (Elizabeth Alexandra Mary of Windsor) (b. 1926), Queen of Gt. Britain and N. Ireland, ascended the throne Feb. 1952 on the death of her father George VI. Her Consort, Prince Philip, Duke of Edinburgh (q.v.), is the son of Prince Andrew of Greece and a descendant of the Danish royal family. They have four children: **Charles, Prince of Wales** (q.v.), **Princess Anne** (b. 1950), **Prince Andrew** (b. 1960), and **Prince Edward** (b. 1964). Princess Anne was styled the Princess Royal in June 1987. She married Commander Tim Laurence in 1992, the first royal remarriage after a divorce since Henry VIII. Prince Charles and Princess Diana were divorced in 1996. In 1997 Diana was killed in a car crash. Prince Edward married Sophie Rhys-Jones in 1999 and took the title Earl of Wessex. In 2007 the Queen became the first British monarch to celebrate a diamond wedding. She became Britain's longest ruling monarch (after Victoria) in September 2015.

Ellis, Havelock (1859–1939), English writer whose *Studies in the Psychology of Sex* was influential in changing the public attitude towards sex.

Emerson, Ralph Waldo (1803–82), American poet and essayist, b. Boston, member of the transcendentalist group of thinkers. Poems include *Woodnotes, Threnody, Terminus etc.*

Emin Pasha, name adopted by **Eduard Schnitzer** (1840–92), a German explorer associated with General Charles Gordon in the Sudan as a medical officer; and governor of the Equatorial Province 1878–89, when he was menaced by the Mahdi and rescued by Stanley.

Emmet, Robert (1778–1803), Irish patriot, led the rising of 1803, was betrayed, and executed.

Empedocles (c. 500–c. 430 B.C.), Greek philosopher, b. Agrigentum in Sicily, founder of a school of medicine which saw the heart as the seat of life, an idea which passed to Aristotle, as did his idea that all matter was composed of four elements.

Engels, Friedrich (1820–95), German socialist, son of a wealthy textile manufacturer, lifelong friend of Karl Marx, with whom he collaborated in writing the *Communist Manifesto* of 1848. Through him Marx acquired his knowledge of English labour conditions.

Epaminondas (c. 418–362 B.C.), Theban general who led the Boeotian League against Sparta in the early 4th cent. B.C. and even defeated her army at the battle of Leuctra in 371 B.C.

Epicurus of Samos (342–270 B.C.), refounded the atomic view of matter put forward by Democritus, and held that peace of mind comes through freedom from fear, the two main sources of which he regarded as religion and fear of death. *See* Epicureanism, Section J.

Epstein, Sir Jacob (1880–1959), sculptor, b. New York of Russian–Polish parents. His work includes *Rima*, in Hyde Park; *Day* and *Night* on the building of London Underground headquarters; *Genesis*, exhibited in 1931; *Lazarus*, in New College, Oxford *etc.*

Equiano, Oluadah (1745–97), African slave who inspired Wilberforce to begin abolition campaign.

Erasmus, Desiderius (1466–1536), Dutch Renaissance humanist, who spent several years in England and was the friend of Dean Colet and Sir Thomas More. He aimed at ecclesiastical reform from within. He thus prepared the way for Luther. His *Praise of Folly* is still widely read.

Erhard, Ludwig (1897–1977), German economist. Chancellor (1963–7) after Adenauer.

Essex, 2nd Earl of (Robert Devereux) (1566–1601), favourite of Queen Elizabeth I in her old age. Unsuccessful as governor-general of Ireland, he returned to England against the Queen's wish; plotted; and was executed.

Ethelbert, King of Kent (560–616). He accepted Christianity on the mission of St. Augustine.

Ethelred II (c. 968–1016), King of England. Unable to organise resistance against the Danish raids, he was called the Unready (from Old Eng. uraed = without counsel).

Etty, William (1787–1849), English artist of historical and classical subjects.

Eucken, Rudolf Christoph (1846–1926), German philosopher of activism. Nobel Prize, 1908.

Euclid, Greek mathematician of the 3rd cent. B.C. Famous for his *Elements*.

Euler, Leonhard (1707–83), Swiss mathematician, remembered especially for his work in optics and on the calculus of variations. He was called by Catherine I to St. Petersburg, 1730–41, and by Frederick the Great to Berlin, 1741–66. He became blind but continued his work.

Euripides (480–406 B.C.), Greek tragic dramatist, who is known to have written about 80 plays of which 18 are preserved, including *Alcestis*, *Medea*, *Iphigenia*, and *Orestes*.

Eusebius (264–340), ecclesiastical historian. His *Ecclesiastical History* gives the history of the Christian church to 324. He also wrote a general history, *Chronicon*.

Evans, Sir Arthur John (1851–1941), English archaeologist, known for his excavations at Knossos in Crete and his discovery of the pre-Phoenician script.

Evans, Dame Edith Mary (1888–1976), English actress, whose celebrated roles included Millamant in *The Way of the World*.

Evans, Sir Geraint Llewellyn (1922–92), much-loved Welsh opera singer. Principal Baritone, Royal Opera House, Covent Garden, 1948–84.

Evans, Gwynfor (1912–2005), major figure in rise of Welsh nationalism. Won 1966 by-election in Carmarthen (first MP for Plaid Cymru). A pacifist.

Evelyn, John (1620–1706), cultured English diarist who gives brilliant portraits of contemporaries. A book collector and librarian who wrote *Sylva*, a manual of arboriculture.

Eyck, Jan van (c. 1389–1441), Flemish painter, whose best-known work is the altarpiece in Ghent cathedral. His brother **Hubert** (c. 1370–1426) is associated with him.

Eysenck, Hans Jürgen (1916–97) Professor of Psychology at the University of London Institute of Psychiatry. His books include *Know Your Own I.Q* (1962) and *Race, Intelligence and Education* (1971).

F

Fabius, the name of an ancient Roman family who played an important part in early Roman history. **Quintus Fabius Maximus Verrucosus** (d. 203 B.C.) saved Rome from Hannibal by strategic evasion of battle; hence his name *Cunctator* (delayer), and the term Fabian policy.

Fabre, Jean Henri Casimir (1823–1915), French naturalist, whose study of the habits of insects was recorded in his *Souvenirs entomologiques*.

Faed, name of two Scottish genre painters, **Thomas** (1826–1900), and **John** (1819–1902). A third brother, **James**, engraved their works.

Fahrenheit, Gabriel Daniel (1686–1736), German physicist, b. Danzig. He introduced the mercury thermometer and fixed thermometric standards.

Fairbairn, Sir William (1789–1874), Scottish engineer. In 1817 he took the lead in using iron in shipbuilding.

Fairfax, 3rd Baron (Thomas Fairfax) (1612–71), parliamentary general in the English civil war, and victor of Marston Moor. In 1650 he withdrew into private life.

Falconer, Hugh (1806–65), British botanist and palaeontologist, b. Forres, Scot.; physician to East India Co.; introduced tea into India.

Falla, Manuel de (1876–1946), Spanish composer whose music is highly individual with a strong folk-song element. See **Section P.**

Faraday, Michael (1791–1867), English experimental physicist, founder of the science of electromagnetism. He was the son of a Yorkshire blacksmith and at 13 became apprenticed to a bookseller in London. In 1813 he became labo-

ratory assistant to Sir Humphry Davy at the Royal Institution, succeeding him as professor of chemistry in 1833. He set himself the problem of finding the connections between the forces of light, heat, electricity, and magnetism and his discoveries, translated by Maxwell (*q.v.*) into a single mathematical theory of electromagnetism, led to the modern developments in physics and electronics. He inaugurated the R.I. Christmas lectures for youngsters.

Farah, Sir Mohamed (Mo) (b. 1987). Britain's most successful track athlete, winning a "double double" of Olympic golds in the 5,000 and 10,000 metres.

Farouk I (1920–65), King of Egypt, 1936–52. He was forced to abdicate after the 1952 coup.

Faulkner, William (1897–1962), American novelist, whose series of novels, *The Sound and the Fury*, *As I Lay Dying*, *Light in August*, *Sanctuary*, depict the American South. Nobel prize 1949.

Fauré, Gabriel Urbain (1845–1924), French composer and teacher. His works include chamber music, nocturnes, and barcarolles for piano, an opera *Pénélope*, some exquisite songs, and *Requiem*. Ravel was among his pupils.

Fawcett, Millicent Garrett (1847–1929), educational reformer and leader of the movement for women's suffrage; one of the founders of Newnham College, Cambridge. Wife of the blind Liberal politician and economist, **Henry Fawcett** (1833–84) and sister of **Elizabeth Garrett Anderson.**

Fawkes, Guy (1570–1606), a Yorkshire catholic, who with Catesby and other conspirators planned the Gunpowder Plot. Though warned, he persisted and was captured and hanged.

Federer, Roger (b. 1981). Swiss tennis ace whose 16th Grand Slam victory (at Wimbledon in 2009) exceeded the record held by Pete Sampras.

Fénelon, François de Salignac de la Mothe (1651–1715), archbishop of Cambrai and author of *Telemachus*.

Ferdinand II of Aragon (1452–1516), who married Isabella of Castile, and with her reigned over Spain, saw the Moors expelled from Spain, equipped Columbus for his discoveries and instituted the Inquisition.

Ferguson, James (1710–76), Scottish astronomer who, from being a shepherd-boy, educated himself in astronomy, mathematics, and portrait painting.

Fermi, Enrico (1901–54), Italian nuclear physicist whose research contributed to the harnessing of atomic energy and the development of the atomic bomb. Nobel prizewinner 1938.

Feynman, Richard (Philips), (1918–88), American physicist, born of working-class Jewish parents. Helped develop the atomic bomb. Won Nobel Prize for Physics (1965) for work on quantum electrodynamics.

Fichte, Johann Gottlieb (1762–1814), German nationalistic and Romantic philosopher who paved the way for modern totalitarianism.

Field, John (1782–1837), Irish composer of nocturnes, pupil of Clementi and teacher of Glinka. His work served as a model for Chopin.

Fielding, Henry (1707–54), English novelist, author of *Tom Jones, Joseph Andrews etc.*

Fields, Gracie (1898–1979). Singer and actress who went from a fish and chip shop in Rochdale to become a famous superstar in Capri.

Fildes, Sir Luke (1844–1927), English painter and woodcut-designer.

Finney, Sir Tom, (1922–2014), footballing legend who played for Preston North End and England.

Finsen, Niels Ryberg (1860–1904), Danish physician who established an institute for light therapy and invented the Finsen ultra-violet lamp. Nobel prizewinner 1903.

Firdausi, *pen-name* of Abu'l Kasim Mansur (940–1020), Persian poet, author of the epic *Shah-Nama* or Book of Kings.

Firth, Sir Raymond (1901–2002), eminent pioneering social anthropologist.

Fisher of Lambeth, Baron (Geoffrey Fisher) (1887–1972), archbishop of Canterbury, 1945–61.

Fisher, Herbert Albert Laurens (1865–1940), English historian and educational reformer.

Fisher, Sir Ronald Aylmer (1890–1962), British scientist who revolutionised both genetics and the philosophy of experimentation by founding the modern corpus of mathematical statistics.

FitzGerald, Edward (1809–83), English poet who translated the *Rubáiyát* of Omar Khayyam (1859).

Fitzroy, Robert (1805–65), British meteorologist, who introduced the system of storm warnings which were the beginning of weather forecasts.

Flammarion, Camille (1842–1925), French astronomer, noted for his popular lectures and books which include *L'Astronomie Populaire*.

Flamsteed, John (1646–1719), the first English astronomer royal, for whom Charles II built an observatory at Greenwich (1675) where he worked for 44 years.

Flaubert, Gustave (1821–80), French novelist, and creator of *Madame Bovary*. Other works were *Salammbô*, *L'Education sentimentale*, and *Bouvard et Pécuchet*.

Flaxman, John (1755–1826), English sculptor, b. York, employed as modeller by Josiah Wedgwood. He then took to monumental sculpture.

Flecker, James Elroy (1884–1915), English poet whose works include *Golden Journey to Samarkand*, *Hassan* (staged in London, 1923), and *Don Juan*, as well as many lyrics.

Fleming, Sir Alexander (1881–1955), Scottish bacteriologist who discovered the antibacterial enzyme lysozyme in 1922 and penicillin in 1928. Full recognition came during the war when Florey separated the drug now used from the original penicillin. Awarded Nobel prize jointly with Florey and Chain, 1945.

Fleming, Sir Ambrose (1849–1945), British scientist whose invention of the radio valve in 1904 revolutionised radio telegraphy and solved problems of radio-telephony. This eventually made possible high quality sound transmission, and thus led to broadcasting and television.

Fletcher, John (1579–1625), English dramatist who collaborated with Francis Beaumont (*q.v.*) in writing many pieces for the stage.

Flinders, Matthew (1774–1814), English navigator and explorer who made discoveries in and around Australia. He sailed through Bass Strait, so called in honour of his surgeon.

Florey, Baron (Howard Walter Florey) (1898–1968), British pathologist, b. Australia. Shared 1945 Nobel prize with Fleming and Chain for work on penicillin.

Fo, Dario (1926–2016), Italian playwright and performance artist, whose plays include *Accidental Death of an Anarchist* (1970) and *Can't Pay? Won't Pay!* (1974). Awarded Nobel Prize 1997.

Foch, Ferdinand (1851–1929), French general, b. Tarbes. In the first world war he halted the German advance at the Marne (1914), and was engaged in the battles of Ypres (1914 and 1915) and the Somme (1916). In 1918 he became supreme commander of the British, French, and American armies and dictated the terms of Allied victory.

Fokine, Michel (1880–1942), Russian dancer.

Fokker, Anthony (1890–1939), Dutch aircraft engineer, b. Java. The Fokker factory in Germany made warplanes for Germany, 1914–18.

Fonteyn, Dame Margot (Mme. Roberto de Arias) (1919–91), prima ballerina of the Royal Ballet seen as the greatest ballerina of her age.

Foot, Michael (1913–2010), British journalist and politician; leader of the Labour Party 1980–83.

Ford, Gerald R. (1913–2006), American Republican President 1974–7; automatically succeeded Richard Nixon when he resigned. The longest-lived of any US President.

Ford, Henry (1863–1947), founder of Ford Motor Company (1903), of which he was president until 1919, when he was succeeded by his son, **Edsel B. Ford** (1893–1943). He was the pioneer of the cheap motor car.

Forester, Cecil Scott (1899–1966), English novelist. Author of the *Captain Hornblower* series.

Forster, Edward Morgan (1879–1970), novelist author of *The Longest Journey*, *A Room with a View*, *Howards End*, *A Passage to India*. O.M. 1969.

Foscari, Francesco (*c.* 1372–1457), Doge of Venice and victor over Milan.

Foster, Lord (Sir Norman Foster) (b. 1935), architect who designed the Berlin Reichstag, Chek Lap Kok airport in Hong Kong, the Great Court of the British Museum and Queen Alia International Airport, Jordan (2012). Life peerage, 1999. O.M. (2015).

Foucault, Michel (1926–84). Philosopher who argued that power is essential to our relationships with others and is in fact the very nature of our existence. Author of *Madness and Civilisation* and *Discipline and Punish*.

Fourier, Charles (1772–1837), French socialist who propounded a system of associated enterprise which although utopian stimulated social reform.

Fourier, Jean Baptiste Joseph (1768–1830), French mathematical physicist. He played an active part in politics, holding administrative posts in Egypt and Isère, yet finding time for his own research, especially on the flow of heat.

Fowler, Sir John (1817–98), was the engineer of the first underground railway (the London Metropolitan) and with his partner Sir Benjamin Baker, of the Forth bridge.

Fox, Charles James (1749–1806), English Whig statesman. Son of the 1st Lord Holland, he entered parliament at 19. He held office only for brief periods between 1770 and 1806, but he upheld the liberal causes of the day (American independence, the French revolution, and parliamentary reform), and was one of the impeachers of Warren Hastings.

Fox, George (1624–91), founder of the Society of Friends, son of a Leicestershire weaver.

Foxe, John (1516–87), English martyrologist, author of *History of the Acts and Monuments of the Church* (better known as *Foxe's Book of Martyrs*).

Frampton, Sir George James (1860–1928), English sculptor of the Peter Pan statue in Kensington Gardens and the Edith Cavell memorial.

France, Anatole (1844–1924), French writer, especially of short stories. Nobel prize 1921.

Francis I (1494–1547), King of France. Brilliant but ambitious and adventurous, he fostered learning and art, and met Henry VIII at the Field of the Cloth of Gold. His rivalry with the Emperor Charles V involved prolonged war, especially in Italy (he was captured at Pavia, 1525). He persecuted the Protestants.

Francis I (b. 1936), succeeded Benedict XVI as Pope in 2013. The first-ever "New World" Pope and the first Jesuit. Former Archbishop of Buenos Aires. His papacy is addressing issues such as poverty, climate change and other environmental concerns.

Francis of Assisi, St. (1181/2–1226), founder of the Franciscan Order. Son of a wealthy silk merchant, in 1208 he turned from a life of pleasure to poverty and the complete observance of Christ's teaching. He and his friars went about preaching the gospel by word and example. He was canonised in 1228.

Francis, Sir Philip (1740–1818), English politician, reputed author of the *Letters of Junius*.

Franck, César Auguste (1822–90), composer and organist, b. at Liège in Belgium. *See* **Section P.**

Franco, Francisco (1892–1975), Spanish general and dictator. He led the Fascist rebellion against the Republican government (1936) and with German and Italian help ended the civil war (1939). He ruled Spain as a dictator.

Franklin, Benjamin (1706–90), American statesman. B. at Boston, he was at first a printer and journalist. He then took an interest in electricity, explained lightning as of electrical origin, and invented the lightning conductor. He was active in promoting the Declaration of Independence in 1773; he negotiated French support; and helped to frame the US constitution.

Franklin, Sir John (1786–1847), English Arctic explorer. His expedition in the *Erebus* and the *Terror* to find the NW passage ended disastrously, and all attempts to find survivors failed. The *Erebus* was found in 2014 and the *Terror* in 2016.

Franks, Baron (Oliver Shewell Franks) (1905–92), British academic, diplomat and banker; British ambassador to USA 1948–52. O.M. 1977.

Fraunhofer, Joseph von (1787–1826), optical instrument-maker of Munich, the first to map the dark lines of the solar spectrum named after him.

Frazer, Sir James George (1854–1941), Scottish anthropologist, author of *The Golden Bough*.

Frederick I (*c.* 1123–90). Holy Roman Emperor, nicknamed Barbarossa. A strong personality, he sought to impose his will on the city-states of northern Italy and the papacy, and was defeated at Legnano in 1176 but was more successful with a conciliatory policy (1183). He had also to contend with opposition at home. He died on the third crusade.

Frederick II (1194–1250), Holy Roman Emperor, grandson of the above, and son of the heiress of Sicily. Brilliant and enlightened, he attracted to his court in Sicily Jewish, Mohammedan, and Christian scholars; founded the university of Naples; was a patron of the medical school of Salerno; wrote a treatise on falconry; and commissioned a code of laws. Politically he was less successful, having trouble with the Lombard cities, and being involved with the papacy especially as regards his delay in going on crusade; but after negotiations with the sultan of Egypt he actually was crowned king of Jerusalem.

Frederick II (the Great) (1712–86), King of Prussia. Having inherited from his father a well-drilled army, in 1740 he seized Silesia from Austria, and retained it through the resulting war and the Seven Years war. He also took part in the partition of Poland. An able administrator and and outstanding general he made Prussia powerful and strengthened its military tradition, but often at great cost. He corresponded with Voltaire and he also played the flute.

French, Sir John, 1st Earl of Ypres (1852–1925), first British commander-in-chief in the first world war; replaced by Sir Douglas Haig in 1915.

Freud, Sigmund (1856–1939), psychiatrist and founder of psychoanalysis; b. Moravia, studied medicine in Vienna, where he lived until 1938 when the Nazi invasion of Austria sent him into exile in London where he died. His theories of the mind illumined the way we think about ourselves. His grandson, the realist painter Lucian Freud, (1922–2011) was awarded the O.M. (1993).

Friedan, Betty (1921–2006), US feminist icon who wrote *The Feminine Mystique* (1963). Founder of National Organisation of Women (NOW).

Friedman, Milton (1912–2006), American economist. Leading proponent of monetarism. The most influential economist since Keynes.

Friel, Brian (1929–2015), outstanding Irish playwright, acclaimed as the 'Irish Chekhov'.

Friese-Greene, William (1855–1921), English inventor of the cinematograph. His first film was shown in 1890. He died in poverty.

Frink, Elisabeth (1930–93), English sculptor whose figurative work made her a much-loved artist.

Frobisher, Sir Martin (1535–94), first British navigator to seek the north-west passage from the Atlantic to the Pacific through the Arctic seas. He is commemorated in Frobisher's Strait. He also fought against the Spanish Armada.

Froebel, Friedrich Wilhelm August (1782–1852), German founder of the Kindergarten system.

Froissart, Jean (1337–1410), French author of *Chronicles* covering the history of Western Europe from 1307 to 1400.

Frost, John (1784–1877), prominent Welsh Chartist; b. Newport.

Frost, Robert (1874–1963), American poet, author of *Stopping by Woods on a Snowy Evening*, *Birches*, *The Death of the Hired Man etc*.

Froude, James Anthony (1818–94), English historian and biographer of Carlyle.

Fry, Christopher (1907–2005), English poet and dramatist of Quaker family; author of *The Lady's Not for Burning*, *Venus Observed*, *The Dark is Light Enough*, *Curtmantle*, *A Yard of Sun etc*.

Fry, Elizabeth (1780–1845), English Quaker prison reformer. She lived at Norwich.

Fry, Roger (1866–1934), English art critic and painter; introduced the work of Cézanne and the post-impressionists into England; author of *Vision and Design*.

Fuchs, Leonhard (1501–66), German naturalist whose compendium of medicinal plants was for long a standard work. He was professor of medicine at Tübingen and the genus *Fuchsia* is named after him.

Fuchs, Sir Vivian Ernest (1908–99), British geologist and explorer; leader of the British Commonwealth Trans-Antarctic Expedition 1957–8, the first to cross the Antarctic continent.

Fuller, Thomas (1608–61), English antiquarian and divine, author of *Church History of Britain*.

Fulton, Robert (1765–1815), American engineer who experimented in the application of steam to navigation, and in 1807 launched the *Clermont* on the Hudson.

Furniss, Harry (1854–1925), caricaturist, b. Wexford. He came to London as a young man, served on the staff of *Punch* and illustrated the works of Dickens and Thackeray.

G

Gaddafi, Muammar (1942–2011). Brutal Libyan dictator whose regime was ended in 2011.

Gade, Niels Vilhelm (1817–90), Danish composer. While studying at Leipzig he met Mendelssohn,

whom he succeeded as conductor of the Gewandhaus orchestra.

Gagarin, Yuri Alexeyevich (1934–68), Soviet cosmonaut, the first man to be launched into space and brought safely back (12 April 1961). Killed in an air crash.

Gainsborough, Thomas (1727–88), English landscape and portrait painter, b. at Sudbury in Suffolk. His portraits are marked by informality and grace.

Gaiseric or Genseric (c. 390–477), king of the Vandals, the ablest of Rome's barbarian invaders. He led his people from Spain into Africa, took Carthage, gained control of the Mediterranean and went on to sack Rome in 455.

Gaitskell, Hugh Todd Naylor (1906–63), Labour politician and economist. Chancellor of the Exchequer 1950–1; leader of the Labour Party 1955–63.

Galbraith, John Kenneth (1908–2006). Eminent professor of economics, b. Canada; his books include *The Affluent Society* (1958), *The Liberal Hour* (1960), *The New Industrial State* (1967), *The Age of Uncertainty* (1977). Ambassador to India 1961–3.

Galdós, Benito Pérez. See Pérez Galdós.

Galen, Claudius (131–201), physician, b. Pergamum (Asia Minor) of Greek parents. He systematised medical knowledge with his idea of purposive creation by the will of God; and thus discouraged original investigation.

Galileo Galilei (1564–1642), Italian scientist whose experimental-mathematical methods in pursuit of scientific truth laid the foundations of modern science. He became professor of mathematics at Pisa university when he was 25 and lectured at Padua for 18 years. He made a number of fundamental discoveries, *e.g.*, in regard to the hydrostatic balance, thermometer, telescope, and foreshadowed Newton's laws of motion. He detected the four major satellites of Jupiter, the ring of Saturn, and the spots of the sun. He supported the superiority of the Copernican over the Ptolemaic theory, and was put under house arrest for so doing.

Galsworthy, John (1867–1933), English novelist and playwright, author of *The Forsyte Saga*, a series of novels dealing with the history of an upper middle-class family. Nobel prize 1932.

Galton, Sir Francis (1822–1911), the founder of eugenics, cousin of Darwin. His early work *Meteorographica* (1863), contains the basis of the modern weather chart. He was an early advocate of using finger-prints for rapid identification, and he applied mathematics to biological problems.

Galvani, Luigi (1737–98), Italian physician and physiologist, whose experiments at Bologna demonstrated the principle of animal electricity.

Gama, Vasco da (c. 1460–1524), Portuguese navigator. Discovered the sea route to India in 1498 by rounding the Cape of Good Hope.

Gandhi, Indira (1917–84), daughter of Nehru, succeeded Shastri in 1966 to become India's first woman prime minister. She suffered a defeat at the polls in 1977 but was spectacularly successful in 1980. Assassinated 1984. Succeeded by her son, **Rajiv Gandhi**, who was assassinated in 1991. His widow, **Sonia**, led Congress to victory in 2004.

Gandhi, Mohandâs Karamchand (Mahatma) (1869–1948), Indian patriot, social reformer and moral teacher. From 1893 to 1914 he lived in South Africa opposing discrimination against Indians. In the movement for Indian independence after 1914 he dominated Congress, instituted civil disobedience, and advocated non-violence; and he sought to free India from caste. After independence he strove to promote the co-operation of all Indians but was assassinated on his way to a prayer meeting. His teaching of non-violence has had great influence.

Garcia, Manuel de Popolo Vincente (1775–1832), Spanish tenor, composer, and singing master. His son **Manuel Patricio Rodriguez** (1805–1906) was tutor to Jenny Lind. His daughters (**Mme. Malibran** and **Mme. Viardot**) were operatic singers.

Garcia Lorca, Federico. See Lorca.

Garibaldi, Giuseppe (1807–82), Italian soldier and patriot, who with Mazzini and Cavour created a united Italy. In 1834 he was condemned to death for helping in a republican plot to seize Genoa, but escaped to S. America. He returned in 1848 to fight for Mazzini but was again forced to flee. In 1851 he returned and gave his support to Cavour, taking part in the Austrian war of 1859. In 1860 with a thousand volunteers he freed Sicily, took Naples, and handed over the Two Sicilies to Victor Emmanuel who was proclaimed king.

Garrick, David (1717–79), English actor and theatrical manager. The giant of the 18th century stage. Brought up at Lichfield, he was taught by Samuel Johnson.

Garrison, William Lloyd (1805–79), American philanthropist who worked to end slavery.

Gaskell, Mrs. Elizabeth Cleghorn (1810–65), English novelist, author of *Mary Barton*, *Cranford*, and a *Life of Charlotte Brontë*. She was brought up by an aunt in Knutsford.

Gates, Bill (William) (b. 1955), computer entrepreneur and philanthropist. Co-founder of Microsoft. The most generous donor in history.

Gaudí, Antoni (1852–1926), architect. Famous for Church of the Holy Family, Barcelona.

Gaulle, Charles de (1890–1970), French general and statesman, first president of the Fifth Republic 1959–69. He fought in the first world war until his capture in 1916. In the second world war he refused to surrender (1940) and raised and led the Free French forces, with headquarters in England. He came to political power in 1958; allowed Algerian independence in 1962 in face of an army and a civilian revolt, initiated closer ties with West Germany (Franco-German treaty 1963), recognised Communist China, withdrew from NATO, building his own nuclear force, vetoed Britain's entry into the Common Market (1963 and 1967); and based his government on personal prestige and the use of the referendum. He was taken by surprise by the 1968 rising. Resigned after losing the 1969 referendum.

Gauss, Karl Friedrich (1777–1855), German mathematician. He spent most of his life at the university of Göttingen where he set up the first special observatory for terrestrial magnetism. He made major contributions to astronomy, mathematics, and physics. The unit of magnetic induction is named after him.

Gautama, Siddhartha (Buddha, the enlightened) (c. 563–c.483 B.C.). B. near Benares, a rajah's son, he gave himself up to the religious life and attracted many disciples. Concerned with man's sorrow and suffering, he planned a movement which could be universally shared, in which kindness to others, including animals, took a leading part. His teaching is summarised in the "four noble truths" and the "eightfold path" (*see* Buddhism, Section J). After his death his teaching spread (with the help of the King Asoka) over much of India and through eastern Asia as far as Japan.

Gautier, Théophile (1811–72), French poet and novelist, author of *Mademoiselle de Maupin*.

Gay, John (1685–1732), poet, author of *The Beggar's Opera* (set to music by Pepusch) and *Polly*.

Gay-Lussac, Joseph Louis (1778–1850), French chemist, who showed that when gases combine their relative volumes bear a simple numerical relation to each other and to the volume of their product, if gaseous (1808), *e.g.*, one volume of oxygen combines with two volumes of hydrogen to form two volumes of water vapour.

Ged, William (1690–1749), Scottish printer who patented stereotyping.

Geddes, Sir Patrick (1854–1932), Scottish biologist and a pioneer in town and regional planning, who invented the term conurbation.

Geikie, Sir Archibald (1835–1924), Scottish geologist. His brother **James** specialised in glacial geology.

Geim, Sir André (b. 1958) Regius Professor of Physics, Manchester University. Nobel Prize for Physics (2010), for the discovery of graphene.

Geldof, Sir Bob (b. 1954), Irish singer and songwriter. Initiator and organiser, Band Aid, Live Aid, Live8 concerts for poverty relief.

Genghis (Chingis) Khan (1162–1227), Mongol conqueror. After years of struggle to make good his succession to his father, he overran much of Asia bringing devastation to his enemies. His original name was Temujin. To his own people, he was a national hero. His burial site has never been found.

Geoffrey of Monmouth (1100–54), chronicler, b. Monmouth, later bishop of St. Asaph.

George I (1660–1727), became King of Great Britain in 1714 as descendant of James I. His chief minister was Sir Robert Walpole. Himself personally undistinguished, his reign saw political development; and in spite of the Jaco-

bite threat (rising in 1715) it began a period of dynastic stability.

George II (1683–1760), son of the above, succeeded in 1727, and survived a more serious Jacobite rising in 1745. His long reign helped the development of constitutional government, for he kept within the limitations of his powers and capacity; and it saw the extension of English power in India and North America.

George III (1738–1820), grandson of George II reigned 1760–1820. Sincere and well-intentioned, but not politically able, he suffered from mental illness due to intermittent porphyria. His reign saw a clash with John Wilkes, the rise of Methodism, and agrarian and industrial revolution; also the loss of the American colonies, the extension of English power in India (Warren Hastings), and long French wars.

George IV (1762–1830), eldest son of George III, reigned 1820–30, having become Prince Regent in 1812. His reign was a time of distress and of demand for reform.

George V (1865–1936), the second son of Edward VII and Queen Alexandra. His elder brother died in 1892 and, in 1901, on his father's accession, he became heir to the throne. He joined the Navy as a cadet in 1877. In 1893 he married Princess Mary of Teck. He succeeded in 1910. In 1932 he began the royal broadcast on Christmas Day.

George VI (1895–1952), second son of George V, was called to the throne in 1936 on the abdication of his elder brother, Edward VIII. His personal qualities gained wide respect. He married Lady Elizabeth Bowes-Lyon (1900–2002) in 1923.

George, Henry (1839–97), American political economist whose "single tax" on land values as a means of solving economic problems is expounded in his *Progress and Poverty* (1879).

George, St., patron saint of England, adopted by Edward III. He is believed to have been martyred by Diocletian at Nicomedia in 303.

German, Sir Edward (1862–1936), composer of light operas whose works (*e.g. Merrie England*) were very popular. He was born Edward German Jones.

Gershwin, George (1898–1937). American jazz pianist and song-writer, composer of *Rhapsody in Blue* and the Negro folk-opera *Porgy and Bess*. His brother **Ira** was a noted lyricist.

Gesner, Conrad (1516–65), Swiss naturalist, b. Zurich. His magnificently illustrated volumes describe animal and vegetable kingdoms.

Getty, Jean Paul (1892–1976), American oil magnate, one of the richest men in the world. Founded J. Paul Getty Museum at Malibu, California.

Ghali, Boutros Boutros (1922–2016). Egyptian diplomat. Secretary-General, United Nations, 1992–96.

Ghiberti, Lorenzo (1378–1455), Florentine sculptor whose bronze doors, beautifying the baptistry in Florence, were described by Michelangelo as fit for the gates of paradise.

Ghirlandaio, Domenico (1449–94), Florentine painter. Most of his frescoes are in Florence, including the cycle of the life of the Virgin and the Baptist in S. Maria Novella. Michelangelo began his apprenticeship in his workshop.

Giacometti, Alberto (1901–66), Swiss sculptor and painter, who worked mainly in Paris and produced abstract symbolic constructions.

Giap, Vo Nguyen (1912–2013), Vietnamese general who defeated the French at Dien Bien Phu (1954) and defied America in the Vietnam War.

Gibbon, Edward (1737–94), English historian of the *Decline and Fall of the Roman Empire*.

Gibbons, Grinling (1648–1720), English woodcarver and sculptor, b. Rotterdam, was brought to the notice of Charles II by Evelyn, the diarist. The choir stalls of St. Paul's and the carving in the Wren library at Trinity College, Cambridge, are his work.

Gibbons, Orlando (1583–1625), English composer of church music. *See also* Section P.

Gibson, Sir Alexander Drummond (1926–95). Founder and music director of the Scottish Opera Company. He was one of the foremost Scottish musicians.

Giddens, Lord (Anthony Giddens) (b. 1938). Director, London School of Economics, 1997–2003. Author, *The Third Way* (1998) and *The Third Way and its Critics* (2000).

Gide, André (1869–1951), French writer of many short novels in which he gives expression to his struggle to escape from his protestant upbringing (*Strait is the Gate*, *The Counterfeiters*). In his memoir *Si le grain ne meurt* he tells the story of his life up to his marriage.

Gielgud, Sir John (1904–2000), actor and director. His career spanned almost eighty years. Celebrated for his beautiful speaking voice, he was a versatile actor, whose most famous rôle was Hamlet. Knighted 1953; C.H. 1977; O.M. 1996.

Gilbert, Sir Alfred (1854–1934). English sculptor. His sculptures include *Eros* in Piccadilly Circus.

Gilbert, Sir Humphrey (1537–83), English navigator. In 1583 he discovered Newfoundland, but was drowned the same year.

Gilbert, William (1540–1603), English physician to Queen Elizabeth. His book *On the Magnet*, published in Latin in 1600, was the first major contribution to science published in England.

Gilbert, Sir William Schwenck (1836–1911), English humorist and librettist, of the Gilbert and Sullivan light operas. First known as author of the *Bab Ballads*, from 1871 he collaborated with Sir Arthur Sullivan, his wit and satire finding appropriate accompaniment in Sullivan's music. Their operas include *H.M.S. Pinafore*, *Patience*, *Iolanthe*, *The Mikado*, *The Gondoliers*, and *The Yeomen of the Guard*.

Giles, Carl Ronald (1916–95), newspaper cartoonist. His work appeared after 1943 in the *Daily Express*.

Gill, Eric (1882–1940), English sculptor and engraver, whose works include the *Stations of the Cross* (Westminster Cathedral), *Prospero and Ariel* (Broadcasting House), *Christ Driving the Moneychangers from the Temple* (Leeds University.)

Gillray, James (1757–1815), English caricaturist who produced over a thousand political cartoons.

Giotto di Bondone (1267–1337), Florentine artist. A pupil of Cimabue, he continued the development away from Byzantine tradition towards greater naturalism. His frescoes survive in the churches of Assisi, Padua, and Florence. He designed the western front of the cathedral at Florence and the campanile.

Gissing, George Robert (1857–1903), English novelist whose works deal with the effect of poverty. The best known is *New Grub Street*.

Giulio Romano or **Giulio Pippi** (*c.* 1492–1546). Italian artist, was a pupil of Raphael. He was also an engineer and architect.

Gladstone, William Ewart (1809–98), English Liberal statesman. B. at Liverpool, he entered parliament in 1832 as a Tory and held office under Peel. From 1852 he served several terms as chancellor of the exchequer and was Liberal prime minister 1868–74, when his legislation included the education act of 1870, the ballot act, the disestablishment of the Church of Ireland and an Irish land act. In 1874 when Disraeli came to power, he temporarily withdrew, but made a come-back in 1879 with his Midlothian campaign. He was again prime minister 1880–5, 1886 and 1892–4; he failed to win home rule for Ireland.

Glazunov, Alexander Constantinovich (1865–1936), Russian composer, pupil of Rimsky-Korsakov. The first of his eight symphonies was composed when he was 16.

Glendower, Owen (*c.* 1350–*c.* 1416), Welsh chief, who conducted guerrilla warfare on the English border. He figures in Shakespeare's *Henry IV*. His Welsh name is *Owain Glyndwr* or *Owain ap Gruffudd*.

Glinka, Mikhail Ivanovich (1804–57), Russian composer, first of the national school, best known for his operas, *A Life for the Tsar*, and *Russlan and Ludmilla*, based on a poem by Pushkin.

Gluck, Christoph Wilibald (1714–87), German composer, important in the development of opera. He studied in Prague, Vienna and Italy, and his first operas were in the Italian tradition; but with *Orfeo ed Euridice* (1762) his style became more dramatic. There followed *Alceste*, *Armide*, and *Iphigénie en Tauride*. *See* **Section P.**

Glyndwr. *See* **Glendower.**

Goddard, Robert Hutchings (1882–1945), American rocket pioneer who achieved (1926) the first rocket flight with a liquid-fuelled engine.

Gödel, Kurt (1906–78), eminent mathematician. Devised Gödel's proof, the vitally important proof of modern mathematics which declares that there will always exist statements that can be neither proven nor disproven in any mathematical system which has a finite number of axioms.

Godfrey of Bouillon (*c.* 1061–1100), Crusader on the first crusade. On capturing Jerusalem took title of protector of the Holy Sepulchre.

Godiva, Lady (1040–80), English benefactress. According to tradition, she obtained from her husband Leofric, Earl of Chester, concessions for the people of Coventry by riding naked through the town.

Godwin, Earl of the West Saxons (d. 1053), was the father of Edith, wife of King Edward the Confessor, and of Harold, last Saxon king.

Godwin William (1756–1836), English political writer and philosopher, author of *Political Justice* (which criticised many contemporary institutions) and a novel *Caleb Williams*. He married **Mary Wollstonecraft** (1759–97), the author of *A Vindication of the Rights of Women*; and their daughter, **Mary Wollstonecraft Godwin** (1797–1851) wrote *Frankenstein* and married Shelley.

Goethe, Johann Wolfgang von (1749–1832), German poet and thinker. B. at Frankfurt-on-Main, his first notable work was a romantic play, *Götz von Berlichingen*, followed by a novel *Werthers Leiden*. In 1776 he became privy councillor to the Duke of Weimar, whom he served for many years. He had wide-ranging interests, and made discoveries in anatomy and in botany. Among his later writings are the play *Iphigenie* and the novel *Wilhelm Meister*. His best-known work is *Faust*.

Gogol, Nikolai Vasilievich (1809–52), Russian novelist and dramatist. His comedy, *The Government Inspector*, satirised provincial bureaucracy; and his novel, *Dead Souls*, deals with malpractice in the purchase of dead serfs.

Golding, Sir William (1911–93), novelist, whose imaginative and experimental fiction includes *Lord of the Flies* (1954) and *The Spire* (1964). Awarded the Nobel Prize for Literature (1983).

Goldsmith, Oliver (1728–74), Irish poet, dramatist and novelist. The son of a poor curate, he came to London in 1756, and eventually joined the circle of Dr. Johnson. Best known for his novel *The Vicar of Wakefield* and his play *She Stoops to Conquer*.

Golovine, Serge (1924–98), a supremely gifted French ballet dancer, equalled only by Nureyev.

Gombrich, Sir Ernst (1909–2001), the most eminent art historian of his time. Born in Vienna.

Goncourt, Edmond Louis Antoine Huot de (1822–96) and **Jules Alfred Huot de** (1830–70), French brothers, remembered for their *Journal des Goncourts*, an intimate account of Parisian society.

Góngora y Argote, Luis de (1561–1627), Spanish poet, b. Córdova. In *Polifemo* and *Soledades* he attempted to express poetry in new forms.

Goodyear, Charles (1800–60), American inventor who discovered the art of vulcanising rubber.

Goossens, Sir Eugene (1893–1962), English conductor and composer of Belgian descent. His compositions include *Judith* and *Don Juan de Mañara*; brother of **Léon**, oboe virtuoso, and of **Sidonie** and **Marie Goossens**, harpists.

Gorbachev, Mikhail (b. 1931). Soviet politician. Succeeded Chernenko (*q.v.*) as General Secretary of the Communist Party, 1985. His accession marked the end of the "old-guard" leadership. Identified with policies of *glasnost* (openness) and *perestroika* (restructuring). President of the USSR, 1990–91. He presided over revolutionary changes both in Eastern Europe and Russia, but faced a growing crisis at home. The abortive coup in 1991 weakened his position, leading to the collapse of the USSR. Nobel Peace Prize, 1990.

Gordimer, Nadine (1923–2014). South African Nobel prize-winning author, a powerful campaigner against apartheid.

Gordon, Charles George (1833–85), Scottish soldier. After service in the Crimea and China, in 1873 he was made governor of the Equatorial provinces of Egypt; and he was a notable governor of the Sudan, 1877–80. When a rising was led by the Mahdi, he was sent out in 1884 to the garrisons in rebel territory. Murdered by the Mahdi's forces on the palace staircase in Khartoum.

Gordon, Lord George (1751–93), agitator, led No-Popery riots in London in 1780.

Gore, Al (b. 1948), US Vice-President under Clinton, 1993–2001. Defeated as Democratic candidate in 2000 presidential elections. Environmental campaigner. Shared Nobel Peace Prize, 2007.

Gorky, Maxim (Alexey Maximovich Peshkov) 1868–1936), Russian writer. His early work was romantic. He spent many years abroad, but returned in 1928, a supporter of the Soviet regime. His later work is marked by social realism.

Gormley, Sir Antony (b. 1950), eminent sculptor, creator of the *Angel of the North*.

Gosse, Sir Edmund (1849–1928), English poet and critic, known for literary studies of the 17th and 18th centuries; and his memoir *Father and Son*.

Gounod, Charles François (1818–93), French composer, known for his operas *Faust* and *Roméo et Juliette*. His lyrical gifts are shown in earlier works, such as *Le Médicin malgré lui* and *Mireille*.

Gower, John (1325–1408), English poet of the time of Chaucer, author of *Confessio Amantis*.

Goya y Lucientes, Francisco José (1746–1828), Spanish painter and etcher b. nr. Saragossa. He became court painter to Charles III in 1786. His portraits are painted with ruthless realism; his series of satirical etchings (*Los Caprichos* and the *Disasters of War*) expose man's inhumanity and the cruelty of his day.

Gracchi, the brothers **Tiberius** (163–133 B.C.) and **Gaius** (153–121 B.C.) who, as Tribunes of the People, tried to reform the system of public landholding and liberalise the franchise at Rome, but were both killed when the Senate suppressed their followers.

Grace, William Gilbert (1848–1915). English cricketer who scored 54,896 runs, including 126 centuries, and took 2,876 wickets.

Graham, Billy (b. 1918), US evangelist who became world-famous for his campaigns.

Grahame, Kenneth (1859–1932), Scottish writer of books for children, including *The Golden Age*, *Dream Days*, and *Wind in the Willows*.

Grahame-White, Claude (1879–1959), the first Englishman to gain an aviator's certificate, 1909.

Gramsci, Antonio (1891–1937). Marxist theorist. A founder of the Italian Communist Party (1921).

Grant, Ulysses Simpson (1822–85), American general of the civil war, and president of the United States from 1869 to 1876.

Granville-Barker, Harley (1877–1946), English dramatist, actor, and producer, who promoted the plays of Ibsen, Shaw, *etc*. His own works include *The Voysey Inheritance*.

Grass, Günter (1927–2015), German novelist and poet. Awarded 1999 Nobel Prize for Literature. His most famous novel is *Die Blechtrommel* (1959; translated as *The Tin Drum*, 1961). His autobiography *Peeling the Onion* (2006) revealed his Waffen SS past. He opposed German reunification.

Grattan, Henry (1746–1820), Irish statesman, who struggled for Irish legislative independence and for Catholic emancipation (though himself a Protestant) and parliamentary reform; but unsuccessfully.

Graves, Robert Ranke (1895–1985), English writer, author of *Goodbye to All That*, and of *I Claudius* and *Claudius the God*; besides poetry.

Gray, Thomas (1716–71), English poet, author of *Elegy written in a Country Churchyard* and *Ode on a Distant Prospect of Eton College*.

Greco, El (Domenikos Theotokopoulos) (1541–1614), one of the most original painters of his time. The Greek (as he was known) was soon forgotten after his death but greatly influenced 20th century painters such as Picasso and Cézanne.

Greeley, Horace (1811–72), American newspaper editor, founder of the New York *Tribune* (1841).

Greenaway, Kate (1846–1901), English artist, who depicted children, especially in book illustrations.

Greene, Graham (1904–91), English novelist and journalist, whose novels (*The Power and the Glory*, *The Heart of the Matter*, *The End of the Affair*, *The Quiet American*, *Our Man in Havana*, *A Burnt-out Case*, *The Comedians*, *The Honorary Consul*), like his plays (*The Complaisant Lover*) and films (*Fallen Idol*, *The Third Man*) deal with moral problems in a modern setting. C.H. (1966), O.M. (1986).

Greer, Germaine (b. 1939). Feminist and writer. Born in Melbourne, Australia. Her most famous work is *The Female Eunuch* (1970) which exposed the misrepresentation of female sexuality by a male-dominated society. Other publications include *The Whole Woman* (1999), *The Boy* (2003) and *Shakespeare's Wife* (2007).

Gregory, St. (*c*. 240–332), converted King Tiridates of Armenia, so founding the Armenian church.

Gregory I (the Great), St. (*c*. 540–604), Pope 590–604, was the last great Latin Father and the forerunner of scholasticism. The main founder of the temporal power and the political influence of the papacy, he also maintained the spiritual claims of Rome, enforcing discipline, encouraging monasticism, defining doctrine *etc*. He sent Augustine on a mission to England.

Gregory VII (Hildebrand) (*c*. 1020–85), Pope 1073–85. He strove for papal omnipotence within the

church and for a high standard in the priesthood (especially by stamping out simony). He also upheld the papacy against the Holy Roman Empire, and the emperor Henry IV did penance for three days in the snow at Canossa.

Gregory XIII (1502–85), Pope 1572–85; introduced the Gregorian calendar.

Gregory, James (1638–75). Scottish mathematician. He invented a reflecting telescope and was the first to show how the distance of the sun could be deduced by observations of the passage of Venus across the disc of the sun. Successive generations of the family reached distinction.

Grenville, Sir Richard (1541–91), English sea captain, who with his one ship engaged a fleet of Spanish war vessels off Flores in 1591, an exploit celebrated in Tennyson's ballad *The Revenge*.

Gresham, Sir Thomas (1519–79), English financier and founder of the Royal Exchange. Son of a Lord Mayor of London, he was an astute moneyfinder for four successive sovereigns, including Queen Elizabeth I. "Gresham's Law" is the statement that bad money drives out good.

Gresley, Sir (Herbert) Nigel (1876–1941), outstanding steam locomotive designer. His A4 class Pacific, *Mallard*, achieved the world speed record.

Greuze, Jean Baptiste (1725–1805), French artist, known especially for his studies of girls. His *Girl with Doves* is in the Wallace Collection.

Grey, 2nd Earl (Charles Grey) (1764–1845), British Whig statesman under whose premiership were passed the Reform Bill of 1832, a bill abolishing slavery throughout the Empire (1833), and the Poor Law Amendment Act, 1834.

Grey, Lady Jane (1537–54), Queen of England for a few days. The daughter of the Duke of Suffolk, she was put forward as queen by protestant leaders on the death of her cousin, Edward VI; but overcome by the legal claimant, Mary Tudor, and executed.

Grieg, Edvard Hagerup (1843–1907), Norwegian composer, b. Bergen. He presented the characteristics of his country's music with strong accentuation. He is best known for his incidental music to *Peer Gynt*.

Griffith, Arthur (1872–1922), the first president of the Irish Free State, 1921; founder of *Sinn Fein*.

Griffith, David Wark. See **Q10**.

Grimaldi, Joseph (1779–1837), British clown, "the father of modern clowning". All clowns are now known as Joeys because of him.

Grimm, the brothers **Jakob Ludwig Karl** (1785–1863), and **Wilhelm Karl** (1786–1859), German philologists and folk-lorists, best known for their *Fairy Tales*. Jakob published a notable philological dictionary, *Deutsche Grammatik*. The brothers also projected the vast *Deutsches Wörtebuch* which was completed by German scholars in 1961.

Grimond, Lord (Joseph) (1913–93), Leader of the Liberal Party, 1956–67.

Grimthorpe, 1st Baron (Edmund Beckett Denison) (1816–1905), horologist who invented the double three-legged escapement for the clock at Westminster, familiarly known as "Big Ben" (the name of the bell). Known as Sir Edmund Beckett.

Gromyko, Andrei Andreevich (1909–89), Soviet diplomat and statesman. President, USSR, July 1985–88, Foreign Minister, 1957–85.

Gropius, Walter (1883–1969), German architect, later a US citizen. He formed the Bauhaus.

Grossmith, George (1847–1912), English actor. With his brother, **Weedon Grossmith**, he wrote *Diary of a Nobody*. His son, **George Grossmith** (1874–1935) was a comedian and introduced revue and cabaret entertainment into England.

Grote, George (1794–1871), English historian, author of a *History of Greece*.

Grotius (Huig van Groot) (1583–1645), Dutch jurist, the founder of international law. He was condemned to life imprisonment for religious reasons, but escaped to Paris, where he wrote *De Jure Belli et Pacis*.

Grouchy, Emmanuel, Marquis de (1766–1847), French general, who served under Napoleon; after Waterloo led defeated army back to Paris.

Grove, Sir George (1820–1900), English musicologist, author of *Dictionary of Music and Musicians*. By profession he was a civil engineer.

Guevara, Ernesto "Che" (1928–67), revolutionary icon. b. Argentina. He took part in the Cuban guerrilla war and became a minister in the Cuban government 1959–65. He was killed while leading guerrillas against US-trained Bolivian troops. His remains were later buried in Cuba in 1997.

Guido Reni (1575–1642), Italian painter of the Bolognese school whose works are characteristic of the Italian baroque of his period and include the *Aurora* fresco in the Rospigliosi palace at Rome, and *Crucifixion of St. Peter* (Vatican).

Gustavus Adolphus (1594–1632), King of Sweden, the "Lion of the North." After a campaign in Poland he entered the Thirty Years' war in support of Swedish interests and Protestant distress, won the battle of Breitenfeld in 1631 and was killed in action the next year.

Gutenberg, Johann (*c.* 1400–68), German printer, b. Mainz, the first European to print with movable types cast in moulds. The earliest book printed by him was the Mazarin Bible (**L72**).

Guy, Thomas (1644–1724), English philanthropist. A printer, he made money by speculation; and in 1722 founded Guy's Hospital in Southwark.

Gwyn, Nell (*c.* 1650–87), English actress and mistress of Charles II by whom she had two sons. Of Hereford origin, she sold oranges in London.

H

Hadid, Dame Zaha (1960–2016) one of the most famous architects of our time. The 'Queen of Curves'.

Hadley, George (1685–1768). He developed Halley's theory of the trade winds by taking into account the effect of the earth's rotation and the displacement of air by tropical heat (1735).

Hadrian (76–138), Roman emperor. A shrewd and ruthless leader, he suppressed revolts, but was also a lover of the arts. He visited Britain *c.* A.D. 121 and built a protective wall between Wallsend-on-Tyne and Bowness-on-Solway.

Hafiz, pseudonym of **Shams ad-Din Mohammed** (d. *c.* 1388), Persian lyrical poet. His principal work is the *Divan*, a collection of short sonnets called *ghazals*. The sobriquet *Hafiz*, meaning one who remembers, is applied to anyone who has learned the Koran by heart.

Hague, Lord. *See* D17.

Hahn, Otto (1879–1968), German chemist and physicist, chief discoverer of uranium fission.

Hahnemann, Samuel Christian Friedrich (1755–1843), German physician who founded homoeopathy (treatment of disease by small doses of drugs that in health produce similar symptoms).

Haig, Douglas, 1st Earl of Bermersyde (1861–1928), British field-marshal, b. Edinburgh. He replaced French as commander-in-chief in France, 1915–19, leading the offensive in August 1918.

Haile Selassie I (1891–1975), Emperor of Ethiopia 1930–74. Proclaimed Emperor after the mysterious death of Empress Zewditu. He spent the years of the Italian occupation 1936–41 in England. Deposed 1974.

Hailsham, Viscount. *See under* Hogg.

Hakluyt, Richard (1553–1616), English writer on maritime discovery. B. in Herefordshire, he spent some time in Paris. From 1582 (when *Divers Voyages* appeared), he devoted his life to collecting and publishing accounts of English navigators, thus giving further impetus to discovery.

Haldane, John Burdon Sanderson (1892–1964), biologist and geneticist, noted not only for his work in mathematical evolutionary theory but for explaining science to the layman. He emigrated to India in 1957. He was the son of **John Scott Haldane** (1860–1936), b. Edinburgh, who studied the effect of industrial occupations upon health.

Haldane, 1st Viscount (Richard Burdon Haldane) (1856–1928). British Liberal statesman. As war minister in 1905 he reorganised the army and founded the Territorials.

Hale, George Ellery (1868–1935), American astronomer, after whom is named the 200-inch reflecting telescope on Mount Palomar.

Halévy, Ludovic (1834–1903), French playwright, who collaborated with Henri Meilhac in writing libretti for Offenbach and Bizet.

Halifax, 1st Earl of (Edward Frederick Lindley Wood) (1881–1959), British Conservative politician; foreign secretary during the period of appeasement of Germany; as Lord Irwin, viceroy of India 1926–31.

Halifax, 1st Marquess of (George Savile) (1633–95), English politician of changeable views, who wrote *Character of a Trimmer*.

Hall, Sir Peter (Reginald Frederick) (b. 1930). Leading

director of plays, films and operas. Director, National Theatre, 1973–88.

Hallam, Henry (1777–1859), English historian, best known for his *Constitutional History*. He was father of Arthur Hallam, friend of Tennyson.

Hallé, Sir Charles (1819–95), German-born pianist and conductor, who settled in Manchester and organised an orchestra of high-class talent. He married the violinist Wilhelmine Neruda.

Halley, Edmond (1656–1742), English astronomer royal 1720–42. He published observations on the planets and comets, being the first to predict the return of a comet (*see* **Section L**). He furthered Newton's work on gravitation, setting aside his own researches. He made the first magnetic survey of the oceans from the naval vessel *Paramour*, 1698–1700. His meteorological observations led to his publication of the first map of the winds of the globe (1686).

Hals, Frans (*c.* 1580–1666), Dutch portrait painter, b. at Mechlin. He is best known for his *Laughing Cavalier* in the Wallace Collection, and for portraits in the Louvre and at Amsterdam.

Hamann, Johann Georg (1730–88), German philosopher. Friend of Kant. An important counter-Enlightenment thinker.

Hamilton, Alexander (1755–1804), American statesman and economist. With Madison and Jay he wrote the *Federalist* (1787). As secretary of the Treasury (1789–95) he put Washington's government on a firm financial footing and planned a national bank. He was the leader of the Federalists, a party hostile to Jefferson. He was killed in a duel.

Hamilton, Emma, Lady (*née* Lyon) (*c.* 1765–1815), a beauty of humble birth who, after several liaisons, was married in 1791 to Sir William Hamilton, British ambassador at Naples. There she met Nelson, and bore him a child, Horatia.

Hamilton, Richard (1922–2011). A founding father of British Pop Art. *See* **N12**.

Hammarskjöld, Dag (1905–61), Swedish Secretary-General of the United Nations, 1953–61. He was killed in an air crash while attempting to mediate in a dispute between Congo and the province of Katanga. Posthumous Nobel peace prize.

Hammond, John Lawrence (1872–1949), English historian of social and industrial history, whose works (with his wife Barbara) include *The Town Labourer* and *The Village Labourer*.

Hammond, Philip. *See* D17.

Hampden, John (1594–1643), English parliamentarian and civil war leader. He refused to pay Charles I's ship money in 1636. When civil war broke out, he raised a regiment and was killed on Chalgrove Field.

Hamsun, Knut, pen-name of Knut Pedersen (1859–1952), Norwegian author who in his youth struggled for existence, visited America twice and earned his living by casual labour. *The Growth of the Soil* won him the 1920 Nobel prize. Other novels are *Hunger* and *Mysteries*.

Handel, George Frederick (1685–1759), German composer, son of a barber-surgeon to the Duke of Saxony; b. Halle, the same year as Bach; spent much of his life in England composing operas and oratorios. His operas, of which there are over 40, include *Atalanta, Berenice* and *Serse*, and his oratorios, of which there are 32, include *Saul, Israel in Egypt, Samson, Messiah, Judas Maccabaeus*, and *Jephtha*. Before he died he became blind and relied upon his old friend and copyist John Christopher Smith to commit his music to paper. *See* **Section P**.

Hannibal (247–182 B.C.), Carthaginian general. He fought two wars against Rome. In the first he conquered southern Spain. In the second he overran Gaul, crossed the Alps, and defeated the Romans in successive battles, especially at Cannae. Thereafter his forces were worn down by Roman delaying tactics; he was defeated by Scipio at Zama and later poisoned himself.

Hardicnut (**Hardicanute**) (1019–42), son of Cnut (Canute), and last Danish king of England.

Hardie, James Keir (1856–1915), Scottish Labour leader, one of the founders of the Labour party. He first worked in a coal-pit; in 1882 became a journalist; and in 1892 was the first socialist to be elected to the House of Commons (for West Ham – South). He edited the *Labour Leader* 1887–1904. He was the first chairman of the parliamentary Labour party, 1906. A pacifist, he opposed the Boer war.

Hardy, Thomas (1840–1928), English novelist and poet, was trained as an architect and practised for some time, but became known in 1871 with *Desperate Remedies*. In 1874 his *Far from the Madding Crowd* was published. There followed a series of novels, including *The Trumpet-Major*, *The Mayor of Casterbridge*, *Tess of the D'Urbervilles*, and *Jude the Obscure*. In 1908 he completed a dramatic poem, *The Dynasts*. See **M23**.

Hargreaves, James (1720–78), English inventor, b. Blackburn. His spinning-jenny was invented in 1764 and became widely used, though his own was broken by spinners in 1768 and his invention brought him no profit.

Harkness, Edward Stephen (1874–1940), American banker and philanthropist, who in 1930 founded the Pilgrim Trust in Gt. Britain.

Harley, Robert, 1st Earl of Oxford and Mortimer (1661–1724), English statesman and collector of MSS. He held office under Queen Anne, and brought a European war to an end with the treaty of Utrecht. After the Hanoverian succession he retired, and formed the Harley MSS. collection, now in the British Museum.

Harold II (1022–66), last Saxon king of England, was son of Earl Godwin. He was chosen king in succession to Edward the Confessor. He had at once to meet a dual invasion. He defeated the Norwegian king at Stamford Bridge; but was himself defeated by William of Normandy at the battle of Hastings (fought at Battle 1066).

Harriman, William Averell (1891–1986), American public official. He was adviser to President Roosevelt and later presidents especially on Marshall Aid and foreign affairs.

Harris, Joel Chandler (1848–1908). American author, creator of Uncle Remus and Brer Rabbit.

Harrison, Frederic (1831–1923), English philosopher and lawyer, author of *The Meaning of History* and *The Philosophy of Common Sense*. He was president of the Positivist Committee.

Harrison, George. *See under* **Beatles**.

Harrison, John (1693–1776), "Longitude Harrison," English inventor of the chronometer, b. near Pontefract, Yorkshire, the son of a carpenter.

Harty, Sir Hamilton (1880–1941), composer and for some years conductor of the Hallé orchestra.

Harun al-Rashid (Aaron the Upright) (763–809), 5th Abbasid caliph of Baghdad. His court was a centre for art and learning, but he governed mainly through his vizier until the latter lost favour and was executed in 803. The *Arabian Nights* associated with him are stories collected several centuries later.

Harvey, William (1578–1657), English physician and rediscoverer of the circulation of the blood. B. at Folkestone, he studied at Padua while Galileo was there, and was physician to James I and Charles I. His treatise on circulation was published in Latin in 1628. Circulation of the blood was already known to the Moors.

Hastings, Warren (1732–1818), English administrator in India. As governor-general of Bengal for the East India Company he revised the finances and administration and put down disorder. On his return to England he was impeached for alleged corruption, and, though acquitted, lost his fortune in his own defence. Later however he received a grant from the company.

Hatshepsut, Queen (*fl.* 1460 B.C.). Ruler of Egypt, 1479–1458 B.C. after the death of her husband-brother Tuthmosis II.

Hauptmann, Gerhart (1862–1946), German dramatist and novelist. B. in Silesia. His play *The Weavers* deals with a revolt of 1844. Other works include *Die versunkene Glocke*, *Der arme Heinrich*, and *Rose Bernd*. Nobel prize 1912.

Havel, Vaclav (1936–2011), Czech playwright, dissident and statesman. Imprisoned, 1979–83. President of Czechoslovakia, December 1989–92. First President of new Czech Republic, 1993–2003.

Havelock, Sir Henry (1795–1857), British general who helped to put down the Indian mutiny.

Hawke, 1st Baron (Edward Hawke) (1705–81), English admiral, who in 1759 defeated the French at Quiberon in a tremendous storm.

Hawking, Stephen William (b. 1942), British theoretical physicist. Lucasian Professor of Mathematics, Cambridge University,1979–2009. Author of *300 Years of Gravitation* (1987), *A Brief History of Time* (1988), *The Universe in a Nutshell* (2001) and *The Grand Design* (2010) (co-authored with

Leonard Mlodinow). C.H. (1989). Sufferer from motor neurone disease.

Hawkins, Sir John (1532–95), English sailor and slave-trader. Born at Plymouth. In 1562 he was the first Englishman to traffic in slaves. Treasurer of the Navy, 1585–88. He helped to defeat the Spanish Armada in 1588, commanding the *Victory*. Died at sea off Puerto Rico, 12 Nov. 1595.

Hawksmoor Nicholas (1661–1736). Architect. Born in Nottinghamshire. Famous for his London churches (*e.g.* Christ Church, Spitalfields).

Hawthorne, Nathaniel (1804–64), American author. His works include *The Marble Faun*, *The Scarlet Letter* and *The House of the Seven Gables*.

Haydn, Franz Joseph (1732–1809), Austrian composer. He has been given the title "father of the symphony." Much of his life was spent as musical director to the princely Hungarian house of Esterhazy. In 1791 and again in 1794 he visited London, conducting his Salomon symphonies. His two great oratorios, *The Creation* and *The Seasons*, were written in old age. See **Section P**.

Hayek, Friedrich August (von) (1899–1992), Austrian economist. The 'father of monetarism.' Strongly influenced development of Thatcherite monetary policies. Shared Nobel Prize for Economics, 1974. C.H. (1984).

Hazlitt, William (1778–1830), English essayist and critic. His writings include *The Characters of Shakespeare's Plays*, *Table Talk*, and *The Spirit of the Age*. His grandson **William Carew Hazlitt** (1834–1913) was a bibliographer and writer.

Healey, Lord (Denis Healey) (1917–2015). Formidable Labour Cabinet Minister. Chancellor of the Exchequer, 1974–79. Previously Defence Secretary, 1964–70. Life Peer, 1992. C.H. (1979).

Heaney, Seamus (1939–2013), Irish poet, whose works include *Death of a Naturalist* (1966) and *North* (1975). Professor of Poetry, Oxford University, 1989–94. Professor of Rhetoric and Oratory, Harvard University, USA. Awarded the Nobel Prize for Literature, 1995. His translation of the Anglo-Saxon epic poem *Beowulf* earned him the Whitbread Book of the Year award. A giant of poetry who spoke for a generation.

Heath, Sir Edward (1916–2005), British statesman, leader of the Conservative Party 1965–75; prime minister 1970–74; leader of the opposition 1965–70, 1974–75. In 1973 he took Britain into the EEC. Order of the Garter, 1992. "Father of the House" 1992–2001.

Hedin, Sven Anders (1865–1952), Swedish explorer of Central Asia; wrote *My Life as Explorer*.

Heenan, John Carmel (1905–76). English Roman Catholic Archbishop of Westminster 1963–76.

Hegel, Georg Wilhelm Friedrich (1770–1831), German idealist philosopher, b. Stuttgart, whose name is associated with the dialectic method of reasoning with its sequence of thesis—antithesis—synthesis. He studied theology at Tübingen with his friend Schelling. He taught philosophy at Jena, Nuremberg, Heidelberg, and Berlin. He produced an abstract philosophical system which was influenced by his early interest in mysticism and his Prussian patriotism. *See* **Dialectical Materialism, Section J**.

Heidenstam, Verner von (1859–1940), Swedish author and poet. Nobel prizewinner, 1916.

Heine, Heinrich (1797–1856), German lyric poet.

Heisenberg, Werner (1901–76), German physicist, noted for his theory of quantum mechanics and the Uncertainty Principle. Nobel Prize, 1932.

Heller, Joseph (1923–99), US novelist, whose celebrated novel is *Catch 22* (1961).

Helmholtz, Herman von (1821–94), German physicist and physiologist. He published his *Erhaltung der Kraft* (Conservation of Energy) in 1847, the year that Joule gave the first clear exposition of the principle of energy. His pupil Heinrich Hertz discovered electromagnetic radiation in accordance with Maxwell's theory.

Heloïse (*c.* 1101–64), the beloved of Abelard (*q.v.*). Her letters to him survive.

Hemingway, Ernest (1898–1961), American novelist of wide influence. His works include *A Farewell to Arms*, *Death in the Afternoon*, *For Whom the Bell Tolls*, *The Old Man and the Sea*. He committed suicide. Nobel prizewinner 1954.

Henderson, Arthur (1863–1935), British Labour politician, b. Glasgow. He worked mainly for disarmament. Nobel peace prize, 1934.

Hendrix, Jimi (1942–70), pioneering rock guitarist, singer and songwriter. A guitar legend.

Henrietta Maria (1609–69), the daughter of Henry IV of France and wife of Charles I.

Henry, Joseph (1797–1878), American physicist and schoolteacher who independently of Faraday discovered the principle of the induced current. The weather-reporting system he set up at the Smithsonian Institution led to the creation of the U.S. Weather Bureau.

Henry I (1068–1135), King of England. The youngest son of William the Conqueror, he ascended the throne during the absence on crusade of his elder brother Robert of Normandy. His long reign brought order and progress.

Henry II (1133–89), King of England. He was son of Matilda, daugher of Henry I, and Geoffrey Plantagenet, count of Anjou; and his lands stretched to the Pyrenees. He was a strong ruler to whom we largely owe the establishment of the common law system and permanent administrative reforms. His conflict with the Church led to the murder of archbishop Becket.

Henry III (1207–72), King of England, succeeded his father John in 1216. Himself devout and simple, his long reign was troubled by a partly factious baronial opposition.

Henry IV (1367–1413), grandson of Edward III and heir to the Duchy of Lancaster, became king of England in 1399. More solid and practical than his cousin Richard II, whom he had supplanted, he consolidated the government.

Henry V (1387–1422), son of Henry IV, succeeded his father as king of England in 1413. A successful commander, he renewed the French war and won the battle of Agincourt, but he died young.

Henry VI (1421–71), son of Henry V, succeeded his father as king of England in 1422 as a baby. Gentle and retiring, he inherited a losing war with France. He founded Eton, and King's College, Cambridge. The Yorkist line claimed the crown from his (the Lancastrian) line, and the Wars of the Roses led to his deposition and death. Ruled 1422–61, 1470–71.

Henry VII (1457–1509) succeeded Richard III as king of England after defeating him in 1485. The first Tudor king, he was firm and shrewd, even avaricious; he built Henry VII's Chapel in Westminster Abbey, and encouraged John Cabot to sail to North America.

Henry VIII (1491–1547), King of England, succeeded his father Henry VII in 1509. A prince of the Renaissance, skilled in music and sports, he loved the sea and built up the navy. His minister Cardinal Wolsey fell when Henry, seeking divorce to obtain a legal heir, rejected papal supremacy and dissolved the monasteries. Ruthless and ostentatious, he executed Sir Thomas More and spent his father's wealth. The father of **Edward VI, Mary I** and **Elizabeth I**.

Henry IV of France (Henry of Navarre) (1553–1610). Prior to becoming king, he was the leader of the Huguenots; and although on being crowned he became a Catholic, he protected the Protestants by the Edict of Nantes. He then became a national king, but was later assassinated by Ravaillac, a religious fanatic.

Henry the Navigator (1394–1460), Portuguese promoter of discovery, son of John I. His sailors discovered Madeira and the Azores.

Henschel, Sir George (1850–1934), singer, composer, and conductor. B. in Breslau, he became a naturalised Englishman. Founder and conductor of the London Symphony Concerts (1886).

Hepplewhite, George (d. 1786), English cabinetmaker whose name is identified with the style which followed the Chippendale period.

Hepworth, Dame Barbara (1903–75). One of the greatest non-figurative sculptors of her time, as in *Contrapuntal Forms* (exhibited at the 1951 Festival of Britain).

Heraclitus of Ephesus (*c.* 540–475 B.C.), Greek philosopher. His discovery of a changing, more democratic, world influenced Parmenides, Democritus, Plato, Aristotle, and Hegel.

Herbert, George (1593–1633), the most purely devotional of English poets. See **M10**.

Hereward the Wake, the last Saxon leader to hold out against the Normans. His base in the fens was captured in 1071 but he escaped. His exploits were written up by Kingsley.

Herodotus (*c.* 485–425 B.C.), Greek historian, called by Cicero, the father of history. He travelled widely collecting historical evidence.

Herrick, Robert (1591–1674), English lyric poet. His poems include *Gather ye Rose Buds, Cherry Ripe*, and *Oberon's Feast*.

Herriot, Edouard (1872–1957), French Radical-Socialist statesman. A scholar, long-time mayor of Lyons. Three times prime minister.

Herschel, Sir John (1792–1871), British astronomer who continued his father's researches and also pioneered photography, a term introduced by him. One of his twelve children introduced fingerprints into criminology.

Herschel, Sir William (1738–1822), German-born astronomer who came to England from Hanover as a musician; father of the above. Unrivalled as an observer, and with telescopes of his own making he investigated the distribution of stars in the Milky Way and concluded that some of the nebulae he could see were separate star systems outside our own. He discovered the planet Uranus in 1781. In 1789 he discovered two of its moons, Enceladus and Mimas.

Hertz, Heinrich Rudolf (1857–95), German physicist, whose laboratory experiments confirmed Maxwell's electromagnetic theory of waves and yielded information about their behaviour.

Herzl, Theodor (1860–1904), founder of modern political Zionism, was b. Budapest. He convened a congress at Basle in 1897.

Hesiod (fl. *c.* 735 B.C.), Greek poet, author of *Work and Days*, which tells of life in the country.

Heyerdahl, Thor (1914–2002), Norwegian anthropologist, famous for crossing the Pacific on the *Kon-Tiki* to demonstrate his belief in links between Peru and Polynesia.

Higgs, Peter (b.1929), physicist whose theory of the 'Higgs particle' was confirmed in 2012. C.H. (2013). Joint winner, Nobel Prize for Physics (2013).

Hildegard von Bingen, St. (1098–1179), medieval Benedictine nun. The 'Sibyl of the Rhine'.

Hill, Octavia (1838–1912), English social reformer concerned with the housing conditions of the poor, a pioneer in slum clearance in London; founder (with Sir Robert Hunter and Canon Rawnsley) of the National Trust.

Hill, Sir Rowland (1795–1879), originator of the penny postal system. He was secretary to the Postmaster-General 1846–54, then chief secretary to the Post Office until 1864.

Hillary, Sir Edmund (1919–2008), New Zealand mountaineer and explorer. Won world-wide fame when he and Sherpa Tenzing (1914–86) were the first to reach the summit of Mt. Everest in 1953. Order of the Garter (1995).

Hindemith, Paul (1895–1963), German composer and viola player. He is associated with the movement in *Gebrauchsmusik*, which regarded music as a social expression. He incurred Nazi hostility and his later life was spent abroad. His numerous works include chamber works, songs, operas, ballet music, symphonies, and the oratorio *Das Umaufhörliche. See also* Section **P.**

Hindenburg, Paul von (1847–1934), German field-marshal. In 1914 he defeated the Russians at Tannenberg. In his old age a national hero, President of the German Reich, 1925–34.

Hinshelwood, Sir Cyril Norman (1897–1967), English chemist. He shared with Prof. Semenov of Russia the 1956 Nobel prize for chemistry for researches into the mechanism of chemical reactions. Pres. Royal Society, 1955–60.

Hippocrates of Chios (fl. *c.* 430 B.C.), Greek mathematician, the first to compile a work on the elements of geometry.

Hippocrates of Cos (fl. *c.* 430 B.C.), Greek physician, whose writings are lost, but who is believed to have established medical schools in Athens and elsewhere, and to have contributed towards a scientific separation of medicine from superstition. Seen as the ideal physician.

Hirohito, Emperor of Japan (1901–89), acceded to the throne in 1926. In 1946 he renounced his legendary divinity. Controversy surrounds his role in Japanese aggression.

Hirst, Damien (b. 1965), controversial contemporary artist who won the Turner Prize in 1995. His "pickled shark" launched the Britart movement.

Hitler, Adolf (1889–1945), German dictator, founder of National Socialism, b. in Austria, son of a customs official. He was in Vienna for 5 years with no regular work before going to Munich in 1913; enlisted in Bavarian infantry in 1914. In post-1918 Germany, he led the extreme-right

Nazi Party. He became Reich chancellor in 1933 and on the death of Hindenburg in 1934 Führer; and commander-in-chief *Wehrmacht* 1935.

Under Hitler, working class movements were ruthlessly destroyed; all opponents—communists, socialists, Jews—were persecuted and murdered. By terrorism and propaganda the German state was welded into a powerful machine for aggression. There followed the occupation of the Rhineland (1936), the annexation of Austria and Czechoslovakia (1938–9), the invasion of Poland and declaration of war by Great Britain and France (1939) and the invasion of Russia (1941). Final defeat came in 1945; on 30 April he committed suicide as the Russians closed in on Berlin.

Hobbes, Thomas (1588–1679), English philosopher who published *Leviathan* in 1651. He favoured strong government and supported the supremacy of the state.

Hobhouse, Leonard Trelawney (1864–1929), English sociologist. His books include *The Theory of Knowledge, Morals in Evolution etc.*

Hobsbawm, Eric (1917–2012), Marxist historian. Author of *The Age of Revolution, The Age of Capital etc.* A peerless social historian. Created C.H. (1998).

Ho Chi-minh (1892–1969), leader of the Vietnam revolutionary nationalist party of Indo-China, which struggled for independence from France. His main purpose was to weld together the nationalistic and communistic elements in Vietnam. He fought to extend his control over South Vietnam, defying the United States.

Hockney, David (b. 1937), one of the most prominent British painters of the post-war generation. Born in Bradford, he moved to California in the 1960s. His massive *Bigger Trees Near Warter 2007* has been acquired by the Tate Gallery. C.H. His work is highly inventive, experimental and subversive. Appointed to Order of Merit (2012).

Hodgkin, Sir Alan (1914–98), British biophysicist working in the field of nerve impulse conduction. He was one of the world's most eminent biophysicists. Nobel prizewinner, 1970; O.M. 1973.

Hodgkin, Dorothy Crowfoot (1919–94), the third woman to win the Nobel prize in chemistry, awarded in 1964 for her X-ray analysis to elucidate the structure of complex molecules. She succeeded in 1969 in determining the crystalline structure of insulin. O.M. (1965).

Hofbauer, Imre (d. 1990), Hungarian-born artist, whose brilliance was portrayed in his compassionate studies of the down-trodden.

Hogarth, William (1697–1764), English engraver and painter, who satirised his time with character, humour, and power, especially in his *Harlot's Progress, Rake's Progress, Marriage à la Mode, Industry and Idleness,* and *The March to Finchley.*

Hogg, Quintin (1845–1903), educationist and philanthropist who purchased the old Polytechnic Institution in 1882 and turned it into a popular college providing education at moderate rates. His grandson, **Lord Hailsham** (1907–2001), was Lord Chancellor 1970–4, 1979–83, 1983–87.

Hokusai, Katsushika (1760–1849), Japanese landscape artist of the Ukiyo-e (popular school).

Holbein, Hans, the elder (c. 1465–1524), German painter, b. Augsburg, father of:

Holbein, Hans, the younger (1497–1543), German painter, b. Augsburg; settled in London 1532. He won the favour of Henry VIII, for whom he painted many portraits. He is also known for his series *The Dance of Death.*

Holden, Charles (1875–1960), British architect, designer of British Medical Association Building, London; Underground HQ; Senate House *etc.*

Holden, Sir Isaac (1807–97), British inventor of woolcombing machinery.

Hölderlin, Johann Christian Friedrich (1770–1843), German poet, friend of Hegel. His works include the novel *Hyperion* and the elegy *Menon's Laments for Diotima.* In his middle years his mind became unhinged.

Holford, Baron (William Graham Holford) (1907–75), British architect and town-planner.

Hollande François (b. 1954). French socialist. President of France, 2012–17.

Holmes, Dame Kelly (b. 1970), British athlete who took historic double at 2004 Olympics (800m and 1,500m titles).

Holmes, Oliver Wendell (1809–94), American author. His writings include *Autocrat of the Breakfast Table, The Professor of the Breakfast Table,* and *The Poet at the Breakfast Table.*

Holst, Gustave Theodore (1874–1934), British composer of Swedish descent whose compositions include *The Planets* suite, *The Hymn of Jesus,* an opera *The Perfect Fool,* and a choral symphony. An outstanding teacher. *See* Section P.

Holyoake, George Jacob (1817–1906), English social reformer and secularist. He wrote a history of the co-operative movement.

Holyoake, Keith Jacka (1904–83), New Zealand politician; prime minister 1960–72.

Home of the Hirsel, Lord (Alex Douglas-Home) (1903–95), British Prime Minister, 1963–64 (after renouncing his peerage as 14th Earl of Home). Foreign Secretary, 1960–63, 1970–74. Created Life Peer, 1974. His younger brother was the playwright **William Douglas-Home** (1912–92).

Homer (c. 700 B.C.), epic poet. He is supposed to have been a Greek who lived at Chios or Smyrna, and has been regarded as the author of the *Iliad* and the *Odyssey,* though this is traditional rather than ascertained fact.

Hood, 1st Viscount (Samuel Hood) (1724–1816), British admiral who in 1793 was in command of the Mediterranean fleet and occupied Toulon.

Hood, Thomas (1799–1845), English poet. His poems include *The Song of the Shirt, The Dream of Eugene Aram* and *The Bridge of Sighs.* He was also a humorist and punster.

Hooke, Robert (1635–1703), English polymath. His inventions include the balance spring of watches. He was also an architect and drew up a plan for rebuilding London after the Great Fire. His *Diary* is published. An inventive genius whose *Micrographia* was the world's first popular science book.

Hooker, Richard (1554–1600), English theologian, author of *Ecclesiastical Polity.* He was Master of the Temple, 1585–91. For his choice of words he was known as "Judicious Hooker".

Hope, Bob (**Leslie Townes**), (1903–2003), legendary entertainer. Born in Eltham, London, but raised in Ohio, USA. The quintessential comedian.

Hopkins, Sir Frederick Gowland (1861–1947), English biochemist, pioneer in biochemical and nutritional research. He first drew attention to the substances later known as vitamins. Pres. Royal Society 1930–5. Nobel prize 1929.

Hopkins, Gerard Manley (1844–89), English poet of religious experience and of a novel style.

Hopkins, Harry (1890–1946), Franklin Roosevelt's personal assistant at foreign conferences, and in the New Deal and Lend-Lease.

Hopkinson, John (1849–98), English engineer. By developing the theory of alternating current and of the magnetic current in dynamos he paved the way to the common use of electricity.

Hoppner, John (1758–1810), English portrait painter, b. Whitechapel, of German parents.

Horace (Quintus Horatius Flaccus) (65–8 B.C.), Roman satirist and poet, son of a Greek freedman. He wrote *Satires, Epodes, Odes,* and *Epistles.* He fought on the republican side at Philippi, but became poet laureate to Augustus.

Horniman, Annie Elizabeth Fredericka (1860–1937), founder of the modern repertory system in England. Her father F. J. Horniman founded the Horniman Museum.

Hosking, Eric (1909–91), famous bird photographer. A highly skilled ornithologist.

Hoskins, William George (1908–92), the great local historian of England and the English. Author of *The Making of the English Landscape* (1955).

Houdini, Harry (Erich Weiss) (1874–1926), American illusionist, son of a Hungarian rabbi. Famed for his escapes from handcuffs.

Housman, Alfred Edward (1859–1936), English poet, author of *A Shropshire Lad;* he was also a classical scholar. His brother Laurence (1865–1959) was a playwright and wrote *Little Plays of St. Francis* and *Victoria Regina.*

Howard, John (1726–90), English prison reformer. Imprisoned in France in wartime, he subsequently investigated English prisons, securing reforms; and later also continental prisons, dying in Russia of gaol fever.

Howard of Effingham, 2nd Baron (Charles Howard) (1536–1624), afterwards Earl of Nottingham; commanded the fleet which defeated the Spanish Armada (1588), and took part in the capture of Cadiz (1596).

Howe, Elias (1819–67), American inventor of the sewing machine.

Howe, Lord. *See* D17.

Howe, Julia Ward (1819–1910), American suffragette, author of *Mine eyes have seen the glory.*

Howe, 1st Earl (Richard Howe) (1726–99), British admiral whose victories over the French in two wars included that off Ushant on 1 June 1794 ("the glorious first of June").

Hoyle, Sir Fred (1915–2001), popular but controversial astronomer who coined the term 'Big Bang' (but denied that it had happened).

Hua Guofeng (1922–2008), b. Hunan, succeeded Mao Tse-tung as Communist Party Chairman, 1976–81.

Hubble, Edwin Powell (1889–1953), American astronomer. With the 100-inch telescope on Mount Wilson he detected the Cepheid variables. The Hubble space telescope was named after him.

Huddleston, Trevor (1913–98), Anglican archbishop who devoted his life to fighting apartheid.

Hudson, Henry (d. 1611), English navigator credited with the discovery of the Hudson river and Hudson Bay, where mutineers turned him adrift to die. He was on a voyage to find a passage by the north pole to Japan and China.

Hudson, William Henry (1841–1922), naturalist, b. Buenos Aires of American parents, naturalised in England (1900). His books include *The Purple Land, Green Mansions,* and *Far Away and Long Ago.* Hyde Park bird sanctuary was established in his memory.

Huggins, Sir William (1824–1910), astronomer who pioneered in spectroscopic photography.

Hughes, Ted (1930–98), English poet. Succeeded Sir John Betjeman as Poet Laureate in 1984. His early poems observed the natural world (as in the collection *The Hawk in the Rain*). O.M. (1998). One of the greatest poets of the 20th century.

Hughes, Thomas (1822–96), English novelist, author of *Tom Brown's Schooldays,* which is based on Rugby school.

Hugo, Victor Marie (1802–85), French poet, dramatist, and novelist, who headed the Romantic movement in France in the early 19th cent. His dramas include *Hernani, Lucrèce Borgia, Ruy Blas,* and *Le Roi s'amuse.* Of his novels *Notre Dame* belongs to his early period, *Les Misérables, Les Travailleurs de la mer,* and *L'Homme qui rit* were written in Guernsey.

Humboldt, Friedrich Heinrich Alexander, Baron von (1769–1859), German naturalist and explorer whose researches are recorded in *Voyage de Humboldt et Bonpland* (23 vols., 1805–34), and *Kosmos* (5 vols., 1845–62). He is now regarded as the father of ecology. He warned of deforestation and intensive farming.

Hume, Cardinal (George) Basil (1923–99), Catholic Benedictine monk. Archbishop of Westminster after 1976. Awarded Order of Merit (1999), the first Catholic prelate to receive this honour.

Hume, David (1711–76), Scottish philosopher. His main works are *Treatise of Human Nature, Dialogues Concerning Natural Religion* and *Enquiry concerning Human Understanding.*

Hunt, Holman (1827–1910), English artist, one of the founders of the Pre-Raphaelite movement. His pictures include *The Light of the World.*

Hunt, Baron (John Hunt) (1910–98), leader of the 1953 British Everest Expedition when Tenzing and Hillary reached the summit.

Hunt, Leigh (1784–1859), English poet and essayist. In 1813 he was fined and imprisoned for libelling the Prince Regent in *The Examiner.*

Hunter, Bob (1941–2005), Canadian pioneering environmental activist who co-founded Greenpeace.

Hus, Jan (1369–1415), Bohemian religious reformer. Strongly influenced by Wyclif, he urged reform both of abuses in the church and of doctrine. Sentenced to death or recantation, he suffered martyrdom on 6 July 1415. His death caused a civil war which lasted many years.

Hussein, King (1935–99), King of Jordan, 1952–99. A symbol of stability in the Middle East.

Hussein, Saddam (1938–2006), dictator of Iraq from 1979 to 2003. Launched the war with Iran in 1980 and the invasion of Kuwait, 1990. The invasion of 2003 ended his regime. He was captured on 13 December 2003 and sentenced to death by hanging after being tried.

Hutton, James (1726–97), an Edinburgh doctor who founded modern geological theory.

Hutton, Sir Leonard (1916–90), foremost English cricketer. Captained England 23 times, scoring 364 in 1938 against Australia.

Huxley, Aldous (1894–1963), English novelist, author of *Brave New World.*

Huxley, Sir Julian (1887–1975), biologist and writer, grandson of T. H. Huxley and brother of Aldous; first director general of UNESCO 1946–8; a founder of the International Union for the Conservation of Nature and the World Wild Life Fund.

Huxley, Thomas Henry (1825–95), English biologist. He started life as assistant-surgeon on H.M.S. *Rattlesnake* and during the voyage (1846–50) studied marine organisms. After the publication of Darwin's *Origin of Species* he became an ardent evolutionist, being known as 'Darwin's Bulldog'. He coined the term "agnostic".

Huygens, Christian (1629–95), Dutch mathematician, physicist, and astronomer, son of the poet **Constantijn Huygens** (1596–1687); discovered the rings of Saturn, invented the pendulum clock, and developed the wave theory of light in opposition to Newton's corpuscular theory.

Hyde, Douglas (1860–1949), Irish scholar, historian, poet, and folk-lorist; first president of Ireland in the 1937 constitution, 1938–45.

Hypatia of Alexandria, most famous woman mathematician of antiquity. She excited the enmity of Christian fanatics. Murdered in A.D. 415.

I

Ibsen, Henrik Johan (1828–1906), Norwegian playwright and poet, who dealt with social and psychological problems and revolutionised the European theatre. His chief works are *Ghosts, The Wild Duck, The Master Builder, A Doll's House, Hedda Gabler* and the poetic drama, *Peer Gynt.*

Ingres, Jean Auguste Dominique (1780–1867), French historical and classical painter. His *La grande odalisque* is in the Louvre.

Innocent III (c. 1160–1216), Pope 1198–1216. He asserted the power and moral force of the papacy over the Emperor Otto IV, Philip II of France, and John of England. He launched the fourth crusade, encouraged the crusade against the Albigensian heretics, and held the 4th Lateran council. His pontificate marks the zenith of the medieval papacy.

Ionesco, Eugene (1912–94), French playwright of the Absurd, b. Romania, whose plays include *The Bald Prima Donna, The Chairs* and *Rhinoceros.*

Iqbal, Sir Muhammad (1877–1938), poet-philosopher, b. Sialkot (Pakistan). He wrote both poetry and prose in Urdu, Persian, and English, and his work is marked by mystic nationalism.

Ireland, John (1879–1962), English composer, popularly known for his setting of Masefield's *Sea Fever,* but also a noted composer.

Irving, Sir Henry (1838–1905), English actor. At the Lyceum theatre from 1871, later with Ellen Terry, he gave notable Shakespearean performances, especially as Shylock and Malvolio. First actor to be knighted.

Irving, Washington (1783–1859), American essayist, whose works include *Tales of a Traveller* and *The Sketch Book* as well as biographies.

Isabella of Castile (1451–1504), reigned jointly with her husband, Ferdinand II of Aragon, over a united Spain, from which the Moors and the Jews were expelled. During their reign the New World was discovered.

Isherwood, Christopher. *See* **M30(1).**

Ismail Pasha (1830–95), grandson of Mehemet Ali, was Khedive of Egypt. Under him the Suez canal was made, but his financial recklessness led to Anglo-French control.

Ismay, 1st Baron (Hastings Lionel Ismay) (1887–1965), British general who was chief of staff to Sir Winston Churchill in the second world war.

Ito, Hirobumi, Prince (1841–1909). Japanese statesman, four times PM. He was assassinated.

Ivan the Great (1410–1505) brought the scattered provinces of Muscovy under one control and put an end to Tartar rule.

Ivan the Terrible (1530–84), crowned as first Tsar of Russia in 1547. An autocratic ruler.

J

Jackson, Andrew (1767–1845), American general who was twice president of the United States.

Jackson, Michael (1958–2009), the 'King of Pop'. One of the greatest entertainers of all time. *See* **P26.**

Jackson, Thomas Jonathan (1824–63), "Stonewall Jackson," was general on the Southern side in the American Civil War; killed at Chancellorsville.

Jacobs, William Wymark (1863–1943), English novelist, b. London, author of humorous sea and other stories.

Jacquard, Joseph Marie (1752–1834), French inventor whose loom provided an effective method of weaving designs.

Jagger, Sir Mick (Michael) (b. 1943), one of the legends of rock music. Formed the Rolling Stones (debut in 1962). The 'ultimate rock and roll rebel'.

Jahangir (1569–1627), 3rd Mogul emperor and patron of art.

James I (1566–1625), King of England (1603–25) and, as James VI, King of Scotland (1567–1625). He was the son of Mary Stuart and succeeded to the English throne on the death of Elizabeth I. His reign saw the Gunpowder Plot of 1605 and the publication of the Authorised Version of the Bible, but it also marked an increasingly critical attitude by the Puritans. Described as "the wisest fool in Christendom."

James II (1633–1701), King of England and, as James VII, King of Scotland (1685–8), was the younger son of Charles I. Personally honest, and an able admiral, he lacked political understanding; and when, having put down Monmouth's rebellion, he tried and failed to obtain better conditions for his fellow Roman Catholics, he was obliged in 1688 to flee the country.

James, Cyril Lionel Robert (1901–89), Trinidadian historian, literary critic, political theorist and cricket writer. Author of *Nkrumah and the Ghana Revolution* (1977) and *Spheres of Existence* (1980).

James, Henry (1843–1916), American novelist. He lived mainly in England. His work, noted for intellectual subtlety and characterisation, includes *The American, Daisy Miller, The Portrait of a Lady, What Maisie Knew, The Spoils of Poynton* etc.

James, William (1842–1910), American psychologist and philosopher, brother of Henry. He was a protagonist of the theory of pragmatism developed by his friend C. S. Peirce, and invented "radical empiricism." His major works are *The Principles of Psychology, The Will to Believe,* and *The Meaning of Truth.*

Janáček, Leoš (1854–1928), Czech composer and conductor, and student of folk music, b. in Moravia, son of a village schoolmaster, creator of a national style. His works include the opera *Jenufa. See* **Section P.**

Jaurès, Jean (1859–1914), French socialist leader and writer. Assassinated by nationalist fanatic, 1914.

Jefferies, Richard (1848–87), English naturalist of poetic perception, b. in Wiltshire, author of *Gamekeeper at Home* and *The Life of the Fields.*

Jefferson, Thomas (1743–1826), American president, 1801–9. He created the Republican Party, by which the federalists, led by Hamilton, were overthrown, and helped to draft the Declaration of Independence. He tried unsuccessfully to bring an end to slavery. He negotiated the Louisiana Purchase of 1803.

Jeffreys, 1st Baron (George Jeffreys) (1648–89), English judge who held the "bloody assize" after Monmouth's unsuccessful rebellion. In 1686 he was sent to the Tower and there died.

Jeffreys, Sir Alec (b. 1950), Professor of Genetics, University of Leicester. He pioneered genetic fingerprinting.

Jellicoe, 1st Earl (John Rushworth Jellicoe) (1859–1935), British admiral. He fought the indecisive battle of Jutland in 1916, after which the German fleet remained in harbour.

Jenkins, Lord (Roy Jenkins) (1920–2003), British politician, b. Wales; Pres. EEC Commission 1977–80; Home Sec. 1965–7; Chanc. of Exchequer 1967–70. Leader, SDP 1982–June 1983. O.M. (1993). Chaired Commission on Voting System, 1997–8.

Jenner, Edward (1749–1823), English physician, b. in Gloucs., pupil of John Hunter. His discovery of vaccination against smallpox (1798) helped to lay the foundations of modern immunology. The 'father of immunology'. he was the first to describe the parasitism of the cuckoo.

Jerne, Niels Kai (1911–94), Danish microbiologist and Nobel laureate.

Jerome, Jerome Klapka (1859–1927), English humorous writer, author of *Three Men in a Boat.*

Jerome, St. (*c.* 331–420), scholar who translated the Bible into Latin (the Vulgate).

Jesus Christ (c. 4 B.C.–A.D. 30). *See* **Section J** under **Christianity.**

Jiang Zemin (b. 1926), Chinese politician. State President of China, 1993–2003. He continued the economic policies of Deng Xiaoping.

Jinnah, Mohammed Ali (1876–1948), Pakistani statesman. B. at Karachi, he became president of the Muslim League, and succeeded in 1947 in establishing the Dominion of Pakistan, becoming its first governor-general.

Joachim, Joseph (1831–1907), Hungarian violinist and composer.

Joan of Arc, St. (Jeanne d'Arc) (1412–31), French patriot, called the Maid of Orleans; of peasant parentage (she was b. at Domrémy), she believed herself called to save France from English domination; and by her efforts Charles VII was crowned at Rheims in 1429. Captured by the Burgundians and sold to the English; burned as a heretic; canonised in 1920. Recent research has cast doubt on many accounts of events in her life.

Jobs, Steve (1955–2011), US computer visionary. Co-founder, Apple, 1976. His devices shaped the way we work and play.

Joffre, Joseph Jacques Césaire (1852–1931), French general. He was commander-in-chief of the French army in the 1914–18 war.

John (1167–1216), youngest son of Henry II, was King of England from 1199. Able but depraved and hopeless in war, he lost Normandy. Baronial opposition to him, under the influence of Archbishop Stephen Langton, acquired a national character, and in 1215 he was obliged to seal Magna Carta. He died of dysentry.

John of Gaunt (1340–99), Duke of Lancaster, son of Edward III and father of Henry IV.

John XXIII, St (1881–1963), elected Pope in 1958, succeeding Pius XII, was formerly Cardinal Angelo Giuseppe Roncalli, patriarch of Venice. He sought to bring the Church closer to modern needs. He was made a saint in 2014.

John Paul II, St. (1920–2005), succeeded Pope John Paul I after his sudden death in 1978; formerly Cardinal Karol Wojtyla, archbishop of Cracow; first Pope to come from Poland. Assassination attempt made 1981. Presided over the Catholic Church during the fall of communism, but grew increasingly conservative with age. Beatified, 1 May 2011. The fastest beatification in church history. He achieved sainthood in 2014. He himself created a record 482 saints during his papacy.

John, Augustus (1878–1961), British painter and etcher, b. in Wales: noted for his portraits.

John, Sir Elton (b. 1947), born Reginald Kenneth Dwight. Rock singer and pianist. Knighted (1998).

Johnson, Amy (1904–41), was the first woman aviator to fly solo from England to Australia.

Johnson, Boris. *See* **D17.**

Johnson, Lyndon Baines (1908–73), President of the United States, 1963–9. He became president on Kennedy's assassination and followed a progressive policy at home, but his achievements were clouded by the war in Vietnam.

Johnson, Samuel (1709–84), English lexicographer and man of letters, b. at Lichfield. His *Dictionary* was published in 1755, and was followed by *Rasselas, The Idler* (a periodical), and *Lives of the Poets.* He was a focus of London literary life of his day. His biographer was James Boswell.

Joliot-Curie, Jean Frédéric (1900–58), and his wife Irène (1896–1956), French scientists who discovered artificial radioactivity. Nobel prizewinners 1935. Joliot-Curie was one of the discoverers of nuclear fission. **Irène** was the daughter of Pierre and Marie Curie. Both were communists, and both died from cancer caused by their work.

Jones, Ernest Charles (1819–69), English Chartist leader and poet.

Jones, Sir Harold Spencer (1890–1960), British astronomer royal, 1935–55. His major research was to determine the mean distance of the earth from the sun, 93,004,000 miles.

Jones, Inigo (1573–1652), architect of the English renaissance who studied in Italy and inspired the use of Palladian forms in England. His buildings include the banqueting hall in Whitehall and the queen's house at Greenwich. He designed furniture and brought the proscenium arch and movable scenery onto our stage. *See* **N17(2).**

Jones, Jack (1913–2009). Lifelong socialist and trade unionist. General Secretary, TGWU, 1969–78.

Jonson, Ben (1573–1637), English poet and dramatist. His plays include *Every Man in his Humour, Volpone* and *The Alchemist*; and his poem *Drink to me only with thine Eyes. See* **M9.**

Josephine, Empress (1763–1814), wife of Napoleon I, *née* de la Pagerie, she was previously married to the Vicomte de Beauharnais. She was divorced from Napoleon in 1809.

Josephus, Flavius (38–c. 100), Jewish historian, author of *History of the Jewish War.*

Joule, James Prescott (1818–89), English physicist, pupil of Dalton, who researched on electromagnetism and determined the mechanical equivalent of heat. See **Section L.**

Jowett, Benjamin (1817–93), English scholar. He translated Plato's *Dialogues*, and he was an influential Master of Balliol College, Oxford.

Jowitt, Earl (William Allen Jowitt) (1885–1957), British Labour politician and Lord Chancellor.

Joyce, James (1882–1941), Irish author, b. Dublin. His *Ulysses* gives a microscopic picture of a day in the life of two Irishmen, and flouted the conventions of his day. Other works include *Portrait of the Artist* and *Finnegans Wake.* He spent most of his life on the Continent. His acclaimed short stories include *Dubliners* (1914).

Julian of Norwich (**Mother Julian**) (c. 1342–1413), author of the long-suppressed *Revelation of Divine Love*, the first book written by a woman in English. A mystic.

Julian the Apostate (331–63), Roman emperor who tried to restore paganism in the empire. He was killed in war against Persia.

Jung, Carl Gustav (1875–1961), Swiss psychiatrist. A pupil of Freud, he later formulated his own system of analytical psychology. See **Section J.**

Junot, Andoche (1771–1813), French general defeated by Wellington in the Peninsular War.

Jusserand, Jean Jules (1855–1932), French author and diplomat, who wrote on English literature and wayfaring life in the Middle Ages.

Justinian I (483–565), Roman emperor in the East. He and his wife Theodora beautified Constantinople, and his general Belisarius was successful in war. He codified Roman law.

Juvenal (60–140), Roman poet and Stoic, remembered for his *Satires.*

K

Kafka, Franz (1883–1924), German-speaking Jewish writer, b. Prague, whose introspective work, the bulk of which was not published till after his early death from tuberculosis, has had a notable influence on later schools, especially the surrealists. It includes the three novels *The Trial, The Castle,* and *America.*

Kālidāsa (c. A.D. 400), chief figure in classic Sanskrit literature. Seven works survive: two lyrics, *Ritu-samhara* (The Seasons), and *Megha-dūta* (Cloud Messenger); two epics, *Raghu-vamsa* (Dynasty of Raghu) and *Kumara-sambhava* (Birth of the War-god); and three dramas, *Sakūntalā, Mālavikāg-nimitra,* and *Vikramorvasīya.*

Kandinsky, Wasily (1866–1944) Russian-born painter, a leader of the *Blaue Reiter* group. A pioneer of abstract art.

Kane, Bob (1915–98), American cartoonist who created Batman, the caped crusader.

Kant, Immanuel (1724–1804), German philosopher, author of *Critique of Pure Reason* (1781), *Critique of Practical Reason* (1788), and *Critique of Judgement* (1790). He came from a Pietist family of Königsberg, where he lectured, but the Prussian government forbade his lectures as anti-Lutheran. He was influenced by the writings of Hamann (*see* **Romanticism, Section J**) and by Rousseau and Hume, and his own work greatly shaped future liberal thought. He believed in the freedom of man to make his own decisions and considered the exploitation of man as the worst evil.

Kapitza, Pyotr (1894–1984), Russian physicist who worked on atomic research with Rutherford at the Cavendish Laboratory, Cambridge, and returned to Russia in 1935. Nobel Prize for Physics, 1978.

Kapoor, Sir Anish (b. 1954). Outstanding British-Indian artist and sculptor. His works include *Cloud Gate* in Chicago. A Turner Prize winner.

Kauffman, Angelica (1741–1807), Anglo-Swiss portrait painter, a foundation member of the Royal Academy and the first woman R.A.

Kaulbach, Wilhelm von (1805–74), German painter who illustrated the works of Goethe and Schiller.

Kaunda, Kenneth (b. 1924), African leader of international standing, son of Christian missionaries. He was president of Zambia, 1964–91.

Kean, Charles John (1811–68), English actor-manager son of **Edmund**. He married Ellen Tree. In the 1850s played with her in spectacular revivals at the Princess's Theatre, London.

Kean, Edmund (1787–1833), English tragic actor. He made his name as Shylock.

Keats, John (1795–1821), English poet who in his short life produced poems notable for richness of imagination and beauty of thought. They include *Odes, Isabella,* and *The Eve of St. Agnes.*

Keble, John (1792–1866), English clergyman associated with the Tractarian movement (*See* **Section J**) and author of *The Christian Year.*

Keller, Helen Adams (1880–1968), American author and lecturer who overcame great physical handicaps (blind and deaf before the age of two) to live an active and useful life.

Kelly, Ned (1855–80), most famous of the Australian bushranger outlaws—to some a revolutionary martyr, to others a cold-blooded killer.

Kelvin of Largs, 1st Baron (William Thomson) (1824–1907), British mathematician and physicist, b. Belfast, known for his work on heat and thermodynamics, and contributions to electrical science and submarine telegraphy. In the domain of heat he stands to Joule as Maxwell stands to Faraday in the history of electrical science. He introduced the Kelvin or Absolute scale of temperature and was one of the original members of the Order of Merit.

Kemble, Fanny (1809–93), actress from a noted theatrical family, her father and uncle respectively being the actors Charles Kemble and John Philip Kemble, and her aunt, Mrs. Siddons.

Kempenfelt, Richard (1718–82), English admiral, who sank with his ship the *Royal George* together with 600 of the ship's company off Spithead when it capsized.

Kempis, Thomas à (1380–1471), name by which the German mystic Thomas Hammerken was known, was a monk of the Augustinian order, whose life was mainly spent in a monastery near Zwolle. The author of *The Imitation of Christ.*

Kennedy, John Fitzgerald (1917–63), President of the USA, 1961–3, the youngest and the first Roman Catholic to be elected; son of a financier. He had world-wide pre-eminence and gave the American people a sense of purpose to meet the challenges of a scientific age. He opposed racial discrimination and initiated a new era of East–West relations; but his foreign policy sowed the seeds of the Vietnam war. He and his brother **Robert** (1925–68) were assassinated, the latter while campaigning for the presidency in 1968. Robert Kennedy was Attorney General, 1961–64 and promoted the Civil Rights Act. The third brother, **Edward** (1932–2009) was a liberal lion, one of the greatest and longest-serving Senators of his generation.

Kent, William (1684–1748), English painter, furniture designer, landscape gardener, and architect, protégé of Lord Burlington, whose buildings include the great hall at Holkham and the Horse Guards, Whitehall.

Kenyatta, Jomo (1893–1978), African leader who became president of Kenya in 1964.

Kepler, Johann (1571–1630), German astronomer and mystic, for a short time assistant to Tycho Brahe whose measurements he used in working out his laws of planetary motion, which are: 1. Planets move round the sun not in circles, but in ellipses, the sun being one of the foci. 2. A planet moves not uniformly but in such a way that a line drawn from it to the sun sweeps out equal areas of the ellipse in equal times. 3. The squares of the period of revolution round the sun are proportional to the cubes of the distances. Newton explained these laws.

Kerensky, Alexander (1881–1970), Russian politician. Prime Minister of Provisional Government, 1917.

Kerouac, Jack (1922–58), American iconic novelist and poet. Champion of the Beat Generation. Born Lowell, Mass. of French-American parents.

Kerry, John (b. 1943), US Democrat. Secretary of State, 2013–17. Defeated in 2004 presidential election.

Ketèlbey, Albert (1875–1959), British composer and conductor of many well-known compositions.

Keyes, 1st Baron (Roger John Brownlow Keyes) (1872–1945), British admiral who led the raid on Zeebrugge in 1918.

Keynes, 1st Baron (John Maynard Keynes) (1883–1946), British economist, who was a Treasury representative at the Versailles peace conference, and published his views in *The Economic Consequences of the Peace*. Author of *Treatise on Money* (1930) and *The General Theory of Employment, Interest and Money* (1936).

Khachaturian, Aram Ilich (1903–78), Armenian-born composer who wrote the popular *Sabre Dance* and *Spartacus* (from which the Love Theme was used in TV's Onedin Line.)

Khomeini, Ayatollah (1900–89), Iranian religious leader. After 16 years in exile, returned to Iran in 1979 after the overthrow of the Shah. Architect of Islamic Republic of Iran. Anti-Western.

Khrushchev, Nikita Sergeyevich (1894–1971), Russian statesman who became leader of the Soviet Union soon after the death of Stalin; first secretary of the Soviet Communist Party, 1953–64; effective leader, 1958–64. After the harsh years of the Stalinist régime he pursued a policy of relaxation in home and foreign affairs.

Kierkegaard, Sören (1813–55), Danish philosopher and religious thinker, whose views have influenced existentialism. His main work is *Either-Or*.

King, Mackenzie (1874–1950), prime minister of Canada, 1921–5, 1926–30, and 1935–48.

King, Martin Luther (1929–68), American clergyman and black civil rights leader; awarded the 1964 Nobel peace prize for his consistent support of the principle of non-violence in the black people's struggle for civil rights. Assassinated at Memphis, Tennessee.

King, Stephen (b. 1947), American writer of horror stories. Born Portland, Maine. His first novel *Carrie* established his world-wide reputation.

Kingsley, Charles (1819–75), English clergyman and novelist, author of *Hypatia*, *Westward Ho!*, *Hereward the Wake* and *The Water Babies*.

Kinnock, Lord (Neil Kinnock), (b. 1942), Labour politician. Leader of the Labour Party 1983–92. Reshaped the party for the 1992 election but resigned after he lost. Later EU Commissioner (with responsibility for Transport), 1995–9. Vice-President of the Commission, 1999–2004.

Kinsey, Alfred (1894–1956). Sexologist. Founder, Institute of Sex Research at Indiana University. His work led to more liberal attitudes to homosexuality, more relaxed divorce laws *etc.*

Kipling, Rudyard (1865–1936), British writer, b. Bombay. His vivid work portrays contemporary British rule in India and includes *The Light that Failed*, *Stalky and Co., Kim*, and the *Barrack Room Ballads*. Among his books for children are the *Just So Stories*, *Puck of Pook's Hill* and the *Jungle Books*. Nobel prize 1907.

Kirchhoff, Gustav Robert (1824–87), German mathematical physicist, who with R. W. Bunsen discovered that in the gaseous state each chemical substance emits its own characteristic spectrum (1859). He was able to explain Fraunhofer's map of the solar spectrum. Using the spectroscope, he and Bunsen discovered the elements caesium and rubidium.

Kissinger, Henry (b. 1923), American Secretary of State 1973–7; inventor of shuttle diplomacy. Shared Nobel peace prize for 1973 with Le Duc Tho.

Kitchener of Khartoum, 1st Earl (Horatio Herbert Kitchener) (1850–1916), English general. In 1898 he won back the Sudan for Egypt by his victory at Omdurman. He served in the South African war. Secretary of State for War, 1914–16. He was drowned on his way to Russia.

Klee, Paul (1879–1940), Swiss artist, whose paintings are delicate dream-world fantasies.

Klemperer, Otto (1885–1973), German-born conductor, renowned as interpreter of the Beethoven symphonies. Expelled by the Nazis he became an American citizen and returned to Europe in 1946. He had been principal conductor of the Philharmonic Orchestra since 1959.

Klimt, Gustav (1862–1918), Viennese painter of such works as *The Kiss, Death and Life, Danaë etc.*

Kneale, Nigel (1922–2006), writer whose paranormal tales included *The Quatermass Experiment*.

Kneller, Sir Godfrey (1646–1723), portrait painter, b. at Lübeck, who settled in England and was patronised by successive English sovereigns.

Knox, John (1514–72), Scottish reformer, b. near Haddington. While in exile at Geneva he was influenced by Calvin. On return to Scotland he was a leader of the reforming party under Mary, Queen of Scots. He wrote a *History of the Reformation in Scotland*.

Koch, Robert (1843–1910), German bacteriologist who discovered the bacillus of tuberculosis.

Kodály, Zoltán (1882–1967), Hungarian composer and teacher. *See* Section P.

Kohl, Helmut (1930–2017), Chancellor of the Federal Republic of Germany until defeated in 1998. First Chancellor of re-united Germany after 1990. Narrowly re-elected Chancellor, 1994. A Christian Democrat who in November 1996 became the longest-serving Chancellor in German history (except for Bismarck).

Kokoschka, Oskar (1886–1980), Austrian portrait and landscape painter. Settled in England.

Korolyov, Sergei (1907–66), Russian space scientist, who designed the world's first earth satellite, manned spaceship and moon rocket.

Kosciusko, Tadeusz (1746–1817), Polish patriot. After fighting in the US War of Independence, he led his people against Russia in 1792 and 1794 in opposition to the partition of Poland.

Kossuth, Louis (1802–94), Hungarian patriot, who in 1848 led a rising of his countrymen against the Hapsburg dynasty, but had to flee to Turkey and later to England.

Kosygin, Alexei Nikolayevich (1904–80), succeeded Khrushchev in 1964 as chairman of the Council of Ministers of the USSR (prime minister).

Krebs, Sir Hans (1900–81), British biochemist, b. Germany. He became Professor of Biology at Oxford in 1954. Nobel prize 1953.

Kreisler, Fritz (1875–1962), Austrian violinist, who composed violin music and an operetta. He became an American citizen in 1943.

Krenek, Ernst (1900–91), Austrian-American composer of partly Czech descent, whose compositions include the jazz opera *Jonny spielt auf*.

Kropotkin, Peter, Prince (1842–1921), Russian anarchist, geographer and explorer, who was imprisoned for favouring the political action of a working men's association, but escaped to England. He wrote on socialistic and geographical subjects. Returned to Russia, 1917.

Kruger, Stephanus Johannes Paulus (1825–1904), Boer leader, who in 1881 was appointed head of the provisional government against Britain, and later president. When the war of 1899–1902 turned against the Boers, he vainly sought help in Europe.

Krupp, Alfred (1812–87), founder of the German gun factories at Essen. He began to make cast steel, and from 1844 specialised in armaments. The firm's factories made the Big Bertha guns which shelled Paris in 1918.

Krylov, Ivan Andreyevich (1768–1844), Russian writer of fables (the Russian La Fontaine).

Kubelik, Jan (1880–1940), Czech violinist who at the age of 12 played in public.

Kublai Khan (1216–94), grandson of Genghis Khan, was the first Mongol emperor of China. He extended the Mongol empire by conquest, and lived in unparalleled splendour. His court was described by Marco Polo and is the subject of a poem by Coleridge.

Kuiper, Gerard Peter (1905–73), Dutch astronomer and founder of modern planetary astronomy. The Kuiper Belt is named after him.

Kun, Bela (1886–*c.* 1939), Hungarian communist revolutionary. Led brief Hungarian government.

L

La Fayette, Marie Joseph Paul Roch Yves Gilbert du Motier, Marquis de (1757–1834), French soldier and statesman. He fought for the colonists in the American War of Independence; and in the 1789 French revolution he proposed a declaration of rights and was commander of the National Guard till his moderation made him unpopular. When the monarchy was restored he was an opposition leader, and took part in the revolution of 1830. Posthumously awarded American citizenship.

La Fontaine, Jean de (1621–95), French poet and fabulist, a friend of Molière, Boileau and Racine.

Lagerlöf, Selma (1858–1940), Swedish novelist and first woman member of the Swedish Academy. Nobel prizewinner 1909.

Lagrange, Joseph Louis, Comte (1736–1813), French mathematician, of Turin and Paris, whose interest in astronomy led him to distinguish two types of disturbance of members of the solar system, the periodic and the secular. He was called by Frederick the Great to Berlin to succeed Euler.

Lalande, Joseph Jerome LeFrançais de (1732–1807), French astronomer, author of *Traité d'astronomie*.

Lamarck, Jean Baptiste Pierre Antoine de Monet de (1744–1829), French biologist whose explanation of evolution was that new organs are brought into being by the needs of the organism in adapting to its environment and that the new characters acquired during its life-time can be passed on to the offspring through heredity, resulting in evolutionary change.

Lamb, Charles (1775–1834), English essayist, b. London. A clerk in the East India Office, he devoted his life to his sister Mary, who was of unstable mind. He is chiefly known for his *Essays of Elia*, and his letters.

Lambert, Constant (1905–51), English composer and critic, and conductor of Sadler's Wells ballet. His *Rio Grande* is in jazz idiom.

Landor, Walter Savage (1775–1864), English writer, b. Warwick, remembered for his *Imaginary Conversations* and poems.

Landseer, Sir Edwin (1802–73), English animal painter. He painted the *Monarch of the Glen* and designed the lions in Trafalgar Square.

Lane, Sir Allen (1902–70), English publisher who founded Penguin Books Ltd. in 1935.

Lane, Edward William (1801–76), English Arabic scholar, translator of the *Arabian Nights*.

Lanfranc (c. 1005–89), ecclesiastic. B. at Pavia, he became a prior in Normandy, and in 1070 an energetic archbishop of Canterbury.

Lang, Andrew (1844–1912), Scottish man of letters, whose output includes poems, fairy-tales *etc*.

Lang, 1st Baron (Cosmo Gordon Lang) (1864–1945), was archbishop of Canterbury, 1928–42.

Langland, William (1330?–1400?), English poet, author of *The Vision of Piers the Plowman. See* **M4**.

Langton, Stephen (1151–1228), archbishop of Canterbury. Adviser to the insurgent barons who induced King John to grant Magna Carta.

Lansbury, George (1859–1940), British Labour politician, founder of the *Daily Herald*.

Lâo Tsze (old philosopher) (c. 600 B.C.), traditional founder of Taoism in China. *See* **Section J**.

Laplace, Pierre Simon, Marquis de (1749–1827), French mathematician and astronomer, author of *Celestial Mechanics* (1799–1825). He believed that the solar system had condensed out of a vast rotating gaseous nebula.

Lara, Brian Charles (b. 1969), West Indies cricketer. Born Trinidad. An accomplished batsman who made the highest-ever score in test cricket (400 not out against England at Antigua in 2004).

Larkin, Philip (1922–85), the 'pre-eminent poet of common experience'. Declined Poet Laureateship, 1984.

La Rochefoucauld, François, Duc de (1613–80), French author of *Reflections and Moral Maxims*.

Larwood, Harold (1904–95), English cricketer, the most celebrated fast bowler of his time. At the centre of the 1932–3 'Bodyline' controversy.

Lasker, Emanuel (1868–1941), German chess player, world champion, 1894–1921.

Lassalle, Ferdinand (1825–64), German socialist who took part in the revolutionary movement of 1848 and organised workers movements.

Lassus, Orlandus (Lasso, Orlando di) (c. 1532–94), Flemish composer and choirmaster, contemporary of Palestrina, writer of *chansons*, madrigals, and sacred music. *See* **Section P**.

Latimer, Hugh (c. 1485–1555), English Protestant martyr, became bishop of Worcester in 1535, and was executed under Queen Mary.

Laud, William (1573–1645), archbishop of Canterbury and adviser to Charles I. His attempt to get conformity for his high church policy made him hated. He was impeached and beheaded.

Lauder, Sir Harry (1870–1950), Scottish comic singer who also wrote *Roamin' in the Gloamin'*.

Laval, Pierre (1883–1945), French politician who collaborated with the Germans, 1940–45.

Lavoisier, Antoine Laurent (1743–94), French chemist, b. Paris, was the first to establish the fact that combustion is a form of chemical action. We owe the word *oxygen* to him.

Law, Andrew Bonar (1858–1923), Conservative politician, prime minister 1922–3.

Lawrence, David Herbert (1885–1930), English poet and novelist, b. Notts., a miner's son. He tried to interpret emotion on a deeper level of consciousness. His works, which have had wide influence, include *The White Peacock, Sons and Lovers, The Rainbow, Women in Love*, and *Lady Chatterley's Lover*; his plays had to wait half a century before coming to the stage in the 1960s.

Lawrence, Sir Thomas (1769–1830), English portrait painter.

Lawrence, Thomas Edward (1888–1935) (Lawrence of Arabia), British soldier who led the Arabs against the Turks in the war of 1914–18, and wrote *The Seven Pillars of Wisdom*. Born in North Wales near Porthmadog.

Leacock, Stephen (1869–1944), Canadian humorist.

Leakey, Mary (1913–96), archaeologist and palaeoanthropologist. *See* **T53(2)**.

Lear, Edward (1812–88), famous author of 'nonsense' verse (*e.g. The Owl and the Pussycat*).

Leavis, Frank Raymond (1895–1978), British critic, who edited *Scrutiny*, 1932–53, and whose works include *The Great Tradition, D. H. Lawrence, Novelist*, and *"Anna Karenina" and Other Essays*.

Leclerc, Jacques Philippe (Philippe, Comte de Hautecloque) (1902–47), French general. He led a Free French force in Africa in the second world war and liberated Paris in 1944.

Le Corbusier (1887–1965), pseudonym of Charles Edouard Jeanneret, Swiss architect, whose books and work (especially his Unité d'Habitation at Marseilles and the Punjab capital at Chandigarh) have influenced town-planning.

Le Duc Tho (1911–90), North Vietnamese politician. Chief negotiator, Vietnam truce talks 1970–3.

Lee of Fareham, 1st Viscount (Arthur Hamilton Lee) (1868–1947), British politician who presented Chequers Court to the nation.

Lee, Sir Christopher (1922–2015), actor famous for playing Dracula and other sinister roles.

Lee, Harper (1926–2016), publicity-shy US authoress of *To Kill A Mocking Bird* (1960) and its sequel *Go Set A Watchman* (2015).

Lee Kuan Yew (1923–2015). First Prime Minister of Singapore, 1959–90. Helped establish prosperity of Singapore, but little opposition was tolerated.

Lee, Laurie (1914–97), poet and writer of autobiographical books about his Gloucestershire childhood and his experiences in Spain in the 1930s. *Cider with Rosie* (1959) has become a modern classic.

Lee, Robert Edward (1807–70), American Confederate general in the Civil War, who made the surrender at Appomattox.

Leech, John (1817–64), Humorous artist and political cartoonist who contributed numerous drawings to *Punch*. He illustrated Surtees' novels and Dickens's *A Christmas Carol*.

Lehár, Franz (1870–1948), Hungarian composer. Among his most popular operettas are *The Merry Widow* and *The Count of Luxembourg*.

Leibniz, Gottfried Wilhelm (1646–1716), German philosopher and mathematician, who invented the differential and integral calculus (1684) independently of Newton whose previous work on the same subject was not published until 1687. Leibniz's nomenclature was adopted.

Leicester, Earl of (Robert Dudley) (1533–88), English soldier, commanded English troops in the Netherlands, 1585–7, without much success, and in 1588 commanded forces assembled against the Armada. He was husband of Amy Robsart.

Leif Ericsson (fl. 1000), discoverer of Vinland on the north-east coast of America; b. Iceland, son of Eric the Red, who colonised Greenland.

Leighton, 1st Baron (Frederic Leighton) (1830–96), English painter whose works include *Paolo and Francesca*. He was also a sculptor.

Leland, John (c. 1506–52). Librarian and antiquarian. The 'father of topography'.

Lely, Sir Peter (Pieter van der Faes) (1618–80), Dutch court painter who settled in London.

Lenin (Vladimir Ilyich Ulyanov) (1870–1924), Russian revolutionary leader and statesman. From 1893 to 1917 he worked underground in Russia and abroad for the revolutionary cause. During this time the Social-Democratic party was formed; within it developed an uncompromising revolutionary group, the Bolsheviks, and of this group Lenin was the leading spirit. In April 1917 he and his fellow exiles returned; after the November revolution he headed the new government having to face both war and anarchy. In 1921 his "new economic policy" somewhat modified the intensive drive towards planned industrialisation. He was born in Simbirsk (later Ulyanovsk) on the middle Volga. He died after his fourth stroke on 21 January 1924.

Lennon, John. *See* **Beatles**.

Leonardo da Vinci (1452–1519), Italian artist and man of science, son of a Florentine lawyer and a peasant. He described himself (when applying to

Lodovico Sforza, Duke of Milan, for the post of city planner) as painter, architect, philosopher, poet, composer, sculptor, athlete, mathematician, inventor, and anatomist. His artistic output is small in quantity, and he is best known for his *Last Supper* in the refectory of Santa Maria delle Grazie in Milan and his *Mona Lisa* in the Louvre. He recorded his scientific work in unpublished notebooks written from right to left in mirror writing. The anatomy of the body (himself carrying out dissections), the growth of the child in the womb, the laws of waves, and the laws of flight, were all studied by him.

Leoncavallo, Ruggiero (1858–1919), Italian composer of the opera *Pagliacci*.

Leonidas was king of Sparta at the time of the invasion of Greece by Xerxes (480 B.C.), and who died defending the pass of Thermopylae.

Lermontov, Mikhail Yurevich (1814–41), Russian poet and novelist, exiled to the Caucasus for a revolutionary poem addressed to Tsar Nicholas I on the death of Pushkin. The poet of the Caucasus. His novel *A Hero of Our Time* was written at St. Petersburg. He lost his life in a duel.

Le Sage, Alain René (1668–1747), French author, b. in Brittany, who wrote *Gil Blas* and *Le Diable Boiteux*. He was also a dramatist and his plays include *Turcaret*.

Lesseps, Ferdinand, Vicomte de (1805–94), French engineer who while serving as vice-consul at Alexandria conceived a scheme for a canal across the Suez isthmus; the work was completed in 1869. He also projected the original Panama canal scheme, which failed.

Lessing, Doris (1919–2013). Novelist, born in Persia. Her works include *The Grass is Singing* (1949), *The Golden Notebook* (1962) etc. C.H. (2000). Nobel Prize for Literature, 2007. A visionary of letters.

Lessing, Gotthold Ephraim (1729–81), German philosopher, dramatist, and critic, noted for his work *Laokoon* and his play *Minna von Barnhelm*.

Leucippus (fl. 440 B.C.), Greek philosopher, the founder with Democritus of atomism, a theory of matter quite nearly that of modern science. One saying survives: "Naught occurs at random, but everything for a reason and of necessity."

Leverhulme, 1st Viscount (William Hesketh Lever) (1851–1925), British industrialist and philanthropist. He founded Lever Bros. which later became Unilever Ltd., and was a practical exponent of industrial partnership. He gave Lancaster House to the nation.

Leverrier, Urbain Jean Joseph (1811–77), French astronomer who, working independently of J. C. Adams of Cambridge, anticipated the existence of the planet Neptune.

Levi, Primo (1919–87). Italian writer. His best-known book is *If this is a man*.

Lévi-Strauss, Claude (1908–2009), French intellectual and social anthropologist, b. Belgium, exponent of the theory of symbolic structures. His major works included *Tristes tropiques*. His structuralist approach dominated philosophical discussion.

Lewis, Sinclair (1885–1951), American writer of novels satirising small-town life and philistinism. His works include *Main Street, Babbitt* and *Elmer Gantry*. Nobel prizewinner 1931.

Liaquat Ali Khan (1895–1951), leader of the Moslem League (1946) and first premier of Pakistan in 1947. He was assassinated.

Lie, Trygve (1896–1968), Norwegian politician. Secretary-General of the United Nations, 1946–52.

Lilburne, John (1614–57), agitator and pamphleteer, leader of the Levellers in Civil War.

Linacre, Thomas (c. 1460–1524), English humanist and physician, who translated Galen's works and founded the College of Physicians.

Lincoln, Abraham (1809–65), American president. Born in Kentucky, he became a lawyer and was returned to Congress from Illinois in 1846. He was a leader of the Republican party which was formed in 1856 to oppose slavery. He became president in 1861, in which year the Confederate States proposed to withdraw from the Union, and war broke out. The phrase "government of the people, by the people, for the people" comes from his Gettysburg speech of 1863. He was assassinated in 1865.

Lind, James (1716–94), pioneer of naval hygiene who realised that citrus fruits cured scurvy.

Lind, Jenny (1820–87), Swedish singer, popular in Europe, and known as the Swedish nightingale.

Lindbergh, Charles Augustus (1902–74), US aviator

who completed the first solo non-stop flight across the Atlantic in the *Spirit of St Louis* (1927). The kidnapping of his baby son took place in 1932.

Linnaeus (1707–78), Swedish botanist, remembered for his system of defining living things by two Latin names, the first being its *genus*, and the second its *species*. His method is expounded in *Philosophia Botanica* (1751). In 1757 he was ennobled as Karl von Linné. He studied, taught and died at Uppsala.

Lippi, Fra Filippo (1406–69), Italian artist, b. Florence. Frescoes in Prato cathedral are his main work. His son **Filippino** (1457–1504) finished Masaccio's frescoes in the Carmine, Florence etc.

Lippmann, Gabriel (1845–1921), French physicist who invented a capillary electrometer. A pioneer in colour photography. Nobel prizewinner 1908.

Lippmann, Walter (1889–1974), American journalist of influence, writing for the New York *Herald Tribune*, 1931–62.

Lipton, Sir Thomas Johnstone (1850–1931), Scottish business man and philanthropist. B. Glasgow, he emigrated to America, but returned to Scotland and established extensive chainstores for groceries. He unsuccessfully competed in yachting for the America's Cup.

Lister, Baron (Joseph Lister) (1827–1912), English surgeon, son of **J. J. Lister** (1786–1869), a microscopist. He founded antiseptic surgery (1865) which greatly reduced hospital mortality.

Liszt, Franz (1811–86), Hungarian pianist and composer. His daughter Cosima became the wife of Hans von Bülow and later of Wagner.

Littlewood, Joan (1914–2002), theatre artist. One of the most influential modern theatre directors. Known as the Mother of Modern Theatre.

Litvinov, Maxim (1876–1952), Russian diplomat. Ambassador in London, then commissar for foreign affairs. Ambassador to the USA, 1941–43.

Livingstone, David (1813–73), Scottish explorer in Africa. He discovered the course of the Zambesi, the Victoria Falls and Lake Nyasa (now Lake Malawi), and roused opinion against the slave trade. At one time believed lost, he was found by Stanley (q.v.) on 10 Nov. 1871. He was obsessive and out of touch with reality.

Lloyd-George of Dwyfor, 1st Earl (David Lloyd George) (1863–1945), Liberal statesman of Welsh origin. He was MP for Caernarvon, 1890–1944; and as chancellor of the exchequer he introduced social insurance, 1908–11. The war of 1914–18 obliged him to become a war premier (superseding Asquith), and he was subsequently one of the main figures at the peace conference. In 1921 he conceded the Irish Free State. His daughter, **Lady Megan Lloyd George**, was an MP for many years.

Lloyd-Webber, Lord (Sir Andrew Lloyd-Webber) (b. 1948), British composer. His musicals include *Jesus Christ Superstar* (1970), *Evita* (1978), *Cats* (1981), *Starlight Express* (1983), the hugely successful *Phantom of the Opera* (1986), *Love Never Dies* etc.

Llywelyn Ap Grufydd (d. 1282), last native prince of Wales. Died in the hostilities against England.

Llywelyn Ap Iorwerth (1173–1240), ablest of the medieval Welsh princes. He united the people against the English.

Locke, John (1632–1704), English liberal philosopher and founder of empiricism, the doctrine that all knowledge is derived from experience. His chief work in theoretical philosophy, *Essay Concerning Human Understanding*, was written just before the revolution of 1688 and published in 1690. Other writings include *Letters on Toleration, Treatises on Government*, and *Education*.

Locke, Matthew (c. 1621–77), English composer, born in Exeter. Composer-in-Ordinary to Charles II.

Lombroso, Cesare (1836–1909), Italian criminologist. His *L'uomo delinquente* was a major work.

Lomonosov, Mikhail Vasilievich (1711–65), Russian philologist and poet who systematised Russian grammar and orthography.

London, Jack (1876–1916), American author of adventure tales such as *Call of the Wild*.

Longfellow, Henry Wadsworth (1807–82), American poet, popular in his lifetime, author of *The Golden Legend* and *Hiawatha*.

Lope de Vega Carpio, Félix (1562–1635), Spanish writer of immense output. First a ballad-writer, he took to play-writing and founded the Spanish drama. The number of his plays is said to have been 1,500, but most are lost.

Lorca, Federico Garcia (1899–1936), Spanish poet and dramatist of Andalusia. Among his works are *Llanto por Ignacio Sánchez Mejías*, an unforgettable lament on the death of a bull-fighter, and *Canción de Jinete* with its haunting refrain, "Cordoba, far away and alone." He was brutally murdered by Franco sympathisers .

Louis IX (1214–70), St. Louis, King of France. Of saintly character, he also carried out practical reforms. He died on crusade.

Louis XIV (1638–1715), King of France. A despotic ruler, builder of Versailles, he also dominated the Europe of his day; but he fought exhausting wars. He revoked the Edict of Nantes which had given religious freedom to the Huguenots since 1598.

Louis XV (1710–74), King of France. Extravagant and self-indulgent, his reign marked a declining period for the monarchy.

Louis XVI (1754–93), King of France. Well-meaning but incapable, he saw the outbreak of the French revolution of 1789, in which he and his queen Marie Antoinette were executed.

Louis, Joe (Joseph Louis Barrow) (1914–81), American Black boxer, who became world heavyweight champion in 1937, successfully defending his title 26 times.

Lovelace, Ada (1815–51), English mathematician and first computer programmer. Daughter of the poet Lord Byron.

Lovelock, James (b. 1919), British scientist best-known for the 'Gaia hypothesis'. His books include *Homage to Gaia: The Life of an Independent Scientist* (2001), *The Revenge of Gaia* (2006), *The Vanishing Face of Gaia* (2009) and *A Rough Ride to the Future* (2014) C.H. (2003).

Low, Archibald Montgomery (1888–1956), British scientist who worked in varied fields, *e.g.* wireless, TV, and anti-aircraft and anti-tank apparatus.

Low, Sir David (1891–1963), Cartoonist, b. New Zealand, worked for the *Evening Standard* and the *Guardian*; creator of Colonel Blimp.

Lowell, Robert (1917–77), American poet, author of the verse play *The Old Glory*, and *Life Studies*, an autobiographical volume in verse and prose.

Lowry, L. S. (Laurence Stephen) (1887–1976), acclaimed painter of bleak urban landscapes (often in Salford). Worked as a rent collector.

Loyola, St. Ignatius (1491–1556), Spanish founder of the Jesuits. See **E7**.

Lucretius (99–55 B.C.), Roman poet, author of *De rerum natura*, a long philosophical poem advocating moral truth without religious belief.

Ludendorff, Erich (1865–1937), German general who directed German strategy in the first world war.

Lugard, 1st Baron (Frederick John Dealtry Lugard) (1858–1945), British colonial administrator in Africa, especially Nigeria, and exponent of the system of indirect rule through native chiefs.

Lukács, Georg (1885–1971), Hungarian writer, Marxist thinker and literary critic. Author of *History and Class Consciousness* (1923), *Studies in European Realism* (1946, Eng. tr. 1950), etc.

Luther, Martin (1483–1546), German Protestant reformer. After spending time in a monastery, he was ordained priest (1507), and lectured at Wittenberg university. In 1517 he protested against the sale of indulgences; and when summoned before the Diet of Worms made a memorable defence. He was protected by the Elector of Saxony, and translated the Bible. See Lutheranism (Section J).

Luthuli, Albert (1899–1967), African non-violent resistance leader, an ex-Zulu chief. Killed in train accident. Nobel prize for peace 1960.

Lutyens, Sir Edwin Landseer (1869–1944), English architect: designed the cenotaph, Whitehall; city plan and viceroy's house, New Delhi, British Embassy, Washington and Liverpool Roman catholic cathedral.

Luxemburg, Rosa (1870–1919), Polish-born German revolutionary leader. Major theoretician of Marxism. Imprisoned for opposition to First World War, 1915–18. Founded German Communist Party in 1918 with Karl Liebknecht, based on earlier Spartacist group. Opposed the nationalism of existing socialist groups. Brutally murdered by counter-revolutionary troops.

Lyell, Sir Charles (1797–1875), Scottish geologist, whose *Principles of Geology* (1830–33) helped to shape Darwin's ideas.

Lynn, Dame Vera (b. 1917), immensely popular singer, the 'Forces' sweetheart' immortalised in *We'll Meet Again* and *White Cliffs of Dover*. She was born in East Ham. Companion of Honour, 2016.

Lysander (d.395 B.C.), Greek war hero who won the

final victory for Sparta in the Peloponnesian War.

Lytton, 1st Baron (Edward George Earle Lytton Bulwer-Lytton) (1803–73), English novelist and playwright, author of *The Last Days of Pompeii*.

M

Maathai, Wangari (1940–2011). Kenyan environmentalist and human rights campaigner. First African woman to be awarded Nobel Peace Prize.

Macadam, John Loudon (1756–1836), Scottish inventor of "macadamising" system of road repair.

MacArthur, Douglas (1880–1964), American general. He defended the Philippines against the Japanese in the second world war, and was relieved of his command in 1951 in the Korean war.

MacArthur, Dame Ellen (b. 1976), English yachtswoman who in February 2005 completed the fastest solo round-the-world voyage.

Macaulay of Rothley, 1st Baron (Thomas Babington Macaulay) (1800–59), English historian, poet and Indian civil servant. His poems include *Lays of Ancient Rome*. In India he reformed the education system.

Macaulay, Zachary (1768–1838), anti-slavery agitator, father of the above.

Macbeth (d. 1057), Scottish king, married Gruoch, granddaughter of Kenneth, king of Alban. He was mormaer of Moray, succeeding Duncan in 1040 after killing him in fair fight. His reign of seventeen years was prosperous, but he was killed by Duncan's son, Malcolm, in 1057. Shakespeare's play is based on the inaccurate *Chronicle* of Holinshed.

McCartney, Sir Paul. See Beatles.

MacDiarmid, Hugh (1892–1978), the pseudonym of Christopher Murray Grieve, Scottish poet, leader of the Scottish literary renaissance; author of *A Drunk Man Looks at the Thistle*.

Macdonald, Flora (1722–90), Scottish Jacobite heroine who saved the life of Prince Charles Edward after the defeat at Culloden in 1746.

Macdonald, Sir John Alexander (1815–91), Canadian statesman, first prime minister of the Dominion of Canada.

MacDonald, James Ramsay (1866–1937), Labour politician of Scottish origin, premier 1924 and 1929–31; also of a coalition 1931–5. His action over the financial crisis of 1931 divided his party.

MacDonald, Malcolm (1901–81), son of above, held positions overseas in the Commonwealth, the last as special representative in Africa.

Machiavelli, Niccolò (1467–1527), Florentine Renaissance diplomat and theorist of the modern state. His book *The Prince* (1513), dedicated to Lorenzo, Duke of Urbino, is concerned with the reality of politics. His *Discourses* is more republican and liberal.

Mackail, John William (1859–1945), British classical scholar, translator of the *Odyssey*.

Mackenzie, Sir Compton (1883–1972), British writer, whose works include *Carnival, Sinister Street*, and a monumental autobiography.

McKinley, William (1843–1901), 25th President of the USA (1897–1901). A Republican, he presided over the Spanish-American War of 1898. Assassinated by an anarchist.

Mackintosh, Charles Rennie (1868–1928). See **G28**.

MacLean, Sorley (Somhairle MacGill-Eain) (1911–96), Gaelic poet. His collected poems, *Choille gu Bearradh (From Wood to Ridge)*, were published in 1989, and won the MacVitie Prize.

McLuhan, Herbert Marshall (1911–80), Canadian author of a number of books, *e.g. The Gutenberg Galaxy, The Mechanical Bride. See* Section J.

Macmillan, Harold. See Stockton, Earl of.

McMillan, Margaret (1860–1931), Scottish educational reformer, b. New York, and pioneer of open-air nursery schools.

Macneice, Louis (1907–63), British poet, playwright, and translator.

Macready, William Charles (1793–1873), British actor and manager, especially associated with Shakespearean roles.

Macron, Emmanuel (b. 1977). President of France after 2017 (the youngest Head of State since Napoleon in 1799). A centrist politician.

Maeterlinck, Maurice (1862–1949), Belgian man of letters, whose plays include *La Princesse Maleine, Pelléas et Mélisande*, and *L'Oiseau Bleu*. Nobel prizewinner 1911.

Magellan, Ferdinand (*c.* 1480–1521), the Portuguese

navigator, and commander of the first expedition (1519) to sail round the world.

Mahfouz, Naguib (1911–2006), the father of the contemporary Egyptian novel. First Arab writer to win the Nobel Prize for Literature (1988).

Mahler, Gustav (1860–1911), Austrian composer and conductor; a writer of symphonies and songs, a classical romantic, much influenced by Anton Bruckner and Wagner. See **Section P.**

Mahavira, Vardhamana Jnatriputra (6th cent. B.C.), Indian founder of Jainism. See **Jainism, Section J.**

Mailer, Norman (1923–2007), U.S. novelist, whose novels include *The Naked and the Dead* (1948) and *The Executioner's Song* (1979). The heavyweight champion of American literature.

Maintenon, Françoise d'Aubigné, Marquise de (1635–1719), second wife of Louis XIV. Her first husband was the poet Scarron.

Major, Sir John (b. 1943), Prime Minister from 1990 to 1997. Leader of the Conservative Party, 1990–97. MP (Con.) Huntingdon, 1979–2001. Foreign Secretary, 1989. Chancellor of the Exchequer, 1989–90. His victory in the 1992 election heralded grave problems for his government. Heavily defeated in 1997. Created Companion of Honour (1999) and awarded Order of the Garter, 2005.

Makarios III (1913–77), Greek Orthodox archbishop and Cypriot national leader. Deported by the British to the Seychelles in 1956, he returned in 1957. First President of Cyprus.

Malibran, Marie Félicité (1808–36), Spanish mezzo-soprano.

Malinowski, Bronisław (1884–1942), Polish-born anthropologist, regarded as the father of modern social anthropology.

Malory, Sir Thomas (c. 1430–71), English writer. From earlier sources and legends of Arthur and the Knights of the Round Table, he compiled the *Morte d'Arthur* printed by Caxton in 1485. See **M6.**

Malpighi, Marcello (1628–94), Italian physician and biologist. Founder of microscopic anatomy.

Malraux, André (1901–76), French novelist and politician. His works include *La Condition humaine, L'Espoir,* and *Psychologie de l'art* (tr. in 2 vols.), *Museum without Walls,* and *The Creative Act*). Served under de Gaulle.

Malthus, Thomas Robert (1766–1834), English clergyman and economist. Wrote *The Principle of Population.* See **Malthusianism, Section J.**

Mandela, Nelson Rolihlahia (1918–2013), President of South Africa, 1994–99, son of chief of Tembu tribe; imprisoned on political grounds 1964–90. His release from prison in February 1990 transformed the political scene in South Africa. Historic agreement (1993) with President De Klerk to form Government of National Unity after multi-party elections. Shared Nobel Peace Prize with De Klerk, 1993. The ANC victory in April 1994 paved the way for him to become President. Honorary Order of Merit, 1995. One of the icons of our time.

Mandelstam, Osip Yemilevich (1891–1938). Russian poet, critic and translator, Perhaps the finest Russian poet of his time, he died *en route* to a Soviet concentration camp.

Manet, Edouard (1832–83), French painter. His Impressionist pictures include *Olympia* and *Un bar aux Folies-Bergères* (the latter at the Courtauld).

Mann, Thomas (1875–1955), German writer who won world recognition at the age of 25 with his novel *Buddenbrooks.* His liberal humanistic outlook had developed sufficiently by 1930 for him to expose national socialism. He left Germany in 1933. Other works are *The Magic Mountain,* and the *Joseph* tetralogy. Nobel prizewinner 1929.

Mann, Tom (1856–1941), British Labour leader for more than fifty years.

Manning, Henry Edward (1808–92), English cardinal; archbishop of Westminster 1865–92. He was an Anglican before he joined Rome.

Mansfield, Katherine (Kathleen Beauchamp) (1890–1923), short-story writer, b. Wellington, New Zealand, whose work was influenced by the short stories of Chekhov. Her second husband was **John Middleton Murry,** literary critic.

Manson, Sir Patrick (1844–1922), Scottish physician, the first to propose that the malarial parasite was transmitted by the mosquito.

Manuzio, Aldo Pio (1450–1515), Italian printer, founder of the Aldine press in Venice which issued books famed for their type and bindings.

Manzoni, Alessandro (1785–1873), Italian novelist and poet, b. Milan. Author of historical novel *I Promessi Sposi* (The Betrothed).

Mao Tse-tung (Mao Zedong) (1893–1976), Chinese Communist leader. B. in Hunan, of rural origin. As a young man he worked as assistant librarian at Peking University. He understood how to win peasant support for a national and progressive movement. Attacked by Chiang Kai-shek, he led his followers by the "long march" to N.W. China, whence later they issued to defeat both Japanese and Chiang and proclaim a People's Republic in 1949, and later to promote the "great leap forward" of 1958–9 (the commune movement). He claimed to stand for an egalitarian democratic society, unbureaucratic, with revolutionary momentum. He promoted the "cultural revolution" (1965–9). His dictatorship led to the deaths of millions. See **Maoism, Section J.**

Marat, Jean Paul (1743–93), French revolution leader, largely responsible for the reign of terror, and assassinated by Charlotte Corday.

Marceau, Marcel (1923–2007), the white-faced clown who was the world's best-known mime artist.

Marconi, Guglielmo Marchese (1874–1937), Italian inventor and electrical engineer who developed the use of radio waves. In 1895 he sent long-wave signals over a distance of a mile, and in 1901 received in Newfoundland the first transatlantic signals sent out by his station in Cornwall, thus discovering that radio waves can bend around the spherically-shaped earth. Nobel prize 1909.

Marcus Aurelius Antoninus (121–180 A.D.), Roman emperor and Stoic philosopher of lofty character, whose *Meditations* are still read.

Marcuse, Herbert (1898–1979), political philosopher. B. Berlin, he emigrated to the U.S. during the Nazi regime. A critic of Western industrial society, he saw the student protest movement as the catalyst of revolution.

Maria Theresa (1717–80), Empress, daughter of the Hapsburg Charles VI. Able and of strong character, she fought unsuccessfully to save Silesia from Prussian annexation. She promoted reforms in her dominions. She married the Duke of Lorraine and had 16 children.

Marie Antoinette (1755–93), Queen of France, was daughter of the above and wife of Louis XVI; accused of treason, she and her husband were beheaded in the French revolution.

Marie Louise (1791–1847), daughter of Francis I of Austria, became the wife of Napoleon and bore him a son (Napoleon II).

Marius, Caius (157–86 B.C.), Roman general who defended Gaul from invasion; later civil war forced him to flee from Rome, and on his return he took terrible revenge.

Mark Antony. See **Antonius, Marcus.**

Markova, Dame Alicia (1910–2005), one of the greatest ballerinas of her time. Born Lilian Alicia Marks. A dancer of great technique and style.

Marlborough, 1st Duke of (John Churchill) (1650–1722), English general, victor of Blenheim, Ramillies, Oudenarde and Malplaquet. His wife, Sarah Jennings, was a favourite of Queen Anne.

Marley, Bob. See **P26(2).**

Marlowe, Christopher (1564–93), English dramatist and precursor of Shakespeare. His plays include *Dr. Faustus, Tamburlaine the Great, Edward II,* and *The Jew of Malta.* His early death was due to a tavern brawl. See **M6(2).**

Márquez, Gabriel García (1928–2014). Colombian author. Nobel prize for Literature. The master of magic realism.

Marryat, Frederick (1792–1848), English author of sea and adventure stories, including *Peter Simple, Mr. Midshipman Easy,* and *Masterman Ready.* A captain in the Royal Navy.

Marshall, George Catlett (1880–1959), American general. U.S. chief of staff 1939–45; originated the Marshall Aid plan. Nobel prize for peace 1953.

Martial, Marcus Valerius (c. 40–104), Roman poet, b. in Spain, remembered for his epigrams.

Marvell, Andrew (1620–78), English poet and political writer. He was Milton's assistant. See **M10.**

Marx, Karl (1818–83), German founder of modern international communism, b. Trier of Jewish parentage. He studied law, philosophy and history at the universities of Bonn and Berlin, and later took up the study of economics. In conjunction with his friend Engels he wrote the *Communist Manifesto* of 1848 for the Communist League of which he was the leader. Because of his revolutionary activities he was forced to leave the continent and in 1849 settled in London. Here, mainly while living at 28 Dean Street, Soho, he wrote *Das Kapital*, a deep analysis of the economic laws that govern modern society. In 1864 he helped found the first International. He ranks as one of the great thinkers of modern times. He was buried in Highgate cemetery. *See* **Marxism, Section J.**

Mary I (1516–58), Queen of England, was daughter of Henry VIII and Catherine of Aragon. A Roman Catholic, she reversed the religious changes made by her father and brother, and about 300 Protestants were put to death. She married Philip of Spain.

Mary II (1662–94), Queen of England with her husband the Dutch William III. As daughter of James II, she was invited to succeed after the revolution of 1688 and expelled her father.

Mary Stuart, Queen of Scots (1542–87), daughter of James V of Scotland and Mary of Guise, she laid claim to the English succession. She was imprisoned in England by Elizabeth and beheaded. Her husbands were the dauphin of France (d. 1560), Lord Henry Stewart Darnley (murdered 1567) and Bothwell.

Masaryk, Jan Garrigue (1886–1948), Czech diplomat. The son of Thomas, he was Czech minister in London 1925–38, and foreign secretary while his government was in exile in London and after it returned to Prague, 1940–8.

Masaryk, Thomas Garrigue (1850–1937), Czech statesman and independence leader. He was the first president of Czechoslovakia, 1918–35.

Mascagni, Pietro (1863–1945), Italian composer of *Cavalleria Rusticana*.

Masefield, John (1878–1967), English poet. His best-known works are *Salt-Water Ballads* (as a boy he ran away to sea), and *Reynard the Fox*. He became poet laureate in 1930.

Maskelyne, John Nevil (1839–1917), English illusionist. He also exposed spiritualistic frauds.

Massenet, Jules Emile Frédéric (1842–1912), French composer of songs, orchestral suites, oratorios, and operas, *e.g. Manon* and *Thaïs*.

Massine, Léonide (1896–1979), Russian dancer, one of Diaghilev's choreographers.

Masters, Edgar Lee (1869–1950), American poet remembered for his *Spoon River Anthology*.

Matisse, Henri (1869–1954), French painter, member of a group known as *Les Fauves* (the wild beasts) for their use of violent colour and colour variation to express form and relief.

Matsys (**Massys**), **Quentin** (1466–1530), Flemish painter, b. Louvain, settled Antwerp. His *Moneychanger, and his Wife* is in the Louvre.

Matthews, Sir Stanley (1915–2000), first footballer to be knighted. He made 880 first-class appearances, 54 for England. Played in the legendary 1953 Cup Final (when Blackpool beat Bolton Wanderers 4–3). One of the greatest of all footballers.

Maugham, William Somerset (1874–1965), British writer, b. Paris. He practised as a doctor till the success of *Liza of Lambeth* (1897) followed by *Of Human Bondage*. A master of the short story, his work reflects his travels in the East. In both world wars he served as a British agent.

Maupassant, Guy de (1850–93), French writer whose novels and short stories show penetrating realism. His stories include *Boule de Suif*, *Le Maison Tellier*, and *La Parure*.

Mauriac, François (1885–1970), French writer whose novels deal with moral problems and include *Le Baiser au Lépreux* and the play *Asmodée*. Nobel prizewinner 1952.

Maurois, André (**Emile Herzog**) (1885–1967), French writer whose works include lives of Shelley and Disraeli.

Maxim, Sir Hiram Stevens (1840–1916), American inventor of the automatic quick-firing gun.

Maxton, James (1885–1946), Scottish Labour politician and pacifist; entered parliament 1922; chairman of ILP 1926–31, 1934–9.

Maxwell, James Clerk (1831–79), Scottish physicist. He wrote his first scientific paper at 15. Became first Cavendish professor of experimental physics at Cambridge. His mathematical mind, working on the discoveries of Faraday and others, gave physics a celebrated set of equations for the basic laws of electricity and magnetism.

May, Peter (**Barker Howard**) (1929–94). English cricketer. The finest post-war batsman produced in Britain. A long-serving and successful captain.

May, Theresa (b. 1956) Conservative politician. Prime Minister after 2016 (only the second

woman to hold the post). Previously Home Secretary (the longest-serving Home Secretary in over a century). The June 2017 election gravely weakened her authority.

Mazarin, Jules (1602–61), cardinal and minister of France was b. in Italy. In spite of opposition from the nobles, he continued Richelieu's work of building up a strong monarchy.

Mazeppa, Ivan Stepanovich (1644–1709), Cossack nobleman, b. Ukraine (then part of Poland, before E. Ukraine passed to Russia, 1667). He fought unsuccessfully for independence allying himself with Charles XII of Sweden against Peter I of Russia (Poltava, 1709). Byron wrote a poem about him.

Mazzini, Giuseppe (1805–72), Italian patriot. B. Genoa, he advocated a free and united Italy, and from Marseilles he published a journal, *Young Italy*. Expelled from the Continent, he took refuge in London in 1837. In 1848 he returned to Italy, and became dictator of the short-lived Roman republic, which was put down by French forces. His contribution to Italian unity was that of preparing the way.

Mbeki, Thabo Mvuyelwa (b. 1942), South African ANC politician who succeeded Nelson Mandela as President in 1999. He resigned in 2008.

Mechnikov, Ilya (1845–1916), Russian biologist who discovered that by "phagocytosis" certain white blood cells are capable of ingesting harmful substances such as bacteria. He shared the 1908 Nobel prize for medicine.

Medawar, Sir Peter Brien (1915–87), British zoologist, author of *The Art of the Soluble* and *The Future of Man*. Nobel prizewinner 1960. O.M. 1981.

Medici, Florentine family of merchants and bankers who were politically powerful and who patronised the arts. **Cosimo the Elder** (1389–1464) was for over 30 years virtual ruler of Florence. His grandson, **Lorenzo the Magnificent** (1449–92), poet, friend of artists and scholars, governed with munificence. His grandson, **Lorenzo**, was father of **Catherine de' Medici**, Queen of France (*q.v.*). A later **Cosimo** (1519–74) was an able Duke of Florence and then Grand-Duke of Tuscany, which title the Medicis held until 1737.

Méhul, Etienne Nicolas (1763–1817), French operatic composer. *Joseph* is his masterpiece.

Meir, Golda (1898–1978), leading member of the Israeli Labour Party, her premiership included the Six Day and Yom Kippur wars.

Meitner, Lise (1878–1969), co-worker of Otto Hahn (*q.v.*) who interpreted his results (1939) as a fission process.

Melanchthon, Philip (1497–1560), German religious reformer, who assisted Luther, and wrote the first Protestant theological work, *Loci communes*. He drew up the Augsburg confession (1530).

Melba, Nellie (Helen Porter Mitchell) (1861–1931), Australian soprano of international repute.

Melbourne, 2nd Viscount (William Lamb) (1779–1848), English Whig statesman, was premier at the accession of Queen Victoria.

Mendel, Gregor Johann (1822–84), Austrian botanist. After entering the Augustinian monastery at Brünn he became abbot and taught natural history in the school. His main interest was the study of inheritance, and his elaborate observations of the common garden pea resulted in the law of heredity which bears his name. His hypothesis (published in 1866) received little attention until 1900.

Mendeleyev, Dmitri Ivanovich (1834–1907), Russian chemist, first to discover the critical temperatures. He formulated the periodic law of atomic weights (1869) and drew up the periodic table (*see* Section T), Element 101 is named after him.

Mendelssohn-Bartholdy, Felix (1809–47), German composer, grandson of Moses Mendelssohn, philosopher. He belongs with Chopin and Schumann to the early 19th cent. classic-romantic school, and his music has delicacy and melodic beauty. He was conductor of the Gewandhaus concerts at Leipzig for a time and often visited England. *See* **Section P.**

Menuhin, Lord (Yehudi Menuhin) (1916–99), famous violinist, b. New York of Russian Jewish parentage. He first appeared as soloist at the age of seven. He was the greatest violinist of his age. Founded a School for musically gifted children. O. M. 1987.

Menzies, Sir Robert Gordon (1894–1978), Australian Liberal statesman, P.M. 1939–41, 1949–66.

Mercator, Gerhardus (Gerhard Kremer) (1512–94), Flemish geographer who pioneered the making of accurate navigational maps. He worked out the map which bears his name in which meridians and parallels of latitude cross each other at right angles, enabling compass bearings to be drawn as straight lines.

Meredith, George (1828–1909), English writer, b. Portsmouth. His novels include *The Ordeal of Richard Feverel*, *The Egoist*, *Evan Harrington*, *Diana of the Crossways*, and *The Amazing Marriage*. Also a gifted poet.

Merkel, Angela (b. 1954). German Christian Democrat politician. First woman Chancellor of Germany, 2005. Re-elected 2009 and again in 2013. Announced intention to stand again in 2017.

Mesmer, Friedrich Anton. *See* Mesmerism, Section J.

Mestrović, Ivan (1883–1962), Yugoslav sculptor of international repute. He designed the temple at Kossovo. He later lived in England, and examples of his work are in London museums.

Metastasio, Pietro (Pietro Bonaventura Trapassi) (1698–1782), Italian librettist who lived in Vienna and provided texts for Gluck, Handel, Haydn, and Mozart.

Metternich, Clemens (1773–1859), Austrian statesman and diplomat. Foreign Minister, 1809–48. Chancellor, 1812–48.

Michelangelo (Michelagniolo Buonarroti) (1475–1564), Italian painter, sculptor and poet. Of a poor but genteel Tuscan family, his first interest in sculpture came through his nurse, wife of a stone-cutter. He became apprenticed to Domenico Ghirlandaio. Like Leonardo, he studied anatomy, but instead of spreading his talents over a wide field, he became obsessed with the problem of how to represent the human body. In him, classical idealism, medieval religious belief, and renaissance energy met. Perhaps his most impressive work is the ceiling of the Sistine Chapel (a surface of about 6,000 square feet), the *Last Judgement* behind the chapel altar, his marble *Pietà* (St. Peter's) the statue of *David* (Academy, Florence), the great figure of *Moses* (San Pietro in Vincoli, Rome), and the four allegorical figures *Day*, *Night*, *Dawn*, *Twilight* (intended for the tombs of the Medici family at San Lorenzo, Florence).

Michelet, Jules (1798–1874), French historian who wrote on France and the revolution.

Michelson, Albert Abraham (1852–1931), American physicist, b. Poland. He collaborated with E. W. Morley in an experiment to determine ether drift, the negative result of which was important for Einstein. Nobel prizewinner 1907.

Mickiewicz, Adam (1798–1855), Polish revolutionary poet, author of *The Ancestors* and *Pan Tadeusz*.

Mies van der Rohe, Ludwig (1886–1969). German architect and designer. One of the greatest 20th-century architects.

Miliband, David. *See* D18.

Miliband, Ed. *See* D18.

Mill, John Stuart (1806–73), English philosopher. A member of Bentham's utilitarian school, he later modified some of its tenets. His main work is *On Liberty*. *The Subjection of Women* supported women's rights. He also wrote *Principles of Political Economy*. Godfather to Bertrand Russell.

Millais, Sir John Everett (1829–96), English artist, b. Southampton; in his earlier years a pre-Raphaelite (*Ophelia*). Later works include *The Boyhood of Raleigh* and *Bubbles*. He married Mrs. Ruskin after the annulment of her marriage.

Miller, Arthur (1915–2005), perhaps the greatest American dramatist of the 20th cent. His plays include *Death of a Salesman*, *The Crucible* etc.

Millet, Jean François (1814–75), French painter of rural life; his works include *The Angelus*.

Millikan, Robert Andrews (1868–1954), American physicist, who determined the charge on the electron and discovered cosmic rays. Nobel prizewinner 1923.

Mills, Sir John (1908–2005), theatrical legend and Oscar winning actor. Knighted in 1976.

Milne, Alan Alexander (1882–1956), English humorist and poet. He remains popular.

Milner, 1st Viscount (Alfred Milner) (1854–1925), British administrator, especially in South Africa; author of *England in Egypt*.

Milosevic, Slobodan (1941–2006), Serbian dictator. A ruthless manipulator of Serbian nationalism. Died while indicted as a war criminal.

Milstein, César (1927–2002) Argentinian-born molecular biologist. Joint Nobel Prize for Medicine, 1984.

Miltiades (d. 489 B.C.), one of the leaders of the Athenian army against the Persians at Marathon.

Milton, John (1608–74), English poet, author of *Paradise Lost*. B. in London, he wrote while still at Cambridge *L'Allegro*, *Il Penseroso*, *Comus*, and *Lycidas*. The Civil War diverted his energies to the parliamentary and political struggle, but during this period he defended in *Aereopagitica* the freedom of the press. After he had become blind he wrote *Paradise Lost* and a sonnet *On His Blindness*. *See* **M10**.

Minot, George Richards (1885–1950), who with W. P. Murphy discovered the curative properties of liver in pernicious anaemia. Shared Nobel prize 1934.

Mirabeau, Gabriel, Honoré Victor Riquetti, Comte de (1749–91), French revolutionary leader. His writings contributed to the revolution of 1789.

Miró, Joan (1893–1983), one of the Catalan surrealist masters of the 20th century. His works include *The Farm*, *The Tilled Field* and *Harlequin's Carnival*.

Mistral, Frédéric (1830–1914), French poet, and founder of a Provençal renaissance. His works include *Lou Trésor dóu Félibrige* and a Provençal dictionary. Nobel prizewinner 1904.

Mitchell, Reginald Joseph (1895–1937), British aircraft designer. Famous for developing the *Spitfire*.

Mithridates (c. 132–63 B.C.), King of Pontus, in Asia Minor; he was defeated by Pompey.

Mitterrand, François Maurice Marie (1916–96), French socialist politician, proclaimed fourth president of the Fifth Republic, 21 May 1981. Re-elected May 1988 for second 7-year term until 1995. The longest serving President of the Fifth Republic. He died of cancer in 1996.

Mobutu Sese Seko (1930–97), brutal and corrupt dictator of Zaïre (Congo), 1965–97.

Modigliani, Amedeo (1884–1920), Italian painter and sculptor, b. Livorno. His portraits and figure studies tend to elongation and simplification. He lived mainly in Paris.

Moffatt, James (1870–1944), Scottish divine who translated the Bible into modern English.

Mohammed (570–632), the founder of Islam (**J27**), received the revelation of the Koran, and the command to preach, at the age of 40. By his constant proclamation that there was only One God he gathered around him a loyal following, but aroused the hostility of other Meccans. The Muslims were forced to flee to Medina in 622, but grew sufficiently to return to Mecca in 630, and establish the Kaaba as the goal of the pilgrimage in Islam.

Molière (Jean Baptiste Poquelin) (1622–73), French playwright. B. in Paris, he gained experience as a strolling player, and subsequently in Paris, partly in the king's service; he wrote an unsurpassed series of plays varying from farce as in *Les Précieuses ridicules* to high comedy. Among his plays are *Tartuffe*, *Le Misanthrope*, and *Le Bourgeois gentilhomme*.

Molotov, Vyacheslav Mikhailovich (1890–1986), Russian commissar for foreign affairs, 1939–49.

Moltke, Helmuth, Count von (1800–91), Prussian general and chief of staff (1858–88) during the period when Prussia successfully united Germany.

Mond, Ludwig (1838–1909), German chemist who in 1867 settled in England as an alkali manufacturer and in partnership with John Brunner successfully manufactured soda by the Solvay process.

Monet, Claude (1840–1926), French painter, leader of the Impressionists, the term being derived in 1874 from his landscape *Impression soleil levant*. He liked painting a subject in the open air at different times of day to show variation in light.

Monk, George, 1st Duke of Albemarle (1608–69), English general and admiral, whose reputation and moderation were mainly responsible for the return of Charles II in 1660.

Monmouth, Duke of (James Scott) (1649–85), English pretender, natural son of Charles II; centre of anti-Catholic feeling against succession of Duke of York (later James II). His troops, mostly peasants, were routed at Sedgemoor (1685) by John Churchill (later Duke of Marlborough). Beheaded on Tower Hill.

Monnet, Jean (1888–1979), French political economist, "father of the Common Market." He drafted the Monnet plan for French economic recovery.

Monroe, James (1758–1831), president of the USA. He propounded the doctrine that the Americas should not be colonised by a European power.

Montagu, Lady Mary Wortley (1689–1762), English writer. From Constantinople where her husband was ambassador she wrote *Letters* (a complete edition was published 1965–7). She introduced the idea of inoculation against smallpox to England.

Montaigne, Michel de (1533–92), French essayist of enquiring, sceptical and tolerant mind.

Montcalm, Louis Joseph, Marquis de (1712–59), French general, who unsuccessfully commanded the French at Quebec against Wolfe.

Montesquieu, Charles-Louis de Secondat, Baron de la Brède et de (1689–1755), French philosopher. His works include *Lettres persanes*, a satire on contemporary life; and *De l'esprit des lois* giving his political philosophy. The latter was based largely, but to some extent mistakenly, on English practice, and its influence led the US constitution to separate the executive (President) from the legislature (Congress).

Montessori, Maria (1870–1952), Italian educationist, who developed an educational system based on spontaneity.

Monteverdi, Claudio (1567–1643), Italian composer who pioneered in opera. His chief dramatic work is *Orfeo* (1607). *See* Section P.

Montezuma II, (Moctezuma) (1466–1520), Aztec emperor of Mexico when the Spanish invaded.

Montfort, Simon de, Earl of Leicester (*c.* 1208–65), English statesman. He led the barons in revolt against the ineffective rule of Henry III, but he differed from other rebels in that he summoned a parliamentary assembly to which for the first time representatives came from the towns. He was killed at Evesham. A notorious anti-Semite.

Montgolfier, the name of two brothers, **Joseph Michel** (1740–1810) and **Jacques Etienne** (1745–99), French aeronauts who constructed the first practical balloon, which flew 6 miles.

Montgomery of Alamein, 1st Viscount (Bernard Law Montgomery) (1887–1976), British field-marshal; commanded 8th Army, N Africa, Sicily, and Italy, 1942–4; C-in-C, British Group of Armies and Allied Armies in Northern France, 1944.

Montrose, Marquess of (James Graham) (1612–50), Scottish general. In the Civil War he raised the Highland clansmen for Charles I and won the battles of Tippermuir, Inverlochy, and Kilsyth; but was finally defeated and executed.

Moody, Dwight Lyman (1837–99), American revivalist preacher, associated with Ira D. Sankey, the "American singing pilgrim."

Moore, George (1852–1933), Irish novelist, author of *Confessions of a Young Man*, *Esther Waters*, and *Evelyn Innes*.

Moore, Henry (1898–1986), English sculptor in semi-abstract style, son of a Yorkshire coalminer. Examples of his work are to be seen all over the world, in the Tate Gallery, St. Matthew's Church, Northampton, the UNESCO building in Paris *etc*.

Moore, Sir John (1761–1809), British general, who trained the infantry for the Spanish Peninsular campaigns and conducted a brilliant retreat to Corunna, where he was mortally wounded after defeating the French under Soult.

Moore, St Patrick (1923–2012), astronomer whose great achievement was to popularise his subject.

Moore, Thomas (1779–1852), Irish poet, author of *Irish Melodies*, *Lalla Rookh*, and *The Epicurean* (novel). He also wrote a life of Byron.

Moravia, Alberto (1907–90), Italian writer. Author of *Woman of Rome*.

More, Sir Thomas (1478–1535), English writer and statesman. In 1529 he succeeded Wolsey as lord chancellor, but on his refusal to recognise Henry VIII as head of the church he was executed. His *Utopia* describes an ideal state. He was canonised in 1935.

Morgan, Sir Henry (*c.* 1635–88), Welsh buccaneer who operated in the Caribbean against the Spaniards, capturing and plundering Panama in 1671. Knighted by Charles II and made deputy-governor of Jamaica.

Morgan, John Pierpont (1837–1913), American financier who built a vast industrial empire.

Morita, Akio (1921–99), Japanese entrepreneur who co-founded the Sony empire (which produced Japan's first tape recorder, transistor radio *etc.*).

Morland, George (1763–1804), painter of rural life.

Morley, 1st Viscount (John Morley) (1838–1923), English biographer and Liberal politician.

Morley, Thomas (*c.* 1557–1603), English composer of madrigals, noted also for his settings of some of Shakespeare's songs. He was a pupil of

Byrd, organist of St. Paul's cathedral, and wrote *Plaine and Easie Introduction to Practicall Music* (1597) which was used for 200 years.

Moroni, Giovanni (1525–78). Italian artist. His best-known work is *The Tailor* (in the National Gallery).

Morris, William (1834–96), English poet and craftsman. His hatred of 19th-cent. ugliness, his belief in human equality, and in freedom and happiness for all, combined to make him a socialist, and he accomplished much for the improvement of domestic decoration. He was a popular lecturer, founded the Socialist League and the Kelmscott Press.

Morrison of Lambeth, Baron (Herbert Morrison) (1888–1965), British Labour statesman. From being an errand-boy, he rose to become leader of the London County Council. Wartime Home Secretary. Deputy Prime Minister, 1945–51.

Morse, Samuel Finley Breese (1791–1872), American pioneer in electromagnetic telegraphy and inventor of the dot-and-dash code that bears his name.

Moss, Sir Stirling (b. 1929), legendary English racing driver who dominated the sport in the 1950s.

Motion, Sir Andrew (b. 1952), poet, critic and biographer. Poet Laureate, 1999–2009. His works include a life of Keats (1997) and *The Customs House* (2012).

Moulin, Jean (1899–1943) French resistance leader who died under Nazi torture.

Mountbatten of Burma, 1st Earl (Louis Mountbatten) (1900–79), British admiral and statesman. In the second world war he became chief of combined operations in 1942. As last viceroy of India, he carried through the transfer of power to Indian hands in 1947 and was the first governor-general of the dominion. His assassination by Irish extremists evoked horror.

Mozart, Wolfgang Amadeus (1756–91), Austrian composer. B. Salzburg, he began his career at four and toured Europe at six. In 1781 he settled in Vienna, where he became a friend of Haydn and where his best music was written. His genius lies in the effortless outpouring of all forms of music. Among the loveliest and grandest works in instrumental music are his three great symphonies in E. flat, G minor, and C (called the "Jupiter"), all written in six weeks in 1788. Three of the greatest operas in musical history are his *Marriage of Figaro* (1786), *Don Giovanni* (1787), and *The Magic Flute* (1791). His last composition, written near to his death, was the *Requiem Mass*. It is now thought he died of dropsy. *See* Section P.

Mugabe, Robert Gabriel (b. 1924), prime minister and president of independent Zimbabwe after 1980. His rule became despotic.

Muggeridge, Malcolm (1903–90), broadcaster and journalist who became an ardent Christian.

Muir, John (1838–1914), Scottish-born US naturalist. A pioneer environmentalist, the 'Patron Saint of National Parks'. Father of the modern environmental movement.

Müller, Sir Ferdinand (1825–96), German-born botanist who emigrated to Australia, where he was director of the Melbourne Botanical Gardens, 1857–73. He introduced the eucalyptus into Europe.

Müller, Friedrich Max (1823–1900), Philologist and orientalist. Born Dessau. A professor at Oxford.

Mulroney, (Martin) Brian (b. 1939), Prime Minister of Canada, 1984–93. First Conservative leader from Quebec in nearly 100 years.

Mumford, Lewis (1895–1990), American writer on town-planning and social problems.

Munch, Edvard (1863–1944), Norwegian painter whose most famous work is *The Scream* (1913).

Munnings, Sir Alfred (1878–1959), English painter, especially of horses and sporting subjects.

Murdoch, Dame Iris (1919–99). *See* **M31.**

Murdock, William (1754–1839), Scottish engineer and inventor, the first to make practical use of coal gas as an illuminating agent (introduced at the Soho works, Birmingham, 1800).

Murillo, Bartolomé Esteban (1617–82), Spanish painter, b. Seville, where he founded an Academy. His early works, such as *Two Peasant Boys* (Dulwich) show peasant and street life; his later paintings are religious, *e.g.*, the *Immaculate Conception* in the Prado.

Murray, Sir Andrew (b. 1987). Scottish-born tennis champion who first won Wimbledon in 2013.

Murray, Gilbert (1866–1957), classical scholar of Australian birth who settled in England. A teacher of Greek at the universities of Glasgow and Oxford, he translated much Greek drama.

Mussolini, Benito (1883–1945), Fascist dictator of Italy 1922–43. From 1935 an aggressive foreign policy (Abyssinia and Spain) was at first successful, and in June 1940 he entered the war on the side of Hitler. Defeat in North Africa and the invasion of Sicily caused the collapse of his government. He was shot dead by partisans while trying to escape to Switzerland.

Mussorgsky, Modest Petrovich (1839–81), Russian composer whose masterpiece is the opera *Boris Godunov* after the play by Pushkin. *See* **P12(1)**.

N

Nabokov, Vladimir (1899–1977). Russian-born writer who settled in England and later America. His most famous novel was *Lolita* 1955). His unfinished novel *The Original of Laura* was published in 2009.

Naipaul, Sir Vidiadhar Surajprasad (b. 1932), Trinidadian novelist and writer, whose novels include *A House for Mr Biswas* (1961) and *The Masque of Africa* (2010). Awarded the Booker Prize for *In a Free State* (1971). Nobel Prize for Literature, 2001.

Nanak (1469–1538), Indian guru or teacher, who tried to put an end to religious strife, teaching that "God is one, whether he be Allah or Rama." *See* **Sikhism, Section J**.

Nansen, Fridtjof (1861–1930), Norwegian explorer. In 1893 his north polar expedition reached the highest latitude till then attained—86° 14′. He was active in Russian famine relief, 1921. Nobel peace prize 1922.

Naoroji, Dadabhai (1825–1917), first Indian to be elected to House of Commons (for Finsbury, 1892–5). An influential critic of the Raj.

Napier, John (1550–1617), Scottish mathematician, b. Edinburgh, invented logarithms (published 1614) and the modern notation of fractions.

Napoleon I (Bonaparte) (1769–1821), French emperor and general, of Corsican birth (Ajaccio). Trained in French military schools, he became prominent in the early years of the revolution, with uncertainty at home and war abroad. In 1796 he became commander of the army in Italy and defeated the Austrians, so that France obtained control of Lombardy. He then led an expedition to Egypt but Nelson destroyed his fleet. After further Italian victories, he made a *coup d'état* in 1799, and in 1804 became emperor. Against continuing European opposition, he defeated the Austrians at Austerlitz, and his power in Europe was such that he made his brothers Joseph, Louis, and Jerome kings of Naples, Holland, and Westphalia; but in Spain he provoked the Peninsular War, and his armies were gradually driven back by the Spanish, helped by Wellington; while his invasion of Russia in 1812 ended in a disastrous retreat from Moscow; and in 1814 the Allies forced him to abdicate and retire to Elba. He emerged again in 1815 to be defeated at Waterloo and exiled to St. Helena. His government at home was firm and promoted some reforms (*e.g.*, legal codification), but the country was weakened by his wars. The imperial idea lingered in France, and Napoleon's remains were brought to Paris in 1840. He married first Josephine Beauharnais and second Marie Louise of Austria. Marie Louise was the mother of **Napoleon II** (1811–32).

Napoleon III (1808–73), son of Napoleon I's brother Louis. He returned to France in the revolution of 1848, and in 1851 came to power by a *coup d'état*. In his reign Paris was remodelled. His foreign policy was adventurous, but when he was manoeuvred by Bismarck into the Franco-Prussian war and defeated at Sedan he lost his throne and retired to England. His wife was Eugénie de Montijo.

Narayan, Rasipuram Kirshnaswamy (1906–2001), one of the greatest Indian novelists and short-story writers. Most of his writing was set in the fictional south Indian town of Malgudi.

Nash, John (1752–1835), English architect who planned Regent Street, laid out Regent's Park, enlarged Buckingham Palace, and designed Marble Arch and the Brighton Pavilion. *See* **N18(2)**.

Nash, Paul (1889–1946), English painter and designer, official war artist in both world wars. Best-known pictures are *The Menin Road* of 1918 and *Totes Meer* of 1941.

Nash, Walter (1882–1968), New Zealand Labour politician; prime minister 1957–60.

Nasmyth, James (1808–90), Scottish inventor of the steam-hammer, which became indispensable in all large iron and engineering works.

Nasser, Gamal Abdel (1918–70), leader of modern Egypt and of the Arab world. He led the 1954 coup that deposed General Neguib. He became president of the Egyptian Republic in 1956 and of the United Arab Republic in 1958. His nationalisation of the Suez Canal in 1956 precipitated a short-lived attack by Britain and France, Israeli-Arab hostility led to the June war of 1967. He constructed the Aswan High Dam.

Navratilova, Martina (b. 1956) Czech-born tennis player of outstanding ability. She won 18 Grand Slam singles, 37 Grand Slam doubles and 149 other championship singles titles.

Ne Win, General (1911–2002), Burmese dictator who reduced his country to ruin under his regime.

Needham, Joseph (1900–95), British biochemist, historian of science and orientalist. Author of the monumental *Science and Civilisation in China*.

Nefertiti (14th cent. B.C.), wife of the heretic Pharaoh Akhenaten. Traditionally considered the most powerful woman in Ancient Egypt. The search continues for her final resting place.

Nehru, Pandit Jawaharlal (1889–1964), Indian national leader and statesman, first prime minister and minister of foreign affairs when India became independent in 1947. A leading member of the Congress Party, during which time he was frequently imprisoned for political activity. He played a part in the negotiations for independence. Under his leadership India made major advances. His daughter was **Indira Gandhi**, (*q.v.*).

Nelson, 1st Viscount (Horatio Nelson) (1758–1805), English admiral. Son of a Norfolk clergyman, he went to sea at 12 and became a captain in 1793. In the French revolutionary wars he lost his right eye in 1794 and his right arm in 1797. Rear-admiral in 1797, he defeated the French at Aboukir Bay in 1798. He was also at the bombardment of Copenhagen in 1801. In 1805 he destroyed the French fleet at Trafalgar, in which battle he was killed. His daring and decision made him a notable commander. He loved Emma Hamilton.

Nernst, Walther Hermann (1864–1941), German scientist who established the third law of thermodynamics that dealt with the behaviour of matter at temperatures approaching absolute zero. Nobel prizewinner 1920.

Nero, Claudius Caesar (A.D. 37–68), Roman emperor, the adopted son of Claudius. He was weak and licentious and persecuted Christians. In his reign occurred the fire of Rome.

Newcomen, Thomas (1663–1729), English inventor, one of the first to put a steam-engine into practical operation. In 1705 he patented his invention, the pumping-engine used in Cornish mines until the adoption of Watt's engine.

Newman, John Henry (1801–90), English priest and writer, who became a cardinal of the Roman Catholic church in 1879, and was a founder of the Oxford Movement. He is best remembered by his *Apologia pro Vita Sua* in which he described the development of his religious thought. He wrote *Lead, kindly Light*, set to music 30 years later by J. B. Dykes, and *The Dream of Gerontius*, set to music of Elgar. Beatification, 2010.

Newton, Sir Isaac (1642–1727), English scientist, b. Woolsthorpe, Lincs. (the year Galileo died). He studied at Cambridge but was at home during the plague years 1665 and 1666 when he busied himself with problems concerned with optics and gravitation. Appointed to the Lucasian chair of mathematics at Cambridge in 1669 and remained there until 1696 when he was appointed Warden, and later Master of the Mint. He was a secret Unitarian and did not marry. His three great discoveries were to show that white light could be separated into a sequence of coloured components forming the visible spectrum; to use the calculus (invented by him independently of Leibniz) to investigate the forces of nature in a quantitative way; and to show by his theory of gravitation (for which Copernicus, Kepler and Galileo had prepared the way) that the universe was regulated by simple mathematical laws.

His vision was set forth in the *Philosophiae Naturalis Principia Mathematica* of 1687, usually called the *Principia*. It was not until 200 years later that Einstein showed there could be another theory of celestial mechanics. He wrote on alchemy and was a religious zealot.

Ney, Michel (1769–1815), French general who served at Jena, Borodino, and Waterloo.

Nicholas II (1868–1918), last emperor and Tsar of Russia, son of Alexander III. His reign was marked by an unsuccessful war with Japan (1904–5), and by the 1914–18 war. Ineffective and lacking ability, he set up a Duma in 1906 too late for real reform. Revolution broke out in 1917. He and his family were shot in July 1918.

Nichols, Cardinal Vincent (b. 1945), Roman Catholic Archbishop of Westminster 2009– . Archbishop of Birmingham, 2000–09. Cardinal, 2014.

Nicholson, Sir William (1872–1949), English artist known for his portraits and woodcuts. His son, **Ben Nicholson**, O.M., (1894–1981) was a giant of English painting, with styles from Cornish landscapes to his controversial white minimalism.

Nicolson, Sir Harold (1886–1968), English diplomat, author, and critic. His wife was **Victoria Sackville-West** (1892–1962).

Niemeyer, Oscar (1907–2012), visionary modernist architect who designed Brasilia (capital of Brazil). One of the greatest contemporary architects.

Niemöller, Martin (1892–1984), German Lutheran pastor who opposed the Nazi regime and was confined in a concentration camp. He was president of the World Council of Churches in 1961.

Nietzsche, Friedrich Wilhelm (1844–1900), German philosopher, in his younger years influenced by Wagner and Schopenhauer. His teaching that only the strong ought to survive and his doctrine of the superman are expounded in *Thus spake Zarathustra*, *Beyond Good and Evil* and *The Will to Power*.

Nightingale, Florence (1820–1910), English nurse and pioneer of hospital reform, who during the Crimean war organised in face of considerable official opposition a nursing service to relieve the sufferings of the British soldiers, who called her "the lady with the lamp." (It was really more of a Chinese lantern). First woman O.M. (1907).

Nijinsky, Vaslav (1892–1950), Russian dancer, one of the company which included Pavlova, Karsavina and Fokine, brought by Diaghilev to Paris and London before the 1914–18 war. In *Les Sylphides*, *Spectre de la Rose* and *L'Après-midi d'un Faune* he won supreme acclaim.

Nikisch, Arthur (1855–1922), Hungarian conductor of the Boston Symphony Orchestra, 1889–93. Piano-accompanist to Elena Gerhardt.

Nimitz, Chester William (1885–1966), American admiral, commanded in the Pacific 1941–5.

Nixon, Richard Milhous (1913–94), Republican president (for two terms) of the U.S., 1969–74. In foreign affairs he negotiated the withdrawal of American troops from S. Vietnam and began a process of reconciliation with China and détente with the Soviet Union. But at home the Watergate conspiracies brought disgrace and an end to his presidency. His resignation in August 1974 rendered the impeachment process unnecessary; he accepted the pardon offered by his successor, President Ford.

Nkomo, Joshua (1917–99), Zimbabwean statesman. Hailed as the 'Father of Zimbabwe' for his leadership of ZAPU which he founded in 1961.

Nkrumah, Kwame (1909–72), Ghanaian leader, first premier of Ghana when his country achieved independence in 1957. Promoted the Pan-African movement; but unsound finance and dictatorial methods led to his overthrow in 1966.

Nobel, Alfred Bernhard (1833–96), Swedish inventor and philanthropist. An engineer and chemist who discovered dynamite, he amassed a fortune from the manufacture of explosives. He founded the Nobel Prizes (*see* **Section L**).

Nolan, Sir Sidney Robert (1917–92), Australian artist and set designer. Best known for his works depicting 19th cent. outlaw Ned Kelly. O.M. 1983.

North, Frederick (1732–92), favourite minister of George III who held the premiership from 1770 to 1782. (He held the courtesy title of Lord North from 1752.) The stubborn policies of George III led to the American war of independence.

Northcliffe, 1st Viscount (Alfred Charles Harmsworth) (1865–1922), British journalist and newspaper proprietor, b. near Dublin. He began *Answers* in 1888 with his brother Harold, (later Lord Rothermere). In 1894 they bought the *Evening News*, and in 1896 the *Daily Mail*. In 1908 he took over *The Times*.

Northumberland, John Dudley, Duke of (1502–53), English politician who attempted to secure for

his daughter-in-law Lady Jane Grey the succession to the throne after Edward VI.

Nostradamus or **Michel de Notre Dame** (1503–66), French astrologer and physician, known for his prophecies in *Centuries*.

Novalis, the pseudonym of Baron Friedrich von Hardenberg (1772–1801), German romantic poet and novelist, whose chief work is the unfinished *Heinrich von Ofterdingen*.

Novello, Ivor (1893–1951), Welsh actor, composer, songwriter *etc*. Born in Cardiff, his original name was David Ivor Davies.

Nozick, Robert (1938–2002). Libertarian philosopher. Author of *Anarchy, State and Utopia* (1974).

Nuffield, 1st Viscount (William Richard Morris) (1877–1963), British motor-car manufacturer and philanthropist. He provided large sums for the advancement of medicine in the university of Oxford, for Nuffield College, and in 1943 established the Nuffield Foundation.

Nureyev, Rudolf Hametovich (1938–93), the most famous ballet dancer of modern times. He defected to the West in 1961.

Nyerere, Julius (1922–99), First premier of independent Tanganyika in 1961; and president. In 1964 he negotiated its union with Zanzibar.

O

Oakeshott, Michael (1901–90). Philosopher famous for his opposition to rationalism.

Oates, Lawrence Edward (1880–1912), English Antarctic explorer. He joined Scott's expedition of 1910, and was one of the five to reach the south pole; but on the return journey, being crippled by frost-bite, he walked out into the blizzard to die.

Oates, Titus (1649–1705), English informer and agitator against Roman catholics.

Obama, Barack (b. 1961), US Democrat. Senator after 2004. Secured Democrat presidential nomination, 2008. Son of a black Kenyan father. Historic election victory (November 2008) to become the first black President of USA in 2009. Awarded Nobel Peace Prize, 2009. Re-elected in 2012 with a narrow but decisive victory. His domestic achievements included welfare reforms (Obamacare) and in foreign policy he healed rifts with Cuba and Iran. Succeeded by Donald Trump.

Obote, Milton (1924–2005), Uganda politician. Twice President of his country, 1966–71 and 1980–85.

O'Casey, Sean (1880–1964), Irish dramatist. Plays include *Juno and the Paycock*, *The Silver Tassie*, *Red Roses for Me*, and *Oak Leaves and Lavender*.

Ockham (Occam), William of (c. 1270–1349), English scholar and philosopher and one of the most original thinkers of all time. He belonged to the Order of Franciscans, violently opposed the temporal power of the Pope, espoused the cause of nominalism and laid the foundations of modern theories of government and theological scepticism. *See* Ockham's razor, Section J.

O'Connell, Daniel (1775–1847), Irish national leader. A barrister, he formed the Catholic Association in 1823 to fight elections; his followers aimed at the repeal of the Act of Union with England, and formed a Repeal Association in 1840; but the formation of the Young Ireland party, the potato famine, and ill-health undermined his position and he died in exile.

O'Connor, Feargus (1794–1855), working-class leader in England, of Irish birth. He presented the Chartist petition in 1848.

O'Connor, Thomas Power (1848–1929), Irish nationalist and journalist, sat in parliament 1880–1929 and founded the *Star*.

Oersted, Hans Christian (1777–1851), Danish physicist who discovered the connection between electricity and magnetism.

Offa (d. 796), king of Mercia (mid-England), was the leading English king of his day, and built a defensive dyke (**E18**) from the Dee to the Wye.

Offenbach, Jacques (1819–80), German-Jewish composer, b. Cologne, settled at Paris. Known for his light operas, especially *Tales of Hoffmann*.

Ohm, Georg Simon (1787–1854), German physicist, professor at Munich, who in 1826 formulated the law of electric current–Ohm's law (*see* **Section L**).

Olivier, Baron (Laurence Kerr Olivier) (1907–89), British actor and director, especially in Shakespearean roles. He also produced, directed, and played in films, including *Henry V*, *Hamlet*, and *Richard III*, and in TV drama. Director of the National Theatre (which opened in 1976) and in 1970 made a life peer. O.M. 1981. He was married to Dame Joan Plowright.

Oman, Sir Charles William (1860–1946), English historian, especially of the Peninsular War.

Omar ibn al Khattab (581–644), adviser to Mohammad, succeeded Abu Bakr as 2nd caliph. In his reign Islam became an imperial power. He died at the hands of a foreign slave.

Omar Khayyám (*c.* 1050–1123), Persian poet and mathematician, called Khayyám (tent-maker) because of his father's occupation. His fame as a scientist has been eclipsed by his *Rubaiyat*, publicised by Edward FitzGerald in 1859.

O'Neill, Eugene Gladstone (1888–1953), American playwright who won success in 1914 with the one-act play, *Thirst*. His later plays include *Anna Christie*, *Strange Interlude*, *Mourning Becomes Electra*, *The Iceman Cometh*. Nobel prize, 1936.

Oppenheimer, J. Robert (1904–67), American physicist who was director of atomic-energy research at Los Alamos, New Mexico, 1942–5, when the atomic bomb was developed but in 1949 he opposed work on the hydrogen bomb on moral grounds.

Orchardson, Sir William Quiller (1835–1910), Scottish painter, b. Edinburgh, best known for his *Napoleon I on board H.M.S. Bellerophon* and *Ophelia*.

Origen (*c.* 185–254), Christian philosopher and Biblical scholar, who taught at Alexandria and Caesarea, and was imprisoned and tortured in the persecution of Decius, 250.

Orpen, Sir William (1878–1931), painter of portraits, conversation pieces, and the 1914–18 war.

Ortega y Gasset, José (1883–1955), Spanish philosopher and essayist, known for his *Tema de Nuestro Tiempo* and *La Rebelión de Las Masas*.

Orwell, George (Eric Arthur Blair) (1903–50), b. India, author of *Animal Farm*, *Nineteen Eighty-Four* and the earlier *Down and Out in Paris*.

Osborne, John (1929–94), playwright, was one of the "Angry Young Men" of the 1950s. His play *Look Back In Anger* (1956) marked a revolution in English theatre. His other plays include *The Entertainer* (1957), *Luther* (1961) and *Inadmissible Evidence* (1965).

Osler, Sir William (1849–1919), Canadian physician. Authority on diseases of the blood and spleen.

Ossietzky, Carl von (1889–1938), German pacifist leader after the first world war; sent by Hitler to a concentration camp. Nobel peace prize 1935.

Oswald, St (*c.* 605–42), seized the Northumbrian throne in 633 and introduced Christianity.

Otto I (the Great) (912–73), founder of the Holy Roman Empire (he was crowned king of the Germans in 936 and emperor at Rome in 962). The son of Henry I of Germany, he built up a strong position in Italy (as regards the papacy) and in Germany where he established the East Mark (Austria).

Otto, Nikolaus August (1832–91). German engineer who built a gas engine (1878) using the four-stroke cycle that bears his name.

Ouida (Maria Louise Ramée) (1839–1908), English novelist of French extraction, whose romantic stories include *Under Two Flags*.

Ovid (43 B.C.–A.D. 18), Latin poet (Publius Ovidius Naso), chiefly remembered for his *Art of Love* and *Metamorphoses*. He died in exile.

Owen, Lord (David Owen). *See* **D18**.

Owen, Robert (1771–1858), Welsh pioneer socialist, b. Montgomeryshire. As manager, and later owner, of New Lanark cotton mills he tried to put his philanthropic views into effect; other communities on co-operative lines were founded in Hampshire and in America (New Harmony, Indiana) but although unsuccessful they were influential in many directions. He inaugurated socialism and the co-operative movement.

Owen, Wilfred (1893–1918), one of the best known poets of World War I. Born in Oswestry.

Owens, Jesse (1913–80), American black athlete whose 1936 Olympic triumph infuriated Hitler.

P

Pachmann, Vladimir de (1848–1933), Russian pianist gifted in the playing of Chopin.

Paderewski, Ignace Jan (1860–1941), Polish pianist and nationalist. He represented his country at Versailles and was the first premier of

a reconstituted Poland. He died in exile.

Paganini, Niccolo (1782–1840), Italian violinist and virtuoso who revolutionised violin technique.

Pahlevi, Mohammed Riza Shah (1919–80), last Shah of Iran. Pro-Western ruler of Iran whose suppression of opposition helped precipitate an Islamic revolution. Went into exile, 1979.

Paine, Thomas (1737–1809), British radical writer and activist, b. Suffolk. Emigrated to America in 1774. Pamphlet, *Common Sense*, in 1776 advocated independence from Britain. First to use expression 'United States'. Returned to Europe in 1787, writing the *Rights of Man* in support of French Revolution. Elected member of French National Convention, 1792; imprisoned for opposing execution of King Louis XVI. Condemned in Britain for treason, he returned to the USA. Also wrote the deist *The Age of Reason*, 1794–5.

Palestrina, Giovanni Pierluigi da (*c.* 1525–94), Italian composer of unaccompanied church music and madrigals. *See* **Section P**.

Palgrave, Sir Francis (1788–1861). English historian and archivist, an early editor of record series. His son **Francis Turner Palgrave** (1824–97) was a poet and critic and edited *The Golden Treasury*; another son, **William Gifford Palgrave** (1826–88) was a traveller and diplomat.

Palissy, Bernard (*c.* 1510–89), French potter who discovered the art of producing white enamel, after which he set up a porcelain factory in Paris which was patronised by royalty.

Palladio, Andrea (1508–80), Italian architect, b. Padua, whose style was modelled on ancient Roman architecture (symmetrical planning and harmonic proportions) and had wide influence; author of *I Quattro Libri dell' Architettura*.

Palmer, Samuel (1805–81), English landscape painter and etcher, follower of Blake whom he met in 1824. *Bright Cloud* and *In a Shoreham Garden* are in the Victoria and Albert Museum.

Palmerston, 3rd Viscount (Henry John Temple) (1784–1865), English Whig statesman. At first a Tory, he was later Whig foreign secretary for many years, and prime minister 1855 and 1859–65. Pursued vigorous foreign policy.

Pancras, St. (d. 304), patron saint of children, was put to death at the age of fourteen in the persecution under Diocletian.

Panizzi, Sir Anthony (1797–1879), Italian bibliographer and nationalist. Taking refuge in England after 1821, he became in 1856 chief librarian of the British Museum, undertook a new catalogue and designed the reading room.

Pankhurst, Emmeline (1858–1928), English suffragette who, with her daughters Christabel and Sylvia, worked for women's suffrage, organising the Women's Social and Political Union.

Panufnik, Sir Andrzej (1914–91), Polish-born composer. His first major work, the *Graduation Concert* was performed in 1935. The first Pole to be knighted.

Paolozzi, Sir Eduardo Luigi (1924–2005), Scottish sculptor and pioneer of Pop Art. Knighted, 1989.

Papin, Denis (1647–1714), French physicist and inventor. He invented the condensing pump, and was a pioneer in the development of the steam-engine. Not being a mechanic, he made all his experiments by means of models.

Paracelsus (Theophrastus Bombastus von Hohenhelm) (1493–1541), Swiss physician whose speculations though muddled served to reform medical thought. He criticised the established authorities, Galen and Aristotle, and experimented and made new chemical compounds. His earliest printed work was *Practica* (1529).

Park, Mungo (1771–1806), Scottish explorer in west Africa, where he lost his life. He wrote *Travels in the Interior of Africa* (1799).

Parker, Joseph (1830–1902), English Congregational preacher, at what became the City Temple.

Parks, Rosa (1913–2005), the "mother of the US civil rights movement" who famously refused to yield her seat on a bus in Montgomery, Alabama, in 1955.

Parnell, Charles Stewart (1846–91), Irish national leader. To draw attention to Ireland's problems, he used obstruction in parliament. He was president of the Land League but was not implicated in crimes committed by some members. His party supported Gladstone, who became converted to Home Rule. His citation in divorce proceedings brought his political career to an end.

Parry, Sir William Edward (1790–1855), English

explorer and naval commander in the Arctic, where he was sent to protect fisheries and also tried to reach the north pole.

Parsons, Sir Charles Algernon (1854–1931), English inventor of the steam-turbine, who built *Turbinia*, the first turbine-driven steamship in 1894.

Pascal, Blaise (1623–62), Frenchman of varied gifts, b. at Clermont-Ferrand. At first a mathematician, he patented a calculating machine. His *Lettres provinciales* influenced Voltaire. In 1654 he turned to religion. *See* **Jansenism, Section J.**

Pasternak, Boris Leonidovich (1890–1960), Russian poet and writer. B. Moscow, he published his first poems in 1931. For some years his time was spent in translating foreign literature, but in 1958 his novel *Dr. Zhivago*, which describes the Russian revolution and is in the Russian narrative tradition, was published abroad, though banned in the USSR. He was awarded a Nobel prize but was obliged to decline it.

Pasteur, Louis (1822–95), French chemist, b. at Dôle in the Jura, whose work was inspired by an interest in the chemistry of life. His researches on fermentation led to the science of bacteriology and his investigations into infectious diseases and their prevention to the science of immunology. The pathological–bacteriological import of his researches came about mainly through his disciples (Lister, Roux, and others) and not directly, though all founded on his early non-medical investigations on organisms of fermentation, *etc.*, which were of great importance in industry, and fundamentally. He spent most of his life as director of scientific studies at the Ecole Normale at Paris. The Institute Pasteur was founded in 1888.

Patmore, Coventry (1823–96), English poet. *The Angel in the House* deals with domesticity. Later became a Roman catholic, and *The Unknown Eros* is characterised by erotic mysticism.

Patrick, St. (387–461), the apostle of Ireland, was born in Britain or Gaul, and after some time on the continent (taken there after his capture by pirates) went as missionary to Ireland, where he fixed his see at Armagh. He wrote *Confessions*.

Patti, Adelina (1843–1919), famous coloratura soprano, b. in Madrid of Italian parents.

Paul VI (Giovanni Battista Montini) (1897–1978), elected Pope in 1963. His encyclical *Humanae Vitae* (1968) condemned contraception. He is now on course for beatification.

Pauli, Wolfgang (1900–58), Austrian-born physicist who first predicted theoretically the existence of neutrinos. Nobel prize 1945.

Pauling, Linus Carl (1901–94), American scientist. Won 1954 Nobel Prize for Chemistry (for work on molecular structure). Won 1963 Nobel Prize for Peace (the only person to receive two Nobel Prizes outright).

Pavarotti, Luciano (1935–2007), Italian operatic tenor. Acclaimed for such roles as Rodolfo in *La Bohème*, the Duke of Mantua in *Rigoletto etc.* He was the world's favourite opera singer.

Pavlov, Ivan Petrovich (1849–1936), Russian physiologist, known for his novel scientific experimental work on animal behaviour, particularly conditioned reflexes and the relation between psychological stress and brain function. Nobel prizewinner 1904. (Russia's first).

Pavlova, Anna (1882–1931), Russian ballerina, b. St. Petersburg, excelling in the roles of *Giselle* and the *Dying Swan*.

Peabody, George (1795–1869), American philanthropist, a successful merchant who lived mainly in London. He promoted education and housing.

Peacock, Thomas Love (1785–1866), English novelist, b. Weymouth. His works included *Headlong Hall* and *Nightmare Abbey*.

Pearson, Lester Bowles (1897–1972), Canadian politician. Prime minister 1963–8.

Peary, Robert Edwin (1856–1920), American arctic explorer, discoverer of the north pole (1909).

Peel, Sir Robert (1788–1850), English Conservative statesman, b. in Lancashire, son of a manufacturer. He first held office in 1811. With Wellington he enacted toleration for Roman catholics in 1829. As home secretary he reorganised London police. He developed a new policy of Conservatism, and in 1846, largely as a result of the Irish famine, he repealed the corn laws but divided his party.

Peierls, Sir Rudolf (1907–95), Wykeham Professor of Physics at Oxford, 1963–74. A founding father of the atomic age.

Peirce, Charles Sanders (1839–1914), American physicist and philosopher, founder of the theory of pragmatism (*see* **Section J**).

Pele (b. 1940), legendary Brazilian footballer. Real name Edson Arantes do Nascimento.

Pence, Mike (b. 1959), US Republican politician. Vice-President since 2017. Former Governor of Indiana.

Penfield, Wilder Graves (1891–1976), Canadian brain surgeon, author of *The Cerebral Cortex of Man, Epilepsy and the Functional Anatomy of the Human Brain*. O.M.

Penn, William (1644–1718), English Quaker and founder of Pennsylvania. The son of Admiral William Penn, he persisted in becoming a Quaker, and on receiving for his father's services a crown grant in America he founded Pennsylvania. He wrote *No Cross, No Crown*.

Penney, Baron (William George Penney) (1909–91), British scientist. His nuclear research team developed the advanced gas-cooled reactor.

Pepys, Samuel (1633–1703), English diarist and naval administrator. His diary, 1660–69, was kept in cipher and not deciphered till 1825. It gives vivid personal details and covers the plague and fire of London. (The first complete version of the diary issued in 1970.) *See* **M11**(2).

Perceval, Spencer (1762–1812), Prime Minister, 1809–12. Assassinated by a deranged bankrupt.

Pereda, José Maria de (1833–1906), Spanish regional novelist (around his native Santander).

Peres, Shimon (1923–2016). Israeli statesman. He built up Israel's military power but pursued peace.

Pérez Galdós, Benito (1843–1920), Spanish novelist and dramatist, who has been compared to Balzac for his close study and portrayal of all social classes, especially in the series of 46 short historical novels *Episodios nacionales*. His longer novels, *Novelas españolas contemporáneas*, some of which are translated, number 31.

Pergolesi, Giovanni Battista (1710–36), Italian composer, best known for his humorous opera *La Serva Padrona* and his *Stabat Mater*.

Pericles (*c*. 490–429 B.C.), Athenian statesman, general, and orator, who raised Athens to a point of its fullest prosperity, and greatest beauty, with the Parthenon, Erechtheum, and other buildings; but he died of plague following the outbreak of the Peloponnesian war.

Perkin, Sir William Henry (1838–1907), English chemist, b. London, who while seeking to make a substitute for quinine discovered in 1856 the first artificial aniline dye, mauve.

Perón, Juan (**Domingo**) (1895–1974), Argentinian populist politician. President, 1946–55. Returned in triumph from exile (1973). His second wife **Eva** (known as **Evita**) was idolized by the masses. His third wife **Isabelita Péron**, succeeded him as President on his death in 1974.

Perry, Frederick John (1909–95), the greatest player in the history of British lawn tennis. Last British player to win singles titles at Wimbledon (1934, 1935 and 1936) until Andrew Murray.

Persius Flaccus Aulus (A.D. 34–62), Roman satirist and Stoic philosopher.

Perugino, Pietro (1446–1524), Italian artist. He worked in the Sistine Chapel at Rome and he taught Raphael.

Perutz, Max Ferdinand (1914–2002), British chemist. Nobel Prize, 1962 (with Sir John Kendrew). Founding father of the world-renowned Laboratory of Molecular Biology at Cambridge.

Pestalozzi, Johann Heinrich (1746–1827), Swiss educational reformer whose theories laid the foundation of modern primary education. He wrote *How Gertrude Educates Her Children*.

Pétain, Henri Philippe (1856–1951), French general and later collaborator. In the first world war he was in command at Verdun. Headed the pro-German Vichy regime in World War II.

Peter I, the Great (1672–1725), emperor of Russia. Son of **Alexei**, he succeeded his brother after some difficulty. He reorganised the army, and, after coming to Deptford to learn shipbuilding, he created a navy. To some extent he westernised Russian social life, and created a new capital at St. Petersburg (1703). In war with Charles XII of Sweden he was at first defeated, but later victorious at Poltava (1709). He married a peasant, Catherine, who succeeded him.

Peter the Hermit (*c*. 1050–1115), French monk who preached the First Crusade, originated by pope Urban II at the council of Clermont. He went on the crusade, but gave up at Antioch.

Petrarch, Francesco (1304–78), Italian poet, son of a Florentine exile. He is chiefly remembered for his poems *To Laura*, but he was also a scholar.

Petrie, Sir Flinders (1853–1942), British egyptologist who excavated in Britain after 1875, Egypt (1880–1924), and Palestine (1927–38). A pioneer of the techniques of modern archaeology.

Pevsner, Sir Nikolaus (1902–83), German-born architectural historian. Author of *The Buildings of England* (46 vols., 1951–74).

Phidias (5th cent. B.C.), Greek sculptor especially in gold, ivory and bronze, worked at Athens for Pericles. No certain examples of his work are extant, but the Elgin marbles in the British Museum may be from his designs.

Philip II of France (1165–1223), son of Louis VII. He went on the Third Crusade with Richard I of England, but in France is mainly remembered for firm government, the recovery of Normandy from England, and the beautifying of Paris.

Philip II of Macedonia (382–336 B.C.), a successful commander, made his the leading military kingdom in Greece. Father of Alexander the Great.

Philip II of Spain (1527–98), succeeded his father Charles V in Spain and the Netherlands, also in Spanish interests overseas. In the Netherlands his strict Roman catholic policy provoked a revolt which ended in 1579 in the independence of the United Provinces. He married Mary Tudor of England; and after her death sent the ill-fated Armada against Elizabeth in 1588.

Philip V of Spain (1683–1746), first Bourbon king, succeeded his great-uncle Charles II and was grandson of Louis XIV. His accession provoked European war.

Phillip, Arthur (1738–1814), first governor of New South Wales. Under his command the first fleet of 717 convicts set sail from Britain to Australia, and with the founding of Sydney in 1788 colonisation of the whole country began.

Phillips, Stephen (1868–1915), English poet who wrote verse dramas, *e.g. Paolo and Francesca*.

Piaf, Edith (1915–63), French singer and actress, renowned for her interpretation of the *Chanson*. Her real name was Edith Giovanna Gassion.

Piast, first Polish dynasty in Poland until the 14th cent. and until the 17th cent. in Silesia.

Piazzi, Giuseppe (1746–1826), Italian who discovered Ceres, the first of the asteroids to be seen by man.

Picasso, Pablo Ruiz (1881–1973) Spanish painter, b. Málaga; received his early training in Catalonia and settled in Paris in 1903. He and Braque were the originators of Cubism (*c.* 1909). His influence over contemporary art is comparable with that exercised by Cézanne (*q.v.*) over the artists of his time. Perhaps the best-known single work is his mural *Guernica*, expressing his loathing of fascism and the horrors of war.

Piccard, Auguste (1884–1962), Swiss physicist, noted for balloon ascents into the stratosphere and for submarine research. In 1960 his son **Jacques** (1922–2008) descended over 7 miles in the Marianas trench in the western Pacific in a bathyscaphe designed and built by his father.

Piggott, Lester (Keith) (b. 1935), outstanding jockey. Won the Derby 9 times, champion jockey 11 times. Rode 4,000th winner in Britain, 14 August 1982.

Piketty, Thomas (b. 1971). Economist, author of *Capital in the Twenty-First Century* (2014).

Pilsudski, Joseph (1867–1935), Polish soldier and statesman who in 1919 attempted by force to restore Poland's 1772 frontiers but was driven back. From 1926 he was dictator.

Pindar (522–443 B.C.), Greek lyric poet.

Pinero, Sir Arthur Wing (1855–1934), English dramatist whose plays include *Dandy Dick*, *The Second Mrs. Tanqueray* and *Mid-Channel*.

Pinochet, Augusto (1915–2006), Chilean dictator who led the 1973 coup and presided over a brutal regime, which became notorious for human rights abuses.

Pinter, Harold (1930–2008), British playwright, whose plays are notable for their spare dialogue, pauses, and sense of menace, *e.g.*, *The Birthday Party* (1957), *The Caretaker* (1959), *The Homecoming* (1965) and *No Man's Land* (1975). His many screenplays include *The French Lieutenant's Woman* (1981), from John Fowles's novel. Created CBE (1966) and a Companion of Honour (2002). Nobel Prize, 2005. A towering literary figure.

Pirandello, Luigi (1867–1936), Italian dramatist and novelist whose plays include *Six Characters in Search of an Author*. Nobel prize 1934.

Pissarro, Camille (1830–1903), French impressionist painter of landscapes; studied under Corot.

Pitman, Sir Isaac (1813–97), b. Trowbridge. Inventor of a system of phonographic shorthand.

Pitt, William (1759–1806), English statesman. Younger son of the Earl of Chatham, (*q.v.*) he entered parliament at 21 and became prime minister at 24 in 1783 when parties were divided and the American war had been lost. He rose to the position, and held office with scarcely a break till his death. An able finance minister, he introduced reforms, and would have gone further, but Napoleon's meteoric rise obliged him to lead European allies in a long struggle against France. He died worn out by his efforts.

Pius XII (1876–1958), elected pope 1939. As Eugenio Pacelli, he was papal nuncio in Germany and later papal secretary of state. It has been argued that he could have taken a stronger line against Nazi war crimes.

Pizarro, Francisco (*c.* 1478–1541), Spanish adventurer, b. Trujillo. After Columbus's earlier discoveries, he conquered Peru for Spain, ending the Inca empire. He was murdered by his men.

Planck, Max (1857–1947), German mathematical physicist, b. Kiel, whose main work was on thermodynamics. In 1900 he invented a mathematical formula to account for some properties of the thermal radiation from a hot body which has since played an important role in physics. Nobel prize 1918. *See* **Quantum theory, Section L**.

Plato (427–347 B.C.), Athenian philosopher, pupil of Socrates, teacher of Aristotle. He founded a school at Athens under the name of the Academy, where he taught philosophy and mathematics. His great work is his *Dialogues*, which includes the *Republic*, the longest and most celebrated. His known writings have come down to us and constitute one of the most influential bodies of work in history.

Playfair, 1st Baron (Lyon Playfair) (1818–98), a far-sighted Victorian who stood for the greater recognition of science in national life. He forsook his profession as professor of chemistry at Edinburgh to enter parliament.

Plimsoll, Samuel (1824–98), English social reformer, b. Bristol. He realised the evil of overloading unseaworthy ships, and as MP for Derby he secured the Merchant Shipping Act, 1876 which imposed a line (the Plimsoll Mark) above which no ship must sink while loading.

Pliny the Elder (A.D. 23–79), Roman naturalist, author of a *Natural History*. He died of fumes and exhaustion while investigating the eruption of Vesuvius. His nephew, **Pliny the Younger** (A.D. 62–113), wrote *Letters* notable for the insight they give into Roman life.

Plisetskaya, Maya (1925–2015), one of the great ballerinas of the Soviet Union.

Plotinus (*c.* 203–*c.* 262), Greek philosopher, was the founder of Neoplatonism, which had considerable influence on early Christian thought.

Plutarch (*c.* 46–120), Greek biographer, whose *Lives* portray 46 leading historical figures (in pairs, a Greek and a Roman whose careers were similar). Although based on myth his *Life of Lycurgus* about life in Sparta had a profound influence on later writers, *e.g.*, Rousseau and the romantic philosophers. He was educated at Athens but visited Rome.

Poe, Edgar Allan (1809–49), American poet and story-writer, b. Boston, Mass. His poems include *The Raven*, *To Helen*, and *Annabel Lee*, and his stories, often weird and fantastic, include *Tales of the Grotesque and Arabesque*.

Poincaré, Raymond Nicolas (1860–1934), French statesman. He was president 1913–20, and as prime minister occupied the Ruhr in 1923.

Pol Pot (1926–98) Evil dictator of Kampuchea (now Cambodia) and mass murderer.

Pole, Reginald (1500–58), archbishop of Canterbury, cardinal of the Roman church and antagonist of the reformation. He opposed Henry VIII's divorce and went abroad in 1532, writing *De Unitate Ecclesiastica*; as a result of which his mother, Countess of Salisbury, and other relatives were executed. Under Mary he became archbishop and died the year she did.

Polo, Marco (1256–1323), Venetian traveller, who claimed to have made journeys through China, India, *etc.*, visiting the court of Kubla Khan, and leaving an account of his travels.

Pompadour, Jeanne Antoine Poisson, Marquise de

(1721–64), mistress of Louis XV of France. She exercised disastrous political influence.

Pompey (106–48 B.C.), Roman commander, who cleared the Mediterranean of pirates, and became triumvir with Caesar and Crassus.

Pompidou, Georges Jean Raymond (1911–74), French administrator and politician who succeeded de Gaulle as president 1969.

Pope, Alexander (1688–1744), English poet, b. London, of a Roman catholic family, and largely self-educated. His brilliant satire was frequently directed against his contemporaries. He is remembered for *The Rape of the Lock*, *The Dunciad*, *Essay on Criticism*, and *Essay on Man*.

Popper, Sir Karl Raimund (1902–94), renowned philosopher of science, b. Vienna; author of *The Open Society and Its Enemies* (1945), *Conjectures and Refutations* (1963), *Objective Knowledge* (1972).

Potter, Beatrix (1866–1943). Famous author and illustrator of books for children (e.g. *The Tale of Peter Rabbit*).

Potter, Dennis (1935–94), television dramatist, wrote many innovative and stimulating plays. These included three six-part serials: *Pennies from Heaven* (1978), *The Singing Detective* (1986) etc.

Potter, Mary (1847–1913), the only Englishwoman to found a religious nursing order, the Little Company of Mary (known as the "Blue Nuns").

Pound, Ezra Loomis (1885–1972), American poet and writer on varied subjects. Noted for his translations of a wide variety of poetry.

Poussin, Nicolas (1593–1665), French painter. He lived in Rome 1624–40, 1642–65. His *Golden Calf* is in the National Gallery.

Powell, Colin (b. 1937). US Secretary of State, 2001–05 (the first black American to hold this office). General who won decisive victory in Gulf War but faced difficult decisions in war on terrorism.

Powell, (John) Enoch (1912–98), English politician, at first Conservative, later Ulster Unionist. A great parliamentarian and renowned orator, his right-wing views on immigration were unacceptable to the party leadership. He was also a Greek scholar.

Powys, John Cowper (1872–1964), English writer, best known for his novel *Wolf Solent* and his essays *The Meaning of Culture* and *A Philosophy of Solitude*. His brothers, **Theodore Francis** (1875–1953) and **Llewelyn** (1884–1939) were also writers.

Prasad, Rajendra (1884–1963), Indian statesman, first president of the Republic of India, 1950–62.

Pratchett, Sir Terry (1948–2015), best-selling author of the Discworld tales. A humourist and fantasist.

Praxiteles (4th cent. B.C.), Greek sculptor, whose main surviving work is *Hermes carrying Dionysus*.

Preece, Sir William Henry (1834–1913), Welsh electrical engineer, associated with the expansion of wireless telegraphy and telephony.

Presley, Elvis (Aron) (1935–77). Legendary rock singer whose songs (Hound Dog, Love Me Tender etc.) sold millions. Buried at Gracelands, Memphis.

Prichard, James Cowles (1786–1848), English ethnologist who perceived that people should be studied as a whole. His works include *Researches into the Physical History of Mankind* and *The Natural History of Man*. He practised medicine.

Priestley, John Boynton (1894–1984), English critic, novelist, and playwright, b. Bradford. His works include the novels *The Good Companions*, *Angel Pavement*, and the plays *Dangerous Corner*, *Time and the Conways*, *I Have Been Here Before*, and *The Linden Tree*, O.M. 1977. He married the writer and archaeologist **Jacquetta Hawkes** (d. 1996) in 1953.

Priestley, Joseph (1733–1804), English chemist who worked on gases, and shared with Scheele the discovery of oxygen. A presbyterian minister, he was for his time an advanced thinker. In 1794 he settled in America.

Prior, Matthew (1664–1721), English poet. In early life he was a diplomat. He was a neat epigrammatist and writer of occasional pieces. His works include *The City Mouse and Country Mouse* and *Four Dialogues of the Dead*.

Pritchett, Sir Victor Sawdon, (1900–97) accomplished novelist, short-story writer and critic. His *Complete Short Stories* were published in 1990 and his *Complete Essays* in 1992. C.H., 1993.

Prokofiev, Serge Sergeyevich (1891–1953), Russian composer, whose music has a strong folk-song element, rich in melody and invention. He wrote operas such as *The Love of Three Oranges*, *The Betrothal in a Nunnery*, *War and Peace*; ballets: *Romeo and Juliet*, *Cinderella*; symphonies, chamber music, and the music for Eisenstein's films *Alexander Nevsky*, *Ivan the Terrible*.

Protagoras (c. 480–411 B.C.), Greek philosopher, chief of the Sophists, noted for his scepticism and disbelief in objective truth, and for his doctrine that "man is the measure of all things."

Proudhon, Pierre Joseph (1809–65), French socialist. In 1840 he propounded the view that property is theft. His main work is *Système des contradictions économiques* (1846).

Proust, Marcel (1871–1922), French psychological novelist, author of a series of novels known under the title of *A la recherche du temps perdu*.

Ptolemy of Alexandria (Claudius Ptolemaeus) (fl. A.D. 140), astronomer and founder of scientific cartography. In the *Almagest* he attempted a mathematical presentation of the paths along which the planets appear to move. His other great work was his *Geographical Outline*.

Puccini, Giacomo (1858–1924), Italian composer, b. Lucca, whose operas include *Manon Lescaut*, *La Bohème*, *Tosca*, *Madam Butterfly*, and *Turandot* (completed by a friend).

Pugin, Augustus (1812–52), Architect whose main work on such Catholic cathedrals as Birmingham and Newcastle aided the Gothic revival. A visionary giant of the Victorian age.

Pupin, Michael Idvorsky (1858–1935), physicist and inventor (telephony and X-rays).

Purcell, Henry (1659–95), English composer, b. Westminster, son of a court musician. Organist of the chapel royal and composer to Charles II. His best works are vocal and choral. *See* **P5**(2).

Pusey, Edward Bouverie (1800–82), English theologian, a leader of the Oxford or Tractarian movement with Keble and at first also with Newman, till the latter became Roman catholic.

Pushkin, Alexander (1799–1837), Russian writer, b. Moscow, whose place in Russian literature ranks with Shakespeare's in English. He wrote in many forms—lyrical poetry and narrative verse, drama, folk-tales and short stories. Musicians have used his works as plots for operas—the fairy romance *Russlan and Ludmilla* was dramatised by Glinka; the verse novel *Eugene Onegin* and the short story *The Queen of Spades* were adapted by Tchaikovsky, and the tragic drama *Boris Godunov* formed the subject of Mussorgsky's opera. He was inspired by the wild beauty of the Caucasus. He was killed in a duel defending his wife's honour.

Putin, Vladimir (b. 1952), President of Russia from January 2000, when he succeeded Yeltsin, to 2008. Prime Minister, 2008–12. Re-elected President, 2012. An authoritarian and nationalist.

Pym, John (1584–1643), English parliamentary leader in opposition to Charles I. He promoted the impeachment of Strafford and Laud.

Pyrrho (c. 360 B.C–270 B.C.), Greek philosopher who established the tradition of scepticism (**J46**). He introduced Buddhist concepts to Greece.

Pythagoras (c. 582–500 B.C.), Greek philosopher, b. on the island of Samos, which he left c. 530 to settle at Croton, a Greek city in southern Italy. He was a mystic and mathematician.

Q

Quasimodo, Salvatore (1901–68), Italian poet of humanity and liberal views whose works include *La vita non è sogno*. Nobel prizewinner 1959.

Quesnay, François (1694–1774), French economist, founder of the physiocratic school. *See* **Section J**.

Quiller-Couch, Sir Arthur Thomas (1863–1944), Known as "Q." Professor of English, Cambridge, 1912–44.

R

Rabelais, François (c. 1495–1553), French satirist. At first in religious orders, he later studied medicine and practised at Lyons. His works are full of riotous mirth, wit and wisdom. The main ones are *Gargantua* and *Pantagruel*.

Rabin, Yitzhak (1922–95) Israeli defence chief and statesman. He was first Prime Minister from 1974–77. Again as Prime Minister he was an architect of the peace process. Assassinated in 1995.

Rachel, Elisa (Élisa Felix) (1821–58), Alsatian Jewish tragic actress (e.g. in Racine's *Phèdre*).

Rachmaninov, Sergey Vasilyevich (1873–1943), Russian composer and pianist, b. Nijni-Novgorod (now Gorki), best known for his piano music, especially his *Prelude. See* **Section P**.

Racine, Jean (1639–99), French tragic poet whose dramas include *Andromaque*, *Iphigénie* and *Phèdre*. An orphan, he was brought up by grandparents who sent him to Port Royal school where he acquired a love of the classics. In Paris he became a friend of Molière, whose company acted his first play, and of Boileau, with whom he became joint historiographer to Louis XIV. *Esther* and *Athalie* were written for Madame de Maintenon's schoolgirls.

Rackham, Arthur (1867–1939), English artist and book-illustrator, especially of fairy tales.

Radhakrishnan, Sir Sarvepalli (1888–1975), Indian philosopher and statesman; President of India 1962–7. He was at one time a professor at Oxford.

Raffles, Sir Thomas Stamford (1781–1826), English colonial administrator who founded a settlement at Singapore in 1819. He founded London Zoo.

Raikes, Robert (1735–1811), English educational pioneer, whose lead in the teaching of children at Gloucester on Sundays led to an extensive Sunday School movement.

Raleigh, Sir Walter (1552–1618), adventurer and writer. He found favour at the court of Elizabeth I, helped to put down the Irish rebellion of 1580, and in 1584 began the colonisation of Virginia, introducing potatoes and tobacco to the British Isles. At the accession of James I he lost favour and was sent to the Tower, where he wrote his *History of the World*. Released in 1615 to lead an expedition to the Orinoco, he was executed when it failed.

Ramakrishna (1836–86), famous Indian mystic.

Raman, Sir Chandrasekhara Venkata (1888–1970), Indian physicist whose main work has been in spectroscopy. For his research on the diffusion of light and discovery of the "Raman effect" he was awarded the 1930 Nobel prize.

Ramanuja (*fl.* A.D. 1125) Indian philosopher, the most revered teacher of the Vaishnava Hindus.

Rameau, Jean Philippe (1683–1764), French composer and church organist whose works on musical theory influenced musical development.

Ramkrishna Paramahamsa (1834–86), one of the great spiritual Hindu teachers of modern India.

Ramón y Cajal, Santiago (1852–1934), Spanish histologist who made discoveries in the structure of the nervous system. Shared 1906 Nobel prize.

Ramsay, Sir William (1852–1916), Scottish chemist, and discoverer with Lord Rayleigh of argon. Later he discovered helium and other inert gases, which he called neon, krypton, and xenon. Nobel prizewinner 1904.

Ramsey, Arthur Michael (1904–88), archbishop of Canterbury, 1961–74, who worked for church unity.

Rand, Ayn (1905–82), Russian-born US novelist and philosopher who propagated the philosophy of Objectivism (*see* **Section J**) in her novels.

Ranke, Leopold von (1795–1886), German historian, one of the first to base his work on methodical research. Author of a *History of the Popes*.

Raphael (Raffaello Santi) (1483–1520) of Urbino was the youngest of the three great artists of the High Renaissance. He was taught at Perugia by Perugino, and then at Florence he came under the influence of Leonardo and Michelangelo. Raphael's Madonnas, remarkable for their simplicity and grace, include the *Madonna of the Grand Duke* (Palazzo Pitti), the *Sistine Madonna* (Dresden) the *Madonna with the Goldfinch* (Uffizi), the *Madonna of Foligno* (Vatican), and the *Ansidei Madonna* (National Gallery). He painted the frescoes on the walls of the Stanza della Segnatura in the Vatican, and designed 10 cartoons for tapestries for the Sistine Chapel. After the death of Bramante, appointed architect for the rebuilding of St. Peter's.

Rasputin, Grigori Yefimovich (1869–1916), Russian peasant from Siberia, a cunning adventurer who at the court of Nicholas II exerted a malign influence over the Tsarina through his apparent ability to improve the health of the sickly Tsarevich Alexis. He was later murdered.

Rathbone, Eleanor (1872–1946), social reformer who championed women's pensions and in her book *The Disinherited Family* set out the case for family allowances.

Rattle, Sir Simon (b. 1955), foremost conductor. Music Director, City of Birmingham Symphony Orchestra, 1991–8. Appointed (1999) first British conductor of Berlin Symphony Orchestra. Music Director, London Symphony Orchestra (after 2017).

Ravel, Maurice (1875–1937), French composer, pupil of Fauré, one of the leaders of the impressionist movement.

Rawlinson, Sir Henry Creswicke (1810–95), English diplomat and archaeologist. He made Assyrian collections now in the British Museum and translated the Behistun inscription of the Persian king Darius. He also wrote on cuneiform inscriptions and on Assyrian history.

Rawls, John (1921–2002), influential American philosopher concerned with justice. Author of *A Theory of Justice* and *Political Liberalism*.

Ray, John (1627–1705), English naturalist. A blacksmith's son, he went to Cambridge, travelled in Europe, and produced a classification of plants. He also wrote on zoology.

Rayleigh, 3rd Baron (John William Strutt) (1842–1919), English mathematician and physicist. He studied sound and the wave theory of light; and with Sir William Ramsay discovered argon. Nobel prizewinner 1904.

Read, Sir Herbert (1893–1968), English poet and art critic. His writings include *Collected Poems*, *The Meaning of Art etc.*

Reade, Charles (1814–84), English novelist. His chief work is *The Cloister and the Hearth*. He also wrote *Peg Woffington*, *It is Never too Late to Mend*, and *Griffith Gaunt*.

Reagan, Ronald (1911–2004). US President, 1981–89; former TV and film star, 1937–66. Governor of California, 1967–74. Won Republican victory, 1980. Re-elected in landslide victory, 1984. His popularity remained, helping ensure the election of George Bush (*q.v.*) as his successor.

Réaumur, René Antoine Ferchault de (1683–1757), French naturalist who invented a thermometer of eighty degrees, using alcohol.

Récamier, Jeanne Françoise (*née* Bernard) (1777–1849), French beauty and holder of a noted salon. Her husband was a banker.

Rees, Lord (Sir Martin Rees) (b. 1942). Astronomer Royal since 1995. Former Master of Trinity College, Cambridge. President of the Royal Society. Order of Merit.

Reeves, Jim (1923–64), internationally-popular country music legend.

Regnault, Henry Victor (1810–78), French chemist and physicist, who worked on gases, latent heat, and steam-engines.

Reith, 1st Baron (John Charles Walsham Reith) (1889–1971), Scottish civil engineer, first director-general of the BBC, 1927–38

Rembrandt (Rembrandt Harmenszoon van Rijn) (1606–69), Dutch painter and etcher, b. Leiden, a miller's son, one of the most individual and prolific artists of any period. His output includes portraits, landscapes, large groups, etchings, and drawings. He settled in Amsterdam establishing his reputation with *The Anatomy Lesson*, painted in 1632. In 1634 he married Saskia, a burgomaster's daughter. *The Night Watch* was painted in 1642; it was not well received and Saskia died the same year, leaving the infant Titus. The path from relative wealth to lonely old age is depicted in his self-portraits. Caring little for convention or formal beauty, his work is characterised by bold realism and spiritual beauty, by vitality and simplicity. His understanding of the play of colour and the effects of light can give his pictures a mystical beauty, as in the atmospheric painting *The Mill*. His figures, even for religious pictures, were taken from real life, the Jews in the etching *Christ Healing* from the Jewish quarter where he lived. He met the misfortunes of later life by withdrawing from society, but it was then that he produced his greatest works.

Renan, Ernest (1823–92), French writer who wrote on religious themes, especially a *Life of Jesus*.

Rendell, Ruth (1930–2015), a prolific crime writer famous for her creation of Chief Inspector Wexford. The 'Queen of crime fiction'.

Reni, Guido. *See* **Guido Reni**.

Rennie, John (1761–1821), Scottish civil engineer who built the old Waterloo and Southwark bridges. He also designed docks at London, Liverpool, Leith *etc.*; constructed Plymouth breakwater; made canals and drained fens.

Renoir, Pierre Auguste (1841–1919), French impressionist painter, b. Limoges. His works include portraits, still-life, landscapes, and groups, including

La Loge, Les Parapluies, La première Sortie, La Place Pigalle. He was later crippled with arthritis.

Reuter, Paul Julius, Freiherr von (1816–99), German pioneer of telegraphic press service, who in 1851 fixed his headquarters in London.

Reymont, Vladislav Stanislav (1868–1925), Polish novelist, author of *The Peasants.* Nobel prize, 1924.

Reynolds, Sir Joshua (1723–92), English portrait painter, b. Plympton, Devon. His portraits, which include *Mrs. Siddons*, are remarkable for expressiveness and colour and he was a sympathetic painter of children. He was first president of the R.A. from 1768 till his death.

Rhodes, Cecil John (1853–1902), English empire-builder. B. at Bishop's Stortford, he went to South Africa for health reasons and there prospered at the diamond mines. He became prime minister of what was then Cape Colony and secured British power in what is now Zimbabwe and Zambia. He withdrew from politics after the failure of the Jameson Raid of 1895. He founded scholarships at Oxford for overseas students.

Ricardo, David (1772–1823), English political economist of Jewish descent. By occupation a London stockbroker, he wrote a major work, *Principles of Political Economy.*

Rice, Condoleezza (b. 1954), US Secretary of State, 2005–09. Former National Security Adviser.

Richard I (1157–99), succeeded his father Henry II as king of England in 1189. A patron of troubadours and a soldier (Lion-heart), he went on the third Crusade and took Acre, but could not recover Jerusalem from Saladin. On his return journey across Europe he was imprisoned and ransomed. He was killed in war with France.

Richard II (1367–1400), son of the Black Prince, succeeded his grandfather Edward III as king of England in 1377. Artistic and able, but erratic and egocentric, he personally at the age of fourteen met the Peasants' Revolt in 1381, making untenable promises. Latterly his rule became increasingly arbitrary, and he was deposed and imprisoned in 1399.

Richard III (1452–85), King of England (1483–5), younger brother of the Yorkist, Edward IV, is believed to have murdered his two nephews in the Tower. He was defeated and killed at Bosworth by the invading Earl of Richmond, who as Henry VII brought to an end the Wars of the Roses, Richard's character is disputed, but he was able and might have been a good ruler. In 2012 his bones were discovered under an old friary in Leicester. He was reburied in Leicester Cathedral on 26 March 2015

Richard, Sir Cliff (b. 1940) Britain's greatest solo singer, 'the first Knight of Pop'. Born Harry Webb in Lucknow, India. His first hit was '*Move It*' in 1958.

Richards, Sir Gordon (1904–86), foremost English jockey who rode 4,870 winners. Knighted in 1953 after he won the Epsom Derby on *Pinza.*

Richardson, Sir Albert Edward (1880–1964), British architect, author of *Georgian Architecture.*

Richardson, Sir Owen Willans (1879–1959), English physicist who worked on thermionics, or emission of electricity from hot bodies. Nobel prizewinner 1928.

Richardson, Sir Ralph David (1902–83), English actor who worked at the Old Vic, on the West End stage, and at Stratford-on-Avon, and appeared in films, including *South Riding, Anna Karenina*, and *The Fallen Idol.*

Richardson, Samuel (1689–1761), English author of *Pamela, Clarissa*, and *The History of Sir Charles Grandison*, exercised considerable influence on the development of the novel.

Richelieu, Armand Jean du Plessis, Duc de (1585–1642), French statesman, cardinal of the Roman church. As minister to Louis XIII from 1624 till his death, he built up the power of the French crown at home in central government, and by his military preparedness and active foreign policy gave France a lead in Europe.

Ridley, Nicholas (1500–55), English Protestant martyr, bishop of Rochester and later of London. He was burnt with Latimer.

Rienzi, Cola di (1313–54), Italian patriot, b. Rome, led a popular rising in 1347 and for seven months reigned as tribune, but had to flee, was imprisoned, and eventually murdered.

Rilke, Rainer Maria (1875–1926), German lyric poet, b. Prague. His work, marked by beauty of style, culminated in the *Duino Elegies* and *Sonnets to Orpheus*, both written in 1922, which

gave a new musicality to German verse. His visits to Russia in 1899 and 1900 and his admiration for Rodin influenced his artistic career.

Rimbaud, Jean Nicolas Arthur (1854–91), French poet, b. Charleville, on the Meuse. In his brief poetic career (4 years from about the age of 16) he prepared the way for symbolism (*Bateau ivre, Les Illuminations*) and anticipated Freud (*Les déserts de l'amour*). He became intimate with Verlaine and at 18 had completed his memoirs. *Une saison en enfer.*

Rimsky-Korsakov, Nikolai Andreyevich (1844–1908), Russian composer whose works include the operas *The Maid of Pskov, The Snow Maiden, Le Coq d'or*, and the symphonic suite *Scheherezade.* He was a brilliant orchestrator and rescored many works, *e.g.* Borodin's *Prince Igor.*

Rizzio, David (1533?–66), Italian musician and secretary of Mary, Queen of Scots. He was murdered in her presence at Holyrood by her jealous husband, Darnley.

Robbia, Luca Della (1400–82), Florentine sculptor who introduced enamelled terra-cotta work.

Roberts of Kandahar, 1st Earl (Frederick Sleigh Roberts) (1832–1914), British general. He took part in the suppression of the Indian Mutiny, in the Afghan war (relieving Kandahar), and when in command in South Africa in the Boer War he relieved Kimberley and advanced to Pretoria.

Robertson, Sir William (1860–1933), the first British soldier to rise from private to field-marshal.

Robeson, Paul (1898–1976), black American singer, b. Princeton, especially remembered for his singing of Negro spirituals, and his appearance in works ranging from *Showboat* to *Othello.*

Robespierre, Maximilien Marie Isidoire de (1758–94), French revolutionary. A country advocate, b. Arras, he was in 1789 elected to the States General and in 1792 to the Convention. He became a leader of the Jacobins, the more extreme party which came to power under stress of war and after the king's execution in 1793. In this crisis, the Committee of Public Safety, of which he was a member and which used his reputation as a cloak, sent many to the guillotine. He opposed the cult of Reason and inaugurated the worship of the Supreme Being. In the reaction from the reign of terror he was denounced, tried to escape, but was guillotined.

Robinson, Mary (b. 1944), President of Republic of Ireland, 1990–97 (1st woman President). Labour politician. Served as UN High Commissioner for Human Rights, 1997–2002.

Robinson, William Heath (1872–1944), English cartoonist and book-illustrator, especially known for his humorous drawings of machines.

Rob Roy (Robert McGregor) (1671–1734), Scottish freebooter who helped the poor at the expense of the rich, and played a lone hand in the troubled times of the Jacobite rising of 1715.

Robsart, Amy (1532–60), English victim (it is believed) of murder. The wife of Robert Dudley, Earl of Leicester, she was found dead at Cumnor Place. Her death was used by Scott in *Kenilworth.*

Rockefeller, John Davison (1839–1937), American philanthropist, b. Richford, N.Y. He settled in Cleveland, Ohio, and with his brother William founded the Standard Oil Company, making a fortune. His philanthropic enterprises are carried on by the Rockefeller Foundation. **Nelson Rockefeller** (1908–79), Vice-Pres. of the United States 1974–7, was his grandson.

Rodin, Auguste (1841–1917), French sculptor, b. Paris. His best-known works include *Le Penseur, Les Bourgeois de Calais*, the statues of Balzac and Victor Hugo, and *La Porte d'Enfer*, a huge bronze door for the Musée des Arts Décoratifs, which was unfinished at his death.

Rodney, 1st Baron (George Rodney) (1719–92), English admiral, who served in the Seven Years War and the War of American Independence; in the latter war he defeated the French fleet under de Grasse.

Rogers, Lord (Sir Richard Rogers) (b. 1933), Architect. Creations include Lloyd's Building and One Hyde Park in London, the Pompidou Centre in Paris and the European Court of Human Rights building in Strasbourg. C.H. (2008).

Roland de la Platière, Manon Jeanne (1754–93), a leading figure in the French revolution. Her husband **Jean Marie** (1734–93), belonged to the more moderate or Girondist party, and when threatened escaped; but she was imprisoned and executed. She wrote *Letters* and *Memoirs.*

B52

Rolland, Romain (1866–1944), French author, whose main work is a ten-volume novel, *Jean Christophe*, the biography of a German musician, based on the life of Beethoven. Nobel Prize, 1915.

Rolls, Charles Stewart (1877–1910), with **Henry Royce** (1863–1933) the co-founders of Rolls-Royce car manufacturers (at Derby in 1907).

Romero y Galdames, Oscar (1917–80), Roman Catholic Archbishop of San Salvador. He was murdered in 1980 while preaching. Nobel Prizewinner. He was beatified in 2015.

Romilly, Sir Samuel (1757–1818), English lawyer and law-reformer, who aimed at mitigating the severity of the criminal law.

Rommel, Erwin (1891–1944), German Field-Marshal. He took part in the 1940 invasion of France, and was later successful in commanding the Afrika Korps till 1944. He committed suicide.

Romney, George (1734–1802), English artist, b. in Lancashire. He painted chiefly portraits.

Röntgen, Wilhelm Konrad von (1845–1923), German scientist who in 1895 discovered X-rays. Nobel prizewinner 1901.

Roosevelt, Franklin Delano (1882–1945), American statesman, a distant cousin of Theodore Roosevelt. During the first world war he held office under Wilson, and though stricken with poliomyelitis in 1921 continued his political career, becoming governor of New York in 1929 and U.S. president in 1933 (the first to hold office for more than two terms), till his death. A Democrat, he met the economic crisis of 1933 with an ambitious policy for a "New Deal". He strove in vain to ward off war. Towards other American countries his attitude was that of "good neighbour." After Pearl Harbor, he energetically prosecuted the war. He kept contact with his people by "fireside talks." His wife **Eleanor** (1884–1962) was a major figure in her own right.

Roosevelt, Theodore (1858–1919), American president. Popular because of his exploits in the Spanish-American war, he was appointed Republican vice-president in 1900, becoming president when McKinley was assassinated. Re-elected 1905. He promoted the regulation of trusts; and his promotion of peace between Russia and Japan gained the Nobel prize, 1906.

Rops, Félicien (1833–98), Belgian artist, known for his often satirical lithographs and etchings.

Ross, Sir James Clark (1800–62), Scottish explorer of polar regions, who accompanied his uncle Sir John, and himself discovered the north magnetic pole in 1831. He commanded the *Erebus* and *Terror* to the Antarctic (1839–43). His discoveries included the Ross ice barrier.

Ross, Sir John (1777–1856), Scottish polar explorer, uncle of the above. He searched for the NW passage and discovered Boothia peninsula.

Ross, Sir Ronald (1857–1932), British Nobel physician, b. India; discovered the malaria parasite.

Rossetti, Dante Gabriel (1828–82), English poet and painter, son of **Gabriele** (1783–1852), an exiled Italian author who settled in London in 1842. With Millais, Holman Hunt and others he formed the Pre-Raphaelite brotherhood which returned to pre-Renaissance art forms. His model was often his wife, Elizabeth Siddal. His poems include *The Blessed Damozel*. His sister **Christina Georgina** (1830–94) wrote poetry, including *Goblin Market*.

Rossini, Gioacchino Antonio (1792–1868), Italian operatic composer. *See* **Section P.**

Rostand, Edmond (1868–1918), French dramatist, whose *Cyrano de Bergerac* made a sensation in 1898.

Rostropovich, Mstislav (1927–2007), one of the greatest virtuoso cellists and conductors. Born in Baku, Azerbaijan. A campaigner for human rights.

Rotblat, Sir Joseph (1908–2005), Polish-born British physicist. Founder of the Pugwash Conferences. Shared 1995 Nobel Prize for Peace.

Rothenstein, Sir William (1872–1945), English portrait painter. His son, **Sir John** (1901–92), was an art historian and director of the Tate.

Rothschild, Meyer Amschel (1743–1812), German financier, founder of a banking family, b. Frankfurt. His five sons controlled branches at Frankfurt, Vienna, Naples, Paris and London (**Nathan Meyer**, 1777–1836). Nathan's son, **Lionel** (1808–79), was the first Jewish MP.

Roubiliac, Louis François (1695–1762), French sculptor who settled in London and carved a statue of Handel for Vauxhall gardens and one of Newton for Trinity College, Cambridge.

Rouget de Lisle, Claude Joseph (1760–1836),

French poet, author of words and music of the *Marseillaise*, revolutionary and national anthem.

Rousseau, Henri (1844–1910), influential French "Sunday" painter, called "Le Douanier" because he was a customs official; self-taught, he was for long unrecognised. He used the botanical gardens for his jungle scenes.

Rousseau, Jean-Jacques (1712–78), French political philosopher and educationist, b. Geneva, herald of the romantic movement. After a hard childhood he met Mme. de Warens who for some years befriended him. In 1741 he went to Paris where he met Diderot and contributed articles on music and political economy to the *Encyclopédie*. *La Nouvelle Héloïse* appeared in 1760, *Emile*, and *Du Contrat Social* in 1762. *Emile* is a treatise on education according to "natural" principles and *Du Contrat Social*, his main work, sets forth his political theory. It begins, "Man is born free and everywhere he is in chains." Both books offended the authorities and he had to flee, spending some time in England. Later he was able to return to France. His views did much to stimulate the French Revolution.

Rowling, Joanne (b. 1965), authoress of the famous Harry Potter novels. The last, *Harry Potter and the Cursed Child* was co-authored 19 years after the first novel. She writes as J.K. Rowling. Her book *The Casual Vacancy* (2012) was her first adult novel. She wrote *The Cuckoo's Calling* (2013), *The Silkworm* (2014) and *Career of Evil* (2015) under the pseudonym Robert Galbraith.

Royce, Henry, *see under* **Rolls, Charles Stewart.**

Rubens, Sir Peter Paul (1577–1640), Flemish painter. B. in exile, his family returned to Antwerp in 1587. He studied in Italy and visited Spain. His range was wide, his compositions vigorous, and he was a remarkable colourist. *Peace and War*, *The Rape of the Sabines*, and *The Felt Hat* are in the National Gallery.

Rubinstein, Anton Grigorovich (1829–94), Russian pianist and composer, who helped to found the conservatoire at St. Petersburg (Leningrad); as did his brother **Nicholas** (1835–81) at Moscow.

Rubinstein, Artur (1887–1982), Polish-born pianist. He moved to the USA during World War II.

Rücker, Sir Arthur (1848–1915), English physicist, who made two magnetic surveys of the British Isles, 1886, and 1891.

Ruisdael, Jacob van (c. 1628–82), Dutch painter of landscapes, b. Haarlem. Several of his works are in the National Gallery, including *Coast of Scheveningen* and *Landscape with ruins*.

Rupert, Prince (1619–82), general, son of Frederick of Bohemia and his wife Elizabeth, daughter of James I of England. He commanded the Royalist cavalry in the English civil war, but was too impetuous for lasting success.

Rushdie, Sir (Ahmed) Salman (b. 1947), controversial author of *The Satanic Verses* (1988 Whitbread Novel Award). Under death sentence (*fatwa*) by ayatollahs until lifted in 1998. He has also published *The Moor's Last Sigh* (set in his native Bombay), *East, West* (a book of short stories), *The Ground Beneath Her Feet* (1999), *Fury* (2001), *Shalimar the Clown* (2005), *The Enchantress of Florence* (2008) and *Two Years Eight Months and Twenty-Eight Nights* (2015). His *Midnight's Children* has been named the greatest Booker winner of all time. He was knighted in 2007.

Ruskin, John (1819–1900), English author and art critic, b. London. His *Modern Painters* in 5 volumes was issued over a period of years, the first volume having a strong defence of Turner. He helped to establish the Pre-Raphaelites. Other notable works include *The Seven Lamps of Architecture*, *The Stones of Venice* and *Praeterita*. *Unto this Last* develops his views on social problems, and he tried to use his wealth for education *etc.* Ruskin College at Oxford is named after him. In 1848 he married Euphemia Gray, but in 1854 she obtained a decree of nullity and later married Millais.

Russell, 3rd Earl (Bertrand Arthur William Russell) (1872–1970), English philosopher, mathematician, and essayist, celebrated for his work in the field of logic and the theory of knowledge, and remembered for his moral courage, belief in human reason and his championship of liberal ideas. He published more than 60 books, including *The Principles of Mathematics* (1903). *Principia Mathematica* (in collaboration with A. N. Whitehead; 3 vols., 1910–13), *The Prob-*

lem of Philosophy (1912), *Mysticism and Logic* (1918), *The Analysis of Mind* (1921), *An Inquiry into Meaning and Truth* (1940) and *History of Western Philosophy* (1945). His *Autobiography* (3 vols.) appeared 1967–9. He was the grandson of Lord John Russell. John Stuart Mill was his godfather. Nobel prize for literature 1950; O.M. 1949.

Russell, 1st Earl (John Russell), (1792–1878), English statesman, third son of the 6th Duke of Bedford. He had a large share in carrying the parliamentary reform bill of 1832. He was Whig prime minister 1846–52 and 1865–6.

Russell of Killowen, 1st Baron (Charles Russell), (1832–1900) British lawyer, b. Ireland; Lord Chief Justice 1894–1900. He defended Parnell.

Rutherford, 1st Baron (Ernest Rutherford) (1871–1937), British physicist, b. New Zealand, eminent in the field of atomic research. His experiments were conducted at Manchester and Cambridge. In 1911 he announced his nuclear theory of the atom and in 1918 succeeded in splitting the atom.

Ruysdael, Jacob van. *See* **Ruisdael.**

Ruyter, Michiel Adrianszoon de (1607–76), Dutch admiral who ranks with Nelson. He fought against England and in 1667 caused alarm by sailing up the Medway as far as Rochester and up the Thames as far as Gravesend. He was mortally wounded at Messina.

S

Saarinen, Eero (1910–61). Finnish-born American architect and furniture designer.

Sachs, Hans (1494–1576), German poet, b. Nuremberg. A shoemaker, he wrote over 6,000 pieces, many (including *Die Wittenbergische Nachtigall*) inspired by the Reformation.

Sachs, Julius von (1832–97), German botanist, founder of experimental plant physiology. He demonstrated that chlorophyll is formed in chloroplasts only in light.

Sadat, Mohammed Anwar El (1919–81), Egyptian statesman, President of Egypt 1970–81. His visit to Israel in Nov. 1977 was a bold and courageous move which led to the Camp David peace treaty with Israel. Assassinated 1981.

Sádi or **Saadi** (Muslih Addin) (c. 1184–1292), Persian poet, b. Shiraz, best known for his *Gulistan* (Flower Garden).

Sagan, Françoise (1935–2004), popular French author. Her most famous novel, *Bonjour Tristesse* (1954) was published when she was only 18.

Sainte-Beuve, Charles Augustin (1804–69), French critic, b. Boulogne. He studied medicine, abandoning it for journalism, and after attempting to write poetry, turned to literary criticism. His work includes *Causeries du lundi* and *Histoire de Port-Royal.*

Saint-Just, Antoine (1767–94), French revolutionary, a follower of Robespierre.

St. Laurent, Louis Stephen (1882–1973), Canadian politician, prime minister 1948–57.

St. Laurent, Yves (1936–2008), leading French fashion designer. The "Pied Piper" of fashion.

Saint-Saëns, Charles Camille (1835–1921), French composer, for 20 years organist at the Madeleine. He wrote symphonic and chamber music and the opera *Samson et Dalila*, which was produced by Liszt at Weimar in 1877. *See* **Section P.**

Saint-Simon, Claude, Comte de (1760–1825), French socialist, who in his *L'Industrie* and *Nouveau christianisme* prepared the way for much later thought.

Saintsbury, George (1845–1933), literary historian and critic. Professor of Rhetoric and English Literature, Edinburgh University (1895–1915).

Sakharov, Andrei Dimitrievich (1921–89), Soviet nuclear physicist and human rights campaigner. Nobel prizewinner 1975.

Saladin (el Melik an-Nasir Salah ed-Din) (1137–93), sultan of Egypt and Syria and founder of a dynasty, who in 1187 defeated the Christians near Tiberias and took Jerusalem. This gave rise to the unsuccessful Third Crusade, in which Richard I of England joined. His great qualities were admired by his opponents. An ethnic Kurd from Tikrit.

Salam, Abdus (1926–96), theoretical physicist and mathematician. Pakistan's first Nobel Laureate.

Salazar, Antonio d'Oliveira (1889–1970), Portuguese dictator, having first been premier in 1932, a new constitution being adopted in 1933. He gave Portugal stability, but refused to bow to nationalism in Portuguese Africa and India.

Salimbene de Adamo (1221–c. 1228), mediaeval chronicler, b. Parma, whose vivid description of life is embodied in his *Cronica.*

Salisbury, 3rd Marquess (Robert Arthur Talbot Gascoyne-Cecil (1830–1903), English Conservative statesman, prime minister 1885–86, 1886–92, 1895–1902, mainly remembered for his conduct of foreign affairs during a critical period.

Salk, Jonas (1914–95), developer of the first effective vaccine against poliomyelitis.

Salmond, Alex *See* **D18.**

Samuel, 1st Viscount (Herbert Samuel) (1870–1963), British Liberal statesman.

Sand, George (1804–76), pseudonym of the French writer Aurore Dupin Dudevant. Her publications are extensive and varied, and include the novel *Mauprat*, rural studies, and an autobiography *Histoire de ma vie*. She was associated with Alfred de Musset and Chopin.

Sanger, Frederick (1918–2013), British scientist noted for his work on the chemical structure of the protein insulin. Nobel prizewinner 1958, and 1980. The father of genomics. C.H. (1981), O.M. (1986).

Sanger, Margaret (1883–1956). American social reformer. Founder of the birth control movement.

Sankey, Ira David (1840–1908), American evangelist and composer, associated with Moody.

San Martin, José de (1778–1850), South American national leader in securing independence from Spanish rule to his native Argentina, Chile and Peru.

Santayana, George (1863–1952), American philosopher and poet, b. Madrid, of Spanish parentage. His books include *The Sense of Beauty, The Life of Reason*, and *The Realms of Being.*

Santos-Dumont, Alberto (1873–1932), Brazilian aeronaut who in 1898 flew a cylindrical balloon with a gasoline engine. In 1909 he built a monoplane.

Sappho of Lesbos (fl. early 6th cent. B.C.), Greek poetess, of whose love poems only three remained until a fourth was discovered in 2005.

Sardou, Victorien (1831–1908), French dramatist popular in his day. Sarah Bernhardt created famous parts in *Fédora, Théodora* and *La Tosca; Robespierre* and *Dante* were written for Irving.

Sargent, John Singer (1856–1922), American painter, b. Florence, who worked mainly in England, especially on portraits.

Sargent, Sir Malcolm (1895–1967), popular British conductor, who conducted the Promenade Concerts from 1950 till his death, and succeeded Sir Adrian Boult as conductor of the BBC Symphony Orchestra, 1950–7.

Sarkozy, Nicolas (b. 1955), President of France, 2007–12. Centre-right politician. Son of an Hungarian immigrant. Defeated in May 2012.

Sartre, Jean-Paul (1905–80), French existentialist philosopher, left-wing intellectual, dramatist, essayist and novelist. His major philosophical work is *L'Etre et le Néant* and his plays include *Les Mouches, Huis Clos, Crime passionel, La Putain respectueuse*, and *Les Séquestrés d'Altona*. Awarded, but declined, the 1964 Nobel prize.

Sassoon, Siegfried (1886–1967), English poet and writer with a hatred of war. He is mainly known for *The Memoirs of a Foxhunting Man*, the first part of the *Memoirs of George Sherston.*

Saunders, Dame Cicely (1918–2005), visionary founder of the modern hospice movement.

Savonarola, Girolamo (1452–98), Florentine preacher and reformer, a Dominican friar, who denounced vice and corruption not only in society but also in the Church itself, especially attacking Pope Alexander VI. He was excommunicated, imprisoned, and with two of his companions, hanged and burned. His passion for reform made him impatient of opposition and incapable of compromise, yet he was a notable figure and commands the respect of later ages. George Eliot's *Romola* portrays him.

Scarlatti, Alessandro (1659–1725), Italian musician who founded the Neapolitan school of opera. He composed over 100 operas, 200 masses, and over 700 cantatas and oratorios. His son **Domenico** (1685–1757) was a harpsichord virtuoso whose work influenced the evolution of the sonata. His chief years were spent at the Spanish court in Madrid. *See* **Section P.**

Scarman, Lord (Leslie George Scarman) (1911–2005), Chairman, Law Commission. Author of Scarman Report on 1981 Brixton Riots.

Scheele, Carl Wilhelm (1742–86), Swedish chemist, discoverer of many chemical substances, including oxygen (c. 1773–but published in 1777 after the publication of Priestley's studies).

Schiaparelli, Giovanni Virginio (1835–1910), Italian astronomer, noted for having observed certain dark markings on the surface of the planet Mars which he called canals.

Schiller, Johann Christoph Friedrich von (1759–1805), German dramatist and poet, b. Marbach in Württemberg, began life as a military surgeon. His play *The Robbers* with a revolutionary theme was successful in 1782 in Mannheim. After a stay at Dresden, where he wrote *Don Carlos*, and at Jena, where he wrote a history of the Thirty Years War, he became the friend of Goethe and removed to Weimar, where he wrote *Wallenstein*, *Mary Stuart*, *The Maid of Orleans* and *William Tell*. He is a leading figure in the European romantic movement.

Schirrmann, Richard (1874–1961), German pioneer of youth hostels. A schoolmaster, in 1907 he converted his schoolroom during holidays to a dormitory. The Verband für deutsche Jugendherbergen was founded in 1913, and the International Youth Hostels Federation in 1932.

Schlegel, Friedrich von (1772–1829), German critic, b. Hanover, prominent among the founders of German Romanticism, whose revolutionary and germinating ideas influenced early 19th-cent. thought. His brother, **August Wilhelm** (1767–1845), made remarkable translations of Shakespeare, Dante, Calderon and Camões.

Schliemann, Heinrich (1822–90), German archaeologist, who conducted excavations at Troy and Mycenae. The subject of numerous biographies mostly based on his own writings which are now viewed with some scepticism.

Schmidt, Helmut (1918–2015), German social democrat (SPD) statesman; succeeded Brandt as Chancellor of West Germany 1974–83.

Schnabel, Artur (1882–1951), American pianist of Austrian birth, regarded as a leading exponent of Beethoven's pianoforte sonatas.

Schoenberg, Arnold (1874–1951), Austrian composer of Jewish parentage who in 1933 was exiled by the Nazi regime and settled in America. Among his works are the choral orchestral *Gurre-Lieder* and *Pierrot Lunaire*. *See* Section P.

Schopenhauer, Arthur (1788–1860), German philosopher, b. Danzig, important historically for his pessimism, and his doctrine that will is superior to knowledge. His chief work is *The World as Will and Idea*. He saw Hegel as a charlatan.

Schröder, Gerhard. (b. 1944), German Social Democrat. Chancellor of Germany, 1998–2005.

Schubert, Franz Peter (1797–1828), Austrian composer, b. Vienna, the son of a schoolmaster, and a contemporary of Beethoven. He wrote not only symphonies, sonatas, string quartets, choral music and masses, but also over 600 songs.

Schulz, Charles (1922–2000), the world's most popular cartoonist, creator of the *Peanuts* strip.

Schumann, Robert Alexander (1810–56), composer of the early 19th cent. German romantic school. He wrote much chamber music, four symphonies, a piano concerto, and choral music, but it is his early piano pieces and songs that give constant delight. His wife **Clara** (1819–96) was one of the outstanding pianists of her time.

Schwarzkopf, Dame Elisabeth (1915–2006), one of the finest and most influential singers of her time. Born in Germany she became a British citizen.

Schweitzer, Albert (1875–1965), Alsatian medical missionary, theologian, musician and philosopher. He resigned a promising European career to found at Lambaréné in French Equatorial Africa a hospital to fight leprosy and sleeping sickness. Nobel peace prize 1952. O.M. 1955.

Scipio, Publius Cornelius (237–183 B.C.), Roman general in the second Punic War, known as Scipio Africanus the elder. **Scipio Africanus the younger** (185–129 B.C.) was an adoptive relative and an implacable opponent of Carthage.

Scott, Charles Prestwich (1846–1931), famous editor (1872–1929) of the *Manchester Guardian*.

Scott, Sir George Gilbert (1811–78), English architect in the Gothic revival. He restored many churches and designed the Albert Memorial and the Martyrs' Memorial at Oxford.

Scott, Sir Giles Gilbert (1880–1960), English architect, grandson of above, designed the Anglican cathedral at Liverpool and planned the new Waterloo Bridge.

Scott, Robert Falcon (1868–1912), English antarctic explorer. He led two expeditions; one

1901–4 which discovered King Edward VII Land; and another 1910–12 which reached the south pole and found the Amundsen records; but while returning the party was overtaken by blizzards and perished just 11 miles from safety. *See also* **Antarctic exploration, Section L.** His son, **Sir Peter Scott** (1909–89), was an artist, ornithologist and pioneeer conservationist The "patron saint of conservation".

Scott, Sir Walter (1771–1832), Scottish novelist and poet, b. Edinburgh. He was educated for the law, but came to know and love the Border country and his interests were literary; and in 1802–3 he issued a collection of ballads, *Border Minstrelsy*. Poems such as *Marmion* and *The Lady of the Lake* followed. His novels appeared anonymously, beginning with *Waverley* in 1814; and continuing with *Guy Mannering*, *The Antiquary*, *Old Mortality*, *Rob Roy*, and *The Heart of Midlothian*. From 1819 he turned also to English history, with *Ivanhoe* and *Kenilworth*. In 1826 he became bankrupt, largely as the fault of his publishing partner.

Scriabin, Alexander (1872–1915), Russian composer and pianist, who relied to some extent on extra-musical factors such as religion, and in *Prometheus* tried to unite music and philosophy.

Seacole, Mary (1805–81), Jamaican businesswoman and nurse. Famous for her nursing of British soldiers in the Crimean War (1854–6), even though the War Office had rejected her help.

Seeley, Sir John Robert (1834–95), English historian, author of a life of Christ, *Ecce Homo*.

Segovia, Andrés (1894–1987), Spanish concert-guitarist. He adapted works by Bach, Haydn, Mozart *etc.* to the guitar.

Seifert, Richard (1910–2001), prolific but controversial architect who designed Centre Point (1966) and the NatWest Tower (1981).

Selfridge, Harry Gordon (1858–1947), American-born merchant who in 1909 opened a new style of department store in Oxford Street.

Semmelweis, Ignaz Philipp (1818–65), Hungarian obstetrician. Pioneered antiseptic methods, thus reducing the incidence of puerperal fever.

Sen, Amartya (b. 1933), Indian-born economist. Awarded 1998 Nobel Prize for Economics. Author of *Poverty and Famines* (1981). Master of Trinity College, Cambridge, 1998–2003. His recent book *The Idea of Justice* appeared in 2009.

Seneca, Lucius Annaeus (c. 4 B.C.–A.D. 65), Roman stoic philosopher who was a tutor to Nero, but lost favour and was sentenced to take his own life.

Senefelder, Alois (1772–1834), Bavarian inventor of lithography about 1796.

Senna, Ayrton (1960–94), Brazilian motor racing champion. The leading driver of his generation, he died in the 1994 San Marino Grand Prix at Imola.

Sentamu, John (b. 1949), Archbishop of York since 2005. First black archbishop in the UK.

Seth, Vikram (b. 1952), Indian novelist whose books include *The Golden Gate: A Novel in Verse* (1986), *A Suitable Boy* (1992) and *An Equal Music* (1999).

Severus, Lucius Septimius (146–211), Roman emperor, and a successful general. On a visit to Britain he suppressed a revolt, repaired Hadrian's Wall, and died at York.

Sévigné, Marie de Rabutin-Chantai, Marquise de (1626–96), French woman of letters. Her letters to her daughter Françoise give a moving picture of fashionable French society.

Sgambati, Giovanni (1841–1914), Italian pianist (pupil of Liszt), composer and teacher, who revived interest in classical instrumental music.

Shackleton, Sir Ernest Henry (1874–1922), British explorer, who made four antarctic expeditions; that of 1909 reached within 100 miles of the south pole. He died on his last expedition.

Shaffer, Sir Peter (1926–2016). Playwright who dominated post-war British theatre. His works include *Equus* and *Amadeus*.

Shaftesbury, 7th Earl of (Anthony Ashley Cooper) (1801–85), English philanthropist largely responsible for legislation reducing the misery of the industrial revolution. He was for 40 years chairman of the Ragged Schools Union.

Shakespeare, William (1564–1616), England's greatest poet and dramatist, b. Stratford-on-Avon. Little is known of his career up to his eighteenth year, when he married Anne Hathaway. He came to London at the height of the English renaissance and soon became connected with the Globe theatre as actor and playwright. Thirty-eight plays comprise the Shakespeare canon. Thirty-six were printed in the First Folio of 1623 (the first collected edition of his dramatic works), of which eighteen had been published during his lifetime in the so-called Quartos. *Henry VI* (3 parts), *The Two Gentlemen of Verona*, *The Comedy of Errors*, *The Taming of the Shrew*, *Richard III*, *Titus Andronicus* and *Love's Labour's Lost* seem to have been the earliest, followed by *Romeo and Juliet*, *A Midsummer Night's Dream*, *Richard II* and *King John*. Then followed *The Merchant of Venice*, *Henry IV* (2 parts), *Henry V*, *Much Ado About Nothing*, *The Merry Wives of Windsor*, and *As You Like It*. Then came some of his greatest plays: *Julius Caesar*, *Troilus and Cressida*, *Hamlet*, *Twelfth Night*, *Measure for Measure*, *All's Well that Ends Well*, *Othello*, *King Lear*, *Macbeth*, *Timon of Athens*, *Antony and Cleopatra* and *Coriolanus*. Shakespeare's career ended with *Pericles*, *Cymbeline*, *The Winter's Tale*, *The Tempest*, *King Henry VIII* and *The Two Noble Kinsmen* (often ascribed to him). In mastery of language, in understanding of character, in dramatic perception, and in use of ritual he has never been surpassed. *See* M7–8.

Shankar, Ravi (1920–2012), Indian sitar virtuoso, the 'godfather of world music'.

Sharon, Ariel (1928–2014), Israeli prime minister after 2001. A towering but controversial figure.

Sharp, Granville (1735–1813), English abolitionist of slavery. Founder of colony of Sierra Leone.

Shastri, Shri Lal Bahadur (1904–66), Indian politician who became prime minister of India after the death of Nehru in 1964. He died of a heart attack at the end of the Tashkent talks.

Shaw, George Bernard (1856–1950), Irish dramatist who conquered England by his wit and exposure of hypocrisy, cant, and national weaknesses, and whose individual opinions found expression in musical criticism, socialist pamphlets and plays. His plays include *Man and Superman*, *Heartbreak House*, *Back to Methuselah*, *Saint Joan*, *The Apple Cart*, and *Buoyant Billions*. In 1884 he joined the newly-born Fabian Society. Nobel prizewinner 1925.

Shelley, Percy Bysshe (1792–1822), English poet, b. Horsham. He was a master of language and of literary form, and a passionate advocate of freedom and of new thought. Sent down from Oxford for his pamphlet *The Necessity of Atheism*, he came under the influence of William Godwin; and, after his first marriage came to an unhappy end, married the latter's daughter, Mary Wollstonecraft, herself a writer. In the same year began his friendship with Byron. His works include *The Revolt of Islam*, The *Masque of Anarchy* (an indictment of Castlereagh), *The Cenci* (a play on evil), and *Prometheus Unbound*, besides lyrics such as *To a Skylark* and *Ode to the West Wind*. He was accidentally drowned while sailing near Spezzia.

Shepard, Alan (1923–98). The first American (and the second man) to fly in space in 1961.

Shepherd, Nan (1893–1981), Scottish novelist and poet.

Sheppard, Hugh Richard (Dick) (1880–1937), Anglican clergyman and pacifist. He made St. Martin-in-the-Fields a centre of social service and also founded the Peace Pledge Union.

Sheraton, Thomas (1751–1806), English cabinetmaker, b. Stockton, whose *Cabinetmaker's Book* promoted neo-classical designs.

Sheridan, Richard Brinsley (1751–1816), British dramatist, b. Dublin. He was a brilliant writer of comedies, especially *The Rivals*, *The Duenna*, *The School for Scandal*, and *The Critic*. He acquired and rebuilt Drury Lane theatre, which reopened in 1794, but was burnt down in 1809; and this, with his lack of business sense, brought him to poverty. He was also in parliament.

Sherman, William Tecumseh (1820–91), American general, who served especially in the Civil War. He took part in the battles of Bull Run and Shiloh, was appointed in 1864 to the command of the southwest, and with 65,000 men marched across Georgia to the sea. In 1865 he accepted Johnston's surrender.

Sherrington, Sir Charles Scott (1857–1952), English scientist, an authority on the physiology of the nervous system. His research led to advances in brain surgery. His principal work is *Integration Action of the Nervous System* (1906). Shared with E. D. Adrian the 1932 Nobel prize.

Shirley, James (1596–1666), English dramatist. His tragedies include *The Traitor*, and his

comedies *Hyde Park*. His death was hastened by the Great Fire.

Sholokhov, Mikhail Aleksandrovich (1905–84), Russian novelist, author of *And Quiet Flows the Don*. Nobel prizewinner 1965.

Shostakovich, Dimitri (1906–75), Russian composer whose music is complex, profound, and deeply significant of the Soviet age in which he lived. *See* **Section P.**

Sibelius, Jean (1865–1957), Finnish composer imbued with national feeling. His works include seven symphonies, a violin concerto, and several tone poems, notably *Finlandia*, and some based on the poem *Kalevala*. *See* **Section P.**

Sickert, Walter Richard (1860–1942), British artist, b. Munich. He was influenced by Degas, and has himself influenced later painters. His *Ennui* is in the Tate Gallery.

Siddons, Sarah (1755–1831), English actress especially in tragic parts. She was the daughter of the manager Roger Kemble.

Sidgwick, Henry (1838–1900), English philosopher who wrote *Methods of Ethics*, and who also promoted women's education, with the foundation of Newnham and Girton colleges at Cambridge.

Sidney, Sir Philip (1554–86), English poet and writer, best remembered for his *Arcadia*, *Apologie for Poetrie*, and *Astrophel and Stella*, all published after his death. Killed at the battle of Zutphen, where he passed a cup of water to another, saying "Thy necessity is greater than mine."

Siemens, Sir William (1823–83), German-born electrical engineer who settled in England and constructed many overland and submarine telegraphs. He was brother of **Werner von Siemens**, founder of the firm of Siemens-Halske.

Sienkiewicz, Henryk (1846–1916), Polish novelist and short-story writer; best known of his historical novels is *Quo Vadis?* Nobel prize, 1905.

Sikorski, Vladislav (1881–1943), Polish general and statesman, prime minister of the Polish government in exile (1939) and commander-in-chief of the Polish forces. Killed in an aircraft accident at Gibraltar.

Simpson, Sir James Young (1811–70), Scottish obstetrician who initiated the use of chloroform in childbirth.

Sinatra, Frank (1915–98), famous singer and actor, a pre-eminent entertainment figure.

Sinclair, Upton (1878–1968), American novelist whose documentary novel *The Jungle* (1906) on the Chicago slaughter yards caused a sensation.

Singer, Isaac Merritt (1811–75), American mechanical engineer who improved early forms of the sewing-machine and patented a single-thread and chain-stitch machine.

Sisley, Alfred (1839–99), French impressionist painter of English origin, who painted some enchanting landscapes, *e.g. Meadows in Spring* (Tate Gallery). Influenced by Corot and Manet.

Sisulu, Walter (1912–2003), South African politician. Secretary-General of the ANC. One of Nelson Mandela's closest allies.

Sitwell, Edith (1887–1964), English poet, a great experimenter in verse forms. *Gold Coast Customs*, *Façade* (set to music by William Walton) and *Still Falls the Rain* are probably best known. She had two brothers, **Osbert** (1892–1969) and **Sacheverell** (1897–1988), both poets and critics.

Slessor, Mary (1848–1915), Scottish missionary (the 'Great Mother') in Calabar, Nigeria.

Slim, 1st Viscount (William Slim) (1891–1970), British soldier who rose from private to fieldmarshal. He commanded the 14th Army in Burma, was chief of the Imperial General Staff 1948–52, and governor-general of Australia 1953–60.

Sloane, Sir Hans (1660–1753), British collector, b. Ireland. He practised in London as a physician. His library of 50,000 volumes and his collection of MSS. and botanical specimens were offered under his will to the nation and formed the beginning of the British Museum.

Slowacki, Julius (1809–49), Polish romantic poet, a revolutionary, he lived in exile in Paris. His work includes the poetic dramas *Kordian*, *Balladyna* and *Lilli Weneda*, written in the style of Shakespeare; and the unfinished poem *King Spirit*.

Smeaton, John (1724–92), English engineer; he rebuilt Eddystone lighthouse (1756–59), improved Newcomen's steam-engine, and did important work on bridges, harbours, and canals. He also invented an improved blowing apparatus for iron-smelting.

Smetana, Bedřich (1824–84), Czech composer, creator of a national style. He was principal conductor of the Prague National Theatre, for which he wrote most of his operas, including *The Bartered Bride* and *The Kiss*. Best known of his other compositions are the cycle of symphonic poems *My Country* and the string quartets *From My Life*. He became totally deaf in 1874, suffered a mental breakdown, and died in an asylum. *See* **Section P**.

Smiles, Samuel (1812–1904), Scottish writer, *b*. Haddington, in early life a medical practitioner, remembered for *Self Help* (1859), and his biographies of engineers of the industrial revolution.

Smith, Adam (1723–90), Scottish economist, *b*. Kirkcaldy. In Edinburgh he published *Moral Sentiments*. Later he moved to London, and his *Wealth of Nations* (1776) is the first serious work in political economy.

Smith. Bessie (1894–1937). Named "Empress of the Blues", Smith was perhaps the greatest and most influential of blues singers. She brought her powerful voice to such songs as "Young Woman's Blues" (1926) and "Back-Water Blues" (1927).

Smith, Sir Grafton Eliot (1871–1937), Australian anatomist who researched the mammalian brain. His works include *The Evolution of Man*.

Smith, Ian (1919–2007), last Prime Minister of white Rhodesia. Declared independence, 1965.

Smith, John (1580–1631), English adventurer who in 1605 went on a colonising expedition to Virginia and was saved from death by the Red Indian Pocahontas.

Smith, John (1938–94), leader of the Labour Party, 1992-94. A much-respected, modernising leader. He is buried on the island of Iona.

Smith, Joseph (1805–44), American founder of the Mormons. He claimed that the *Book of Mormon* was revealed to him. In 1838 feeling against the Mormons culminated in a rising and Smith was murdered. He was succeeded by Brigham Young. *See* **Mormonism, Section J**.

Smith, Sydney (1771–1845), Anglican divine and journalist, who founded the *Edinburgh Review* and supported Catholic emancipation.

Smith, William (1760–1839), English surveyor and canal-maker, the first to map the rock strata of England and to identify the fossils peculiar to each layer. The father of world geology.

Smith, Sir William Alexander (1854–1914), Scottish founder of the Boys' Brigade (1883), the oldest national organisation for boys in Britain.

Smith, William Robertson (1846–94), Scottish biblical scholar whose "Bible" contribution to the 9th edition of *The Encyclopaedia Britannica* resulted in an unsuccessful prosecution for heresy.

Smollett, Tobias George (1721–71), Scottish novelist whose work is noted for satire and coarse humour. His main novels are *Roderick Random*, *Peregrine Pickle*, and *Humphrey Clinker*.

Smuts, Jan Christian (1870–1950), South African statesman and soldier. B. in Cape Colony, during the Boer War he fought on the Boer side. He was premier of the Union 1919–24, 1939–48, and worked for Commonwealth cooperation, but his party was defeated in 1948 by Malan's Nationalists.

Smyth, Ethel Mary (1858–1944), English composer and suffragette. Works include operas (*The Wreckers* and *The Boatswain's Mate*) and a *Mass in D*.

Snow, Baron (Charles Percy Snow) (1905–80), English physicist and novelist, author of the essay *The Two Cultures and the Scientific Revolution*, and *Strangers and Brothers* (11 vols.).

Snyders, Frans (1597–1657), Flemish still-life and animal painter who studied under Breughel.

Soane, Sir John (1753–1837), English architect who designed the Bank of England. He left the nation his house and library in Lincoln's Inn Fields (Soane Museum). 'The architect's architect'. *See* **N19**(1).

Sobers, Sir Garfield (b. 1936), West Indies and Nottinghamshire cricketer who ranks as one of the greatest all-rounders. Knighted 1975.

Socinus or **Sozzini Laelius** (1525–62), Italian founder of the sect of Socinians, with his nephew **Faustus** (1539–1604). Their teachings resemble those of Unitarians.

Socrates (470–399 B.C.), Greek philosopher and intellectual leader, was the son of a sculptor of Athens. He distinguished himself in three campaigns (Potidaea, Delium, and Amphipolis). Returning to Athens, he devoted himself to

study and intellectual enquiry, attracting many followers; through these, especially Xenophon and Plato, we know of his teachings, for he wrote nothing. In 399 B.C. he was charged with impiety and with corrupting the young, found guilty, and accordingly died by drinking hemlock. He put ethics at the core of his philosophy.

Soddy, Frederick (1877–1956), English chemist, who in Glasgow about 1912 laid the foundation of the isotope theory. Nobel prizewinner 1921.

Solon (638–558 B.C.), Athenian lawgiver, who in a time of economic distress cancelled outstanding debts, and introduced some democratic changes.

Solti, Sir Georg (1912–97), one of the great conductors of his time. Music director of Covent Garden and Chicago Symphony Orchestra.

Solzhenitsyn, Alexander Isayevich (1918–2008), Russian novelist, b. Rostov-on-Don; author of *One Day in the Life of Ivan Denisovich*, a documentary novel depicting life in one of Stalin's prison camps where he spent many years of his life. He was expelled from the Soviet Writers' Union in 1969, and from his country in 1974, returning in 1994. Nobel prize 1970. Elected to Russian Academy of Sciences, 1997. A trenchant critic of western materialism. He was the conscience of Russia

Somerset, Duke of (Edward Seymour) (1506–52), lord protector of England in the time of the young Edward VI, but he fell from power and was executed.

Somerville, Mary (1780–1872). Pioneering Scottish mathematician and astronomer whose works include *The Mechanism of the Heavens* (1831). Somerville College, Oxford, is named after her.

Sondheim, Stephen (b. 1930). US lyricist for musicals, including "West Side Story" (1958), "A Little Night Music" (1973) and "Into the Woods" (1987).

Soper, Lord (Donald Soper) (1903–98), Methodist preacher and campaigner for socialism.

Sophocles (495–406 B.C.), Athenian dramatist, who was awarded the prize over Aeschylus in 468. Of over a hundred plays of his, the only extant ones are *Oedipus the King*, *Oedipus at Colonus Antigone*, *Electra*, *Trachiniae*, *Ajax*, *Philoctetes*.

Sopwith, Sir Thomas (1888–1989), British designer of 'Sopwith Camel' biplane.

Sorel, Georges (1847–1922), French advocate of revolutionary syndicalism, author of *Reflections on Violence* (1905). The irrational aspects of his philosophy (derived from Bergson) appealed to Mussolini and the Fascists.

Soult, Nicolas Jean de Dieu (1769–1851), French general who fought under Napoleon in Switzerland and Italy, at Austerlitz, and in Spain.

Sousa, John Philip (1854–1932), American bandmaster and composer of some stirring marches.

Southey, Robert (1774–1843), English poet and historian. In 1803 he settled near Coleridge at Keswick, and in 1813 became poet laureate. His best work was in prose: histories of Brazil and of the Peninsular War; lives of Nelson, Wesley, *etc.* He wrote the anti-war poem *After Blenheim* (1796).

Southwell, Robert (1561–95), English poet and Jesuit martyr, beatified 1920.

Soyinka, Wole (b.1934). Nigeria's foremost man of letters and the conscience of the nation.

Spaak, Paul Henri (1899–1972), Belgian statesman and advocate of European Union.

Spark, Dame Muriel (1918–2006), Scotland's most important modern novelist. Her most famous work is *The Prime of Miss Jean Brodie* (1961).

Spartacus (d. 71 B.C.), Thracian rebel. A Roman slave and gladiator in Capua, he escaped and headed a slave insurrection, routing several Roman armies, but was defeated and killed by Crassus.

Speke, John Hanning (1827–64), British explorer. In 1858 he discovered the Victoria Nyanza; in 1860 with Grant he traced the Nile flowing out of it.

Spelling, Aaron (1923–2006), the most successful TV producer in American history (from *Starsky and Hutch* to *Dynasty*).

Spence, Sir Basil Urwin (1907–76), Scottish architect, mainly known for the new Coventry cathedral, for Hampstead civic centre and for university architecture. O.M. 1962.

Spencer, Herbert (1820–1903), English philosopher. B. Derby, he was at first a civil engineer, then a journalist (sub-editor of the *Economist*), when he wrote *Social Statics*. He coined the phrase (1852) "the survival of the fittest" and his *Principles of Psychology* (1855), published four years earlier than Darwin's *Origin of Species*, expounded doctrines of evolution. Author of the ten-volume *Synthetic Philosophy*.

Spencer, Sir Stanley (1891–1959), English artist of visionary power. His two pictures of the *Resurrection* are in the Tate Gallery. He also painted Cookham regatta.

Spender, Sir Stephen (1909–95), poet and critic, first made his name as one of the politically committed poets of the 1930s. He was co-editor of *Encounter* 1953–67 and Professor of English, University College, London 1970–77.

Spengler, Oswald (1880–1936), German historicist who held that every culture is destined to a waxing and waning life cycle and that the West European culture was entering its period of decline. His principal work is *The Decline of the West*. His views prepared the way for national socialism.

Spenser, Edmund (1552–99), English poet, b. London and educated at Cambridge. His *Shepheards Calendar* appeared in 1579. In 1580 he went to Ireland as the lord deputy's secretary, and later acquired Kilcolman castle, where he wrote most of his main work, *The Faerie Queene*. His castle was burnt in an insurrection in 1598, when he returned to London. He is called "the poet's poet." *See* **M6(2)**.

Spinoza, Baruch (1632–77), Dutch philosopher, b. Amsterdam, whose parents came to Holland from Portugal to escape the Inquisition. An independent thinker, his criticism of the Scriptures led to his being excommunicated from the synagogue. He supported himself by grinding and polishing lenses. He owed much to Descartes but was mainly concerned with religion and virtue. His philosophical theories are set out in the *Ethics* (published posthumously).

Spock, Dr Benjamin (1903–98). Paediatrician and child psychologist. Author of *Baby and Child Care* (1946).

Spofforth, Reginald (1770–1827), English writer of glees, including *Hail, Smiling Morn.*

Springsteen, Bruce (b. 1949). Leaving behind the "new Dylan" tag of the early 1970s, Springsteen produced a series of thoughtful and atmospheric rock albums between 1978 and 1982. He went on to become one of the most successful artists of the 1980s with albums such as "Born in the USA' (1984) and "Tunnel of Love" (1987).

Spurgeon, Charles Haddon (1834–92), English Baptist who preached at the vast Metropolitan Tabernacle, London, from 1861 (burnt down 1898).

Staël, Anne Louise, Baronne de Staël-Holstein (1766–1817), French writer. Daughter of the finance minister, Necker, she married the Swedish ambassador, and kept a salon. Her *Lettres sur Rousseau* appeared in 1788. After the revolution she lived partly abroad, partly in France, and after a visit to Italy wrote her novel *Corinne* (1807).

Stalin (Joseph Vissarionovich Djugashvili) (1879–1953), Soviet dictator who for nearly 30 years was leader of the Russian people. He originally studied at Tiflis for the priesthood, but became an active revolutionary and took part in the civil war after 1917. After Lenin's death, he ousted Trotsky and became the outstanding figure. He modernised agriculture on socialist lines by ruthless means, and his series of five-year plans from 1929 made Russia an industrial power. His regime carried out mass murder, show trials and the ruthless purges of the 1930s. Under Stalin, the famine in Ukraine claimed millions of lives. On the German invasion in 1941 he assumed military leadership; and later attended Allied war conferences. After his death a process of 'de-Stalinisation' began.

Stanford, Sir Charles Villiers (1852–1924), Irish composer of instrumental, choral, operatic, and other music.

Stanley, Sir Henry Morton (1841–1904), British explorer, b. Denbigh, N. Wales. He fought for the Confederates in the US Civil War. He then became a correspondent for the *New York Herald*, was commissioned to find Livingstone, and did so in 1871 at Ujiji, and with him explored Lake Tanganyika. In 1879 he founded the Congo Free State. His works include *Through the Dark Continent* and an *Autobiography*.

Stark, Freya Madeline (1893–1993), British writer and explorer of the Arab world.

Stead, William Thomas (1849–1912). Editor, *Pall Mall Gazette*. Campaigned against child prostitution.

Steel, Lord (Sir David Steel) (b. 1938), Liberal (Lib. Dem.) MP, 1965–97. Leader, Liberal Party, 1976–88. First Presiding Officer (Speaker) of Scottish Parliament, 1999–2003.

Steele, Sir Richard (1672–1729), British essayist, b. Dublin. He founded the *Tatler* (1709–11), to which Addison also contributed, and later the *Spectator* (1711–12) and the *Guardian* (1713).

Steen, Jan (1626–79), Dutch genre painter, b. Leiden, son of a brewer. *The Music Lesson* and *Skittle Alley* are in the National Gallery, the *Lute Player* in the Wallace collection.

Steer, Philip Wilson (1860–1942), English painter, especially of landscapes and of portraits.

Stefansson, Vilhjalmur (1879–1962), Canadian arctic explorer of Icelandic parentage; author of *Unsolved Mysteries of the Arctic*.

Stein, Sir Aurel (1862–1943), British archaeologist, b. Budapest. He explored Chinese Turkestan.

Steiner, Rudolf (1861–1925), founder of anthroposophy. *See* **Section J.**

Stendhal, pseudonym of Marie Henri Beyle (1783–1842), French novelist, b. Grenoble. He was with Napoleon's army in the Russian campaign of 1812, spent several years in Italy, and after the revolution of 1830 was appointed consul at Trieste, and afterwards at Civitavecchia. In his plots he recreates historical and social events with imaginative realism and delineates character with searching psychological insight. His main works are *Le Rouge et le Noir*, and *La Chartreuse de Parme*.

Stephen (1105–54), usurped the crown of England from Henry I's daughter in 1135; and, after anarchy, retained it till his death.

Stephen, Sir Leslie (1832–1904), English writer, critic, and biographer. He edited the *Cornhill Magazine* (1871–82), and the *Dictionary of National Biography* (1882–91). Father of Virginia Woolf.

Stephenson, George (1781–1848), English engineer; a locomotive designer, b. at Wylam near Newcastle, a colliery fireman's son. As engine-wright at Killingworth colliery he made his first locomotive in 1814 to haul coal from mines. He and his son Robert built the *Locomotion* for the Stockton and Darlington Railway (1825), the first locomotive for a public railway. His *Rocket* at 30 miles an hour won the prize of £500 in 1829 offered by the Liverpool and Manchester Railway. He also discovered the principle on which the miners' safety lamp was based. First president of the Institution of Mechanical Engineers. Known as the 'Father of the Railways'.

Stephenson, Robert (1803–59), English engineer, son of the above, engineered railway lines in England and abroad, and built many bridges including the Menai and Conway tubular bridges.

Sterne, Laurence (1713–68), English novelist and humorist. His main works are *Tristram Shandy* and *A Sentimental Journey*. He led a wandering and unconventional life, dying in poverty.

Stevenson, Adlai (1900–65), American politician, an efficient governor of Illinois, 1949–53; ambassador to the UN, 1960–5, and unsuccessful presidential challenger to Eisenhower 1952 and 1956.

Stevenson, Robert (1772–1850), Scottish engineer and builder of lighthouses, who invented "intermittent" and "flashing" lights.

Stevenson, Robert Louis (1850–94), Scottish author, b. Edinburgh. He suffered from ill-health and eventually settled in Samoa. His main works are *Travels with a Donkey*, *Treasure Island*, *Kidnapped*, *Dr. Jekyll and Mr. Hyde*, and *The Master of Ballantrae*.

Stiglitz, Joseph Eugene (b. 1943), American Professor of Economics. Author of such influential works as *Globalization and its Discontents* (2000), *The Roaring Nineties* (2003), *Making Globalisation Work* (2006) *etc*. Nobel Prize for Economics, 2001.

Stinnes, Hugo (1870–1924), German industrialist who built up a huge coalmining, iron and steel, and transport business, and later entered politics.

Stirling, James (1926–92), one of the great British architects of the 20th century.

Stockton, Earl of (Harold Macmillan) (1894–1986), British Conservative statesman, prime minister 1957–63; During his premiership came the crises of the Berlin Wall and the Cuban missiles (in which his personal diplomacy played an influential role), de Gaulle's veto to our entry into Europe, the signing of the Partial Test-Ban Treaty and his "wind of change" speech hailing African independence. Earl of Stockton, 1984.

Stoker, Bram (Abraham Stoker) (1847–1912), Irish author of the horror story *Dracula* and *Personal Reminiscences of Henry Irving*.

Stokes, Sir George Gabriel (1819–1903), Irish mathematician and physicist to whom is due the modern theory of viscous fluids and the discovery that rays beyond the violet end of the spectrum (the ultra-violet rays) produce fluorescence in certain substances.

Stopes, Marie Carmichael (1880–1958), English pioneer advocate of birth control. Her *Married Love* appeared in 1918, and she pioneered birth control clinics.

Stoppard, Sir Tom (b. 1937), playwright, whose witty and inventive plays include *Rosencrantz and Guildenstern are Dead* (1966), *Jumpers* (1972), *Arcadia* (1993) and *The Invention of Love* (1997) and *The Hard Problem* (2015). O.M. (2000).

Stowe, Harriet Beecher (1811–96), American author of *Uncle Tom's Cabin* (1852), written to expose slavery.

Strachey, John St. Loe (1901–63), English Labour politician and writer. He held office 1945–51.

Stradivari, Antonio (1644–1737), Italian maker of violins, b. Cremona, first in his art.

Strafford, 1st Earl of (Thomas Wentworth) (1593–1641), English statesman. He supported Charles I with a "thorough" policy, both as president of the north and as lord deputy in Ireland, where he introduced flax. His efficiency made him a special target when parliament met, and he was impeached and executed.

Strauss, David Friedrich (1808–74), German theologian, whose *Life of Jesus* attempted to prove that the gospels are based on myths.

Strauss, family of Viennese musicians. Johann Strauss (1804–49), the elder, was a composer of dance music, who with Joseph Lanner established the Viennese waltz tradition. His son, **Johann Strauss** (1825–99), the younger, although not so good a violinist or conductor as his father, was the composer of over 400 waltzes, which include *The Blue Danube* and *Tales from the Vienna Woods*. Two of his brothers, **Josef Strauss** (1827–70) and **Eduard Strauss** (1835–1916) were also composers and conductors.

Strauss, Richard (1864–1949), German composer and conductor, the son of a horn player in the opera orchestra at Munich. He succeeded von Bülow as court musical director at Meiningen. His works include the operas *Salome*, *Elektra*, and *Der Rosenkavalier*, the symphonic poems *Don Juan*, *Till Eulenspiegel*, and *Don Quixote*, and many songs. *See* **Section P.**

Stravinsky, Igor (1882–1971), Russian composer and conductor, pupil of Rimsky-Korsakov. His ballets *The Fire Bird* (1910). *Petrushka* (1911), representative of his early romantic style, and the revolutionary *The Rite of Spring*, which caused a furore in 1913, were written for the ballet impresario Diaghilev. He adopted a neo-classical style in later works, for example, in the ballets *Pulcinella* and *Apollo Musagetes* and the opera-oratorio *Oedipus Rex.* He brought new vigour and freedom to rhythm. He became a French citizen in 1934 and a US citizen in 1945. *See* **Section P.**

Strindberg, Johan August (1840–1912), Swedish writer of intense creative energy. His work is subjective and reflects his personal conflicts. He produced some 55 plays as well as novels, stories, poems, and critical essays. *Lucky Peter*, *Gustav Adolf*, *Till Damascus*, *The Father*, *Miss Julie* are some of his plays.

Styron, William (1925–2006), American novelist whose acclaimed works included *Sophie's Choice* (1979) and *The Confessions of Nat Turner* (1967).

Suckling, Sir John (1609–42), English poet, author of *Why so pale and wan?* He invented cribbage.

Sudermann, Hermann (1857–1928), German writer of plays and novels, including *Frau Sorge* (translated as Dame Care).

Suharto, General (1921–2008). Authoritarian president of Indonesia from 1968 to 1998.

Sukarno, Ahmed (1901–70). The founding father of Indonesia. An authoritarian president, 1950–68.

Sulaiman the Magnificent (1494–1566), Ottoman Sultan, conqueror, and patron of art and learning, who dominated the eastern Mediterranean but failed to capture Malta.

Sulla (138–78 B.C.) Roman general, he supported the oligarchy of the Senate against the demagogues Marius (Julius Caesar's uncle) and Cinna and established himself dictator in 82 B.C.

Sullivan, Sir Arthur Seymour (1842–1900), famous composer, mainly known for the music he wrote

for light operas with W. S. Gilbert as librettist, especially *The Pirates of Penzance*, *Patience*, *The Mikado*, *The Yeomen of the Guard* and *The Gondoliers*. He also wrote sacred music, some of which remains very popular. He and George Grove discovered Schubert's lost *Rosamunde* music.

Sully, Maximilien de Béthune, Duc de (1560–1641), French statesman, finance minister to Henry IV.

Summerson, Sir John (1904–92), the greatest British architectural historian of his generation.

Sumner, Mary (1828–1921), founder of the Mothers' Union to help promote the virtues of family life.

Sun Yat Sen (1867–1925), Chinese revolutionary, idealist and humanitarian. He graduated in medicine at Hong Kong, but after a rising failed in 1895 he lived abroad, planning further attempts, which succeeded in 1911 when the Manchus were ousted and he became president.

Sutherland, Graham Vivian (1903–80), British artist. He painted the 80th birthday portrait of Winston Churchill for parliament, and designed the tapestry for Coventry cathedral. O.M. 1960.

Sutherland, Dame Joan (1926–2010), Australian operatic soprano who achieved international fame (*e.g.* in Handel's Samson). Known as *La Stupenda.*

Suu Kyi, Aung San (b. *c.* 1945), Opposition leader in Myanmar (Burma). Nobel Peace Prize, 1991. She was at last released from house arrest by the military junta on 13 November 2010. Her party won a landslide victory in the 2015 elections.

Svevo, Italo (1861–1928). Italian author. He wrote *Confessions of Zeno.*

Swan, Sir Joseph Wilson (1829–1914), British scientist who shares with Edison the invention of the incandescent electric lamp.

Swedenborg, Emanuel (1689–1772), Swedish author of *Arcana Coelestia*, *The Apocalypse Revealed*, *Four Preliminary Doctrines*, and *The True Christian Religion.* His works became the scriptures of his followers, the Swedenborgians.

Sweelinck, Jan Pieterszoon (1562–1621), Dutch organist and composer of sacred music. In his fugues he made independent use of the pedals, and prepared the way for Bach. *See* **Section P.**

Swift, Jonathan (1667–1745), English satirist, b. Dublin of English parents. He crossed to England in 1688 to become secretary to Sir William Temple, and took Anglican orders, but did not obtain promotion. His *Tale of a Tub* and *The Battle of the Books* appeared in 1704. At first active in Whig politics, he became Tory in 1710, writing powerful tracts such as *Conduct of the Allies* (1711). In 1714 he retired to Ireland as Dean of St. Patrick's. His devoted women friends followed him—Hester Johnson (d. 1728), the Stella of his *Journal*, and Esther Vanhomrigh (d. 1723), the Vanessa of his poetry. Here he wrote *Gulliver's Travels* (1726) and *The Drapier's Letters.*

Swinburne, Algernon Charles (1837–1909), English poet and critic. He first won attention with a play, *Atalanta in Calydon*, in 1865, followed by *Poems and Ballads.* Later followed *Songs before Sunrise*, *Bothwell*, and *Mary Stuart.*

Swithin, St. (d.862), English saint and bishop of Winchester. A mentor to King Alfred.

Symonds, John Addington (1840–93), English author who wrote on the Italian Renaissance.

Synge, John Millington (1871–1909), Irish poet and playwright, author of *Riders to the Sea* and *The Playboy of the Western World.*

Szymborska, Wislawa (1923–2012). Polish poet, the 'Mozart of poetry'. Nobel Prize, 1996.

T

Tacitus, Gaius Cornelius (c. 55–120), Roman historian. His chief works are a life of his father-in-law Agricola, and his *Histories* and *Annals.*

Taft, William Howard (1857–1930), 27th President of the United States (1909–13). A Republican, he supported the policies of his predecessor Theodore Roosevelt. He later served on the US Supreme Court as Chief Justice (1921–30), the only man ever to hold both offices.

Tagore, Rabindranath (1861–1941), Bengali poet and philosopher who tried to blend east and west. Nobel prize 1913 (first non-European recipient).

Talbot, William Henry Fox (1800–77), English pioneer of photography which he developed independently of Daguerre. He also deciphered the cuneiform inscriptions at Nineveh.

Talleyrand-Périgord, Charles Maurice de (1754–1838), French politician and diplomat, led a mission to England in 1792 and was foreign minister from 1797 until 1807. He represented France at the Congress of Vienna.

Tallis, Thomas (c. 1510–85), English musician, with Byrd joint organist to the chapel royal under Elizabeth. He has been called the father of English Cathedral choral music.

Tamerlane (Timur the Lame) (1336–1405), Mongol conqueror. Ruler of Samarkand, he conquered Iran, Transcaucasia, Iraq, Armenia, and Georgia, and invaded India and Syria. He defeated the Turks at Angora, but died marching towards China. A ruthless conqueror, he was also a patron of literature and the arts. The line of rulers descended from him are the Timurids. He is the subject of a play by Marlowe.

Tarquinius: two kings of Rome came from this Etruscan family; **Lucius the Elder** (d. 578 B.C.); and **Lucius Superbus,** or the proud, (d. 510 B.C.) whose tyranny provoked a successful rising and brought an end to the monarchy.

Tartini, Giuseppe (1692–1770), Italian violinist, who wrote *Trillo del Diavolo*. He discovered the "third sound" resulting from two notes sounded together.

Tasman, Abel Janszoon (1603–59), Dutch navigator despatched by Van Diemen. He discovered Tasmania or Van Diemen's Land, and New Zealand, in 1642.

Tasso, Torquato (1544–95), Italian epic poet, b. Sorrento, author of *Gerusalemme Liberata*. He also wrote plays, *Aminta* and *Torrismondo*.

Tawney, Richard Henry (1880–1962), British historian, b. Calcutta, pioneer of adult education, and leader of socialist thought—the first critic of the affluent society.

Taylor, Alan John Percivale (1906–90), English historian. Broadcaster, lecturer and radical. Author of such noted works as *English History, 1914–45* and *The Origins of the Second World War*.

Taylor, Sir Geoffrey Ingram (1886–1975), British scientist, noted for his work on aerodynamics, hydrodynamics, *etc*. O.M. 1969.

Taylor, Jeremy (1613–67), English divine, b. Cambridge, author of many religious works, of which the chief are *Holy Living* and *Holy Dying*.

Taylor, Zachary (1784–1850), 12th President of the United States (1849–50). Formerly commander of the American forces during the Mexican War of 1846–48, he opposed the extension of slavery into the western territories of the USA.

Tchaikovsky, Peter Ilyich (1840–93), Russian composer. His music is melodious and emotional and he excelled in several branches of composition. Among his works are the operas *Eugene Onegin* and *The Queen of Spades* (both from stories by Pushkin), symphonies, including the *Little Russian* and the *Pathétique*, ballets, including *Swan Lake*, *The Sleeping Beauty*, and *The Nutcracker*, the fantasies *Romeo and Juliet*, and *Francesca da Rimini*, the piano concerto in B flat minor, the violin concerto in D, and numerous songs. *See* **Section P.**

Tedder, 1st Baron (Arthur William Tedder) (1890–1967), British air marshal. Deputy supreme commander under Eisenhower for the invasion of Europe.

Teilhard de Chardin, Pierre (1881–1955), French palaeontologist and religious philosopher. He went on expeditions in Asia, but his research did not conform to Jesuit orthodoxy. His main works were published posthumously, *The Phenomenon of Man* and *Le Milieu Divin*.

Telemann, Georg Philipp (1681–1767), German composer, b. Magdeburg. His vitality and originality of form are appreciated today after a long period of neglect. His works include church music, 46 passions and over 40 operas, oratorios *etc*.

Telford, Thomas (1757–1834), Scottish engineer. He built bridges (two over the Severn and the Menai suspension bridge), canals (the Ellesmere and Caledonian canals), roads, and docks.

Tell, William, legendary Swiss patriot, reputedly required by the Austrian governor Gessler to shoot an apple from his son's head, and the subject of a play by Schiller. The story is late, but the Swiss confederation did first arise in the 14th cent. with Schwyz, Uri, and Unterwalden.

Temple, Frederick (1821–1902), English divine. He was headmaster of Rugby, 1857–69, and archbishop of Canterbury, 1897–1902.

Temple, William (1881–1944), English ecclesiastic, son of above, was a leading moral force in social matters and a worker for ecumenism. He was headmaster of Repton, 1910–14, and became archbishop of Canterbury in 1942. An outstanding national and international figure.

Temple, Sir William (1628–99), English diplomat and writer, was instrumental in bringing about the marriage of Princess Mary with William of Orange. Swift was his secretary.

Templewood, 1st Viscount (Samuel John Gurney Hoare) (1880–1959), British Conservative politician. He piloted the India Act while secretary for India, 1931–5; and as foreign secretary he negotiated an abortive pact with Laval.

Tendulkar, Sachin (b. 1973), the most prolific runscorer in Test cricket (15,921 runs). A boy genius who first played for India in 1989 (aged 16). The first batsman to score a double century in one-day cricket (2010) and the first to score 15,000 runs in Test cricket (2011). He retired in 2014.

Teniers, David, the elder (1582–1649), and **the younger** (1610–94), Flemish painters of rural life and landscape. The elder lived at Antwerp and the younger at Brussels.

Tenniel, Sir John (1820–1914), English artist, principal cartoonist for *Punch* 1864–1901 and illustrator of Lewis Carroll's *Alice* books.

Tennyson, 1st Baron (Alfred Tennyson) (1809–92), English poet-laureate, b. Somersby, Lincs. A master of language, his publications extended over 60 years. *In Memoriam* reflects his grief for his friend Arthur Hallam. Apart from his lyrics, his longer works include *The Princess*, *Maud*, *Idylls of the King*, and *Enoch Arden*.

Tenzing Norgay Sherpa (1914–86), Nepalese sherpa. On his seventh Everest trip reached the summit with Edmund Hillary (*q.v.*) on 29 May 1953.

Terence, Publius Terentius Afer (c. 184–159 B.C.), a Latin poet and dramatist, an African (Berber), who rose from the position of a slave.

Teresa, Mother (1910–97), Albanian-born Catholic whose work in Calcutta (Kolkata) won world-wide acclaim. Beatified, 2003. She was proclaimed a saint in September 2016. The 'Saint of the Gutters'.

Teresa, St. (1515–82), influential Spanish religious reformer and writer, b. Avila, a woman of boundless energy and spiritual strength. She entered the Carmelite order about 1534, established a reformed order in 1562 (St. Joseph's, Avila), and also founded, with the help of St. John of the Cross, houses for friars. Her writings include *The Way of Perfection* and *The Interior Castle*.

Terry, Ellen Alice (Mrs. James Carew) (1848–1928), English actress, especially in Shakespearean parts with Sir Henry Irving.

Tertullian Quintus (c. 160–220), Carthaginian theologian whose works, especially *Apologeticum*, have profoundly influenced Christian thought.

Tesla, Nikolai (1856–1943), Yugoslav physicist and inventor; went to America 1883; pioneer in high-tension electricity.

Tetrazzini, Luisa (1871–1940), Italian soprano, especially successful in *Lucia di Lammermoor*.

Tetzel, John (c. 1465–1519), German Dominican preacher, whose sale of indulgences for St. Peter's building fund provoked Luther.

Thackeray, William Makepeace (1811–63), English novelist, b. Calcutta, author of *Vanity Fair*, *Pendennis*, *Esmond*, *The Newcomes*, *The Virginians*, *Philip*, and *Lovel the Widower*. He edited the *Cornhill Magazine* from the first number in 1860, his most notable contributions being *Roundabout Papers*. He also wrote *Yellowplush Papers* and *The Book of Snobs* and lectured on *The English Humorists* and *The Four Georges*.

Thales of Miletus (c. 624–565 B.C.), earliest of the Greek scientists, he created a sensation by his prediction of an eclipse of the sun, which was visible at Miletus in 585 B.C. He saw water as the basis of all material things, and in his mathematical work enunciated natural laws.

Thant, Sithu U (1909–74), Burmese diplomat; secretary-general of the UN 1962–72.

Thatcher, Baroness (Margaret Hilda Thatcher) (1925–2013), leader of the Conservative Party 1975–90; prime minister, 1979–90; first woman to lead a western democracy; secured landslide victory, June 1983; MP (Finchley), 1959–92. Historic third successive election victory, June 1987. On 3 Jan 1988 became longest serving P.M. since Asquith. By 1990 she faced growing unpopularity. Deserted by many in her party, she resigned on 28 November 1990. Created Baroness Thatcher of

Kesteven, 1992. Order of the Garter (1995).

Themistocles (c. 523–458 B.C.), Athenian soldier and statesman. He fortified the harbour of Piraeus and created a navy, defeating the Persians at Salamis in 480 B.C. He prepared the way for later greatness, but fell from power and died in exile.

Theocritus (c. 310–250 B.C.), Greek poet, especially of pastoral subjects. His short poems came to be called *Idylls*.

Theodoric the Great (455–526), King of the East Goths, who conquered Italy. Himself an Arian, he practised toleration, and his long reign was peaceful and prosperous.

Theodosius the Great (346–95), Roman emperor of the East (the Empire being divided in 364). He was baptised as a Trinitarian, issuing edicts against the Arians, and after a judicial massacre at Thessalonica he did penance to (St.) Ambrose.

Theophrastus (c. 372–287 B.C.), Greek philosopher, who succeeded Aristotle as teacher at Athens and inherited his library. Best known for his botanical works and his *Characters* (moral studies).

Thesiger, Sir Wilfred (1910–2003), English explorer of Arabia's Empty Quarter.

Thierry, Augustin (1795–1856), French historian, known for his *History of the Norman Conquest*.

Thiers, Louis Adolphe (1797–1877), French statesman and historian. After a varied political career, he became president in 1871, helping to revive France after defeat. He wrote a history of the Revolution.

Thomas, Dylan (1914–53), Welsh poet, whose highly individual *Eighteen Poems* (1934) brought him instant recognition. There followed *Twenty-five Poems* and *Deaths and Entrances*. *Under Milk Wood*, a play for voices, has more general appeal. He was born in Swansea. A Welsh icon.

Thompson, Sir D'Arcy Wentworth (1860–1948), Scottish zoologist whose *On Growth and Form* (1917) has influenced biological science.

Thomson, Sir George Paget (1892–1975), English physicist, son of Sir J. J. Thomson; author of *The Atom, Theory and Practice of Electron Diffraction*, *The Inspiration of Science*. Nobel prizewinner 1937.

Thomson, James (1700–48), Scottish poet who wrote *The Seasons* and *The Castle of Indolence*.

Thomson, James (1834–82), poet and essayist, b. near Glasgow. Wrote *The City Of Dreadful Night*.

Thomson, Sir Joseph John (1856–1940), English physicist and mathematician, leader of a group of researchers at the Cavendish laboratory, Cambridge. He established in 1897 that cathode-rays were moving particles whose speed and specific charge could be measured. He called them corpuscles but the name was changed to electrons. This work was followed up by the study of positive rays which led to the discovery of isotopes, whose existence had earlier been suggested by Soddy. Nobel prize 1906.

Thoreau, Henry David (1817–62), American essayist and nature-lover, who rebelled against society and lived for a time in a solitary hut. His chief work is *Walden*. He was a friend of Emerson.

Thorez, Maurice (1900–64), French communist leader from 1930 and after the second world war.

Thorndike, Dame Sybil (1882–1976), English actress. She made her début in 1904, and played in Greek tragedies, in the plays of Shakespeare and Shaw, and in Grand Guignol. Her husband was Sir Lewis Casson.

Thornycroft, Sir William Hamo (1850–1925), English sculptor, whose works include a statue of General Gordon in Trafalgar Square.

Thorpe, Sir Thomas Edward (1845–1925), English chemist who researched in inorganic chemistry and with his friend Arthur Rücker made a magnetic survey of the British Isles.

Thorwaldsen, Bertel (1770–1844), Danish sculptor. Works include the Cambridge statue of Byron.

Thucydides (c. 460–399 B.C.), Greek historian, especially of the Peloponnesian War in which he himself fought. He was not merely a chronicler, but saw the significance of events and tried to give an impartial account. The speeches attributed by him to leaders include the beautiful funeral oration of Pericles.

Tiberius, Claudius (42 B.C.–A.D. 37), Roman emperor who succeeded Augustus. His early reign was successful but his later years were marked by tragedy and perhaps insanity. He is the Tiberius of Luke 3.1.

Tiepolo, Giambattista (1696–1770), one of the greatest painters in Venetian history. A flamboyant Rococo artist.

Tillett, Benjamin (1860–1943), English trade-union leader, especially of a dockers' strike in 1889 and a transport-workers' strike in 1911.

Tillotson, John (1630–94), English divine, a noted preacher. Archbishop of Canterbury, 1691–94.

Tindal, Matthew (1655–1733), English deist, author of *Christianity as old as the Creation*.

Tintoretto (1518–94), Venetian painter whose aim it was to unite the colouring of Titian with the drawing of Michelangelo. His numerous paintings, mostly of religious subjects, were executed with great speed, some of them on enormous canvases. His *Origin of the Milky Way* is in the National Gallery. His name was Jacopo Robusti, and he was called Il Tintoretto (little dyer) after his father's trade.

Tippett, Sir Michael Kemp (1905–98), English composer whose works include the operas *The Midsummer Marriage*, *King Priam*, and *Knot Garden*, and the song-cycles *Boyhood's End* and *The Heart's Assurance*. O.M. 1983. *See* Section P.

Titian (Tiziano Vecelli) (c. 1487–1576), Venetian painter. He studied under the Bellinis and was influenced by Giorgione, for example, in his frescoes at Padua. His mature style is one of dynamic composition and full colour, as in his *Bacchus and Ariadne* (National Gallery). Among his principal works are *Sacred and Profane Love* (Borghese Gallery, Rome), and some in the Prado. A giant of European painting.

Tito (Josip Broz) (1892–1980), Yugoslav leader, b. Kumrovec. In 1941 he organised partisan forces against the Axis invaders and liberated his country. In 1945 he became the first communist prime minister and in 1953 president. He successfully pursued an independent line .

Titus (A.D. 39–81), Roman emperor, son of Vespasian, ended the Jewish war with the capture of Jerusalem. He completed the Colosseum.

Tizard, Sir Henry Thomas (1885–1959), English scientist and administrator. He was chairman of the Tizard Committee that encouraged the birth of radar before 1939. He was chief scientific adviser to the government, 1947–52.

Tocqueville, Alexis, Comte de (1805–59), French liberal politician and historian, author of *Democracy in America*, still relevant reading.

Todd, 1st Baron (Alexander Robertus Todd) (1907–97), Scottish biochemist, noted for his work on the structure of DNA. Nobel prizewinner 1957; Pres. Royal Society 1975. O.M. (1977).

Todd, Sir Garfield (1908–2002), Rhodesian missionary and statesman. As Prime Minister of Southern Rhodesia supported black rule.

Tolkien, John Ronald Reuel (1892–1973). Academic and writer. Professor of English language and literature at Oxford, 1945–59. Famous as creator of *The Hobbit* (1937), *The Lord of the Rings* (3 vols, 1954–5) and *The Silmarillion* (1977).

Tolstoy, Leo Nikolayevich, Count (1828–1910), Russian writer and philosopher, b. Yasnaya Polyana. Of noble family, he entered the army and fought in the Crimean War. Beginning with simple, natural accounts of his early life (*Childhood* and *Boyhood*), he proceeded to articles on the war, and so eventually to perhaps his best work, the long novel *War and Peace*, followed by *Anna Karenina*. Increasingly preoccupied with social problems, he freed his serfs before this was done officially, and refused to take advantage of his wealth. His later works include *The Kreutzer Sonata* and *Resurrection*.

Tonypandy, Viscount (George Thomas) (1909–97), Speaker of the House of Commons, 1976–83.

Tooke, John Horne (1736–1812), English politician and pamphleteer, was a supporter of Wilkes and later of Pitt. He was tried for high treason, but was acquitted.

Torquemada, Tomas de (1420–98), first inquisitor-general of Spain.

Torricelli, Evangelista (1608–47), Italian physicist, pupil of Galileo. He invented the barometer and improved both microscope and telescope.

Toscanini, Arturo (1867–1957), Italian conductor, b. Parma. With a remarkable musical memory, he was both exacting and self-effacing.

Toulouse-Lautrec, Henri de (1864–1901), French painter, whose pictures portray with stark realism certain aspects of Parisian life in the nineties, especially the *Moulin Rouge* series.

Many are in the Musée Lautrec at Albi. His life was marred by alcoholic and sexual excesses.

Tovey, Sir Donald Francis (1875–1940), English pianist and composer. His compositions include chamber music, a piano concerto, and an opera *The Bride of Dionysus*.

Townshend, Sue (1946–2014), Leicester-born comic writer whose famous creation was Adrian Mole.

Toynbee, Arnold (1852–83), English historian and social reformer. The settlement Toynbee Hall was founded in his memory.

Toynbee, Arnold Joseph (1889–1975), nephew of above, English historian, known mainly for his 10-volume *A Study of History*, an analysis of many civilisations. He was for 30 years director of the Institute of International Affairs.

Tradescant, John (d. 1638) and **Tradescant, John** (1608–62), father and son who were pioneer gardeners and naturalists.

Traherne, Thomas (c. 1636–74), English religious poet; author of *Centuries of Meditations*.

Trajan (c. 53–117), Roman emperor, was a successful general and administrator. Born in Spain.

Tree, Sir Herbert Beerbohm (1853–1917), English actor-manager of the Haymarket theatre until 1897 when he built His Majesty's theatre. **Sir Max Beerbohm** was his half-brother.

Trenchard, 1st Viscount (Hugh Montague Trenchard) (1873–1956), British air-marshal. He served with the Royal Flying Corps in the first world war. The first air marshal of the RAF.

Trent, 1st Baron (Jesse Boot) (1850–1931), drug manufacturer, b. Nottingham. He built up the largest pharmaceutical retail trade in the world.

Trevelyan, George Macaulay (1876–1962), English historian, known for his *English Social History*.

Trevelyan, Sir George Otto (1838–1928), English liberal politician, father of above. He wrote a life of his uncle Lord Macaulay.

Trevithick, Richard (1771–1833), English mining engineer and inventor, b. near Redruth, Cornwall. His most important invention was a high-pressure steam-engine (1801) and he is commonly (and rightly) acknowledged as the inventor of the steam locomotive for railways.

Trollope, Anthony (1815–82), English novelist. His early life was a struggle, the family being supported by his mother's writings. His own career was in the post office, but by strict industry he produced many novels especially portraying clerical life (the *Barchester* series) and political life (the Palliser Novels).

Trotsky, Leo (Lev Davidovich Bronstein) (1879–1940), Russian revolutionary, b. of Jewish parents in the Ukraine, one of the leaders of the Bolshevik revolution. He led the Russian delegation at the Brest-Litovsk conference. He differed from Stalin on policy, believing in "permanent revolution," according to which socialism could not be achieved in Russia without revolutions elsewhere, and was dismissed from office in 1925 and expelled from the Communist party in 1927. In 1929 he took up exile in Mexico where he was assassinated in 1940.

Trudeau, Pierre Eliott (1919–2000), Liberal prime minister of Canada 1968–79, 1980–84. His son **Justin Trudeau** went on to become Prime Minister.

Trueman, Fred (1931–2006), Yorkshire and England cricketer. The first man to take 300 Test wickets. One of the greatest fast bowlers.

Truman, Harry S. (1884–1972), U.S. President, 1945–53. He inherited the presidency on Roosevelt's death in 1945 when he took the decision to drop the first atom bomb, and he won the election of 1948. He intervened in Korea and dismissed General MacArthur.

Trump, Donald (b.1946). Right-wing Republican who won the 2016 election to become the 45th President of the United States. A billionaire businessman turned populist politician.

Tubman, Harriet (1820–1913). Afro-American woman famous for shepherding slaves to freedom before the Civil War.

Tudjman, Franjo (1922–99), authoritarian President of Croatia, the father of modern Croat nationalism.

Tulsi Das (1532–1623), Indian poet whose masterpiece *Ram-Charit-Mānas* (popularly known as the *Ramayana* and based on the Sanskrit epic of *Vālmīki*) is venerated by all Hindus.

Turenne, Henri de la Tour d'Auvergne, Vicomte de (1611–75), French commander who was successful in the Thirty Years' War.

Turgenev, Ivan Sergeyvich (1818–83), Russian novelist, friend of Gogol and Tolstoy, who spent part of his life in exile. His works include *Fathers and Children*, *Smoke*, and *Virgin Soil*.

Turing, Alan Mathison (1912–54), computer genius. Developed concept (1936) of Turing machine. He may have committed suicide after being victimised for being homosexual. Royal Pardon, 2013.

Turner, Joseph Mallord William (1775–1851), English landscape painter, b. London, a barber's son. He entered the Royal Academy and was at first a topographical watercolourist. Later he turned to oil and became a master of light and colour, achieving magical effects, especially in depicting the reflection of light in water. His works include *Crossing the Brook*, *Dido building Carthage*, *The Fighting Temeraire*, *Rain, Steam and Speed*. He also made thou-sands of colour studies. He encountered violent criticism as his style became more abstract which led to Ruskin's passionate defence of him in *Modern Painters*. His art also depicted machines and technology. He bequeathed his work to the nation.

Tussaud, Marie (1761–1850), Swiss modeller in wax who learnt from her uncle in Paris, married a Frenchman, and later came to England where she set up a permanent exhibition.

Tutankhamen (d. c. 1327 B.C.), Egyptian pharaoh of the 18th dynasty, son-in-law of Akhenaten, whose tomb was discovered by Howard Carter in 1922, with the mummy and gold sarcophagus intact. He died when he was 18, possibly murdered. He suffered from epilepsy.

Tutu, Desmond Mpilo (b. 1931), South African Archbishop of Cape Town, 1986–96. Nobel Peace Prize, 1984. Outstanding opponent of apartheid.

Twain, Mark (Samuel Langhorne Clemens) (1835–1910), American humorist. His *Innocents Abroad* was the result of a trip to Europe. His works include *A Tramp Abroad*, *Tom Sawyer*, *Huckleberry Finn*, and *Pudd'nhead Wilson*.

Tweedsmuir, 1st Baron (John Buchan) (1875–1940), Scottish author of biographies, historical novels, and adventure stories, including *Montrose* and *Thirty-nine Steps*. He was governor-general of Canada 1935–40.

Tyler, John (1790–1862), 10th President of the United States (1841–45). Formerly Vice-President to his Whig predecessor William Henry Harrison; his Administration concluded with Great Britain the Webster-Ashburton Treaty of 1842 fixing the eastern border between the US and Canada.

Tyler, Wat (d. 1381), English peasant leader. He was chosen leader of the Peasants' Revolt of 1381, and parleyed at Smithfield with the young king Richard II, but was killed.

Tyndale, William (c. 1494–1536), English religious reformer, translator of the Bible. He had to go abroad, where he visited Luther and his New Testament was printed at Worms. When copies entered England they were suppressed by the bishops (1526). His Pentateuch was printed at Antwerp, but he did not complete the Old Testament. He was betrayed, arrested, and executed. Unlike Wyclif, who worked from Latin texts, he translated mainly from the original Hebrew and Greek and his work was later to become the basis of the Authorised Version of the Bible.

Tyndall, John (1829–93), Irish physicist whose wide interests led him to research on heat, light, and sound, and on bacteria-free air and sterilisation. He discovered why the sky is blue (Tyndall effect) and pioneered popular scientific writing, *e.g.*, *Heat as a Mode of Motion*.

U

Ulanova, Galina (1910–98), the greatest Soviet ballerina of her time. With the Kirov Ballet in Leningrad from 1928–44 and then at the Bolshoi Theatre in Moscow where she was the *prima ballerina assoluta* for 16 years. Her artistry lay in combining effortless technique with a talent for acting which created living personalities out of her roles.

Ulbricht, Walter (1893–1973), East German statesman. Communist leader who ordered the building of the Berlin Wall.

Unamuno, Miguel de (1864–1936), Spanish philosopher, poet, essayist, and novelist, author of *El Sentimiento Trágico de la Vida* (The Tragic Sense of Life).

Undset, Sigrid (1882–1949), Norwegian novelist, author of *Jenny*, *Kristin Lavransdatter*, and *Olav Audunsson*. Nobel prizewinner 1928.

Unwin, Sir Raymond (1863–1940), English architect of the first garden city at Letchworth in Hertfordshire.

Updike, John (1932–2009), one of America's greatest novelists who chronicled sex and divorce in the USA. Author of *The Witches of Eastwick* and *Couples*. A double Pulitzer prize-winner.

Ursula, St., said in late legend to have been killed at Cologne with many companions while on pilgrimage. It arose from a 4th cent. inscription which simply referred to virgin martyrs.

Usher or **Ussher, James** (1581–1656), Irish divine who in 1625 became archbishop of Armagh. He placed the creation at 4004 B.C.

Ustinov, Sir Peter (1921–2004), gifted and much-loved raconteur, entertainer, actor and writer. An ambassador of laughter.

V

Valentine, St., was a christian martyr of the reign of the emperor Claudius II (d. A.D. 270). The custom of sending valentines may be connected with the pagan festival of Lupercalia.

Valéry, Paul (1871–1945), French poet and essayist, strongly influenced by the symbolist leader, Mallarmé. His poems include *La jeune Parque*, *Charmes*, and *Le cimetière marin*.

Van Allen, James (1914–2006), pioneer US astrophysicist who discovered the belts of trapped energy particles surrounding the Earth (and which are named after him).

Vanbrugh, Sir John (1664–1726), English architect and playwright. His buildings include Blenheim Palace and his plays *The Provok'd Wife*.

Van Buren, Martin (1782–1862), 8th President of the United States (1837–41). Formerly Vice-President to his Democratic predecessor Andrew Jackson, he opposed the annexation of Texas to the US for fear of increasing the power of the South.

Vancouver, George (1758–98), British navigator who served under Captain Cook, also doing survey work, and who sailed round Vancouver island.

Vanderbilt, Cornelius (1794–1877), American merchant and railway speculator who amassed a fortune and founded a university at Nashville. His son, **William Henry Vanderbilt** (1821–85), inherited and added to it.

Van Dyck, Sir Anthony (1599–1641), Flemish painter, b. Antwerp. He studied under Rubens, travelled in Italy, and then settled in England with an annuity from Charles I. He excelled in portraits, especially of Charles I and Henrietta Maria, and of their court.

Vane, Sir Henry (1613–62), English parliamentary leader during the civil war period. He was executed in 1662.

Van Gogh, Vincent (1853–90), Dutch painter of some of the most colourful pictures ever created. With passionate intensity of feeling he painted without pause whatever he found around him—landscapes, still life, portraits; his was a truly personal art. His life was one of pain, and often despair, and in the end he committed suicide (but this is now disputed by some scholars).

His *Sunset At Montmajour* was declared to be genuine in 2013.

Varah, Chad (1911–2007), the inspirational founder of the Samaritans in 1953.

Vauban, Sebastien de Prestre de (1633–1707), French military engineer, whose skill in siege works (*e.g.*, at Maestricht 1673) was a factor in the expansive wars of Louis XIV. He protected France with fortresses and also invented the socket bayonet.

Vaughan Williams, Ralph (1872–1958), English composer, b. Gloucestershire. After Charterhouse and Cambridge he studied music in Berlin under Max Bruch and, later in Paris, under Ravel. He wrote nine symphonies besides a number of choral and orchestral works, operas (including *Hugh the Drover*, *Riders to the Sea*), ballets, chamber music, and songs. See **Section P.**

Velasquez, Diego (*c.* 1460–1524), Spanish conquistador, first governor of Cuba.

Velasquez, Diego Rodriguez de Silva y (1599–1660), Spanish painter, b. Seville, especially of portraits at the court of Philip IV, and also of

classical and historical subjects. He made two visits to Italy (1629–31, 1649–51), studying the Venetian painters, especially Titian, which hastened the development of his style. Among his masterpieces are *The Maids of Honour*, *The Tapestry Weavers* (both in the Prado), the Rokeby Venus and a portrait of Philip IV (both in the National Gallery), the landscape views from the Villa Medici (Prado) and *Juan de Pareja* (sold in London in 1970 for £2·25 million).

Venizelos, Eleutherios (1864–1936), Greek statesman, b. Crete. He became prime minister in 1910 and held this office intermittently. He promoted the Balkan League (1912), forced the king's abdication (1917), and brought Greece into the war on the Allied side, securing territorial concessions at the peace conference, but his expansionist policy in Turkish Asia was a failure.

Ventris, Michael (1922–56). Pioneering linguist who deciphered the Linear B script. Born Wheathampstead, Hertfordshire, he was killed in a road accident.

Verdi, Giuseppe (1813–1901), Italian composer, b. near Busseto in the province of Parma. His early works include *Nabucco*, *Ernani*, *I Due Foscari*, and *Macbeth*; a middle period is represented by *Rigoletto*, *Il Trovatore*, *La Traviata*, *Un Ballo in Maschera*, and *Don Carlos*; to the last period belong *Aida*, *Otello*, and *Falstaff* (produced when he was 80). See **Section P.**

Verlaine, Paul (1844–96), French poet, one of the first symbolists, also known for his memoirs and confessions. His works include *Poèmes saturniens*, *Fêtes galantes*, *Sagesse*, and *Romances sans paroles*. He was imprisoned in Belgium for shooting and wounding his friend Rimbaud. He died in poverty in Paris.

Vermeer, Jan (1632–75), Dutch painter, b. Delft. His main paintings are of domestic interiors, which he makes into works of art, as in *Lady at the Virginals* (National Gallery). However, his tranquil images in fact mask his own life of turmoil.

Verne, Jules (1828–1905), French writer of science fiction, including *Five Weeks in a Balloon*, *Twenty Thousand Leagues Under the Sea*, *Round the World in Eighty Days*.

Vernier, Pierre (1580–1637), French inventor of the small sliding scale which enables readings on a graduated scale to be taken to a fraction of a division.

Veronese, Paolo (1528–88), Italian painter of the Venetian school, whose works include *Marriage Feast at Cana in Galilee*, *The Feast in the House of Simon*, and *The Presentation of the Family of Darius to Alexander*, *His Adoration of the Magi* is in the National Gallery.

Veronica, St., legendary woman who was said to hand her kerchief to Christ on the way to Calvary, to wipe his brow, and his impression was left on the kerchief. In its present form her legend dates from the 14th cent.

Verwoerd, Hendrik Frensch (1901–66), South African politician, b. Amsterdam, exponent of the policy of apartheid; prime minister 1958–66. He was assassinated.

Vespasian, Titus Flavius (A.D. 9–79), Roman emperor. He was sent by Nero to put down the Jews and was proclaimed by the legions. He began the Colosseum.

Vespucci, Amerigo (1451–1512), Florentine explorer, naturalised in Spain, contractor at Seville for Columbus. He later explored Venezuela. The use of his name for the continent arose through a mistake.

Vico, Giambattista (1688–1744), Italian philosopher of history and of culture, b. Naples. His ideas were developed in his *Scienza nuova* (science of history) but it was not until our own day that his originality was fully recognised.

Victor Emmanuel II (1820–78), first king of Italy. King of Sardinia, he was proclaimed king of Italy in 1861 after the Austrians had been defeated and Garibaldi had succeeded in the south. Rome was added in 1870.

Victoria (1819–1901), Queen of the United Kingdom of Gt. Britain and Ireland and Empress of India, was granddaughter of George III and succeeded her uncle, William IV, in 1837. In 1840 she married Prince Albert of Saxe-Coburg-Gotha, who died in 1861. Conscientious, hard-working, and of strict moral standards, she had by the end of a long life (jubilees 1887 and 1897) won much affection. Her reign saw great industrial growth and imperial expansion. She is buried in the Royal Mausoleum at Frogmore (near Windsor). She was the first British monarch to travel by train. She reigned through 15 general elections and was served by 10 prime ministers.

Vigée Le Brun, Elisabeth (1755–1842), the most significant female painter of the 18th cent.

Villeneuve, Pierre de (1763–1806), French admiral defeated by Nelson at Trafalgar and captured along with his ship, the *Bucentaure*.

Villon, François (1431–?1463), French poet, b. Paris, who lived at a turbulent time at the close of the Hundred Years War. After fatally stabbing a man in 1455 he joined the *Conquillards*, a criminal organisation. They had a secret language (the *jargon*) and it was for them that he composed his ballads.

His extant works consist of the *Petit Testament* (1456), originally called *Le Lais*, and the *Grand Testament* (1461), masterpieces of medieval verse.

Virgil (Publius Vergilius Maro) (70–19 B.C.), Roman epic poet, b. at Andes near Mantua, he went to Rome to obtain redress for the military confiscation of his farm. He was patronised by Maecenas, and wrote his pastoral *Eclogues*, followed by his *Georgics*. His best-known work, the *Aeneid*, deals with the wanderings of Aeneas after the fall of Troy till his establishment of a kingdom in Italy.

Vivaldi, Antonio (1678–1741), Venetian composer, violin master at the Ospedale della Pieta. His output of orchestral works was prolific and Bach arranged some of his violin pieces for the harpsichord. *See* Section P.

Volta, Alessandro (1745–1827), Italian physicist of Pavia, who, working on the results of Galvani, invented the voltaic pile, the first instrument for producing an electric current. It provided a new means for the decomposition of certain substances. His name was given to the volt, the unit of electrical potential difference.

Voltaire (François Marie Arouet) (1694–1778), French philosopher and writer. His first essays offended the authorities, and he spent the years 1726–9 in England, where he wrote some of his dramas. Returning to France, he published his *Philosophical Letters*, which aroused the enmity of the priesthood. At this juncture, the Marquise du Châtelet offered him the asylum of her castle at Cirey, and for the next 15 years he made this his home, writing there his *Discourses of Man, Essay on the Morals and Spirit of Nations, Age of Louis XIV*, etc. His most celebrated book was *Candide*, in which he attacked the theory of Optimism. Its observations include *"pour encourager les autres"* (about Admiral Byng's execution) and its final message: *"il faut cultiver notre jardin."*

Vondel, Joost van don (1587–1679), Dutch poet who lived at Amsterdam. Most of his dramas are on biblical subjects, and the two most famous are *Jephtha* and *Lucifer*.

Vonnegut, Kurt (1922–2006). American literary idol whose works became counter-culture classics.

Voroshilov, Klimentiv Efremovich (1881–1969), Soviet general who commanded the Leningrad defences in 1941. USSR president, 1953–60.

Vries, Adriaen de (1556–1626), Dutch Mannerist sculptor whose works include *Christ in Distress*.

Vyshinsky, Andrei Yanuarievich (1883–1954), Soviet jurist and diplomat; conducted the prosecution of the infamous Moscow treason trials, 1936–8.

W

Wade, George (1673–1748), English general and military engineer who, after the rising of 1715, pacified the Scottish highlands, constructing military roads and bridges. In the 1745 rising Prince Charles' forces evaded him.

Wagner, Richard (1813–83), German composer, b. Leipzig. He achieved a new type of musical expression in his operas by the complete union of music and drama. He made use of the *Leitmotif* and was his own librettist. His originality (and involvement in the 1848 revolution) aroused opposition, and he was exiled for some years. But he was supported by loyal friends, including

Liszt, the young King Ludwig of Bavaria, and Nietzsche. He began the music of the *Ring des Nibelungen* in 1853, but it was not until 1876 that the whole of the drama (Rheingold, Valkyrie, Siegfried, Götterdämmerung) was performed at Bayreuth under the conductor Hans Richter.

Other operas are *The Flying Dutchman, Rienzi, Tannhäuser, Lohengrin, Tristan und Isolde, Die Meistersinger von Nürnberg,* and *Parsifal,* a religious drama. He married Liszt's daughter Cosima.

Walcott, Derek (1930–2017), West Indian poet and playwright, whose works include *Collected Poems 1948–1984* (1986) and *Omeros* (1990). He won the Nobel Prize for Literature (1992).

Waldheim, Kurt (1918–2007), Austrian diplomat; succeeded U Thant as secretary-general of the UN, 1972–81. President of Austria, 1986–92. His career was tainted by his Nazi past.

Walesa, Lech (b. 1943), Polish trade unionist. Shipyard worker in Gdansk. Leader of *Solidarity*. Awarded 1983 Nobel Peace Prize. President of Poland, 1990–95. Retired from politics, 2000.

Waley, Arthur (1889–1966), English orientalist, known for his translations of Chinese and Japanese poetry and prose. The first to bring the literature of those countries to the western world.

Walker, George (1618–90), hero of the siege of Londonderry in 1688, who kept the besiegers at bay for 105 days.

Wallace, Alfred Russel (1823–1913), British naturalist, b. Usk, Monmouth, joint author with Darwin of the theory of natural selection. In 1858, while down with illness in the Moluccas, he sent a draft of his theory to Darwin in England who was amazed to find that it closely agreed with his own theory of evolution which he was on the point of publishing. The result was a reading of a joint paper to the Linnean Society.

Wallace, Edgar (1875–1932), English novelist and playwright, known for his detective thrillers.

Wallace, Sir Richard (1818–90), English art collector and philanthropist. His adopted son's wife bequeathed his collection to the nation (Wallace Collection, Manchester Square, London).

Wallace, Sir William (c. 1274–1305), Scottish patriot. He withstood Edward I, at first successfully, but was defeated at Falkirk, taken to London and brutally murdered. He is now a cultural icon.

Wallenstein, Albrecht von (1583–1634), German soldier and statesman during the Thirty Years War. An able administrator of his own estates, he sought the unity of Germany, but was distrusted and eventually assassinated.

Waller, Edmund (1606–87), English poet of polished simplicity, author of *Go, lovely rose.*

Wallis, Sir Barnes Neville (1887–1979), British scientist and inventor whose many designs include the R100 airship, the Wellington bomber, the swing-wing aircraft, and the "bouncing bomb" that breached the Ruhr dams in 1943.

Wallis, John (1616–1703), English mathematician who introduced the symbol for infinity.

Walpole, Horace, 4th Earl of Orford (1717–97), younger son of Sir Robert Walpole, English writer, chiefly remembered for his *Letters,* his *Castle of Otranto,* and his "Gothic" house at Strawberry Hill.

Walpole, Sir Hugh Seymour (1884–1941), English novelist, b. New Zealand. His works include *Fortitude, The Dark Forest,* and *The Herries Chronicle.*

Walpole, Sir Robert, 1st Earl of Orford (1676–1745), English Whig statesman, who came to office soon after the Hanoverian succession and is considered the first prime minister.

Walter, Bruno (1876–1962), German-American conductor, especially of Haydn, Mozart, and Mahler.

Walter, John (1776–1847), English newspaper editor. Under him *The Times,* founded by his father John Walter (1739–1812), prospered.

Walton, Izaak (1593–1683), English writer, especially remembered for *The Compleat Angler,* first published in 1653. He also wrote biographies of Donne, Hooker, and George Herbert. Known as the "father of angling".

Walton, Sir William Turner (1902–83), English composer, whose works include concertos for string instruments, two symphonies, two coronation marches, *Façade* (setting to Edith Sitwell's poem), and an oratorio, *Belshazzar's Feast.* O.M. 1967.

Warbeck, Perkin (1474–99), Flemish impostor, b. Tournai, who claimed to be the younger son of Edward IV with French and Scottish backing, but failed and was executed.

Warhol, Andy (1927–87), controversial American pop artist and film-maker. The 'father of Pop Art'.

Warne, Shane (b. 1969). For many (and certainly for all Australians) the greatest spinner to have played the game of cricket. He was the first bowler to have taken over 700 Test wickets. His tally has now been overtaken by the Sri Lankan Muttiah Muralithan.

Warwick, Earl of (Richard Neville) (c. 1428–71), "the kingmaker." At first on the Yorkist side in the Wars of the Roses, he proclaimed Edward IV king; but later changed sides and restored the Lancastrian Henry VI. Killed at Barnet in 1471.

Washington, Booker Taliaferro (1858–1915), American black educationist, author of *Up from Slavery*.

Washington, George (1732–99), first U.S. president. B. in Virginia, of a family which originated from Sulgrave, Northants., he served against the French in the Seven Years War. When the dispute between the British government and the Americans over taxation came to a head, he proved a successful general, and Cornwallis's surrender to him at Yorktown in 1781 virtually ended the war. In 1787 he presided over the Philadelphia convention which formulated the constitution, and was president 1789–97.

Watson, John Broadus (1878–1958), American psychologist, an exponent of behaviourism. *See* **Behaviourism, Section J.**

Watson-Watt, Sir Robert (1892–1973), Scottish physicist, who played a major part in the development of radar.

Watt, James (1736–1819), Scottish engineer and inventor, b. Greenock. He made important improvements to Newcomen's steam-engine by inventing a separate condenser (applying Black's discoveries (1761–4) on latent heat) and other devices based on scientific knowledge of the properties of steam. He was given support by Matthew Boulton, a capitalist, and settled down in Birmingham with him. He defined one horse-power as the rate at which work is done when 33,000 lb are raised one foot in one minute. He also constructed a press for copying manuscripts. The watt as a unit of power is named after him.

Watteau, Jean Antoine (1684–1721), French painter. He painted pastoral idylls in court dress. His works include *Embarquement pour Cythère* in the Louvre. He died of tuberculosis.

Watts, Isaac (1674–1748), English hymn-writer, author of *O God, our help in ages past*.

Watts-Dunton, Walter Theodore (1836–1914), English poet and critic, friend of Swinburne whom he looked after until his death in 1909.

Waugh, Evelyn (1902–66), English satirical writer, author of *Vile Bodies, The Loved One, Brideshead Revisited, Life of Edmund Campion, The Ordeal of Gilbert Pinfold*, and an autobiography, *A Little Learning*.

Wavell, 1st Earl (Archibald Percival Wavell) (1883–1950), British field marshal. He served in the first great war on Allenby's staff and in the second he commanded in the Middle East 1939–41, defeating the Italians; and in India 1941–3. He was viceroy of India 1943–7.

Webb, Matthew (1848–83), English swimmer, the first to swim the English Channel (1875).

Webb, Sidney James, Baron Passfield (1859–1947), and his wife **Beatrice,** *née* Potter (1858–1943), English social reformers and historians. They combined careful investigation of social problems (their books include *History of Trade Unionism* and *English Local Government*) with work for the future; they were members of the Fabian Society, launched the *New Statesman*, and helped to set up the London School of Economics. He held office under Labour.

Weber, Carl Maria Friedrich Ernst von (1786–1826), German composer, who laid the foundation of German romantic opera. His reputation rests principally on his three operas, *Der Freischütz, Euryanthe*, and *Oberon*. He was also an able pianist, conductor, and musical director. *See* **Section P.**

Webster, Daniel (1782–1852), American statesman and orator. He held office more than once and negotiated the Ashburton Treaty which settled the Maine–Canada boundary.

Webster, Noah (1758–1843), American lexicographer, who published an *American dictionary*

of the English language.

Wedgwood, Dame Cicely Veronica (1910–97), English historian, author of *William the Silent, Thomas Wentworth, The Thirty Years' War, The King's Peace, The Trial of Charles I*; a member of the Staffordshire pottery family. O.M. 1969.

Wedgwood, Josiah (1730–95), English potter, who at his Etruria works near Hanley produced from a new ware (patented 1763) pottery to classical designs by Flaxman, and gave pottery a new impetus.

Wei Jingsheng (b. 1951), Chinese human rights campaigner. Imprisoned, 1979–93, for his political beliefs. Imprisoned again, 1995, then exiled.

Weill, Kurt (1900–50), German composer of satirical, surrealist operas, including *Die Dreigroschenoper* and *Mahagonny* (librettist Brecht). His wife, the Viennese actress Lotte Lenya (d. 1981) will be remembered for her singing of the Brecht songs and the interpretation of her husband's works. They left Europe for the United States in 1935.

Weingartner, Felix (1863–1942), Austrian conductor, also a composer and writer of a text book on conducting.

Weismann, August (1834–1914), German biologist. He worked on the question of individual variability in evolution, stressing the continuity of the germ plasm and rejecting the idea of inheritance of acquired characteristics.

Weizmann, Chaim (1874–1952), Israeli leader, b. Motol, near Pinsk (now in Belarus). He came to England in 1903 and taught biochemistry at Manchester. He helped to secure the Balfour Declaration (1917). In 1948 he became first president of Israel.

Welby Justin (b. 1956), Archbishop of Canterbury since 2013. Bishop of Durham, 2011–12. A former oil company executive.

Welensky, Roland (Roy) (1907–91), Deputy Prime Minister and Minister of Transport of the Central African Federation, 1953–56. He then became Prime Minister and Minister of External Affairs. He remained Prime Minister until the break-up of the Federation in 1963.

Wellesley, Marquess (Richard Colley Wellesley) (1760–1842), British administrator. He was a successful governor-general of India, and was brother of the Duke of Wellington.

Wellington, 1st Duke of (Arthur Wellesley) (1769–1852), British general. B. in Ireland, he joined the army and gained experience in India. In the Peninsular War he successfully wore down and drove out the invading French. When Napoleon escaped from Elba, Wellington defeated him at Waterloo. Thereafter he took some part in politics as a Tory, but in the last resort was capable of accepting change.

Wells, Herbert George (1866–1946), English author. B. London, he was at first a teacher. He believed in progress through science, and became one of the most influential writers of his time. His long series of books includes romances of the Jules Verne variety (*The Time Machine, The Island of Dr. Moreau, The Invisible Man*), sociological autobiography (*Love and Mr. Lewisham, Kipps, Tono-Bungay, The History of Mr. Polly, Mr. Britling Sees it Through*), as well as popular education (*Outline of History, The Science of Life, The Work, Wealth and Happiness of Mankind, The Shape of Things to Come, The Fate of Homo Sapiens*). He was a founder member of the Fabian Society.

Wells, Horace (1815–48), US dentist, the first to use laughing gas as an anaesthetic in dentistry (1844).

Wenceslaus, St. (907–929), Patron saint of the Czechs. A Christian ruler, murdered by his brother Boleslav on his way to Mass. The 'Good King' of the Christmas carol.

Wesker, Sir Arnold (1932–2016), English playwright best-known for such political and social dramas as *Chicken Soup with Barley* and *Chips with Everything*. The 'kitchen-sink playwright'.

Wesley, Charles (1707–88), English hymnwriter. He was the companion of his brother John, and wrote over 5,500 hymns, including *Love divine* and *Jesu, lover of my soul*.

Wesley, John (1703–91), English evangelist and founder of Methodism (at first a nickname applied to friends of himself and his brother), b. at Epworth. After a trip to Georgia and after encountering Moravian influence, he began to teach on tour, covering in over 50 years more than 200,000 miles and preaching over 40,000 sermons. He made religion a live force to many ignorant folk of humble station who could only be reached by a new and direct challenge. He made a feature of the Sunday school and increased the use of music (the brothers' first hymnbook appeared in 1739). He did not plan separation from the Anglican church, though it was implicit in his ordination of a missionary, and it took place after his death. *See also* **Methodism, Section J.**

Westermarck, Edward Alexander (1862–1939), Finnish sociologist. His works include *History of Human Marriage, Origin and Development of the Moral Ideas*, and *The Oedipus Complex.*

Westinghouse, George (1846–1914), American engineer who invented an air-brake for railways (1868) called by his name, and pioneered the use of high tension alternating current for the transmission of electric power.

Westmacott, Sir Richard (1775–1856), English sculptor of Achilles in Hyde Park.

Wharton, Edith (1862–1937), American novelist and friend of Henry James. Her works include *House of Mirth* and *Custom of the Country.*

Whately, Richard (1787–1863), English arch-bishop of Dublin. He wrote treatises on *Rhetoric* and *Logic.*

Wheatstone, Sir Charles (1802–75), English physicist, one of the first to recognise Ohm's law. In 1837 he (with W. F. Cooke) patented an electric telegraph. He also introduced the microphone.

Wheeler, Sir Charles (1892–1974), English sculptor, especially on buildings. President, R.A., 1956–66.

Wheeler, Sir Mortimer (1890–1976), notable archaeologist who popularised his subject.

Whistler, James Abbott McNeill (1834–1903), American artist. B. at Lowell, he studied in Paris and settled in England. He reacted against the conventions of his day, and Ruskin's uncomprehending criticism of his work resulted in a lawsuit. Among his main works are studies of the Thames, and a portrait of his mother, now in the Louvre.

White, Sir George Stuart (1835–1912), British general. Defended Ladysmith in the Boer War.

White, Gilbert (1720–93), a father of English ecology. His book *The Natural History and Antiquities of Selborne*, was published in 1789.

White, Patrick (1912–90), Australian novelist whose books include *The Aunt's Story, Riders in the Chariot, The Solid Mandala* and *The Eye of the Storm.* Nobel prize 1973.

Whitefield, George (1714–70), English evangelist, b. Gloucester. He was at first associated with the Wesleys, but differed from them on predestination. His supporters built him a "Tabernacle" in London, and he had other chapels elsewhere. He founded no lasting sect.

Whitehouse, Mary (1910–2001), tireless campaigner against screen sex and violence.

Whitelaw, Viscount ((William Whitelaw) (1918–99), Deputy Prime Minister under Thatcher.

Whitgift, John (1530–1604), archbishop of Canterbury in the time of Elizabeth I (from 1583). His policy helped to strengthen Anglicanism.

Whitman, Walt (1819–92), American poet, b. Long Island. He led a wandering life and did hospital work in the Civil War. He aimed at forming a new and free American outlook. His works include *Leaves of Grass, Drum Taps,* and *Democratic Vistas.*

Whittier, John Greenleaf (1807–92), American Quaker poet, b. Haverhill, Mass. He wrote against slavery (*Justice and Expediency*), turning to poetry after the Civil War, especially remembered for *Snow-bound.*

Whittington, Richard (*c.* 1358–1423), famous English merchant. Son of a Gloucestershire knight, he became a London mercer and was mayor of London 1398, 1406, 1419. The cat legend is part of European folklore.

Whittle, Sir Frank (1907–96), 'the father of jet flight'. The first flights of Gloster jet propelled planes with Whittle engines took place in 1941. O.M. (1986).

Whymper, Edward (1840–1911), English wood-engraver and mountaineer. He was the first to climb the Matterhorn.

Wiesel Elie (1928–2016). Auschwitz survivor who later won the Nobel Peace Prize. One of the great moral voices of our time.

Wiesenthal, Simon (1908–2005), Nazi-hunter who devoted his life to bringing Nazi murderers to

justice. The "conscience of the Holocaust".

Wilberforce, William (1759–1833), English philanthropist, b. Hull. He was the parliamentary leader of the campaign against the slave trade, abolished in 1807. He then worked against slavery itself.

Wilcox, Ella Wheeler (1855–1919), American writer of romantic sentimental verse.

Wilde, Oscar Fingall (1854–1900), Irish author and dramatist, son of a Dublin surgeon and leader of the cult of art for art's sake. His works include poems, fairy-tales, short stories, and witty plays—*Lady Windermere's Fan, A Woman of No Importance, An Ideal Husband,* and *The Importance of Being Earnest.* After an ill-advised libel action which failed, he was subsequently convicted of homosexual practices and imprisoned for two years, when he wrote *The Ballad of Reading Gaol.*

Wilder, Thornton Niven (1897–1975), American author and playwright. Among his books are *The Bridge of San Luis Rey* and *Ides of March.*

Wilhelm, Kaiser. *See* **William I, II** *etc.*

Wilkes, John (1727–97), English politician. A Whig, he violently attacked George III in his paper the *North Briton,* and as a result of unsuccessful proceedings against him, general warrants were determined illegal. He was again in trouble for obscene libel; his defiance of authority brought him popularity, and he was four times re-elected to parliament but refused his seat, until his opponents gave way. He helped to establish freedom of the press.

Willcocks, Sir David (1919–2015),conductor and composer who made the annual Festival of Nine Lessons and Carols from King's College, Cambridge a national institution. Often called the nation's choirmaster.

Willcocks, Sir William (1852–1932), British engineer, b. India, who carried out irrigation works in India *etc.* He built the Aswan dam (1898–1902).

Willett, William (1856–1915), English advocate of "daylight savings," adopted after his death.

William I of England (1027–87), the "Conqueror," Duke of Normandy, claimed the English throne as successor to Edward the Confessor, and defeated Harold II at Hastings in 1066. An able commander and a firm ruler, he crushed Saxon resistance, especially in the north, transferred most of the land to his Norman followers, and drew England into closer relations with the continent, as did his archbishop Lanfranc. He ordered the Domesday survey.

William II of England (1056–1100), the Conqueror's son, surnamed Rufus, succeeded in 1087. Capricious and self-indulgent, his reign was troubled, and he was shot (by accident or design) while hunting in the New Forest.

William III of England (1650–1702), King of England, Scotland, and Ireland (1689–1702), son of William II of Orange and Mary, daughter of Charles I. He married Mary, daughter of the Duke of York (later James II) while stadtholder of Holland. In 1688, when James had fled the country, he was invited to succeed and he and Mary became joint king and queen. The revolution of 1688 brought to England tolerance of Protestant worship, but William was mainly concerned with war against France, ended in 1697.

William IV of England (1765–1837), third son of George III, succeeded his brother George IV in 1830; called the "sailor king." The reform bill of 1832 and other reform measures were carried without obstruction from him.

William I of Germany (1797–1888), King of Prussia and first German emperor. He succeeded to the throne in 1861 and continued resistance to reform, appointing Bismarck as chief minister, and supporting him through the Austro-Prussian and Franco-Prussian wars. His personal character was simple and unassuming.

William II of Germany, the Kaiser (1859–1941), King of Prussia and German emperor from 1888, was grandson of William I and of Queen Victoria. He was intelligent but impetuous, and believed in military power. He dismissed Bismarck. In 1914 his support of Austria helped to precipitate European war, and the resulting defeat brought his abdication, after which he lived in retirement at Doorn in Holland.

William the Silent (1533–84), Dutch national leader. Prince of Orange, he led the revolt of the Protestant Netherlands against the rule of the Spanish Philip II. The union of the northern provinces was accomplished in 1579, and Spanish rule was renounced by 1584, in which year William was assassinated.

Williams, Sir Bernard (1929–2003), a brilliant and humane thinker, the outstanding moral philosopher of his age.

Williams, Eric (1911–81), the first Prime Minister of independent Trinidad and Tobago. He led his country to independence. His policy of "empirical socialism" saw his country prosper.

Williams, Sir George (1821–1905), founder of the Young Men's Christian Association.

Williams, Raymond (1921–88), one of the towering Welsh socialist thinkers of the 20th cent. Author of *Culture and Society* (1958) *etc*. A critic and novelist.

Williams, Rowan (b.1950), the Archbishop of Canterbury, 2002–12. An eminent theologian and profound thinker. Archbishop of Wales, 2000–02. Bishop of Monmouth, 1992–2000.

Williams, Tennessee (1911–83), pseudonym of the great American playwright Thomas Lanier Williams. Famous for *A Streetcar Named Desire* and *Cat on a Hot Tin Roof*.

Williams, William (1717–91), leading Welsh hymn writer. Born at Pantycelyn, nr. Llandovery. His best-known hymn is *Guide Me O Thou Great Jehovah*.

Willis, Ted (**Lord Willis**) (1914–92), socialist politician and playwright. His best-known play was *Woman in a Dressing Gown* (1962), and he created the TV series, *Dixon of Dock Green* (1953–75).

Wilson, Sir Angus (1913–91), British novelist and man of letters.

Wilson, Edmund (1895–1972), American critic, author of *Axel's Castle* (1931), *The Triple Thinkers* (1938), *The Wound and the Bow* (1941), *To the Finland Station* (1940), *The Shores of Light* (1952), *The Dead Sea Scrolls* (1955).

Wilson of Rievaulx, Lord (Sir Harold Wilson) (1916–95), British statesman, leader parl. Labour Party 1963–76; prime minister 1964–6, 1966–70, 1974–6. Entered parliament 1945 as member for Ormskirk; elected for Huyton 1950–83. Returned as Prime Minister on four occasions. Resigned March 1976. Founder of the Open University. He is buried in the Scilly Islands, his favourite holiday destination.

Wilson, Richard (1714–82), British landscape painter. Admired by Turner and Constable. He was born at Penegoes in Wales.

Wilson, Thomas Woodrow (1856–1924), American statesman. He was US president 1913–21, brought America into the first world war and advocated the League of Nations, but was not a successful negotiator at the peace conference and could not carry his country into the League. He introduced prohibition and women's suffrage.

Wingate, Orde Charles (1903–44), leader of the Chindit forces engaged behind the Japanese lines in Burma during the second world war.

Winifred, St., the 7th cent. patron saint of North Wales, said in late legend to have been killed by her rejected suitor, Prince Caradoc, but restored by her uncle.

Winton, Sir Nicholas (1909–2015). The 'British Schindler' who saved 669 children from concentration camps in Nazi-occupied Czechoslovakia in 1939. Eight trains took the children to foster parents in London.

Wiseman, Nicholas Patrick (1802–65), cardinal, b. in Spain of an Irish family. In 1850 on the restoration in England of the Catholic hierarchy he became first archbishop of Westminster.

Wittgenstein, Ludwig Josef Johann (1889–1951), Austrian linguistic philosopher whose main works were the *Tractatus Logico-Philosophicus* of his early period, much admired by Russell, and the *Philosophical Investigations*.

Wodehouse, Sir Pelham Grenville (1881–1975), English humorist, creator of Jeeves in the Bertie Wooster stories. He became a US citizen.

Wolf, Friedrich August (1759–1824), German scholar, a founder of scientific classical philology.

Wolf, Hugo (1860–1903), Austrian song-writer. In his settings of over 300 German lyrics, including many of Mörike and Goethe, he achieved union of poetry and music. See **Section P.**

Wolfe, James (1727–59), British general, b. Westerham. He showed early promise in the Seven Years' War, and was given command of the expedition against Quebec, which in spite of its strong position he captured, but lost his life.

Wollstonecraft, Mary (1759–97), feminist and writer. She was most famous for her work *A Vindication of the Rights of Women* (1792), a protest against the limited openings for women. See **Feminism, Section J**.

Wolsey, Thomas (*c*. 1475–1530), English cardinal. A butcher's son at Ipswich, he entered the church, becoming archbishop of York and cardinal, while in the same year (1515) he became Henry VIII's lord chancellor. But in spite of his ability he was unable to secure papal sanction for the king's divorce from Catherine of Aragon, and fell from power and died.

Wood, Sir Henry Joseph (1869–1944), English conductor, founder of the Promenade Concerts which he conducted from 1895 till his death.

Woodcock, George (1904–79), trade union leader. TUC general secretary 1960–69; first chairman, Commission on Industrial Relations, 1969–71.

Woods, Donald (1933–2001), South African journalist whose friendship with Steve Biko inspired the film *Cry Freedom*.

Woods, Granville (1856–1910), black American inventor of induction telegraph system (1887). Known as the "Black Edison".

Woodsworth, James Shaver (1874–1942), Canadian politician, parliamentary leader of the Co-operative Commonwealth Federation.

Woodville, Elizabeth (1437–91), wife of Edward IV. Her daughter Elizabeth married Henry VII.

Woolf, Virginia (1882–1941), English writer, daughter of Sir Leslie Stephen and wife of Leonard Woolf with whom she founded the Hogarth Press. Her works include *To the Lighthouse, Mrs. Dalloway, The Waves, A Room of One's Own*.

Wootton of Abinger, Baroness (Barbara Frances Wootton) (1897–1988), English social scientist.

Wordsworth, William (1770–1850), English poet, b. Cockermouth. He went to Cambridge, and in 1798 with Coleridge issued *Lyrical Ballads*, a return to simplicity in English poetry. He settled at Grasmere with his sister Dorothy (1771–1855), to whose insight his poems owe much. Among his best works are his sonnets and his *Ode on the Intimations of Immortality*, besides his *Prelude*.

Wren, Sir Christopher (1632–1723), English architect, b. Wiltshire. After the great fire (1666) he prepared an abortive plan for rebuilding London, but did in fact rebuild St. Paul's and more than fifty other city churches, including St. Stephen, Walbrook, and St. Mary-le-Bow. Other works include Chelsea Hospital, portions of Greenwich Hospital, the Sheldonian theatre, Oxford, and Queen's College library, Oxford. He had wide scientific interests (he was professor of mathematics at Gresham College, London, and professor of astronomy at Oxford) and helped found the Royal Society. See **N18(1)**.

Wright, (**William Ambrose**) **Billy** (1924–94), the golden-boy of post-war English football. A former captain of Wolves and England, he won 105 caps for England, captaining his country 90 times.

Wright, Frank Lloyd (1869–1959), American architect, initiator of horizontal strip and all-glass design. Buildings include the Imperial Hotel, Tokyo, and the Guggenheim Museum, New York.

Wright, Orville (1871–1948), American airman who with his brother **Wilbur** (1867–1912) in 1903 was the first to make a controlled sustained flight in a powered heavier-than-air machine, flying a length of 852 ft. at Kitty Hawk, N.C.

Wright, Richard (1908–60), black American novelist. Author of *Native Son* (1940) a pioneering novel of black revolt. A later work *The God That Failed* reflects his disillusion with communism.

Wu, Empress (Wu Zhao) (*c*. 625–706). Empress of China of the Tang dynasty. The only woman ever to have become emperor of China. Seized the title Empress in 690 after a reign of terror. A visionary who appointed China's first female prime minister. Forced to abdicate, 705.

Wyatt, James (1746–1813), English architect who built Fonthill Abbey.

Wyatt, Sir Thomas (1503–42), English poet (and diplomat) who introduced the sonnet from Italy. See **M6(2)**.

Wyatt, Sir Thomas the younger (*c*. 1520–54), son of above, unsuccessfully led a revolt against Queen Mary on behalf of Lady Jane Grey.

Wycherley, William (1640–1715), English drama-tist of the Restoration period. A master of satiric comedy, his plays include *Love in a Wood*, *The Plain Dealer* and *The Country Wife*.

Wyclif, John (*c.* 1320–84), English religious re-former. He taught at Oxford, later becoming rector of Lutterworth. He insisted on inward religion and attacked those practices which he thought had become mechanical. His fol-lowers, called Lollards, were suppressed, partly for political reasons. The Wyclif Bible, the first translation of the Latin Vulgate into English, was mainly the work of his followers at Oxford.

Wykeham, William of (1324–1404), English churchman. He held office under Edward III and became bishop of Winchester in 1367. He founded New College, Oxford, and Winchester School, and improved Winchester cathedral.

Wyllie, William Laine (1851–1931), English mar-ine painter of *The Thames Below London Bridge*.

Wyspianski, Stanislav (1869–1907), Polish poet, dramatist and painter. His plays include *The Wedding*, *Liberation*, and *November Night*.

X

Xavier, St. Francis (1506–52), "apostle of the Indies," b. at Xavero in the Basque country. He was associated with Loyola in founding the Jesuits, and undertook missionary journeys to Goa, Ceylon, and Japan.

Xenocrates (*c.* 395–314 B.C.). Greek philosopher and scientist. A pupil of Plato. His interests embraced astronomy and natural science but very few of his writings survive.

Xenophanes (*c.* 570–*c.* 480 B.C.) Greek poet, religious thinker and philosopher. His interests included the observation of fossils.

Xenophon (444–359 B.C.), Athenian general and historian. He commanded Greek mercenaries under the Persian Cyrus, and on the latter's death safely marched the Ten Thousand home through hostile country. His chief works are the *Anabasis*, the *Hellenica*, and *Cyropaedia*.

Xerxes (*c.* 519–465 B.C.), King of Persia, was son of the first Darius. In 481 B.C. he started on an expedition against Greece when, according to Herodotus, he had a combined army and navy of over two and a half million men. He defeated the Spartans at Thermopylae, but his fleet was overcome at Salamis. He reigned from 485 to 465 B.C. and met his death by assassination.

Xi Jinping (b. 1953) Chinese politician. Head of state since 2013.

Ximénes de Cisneros, Francisco (1436–1517), Spanish statesman and churchman. He be-came cardinal in 1507; carried out monastic reforms; and directed preparation of a polyglot bible, the *Complutensian*; but as inquisitor-general he was fanatical against heresy. He was adviser to Queen Isabella; in 1506 regent for Queen Juana. He also attempted to conquer Oran.

Y

Yeats, William Butler (1865–1939), Irish lyric poet and playwright, b. near Dublin, a leader of the Irish lit-erary revival. His plays were performed in the Abbey Theatre (which with **Lady Gregory** (1852–1932) he helped to found), and include *Cathleen Ni Houlihan*, *The Hour Glass*, and *Deidre*. A complete edition of the *Collected Poems* appeared in 1950. County Sligo provided the inspiration for most of his work (he spent many summers there). Probably Ireland's most influential poet.

Yeltsin, Boris Nikolayevich (1931–2007), Russian politician. President, 1990 to 1999, of the Russian Federation. At first an ally of Gorbachev (*q.v.*) then a rival. Yeltsin's role in opposing the August 1991 coup strengthened his power and under-mined the old USSR. Architect of the Common-wealth of Independent States. He overcame the 1993 communist rising in Moscow. Dubbed 'the man who buried communism'. The euphoria of the early 1990s rapidly turned to disillusion.

Yonge, Charlotte Mary (1823–1901), English novel-ist. Influenced by Keble, she wrote novels which faithfully reflect some aspects of Victorian life; one such is *The Daisy Chain*. She also wrote historical fiction *e.g. The Dove in the Eagle's Nest*.

Young of Dartington, Lord (Michael Young) (1915–2002), an inspired innovator who helped create the Open University and the Consumers' Association.

Young, Brigham (1801–77), American Mormon leader, and president in 1844 after the founder's death. He was a main founder of Salt Lake City. He practised polygamy. See **Section J**.

Young, Francis Brett (1884–1954), English novel-ist, author of *My Brother Jonathan* and *Dr. Bradley remembers*.

Young, James (1811–83), Scottish chemist, b. Glasgow, whose experiments led to the manu-facture of paraffin oil and solid paraffin.

Young, Thomas (1773–1829), English physicist, physician and Egyptologist, b. Somerset, of Quaker family. He established the wave theory of light and its essential principle of interference, put forward a theory of colour vision, and was the first to describe astigmatism of the eye. He was largely responsible for deciphering the inscrip-tions on the Rosetta stone.

Younghusband, Sir Francis Edward (1863–1942), English explorer and religious leader. He ex-plored Manchuria and Tibet. He founded the World Congress of Faiths in 1936 (*see* **Section J**).

Yousafzai, Malala (b. 1997). Born in Mingora. Pakistani child rights and educationalist activist. Shot by the Taliban. Joint winner of 2014 Nobel Peace Prize (at age of 17, the youngest recipient ever).

Ypres, 1st Earl of. *See* **French.**

Ysaÿe, Eugène (1858–1929), Belgian violinist and conductor, noted chiefly for his playing of the works of Bach and César Franck.

Yukawa, Hideki (1907–81), Japanese physicist, who received the 1949 Nobel prize for predict-ing (1935) the existence of the meson. Japan's first Nobel laureate.

Yunus, Muhammad (b. 1940). Bangladeshi econo-mist, the "Adam Smith of poverty". Nobel Prize-winner (with Grameen Bank) 2006. Author of the highly-influential books *Creating a World Without Poverty* (2007) and *Building Social Business* (2010).

Z

Zadkiel (angel in rabbinical lore), pseudonym of two astrologers: **William Lilly** (1602–81) and **Richard James Morrison** (1794–1874).

Zadkine, Ossip (1890–1967), Russian-born sculptor who made play with light on concave surfaces.

Zaharoff, Sir Basil (1849–1936), armaments mag-nate and financier, b. Anatolia of Greek parents. He was influential in the first world war.

Zamenhof, Ludwig Lazarus (1859–1917), Polish-Jew who invented Esperanto. He was by profes-sion an oculist.

Zappa, Frank (1940–93). Idiosyncratic and contro-versial composer, guitarist and bandleader. His most praised work includes "Freak Out!" (1966), "Waka/Jawaka" (1972) and "Make a Jazz Noise Here" (1991).

Zatopek, Emil (1922–2000), Czech athlete, the greatest distance runner of the 20th century.

Zeno of Citium (?342–270 B.C.), philosopher, founder of the Stoic system. He left Cyprus to teach in Athens.

Zeppelin, Ferdinand, Count von (1838–1917), German inventor of the dirigible airship, 1897–1900. It was used in the first world war.

Zeromski, Stefan (1864–1925), Polish novelist, author of *The Homeless*, *The Ashes*, *The Fight with Satan*.

Zhao Ziyang (1919–2005), Chinese Communist leader. Advocate of economic reform. Ousted for moderate views after Tiananmen Square.

Zhukov, Georgi Konstantinovich (1896–1974), Soviet general, who led the defence of Moscow and Stalingrad and lifted the siege of Leningrad in the second world war. He accepted the German surrender in 1945. The most decorated general officer in Russian and Soviet history.

Zhukovsky, Vasily Andreyevich (1783–1852), Russian poet and translator of German and English poets. For many years he was tutor to the future Tsar Alexander II.

Zog, King (1895–1961), the first King of Albania after 1928. In exile after Italian invasion.

Zola, Emile Edouard (1840–1902), French novelist, b. Paris, of Italian descent. His series, *Les Rougon-Macquart*, portrays in a score of volumes (the best known of which are perhaps *L'Assommoir*, *Nana* and *Germinal*) the fortunes of one family in many aspects and in realistic manner. He had the moral courage to champion Dreyfus.

Zorn, Anders Leonhard (1860–1920), Swedish sculptor, etcher, and painter.

Zoroaster (Zarathustra) (fl. 6th century. B.C.), the Persian founder of the Parsee religion. He was a monotheist, and saw the world as a struggle between good (Ahura Mazda) and evil (Ahriman). *See* **Zoroastrianism, Section J.**

Zoshchenko, Mikhail (1895–1958), Russian writer of humorous short stories, which include *The Woman who could not Read and other Tales* and *The Wonderful Dog and other Stories.*

Zosimus (fl. *c.* 300), the first known alchemist.

He lived in Alexandria.

Zuccarelli, Francesco (1702–88), Italian artist of fanciful landscapes. He spent many years in London and was elected a founder member of the R.A. (1768).

Zuckermann, Baron (Solly Zuckermann) (1904–93), British biologist; chief scientific adviser to British governments; 1940–71. Author of *Scientists and War etc.* O.M. 1968.

Zuma, Jacob (b. 1942). South African politician. President of South Africa since May 2009. His period in office has been blighted with extensive corruption and marked economic decline.

Zwingli, Ulrich (1484–1531), Swiss religious reformer. He taught mainly at Zurich, where he issued a list of reformed doctrines, less extreme than those of Calvin.

Zwirner, Ernst Friedrich (1802–61), German architect who restored Cologne cathedral.

BACKGROUND TO WORLD AFFAIRS

This section provides a wide-ranging chronology of major events in important countries in key areas of the world. Each country is arranged alphabetically within different areas of the world, from Europe and the Middle East to the Americas. There is also a detailed account of the history and evolution of the European Union.

TABLE OF CONTENTS

BACKGROUND TO WORLD AFFAIRS

I. THE NEW EUROPE

Note. For the background history and development of the European Union, *see* C27–30.

AUSTRIA.

Chronology of Key Events.

1920 Republic of Austria established.
1932 Dollfuss becomes chancellor.
1934 Socialist rising defeated; abortive Nazi coup; Dollfuss assassinated.
1938 Incorporated into Germany under *Anschluss.*
1945 Under joint British, American, Soviet occupation.
1955 Independent and neutral state established.
1970 Kreisky becomes chancellor.
1986 Waldheim becomes president.
1992 Klestil succeeds Waldheim as president.
1995 Joins EU.
1999 Right-wing Freedom Party makes gains in elections.
2000 Freedom Party joins coalition government; EU diplomatic sanctions.
2004 Fischer elected president.
2005 Ratifies EU constitution.
2007 Social Democrats form coalition with conservative People's Party following elections.
2008 Social Democrat-Centre Party coalition collapses but is reformed under Werner Faymann following elections in which far-right parties make gains.
2009 Far-right Freedom Party and Alliance for the Future of Austria merger in Carinthia presages possible national fusion.
2010 Social Democrat Fischer re-elected president; unemployment below 4%.
2011 Coalition intensifies spending cuts and specifies a constitutional debt limit.
2012 Tighter rules on political donations following corruption scandals.
2013 Referendum rejects changes to military conscription. Governing coalition parties win sufficient election votes to retain power.
2014 Chancellor Faymann appoints new cabinet. Chancellor warns against further sanctions on Russia.
2015 Major defence spending cuts. Ban on foreign funding of mosques and imams; fence on border with Slovenia to halt refugees.
2016 Surprise resignation of Chancellor Faymann. Christian Kern appointed Chancellor; Green-supported Alexander Van der Bellen elected President.
2017 Ministers call for end to 'failed' European asylum policy.

BELGIUM.

Chronology of Key Events.

1830 Independence from Netherlands.
1914–18 Under German occupation.
1940–44 Under German occupation.
1951 King Leopold III abdicates in favour of son Baudouin.
1957 A founder member of European Economic Community.
1993 Divided in three administrative regions of Dutch-speaking Flanders, French-speaking Wallonia and bi-lingual Brussels; Albert II succeeds Baudouin.
1999 Adopts Euro as currency; centre-left coalition under Verhofstadt.
2003 Centre-left coalition under Verhofstadt returns in elections.
2005 Far-right Flemish Bloc successes in local and regional elections.
2007 No government for 100 days following Conserva-

tive gains in elections; division of country muted; Verhofstadt forms interim government.
2008 Yves Leterme forms coalition government but resigns following failure of proposed devolution programme.
2009 Herman van Rompuy forms caretaker government. Troop commitment in Afghanistan increases; Leterme succeeds Rompuy as prime minister.
2010 Collapse of Leterme government (April). June general election results in political stalemate; public debt reaches 100% of GDP, unemployment 8·5%.
2011 King Albert orders caretaker government to make cuts to meet public debt. Elio Di Rupo forms coalition after 535-day deadlock.
2012 Separatist Flemish Nationalist Party local election gains.
2013 King Albert II abdicates and is succeeded by his son Philippe.
2014 Senate extends euthanasia right to terminally ill children. Michel forms coalition government.
2015 Deaths and arrests in police anti-Islamist terror raids. Unions mount anti-austerity protests; increased anti-terror precautions.
2016 Deadly terrorist attacks hit airport at Brussels as well as metro station. Unions protest over government threats to workers' rights.
2017 Government urges EU to adopt anti-terrorist passenger tracking system.

FRANCE.

Chronology of Key Events.

1946 The Fourth Republic is established.
1951 Joins the European Coal and Steel Community.
1954 Relinquishes Indo-China following defeat at Dien Bien Phu; Algeria begins war for independence.
1956 Allies with Britain and Israel against Egypt during Suez events.
1957 Founder member of the European Economic Community.
1958 Fourth Republic collapses; de Gaulle establishes Fifth Republic.
1962 Algeria wins independence.
1968 Student riots and workers' strikes bring country close to revolution.
1969 De Gaulle resigns; Pompidou succeeds as president.
1974 Giscard d'Estaing becomes president.
1981 Socialist Mitterrand becomes president.
1986 'Cohabitation' between left president Mitterrand and right prime minister Chirac follows elections.
1988 Mitterrand re-elected.
1995 Chirac elected president.
1997 Socialist Jospin becomes prime minister.
2002 Chirac re-elected as President after substantial first round National Front vote.
2003 Opposition to Iraq invasion.
2004 Socialists triumph in elections; unions oppose labour reforms.
2005 European constitution rejected in referendum; ethnic minority riots in Paris and other cities.
2006 Student and worker protests against proposed labour legislation.
2007 Sarkozy elected President; centre-right parliamentary election victory.
2008 Ratifies Lisbon Treaty on EU reform.
2009 Rejoins NATO military command.
2010 Ruling UMP setback in regional elections; €45 billion spending cuts; mass protests over pension changes.
2011 Face veil banned; further public spending cuts.
2012 Socialist Hollande defeats Sarkozy in presidential election. Jean-Marc Ayrault becomes prime minister.

2013 Intervention in Mali against Islamist rebels; anti-gay marriage protests. Second recession in four years.

2014 President Hollande calls for nuclear power output cut. Socialist reverse in local elections. Valls appointed prime minister; National Front wins Senate seats.

2015 Islamist terrorist attacks in Paris. Bombing raids on Syria; ISIS terror attack in Paris kills 130; state of emergency declared; Front National setback in regional elections.

2016 Country's 22 regions reduced to 13; growing Jewish emigration. Government weakens workers' rights despite protests; 85 die in Nice terrorist attack; Bernard Cazeneuve replaces Valls as prime minister.

2017 In presidential election, Emmanuel Macron emerges as surprise winner.

GERMANY.

Chronology of Key Events.

1945 Defeated and occupied by Allies.

1948 British, French and US zones become Federal Republic of Germany and Soviet zone becomes German Democratic Republic.

1955 Cold War divisions solidify as East Germany joins the Warsaw Pact, West Germany the North Atlantic Treaty Organisation (NATO).

1957 West Germany is a founder member of the European Economic Community.

1961 East Germany builds the Berlin Wall to prevent flight of refugees.

1969 West German Social Democrat Chancellor Brandt attempts to improve East-West relations.

1973 West and East Germany become UN members.

1982 Christian Democrat Kohl becomes West German Chancellor.

1987 East German Chancellor Honecker pays official visit to West Germany.

1989 Berlin Wall dismantled.

1990 Germany unified under Chancellor Kohl.

1994 Kohl re-elected; all foreign troops leave Berlin.

1998 Schroeder forms Socialist-Green coalition.

2000 Kohl resigns as Christian Democrat president over funding scandal.

2002 Euro replaces mark as currency; Socialist-Green coalition returns in elections.

2004 Demonstrations against proposed welfare cuts.

2005 European constitution ratified; Merkel leads post-election 'grand coalition' of CDU, CSU and SPD.

2008 Officially in recession; CDU/CSU setback in regional elections.

2009 Out of recession; Merkel's coalition wins general election.

2010 Mrs Merkel says multi-culturalism has failed; economy grows 3·6%.

2011 Phasing out of nuclear power plants begins.

2012 President Wulff resigns; Joachim Gauck elected.

2013 Opposition mounts over EU bailouts. Merkel forms post-election coalition with Socialists.

2014 EU Commission says German benefits law is anti-immigrant.

2015 Minimum wage introduced; anti-Islam demonstrations. Merkel's welcome to refugees criticised as over a million arrive; jets deployed in Syria.

2016 Stricter rules on asylum seekers; Merkel increasingly isolated over policy.

2017 Security tightened following Berlin terror attack.

IRELAND.

Chronology of Key Events.

1916 Abortive Easter Rising against British rule.

1921 26 counties Free State established under Anglo-Irish Treaty; six counties of Northern Ireland remain British.

1922 Civil war as Anglo-Irish Treaty opposed by de Valera and followers.

1949 Eire leaves Commonwealth, becomes Republic of Ireland.

1957 De Valera returns as prime minister, declares unification of Ireland must be voluntary; Sinn Fein leaders arrested.

1969 Violence begins in Northern Ireland.

1973 Joins European Economic Community.

1985 Signs Anglo-Irish Agreement on governance of Northern Ireland.

1993 Anglo-Irish Downing Street Declaration proposes Northern Ireland talks when violence ends.

1998 Referendum approves Good Friday Agreement on Northern Ireland settlement.

1999 Adopts Euro as currency; cross border co-operation with Northern Ireland begins.

2002 Fianna Fail-Progressive Democrat coalition re-elected.

2006 Government proposes using name Eire at EU meetings.

2007 Fianna Fail forms coalition with Progressive Democrats and Greens.

2008 Prime Minister Ahern resigns following financial allegations; succeeded by Brian Cowen; referendum rejects European Union Lisbon treaty.

2009 Drastic public spending cut as economic crisis takes hold and unemployment rises; referendum endorses Lisbon Treaty following previous year's rejection.

2010 EU-IMF €85 billion rescue package and austerity budget as deficit crisis continues; unemployment over 13%

2011 Cowen resigns as Fianna Fail leader but remains as prime minister; crucial General Election held on 25 February. Defeat for Fianna Fail. Enda Kenny prime minister following Fine Gael election victory; Labour's Michael Higgins elected president; further austerity measures.

2012 Referendum accepts European Fiscal Compact budget rules; demonstrations against austerity budget.

2013 Limited right to abortion introduced; leaves EU/IMF bailout programme.

2014 Reform Alliance formed by breakaway Fine Gael members. Centre-right Reform Alliance set up.

2015 Prime minister Kenny says recovery fragile. Referendum approves same-sex marriage.

2016 Deadlock in General Election. 1916 Easter Rising commemoration. Fianna Fail forms minority government under Enda Kenny.

2017 Citizens' Assembly calls for abortion law reform.

ITALY.

Chronology of Key Events.

1946 Republic proclaimed following a referendum.

1948 New constitution introduced; Christian Democrats begin long run of power.

1949 Joins NATO.

1951 Joins European Coal and Steel Community.

1955 Becomes a member of the United Nations.

1957 Founder member of the EEC.

1963 Socialists join Christian Democrat led coalition under Moro.

1976 Communist Party makes election gains.

1978 A period of near civil war; Moro, architect of left-right unity, kidnapped and killed by the Red Brigades.

1980 Over 80 killed in far right bombing at Bologna.

1981 Cabinet resigns over P2 Masonic lodge scandal, opening of campaign against corruption.

1983 Craxi becomes first post-war Socialist prime minister.

1984 Roman Catholicism ceases to be state religion under concordat with Vatican.

1991 Communist Party splits.

1992 Revelations of corruption involving all major political parties.

1994 Short-lived Freedom Alliance of Berlusconi's *Forza Italia*, the Northern League and neo-fascist National Alliance.

1995 Government of technocrats under Dini imposed austerity budget.

1996 Prodi becomes head of Centre-left Olive Tree alliance government.

2001 Victory for Berlusconi in general election. Referendum approves more regional autonomy.

2002 Euro replaces lira as currency.

2003 Parliament grants Berlusconi immunity from corruption charges.

2004 Constitutional court withdraws Berlusconi's immunity; not guilty verdict.

2005 Parliament ratifies European constitution.

2006 Centre-left coalition led by Prodi wins elections.
2007 Prodi resigns following Senate defeat but wins confidence vote.
2008 Officially in recession; Berlusconi premier following election victory.
2009 Constitutional court removes Berlusconi's immunity from prosecution.
2010 Ruling coalition loses parliamentary majority following defections.
2011 €54 billion austerity package; Berlusconi resigns, replaced by Mario Monti at head of technocrat administration.
2012 Deregulation reforms introduced; credit rating downgraded to A-.
2013 Political uncertainty follows inconclusive elections. Letta succeeds Bersani as prime minister; Napolitano re-elected president; Berlusconi faces imprisonment.
2014 'Pitchfork Movement' anti-austerity protests in Rome. Prime minister Letta resigns; Renzi forms left-right coalition.
2015 President Napolitano retires. Succeeded by Sergio Mattarella. Electoral reform introduced to stabilise legislature; labour law reforms make dismissal easier.
2015 Berlusconi plans to relaunch Forza Italia. The Senate approves limited same-sex civil unions. Prime minister Renzi resigns after losing constitutional reform referendum, succeeded by Paolo Gentiloni.
2017 Harder line on migrant repatriation.

SPAIN.

Chronology of Key Events.

1936–39 Spanish Civil War ends in Nationalist victory under Franco.
1955 Spain admitted to UN.
1959 ETA founded to campaign for independent Basque homeland.
1973 Prime minister Admiral Luis Carrero Blanco assassinated by Basque nationalists.
1975 Franco dies; monarchy restored with King Juan Carlos as head of state.
1977 First free elections since 1936.
1978 New constitution introduces a parliamentary monarchy.
1980 Basque country and Catalonia elect regional assemblies.
1981 Un successful military coup attempt.
1982 Socialist government elected.
1986 Spain joins European Community.
1996 Jose Maria Aznar becomes prime minister of right-wing Popular Party/Catalan nationalist coalition.
1997 Demonstrations against rising Basque nationalist violence.
1998 ETA announces ceasefire.
1999 ETA talks with government collapse.
2000 ETA renews violence; landslide election victory for Popular Party.
2001 Spain and Britain agree to reach settlement on Gibraltar.
2002 Euro replaces peseta as currency.
2004 Terrorist bombs in Madrid kill 191; Zapatero forms government following Socialist election victory; troops withdraw from Iraq.
2005 Referendum approves European constitution; ETA bomb in Madrid; government offers negotiations.
2006 Proposals to extend Catalan autonomy; ETA declare ceasefire; government suspends peace moves after further bombing.
2007 Government declares peace process with ETA at an end.
2008 Socialists return in election with 169 seats to Popular Party's 153.
2009 Renewed ETA terrorism; unemployment rises as financial crisis intensifies.
2010 Anti-austerity demonstrations; ETA ceasefire.
2011 Popular Party wins general election; Rajoy becomes premier; further public spending cuts.
2012 Unemployment reaches 22·8 %; continuing anti-cuts protests. Government condemns growing Catalan independence demands.
2013 Royal Family and governing People's Party financial scandal allegations.
2014 King's daughter faces tax evasion charges. King Juan Carlos abdicates, succeeded by Felipe VI.
2015 Princess Cristina fraud trial. Electoral change as new anti-austerity Podemos and liberal Cuidadanos parties advance; Catalan separatists strengthened.
2016 Mariano Rajoy forms minority coalition after months of deadlock.
2017 Government warns Catalonia against independence referendum.

BULGARIA.

Chronology of Key Events.

1908 Declares independence.
1944 Communists take power following liberation from German occupation.
1947 One-party state established.
1989 Multi-party system established; opposition Union of Democratic Forces (UDF) formed.
1990 Former Communist Bulgarian Socialist Party (BSP) wins elections.
1991 UDF wins elections.
1993 Programme of privatisation begins.
1994 BSP returned to office.
1997 UDF returns to office after economic crisis.
2001 Party of former King Simeon II wins elections; Simeon becomes prime minister.
2004 Joins NATO.
2005 BSP forms coalition government after election victory.
2007 Joins EU.
2008 EU suspends subsidies following government failure to combat corruption.
2009 Anti-government riots as economic situation worsens. Boyko Borisov becomes minister of a centre-right government following Socialist election defeat.
2010 EU issues positive report on government anti-corruption measures; unemployment at 10 %.
2011 Socialist Party alleges presidential election irregularities following defeat by Rosen Plevneliev of the Citizens for European Development.
2012 'Fracking' method of extracting shale gas banned.
2013 Prime minister Borisov resigns following anti-austerity protests; Oresharski heads technocrat government after elections.
2014 Nationalist Party activists harass Roma and immigrants. Borisov heads coalition government following elections.
2015 Finance minister calls for Eurozone membership talks. Fence on Turkey border extended to curb refugees.
2016 Tensions in ruling coalition. Compulsory voting introduced; Socialist-backed Rumen Radev wins presidential election.
2017 Construction of nuclear power plant rejected.

CROATIA.

Chronology of Key Events.

1918 Becomes part of the Kingdom of Serbs, Croats and Slovenes (later Yugoslavia).
1945 Becomes a republic of the Yugoslav Socialist Federation.
1991 Declares independence following break-up of Yugoslavia; Croat Serbs seize a third of the country.
1992 UN peacekeeping force deployed; involved in war with Bosnian Serbs and Muslims; Franjo Tudjman elected president.
1995 War in Bosnia ends with Dayton peace agreement; Tudjman re-elected president (dies 1999).
2000 Social democrats and liberals form coalition.
2003 Croatian Democratic Union (HDZ) forms minority government.
2006 European Commission says Croatia not ready for EU membership because of corruption and attitude to minorities.
2007 HDZ forms coalition government following elections.
2008 European Commission demands anti-corruption action before Croatia is considered for EU membership.
2009 Joins NATO; Jadranka Kosor succeeds Ivo Sanader as prime minister; EU entry negotiations begin.
2010 Social Democrat Ivo Josipovic elected president. Relations improve with Slovenia and Serbia; unemployment over 16 %.
2011 Agreement in principle for Croatia's entry into EU in 2013. Ruling Croatian Democratic

Union investigated for corruption; centre-left coalition under Zoran Milanovic wins elections; signs treaty to join EU, subject to ratification.
2012 Croatia votes in referendum (22 January) to join EU.
2013 EU membership from 1 July. Government austerity programme to reduce deficit.
2014 Tax and customs fraud agreement with Slovenia. EU instructs government to halve budget deficit.
2015 Kolinda Grabar-Kitarović elected first woman President. Hung parliament following election.
2016 Croatian Democratic Union heads coalition government. Croatian Democratic Union heads coalition government following elections.
2017 Further moves towards joining Euro.

ROMANIA.
Chronology of Key Events.

1947 Soviet-backed People's Republic established.
1952 Communist leader Gheorghiu-Dej becomes prime minister.
1955 Joins Warsaw Pact.
1965 Ceausescu becomes party leader and weakens ties with Soviet Union.
1987 Anti-government protests quelled by army.
1989 Government overthrown; Ceausescu and wife executed; Iliescu leads National Salvation Front.
1990 Iliescu elected president, Roman becomes reforming prime minister.
1991 Roman replaced by Stolojan following anti-government riots.
1996 Centre-right election victory; Constantinescu becomes president, Ciorbea prime minister
2000 Iliescu re-elected president; Nastase heads minority government.
2004 Joins NATO; Basescu elected president; Tariceanu becomes prime minister.
2007 Joins EU, which insists on agricultural reforms.
2008 EU issues warning over failure to combat corruption; Theodor Stolojan attempts to form government after inconclusive elections. Emil Boc forms coalition but loses confidence vote; Boc remains as head of interim administration pending elections; President Traian Basescu narrowly re-elected.
2009 Basescu re-elected president; Emil Boc forms coalition government.
2010 Austerity measures provoke public sector workers' protests; unemployment over 8%. EU demands further action against organised crime and corruption.
2012 Resignation of Prime Minister Emil Boc. Social Liberal Union coalition wins elections, Victor Ponta becomes prime minister.
2013 Charges of irregularities in 2012 presidential referendum.
2014 Former prime minister Nastase imprisoned on bribery charges. Iohannis elected President.
2015 Iohannis declares 'full Europeanisation' project. Prime minister Ponta resigns after prolonged financial scandal.
2016 World Bank aid to reform pubic administration. US missile defence system installed.
2017 Social Democrat-led coalition with Sorin Grindeanu as prime minister.

SLOVAKIA.
Chronology of Key Events.

1993 Divides from Czech Republic on break-up of Czechoslovakia; Kovac elected president, Meciar prime minister.
1998 Parliament fails to choose successor to Kovac; Meciar takes temporary powers; ousted in election and succeeded by reformist Dzurinda.
1999 Schuster elected president.
2001 New constitution to prepare for entry to NATO and EU.
2002 Dzurinda returns as head of centre-right coalition.
2004 Joins NATO and EU; Gasparovic president.
2006 Three party coalition government under left-wing populist Fico.
2007 Financial scandal rocks government.
2009 Slovakia adopts the Euro (1 Jan.). Ivan Gasparovic re-elected president.

2010 Election results in centre-right coalition government under Iveta Radicova; unemployment over 11%.
2011 Radicova's coalition falls after losing vote on more powers for EU bailout fund; opposition subsequently support bill in exchange for early elections.
2012 Opposition Social Democrats win general election.
2013 Criticism of lack of independence of judiciary. European Commission criticises anti-Roma measures.
2014 Andrej Kiska elected President. Russian gas supplies threatened by Ukraine crisis. Anti-refugee demonstrations.
2016 Prime minister Fico says no Muslim migrants will be accepted. Direction-Social Democracy heads coalition government following elections; Slovakia takes rotating EU presidency.
2017 Co-operation agreement with Czech Republic over airspace protection.

POLAND.
Chronology of Key Events.

1918 Becomes independent state.
1939 Occupied by Germany and Soviet Union.
1947 Becomes a Communist state.
1955 Joins Warsaw Pact.
1980 Anti-Communist Solidarity trade union formed by Lech Walesa.
1981–3 Martial law under Gen. Jaruzelski.
1990 Walesa elected president of Poland; privatisation programme begins.
1992 Soviet troops withdraw.
1997 New constitution adopted.
1999 Joins NATO.
2004 Joins EU.
2005 Lech Kaczynski of Law and Justice party (PiS) becomes president.
2006 President Kaczynski's brother Jaroslaw becomes prime minister of PiS-led coalition.
2007 Coalition collapses; Civic Platform wins election.
2008 Former Communist leader, General Jaruzelski, faces trial.
2009 IMF grants one-year credit of $20·6 billion.
2010 President Lech Kaczynski and top officials killed in air crash; Civic Platform's Bronislaw Komorowski elected president.
2011 Russian enquiry blames Polish pilot for 2010 air crash; Tusk's Civic Platform wins second term in coalition with Peasants' Party.
2012 Opposition Law & Justice Party supporters mount protests in capital.
2013 Union-led anti-government demonstrations; Tusk shuffles cabinet.
2014 Government boosts public investment in infrastructure and energy. Ewa Kopacz prime minister as Tusk becomes European Council President.
2015 Defence minister says Poland not threatened by Russian attack. Conservative Andrzej Duda defeats President Komorowski; Law and Justice party wins majority in national elections.
2016 Government takes control of state media and curbs authority of constitutional court. Abortion ban rejected following demonstrations; opposition accuses government of undermining constitution and free media.
2017 US troops deployed on Russian border.

THE CZECH REPUBLIC (CZECHIA).
Chronology of Key Events.

1993 Following 'velvet divorce' from Slovak Republic, Vaclav Havel elected President; privatisation programme introduced.
1996 Vaclav Klaus confirmed as head of coalition government in first general election.
1997 Klaus resigns following criticisms of economic policies; Social Democrat Milos Zeman forms minority government following inconclusive elections.
1998 Havel re-elected President.
1999 Joins NATO.
2002 Social Democrat Vladimir Spidla forms coalition government with Christian Democrats and Freedom Union.
2003 Klaus replaces Havel as President; referendum supports entry to EU.
2004 Joins EU; Stanislav Gross replaces Spidla at head of coalition government.

2005 Paroubek replaces Gross as prime minister following financial scandal; entry to Euro delayed.
2006 Months of political stalemate following inconclusive elections.
2007 Topolánek forms centre-right coalition government.
2009 Government resigns; Jan Fischer heads interim administration pending elections; Lisbon Treaty approved.
2010 Petr Necas's Civic Democrats lead centre-right coalition; public spending cuts provoke demonstrations.
2011 Withdraws from US missile defence programme.
2013 Social Democrat Milos Zeman wins first direct presidential elections. Government falls in corruption scandal; inconclusive election.
2014 Social Democrat coalition with Christian Democrats and ANO. Velvet Revolution 25th anniversary marked by pro- and anti-government demonstrations. Prime minister Sobotka criticises President Zeman's claim that refugees represent 'organised invasion'.
2016 Co-operation agreement with Albania. 'Czechia' adopted as country's official English name; government accuses Russia of propaganda war.
2017 President Zeman urges Czechs to arm themselves against terrorist threats.

HUNGARY.

Chronology of Key Events.

1949 Communist state declared; industry and agriculture comes under state control.
1956 Anti-Soviet uprising crushed; prime minister Nagy captured and later executed by Communists; Kadar becomes head of government.
1968 New Economic Mechanism introduces market socialism.
1988 Karoly Grosz replaces Kadar; opposition Hungarian Democratic Forum formed.
1989 Communist state collapses; transition to multi-party state begins.
1990 Centre-right coalition forms government; withdraws from Warsaw Pact.
1991 Soviet troops leave.
1994 Coalition of liberals and former Communists win elections.
1997 Joins NATO; EU membership negotiations begin.
1998 Viktor Orban leads centre-right coalition government.
2000 Peter Medgyessy forms centre-left coalition.
2003 Referendum approves joining EU on 46% turnout.
2004 Joins EU; Ferenc Gyurcsany replaces Medgyessy as prime minister.
2006 Gyurcsany forms Socialist-led coalition after elections; violent demonstrations following his admission that he had lied about the economy.
2009 Mounting financial crisis; resignation of Gyurcsany.
2010 Fidesz-Christian Democratic People's Party alliance wins elections; far-right Jobbik gains seats; IMF suspends loan negotiations over failure to disclose deficit reduction plans.
2011 New conservative constitution arouses opposition criticism; government amends media law under European Commission pressure.
2012 Janos Ader of Fidesz elected President following Schmitt's resignation.
2013 European Commission alleges constitution conflicts with EU values.
2014 Nuclear co-operation agreement with Russia. Fidesz and Christian Democrat election successes. Prime minister Orban criticises 'liberal democracy'.
2015 Anti-government demonstrations. EU criticises anti-immigrant campaign; barrier with Serbia to halt refugees.
2016 Prime minister Orban says all refugee entry into EU must stop. Low turnout referendum supports rejection of EU migrant relocation plan.
2017 Minister says illegal immigration a danger to Europe; crackdown on civil society groups.

2. RUSSIA AND THE BALKANS

RUSSIA.

1999 Victory for Unity in elections (Dec.). Followed by resignation of Yeltsin. Succeeded by Putin.
2000 Putin trounces Communists in presidential election.
2001 Friendship treaty with China.
2002 Agreement with US on nuclear weapons reduction.
2003 Chechens vote to remain in Russian Federation in disputed referendum; Chechen separatist violence continues; pro-Putin United Russia wins sweeping victory in Duma elections.
2004 Putin re-elected by landslide.
2005 State takes control of Gazprom gas giant.
2006 Gas supply to Ukraine temporarily curtailed in political dispute; economic agreement signed with China.
2007 President Putin's United Russia party triumphs in widely criticised elections.
2008 Medvedev succeeds Putin as president with 70% of vote.
2009 Rigging allegations following ruling United Russia successes in local elections.
2010 Agreement with US on nuclear weapons reductions; Chechen separatist terrorist attacks.
2011 United Russia setback in Duma elections.
2012 Putin wins presidential election. 'Pussy Riot' dissidents jailed for hooliganism; Russia joins World Trade Organisation.
2013 Terrorist bombings in Volgograd.
2014 Proposal to reinstate 'none of the above' in federal elections. Occupation of Crimea. 30-year gas deal with China; EU & US sanctions over Ukraine weaken economy.
2015 Eurasian Economic Union with Belarus and Kazakhstan. Duma approves deployment of armed forces overseas; air strikes in Syria; Russia imposes sanctions after shooting down of jet over Turkey.
2016 Putin says NATO a threat to Russian security. Ruling United Russia increases majority in elections as turnout falls to 40%.
2017 Aircraft and warships withdrawn from Syria.

BELARUS.

1991 Independence from Soviet Union.
1994 Pro-Russian Lukashenko becomes president.
1997 Agreement with Russia on merging of currency and tax system.
2001 Lukashenko returned in widely criticised election.
2002 Lukashenko rejects proposed union with Russia.
2004 Protests following opposition failure to win seats in widely criticised parliamentary elections.
2006 Lukashenko re-elected; opposition leaders arrested; EU imposes diplomatic sanctions.
2007 Demonstrators demand Lukashenko's resignation.
2008 International criticism of parliamentary elections when President Lukashenka's supporters win all seats.
2009 President Lukashenko visits Vatican after EU lifts travel ban to encourage reform.
2010 President Lukashenko re-elected in widely disputed poll.
2011 EU and US impose sanctions following disputed presidential elections; opposition presidential candidate imprisoned; anti-government demonstrations.
2012 Mounting tension with EU over human rights.
2013 Threats to leave Russian-controlled Eurasian Union.
2014 Negotiations on installation of Russia air base.
2015 Eurasian Economic Union with Russia and Kazakhstan. President Lukashenko wins fifth term against cowed opposition.
2016 EU doubles aid to Belarus. Governing parties overwhelmingly returned in disputed elections.
2017 Visa-free entry for 80 countries to encourage tourism. Street protests against regime.

UKRAINE.

Chronology of Key Events.

1941–4 Five million die under German occupation.
1986 Major accident at Chernobyl nuclear power plant.
1991 Independence from Soviet Union.
1994 Kuchma elected president.

2002 Hung parliament following elections; demonstrators demand Kuchma's resignation alleging electoral fraud.

2004 'Orange Revolution' by supporters of Yushchenko after Yanukovych declared president; Yushchenko wins re-run election.

2005 Tymoshenko appointed prime minister; dismissed and replaced by Yekhanurov after corruption allegations against officials.

2006 Russia temporarily cuts gas supply; Yanukovych's party wins elections, with Tymoshenko's second and President Yushchenko third; Yanukovych leads coalition government with Socialists and Communists.

2007 Power struggle between president and prime minister; President Yushchenko calls inconclusive elections; Tymoshenko appointed prime minister.

2008 Gas dispute with Russia resolved; continuing turmoil in weak coalition government.

2009 10-year agreement signed with Russia following renewed dispute over gas supply.

2010 Presidential election won by the pro-Russian Viktor Yanukovytch amid claims of fraud. Mykola Azarov replaces Tymoshenko as premier; agreement with Russia on lease of Black Sea port of Sebastopol.

2011 Former prime minister Tymoshenko imprisoned for abuse of office.

2012 Party of the Regions wins flawed elections.

2013 Demonstrations against withdrawal from EU Association Agreement.

2014 President Yanukovych ousted; interim government formed; Russia occupies Crimea; tension in eastern Ukraine. Crimea referendum backs joining Russia; Poroshenko elected pro-Western President; Russia accused of military involvement in Ukraine; abortive ceasefire efforts.

2015 EU attempts to revive peace talks. Further tension with Russia; NATO agrees to modernise Ukraine's military.

2016 Illegal to deny former Communist regime's 'criminal nature'; free trade agreement with EU. Volodymyr Groysman succeeds Yatsenyuk as prime minister; continuing deadlock over fighting in eastern regions.

2017 Government sues Russia in International Criminal Court for 'terrorism' and 'discrimination'.

SERBIA.

Chronology of Key Events.

1991–2 Yugoslavia confined to Serbia and Montenegro following breakaway of six former republics; civil war; UN Security Council votes to establish peacekeeping force.

1992 Federal Republic of Yugoslavia proclaimed by Serbia and Montenegro; sanctions and naval blockade imposed to end Yugoslav operations in Bosnia; Yugoslavia expelled from UN; Slobodan Milosevic elected President.

1995 Serbia, Croatia and Bosnia sign Dayton Accord to end war in Bosnia.

1998 Guerrilla war begins in predominantly Albanian Kosovo.

1999 NATO launches air attacks on Yugoslavia to force withdrawal from predominantly Albanian Kosovo; Serbian economy collapses; Montenegro proposes separation.

2000 Vojislav Kostunica takes office following revolt against Milosevic's refusal to accept election defeat; Milosevic arrested.

2001 Milosevic faces UN International Criminal Tribunal; sanctions lifted.

2002 Yugoslav Republic renamed Serbia and Montenegro, a loose union, with Svetozar Marovic as president.

2003 Serb prime minister Zoran Djindjic assassinated; ultra-nationalist Socialist and Radical electoral revival in Serbia.

2004 Serb-Albanian ethnic clashes in Kosovo; former Yugoslav president Vojislav Kostunica becomes Serbian prime minister in centre-right coalition; Boris Tadic elected Serbian president.

2006 Montenegro forms republic independent of Serbia; referendum boycotted by Albanians opposes Kosovan independence.

2007 Serb Nationalists strongest party following elections.

2008 Independence for Kosovo triggers collapse of Serbian government. Pro-European parties returned in general election.

2009 IMF and Russia provide loans to meet budget deficit.

2010 Attempts to improve relations with neighbouring former Yugoslavia states; application for EU membership passed to European Commission.

2011 Talks open with Kosovo, though Serbia refuses to accept independence.

2012 EU leaders formally declare Serbia a membership candidate. Tomislav Nikolic elected president; Ivica Dačić appointed prime minister.

2013 Agreement with Kosovo on improved relations.

2014 EU accession negotiations begin. Vučić forms centre-right government after Progressive Party election victory.

2015 Prime minister visits Kosovo to improve relations. EU brokered deal on treatment of Serb minority in Kosovo.

2016 Official register says Serbia has 107 political parties. Ruling Progressive and Socialist coalition re-elected.

2017 European Parliament calls for action on corruption and media freedom on path to EU membership.

BOSNIA AND HERZEGOVINA.

Chronology of Key Events.

1918 Part of Kingdom of Serbs, Croats and Slovenes (later Yugoslavia) following collapse of Austro-Hungarian Empire.

1941 Annexed by Nazi puppet state of Croatia.

1945 Becomes a republic in Yugoslav Socialist Federation.

1991 Coalition government formed following post-Communist collapse elections; divisions grow between Serbs, Croats and Muslims.

1992 Muslim dominated government under President Izetbegovic; Bosnian Serbs proclaim a separate republic; bitter fighting and ethnic cleansing.

1993 Clashes between Muslims and Bosnian Croats.

1995 Massacre at Srebrenica by Bosnian Serbs; Dayton agreement establishes separate Muslim-Croat and Serb territories; UN peacekeeping force deployed.

2000 Moderates elected in Muslim-Croat area, nationalists in Serb area; coalition government formed.

2003 EU takes over peacekeeping from UN.

2004 Bosnian force deployed in Iraq.

2006 Serbs vote to leave Muslim-Croat state.

2007 Bosnian Serb Nikola Spiric heads short-lived coalition government.

2008 Local election results show the country remains torn by ethnic division.

2009 Constitutional reform conference organised by EU and United States collapses.

2010 Dodik's Serb nationalist party and Lagumdzija's multi-ethnic party attempt co-operation after emerging as major forces in elections.

2011 Uncertainty follows indecisive election result; ethnic tensions mount.

2012 Vjekoslav Bevanda prime minister with Croat, Muslim and Serb agreement.

2013 Police search government offices in anti-corruption drive.

2014 Investigation into criminal tax evasion by 2,000 companies. Mass protests over unemployment and corruption.

2016 Prime minister Zvizdic says Bosnia will make EU application. EU membership application formally accepted.

2017 World Bank €50 million loan to create private sector jobs.

ALBANIA.

Chronology of Key Events.

1944 Enver Hoxha becomes Communist leader following liberation from German occupation.

1951 Abortive US backed anti-Communist invasion.

1955 Joins Warsaw Pact.

1961 Allies with China after ideological break with Soviet Union.

1978 China ends economic support.

1985 Hoxha succeeded by Ramiz Alia.
1991 Communists win office in first free multi-party elections.
1992 Democratic Party wins elections; Sali Berisha elected president.
1996 Democratic Party returned in allegedly fraudulent elections.
1997 Kosovo crisis begins; Socialist-led coalition takes office following financial crisis; Rexhep Mejdani becomes president.
2001 Socialists re-elected.
2002 Alfred Moisiu elected president.
2003 Negotiations on EU membership begin.
2004 Demonstrations over economic conditions.
2005 Former president Berisha becomes PM.
2007 US President Bush visits; Bamir Topi elected president.
2009 Application lodged to join EU. Joins NATO. Sali Berisha's centre-right coalition narrowly wins election.
2010 Socialist civil disobedience campaign as dispute over 2009 election continues.
2011 Protestors demand fall of government following deputy prime minister's resignation over corruption allegations.
2012 Government and opposition agree co-operation on seeking EU entry.
2013 Edi Rama prime minister following Socialist landslide election victory.
2014 Joint session of Albanian and Kosovo governments. European Commission recommends Albania for future EU membership.
2015 Agriculture minister proposes common food market with Kosovo. Socialist government proposes privatisation of state oil business.
2016 Co-operation agreement with Czech Republic. Ruling Socialists seek more control over online media.
2017 Finance minister Ahmetaj says economy in positive growth cycle.

TURKEY.

Chronology of Key Events.

1923 Republic proclaimed with Ataturk as president.
1950 Opposition Democratic Party wins first free elections.
1952 Joins NATO.
1960 Military coup.
1971 Prime minister Demirel forced to resign by army.
1974 Invasion of northern Cyprus.
1980–3 Military rule.
1984 Kurds begin guerrilla war.
1993 Tansu Ciller first woman prime minister.
1995 Centre-right parties form anti-Islamist coalition following Islamist Welfare Party gains in election.
1996 Erbakan heads coalition government.
1997 Centre-right coalition under Yilmaz after army intervention.
1998 Welfare Party outlawed; Ecevit becomes PM.
2002 Islamist Justice and Development Party (AK) wins elections; Gul becomes prime minister.
2003 AK leader Erdogan becomes prime minister.
2005 Negotiations on EU entry begin.
2007 Secularist demonstrations in Ankara to prevent Erdogan running for presidency; AK wins parliamentary elections; Gul elected president; preparations to invade Iraq in pursuit of Kurd guerrillas.
2008 Constitutional amendment allows women to wear Islamic headscarf in universities; troops deployed in northern Iraq; constitutional court rejects attempt to ban ruling Justice & Development party; trial begins of nationalist group accused of plotting coup.
2009 Ruling Justice & Development Party setback in local elections; agreement with Armenia to improve relations; renewed tension between government and army.
2010 Officers charged over coup plot; strained relations with Israel over Gaza blockade; referendum accepts constitutional amendments, including reform of judiciary; Erdogan criticises EU, as Turkish entry remains stalled.
2011 General election won by ruling Justice & Development Party; 250 officers charged with anti-government conspiracy; clashes with separatist Kurdistan Workers' Party (PKK) intensify; government adopts increasingly pro-Palestinian and anti-Israel stance.

2012 Former army chief accused of coup plot; Council of Europe expresses human rights concerns; NATO to deploy Patriot missiles on border with Syria.
2013 Anti-government protests; military officers imprisoned for coup plot; EU membership talks resume.
2014 Prime minister Erdoğan says corruption investigation is 'judicial coup'. Foreign forces allowed use of bases for anti-Islamist action in Iraq and Syria; Erdoğan elected President in criticised contest.
2015 Prime minister Davutoğlu accuses Israel's Netanyahu of crimes against humanity. President Erdogan calls two elections to secure AKP majority; tension with Russia over shooting down of jet; EU payment and entry talks pledge to curb refugees.
2016 ISIS bomb in Istanbul kills tourists; demand for more EU aid in refugee crisis. Sweeping civil liberties restrictions, arrests and dismissals following attempted military coup; improved relations with Russia; deeper involvement in Syrian war.
2017 Referendum outcome strengthens position of President Erdogan.

3. THE MIDDLE EAST

Chronology of War and Peace since 1948.

1948 State of Israel proclaimed; war between Israel and its Arab neighbours; 700,000 Palestinian Arabs become refugees.
1956 Israel invades Sinai with British and French backing following Egypt's nationalisation of the Suez Canal.
1964 Palestinian Liberation Organisation (PLO) founded; it is reformed under Arafat in 1967.
1967 Israel captures Sinai, the Gaza Strip, the Golan Heights, the West Bank and East Jerusalem during 'Six Day War' against Egypt, Syria and Jordan; United Nations Resolution 242 orders Israel to withdraw from the occupied territories.
1972 Palestinians kill Israeli athletes at the Olympic Games as part of growing terrorist campaign.
1973 Egypt and Syria attack Israel in 'Yom Kippur War' but fail to recapture Sinai and the Golan Heights.
1978 Israel temporarily occupies southern Lebanon to protect her northern frontier; Israel agrees to return Sinai to Egypt under 'Camp David Accord' between Egypt, Israel and the USA.
1982 Israel invades southern Lebanon to oust PLO guerrillas; Israeli-backed Christian militia in Lebanon massacres Palestinian refugees.
1983 Israel begins a phased withdrawal from most of southern Lebanon.
1987 Palestinian 'intifada' (uprising) mounted against Israeli occupation of the West Bank and Gaza; over 20,000 are killed or wounded.
1988 PLO leader Yasser Arafat renounces terrorism and recognises Israel as a state; US begins discussions with PLO.
1993 Following secret negotiations, the PLO and Israeli prime minister sign a declaration by which Israel recognises the PLO and agrees to give limited Palestinian autonomy in occupied Gaza and the West Bank.
1994 Israel and Jordan sign a peace treaty; Israel and the PLO agree on implementation of the 'Oslo Accords'; Israel will withdraw from 60% of Gaza and the West Bank town of Jericho; there is to be a five year negotiation on further withdrawals and the future of Jerusalem; Arafat becomes head of a new Palestinian National Authority in Gaza.
1995 Palestinian authority is extended over most of the West Bank under the Taba Agreement; Israel begins peace negotiations with Syria; talks are suspended following attacks by Palestinian terrorist group Hamas.
1996 Binyamin Netanyahu, an opponent of concessions, becomes Israeli prime minister; a ban on the construction of further Jewish settlements in Gaza and the West Bank is lifted.
1997 There are renewed terrorist attacks by the Palestinian group Hamas.

1998 Under US pressure, Netanyahu signs the Wye Accord agreeing to further Israeli withdrawals.

1999 Israel suspends the Wye Accord as Netanyahu's coalition splits over implementation; death of King Hussein of Jordan threatens delays; talks resume as Ehud Barak becomes Israeli prime minister and freezes further Jewish settlement around Jerusalem; Barak opens negotiations with Syria.

2000 Renewal of the *intifada* leads to escalating violence.

2001 US mediator calls on Israel to withdraw from recently occupied territory and Arafat to act firmly against militants; President Bush declares support for establishment of a Palestinian state; ceasefire negotiated.

2002 Hamas attack on Israeli troops ends ceasefire; Arafat promises free elections to Palestinian Assembly; President Bush calls for greater Palestinian democracy and Arafat's removal.

2003 Likud re-elected in Israeli elections; Labour refuse to enter into coalition, expressing doubts about Sharon's commitment to peace; Abbas appointed Palestinian prime minister; Abbas and Sharon agree ceasefire; Israel withdraws from parts of West Bank and Gaza; Hamas ends ceasefire; Abbas replaced by Qurei.

2004 Arafat blames Israeli settlements and security barrier for undermining peace hopes; President Bush supports Israeli proposal to withdraw from Gaza but maintain control of West Bank; Arafat dies and is succeeded as president of Palestinian Authority by Abbas.

2005 London conference convened by Blair achieves little; Israel withdraws from Gaza.

2006 Hamas win Palestinian elections; newly elected prime minister Haniya repeats Hamas refusal to recognise Israel; renewed tension following Israel's invasion of Lebanon and clashes in Gaza; new Israeli prime minister Olmert meets Abbas.

2007 US Secretary of State Rice tours Middle East; Arab League states offer Israel recognition in exchange for return to 1967 borders.

2008 President Bush calls on Israel to withdraw from territories occupied in 1967 and on the Palestinians to make concessions; Mr Abbas and Mr Olmert agree, but fail to sign, a peace treaty by the end of the year.

2009 President Obama declares he will work 'aggressively' to achieve peace; the new Israeli prime minister, Mr Netanyahu, initially resists President Obama's appeals to freeze construction of new settlements in the occupied West Bank but agrees a temporary cessation in December.

2010 Mr Netanyahu says Israel intends to retain parts of the West Bank in perpetuity; indirect talks between Israel and the Palestinians resume in May; Mr Abbas and Mr Netanyahu meet in August; further negotiations falter as Israel rejects President Obama's plea to extend the settlement construction freeze; Mr Netanyahu refuses unless the Palestinians formally acknowledge Israel is a Jewish state.

2011 Leaked documents reveal the extent of concessions offered by Palestinians in past negotiations, including acceptance of illegal Israeli settlements in occupied East Jerusalem. Israeli prime minister Netanyahu reluctantly agrees with President Obama that future Palestinian state should be broadly based on 1967 borders.

2013 First Palestinian-Israeli peace talks since 2000 soon falter.

2014 US Secretary of State Kerry attempts to revive peace talks. Israel suspends talks when Fatah and Hamas make unity pact; Pope Francis urges Peres and Abbas to work for peace.

2015 Former UK prime minister Blair resigns as peace envoy; President Abbas says Palestinian Authority will not comply with Oslo accords as Israel does not abide by them; growing violence between Palestinians and Israelis.

2016 UN Security Council calls on Israel to halt further settlement in occupied territories. US Secretary of State Kerry says hope for a two state solution is in 'serious jeopardy'.

2017 Foreign ministers at Paris peace conference urge progress towards a two state agreement. Israel does not attend and UK refuses to sign final communique.

ISRAEL.

Chronology of Key Events.

1948 State of Israel proclaimed, with Ben Gurion as prime minister; war with Arab neighbours.

1949 Defeat of Arabs sees Israel increase a third in area.

1956 Attacks Egypt with Britain and France.

1963 Eshkol succeeds Ben Gurion as prime minister.

1967 Defeats Egypt, Syria and Jordan in Six-Day War; occupies Sinai, Golan Heights, Gaza, West Bank and East Jerusalem; UN Resolution 242 demands withdrawal.

1969 Golda Meir becomes prime minister.

1973 Defeats Egypt and Syria in Yom Kippur War.

1974 Rabin becomes prime minister.

1977 Begin defeats Rabin in general election, ending 29 years of Labour government; visit of Egyptian President Sadat opens peace negotiations.

1979 Camp David Agreement with Egypt.

1980 Jerusalem declared capital of Israel.

1982 Invades Lebanon to defeat Palestinian guerrillas.

1984 Labour leader Peres forms coalition with Likud.

1986 Shamir succeeds Peres as prime minister.

1987 Palestinian *intifada* (uprising) begins in occupied territories.

1993 Oslo Agreement outlines Palestinian autonomy in West Bank and Gaza on 'peace for land' principle.

1994 Peace treaty with Jordan.

1995 Oslo 2 Agreement; prime minister Rabin assassinated; succeeded by Peres.

1996 Palestinian terrorism threatens peace process; Natanyahu becomes prime minister.

1998 Wye River agreement on Israeli withdrawal from West Bank; Netanyahu abandons agreement alleging Palestinian failure to end terrorism.

1999 Labour-led coalition under Barak.

2000 Peace talks collapse; second Palestinian *intifada* begins.

2001 Sharon becomes prime minister; renewed attacks on Palestinian territories.

2003 Withdrawals from parts of West Bank and Gaza; construction of security barrier through West Bank; Likud wins elections.

2004 Sharon proposes withdrawal from Gaza.

2005 Withdrawal from Gaza; Sharon forms new party, Kadima.

2006 Sharon suffers stroke, Olmert becomes prime minister; Kadima-Labour coalition formed following elections; troops invade Lebanon following Hizbollah capture of soldiers.

2007 Calls for Olmert's resignation over conduct of Lebanon war.

2008 Olmert resigns as premier; attack on Gaza in response to Palestinian missile attacks.

2009 Likud's Netanyahu forms coalition government following elections.

2010 Netanyahu declares Israel will permanently retain parts of West Bank.

2011 Demonstrations over rising living costs; tension with Egypt.

2012 Public sector general strike; growing threats against Iran.

2013 Netanyahu remains prime minister but elections see centre party gains. Cross border clashes with Syria; further east Jerusalem settlements approved.

2014 Former general and politician Ariel Sharon dies aged 85. Rivlin becomes President; Israel declared a Jewish state; 50-day Operation Protective Edge against Gaza following death of three youths.

2015 Netanyahu again returned in elections, forming coalition after surprise election victory; mounting violence between Palestinians and Israelis in Jerusalem and West Bank.

2016 Relations restored with Turkey. Premier Netanyahu says Israel will retain occupied Syrian Golan Heights; calls UN resolution opposing occupied territories settlements 'shameful.'

2017 Expansion of settlement building in occupied West Bank and East Jerusalem.

EGYPT.

1952 Muhammad Najib deposed King Farouk; becomes president and prime minister in Free Officers' Movement coup.

1953 Republic declared.
1954 Nasser becomes prime minister; later president. Last British forces leave.
1956 Britain, France and Israel invade following Suez Canal nationalisation.
1958 Forms United Arab Republic with Syria (abandoned 1961).
1967 Defeated by Israel in Six-Day War.
1970 Sadat becomes president on Nasser's death; Aswan Dam completed.
1973 Yom Kippur war with Israel.
1978 Camp David Accords signed.
1979 Peace treaty with Israel; expelled from Arab League.
1981 Sadat assassinated by Islamic fundamentalists; succeeded by Mubarak.
1989 Rejoins Arab League.
1995 Mubarak survives assassination attempt; his National Democratic Party (NDP) wins overwhelmingly in elections seen as rigged.
1998 Foreign tourists killed in terrorist attack.
1999 Mubarak survives assassination attempt; returned to office in referendum with 95 % of vote.
2000 NDP retains majority in People's Assembly elections.
2002 Contacts with Israel suspended in support of Palestinians.
2003 Protests over US/British invasion of Iraq.
2005 Anti-government demonstrations; Mubarak wins fifth term in low turn-out election; opposition Muslim Brotherhood candidates make gains in Assembly elections.
2006 Emergency laws in force since 1981 extended two years; Mubarak promises political reform.
2007 Mubarak criticises execution of Saddam in Iraq.
2008 Muslim Brotherhood members imprisoned for opposition activities.
2010 Ruling NDP wins disputed elections.
2011 Mubarak forced out by anti-government demonstrations; first free elections held.
2012 Muslim Brotherhood's Freedom and Justice Party takes 47 % of vote and the Al-Nour Party 25 %. Mohammed Morsi elected president; former President Mubarak sentenced to life imprisonment; voters approve new constitution.
2013 Mubarak faces retrial as court overturns conviction. President Morsi deposed by army; Muslim Brotherhood banned.
2014 New constitution approved in low turnout referendum; wave of bomb attacks. 838 Muslim Brotherhood supporters sentenced to death; former army chief Abdul Fattah al-Sisi wins presidential election.
2015 Mubarak's embezzlement conviction overturned; renewed pro-democracy protests. Egypt bombs ISIS bases in Libya; former President Morsi sentenced to death; ISIS attacks in north Sinai; elections give pro-President al-Sisi alliance legislative control.
2016 Legislature meets for first time since 2012 coup. ISIS terrorist attacks; IMF grant $12 billion loan; death sentence on former President Morsi overturned.
2017 Economic reforms, including subsidy reductions, in return for IMF loan.

THE PALESTINIANS.

Chronology of Key Events.

1949 700,000 Palestinians become refugees from new state of Israel.
1964 Palestine Liberation Organisation (PLO) formed.
1965 Fatah (Movement for the Liberation of Palestine) begins guerrilla actions against Israel.
1967 Israeli victory in Six-Day War and occupations of Arab territory radicalise Palestinian resistance.
1968 PLO adopts demand for Palestinian homeland.
1969 Yasser Arafat elected PLO chairman.
1970 Black September aircraft hijackings; Jordan attacks Palestinian leadership.
1974 Arafat addresses UN; Arab summit declares PLO the 'sole and legitimate representative' of the Palestinians.
1982 Israel invades Lebanon to oust Palestinian guerrillas.

1987 First Palestinian *intifada* (uprising) in Israeli-occupied territories begins.
1988 Arafat rejects terrorism, accepts Israel's right to exist.
1990 Arafat loses Gulf states' support by backing Iraq's invasion of Kuwait.
1993 Arafat and Israeli prime minister Rabin agree on limited Palestinian self-rule in West Bank and Gaza.
1994 Arafat becomes head of Palestinian Authority in Gaza.
1995 Arafat and Rabin sign aborted agreement on West Bank.
1996 Palestinian suicide bombings in Israel undermine peace process; Arafat moves against Hamas militants.
1998 Arafat and Netanyahu sign Wye River agreement on phased Israeli West Bank withdrawal; Israel abandons, accusing Arafat of not meeting security promises.
1999 Arafat agrees with Israeli prime minister Barak on September 2000 deadline for peace treaty.
2000 US-brokered peace negotiations at Camp David collapse; Palestinians begin second *intifada* following alleged provocation by Israeli opposition leader Sharon.
2001 Rising death toll in Israeli-Palestinian conflict.
2002 Arafat besieged by Israelis in presidential compound; Palestinian suicide bombings escalate.
2003 Arafat appoints Abbas (Abu Mazen) as prime minister under international pressure; Abbas resigns as Arafat refuses to relinquish security powers; Qurei (Abu Ala) succeeds; Palestinians accept US-backed 'road map' to peace.
2004 Increasing Palestinian dissatisfaction with Arafat and Palestinian Authority corruption; Arafat dies. Hamas makes gains against Fatah in municipal elections.
2005 Former prime minister Abbas wins landslide victory in presidential election.
2006 Hamas ousts Fatah in elections; Haniya becomes prime minister; Israeli troops return to Gaza; Hamas and Fatah agree on national unity government but clashes continue.
2007 National unity government collapses; Hamas forms administration in Gaza.
2008 Israeli invasion of Gaza.
2009 Following longstanding economic blockade, Israel invades Gaza in response to rocket attacks.
2010 By end of year over 100 countries recognised Palestine as a state within the 1967 borders.
2011 Hopes of Fatah-Hamas unity government thwarted; Abbas urges UN to recognise Palestinian state.
2012 Reaffirmation that peace talks cannot resume until Israel ends settlement construction in West Bank and east Jerusalem. Hamas military leader killed by Israelis in Gaza; cross border clashes; UN general assembly recognises Palestine as state.
2013 Prime minister Fayyad resigns; successor Hamdallah soon quits.
2014 US increases annual aid to $440 million. Fatah and Hamas unity government formed; over 2,000 die in Israeli attack on Gaza; Sweden recognises Palestinian state.
2015 Palestine becomes member of the International Criminal Court. Vatican formally recognises Palestinian state. President Abbas says Palestine will not comply with Oslo accords as Israel does not abide by them.
2016 Growing criticism of Abbas leadership. Municipal elections postponed.
2017 Palestinian Authority and Hamas agree on formation of unity government.

LEBANON.

1944 Gains independence from France.
1958 US troops intervene in civil war.
1975–90 Further civil war in which Syria and Israel invade.
1990 Government of national reconciliation formed.
1992 Rafik Hariri becomes prime minister.
1996 Israel bombs Hizbollah guerrilla bases in south.
1998 Emile Lahoud becomes president.
2000 Israeli forces withdraw.
2005 Anti-Syrian rallies following assassination of Hariri; Syria withdraws.
2006 Israel invades following Hizbollah capture of soldiers.

2007 Demonstrations demand government's resignation; parliament fails to elect successor to President Lahoud.
2008 Parliament elects army head Michel Suleiman as president; Fouad Siniora prime minister of national unity government.
2009 Saad Hariri prime minister of unity government following his 14 March coalition election victory; talks with Syrian President Assad.
2010 Border clash with Israel; Iranian President Ahmadinejad's visit intensifies sectarian tension.
2011 Hezbollah and allies leave government; Najib Mikati forms new administration.
2012 Syrian conflict threatens government stability as Sunni Muslims and Alawites clash.
2013 Sectarian clashes over Syrian conflict; elections postponed.
2014 Prime minister Hariri forms coalition after long deadlock. Over one million Syrian refugees; border clashes with ISIS.
2015 Restrictions on entry of Syrian refugees. Clashes as violence spreads from Syria; failure by legislature to elect President.
2016 Over 1·5 million Syrian refugees in country. Michel Aoun becomes President after months of deadlock.
2017 Restored relations with Saudi Arabia.

IRAN.

1941 Pro-German Shah ousted by Allies; replaced by son Mohammad Reza Pahlavi.
1950 Radical nationalist Mohammad Mossadeq becomes prime minister.
1951 Oil industry nationalised; power struggle between Shah and Mossadeq.
1953 Shah ousts Mossadeq with Western support.
1963 Shah begins "White Revolution" of land reform and social modernisation; uses secret police against opponents.
1973 Martial law imposed as resistance grows.
1979 Shah exiled; Islamic Republic declared under fundamentalist Ayatollah Khomeini.
1980 Government begins radical nationalisation programme; war with Iraq.
1988 War with Iraq ends.
1989 Ayatollah Khomeini dies; Ayatollah Khamenei becomes supreme leader; Ali Akbar Rafsanjani becomes president.
1995 US imposes trade sanctions, alleging Iran sponsors terrorism.
1997 Reformist Mohammad Khatami wins landslide presidential election.
1999 Pro-democracy riots in Tehran.
2000 Reformists win parliamentary majority; conservatives attempt to thwart election result; judiciary bans reformist press.
2001 President Khatami re-elected.
2002 Denounced as part of an 'axis of evil' by President Bush.
2003 Reformist candidates fare badly in local elections. Growing disappointment with Khatami.
2004 Low turnout in the Majlis elections as many reformist candidates excluded; conservatives win control; President Bush threatens action over alleged nuclear weapons development.
2005 Ultra-conservative Ahmadinejad elected President.
2006 Confrontation grows over nuclear issue; increasing discontent over government's failure to reduce unemployment.
2007 Ayatollah Khamenei warns US against attacking Iran.
2009 Mass opposition protests suppressed.
2010 UN imposes further sanctions over alleged nuclear programme.
2011 Opposition demonstrations; open tension between Ahmadinejad and Supreme leader Ayatollah Khamenei.
2012 Setback for Ahmadinejad as conservatives gain in elections. International Atomic Energy Agency declares no progress in talks on nuclear programme.
2013 Reformist Rouhani elected president.
2014 International sanctions eased after deal to curb nuclear programme. Rouhani offers Iraq aid against Sunni insurgents.
2015 Breakthrough with USA over nuclear talks. Aid to Iraq in anti-ISIS campaign; nuclear activity agreement with 'group of six' powers.

2016 Tension with Saudi Arabia over executions; international sanctions lifted. Reformists make gains in elections. Retaliation threatened over US Senate vote to extend Iran Sanctions Act.
2017 Military spending increased to 5% of national budget.

IRAQ.

Chronology of Key Events.

1932 Gains independence from British control.
1958 General Karim Qasim overthrows monarchy.
1966 General Muhammad Arif becomes president.
1968 Arif is overthrown by General Ahmad Hasan al-Bakr.
1972 Signs Treaty of Friendship and Co-operation with Soviet Union; nationalises Iraq Petroleum Company.
1974 Grant of limited autonomy to Kurds rejected by Kurdistan Democratic Party.
1979 Saddam Hussein becomes president.
1980 War with Iran.
1988 War with Iran ends; Iraq uses chemical weapons against Kurds.
1990 Invades Kuwait.
1991 Defeated in Gulf War; UN safe haven established in north to protect Kurds; 'no flight' zone later set up in south.
1995 UN allows partial resumption of oil exports to buy medicine and food; referendum returns Saddam Hussein as president for seven years.
1998 Ends co-operation with UN supervision of weapons destruction; Britain and US launch bombing campaign.
2000 Rejects weapons inspection proposals; Iraq halts oil exports following dispute with UN.
2001 US threatens action if links found with 11 September terrorist attacks.
2002 Government denies possession of weapons of mass destruction; UN orders admission of inspectors; exile opposition prepares for return.
2003 US and British coalition invades; Saddam Hussein captured.
2004 Nominal control handed to interim government; anti-coalition and sectarian violence intensifies.
2005 Talabani becomes President following elections; parliamentary elections show stark divisions between Shia, Sunni and Kurdish regions; Nuri al-Maliki becomes prime minister.
2006 Civil war feared as Shia-Sunni conflict mounts; Saddam Hussein executed following trial.
2007 US 'surge' to curb continuing insurrection.
2009 Provincial elections held.
2010 Talabani president and Nouri al-Maliki prime minister following elections; US ends combat operations;
2011 US completes combat troop withdrawal; sectarian violence heightens.
2012 Continuing attacks on Shia areas raise fears of sectarian conflict.
2013 Sunni-Shia sectarian clashes intensify.
2014 Islamic militants seize cities of Fallujah and Ramadi. Islamic State (ISIS) declares captured territory a caliphate.
2015 US-led coalition air strikes on ISIS territory. Continuing drive against ISIS; government anti-corruption and sectarianism campaign.
2016 ISIS intensify terrorist attacks in capital. Fallujah recaptured from ISIS; protests over government corruption; ISIS lose then retake Palmyra; army advance on Mosul.
2017 Nuclear programme for peaceful purposes restored.

SYRIA.

Chronology of Key Events.

1970 Assad seizes power
1971 Assad elected president.
1973 War with Israel.
1974 Agreement signed with Israel.
1975 Assad offers Israel peace treaty in return for withdrawal from occupied territories.
1976 Intervenes in Lebanese civil war.
1980 Muslim Brotherhood assassination attempt on Assad.
1982 Army suppresses Muslim Brotherhood uprising; clashes with Israel in Lebanon.
1990 Joins the US-led coalition against Iraq.
1991 Holds abortive talks with Israel.

2000 Assad dies; succeeded by son Bashar.
2001 Becomes member of UN Security Council.
2002 President Bush accuses Syria of being part of an 'axis of evil'.
2003 US accuses Syria of developing chemical weapons and threatens sanctions; Mohammed Naji al-Otari becomes prime minister.
2004 US imposes sanctions; UN calls for withdrawal from Lebanon.
2005 Troops leave Lebanon; UN implicates Syria in murder of former Lebanese prime minister.
2006 Relations restored with Iraq; number of Iraqi refugees mounts.
2007 Israel bombs alleged nuclear facility site; dissidents jailed.
2008 Efforts to end diplomatic isolation.
2009 Diplomatic ties with Iraq restored.
2010 Diplomatic relations restored with US.
2011 Anti-government protests; Arab League criticises repression; opposition forms Syrian National Council.
2012 EU recognises National Coalition for Syrian Revolutionary & Opposition Forces as representative body.
2013 Western-backed Syrian Free Army loses ground to Islamists; alleged chemical weapons use prompts Western threats; agreement to destroy weapons.
2014 Peace talks open in Geneva. Assad wins disputed election; peace talks falter; US and Arab states bomb Islamic State controlled areas.
2015 UN proposes local ceasefires. Continuing rebel and ISIS offensives; Russia bombs rebels and ISIS.
2016 Peace efforts falter; Russian and Iranian backed government forces retake Aleppo.
2017 Russia-Turkey broker peace agreement.

SAUDI ARABIA.

Chronology of Key Events.

1982 Khalid succeeded by brother Fahd.
1990 Supports Gulf War against Iraqi invasion of Kuwait.
1992 Fahd announces mild democratic reforms.
1993 Consultative Council (Majlis al-Shura) comprising members selected by King inaugurated.
1995 Crown Prince Abdullah effective ruler following Fahd's stroke.
1996 Fahd resumes power; bomb attack on US base.
1997 Consultative Council enlarged.
2000 Amnesty International condemns treatment of women.
2001 Anti-terrorism and crime security pact with Iran signed.
2003 Following the Iraq war, the US announced a withdrawal of its forces from Saudi Arabia. King Fahd announces limited constitutional reforms.
2004 Terrorist attacks in April, May, June and December.
2005 King Fahd dies; Abdullah succeeds; World Trade Organisation invites membership.
2006 Alleged al-Qaeda members killed by police.
2007 Decree orders reform of judicial system.
2009 Dismissal of conservatives from key posts marks continuing modernization.
2010 US concern that country funds Sunni international terrorism.
2011 Pro-democracy demonstrations; Saudi troops deployed against protesters in Bahrain.
2012 Defence minister Prince Salman bin Abdulaziz becomes heir apparent to throne.
2013 Women join all-male consultative council; government declines seat on UN Security Council.
2014 Nuclear power negotiations with France and Japan. Saudi Arabia joins US air attacks on Islamist bases in Syria.
2015 International protests over flogging sentence on liberal website blogger; King Abdullah dies, succeeded by Salman. King's nephew Mohammed bin Nayef named Crown Prince; first women elected in municipal elections; Saudi Arabia forms 34 Islamic state anti-terrorism coalition.
2016 Execution of 47 alleged terrorists including leading Shia cleric heightens tension with Iran. Involvement in Yemen war intensifies; King Salman's 'Vision 2030' attempts to reduce reliance on oil production; ISIS bombings.
2017 Further crackdown on human rights activists.

YEMEN.

Chronology of Key Events.

1918 North Yemen independent as Ottoman Empire collapses.
1967 Southern Yemen (formerly Aden) independent from Britain.
1970s Frequent conflict between north and south.
1990 North and south establish United Republic of Yemen under Ali Abdallah Saleh.
1994 Northern troops re-occupy south following secession attempt.
2000 Al-Qaeda attack on US naval vessel kills 17; British Embassy bombed.
2001 President Saleh assures US of support in war on terrorism.
2004 Clashes between government forces and northern Shia rebels.
2008 18 die in suspected al-Qaeda attack on US Embassy.
2009 Yemen and Saudi wings of al-Qaeda merge into al-Qaeda in the Arabian Peninsula (AQAP); renewed clashes with northern Shia rebels.
2010 Appeal to US for aid against al-Qaeda; ceasefire with northern Shia rebels.
2011 Anti-government demonstrations; President Saleh offers to stand down in 2012; unity government formed.
2012 Abdrabbuh Mansour Hadi succeeds Saleh. Continuing terror attacks by al-Qaeda allies.
2013 Attempts to draft new constitution; US drone attacks on al-Qaeda intensify.
2014 Hundreds die in Shia-Sunni clashes in north. Shia Houthi rebels capture capital.
2015 Government-Houthi clashes intensify; President Hadi resigns. Houthi advances lead to Saudi military response. ISIS terror attacks; Saudi Arabian-led coalition air strikes on Houthi targets; President Hadi returns.
2016 Faltering peace talks between government and Houthi. Saudi-led coalition and US attacks on Houthi continue.
2017 Efforts to end military stalemate and begin talks.

4. SOUTH ASIA

INDIA.

Chronology of Key Events.

1947 Gains independence from Britain.
1948 War with Pakistan over disputed Kashmir.
1951 Congress Party wins first elections under Jawaharlal Nehru.
1962 Defeated in border war with China.
1965 War with Pakistan over Kashmir.
1966 Indira Gandhi becomes prime minister.
1971 War with Pakistan.
1974 Explodes first nuclear weapon.
1975 Indira Gandhi declares state of emergency following conviction for electoral irregularities.
1977 Congress Party election defeat; Gandhi forms splinter Congress (I).
1980 Congress (I) wins election.
1984 Troops attack Golden Temple to eject Sikh militants; Gandhi assassinated by Sikhs; son Rajiv succeeds.
1987 Sends peacekeeping force to Sri Lanka.
1989 Congress defeated in general election.
1991 Rajiv Gandhi assassinated; prime minister Rao begins economic reform.
1992 Hindu-Muslim sectarian violence.
1996 Hindu nationalist Bharatiya Janata Party (BJP) largest single party following elections.
1998 BJP heads coalition government under Atal Behari Vajpayee; nuclear weapons tests.
1999 Clash with Pakistan over Kashmir.
2000 Continued clashes with guerrillas in Kashmir; long range missile test.
2002 Increased tension with Pakistan over Kashmir dispute.
2003 Agreement with Pakistan on Kashmir ceasefire.
2004 Congress-led United Progressive Alliance trounces BJP in elections.
2005 40-year border dispute with China ends.
2006 Rural anti-poverty programme launched.
2007 Renewed efforts to resolve Kashmir dispute with Pakistan.
2008 Mumbai terrorist attacks.

2009 General election held. Decisive win for Congress Party and allies.

2010 Diplomatic contacts with Pakistan renewed.

2011 Government says India had recovered from global financial crisis; renewed anti-corruption measures.

2012 Long range missile capable of carrying nuclear warhead successfully tested. Former finance minister Pranab Mukherjee becomes President.

2013 Gang rape case highlights women's rights issues; Supreme Court rejects homosexuality decriminalisation.

2014 General election won with landslide majority for Narendra Modi and his BJP-led coalition. India third largest world economy.

2015 10-year defence agreement with US renewed. Ruling BJP setback in Delhi state elections; prime minister Modi meets Pakistan leader for first time in a decade; clashes with Pakistan in Kashmir.

2016 Modi launches the 'Startup India' campaign. Defence and energy agreements with France and Russia; recall of all 500 and 1,000 rupee notes provokes crisis.

2017 Oxfam reports top 1% own 58% of country's wealth.

SRI LANKA.

Chronology of Key Events.

1948 Gains independence from Britain.

1956 Bandaranaike becomes prime minister.

1959 Bandaranaike assassinated; succeeded by his widow.

1965 United National Party wins elections.

1970 Mrs Bandaranaike returns to power.

1971 Student-led Marxist revolt.

1972 Changes name to Sri Lanka; Buddhism becomes country's religion.

1976 Liberation Tigers of Tamil Eelam (LTTE) formed in Tamil north and east of country.

1977 Tamil United Liberation Front gains all seats in Tamil area.

1983 Fighting begins between army and LTTE.

1985 First attempt at peace talks between government and LTTE fails.

1987 Government forces push LTTE back into northern city of Jaffna; offers limited local government to Tamils; Indian peacekeeping force deployed.

1988 Sinhalese JVP campaign against Indian involvement.

1990 Indian troops withdraw; escalating violence between army and separatists.

1991 LTTE implicated in assassination of Indian premier Gandhi.

1993 President Premadasa assassinated by LTTE.

1994 President Kumaratunga opens peace talks with LTTE.

1995 Peace talks collapse; major government offensive.

1996 State of emergency after LTTE bomb attacks in capital.

1997 Government offensive against LTTE.

1998 LTTE military successes.

1999 President Kumaratunga re-elected.

2000 President Kumaratunga's People's Alliance wins general elections; Norway offers mediation; government rejects LTTE ceasefire offer.

2002 Ceasefire agreed as preliminary to peace talks.

2003 Tamil Tigers withdraw from peace talks.

2004 First terrorist bombing in Colombo since 2001; over 30,000 die in tsunami.

2005 Former prime minister Rajapakse wins presidential election.

2006 Renewed fighting between government forces and Tamil Tigers.

2007 Violent stalemate between government and Tamil Tigers continues.

2009 26-year war with Tamil Tiger separatists ends.

2010 President Rajapaksa's United People's Freedom Alliance defeats United National Front in elections.

2011 Government rejects UN report on human rights violations in final stages of civil war; proposals to lift wartime emergency laws.

2012 Opposition leader Sarath Fonseka freed from imprisonment.

2013 Chief Justice dismissed; UN Human Rights Commissioner accuses government of repression.

2014 US war crimes official urges investigation of human rights abuses. Entry refused to UN team investigating war crimes allegations.

2015 Sirisena defeats incumbent Rajapaksa in presidential election. Sirisena declares commitment to national reconciliation.

2016 Plans to draft new inclusive constitution. Government announces intention of removing military involvement by 2018; country declared free of malaria.

2017 Violent protests over Chinese plans to build a port and industrial zone.

PAKISTAN.

Chronology of Key Events.

1947 Established as a Muslim state on the independence of India from Britain.

1948 First war with India over disputed Kashmir.

1956 Proclaimed an Islamic republic.

1958 General Ayub Khan seizes power and proclaims martial law.

1960 Khan becomes president.

1965 War with India over Kashmir.

1969 Khan is succeeded by General Yahya Khan.

1971 War with India; East Pakistan secedes to establish Bangladesh.

1972 Zulfiqar Ali Bhutto becomes prime minister.

1977 Military coup by General Zia ul'Haq.

1985 Martial law lifted and political activity legalised.

1988 Zia killed in air crash; Benazir Bhutto's Pakistan People's Party wins elections.

1989 Bhutto dismissed for corruption; Nawaz Sharif succeeds.

1991 Islamic Sharia law incorporated into legal code.

1993 Sharif resigns as prime minister; Bhutto succeeds.

1996 Bhutto government dismissed for alleged corruption.

1997 Sharif's Pakistan Muslim League wins elections.

1998 Nuclear weapons tests.

1999 Clash with India over Kashmir; General Musharraf seizes power.

2000 Musharraf promises gradual restoration of democracy.

2002 Musharraf secures 5-year renewal in referendum (he was the only candidate).

2003 Agreement with India on Kashmir ceasefire; Musharraf escapes assassination attempt.

2004 Readmitted to Commonwealth; Musharraf reneges on promise to relinquish post as army chief.

2005 Agreements with India on Kashmir and missile testing.

2006 Anti-American demonstrations following deaths in US missile attack on border with Afghanistan.

2007 President Musharraf imposes state of emergency; former prime minister Benazir Bhutto assassinated.

2008 Musharraf stands down; Asif Zardari elected president.

2009 Military operation against Taliban in Swat Valley.

2010 Terrorism incidents intensify; constitutional changes shift powers to prime minister.

2011 Al-Qaeda leader Osama bin Laden killed by US in Pakistan.

2012 Military coup fears after prime minister criticises army chiefs. Raja Pervez Ashraf becomes prime minister.

2013 Supreme Court orders Ashraf's arrest. Sharif prime minister in Muslim League election victory; Mamnoon Hussain becomes president.

2014 China lends $6·5 billion for plant construction in nuclear power deal. Former President Musharraf charged with high treason; government talks with Taliban; Taliban school massacre.

2015 Military tribunals for terror suspects; clashes with India in Kashmir. Taliban attacks in Sindh and Peshawar; government demands British return of Koh-i-noor diamond.

2016 Arms purchase deal with China. Military acknowledges ISIS militants are active in country.

2017 First submarine-based missile with nuclear potential launched

BANGLADESH.

1947 Gains independence from Britain; split into East and West.

1949 Awami League founded to campaign for East Pakistan autonomy.

1970 Awami League wins election victory in East Pakistan; government in West Pakistan refuses to accept result.

1971 East Pakistan declares independence as Bangladesh under Sheikh Mujibur Rahman; Pakistan troops defeated with Indian backing.

1974 State of emergency declared as unrest grows.

1975 Sheikh Mujib becomes president; assassinated in military coup; martial law imposed.

1977 General Zia Rahman becomes president; Islamic constitution adopted.

1979 Zia's Bangladesh National Party (BNP) wins elections.

1981 Zia assassinated in abortive military coup; Abdus Sattar succeeds.

1982 General Ershad leads military coup; constitution suspended.

1983 Ershad becomes president.

1986 Parliamentary and presidential elections; Ershad ends martial law.

1987 State of emergency following opposition demonstrations.

1988 Islam becomes state religion.

1990 Ershad resigns.

1991 Begum Khaleda Zia becomes prime minister.

1996 Awami League election victory; Sheikh Hasina Wajed becomes prime minister.

1997 Opposition BNP opens strike campaign against government.

2000 Tension with Pakistan over attitudes to 1971 independence war.

2001 Border clashes with India; Hasina hands power to caretaker authority.

2002 Ahmed becomes president following Chowdhury's resignation.

2004 Opposition mounts general strikes to oust government; failed assassination attempt on Awami League leader Hasina.

2005 Terrorist bombings by banned Islamic group.

2006 Opposition Awami League ends boycott of parliament.

2007 Elections postponed; state of emergency declared.

2008 Elections won by Awami League.

2009 Over 70 dead in border guards' mutiny over conditions.

2010 Former army officers executed for the 1975 murder of founding prime minister Sheikh Mujibur Rahman; Jamaat-e-Islami party banned for violating secularism embodied in constitution.

2011 Social and economic problems mount as thousands of migrant workers are forced to return home by Middle East upheavals.

2012 Army command claims coup plans thwarted; Jamaat-e-Islami leaders charged with war crimes in 1971 independence war.

2013 Abdul Hamid becomes president; vetoes bill banning criticism of Islam.

2014 Governing Awami League wins election boycotted by opposition BNP. Opposition leaders face corruption charges.

2015 Government and opposition supporters clash on streets. Jaamat-e-Islami leaders executed for 1971 war crimes; continuing attacks on Shia Muslims and Christians.

2016 World Bank $100 million for primary education. ISIS terrorism in Dhaka; mounting attacks on secularists.

2017 Former prime minister Zia tried for alleged corruption.

AFGHANISTAN.

1919 Gains independence after third war against Britain.

1933 Zahir Shah becomes king.

1953 Prime minister Mohammed Daud heads reforming government until ousted in 1963.

1964 Power struggles follow introduction of constitutional monarchy.

1973 Republic declared following coup by Daud.

1978 Daud overthrown by left-wing People's Democratic Party; Islamic conservative revolt.

1979 Hafizullah Amin wins left power struggle in Kabul but is executed following Soviet invasion.

1980 Soviet Union installs Babrak Karmal as ruler; resistance from mujahedin groups backed by US, Pakistan, Saudi Arabia and Iran intensifies.

1985 Pakistan-based mujahedin forces unite.

1986 Najibullah replaces Karmal as head of government.

1989 Soviet Union withdraws; civil war intensified.

1992 Najibullah falls; rival militias compete for power.

1993 Mujahedin groups unite around President Burhanuddin Rabbani.

1996 Islamic fundamentalist Taliban forces capture Kabul; recognised as government by Pakistan and Saudi Arabia; Rabbani flees to join Northern Alliance.

1998 US bombs alleged bases of terrorist Osama bin Laden.

1999 UN embargo and sanctions imposed to secure trial of Osama bin Laden.

2001 Invasion of Afghanistan. Hamid Karzai becomes head of interim government.

2002 UN International Security Assistance Force deployed to combat Taliban and al-Qaeda; Karzai appointed interim president.

2004 New constitution adopted; President Karzai elected with 55% of vote.

2005 Low turnout in elections to new parliament.

2006 Anti-US demonstrations in Kabul; NATO takes responsibility for military operations against Taliban.

2009 Presidential election won by Karzai.

2010 NATO launches offensive in Helmand; legislative elections riven by fraud.

2011 Taliban assassinate prominent figures; tense relations with Pakistan.

2012 Further moves towards peace talks between government, Taliban and US. US promises 10 years development aid following troop withdrawal.

2013 Afghan forces take over security from NATO.

2014 Karzai refuses security pact with US without Taliban peace deal. Power sharing with Ghani as President, Abdullah as chief executive; UK and US end combat operations.

2015 Ghani appoints cabinet, including three women. Around 10,000 US troops to remain in country as advisors; informal government-Taliban talks in Qatar; Taliban take major city of Kunduz.

2016 Renewed peace talks. NATO troops to remain in country; peace agreement with militant Hezb-e-Islami group; mounting internal threat from ISIS.

2017 US troops redeployed to combat Taliban.

5. THE FAR EAST

CHINA.

Chronology of Key Events.

1949 Chinese People's Republic proclaimed with Mao Zedong as Chairman of the Republic.

1950 Chinese troops intervene in Korean War against United Nations forces.

1951 China occupies Tibet.

1953 Main industries nationalised under first Five Year Plan.

1956 Mao's 'let a hundred flowers bloom' campaign raises disappointed hopes of intellectual freedom.

1958 Second Five Year Plan introduces 'Great Leap Forward' to industrialise China and build agricultural communes; widespread famine follows.

1960 China accuses Soviet Union of ideological 'revisionism'.

1962 War with India over border dispute.

1964 China explodes atomic bomb.

1966 Mao opens Cultural Revolution, encouraging Red Guards to attack his political opponents.

1969 Border clashes with Soviet Union.

1971 China joins the United Nations, replacing Taiwan (Nationalist China) as a permanent member of the Security Council.

1976 Mao dies; new Chairman and prime minister Hua Guofeng moves against Mao's widow, Jiang Qing, and her 'Gang of Four' allies.

1977 Economic pragmatism introduced; Jiang Qing expelled from party and imprisoned.

1978 China opens diplomatic relations with United States.

1979 China invades Vietnam; demonstrators in Beijing call for greater political freedom.

1983 Economic reformer Deng Xiaoping increases influence.

1984 Economic modernisation continues with

weakening of collectivism in agriculture and industry.

1987 Zhao Zinyang replaces Hu Yaobang as prime minister in apparent backlash against reform.

1989 Increasing demands by students and workers for democracy culminate in Tiananmen Square massacre in Beijing; Zhao Zinyang replaced by Jiang Zemin in a party purge.

1990 Finance minister reports soaring unemployment and falling foreign investment.

1993 New constitution declares the establishment of a 'social market economy'; peasant riots over rising prices.

1995 Five Year Plan calls for doubling gross national product by 2000.

1997 Deng Xiaoping dies; Hong Kong returned by Britain; increasing protests against unemployment and corruption; Party Congress sets programme for rapid privatisation of remaining state industries; US President Clinton criticises China's human rights record.

1998 China intensifies privatisation of state enterprises and the campaign against corruption; chief economic planner Zhu Rongji becomes prime minister; China and Europe hold first economic summit meeting; Taiwan rejects an offer of reunification with autonomy.

1999 Government slows economic reform in the face of soaring unemployment; there are mass arrests of dissidents in the run-up to the Republic's 50th anniversary; China agrees to join the World Trade Organisation; President Jiang declares China will complete the transition to a 'socialist market system' within a decade.

2000 Government intensifies anti-corruption campaign.

2001 Joins Shanghai Co-operation Organisation with Russia and Central Asian states; joins World Trade Organisation.

2002 US accuses China of planning invasion of Taiwan; Hu Jintao replaces Jiang Zemin as head of Communist Party.

2003 Hu Jintao becomes President; first manned spacecraft launched; constitutional changes to protect private property signal abandonment of communism.

2005 Strained relations with Japan; military exercises with Russia.

2006 African heads of state conference in Beijing symbolises China's expanding international reach.

2007 EU warns that arms embargo would continue because of human rights record.

2008 Protests in Tibet and western provinces suppressed; China mounts Olympic Games; infrastructure spending to avoid economic downturn.

2009 Ethnic clashes in Xinjiang province; improved relations with Taiwan; easing of one-child policy.

2010 Diplomatic clashes with Japan and US.

2011 Overtakes Japan as second largest economy; protests at repression of dissidents.

2012 Free trade negotiations begin with Japan and South Korea. Xi Jinping succeeds Hu Jintao as Communist Party leader.

2013 Tension with Japan over disputed islands; one child policy eased.

2014 High speed missile test; foreign fishing vessel access to disputed sea restricted. Uighur separatist terrorist attacks; pro-democracy demonstrations in Hong Kong; gas deal with Russia.

2015 Measures to curb credit boom. Growth lowest for 20 years; free trade agreement with Australia; historic high-level talks with Taiwan; one-child policy ends after 35 years.

2016 Central bank props up ailing stock market; government warns Taiwan not to seek independence. Economic growth continues to slow; International Court criticises actions in South China Sea; two separatists banned from taking seats in Hong Kong legislature.

2017 President Xi praises globalisation and warns against trade wars.

JAPAN.

Chronology of Key Events.

1945 Surrenders to Allies following atom bomb attacks.

1947 New constitution introduced.

1952 US military government ends.

1955 Liberal Democratic Party (LDP) begins over 30 years as ruling party.

1956 Joins UN.

1972 Opens diplomatic relations with China.

1989 Emperor Hirohito dies; Akihito succeeds.

1993 LDP loses power amidst bribery allegations and economic failure.

1994 Coalition government falls; LDP/Socialist led administration formed.

1996 Tension with United States over military bases in Okinawa; LDP forms minority government.

1997 Economic recession intensifies.

1998 LDP's Keicho Obuchi becomes prime minister.

2000 Yoshiro Mori succeeds Obuchi as prime minister; LDP-led coalition elected; Diet calls for review of pacifist constitution.

2001 Junichiro Koizumi succeeds Mori.

2003 LDP-led coalition returned to power in lower house elections.

2004 Troops deployed in Iraq; applies for permanent UN Security Council seat.

2005 Strained relations with China; LDP-led coalition wins snap election called by Koizumi after party opposition to reforms.

2006 Shino Abe succeeds Koizumi as prime minister; establishment of defence ministry symbolises growing national assertiveness.

2007 Yasuo Fukuda prime minister after Abe resigns.

2008 Fukuda resigns; Taro Aso succeeds him.

2009 Opposition DPJ ends almost 50 years of LDP rule in election landslide; Yukio Hatoyama heads coalition.

2010 Hatoyama resigns, succeeded by Naoto Kan.

2011 Nuclear power curbed following Fukushima disaster; Yoshihiko Noda prime minister following Kan's resignation.

2012 Liberal Democrat election victory; Shinzo Abe becomes prime minister.

2013 Government introduces $116 billion stimulus package. Tension with China prompts increased military spending.

2014 Prime minister Abe proposes end to 'self defence only' constitution clause; calls on China to curb military spending. Ban on armed forces overseas deployment ended; LDP-led coalition election victory.

2015 $26 billion public spending stimulus; largest ever defence budget. Protests over legislation allowing troop deployment overseas; voting age lowered to 18; nuclear power generation resumes.

2016 Military presence in East China Sea increases. Further economic stimulus package; increased military spending; Abe apologises for 1941 Pearl Harbor attack.

2017 Criticism of long hours 'overwork' culture.

KOREA.

Chronology of Key Events.

1945 Korea is divided by the United States and the Soviet Union into southern and northern zones after being controlled by Japan for 40 years.

1950 North Korean attack on South Korea leads to United Nations military intervention.

1953 The Korean War ends in a stalemate; tense relations between north and south continue for two decades.

1972 Inconclusive discussions open between South and North Korea.

1991 North and South Korea agree on mutual recognition.

1994 Diplomatic progress is stalled on the death of North Korean dictator Kim Il Sung.

1995 Kim Jong Il succeeds his father as North Korean dictator; the country is devastated by famine.

1998 Newly elected South Korean president Kim Dae-jung launches a 'sunshine diplomacy' campaign to promote harmony between the two states; tension rises as North Korea begins missile tests over Japan.

1999 North Korea proposes discussions on unification; the United States lifts trade sanctions but expresses concern at missile development.

2000 Historic meeting of leaders of South Korea and North Korea.

2002 President Bush accuses North Korea of being

part of an 'axis of evil'; tension mounts over nuclear weapons programme.

2003 North Korea withdraws from Nuclear Non-Proliferation Treaty; discussions over nuclear issue with US and China begin.

2004 North Korea withdraws from talks.

2005 North Korea says it has defensive nuclear weapons; offers to relinquish them in return for economic aid.

2006 North Korea tests long-range missile and claims to have conducted nuclear test.

2007 North Korea agrees to admit international nuclear observers and to close nuclear reactor.

2008 Renewed military tensions.

2009 Successful North Korean underground nuclear test; UN imposes stronger sanctions.

2010 Attack on South Korean naval vessel heightens tension.

2011 Kim Jung-on succeeds Kim Jong-il on latter's death.

2012 US withdraws food aid after abortive test launch of long-range missile. Agricultural reforms; UN condemns space satellite launch.

2013 North Korea detonates third nuclear weapon; leader's uncle executed for alleged coup plot.

2014 North rejects South Korean family reunion visits proposal. Troops exchange fire across border.

2015 Kim Jong-un offers talks with south; military service for women introduced. Yongbyon nuclear plant re-opens; US heightens sanctions.

2016 North Korea claims successful hydrogen bomb detonation. Kim Jong-un rules out nuclear first strike; Workers' Party holds first congress since 1980; further nuclear warhead tests.

2017 South Korean political/business corruption scandal intensifies. Assassination in Malaysia of Kim Jong-nam, (estrange) half-brother of North Korea's Leader.

BURMA (MYANMAR).

Chronology of Key Events.

1948 Burma, a British colony since 1886, becomes independent.

1962 Prime minister U Nu is deposed in a military coup led by General Ne Win; a long period of repression follows.

1988 Ne Win is overthrown in student-led riots but many are killed by the State Law and Order Restoration Council (SLORC) as it takes power; the country's name is changed to Myanmar.

1989 Opposition National League for Democracy (NLD) leader Aung San Suu Kyi is placed under house arrest.

1990 NLD wins a landslide victory in the first elections for 30 years; SLORC annuls the elections and retains power.

1991 Aung San Suu Kyi is awarded Nobel Peace Prize.

1995 Aung San Suu Kyi is released from house arrest but restrictions continue.

1996 There are widespread student demonstrations against the regime; all universities are closed.

1997 SLORC renames itself the State Peace and Development Council (SPDC) and attempts economic reform.

1998 NLD sets up a shadow parliament of members elected in 1990; opposition activists are arrested.

1999 The International Labour Organisation condemns the use of slave labour in Burma; the World Bank demands political and human rights reforms; the government intensifies long-running action against Karen National Union guerrillas on border with Thailand.

2000 Continued international condemnation of the regime.

2001 Major changes to ruling State Peace and Development Council.

2002 Aung San Suu Kyi released from house arrest.

2003 Aung San Suu Kyi in protective custody following pro-democracy demonstrations.

2004 National League for Democracy boycotts government constitutional convention; Khin Nyunt dismissed as prime minister.

2005 Government declares country moving towards democracy; Aung San Suu Kyi's confinement extended.

2006 Major offensive against Karen National Liberation Army, which had waged independence campaign since 1949.

2007 Association of South East Asian Nations calls for democratic reform.

2008 Referendum on a draft constitution.

2009 Aung San Suu Kyi meets military leaders.

2010 Military Union Solidarity & Development Party wins landslide victory in elections boycotted by NLD; Suu Kyi freed from house arrest.

2011 Thein Sein becomes President of ostensibly civilian government.

2012 Suu Kyi elected in NLD by-election victories; EU suspends sanctions. President Thein Sein brings economic reformers into government.

2013 Buddhist-Muslim clashes; state newspaper monopoly ends; political prisoners released.

2014 Protesters demand end to political arrests; Japan pledges $96 million aid. US sanctions continue; government amnesties 3,000 prisoners.

2015 Continuing criticism of human rights violations. Opposition National League for Democracy wins elections.

2016 Htin Kyaw becomes President (effectively a proxy for Aung San Suu Kyi). US lifts sanctions; rising number of political prisoners.

2017 Clashes with Kachin Independence Army intensify; Japan makes $824 million loan.

VIETNAM.

Chronology of Key Events.

1946 Communist-led independence war against France begins.

1954 Independent Vietnam divided between North and South.

1957 Communist-led rebellion in South begins.

1960 US military aid to South begins.

1964 US intensifies military involvement and bombs North.

1967 US forces in South reach 500,000.

1968 Tet Offensive weakens US commitment to war.

1973 US withdraws troops.

1976 Socialist Republic proclaimed as North occupies South.

1979 Invades Cambodia and ousts Khmer Rouge.

1986 Economic reforms introduced.

1992 New constitution adopted.

1995 Diplomatic relations restored with US.

2001 Trade links with US restored.

2007 Further economic reform; joins World Trade Organisation.

2009 Pro-democracy activists imprisoned.

2010 Ruling Communist Party admits widespread corruption.

2011 Oil and gas exploration deal with India; party congress reappoints Nguyen Tan Dung as prime minister; pressure on dissidents intensifies.

2012 Communist Party leader admits corruption in state-owned enterprises.

2013 Curbs on freedom of expression and internet use intensify.

2014 China accused of violating Vietnamese sovereignty in East China Sea. Trade talks with US; tension with China intensifies.

2015 Ban on same-sex marriage ends. Extension of press censorship; free trade agreement with South Korea.

2016 Ruling Communist Party leadership changes. US ban on arms sales lifted.

2017 Effort to ease tensions with China over South China Sea islands.

INDONESIA.

1945 Indonesia declares independence from the Netherlands (recognised in 1949).

1957 President Sukarno introduces 'guided democracy', replacing the elected parliament with an appointed legislature.

1965 Thousands are killed as the Communist Party is banned following an attempted coup.

1966 General Suharto seizes power in an army coup and introduces a 'New Order'; he is elected president by a puppet People's Consultative Assembly in 1968.

1976 Occupation of the former Portuguese colony of East Timor provokes resistance; a separatist campaign begins in Aceh province.

1991 There is international condemnation of a massacre of East Timor demonstrators by Indonesian troops.

1996 Despite growing opposition, the ruling Golkar is returned to power with an increased majority.

1998 President Suharto resigns following intensifying opposition in the wake of economic crisis and is succeeded by President Habibie.

1999 Abdurrahman Wahid is elected President; East Timor referendum vote for independence provokes anti-separatist violence; growing separatist movements throughout Indonesia.

2000 Government threatened with financial scandal; corruption charges against Suharto fail; Irian Jaya separatists intensify campaign.

2001 Ethnic violence mounts; Wahid dismissed over corruption and incompetence charges; Sukarnoputri succeeds following clashes between rival supporters.

2002 East Timor independent; greater autonomy for Irian Jaya; agreement with separatist Free Aceh Movement (GAM); terrorist bombing in Bali kills 202.

2003 Clashes with GAM separatists; terrorists bomb Jakarta.

2004 Golkar election successes; President Megawati Sukarnoputri ousted in elections by Susilo Bambang Yudhoyono; over 200,000 die in tsunami.

2005 Aceh granted autonomy under peace agreement.

2006 Report accuses Indonesia of responsibility for over 100,000 deaths during East Timor occupation; former rebel leader Irwandi Yusuf elected governor of Aceh province.

2009 Truth Commission Report published. President Yudhoyono's Democratic Party wins largest share of seats in legislative elections and he is re-elected to office.

2010 Military operations continue against banned Jemaah Islamiah movement as leader is accused of plotting President Yudhoyono's assassination.

2011 Religious tensions heighten; radical Islamic cleric Abu Bakar Basyir imprisoned for terrorism, including 2002 Bali bombing.

2012 Umar Patek imprisoned for role in 2002 Bali bombing.

2013 Fuel subsidy cuts trigger protests; Netherlands apologises for 1940s independence war excesses.

2014 Ban imposed on mineral exports. Joko Widodo elected President.

2015 Government widens anti-poverty programme. Tension with Australia, Brazil and Netherlands over execution of drug traffickers; agreement with Malaysia on shelter for refugees.

2016 ISIS mount first terror attack in Jakarta. Chinese Christian governor of Jakarta faces blasphemy charges as 'political Islam' grows.

2017 Ban on unprocessed mineral exports eased.

6. AFRICA

Chronology of Events since 1957.

1957 Independence of Ghana under Nkrumah begins era of European decolonisation.

1958 Guinea becomes independent.

1960 Independence of Nigeria, Cameroon, Togo, Mali, Senegal, Belgian Congo, Somalia, Dahomey (now Benin), Niger, Upper Volta (now Burkina Faso), Ivory Coast, Chad Republic, Central African Republic, Congo Brazzaville, Gabon, and Mauritania; black South Africans massacred at Sharpeville; African National Congress (ANC) banned.

1961 Angolan independence struggle against Portugal begins; Sierra Leone and Tanganyika (later Tanzania) become independent; South Africa leaves Commonwealth; guerrilla resistance to apartheid regime begins.

1962 Uganda, Burundi and Rwanda gain independence.

1963 Organisation of African Unity formed; Guinea-Bissau independence struggle against Portugal begins; Kenya becomes independent.

1964 Malawi and Zambia gain independence; Mandela sentenced to life imprisonment in South Africa; Mozambique struggle against Portugal begins.

1965 Gambia becomes independent; Southern Rhodesia white regime declares illegal unilateral independence; Mobutu seizes power in Congo (renamed Zaïre in 1971).

1966 African resistance to white Rhodesian regime begins; South West Africa People's Organisation begins armed struggle against South African occupation; Botswana and Lesotho gain independence; Nkrumah ousted in Ghana coup.

1967 Biafran secession begins civil war in Nigeria (ends 1970).

1968 Emperor Haile Selassie of Ethiopia overthrown in military coup; Guinea-Bissau gains independence.

1969 Amin seizes power in Uganda (ousted in 1979).

1975 Economic Community of West African States formed; Angola, Mozambique and Cape Verde gain independence; civil war breaks out in Angola (ends 1994).

1976 Civil war in Mozambique (ends 1992); black South African protestors killed in Soweto.

1980 Mugabe wins first free elections in Zimbabwe.

1981 Long-running civil war begins in Somalia.

1984 900,000 die in Ethiopian famine.

1989 Civil war begins in Liberia.

1990 Namibia gains independence from South Africa; ban on black political organisations ends in South Africa.

1991 Apartheid ends in South Africa.

1992 Rawlings wins first democratic elections in Ghana.

1993 Southern African Development Community established.

1994 Mandela becomes President in first South African multi-racial elections; massacre of Hutus by Tutsis in Rwandan civil war.

1996 Civil war breaks out in Zaïre (now Democratic Republic of Congo).

1997 Kofi Annan becomes first black African United Nations secretary general; Mobutu ousted in Zaïre.

1998 Border war between Ethiopia and Eritrea; United States bombs Sudan for alleged terrorist links.

1999 Obasanjo wins Nigerian presidential election.

2000 Kufuor wins presidential election in Ghana; Islamic law (sharia) introduced in parts of Nigeria.

2001 OAU dissolved, replaced by the African Union.

2002 Mugabe approves confiscation of white-owned farms in Zimbabwe.

2003 Transitional government of national reconciliation formed in Congo Democratic Republic (formerly Zaïre).

2004 Commission for Africa, a British initiative to confront the continent's problems, holds first meeting in Ethiopia.

2005 Britain calls on wealthy nations to write off African debts; President Bush pledges to double aid to Africa by 2010; African Union leaders discuss regional political integration.

2006 China and 48 African states agree on economic and political partnership; African leaders launch campaign to guarantee every child education by 2015; Zambian President Levy Mwanawasa elected for second term.

2007 Libyan leader Col. Gaddafi urges formation of unified African army; Sidi Ould Cheikh Abdallahi wins Mauritania's first democratic elections; Ernest Bai Koroma elected Sierra Leone president.

2008 Coalition government in Kenya following election dispute; Ugandan government signs peace agreement with Lord's Resistance Army; Mohamed Ould Abdelaziz ousts Mauritanian president in military coup; Moussa Dadis Camara seizes power in Guinea in military coup.

2009 Ali Bongo Ondimba becomes Gabon president following rigged elections; China pledges $10 billion loans to Africa; Namibia's President Hifikepunye Pohamba wins second term.

2010 Alpha Condé's election as president restores civilian rule to Guinea; military coup ousts Niger president Mamadou Tandja; Kenya adopts new constitution; Laurent Gbagbo refuses to quit as Ivory Coast president despite election defeat by Alassane Ouattara.

2011 Civilian rule restored in Niger with election to presidency of Mahamadou Issoufou; French troops arrest Ivory Coast's President Gbagbo and place the elected President Ouattara in office; Michael Sata elected Zambian president; Liberian President Ellen Johnson Sirleaf re-elected for second term; popular risings across North Africa (Tunisia, Egypt, Libya).

2012 Joyce Banda becomes Malawi President on death of Mutharika; governing MPLA and President dos Santos returned in Angola elections; Sierra Leone President Koroma wins second term; Islamist rebels consolidate control in northern Mali; Uganda accused of aiding M23 rebels in Democratic Republic of Congo; Macky Sall elected Senegal President.

2013 Uhuru Kenyatta wins Kenya presidential election; French troops aid Mali government against Islamist rebels; Seleka rebels under Michel Djotodia seize power in Central African Republic; tension between Mozambique government and Renamo opposition; Uganda introduces anti-gay legislation.

2014 Hery Rajaonarimampianina becomes Madagascar President; Ebola outbreak in Guinea, spreads to Sierra Leone and Liberia; Peter Mutharika elected Malawi President; Mauritanian President Abdelaziz re-elected as opposition boycott election; UN peacekeeping mission as Mahamat Kamoun heads transitional government in Central African Republic; ruling FRELIMO win Mozambique legislative and presidential elections; Gambia withdraws from Commonwealth; Botswana Democratic Party wins elections; SWAPO's Hage Geingob elected Namibian President.

2015 Human rights groups launch secure website for whistleblowers; Chinese foreign minister denies 'empire building' in Africa; survey finds Botswana most prosperous African state; Lungu becomes Zambian President. Islamic militants kill over 140 in Kenyan university attack; Burkina Faso and Niger resolve long-running border dispute; John Magufuli elected Tanzanian President; Islamist terrorist attacks in Mali; Gabon government lifts opposition party ban; President Condé of Guinea wins second term; President Jammeh of Gambia declares Islamic republic.

2016 President Deby of Chad re-elected for fifth term; President Mbasogo of Equatorial Guinea returned as opposition boycotts election; President Bongo of Gabon re-elected; President Lungu of Zambia returned and his Patriotic Front wins National Assembly majority; Gambian President Jammeh refuses to accept electoral defeat by Adama Barrow.

2017 Ivory Coast soldiers revolt over pay; Namibian descendants of Herero and Nama people sue Germany over genocide in 1904-8 repression; suicide bomber kills over 70 in Mali; Gambian President Jammeh forced into exile.

ETHIOPIA.

Chronology of Key Events.

1896 Defeats Italians at Adowa to retain independence.

1930 Haile Selassie becomes Emperor.

1936 Italy annexes Ethiopia (Abyssinia) and retains control until 1941.

1952 Eritrea federates with Ethiopia; annexed in 1962.

1974 Serious famine; Haile Selassie overthrown in a coup by Teferi Benti.

1977 Colonel Mengistu seizes power in a military coup; Benti killed; 'Red Terror' against opponents begins.

1978 Tigre People's Liberation Front begins autonomy campaign.

1985 Serious famine.

1987 New constitution; Mengistu elected president.

1991 Mengistu flees after capital captured by Ethiopian People's Revolutionary Democratic Front.

1993 Eritrea becomes independent from Ethiopia.

1994 Republic of Ethiopia established under new constitution.

1995 Negasso Gidada becomes president and Meles Zedawi prime minister.

1999 Border war with Eritrea.

2000 Serious famine; ceasefire with Eritrea.

2001 Withdraws troops from Eritrea.

2003 Refuses to accepted independent commission border decision.

2004 Rural resettlement programme begins.

2005 Opposition successes against governing Ethiopian People's Revolutionary Democratic Front in elections; violent demonstrations over electoral irregularities; mass arrests of opposition members.

2006 Troops deployed in Somalia to support transitional government against Islamists; rising tension with Eritrea.

2007 Border dispute with Eritrea continues; opposition boycotts elections.

2008 Government promises to withdraw troops from Somalia.

2009 Ogaden National Liberation Front rebels claim successes in continuing fighting.

2010 Ruling EPRDF wins majority in disputed elections.

2011 Tension as government declares support for Eritrean rebels.

2012 Government denies continuing military presence in Somalia. Prime minister Zenawi dies; Haile Mariam Desalegne succeeds.

2013 Negotiations with Egypt and Sudan on Nile dam project.

2014 Government claims to have created four million jobs in past three years.

2015 Agreement with Egypt on Nile dam project. government calls for African withdrawal from International Criminal Court. Ruling EPRDF wins election; Obama first US president to visit country.

2016 Plans to expand capital scrapped after deaths in protests. African Union urges restraint in government repression of opposition protests; state of emergency declared.

2017 Two-year term as UN Security Council member begins.

SOMALIA.

1960 Independence from Britain and Italy.

1964 Border war with Ethiopia.

1969 Muhammad Siad Barre takes power in military coup.

1977–88 War with Ethiopia.

1991 Barre overthrown by opposition clans.

1992–94 UN peacekeeping force deployed.

2000 Transitional government established but opposed by warlords.

2004 New transitional government formed in Kenya.

2006 Transitional government holds first session in Somalia; Somali Council of Islamic Courts (SCIC) militia dominate capital and south of country; Ethiopian troops assist government in ousting them.

2007 President Abdullahi Yusuf returns; US air strikes on al-Qaeda outposts.

2008 Somali pirate activity increases; President Yusuf resigns.

2009 Sheikh Sharif Sheikh Ahmed becomes president, Omar Abdirashid Ali Sharmarke prime minister; state of emergency as violence intensifies.

2010 Al-Shabab militants ally with al-Qaeda; Mohamed Abdullahi becomes prime minister.

2011 Transitional government term extended further three years.

2012 New constitution; Hassan Sheikh Mohamoud becomes President.

2013 US recognises government and offers aid.

2014 US announces deployment of military advisers; Kenya bombs suspected terrorist base.

2015 East African foreign ministers meet in capital to discuss stabilisation. Kenya bombs al-Shabab bases following killing of 148 Christian students.

2016 UN says Somalia no longer a 'failed state'; al-Shabab overrun African Union base. African Union increases peacekeeping presence; widely criticised elections.

2017 UN reports growing food and water shortages.

ALGERIA.

1962 Gains independence from France.

1963 Ahmed Ben Bella elected first president.

1965 Houari Boumedienne overthrows Ben Bella.

1976 Boumedienne becomes president; introduces

socialist constitution; National Liberation Front sole party.

1978 Chadli Bendjedid becomes military-backed president.

1986 Strikes and riots over unemployment.

1989 Opposition parties legalised; Islamic Salvation Front (FIS) established.

1991 FIS wins first round of elections.

1992 National People's Assembly dissolved; Higher State Council under Mohamed Boudiaf takes power; FIS clashes with troops; Armed Islamic Group formed; FIS banned; Boudiaf assassinated.

1995 Liamine Zeroual elected president.

1996 Referendum approves constitutional changes.

1997 Democratic National Rally wins elections.

1999 Abdelaziz Bouteflika elected president; government talks with FIS armed wing, the Islamic Salvation Army.

2000 Continuing violence; 100,000 killed since 1992.

2001 Berber Rally for Culture and Democracy leaves government following Berber/army clashes; government makes concessions.

2002 Ali Benflis's National Liberation Front wins in general elections.

2004 President Bouteflika wins second term.

2005 Referendum supports amnesty for Islamist insurgents and reconciliation programme.

2006 Amnesty period begins; Islamic Salvation Front leader urged rebels to lay down arms. Al-Qaeda Organisation in the Islamic Maghreb terrorist attacks intensify; governing parties retain majority in elections.

2008 Terrorism incidents continue; constitutional changes allow President Bouteflika to run for a further term.

2009 President Bouteflika wins third term.

2010 Joint military command established with Mauritania. Mali and Niger to combat al-Qaeda Organisation in the Islamic Maghreb.

2011 Anti-Bouteflika protests repressed; 19-year state of emergency lifted; further terrorist bombings; Bouteflika promises independent broadcasting media.

2012 Ruling FLN/RND coalition holds power in elections.

2013 Islamist militants take foreign engineers hostage. Military action against al-Qaeda activists intensifies.

2014 Training for Libyan police and troops follows joint border agreement. President Bouteflika returned for fourth term.

2015 Protests over shale-gas exploitation in south. Continuing Arab-Berber clashes and Islamist attacks; falling oil prices threaten public spending.

2016 Constitutional reform to limit presidential term. Growing concerns over President Bouteflika's heath and Islamist threat.

2017 Protests over government austerity measures.

SUDAN.

Chronology of Key Events.

1956 Sudan gains independence from Britain and Egypt.

1958 General Abbud ousts civilian government.

1962 Civil war begins in the south.

1964 Abbud overthrown; national government established.

1969 Ja'far Numayri leads military coup.

1972 South becomes self-governing region.

1978 Oil discovered in south.

1983 Numayri introduces *sharia* (Islamic law), provoking rebellion in the predominantly Christian and animist south.

1985 Numayri deposed; Transitional Military Council formed.

1986 Civilian coalition government established.

1989 Military coup.

1993 Omar al-Bashir becomes president.

1998 US bombs pharmaceutical factory in Khartoum.

1999 Bashir dissolves National Assembly; declares state of emergency; oil exports begin.

2000 Bashir returned in disputed elections.

2001 Sudan People's Liberation Army (SPLA) rebels in south threaten attack on oil workers; Libya and Egypt mediate in civil war; US sanctions.

2002 SPLA begins negotiations with government.

2003 Bashir and SPLA leader John Garang meet for talks.

2004 Army confronts Darfur region rebellion; UN accuses pro-government Janjaweed Arab militia of slaughtering Africans in area.

2005 Government and southern rebels sign power-sharing peace agreement; newly appointed vice president killed in accident; accusations of genocide in Darfur.

2006 Government and main Darfur rebel group reach peace agreement but killings continue.

2007 UN proposes strengthening African Union peace force.

2008 UN assumes control of Darfur peace force; International Criminal Court (ICC) calls for President Bashir's arrest for war crimes in Darfur.

2009 ICC issues arrest warrant for President Bashir; UN declares end to six-year Darfur war between government and rebels; legislature passes law authorising referendum on independence for South Sudan.

2010 President Bashir returned in first elections for 24 years in widely criticised poll; ICC issues arrest warrant against Bashir for genocide.

2011 South Sudan gains independence following referendum; continuing clashes in South Kordofan state.

2012 Clashes continue with South Sudan over border oil fields.

2013 Oil production agreement with South Sudan; fighting in South Sudan after coup attempt. Humanitarian crisis.

2014 Ruling National Congress Party proposes lifting media restrictions.

2015 Government to host South Sudan civil war peace talks. Bashir returned in election boycotted by main opposition; Bashir ignores court order to remain in South Africa to face war crime charges.

2016 Referendum on status of Darfur. Military accused of 'scorched earth' tactics in Darfur.

2017 US eases trade sanctions after 20 years.

TUNISIA.

1956 Gains independence from France with Bourguiba as prime minister.

1957 Monarchy ousted; republic under President Bourguiba.

1975 Bourguiba becomes President for life.

1977 50 die in anti-government riots.

1981 National Front coalition wins 95 % of vote in first multi-party elections.

1983 Riots over rising food prices.

1987 Zine El Abidine Ben Ali ousts Bourguiba.

1989 Ben Ali wins uncontested presidential election.

1994 Ben Ali re-elected with 99 % of vote.

2004 Ben Ali wins fourth term with 94 % of vote.

2007 Clashes between security force and Islamists.

2009 Ben Ali wins fifth term; his Constitutional Democratic Rally (RCD) wins rigged legislative elections.

2010 Growing unrest over unemployment and inflation triggers 'Jasmine Revolution'.

2011 President Ben Ali flees; moderate Islamist Ennahda heads coalition following elections to constituent assembly; dissident Moncef Marzouki becomes President.

2012 Former President Ben Ali sentenced to life imprisonment *in absentia*; demonstrations against moves to reduce women's rights.

2013 Prime minister Jebali resigns after protests over opposition leader's assassination; succeeded by Ali Laarayedh.

2014 Laarayedh resigns, prompting elections. State of emergency lifted; Beji Caid Essebsi elected President.

2015 Habib Essid appointed prime minister. Many killed in Jihadist attack on Tunis museum. Islamist terrorists kill tourists in beach and museum attacks.

2016 Moderate Islamist Ennahda party gains majority in parliament. Habib Essid ousted as prime minister, succeeded by Youssef Chahed.

2017 Electoral Commission head says transition to democracy blocked; government seeks EU help against terrorism.

LIBYA.

1951 Becomes independent under King Idris.
1969 Gaddafi seizes power in military coup, nationalises oil.
1970 British and US bases closed.
1977 Renamed Great Socialist People's Libyan Arab Jamahiriyah.
1984 British police officer killed outside London embassy; UK severs relations.
1992 UN sanctions over alleged Libyan involvement in 1988 Lockerbie attack.
1999 Sanctions suspended when Libya hands over Lockerbie suspect for trial; UK restores relations.
2003 UN lifts sanctions; Libya ends weapons of mass destruction development.
2006 Diplomatic relations restored with US.
2009 Scotland releases Lockerbie bomber on health grounds.
2010 Agreement signed with EU on curbing illegal immigration.
2011 Gaddafi killed after overthrow in revolution.
2012 National Forces Alliance largest party following elections; US ambassador killed in militia attack; Ali Zidan becomes prime minister.
2013 Government moves against militias as security situation worsens; national assembly declares Islamic law basis of all legislation.
2014 Minister assassinated in Sirte; US begins training troops. Zidan dismissed; UN and diplomats withdraw as situation worsens.
2015 Army-militia ceasefire as factions open talks in Geneva. UN plan for national unity government collapses.
2016 ISIS terrorist attacks intensify.Precarious UN-backed 'Government of National Accord' established; abortive coup attempt.
2017 Attempt to resolve country's instability by Algeria, Egypt and Tunisia.

NIGERIA.

Chronology of Key Events.

1960 Nigeria becomes independent.
1963 Nigeria becomes a republic within the British Commonwealth.
1966 Civilian government overthrown in military coup by Major General Aguiyi Ironsi, who is then ousted by Colonel Yakuba Gowon.
1967 Biafra secedes, opening a three year civil war.
1970 Civil war ends with the surrender of Biafra.
1975 Gowon is overthrown in a bloodless coup by Brigadier Murkata Muhammed.
1976 Muhammed is assassinated and succeeded by General Olesegun Obasanjo.
1979 Nigeria returns to civilian rule under Shehu Shagari.
1983 Shagari is ousted by Major General Mohammadu Buhari.
1985 Buhari is overthrown by Major General Ibrahim Babangida.
1986 Babangida promises to restore civilian rule in 1990 but later postpones this to 1992.
1988 Rioting against the military government.
1989 Ban on political activity is lifted; two state-sponsored parties are formed.
1990 Unsuccessful coup against Babangida.
1992 The Social Democratic Party (SDP) wins legislative elections.
1993 SDP candidate Moshood Abiola elected President but military regime refuses to accept result; Babangida hands power to Ernest Shonekan as interim President but he is ousted by General Sani Abacha.
1995 Abacha promises restoration of civilian rule in 1998; Europe imposes economic sanctions following execution of Ken Saro-Wiwa.
1997 Multi-party municipal elections are held.
1998 Widespread boycott of legislative elections; Abacha dies in mysterious circumstances; his successor Olesegun Obasanjo promises to restore civilian rule.
1999 Obasanjo's People's Democratic Party (PDP) wins elections and Obasanjo becomes President; stability is threatened by growing ethnic conflict.
2003 Obasanjo's ruling party wins elections. Obasanjo re-elected president.

2004 State of emergency following Christian-Muslim clashes.
2005 Two-thirds of country's foreign debt written off by lenders; constitutional reform conference; attacks on pipelines in Niger Delta and further religious clashes.
2006 Senate rejects proposal to allow President Obasanjo a third term.
2007 Umaru Yar'Adua wins widely disputed presidential election.
2008 Attacks by the Movement for the Emancipation of the Niger Delta (MEND) intensify; renewal of sectarian violence in central Nigeria.
2009 MEND ends ceasefire and attacks commercial capital Lagos; sectarian clashes.
2010 Goodluck Johnson becomes President on death of Yar'Adua; terrorist attacks during independence celebrations.
2011 Johnson wins presidential election with 60 % of vote; Boko Haram intensify sectarian attacks.
2012 Bloody Boko Haram attacks continue in north. President Jonathan dismisses defence minister as Islamist attacks continue.
2013 State of emergency in north as Boko Haram Islamist militancy intensifies; key ruling party governors defect to opposition.
2014 Fears that Boko Haram rising may spread to 16 of country's 36 states. Joint action with Niger, Cameroon, Chad and Benin to combat Boko Haram.
2015 Boko Haram kill over 2,000 in Baga massacre. Muhammadu Buhari wins presidential election; Nigeria commands unified regional force to confront Boko Haram.
2016 $2 billion arms corruption scandal. President Buhari announces 20 % public spending increase to stimulate economy.
2017 Effort launched to end hunger in country by 2030.

GHANA.

Chronology of Key Events.

1957 Independence from Britain under prime minister Kwame Nkrumah.
1960 Becomes a republic; Nkrumah elected president.
1966 Military coup ousts Nkrumah.
1969 Civilian government restored under Kofi Busia.
1972 Military seize power.
1979 Military ruler Jerry Rawlings hands power to civilian President Hilla Limann.
1981 Rawlings ousts Limann in coup.
1992 Rawlings elected president under new constitution.
1996 Rawlings re-elected, defeating John Kufuor.
2000 Kufuor wins presidency, defeating John Atta Mills.
2004 Kufuor re-elected.
2007 Offshore oil discovery promises economic expansion.
2008 Mills narrowly elected president, defeating Nana Akufo-Addo.
2009 IMF grants $600 million three-year loan.
2010 Offshore oil production begins.
2011 Further oil discoveries off the coast.
2012 John Mahama becomes President on death of John Atta Mills.
2013 Mahama wins election as opposition dispute result.
2014 Troops deployed for South Sudan peacekeeping. Demonstrations over economic conditions.
2015 Government denies country returning to Highly Indebted Poor Countries league. IMF makes $918 million three-year credit available to stabilise economy.
2016 Demonstrations over rising prices in run-up to elections. Opposition candidate wins presidential election.
2017 Nana Akufo-Addo sworn in as President.

CONGO.

Chronology of Key Events.

1960 Congo gains independence from Belgium; there is immediate political upheaval.
1965 General Mobutu seizes power and rules as dictator; civil war continues until 1967.

1971 The country is renamed Zaïre.

1977 Anti-Mobutu forces unsuccessfully invade from Angola.

1990 President Mobutu promises democracy under international pressure.

1996 Zaïre is drawn into the Central African turmoil triggered by the Rwandan civil war.

1997 President Mobutu flees as rebels advance; long-term rebel leader Lauren Kabila takes power and the country is renamed the Congo.

1998 There is renewed civil war as rebel forces backed by Uganda and Rwanda advance; Angola, Zimbabwe and Namibia support Kabila.

1999 The combatants agree a ceasefire but violence soon resumes.

2001 Assassination of Kabila, who is succeeded by his son. Continued pressure to secure peace.

2002 Peace treaty promises end to 4-year civil war.

2003 President Kabila inaugurates a power-sharing administration including former anti-government rebels.

2004 Further clashes following a coup attempt.

2005 New constitution approved in referendum.

2006 President Kabila defeats Jean-Pierre Bemba in elections.

2007 Joins revived Great Lakes Economic Community with Rwanda and Burundi; border dispute with Uganda.

2008 Fighting with Tutsi rebels under Laurent Nkunda; UN strengthens peacekeeping force.

2009 Operation with Rwanda against Nkunda, who is arrested; President Kabila amnesties rebels in east of country.

2010 Government pressure on UN to withdraw peacekeepers; $8 billion debt relief from IMF and World Bank.

2011 New constitution strengthens President Kabila's position; Kabila defeats Tshisekedi in disputed presidential election.

2012 UN peacekeeping force supports government offensive against M23 rebels.

2013 M23 rebels end insurgency following defeat; UN/army offensive against Rwandan rebels in east.

2014 Troops clash with secessionist rebels in Katanga.

2015 Joint action with UN force against Hutu rebels in east. Violent protests over legislation to allow President Kabila third term.

2016 UN warns of violence in run-up to elections. Violent protests as President Kabila refuses to stand down, postponing elections.

2017 Government and opposition agreement on Kabila relinquishing office.

1990 ANC leader Mandela is released from prison.

1994 Mandela is elected President in South Africa's first multi-racial elections and heads a government of national unity.

1996 South Africa adopts a new constitution; the white National Party withdraws from the government of national unity and goes into decline.

1998 Truth & Reconciliation Commission—established to investigate the causes and results of apartheid—issues report after two years of hearings.

1999 ANC strengthens its position in elections, taking 66% of the vote, enabling the party to amend the constitution; Thabo Mbeki succeeds Mandela as President.

2004 ANC takes 70% of vote in elections; President Mbeki re-elected.

2005 President Mbeki dismisses ANC deputy leader Jacob Zuma following corruption allegations.

2006 Government suggests possible expropriation of white land for redistribution; Zuma reinstated as ANC deputy.

2007 Convincing ANC election victory; Zuma formally elected president.

2007 Public sector workers strike; Zuma elected ANC chairman.

2008 Attacks on foreign workers; Zuma absolved of corruption.

2009 ANC wins general election; Zuma becomes President; country goes into recession.

2010 Opposition Democratic Alliance local election successes.

2011 Ministers dismissed for corruption; ANC youth leader Julius Malema suspended for bringing party into disrepute.

2012 ANC centenary celebrations. Police kill 34 striking miners near Marikana.

2013 Report alleges worsening corruption; Mandela dies aged 95.

2014 300,000 strong metalworkers' union splits from ANC. Ruling ANC reduced majority in elections; President Zuma re-elected.

2015 Government moves against Zimbabwean migrants. President Zuma plans ban on foreign farm ownership to aid land redistribution; anti-government demonstrations after three finance ministers appointed in one week.

2016 Agriculture trade dispute with US resolved. ANC setback in municipal elections as Democratic Alliance makes gains; President Zuma survives third no confidence vote following corruption allegations.

2017 President Zuma urges ANC to choose woman leader.

SOUTH AFRICA.

Chronology of Key Events.

1948 The National Party takes office on a programme of apartheid or 'separate development'.

1952 A 'defiance campaign' against apartheid is organised by the African National Congress (ANC).

1955 Black, Indian and Coloured organisations adopt a Freedom Charter calling for a multiracial South Africa; eviction of the black population from designated 'white' areas begins.

1958 Progress of apartheid intensifies with the election of President Verwoerd; process of establishing 'independent' black homelands begins.

1960 76 black demonstrators against the Pass laws are killed in the Sharpeville Massacre.

1961 ANC forms Umkhonto we Sizwe (Spear of the Nation) to wage armed resistance.

1964 Nelson Mandela and other ANC activists are imprisoned for life following the Rivonia treason trial.

1976 Demonstrations in Soweto open a new phase of anti-apartheid agitation in which over 1,000 people are killed.

1984 State of virtual civil war in black townships; international companies begin withdrawing from South Africa.

1986 President Botha declares that South Africa has 'outgrown' apartheid.

1989 President de Klerk succeeds Botha and promises reform.

ZIMBABWE.

Chronology of Key Events.

1923 British colony of Southern Rhodesia is granted self-government under white rule.

1965 The white government illegally declares independence from Britain to avoid black majority rule.

1966 Guerrilla war against the white regime begins.

1977 The 'front line' African states step up support for liberation forces.

1979 The country is renamed 'Zimbabwe-Rhodesia' as a transitional government is established.

1980 The independent Republic of Zimbabwe is formed with resistance leader Robert Mugabe as prime minister.

1986 Mugabe's ZANU-PF wins an overwhelming majority in elections; he announces that he intends to create a one-party state.

1987 Mugabe becomes executive President with sweeping powers under a new constitution.

1990 Mugabe is re-elected as President and ZANU-PF wins the majority of seats in multi-party elections.

1992 The Land Acquisition Act allows the confiscation of white-owned farms for redistribution.

1996 Mugabe is re-elected President following the withdrawal of opposition candidates; Zimbabwe formally abandons Marxism-Leninism as a state ideology.

1997 As popular discontent grows, Zimbabwe faces a wave of strikes; Mugabe threatens to confiscate 12·3 million acres of white-owned land.

1998 There is rioting in Harare and a nationwide general strike over unemployment and widespread economic breakdown; concern grows over Zimbabwe's increasing involvement in the Congo civil war.

1999 International aid donors withdraw their support for Zimbabwe; there are demonstrations against Mugabe's proposed constitutional reforms; trade union leader Morgan Tsvangirai launches a Movement for Democratic Change to contest elections due in 2000.

2002 Mugabe re-elected president in flawed election. Expulsion of Zimbabwe from Commonwealth.

2003 Nationwide strike and mass arrests. Zimbabwe withdraws from Commonwealth.

2004 International sanctions intensify.

2005 Ruling ZANU-PF wins majority in widely criticised elections; IMF reports continuing economic decline.

2006 Life expectancy estimated at 30, the world's lowest.

2008 National Unity government formed after disputed elections; Mugabe remains president, Morgan Tsvangirai becomes executive prime minister.

2009 Tsvangirai sworn in as power-sharing administration prime minister.

2010 Tsvangirai accuses Mugabe of failing to consult unity government partners.

2011 EU sanctions on leading politicians eased; Tsvangirai says ZANU-PF attacks making co-operation unworkable.

2012 EU lifts some sanctions on leaders; Tsvangirai threatens to quit unity government over violence against his supporters.

2013 Referendum approves new constitution. Mugabe wins seventh term; US refuses to lift sanctions without political reform.

2014 Mrs Mugabe made head of Zanu-PF Women's League; Vice-President Mujuru dismissed for alleged assassination plot.

2015 Whites to be allowed to co-own farm land. President Mugabe chairs African Union, awarded Confucius Peace Prize by China; Zimbabwe dollar phased out.

2016 Journalists jailed for criticising government. Mounting protests against Mugabe regime; loyalist War Veterans' Association withdraws support.

2017 Growing crisis as businesses threaten to close.

7. NORTH AMERICA

THE UNITED STATES.

Chronology of Key Events.

1963 Kennedy assassinated; succeeded by Johnson.

1964 Gulf of Tonkin resolution allows Johnson to escalate Vietnam War; racial segregation is outlawed

1965 Watts Riots; Johnson attempts to build 'Great Society' with civil rights and welfare legislation.

1968 Growing opposition to intensifying Vietnam War; Martin Luther King and Robert Kennedy assassinated; Republican Nixon wins election.

1969 Gradual withdrawal from Vietnam begins.

1970 Invasion of Cambodia.

1972 Nixon defeats Democrat McGovern in presidential election; Nixon makes historic visit to China; 'Watergate' scandal begins.

1973 Vice-President Agnew resigns; replaced by Ford; Treaty of Paris ends US involvement in Vietnam.

1974 Nixon resigns; replaced by Ford.

1976 Democrat Carter defeats Ford in presidential election.

1978 Establishes diplomatic relations with China.

1979 Negotiates Camp David peace accord between Egypt and Israel.

1980 Reagan defeats Carter in presidential election.

1981 Reagan survives assassination attempt.

1983 Invades Grenada; Reagan announces proposed 'Star Wars' strategic defence initiative.

1984 Reagan re-elected.

1986 Bombs Libya for alleged terrorist involvement; 'Irangate' scandal reveals illegal arms sales to Iran to fund war in Nicaragua.

1988 Republican Bush elected president.

1989 Invasion of Panama to oust president.

1991 Leads coalition to force Iraq from Kuwait.

1992 Signs treaty with USSR formally ending Cold War; Democrat Clinton defeats Bush in presidential election.

1994 Clinton's health care reforms rejected by Congress; Clinton faces corruption and sexual impropriety allegations.

1996 Clinton re-elected.

1998 Bombs Afghanistan and Sudan in response to terrorism and also Iraq; Clinton impeached; acquitted in 1999.

1999 Leads bombing of Yugoslavia; returns control of Panama Canal to Panama.

2000 Republican Bush defeats Democrat Gore in disputed presidential election.

2001 Terrorist attacks on New York City and Washington DC; invasion of Afghanistan; Patriot Act gives government sweeping powers.

2002 President Bush describes Iraq, Iran and North Korea as part of an 'axis of evil'.

2003 Invasion of Iraq in pursuit of alleged weapons of mass destruction.

2004 President Bush wins second term; Republicans dominate the Senate and the House of Representatives.

2005 Hurricane Katrina aftermath raises questions about treatment of black Americans; growing unpopularity of Republicans following scandals and disillusion over Iraq war.

2006 Mid-term elections give Democrats control of Senate and House of Representatives.

2007 Domestic spending cut to meet cost of war; 'surge' of troops deployed in Iraq.

2008 Victory for Obama.

2009 Obama signs $787 billion economic stimulus package; offers 'new beginning' with Muslim world and 'new partnership' with Latin America.

2010 Health care reform bill passed against Republican opposition; new nuclear arms reduction treaty agreed with Russia; Republican gains in mid-term elections.

2011 US troops kill al-Qaeda leader Osama bin Laden in Pakistan; 'Occupy Wall Street' anti-capitalist protests.

2012 Obama announces defence cuts; Obama declares support for gay marriage; Obama re-elected; massacre at a Connecticut school prompts gun law reform calls.

2013 Senate budget deal avoids 'fiscal cliff.' Boston marathon terrorist attack. Kerry replaces Clinton as Secretary of State; leaks reveal extent of National Security Agency surveillance; federal government departments shutdown in clash over Affordable Care Act implementation.

2014 Obama announces NSA surveillance reforms, promises action on inequality. Riots over police shooting of unarmed black men; Republicans control Senate and House of Representatives following elections; report condemns CIA interrogation practices; links resumed with Cuba.

2015 Obama says 15-year shadow of war and economic crisis has passed. Historic meeting of Obama and Cuban leader. Troops to remain in Afghanistan; US and Cuban Presidents meet for first time in over 50 years, embassies re-open; troops deployed in Syria to assist rebels fighting ISIS; Supreme Court declares same sex marriage constitutional.

2016 Obama plans to tighten gun control, regrets leaving country more polarised in final State of the Union speech. Trump defeats Clinton in Presidential election; Republicans control Senate and House of Representatives.

2017 Trump sworn in as 45th President; issues executive orders on healthcare, a missile defence system, the Trans-Pacific Partnership, immigration, refugees and a wall with Mexico.

CANADA.

Chronology of Key Events.

1867 Dominion of Canada established.

1931 Canada gains autonomy under Statute of Westminster.

1949 Founding member of NATO.

1964 New flag adopted.

1967 French President de Gaulle declares 'Vive le Quebec libre' (Long live free Quebec).

1968 Liberal Pierre Trudeau becomes prime minister; Parti Quebecois (PQ) formed to campaign for Quebec independence.

1970 Quebec separatists kidnap British official.
1976 PQ wins elections in Quebec.
1980 Referendum rejects Quebec's independence.
1984 Progressive Conservative Mulroney becomes prime minister.
1992 Negotiations with US and Mexico on a North American Free Trade Agreement (NAFTA).
1993 Mulroney succeeded by Kim Campbell, Canada's first female prime minister; NAFTA treaty ratified; Liberal Jean Chrétien becomes prime minister following elections.
1995 Quebec referendum narrowly rejects independence.
1997 Chrétien returned with reduced majority.
2000 Chrétien re-elected prime minister.
2003 Supports US-led invasion of Iraq; Parti Quebecois loses to Liberals in Quebec provincial elections; Paul Martin replaces Jean Chrétien as prime minister.
2004 Martin returns as prime minister but Liberals lose overall majority.
2005 Government loses confidence vote.
2006 Conservatives under Stephen Harper form minority government after elections.
2008 Conservatives fail to win majority in elections; Harper forms third minority government.
2009 Parliament passes budget with economic stimulus measures; government denies cover-up of torture by troops in Afghanistan.
2008 Conservatives form minority government following election setback.
2009 Parliament passes economic stimulus package.
2010 Fails to secure seat on UN Security Council.
2011 Government defeated in confidence vote but gains majority in subsequent election; withdraws from Kyoto Protocol on climate change.
2012 Prime minister urges improved government relations with indigenous population.
2013 Budget emphasises eliminating federal deficit. Trade agreement with EU; claims North Pole and surrounding waters.
2014 Military operations end in Afghanistan; advisers deployed in Iraq; two soldiers killed by Islamist terrorists.
2015 Supreme Court rules oath of allegiance to Queen still required for citizenship applications. Liberals under Justin Trudeau win surprise election victory; participation in air war on ISIS in Iraq and Syria ends.
2016 Canada presses for nuclear non-proliferation. Comprehensive Economic and Trade Agreement (CETA) signed with EU.
2017 150th anniversary of Dominion of Canada celebrated.

8. SOUTH AMERICA

Chronology of Key Events.

1929 National Revolutionary Party (later the Institutional Revolutionary Party—PRI) formed in Mexico; retains power for 70 years.
1934 Mexican President Carderas introduces radical reform programme.
1937 Getulio Vargas seizes power in Brazil with military support; institutes authoritarian reformist regime.
1943 Military coup in Argentina; Brazil joins Allies in World War Two.
1945 Argentina declares war on Germany and Japan; Vargas ousted in Brazil.
1946 Peron elected Argentine president; re-elected in 1951.
1951 Former dictator Vargas elected Brazilian president.
1955 Military coup ousts Argentine President Peron.
1956 Period of economic growth in Brazil begins under President Kubitschek.
1959 Fidel Castro takes power in Cuban revolution.
1961 US backs Bay of Pigs invasion of Cuba; Cuba allies with USSR.
1964 Brazilian left-wing President Goulart ousted by military.
1966 General Ongania imposes military rule in Argentina.
1968 Student demonstrations violently suppressed in Mexico City.
1970 Allende becomes world's first democratically elected Marxist president in Chile; begins reform programme.
1973 General Pinochet ousts Allende in CIA-backed coup; establishes a dictatorship.

1974 Limited political activity restored to Brazil by President Geisel.
1976 General Videla seizes power in Argentina; regime wages 'Dirty War' against opponents.
1981 General Galtieri leads military coup in Argentina.
1982 Argentina invades Falklands (Malvinas); ejected by Britain.
1983 Civilian rule restored in Argentina.
1985 Neves elected as first civilian president in Brazil since 1964.
1988 New Brazilian constitution reduces presidential powers.
1989 Argentine President Menem introduces austerity programme; re-elected in 1995.
1993 Mexico joins Canada and US in North American Free Trade Agreement (NAFTA); Cuba introduces market reforms.
1994 Zapatista National Liberation Army (EZLN) rising begins in Mexico; Cardoso elected Brazilian president on pledge to stem inflation and introduce land reform.
1996 US trade embargo on Cuba made permanent.
1997 PRI loses majority in Mexican elections.
1999 Centre-left President de la Rua elected in Argentina faces economic problems; Brazilian President Cardoso elected for a second term.
2000 PRI ousted in Mexican elections; Alliance for Change leader Fox becomes president; demonstrations and strikes in Argentina; indigenous population mounts protests at Brazil's 500th anniversary celebrations.
2001 Chilean court suspends human rights charges against Pinochet on health grounds. Left-wing Alejandro Toledo elected as President of Peru.
2002 Colombia elects centre-right Alvaro Uribe as President; Ecuador elects left-wing government of Lucio Gutierrez; Brazil elects left-wing President Ignacio Lula da Silva.
2003 Centre-right Carlos Mesa becomes Bolivian President; Nicanor Duarte Frutos elected centre-right President of Paraguay; centre-left Ricardo Lagos elected in Chile.
2004 Centre-left President Tabare Vazquez elected in Uruguay.
2005 Socialist Evo Morales wins Bolivian presidential election; civilian authority over military commanders restored in Chile; President Toledo guilty of electoral fraud in Peru.
2006 Michelle Bachelet elected Chile's first woman president; Rene Preval elected President of Haiti; land reform and gas nationalisation in Bolivia; conservative Felipe Calderon elected Mexican president; Alan Garcia elected Peruvian president.
2007 Rafael Correa wins Ecuador presidential election; parliament of the Mercosur trade bloc inaugurated in Montevideo, Uruguay; Venezuelan President Chavez loses referendum on extending powers; Cristina Fernandez succeeds husband as Argentine president following election victory.
2008 Alvaro Colom elected Guatemala's first left-wing president; Union of South American Nations (Unasur) established by 12 Latin American states; 60-year rule of Partido Colorado in Paraguay ends with presidential election victory of former bishop Fernando Lugo.
2009 New Bolivian constitution extends rights of indigenous population following referendum; former left-wing rebel Jose Mujica elected president of Uruguay; Colombia grants United States access to military bases in war on drugs trafficking; Chile-Peru border dispute.
2010 Juan Manuel Santos elected Colombian president; Laura Chinchilla elected first Costa Rican female president; Dilma Rousseff elected first female Brazilian president; Sebastián Piñera defeats former President Eduardo Frei in Chilean presidential election; Raul Castro institutes market reforms in Cuba.
2011 Left-wing Ollanta Humala wins presidential election in Peru; Brazil and Bolivia sign agreement on combating drug trade; Uruguay revokes amnesty protecting officials implicated in 1973-85 dictatorship; violent student protests in Chile; Revolutionary Armed Forces of Colombia (FARC) leader Alfonso Cano killed;
2012 Colombia government sets out conditions for peace talks with rebel FARC; Chile outlaws sexual orientation discrimination; Franco replaces Lugo as Paraguay President following latter's impeachment; Ecuador grants political

asylum to Wikileaks founder Assange; Uruguay becomes first Latin American country after Cuba to legalise abortion.

2013 Bachelet elected Chilean President with 62% of vote; Cartes elected Paraguay President as his party takes control of legislature.

2014 Colombian President Santos re-elected; President Morales of Bolivia wins third term; Chilean students demand education reforms; UN sets new Peru-Chile maritime boundary; Vasquez elected President of Uruguay; FARC guerrillas in Colombia declare ceasefire.

2015 Guatemalan President Molina resigns over corruption allegations; Jimmy Morales wins subsequent election; Colombian government and FARC establish truth commission; former general David Granger elected President of Guyana; National Democratic Party wins majority in Surinam elections; Chilean President Bachelet eases abortion ban.

2016 Argentina, UK and local representatives agree on additional air service to Falklands (Malvinas); Pedro Kuczynski narrowly wins Peruvian presidential election; Bolivia referendum rejects allowing President Morales a further term.

2017 Chile moves to decriminalise abortion; Uruguay signs customs co-operation agreement with India; Bolivia and Paraguay agreement on future rail link; Colombia begins talks with ELN rebels.

ARGENTINA.

Chronology of Key Events.

1816 Independence from Spain.
1946 Peron elected president.
1951 Peron re-elected.
1955 Military coup ousts Peron.
1966 Gen. Onganía imposes military rule.
1973 Peron briefly in power, succeeded by wife.
1976 Gen. Videla seizes power; regime wages 'dirty war' against opponents.
1981 Gen Galtieri seizes power in coup.
1982 Invades Falklands ('Malvinas'); ejected by Britain.
1983 Civilian rule restored.
1989 Peronist President Menem elected; introduces austerity programme.
1995 Menem re-elected.
1999 Centre-left President de la Rua elected; severe economic problems.
2000 Demonstrations and strikes against austerity policies.
2001 Government defers payment of international debt; budget cuts provoke general strike; succession of presidents.
2002 Peronist President Duhalde says banking system collapsing; unemployment reaches 20%.
2003 Peronist President Kirchner elected.
2006 Debt to International Monetary Fund cleared with assistance from Venezuela.
2007 Former President Kirchner's wife elected president.
2008 Legislature approves plan to nationalise pension funds.
2009 Ruling centre-left Front for Victory suffers setback in legislative elections.
2010 Restrictions imposed on shipping to Falklands (Malvinas).
2011 President Kirchner calls for negotiations over the Falklands (Malvinas); re-elected president with 54% of vote.
2012 President Kirchner denounces British over Falklands on 30th anniversary of 1982 war, accusing Britain of 'militarising' the area.
2013 President Kirchner calls for negotiations over Falklands/Malvinas. Ruling Front for Victory losses in mid-term elections; left-wingers appointed to major government posts.
2014 Action threatened against oil drilling off disputed Falklands. Debt default for third time in 25 years.
2015 All public transport to carry sign 'Las Islas Malvinas son Argentinas'. The Conservative Mauricio Macri defeats Peronist Daniel Scioli in presidential election.
2016 Government calls for negotiations over future of the Falklands (Malvinas). Trade union demonstrations against austerity; former military dictator Bignone jailed for operating 1970s death squad.
2017 $6 billion loan from international banks.

BRAZIL.

Chronology of Key Events.

1822 Independence from Portugal.
1889 Republic established.
1937–45 Military dictatorship under Vargas.
1964–85 Under military rule.
1985 Civilian rule re-established.
1989 Fernando Collor de Mello elected president.
1994 Fernando Henrique Cardoso becomes president; land reform instituted.
2002 Luiz Inacio Lula da Silva ('Lula') elected president promising economic and political reform.
2004 Landless workers' movement occupies estates; demonstrations against conservative economic policy
2005 Lula apologises for corruption in ruling Workers' Party.
2006 Lula re-elected.
2007 Lula announced tax cuts and reduced public spending.
2008 Foot-and-mouth hampers beef exports; abortion legalisation rejected.
2009 Truth commission established on 1964–85 military dictatorship.
2010 Workers' Party candidate Dilma Rousseff elected first female president.
2011 Senior ministers resign following corruption allegations.
2012 Truth Commission begins hearings on 1964-85 military dictatorship; tax cuts in effort to revive economy.
2013 Former President Lula faces corruption allegations. Protests against rising transport fares and deteriorating public services.
2014 Land disputes between indigenous population and farmers intensify. President Rousseff wins second term.
2015 Rousseff promises anti-corruption action. Demonstrators demand Rousseff's resignation over oil corruption scandal; $17 billion austerity package; Rousseff faces impeachment proceedings.
2016 Violent clashes in cities over bus fare rises. Zika virus epidemic. President Rousseff impeached and dismissed, replaced by Michel Terner; austerity package freezes social spending for 20 years; anti-government demonstrations.
2017 Many deaths in continuing prison gang wars.

VENEZUELA.

Chronology of Key Events.

1811 Independence from Spain.
1947–8 President Gallegos overthrown after eight months by US-backed military coup.
1973 Leoni elected president; steel nationalised.
1989 Perez elected president; riots over austerity policies.
1992 Two abortive military coups by Col. Hugo Chavez.
1995 Caldera elected president.
1998 Chavez elected president.
2001 Chavez announces reforms to land and oil industry under extra-parliamentary powers.
2002 Chavez temporarily ousted in military coup.
2003 Chavez returned with 59% of vote.
2005 Reforms introduced to redistribute large estates; opposition boycotts National Assembly elections.
2006 Chavez wins third term with 63% of vote.
2007 Chavez announces plans to nationalise energy and telecommunications; granted power to rule by decree for 18 months.
2008 President Chavez issues decrees enlarging state role in economy.
2009 Referendum lifts limits on terms in office, paving way for Chavez to stand again.
2010 Currency devalued; opposition Democratic Unity legislative election gains.
2011 Concerns over President Chavez's health following treatment in Cuba.
2012 President Chavez elected to fourth term with 55% of vote.
2013 Chavez dies; Nicolas Maduro wins presidential

election. Armed forces deployed against violent criminals; workers' militia established.

2014 President Maduro urges co-ordinated action against violent crime. Oil price fall weakens economy.

2015 China offers $20 billion infrastructure investment. Rising tension with US; Democratic Unity National Assembly elections win ends 16 years of Socialist control.

2016 Maduro attempts to weaken Assembly powers. Government declares economic emergency, devalues currency and increases petrol price; anti-government protests.

2017 Opposition attempts to remove President Maduro from office.

9. AUSTRALASIA

AUSTRALIA.

Chronology of Key Events.

1901 Commonwealth of Australia established, unifying the country.

1931 Labour government defeated.

1941 War in Pacific closens relationship with USA.

1948 Australia encourages European immigration; over two million arrive in next three decades.

1950 Australian troops join UN force in Korean War.

1965 Australia sends troops to support US in Vietnam War.

1967 Referendum votes to delete from Constitution words that referred to "Aboriginal race" and "Aboriginal natives".

1975 Dismissal of Whitlam's Labour government by governor-general calls relationship with Britain into question.

1986 Australian law becomes independent of British legal and parliamentary system under Australia Act.

1992 Citizenship Act removes obligation to swear oath of allegiance to British Crown.

1993 Labour wins elections under Keating; Native Title Act grants Aborigines compensation for lost land.

1996 Liberals form coalition with National Party under Howard.

1998 Liberal-National coalition re-elected with reduced majority; constitutional convention votes to replace monarchy with president elected by Parliament.

1999 Referendum vote to retain monarchy by 55 % to 45 %.

2000 Accused by UN human rights committee of discriminating against Aborigines.

2001 Howard re-elected in November elections.

2002 88 Australians killed in Bali terrorist bombing.

2003 Senate no-confidence resolution on Howard over involvement in Iraq invasion.

2004 Race riots in Sydney; government announces cruise missile programme; Howard wins fourth term as prime minister.

2005 Troops deployed in Afghanistan; racial clashes in Sydney.

2006 Troops sent to Solomon Islands and East Timor; gas and oil treaty with East Timor.

2007 Landslide election victory for Kevin Rudd. Defeat for Howard.

2008 Mr Rudd declares worldwide economic crisis a 'failure of capitalism'.

2009 Government announces curb on immigration and economic stimulus measures.

2010 Rudd ousted by Julia Gillard; hung parliament follows elections.

2011 Economy grows; US to station marines on north coast.

2012 Gillard thwarts Rudd's abortive leadership challenge. Controversial carbon tax introduced.

2013 Australian troops leave Afghanistan. Gillard ousted as Labor leader by Rudd, who goes on to election defeat by Liberal-National coalition under Abbott.

2014 UN warns action against asylum seekers may breach international law. Appointment of knights and dames restored; Japan trade deal.

2015 Controversy over knighthood for Prince Philip. Malcolm Turnbull replaces Tony Abbott as Liberal leader and prime minister; free trade agreement with China.

2016 Growing political support for Australia to become a republic. Incumbent Liberal-National coalition wins narrow majority over Labor; terrorist plot uncovered.

2017 Health Minister resigns over expenses scandal; first indigenous cabinet minister, Ken Wyatt, appointed.

NEW ZEALAND.

Chronology of Key Events.

1907 Becomes dominion within British Empire.

1947 Gains full independence from Britain.

1951 Joins Anzus Pacific security treaty with Australia and US.

1984 Labour government elected, prime minister Lange institutes sweeping economic reforms.

1985 Refuses entry to nuclear-powered or armed ships.

1986 US ends obligations under Anzus pact.

1989 Palmer replaces Lange as prime minister.

1990 National Party defeats Labour; Bolger becomes prime minister.

1993 National Party narrowly re-elected; proportional representation introduced.

1997 Shipley becomes first woman prime minister; National Party in coalition with New Zealand First.

1998 Government ordered to return land to its Maoris.

1999 Clark becomes prime minister following Labour election victory.

2002 Prime minister Clark apologises to Samoa for colonial ill-treatment; Clark wins second term in elections.

2003 Troops deployed in the Solomon Islands with Australia.

2004 Government survives confidence vote over proposals to nationalise seabed against Maori opposition.

2005 Clark wins third term in narrow victory over National Party.

2008 National Party wins election.

2011 Earthquake hits Christchurch.

2012 Three soldiers killed in Afghanistan brings deaths to ten since 2003.

2013 Same-sex marriage legalised. Cunliffe replaces Shearer as Labour leader; voters reject state asset sales in non-binding referendum.

2014 Deployment of troops in Afghanistan extended till end of 2014. National Party heads minority coalition after elections.

2015 Referendum on national flag change proposed. Troops deployed to train Iraqi army in anti-ISIS operations.

2016 Free trade Trans-Pacific Partnership Agreement signed in Auckland; New Zealand votes to retain the national flag. Bill English becomes prime minister following Key's resignation.

2017 English optimistic about future trade talks with UK.

SPECIAL TOPIC

THE HISTORY AND DEVELOPMENT OF THE EUROPEAN UNION, 1957–2017

Chronology of Early Events.

1951 France, West Germany, Italy, Belgium, Luxembourg & the Netherlands (the Six) form European Coal and Steel Community (ECSC).

1957 The Six form the European Economic Community (EEC) under Treaty of Rome.

1962 Common Agricultural Policy established.

1963 President de Gaulle vetoes UK application to join EEC.

1973 UK, Ireland and Denmark join EEC (Greece 1981, Spain & Portugal 1986).

1989 Single European Act.

1991 Maastricht Treaty sets timetable for economic and monetary union.

1993 Single European Market comes into effect.

1995 Austria, Finland and Sweden join.

1997 Amsterdam Treaty prepares for membership enlargement to Eastern Europe.

1999 11 states adopt Euro as currency.

2000 Treaty of Nice increases centralised decision-making but allows national vetoes on tax and social security.

2004 Expansion of the EU (May) brings 10 new members. Draft EU Constitution agreed.

2007 Romania and Bulgaria joined. Treaty of Lisbon (Reform Treaty) signed.

2008 Referendum in Ireland rejects Treaty of Lisbon.

2009 Second Irish referendum votes in favour of Lisbon Treaty. Serbia applies for EU membership. Slovakia becomes 13th EU member to adopt euro.

2010 Ireland requires crisis bailout. Followed later by Greece and Cyprus in 2012.

2011 Estonia joins euro.

2013 Growing opposition to bailouts in Germany.

2014 Continued rise of anti-EU UKIP in Britain.

2015 Victory of the Greek anti-austerity party pledged to renegotiate bailout terms.

2016 Massive refugee influx tests Schengen Accord. British referendum rejects continued membership of the EU (*see* D22). Juncker calls for creation of an EU military headquarters.

Note: Following the outcome of the referendum in June 2016, the relationship of Britain and the EU may radically change. The exact future of that relationship is not yet settled, but some aspects of the information given below will alter.

The Background.

The European Union, which now incorporates almost all of western and much of central Europe, has grown out of a rare marriage of political idealism and political realism nurtured by considerable pragmatism.

The political idealism was focused, and largely remains focused, in the core continental states of western Europe—France, Germany and Italy. All three experienced defeat and occupation at some stage of the Second World War, and France and Germany had fought three wars in less than 80 years. The very concept of the nation state was perceived as flawed. The founding fathers of what was to become the European Union—Jean Monnet and Robert Schuman in France, Paul-Henri Spaak in Belgium, Konrad Adenauer in West Germany and Alcide de Gasperi in Italy—saw the future as lying rather in an ever closer integration of their peoples which would literally make another war impossible. They were also highly conscious of a very substantial common cultural heritage.

Realism and Idealism.

Political realism, however, was no less important than idealism. Integration was seen by Germany's neighbours as their surest defence against future German expansionism and by West Germany as its surest route to restored international respectability.

It was also favoured by the Benelux countries (Belgium, Netherlands and Luxembourg), who feared nothing more than a renewed conflict between their two great neighbours. Moreover, the perceived threat from the Soviet Union prompted unification in the economic as much as in the military sphere and some were to see the future European institutions as NATO's economic and political arm in Europe.

These twin impulses of idealism and realism were, however, to be associated with considerable flexibility and pragmatism. There has never been a blueprint for European integration, let alone unity, and the organs of what is now the EU have evolved significantly in response to changing political pressures from the member states. The consistent thread has been the core belief that economic integration is the surest route to wider integration, with the single market being the keystone to the whole structure.

The First Practical Moves: The Messina Conference.

The first practical move towards integration was the creation of the European Coal and Steel Community (ECSC) in 1952, which pooled the Belgian, Dutch, French, Italian, Luxembourg and West German raw materials essential for waging traditional warfare, but the real birth of what is now the EU was heralded at the Messina Conference of 1955. Representatives of the six ECSC member states there agreed to establish the common market in goods, people and services which came into force as the European Economic Community in January 1958 following the signing of the Treaty of Rome the previous year.

The British Attitude.

To the considerable disappointment of many in the six states, the British held themselves aloof for reasons which remain familiar. The British did not feel "European", they had been neither defeated nor occupied in the Second World War, and they trusted their nation state, sympathising with the view of the then leader of the Labour Party, Hugh Gaitskell, that entry into the "common market" would be the end of a thousand years of history.

Many felt more affinity with the United States or the Commonwealth, particularly perhaps on the right, and a number on the left suspected that the rules of the market would make it impossible to build socialism in Britain. Moreover, the British did not believe that the "common market" would work and instinctively saw moves towards European integration as a threat. They, therefore, actively promoted the European Free Trade Association as an alternative, but to no lasting avail. The "common market" did work, while the British economy comparatively lost ground. However, the European Economic Community proved an irresistible magnet to its neighbours, with the British themselves, together with Denmark and the Republic of Ireland, being in the first wave of new members in 1973. Greece joined in 1981, and Spain and Portugal in 1986. The former East Germany became a member on German unification in 1990. Austria, Finland and Sweden followed in 1995. Only oil-rich Norway, remote Iceland, and traditionally neutral Switzerland remained outside.

The 1975 British Referendum.

Although the referendum on British membership of the European Community was conclusive, British motivation was essentially economic. There was little understanding of, or sympathy with, the concept of integration, and that situation has changed little in the years since them. Sir Edward Heath and Lord Jenkins of Hillhead remained the only two major political office holders to give it consistent support. A further difficulty is that the British were, and are, ill at ease with the institutional framework of the Community, now Union, which reflects continental rather than UK practice. Their reserve is focused on the Commission, which is the EU's Brussels based civil service headed by the commissioners and a commission president, all nominated by the member states.

The EU Commission.

Although the Commission must swear loyalty to the Union as a whole, the most effective presidents are normally those who can rely on the political support of at least one major member state. Current and former presidents are listed on **D15**.

The Commission was envisaged by the founding fathers as "the motor of the Community" and, in accordance with French practice, it promotes legislation on its own initiative as well as at the request of the other EU institutions. The relevant commissioners also represent and speak for the EU in international negotiations. It is often alleged that these characteristics make the Commission anti-democratic but such criticisms ignore the fact that the Commission has no power of decision. That power has largely lain with the council of ministers, whose membership reflects the topic under discussion (energy, environment, finance *etc.*) and is composed of the ministers of the member states, in consultation with the European Parliament.

The European Parliament.

The Parliament, which meets in Strasbourg, is one of the original institutions of the Union, and was envisaged as its source of direct democratic legitimacy. Initially nominated, it has been directly elected since 1979, and it has grown steadily in significance. Since the enactment of the 1997 Treaty of Amsterdam it has shared the power of decision on a wide range of issues, including the environment, with the council of ministers. For all these advances it is yet to establish itself fully.

Despite, and sometimes even because of, its real impact on many sectors of policy-making, it is suspect to many national governments, widely resented by other parliamentarians and a subject of general indifference for the public. Following the admission of Croatia to the EU it now has 766 members (MEPs). The 2014 elections to the European Parliament were the last in which Britain voted for MEPs.

Party Groupings.

The Parliament, like the Commission, operates in a fundamentally non-British way. A combination of differing national political traditions, the use of proportional representation, and in some countries very fluid political groupings, means that majorities have to be assembled issue by issue. There is no equivalent to the Westminster model whereby a disciplined majority provides and supports the government for a period of up to 5 years. Instead, there are usually about eight transnational groupings, of which the socialists have usually been the largest and the most organised. The British Conservatives worked somewhat less readily with the continental Christian Democrats under the banner of the European People's Party, but they left in 2009 to join the newly-formed European Conservatives and Reformists. The Liberals, the Greens, and the UK Independence Party participate in comparable groupings.

The European Council.

The Treaty of Rome envisaged a balance between Commission, Parliament and council of ministers but it has been supplemented by the rapid growth in importance of the European Council, which brings together heads of government every six months. It is these summit meetings which determine the future direction of the EU and attempt to resolve the major tensions between member states and between sectoral policies. The chairmanship of the European Council and the council of ministers (the "presidency") is held by the member states for six month terms in rotation. Eurosceptic opinion often argues that the European Council, representing as it does the national governments alone, is the only legitimate form of European co-operation, and would abolish both the Parliament and the pro-active role of the Commission. It seems unlikely, however, that other member states would ever agree to such a radical course of action.

Other Specialised Bodies.

The major institutions described are supported by a range of more specialised bodies of which the more important include the Economic and Social Committee in Brussels, which is a consultative body composed of employer, employee and public interest representatives, the European Investment Bank in Luxembourg and the Court of Auditors, also based in Luxembourg, which conducts rigorous reviews of the effectiveness of EU programmes. The Commission is obliged to respond publicly and in writing to the Auditors' criticisms. The most important of the Luxembourg based institutions, however, is the European Court of Justice, which resolves conflicts between EU legislative acts and has the power to levy heavy fines on member states for non-compliance with EU legislation.

Expanding the EU: The Copenhagen Summit.

The EU opened accession negotiations with the Czech Republic, Cyprus, Estonia, Hungary, Poland and Slovenia in 1998, and at the Helsinki summit in December 1999 it agreed to open negotiations with all the other applicants for membership as well, namely Bulgaria, Latvia, Lithuania, Malta, Romania, Slovakia and Turkey.

Those negotiations were complex but the EU decided at the Copenhagen summit in December 2002 that, except in the cases of Bulgaria, Romania and Turkey, they had advanced sufficiently to offer the candidate countries membership in 2004. Bulgaria and Romania joined on 1 January 2007 but the possible entry of Turkey has so far not been resolved.

The Nice Summit.

It was at the Nice Summit in December 2000 that the EU seriously grappled with the political consequences of enlargement for the first time. Nevertheless, some changes were accepted without which enlargement would have meant paralysis. Qualified majority voting in the Council of Ministers was to be extended to 35 more areas, mostly minor but including the appointment of the president of the Commission. The number of votes available for both current and future member states was changed by agreement to a potential total of 342 with 27 member states. 255 votes are needed for a qualified majority, but there is also provision for a blocking minority of 88 votes.

The reallocation of votes protected the interests of the then four larger member states—France, Germany, Italy and the UK—who had 29 votes each, but a further, reserve provision confers a modest advantage on Germany with its appreciably larger population. The provision enables any member state to invoke a clause requiring the support of 62% of the EU population for any decision reached by a qualified majority vote. The importance of the provision may prove primarily symbolic in recognising united Germany's prime status in the EU of the twenty-first century, and it may actually contribute with other reserve provisions to making EU decision-making harder. Lastly, the larger member states agreed to forego from 2005 their right to nominate a second Commissioner, and each new member state will have a right to nominate a Commissioner until a total of 27 is reached.

The Proposed EU Constitution.

These wider practical and strategic considerations have a direct bearing on the seemingly unrelated issue of the EU constitution. Originally conceived as a means at one and the same time of codifying and simplifying the numerous agreements, practices and treaties which have accompanied the European Union since its foundation under the Treaty of Rome in 1957, and of allowing the Union to cope with the challenge of enlargement, a draft was produced in 2003 by a constitutional convention chaired by the former French president, Valéry Giscard d'Estaing. Initially considered at an acrimonious Summit in Brussels in December 2003 which collapsed under a dispute over national voting rights, it was finally adopted at a scarcely less acrimonious Summit on 18 June 2004.

The 2005 Referendum Bombshells.

In mid-2005 the EU was suddenly thrown into turmoil by the referendum outcome in France and the Netherlands on the proposed EU constitution. On 29 May, France voted no by 55% to 45%. For France, one of the six founding members of the European Community, to vote no was a disaster. On 1 June the Netherlands rejected the proposed constitution by a landslide (62% to 38%). If the reasons for the Dutch rejection were perhaps different (many Dutch feared loss of sovereignty and were angry at their level of EU Budget contributions), the consequences were the same. Europe, and the vision of integration, was in turmoil.

Within a few days in the early summer of 2005, the EU had suddenly faced one of the most profound crises in its history.

The 2007 Reform Treaty (Treaty of Lisbon).

The paralysis in the EU following the referendum bombshells lasted until the June 2007 Brussels Summit where agreement was finally reached on a proposed compromise Reform Treaty. Its main provisions were the creation of a new full-time post of President to chair European Council meetings (to be held for 2½ years and renewable for an extra term), a smaller European Commission from 2014, a new post of EU Foreign Minister, a maximum total of 96 MEPs from any single country, a Charter on Fundamental Rights (with Britain granted an opt-out), an extension of qualified majority voting (again with a British opt-out) and a compromise deal on voting rights (to satisfy Poland). The Reform Treaty became the Treaty of Lisbon when all EU members signed up to it at the end of 2007. However, the rejection of the Lisbon Treaty by Irish voters in a referendum in 2008 caused a renewed paralysis over the EU's future direction. However, a second referendum in October 2009 reversed this vote. The first President of the European Council was the Belgian Herman van Rompuy.

The Euro Crisis: The Greek Deficit.

The European Union was dominated by the impact of the global financial crisis and the threat to the stability, if not the survival, of the Euro. In late 2009 the Greek government admitted the extent of the country's deficit. The German chancellor, Mrs Merkel, argued forcefully that Europe would not support the Greek economy until the government introduced stringent austerity measures. Greece announced severe public spending cuts in March 2010, provoking violent protests, and in May was granted a €110 billion three-year rescue package. The 27 EU members agreed on 9 May on *ad hoc* arrangements to protect the Euro from the threat of sovereign insolvencies by making available assistance from a fund made up of €440 billion from the Eurozone states (raised through bond sales), €250 billion from the International Monetary Fund and €60 billion from the wider EU.

The Crisis in Ireland and Portugal.

Attention then turned to Ireland where the government revealed in September that the continuing cost of supporting failing banks had pushed the budget deficit to 32% of GDP. An EU summit in October agreed a reform plan aimed at preventing a recurrence of the sovereign debt crisis by strengthening each state's budget discipline, thereby effectively co-ordinating economic policies and establishing a permanent Eurozone crisis resolution mechanism. This implied a drastic revision of the Lisbon Treaty. As the Irish crisis intensified, European finance ministers agreed in November to provide a €85 billion rescue package, €50 billion of which was to enable the government to maintain essential public spending. There were growing fears in late 2010 that the crisis would spread to the weaker Eurozone members, Portugal, Spain, Italy and Belgium. In December EU leaders formalised the May agreement into a permanent European Financial Stability Facility (EFSF) from 2013. In January 2011 Germany's finance minister rejected European Commission President Jose Manuel Barroso's proposal to increase the EFSF fund's size.

The resignation of the Portuguese prime minister in March following rejection of his government's proposed austerity budget made an EU bailout package similar to that of Greece and Ireland almost a certainty.

Fiscal Compact and Greek Turmoil.

The developing crisis threatened not only the survival of the Euro as a common currency, but also the European Union itself. In November 2011 Chancellor Merkel of Germany declared, 'Europe is in perhaps its most difficult hour since World War Two'. In the course of the year, the governments of Ireland, Portugal, Spain, Greece and Italy collapsed under the burden of sovereign debt, the latter two replaced by unelected 'technocratic' administrations. Numerous summit meetings, dominated by Chancellor Merkel and French President Sarkozy, served only to demonstrate that Europe's politicians had little idea of how to resolve the crisis. In October they constructed yet another package of measures to avoid economic collapse, followed in December by agreement - with Britain demurring - on closer fiscal integration across the Eurozone, with strict and enforceable tax and spending rules. Such an austerity programme, some commentators said as 2012 opened, posed the danger of pushing Europe back into recession and preventing any future expansionary policy.

The new fiscal compact was signed by 25 EU countries on 2 March 2012, only Britain and the Czech Republic standing aside, as unemployment in the Eurozone reached a record high of 10·7%.

In May 2012, following an inconclusive election in Greece, European stock markets plunged as fears of a Greek Eurozone exit rapidly grew. In September, in an attempt to reassure the markets, the European Central Bank unveiled a program under which the bank would buy unlimited quantities of government bonds from troubled eurozone members (provided assistance had first been sought from Europe's bailout facility).

The 2014 Elections.

Much attention was centred on how Europe would vote in the 2014 elections, not least over how well Eurosceptic parties would fare at the polls. In the event, the fears of a Eurosceptic upsurge were justified. The National Front topped the poll in France (the first time it had ever won a nationwide vote) whilst extremist parties did well in Denmark, Austria and Greece. There was particular interest concerning how well the extreme right in France would perform and also the resurgent UKIP in Britain. A further factor concerned the unrest in Ukraine, where Russia had annexed the Crimea and had helped foment nationalist fervour in eastern Ukraine. Would other extremist nationalist groups in eastern Europe, such as Jobbik in Hungary, also benefit?

In Britain, the Eurosceptic UKIP came top of the poll, winning 24 seats. The pro-European Liberal Democrats were virtually wiped out. The voters of Europe had delivered a damning verdict – even if turnout was only marginally up on 2009.

The Advent of Juncker.

Former Luxemburg prime minister Jean-Claude Juncker succeeded José Manuel Barroso as President of the European Commission in November 2014, despite controversy over his role in Luxemburg's position as a centre for corporate tax avoidance. The Swiss National Bank's abandonment of franc-euro parity underlined the euro's fragility. In January 2015 the European Central Bank launched a €1·1 trillion quantitative easing programme in an effort to revive the sluggish Euro-economy.

The Greek crisis provided evidence of how the EU, led by Germany, could deal with a member state threatening not only the Euro but also the EU as an institution. Greece went through two elections, a referendum, and protracted bailout negotiations before reluctantly accepting an austerity programme that enabled the country to retain the Euro as a currency and remain in the EU. More widely, the pace of EU economic recovery in 2015 was irregular, though European Central Bank quantitative easing boosted export industries through a weak Euro.

The Refugee Crisis.

Far more endangering to EU stability was the refugee crisis that took a dramatic turn in 2015. The flow of refugees – by sea across the Mediterranean and by land through the Balkans – intensified until by August 2015 the United Nations estimated 3,000 a day were entering the Balkans en route in most cases to northern Europe. A reluctant agreement in September to distribute refugees across member states made slow progress. Of the estimated million asylum seekers arriving in 2015, half fled Syria and a quarter Afghanistan. Germany, which initially welcomed those in flight, estimated that over a million asylum seekers entered the country by the year's end. The crisis called into question a core element of the EU project, 'free movement of people' under the 1995 Schengen Convention. In July 2015 Hungary erected a fence to prevent refugees crossing from Serbia. Austria, Slovakia, Sweden, Denmark and Italy temporarily reintroduced border controls, while Germany restricted entry from Austria and tightened conditions. In January 2016 the French prime minister, Manuel Valls, declared the refugee crisis was putting the concept of Europe in danger.

Other Developments.

After protracted negotiations, the EU and Canada finalised the Comprehensive Economic and Trade Agreement in October 2016 and in December Cuba and the EU signed an accord to normalise relations.

The 2016 British Referendum and after.

For the background to the in-out referendum held in Britain on 23 June 2016 and an analysis of the outcome, *see* **D22.** Following the referendum, the new Prime Minister, Theresa May, began taking the necessary steps to trigger Article 50 and so begin the formal withdrawal process of the UK from the European Union. On 29 March 2017 that process was formally begun.

MEMBERSHIP OF THE EUROPEAN UNION (as at May 2017)			
Country	**Date of Joining**	**Country**	**Date of Joining**
Austria	1 January 1995	Italy*	1957
Belgium*	1957	Latvia	1 May 2004
Bulgaria	1 January 2007	Lithuania	1 May 2004
Croatia	1 July 2013	Luxembourg*	1957
Cyprus	1 May 2004	Malta	1 May 2004
Czech Republic	1 May 2004	Netherlands*	1957
Denmark	1 January 1973	Poland	1 May 2004
Estonia	1 May 2004	Portugal	1 January 1986
Finland	1 January 1995	Romania	1 January 2007
France*	1957	Slovakia	1 May 2004
Germany*	1957	Slovenia	1 May 2004
Greece	1 January 1981	Spain	1 January 1986
Hungary	1 May 2004	Sweden	1 January 1995
Ireland	1 January 1973	United Kingdom**	1 January 1973

*Original founding member.** Negotiations for withdrawal now underway.

BRITAIN TODAY

This section provides a compact reference work of key facts and figures for an understanding of the background to government and politics in Britain today. It is fully revised each year to take account of the most recent political developments. There is material on elections, parliament, political parties, the Cabinet, trade unions, local government, the civil service, pressure groups *etc*. There is also an outline summary of events up to the historic referendum of June 2016, the advent of Theresa May as Prime Minister and an analysis of the 2017 general election which resulted in a hung parliament.

TABLE OF CONTENTS

BRITAIN TODAY

THE MONARCHY

The Queen is a constitutional monarch. In law she is the head of the executive, an integral part of the legislature, head of the judiciary, commander-in-chief of the armed forces and temporal head of the Church of England. In practice, the Queen's role is purely formal; she reigns, but she does not rule. In all important respects she acts only on the advice of her ministers. However, she still plays an important role symbolically. *See also* G3–4.

GENERAL ELECTIONS

For electoral purposes the United Kingdom is divided into 650 constituencies each returning one MP to the House of Commons. Scotland returns 59 MPs. In the 2010 election 79 old constituencies ceased to exist, 83 were created. There were no changes in 2015 or in 2017. In 2011, a law requiring a reduction in the number of MPs to 600 was passed, but in 2013 when a boundary review was blocked by the Liberal Democrats, no action was taken.

All British subjects and citizens of the Irish Republic are entitled to vote provided they are 18 years old and over and are included on the electoral register which is compiled annually. Each person is now responsible for ensuring his or her name is on the electoral register (previously it was the head of the household). For the September 2014 referendum in Scotland 16- and 17-year olds were given the vote. Expatriates (around 5·6 million of them) can vote in UK and EU elections, (the old 15-year time limit is planned to be scrapped).

Postal votes were introduced for servicemen in 1918 and in 1948 for any voter with a justifiable reason (*e.g.* absence from home). Trials of on-line voting have been proposed. It is also proposed that voters should have to produce ID when they go to vote.

Voting in Britain is not compulsory (unlike such countries as Australia, Austria, Belgium or Greece).

The main exceptions to those allowed to vote are members of the House of Lords and those incapacitated through insanity or imprisonment (although certain relaxations of these rules are currently being proposed for less serious offenders).

Anyone who is entitled to vote and aged at least 18 may stand as a candidate, the exceptions being undischarged bankrupts, together with holders of certain public offices. Anglican clergy may now serve as MPs.

All candidates have to pay a deposit of £500, which is forfeited unless they receive 5 % of the votes cast. In each constituency the winning candidate has (under the present voting system) only to obtain a simple majority.

General Elections since 1959

VOTES CAST (thousands)

	Conservative	Labour	Liberal*	Communist	Plaid Cymru	SNP	Others
1959	13,750	12,216	1,639	31	78	22	125
1964	12,023	12,206	3,093	46	70	64	168
1966	11,418	13,095	2,328	62	61	128	171
1970	13,145	12,198	2,117	38	175	307	384
1974 (Feb.)	11,910	11,646	6,059	33	171	632	958
1974 (Oct.)	10,501	11,457	5,347	17	166	840	897
1979	13,698	11,532	4,314	17	133	504	1,024
1983	12,991	8,437	7,775	12	125	331	952
1987	13,761	10,030	7,340	6	124	417	859
1992	14,092	11,563	6,003	–	154	630	1,178
1997	9,590	13,550	5,243	–	161	622	2,440
2001	8,355	10,740	4,813	–	196	464	1,794
2005	8,772	9,556	5,982	–	174	412	2,234
2010	10,728	8,609	6,833	–	165	491	2,862
2015	11,335	9,344	2,416	–	182	1,454	**
2017	13,650	12,850	2,360	–	164	980	***

* 1983 and 1987 figures for Liberals include the SDP total. Recent figures are for Liberal Democrats.
** The largest votes in this category were UKIP (3,881,129) (12·6 %) and Greens 1,157,613 (3·8 %).
*** The largest votes in 2017 in this category were UKIP (590,000), followed by the Greens.

SEATS WON

	Conservative	Labour	Liberal*	Communist	Plaid Cymru	SNP	Others (GB)	Others (NI)	Total
1959	365	258	6	0	0	0	1	0	630
1964	304	317	9	0	0	0	0	0	630
1966	253	364	12	0	0	0	0	1	630
1970	330	288	6	0	0	1	1	4	630
1974 (Feb.)	297	301	14	0	2	7	2	12	635
1974 (Oct.)	277	319	13	0	3	11	0	12	635
1979	339	269	11	0	2	2	0	12	635
1983	397	209	23	0	2	2	0	17	650
1987	376	229	22	0	3	3	0	17	650
1992	336	271	20	0	4	3	0	17	651
1997	165	419	46	3	4	6	1	18	659
2001	166	413	52	0	4	5	1	18	659
2005	198	356	62	0	3	6	3	18	646
2010	307	258	57	0	3	6	1	18	650
2015	331	232	8	0	3	56	2	18	650
2017	318	262	12	0	4	35	1	18	650

Others (NI): Ulster Unionists regarded as Conservatives 1929–70.
* 1983 and 1987 figures for Liberals include SDP MPs. Since 1992 figures are for the Liberal Democrats.

By-Elections 1979–June 2017

Parliament	Government	No. of By-elections	Changes	Con. +	Con. –	Lab. +	Lab. –	Lib. Dem.* +	Lib. Dem.* –	Others +	Others –
1979–83	Con.	20	6	1	4	1	1	4	1	—	—
1983–87	Con.	31†	6	—	4	1	1	4	—	1	1
1987–92	Con.	24	8	—	7	4	1	3	—	1	—
1992–97	Con.	18	9	—	8	3	—	4	—	2	1
1997–01	Lab.	17	2	—	—	—	—	1	—	1	1
2001–05	Lab.	6	2	—	—	—	2	2	—	—	—
2005–10	Lab.	14	4	2	—	—	4	1	—	1	—
2010–15	Con./LibDem	20	4	—	3	1	1	—	—	3	—
2015–17	Con.	11††	1	—	1	—	—	1	—	—	—

* Liberal 1945–79; Alliance (Liberal and SDP) 1979–89, Liberal Democrat after 1990.
† Includes 15 by-elections held in Northern Ireland in January 1986 following Unionist resignations.
†† From May 2015 to June 2017 only one seat changed hands (Richmond Park).

General elections must be held every five years. If a seat falls vacant between general elections a by-election is held on a date usually chosen by the party which previously held the seat. Elections have generally been held on Thursdays.

Electoral Reform

As part of the Conservative–Liberal Democrat Coalition Agreement, a referendum on whether to adopt the AV system was proposed. Despite opposition in Parliament, this was duly held on 5 May 2011. The AV system was rejected by 67·9 % to 32·1 %.

First Past The Post (FPTP): the current system used to elect MPs—whoever gets the most votes in a constituency wins.

Alternative Vote (AV): a system whereby candidates are ranked by electors and redistributed until a candidate with 50 % support emerges.

AV-plus: *(see above)*

Additional Member System (AMS): The system used for the Scottish Parliament and Welsh Assembly. Essentially FPTP with top-up list elected by proportional representation

Single Transferable Vote (STV): Multi-member seats elected by proportional representation—system favoured by Liberal Democrats. Used in Scottish local elections (since 2007).

TURNOUT AND MAJOR PARTY SHARE

Turnout (%)		Share of Poll (%)		
		Conservative	Labour	Liberal
1945	73	40	48	9
1950	84	44	46	9
1951	83	48	49	3
1955	77	50	46	3
1959	79	49	44	6
1964	77	43	44	11
1966	76	42	48	9
1970	72	46	43	8
1974 (Feb.)	78	38	37	19
1974 (Oct.)	73	36	39	18
1979	76	44	37	14
1983	73	42	28	26*
1987	75	42	31	23*
1992	78	42	34	18**
1997	72	31	43	17**
2001	59	32	41	18**
2005	61	33	36	22½**
2010	65	36	29	23**
2015	66	37	30	8**
2017	69	42	40	7**

* includes SDP figures.   ** Liberal Democrats

POLITICAL PARTIES

For their background, *see under* Conservatism, Liberalism and Socialism in **Section J**.

Party Leaders

In 1993, Labour adopted a more democratic system for electing future leaders. This system was used to elect Tony Blair in 1994 after the death of John Smith. Gordon Brown was elected unopposed in 2007 while in 2010 the leadership election was narrowly won by Ed Miliband (who defeated his brother David). The one-member, one-vote system was adopted in March 2014.

In the 2015 leadership election, when members, registered supporters and affiliated supporters could vote, the comfortable victor was Jeremy Corbyn with 59·5 % of the vote. In the 2016 leadership election, when Owen Smith challenged Jeremy Corbyn, only members who had signed up before 12 January 2016 could vote. Corbyn took 61·8 % of the vote.

The Social and Liberal Democrat leader is elected by party members nationally. The last leadership election (in 2015) followed the general election rout. Tim Farron beat Norman Lamb.

Changes to the method of electing a Conservative leader were adopted after the 1997 defeat. A new system was used to elect Iain Duncan Smith in September 2001. Two candidates (selected by Conservative MPs) were chosen by a ballot of all party members. In 2003, following the resignation of Iain Duncan Smith, Michael Howard was elected unopposed. Despite much debate, in 2005 two candidates chosen by Conservative MPs were voted for by party members. David Cameron beat David Davis (134,446 votes to 64,398).

When David Cameron stood down in 2016 after the referendum defeat, Theresa May easily won most support among the MPs. Her last rival withdrew, so party members were not balloted.

Leaders *(on 8 June 2017)*

Conservative	Mrs Theresa May
Liberal Democrat	Mr Tim Farron**
Labour	Mr Jeremy Corbyn
UKIP	Mr Paul Nuttall*
Greens	{ Ms Caroline Lucas { Mr Jonathan Bartley
SNP	Ms Nicola Sturgeon
Plaid Cymru	Ms Leanne Wood
DUP	Ms Arlene Foster

* Resigned, 9 June 2017
** Resigned, 14 June 2017

Conservative Party Leaders

1975–90	Mrs M Thatcher
1990–97	(Sir) J Major
1997–01	W Hague
2001–03	I Duncan Smith
2003–05	M Howard
2005–16	D. Cameron
2016–	Ms. T. May

Labour Party Leaders

1983–92	N Kinnock
1992–94	J Smith
1994–2007	A Blair
2007–10	G Brown
2010–15	E Miliband
2015–	J Corbyn

Liberal Party Leaders (1945–88)

1945–56	C Davies
1956–67	J Grimond
1967–76	J Thorpe
1976–88	D Steel

Social and Liberal Democratic Party Leaders

1988–99	P Ashdown
1999–06	C Kennedy
2006–07	Sir M Campbell
2007–15	N Clegg
2015–17	T Farron

Party Officers

Conservative Party

Chairman of the Party Organisation
(appointed by the Leader of the Party)

1995–97	Dr B Mawhinney
1997–98	Lord Parkinson
1998–01	M Ancram
2001–02	D Davis
2002–03	Ms Theresa May
2003–05	{ Dr Liam Fox
	{ Lord Saatchi
2005–07	F Maude
2007–09	Ms Caroline Spelman
2009–10	E Pickles
2010–12	{ Baroness Warsi
	{ Lord Feldman
2012–16	{ Lord Feldman
	{ Grant Shapps (to 2015)
2016–	Sir P McLoughlin

Chairman of Conservative (Private) Members'
Committee (or the 1922 Committee)

1984–92	Sir C Onslow
1992–97	Sir M Fox
1997–01	Sir A Hamilton
2001–10	Sir M Spicer
2010–	G Brady

Labour Party

General Secretary

2001–04	D Triesman
2004–06	M Carter
2006–07	P Watt
2008–11	R Collins
2011–	I McNicol

Social and Liberal Democratic Party

President
(election by Party members)

1988–90	I Wrigglesworth
1990–94	C Kennedy
1994–98	R Maclennan
1998–00	Baroness Maddock
2000–04	Lord Dholakia
2004–08	S Hughes
2008–12	Baroness Scott
2012–14	T Farron
2015–	Baroness Brinton

PARLIAMENT

Parliament consists of the Queen, the House of Lords and the House of Commons. Over the centuries the balance between the three parts of the legislature has changed such that the Queen's role is now only formal and the House of Commons has established paramountcy over the House of Lords. Because of the party system the initiative in government lies not in Parliament but in the Cabinet. But Parliament, and especially the Commons, has important functions to play not only as the assembly to which the government is ultimately responsible but also in legitimising legislation, voting money and in acting as a body in which complaints may be raised.

House of Lords

Composition. The old House of Lords comprised *c.* 1,240 peers before its reform (when most of the hereditary peers were removed). These consisted of 26 bishops and archbishops, 10 Lords of Appeal, over 400 Life Peers and more than 760 hereditary peers. No new hereditary peers were created between 1964 and 1983. After then, there were only 3: Viscounts Tonypandy (George Thomas) and Whitelaw, and the Earl of Stockton (Harold Macmillan). Less than 300 peers attended more than one-third of the Lords' proceedings, although 621 peers voted in the debate over Maastricht. Women were allowed to sit in the House of Lords for the first time following the 1958 Life Peerages Act. The Law Lords now sit in the Supreme Court. The Lords Spiritual (Women) Act now provides for women bishops to take their seat.

Reform. The most recent proposals in the long-running attempts to reform the House of Lords were put forward by the Coalition Government in June 2012. The Lords would be turned into a mainly elected chamber with its membership reduced to 450. Some 80% would be elected for 15-year terms.

However, faced with intractable opposition from many Conservative backbenchers, it became clear that these proposals could not pass through parliament. The plans were formally shelved in September 2012. Lord Strathclyde was appointed to lead another review into the role of the Lords. His review was released in 2016 but its proposals were shelved.

Under the 2014 House of Lords Reform Act, peers can for the first time ever retire permanently. Also, peers who have been convicted of a serious crime can be expelled.

In early 2017 there were around 255 Conservative peers, 210 Labour and 105 Liberal Democrats. Crossbenchers number *c.* 175. The number of peers in the Lords is now over 875 (including the 26 Bishops). It is now the second biggest legislative chamber in the world. Not all these peers are active. There are 2 Plaid Cymru peers, 2 UKIP and just one Green.

The Lord Speaker. Until 2006, the Lord Chancellor acted as Speaker of the House of Lords. The new post of Lord Speaker was first filled in June 2006, when Baroness Hayman was elected. The Speaker, currently Lord Fowler, sits on the Woolsack.

Functions. (1) Legislation. Some bills on subjects which are not matters of partisan controversy are initiated in the Lords. It also examines in detail many bills which originated in the Commons, but its part is limited by the Parliament Acts, under which it cannot require the Commons to agree to amendments nor delay a bill indefinitely.

(2) Debate. The Lords provides a forum for men and women, distinguished in most fields of national life, to discuss issues of importance free from the reins of party discipline.

(3) Court of Appeal. From 1876 to 2009 the Lords was the highest court of appeal. Only the Law Lords participated in this. This function, however, ceased when the new Supreme Court (based in the former Middlesex Guildhall) began work in 2009.

House of Commons

Composition. At the May 2015 general election there were 650 MPs elected (533 in England, 59 in Scotland, 40 in Wales and 18 in Northern Ireland). These total should be reduced to 600 for 2020.

The Speaker. Its proceedings are presided over by the Speaker, who is elected by MPs, usually at the beginning of each session. Betty Boothroyd (the first woman Speaker) was elected in 1992. After her resignation in 2000, Michael Martin was elected. He resigned on 21 June 2009 after mounting criticism of his conduct amid the expenses scandal. He was succeeded by John Bercow, who defeated Sir George Young by 322 votes to 271 in the third round of a secret ballot. Mr. Bercow is now the highest-paid MP.

Frontbenchers and Backbenchers. MPs sit on parallel rows of seats, known as benches, with those who support the government on one side of the chamber and the rest on the other. Members of the government and the Opposition spokesmen are known as "frontbenchers"; other MPs are "backbenchers".

Functions. (1) Legislation. There are two types of legislation—*public acts*, most of which are introduced by the government, but which can also be introduced by individual MPs, and *private acts*, which confer special powers on bodies such as local authorities in excess of the general law and which are subject to special procedures.

All public legislation must pass through the following stages before becoming law:

First Reading. The bill is formally introduced.

Second Reading. The general principles of the bill are debated and voted.

Committee Stage. Each clause of the bill is debated and voted.

Report Stage. The bill is considered as it was reported by the committee, and it is decided whether to make further changes in individual clauses.

Third Reading. The bill, as amended, is debated and a final vote taken.

The Other House. The bill has to pass through all the same stages in the other House of Parliament.

Royal Assent. The Queen gives her assent to the bill which then becomes law.

(2) Scrutiny of government activities. There are a number of opportunities for the opposition and the government's own back-benchers to criticise government policy. They can question ministers on the floor of the House; they can table motions for debate and speak in debates initiated by the government; and they can take part in one of the select committees set up to scrutinise government activity.

(a) *Committees.* The House of Commons uses committees to assist it in its work in various ways. They are of two types:

(b) *Standing Committees.* A standing committee is a miniature of the House itself, reflecting its party composition, and consists of between 20 and 50 MPs. Its function is to examine the Committee Stage of legislation. Usually seven or eight such committees are needed.

(c) *Select Committees.* A select committee is a body with special powers and privileges to which

HER MAJESTY GOVERNMENT
Members of the Conservative Cabinet, (after the June 2017 reshuffle)

Prime Minister and First Lord of the Treasury	Theresa May
First Secretary of State and Minister for the Cabinet Office	Damian Green
Chancellor of the Exchequer	Philip Hammond
Home Secretary	Amber Rudd
Secretary of State for Foreign and Commonwealth Affairs	Boris Johnson
Secretary of State for Defence	Sir Michael Fallon
Lord Chancellor and Secretary of State for Justice	David Lidington
Secretary of State for Education and Minister for Women and Equalities	Justine Greening
Secretary of State for exiting the European Union	David Davis
Secretary of State for International Trade and President of the Board of Trade	Liam Fox
Secretary of State for Business, Energy and Industrial Strategy	Greg Clark
Secretary of State for Health	Jeremy Hunt
Secretary of State for Work and Pensions	David Gauke
Secretary of State for Transport	Chris Grayling
Secretary of State for Communities and Local Government	Sajid Javid
Lord President of the Council and Leader of the House of Commons	Andrea Leadsom
Lord Privy Seal and Leader of the House of Lords	Baroness Evans
Secretary of State for Scotland	David Mundell
Secretary of State for Wales	Alun Cairns
Secretary of State for Northern Ireland	James Brokenshire
Secretary of State for Environment, Food and Rural Affairs	Michael Gove
Secretary of State for International Development	Priti Patel
Chief Secretary to the Treasury	Elizabeth Truss
Chancellor of the Duchy of Lancaster (and Chairman of the Conservative Party)	Sir Patrick McLoughlin
Secretary of State for Culture, Media and Sport	Karen Bradley
Attorney General	Jeremy Wright
Chief Whip (House of Commons)	Gavin Williamson

Note: This list excludes some less senior posts as well as those who do not normally attend Cabinet on a regular basis.

Principal Ministers 1916–1964

Prime Minister	Chancellor of the Exchequer	Foreign Secretary	Home Secretary	Leader of the House of Commons
1916–22 D Lloyd George	A Bonar Law A Chamberlain Sir R Horne	A Balfour Earl Curzon	Sir G Cave E Shortt	A Bonar Law A Chamberlain
1922–23 A Bonar Law	S Baldwin	Earl Curzon	W Bridgeman	A Bonar Law
1923–24 S Baldwin	S Baldwin N Chamberlain	Earl Curzon	W Bridgeman	S Baldwin
1924 J R MacDonald	P Snowden	J R MacDonald	A Henderson	J R MacDonald
1924–29 S Baldwin	W Churchill	(Sir) A Chamberlain	Sir W Joynson-Hicks	S Baldwin
1929–35 J R MacDonald	P Snowden N Chamberlain	A Henderson Marquis of Reading Sir J Simon	J Clynes Sir H Samuel Sir J Gilmour	J R MacDonald
1935–37 S Baldwin	N Chamberlain	Sir S Hoare A Eden	Sir J Simon	S Baldwin
1937–40 N Chamberlain	Sir J Simon	A Eden Viscount Halifax	Sir S Hoare Sir J Anderson	N Chamberlain
1940–45 W Churchill	Sir K Wood Sir J Anderson	Viscount Halifax A Eden	H Morrison Sir D Somervell	C Attlee * Sir S Cripps A Eden
1945–51 C Attlee	H Dalton Sir S Cripps H Gaitskell	E Bevin H Morrison	C Ede	H Morrison C Ede
1951–55 Sir W Churchill	R Butler	Sir A Eden	Sir D Maxwell-Fyfe G Lloyd George	H Crookshank
1955–57 Sir A Eden	R Butler H Macmillan	H Macmillan S Lloyd	G Lloyd George	R Butler
1957–63 H Macmillan	P Thorneycroft D Heathcoat Amory S Lloyd R Maudling	S Lloyd Earl of Home	R Butler H Brooke	R Butler I Macleod
1963–64 Sir A Douglas-Home	R Maudling	R Butler	H Brooke	S Lloyd

* Churchill deputed day to day business to Attlee.

Principal Ministers 1964–June 2017

	Prime Minister	Chancellors	Foreign Secretary	Home Secretary	Leader of the House of Commons
1964–70	H Wilson	J Callaghan R Jenkins	P Gordon Walker M Stewart G Brown M Stewart	Sir F Soskice R Jenkins J Callaghan	H Bowden R Crossman F Peart
1970–74	E Heath	I Macleod A Barber	Sir A Douglas-Home	R Maudling R Carr	W Whitelaw R Carr J Prior
1974–76	H Wilson	D Healey	J Callaghan	R Jenkins	E Short
1976–79	J Callaghan	D Healey	A Crosland D Owen	R Jenkins M Rees	M Foot
1979–90	Mrs M Thatcher	Sir G Howe N Lawson J Major	Lord Carrington F Pym Sir G Howe J Major D Hurd	W Whitelaw L Brittan D Hurd D Waddington	N St John-Stevas F Pym J Biffen J Wakeham Sir G Howe J MacGregor
1990–97	J Major	N Lamont K Clarke	D Hurd M Rifkind	K Baker K Clarke M Howard	J MacGregor A Newton
1997–2007	A Blair	G Brown	R Cook J Straw Ms M Beckett	J Straw D Blunkett C Clarke J Reid	A Taylor M Beckett R Cook J Reid P Hain G Hoon J Straw
2007–10	G Brown	A Darling	D Miliband	Ms J Smith* A Johnson	Ms H Harman
2010–16	D Cameron**	G Osborne	W Hague P Hammond	Ms T May	A Lansley W Hague C Grayling
2016–	Mrs T May	P Hammond	B Johnson	Ms A Rudd	D Lidington Ms A Leadsom

* A separate Ministry of Justice was created in May 2007.
** In the Coalition Government from 2010 to 2015, Nick Clegg was Deputy Prime Minister.

the House has delegated its authority for the purpose of discovering information, examining witnesses, sifting evidence and drawing up conclusions which are then reported to the House. A few select committees are established *ad hoc*, but the majority are semi-permanent.

There are a variety of select committees, each one scrutinising the work of one or two government departments (*e.g.* Agriculture, Foreign Affairs, Treasury and Civil Service); and various others including, the following: European Legislation, Members' Interests, Parliamentary Commissioner for Administration, Privileges, Public Accounts *etc.*

Central Government

The executive work of central government is performed by the Prime Minister and the other ministers of the Crown. The power of executive action is not given to a government department as a corporate body but to the minister individually, who is responsible for the exercise of his duties legally to the Queen and politically to Parliament. For this reason, all ministers must be members of either the Commons or the Lords.

The Cabinet

At the head of the government structure is the Cabinet, which consists of the leading members of the majority party in the Commons, selected by the Prime Minister. Most Cabinet ministers are the heads of government departments, which are staffed by civil servants, but there are usually some without departmental responsibilities. Although legally ministers are individually responsible for the exercise of government powers, politically it is accepted that the Cabinet is collectively responsible for government policy. It thus acts as a unity, and a minister who disagrees with the Cabinet must either resign or remain silent.

HER MAJESTY'S OPPOSITION

The leader of the largest party opposed to the government is designated Leader of Her Majesty's Opposition and receives an official salary. The leading spokesmen of the Opposition meet together as a committee and are generally known as the Shadow Cabinet. A Conservative Shadow Cabinet, officially known as the Leader's Consultative Committee, is selected by the leader of the party.

Labour Shadow Cabinets, officially known as the Parliamentary Committee, which used to be elected by the Parliamentary Labour Party until 2011, are now appointed by the Leader.

OTHER EXECUTIVE BODIES

A large number of semi-autonomous agencies have been established to carry out functions on behalf of the government, usually because a particular function is considered to be unsuitable for a normal government department. In this category are bodies such as the British Broadcasting Corporation and the Commission for Racial Equality which need to be insulated from the political process, and the former nationalised industries, most of which were managed by public corporations so as to secure managerial flexibility. Some public control over these bodies was maintained by means of various powers which ministers possessed.

THE CIVIL SERVICE

The civil service is the body of permanent officials who, working in the various departments, administer the policy of central government. In early 2017 it consisted of *c.* 398,000 full-time and part-time staff, 140,000 fewer than a decade earlier.

MAJOR FIGURES IN THE LABOUR SHADOW CABINET
(at the time of the June 2017 Election)

Leader of the Party	Jeremy Corbyn
Deputy Leader and Shadow Culture Secretary	Tom Watson
Shadow Chancellor	John McDonnell
Shadow Foreign Secretary	Emily Thornberry
Shadow Home Secretary	Diane Abbott
Shadow Business Secretary	Rebecca Long-Bailey
Shadow Employment Secretary	Jack Dromey
Shadow Health Secretary	Jon Ashworth
Shadow Defence Secretary	Baroness Chakrabarti
Shadow Environment, Food and Rural Affairs	Sue Hayman
Shadow Brexit Secretary	Sir Keir Starmer
Shadow Chief Whip	Nick Brown
Shadow Communities Secretary	Roberta Blackman-Woods
Shadow Housing Secretary	John Healey
Shadow Scottish and Northern Ireland Secretary	David Anderson
Shadow Welsh Secretary	Christina Rees
Shadow Education Secretary	Angela Rayner
Shadow Leader of the House	Valerie Vaz
Shadow Leader of the Lords	Baroness Smith of Basildon
Shadow Chief Whip (in the Lords)	Lord Bassam
Shadow Women and Equalities	Sarah Champion
Shadow Economic Secretary to the Treasury	Jonathan Reynolds
Shadow Attorney General	Nia Griffith
Shadow Lord President of the Council and Shadow Minister for the Cabinet Office	Jon Trickett
Shadow Chief Secretary to the Treasury	Peter Dowd

Over 80% of the civil service now work outside Greater London, mainly in the regional and local offices of departments such as Health, Work and Pensions, Education and Skills, Revenue and Customs *etc.*

The political head of each department is a minister, but, as he often has no previous experience of the field to which he is appointed and his tenure of office may be fairly short-lived, great responsibility falls on the shoulders of the permanent civil servants in his department. Civil servants remain largely anonymous and their relationship with their minister is a confidential one. They are non-political in the sense that they serve all political parties impartially.

Senior Civil Servants

Some lists of major heads are given below.

Head of the Diplomatic Service

1953–57	Sir I Kirkpatrick
1957–62	Sir F Hoyer Millar
1962–65	Sir H Caccia
1965–68	Sir S Garner
1968–69	Sir P Gore-Booth
1969–73	Sir D Greenhill
1973–75	Sir T Brimelow
1975–82	Sir M Palliser
1982–86	Sir A Acland
1986–91	Sir P Wright
1991–94	Sir D Gillmore
1994–97	Sir J Coles
1997–02	Sir J Kerr
2002–06	Sir M Jay
2006–10	Sir P Ricketts
2010–15	Sir S Fraser
2015–	Sir S McDonald

Secretary to the Cabinet

1963–73	Sir B Trend
1973–79	Sir J Hunt
1979–88	Sir R Armstrong
1988–98	Sir R Butler
1998–02	Sir R Wilson
2002–05	Sir A Turnbull
2005–11	Sir G O'Donnell
2011–	(Sir) J Heywood

Head of the Home Civil Service

1968–74	Sir W Armstrong
1974–78	Sir D Allen
1978–81	Sir I Bancroft
1981–83	{Sir R Armstrong {Sir D Wass
1983–88	Sir R Armstrong
1988–98	Sir R Butler
1998–02	Sir R Wilson
2002–05	Sir A Turnbull
2005–11	Sir G O'Donnell
2011–14	Sir R Kerslake

Permanent Secretary to the Treasury

1962–63	{Sir N Brook {Sir W Armstrong
1963–68	{Sir L Helsby {(Sir) W Armstrong
1968	{Sir W Armstrong {Sir D Allen
1968–74	Sir D Allen
1974–83	Sir D Wass
1983–91	Sir P Middleton
1991–98	Sir T Burns
1998–02	Sir A Turnbull
2002–05	Sir G O'Donnell

2005–16	Sir N Macpherson
2016–	Sir T Scholar

LOCAL GOVERNMENT

Local government in the United Kingdom is the creation of Parliament. Its structure is laid down by Parliament, and local authorities may only exercise those powers which Parliament either commands or permits them to exercise. Their functions include responsibility for all education services, except further and higher education, most personal welfare services, housing, public health, environmental planning, traffic management and transport, all subject to some central government control.

Directly-Elected Mayors/Devolution of Power

Draft legislation in 2000 proposed a major shake-up of the running of town halls, opening up the prospect of directly-elected mayors with wide-ranging executive powers. The first directly-elected Mayors were voted for in 2002. Many more cities (such as Leicester) now have directly elected Mayors.

An elected Mayor with sweeping powers was proposed for Greater Manchester in 2014. The new metro-mayors were elected in such places as Manchester, Liverpool and the West Midlands in May 2017.

First-Tier Authorities. See D11.

London

In London and the six metropolitan areas there was, after April 1986 (when the Greater London Council and the metropolitan county councils were abolished), a single-tier system with a few special bodies undertaking county-wide functions.

A referendum on the future government of London was held on 7 May 1998 when voters decided they wanted a new Greater London Assembly (GLA) and a directly elected Mayor. Londoners chose their first directly-elected Mayor on 4 May 2000 (electing the Independent candidate, Ken Livingstone). The second elections for the GLA were held in June 2004, when Ken Livingstone was re-elected (now standing as the Labour candidate). The third elections took place in 2008. The winner was the Conservative Boris Johnson, who won again in 2012.

In the 2016 election, the two main contenders were Zac Goldsmith (Conservative) and Sadiq Khan (Labour). Sadiq Khan won (the first Muslim to do so).

The London Assembly, with 25 members, holds the Mayor to account.

Regional Assemblies

As a result of the Regional Assemblies (Preparations) Act, a referendum was held in north-east England on 4 November 2004. The outcome was a decisive rejection of a regional assembly, with 696,519 votes against an assembly (78%) and 197,310 for (22%). Future referendums on regional assemblies in England were then abandoned.

Wales, Scotland and Northern Ireland

In Wales, 22 all-purpose councils replaced the 8 counties and 37 district councils. Elections to these councils first took place in 1995. There are calls to reduce these 22 councils to just 8 or 9. *See* **D11**.

In Scotland, 29 single-tier authorities replaced the existing 2-tier structure after April 1996. These new authorities were first elected in April 1995. There are single-tier island councils in Orkney, Shetland and the Western Isles. *See* **D11**.

In Northern Ireland, reorganisation has now resulted in 11 new super-councils (with 462 seats). These became fully operational in 2015. *See* **D11**.

First-tier Authorities (as at May 2017)

This list excludes Avon, Cleveland and Humberside which were abolished in April 1996. Since April 1995 the Isle of Wight has been a unitary authority, whilst Hereford and Worcester has been reorganised and Berkshire has lost its old status. North Yorkshire has become a unitary authority. In 2009 the old county councils of Bedfordshire, Cheshire, Cornwall, Durham, Northumberland, Shropshire and Wiltshire were reorganised into unitary authorities. They are also excluded from this list.

ENGLAND

Selected Non-Metropolitan Counties

Buckinghamshire	Leicestershire
Cambridgeshire	Lincolnshire
Cumbria	Norfolk
Derbyshire	Northamptonshire
Devon	Nottinghamshire
Dorset	Oxfordshire
East Sussex	Somerset
Essex	Staffordshire
Gloucestershire	Suffolk
Hampshire	Surrey
Hertfordshire	Warwickshire
Kent	West Sussex
Lancashire	Worcestershire

WALES

The following 22 unitary authorities took up their duties on 1 April 1996.

Aberconwy and Colwyn	Merthyr Tydfil
Anglesey	Monmouthshire
Blaenau Gwent	Neath and Port Talbot
Bridgend	Newport
Caernarfonshire and Merionethshire	Pembrokeshire
Caerphilly	Powys
Cardiff	Rhondda, Cynon, Taff
Cardiganshire	Swansea
Carmarthenshire	Torfaen
Denbighshire	Vale of Glamorgan
Flintshire	Wrexham

SCOTLAND

The following 32 unitary authorities took up their duties on 1 April 1996.

Aberdeenshire	Fife
Angus	Highland
Argyll and Bute	Inverclyde
Borders	Midlothian
City of Aberdeen	Moray
City of Dundee	North Ayrshire
City of Edinburgh	North Lanarkshire
City of Glasgow	Orkney Islands Council
Clackmannan	Perthshire and Kinross
Dumbarton and Clydebank	Renfrewshire
Dumfries and Galloway	Shetland Islands Council
East Ayrshire	South Ayrshire
East Dumbartonshire	South Lanarkshire
East Lothian	Stirling
East Renfrewshire	Western Isles Islands Council
Falkirk	West Lothian

NORTHERN IRELAND

The following 11 authorities became fully operational after 2015.

Antrim and Newtownabbey	Lisburn and Castlereagh
Armagh, Banbridge and Craigavon	Mid and East Antrim
Belfast	Mid Ulster
Causeway Coast and Glen	Newry, Mourne and Down
Derry and Strabane	North Down and Ards
Fermanagh and Omagh	

Metropolitan Councils in England

	Name	Political control (2017)
London	Barking & Dagenham	Lab.
	Barnet	Con.
	Bexley	Con.
	Brent	Lab.
	Bromley	Con.
	Camden	Lab.
	Croydon	Lab.
	Ealing	Lab.
	Enfield	Lab.
	Greenwich	Lab.
	Hackney	Lab.
	Hammersmith and Fulham	Lab.
	Haringey	Lab.
	Harrow	Lab.
	Havering	Con.
	Hillingdon	Con.
	Hounslow	Lab.
	Islington	Lab.
	Kensington and Chelsea	Con.
	Kingston-on-Thames	Con.
	Lambeth	Lab.
	Lewisham	Lab.
	Merton	Lab.
	Newham	Lab.
	Redbridge	Lab.
	Richmond-on-Thames	Con.
	Southwark	Lab.
	Sutton	Lib Dem.
	Tower Hamlets	NOM.
	Waltham Forest	Lab.
	Wandsworth	Con.
	Westminster	Con.
Greater Manchester	Bolton	Lab.
	Bury	Lab.
	Manchester	Lab.
	Oldham	Lab.
	Rochdale	Lab.
	Salford	Lab.
	Stockport	NOM.
	Tameside	Lab.
	Trafford	Con.
	Wigan	Lab.
Merseyside	Knowsley	Lab.
	Liverpool	Lab.
	St. Helens	Lab.
	Sefton	Lab.
	Wirral	Lab.
South Yorkshire	Barnsley	Lab.
	Doncaster	Lab.
	Rotherham	Lab.
	Sheffield	Lab.
Tyne & Wear	Gateshead	Lab.
	Newcastle-upon-Tyne	Lab.
	North Tyneside	Lab.
	South Tyneside	Lab.
	Sunderland	Lab.
West Midlands	Birmingham	Lab.
	Coventry	Lab.
	Dudley	NOM.
	Sandwell	Lab.
	Solihull	Con.
	Walsall	NOM.
	Wolverhampton	Lab.
West Yorkshire	Bradford	Lab.
	Calderdale	NOM.
	Kirklees	NOM.
	Leeds	Lab.
	Wakefield	Lab.

THE SCOTTISH PARLIAMENT

Voting took place on 5 May 2016 for the fifth elections to the Scottish Parliament. The outcome was again a very strong performance by the SNP, who dominated the Parliament, albeit without an over-all majority (63 seats out of 129). Labour was reduced to 24 seats, a loss of 13. This was its worst-ever result. It suffered the added humiliation of being forced into third place by the Conservatives under Ruth Davidson who polled significantly better than for many years (finishing with 31 seats). The Greens secured 6 seats, pushing the Liberal Democrats into fifth place.

Party	Seats	Gain/Loss
SNP	63	−6
Con	31	+16
Labour	24	−13
Green	6	+4
Lib Dem	5	
	129	

THE WELSH ASSEMBLY

Voting took place on 5 May 2016 for the fifth elections to the Welsh Assembly. Labour was once again the leading party, despite a fall in its share of the vote from 43 to 35 %, securing 29 seats. Plaid Cymru was in second place with 12 seats, just ahead of the Conservatives with 11. UKIP achieved a significant success, taking 7 seats (the first seats it had ever won in the Assembly). The Liberal Democrats only returned one solitary member, a sign of their continuing weakness in Wales. The most significant personal victory was in Rhondda, won by Plaid Cymru leader Leanne Wood.

Party	Seats	Gain/Loss
Labour	29	−1
PC	12	+1
Cons	11	−3
UKIP	7	+7
Lib Dem	1	−4
	60	

REDRESS OF GRIEVANCES

In the first instance most citizens who are aggrieved by the decision of a public body take up their complaint with the body concerned. If this does not satisfy them they have a number of options which vary according to the type of body and the nature of their complaint.

Central Government

1. MPs. MPs may be contacted by letter, and many of them hold regular surgeries in their cons-tituencies. On receipt of a complaint they can write to the minister in charge of the department concerned or ask a question in Parliament. If the complainant alleges maladministration (*e.g.*, arbitrary action, undue delay) this can be referred to the *Parliamentary Commissioner for Administration* (usually known as the *Ombudsman*). The powers and responsibilities were set out in the Parliamentary Commissioner Act, 1967. In 2016 the Public Service Ombudsman Bill proposed a merger of the Health, Local Government and Parliamentary Ombudsmen.

Parliamentary Commissioner for Administration

(and Health Service Commissioner since 1973)

1967–71	Sir Edmund Compton
1971–76	Sir Alan Marre
1976–78	Sir Idwal Pugh
1979–85	Sir Cecil Clothier
1985–90	Sir Anthony Barrowclough
1990–96	Sir William Reid
1997–02	Sir Michael Buckley
2002–12	Ms Ann Abraham
2012–	Dame Julie Mellor

Parliamentary Commissioner for Standards

(established in 1995 after the Nolan Report)

1995–98	Sir Gordon Downey
1998–02	Ms Elizabeth Filkin
2002–08	Sir Philip Mawer
2008–14	Mr John Lyon
2014–	Ms Kathryn Hudson

2. Tribunals and Inquiries. In certain areas of government (*e.g.*, social security), special tribunals exist to adjudicate on disputes between citizens and government. In others (*e.g.*, planning) an inquiry can be set up. In both cases the machinery is less formal and more flexible than the ordinary courts.

3. Courts of Law. On certain restricted matters (*e.g.*, that a public body has acted outside its lawful powers), citizens have recourse to ordinary courts.

Local Government

1. Councillors. Local councillors can be con-tacted in the same way as MPs. They can also refer complaints of maladministration to a *Commissioner for Local Administration* (or local Ombudsman). There are five commissioners, three in England and one each in Scotland and Wales.

2. Tribunals and Inquiries (as above).

3. Courts of Law (as above).

Other Bodies

1. National Health Service. *See* **Z5–6**.

2. Privatised Industries. In former nationalised industries, independent regulatory bodies have been created (*e.g.* Ofwat for water).

PRESSURE GROUPS

Large numbers of groups exist to exert pressure on government by direct consultation with minis-ters and civil servants, lobbying Parliament and general publicity campaigns. Some exist to de-fend interests such as labour, business or con-sumers; others promote particular causes such as the prevention of cruelty to children or the banning of blood sports. Of great importance are the groups representing labour and business.

Recent Growth

In recent years, British pressure groups have exhibited dynamism, spontaneity, and in many cases rapidly growing memberships, and they influence policy at local, national and international levels. Issues surrounding environmental policy, for example, from animal rights to renewable energy and food production, have risen up the political agenda chiefly because of the work of pressure groups concerned with them. However, they have also been accused on the one hand of secrecy, self-interest and even corruption; on the other of ineffectiveness and superficiality.

Types of Pressure Group

The diverse range of pressure groups runs from 'insiders' – well-established organisations in regular direct, and often private, contact with the government – to 'outsiders' – those not enjoying government sympathy and who appeal to the public via the media as a way of applying pressure to decision-makers, sometimes using direct action to attract attention. Members of a small group campaigning for family law reform called 'Fathers for Justice' became notorious after scaling the walls of Buckingham Palace in fancy dress, throwing purple powder at the Prime Minister in the Commons, and handcuffing themselves to a junior minister.

Trade Unions

In 1980, 49 % of the workforce belonged to a trade union. This percentage has declined and by early 2017 there were *c.* 6·3 million members of a trade union or staff association. Nearly three in five public sector employees are in a union, but only one in seven private sector employees. Increasingly, unions have formed large "super-unions".

The merger of the Transport and General Workers Union (T&G) with Amicus on 1 May 2007 created the biggest trade union in Britain (with 1·5 million members). The new union (named Unite) has now formed a merger with North America's United Steelworkers. The new body (formed in 2008) is called Workers Uniting.

Other large unions include Unison (with around 1·3 million members and formed in 1993 from a merger of Nalgo, Nupe and Cohse) and the GMB (the General, Municipal and Boilermakers Union) which has around 640,000 members. USDAW has 400,000 members and the CWU 200,000. UCATT now plans to merge with Unite. The three big teaching unions are planning to come together in the new National Education Union.

The Conservative Government has secured the passage of its Trade Union Act. Under it, strikes can only go ahead when there has been a ballot turnout of over 50 %. In fact the number of workers taking strike action had reached a record low in 2015. A total of 81,000 people went on strike, the lowest since records first began in 1893.

Relations with the Labour Party

The TUC maintains a close relationship with the Labour Party, providing funds for both the national headquarters and local offices. This close relationship has in the past been reflected in the unions' direct involvement in the making of government economic policy, as in the 'Social Contract' of 1975.

Recently, the historic links between the unions and the Labour Party have come under renewed scrutiny – particularly over selection of parliamentary candidates. At a Labour Party conference in March 2014 the automatic affiliation of thousands of union members into the party was ended.

Trades Union Congress (TUC)

The major unions, representing over 80 % of total union membership, are affiliated to the Trades Union Congress, which is the federal body of the trade union movement, representing its views to government and others, and giving assistance on questions relating to particular industries.

TUC General Secretaries (since 2000)

1993–03	J Monks
2003–12	B Barber
2013–	Ms F O'Grady

Business

The peak organisation representing business is the *Confederation of British Industry*, formed in 1965. Its members comprise many thousand individual enterprises and numerous representative organisations (employers' organisations, trade associations *etc.*).

Business is also represented by large numbers of associations which promote the interests of individual industries and sectors.

Director-Generals of the CBI (since 2000)

2000–06	(Lord) Digby Jones
2006–10	Sir R Lambert
2011–15	J Cridland
2015–	Ms Carolyn Fairbairn

THE MEDIA

1. Principal Newspapers

The British are more committed to the reading of newspapers than any other country in Europe. Although newspaper sales are steadily declining, annual sales each day of national and regional newspapers are now around 15 million (and to these figures should be added the many millions of copies of weekly papers and free newspapers). The free *Metro* was launched in 1999 in London.

The Independent Press Standards Organisation (IPSO) oversees the press.

Ownership

The largest grouping is News International. Owned by Rupert Murdoch it possesses *The Sun, The Times*, the *Sunday Times*, and the *News of the World* (this was closed in 2011 amid the phone hacking scandal). *The Sun on Sunday* was launched in February 2012. It also owns extensive interests in the US and Australia and is a global media group.

The Trinity Mirror Group follows with *The Mirror*, the *Sunday Mirror*, the *People* and the *Daily Record* (published in Scotland). On 29 February 2016 it launched the *New Day* daily newspaper, but this closed after nine weeks.

Northern and Shell is the owner of *The Express, Express on Sunday*, and *Daily Star*. Associated Newspapers owns the *Daily Mail, Mail on Sunday*, and large regional holdings, including the *Evening Standard* in London. Smaller companies are the Telegraph Media Group, owning the *Daily Telegraph* and *Sunday Telegraph*; Guardian Media Group owns *The Guardian, The Observer* and local newspapers. The *Financial Times* is owned by Japanese media giant Nikkei.

The Independent is now a digital format only newspaper. Its sister paper, the *i*, has been acquired by Johnston Press, which also publishes *The Yorkshire Post* and *The Scotsman*.

2. Broadcasting

British Broadcasting Corporation

Established in 1926 as a public service body and financed by licence fees paid by all owners of TV sets. It used to be directed by a board of governors appointed by the government. Major recent changes include the abolition of the old structure of governors and a commitment to retain the licence fee for 10 years. From 2007 the BBC Trust replaced the former Board of Governors. In May 2016 a White Paper on the future of the BBC was published under which the BBC Trust would be replaced.

Under the new 11-year Royal Charter, which began in 2017, a new unitary BBC Board replaced the former BBC Trust. Its chairman is Sir David Clementi.

Independent Television

There are numerous independent regional TV licensees which comprise the ITV network. The ITC (Independent Television Commission) awards licences for a minimum of 10 years.

Ofcom

Ofcom brings together the work previously done by such bodies as the Broadcasting Standards Commission, the Radio Authority, Oftel, the Independent Television Commission *etc.* It acts as a super-regulator for the communications industry.

SCOTLAND, WALES AND NORTHERN IRELAND

Scotland

Most central government functions here were the responsibility of a single department, the Scottish Office, based in Edinburgh and represented in the Cabinet by the Secretary of State for Scotland. On many matters special Scottish legislation was enacted by Parliament and administrative structure (*e.g.* the local government system) and practice (*e.g.* the educational system) differ from that in England.

The Labour Government elected in May 1997 established a 129-member Scottish Parliament (following a 'Yes' vote on the issue on 11 September). Of those voting 74·3% voted in favour of a Scottish Parliament with 63·5% backed tax raising powers.

The Parliament, first elected on 6 May 1999, has devolved powers over such areas as education, health, law and local government. Foreign, defence, security and constitutional issues remain at Westminster.

The Scottish Parliament is able to increase or decrease tax (*see below*). Some of the MPs are elected from a party list (*see* **D**13). Donald Dewar became First Minister in 1999, to be succeeded after his untimely death in October 2000 by Henry McLeish. He in turn was replaced in November 2001 (following his resignation) by Jack McConnell. In May 2007 Alex Salmond became the first SNP politician to become First Minister. The current (2017) First Minister is Nicola Sturgeon.

The Calman Commission, set up in 2008 to improve how Scottish devolution works, recommended in 2009 increased tax and borrowing powers for Holyrood. The Scotland Act put this into law.

A referendum on the question of independence for Scotland, held in September 2014, rejected independence by 55% to 45%. Further devolution was the subject of the all party Smith Commission. Such powers as the setting of income tax rates, lowering the voting age, granting a proportion of VAT raised in Scotland to Holyrood, full devolution of air passenger duty *etc.* were agreed. The agreed new powers have now become law.

Legislation paving the way for a second referendum has been agreed by Holyrood.

Wales

The Welsh Office, based in Cardiff and represented in the Cabinet by the Secretary of State for Wales, performed many central government functions in Wales but its responsibilities were narrower than its Scottish counterpart. In other respects too government in Wales resembled more closely that in England.

The Labour Government elected in May 1997 created a Welsh Assembly, following a very close referendum vote in favour. Of the 22 voting areas, 11 voted in favour, 11 voted against in the referendum on 18 September 1997 (the final figures were 'Yes', 559,419; 'No', 552,698; majority, 6,721). On a turnout of 50·1%, 50·3% had voted in favour. A massive 'yes' vote in Carmarthenshire decided the outcome.

The 2006 Government of Wales Act altered the functions and status of the National Assembly. The Assembly and the Government were formally separated and the Assembly can now formulate its own legislation.

In 2009 the All Wales Convention proposed a referendum on the question of giving more powers to the Assembly. This was held on 3 March 2011 and resulted in a substantial yes vote. Bill New powers over energy, transport and local government, including the power to choose the voting age in Assembly elections, have now been devolved. A land transaction tax to replace stamp duty becomes law in 2018 (the first Welsh tax in 800 years).

Northern Ireland

From 1921 until 1972 Northern Ireland was governed under the scheme of devolution embodied in the Government of Northern Ireland Act 1920. This created the Northern Ireland Parliament, generally known as Stormont after its eventual location. Executive powers were formally vested in the Governor of Northern Ireland, but were in effect performed by a Prime Minister and small cabinet, responsible to Stormont.

Devolved Government

The onset of troubles in the province led the UK Government in 1972 to suspend the Government of Northern Ireland Act. After then, apart from a period of four months in 1974, Northern Ireland was ruled direct from Westminster, the powers of government being vested in the Secretary of State for Northern Ireland. This changed in 1999 with the return of devolved government. However devolved government has been suspended on frequent occasions (for three months in 2000, twice briefly in 2001 and again on 14 October 2002). The Assembly elections of 7 March 2007 were an attempt to pave the way for a return to devolved government. Devolved government was finally restored on 8 May when Ian Paisley became First Minister with Martin McGuinness as his Deputy. In 2015 Peter Robinson (DUP) resigned as First Minister. He was succeeded by Arlene Foster, the first woman to hold the post.

However, Northern Ireland faced a political crisis in January 2017 with the resignation of Martin McGuinness as Deputy First Minister and the calling of elections for March. These resulted in renewed deadlock.

BRITAIN AND EUROPE

The UK is still currently participating in the EU. After Britain completes its withdrawal from the EU all this will of course change.

Council of Ministers and Commission

The Council of Ministers has been the decision-making body within the Union, consisting of representatives of the 27 member states (25 before 2007 when Bulgaria and Romania joined), each government delegating one of its ministers according to the business under discussion. The principal UK delegate is the Foreign Secretary. Under the terms of the Lisbon Treaty, the European Council became an integral part within the EU and is now the senior body. The posts of President of the European Council and High Representative for Foreign Affairs and Security were also created.

The Commission heads a large bureaucracy in Brussels which submits proposals to the Council of Ministers, implements its decisions, and has powers of its own to promote the Community's interests. Its members are appointed by agreement among the member states for 4-year renewable terms. Members are pledged to independence of national interests.

President of the European Council:

Donald Tusk (Poland) (2014–)

High Representative for Foreign Affairs and Security:

Ms Federica Mogheriti (Italy) (2014–)

Presidents of the Commission

1958–66	Walter Hallstein (West Germany)
1966–70	Jean Rey (Belgium)
1970–72	Franco Malfatti (Italy)
1972–73	Sicco Mansholt (Netherlands)
1973–77	Francois-Xavier Ortoli (France)
1977–81	Roy Jenkins (UK)
1981–85	Gaston Thorn (Luxembourg)
1985–95	Jacques Delors (France)
1995–99	Jacques Santer (Luxembourg)
1999–04	Romano Prodi (Italy)
2004–14	Sr Durão Barroso (Portugal)
2014–	Jean-Claude Juncker (Luxembourg)

European Parliament

Apart from general powers of supervision and consultation, the Parliament can dismiss the Commission and has some control over the Community Budget. Until 1979 it consisted of members nominated by the national parliaments of the member states. The first direct elections were held in June 1979, the second in June 1984, and the third in June 1989. The fourth elections were held in June 1994, when Britain elected 87 MEPs, 6 more than in 1989. Five extra seats were given to England and one to Wales. The sixth elections were in June 2004, when Britain elected 78 MEPs (down from 87 due to the enlargement of the EU).

In order to vote, you must be over 18 and registered. EU citizens resident in the UK can also vote (but they have to fill in an additional registration form). They are not allowed to vote in more than one country.

Elections, 1999–2014

For the elections in June 1999 the European Parliament constituencies, which used to elect one member, were replaced by large multi-member constituencies (or regions). London, for example, became one constituency instead of the former ten. Electors voted not for an individual candidate but for a party list of candidates. These elections represented the first time proportional representation had been used nationwide.

In the elections of June 2004 the number of UK MEPs was reduced from 87 to 78 (owing to the enlargement of the EU). In June 2009 this total was further reduced to 72. The results for 1999, 2004 and 2009 are set out below. The last elections were in May 2014. Following the EU referendum vote of June 2016, no further elections involving the UK will be held.

Party	1999 Seats	2004 Seats	2009 Seats	2014 Seats
Cons	36	27	25	19
Lab	29	19	13	20
Lib Dems	10	12	11	1
UKIP	3	12	13	24
Green	2	2	2	3
BNP	0	0	2	0
Nats	4	3	3	3
Others (NI)	3	3	3	3

The 2016 Referendum

For the background and result of the historic 23 June referendum, see **D22**.

BRITAIN AND THE UN

Britain was one of the founding members of the United Nations Organization which was created in 1945. The UN currently has 193 member states (South Sudan having joined in 2011). The Vatican is not a UN member, neither is Taiwan, nor is Kosovo which declared its independence in February 2008. Palestine was recognised as a non-member state with observer status in 2012.

General Assembly in which each member state has one vote and which normally meets once a year.

Security Council which has five permanent members (China, France, Russia, UK, USA) and ten non-permanent members elected for two years.

Also linked with the UN are various international organizations, including the International Court of Justice (based in the Hague), the International Labour Organization (based in Geneva), the Food and Agriculture Organization (based in Rome), the UN Educational, Scientific and Cultural Organization (based in Paris) and the World Health Organization (based in Geneva).

Secretary-General: Mr António Guterres (Portugal) (2017–).

WHO'S WHO IN BRITISH POLITICS 1997–2017
(for MPs, present constituency only is given)

Ashdown, Lord, b. 1941; MP (Lib) 1983–8, (SLD) 1988–2001 (Yeovil); Leader, Social and Liberal Democratic Party from 1988 to 1999. High Representative, Bosnia, 2002–05. Companio of Honour, 2015.

Balls, Ed, b. 1967; MP (Lab) Morley and Outwood 2010–15; (formerly Normanton); Secretary of State for Children, Schools and Families, 2007–10. Labour leadership candidate, 2010. Shadow Home Secretary, 2010–11; Shadow Chancellor, 2011–15.

Beckett, Margaret, b. 1943; MP (Lab) 1974–9 and since 1983 (Derby South); Deputy Leader 1992–4; Shadow Health Secretary, 1994–5; Trade and Industry, 1995–7. President of the Board of Trade and Secretary of State for Trade and Industry, 1997–8. Leader of the House of Commons, 1998–2001. Environment, Food and Rural Affairs Secretary, 2001–06; Foreign Secretary, May 2006–June 2007. Housing Minister, 2008–09.

Benn, Hilary, b. 1953; MP (Lab) Leeds Central 1999– . Shadow Foreign Secretary, 2015–16. Son of Tony Benn.

Bennett Natalie, b. 1966; Journalist and editor. Leader of the Green Party, 2012–16.

Bercow, John, b. 1963; MP (Con) Buckingham since 1997. Elected 157th Speaker of the House of Commons after 2009.

Blair, Tony, see Section B.

Blunkett, Lord (David Blunkett), b. 1947; MP (Lab), 1987–2015, (Sheffield Brightside and Hillsborough). Shadow Health spokesman 1992–5. Shadow Education and Employment spokesman, 1995–7. Secretary of State for Education and Employment, 1997–2001. Home Secretary, 2001–04 (resigned). Secretary of State for Work and Pensions, 2005 (May–November) (resigned).

Boothroyd, Baroness, b. 1929; MP (Lab) 1973–2000 (West Bromwich until 1974, then West Bromwich West). Speaker of the House of Commons 1992–2000. (As Betty Boothroyd, the first woman to be elected Speaker). Life Peer, 2000. O.M. (2005).

Brown, Gordon, see Section B.

Burnham, Andy, b. 1970; MP (Lab) Leigh, 2001–17. Ministerial posts as Chief Secretary to the Treasury, 2007–08. Culture Secretary, 2008–09. Secretary of State for Health, 2009–10. Unsuccessful leadership contender, 2015. Elected Mayor of Greater Manchester, 2017.

Cable, Sir Vince, b. 1943; MP (Lib Dem) Twickenham 1997–2015, 2017–. Deputy Leader of the Liberal Democrats, 2006–10. Economic Affairs spokesman, 2003–10. Secretary of State for Business, 2010–15.

Cameron, David, see B12.

Campbell Lord, (Sir Menzies Campbell), b. 1941; MP (Lib, then Lib Dem) Fife North East, 1987–2015. Spokesman on Foreign Affairs, 1997–2006. Deputy Leader, 2003–06. Leader, 2006–07. C. H. (2013).

Clarke, Charles, b. 1950; MP (Lab) Norwich South 1997–2010; President, NUS, 1975–7; Minister without Portfolio and Chairman of the Labour Party, 2001–02; Secretary of State for Education and Skills 2002–04. Home Secretary, 2004–May 2006.

Clarke, Kenneth, b. 1940; MP (Con) since 1970 (Rushcliffe); Paymaster General 1985–7, Chancellor of the Duchy of Lancaster 1987–8, Secretary of State for Health 1988–90, for Education 1990–92. Home Secretary 1992–3, Chancellor of the Exchequer 1993–7. Defeated for Conservative leadership, 1997. Defeated again in 2001 and 2005. Returned to Shadow Cabinet as Business Secretary, 2009. Lord Chancellor (and Justice Secretary), 2010–12. Minister without Portfolio, 2012–14. Companion of Honour, 2014. Father of the House after 2017.

Clegg, Nick, b. 1967; MP (Lib Dem) Sheffield Hallam 2005–17. MEP (Lib Dem) East Midlands, 1999–2004. Liberal Democrat Shadow Home Secretary, 2006–07. Leader of the Liberal Democrats, 2007–15. Deputy Prime Minister in the Conservative-led Coalition, 2010–15. Resigned as Leader, May 2015.

Cook, Robin, (1946–2005); MP (Lab) 1974–2005 (Livingston); Shadow spokesman on Health 1987–92; Shadow Trade and Industry spokesman, 1992–4. Shadow Foreign Secretary, 1994–7. Foreign Secretary, 1997–2001. Leader of the House of Commons, 2001–03. Resigned, 17 March 2003.

Cooper, Yvette, b. 1969; MP (Lab) Pontefract and Castleford since 1997. Chief Secretary to the Treasury, 2008–10. Shadow Home Secretary, 2010–15. Married to Ed Balls. Contender for Labour leadership, 2015.

Corbyn, Jeremy, b. 1949; MP (Lab) Islington North, 1983– . Elected Leader of the Labour Party, September 2015. On the left of the party.

Darling, Lord (Alistair Darling), b. 1953; MP (Lab) Edinburgh SW 2005–15 (previously Edinburgh Central, 1987–2005). Secretary of State for Trade and Industry, 2006–07. Chancellor of the Exchequer, June 2007–May 2010. Leader of the No campaign in 2014 Scottish referendum.

Davidson, Ruth, b. 1978, MSP (Con) for Glasgow since May 2011. Leader of the Scottish Conservative Party since November 2011, overseeing a major revival in its fortunes.

Davis, David, b. 1948: MP (Con) Boothferry, 1987–97. Haltemprice and Howden since 1997. Chairman of the Conservative Party, 2001–02: Shadow Deputy Prime Minister, 2002–03: Shadow Home Secretary, 2003–08. Secretary of State for exiting the European Union, 2016–.

Dewar, Donald, (1937–2000). MP (Lab) 1966–70 and 1978–2000 (Glasgow Garscadden). First elected to Shadow Cabinet 1984; Opposition Chief Whip 1995–7. Secretary of State for Scotland 1997–9; Chosen to lead Labour in Scottish Assembly, 1998. Scotland's First Minister 1999–October 2000.

Duncan Smith, Iain, b. 1954; MP (Con) Chingford 1992–7, Chingford and Woodford Green since 1997. Shadow Social Security spokesman, 1997–9. Shadow Defence spokesman, 1999–2001. Right-wing Eurosceptic who won 2001 leadership contest. Lost support of his party; resigned, Oct. 2003. Secretary of State for Work and Pensions, 2010–16. Resigned, 2016.

Farage, Nigel, b. 1964; MEP after 1999. Leader, UKIP (United Kingdom Independence Party), 2006-09, 2010–15. He failed to become an MP, May 2015. He resigned as leader in May 2015, but then withdrew his resignation. Resigned as Leader after EU referendum, 2016.

Farron, Tim, b. 1970; MP (Lib Dem) Westmoreland and South Lakeside, 2005– . Succeeded Nick Clegg as Liberal Democrat leader, 2015. Resigned, June 2017.

Foster, Arlene, b. 1970; Northern Ireland Assembly MP for Fermanagh and South Tyrone, 2003-. First Minister of Northern Ireland, Jan. 2016–Jan. 2017. Leader, Democratic Unionist Party, Dec. 2015-.

Fox, Liam, b. 1961: MP (Con) North Somerset (formerly Woodspring) since 1997, Co-Chairman, Conservative Party, 2003–05. Appointed Shadow Foreign Secretary, May 2005: Shadow Defence Secretary, 2005–10. Secretary of State for Defence in the Coalition. Currently Secretary of State for International Trade and President of the Board of Trade.

Gove, Michael, b. 1967; MP (Con) Surrey Heath since 2005, Secretary of State for Education, 2010–14. Chief Whip, 2014–15. Lord Chancellor and Justice Secretary; 2015–16. Unsuccessful leadership candidate, 2016. Appointed Environment Secretary, June 2017.

Green, Damian, b. 1956; MP (Con) Ashford, 1997–; Major promotion as First Secretary of State and Minister for the Cabinet Office, June 2017. Friend and ally of Theresa May.

Hague, Lord (William Hague), b. 1961; MP (Con) 1989–2015 (Richmond, Yorks); Secretary of State for Wales, 1995–7. Leader of the Conservative Party, 1997, following election defeat of John Major, but resigned (8 June 2001) after his own election defeat. Shadow Foreign Secretary, Dec 2005–10. Secretary of State for Foreign Affairs, 2010–14. Leader of the House of Commons, 2014–15.

Hammond, Philip, b. 1955, MP (Con), Runnymede and Weybridge since 1997. Secretary of State for Defence, 2011–14 Foreign Secretary, 2014–16. Appointed Chancellor of the Exchequer, 2016.

Harman, Harriet, b. 1950; MP (Lab) since 1982 (Camberwell & Peckham). Secretary of State for Social Security, 1997–8. Solicitor-General 2001–05; Minister of State, Constitutional Affairs, 2005–07. Elected Labour Party Deputy Leader, June 2007. Leader of the House and Minister for Women, 2007–10. Acting Labour leader, 2010, and in 2015. The longest-serving constituency woman MP.

Hattersley, Lord, b. 1932; MP (Lab) 1964–97 (Birmingham Sparkbrook); Secretary of State for Prices and Consumer Protection 1976–9; Shadow Home Secretary 1987–92; Deputy Leader, 1983–92.

Heseltine, Lord, b. 1933; MP (Con) 1966–2001 (Henley); Secretary of State for the Environment 1979–83; for Defence 1983–6; for the Environment 1990–92. Secretary of State for Trade and Industry 1992–5; Deputy Prime Minister 1995–7.

Howard, Lord, b. 1941; MP (Con) 1983–2010 (Folkestone and Hythe); Secretary of State for Employment 1990–92, for the Enviroment, 1992–3. Home Secretary, 1993–7. Shadow Foreign Secretary 1997–9. Shadow Chancellor, 2001–03. Leader of the Conservative Party after November 2003. Announced he would resign as Leader, May 2005. Life Peerage, 2010. Companion of Honour (2011).

Howe, Lord, (1926–2015); MP (Con) 1964–6 and 1970–92 (Surrey East); Solicitor-General 1970–2, Minister for Trade and Consumer Affairs 1972–4, Chancellor of the Exchequer 1979–83, Secretary of State for Foreign and Commonwealth Affairs 1983–9, and Leader of the House of Commons (and Deputy Prime Minister) 1989–90. C.H.

Huhne, Chris, b. 1954; MP (Lib Dem) Eastleigh 2005–13. MEP (Lib Dem) South East, 1999–2004. Fought Liberal Democrat leadership, 2006, 2007. Secretary of State for Energy and Climate Change, 2010–12. Resigned, 3 February 2012 from Cabinet. Resigned as MP, February 2013.

Hume, John, b. 1937; MP (SDLP) Foyle 1983–2005. Leader, Social Democratic and Labour Party, 1979–2001. MEP (SDLP) Northern Ireland, 1979–2004. Declined to stand for Irish Presidency, 1997. Shared 1998 Nobel Peace Prize (with David Trimble).

Hurd, Lord, b. 1930; MP (Con) 1974–97 (Witney); Minister of State, Foreign Office 1979–83, Home Office 1983–4, Secretary of State for Northern Ireland 1984–5, for Home Department 1985–9, and for Foreign and Commonwealth Affairs, 1989–95.

Johnson, Alan, b. 1950; MP (Lab) 1997–2017 (Hull West and Hessle); Secretary of State for Health, 2007–09. Home Secretary, 2009–10. Shadow Chancellor, 2010–11. Resigned, January 2011.

Johnson, Boris, b. 1964; Conservative politician. Editor, *The Spectator*, 1999–2005. Elected Mayor of London, 2008. Re-elected, 2012. MP (Con) Uxbridge and South Ruislip since 2015 (first elected for Henley in 2001). A leading figure in Brexit. Appointed Foreign Secretary, 2016.

Kennedy, Charles, (1959–2015); MP (Lib Dem) Ross, Skye and Lochaber 2005–15. Previously SDP (then Lib Dem) MP for Ross, Cromarty and Skye, 1983–97; Ross, Skye and Inverness West, 1997–2005. President, Liberal Democrats, 1990–94. Leader of Liberal Democrats, 1999–2006 (Jan).

Khan, Sadiq, b. 1970; MP (Lab) Tooting, 2005–2016. First Muslim to attend Cabinet. Won election as Mayor of London (May 2016). First Muslim to hold this post.

Kinnock, Lord, *see* Section B.

Lawson, Lord, b. 1932; MP (Con) (Feb.) 1974–92 (Blaby); Financial Secretary to the Treasury 1979–81, Secretary of State for Energy 1981–3, Chancellor of the Exchequer 1983–9.

Livingstone, Ken, b. 1945; MP (Lab) 1987–2001 (Brent East). Leader, Greater London Council, 1981–6. Won election as Independent candidate for Mayor of London, May 2000. Re-elected Mayor (June 2004) as Labour candidate. Defeated, 2008, by Boris Johnson. (and again defeated, 2012).

Lucas, Caroline, b. 1960; MP (Green) Brighton Pavilion since 2010. MEP, 1999–2010. President, Green Party, 2009–10. First elected Green MP in the United Kingdom. Re-elected, 2015. Leader of Green Party (job share with Jonathan Bartley) again from 2016.

McConnell, Lord, b. 1960; MSP (Lab) Motherwell and Wishaw after 1999. Minister for Finance, Scottish Executive, 1999–2001. First Minister 2001–07. Life Peerage, 2010.

McDonnell John, b. 1951; MP (Lab) Hayes and Harlington, 1997–   . Unsuccessful leadership bid, 2007. Shadow Chancellor of the Exchequer after 2015. On the left of the party.

Mandelson, Lord, b. 1953; MP (Lab) Hartlepool, 1992–2004. Opposition Whip, 1994–7. Minister of State, Cabinet Office, 1997–8; Secretary of State for Trade and Industry, 1998. Resigned, December 1998. Secretary of State for Northern Ireland, 1999–2001. Second resignation, 24 January 2001. European Commissioner, 2004–08. Secretary of State for Business, 2008–10 (with title First Secretary of State, 2009–10).

May, Theresa, *See* **Section B**.

Michael, Alun, b. 1943; MP (Lab) Cardiff South and Penarth after 1987. Minister of State, Home Office, 1997–8. Secretary of State for Wales, 1998–9. First Minister, Welsh Assembly, 1999–February 2000. Rural Affairs Minister, June 2001–05. Police Commissioner for South Wales, 2012.

Milburn, Alan, b. 1958; MP (Lab) Darlington, 1992–2010. Chief Secretary to the Treasury, 1998–9. Secretary of State for Health, 1999–2003. Chancellor of the Duchy of Lancaster, 2004–05. Adviser on social mobility to PM, 2009–10.

Miliband, David, b. 1965; MP (Lab) South Shields, 2001–13. Secretary of State for Environment, Food and Rural Affairs, 2006–07. Foreign Secretary, 2007–10. Defeated in 2010 Labour leadership election by his younger brother, **Ed Miliband** (*q.v.*). He resigned as an MP in March 2013.

Miliband, Ed, b. 1969; MP (Lab) Doncaster North, 2005–. Chancellor of the Duchy of Lancaster and Minister for the Cabinet Office, 2007–08. Secretary of State for Energy and Climate Change, 2008–10. Leader of the Labour Party, September 2010–May 2015.

Morgan, Rhodri, (1939–2017); MP (Lab) 1987–2001 (Cardiff West). First Minister, Welsh Assembly, 2000–09.

O'Grady, Frances, b. 1959; Deputy General Secretary, TUC, 2003–12. General Secretary, 2013–.

Osborne, George, b. 1971; MP (Con) Tatton 2001–17. Appointed Shadow Chancellor, May 2005. Chancellor of the Exchequer after May 2010 (the youngest of the modern era). Also First Secretary of State, 2015–16. Resigned, 2016. Companion of Honour, 2016.

Owen, Lord, b. 1938; MP (Lab) 1966–81, (SDP, Ind. Soc. Dem. after 1990) 1981–92 (Plymouth Devonport); Secretary of State for Foreign and Commonwealth Affairs 1977–9; co-founder of Social Democratic Party 1981 and Leader 1983–7 and from 1988 until its dissolution in 1990. Co-Chairman, Peace Conference on ex-Yugoslavia, 1992–5. Created Companion of Honour, 1995.

Paisley, Rev. Ian, (1926–2014); MP (Prot. Unionist 1970–4, Democratic Unionist 1974–2010) (Antrim North); MEP, 1979–2004; member of Stormont 1970–2, NI Assembly 1973–5, NI Constitutional Convention 1975–6, NI Assembly after 1982. First Minister in power-sharing government, 2007–08. Life Peerage, 2010 (taking the title Lord Bannside).

Portillo, Michael Denzil Xavier b. 1953; MP (Con) Dec, 1984–97 (Southgate). Chief Secretary to the Treasury, 1992–5. Secretary of State for Defence, 1995–7. Defeated in 1997 election. Returned to parliament in Kensington and Chelsea by-election, November 1999. Shadow Chancellor of the Exchequer 2000–2001. Unsuccessful leadership candidate, 2001. Left

the House of Commons, 2005.

Prescott, Lord (**John Prescott**), b. 1938; MP (Lab) 1970–2010 (Hull East); Shadow spokesman on Transport, 1988–93; on Employment, 1993–4. Deputy Leader of the Labour Party, 1994–2007. Deputy Prime Minister, and Secretary of State for Environment, Transport and the Regions, 1997–2001. Remained Deputy Prime Minister after 2001 and 2005 elections with title First Secretary of State (no departmental duties after May 2006). Retired, 2007. Longest-serving Deputy Prime Minister. Life Peerage, 2010.

Reid, Lord (**John Reid**), b. 1947; MP (Lab) Motherwell North, 1987–97, Hamilton North and Bellshill, 1997–2005; Airdrie and Shotts, 2005–10; Secretary of State for Scotland, 1999–2001; Secretary of State for Northern Ireland, 2001–02; Chairman of the Labour Party and Minister without Portfolio, 2002–03. Secretary of State for Health, 2003–05. Defence Secretary, 2005–06. Home Secretary, 2006–07. Life Peerage, 2010.

Rifkind, Sir Malcolm, b. 1946; MP (Con) Edinburgh Pentlands, Feb 1974–97; Kensington, 2005–15; Secretary of State for Scotland, 1986–90; for Transport, 1990–92; for Defence, 1992–5; Foreign Secretary, 1995–7. Shadow Work and Pensions Secretary, 2005 (May–Dec).

Robertson, Lord, b. 1949; MP (Lab) Hamilton South, 1978–99. Secretary of State for Defence, 1997–9. Secretary-General of NATO, 1999–2003.

Robinson, Peter, b. 1948; MP (DUP) Belfast East 1979–2010. Deputy Leader, DUP, 1979–87, 1998–2008. Succeeded Ian Paisley as Leader, 2008. First Minister, NI Assembly, after 2008. Resigned in 2015.

Rudd, Amber, b. 1963, MP (Con) Hastings and Rye since 2010. Secretary of State for Energy and Climate Change, 2015–16. Appointed Home Secretary, 2016.

Salmond, Alex, b. 1954; MP (SNP) 1987–2010 (Banff and Buchan); Leader of SNP, 1990–2000, 2004–10. On left of party. MSP (SNP) Gordon since 2007 (previously Banff and Buchan, 1999–2001). Elected First Minister, May 2007. Won historic victory, May 2011, in Scottish Parliament elections. He resigned as First Minister and SNP Leader after September 2014 referendum defeat. Returned to Westminister as MP for Gordon, 2015–17.

Straw, Jack, b. 1946; MP (Lab), 1979–2015 (Blackburn); Shadow Home Secretary under Tony Blair. Home Secretary, 1997–2001. Foreign Secretary, 2001–06. Leader of the House, 2006–07. Lord Chancellor and Minister of Justice, 2007–10.

Sturgeon, Nicola, b. 1970; SNP First Minister of Scotland since 2014 (having previously been Deputy First Minister for 10 years). Succeeded Alex Salmond. MSP since 1999. Leader of the SNP.

Trimble, Lord, b. 1944; MP (Ulster Unionist) from 1990 by-election to 2005 (Upper Bann). Leader of the Ulster Unionists, 1995–2005. First Minister in Northern Ireland Assembly, 1998–2006. Shared 1998 Nobel Peace Prize (with John Hume). Defeated in May 2005 election. Life Peerage, 2005. Joined Conservative Party, 2007.

Truss, Elizabeth, b. 1975; MP (Con) SW Norfolk since 2010. Secretary of State for Environment, Food and Rural Affairs, 2014–16. Lord Chancellor and Secretary of State for Justice, 2016–17. (the first woman Lord Chancellor). Appointed Chief Secretary to the Treasury, June 2017.

Watson, Tom, b. 1967; MP (Lab) West Bromwich East, 2005–   . Deputy Leader of the Labour Party since 2015. Led campaign against phone hacking and historic child sex abuse.

Williams, Baroness, b. 1930; MP (Lab) 1964–79, (SDP) 1981–3; Secretary of State for Prices and Consumer Protection 1974–6 and for Education and Science 1976–9; Member Labour Party NEC 1970–81; co-founder of Social Democratic Party 1981 and President 1982–8; joined SLDP, 1988. Leader, Liberal Democrats, House of Lords, 2001–04. One of the 'Gang of Four'. Created C.H. (2017).

GLOSSARY OF PUBLIC AFFAIRS

Academies *See* **Free Schools**.

Anglo-Irish Agreement Agreement on Northern Ireland reached by Mrs Thatcher and the Irish premier Garret Fitzgerald on 15 November 1985. The Agreement recognised the right of the Northern Irish people to decide their own destiny but gave the Irish government a consultative role in the province's affairs through an Intergovernmental Conference where political, legal and security matters would be discussed. The Agreement was angrily received by the Unionist MPs who subsequently boycotted the Commons in protest.

Asylum Seeker A person who applies for refugee status because he or she has, in the words of the 1951 United Nations Convention on Refugees, 'a well-founded fear of persecution' on the grounds of 'race, religion, nationality, membership of a particular social group or political opinion.' States that have signed the convention are obliged to grant refugee status to anyone who meets one of these five grounds. The Immigration & Asylum Act 1999, in force since April 2000, made it very difficult for asylum seekers to enter Britain legally. The massive influx of refugees from Middle East conflicts brought the issue to the fore again in 2015.

Black Wednesday Heavy selling of the pound on the money markets in 1992 prompted the raising of the base rate twice on 16 September to 15 %. When this failed to preserve sterling's value relative to the Deutschmark, Chancellor of the Exchequer Norman Lamont withdrew Britain from the Exchange Rate Mechanism (ERM) and effectively devalued the pound. Despite the longer term beneficial effect on the British economy, the crisis with its underlying impression of drift and weak leadership undermined the position of John Major and led to Norman Lamont's eventual resignation.

Bloody Sunday. *See* **Saville Report**.

Brexit Acronym for British exit (from the European Union). This highly-complex process (invoking Article 50) is now underway following the 2016 referendum.

Brighton Bombing On 12 October 1984 a Provisional IRA bomb exploded at the Grand Hotel, Brighton, during the Conservative party conference, killing five people (including a Conservative MP), and seriously injuring Norman Tebbit and his wife.

Brixton Riots Rioting broke out on 11 April 1981 following an incident in the week-long "Operation Swamp" mounted by police against street crime but which the local black population saw as unnecessarily provocative. During three days of rioting black and white youths fought the police, burnt buildings and vehicles and looted the central shopping area. Further riots broke out in Toxteth, Southall, Handsworth, Manchester and a wide range of towns in July. There was further rioting in Brixton on 28 September 1985 (following the accidental shooting of a black woman by police) and again in 1995 after the death of a young black man in custody.

Butler Enquiry Conducted under Lord Butler of Brockwell, a former senior civil servant, into the use of intelligence on Iraq's alleged possession of weapons of mass destruction (WMD) in the run-up to the 2003 invasion of Iraq. Appointed in February 2004, the enquiry reported on 14 July 2004, concluding that intelligence justifying the invasion had been unreliable and criticising the claim in a 2002 dossier that Iraq could launch a WMD attack in 45 minutes. However, Butler attached no blame to any individual and the report was widely criticised as a 'whitewash'.

Cash for Peerages Allegations emerging in 2006 that the Labour government had nominated for peerages individuals who had used a loophole in electoral law over financial contributions by making large loans to the Labour party. The Metropolitan Police arrested (and subsequently released without charge) Labour fundraiser Lord Levy and questioned the prime minister, Mr Blair, his personal staff and members of the Conservative and Liberal Democrat parties. Although the Crown Prosecution Service announced in July 2007 that nobody would be charged, the affair added to growing disillusionment with Mr Blair and his government.

Chilcot Enquiry Launched in July 2009, chaired by the former senior civil servant, Sir John Chilcot to identify lessons to be learned from the 2003 Iraq invasion. The enquiry took written and oral evidence from leading political, military and civil service figures involved in the decision to invade and the subsequent conflict. Hearings began in autumn 2009, were suspended during the general election, and resumed in 2011. There was anger that the report was not finally due for publication until 6 July 2016.

Credit Crunch Term meaning a severe credit shortage, used to describe the response of the banks in 2007 to the 'sub-prime' mortgage crisis when it became apparent they had made many unsafe loans that were unlikely to be repaid by borrowers. In addition, many domestic and foreign holders of capital withdrew their deposits. In response to both, banks tightened conditions on further lending or ceased lending altogether, provoking a recession.

Downing Street Declaration Agreement on 15 December 1993 between Mr Major and Irish prime minister Albert Reynolds offering Provisional Sinn Fein participation in multi-party talks on the future of Ireland within three months of a permanent end to IRA terrorism. Although unification could not take place without Unionist agreement, the British government took a near-neutral stance on its possibility. The Declaration followed meetings between Sinn Fein president Gerry Adams and SDLP leader John Hume (and the revelation of previous secret contacts between the government and Sinn Fein). Hopes of immediate peace were disappointed but Provisional IRA announced a ceasefire on 31 August 1994. This ceasefire ended in February 1996.

Falklands War Fought to restore the 2,000 population on the Falklands (Malvinas) Islands to British control following invasion by Argentine forces on 2 April 1982. A 6,000 strong military and naval task force crossed the Atlantic, landed on 21 May and captured the capital Port Stanley on 14 June, forcing the Argentine surrender.

Freedom of Information Act Legislation passed in 2000, coming into force on 1 January 2005, giving members of the public the right to request and receive information from public bodies (for example, government departments and local authorities) about their activities, though there was criticism of the number of exemptions built into the Act. The provision for ministerial veto was used to prevent the release of Cabinet minutes covering the 2003 Iraq invasion and devolution. An Information Commissioner oversees functioning of the Act. A separate Freedom of Information (Scotland) Act 2002 covers public bodies in Scotland.

Free Schools Schools directly funded by the government, but operating as independent academies outside local authority control, announced by the Education Secretary in 2010, to be run by charities, private businesses, religious groups, parents and teachers and able to operate outside the National Curriculum and to set their own pay and conditions for teachers. By May 2015 255 had opened and around 150 more were planned. It is planned to make all failing schools under local authority control into academies.

Gibraltar Dispute. Under the terms of the 1713 Treaty of Utrecht, Gibraltar was ceded to Britain in perpetuity. It has remained an important British possession ever since (and a major naval base). Spain has repeatedly attempted to secure its return (from 1779 to 1783 it was besieged by Spain) but the local people are equally determined to stay British.

Gibraltar is one of the "Pillars of Hercules" and (from 711 to 1462) was ruled by the Moors.

Good Friday Agreement A stage in the Northern Ireland peace process, the agreement was signed on 10 April 1998 and contained sections on the internal structure of Northern Ireland (including an elected Assembly and power-sharing), the north's relations with the Republic of Ireland (including a number of North–South bodies), and relations between the Republic and the United Kingdom (which included a Council of the British Isles). There were additional sections on constitutional and human rights, decommissioning of weapons, security, policing and prisoners. The Agreement was put to a referendum in Northern Ireland and the Republic on 22 May 1998. Of those who voted, 94·39 % supported the agreement in the Republic and 71·12 % also voted for it in the north.

Greater London Authority (GLA) A strategic authority for London, partly a replacement for the Greater London Council abolished by the Conservative government in 1986. The 1998 Greater London Authority Act provided for an elected mayor and a 25-member GLA covering the 32 London boroughs (both ratified in a referendum held in May 1998). The GLA has a £3 billion annual budget and has responsibility for transport, the environment, planning, the police, fire services and economic regeneration. The first elections for mayor and GLA members – under a form of proportional representation – were held in May 2000.

Healthrow Airport *See* **L52**.

Human Rights Act The Act, which received Royal Assent in 1998 and came into force on 2 October 2000, absorbs into United Kingdom law rights set out in the European Convention on Human Rights, making it unlawful for any public body to act in contravention of those rights and enabling an individual to seek a remedy in a United Kingdom court rather than, as previously, having to go to the European Court of Human Rights in Strasbourg. A court cannot override an Act of Parliament but can issue a declaration that an action is incompatible with the Human Rights Act.

Hutton Report Issued by Lord Hutton of Bresagh, a senior judge, following his enquiry into the circumstances surrounding the death in July 2003 of government weapons adviser Dr David Kelly. Kelly had been identified as the source of a story on BBC radio that the government had exaggerated intelligence on Iraq's possession of weapons of mass destruction before the 2003 invasion. There was speculation about the responsibility for his death. Hutton said in his January 2004 report that Kelly's death had been self-inflicted and no one else was involved. Hutton's criticism of the way the BBC had handled matters led to the resignation of the director-general.

Independent Parliamentary Standards Authority (IPSA) Body established under the Parliamentary Standards Act 2009 after revelations of the abuse by some Members of Parliament of their expenses and allowances system. IPSA sets and monitors MPs' salaries, expenses and allowances, pays MPs' staff, and established procedures for investigating complaints about MPs. There were early complaints from MPs about the cost of IPSA's operations and the body's complex procedures. The current head is Ruth Evans.

Iraq War March Protest march in London on 16 February 2003 organised by the Stop the War Coalition, the Campaign for Nuclear Disarmament and the Muslim Association of Great Britain as an attack on Iraq by Britain and the United States appeared imminent. An estimated one million people participated, making the event the largest such demonstration in London's history. Similar marches were mounted in 60 cities throughout the world. The controversial invasion of Iraq began on 20 March.

Legg Report Issued by Sir Thomas Legg, a former senior civil servant, in February 2010 following an audit of MPs' expenses claims made between 2004 and 2008 after revelations of abuses by MPs, particularly over second home allowances. Legg recommended that 390 MPs (reduced to 373) should repay a total of £1·3 million (reduced to £1·12 million). The three party leaders, Mr Brown, Mr Cameron and Mr Clegg were among those making repayments. Legg criticised both MPs and the system.

MPs' Expenses Scandal Abuse by MPs of the allowances and expenses system revealed by the *Daily Telegraph* in 2009 led to widespread anger and a growing cynicism about the political class, particularly as Parliament had attempted to prevent disclosure under the Freedom of Information Act. MPs repaid over a million pounds and some were forced to stand down at the 2010 general election, while others lost their seats. A number faced criminal charges and the first to be tried were imprisoned in 2011.

Nolan Committee The Committee on Standards in Public Life set up in 1994 under the chairmanship of Lord Nolan following a series of "sleaze" events. One of its recommendations was to set up the office of Parliamentary Commissioner for Standards.

'Non-dom' British and overseas citizens living in the United Kingdom can secure non-domiciled status by claiming an overseas residence as their base. This enables them to avoid taxation on earnings from outside the UK. The issue came to prominence because of the non-dom status of Lord Ashcroft, the multi-millionaire Conservative party deputy chairman and substantial donor to party funds. The government introduced an annual £30,000 levy on non-doms in 2008.

Opting Out Right of a school to leave local education authority control if a majority of parents and governors vote to do so, introduced in the 1988 Education Reform Act.

Prevention of Terrorism Act 2005 Legislation to overcome a 2004 Law Lords' decision that detaining terrorism suspects without trial was incompatible with the Human Rights Act. The 2005 Act introduced 'control orders' empowering ministers to restrict the liberty of suspects through a form of house arrest. In 2006 a High Court judge ruled the orders 'an affront to justice', though the Court of Appeal later said the orders did not infringe the right to fair trial. The Liberal Democrats pledged in the 2010 general election to end control orders but in January 2011 the coalition government proposed only to reform the system.

Privatisation *See* **Section L**.

Public Private Partnerships (PPP) Collaboration between public bodies, for example, local authorities or central government, and private business. PPP is at the centre of attempts by the Labour government since 1997 to revive public services and is based on the belief that private companies are more efficient and managerially effective than public bureaucracies. Advocates say that if privatisation represents a take-over of a publicly-owned asset, PPP is closer to a merger, with both sides sharing risks and reaping benefits. PPP is an important aspect of the Private Finance Initiative.

Saville Report Report of an enquiry chaired by Lord Saville of Newdigate, an English judge, into events surrounding the killing by the Parachute Regiment of 13 people at a civil rights demonstration in Derry on 30 January 1972. Established in 1998, the enquiry began hearings in 2000 and issued a final report on 15 June 2010. Saville found solders had opened fire without justification on unarmed civilians posing no threat. The prime minister, Mr Cameron, apologised in the House of Commons on behalf of the British government. There were criticisms of the enquiry's length and cost, of £400 million.

7 July 2005 Bombings Co-ordinated suicide bomb attacks by four terrorists allegedly associated with al-Qaeda on three Underground trains and a bus in the London rush hour. 52 people (and the four terrorists) died and over 750 people were injured. An attempt on 21 July to detonate four further bombs on public transport failed. The government rejected calls for a public enquiry into the 7 July events, particularly into what previous intelligence the security authorities had on the bombers.

Scarman Report Lord Scarman was appointed to investigate the causes of the April 1981 Brixton riots and other disturbances. His report defended the measures police had taken but pointed to the need for more ethnic minority police officers, for the screening of recruits for racist attitudes and the dismissal of proven racist officers, greater consultation with local communities, more police on the beat, and regulation of police search powers.

Trident *See* **Submarines, L103**.

West Lothian Question A key argument (named after the anti-devolution Labour MP Tam Dalyell who represented West Lothian) in the debates of the 1970s on devolution. In essence, Dalyell asked why an MP for a Scottish constituency could vote at Westminster on English issues, but an MP for an English constituency could not vote on Scottish issues. In the 1990s, devolution went ahead but the question was never really answered. It received renewed attention as more powers were devolved to Holyrood after the 2014 referendum, provoking the call for English votes for English Laws.

THE POLITICAL RECORD SINCE 2005.

2005   Parliament dissolved in readiness for an election (11 April). Labour win historic third term victory (Labour 356 seats, Conservatives 197, Liberal Democrats 62, SNP 6, Plaid Cymru 3, Others 21). Best Liberal Democrat result since 1923. Resignation of Michael Howard as Conservative leader (replaced by David Cameron). Series of terrorist attacks cripple the heart of London (7 July). IRA announce decommissioning of arms. Growing speculation over future of Tony Blair as Prime Minister.

2006   Labour lose Dunfermline and West Fife by-election to Liberal Democrats (9 February). Further Labour local election losses (May) are followed by Cabinet reshuffle: Margaret Beckett becomes Foreign Secretary and John Reid Home Secretary. Growing leadership debate in Labour ranks. Tony Blair questioned by police in "Cash for Peerages" allegations.

2007   House of Commons votes for a fully-elected chamber in debate on House of Lords reform (7 March). Largest backbench rebellion yet (95 Labour MPs vote against government) (14 March). New Ministry of Justice to be created. Further Labour local election reverses. Tony Blair announces (10 May) he will stand down as Prime Minister on 27 June.

2008   Northern Rock nationalised (Feb.); Labour's worst local election results for 40 years include London mayoral defeat (May); leadership challenge speculation following Labour by-election disasters (July); Chancellor warns Britain faces worst economic crisis for 60 years (Sept.); part nationalisation of three major banks in £37 billion rescue (Oct.); largest annual FTSE fall for over 20 years (Dec.).

2009   Interest rate cut to 1·5 % as Britain goes into recession (Jan.); interest rate falls to unprecedented 0·5 % (Mar.); scandal over MPs' excessive expenses claims (May); further Labour setback in local elections and party is pushed into third place in European elections (June); Chilcot enquiry into Iraq war opens as bulk of British troops withdraw (Nov.); economy comes out of recession (Nov.).

2010   Abortive coup against Brown leadership (Jan.); Budget forecasts £167 billion borrowing in 2009–10, stresses government role in dealing with economic crises (Mar.); general election (6 May) inconclusive with Conservatives (36·1 % of vote) taking 306 seats, Labour (29 %) 258, and Liberal Democrats (23 %) 57; Brown announced resignation in attempts to ease Labour coalition negotiations with Liberal Democrats. Tories and Lib Dems form coalition under Cameron, with Clegg as deputy prime minister (May); Ed Miliband elected Labour leader (Sept.); Chancellor Osborne announces £81 billion cuts (Oct.); violent protests against university tuition fee rises (Nov.).

2011   VAT rises to 20 % (Jan.); referendum approves further Welsh National Assembly powers (Mar.); referendum rejects electoral reform by 67·9 % to 32·1 % (May); UK military operations in Iraq end (May); controversial NHS reforms modified (June); *News of the World* closed in phone hacking scandal (July); police shooting of London man provokes serious riots (Aug.); Defence Secretary Fox forced to resign (Sept.); Leveson Enquiry into British media opens (Nov.); Chancellor announces further austerity measures (Nov.); Britain vetoes EU treaty change on Eurozone crisis. (Dec.)

2012   Top income tax rate cut from 50 % to 45 % in budget (Mar); NHS reform bill receives Royal Assent (Mar.); economy returns to recession

(Apr.); Labour gains in local elections, Johnson re-elected London Mayor (May); First Minister Salmond launches Scottish independence 'Yes' campaign (May); Tory backbenchers force abandonment of House of Lords reform (July); sweeping reform of secondary school exams (Sept.); Edinburgh Agreement on terms of 2014 Scottish independence referendum (Oct); TUC anti-austerity protests (Oct.); low turnout in English and Welsh police commissioner elections (Nov.); Labour gains Tory seat in three by-election wins (Nov.); Leveson Enquiry into media recommends new regulatory body (Nov.); Chancellor says austerity will continue until 2018 (Dec.).

2013   Cameron promises EU membership referendum by 2017 (Jan.); government Commons defeat on constituency boundary changes (Jan.); UK loses AAA debt status (Feb.); former prime minister Thatcher dies (Apr.); Labour and UKIP local elections gains (May); same-sex marriage legalised in England and Wales (July); Commons rejects military intervention in Syria (Aug.); Labour leader Miliband promises future energy price freeze (Sept.); controversial draft Royal Charter on press self-regulation (Oct.); first UK nuclear plant construction since 1995 approved (Oct); privatized Royal Mail shares go on sale (Oct.); Scottish Government White Paper on independence (Nov.); Chancellor says economy recovering but further spending cuts required (Dec.).

2014   Cabinet divisions over Chancellor's proposed £12 billion benefits cuts (Jan.); inquest finds Mark Duggan, whose shooting provoked 2011 riots, lawfully killed by police (Jan.); inflation falls to 2 %, unemployment to 7·1 % (Jan.); Cameron says 'money no object' to deal with flood damage (Feb.); Home Secretary announces enquiry into police spying on Stephen Lawrence family (Mar.); tax and pensions changes in Budget (Mar.); Culture Secretary Maria Miller resigns in expenses scandal (Apr.). European elections (May) Former Downing St spokesman and tabloid editor Coulson guilty of phone hacking conspiracy (June); Cabinet reshuffle (July); Tory MP Carswell defects to UK Independence Party (UKIP) (Aug.); Scotland votes 55 %-45 % against independence on 88 % turnout (Sept.); Salmond resigns as Scottish First Minister (Sept.); Parliament approves air strikes against ISIS in Iraq by 524-43 (Sept.); Tory MP Reckless defects to UKIP (Sept.); Carswell wins Clacton for UKIP (Oct.); Labour narrowly hold Heywood & Middleton (Oct.); the British military mission in Afghanistan ends (Oct.); Sturgeon elected SNP leader (Nov.); Reckless wins Rochester & Strood for UKIP (Nov.); Chancellor's Autumn Statement shows failure to hit target of clearing deficit by 2015 and falling tax receipts (Dec.); Murphy elected Scottish Labour leader (Dec.)

2015   Buckingham Palace denies sexual impropriety by Prince Andrew (Jan.); Archbishops of Canterbury and York attack growing inequality (Jan.); Chilcot Iraq war enquiry report delayed until after May election (Jan.) English health charity King's Fund says coalition NHS reforms 'disastrous' (Feb.); HMRC criticised for inaction over alleged HSBC involvement in UK tax evasion (Feb.); former Foreign Secretaries Sir Malcolm Rifkind (Tory) and Jack Straw (Labour) in cash for access scandal (Feb.); Church of England calls for new moral vision in British politics (Feb.); UK inflation falls to 0 % (Feb.); Dudley North Tory candidate resigns after alleged conspiracy with far-right English Defence League (Mar.); Cameron says if elected he will stand down after second term as Prime Minister (Mar.). Conservatives win general election with 331 seats, Labour

232, SNP 56, Liberal Democrats 8; Labour and Lib Dem leaders resign; UKIP's leader resigns, then stays (May); Cameron begins pre-referendum EU reform campaign at Riga summit (May); former Lib Dem leader Charles Kennedy dies, aged 55 (June); anti-austerity demonstrations in major cities (June); 800th anniversary of King John's sealing of Magna Carta commemorated (June); Chancellor announces further benefits cuts and £9 National Living Wage in 2020 (July); Tim Farron elected Lib Dem leader (July); Cameron says UK will take an extra 20,000 refugees by 2020 (Sept.); Jeremy Corbyn elected Labour leader (Sept.); government restricts Scottish MPs' Commons voting rights under 'English Votes for English Laws' (Oct.); Commons rejects SNP motion opposing Trident renewal (Nov.); Chancellor retreats on tax credits cuts in Autumn Statement (Nov.); Commons authorises air strikes in Syria (Dec.); Labour hold Oldham West in by-election (Dec.) criticism of awards to Tory cronies in New Year's honours (Dec.).

2016   Cameron suspends Cabinet collective responsibility in EU referendum campaign (Jan.); shadow cabinet reshuffle and resignations (Jan.); Chancellor warns economy faces 'cocktail of threats' (Jan.); MPs support idea of anthem for England (Jan.); Health Secretary Hunt imposes junior doctors' contract against background of strikes (Feb.); MPs reject England-only anthem (Mar.); growth forecast down in budget, public spending to fall to 36·9% of GDP by 2020, all schools to become academies (Mar.); Budget unravels as Work & Pensions Secretary Iain Duncan Smith resigns (Mar.); troops to be deployed in Tunisia (Mar.) £7·20 per hour national living wage comes into

effect (Apr.); Labour party anti-Semitism row (Apr.); local government, London mayor, Scottish Parliament and Northern Ireland and Welsh Assembly elections (May); plain packaging for cigarettes introduced (May); Labour MP Jo Cox murdered (June); Labour hold Tooting in by-election (June); 51·9% to 48·1% referendum vote to leave EU (June); Labour MPs 172 to 40 no confidence vote in leader Corbyn (June); Chilcot Inquiry report into Iraq War published (July); Theresa May succeeds Cameron as Tory leader and prime minister (July); Bank of England cuts interest rate to record low 0·25% (Aug.); May lifts ban on new grammar schools (Sept.); government approves Hinkley Point C nuclear power plant (Sept.); Corbyn re-elected Labour leader with 61·8% of vote (Sept.); Tories hold Witney in by-election (Oct.); Paul Nuttall elected UKIP leader (Nov.); Lib Dems take Richmond Park in by-election (Dec.). Government admits Saudi Arabia used British-made cluster bombs in Yemen. (Dec.)

2017   UK ambassador to EU Sir Ivan Rogers resigns after criticising government, succeeded by Sir Tim Barrow (Jan.); Northern Ireland deputy first minister McGuinness resigns, collapsing power-sharing government (Jan.); May denies NHS crisis but demands GP surgeries open seven days a week (Jan.); May sets out key objectives in EU negotiations (Jan.); government embarrassment over revelation of aborted Trident missile test (Jan.); Michelle O'Neill named new Northern Ireland Sinn Féin leader (Jan.); Supreme Court rules Parliament must vote to trigger Article 50 on leaving EU (Jan.). Government publishes two-clause Article 50 Bill. (Jan.);

SPECIAL TOPICS

THE 2016 REFERENDUM

Historical Background

Over the last four decades the use of the referendum has become a familiar part of British politics. Prior to the 1975 referendum, the national referendum had not been used in Britain (though its use was common in Europe in such countries as France). In the 1975 referendum, the outcome was a clear victory for the pro-EU camp (67·2% in favour, 32·8% against on a turnout of 64%). Subsequent referenda on devolution for Scotland and Wales were held on 1 March 1979.

During the Thatcher and Major eras (1979-1997) no other referenda were held. But with the advent of Labour under Tony Blair in 1997 further referenda were held in Scotland and Wales (on 11 September 1997 and 18 September 1997 respectively). A referendum on establishing a Greater London Authority was held in May 1998. Much more recently, a referendum on the Alternative Vote was held in May 2011 (with the voters rejecting the proposal) and a referendum on Scottish Independence was held in September 2014 (with a narrow rejection of Independence).

The EU Referendum

The June 2016 EU referendum was the consequence of a pledge by the Conservatives prior to the 2015 general election to hold a referendum if they came to power. It did not stop the Conservatives (even at Cabinet level) taking opposing sides. All major parties supported the 'Remain' campaign. The 'Out' campaign featured UKIP (led by Nigel Farage), as well as many prominent Conservatives (such as Boris Johnson, Iain Duncan Smith and Michael Gove) and some Labour MPs. But the real unknown was how the electorate would vote (especially with the voters wary of opinion polls after they failed to predict the 2015 election outcome).

The campaign officially began on 15 April. The two organisations recognised as the bodies able to spend campaign money were Britain Stronger in Europe and Vote Leave.

The campaign itself was partly overshadowed by

the elections for the Scottish Parliament, Welsh Assembly etc.

The Outcome

When the final votes had been counted, the United Kingdom had voted narrowly but decisively for the Leave campaign. A record 46,499,537 votes were eligible to go the polls. Overall, 51·9% voted to leave the EU, 48·1% to remain. The turnout was 72·2% (higher than in the 2015 General Election) and also higher than the 64·5% turnout in the 1975 EU referendum. In all, 33,578,016 voted. The votes cast to leave were 17,410,000, those to remain were 16,140,000. It was the highest *national* turnout since 1997.

However, these figures disguised some very marked differences across the UK. Both Scotland and Northern Ireland voted to remain in the EU (not a single Scottish voting area voted for Leave). But both England and Wales voted to quit the EU, as shown below:

	Leave %	Remain %
England	53	47
N.Ireland	44	56
Scotland	38	62
Wales	53	47

The much greater population of England carried the day for the Leave campaign.

The Regional Vote in England

Within England itself, there were very marked variations. These are reflected in the table below:

Region	% Voting to Leave
South-West	52·7
South-East	51·8
London	40·1
Eastern	56·5
West Midlands	59·3
East Midlands	58·8
Yorkshire-Humber	57·7
North-West	53·7
North-East	58·0

As the table on **D**22 shows, such industrial areas as the West Midlands and the North East came out most strongly to leave, whilst London was the only English region to vote to remain.

The Constituencies

Just as with the regions, individual constituencies across the United Kingdom registered major differences. Thus the Leave constituency strongholds, all in England, were heavily concentrated in Eastern England (Essex, East Anglia and Lincolnshire) together with some old industrial areas (Mansfield, Bolsover). The Remain strongholds (apart from the exceptional case of Gibraltar) were heavily concentrated in London, in inner city areas such as Hackney, Lambeth and Camden.

The Aftermath

If the result of the referendum had been dramatic, so also was its aftermath. David Cameron immediately announced his intention to stand down as Prime Minister, once his party had completed a leadership election. In the event, Theresa May became the new Conservative leader without the need for a vote involving party members. As UKIP faced mounting internal problems, and Jeremy Corbyn was easily re-elected Labour leader, it was clear Britain was entering a new political era.

THE 2017 GENERAL ELECTION

The Background

The announcement of a snap general election came as a complete surprise, not least because the Prime Minister had repeatedly denied there would be such an event.

One result was a fall in the total number of candidates to 3,307, down 664 from 2015. The Conservatives contested 637, Labour 631, the Liberal Democrats 629 and UKIP 377 (down from 624). The Greens put up 468. The SNP and Plaid Cymru fought all the seats in Scotland and Wales respectively.

The Campaign

At the start of the campaign the opinion polls had shown the Conservatives with a commanding lead over a divided Labour Party. The Liberal Democrats showed only patchy signs of local support and the UKIP vote seemed to be collapsing. However, major blunders in the Conservative manifesto launch and a steady rise in support for Labour suggested a closer result than many had predicted after a campaign overshadowed by deadly terrorist attacks.

The Outcome

The final results produced a political sensation. Instead of a healthy Conservative majority, the outcome was a hung parliament. The final tally of seats left the Conservatives on 318, Labour with 30 gains on 262, the SNP on 35 and the Liberal Democrats on 12. The next largest party was the DUP in Northern Ireland on 10. Turnout rose to 68.7% (from 66.1% in 2015), boosted by larger numbers of young people voting. Swing varied enormously. The best Labour results were in areas that had voted Remain in the referendum, the best Conservative results in seats where they captured UKIP votes. Labour made remarkable gains, such as Canterbury, Stroud and Kensington, while the Conservatives took Mansfield, NE Derbyshire and Stoke-on-Trent South. Prominent election casualties included Nick Clegg (the former Deputy Prime Minister) and Alex Salmond. The Liberal Democrats lost 5 seats but gained 8 (returning Sir Vince Cable in Twickenham). Both UKIP and the Greens fared badly. The Greens returned Caroline Lucas again in Brighton Pavilion but fell back elsewhere. UKIP won nothing and their support evaporated. Their leader, Paul Nuttall, resigned once the results were known.

Scotland and Wales

In Wales, Labour reasserted its dominance, taking 3 seats from the Conservatives. Plaid Cymru captured Ceredigion, the last Liberal Democrat seat. In Scotland, the political map was redrawn as the SNP suffered a major reverse (down from 56 seats in 2015 to 35 in 2017). Their casualties included Alex Salmond and Angus Robertson, the party's leader at Westminster. Most of the losses were to Conservatives (who enjoyed there best result since 1983 with 13 seats) but Labour and the Liberal Democrats also enjoyed gains.

Northern Ireland

The election saw dramatic developments in Northern Ireland, with the DUP taking 10 seats and Sinn Fein 7. Both the SDLP and the Ulster Unionists (the two main historic parties for much of the post-war period) failed to return any MPs to Westminster.

The Aftermath of the Election

Despite the commanding Conservative lead at the start of the campaign, the election produced a hung parliament. An unwanted election had also resulted in an outcome no one wanted. Although the Conservatives moved to stay in power by seeking support from the Democratic Unionist Party, most political observers believed that the Prime Minister had been badly, if not fatally, weakened. It seemed Britain was entering a new period of political uncertainty.

THE COMMONWEALTH, 2017

The Commonwealth is a free association of 54 independent member nations. *See also* **L18**.

Country	Capital	Status	Joined
1. Antigua and Barbuda	St. John's	M	1981
2. Australia	Canberra	M	1931
3. The Bahamas	Nassau	M	1973
4. Bangladesh	Dhaka	R	1972
5. Barbados	Bridgetown	M	1966††††
6. Belize	Belmopen	M	1981
7. Botswana	Gaborone	R	1966
8. Brunei	Bandar Seri Begawan	M*	1984
9. Cameroon	Yaoundé	R	1995
10. Canada	Ottawa	M	1931
11. Cyprus	Nicosia	R	1961
12. Dominica	Roseau	R	1978
13. Fiji	Suva	R	1970†††
14. Gambia	Banjul	R	1965
15. Ghana	Accra	R	1957
16. Grenada	St. George's	M	1974
17. Guyana	Georgetown	R	1966
18. India	New Delhi	R	1947
19. Jamaica	Kingston	M	1962††††
20. Kenya	Nairobi	R	1963
21. Kiribati	Tarawa	R	1979
22. Lesotho	Maseru	M*	1966
23. Malawi	Lilongwe	R	1964
24. Malaysia	Kuala Lumpur	M*	1957
25. Maldives	Male	R	1982†††††
26. Malta	Valletta	R	1964
27. Mauritius	Port Louis	R	1968
28. Mozambique	Maputo	R	1995
29. Namibia	Windhoek	R	1990
30. Nauru	Nauru	R	1968
31. New Zealand	Wellington	M	1931
32. Nigeria	Abuja	R	1960†
33. Pakistan	Islamabad	R	1947*
34. Papua New Guinea	Port Moresby	M	1975
35. Rwanda	Kigali	R	2009
36. St. Kitts and Nevis	Basseterre	M	1983
37. St. Lucia	Castries	M	1979
38. St. Vincent and the Grenadines	Kingstown	M	1979
39. Samoa	Apia	M*	1970
40. Seychelles	Victoria	R	1976
41. Sierra Leone	Freetown	R	1961
42. Singapore	Singapore	R	1965
43. Solomon Islands	Honiara	M	1978
44. South Africa	Pretoria	R	1931**
45. Sri Lanka	Colombo	R	1948
46. Swaziland	Mbabane	M*	1968
47. Tanzania	Dodoma	R	1961
48. Tonga	Nuku'Alofa	M*	1970
49. Trinidad and Tobago	Port of Spain	R	1962
50. Tuvalu	Funafuti	M	1978(S)
51. Uganda	Kampala	R	1962
52. United Kingdom	London	M	1931
53. Vanuatu	Port Vila	R	1980
54. Zambia	Lusaka	R	1964
(Zimbabwe	Harare	R	1980)††

M = Monarchy under Queen Elizabeth, represented by Governor-General (except UK).
M* = Country with its own monarchy. Brunei is a Sultanate.
R = Republic.
(S) = Special Member.
* = Pakistan left in 1972, rejoining in 1989. It was suspended, 1999–2004, 2007–08.
** = South Africa left in 1961, rejoining in 1994.
† = Membership suspended from 1995 to 1999.
†† = Zimbabwe left the Commonwealth in 2003.
††† = Membership suspended in 2000 and again after 2006 military coup.
†††† = Both Jamaica and Barbados have announced plans to become a Republic.
††††† = The Maldives left the Commonwealth in October 2016.

United Kingdom Overseas Territories

Anguilla
Bermuda
British Antarctic Territory
British Indian Ocean Territory
British Virgin Isles
Cayman Islands
Dhekelia (Cyprus)
Falkland Islands and Dependencies
(South Georgia, South Sandwich Islands)
Gibraltar
Montserrat
Pitcairn Islands Group
St. Helena and Dependencies (Ascension, Tristan da Cunha)
Turks and Caicos Islands

Territories of Member Countries

Australia Norfolk Island, Heard Island, McDonald Islands, Cocos (Keeling) Islands, Christmas Island, Asmore and Cartier Islands, Coral Sea Islands   *New Zealand* Cook Islands, Niue, Tokelau Islands

The Channel Islands and the Isle of Man are dependent territories of the crown and do not form part of the United Kingdom. They have their own legislative assemblies and legal and administrative systems.

THE HISTORICAL WORLD

This popular section in *Pears* provides a wide variety of historical facts and figures, ranging from landmark wars and treaties to key terms and events. There is also a concise guide to historic places to visit in Britain. Also outlined are some of the great archaeological discoveries of the last 60 years, including famous sites from Angkor Wat and Babylon to Great Zimbabwe and the Valley of the Kings. For a chronology of world events from the earliest times to the present day, see Section A. For biblical history, see Section H.

TABLE OF CONTENTS

PART I. HISTORICAL GLOSSARY

A

Abdication. The term usually refers to the renunciation of the royal office by a reigning monarch. Both Edward II (1327) and Richard II (1399) were forced to abdicate, James II left the throne vacant without waiting for a formal deposition, and the abdication of Edward VIII was effected by the Declaration of Abdication Act, 1936. Since 1688 when Parliament declared James II to have abdicated, no monarch can abdicate without the consent of Parliament.

Angevin Dynasty includes the Plantagenet kings from Henry II to Richard II. The name came from Henry II's father, Geoffrey, Count of Anjou.

Annates were acknowledgments formerly paid to the Popes by way of fee or tax in respect of ecclesiastical preferment and consisted usually of a proportion of the income ("first-fruits") of the office. Introduced into England in the 13th cent.; annexed to the Crown under Henry VIII; transferred to a perpetual fund for the benefit of poorer clergy in 1704. *See* **Queen Anne's Bounty.**

Anschluss, German term for the union of Austria and Germany achieved in March 1938. Pressure for the union of the two war allies, building up since the fall of the Habsburg monarchy in 1918, increased when Hitler, an ardent advocate of union, became German Chancellor in 1933.

Appeasement Policy. The name of the policy during 1937 and 1938 of yielding to the demands of Hitler and Mussolini in the hope that a point would be reached when the dictators would co-operate in the maintenance of peace. The policy culminated in the Munich Agreement (which was the subject of much criticism) after a series of concessions including the recognition of the Italian conquest of Abyssinia and the German annexation of Austria. The policy was finally demonstrated as futile when Hitler seized Czechoslovakia in March 1939.

Armada, Spanish, the naval expedition fitted out by Philip II of Spain in 1588 against England, commanded by the Duke of Medina Sidonia. It comprised 127 ships, was manned by 8,000 sailors and carried 19,000 soldiers and more than 2,000 cannon. Against this formidable force Elizabeth had only 80 ships, manned by 9,000 sailors, under Lord Howard of Effingham, under whom served Drake, Hawkins and Frobisher.

The British Fleet awaited the Armada off Plymouth, and at Tilbury there was a considerable defensive land force under the command of the Earl of Leicester. On 19 July the ships of the Armada were sighted off the Lizard, disposed in a crescent 11 km long from horn to horn. The excellent manoeuvring of the English, their fire-ships and a gale from the N.W. combined so effectively to cripple the Spanish ships that the Armada was scattered, reaching home via the North of Scotland. It was impossible to embark the army of Parma waiting in the Netherlands. Elizabeth had a medal struck inscribed, "God blew and they were scattered".

Assassination, treacherous murder for political ends, usually of a ruler or distinguished person. Among the most notable: Julius Caesar, 44 B.C.; Thomas Becket, 1170; David Rizzio, 1566; William the Silent, 1584; Henry IV of France, 1610; Jean Paul Marat, 1793; Abraham Lincoln, 1865; Alexander II of Russia, 1881; Archduke Francis Ferdinand of Austria, 1914; Mahatma Gandhi, 1948; President John F. Kennedy, 1963; Malcolm X, 1965; Dr. Verwoerd, 1966; Dr. Martin Luther King, 1968; Senator Robert Kennedy, 1968; Lord Mountbatten, 1979; John Lennon, 1980; Pres. Sadat, 1981; Indira Gandhi, 1984; Olof Palme, 1986; Rajiv Gandhi, 1991; Yitzhak Rabin, 1995; Pim Fortuyn (Dutch far-right politician), 2002; Sheikh Ahmed Yassin (founder of Hamas), 2004, the Lebanese leader Rafik Hariri in 2005, the Pakistani opposition leader Benazir Bhutto in 2007 and the former Afghan President Burhanuddin Rabbani in 2011.

B

Balance of Power was the doctrine in British policy whereby European groups should be so balanced as to prevent the emergence of a dominating Power. Thus the balance was maintained between the Triple Alliance (Germany, Austria and Italy) and the Triple Entente (Great Britain, France and Russia) and preserved peace from 1871 to 1914. After the first world war there was support of Germany's recovery to counterweigh the possible French hegemony; but when Germany's power grew under Hitler leading to the second world war, Britain, France and Russia again became allies.

Barbarossa, the code-name for the German attack on the Soviet Union on 22 June 1941.

Bartholomew, Massacre of St., occurred in Paris on the night of 24 August 1572, when over two thousand Huguenots were massacred by order of the Catholic French Court.

Berlin Wall, construction formerly dividing Berlin. Symbol of the Cold War from 1961 to 1989.

Bill of Rights, or Declaration of Rights, was the document setting forth the conditions upon which the British throne was offered to William and Mary in 1688. This was accepted and ultimately became an Act of Parliament.

Black Death, the plague which swept across Europe in the years 1348–50, beginning in the ports of Italy, brought in by merchant ships from Black Sea ports. It was the worst scourge man has ever known; at least a quarter of the European population was wiped out in the first epidemic of 1348. It reached England in the winter of that year. The disease was transmitted to man by fleas from what some scientists now believe were gerbils from central Asia, though this was not known at the time, the specific organism being *Bacillus pestis.* The disease continued to ravage Europe in recurrent outbreaks up to the late 17th cent. The epidemic in England in 1665 wiped out whole villages and one-fifth of London's population, then estimated at 460,000. Samuel Pepys wrote a grim account of it in his *Diary.* Recently, some studies have suggested the plague was in fact *pneumonic* plague, a mutation from *bubonic* plague. *See also* **Labourers, English Statute of.**

Black Hole of Calcutta, the name given to the place where a captured British garrison was confined in 1756, during the struggle for India between the French and British. Into a confined space, about 6 m square, 146 persons were driven and only 23 were found alive the next morning. The authenticity of the story has been called into question.

Bloody Assizes, the assizes conducted in 1685 by George Jeffreys, Lord Chief Justice, at which participants in the Duke of Monmouth's rebellion against King James II were tried. They were marked by relentless cruelty.

Boer War lasted from 11 October 1899, when the Boers invaded Natal, to 31 May 1902, when the Treaty of Vereeniging ended hostilities. At first the operations of the British troops in Cape Colony were unsuccessful and disastrous reverses were sustained. Lord Roberts was then sent out as Commander-in-Chief, with Lord Kitchener as Chief-of-Staff, and from February 1900, when Kimberley was relieved and Cronje was compelled to surrender and Ladysmith and Mafeking were relieved, the military defeat of the Boers was inevitable by 1902.

Boston Tea Party, an incident which occurred on 16 December 1773, on board some tea-ships in Boston Harbour. High taxation imposed by the British Parliament under George III had caused bitter feelings, and instigated by popular meetings, a party of citizens, disguised as Indians, boarded the tea-ships and threw the tea overboard. This was a prelude to the American War of Independence (1775–83) which resulted in Britain's loss of her American colonies.

C

Capet, the family name of the royal house of France, founded by Hugh Capet in 987, with its collateral branches. The main line of the dynasty came to an end in 1328 with the death of Charles IV when the throne passed to the related house of Valois. The direct Valois line ended in 1498 with the death of Charles VIII. The first of the Bourbon line was Henry IV whose descendants ruled France (except during the Revolution and the Napoleonic era) until 1848.

Carbonari, members of a secret political society originating in Naples, and at one time very numerous. Their chief aim was to free Italy from foreign rule, and they exerted considerable influence in the revolutionary movements in the first half of the 19th cent. Their name comes from the charcoal-burners (*carbonari*).

Carolingians, dynasty of Frankish rulers founded in the 7th cent. The family was at its height when represented by Charlemagne. It ruled, with interruptions, until 987 when the Capetian dynasty succeeded.

Cavalier, a name adopted during the troubles of the Civil War to designate the Royalist party; it is also used generally in reference to a knightly, gallant or imperious personage.

Chouans, the name given to the band of peasants, mainly smugglers and dealers in contraband salt, who rose in revolt in the west of France in 1793 and joined the royalists of La Vendée. Balzac gives a picture of the people and the country in which they operated in his novel *Les Chouans*. They used the hoot of an owl as a signal—hence the name.

Commune of Paris has twice played a dramatic part in the history of France. In 1792 it was able, through its control of the administrative organisation of Paris, to override the National Assembly. In 1871, after the withdrawal of the Prussian troops, it tried to assert its authority. Public buildings were destroyed by members of the Commune and civil war raged during April and half May, but Government troops savagely suppressed the rising.

Concordat, an agreement of convention between the Pope and a secular government regarding ecclesiastical matters. The Concordat of Worms in 1122 between Calixtus II and the Emperor Henry V was famous as deciding a long struggle in regard to investiture. In 1801, Napoleon concluded a concordat with Pius VII defining the restored relations between the head of the Church and the French Roman Catholics.

Convention Parliaments, terms used to describe the Parliaments of 1660 (after the dissolution of the Long Parliament) and 1689, (summoned by William of Orange).

Corn Laws were statutes intended for the benefit of British agriculture, and restricted import and export of grain. From the 14th to the mid-19th cent. such laws were in force, and were often of a stringent nature. They became so oppressive and caused corn to reach so high a price that the poorer classes were plunged into distress. A powerful anti-corn law agitation was organised of which Cobden, Bright and Villiers were the leaders, and Sir Robert Peel in 1846, at the time of the Irish potato famine, carried through free trade. The repeal of the Corn Laws marked an important phase in the transformation of an agricultural to an industrial Britain.

Crimean War (1853–56). This conflict between Russia and the allied powers of Turkey, Britain, France and Sardinia, was connected with the Eastern Question (*q.v.*) and the desire of Russia for a port on the Mediterranean. Chief engagements were the Alma, Balaclava and Inkerman. Fighting virtually ceased with fall of Sevastopol in September 1855. The Treaty of Paris was signed 30 March 1856.

Crusades were military expeditions undertaken by some of the Christian nations of Europe with the object of ensuring the safety of pilgrims visiting the Holy Sepulchre and to retain in Christian hands the Holy Places. For two centuries nine main crusades were launched: First, 1095–99, under Godfrey of Bouillon, which succeeded in capturing Jerusalem; Second, 1147–49, led by Louis VII of France, a dismal failure, which ended with the fall of Jerusalem; Third, 1180–92, in which Richard I of England took part, making a truce with Saladin; Fourth, 1202–4, led by French and Flemish nobles, a shameful expedition, resulting in the founding of a Latin empire in Constantinople; Fifth, 1217–21, led by John of Brienne; Sixth, 1228–29, under the Emperor Frederick II; Seventh, 1248–54, under St. Louis of France; Eighth,

1270, under the same leadership, but cut short by his death on an ill-judged expedition to Tunis; Ninth, 1271–72, led by Prince Edward of England, which accomplished nothing. Thousands of lives were sacrificed in these enterprises which frequently degenerated into an orgy of killing against the followers of Islam and which were an excuse to seize territory.

The chief material beneficiaries were the Italian maritime cities; the chief spiritual beneficiary was the Pope.

Other famous (or infamous) crusades included the Albigensian Crusade (*see* **J3**), the Spanish crusade against the Moors and the Northern Crusades conducted by the Teutonic Knights in the Baltic.

D

Danegeld, tax imposed in England in Anglo-Saxon times to raise funds for resisting the Danes or to buy them off. Edward the Confessor abolished the tax, but it was revived by the Conqueror and subsequently retained, under another name, after the danger from the Danes was past. It is the basis of all taxation in this country.

Danelaw, the law enforced by the Danes in the kingdoms of Northumbria, East Anglia, and in the districts of the five (Danish) boroughs—lands grouped round Leicester, Nottingham, Derby, Stamford and Lincoln—which they occupied during the Viking invasions of the 9th and 10th cent. The country occupied was also called the Danelaw or Danelagh.

Dauphin, the title borne by the eldest sons of the Kings of France from 1349 to 1830.

D-Day, the allied invasion of Normandy on 6 June 1944 which began the liberation of France in World War II. Allied troops landed on the coast of Normandy between the river Orne and the Cotentin peninsula, in the largest ever seaborne invasion. Three divisions from the Canadian and British army landed on 'Gold', 'Juno', and 'Sword' beaches and two divisions of the American First Army at 'Omaha' and 'Utah' beaches. After a fierce battle on 'Omaha' a substantial beach-head—24 miles long and 4 miles deep—was established by nightfall.

Declaration of Independence was an act by which the American Congress, on 4 July 1776, declared the American colonies to be independent of Great Britain. "Independence Day" is a holiday in the United States.

Declaration of Rights. *See* Bill of Rights.

Diet, in German history, an assembly of dignitaries or delegates called together to debate upon and decide important political or ecclesiastical questions. The most famous imperial Diets were those held at Worms (1521), Speyer (1529), and Augsburg (1530), all of which dealt with matters arising from the Reformation.

Doge, the chief magistrate in the old republics of Venice (697–1797) and Genoa (1339–1797, 1802–5).

Domesday Book is the famous register of the lands of England framed by order of William the Conqueror. According to Stowe, the name was derived from *Domus dei*, the name of the place where the book was deposited in Winchester Cathedral; though by others it is connected with doom in the sense of judgment. Its compilation was decided upon in 1085, in order that William might compute what he considered to be due to him in the way of tax from his subjects.

William sent into each county commissioners to make survey. They were to inquire the name of each place, the possessor, how many hides of land were in the manor, how many ploughs were in demesne, how many homagers, villeins, cottars, serving men, free tenants, and tenants in soccage; how much wood, meadow, and pasture; the number of mills and fish ponds; what had been added to or taken away from the place; what was the gross value at the time of Edward the Confessor. It was a meticulous survey.

The record, which did not take in Northumberland, Cumberland, Durham and parts of Lancashire and Westmorland, was completed in 1086, and was comprised in two volumes—one a large folio, sometimes called the Little Domesday, which deals with Essex, Norfolk and

Suffolk, the other a quarto, sometimes called the Great Domesday. The first is written on 384 double pages of vellum in one and the same hand, and in a small but plain character, each page having a double column. The quarto is written on 450 pages of vellum, but in a single column and in a large, fair character. The original is kept in the National Archives at Kew. Since 2006 it has been available online at nationalarchives.gov.uk/ domesday. See also Danegeld.

Durbar, a term used in India from the Persian word *darbár* meaning "court" or "audience". The word was applied to great gatherings like Lord Lytton's durbar in 1877 and the Delhi durbar of 1911.

E

Eastern Front, the battlefront between Russia and Germany in both World Wars.

Eastern Question, a term formerly applied to the problems arising from the instability of the Ottoman Empire and its relations with the other nations of Europe. Later connected with other problems of the Near East such as the possession of Constantinople and rivalries in the Balkans.

East India Company was incorporated by Elizabeth in 1600. In 1613 the Company set up a factory at Surat, India, and in 1662 Bombay came under the Company's influence and developed into an important trading port. Dupleix wanted to establish French power in India and a struggle for supremacy took place. Clive gained the victory for England and thenceforward British dominion in India remained undisputed except by native princes. In 1772 Warren Hastings was appointed the first Governor-General and in 1784 Pitt's India Act established a Board of Control for the India Company.

A great increase of trade resulted, and this rule continued down to 1858, when, as a result of the mutiny, the Crown assumed the sovereignty. British dominion ended in 1947.

F

Farmer-General, the name given to the financiers who in the days of the old French monarchy farmed certain taxes, contracting to pay the Government a fixed sum yearly, on condition that the unspecified taxes were collected and appropriated by themselves. The revolution of 1789 swept the Farmer-General away.

Fifth Column. When Franco, the Spanish dictator, revolted against the Spanish Republic in 1936 and attacked Madrid with four armies, his commander, General Mola declared that a group of fascists within the city was assisting the besiegers. The term is used to describe a body of spies behind a fighting front.

Fire of London, of 1666, extended from East to West, from the Tower to the Temple church, and northward to Holborn Bridge. It broke out in a baker's shop in Pudding Lane, and lasted four days, and destroyed 87 churches, including St. Paul's Cathedral, and many public buildings, among them the Royal Exchange, the Custom House and the Guildhall. In the ruins were 13,200 houses and 400 streets. About 100,000 people were made homeless yet in about 10 years all the houses had been rebuilt. The plague had not disappeared from London when the fire occurred.

Four Freedoms, a phrase coined by President Roosevelt in January 1941, embodying what should be the goal of the Allies. They were (1) Freedom of speech and expression; (2) Freedom of every person to worship God in his own way; (3) Freedom from want; (4) Freedom from fear.

Franco-German War (1870–71) was opened by a declaration of war by Napoleon III, but the Germans who were better prepared than the French, won victory after victory. On 12 September Napoleon with 104,000 men were made prisoners at Sedan, a republic was then proclaimed, and Paris sustained a four months' siege. In the end France ceded Alsace and part of Lorraine to Germany, who claimed a war indemnity of £200 million. Revenge for the loss of these territories was important in French politics.

Franklin, in feudal times a country landowner who was independent of the territorial lord, and performed many of the minor functions of local government, *e.g.* serving as magistrate.

G

Gabelle. French tax on salt, first levied in the 14th-century. Nobility, clergy and certain towns and provinces were exempt while elsewhere it was strictly imposed and proved both burdensome and unpopular. It was abolished in 1791.

Gavelkind, an old English custom of land tenure in Kent and other places in England, whereby on the death, intestate, of a property owner his property is subsequently divided equally among his children.

Geneva Convention, an agreement made by the European Powers at Geneva in 1864, establishing humane regulations regarding the treatment of the sick and wounded in war and the status of those who minister to them. All persons, hospitals, hospital ships are required to display the Geneva cross—a red cross on a white ground. A second conference held at Geneva in 1868 drew up a supplementary agreement. A major result of this Convention was the later birth of the International Red Cross.

Gordon Riots of 1780 were an anti-popery agitation fomented by Lord George Gordon. Called also "No-Popery Riots".

Guelph and Ghibelline, italianised forms of the German words "Welf" and "Waiblingen", the names of two rival princely families whose conflicts made much of the history of Germany and Italy during the Middle Ages. The feuds between these two factions continued in Italy during the campaigns of Emperor Frederick I, and later developed into the fierce struggles of the 13th cent. between emperor and pope. In Italy the Ghibellines supported the side of the German emperors and the Guelphs the cause of the Pope. The present Royal Family of England and other Northern monarchies are descended by different routes from the Guelph George I, Duke of Brunswick-Lüneburg of the House of Hanover.

Gunboat diplomacy, the use of naval power to achieve foreign policy ends—invariably by a stronger against a weaker state—associated particularly with Lord Palmerston's second period at the Foreign Office from 1846 to 1851 and with American policy towards the Caribbean in the 20th century.

Gunpowder Plot was a conspiracy by a desperate band of Roman Catholics in the reign of James I to avenge the harsh treatment to which Catholics were subjected. Barrels of gunpowder were secreted in the vaults underneath the Houses of Parliament, and it was proposed to fire these when the King and his Ministers assembled on 5 November 1605. The plot was betrayed and Guy Fawkes and his co-conspirators were arrested and executed. The date serves to perpetuate the ancient custom of burning the effigy of Fawkes.

H

Habsburg (Hapsburg), the former ruling house of Austria, 1282–1918; held title of Roman Emperor, 1438–1806, except for 1740–5. The aggrandisement of the Habsburg family was mainly brought about by a series of fortunate marriages. In 1521 when the Habsburg power was at its zenith, Charles V divided his dominions into two branches—Austrian Habsburg and Spanish Habsburg. The Habsburg Danubian Monarchy dates from 1526 when the Hungarian and Bohemian crowns were united with the Austrian patrimony of the Habsburg. The union lasted 400 years.

The assassination of the heir to the Habsburg thrones, Francis Ferdinand, at Sarajevo in 1914, provoked the outbreak of the first world war. Francis Joseph's great-nephew, Charles, went into exile in 1918.

Hampton Court Conference, presided over at Hampton Court Palace by James I in 1604 and which brought about his authorised translation of the Bible, had an important bearing on the religious differences of the time. James refused to grant tolerations to the Puritans. This sowed the seeds of civil war. Following the conference three hundred English Puritan clergy were ejected from their livings.

Hanaper Office, a former Chancery office, deriving its name from the fact that its writs and papers were kept in a hanaper (hamper). The Chancellor's office thus came to be known as the Hanaper. The Comptrollers of the Hanaper were abolished in England in 1842.

Hanoverians, Royal dynasty which ruled Great Britain and Ireland, from 1714 to 1901. From the Brünswick-Luneburg branch of the Guelph family, they took their name from the German state of Hanover where they were Electors of the Holy Roman Empire. Their succession to the English, and later British, crown was secured by the 1710 Act of Settlement. In 1837 the crown of Hanover went to the uncle of Queen Victoria, Ernest, Duke of Cumberland and the personal union of the Hanoverian and British crowns ceased.

The British Hanoverian monarchs were George I (ruled 1714–27); his son George II (1727–60); George III, grandson of George II (1760–1820); his eldest son George IV (1820–30 and Prince Regent from 1812); William IV, third son of George III (1830–37) and Queen Victoria, granddaughter of George III (1837–1901).

Hanseatic League was a confederation of North German towns established about 1241 for purposes of mutual protection in carrying on international commerce. The League became so powerful that it was able to dominate the foreign trade of Norway, Sweden, Denmark, and even to some extent of London. A branch was established in London and had its guild hall in Cannon Street for hundreds of years. The League existed until the mid 17th cent.

Hamburg, Lübeck and Bremen are the only cities which, as free ports, still by commercial courtesy retain the name of Hanse towns. *Hansa* is Old High German for Association or Merchants' Guild.

Hearth-Money was a tax laid on hearths (in all houses paying the church and poor rates). Charles II introduced it in 1662, and it was repealed in the reign of William and Mary.

Heptarchy, a word derived from the Greek *hepta*, seven, and denoting the seven kingdoms (*archai*) into which Anglo-Saxon England was divided before 900. The seven were Kent, Essex, Sussex, Wessex, Mercia, East Anglia and Northumbria.

Holy Alliance, an alliance ostensibly for conserving religion, justice and peace in Europe, but used for repressing popular tendencies towards constitutional government. Formed by Alexander I of Russia, Francis I of Austria and Frederick William III of Prussia, at Paris on 26 September 1815. Subsequently joined by all the sovereigns of Europe, except the Pope and the King of England. It ended after the 1830 revolution in France.

Holy Roman Empire, the title traditionally given (although the term "Holy" does not appear in a document until 1157) to the revived Empire when the German king Otto I was crowned in Rome by Pope John XII in 962. It endured until Napoleonic times (1806) two years after Francis II had assumed the title of Emperor of Austria.

Hospitallers, Knights, were of the order of St. John of Jerusalem, at first devoted to the aid of the sick, but afterwards military monks, who became prominent figures in the Crusades of the 12th cent. They adopted the Benedictine black habit with the eight-pointed cross worn by the modern St. John Ambulance Brigade. In 1309 they took Rhodes, but were expelled by the Ottomans in 1522. In 1530 the emperor Charles V gave them the island of Malta, which as Knights of Malta, they held until 1798, when they were finally forced out by Napoleon. The Knights still survive as a sovereign order, with headquarters in Rome. *See* **Templars** and **Teutonic Order.**

Huguenots, a name applied to the French Protestant communities of the 16th and 17th cent. Henry of Navarre, by the Edict of Nantes in

1598, granted them religious freedom, but more than a quarter of a century before—24 August 1572—thousands had been put to death in the massacre of St. Bartholomew. The revocation of the Edict of Nantes by Louis XIV in 1685 drove thousands into exile in England, Holland, Germany and America.

Hundred, the ancient divisonal name given to a portion of a county for administration or military purposes. It is supposed to imply the territory occupied by a hundred families; or the space of a hundred hides of land, or the capacity of providing 100 soldiers. Each hundred had its hundred court, with powers similar to those of a manor court, but this was abolished in 1867 by the County Court Act.

Hundred Days, the interval of time between Napoleon Bonaparte's entry into Paris after his escape from Elba and his departure after his abdication, extending from 20 March 1815 to 28 June. During this period occurred the battle of Waterloo (*q.v.*) on 18 June.

Hundred Years' War, a term applied to the almost incessant contest between England and France, lasting from 1338 to 1453, including such famous battles as Crécy, Poitiers and Agincourt, and engaging successively Edward III, Henry V and Henry VI, among English kings.

Huns, a fierce Asiatic race which swept over eastern Europe in the 4th cent. Under Attila about the middle of the 5th cent, they obtained control of a large portion of central and eastern Europe, forcing even Rome to pay tribute. Their defeat at Châlons-sur-Marne in 451 and the death of Attila in 453 ended their empire.

I

Impeachment, a special arraignment, usually before Parliament or other high tribunal, of a person charged with some offence against the State. The custom in England was for the impeachment to be made in the House of Commons, and the trial to be before the House of Lords. The first instance occurred in 1376 when Lord Latimer was impeached. With present parliamentary procedure, impeachment is no longer necessary, since the Cabinet is responsible for the individual actions of its ministers, who, acting as a team, must carry the Commons with them, or resign, when it falls to the Leader of the Opposition to form a new Cabinet.

Other famous impeachments were those of the Lord High Chancellor Francis Bacon (1621), Earl of Strafford and Archbishop Laud (1640), Warren Hastings (1788), the last being that of Lord Melville (1805). Under the constitution of the United States the President may be impeached by the House of Representatives and tried by the Senate. The first case was that of President Andrew Johnson who was saved from impeachment in 1868 by one vote.

President Clinton became only the second president in US history to be impeached in December 1998. The trial ended in February 1999 with his acquittal.

Impressment, the forced seizure of persons for military service resorted to by many countries before the establishment of conscription. Press gangs forcibly recruited men for British warships especially during the Napoleonic wars, but such measures were abandoned after *c* 1850.

Incas. *See* **L57.**

Indian Revolt (Mutiny). This turning-point in the history of modern India occurred in 1857–58. The ostensible cause was the serving out to the native troops of cartridges greased with animal fat, for contact with this was forbidden both by the Hindu and Muslim faiths. A rebellious feeling, however, had long been developing, and when the Sepoys at Meerut in May 1857 refused to obey the English officers, overpowered and put them to death, the revolt spread like wildfire.

The rebels took Delhi and Lucknow, and for many months massacres and atrocities were committed. Order was restored in autumn 1858 when the governing power was transferred from the East India Company to the Crown.

Indulgence, Declaration of, was the proclamation by which James II suspended the penal laws against Roman Catholics and Dissenters. It was issued in 1688, but the clergy as a body refused to obey, and the trial of the Seven Bishops and their acquittal by a jury followed. An invitation was thereupon sent to William of Orange to become King.

Industrial Revolution. The name, first given by Engels in 1844, to describe the radical changes that took place in Britain during *c.* 1730–1850 to transform a mainly agricultural country into one predominantly industrial. It began with the mechanisation of the textile industry (Hargreave's spinning jenny, 1764, Arkwright's water-frame, 1769, Crompton's mule, 1770, and Watt's steam-engine, 1785), with subsequent major developments in mining, transport and industrial organisation. It was based on Britain's rich mineral resources, particularly coal and iron ore. With the use of the steam-engine as power, industry became concentrated round the coalfields and the great new industrial towns developed—Birmingham, Manchester, Newcastle and Glasgow. Britain became supreme in constructional ironwork (Telford, George and Robert Stephenson).

Canals, bridges, railways and ships were built, and great advances were made in the practical application of scientific principles. Aided by colonial exploitation Britain became the most prosperous country in the world. The new industrial capitalists began to replace the country squires as ruling class.

Iron Curtain. In a speech at Fulton, USA, on 5 March 1946, Sir Winston Churchill used this phrase to describe the dividing line behind which, he said, lie all the capitals of the ancient States of Central and Eastern Europe—Warsaw, Berlin, Prague, Vienna, Budapest, Belgrade, Bucharest and Sofia. The Iron Curtain was symbolised by the Berlin Wall (dividing that city in half) and the rival military groupings of NATO and the Warsaw Pact. The dramatic changes in Eastern Europe after 1989 and the collapse of the Soviet Union in 1991 ended all this as some former Communist countries became members of the EU and NATO.

Ironsides. Cromwell's special troopers, so called because of their solidity and firmness in battle.

Irredentists, a political party organised in Italy about 1878 with the object of incorporating within Italy neighbouring regions. Also a person, group or party advocating policies for the restoration of their country of lost territory.

J

Jacobins, a French revolutionary club or party, formed in 1789, and accustomed to meet at a Jacobin convent, hence the name. It became a controlling force in the Revolution, especially in the movement which led to the Terror. Robespierre was its chief spokesman.

Jacobites, adherents of the Stuart cause after the abdication of James II. First James himself, then his son (the Old Pretender), and later his grandson (the Young Pretender) tried to fan the flame of rebellion in Scotland and Ireland, but after the defeat at Culloden on 16 April 1746 the cause was lost. Also the name of the monophysite heretics of Syria, so named after their leader Jacobus Baradaeus in the 6th cent. A.D.

Janissaries, an élite band of Ottoman foot soldiers who acted as the Sultan's bodyguard. They were conscripts, raised by the "tribute of children" from conquered Christian countries, mainly Serbia and Albania. First recruited under Murad I (14th cent.). They were not allowed to marry. They gained great power under the Ottoman Empire. In 1826 the Sultan Mahmud II had them massacred.

Jesuits. Members of the Roman Catholic teaching order, the Society of Jesus, founded in Paris by Ignatius Loyola in 1540 as a spearheading force in the counter-reformation. Its strict organization made it very powerful and at various times it has played an important part in politics. A long and rigorous course of study is prescribed before an applicant is admitted into the privileges of full membership. The first-ever Jesuit Pope was Francis I, elected in 2013. In the UK, Jesuit numbers have fallen sharply.

K

Kaiser. Title of the German emperor, assumed by the kings of Prussia following German unification in December 1870.

Kamikaze. Japanese suicide-planes in World War II which, laden with bombs, were flown directly into Allied warships. The name derives from a legendary occasion in the 13th century when the fleet of Kublai Khan was destroyed by a typhoon while preparing for the invasion of Japan.

The first kamikaze attacks were made in November 1944 on US warships in Leyte Gulf.

L

Labarum, the standard of Constantine the Great, adopted after his conversion to Christianity, marked with his seal and represented upon the coinage.

Labourers, English Statute of, was passed 1350–51, with the object of compelling labourers to accept a certain rate of wages and not leave their employers' service, the Plague having rendered labourers so scarce that they were in great demand and had been insisting on higher pay. These acts were bitterly opposed and led to the "Peasants' Revolt", headed by Wat Tyler.

Land League, an association formed in 1879, with Parnell as president, for compelling a reduction in the rents of land, and a reconstruction of the land laws in Ireland, and in case of non-compliance refusing to pay rent. For a time this League exercised great political influence and was an important aid to the Home Rule movement.

Leagues, or combinations of kings, countries, communities, have been frequent since the kings of Canaan united against the Israelites. Among the most famous leagues may be mentioned the Holy or Catholic League, which prevented the recognition of Henry IV as King of France until he became a Roman Catholic; and the League of Augsburg against Louis XIV of France in 1686.

League of Nations, was founded on 10 January 1920, with the object of promoting international peace and security. The original members were the signatories to the Peace Treaties at Versailles, and membership grew to fifty-three as new nations and ex-enemy States were admitted. Two notable absentees were the United States and Soviet Russia, the latter not being represented until 1934. Germany was a member from 1926 to 1933. The League had an Assembly which met at Geneva every year and a Council which met five or six times a year. The Permanent Court of International Justice (now under the UN) sits at The Hague. The League held its last Assembly at Geneva in April 1946. Its place was taken by the United Nations.

The International Labour Organisation, set up by the League of Nations, met in April 1944 at Philadelphia and resumed its work at Geneva under the UN in 1946.

Legion, a body of Roman troops, varying in numbers at different periods. A legion was divided into 10 cohorts, and every cohort into three maniples. Three legions composed the Roman army of occupation in Britain.

Lend-Lease. During the earlier phases of the second world war the bulk of British investments in the USA had to be either sold or pledged to Americans in payment for dollar supplies. After the United States entered the war this drain was stopped by the Lend-Lease arrangement, under which Great Britain met the costs of American consumption in Great Britain, while the United States paid for British supplies from America. This arrangement was abruptly terminated on the ending of hostilities; and Great Britain and other belligerent countries found themselves without means of paying in dollars for indispensable American supplies, including the foodstuffs, materials and capital goods needed for economic reconstruction. In these circumstances Great Britain negotiated with the United States and also with Canada a large loan, which was used for buying dollar supplies and played an important part in helping the West European economies to maintain themselves and feed their people while they were carrying through the earlier stages of post-war reconstruction. These loans involved large charges for interest and amortisation in future years, but proved far too small to meet the dollar deficit for more than a short period. In face of this the USA launched the Marshall Plan.

Lettres de Cachet, sealed letters which the kings of France issued to their agents to secure the imprisonment of distrusted or disliked persons without trial. Abolished in 1789.

Levée, a State reception held by the Sovereign or his representative and attended by men only.

Levellers. See Section **J**.

Locarno, Treaty of. See **E27**.

Long Parliament (1640–60), marked the end of Charles I's 11-year attempt to govern without Parliament. It carried through what has come to be called "the English Revolution" and was the parliament of the civil war (1642–49).

Luddites, a combination of workmen formed in 1811, in a period of great distress, with the object of destroying the new textile machinery then being largely adopted, which they regarded as the cause of their troubles. Their first outbreak was at Nottingham, and was stated to have been started by a young apprentice named Ned Ludd.

Afterwards, serious Luddite riots occurred in various parts of the country, especially in West Yorkshire, where many people were killed, mills were destroyed and numbers of rioters were tried and executed. Charlotte Brontë used the period in her novel, *Shirley.*

M

McCarthyism, the term given to the wave of anti-Communist hysteria, associated with the name of Senator McCarthy (1908–57). The campaign lasted from early 1947 to late 1954.

Magna Carta was sealed by King John at Runnymede on 15 June 1215, in obedience to the insistent demands of the barons and has been confirmed many times by later monarchs, even though 60 of its 63 clauses have since been repealed. Its text ran to over 4,000 words. It was in part a reactionary document. It laid down what the barons took to be the recognised and fundamental principles for the government of the realm and bound king and barons alike to maintain them. Its main provisions were that no man should be punished without fair trial, that ancient liberties generally should be preserved, and that no demands should be made by an overlord to his vassal (other than those recognised) without the sanction of the great council of the realm.

A sister document, the Charter of the Forest, was signed in 1217 by Henry III.

Mahdi an Arab leader of great influence, invested with powers akin to those of a Messiah in the Muslim mind. The title was taken by Mohammed Ahmed, who overran the Egyptian Sudan, and in 1885 captured Khartoum.

Mamluks, commonly known as Mamelukes, were originally—in the 13th cent.—a bodyguard of Turkish and Circassian slaves in the service of the Sultan of Egypt, and attained such influence that in 1250 they were strong enough to appoint one of their own body to the throne of Egypt. After that a succession of Mamluk Sultans reigned down to 1517. Then the Turks annexed Egypt, and the Mamluks were taken into the service of the Beys. They again came to the front after Napoleon's conquest of Egypt, but in 1811 they were massacred by order of Mehemet Ali.

Manchus, originally nomads inhabiting northern Manchuria who invaded China early in the 17th cent. A Manchu dynasty occupied the imperial throne of China from 1644 to 1911.

Maquis, name of the dense scrub in Mediterranean France and Corsica, providing good cover for bandits and outlaws. The French resistance movement, 1940–45, adopted the name Maquis.

Marprelate Tracts, seditious pamphlets written with great maliciousness by a group of Elizabethan puritans about 1586, and intended to discredit the episcopacy, caused a great sensation in their time, and led to the execution of their supposed author, John Penry.

Marston Moor. See **E18**.

Martello Towers, circular forts erected on the coasts of England, Ireland and the Channel Isles early in the 19th cent. as defences against the threatened Napoleonic invasion. So called from the circular fort at Mortella (Corsica), which resisted an English sea attack in 1794.

"Mary Rose". See **E18**.

Mau-Mau, a secret, violent, anti-European, movement among the Kikuyu tribe of Kenya, 1953–57. Mau-Mau was a symptom of insecurity and discontent; emergency powers were lifted in 1959, and reforms were instituted. Kenya attained independence in 1963 under Jomo Kenyatta.

"Mayflower". See Pilgrim Fathers, **E9**(1).

Merovingians, the name given to the family that ruled over France from about 500 to 750. Clovis was first of the line and Childeric the last. The "long-haired kings" have become the centre of much recent speculative history.

Middle Ages (c. A.D. 400–1500), usually considered to be the period between the decline and fall of the Western Roman Empire and the fall of Constantinople to the Turks in 1453.

The period covers (a) an earlier part ending with the 12th cent. (sometimes called the Dark Ages) when science was dead, when theology was the main preoccupation, and when the language of the learned West was Latin; and (b) a later age of Arabian influence when alchemy and astrology (at that time indistinguishable from astronomy) were central interests, technology was advancing, and Greek learning was transmitted by Arab scholars.

Characteristic features of the medieval scene were monasticism (**Section J**), the Crusades (q.v.), Gothic art (q.v.), feudalism (**Section J**), and the supremacy of Islam in the field of learning. The period came to an end with the decline of Christendom and the start of the Renaissance.

The term "Middle Ages" was coined by the 17th-century German historian Christoph Keller.

Millenary Petition was presented to James I in 1603, on behalf of nearly 1000 Puritan Ministers against certain of the rites and ceremonies of the Church of England. The Hampton Court Conference was the outcome of this petition.

Ming, the dynasty which ruled imperial China from 1368 to 1644 (before the Manchus took power).

Mogul. See **Mughal.**

Monroe Doctrine, a principle of American policy declining any European intervention in political affairs of the American continent, outlined by President Monroe in 1823. At the same time interference was disclaimed with existing European colonies in the Western Hemisphere. The American Civil War hampered the application of the doctrine for some time, but afterwards the United States firmly insisted on it.

Mughal, the dynasty founded by Babur in 1526 which ruled Muslim India until the 18th century. Fierce warriors, who claimed descent from Genghis Khan. They were also poets, traders and scholars.

Munich Agreement. See **E28**.

N

Nantes, Edict of, was a decree promulgated by Henry IV of France in 1598, giving full freedom of worship to the Protestants of the country. It was the revocation of this edict in 1685 by Louis XIV that drove hundreds of thousands of French Huguenots abroad.

Naseby, Battle of. See **E18**.

National Assembly, the name taken by the body responsible for the opening stages of the French Revolution and subsequently by other sovereign bodies in France and elsewhere.

National Covenant, an oath and declaration subscribed to by the Scottish Presbyterians in 1638 to maintain their religion against Charles I.

NATO. See Section **L**.

Nazi. A member of the *Nationalsozialistische Deutsche Arbeiter Partie* (German National Socialist Workers' Party). The title was adopted by the former German Workers' Party at Munich in October 1920. The party's philosophy was similar to the romantic right-wing authoritarianism of Italian Fascism but after Hitler became leader he imposed his anti-semitic, racialist doctrines. The Nazi party expanded rapidly between

1930–32 due to the mass unemployment of the depression and on 30 January 1933 Hitler became Chancellor. In February 1932 party membership stood at two million. In 1945 the party disintegrated and it was outlawed by the constitution of the German Federal Republic. *See also* **J37.**

New Deal. The measures taken by President Roosevelt in the USA in 1933 to overcome the great economic crisis which broke out at the end of 1929 and to restore the social security threatened by it. The measures were drawn up by a group of experts called a Brains Trust and they provided for recovery by a programme of public works, including large-scale construction of houses and large-scale assistance to farmers. Loans were granted and authorities formed which reduced the workless from 17 millions to between 7 and 10 millions.

Nuremberg Trial. On 21 November 1945, an International Military Tribunal, consisting of one American, one British, one Russian and one French member, began the trial of twenty-four Nazi leaders. Twelve were condemned to hanging of whom ten were hanged on 16 October 1946. Goering committed suicide; Bormann is now dead; Papen, Schacht and Fritsche were acquitted. The rest received terms of imprisonment.

O

Octarch, the kings of the English heptarchy, Hengist (455) was the first, Egbert (800) the last.
Offa's Dyke. *See* **E18.**
Oléron Laws *or* **Judgments,** were a code of maritime laws, introduced into England in the reign of Richard I in the 12th cent. Oléron is an island off the west coast of France, opposite the mouth of the Charente.
Oriflamme, the name of the original banner of the abbey of St. Denis, and adopted by Louis VI as his standard. It remained the national emblem of France for three centuries. The flag was of red silk, the outer edge cut in the form of flames.

P

Palatinate, a term formerly applied to two German regions, historically related, the Upper and Lower Palatinates. Now provinces of Bavaria. In medieval England the term was applied to semi-autonomous areas such as Durham.
Pale, the name given to the part of Ireland colonised by the English and comprising portions of the counties of Louth, Dublin, Meath and Kildare. The Anglo-Norman rulers were styled "Lords of the Pale".
Patricians, the aristocracy of ancient Rome.
Peasants' Revolt, term for the series of uprisings in England in 1381 in protest at the poll tax. In Kent, rebels led by Wat Tyler seized Rochester Castle. They then joined the men of Essex and entered the City of London on 13 June 1381, destroying various properties, including that of John of Gaunt, Duke of Lancaster (1340–99), who was widely blamed for the discontent.
The next day, King Richard II met the Essex bands at Mile End and agreed on a general pardon, the abolition of villeinage and various commercial and economic reforms. Meanwhile the Kentish men had seized the Tower of London and killed Simon Sudbury, Chancellor and Archbishop of Canterbury, and the Treasurer, Sir Robert Hales. By September the government had recovered control of the country and the promises made by Richard during the crisis were never fulfilled. Many artisans and merchants also joined these uprisings.
Peninsular War lasted from 1808 to 1814. Fought in Spain and Portugal by the British, Spanish and Portuguese forces, chiefly under Wellington, against the French. The latter were defeated.
Pilgrimage of Grace (1536), the rising in Lincolnshire and Yorkshire in the reign of Henry VIII against religious innovations and the dissolution of the smaller monasteries, which overlapped with discontents caused by taxation, rising prices, enclosures and land speculation. The insurrection was followed by many executions.
Pilgrim Fathers, the 101 English Puritans who, after living some years in exile in Holland, to escape persecution in their own country, set sail for America in the *Mayflower*, 6 September 1620, landing at Plymouth, Mass., 4 December. They founded the settlement of Plymouth, and are regarded as the pioneers of American colonisation although 13 years earlier a small Virginian colony had been established.
Plantagenets, the kings who reigned in England between 1154 and 1485 and included the Houses of Lancaster and York. More correctly they are styled Angevins, from Anjou, of which Geoffrey, father of Henry II, was Count. His badge was a sprig of broom (*Planta genista*).
Pogrom. Russian word meaning "destruction". First used to describe the Czarist attacks on the Jews in 1881 in Russia. In 1938 Hitler ordered a general pogrom which led on to the holocaust.
Poitiers, Battle of, was fought on 19 September 1356, during the Hundred Years' War, when Edward the Black Prince gained a complete victory over John, King of France, who was taken prisoner and brought to London.
Pontifex, the title assigned in ancient Rome to members of the college of pontifices. "Pontifex maximus" was the official head of Roman religion. It was as "pontifex maximus" that Julius Caesar revised the calendar in 46 B.C., and when after the rise of Christianity the Popes took over the title the revision fell to them.
Potato Famine. Term for the disaster in Ireland in 1845 and 1846 when the failure of the potato crop led to a million deaths from starvation.
Potsdam Agreement was signed by Truman, Stalin and Attlee in August 1945. By this Agreement a Council of Foreign Ministers was established, representing the five principal Powers: China, France, Soviet Russia, the United Kingdom and United States of America, with the task of drawing up the peace treaties for submission to the United Nations. It laid down, *inter alia*, that German militarism and Hitlerism should be destroyed and that industrial power should be reduced. The Potsdam Agreement became a dead letter with the creation of a communist régime in the Russian zone of Germany, and marked the beginning of the "cold war".
Press-Gang, a body of sailors employed to impress men into naval service, frequently resorted to in England, especially during the Napoleonic Wars. Press gangs were not used after about 1850.
Prud'hommes (Prudent Men), **Councils of,** were French trade tribunals, of masters and workmen, formed to decide on disputes. Originally mediaeval, they were revived by Napoleon in 1806, and carried on by the Third Republic.
Putney Debates. The debates during the English Civil War when the Roundhead (*q.v.*) rank and file argued their case for a democratic state that would boast male suffrage, religious toleration, parliamentary reform and rights of property.

Q

Queen Anne's Bounty, established by Queen Anne in 1704 for the augmentation of the maintenance of the poor clergy. Since 1 April 1948 Queen Anne's Bounty and the Ecclesiastical Commissioners ceased to exist and became embodied in the Church Commissioners for England.
Quisling, term which came into use during the second world war to denote traitor, collaborator or fifth-columnist. After Vidkun Quisling, who became head of the puppet government after the German invasion of Norway in 1940.

R

Reform Acts. The first was the great Reform Act of 1832, introduced by Lord John Russell and enacted under the Whig administration of Lord Grey. In addition to a sweeping redistribution of seats, this Act greatly extended the franchise but still left many people without the right to vote. The second Act, passed by Disraeli in 1867, by giving the vote to workers in towns, established household suffrage. A third Act, passed in 1884 under a Gladstone ministry, removed the distinction between borough and county franchise and enfranchised agricultural workers, giving the vote to all men over 21.

Women had to wait until 1918 to get the vote at the age of 30. The Representation of the People (Equal Franchise) Act, 1928, gave them the right to be registered as Parliamentary electors at the age of 21, thus making England into a true democracy. The Representation of the People Act, 1948, abolished the representation of the universities and the separate representation of the City of London and the business-premises vote. The Representation of the People Act, 1969, reduced the voting age to 18.

Roses, Wars of the (1455–85), between the rival houses of York and Lancaster, for the possession of the English crown, began in the reign of Henry VI and ended with the death of Richard III on Bosworth Field. The emblem or badge of the Lancastrians was the red rose and of the Yorkists the white rose. All rivalry between The Roses ended by the marriage of Henry VII, the Lancastrian, with the Princess Elizabeth, daughter of Edward IV, the Yorkist.

Roundhead. In the reign of Charles I and later, a Puritan or member of the Parliamentary party who wore his hair cut short. It was originally a term of derision applied by the Royalists, who usually wore ringlets. The Royalists were popularly known as Cavaliers.

Round Towers, high circular towers with conical roof and massive masonry walls, built during the early Middle Ages (c. 10th cent.). It is believed they served as refuges and lookouts. These buildings are numerous in Ireland, and two remain in Scotland (Brechin and Abernethy).

S

Salic Law was probably instituted in France in the 5th cent. for the purpose of excluding females from inheriting the Crown. The Bourbons introduced the same law into Spain, but this was abolished by decree in 1830 to enable Isabella II to succeed.

Sans-culottes (French = without knee breeches), a term applied by the aristocrats to the revolutionary leaders during the French Revolution who wore long trousers instead of knee breeches.

Saracen, the name given in classic times to the Arab tribes of Syria and adjacent territories. In the Middle Ages the current designation among Christians for their Muslim enemies.

Sassanides were a dynasty of Persian rulers descended from Artaxerxes from 226 to 625.

Saxons, a Teutonic race originally inhabiting what is now Holstein. By the 7th cent. they had, with the Angles and Jutes, conquered and colonised most of England. The three main Anglo-Saxon kingdoms were Northumbria, Mercia and Wessex. The Saxons first arrived c. 449 A.D.

Serfs, the name given to the peasants formerly existing in Russia, who answered to the condition of the feudal "villeins" of England. They were attached to the soil and were transferred with it in all sales or leases. Serfdom existed in Prussia until 1807 and in Russia until 1861.

Settlement, Act of, passed in 1701, assigned the Crown to the House of Hanover in case of Anne's death without children. The decision represented the determination of the squires and the Anglican Church never again to trust themselves to a Roman Catholic king. Talks are now underway to amend the Act. The Act has been amended by the more recent Succession to the Crown Act. *See also* **G25**.

Seven Years War was waged by Frederick the Great and England against Austria, France, and Russia, from 1756 to 1763. It resulted in the retention of Silesia by Prussia, the breaking of French power in India and the strengthening of the British Indian Empire.

Sicilian Vespers, the term applied to the terrible massacre of French people in Sicily in 1282. The French under Charles of Anjou were then in occupation of the island and had been guilty of many cruelties. It began at Palermo on Easter Monday at the hour of vespers and resulted in the expulsion of the French king and the introduction of Spanish rule.

Six Articles, The Statute of the, was passed in 1539 to compel adhesion to Roman Catholicism. Those who refused to subscribe to the Articles were treated as heretics. The Act was repealed in 1547.

South Sea Bubble, the name given to a series of financial projects which began with the formation of the South Sea Company in 1711 and ended nine years later in disaster after a mania of speculation. The idea behind the parent scheme was that the state should sell certain trading monopolies in the South seas in return for a sum of money to pay off the National Debt (which stood at £51,300,000 in 1719 when the scheme started). The idea fascinated the public, fabulous profits being dreamt of, and the price of the stock rose out of all proportion to the earnings of the Company. Many dishonest speculative ventures sprang up in imitation with the inevitable result that thousands were ruined. All classes had joined in the gamble and a Committee of Secrecy set up by the House of Commons in December 1720 to investigate the Company proved that there had been fraud and corruption on a large scale. Sir Robert Walpole dealt with the crisis.

Spanish Armada. *See* **Armada.**

Spartacists. A group of radical German socialists, active from early summer 1915, who founded the German Communist Party (KPD) in 1918. Following a week of street violence in Berlin in January 1919, their leaders were either imprisoned or murdered by members of the Freikorps. The Spartacists were led by Rosa Luxemburg and Karl Liebknecht, both of whom opposed what they saw as the Revisionist tendencies of the German Social Democratic Party. Their name was taken from that of Spartacus, leader of a slave revolt against Rome in 73 B.C.

Star Chamber, an ancient tribunal of state in existence in 1487 and possibly earlier, charged with the duty of trying offences against the government, unfettered by the ordinary rules of law. It was in effect a Privy Council entrusted with judicial functions. Under Charles I the Star Chamber was used by the King and his party to persecute opponents; and in 1641 a Bill carried in both Houses abolished it.

States-General, national assembly in which the chief estates of the realm were represented as separate bodies. In France the states-general consisted of three orders, clergy, nobility and commons. Philip IV first summoned it in 1302 to support him in his quarrel with Pope Boniface VIII. While absolute monarchy was establishing itself it met rarely, and not at all from 1614 until 1789, when it was convoked as a last resort by Louis XVI. But when it met it declared itself the National Assembly which marked the beginning of the revolution.

Statute of Westminster, 1931. An Act of parliament which gave a basis of equality to the British Dominions. The Dominions as well as the United Kingdom were defined by the Balfour Memorandum of 1926 as "autonomous communities within the British Empire, equal in status, in no way subordinate one to another in any aspect of their domestic or external affairs, though united by a common allegiance to the Crown, and freely associated as members of the British Commonwealth of Nations". The Statute was the sequel. The Dominions are sovereign States governed solely by their own Parliaments and Governments.

Suffragette, member of the Women's Suffrage Movement who in the early part of the 20th century agitated to obtain the parliamentary vote. The movement partly succeeded in 1918, when women of 30 were given the vote. In 1928 a Bill was passed which granted equal suffrage to men and women. Among leaders of the Women's Suffrage Movement were Mrs. Pankhurst and her two daughters, Sylvia and Dame Christabel, Mrs. Fawcett, Annie Kenney and others.

T

Taiping Rebellion, 1850–64, the most famous of China's many peasant uprisings. It took place in Hunan and was savagely suppressed with the help of foreign powers.

Tallage, in Norman times, were taxes levied by the Crown upon lands of the royal demesnes. The levying of tallage was taken away in 1340.

Tammany, an organisation founded in New York (c. 1786) and formed from a benevolent society named after an Indian chief. It came to exert a powerful influence over political movements in that city. The leaders of the organisation used their power when their party was successful at the polls to appoint their nominee to every prominent office, and exacted bribes for concessions and privileges, and generally Tammany rule has meant wholesale corruption.

Tiers Etat, the lowest of the three estates of the realm as reckoned in France—nobility, clergy and commons (*tiers état*)—prior to the Revolution.

Tolpuddle Martyrs. *See* E20.

Trafalgar, Battle of. *See* E27.

Trebuchet. A giant siege engine used in medieval warfare.

Trent, Council of, the longest and one of the most important in the history of the Roman Catholic Church, was convened to combat the doctrines of Martin Luther. It first sat in 1545, the last sitting being in 1563. At this Council the general policy, principles and dogmas of the Roman Catholic Church were settled.

Triumvirate, a term used to denote a coalition of three persons in the exercise of supreme authority. The first Roman triumvirate was that of Pompey, Julius Caesar and Crassus, 60 B.C.; the second was that of Mark Antony, Octavus and Lepidus, 43 B.C.

Tudor Period extends from 1485 to 1603. The first Tudor sovereign was Henry VII, descended from Owen Tudor; then followed Henry VIII, Edward VI, Mary and Elizabeth, last of the line.

Turnpikes, privately-owned toll roads, run by trustees, which became increasingly common as a means of improving road transport in Britain from the late seventeenth century. Some produced opposition and rioting, though they are considered to have contributed to improving journey times for passengers, mails, and goods.

U

Uhlan, a light cavalry soldier armed with lance, pistol, and sabre and employed chiefly as skirmisher or scout. Marshal Saxe had a corps of them in the French Army; and in the Franco-German war of 1870 the Prussian Uhlans won fame.

Union of Soviet Socialist Republics (USSR). The Union of Soviet Socialist Republics was formally constituted on 6 July 1923, covering most of the old Russian Empire overthrown in the Communist revolution of 1917, minus the territories which formed Finland, Poland, the Baltic Republics and East Prussia. With the fall of communism, it collapsed in 1991.

Union, Treaty of, was the treaty by which Scotland became formally united to England, the two countries being incorporated as the United Kingdom of Great Britain, the same Parliament to represent both, Scotland electing sixteen peers and forty-five members of the House of Commons. Uniformity of coins, weights, and measures was provided for, Scottish trade laws and customs were assimilated to those of England, and as regards religion and the practices of the law, Scotland was to continue as before. This Act was ratified on 1 May 1707.

United Irishmen. Society formed by Wolfe Tone in 1791 to unite Irish Catholics and the republican northern Protestants in attempts to force reform on Grattan's parliament. It drew support from both northern Presbyterians and from Catholic peasants in the south and soon turned to revolutionary means to secure independence. Its leaders were arrested on the eve of an attempt to seize Dublin with French help in March 1798; after further sporadic outbursts of violence the movement was suppressed.

United Provinces. The seven Dutch-speaking provinces of Friesland, Gelderland, Gröningen-Drente, Holland, Utrecht, Zeeland, and Overijssel which—in alliance with ten other Spanish occupied provinces—fought a war of independence from 1568 until their independence as the Dutch Republic was recognized in 1648.

V

Versailles, Treaty of. The Peace Treaty, 28 June 1919, ending the first world war. The first half was devoted to the organisation of the League of Nations. Among the territorial changes Germany ceded Alsace-Lorraine to France, Posen and the Corridor to Poland. Germany undertook to dis-

arm, to abolish universal military service, to keep only a small army of 100,000 and a small navy. Her colonies were to be shared out among the Allies under League Mandates. Reparations were to be paid, but were gradually reduced and entirely ceased in 1932. Hitler took unilateral action against the Treaty especially in regard to rearmament and the annexation of Austria. Italy also resented the provisions of the Treaty.

Vienna Congress, sat at Vienna from September 1814 to June 1815, and settled the delineation of the territories of the various European nations after the defeat of Napoleon. The Treaty of Vienna which resulted gave Sri Lanka, Mauritius, Cape Colony, Heligoland, Malta and part of Guyana to England; Belgium, Holland and Luxemburg were united in the Kingdom of the Netherlands; Austria took Lombardy-Venetia; Russia took part of Poland; and Prussia, part of Saxony and the Rhenish province. Except for one or two changes the treaty was maintained virtually intact for over forty years.

Vikings. *See* L114.

W

Wapenstake, the ancient name given in the northern counties to territorial divisions corresponding to the Hundreds of southern counties.

War Communism. Bolshevik policy in 1918 to meet the pressures of civil war and economic collapse, including nationalization of larger enterprises and a state monopoly of exchange; the partial militarization of labour, and the forced requisition of agricultural produce. War Communisms's unpopularity and failure led to the New Economic Policy in March 1921.

War criminal. A concept first enunciated in the 'Hang the Kaiser' campaign at the end of World War I. In the 1946 Nuremberg Trials 177 Nazis were indicted as war criminals for genocide and planning agressive war, new and controversial concepts in international law. Ten were sentenced to death.

Warsaw Pact, Eastern European Mutual Assistance Treaty, signed in Warsaw on 14 May 1955 by Albania, Bulgaria, Czechoslovakia, East Germany, Hungary, Poland, Romania and the USSR. A Soviet response to West Germany's joining NATO in October 1954, it reaffirmed the USSR's hold over eastern Europe following agreement to withdraw all occupying forces from Austria. The treaty established a unified command structure controlled from Moscow and obliged all signatories to give armed help to any co-signatory who was attacked. Albania formally withdrew in September 1968. Their only joint military action was the occupation of Czechoslovakia in 1968. With the collapse of communism, the Pact ended on 1 July 1991.

Waterloo, Battle of. *See* E27.

Weimar. Town where the German National Constituent Assembly met in February 1919, which gave its name to the constitution drawn up in July and hence to the German Republic of 1919–33. The economic problems of the Weimar Republic—hyper-inflation followed by mass unemployment—undermined its authority and facilitated the rise of Hitler and the Nazis. In March 1933 Hitler suspended the Weimar constitution to make way for the Third Reich.

Weltpolitik. New trend in German foreign policy which emerged at the end of the 19th century when Kaiser Wilhelm II determined to transform the country into a first-rank global power. Ultra-nationalistic fervour was combined with internal social and economic forces to promote a new interest in colonial expansion, German participation in the scramble for China and the foundation of a powerful navy. The term is sometimes applied with a more general meaning.

Witan or **Witenagemot,** the name given to the king's council of "wise men" in Anglo-Saxon times, composed of the archbishops, bishops, abbots of the greater abbeys, earldormen and influential thanes.

Wounded Knee. Scene of the massacre of at least 200 Hunkpapa Sioux, mostly women and children, by a unit of the US Seventh Cavalry shortly after Christmas 1890. The events at Wounded Knee Creek, South Dakota, now symbolize the end of the Plains Indians' resistance to American expansion.

PART II. HISTORIC BRITAIN

This section provides a wide-ranging guide to a selection of places to visit relating to interesting people, events and developments in British history. The references at the end of each entry will provide more information about visiting a site: location, opening times, *etc.* The website addresses of the following organisations, which appear most frequently in the text, are: National Trust – www.nationaltrust.org.uk; English Heritage – www.english-heritage.org.uk; National Trust for Scotland – www.nts.org.uk; Historic Scotland – www.historic-scotland.gov.uk; CADW: Welsh Historic Monuments – www.cadw.wales.gov.uk

A

Abbey Road, London NW8. A road in St John's Wood where EMI opened the first purpose-built recording studios in 1931. In the 1960s The Beatles made many hit records there and put it on the map in 1969 by calling the last album they recorded as a group *Abbey Road.* The pedestrian crossing that features on the album cover is getting Grade-II listed status. The studios opened to the public for the first time for a festival of films scored at Abbey Road in spring 2005. In 2010 the studios were given a Grade II listing. (www.abbeyroad.co.uk)

Abbotsford, Borders. Scottish baronial-style house on the River Tweed near Melrose, completed in 1824 for the novelist and poet, Sir Walter Scott. His study and library, containing some 9,000 rare books, are particularly atmospheric. (www.scottsabbotsford.co.uk) Scott is also commemorated by the Scott Monument, a Gothic spire designed by George Meikle Kemp, with a statue of Scott by Sir John Steell. It was inaugurated in 1846 in East Princes Street Gardens, Edinburgh. There are 287 steps to the top.

Alnwick Castle, Northumberland. Home of the Percy family, the Earls and Dukes of Northumberland, since 1309. Known as 'the Windsor of the North', it features as Hogwarts school in the Harry Potter films. (www.alnwickcastle.com) New gardens, created by the Duchess of Northumberland, were opened in 2002. (www.alnwickgarden.com)

Althorp, Northamptonshire. Home of the Spencer family for more than 500 years. In 1997 a small island in the middle of the 'Round Oval' lake at Althorp was chosen as the final resting place of Diana, Princess of Wales, by her brother, Earl Spencer. There is an exhibition in the stable block commemorating her life and also her work. (www.althorp.com)

Antonine Wall, Falkirk. Roman defensive works, stretching 60 kms from the Clyde to the Firth of Forth, were begun in A.D. 142, in the reign of Emperor Antoninus Pius. The wall consisted of a turf rampart on stone foundations, with a timber palisade on top, a wide ditch in front and a Military Way running behind. By A.D. 180 the Romans had withdrawn to Hadrian's Wall. The best-preserved sections of ditch and rampart, together with the earthworks of Rough Castle fort, can be seen west from Falkirk, around Bonnybridge. Created a UNESCO World Heritage Site in 2008. (Historic Scotland)

Apsley House, London W1. The London residence of the Duke of Wellington at Hyde Park Corner ('Number 1, London'). The house contains many trophies of his career. (English Heritage) Wellington is also associated with Stratfield Saye House and Walmer Castle, *q.v.*

Avebury Stone Circles, Wiltshire. The principal circle, the largest in the world, dates from around 2500 B.C., and originally had 98 standing stones (only 27 now remain). With its surrounding ditch and outer bank, it covers 12 hectares. In 1986 Avebury was designated part of a UNESCO World Heritage Site, together with Stonehenge. There is a museum, named after Alexander Keiller who investigated the site in the 1930s. (National Trust) *See also* **E35.**

B

Badbury Rings, Dorset. An Iron Age hill fort near Wimborne Minster, acquired by the National Trust in 1982. It consists of three concentric earth ramparts, enclosing an area planted with trees in the 18th century. It is one of the sites suggested for the battle of Mount Badon in the early 6th century when the Britons under Arthur won a great victory over the Saxons. (National Trust)

Balmoral Castle, Aberdeenshire. The estate was purchased by Prince Albert for Queen Victoria in 1852, and the new house was built in the Scottish baronial style in 1853–56. Since then it has been 'a favourite home to successive generations of the Royal Family.' The grounds and the largest room in the castle, the ballroom, are open to the public. (www.balmoralcastle.com)

Bannockburn, Stirling. Site of the battle on 24 June 1314 when King Edward II's army, attempting to relieve Stirling Castle, was heavily defeated by the Scots under Robert the Bruce. The traditional location of Robert the Bruce's command post is marked by the Borestone and a bronze equestrian statue of the Scottish King by Pilkington Jackson, unveiled in 1964. There is a renovated Heritage Centre. (National Trust for Scotland)

Banqueting House, London SW1. All that remains of the great Whitehall Palace, destroyed by fire in 1698. It was designed by Inigo Jones and completed in 1622. The magnificent ceiling paintings were added by Rubens in the 1630s. In 1649 King Charles I was executed on a platform in front of the building. (www.banqueting-house.org.uk)

Barnet, Greater London. The battle of Barnet in the Wars of the Roses took place at Monken Hadley, just to the north of Barnet, on 14 April 1471. The Yorkists defeated the Lancastrians. The stone obelisk beside the A1000 road was erected in 1740; according to the inscription it marks the site of the battle where the Lancastrian leader, Warwick the Kingmaker, 'was defeated and slain.' (www.btlse.co.uk)

Bath, Bath & NE Somerset. Bath is an historical *tour de force* with the remains of the baths of Roman Aquae Sulis, the Abbey – the 'Lantern of the West' – and the magnificent architecture of the Georgian spa town. UNESCO recognised the city as a whole as a World Heritage Site in 1987. (www.visitbath.co.uk)

Battle Abbey, East Sussex. This was the site, about 10 kms north-west of Hastings, where Duke William's invading Norman army defeated King Harold's Anglo-Saxons on 14 October 1066. William founded Battle Abbey in 1070 to atone for the loss of life during his conquest of England. The exact site of the battle remains hotly debated.

Beaulieu Abbey, Hampshire. A Cistercian Abbey was founded here in 1204. The Great Gatehouse became the home of the Montagu Family – Palace House – in 1538 after the Dissolution. In the grounds of Beaulieu Abbey one of the most influential features of life in the 20th century – the motorcar – is celebrated in the National Motor Museum, which opened to the public in 1972. (www.beaulieu.co.uk)

Beaumaris Castle, Isle of Anglesey. Construction of this, the last of King Edward I's Welsh castles, began in 1295. Not as impressive as Caernarvon or Harlech when viewed from a distance, it is probably the strongest and best-preserved concentric castle in Britain. It is one of the components of the Edwardian castles and town walls World Heritage Site, listed by UNESCO in 1987. (CADW)

Belfast, HMS, London SE1. The last survivor of the Royal Navy's heavy cruisers is moored by Tower Bridge and preserved as part of the Imperial War Museum. She was launched in 1938, and took part in convoy work, the battle of North Cape and the D-Day bombardment of Normandy. Exploring HMS *Belfast* gives an insight into what life was like in a great warship during the Second World War. (www.hmsbelfast.org.uk)

Berkeley Castle, Gloucestershire. A 12th-century castle that has been home to the Berkeley family since 1153. It is best known for the brutal murder of Edward II in 1327, and visitors can see the King's place of imprisonment. According to *1066 and All That*, 'horrible screams' were heard from the castle and the next day Edward was 'horribly dead'. (www.berkeley-castle.com)

Bignor Roman Villa, West Sussex. The villa, which lay close to Roman Stane Street, was discovered by a farmer ploughing his land in 1811. It was occupied from the 2nd to the 4th century, and was one of the largest in Britain, covering two hectares. It has some exceptional mosaics, including one that runs for 24 metres in all and is thought to be the longest in the country. (www.romansinsussex.co.uk)

Bladon, Oxfordshire. When Sir Winston Churchill died in 1965 he was buried with his parents in the churchyard of St Martin's, Bladon, on the south side of Blenheim Park. When Lady Churchill died in 1977, she was buried beside him. (www.blenheimpalace.com)

Blaenavon, Torfaen. This Welsh town was designated a World Heritage Site by UNESCO in 2000 on the grounds that it constituted an 'outstanding and remarkably complete example of a 19th century industrial landscape.' Centrepiece of this landscape today is the Big Pit colliery. It closed in 1980 and is now the National Mining Museum of Wales. Visitors can descend the 86 metres to the pit floor and be given a guided tour by a former miner. (www.nmgw.ac.uk)

Blenheim Palace, Oxfordshire. Home of the Dukes of Marlborough, and birthplace of Sir Winston Churchill in 1874. It was designed by Sir John Vanbrugh and presented to the first Duke to mark his victory over the French and Bavarians at Blenheim in 1704. The tapestries depicting Marlborough's victories are an outstanding exhibit. The Palace was designated a UNESCO World Heritage Site in 1987. (www.blenheimpalace.com)

Bletchley Park, Milton Keynes. Home of the Government Code and Cipher School in the Second World War and the 'birthplace of modern computing.' The team at Bletchley, including figures such as Turing, broke the German 'Enigma' machine ciphers and produced the top secret 'Ultra' information that helped to win the war. The whole operation remained secret until the 1970s. The Bletchley Park Trust was formed in 1992 and the site opened as a museum in 1994. (www.bletchleypark.org.uk)

Bodiam Castle, East Sussex. The castle was built by Sir Edward Dallingrigge in 1385 to defend the area against French raiders. It was bought by Lord Curzon in 1917, restored and given to the National Trust. Today, as the handbook says, it is 'the perfect example of a late-medieval moated castle.' (National Trust)

Boscobel House, Shropshire. The future King Charles II hid here, famously spending the day up an oak tree, after his defeat at the battle of Worcester in 1651. (English Heritage) Another of the royal fugitive's hiding places was a priest's hole at Moseley Old Hall, which was acquired by the National Trust in 1962.

Bosworth Field, Leicestershire. King Richard III (*see* **B51**) was defeated and killed here by Henry Tudor on 22 August 1485, gaining the distinction of being the last English king to die leading his soldiers into battle. There is a Visitor Centre and battlefield trail on the site, though the latest research, including the discovery of primitive bullets and cannonballs, suggests that the battle was actually fought two miles away. (www.bosworth battlefield.com)

Brading Roman Villa, Isle of Wight. A 3rd century Roman villa, once at the heart of a prosperous farming estate. Discovered in 1879, it has some fine mosaics, including a head of Medusa surrounded by other classical mythological figures. (www.bradingromanvilla.org.uk)

Brantwood, Cumbria. The Victorian writer and artist, John Ruskin, lived in this house from 1872 to 1900. It lies on the eastern side of Coniston Water, and contains some of Ruskin's paintings, furniture and books. (www.brantwood.org.uk)

Bristol Temple Meads, City of Bristol. When Isambard Kingdom Brunel (*q.v.*) designed the Old Station at Temple Meads for the Great Western Railway in 1839, it was one of the first main line railway termini to be built in Britain. It remained in use until the 1960s. It is now a Grade I listed building, and since 2002 it has been the home of the British Empire and Commonwealth Museum. (www.empiremuseum.co.uk)

Broadlands, Hampshire. An elegant Palladian mansion on the banks of the River Test, which was the birthplace and home of the Victorian Prime Minister, Lord Palmerston. The house is particularly associated with a later resident, Lord Mountbatten. He opened the house to the public in 1979, only months before he was assassinated by the IRA. There is an exhibition telling the story of Mountbatten's career. (www.broadlands.net)

Brooklands, Surrey. The birthplace of British motorsport and aviation. The world's first motor-racing circuit was built here in 1907. Today many of the original buildings and the race-track form part of a museum, which has a fine collection of historic vehicles *etc*. (www.brooklandsmuseum.co)

Brownsea Island, Dorset. In 1907 Robert Baden-Powell held a camp on the island from which developed the Scouting and Guiding movement. The island is located in Poole Harbour and was acquired by the National Trust in 1962. Part of the island is leased to the Dorset Wildlife Trust as a nature reserve. (National Trust)

Buckingham Palace. *See* Section L.

Burghley House, Lincolnshire. The house was completed in 1587 for Sir William Cecil, later Lord Burghley, principal adviser and Lord High Treasurer to Queen Elizabeth I. The house has a large collection of art, porcelain and furniture. The 120-hectare deer park was landscaped by Capability Brown. Burghley is near the attractive old town of Stamford. (www.burghley.co.uk)

C

Cabinet War Rooms, London SW1. Work began in 1938 on creating emergency underground accommodation beneath government offices in Whitehall in anticipation of enemy bombing raids on London. Today visitors can see what became the nerve centre of the war effort during the Second World War, including the Map Room, Cabinet Room and also Churchill's bedroom. A fascinating Churchill Museum opened in 2005. (www.iwm.org.uk)

Cadbury Castle, Somerset. An Iron Age hill fort with massive earth ramparts covering 7 hectares. It is one of the leading candidates for the historical site of Arthur's headquarters, 'Camelot'. Extensive archaeological excavations in the 1960s showed that the site had been re-fortified in the Arthurian period, and revealed the remains of a large feasting hall. The site is known to have been a royal mint in the time of Aethelred the Unready. (www.time-scapes.co.uk)

Caerleon, Newport. Known to the Romans as Isca Silurum, this was an important Roman military base and headquarters of the 2nd Legion Augusta from A.D. 75 to 300. There are baths, a well-preserved amphitheatre and barrack blocks. (CADW). There is a Roman Legionary Museum. (www.nmgw.ac.uk)

Caernarvon Castle, Gwynedd. Work on the most impressive and costliest of Edward I's castles began in 1283 and continued for fifty years. The unusual polygonal towers, particularly the Eagle Tower, and the bands of coloured stone are said to have been inspired by Constantinople. Edward I created his son Prince of Wales here in 1301; the investiture of Prince Charles took place in 1969. It is a UNESCO World Heritage Site. (CADW)

Caerphilly Castle, Caerphilly. The castle's land and water defences cover some 12 hectares, making it the second largest castle in Britain after Windsor Castle. It was begun in 1268 by the King's son-in-law, Gilbert de Clare, and was one of the first concentric castles in the country. (CADW)

Cambridge University. *See* **Section L**.

Canterbury Cathedral, Kent. The Cathedral was founded by St Augustine, who arrived in Kent in A.D. 597 to convert the people to Christianity. Archbishop Lanfranc began building the present Cathedral in 1070. It became a place of pilgrimage after the murder of Archbishop Thomas Becket in 1170. The central tower, called Bell Harry Tower, dates from the late 15th century. In 1988 the Cathedral, together with the remains of St Augustine's Abbey and St Martin's Church, the oldest church in England still in use, were designated a World Heritage Site by UNESCO. (www.canterbury-cathedral.org)

Carisbrooke Castle, Isle of Wight. A castle with fortifications of many periods, ranging from the Norman motte surmounted by a 12th century shell keep, to the late 16th century artillery bastions. Charles I was held prisoner here in 1647–48. The original window that proved too narrow and foiled one of his escape attempts was replaced in the 19th century. (English Heritage)

Castle Howard, North Yorkshire. The house was constructed mainly between 1701 and 1712 for Charles Howard, 3rd Earl of Carlisle. It was the first building designed by playwright Sir John Vanbrugh, who went on to design Blenheim Palace. The façade is dominated by the dome, restored after a disastrous fire in 1940. There is an arboretum, called 'Kew at Castle Howard'; it opened to the public in 1999, and is a joint venture with the Royal Botanic Gardens at Kew. (www.castlehoward.co.uk)

Castlerigg Stone Circle, Cumbria. Near Keswick, this is thought to be one of the earliest stone circles in Britain. There are 38 stones in the circle, and a rectangle of 10 stones within it. The antiquarian, William Stukeley, popularised the linking of it with the Druids in the 18th century. John Keats visited the Circle in 1818, and in his poem *Hyperion* referred to it as 'a dismal cirque of Druid stones upon a forlorn moor.' (National Trust)

Chartwell, Kent. Sir Winston Churchill bought the house in 1922, and it was his family home until his death in 1965. The National Trust, which acquired the house in 1946, has left the interior and the gardens much as they were in Churchill's day. Many of Churchill's paintings and the brick walls he built can be seen. (National Trust)

Chatham Historic Dockyard, Kent. This was the site of an important Royal Dockyard on the River Medway from 1613 up to its closure in 1984. It covered 32 hectares and is said to be the most complete dockyard from the age of sail in the world. Over 400 Royal Navy ships were built there, including HMS *Victory*. Three historic warships are preserved there – HMS *Gannet* (1878),

HMS *Cavalier* (1944) and HM Submarine *Ocelot* (1962) – together with the national collection of lifeboats. (www.chdt.org.uk)

Chatsworth, Derbyshire. A baroque mansion that is the family home of the Cavendishes, the Dukes of Devonshire. In addition to all that the house has to offer, the grounds have magnificent water features, including the early 18th century cascade and the Emperor Fountain, designed and constructed in the 1840s by Joseph Paxton (of Crystal Palace fame), who was the head gardener at Chatsworth. On an autumn day the view of the house from the bridge across the River Derwent is especially beautiful. (www.chatsworth.org)

Chedworth Roman Villa, Gloucestershire. The villa was one of the largest in the country, lying close to the Fosse Way in rich farming country. It was first excavated in 1864, and the site includes mosaics, bathhouses, hypocausts and a water shrine. (National Trust)

Cirencester, Gloucestershire. Known to the Romans as Corinium, this was the second largest city in Roman Britain after London. Sections of the walls can be seen, together with the remains of a 9,000-seater amphitheatre. (English Heritage) There are fine mosaics and sculptures in the Corinium Museum. (www.cotswold.gov.uk)

Cissbury Ring, West Sussex. This Iron Age hill fort lies on the South Downs to the north of Worthing and covers an area of 26 hectares. There is evidence of extensive mining of flint for making tools. (National Trust)

Claydon House, Buckinghamshire. The site has been the home of the Verney family since 1620. The present house was built in the 18th century. Florence Nightingale was the sister-in-law of the 2nd Baronet, Sir Harry Verney, and her bedroom and various mementoes have been preserved. (National Trust)

Clifton Suspension Bridge, Bristol. The bridge across the Avon Gorge was designed by Isambard Kingdom Brunel. The foundation stone was laid in 1831, but political and financial difficulties led to the abandonment of the project in 1843, with only the towers built. It was finally completed in 1864, five years after Brunel's death. At 214 metres, it had the longest suspended span in the world. There are guided tours of the bridge. (www.clifton-suspension-bridge.org.uk)

Colchester, Essex. The Roman city was known as Camulodunum. Relics of that period include the Balkerne Gate, the largest surviving Roman gateway in Britain. Colchester Castle, an important visitor attraction which now houses a museum with displays of Roman artefacts, was built by the Normans on the vaults of the Roman Temple of Claudius, and had the largest keep in Europe. (www.colchestermuseums.org.uk)

Conwy Castle, Conwy. The castle and town walls were built by King Edward I in 1283–87, and are today part of a UNESCO World Heritage Site. The town walls, with their 21 towers, are the best-preserved in Britain. The aerial photographs and artist's impressions in the CADW guidebook give a good idea of the whole site. (CADW)

Corfe Castle, Dorset. Before the present castle was built this was the site of the murder of King Edward the Martyr by his step-mother Elfryda in A.D. 978. In the Middle Ages it was a royal fortress, palace, treasury and prison. Held for the Royalists in the English Civil War, it withstood a siege in 1643, but was captured by treachery at the end of a second siege in 1646. It was then thoroughly 'slighted' on Parliament's orders, leaving us with one of the most impressive ruins in the country. (National Trust)

Cornish Mining Landscape, Cornwall. In 2006 UNESCO accorded World Heritage Site status to the tin and copper mining buildings and landscapes of Cornwall and west Devon, developed between 1700 and 1914. There are ten separate locations for these pioneering industries, including Geevor Tin Mine (www.geevor.com) and various National Trust sites such as the Levant Mine and Beam Engine.

Coventry Cathedral, Coventry. The cathedral stands beside the remains of the 13th century St Michael's Cathedral, which was destroyed by German bombers on the night of 14 November 1940. The new cathedral was designed by Sir Basil Spence and consecrated in 1962. It is notable for its Graham Sutherland altar tapestry, John Piper stained glass and Sir Jacob Epstein's bronze sculpture of St Michael subduing the devil. (www.coventrycathedral.org.uk)

Cragside, Northumberland. This Victorian mansion was designed by Richard Norman Shaw for the inventor, engineer and arms manufacturer, William Armstrong. It was the first house in the world to be lit by hydro-electricity. Armstrong landscaped the grounds, with woodlands and one of the largest rock gardens in Europe. It was acquired by the National Trust in 1977. (National Trust)

Culloden Moor, Highland. Site of the last major battle on British soil. On 16 April 1746 Prince Charles Edward Stuart led his clansmen to defeat at the hands of the Duke of Cumberland's Hanoverian forces, ending the Jacobite Rebellion.
There are a number of features to see on the battlefield, such as the Memorial Cairn, the Cumberland Stone and the Graves of the Clans. The National Trust for Scotland opened the new Culloden Battlefield Memorial Centre at the end of 2007. (www.nts.org.uk/Culloden)

Cutty Sark, London SE10. This famous tea clipper was built at Dumbarton on the Clyde in 1869. Her fastest time to London from the Far East round the Cape was 107 days in 1871. She opened to the public at Greenwich in 1957. Whilst undergoing construction work the ship was badly damaged by fire in May 2007. Renovation was completed in 2012 and she was re-opened to the public. She took her name from the Scottish phrase for an undergarment. (www.cuttysark.org.uk)

D

Deal Castle, Kent. A fine example of the coastal defences built by King Henry VIII in 1539–40. It is a castle for the artillery age, with a low profile and rounded bastions capable of mounting more than 100 guns. The cloverleaf design was already out of fashion when Henry built his castle at Southsea in Hampshire in 1545, incorporating angled rather than rounded bastions. (English Heritage)

Derwent Valley Mills, Derbyshire. The Derwent Valley, south of Matlock, is an important area for industrial archaeology. The Derwent Valley Mills were designated a UNESCO World Heritage Site in 2001. Cromford Mill, established by Sir Richard Arkwright in 1771, was the first water-powered cotton spinning mill. Historians refer to it as 'the true blueprint for factory production.' (www.derwentvalleymills.org)

Dover Roman Painted House, Kent. An unusual relic of Roman Britain, the painted house, which was discovered in 1970, is thought to have been built about A.D. 200 as a hotel for official visitors arriving in Britain. It has unique frescoes relating to Bacchus. The Roman name for Dover was Portus Dubris, and the remains of the pharos, a Roman lighthouse, can also be seen in Dover Castle. (www.romans-in-Britain.org.uk)

Dover Castle and Wartime Tunnels, Kent. The massive stone keep was built by King Henry II in the 1180s. The castle withstood – just – a lengthy siege by Prince Louis of France and rebel barons in 1216. Today the keep has displays relating to the siege and also to the arrival of Henry VIII's court in 1539. Dover Castle is also the site of tunnels that were the nerve centre for Admiral Ramsay to mastermind the Dunkirk evacuation in 1940. There is a statue of Ramsay, unveiled in 2000. (English Heritage)

Down House, Greater London. This early 18th century house at the village of Downe was Charles

Darwin's family home from 1842 until his death in 1882. It was in the study here that he wrote his revolutionary treatise, *On the Origin of Species by Means of Natural Selection* (1859). The bedroom is to be painstakingly recreated. (English Heritage)

Durham Castle and Cathedral, Durham. The castle and cathedral on their impressive site above the River Wear were designated a UNESCO World Heritage Site in 1986. The castle was begun by William the Conqueror in 1072, and was the residence of the Prince Bishops of Durham until the 1830s, when they made way for the newly-established university. The cathedral dates from the first half of the 12th century and is regarded as the finest example of Norman architecture to be found in England. (www.durham.gov.uk)

E

Edgehill, Warwickshire. The first major battle of the English Civil War was fought to the south of Kineton on 23 October 1642. The result was inconclusive. There is a monument beside the Kineton-Banbury Road, but access to the battlefield is restricted. (www.battlefieldstrust.com)

Edinburgh Castle, City of Edinburgh. The Old Town, with the castle as its dominating feature, and the New Town, which dates from the 18th and 19th centuries, were together designated a World Heritage Site by UNESCO in 1995. The castle has been a royal residence since the 11th century, and the oldest surviving feature is St Margaret's Chapel, built in 1076. There have been 26 sieges in the castle's history. (www.Edinburgh.gov.uk)

Elstow, Bedfordshire. John Bunyan was born here in 1628. In neighbouring Bedford there is a John Bunyan Museum, and the sites of his home and the county gaol, where he wrote *Pilgrim's Progress*. There is also a statue of Bunyan, dating from 1874. (www.britainexpress.com)

Epworth Old Rectory, North Lincolnshire. The Queen Anne house where the founding fathers of Methodism, John and Charles Wesley, were brought up is preserved by the World Methodist Council as the home of the Wesleys, with items of family memorabilia and other relics on display. (www.epwortholdrectory.org.uk) Wesley's Chapel, House and Museum of Methodism are in City Road, London EC1. (www.wesleyschapel.org.uk)

Eton College, Windsor and Maidenhead. The College was founded by Henry VI in 1440, making it the second oldest in England after Winchester. The Chapel, which is one of the finest examples of Perpendicular architecture in England, was built between 1449 and 1482. (www.etoncollege.com)

Eyam, Derbyshire. The village has gone down in history because of an act of communal self-sacrifice in the 17th century. In 1665 cloth sent from London to the village tailor, George Vicars, brought the plague with it. The rector, William Mompesson, persuaded the villagers to quarantine themselves. 260 out of 350 inhabitants died over the next year. Eyam Museum tells the story, and the tombstones and memorial plaques show the impact of the plague on individual families. (www.eyammuseum.demon.co.uk)

F

Fishbourne Roman Palace, West Sussex. The palace, which was built A.D. 75–100, was discovered by workmen digging a new water main in 1960.The scale and quality of the palace, with a hundred rooms and some of the country's finest mosaic floors, has led to its being identified with Cogidubnus, a local British ruler and ally of Rome. The re-created Roman garden is a feature of the palace. (www.sussexpast.co.uk)

Flodden Field, Northumberland. An English army under the Earl of Surrey defeated the invading Scots, led by King James IV, south of the village of Branxton on 9 September 1513. James was killed. There is a large granite memorial cross on Piper's Hill, Branxton, where the English right wing formed up, and an exhibition at the nearby English Heritage property, Etal Castle. (www.flodden.net)

Fountains Abbey and Studley Royal, North Yorkshire. The ruins of the Cistercian abbey, founded in 1132, are the largest such remains in Europe. In the 18th century the Aislabie family made the abbey the focal point of their landscaped water gardens at Studley Royal. Also on the site are Fountains Hall, Fountains Hall, built 1598–1604 using stone from the abbey, and St Mary's Church, 'a masterpiece of the Victorian Gothic style' by William Burge. The whole assemblage was designated a UNESCO World Heritage Site in 1986. (www.fountainsabbey.org.uk)

G

Gad's Hill Place, Kent. Charles Dickens had admired this 18th century house to the north of Rochester as a boy and bought it in 1856. He lived there until his death in 1870. The house is now a school, but is open regularly to the public. Dickens sometimes wrote in a small Swiss chalet he had built in the garden, and this can be seen at Eastgate House in Rochester, formerly the Charles Dickens Centre. (www.medway.gov.uk)

Amongst many other Dickens-related sites in the country, the house where Dickens was born in 1812 is preserved as a museum in Portsmouth. (www.charlesdickensbirthplace.co.uk)

Glencoe, Highland. Glencoe is now a popular place for walking and climbing, but historically speaking it is notorious for the breach of hospitality that occurred on 13 February 1692 when Campbells and English troops quartered on the Macdonalds of Glencoe massacred 38 of their hosts. There is a National Trust for Scotland Visitor Centre. (National Trust for Scotland)

Glenfinnan, Highland. Here at the head of Loch Shiel on 19 August 1745 Prince Charles Edward Stuart raised his standard to mark the beginning of the Jacobite Rebellion. The Glenfinnan Monument, a tower with the figure of a highlander on top, was designed by James Gillespie Graham and erected in 1815 by Alexander Macdonald of Glenaladale. The inscription on the monument refers to the rebellion as 'that arduous and unfortunate enterprise.' (National Trust for Scotland)

Grasmere, Cumbria. Dove Cottage at Grasmere was home to the poet, William Wordsworth, and his family from 1799 to 1808. The cottage and associated Wordsworth Museum are run by the Wordsworth Trust. (www.wordsworth.org.uk) Nearby Rydal Mount, overlooking Rydal Water, was Wordsworth's home from 1813 to his death in 1850. Wordsworth was a keen landscape gardener and the garden remains much as he designed it. (www.rydalmount.co.uk)

***Great Britain*, SS,** City of Bristol. Designed by Isambard Kingdom Brunel and built in Bristol in 1843, this was the world's first iron, screw-propelled, ocean-going passenger ship. After being abandoned in the Falklands in 1886, she was eventually brought back in 1970 and carefully restored in the dock at Bristol where she was built. (www.ssgreatbritain.org)

Greenwich, London SE10. The Old Royal Observatory, built for King Charles II by Wren in 1675, is a good place to look down on all the historic buildings this site has to offer, including the Queen's House, designed by Inigo Jones in 1616, the Old Royal Naval College and the National Maritime Museum. 'Maritime Greenwich' was listed by UNESCO as a World Heritage Site in 1997, on the grounds that the historic buildings and the park symbolised 'English artistic and scientific endeavour in the 17th and 18th centuries.' (www.greenwichwhs.org.uk)

Grime's Graves, Norfolk. The largest Neolithic flint mines in Europe. It was given the name by the

Anglo-Saxons, 'Grim' being a nickname for Woden. With hard hats provided, visitors can descend by ladder into the workings. It is also a Site of Special Scientific Interest because of the range of flora and fauna to be found there. (English Heritage)

H

Hadrian's Wall. *See* Section L.

Hambledon, Hampshire. This was 'the cradle of English cricket' in the 18th century when the local club became the accepted authority on the game. There is a large stone memorial, erected in 1908, on nearby Broadhalfpenny Down, marking the site of the Hambledon Cricket Club's ground, *c.* 1750–87. The old pub opposite, The Bat and Ball, served as the club's pavilion and has a collection of cricket memorabilia on display. (www.hambledon-hants.com)

Hampton Court Palace, Greater London. Cardinal Wolsey began building the Palace in 1514, but it passed to Henry VIII when Wolsey fell from power and was a favourite royal residence for 200 years. Sir Christopher Wren carried out alterations for William and Mary at the end of the 17th century and the famous maze dates from 1690. (www.hampton-court-palace.org.uk)

Hardwick Hall, Derbyshire. Designed by Robert Smythson for Bess of Hardwick in the 1590s, its expanse of windows gave rise to the tag, 'Hardwick Hall, more glass than wall.' (National Trust) In the grounds are the ruins of Hardwick Old Hall, which was only just being completed when Bess began work on her prestigious new house. (English Heritage)

Hardy's Cottage, Dorset. The cottage where the novelist and poet, Thomas Hardy, was born in 1840 and wrote his early novels is at Higher Bockhampton, near Dorchester. It is owned by the National Trust, as is Max Gate, the house in Dorchester that Hardy designed and lived in from 1885 to his death in 1928. Also in Dorchester there is a statue of Hardy by Eric Kennington (1931) and a large Hardy collection, including a reconstruction of his study, at the County Museum. (www.dorsetcountymuseum.org)

Harlech Castle, Gwynedd. Although the sea in Tremadog Bay has now receded, this is still the most dramatically sited of Edward I's castles. It was completed by veteran castle builder, James of St George, in 1290. It has been part of a UNESCO World Heritage Site since 1986. (CADW)

Hatfield House, Hertfordshire. One of the largest Jacobean houses in England, it was built 1607–11 for King James I's Chief Minister, Robert Cecil, 1st Earl of Salisbury. In the grounds is the Great Hall of the Royal Palace of Hatfield where young Queen Elizabeth I spent some of her childhood. (www.hatfield-house.co.uk)

Haworth Parsonage, Bradford. This was the home of the Bronte family from 1820 to 1861. Its moorland setting 'had a profound influence on the writing of Charlotte, Emily and Anne Bronte.' It has been owned by the Bronte Society since 1928, and is known as the Bronte Parsonage Museum. (www.bronte.org.uk)

Hever Castle, Kent. This 13th century castle with its double moat has a special place in English history as the childhood home of Henry VIII's second wife, Anne Boleyn. In 1903 it was purchased and restored by the American millionaire, William Waldorf Astor, later the first Lord Astor of Hever. (www.hevercastle.co.uk)

Highgate Cemetery, London N6. The most impressive of seven large commercial cemeteries created around London in the mid-19th century. The West Cemetery opened in 1839 and the extension of the East Cemetery in 1854. At least 850 notable people are buried in the cemetery, but it is still probably most famous as the burial place of Karl Marx. (www.highgate-cemetery.org/index.asp)

Hod Hill, Dorset. An Iron Age hill fort, covering some 21 hectares. It was one of the hill forts captured by the future Emperor Vespasian. Excavations in the 1950s showed a concentration of ballista bolts around the south-eastern entrance, indicating the likely line of the Roman assault. The hill fort is unusual in that there are the ramparts of a Roman fort in the north-west corner. Nearby Hambledon hill fort is also worth the climb. (National Trust)

Holkham Hall, Norfolk. A classic Palladian mansion, in a beautiful setting near the Norfolk coast. It was designed by William Kent, and built 1734–64 for Thomas Coke, 1st Earl of Leicester. His great-nephew, Thomas William Coke, first pioneered the Norfolk four-course crop rotation system. (www.holkham.co.uk)

Holyroodhouse, Palace of, City of Edinburgh. Founded as a monastery in 1128, the Palace is the Queen's official residence in Scotland. It is situated at the opposite end of the Royal Mile from the Castle, against the backdrop of Arthur's Seat. Mary, Queen of Scots lived there 1561–67. The Queen's Gallery displays works of art from the Royal Collection. (www.royal.gov.uk)

Houghton Hall, Norfolk. A Palladian mansion built for Britain's first Prime Minister, Sir Robert Walpole, between 1722 and 1735. It was designed by James Gibbs, with interiors by William Kent. It is now the home of the Marquess of Cholmondeley. (www.houghtonhall.com)

Hughenden Manor, Buckinghamshire. Home of the Victorian Prime Minister and novelist, Benjamin Disraeli, Earl of Beaconsfield, from 1848 to his death in 1881. It still contains many of his possessions. Disraeli's grave can be seen in Hughenden churchyard. A monument erected to him by Queen Victoria is in the church. (National Trust)

Huntingdon, Cambridgeshire. Oliver Cromwell was born here in 1599, and he was briefly its MP. He was educated at the local grammar school (as was Samuel Pepys), and this is now a Cromwell Museum. (www.cambridgeshire.gov.uk) Oliver Cromwell's House in Ely, where he lived 1636–47, can also be visited. (www.ely.org.uk)

I

Iona, Island of, Argyll and Bute. A small island off the south-west of the Isle of Mull. St Columba arrived from Ireland in A.D. 563 and established a monastery before setting out to convert Scotland to Christianity. It was destroyed by Norse raiders, but in 1203 St Mary's Abbey, a Benedictine foundation, was established. It was restored in the early 20th century. The Iona Community, an ecumenical Christian community, was founded in 1938. (Historic Scotland/National Trust for Scotland)

Ironbridge, Telford and Wrekin. The bridge across the River Severn was the world's first iron bridge. It was cast at Coalbrookdale by local ironmaster, Abraham Derby, and erected in 1779. It is the centrepiece of the Ironbridge Gorge UNESCO World Heritage Site (1986), where nine museums and historic sites tell the story of the major part played by the area in the Industrial Revolution. (www.ironbridge.org.uk)

J

Jane Austen's House, Hampshire. The house at Chawton where Jane Austen lived with her mother and her sister, Cassandra, from 1809 until shortly before her death in 1817. It was there that she wrote or revised her most famous novels. The house where she died in College Street, Winchester, is a private house but is marked by a plaque. She is buried in the nearby cathedral. (www.janeaustenmuseum.org.uk)

Jarrow, South Tyneside. St Paul's Monastery was founded in A.D. 681 and it was there that Britain's first historian, the Venerable Bede, completed his *Ecclesiastical History of the English People* in A.D. 731. There is a museum of early medieval Northumbrian history, called 'Bede's World', which includes displays of finds from excavations of the monastery. (www.bedesworld.co.uk)

K

Kedleston Hall, Derbyshire. Home of the Curzon family since the 12th century, the present Palladian mansion was designed by Robert Adam and completed in 1765. Probably the best-known occupant was the statesman, Lord Curzon, the 'most superior person', who was Viceroy of India 1899–1905 and also Foreign Secretary 1919–25. (National Trust)

Kenilworth Castle, Warwickshire. The mellow red sandstone remains are said to constitute the largest castle ruin in England. The castle was begun in the early 12th century, but probably its greatest moment of glory came in 1575 when Robert Dudley, Earl of Leicester, lavishly entertained Queen Elizabeth and her court for nineteen days. (English Heritage)

Kew Gardens. *See* Section L.

L

Lacock Abbey, Wiltshire. Medieval cloisters testify to the fact that this is a country house created out of the buildings of a nunnery following the Dissolution in the 1530s. In the 19th century it was home to the 'father of modern photography', William Henry Fox-Talbot, and a photographic museum describes his pioneering work. (National Trust)

Lichfield, Staffordshire. The house where Samuel Johnson was born in 1709 is now a museum which is devoted to his life and work. (www.lichfield.gov.uk/sjmuseum) Also open to the public is the 18th century town house in Gough Square, London EC4, where Dr Johnson compiled his famous dictionary, published in 1755. (www.drjh.dircon.co.uk)

Lincoln Castle and Cathedral, Lincolnshire. The cathedral, with its triple towers, dominates the city. It was built 1185–1280, after an earthquake destroyed the Norman cathedral. At 83 metres, the central tower is the highest in England. The castle, which faces the cathedral, was begun by William the Conqueror in 1086. One of the four surviving copies of the Magna Carta is on display. The castle was reopened in June 2015 after a £22m. refurbishment. (www.lincolnshire.gov.uk)

Lindisfarne, Northumberland. One of the cradles of Christianity in Anglo-Saxon England. Settled by St Aidan in A.D. 635, Lindisfarne is especially associated with St Cuthbert and with the 8th century illuminated manuscript, the Lindisfarne Gospels, on display at the British Library. There are the sandstone ruins of the 11th century priory, dissolved by Henry VIII. The island's Tudor castle was converted into an Edwardian country house and garden by Edwin Lutyens and Gertrude Jekyll. (English Heritage/National Trust)

Liverpool Cathedrals, Liverpool. The Anglican and Catholic Cathedrals provide a fascinating contrast in 20th century church architecture. The gothic revival Anglican Cathedral is the largest in Britain. Designed by Sir Giles Gilbert Scott, it was begun in 1904, consecrated in 1924 but not finally completed until 1980. The ultra-modern Catholic Metropolitan Cathedral of Christ the King was designed by Frederick Gibberd, after an earlier Lutyen's plan had been abandoned on the grounds of cost, and completed in 1967. (www.liverpoolcathedral.org.uk) and see also (www.liverpoolmetrocathedral.org.uk)

Liverpool and the Beatles, Liverpool. The Beatles made their debut appearance at the Cavern Club on 21 February 1961. In 1995 the National Trust acquired the boyhood home of Paul McCartney in Allerton, where he and John Lennon wrote many of their early songs. Then in 2002 the Trust acquired John Lennon's home, 'Mendips', in Woolton, and the two houses can now be visited. (National Trust)

Liverpool 'Maritime Mercantile City', Liverpool. The waterfront area of the City was recognised as a World Heritage Site by UNESCO in 2004 because of its role in the development of the British Empire and the world trading system, and as a pioneer in dock technology and port management in the 18th and 19th centuries. The focal point of the waterfront is the trio of buildings at the Pier Head – the Royal Liver Building, the Cunard Building and the Port of Liverpool Building. (www.liverpoolworldheritage.com)

Longleat, Wiltshire. One of the best examples of high Elizabethan architecture, Longleat was designed by Robert Smythson for Sir John Thynne in the 1570s. The 6th Marquess of Bath became the first stately home owner to open to the paying public on a regular basis in 1949, and the famous Safari Park with the Lions of Longleat opened in 1966. The 7th Marquess has added his own fantasy murals in the Private Apartments to the portfolio of other attractions. (www.longleat.co.uk)

Lord's Cricket Ground, London NW8. The ground of the Marylebone Cricket Club (MCC) was moved to this site in 1814 by a Yorkshireman, Thomas Lord. By the mid-19th century the MCC was the premier club and by the 20th century the governing body of the sport. There are tours and a museum, which displays the famous urn containing 'the ashes'. (www.lords.org).

Lullingstone Roman Villa, Kent. The villa was built around A.D. 100 and enlarged over the next 300 years. Excavations began in 1949, and have revealed mosaics, an extensive bath complex and an early Christian chapel. (English Heritage)

M

Maiden Castle, Dorset. The best known of the country's Iron Age hill forts was the capital of the Durotriges. It covers 19 hectares, and the complex of earthworks protecting the eastern entrance is particularly impressive. It was stormed in A.D. 43 by the 2nd Legion Augusta under the future Emperor Vespasian. A skeleton with a Roman catapult bolt lodged in the spine was found during Sir Mortimer Wheeler's excavations in the 1930s and can be seen at the Dorset County Museum in Dorchester. (English Heritage)

Marston Moor, North Yorkshire. The largest battle of the English Civil War took place between Long Marston and Tockwith on 2 July 1644. The two-hour battle resulted in a decisive victory for the forces of Parliament and the Scots over the Royalists. There is a 1939 stone monument on the battlefield. (www.battlefieldstrust.com)

Mary Rose, City of Portsmouth. Henry VIII's favourite warship, *Mary Rose*, sank in the Solent on 19 July 1545 with a French invasion fleet in sight. Her remains were raised in 1982 and went on display at Portsmouth historic dockyard, together with hundreds of artefacts and other material that form a unique 'Tudor time capsule'. The ship's hull was reopened to the public in 2013 after the completion of a major new museum housing both the hull and many of the 19,000 artefacts. In 2016 the whole ship was revealed in her full glory. (www.maryrose.org)

Menai Suspension Bridge, Isle of Anglesey. The bridge linking the Isle of Anglesey to the mainland was built by Thomas Telford to improve the London to Holyhead route and was opened in 1826. It had a central span of 176 metres and was the world's first large-scale iron suspension bridge. (www.anglesey-history.co.uk)

Mey, Castle of, Highland. The most northerly castle on the British mainland, it was originally built between 1566 and 1572. It was purchased by the Queen Mother in 1952. She restored the castle and the gardens, which are protected from the elements by a 3·5-metre high wall, known as the 'Great Wall of Mey.' The Castle of Mey is now open to the general public for part of the year. (www.castleofmey.org.uk)

Milton's Cottage, Buckinghamshire. A 16th century cottage at Chalfont St Giles, where John Milton came to live in 1665 to escape the plague in London. Although blind, Milton completed *Paradise Lost* and began work on *Paradise Regained* during his time at the cottage. There are four museum rooms and an attractive cottage garden. (www.miltonscottage.org)

N

Naseby, Northamptonshire. The most decisive battle of the English Civil War was fought on 14 June 1645 between Naseby and Sibbertoft. The Parliamentary forces under Cromwell and Fairfax defeated the Royalists under the King and Prince Rupert. There are two memorials to the battle – the Fitzgerald Obelisk, erected in 1823, and a 1936 monument. (www.battlefieldstrust.com)

New Lanark, South Lanarkshire. New Lanark was established as a cotton-spinning village on the Clyde in 1785 by philanthropist, David Dale. His son-in-law, Robert Owen, was mill manager 1800–25, and made improvements in working conditions, housing and education. The evidence at New Lanark today of Owen's pioneering work in developing a model industrial community led to its listing as a World Heritage Site by UNESCO in 2001. (www.newlanark.org)

Newstead Abbey, Nottinghamshire. The Abbey, which was originally founded in the 12th century, became the seat of the Byron family after the Dissolution in 1540. The poet Lord Byron inherited it in 1798, but financial problems led him to sell it in 1818. His apartments, documents and artefacts can be seen at the Abbey.

O

Offa's Dyke. Offa, King of the Mercians, may have had this earthwork constructed from c. A.D. 785. It stretched from Prestatyn in the north to the Severn Estuary in the south. However, recent research suggests it may have been built back in the 4th cent. Offa's Dyke Path is a British National Trail, 270 kms in length, which broadly follows the earthwork and was inaugurated in 1971. At about the midway point, at Knighton in Powys, there is a visitor centre run by the Offa's Dyke Association. One of the best-preserved sections lies to the north in the Clun area. (www.offasdyke.co.uk)

Orkney Islands. 'The Heart of Neolithic Orkney' was designated a World Heritage Site by UNESCO in 1999, on the grounds that it provided 'outstanding testimony to the cultural achievements of the Neolithic peoples of northern Europe.' The important Neolithic monuments include a large chambered tomb, ceremonial stone circles and the outstanding settlement of Skara Brae, which was occupied from around 3100 to 2500 B.C. It comprises one of the best preserved groups of prehistoric houses in Europe. (Historic Scotland)

Osborne House. *See* Section L.

P

Peterloo Massacre, Manchester. The 'massacre' took place on 16 August 1819 when 60,000 people gathered on St Peter's Fields, Manchester, to demand parliamentary reform and the repeal of the Corn Laws. Magistrates decided to disperse the crowd, and 11 people were killed by the yeomanry cavalry. The episode is commemorated by a plaque on the former Free Trade Hall (now an hotel) that was later built on the site. (www.manchester2002-uk.com)

Plymouth Hoe, Devon. According to legend it was on Plymouth Hoe that Sir Francis Drake insisted on finishing his game of bowls before sailing to meet the Spanish Armada in 1588. The statue of Drake on the Hoe was unveiled in 1884. Buckland Abbey, to the north of Plymouth, was Drake's home and has been owned by the National Trust since 1948. (www.plymouthdata.info)

Pontcysyllte Aqueduct and Canal, Clwyd. This engineering masterpiece of the Industrial Revolution was recognised by UNESCO as a World Heritage Site in 2009. It was constructed by Thomas Telford and William Jessop between 1795 and 1805. The 307-metre long aqueduct consists of a cast iron trough raised above the valley of the River Dee on nineteen slender masonry piers. It is still operational and those with a head for heights can cross in a narrowboat or walk the towpath. (www.waterscape.com)

Portchester Castle, Hampshire. The Romans built a massive fort here at the end of the 3rd century, with 20 bastions and walls 6 metres high. Today it is the best-preserved of the Saxon Shore forts. In the 12th century Henry II built a square keep in the north-east corner. There is a good view of Portsmouth harbour from the top of the keep, although this has been somewhat superseded by the opening of Portsmouth's Spinnaker Tower in 2005. (English Heritage)

Portsmouth Historic Dockyard and Fortifications, City of Portsmouth. King Henry VII had the world's first dry dock built here in 1495–96, and Portsmouth grew into the country's premier naval base. It had to be protected, and fortifications of many periods are preserved at and around Portsmouth. One of the Victorian forts on Portsdown hill – Fort Nelson – appropriately displays the Royal Armouries' artillery collection. (www.hants.gov.uk/discover/navdef.html)

R

Richborough Roman Fort, Kent. Although the sea has now receded, this was once the main port of entry into Britain for the Romans, who called it Rutupiae. The foundations can be seen of a great monumental archway through which the Emperor Claudius is said to have ridden on an elephant when he visited Britain. The remains of the Saxon Shore fort and the amphitheatre date from the 3rd century. (English Heritage)

Rievaulx Abbey, North Yorkshire. Founded in 1131, this was the first Cistercian Abbey in the north of England and became one of the richest. It was dissolved by Henry VIII in 1538. (English Heritage) Above the abbey ruins are Rievaulx Terrace and Temples, a landscaped promenade laid out in the 18th century. (National Trust)

Rochester Castle, Kent. The square keep, which is 38 metres high, was built around 1127, and is an outstanding example of Norman military architecture. In 1215 King John besieged the castle, which was held by the rebel barons. He undermined and brought down one corner of the keep, but even then the defenders held out for another two months. (English Heritage)

Royal Pavilion Brighton, Brighton and Hove. It was built by John Nash for the Prince Regent, later King George IV, between 1815 and 1823. The Indian-style exterior and Chinese-inspired interiors are beautiful. Queen Victoria sold it to the town in 1850. (www.royalpavilion.org.uk)

Rufus Stone, Hampshire. A memorial near the village of Minstead in the New Forest, which is said to mark the place where the oak tree stood that was indirectly responsible for the death of King William II. An arrow shot by Sir Walter Tyrell, while out hunting with William Rufus on 2 August 1100, glanced off the tree and hit and killed the King. (www.new-forest-tourism.com)

Runnymede, Surrey. The riverside meadow where King John put his seal to Magna Carta on 15 June 1215 has been owned by the National Trust since 1931. The American Bar Association erected a Grecian-style temple to commemorate Magna Carta in 1957. Nearby are the Second World War Commonwealth Air Forces Memorial and the John F Kennedy Memorial. (National Trust)

S

St Albans, Hertfordshire. Known to the Romans as Verulamium, this was the third largest city in Roman Britain. Verulamium Museum tells the story of the Roman city, where the first British Christian martyr, St Alban, was executed around A.D. 250. (www.stalbansmuseums.org.uk) Nearby, the Roman Theatre, built in A.D. 140 with a stage rather than as an amphitheatre, is unique in Roman Britain. (www.romantheatre.co.uk)

St Ives, Cornwall. St Ives has been a popular location for artists since Victorian times. The Tate Gallery opened a branch overlooking Porthmeor Beach in 1993, focussing on the post-war modern movement. One of the leading figures was Barbara Hepworth, and there is now a museum and sculpture garden at the house where she lived 1949–75. (www.tate.org.uk)

St Paul's Cathedral. *See* **Section L.**

Salisbury Cathedral, Wiltshire. The foundation stone of the Cathedral was laid in 1220 when the clergy moved from the original settlement of Old Sarum. (English Heritage) The Cathedral was completed in 1258. In the first half of the 14th century the tower was raised and the spire added, making the total height 123 metres, the tallest in Britain. (www.salisburycathedral.org.uk)

Saltaire, Bradford. The philanthropic industrialist, Sir Titus Salt, founded this town on the River Aire as a model village for the workers in his factory, Salt's Mill, which was the largest in the world when it opened in 1853. As a 'complete and well-preserved industrial village of the second half of the 19th century', its importance was recognised as a World Heritage Site by UNESCO in 2001. (www.saltaire.yorks.com)

Sandham Memorial Chapel, Hampshire. There are many memorials to those who died in the First World War, but one of the most impressive is this red-brick chapel at the village of Burghclere. It was erected in the 1920s as a memorial to H W Sandham by his sister. It is famous for the murals by Stanley Spencer, which were inspired by his own experiences serving in the Royal Army Medical Corps in Salonika. (National Trust)

Sandringham, Norfolk. The estate was purchased by Queen Victoria in 1862 for her eldest son, Edward, and the new house was completed in the neo-Jacobean style in 1870. Sandringham opened to the public for the first time in 1977. The first car owned by a British monarch, a 1900 Daimler Phaeton, bought by the future King Edward VII in 1900, can be seen by visitors on display here. (www.sandringhamestate.co.uk)

Scapa Flow, Orkney Islands. The large sheltered anchorage was the main base of the Royal Navy's Home Fleet in the two world wars. The German High Seas Fleet scuttled itself there in 1919. In 1939 German submarine U-47 penetrated the defences and sank HMS *Royal Oak*, with the loss of 833 lives. The Churchill Barriers were built to increase security by Italian prisoners-of-war, who also created a chapel out of Nissen Huts. (www.orkneyheritage.com)

Seaford Martello Tower, East Sussex. Martello Tower No 74 at Seaford is an example of the chain of 103 Martello Towers built as a defence against invasion around the south and east coasts during the Napoleonic Wars. It was the last to be completed, and is now a local history museum. (www.martello-towers.co.uk)

Sedgemoor, Somerset. Site of the last battle on English soil, which was fought near the village of Westonzoyland on 6 July 1685. The Duke of Monmouth, illegitimate son of King Charles II, was defeated and later beheaded after this unsuccessful attempt to seize the throne. There is a memorial to those who died in the battle and those who were subsequently punished for taking part in the uprising. (www.battlefieldstrust.com)

Segontium Roman Fort, Gwynedd. The remains of a Roman fort at Caernarvon, established around A.D. 78. Its strategic importance meant that it was manned until the end of the 4th century, longer than any other Roman fort in Wales.

Selborne, Hampshire. The pioneering naturalist, the Rev Gilbert White, lived in the house called 'The Wakes' at Selborne from 1729 to his death in 1793. He published his book, *The Natural History and Antiquities of Selborne*, in 1788. The house is also home to a museum devoted to the Oates family, especially Captain Lawrence Oates, who died in 1912 on Scott's Antarctic expedition. His family funded the purchase of the house and the subsequent opening of it to the public in 1955. (www.gilbertwhiteshouse.org.uk)

Silbury Hill, Wiltshire. An extraordinary artificial prehistoric mound, rising to a height of 40 metres. It is probably the largest prehistoric mound in the world. Archaeological investigations have so far failed to establish its original purpose. Soil erosion means that it is no longer possible to climb the mound. It is part of the Avebury/Stonehenge World Heritage Site. (English Heritage)

Silchester, Hampshire. The site of the Roman town of Calleva Atrebatum. It had earlier been an Iron Age settlement, but it was abandoned after the Romans left and never reoccupied. Today it is possible to walk the 2.8 kms circuit of the town walls, built about A.D. 270, which are still 4 metres high in places. There are the remains of a large amphitheatre just outside the walls. The area within the walls, some 40 hectares in extent, contained some substantial buildings, but their remains are buried beneath pastureland to protect them. There are displays at Reading Museum. (English Heritage)

Skara Brae. *See* **Orkney, E18.**

Stamford Bridge, East Riding of Yorkshire. Site of the battle by the River Derwent on 25 September 1066 when King Harold crushed an invasion by his brother, Tostig, and King Harold Hardrada of Norway, who both died. Three days later Duke William of Normandy landed at Pevensey. (www.battlefieldstrust.com)

Stirling Castle, Stirling. The castle was begun in the early 12th century, and has served as a fortress, royal residence, prison and barracks. Most of what can be seen today dates from the 15th and 16th centuries. It was besieged often. It was Edward II's attempt to lift a siege that ended in disaster at Bannockburn in 1314. (Historic Scotland)

Stonehenge, a remarkable collection of Bronze Age monuments on Salisbury Plain. The site which contains ditches, earthwork-banks and megaliths (large stones) has long been recognised for its architectural innovations (the trillithon or free-standing arch and the circle of dressed and lintelled stone blocks) and for its astronomical, numerical and geometrical properties. The building and rebuilding, according to modern archaeological research, lasted from about 2300 to 1600 B.C. It became a World Heritage Site in 1986. Another prehistoric monument nearby was found in 2010.

It is still not known who built Stonehenge or what its true purpose was. Excavations in 2008 have lent weight to the theory that it may have been primarily a place of healing. Recent discoveries in 2012 have also revealed 72 Bronze Age carvings chipped into the stones. *See* **E35.**

Stratfield Saye House, Hampshire. Home to the Dukes of Wellington since 1817. Plans to pull the old house down and build a 'Waterloo Palace', to emulate Blenheim Palace, were abandoned in 1821 on grounds of cost.

There is a Wellington Exhibition featuring the first Duke's massive funeral carriage. The grave of 'Copenhagen', the chestnut stallion Wellington rode at Waterloo, can be seen in the grounds. (www.stratfield-saye.co.uk)

Stratford-on-Avon, Warwickshire. The Shakespeare Birthplace Trust owns five houses associated with Shakespeare in and around Stratford-on-Avon. The centrepiece is the house where he was born in 1564. His tomb can be seen in Holy Trinity Church. The Shakespeare Memorial Theatre dates from 1932, replacing the Victorian theatre that burnt down. After a major redevelopment, it was re-opened in 2011. (www.shapespeare.org.uk)

Sudeley Castle, Gloucestershire. The castle was briefly home to King Henry VIII's sixth wife, Katherine Parr, after the King's death. She married Sir Thomas Seymour, but died in 1548 after giving birth to a daughter. During the English Civil War Prince Rupert made it his HQ and it was reduced to a ruin by parliamentary forces as a consequence. (www.sudeleycastle.co.uk)

Sutton Hoo, Suffolk. When one of a group of low grassy mounds above the River Deben near Woodbridge was excavated in 1939, an Anglo-Saxon ship burial containing priceless treasures was discovered. It is thought to have been the burial of Raedwald, King of the East Angles, who died in A.D. 625. The site was given to the National Trust in 1998. A fine Visitors' Centre, with an exhibition hall containing a full-size reconstruction of the ship burial, opened in 2002.

T

Tattershall Castle, Lincolnshire. The Great Tower, 34 metres high, is 'one of the masterpieces of medieval brickwork.' It was built 1434–46 for Henry VI's Lord Treasurer, Ralph, 3rd Baron Cromwell. The castle was restored by Lord Curzon before the First World War. (National Trust)

Tewkesbury, Gloucestershire. The scene of one of the most decisive battles of the Wars of the Roses, when the Yorkists under King Edward IV defeated the Lancastrians on 4 May 1471. After a Public Inquiry in 1998 plans for housing development on the Gastons, the field thought to have been at the heart of the battle, were turned down. (www.tewkesbury.org.uk/battlefield)

Tintern Abbey, Monmouthshire. This Cistercian Abbey on the River Wye was founded in 1131. It was dissolved by King Henry VIII in 1536, but much of the 13th century church has survived. In the late 18th century the ruins attracted poets and artists, such as Wordsworth and Turner.

Tolpuddle, Dorset. Here in 1834 six agricultural labourers were prosecuted for forming a trade union and transported to Australia. To mark the centenary of the Tolpuddle Martyrs, the TUC built six memorial cottages in 1934, and there is now a museum. The village green with the Martyrs' Tree, a sycamore beneath which the men gathered to meet, is owned by the National Trust. (www.tolpuddlemartyrs.org.uk)

Tower of London was built as a fortress by William the Conqueror. It was a royal palace in the Middle Ages and later used as a garrison and prison. Many distinguished prisoners were executed there, or on the neighbouring Tower Hill, including Anne Boleyn, Catherine Howard, Lady Jane Grey, the 2nd Earl of Essex and the Duke of Monmouth. The Chapel Royal of St Peter ad Vincula in the Tower was built in 1105 and took its present shape in the reign of Henry VII.

The Crown Jewels are kept at the Tower, and in the Armoury a fine collection of armour is preserved. The staff (in Tudor dress) are called Yeomen Warders of the Tower. Over 2 million people visit the Tower every year.

Towton, North Yorkshire. A battle in the Wars of the Roses, which took place between Towton and Saxton on 29 March 1461. It was fought in a blizzard, and the Yorkists were victorious over the Lancastrians in one of the bloodiest battles on English soil. In 2005 the Towton Battlefield Society erected a new memorial to the dead of Towton. It is located in Saxton churchyard. (www.towton.org.uk)

U

Uffington White Horse, Oxfordshire. This stylised horse is probably the oldest chalk-cut hill figure in Britain. White Horse Hill forms part of the ancient Ridgeway Path and on top there is an Iron Age hill fort, Uffington Castle. Nearby is a mound called Dragon Hill where legend says St George killed the dragon. (National Trust)

V

Victory, HMS, City of Portsmouth. HMS *Victory* was laid down at Chatham Dockyard in 1759, and launched in 1765 as a 1st rate 104-gun ship-of-the-line. She was Nelson's flagship at the battle of Trafalgar on 21 October 1805, and the focal point of the bicentenary celebrations in 2005. She has been open to the public in dry dock at Portsmouth since 1928. A long-term restoration scheme began at the end of 2011. It has been calculated that 6,000 oaks went into the building of the ship. (www.hms-victory.com)

W

Walmer Castle, Kent. One of Henry VIII's coastal defence forts of 1539–40, but probably more famous as the official residence of the Lord Warden of the Cinque Ports since 1708. The Duke of Wellington held the post for 23 years, and the armchair in which he died at the castle in 1852 is on display. (English Heritage)

Warrior, HMS, City of Portsmouth. Launched in 1860, she was the world's first iron-hulled armoured warship. Restored at Hartlepool, she has been on display at Portsmouth historic dockyard since 1987, providing a unique picture of life on a Victorian warship. (www.hmswarrior.org)

Warwick Castle, Warwickshire. The building of this castle began around 1068, but what can be seen today mainly dates from the 14th century, with much re-working from later periods. It was acquired by the Tussauds Group in 1978, and one of the features is a waxwork tableau of guests at a weekend house-party in 1898, including the Prince of Wales, later King Edward VII. (www.warwick-castle.co.uk)

West Kennet Long Barrow, Wiltshire. This chambered tomb dates from around 3250 B.C. The earth mound is built over giant stones and is 104 metres long. It is part of the Stonehenge/Avebury World Heritage Site listed by UNESCO in 1986. (English Heritage/National Trust)

Westminster Abbey stands on the site of an old church and Benedictine foundation of the 7th cent. It was rebuilt under Edward the Confessor, and again under Henry III, and important additions were made by Edward II, Edward III, Richard II, Richard III and Henry VII, the latter erecting the beautiful eastern chapel in the perpendicular style which bears his name. The west towers and gable were designed by Hawksmoor (1661–1736). The Abbey contains tombs of 17 English monarchs, of the Unknown Warrior *etc*.

Whitby Abbey, North Yorkshire. The Abbey was founded by St Hilda in A.D. 657, and is best remembered in English history for the Synod of Whitby in A.D. 664, when King Oswy of Northumbria decided to follow the Roman rather than the Celtic church in matters such as the dating of Easter. Today's ruins are those of the 13th century Benedictine Abbey. The Whitby Abbey Cholmley House Visitor Centre opened in 2002. (English Heritage)

Wilton House, Wiltshire. Home of the Earls of Pembroke. The original Tudor house was rebuilt in the 17th century by Inigo Jones and his nephew, John Webb. The Double Cube Room is one of the finest extant state rooms in England. (www.wiltonhouse.com)

Winchester Cathedral, Hampshire. Work on the Cathedral began in 1079, and at 169 metres in length, it is the longest medieval church in Europe. It was originally built on marshland and it has the distinction of being saved from collapse by a diver, William Walker, who, between the years 1906 and 1912, replaced the rotting timber raft on which it rested by cement foundations. (www.winchester-cathedral.org.uk)

Windmill Hill, Wiltshire. A causewayed enclosure dating from around 2500 B.C., with three concentric rings enclosing 8 hectares, Windmill Hill has given its name to the culture of the Neolithic farmers who arrived in southern England from the continent 5000 years ago. It is part of the Avebury/Stonehenge World Heritage Site, listed by UNESCO in 1986. (National Trust)

Windsor Castle, the famous British royal residence on the banks of the Thames, as it now stands, was mainly built by Henry III, though a royal residence had existed there from the time of the Conqueror. Additions were made by Henry VIII, Elizabeth and Charles II. Windsor Park and Forest comprise over 5,200 ha. A serious fire in 1992 caused very extensive damage, destroying St. George's Hall and gutting the Queen's Chapel. After completion of restoration work costing £40m, visitors were readmitted in 1997. The famous Round Tower reopened to the public in 2011 (for the first time in nearly four decades). It is the oldest official royal residence in the world.

Woburn Abbey, Bedfordshire. Originally a Cistercian Abbey, the Dukes of Bedford have lived here since 1547. As well as the treasures the house contains, the 1,200-hectare deer park has the largest breeding herd of rare Père David's deer in the world. (www.woburnabbey.co.uk)

Woolsthorpe Manor, Lincolnshire. This small 17th century farmhouse to the south of Grantham was the birthplace and family home of the scientist and philosopher, Sir Isaac Newton. He formulated some of his major works here during the plague years 1665–67 when Cambridge University was closed. The apple tree that inspired his theory of gravity is said to have been in the garden. (National Trust)

Worcester, Worcestershire. The site of the last battle of the English Civil War, which took place on 3 September 1651 and resulted in defeat for Prince Charles' army of Scots at the hands of Cromwell's New Model Army. A 15th century timber-framed building, the Commandery, was the Royalist headquarters, and now has displays interpreting the battle. (www.worcestercitymuseum.org.uk)

Wordsworth House, Cumbria. Georgian town house at Cockermouth where William Wordsworth was born in 1770. The house and garden have been recreated to suit the period when William and his sister, Dorothy, grew up there. (National Trust)

Wroxeter, Shropshire. The Romans called their city here Viroconium Cornoviorum. It lay on Watling Street and was the fourth largest city in Roman Britain. The remains of the public baths, constructed A.D. 120–150, and particularly part of the original south wall of the basilica, are reminders of past glories. (English Heritage)

Y

York Minster, one of the oldest and finest of English cathedrals, is 160 m long, its nave is 73 m broad, and the central tower is 66 m high. The present edifice, in parts, dates back to the 12th cent., but a church stood on the site in the 7th cent. In 1829 it was set on fire by a lunatic, Jonathan Martin.

PART III. DICTIONARY OF MODERN WARS SINCE 1914

Introduction

This section in *Pears* brings together brief accounts of some of the more important conflicts in the world, from the outbreak of the First World War (the "Great War") in 1914 to such current conflicts as the civil war in Syria.

First World War 1914–18.

On 28 July 1914 Austria-Hungary declared war on Serbia, whom she blamed for the assassination of the Austrian heir to the throne a month earlier. Austria was supported by her ally Germany, but they were faced by the "Entente" powers, Russia, France and Britain. In late 1914 the Germans failed to capture Paris despite the boldness of their invasion plan (the Schlieffen Plan), and the war settled into the deadlock of trench warfare on the Western Front. In the East the Germans defeated the Russian invasion of East Prussia at Tannenberg and the Masurian Lakes.

In 1915 the Entente tried to break the deadlock on the Western Front by expeditions to the Dardanelles and Salonika in southeast Europe, and by inducing Italy to attack Austria, but to no avail. In 1916 both sides launched grand offensives on the Western Front, the Germans against Verdun and the Allies on the Somme, but despite enormous casualties the deadlock continued. At sea the British and Germans fought the drawn battle of Jutland.

In 1917 both sides were given hope, the Germans by the Russian Revolution (which eventually removed Russia from the war) and the Allies by the United States' entry into the war. The next year proved decisive. The Germans launched a last great offensive (the Spring Offensive) in 1918 but this was halted and US support tipped the scales the Allied way.

Germany agreed to an armistice in November. Her allies, Austria and Turkey, had already given up the fight, the Austrians defeated at Vittorio Veneto in Italy and the Turks defeated by the British in Palestine and Mesopotamia. Although the major engagements were fought in Europe, British and Arab forces fought major campaigns against the Turks in Arabia and Palestine and Mesopotamia. In Africa, the German colonies of South West Africa and Tanganyika were also the scene of fighting. In the Far East Japanese forces seized the German base of Kiaochow.

Greek–Turkish War 1920–23.

By the Treaty of Sèvres, 1920, the Allies handed territory in Asia Minor to Greek control, but the Turks refused to accept this change, and General Mustapha Kemal resisted the Greek occupation. In 1922 he drove the Greeks from their last stronghold at Smyrna, secured control of the area around Constantinople and overthrew the Ottoman Sultan. In 1923 the Allies renegotiated the peace treaty with Turkey at Lausanne.

Spanish Civil War 1936–9.

The war began in 1936 with a revolt by the Fascist General Franco against the Republic which had succeeded the Monarchy in 1931. Germany and Italy aided the rebels who besieged Madrid for over 2 years. An International Brigade was formed to help the Republic, but the Spanish Government was faced by the greater part of the Army, and very effective assistance from Italy and Germany.

The Fascist powers seized the opportunity to have a curtain-raiser to the world conflict which they intended to precipitate. After a total loss of a million men the Fascists overpowered the Republic.

Sino–Japanese War 1937–45.

In July 1937 the Japanese seized upon the pretext of fighting between Chinese and Japanese troops at the Marco Polo Bridge in Beijing to launch an all-out invasion of China, which the Japanese dubbed the China Incident. The Japanese seized Shanghai after fierce fighting and took Nanjing and Guangzhou (Canton). The Chinese government was forced to abandon most of the Chinese coast and set up its capital in Chongqing (Chungking). Japanese forces were unable to conquer the whole of China, being resisted both by Nationalist Chinese troops under Chiang Kai-shek and increasingly by the Communist forces under Mao Tse-tung.

Over half of all Japanese forces were still involved in China when war with the USA and Britain broke out in 1941. The USA gave assistance to the Chinese forces by airlifts from India. Communist forces waged a mainly guerrilla war in north China, while the Nationalists stood on the defensive in the southwest. Clashes between the Nationalist and Communist forces in the run-up to Japanese surrender in August 1945 prefigured the struggle for control of China which brought civil war and eventual Communist triumph.

Russo-Finnish War 1939–40, 1941–4.

War broke out on 30 November 1939 over Russian claims to Karelia, but Finnish resistance under Mannerheim led to several Russian defeats before Finland was forced to make peace and to cede territory in Karelia and the northern border area with Russia. In June 1941 the Finns joined the Germans in war against Russia, fighting mainly on the Karelian front north of Leningrad. Finland made peace with Russia in 1944, when the defeat of Germany seemed inevitable.

Second World War 1939–45.

German forces invaded Poland on 1 September 1939, which led to declarations of war by Britain and France on 3 September. The Germans invaded the Low Countries on 10 May 1940, and France was compelled to sign an armistice on 22 June. The British army was evacuated from Dunkirk, while in the "Battle of Britain" the German *Luftwaffe* failed to defeat the RAF and establish air superiority which would have made an attempted invasion of Britain possible. Italy declared war on 10 June 1940, and Britain attacked Italian forces in North Africa. For over a year Britain and her Empire stood alone against the Axis powers.

In 1941, however, the war was vastly extended, Japan joining the Axis and Russia, China and America joining Britain. The Japanese rapidly overran many of the European colonies in Southeast Asia, but Hitler's invasion of Russia (June 1941) eventually proved a decisive mistake. In 1942 the Germans were defeated in North Africa and Russia, in 1943 the Allies invaded Italy, and in 1944 Britain and America opened the "Second Front" in France. The Allies linked up with the Russians on the Elbe on 28 April 1945 and the Germans accepted unconditional surrender terms on 7 May.

In the Far East, major Japanese forces remained committed to the indecisive war in China, but American forces in the "island-hopping" campaign in the Pacific, and British forces via Burma, inflicted defeats on the Japanese forces. A huge bombing and submarine offensive had brought Japan near to defeat when atomic bombs were dropped on Hiroshima and Nagasaki in early August 1945. Japan surrendered on 14 August 1945.

Chinese Civil War 1945–9.

Civil war between the Nationalist government under Chiang Kai-shek and the Communist forces resumed after the defeat of Japan in August 1945. Through the mediation of General Marshall, a truce was arranged on 14 January 1946. It broke down and US supplies to the Nationalists were halted on 29 July 1946. A Nationalist offensive in Shaanxi took the Communist capital, Yan'an, on 19 March 1947, but it was retaken in April 1948.

As Communist forces advanced, Peking (Beijing) fell on 22 January 1949, Nanjing on 22 April 1949 and Shanghai on 27 May 1949. Mao Tse-tung proclaimed the People's Republic of China on 1 October 1949. The Nationalists withdrew to Taiwan on 7 December 1949.

Indo-China War 1946–54.

Following the surrender of Japan, Ho Chi Minh proclaimed the Democratic Republic of Vietnam at Hanoi on 2 September 1945. French and British forces regained control in Saigon, and after negotiations, French troops entered Hanoi on 16 March 1946.

After French naval forces shelled the Vietnamese quarter of Hai Phong on 23 November 1946, an abortive Viet Minh uprising took place in Hanoi on 19 December 1946.

Guerrilla warfare grew into full-scale conflict between the French and the Viet Minh forces under General Giap. On 20 November 1953 the French established a forward base at Dien Bien Phu to lure the Viet Minh into a set-piece battle, but the garrison of 15,000 men was overwhelmed on 7 May 1954. An agreement for a ceasefire and the division of the country at latitude 17°N was signed at the Geneva Conference on 27 July 1954.

The Cold War 1947–89.

The term was first used in a US Congress debate on 12 March 1947 on the doctrine expounded by Harry S. Truman (1894–1972) promising aid to "free peoples who are resisting attempted subjugation by armed minorities or by outside pressures". A direct product of the civil war in Greece (1946–9), the doctrine bore the wider implication that the USA would actively respond anywhere in the world to what it saw as direct encroachment by the USSR.

The practical division of Europe occurred as a result of the Eastern European states' rejection of US Marchall Aid, often under pressure from the Soviet Union, and their subsequent membership of Comecon. This division into two hostile camps was completed by the creation of NATO in 1949–50 and the Warsaw Pact in 1955. The Cold War between the USSR and the USA continued into the 1970s before being superseded by a period of détente.

The main crises within the Cold War period were the Russian invasion of Hungary in 1956; of Czechoslovakia in 1968; the Berlin Blockade of 1948, and the Cuban Missile Crisis of 1962. Western outrage at these supposed manifestations of Soviet expansion was tempered by the British and French involvement in Suez in 1956, and the US involvement in Vietnam during the 1960s and early 1970s. The advent of Gorbachev in Russia and the events of 1989 in Eastern Europe are regarded as marking the end of the Cold War.

Indo–Pakistan War 1947–9.

A rebellion of the Muslim majority in Kashmir led the Hindu maharajah to accede to the Indian Union, and Indian troops were flown into Kashmir on 27 October 1947. Pakistan sent aid to the Muslim Azad ('free') Kashmir irregulars, and Pakistan army units crossed into Kashmir in March 1948. An undeclared state of war between India and Pakistan continued until UN mediation brought about a ceasefire on 1 January 1949. India formally annexed Kashmir on 26 January 1957.

War occurred again in 1965 (over the Rann of Kutch) and in 1971 (over events in East Pakistan). See **E24**.

Arab–Israeli War 1948–9.

Israel was invaded by the armies of its Arab neighbours on the day the British Mandate ended, 15 May 1948. After initial Arab gains, Israel counter-attacked sucessfully, enlarging its national territory. Only the British-trained Arab Legion of Jordan offered effective opposition. Separate armistices were agreed with Egypt (23 February 1949), Jordan (3 April 1949) and Syria (20 July 1949).

Korean War 1950–53.

North Korean troops invaded the South on 25 June 1950. The UN decided to intervene following an emergency session of the Security Council, which was being boycotted by the Soviet Union. The first US troops landed at Pusan airport on 1 July 1950. General MacArthur mounted an amphibious landing at Inchon on 15 September 1950, and Seoul was recaptured on 26 September. The advance of UN forces into North Korea on 1 October 1950 led to the entry of China into the war on 25 November 1950. Seoul fell to the Chinese on 4 January 1951, but was retaken by UN forces on 14 March 1951. General MacArthur was relieved of his command on 11 April 1951 after expressing his desire to expand the war into China. Truce talks began on 10 July 1951, and an armistice was finally signed at Panmunjon on 27 July 1953.

Hungarian Uprising 1956.

Student demonstrations in Budapest on 23 October 1956 (following a workers' revolt in Poland in June) led to a general uprising against the Communist government of Erno Gero. On 27 October Soviet troops were withdrawn from Budapest. On 1 November 1956 Imre Nagy, the new Prime Minister, announced Hungary's withdrawal from the Warsaw Pact and asked the United Nations to recognize its neutrality. Soviet reinforcements surrounded Budapest and entered the city early on 4 November. Resistance ended on 14 November 1956.

Suez Invasion 1956.

Egypt nationalized the Suez Canal on 26 July 1956. After secret talks with Britain and France, Israel invaded Sinai on 29 October 1956. When Egypt rejected a ceasefire ultimatum by France and Britain, their air forces began to attack Egyptian air bases on 31 October. On 5 November British and French forces invaded the Canal Zone.

Pressure from the United Nations and world opinion forced a ceasefire at midnight on 6/7 November 1956.

Vietnam War 1959–75.

The Communists in South Vietnam (the Viet Cong) built up their strength and launched their first attack on the South Vietnamese armed forces on 8 July 1959 near Bien Hoa, killing two advisers. A state of emergency was proclaimed in the south on 19 October 1961. After attacks on the USS *Maddox* and *Turner Joy*, the US Congress passed the Gulf of Tonkin resolution on 7 August 1964, giving President Johnson wide military powers in South Vietnam. The sustained bombing of North Vietnam by US aircraft (Operation Rolling Thunder) began on 7 February 1965. The first US combat troops landed at Da Nang on 8 March 1965 and engaged the Viet Cong on 15 June.

On 30 January 1968, Communist forces launched their Tet Offensive with heavy attacks on Saigon, Hué and 30 provincial capitals. On 31 March 1968 President Johnson announced the end of the bombing of the north, and on 13 May 1968 peace discussions began in Paris. On 25 January 1969 these discussions were transformed into a formal conference. US and South Vietnamese troops invaded Cambodia in 1970, and the South Vietnamese made an incursion into Laos in 1971. A new Communist offensive against the south began on 30 March 1972, and this led to a resumption of US bombing of the north on 6 April. The last US ground combat units were withdrawn on 11 August 1972. US bombing was halted on 15 January 1973, and a peace agreement was signed in Paris on 27 January. Two years later, a North Vietnamese offensive, which began on 6 January, overran the South, and Saigon was occupied on 30 April 1975.

Sino-Indian War 1962.

After a series of incidents in the disputed border areas, Chinese forces attacked on 20 October 1962 and drove the Indian forces back on the northeast frontier and in the Ladakh region. India declared a state of emergency on 26 October 1962, and launched an unsuccessful counter-offensive on 14 November 1962. On 21 November, the Chinese announced that they would cease fire all along the border and withdraw 12½ miles behind the line of actual control that existed on 7 November 1959. No further fighting took place and the ceasefire held firm.

Nigerian Civil War 1967–70.

On 30 May 1967 the military governor of the Eastern Region of Nigeria, Colonel Ojukwu, declared the Ibo homeland an independent sovereign state under the name of the Republic of Biafra. Troops of the Nigerian federal army attacked across the northern border of Biafra on 7 July 1967. The Biafrans invaded the neighbouring Mid-West Region on 9 August 1967. The federal army recaptured Biafra on 22 September 1967, and Port Harcourt fell on 20 May 1968. Supply shortages and starvation finally led to the collapse of Biafran resistance after a four-pronged federal attack in December 1969. The Biafran army surrendered on 15 January 1970.

The Six Day War 1967.

Israel decided on a pre-emptive strike following Egypt's request for the withdrawal of the UN peace-keeping force from Sinai on 16 May, the closure of the Gulf of Aqaba to Israeli shipping on 22 May, and the signature of an Egyptian–Jordanian defence pact on 30 May.

On 5 June 1967 Israel launched devastating air attacks on Egyptian air bases. Israeli forces then invaded Sinai and reached the Suez Canal on 7 June. By nightfall on 7 June Jordan had been defeated and Jerusalem and the West Bank were in Israeli hands. On 9 June Israeli troops attacked Syria and occupied the Golan Heights. A ceasefire was agreed on 10 June 1967.

Indo–Pakistan War and Bangladeshi War of Independence, 1971.

Elections in December 1970 resulted in a landslide victory in East Pakistan for the Awami League. On 26 March 1971 Sheikh Mujibur Rahman, the head of the League, proclaimed East Pakistan an independent republic under the name of Bangladesh. He was arrested and West Pakistani troops and locally raised irregulars, *razakars*, put down large-scale resistance on 10 May 1971. Awami League fighters, the *Mukti Bahini*, began a guerrilla campaign, and clashes between India and Pakistan increased as millions of refugees fled into India. President Yahya Khan declared a state of emergency in Pakistan on 23 November 1971. On 3 December 1971 the Pakistani air force launched surprise attacks on Indian airfields. On 4 December some 160,000 Indian troops invaded East Pakistan. Pakistani forces in East Pakistan surrendered on 16 December 1971, and a general ceasefire came into effect the following day.

Since 1971 Indo-Pakistan relations have remained strained with intermittent hostilities.

Yom Kippur War 1973.

On 6 October 1973, the day of a Jewish religious holiday, Egyptian forces crossed the Suez canal, overwhelming Israel's Bar-Lev defence line in a well-planned surprise attack. Syrian forces attacked the Golan Heights, but initial gains were surrendered by 12 October.

In a daring counter-stroke on 15 October 1973, Israeli forces crossed to the west bank of the Suez Canal and encircled the Egyptian Third Army. A ceasefire became effective on 24 October 1973.

Iran–Iraq War 1980–88.

Hoping to exploit the instability of Iran after the fall of the Shah, Iraq abrogated the Algiers pact of 1975, by which it had been forced to accept joint control of the Shatt al-Arab waterway, and invaded Iran on 12 September 1980. Khorramshahr fell on 13 October, 1980, but the Iranian government did not collapse and its armed forces began to counter-attack successfully. Each side bombed the other's oil installations and attacked international shipping in the Gulf. Iran rejected Iraq's ceasefire overtures as the military stalemate deepened. On 9 January 1987 Iran launched a major offensive – codenamed Karabala-5 – with the aim of capturing Basra. The Iranians advanced some distance towards their objective, while suffering heavy casualties. In 1987 and 1988 Iraq made major advances and a ceasefire was organized in August 1988. The war is estimated to have cost almost a million casualties, with some of the heaviest land-fighting since the Second World War.

Falklands War 1982.

On 2 April 1982 the Argentine dictatorship, under General Galtieri, launched a successful invasion of the islands, forcing its garrison of 18 Royal Marines to surrender. Argentine forces also seized the island of South Georgia. On 5 April a British Task Force set sail to recapture the islands and on 7 April an exclusion zone of 200 miles was declared around the island. On 25 April South Georgia was recaptured and on 1 May air attacks began on the Argentine garrison on the Falklands. The next day the Argentine cruiser *Belgrano* was sunk by a British submarine and on 4 May HMS *Sheffield* was hit by an Exocet missile.

On 21 May British troops went ashore at San Carlos. Two British frigates, the *Ardent* and *Antelope*, were sunk and others damaged by air attack, but British troops took Darwin and Goose Green by the end of May and on 11–14 June an attack on Port Stanley led to the surrender of the Argentine forces.

Gulf War 1990.

On 2 August Iraq invaded Kuwait. UN Resolution 660, condemning the invasion and calling for immediate and unconditional withdrawal, was passed the same day. The USA ordered naval forces to the Gulf on 3 August and sent troops to Saudi Arabia on 7 August (Operation Desert Shield). UN Resolution 661, imposing economic sanctions on Iraq, was passed on 6 August. On 8 August Iraq announced the annexation of Kuwait. On 29 November UN Resolution 678 sanctioned the use of force if Iraq had not withdrawn by 15 January 1991. Britain joined the Allied armies (led by the USA), contributing land, sea and air forces.

The Allied offensive against Iraq (Operation Desert Storm) began shortly before midnight on 16 January. The Allied ground offensive began on 24 February. Kuwait City was entered by the Allies on 26 February. With Kuwait liberated and the Iraqi army defeated, US President Bush ordered a ceasefire, which came into effect on 28 February. During the conflict, Allied forces lost 166 killed, 207 wounded and 106 missing or captured. Iraqi losses were estimated by some to be 200,000.

Yugoslavian Civil War (Serbo–Croat War) 1991–5.

Declarations of independence by the former Yugoslav Republics of Slovenia and Croatia led to clashes on Slovenia's borders from July 1991, followed by heavy fighting on Croatian territory between Croatian militia and Serbian irregulars (*chetniks*) backed by the Yugoslav Federal Army. The main centres of fighting were eastern and central Croatia and the Adriatic coast around Dubrovnik.

Yugoslavia officially ceased to exist in January 1992 and Slovenia and Croatia were recognized as independent states. On 29 February 1992 Muslim leaders in Bosnia-Herzegovina declared independence. Bosnian Serbs and the Serbian leadership in Belgrade rejected this, and war began on 6 April with the opening of the siege of the capital Sarajevo.

Serbs were accused of "ethnic cleansing" to secure territorial domination, and a UN trade embargo was imposed on Serbia on 31 May. Peace talks in Geneva, mediated by Lord Owen and Cyrus Vance, began on 26 August. On 16 November a UN naval blockade was mounted against Serbia and Montenegro. Fighting continued as a further peace conference was held in Geneva on 22–3 January 1993. Serbs attacked Muslim enclaves at Srebenica and Goradze. Numerous peace talks collapsed. In 1995 Croatia launched major offensives and an uneasy peace accord was signed at Dayton, Ohio. An estimated 200,000 people died in the Civil War.

Russo-Chechnya War 1994–96 and after 1999.

Russian troops were ordered into Chechnya in December 1994 to end the rebel republic's bid for independence. Fighting ensued for 21 months as Russian troops failed to subdue the population. The fighting was the worst on Russian soil since the Second World War, with Grozny, the Chechnya capital, razed to the ground. The Russian army suffered a major loss of face. On 31 August 1996 Russia and Chechnya signed a peace deal, freezing the issue of independence for five years. In January 1997 the withdrawal of all Russian troops from Chechnya was completed.

However, partly provoked by Chechen support for guerrillas in the adjacent Caucasus region of Dagestan, and partly because of terrorist bomb outrages in Russia itself, a renewed Russian offensive was launched against Chechnya in September 1999. Massive Russian aerial bombardment was followed by a major ground offensive against Grozny launched on 25 December 1999.

Zaïre Civil War 1996–97, 1998–2002.

In October 1996 the Alliance of Democratic Forces for the Liberation of Congo-Zaïre – led by President Mobutu Sésé Séko's long-term opponent Laurent Kabila – launched an attack on the Zaïrean army in alliance with anti-Mobutu Tutsi guerrillas and forces seeking autonomy for the Shaba and Kasai provinces. Kabila's troops were supported during the campaign by Rwanda and Uganda while Mobutu strengthened his army with white mercenaries. After a rapid advance through the country, the capital Kinshasa fell to Alliance forces in May 1997. Kabila declared himself head of state, renaming the country the Democratic Republic of the Congo. Renewed civil war from 1998 to 2002 cost over 3 million lives and in parts of eastern Congo war continues to remain endemic.

The Balkan War 1999.

Conflict in Kosovo, until 1989 an autonomous province in "rump" Yugoslavia mainly inhabited by Kosovar Albanians, gradually intensified as Serbian forces embarked on a policy of ethnic cleansing. The Serbian leader Slobodan Milosevic ignored a series of NATO warnings during 1998. On 24 March 1999 NATO forces (including British aircraft) launched air strikes against Yugoslavia. Cruise missile attacks followed. Milosevic intensified his ethnic cleansing policy, producing a human tide of refugees into Macedonia and Albania. NATO air strikes were marked by a series of calamitous errors (including the missile attack on the Chinese embassy in Belgrade on 8 May) and a serious worsening of relations with Russia. Eventually air power (backed by a threat of a land offensive) caused Milosevic to sue for peace and a mainly NATO peace-keeping force (KFOR, with some Russian troops) was stationed in Kosovo.

The War on Terror since 2001.

The term given to the military response by the United States and its allies to the 11 September attack on New York, believed to be by al-Qaeda under the direction of Osama bin Laden. Afghanistan, a stronghold of militant Islamists under the Taleban regime, was perceived as an immediate target. A war to overthrow the Taleban quickly followed (see below). Another target in America's sights was Iraq under Saddam Hussein. Coalition forces attacked Iraq in 2003 (see below). Meanwhile, although no further major terrorist attack took place in the United States, al-Qaeda and similar militant Islamist groups launched attacks elsewhere (e.g. bombings in London, Bali and Madrid, and major attacks on Indian cities such as Mumbai). A renewed war against a revived Taleban began in Afghanistan which spilled across the Pakistan border into such areas as the Swat Valley. The "War on Terror" remains ongoing. It has moved to such countries as Yemen and Somalia. The death of Osama bin Laden in 2011 has not ended the terrorist threat. A new phase opened in 2014 with the onset of ISIS.

The Afghan Conflict, 2001–14.

After the 11 September 2001 assault on America (carried out by the al-Qaeda terror group headed by Osama bin Laden), US and British forces launched attacks on Afghanistan on 7 October 2001. Air attacks were launched from Pakistan and bases in central Asia, while allied forces assisted Northern Alliance rebels within Afghanistan. The Taleban regime rapidly fell: Hera was gained on 12 November, Kabul on 18 November and Kandahar in December. Pockets of resistance by al-Qaeda and Taleban forces continued to resist ISAF (the International Security Assistance Force) and the 8,000-strong US forces in Afghanistan.

Following the invasion of Iraq (see below) fighting by an increasingly strong Taleban steadily mounted. The British troops deployed in Helmand Province suffered increasing casualties, while American troop numbers in the country surged to counter the renewed threat. Most foreign combat troops left the country by 31 December 2014. However, the future of the country remains as uncertain as ever and foreign troops have had to remain longer. British fatalities in the war were 456. Total foreign coalition casualties were around 3,500.

Invasion of Iraq (the Second Gulf War) 2003.

Following unsuccessful attempts to persuade the regime of Saddam Hussein to comply with UN resolutions on disarmament, US-led forces invaded Iraq in March 2003. The attack opened on 20 March with the bombing of Baghdad and central Iraq, followed by the movement of American and British troops in the south to secure the oilfields and the port of Umm Qasr. As the Americans moved north towards Baghdad, bypassing obstacles where resistance proved stronger than expected, British troops began a slow campaign to take Iraq's second city of Basra.

Forecasts that the Iraqi people would rise against Saddam Hussein and that the regime's collapse would be speedy were confounded. On 3 April American forces reached the airport close to the capital and on 6 April Basra fell to British troops. American troops began their decisive entry into Baghdad on 7 April. The Saddam Hussein regime had effectively ended, but an increasingly bloody insurgency against the occupation forces developed during 2004. American forces finally withdrew from Iraq in December 2011, having lost 4,488 men in the conflict. The number of British soldiers killed was 179.

The descent of Iraq into civil war in 2014, and the victories of jihadist ISIS forces in the north, led to renewed US-led air strikes in August.

Syrian Civil War, 2015–.

The war began in 2011 with an uprising against the brutal regime of President Bashar al-Assad. By 2015, although the government had lost control of much of Syria, the conflict had become highly complex. Sunnis fought Shia, the fundamentalist Islamic State (ISIS) fighters seized swathes of territory, the Kurds fought their own independence struggle and outside powers, notably Turkey, Russia and the United States were all involved. The war has created over five million refugees. By early 2017 Assad's forces had regained much ground. In response to Assad's use of chemical warfare, America launched a missile strike in April 2017.

PART IV. FAMOUS MODERN BATTLES

Anzio (23 January 1944) An initial Anglo-American landing 60 miles behind the front took German forces by surprise but the Allies were rapidly contained in the immediate bridgehead, the attack failing in its objective of speeding the advance up Italy.

Ardennes (16 December 1944 to 3 January 1945). German effort to break the momentum of the Allied advance by piercing their lines, capturing Antwerp and blocking supplies. The initial drive broke through but the Allies held, counterattacking on 3 January 1945 against a now exhausted enemy.

Arnhem (17 to 26 September 1944) Allied attempt to make an early thrust into Germany by landing British airborne forces to hold a Rhine bridge while British Second Army advanced to link up. Meeting unexpectedly heavy opposition, the attackers were unable to hold their ground long enough.

Austerlitz (2 December 1805) Napoleon decisively defeated numerically superior Russian and Austrian armies, France losing 17,300 of 70,000 men with Allied casualties 18,500 from 86,000. As Russia retreated homewards, Austria made peace on French terms.

Balaclava (25 October 1854) Russian attack on British Crimean War base stemmed by a Highland Regiment and the cavalry's Heavy Brigade in an inconclusive battle. Remarkable for the mistaken and celebrated Charge of the Light Brigade.

Bosworth Field See **E13**

Boyne, The (1 to 11 July 1690) James II, having lost the English throne to William and Mary in the 1688 Revolution, attempted to recapture it by landing in Ireland with a French army, but having unsuccessfully beseiged Derry and met defeat by William, fled to France.

Britain (10 July to 31 October 1940) Air attack on Britain launched by Germany with 3 to 1 superiority as part of invasion plans, aimed at shipping, airfields and towns. RAF pilots shot down 1,733 German planes for the loss of 915, the high point coming on 15 August when 75 Luftwaffe aircraft were destroyed. With invasion postponed, Germany turned to night-bombing of civilian targets.

Caporetto (24 October to 4 November 1917) Collapse of Italian armies on the River Isonzo in the face of an Austro-German offensive, the situation being retrieved only by a stiffening of British and French forces. 300,000 Italians were captured and as many deserted, the sense of shame encouraging post-war Fascism.

Cassino See **A16**

Culloden Moor See **E15**

Dettingen (16 to 27 June 1743) With Britain taking an anti-French line in the dynastic War of the Austrian Succession, George II, leading allied British, Dutch, Austrian, Hanoverian and Hessian forces, defeated the French, the last occasion on which an English king personally accompanied his army into battle.

Dien Bien Phu (13 March to 7 May 1954) French airborne troops fortifed this North Vietnam village, intending to draw General Giap's Viet Minh guerrillas into a conventional fixed battle, but were themselves besieged and bombarded into surrender, the loss provoking an armistice in two months and the collapse of French power in Indo-China. See also **E23**

Dunkirk (27 May to 4 June 1940) Almost 340,000 British and French troops, retreating from the German armoured advance as Belgian forces collapsed and French resistance wavered, were successfully ferried from the beaches across the Channel to England.

El Alamein Two battles between British and Commonwealth 8th Army and German – Italian forces in 2nd World War North African campaign. First, 30 June to 25 July 1942, a defensive action in which Auchinleck held Rommel's attack into Egypt. Second, 23 October to 4 November

in which Montgomery led the drive which ultimately pushed the Axis armies from North Africa.

Flodden Field See **E15**

Gallipoli (25 April 1915 to 9 January 1916) A British, Australian and New Zealand forces' attempt to break the Western stalemate by landing in Turkey, threatening Constantinople and easing pressure on Russia. The landing, expected by the Turks, met with heavy resistance, degenerating into protracted and bloody fighting. A further landing at Suvla in August suffered a similar fate and a decision to withdraw was made in December.

Gettysburg (1 to 3 July 1863) American Civil War battle. General Lee's Confederate armies attempted to carry the fighting into Union territory but were held and defeated at Gettysburg, the turning point of the American Civil War. In November at the military cemetery Lincoln made his celebrated Gettysburg Address.

Jena (14 October 1806) Divided Prussian armies defeated in two actions by Napoleon and Davout which, followed by the fall of the capital Berlin, exposed the depth of Prussia's economic and political weakness and led to the temporary waning of Prussia as a European military power of any consequence.

Jutland (31 May to 1 June 1916) The long-awaited engagement between the British Grand Fleet and German High Seas Fleet in the North Sea. Though the British appeared to come off worst in terms of ships lost, it was the German fleet which retired, never to risk leaving harbour again for the duration of the war.

Leipzig (16 to 19 October 1813) "Battle of the Nations". An overwhelming combination of Austrian, Russian and Prussian forces smashed Napoleon's armies, the remnants of which fell back to the Rhine to leave Germany liberated.

Marne, The A river, the scene of two World War One battles. First, 5 to 9 September 1914 in which French and British armies counter-attacked and then repulsed advancing German forces which were within sight of Paris. Second, 15 July to 7 August 1918 when Franco-American forces held off the final German offensive of the war, beginning an advance which led to the Armistice.

Midway Islands (4 June 1942) The central sea clash between the United States and Japan fought almost entirely by carrier-borne aircraft, with America losing one carrier to Japan's four, and which marked the turning point ending the Japanese Pacific advance.

Naseby See **E18**

Navarino (20 October 1827) When Turkey ignored British, French and Russian demands that she make peace in the Greek War of Independence, their ships attacked in the Turkish-Egyptian fleet, sinking 50 vessels and securing Greek autonomy.

Nile, The (1 August 1798) British under Nelson destroyed the bulk of a French fleet that had carried Napoleon's by then abandoned Levant Army to Egypt, cutting the force off from any hope of relief.

Pearl Harbor (7 December 1941) While Japanese diplomats negotiated in Washington, her carrier-based aircraft launched a surprise attack on the US naval base in Hawaii, sinking or damaging 19 ships, destroying 180 aircraft and killing over 2,000. The United States declared war the following day, Germany and Italy declaring war on her three days later.

Sadowa (3 July 1866) Moltke's army defeated the Austrians in the main battle of the Austro-Prussian War, shattering further Austrian resistance, ending her influence in Germany and announcing the beginning of Prussian dominance in Central Europe. Sometimes called Sadowa-Koniggratz.

Saratoga (17 October 1777) The British having divided their armies and then lost contact, Burgoyne's force marching south from Canada became isolated, surrendering to the Americans, a disaster which encouraged the French to join against Britain in the American War of Independence.

Sedan (1 to 2 September 1870) French under Marshal McMahon caught and overwhelmed by German army at fortress of Sedan with Napoleon III personally surrendering, ending the authority of the 2nd Empire and leading to the proclamation of the French 3rd Republic.

Sedgemoor See **E19**

Somme, The (1 July to 18 November 1916) British attempt with French support to break through German trenches on a 20-mile front in NW France. At a cost of 600,000 casualties – the British losing 20,000 dead on 1 July alone – the Allies, despite equally heavy German losses, advanced at most ten miles.

Stalingrad (5 September 1942 to 1 February 1943) German forces reached their furthest point east at Stalingrad where they were held down in heavy street fighting until surrounded by Russian armies led by Zhukov. Cut off from relief, their commander von Paulus was forced to surrender with 91,000 troops.

Tannenberg (26 to 30 August 1914) The first of two battles in which Germany defeated the sole Russian incursion into her territory during World War One, surrounding and capturing a Russian army of 100,000. At the nearby Masurian Lakes in a three day battle beginning on 10 September a second Russian army of 125,000 was defeated and taken prisoner.

Trafalgar (21 October 1805) British under Nelson defeated the Franco-Spanish fleet – including shipping collected for an invasion of England – off south-west coast of Spain. Though Napoleon had already abandoned his invasion plans, the victory, in which Nelson was killed, confirmed British naval predominance in Europe.

Tsushima (27 to 28 May 1905) The ill-equipped and badly led Russian Baltic Fleet, sailing round the world to isolate Japanese forces in Manchuria, was destroyed by a Japanese fleet which suffered few casualties, leading Russia to seek a cessation of hostilities, this humiliation encouraging the Russian Revolution of 1905.

Verdun (21 February to 16 December 1916) German forces suffered 450,000 casualties in an attempt to break through on a 15-mile front to capture French fortifications and shatter their morale. Despite German failure, the French – who lost 550,000 men – suffered the longer term blow to their morale.

Waterloo (18 June 1815). The British army under Wellington inflicted the final defeat on Napoleon, destroying his hopes of retrieving power after escaping from exile in Elba. The appearance of the Prussians under Blucher in the evening decided the outcome and Napoleon fled, abdicating 4 days later.

Worcester See **E21**

Yorktown (19 October 1781) An apparently successful British army, cut off in Virginia by French command of the coastal sea, was forced to surrender to American-French troops, effectively ending the American War of Independence and precipitating the fall of Lord North's government in London.

Ypres Belgian town, the scene of protracted fighting and four specific battles in World War One. From 12 October to 11 November 1914 German forces failed to capture the town, being repelled again in an offensive opened using poison gas from 22 April to 24 May 1915. From 31 July to 6 November 1917 the British mounted a bloody but fruitless attack, suffering 300,000 casualties. In September 1918 British troops advanced in the area as part of the final push against the retreating German armies.

PART V. TREATIES AND ALLIANCES

Anglo-French Entente ("Entente Cordiale") (8 April 1904) Resolving outstanding territorial issues in Africa, the Far East and Egypt, symbolising the beginning of a warmer phase in Anglo-French relations and, while not overtly an anti-German compact, leaving open the possibility of France in June 1940. Remained operative till the collapse of France in June 1940.

Anglo-Irish Treaty (6 December 1921) Agreement leading to the 1922 Irish Free State Act, granting 26 Southern Irish counties independent dominion status, six northern counties remaining part of the United Kingdom with limited self-government, but resisted in the south by de Valera's republicans, civil war ensuing till 1923.

Anglo-Russian Entente (31 August 1907) Though never as close as the "Entente Cordiale" (*q.v.*) through a British domestic wariness towards the Tsarist political system, nevertheless settled differences over Afghanistan, Persia and Tibet and aided Russian industrial development by opening the way to British investment.

Anti-Cominterm Pact An agreement on joint anti-Communist attitudes and measures signed by Germany and Italy (25 November 1936), Hungary (February 1939) and Franco's Spain (April 1939) and interpreted to be a loose alliance aimed as much against the Western democracies as against Communism.

Anzus Pact (1 September 1951) Australian, New Zealand and United States agreement to provide military assistance if either were attacked in the Pacific, demonstrating the two Commonwealth powers increasing diplomatic independence from Britain and America's developing Far East policy.

Atlantic Charter (14 August 1941) A joint Anglo-American declaration of war aims arising from talks between Churchill and Roosevelt, setting out the principles of "a better future for the world" based on democracy and the abandonment of the use of force.

Brest-Litovsk, Treaty of (3 March 1918) Russia was

compelled by Germany and Austria-Hungary to relinquish Russian Poland, Lithuania, Latvia, Estonia and to recognise the independence of Finland, Ukraine and Georgia, Russia losing 34% of her population, 54% of industry and 90% of coal mines with massive reparations imposed upon her. Annulled by the later Treaty of Versailles (**E11**) settling the First World War.

Entente Cordiale See **Anglo-French Entente**

Frankfurt, Treaty of (10 May 1871) Defeated in war, France ceded the province of Alsace and the bulk of Lorraine to Prussia, with an army of occupation imposed until reparations of five billion francs were paid.

Kanagawa, Treaty of (31 March 1854) An agreement with the United States by which Japan granted facilities to American traders in two ports, beginning the opening up of Japan to Western influences.

Kellogg Pact (27 August 1928) Also known as the Kellogg-Briand Pact after the American and French ministers instrumental in its formulation, with most world powers condemning recourse to war as a means of settling disputes and undertaking to find peaceful methods of resolution.

Lateran Treaties (11 February 1929) The Italian state recognised the independence of the papal Vatican State, acknowledged the position of the Church in Italy and agreed to pay compensation for Papal State territories seized in the reunification of the 1870s.

Locarno, Treaty of (16 November 1925) Britain, France, Germany, Italy and Belgium undertook to maintain the integrity of Western European frontiers and to refrain from the use of force against one another, with Britain and Italy acting as overall guarantors and Germany acknowledging the demilitarisation of the Rhineland. Ended when Hitler reoccupied the Rhineland unhindered in 1936.

London, Treaty of (19 April 1839) The Netherlands, Belgium's former ruler, acknowledged Belgian independence, with Britain, Prussia, Russia and Austria providing collective guarantees, the breaking of which by the German invasion of August 1914 provoked Britain's declaration of war.

London, Treaty of (26 April 1915) To encourage Italy to join them in war against the Central Powers, Britain, France and Russia secretly promised her Austrian and Turkish territory, together with African colonies, but the agreement was repudiated at the 1919 Peace Conference, Italy receiving far less than she had hoped for.

Munich Agreement (29 September 1938) Attempt to resolve the European crisis through the appeasement of Hitler's demands by allowing Germany to take possession of the German-speaking Sudeten area of Czechoslovakia with the agreement of Britain, France and Italy. Initially hailed as "peace for our time" (by Neville Chamberlain, the British Prime Minister) but doubts soon set in, these being confirmed when Hitler occupied the remainder of Czech territory in March 1939.

Nanking, Treaty of This treaty ended the "Opium War" with China in 1842 ceding Hong Kong to Britain and agreeing to open the "treaty ports" of Amoy, Canton, Foochow, Nangpo and Shanghai to British traders, marking the beginning of developing Western interests in China.

Nazi-Soviet Pact (23 August 1939) A 10-year non-aggression treaty between Germany and the Soviet Union with each to remain neutral if the other were engaged in war, secret protocols designating respective spheres of influence in Eastern Europe. It signalled the German intention to attack a now isolated Poland and was broken when Hitler attacked Russia in June 1941.

Potsdam Agreement *See* **E9**

Rapallo, Treaty of (16 April 1922) A surprise agreement, largely symbolic but nonetheless disconcerting to Britain and France, on co-operation, friendship and trade between Germany and Russia – the "outsiders" of European diplomacy.

Reinsurance Treaty (18 June 1887) A secret agreement (not renewed after 1890), Germany and Russia promising neutrality in war unless Germany attacked France or Russia moved against Austria-Hungary, Russia being further guaranteed German backing if Bulgaria countered any Russian move against the Turkish Straits.

Rome, Treaty of *See* **Section C, Part I**

St Germain, Treaty of (10 September 1919) Allied peace terms with Austrian Republic, Austria losing all non-German areas, ceding territory and population to Czechoslovakia, Italy, Poland, Romania and Yugoslavia, union with Germany being forbidden, her army limited to 35,000 and reparations imposed.

San Stefano, Treaty of (3 March 1878) Ended the Russo-Turkish War, creating an independent Bulgaria, confirming the autonomy of Montenegro, Serbia and Romania and ceding Turkish Caucasus territory to Russia. Britain and Austria saw it as excessively favourable to Slav interests and later modified it at the Congress of Berlin.

Triple Alliance (20 May 1882) A secret agreement contrived by Bismarck to isolate the French, with Germany and Austria-Hungary promising to support Italy if France attacked her, while Italy would come to Germany's aid if she were attacked by France. Renewed every five years until 1915, when Italy – encouraged by the Treaty of London (q.v.) – declared war on both her former partners.

Triple Entente (3 September 1914) Britain, France and Russia guaranteed not to conclude a separate peace with the Central Powers, with whom they were all at war, but the Bolsheviks broke the agreement after the 1917 Revolution, ending hostilities at Brest Litovsk (q.v.)

Vereeniging, Treaty of (31 May 1902) Concluding the Boer War, Britain annexed the Boer territories of Transvaal and Orange Free State, promising self-government (granted in 1907), and made payment of £3 million to aid rebuilding of damaged Boer farms.

Versailles, Treaty of *See* **E11**

Warsaw Pact *See* **E11**

PART VI. SELECTED EUROPEAN RULERS

RUSSIA

Tsars (House of Romanov)

	Succeeded
Peter I (the Great)	1682
(took the title of Tsar, or Emperor in 1721)	
Catherine	1725
Peter II	1727
Anne	1730
Ivan VI	1740
Elizabeth	1741
Peter III (deposed)	1761
Catherine II (the Great)	1762
Paul I (murdered)	1796
Alexander I	1801
Nicholas I	1825
Alexander II (assassinated)	1855
Alexander III	1881
Nicholas II (deposed by revolution 1917, executed with his family 1918)	1894

Premiers of Provisional Government

Prince Georgi Lvov	1917
Alexander Kerensky	1917

Leaders of the USSR

After the Bolshevik Revolution of November 1917 though the actual personality holding power was usually clear, the title varied.

Vladimir Lenin – Premier (died Jan 1924)	1917

A power struggle ensued after the death of Lenin between Joseph Stalin and Leon Trotsky. Stalin, General Secretary of the Communist Party, ruled with Zinoviev and Kameniev through a "troika" until Trotsky's position had been weakened. Stalin then acted with Rykov and Kalinin against Zinoviev. By 1927 Stalin was in authority, acting solely through his Party position and no State title.

Joseph Stalin – Premier	1941
Nikita Khrushchev – First Party Secretary (after Stalin's death)	1953
Georgi Malenkov – Premier	1953

Khrushchev used his authority to demote Malenkov to deputy premier in February 1955, Marshal Nikolai Bulgarin taking the position. In March 1958 Bulganin resigned, Khrushchev succeeding while retaining his Party office. He was ousted from both in 1964

Leonid Brezhnev – First Party Secretary	1964
Aleksei Kosygin – Premier (resigned 1980)	1964

Brezhnev became President in June 1977, the Constitution having been revised to make this post more than purely titular, Brezhnev also retaining his Party office. He died in November 1982

Yuri Andropov – President and Party Secretary (died 1984)	1982
Konstantin Chernenko – Party Secretary	1984
Mikhail Gorbachev – until the fall of the Soviet Union	1985

Presidents of Russia (since 1991)

Boris Yeltsin	1991 (to 31 December 1999)
Vladimir Putin	2000
Dmitri Medvedev	2008
Vladimir Putin	2012

GERMANY
(Prussia prior to 1871)

Prussia (Head of State)	Reigned
Frederick I	1701–13
Frederick William I	1713–40
Frederick II (The Great)	1740–86
Frederick William II	1786–97
Frederick William III	1797–1840
Frederick William IV	1840–61

Second Reich

William I	1861–88
(Germany unified and the Reich proclaimed 1871)	
Frederick III	1888
William II	1888–1918
(Abdicated)	

Weimar Republic

	Term of Presidential office
Frederick Ebert	1919–25
Paul von Hindenburg-Beneckendorff	1925–34

Third Reich

Adolf Hitler – became Chancellor 1933. On President Hindenburg's death in 1934 combined offices and took role of Führer and Reichskanzler.

Federal Republic (West Germany prior to reunification)

Chancellors

Konrad Adenauer	1949–63
Ludwig Erhard	1963–66
Kurt Georg Kiesinger	1966–69
Willy Brandt	1969–74
Helmut Schmidt	1974–82
Helmut Kohl	1982–98
Gerhard Schröder	1998–2005
Angela Merkel	2005–*

*Sought a fourth term in office.

FRANCE
(Monarchs and Heads of State)

Rulers for the early period are listed by dynasty.

The Capets	Year of Accession
Hugh	987
Robert II	996
Henry I	1031
Philip I	1060
Louis VI	1108
Louis VII	1137
Philip II	1180
Louis VIII	1223
Louis IX	1226
Philip III	1270
Philip IV	1285
Louis X	1314
Philip V	1316
Charles IV	1322

House of Valois

Philip VI	1328
John II	1350
Charles V	1364
Charles VI	1380
Charles VII	1422
Louis XI	1461
Charles VIII	1483
Louis XII	1498
Francis I	1515
Henry II	1547
Francis II	1559
Charles IX	1560
Henry III	1574

House of Bourbon

Henry IV	1589
Louis XIII	1610
Louis XIV	1643
Louis XV	1715

Louis XVI	1774

(Following the 1789 revolution, Louis XVI was beheaded in 1793; his son described as Louis XVII died in prison and never ascended to the throne)

First Republic

National Convention	1792
Directory	1795
Consulate	1799

(Napoleon Bonaparte First Consul, elected Consul for life in 1802)

First Empire

Napoleon I	1804
(Abdicated)	

Bourbon Restoration

Louis XVIII	1814
Charles X	1824
(Deposed by revolution in 1830)	

House of Orleans

Louis-Philippe	1830

Second Republic

Louis Napoleon Bonaparte – President	1848

Second Empire

Napoleon III	1852
(Deposed)	

Third Republic	Elected President
Louis Thiers	1871
Marshal Patrice de MacMahon	1873
Paul Grevy	1879
M. Sadi-Carnot	1887
(Assassinated in 1894)	
Jean Casimir-Perier	1894
Francois Faure	1895
Emile Loubet	1899
C. Armand Fallieres	1906
Raymond Poincare	1913
Paul Deschanel	1920
Alexandre Millerand	1920
Gaston Doumergue	1924
Paul Doumer	1931
(Assassinated in 1932)	
Albert Lebrun	1932

Vichy Government	Chief of State
Henri Pétain	1940

Provisional Government

Charles de Gaulle	1944
Felix Gouin	1946
Georges Bidault	1946

Fourth Republic	Elected President
Vincent Auriol	1947
René Coty	1954

Fifth Republic

Charles de Gaulle	1959
Georges Pompidou	1969
Valery Giscard d'Estaing	1974
François Mitterrand	1981
Jacques Chirac	1995
Nicolas Sarkozy	2007
François Hollande	2012
Emmanuel Macron	2017

SPAIN
(Monarchs and Heads of State)

	Succeeded
Charles I	1520
(abdicated)	
Philip II	1556
Philip III	1598
Philip IV	1621

Charles II	1665
Philip V	1700
Ferdinand VI	1746
Charles III	1759
Charles IV	1788
(abdicated)	
Ferdinand VII	1808

Napoleon occupied Spain and made his brother Joseph king, Joseph being ousted in 1813.

Ferdinand VII	1814
Isabella II	1833

(threatened by revolution in 1843 and a seven year civil war, Isabella retaining the throne with the support of her generals until 1868)

Amadeo elected King by the Cortes	1870
(abdicated)	

First Spanish Republic (1873–74)

Spain had four Presidents in one year

The Bourbon Restoration

Alphonso XII	1875
Alphonso XIII	1885

(his mother Maria Christina acting as Regent till 1902)

Dictatorship of General Primo de Rivera 1923, which fell in 1930, followed by revolution in which Alphonso fled without formal abdication and which ended the monarchy.

Second Spanish Republic	President
Niceto Alcala Zamora	1931

Manuel Azaña	1936

(resigned with the defeat of the Republicans by the Nationalists in Civil War)

The Franco Dictatorship

Francisco Franco, Chief of State	1939
(died 1975)	

Restoration of the Monarchy

Juan Carlos	1975
Felipe VI	2014

ITALY
(Rulers and Heads of State)

	Succeeded
Victor Emmanuel	1861
Umberto I	1878
(assassinated)	
Victor Emmanuel III	1900
(abdicated 1945)	

Benito Mussolini: became Fascist Prime Minister 1922; made the King Emperor of Ethiopia 1937; deposed 1943.

Umberto II	1946

The Republic

Italy became a Republic by plebiscite in 1946. The first president of the Italian Republic was de Gasperi (Acting President).

PART VII. ARCHAEOLOGY

GREAT ARCHAEOLOGICAL DISCOVERIES SINCE 1960

Introduction.

Although such a title for this article may appear self-explanatory, it actually serves to hide some profound controversies about the whole nature of archaeology. The general public, for example, may tend to equate "great" with "treasure" and the "spectacular" – the stuff of blockbuster exhibitions. The professional archaeologist, however, is focused on how man has evolved and how he has lived, and may well find a few pieces of bone, scattered tools and some broken pottery more informative and more exciting than, say, a pile of gold coins. Indeed, some archaeologists would go so far as to dismiss some treasure hoards as being of interest only to the art historian. This may be an extreme view, but greatness remains in the eye of the beholder.

New Interpretations.

"Discovery" is similarly ambiguous, because it cannot be confined to the objects exposed during the traditional archaeological dig or found by expeditions through unmarked desert, jungle or mountain. It must also include discoveries of the mind. Learning how to read a previously indecipherable inscription, manuscript or tablet is amongst the greatest of discoveries because it enables us to approach a civilisation on its own terms for the first time. The same can be said of those leaps of vision which provide us with a whole new interpretation of the past on the basis of a fresh and often controversial review of evidence old and new.

New Scientific Techniques.

"Discoveries" should also arguably include the invention or dramatic refinement of the new scientific techniques, which have, for example, enabled archaeology to model agricultural, climatic and population cycles with a sophistication unimaginable 50 years ago. Excavation is now often preceded by *soil resistivity surveys* which, by identifying likely foundations, direct archaeologists to those areas most likely to be fruitful for detailed examination. *Dendrochronology*, which has only become routinely available to British archaeologists in the last 45 years, can, by examining the annual growth rings of trees, reveal not only the age of the specimen timber but also the fluctuating climatic conditions during the specimen's lifespan.

Developments in laser technology are also now revealing structures underground, once hidden for centuries.

The advent of computers from the 1960s onwards has greatly facilitated the application of all such techniques, and notably encouraged the execution of simulation studies.

Most remarkable of all perhaps is the development of *potassium-argon dating* which, by dating the volcanic deposits in which remains have been found, can also put a date, sometimes of more than a million years old, on the earliest hominid remains yet discovered.

At the other extreme, but not necessarily less important, are finds by metal detector owners, of whom there are 10,000 in England and Wales.

The Frontiers of Archaeology.

Last, but not least, the concept of archaeology itself has its own ambiguities. It can be used, or misused depending on one's point of view, to promote national and political agendas. It incorporates highly controversial approaches such as archaeoastronomy, which argues that the complex mathematical relationship between the heavenly bodies and the layout of a number of ancient monuments is deeply purposeful and the reverse of coincidental. It has also expanded from its original province to cover what is known as industrial archaeology, with such current concerns as steam railway preservation and the restoration of the canal network.

The following selection of discoveries is worldwide in scope, although it takes a particular interest in Britain. It tries to respect the different possible interpretations of great discoveries which have been discussed but it is inevitably subjective. It is organised chronologically, which avoids the invidious comparative ranking of discoveries but at the expense of cutting across cultural periods and geographical areas.

A Chronology of Discovery.

1960

The discovery of Fishbourne Roman Palace just west of Chichester, West Sussex. Covering some ten acres in all, it remains the largest Roman building yet discovered north of the Alps. It is believed to have been constructed for Togidubnus (Cogidubnus), a native client king honoured by the Romans with the aristocratic rank of *legatus augusti*, as a reward for his, and his tribe's, support at the time of the Roman conquest of Britain by Claudius in A.D. 43.

Later excavations between 1995 and 2002 have established the late Iron Age occupation of the site and pointed to the possibility of a Roman military or trading enclave there prior to the Roman invasion. There has been consequential speculation that the main thrust of the A.D. 43 invasion could have been through, or focused on, Fishbourne, rather than at Richborough, Kent, as conventionally believed.

1961

(i) The discovery in the Olduvai Gorge, Tanzania, of the remains of *homo habilis*. At 1·7 million years old, they were the oldest remains of the genus *homo* yet found. *See also* **T52–5**.

A fossil jawbone of *homo habilis*, found near Lake Turkana, Kenya, in 2007, dated at 1·44 million years old, virtually disproves, though, the earlier belief that *homo habilis* was a direct ancestor of *homo sapiens*.

(ii) The excavation of Çatal Hüyük in central Turkey, which proved to be one of the very earliest towns yet identified. Dated at between 6,230 and 5,400 B.C., it covered 50 acres (21 hectares) and comprised hundreds of mud-brick and timber houses, many with bright mural decorations and a remarkable number with clay bull heads on the wall. These cult objects were paralleled by numerous figurines of the mother goddess giving birth. A hunting shrine was also identified, with a painted frieze illustrating a deer hunt.

The neolithic (New Stone Age) town, however, had no streets and access to the houses appears to have been through the roofs. The dead were buried, often with grave goods, below the house floors. There was much evidence of trade with quite distant areas, and the wealth of Çatal Hüyük may have been attributable to its domination of the trade in obsidian (volcanic glass).

(iii) The Swedish warship, *Vasa* (originally *Wasa*), which sank on her maiden voyage in 1628, is raised from 100 feet of water near Beckholmen in Stockholm harbour. She could carry 100 seamen, 20 gunners and 300 soldiers. The sculpture of the stern decoration is outstanding, but the workmanship and degree of preservation of the ship as a whole, which is displayed near where she sank, is remarkable.

Her successful raising stimulated the equally successful attempt to raise the *Mary Rose* in 1982 (*see* **E32**).

1963–65

The uncovering of the remains of the Jewish zealots in the former royal citadel of Masada, built by King Herod on a rock dropping 1,300 feet sheer to the Dead Sea, Israel. The zealots had used Masada as a base for harrying the Romans in the years following the great Jewish rebellion of A.D. 66.

That rebellion had been punished by the sack of Jerusalem, the destruction of the Temple and the expulsion from the country of much of the Jewish population. Masada itself had been besieged by the Romans and according to the contemporary historian, Josephus, in A.D. 73 the 960 defenders, men, women and children, chose to commit suicide en masse rather than surrender to the Romans.

The excavations were widely seen in Israeli nationalist terms, but later scholarship has cast considerable doubt on both the veracity of Josephus and the interpretation put on some of the finds.

1965

The excavation of the mesolithic (Middle Stone Age) settlement of Lepenski Vir on the banks of the River Danube near the Iron Gates Gorge, Serbia. First inhabited in about 8,000 B.C., it established that permanent settlements had developed in Europe prior to the rise of the early civilisations. Many of the houses contained a fish-head sculpture

near the hearth, which may possibly have represented a fish deity.

1967–72

The exposure of the exceptionally well-preserved remains of the great hall of the Roman legionary fortress established in York in about A.D. 72. The exposure resulted from the excavations necessary for the strengthening of the foundations and fabric of York Minster. Rediscovery in 1967 of Pavlopetri, the world's oldest submerged city.

1969

The discovery in an eroding sand dune on the eastern side of the dried-up Lake Mungo in New South Wales, Australia, of the world's oldest known cremation burial. It was of a female and is dated at about 24,000 B.C.

1974

(i) The discovery at Hadar, Ethiopia, of "Lucy", at 3 million years old the earliest hominid yet found. (*See* Olduvai Gorge discovery of 1961, *above*, for explanation of "hominid".) Scientifically *Australopithecus afarensis*, "Lucy" was 3 feet 7 inches (1·1 m) tall, and the survival of 40 % of her skeleton was as remarkable as its age.

(ii) The uncovering of the pits containing some 8,000 life-sized warriors in fired clay, the so-called "terracotta army", guarding the burial mound of China's first emperor, Qin Shihuangdi, near Xi'an, China. Dating from the third century B.C., the warriors have a standardised body but unique features and expressions. They are drawn from all levels of military society, ranging from generals to infantrymen, and appear tall, strong, healthy and ready for battle. They were accompanied by more than 600 horses in clay and more than 100 war chariots. All the warriors are individual, with distinct expressions and uniforms, weapons, armour and even hairstyles according to rank.

1976

Excavations at the Coppergate (the Norse for "street of the smiths", York, uncover Jorvik, the tenth-century Viking town. The houses were a focus for craft production, with evidence of carpentry, and of cloth, bone, leather and metal working.

1977

The uncovering of the "princely tomb" of Hochdorf, near Stuttgart, Germany. Dating from the Celtic Hallstatt period, c. 550–500 B.C., it was just one of a number of such tombs surrounding the contemporaneous mountain fort of the Hohenasperg, but the only one not to have been robbed in antiquity. Such parallels have led to its being compared with the tomb of Tutankhamen.

Excavation of the largely eroded barrow revealed the body of a man resting on a bronze recliner and wearing a conical hat of birchbark. His clothes and body were adorned with gold brooches, cuffs and hammered gold hoops. It was the recliner, however, unique in Celtic Europe, which was probably the most spectacular find. Covered in furs and textiles, its seat was supported by eight female figures in bronze, and the back and sides embossed, again in bronze, with wagon and dance scenes.

On the other side of the burial chamber stood a wooden four-wheeled wagon sheathed in iron, nearly 15 feet (4·5 m) long in all, with the harnessing for two horses and huge ten-spoke wheels to carry its lightweight platform.

1978

(i) The exposure of the "Laetoli footprints", two trails of fossilised hominid footprints about 3·7 million years old, at Laetoli, just south of the Olduvai Gorge in northern Tanzania. The footprints were important because they confirmed that two-legged walking in the modern human manner had evolved before either larger brain capacity or the use of stone tools 2·5 million years ago. The reverse had been expected.

The prints were probably made by two members of the hominid group classified as *Australopithecus*, akin to "Lucy" found at Hadar, Ethiopia, in 1974 (*q.v.*). It is generally believed that our own hominid genus, *homo*, evolved from *Australopithecus*.

(ii) The Mayan hieroglyphs of Mexico are finally fully deciphered after some decades of research.

1982

The raising from 45 feet of water off Portsmouth, Hampshire, of the *Mary Rose*, Henry VIII's flagship, which capsized in July 1545 when preparing to use its guns in earnest, against the French, for the first time. It is said that Henry himself saw the disaster, in which almost 700 crewmen died, from the adjacent Southsea Castle.*See* **E18**.

1988

The finding on the site of ancient Nimrud in Iraq of the treasures of the Assyrian queens, dating from the eighth century B.C. The richest, third, tomb contained gold and silver objects weighing some 50 lb (23 kg) including a gold crown, a golden ewer, gold plate and jewellery. The second tomb contained another gold crown and a profusion of gold anklets, armlets, earrings, finger rings *etc.*

1991

(i) The finding by a diver of the Casquer cave near Marseille, France. Four-fifths of the cave had been long flooded and its cave art destroyed but above the water level there survived 187 paintings of animals together with representations of a dead man and of the male and female sexual organs. They dated from the two periods of occupation, 27,000 and 19,000 years ago.

(ii) The discovery of the 5,000-year-old "Iceman". *See* **Ice Man, L56**.

(iii) The discovery at Abydos in Middle Egypt of the oldest built boats yet known, dating from the period 2950–2650 B.C. The fourteen vessels, built as funerary boats, were encased in brick structures and were to serve the pharaoh in the afterlife.

1992

The finding of the Hoxne Hoard in a Suffolk field. It was the largest late Roman hoard yet found in Britain, and it comprised 15,234 gold and silver coins together with pieces of jewellery.

1993

The recovery of the earliest surviving English panel paintings. Originating in the redecoration of the Royal State Bedchamber in the Palace of Westminster for Henry III after 1263, they were removed from the Palace in 1816 and thus escaped destruction in the great fire of 1834, which destroyed the whole palace except for Westminster Hall.

1993–96

The discovery in Eartham gravel pit near Boxgrove, east of Chichester, West Sussex, of the earliest human remains yet found in Britain. Most exceptionally, the remains were associated with such evidence for human behaviour and ecology as butchery, hunting and the manufacture of flint tools. Although only a left tibia and two teeth have been found, "Boxgrove Man" appears to have been an archaic human, similar, or identical, to "Heidelberg Man", discovered in Germany in 1907 and characterised by large brow ridges, sloping forehead and a heavy chinless jaw, living between 524,000 and 478,000 years ago.

"Heidelberg Man" is likely to have been the ancestor of both modern man, *homo sapiens*, and "Neanderthal Man", *homo neanderthalis*, who became extinct about 28,000 years ago. *See also* **T55**(1).

1994

The finding of the Chauvet cave in France, with its 420 paintings and engravings of animals on the rock walls, most dating from 32,000–30,000 years ago and the remainder from 27,000–26,000 years ago. It is one of the most densely decorated caves in Europe.

1996

(i) The discovery of Caral, the oldest site of civilisation in Peru and in the Americas as a whole. Situated in the Supe valley, in the coastal lands north of Lima, it is believed to date from about 2,600 B.C. Its pyramids and plazas have parallels in the Ancient Egypt and Ancient Mesopotamia (modern Iraq) of the time, but no evidence of cross-fertilisation has ever been found.

(ii) The discovery by underwater archaeologists of the ruins of the classical cities of Canopus and Haraclelon in Aboukir Bay, off Alexandria, Egypt. The ruins dated from the sixth century B.C. through to the Byzantine period.

(iii) The discovery of the "Valley of the Golden Mummies" at Bahariya Oasis, 375 km south-west of Cairo, Egypt. A significant number of the 10,000 mummies found were sheathed in gold.

1999

(i) The finding of the Cascajal block in Mexico, bearing the oldest writing yet found in the New World. It is from the Olmec period and is believed to date from about 900 B.C., but the script is yet to be deciphered.

(ii) The unearthing of the Spillings Silver Hoard, the largest Viking treasure yet found, on the Swedish Baltic island of Gotland. The Hoard comprised three deposits, weighing some 87 kg in all, of a total of 14,300 silver coins, almost all of Arabic origin and dating from the Viking period. Gotland was a great centre of Viking trade.

2002

The discovery of the "Amesbury Archer" near Stonehenge, Wiltshire, dating from about 2,500 B.C. The inclusion with the body of the earliest known gold ornaments in Britain, together with copper knives, boar's tusks, and flint tools *etc.*, make it the richest early Bronze Age burial in Europe.

2006

The publication of the so-called "Gospel of Judas". It formed part of the *Codex Tchacos*, found in the 1970s in a cave used for a burial in Middle Egypt, and was written in Coptic, the late form of the Ancient Egyptian language, probably in the third century A.D. It is, though, clearly translated from a Greek text of perhaps a century earlier. The Gospel is written from a standpoint sympathetic to Judas Iscariot, but its value is controversial.

2009

(i) The uncovering of what is believed to be the rotating dining room (*coenatio rotunda*) of the Emperor Nero's first-century Golden House palace (*domus aurea*) on the Palatine Hill in Rome.

(ii) The discovery with a metal detector of the seventh-century Anglo-Saxon Staffordshire Hoard.

2012

The Grouville Hoard, the world's largest hoard of Celtic coins, found in Jersey in the Channel Islands.

2013

Archaeologists claim to have found Ciudad Blanca ("The White City") in an unexplored region of Honduras. Artefacts such as stone were-jaguars found in the "City of the Monkey God." Confirmation that bones found in Leicester in 2012 were those of Richard III.

2014–17

(i) Fears for more archaeological desecration after militants raze parts of Nimrud, Hatra and Palmyra.

(ii) Sensational discovery of Durrington Walls, a massive 'superhenge' (four times larger than nearby Stonehenge) now buried below the surface. One of the largest stone monuments of ancient Europe.

(iii) Bronze Age treasures discovered at Must Farm near Peterbrough. Dubbed 'Britain's Pompeii'.

(iv) The authentication and publication in 2015 of a missing part of Tablet 5 of the Babylonian Epic of Gilgamesh, unearthed in 2011, adds significantly to the overall sense of the Epic, which is one of the world's oldest surviving works of literature.

(v) Discovery of what is believed to be the oldest known jewellery ever found in Britain (*c.* 11,000 years old) near Scarborough in Yorkshire.

FAMOUS ARCHAEOLOGICAL SITES

This section aims to present a selection of those sites which have contributed most to our understanding of human history. Some, like Peru's Machu Picchu, are visually spectacular; others, like Iraq's Nineveh, are mounds of earth whose discovered treasures are now in museums. Some, like Italy's Pompeii and Herculaneum, are as comprehensively understood as is a modern Italian town.

It has to be recognised that some of the world's greatest potential sites may be under vibrant modern cities, where full excavation is effectively impossible. Alexandria, Damascus, Istanbul and Jerusalem are four such cities, although in the last three cases there is treasure enough above ground. An exception can be made for Athens and Rome which had both dramatically declined in urban importance until quite recent times, thus minimising new construction. Rome is unique in that Mussolini in the 1920s and 1930s cleared many later buildings so as to reveal more fully the plan and the ruins of Ancient Rome and thus create the "city-museum" we know today.

Angkor Wat (north-western Cambodia).

The site of what was the capital of the Khmer empire between the ninth and fifteenth centuries. Its most famous monuments are Angkor Wat and Angkor Thom, temple complexes built during the twelfth and at the beginning of the thirteenth centuries respectively. Angkor Wat is the largest religious monument in the world. One of the most sophisticated of south-east Asia, the Khmer empire covered the length of the Indochinese peninsula and extended westwards from Vietnam to the Bay of Bengal.

Angkor was both an administrative and a religious capital, and was planned as a symbolic universe based on the traditional cosmology of Hindu India. Angkor Wat itself was built as a funerary temple in which the king's remains were symbolically identified with the Hindu god, Vishnu.

The city of Angkor was abandoned after being sacked by Thai forces in 1431, but the temple of Angkor Wat passed into the care of Buddhist monks and became a major site of pilgrimage.

In 2013 a vast ruined city surrounding Angkor Wat was uncovered, revealing that Angkor was the most extensive city of the medieval world until climate change destroyed its water supply. Laser technology continues to reveal vast medieval cities buried beneath the tropical forest floor.

Athens, the Acropolis (Greece).

The hill which formed the core of classical Athens and on which some of its most famous buildings, notably the Parthenon (the Maiden), still stand. Constructed in the fifth century B.C. to replace an earlier structure destroyed by the Persians, the Parthenon was erected as a temple to Athena, the patron goddess of the city, and is viewed by many as still the greatest of Europe's buildings, only rivalled world-wide by India's Taj Mahal. Adjacent to the Parthenon are the Erechtheum, once the temple of Athena and Poseidon, and deservedly famous for its delightful Porch of the Maidens, and the small Temple of Victory. At the foot of the Acropolis are the theatre and a little further away the *agora* or market place.

For all its cultural pre-eminence, the political dominance of classical Athens was comparatively short-lived. By 338 B.C., the leadership of Greece had passed to Macedonia and within two years to its young king, Alexander the Great. The fate of the Acropolis was to be chequered. The Parthenon had its central portion blown out in 1687 when a Venetian shell hit the Ottoman Turkish powder magazine inside. The Turks in the same period demolished the Temple of Victory to create a battery, only for it to be rebuilt by newly independent Greece after 1835. Not least, much of the Parthenon frieze was purchased from the Turkish imperial authorities by Lord Elgin and is preserved as the Elgin Marbles (*see* **L36**) in the British Museum. Greece presses for their return.

Babylon (Atlal Babil) (near Al-Hillah, central Iraq).

At the height of its splendour in the seventh century B.C., Babylon was the largest city in the world, covering 2,500 acres, and we have a detailed description of it by the Greek historian, Herodotus, to supplement the evidence of archaeology and the surviving extensive ruins. The ziggurat associated with the great Temple of Marduk was the original Tower of Babel, and a Processional Way led from it to the Ishtar Gate. The walls of the Way were decorated with enamelled lions, which may still be seen though without the enamelling, but the Gate is now in Berlin's Pergamon Museum. The site of the famous Hanging Gardens, one of the Seven Wonders of the World, was probably within the royal palace. "The Lion of Babylon", a statue more than life-size and of probable Hittite origin, has stood near the Ishtar Gate since antiquity.

Later in its foundation than Nineveh (*q.v.*) or Ur (*q.v.*), Babylon really entered history with the reign of Hammurabi (1792–1750 B.C.) who made it the capital of a kingdom covering much of modern Iraq. Hammurabi is particularly remembered for his eponymous code, from which the famous biblical "an eye for an eye and a tooth for a tooth" was almost certainly derived. The stela found in Babylon on which the code is inscribed is now in the Louvre in Paris.

Babylon remained a capital until the beginning of the first millennium, but some centuries of intermittent disorder preceded its flowering and rebuilding under Nebuchadnezzar II in the seventh century B.C. Its splendour survived capture by the Persians in 539 B.C. and then by Alexander the Great in 331 B.C., who had intended to make Babylon the capital of his empire. In fact he died in Nebuchadnezzar's palace in 323 B.C., after which the city went into rapid decline.

Carthage (near Tunis) (Tunisia).

Certainly not the most imposing of sites, from the point of view of its physical remains, but one of the most evocative and charming, situated above the Mediterranean. Such structures as remain are the ruins of the Roman city, but the underlying Punic city of Hannibal, founded by the Phoenicians in 814 B.C., can still be traced and the rich finds from both the Punic and Roman cities are displayed in the Bardo Museum of Tunis.

The particularly evocative atmosphere of Carthage springs to no small degree from our extremely detailed knowledge of the destruction of the Punic city by the Romans in 146 B.C. The insistence of the elderly Cato at every meeting of the Roman Senate that *Delenda est Carthago* (Carthage must be destroyed) became proverbial, and the most learned man of the time, Polybius, who had been the tutor of the Roman general Scipio and had remained his friend, and who also knew the Carthaginian leader, Hasdrubal, left an intimate eye-witness account of its horrifying end.

The city was refounded by the Romans in 122 B.C. and soon came to rival Alexandria and Antioch in its prosperity, before entering into a long period of decline and ultimate replacement by the Arab foundation of Tunis.

Harappa. (*see* Mohenjo-Daro).

Knossos (near Iráklion, Crete) (Greece).

The capital of Crete's Minoan civilisation from *c.* 2000 to *c.* 1450 B.C., by which time the civilisation had expanded into mainland Greece and transmuted into the specifically Greek culture known as Mycenean (*see* **E34**).

The site of Knossos is most famous for the remains of the second palace, the palace of Minos, built in about 1700 B.C., of which the throne room with the gypsum chair of the kings of Knossos survives, as do the spirited and naturalistic fresco paintings, albeit substantially restored. Although the influence of Egypt was strong, the Cretan palaces were largely unplanned and it was the resulting maze-like effect which no doubt gave rise to the legend of Theseus and the Labyrinth. Nevertheless, the palace at Knossos has been described as the first real architecture in the northern Mediterranean. It was surrounded by a city housing perhaps as many as 80,000 people.

The city, together with a number of other Minoan settlements, was destroyed by fire in *c.* 1450 B.C., and many associate that destruction with the devastating volcanic eruption of Santorini (Thera) in the Aegean at that time. More fancifully, others have linked the end of Knossos with the legend of Atlantis.

Leptis Magna (Libya).

The site of first a Phoenician and then a Roman city on the Mediterranean coast with some of the world's finest surviving Roman remains, both from the point of view of their quality and of their state of preservation. The finest date from the time of the emperor Septimus Severus, who was born there and ruled A.D. 193–211, and of his son Caracalla. Amongst them are the rebuilt harbour, a 12-mile aqueduct, and the new quarter by the Wadi Labdah focused on a quarter-mile monumental street leading to a circular piazza with the forum and a hundred-foot high basilica.

The city, which was already in serious decline, was essentially abandoned after the Arab conquest of A.D. 642.

Luxor (Al-Uqsur) (Karnak, Upper Egypt).

Thebes, the capital in the Imperial period, c. 1580–1150 B.C., lay on both sides of the Nile, but is more familiar now as the site of the great temple complexes of Luxor and Karnak on the eastern bank of the river. The Egyptian Empire in its 400-year existence stretched from the River Euphrates to the Fourth Cataract of the Nile in what is now the Sudan.

The Temple of Amon at Karnak stretches nearly a quarter of a mile back from its river frontage, and although its most imposing part dates from the Imperial era and the reigns of Queen Hatshepsut, the first great woman in history to be known to us, and Thutmose III, perhaps the first great general, its construction occupied nearly 2,000 years. The Great Hall alone at 338 feet wide and 170 feet deep is comparable in area with the cathedral of Notre Dame in Paris and enough survives to convey the force of the original. The temples of Luxor are almost as impressive. The temples were linked, and remain linked, by long avenues of sphinxes, making Thebes the world's first "monumental city".

The temples of Egypt may not have the aesthetic perfection of their Greek successors but the engineering skill behind their construction, the sheer massiveness which has aided their survival, and the scale and quality of the accompanying sculpture, allied with the beauty of the situation beside the Nile, make them perhaps the most awe-inspiring of the world's great sites. The Temple of Karnak is the second most popular tourist attraction in Egypt after the Great Pyramid at Giza.

Machu Picchu (Peru).

Surely the most scenically spectacular of all archaeological sites, the city of Machu Picchu was designed as a residence for the governor and his bureaucracy in a conquered area of the Inca Empire. Comprising two to three hundred buildings, it sits on a hill in the heart of the Peruvian Andes dominating the Valley of Urubamba and was accessible only on the south side. The most noteworthy structures, which date back to the fifteenth and sixteenth centuries, include the round temple and the "Three Windows" which are believed to represent the three caves from which according to legend, the Inca race sprang. Equally striking are the elaborate agricultural terraces below the city.

The city was never found by the Spanish conquerors, perhaps because it was hidden from the valley on three sides, and was, therefore, preserved, but it appears to have been abandoned after the final defeat of the Inca Empire in 1572.

Mexico City, Templo Mayor (Mexico).

The area surrounding the great Templo Mayor pyramid, which lay at the heart of the ancient Aztec capital of Tenochtitlán and which became the centre of the subsequent Spanish imperial capital of Mexico City. The sacred precinct, or Teocalli, measured some 300 m² with the Templo Mayor in the centre of the east side, and is now an open air museum. The pyramid was originally surmounted by two tower temples, which ensemble the conqueror, Cortés, described as being higher than the Cathedral of Seville.

The Teocalli has been the site of major finds since the end of the eighteenth century and continues to be so. Amongst the best-known are a huge statue of a jaguar, one of the heads from the great decorative serpent sculptures of the staircase to the Temple of Huitzilopochtli, and a huge stone sculpture of Coyolxauhqui, goddess of the moon.

Mohenjo-Daro (Sind province, southern Pakistan).

The site of what was the largest city of the Indus Valley Civilisation, the earliest known urban civilisation of the Indian sub-continent and the oldest known civilisation after those of Mesopotamia and Egypt, extant between c. 2700 and 1700 B.C. The city, comparable to its partner at Harappa, was three miles round and was planned in regular settlement blocks, of which one was a citadel with ritual purposes. Many of the houses had an upper storey or accessible roof and bathrooms with drains and sanitation. Merchants from both Mohenjo-Daro and Harappa traded with Ur (see E35), probably exporting cotton, but the importance of Mohenjo-Daro was not recognised by archaeologists until 1922. Now the site is suffering serious decay.

Mycenae (south-west of Corinth, Greece).

The site of the first mainland Greek city, which became the dominant power in the Aegean following the destruction of Knossos (q.v.) in c. 1450 B.C. Although the site dates back to the Early Bronze Age, the surviving impressive remains are of the Late Bronze Age (1400–1100 B.C.).

The most significant include: the Lion Gate at the entrance to the citadel; the palace itself; "the house of the columns", which was originally three storeys high; and the so-called Treasury of Atreus, in fact a tomb chamber 45 foot high and 120 foot long. The rich finds at Mycenae were primarily the achievement of the German archaeologist, Heinrich Schliemann, who also excavated Troy (q.v.). The most famous and most spectacular of the many pieces of jewellery and metalwork found is the gold funeral mask wrongly attributed by Schliemann to Agamemnon but actually dating back to the early fifteenth century B.C., some 200–300 years before the Trojan War. The mask is now in the National Museum in Athens.

According to Homer's Iliad, Agamemnon was the king of Mycenae who led the Greeks to victory in that War. Mycenae was destroyed, perhaps by Dorian Greeks, in c. 1000 B.C., but survived as a small city-state for about another 1,000 years.

Nineveh (opposite Mosul, northern Iraq).

Visually unimpressive, the mound of Nineveh nevertheless marks the remains of the oldest and most populous city of Ancient Assyria. Occupation of the site probably dates back to the seventh millennium B.C., but the earliest major find is a life-size bronze head deemed to be the finest metal sculpture ever found in Iraq, probably representing King Sargon of Akkad (c. 2334–c. 2279 B.C.) or possibly King Naram-Sin (c. 2254–c. 2218 B.C.). It was placed in the Iraqi Museum in Baghdad.

The architectural splendour of Nineveh, however, was attributable to the later Assyrian kings, notably Sennacherib in c. 700 B.C. His city covered 1,800 acres and entry was through 15 great gates, with water being supplied by 18 canals. The city wall was some 7½ miles long. The most important buildings to have been excavated are the palaces of Sennacherib and his grandson, Assurbanipal. The former contained at least 80 rooms and the human-headed bulls flanking many of the principal doorways were a particular feature. That of Assurbanipal contained his celebrated library with a priceless collection of some 20,000 cuneiform-inscribed tablets on religious and scientific as well as literary topics. The most important literary work is the text of the Epic of Gilgamesh, known otherwise only in fragments. Both palaces were adorned with the intensely vigorous stone reliefs of warfare and hunting, which like the tablets from the library are amongst the treasures of the British Museum.

The city's splendour was, however, shortlived. In 612 B.C. it was sacked by the Babylonians, Scythians and Medes, although it survived as an insignificant township until as late as the sixteenth century A.D.

Persepolis (Takht-i Jamshid) (near Shiraz, Iran).

The royal capital of Achaemenid Iran founded by Darius I the Great in the sixth-fifth centuries B.C.

The site is dominated by a large terrace, up to 41 feet above the ground and some 1,600 feet long and 1,000 feet wide, approached on its western side by a sumptuous double stairway in two flights of 111 stone steps, shallow enough to be ridden comfortably by a horseman. The terrace supported numerous very large stone buildings constructed without mortar, of which the thirteen great columns, 65 feet high, which still stand in the audience hall, the Hall of a Hundred Columns (*apadana*), of Darius the Great are the most impressive remains.

The most memorable feature of Persepolis, however, is the wonderfully preserved reliefs which adorn the stairway in particular as an integral part of the architectural design. The processions of figures bearing tribute can be criticised as being repetitive but they impress by their sheer number and have moved away from the two-dimensional sculpture familiar from Nineveh (*q.v.*) towards a much more three-dimensional style, inspired by familiarity with Greek art.

The ruins of the city are complemented by the elaborately carved royal tombs cut high into the rock face at Naqsh-i-Rustam eight miles away, which include that of Darius the Great himself.

Persepolis, containing what have been described as the most magnificent buildings the East had ever produced, was destroyed by Alexander the Great in 330 B.C. in what some sources say was a drunken revel. He certainly regretted the destruction later. The Persians arguably had their revenge when Alexander turned his vast new empire into an oriental despotism, with enduring implications for the Roman, Byzantine and Russian Empires which were to follow, rather than a democracy along Classical Greek lines.

Pompeii and Herculaneum (near Naples, Italy).

The twin towns of Pompeii and Herculaneum (Ercolaneo) comprise perhaps the most famous archaeological site in the world, because the suddenness of the eruption of Vesuvius in A.D. 79 not only preserved such delicate artefacts as wall paintings to an unparalleled degree, but also preserved a living community, suddenly struck down. Walking into Pompeii has parallels with reality TV or the "fly on the wall" documentary. It is what makes the site unique.

Pompeii was a prosperous trading town but not of particular strategic significance. Its buildings are too numerous to list, but an exception must be made for the Villa of the Mysteries outside the town walls, which contains perhaps the most famous painting of antiquity – a series of almost perfectly preserved frescoes interpreted as representing the rites of initiation into the Dionysiac mysteries.

Research shows the ancient Pompeiians enjoyed a healthy diet of vegetables, fish and cereals.

Herculaneum was a market town rather than a trading town like Pompeii, and its quietness made it a favourite retreat of the Roman aristocracy, whose domestic wealth contrasted strongly with the poor properties of the locals. It was covered by a lava flow some 60 feet deep, much deeper than at Pompeii, and much remains unexcavated under the town of today which dates from medieval times.

Much has been conserved *in situ* in both towns, but much also has been transferred to the National Archaeological Museum of Naples which should be visited in conjunction with the twin sites.

Rome, the Forum (Italy).

The whole city of Rome can be described as one of the world's greatest archaeological sites, but the forum, or more correctly the series of *fora* (Latin) or *fori* (Italian)), can be given pride of place, partly because they were the focus of Ancient Rome and partly because of the opening in 1932 of the one kilometre long Via dei Fori Imperiali, which gives remarkable access to the various imperial fora as well as to the cleared markets of Trajan.

The markets of Trajan were originally a graceful part of the forum built by that emperor, which was more than 620 feet wide and was specifically designed to provide Rome with a structural "backbone" and give axial symmetry to the previously somewhat haphazard succession of the old forum

and then the "new" fora of Caesar Augustus, Nerva and Vespasian.

It is nevertheless the "old" forum which has the most familiar associations. The *rostra* or platform at the northern end was where Cicero and other orators addressed the people. The golden milestone marked the point of departure of all the great roads of the Empire. Julius Caesar was famously assassinated in the adjacent theatre during a meeting of the Senate in 44 B.C.

It is, though, the extant portico of the temple of Saturn, the circular temple of Vesta where the Vestal Virgins kept the sacred flame of Rome continually burning, and the columns of the temple of Castor and Pollux, together with the arches of Titus and Septimius Severus at the edges, which speak to the visitor of the splendour of the imperial fora.

Stonehenge, Avebury and Silbury Hill (Wiltshire, England).

Strictly speaking three distinct sites, they are so related that they may be considered together.

Stonehenge must be the most famous prehistoric monument of western Europe with its concentric circles of great stones, the most impressive being the sarsen circle of thirty upright stones all once supporting a corresponding number of lintels. The monument in its present form dates back to the Wessex Culture of the sixteenth and fifteenth centuries B.C., but the still visible early bank, ditch and post holes, known as Aubrey holes, could date back even before 3000 B.C. It is even possible that the great stones now in the centre of the site originally stood around the centre and were moved to their present position many centuries later.

Despite massive research, the original purpose of Stonehenge remains a mystery. However, it may have been a graveyard for chiefs or a centre of healing (there are warm springs nearby) or have some kind of astronomical purpose. Its "bluestones" appear to have been transported from the Preseli Mountains of Wales, indicating its great significance to its builders. These 'bluestones' also have strong acoustic properties. It does, though, certainly long predate the Celtic druids now associated with the site. Another prehistoric site nearby was discovered in 2010 and it is now clear the area around Stonehenge is teeming with previously unseen archaeology, as witnessed by the discovery of Durrington Walls (*see* **E32(2)**).

The 125 to 130-foot high earthen mound covering 5½ acres close to nearby Avebury, known as Silbury Hill, is as impressive in its way and equally mysterious. (*see* **E20(1)**) Dating back to *c*. 2500 B.C. it may have been a great burial mound but no burial has ever been found and early inexpert investigations may have destroyed crucial evidence.

The site of Avebury itself, with its smaller, undressed sarsen stones, does not have the visual impact of Stonehenge but its size of 28 acres and the 100 pairs of standing stones forming the 1¼ mile Avenue from it to Overton Hill are remarkable. The Avenue dates from between 1900 and 1600 B.C.

Troy (north-western Anatolia, Turkey).

Commanding the southern entrance to the Dardanelles and the land route to Europe along the Anatolian coast, the site was of the highest strategic significance in ancient times. As the scene of the Trojan War in Homer's "Iliad" it was long believed by many to be fictional, but excavations by the German archaeologist, Heinrich Schliemann, between 1870 and 1890 firmly established that Homeric Troy lay below the 100-foot high mound known to the Turks as Hisarlik.

Nine successive layers of occupation were identified, with Troy I-V dating from 3000–1900 B.C.; Troy VI and VII date from 1900–1100 B.C.; Troy VIIa may have been at its peak *c*. 1260–1240 B.C., and its destruction by fire strongly suggests that it was the Troy captured by the Greeks of Homer's epic. Troy VIII and IX are the successive Greek and Roman cities prior to Troy's decline after the founding of Constantinople (Istanbul) in A.D. 324.

The find of gold jewellery in Troy II, identified as "Priam's treasure" by Schliemann, thus predates the Trojan War by some centuries. (*See* Mycenae, **E34**).

Ur (Tell el Muqayyar) (near An-Nasiriyah, Iraq).

Claimed by the biblical book of Genesis as the

home of Abraham, the city was founded in the fourth millennium B.C. and knew some three periods of major importance, of which Abraham's in the eighteenth century B.C. would have been only the last. It is also possible that the biblical legend of the Flood had its origins in a major inundation of the Tigris-Euphrates delta below Ur in the city's first period of settlement.

It was in the twenty-ninth to the twenty-fourth centuries B.C., however, that the Sumerian kings of Ur established their dominance over what is now southern Iraq and the city achieved the previously quite unsuspected level of civilisation and artistic brilliance which caused international astonishment when the royal tombs were excavated in the late 1920s and early 1930s. Amongst the spectacular grave goods uncovered was the offering-stand in the form of a goat, known as "the Ram caught in the thicket", which is now in the British Museum.

It was the second period of major importance, between the twenty-second and twenty-first centuries B.C., which saw the construction of the celebrated "ziggurat", a three-storeyed stepped pyramid of mud brick which had a small shrine at the summit dedicated to the moon god. It remains an impressive sight across the featureless desert and its construction is remarkable in that there is not a single straight line in the structure. The impression of strength is derived from total reliance on barely perceptible convex curves – a technique to be used much later by the architects of the Parthenon in Athens (*q.v.*).

In the third period, between the twenty-first and ninth centuries B.C., Ur had lost its status as a capital but prospered as a centre of sea-borne foreign trade. At the very end of the period Nabonidus, the last king of Babylon (*q.v.*) (556–539 B.C.), increased the height of the "ziggurat" to seven storeys.

Ur was subsequently abandoned, perhaps because of the change of course of the Euphrates which reduced the fertile, irrigated area to desert.

Valley of the Kings (Biban el-Moluk) (near Luxor, middle Egypt).

The Valley of the Kings, a donkey ride from Luxor, is the desert valley in which the tomb of Tutankhamen was famously found in 1922. There are, however, more than forty galleries hewn into the rock, and the uniqueness of Tutankhamen's tomb was that it was the only one not to have been robbed in antiquity. The bodies of a number of the other pharaohs had been repeatedly moved after the robbery of their tombs before being placed in a secret chamber discovered in 1881.

The direct interest of the site for the modern visitor, however, is the superb wall paintings which adorn many of the tombs and which are perfectly preserved as a result of the dry climate and the absence of sunlight. Adorning the tombs of nobles and high functionaries and not just pharaohs, the paintings show a new naturalism of the Eighteenth Dynasty (1375–1202 B.C.) in the portrayal of feasts, music and dancing, hunting and rural life. Even in the funeral scenes there is a previously unknown element of personal grief. Corridors and chambers beneath the surface extend for around two miles.

(Great) Zimbabwe (near Nyanda, Zimbabwe).

Although our species, homo sapiens, appears to have originated in Africa, and Egypt was one of the two countries to see the birth of advanced civilisation, the number of true archaeological sites in sub-Saharan Africa is comparatively small.

The best-known is (Great) Zimbabwe, a complex of stone buildings and walls dating in parts from the eighth century A.D. and covering more than 60 acres. There are smaller parallels to the complex elsewhere in the country and in Mozambique. It was the centre of the empire of the Karanga people, who traded on the seaboard of the Indian Ocean, between the eleventh and fifteenth centuries A.D., and it remained in use until at least the seventeenth century. The stability of the stones without any use of mortar is particularly noteworthy.

Among the lesser known sites in sub-Saharan Africa is Ife, Nigeria, capital of the Yoruba people. It dates from the 13th–15th centuries and is celebrated for its sculptures. The sculpted heads, thought to be of ancestors or chiefs, were mounted on wooden effigies and used in funerary rituals in the sacred groves.

GENERAL COMPENDIUM

A collection of useful tables and data on a variety of unrelated subjects, such as the British monarchy, Prime Ministers from 1721 to 2016, rulers of the Roman world, United States Presidents, assorted recent words, winners of the Nobel Prizes, major literary awards, Roman numerals, the Chinese calendar, foreign phrases, national currencies, the letters of the Greek alphabet, some common legal terms, 2017/18 tax rates, selected famous ships and a glossary of popular antiques.

TABLE OF CONTENTS

GENERAL COMPENDIUM

ENGLISH MONARCHS
(A.D. 827–1603)

Monarch	Accession	Died	Age	Reigned

I.—BEFORE THE CONQUEST.
SAXONS AND DANES

Monarch	Accession	Died	Age	Reigned
Egbert	827	839	—	12
Ethelwulf	839	858	—	19
Ethelbald	858	860	—	2
Ethelbert	858	865	—	7
Ethelred	865	871	—	6
Alfred the Great	871	899	50	28
Edward the Elder	899	924	54	25
Athelstan	924	939	45	15
Edmund	939	946	25	7
Eadred	946	955	32	9
Eadwig	955	959	18	3
Edgar	959	975	32	17
Edward the Martyr	975	978	17	3
Ethelred II ("the Unready")	978	1016	48	37
Edmund Ironside	1016	1016	27	Apr.–Nov.
Canute the Dane	1017	1035	40	18
Harold I	1035	1040	—	5
Hardicanute	1040	1042	24	2
Edward the Confessor	1042	1066	62	24
Harold II	1066	1066	44	Jan.–Oct.

II.—FROM THE CONQUEST TO THE PRESENT DAY.
NORMANS

Monarch	Accession	Died	Age	Reigned
William I	1066	1087	60	21
William II	1087	1100	43	13
Henry I	1100	1135	67	35
Stephen, Count of Blois	1135	1154	50	19

PLANTAGENETS

Monarch		Accession	Died	Age	Reigned
Henry II		1154	1189	56	35
Richard I		1189	1199	42	10
John		1199	1216	50	17
Henry III		1216	1272	65	56
Edward I		1272	1307	68	35
Edward II		1307	dep. 1327	43	20
Edward III		1327	1377	65	50
Richard II		1377	dep. 1399	34	22
Henry IV	Lancaster	1399	1413	47	13
Henry V		1413	1422	34	9
Henry VI		1422	dep. 1461	49	39
Edward IV	York	1461	1483	41	22
Edward V		1483	1483	13	Apr.–June
Richard III		1483	1485	32	2

TUDORS

Monarch	Accession	Died	Age	Reigned
Henry VII	1485	1509	53	24
Henry VIII	1509	1547	56	38
Edward VI	1547	1553	16	6
Jane	1553	1554	17	9 days
Mary I	1553	1558	43	5
Elizabeth I	1558	1603	69	44

THE BRITISH MONARCHY
(1603 to the present day)

Monarch	Accession	Died	Age	Reigned (years)
STUARTS				
James I (VI of Scotland)	1603	1625	59	22
Charles I	1625	beh. 1649	48	24
COMMONWEALTH DECLARED, MAY 19, 1649				
Oliver Cromwell, Lord Protector . . .	1653–8	—	—	—
Richard Cromwell, Lord Protector . . .	1658–9	—	—	—
STUARTS (RESTORATION)				
Charles II	1660	1685	55	25
James II (VII of Scotland)	1685	dep. 1688	68	3
Interregnum Dec. 11, 1688 to Feb. 13, 1689				
William III and Mary II	1689	1702	51	13
		1694	33	6
Anne	1702	1714	49	12
HOUSE OF HANOVER				
George I	1714	1727	67	13
George II	1727	1760	77	33
George III	1760	1820	81	59
George IV	1820	1830	67	10
William IV	1830	1837	71	7
Victoria	1837	1901	81	63
HOUSE OF SAXE-COBURG				
Edward VII	1901	1910	68	9
HOUSE OF WINDSOR				
George V	1910	1936	70	25
Edward VIII	1936	Abd. 1936	77	325 days
George VI	1936	1952	56	15
Elizabeth II	1952			

SCOTTISH MONARCHS
(1034–1603)

Monarch		Accession	Died
Duncan I	Son of Malcolm II	1034	1040
Macbeth	Slew Duncan in 1040	1040	1057
Malcolm III (Canmore)	Son of Duncan I	1058	1093
Donald Ban	Brother of Malcolm Canmore	1093	—
Duncan II	Son of Malcom Canmore, by first marriage	1094	1094
Donald Ban	Restored	1094	1097
Edgar	Son of Malcolm Canmore, by second marriage	1097	1107
Alexander I	Son of Malcolm Canmore	1107	1124
David I	Son of Malcolm Canmore	1124	1153
Malcolm IV (the Maiden)	Son of Henry, eldest son of David I	1153	1165
William I (the Lion)	Brother of Malcolm the Maiden	1165	1214
Alexander II	Son of William the Lion	1214	1249
Alexander III	Son of Alexander II, by second marriage	1249	1286
Margaret, Maid of Norway	Daughter of Eric II of Norway, granddaughter of Alexander III	1286	1290
John Baliol	Grandson of eldest daughter of David, Earl of Huntingdon, brother of William the Lion	1292	1296
Robert I (Bruce)	Great-grandson of 2nd daughter of David, Earl of Huntingdon, brother of William the Lion	1306	1329
David II	Son of Robert I, by second marriage	1329	1371
Robert II (Stewart)	Son of Marjorie, daughter of Robert I by first marriage, and Walter the Steward	1371	1390
Robert III	(John, Earl of Carrick) son of Robert II	1390	1406
James I	Son of Robert III	1406	1437
James II	Son of James I	1437	1460
James III	Eldest son of James II	1460	1488
James IV	Eldest son of James III	1488	1513
James V	Son of James IV	1513	1542
Mary	Daughter of James V, by second marriage	1542	1587
James VI (ascended the Throne of England 1603)	Son of Mary, by second marriage	1567	1625

BRITISH PRIME MINISTERS

George II, 1727–60

Sir Robert Walpole	Whig	1721–42
Earl of Wilmington	Whig	1742–3
Henry Pelham	Whig	1743–54
Duke of Newcastle	Whig	1754–6
Duke of Devonshire	Whig	1756–7
Duke of Newcastle	Whig	1757–60

George III, 1760–1820

Duke of Newcastle	Whig	1760–2
Earl of Bute	Tory	1762–3
George Grenville	Whig	1763–5
Marquis of Rocking-ham	Whig	1766
Earl of Chatham	Tory	1766–8
Duke of Grafton	Whig	1766–9
Lord North	Tory	1770–82
Marquis of Rocking-ham	Whig	1782
Earl of Shelburne	Whig	1782–3
Duke of Portland	Coalition	1783
William Pitt	Tory	1783–1801
Viscount Sidmouth	Tory	1801–4
William Pitt	Tory	1804–6
Lord Grenville	Whig	1806–7
Duke of Portland	Tory	1807–9
Spencer Perceval	Tory	1809–12

George IV, 1820–30

Earl of Liverpool	Tory	1812–27
George Canning	Tory	1827
Viscount Goderich	Tory	1827
Duke of Wellington	Tory	1827–30

William IV, 1830–7

Earl Grey	Whig	1830–4
Viscount Melbourne	Whig	1834
Sir Robert Peel	Tory	1834–5
Viscount Melbourne	Whig	1835–7

Victoria, 1837–1901

Viscount Melbourne	Whig	1837–41
Sir Robert Peel	Tory	1841–6
Lord John Russell	Whig	1846–52
Earl of Derby	Tory	1852
Earl of Aberdeen	Peelite	1852–5
Viscount Palmerston	Liberal	1855–8
Earl of Derby	Tory	1858–9
Viscount Palmerston	Liberal	1859–65
Earl Russell	Liberal	1865–6
Earl of Derby	Conservative	1866–8
B. Disraeli	Conservative	1868
W. E. Gladstone	Liberal	1868–74
B. Disraeli	Conservative	1874–80
W. E. Gladstone	Liberal	1880–5
Marquis of Salisbury	Conservative	1885–6
W. E. Gladstone	Liberal	1886
Marquis of Salisbury	Conservative	1886–92
W. E. Gladstone	Liberal	1892–4
Earl of Rosebery	Liberal	1894–5
Marquis of Salisbury	Conservative	1895–1901

Edward VII, 1901–10

Marquis of Salisbury	Conservative	1901–2
A. J. Balfour	Conservative	1902–5
Sir H. Campbell-Bannerman	Liberal	1905–8
H. H. Asquith	Liberal	1908–10

George V, 1910–36

H. H. Asquith	Liberal	1910–15
H. H. Asquith	Coalition	1915–16
D. Lloyd George	Coalition	1916–22
A. Bonar Law	Conservative	1922–3
S. Baldwin	Conservative	1923–4
J. R. MacDonald	Labour	1924
S. Baldwin	Conservative	1924–9
J. R. MacDonald	Labour	1929–31
J. R. MacDonald	National	1931–5
S. Baldwin	National	1935–6

George VI, 1936–52

S. Baldwin	National	1936–7
N. Chamberlain	National	1937–39
N. Chamberlain	War Cabinet	1939
W. S. Churchill	War Cabinet	1940–45
W. S. Churchill	Caretaker	1945
C. R. Attlee	Labour	1945–51
Sir W. S. Churchill	Conservative	1951–2

Elizabeth II, 1952–

Sir W. S. Churchill	Conservative	1952–5
Sir A. Eden	Conservative	1955–7
H. Macmillan	Conservative	1957–63
Sir A. Douglas-Home	Conservative	1963–4
H. Wilson	Labour	1964–70
E. Heath	Conservative	1970–4
H. Wilson	Labour	1974–6
J. Callaghan	Labour	1976–9
Mrs. M. Thatcher	Conservative	1979–90
J. Major	Conservative	1990–97
A. Blair	Labour	1997–2007
G. Brown	Labour	2007–10
D. Cameron	Con/Lib Dem	2010–15
D. Cameron	Conservative	2015–16
Mrs. T. May*	Conservative	2016–

*Minority administration after June 2017

PRESIDENTS OF THE UNITED STATES

The terms are for four years; only President F. D. Roosevelt has served more than two terms.

1. George Washington	Fed.	1789–97
2. John Adams	Fed.	1797–1801
3. Thomas Jefferson	Rep.	1801–9
4. James Madison	Rep.	1809–17
5. James Monroe	Rep.	1817–25
6. John Quincey Adams	Rep.	1825–9
7. Andrew Jackson	Dem.	1829–37
8. Martin Van Buren	Dem.	1837–41
9. William H. Harrison†	Whig	1841
10. John Tyler	Whig	1841–5
11. James K. Polk	Dem.	1845–9
12. Zachary Taylor†	Whig	1849–50
13. Millard Fillmore	Whig	1850–3
14. Franklin Pierce	Dem.	1853–7
15. James Buchanan	Dem.	1857–61
16. Abraham Lincoln*	Rep.	1861–5
17. Andrew Johnson	Dem.	1865–9
18. Ulysses S. Grant	Rep.	1869–77
19. Rutherford B. Hayes	Rep.	1877–81
20. James A. Garfield*	Rep.	1881
21. Chester A. Arthur	Rep.	1881–5
22. Grover Cleveland	Dem.	1885–9
23. Benjamin Harrison	Rep.	1889–93
24. Grover Cleveland	Dem.	1893–7
25. William McKinley*	Rep.	1897–1901
26. Theodore Roosevelt	Rep.	1901–9
27. William Howard Taft	Rep.	1909–13
28. Woodrow Wilson	Dem.	1913–21
29. Warren G. Harding†	Rep.	1921–3
30. Calvin Coolidge	Rep.	1923–9
31. Herbert C. Hoover	Rep.	1929–33
32. Franklin D. Roosevelt†	Dem.	1933–45
33. Harry S. Truman	Dem.	1945–53
34. Dwight D. Eisenhower	Rep.	1953–61
35. John F. Kennedy*	Dem.	1961–3
36. Lyndon B. Johnson	Dem.	1963–9
37. Richard M. Nixon††	Rep.	1969–74
38. Gerald R. Ford	Rep.	1974–7
39. James Carter	Dem.	1977–81
40. Ronald Reagan	Rep.	1981–9
41. George Bush	Rep.	1989–93
42. William J. Clinton	Dem.	1993–2001
43. George W. Bush	Rep.	2001–09
44. Barack Obama	Dem.	2009–17
45. Donald Trump	Rep.	2017–

*Assassinated; †Died in office. ††Resigned.

FOREIGN PHRASES

Fr., French.   Gr., Greek.   Ger., German.   It., Italian.   L., Latin.   Sp., Spanish

à bas (Fr.), down, down with.
ab extra (L.), from without.
ab incunabilis (L.), from the cradle.
ab initio (L.), from the beginning.
ab intra (L.), from within.
à bon chat, bon rat (Fr.), to be a good cat, a good rat; well attacked and defended; tit for tat; a Rowland for an Oliver.
à bon marche (Fr.), cheap, a good bargain.
à bras ouverts (Fr.), with open arms.
absente reo (L.), the accused being absent.
absit invidia (L.), let there be no ill-will; envy apart.
ab uno disce omnes (L.), from one specimen judge of all the rest; from a single instance infer the whole.
ab urbe conditâ (L.), from the building of the city; *i.e.*, Rome.
a capite ad calcem (L.) from head to heel.
à chaque saint sa chandelle (Fr.), to each saint his candle; honour where honour is due.
à cheval (Fr.), on horseback.
à compte (Fr.) on account; in part payment.
à corps perdu (Fr.), with might and main.
à couvert (Fr.), under cover; protected; sheltered.
ad astra (L.), to the stars.
ad calendas Græcas (L.), at the Greek calends; *i.e.*, never, as the Greeks had no calends in their mode of reckoning.
à demi (Fr.), by halves; half-way.
a Deo et rege (L.), from God and the king.
ad hoc (L.), arranged for this purpose; special.
ad hominem (L.), to the man; to an individual's interests or passions; personal.
adhuc sub judice lis est (L.), the case has not yet been decided.
a die (L.), from that day.
ad infinitum (L.), to infinity.
ad interim (L.), in the meantime.
ad libitum (L.), at pleasure.
ad modum (L.), after the manner of.
ad nauseam (L.), to disgust or satiety.
ad referendum (L.), for further consideration.
ad rem (L.), to the purpose; to the point.
ad valorem (L.), according to the value.
affaire d'amour (Fr.), a love affair.
affaire d'honneur (Fr.), an affair of honour; a duel.
affaire de cœur (Fr.), an affair of the heart.
à fortiori (L.), with stronger reason.
à gauche (Fr.), to the left.
à genoux (Fr.), on the knees.
à haute voix (Fr.), aloud.
à huis clos (Fr.), with closed doors; secretly.
à belle étoile (Fr.), under the stars; in the open air.
à la bonne heure (Fr.), well timed; all right; very well; as you please.
à l'abri (Fr.), under shelter.
à la mode (Fr.), according to the custom or fashion.
à la Tartuffe (Fr.), like Tartuffe, the hero of a celebrated comedy by Molière; hypocritically.
al fresco (It.), in the open air; out-of-doors.
al più (It.), at most.
alter ego (L.), another self.
à merveille (Fr.), to a wonder; marvellously.
amor patriæ (L.), love of country.
amour-propre (Fr.), self-love, vanity.
ancien régime (Fr.), the ancient or former order of things.
anguis in herba (L.), a snake in the grass.
anno Christi (L.), in the year of Christ.
anno Domini (L.), in the year of our Lord.
anno mundi (L.), in the year of the world.
annus mirabilis (L.), year of wonders; wonderful year.
ante bellum (L.), before the war.
ante lucem (L.), before light.
ante meridiem (L.), before noon.
à outrance (Fr.), to the utmost; to extremities; without sparing.
à pied (Fr.), on foot.
à point (Fr.), to a point, just in time, exactly right.

a posse ad esse (L.), from possibility to reality.
ariston metron (Gr.), the middle course is the best; the golden mean.
arrière-pensé (Fr.), hidden thought; mental reservation.
au courant (Fr.), fully acquainted with.
audi alteram partem (L.), hear the other side.
au fait (Fr.), well acquainted with; expert.
au fond (Fr.), at bottom.
auf Wiedersehen! (Ger.), till we meet again.
au pis aller (Fr.), at the worst.
au revoir (Fr.), adieu; till we meet again.
aut vincere aut mori (L.), either to conquer or to die; death or victory.
a verbis ad verbera (L.), from words to blows.
a vinculo matrimonii (L.), from the bond of matrimony.
à volonté (Fr.), at pleasure.
à vostra salute (It.)
à votre santé (Fr.)   } to your health.
a vuestra salud (Sp.)
bas bleu (Fr.), a blue-stocking; a literary woman.
beau monde (Fr.), the world of fashion.
beaux esprits (Fr.), men of wit, gay spirits.
beaux yeux (Fr.), fine eyes; good looks.
ben trovato (It.), well or cleverly invented.
bête noire (Fr.), a black beast; a bugbear.
bon gré mal gré (Fr.), with good or ill grace; willing or unwilling.
bonhomie (Fr.), good-nature; artlessness.
bonne bouche (Fr.), a delicate or tasty morsel.
bon vivant (Fr.), a good liver; a gourmand.
brutum fulmen (L.), a harmless thunderbolt.
canaille (Fr.), rabble.
candida Pax (L.), white-robed Peace.
casus belli (L.), that which causes or justifies war.
causa sine qua non (L.), an indispensable cause or condition.
caveat emptor (L.), let the buyer beware (or look after his own interest).
cela va sans dire (Fr.), that goes without saying; needless to say.
ceteris paribus (L.), other things being equal.
chacun à son goût (Fr.), every one to his taste.
cogito, ergo sum (L.), I think, therefore I exist.
comme il faut (Fr.), as it should be.
compos mentis (L.), sound of mind; quite sane.
compte rendu (Fr.), an account rendered; a report or statement drawn up.
conditio sine qua non (L.), a necessary condition.
conseil de famille (Fr.), a family consultation.
consensus facit legem (L.), consent makes the law.
consilio et animis (L.), by wisdom and courage.
consilio et prudentia (L.), by wisdom and prudence.
constantia et virtute (L.), by constancy and virtue.
contra bonos mores (L.), against good manners.
contretemps (Fr.), an unlucky accident; a hitch.
cordon bleu (Fr.), blue ribbon; a cook of the highest class.
cordon sanitaire (Fr.), a line of guards to prevent the spreading of contagion or pestilence.
corpus delicti (L.), the body or substance of a crime or offence.
corrigenda (L.), things to be corrected.
coup de grâce (Fr.), a sudden decisive blow in politics; a stroke of policy.
coup de soleil (Fr.), sunstroke.
credat Judæus Apella (L.), let Apella, the superstitious Jew, believe it (I won't); tell that to the marines.
cucullus non facit monachum (L.), the cowl does not make the friar.
cui bono? (L.), For whose advantage is it? to what end?
culpam pœna premit comes (L.), punishment follows hard upon crime.
cum grano salis (L.), with a grain of salt; with some allowance.
cum privilegio (L.), with privilege.
currente calamo (L.), with a fluent pen.
da locum melioribus (L.), give place to your betters.

damnant quod non intelligunt (L.), they condemn what they do not comprehend.

data et accepta (L.), expenditures and receipts.

de bon augure (Fr.), of good augury or omen.

de bonne grâce (Fr.), with good grace; willingly.

de die in diem (L.), from day to day.

de facto (L.), in point of fact; actual or actually.

dei gratia (L.), by God's grace.

de jure (L.), from the law; by right.

de mal en pis (Fr.), from bad to worse.

de novo (L.), anew.

deo volente (L.), God willing; by God's will.

de profundis (L.), out of the depths.

dernier ressort (Fr.), a last resource.

deus ex machina (L.), one who puts matters right at a critical moment; providential intervention.

dies non (L.), a day on which judges do not sit.

distingué (Fr.), distinguished; of genteel or elegant appearance.

dolce far niente (It.), a sweet doing-nothing; sweet idleness.

double entente (Fr.), a double meaning; a play on words.

dramatis personæ (L.), characters of the drama or play.

dum spiro, spero (L.), while I breathe, I hope.

ecce homo! (L.), behold the man!

eheu! fugaces labuntur anni (L.), alas! the fleeting years glide by.

einmal ist keinmal (Ger.), just once doesn't count.

en avant (Fr.), forward.

en badinant (Fr.), in sport; in jest.

en déshabillé (Fr.), in undress.

en famille (Fr.), with one's family; in a domestic state.

enfant terrible (Fr.), a terrible child, or one that makes disconcerting remarks.

enfin (Fr.), in short; at last; finally.

en passant (Fr.), in passing; by the way.

en plein jour (Fr.), in broad day.

en rapport (Fr.), in harmony; in agreement; in relation.

en règle (Fr.), according to rules; in order.

entente cordiale (Fr.), cordial understanding, especially between two states.

entre nous (Fr.), between ourselves.

en vérité (Fr.), in truth; verily.

e pluribus unum (L.), one out of many; one composed of many.

esprit de corps (Fr.), the animating spirit of a collective body, as a regiment, learned profession or the like.

et sequentes, et sequentia (L.), and those that follow.

et tu, Brute! (L.), and thou also, Brutus!

ex animo (L.), heartily; sincerely.

ex capite (L.), from the head; from memory.

ex cathedra (L.), from the chair or seat of authority, with high authority.

exceptio probat regulam (L.), the exception proves the rule.

ex curia (L.), out of court.

ex dono (L.), by the gift.

exeunt omnes (L.), all go out or retire.

exit (L.), he goes out.

ex mero motu (L.), from his own impulse, from his own free will.

ex nihilo nihil fit (L.), out of nothing, nothing comes; nothing produces nothing.

ex officio (L.), in virtue of his office.

ex post facto (L.), after the deed is done; retrospective.

face à face (Fr.), face to face.

façon de parler (Fr.), manner of speaking.

faire bonne mine (Fr.), to put a good face upon the matter.

fait accompli (Fr.), a thing already done.

fama clamosa (L.), a current scandal; a prevailing report.

faute de mieux (Fr.), for want of better.

faux pas (Fr.), a false step; a slip in behaviour.

festina lente (L.), hasten slowly.

fiat justitia, ruat cœlum (L.), let justice be done though the heavens should fall.

fiat lux (L.), let there be light.

fide et amore (L.), by faith and love.

fide et fiduciâ (L.), by fidelity and confidence.

fide et fortitudine (L.), with faith and fortitude.

fidei defensor (L.), defender of the faith.

fide non armis (L.), by faith, not by arms.

fide, sed cui vide (L.), trust, but see whom.

fides et justitia (L.), fidelity and justice.

fides Punica (L.), Punic faith; treachery.

filius nullius (L.), a son of nobody; a bastard.

finis coronat opus (L.), the end crowns the work.

flagrante bello (L.), during hostilities.

flagrante delicto (L.), in the commission of the crime.

floreat (L.), let it flourish.

fons et origo (L.), the source and origin.

force majeure (Fr.), irresistible compulsion; war, strike, Act of God, *etc.*

forensis strepitus (L.), the clamour of the forum.

fortuna favet fortibus (L.), fortune favours the bold.

functus officio (L.), having performed one's office or duty; hence, out of office.

gaudeamus igitur (L.), so let us be joyful!

genius loci (L.), the genius or guardian spirit of a place.

gradu diverso, via una (L.), the same road by different steps.

grande parure } (Fr.), full dress.
grande toilette }

guerra al cuchillo (Sp.), war to the knife.

Hannibal ante portas (L.), Hannibal before the gates; the enemy close at hand.

hiatus valde deflendus (L.), a chasm or deficiency much to be regretted.

hic et nunc (L.), here and now.

hic et ubique (L.), here and everywhere.

hic jacet (L.), here lies.

hic labor, hoc opus est (L.), this is a labour, this is a toil.

hic sepultus (L.), here buried.

hoc genus omne (L.), all of this sort or class.

hoi polloi (Gr.), the many; the vulgar; the rabble.

hominis est errare (L.), to err is human.

homme de robe (Fr.), a man in civil office.

homme d'affair (Fr.), a man of business.

homme d'esprit (Fr.), a man of wit or genius.

honi soit qui mal y pense (O. Fr.), evil to him who evil thinks.

honores mutant mores (L.), honours change men's manners or characters.

hors de combat (Fr.), out of condition to fight.

hors de propos (Fr.), not to the point or purpose.

hors d'œuvre (Fr.), out of course; out of order.

ich dien (Ger.), I serve.

idée fixe (Fr.), a fixed idea.

id est (L.), that is.

il a diable au corps (Fr.), the devil is in him.

Ilias malorum (L.), an Iliad of ills; a host of evils.

il penseroso (It.), the pensive man.

il sent le fagot (Fr.), he smells of the faggot; he is suspected of heresy.

imperium in imperio (L.), a state within a state; a government within another.

in actu (L.), in act or reality.

in articulo mortis (L.), at the point of death; in the last struggle.

in capite (L.), in chief.

in curia (L.), in court.

index expurgatorius } (L.) a list of books prohibited
index prohibitorius } to Roman Catholics.

in esse (L.), in being; in actuality.

in extenso (L.), at full length.

in extremis (L.), at the point of death.

in memoriam (L.), to the memory of; in memory.

in nubibus (L.), in the clouds.

in omnia paratus (L.), ready for everything.

in petto (It.), in (my) breast; to one's self.

in re (L.), in the matter of.

in sano sensu (L.), in a proper sense.

in situ (L.), in its original situation.

in vino veritas (L.), there is truth in wine; truth is told under the influence of intoxicants.

ipse dixit (L.), he himself said it; a dogmatic saying.

ipsissima verba (L.), the very words.

ipso facto (L.), in the fact itself.

ipso jure (L.), by the law itself.

jacta est alea (L.), the die is cast.

je ne sais quoi (Fr.), I know not what.

joci causa (L.), for the sake of a joke.

labor omnia vincit (L.), labour conquers everything.

l'allegro (It.), the merry man.

lapsus linguæ (L.), a slip of the tongue.

lares et penates (L.), household goods.

laus Deo (L.), praise to God.

le beau monde (Fr.), the fashionable world.

lector benevole (L.), kind or gentle reader.

le jeu n'en vaut pas la chandelle (Fr.), the game is not worth the candle; the object is not worth the trouble.

le mot de l'énigme (Fr.), the key to the mystery.

le point du jour (Fr.), daybreak.

lèse-majesté (Fr.), high-treason.

lettre de cachet (Fr.), a sealed letter containing private orders; a royal warrant.

lex loci (L.), the law or custom of the place.

lex non scripta (L.), unwritten law; common law.

lex scripta (L.), written law; statute law.

locum tenens (L.), a deputy.

lucri causa (L.), for the sake of gain.

magnum opus (L.), a great work.

mala fide (L.), with bad faith; treacherously.

mal à propos (Fr.), ill-timed; out of place.

malgré nous (Fr.), in spite of us.

malheur ne vient jamais seul (Fr.), misfortunes never come singly.

malum in se (L.), evil or an evil in itself.

mardi gras (Fr.), Shrove Tuesday.

mariage de convenance (Fr.), marriage from motives of interest rather than of love.

mauvais goût (Fr.), bad taste.

mauvaise honte (Fr.), false modesty.

mea culpa (L.), my fault; by my fault.

me judice (L.), I being judge; in my opinion.

mens agitat molem (L.), mind moves matter.

mens legis (L.), the spirit of the law.

mens sana in corpore sano (L.), a sound mind in a sound body.

meo periculo (L.), at my own risk.

meo voto (L.), according to my wish.

mise en scène (Fr.), the getting up for the stage, or the putting on the stage.

modus operandi (L.), manner of working.

more suo (L.), in his own way.

motu proprio (L.), of his own accord.

multum in parvo (L.), much in little.

mutatis mutandis (L.), with suitable or necessary alteration.

nervus probandi (L.), the sinews of the argument.

nihil ad rem (L.), irrelevant.

nil desperandum (L.), there is no reason to despair.

noblesse oblige (Fr.), rank imposes obligations; much is expected from one in good position.

nolens volens (L.), willing or unwilling.

nom de guerre (Fr.), a false or assumed name.

non compos mentis (L.), not of sound mind.

non sequitur (L.), it does not follow.

nosce te ipsum (L.), know thyself.

nota bene (L.), mark well.

nudis verbis (L.), in plain words.

obiter dictum (L.), a thing said by the way.

omnia vincit amor (L.), love conquers all things.

ora pro nobis (L.), pray for us.

O tempora! O mores! (L.), O the times! O the manners (or morals)!

oui-dire (Fr.), hearsay.

padrone (It.), a master; a landlord.

par excellence (Fr.), by way of eminence.

pari passu (L.), at an equal pace or rate of progress.

particeps criminis (L.), an accomplice in a crime.

pas de quoi (Fr. abbrev. Il n'y a pas de quoi), don't mention it.

passim (L.), everywhere; in all parts of the book, chapter, etc.

pâté de foie gras (Fr.), goose-liver paté.

pater patriæ (L.), father of his country.

patres conscripti (L.), the conscript fathers; Roman senators.

pax vobiscum (L.), peace be with you.

per ardua ad astra (L.), through rough ways to the stars; through suffering to renown.

per capita (L.), by the head or poll.

per contra (It.), countrariwise.

per diem (L.), by the day; daily.

per se (L.), by itself; considered apart.

pied-à-terre (Fr.), a resting-place; a temporary lodging.

pis aller (Fr.), the worst or last shift.

plebs (L.), the common people.

poco a poco (It.), little by little.

poste restante (Fr.), to remain in the post-office till called for.

prima facie (L.), at first view or consideration.

primus inter pares (L.), first among equals.

pro forma (L.), for the sake of form.

pro patria (L.), for our country.

pro tanto (L.), for so much; for as far as it goes.

pro tempore (L.), for the time being.

quid pro quo (L.), one thing for another; tit for tat; an equivalent.

qui m'aime, aime mon chien (Fr.), love me, love my dog.

qui tacet consentit (L.), he who is silent gives consent.

quod erat demonstrandum (L.), which was to be proved or demonstrated.

quod erat faciendum (L.), which was to be done.

quod vide (L.), which see; refer to the word just mentioned.

quo jure? (L.), by what right?

raison d'être (Fr.), the reason for a thing's existence.

re (L.), in the matter or affair of.

reculer pour mieux sauter (Fr.), to draw back in order to make a better spring.

reductio ad adsurdum (L.), the reducing of a position to a logical absurdity.

requiescat in pace (L.), may he (or she) rest in peace.

respice finem (L.), look to the end.

respublica (L.), the commonwealth.

revenons à nos moutons (Fr.), let us return to our sheep; let us return to our subject.

re vera (L.), in truth.

sans peur et sans reproche (Fr.), without fear and without reproach.

sans rime ni raison (Fr.), without rhyme or reason.

sans souci (Fr.), without care.

sartor resartus (L.), the botcher repatched; the tailor patched or mended.

sauve qui peut (Fr.), let him save himself who can.

savoir-faire (Fr.), the knowing how to act; tact.

savoir-vivre (Fr.), good-breeding; refined manners.

semper idem (L.), always the same.

seriatim (L.), in a series; one by one.

sic passim (L.), so here and there throughout; so everywhere.

sicut ante (L.), as before.

sine die (L.), without a day being appointed.

sine mora (L.), without delay.

sine qua non (L.), without which, not; indispensable condition.

sotto voce (It.), in an undertone.

spirituel (Fr.), intellectual; witty.

stet (L.), let it stand; do not delete.

sub judice (L.), under consideration.

sub pœna (L.), under a penalty.

sub rosa (L.), under the rose; privately.

sub voce (L.), under such or such a word.

sui generis (L.), of its own or of a particular kind.

summum bonum (L.), the chief good.

tableau vivant (Fr.), a living picture; the representation of some scene by a group of persons.

tant mieux (Fr.), so much the better.

tant pis (Fr.), so much the worse.

tempora mutantur, nos et mutamur in illis (L.), the times are changing and we with them.

tempus fugit (L.), time flies.

tête-à-tête (Fr.), together in private.

tiers état (Fr.), the third estate; the commons.

to kalon (Gr.), the beautiful; the chief good.

to prepon (Gr.), the becoming or proper.

tour de force (Fr.), a feat of strength or skill.

tout à fait (Fr.), wholly; entirely.

tout à l'heure (Fr.), instantly.

toute de suite (Fr.), immediately.

tu quoque (L.), thou also.

ubique (L.), everywhere.

ubi supra (L.), where above mentioned.

ultra licitum (L.), beyond what is allowable.

ultra vires (L.), beyond powers or rights conferred by law.

urbi et orbi (L.), to the city (Rome), and the world.

utile dulci (L.), the useful with the pleasant.

ut infra (L.), as below.

ut supra (L.), as above stated.

vade in pace (L.), go in peace.

variæ lectiones (L.), various readings.

variorum notæ (L.), the notes of various commentators.

vede et crede (L.), see and believe.

veni, vidi, vici (L.), I came, I saw, I conquered.

verbatim et literatim (L.), word for word and letter for letter.

verbum sat sapienti (L.), a word is enough for a wise man.

ver non semper viret (L.), spring is not always green.

vexata quæstio (L.), a disputed question.

via media (L.), a middle course.

via trita, via tuta (L.), the beaten path is the safe path.

vice versa (L.), the terms of the case being reversed.

videlicet (L.), that is to say; namely.

vi et armis (L.), by force of arms; by main force; by violence.

vigilate et orate (L.), watch and pray.

vita brevis, ars longa (L.), life is short; art is long.

viva regina! (L.), long live the queen!

vivat rex! (L.), long live the king!

viva voce (L.), by the living voice; orally.

voilà (Fr.), behold; there is; there are.

voilà tout (Fr.), that's all.

volo, non valeo (L.), I am willing, but unable.

vox populi, vox Dei (L), the voice of the people is the voice of God.

MAJOR NATIONAL CURRENCIES

(as in mid-2017)

Country	Currency
Albania	Lek
Argentina . . .	Peso
Australia . . .	Dollar
Austria	Euro
Belgium/Lux. . .	Euro
Belize	Dollar
Bolivia	Peso Boliviano
Brazil	Real
Bulgaria	Lev
Burma (Myanmar) .	Kyat
Canada	Dollar
Chile	Peso
China	Yuan
Colombia . . .	Peso
Costa Rica . .	Colón
Czech Republic .	Koruna
Denmark . . .	Krone
Dominican Republic .	Peso
Ecuador . . .	Dollar
Egypt	Pound
El Salvador . .	Dollar
Ethiopia . . .	Birr
Finland . . .	Euro
France	Euro
Germany . . .	Euro
Guatemala . . .	Quetzal
Guyana . . .	Dollar
Haiti	Gourde
Hungary . . .	Forint
Iceland . . .	Króna
India	Rupee
Indonesia . . .	Rupiah
Iran	Rial
Iraq	Dinar
Ireland . . .	Euro
Israel . . .	New Shekel
Italy	Euro
Jamaica . . .	Dollar
Japan	Yen
Jordan . . .	Dinar
Kenya	K. Shilling
Lebanon . . .	Pound
Malaysia . . .	Ringgit
Malta	Euro
Mexico . . .	Peso
Netherlands . .	Euro
New Zealand . .	Dollar
Nicaragua . . .	Córdoba
Nigeria . . .	Naira
Norway . . .	Krone
Pakistan . . .	Rupee
Panama . . .	Balboa
Paraguay . . .	Guaraní
Peru	Nuevo Sol
Philippines . .	Peso
Poland . . .	Zloty
Portugal . . .	Euro
Romania . . .	New Leu
Russia	Rouble
Saudi Arabia . .	Riyal
Slovenia . . .	Euro
South Africa . .	Rand
Spain	Euro
Sri Lanka . . .	Rupee
Sweden . . .	Krona
Switzerland . .	Franc
Syria	Pound
Tanzania . . .	T. Shilling
Thailand . . .	Baht
Trinidad and Tobago .	T.T. Dollar
Tunisia . . .	Dinar
Turkey	Lira
Ukraine . . .	Hryvnia
United Arab Emirates .	Dirham
USA	Dollar
Uruguay . . .	Peso
Venezuela . . .	Bolívar
Vietnam . . .	Dong
Zambia . . .	Kwacha
Zimbabwe . . .	Dollar

ROMAN NUMERALS

I .	.	.	.	. 1		LXX .	.	.		70
II	.	.	.	. 2		LXXX .	.			80
III	.	.	.	. 3		LXXXVIII	.			88
IV	.	.	.	. 4		XC .	.			90
V.	.	.	.	. 5		C .	.	.		100
VI	.	.	.	. 6		CX .	.			110
VII	.	.	.	. 7		CXI	.			111
VIII	.	.	.	. 8		CXX .	.			120
IX	.	.	.	. 9		CC .	.			200
X	.	.	.	.10		CCXX	.			220
XI	.	.	.	.11		CCC .	.			300
XII	.	.	.	.12		CCCXX	.			320
XIII	.	.	.	.13		CD .	.			400
XIV	.	.	.	.14		D .	.	.		500
XV	.	.	.	.15		DC .	.			600
XVI	.	.	.	.16		DCC .	.			700
XVII	.	.	.	.17		DCCC .	.			800
XVIII	.	.	.	.18		CM .	.			900
XIX	.	.	.	.19		CXM .	.			990
XX	.	.	.	.20		M .	.	.		1000
XXX	.	.	.	.30		MD .	.			1500
XL	.	.	.	.40		MDCCC .	.			1800
L.	.	.	.	.50		MM .	.			2000
LV	.	.	.	.55		MMXVIII .				2018
LX	.	.	.	.60		MMXX .	.			2020

INTERNATIONAL TIME-TABLE (GMT)

The following table gives times around the world.

Place	Time h	Place	Time h
Adelaide	21 30	Melbourne	22 00
Amsterdam	13 00	Montreal	07 00
Ankara	14 00	Moscow	15 00
Athens	14 00	Mumbai	17 30
Auckland (NZ)	24 00	(Bombay)	
Beijing	20 00	Nairobi	15 00
Belgrade	13 00	New York	07 00
Berlin	13 00	Oslo	13 00
Brisbane	22 00	Ottawa	07 00
Brussels	13 00	Panama	07 00
Budapest	13 00	Paris	13 00
Buenos Aires	09 00	Perth (WA)	20 00
Cairo	14 00	Prague	13 00
Cape Town	14 00	Quebec	07 00
Chicago	06 00	Rangoon	18 30
Copenhagen	13 00	Rio de Janeiro	09 00
Gibraltar	13 00	Rome	13 00
Helsinki	14 00	San Francisco	04 00
Hobart	22 00	St. John's (NF)	08 30
Hong Kong	20 00	Singapore	20 00
Istanbul	14 00	Stockholm	13 00
Jerusalem	14 00	Sydney	22 00
Kolkata	17 30	Tehran	15 30
(Calcutta)		Tokyo	21 00
London	12 00	Toronto	07 00
Madeira	12 00	Vancouver	04 00
Madrid	13 00	Vienna	13 00
Malta	13 00	Winnipeg	06 00
Mauritius	16 00	Yokohama	21 00

GREEK ALPHABET

A	α	Alpha	N	ν		nu
B	β	beta	Ξ	ξ		xi
Γ	γ	gamma	O	o		omicron
Δ	δ	delta	Π	π		pi
E	ε	epsilon	P	ρ		rho
Z	ζ	zeta	Σ	σ		sigma
H	η	eta	T	τ		tau
Θ	θ	theta	Y	υ		upsilon
I	ι	iota	Φ	φ		phi
K	κ	kappa	X	χ		chi
Λ	λ	lambda	Ψ	ψ		psi
M	μ	mu	Ω	ω		omega

COMMON LEGAL TERMS

Note: A term that applies only in Scotland is noted accordingly.

Accused The person in court charged with a criminal offence, also known as the *defendant*.

Arbitration Agreeing to settle a dispute through a third party to avoid the trouble and expense of court proceedings. (*See also* **Mediation**).

Bail A sum of money paid or pledged to guarantee that an accused person will appear in court and so will not be held in prison pending trial.

Barrister A lawyer who is qualified to speak in a higher court, unlike a solicitor. In Scottish courts the term advocate is used.

Brief Written instructions given by a solicitor to a barrister appearing in a court case. The word has become a popular synonym for barrister.

Case law The body of law built up through previous court cases rather than parliamentary legislation. (*See* **Statute law**).

Civil law The law dealing with non-criminal disputes.

Claimant Person pursuing a civil case in court, formerly known as the *plaintiff*. The opponent is known as the *defendant*.

Committal proceedings Hearing in a magistrates' court to determine whether an alleged crime is sufficiently serious in nature to go to the Crown court for a jury trial.

Compensation order Order made by a court for a convicted criminal to compensate the victim of the offence.

Contempt of court Offence committed by abusing a judge in court, disobeying a court order or interfering in the judicial process.

Coroners' court Court that determines the cause of sudden or unnatural deaths. In Scotland the sheriff court deals with these matters.

County court Court in which civil (non-criminal) cases are heard by a judge.

Court of Appeal Court that hears appeals against the decision of the High Court and the Crown Court in civil and criminal cases.

Court of Session Highest civil court in Scotland, dealing with serious cases and acting as a court of appeal.

Cross examine To question a witness for the opposing side in a court case.

Crown court Court in which a judge – sometimes sitting with jury – hears more serious criminal cases.

Damages Money the court orders a loser in a case to pay as compensation for loss or injury.

Defamation Damaging a person's reputation in writing or in speech. (*See* **Libel** and **Slander**).

Defence, the Barrister (advocate in Scotland) or solicitor who represents the defendant (the accused) in court.

Executor Man (executrix if female) appointed in a will to deal with settling the estate after death. (*See also* **Probate**).

Habeus corpus Writ issued by a judge challenging the legality of a person's detention.

High Court Court that hears civil cases and deals with appeals in criminal cases.

High Court of Justiciary Court in Scotland in which a judge and jury deal with serious criminal cases, including murder. It also acts as an appeal court.

Injunction Order made by a court to prevent an action being taken.

Jury Twelve members of the public (15 in Scotland), randomly selected from the voters' register, who hear evidence in court and determine whether the accused is guilty or not guilty.

Justice of the Peace (**JP**) A non-professional person (also known as a magistrate) who hears cases in the lower courts. Known as sheriff in Scotland.

Justice of the Peace court Formerly the district court, the court deals with less serious criminal offences in Scotland.

Libel Defamation in writing. (*See* **Defamation**).

Magistrates' court Court in which a district judge or justice of the peace hears criminal cases and some civil cases. There are no juries. (*See also* **Sheriff court**).

Mediation Attempt by a third party to secure agreement between a couple whose marriage has broken down on, for example, the division of assets and future care of children.

Mens rea A person's intention to commit a crime with the understanding that he or she is carrying out a wrongful act.

Oath Promise made in court to tell the truth, sworn on the Bible or other sacred text. It is also possible to "affirm".

Perjury Lying in evidence to a court after swearing an oath to be truthful. (*See also* **Oath**).

Probate Authority granted by the Probate Registry for an executor of a will to settle the deceased's estate. (*See also* **Executor**).

Probation Sentence made by a court as an alternative to imprisonment. Under the terms of an order, a probation officer is appointed to supervise the convicted person for up to three years.

Procurator fiscal An officer of the sheriff court in Scotland who initiates criminal investigations and conducts prosecutions and enquiries into sudden deaths.

Prosecution Barrister or solicitor who presents the case against the accused in court.

Remand Being held in custody or allowed liberty on bail while awaiting trial for an alleged criminal offence. (*See also* **Bail**).

Sequestration Court order that a person's property should be seized.

Sheriff court Court that hears civil and criminal cases in Scotland. A jury sometimes decides a criminal case.

Slander Defamation in spoken word. (*See* **Defamation**).

Small Claims court Part of the county court (sheriff court in Scotland) dealing with minor civil claims. The process is simpler than an ordinary court case and neither party can claim costs.

Solicitor Lawyer who advises clients and, where there is a court hearing, prepares material for the case. Solicitors can speak in lower courts.

Statute law Law established by parliamentary legislation. (*See* **Case law**).

Summons Official order to attend court for a case.

Sub judice Rule limiting discussion outside court of issues being considered in a case to avoid influencing or prejudicing matters.

Tort Action that causes harm to a person and can lead to a claim for damages.

Verdict Decision reached by a jury. The verdict is guilty or not guilty, but in Scotland the jury can also find a charge not proven where innocence is in

doubt but the prosecution's case has been insufficiently convincing.

Vexatious litigant Person who persistently attempts court action over matters with scant prospect of success.

Warrant Document issued by a magistrate authorising an arrest or search of property.

Youth court Part of the magistrates' court dealing with cases involving young people aged under 17.

POPES (Since 1800)

Pius VII	1800	Pius XI	1922
Leo XII	1823	Pius XII	1939
Pius VIII	1829	John XXIII	1958
Gregory XVI	1831	Paul VI	1963
Pius IX	1846	John Paul I	1978
Leo XIII	1878	John Paul II	1978
St. Pius X	1903	Benedict XVI	2005
Benedict XV	1914	Francis I	2013

ARCHBISHOPS OF CANTERBURY
(Since the Reformation)

1533	Thomas Cranmer	1783	John Moore
1556	Reginald Pole	1805	Charles Manners Sutton
1559	Matthew Parker	1828	William Howley
1576	Edmund Grindal	1848	John Bird Sumner
1583	John Whitgift	1862	Charles Thomas Longley
1604	Richard Bancroft	1868	Archibald Campbell Tait
1611	George Abbot	1883	Edward White Benson
1633	William Laud	1896	Frederick Temple
1660	William Juxon	1903	Randall Thomas Davidson
1663	Gilbert Sheldon	1928	Cosmo Gordon Lang
1678	William Sancroft	1942	William Temple
1691	John Tillotson	1945	Geoffrey Francis Fisher
1695	Thomas Tenison	1961	Arthur Michael Ramsey
1716	William Wake	1974	Frederick Donald Coggan
1737	John Potter	1980	Robert Runcie
1747	Thomas Herring	1991	George Carey
1757	Matthew Hutton	2002	Rowan Williams
1758	Thomas Secker	2013	Justin Welby
1768	Hon. Frederick Cornwallis		

ARCHBISHOPS OF YORK (Since 1900)

1891	William Maclagan	1961	Donald Coggan
1909	Cosmo Gordon Lang	1975	Stuart Blanch
1929	William Temple	1983	John Habgood
1942	Cyril Garbett	1995	David Hope
1956	Arthur Michael Ramsey	2005	John Sentamu

ARMED FORCES: TRADITIONAL RANKS

	Royal Navy		*Army*		*Royal Air Force*
1	Admiral of the Fleet	1	Field Marshal	1	Marshal of the RAF
2	Admiral	2	General	2	Air Chief Marshal
3	Vice-Admiral	3	Lieutenant-General	3	Air Marshal
4	Rear-Admiral	4	Major-General	4	Air Vice-Marshal
5	Commodore (1st & 2nd class)	5	Brigadier	5	Air Commodore
6	Captain	6	Colonel	6	Group Captain
7	Commander	7	Lieutenant-Colonel	7	Wing Commander
8	Lieutenant-Commander	8	Major	8	Squadron Leader
9	Lieutenant	9	Captain	9	Flight Lieutenant
10	Sub-Lieutenant	10	Lieutenant	10	Flying Officer
11	Acting Sub-Lieutenant	11	Second Lieutenant	11	Pilot Officer

RULERS OF THE ROMAN WORLD
(from 753 B.C. to 363 A.D.)

The Kingdom

753	Romulus (Quirinus)
716	Numa Pompilius
673	Tullus Hostilius
640	Ancus Marcius
616	L. Tarquinius Priscus
578	Servius Tullius
534	L. Tarquinius Superbus

The Republic

509	Consulate established
509	Quaestorship instituted
498	Dictatorship introduced
494	Plebeian Tribunate created
494	Plebeian Aedileship created
444	Consular Tribunate organized
435	Censorship instituted
366	Praetorship established
366	Curule Aedileship created
362	Military Tribunate elected
326	Proconsulate introduced
311	Naval Duumvirate elected
217	Dictatorship of Fabius Maximus
133	Tribunate of Tiberius Gracchus
123	Tribunate of Gaius Gracchus
82	Dictatorship of Sulla
60	First Triumvirate formed (Caesar, Pompeius, Crassus)
46	Dictatorship of Caesar
43	Second Triumvirate formed (Octavianus, Antonius, Lepidus)

The Empire

27	Augustus (Galus Julius Caesar Octavianus)
14	Tiberius I
37	Gaius Caesar (Caligula)
41	Claudius I
54	Nero
68	Galba
69	Galba; Otho, Vitellius
69	Vespasianus
79	Titus
81	Domitianus

96	Nerva
98	Trajanus
117	Hadrianus
138	Antoninus Pius
161	Marcus Aurelius and Lucius Verus
169	Marcus Aurelius (alone)
180	Commodus
193	Pertinax; Julianus I
193	Septimius Severus
211	Caracalla and Geta
212	Caracalla (alone)
217	Macrinus
218	Elagabalus (Heliogabalus)
222	Alexander Severus
235	Maximinus I (the Thracian)
238	Gordianus I and Gordianus II; Pupienus and Balbinus
238	Gordianus III
244	Philippus (the Arabian)
249	Decius
251	Gallus and Volusianus
253	Aemilianus
253	Valerianus and Gallienus
258	Gallienus (alone)
268	Claudius II (the Goth)
270	Quintillus
270	Aurelianus
275	Tacitus
276	Florianus
276	Probus
282	Carus
283	Carinus and Numerianus
284	Diocletianus
286	Diocletianus and Maximianus
305	Galerius and Constantius I
306	Galerius, Maximinus II, Severus I
307	Galerius, Maximinus II, Constantinus I, Licinius,Maxentius
311	Maximinus II, Constantinus I, Licinius, Maxentius
314	Maximinus II, Constantinus I, Licinius
314	Constantinus I and Licinius
324	Constantinus I (the Great)
337	Constantinus II, Constans I, Constantius II
340	Constantinus II and Constans I
361	Julianus II (the Apostate)
363	Jovianus

Note: In 364 the Empire was divided between the brothers Valentinian (in the West) and Valens (East).

MAJOR PLACE NAMES OF ROMAN BRITAIN

Andover	Levcomagus	Gloucester	Glevum
Bath	Aquae Sulis	Ilchester	Lindinus
Cambridge	Durolipons	Leicester	Ratae Coritanorum
Caernarvon	Segontium	Lincoln	Lindum
Canterbury	Durovernum	London	Londinium
Carlisle	Luguvalium	Manchester	Mamucium
Carmarthen	Moridunum	Northwich	Condate
Catterick	Cataractonium	Pevensey	Anderita
Chelmsford	Caesaromagus	Richborough	Rutupiae
Chester	Deva	Rochester	Durobrivae
Chichester	Noviomagus Regnensium	St. Albans	Verulamium
Cirencester	Corinium Dobunnorum	Silchester	Calleva Atrebatum
Colchester	Camulodunum	South Shields	Caer Urfa
Doncaster	Danum	Towcester	Lactodorum
Dorchester	Durnovaria	Wight. I. of	Vectis
Dover	Portus Dubris	Winchester	Venta Belgarum
Dunstable	Durocobrivae	Wroxeter	Viroconium Cornoviorum
Exeter	Isca Dumnoniorum	York	Eboracum

DIGEST OF NEW WORDS

Introductory Note.

This is a selection of words or phrases, formal and informal, that have become widely used over the past thirty years or so. Many of them existed before that time but now have fresh meanings and implications.

Developments in communication, medicine, politics and technology, for example, have led to a number of additions to our vocabulary. But only time will tell which of these neologisms will survive.

With new words always being added to the English language, it is little surprise that linguists recorded the millionth word in the English language back in 2009. It is estimated that a new word is added to the English language every 98 minutes.

acid house: a type of 'house' music (*q.v.*) played loud with a fast rhythmic beat, often associated with drug-taking by young people at parties in clubs.

additive: a chemical substance added to food or drink for preservation, colour, *etc.*, and denoted by E (European) numbers on labels.

aerobics: rhythmical physical exercises, often practised in groups, to improve physical fitness.

Aga saga: a novel about middle-class, professional people usually living in a rural area (perhaps with an Aga stove in their kitchen). One novelist associated with this genre is Joanna Trollope.

ageism: discrimination in employment against people considered to be too old. Cf. 'sexism.'

-aid: a suffix denoting a scheme or organisation for raising funds for charity, made famous by Bob Geldof's Live Aid campaign in 1985 to relieve African famine.

airhead: an American term for a stupid person.

alcopops: drinks consisting of soft drinks, such as lemonade, mixed with a small percentage of alcohol.

anal retentive: excessively constrained or parsimonious (from Freudian theory).

angioplasty: surgical treatment of a damaged blood-vessel usually by means of unblocking a coronary artery.

anorak: a boring person, usually a young male, obsessed with a solitary hobby or pastime, such as trainspotting. His typical garment is an anorak.

app: in computing, an application program.

aromatherapy: a form of alternative medicine using aromatic oils.

-babble: a suffix denoting jargon in a particular field, *e.g.*, psychobabble, technobabble.

bankable: ensuring a profit, especially when applied to a film star or a theatrical show.

Barbour: the trade name of a fashionable waxed jacket.

Belieber: a fan of 'bad boy' pop star Justin Bieber.

bimbo: an attractive young woman (typically 'a dumb blonde'), especially one accompanying a well-known man, such as a pop star.

biodegradable: able to decompose naturally by means of bacteria.

bitcoin: an online digital cryptocurrency. It can be used to buy goods and services online. Transactions are almost untraceable.

Blackberry thumb: repetitive strain injury caused by over-use of mobiles to send e-mails.

bonding: deliberately forming a strong emotional link between individual people, *e.g.*, parent and child.

bootleg: an adjective originally applied to illegally made liquor and now extended to describe illegally made recordings and video tapes.

Boris bikes: the cycles now available to rent in London, named after the Mayor of London, Boris Johnson.

Brexit: term for the potential departure of Britain from the European Union.

brinner: an evening meal made essentially from breakfast ingredients.

bubble tea: a Taiwanese drink of tea, ice and tapioca pearls that look like bubbles.

bum-bag: a pouch on a belt for money and valuables.

bung: money secretly given as a bribe or reward, especially in the world of sport.

bungee jumping: jumping from a great height while held by an elasticated cable.

burkini: women's swimwear designed to respect Islamic traditions and modesty.

bypass: a surgically constructed artery to take blood past a blocked artery.

carpet-bagger: one who invests in a building society to receive bonuses when the society becomes a bank.

-challenged: a suffix used euphemistically in politically correct English to denote disability, *e.g.*, visually or mentally challenged.

chattering classes: liberal, middle-class people constantly expressing opinions at social gatherings or through the media.

chav: derogatory term applied to young working-class people wearing casual sports clothing.

chillax: a combination of chilling-out and relaxation.

Chollywood: the Chinese film industry.

CJD: Creutzfeldt-Jakob Disease, a degenerative and fatal disease of the brain.

cliometrics: statistical analysis used in historical studies.

clone: a genetically identical copy of an animal, but also used more generally and often pejoratively to denote any exact copy.

corpse: among actors, to forget lines or to spoil them by involuntary giggling.

cottaging: frequenting public lavatories for gay sex.

couch potato: someone who sits and watches TV for many hours or who indulges in other passive pleasures.

crack: a potent form of cocaine.

crowdfunding: investment done via the Internet of small amounts by large number of people in business ventures.

crumblie: an old person even older than a wrinklie (*q.v.*).

cursor: a flashing device on a computer screen to mark positions.

cyberchondria: healthy people who feel they have the symptoms of an illness after reading about it on the Internet.

dark web: parts of the Internet accessible only using special software.

deselect: to refuse to choose a parliamentary candidate again.

designer label: a label, often visible, denoting a fashionable and expensive designer of a garment, hence used as an adjectival phrase, as in 'designer label dress.'

digital detox: a period during which a person refrains from using electronic devices.

digital native: a person who has used computers since childhood.

dinky: an acronym for 'double income no kids,' describing a well-off young professional couple.

doorstep: to canvass or wait outside a door to get photographs or interviews.

doughnutting: people surrounding a speaker (*e.g.*, on TV) to give the impression of a large audience.

downsize: to reduce in size, usually referring to the number of employees (often, that is, to sack them).

dumb down: to simplify and make less demanding, often in the hope of finding a wider audience.

eco-friendly: beneficial or harmless towards the natural environment (*e.g.* **ecotown**).

ecstasy: an hallucinogenic drug.

El Niño: a periodical warming of the ocean off the coast of northern Peru that can result in drastic changes to the weather elsewhere.

e-mail (email): electronic mail, conveyed by computer from sender to reader.

electrosmog: electro-magnetic fields emitted by computers and mobiles.

emoji: in electronic communication, a small digital icon or image used to express an emotion or idea.

europhile and **eurosceptic:** a supporter and opponent respectively of the closer integration of the UK with the other countries of the European Union.

feng shui: an ancient Chinese art involving spirit influences that decide the most advantageous sites for buildings and the best disposition of lighting, furniture, *etc.* From the Chinese '*feng*' (wind) and '*shui*' (water).

filofax: a small loose-leaf filing system often contained in a wallet, associated with yuppies (*q.v.*) of the 1980s.

fist bump: a popular form of greeting, replacing the high-five (*q.v.*) and handshake.

foodie: someone deeply or obsessively interested in food, often used negatively.

Footsie: the popular pronunciation of FTSE, the Financial Times/Stock Exchange index of the shares of 100 public companies.

fracking: hydraulic fracturing, a technique used to extract shale gas.

fromage frais: a soft, low-fat cheese, used in desserts.

fudge: an unsatisfactory, vague compromise, as in political decisions. Sometimes found in the phrase 'fudge and mudge.'

futon: a Japanese-style mattress or bed.

gap year: the year, sometimes spent travelling abroad, between leaving school and entering university.

-gate: a suffix attached to a place name to denote a scandal, after the Watergate scandal of 1972 (*e.g.*, Irangate, Whitewatergate).

gazump: to increase the price of a house after accepting an offer and before contracts are signed. Its opposite, rarely found, is 'gazunder.'

generation square: today's young people who spurn drink and drugs.

gentrification: raising the social status or improving the appearance of an area or a building.

glam-ma: a glamorous granny.

glamping: luxury camping in comfort.

glitterati: rich and fashionable people, such as film or pop stars, especially at publicised social gatherings (*e.g.*, first nights).

Globish, the universal English language, perhaps spoken by a Chinaman to a Mexican.
google: As a verb, to search the Internet for data.

grandtrepreneurs: the over-60s going back into business, starting new careers *etc.*

graphic novel: a novel in pictures.

greenhouse effect: the raising of atmospheric temperature because of pollution that prevents heat from escaping.

grey gappers: the pensioners who spend their time globetrotting.

gripe sites: websites set up as a forum for people to air grievances about an organisation.

hackette: pejorative term for a female journalist.

handbag: to attack or coerce with forceful words. Often associated with Margaret Thatcher when she was Prime Minister (1979–90).

hands on: an adjectival phrase denoting direct practical experience.

happy clappy: a term for evangelical Christian groups who practise enthusiastic communal singing and movement.

high five: slapping palms with hands held high to celebrate an achievement, *e.g.* in sports such as football.

homophobia: prejudice against homosexuals.

house music: fast, loud pop music with a strong beat.

hoverboard: essentially a battery-powered skateboard. The latest street craze.

HRT: hormone replacement therapy, given to women during or after the menopause.

hunk: a well-built, handsome man. Hence, 'hunky,' the adjective.

hygge: Danish term for warmth, cosiness and conviviality.

icon: a symbol on a computer screen; a person or thing idolised by people for supremely representative qualities.

insider dealing: illegally using inside knowledge when dealing in stocks and shares.

iPod: the best selling music player from Apple, featuring an innovative interface and design, with a high storage capacity for media files. Newer models include photo browsing and video playback.

junk food: food, usually fast food, of little nutritional value.

junk mail: unsolicited brochures, circulars, *etc.* sent through the post.

karaoke: singing to a prerecorded accompaniment, especially in a pub or club. (Japanese for 'empty orchestra').

keyhole surgery: surgery performed through a tiny incision in the body.

laddish: applied to assertively male behaviour by young men, typically obsessed with lager and football.

lager lout: a drunken hooligan indulging in noisy and violent behaviour.

liposuction: the process of sucking out fat from the body in cosmetic treatments.

lite: a spelling of 'light,' describing food and drink low in calories.

logocentrism: concentration on the words themselves in a text rather than subject-matter and context.

luvvy: a mocking term for an actor, popularised in *Private Eye*, the satirical periodical.

lycra: a lightweight synthetic fibre used as a fabric (in sportswear, for example).

macho: aggressively male.

mailshot: an item of unsolicited advertising mail sent by post.

make over: improvement of a person's appearance by means of cosmetics, hair-styling, *etc.*

McJob: low-paid, repetitive dead end work.

meltdown: a sudden disastrous collapse in a nuclear reactor, applied metaphorically to other situations, such as a failure in the stock market.

menu: the list of items or instructions on a computer screen.

microwav(e)able: suitable for cooking in a microwave oven.

minder: someone, usually male, employed as a bodyguard or protector. Popularised by the TV series of that name in the 1980s and 1990s.

moobs: unusually prominent breasts on a man.

Moocs: Acronym for Massive Open Online Courses, a major form of distance learning.

mooning: exposing the bare buttocks in public as a joke or an insult.

mouse: the manual device used to position the cursor on a computer screen.

mousemat: the pad on which the mouse (*see above*) is moved by hand.

MP3 player: generic name for a portable data file based music player. MP3 is the dominant encoding standard (from the MPEG working group) but many players work with other formats, often including DRM features.

MSP: a member of the Scottish Parliament.

naff: either a euphemistic verb ('naff off') or an adjective meaning unfashionable and without style.

nanny state: overprotective and fussy government seeking to control people's lives for reasons of so-called safety.

narratology: the study of narratives.

NBD: no big deal.

nerdic: the collection of buzz words and terms used by computer addicts.

Nikkei Index: the index of shares on the Tokyo Stock Exchange (an acronym from Nihon Keizai Shimbun, the principal Japanese financial newspaper).

nimby: someone who opposes building or similar developments in his locality (an acronym from 'not in my back yard').

nuke: to use nuclear weapons.

nutribabble: diets sold to the public that have no nutritional value.

octocopter: a remote-controlled flying camera.

omnishambles: a complete mess.

open-collar worker: someone who works mainly from home.

out: denoting the open avowal of homosexuality, as in the phrasal verb, 'to come out.'

overshare: being for too forthcoming about your personal life.

ozone-friendly: applied to products, *e.g.*, aerosols, that contain no chemicals harmful to the ozone layer.

pacemaker: an electronic device installed in the body to correct the functions of the heart.

paintball: a game involving firing paint-covered pellets at opponents.

paparazzi: photographers for the mass media who constantly follow and often harass celebrities.

parascending: a sport in which people wearing parachutes are towed behind a speedboat (or other vehicle) so that they reach enough speed to ascend.

patriarchal: pertaining to male-dominated culture and society, especially as perceived by feminist critics.

p.c.: politically correct: personal computer.

pecs: an abbreviation for 'pectoral muscles,' especially on the male body.

personal organiser: a pocket-sized computer or loose-leaf wallet for storing information. *Cf.* 'filofax,' above.

photocopiable: sometimes specifically applied to texts that may be photocopied without paying copyright fees.

PIN: acronym for the 'personal identification number' used by customers using cash dispensers *etc.*

plonker: a stupid or foolish person. Popularised in the TV comedy series, 'Only Fools and Horses.'

plummy: pejorative adjective describing a patrician accent or tone of voice.

Polish Plumber: term currently in vogue for a worker from Eastern Europe in the UK, especially from the old communist countries now part of the EU.

post-truth: a situation where fact or reason takes second place to appeals to emotion and personal beliefs.

Quorn: a brand of vegetable protein, used as a substitute for meat.

rabbit: to keep on talking inconsequentially.

radicchio: a type of chicory with reddish-purple leaves used in salads.

rap: words spoken rapidly and rhythmically with an instrumental backing.

reflexology: a therapy in alternative medicine using gentle pressure on the hands and feet.

refusenik: one who refuses to obey orders (originally a Russian dissident).

road rage: anger and sometimes violence displayed by car drivers.

roll over: the prize money accumulating in the twice-weekly National Lottery if the jackpot is not won.

sad: an acronym for 'seasonal affective disorder.'

salami technique: a fraud carried out bit by bit, often by means of a computer.

sarnie: a colloquialism for 'sandwich.'

sat nav: device used in a car which includes information about the road network, allowing for computer assisted navigation.

scratch card: a card that reveals numbers or symbols (which may win money or prizes) when the coverings are scratched off.

screenager: young people reared on a world of screens – TV, computers, mobiles.

scrunch: to crush the hair for a particular hair style.

segway: transportation device for a single individual, featuring two wheels and an electric motor. The passenger rides standing up and steers by leaning their body in the desired direction of travel. Balance is maintained with a sophisticated configuration of gyroscopes.

selfie: self-portraits, a photograph of yourself taken at arm's length.

showmance: a faked showbiz romance.

skunk: a most potent and potentially dangerous form of cannabis.

sledging: verbal abuse or intimidation used by players on the cricket field.

smart card: a plastic card incorporating a microprocessor which can be read electronically for cash transactions or other services.

smart phone: mobile phone with extra functionality and input devices.

smirting: a combination of flirting and smoking, especially outside buildings or pubs where smoking inside is banned.

soundbite: an extract, intended to be memorable, from a speech broadcast on radio or TV.

spin doctor: one who presents or contrives a favourable image of a politician, especially during elections.

spornosexuals: young men striving for gym-fit picture-perfect bodies. A product of the selfie generation.

staycation: term in vogue in the credit crunch meaning to holiday in the UK, not abroad.

steaming: rushing in a gang in and out of shops in order to steal.

streetwise: knowledgeable and cynical regarding aspects of city life.

stretch limo: an extra-long limousine for ceremonial occasions, such as a wedding.

Strimmer: a proprietary name for an electric grass trimmer.

strippagram or **strippogram:** a message delivered by someone who performs a striptease in front of the recipient.

surfing: exploring the contents of the Internet; also riding dangerously on the outside of a train.

surtitle: words of a libretto or playscript (usually in translation) displayed above the stage.

switch: computerised system of transferring money by means of a debit card.

swofties: single women over fifty.

tagging: using electronic markers on goods to prevent theft or on criminals to trace their movements.

tamagotchi: a Japanese word for an electronic toy, sometimes called a cyberpet, which needs regular attention to keep it "alive." (From the Japanese, '*tamago*,' an egg).

terrestrial: an adjective applied to TV or radio transmission to distinguish it from satellite transmission.

texting: the sending of written messages from a mobile phone or similar device.

thirty-something: applied to people, especially professional people, who are between thirty and forty years old. Popularised by an American TV series of that name first shown in 1987.

-thon: a suffix (from the ending of 'marathon') to denote something of long duration, as in 'telethon,' a TV programme lasting several hours with the purpose of raising money for charity.

tokenism: choosing someone on a panel, *etc.* to give the impression of political correctness (*e.g.*, a woman or a person from an ethnic minority).

tombstoning: the craze for jumping into water from a great height.

tweeting: verb derived from Twitter, a social networking site where people can communicate in text messages. The 140-character limit no longer applies. Prolific users are known as the **Twitterati**.

twerking: dancing to popular music in a raunchy, sexually-provocative manner.

twitching: obsessive bird-watching in order to spot rare species.

Uber: a mobile phone app used for hailing minicabs. While many find it easy and convenient, licensed taxi drivers are bitterly-opposed.

unleaded: applied to petrol free from lead.

unwaged: unemployed and hence earning no wages.

user friendly: easy to operate.

vapers: users of e-cigarettes.

video nasty: a horror video film.

video phone: any device capable of providing visual as well as audible communication remotely. A range of solutions are now available that typically combine internet telephony with web cams (*q.v.*).

virus: a device which can be used to sabotage a computer system.

vuvuzela: the noisy instrument, derived from a horn, popular in the 2010 Football World Cup.

wannabe: someone who wants to be special in some way.

web cam: a low-resolution video camera connected to a computer. Often permanently linked to the Internet to provide a continuously updated view, of a famous landmark, for example.

wheelie bin: a large dustbin on wheels.

wii: video game console manufactured by Nintendo, famous for its innovative control device – the Wii remote – which works by detecting movement rather than button presses.

wimmin: a feminist spelling of 'women,' sometimes used mockingly by anti-feminists.

wok: a pan used in Chinese cookery.

wrinklie: an old person. *See* 'crumblie,' above.

yolo: you only live once.

yuppie: a young urban (or upwardly mobile) professional, an acronym associated with the 1980s.

zapper: a remote-control unit.

zero hours: contract requiring a worker to be available for work at certain times with no obligation that the employer will find him or her work.

zero tolerance: refusal to tolerate any illegal activity.

zombie company: a company struggling to survive financially, only existing by paying off the interest on their loans.

zombie knives: curved blades with serrated edges. Often used by criminals and banned in 2016.

THE NOBEL PRIZES

The Nobel Foundation was established at the start of the 20th century to give effect to the wishes expressed by Alfred Nobel in his will. Alfred B Nobel (1833–96) was the inventor of dynamite and bequeathed $9,000,000 to the Foundation. The award of a Nobel Prize is accepted as the highest form of international recognition in the fields in which it is given: physics, chemistry, medicine, literature, peace and, since 1969, economics.

The Royal Academy of Science in Sweden picks the prizewinners in physics, chemistry and economics. The medical faculty of Stockholm's Caroline Institute chooses the winner in the field of physiology or medicine. The Swedish Academy of Literature names the winner in the field of literature.

The Norwegian parliament elects a committee of five persons to select the winner of the prize for peace. The first Nobel Prizes were awarded in 1901. The current value of a Nobel Prize is *c.* £700,000.

CHEMISTRY

This was first awarded in 1901. The following Britons received the award prior to 1945:

1904	Sir William Ramsay
1908	Ernest Rutherford (NZ-born)
1921	Frederick Soddy
1922	Francis W. Aston
1928	Arthur Harden (with Hans von Eulor-Chelpin) (Swe, German-born)
1937	Walter N. Haworth (with Paul Karrer) (Swi, Russian-born)

Winners since 1945 have been:

1945	Artturi I. Virtanen (Fin)
1946	James B. Sumner (USA)
	John H. Northrop (USA)
	Wendell M. Stanley (USA)
1947	Sir Robert Robinson (GB)
1948	Arne W. K. Tiselius (Swe)
1949	William F. Giauque (USA)
1950	Kurt Alder (Ger)
	Otto P. H. Diels (GDR)
1951	Edwin M. McMillan (USA)
	Glenn T. Seaborg (USA)
1952	Archer J. P. Martin (GB)
	Richard L. M. Synge (GB)
1953	Hermann Staudinger (GDR)
1954	Linus C. Pauling (USA)
1955	Vincent du Vigneaud (USA)
1956	Sir Cyril N. Hinshelwood (GB)
	Nikolai N. Semenov (USSR)
1957	Lord Todd (Alexander R. Todd) (GB)
1958	Frederick Sanger (GB)
1959	Jaroslav Heyrovsky (Cze)
1960	Willard F. Libby (USA)
1961	Melvin Calvin (USA)
1962	Sir John C. Kendrew (GB)
	Max F. Perutz (GB, Austrian-born)
1963	Giulio Natta (Ita)
	Karl Ziegler (GDR)
1964	Dorothy Crowfoot Hodgkin (GB)
1965	Robert B. Woodward (USA)
1966	Robert S. Mulliken (USA)
1967	Manfred Eigen (Ger)
	Ronald G. W. Norrish (GB)
	Sir George Porter (GB)
1968	Lars Onsager (USA, Norwegian-born)
1969	Derek H. R. Barton (GB)
	Odd Hassel (Nor)
1970	Luis F. Leloir (Arg, French-born)
1971	Gerhard Herzberg (Can, German-born)
1972	Christian B. Anifinsen (USA)
	Stanford Moore (USA)
	William H. Stein (USA)
1973	Ernest Otto Fischer (GDR)
	Geoffrey Wilkinson (GB)
1974	Paul J. Flory (USA)
1975	John W. Cornforth (GB)
	Vladimir Prelog (Swi, Yugoslavian-born)
1976	William N. Lipscomb Jr (USA)
1977	Ilya Prigogine (Bel, Russian-born)
1978	Peter Mitchell (GB)
1979	Herbert C. Brown (USA)
	Gerry Wittig (GDR)
1980	Frederick Sanger (GB)
	Paul Berg (USA)
	Walter Gilbert (USA)

1981	Roald Hoffman (USA)
	Kenichi Fukui (Jap)
1982	Aaron Klug (GB)
1983	Henry Taube (USA)
1984	R. Bruce Merrifield (USA)
1985	Herbert A. Hauptman (USA)
	Jerome Karle (USA)
1986	Dudley Herschbach (USA)
	Yuan T. Lee (USA)
	John C. Polanyi (Can)
1987	Donald J. Cram (USA)
	Charles J. Paderson (USA)
	Jean-Marie Lehn (Fra)
1988	Johan Deisenhofer (Ger)
	Robert Huber (Ger)
	Hartmut Michel (Ger)
1989	Thomas R. Cech (USA)
	Sidney Altman (USA)
1990	Elias J. Corey (USA)
1991	Richard R. Ernst (Swi)
1992	Rudolph Marcus (USA, Canadian-born)
1993	Michael Smith (Can, British-born)
	Kary Mullis (USA)
1994	George A. Olah (USA)
1995	Paul Crutzen (Hol)
	Mario Molina (USA)
	Sherwood Rowland (USA)
1996	Harold Croto (GB)
	Robert Curl (USA)
	Richard Smalley (USA)
1997	John Walker (GB)
	Paul Boyer (USA)
	Jens Skou (Den)
1998	John Pople (USA, UK born)
	Walter Kohn (USA)
1999	Ahmed Zewail (USA, Egyptian-born)
2000	Alan Heeger (USA)
	Alan MacDiarmid (USA, NZ-born)
	Hideki Shirakawa (Jap)
2001	Barry Sharpless (USA)
	William Knowles (USA)
	Ryoji Noyori (Jap)
2002	John Fenn (USA)
	Koichi Tanaka (Jap)
	Kurt Wietrich (Swi)
2003	Peter Agre (USA)
	Roderick MacKinnon (USA)
2004	Aaron Ciechanover (Isr)
	Avram Hershko (Isr)
	Irwin Rose (USA)
2005	Yves Chauvin (Fr)
	Richard Schrock (USA)
	Robert Grubbs (USA)
2006	Robert Kornberg (USA)
2007	Gerhard Ertl (Ger)
2008	Martin Chalfie (USA)
	Roger Tsien (USA)
	Osamu Shimomura (Jap)
2009	Venkatraman Ramakrishnan (UK)
	Thomas Steitz (USA)
	Ada Yonath (Isr)
2010	Richard Heck (USA)
	Ei-ichi Negishi (Jap)
	Akira Suzuki (Jap)
2011	Daniel Shechtman (Isr)
2012	Brian Kobilka (USA)
	Robert Lefkowitz (USA)
2013	Michael Levitt (USA/UK)
	Martin Karplus (USA/Aus)
	Arieh Warshel (USA/Isr)
2014	Eric Betzig (USA)
	William Moerner (USA)
	Stefan Hell (Ger)
2015	Tomas Lindahl (Swe)
	Paul Modrich (USA)
	Aziz Sancar (Tur/USA)
2016	Jean-Pierre Sauvage (Fr)
	Sir Fraser Stoddart (GB)
	Bernard Feringa (Hol)

ECONOMICS

The most recent Prize, established in 1969.

Winners have been:

1969	Ragnar Frisch (Nor)
	Jan Tinbergen (Hol)

1970	Paul A. Samuelson (USA)
1971	Simon Kuznets (USA)
1972	Kenneth J. Arrow (USA)
	Sir John R. Hicks (GB)
1973	Vassily Leontief (USA) (Russian-born)
1974	Gunnar Myrdal (Swe)
	Friedrich A. von Hayek (Aut)
1975	Leonid V. Kantorovich (USSR)
	Tjalling C. Koopmans (USA) (Dutch-born)
1976	Milton Friedman (USA)
1977	Bertil Ohlin (Swe)
	James Edward Meade (GB)
1978	Herbert Simon (USA)
1979	Sir Arthur Lewis (GB) (St Lucien-born)
	Theodore W. Schultz (USA)
1980	Lawrence Klein (USA)
1981	James Tobin (USA)
1982	George J. Stigler (USA)
1983	Gerard Debreu (USA)
1984	Sir Richard Stone (GB)
1985	Franco Modigliani (USA, Italian-born)
1986	James M. Buchanan (USA)
1987	Robert M. Solow (USA)
1988	Maurice Allais (Fra)
1989	Trygve Haavelmo (Nor)
1990	Harry M. Markowitz (USA)
	William F. Sharpe (USA)
	Merton H. Miller (USA)
1991	Ronald H. Coase (GB/USA)
1992	Gary Becker (USA)
1993	Robert W. Fogel (USA)
	Douglass C. North (USA)
1994	John Nash (USA)
	Reinhard Selter (Ger)
	John Harsanyi (USA)
1995	Robert E. Lucas (USA)
1996	James Mirrlees (GB)
	William Vickrey (Can)
1997	Robert Merton (USA)
	Myron Scholes (USA)
1998	Amartya Sen (Ind)
1999	Robert Mundell (USA, Canadian-born)
2000	James J. Heckman (USA)
	Daniel L. McFadden (USA)
	Joseph Stiglitz (USA)
2001	George Akerlof (USA)
	Michael Spence (USA)
2002	Daniel Kahnemann (USA/Isr)
	Vernon Smith (USA)
2003	Robert Engle (USA)
	Clive Granger (GB)
2004	Finn Kydland (Nor)
	Edward Prescott (USA)
2005	Thomas Schelling (USA)
	Robert Aumann (USA/Isr)
2006	Edward Phelps (USA)
2007	Leonid Hurwicz (USA)
	Eric Maskin (USA)
	Roger Myerson (USA)
2008	Paul Krugman (USA)
2009	Elinor Ostrom (USA)
	Oliver Williamson (USA)
2010	Peter Diamond (USA)
	Dale Mortensen (USA)
	Christopher Pissarides (GB/Cyp)
2011	Thomas Sargent (USA)
	Christopher Sims (USA)
2012	Alvin Roth (USA)
	Lloyd Shapley (USA)
2013	Eugene F. Fama (USA)
	Lars Peter Hansen (USA)
	Robert Shiller (USA)
2014	Jean Tirole (Fra)
2015	Sir Angus Deaton (GB)
2016	Oliver Hart (UK/USA)
	Bengt Holmstrom (Fin)

LITERATURE *See* **G20**.

MEDICINE

The Nobel Prize for Medicine dates from 1901. Up to 1945 the following British persons were winners:

1902	Sir Ronald Ross
1922	Archibald V. Hill
1929	Sir Frederick G. Hopkins (joint)
1932	Edgar D. Adrian
	Sir Charles S. Sherrington
1936	Sir Henry H. Dale

Winners since 1945 have been:

1945	Sir Alexander Fleming (GB)
	Ernst B. Chain (GB, German-born)
	Sir Howard W. Florey (GB, Australian-born)
1946	Hermann J. Muller (USA)
1947	Carl F. Cori (USA, Czech-born)
	Gerty T. Cori (USA, Czech-born)
	Bernardo A. Houssay (Arg)
1948	Paul H. Müller (Swi)
	Walter R. Hess (Swi)
1949	Antonio Moniz (Por)
	Philip S. Hench (USA)
1950	Edward C. Kendall (USA)
	Tadeus Reichstein (Swi, Polish-born)
1951	Max Theiler (USA, S. African-born)
1952	Selman A. Waksman (USA)
1953	Hans A. Krebs (GB, German-born)
	Fritz A. Lipmann (USA, German-born)
1954	John F. Enders (USA)
	Frederick C. Robbins (USA)
	Thomas H. Weller (USA)
1955	Alex H. T. Theorell (Swe)
1956	André F. Cournand (USA, French-born)
	Werner Forssmann (Ger)
	Dickinson W. Richards Jr (USA)
1957	Daniel Bovet (Ita, Swiss-born)
1958	George W. Beadle (USA)
	Edward L. Tatum (USA)
	Joshua Lederberg (USA)
1959	Arthur Kornberg (USA)
	Severo Ochoa (USA, Spanish-born)
1960	Sir F. Macfarlane Burnet (Aus)
	Peter B. Medawar (GB, Brazilian-born)
1961	Georg von Békésy (USA, Hungarian-born)
1962	Francis H. C. Crick (GB)
	James D. Watson (USA)
	Maurice H. F. Wilkins (GB, NZ-born)
1963	Sir John C. Eccles (Aus)
	Alan L. Hodgkin (GB)
	Andrew F. Huxley (GB)
1964	Konrad E. Bloch (USA)
	Feodor Lynen (Ger)
1965	François Jacob (Fra)
	André Lwoff (Fra)
	Jacques Monod (Fra)
1966	Charles B. Huggins (USA)
	Francis Peyton Rous (USA)
1967	Ragnar Granit (Swe, Finnish-born)
	Haldan Keffer Hartline (USA)
	George Wald (USA)
1968	Robert W. Holley (USA)
	Har Gobind Khorana (USA, Indian-born)
	Marshall W. Nirenberg (USA)
1969	Max Delbrück (USA, German-born)
	Alfred D. Hershey (USA)
	Salvador D. Luria (USA, Italian-born)
1970	Julius Axelrod (USA)
	Ulf von Euler (Swe)
	Bernard Katz (GB)
1971	Earl W. Sutherland Jr (USA)
1972	Gerald M. Edelman (USA)
	Rodney Porter (GB)
1973	Karl von Frisch (Aut)
	Konrad Lorenz (Aut)
	Nikolaas Tinbergen (GB, Dutch-born)
1974	Albert Claude (USA, Luxembourg-born)
	Christian René de Duve (Bel)
	George Emil Palade (USA, Romanian-born)
1975	David Baltimore (USA)
	Howard Martin Temin (USA)
	Renato Dulbecco (USA, Italian-born)
1976	Baruch S. Blumberg (USA)
	D. Carleton Gajdusek (USA)
1977	Rosalyn S. Yalow (USA)
	Roger C. L. Guillemin (USA, French-born)
	Andrew V. Schally (USA)
1978	Werner Arber (Swi)
	Daniel Nathans (USA)
	Hamilton Smith (USA)
1979	Dr Hounsfield (GB)
	Allan Cormack (USA)
1980	Baruy Benacerraf (Ven)
	Jean Dausset (Fra)
	George Snell (USA)
1981	Roger W. Sperry (USA)
	David H. Hubel (USA)
	Torsten N. Wiesel (Swe)
1982	Sune Bergstrom (Swe)
	Bengt Samuelsson (Swe)
	John R. Vane (GB)

1983	Barbara McClintock (USA)
1984	{ Cesar Milstein (GB, Argentinian-born) { Georges J. F. Kohler (Ger) { Niels K. Jerne (GB, Danish-born)
1985	{ Michael S. Brown (USA) { Joseph L. Goldstein (USA)
1986	{ Rita Levi-Montalcini (USA, Italian-born) { Stanley Cohen (USA)
1987	Susumu Tonegawa (Jap)
1988	{ Gertrude B. Elion (USA) { George H. Hitchings (USA) { Sir James Black (GB)
1989	{ J. Michael Bishop (USA) { Harold E. Varmus (USA)
1990	{ Joseph E. Murray (USA) { E. Donnall Thomas (USA)
1991	{ Edwin Neher (Ger) { Bert Sakmann (Ger)
1992	{ Edwin Krebs (USA) { Edmond Fischer (USA)
1993	{ Richard Roberts (GB) { Phillip Sharp (USA)
1994	{ Alfred G. Gilman (USA) { Martin Rodbell (USA)
1995	{ Edward B. Lewis (USA) { Christiane Nüesslein-Volhard (Ger) { Eric F. Wieschaus (USA)
1996	{ Peter Doherty (Aus) { Rolf Zinkernagel (Swi)
1997	Stanley Prusiner (USA)
1998	{ Robert Furchgott (USA) { Louis Ignarro (USA) { Ferid Murad (USA)
1999	Günter Blobel (USA, German-born)
2000	{ Arvid Carlsson (Swe) { Paul Greengard (USA) { Eric Kandel (USA)
2001	{ Sir Paul Nurse (GB) { Tim Hunt (GB) { Leland Hartwell (USA)
2002	{ John Sulston (GB) { Robert Horvitz (USA) { Sydney Brenner (USA)
2003	{ Sir Peter Mansfield (GB) { Paul C. Lauterbur (USA)
2004	{ Richard Axel (USA) { Linda Buck (USA)
2005	{ Barry Marshall (Aus) { Robin Warren (Aus)
2006	{ Andrew Fire (USA) { Craig Mello (USA)
2007	{ Sir Martin Evans (GB) { Mario Capecchi (USA, Italian-born) { Oliver Smithies (USA, GB-born)
2008	{ Françoise Barre-Sinoussi (Fr) { Luc Montagnier (Fr) { Harald zur Hausen (Ger)
2009	{ Elizabeth Blackburn (USA) { Carol Greider (USA) { Jack Szostak (USA)
2010	Robert Edwards (GB)
2011	{ Ralph Steinman (USA, Canadian-born) { Bruce Beutler (USA) { Jules Hoffman (Fr)
2012	{ Sir John Gurdon (GB) { Shinya Yamanaka (Jap)
2013	{ James Rothman (USA) { Randy Schekman (USA) { Thomas Sudhof (Ger)
2014	{ John O'Keefe (US-born) { May-Britt Moser (Nor) { Edvard Moser (Nor)
2015	{ Youyou Tu (Chi) { Satoshi Omura (Jap) { William C. Campbell (USA)
2016	Yoshinori Ohsumi (Jap)

PEACE

The first Nobel Prize was awarded in 1901 to Jean Henri Dunant, the Swiss founder of the Red Cross, and Frederic Passy, a French advocate of international arbitration. The prize was not awarded in 1948, 1955, 1956, 1966, 1967 and 1972.

Winners since 1945 have been:

1945	Cordell Hull (USA)
1946	{ Emily G. Batch (USA) { John R. Mott (USA)
1947	{ Friends Service Council (GB) { American Friends Service Committee (USA)

1949	Lord John Boyd Orr (GB)
1950	Ralph J. Bunche (USA)
1951	Léon Jouhaux (Fra)
1952	Albert Schweitzer (Fra, German-born)
1953	George C. Marshall (USA)
1954	Office of the UN High Commission for Refugees
1957	Lester B. Pearson (Can)
1958	Georges Pire (Bel)
1959	Philip J. Noel-Baker (GB)
1960	Albert J. Luthuli (SAf)
1961	Dag Hammarskjöld (Swe) (posthumous)
1962	Linus C. Pauling (USA)
1963	{ International Committee of the Red Cross { Red Cross Societies League
1964	Martin Luther King Jr (USA)
1965	United Nations Childrens Fund (UNICEF)
1968	René Cassin (Fra)
1969	International Labour Organization (ILO)
1970	Norman E. Borlaug (USA)
1971	Willy Brandt (FRG)
1973	{ Henry A. Kissinger (USA, German-born) { Le Duc Tho (NViet)
1974	{ Eisaku Salo (Jap) { Sean MacBride (Ire)
1975	Andrei D. Sakharov (USSR)
1976	{ Betty Williams (GB) { Mairead Corrigan (GB)
1977	Amnesty International
1978	{ Anwar el Sadat (Egy) { Menachem Begin (Isr)
1979	Mother Teresa of Calcutta (Alb)
1980	Adolfo Pérez Esquivel (Arg)
1981	UN High Commission for Refugees
1982	{ Alva Myrtal (Swe) { Alfonso Garcia Robles (Mex)
1983	Lech Walesa (Pol)
1984	Archbishop Desmond Tutu (SAf)
1985	International Physicians for the Prevention of Nuclear War
1986	Elie Wiesel (USA, Romanian-born)
1987	President Oscar Arias Sanchez (CoR)
1988	UN Peacekeeping Forces
1989	Dalai Lama (Tib)
1990	Mikhail Gorbachev (USSR)
1991	Aung San Suu Kyi (Mya)
1992	Rigoberta Menchu (Gua)
1993	{ F. W. de Klerk (SAf) { Nelson Mandela (SAf)
1994	{ Yitzak Rabin (Isr) { Yasser Arafat (Pal) { Shimon Peres (Isr)
1995	{ Joseph Rotblat (GB, Polish-born) { Pugwash Conferences
1996	{ Carlos Felipe Belo (Timor) { José Ramos-Horta (Timor)
1997	{ International Campaign to Ban Landmines { Jody Williams (USA)
1998	{ John Hume (UK) { David Trimble (UK)
1999	Médecins sans Frontières (Fra)
2000	Kim Dae-jung (S Kor)
2001	{ Kofi Annan (Gha) { United Nations
2002	Jimmy Carter (USA)
2003	Shirin Ebadi (Iran)
2004	Wangari Maathai (Ken)
2005	{ International Atomic Energy Agency { Mohamed ElBaradei
2006	{ Muhammad Yunus (Ban) { Grameen Bank
2007	{ Al Gore (USA) { Intergovernmental Panel on Climate Change
2008	Martti Ahtisaari (Fin)
2009	Barack Obama (USA)
2010	Liu Xiaobo (China)
2011	{ Ellen Johnson Sirleaf (Lib) { Leyman Gbowee (Lib) { Tawakul Karman (Yem)
2012	European Union
2013	Organisation for the Prohibition of Chemical Warfare (OPCW)
2014	{ Malala Yousafzai (Pak) { Kailash Satyarthi (Ind)
2015	National Dialogue Quartet (Tunisia)
2016	Juan Manuel Santos (Colombia)

PHYSICS

The first Nobel Prize for Physics was awarded in 1901 to Wilhelm C. Roentgen of Germany. Among the British recipients before 1945 were:

1904	Lord Rayleigh (John W. Strutt)		
1906	Sir Joseph John Thomson	1981	Nicolaas Bloemergern (USA)
1915	Sir William H. Bragg		Arthur Schawlow (USA)
1917	Charles G. Barkla	1982	Kenneth Wilson (USA)
1927	Charles T. R. Wilson (*joint award*)	1983	Subrahmanyan Chandrasekhar (USA)
1928	Owen W. Richardson		William Fowler (USA)
1933	Paul A. M. Dirac (*joint award*)	1984	Carlo Rubbia (Ita)
1935	Sir James Chadwick		Simon van der Meer (Hol)
1937	George P. Thomson (*joint award*)	1985	Klaus von Klitzing (Ger)
		1986	Erns Ruska (Ger)
			Gerd Binnig (Ger)
			Heinrich Rohrer (Swi)
		1987	Georg Bednorz (Ger)
			Alex Müller (Swi)
		1988	Leon M. Lederman (USA)
			Melvin Schwartz (USA)
Winners since 1945 have been:			Jack Steinberger (Ger)
		1989	Norman Ramsey (USA)
1945	Wolfgang Pauli (USA)		Hans Dehmelt (USA)
1946	Percy Williams Bridgman (USA)		Wolfgang Paul (Ger)
1947	Sir Edward V. Appleton (GB)	1990	Jerome Friedman (USA)
1948	Patrick M. S. Blackett (GB)		Henry Kendall (USA)
1949	Hideki Yukawa (Jap)		Richard Taylor (Can)
1950	Cecil F. Powell (GB)	1991	Pierre-Giles de Gennes (Fra)
1951	Sir John D. Cockcroft (GB)	1992	Georges Charpak (Fra)
	Ernest T. S. Walton (Ire)	1993	Russell Huise (USA)
1952	Felix Block (USA, Swiss-born)		Joseph Taylor (USA)
	Edward Purcell (USA)	1994	Bertram N. Brockhouse (Can)
1953	Fritz Zernike (Hol)		Clifford G. Shull (USA)
1954	Max Born (GB, German-born)	1995	Frederick Reines (USA)
	Walther Bothe (FRG)	1996	Douglas Osheroff (USA)
1955	Polykarp Kusch (USA, German-born)		David Lee (USA)
	Willis E. Lamb (USA)		Robert Richardson (USA)
1956	John Bardeen (USA)	1997	Claude Cohen-Tannoudji (Fra)
	Walter H. Brattain (USA)		Steven Chu (USA)
	William Shockley (USA)		William Phillips (USA)
1957	Tsung-Dao Lee (USA, Chinese-born)	1998	Robert Laughlin (USA)
	Chen Ning Yang (USA, Chinese-born)		Daniel Tsui (USA)
1958	Paval A. Cherenkov (USSR)		Horst Störmer (Ger)
	Ilya M. Frank (USSR)	1999	Gerardus 't Hooft (Hol)
	Igor J. Tamm (USSR)		Martinus Veltman (Hol)
1959	Owen Chamberlain (USA)	2000	Zhores Alferov (Rus)
	Emilio G. Segrè (USA, Italian-born)		Herbert Kroemer (USA)
1960	Donald A. Glaser (USA)		Jack Kilby (USA)
1961	Robert Hofstadter (USA)	2001	Eric Cornell (USA)
	Rudolf L. Mössbauer (FRG)		Carl Wiemann (USA)
1962	Lev D. Landau (USSR)		Wolfgang Ketterle (Ger)
1963	Maria Goeppert-Mayer (USA)	2002	Raymond Davis Jnr (USA)
	J. Hans D. Jensen (FRG)		Masatushi Koshiba (Jap)
	Eugene P. Wigner (USA)		Riccardo Giaconni (USA)
1964	Nikolai G. Basov (USSR)	2003	Anthony Leggett (GB)
	Aleksandr M. Prokhorov (USSR)		Alexei Abrikosov (Rus)
	Charles H. Townes (USA)		Vitaly Ginzburg (USA)
1965	Richard P. Feynman (USA)	2004	David Gross (USA)
	Julian S. Schwinger (USA)		David Politzer (USA)
	Sin-itiro Tomonaga (Jap)		Frank Wilczek (USA)
1966	Alfred Kastler (Fra)	2005	Roy Glauber (USA)
1967	Hans A. Bethe (USA, German-born)		John Hall (USA)
1968	Luis W. Alvarez (USA)		Theodor Haensch (USA)
1969	Murray Gell-Man (USA)	2006	John Mather (USA)
1970	Hannes O. G. Alfven (Swe)		George Smoot (USA)
	Louis E. F. Néel (Fra)	2007	Albert Fert (Fr)
1971	Dennis Gabor (GB, Hungarian-born)		Peter Grünberg (Ger)
1972	John Bardeen (USA)	2008	Yoichiro Nambu (USA, Japanese-born)
	Leon N. Cooper (USA)		Makoto Kobayashi (Jap)
	John R. Schrieffer (USA)		Toshihide Maskawa (Jap)
1973	Ivar Giaever (USA, Norwegian-born)	2009	Charles Kuen Kao (UK/USA)
	Leo Esaki (Jap)		Willard Sterling Boyle (USA)
	Brian D. Josephson (GB)		George Smith (USA)
1974	Antony Hewish (GB)	2010	Andrei Geim (Rus) (UK-based)
	Sir Martin Ryle (GB)		Konstantin Novoselov (Rus)
	L. James Rainwater (USA)		(UK-based)
1975	Aage Bohr (Den)	2011	Saul Perlmutter (USA)
	Ben Roy Mottelson (Den, USA-born)		Adam Reiss (USA)
1976	Burton Richter (USA)		Brian Schmidt (Aus)
	Samuel C. C. Ting (USA)	2012	Serge Haroche (Fra)
1977	John H. Van Vleck (USA)		David Wineland (GB)
	Philip W. Anderson (USA)	2013	Peter Higgs (GB)
	Sir Nevill F. Mott (GB)		François Englert (Bel)
1978	Piotr Leontevich Kapitsa (USSR)	2014	Isamu Akasaki (Jap)
	Arno A. Penzias (USA, German-born)		Hiroshi Amano (Jap)
	Robert W. Wilson (USA)		Shuji Nakamura (Jap)
1979	Abdus Salam (GB)	2015	Takaaki Kajita (Jap)
	Sheldon Glashow (USA)		Arthur McDonald (Can)
	Steven Weinberg (USA)	2016	David Thouless (UK)
1980	James W. Cronin (USA)		Duncan Haldane (UK, USA-based)
	Val Fitch (USA)		Michael Kosterlitz (UK, USA-based)

LITERARY PRIZES

This section provides information on some of the main literary prizes awarded in the UK, along with details of the Nobel Prize for Literature.

The Nobel Prize for Literature

The most prestigious literary prize in the world, the Nobel is one of the five annual prizes awarded since 1901 under the terms of the will of the Swedish chemist Alfred Nobel (1833–96). Nobel's will stipulated that one of the prizes should be given to the person who 'in the field of literature shall have produced the most outstanding work in an ideal direction'. British Nobel Literature laureates have included Rudyard Kipling (1907), W.B. Yeats (1923), George Bernard Shaw (1925), John Galsworthy (1932), T.S. Eliot (1948), Sir Winston Churchill (1953), William Golding (1983), V.S. Naipaul (2001) and Harold Pinter (2005).

Winners since 1991 have been:

1991 Nadine Gordimer
1992 Derek Walcott
1993 Toni Morrison
1994 Kenzaburo Oe
1995 Seamus Heaney
1996 Wislawa Szymborska
1997 Dario Fo
1998 José Saramago
1999 Günter Grass
2000 Gao Xingjian
2001 V.S. Naipaul
2002 Imre Kertész
2003 J.M. Coetzee
2004 Elfriede Jelinek
2005 Harold Pinter
2006 Orhan Pamuk
2007 Doris Lessing
2008 Jean-Marie Gustave Le Clézio
2009 Herta Müller
2010 Mario Vargas Llosa
2011 Tomas Tranströmer
2012 Mo Yan
2013 Alice Munro
2014 Patrick Modiano
2015 Svetlana Alexievich
2016 Bob Dylan

The Man Booker Prize (formerly the Booker Prize)

Established in 1969, the Booker is the UK's leading prize for a work of fiction. It is awarded annually for the best full-length novel written in English by a citizen of the UK or the Commonwealth. It was sponsored for many years by Booker plc. In 2002 the organization and administration of the Prize was transferred to a newly registered charity, the Booker Prize Foundation. The financial services conglomerate, the Man Group, became its new sponsor, renaming it the Man Booker Prize and more than doubling the prize money awarded to the winning book to £50,000, so that at that time the Booker once again became Britain's richest literary prize. Since 2014 there has been no geographical limit concerning who may be awarded the prize.

Winners since 1985 have been:

1985 Keri Hulme, *The Bone People*
1986 Kingsley Amis, *The Old Devils*
1987 Penelope Lively, *Moon Tiger*
1988 Peter Carey, *Oscar and Lucinda*
1989 Kazuo Ishiguro, *The Remains of the Day*
1990 Antonia Byatt, *Possession*
1991 Ben Okri, *The Famished Road*
1992 Michael Ondaatje, *The English Patient* and
    Barry Unsworth, *Sacred Hunger* (joint winners)
1993 Roddy Doyle, *Paddy Clarke Ha Ha Ha*
1994 James Kelman, *How Late It Was, How Late*
1995 Pat Barker, *The Ghost Road*
1996 Graham Swift, *Last Orders*
1997 Arundhati Roy, *The God of Small Things*
1998 Ian McEwan, *Amsterdam*
1999 J.M. Coetzee, *Disgrace*
2000 Margaret Atwood, *The Blind Assassin*
2001 Peter Carey, *True History of the Kelly Gang*
2002 Yann Martel, *Life of Pi*
2003 D.B.C. Pierre, *Vernon God Little*

2004 Alan Hollinghurst, *The Line of Beauty*
2005 John Banville, *The Sea*
2006 Kiran Desai, *The Inheritance of Loss*
2007 Anne Enright, *The Gathering*
2008 Aravind Adiga, *The White Tiger*
2009 Hilary Mantel, *Wolf Hall*
2010 Howard Jacobson, *The Finkler Question*
2011 Julian Barnes, *The Sense of an Ending*
2012 Hilary Mantel, *Bring up the Bodies*
2013 Eleanor Catton, *The Luminaries*
2014 Richard Flanagan, *The Narrow Road to the
    Deep North*
2015 Marlon James, *A Brief History of Seven Killings*
2016 Paul Beatty, *The Sellout*

Peter Carey, J.M. Coetzee and Hilary Mantel share the distinction of being the only three authors to have won the Prize twice. Prior to winning in 2000, Margaret Atwood had been short-listed on three previous occasions. In 1993, Rushdie's *Midnight's Children* was awarded the Booker of Bookers (the 'Best of Twenty Five Years of the Booker Prize').

The Man Booker International Prize

Awarded biennially for a writer's body of work.

2005 Ismail Kadaré	2011 Philip Roth
2007 Chinua Achebe	2013 Lydia Davis
2009 Alice Munro	2015 Laszlo Krasnahorkai

The Orange Prize for Fiction / Bailey's Women's Fiction Prize

The Orange Prize was introduced in 1996, to help remedy the perceived neglect of women writers shown by the UK's major literary prizes. It is awarded annually for a novel written by a woman and published in the UK and is open to women of all nationalities. Prize renamed in 2007. The last Orange-sponsored prize was awarded in 2012.

It became the privately sponsored £30,000 Bailey's Women's Fiction Prize. Bailey's ceased sponsoring the prize after 2017. The first winner (2013) was A.M. Homes for *May We Be Forgiven*. The 2014 winner was Elmear McBride for *A Girl is a Half-Formed Thing* and in 2015 Ali Smith won with *How to be Both*. The last winner was Naomi Alderman, *The Power*.

Winners of the Orange Prize were:

1996 Helen Dunmore, *A Spell of Winter*
1997 Anne Michaels, *Fugitive Pieces*
1998 Carol Shields, *Larry's Party*
1999 Suzanne Berne, *A Crime in the Neighbourhood*
2000 Linda Grant, *When I Lived in Modern Times*
2001 Kate Grenville, *The Idea of Perfection*
2002 Anna Patchett, *Bel Canto*
2003 Valerie Martin, *Property*
2004 Andrea Levy, *Small Island*
2005 Lionel Shriver, *We Need to Talk About Kevin*
2006 Zadie Smith, *On Beauty*
2007 Chimamanda Ngozi Adichie, *Half of a Yellow Sun*
2008 Rose Tremain, *The Road Home*
2009 Marilynne Robinson, *Home*
2010 Barbara Kingsolver, *The Lacuna*
2011 Téa Obreht, *The Tiger's Wife*
2012 Madeleine Miller *The Song of Achilles*

The David Cohen Prize

Unlike Britain's other major literary awards, the David Cohen British Literature Prize in the English Language is awarded for lifetime achievement. It has been awarded biennially since 1993 and is funded by the David Cohen Family Trust and the Arts Council, who administer the Prize. Members of the public are invited to nominate winners. A proportion of the prize money is allocated to the encouragement of younger writers and readers at the winner's choosing.

Winners so far have been:

1993 V.S. Naipaul
1995 Harold Pinter
1997 Muriel Spark
1999 William Trevor
2001 Doris Lessing
2003 Beryl Bainbridge and Thom Gunn

2005 Michael Holroyd
2007 Derek Mahon
2009 Seamus Heaney
2011 Julian Barnes
2013 Hilary Mantel
2015 Tony Harrison

The Costa (formerly Whitbread) Book Awards

The Whitbread Book Awards were founded in 1971, with awards being made in five categories: best book, best first book, best biography, best poetry collection and best children's book. Their format changed in 1985, when the Whitbread Book of the Year, widely regarded as Britain's most important literary prize after the Booker, was introduced. Between 1996 and 1998 the Children's Book of the Year was a separate award in its own right. From 1999 to 2001, this separate award continued, but with the Children's Book of the Year subsequently being judged against the other categories for overall Book of the Year. From 2002 it once again became one of five categories, with its winner competing for the overall title of Book of the Year.

The awards were sponsored by Whitbread plc and administered by the Bookseller's Association of Great Britain and Ireland. They are open to authors who have been resident in the UK or Ireland for over six months of the previous three years. Costa took over the Prize in 2006.

Winners of the overall Book of the Year have been:

1985 Douglas Dunn, *Elegies* (Poetry)
1986 Kazuo Ishiguro, *An Artist of the Floating World* (Novel)
1987 Christopher Nolan, *Under the Eye of the Clock* (Biography)
1988 Paul Sayer, *The Comforts of Madness* (First Novel)
1989 Richard Holmes, *Coleridge: Early Visions* (Biography)
1990 Nicholas Mosley, *Hopeful Monsters* (Novel)
1991 John Richardson, *A Life of Picasso* (Biography)
1992 Jeff Torrington, *Swing Hammer Swing!* (First Novel)
1993 Joan Brady, *Theory of War* (Novel)
1994 William Trevor, *Felicia's Journey* (Novel)
1995 Kate Atkinson, *Behind the Scenes at the Museum* (First Novel)
1996 Seamus Heaney, *The Spirit Level* (Poetry)
1997 Ted Hughes, *Tales from Ovid* (Poetry)
1998 Ted Hughes, *Birthday Letters* (Poetry)
1999 Seamus Heaney, *Beowulf* (Poetry)
2000 Matthew Kneale, *English Passengers* (Novel)
2001 Philip Pullman, *The Amber Spyglass* (Children's Book of the Year)
2002 Claire Tomalin, *Samuel Pepys: The Unequalled Self* (Biography)
2003 Mark Haddon, *The Curious Incident of the Dog in the Night-Time* (Novel)
2004 Andrea Levy, *Small Island* (Novel)
2005 Hilary Spurling, *Matisse: The Master* (Biography)
2006 Stef Penney, *The Tenderness of Wolves* (Novel)
2007 A. L. Kennedy, *Day*
2008 Sebastian Barry, *The Secret Scripture*
2009 Christopher Reid, *A Scattering*
2010 Jo Shapcott, *Of Mutability*
2011 Andrew Miller, *Pure*
2012 Hilary Mantel, *Bring out the Bodies*
2013 Nathan Filer, *The Shock of the Fall*
2014 Helen Macdonald, *H is for Hawk*
2015 Frances Hardinge, *The Lie Tree*
2016 Sebastian Barry *Days Without End*

The *Guardian* Fiction Award and The *Guardian* First Book Award

First awarded in 1965, the *Guardian* Fiction Award was one of the UK's most important fiction prizes. It was awarded for both novels and short story collections. In 1999 it was replaced by the Guardian First Book Award, which is not restricted to works of fiction.

Winners of the *Guardian* Fiction Award from 1980 onwards have been:

1980 J.L. Carr, *A Month in the Country*
1981 John Banville, *Kepler*
1982 Glyn Hughes, *Where I Used to Play on the Green*
1983 Graham Swift, *Waterland*
1984 J.G. Ballard, *Empire of the Sun*
1985 Peter Ackroyd, *Hawksmoor*
1986 Jim Crace, *Continent*
1987 Peter Benson, *The Levels*
1988 Lucy Ellmann, *Sweet Desserts*
1989 Carol Lake, *Rose-Hill: Portrait from a Midlands City*
1990 Pauline Melville, *Shape-Shifter*
1991 Alan Judd, *The Devil's Own Work*
1992 Alasdair Gray, *Poor Things*
1993 Pat Barker, *The Eye in The Door*
1994 Candia McWilliams, *Debatable Land*
1995 James Buchan, *Heart's Journey in Winter*
1996 Seamus Deane, *Reading in the Dark*
1997 Anne Michaels, *Fugitive Pieces*
1998 Jackie Kay, *Trumpet*

Winners of the *Guardian* First Book Award have been:

1999 Philip Gourevitch, *We Wish to Inform You that Tomorrow We Will Be Killed with Our Families*
2000 Zadie Smith, *White Teeth*
2001 Chris Ware, *Jimmy Corrigan: The Smartest Kid on Earth*
2002 Jonathan Safron Foer, *Everything Is Illuminated*
2003 Robert Macfarlane, *Mountains of the Mind*
2004 Armand Marie Leroi, *Mutants*
2005 Alexander Masters, *Stuart: A Life Backwards*
2006 Yiyun Li, *A Thousand Years of Good Prayers*
2007 Dinaw Mengestu, *Children of the Revolution*
2008 Robert Macfarlane, *Mountains of the Mind*
2009 Petina Gappah, *An Elegy for Easterly*
2010 Alexandra Harris, *Romantic Moderns*
2011 Siddhartha Mukerjee, *The Emperor of All Maladies: A Biography of Cancer*
2012 Kevin Powers, *The Yellow Birds*
2013 Donal Ryan *The Spinning Heart*
2014 Colin Barrett *Young Skins*
2015 Andrew McMillan *Physical*

Discontinued 2016. No further awards.

The T. S. Eliot Prize

The T. S. Eliot Prize is administered by the Poetry Book Society, of which Eliot was a founding member in 1953. It was inaugurated in 1993 to celebrate the Society's fortieth anniversary and is awarded to the best new collection of poetry published in the UK or the Republic of Ireland the previous calendar year.

Winners since 2000 have been:

2000 Michael Longley, *The Weather in Japan*
2001 Anne Carson, *The Beauty of the Husband*
2002 Alice Oswald, *Dart*
2003 Don Paterson, *Landing Light*
2004 George Szirtes, *Reel*
2005 Carol Ann Duffy, *Rapture*
2006 Seamus Heaney, *District and Circle*
2007 Sean O'Brien, *The Drowned Book*
2008 Jen Hadfield, *Nigh-No-Place*
2009 Philip Gross, *The Water Table*
2010 Derek Walcott, *White Egrets*
2011 John Burnside *Black Cat Bone*
2012 Sharon Olds, *Stag's Leap*
2013 Sinéad Morrissey, *Parallax*
2014 David Harsent *Fire Songs*
2015 Sarah Howe *Loop of Jade*

FAMOUS SHIPS

Achille Lauro. An Italian cruise ship that was hijacked off Egypt by four members the Palestine Liberation Front in October 1985. A wheelchair-bound American, Leon Klinghoffer, was murdered before the hijackers surrendered in return for safe passage.

Amethyst, HMS. During the Chinese civil war in April 1949 this Royal Navy frigate was en route to Nanking on the Yangtse River when she was shelled and detained by the Communist forces. She succeeded in escaping, and her exploits were made into the 1957 film 'Yangtse Incident: The Story of HMS *Amethyst*.'

Amistad. In 1839 this schooner was seized by the African captives being transported in her from Cuba into slavery. They were taken into American custody and their legal status became the subject of a battle in the courts. The episode was made into the film 'Amistad' by Steven Spielberg in 1997.

Arizona, USS. American battleship that was sunk by the Japanese at Pearl Harbor on 7 December 1941. She remains *in situ* as a memorial to the 1,177 crew members who lost their lives.

Ark Royal, HMS. The name of three of the Royal Navy's purpose-built aircraft carriers. The first was launched in 1938, helped sink the *Bismarck* but was sunk by a German U-boat in the Mediterranean in 1941. The second was launched in 1950, in commission 1955–79 and scrapped in 1980. The third was launched in 1981, becoming the Fleet Flagship.

Aurora. This Russian cruiser took part in the battle of Tsushima against the Japanese in 1905 and in the 1917 October Revolution at St Petersburg. She is preserved as a museum ship on the River Neva at St Petersburg.

Beagle, HMS. Scientist Charles Darwin took part in the ship's survey expedition to South America and the Pacific 1831–6. The voyage, particularly the visit to the Galapagos Islands, led Darwin to formulate his ideas on evolution.

Belfast, HMS. *See* E13.

Bellerophon, HMS. A 74-gun warship that fought at the battle of Trafalgar. She is best known for the fact that Napoleon surrendered to her captain and was held on board after his defeat at Waterloo in 1815, before he was shipped to St Helena.

Bismarck. Germany's largest World War II battleship, which was located and destroyed by the Royal Navy on 27 May 1941. The story was told in the classic 1960 war film 'Sink the Bismarck!'

Bounty, HMS. This ship acquired notoriety in 1789 when some of her crew, led by Fletcher Christian, mutinied soon after leaving Tahiti and seized the ship from the captain, William Bligh.

Britannia, HM Yacht. The last Royal Yacht was launched in 1953 and retired in 1997. She is moored in Leith Harbour, Edinburgh, as a visitor attraction.

Conqueror, HMS. Nuclear-powered submarine, in service with the Royal Navy 1971–90. During the Falklands War she torpedoed and sank the Argentinian cruiser *General Belgrano* on 2 May 1982.

Constitution, USS. A US Navy frigate, nicknamed 'Old Ironsides', which was launched in 1797. She is berthed as a museum ship at Charlestown Navy Yard, Boston, and is the oldest warship in the world that is still in commission and afloat.

Cutty Sark. *See* E15.

Discovery, RRS (Royal Research Ship). Launched in 1901, she undertook the British National Antarctic Expedition, led by Captain Robert Scott, in 1901–4. She is at present preserved at Dundee where she was built.

Dreadnought, HMS. The first of the Royal Navy's 'all-big-gun' battleships and powered by steam turbines, she heralded a revolution in warship design when she was launched in 1906. She was scrapped in 1923.

Empire Windrush. Originally a German cruise ship, this vessel brought the first 500-strong group of immigrants from the Caribbean to settle in Britain in 1948.

Endeavour, HM Bark, Captain James Cook's ship on his first voyage of exploration to Australia and New Zealand in 1768–71. It was sunk in the American Revolutionary War off Rhode Island.

Endurance. Norwegian-built vessel in which Sir Ernest Shackleton sailed to explore the Antarctic in 1914. She was trapped by pack ice in the Weddell Sea and sank the following year.

Exodus 1947. The ship attempted to take more than 4,000 Jewish refugees from France to Palestine, then under British mandate, in 1947. She was intercepted by the Royal Navy, and the refugees were sent back to Europe.

Exxon Valdez. An Exxon Corporation tanker that caused an ecological disaster in 1989 when she hit a reef in Prince William Sound, Alaska, and spilled 9 million gallons of crude oil.

Fram. Specially designed to overcome the pressure of pack ice, this three-masted schooner was used by Norwegian explorers such as Nansen and Amundsen on their expeditions to the Arctic and Antarctic, 1893–1912. She is preserved as a museum ship in Oslo.

Golden Hind. English galleon, originally called the *Pelican*, in which Sir Francis Drake circumnavigated the globe, 1577–80.

Great Britain, SS. *See* E16.

Great Eastern, SS. Iron steamship designed by Isambard Kingdom Brunel to be able to reach India and Australia without re-coaling. She was the largest ship ever built when she was launched in 1858. After a chequered career, she was scrapped in 1889.

Great Western, SS. Steamship launched in 1837. Designed by Isambard Kingdom Brunel for the trans-Atlantic route. After working as a troopship in the Crimean War, she was broken up in 1856.

Gypsy Moth IV. A 54-foot ketch that was designed and built for Sir Francis Chichester, who carried out his single-handed circumnavigation in her, 1966–7.

Harmony of the Seas. Currently, the largest cruise ship ever built. It can carry 6,780 passengers with a crew of 2,300. With 23 swimming pools it is 361 metres long (equivalent to 10 London buses).

Herald of Free Enterprise. A Townsend Thoresen cross-Channel car ferry that sailed from Zeebrugge on the night of 6 March 1987 with her bow doors open. She capsized with the loss of 193 lives.

Holland 1. The first submarine commissioned by the Royal Navy in 1901. She is now preserved at the RN Submarine Museum, Gosport.

Hood, HMS. Royal Navy battlecruiser commissioned in 1920. Pride of the pre-war navy, she was sunk by the German battleship *Bismarck* in the battle of the Denmark Strait on 24 May 1941.

Kelly, HMS. Royal Navy destroyer commissioned in August 1939 and commanded by Lord Louis Mountbatten until she was sunk during the battle for Crete on 23 May 1941.

Kon-Tiki. A raft made of balsa logs on which Norwegian anthropologist Thor Heyerdahl sailed from South America across the Pacific to Polynesia in 1947 to prove his theory that the Polynesians came from South America. The raft is preserved at the Kon-Tiki Museum in Oslo.

La Gloire. French warship launched in 1859. As the first ironclad battleship she brought about a revolution in naval architecture.

Lancastria, **RMS**. Cunard liner that was launched in 1920 and requisitioned as a troopship in 1940. On 17 June 1940 she was bombed and sunk by German aircraft off the port of St Nazaire whilst evacuating civilian refugees and service personnel following the fall of France. There were 2,477 survivors and 1,738 known dead, but it is generally held that at least 4,000 lost their lives in what was the most costly British maritime disaster of the Second World War.

Lively Lady. This 36-foot yacht was built in Calcutta in 1948. Portsmouth greengrocer Sir Alec Rose carried out his solo circumnavigation in her in 1967–68.

Lusitania, **RMS**. Cunard ocean liner that was torpedoed and sunk by German submarine U-20 off the coast of Ireland on 7 May 1915. 1,198 lives were lost, including 128 citizens of the United States, provoking outrage there against Germany.

Maine, **USS**. American armoured cruiser that sank in Havana harbour, Cuba (then a Spanish colony) as a result of an unexplained explosion on 15 February 1898, with the loss of 266 lives. This gave rise to the slogan 'Remember the Maine and to Hell with Spain!' and precipitated the Spanish-American War.

Marchioness. In the early hours of 20 August 1989 a private party was taking place on this Thames pleasure boat, when she was struck by the dredger *Bowbelle*. She sank and 51 people died.

Mary Celeste. Mystery still surrounds what happened to the crew of this American brigantine found abandoned in the Atlantic in December 1872, en route from New York to Italy with a cargo of alcohol.

Mary Rose. *See* **E18**.

Mayflower. The ship that took the settlers known as the Pilgrim Fathers from Plymouth in Devon to New England in 1620.

Missouri, **USS**. Commissioned in June 1944, this was the last battleship to be completed for the US Navy. The Japanese signed the Instrument of Surrender on board in Tokyo Bay on 2 September 1945. She is preserved as a museum ship at Pearl Harbor.

Nautilus, **USS**. Commissioned by the US Navy in 1954 as its first nuclear-powered submarine. She is preserved as a museum at Groton, Connecticut.

Potemkin. Russian battleship of the Black Sea Fleet whose crew mutinied during the Revolution of 1905. The episode was the subject of Sergei Eisenstein's silent film 'Battleship Potemkin' in 1925.

PT-109. US Navy Motor Torpedo Boat commanded in the Pacific in World War II by the future president John F. Kennedy. In August 1943 she was run down by a Japanese destroyer, *Amagiri*. Kennedy was awarded the Navy and Marine Corps Medal for his actions after the sinking.

Queen Anne's Revenge. The flagship of the pirate Edward Teach, known as Blackbeard, in 1717–18. What is thought to be the wreck of the ship was found off the coast of North Carolina in 1996.

Queen Elizabeth (QE) 2, **RMS**. Cunard ocean liner, launched in 1967 and in service from 1969 to 2008 when she retired to become a floating hotel in Dubai.

Queen Elizabeth, **RMS**. When she was launched in 1938, this Cunard ship was the largest passenger liner ever built. She was in service from 1940 (as a

troopship) to 1968. After a fire, she was scrapped at Hong Kong in 1975.

Queen Mary, **RMS**. Cunard ocean liner, launched in 1934 and in service 1936 to 1967. She is now berthed in Long Beach, California as a visitor attraction and hotel.

Queen Mary 2, **RMS**. Launched in 2003, she is the largest ocean liner ever built and the flagship of the Cunard Line.

Rainbow Warrior. Greenpeace vessel that was sunk by explosive devices planted by the French secret service at Auckland, New Zealand, in 1985. A member of the crew was killed. At the time *Rainbow Warrior* was taking part in protests against French nuclear tests in the Pacific.

Revenge. English galleon captained by Sir Richard Grenville that was cut off and captured by the Spanish off the Azores in 1591. Her heroic fight was immortalised by Tennyson in his poem 'The Revenge: A Ballad of the Fleet' (1878).

Santa Maria. Flagship of the trio of ships that took part in Christopher Columbus' first voyage across the Atlantic to the New World in 1492. The other two ships were the *Pinta* and the *Nina*.

Tamzine. This 15-foot fishing boat was the smallest of the 'Little Ships' that took part in the Dunkirk evacuation in 1940. She is preserved at the Imperial War Museum in London.

Temeraire, **HMS**. 98-gun ship that fought at the battle of Trafalgar in 1805, but is best remembered as the subject of J.M.W. Turner's painting 'The Fighting Temeraire' (1838), showing her being towed by a paddle steamer to be broken up.

Titanic, **RMS**. White Star Line passenger liner that struck an iceberg on her maiden voyage across the Atlantic and sank early on 15 April 1912. 1,517 lives were lost. Her remains were located in 1985. New research suggests a fire on the *Titanic* may have played a major role.

Torrey Canyon. Supertanker that struck a reef between Cornwall and the Scilly Isles in 1967. Her cargo of crude oil caused major pollution and damage to wildlife.

Trincomalee, **HMS**. Royal Navy frigate built in India and launched in 1817. She is preserved as a museum ship at Hartlepool, and is the oldest British warship still afloat.

Vasa. Warship built for King Gustaphus Adolphus of Sweden that capsized on her maiden voyage in 1628. She was salvaged in 1961 and is on display in Stockholm.

Victory, **HMS**. *See* **E20**.

Warrior, **HMS**. *See* **E21**.

White Ship. When this ship foundered in the English Channel in 1120, the son and heir of King Henry I, William Adelin, was drowned. It was said that King Henry 'never smiled again.'

Yamato. Imperial Japanese Navy warship launched in 1940. The *Yamato* and her sister ship, *Musashi*, were the largest and most powerful battleships ever built. She was sunk by US aircraft off Okinawa on 7 April 1945.

Yorktown, **USS**. Named after her predecessor sunk at the battle of Midway in 1942, this US aircraft carrier was launched in 1943 and served in the Pacific during the closing stages of World War II. Decommissioned in 1970, she is at present preserved as a museum ship at Mount Pleasant, South Carolina.

ORDER OF SUCCESSION
(as at June 2017)

The ten persons in line of succession to the throne of the United Kingdom are listed below. Under the new Succession to the Crown Act the first child born to the Duchess of Cambridge, whether a boy or girl, became third in line to the throne.

1 The Prince of Wales
2 Prince William of Wales
3 Prince George of Cambridge
4 Princess Charlotte of Cambridge
5 Prince Henry of Wales (known as Harry)
6 The Duke of York
7 Princess Beatrice of York
8 Princess Eugenie of York
9 The Earl of Wessex
10 The Viscount Severn

THE PHONETIC ALPHABET

A	Alpha	J	Juliet	S	Sierra
B	Bravo	K	Kilo	T	Tango
C	Charlie	L	Lima	U	Uniform
D	Delta	M	Mike	V	Victor
E	Echo	N	November	W	Whiskey
F	Foxtrot	O	Oscar	X	X-Ray
G	Golf	P	Papa	Y	Yankee
H	Hotel	Q	Quebec	Z	Zulu
I	India	R	Romeo		

CHINESE CALENDAR

Each successive year in the Chinese Calendar is named after one of 12 animals. The year 2017 was the year of the rooster.
Thereafter they are as follows:

2018	Dog	2021	Ox
2019	Pig	2022	Tiger
2020	Rat	2023	Rabbit

PATRON SAINTS

Among the many Patron Saints of countries are those listed below:

Australia	Our Lady Help of Christians
Belgium	Joseph
Canada	Joseph, Anne
Denmark	Asgar, Canute
England	George
France	Several*
Germany	Boniface, Michael
Greece	Nicholas, Andrew
Hungary	Stephen, Our Lady
India	Our Lady of the Assumption
Ireland	Patrick
Italy	Francis of Assisi, Catherine of Siena
Netherlands	Willibrord
New Zealand	Our Lady Help of Christians
Norway	Olaf
Poland	Our Lady of Czestochowa, Casimir, Stanislaus
Portugal	Cyriacus
Russia	Andrew, Nicholas, Thérèse of Lisieux
Scotland	Andrew, Columba
South Africa	Our Lady of the Assumption
Spain	James, Theresa
Sweden	Bridget, Eric
Wales	David
West Indies	Gertrude

* Unofficial patron saints include Joan of Arc, Denys, Louis, Thérèse and Our Lady of the Assumption.

HINDU CALENDAR

Month	Days	Month	Days
Caitra	30*	Asvina	30
Vaisakha	31	Kartika	30
Jyaistha	31	Agrahayana	30
Asadha	31	Pausa	30
Sravana	31	Magha	30
Bhadra	31	Phalguna	30

* In a leap year Caitra has 31 days.

EASTER DAY
(and associated Church Festival Dates)*

Year	Ash Wednesday	Easter Day	Ascension Day	Whit Sunday
2018	14 February	1 April	10 May	20 May
2019	6 March	21 April	30 May	9 June
2020	26 February	12 April	21 May	31 May
2021	17 February	4 April	13 May	23 May
2022	2 March	17 April	26 May	5 June
2023	22 February	9 April	18 May	28 May
2024	14 February	31 March	9 May	19 May
2025	5 March	20 April	29 May	8 June

* For a note on the origin of Easter and the dates on which it can fall, *see* **L34**.

SIGNS OF THE ZODIAC

Sign	Symbol	Dates
Aries	The Ram	21 March–19 April
Taurus	The Bull	20 April–20 May
Gemini	The Twins	21 May–21 June
Cancer	The Crab	22 June–22 July
Leo	The Lion	23 July–22 August
Virgo	The Virgin	23 August–22 September
Libra	The Balance	23 September–23 October
Scorpio	The Scorpion	24 October–21 November
Sagittarius	The Archer	22 November–21 December
Capricorn	The Goat	22 December–19 January
Aquarius	The Water Bearer	20 January–18 February
Pisces	The Fishes	19 February–20 March

ANTIQUES GLOSSARY

Acanthus, a thistle-like plant which grows abundantly in the Mediterranean countries, and which has inspired decorators from classical antiquity to modern times to fine leaf ornaments. The acanthus appears on Corinthian columns on Greek and Roman temples, it lends its rhythm to stone carvings on medieval cathedrals, and runs in friezes on innumerable Renaissance buildings and art objects. During the Baroque, it appears, rich and majestic, handled with particular grandeur in England by Grinling Gibbons (1648–1721). In the revival styles of the 19th cent., the acanthus appears in all kinds of connections.

One reason for the never-ending popularity of the acanthus is that it can be adapted to almost any shape, to fit the capital of a column as well as a frieze or an "un-ending" flat pattern. And it can be interpreted in any material, carved in stone or wood, printed and painted, woven in silk, wrought in iron—the possibilities are endless.

Animaliers (Fr. = "animal makers"), term used to describe the group of French 19th cent. sculptors who specialised in the modelling of animals. They made them singly or in pairs to form a group and the animals are described in much naturalistic detail and always in vigorous movement, leaping, running, fighting. They are cast in bronze, in dimensions small enough for them to be used as table ornaments. The originator of the genre was Antoine-Louis Baryc (1796–1875)

The quality of the works of *les animaliers* can vary greatly, and there has been much recasting of good models, with results which are inevitably imperfect.

Aquamanile (Lat. *aqua* = water and *manus* – hand), an ewer of brass or bronze used for ceremonial hand-washing for church or lay purposes during the Middle Ages. One popular and picturesque version has the shape of a standing lion. Its body contains the water, which can be poured out through a spout concealed in its tongue, while the tail is twirled up to serve as handle.

Arabesque, a decorative motif consisting of curved and interlacing lines, symmetrically arranged: a stylised interpretation of branches, tendrils and leaves as seen in nature. As the name suggests, the motif was invented by the Arabs, who used it for hundreds of years, partly because the representation of beings, animal or human, was not permitted by their culture. Arabesques were used most impressively to cover large areas, like tiled walls and carpets. From the Renaissance onwards, the Europeans adapted the arabesque to decorate inlaid furniture, ceramic plates and tiles and textiles.

Arita. *See* **Imari.**

Automobile mascots, sculptured ornaments affixed to the bonnet of motor-cars. They came into fashion immediately after the first world war, when fast cars became symbols of the modern age of streamlined speed. The mascots have been made in a variety of materials, silver or silver plate, brass and bronze, cast glass. The figures usually suggest speed (girls' heads or figures facing the oncoming wind with ecstatic joy) or power (prancing horses, falcons' heads). They have become increasingly collectable.

Biscuit (Fr. = "twice baked"), porcelain (*see* **L88**) which has been fired but not glazed. This gives a matted marble-like surface, and *biscuit* has been widely used for porcelain sculpture.

Blanc-de-Chine, a kind of Chinese porcelain, made into vessels or figures, covered with a fine, milky-white glaze and otherwise unornamented. Within the great ceramic history of China, *blanc-de-Chine* represents a distinctive and strictly limited group. It was made during the 18th, 19th and 20th centuries in Të-Hua in Fukien province. Much of it was exported to Europe. The serene figure of the female

deity Kuan-Yin has always been very popular in the West, and many models have been made, varying from the exquisite to the clumsy and angular. Of great interest are also the groups of Europeans with their Chinese servants, made in Të-Hua for the Western market.

Boulle (**Buhl**) furniture, a luxurious kind of case furniture, first made in Paris by the Court cabinet-maker André-Charles Boulle (Buhl is the Germanised form) (1642–1732). Cupboards, chests, clocks, *etc.* are veneered with tortoiseshell and inlaid with patterns in bronze.

The technique was practised in Paris throughout the 18th cent. by the sons and successors of André-Charles Boulle, and later by imitators in many countries. Boulle furniture has been made right up to recent times.

Britannia Metal, a soft variety of pewter compounded of tin, antimony and copper. It was first made in Sheffield during the late 18th cent. under the name of White Metal and used as a cheap substitute for pewter. The name Britannia Metal was introduced in 1817. By the 1840s it was increasingly being electroplated (*q.v.*) with silver. Such wares are frequently marked EPBM = Electro Plated Britannia Metal, the letters being placed in separate oval frames to simulate hallmarks on silver. The metal and its markings continued in use well into the 20th cent.

Bullet teapot, a modern collectors' term for silver teapots, as first made by Huguenot goldsmiths in London at the time of Queen Anne, with the body and its cover made in the form of a sphere, with a low foot and a spout of silver and a black wooden handle. Bullet teapots were also made after the reign of Queen Anne, and the shape was eventually translated into porcelain and earthenware, in England and on the Continent.

Cameos are cut from stones or from shells which have natural layers of different colours, so that the ornaments stand in high relief as well as in a contrasting colour against the background. The Italians have always been masters in cameo-cutting. During the 19th cent. they had a large production of shell cameos with white figures on a brown ground, the whole mounted in gold or silver and used as brooches. Today cameos are being mass-produced in manmade materials in imitation of the genuine articles.

Candlesticks have of course been household necessities as long as candles were main means of lighting. Over the ages people have rigged up all kinds of cheap and simple candleholders, but the handsome tall candlestick on a steady foot has existed since the late Middle Ages. They have been made in brass and pewter, silver or Sheffield plate in ever-varying forms.

Cased glass, a technique whereby clear or coloured glass is covered by a layer of glass in a different shade; when patterns are cut through the top layer the inner core will be revealed and interesting colour effects and contrasts result. The most famous piece of cased glass in history is the Portland Vase, of Roman make (1st cent. A.D.) now in the British Museum (*see* **Section N**).

Celadon, a soft greyish-green coloured glaze, widely used on Chinese pottery and porcelain from the Sung period (960–1279) and well into the 19th cent. The name was given it by the Europeans: in Honoré d'Urfé's 17th cent. pastoral romance "L'Astreé" a shepherd called Celadon wore a costume of this subtle and beautiful colour. The French imported a lot of Celadon ware from China during the 18th cent., and the best pieces were mounted in elaborate bronze.

Champlevé. *See* **Enamel.**

Chinoiserie, ornamentation used in 17th, 18th and

early 19th cent. Europe, which made wide use of Oriental themes: "chinamen", pagodas, bells, parasols, dragons and the like. Chinoiserie was preferably used on porcelain, silks and lacquered furniture, materials which were admiringly associated with China and the East. It was also expressed in architecture, in garden houses in pagoda and pavilion style, the Pagoda in Kew Gardens, built in 1762 by Sir William Chambers, being a famous example. Chinoiserie was based on an incomplete knowledge of the Oriental models, and this gave full scope for imagination and caprice on the part of the European designers. The best examples date from early and mid 18th cent., the rococo versions being particularly charming and suggestive of "the dream of Cathay".

Chippendale Furniture was introduced in the reign of George I by Thomas Chippendale, a cabinetmaker from Yorkshire who migrated to London and set up for himself in St. Martin's Lane, Charing Cross (*see* **B15**). He was fonder of inventing designs for furniture than of making it, and in 1752 published a book of patterns; the London furniture-makers of the day soon began to model their work upon it.

Cloisonné. *See* **Enamel.**

Clutha glass, decorative vessels of tinted glass, made during the 1890s by the Glasgow firm of James Couper & Sons to designs by Christopher Dresser. The glass, usually amber or green, is made purposely rough and "primitive" with bubbles and striations, and formed into free, furnace-worked shapes. Occasionally other colours were added. The more elaborate examples are marked underneath in acid-etching with C L U T H A and name of producer and designer.

Cranberry glass, a modern collectors' term for Victorian glass of a deep red colour. It is reminiscent of the famous 17th-cent. ruby glass, but it is less brilliantly red and was cheaper to make. It had its great vogue during the latter part of the 19th cent., and was used for all manner of objects, often combined with clear glass in handles, stems and the like.

Creamware, a ceramic material which has a cream-coloured glaze over a solid and resistant body, the clay usually containing calcined flint. Creamware was developed in Staffordshire during the middle years of the 18th cent., and brought to perfection in the course of the 1760s by Josiah Wedgwood. He formed the new ware into shapes which were at the same time practical and handsome, suitable for every household, and with a distinctive touch of the Neo-Classical style which was just coming into fashion. When his product was complete and perfect, he appealed to Royalty for patronage, and received permission to call his invention Queen's Ware.

Soon creamware was put into production by most Staffordshire firms, and, most importantly, by the factory at Leeds, which became a major producer. Because of its excellent ceramic qualities, its elegant appearance and reasonable price, creamware became the standard material for plates, dishes and the like all over the world, and by the beginning of the 19th cent. it was being widely produced on the Continent. The rise of creamware meant the decline of faience (*q.v.*).

English creamware was long the basis for most of the ceramic tableware used in the world.

Cymric silver, jewellery, table-silver and plate in a "Celtic" variety of the Art Nouveau (*see* **N3**), made by various designers and producers to the orders of Liberty's of Regent Street and sold in their shop. The objects were serially produced, but looked hand-made, with a wide use of enamelling, stones and "hammered" surfaces. Many examples have the word CYMRIC struck next to maker's mark. The best period for Cymric silver was *c.* 1900–12, but the genre was not finally given up until 1927. *See also* **Tudric pewter.**

Davenport, a special type of writing desk, originally made for travelling, small in size, with a sloping top

and three or four drawers opening to the side. According to tradition, it got its name from one Captain Davenport, who ordered such a desk from Gillow's in Lancaster in the early 19th cent. This is, however, apparently apocryphal, for the type has now been traced back to the late 18th cent. The early examples are compact in shape and devoid of ornamentation. But as the 19th cent. proceeded, the type became popular as a lady's desk, and it was provided with pigeon-holes on top and richly ornamented in Neo-Rococo. Most of the extant examples are veneered with mahogany. Davenports remained in regular use until the end of the Victorian age.

Dolls have for a long time been important collectors' items. Connoisseurs distinguish expertly between dolls with heads of wax or bisque (= biscuit, *q.v.*). Eyes, wigs and of course clothes also influence prices, and so do marks and makers' signatures. The dolls which change hands date almost exclusively from the 19th and 20th cents. Related material like doll's-house furniture and toys is normally included in the sales. Anybody interested in this highly specialized branch of collecting is advised to study the Christie catalogues and the literature that has grown up around the subject.

Electroplating. The process of coating one metal with another by the use of an electric current was invented during the early years of the 19th cent., but became widely used, especially in Sheffield and Birmingham, after 1840 when the Birmingham firm of Elkington patented their method for coating copper with silver in this manner. Eventually nickel silver, compounded of nickel, copper and zinc, was increasingly employed as a base for the silver plating, and the products were marked EPNS = Electro Plated Nickel Silver, the letters being sometimes placed in separate oval frames to simulate hallmarks on silver. This ware was widely used until the 1920s and 1930s.

Enamel, is glass, usually brilliantly coloured, which has been crushed to powder and mixed with oily fluids. It is applied to metal, pottery and glass for decorative purposes.

When applied to faience (*q.v.*) or porcelain (*q.v.*), the enamels are painted on to the glazed surface, the object is fired at a moderate temperature and the colours will be permanently fixed. Similar methods are used for enamelling on glass, both vessels and windows, and for enamelling on enamelled surfaces, as practised so charmingly in Birmingham and Bilston during the 18th cent.

When applied to the hard, smooth surfaces of metals, special methods are needed to prevent the colours from running. Among the most important are:

Champlevé: the outlines of the pattern are engraved or cut into the surface, and the enamel is poured into the grooves.

Cloisonné: the outlines of the pattern are drawn up by tiny dividing walls which are soldered on to the surface, and the enamels are poured into the spaces in between.

Plique-à-jour: enamels are filled into the empty spaces in a carefully prepared net of metal threads.

Enamelling has been practised with mastery in ancient, medieval and modern times. The Chinese and Japanese have used enamels on copper and brass in complex combinations for several hundred years. During the 19th century French artist-craftsmen used all techniques most delicately, while Russian enamelling of the same period is picturesque and robust, and became widely influential.

Épergne, centrepiece for the luxuriously laid table, carrying baskets and bowls for sweets, nuts, fruit, macaroons and the like. It is an 18th-cent. invention, and was at first made in silver, later in colourful porcelain or earthenware, in glass and eventually in Sheffield plate. Its purpose was always more to be ornamental than useful, and in the making of épergnes, goldsmiths, potters and glassmakers let their fancy roam freely, whether making them in rococo or neo-classical form or as Chinoiserie (*q.v.*).

Etagère. *See* **Whatnot.**

Fabergé, Peter Carl (1846–1920). Russian goldsmith. From 1870 onwards his firm in St. Petersburg produced great quantities of luxury goods, mostly miniature objects such as gold boxes, picture frames, cigarette cases, umbrella handles, all finely wrought, richly enamelled and some even set with precious stones. Famous are his Easter eggs, which, when opened, are found to contain a tiny model of a carriage, a string of miniature pictures framed in gold and skilfully folded, and the like. The firm also made miniature figures of animals carved in semi-precious stones such as agate and neophryte, and other varieties of super sophisticated luxury trinkets.

Fabergé's products had a rich, aristocratic and international clientèle, with the Imperial family as the keenest patrons of all. He employed a large staff of first-rate goldsmiths, and had a phenomenal commercial success, running branches in Moscow, Odessa, Kiev and for a time also in London. The whole structure collapsed with the revolution in 1917. Fabergé products are sometimes marked with his name in Russian characters and the mark of the workmaster, under whose supervision the object was made.

Faience, a ceramic ware of porous, lightweight, fired clay covered with a milky-white, non-transparent tin glaze. It began as an imitation of Chinese porcelain, and was usually decorated with coloured ornamentation. As the painted motifs have to be applied directly on to the wet glaze to be fired with it, the colours are absorbed into the damp surface as if it were blotting-paper, and the painter has to work fast, without changing his mind or correcting his work. This gives to faience painting an imminence, at times a nonchalance, which is its greatest charm.

The name faience is derived from Faenza, the name of a north Italian town, which has had a large and important output from the 15th cent. to this day. But Faenza was only one of many centres in Italy to produce this kind of ware during the Renaissance, which in some contexts is described as Maiolica (*q.v.*).

The word faience is applied more specifically to tin-glazed ceramic ware made in northern Europe during post-Renaissance times.

Fairings (lit, a gift bought from a fair), small porcelain groups telling simple stories of a sentimental or gross kind, with titles painted on the base like "The Orphan" or "The Wedding Night". They were made for the English market in Germany from the late 19th cent. until 1914, the firm of Conta & Böhme in Saxony being particularly productive. They were cheap to buy at the time, today they are collectors' items. They have been made in modern copies.

Friggers, objects made by glassblowers outside working hours. Some were made by apprentices in training, others by highly-skilled and experienced men, who could display their personal fancies and idiosyncracies more freely when "friggering" than when working on instructions to produce commercial goods.

Furnace-work, the forming and decorating of vessels by the glassblower in front of his furnace, while the glass is still hot and pliable.

Gallé, Emile (1846–1904) of Nancy in Lorraine, maker of art glass, decorative pottery and luxury furniture, and a main exponent of Art Nouveau (*see* **N3**) in Europe. Gallé began making decorative glass during the 1870s, and at the Paris exhibition in 1889 he created a world sensation with his imaginative and technically complex art glass. In that year he began the production of carved and inlaid furniture, while he went on developing his glassmaking to ever greater heights of intricacy and sophistication. Flowers, leaves and insects were the chief decorative themes, and texts from contemporary poets were sometimes integrated into the patterns. He invented endless variations and combinations of coloured glass, many models being produced in a personal version of the cased glass technique (*q.v.*).

The output of his factories was enormous, and while the standardized cased glass models made for the commercial market may become monotonous, those composed for individual clients in one to five copies are marvels of beauty and originality. Every item that left the works in Nancy was marked with his full name.

Pottery production, which was never very important, seems to have ended in 1892 and furniture making finished with his death. But the glassmaking plant carried on until 1935, making standardized cased glass in an ever more repetitive manner, and still signed with his name. This long posthumous production of indifferent glass has done much to lower his reputation.

Goss, ware from the Staffordshire pottery, founded by W. H. Goss in 1858 and active until the Second World War. Its fame is mainly built on the masses of miniature models in porcelain of objects of local fame or association, with the arms of the locality printed in colours, like the Coronation Chair with the arms of Westminster.

Goss mementoes have been collected systematically since before the First World War.

The firm also produced statuettes in Parian (*q.v.*), models of the houses of famous men and many other small, toy-like objects.

Imari, a port on the Japanese island of Kyushu, whence porcelain made at the nearby production centre of Arita was exported in large quantities. The name applies particularly to the wares made from the 17th cent. and until recently, with red and dark blue ornaments on a white ground, accompanied by plenty of gilding: in essence the style changed little over the long period when Imari porcelain enjoyed its great popularity in the West.

The best examples are very fine, while other pieces made in the later stages can often be somewhat crude.

Isnik pottery, a kind of faience (*q.v.*), made in Isnik in Anatolia between *c*. 1550 and 1700. Characteristic are the bold floral designs in brilliant blues, greens and tomato reds, which decorate plates and dishes, bowls, ewers and tiles. Isnik pottery was made in great quantities.

Kelmscott Press, a printing press set up in 1890 by William Morris (*see* **B43**) in a cottage in Hammersmith. Here he produced *c*. 50 books from handcut and specially designed type, on handmade paper, every page being most carefully laid out with exquisite borders and vignettes. Medieval illuminated manuscript books and early printed books were his chief sources of inspiration. The Kelmscott Press finished working in 1896, two years after Morris's death. Morris's work sparked off a long-lasting revival in fine book production at home and abroad.

The press was named after Kelmscott Manor in Gloucestershire, which Morrris had acquired as a summer home in 1871. He is buried in the village church, and the Manor, which contains many Morris memories, is open to the public.

Macdonald, Margaret. *See* **Mackintosh, Charles Rennie.**

Mackintosh, Charles Rennie (1863–1928), Scottish architect and designer. From the late 1890s until the First World War he designed several important buildings in Glasgow and elsewhere in Scotland, and he also composed complete interiors, including the furniture, clocks, light-fittings, *etc*. His taste for what was simple and rectilinear was remarkably advanced for his time, and perfectly attuned to the new sober intellectual style that was emerging on the Continent. At exhibitions in Vienna in 1900 and in Turin in 1902 he gained enthusiastic international recognition. He married Margaret Macdonald (1865–1933), an important artist and designer in her own right.

Mahogany, a very hard wood with a fine grain and distinctive markings. Because it is so hard, carved work retains its precision even after years of wear. Mahogany can also be polished to a wonderfully high gloss and sparkle. Because of these qualities it has been widely used for fine furniture ever since it was first imported into Europe early in the 18th cent. The dark Cuban mahogany (Swietenia) was first used most widely, later much fine mahogany (Khaya) from Africa was in demand. The English were the first to use mahogany for furniture, and it gave distinctive character to many of their finest 18th cent. products, like the chairs in the styles of Chippendale and Hepplewhite (*q.v.*) and, as veneers, on chests and cupboards.

Maiolica, a ceramic ware with a white tin glaze and decorated with painted figures, often with a metallic lustre sheen. The name itself appears to have been derived from Majorca because ware of this kind by Spanish-Moorish potters was largely imported into Italy, the ships arriving by way of this island. The name has been retained for tin-glazed ware with painted decoration made in various Italian centres during the Renaissance, but it can also be defined as Faience (*q.v.*).

Majolica, a ceramic ware of the 19th cent., invented at the Minton factory in 1849, and imitated all over Europe within a short time. It is a kind of earthenware, suitable for bold modelling on a large scale, and when covered with colourful glazes in greens and browns, particularly well suited for outdoor goods, *jardinières* on tall stands or decorative sculptures. Majolica tiles became extremely popular for covering halls, kitchens, *etc.* Some of them are handsomely provided with relief decoration, while the fact that they could easily be washed down with water added to their popularity.

Marquetry, inlaid work of woods in contrasting colours. The patterns can be geometrical (and this is particularly suitable when marquetry is used for floors), but the technique can also be applied to veneered furniture, with delicate motifs of flowers, animals or human figures with lively curves and much fine detail.

Mary Gregory glass, an imprecise but generally accepted term used to describe a group of 19th cent. coloured glass decorated in opaque white enamels with pretty pictures of children playing and the like. The genre probably originated in Bohemia, but it was widely produced also in Britain and in the USA. Mary Gregory is believed to have been an American glass painter, but nothing is known of her life or personality, and no existing piece of glass can be ascribed to her.

Netsuke, a clasp or sliding toggle, used on the sash of the Japanese kimono, to carry a small bag or box for the little necessities of daily life. Netsuke can be made in a variety of materials, wood, horn, ivory, bamboo, *etc.*; and carved into sculptured forms or covered with black lacquer ornamented with pictures in gold. The subjects of the decorations are usually taken from Japanese folklore or mythology. Netsuke have been collectors' items for many decades.

Niello, a method for decorating silver. A line pattern is engraved into the silver surface, and the lines are filled with an alloy of metals, which produces a black colour. The black makes a handsome contrast to the whiteness of the silver, and niello has been one of the most ancient ways of ornamenting the precious metal, having been used in classical antiquity as well as in pre-Christian and medieval Europe. Later, it gave way to more sophisticated methods of decoration.

Opaline, modern collectors' word used to describe an important group of French 19th cent. ornamental glass. *Opaline* is made of opaque, usually milky-white glass with an opalescent sheen. The best *opaline* is the earliest, which dates from the Napoleonic period and the Restoration. It comes in vases, urns, ewers and the like, severely Neo-Classical in shape and frequently mounted in brass or bronze. After *c*. 1830, the shapes become less austere, and the glass is sometimes tinted into pastel shades. *Opaline* became widely used for dainty flacons for ladies' boudoirs and decorated with gilding and pretty painted flowers. After *c*. 1860 the whole genre degenerated; the opalescent glass was replaced by a grey and dull kind of material, and decorations in relief were produced by machine-

pressing. *Opaline* with painted decorations was also made in England.

Papier-mâché (French, literally: "chewed paper"), one of the earliest man-made materials, produced from pulped paper, rags, chalk, sand and glues. After mixing and preparation, it becomes plastic and can be pressed and formed into any variety of shapes. When covered in black varnish, inlaid with mother-of-pearl, gilt and painted, it becomes very attractive. *Papier-mâché* was invented in England in the late 18th cent., and Birmingham became an important centre of production. It was particularly well suited for trays, covered boxes and other small and medium-sized objects, but by the middle of the 19th cent. whole pieces of furniture of *papier-mâché* were also being made. By this time, the taste for it had spread to the Continent, and it was soon being widely produced in Europe.

The fashion for *papier-mâché* declined towards the end of the century, when the market was being flooded by so many new inventions of materials and processes.

Parian ware, a kind of opaque white porcelain with a surface that gives an illusion of marble. It was invented in England *c*. 1845, and used by many porcelain factories for the production of statuettes, groups and busts in sculptured forms for use as ornaments for parlours; it was sometimes called "statuary porcelain". Parian ware was imitated, name and all, in many European countries and in the USA.

The name is derived from Paros, a Greek island which in classical antiquity provided a particularly fine marble, much sought after by sculptors.

Pastille burners, miniature models of buildings, made of Staffordshire earthenware, glazed and painted, and often of fantastic shapes, with plenty of window openings. When a pastille was burned inside, the windows lit up prettily. These Victorian pieces of amusement were made in quantity from *c*. 1835 onwards. In their period they cost a few shillings, today they fetch high prices at auctions and in shops.

Plique-à-jour. *See* **Enamel**.

Porcelain. The word is thought to be derived from the Italian *porcellana*, indicating the texture of a piglet. The majority of porcelain made on the continent was of "hard-paste", or true porcelain, similar to that discovered by the Chinese as early as the T'ang Dynasty (A.D. 618–907). It was composed of *kaolin* (china-clay) and *petuntse* (china-stone) which when fired in a kiln at a temperature of *c*. 1300°C became an extremely hard and translucent material. The old recipe for "hard-paste" porcelain remained a secret of the Chinese until 1709, when it was rediscovered in Europe by Johann Böttger of the Meissen factory (popularly known as Dresden). Aided by disloyal Meissen workmen, factories were later established at Vienna, Venice and in many parts of Germany. Plymouth and Bristol were the only English factories to produce this type of porcelain, from 1768 to 1781. Elsewhere, both in England and France, the material manufactured was known as "soft-paste" or artificial porcelain which was made by blending varying white-firing clays with the ingredients of glass. The French factory of Sèvres began to make some hard-paste porcelain by 1768 and by the 19th cent. such porcelain was the only type being made throughout the whole of the continent. In England Josiah Spode is credited with the introduction of "bone-china" about 1794. This hybrid-paste was quickly adopted by many factories and remains popular.

Printed decoration on pottery, the most usual kind of ornamentation for table-services of earthenware throughout the 19th cent. and into modern times. In its simplest form the process worked like this: The pattern or motif desired was engraved into a steel or copper plate, printed on to a piece of thin paper, and from there transferred on to the piece of pottery (thence the expression transfer printing). In the kiln the colour was fixed to the surface. The method was perfected by a Liverpool printer. John Sadler, and put into commercial use on Wedgwood creamware (q.v.) c. 1760. Sadler & Green, as the firm became in 1763, executed printing on ware from many potteries in the Midlands. It was active until 1799, but by that time most potteries had acquired their own printing equipment.

During the 19th cent. printing was constantly improved upon, to give richer and more finely shaded colours. While early printing is usually done in black, blue became the favourite colour of the 19th cent. By 1840 it was possible to produce multi-coloured printed patterns. Printing on pottery was practised outside Britain from the late 18th cent. See **Willow pattern**.

Puzzle-jug, a ewer or tankard facetiously made with a perforated neck and other unexpected leakages, so that whoever drank from it would find the contents spilling down their clothes. The type was made in pottery during the 17th and 18th cents., and reflects the love of practical jokes of the period.

Roemer, the wineglass with the most ancient history. It has a rounded bowl, a broad hollow stem with "strawberries" or prunts, and a tall foot made of coiled-up glass thread. The basic shape is known from classical antiquity as well as from southern and eastern Europe during the mediæval period. During the Renaissance it was revived in the Rhine area and became the classic vessel for the drinking of Rhenish wines, a role it has retained to this day.

The early examples are of rough green glass, but during the 17th cent., Roemers were sometimes made from fine, crystal-clear glass or from glass purposely tinted into a bright green. The tradition of the green glass for German wines dates from this period. The 19th cent. saw a revival of the ancient form, in a number of new varieties. Modern Roemers have the rounded bowl, the prunts and the tall stem with horizontal lines. They are usually made of tinted glass in green or mauve or brown, and sometimes vineleaves are engraved on the bowl.

Satinwood, an exotic kind of wood, blond in colour, with a fine grain and a silky sheen. From c. 1770 until c. 1800 it was widely used for small and exquisite pieces of furniture in the Adam Style. Rarer than mahogany, satinwood was used mainly for veneering and throughout the 19th cent. for small inlaid motifs on less expensive woods. During the 18th cent. satinwood was imported mainly from the West and East Indies, though it has also been found in Tasmania and Florida. During the Edwardian period satinwood furniture enjoyed a brief revival.

Sewing table, came into fashion c. 1820. It usually stands on a pedestal with three feet, the table itself being oval, octagonal or of some other interesting shape, prettily made with a lift-up lid covering neat little compartments for silks, thimbles, etc., usually a pin-cushion and perhaps a mirror. Underneath is a bag to hold the work in hand. Much fine work of inlay, painting and upholstery was lavished on these charming pieces of ladies' furniture.

Shaving bowl, of the approximate shape of a large soup plate with a segment cut out of the edge so that the barber could hold it comfortably under the chin of his client while applying lather to his face. Shaving bowls date mainly from the late 17th and 18th cents. Some are made of pewter, but the majority are of faience or porcelain, occasionally with painted decorations in the form of barbers' requisites, like combs, scissors, knives, saws and lancets, barbers of the period acting also as surgeons.

Sheffield plate, a substitute for solid silver, consisting of a copper base coated on both sides with silver, the whole fused into one indissoluble whole and rolled into plate from which the desired objects are formed. The method was invented in Sheffield by Thomas Bolsover c. 1742. The new, cheap, silver-like plate became very popular, and was soon being widely produced not only in Sheffield, but in Birmingham, London, Edinburgh and elsewhere, and by firms outside Britain. The special character of the fused plate imposed certain limits on the makers. The normal goldsmith's methods of decorating by engraving and chasing were not suitable, while wirework came out beautifully, as did orna-

mental borders and ornaments, cast separately and soldered on to the plated body.

Sheffield plate had its finest period from c. 1780 onwards, when technical methods had been perfected and aesthetic possibilities exploited to the full. By c. 1840 it was ousted by even cheaper silver substitutes (see **Britannia Metal and Electroplating**).

Today objects of old Sheffield plate are sought-after antiques. The old methods have, however, been revived in modern times in traditional shapes.

Ship-bowls, made of faience (q.v.) in sea-ports such as Bristol, Liverpool and Hamburg were made for sale to visiting sea-captains. The bowls are usually decorated in blue with the picture of a sailing-ship in the centre, and with the name of the captain and his vessel on the rim. The ship pictures are conventional, and should not be accepted as "portraits" of the ships named. The genre belongs mainly to the 18th cent.

Snuffers, used for snuffing candles and formed like a pair of scissors with a small, square box positioned on one of the blades to catch the glowing, smoking wick-end. Examples survive from the late 17th cent., and they remained in use as long as candles were a normal kind of lighting in the home. Snuffers were usually made of brass or steel.

Transfer printing. See **Printed decoration on pottery**.

Tudric pewter, was made by the Birmingham firm of Haseler to designs by various artists under the sponsorship of Liberty's of Regent Street, who sold it in their shop. The style is a "Celtic" variety of the Art Nouveau (see **N3**), and many of the preserved examples are stamped TUDRIC. The best period was c. 1800–1914, but the production lingered on until well into the 1930s. See **Cymric silver**.

Tunbridge ware, small wooden objects, some turned (cups, bowls and dishes), most of them joined and inlaid (boxes, gaming boards and the like), made mostly from local woods by local craftsmen in Tunbridge Wells and sold in quantity to visitors who flocked to take the waters at the spa. Tunbridge work is mentioned in documents from the late 17th cent., but the most productive period was from c. 1820 to 1870. Occasionally products bear makers' labels. Some London firms produced woodwork in the Tunbridge style in the 18th cent., and called it "Tunbridge Ware" in their advertisements.

Whatnot, a piece of furniture made of three to five shelves or trays, placed one above the other between four corner-supports. The whatnot, which in France is called an elagère, became fashionable during the early part of the 19th cent. for the display of ornaments. Today it seems to epitomise one aspect of Victorian life, the love of fancy objects.

Willow pattern, the most popular of all printed (q.v.) motifs for table-ware. It consists of a chinoiserie (q.v.) island landscape with a bridge and figures and a willow-tree bending over it, on the island pavilions, on the water a houseboat, in the air flying birds. It was probably invented in the late 18th cent., nobody knows by whom. The only dated example is from 1818. With small variations it has been used to this day, usually printed in blue, occasionally in mauve, and more rarely in yet other colours. Various romantic anecdotes which it is supposed to illustrate are all inventions.

Wing-glass, an ornamental glass with freely furnace-worked "wings" added to the stem. The ornaments may be formed as ropes twisted into fantastic curves and convolutions, or as figures of eight or related forms. The details are frequently made in bluish-green against otherwise clear and colourless glass. Wing-glasses were made most expertly by Italian glass-makers at work in northern Europe from c. 1550 to 1650. They have been widely copied in German and Belgian factories within the last 150 years.

The shapes may have been very faithfully produced, but the faultless perfection of the modern material give them away as modern copies.

TAXES

Taxation permeates almost every aspect of financial life. In addition, the entire subject is exceedingly complex, and the tax system is altered or amended at least once a year. All taxes are paid to HM Revenue and Customs (HMRC).

For reasons which are largely historical, taxes are often divided into *direct* and *indirect* taxes.

There are four main types of direct taxation:

1. **Income tax**
2. **Capital gains tax**
3. **Inheritance tax (formerly Capital transfer tax)**
4. **Corporation tax**

National Insurance Contributions are a form of tax. (*See* **G34**). There are plans to merge National Insurance (now called Earnings Tax) and Income Tax.

Indirect taxes include:

1. **Value added tax**
2. **Customs & excise duties**
3. **Car tax**
4. **Stamp duties**

INCOME TAX

If you are resident in the United Kingdom tax is levied on your income whether it originates in the UK or from overseas. Even if you are not resident, tax is still levied on any income you have which originates in the UK. Tax is charged for each year of assessment; that is the year from 6 April to the following 5 April.

Income Subject to Tax.

Most types of income are taxable. They include:

Income from employment. This includes wages, bonuses, commission. tips and benefits in kind.

Income from self-employment, business, professions and vocations.

Interest, dividends and annuities.

Rent.

Pensions.

Income not Subject to Tax.

A few types of income are not subject to tax:

Interest on National Savings Certificates and increases in the value of Index-Linked National Savings Certificates. Also, interest from the Save-As-You-Earn scheme is exempt and income from Individual Savings Accounts (ISAs).

Social security benefits that are not taxable include attendance allowance, child benefit, Christmas bonus for pensioners, disability living allowance, disability working allowance, invalidity pension, maternity allowance, mobility allowance, one parent benefit, severe disablement allowance, sickness benefit (but not statutory sick pay) and youth training scheme allowance.

Educational grants and awards.

Compensation for loss of employment—up to £30,000. There are plans to end this.

War widows' pensions.

Wound and disability pensions.

Any wins from gambling, and also Premium Bond prizes.

Profit-related pay, within certain limits.

Rent under the 'rent a room' scheme up to £7,500.

Personal Allowances and Rates of Tax.

Almost everyone is entitled to at least one personal allowance which may be deducted before tax is levied on the remainder of a person's income. The current allowances are shown in Table 1.

The basic personal allowance is available to individuals generally and there are two levels of higher personal allowances for taxpayers aged 65 or more. The current (2017/18) basic personal allowance is £11,500. This will rise to £12,500 by 2020.

The higher-rate threshold rose from £43,000 in 2016/17 to £45,000 for 2017/18 (although it stays at £43,000 in Scotland).

A new 50% band on incomes over £150,000 began in April 2010. This was reduced to 45% from April 2013. Income tax relief for high earners is now capped at £50,000 annually (except for charity donations).

Note: A new **Personal Savings Allowance** came into force from April 2016. Basic rate taxpayers will not pay tax on their first £1,000 of savings interest (higher rate taxpayers £500). A new **Dividend Allowance** allows investors to earn the first £5,000 a year in dividends tax free (but some high tax rates apply above this limit). There are plans to reduce this to £2,000 from April 2018.

Readers should also note that in Scotland different rates of income tax may apply.

ASSESSMENT AND COLLECTION

The administration of income tax is essentially divided into two parts: assessment and collection. The "assessments" for tax are the responsibility of inspectors of taxes. When an individual's tax has been assessed the information is then passed to a collector of taxes who actually sends out the bill. If you receive a tax bill which you think is wrong you should contact the inspector. The collector has no power to amend the bill, his or her job is to collect the amounts decided between you and the inspector.

Income is now divided into six groups known as "schedules.":

1. **Schedule A**: Income from property.

2. **Schedule B**: Income from commercial woodlands. Schedule B was abolished in 1988.

3. **Schedule C**: Certain interest and annuities paid out of public revenue.

4. **Schedule D**: Income from trades, businesses and professions. Also included are interest, rents and income not covered by other schedules.

5. **Schedule E**: This is the schedule that affects most people as it covers wages and salaries. It also deals with pensions.

6. **Schedule F**: Dividends *etc.* by companies.

Pay-As-You-Earn.

By far the largest schedule is Schedule E. Nearly all Schedule E income is taxed through the Pay-As-You-Earn (PAYE) system. PAYE is the method used to deduct tax from wages, salaries and some pensions. PAYE is operated on a cumulative basis. This means that your earnings, tax paid and so on are accumulated throughout the tax year.

SELF-ASSESSMENT

Self-assessment was introduced for those receiving income tax returns from 1997. It is a different way of calculating and paying tax which has been used in many other countries for some time. The main difference with the previous system is that a greater responsibility is placed on taxpayers to keep records, to complete their tax returns properly and to send them back on time. For taxpayers who are late there are penalties.

Self-assessment tax returns contain different schedules which apply to different sorts of income received by taxpayers. They are designed to allow taxpayers to be able to work out their own tax. There is also a guide which should be read carefully before completing the return.

With self-assessment, the process is stricter than before. Not all taxpayers are required to complete a tax return but they should all keep the necessary records to enable them to do so if required. If taxpayers receive income or capital gains which should be taxed and have not been, they are required to inform the Inland Revenue within six months of the end of the tax year, that is by 5 October. Most tax returns are sent out in April each year. If taxpayers wish the Inland Revenue to calculate their tax for them they should submit their returns by 30 September. If the taxpayer does the calculation the return does not have to be submitted until 31 January.

The Deadline.

If the tax return is not submitted by 31 January then a fixed penalty of £100 is applied. If the return is still outstanding six months later a further penalty of £100 becomes due. These penalties are scheduled to rise. The Inland Revenue is able to ask the Commissioners of Income Tax to apply further penalties. Interest is charged on overdue tax. There is also a 5 per cent penalty for tax outstanding at the end of February and another 5 per cent on any tax still outstanding by 31 July.

Some Basic Advice.

It is very worthwhile keeping a tax file containing all the information relevant to your tax affairs. The whole process of completing a tax return is much simpler if you keep all the relevant documents close together. These documents include items such as: P60 (from your employer); dividend advice slips; receipts for expenses. You may also be asked by the inspector to submit detailed records supporting expense claims. A second point is to keep a copy of your return. A photocopy is perhaps the best method of doing this. Alternatively, you can keep a separate record of what you put in the return as you go along.

Contacting the Tax Office.

If you get into difficulties with your return, you can always contact tax office whose address appears on the front of the form. If you wish to call personally, most tax offices are open for public enquiries between 10 am and 4 pm. But remember to take your tax file with you. It does not matter if you wish to make a personal call and your tax office is hundreds of miles away. This is often the case with Londoners and people who work for large nationwide companies. You can always call at a local office and in London there are special PAYE enquiry offices. (Their addresses are in the telephone directory.) Most enquiries can be handled without recourse to your official file. If the file is needed, the Inland Revenue can arrange to have it sent to a local office.

Note. In his Budget of March 2015, the Chancellor promised a major simplification of tax collection that would end the need for around ten million people to complete an annual tax return. These new digital—tax accounts are being phased in over 5 years.

CAPITAL GAINS TAX

When you dispose of an asset or possession you may make a capital gain or a capital loss. An asset is property of any kind. It includes both property in the UK and property overseas.

You are considered to have disposed of an asset if you sell it, lose it, exchange it or give it away. However, the transfer of a possession between a husband and wife who are not separated is not considered to be a disposal.

Tax-free Gains.

Your home (but *see below*).

Personal possessions, household goods and other chattels, provided that each item is worth £6,000 or less at the time of the disposal. A set of goods, for example a pair of vases, is counted as one. (*Chattels* means tangible, movable property.)

Animals, private cars, caravans and boats. Also other chattels which are wasting assets; that is assets expected to last 50 years or less.

Life assurance policies.

National Savings Certificates, British Savings Bonds and Save-As-You-Earn.

British government stocks if owned for more than one year or inherited. This exemption has been extended to corporate bonds (*e.g.* debentures) which are issued after 13 March 1984 and held for at least twelve months.

British money.

Foreign currency for personal or family use.

Winnings from betting or from Premium Bonds.

Gifts to charities.

Gifts to certain institutions such as the National Trust and the British Museum.

Your Own Home.

When you sell your house any capital gains you make will normally be exempt from tax. This exemption applies (within certain limits) if you let part of your home. However, there are a number of circumstances in which you may get only partial exemption. For example, if you use part of your home for business you may not be allowed full exemption from capital gains tax. These circumstances are described in more detail in the Inland Revenue publication CGT1, *Capital Gains Tax—An Introduction.* You should enter any gains from the disposal of your house on your tax return in case they are not wholly exempt.

Capital Losses.

Your capital gains can be reduced by deducting allowable losses. An allowable capital loss is usually one which would have been taxable if it had been a gain. For example, a loss on an item which is exempt, such as your car, would *not* be considered an allowable loss. If your losses exceed your gains in the tax year you can carry the balance forward to set against gains in future years. You can also deduct allowable expenditure from your capital gains (or add them to your capital losses). Allowable expenditure includes the costs of acquiring or disposing of an asset; for example, commission, conveyancing costs and advertising. It also includes expenditure which increases the value of the asset, such as improvements to property.

Working Out Your Gain.

Normally your capital gain (or loss) is the amount you receive when disposing of the asset *minus* the original amount you paid for it. If you give the asset away, the market value at the time of disposal is used instead. The same method is used if you were originally given the asset, or if you inherited it.

If you buy batches of the same share at different prices the cost of each share is considered to be the average cost. For example, suppose you purchase 100 shares in a company for £200. Three months later you buy a further 100 of the same shares for £300. You would then have a total of 200 shares which cost you £500. The average cost is, therefore, £2·50 per share. When you sell all or some of these shares the calculation of your gain or loss will be based on this average cost.

The Rates of Capital Gains Tax.

From its introduction in 1965 to 1988, capital gains tax was levied at a flat rate of 30 per cent. After 6 April 1999 capital gains were charged at an individual's income tax rate for savings income. However the tax is only applied to a person's gains over £10,900 from April 2013, £11,000 from April 2014 and £11,100 from April 2015. This amount usually rises each year in line with inflation. Beyond this amount a single rate of capital gains tax of 10% now applies (20% for higher rate taxpayers since April 2016). Higher rates apply to buy-to-let landlords and owners of second properties. Gains accruing prior to April 1982 are exempt. Capital gains tax on business assets is treated separately. Advice should be sought.

INHERITANCE TAX

Inheritance tax emerged from the remains of the previous capital transfer tax in March 1986. Capital transfer tax applied to transfers of capital made both during life and on a person's death.

Capital transfer tax had replaced the old estate duty which was imposed on property passing at death, and gifts made within 7 years before death. The position has now turned full circle because, essentially, inheritance tax, like the old estate duty, is levied on transfers between individuals made on the death of the donor, or up to 7 years before death.

The Tax.

Inheritance tax is payable on transfers made on or after 18 March 1986 on transfers made at death or in the years preceding death. Certain gifts, most of which are listed below, are exempt from tax. All other gifts which are not exempt and which are made within 7 years of death are taxable as soon as the total amount of taxable transfers exceeds the threshold for tax. Rates for 2008/2009 were £312,000 and for 2011/2012 £325,000. This £325,000 threshold has since been frozen.

In the case of married couples, a widow or widower can leave twice this amount (currently £650,000) by using up the £325,000 relief of the deceased partner. These inheritance tax allowances became transferable from 9 October 2007.

A new Family Home Allowance was introduced from April 2017. It adds to the inheritance tax allowance of some people. It is being phased in gradually, starting at £100,000 in 2017–18 and rising to £125,000 in 2018–19, £150,000 in 2019–20 and £175,000 in 2020–21.

The March 2011 Budget proposed a reduction in inheritance tax from 40 % to 36 % for those who leave a minimum of 10 % of their estate to a good cause.

Furthermore, there are rules, similar to those operated under estate duty, which apply where the donor continues to enjoy some benefit from a gift even after it has been "given away". For example, this might apply where a person gives his or her home to the children, but continues to live in it. If this happens, for the purpose of inheritance tax, the gift will normally be treated as if it had been given on the date such enjoyment finally ceases.

The method of valuing assets largely continues on from the previous capital transfer tax and estate duty. Assets are usually valued at the price they would fetch on the open market at the time of the transfer.

The value of the estate on death will be taxed as the top slice of cumulative transfers in the 7 years before death. (For capital transfer tax the cumulation period was 10 years.)

Tax Relief.

Since 2001/2002 the tax has been levied at a single rate of 40 per cent on transfers over the legal threshold. However, where gifts are made between individuals more than 3 years before the death of the donor the rate of tax is reduced by the relevant percentage given in Table 3. Different rules apply to gifts into and out of trust, discretionary trust charges and gifts involving companies.

TABLE 3. *Relief for Lifetime Transfers*

Years between gift and death	Percentage of full charge
0–3	100
3–4	80
4–5	60
5–6	40
6–7	20
Over 7	0

Exempt Transfers and Other Reliefs.

Certain transfers are eligible for exemption. They include the following:

Transfers up to £3,000 in any one year (unused relief may be carried forward for one year only).

Small gifts of up to £250 to any one recipient in any tax year.

Gifts made as part of normal expenditure.

Marriage gifts as follows:

Parents	£5,000 each
Grandparents	£2,500 each
Bride and groom	£2,500 to each other
Other people	£1,000 each

Transfers between husband and wife if the recipient is domiciled in the United Kingdom.

Gifts to charities and political parties. A "political party' is defined as one with two MPs, or one MP and not less than 150,000 votes for its candidates at the last general election.

Gifts for national purposes, *e.g.* to the National Trust, National Gallery, universities, museums *etc.*

There is also some relief for business assets, agri-cultural land and shares which represent a controlling interest in a company. In addition, a certain amount of relief is available for minority shareholdings in unquoted companies.

Administration and Collection.

The responsibility for the administration of inheritance tax lies with the Revenue, and the procedures for assessment, appeals and penalties are similar to those for income tax. Responsibility for dealing with Revenue enquiries about transfers made before death lies with the personal representatives of the deceased. Where a person's death creates tax liability on gifts previously made, the main responsibility for the tax falls on the recipient, but with recourse to the donor's estate if necessary.

VALUE ADDED TAX

Value Added Tax (VAT) is levied on most goods and services. The standard rate of 17·5 per cent was reduced to 15 per cent for the temporary period 1 December 2008 to 31 December 2009. On 1 January 2010 the rate returned to 17·5 %. It rose to 20 % on 4 January 2011. For most people it is simply included in the selling price. Anyone with a business over a certain threshold (currently £85,000) must register with HM Revenue and Customs.

The way VAT works is that it is charged at each stage of production but businesses may deduct any VAT they have been charged on their inputs. There are some concessions in the form of a reduced rate of VAT, zero-rating and exemption.

Reduced Rate.

A reduced rate of VAT applies to the following:

Supplies of domestic fuel or power.
Installation of energy-saving materials.
Grant-funded installation of heating equipment or security goods or connection of gas supply.
Children's car seats.
Residential conversions.
Residential renovations and alterations.
Contraceptives

Zero-Rating.

Goods and services that are "zero-rated" are in principle subject to VAT but the rate applying to them is zero. This means that while VAT is not charged on these goods, businesses can still recover VAT paid on their own purchases. The effect of this arrangement is that zero-rated goods and services should be entirely free of tax. The groups of items treated in this way are:

Food – of a kind used for human consumption and animal feeding stuffs but not "meals out", hot takeaway food and drink, ice cream, confectionary, beverages, pet foods *etc.*
Sewerage services and water.
Books etc.
Talking books for the blind and handicapped and wireless sets for the blind.
Construction of buildings *etc.*
Protected buildings.
International services.
Transport.
Caravans and houseboats.
Gold.
Bank notes.
Drugs, medicines, aids for the handicapped etc.
Imports, exports, etc.
Charities etc.
Clothing and footwear for young children and protective equipment.
Supplies to hospices, rescue and air ambulance charities
Women's sanitary products.

Exempt Supplies.

Exempt goods and services are not subject to VAT, even in principle. A business cannot take any credit for VAT paid on the supplies used to produce exempt goods. Exemption is therefore less advantageous than zero-rating, but if a good falls into both categories it is zero-rated. Exempt items include:

Land.
Insurance.

Postal services.
Betting, gaming and lotteries.
Finance.
Educational.
Health and welfare.
Burial and cremation.
Subscription to trade unions, professional and other public interest bodies.
Sport, sports competitions and physical education.
Works of art etc.
Fund-raising events by charities etc.

NATIONAL INSURANCE (EARNINGS TAX) CONTRIBUTIONS

There are four classes of Earnings Tax contribution. Class 1 relates to employees and is paid by both employers and employees. Class 2 is payable by the self-employed (abolition of these takes effect in 2018). It was a flat-rate contribution on self-employed lower earnings of £2·80 a week. Earnings above £5,965 pay this. Class 3 is voluntary and is to help people protect their entitlement to the basic state pension if they do not pay enough Class 1 or Class 2 contributions. The March 2017 Budget controversially proposed raising the 9% rate of Class 4 contributions for those on earnings over £8,060 to 10% in April 2018 and to 11% in April 2019. This proposal was later withdrawn.

Class 1 Employee Contribution Rates.

Thresholds for tax-free allowances for Earnings Tax will in future rise in line with the Consumer Prices Index (CPI) rather than the Retail Prices Index. In 2017/18 there was a 12% band on income up to £45,000 per year, falling to 2% above £45,000. Lower earnings (below £155 per week) pay a nil band.

ISAs

The March 2012 Budget enabled savers using tax-free ISAs to increase their total to £11,280 from April 2012 (£5,640 in a Cash ISA) and to £11,520 from April 2013 (£5,760 in a Cash ISA). A major boost to savers came with the introduction of new ISAs (NISAs) from July 2014 raising the limit to £15,000 (all of which could be in a cash ISA if so desired). This was raised to £15,240 from April 2015. It was raised to £20,000 in April 2017. Anyone over the age of 16 can open a cash ISA.

Transferring an ISA to a surviving partner is no longer taxed and "flexible ISAs" were introduced in 2015 (allowing money to be taken out and put back in).

Junior ISAs began in November 2011. With a current limit of £4,128, they run alongside Child Trust Funds. Child Trust Funds can now be moved to Junior ISAs.

New Help to Buy ISAs were introduced in 2015 allowing young couples to save up to £12,000. For every £200 the government adds £50 up to a £3,000 maximum. People have until November 2019 to open an Help to Buy ISA.

New Lifetime ISAs (LISAs) began in April 2017. Available only to those aged 18–40, it allows investment of up to £4,000 a year. The Government will also boost the total saved by 25%. The scheme is intended for house purchase or retirement and penalties apply for other uses or early cashing in.

THE COUNCIL TAX

The council tax was introduced in April 1993. The tax is based on property but there is also a personal element. The property element is assessed using a system of banding which is constructed around average property values. Every home in Britain is allocated to one of eight bands according to its value. Properties in the same band in a local authority area are assessed to tax on the same basis. The tax levied on homes in the highest band is limited to two and a half times the amount levied on homes in the lowest band.

The assessment to tax begins with the assumption that each home contains two adults, but households of three or more adults are not charged extra. However a personal element remains in that single adult households receive a discount of 25 per cent of the basic charge. Discounts are also extended to students. If the first or second adult in a household is a student, a student nurse or Youth Training trainee, he or she is entitled to a personal discount. So, for example, in a household of students and no other adults, two 25 per cent discounts are available.

For individuals with a second home, the tax should be reduced by two personal discounts so that only half the usual charge would apply.

People on low incomes may be entitled to Council Tax Benefit. The claim form for Income Support also includes a claim form for Council Tax Benefit. For those not claiming Income Support a claim form should be available from the Council, or Regional Council in Scotland.

Valuation and Appeals.

The value of each home for the purposes of council tax is the value on 1 April 1991. This is worked out on the basis of the amount the home could have been sold for on the open market if it had been sold on 1 April 1991. Each home is put in one of the eight bands shown below. The amount of council tax payable is then calculated on the basis of the band in which your home is placed.

COUNCIL TAX VALUATION BANDS

Band	£
A	Up to 40,000
B	40,001–52,000
C	52,001–68,000
D	68,001–88,000
E	88,001–120,000
F	120,001–160,000
G	160,001–320,000
H	Over 320,000

It is not possible, or course, to appeal against the amount of council tax your council decides to raise. However, there are some grounds for appeal. One of these is where there has been a *material change* in the value of the home. This may arise, for example, because part of the dwelling has been demolished. There is no appeal on the grounds that there has been a general movement in house prices.

STAMP DUTY

Recent budgets have seen major changes to how Stamp Duty works. Under the old system, the same rate of tax was charged on the whole purchase price, rising at the different thresholds. At present the system works as follows. No tax is payable on houses worth less than £125,000. Two per cent is then payable on the portion of any value between £125,000 and £250,000. Five per cent is then payable on the portion between £250,000 and £925,000. Above £925,000 ten per cent is payable up to £1·5 million and 12 per cent above this.

Since April 2016 a 3% surcharge has been imposed on the purchase of second homes and buy-to-let properties. This does not apply to caravans or canal boats.

Readers should note that different rates may apply in Scotland. Wales plans to replace Stamp Duty with a different tax.

BIBLICAL GLOSSARY

This section provides an easy to use treasure-house of information about the biblical world. It presents a concise and valuable guide to the people, places and events which have had so much influence on the course of history (with a short note on the history of the Bible itself and also the Apocrypha). There is also a map of the biblical land of Palestine, from Sidon in the north to Beersheba in the south.

THE LAND OF PALESTINE

N.B. This map does not represent Palestine as it was at any one period of history. It shows most of the Palestinian locations mentioned in the text from whatever period.

BIBLICAL GLOSSARY

THE BIBLE

Introduction

There is a sense in which the Bible is part of every person's heritage. Though it is sometimes claimed that we are now living in a post-Christian era, the marks of a Christian culture are part of our everyday experience: the great cathedrals of our cities, the parish churches and village chapels of our countryside. At the root of this culture is the revelation of God offered by the Bible.

It is not, however, an easy book. The modern reader has to bridge a major time-gap of at least 2,000 years (often much more) and enter into an alien culture if he or she is to become familiar with the biblical world. It is astonishing how many Christians have succeeded in making this transition with little or no help, and found that the Bible can still speak across the barriers of time and space. But today it should not be necessary for anyone to read the Bible unaided. During the 20th century our understanding of the way the biblical writers worked, of the cultural background against which their lives were set, and of the wider historical, social and religious background of the surrounding nations all increased enormously.

Composition of the Bible

The Bible includes the Hebrew sacred Scriptures (Old Testament) and those held sacred by the Christians (New Testament). The Old Testament—the prehistoric portion—consists of 39 books, and is divided into three parts: (1) the Law, (2) the Prophets, (3) Miscellaneous Writings. The Old Testament was written in Hebrew except for parts of Ezra and Daniel, which were in Aramaic.

It was not until the 9th century A.D. that a complete Hebrew text was made, the so-called Massoretic text. Before that the main versions were the Alexandrian Greek translation (Septuagint) made in the 2nd cent. B.C. and St. Jerome's Latin Vulgate of the 4th cent. A.D. (It was Jerome who used the Latin word "testament" (formed from *testis* = a witness).) Portions were translated into the Anglo-Saxon in the 8th cent. and the Venerable Bede put the greater part of St. John's gospel into English, but it was not until 1535 that a complete, printed English version appeared—the Coverdale Translation.

The Authorised Version

The Authorised Version dates from 1611 in the reign of James I, and its beautiful phraseology has given it a lasting appeal. The Revised Version dates from 1885. *The New English Bible*, with the Apocrypha, was published in 1970. It is a new translation in plain English prose of the earliest Hebrew, Aramaic, and Greek manuscripts. The finding of the Dead Sea Scrolls (*see* **H24**) added much to our knowledge of Scripture.

The Apocrypha

These "hidden writings" are the books which were included in the Septuagint (Greek) and Vulgate (Latin) versions of the Old Testament but excluded from the sacred canon at the Reformation by the Protestants on the grounds that they were not originally written in Hebrew nor regarded as genuine by the Jews. The books include: 1 and 2 Esdras, Tobit, Judith, additions to Esther, Wisdom of Solomon, Ecclesiasticus, Baruch, Song of the Three Holy Children, History of Susannah, Bel and the Dragon, Prayer of Manasses, 1 and 2 Maccabees. The term is usually applied to the additions to the Old Testament, but there are also numerous Christian writings of the same character. The apocryphal First Book of Enoch (the seventh patriarch in the Book of Genesis) was used at first in the Christian Church and is still accepted in Ethiopia.

ABBREVIATIONS USED IN GIVING BIBLICAL REFERENCES

Acts	Acts	Isaiah	Is	Nehemiah	Neh
Amos	Amos	James	Jas	Numbers	Num
Chronicles	Chr	Jeremiah	Jer	Obadiah	Obad
Colossians	Col	Job	Job	Peter	Pet
Corinthians	Cor	Joel	Joel	Philemon	Phlm
Daniel	Dan	John	Jn	Philippians	Phil
Deuteronomy	Deut	Jonah	Jon	Proverbs	Prov
Ecclesiastes	Ecc	Joshua	Josh	Psalms	Ps
Ephesians	Eph	Jude	Jude	Revelation	Rev
Esther	Esth	Judges	Judg	Romans	Rom
Exodus	Ex	Kings	Kgs	Ruth	Ruth
Ezekiel	Ezek	Lamentations	Lam	Samuel	Sam
Ezra	Ezra	Leviticus	Lev	Song of Songs	Song
Galatians	Gal	Luke	Lk	Thessalonians	Thes
Genesis	Gen	Malachi	Mal	Timothy	Tim
Habakkuk	Hab	Mark	Mk	Titus	Tit
Haggai	Hag	Matthew	Mt	Zechariah	Zech
Hebrews	Heb	Micah	Mic	Zephaniah	Zeph
Hosea	Hos	Nahum	Nah		

A

Aaron. The elder brother of Moses, he was appointed by God to be Moses' spokesman in the negotiations with the Egyptian Pharaoh for the release of the Jews (Ex 4:14). After the exodus, in Moses' absence, he made a golden calf for the people to worship (Ex 32:1-6). In spite of this lapse, tradition regards him as Israel's first High Priest (Ex 29:1-7).

Abednego. One of three young men who, according to the book of Daniel, survived being thrown into a blazing furnace for refusing to worship a gold statue set up by King Nebuchadnezzar (Dan 3:1-27).

Abel. The second son of Adam and Eve, he was killed by his elder brother Cain out of jealousy because God found Abel's offering of a lamb more acceptable than his offering of grain (Gen 4:1-8). The story probably reflects a feeling among traditionalists that the Jews had been corrupted by the agricultural civilisation of Canaan, and were less acceptable to God than when they had been shepherds.

Abiathar. When his father Ahimelech was killed by Saul for his unwitting involvement in David's escape, Abiathar fled to join David's outlaw band (1 Sam 22:16-23). He subsequently became David's High Priest, but was banished by Solomon because he supported Adonijah in the struggle for succession to the throne (1 Kgs 1:5-7, 26-27).

Abijah. King of Judah (915-913 B.C.).

Abner. Saul's commander-in-chief. After Saul's death he supported Ishbosheth, his only surviving son, as king of Israel, but soon became disenchanted with him. He was negotiating with David to transfer the allegiance of the northern tribes to him when he was murdered by David's commander, Joab, in pursuance of a family quarrel (2 Sam 3:6-27).

Abraham. Abraham, originally known as Abram, is regarded as the father of the Jewish people. He is the first person to be referred to as a Hebrew.

While there are doubtless legendary elements in the stories told of him, there is no reason to question his historical existence, probably in the period 2000-1800 B.C. Through the stories of Abraham run two complementary themes: God's promises and Abraham's faith. God promises to Abraham that he will have numerous descendants, that they will occupy the land of Canaan and that they will be a source of blessing to all mankind (Gen 12:1-3). Abraham responds to these promises with faith, shown in his willingness to set out for the promised land not knowing where he is being led, and to sacrifice his son Isaac when he thinks this is what God requires.

Neighbouring peoples (*e.g.* the Moabites) still practised child sacrifice a thousand years later, and this story, as well as indicating Abraham's faith, reflects the early understanding of the Jews that God did not require human sacrifice.

Absalom. David's third son. After his sister Tamar had been raped by his elder half-brother Amnon, he plotted revenge and eventually had Amnon killed (2 Sam 13). As a result he had to flee to the small state of Geshur which his grandfather ruled. After three years he was permitted to return at the instigation of David's general, Joab, who probably felt that Amnon had only got his due punishment. He then proceeded to plot against his father, sowing seeds of discontent among the northern tribes especially (2 Sam 15:1-6) and finally raised an army to march on Jerusalem. David withdrew across the Jordan, gained time to organise loyal forces and crushed the rebels. In the decisive battle Absalom was killed by Joab, even though David had expressly instructed that he should not be harmed (2 Sam 18:6-15).

Acts of the Apostles. The book is clearly a sequel to Luke's gospel, being addressed to the same person, Theophilus, and referring to an earlier work which described "the things that Jesus did and taught from the time he began his work until the day when he was taken up to heaven." It is invaluable for the insight it gives into the first thirty years of the Christian church. Peter and Paul are the leading personalities in the book, yet the theme is not one of human heroes but of God at work among the community of believers through the gift of the Holy Spirit. The somewhat surprising ending, with Paul under house arrest in Rome, has led many to wonder whether the work was unfinished or a third volume planned, yet in some ways this is a most fitting conclusion—Paul in spite of everything proclaiming the good news at the very heart of the Roman empire.

Adam. The name is simply the Hebrew for "man". Adam is therefore to be thought of not as the first man in a historical sense but as the symbolic prototype of all mankind.

Adonijah. The fourth son of David. As the eldest surviving son by the time his father reached old age, he expected to succeed to the throne and had himself declared king by Abiathar and Joab before David's death. David, however, nominated Solomon to succeed him and Solomon soon found occasion to accuse Adonijah of treachery and have him put to death (1 Kgs 1:5-53, 2:13-25).

Agrippa. *See* **Herod Family.**

Ahab. King of Israel (869-850 B.C.). The son of Omri, who arranged his marriage to Jezebel, daughter of the king of Tyre, as part of his policy of friendly relations with Phoenicia. His chief fault was his failure to curb the excesses of his wife, who was determined to supplant the worship of Yahweh with the worship of her own god, Baal Melkart. He ignored the advice of the prophet Micaiah to go to battle against the Syrians at Ramoth-Gilead, where he was fatally wounded by an arrow.

Ahaz. King of Judah (735-715 B.C.). Ahaz came to the throne at a moment of crisis. King Pekah of Israel and King Rezin of Damascus had formed an allegiance against the powerful Assyrians, and were threatening to attack Judah if she did not join them. In desperation, and against the advice of Isaiah, he appealed to the Assyrians for help. This he received, but at the cost of becoming an Assyrian vassal. He is criticised by the biblical historians for taking part in idolatrous practices, and is even said to have sacrificed his own son (2 Kgs 16:1-4).

Ahaziah. (1) King of Israel (850-849 B.C.). The son of Ahab, within two years of coming to the throne he fell from a balcony and never recovered from his injuries (2 Kgs 1:2).

(2) King of Judah (842 B.C.). The son of Jehoram, he had the misfortune to be visiting his father's namesake, Jehoram king of Israel, at the time of Jehu's rebellion in which he was killed (2 Kgs 9:27-28).

Ahijah. A prophet from Shiloh who predicted the division of the kingdom after Solomon's death by tearing his robe into twelve pieces and giving ten of them (representing ten tribes) to Jeroboam, later to be the first king of the breakaway state of Israel (1 Kgs 11:29-40).

Ahimelech. The priest at Nob who unwittingly assisted David's escape from Saul by giving him food and a sword. He was subsequently killed by Saul together with all other priests at Nob.

Alexandria. Though only mentioned four times in the Bible (all the references being in Acts), Alexandria had a large Jewish community almost from its foundation in 332 B.C. by Alexander the Great, and it was here that the Septuagint, the Greek translation of the Old Testament, was made during the third and second centuries B.C.

Amalekites. A nomadic people who lived in the desert regions to the south of Israel. They attacked the Israelites during their march from Egypt to the promised land, and were later attacked and defeated by both Saul and David .

Amaziah. King of Judah (800-783 B.C.). After succeeding in regaining territory earlier lost to the Edomites, Amaziah got into an unnecessary and disastrous quarrel with King Jehoash of Israel from which he emerged the clear loser. He was eventually assassinated at Lachish, whence he had fled, having heard of a plot against his life.

Ammonites. A trans-Jordanian tribe frequently at war with the Israelites. It was in action against the Ammonites that Saul proved his powers of leadership (1 Sam 11:1-15), and although David seems to have established good relations with King Nahash of Ammon, his son insulted David's envoys and bitter hostilities ensued. David ultimately took the Ammonite crown, but only after a long struggle (1 Sam 10:1-11:1, 13:26-31).

Amon. King of Judah (642-640 B.C.). The son

of the hated Manasseh, he was soon assassinated for continuing in his father's idolatrous ways.

Amos. The first of the great reforming prophets of the eighth century B.C., we know relatively little about the man himself as opposed to what he taught. A herdsman and grower of figs from Tekoa in Judah, he prophesied in the cities of Israel to which he perhaps travelled to sell his produce. His prophetic career may have lasted as little as a few months sometime during the period 760–750 B.C.

Amos was appalled by a society in which an affluent minority exploited the poverty-stricken majority. Loans would be made to the poor, and when they were unable to repay them, their houses and land would be seized, or their children sold into slavery to pay off the debt. The use of false weights and measures by the merchants was commonplace, and bribery in the courts ensured that no case against them would ever succeed. Yet these same merchants made lavish sacrifices to God at the national shrines of Gilgal and Bethel.

The message of Amos is uncompromising, and needs to be balanced by the words of later prophets who saw the possibility of redemption as well as judgement. His importance is immense, as the man who proclaimed with a new clarity the incompatibility of worshipping God and exploiting one's fellow men.

Ananias. (1) A member of the early church who sold some property and gave part of the proceeds to the church, but claimed to have given all. Peter accused him of lying to God, and he fell down dead (Acts 5:1–6).

(2) A Christian in Damascus who, in response to a vision, went and baptised Saul following his conversion (Acts 9:10–19).

(3) The Jewish High Priest before whom Paul appeared after his arrest in the temple at Jerusalem (Acts 23:1–5).

Andrew, St. The brother of Simon Peter and one of the first disciples. His feast day is 30 November. Patron Saint of Scotland.

Annas. Though he had retired from the High Priesthood before the time of Jesus' trial, Annas continued to exercise influence through his son-in-law and successor, Caiaphas.

Annunciation, Feast of the (25 March), is a Church festival commemorating the message of the incarnation of Christ brought by the angel Gabriel to the Virgin Mary, hence the title Lady Day.

Antioch. (1) The capital of the Roman province of Syria and an important centre of early Christianity. It was here that disciples were first called Christians, and it was this church that sent Paul and Barnabas out on the first missionary journey (Acts 13:1–3).

(2) A city in Pisidia (part of Asia Minor) visited by Paul on his first missionary journey.

Apocalypse. Prophetic description of the end of the world from the Greek word meaning "revelation". Apocalyptic writings are those dealing with revelation and prophecy, more especially the Revelation of St. John.

Apocrypha. See **Introduction, H3.**

Apollos. A Jew from Alexandria who proclaimed the gospel in Ephesus but only knew about John's baptism as opposed to Christian baptism in the Holy Spirit. After Prisca and Aquila had explained Christianity more fully to him he went on to Corinth where, unfortunately, opposing factions developed according to whether they "followed" Apollos or other teachers.

Apostles. The twelve apostles who were disciples of Jesus were: Simon Peter and Andrew (his brother), James and John (sons of Zebedee), Philip, Bartholomew, Thomas, Matthew, James, Thaddaeus, Simon, and Judas Iscariot. After the Ascension Matthias was chosen to take the place of Judas. St. Paul was the leading apostle in the mission to the Gentiles, though he was not one of the twelve. St. Barnabas has also been called an apostle.

Apostolic Fathers were the immediate disciples or followers of the apostles, especially such as left writings behind. They included Barnabas, Clement of Rome, Ignatius of Antioch, Hermas, Papias of Hieropolis and Polycarp.

Aquila. A Jew who, with his wife Prisca, was expelled from Rome by an edict of Claudius and settled in Corinth. Here they welcomed Paul, and later worked with him in Ephesus.

Aramaeans. See **Syrians.**

Aramaic Languages, the Semitic dialects current in Mesopotamia and the regions extending south-west from the Euphrates to Palestine from about the 12th cent. B.C. until after the rise of Islam, when Aramaic was superseded by Arabic. Both Aramaic and Greek were spoken in Palestine during the time of Christ.

Areopagus. An open space in Athens, often used for public debates, and where Paul addressed the Athenians (Acts 17:16–34).

Ark of the Covenant. An ornate wooden chest believed to contain the stone tablets on which the ten commandments were written. It accompanied the Israelites throughout their nomadic wanderings and was then kept at Shiloh during the early years of the occupation of Palestine. Brought by the Israelites to encourage them in battle against the Philistines at Aphek, it was in fact captured, but the Philistines soon returned it, attributing a series of disasters to its presence. David brought it to Jerusalem, where Solomon eventually enshrined it in the temple. It is presumed to have remained there until the temple was destroyed by the Babylonians in 586 B.C.

Artemis. A Greek goddess identified with the Roman Diana. See **I5.**

Asa. King of Judah (913–873 B.C.).

Ascension. Although this is the word normally used to describe Jesus' departure from the earth, its significance is metaphorical rather than literal. It signifies the return of Jesus to God, and the taking up again of the power and authority he voluntarily laid down in order to share the human experience (Acts 1:6–11).

Ashdod. One of the five Philistine city-states.

Asher. (1) The eighth son of Jacob, his second by Zilpah, Leah's slave-girl.

(2) The tribe of Asher which occupied fertile land along the coastal plain north of Mt. Carmel.

Ashkelon. One of the five Philistine city-states.

Assyria. A major power to the north-east of Israel for over two centuries. As early as 853 B.C. Ahab had to meet the threat of an Assyrian invasion, though it was not until the accession of Tiglath-pileser III to the Assyrian throne in 745 B.C. that Assyria took a dominating role in the affairs of Palestine. By 721 B.C. the northern kingdom of Israel had become an Assyrian province and the southern kingdom of Judah was paying heavy tribute. An attempt by Hezekiah to become independent from Assyria in 705 B.C. was punished by an invasion in which all the fortified cities of Judah except for Jerusalem itself were taken and destroyed. Judah remained subservient to Assyria until the Assyrian empire began to break up under pressure from the Medes and the Babylonians c. 630 B.C.

Athaliah. Queen of Judah (842–837 B.C.). The wife of Jehoram, king of Judah and mother of Ahaziah, who succeeded him. When Ahaziah lost his life in Jehu's rebellion, Athaliah seized the throne and put to death all male members of the royal family except for Joash, one of Ahaziah's sons who was hidden by his aunt. After six years in hiding he was proclaimed king by forces acting on the instructions of Jehoiada the priest, and Athaliah was killed.

Athens. Visited by Paul on his second missionary journey. The sermon he preached there (Acts 17:16–34) is notable for its attempt to speak to Greek thinkers in terms they would find familiar, but his success was slight and Athens was never a major centre of Christianity.

Atonement, Day of. The most solemn day of fasting in the Jewish calendar. The High Priest went into the most sacred part of the temple (the only day of the year on which this was permitted) to make a special offering in expiation of the sins of the people. These sins were symbolically transferred to a goat (the "scape-goat") which was then driven out into the wilderness.

B

Baal. The Hebrew word itself means simply "master", "owner" or "husband", and it was used as a general term for foreign gods, but especially for the Canaanite fertility god. Although the debased sexual practices associated with the worship of this god were fiercely condemned by Hebrew writers, it was probably through contact with Canaanite religion that the people of Israel came to view their own God as creator and lord of the world of nature.

Baasha. King of Israel (900–877 B.C.), involved in a border dispute with Asa, king of Judah.

Babel, Tower of. The significance of the story is mythological rather than historical. Partly it is an attempt to explain the variety of human languages, but it also reflects a view long held in certain sectors of Israelite society that man's close relationship with God was broken once he began to build cities and become, in his own eyes, self-sufficient.

Babylonians. When the Babylonians and Medes destroyed Assyria they divided her empire between them, with the Babylonians taking the southern portion. They therefore took over from the Assyrians the dominating role in Palestinian affairs from 605 B.C. Rebellions against Babylonian overlordship in 598 B.C. and 589 B.C. were disastrously unsuccessful, the latter resulting in the destruction of Jerusalem and its temple and the exile of many of its people in 586 B.C. (the Babylonian Captivity). In 538 B.C. the exiles were permitted to return to Jerusalem when Babylon was taken by Cyrus.

The term is also applied to the period 1309–78 when the papacy moved to Avignon.

Baptism. The origins of baptism are obscure. John the Baptist baptised as a sign of repentance (Mk 1:4–5), and the Jews are known to have used a form of baptism as a means of entry to the Jewish faith for non-Jews, though it is uncertain whether or not this custom was established before John started baptising. There is no record of Jesus baptising anyone, yet it seems to have been established as the mode of entry into the Christian church from earliest times (Acts 1:38). Baptism was first administered to adult believers, or sometimes to whole families on the conversion of the head of household (Acts 16:33), and from this seems to have sprung the practice of baptising infants of Christian parents.

Barabbas. According to an established custom of releasing a prisoner at Passover time, Pilate set free Barabbas in preference to Jesus on the insistence of the crowd (Jn 18:38–40).

Barnabas. A prominent member of the early church, invariably exerting an influence for good at crucial moments. He was the first to befriend Paul in Jerusalem after his conversion (Acts 9:26–27). Sent by the Jerusalem church to report on work among the Gentiles which had begun in Syrian Antioch, he made a favourable recommendation, remained himself to continue the work and brought Paul to join him (Acts 11:19–26). He was Paul's companion on the first missionary journey (Acts 13:1–3), but did not accompany him on the second journey for characteristic reasons. Paul did not want to take John Mark, who had failed them on the first journey, while Barnabas wanted to give him a second chance. Significantly Paul was later to become reconciled to John Mark, thus confirming Barnabas' judgement (2 Tim 4:11).

Bartholomew. One of the twelve disciples. See **Nathaniel.**

Baruch. Acted as scribe to Jeremiah and read out a message from Jeremiah in the temple precincts at a time when Jeremiah himself had been banned from speaking there (Jer 36:1–8).

Bathsheba. The wife of Uriah, an officer in King David's army. Because she was expecting a child by David, he gave orders that Uriah be left in an exposed position during the fighting against the Ammonites, and he was killed. Bathsheba's child died in infancy, but she subsequently bore Solomon (2 Sam 11:2–12:25).

Beersheba. A town on the southernmost border of Judah: hence the expression "from Dan to Beersheba" to mean the whole of Israel.

Bel and the Dragon is the title of certain supplementary chapters to the "Book of Daniel" of an apocryphal character. First appeared in the Septuagint, but the Jewish Church did not accept it as inspired. In 1546 the Council of Trent declared it to be canonical.

Belshazzar. The last king of Babylon before its capture by the Persian monarch Cyrus in 539 B.C. Mentioned in the Bible only in the book of

Daniel, particularly in the dramatic story of his downfall recorded in the fifth chapter.

Benjamin. (1) The twelfth son of Jacob, his second by Rachel, who died giving birth to him.

(2) The tribe of Benjamin, occupying a relatively small area just north of Judah.

Bernice. The sister of Herod Agrippa II, she heard with him Paul's defence of his conduct before the Roman governor Festus.

Bethany. A village just outside Jerusalem, the home of Lazarus, Martha and Mary. Here Jesus stayed on his final visit to Jerusalem.

Bethesda. A pool in Jerusalem believed to have healing properties, particularly when the waters were disturbed. The scene of one of Jesus' healing miracles in John 5:1–9.

Bethlehem. A town in Judaea some five miles south of Jerusalem and known from before King David's time. Chiefly famous as the birthplace of Jesus, although some scholars now believe it more likely he was born near Nazareth, in Bethlehem of the Galilee.

Bible. See **H3**.

Bildad. The second of Job's three "comforters".

Booths. See **Tabernacles.**

C

Caesarea. A city on the Palestinian coast built by Herod the Great and named after Caesar Augustus. The Roman governors of Palestine had their residence in Caesarea, and it was here that Paul was tried before Felix and Festus, spending the intervening two years under arrest (Acts 24:1–26:32).

Caiaphas. The High Priest during the time of Jesus' ministry, who presided at his examination before the Jewish Council.

Cain. See **Abel.**

Cana. A village in Galilee where Jesus attended a wedding celebration and, according to John 2:1–11, turned water into wine.

Canaanites. The people who occupied the territory subsequently taken over by the people of Israel. Their civilisation was materially more advanced than that of the people of Israel, but morally they lagged far behind and their cultic practices are condemned by biblical writers. Around 1800 B.C. they invented the alphabet.

Capernaum. A little frontier town by the Sea of Galilee which for a time was the centre of Jesus' ministry. It was here that he called Matthew (Mt 9:9) and performed a number of healings including the centurion's servant (Lk 7: 1–9).

Carmel. The culmination of a spur branching westwards from the main north–south mountain range of Palestine and almost reaching the coast. It was the scene of Elijah's confrontation with the prophets of Baal (1 Kgs 18:19–40).

Chaldeans. See **Babylonians.**

Christ. See **Jesus** and **Messiah.**

Christian. A nickname, first used in Syrian Antioch (Acts 11:26), which gradually became the normal way of describing a follower of Christ. Elsewhere in the New Testament, Christians are referred to as followers of "the Way", Nazarenes or simply the saints.

Chronicles, Books of. These books give an account of the history of the Jews from the death of Saul to the return from the exile. They are therefore largely a retelling of events already recorded by earlier authors in the books of Samuel and Kings. The purpose of the chroniclers seems to have been to reassure their people of God's care for them in spite of the adversities recently suffered, and this leads them to present an unjustifiably rosy view of Israel's history (e.g. glorifying David's reign and glossing over his weaknesses). Consequently most scholars prefer to rely on the earlier and more sober accounts in Samuel and Kings, but, treated with caution, the information in Chronicles provides a useful supplement to them.

Colossians, Letter to the. As far as is known, Paul himself never visited Colossae, but the church there had been founded by Epaphras, a close associate of Paul (Col 1:7). Perhaps he felt some responsibility for the Colossian Christians because of this. The letter was probably written during Paul's imprisonment in Rome and appears to be a response to reports of false teachers in Colossae. These teachers suggest that there is a special kind of knowledge (over and above the knowledge of Christ) which is necessary for salvation, and they advocate an ascetic way of life. Paul's reply stresses that Christ alone is all-sufficient for the needs of his readers.

Commandments. There are, of course, many commandments in the Bible, but the ten commandments which God is said to have given to Moses on Mount Sinai have a special place.

They are seen as the basis of God's agreement with the people of Israel and, significantly, combine religious and social obligations. *See also* **Decalogue, H8.**

Corinth. Strategically situated at a major junction of trading routes, Corinth in New Testament times was a wealthy city which not even Athens could match in importance among the cities of Greece. It also had an evil reputation, however, because of its notoriously lax moral standards. Both its importance and its depravity may have commended it to Paul as a place to preach the Christian gospel. He spent 18 months there about A.D. 50 (Acts 18:1–18), and made at least one further visit, possibly two. His letters to the church at Corinth show that he was passionately concerned about its welfare.

Corinthians, Letters to the. Although Paul's correspondence with the Corinthians is collected into two letters in the New Testament, most scholars are agreed that they include parts of four separate communications, as follows:

(1) A letter of warning against pagan influences, a fragment of which appears in 2 Corinthians 6:14–7:1 and which is referred to in 1 Corinthians 5:9–13.

(2) The letter now known as 1 Corinthians.

(3) An extremely severe letter partly preserved in 2 Corinthians 10–13.

(4) A much more relaxed letter, perhaps showing relief that the severe letter had had the desired effect, and preserved in 2 Corinthians 1–9.

The letters afford valuable insights into the problems which faced a small Christian community set in a pagan environment, and into the relationship between Paul and a church which nearly drove him to distraction because of its waywardness and the depth of his concern for it.

Cornelius. A Roman centurion whose baptism by Peter represented an important step in the progress of the Christian church from a Jewish sect to a universal faith (Acts 10).

Covenant. The concept of the covenant—an agreement between God and man—is implicit throughout the Old Testament. The first explicit reference comes in the story of Noah where God makes a covenant to save Noah and his family from the impending flood and subsequently agrees never again to send such a flood upon the earth. God then makes a covenant with Abraham to establish his descendants as a chosen people, though it should be noted that they are chosen to bring God's blessing to all nations (Gen 12:3). It is however, the covenant made at Sinai after the exodus that is regarded as the most important. In this covenant God offers the people of Israel a special place in his plans if they will serve him alone and obey his commandments (Ex 19:5–6).

Again it is noteworthy that the people of Israel are to serve God as priests, *i.e.* as people who mediate the knowledge of God to others.

Covenant, Book of the. In 622 B.C. during the course of repairs on the temple, a scroll was discovered which is described as the Book of the Covenant. When this was brought to King Josiah he realised that his people had failed to live up to God's demands, and set in motion the most far-reaching religious reforms ever known in Judah. These included the suppression of all pagan cults, an edict that in future sacrifice could only take place in the temple in Jerusalem, and the re-institution of the Passover which had apparently not been celebrated for many years (2 Kgs 22:3–23:23). The close similarities between these measures and instructions contained in the book of Deuteronomy suggest that the Book of the Covenant was in fact the first edition of Deuteronomy.

It is thought to have been written by pious Jews during the evil reign of Manasseh (687–642 B.C.) as a re-statement and amplification of the covenant with Moses. Not daring to publish it

openly at the time, they hid it in the temple, hoping that it would later be discovered and acted upon.

Creation. There are two creation stories in the Old Testament, a primitive version which nevertheless has considerable charm starting at Genesis 2:4, and the more familiar version with which Genesis begins, but which is actually later in origin. *See also* **Genesis.**

Cross. The supreme symbol of the Christian faith because it represents the depths of suffering Jesus was prepared to embrace in order to save mankind by inaugurating God's Kingdom upon earth. Crucifixion was the normal method of execution for those who did not possess Roman citizenship, and because the wounds inflicted were not in themselves very serious, a strong man could take days to die. According to Mark 15:44, Pilate was surprised that Jesus had died within hours.

Cyrenius. *See* **Quirinus.**

Cyrus (*c.* 559–530 B.C.). The Persian king who overthrew the Babylonian empire and allowed the exiled Jews to return to their homeland.

D

Damascus. An ancient city, the capital of Syria. In the Old Testament, in fact, Damascus and Syria are synonymous. It was on his way to Damascus to persecute the Christian community there that Paul had his conversion experience.

Dan. (1) The fifth son of Jacob, his first by Bilhah, Rachel's slave-girl.

(2) The tribe of Dan, occupying a small area north of Judah and west of Benjamin.

(3) The city of Dan in the far north of Israel; hence the expression "from Dan to Beersheba" meaning the whole of Israel.

Daniel. Almost certainly written between 167 and 164 B.C., Daniel is one of the last of the books of the Old Testament chronologically. At this time the Greek ruler Antiochus Epiphanes was attempting systematically to destroy the Jewish religion. The book was written to encourage the resistance movement with stories of Daniel and his friends, who refused to compromise in religious matters during the Babylonian captivity some four hundred years earlier. The second half of the book contains obscure visions which appear to predict the ultimate downfall of pagan empires and the triumph of the people of God.

David. King of Israel from about 1000 to about 960 B.C. It is not clear whether David first came to Saul's attention as a skilled musician able to soothe him in his depressions (1 Sam 16:17–23) or as the shepherd boy who killed the Philistine champion Goliath (1 Sam 17:12–51). In either case he soon showed his military skill, and before long was receiving adulation greater than Saul himself (1 Sam 18:7). Saul's insane jealousy forced David to flee from his court and become an outlaw, eventually offering his services, and those of the 600 men who had joined him, to the Philistines as a way of keeping out of Saul's clutches (1 Sam 27:1–4).

Whilst nominally a Philistine vassal, David attacked traditional enemies of Israel such as the Amalekites, and distributed his booty among the tribe of Judah, thus indicating that his change of allegiance was a temporary expedient (1 Sam 30:1–31). When Saul was killed in battle David was immediately accepted as king of Judah (2 Sam 2:4), but the northern tribes were ruled by Saul's son, Ishbosheth, until he was assassinated by two of his officers.

As king of all Israel David rapidly subdued the Philistines (2 Sam 5:17–25), and soon turned his attention to the Ammonites, who had insulted his ambassadors (2 Sam 10:1–5). During the Ammonite war he successfully beat off a Syrian attack and subsequently annexed much Syrian territory. He also conquered the Moabites and the Edomites east of the Jordan. In the end he ruled an empire stretching some 725 kilometres from north to south and 185 kilometres from east to west.

David was not just a brilliant military tactician however. He was a statesman who understood the need for national unity and the crucial part to be played by his people's religion in achieving this. He established his capital in Jerusalem because it was close to the boundary between Judah and the northern tribes, and did not actually belong to any of the tribes, being still in the hands of the Jebusites. This was presumably to avoid inter-tribal jealousy. Although he did not build a temple, he brought the ark of the covenant to Jerusalem, thus establishing it as a religious centre and not just an administrative capital.

David's later years were marred by struggles among his sons to gain the throne, and he seems to have been uncharacteristically weak and indecisive in dealing with them.

Dead Sea Scrolls. *See* Scrolls, H24.

Deborah, Song of. If this hymn of triumph over the enemy commander, Sisera, was composed at the time of the events, as seems likely, it dates from before 1100 B.C. and is therefore one of the oldest fragments of literature in the Old Testament (Judg 5:2–31).

Decalogue. the name given to the Ten Commandments of the Old Testament. There are two versions of them, differing in detail: Exodus xx. 2–17 and Deuteronomy v. 6–21. They are of Hebrew origin and are recognised by Jews and Christians as the divine law given by God to Moses on Mt. Sinai. Most of them are prohibitions in contrast to the beatitudes (pronounced by Christ in the Sermon on the Mount) which are positive, *e.g.*, Blessed are the merciful.

Dedication, Feast of. A feast to commemorate the rededication of the temple following its desecration by the Greek ruler Antiochus Epiphanes in 168 B.C.

Deluge, a flood, commonly applied to the story of Noah and the Ark in the Bible. A similar tradition can be found in the mythology of many ancient peoples. Mesopotamian cuneiform tablets recount the story of a great flood with an Ark. Other flood stories occur in Egypt, Greece, Syria, India and even Australia.

Demetrius. A silversmith of Ephesus who stirred up trouble for the Christian community because the success of Christianity was affecting the trade of those who made silver models of the temple of Artemis (or Diana), the local goddess.

Deuteronomy. *See* Covenant, Book of the.

Devil. Contrary to popular opinion, the devil has a very minor role in the biblical writings. In the book of Job, Satan is counsel for the prosecution at the court of God, and therefore not a figure of evil as such. At the beginning of Jesus' ministry the devil appears in the role of tempter (Lk 4:1–13) and elsewhere as the adversary of God (1 Jn 3:8).

Diana. *See* Artemis.

Diaspora. *See below under* Dispersion.

Dispersion (Greek Diaspora). Over a period of centuries many Jews left Palestine for a variety of reasons. Some left in times of famine to seek food elsewhere, some fled from invading armies or were forcibly exiled, others went voluntarily to set up business in the major centres of commerce. By New Testament times these Jews of the Dispersion outnumbered those in Palestine, and there were few cities round the eastern Mediterranean without a sizeable Jewish colony. It is no accident that some of the most important figures in the early church—Stephen, Philip, Barnabas and Paul, for example—were Jews of the Dispersion, for their circumstances made them less fettered by tradition and more open to new thinking.

Dorcas. A Christian woman who lived in Joppa and was renowned for her good deeds among the poor. According to Acts 9:36–42 Peter restored her to life after she had died.

E

Ecclesiastes. A strange book to find in the Bible because of its apparently unrelenting pessimism. The burden of the author's message seems to be that there is no fulfilment to be found in human existence.

Edomites. Recognised as relations of the Jews because of their alleged descent from Esau, the Edomites were nevertheless often in conflict with the people of Israel. Their territory extended from the southern end of the Dead Sea to the Gulf of Aqaba, and was of importance because of its copper mines and because it afforded access to African trade routes via the Red Sea. David conquered the Edomites and Solomon made full use of the strategic advantages thus gained, but they gradually reasserted their independence and were never again completely subjugated by the people of Israel.

Egypt. Although the influence of Egypt on Palestinian affairs was less dramatic than that of the Mesopotamian empires of Assyria and Babylonia, it was far more persistent. From very early times the story of the Jews is linked with Egypt, and the great event of Jewish history is the escape from Egyptian captivity. During the period when Assyria and Babylon were at the height of their power, Egypt used the Palestinian states to foment trouble against them, promising assistance if they rebelled against their Mesopotamian overlords. The promised assistance did not always materialise, however, and when it did it was inadequate. After the destruction of the temple by the Babylonians in 586 B.C. a considerable number of Jews sought refuge in Egypt, and it was in Egypt during the third and second centuries B.C. that the Greek translation of the Old Testament was made. References to Egypt in the New Testament are far fewer, though Joseph and Mary are said to have fled there to protect their child from the wrath of Herod.

Ekron. One of the five Philistine city-states.

Elah. King of Israel (877–876 B.C.).

Eli. The priest who brought up Samuel.

Elihu. A young man who, after Job's three "comforters" had failed to persuade him of the error of his ways, made another attempt to do so (Job 32).

Elijah. A prophet from Tishbe in Gilead, Elijah is rightly considered one of the great figures of the Old Testament. He was the supreme champion of Israel's God at a time when Jezebel was trying to substitute the worship of her own god, Baal Melkart. This epic struggle is epitomised by the confrontation between Elijah and the prophets of Baal on Mount Carmel (1 Kgs 18:19–40). While many different interpretations of this story have been offered, ranging from the absolutely literal to the purely legendary, there can be no doubt whatever that the conflict it represents was real. Apart from this, however, the Elijah stories contain many pointers towards a more complete understanding of God. On Mount Horeb (Sinai) he realised that God was to be found in quiet reflection rather than in dramatic natural events, and the instructions he received there showed that God's power extended beyond Israel to the surrounding nations (1 Kgs 19:8–16). The encounter with King Ahab over Naboth's vineyard (1 Kgs 21:1–24), while not proclaiming anything new, is a forceful restatement of God's concern with social justice, and clearly anticipates the work of Amos.

Eliphaz. The first of Job's three "comforters".

Elisha. Though he is inevitably linked with his master and predecessor Elijah, Elisha is a very different character. More miraculous incidents are recorded about Elisha, yet many of them are trivial, e.g. recovering an axe-head from the river Jordan (2 Kgs 6:1–7), and the effect is to diminish rather than enhance his stature. Whereas Elijah was a largely solitary figure spending long periods in the wilderness, Elisha associated freely with the communities of prophets and lived in the capital city, Samaria, for at least part of his career. Though not always in sympathy with the kings of Israel, he advised them in military matters. He added little or nothing to the understanding of God achieved by Elijah, but some of the ways in which he exemplified that understanding are notable, e.g. the breadth of concern shown in the healing of Naaman, the commander of the Syrian army.

Elizabeth. The mother of John the Baptist and a relative of Mary, mother of Jesus.

Emmanuel. The name, meaning "God with us", is in fact used in a prophecy of Isaiah to King Ahaz during a time of crisis. Isaiah says that a young woman will conceive and bring forth a son, whom she will name Emmanuel. He is saying, in effect, that in nine months' time the situation will have improved so much that parents will give their children a name expressive of God's care for his people. Though the immediate prophecy, therefore, refers to events in the immediate future, it is not surprising that Christians should have seen in these words the foreshadowing of God's presence with his people in Christ (Mt 1:22–23).

Enoch, Book of. See Aprocrypha, H3.

Epaphras. An associate of Paul who founded the church at Colossae (Col 1:7).

Epaphroditus. A Christian from Philippi who was sent by the Philippian church to render assistance to Paul during imprisonment, probably in Rome. While with Paul he had a serious illness and Paul thought it best to send him back home possibly taking the letter to the Philippians with him (Phil 2:25–30).

Ephesians, Letter to the. Although apparently written by Paul, there is considerable doubt as to the authorship of this letter. It was not uncommon in those times for a follower of a great teacher to write in the teacher's name and, far from being considered fraudulent, this was regarded as a mark of respect. The style of writing is not quite as in Paul's other letters, themes are introduced which appear nowhere else in his correspondence, and there is a remarkable absence of personal greetings considering that Paul had spent two years in Ephesus. If the author were not Paul, however, he was clearly well acquainted with Paul's writings, especially the letter to the Colossians, parts of which are quoted almost verbatim. The first part of the letter emphasises the unity of Christian believers, whose common life in Christ overrides all human distinctions, and the glory of the church which, whatever its human weaknesses, is Christ's body. The second part of the letter draws out the implications of this view of the church for practical living.

Ephesus (in Asia Minor). The capital of the Roman province of Asia and an important trading centre, Ephesus was famous for its temple of Artemis (Diana). It had a substantial Jewish population, and soon became an important centre of Christianity. Paul visited Ephesus as he returned from his second missionary journey (Acts 18:19–21) and subsequently spent two years there (Acts 19:1–10).

Ephraim. (1) Although he was Joseph's second son, he received from Jacob his grandfather the blessing normally due to the eldest, and established an important tribe (Gen 48:17–19).

(2) It appears that Joseph never had a tribe named after him, but he gave rise to two of the tribes of Israel, named after his sons Manasseh and Ephraim. The tribe of Ephraim occupied fertile land running down to the Mediterranean coast north of Dan and Benjamin and south of Manasseh. Its significance in the affairs of Israel was such that the northern kingdom was often referred to as Ephraim.

Epicureans. A school of Greek philosophers with whom Paul debated in Athens (Acts 17:18).

Epiphany, a Christian festival celebrated on 6 January, originally an old solstice festival, celebrating the birth of light.

Esau. The first-born son of Isaac, he sold the birthright which was his by tradition to his younger brother, Jacob, for a bowl of soup. He is regarded as the ancestor of the Edomites.

Essenes. See Section J.

Esther. Dated between 150 and 100 B.C., the book of Esther describes how a Jewish heroine of that name became queen to the Persian king, Xerxes, and was able to save her people from the evil plotting of one Haman. The book makes no mention of God at all, and it appears to have gained its place in the Old Testament purely as an expression of nationalist sentiments. The deliverance from Haman is still celebrated by Jews in the feast of Purim.

Eve. Adam's partner (Gen 2:21–24, 3:20). As Adam should be thought of as a symbolic prototype of mankind, so is Eve the typical woman rather than the first woman.

Exile. The term usually refers to the exile of the leading Jewish people in Babylon between 586 and 538 B.C., though there had been an earlier deportation in 597 B.C. This experience was of great importance to the Jews for a number of

reasons. They had to learn how to worship God without the temple and without sacrifice, and so it was here that forms of worship developed which were based on the recollection of the way God had led them throughout their history. This in turn stimulated interest in writing down their history, and it was during the exile that much of the editorial work on the historical books of the Old Testament was done. On the negative side, the Jews became more exclusive during the exile because of fears that intermarriage would result in the loss of their religious and national identity. The Jews, therefore, emerged from the exile purified but also hardened in a way that was not entirely to the good.

Exodus. The name given to the escape of the people of Israel from Egypt, an escape always seen as the supreme symbol of God's concern for them and an event still celebrated annually by Jews in the feast of the Passover. While some allowance has to be made for exaggeration of the incidents leading up to the escape, there is no reason to doubt the essential historical truth of the account. It appears that, originally having gone to Egypt because of famine in Palestine, the Jews had become slave-labourers working on Egyptian building projects. They were freed from this oppression about 1250 B.C. under the leadership of Moses with the assistance of a remarkable sequence of events known as the plagues of Egypt (Ex 7:14–12:36). The pursuing Egyptian army fell into a panic as their chariots sank in the waters of a shallow swamp, successfully crossed on foot by the Israelites, in the area of the Suez canal today. Whatever our interpretation of these events, the people of Israel ascribed them to God.

Exodus, Book of. As its name implies the book of Exodus tells the story of the Jews' escape from Egypt, but it contains much else of importance besides. It includes the account of God's covenant with the people of Israel at Sinai based on the ten commandments. It also gives instructions about the construction of the ark and of the tent in which it is to be housed, as well as directions concerning worship.

Ezekiel. Ezekiel is probably the most difficult of the major prophets for the modern reader to come to grips with. Among the Jews deported to Babylon in the first exile of 597 B.C., his call to be a prophet came in Babylon and the whole of his prophetic ministry was carried out there, though his prophecies are directed to his people in Jerusalem as well as to the exiles. Many of the messages of Ezekiel are in the form of symbolic visions of great complexity; in fact, Ezekiel has been called "the father of apocalyptic", a kind of visionary writing represented elsewhere in the Bible by the books of Daniel and Revelation. The Old Testament book stresses the responsibility of the individual before God, rather than the people as a corporate body (Ezek 18:1-4), looks forward to the restoration of his people (Ezek 37:1-14) and presents a vision of the future temple and its worship (chapter 40 onwards). This interest in ritual, the result of his priestly status (Ezek 1:1) is in sharp contrast to earlier prophets who tend to condemn ritual, or at least the insincerity of ritual without righteousness.

Ezra. A lawyer who led a party of exiles to Jerusalem from Babylon about 460 B.C. (Ezra 7:1-9) and played a major role in the re-establishment of the worship of the temple. Unfortunately he shows the hard-line tendencies some of the Jews developed in exile, to the extent of insisting that Jews who had married foreign wives should get rid of them and their children. The book of Ezra relates events from the first return of exiles in 538 B.C. up to those in which Ezra himself was involved. It is not clear how much of the book is the work of Ezra.

F

Fathers of the Church. Early writers who laid the foundations of Christian ritual and doctrine. The earliest were the Apostolic Fathers (q.v.). The Four Fathers of the Latin Church were St.

Ambrose, St. Jerome, St. Augustine and St. Gregory the Great. The Four Fathers of the Greek Church were St. Basil, St. Gregory Nazianzen, St. John Chrysostom and St. Athanasius.

Felix. The Roman governor of Judaea from about A.D. 52 to 58, he had a Jewish wife and was apparently well informed about the Christian way (Acts 24:22–25). He kept Paul in custody for two years, having no cause to condemn him but unwilling to release him for fear of opposition from the Jewish leaders (Acts 24:27).

Festivals. *See* separate entries under **Dedication, Feast of; New Year; Passover; Tabernacles, Feast of; Weeks, Feast of.**

Festus. The Roman governor of Judaea who succeeded Felix about A.D. 58. He seems to have behaved with absolute correctness in his dealings with Paul, and would probably have set him free had not Paul taken the matter out of his hands by appealing to Caesar.

Flood. *See* **Deluge.**

G

Gabriel. The literal meaning of the name is simply "man of God". In Jewish tradition one of seven archangels, he is said to have announced the birth of John the Baptist to Zechariah (Lk 1:5–20) and of Jesus to Mary (Lk 1:26–38).

Gad. (1) Jacob's seventh son, his first by Zilpah, Leah's slave-girl.

(2) The tribe of Gad, holding territory east of the Jordan, north of that occupied by Reuben.

Galatia. The ancient kingdom of Galatia was in central Asia Minor, but the Roman province of the same name included a much larger area reaching down to the Mediterranean coast. Paul visited several towns within the Roman province on his first missionary journey.

Galatians, Letter to. One of the earliest of Paul's letters, probably written in *c.* A.D. 54, though some scholars would date it to A.D. 49, making it the first of all his surviving letters. It was written, almost certainly, to the churches Paul founded in the Roman province of Galatia on his first missionary journey, and is unusual in being addressed to a group of churches rather than a single church. The purpose in writing is very clear: Paul has been told that there are people going round the churches claiming that circumcision and the acceptance of the Jewish law is a necessary part of Christianity. Paul writes with the utmost urgency and vigour to refute these claims. He himself had been a Pharisee and knew that the attempt to satisfy God by perfect obedience to the law was impossible. It was faith in Christ which had liberated him from that futile pursuit, and the last thing he wanted was to see anyone persuaded into taking up something he had only discovered by long and painful experience to be of no value.

Galilee. The area west of the Sea of Galilee (actually an inland lake some 20 km long) where Jesus was brought up and spent much of his ministry. In the time of Jesus it formed the northern part of the Roman province of Galilee and Peraea, governed by Herod Antipas.

Gallio. The proconsul of the Roman province of Achaia before whom Paul was accused during his eighteen-month stay at Corinth (Acts 18:12– 17). An inscription from Delphi establishes that Gallio was in Corinth by A.D. 52, probably having been appointed the previous year. It is implied (though not definitely stated) in Acts that Paul's trial took place soon after Gallio's arrival, and if this is accepted it fixes Paul's ministry in Corinth within a year or so, providing a useful fixed point in the chronology of the early church.

Gamaliel. A well-known Jewish teacher who numbered Paul among his pupils (Acts 22:3), and who argued in the Jewish Council against trying to stamp out Christianity on the grounds that history would show whether it was a movement from God or a worthless novelty (Acts 5:34–40).

Gath. One of the five Philistine city-states.

Gaza. The southernmost of the five Philistine city-states.

Gedaliah. When Zedekiah, the last king of Judah, was taken in chains to Babylon in 586

B.C., the Babylonians appointed Gedaliah as governor. Though in his brief spell of office he seems to have acted with wisdom and humanity, he was soon assassinated by supporters of the royal house who regarded him as a traitor (2 Kgs 25:22–26).

Gehazi. Elisha's servant, condemned by Elisha for accepting gifts against his instructions from the healed Syrian commander, Naaman (2 Kgs 5:19–27).

Genesis. As the name implies, the first book of the Bible. Chapters 1–11 contain the acounts of the creation and the stories of Adam and Eve, Cain and Abel, Noah and the tower of Babel. These stories, though they may have some basis in historical fact, are important mainly for their mythological value. They are to be seen as parables, conveying in a vivid and often entertaining way, the convictions of their authors on immensely important matters—the nature of God, the nature of the universe and the nature of man. From chapter 12 onwards, with the entrance of Abraham into the story, the book is dealing with historical figures, however much allowance may have to be made for the inevitable legendary accretions acquired during centuries of handing down by word of mouth.

Gentiles. The word usually translated as Gentiles means literally "the peoples" or "the nations", *i.e.* the peoples other than the people of Israel. The Bible shows ambivalent attitudes among the Jews towards Gentiles. The covenants with Abraham and Moses both stress that the people of Israel are to be a blessing to "the nations", but during and following the exile the fear of religious and ethnic absorption made the Jews increasingly exclusive. Even in the early church there was a long and sometimes acrimonious debate before the mission to the Gentiles was accepted by all as an inevitable implication of Christian belief. It was this crucial decision which made Christianity a universal faith and no longer just a sect within Judaism.

Gethsemane. An olive grove on the western slopes of the Mount of Olives, facing Jerusalem across the Kidron valley, it was apparently Jesus' custom to go there with his disciples to avoid the crowds, and it was there that he was arrested (Mk 14:32–52).

Gibeah. A town some 7 km north of Jerusalem which was Saul's capital throughout his reign.

Gideon. Before the monarchy was established, the people of Israel relied on inspired leaders, known as judges, to raise armies and cope with enemy aggression as the need arose. Gideon was one such leader, renowned for his victory over the Midianites (Judg 7:1–22).

Gilgal. (1) A town on the west bank of the Jordan, just north of the Dead Sea, where the people of Israel first entered the "promised land" and Saul was later proclaimed king.

(2) A settlement north of Bethel where there was a community of prophets in the time of Elijah and Elisha (2 Kgs 2:1, 4:38).

God. The existence of God is never discussed in the Bible; it is simply assumed from start to finish. But if the biblical authors never question God's existence, they do question what sort of God he is and, as one would expect of a varied group of writers working over a period of many centuries, they do not all arrive at the same conclusion. Samuel believed that God demanded the total destruction of Israel's ancient enemy the Amalekites, severely criticised Saul because he had spared the life of Agag the Amalekite king, and himself cut him to pieces (1 Sam 15:1–33). The writer of 2 Kings 2:23– 24 believed that God had punished some boys who had made fun of Elisha by causing them to be mauled by bears. Clearly these are primitive views of God.

In spite of these relics of an early religion, however, the Bible as a whole presents a remarkably unified view of God, with most of the key concepts established at quite an early date in Israel's history. The "otherness" of God is expressed in the idea that no man could look upon the face of God and live (Ex 33:20) or that anyone who touched the ark, representing God's presence, would be struck dead (2 Sam 6:6–8). Later on these primitive attempts to express belief in a God whose ways are unsearchable, whose powers are unlimited, whose holiness is literally aweful, and who is as far removed from man as the heavens are from the earth, find nobler expression in such passages as the call vision of Isaiah (Is 6:1–8) and many of the Psalms. But the God of the Bible, though far removed from man in his wisdom, power and purity, is never remote. From the very earliest stories in the Bible he is a God who involves himself in the life of men, both making demands on them and caring for them. What he demands from men is justice in their dealings with each other. The ten commandments (Ex 20:1–17) form the basis of the moral code by which men are to live, and it is significant that even the king is subject to these demands and open to criticism for failure (1 Kgs 21:17–19) unlike other monarchs of the day who were a law unto themselves. What he offers men is a constant concern for their welfare, seen at an early stage in the exodus and expressed most movingly among Old Testament writers by the prophet Hosea, who daringly compares God to a faithful husband whose love for his wife does not waver in spite of her infidelity. So the thinkers of the Old Testament prepared the way for one whose moral demands reached new and greater heights in the commandment to "love your enemies and do good to those who hate you".

Golgotha. The name of the place where Jesus was crucified, the word means "skull". Whether this is a reference to the shape of the hill or an indication that executions had long been carried out there is uncertain, as is the location.

Goliath. A Philistine warrior of enormous stature supposedly killed by David, though 2 Samuel 21:19 says that it was Elhaman who killed Goliath, and it seems possible that tradition transferred this exploit to David.

Gomorrah. One of five cities described in Genesis 14:3 as occupying the valley of Siddim. The location is not quite certain, but is thought to be covered now by the southern part of the Dead Sea. Notorious for its wickedness, the city was destroyed by burning sulphur according to Genesis 19:24–25.

Gospels. Those key portions of the New Testament which deal with the life, death, resurrection and teachings of Christ. They are the gospels of Matthew, Mark, Luke and John, all probably compiled in the later part of the 1st cent. The first three are called the *synoptic gospels* because of their general unity of narrative. Mark was probably the first to be written and John the last, and it is to Mark that scholars have turned for the most reliable source of the life of Jesus.

The word *gospel* comes from two Anglo-Saxon words *gode* (good) and *spell* (tidings), a translation of the Greek *evangelion* = evangel, evangelist.

Greeks. Apart from its literal meaning, the word is often used in the New Testament as a general word for non-Jews. Thus in Romans 1:16 Paul says that the gospel is the saving power of God for "the Jew first but the Greek also". Some modern versions use the translation "Gentile" when this is the sense intended.

H

Habakkuk. A prophet whose ministry coincided with the rise to power of the Babylonians in the closing years of the seventh century B.C. The Old Testament book views the ascendency of the Babylonians as an act of God, but nevertheless questions how God can countenance such ruthless people, and declares that they are doomed, whereas "the righteous shall live by faith".

Hagar. The slave-girl of Abraham's wife Sarah. When it seemed that Sarah would never have a child, Hagar was given to him to bear his children, and gave birth to Ishmael (Gen 16:1–4, 15). After the birth of Sarah's own son, Isaac, she sent Hagar and Ishmael away, but God promised Abraham that Ishmael would become the father of a nation.

Haggai. A prophet who prophesied about 520 B.C. some twenty years after the first Jews had returned from the exile to Jerusalem. He said that the reason for the poor harvests the people were getting was their failure to make a start

on rebuilding the temple, and encouraged them to begin the rebuilding programme.

Haman. The villain of the book of Esther, an official at the Persian court who schemed to bring about the destruction of the Jews.

Hannah. The mother of Samuel, she was childless for many years and therefore considered to be out of favour with God. She made a promise that if God granted her a son she would dedicate him to the service of his sanctuary at Shiloh (1 Sam 1:1–28).

Hazael. An army officer who came to the Syrian throne shortly before 840 B.C. by suffocating the ruling monarch, Benhadad, in his bed. Elijah had been instructed to anoint Hazael king of Syria, but had not been able to do so before his death. Elisha is said to have told Hazael that he would become king, though he did not apparently anoint him (2 Kgs 8:7–15). Hazael was to be a scourge to Israel throughout his long reign, and it is significant that the people of Israel were prepared to see even an enemy who oppressed them as God's appointed agent.

Hazor. A large town in the far north of Israel, one of those which Solomon specially fortified and made into a garrison town for his chariot forces (1 Kgs 9:15–19).

Hebrew. The language in which the Old Testament was written. Over the last sixty years, archaeological work has brought to light a vast quantity of texts in Hebrew or closely related Semitic languages, and this has greatly increased our knowledge.

Hebrews, Letter to the. Although traditionally ascribed to Paul, it has long been recognised that this is not one of Paul's letters, being quite unlike Paul's writing in both style and content. The main theme of the letter is an interpretation of the significance of Jesus' life and teaching based on the concept of priesthood—Jesus as the supreme mediator between God and man. It is most famous for its eleventh chapter on the nature of faith. The obviously Jewish outlook of the writer has led most commentators to assume that the letter was destined for a community of Jewish Christians, as the title implies, but even this has been questioned and it has to be said that authorship, destination and circumstances of writing remain conjectural.

Hebron. A city in the territory of Judah, it was David's capital for a time before the northern tribes accepted him as king and he established Jerusalem as the new religious and administrative centre.

Hermon. At over 2,800 m., Mt Hermon is the highest point in Palestine and also represents the far north-eastern frontier of Israel at the height of her power. It is considered by some to be the scene of the transfiguration because of its proximity to Caesarea Philippi.

Herod Family. Four Herods of four different generations are mentioned in the New Testament, in addition to Philip, who was also a member of the family. Herod the Great ruled the whole of the territory of the Jews (under Roman authority) from 37 B.C. to 4 B.C. He was the Herod ruling at the time of the birth of Jesus (which was incorrectly calculated when the Christian calendar was established: hence the anomaly of Jesus' birth taking place "before Christ"). Although suspicious and intolerant by nature, he kept his country free from conflict for 35 years, which was no mean achievement. He was a master architect and astute ruler. In 2015 excavations at Herodium, 10 miles south of Jerusalem, revealed the dramatic entrance to his palace.

Although certainly guilty of cruelty, his massacre of the innocents is not accepted by many historians. His tomb has been located.

On his death, his kingdom was divided between his three sons, Archelaus, Herod Antipas and Philip. Archelaus, however, was soon deposed in A.D. 6 and his territory came under the direct rule of a Roman governor. Herod Antipas, the Herod who had John the Baptist killed and before whom Jesus was tried, continued to rule Galilee and Peraea until his banishment in A.D. 39. Philip ruled Ituraea and Trachonitis until his death in A.D. 34. The territories of both Herod Antipas and Philip passed to Herod Agrippa I, who persecuted the Church and had James put to death (Acts 12:2). He himself died in A.D. 44 and was succeeded by Herod Agrippa II, the king before whom Paul appeared in Acts 25.

Herod the Great

Artistobulus	Antipas (tetrarch of Galilee) Mk 6:14	Archelaus	Philip (tetrarch of Decapolis)

Herod Agrippa I Acts 12:1	Herodias Mk 6:17	

Herod Agrippa II Acts 25:13	Bernice Acts 25:13	Drusilla Acts 24:24

Herodias. Originally the wife of Philip (not the tetrarch), she was subsequently married to his half-brother Antipas. It was John the Baptist's objection to this marriage which brought about his imprisonment and eventual death (Mk 6:14–29).

Hezekiah. King of Judah (715–687 B.C.). Hezekiah came to the throne as a vassal of Assyria as his father, Ahaz, had been. The Assyrian ruler, Sargon II, was having difficulties elsewhere in his empire, however, and Hezekiah soon removed Assyrian religious objects from the temple, a step he might have hesitated to take but for the temporary Assyrian weakness. He also attacked the old Canaanite places of worship which were still used, and broke a bronze serpent allegedly made by Moses before which incense was burned. The exact extent of his religious reforms is uncertain, but it is clear that they were far-reaching. In spite of his removal of Assyrian cult objects from the temple,

Hezekiah did not join other small Palestinian states, led by the Philistine city of Ashdod, in rebellion against the Assyrians in 713 B.C., perhaps because Isaiah opposed the enterprise. In 705 B.C., however, when Sargon II died, Hezekiah did refuse tribute to Assyria.

Facing troubles elsewhere, it was 701 B.C. before the new king Sennacherib was able to move against Judah. When he did, he devastated 46 of Judah's fortresses and, in the words of his own inscription, shut up Hezekiah in Jerusalem "like a bird in a cage". What happened at this point is not clear. 2 Kings 18:14–16 says that Sennacherib demanded vastly increased tribute and Hezekiah meekly agreed. 2 Kings 18:17–19:37, however, relates how Hezekiah defied Sennacherib and the Assyrian had to return home after his army had been struck down by some mysterious agency. No attempt to reconcile these conflicting statements is entirely satisfactory, and this has led some scholars to suggest that the account of Hezekiah's successful defiance relates to a second invasion about 688 B.C. There is no corroborative evidence for this however.

Hinnom. A deep valley south-west of Jerusalem where child sacrifice was carried out according to Jeremiah 7:30–34. It is not clear from Jeremiah when this occurred (at no time was it a normal feature of Jewish religion), but it may have been during the long and evil reign of Manasseh (687–642 B.C.).

Hittites. A people referred to many times in the early period of Old Testament history from the time of the patriarchs to the establishment of the monarchy.

Hosea. Hosea prophesied in the northern kingdom of Israel shortly after Amos (i.e. from about 750 B.C. onwards) during a period of political anarchy which was eventually to lead to the end of Israel as an independent kingdom in 721 B.C. His prophetic message is coloured throughout by his own experience of marriage, though the facts about his marriage are disputed, the evidence being ambiguous on many points. The most commonly accepted view is that his wife Gomer was unfaithful to him and eventually left him to become a prostitute. Falling upon hard times, she was sold into slavery, from which Hosea bought her back,

attempting to reform her by keeping her in seclusion for a period of time. Such a view certainly accords well with Hosea's daring portrayal of God as the faithful and persistent lover who will not abandon his faithless wife Israel. Although Hosea's message is therefore supremely hopeful, being based on the constant love of God for his people, it is not lacking in stern warnings of judgement, for the concept of God's love does not exclude the possibility of corrective punishment and Hosea is utterly appalled by the idolatry and unrighteousness of his people.

Yet even God's judgement is seen as something positive, as a necessary step towards the re-establishment of a relationship between God and his people which is based on faithfulness on both sides.

Hoshea. King of Israel (732–724 B.C.). The last king of Israel, Hoshea came to the throne by the assassination of his predecessor Pekah. It was a period of Assyrian domination and for a while Hoshea wisely remained subservient to his Assyrian masters. When the capable Assyrian ruler Tiglath-pileser III died in 727 B.C., however, Hoshea made an alliance with Egypt and withheld tribute. The new Assyrian king Shalmaneser V, attacked and overran Israel, taking Hoshea captive in 724 B.C., though the capital city, Samaria, held out against the Assyrians until 721 B.C. Thereafter Israel was an Assyrian province.

I

Iconium. A city in the Roman province of Galatia visited by Paul and Barnabas on Paul's first missionary journey (Acts 13:51–14:6).

Immanuel. *See* **Emmanuel.**

Isaac. The son of Abraham and Sarah, he was nearly sacrificed to God until God showed Abraham that he did not require child sacrifice (Gen 22:1–14). His wife Rebecca bore him twin sons, Esau and Jacob, whose descendants became the Edomites and the people of Israel respectively.

Isaiah. It has long been recognised that the book of Isaiah is the work of three major prophets, often known for convenience as first, second and third Isaiah.

First Isaiah, also sometimes called Isaiah of Jerusalem, prophesied from "the year that King Uzziah died" (i.e. 742 B.C.) until at least the end of the eighth century B.C., and his work occupies chapters 1–39 of the book which bears his name. It has been said that Isaiah was more of a statesman than a prophet because of the close interest he took in Judah's affairs, and especially her foreign policy. Thus, when King Ahaz was threatened by Pekah of Israel and Rezin of Syria, Isaiah advised against taking panic measures because he believed the threat would be short-lived. Ahaz, however, ignored his advice, appealed to Assyria for help and became an Assyrian vassal for the remainder of his reign.

Later Isaiah was to warn King Hezekiah against becoming involved in rebellion against Assyria led by the Philistine city-state of Ashdod, and this time his advice was heeded. He also constantly spoke out against reliance on Egyptian help against the Assyrians. But to call Isaiah a statesman rather than a prophet is to ignore the religious foundations of his political advice. He believed in a God whose control of history was absolute. He also believed that his people's difficulties were the result of their failure to put their trust in God and to meet his moral demands in their social life. For him, therefore, the way to solve their problems was to put these things right. Political intrigues and alliances with foreign nations were not only worthless but diverted attention from the real issues. For much of his career Isaiah regarded the Assyrians as instruments of God's judgement, and consequently argued that resistance to them was futile, but towards the end of his life he encouraged King Hezekiah in defying them, perhaps feeling that his people had now received sufficient punishment and certainly believing that the arrogance of the Assyrians must in its own time come under God's judgement.

Second Isaiah, the author of chapters 40–55 of the prophetic book, was a prophet of the exile. Like the earlier Isaiah he had a profound belief in the utter sovereignty of God, and expresses this in some of the most beautiful and exalted language in the Old Testament. His most important contribution to religious thought, however, comes in the sections which speak of a suffering servant of the Lord. These passages are enigmatic, and it is not clear whether Isaiah was speaking of a past, present or future figure. What is important is the insight—while astonishing in his time—that a man who set himself to serve God faithfully might be despised, reviled and rejected and that God might somehow bring healing to his people through such a person. Whatever Isaiah himself intended, it is hardly surprising that Christians equate the suffering servant with Christ.

Third Isaiah, responsible for chapters 56–66, mostly addresses people back in Jerusalem after the exile, offering them encouragement through his belief in a God who keeps his promises. It may seem strange to us that the work of three different prophets, living at different times, should have been combined in this way in one book under one name, yet the book does show a fundamental unity of outlook, especially in its proclamation of God's sovereignty. It seems possible that the first Isaiah left behind a group of disciples which continued in existence long after his death, a group which included the two later authors and which was responsible for the editing of the book of Isaiah as we know it.

Isaiah is sometimes called the 'Prince of the Prophets'.

Ishbosheth. The only one of Saul's four sons to survive his final tragic battle against the Philistines, Ishbosheth was accepted as king by the northern tribes while Judah proclaimed David as its king (2 Sam 2:8–11). David carefully avoided open confrontation with Ishbosheth while constantly weakening his position by diplomatic pressure. Abner, Saul's general, soon defected and Ishbosheth was later murdered in his bed by two of his officers (2 Sam 4:5–7).

Ishmael. The son Abraham had by Hagar, Sarah's slave-girl, when it seemed that Sarah herself would have no children (Gen 16:1–4, 15). After Sarah had Isaac, Hagar and Ishmael were driven out (Gen 21:9–20).

Israel. In the first instance this is the name given to Jacob by his mysterious opponent in the wrestling match at Peniel (Gen 32:22–28). His descendants therefore became the children of Israel, or simply Israel. When, after Solomon's reign, the northern tribes rebelled against his son Rehoboam, the term was reserved for the northern kingdom as opposed to the southern kingdom of Judah. Sometimes the term "all Israel" is used of the undivided kingdom to distinguish this usage from the later use for the northern kingdom only.

Issachar. (1) The ninth son of Jacob, his fifth by Leah.

(2) The tribe of Issachar which occupied a fairly small area west of the Jordan and south of the Sea of Galilee.

J

Jabesh-Gilead. A town just east of the Jordan which Saul delivered from the Ammonites (1 Sam 11:1–11). In gratitude the men of Jabesh-Gilead rescued the bodies of Saul and his sons from the Philistines and took them back to give them a decent burial.

Jacob. One of twin brothers, Jacob nevertheless had no claim on his father's property or the special blessing reserved for the eldest son because he was the second from his mother's womb. However, he first got his brother, Esau, to agree to sell his birthright (Gen 25:29–33) and then tricked his blind father Isaac into giving him the blessing (Gen 27:1–29). He fled from his father's wrath to his uncle Laban, in whom he met someone almost as crafty as himself. He served Laban for seven years for his younger daughter Rachel, only to find after his marriage that he had been given the elder daughter Leah (Gen 29:15–26). He then had to serve another seven years for Rachel. Nevertheless, Jacob prospered with Laban and returned a wealthy man to be reconciled with Esau (Gen 33:1–4). Bilhah and Zilpah were concubines of the Hebrew patriarch. He ended his days in Egypt as the guest of his eleventh son, Joseph (Gen 47:11–12). The stories of Jacob which do not gloss over his failings, show a man who is often self-centred and careless about God in his early years, but who comes to see that God has plans for him and has in fact been caring for him throughout his life.

Jahweh. *See* **Yahweh.**

James. (1) One of the three disciples who were with Jesus on the mount of transfiguration (Mk 9:2–9). The brother of John and a son of Zebedee, he was later killed by Herod Agrippa.

(2) Another disciple, the son of Alphaeus, of whom nothing more is known (Mk 4:18).

(3) The brother of Jesus who apparently became an apostle after a special resurrection appearance to him (1 Cor 15:7, Gal 1:19) and subsequently became leader of the Jerusalem church (Acts 15:13–21).

James, Letter of. Though some have identified the author as James the brother of Jesus, this can only be speculation, nor is there any clear indication to whom the letter was first addressed. It is a set of practical instructions on how to live the Christian life, and its emphasis on deeds (as opposed to Paul's emphasis on faith) led Luther to dismiss it as "a letter of straw". In reality, however, there is no conflict; for both James and Paul righteousness is a product of faith.

Jebusites. The original inhabitants of Jerusalem, they were not conquered by the people of Israel when they occupied Canaan but remained as an independent city-state. David took the city, however, by sending his men along a water tunnel, and established his capital there.

Jehoahaz. (1) King of Israel (815–801 B.C.). The son of Jehu, Jehoahaz was an ineffective ruler and spent the whole of his reign under Syrian domination.

(2) King of Judah (609 B.C.). The unfortunate Jehoahaz succeeded his father Josiah who had been killed in battle with the Egyptians. He was almost immediately deposed by the Egyptians in favour of his brother Eliakim, who took the throne-name Jehoiakim.

Jehoash. King of Israel (801–786 B.C.). A strong ruler who regained from Syria all the territory lost by his father Jehoahaz, and who also defeated King Amaziah of Judah after being provoked into a quarrel he did not seek.

Jehoiachin. King of Judah (598–597 B.C.). Jehoiachin came to the throne when a Babylonian army was already on the march against Jerusalem because of his father Jehoiakim's rebellion. Within three months he surrendered the city and was taken into exile where he spent the rest of his life.

Jehoiakim. King of Judah (609–598 B.C.). Placed on the throne by the Egyptians after they had killed his father Josiah in battle and deposed his elder brother Jehoahaz, Jehoiakim remained a vassal of Egypt until 605 B.C. when the Egyptians were routed by the Babylonians. He transferred his allegiance to Babylon, but in 601 B.C. another battle between the Egyptians and Babylonians on the Egyptian frontier resulted in the withdrawal of the Babylonian armies to reorganise. Interpreting this as weakness, Jehoiakim rebelled. In December 598 the Babylonians marched against him, and in the same month Jehoiakim died, possibly by assassination (this may be implied by Jeremiah 22:18, 36:30). Jeremiah, himself forced into hiding by Jehoiakim, is scathing in his criticism of the king as one who callously exploited his people and shed much innocent blood.

Jehoram. (1) King of Israel (849–842 B.C.). A son of Ahab, he actually succeeded his brother Ahaziah, who died after a short reign leaving no sons. During his reign the Moabites successfully rebelled against him, and the war against Syria, in which Ahab had lost his life, dragged on. It was while recovering from wounds received in the Syrian war that he was killed in Jehu's coup.

(2) King of Judah (849–842 B.C.). Like his contemporary and namesake in Israel, Jehoram of Judah lost territory to his enemies in Edom and also on the Philistine frontier. He was married to Ahab's sister (or possibly daughter) Athaliah, who was to seize the throne after the death of their son Ahaziah.

Jehoshaphat. King of Judah (873–849 B.C.). A capable ruler who allied himself with Omri and Ahab, his contemporaries in Israel, to subjugate enemies across the Jordan and, with rather less success, keep the Syrians at bay. In 2 Chronicles 19:4–11 we are told of a reform of the judicial system he carried out, and it seems from 2 Kings 3:14 that Elisha held him in considerable respect.

Jehu. Jehu was anointed king while serving as commander of Jehoram's army by one of the prophets acting on Elisha's instructions (2 Kgs 9:1–10). He promptly killed Jehoram, who was recovering from wounds in Jezreel, King Ahaziah of Judah who had the misfortune to be visiting him at the time, and the evil Jezebel who, as queen mother, still exercised considerable influence. He went on to exterminate every surviving member of the royal family and the worshippers of Baal. In so doing he broke the alliance with Judah, on which Israel's defence against her enemies largely depended, and deprived the nation of many of its leading figures. In spite of the ferocity of his coup, he was unable to withstand the aggression of Hazael, king of Syria, and lost all his territory across the Jordan.

Jephthah. One of the inspired leaders of Israel known as judges, before the days of the monarchy. He defeated the Ammonites, having made a vow to sacrifice the first living thing he met on his return if God gave him victory. In consequence he was compelled to sacrifice his own daughter (Judg 11:1–39).

Jeremiah. Jeremiah was numerous to be a prophet as a young man about 630 B.C. and prophesied until after the fall of Jerusalem to the Babylonians in 586 B.C. His long prophetic ministry therefore spanned the last years of Judah as an independent kingdom. His early prophecies paint a terrifying picture of impending disaster (Jer 5:23–31) which, in the short term at least, never materialised and made Jeremiah feel that God had made a laughing stock of him.

Among the numerous fascinations of the book of Jeremiah are the frankness of the prophet's conversations with God and his reflections on how to distinguish true prophecy from false. When Josiah carried out his great religious reforms in 622 B.C. Jeremiah supported them and thus aroused the anger of his family, who were priests at Anathoth just outside Jerusalem and probably objected to the ban on sacrificial worship except in the temple.

Although he was a supporter of the reforms initially, Jeremiah soon saw their limitations or even dangers: because the external forms of Judah's religion had been regularised people might become complacent, failing to realise that what God really required was a change of heart. It was this that led Jeremiah to speak of a new covenant written in men's hearts (Jer 31:31–34). From Jehoiakim's time onwards Jeremiah became increasingly unpopular because of his insistence that the presence of the temple would not save the Jews from the Babylonians, contrary to the accepted doctrine that God would never permit his city to be taken or his temple destroyed (Jer 26:1–11). During the siege of Jerusalem he was imprisoned and nearly killed as a traitor because he constantly advocated surrender and was suspected of deserting to the Babylonians.

When Jerusalem finally fell, Jeremiah was permitted to remain rather than being taken into exile on the express instructions of King Nebuchadnezzar (Jer 39:11–14). After the murder of the newly appointed governor, Gedaliah, Jeremiah was taken against his will to Egypt by the remaining officials who fled there. Here he ended his days. In spite of the almost unrelieved tragedy of his life, Jeremiah was not without hope. At the height of the siege of Jerusalem he bought a plot of land from a kinsman as a symbol that people would one day have the confidence to engage in business again (Jer 32:1–15), and he wrote a letter to the first group of exiles, taken to Babylon in 597 B.C., declaring that the future of the nation was in their hands and that God had plans for their welfare (Jer 29:1–14).

Jericho. A very ancient city a few miles west of the Jordan, it was the first stronghold to be captured by Joshua after crossing the river. In Elijah's time it was the home of a company of prophets (2 Kgs 2:4–5), and in the gospels it is the setting for the healing of blind Bartimaeus and the rehabilitation of Zacchaeus (Lk 18:35–19:9).

Jeroboam I. King of Israel (922–901 B.C.). Jeroboam first appears as one of Solomon's officials in charge of forced labour. Told by the prophet Ahijah that he would receive ten of the twelve tribes of Israel, he became a marked man and had to flee to Egypt to escape Solomon's wrath (1 Kgs 11:26–40). After Solomon's death he returned to lead the northern tribes in their revolt against Rehoboam, and became the first king of the northern kingdom (1 Kgs 12:1–20). He established a capital at Shechem initially, but later moved to Tirzah, which remained the capital until the reign of Omri. Clearly he could not have his people going to the Jerusalem temple to worship, since the cult there celebrated amongst other things, God's eternal covenant with the house of David. He therefore established two rival centres at the ancient shrines of Dan and Bethel, and in each of them placed a golden calf. The significance of these animals is not in fact clear, but the biblical writers assume that they were idols and the name of Jeroboam is always associated by them with idolatry (1 Kgs 12:26–30).

Jeroboam II. King of Israel (786–746 B.C.). Long-lived and capable, in human terms Jeroboam II must be judged one of the most successful kings the northern kingdom ever had. The biblical record gives few details but states that he "restored the border of Israel from the entrance to Hamath as far as the Sea of Arabah" (2 Kgs 14:25). It appears from this that his north-eastern border stood where it had been in Solomon's time.

The books of Amos and Hosea give a vivid picture of social conditions during Jeroboam's reign, a picture of great prosperity, but prosperity confined to a fortunate minority who cared little for the fate of the masses.

Jerusalem. An ancient city originally occupied by the Jebusites but captured from them by David. It made an ideal capital because of its military strength, because it was near the border between Judah and the northern tribes who were now being brought together again under David's rule, and because it did not actually belong to any of the tribes, having remained as an independent enclave until David took it. As time went on it acquired a mystical significance as the city of God, with the temple as his dwelling-place. This mystique was partly, though not entirely, destroyed by the experience of the exile, which showed that Israel's faith could survive without Jerusalem and its temple.

Jesse. The father of David (1 Sam 16:1).

Jesus. Without doubt more words have been written about Jesus than any other figure in history, and the debate still continues, not only about the historical facts but about their significance. It is impossible in a short article to do justice to the complexity of the issues arising from the life of this man, but the main facts of his public ministry may be stated with some certainty.

The existence of Jesus, as a religious leader put to death by the Romans at the instigation of the Jewish authorities, is attested by the contemporary Jewish historian Josephus. For the details of his life and teaching we have to rely mainly on the four gospels written some 35 to 65 years after his death. The earliest of these, Mark, does not record the birth of Jesus and the birth stories contained in Luke and Matthew are important more for their symbolic value than for their contribution to our historical knowledge. They do establish the date of Jesus' birth as about 4 B.C. (the obvious anomaly is due to the fact that when the

Christian calendar was established much later the date of Jesus' birth was miscalculated).

Virtually nothing is known about his life until he was nearly thirty when he received baptism from John the Baptist and was confirmed in his conviction that God had entrusted him with a special mission and he retired to the wilderness to reflect upon it (Lk 3:21–22, 4:1–13). When he returned he declared his manifesto in the synagogue at Nazareth using some words of Isaiah, "to bring good news to the poor, to proclaim liberty to the captive and recovery of sight to the blind, to set free the oppressed, and to announce that the time has come when God will save his people". He proceeded to put this manifesto into practice in both words and actions.

Jesus believed that the Kingdom of God foreshadowed in the Old Testament was about to be realised and his teaching was to prepare people for that Kingdom which he described in his parables. "Unless a man has been born again he cannot see the Kingdom of God" (Jn 3:3). Wherever he went he healed the sick.

Whether these were miracles in the sense that normal physical laws were set aside is, of course, open to question, but they are such an integral part of the gospel records that they cannot be ignored. It seems clear that Jesus was able to heal people who could not otherwise be healed in his day, and drove himself to exhaustion in doing so, thus demonstrating in practice the love of God he preached. Inevitably this made him popular, in the end embarrassingly so, for the people came to have expectations of him which he had no intention of fulfilling (Jn 6:14–15). As it became clear that he was not going to lead his countrymen in throwing off the the yoke of Roman rule, disillusionment set in.

It had also become clear that alongside the tremendous assurance of God's unwavering love Jesus set demands far harder to meet than those of the Old Testament. What other teacher had ever required that they should love their enemies and do good to those who hated them (Mt 5:43–48)? The religious authorities had never shared the popular enthusiasm for Jesus, partly because of his disregard for sabbath rules (Mk 2:23–3:6) but even more so because the note of authority in his teaching put them to shame and seemed to imply a special relationship with God (Mk 2:1–12). Jesus, well aware that their net was closing in around him, set out for Jerusalem for the final confrontation (Lk 9:51). Here, having failed to trap him by any legal method the authorities arrested him by night with the connivance of Judas (Mk 14:43–46), condemned him in their own court on the charge of blasphemy (Mk 14:55–64) and rushed him before the Roman governor on charges of political subversion (Mk 15:1–5). Within hours he was dead, executed by crucifixion (Mk 15:24–37).

Yet not long afterwards his followers, who had gone to ground after his arrest, were boldly proclaiming his message regardless of the risks and declaring that death had been unable to hold him fast (Acts 2:22–24). In all the inevitable questioning over the resurrection of Jesus one fact seems beyond dispute: that his disciples were prepared to stake their lives on its reality.

Jethro. A Midianite priest whose daughter Zipporah was married to Moses (Ex 2:16–22). He also advised Moses on the setting up of a judicial system after the exodus (Ex 18:13–26).

Jezebel. A Phoenician princess who was married to Ahab, probably as part of his father Omri's policy of friendly relations with the Phoenicians for trade purposes. She was a fanatical devotee of the Phoenician Baal Melkart and made strenuous efforts to introduce his worship to Israel, equally strenuously opposed by Elijah (1 Kgs 18:19–40). Her involvement in Naboth's unjust execution (1 Kgs 21:1–15) shows a completely despotic view of the king's rights. She outlived Ahab and continued to exercise an evil influence as queen mother during the reigns of his sons Ahaziah and Jehoram until killed in Jehu's rebellion.

Jezreel. A city which seems to have been used as a second capital by the kings of Israel about the time of Ahab. It was here that Jehoram

went to recover from his wounds received in the Syrian wars and where he was killed, together with Jezebel, in Jehu's coup (2 Kgs 9:14–35). Hosea named his first child Jezreel as a symbol of judgement on the house of Jehu for its unnecessary brutality (Hos 1:3–4).

Joab. David's commander-in-chief and a considerable influence upon him. It was he who persuaded David to accept Absalom back from exile (2 Sam 14:1–24), though after Absalom's death he took David to task for showing excessive grief over his rebellious son rather than gratitude to those who had been loyal to him (2 Sam 19:1–8).

As David's life drew to a close Joab backed Adonijah as his successor, but David nominated Solomon, who subsequently had Joab killed (1 Kgs 1:5–6, 2:28–34).

Joash. King of Judah (837–800 B.C.). The only son of Ahaziah to escape Athaliah's slaughter, he was kept in hiding for six years and then proclaimed king at the age of seven on the instructions of Jehoiada the priest (2 Kgs 11:1–11). Under Jehoiada's influence he made repairs to the temple, but according to Chronicles 24:17–22 he showed a very different character once Jehoiada was dead. Certainly he must have aroused the hatred of his subjects, as he was eventually assassinated.

Job. The book of Job is a protest against the commonly accepted view that God rewards the good with prosperity and punishes the wicked with suffering. It postulates the case of a man who had led a blameless life (Job's personal code of conduct described in chapter 31 is astonishing in its closeness to the ideals later proclaimed by Jesus) who nevertheless suffers every conceivable disaster from the death of his children to painful and disfiguring illness. The major part of the book consists of dialogue between Job and three of his friends (later joined by a fourth).

The friends try to convince Job that he must have done something to deserve his misfortunes, while Job continues to protest his innocence and cannot accept this explanation of his suffering. The book does not arrive at any specific answer to the problem of innocent suffering but rejects facile solutions, declaring in majestic poetry that God is far greater than human understanding can encompass.

Joel. The book of Joel tells us nothing about the author except his father's name, and there is no clear indication when he lived, though a date in the fifth or fourth century B.C. is likely. The prophet regards a severe infestation of locusts as a sign of God's judgement on his people, and calls them to repent. He looks forward to a time when God will pour out his spirit on everyone, men and women, young and old alike, a passage quoted by Peter on the first Whit Sunday.

John. (1) John the Baptist. A kinsman of Jesus, he was also his forerunner, preaching repentance to all who would listen and baptising them in the Jordan as a symbol of the new way of life to which they committed themselves (Lk 3:3–14). Jesus accepted baptism from John but then embarked on a very different kind of ministry. It is clear, however, that the two men regarded each other with the greatest respect (Lk 7:18–28). John was imprisoned by Herod Antipas for criticising his marriage to his half-brother's wife Herodias, and it was Herodias who eventually engineered his execution (Mk 6:17–28).

(2) The brother of James, a son of Zebedee and one of the inner group of disciples who were with Jesus on the mount of transfiguration. Though the identification between John and "the disciple whom Jesus loved" in John's gospel is not certain, it is widely assumed. In the early days of the Christian church he was a prominent leader with Peter (Acts 3:1–10, 4:1–21) but we hear relatively little of him afterwards. His connection with the writing of the fourth gospel is problematic (see below).

John, Gospel of. The fourth gospel is clearly different from the other three even to the casual reader. To name only the most obvious difference, whereas the teaching of Jesus in the first three gospels is in the form of short pithy sayings or vivid parables, in John it appears as long philosophical discourses. The gospel is not therefore so much an account of the life of Jesus as an interpretation of its significance. But although the author has deliberately and freely recast the teaching of Jesus into a more explicitly theological form, this does not mean that he is not concerned with the historical truth; indeed, the leading British New Testament scholar of recent times has argued that in some respects the historical information in the fourth gospel is superior to that in the other three. The author then was a man of great intellectual stature who had long reflected on the significance of Jesus, and was capable of expressing his conclusions in a form more akin to Greek philosophical writing than traditional Jewish teaching, but who was also in contact with a good historical source independent of the other three gospels. John the disciple of Jesus, with his humble background as a Galilean fisherman, seems an unlikely author, but may well have been the source of the author's historical information.

John, Letters of. The three letters of John show many similarities with the fourth gospel in their vocabulary, style and thematic content, but there are some difficulties in ascribing them to the same author. If they were not by the author of the fourth gospel they were certainly written by someone thoroughly steeped in his way of thinking. The first letter is concerned with a form of false teaching which claims that there is a special way of knowing God open only to the initiated, that Jesus was not truly a physical person and that morality, having nothing to do with actions in the physical world has nothing to do with religion. In opposing this heresy John insists on the physical reality of Jesus and declares that knowing God is inseparable from loving others. Whereas the first letter appears to be a "circular" for general dissemination among the churches, the second is addressed to "the dear lady and her children"—probably a local church. It is much shorter but deals with the same false teaching.

The third letter is addressed to an individual, Gaius, encouraging him and warning him against one Diotrephes.

Jonadab. The son of Rechab, he seems to have been the real founder of the Rechabites who tried to maintain the way of life of their forefathers, living in tents rather than houses and not planting crops or vineyards or drinking wine. Apart from this the only information we have on Jonadab is that he helped Jehu in his seizure of the throne (2 Kgs 10:15-17).

Jonah. The book of Jonah is in effect a short story, making a very important point in a humorous way. The essence of the story is Jonah's reluctance to preach to the people of Nineveh, the Assyrian capital, in case they listen to him and consequently enjoy the benefits of God's favour! His attempt to flee to a distant place out of God's reach is foiled by a storm and the great fish which conveniently deposits him on the Palestinian shore once more. Realising that he has no option but to do as God has told him, he goes and preaches to the people of Nineveh, who, as he had feared, repent of their evil and turn to God. Jonah consequently sulks over God's failure to punish them for their previous sins until God shows him how unreasonable his attitude is. The book is thus a witty but serious appeal to the Jews to broaden their conception of God and to rejoice in his concern for other nations. In spirit it comes close to several of the parables of Jesus, *e.g.* the parable of the prodigal son and his elder brother who refuses to rejoice over the return of the lost one.

Jonathan. One of the four sons of Saul whose reckless daring was largely responsible for a victory over the Philistines at the pass of Michmash (1 Sam 14:1-23). He is best known, however, for his unwavering friendship with David which survived his father's intense jealousy and David's ultimate exile (1 Sam 19:1-7, 20:1-42). He was killed, together with his father and two other brothers, in battle against the Philistines (1 Sam 31:1-4).

Joppa. A port on the Palestinian coast where Peter was staying when he had his vision showing him that there was no distinction between Jew and Gentile in God's sight (Acts 10:9-23).

Joram. *See* Jehoram.

Jordan. The river Jordan runs north-south from the foot of Mount Hermon to the Dead Sea through a rift valley which is below sea level for the greater part of its length. It forms a natural division between the central highlands of Palestine to the west and the plateau of the Transjordanian desert to the east. As well as being a natural barrier it is also a psychological one, the crossing of the Jordan having the same sort of significance for the people of Israel as the crossing of the Rubicon for Julius Caesar—a decisive step on the road to conquest.

Joseph. (1) The eleventh son of Jacob, his first by Rachel. A precocious child who provoked the enmity of his brothers, he was taken and sold as a slave in Egypt by Ishmaelite or Midianite traders. Not only is the story confused on this point but also as to whether he was sold to the traders by his brothers or rescued by the traders from a pit where his brothers had left him (Gen 37:12-35). After various vicissitudes in Egypt he gained high office by his power to interpret dreams, and in this position he was able both to help and test his brothers incognito when they came seeking corn in time of famine (Gen 41:1-45:14). Eventually he brought his father and brothers to live in Egypt (Gen 47:11-12). While there is no reason to doubt that the Joseph stories have a historical basis, they may well have been embellished in order to drive home the theological point made in Joseph's words to his brothers when he revealed his identity: "so it was not really you who sent me here but God" (Gen 45:8). Joseph gave rise to two of the tribes of Israel named after his sons Ephraim and Manasseh.

(2) The husband of Mary. Information on Joseph is sparse. He was a descendant of David (Mt 1:20), and worked as a village carpenter in Nazareth (Mt 13:55). He is not mentioned after the visit to Jerusalem when Jesus was twelve (Lk 2:41-51), and it seems a reasonable supposition that he had died before Jesus began his public ministry. This has led to the tradition, not necessarily true, that he was much older than Mary.

(3) Joseph of Arimathea. A rich Jew who was a member of the Jewish Council but who sympathised with Jesus and his cause. After Jesus' execution he requested the body from Pilate and had it buried in his own rock-hewn tomb (Mk 15:42-46).

Joshua. The book of Joshua takes its name from Moses' successor and records the invasion and settlement of Canaan by the people of Israel under his leadership. While it includes some very early material, the book has been extensively edited and did not reach its final form until centuries after the events it describes. It is generally considered that the picture it presents is a simplified one, representing the invasion of Canaan as a single co-ordinated campaign with Joshua as commander-in-chief. In fact, the likelihood is that the occupation was far more haphazard, with some of the tribes at least acting independently and Joshua commanding only the most successful part of the invasion forces. In particular there are indications in Joshua 15:13-14 and Judges 1:11-21 that the southern tribes of Judah, Simeon and Benjamin may have operated in isolation from the main body with a man called Caleb as their leader. The most famous incident in the conquest is undoubtedly the battle of Jericho, and controversy still rages on what actually happened on this occasion (Josh 6:1-20). In spite of the unresolved historical questions, the character of Joshua emerges clearly—a man of simple faith who believed that God had given the land of Canaan to the people of Israel and would continue to support them if they remained true to him.

Josiah. King of Judah (640-609 B.C.). Josiah is chiefly remembered for the great religious reform he carried out in 622 B.C. following the discovery in the temple of a Book of the Covenant which made him realise how far short his people had fallen from the standards God demanded. He closed down all pagan altars and, in order to prevent irregularities, decreed that sacrifice could only be offered in the temple in Jerusalem. These measures were extended even to parts of the old northern kingdom of

Israel, indicating the degree of freedom Josiah enjoyed due to the preoccupation of the Assyrians with survival against the Medes and Babylonians. He also reinstated the celebration of the Passover which had apparently lapsed (2 Kgs 23:1–23). In 609 B.C. the Egyptians marched through Judah on their way to render assistance to the beleaguered Assyrians, preferring to maintain a weakened Assyria in power than to face a strong Babylon. Josiah tried to stop them and was killed in battle at Megiddo.

Jotham. King of Judah (742–735 B.C.). The son of Uzziah, Jotham ruled as co-regent with his father as his father had contracted "leprosy" (*i.e.* a disfiguring skin disease, not necessarily leprosy as it is known today), and could not carry out public duties. Little is said about Jotham except that he continued the good work of his father, building the upper gate of the temple. At the end of his reign he was under pressure from Pekah of Israel and Rezin of Syria to join an anti-Assyrian coalition, but this problem was left to his successor Ahaz.

Judaea. Like many names which denote an area, the term Judaea is used differently at different times. Its most common usage, however, is to denote the Roman province of Judaea, the area of southern Palestine which from A.D. 6 onwards came under the rule of a Roman governor rather than a member of the Herod family. It was this province which was governed by Pontius Pilate and later by Felix and Festus.

Judah. (1) Fourth son of both Jacob and Leah.
(2) The tribe of Judah which occupied a large area to the west of the Dead Sea and as far as the Egyptian frontier.
(3) The name of the southern kingdom after the northern tribes had broken away under Jeroboam I. While its boundaries coincided roughly with the old tribal area of Judah, it also included most of the territory of Benjamin.

Judas. (1) Judas, son of James, a disciple of Jesus about whom nothing else is known.
(2) Judas Iscariot, the disciple of Jesus who betrayed him. John 12:4–6 states that he was in charge of the common purse used by the disciples and stole from it, but apart from that there is little information on him prior to his act of betrayal. After betraying Jesus for 30 pieces of silver (Mt 26:14–16) he returned the money and committed suicide (Mt 27:3–5). His motives will always remain a matter of speculation. The most charitable view is that he was trying to force Jesus into a position where he would have to perform a dramatic miracle to save himself, thus convincing the sceptics, and he never anticipated that Jesus would let himself be killed.

Judas, Gospel of. An ancient Coptic manuscript, found in the 1970s in Egypt. Hailed as an authentic copy of a lost Gospel and portraying Judas, not as a traitor, but as carrying out Christ's plan.

Jude, Letter of. A short letter warning of the dangers of false teaching and the judgement which will befall those who distort the Christian message. Though it has been suggested on the basis of Mark 6:3 that the author was one of the brothers of Jesus, this is by no means certain.

Judge. The term is used in several senses in the Old Testament, including the modern sense of one who arbitrates in a legal dispute or enforces the law. There is, however, an important special use of the term to describe men like Gideon, Jephthah and Samson who exercised leadership among the tribes of Israel, especially in times of danger, during the period between the settlement of Canaan and the establishment of the monarchy. Their authority was regarded as God-given and was entirely personal, *i.e.* it did not extend to their sons. In many ways they acted as kings, but for a long time the establishment of a recognised monarchy was resisted on the grounds that it would be a denial of God's sovereignty (Judg 8:22–23).

Judges, Book of. This book deals with the history of the people of Israel during the period of the Judges, *i.e.* from the death of Joshua until shortly before the anointing of Saul as Israel's first king. It contains some material (*e.g.* the song of Deborah in chapter five) which is contemporaneous with the events described, and therefore of enormous historical value, though like all the historical books of the Old Testament it was not edited into its final form until centuries later.

Much of the book is concerned with the battles for survival against hostile tribes, but as in all the writings of the Old Testament the uniting theme is a theological one, tracing in Israel's history a recurring cycle of disobedience, oppression, repentance *etc.*

K

Kenites. A tribe which lived in southern Palestine and, unlike many of the surrounding tribes enjoyed friendly relations with the people of Israel, perhaps because they had religious affinities with them. Moses' father-in-law, Jethro, was a Kenite (Judg 1:16) and the Rechabites who long persisted as an ascetic group among the people of Israel appear to have been closely connected with the Kenites (1 Chr 2:55).

Kidron. A stream running through a deep valley to the east of Jerusalem and separating the city from the Mount of Olives.

Kings, Books of. The two books of Kings are the major source for nearly 400 years of the history of the people of Israel, from the accession of Solomon around 960 B.C., through the division of the kingdom on Solomon's death and the end of the northern kingdom after the fall of Samaria in 721 B.C., to the destruction of Jerusalem and the exile of the leading people by the Babylonians in 586 B.C. Like all the historical books of the Old Testament, it is a composite work containing material of different ages and not reaching its final form until centuries after some of the incidents described. Many of the major events recorded, however, can be confirmed by archaeological evidence from other sources, *e.g.* the Moabite stone, an inscription of Mesha, king of Moab, which describes relations between his people and the northern kingdom of Israel about the time of Jehoram and, except in minor details, agrees with the biblical record.

The interest of the authors of Kings was not in history as an academic exercise, however, but history as it revealed the hand of God, and the kings of Israel and Judah are therefore judged by their loyalty to Yahweh, and the fortunes of their people are related to this.

On this criterion all the kings of Israel are judged to have failed, but among the kings of Judah, Uzziah, Hezekiah and Josiah especially are regarded as good kings.

L

Laban. Jacob's uncle and the father of Leah and Rachel.

Lachish. An important city and stronghold about 50 km south-west of Jerusalem. Against both the Assyrians in 701 B.C. and the Babylonians in 587 B.C. it proved its defensive strength, in the latter campaign holding out longer than any other city except Jerusalem itself. Important archaeological finds have been made there, including the Lachish letters written in the heat of the Babylonian invasion.

Lamentations, Book of. Traditionally known as the Lamentations of Jeremiah, there is in fact no evidence to connect them with the prophet. The book is a collection of fine poems mourning the devastation of Jerusalem in 586 B.C. The third chapter expressed hope for the future, however, and the fifth is a prayer for mercy.

Laodicea. A city of Asia Minor near Colossae. The church there is referred to in Revelation 3:14–22 and criticised for its lukewarmness. There is particular irony in the author's claim that the church is blind, for Laodicea was famed for an eye ointment made there. It appears from Colossians 4:16 that Paul wrote a letter to Laodicea, though he never visited it as far as is known.

Last Supper. *See* **Lord's Supper.**

Lazarus. (1) The brother of Martha and Mary whom, according to John 11:17–44, Jesus raised to life again.

(2) The poor beggar in Jesus' parable of the rich man and Lazarus (Lk 16:19–31).

Leah. The elder daughter of Laban and first wife of Jacob. She bore six of Jacob's twelve sons.

Levi. (1) The third son of both Jacob and Leah.
(2) *See* **Matthew**.

Levites. It appears that the descendants of Levi never possessed any tribal territory of their own but were dispersed among the other tribes. At an early stage, by a process which is far from clear, they were associated with the priesthood, and it became the custom that only Levites could be priests, although not all Levites were. Later the term was used for an order of temple assistants with lower status than priests, as in the parable of the good Samaritan.

Leviticus. As the name of the book implies it is almost entirely concerned with Levitical or priestly duties (*see* above), the offering of worship and sacrifice, the maintenance of ritual purity and the proper response to God's holiness. To the modern reader who does not accept the need for physical sacrifice as part of worship, much of it may appear irrelevant or even repugnant, yet it represents a real desire to give to God the respect properly due to him, and it is not completely taken up with obscure ritual instructions, for it includes the words quoted with approval by Jesus, "love your neighbour as you love yourself " (Lev 19:18).

Lord's Prayer. This brief prayer, given by Jesus in response to a request from his disciples (Lk 11:1), is highly characteristic of his thought. It first places God at the centre of the worshipper's life and only then concerns itself with human needs, asking only for the basic physical requirements of food and the spiritual necessities of forgiveness and strength under testing.

Lord's Supper. The name given both to the last meal Jesus had with his disciples and to its re-enactment by the Christian community subsequently. The earliest account of the meal occurs in 1 Corinthians 11:23–26, and it is clear from the fact that Paul was instructing the Corinthian church in the proper celebration of the Lord's Supper that it was an established part of Christian worship by the mid-fifties A.D. Accounts are also given in the first three gospels. While John does not describe the meal itself, his treatment of the feeding of the five thousand is given strong sacramental overtones (Jn 6:25–58) which suggest a knowledge of the Lord's Supper. It is impossible to reconstruct with certainty the exact words of Jesus on this occasion, but it seems clear that he linked the breaking of bread and sharing of wine with his approaching sacrifice and ultimate triumph, and also with the new covenant (or new relationship) between God and man foreseen by Jeremiah (Mk 14:22–25).

Lot. A nephew of Abraham who journeyed with him to Canaan. Eventually they had to separate because their herds were too big to remain together, and Lot chose the plain of the Jordan near the Dead Sea as his territory. Escaping from the destruction of Sodom and Gomorrah his wife is said to have looked back and been turned into a pillar of salt (Gen 19:26).

Luke. Luke is referred to only three times in the New Testament, but is of special interest as being almost certainly the author of the third gospel and the book of Acts (*see below*). Only one of the references, that in Colossians 4:14, gives any information other than his name. Here he is spoken of as "our dear doctor", and since Paul has earlier named three people as the "only Jewish converts who work with me" it follows that Luke was a Gentile.

Luke, Gospel of. The question of the authorship of this gospel is closely linked to that of Acts, which is clearly a sequel to the gospel, being addressed to the same person Theophilus. The author of Acts sometimes uses the first person plural, showing that he was present himself for certain parts of the story, including Paul's crossing from Troas to Philippi on his second missionary journey and his voyage to Rome as a prisoner. It seems likely, therefore, that he would be among the people Paul names as his co-workers in his letters and, by a process of elimination, Luke emerges as the strongest candidate. Since there is also a tradition going back to the second century that Luke was the author of the third gospel this seems a near certainty. About half the material in Luke's gospel comes from Mark (in those days copying another author's work, far from being considered unethical, was regarded a mark of respect), and some of the remainder comes from a collection of the sayings of Jesus which Matthew evidently used as well. Luke had other sources of his own, however, and it is to him that we owe the preservation of some of Jesus' best-loved parables including those of the good Samaritan and the prodigal son.

He also gives us the story of Zacchaeus and the account of the two disciples on the road to Emmaus. He lays special emphasis on Jesus' concern for Gentiles and outcasts.

Lydia. A resident of Philippi and dealer in the purple-dyed cloth for which that area was famous, she was Paul's first convert there and opened her house to him and his companions.

M

Macedonia. A Roman province including parts of northern Greece, Albania and Serbia with Philippi as its chief city. It was here that Paul first preached in Europe (as opposed to Asia Minor) in response to a vision of a man of Macedonia asking for his help (Acts 16:9–12).

Magi, the 'wise men' from the East who presented gifts to the infant Jesus at Bethlehem. Only tradition suggests there may have been three and may have been kings.

Magnificat, the hymn of the Virgin Mary, given in Luke 1, 46 beginning in the Vulgate with the words "Magnificat anima mea Dominum" ("My soul doth magnify the Lord").

Malachi. The book of Malachi clearly comes from some time after the reconstruction of the temple following the Babylonian exile. A probable date would be the first half of the fifth century B.C. The prophet takes his people to task for their laxity in the worship of God and their failure to obey the terms of God's covenant. He warns of God's judgement but also speaks of his saving power (Mal 4:2–3).

Malta. Paul was shipwrecked and spent the rest of the winter here on his journey to Rome.

Manasseh. (1) The elder of Joseph's two sons.
(2) The tribe of Manasseh, which occupied a large area on both banks of the Jordan to the north of Ephraim.
(3) King of Judah (687–642 B.C.). Regarded as the worst king in Judah's history, he actively promoted Assyrian and other pagan religious practices, sacrificed his own son and "killed so many innocent people that the streets of Jerusalem were flowing with blood" (2 Kgs 21:16).

Manna. The name of the food which God is said to have provided for the people of Israel during their wanderings in the wilderness (Ex 16:1–31). It is thought to have been a secretion formed by insects feeding on the scrublands of the desert.

Mark. The house of John Mark's mother, Mary, appears to have been the headquarters of the Jerusalem church (Acts 12:12). Paul and Barnabas took him to work with them in Antioch (Acts 12:25) and subsequently on the first missionary journey (Acts 13:5). He left them at Perga to return to Jerusalem, however, and this led to Paul refusing to take him on his second journey, with the consequence that Barnabas took him to Cyprus instead (Acts 15:36–40). It is clear from Colossians 4:10 and other references that Mark later became a close associate of Paul, and we are also told here that he was Barnabas' cousin. *See also below*.

Mark, Gospel of. There is a tradition dating back to A.D. 135 that the second gospel was written by Mark on the basis of Peter's memories of the life and teaching of Jesus. It seems probable that Mark collected these reminiscences shortly before Peter's death in Nero's persecution of A.D. 64 and published his gospel in Rome soon afterwards. While the identification of this Mark with John Mark cannot be absolutely certain, it seems highly likely, since John Mark knew Peter from the early days in Jerusalem. The view that the gospel is based on the first-hand information of an eye-witness is borne out by the many vivid details it contains—details often omitted by Luke and Matthew when they later used Mark's work as a basis for their own. They had other material to include and economised on unnecessary detail. Mark's gospel is of special value, therefore, as the one with most direct links with the events described.

Martha. The sister of Mary and Lazarus, who gave Jesus hospitality at her home in Bethany just outside Jerusalem (Lk 10:38-41, Jn 11:1).

Mary. (1) The mother of Jesus. Our knowledge of Jesus' mother is very limited. The birth stories present her as a pious girl, open to God's bidding. Luke's account of the visit to Jerusalem when Jesus was twelve shows her anxious and somewhat uncomprehending at her unusual son (Lk 2:41-51), and it is later suggested (Mk 3:21) that she may have attempted to restrain Jesus in his public ministry. John records that she was present at the crucifixion, and that Jesus entrusted her to the "beloved disciple". By this time she must have been old by current standards and may well have died soon after.

(2) The sister of Martha and Lazarus, who was praised for her sense of priorities in listening to Jesus (Lk 10:38-41).

(3) Mary Magdalene. A woman whom Jesus cured of "seven demons" (Lk 8:2), and who became one of those who travelled with Jesus and his disciples ministering to their needs. She was present at the crucifixion, was among a group which discovered the empty tomb and was a witness of the resurrection (Mk 15:40, 16:1, Jn 20:11-18). The tradition which identifies her with the sinful woman of Luke 7:37 is wholly without foundation. In the Gnostic Gospels she is a key player in the Easter story.

(4) The mother of James and Joseph. Another woman who followed Jesus to Jerusalem, witnessed his crucifixion and saw the empty tomb (Mk 15:40, 47, 16:1).

(5) The mother of John Mark (Acts 12:12).

Massorah, a collection of criticisms on the Hebrew text of the Scriptures and rules for its correct interpretation.

Matthew. Also called Levi, Matthew was a tax collector before becoming one of the twelve disciples (Mt 9:9-13, cf. Mk 2:13-17).

Matthew, Gospel of. It is highly unlikely that the author of the gospel was the disciple Matthew, since he draws heavily on Mark for much of his material, and this would have been unnecessary for an eyewitness of the events. Like Luke, he also uses a collection of the sayings of Jesus in addition to some material of his own (e.g. the parable of the sheep and the goats). It is clear that the author was a Jewish Christian who was concerned among other things to stress the continuity between the Christian church and the old community of the people of Israel. Significantly, Matthew traces the ancestors of Jesus back to Abraham, whereas Luke traces them back to Adam, the symbolic father of the whole human race, and Matthew frequently states that events occurred in order to fulfil Old Testament prophecies. He arranges most of his material in five sections, possibly a conscious imitation of the Pentateuch (the five books of teaching which begin the Old Testament and have a special status among the Old Testament writings for Jews). Each section begins with a narrative and continues with the teaching of Jesus. It is the teaching of the first main sections in chapters 5-7 which constitutes the so-called Sermon on the Mount.

Megiddo. A city of strategic importance controlling the pass through the Carmel ridge from the coastal plain on the south to the Plain of Esdraelon on the north side. It was fortified by Solomon, and it was here that King Josiah lost his life in battle against the Egyptians.

Melchizedek. A king and priest who gave hospitality to Abraham (Gen 14:18-20) and who is referred to by the author of Hebrews as a forerunner of Christ, himself a priest-king.

Menahem. King of Israel (745-738 B.C.). Menahem secured the throne by the murder of his predecessor Shallum and a bloody struggle against his opponents. He gave tribute to the Assyrian ruler Tiglath-pileser III, hoping both to forestall any Assyrian designs on his territory and gain support to keep him in power. He raised the money by unpopular taxation.

Mephibosheth. A crippled son of Jonathan who

was befriended by David (2 Sam 9:1-13), though he later entertained hopes of gaining the throne as the only remaining descendant of Saul (2 Sam 16:3). Perhaps because this was by now a totally unrealistic hope, David chose to overlook the matter (Sam 19:24-30).

Mesha. The king of Moab during Jehoram's reign, he succeeded in regaining much territory from Israel, according to an ancient inscribed stone known as the Moabite stone (see below). This is consistent with 2 Kings 3:27, which implies that after a highly successful campaign against Mesha, the Israelite forces were unnerved by Mesha's sacrifice of his son and withdrew, having failed to bring the rebel into subjection.

Meshach. One of the three young men who, according to the book of Daniel, survived being thrown into a blazing furnace for refusing to worship a gold statue set up by King Nebuchadnezzar (Dan 3:1-27).

Mesopotamia. The fertile area between the rivers Tigris and Euphrates. It was from here that Abraham came. It was also the land of the Assyrians and Babylonians.

Messiah. The Hebrew word means "anointed one" and therefore implies kingship. "Christ" is the Greek equivalent. The concept of a Messiah has a complex background, but essentially it was born out of Israel's calamitous history and a sense of disillusionment with her leaders. As a result of these factors the hope grew up of a future leader who would truly be God's representative and would consequently restore his people to the position of power and prosperity they enjoyed under David and Solomon. The balance between his spiritual and political functions seems to have been viewed differently by different groups, however, which may well explain why Jesus was apparently prepared to accept the title from his disciples (in a spiritual sense) while forbidding its general use for fear of misunderstanding.

Micah. A contemporary of Isaiah prophesying in the southern kingdom of Judah towards the end of the eighth century B.C., Micah pronounces God's judgement on his people for their failure to establish a just society and declares that not even the temple will be spared in the general destruction (Mic 3:12). His book is best known for its simple but searching statement of God's requirements: to do what is just, to show constant love and to walk in humble fellowship with God (Mic 6:8). Many scholars consider that the more hopeful elements in the book of Micah are later editorial insertions, and on this view Micah must be considered primarily as a prophet of judgement like Amos before him in the northern kingdom.

Micaiah. A prophet who, in contrast to the 400 court prophets, predicted disaster for King Ahab if he went to take Ramoth-Gilead from the Syrians (1 Kgs 22:1-35).

Miletus. A port near Ephesus. Paul called the leaders of the Ephesian church to meet him here on his last journey to Jerusalem, and warned them against false teachers (Acts 20:17-38).

Miriam. The elder sister of Moses, she is referred to as a prophetess when she leads the women of Israel in a song and dance of triumph after the crossing of the sea on the escape from Egypt.

Moabite Stone, a stone of the 9th cent. B.C. containing the earliest known inscription in Phoenician characters, and discovered in the highlands of Moab in 1868. It is now in the Louvre, Paris. It records the campaign between Moab and Israel (c. 850 B.C.) (2 Kings 3:27).

Moabites. Occupying land east of the Dead Sea, the Moabites were generally hostile to the people of Israel. David conquered them, but they reasserted their independence in the period of weakness after the division of the kingdom, only to be subjugated again later by Omri. They were finally led to independence by Mesha while Jehoram was king of Israel.

Molech. A Canaanite god whose worship involved child-sacrifice. King Manasseh apparently worshipped him (2 Kgs 21:6), but Josiah desecrated the site of these sacrifices to prevent them happening again (2 Kgs 23:10).

Mordecai. The cousin and foster-father of Queen Esther (Esth 2:6-7).

Moses. If Abraham is the father of the Jewish race, Moses is the founder of Jewish religion.

This does not mean, however, that the religion he established had no antecedents, but it was under Moses that it achieved its definitive form. While it is admittedly difficult to disentangle fact from legend in many of the stories of Moses, there is no reason to doubt their essential historical basis as recollections of the great leader who took the people of Israel from slavery in Egypt to the threshold of the promised land, and in the process firmly established their religious traditions. At the centre of Moses' religion is the concept of the covenant, an agreement between God and the people of Israel whereby God gives them a special position of responsibility in his plans and they pledge him their loyalty and obedience. This obedience is to be expressed not only in worship but also in behaviour towards others.

N

Naaman. Commander of the Syrian army, cured of "leprosy" by Elisha (2 Kgs 5:1–19).

Naboth. Owner of a vineyard adjoining King Ahab's palace, he was put to death on false evidence at Jezebel's instigation so that Ahab could take the property in the absence of an heir (1 Kgs 21:1–16).

Nadab. King of Israel (901–900 B.C.). Assassinated within two years of his accession by Baasha whilst fighting the Philistines at Gibbethon (1 Kgs 15:27).

Nahum. The book is a poem exulting in the fall of the Assyrian capital Nineveh, which is seen as an example of God's judgement on a nation which had long taken for granted its dominant position and gave no thought to the suffering of its subject peoples. Nineveh fell in 612 B.C.

Naphtali. (1) The sixth son of Jacob, his second by Bilhah, Rachel's slave-girl.
(2) The tribe of Naphtali, occupying territory to the north and west of the Sea of Galilee.

Nathan. A prophet who advised David not to build a permanent temple in Jerusalem and rebuked him for his misconduct with Bathsheba. Nevertheless, he backed Bathsheba's son, Solomon, in the struggle for succession. It was largely through him that David was eventually persuaded to declare himself in Solomon's favour (1 Kgs 1:11–40).

Nathanael. Often identified with Bartholomew, since John omits all mention of Bartholomew but names Nathanael as one of the disciples. Brought to Jesus by Philip (who is linked with Bartholomew in the other gospels), Jesus referred to him as "a true Israelite in whom there is nothing false" (Jn 1:47).

Nativity. There are three nativity festivals of the Church: Christmas, 25 December, festival of birth of Christ; birthday of the Virgin Mary (8 Sept.); and St. John the Baptist (24 June).

Nazareth. The home of Joseph and Mary, and the place where Jesus lived until he began his itinerant ministry. Until then this small Galilean town was of no importance and is not even mentioned in the Old Testament. Today it has the largest Arab population of any town in Israel.

Nazirite. A person dedicated to God's service and following an ascetic rule of life involving abstinence from alcohol and refusal to cut hair amongst other things. Samson was a Nazirite and John the Baptist may have been.

Nebuchadnezzar. The Babylonian ruler (605–562 B.C.) under whose orders Jerusalem was taken and destroyed and the people exiled in 586 B.C. By the standards of his day he was not excessively ruthless, and it could be argued that only the intransigence of the Jews compelled him to treat them with severity.

Nehemiah. A Jewish exile who became cupbearer to the Persian king Artaxerxes and was allowed by him to go to Jerusalem as governor about 445 B.C. in order to accelerate reconstruction of the nation's life.
The book of Nehemiah relates how he overcame opposition to get the walls of Jerusalem rebuilt. It also tells how Ezra read the law aloud to the people and got them to agree to keep it.

New Year. Originally the Jewish New Year began in the autumn, but during the exile the Babylonian New Year starting in the spring was adopted. The autumn New Year was still maintained for cultic purposes, however, and there has been much speculation, based on strong but circumstantial evidence mainly from the Psalms, over the possibility that the autumn New Year was the occasion of a major religious festival celebrating and renewing the covenant.

Nicene Creed, a summary of the principles of Christian faith, first issued in 325 by the Council of Nicaea (summoned by the emperor Constantine the Great) for the purpose of thwarting the Arian heresy and asserting the godhead of Christ. Date of Easter fixed at Council of Nicaea.

Nicodemus. A member of the Jewish Council who sympathised with Jesus and came to see him by night—presumably fearful of associating with him openly (Jn 3:1–12). He objected to the Council condemning Jesus without giving him a chance to defend himself (Jn 7:50–51) and helped Joseph of Arimathea to give Jesus a decent burial (Jn 19:39–42).

Nineveh. The capital of Assyria until its destruction by the combined forces of the Medes and Babylonians in 612 B.C. It was legendary for its size and sinfulness (Jon 1:2).

Noah. While the story of Noah may have a historical basis, its primary value lies in what it says about God. It shows God as one who does not fully carry out the judgement which man's sinfulness deserves, but in his generosity makes a new start possible. For Noah's Ark, see Deluge.

Numbers, Book of. The name of the book refers to two censuses of the people of Israel recorded in it, one just before they left Mount Sinai and the other about a generation later. The book covers the history of the people of Israel from the exodus until just before the crossing of the Jordan and lays down rules for everyday life.

O

Obadiah. (1) A high official under King Ahab who tried to protect loyal worshippers of Yahweh against the persecution of Queen Jezebel.
(2) A prophet who wrote sometime after the fall of Jerusalem in 586 B.C., condemning the Edomites for taking advantage of Judah's plight to settle old scores, and predicting final victory for the people of Israel.

Omri. King of Israel (876–869 B.C.). Although Omri is only given six verses in the books of Kings (1 Kgs 16:23–28), and is condemned for leading his people into idolatry, he was a capable ruler who in a relatively short reign established good relations with both Judah and the Phoenician states, subjugated enemies east of the Jordan and built a new capital, Samaria.

Onesimus. A runaway slave who was converted by Paul and sent back to his master Philemon, bearing with him the letter of that name.

P

Palestine. Derived from "Philistine", the name originally referred only to the southern part of the coastal plain around the Philistine cities, but it came to be used for the whole of the area bordering the eastern Mediterranean from the Lebanon southwards to the Egyptian frontier and across to the desert land of Transjordan.

Paraclete (the Holy Ghost, or Comforter), the name used in the English translations of St. John's Gospel, and adopted by Abelard to designate the convent in Champagne founded by him, of which Héloïse became the abbess.

Paradise. A Persian word used by the translators of the Old Testament to designate the Garden of Eden, and since meaning any place of happiness.

Passover. The important Jewish festival (Pesach) celebrated in spring by a special meal. Originally it probably derived from a custom of sacrificing the first lamb of the new season, but it became associated with the deliverance from slavery in Egypt, and it is as a way of remembering this that it has been celebrated ever since. It is followed by a week of eating unleavened bread, also in memory of the escape from Egypt. It is a time for family, and the highlight is the Seder meal during which the Haggadah, or Telling will be recounted.

Paul. We know more about Paul than about any other leader of the early church, our information coming both from Acts and his own letters. Born in Tarsus in Asia Minor, he was brought up in strictest Jewish tradition and studied under the renowned teacher, Gamaliel. He considered it his duty to persecute the Christian community, and was present at the stoning of Stephen, whose saintly behaviour towards his executioners almost certainly sowed the first seeds of doubt in his mind. These doubts culminated in a shattering conversion experience as he travelled to Damascus to continue his persecution of the Christians there. It was not until many years had elapsed, however, that Paul emerged as the leading figure in the mission to the Gentiles, and he did so at the instigation of Barnabas, who sent for him to help in the work at Antioch. Soon the church decided to send Paul and Barnabas on a missionary journey which took them first to Cyprus and then into the Roman province of Galatia. By this time some of the Jewish Christians were becoming alarmed at the large number of Gentile converts, and on their return they went to a gathering in Jerusalem to thrash out questions of policy with regard to the admission of Gentiles to the church. Here, Paul, more aware than anyone else of the futility of the Jewish law, strongly resisted the imposition of Jewish customs on Gentile converts, and appears to have won, though the argument was to rumble on for many years.

Soon he undertook a second missionary journey with Silas, in the course of which he founded the first church in Europe at Philippi and stayed for eighteen months in Corinth. On a third journey he spent two years in Ephesus before revisiting the churches founded earlier during his second journey. On a visit to Jerusalem at the end of his third journey he was arrested by Roman guards during a disturbance in the temple courtyard when Jews alleged that he had taken Trophimus, a Gentile from Ephesus, into the temple. After two years' imprisonment during which he was neither condemned nor declared innocent, Paul appealed to Caesar and was duly sent to Rome. We are told in Acts 28:30 that he was there for two years, presumably waiting for his accusers to present a case against him, and this may imply that he was then released, since the rule was that a case must be presented within two years. But this is not certain, and tradition has it that he died, together with Peter, in Nero's persecution of A.D. 64.

From about the year A.D. 50 onwards Paul wrote numerous letters, mainly to churches he had founded, but occasionally to churches he had not visited himself, and some of these letters form a substantial part of the New Testament. Some have accused Paul of complicating the simple gospel preached by Jesus, yet the church today may owe its very existence to Paul's clear understanding that Christianity could not just remain an offshoot of Judaism, but must become a universal religion.

Pekah. King of Israel (737–732 B.C.). Seizing the throne by assassinating his predecessor, Pekah immediately entered an anti-Assyrian coalition with his Syrian neighbour Rezin. Together they made threats against Ahaz, king of Judah, who soon appealed to the Assyrians for help. In 733 B.C. Tiglath-pileser III attacked Israel, capturing many cities and deporting much of the population. It was possibly only Pekah's assassination by Hoshea, who promptly surrendered, which saved Israel from further destruction.

Pekahiah. King of Israel (738–737 B.C.). Assassinated after a short period by Pekah, probably because of discontent with his policy of submission to Assyria.

Pentateuch. The first five books of the Old Testament, having special significance for the Jews as the Torah, the basis of Jewish law.

Pentecost. *See* Weeks, Feast of.

Peter. The undisputed leader of the disciples, and of the Christian church during its earliest days. A Galilean fisherman, he was brought to Jesus by his brother Andrew and quickly became one of the inner group of disciples. He showed his leadership in his declaration of faith in Jesus as the Christ at Caesarea Philippi, and it was here that Jesus added the name Peter (the rock) to his original name Simon. After Jesus' arrest he denied all knowledge of him, but it could be

argued that he was only exposed to this temptation because he had had the courage to follow Jesus to the High Priest's house. He was the first disciple to enter the empty tomb and preached the first Christian sermon on the day of Pentecost. He was also instrumental in paving the way for Gentiles to enter the church through the baptism of the Roman centurion Cornelius and his subsequent defence of this action (Acts 10:1–11:18). It is unfortunate, though understandable, that the emphasis in the second half of Acts on the work of Paul leave us in ignorance as to the subsequent development of Peter's ministry. Tradition has it that he founded the church in Rome, and died there in Nero's persecution of A.D. 64.

Peter, Letters of. There is considerable doubt whether either of these letters is by the disciple Peter, or indeed whether they are by the same author. The first letter is written to encourage Christians in Asia Minor who are suffering or are likely to suffer, for their Christian faith. If this were written during a specific period of persecution it would almost certainly have been that under the Roman emperor Domitian (A.D. 81–96), since Nero's persecution does not appear to have extended far beyond the capital, and this would rule out authorship by Peter if he had died in A.D. 64. The second letter, which shows a detailed knowledge of the letter of Jude, is a general warning against false teachers. Many scholars date it as the latest document in the New Testament, around the second century.

Pharaoh. The title of the kings of Egypt. The Pharaohs under whom the people of Israel served as forced labourers have not been identified with certainty, but the likelihood is that the Pharaoh at the time of the exodus was Rameses II (reigned 1304–1237 B.C.).

Pharisees. One of the chief sects within Judaism at the time of Jesus. The movement started as an attempt to bring everyday life more closely into conformity with the law of Judaism, so that religious observance became an integral part of daily living. Jesus would hardly have quarrelled with this aim, but the effect had been to emphasise trivial details and lose sight of basic principles. It was this, and the sense of self-righteousness so often engendered, that Jesus criticised in the Pharisees.

Philemon, Letter to. A short personal letter from Paul to a member of the church at Colossae. Onesimus, Philemon's slave, had run away to Rome, where he came into contact with Paul. Paul would have liked to keep him as he was proving so useful, but felt bound to return him to Philemon, begging Philemon to welcome him back not just as a slave but as a Christian brother.

Philip. (1) Ruler of Ituraea and Trachonitis (4 B.C.–A.D. 34). *See* **Herod family.**

(2) One of the twelve disciples about whom little is known, although John's gospel gives him slightly greater prominence than the other three (Jn 1:43–46, 12:20–22, 14:8–9).

(3) One of the seven deacons appointed to organise the distribution of resources in the system of sharing goods adopted by the early church in Jerusalem (Acts 6:1–6). In fact, he quickly became a notable evangelist, working among the Samaritans and also in southern Palestine, where he converted an Ethiopian official travelling home, before settling in Caesarea, where he still lived nearby thirty years later (Acts 8:4–40, 21:8).

Philippi. A city of Macedonia where Paul first preached in Europe (Acts 16:12).

Philippians, Letter to the. Unlike many of Paul's letters, the letter to the church at Philippi does not seem to have been written with any particular object in mind—to combat false teaching (Galatians) or pave the way for a possible future visit (Romans). It is simply keeping in touch with old friends, for the church at Philippi had apparently been the first to give Paul financial support so that he could be a full-time missionary without the necessity of plying a trade (Phil 4:15–16). Although he warns the Philippian Christians to be on their guard against any attempt to impose Jewish customs on them (Phil 3:2–7), he seems confident of their ability to maintain their Christian life against any opposition it encounters. The whole atmosphere of the letter is one of gratitude, joy and peace, all the more remarkable as Paul was in prison and possibly close to death as he wrote (Phil 1:20–24).

Philistines. A people who came from Crete or the Aegean islands to settle on the coastal plain of Palestine about the same time that the people of Israel were entering Canaan from the east. They were organised in five main city-states and were a serious threat to the Israelites because of their iron weapons (Israel being still in the Bronze Age), their use of chariots and their military form of government. After the period of acute antagonism which was brought to a close by David's unchallengeable superiority, they lived relatively peacefully apart from occasional incidents until, sometime after the exile, the Philistines disappeared as an independent entity. Recent evidence from a Philistine cemetery suggests they were a more cultured people than previously thought.

Phoenicia. A term used to describe the coastal area north of Mount Carmel which is now the Lebanon. It was never a kingdom as such, but included a number of city-states, of which Tyre was the most important. The Phoenicians were seafarers and traders and times of prosperity in Israel often hinged upon good relations with Phoenicia, as in Solomon's reign. Their trade routes extended from Palestine to Portugal.

Pilate, Pontius. The Roman governor of Judaea at the time of Jesus' execution, he does not seem to have handled the admittedly difficult task of governing the Jews particularly well. All the gospels represent him as resisting the death sentence on Jesus, however, and only passing it under Jewish pressure. John implies that the Jews had some kind of hold over Pilate: possibly because of previous blunders he could not afford to antagonise the Jews again. In fact, he was recalled to Rome c. A.D. 36, tried and imprisoned.

Priest. In the early period of Jewish religion there were no priests. The head of the family would perform any religious functions necessary. Samuel, however, is said to have condemned Saul for offering sacrifice, thereby usurping his proper function (1 Sam 13:8–14). This suggests that by now a specific priestly role was recognised. It was with the construction of the temple and the development of more elaborate rituals that a priesthood became essential, though it was the offering of sacrifice which remained the primary function.

Prisca. See **Aquila.**

Prophet. What marks a person out as a prophet has been much debated. The prophets of Baal on Mount Carmel present an extremely unedifying spectacle as they dance and cut themselves to invoke the power of their god (1 Kgs 18:26–29), yet there were prophets in Israel whose behaviour was not dissimilar (1 Sam: 10:10–13). There is clearly a vast gulf between such people and men of the calibre of Amos, Hosea or Jeremiah. The one thing they have in common is their enthusiasm for God. It is possible to trace the gradual transition from these primitive prophets who expressed themselves in emotional outbursts to the great religious thinkers of later times but to sum up the difference in terms of emotions against intellect (or any other pair of contrasting qualities) is an over-simplification. Possibly the best short definition of a prophet is "one who is convinced that God has something to say through him". Although prophets were expected to have knowledge of future events, this is not an essential part of the Hebrew concept of prophecy.

Proselyte. One who was not a Jew by birth but who, by circumcision and a form of baptism, had become a Jew by faith.

Proverbs, Book of. This is basically a collection of short sayings offering advice on how to act in everyday situations, but, as with all the biblical writings, it emphasises an important theological belief—that all true wisdom comes from God and is based on respect for him. The sayings are ascribed to Solomon, who may indeed be responsible for some of them, but the compilation of the book took place centuries after his death and incorporated much later material.

Psalms, Book of, for many years attributed to David, but present-day scholars are of the view that the psalms were written by a series of authors at different times and for different purposes, and that few, if any, were written by David. The Holy Scriptures contain 150.

It is a truism to say that the Psalms are the hymn book of the Old Testament. If the Psalms were collected for use in corporate worship, we need to ask for each Psalm, "On what sort of occasion would these have been appropriate sentiments to express?" This approach has led to some interesting conclusions about the worship of the people of Israel, and greatly illuminated the Psalms themselves. For the ordinary reader, however, the attraction of these poems remains what it has always been—their expression of a wide range of human emotions within an overall context of faith in God.

Publicans. See **L89.**

Publius. The chief official (his exact status is unclear) on Malta where Paul was shipwrecked. Paul cured his father of a fever (Acts 28:7–10).

Q

Quirinus (Cyrenius). Described by Luke as the governor of Syria at the time of Jesus' birth, though if this took place in the reign of Herod the Great, Luke is wrong on this point. He later had two terms of office as governor of Syria, but at this time commanded the Roman army there.

R

Rabbah. The Ammonite capital, captured by David. During the siege of Rabbah David arranged for Uriah to be left exposed to the enemy, in order to marry his wife Bathsheba.

Rabbi. Sometimes translated "teacher", but implying rather more than this. It is a respectful title, suggesting that the one who uses it accepts the authority of the one to whom it is used. In John's gospel Jesus is addressed in this manner several times.

Rachel. Laban's younger daughter and Jacob's second wife, though she was his first choice. She bore him Joseph and Benjamin.

Rahab. A prostitute of Jericho who concealed two spies sent by Joshua, and was subsequently spared when the other inhabitants were slaughtered (Josh 1:1–21, 6:22–25).

Rameses. An Egyptian city where Israelite slave labour was used, and from which the people of Israel started out on the exodus. It was on the eastern edge of the Nile delta, and is generally identified with a city earlier known as Avaris and later as Tanis.

Ramoth-Gilead. A town on the border between Israel and Syria which was the scene of bitter fighting between these traditional enemies. It was here that Ahab died, and that Jehoram received the wounds from which he was recovering at the time of Jehu's coup.

Rebecca. The sister of Laban, wife of Isaac, and mother of the twins Esau and Jacob.

Rechabites. The descendants of Rechab, about whom we know nothing except that he was the father of Jonadab, who laid down the rules of the Rechabite community. He insisted that they lived in tents and refrained from alcohol, thus trying to protect them against the corrupting influences of Canaanite civilisation. Jeremiah commends the Rechabites for their faithfulness to these principles, in contrast to the lack of faithfulness found elsewhere among the people of Israel (Jer 35:1–17).

Red Sea. The name translated as "Red Sea" in older versions of the Bible is not always to be equated with the Red Sea as known today. References in the exodus story may be to a shallow inland lake in the region now cut through by the Suez Canal, and in 1 Kings 9:26 the reference is to the Gulf of Aqaba, rather than the Red Sea itself.

Rehoboam. King of Judah (922–915 B.C.). The son of Solomon, Rehoboam refused to listen to the grievances of his people at the beginning of his reign and as a consequence was faced with rebellion by the ten northern tribes under Jeroboam's leadership. Rehoboam was unable to prevent the division and soon gave up any attempt to reassert his authority over Israel.

He lost nearly all his foreign territory, was invaded by the Egyptians and had to ransack his treasury to pay the tribute demanded.

Resurrection. It is quite clear from the book of Acts that the resurrection of Jesus was the central theme of early Christian preaching. It is equally clear that those who proclaimed the resurrection in this way stood a considerable risk of sharing the fate of their leader. It follows that they must have been absolutely certain in their own minds of the truth and importance of their claims. Because these claims are admittedly extraordinary, it is natural that people should have sought explanations in terms of natural causes, but no such explanation has proved entirely satisfactory. In any case, an extraordinary event is needed to explain the transformation in the behaviour of the disciples. Among those who believe in the resurrection it is, of course, possible to find a wide variety of interpretations as to what exactly took place.

Reuben. (1) The first-born son of both Jacob and Leah.

(2) The tribe of Reuben, which occupied an area on the eastern shore of the Dead Sea between Ammonite and Moabite territory.

Revelation, Book of. Without doubt the most difficult book in the New Testament for modern readers because its thought-forms and imagery are so remote from those to which we are accustomed. Written during a time of persecution, probably that of the emperor Domitian in the last decade of the first century, it declares in highly metaphorical language that the stage of human history is set in the context of an eternal scheme of things, in which God reigns supreme. Whatever their present sufferings, ultimate victory is assured to those who put their trust in Jesus. The writer describes himself as John, and some scholars have identified him with the disciple John, but there is no solid evidence for this. There is no question of the writer being the author of John's gospel or the letters of John.

Rezin. King of Syria (about 740–732 B.C.). An ally of Pekah, king of Israel, against the Assyrians. Together they threatened to attack Judah if King Ahaz would not join their coalition. Rezin was killed by the Assyrians when they finally took his capital, Damascus.

Romans. The Roman empire provides the context in which the events of the New Testament took place. Many Jews hated the Romans, and there were frequent misguided attempts at rebellion which culminated in the revolt of A.D. 66 and the eventual destruction of Jerusalem by the Romans in A.D. 70. In spite of occasional persecution, Roman rule was generally helpful to the spread of Christianity through its good communications and political stability.

Romans, Letters to the. Paul's letter to the Romans was written to an already flourishing church which he did not know personally. Its purpose was apparently to pave the way for further missionary work in the western Mediterranean, using Rome as a base. Paul seems to feel it necessary to lay before the Roman church the gospel that he preaches, and this letter provides the most coherent statement of his theology that we possess. Its great emphasis is on faith in Jesus as the sole necessity for reconciliation with God.

Rome. The capital of the Roman empire, a church seems to have been established there at an early but unknown date. Tradition says it was founded by Peter, but there is no biblical evidence for this. Paul spent two years there under arrest and, again according to tradition, died with Peter in Nero's persecution.

Ruth. The book of Ruth is one of the gems of the Old Testament. It tells how Ruth, the Moabite widow of an Israelite husband, decides to accompany her widowed mother-in-law, Naomi, back to her home town of Bethlehem. In so doing Ruth accepts Israel's God as her own. Boaz, a kinsman of Naomi, notices Ruth gleaning the remains of his barley field and ultimately marries her, and they give birth to Obed, David's grandfather. The story is a parable (as is suggested by the names of the chief characters, all of them symbolic), but may rest on a historical fact, for much of the point of the story depends on Ruth being David's great-grandmother, and

if this were made up the point would be lost. The book is essentially a plea for tolerance of mixed marriages, and as such it shows a liberality of outlook matched in the Old Testament only by the book of Jonah. Attempts to date the book have proved very difficult, but the most likely period is shortly after the exile, when the Jewish community was becoming more exclusive.

S

Sabaoth, a Hebrew word, meaning an army or host, and applied sometimes to the Supreme Being, *e.g.*, "the Lord of Hosts" (Rom. ix. 29).

Sabbath. The observance of the sabbath as a day of rest and worship goes back at least to the time of Moses, yet it was only during the exile that it came to assume the importance it has had ever since for Jews. Deprived of temple worship, and living among aliens, strict sabbath observance became the identifying characteristic of a good Jew. By Jesus' time the number of rules about the sabbath was enormous, and while Jesus clearly supported the principle of the sabbath, he would not let his work be hindered by such petty rules. This became one of the major sources of friction between him and the Pharisees.

Sacrifice. Although the Jews came to realise at an early stage that God did not require human sacrifice (Gen 22:9–14), animal sacrifice continued to be part of their worship until the destruction of Herod's temple by the Romans. Many of the prophets questioned the value of the practice, however, declaring that what God really wanted was justice and compassion in all men's dealings with their fellows.

Sadducees. A major party within Judaism at the time of Jesus. They were mainly of priestly background and, because many of them occupied positions which depended on the good will of the Romans, they generally favoured a conciliatory approach. Unlike the Pharisees, many of whom commanded respect by their conscientiousness, the Sadducees were liked by no one.

Salome. One of the women who had followed Jesus from Galilee to Jerusalem, watched the crucifixion and saw the empty tomb.

Samaria. Originally the name referred to the new capital city built by Omri, king of Israel. It was increasingly used, however, as another term for the northern kingdom as a whole. After the kingdom had ceased to exist it denoted an area corresponding to the central part of the old kingdom.

Samaritan. An inhabitant of Samaria. The Jews considered Samaritans to be excluded from their ranks because, following the deportation of many Samaritan citizens by the Assyrians in 721 B.C. and the establishment of people from other parts of the Assyrian empire on their soil, many mixed marriages had taken place. Since the northern kingdom had always been considered idolatrous by southern Jews, this put them both religiously and socially beyond the pale.

Samson. A Nazirite, and one of the most famous of the judges. He seems to have had more valour than discretion, however, and provoked the Philistines needlessly (Judg 15:1–6). He paid for this unnecessary bravado with his life (Judg 16:4–30).

Samuel. Samuel was the last great leader of Israel before the establishment of the monarchy, and a unique figure combining the functions of prophet, priest, judge and even ruler. Undoubtedly the most significant part of his work was the creation of the monarchy, but unfortunately the role he played in this is far from clear. There are two conflicting accounts interwoven in 1 Samuel. One represents Samuel privately anointing Saul as king on God's instructions, and later arranging for a public acclamation of his kingship when he has proved himself in battle. The other suggests that the people demanded a king against Samuel's advice and that only under protest did he arrange a system for choosing a king by lots. Whatever his initial attitude, his support for Saul was soon withdrawn when Saul offered sacrifice instead of waiting for Samuel to do it (1 Sam 13:8–14) and failed to destroy totally the Amalekites according to Samuel's instructions (1 Sam 15:13–23). It seems clear that Samuel came to regard Saul as one who was usurping God's position, and his hostility did much to break the man who, willingly or otherwise, he had created king.

Samuel, Books of. The two books of Samuel cover an epoch-making period in Israel's history. They trace the development of a loose confederation of tribes, without any established form of government, into a considerable empire under a dynastic ruler. Like all the historical books, they contain material from a variety of sources, some much closer to the events than others. We are fortunate, however, to have in 2 Samuel 9–20 (and continuing in 1 Kings 1–2) a continuous source which is widely recognised as the finest piece of history writing of its time from anywhere in the world. The author deals with the reign of David in such a way that he can only have been a close associate of the king himself. Not only does he describe in detail David's conversations with his advisers, but he does it so vividly that the characters of the major participants are laid open to scrutiny. He is quite remarkable in his absence of bias. He paints a sympathetic portrait of David but does not gloss over his failings.

Sanhedrin. A council meeting under the High Priest at Jerusalem which had ultimate authority in religious and legal matters except for the power to pass the death penalty. This was why the Jews had to take Jesus before Pilate. The stoning of Stephen appears to have been a flagrant violation of this restriction. How and when the Sanhedrin was established is uncertain, but it came to an end with the destruction of Jerusalem in A.D. 70.

Sarah. Wife of Abraham and mother of Isaac. One of a number of women in the Bible whose child was seen as a special mark of God's favour because it came late in life.

Saul. (1) As the first king of Israel shortly before 1000 B.C., Saul faced a near impossible task, and his undoubted courage in battle was not an adequate qualification. The people of Israel wanted a king to defend them from their enemies, especially the Philistines, but they were not yet ready to give up their tribal independence, or support a permanent army as opposed to a constantly changing collection of volunteers. So he occupied an uncomfortable position in which more was expected of him than of the judges of old, but without any constitutional means of exercising his authority.

When Samuel, a powerful influence on public opinion, withdrew his support, Saul clearly felt exposed and vulnerable, and the popularity of the young hero David increased his sense of insecurity. When David fled from his jealousy, helped unwittingly by the priest Ahimelech, Saul's slaughter of Ahimelech and his household was widely regarded as unjust, and must have alienated the priesthood. Thereafter much of his time and energy was diverted into hunting down David when it could have been more usefully employed in other ways. His final battle was an act of desperation, meeting the Philistines on level ground at the foot of Mount Gilboa, where their chariots gave them a decisive advantage. In the early years of his reign he seems to have enjoyed success, however, ejecting the Philistines from the central mountain range and, temporarily at least, being sufficiently free from the Philistine threat to strike at other enemies across the Jordan and far to the south. When he died there seems to have been no move to dispense with a king, so in spite of his ultimate failure, he seems to have achieved the acceptance of the monarchy by his people, paving the way for his successors.

(2) The Hebrew name by which Paul was known before his conversion. He may have taken the Roman form of his name to signify that he was "a new man in Christ", or possibly in order to identify himself with the Gentiles.

Scapegoat. A goat on which the sins of all the people were symbolically laid before driving it out into the wilderness. This happened annually on the Day of Atonement (Lev 16:20–22).

Scribes. The scribes were the professional interpreters of the law from the exile onwards.

Many of them were also Pharisees, and the two are often linked in the New Testament.

Scripture. The term can be applied to any body of writings, but in the New Testament (where it is sometimes used in the plural) it invariably refers to the Old Testament. The use of the term by Christians to signify the Bible as a whole naturally came later.

Scrolls, Dead Sea. A collection of about 1,000 fragments, the first of them discovered in 1947, from caves near the Dead Sea. Written between 170 B.C. and A.D. 70, some of them relate to the life of the ascetic community to which they belonged and others are parts of the Old Testament. Surprisingly the most ancient manuscripts of the Old Testament previously known were medieval, yet the differences in the text are mostly insignificant. New techniques using ultra-bright light may enable more of the documents to be read. Another cave was discovered in 2017, but it had been looted.

Sennacherib. The king of Assyria who invaded Judah in 701 B.C., destroyed 46 of its fortified cities and shut up Hezekiah "like a bird in a cage" (to use the words of his own inscription). He did not take Jerusalem, but it is not clear whether this was because of a disaster in the Assyrian camp or because Hezekiah accepted his punitive terms of surrender.

Septuagint. The Greek translation of the Old Testament, so called because of a tradition that it was made by 72 scribes. The Latin *septuaginta* actually means 70, and hence the use of LXX as an abbreviation. It was made by Alexandrian Jews between 250 B.C. and 100 B.C. from Hebrew texts now lost. There are many differences between the Septuagint and the Massoretic version (A.D. 900), and therefore it is of great value for textual criticism.

Seven Champions of Christendom, were St. George of England, St. Andrew of Scotland, St. Patrick of Ireland, St. David of Wales, St. James of Spain, St. Denis of France, and St. Antony of Italy.

Seven Churches of Asia, referred to in the Revelation of St. John, were those of Ephesus, founded by St. Paul in 57, Smyrna, Pergamos, Thyatira, Sardis, Philadelphia (Lydia) and Laodicea (Phrygia), all in W. Asia Minor.

Shadrach. One of three young men, who according to the book of Daniel, survived being thrown into a blazing furnace for refusing to worship a gold statue set up by King Nebuchadnezzar.

Shallum. King of Israel (745 B.C.). He came to the throne by assassinating his predecessor and died in the same manner a month later.

Shaphan. The high official of King Josiah who took the Book of the Covenant from the temple and read it to him (2 Kgs 22:3–10). His family later protected Jeremiah, particularly during Jehoiakim's reign.

Sheba, Queen of. Sheba, in the Arabian peninsula, was a trading nation. The visit of the Queen of Sheba to Solomon (1 Kgs 10:1–10, 13) was probably a trade mission, with Solomon offering copper in exchange for spices.

Shechem. A town with ancient religious connections, since Jacob is said to have built an altar there (Gen 33:18–20). Centrally situated on the borders of Ephraim and Manasseh, it was the first capital of the northern kingdom.

Shiloh. A town where the tabernacle was taken after the occupation of Canaan and which became the site for a permanent temple, the central sanctuary for the confederation of Israelite tribes before the monarchy (1 Sam 1:3). Jeremiah refers to the destruction of this temple, most probably by the Philistines.

Sidon. Next to Tyre, the most important city of Phoenicia and a good port.

Silas. Sent with Paul and Barnabas to present the findings of the Council of Jerusalem to the church at Antioch, he subsequently became Paul's companion on the second missionary journey (Acts 16:22–41). Probably to be identified with the Silvanus mentioned in some of Paul's letters.

Siloam. The name of a pool within the city walls of Jerusalem, fed from a spring outside by a tunnel some 620 m long. The tunnel was cut by Hezekiah (2 Chr 32:30) and still exists.

Simeon. (1) The second son of Jacob and Leah.

(2) The tribe of Simeon which originally possessed territory south of Judah but was then absorbed into its neighbour.

Simon. (1) *See* **Peter.**

(2) **Simon the Zealot,** one of the twelve disciples, whose name suggests that he started at least with very different political ideals from Jesus (Mk 3:18).

(3) **Simon the Pharisee.** The man with whom Jesus was eating when a sinful woman anointed him (Lk 7:36–47).

(4) **Simon of Cyrene.** The man who was compelled to carry Jesus' cross (Mk 15:21).

(5) **Simon Magus.** A miracle-worker in Samaria who, when he saw the effects of the Holy Spirit on a group of converts Peter and John had laid hands on, tried to buy this power from them (Acts 8:9–24).

Sinai. The peninsula between the Gulf of Suez and the Gulf of Aqaba which was the first objective on the exodus from Egypt. Mount Sinai (also called Horeb) has not been identified with certainty. If the giving of the law was accompanied by volcanic activity, as elements of the account suggest, a site on the eastern side of the Gulf of Aqaba (and therefore not on the Sinai peninsula at all) is more likely.

Smyrna. An important city on the Aegean coastline of Asia Minor. The book of Revelation (Rev 2:8–11) refers sympathetically to the church there and its steadfastness under persecution, but we know little else about it.

Sodom. A city of evil reputation, probably to be located in an area now covered by the southern part of the Dead Sea. The city was destroyed by burning sulphur (presumably a volcanic disturbance) according to Genesis 19:24–25.

Solomon. King of Israel (*c.* 960–922 B.C.). Solomon is traditionally regarded as a wise king, yet by the end of his reign his subjects were seething with discontent, and it would have taken a man of exceptional ability to win back their loyalty. Rehoboam, his son, was not such a man, and so the great empire of Solomon was reduced almost overnight to two insignificant states. For this Solomon must take much of the blame. His reputation for wisdom is not without foundation, however. Inheriting a large and relatively peaceful empire from his father, David, he was never in serious danger from enemies, though he strengthened his defences and added chariots to his army just in case.

Solomon was thus able to concentrate on economic policy and proved a genius at exploiting his position across a number of major trade routes as well as developing the copper mines south of the Dead Sea. The wealth generated by this economic development went into building his own palace and its ancillary buildings and the first temple. He allowed himself to get carried away by the splendour of his own designs, however, and got into such debts that not even heavy taxation could pay them and he had to give away territory to his neighbour Hiram, king of Tyre, in payment for the supply of cedar wood (1 Kgs 9:10–11). These measures, together with the system of forced labour introduced to man the copper mines and the building projects, were exceedingly unpopular. So was his marriage to foreign wives (often in pursuance of trade agreements) and his tolerance of their pagan religions. Less obviously the reign of Solomon saw the beginnings of an insidious trend towards the concentration of power in the hands of a small number of people, which led ultimately to the kind of social injustice so fiercely condemned by the prophets.

That Solomon was clever is beyond dispute; whether he was wise may be debated.

Sosthenes. The leader of the synagogue at Corinth who was beaten by the Jews (Acts 18:17). The reason for this is not stated. Possibly he had shown sympathy towards Christianity, since a Sosthenes is associated with Paul in the writing of 1 Corinthians.

Stephen. Appointed originally as one of the seven administrators of the charitable work of the Jerusalem church (Acts 6:1–6), Stephen soon showed himself a powerful advocate of the Christian faith. He was brought before the Jewish Council on charges of denigrating the temple and denying the necessity for the law of Moses, and was illegally executed by stoning, the traditional Jewish method (Acts 6:8–60).

Stoics. Members of a Greek school of philosophers who believed in the suppression of the emotions so as to remain unaffected by life's adversities. Paul debated with the Stoics in Athens (Acts 17:18).

Stoning. The method of execution among the Jews, and the prescribed penalty for 18 crimes. The accusers were required to throw the first stone (Deu 17:5–7, *see* John 8:7 for Jesus' reaction to this rule).

Sychar. According to John 4:5–6 the site of Jacob's well. Usually identified with Shechem.

Synagogue. The development of synagogue worship was a response to three things: the law forbidding sacrifice except in the Jerusalem temple, the destruction of the temple in 586 B.C. and the dispersion of the Jews. As a result, the offering of sacrifice could no longer be a regular way of worship and a non-sacrificial form of worship had to be developed. This was based on the reading and exposition of the Law, interspersed with psalms and prayers, and it set the pattern for later Christian worship.

Synoptists. The writers of the first three Gospels whose narratives in the main agree, though Matthew and Luke add material not found in Mark; all three differ from John's Gospel.

Syrians. Also known as Aramaeans, these people were Israel's immediate north-eastern neighbours. At one time forming several small kingdoms, they gradually coalesced into a single state which was frequently at war with Israel. Syria became a province of Assyria after the destruction of Damascus, the capital, in 732 B.C.

T

Tabernacle. The name given to the "tent of meeting", the place where Moses met with God and which represented God's presence among his people. An elaborate structure, it was in effect a travelling temple.

Tabernacles, Feast of. Known also as the Feast of Booths, the festival was both a celebration of the grape harvest and a recollection of the wilderness wanderings, symbolised by people living in temporary shelters (booths) throughout the week.

Tarsus. A city in Asia Minor which was the home of Paul. It had a large Jewish population, but was also noted for its Greek philosophers, and it was this dual background that equipped Paul especially to be a missionary to the Gentiles.

Temple. There were three successive temples in Jerusalem. Solomon's temple, the first, was destroyed by the Babylonians in 586 B.C. After the exile a second temple was built, but due to the circumstances of the time this seems to have been a relatively poor affair. Then in 19 B.C. Herod the Great began work on the third temple, a large and imposing structure in every way. Though substantially complete by Jesus' time the finishing touches were not added until about A.D. 60. Ten years later it was destroyed by the Romans.

Ten Commandments. *See* **Commandments.**

Tertullus. A Roman or Romano-Jewish lawyer whom the Jewish Council employed to present the case against Paul before Felix (Acts 24:1–9).

Tetrarch. Both Herod Antipas and Philip were known as tetrarchs because they each received roughly a quarter of Herod the Great's kingdom (the other half going to Archelaus).

Thaddeus. One of the twelve disciples (Mk 3:18), known in Luke as Judas, son of James.

Thessalonians, Letters to the. The two letters of Paul to the Thessalonians are the earliest writings in the New Testament unless, as some scholars think, Galatians came earlier. They were written from Corinth, within a short time of each other, about A.D. 52. Amongst other things they show that the church at that time still expected the second coming of Christ in a literal form quite shortly, and that this expectation had led to undesirable behaviour such as refusal to work any more. Although Paul's correspondence with the Corinthians two to three years later shows that he still thought in terms of a second coming then, it is not a theme which occurs in his later letters.

Thessalonica. The capital of Macedonia in northern Greece, the city was visited by Paul during his second missionary journey (Acts 17:1–9) and presumably on the short tour he made of the Greek churches following his ministry in Ephesus (Acts 20:1–6).

Thomas. One of the twelve disciples well characterised in John's gospel, where he appears as loyal but slow to learn. His confession of Jesus as "My Lord and my God" after the resurrection identifies Jesus with God more clearly than any other statement in the gospels, however (Jn 20:28).

Tiglath-pileser III. King of Assyria (745–727 B.C.). It was Tiglath-pileser who established the Assyrian dominance of Palestine which was to last well over a century. It was to him that Ahaz of Judah appealed for help against Israel and Syria, both of which were invaded and devastated.

Timothy. Born of a Jewish mother and Greek father, Timothy was a native of Lystra. When Paul revisited the city at the start of his second missionary journey he asked Timothy to join him. From this time onwards he was constantly with Paul, or working elsewhere under Paul's oversight, and only three of the letters ascribed to Paul do not mention him.

Timothy, Letters to. There are difficulties in ascribing to Paul the two letters to Timothy. The style is not quite like Paul's, and the more formal organisation of the church suggests a later period. The most probable view is that they do contain fragments of personal notes written by Paul to Timothy, but that these have been used by a later author as the basis for general advice to church leaders. Similar considerations apply to the letter to Titus, which is often linked with the two letters to Timothy under the title of the Pastoral Letters.

Titus. A companion and co-worker of Paul, he seems to have been particularly involved in Paul's correspondence with Corinth, carrying his letters and acting as his representative (2 Cor 7:7, 8:16–17).

Titus, Letter to. *See* Timothy, Letters to.

Tongues, Speaking with. An outpouring of incomprehensible sounds which often accompanied a state of religious excitement in New Testament times, and still occurs in some churches today. The implication that the disciples actually spoke in foreign languages on the day of Pentecost is probably intended as a way of symbolising the universal relevance of the gospel. Paul warned against giving undue emphasis to this gift of the Spirit (1 Cor 14).

Tower of Babel. *See* Babel, Tower of.

Tribes of Israel. Traditionally descended from the twelve sons of Jacob, the number remained twelve in spite of some changes. The descendants of Joseph in fact formed two tribes, named after his sons Ephraim and Manasseh, whereas Simeon quickly became absorbed into Judah.

Tyre. The principal city of Phoenicia, and the centre of a city-state. The kings of Tyre were often on good terms with the kings of Israel, and the two nations traded to their mutual advantage (1 Kgs 5:1–11).

U

Unclean Foods. By long established tradition the Jews did not eat (and still do not eat) certain foods which were ritually unclean. This, and the fact that every meal was seen as a family religious occasion, meant that Jews rarely sat down at table with Gentiles. When Jewish and Gentile Christians began to associate with one another this was one of the difficulties they had to face (Rom 14:14–15).

Unleavened Bread. *See* Passover.

Ur. The home town of Abraham, sited in the southern part of the fertile flood-plain of the Tigris–Euphrates river system.

Urim and Thummim. Two objects used by a priest to determine God's will. It is not known how they were used, but the technique was probably to ask specific questions, to which the objects, on being thrown like dice, would then give a "yes" or "no" answer (1 Sam 14:41).

Uzziah. King of Judah (783–742 B.C.). Long-lived, capable and with the welfare of his people at heart, Uzziah was one of the better kings of Judah. He repaired and strengthened the defences of Jerusalem, re-equipped his army (with slings for hurling stones among other things), attacked the Philistine cities and recaptured from the Edomites the important port of Elath on the Gulf of Aqaba (2 Chr 26:1–15). Towards the end of his reign he was stricken by a skin disease and his public duties were taken over by his son Jotham.

W

Weeks, Feast of. Also known as Pentecost, the feast came at the end of the wheat harvest and later was associated with the giving of the Law on Sinai. It was during this feast that the apostles received the gift of the Holy Spirit (Acts 2:1–4).

Wisdom Literature. A name applied to books such as Proverbs, Job and Ecclesiastes which discuss philosophical issues or offer practical advice for living. There is a parallel literature from other middle-eastern civilisations, but the Hebrew literature is unique in its emphasis on the knowledge of God (and not merely academic knowledge but the knowing that comes from a relationship) as the basis of all wisdom.

Y

Yahweh. The proper name of the God of Israel was written as YHWH, there being no vowels in Hebrew. How it would have been pronounced (in fact it was considered too sacred ever to be spoken aloud) is a matter of speculation, but modern opinion favours Yahweh. Jehovah is an earlier attempt to render the same name.

Z

Zacchaeus. A tax collector of Jericho who became a follower of Jesus and generously compensated all those he had previously cheated (Lk 19:1–10).

Zadok. He appears to have been High Priest jointly with Abiathar during David's reign, but when Abiathar was banished by Solomon for supporting Adonijah in the struggle for succession, Zadok became the sole High Priest.

Zebulum. (1) The tenth son of Jacob, his sixth by Leah.
(2) The tribe of Zebulum which occupied a fairly small area of northern Israel surrounded by Manasseh, Issachar, Naphtali and Asher.

Zechariah. (1) King of Israel (746–745 B.C.). The son of Jeroboam II, he was assassinated by Shallum.
(2) A prophet who wrote chapters 1–8 of the book of Zechariah about 520 B.C. His prophecies look forward to the restoration of the temple and the new age about to dawn. Chapters 9–14 are from a later date.
(3) The father of John the Baptist.

Zedekiah. King of Judah (597–586 B.C.). The uncle of his predecessor Jehoiachin, he was placed on the throne by the Babylonians when Jehoiachin surrendered to them in 597 B.C. and was deported. In 589 B.C. Zedekiah himself rebelled and so precipitated the final crisis in the history of Judah. After Jerusalem fell in 586 B.C. he fled, but was captured, and after watching all his sons killed he was blinded and taken in chains to Babylon.

Zephaniah. A contemporary of Jeremiah, Zephaniah threatened a day of judgement against his people, primarily because of their unfaithfulness in worshipping other gods, but also he looked forward to repentance and restoration.

Zimri. King of Israel (876 B.C.). After assassinating his predecessor Elah, Zimri ruled for only seven days before committing suicide in order to avoid being murdered by Omri.

Zion. Originally just the name of one of the hills on which Jerusalem is built, it came to be a symbolic term indicating the dwelling-place of God and associated with the belief that he would always protect Jerusalem.

Zophar. The third of Job's "friends" (Job 11).

MYTHS AND LEGENDS

This popular section gives a brief guide to the ancient myths and legends of Greece and Rome. There is also an outline introduction to the gods and sagas of Norse tradition, from Odin and Thor to Valhalla and Ragnarok. Great artists and writers throughout the ages have enriched their work by reference to these endearing tales of the ancient world and some basic knowledge of them is vital to the full appreciation of our art and literature.

CLASSICAL MYTHOLOGY

A

Abas. In Greek mythology either (1) the son of Celeus and Metanira. His mockery of Demeter (*q.v.*) as she drank resulted in his being turned into a lizard, or
    (2) the twelfth king of Argolis who owned a magic shield from which he derived authority. He was the father of Acrisius (*q.v.*) and Proetus (*q.v.*).

Abderus. The friend of Heracles (*q.v.*) in whose care Heracles left the mares of Diomedes (*q.v.*). The horses ate him and Heracles founded Abdera, a coastal town in Thrace, in his honour.

Absyrtus (or **Apsyrtus**). Half brother of the sorceress Medea (*q.v.*). When Aëtes pursued Jason (*q.v.*) and Medea, in order to recover the golden fleece, Medea slew the boy, cut his corpse into pieces and tossed the pieces into the sea. Because Aëtes stopped his ship to collect the pieces of his son for burial Jason and Medea were able to escape.

Abyla. *See* **"Pillars of Hercules"**.

Acamas. Son of Theseus (*q.v.*) and Phaedra (*q.v.*), brother of Demophon (*q.v.*). He went to Troy (*q.v.*) with Diomedes (*q.v.*) to demand the return of Helen (*q.v.*). He and his brother also rescued their grandmother Aethra, who had been Helen's slave, when Troy fell.

Acastus. Son of Pelias King of Iolcos and one of the Argonauts (*q.v.*). When Medea (*q.v.*) caused his father's death he banished her and Jason (*q.v.*). Showed hospitality to Peleus (*q.v.*) but suspecting him of advances towards his wife he left Peleus to die at the hands of the Centaurs (*q.v.*). Later Peleus returned to slay the couple. Acastus was the father of Laodamia (*q.v.*).

Acestes. In Roman mythology a chieftain of Trojan descent who had settled in Sicily prior to the arrival of Aeneas (*q.v.*).

Achelous. A great river god, the son of Oceanus (*q.v.*) and Tethys (*q.v.*). By defeating Achelous Heracles (*q.v.*) won the hand of Deianeira (*q.v.*) daughter of Oeneus (*q.v.*).

Acheron. A real river of Epirus flowing into the Ionian Sea. Part of it runs underground which may account for its position in Greek mythology. Here it is the "river of grief " which flows in the underworld of the dead.

Achilles. A Greek warrior who is the principal character of the *Iliad*. The son of Peleus (*q.v.*) King of the Myrmidones at Phthia in Thessaly and Thetis (*q.v.*) one of the Nereides (*q.v.*). As a baby his mother dipped him in the Styx (*q.v.*) making him invulnerable save for his heel, by which she held him. He was educated in the arts of war and hunting, and in morality, by Cheiron.

His mother, knowing that he would die at Troy (*q.v.*) tried to prevent him joining the Greek expedition there by disguising him as a girl and sending him to the court of Lycomedes, King of Scyros. Here Lycomedes' daughter Deidamia, bore him a son, Neoptolemus (*q.v.*). Odysseus (*q.v.*) learned of this subterfuge and visited Lycomedes' court disguised as a merchant. While the king's daughters and the disguised Achilles were surveying his wares he suddenly produced swords which Achilles eagerly clasped, thus revealing himself. Achilles proved himself the most formidable warrior at Troy. At Tenedos on the way to Troy he killed King Tenes and his father Cyncus and by raiding Aeneas' (*q.v.*) cattle prompted him to join the Trojan forces. In the tenth year of the war Achilles quarrelled with Agamemnon (*q.v.*) over the captive girl Briseis and withdrew from the fighting. However he loaned his armour to Patroclus, his cousin and friend who was slain by Hector (*q.v.*). His death prompted Achilles to cease sulking in his tent and to return to the fray. Thetis gave him new armour made by Hephaestus (*q.v.*) and wearing this he slew Hector. He also killed Penthesilea (*q.v.*) and the

Greek Thersites (*q.v.*). After killing Memnon (*q.v.*) Achilles was shot in his vulnerable ankle at a battle near the Scaean gate (*q.v.*) Odysseus and Ajax (*q.v.*) recovered his body and argued over his armour.

Acis. In later Greek legend the young son of Faunus (*q.v.*) and a river nymph. He loved the sea-nymph Galatea (*q.v.*) and was killed by his jealous rival Polyphemus (*q.v.*). According to Sicilian tradition he was then turned into the river of the same name which runs at the foot of Mount Etna. This tradition first appears in the writing of Theocritus (*q.v.*) and later in Ovid's (*q.v.*) "Metamorphoses". It inspired paintings by Poussin and Claude and the opera *Acis and Galatea* by Handel.

Acrisius. Son of Abas (*q.v.*), twin brother of Proetus (*q.v.*) and King of Argos. Warned by an oracle that the son of his daughter Danaë (*q.v.*) would kill him he had her locked up in a brazen tower. But this was to no avail because Zeus (*q.v.*) visited her and fathered Perseus (*q.v.*), Acrisius then cast mother and son adrift on the sea, locked in a chest. Years later Perseus returned to Argos causing Acrisius to flee to Larissa. However Perseus, visiting Larissa to take part in the games, accidentally killed him with a discus.

Acropolis. In general terms a high citadel found in all Greek cities. The best known acropolis is that at Athens which was first inhabited around 2000 B.C. From time immemorial it was dedicated to Athene (*q.v.*).

Actaeon. Mythical huntsman and grandson of Cadmus (*q.v.*) of Thebes. Artemis (*q.v.*) turned him into a stag, torn to pieces by his own hounds because he inadvertently spied her bathing. The story is recounted in Ovid's (*q.v.*) "Metamorphoses" and recalled in the works of Titian, Veronese, Poussin, Rembrandt, Gainsborough and Parmigiano.

Admetus. King of Pherae in Thessaly and husband of the beautiful Alcestis (*q.v.*). Apollo (*q.v.*) offered to allow Admetus to avoid death if one of his family would die in his place. Alcestis offered herself but according to legend either Persephone (*q.v.*) refused the self-sacrifice or Heracles (*q.v.*) rescued Alcestis from Hades (*q.v.*). This forms the theme of one of Euripides' best known plays and Gluck's opera *Alceste* (in which Apollo not Heracles saves her).

Adonis. A Syrian deity associated with the mystery of vegetation. He was a beautiful Cypriot youth, the son of Myrrha and her father. For this incest Myrrha was turned into a tree. Nine months later Adonis was born from the bark of the tree, taken up by Aphrodite (*q.v.*) and placed in the care of Persephone (*q.v.*). He spent alternate parts of the year with Persephone and Aphrodite who loved him. He was killed by a boar sent by Artemis (*q.v.*). Shakespeare's *Venus and Adonis* is based on Ovid's (*q.v.*) version of the tale while Shelley's elegy on the death of Keats, *Adonais*, derives its title from Bion's *Lament for Adonis*. Adonis was painted by Titian, Veronese and Poussin.

Adrastus. Son of Talaus and King of Argos. An oracle told him that his offspring would be a lion and a boar and in accordance with this he gave his daughter Argia to Polynices (*q.v.*) and her sister to Tydeus (*q.v.*) who bore images of these animals on their shields. He attempted to restore Polynices to his throne at Thebes (*see* **Seven against Thebes**). He survived this adventure—some say due to his magic horse Arion (*q.v.*)—and led a second expedition of the Epigoni, *q.v.*) against Thebes, dying of grief when he heard that his son Aegialeus had fallen in the attack.

Aeacides. The descendants of Aeacus (*q.v.*).

Aeacus. Son of Zeus and Aegina and King of the Myrmidones. The Myrmidones were originally ants, transformed into men by Zeus at the request of Aeacus. He aided Poseidon (*q.v.*) and Apollo (*q.v.*) in the construction of the walls of Troy. He had two sons, Peleus (*q.v.*) and Telamon (*q.v.*) by his wife Endeis. He was also the father of Phocus (q.v.) by a Nereid. Aeacus later exiled Peleus (future father of Achilles) for the murder of Phocus. A model of virtue and piety, Aeacus was made one of the three judges of the Underworld.

Aeaea. In the *Odyssey* the island home of Circe (q.v.).

Aedon. In Greek mythology the wife of Zethus, king of Thebes. She was jealous of Niobe, wife of Zethus' brother Amphion (q.v.). In trying to murder Niobe's son she killed her own son Itylus by mistake. In pity Zeus (q.v.) turned her into a nightingale whose song still mourns Itylus.

Aegaeon. Alternative name for Briareus (q.v.).

Aegeus. King of Athens and father of Theseus (q.v.) by Aethra (q.v.) daughter of Pittheus king of Troezen. She brought Theseus up secretly at her father's court, during which time Aegeus married Medea (q.v.). When Theseus finally returned to his father's court Medea fled. Before Theseus went to slay the Minotaur (q.v.) he and Aegeus agreed that he would hoist a white sail when returning to Athens to signal his success.

On returning Theseus forgot to do this and Aegeus seeing a black sail on his son's ship supposed him dead and, in grief threw himself into the sea, henceforth called the Aegean.

Aegisthus. The son of Thyestes (q.v.) by his daughter Pelopia. Pelopia exposed the baby but it was rescued by her husband Atreus (q.v.) who believed it to be his own son. Atreus was king of Mycenae and when Thyestes, an enemy, returned in later years he ordered Aegisthus to kill him. But father and son recognised each other and Aegisthus killed Atreus. Thyestes became king of Mycenae but Atreus had had two sons by Aerope, Menelaus (q.v.) and Agamemnon (q.v.). Agamemnon expelled Thyestes and reclaimed his father's throne. While Agamemnon was at Troy (q.v.) Aegisthus seduced his wife Clytemnestra (q.v.) and helped her murder him on his return. These two murderers of Agamemnon now ruled Mycenae. But at the urging of his sister Electra (q.v.) (whom Aegisthus would have liked to kill and whom he forced to marry a peasant) Agamemnon's son Orestes (q.v.) and his friend Pylades (q.v.) returned from exile in Phocis and with Electra's help avenged their father, slaying Aegisthus and Clytemnestra.

Aeneas. The Trojan hero regarded by the Romans as their ancestor. The son of Anchises (q.v.) and Aphrodite (q.v.). Led the survivors of the Trojan War to Italy. The lover of Dido. *See under* **Aeneid.**

Aeneid. Virgil's (q.v.) unfinished epic poem. In 12 volumes, it is written to honour Rome, to increase the prestige of Augustus (by recalling the deeds of his supposed ancestor) and to foretell prosperity to come. It describes Aeneas' (q.v.) wanderings after Troy fell, recounting his stay in Carthage and love for Dido (q.v.) the funeral games of his father Anchises (q.v.) in Sicily, a journey to the Underworld to visit his dead father's spirit and his arrival at the mouth of the Tiber where he landed on the Latin shore. Here he fought wars with the Latins and their allies before finally defeating Turnus the Rutulian prince and uniting the races by marrying Lavinia the Latin princess. He founded Lavinium, named in her honour.

Aeolian Isles. The present Aeolian Isles are off the North East of Sicily, forming part of the Liparia group. They are mentioned in the *Odyssey.*

Aeolus. In Greek mythology (1) the son of Helen and ruler of Thessaly, believed to be the brother of Dorus and Xuthus (q.v.) and the ancestor of the Aeolians or Aeolic Greeks.

(2) The son of Poseidon (q.v.) and ruler of the Aeolian isles (q.v.). Zeus (q.v.) made him guardian of the winds. He gave Odysseus (q.v.) a bag of winds which his men let loose and which blew the ship off course.

Aeschylus. *See* **Section B.**

Aetolus. Legendary conqueror of Aetolia. The son of Endymion (q.v.) king of Elis, he was banished across the Corinthian Gulf after accidentally killing Apis in a chariot race.

Agamemnon. Son of Atreus (q.v.) and Aerope, brother of Menelaus (q.v.) and king of Mycenae. He married Helen's (q.v.) half-sister Clytemnestra (q.v.) and commanded the Greek forces at Troy (q.v.). Before the Greek fleet could leave Aulis to sail for Troy he had to sacrifice his daughter Iphigenia (q.v.). At Troy he quarrelled with Achilles (q.v.) when he seized Briseis from Achilles. He did this because Apollo (q.v.) had forced him to return Chryseis to her father, the Trojan Chryses (q.v).

On his return to Mycenae he was murdered by Aegisthus (q.v.) and Clytemnestra. Clytemnestra attacked him with an axe while he was bathing. This occurred despite the warning given to Agamemnon by Cassandra (q.v.) whom he had brought back from Troy as his mistress. He was avenged by his children Orestes (q.v.) and Electra (q.v.). The story inspired Aeschylus' (q.v.) trilogy *Orestia.*

Aganippe. A fountain at the foot of Mt. Helicon, sacred to the Muses (q.v.) who are sometimes called Aganippides. It inspired those who drank from it. The fountain of Hippocrene, also sacred to the Muses, was known as Aganippis.

Agathyrsans. In the *Aeneid* (q.v.) a tribe in Thrace.

Aglaia. "The bright one": one of the Graces (q.v.).

Aides or Aidoneus. Hades (q.v.).

Ajax. (Greek Aias) In Greek legend two Ajaxes appear. The first was the son of King Telamon of Salamis. He killed Teuthras King of Teuthrania, an ally of Troy (q.v.) and took his daughter Tecmessa. At Troy he fought all day with Hector (q.v.) and at the end of the duel they exchanged gifts, Hector giving him a sword. With Menelaus (q.v.) he rescued the body of Patroclus (q.v.) and with Odysseus (q.v.) killed Glaucus and rescued the body of Achilles. Homer (q.v.) says the pair quarrelled over the armour and that Odysseus killed him. Later, when Odysseus summoned the spirits of the dead Ajax held aloof. But Sophocles (q.v.) in his *Ajax* calls on another tradition in which Ajax, disappointed at not being given the Palladium (q.v.) or Troy when the city fell, went mad, killing the Greek sheep under the delusion they were his rivals before impaling himself on the sword Hector had given him. The other Ajax was the son of Oileus, king of the Locrians. He was courageous but blasphemous. When Troy was sacked he dragged Cassandra (q.v.) from the altar of Athene (q.v.) where she sought refuge and gave her to Agamemnon (q.v.). On his return to Greece Poseidon (q.v.) saved him from shipwreck in a storm sent by Athene. Taking shelter on a rock he boasted himself more powerful than the goddess. She commanded Poseidon to crack the reef with his trident and Ajax drowned.

Alba Longa. The Latin city founded by Ascanius (q.v.) in the Alban Hills. In fact, as well as legend, Alba was the mother city of Rome which was probably founded as one of her western outposts. Alba was capital of the Latin League, a confederation of Latin states, but was eventually supplanted by Rome.

Alcaeus. *See* **Alcmene.**

Alcestis. Daughter of Pelias (q.v.) and the only one of his daughters not to follow Medea's (q.v.) advice and boil him alive. Married Admetus (q.v.) and was devoted to him.

Alcides. Another name for Heracles (q.v.) whose grandfather was reputed to be Alcaeus.

Alcinous. King of the mythical Phaeacians of the isle of Scheria. A grandson of Poseidon (q.v.), he married Arete his own sister. Father of the beautiful Nausicaa (q.v.). He entertained Odysseus and gave him a ship. He was also said to have entertained the Argonauts and refused to return Medea to her father. Scheria has been identified with Corfu.

Alcmaeon. In myth the son of Amphiaraus (q.v.) and Eriphyle (q.v.). One of the Epigoni (q.v.).

Alcmene. The wife of Amphitrion (q.v.) son of Alcaeus. Her brothers had been slain by the Taphians and she would not consummate her marriage until Amphitrion avenged them. While he was away warring with the Taphians Zeus (q.v.) appeared in his likeness and fathered Heracles (q.v.) upon her. Hermes (q.v.) was ordered to delay the dawn in order that Zeus might take his time—an amusing situation which had appealed to Plautus, Molière and Dryden. Later that night the real Amphitrion returned and fathered Iphicles (q.v.).

In his *Amphitryon 38* Jean Giraudoux claims 37 versions of the tale have preceded him. On the death of Amphitrion Alcmene married Rhadamanthus (q.v.).

Alcyone or Halcyone. (1) Leader of the Pleiades (q.v.), daughter of Atlas (q.v.) and Pleione.

(2) The daughter of Aeolus (q.v.) and wife of Ceyx. When Ceyx was lost at sea she drowned herself in sorrow. The sympathetic gods turned the pair to kingfishers which supposedly bred during the winter solstice. Then Aeolus forbids the wind to blow leaving the Aegean calm while they build and sit on their nest. This is the time of year

called the "Halcyon days". The story is told in Ovid's (q.v.) "Metamorphoses" and Chaucer's "Book of the Duchess".

Alecto. One of the Erinnyes (q.v.).

Alexander the Great. See Section B.

Amalthea. The she-goat which nursed the infant Zeus in the Dictaean cave in Crete. As a reward she was placed among the stars as Capricorn while one of her horns which had broken off became the Cornucopia, or horn of plenty.

Amazons. Mythical race of female warriors at one time believed by the Greeks to live in Thrace or Asia Minor. As the Greeks' knowledge of the world grew, so the homeland of the Amazons was held to be more distant. In the *Iliad* (q.v.) Priam (q.v.) is said to have warred with them, though they came to the aid of Troy (q.v.). Achilles (q.v.) slew their queen Penthesilea (q.v.). Heracles (q.v.) fought with them and seized the girdle of the queen Hippolyte (q.v.) while Theseus (q.v.) carried off either Hippolyte or Antiope (q.v.). Theseus' act caused the Amazons to invade Attica but Theseus defeated them in the streets of Athens. In antiquity it was thought they amputated their right breast (Greek *mazos*) in order to hold a bow better.

Ambrosia. The food of the Olympians which gave immortality.

Ammon. The Egyptian god Amun was known to the Greeks from the 7th century B.C. when they came into contact with his cult at the Siwa oasis. They identified him with Zeus. Alexander the Great consulted the oracle of Zeus and Ammon was recognised as the son of Zeus by the priests of the oracle. A legend grew up that Alexander was begotten by Ammon in the form of a snake.

Amphiaraus. See **Seven Against Thebes**.

Amphion. Twin brother of Zethus, sons of Zeus (q.v.) and Antiope (q.v.). Antiope was married to Lycus King of Thebes who divorced her. She was cruelly treated by his second wife Dirce. The twins were raised by herdsmen on Mt. Cithaeron. When they reached manhood they avenged their mother by killing Zethus and tying Dirce to the horns of a wild bull. The fountain into which her body was thrown henceforth bore her name. The twins now took possession of Thebes and built the fortifications below the Cadmea. Amphion, who had been given a lyre by Hermes (q.v.) played so skilfully that the stones moved into place of their own accord. They ruled jointly, Zethus marrying Thebe who gave her name to the city, and Amphion marrying Niobe (q.v.).

Amphitrion. Son of Alcaeus, husband of Alcmene (q.v.) and father of Iphicles (q.v.). Foster father of Heracles (q.v.). When Heracles killed his teacher Linus with Linus' own lyre, Amphitrion sent him away to keep cattle. Later Amphitrion was killed helping Heracles defeat the Minyans.

Amphitrite. The daughter of Nereus (q.v.) leader of the Nereides (q.v.). Persuaded by Delphinos to accept Poseidon (q.v.) (Delphinos was rewarded by having her image placed amongst the stars as the Dolphin). By Poseidon she was mother of Triton (q.v.). Her hatred of Scylla (q.v.), Poseidon's daughter by another, led her to turn Scylla into a monster with six barking heads and twelve feet.

Amphitroniades. Another name for Heracles (q.v.) whose putative father was Amphitrion (q.v.).

Amyclae. One of the most sacred sites in the Peloponnese, a sanctuary a few miles from Sparta consecrated to Hyacinthus (q.v.).

Anchises. A cousin of Priam (q.v.). For his piety he was allowed to sleep with Aphrodite (q.v.) who bore him Aeneas. When Troy (q.v.) fell Aeneas carried his father (now blind) to safety through the Dardanian gate of the city. He died in Sicily and was buried in the *Aeneid* (q.v.) he appears among the blessed spirits of the dead to foretell Rome's greatness. *Aeneas carrying his Father* is an early work of Bernini.

Ancus Martius. The legendary fourth king of Rome who succeeded Tullus Hostilius. A grandson of Numa Pompilius (q.v.) he ruled from 640 to 616 B.C. He was very religious but also succeeded in defeating the Latins. He was succeeded by Tarquin the Elder.

Andromache. A Trojan princess, wife of Hector (q.v.) and by him mother of Astyanax. When Troy fell her son was thrown from the city walls, despite her spirited defence of him with a pestle. She was carried off to Epirus by Neoptolemus (q.v.) and here married his brother in law Hellenus and

became joint ruler. She also had a son by Neoptolemus and was threatened by his jealous wife Hermione (see Racine's *Andromaque*). Her days were ended at Pergamum, the city founded by her and Neoptolemus' son, Molossus. In historic times the Molossi claimed descent from Molossus and Neoptolemus.

Andromeda. See **Cassiopeia**.

Antaeus. A Libyan giant, son of Poseidon (q.v.) and Ge (q.v.). An invincible wrestler until Heracles (q.v.), realising he drew his strength from his mother, held him in the air and squeezed him to death. He is featured in a painting by Pollaiuolo in Florence.

Antenor. The wisest of the Trojans. Priam (q.v.) sent him to reclaim Hesione from Telamon after Heracles (q.v.) sacked Troy (q.v.). He advised the Trojans to return Helen (q.v.) to Menelaus (q.v.) but they refused. His hatred for Deiphobus (q.v.) led him to help the Greeks steal the Palladium (q.v.). The husband of Theano and father of Laocoön (q.v.). After Troy fell he and his wife went to Italy and founded either Venice or Padua.

Antigone. Daughter of Oedipus (q.v.) and Jocasta (q.v.) she accompanied her father into exile (recalled in Sophocles' *Oedipus at Colonus*). After his death she returned to Thebes where her brother Eteocles (q.v.) and Polynices (q.v.) were warring on each other. Both perished in battle and her uncle Creon (q.v.) seized power. Because Polynices had fought against his own country Creon refused him burial. Antigone defied Creon and buried her brother with full rites and was imprisoned in a cave for doing so. Here she hung herself, and her betrothed, Creon's son Haemon, committed suicide in despair. The story and the ethical principles it raises are the basis of Sophocles' *Antigone*. In his work of the same name Anouilh reconsiders the arguments involved.

Antilochus. Son of Nestor (q.v.) a valiant Greek warrior at Troy (q.v.). Too young to sail from Aulis when the expedition began he arrived later. Slain by Memnon (q.v.) while defending his father.

Antinous. See **Odysseus**.

Antiope. (1) An Amazon, sister of Hippolyte (q.v.). According to some legends she was carried off by Theseus (q.v.), perhaps with the aid of Heracles (q.v.) and bore him Hippolytus (q.v.).

(2) A Theban princess who bore Amphion (q.v.) and Zethus to Zeus (q.v.) who visited her in the form of a satyr (q.v.). Her father exposed the children on Mt. Cithaeron. She was badly treated and imprisoned by Lycus and his wife Dirce (Lycus was either her husband, who divorced her to marry Dirce, or her uncle). She was later freed and avenged by her twin sons. Titian, Correggio and Watteau have all painted Zeus visiting Antiope as a satyr.

Aphaia. A goddess worshipped in Aegina and identified with the Cretan Britomartis.

Aphrodite. The goddess of love, desire and procreation, known to the Romans as Venus. She sprang from the seed of Uranus (q.v.), rising naked from the sea at Paphos in Cyprus. However, Homer (q.v.) holds her to be the daughter of Zeus (q.v.) and Dione, and makes her the wife of Hephaestus (q.v.). She was not faithful to Hephaestus, but bore children by Ares (q.v.), Poseidon (q.v.), Dionysus (q.v.), and Hermes (q.v.). She loved the mortals Adonis (q.v.) and Anchises (q.v.) by whom she bore Aeneas (q.v.), and tempted Paris (q.v.) to desert Oenone. It was to her that Paris gave the golden apple of discord, she being the "fairest" goddess. In return she promised him the most beautiful woman in the world. Around her waist she wore a magic girdle which made her beautiful and irresistibly desirable.

Apis. The sacred bull of Memphis which the Egyptians worshipped as a god.

Apollo. Son of Zeus (q.v.) and the mortal Leto; twin brother of Artemis (q.v.). As a child he killed the she-dragon Python on Mt. Parnassus and took over her role as the oracle at Delphi. Hence he was sometimes known as the Pythian or as Loxias "the Ambiguous". He was also a symbol of light and was known as Phoebus or "shining". Apart from being god of prophecy he was a god of song and music, having been given the lyre by Hermes.

He was the leader of the Muses (q.v.) and was sometimes called Musagetes. He could be a destroyer (he is always portrayed with bow and arrows) and sent plagues amongst the Greeks at Troy, but was also protective against evil and was father of Asclepius (q.v.). When Zeus slew Asclepius he retaliated by slaying the Cyclops (q.v.)

and was punished by being sent as a servant to Admetus (*q.v.*) of Pherae in Thessaly. Prior to this Zeus had sent him as a bondsman to King Laomedan whom he helped to build the walls of Troy. This was punishment for his part in a conspiracy (led by Hera, Poseidon and himself) against Zeus. He loved Hestia (*q.v.*) but also seduced the nymph Dryope and attempted to seduce Daphne. When Daphne protested she was turned into a laurel tree. Amongst mortal women he at one time loved Cassandra (*q.v.*). With his sister Artemis he shot the giant Tityus, whom the jealous Hera sent to violate Leto; it was he who shot the vulture which tormented Prometheus and he also helped Paris (*q.v.*) shoot Achilles (*q.v.*). He was identified with the sun-god by later writers but in Homer (*q.v.*) he and Helios (*q.v.*) are quite distinct.

Arachne. A Lydian maiden who competed with Athene (*q.v.*) at a weaving contest. When she won the angry goddess forced her to hang herself before turning her into a spider and her weaving into a cobweb.

Arcadia. Green but mountainous region, isolated in the centre of the Peloponnese. Its inhabitants were primitive shepherds and peasants.

Arcas. The son of Zeus (*q.v.*) and Callisto (*q.v.*) who gave his name to Arcadia (*q.v.*).

Ares. The son of Zeus (*q.v.*) and Hera (*q.v.*) and the god of war. Associated with Mars, by the Romans. He was disliked by all the gods save Hades (*q.v.*) and Eris (*q.v.*) because of his love of battle for its own sake. He loved Aphrodite (*q.v.*), and Hephaestus (*q.v.*) once caught the pair in an invisible net exposing them to the ridicule of the other gods.

The father of Penthesilea by Otrere. He was once defeated by Heracles (*q.v.*), was wounded by Diomedes (*q.v.*) and imprisoned for 13 months (till Hermes (*q.v.*) released him) in a brazen vessel by the Aloeidae (*q.v.*). Athene (*q.v.*) got the better of him on several occasions. He once stood trial on the site of the Areopagus.

Arethusa. A river and a river goddess of southern Greece. She was pursued under the sea to Sicily by the river god Alpheus. In Sicily she was identified with Artemis and a cult of Artemis Arethusa flourished at Syracuse.

Argo. A fifty-oared ship built for Jason (*q.v.*) by Argus. In its prow Athene (*q.v.*) fitted an oracular beam.

Argonauts. The heroes who sailed with Jason (*q.v.*) in the Argo (*q.v.*) to fetch the golden fleece from Colchis. Their ranks included Heracles (*q.v.*), Orpheus (*q.v.*) Castor and Polydeuces (*q.v.*) Echion, Idas (*q.v.*) and Lynceus (*q.v.*). The voyage was an adventurous one and after dallying at Lemnos they passed through the Hellespont and reached Mysia. Here Hylas (*q.v.*) was lost and Heracles stayed to look for him. At some point the Sirens (*q.v.*) were passed with the help of Orpheus (*q.v.*) and at Bebrycos Polydeuces (*see* **Castor**) slew Amycus. In Thrace they rid Phineus (*q.v.*) of the Harpies (*q.v.*) and in return were told how to navigate the Symplegades (*q.v.*).

Argus. (1) The builder of the Argo (*q.v.*).

(2) A hundred-eyed giant set by Hera (*q.v.*) to watch Io (*q.v.*).

(3) The faithful hound of Odysseus (*q.v.*).

Ariadne. The daughter of Minos (*q.v.*) and Pasiphae (*q.v.*). She helped Theseus (*q.v.*) but he abandoned her at Naxos when Dionysus (*q.v.*) fell in love with her. He married her and gave her a crown of seven stars which became a constellation after her death.

Arimaspi. A mythical people of the Scythian steppes said to be neighbours of the Hyperboreans. They had one eye and constantly fought a group of griffins for the gold they guarded. Herodotus (*q.v.*) tells of a poem by Aristeas, a priest of Hyperborean Apollo, about them. Aristeas is clearly a *shaman*, able to separate body and soul and to be in two places at once. Aeschylus (*q.v.*) refers to them when describing Io's (*q.v.*) wanderings.

Arion. A fabulous horse, the offspring of Demeter (*q.v.*) and Zeus (*q.v.*). Demeter had taken the form of a mare and Zeus raped her in the form of a horse. She also gave birth to the nymph Despoena and possibly Persephone (*q.v.*) at the same time as Arion. It saved Adrastus (*q.v.*) at the siege of Thebes.

Aristaeus. The son of Apollo (*q.v.*) and a Lapith (*see* **Lapithae**) girl Cyrene. A minor deity, the protector of cattle, fruit trees and bee-keepers. Virgil (*q.v.*) makes Cyrene a nymph and says that Aristaeus fell in love with Eurydice who died of a snake bite she received while fleeing from him. In

punishment all his bees were killed. Cyrene sought the advice of Proteus (*q.v.*) and Aristaeus made sacrifices of cattle to placate the nymphs. Nine days later he found fresh swarms in the carcasses.

Aristophanes. *See* **Section B**.

Artemis. The daughter of Zeus (*q.v.*) and Leto (*q.v.*) twin sister of Apollo (*q.v.*). Her Roman counterpart was Diana. She was often conflated with Hecate (*q.v.*) and Selene (*q.v.*), the moon goddess. A goddess of the chase and protectress of children and young animals. She was also treated as a mother or earth goddess in the Asian tradition and was worshipped orgiastically at Ephesus. She was generally portrayed with a bow and arrow, made by Hephaestus (*q.v.*), and like Apollo could spread the plague and death. With her arrows she punished impiety (*e.g.* Niobe). A virgin who sternly protected her own chastity, she was known to punish unchastity in others *e.g.* Callisto (*q.v.*).

Ascanius. The son of Aeneas (*q.v.*) and Creusa, who escaped from Troy (*q.v.*) with his father. Another tradition makes his mother the Latin princess Lavinia. He succeeded his father as king and made Alba Longa (*q.v.*) his capital.

Asclepius or **Aesculapius.** The son of Apollo (*q.v.*) and Coronis, a god of healing whose worship spread to Rome after a plague in 293 B.C. He was taught healing by Cheiron the centaur (*q.v.*). Once he brought a dead man back to life and Zeus (*q.v.*) punished him, killing him with a thunderbolt. At Apollo's request he was placed among the stars.

Asopus. A river god, the son of Oceanus (*q.v.*) and Tethys (*q.v.*). The father of Evadne, Euboea and Aegina.

Astraeus. A Titan (*q.v.*) and by Eos the father of the beneficent winds. According to other traditions he also fathered the stars.

Astyanax. The son of Hector (*q.v.*) and Andromache (*q.v.*). He was a sensitive child frightened by the plume of his father's helmet. When Troy (*q.v.*) fell Andromache struggled to protect him but Neoptolemus (*q.v.*) threw him from the city walls. Another tradition says she took him to Neoptolemus' court in Epirus.

Atalanta. The Boeotian Atalanta was the daughter of Schoeneus and wife of Hippomenes, the Arcadian Atalanta, the daughter of Iasus and Clymene and wife of Milanion. Similar tales were told of her in both traditions. She was exposed by her father and suckled by a bear sent by Artemis (*q.v.*) with whom she was sometimes identified. She became a famous huntress and hunted the Calydonian Boar (*q.v.*). Though vowed to virginity she bore Meleager (*q.v.*) a son. She refused to marry any suitor except he who beat her in a foot race. Hippomenes (or Milanion) did this by placing three golden apples, gifts from Aphrodite (*q.v.*) in her path, causing her to stop and collect them.

Athamas. The son of Aeolus and king of Orchomenus in Boeotia. He loved Ino (*q.v.*) who bore him Learchus and Melicertes, but Hera (*q.v.*) forced him to marry Nephele who bore him Phrixus and Helle (*q.v.*). Hera drove him mad because he sheltered Dionysus (*q.v.*) and he killed Learchus. Ino flung herself into the sea with Melicertes and both became sea deities. Ino became Leucothea and Melicertes became Palaemon. Athamas fled to Thessaly.

Athene or **Athena.** Identified with Minerva by the Romans. The daughter of Zeus (*q.v.*) and Metis (*q.v.*). Though it was foretold she would be a girl, an oracle said that if Metis bore another child it would be a son who would depose Zeus. He then swallowed Metis and later suffered a terrible headache near Lake Triton. Hermes (*q.v.*) knew the cause and persuaded Hephaestus (*q.v.*) to cleave Zeus' skull. Out sprang Athene fully armed. She was the goddess of wisdom and patron of arts and crafts, a protectress of agriculture and also a warrior. Moreover, she was a virgin (*see* **Pallas**). She disputed possession of Athens with Poseidon (*q.v.*): he offered the city the horse, Athene the olive which was judged to be the better gift.

Henceforth she was patron of the city which was a centre of her cult. Her epithet "glaucopis" meant "bright-eyed" or "owl-faced" and in the *Odyssey* (*q.v.*) she assumed the form of a bird. Athenian coins bore an owl and the saying "Owls to Athens" meant the same as "Coals to Newcastle". She was worshipped on the Acropolis. A defender of all heroes who worked for the good of mankind, *e.g.* Heracles (*q.v.*).

Atlantiades. Another name for Hermes (*q.v.*) whose mother Maia was the daughter of Atlas (*q.v.*).

Atlantis. A legendary island said to be to the west of the Pillars of Hercules (q.v.). Its inhabitants, once powerful and virtuous, became wealthy and degenerate and were conquered by the Athenians. Later the island sank beneath the ocean in a day and a night. It may be that the island Plato speaks of in *Timaeus* was part of Crete or some other island which suffered when a volcano on Suntorini (ancient Thera) erupted.

Atlas. A Titan (q.v.) the son of Iapetus and Clymene and brother of Prometheus (q.v.) and Epimetheus. For his part in the Titanomachia (q.v.) he was condemned to carry the sky on his shoulders and stood holding it far to the west of the Pillars of Hercules (q.v.). For a brief time Heracles (q.v.) shouldered his burden. It is said Perseus (q.v.) turned him to stone with Medusa's (q.v.) head and he was identified with Mt. Atlas in North-West Africa. The father of Calypso (q.v.) and the Pleiades (q.v.).

Atreus. See **Thyestes**.

Attis. A god of vegetation whose cult originated in Phrygia and involved a festival of death and resurrection in the Spring. A consort of Cybele (q.v.) according to one tradition he castrated himself in a religious frenzy and became head of her college of eunuch priests.

Augeas. A king of Elis with more sheep and cattle than any other man. Heracles (q.v.) was given the task of cleansing his filthy stables (the Augean stables) which had not been cleared for many years. Heracles promised to cleanse them in a day in return for one tenth of the cattle. He did so by diverting the rivers Peneius and Alphaeus through them but Augeas refused to pay him. Heracles later invaded Elis, killed Augeas, his sons and their allies the Moliones and destroyed the city of Pylus which had also helped Augeas. One tradition says he spared Augeas.

Aurora. The Roman goddess of the dawn, associated with the Greek Eos (q.v.).

Autolycus. The son of Hermes (q.v.) and Chione, father of Anticleia and thus grandfather of Odysseus (q.v.). Also grandfather of Sinon (q.v.). He was renowned for trickery, cunning and theft.

Aventine. One of the hills of Rome and the southernmost. It was close to the Tiber, was outside the pomerium and was associated with the "plebians".

Avernus, Lake. The modern Lago di Averno near Naples, thought to be an entrance to the Underworld. This is how Aeneas (q.v.) was told to enter Hades (q.v.). Agrippa linked it with the Lucrine Lake while building the harbour of Portus Julius.

B

Bacchae. The female followers of the cult of Bacchus or Dionysus whose worship was characterised by wine-induced frenzies of a mystic nature. At the height of such frenzies they believed themselves to be at one with the god. Also known as Bacchantes, Maenads and Thyiads.

Bacchoi. Male equivalent of the Bacchae.

Bacchus. Latin name for Dionysus (q.v.).

Bassaris. A Bacchante (See **Bacchae**).

Baucis. See **Philemon**.

Bellerophon. Son of Glaucus (q.v.) King of Corinth. He killed one Bellerus and fled to Tiryns where Anteia, wife of the King Proetus falsely accused him of trying to seduce her. Proetus sent him to his father-in-law Iobates with a letter requesting Iobates to kill the bearer of it. Reluctant to kill a guest Iobates sent him to kill the Chimaera (q.v.). Capturing Pegasus (q.v.) with a golden bridle given to him by Athene (q.v.) he was able to accomplish the task. He was then sent to fight the Amazons (q.v.) and again triumphed. On his return to Tiryns he survived an ambush set by Iobates and finally persuaded the king of his innocence. Iobates made him his heir.

One tradition says Bellerophon presumed to rise to Olympus on Pegasus but Zeus sent a gadfly which stung the horse. Pegasus threw Bellerophon to earth but itself entered Olympus.

Belus. One of Poseidon's (q.v.) sons and father of Danaus (q.v.), Cepheus (q.v.) and Aegyptus.

Biton and Cleobis. Sons of a priestess of Hera (q.v.) in Argos who drew their mother's chariot several miles to the goddess's temple when no oxen could be found. Their mother asked Hera to bestow on them the best of gifts for mortals, and they died in their sleep in the temple.

Boeotia. Region of northern Greece; the capital city was Thebes.

Bona Dea. A Roman fertility goddess. Only women worshipped her. Cicero (q.v.) recounts an occasion when his opponent Clodius (q.v.), disguised as a woman, entered an annual nocturnal ceremony of her worshippers over which the chief magistrate's wife presided.

Boreas. The Roman Aquilo; the north wind in Greek mythology. Son of Astraeus (q.v.) and Eos (q.v.) and brother of the other beneficent winds Zephyrus (q.v.), Notus (q.v.) and Eurus (q.v.). A friend of Athens who destroyed Xerxes' (q.v.) fleet. He carried off Oreithyia, daughter of Erechtheus king of Athens who bore him two sons Zetes (q.v.) and Calais (q.v.) and two daughters, Chione and Cleopatra, wife of Phineus.

Brauron. Site on the east coast of Attica. Centre of a cult of Artemis (q.v.). It was believed the locals had killed a she-bear, an animal sacred to the goddess, and that she demanded they worship her on the site, and that girls between the ages of 7 and 11 serve her and live in her temple. Also believed to be the burial place of Iphigenia (q.v.) after her sacrifice at Aulis.

Briareus or **Aegaeon.** One of the Hecatoncheires (q.v.).

Briseis. See **Achilles**.

Brontes. One of the Cyclopes (q.v.).

Brutus, Lucius Junius. According to a Roman tradition accepted by Livy (q.v.) the liberator of Rome from the Etruscan kings following the rape of Lucretia (q.v.). Also the first Roman consul in 509 B.C. He ordered the execution of his own sons when they became involved in a conspiracy to restore the monarchy.

C

Cacus. In Roman tradition this fire-breathing giant and his sister Caca were children of Vulcan (q.v.) who lived on the Palatine hill (q.v.), although Virgil in book 8 of the *Aeneid* (q.v.) makes it the Aventine (q.v.). Virgil tells how Cacus stole the cattle of Geryon (q.v.) from Hercules (q.v.) who pursued Cacus back to his cave, tracking him by the cattle's mooing. There he slew Cacus. This event has been portrayed in a painting by Poussin and a statue by Bandinelli in the Signoria, Florence.

Cadmus. Son of Agenor, king of Phoenicia and grandson of Poseidon (q.v.). When Zeus (q.v.) carried off his sister Europa (q.v.) he went to look for her but was told by the Delphic oracle (see Apollo) to relinquish the search and to follow a magical cow. Where the cow lay down he was to found a city. The place where it sank became the site of the Cadmea, the citadel of Thebes. Here Cadmus slew the dragon guarding the spring of Ares and on her advice sowed its teeth. The Sparti (q.v.) sprang up. Cadmus married Harmonia (q.v.) and their wedding was attended by the gods. Their children included Autonoe, Ino, Semele (q.v.) Agave Polydoros (q.v.) and Illyrius. In old age Cadmus, who had introduced the use of letters to Greece from Phoenicia, gave up his throne to his grandson Pentheus and went to reign in Illyria. Later he and Harmonia were received into Elysium (q.v.) in the form of serpents.

Caeneus. Originally the nymph Caenis turned into a man at her own request by Poseidon (q.v.). Accompanied the Argonauts (q.v.) and hunted the Calydonian Boar (q.v.). Invulnerable to normal blows he was killed by the Centaurs (q.v.) in their battle with the Lapithae (q.v.) when they buried him beneath a pile of trees. His soul left the body as a bird and in the Underworld again became female.

Calais. Twin brother of Zetes. Winged sons of Boreas (q.v.) and Oreithyia, they accompanied the Argonauts (q.v.) and drove off the Harpies (q.v.), tormenting Phineus (q.v.) husband of their sister Cleopatra.

Calchas. A renegade Trojan seer who helped the Greeks at Troy (q.v.). He foretold that Troy would not fall without Achilles' (q.v.) presence and that the sacrifice of Iphigenia (q.v.) was necessary to secure a favourable wind. It was he who advised Agamemnon to return the girl Chryseis to her father the Trojan priest Chryses. This caused Agamemnon to seize Briseis and sparked the quarrel with Achilles. Calchas later died of grief when surpassed in prophecy by Mopsus, a mysterious mythical figure who was also said to have sailed with the Argonauts (*q.v.*).

Calipe. See **Pillars of Hercules**.

Calliope. See **Muses**.

Callirhoë. Daughter of the river god Achelous (*q.v.*) and wife of Alcmaeon (*q.v.*). Alcmaeon gave her the necklace and robe of Harmonia (*q.v.*).

Callisto. Daughter of Lycaon (*q.v.*). One of Artemis' (*q.v.*) huntresses. She bore Arcas (*q.v.*) to Zeus (*q.v.*) who sought to conceal their affair from Hera (*q.v.*) by turning Callisto into a bear. Realising the ruse Hera had the bear hunted down but Zeus saved her and placed her amongst the stars as Arctos. Others say that Artemis turned her into a bear and Arcas hunted her. In this version Callisto became the Great Bear constellation and Arcas the Little Bear.

Calydonian Boar. A savage boar which Artemis (*q.v.*) sent to ravage Calydon because its king, Oeneus (*q.v.*) had not offered her proper sacrifice (*see also* Atalanta and Meleager). Pausanias (*q.v.*) tells of a story of long tusks found at Tegea, seen by Augustus and taken to Rome.

Calypso. A nymph of Ogygia who tended Odysseus (*q.v.*) there for eight years until Zeus (*q.v.*) ordered her to send him home to Ithaca. The name means "hidden" and she may have been a death goddess. At one point she offers the hero eternal youth, but he refuses, preferring real life. She bore him two sons.

Camilla. The Roman equivalent of an Amazon (*q.v.*) —a female warrior.

Capaneus. See **"Seven Against Thebes"**.

Capricorn. See **Amalthea**.

Cassandra. Daughter of Priam (*q.v.*) and Hecuba and twin of Helenus. She was given the gift of prophecy by Apollo (*q.v.*) but when she disappointed him he decreed that no one would ever believe her prophecies. Several times her important warnings went unheeded, *e.g.* against Paris (*q.v.*) going to Sparta, and against the wooden horse (*q.v.*). She was taken as a slave by Agamemnon (*q.v.*) when Troy (*q.v.*) fell and became his mistress. She was murdered with him by Clytemnestra (*q.v.*).

Cassiopeia. The wife of Cepheus and mother of Andromeda. Her boast that Andromeda was more beautiful than the Nereids (*q.v.*) caused Poseidon (*q.v.*) to send a monster to ravage the kingdom. Only the sacrifice of Andromeda could prevent this. Perseus (*q.v.*), who found her chained naked to a rock by the sea, offered to save her life if she would become his wife. Cepheus and Cassiopeia agreed to this and Perseus slew the beast. Her parents then attempted to renege on their promise, claiming Andromeda was promised to another.

At her wedding to Perseus the other suitor and his followers attempted to seize the bride but Perseus turned them all to stone with the head of Medusa (*q.v.*). The images of Cepheus and Cassiopeia were set amongst the stars by Poseidon.

Castalian Spring. Sacred spring on Mt. Parnassus, near the site of the Delphic oracle. Here the young girl Castalia drowned herself to avoid Apollo's (*q.v.*) advances.

Castalides. A name for the Muses (*q.v.*).

Castor and Polydeuces. (*Latin* "**Pollux**") The "Dioscuri". The twin "Sons of Zeus", brothers of Helen (*q.v.*) and the sons of Leda (*q.v.*) the wife of Tyndareus of Sparta. One tradition says that they were born from an egg, like Helen, after Zeus had visited Leda in the form of a swan. Others say only Polydeuces was Zeus' son and that Castor being the son of Tyndareus was a mere mortal. Castor was a famous horse tamer and Polydeuces a great boxer. Sailing with the Argonauts (*q.v.*) Polydeuces slew Amycus son of Poseidon (*q.v.*) who lived on the isle of Bebrycos. Amycus was a renowned boxer who killed travellers by challenging them to a boxing match. They also hunted the Calydonian boar (*q.v.*). The Dioscuri fought a mortal battle with their cousins the twins Idas and Lynceus. Zeus then killed Idas but Polydeuces begged to die with his brother. However Zeus decided they should live alternate days with the gods and under the earth. Their image was placed amongst the stars as Gemini. Poseidon gave them power over the wind and waves and they became protectors of seafarers.

They were said to have appeared on horseback to help the Romans against the Latins in the battle of Lake Regillus in 484 B.C., after which their cult was adopted at Rome.

Centaurs. A race of savage creatures, half-man, half-horse which inhabited the woodlands and mountains, particularly those of Thessaly. They were the offspring of Ixion and a cloud. In Homer (*q.v.*) the centaurs appear as representatives of primitive desires, fighting, drinking and womanising, but later they are only portrayed as turning to violence when drunk. When they tried to abduct Deidamia (*q.v.*) from her wedding, they became involved in a famous battle with their neighbours the Lapithae (*q.v.*).

Centimani. See **Hecatoncheires**.

Cephalus. Husband of Procris who was carried off by Eos (*q.v.*). Eos released him but Procris, suspicious of the time he spent hunting, followed him into the woods. Hearing him praying for a breeze she supposed it to be his mistress (the Roman equivalent of Eos was Aurora, the Latin for breeze aura). Moving closer she was struck by his spear, which never missed, and killed.

The story is told by Hesiod and Ovid and inspired paintings by Poussin and Claude.

Cepheus. King of Tegea and one of the Argonauts (*q.v.*). He and most of his 20 sons were killed helping Heracles (*q.v.*) fight Hippocoon.

Cerberus. A huge and savage dog, the offspring of Echidne (*q.v.*) and Typhon (*q.v.*) which guarded the entrance to Hades (*q.v.*). He is usually said to have had three heads, but Hesiod gives him fifty. His back was covered with serpents' heads and he had a snake for a tail.

Heracles (*q.v.*) dragged him from the Underworld; Orpheus (*q.v.*) charmed him with music when seeking Eurydice while Aeneas (*q.v.*) drugged him with a cake of honey and narcotics, hence "a sop to Cerberus".

Cercyon. A son of Hephaestus (*q.v.*) reigning near Eleusis. Here he challenged all travellers to a wrestling match and killed them, until he challenged Theseus (*q.v.*) and was killed himself.

Ceres. Ancient Italian corn-goddess worshipped in a temple on the Aventine. Games and a spring festival, the Ceriala, were held in her honour. She was associated with Demeter (*q.v.*) from an early date and her daughter Proserpina with Persephone.

Ceryneian Hind. A creature with brazen feet and golden antlers. One of Heracles' (*q.v.*) tasks was to catch it alive. He pursued it for a year and caught it without shedding blood by pinning its forelegs together with an arrow.

Chalybes. Mythical inhabitants of north Asia Minor said to have invented iron working.

Chaos. In Greek creation myth Chaos was the infinite space existing before creation. From Chaos sprang Ge (*q.v.*), the Earth.

Charities. Also called the Gratiae or Graces by the Romans. They were originally divinities of nature. In the *Iliad* (*q.v.*) only one Charity is personified, Charis, wife of Hephaestus (*q.v.*). Later the three Graces appear, Aglaia, Thalia and Euphrosyne, friends of the Muses (*q.v.*) with whom they inhabited Mt. Olympus.

Charon. The surly ferryman who transported the dead across the Styx (*q.v.*) to Hades (*q.v.*). He only transported them if they had received the correct funeral rite and if their relatives had placed a small coin, his fare, under the tongues. However Heracles (*q.v.*) forced his passage and Orpheus (*q.v.*) charmed his with his lyre.

Amongst the Etruscans (*q.v.*), as in modern Greek folklore, he was regarded as a synonym or figure of death. Virgil (*q.v.*) portrays him with unkempt white hair and eyes of fire in the 6th book of the *Aeneid*.

Charybdis and Scylla. Two monsters guarding the Straits of Messina. Charybdis swallowed the sea and vessels on it, three times a day, regurgitating what she swallowed each time. Opposite was Scylla, the daughter of Poseidon (*q.v.*) by a mortal, whom the jealous Amphitrite (*q.v.*) turned into a monster with six barking heads and twelve feet.

Odysseus (*q.v.*) was forced to pass between the two evils and the equally undesirable choice between the pair has become proverbial.

Cheiron. Also called Chiron. A centaur (*q.v.*). A son of Cronus (*q.v.*) and Philyra, hence he is sometimes referred to as Philyrides. Unlike his fellow centaurs a wise and kindly being who learnt music, medicine, hunting and prophecy from Apollo (*q.v.*) and Artemis (*q.v.*). This learning he imparted to numerous heroes including Achilles (*q.v.*), the Dioscuri (*q.v.*), Jason (*q.v.*) and Peleus (*q.v.*). An immortal, he was accidentally wounded by the poisoned arrow of his friend Heracles (q.v.). In pain he longed for death.

By surrendering his immortality he was relieved of life and suffering and placed among the stars as Sagittarius.

Chimeira. A monster with a lion's head, goat's body and a serpent for a tail. It could breathe fire. The offspring of Echidne (q.v.) and Typhon (q.v.), though some say it was begot by the Sphinx (q.v.) and Orthrus (q.v.). It was killed by Bellerophon (q.v.) while ravaging Lycia. The beast gave us the word "chimera" or fanciful notion.

Chryseis. (Cressida) Daughter of the Trojan seer and priest of Apollo (q.v.). Chryseis was captured by Agamemnon (q.v.) who refused to ransom her. Apollo then sent a plague on the Greek camp and when Calchas (q.v.) explained the cause Agamemnon released her. He then seized Briseis thus causing the quarrel with Achilles (q.v.). The medieval *Roman de Troie* tells how Troilus loved her, but she left him for Diomedes (q.v.).

This is the basis of Chaucer's *Troilus and Criseyde* and Shakespeare's *Troilus and Cressida*.

Chrysippus. The son of Pelops (q.v.), murdered by his half-brother Atreus (q.v.) and Thyestes (q.v.) at the instigation of his step-mother Hippodameia.

Chthonius. *See* Spartii.

Circe The daughter of Helios (q.v.) and Perse. A sorceress living on the island of Aeaea (Virgil (q.v.) identifies it with Circeii in Campania (q.v.)). She turned Odysseus' (q.v.) men into swine but he resisted by use of the herb "moly" given to him by Hermes (q.v.). Having forced her to restore his men he stayed a year with her and she advised him on his trip to the Underworld and return to Ithaca. She had a son, Telegonus by him and later married his son by Penelope (q.v.), Telemachus (q.v.).

In the *Argonautica* of Apollonius of Rhodes she purifies Jason (q.v.) and Medea (q.v.) of murder on their return from Colchis.

She was worshipped in Campania in the form of Feronia.

Cisseus. Father of Hecabe (q.v.).

Claros. Site of a shrine and oracle of Apollo (q.v.) to the south of Smyrna.

Cleobis. *See* Biton.

Clio. *See* Muses.

Cloacina. Ancient Roman divinity of "purification", later identified with Venus.

Cloelia. A Roman girl, legendary for having escaped from Porsenna (q.v.) when taken hostage and swimming back to Rome across the Tiber.

Clotho. One of the Fates (q.v.). She pulled the Limbs of Pelops (q.v.) from the cauldron in which they were to be boiled, thus enabling his restoration to life.

Clytemnestra. Daughter of Tyndareus (q.v.) and a half-sister of Helen (q.v.) and Castor and Polydeuces (q.v.). Wife of Agamemnon (q.v.) by whom she bore Orestes (q.v.), Iphigenia (q.v.) and Electra (q.v.). While Agamemnon was at Troy (q.v.) she began an affair with Aegisthus (q.v.) and on his return the pair murdered him. She was killed by Orestes. Her murder of Agamemnon should be seen in the context of his infidelity with Cassandra (q.v.) and others and his sacrifice of Iphigenia. This is how Strauss views the matter in his opera *Elektra*.

Cocles. The "one-eyed", a nickname of Horatius (q.v.) who kept the bridge across the Tiber.

Cocytus. The river of wailing in Hades (q.v.).

Coeus. One of the Titans (q.v.).

Cornelia. Mother of the "Gracchi", daughter of Scipio Africanus and a model of what Romans of the Republic thought a matron should be. On the deaths of her sons she withdrew to Misenum and her home became a centre of culture. She appears in Plutarch's (q.v.) *Lives* of her sons and he tells us that when a visitor asked to see her jewels she presented her sons saying "These are my jewels".

Coronis. Thessalian princess made pregnant by Apollo (q.v.) but who fell in love with an Arcadian youth. Learning of this from a crow, Apollo sent Artemis (q.v.) to kill her. The unborn child was snatched from her and given to Cheiron (q.v.) to rear. The child was Asclepius (q.v.).

Corybantes. Priests of Rhea (q.v.) or Cybele (q.v.) in Phrygia and Asia Minor. Known for their dancing and performance of wild rites to the sound of drums and cymbals.

Corydon. Common Arcadian shepherd's name but

in Virgil's (q.v.) second *Eclogue* the shepherd Corydon laments his "faithless Alexis". From this Corydon became a symbol of homosexual love.

Creon. A "ruler" or "prince" and the name often given to subsidiary characters in Greek legend, *e.g.* the brother of Jocasta (q.v.) who succeeds Oedipus (q.v.). *See also* **Jason**.

Cretan Bull. A magnificent white bull sent by Poseidon (q.v.) to Minos (q.v.) for sacrifice. Minos' wife Pasiphaë (q.v.) so admired the bull she had Daedalus (q.v.) construct a hollow cow for her to get inside. She then mated with the bull and later bore the Minotaur (q.v.). Minos also admired the bull and rather than sacrifice it, substituted another bull. The original bull escaped to ravage Crete until captured by Heracles (q.v.) and taken to Eurystheus (q.v.). Eurystheus freed it and it ravaged Greece until captured by Theseus (q.v.) at Marathon (q.v.) and sacrificed to Athene (q.v.).

Creusa. Feminine equivalent of Creon. The most famous is the daughter of Priam (q.v.), first wife of Aeneas (q.v.) and mother of Ascanius. She was lost in the escape from Troy (q.v.) when the city fell. When Aeneas looked for her he met only her ghost who bid him go forward to meet his destiny.

Croesus. Last king of Lydia who in the mid-6th century B.C. amassed a great fortune. His wealth is proverbial. Regarded as a model of piety for his gold offerings to Apollo (q.v.) at Delphi (q.v.). He met Solon and tried to persuade him to admit that Croesus was the happiest of men. Solon refused, saying that no man could be considered happy till his life had ended. The Delphic oracle told him that a great empire would fall if he invaded Persia. His own did.

The Persian king Cyrus ordered him to be burnt alive but he called on Solon's name and told Cyrus of Solon's sayings. Cyrus pardoned him and made him an adviser.

A later tradition says Apollo saved him and carried him to the land of the Hyperboreans.

Crommyum, Sow of. Wild sow slain by Theseus (q.v.).

Cronus. The son of Uranus (q.v.) and Ge (q.v.). The youngest of the twelve Titans (q.v.). When Ge stirred the Titans to revolt against Uranus she gave Cronus a flint sickle with which he castrated his father. Having deposed Uranus, Cronus reigned supreme and consigned the Cyclopes (q.v.) and the Hecatoncheires (q.v.) to Tartarus (q.v.). He married his sister Rhea (q.v.) and by her was father of Hestia (q.v.), Demeter (q.v.), Hera (q.v.), Poseidon (q.v.), Hades (q.v.) and Zeus (q.v.). Mindful of a curse by Uranus and Ge that he too be deposed by his own son, he swallowed each child at birth. But Rhea gave him a stone to swallow instead of Zeus and later gave him an emetic forcing him to regurgitate his other children. They now joined Zeus in a war on Cronus and the Titans. The Cyclopes aided them and gave Zeus the thunderbolt, Poseidon the trident and Hades a helmet of darkness or invisibility. Cronus was defeated and the Titans were consigned to Tartarus.

Cupid or **Amor.** Roman god of love, identified with the Greek Eros (q.v.).

Curetes. Priests of Rhea (q.v.) who drowned the cries of the infant Zeus (q.v.) as he lay in the Dictaean Cave by the clashing of their weapons. This prevented Cronus (q.v.) finding and devouring him. They were half-divine and in later times were conflated with the Corybantes (q.v.) who were also believed to be half-divine. All became part of Dionysus' ritual.

Cybele. The mother goddess of Phrygia where she and her lover Attis (q.v.) were worshipped in orgiastic rites and purification ceremonies including bathing in the blood of a sacrificed bull. Her symbol was a black stone and this was brought to Rome from Pessinus in 204 B.C. However it was only during the reign of Claudius that Roman citizens were allowed to serve as her priests and the oriental eunuchs serving her cult were always frowned upon. Her worship is described by Lucretius (q.v.) in book 2 and Catullus in his *Attis*.

Artists of the classical world portray her with a crown of towers, a libation dish and tambourine, flanked by lions to show her control of wild nature.

Cyclops. Generally known to the Greeks as one-eyed giants living in a distant country, perhaps Sicily. In Homer (q.v.) the Cyclops Polyphemus is a man-eating son of Poseidon (q.v.), made drunk and blinded by Odysseus (q.v.) and his men whom he had captured and meant to eat. Hesiod (q.v.) refers to three Cyclops but describes them as Titans (q.v.). The three (Brontes, Steropes and Arges) were sons of Ge (q.v.) and Uranus (q.v.) who made weapons for Zeus (q.v.), Poseidon and Hades (q.v.) (see **Cronus**).

Other traditions make them skilled craftsmen helping Hephaestus (q.v.) at his Sicilian forge. They were also builders of cities including Athens and the walls of Tiryns.

Cyllenius. Another name for Hermes (q.v.) who was said to have been born on Mt. Cyllene in southern Greece.

Cyncus. "The Swan", a mythical king of Liguria who loved Phaeton (q.v.) and was turned into a swan.

Cynthia. A name given to Artemis (q.v.). She and Apollo (q.v.) were thought to have been born on Mt. Cynthus in Delos and were thus referred to as Cynthia and Cynthus.

Cyrene. In myth the mother of Aristaeus (q.v.) by Apollo (q.v.) who carried her to Libya where she gave her name to the city of Cyrene.

Cythera. An island off the south-east coast of Greece noted for its sanctuary of Aphrodite (q.v.). She was thus referred to as "the Cytherean".

D

Dactyli. Greek equivalent of the Roman Chalybes (q.v.) the mythical beings who lived on Mt. Ida in northern Asia Minor and invented iron-working.

Daedalus. Mythical Athenian craftsman. His jealousy of his nephew Perdix or Talos, who was said to have invented the saw, caused him to throw Perdix from Athene's (q.v.) temple on the Acropolis (q.v.). Having thus committed murder he fled to Crete. Here he arranged the liaison between Pasiphaë (q.v.) and the Cretan Bull (q.v.) which produced the Minotaur (q.v.). Then, to conceal what had transpired from Minos (q.v.) he built the famous labyrinth to hide the Minotaur. When Minos discovered the truth he imprisoned Daedalus and his son Icarus in the labyrinth. Pasiphaë released them and Daedalus invented wings which, when attached to their shoulders by wax, enabled him and his son to fly. However Icarus flew too near to the sun, the wax melted, and he fell to his doom in the Icarian sea. Daedalus reached Cumae and then went to Sicily. Here King Cocalus welcomed him and when Minos arrived in pursuit Cocalus' daughters helped Daedalus kill him. In Sicily Daedalus was credited with many wonderful buildings including a honeycomb of gold for Aphrodite's (q.v.) temple on Mt. Eryx.

His name has become synonymous with ingenuity and skill, hence "Daedal" and "daedalian" in the English language.

Damocles. Member of the court of Dionysius I, tyrant of Syracuse. Cicero tells how the tyrant had him eat a sumptuous dinner while a sword was suspended by a hair over his head. This illustrated the luxurious but precarious life style of the tyrant and "the sword of Damocles" has become proverbial.

Danaë. A princess of Argos, daughter of King Acrisius (q.v.). An oracle told the king that Danaë's son would kill him so he imprisoned her in a brazen tower. Zeus (q.v.) visited her in a shower of gold and fathered Perseus (q.v.). Acrisius cast them adrift in a box and they came to Seriphos. They were found by the fisherman Dictys and taken to the king Polydectes. He wished to marry Danaë and so, to get Perseus out of the way, sent him to fetch the head of Medusa (q.v.). Danaë was saved from Polydectes' advances when Perseus returned and, showing the head, turned him to stone.

Danai. A general name used by Homer for the Greeks assembled at Troy. It was meant to perpetuate the memory of a common ancestor, Danaus (q.v.).

Danaus. A king of Libya and the father of 50 daughters, the "Danaïdes". His brother Aegyptus, who had 50 sons, wanted a mass marriage, but Danaus fled with his daughters to Argos where he became king. Eventually Aegyptus' sons followed and demanded the "Danaïdes". Danaus agreed but gave each daughter a weapon with which they slew their husbands on the wedding night. All, that is, save Hypermestra who spared Lynceus. Lynceus killed Danaus and became king of Argos. In the Underworld the Danaïdes were condemned to carry water in sieves for ever. The story is told

by Pindar (q.v.) and the Danaïdes form the chorus in Aeschylos' (q.v.) Suppliants.

Daphne. The daughter of the river god Peneus or Ladon. A nymph pursued by Apollo (q.v.). To escape him she prayed either to her father or to the Earth to be turned into a laurel tree, which she was. Apollo made himself a laurel wreath as consolation and it became the prize at the Pythian Games held in his honour.

Daphnis. The son of Hermes (q.v.) and a nymph. She abandoned the infant but he was raised by Sicilian shepherds. Pan (q.v.) taught him the pipes and he was the originator of pastoral poetry. Later he was unfaithful to a nymph who loved him and in revenge she blinded him. His father ordered forth the fountain of Daphnis near Syracuse in his honour.

Dardanus. The son of Zeus (q.v.) and the Pleiad (q.v.) Electra. He founded Dardania on land given to him by Teucer. He was grandfather of Tros, great grandfather of Ilus (q.v.) and Ganymede (q.v.). Hence an ancestor of the Trojans who were sometimes called Dardanids, Dardans or Dardonians. Roman legend sometimes envisages him migrating to Dardania from Italy.

Deianeira. The daughter of Oeneus, king of Calydon and the wife of Heracles (q.v.) who won her hand by defeating the river god Achelous (q.v.). She bore him a son Hyllus. After accidentally killing Eunomus, Heracles took her and Hyllus into voluntary exile. When they came to cross the River Evenus the centaur (q.v.) Nessus offered to transport her on his back. However he tried to rape her and was killed by Heracles. As he lay dying he told her to take his blood as it was a charm which would keep Heracles in love with her. Later Heracles won Iole, daughter of Eurytus King of Oechalia, in an archery contest. When Eurytus refused to surrender Iole Heracles invaded Oechalia and defeated him. He then ordered Deianeira to send him a white shirt which he was to wear at a thanksgiving sacrifice to Zeus (q.v.). Deianeira, jealous of Iole, dipped the shirt in the blood of Nessus. But the blood was poisonous and when Heracles donned the shirt it burned his body and attempts to pull it off tore pieces of flesh from the hero. In agony he ordered Hyllus to build a funeral pyre on which he would find quick death and release from the pain. He also had Hyllus marry Iola. Deianeira, horrified at the result of her action, hanged herself.

The story forms the plot of Sophocles' Women of Trachis.

Deidamia. The maiden who fell in love with Achilles (q.v.) and bore him Neoptolemus (q.v.).

Deiphobus. See **Helen** and **Helenus**.

Delis, Delius. Epithets of Artemis (q.v.) and Apollo (q.v.) who were born on Delos (q.v.).

Delos. Site of the important Ionian shrine of Apollo (q.v.). Here he was known as Phoebus ("the shining") or Lycius. When the jealous Hera (q.v.) pursued Leto (q.v.) she sought asylum where she could give birth to Apollo, her son by Zeus (q.v.). Delos, which was so poor it could lose nothing to Hera's wrath, accepted her.

Delphi. Site of Apollo's (q.v.) Dorian shrine and the most famous centre of his worship. Here he took his prophetic role having replaced Python. The oracle, located near the Castalian spring, was supposed to contain the omphalos or navel store of the Earth. A priestess, the Pythia, sat on a tripod chewing the intoxicating laurel leaf and voicing her utterances. Intoxicating vapours also issued from a chasm in the shrine. In this role Apollo was known as Loxias "the Ambiguous". (See **Croesus**). The priests of the shrine were not incorruptible and were known to take sides, e.g. with Sparta against Athens and with Philip of Macedon against Greece. The oracle had greatest influence during the period of overseas colonisation when its advice on location of colonies was always sought. The oracle encouraged Rome to defy Hannibal but was looted by Sulla. Nero visited it and Hadrian tried in vain to revive its prestige. Its decline came with the advance of Christianity and the growing interest in astrology as a means of prophecy. The temples at Delphi were sacked by Alaric in A.D. 396. Apollo's temple with its inscribed maxims "Know thyself" and "Nothing in excess" had stood on the highest point of Mt. Parnassus and had housed the sepulchre of Bacchus (q.v.) who was also worshipped at Delphi.

Demeter. The counterpart of the Roman Ceres, a Greek corn-goddess responsible for the fertility of the earth. The daughter of Cronus (*q.v.*) and Rhea (*q.v.*) she became mother of Persephone (*q.v.*) or Kore ("the maiden") by her brother Zeus (*q.v.*). A 7th century B.C. Homeric *Hymn to Demeter* tells how Hades (*q.v.*) carried off Persephone from Eleusis twelve miles from Athens (Ovid says she was taken while gathering poppies in Sicily). Demeter scoured the earth for her until Helios (*q.v.*) told her what had occurred. She then shunned Olympus (*q.v.*) and wandered the earth, forbidding it to bring forth fruit and therefore threatening famine. Zeus finally agreed that Persephone could leave Hades provided she had not eaten in the Underworld. Hades agreed to let her go but tempted her into eating a pomegranate. She thus had to spend half a year with him in the Underworld and half with Demeter. Demeter again made the earth fertile but turned Ascalaphus, who had seen and reported Persephone eating the pomegranate, into an owl. She punished those who had been unkind to her during her wandering (*see* **Abas**) but rewarded those who had treated her hospitably. She taught Triptolemus, another son of Celeus (*q.v.*) the art of agriculture and gave him an ear of corn whose virtues he revealed to his fellow men. The Eleusian Festival was held in Demeter's honour from the 6th century B.C. and there was an annual procession from Eleusis to Athens.

Those who spoke Greek were initiated into the mysteries of her cult. The Thesmophoria, a celebration of the foundation of laws, was held in her honour in many cities.

Demophon (1) The son of Theseus (*q.v.*) and Phaedra (*q.v.*) brother of Acamas (*q.v.*). He helped rescue his grandmother Aethra who had been Helen's (*q.v.*) slave, when Troy (*q.v.*) fell. Phyllis, a Thracian princess, loved him and committed suicide when he left her to visit Athens. She was then transformed into a tree.

(2) The son of Celeus and Metaneira. Demeter (*q.v.*) tried to reward the pair for their kindness to her by making Demophon immortal. To achieve this he had to be suspended above a fire, but Metaneira cried out thus breaking the spell and he perished.

Deucalion. The son of Prometheus (*q.v.*), husband of Pyrrha and father of Hellen. He was thus the ancestor of the Greeks. When Zeus (*q.v.*) decided to flood the earth in order to destroy mankind they escaped in an ark which finally made land on Mt. Parnassus. The couple prayed to Themis (*q.v.*) that mankind be restored and were told to scatter their mother's bones behind them. They took this to mean stones, the skeleton of Mother Earth. The rocks Deucalion scattered became men; those Pyrrha scattered became women.

Diana. Italian goddess of woods, women, childbirth and later, by association with the Greek Artemis (*q.v.*), the moon. Her cult was originally centred on the volcanic Lake Nemi at Aricia. The lake was known as Diana's mirror. The priest here, known as the rex, was always a runaway slave who had murdered his predecessor.

A temple of Diana, said to have been founded by Servius Tullius also stood on the Aventine.

Dictaean Cave. A cave on Mt. Dicte in Crete, the reputed childhood home of Zeus (*q.v.*). Hence he was known as Dictaeus.

Dictys. (1) The sailor who found Perseus (*q.v.*) and his mother Danaë (*q.v.*) adrift at sea in a chest.

(2) A Cretan said to have accompanied Idomeneus (*q.v.*) to the Trojan war. His diary of the war was supposedly buried near Cnossos and found in the reign of Nero.

Dido. A daughter of the king of Tyre originally called Elissa. Her husband Sychaeus was murdered but with a few followers she escaped to Libya and founded Carthage. Local legend said she burnt herself on a funeral pyre to avoid marrying Iarbas, a native king. The Roman version, given in the *Aeneid* takes Aeneas (*q.v.*) to Carthage where Dido's unrequited love for him results in her death. Aeneas abandons her to fulfil his destiny as ancestor of Rome.

Didyma. A great sanctuary of Apollo (*q.v.*) at Miletus.

Dindyma. Mountain in Asia Minor and a centre of the Cybele's (*q.v.*) cult.

Diomedes. (1) A king of the Bistones in Thrace who possessed man-eating mares. A labour of Heracles (*q.v.*) was to bring them to Eurystheus (*q.v.*). This he did by stealing them and beating off his pursuers. But while he was busy fighting, the mares devoured his friend Abderus. Heracles founded the city of Abdera in his honour. Eurystheus freed the horses on Mt. Olympus (*q.v.*) where wild beasts devoured them.

(2) The son of Tydeus, king of Argos. One of the Epigoni (*q.v.*). He also went to Troy (*q.v.*) and was a companion of Odysseus (*q.v.*). With Odysseus he sailed to fetch Achilles (*q.v.*) and later Neoptolemus (*q.v.*). He encouraged Agamemnon (*q.v.*) to sacrifice Iphigenia (*q.v.*) and helped Odysseus capture the Trojan spy Dolon. He wounded Aeneas (*q.v.*) and Aphrodite (*q.v.*) as she saved the Trojan. He also wounded Ares. He returned from Troy to find his wife had been unfaithful and went to settle in Daunia in Italy. Here he married Euippe, daughter of king Daunus. He was buried on one of the Diomedan islands.

Dionysus. The Roman Bacchus. Also called Bromius "the Boisterous". The son of Zeus (*q.v.*) and Semele, a mortal, Zeus visited her in the guise of a mortal but when she was six months pregnant the jealous Hera (*q.v.*) came to her as an old woman. She advised Semele to demand her lover appear in his true form. Zeus unwillingly agreed to do so and Semele was consumed by fire. The unborn child was sewn up in Zeus' thigh to be born as Dionysus. The child was given into the care of Athamas and Ino. He was disguised as a girl but Hera learned the truth and drove Athamas mad, causing him to kill his own son. Hermes (*q.v.*) then took Dionysus to Mt. Nysa in India where he was raised by nymphs. Zeus placed their images in the stars as the Hyades. Here he was taught the use of the vine by his tutor Silenus and his satyrs and here he invented wine. As an adult he journeyed through India, Egypt, Syria and Asia accompanied by a wild following of Maenads or Bacchae and Satyrs. As he went he founded cities and taught cultivation of the vine.

When he reached Thrace, Lycurgus, king of the Edones, opposed him but was driven mad by Rhea (*q.v.*) and slew his own son. His people then had him torn apart by horses. King Pentheus of Thebes also opposed Dionysus and was torn apart by crazed Bacchae whose ranks included his mother and sisters. Entranced they took him for a wild animal. Sailing to Naxos Dionysus was captured by pirates for sale as a slave. He became a lion and turned the oars to serpents. Ivy grew on the mast. The terrified pirates jumped overboard and became dolphins. At Naxos he married Ariadne (*q.v.*) whom Theseus (*q.v.*) had deserted.

He was eventually received into Olympus as a god, replacing Hestia (*q.v.*). He fetched his mother to Olympus from the Underworld and she was henceforth known as Thyone. Dionysus was the god of wine and intoxicating herbs like ivy and laurel. He was also the god of tillage and law giving. He was worshipped at Delphi (*q.v.*) and in the spring festival, the Great Dionysia.

In Rome the mysteries of his cult were a closely guarded secret. His followers worshipped him in communal wine-induced frenzies and the ritual involved sacrifice of animals, flagellation and a mystical marriage of novices with the god.

Dioscuri. *See* **Castor and Polydeuces.**

Dirce. *See* **Antiope.**

Dis or **Orcus.** Hades (*q.v.*).

Dodona. Site of an oracle of Zeus (*q.v.*) in north west Greece near modern Janina. It was associated with the union of Zeus and Dione, a minor goddess. The oracle centred on an oak and messages were transmitted by the rustling branches and cooing of pigeons nesting in it. The priests were "Selloi" who slept on the ground and walked barefoot. It was visited by Croesus (*q.v.*) and Alexander the Great offered the sanctuary a large sum of money.

Dryope. The daughter of King Dryops. Apollo (*q.v.*) seduced her and she was carried off by the Hamadryads (nymphs of trees).

E

Echidne. A mythical creature, half-woman, half-serpent. Mother by Typhon (*q.v.*) of the Chimaera (*q.v.*), Sphinx (*q.v.*), Cerberus (*q.v.*), Hydra (*q.v.*), Nemean Lion, Orthrus (*q.v.*), and Ladon. Slain by Argus.

Echion. A son of Hermes (*q.v.*). An Argonaut (*q.v.*) who took part in the hunt of the Calydonian boar (*q.v.*).

Echo. A nymph who occupied Hera's (*q.v.*) attention by incessant talk while Zeus (*q.v.*) enjoyed himself with the other nymphs. In punishment Hera deprived her of the power of speech except to repeat the words of others. Echo loved Narcissus who refused her. Heart-broken she pined away to nothing, only her voice remaining. Artemis (*q.v.*) punished Narcissus for his heartlessness by making him fall in love with his own reflection. Despairingly he committed suicide and was turned into a flower.

Egeria. An Italian goddess or nymph whose worship was connected with that of Diana (*q.v.*). She was associated with water. It was believed she advised Numa Pompilius (*q.v.*) especially on religious matters and Livy tells us they met in a sacred grove near Rome.

Eileithyia. A goddess of childbirth whom the Greeks associated with Artemis and the Romans with Juno (*q.v.*).

Elatus. The father of Caeneus and one of the Lapithae (*q.v.*).

Electra. (1) A Pleiad (*q.v.*).
  (2) The daughter of Agamemnon (*q.v.*) and Clytemnestra (*q.v.*). Treated as a slave by her mother and Aegisthus (*q.v.*) she later helped her brother Orestes (*q.v.*) and his friend Pylades (*q.v.*) avenge their father and married Pylades. This is the basis of Euripedes' *Electra* and Strauss's *Elektra*. Freud gave the name "Electra complex" to female fixation on the father, the opposite of the "Oedipus complex".

Electryon. The son of Perseus (*q.v.*) and Andromeda (*q.v.*). King of Mycenae and father of Alcmene (*q.v.*) wife of Amphitrion (*q.v.*).

Eleusis. A sacred site twelve miles west of Athens facing Salamis. Here Celeus received Demeter (*q.v.*). Games and an oracle were found there. A cult involving "Mysteries" was centred there and administered by two families, the Eumolpidae and Kerykes. Ceremonies were held twice a year in Spring and Autumn and initiation to the mysteries, of which we know little, was open to all men, Greek or not, free or slave, who had not committed murder.

Elissa. *See* Dido.

Elpenor. One of Odysseus' (*q.v.*) crew who fell off the roof of Circe's (*q.v.*) palace while sleep-walking and broke his neck. When Odysseus visited the Underworld his shade begged for cremation and a burial mound in which his oar was to be planted.

Elysium. A blessed abode of the dead, placed by Homer near the Underworld but not in Hades (*q.v.*). The virtuous went here after death. It was a land of warmth never knowing cold or snow. Later it was associated with "Fortunate Isles" holding "Elysian Fields" which were believed to be far to the west, beyond the Pillars of Hercules (*q.v.*).

Empusae. Daughters of Hecate (*q.v.*). They were demons with the haunches of an ass who wore brazen slippers. Able to turn themselves into cows, bitches or young maidens, as the latter they lay with young men and sucked their blood as they slept.

Enceladus. A son of Ge (*q.v.*). One of 24 giants (*q.v.*) with serpents' tails whom Alcyoneus led in an assault on Olympus (*q.v.*). Buried under Mt. Etna in Sicily as a punishment.

Endymion. Either a shepherd of Caria or an Aeolian youth who became king of Elis. As he slept in a cave Selene (*q.v.*) the moon saw him and descended to kiss him. Captivated by his looks she made him fall into a dreamless everlasting sleep so that she could always gaze upon him. His son Aetolus conquered Aetolia.

Enipeus. A river god, beloved of Tyro (*q.v.*).

Eos. The goddess of the dawn, the Romans identified her with Aurora (*q.v.*). The daughter of Hyperion (*q.v.*) and Theira and sister of Helios (*q.v.*). She drove the chariot of Helios each morning to announce his arrival and traversed the sky with him as Hemera before landing in the west as Hespera. The wife of Astraeus and by him mother of the stars and all the winds save the east. She carried off several handsome youths including Orion (*q.v.*), Cephalus (*q.v.*), and Tithonus to whom she bore Memnon (*q.v.*). She requested Zeus (*q.v.*) to make Tithonus immortal but forgot to ask for eternal youth and as he aged he shrank to a cicada.

Epaphus. The son of Zeus (*q.v.*) and Io who ruled

Egypt and was said by some to be the sacred bull of Egypt, Apis (*q.v.*).

Epeius. A cowardly son of Panopeus who built the Trojan Horse.

Ephialtes. One of the 24 giants (*q.v.*) led by Alcyoneus. (*See also* **Otus**).

Epidaurus. Site of a famous sanctuary of Asclepius (*q.v.*) built in the 6th century B.C. Here pilgrims could see the tomb of the god.

Epigoni. Descendants of the "Seven against Thebes" (*q.v.*) who also attacked the city ten years after their fathers had done so. They were assembled by Adrastus (*q.v.*) and their ranks included his own son Aegialeus, Diomedes son of Tydeus, Sthenelus son of Capaneus and Eradne and Therseander. Like his father Polynices (*q.v.*) Therseander bribed Eriphyle (*q.v.*) into persuading Alcmaeon into joining the assault on Thebes. Aegialeus died at the walls of the city but the Theban prophet Teiresias advised the citizens to leave the city at night as he had foreseen the Argives (*i.e.* the Epigoni), capturing an empty city. He died next morning drinking from the well of Tilphussa. Adrastus died of grief hearing of his son's death while the remaining Epigoni were left holding an empty city. Alcmaeon went home to take revenge on Eriphyle (*q.v.*).

Erebos. A deep chasm in the Underworld.

Erebus. "Darkness", the son of Chaos (*q.v.*) and father of Aether and Hemera by "Night", his sister. Some traditions hold that the Fates (*q.v.*) were daughters of Erebus and Night and that they held sway even over Zeus (*q.v.*).

Erechtheus. Son of Pandion and grandson of Erichthonius (*q.v.*) with whom he is sometimes confused or identified. Both were reared by Athene (*q.v.*) and were associated with serpents. Both were mythical kings of Athens. When the Eleusians led by Eumolpus, a son of Poseidon (*q.v.*), invaded Athens, Erechtheus was told by an oracle to sacrifice his daughter Otonia. He did so and her sisters Protogonia and Panora also sacrificed themselves. He slew Eumolpus and was slain by lightning from either Poseidon or Zeus (*q.v.*).

Erichthonius. A son of Hephaestus (*q.v.*) by Athene (*q.v.*). The child was concealed in a chest by the normally chaste Athene and entrusted to the daughters of Cecrops of Athens who were forbidden to open it. However they did so and finding a serpent inside went mad and leaped to their death from the Acropolis (*q.v.*). Erichthonius eventually succeeded Cecrops as King of Athens and was grandfather of Erechtheus. It was said Erichthonius was the founder of the Panathenaean games in honour of Athene and that he was the first man to harness a team of four horses to a single chariot.

Eridanus. An Italian river god, later thought to be the River Po.

Erigone. The daughter of Icarius. Led to her father's grave by his faithful pet hound Maera, she hanged herself from the tree beneath which she lay.

Erinnyes. Three daughters of Mother Earth whom she conceived by the blood of Uranus (*q.v.*) when Cronus (*q.v.*) castrated him. They personified the conscience and were powerful divinities who punished crimes of sacrilege, especially matricide. They pursued Alcmaeon (*q.v.*) and drove Orestes (*q.v.*) mad and into exile. These winged creatures had serpent hair and lived in the Underworld. Their names were Alecto, Magaera and Tisiphone. Orestes was acquitted by Athene (*q.v.*) of matricide following his defence by Apollo (*q.v.*). To pacify the Erinnyes Athene gave them a grotto at Athens where they received libations and sacrifices. Henceforth they were euphemistically referred to as the Eumenides or "kindly ones".

Eriphyle. The sister of Adrastus (*q.v.*) and wife of the seer Amphiarus. Mother of Alcmaeon (*q.v.*). Polynices (*q.v.*) bribed her into persuading Amphiarus into joining the Seven Against Thebes (*q.v.*) despite the seer's prophecy that only Adrastus would survive their expedition. She received the necklace of Harmonia (*q.v.*) for this. Later Thersander bribed her with the magic robe of Harmonia into persuading Alcmaeon to join the Epigoni (*q.v.*). On returning from Thebes Alcmaeon slew her for her selfish deceit.

Eris. A female divinity personifying Quarrels and Strife for the Greeks.

Eros. The Greek god of love, identified with the Roman Cupid (*q.v.*) or Amor. A son of Aphrodite (*q.v.*), whom he often accompanied, by either her father Zeus (*q.v.*) or Hermes (*q.v.*). His half-brother was Anteros, son of Aphrodite and Ares (*q.v.*) who personified mutual love. It was only from the 4th century B.C. onwards that he came to be represented as a winged boy firing arrows of love which could wound both men and gods. (*See* **Psyche**).

Erymanthian Boar. A giant wild boar from Mt. Erymanthus which was ravaging the region of Psophis until captured by Heracles (*q.v.*). Whilst performing this task he was given wine made by Dionysus (*q.v.*) by the centaur Pholus. A dispute broke out with other centaurs, eager as ever for their share of the drink, and in the resulting battle Heracles accidentally wounded his friend Cheiron (*q.v.*). He caught and chained the boar in a snow drift and delivered it to Eurystheus (*q.v.*) before going to join the Argonauts (*q.v.*).

Erysichthon. Son of Triopas. He was punished with an insatiable hunger by the goddess Demeter (*q.v.*) for felling trees in one of her sacred groves.

Eryx. Mythical Sicilian hero. A son of Venus (*q.v.*) and a renowned boxer. The mountain near modern Trapani is named after him.

Eteocles. *See* **Seven Against Thebes.**

Etruscans. *See* Section L.

Eumneus. Born of royal birth but given to Phoenician slave traders, Eumneus' story is told in Book 15 of the *Odyssey*. He became Odysseus' (*q.v.*) faithful swineherd.

Eumolpus. "The good singer", son of Poseidon (*q.v.*) and Chione. Chione threw him into the sea at birth but Poseidon saved him and he was raised at the court of King Tegyrius of Thrace before becoming a priest of Demeter (*q.v.*) and Persephone (*q.v.*) at Eleusis. Here he initiated Heracles (*q.v.*) into the mysteries and taught the hero the lyre. He later made war on Athens and was slain by Erechtheus (*q.v.*).

His descendants became hereditary priests of the Eleusian mysteries.

Euphorbus. Son of Panthous, a Trojan who wounded Patroclus (*q.v.*) before he was slain by Hector (*q.v.*).

Euphrosyne. One of the Charities or Graces (*q.v.*).

Euripides. *See* Section B.

Europa. Daughter of Agenor and Telephassa and a grand-daughter of Poseidon (*q.v.*). While she was on the sea-shore Zeus (*q.v.*) appeared in the form of a white bull and when she jumped on his back carried her off to Crete where he fathered three sons on her, Minos (*q.v.*), Rhadamanthus (*q.v.*) and Sarpedon (*q.v.*). The Cretan king married her and adopted the children. Zeus gave her a necklace fashioned by Hephaestus (*q.v.*) which rendered the wearer irresistibly beautiful.

Eurystheus. A grandson of Perseus (*q.v.*). He was conceived shortly after Heracles (*q.v.*) but when Zeus (*q.v.*) boasted that Heracles would rule the House of Perseus, Hera (*q.v.*) in her jealousy extracted a promise from Zeus that the next son born to the House of Perseus would be its ruler. She then delayed the birth of Heracles until after that of Eurystheus. Later, after Heracles had slain his children in a fit of madness he was told by the oracle to serve Eurystheus in order to be cleansed of guilt. Eurystheus, a cowardly and contemptible creature, set him twelve labours. After Heracles' death he decided to expel the Heracleidae (*q.v.*) or descendants of Heracles from Greece but they sheltered at Athens. Eurystheus attacked the city but was resisted by Theseus (*q.v.*), Iolaus (*q.v.*) and Hyllus (*q.v.*). An oracle demanded the sacrifice of one of Heracles' children and Macaria slew herself. Eurystheus was then defeated and slain by Alcmene.

Eurus. The South-East wind, son of Astraeus (*q.v.*) and Eos.

Euryale. One of the Gorgons (*q.v.*).

Eurydice. The wife of Orpheus (*q.v.*). She died from a snake bite and Orpheus followed her to the Underworld. Hades (*q.v.*) delighted by Orpheus' lyre playing allowed him to take her back to life provided he did not look back. Unfortunately at the gates of the Underworld the anxious Orpheus could no longer resist the temptation to gaze on her beauty nor acquiesce in her accusations of indifference. He turned round to see her and she was lost to him.

Eurytus. *See* **Deianeira.**

Euterpe. Muse of music and lyric poetry.

Evadne. The daughter of Iphis and wife of Capaneus who killed herself on the funeral pyre of the Seven against Thebes (*q.v.*).

Evander. A mythical king of Arcadia who settled in Italy on the future site of Rome.

Evenus. The father of Marpessa. When Idas carried her off he drowned himself in the river which henceforth bore his name.

F

Fates. The personifications of impersonal destiny who sometimes seem to control even Zeus (*q.v.*), at others merely to perform his will. The concept developed of three Moirae (*Latin* Parcae) daughters of Zeus and Themis (*q.v.*), or of Erebus (*q.v.*) and Night. The first, Clotho, spins the thread of life, Lachesis measures it, and Atropus cuts it. With Hermes (*q.v.*) they composed the Alphabet.

Faunus. An Italian god of the flocks, herds and wild countryside, later identified with Pan (*q.v.*). In this context he had a human head and torso with goat legs and waist. He lived in Arcadia (*q.v.*). He had a shrine on the Palatine Hill. He is sometimes regarded not as one god but as numerous spirits of the woods or "fauns".

Faustulus. A kindly shepherd who, with his wife Acca Larentia, raised Romulus (*q.v.*) and Remus (*q.v.*). His name relates to Faunus (*q.v.*) and his wife's to Lares (*q.v.*) respectively the pastoral god of Latium and the tutelary deities of the Roman home. Up to Cicero's time Romans proudly pointed to a hut on the Palatine which was said to be that where Faustulus raised Romulus but, embarrassingly, a hut with similar claims also stood on the Capitol.

Fidius. Dius Fidius was a name for Jupiter (*q.v.*) as guarantor of Good Faith.

Flora. Italian goddess of flowers and the spring, worshipped at Rome from the mid 3rd century B.C. Ovid tells us the April festival in her honour, "Ludi Florales" was one of drunken boisterousness. As an earth nymph called Chloris she was pursued by Zephyr (*q.v.*) and changed into Flora whose breath spread flowers across the fields.

The scene has been a subject for Botticelli, Titian and Poussin.

Fortuna. Roman goddess identified with Tyche (*q.v.*).

Fortunate Isles. *See* **Elysium.**

G

Gaea or Ge. The "Earth" who sprang from Chaos (*q.v.*). She was mother of Uranus (*q.v.*), the heavens, and Pontus the sea. By Uranus she was mother of the Hecatoncheires (*q.v.*), the Cyclopes (*q.v.*), the Titans (*q.v.*) and Themis (*q.v.*). When Uranus condemned the Cyclopes to Tartarus (*q.v.*) she instigated rebellion by the Titans and gave Cronus (*q.v.*) the flint sickle with which he castrated Uranus. From the blood which fell on her she bore Erinnyes (*q.v.*) and from the blood which fell into the sea came Aphrodite (*q.v.*). By Tartarus she was mother of Typhon (*q.v.*). She gave Hera (*q.v.*) a tree of golden apples which was guarded by the Hesperides (*q.v.*).

The Romans identified her with their own earth goddess Tellus.

Gaetulians. A mythical savage tribe which the Romans placed in North Africa.

Galatea. (1) A sea nymph who loved the Sicilian shepherd Acis (*q.v.*). She was pursued by the Cyclops Polyphemus and to escape him threw herself into the sea off Sicily. She turned Acis into a river.

(2) *See* **Pygmalion.**

Ganymede. The most handsome of youths, the son of Tros (*q.v.*) and Callirhoë. Zeus (*q.v.*) loved the youth and taking the form of an eagle carried him off to become cup-bearer of the gods, leaving Tros two white horses in compensation. A subject for Correggio, Rubens, and Rembrandt.

Garamantians. Mythical North African tribe appearing in the *Aenead* (*q.v.*).

Ge. *See* **Gaea.**

Geryon. A three-bodied monster living on the island of Erythia far to the west of the known world.

Here he kept cattle guarded by Eurytion, son of Ares (q.v.) and Orthrus (q.v.). Heracles (q.v.) was sent to steal the cattle by Eurystheus (q.v.) and on his way to Erythia erected the "Pillars of Hercules" (q.v.), before sailing, on a boat provided by Helios (q.v.), to the island. He overcame Eurytion, Orthrus and Geryon and fetched the cattle to Eurystheus.

Giants (Gigantes). (1) The sons of Ge (q.v.) and Uranus (q.v.), twenty-four giants with serpents' tails who, to avenge the imprisonment of their brothers the Titans (q.v.), attacked the gods on Mt. Olympus (q.v.). Their leader was Alcyoneus and their ranks included Porphyrion, Ephialtes, Pallas, Minas, Enceladus and Polybotes. The gods finally triumphed due to the help of Heracles (q.v.) and the giants were buried under various volcanoes in punishment.

(2) In another version two giants, Ephialtes and Otus, the sons of Iphimedeia and Poseidon (q.v.), but called the Aloeidae after the name of Iphimedeia's husband Aloeus, attacked Olympus. At an early age the two imprisoned Ares (q.v.), then swearing to rape Hera (q.v.) and Artemis (q.v.) they stacked Mt. Pelion on top of Mt. Ossa in order to climb to the heavens. But Artemis lured them to Naxos and disguised as a doe leapt between them and they slew each other by accident. In Hades (q.v.) they were tied by vipers to a pillar back to back.

Glauce. Or Creusa, daughter of Creon. For her Jason (q.v.) forsook Medea (q.v.) and in revenge the sorceress sent Glauce a garment which enveloped her in flames and also killed Creon.

Glaucus. (1) King of Corinth, son of Sisyphus and Merope and father of Bellerophon (q.v.). He fed his horses on human flesh but Aphrodite (q.v.) caused them to devour Glaucus himself because he mocked her.

(2) His great-grandson, the grandson of Bellerophon who fought for the Trojans and was slain by Ajax (q.v.).

(3) The son of Minos (q.v.) and Pasiphaë (q.v.) who was drowned in a barrel of honey. The seer Polyides found the corpse and was entombed with the boy for failing to restore him. Both were saved when a serpent revealed a magic herb which resurrected Glaucus.

(4) A Boeotian fisherman who pursued Scylla (q.v.) and was turned into a sea god on eating a magic herb.

Golden Age. A concept of Hesiod's who lists four ages of man in his *Works and Days*: golden, silver, bronze and iron. Horace, Virgil, and Ovid also refer to it. A tranquil time when Cronus (q.v.) ruled as the ideal king.

Golden Bough. A gift Aeneas (q.v.) had to take to Proserpina (q.v.) before he could enter the Underworld. Also associated with the cult of Diana (q.v.) at Aricia where a runaway slave had to break the bough from a sacred tree before killing the priest and taking his place. Subject of a painting by J. W. M. Turner.

Gordian Knot. Gordius was a peasant who was acclaimed king of Phrygia by the inhabitants when he appeared in a wagon. An oracle had prophesied that the new king would appear thus. In thanksgiving he dedicated the cart to Zeus (q.v.) in the acropolis of Gordium. An oracle prophesied that he who untied the complex knot joining the yoke and pole would rule all Asia. It was eventually severed by Alexander the Great.

Gorgons or **Gorgones.** Three beautiful sisters, Medusa (q.v.), Stheno and Euryale, daughters of Phorcys and Ceto. Medusa slept with Poseidon (q.v.) in a temple of Athene (q.v.) and was transformed into a winged monster with serpent hair and brazen claws by the goddess as punishment. She could turn those who looked on her to stone. The Gorgons were sisters of the Graeae (q.v.). *See also* Perseus.

Graces (also **Gratiae**). *See* Charities.

Graeae. Sisters of the Gorgons (q.v.) who lived on Mt. Atlas. The three old women possessed only one eye and one tooth which they shared, passing them from one to the other. Perseus (q.v.) stole the eye and thus forced them to reveal the whereabouts of Medusa (q.v.) and also of the Stygian nymphs who gave him the winged sandals, magic wallet and helmet of Hades which Hermes (q.v.) said he needed in order to slay Medusa.

Gyes or **Gyges.** One of the Hecatoncheires (q.v.).

H

Hades. (1) The son of Cronus (q.v.) and Rhea (q.v.) brother of Zeus (q.v.) and Poseidon (q.v.). The Cyclopes (q.v.) gave him a helmet of darkness which made him invisible. When he and his brothers threw lots for their kingdoms Hades won the Underworld, home of the dead. His name was later extended to his realm itself. He was one of the few gods to like Ares (q.v.) and Hermes (q.v.) was his herald, conducting the shades of the dead to the Underworld. Because his name was too dread to mention he was often called "Pluto" (q.v.). No favours were expected of him so no temples were dedicated to him. He abducted Persephone (q.v.) and also chased the nymph Minthe (whom the jealous Persephone turned into a mint plant) and Leuce, who was turned into the white poplar.

(2) His realm, the Underworld, land of the dead. Its deepest reaches were called Tartarus (q.v.). Hades and Persephone ruled over it. Persephone was accompanied by Hecate (q.v.). There were five rivers in Hades, the Styx, Acheron, river of woe, Phlegethon, river of flame, Lethe, river of forgetfulness and Cocytus river of wailing. Three judges Minos (q.v.), Aeacus (q.v.) and Rhadamanthus (q.v.) decided on what would happen to souls, sending the evil for punishment, the virtuous to Elysium (q.v.) and those who had led indifferent lives to the drab asphodel fields.

Harmonia. The daughter of Ares (q.v.) and Aphrodite (q.v.) and the wife of Cadmus (q.v.). The gods attended their wedding and Aphrodite gave her the necklace which Zeus (q.v.) had given to Europa (q.v.). It had been made by Hephaestus (q.v.) and conferred irresistible beauty on the wearer. Athene (q.v.) gave her a robe which conferred divine dignity on its possessor. The couple had three children, Autonoe, Ino and Semele (q.v.). After Cadmus had resigned his throne to Pentheus (q.v.) the couple left Thebes and were eventually, in the form of serpents, received in Elysia (q.v.). The necklace and robe were later used to bribe Eriphyle.

Harpalyce. A mythical princess of Thrace, a fierce warrior and huntress.

Harpies (Greek "snatchers"). Originally spirits of the wind, in Homer they appear to carry people off to their death. Later they are portrayed as female creatures with the body of a bird and the upper torso and head of a human, sent by the gods to torment mortals. They snatched and carried off people for their food.

Hebe. A personification of the Greek word for youth, the daughter of Zeus (q.v.) and Hera (q.v.). She was cupbearer to the gods until replaced by Ganymede (q.v.). Her Roman counterpart was Juventas. She married Heracles (q.v.) after his apotheosis.

Hecabe or **Hecuba.** The second wife of Priam (q.v.) who bore him 19 sons including Hector (q.v.) and Paris (q.v.). By Apollo (q.v.) the mother of Troilus (q.v.). Taken as a slave by Odysseus (q.v.) when Troy (q.v.) fell. Priam had entrusted their youngest son Polydorus, plus much gold, to Polymester, king of the Thracian Chersonese. He had murdered Polydorus and thrown his body into the sea. When Odysseus took her to the Thracian Chersonese she found the body, killed Polymester and his two sons, and escaped in the form of a bitch, Maera.

Hecate. An ancient goddess, later closely associated with Artemis (q.v.). Originally she was venerated by women, she was powerful in Heaven, Earth and the Underworld. But primarily she was seen as a goddess of the Underworld and companion of Persephone (q.v.). She was represented holding torches and accompanied by wolves. She was most formidable at the full moon with which she was associated. A practitioner of sorcery her image was worshipped at crossroads where she was portrayed with three heads or three bodies.

Hecatoncheires. The sons of Ge (q.v.) and Uranus (q.v.), three 100-handed giants called Cottus, Gyes or Gyges and Briareus or Aegaeon.

Hector. The eldest son of Priam (q.v.), Trojan hero of the Trojan War. Husband of Andromache (q.v.) and father of Astynax. He fought the great Ajax (q.v.) until nightfall when the two exchanged gifts. He slew Patroclus and in turn was slain by Achilles (q.v.) who dragged his body round the walls of Troy (q.v.). Priam begged for the corpse and his funeral is the closing scene of Homer's *Iliad*. A chivalrous warrior.

Helen. The daughter of Leda (q.v.) by Zeus (q.v.), hatched from an egg, and the sister of Clytemnestra (q.v.), Castor and Polydeuces (q.v.) (known as the Dioscuri). She was raised at the court of Leda's husband, Tyndareus of Sparta. As a child she was abducted by Theseus (q.v.) and Pirithous (q.v.) but being too young to marry, was left with Theseus' mother Aethra. The Dioscuri rescued her and Aethra became her slave. The most beautiful of women she had many suitors who swore to defend her chosen husband, Menelaus (q.v.). She was taken by Paris (q.v.) to Troy (q.v.) thus causing the Trojan war (q.v.) and "launching a thousand ships" (of the Greeks who went to reclaim her). When Paris died Helenus (q.v.) and Deiphobus quarrelled for her, the latter forcibly marrying her. By then she was homesick for Sparta and when Odysseus (q.v.) entered Troy in disguise told him so and gave him information useful to the Greek cause. When Troy fell Deiphobus was killed and mangled by Odysseus and Menelaus, but when Menelaus chased her, sword drawn, to punish her, she calmed him by baring her breast.

In the *Odyssey* she was reconciled to Menelaus and became a domesticated and faithful wife. She bore him a daughter, Hermione. It appears that Helen may have been a pre-Greek goddess associated with birds and trees. Various tales are told of her. Stesichorus says that only her phantom went to Troy: the real Helen went to Egypt.

Another legend says that at her death she was carried off to live eternally with Achilles (q.v.) on a "white isle". Others suggest that her mother was not Leda but Nemesis (q.v.).

Helenus. The son of Priam (q.v.) and Hecabe (q.v.), twin of Cassandra (q.v.) and a prophet. He quarrelled with his brother Deiphobus over Helen (q.v.) and when the latter forcibly married her fled Troy (q.v.) and was captured by Odysseus (q.v.). Calchas (q.v.) had said that only Helenus knew the secret oracles of how Troy would fall. He told Odysseus that the city would be taken in the summer if a bone of Pelops (q.v.) were brought to the Greeks, if Neoptolemus (q.v.) joined them, and if the Palladium (q.v.) were stolen. These things were done. After the war he was taken by Neoptolemus and prophesied a safe route home for him.

When Neoptolemus settled in Epirus he gave part of the kingdom to Helenus who married Andromache (q.v.).

Helicon. A mountain in Boeotia (q.v.) sacred to Apollo (q.v.) and inhabited by the Muses (q.v.) who were thus called respectively Heliconiades and Heliconides.

Helios. Equates to the Roman "Sol". A Titan later identified with Hyperion and Apollo (q.v.), though some traditions make him the son of Hyperion and Theia. A sun-god, his chariot was drawn across the sky each day by four horses and at night he returned to the east floating on the stream of Ocean, which surrounded the earth, in a large cup. The husband of Rhode by whom he had seven sons and a daughter, Pasiphaë. He was father of Phaeton (q.v.) by Clymene and of Circe (q.v.) by Perse. He reputedly saw all, but missed Odysseus' (q.v.) men stealing his cattle. When he shone too brightly Odysseus (q.v.) fired an arrow at him. Admiring the hero's boldness he lent him his cup or boat with which to travel to Erythia. It was he who told Demeter (q.v.) that Hades (q.v.) had abducted Persephone (q.v.).

Hellas, Hellenes, Hellenism. The Greeks of the classical period termed themselves Hellenes and their country Hellas (in contrast to Homer's "Achaeans"). They traced their common descent from Hellen (q.v.) an eponymous hero. In modern times Hellenism refers to the culture flourishing in Greece, the Aegean isles, the Ionian coast of Asia Minor and Magna Graecia between the first Olympiad in 776 B.C. and the death of Alexander the Great in 323 B.C.

Hellen. Eponymous ancestor of the Greeks or Hellenes (q.v.), the son of Pyrrha and Deucalion (q.v.). His sons were Aeolus, Dorus and Xuthus.

Hephaestus. One of the Olympian gods, the son of Zeus (q.v.) and Hera (q.v.). The god of fire and metal work, known to the Romans as Vulcan (q.v.). He was hated by Hera because he was lame and she threw him down from Olympus and he

landed in the sea where Thetis (q.v.) and Eurynome cared for him. Nine years later Hera accepted him back but Zeus, angry with him for taking Hera's side in a quarrel, again cast him down. He was a day falling and landed on Lemnos. On returning to Olympus he sought to keep the peace between Zeus and Hera. The other gods always laughed at his lameness. His workshop was said to be on Olympus or else in Sicily, where the Cyclopes (q.v.) helped him in his labours. He made palaces for all the gods, the necklace of Harmonia (q.v.), the armour of Achilles (q.v.) and a wide variety of other wonderful articles. He was married either to Charis or to Aphrodite (q.v.) who deceived him with Ares (q.v.).

Hera. The Roman Juno, daughter of Cronus (q.v.) and Rhea (q.v.), sister and wife of Zeus (q.v.). A pre-Hellenic goddess, originally having power over all living things and vegetable life, she gradually lost these functions and eventually was only the goddess of marriage and childbirth. She was the mother of Ares (q.v.), Hephaestus (q.v.), Hebe (q.v.) and Ilythia (q.v.) by Zeus. Her virginity was renewed annually by bathing in a magical spring near Argos. Though she was the goddess of marital fidelity she had difficulty controlling the amorous adventures of her own husband (who had wooed her in the form of a cuckoo) and was violently jealous of his many affairs and cruel to her rivals and their offspring, e.g. Semele, Leto, Alcmene and Heracles. She once led a conspiracy against Zeus in which Poseidon (q.v.) and Apollo (q.v.) participated. Zeus was enchained and when he was freed he punished her by suspending her from the sky by the wrists with an anvil on each ankle. She helped Jason (q.v.) but was opposed to the Trojans because Paris (q.v.) did not give her the apple of discord. Her name means "lady".

Heracleidae. The children of Heracles (q.v.). Eurystheus (q.v.) attempted to expel them from Greece but failed.

Heracles. A hero who later became a god, a figure popular all over Greece and in Italy where the Romans knew him as Hercules. The son of Alcmene (q.v.) and Zeus (q.v.) and half-brother of Iphicles (q.v.). Alcmene fearing Hera's (q.v.) jealousy exposed him but by mistake Hera nursed him. After he had been returned to his mother Hera sent two snakes to kill him in his cradle, but he strangled them. He was taught to fight by Castor (q.v.), to play the lyre by Eumalpus, to wrestle by Autolycus (q.v.) and the art of archery by Eurytus. Linus also tried to teach him to play the lyre but, when he censured his awkward pupil, Heracles killed him with his own instrument. Amphitrion (q.v.) then sent him to keep cattle.

Aged 18, after a 50-day chase, he killed a huge lion on Mt. Cithaeron because it had been ravaging the herds of Amphitrion and Thespius. He did this with a wild olive club and later wore the pelt everywhere, though some other sources say he wore the pelt of the Nemean lion. In reward Thespius gave him his 50 daughters. At Thebes he defeated the Minyan heralds of Orchomenus who had come to demand tribute. Creon, king of Thebes, rewarded him by giving him his daughter Megara or Megera who bore him several children. His half-brother Iphicles married Creon's youngest daughter. Hera now made him mad and he killed his own children and two of Iphicles'. At Delphi the Pythia (q.v.), calling him Heracles for the first time, sent him to serve, for 12 years, his wretched cousin Eurystheus (q.v.) in order to purify himself of the murder. At the end of that time he would become immortal. With his nephew Iolaus (q.v.) as companion he embarked on 12 labours set by Eurystheus.

These were to fetch the pelt of the Nemean lion, to kill the Hydra of Lerna (q.v.), to capture alive the Ceryneian Hind (q.v.), to capture alive the Erymanthian Boar (q.v.), to cleanse the stables of Augeas (q.v.), to drive off the Stymphalian Birds (q.v.), to capture the Cretan Bull (q.v.), to fetch the horses of Diomedes (q.v.), to fetch the girdle of Hippolyte (q.v.), to steal the cattle of Geryon (q.v.), to fetch the golden apples of the Hesperides (q.v.) and to bring back Cerberus.

After capturing the Erymanthian Boar he had joined the Argonauts (q.v.) but his squire Hylas was spirited off by the Naiads (q.v.) while fetching water at Cios in Mysia and Heracles left the expedition to search for him. Having completed his service for Eurystheus he returned to Thebes and

here gave Megara to Iolaus. But Hera again
drove him mad and he killed Megara and her children. Some traditions say he also killed himself
and his family. He now desired to marry Iole
daughter of his friend Eurytus of Oechalia and
won her in an archery contest. But Eurytus
refused to surrender her because Heracles had
slain his own children. The incident ended in
Heracles killing Iphitus (*q.v.*) but he later seized
Iole. To purify himself of this murder he went to
serve Omphale (*q.v.*). After serving her he and
Telamon saved Hesione, daughter of Laomedon
(*q.v.*) and sacked Troy (*q.v.*). Heracles gave Hesione to Telamon and ransomed Priam (*q.v.*). Next
he made war on Augias and Neleus (*q.v.*) and
then on Hippocoon who had helped Neleus. In this
he was assisted by Cepheus (*q.v.*) and he restored
Tyndareus (*q.v.*). At this time he seduced the
priestess Auge, daughter of Aleus king of Tegea,
who bore him a son, Telephus. Now he married
Deianeira (*q.v.*) who inadvertently caused his
death.

As Heracles ascended his funeral pyre, to be
burned alive he gave his bow and quiver to
Philoctetes (*q.v.*) who kindled the flame but thunderbolts demolished the pyre and he was carried
on a cloud to Olympus. Here he was reconciled to
Hera and married Hebe (*q.v.*), himself becoming
an immortal. Numerous other legends concerning
Heracles exist. We are told he rescued Alcestis
(*q.v.*), helped the gods defeat the Giants (*q.v.*),
defeated Antaeus (*q.v.*) and, when the Delphic
Oracle would not give him an answer seized the
sacred tripod and struggled with Apollo for it.

Xenophon tells us that before beginning his
adventures Heracles was confronted by two beautiful women, one offering a life of ease, the other
of service to mankind and he had to choose between
the two. Other writers tell of him having to choose
between two roads offering similar alternatives to
the women. From a mighty and boisterous hero
the picture of Heracles gradually developed into a
morality tale of selfless service and fortitude
eventually rewarded and for this reason the Stoic
philosophers of Rome idealised him.

Hercules. *See* **Heracles.**

Hermaphroditus. The son of Hermes (*q.v.*) and
Aphrodite (*q.v.*) who refused the advances of the
nymph Salmacis. Her request that their bodies be
joined in one was then granted by the gods. The
name gives us the word "hermaphrodite", a being
with the characteristics of both sexes.

Hermes. The Roman Mercury. Originally a god of
fertility. The son of Zeus (*q.v.*) and Maia, daughter
of Atlas (*q.v.*). He was born on Mt. Cyllene (hence
he was sometimes referred to as Cyllenius). While
still hours old he left the cradle and stole Apollo's
(*q.v.*) cattle. He invented the lyre by stringing a
tortoise shell with cow-gut and gave it to Apollo.
This calmed Apollo's wrath and the two became
friends. Zeus made him messenger of the gods and
gave him his winged sandals (the Alipes), broad-
brimmed hat (the Petasus) and herald's staff
(caduceus) originally entwined with two white
ribbons, later represented as entwined snakes. He
conducted the souls of the dead to Hades (*q.v.*)
and in this role was known as Psychopompus. The
patron of travellers, traders and thieves and the
father of Autolycus the thief, by Chione, and of
Echion herald of the Argonauts (*q.v.*). He was the
father of Pan (*q.v.*) by Penelope (*q.v.*) and a companion of the Muses (*q.v.*). He helped the Fates
compose the alphabet, invented the musical scale,
weights and measures and olive cultivation. A god
of dice games.

As herald he was eloquent and in *Acts* ch. XIV
St. Paul, who spoke in tongues more than any
man, is mistaken for him.

Hermione. The daughter of Helen (*q.v.*) and
Menelaus (*q.v.*). Betrothed by Tyndareus (*q.v.*) to
Orestes (*q.v.*) but given to Neoptolemus (*q.v.*) by
Menelaus.

Hero. A priestess of Aphrodite (*q.v.*) at Sestos. Her
lover Leander (*q.v.*) used to swim the Hellespont
each night to see her but drowned when a storm
extinguished the light she used to guide him. She
then drowned herself. The subject of a play by
Marlowe and paintings by Rubens and Turner.

Herodotus. *See* **Section B.**

Heroes. To the Greeks a hero was the son of a
mortal or divinity who was essentially superior to
other men. They were venerated and received
sacrifices because they were believed to help the

living. Thus Theseus (*q.v.*) was supposed to have
helped the Athenians at Marathon. "Heroic
poetry" was epic poetry, telling of their deeds.

Hesiod. *See* **Section B.**

Hesperides. "The daughters of evening" who
lived in a land at the end of the world, far to the
west. These maidens guarded a tree belonging to
Hera (*q.v.*) which bore golden apples. They were
assisted by a dragon, Ladon. Ge (*q.v.*) had given
the tree to Hera on her wedding day. On the
advice of Prometheus (*q.v.*) Heracles (*q.v.*) (who
had been sent to get the apples by Eurystheus
(*q.v.*)) persuaded Atlas (*q.v.*) to fetch three apples
while he shouldered Atlas' burden. Atlas then
refused to take the sky back on his shoulders but
Heracles tricked him into doing so. On his return
journey Heracles slew Antaeus (*q.v.*). Eurystheus
gave the apples back to Heracles and he passed
them to Athene to return to the Hesperides.

Hesperus. The evening star, the Greek form of the
Latin vesper or evening.

Hestia. The sister of Zeus (*q.v.*) and Hera (*q.v.*), the
goddess of the hearth worshipped by every family.
Though Poseidon (*q.v.*) and Apollo (*q.v.*) tried to
seduce her she swore to Zeus always to remain a
virgin. The Romans worshipped her counterpart,
the goddess Vesta (*q.v.*).

Hippodamia. (1) The daughter of Oenomaus, king of
Elis. An oracle said he would die at the hands of
his son-in-law so he challenged all her suitors to a
chariot race. Victory meant they could marry
Hippodamia, defeat meant death. His horses
were the gifts of his father Ares (*q.v.*). However
Pelops (*q.v.*) engineered his death and married
Hippodamia.

(2) The wife of Pirithous (*q.v.*). When a drunken
centaur (*q.v.*) abducted her on her wedding day
the battle between the Lapithae (*q.v.*) and
Centaurs occurred.

Hippolyte. A queen of the Amazons (*q.v.*) and sister
of Antiope. Heracles (*q.v.*) had to fetch her golden
girdle for Eurystheus. At first he was well received
but Hera (*q.v.*) stirred the Amazons against him
and in the fight he slew Hippolyte and took the
girdle. Returning home he saved Laomedon's
(*q.v.*) daughter Hesione. Another legend says
Theseus (*q.v.*) abducted Hippolyte who bore him
the son Hippolytus (*q.v.*).

Hippolytus. The son of Theseus (*q.v.*) and the
Amazon Hippolyte (*q.v.*) or her sister Antiope
(*q.v.*). When Theseus married again to Phaedra
(*q.v.*), sister of Ariadne (*q.v.*), Phaedra fell in
love with her stepson and committed suicide when
he refused her. She left a note falsely accusing
Hippolytus. Theseus prayed to Poseidon (*q.v.*)
who was under an obligation to him, that
Hippolytus would die the same day. Poseidon then
sent a sea-monster which scared the youth's horses
and he was dragged to death behind his chariot.

Homer. *See* **Section B.**

Horae. The "hours", three daughters of Zeus
(*q.v.*) and Themis (*q.v.*) and tutelary goddesses
of nature and the seasons. They were bound to the
soil and promoted fertility. Thus they were
important and are involved in solemn oaths.
However they rarely appear except in attendance
on other gods and have no "adventures".

Horatii. Three Roman brothers whose tale is told by
Livy. In the mid 7th century B.C. while Rome was
ruled by Tullus Hostilius the city of Alba Longa
(*q.v.*) was destroyed and its population transferred
to Rome. According to legend the Horatii challenged the three Alban champions, the Curatii, to a
sword battle. Two Horatii were killed but the third
slew all the Curatii. On returning to Rome he met his
sister, who had been engaged to one of the Curatii,
weeping. He stabbed her to death. After ceremonies
of expiation Tullus acquitted him of murder.

Horatius Cocles. Another of the Horatii family, the
"one-eyed" (Cocles). In the 6th century B.C. he
held the Etruscans at bay on the wooden Sublican
bridge into Rome until it was pulled down beneath
him. He then swam the Tiber to safety. The subject of a *Lay* by Macaulay.

Hyacinthus. A Peloponnesian youth loved by Apollo
(*q.v.*) who was killed when the jealous Zephyrus
(*q.v.*) diverted a discus to hit him. From his blood
sprang the "hyacinth" flower. He had a shrine at
Amyclae in Laconia and a three-day festival, the
Hyacinthia, was held in his honour at Sparta.

Hyades. Nymphs who cared for Dionysus (*q.v.*) as
a child on Mt. Nysa. Zeus (*q.v.*) placed their images
in the sky as the "rain stars", part of the constel-

lation of Taurus which rises at midnight in the rainy season.

Hydra of Lerna. The "water snake", offspring of Echidne (q.v.) and Typhon (q.v.) and raised by Hera (q.v.). It was a monster with the body of a dog and 9 serpent heads. Heracles (q.v.) was sent to kill it by Eurystheus (q.v.). It lived at the source of the River Amymone in the swamp of Lerna. As Heracles lopped off a head two more grew. He also had to crush a giant crab which Hera placed among the signs of the zodiac. Finally he crushed the Hydra's heads with his club and Iolaus (q.v.) burned them to stop them regrowing. He dipped his arrows in the beast's blood thereby making them poisonous.

Hygeia. The wife or daughter of Asclepius (q.v.), a goddess of health.

Hylas. See **Heracles**.

Hyllus. The son of Heracles (q.v.) and Deianeira (q.v.). He conducted Heracles to his funeral pyre. Either he or Iolaus (q.v.) defeated Eurystheus (q.v.). Eventually he was slain by Echemus, king of Tegea.

Hymen. God of weddings.

Hyperboreans. A mythical race living far to the north, behind Boreas (q.v.) i.e. at the place where the north wind originates. Apollo (q.v.) spent time with them before going to Delphi and spent the winter months with them. A Hyperborean soothsayer, Olen, installed Apollo's oracle at Delphi. Their land was supposed to have perpetual sunshine and was a land of plenty, an earthly paradise where men lived in peace and ease on the fruits of the earth. Herodotus tells us that one of their priests, Aburis, travelled the world on a golden arrow and never needed to eat. He places their land in Southern Russia.

Hypenor. One of the Spartii (q.v.).

Hyperion. A Titan (q.v.) and sun-god, father of Helios (q.v.), Selene (q.v.) and Eos (q.v.), the sun, moon and dawn. In Keats' poem he is the last of the old gods to be deposed, the young Apollo (q.v.) taking his place.

Hypermestra. See **Danaus**.

Hypnus. The god of sleep.

I

Iacchus. Alternative name for Dionysus (q.v.) used in the Eleusian mysteries where he was regarded as the son of Zeus (q.v.) and Demeter (q.v.), not Semele (q.v.).

Iapetus. A Titan (q.v.), father of Prometheus (q.v.), Atlas (q.v.) and Epimetheus.

Iasion. Or Iasius or Iasus, the son of Zeus (q.v.) and Electra (q.v.), lover of Demeter (q.v.) who bore him a son Pluton. Zeus in his jealousy slew him with a thunderbolt.

Icarius. Father of Erigone. An Athenian to whom Dionysus (q.v.) taught cultivation of the vine and who gave wine to a band of shepherds. Mistaking drunkenness for witchcraft they slew him.

Icarus. See **Daedalus**.

Idaea. A nymph, mother of Teucer (q.v.) by Scamander (q.v.) of Crete.

Idas. The twin of Lynceus and a son of Poseidon (q.v.). He abducted Marpessa in a chariot given to him by Poseidon and fought Apollo (q.v.) for possession of her. Given the choice by Zeus (q.v.) she chose Idas. He and Lynceus took part in the voyage of the Argonauts (q.v.) and the hunt of the Calydonian boar (q.v.) and were killed in battle with their cousins the Dioscuri (q.v.).

Idomeneus. King of Crete who contributed 100 ships to the expedition against Troy (q.v.). Virgil adds that on his return from Troy he was caught in a storm and vowed to sacrifice the first person he met to Poseidon (q.v.) in return for safe passage. This proved to be his son and the sacrifice brought a pestilence on Crete. Idomeneus was banished to Calabria in Italy.

Ilia. A priestess of Vesta (q.v.) also called Rhea Silvia. The mother of Romulus (q.v.) and Remus.

Iliad. Homer's epic poem on the siege of Troy (q.v.). Although it hints at earlier and later events it covers only a period of weeks in the tenth year of the war, recounting Achilles' (q.v.) quarrel with Agamemnon (q.v.), the death of Patroclus (q.v.) and the death of Hector (q.v.). It ends with Achilles returning Hector's (q.v.) body to Priam (q.v.). Although many gods and heroes appear, Achilles and Hector are the main protagonists.

Ilioneus. An old and venerated Trojan who accompanied Aeneas (q.v.).

Ilithyiae. Daughters of Hera (q.v.) who helped women in childbirth. Later only one goddess, Ilithyia, is mentioned in this connection.

Ilus. (1) The son of Tros (q.v.) and father of Laomedon (q.v.). An ancestor of the Trojans.

(2) Original name of Ascanius (q.v.) son of Aeneas (q.v.) and Creusa.

Inachus. The first king of Argos, son of Oceanus (q.v.) and Tethys. A river was named after him.

Ino. The daughter of Cadmus (q.v.) and Harmonia (q.v.), sister of Cadmus, Agave, Polydoras, Illyrus and Semele. She helped to rear Dionysus (q.v.) and her husband Athamas (q.v.) was punished for it by Hera (q.v.) who drove him into madness and the murder of his own children. Ino, Autonoe and Agave were Bacchae (q.v.) and they slew Pentheus, the son of Agave and heir to Cadmus, for opposing the worship of Dionysus. Ino committed suicide (see **Athamas**) and became a sea deity.

Io. The daughter of Inachus. Zeus (q.v.) loved her and turned her into a white heifer to deceive the jealous Hera (q.v.). He did not succeed in this and Hera set the hundred-eyed Argus to watch the heifer. But Hermes (q.v.) at Zeus' command cut off his head and placed his eyes in the tail of the peacock. He also sent a gadfly whose sting caused Io to wander the earth till she reached Egypt. On her wanderings she gave her name to the Ionian sea and to the Bosphorus ("ford of the cow"). In Egypt Zeus restored her to human form and she bore him a son, Epaphus, an ancestor of Danaus.

Iobates. See **Bellerophon**.

Iolaus. Son of Iphicles (q.v.) and nephew of Heracles (q.v.) to whom he was charioteer and constant companion. He helped Heracles kill the Hydra (q.v.) and perform his other labours and in return Heracles gave him his wife Megara. He also sent Iolaus as the leader of his sons by the daughters of Thespius to settle in Sardinia.

Iolcus. The kingdom of Jason's (q.v.) father Aeson, usurped by his half brothers Pelias and Neleus.

Iole. See **Deianeira**.

Ion. The son of Xuthus and Creusa, brother of Achaeus. In Euripides' play Ion he is the son of Creusa and Apollo (q.v.) who is carried off to Delphi (q.v.), as a baby but is eventually restored to Creusa and adopted by Xuthus. The eponymous ancestor of the Ionian Greeks.

Iphicles. (1) One of the Argonauts (q.v.).

(2) The son of Amphitrion (q.v.) and Alcmene (q.v.) a night younger than Heracles (q.v.). The father of Iolaus (q.v.). He married the youngest daughter of Creon of Thebes when Heracles married Megara.

Iphigenia. The daughter of Agamemnon (q.v.) and Clytemnestra (q.v.), sacrificed by her father at Aulis to get a favourable wind for the Greek fleet sailing to Troy (q.v.). Euripides cites another tradition in which Artemis (q.v.) substituted a doe for Iphigenia at the last moment and carried her off to Tauris. Later Orestes (q.v.) found Iphigenia on the Tauric Chersonese and brought her home to Greece.

Iphitus. A son of Eurytus who argued that his father should deliver Iole (see **Deianeira**) to Heracles (q.v.). But in a rage Heracles slew him and though purified of the murder was told by an oracle to sell himself into slavery and give the proceeds to Iphitus' family.

Irene. The daughter of Zeus (q.v.) and Themis (q.v.), goddess of peace and one of the Horae (q.v.). The Romans identified her with Pax.

Iris. The personification of the rainbow and, in later myth, a messenger of the gods, particularly Hera (q.v.).

Isis. An Egyptian goddess, wife of Osiris and mother of Horus. In Hellenistic times she became one of the most important deities of the Mediterranean world, her cult arriving in Rome by the time of Augustus. Here the features of her worship, Egyptian priests, processions, initiation ceremonies etc. were described by Apuleius in his Golden Ass. One of her temples is preserved at Pompeii.

Ismene. The daughter of Oedipus (q.v.) and Jocasta (q.v.). She followed her father and her sister Antigone (q.v.) into exile.

Issa. The daughter of Macareus and his sister Canace, beloved by Apollo (q.v.).

Isthmian Games. Quadrennial games held at Corinth in honour of Poseidon (q.v.).

Ithaca. The island home of Odysseus (*q.v.*), one of the Ionian islands.

Itys, Itylus. *See* Procne.

Iulus. A name used for Ascanius (*q.v.*) by Virgil to indicate the descent of the Julian clan from Aeneas (*q.v.*).

J

Janus. A god of beginnings or new ventures, worshipped at Rome. He had a flamen (sacred priest) and was very important but the origin and nature of his worship is obscure. He had two faces and may represent the assimilation of an eastern god and an Etruscan deity. Also associated with doorways and thresholds.

Jason. Son of Aeson, rightful king of Iolcus who was usurped by his half-brothers, Pelias and Neleus. The infant Jason was smuggled out of Iolcus and reared by Cheiron (*q.v.*) while Pelias expelled Neleus and ruled alone. When Jason returned to claim his birthright Pelias sent him to fetch the Golden Fleece from Colchis. This was the fleece of the ram on which Phrixus (*q.v.*) had escaped and which he had given to Aëtes, king of Colchis. Its presence was the cause of Colchis' prosperity and it hung from an oak tree in the grove of Ares (*q.v.*) where a dragon guarded it. After numerous adventures Jason and his Argonauts (*q.v.*) arrived at Colchis and Aëtes promised Jason the fleece if he could yoke two fire-breathing bulls with brazen feet made by Hephaestus (*q.v.*), and sow the grove of Ares with dragons' teeth left by Cadmus of Thebes (*q.v.*). Medea (*q.v.*) the sorceress gave him a fire-proof lotion which allowed him to complete the task and when her father Aëtes refused to give up the fleece, charmed the dragon to sleep while Jason stole it. Pursued by Aëtes the couple escaped when Medea murdered her half-brother Absyrtus and dropped pieces of his corpse into the sea, causing Aëtes to stop and collect them. They were purified of the murder by Circe (*q.v.*). At Iolchus Pelias had forced Aeson to commit suicide and in revenge Medea persuaded Pelias' daughters to boil their father alive pretending it would restore his youth.

The couple were banished because of this and went to Corinth. Here Jason abandoned Medea for Glauce (*q.v.*) whom Medea killed. Jason took his own life though one tradition holds he was killed by the falling prow of the Argo (*q.v.*).

Jocasta. Daughter of Menoeceus, wife of Laius king of Thebes and mother of Oedipus (*q.v.*). When her unwitting incest with Oedipus brought a plague on Thebes Menoeceus sacrificed himself in answer to an oracle demanding the life of one of the Sparti (*q.v.*) *i.e.* a descendant of the "sown men". Jocasta hanged herself when she learned the truth of her marriage to Oedipus.

Jove. Alternative name for Jupiter (*q.v.*).

Juno. Italian goddess of womanhood and childbirth, associated by the Romans with the Greek Hera (*q.v.*) and regarded as the consort of Jupiter (*q.v.*).

Jupiter. Originally an Italian sky-god, later regarded by the Romans as *Dies Pater*—"Father Day", god of the day. Later still identified with Zeus (*q.v.*). His cult was introduced to Rome by the Etruscans and the temple to Jupiter Optimus Maximus (Best and Most High) stood on the Capitol. His *flamen*, the *flamen* Dialis was the most important of the college.

He was guarantor of the *imperium* and city of Rome and triumphs were an act of Jupiter worship. Worshipped in various capacities as *Stator* (he who founds or maintains), *Teretrius* (he who strikes), *Ultor* ("Avenger") and also *Tonans* ("Thunderer").

Juturna. (1) An Italian goddess of springs and streams.

(2) The sister of Turnus (*q.v.*).

Juventas. Italian goddess identified with Hebe (*q.v.*).

L

Labdacus. Mythical king of Thebes; a descendant of Cadmus (*q.v.*) and an ancestor of Oedipus (*q.v.*).

Lachesis. One of the Fates (*q.v.*).

Laelaps. A fleet-footed hound given to Procris by Cephalus (*q.v.*).

Laertes. The king of Ithaca, father of Odysseus (*q.v.*) by Anticleia, daughter of the thief Autolycus (*q.v.*). While Odysseus was at Troy (*q.v.*) Penelope's (*q.v.*) suitors forced him to retire to the country.

Laestrygones. A race of giant cannibals ruled by Lamus. At Telepylos, their capital city, Odysseus (*q.v.*) lost all but one of his twelve ships to them. Homer says their summer nights were so short that shepherds going out with their flocks in the morning met those returning at sunset. Traditionally located in eastern Sicily or at Formiae in central Italy.

Laius. *See* Oedipus.

Lamia. One of the Empusae, daughter of Belus.

Lamus. *See* Laestrygones.

Laocoön. A Trojan prophet, son of Antenor and a priest of Apollo (*q.v.*) and Poseidon (*q.v.*). He warned the Trojans against the Wooden Horse (*q.v.*) and flung a spear at it. However he had angered Apollo by breaking his vows of celibacy and the god now sent two sea serpents which crushed him and his two sons. A famous group of statues depicting the scene, carved in Rhodes *c.* 25 B.C., now stands in the Vatican museum. The Trojans disastrously drew the wrong conclusion *viz.* that his death was punishment for striking the horse.

Laodamia. The daughter of Acastus and wife of Protesilaus of Thessaly, the first Greek ashore at Troy (*q.v.*) though he knew from an oracle the first Greek to land would die. Homer says he left his wife mourning and his house unfinished but Catullus, Virgil and Ovid follow another tradition in which she begged the gods that Protesilaus might return to life for three hours. When he died a second time she committed suicide. Wordsworth's poem *Laodamia* takes the tale as its subject.

Laodice. (1) A daughter of Priam (*q.v.*), sister of Cassandra (*q.v.*) and wife of Helicaon. When Troy (*q.v.*) fell the earth swallowed her.

(2) Alternative name for Electra (*q.v.*), Agamemnon's (*q.v.*) daughter.

Laomedon. The son of Ilus (*q.v.*), king of Troy (*q.v.*) and father of Hesione and Priam (*q.v.*). Apollo (*q.v.*) and Poseidon (*q.v.*) helped him build the walls of Troy and he refused to pay them. Poseidon then sent a sea monster to devour Hesione but Heracles (*q.v.*) saved her. Laomedon then refused to pay Heracles the agreed white horses left by Zeus (*q.v.*) in exchange for Ganymede (*q.v.*). Heracles and Telamon then sacked Troy and slew Laomedon and all his sons save Priam (*q.v.*).

Lapis Niger. Black marble paving in the Roman Forum said to cover the tomb of Romulus (*q.v.*).

Lapithae or **Lapiths.** Mythical tribe of Thessaly, governed by Pirithous, son of Ixion (*q.v.*) and thus half-brothers to the Centaurs (*q.v.*). At the wedding of Pirithous and Hippodamia, attended by Theseus (*q.v.*) a centaur tried to abduct the bride and a famous battle between the Lapithae and Centaurs ensued. It is described by Ovid and is depicted in the Parthenon and the frieze of Apollo's (*q.v.*) temple at Bassae. It is also the subject of a sculptured frieze by Michelangelo.

Lares. Originally fertility gods, worshipped by the Romans privately in the home and semi-publicly at crossroads. They were represented as youths with handfuls of fruit who wandered the farmstead incessantly whirling round and round. They kept away maleficent demons and ensured the prosperity of the family home. Each month they received offerings of oat cakes, milk, honey and flowers. Generally associated with the Penates, the spirits who guarded the household stores. Together the guardians of the hearth and home.

Larissa. A city in Thessaly near modern Volos. Reputed birthplace of Achilles (*q.v.*) hence his nickname "the Larissaen".

Lars Porsenna. Legendary Etruscan chief whom Livy tells us besieged Rome on behalf of the exiled Tarquinius Superbus. Lars means "overlord" and he is probably a symbol of Etruscan suzerainty over Rome. (*See* **Horatius Cocles**).

Latinus. Eponymous king of the Latini or Latins in Italy. Hesiod makes him the son of Odysseus (*q.v.*) and Circe (*q.v.*). Virgil makes him the son of Faunus (*q.v.*). Livy and Virgil portray him as opposing the settlement of Aeneas (*q.v.*) and the Trojans in Italy but then agreeing Aeneas should marry his daughter Lavinia. He next helps Aeneas fight Turnus king of the Rutuli, to whom Lavinia had been promised. Livy says he died in battle and Aeneas became king of the Latins; Virgil that he survived to celebrate the marriage and uniting of Latins and Trojans.

Leander. Mythical youth who drowned while swimming to meet Hero (q.v.).

Leda. Daughter of Thestius and wife of Tyndareus king of Sparta. Seduced by Zeus (q.v.) in the form of a swan she gave birth to two eggs, from one of which hatched Helen (q.v.) and Polydeuces (q.v.) from the other, Castor (q.v.) and Clytemnestra (q.v.). One tradition says that Helen was the daughter of Nemesis (q.v.) who left the egg for Leda to incubate.

Lemnos. A small island at the mouth of the Hellespont, home at one time of a primitive people known to the Greeks as the Pelasgi. Hephaestus (q.v.) was said to have landed on the island when Zeus (q.v.) hurled him out of heaven and supposedly had a forge here.

Lethe. "Forgetfulness", one of the rivers of the Underworld whose waters induced amnesia in those who drank of them. Virgil holds that here souls forgot their past prior to reincarnation and Ovid says that it flowed round the "cave of sleep".

Leto. Known to the Romans as Latona. The daughter of the Titans (q.v.) Coeus and Phoebe and the mother of Apollo (q.v.) and Artemis (q.v.) by Zeus (q.v.). While she carried the unborn gods the jealous Hera (q.v.) forced her to wander the earth until she finally gave birth to them at Ortygia, henceforth called Delos (q.v.). Hera sent the giant Tityus (q.v.) to rape her but her children slew him with their arrows. See also Niobe.

Leuce. A nymph loved by Hades (q.v.) who turned her into a white poplar tree.

Leucippus. (1) King of Messenia whose daughters Hilaera and Phoebe were abducted by the Dioscuri (q.v.) and whose brothers Idas (q.v.) and Lynceus (q.v.) fought to save them.

(2) The son of Oenomaus who loved Artemis (q.v.) To be near her he disguised himself as a nymph but when Apollo (q.v.) advised the nymphs to bathe naked he was discovered and torn to pieces by them.

Leucothea. Originally Ino, daughter of Cadmus (q.v.) and wife of Athamas who helped Zeus (q.v.) save Dionysus (q.v.) at the death of Semele (q.v.). In revenge Hera (q.v.) drove her mad and she leapt into the foaming sea to become the sea deity Leucothea—"the white goddess". In this role she helped Odysseus (q.v.) land on Scheria. Her son was Palaemon, a minor sea god.

Liber Pater. An ancient Italian god of the vine, early identified with Bacchus (q.v.) by the Romans.

Lichas. The herald of Heracles (q.v.) who took the shirt of Deineira (q.v.) to him. In his agony Heracles took him by the ankle, swung him round three times and threw him into the Euboean Sea where he became a rock of human shape which henceforth bore his name.

Linus. (1) The son of Psamathe of Argos and Apollo (q.v.). Fearful lest her father learn of her liaison with the god she exposed the baby who was reared by shepherds but later killed by her father's hounds. When her distress revealed her secret her father condemned her to death but Apollo sent a plague to the city which only abated when the Argives propitiated mother and son with dirges called linoi.

(2) The son of a Muse who was so gifted musically that the jealous Apollo killed him.

(3) Heracles' (q.v.) music tutor whom Heracles slew in a rage with his own lyre.

Lotophagi. ("The Lotus eaters"). A mythical people living on lotus fruit which induced trances and forgetfulness and made the eater lose any desire to return home. They gave the fruit to Odysseus' (q.v.) men. Herodotus placed them in western Libya, possibly the island of Jerba.

Luceres. One of the original three tribes into which Rome was divided and which were believed to date back to Romulus (q.v.). The other tribes were the Ramnes and Tities.

Lucifer. The "light bringer", the name given to the planet Venus which can be seen before dawn. In the evening sky the Greeks called it Hesperus.

Lucretia. Wife of Tarquinius Collatinus whose rape by Sextus, son of Tarquinius Superbus led her to stab herself in shame. Junius Brutus then swore by her spirit to expel the Tarquins which he did. The story is told by Livy and Ovid and inspired Shakespeare's poem The Rape of Lucrece and Brit-

ten's opera The Rape of Lucretia. A subject also for Titian, Botticelli, Tintoretto and Veronese.

Lucretius. See Section B.

Lycaon. A mythical character who tricked Zeus (q.v.) by feeding him human flesh. Zeus killed him and all his sons save Nyctinus by lightning or turned them into wolves, hence Lycanthropy. See J30.

Lycomedes. The king of Scyros who murdered Theseus (q.v.). It was to his court that Thetis (q.v.) sent Achilles (q.v.), and Lycomedes' daughter Deidamia bore Achilles his son Neoptolemus (q.v.).

Lycurgus (1) Mythical king of Thrace who was made blind and mad for opposing the worship of Dionysus (q.v.).

(2) Mythical founder of the Spartan constitution and military regime, first mentioned by Herodotus and subject of a Life by Plutarch. Some traditions say the Pythia at Delphi gave him the constitution, others that he devised it while in Crete. In Sparta he was worshipped as a god.

Lynceus. (1) See Danaus.

(2) Twin of Idas (q.v.) noted for his keen eyesight.

Lyrnessus. City near Troy (q.v.) sacked by Achilles (q.v.).

M

Macareus. See Issa.

Macaria. See Eurystheus.

Machaon. The son of Asclepius the physician (q.v.).

Maenads. See Bacchae.

Maia. The daughter of Atlas (q.v.) and Pleione, eldest of the Pleiades (q.v.) and the most beautiful. By Zeus (q.v.) the mother of Hermes (q.v.). The Romans identified her with spring and as a nature goddess gave her name to the month of May.

Manes. "The good ones", the Roman name for the spirits of the dead, regarded as a collective divinity, Di Manes. On certain days they could leave the Underworld and were capable of great mischief. Thus they demanded propitiatory ceremonies at funerals and on set days when the head of the house, the paterfamilias, would go into the night and cast boiled beans to them. The Roman poets applied the term also to the gods of the Underworld and to the Underworld itself.

Marpessa. See Idas. The daughter of the river god Evenus.

Mars. Roman god of war, at one time also associated with agriculture. Later completely identified with Ares (q.v.).

Marsyas. A Phrygian, in some traditions a silenus (q.v.), who found the flute invented and discarded by Athene (q.v.). He challenged Apollo (q.v.) to a music contest, judged by the Muses (q.v.). Apollo won and had him flayed alive. The tears of the woodland spirits and animals which wept for him formed the river Meander.

Medea. The niece of Circe (q.v.) and daughter of Aëtes of Colchis some say by Hecate (q.v.). She loved Jason (q.v.) and helped him steal the Golden Fleece, murdering her half-brother in their escape. Having cut a goat in pieces, boiled them and pulled forth a lamb she persuaded the daughters of Pelias to boil him, causing his death.

When Jason left her for Glauce (q.v.) she caused her death and slew her sons by Jason. She then escaped in a chariot drawn by winged serpents to Athens. Here she married Aegeus (q.v.). When Theseus (q.v.) returned she tried to poison him to secure the succession of her own son Medus (q.v.) but Aegeus recognised Theseus and saved him.

She fled to wander the earth: some say she returned to Colchis and was reconciled to her father, others that she went to Asia Minor where her son gave his name to the Medes. She became an immortal.

Medus. Son of Medea (q.v.) and Aegeus (q.v.) eponymous ancestor of the Medes.

Medusa. See Gorgons. Slain and beheaded by Perseus (q.v.) as she slept. From her corpse sprang forth the fully grown Pegasus (q.v.) and the warrior Chrysaor.

Megaeia. One of the Erinnyes (q.v.).

Megara or **Megaera.** The eldest daughter of Creon of Thebes. Wife of Heracles (q.v.) and bore him several children. Later married Iolaus (q.v.) though one tradition says Eurystheus tried to kill her and Heracles instead killed Eurystheus. In revenge Hera (q.v.) drove Heracles mad and he killed Megara and his children.

Melampus. Son of Amythaon, a seer who introduced the worship of Dionysus (q.v.) to Greece. He and his brother Bias cured the women of Argos (including the daughter of the king, Proctus) of madness and received two thirds of his kingdom in reward.

Meleager. The son of Oeneus and Althaea. The Fates (q.v.) told his mother he would only die when a certain brand, which was on the fire, was burned. She extinguished and hid it. Meleager was one of the Argonauts (q.v.) and organised the hunt of the Calydonian Boar (q.v.). He fell in love with Atalanta who joined the hunt and having killed the boar himself gave her the hide on the pretext she had touched it first. This set the hunters quarrelling and in the dispute he killed his uncles, brothers of Althaea. She cursed their murderer, not realising the truth, and when she learned the Erinnyes (q.v.) were persecuting him because of the curse burned the brand and committed suicide. Her daughters (save Gorge and Deianeira) were turned into guinea-hens by Artemis. The son of Meleager and Atlanta was Parthenopaeus.

Melpomene. The Muse of Tragedy.

Memnon. The son of Eos (q.v.) and Tithonus, half-brother of Priam (q.v.). The king of Ethiopia who helped the Trojans and killed many Greeks. Achilles (q.v.) met him in single combat while Zeus (q.v.) weighed their fates in the balance. Achilles slew him but Zeus answered his mother's request that he be honoured by having the birds called *Memnonides* rise above his funeral pyre, then fall as a sacrifice. They annually visited his tomb on the Hellespont though one tradition says he survived the war and ruled five generations in Ethiopia before becoming an immortal.

The Greeks assumed many monuments, which they called *Memnonia*, were dedicated to him including a huge statue in Egyptian Thebes.

Menelaus. Son of Atreus, younger brother of Agamemnon (q.v.) and husband of Helen (q.v.). When her father chose him from amongst many suitors he made the others swear to help him in any misfortune. He was thus able to summon the Greek forces for the war on Troy (q.v.). At one stage in the war he fought a duel with Paris (q.v.) to decide the war and was winning until Aphrodite (q.v.) carried Paris off. Because he failed to sacrifice to Athene (q.v.) he took eight years to return from Troy to Sparta.

Menoeceus. (1) *See* Jocasta.

(2) *See* Seven against Thebes.

Mentor. Friend and adviser of Odysseus (q.v.) who was too old to go to Troy (q.v.) and remained at Ithaca to watch over Odysseus' interests. Athene (q.v.) took his form to guide Telemachus' (q.v.) search for his father. The name is now synonymous with a trusted counsellor.

Mercury. The Roman equivalent of Hermes (q.v.).

Merope. A Pleiad. Wife of Sisyphus.

Metis. Counsellor of the young Zeus (q.v.) and his first wife. Mother of Athene (q.v.). Herself the daughter of Oceanus (q.v.) and Tethys.

Midas. Son of Gordius. *See* Gordian Knot. His hospitality to Silenus (q.v.) led Dionysus (q.v.) to grant him any wish: he wished that all he touched would turn to gold. When even his food became gold he begged to be relieved of his gift—and was—by bathing in the River Pactolus which was henceforth rich in gold. When he judged Pan (q.v.) a better musician than Apollo (q.v.) the latter gave him asses' ears which he hid under his hat. Only his barber knew, but when his barber told a hole in the ground, reeds grew from it which, via the wind, revealed his secret to the world.

Milanion. Husband of Atalanta (q.v.).

Miletus of Crete. The son of Aria and Apollo (q.v.), a beautiful youth over whom Minos (q.v.) and his brothers Rhadamanthus (q.v.) and Sarpedon quarrelled. Miletus chose Sarpedon and to escape Minos' jealousy they fled to Asia Minor where Miletus founded the city Miletus which bore his name.

Minerva. Etruscan goddess of wisdom, the arts and crafts. The Romans identified her with Athene (q.v.).

Minos. The son of Zeus (q.v.) and Europa (q.v.), brother of Rhadamanthus (q.v.) and Sarpedon (q.v.). Ruler of Crete and supported in this by Poseidon (q.v.) who gave him a magnificent white bull. *See* Cretan Bull. He gave Crete her laws and defended the island with the aid of Talos, a brazen

giant with a bull's head. He pursued the nymph Britomartis for nine months but she leapt into the sea. Artemis (q.v.) deified her and the two shared the epithet Dictynna. While besieging Nisa, the port of Megara, Scylla, the daughter of the king Nisus fell in love with Minos and cropped her hair on which Nisus' life depended. She let Minos into the city but he was repulsed by her parricide and deserted the girl who swam after his ship. According to one tradition her father's spirit in the form of an eagle seized her and she was transformed into the Ciris bird; according to another tradition Minos drowned her and she became a fish. Minos married Pasiphaë (q.v.) who bore him Ariadne (q.v.), Androgeos and Phaedra. When Androgeos won all the events at the Panathenaic games Aegeus (q.v.) had him murdered and in revenge Minos extracted a tribute of seven Athenian youths and maidens who were devoured by the Minotaur (q.v.).

He was killed by the daughters of Cocalus of Sicily while pursuing Daedalus (q.v.) and became one of the three judges of the Underworld.

Minotaur. Offspring of Pasiphaë (q.v.) and the Cretan Bull (q.v.) which had the head of a bull and body of a man. It lived in a labyrinth devised by Daedalus (q.v.) where it devoured the maidens and youths of Athens delivered in tribute to Minos (q.v.). It was slain by Theseus (q.v.).

Minyans or Minyae. Prehistoric inhabitants of Boeotia (q.v.) and Thessaly whose reputed ancestor was Minyas.

Misenus. Trumpeter of Aeneas (q.v.) who was drowned by a Triton (q.v.) and buried in the Bay of Naples at the port which then bore the name Misenum (the modern Capo Miseno). From the time of Agrippa Misenum was a major Roman naval station.

Mithras. An Iranian deity whose worship was developed in Persia and spread throughout the Middle East. Known to the Greeks from the time of Herodotus his worship spread to Rome under the Republic and from the 2nd century A.D. spread throughout the empire. Mithras was linked with astrology and appears to have been linked with the sun following a fight with the sun-god. But the core of his cult was that man or the soul had fallen from grace and that Mithras could bring redemption and thus eternal life. Very popular with the Roman legions. Mithras was the one serious contender with Christianity for religious supremacy. His ritual involved seven stages of initiation and secret ceremonies conducted in underground caves or artificial subterranean chambers such as that found in London. These temples were called mithraea.

Mnemosyne. "Memory", the daughter of Uranus (q.v.) and by Zeus (q.v.) the mother of the Muses (q.v.).

Moirae or Moerae. *See* Fates.

Monoecus. "The lone dweller", Latin name for Heracles (q.v.) who was said to have dwelt alone for a time in the region of modern Monte Carlo.

Mopsus. The son of Apollo (q.v.) and Manto, daughter of Teiresias. When he beat Calchas (q.v.) in prophecy Calchas died of grief.

Morpheus. The Greek *Hypnos*. The son of the god of "Sleep". A god who sends dreams and visions of human form. In Ovid's *Metamorphoses*, "Sleep" sends him to Alcyone (q.v.) in the form of her dead husband.

Musaeus. A mythical poet who succeeded Orpheus (q.v.), the first poet.

Muses or Musae. The daughters of Zeus (q.v.) and Mnemosyne (q.v.) who presided over the arts and sciences. Originally three in number, Hesiod later names nine. Clio was muse of history, Euterpe of lyric poetry and music, Thalia of comedy, Melpomene of tragedy, Terpsichore of song and dance, Erato of mime, Polyhymnia or Polymnia of the hymn, Calliope of epic poetry and Urania of astronomy, though the attributions vary.

Myrmidons or Myrmidones. Tribe of southern Thessaly which provided Achilles' (q.v.) contingent at Troy.

Myrtilus. The son of Hermes (q.v.). The charioteer of Oenomaus whose death he caused by removing the lynch pin of his chariot and substituting a wax replica. He did this because Pelops (q.v.) had bribed him with the promise of half his kingdom, but instead Pelops flung him into the sea. He cursed the House of Pelops as he died and his father placed him amongst the stars.

N

Naiads or **Naiades.** Fresh-water nymphs in Greek mythology. They carried off Hylas (q.v.).

Narcissus. See Echo.

Nauplius. A king of Euboea who lured ships returning from Troy (q.v.) to their doom on the promontory of Caphareus by lighting misleading fires.

Nausicaa. Daughter of Alcinous, king of the Phaeacians who found Odysseus (q.v.) after a shipwreck while playing ball with her friends on the beach. She looked after him and her father gave him a ship.

Nectar. The drink of the Greek gods which conferred immortality.

Neleus. Twin of Pelias (q.v.), sons of Poseidon (q.v.) and the nymph Tyro. The twins were exposed by their mother but reared by a horse breeder. When Tyro married Cretheus, king of Iolcus, he adopted the boys who were thus half-brothers of Aeson. Pelias then later seized the kingdom, imprisoned Aeson and expelled Neleus who went to Pylus with Bias and Melampus and became its king. He and all twelve of his sons bar Nestor (q.v.) were killed by Heracles (q.v.) for aiding Augias (q.v.) in his war against Heracles.

Nemesis. Greek goddess, daughter of Oceanus. Originally she was envisaged as allotting to men their share of happiness and unhappiness, thereby chastening the over-fortunate. Later she was portrayed as the punisher of crime, the goddess of retribution. Some say she laid the egg from which Helen (q.v.), Clytemnestra (q.v.) and the Dioscuri (q.v.) were born. She had a sanctuary at Rhamnus from around 430 B.C.

Nemi. A lake in the Alban mountains, site of a sanctuary and sacred wood of Diana (q.v.).

Neoptolemus. Also called Pyrrhus, a son of Achilles (q.v.) and Deidamia. Odysseus (q.v.) and Diomedes (q.v.) persuaded his grandfather Lycomedes to let him go to Troy (q.v.) after his father's death. He was one of the Greeks inside the Wooden Horse. He slew Polites, the son of Priam (q.v.) and Hecuba (q.v.) before their eyes. He killed Priam at the altar of Zeus, smashed the skull of Astyanax (q.v.), Hector's (q.v.) child, and sacrificed Polyxena, Priam's daughter, on his father's tomb. He was given Andromache (q.v.) but back in Greece married Hermione (q.v.) with the blessing of Menelaus (q.v.) despite her prior betrothal to Orestes (q.v.).

When their marriage proved barren he went to Delphi (q.v.) to consult the oracle and was slain either by Orestes or the priests of Apollo.

Nephele. A phantom conjured up by Zeus (q.v.) to deceive Ixion. She later married Athamas.

Neptune. Italian sea-god whom the Romans identified with Poseidon (q.v.).

Nereids or **Nereides.** Fifty beautiful sea nymphs, the daughters of Nereus (q.v.) and Doris, of whom the most famous were Amphitrite (q.v.) and Thetis (q.v.).

Nereus. An ancient and benevolent sea god, the son of Pontus (the sea) and Ge (q.v.). Husband of Doris, the daughter of Oceanus (q.v.) by whom he was father of the Nereids (q.v.).

Nero. See Section B.

Nessus. See Deianeira.

Nestor. King of Pylos, only one of Neleus' (q.v.) twelve sons spared by Heracles. He participated in the Calydonian Boar (q.v.) hunt and the battle of Lapithae (q.v.) and Centaurs (q.v.). The oldest of the Greeks at Troy (q.v.) he was famous for his eloquence and wisdom. The father of Antilochus, a friend of Achilles (q.v.) and one of the bravest Greeks at Troy. Nestor was the only Greek to return home without mishap.

Nike. Goddess of Victory, not only in war but in musical and athletic competitions in Hesiod's *Theogony*, the daughter of the Titan Pallas and Styx. A minor deity, later envisaged not as one goddess but as several spirits, represented as young girls with wings who flew across the heavens to carry the crown to the victor. Zeus honoured Nike for helping the Olympian gods in the Titanomachia (q.v.). She was sometimes identified with Athene.

Niobe. Daughter of Tantalus, sister of Pelops (q.v.) and wife of Amphion (q.v.) by whom she had seven sons and seven daughters (according to Ovid, Homer makes it six of each). She boasted of being superior to Leto (q.v.) who only had two children

and in revenge Apollo (q.v.) slew her sons and Artemis (q.v.) her daughters. She wept for nine days and nights and Zeus (q.v.) then turned her into a stone on Mt. Sipylus.

Nisus. See Minos.

Nomius. "The pasturer", a name given to Pan (q.v.), Apollo (q.v.) and Hermes (q.v.) in their roles as protectors of flocks and pastures.

Notus. The south-west wind, known to the Romans as Auster. The son of Astraeus (q.v.) and Eos (q.v.).

Numa. The name of two Italian warriors in the *Aeneid*.

Numa Pompilius. Legendary king of Rome. The second king, successor of Romulus (q.v.) he was said to have ruled between 717 and 673 B.C. Said to be of Sabine (q.v.) origin he reorganised Roman religion under the guidance of Egeria (q.v.). He was said to have been initiated into the mysteries of Pythagoras, an obvious anachronism as he predates Pythagoras' 6th century visit to Italy, but his reputed religious reforms signify a new strand in Roman religion, a disinterested search for knowledge as opposed to inspired action.

He founded the cult of Janus (q.v.), organised the priests in *collegia* and established the flamens, and reorganised the Salii whose war dances in honour of Mars (q.v.) reflected a very ancient Italic rite.

He also appointed the Pontifex Maximus, a high priest with responsibility for ensuring religious rites were properly performed and for preventing the growth of undesirable foreign cults. He also reformed the Roman calendar to achieve the maximum coincidence of lunar and solar cycles.

Numicius. A sacred river in Latium between Ardea and Lavinium.

Numitor. The grandfather of Romulus (q.v.) and Remus (q.v.).

Nymphae or **Nymphs.** Minor deities, the spirits of nature. These daughters of Zeus (q.v.) were semi-mortal and were generally benevolent, though they could be malevolent particularly to unresponsive lovers. Each was the tutelary deity of a rock, tree, cave or fountain and was better known to the local peasants than the great gods of Olympus (q.v.).

Lavishly decorated monumental fountains (a "*nymphaeum*") were dedicated to the nymphs by both Greeks and Romans.

Nysa, Mt. Mountain in Libya where, according to tradition, Dionysus (q.v.) was raised.

O

Oceanides. Sea nymphs (q.v.) of the ocean, daughters of Oceanus (q.v.). Hesiod says they were 40 in number.

Oceanus. One of the Titans (q.v.), the son of Ge (q.v.) and Uranus (q.v.). The only Titan not to revolt against Uranus (q.v.). In Aeschylus' *Prometheus Bound* he preaches submission to the authority of Zeus (q.v.). He was seen originally as the river encircling the world from which all rivers and seas sprang. He is thus depicted as the rim on Achilles' (q.v.) shield. The husband of Tethys and by her father of, among others, Metis.

Odysseus. The hero of Homer's *Odyssey*, itself the model for James Joyce's *Ulysses*, Ulysses being the Roman name for him. The son of Laertes, king of Ithaca, and Anticleia, daughter of the wily thief Autolycus. However, one tradition makes him the son of Sisyphus (q.v.). He married Penelope (q.v.). Warned by an oracle not to go to Troy (q.v.) he feigned madness when the heralds arrived by sowing salt, but when Palamedes placed his son Telemachus (q.v.) before the plough he was forced to disclose his sanity and join the expedition. Later, at Troy, he avenged himself by having a letter signed in Priam's (q.v.) hand placed in Palamedes' tent. The letter was found and Palamedes was stoned to death. But Odysseus himself tricked Achilles (q.v.) into revealing his true identity and joining the expedition. At Troy Odysseus and Diomedes (q.v.) entered the city at night to kill Rhesus the Thracian and steal his white horses, because it was prophesied that if they drank of the Scamander (q.v.) Troy would not fall. He quarrelled with Ajax (q.v.) over the armour of Achilles and some say he killed him. He captured Helenus and from him learned the secret oracles which told how Troy would fall. In accordance with these he stole the Palladium of Athene (*q.v.*). It was also Odysseus who devised the stratagem of the Wooden Horse. When Troy fell he took Hecuba (*q.v.*) as a slave. His journey home lasted ten years and involved many adventures. He first went to Cicones to procure jars of sweet wine and then visited the Lotophagi (*q.v.*). After leaving them he landed in Sicily where he blinded Polyphemus the Cyclops (*q.v.*). Next he visited Aeolus (*q.v.*) and as a result was blown off course and lost all his ships save one at Telepylos. In this he reached Aeaea, land of Circe (*q.v.*) and on her advice sought the aid of Teiresias, a dead seer in the Underworld. In the land of the Cimmerians he summoned Teiresias' shade, and also those of his mother and former comrades, though Ajax (*q.v.*) held aloof. Then, with Circe's counsel he navigated the Scylla and Charybdis (*q.v.*) and neutralised the spell of the Sirens (*q.v.*) by blocking his crew's ears with wax but having himself tied to the mast that he might hear their song. At Thrinacia his men slaughtered the cattle of Helios (*q.v.*) and were punished by Zeus (*q.v.*), all but Odysseus dying in a subsequent shipwreck.

He drifted to Ogygia on flotsam, where he spent eight years with the nymph Calypso (*q.v.*). On a raft he made land at Scheria, was found by Nausicaa (*q.v.*) and given a ship to Ithaca (*q.v.*). Here he was recognised by Eumaeus (*q.v.*) despite his disguise as a beggar. He found Laertes in the country and Penelope (*q.v.*) besieged by suitors.

This drunken and unruly crew were headed by one Alcinous, their most persistent member. Penelope had kept them at bay by promising to marry one of them when she had finished weaving a robe for Laertes: a robe she unpicked each night. But betrayed by her servants she was now being forced to choose a husband.

Meanwhile Telemachus (*q.v.*) who had sailed away to find Odysseus returned to find him with Laertes and they plotted revenge. Still dressed as a beggar Odysseus entered the palace and was recognised only by his nurse Eurycleia and his faithful hound Argus which died on seeing his long lost master. Penelope now announced she would marry the suitor who could fire Odysseus' bow. Only he was able to bend and string it. The suitors having failed Odysseus strung the bow and with Telemachus slew the suitors.

The *Odyssey* ends when Athene (*q.v.*) reconciles the hero and the kinsmen of the suitors who were seeking revenge. Teiresias had prophesied that Odysseus had to go on another journey to appease Poseidon (*q.v.*) for the blinding of his son Polyphemus and would then live to an old age until death came from the sea.

One tradition tells how Telegonus, Odysseus' son by Circe came looking for his father, landed and began plundering for supplies. Odysseus and Telemachus gave battle and Telegonus killed Odysseus, not recognising his father. He also took Telemachus and Penelope to Aeaca where Circe married Telemachus and he himself married Penelope.

Odyssey. *See under* **Odysseus.**

Oedipus ("Swollen-foot"). The son of Laius, king of Thebes, and Jocasta (*q.v.*). The Delphic oracle said Laius would be killed by his son so he had the baby exposed on Mt. Cithaeron with a nail driven through its feet—hence "Oedipus". But he was found by a shepherd and raised by Polybus, king of Corinth, as his own son. As an adult Oedipus learned from the oracle that he would kill his own father and marry his own mother and believing himself the son of Polybus, left Corinth. He met Laius on the road and killed him in a quarrel. Laius had been on his way to Delphi to seek advice on ridding Thebes of the Sphinx (*q.v.*). This Oedipus did and was made king by the Thebans. He married Jocasta and they had four children, Eteocles (*q.v.*), Polynices (*q.v.*), Antigone (*q.v.*) and Ismene (*q.v.*). When Thebes suffered a plague because of their incest Oedipus contacted the seer Teiresias and learned whose son he was. When she heard the truth Jocasta hanged herself and Oedipus blinded himself with the pins from her dress. With Antigone and later Ismene he went into exile at the grove of the Eumenides (*see* **Erinnyes**) at Colonos in Attica. Here he was received by the gods, having first cursed the sons who had neglected him, saying they would divide

their kingdom by the sword.

Oeneus. King of Pleuron and Calydon, husband of Althaea and father of Tydeus (*q.v.*), Meleager (*q.v.*), Gorge and Deineira (*q.v.*). His realm was seized by his nephews but his grandson Diomedes (*q.v.*) avenged him and put Andraemon, husband of Gorge, on the throne. He accompanied Diomedes to the Peloponnesus where he was killed by two nephews who had escaped Diomedes. Deineira (*q.v.*) married Heracles (*q.v.*).

Oenomaus. A son of Ares (*q.v.*), king of Elis. An oracle said he would be killed by his son-in-law. Therefore he challenged all his daughter's suitors to a chariot race and if they won they would marry his daughter Hippodameia: if they lost they were put to death. His own chariot was drawn by wind-born horses, a gift of Ares. He was murdered by Myrtilus at the instigation of Pelops (*q.v.*).

Oenone. A nymph who loved Paris (*q.v.*). He deserted her for Helen (*q.v.*) and when he was wounded by Philoctetes (*q.v.*) she refused to help him. Then, in remorse at his death, she committed suicide.

Oileus. One of the Argonauts (*q.v.*), father of Ajax.

Olympia. A small province in the western Peloponnesus, isolated from the centre and east of the Peloponnesus by high mountains. The site of a major sanctuary of Zeus (*q.v.*) whose worship replaced that of an early female divinity in the 9th century B.C. However, it was not till about 470 B.C. that a magnificent temple was built to Zeus. From 776 B.C. though, the Olympic games had been celebrated at Olympia in honour of Zeus. These quadrennial contests were international in character and an international truce accompanied their celebration. The prestige of the games was great and from 776 Greek chronology was based on the games, an "Olympiad" being a four-year cycle. Hence Olympiad 12, 1 denoted the 1st year in a four-year period after 11 previous Olympiads. If the number of Olympiads is multiplied by 4 and deducted from 776 we have our date *e.g.* $11 \times 4 = 44$, subtracted from 776 is 732 B.C.

Olympius. A term for any deity or muse inhabiting Olympus and not the Underworld.

Olympus, Mt. The highest peak in Greece on the borders of Thessaly and Macedonia. Its 2975 m are almost inaccessible and it was not climbed until 1913. It was believed to be the home of the twelve Olympian gods.

Omphale. Queen of Lydia and widow of Tmolus who purchased Heracles (*q.v.*) as a slave. He served her for three years and one tradition says he dressed as a woman and swapped clothes with Omphale during this period.

Ops. Roman goddess of plenty, a consort of Saturn (*q.v.*) and the personification of abundance.

Orcus. The Roman name for Hades (*q.v.*) and for his realm.

Orestes. The son of Clytemnestra (*q.v.*) and Agamemnon (*q.v.*). As a child he was smuggled out of Mycenae by his sister Electra (*q.v.*) when Clytemnestra and Aegisthus (*q.v.*) seized power. He took refuge at the court of king Strophius in Phocis, becoming a close friend of Pylades (*q.v.*), the king's son. When of age he, Pylades and Electra killed Aegisthus and Clytemnestra, and Orestes was punished for his matricide by the Erinnyes (*q.v.*). He fled to the Acropolis of Athens and embraced the image of the goddess. Athene (*q.v.*) then summoned the Areopagus to judge his case. Apollo (*q.v.*), whose oracle had encouraged his crime, defended him on the grounds that fatherhood was more important than motherhood. Athene's casting vote found him innocent. Another tradition says Apollo told him he could be free of the Erinnyes by fetching the statue of Artemis (*q.v.*) from the Tauric Chersonese. Orestes and Pylades went to Tauris and were seized by the natives for sacrifice to Artemis. But it transpired that his sister Iphigenia (*q.v.*) was the priestess and she helped them steal the statue and return to Greece. They met Electra and went on to Mycenae where Orestes killed Aegisthus' son and became king. Later he slew his rival Neoptolemus (*q.v.*) and married his cousin Hermione.

Oreithyia. *See* **Boreas.** He turned her into a wind.

Orion. A giant, son of Poseidon (*q.v.*) who was a renowned hunter and very handsome. He loved Merope, daughter of Oenopion of Chios and was promised her hand in return for ridding Chios of wild animals. This he did but Oenopion would not give up Merope which led Orion to seduce her. Oenopion, with the help of his father Dionysus, blinded Orion who was told by the oracle he could only recover his sight by going to the east and gazing on the sun as it rose. This he did with the help of Hephaestus (q.v.) and once there Eos (q.v.) fell in love with him and Helios (q.v.) restored his sight. Later he joined Artemis (q.v.) in a hunt. Apollo (q.v.) angry at his boasting that he would kill all the wild beasts and afraid he would seduce Artemis contrived his death at the unwitting hands of Artemis. She placed his image in the stars, his constellation rising with the sun at the autumnal equinox.

Orpheus. The son of king Oeagrus of Thrace and Calliope (q.v.). The Greeks regarded him as the first great poet. He could enchant the beasts and trees with his lyre, a gift from Apollo (q.v.). After returning from the voyage of the Argonauts (q.v.) he married Eurydice (q.v.). His grief at losing her after redeeming her from Hades (q.v.) led to a failure to honour Dionysus (q.v.) at a Bacchanalia and he was torn to pieces by Bacchae (q.v.). The muses buried the pieces at the foot of Mt. Olympus (q.v.) save his head which was thrown into the River Hebrus still singing. The head and his lyre eventually floated to Lesbos (q.v.) and were finally placed amongst the stars at the request of Apollo and the Muses. *See also* **Orphism, Section J.**

Orthrus. A giant two-headed dog, the offspring of Typhon (q.v.) and Echidne (q.v.) and, some say, the father of the Sphinx (q.v.) and Chimaera (q.v.). It was set to watch the oxen of Geryon (q.v.) and was slain by Heracles (q.v.).

Ortygia (1) Port of Syracuse in Sicily.
(2) Port of Delos (q.v.), birthplace of Artemis (q.v.).

Otus and Ephialtes. Twin sons of Iphimedeia and Poseidon (q.v.), named Aloeidae after their mother's later husband Aloeus. At an early age they imprisoned Ares (q.v.) and later swore to rape Hera (q.v.) and Artemis (q.v.). In a vain effort to achieve this they placed Mt. Pelion on top of Mt. Ossa and attacked Heaven. But Artemis induced them to seek her at Naxos. Here she leapt between them in the form of a doe and they accidentally slew each other. In Tartarus (q.v.) their shades were tied back to back by bonds of vipers.

Ovid. *See* **Section B.**

P

Palaemon. A sea god, the son of Athamas and Ino who was originally named Melicertes.

Palamedes. *See* **Odysseus.**

Pales. Italic deity of flocks and herds, worshipped on the Palatine.

Palicus. An obscure god or hero worshipped in Sicily and mentioned in the *Aeneid* (q.v.).

Palinurus. "Wind Astern", the helmsman of Aeneas. He managed the ship between the Scylla and Charybdis (q.v.) and in the storm off the coast of Carthage but later fell asleep and into the sea. He was cast ashore but murdered by local tribesmen. His shade begged Aeneas for carriage across the Styx (q.v.) so it could be at rest, but the Sybil refused as he had not been properly buried. However she promised him a shrine, Capo Pulinuro in Lucania near modern Salerno.

Palladium. A mythical statue of Athene given to Dardanus (q.v.) by Zeus (q.v.) to ensure the protection of Troy. By one tradition it was stolen by Odysseus (q.v.) and Diomedes (q.v.). By another Aeneas (q.v.) saved it and brought it to Rome where it saved the city several times in its early years.

Pallas. (1) A title of Athene (q.v.) given to her by the Achaens. Pallas, Kore and Parthenos signify a virgin, maiden or girl.
(2) One of the 24 Giants (q.v.) who rebelled against Zeus (q.v.).
(3) A brother of Aegeus (q.v.). *See also* **Theseus.**
(4) An ancestor of Evander (q.v.).
(5) Evander's son who went to follow Aeneas.

Pan. A god, half-man, half-goat, said by some to be a son of Zeus (q.v.) by others to be the son of Hermes (q.v.) and Penelope with whom he inhabited Arcadia. He was a patron of shepherds and herdsmen and a lover of mischief. When not frolicking with the nymphs he liked to startle peasants and flocks inspiring "panic". He loved and pursued Syrinx whose flight from him resulted in her being transformed into a reed from which he

made a seven-piped flute, the syrinx. He also seduced Selene (q.v.). Sometimes identified with the Roman Faunus (q.v.).

Pandarus. A Trojan archer who broke a truce by shooting at the Greeks. In Chaucer's *Troilus and Criseyde* and Shakespeare's *Troilus and Cressida* he is Cressida's uncle and the lovers' go-between. The word "pandar" is derived from his name for this reason.

Pandora. "All gifts", the first woman fashioned and given life by Hephaestus (q.v.) and Athene (q.v.). Zeus (q.v.) sent her to punish man after Prometheus (q.v.) had given him fire. She married the brother of Prometheus, Epimetheus. Her curiosity led her to open a box which it was forbidden to touch, and from it sprang all the evils and diseases which beset mankind. Only hope was left at the bottom of the box.

Parcae. The Roman equivalent of the "Fates" or Horae.

Paris. Son of Priam (q.v.) and Hecuba (q.v.) who dreamed during her pregnancy that she would bring forth a blazing firebrand. As a child he was exposed on Mt. Ida. Raised by shepherds he was named Paris or sometimes Alexander ("defender of men") because of his courage. He loved and deserted Oenone (q.v.) who eventually caused his death. Promised the fairest of women by Aphrodite (q.v.) if he gave her the apple of discord, he did as she bade. Reunited with his parents he then left for Sparta whence he seduced Helen (q.v.) thus starting the Trojan War. At one point in the war Aphrodite saved him from death in a duel with Menelaus.

He shot the arrow which slew Achilles (q.v.) at the Scaean Gate but was himself mortally wounded by Philoctetes (q.v.).

Parnassus, Mt. 2461 m peak in the Pindus range, north-east of Delphi (q.v.). Home of Apollo (q.v.) and the Muses (q.v.) hence the name "Montparnasse" for the hill in Paris on which centred the university and cultural life of that city. On the original's slopes were also the Corycian Cave, a centre of the Bacchae (q.v.).

Parthenon. *See* **Section L.**

Parthenope. A nymph whose body was said to have washed up at Neapolis (Naples) around 600 B.C. She gave her name to the short-lived Parthenopean Republic of Naples established by Napoleon in 1799.

Parthenopeus. *See* **Seven Against Thebes.**

Parthenos. *See* **Pallas.**

Pasiphaë. Daughter of Helios (q.v.) and Persë, and wife of Minos (q.v.). Mother of the Minotaur (q.v.) by the Cretan Bull (q.v.) and of many children, including Ariadne (q.v.), Glaucus and Phaedra, by Minos.

Patroclus. Cousin and bosom companion of Achilles (q.v.) whom he met at the court of Peleus (q.v.) while in exile for an accidental murder. Slain by Hector (q.v.) while wearing Achilles' armour, his death persuaded Achilles to re-enter the Trojan War.

Pausanias. Spartan king who intervened to moderate Lysander's arrogant attitude towards Athens and other Greek cities after the Peloponnesian War.

Pegasus. Winged horse, offspring of Poseidon (q.v.) and Medusa (q.v.). It was captured by Bellerophon (q.v.) at the fountain of Pirene and helped him slay the Chimaera (q.v.). It struck Mt. Helicon with its hoof and brought forth the spring of Hippocrene, sacred to the Muses.

Peleus. The son of Aeacus, king of Aegina. With his brother Telamon he killed their half-brother Phocus and the two were expelled to Phthia in Thessaly by Aeacus. Here Eurytion purified them of murder. They took part in the Calydonian Hunt when they accidentally killed Eurytion. They then fled to the court of Acastus (q.v.) of Iolcis. Zeus (q.v.) married him to Thetis (q.v.) though he himself loved Thetis. This was because the oracle foretold that her son would be greater than his father.

Their son was Achilles (q.v.). All the gods save Eris (q.v.) were invited to the wedding and in revenge she cast the Apple of Discord. Peleus later ruled the Myrmidones at Phthia.

Pelias. *See* **Jason.**

Pelicles. Son of Peleus *i.e.* Achilles (q.v.).

Peloponnesus. The "island of Pelops" (q.v.), the large southern peninsular of mainland Greece, attached to northern Greece by the Corinthian isthmus.

Pelops. Son of Tantalus (q.v.) king of Lydia. Tantalus cut him in pieces and served him to the gods at a meal. Only Demeter (q.v.) grieving for Persephone *(q.v.)* did not realise and she ate Pelops' shoulder. Zeus *(q.v.)* restored him to life by having Hermes *(q.v.)* boil him in a pot. Demeter gave him an ivory shoulder, said to be the birthmark of his descendants. His shoulder blade was later taken to Troy *(q.v.)* by the Greeks as the oracle said this was necessary if the city were to fall. He married Hippodamia.

Pelorus. One of the Sparti *(q.v.)*.

Penates. Roman deities of the home, confused from early times with the *genius* and the Lares. Eventually a wide variety of deities, *e.g.* Mars, Mercury, Venus, were regarded as *"di Penates"* that is, "guardians of the hearth".

Penelope. The wife of Odysseus *(q.v.)*, usually seen as a symbol of fidelity. One tradition in the Peleponnesus made her adulterous and the mother of Pan *(q.v.)* by Hermes *(q.v.)* or by all of her many suitors.

Peneus. The son of Oceanus *(q.v.)* and Tethys. A river god and father of Daphne *(q.v.)* and Cyrene *(q.v.)*. Identified with the River Peneus in Thessaly.

Penthesilea. Daughter of Otrere and Ares *(q.v.)*, queen of the Amazons *(q.v.)* who helped the Trojans. Slain by Achilles *(q.v.)* they fell in love as she died and he later mourned her. When the wretched Thersites mocked his grief Achilles slew him which caused his kinsman Diomedes *(q.v.)* to throw her corpse into the Scamander. It was retrieved and honourably buried.

Pentheus. Grandson of Cadmus *(q.v.)* and king of Thebes. The subject of Euripides' *Bacchae*. He refused to allow Dionysus *(q.v.)* into the city but the god, in disguise, persuaded him to dress as one of the Bacchae *(q.v.)* and watch their orgies. He was then torn to pieces by the Bacchae, led by his own mother who was in a trance.

Perdix (or Talos). *See* Daedalus.

Periclymenus. The son of Neleus *(q.v.)* and brother of Nestor *(q.v.)*. An Argonaut *(q.v.)* he could assume any form he chose. Slain by Heracles *(q.v.)*.

Periphetes. A giant residing at Epidaurus who murdered travellers with an iron club. Slain by Theseus *(q.v.)* who henceforth carried his club.

Perse. The daughter of Oceanus *(q.v.)*. Wife of Helios *(q.v.)* to whom she bore Circe *(q.v.)*, Pasiphaë *(q.v.)*, Aeetes and Perses *(q.v.)*.

Persephone. Daughter of Zeus *(q.v.)* and Demeter *(q.v.)*. She spent the winter months with Hades *(q.v.)* when nothing grew and with Demeter she spent the fertile months. Thus she was a goddess of vegetation. She was also queen of the Underworld and was a symbol of death. Known to the Romans as Proserpina. Her companion in the Underworld was Hecate *(q.v.)*.

Perses. The son of Helios *(q.v.)* and Perse *(q.v.)* father of Hecate *(q.v.)*.

Perseus. Grandson of Acrisius *(q.v.)* king of Argos and the son of Zeus *(q.v.)* and Danae *(q.v.)*. Raised at the court of Polydectes who sent him to fetch the head of Medusa *(q.v.)*. Hermes *(q.v.)* gave him a sickle with which to do this and told him how, via the Graeae *(q.v.)* he could procure Hades' *(q.v.)* helmet of invisibility, winged sandals and a magic wallet to help him in the task. Once he had the head he petrified the Titan Atlas *(q.v.)* with it. He then flew to Aethiopia where he found Andromeda *(see* **Cassiopeia**). Returning to Seriphos he slew Polydectes, made Dictys *(q.v.)* king and returned to Argos. He went on later to exchange the kingdom of Argos for that of his cousin Megaperthes of Tiryns.

Phaebus ("Shining"). A name used for Apollo *(q.v.)* at Delos *(q.v.)* where he was associated with Artemis *(q.v.)*.

Phaedra. The daughter of Minos *(q.v.)* and wife of Theseus *(q.v.)* to whom she bore Acamas and Demephon. *See also* **Hippolytus**.

Phaeton. The son of Helios *(q.v.)* and Clymene. Helios let him drive the chariot of the sun across the sky but he lost control of it and was killed by a thunderbolt from Zeus *(q.v.)* for almost setting the world on fire. He fell into the River Po and his sisters who mourned him were turned into poplar or alder trees and their tears into amber.

Phalanthus. Mythical founder of Tarentum in Italy.

Philemon. The husband of Baucis. This old Phrygian couple once received Zeus *(q.v.)* and Hermes *(q.v.)* with great hospitality.

Philoctetes. The son of Poecas, nephew of Protesilaus, and companion of Heracles *(q.v.)*. He lit Heracles funeral pyre and received his bow and arrows. On the way to Troy *(q.v.)* one of the poisoned arrows wounded him, or he was bitten by a snake on the island of Tenedos. The smell of the wound became so offensive that on the advice of Odysseus *(q.v.)* he was left on Lemnos. Later an oracle revealed that Troy would not fall till the bow and arrows of Heracles were brought to the Greeks and Odysseus and Diomedes *(q.v.)* fetched him to Troy. Here either Machaon or Podalirius, the sons of Asclepius *(q.v.)* cured him of his wound. He slew Paris *(q.v.)* and later settled in Italy.

Philomela. *See* **Procne**.

Phineus. King of Salmydessus in Thrace and the son of Agenor. He first married Cleopatra, then Idaca who falsely accused her stepsons of improper advances. Phineus imprisoned them and was made blind and pursued by the Harpies *(q.v.)*. Eventually the Argonauts *(q.v.)* whose ranks included Zetes and Calais, Cleopatra's brothers, slew the Harpies. Phineus freed the stepsons and told Jason *(q.v.)* what course to set.

Phlegethon ("Blazing"). A river of the Underworld called the "river of flames" by Plato. The shades of those who had committed crimes of violence against their kin were roasted in it until they received forgiveness.

Phlegyas. A king of the Lapithae *(q.v.)* who burnt Apollo's *(q.v.)* shrine at Delphi and was punished for it in the Underworld by having to sit beneath a huge rock which was liable to fall at any time.

Phocis. Small mountainous province of northern Greece which held the oracle of Delphi.

Phocus. *See* **Peleus**.

Phoebe ("Bright"). In early myth the daughter of Heaven and Earth and mother of Leto *(q.v.)*. Later identified with Artemis *(q.v.)* the moon-goddess.

Phoenix ("Red"). (1) Companion and tutor of Achilles *(q.v.)* who tried to reconcile him with Agamemnon *(q.v.)*.

(2) The brother of Cadmus *(q.v.)* and Europa *(q.v.)*, eponymous ancestor of the Phoenicians.

(3) A mythological bird which died on a funeral pyre every 500 years before rising again from the ashes.

Phorcys. A sea-god, the father of Echidne *(q.v.)*, Ladon, the Gorgons *(q.v.)* and the Graeae *(q.v.)*.

Phrixus and Helle. Brother and sister, the children of Athamas king of Aeolia. Their stepmother, Ino *(q.v.)*, had engineered their sacrifice by Athamas out of jealousy but they escaped on a flying ram with a golden fleece sent by Zeus *(q.v.)*. Helle fell off into what was henceforth the Hellespont, but Phrixus reached Colchis and sacrificed the ram to Zeus *(see* **Jason**). The ram's image was placed amongst the stars as Aries.

Phyllis. *See* **Demophon**.

Picus. An ancient Italian god represented as a woodpecker *i.e.* "*picus*".

Pierides. A name applied to the Muses *(q.v.)*. It was derived from the inhabitants of Pieria, on the south coast of Macedonia, who were noted for their worship of the Muses.

Also a name for nine daughters of Pierus king of Macedonia who were defeated in a contest by the Muses and turned into birds.

Pillars of Hercules. Two pillars, Calpe and Abyla, erected on either side of the straits of Gibraltar by Heracles *(q.v.)*.

Pilumnus. An ancient minor Italian god, "the spearman".

Pindar. *See* **Section B.**

Pirithous. Son of Ixion *(q.v.)* and Dia, companion of Theseus *(q.v.)* and king of the Lapithae *(q.v.)*. He led the fight on the Centaurs *(q.v.)*. On the death of his wife Hippodamia he and Theseus abducted the young Helen *(q.v.)* of Troy. She fell by lot to Theseus who, in return and despite misgivings, promised to help Pirithous abduct a daughter of Zeus *(q.v.)* for himself. They attempted to abduct Persephone *(q.v.)* from the Underworld but Hades *(q.v.)* chained them to a rock. Heracles *(q.v.)* later freed Theseus but Pirithous was left to suffer torment for his sins.

Pleiades. The seven daughters of Atlas *(q.v.)* and Pleione and companions of Artemis *(q.v.)*. Zeus *(q.v.)* turned them into doves and placed their image in the stars to save them from the attentions of Orion *(q.v.)* who pursued them for five years. A group of seven poets in 3rd century B.C. Alexandria also called themselves the Pleiad.

Plutarch. *See* **Section B.**

Pluto. (1) A Roman name for Hades *(q.v.)*, "the rich one" who owns the riches of the earth itself.

(2) A nymph who was mother of Tantalus (*q.v.*) by Zeus (*q.v.*).

Podarces. (1) *See* **Priam**.

(2) Son of Iphiclus, leader of the Thessalians who fought at Troy (*q.v.*).

Polites. A son of Priam (*q.v.*) and Hecabe (*q.v.*), slain before their eyes by Neoptolemus (*q.v.*).

Pollux. The Roman name for Polydeuces. *See* **Castor**.

Polydeuces. *See* **Castor**.

Polydorus. (1) The son of Cadmus (*q.v.*) and Harmonia and ancestor of Oedipus (*q.v.*) and other great Theban kings.

(2) The youngest son of Priam (*q.v.*) and Hecabe (*q.v.*).

Polymnia. *See* **Muses**.

Polynices. The son of Jocasta and Oedipus (*q.v.*), brother of Eteocles (*q.v.*), Antigone (*q.v.*) and Ismene (*q.v.*). *See also* **Seven Against Thebes**. When Creon refused to allow his burial Antigone (*q.v.*) disregarded the order and buried the corpse.

Polypemon. Also known as Procrustes, "the stretcher'. A robber who tied travellers to a bed and if they were too tall he cut off their legs; if too short he put them on a rack. Theseus (*q.v.*) did the same to him.

Polyphemus. *See* **Cyclopes and Galatea**.

Polyxena. The daughter of Priam (*q.v.*) and Hecuba (*q.v.*) beloved by Achilles (*q.v.*) whose shade requested her sacrifice by Neoptolemus (*q.v.*) after Troy's (*q.v.*) fall. This is the theme of Euripedes' *Hecabe*.

Pomona. An Italian goddess of tree-fruits (*poma*) *e.g.* apples. She was a minor deity but had her own priest and sanctuary near Rome. Ovid links her with Vertumnus, an Etruscan god with the power to change his shape. He was god of the changing seasons and the ripening fruits of autumn, and also of money changing. *Vertere* means "change" in Latin. He loved Pomona and pursued her disguised as a harvester, vine-dresser, herdsman and old woman, but only won her when he appeared as himself. His statue stood in the Vicus Tuscus, a busy street of brothels and shops named after him as an Etruscan.

Pontus. The sea, offspring of Ge (*q.v.*) the earth.

Pontus Euxinus. The "Hospitable Sea", the Greek name for the Black Sea. The name was an attempt to flatter and placate a hostile sea which was much feared by sailors.

Porphyrion. *See* **Giants**.

Porsenna. *See* **Lars Porsenna**.

Portunus. A Roman sea-deity associated with harbours.

Poseidon. The Roman Neptune, the god of earthquakes, and later of the sea. The eldest son of Cronus (*q.v.*) and Rhea. When he and Zeus (*q.v.*) and Hades (*q.v.*) cast lots for their realms he won the sea and had an underwater palace near Aegae in Euboea. Here he kept horses with brazen hoofs and gold manes who drew his chariot across the sea. Its passage calmed the sea. Poseidon created the horse and invented the bridle. As a horse he raped Demeter (*q.v.*) who was disguised as a mare. Their offspring was the horse Arion and the nymph Despoena and, some say, Persephone (*q.v.*). He resented Zeus (*q.v.*) and helped Hera (*q.v.*) and Apollo (*q.v.*) enchain him. In punishment Zeus made him a servant of Laomedon (*q.v.*) and he built the Neptunilia Pergama, the walls of Troy. He helped the Greeks at Troy but hated Odysseus (*q.v.*) who blinded Polyphemus (*q.v.*). He disputed the possession of Athens with Athene (*q.v.*) and lost, but Zeus gave him the Isthmus of Corinth instead. Here the Isthmian games were held in his honour. He married Amphitrite (*q.v.*). By mortal women he had many children including Pegasus (*q.v.*) and the Aloeidae (*q.v.*).

He is usually portrayed with a trident which he used to shake the earth.

Priam. The son of Laomedon (*q.v.*) and husband of Hecuba (*q.v.*). Originally called Podarces his name was changed to Priam *i.e.* "ransomed" because Heracles (*q.v.*) spared him and sold him to Hesione (*q.v.*) his sister. He had fifty sons and fifty daughters, nineteen of whom were by Hecuba and included Hector (*q.v.*), Paris (*q.v.*), Helenus (*q.v.*) and Cassandra (*q.v.*). He begged Achilles (*q.v.*) to return Hector's body. Eventually slain at the altar of Zeus (*q.v.*) by Neoptolemus (*q.v.*).

Priapus. The son of Dionysus (*q.v.*) and Aphrodite (*q.v.*). A fertility god whose worship spread from the Hellespont to Greece and later Rome, though he was never taken seriously. He was often por-

trayed in the form of a red-faced scarecrow with a large detachable phallus and in this role was used to scare birds. The phallus became a truncheon to ward off other intruders. He was also a protector of cultivated gardens and a god of sailors. In Petronius' *Satyricon* he pursues the hero Encolpius and makes him impotent. Horace and Martial write of him lightheartedly and 85 obscene poems about him - "*priapeia*' - exist of unknown authorship. His sacrificial animal was the donkey, a symbol of lust.

Procne. The daughter of Pandion, king of Athens. Pandion gave her to Tereus in return for his assistance and they had a son Itys. But Tereus wanted her sister Philomela. He made Procne a slave and tore out her tongue, then seduced Philomela saying Procne was dead. Procne could only alert her sister and be free by stitching a message to her robe. Once free she slew Itys, cooked pieces of the corpse and fed it to Tereus. When Tereus learnt what had happened he chased the sisters with an axe but the gods turned him into a hawk, Procne into a swallow and Philomela a nightingale though some traditions say it was Philomela who lost her tongue and became a swallow.

Procris. Daughter of Erectheus of Athens and the wife of Cephalus. Eos (*q.v.*) who also loved Cephalus showed him that Procris was easily seduced in return for gold. Procris then fled to Crete and lived for a time with Minos (*q.v.*). On returning to Athens disguised as a youth she brought with her a hound and spear, gifts from Artemis (*q.v.*), which never missed their quarry. Cephalus so wanted the gifts that the couple were reconciled. But Procris suspected Cephalus of having an affair with Eos and followed him on a hunt where he accidentally killed her with the spear.

Procrustes. *See* **Polypemon**.

Proetus. The son of Abas (*q.v.*) king of Argolis. His twin brother Acrisius (*q.v.*) expelled him and he fled to Lydia where he married Anteia (also called Stheneboea) daughter of king Iobates (*see* **Bellerophon**). He later returned to Argolis and forced Acrisius to give him half the kingdom. He ruled from Tiryns whose huge walls he built with the aid of the Cyclopes (*q.v.*). Eventually gave two thirds of his kingdom to Melampus (*q.v.*) and Bias.

Prometheus. A Titan (*q.v.*) and the brother of Epimetheus (*q.v.*) or "afterthought" and Atlas (*q.v.*). Sometimes said to be the maker of mankind. He supported Zeus (*q.v.*) against his brother Titans but stole fire from Olympus and gave it to men. This angered Zeus who took revenge on man through Pandora (*q.v.*) and punished Prometheus by chaining him to a rock in the Caucasus. Here an eagle tore at his liver each day. The liver was renewed daily and Prometheus suffered this torment until Heracles (*q.v.*) rescued him.

Proserpina. Roman counterpart of Persephone (*q.v.*).

Proteus. A sea god and a subject of Poseidon (*q.v.*). He had the power of prophecy and could change his form. He would avoid prophecy by changing form until tightly gripped; then he appeared in his true shape and spoke the truth. Said to live on the isle of Pharos in the Nile Delta. Menelaus (*q.v.*) mastered him while returning from Troy (*q.v.*) and forced him to reveal the way to Sparta.

Psyche. In Greek literature, the "soul" personified, often portrayed as a butterfly. As the centre of emotion she was tormented by "*eros*". Her beauty made Aphrodite (*q.v.*) jealous and she sent Eros (*q.v.*) to torment her. Instead he fell in love with her though he would not let her see him or disclose his identity. But at the bidding of her two sisters she sought to discover who he was. For the first time she saw him, holding a candle above him as he slept, but hot wax fell on him. He woke and left her to seek him. After many trials she found him, became immortal and was united with Eros for ever.

Pygmalion. (1) The king of Tyre and brother of Dido (*q.v.*).

(2) The king of Cyprus who made and fell in love with a maiden's statue. Aphrodite (*q.v.*) answered his prayers and gave the statue life as the girl Galatea. They married and had two sons, Paphus and Metharme. In some versions of the tale he is a sculptor. The basis of Shaw's *Pygmalion* and the musical *My Fair Lady*.

Pylades. Husband of Electra (*q.v.*). *See also* **Orestes**.

Pyramus and Thisbe. The lovers in a tale by Ovid which he heard in the East. Living in Babylon they are forbidden to meet but converse through a chink in a wall. They arrange a meeting at the tomb of Ninus but Thisbe, arriving first, was chased away by a lion and dropped her veil. Finding this, Pyramus thought her dead and committed suicide. She returned and slew herself on his sword. Since that time the nearby mulberry has borne fruit the colour of blood. This is the basis of Bottom's tale in Shakespeare's *A Midsummer Night's Dream*.

Pyrrhus. Another name for Neoptolemus.

Pythia. The priestess of Apollo (*q.v.*) at Delphi (*q.v.*).

Python. A she-dragon of Mt. Parnassus who controlled the oracle at Delphi (*q.v.*). The boy Apollo (*q.v.*) slew her and the Pythia (*q.v.*) took over her task of giving voice to oracles.

Q

Quirinus. A very ancient Roman deity whose cult was centred on the Quirinal. The Romans eventually forgot his original character and he was identified with Mars (*q.v.*) in classical times, though Romulus (*q.v.*) was also supposed to have adopted the name after his deification.

R

Rape of the Sabine Women. An episode recounted by Livy and Ovid to explain the intermarriage of the Roman settlers and natives. Romulus (*q.v.*) and his followers invited the surrounding tribes to celebrate a festival in the Circus Maximus then carried off the native girls. War broke out but the Sabine women, who had been well treated, intervened to restore peace.

The event has been the subject of paintings by Poussin and Rubens and of a group of statues by Giovanni da Bologna.

Remus. *See* Romulus.

Rhadamanthus. The son of Zeus (*q.v.*) and Europa (*q.v.*), brother of Minos (*q.v.*) and Sarpedon (*q.v.*). Once the ruler of part of Crete but Minos forced him to flee to Boeotia (*q.v.*). Famed for his wisdom and justice he was made one of the judges of the Underworld after his death. He married Alcmene (*q.v.*) on the death of Amphitrion (*q.v.*).

Rhea. (1) A Titaness, daughter of Ge (*q.v.*) and Uranus (*q.v.*). *See* Cronus.

(2) *See* Romulus.

Rhesus. A Thracian king who helped the Trojans. An oracle said that if his magnificent snow-white horses ate the grass of the Trojan plain and drank of the River Scamander Troy would not fall. Diomedes (*q.v.*) and Odysseus (*q.v.*) raided his camp, slew him, and stole the horses.

Rhodos/Rhode. The daughter of Poseidon (*q.v.*), wife of Helios (*q.v.*).

Rome. The "eternal city" sited on the banks of the Tiber. Traditionally founded in 753 B.C. (year 1 of the Roman calendar) by Romulus (*q.v.*). It only really became a city in the 6th century under the Tarquins. Under the Republic it had a population of two or three hundred thousand, of 450,000 by the time of Augustus and 1,000,000 under the Antonines, though the population was occasionally reduced by wars, fires and plagues.

Romulus. The legendary founder of Rome (*q.v.*), twin brother of Remus and together the sons of Rhea or Rhea Silvia. She was the daughter of Numitor, king of Alba Longa (*q.v.*) who was deposed by his brother. Her uncle compelled her to become a Vestal Virgin (*q.v.*) but she bore Romulus and Remus, according to her, by Mars (*q.v.*). Her uncle then imprisoned her and threw the babies into the Tiber. The shepherd Faustulus (*q.v.*) found a wolf suckling them and reared them. When they reached manhood they returned to Alba Longa, restored Numitor to the throne and set off to found a city of their own. They went to the site of Rome and decided to consult the gods. Romulus chose the Palatine Hill, his childhood home, as the centre of the city, Remus the Aventine (*q.v.*). The gods favoured Romulus, sending him an extraordinary omen of twelve vultures, Remus only six. Thus Romulus was given the honour of founding Rome which he did by ploughing a furrow around the Palatine. As he commenced

building the city wall Remus derisively jumped over it, a quarrel ensued and Romulus slew him. Romulus took in fugitives in order to populate the city, found them wives by the "Rape of the Sabine women" (*q.v.*) and reigned for forty years before disappearing in a whirlwind on the Campus Martius.

He was deified and identified with the Sabine god Quirinus (*q.v.*).

Rubicon. *See* Section L.

S

Sabines. A branch of the Samnite race and one of the Sabellian peoples who occupied the Etruscanised area on the middle valley of the Tiber around Falerii. To the south of Rome they held the mountainous land between Rome and Campania. They were a constant threat to early Rome and the tradition that one Titus Tatius, a Sabine prince, was offered joint rule by Romulus (*q.v.*) may indicate a period of Sabine occupation or domination of Rome.

Sabinus. A mythical Sabine king.

Salmoneus. The son of Aeolus (*q.v.*) and brother of Sisyphus (*q.v.*). The founder of Salmone. His pride led him to emulate the thunder and lightning of Zeus (*q.v.*) who slew him and crushed his city with a thunderbolt.

Sarpedon. The son of Zeus (*q.v.*) and Europa (*q.v.*), brother of Minos (*q.v.*) and Rhadamanthus (*q.v.*). The three brothers quarrelled over the love of the youth Miletus (*q.v.*). Sarpedon went to Asia Minor and became king of the Lycians after helping king Cilix of Cilicia defeat them. Zeus allowed him to live three generations and he helped Troy (*q.v.*) in the Trojan war. Patroclus (*q.v.*) slew him.

Saturn. From *Satus* i.e. "sown". Ancient Mediterranean god of agriculture, possibly of Ligurian origin and particularly revered in Sardinia (*q.v.*) and Africa (*q.v.*). Later identified with Cronus (*q.v.*) who supposedly emigrated to Italy after being deposed by Zeus (*q.v.*). Here he presided over a mythical "Golden Age". His temple in Rome was consecrated in 497 B.C. and housed the state treasury. His festival, the Saturnalia, was celebrated near the winter solstice, originally on 17 December but from the 4th century A.D. on New Year's Day. During the celebrations complete licence was given, slaves took the place of their masters, presents were given, a "Lord of Misrule" appointed and merrymaking and disorder of every kind was rife. It may be that in primitive times his worship involved the sacrifice of humans because in classical times rush dummies in human shape (*argei*) were flung into the Tiber each year on 15 May in his honour.

Satyrs. Young spirits of wildlife, the woods and hillsides. Sons of Hermes (*q.v.*) closely associated with Dionysus (*q.v.*). They were possessed by lechery and a love of wine and embodied the fertile force of nature. Usually they were personified with pointed ears, horns and a tail like Pan's (*q.v.*).

Scaean Gate. The "left hand", the gate in the walls of Troy (*q.v.*) where Achilles (*q.v.*) fell.

Scamander, River. River in Asia Minor near Troy (*q.v.*), originally called the Xanthus. Its name was changed when the mythical Scamander (*q.v.*) of Crete founded a colony in Phrygia and jumped into the river.

Scamander. One-time king of Crete, father of Teucer (*q.v.*) by the nymph Idaea and therefore an ancestor of the Trojans.

Sciron. A robber who dwelt on the border of Attica and Megara. He preyed on travellers and forced them to wash his feet on the Scironian rock. He then kicked them off the rock into the sea to be eaten by a giant turtle. Theseus (*q.v.*) slew him.

Scylla. (1) *See* Minos.

(2) *See* Charybdis.

Scyrus. Aegean isle, half-way between Lesbos and Euboea and off the major trade routes. It was of no importance save in legend: here Achilles (*q.v.*) was hidden by Lycomedes. It was also here that Lycomedes threw Theseus (*q.v.*) from a rock while the hero was in voluntary exile from Athens after giving the city its first constitution. In 470 B.C. Cimon expelled the local populace in order to install Athenian colonists. At the same time he found the reputed body of Theseus and took it back to Athens amidst great pomp.

Selene. Eastern goddess whom the Greeks identified with Artemis (*q.v.*) and the Romans with Diana (*q.v.*) or the older moon goddess Luna. Both also identified her with Hecate (*q.v.*), thus the moon became associated with sorcery.

Semele. *See* **Dionysus.**

Semiramis. The wife of Ninus. These two were the mythical founders of Ninus or Nineveh.

Seven Against Thebes. Oedipus (*q.v.*) cursed his sons for neglecting him, saying they would divide their kingdom by the sword. To avoid this Eteocles and Polynices agreed to rule in turn but Eteocles then refused to give up the throne when his term expired. Polynices sought the help of Adrastus (*q.v.*) king of Argos and married his daughter Argia while her sister married Tydeus son of Oeneus of Calydon who was in exile because of a murder he had committed. Amphiaraus the seer (brother-in-law of Adrastus) prophesied death for all who marched on Thebes save Adrastus. But on the advice of Tydeus, Polynices bribed Eriphyle into persuading Amphiaraus to join them. These four were joined by Capaneus, Hippomedon and Parthenopaeus. The seven were initially successful but Teiresias (*q.v.*) prophesied that a The ban royal prince must sacrifice himself to save the city and Menoeceus did so. The fortunes of the seven now waned. Zeus (*q.v.*) killed Capaneus with a thunderbolt as he stormed the city walls. Tydeus was wounded by Melanippus but Athene (*q.v.*) intended to save him with an elixir from Zeus. But Amphiaraus, who had a grudge against him, persuaded him to drink the brains of Melanippus which so disgusted Athene she let him die. Hippomedon and Parthenopaeus were also slain. Polynices now fought a duel with Eteocles to settle the matter and both were mortally wounded. Amphiaraus was swallowed up by the earth and only Adrastus survived. *See also* **Antigone** and **Epigoni.**

Seven Hills of Rome. The Quirinal, Viminal, Esquiline, Caelian, Capitoline, Palatine and Aventine.

Seven Kings of Rome. Traditionally said to be Romulus, Numa Pompilius, Tullus Hostilius, Ancus Martius, Tarquinius Priscus, Servius Tullius and Tarquinius Superbus.

Seven Sages of Greece. Usually held to be Thales of Miletus, Bias of Priene, Solon, Chilo of Sparta who brought the bones of Orestes (*q.v.*) to Sparta, Periander of Corinth, Pittacus of Mytilene, a democrat, contemporary of Solon and opponent of Alcaeus, and Cleobulus of Rhodes.

Sibyl (Sibylla). A priestess and prophetess who uttered oracles. Localised in several places the term came to be used generically of many sibyls and Varro lists ten. The most famous was at Cumae in Campania and she told Aeneas (*q.v.*) how to enter the Underworld. Ovid says she was seven generations old when Aeneas met her and that Apollo (*q.v.*) had granted her request to live as many years as there were grains in a handful of sand. But she had forgotten to seek eternal youth and was now withered with age. In Petronius' *Satyricon* she hangs in a bottle and when asked what she wants replies "I want to die".

Sibylline Books. A Roman tradition tells how a sibyl (*q.v.*) offered Tarquinius Priscus nine prophetic books which he refused to buy at the price. She destroyed three and he still refused them; she burnt three more and he took the remaining three at the price demanded for the nine. Special priests kept them and they were consulted only when the Senate authorised it in time of need. In 83 B.C. the originals were destroyed by fire but replaced by new ones. Many later additions were made including Jewish and Christian forgeries and fourteen still exist. They were last consulted in the 4th century A.D. and shortly afterwards Stilicho had them burnt. The original books instructed the Romans to convey the sacred stone of Cybele to Rome.

Sigeum. Part of Troy (*q.v.*). Hence the Dardanelles were known as the "straits of Sigeum".

Sileni, Silenus. Scholars distinguish between *sileni* and satyrs (*q.v.*) but the two are very similar and the Greeks themselves seem to have made no distinction. They are regarded as companions of Dionysus (*q.v.*) and have pointed ears, flat noses and the tail of a horse or goat. By the 6th century B.C. one of their number, Silenus, stands out from his fellows for his wisdom and is sometimes said to have been the tutor of Dionysus. His special

knowledge comes from wine drinking and like his fellows he is usually drunk. An old man with horse-ears and tail he proves a good raconteur when captured, though something of a comic drunkard.

Silvanus. Ancient Italian god, a protector of uncultivated land.

Sinis or **Sinnis.** A robber of the Corinthian Isthmus who killed travellers by tying them to the tops of fir trees tied to the ground and then releasing the trees. Theseus (*q.v.*) slew him in the same fashion.

Sinon. A cousin of Odysseus (*q.v.*) and grandson of Autolycus the thief. When the Greeks pretended to leave Troy (*q.v.*) he remained in camp and persuaded the Trojans that the wooden horse was a gift in atonement for the theft of Athene's Palladium (*q.v.*). Once the horse was inside Troy he signalled the Greek fleet to return.

Sirens. In Homer two sisters who lure sailors to their death by their singing. Odysseus (*q.v.*) and the Argonauts (*q.v.*) withstood their fatal charms, the latter because Orpheus (*q.v.*) outsang them. They have been associated with the modern Galli islands. In non-Homeric tradition their number varies and they are portrayed as having the bodies of birds and heads of either sex. Some say they were daughters of Ge (*q.v.*) and companions of Persephone (*q.v.*) who escorted the dead to the Underworld. They were said to feed on the dead. Later they are given the heads of beautiful women and sing to console the dead they escort. Finally they lose their funerary and evil nature and develop fishes' tails like mermaids.

Sisyphus. The son of Aeolus and husband of the Pleiad Merope who bore him Glaucus. He was an ancestor of Bellerophon (*q.v.*) and also seduced Anticleia, mother of Odysseus (*q.v.*) and may have been his father. The founder of Ephyra (later Corinth) and an infamous rogue and knave he was condemned in the Underworld perpetually to push a large stone, uphill, only to see it always roll down, hence the term "labour of Sisyphus' to denote a futile task.

Sophocles. *See* **Section B.**

Spartii. "The sown men" who sprang up when Cadmus (*q.v.*) sowed the dragon's teeth. They were fully armed and fought amongst themselves until only five remained, Echion, Udaeus, Chthonius, Hyperenor and Pelorus. These helped Cadmus build the Cadmea, citadel of Thebes, and were ancestors of the Thebans. The title was also given to their descendants. Cadmus saved some of the teeth and Jason (*q.v.*) had to sow these to get the Golden Fleece.

Sphinx. A fabulous monster with a human head and the body of a lion. In Egyptian mythology where it originates it could be of either sex but in Greek myth is a female and lives north of Thebes. It was the offspring of Echidne (*q.v.*) and Typhon (*q.v.*) or possibly Orthrus (*q.v.*) and the Chimaera (*q.v.*) and plagued Thebes by strangling and devouring all who could not answer her riddle: what walks on four legs at dawn, two at noon and three in the evening? Oedipus (*q.v.*) answered correctly that it was man who first crawls, then walks upright and finally uses a stick in old age. The sphinx then leapt from her rock and was dashed to pieces.

Stentor. Greek herald in the Trojan war who supposedly had a voice equal to that of fifty men. He died after Hermes (*q.v.*) beat him in a shouting match. His name gives us the word "stentorian' meaning extremely loud.

Steropes. One of the Cyclopes (*q.v.*).

Stheneboea. Another name for Anteia. *See* **Bellerophon.**

Sthenelus. (1) A king of Mycenae, the son of Perseus (*q.v.*) and Andromeda (*q.v.*). The husband of Nicippe by whom he was the father of Alcinoe, Medusa (*q.v.*) and Eursytheus (*q.v.*).

(2) The son of Capaneus and Evadne, a companion of Diomedes (*q.v.*) and one of the Epigoni (*q.v.*). One of the Greeks in the Wooden Horse (*q.v.*).

(3) A Trojan and companion of Aeneas (*q.v.*).

Stheno. One of the Gorgones (*q.v.*).

Strymon. River in Thrace, believed by the Greeks to be the home of the crane.

Stymphalian Birds. Monsters inhabiting Lake Stymphalus, a marshy area in northern Arcadia. They were huge birds with bronze beaks and claws that ate human flesh. They used their feathers as arrows. The birds were sacred to Ares (*q.v.*) but Heracles (*q.v.*) startled them with bronze castanets provided by Athene (*q.v.*) and shot them. Some say they flew to the Black Sea and were found there by the Argonauts (*q.v.*).

Styx. The river of "hate" in the Underworld and flowing several times around its perimeter. When dipped in it Achilles (*q.v.*) was made invulnerable. Ghosts could only cross it if they paid Charon (*q.v.*) to ferry them across and for this purpose a coin was placed beneath the tongue of corpses. On its far bank was Cerberus (*q.v.*). Aristophanes (*q.v.*) and others describe it as a marsh rather than a river though Herodotus (*q.v.*) identifies it with a trickle from the rock near Pheneus. Generally it was associated with the cascade on Mt. Chelmos further west whose cold waters stain the rock black. Plutarch and Arrian say Alexander the Great was poisoned by water from here brought to him in a mule's hoof.

Sul or **Sulis.** A Celtic deity identified with Minerva (*q.v.*) by the Romans. The patron of Aquae Sulis.

Symplegades. Floating islands, like icebergs, at the entrance to the Bosphorus. They clashed together and crushed ships. Jason (*q.v.*), on the advice of Phineus, let loose a dove which made them recoil and as they did so the Argo (*q.v.*) slipped between them. Henceforth they remained stationary.

Syrinx. An Arcadian nymph. *See* **Pan.**

T

Talaus. The father of Adrastus (*q.v.*).

Talos. (1) A mythical brazen giant with a bull's head said to protect Crete.

(2) *See* **Daedalus.** Another name for Perdix.

Tantalus. A wealthy king, the son of Zeus (*q.v.*) and the nymph Pluto. The father of Pelops, Broteas and Niobe. He was favoured by Zeus and was invited to Olympian banquets but stole nectar (*q.v.*) and ambrosia (*q.v.*) and revealed Zeus' secrets. He received the golden dog made by Hephaestus (*q.v.*) for Rhea (*q.v.*) (which had watched Zeus' cradle) from Pandareus. This incensed the gods but Tantalus denied having seen it. Pandareus was then put to a miserable death and his daughters were abducted by the Harpies (*q.v.*). His numerous other crimes included serving Pelops (*q.v.*) as a meal to the gods.

For this he was punished in the Underworld, either by being placed beneath a huge rock which constantly threatened to fall and crush him or by being placed in a lake the waters of which receded whenever he tried to drink, while above his head were boughs of fruit "tantalisingly" behind his reach.

Tarchon. Legendary ancestor of the Etruscan "Tarquins" who lead a group of emigrants from Lydia to Italy and there founded Tarquinii and other Etruscan cities. He became an ally of Aeneas (*q.v.*).

Tarpeia. The daughter of Tarpeius, commander of the Roman garrison on the Capitol during the Sabine (*q.v.*) wars shortly after Rome's foundation. Her story is told by Livy. She treacherously offered to show the way into the citadel if the Sabine chief Tatius would give her that which his men "wore on their shield arms". By this she meant gold torques but instead the Sabines crushed her to death with their shields. The tale is an attempt to account for the name of the Tarpeian Rock (*q.v.*).

Tarpeian Rock. A precipice on the south-west corner of the Capitol from which traitors and other condemned criminals were thrown to their death. The last victim was an equestrian implicated in a conspiracy against Claudius in 43 A.D.

Tartarus. (1) Another name for Hades (*q.v.*) though in Homer it refers to the deepest reaches of the Underworld, a place of punishment to which the Titans (*q.v.*) and Centimani (*q.v.*) were consigned by Cronus (*q.v.*).

(2) Also the name of a son of Ge (*q.v.*) who was father, by his mother, of the monster Typhon (*q.v.*).

Teiresias or **Tiresias.** A blind Theban prophet, who, while young, had come upon Athene (*q.v.*) bathing in the nude. She had therefore blinded him but in compensation gave him the gift of prophecy. He revealed to Oedipus (*q.v.*) the truth of his incest. He helped Thebes against the Seven (*q.v.*) then died after drinking from the well of Tilphussa.

Odysseus (*q.v.*) consulted his shade in the land of the Cimmerians.

Telamon. The son of Aeacus and brother of Peleus (*q.v.*). After the two murdered their half-brother Phocus, his father expelled him to Salamis where he married Glauce and later succeeded her father as king. Next he married Periboea of Athens and she bore him Ajax (*q.v.*). A friend of Heracles (*q.v.*) and with him sacked Troy (*q.v.*). He carried off Hesione who bore him Teucer and his refusal to return her to her brother Priam (*q.v.*) was one cause of the Trojan war.

Telchines. Mythical beings, artists in metal work who made a sickle for Cronus (*q.v.*) and the trident for Poseidon (*q.v.*). They raised the infant Poseidon. At times they were destructive and interfered with the weather. They annoyed Zeus (*q.v.*) who drowned a number of them in a flood, and Apollo (*q.v.*) who took the form of a wolf to savage them.

Telemachus. *See* **Odysseus.**

Telephassa. The mother of Europa (*q.v.*) and Cadmus (*q.v.*) by Agenor.

Telephus. The son of Heracles (*q.v.*) and Auge (a priestess and daughter of Aleus, king of Tegea). Abandoned as a child, the Delphic oracle later directed him to the court of king Teuthras in Mysia where he found his mother married to Teuthras. He later succeeded Teuthras and married Laodice, daughter of Priam (*q.v.*). When the Greeks on their way to Troy (*q.v.*) landed in Mysia he repulsed them, but Dionysus (*q.v.*) caused him to trip on a vine and Achilles (*q.v.*) wounded him. An oracle told him he could only be cured by the one who wounded him while the Greeks were told they could not take Troy without his help. He therefore went to Achilles who cured the wound with rust from his spear and in return Telephus showed the Greeks the route to Troy.

Tempe. A vale in Thessaly where Apollo (*q.v.*) pursued Daphne (*q.v.*) and was purified of the killing of Python.

Tenedos. Small island off the coast of Asia Minor, south west of Troy (*q.v.*). Here Achilles (*q.v.*) slew king Tenes (*q.v.*) and his father Cyncus and here Philoctetes (*q.v.*) was wounded.

Tenes. The son of Apollo (*q.v.*) though reputed to be son of Cycnus, king of Colonae in Troas. His stepmother attempted to seduce him and, when he refused her, made false accusations against him. Cycnus then put Tenes and his sister Hemithea into a chest and cast it adrift at sea. It washed up on the isle of Leucophrys where Tenes became king and gave his name to the island, Tenedos (*q.v.*).

Tereus. *See* **Procne.**

Terpsichore. The muse of song and choral dance, portrayed with a lyre and plectrum.

Teucer. (1) The son of Scamander (*q.v.*) and the nymph Idaca. He gave the land to Dardanus (*q.v.*) on which Dardanus built Dardania. An ancestor of the Trojans.

(2) The son of Hesione and Telamon, half brother of Ajax (*q.v.*) behind whose shield he fought at Troy (*q.v.*).

Teucri. Name for the Trojans derived from that of their ancestor Teucer (*q.v.*).

Teuthras. *See* **Telephus.** The father of the girl Tecmessa. Ajax (*q.v.*) raided the Thracian Chersonese, slew him and abducted Tecmessa.

Tethys. A Titaness, mother of Oceanus (*q.v.*) of Metis.

Thalia. (1) Muse of comedy.

(2) One of the Charities (*q.v.*).

Thebe. The wife of Zethus, who gave her name to Thebes.

Themis. A Titaness, the daughter of Ge (*q.v.*) and Uranus (*q.v.*) and sister of Cronus (*q.v.*). The wife of Zeus (*q.v.*) before Hera (*q.v.*), she bore him the Horae (*q.v.*) and Moerae (*q.v.*). She determined religious rites, instituted laws and was the first to distinguish between that which was permitted and that which offended the divine order. Hence she became the personification of justice and represented the incarnation of divine law.

Therseander. *See* **Epigoni.**

Theocritus. *See* **Section B.**

Thersites. A low-minded, ugly and mean spirited wretch amongst the Greek forces at Troy (*q.v.*). He accused Agamemnon (*q.v.*) of prolonging the war to serve his own interest until Odysseus (*q.v.*) beat him into silence.

Theseus. The son of Aethra, a princess of Troezen, by Aegeus (*q.v.*) though one tradition says Poseidon (*q.v.*) fathered him in the form of a bull.

Aegeus left her after seducing her but showed her a rock under which he had hidden his sword and sandals. Theseus was raised secretly by his mother at her father's court, and when he reached adolescence lifted the rock to claim Aegeus' sword and sandals. With these he set off for Athens and on the way had many adventures, slaying the wild sow of Crommyum, Sciron (q.v.), Periphetes (q.v.), Cercyon and Procrustes (q.v.). Arriving at Athens Aegeus recognised the sword and sandals and accepted him as his son despite the plots of Medea.

Theseus then scattered the Pallantides, fifty nephews of Aegeus and the sons of Pallas who hoped to claim the throne themselves. Next he captured the Cretan Bull (q.v.). But his greatest task was to go voluntarily to Crete to slay the Minotaur (q.v.). As one of the tribute demanded by Minos (q.v.) he was to be sacrificed to the monster but Minos' daughter Ariadne fell in love with him and gave him a sword with which to slay the beast and a thread by which he could retrace his steps through the massive labyrinth in which it lived. The couple then fled to Naxos where he left Ariadne and where she was loved by Dionysus (q.v.) whose sacred island it was. Aegeus tragically killed himself on Theseus' return and the hero then became king of Athens. Either alone or with Heracles (q.v.) he invaded the land of the Amazons and carried off either Antiope or Hippolyte. The Amazons attacked Athens but Theseus defeated them in the middle of Athens. By the Amazon queen he became father of Hippolytus (q.v.). Later he married Phaedra and was father by her of Acamas and Demophon (q.v.). A close friend of Pirithous (q.v.), the two shared many adventures. Eventually he returned again to Athens but was ousted by Menestheus and retired to Scyros where, for some reason he was murdered by Lycomedes.

Unlike Heracles, Theseus was not worshipped throughout the Hellenistic world but was very much an Athenian hero and his reputed bones were brought to the city from Scyros in historical times. He is said to have gathered the villages of Attica into one state by the process of synoecismus.

Thetis. A Nereid (q.v.) who was raised by Hera (q.v.) and remained attached to her. Zeus (q.v.) and Poseidon (q.v.) desired her but it was foretold that her son would be greater than his father. She was thus forced to marry a mortal, Peleus (q.v.), but only after she had tried to avoid him by changing her shape, becoming various animals including a lion. Their wedding on Mt. Pelion was attended by all the gods save Eris (q.v.). They had a number of children who were killed when Thetis tried to make them immortal by throwing them into the fire. Peleus snatched their seventh child, Achilles (q.v.), from her as she tried yet again. Instead she dipped him in the Styx (q.v.). Angry at not giving birth to an immortal she left Peleus to live with her sister Neireids. She cared for Hephaestus (q.v.) when Zeus threw him into the sea, and for Dionysus (q.v.) though she and Briareus (q.v.) freed Zeus when the other gods enchained him.

Thoas. The son of Andraemon king of Calydon who took forty ships to Troy (q.v.) and was one of the Greeks in the Wooden Horse (q.v.).

Thyades. See **Thyia**.

Thyestes. The son of Pelops (q.v.) and Hippodamia and brother of Atreus, ancestor of the illustrious Atridae family. He and Atreus murdered their half-brother Chrysippus and fled to Mycenae. Here Atreus seized the kingdom and banished Thyestes. Thyestes had seduced Atreus' second wife Aerope and he now tricked Atreus into killing Pleisthenes, his son by his first wife. In revenge Atreus lured Thyestes to Mycenae, slew his three sons and served them to him. Thyestes unknowingly ate them. Not surprisingly he cursed the house of Atreus on learning the truth. The Delphic oracle told Thyestes he could get revenge by fathering a son on his own daughter Pelopia, a priestess at the court of Threspotus of Sicyon. He raped her and Atreus later married her, believing her to be the daughter of Threspotus. He raised Thyestes' son Aegisthus as his own.

Thyia. The first woman to worship and sacrifice to Dionysus (q.v.). She gave her name to the Attic women who participated in the orgies of Dionysus at Parnassus, the Thyiades. These women were also called Thyades, "raging women", a similar name but of different origin.

Thyone. See **Semele**.

Thyrsus. A wand carried by the Maenads, covered with ivy wreaths and surmounted by a fir cone.

Tiryns. City reputedly founded by Proetus (q.v.) and built with the help of the Cyclopes (q.v.). The actual site is a mound 300 yd long on the Gulf of Argolis. It was first inhabited in the 3rd millennium B.C. and held a chief's residence and town. Around 1600 B.C. a larger palace was built and ramparts constructed. In the 14th and 13th centuries the rampart was rebuilt and enlarged. Its impressive ruins remain.

Tisiphone. One of the Eumenides (q.v.).

Titanesses. Sisters of the Titans (q.v.), daughters of Ge (q.v.) and Uranus (q.v.). Their numbers included Rhea (q.v.), Themis (q.v.), Tethys and Mnemosyne.

Titanomachia. The ten-year war, waged in Thessaly by Zeus (q.v.) and the Olympian gods against Cronos (q.v.) and the Titans (q.v.) led by Atlas (q.v.). Ge (q.v.) promised Zeus (who had usurped his Titan father Cronos) victory if he would free the Cyclopes (q.v.) and Hecatoncheires (q.v.) from Tartarus (q.v.). He did and the Cyclopes gave him the thunderbolt, Hades (q.v.) a helmet which conferred invisibility and Poseidon a trident. The three overcame Cronos and the Hecatoncheires stoned the other Titans who were defeated and consigned either to Tartarus or an island far to the west. Here the Hecatoncheires guarded them. Atlas was made to carry the sky as punishment but the Titanesses (q.v.) were spared. The war is the basis of Keats' Hyperion.

Titans. The sons of Ge (q.v.) and Uranus (q.v.). There were twelve of them though the lists given of their names are inconsistent. The most often named are Cronus (q.v.), Oceanus (q.v.), Hyperion, Iapetus and Atlas (q.v.). Brothers of the Titanesses (q.v.). When Uranus consigned the Cyclopes (q.v.) to Tartarus (q.v.) Ge persuaded Cronos and his brother Titans to depose Uranus. The Titans were in turn deposed in the Titanomachia (q.v.).

Tithonus. The son of Laomedon and Strymor and a half-brother of Priam (q.v.). By Eos (q.v.) the father of Memnon (q.v.). Eos begged Zeus (q.v.) to make him immortal, which he did, but forgot to ask for perpetual youth. Tithonus grew older and older until Eos tired of looking on him, turned him into a cicada and locked him in a cage.

Tities. One of the three primitive tribes of Rome.

Tityus. A giant son of Ge (q.v.) sent by Hera (q.v.) to violate Leto (q.v.) but Artemis (q.v.) and Apollo (q.v.) slew him with their arrows. In Hades (q.v.) he was pegged to the ground (he covered nine acres) while two vultures picked at his liver.

Tleopolemus. A son of Heracles (q.v.) who settled in Argos and later Rhodes.

Triptolemus. See **Demeter**.

Triton. The son of Poseidon (q.v.) and Amphitrite (q.v.) though sometimes several tritons are spoken of. He was a merman, his upper body being human, the lower fish. He blew a shell-trumpet, the concha, to calm the waves and Ovid tells us that he blew the concha to order the waters to recede after the Flood. (See **Deucalion**).

Troilus. A young son of Priam (q.v.) slain by Achilles (q.v.). His romance with Cressida is a medieval invention.

Trojan War. The ten-year siege of Troy (q.v.) and its eventual sack by Greek forces under Agamemnon (q.v.). The combined forces sought to restore Helen (q.v.) to Menelaus (q.v.). The story of the war is told in Homer's Iliad where Achilles (q.v.) is the major hero of the Greeks and Hector (q.v.) of the Trojans. According to Homer the war was ended by the Wooden Horse (q.v.) concocted by Odysseus (q.v.). The war is usually placed by tradition as occurring in the 12th century B.C. The war is not a purely mythical episode. Archaeological evidence from the site of Troy shows that the city occupying the seventh stratigraphical layer was destroyed by fire, though probably in the 14th century B.C. Archaeology also confirms the Iliad's description of the main towns in Trojan civilisation together with its picture of the Greek people and army.

Trophonius and **Agamedes.** Sons of Erginus who built a temple for Apollo (q.v.) at Delphi. They were rewarded by living merrily for six days and dying in their sleep on the seventh. Trophonius later had an oracle of his own at Lebadeia in Boeotia. Here, according to Pausanias, the questioner underwent a complex initiation, was dressed as a sacrificial victim and (carrying a honey-cake to placate the Underworld divinities) descended into a pot-hole. An underground stream swept him along some distance before he was returned to the light having heard invisible speakers in the cavern. Not surprisingly the questioner would look dazed and dejected and it became common to speak of a gloomy person as one who had been consulting Trophonius.

Tros. (1) The grandson of Dardanus (*q.v.*) and father of Ilus (*q.v.*) and Ganymede (*q.v.*). An ancestor of the Trojans, he gave his name to Troy (*q.v.*).

(2) A small town absorbed by the city of Troy (*q.v.*).

Troy. Also called Ilium, a city of Asia Minor near the sea not far from the straits of the Dardanelles. From its position the inhabitants could watch the sea traffic between the Aegean and Sea of Marmara. Many traders off-loaded cargo and used the land route to bypass the dangerous straits. Hence in the late 3rd millennium B.C. Troy became very prosperous from trade, a prosperity which returned at various periods in the 2nd millennium. In 1870 the German Heinrich Schliemann, an amateur archaeologist, sought the site near modern Hissarlik in Turkey. He found it and later excavations have distinguished nine strata of occupations, the richest dating from 2200 B.C. and the 7th showing signs of destruction by fire (*See* **Trojan War**). From the 14th century B.C. the site was of little importance until the Roman occupation when, as Ilium Nevum, it played a large part in provincial life. Homer's Troy had probably absorbed three neighbouring towns, Tros (*q.v.*), Dardania and Ilium and the names of three tribes, Ilians, Trojans and Dardanians are represented in the myths of its foundation.

Tyche or **Tuche.** The Roman "Fortuna", and always more popular in Rome. A daughter of Zeus (*q.v.*) and the goddess of luck who bestowed or denied gifts to men according to her whims. She often accompanied Pluto (*q.v.*). She is portrayed juggling a ball, symbolising the instability of fate, or with a rudder to guide men's affairs.

Tydeus. Son of Oeneus and Calydon, husband of Deipyle. After committing a murder in his youth he fled to the court of Adrastus (*q.v.*). *See* **Seven Against Thebes.**

Tyndareus. The brother of Hippocoon who deposed him as king of Sparta, but Heracles (*q.v.*) reinstated him. Helen (*q.v.*) was brought up at his court (she was his wife Leda's (*q.v.*) child by Zeus (*q.v.*)). Helen married Menelaus (*q.v.*) who succeeded Tyndareus. Tyndareus had had all the Greek nobles who sought Helen's hand swear an oath to defend her chosen husband. This was the reason why the Greeks allied in support of Menelaus in the Trojan War (*q.v.*). Tyndareus also helped Agamemnon (*q.v.*) expel Thyestes (*q.v.*) and regain his throne.

Typhon. The monstrous offspring of Ge (*q.v.*) and Tartarus (*q.v.*), whose eyes could expel fire and whose limbs ended in snakes' heads. He attacked Olympus and the gods fled to Egypt disguised as animals, Zeus (*q.v.*) as a ram, Apollo (*q.v.*) as a cow, Dionysus (*q.v.*) as a goat, Hera (*q.v.*) as a white cow, Artemis (*q.v.*) as a cat, Aphrodite (*q.v.*) as a fish, Ares (*q.v.*) as a boar and Hermes (*q.v.*) as an ibis. Athene (*q.v.*) did not flee and persuaded Zeus to fight. In a great struggle Zeus was saved by Hermes and Pan (*q.v.*) and then defeated Typhon with his thunderbolts. He was then buried under Mt. Etna. By Echidne (*q.v.*) Typhon was father of a variety of monsters.

Tyro. A nymph, mother of Pelias (*q.v.*) and Neleus (*q.v.*) by Zeus (*q.v.*) and of Aeson by Cretheus. The grandmother of Jason (*q.v.*).

U

Udaeus. One of the Spartii (*q.v.*).

Ulysses. The Roman name for Odysseus (*q.v.*).

Urania. The Muse of Astronomy.

Uranus. The Sky, offspring of Ge (*q.v.*) the earth and brother of Pontus, the sea. The father by Ge of the Hecatoncheires (*q.v.*), the Cyclopes (*q.v.*) and the Titans (*q.v.*). He threw the rebellious Cyclopes into Tartarus (*q.v.*). Ge then persuaded the Titans to rise against their father and avenge their brothers. She gave Cronos (*q.v.*) a flint sickle with which he castrated Uranus. The blood of Uranus which fell to earth produced the Erinyes and the blood which fell into the sea produced Aphrodite (*q.v.*). Uranus was deposed but cursed Cronos that his own children depose him.

V

Venus. Originally an Italian deity whose name meant "beauty" or "charm", she was a goddess of vegetable rather than animal fertility. She became identified with Aphrodite (*q.v.*) by way of Aphrodite's cult at Mt. Eryx in Sicily, said to have been founded by Aeneas (*q.v.*) on the death of Anchises (*q.v.*). In 217 B.C. Venus Erycina was given a temple at Rome and became completely associated with Aphrodite taking on her functions and attributes. She was patron goddess of Sulla and Pompey. In the imperial cult she played a very important role as the Julian family claimed descent from Aeneas and therefore Aphrodite. In this context she was Venus Genetrix, creator of all things, the universal mother and life giver.

Vesta. A primitive Roman goddess of the hearth, the counterpart of Hestia (*q.v.*). She was worshipped in each Roman house and officially in a circular temple in the Forum. The temple held a fire, said to have come from Troy (*q.v.*) which could never be allowed to go out. It was tended by the Vestal Virgins (*q.v.*). Her cult was purely Italian and never spread to the provinces.

Vestal Virgins. A college of priestesses of the cult of Vesta (*q.v.*). There were originally four of them, later six and finally seven. Candidates for the college were chosen at between six and ten years of age; both their parents had to be alive and they underwent a prolonged special training. They served for thirty years under the control of the Pontifex Maximus and during all this period had to remain virgins. The punishment for unchastity was burial alive. However they were highly honoured and had great privileges. For instance they could save from execution any criminal they met on the way to his death. They lived in a large residence near the temple of Vesta.

The sacred fire of Vesta was tended by Vestal Virgins up to the 4th century A.D.

Victoria. The Roman goddess of victory, corresponding to the Greek *Nike* (*q.v.*).

Virgil. *See* **Section B.**

Vulcan. The Roman god of fire, identified with Hephaestus (*q.v.*) and sometimes called Mulciber, "the smelter". His name gives us the word "volcano".

W

Wooden Horse of Troy. The "Trojan Horse", a stratagem devised by Odysseus (*q.v.*) which ended the Trojan War (*q.v.*). The Greeks had Epeius, son of Panopeus, build a large wooden horse. Athene (*q.v.*) helped him and it bore an inscription dedicated to her. Then twenty-three or more Greeks including Odysseus, Neoptolemus (*q.v.*), Sthenelus and Thoas hid inside it. The rest of the Greek force then burnt their camp and put to sea leaving only the wily Sinon (*q.v.*) to trick the Trojans into dragging the horse into Troy. (*See also* **Laocöon**).

Inside the city Helen patted the horse and called out the names of those she suspected were inside it, but she was accompanied by the Trojan prince Deiphobus and Odysseus stopped the Greeks answering. At night the Greek fleet returned, Sinon let the men out of the horse, the gates of Troy were opened and the city was sacked.

X

Xenophon. *See* **Section B.**

Xuthus. The son of Hellen and husband of Creusa, the daughter of Erectheus, king of Athens. By her the father of Achaeus and Ion. On the death of

Erectheus Xuthus was asked to determine which of the king's sons should succeed him. He chose Cecrops and was expelled to Achaia by the other heirs. Euripides (q.v.) makes Ion the son of Apollo (q.v.) and Creusa.

Z

Zagreus. A son of Zeus (q.v.). He was torn apart and eaten by Titans (q.v.) except for his heart which Athene (q.v.) saved. He is sometimes identified with Dionysus (q.v.).

Zephyrus. The son of Astraeus and Eus. He was the west wind, originally imagined, like all winds, in the form of a horse. The father of Xanthus and Balius, the talking horses of Achilles (q.v.) which Poseidon (q.v.) had given to Peleus (q.v.) as a wedding gift. The husband of Iris (q.v.). He deflected the discus which killed Hyacinthus (q.v.). His Roman counterpart was Favonius.

Zetes. See Calais.

Zethus. See Amphion.

Zeus. The son of Cronos (q.v.) and Rhea (q.v.). He deposed his father and defeated the Titans (q.v.). Then he and his brothers Hades (q.v.) and Poseidon (q.v.) cast lots for their kingdoms and Zeus won the sky. The earth was common to all. Zeus was the king of the gods and was identified with Jupiter by the Romans. He was the father of men. In early legend his consort is Dione, but his consort on Mt. Olympus (q.v.) is the jealous Hera (q.v.). He first married Hetis who bore him Athene (q.v.) and his second wife was Themis (q.v.) who bore him the Horae and Maerae. Hera bore him Ares (q.v.), Hebe (q.v.) and Hephaestus (q.v.). His sister Demeter (q.v.) bore him Persephone (q.v.) and Eurynome bore him the Charities (q.v.) while by Mnemosyne he was father of the Muses (q.v.). By mortal women he was father of Hermes (q.v.), Apollo (q.v.) and Artemis (q.v.) and Dionysus (q.v.). Given the thunderbolt by the Cyclopes (q.v.) he was known as the thunderer.

SPECIAL TOPIC

NORSE MYTHOLOGY

Introduction.

The Norse myths have never enjoyed in Britain the same cultural esteem and popularity as the myths of Greece and Rome. At best they have been deemed inferior, more normally they have been simply ignored. The celebrated nineteenth-century designer, William Morris, is perhaps the only well-known Briton to have taken them with real seriousness.

There are a number of possible causes of this neglect. We know very little, for example, about the associated religious observances and rites, which would have given them meaning to the individual. They may never even have truly developed. Julius Caesar, writing of the Germanic peoples as a whole more than one thousand years before Scandinavia was converted to Christianity, observed that they had no priests comparable to the Celtic druids and had little interest in ritual. He believed that they found religious significance rather in the depths of the forests.

Their Relative Inaccessibility.

Moreover, the Norse myths have never exercised the direct influence on art and literature that their classical counterparts have done. This may be explained to no small degree by their inaccessibility until comparatively recent times. The myths of the Germanic peoples—encompassing the Anglo-Saxons, the Germans, and the Scandinavians or Vikings—remained a living tradition longest in Viking Iceland which was one of the last places in Europe to be converted to Christianity. We owe their preservation to a Christian priest, Saemund, who wrote down the Elder Edda, in which the oral traditions were collected, and to Snorri Sturluson who at the beginning of the thirteenth century wrote a guide to the myths for poets. Both wrote in Old Icelandic, hence our designation of the myths as specifically Norse myths. The Icelandic language, however, was virtually unknown outside its remote homeland until the end of the eighteenth century.

The Case of Beowulf.

Mention must also be made of the Anglo-Saxon epic poem Beowulf. It necessarily stands somewhat apart by virtue of the seventh-century date of its composition and its preservation in a language other than Icelandic, but there are numerous cross-references in it to specifically Norse mythology.

Norse Myths and our Ancestors.

Such causes, though, do not make the neglect of the myths any less regrettable, for a wide range of reasons. One of the most important is that although they were preserved specifically as the myths of the early Scandinavians, most familiar to us as the feared Vikings of the tenth and eleventh centuries, they were common, with variations over time and from place to place, to the early Germanic peoples as a whole, including the Anglo-Saxons, the direct ancestors of the modern English. They are thus the best reflection we have of the thought-world of our earliest ancestors. It is a thought-world which has literally left its mark. If the global worship of the sun and moon has given us Sunday and Monday, then the father of the gods, Odin, in his Anglo-Saxon form of Woden, has given us Wednesday, his son Thor has given us Thursday, and his wife Freya has given us Friday. Tuesday takes its name from the goddess Tiwe, only known from Anglo-Saxon sources. Freya has also bequeathed the German *Frau* and Swedish *Fru*, both meaning "Mrs."

Place Names and Norse Mythology.

English place names similarly preserve this mythological heritage. Wednesbury and Wednesfield, both in the West Midlands, preserve the name of Woden; Thoresby, Thoresway and Thorganby, all in Lincolnshire, and Thorlby and Thormanby in North Yorkshire, preserve the name of Thor through the personal name of the original Viking settler. They remind us similarly, as does the prevalence of the Scandinavian ending "by", meaning village, of the very extensive settlement by the Vikings of the eastern counties. Thundersley in Essex not only preserves the name of Thor in its Anglo-Saxon form of Thunor but vividly recalls the thunder which he created through the crash of his hammer on his anvil.

Not least, Odin or Woden had the alternative name of "Grim" and the prehistoric earthworks across England known as Grimsditch or Grimsdyke and Grimes Graves record the readiness of the early Anglo-Saxon settlers to attribute anything marvellous to the greatest of their gods.

The Bleak Norse World.

This geographical legacy gives an invaluable insight into the establishment of the English nation we know today, but the myths live on much more significantly in the essentially subconscious psychological continuities. Their world was a bleak one, overshadowed by a sense of doom and foreboding and the threat of Ragnarok, Wagner's *Götterdämmerung*, the twilight of the gods. The image of Hel, the ruler of the underworld, who was semi-decomposed with the face and trunk of a living woman but the legs and thighs of a dead one, conveys some of its grimness. We have inherited such words as hell and grim for good reason—some might even prefer the Christian tradition of the fiery furnace!

The Divine Actors.

The myths were complex although, at least by the time they were written down, coherent. The main protagonists are set out later in the Glossary.

The Psychological Heritage.

One can see the psychological continuity of this bleak world, full of doom and foreboding, in the black humour which comes so naturally to the English but is so alien, for example, to the French, and the thread of the sombre and the macabre which permeates so much Germanic literature, whether it be Shakespeare, the German Romantics, or such Scandinavian dramatists as Ibsen and, particularly, Strindberg.

Rather remarkably, 80 % of Icelanders allegedly still believe in the existence of elves, and roads have been rerouted to avoid them. Other manifestations of the enduring mind-set of the myths may be more controversial. Parallels have been drawn between the impending catastrophe of Ragnarok and the medieval German obsession with the Last Judgement, which was a major inspiration of the greatest German painting, Matthias Grünewald's Issenheim altarpiece, now preserved in the Alsatian city of Colmar.

It is also certainly the case that modern European environmentalism owes much to the Germanic sense of the religious significance of the forest noted by Caesar. The German Green Party became a political party of lasting significance in response to growing national alarm at the death of German forests as a consequence of sulphur pollution.

A Greatness of Soul.

The myths of the north may have been bleak but they were never ignoble. The nineteenth-century English writer, Thomas Carlyle, maintained that they "have a truth in them, an inward perennial truth and greatness. It is a greatness not of mere body and gigantic bulk, but a rude greatness of soul." Perhaps its finest expression in English is in the Anglo-Saxon poem "The Battle of Maldon", commemorating, slightly ironically, the defeat of the now Christianised Anglo-Saxons at the hands of the Vikings, when the Anglo-Saxon warrior exhorts his comrades: "Thought shall be the harder, heart the keener, courage the greater, as our might lessens." A similar spirit has even been seen in the ferocious German resistance in the Second World War, continuing long after the War was clearly lost.

A Source of Inspiration Missed?

A rather different reason to regret the neglect of the Norse myths is suggested by comparing a hope expressed by William Morris with the reality of Wagner's triumph in composing his operatic masterpiece *Der Ring der Nibelungen*, or simply "The Ring". Morris maintained: "This is the great story of the North, which should be to all our race what the Tale of Troy was to the Greeks—to all our race . . . when the change of the world has made our race nothing more than a name of what has been—a story too—then should it be to those that come after us no less than the Tale of Troy has been to us." Such a hope has an unfashionable sound at the beginning of the twenty-first century but even the most superficial acquaintance with Richard Wagner's operatic cycle, widely valued as one of the world's greatest cultural achievements, gives rise to a suspicion that a great source of inspiration has been missed by so many others. The suspicion is not diminished by a consciousness of the limited relevance of so much classical imagery to northern climes. The inspiration there has been, as in the novels of J.R.R. Tolkien, is at most tangential.

Wagner and Norse Mythology.

Wagner drew on some specifically German legends, but the proceedings are dominated by Wotan (Odin or Woden), the father of the gods, Freya, his wife, and Brünnhilde, his daughter. Wagner uses the myths for his own purposes, but in so doing he reminds us, as have the countless writers and artists who have reinterpreted the classical myths, that myths are more than legends. Legends are usually rooted in historical fact, however distorted by time. Myths, however, are an attempt to understand the human condition and, as such, exist outside time. Wagner's Wotan is the quintessential father—stern but caring. Freya is the quintessential jealous wife, hurt and outraged by her husband's compulsive pursuit of the latest pretty face glimpsed on earth. Brünnhilde is the eternal disobedient daughter. Age is permanently threatened by the youth which will supplant it.

Moreover the Norse myths provided Wagner with a vision which the classical myths had apparently lost: a vision in which the gods themselves would come to an end. *Götterdämmerung*, the Twilight of the Gods, the last of the Ring cycle, sees decay of the earth and the heavens in which the gods perish as surely as the world beneath.

The Sense of Divine Impotence.

The vision is as powerful as that of Dante's Divine Comedy, although obviously the reverse of Christian, but the concept of the ultimate impotence of the gods is found likewise at the opposite end of the Indo-European world, in Hindu India. There is a celebrated passage in the Rig-Veda, a sacred Sanskrit text dating from 1500–900 B.C., on the subject of creation, which concludes:

Only he who is overseer in highest heaven knows,
He only knows, or perhaps he does not know!

Parallels with Classical Mythology.

This sense of divine ignorance or impotence, which contrasts so strongly with the omnipotent deity of Judaism, Christianity and Islam, underlines another reason for valuing the Norse myths. The gods of the Germanic world, of the classical world and of India were all intimately related, and originally the same. Thor is paralleled by the Latin Vulcan, Freya by the Latin Venus and Greek Aphrodite, all voluptuous goddesses of love. Where those of Europe diverged from those of India was in making one god, in practice a "father god", the ruler of the rest, call him Zeus, Jupiter or Odin-Woden.

The Norse myths open a window not just on the thought-world of our own Germanic ancestors, but also on that of their ancestors across Europe, Iran and India whom we can otherwise approach only through archaeology.

An Untapped Potential?

Norse mythology and religion, moreover, were not static, and one last reason for valuing them is the light they throw on European man's deepest psychological needs in the absence of Christianity. One of the more unpredictable developments was a growing belief that Ragnarok would not mark the total end of the world and the gods and their submission to Jormungand, the immense world serpent, but that a fair, green new world would arise out of the water, and that several of the gods would survive, including Baldr who would return from the dead. A second was that Thor became an increasingly personal deity and by the end of the Viking period had become a greater god than his father, Odin. The magic hammer, Mjollnir, with which he wielded destruction was also a force for fertility and resurrection.

Were these echoes of distant Christianity or was Christianity, when it arrived, itself but a further response to existing aspiration and even faith? We can never know, but the parallel myths of India were to flourish until our own time, associated with the imposing wealth of religious mysticism and philosophy which is the great creation of Hinduism. The religious potential of the north could have proved similarly unexpected.

GLOSSARY

Note: Some mythological names have come down to us from different sources and are not, therefore, spelt consistently. Moreover, the Germanic languages were highly inflected and names varied accordingly, *e.g.* Kriemhild, Kriemhilde, Kriemhilden (Gudrun). The more significant variations include Balder and Baldr; Brynhild, Brünhild, Brünnhilde and Prünhilt; Thonur and Thor; and Woden and Wotan.

Ægir. The god of the sea, sometimes known by the epithet "the ale-brewer".

Æsir. Generic name for the gods led by Odin (*q.v.*).

Alfheim. The elvish homeland. *See* **Elves.**

Andvari. Loki (*q.v.*) compelled this dwarf (*q.v.*) to surrender his hoard of gold. Andvari put a curse of death on a ring from this treasure: the curse was eventually responsible for the death of Sigurd (*q.v.*).

Angrboda. "Bearer of Grief". Loki's (*q.v.*) consort, a frost giantess and mother of Fenrir (*q.v.*), the Midgard serpent (*q.v.*) and Hel (*q.v.*).

Apples of Youth. (Golden Apples of Idunn). Magical fruit which preserved the gods' eternal youth. Under duress, Loki (*q.v.*) stole them for the giant Thjazi (*q.v.*). The Æsir (*q.v.*) promptly began to age and soon found Loki out. He was then forced to recapture the apples, which he successfully did disguised as a falcon.

Asgard. Home of the gods led by Odin (*q.v.*).

Baldr. His name means "lord". A warrior hero of celestial birth. Snorri Sturluson identified him as Odin's (*q.v.*) blond son "the shining sky-god". However, there is no evidence that Baldr was part of traditional Germanic myth. His mother the goddess Frigg (*q.v.*) ensured his invulnerability on earth by asking all terrestrial things to swear they would not hurt him. Subsequently, the Æsir (*q.v.*) tested him with spears and stones. According to Snorri, the troublemaker Loki (*q.v.*) discovered that mistletoe had not been accounted for and provided the blind god Hod (*q.v.*) with a dart made of this wood. Once shot at Baldr, the dart killed him and he descended to Hel (*q.v.*).

There is also some variation in this story with the writer Saxo Grammaticus suggesting that Hod alone was responsible for Baldr's death. The detail of the mistletoe may be a late addition, possibly a misunderstanding caused by the name of the magic sword *Mistilleinn*, with which Hod killed Baldr in Saxo's account. Baldr is sometimes seen as a Christ-like figure due to his lead role in the "resurrection" of the world after Ragnarok.

Baugi. The brother of the giant Suttung (*q.v.*). He helped Odin (*q.v.*) steal the Mead-of-Inspiration (*q.v.*) from his brother.

Bragi. The god of poetry, possibly a personified facet of Odin (*q.v.*). Married to Idunn (*q.v.*).

Brynhild. A beautiful Valkyrie (*q.v.*) released from a curse of sleep in a ring of fire by Sigurd (*q.v.*). Despite falling in love with Brynhild, Sigurd subsequently married Gudrun (*q.v.*) due to the effects of a magic drink, and then convinced his foster brother Gunnar (*q.v.*) to seek Brynhild's hand. However, Gunnar could not enter the ring of fire, so Sigurd adopted his likeness and wooed Brynhild as his brother. Brynhild became aware of the trick and vowed to revenge herself on her former lover. Pressed by Gunnar and his brother Hegni, her brother-in-law Guttorm killed Sigurd whilst he was in bed, but she was then overwhelmed with remorse and killed herself on Sigurd's funeral pyre. Her story is told in the Old Norse *Volsunga Saga* (*q.v.*) and the Germanic *Nibelungenlied* (*q.v.*), where she is called Prünhild.

Disir. The Norse goddesses.

Draupnir. Odin's (*q.v.*) gold ring. The origin of all others.

Dwarves. Swarthy elves (*q.v.*), naturally treacherous, who lived underground. Also known as trolls.

Elves. Supernatural creatures below the level of gods. There were two types of elves: swarthy ones who dwelt within the earth and brilliant ones who lived in Alfheim (*q.v.*).

Fafnir. The brother of Regin (*q.v.*), originally a man but then transformed into a dragon. At Regin's request, Sigurd (*q.v.*) killed Fafnir and ate his heart. He and Regin thus obtained the hoard of gold which the dragon guarded. The story is in the *Volsunga Saga* (*q.v.*) and the *Nibelungenlied* (*q.v.*).

Farbauti. A giant and the father of Loki (*q.v.*).

Fenrir. The wolf-son of Loki (*q.v.*) and Angrboda (*q.v.*). The gods heard that he would one day destroy the world and so attempted to tie him up. However, Fenrir repeatedly broke out of his chains and eventually the gods turned to the dwarves (*q.v.*) to make a magical fetter. Fenrir

took his chaining up as a challenge and agreed to accept the dwarves chain, but only on condition that one of the gods put their hand into his mouth in case it was a trick. Only Tyr (*q.v.*) had the courage to do so and when Fenrir found he was trapped, lost his hand, bitten off by the wolf.

Fitela. Nephew of Sigmund (*q.v.*).

Fjorgyn. A goddess of fertility and the mother of Thor (*q.v.*).

Freyja. The chief Vanir (*q.v.*) goddess, a symbol of promiscuity and fertility. Daughter of Njord (*q.v.*) and twin sister of Freyr (*q.v.*). Her most prized possession was the *Brisingamen* necklace. One of her magical powers was her ability to turn into a falcon at will. The Frost Giants (*q.v.*) made repeated attempts to win her. She married Od (*q.v.*).

Freyr. Son of Njord, twin brother of Freyja and one of the greatest of the Vanir (*q.v.*). His cult was associated with fertility and often linked with horses and boars (established fertility symbols). Freyr also had connections with the sea. He married the giantess Gerd (*q.v.*).

Frigg. Odin's (*q.v.*) wife, a fertility goddess linked with Freyja (*q.v.*), with whom she is sometimes confused. Frigg seems to have represented the maternal side of fertility, Freyja the more promiscuous. Frigg was the mother of Baldr (*q.v.*). She was said to know the fate of all men.

Frija. Wife of Woden (*q.v.*).

Frost Giants. The enemies of the Æsir (*q.v.*). Springing from the feet of the giant Ymir (*q.v.*) all the Frost Giants died when Ymir was killed by the Æsir, with the exception of Bergelmir. Bergelmir fostered a new race who lived in Iotunheim.

Garm. The hound of Hel (*q.v.*), possibly an alternative version of Fenrir (*q.v.*).

Gerd. Wife of Freyr (*q.v.*) and daughter of the giant Gymir.

Gimli. The gilded hall in Asgard (*q.v.*) to which good men went after death.

Ginnungagap. The original space between Muspellsheim (*q.v.*) and Niflheim (*q.v.*).

Gudrun. In *Volsunga Saga*, Sigurd's (*q.v.*) wife and one of the Nibelungs. On his death she married Atli. She is known as Kriemhilt in the *Nibelungenlied* (*q.v.*).

Gunnar. The foster-brother of Sigurd (*q.v.*) and husband of Brynhild (*q.v.*).

Heimdall. The guardian of Asgard (*q.v.*) and offspring of "nine giantesses". Associated with Freyja (*q.v.*) and possibly one of the Vanir (*q.v.*), he will be the herald of Ragnarok (*q.v.*). Heimdall was the enemy of Loki (*q.v.*).

Hel. The daughter of Loki and the frost goddess Angrboda. The ruler of the underworld where she was more powerful than Odin, although banished there by him.

Helgrind. The gate between the world and the underworld.

Hod. The blind god who killed Baldr (*q.v.*).

Hreidmar. The father of Fafnir (*q.v.*) and Regin (*q.v.*). by whom he was murdered.

Idunn. Goddess and guardian of the Apples of Youth (*q.v.*). Married to Bragi (*q.v.*).

Iotnar. The race of the giants, probably envisaged as types of demons or trolls.

Iotunheim. The land of the Frost-Giants (*q.v.*).

Irminsul. The central pillar of the world. *See* **Yggdrasil.**

Kvasir. After a great battle between the Æsir (*q.v.*) and the Vanir (*q.v.*), peace was made and sealed by all parties spitting into a cauldron. From this spittle the gods made Kvasir, a being of supreme wisdom. However, Kvasir was killed by two dwarves (*q.v.*) who brewed the Mead-of-Inspiration (*q.v.*) from a mixture of his blood and honey.

Loki. Part god, part demon and the son of the giant Farbauti (*q.v.*). Loki was a mischievous god of ambivalent loyalties, whose cheekiness resulted in him often being portrayed in comic terms. He was a master of disguise and shape-changing. Loki was central in the killing of Baldr (*q.v.*) and was consequently punished by the Æsir (*q.v.*) by being bound beneath the dripping jaws of a venomous snake. His writhing produces earth tremors and he will remain in agony until Ragnarok (*q.v.*). He married Sigyn (*q.v.*).

Mead-of-Inspiration. A drink-inspiring poetic eloquence and wisdom, brewed by dwarves (*q.v.*) from the blood of Kvasir (*q.v.*). Suttung (*q.v.*) took the Mead from the dwarves as compensation for the death of his father and killing of his mother. Through trickery it finally came to Odin (q.v.).

Midgard. The world of men or "middle earth". Made by the Æsir (q.v.) from the body of Ymir (q.v.).

Midgard Serpent. The world serpent, which coils around the earth and keeps it in place. Twice (inconclusively) pitted against Thor (q.v.), the two will once again face each other at Ragnarok (q.v.) when the serpent will rise from the sea and flood the earth. The Midgard serpent seems to have been generally seen as a malevolent creature.

Mimir. One of the Æsir (q.v.) and possibly a giant. Mimir was sent with Hoenir as a hostage to the Vanir (q.v.) as part of a truce package. However, the Vanir killed him by cutting off his head, which they then returned to Odin (q.v.). Odin enchanted the head and gave it powers of speech. Mimir's head could then tell hidden things and Odin regularly consulted it.

Mimir, the Spring of. A font of wisdom for all who drank from it, situated below the root of Yggdrasil (q.v.) in the land of the Frost Giants (q.v.). Odin gave up one of his eyes as the price for obtaining a drink from it. There is some confusion as to whether this Mimir is the same as the beheaded giant (q.v.). It may be that Mimir is here used as a general term for "giants".

Mjollnir. Thor's (q.v.) magic hammer, made by dwarf (q.v.) craftsmen.

Muspell. A personification of Muspellsheim (q.v.). Muspell's sons fight on the side of the fire giant Surt (q.v.) at Ragnarok (q.v.).

Muspellsheim. The southern part of the world, an area of fire and light in opposition to Niflheim (q.v.). The home of the Muspell (q.v.). Sparks from Muspellsheim melted the ice of Niflheim and created the first life, the giant Ymir (q.v.).

Nanna. The wife of Baldr (q.v.).

Nibelungenlied. The medieval German epic poem telling the story of the father and son heroes Siegmund (Norse Sigmund) and Siegfried (Sigurd). The same material is also found in the Old Norse Volsunga Saga (q.v.).

Nidhogg. A voracious dragon who steals corpses. Also the name of the snake which gnaws at one of the roots of Yggdrasil (q.v.).

Niflheim. The northern part of the world, an area of ice and darkness in opposition to Muspellsheim (q.v.). Niflheim was the kingdom of Hel (q.v.), the goddess of the dead.

Njord. God of seafaring, fishing and plenty. He married the giantess Skadi (q.v.).

Norns. The three guardians of the Well of Urd—the Spring of Fate—at the foot of Yggdrasil (q.v.). They were named Urd (past), Verdandi (present) and Skuld (future). See also **Wyrd**.

Od. The husband of Freyja (q.v.), whom he later abandoned.

Odin. The greatest of the gods and the father of the divine family. The personification of the air, the god of wisdom, and the spirit of the universe. His blue cloak flecked with grey symbolised the sky. He was also venerated as the father of the slain, the Einherjar, whom he gathered with him in Valhalla in preparation for Ragnarok, the final battle on the Vigrid Plain when nearly all would die in the struggle between the gods and the frost giants. He himself would be killed by the wolf, Fenrir, the offspring of the fire god, Loki, and the giant frost goddess, Angrboda.

He was traditionally one-eyed and was also the inspiration of the berserkers, the frenzied and fearsome warriors who fought naked and fathered the English phrase "to go berserk".

Ragnarok. The apocalyptic doom of the gods, when Fenrir (q.v.) will eat the sun and moon and a monstrous anarchy will be set loose on the world. The inhabitants of the underworld will rise, the Midgard serpent (q.v.) will rise from the sea and flood the earth, the Æsir (q.v.) will fight a final battle: Odin (q.v.) against Fenrir, Thor (q.v.) against the Midgard serpent, Freyr (q.v.) against Surt (q.v.), Tyr (q.v.) against Garm (q.v.), Heimdall (q.v.) against Loki (q.v.). Of these combatants only the fire-god Surt will survive and he will engulf the world in flames, killing everyone. However, the earth will rise again, be repopulated by those who had hidden inside Yggdrasil (q.v.), and Baldr (q.v.) will return from the dead to rule the sons of the gods.

Ran. Goddess of the sea and wife of Ægir (q.v.).

Regin. Fafnir's (q.v.) duplicitous brother. He betrayed Fafnir with Sigurd (q.v.) to obtain his hoard of gold. He also intended to trick Sigurd out of his share, but was killed by him instead.

Siegfried. See Sigurd.

Siegmund. See Sigmund.

Sif. The wife of Thor (q.v.), notable for her golden hair.

Sigmund. Germanic hero of Volsunga Saga (q.v.) and father of Sigurd (q.v.). In Beowulf (q.v.) it is he, not his son, who kills the dragon Fafnir (q.v.). He corresponds to Siegmund in the Nibelungenlied (q.v.).

Sigtyr. God of victory, a title for Odin (q.v.).

Sigurd. One of the heroes of Volsunga Saga (q.v.). The posthumous son of Sigmund (q.v.) and slayer of the dragon Fafnir (q.v.). He is known as Siegfried in the Nibelungenlied (q.v.). See also **Brynhild** and **Gudrun**.

Signy. The wife of Loki (q.v.). She attempted to catch the poison dripped over Loki as a punishment for his involvement in the death of Baldr (q.v.).

Skadi. Giantess, daughter of Thjazi (q.v.) and the wife of Njord (q.v.).

Skuld. One of the Norns (q.v.).

Sleipnir. Odin's (q.v.) great eight-legged stallion—the offspring of Loki (q.v.)—used by his son Hermod to rescue Baldr (q.v.) from Hel (q.v.).

Surt. The giant fire-god of Muspellsheim (q.v.), who will destroy the earth at Ragnarok (q.v.).

Suttung. The son of Gilling and sometime owner of the Mead-of-Inspiration (q.v.).

Thjazi. A giant who obtained the Apples of Youth (q.v.). When Loki (q.v.) recaptured them for the Æsir (q.v.), Thjazi pursued him in the form of an eagle. However, the Æsir singed his wings and easily killed him.

Thor. The son of Fjorgyn (q.v.) and the champion of the Æsir (q.v.). He wore iron gloves and wielded the terrible hammer Mjollnir (q.v.) in the defence of Asgard (q.v.). Thor was often associated with thunder and violence, being a highly irascible god; however, he also appears in a number of comic stories. He will confront the Midgard serpent (q.v.) at Ragnarok (q.v.).

Thunor. The Anglo-Saxon god of thunder, often associated with oak trees.

Tyr. A Norse god, equivalent to the Germanic Tiwaz (see Odin). The brave and wise god of war, he captured Fenrir (q.v.), but sacrificed one of his hands to secure the wolf. The boldest of the gods, according to Snorri Sturluson.

Ull. One of the Æsir (q.v.), associated with archery and skiing.

Urd. One of the Norns (q.v.).

Utgarthar-Loki. Giant and opponent of Thor (q.v.) who challenged him to a series of tests and won by means of misleading magic.

Valhalla. The great hall of battle-dead heroes presided over by Odin (q.v.). The inhabitants feast all night on pork and mead, milked from the goat Heidrun which lived on the roof of the hall.

Vali. Odin's (q.v.) son by Rind. He will survive Ragnarok (q.v.).

Valkyries. Terrible figures associated with bloody battles and death, sometimes seen as riding wolves and stalking battlefields. The Valkyries often represented Fate—their name means "Choosers of the Slain". They included Brynhild (q.v.), Hild, Hlok, Gud and Herfjotur.

Vanir. The race of Njord (q.v.), Freyr (q.v.) and Freyja (q.v.), a group of gods particularly associated with fertility. They were often in opposition to the Æsir (q.v.).

Verdandi. One of the Norns (q.v.).

Volsung. Founder of the Volsungs, the family of Sigmund (q.v.) and Sigurd (q.v.).

Volsunga Saga. Icelandic prose account of the Volsungs, including the heroes Sigmund (q.v.) and Sigurd (q.v.). Analogous with the German Nibelungenlied (q.v.).

Voluspá. Icelandic poem telling of the creation and destruction of the world.

Wayland (Weland). The Anglo-Saxon smith of the gods, known as Volund (q.v.) in Icelandic and the equivalent of the Roman Vulcan.

Woden (Wodan, Wotan). "Master of Fury", an Anglo-Saxon analogue of the Norse god Odin (q.v.). Woden was seen as the leader of sky warriors, a master of the powers of darkness and death and a god of variable favour. Also known by many other names in Norse myth.

Wyrd. The Anglo-Saxon Fate, equivalent to the

Norse Urd (*q.v.*). Wyrd was an arbitrary, inexorable and at times malevolent force presiding over all men's destinies. A key concept in Old English heroic verse.

Yggdrasil. The great ash tree, central to the world. Its tree roots went into Asgard (*q.v.*), Iotunheim (*q.v.*) and Niflheim (*q.v.*). Its boughs encompassed heaven and earth. At its foot was the Well of Urd (*q.v.*) and beneath its roots were the Spring of Mimir (*q.v.*) and Hvergelmire, the source of all rivers. After Ragnarok (*q.v.*), the new world will be created by those who had sheltered inside Yggdrasil.

Ymir. An ice giant, the result of the contact between the fire of Muspellsheim (*q.v.*) and the ice of Niflheim (*q.v.*). From Ymir came the first man and woman and the Frost Giants (*q.v.*). He was killed by the Æsir (*q.v.*).

IDEAS &
BELIEFS

This section explains many of the ideas and beliefs that dominated our history during the centuries. The arrangement is alphabetical and the subjects covered range from a world-wide spectrum of religious and philosophical terms to the major political controversies and ethical debates which have helped to shape contemporary thought.

IDEAS AND BELIEFS

This section explains many of the ideas and beliefs which people have held at different periods in history. Beliefs may be true or false, meaningful or totally meaningless, regardless of the degree of conviction with which they are held. Since man has been moved to action so often by his beliefs they are worth serious study. The section throws a vivid light on human history.

Humans have has always felt a deep need for emotional security, a sense of "belonging". This need has found expression in the framing of innumerable religious systems, nearly all of which have been concerned with man's relation to a divine ruling power. There is also to be found in man an irresistible curiosity which demands an explanation of the world in which he finds himself. This urge to make the world intelligible takes him into the realm of science where the unknown is the constant challenge. Science is a creative process, always in the making, since the scientist's conjectures are constantly being submitted to severe critical tests. Basic scientific ideas are discussed in **Section T**.

A

Abortion is the ending of the life of a foetus after conception and before birth. Is this ever morally right? After 1967 there was a liberalization of abortion laws throughout Europe, but opponents have not given up the argument, making abortion a bitter ethical issue. The Roman Catholic church in particular is strongly opposed to it. Defenders of abortion argue that an embryo is very different from us and that there is little difference between an early abortion and contraception. Opponents focus on the later stages of pregnancy. They talk of 'the unborn child' and claim that abortion is the deliberate killing of an innocent human being and in the same category as murder. So the debate is often about drawing the line as to where one becomes a human being or person. The debate is particularly acrimonious in the USA.

The 1967 Abortion Act (in the UK) legalised abortion until 28 weeks. The 1990 Human Fertilisation and Embryo Act reduced this time limit to 24 weeks. In 2015 the Irish Republic voted to legalise abortion in a referendum (but Northern Ireland still lags behind).

Activists, those in a political movement who insist on taking active steps towards their objectives rather than merely putting forward a programme. Lately activism has become an increasingly common facet of political life. This is probably because the undeniably rapid social changes which are taking place across the world at the moment are not generally being followed by appropriate shifts in political structures and ideals.

Acupuncture, a unique medical system originating in China and based on the established therapeutic effects of implanting fine gold needles in specific parts of the body. The site of needle implantation is decided according to traditional texts. The apparent lack of any logical relationship between the implantation sites and any known physiological or anatomical systems within the body once caused acupuncture to be held in low regard by Western medicine. Indeed it was certainly true that acupuncture and other similar practices tended to flourish in parts of the world where orthodox medicine has made little progress or where doctors and trained staff are scarce.

Recent years however have seen a curious and unexpected revival of interest in acupuncture in Europe and America. Chinese medicine has now used acupuncture for over 2000 years.

In Britain there is now a growing number of acupuncturists registered with the British Acupuncture Council. Increasingly the British Medical Association (BMA) is endorsing acupuncture as studies show its beneficial effects are similar to Western medicines.

Adlerian Psychology. In 1911 the Viennese psychoanalyst Alfred Adler (1870–1937) together with his colleague Carl Gustav Jung broke with their friend Sigmund Freud over disputes concerning the latter's theoretic approach to psychoanalysis. Jung and Adler were themselves shortly also to part company, each to set up and develop his own "school".

Adler's system of psychotherapy is based on the idea, not of sex as a driving force as in the case of Freud, but on the concept of "compensation" or a drive for power in an attempt to overcome the "inferioritycomplex" which he held to be universal inhuman beings. The child naturally feels inferior to adults, but bullying, making him feel insignificant or guilty or contemptible, even spoiling, which makes him feel important within the family but relatively unimportant outside, increases this feeling. Or the child may have physical defects: he may be small or underweight, have to wear glasses, become lame, be constantly ill, or stupid at school. In these ways he develops a sense of inferiority which for the rest of his life he develops a technique to overcome.

This may be done in several ways: he may try to become capable in the very respects in which he feels incompetent—hence many great orators have originally had speech defects; many painters poor eyesight; many musicians have been partially deaf; like Nietzsche, the weakling, he may write about the superman, or like Sandow, the strong man, be born with poor health.

On the other hand he may overdo his attempt and overcompensate. Hence we have the bully who is really a coward, the small man who is self-assertive to an objectionable degree (Hitler, Napoleon, Stalin, and Mussolini were all small men) or the foreigner who like three of these men wanted to be the hero of his adopted country—Hitler the Austrian, Napoleon the Italian, Stalin the Georgian.

But what about the man who can do none of these things, who continues to fail to compensate? He, says Adler, becomes a neurotic because neurosis is an excuse which means "I could have done so-and-so but . . ." It is the unconscious flight into illness—the desire to be ill. Adler's treatment involves disclosing these subterfuges we play on ourselves so that we can deal with the real situation in a more realistic way.

Adlerian psychoanalysis still attracts supporters, but its golden days were when the founder was at the head of the movement in the USA, when his views were considered to provide a more "acceptable" theory of the mind than the controversial theories of Freud with their strong sexual orientation.

Adventists, a group of American religious sects, the most familiar being the Seventh-Day Adventist Church, which observes Saturday as the true Sabbath. Today, it has more than 6 million members throughout the world. It shares with other Adventists a belief in the imminent second coming of Christ (a doctrine fairly widespread in the USA during the early decades of the 19th cent. when the end of the world was predicted by William Miller for 1843, then for 1844). Modern Adventists content themselves with the conviction that the "signs" of the Advent are multiplying, the "blessed event" which will solve the world's ills. Believers will be saved, but the sects differ as to whether the unjust will be tortured in hell, annihilated, or merely remain asleep eternally.

Agnosticism. See God and Man.

Albigenses, also known as Cathars. French heretical sect (named after the town of Albi in Provence) which appeared in the 11th cent. to challenge the Catholic Church on the way true Christians should lead their lives. They followed a life of extreme asceticism in contrast to the local clergy and their faith was adopted by the mass of the local population, especially in Toulouse. Condemned as heretics by Pope Innocent III, the sect was exterminated in the savage Albigensian Crusade (1208–29), initially led by Simon de Montfort. (In his thoroughness, de Montfort also succeeded in destroying the high culture of the Troubadours.)

Alchemy, ancient art associated with magic and astrology in which modern chemistry has its roots. The earliest mention of alchemy comes from ancient Egypt but its later practitioners attributed its origins to such varied sources as the fallen angels of the Bible, to Moses and Aaron, but most commonly to Hermes Trismegistus, often identified with the Egyptian god Thoth, whose knowledge of the divine art was handed down only to the sons of kings (*cf.* the phrase "hermetically sealed").

Its object was the transmutation of metals. Egyptian speculation over this reached its height during the 6th cent. in the Alexandrian period. Brought to Western Europe by the Muslims, one of its most famous Arab exponents was Jabir (*c.* 760–*c.* 815), known to the Latins as Geber, who had a laboratory at Kufa on the Tigris. One school of early Greek philosophy held that there was ultimately only one elemental matter of which everything was composed. Such men as Albertus Magnus (1206–80) and Roger Bacon (1214–94) assumed that, by removing impurities, this *materia prima* could be obtained. Although Bacon's ideas were ahead of his time, he firmly believed in the philosopher's stone, which could turn base metals into gold, and in an elixir of life which would give eternal youth.

Alternative Medicine includes treatments such as acupuncture (**J2**), homoeopathy (*see* **J26**), reflexology, chiropractic, aromatherapy and yoga. A Natural Healthcare Council has been established to regulate complementary therapies for the first time. Since 2011, all herbal medicines sold over the counter must be approved and registered.

Amish. *See* **Mennonites.**

Anabaptists. *See* **Baptists.**

Analytical Psychology, the name given by Carl Gustav Jung (1875–1961) of Zürich to his system of psychology, which, like Adler's (*see* **Adlerian Psychology**), took its origin from Freud's psychoanalysis from which both diverged in 1911. Briefly, Jung differed from Freud: (1) in believing that the latter had laid too much emphasis on the sexual drive as the basic one in man and replacing it with the concept of *libido* or life energy of which sex forms a part; (2) in his theory of types: men are either extrovert or introvert (*i.e.* their interest is turned primarily outwards to the world or inwards to the self), and they apprehend experience in four main ways, one or other of which is predominant in any given individual—sensing, feeling, thinking, or intuiting; (3) in his belief that the individual's unconscious mind contains not only repressed materials which, as Freud maintained, were too unpleasant to be allowed into awareness, but also faculties which had not been allowed to develop—*e.g.*, the emotional side of the too rational man, the feminine side of the too masculine one; (4) in the importance he attaches to the existence of a collective unconscious at a still deeper level which contains traces of ancient ways of thought which mankind has inherited over time.

These are the *archetypes* and include primitive notions of magic, spirits and witches, birth and death, gods, virgin mothers, resurrection, *etc.* In the treatment of the neuroses Jung believed in the importance of (*a*) the present situation which the patient refuses to face; (*b*) the bringing together of conscious and unconscious and integrating them.

In the 1940s and 1950s interest in Jung's ideas waned, at least in academic circles, as the emphasis among experimental psychologists shifted closer and closer to the "hard" scientific line. This was also true in the field of psychoanalysis where the Jungian as opposed to the Freudian point of view became progressively less popular. At the present time this trend is beginning to reverse, and while Jung's

offbeat views on astrology, telepathy, *etc.*, are still unfashionable, a reappraisal of the significance of his views on the nature of the unconscious is taking place and many psychologists feel that his contribution to our understanding of the nature of human mental processes has been greatly underrated.

Anarchism, a political philosophy which holds, in the words of the American anarchist Josiah Warren (1798–1874), an early follower of Robert Owen, that "every man should be his own government, his own law, his own church."

The idea that government interference or even the mere existence of authority is inherently bad is as old as Zeno, the Greek Stoic philosopher, who believed that compulsion perverts the normal nature of man. William Godwin's *Enquiry Concerning Political Justice* (1793) was the first systematic exposition of the doctrine. Godwin (father-in-law of Shelley) claimed that man is by nature sociable, co-operative, rational, and good when given the choice to act freely; that under such conditions men will form voluntary groups to work in complete social harmony.

Such groups or communities would be based on equality of income, no state control, and no property: this state of affairs would be brought about by rational discussion and persuasion rather than by revolution.

Proudhon. The French economist Proudhon (1809–65) was the first to bring anarchism to the status of a mass movement. In his book *What is Property?* he stated bluntly that "property is theft" and "governments are the scourge of God". He urged the formation of co-operative credit banks where money could be had without interest and goods would be exchanged at cost value at a rate representing the hours of work needed to produce each commodity. Like Godwin, he disapproved of violence but, unlike Marx, disapproved of trade unions as representing organised groups.

Bakunin and Kropotkin. In communistic anarchism these ideas were combined with a revolutionary philosophy, primarily by the Russians Michael Bakunin (1814–76) and Peter Kropotkin (1842–1921) who favoured training workers in the technique of "direct action" to overthrow the state by all possible means, including political assassination. In 1868 anarchists joined the First International which broke up a few years later after a bitter struggle between Bakuninists and Marxists. Subsequently small anarchist groups murdered numerous political figures.

Anarchism and communism differ in three main ways: (1) anarchism forms no political party, rejects all relationship with established authority, and regards democratic reform as a setback; (2) communism is against capitalism, anarchism against the state as such; (3) both have the final goal of a classless society, but anarchism rejects the idea of an intermediate period of socialist state control accepted by communism. Philosophical anarchists, such as the American writer Henry David Thoreau (1817–62), were primarily individualists who believed in a return to nature, the non-payment of taxes, and passive resistance to state control; Thoreau thus strongly influenced Gandhi as did the Christian anarchist Tolstoy.

Spain. Although active in the 1917 Russian Revolution, where it opposed Bolshevik dictatorship, anarchism has had only limited political influence. Its most notable achievement was in the anarcho-syndicalist trade union, the CNT, which had mass support in parts of Spain and which developed agricultural and industrial workers' control in the early stages of the 1936–9 civil war. There was a revival in the 1960s student movement, particularly in the 1968 French events, and the anti-capitalist and anti-globalisation movement of recent years has shown renewed interest. See also **Syndicalism.**

Anglicanism. *See* **Church of England.**

Anglo-Catholicism. To Queen Elizabeth I the Church of England was that of the "middle way" in which human reason and common-sense took their place beside Scripture and Church authority. The extent to which these various factors are stressed creates the distinctions between "high" and "low" church.

Anglo-Catholics tend to reject the term "Protestant" and to stress the term "Catholic" and, although few accept the infallibility of the Pope some Anglo-Catholic churches have introduced much or all of the Roman ritual and teach Roman dogmas. The ordination in March 1994 of the first women priests to the Anglican ministry caused over 200 former Anglican clergy (many of them married) to be received into the Catholic Church. *See* **Catholicism, Tractarianism**.

Animal Rights. *See* **Anti-vivisection (J5)**.

Animism. To early man and in less developed societies the distinction between animate and inanimate objects was not always obvious—it is not enough to say that living things move and non-living things do not, for leaves blow about in the wind and streams flow down a hillside. In the religions of early societies, therefore, we find a tendency to believe that life exists in all objects from rocks and pools to seas and mountains. This belief is technically known as *animatism*, which differs from *animism*, a somewhat more sophisticated view which holds that natural objects have no life in themselves but may be the abode of dead people, spirits, or gods who occasionally give them the appearance of life.

The classic example of this, of course, is the idea that an erupting volcano is an expression of anger on the part of the god who resides in it.

Anthropomorphism, the attribution of human form, thoughts or motives to non-human entities or life forms from gods to animals. At one end this can be summed up in the once widespread image of God as a "white-bearded old gentleman sitting on a cloud." At the other end is the very common tendency to invest domestic animals and pets with man-like wishes and personalities. At both extremes the belief could be seriously misleading. Firstly, it could be very unwise to assume that God, if he exists, necessarily thinks as humans do and has human interests at heart. Secondly, we shall learn very little about animal behaviour if we look upon them as mere extensions of our own personality, and we do them less than justice if we see them simply as human beings of diminutive intelligence.

Anthroposophy, a school of religious and philosophical thought based on the work of the German educationist and mystic Rudolf Steiner (1861–1925). Steiner was originally an adherent of Madame Blavatsky's theosophical movement (*cf* Theosophy) but in 1913 broke away to form his own splinter group, the Anthroposophical Society. Steiner was much influenced by the German poet and scientist, Goethe, and believed that an appreciation and love for art was one of the keys to spiritual development. One of the first tasks of his new movement was the construction of a vast temple of arts and sciences, known as the Goetheanum, to act as the headquarters of the society. This structure, which was of striking and revolutionary architectural style, was unfortunately burnt down in 1922 to be replaced by an even more imaginative one which today is one of the most interesting buildings of its kind in the world.

Anthroposophy, which continued to expand following its founder's death, is well-established in various parts of the world with specialised, and often very well equipped, schools and clinics which propagate the educational and therapeutic theories of the movement. These, which include the allegedly beneficial powers of music, coloured lights, *etc.*, have made an increasing impact on modern educational ideas, but the schools have acquired a reputation for success in the training of mentally handicapped children. Today there are more than 750 Steiner schools worldwide, many clinics and homes for the handicapped, adult education centres, an international management consultancy, and several hundred thousand acres under biodynamic cultivation without the use of chemical pesticides, herbicides, or fertilizers. Interesting work continues to be done, in pharmacology, botany, mathematics and physics, and architecture.

New banking systems, operating rather like credit unions, have arisen (Mercury in Britain, Prometheus in New Zealand).

Anticlericalism, resentment of priestly powers and privileges, traceable in England to Wyclif's insistence in the 14th cent. on the right of all men to have access to the Scriptures. The translation of the Bible into the common tongue was a great landmark in the history of the Bible and the English language. Wyclif's principles were condemned by the Roman Church of his time but were readily accepted during the Reformation. Tudor anticlericalism arose from motives ranging from a greedy desire to plunder the riches of the Church to a genuine dislike of the powers of the priesthood whose spiritual courts still had the right to decide on points of doctrine or morals in an age when the layman felt he was well able to decide for himself. In innumerable ways the Church was permitted to extort money from the laity. It is generally agreed that the final submission of church to state in England was motivated quite as much by anticlericalism as by Protestantism.

The rise of the Reformed churches in England satisfied the people generally and anticlericalism never became the fixed principle of permanent parties as happened in France and Italy.

Antiglobalisation is either scepticism of the existence of globalisation (*q.v.*), or opposition to globalisation. Scepticism of globalisation rejects the view that globalisation is new and intrinsically different, and points to the long history of global trade, exchange of ideas and culture, and international treaties and laws. Such sceptics also point to the continued importance of nation states as many groups continue to strive for nationhood, and global free trade struggles with national protected markets and economic subsidies. Opponents regard globalisation as a cloak for the expansion of western, and particularly American economic, political and social power. Some opponents promote an alternative form of globalisation where solidarity and cooperation defeat private capital and western strategic interests. Such has been the motivation of the antiglobalisation protests in London, Seattle and Genoa in recent years.

Antisemitism, a term which gained currency about the middle of the 19th century to those who were anti-Jewish in their outlook. Although this attitude was prevalent for religious reasons throughout the Middle Ages, modern antisemitism differed (*a*) in being largely motivated by economic or political conditions, and (*b*) in being doctrinaire with a pseudo-scientific rationale presented by such men as Gobineau (1816–82) and Houston Stewart Chamberlain (1855–1927), and later by the Nazi and Fascist "philosophers".

It was evident in Russia and Hungary with the pogroms of 1882.It was later to spread south and westwards where, in France, the Dreyfus case provided an unsavoury example in 1894. Thousands of Jews from Eastern Europe fled to Britain and America during this period; for in these countries antisemitism has rarely been more than a personal eccentricity. During the Second World War the murder of six million Jews by the Nazis and their accomplices led to a further exodus to various parts of the world and finally to the creation of the state of Israel.

But there are social causes too and politicians in some lands are well versed in the technique of blaming unsatisfactory conditions (which they themselves may have in part produced) upon minority groups and persuading others to do the same. Historically, the Jew was ideally suited for this role of scapegoat; (1) in the Middle Ages when usury was forbidden to Christians but not to Jews, the latter often became moneylenders incurring the opprobrium generally associated with this trade; (2) many trades being closed to Jews, it was natural that they concentrated in others, thus arousing suspicions of "influence" (*i.e.* Jews are felt to occupy a place in certain trades and professions which far exceeds their numerical proportion to the population as a whole); (3) even with the ending of ghetto life, Jews often occupy *en masse* some parts of cities rather than others and this may lead to resentment on the part of the original inhabitants who begin to feel themselves dispossessed; (4) Jews tend to form a closed society and incur the suspicions attached to all closed societies within which social contacts are largely limited to members; marriage outside the group is forbidden or strongly disapproved of, and the preservation, among the orthodox, of cultural and religious barriers tends to isolate them from their fellow citizens. After 1990, with the political changes in Russia and Eastern Europe, neo-fascists began a resurgence of anti-semitism. Acts of anti-semitism continued to rise after the economic crisis of 2007. Anti-semitism in Europe has now reached its highest level in decades.

Anti-Slavery International, the world's oldest human rights organisation (founded in 1839). It is the successor to the British and Foreign Anti-Slavery Society. Slavery was abolished in the British Empire in 1839. There are even today an estimated 40 million people living in slavery, in countries such as Mauritania, India, Pakistan, Haiti, Benin *etc.*, according to the 2016 Global Slavery Index. Slavery includes debt bondage, forced marriage, human trafficking and child exploitation. A Moden Slavery Act was passed in 2015 which established the first anti-slavery commissioner.

Anti-vivisection, opposition to scientific experimentation upon live animals based, according to its supporters, both on the moral grounds of the suffering imposed, and also on the grounds that many doctors and scientists of repute have rejected the value of information gained in this way. It is true that the protagonists of the movement during its early days in the mid-19th cent. included a number of eminent physicians and surgeons. Many people today remain deeply concerned about the moral problems of vivisection, even though without animal experiments we would be unable to test out new drugs for safety before using them on human beings. There are in Britain many active anti-vivisection societies. Much of their work is co-ordinated through the British Council of Anti-Vivisection Societies. In Britain, experiments on live animals are covered by the 1986 Animals (Scientific Procedures) Act. Worldwide over 200 million animals are killed in experiments each year.

Many people would like the number of experiments on animals reduced and the law changed to prohibit any experiments in which there is any risk of inflicting suffering. Recent years have seen an upsurge in support for such organisations. The 2006 Animal Welfare Act set out the needs of a pet to protect its physical and mental health.

Recent years have also seen moves to outlaw the use of wild animals in circuses, to reduce the use of animals to test cosmetic products and to insist animals killed in abattoirs are first stunned.

Apartheid. An Afrikaans word meaning "apartness", which refers to the policy of total racial discrimination between black and white South Africans as enforced by successive governments of that country from 1948 until the early 1990s when the system was dismantled. At its height, apartheid was an inhuman system which denied even the most basic human rights to the Africans.

In January 2000 a far-reaching Equality Bill was introduced in South Africa which sought finally to end the legacy of apartheid.

Arianism, formed the subject of the first great controversy within the Christian Church over the doctrine of Arius of Alexandria (d. 336) who denied the divinity of Christ. The doctrine, although at first influential, was condemned at the Council of Nicaea (325), called by the Emperor Constantine, at which Arius was opposed by Athanasius, also of Alexandria, who argued the now orthodox view that the Son is of one substance with the Father.

Arius was banished but the heresy persisted until the 7th cent., especially among the barbarians, the Goths, Vandals and Lombards. Disbelief in the divinity of Christ has formed part of the doctrine of many sects since (*e.g.*) **Unitarianism** (*q.v.*).

Arminianism. A theological movement in Christianity, based on the teachings of the Dutch theologian Jacob Harmensen (or Hermansz) (1560–1609), whose name was Latinised as Jacobus Arminius. He reacted against the Calvinist doctrine of predestination. His followers formulated his three main beliefs as: divine sovereignty was compatible with real freewill in man; Christ died for all men (and not only the elect); and all who believe in him can be saved. Arminianism had an important influence on John Wesley and through him on Methodism.

Asceticism. The practice of self-discipline of both mind and body in order to achieve a spiritual ideal or goal. From the Greek *askein,* to practise or exercise. The term originally referred to the training carried out by athletes. The concept was

then transformed into the idea of training for wisdom. This view is clearly articulated in Plato, who argued that one must free oneself from the desires of the body in order to achieve full spiritual insight. Since all religions exalt the soul over the body, the spiritual over the material, and eternal life over this world, they all have traces of asceticism. In many of them, there are adherents who have gone beyond self-denial to self-punishment. Important features of ascetic movements are celibacy, abdication of worldly possessions, abstinence and fasting.

Asceticism has been very important in Christianity, most notably in the monastic movement (*see* **Monasticism**), though practices varied widely among monks, from the extravagant austerity of Egyptian hermits to the work-oriented community life of the Benedictines. Since the rise of Protestantism, however, extreme austerity has been less favoured. Hinduism also has a strong tradition of asceticism, and there are elements in Buddhism and Islam.

Assassins, a sect of Muslim Shi'ites, founded by the Persian Hasan i Sabbah (*c.* 1090), which for more than two centuries established a rule of terror all over Persia and Syria. The coming of the Mongols in 1256 destroyed them in Persia and the Syrian branch suffered a similar fate at the hands of the then Mamluk sultan of Egypt, *c.* 1270. It was a secret order, ruled over by a grand master, under whom the members were strictly organised into classes, according to the degree of initiation into the secrets of the order. The devotees, belonging to one of the lower groups, carried out the actual assassinations under strict laws of obedience, and total ignorance of the objects and ritual of the society. It is believed that these devotees were given ecstatic visions under the influence of hashish, whence the term *hashshashin,* corrupted to "assassin".

Assisted Dying. *See* **Euthanasia.**

Associationism. In psychology, the Associationist school of the 19th cent. accepted the association of ideas as the fundamental principle in mental life. It was represented in Britain by the two Mills and Herbert Spencer, in Germany by J. F. Herbart (1776–1841). To these, mental activity was nothing but the association of "ideas" conceived of as units of both thought and feeling—the emotion of anger or the perception of a chair were both "ideas"—and apart from them the self did not exist. Personality was simply a series of these units coming and going, adding to or cancelling each other out, in accordance with rigid scientific laws.

Astrology was once the best available theory for explaining the course of human life and bears much the same historical relationship to astronomy as alchemy does to chemistry.

Originally it was divided into two branches: (1) **Natural Astrology** which dealt with the movements of the heavenly bodies and their calculations, and (2) **Judicial Astrology** which studied the alleged influence of the stars and the planets on human life and fate. It was the former that developed into modern astronomy; the latter was, and remains, a myth.

Astrology owes most to the early Babylonians (or Chaldeans) who readily accepted the idea that divine energy is manifested in the movements of the sun and planets. Gradually this concept became enlarged and the relative positions of the planets both in relation to each other and to the fixed stars became important together with the idea of omens—that, if a particular event occurred whilst the planets were in a particular position, the recurrence of that position heralded a recurrence of the same sort of event.

The planets became linked with almost every aspect of human life. They were bound up with the emotions, with parts of the body, so that astrology played quite a large part in medicine up to late medieval times. Not only was the position of the planet to be considered but also the particular sign of the zodiac (or house of heaven) it was occupying, and it was believed possible to foretell the destiny of an individual by calculating which star was in the ascendant (*i.e.* the sign of the zodiac nearest the eastern horizon and the star which arose at that precise moment) at the time of his birth.

Astrology was popular among the Egyptians, the Romans (whose authorities found the

Chaldean astrologers a nuisance and expelled them from time to time), and in the Middle Ages.

Atheism. See God and Man.

Atlantis, a mythical empire supposed to have lain somewhere between Europe and America and a centre of advanced civilisation before it was inundated by some great natural catastrophe in pre-Christian times. Plato made use of the myth. Some believe the myth was based on the eruption of Santorini, an island in the Eastern Mediterranean.

Atomism. In philosophy, the atomists were a group of early Greek thinkers, the most important of whom were Leucippus (fl. c. 440 B.C.) and his younger contemporary Democritus (c. 460–370 B.C.). Prior to these men, although it had been agreed that matter must be composed of tiny ultimate particles and that change must be due to the manner in which these mingled or separated from each other, it was supposed that there existed different types of particle for each material—e.g. for flesh, wood, hair, bone. The atomists taught that atoms were all made of a single substance and differed only in the connections (pictured as hooks, grooves, points, etc.) which enabled them to join each other in characteristic ways. Theirs was the first move towards modern atomic theory and a predecessor of the modern concept of chemical linkages.

Authoritarianism, a dictatorial form of government as contrasted with a democratic one based on popular sovereignty.

Automatism, the production of material, written or spoken in "automatic" fashion—i.e., apparently not under the conscious or volitional control of the individual. This psychologically perplexing phenomenon has occurred from time to time throughout the history of literature and art, and while it has occasionally produced work of great merit (much of William Blake's poetry, Coleridge's "Kubla Khan", etc.) the bulk of it is indifferent and often simply rubbish. Spiritualists claim that the work is produced under the direct guidances of the spirit world, and their argument once attracted considerable attention through the compositions of the pianist Rosemary Brown who, with little or no academic background in musical theory, produced a number of "original" piano pieces allegedly composed by Beethoven, Mozart, etc., from the astral plane. While few music critics denied Mrs. Brown's honesty and integrity, most consider her work to be clever pastiche and barely comparable in quality to the masterworks of the dead composers.

Nevertheless automatism wants some explaining, and most psychologists today defer judgement, taking the view that it serves to remind us of the fund of material which lies in the unconscious mind, and which is prone to pop up from time to time without warning.

Ayurveda (Sanskrit, the Science of Life), a philosophy based on divine Hindu writings, which seeks to prolong both physical and spiritual life and health.

B

Baconian Method, the use of the inductive (as opposed to the deductive or Aristotelian) method of reasoning as proposed by Francis Bacon in the 17th cent. and J. S. Mill in the 19th cent. Deduction argues from supposedly certain first principles (such as the existence of God or Descartes's "I think, therefore I am") what the nature of the universe and its laws *must* be, whereas the only means of obtaining true knowledge of the universe, in Bacon's view, was by the amassing of facts and observations so that when enough were obtained the certain truth would be known in the same way that a child's numbered dots in a playbook joined together by a pencilled line create a picture. However, this is not the way science progresses in practice. Bacon had underrated the importance of hypothesis and theory and overrated the reliability of the senses. In discussing the scientific tradition, Sir Karl Popper in his book, *Conjecture and Refutations*, says: "The most

important function of observation and reasoning, and even of intuition and imagination, is to help us in the critical examination of those bold conjectures which are the means by which we probe into the unknown." Two of the greatest men who clearly saw that there was no such thing as an inductive procedure were Galileo and Einstein.

Bahá'í Faith. Although its origins lie within Islam, the Baha'i movement today considers itself to be the fourth branch of the Western Monotheistic Tradition. Believing that God's revelation to mankind did not end with the Prophet Muhammad, Baha'is revere two further figures, Bab and Baha'u'lla. It was begun in 1844 by a Persian Muslim, Mirza Ali Muhammad, who pronounced himself to be Bab, 'The Gate', who would be a forerunner for a greater prophet. Upon his execution in 1850, one of his closest followers Mirza Husayn-Ali Nuri, also known as Baha'u'lla, 'The Glory of God' took over the community and in 1863 announced that he was the promised one. Baha'is revere the holy writings of both figures and believe them to be the first-hand writings of God's own messengers.

The fundamental beliefs of the faith relate to God sending a messenger in every generation to bring together the teachings of those who have gone before. It prides itself in inclusion, having no priesthood or liturgy and a structure based on gender and race equality as well as absolute democracy.

Although at times plagued by internal disputes, it claims that the message of Baha'u'lla is for the whole of mankind. An emphasis is placed on the education of all, traditional family values and healthy living, including the recommendation of vegetarianism.

The Baha'i faith has suffered repeated severe persecution in Iran (the country of its birth) since the 1979 revolution (over 200 have been executed, hundreds more imprisoned). They are most numerous in India (1·8 million).

Baptists, a Christian denomination whose distinctive doctrines are that members can only be received by baptism "upon the confession of their faith and sins" and that "baptism is no wise appertaineth to infants." Baptism is therefore by total immersion of adults. Modern Baptists base their doctrines upon the teaching of the Apostles and some hold that the Albigenses (q.v.) maintained the true belief through what they regarded as the corruption of the Roman Church in medieval times. On the other hand any connection with the Anabaptist movement during the Reformation is rejected and the beginning of the modern Church is traced to John Smyth, a minister of the Church of England who in Amsterdam was influenced by the Arminians (q.v.) and Mennonites. Smyth died in 1612 when the first Baptist church in England was built at Newgate.

This, the "General" Baptist Church, rejected Calvinistic beliefs and held the Arminian doctrine of redemption open to all, but some years later a split occurred with the formation of the "Particular" Baptist Church which was Calvinist in doctrine. In 1891 the two bodies were united in the Baptist Union and today the sect is spread throughout the world, notably in the United States. There are less than 150,000 Baptists in Great Britain.

Anabaptism. This movement began in Zurich, Switzerland, in 1525, when Conrad Grebel, Felix Manz and Jörg Blaurock, their hearts moved by their failure to live according to the Gospel, decided to give their lives to following Christ's teaching, whatever the cost. The movement spread widely in Switzerland, Germany and Holland in the 16th century, and its followers suffered martyrdom by fire, water and the sword for the sake of their faith. They met with further condemnation and persecution because of the excesses of a violent and radical group, known as the Münster Anabaptists, whom they disowned.

The wider movement was non-violent and stood for baptism on confession of faith, love to one's enemies and obedience to the Spirit of Christ's Sermon on the Mount. This movement is the spiritual precursor of several of the Peace Churches of today: the Hutterians (named after their founder, Jakob Hutter), the Mennonites (after Menno Simons), and, later, the Amish.

The most radical of these groups is that of the Hutterian Brethren, who live, work, and hold their goods in common like the first Christians.

Beat Generation, a term first used by the American writer Jack Kerouac (1922–69), author of *The Town and the City* and *On the Road*, to define various groups spread across the face of the country, but notably in New York and San Francisco, who, belonging to the post-war generation, represented various rebellious attitudes to authority.

Behaviourism, a school of psychology founded in 1914 by J. B. Watson (1878–1958), an animal psychologist at Johns Hopkins University, Baltimore. Its main tenet was that the method of introspection and the study of mental states were unscientific and should be replaced by the study of behaviour. When animals or human beings were exposed to specific stimuli and their responses objectively recorded, or when the development of a child, as seen in its changing behaviour, was noted, these alone were methods which were truly scientific. Watson contributed an important idea to psychology and did a great deal towards ridding it of the largely philosophical speculations of the past. But he also went to absurd extremes, as in his view that thought is nothing but subvocal speech, consisting of almost imperceptible movements of the tongue, throat, and larynx (*i.e.*, when we think, we are really talking to ourselves), and his further opinion that heredity is, except in grossly abnormal cases, of no importance. He claimed that by "conditioning", the ordinary individual could be made into any desired type, regardless of his or her inheritance.

Pavlov. The work of Ivan Pavlov began about 1901, but was unknown in America until about ten years later, and it was through another Russian, Vladimir Bekhterev, that the concept of "conditioning" was introduced into the country. Bekhterev's book *Objective Psychology*, describing his new science of "reflexology", was translated in 1913 and played a great part in the development of Behaviourist ideas.

The conditioned reflex became central to Watson's theory of learning and habit, formation (*e.g.*, he showed that a year-old child, at first unafraid of white rats, became afraid of them when they came to be associated with a loud noise behind the head).

Finally all behaviour, including abnormal behaviour, came to be explained in terms of conditioned responses; these were built up by association on the infant's three innate emotions of fear, rage, and love, of which the original stimuli were, for the first, loud noises and the fear of falling; for the second, interference with freedom of movement; and for the third, patting and stroking.

Because of its considerable theoretical simplicity and its implicit suggestion that human behaviour could be easily described (and even modified or controlled), Pavlovian psychology appeared very attractive to the Communist regime in Russia, and before long it became the "official" dogma in universities and research laboratories. Whereas in America and Western Europe its severe limitations became gradually apparent, in the former USSR these were ignored or disguised for ideological reasons with the inevitable outcome that Soviet psychology failed to evolve and, at one stage, seemed to be no more than a pallid offshoot of physiology. In non-Communist countries simple Watsonian behaviourism evolved into more sophisticated studies of animal learning, largely pioneered by the Harvard psychologist, Skinner. These techniques, which have shown that animals, from monkeys to rats, may be taught to solve a remarkable range of physical problems (such as pressing complex sequences of buttons or levers to escape from a cage) have themselves turned out to be rather disappointing in terms of advancing our general understanding of the workings of the human and animal brain. There is a growing feeling among psychologists that the real keys to the understanding of mankind will only be found through the study of man himself, and not his simpler animal cousins. *See also* **Gestalt Psychology.**

Benthamism. *See* **Utilitarianism.**

Bermuda Triangle, an area of sea, bounded by Bermuda, Florida and Puerto Rico where unexplained disappearances of aircraft and ships have led to many fanciful theories. Natural phenomena are the most likely explanation.

Bioethics, the application of ethics to such fields as the biological sciences, medicine, healthcare *etc.* as well as the debate on which policies should be approved by government in these areas.

Biopsychology, the study of the biological and physiological bases of behaviours and psychological processes. It is considered to be a branch of neuroscience and includes the study of: the structure and development of the nervous system; the effects of hormones and other chemicals on neural activity; the effects of drugs, surgery and electrical manipulation on the central nervous system; and the genetics and heritability of behavioural traits.

Bolshevism. When the Russian Social Democratic Party at a conference held in London in 1903 split over the issue of radicalism or moderation, it was the radical faction headed by Lenin which polled the majority of votes. The Russian for majority is *bolshinstvo* and for minority *menshinstvo*; hence the radicals became known as Bolsheviks and the moderates as Mensheviks. Bolshevik was sometimes used (wrongly) in a derogatory way to include all communists (after the Bolshevik seizure of power in Russia in October 1917). *See* **Communism, Marxism.**

Brahmanism. A religion of ancient India which evolved out of the Vedas about 1000–800 B.C. and is still powerful today. It provides the orthodox core of traditional Hinduism. Characteristics of the faith were elaborate ceremonies, material offerings, animal sacrifice, a dominant priestly caste (the Brahmins), and a development of the idea of Brahman as the eternal, impersonal Absolute Principle. *See also* **Hinduism.**

Buchmanism. *See* **Moral Re-Armament.**

Buddhism, one of the great Oriental religions. It arose against the background of Brahmanism in north India in the 6th cent. B.C., its founder being the Sākyan prince Siddhattha Gotama, known as the Buddha or "Enlightened One". Distressed by the problem of human suffering from which even death allowed no escape—since Buddha accepted a doctrine of a cycle of lives—he left his palace and his beloved family to become a religious mendicant and ascetic, studying for six years the beliefs of Brahmin hermits and self-torturing recluses. After this long search he sat down under a tree (the Banyan tree, which became known as the Bo-tree or tree of enlightenment because of his enlightenment) and finally came to understand the cause and release from suffering.

The result of his meditations are found in the "four noble truths" which are: (1) that all living is itself suffering; (2) suffering is caused by desire; (3) suffering ceases when desire is eradicated; (4) that it can be destroyed by following the "noble eightfold path" whose steps are: right views; right thought; right speech, plain and truthful; right conduct, including abstinence not only from immorality and the taking of life, whether human or animal; right livelihood, harming no one; right effort, always pressing on; right awareness of the present; and lastly, right meditation. The more man acquires merit by following these rules in his chain of lives, the sooner is *Nirvana* attained; he loses his individuality, not by annihilation, but "as the dewdrop slips into the shining sea," by merging with the universal life.

Buddhism teaches a way of liberation through ethics and meditation. In many Buddhist nations no word exists for the concept of an Almighty God, which was neither affirmed nor denied by Buddha himself but simply ignored. Nor did Buddha claim to be other than a man, although prayers were made to Buddha, ritual developed, sacred relics preserved under stupas, and the belief in a succession of Buddhas introduced; the sacred writings (*Tripitaka*) are divided into three parts; *Suttanta*, *Abhidhamma* and *Vinaya*. *Suttanta* are mostly teachings in everyday language, *Abhidhamma* are teachings using the analytical method and the *Vinaya* is the monastic rule for monks. They were gathered by devotees at various councils—the first held after the death of Buddha at the age of 80, a third at the order of King Asoka in 244 B.C. The founder himself wrote nothing.

Buddhism spread to Sri Lanka, Nepal, Tibet, Mongolia, Indo-China, Myanmar (Burma), Thailand, China, and Japan, although on the whole losing influence in its old stronghold of the Indus Valley in India. In Tibet, Buddhism developed into Lamaism (q.v.). In Sri Lanka, Burma, Thailand etc., it persisted in its pure form (the Theravada), while in China and Japan it developed into the Mahayana. Nowadays, there are over 494 million Buddhists world-wide, with over 250,000 in Britain. The greatest number live in China (c. 250 million), where there has been a major revival. Buddhism is the state religion in Cambodia. Fragments of the oldest known Buddhist manuscript (the religion's equivalent to the Dead Sea Scrolls) were discovered by the British Library in 1996. The largest Buddhist temple in the world is in Magelang in Java.

In 2013, excavations at the site believed to be the birthplace of Buddha produced evidence dating back to the 6th cent. B.C.

Buddhism is now advocating a more secular version of its religion to adapt to the needs of modern society.

Bushido, the traditional code of honour of the Samurai or Japanese military caste corresponding to the European concept of knighthood and chivalry. Bushido evolved in the 12th cent. Even today it is a potent influence among the upper classes, being based on the principles of simplicity, honesty, courage, and justice.

C

Cabala (**Kabbalah**), originally a collection of Jewish doctrines about the nature of the Universe, supposedly handed down by Moses to the Rabbis, which evolved into a kind of mystical interpretation of the Old Testament. Students of the history of religious belief have found its origins to be in fact extremely obscure, and some aspects appear to have been lifted from ancient Egyptian sources. Skilled Cabalists hold that the system contains a key to biblical interpretation based on the numerical values of the words and letters of the Scriptures which reveal hidden depths of meaning behind the allegorical Old Testament stories. This 'received' teaching is now enjoying a major revival (e.g. in the USA).

Caliph, The title of Muslim rulers, successors to Mohammed. In 680 it became hereditary in the Umayyad line until 750. It then passed to the Abbasids. The title was later taken by various rulers, notably the Ottomans until 1924.

Calvinism, the branch of Protestantism founded basically (although preceded by Zwingli and others) by Jean Chauvin (1509-64), who was born in Noyon in Picardy. John Calvin, as he is usually called, from the Latin form of his name, Calvinius, provided in his Institutions of the Christian Religion the first logical definition and justification of Protestantism, thus becoming the intellectual leader of the Reformation as the older Martin Luther was its emotional instigator. The distinctive doctrine of Calvinism is its dogma of predestination which states that God has unalterably destined some souls to salvation to whom "efficacious grace and the gift of perseverance" is granted and others to eternal damnation. Calvinism, as defined in the Westminster Confession, is established in the Reformed or Presbyterian churches of France, Holland, Scotland, etc., as contrasted with the Lutheran churches, and its harsh but logical beliefs inspired the French Huguenots, the Dutch in their fight against Spanish Catholic domination, and the English Puritans. The rule set up under Calvin's influence in Geneva was marred by the burning at the stake of the anatomist Servetus for the heresy of "pantheism", i.e. Unitarianism.

Perhaps its greatest single influence outside the Church was the result of Calvinist belief that to labour industriously was one of God's commands. This changed the medieval notions of the blessedness of poverty and the wickedness of usury, proclaimed that men should shun luxury and be thrifty, yet implied that financial success was a mark of God's favour. In this way it was related to the rise of capitalism either as cause or effect.

Max Weber, the German sociologist, believed that Calvinism was a powerful incentive to, or even cause of, the rise of capitalism (q.v.): Marx, Sombart and Tawney asserted the reverse view—

that Calvinism was a result of developing capitalism, being its ideological justification.

Capitalism is an economic system under which the means of production and distribution are owned by a relatively small section of society which runs them at its own discretion for private profit. There exists, on the other hand, a propertyless class of those who exist by the sale of their labour power. Modern capitalism, in the form Marxists refer to it, arose towards the end of the 18th cent. in England where the early factory owners working with small-scale units naturally approved of free enterprise and free trade. But free enterprise has no necessary connection with capitalism; by the beginning of the 20th century monopolies were developing and state protection against foreign competition was demanded. Capitalism is opposed by those who believe in socialism (q.v.), first, for the moral reasons that it leads to economic inequality and the exploitation of labour and the consuming public, and that public welfare rather than private profit should motivate the economic system; secondly, for the practical reason that capitalism has led to recurrent economic crises.

Cartomancy, the art of fortunes or predicting the future by playing cards or by the Tarot pack.

Caste System. See **Hinduism.**

Cathars. See **Albigenses.**

Catholic Reformation. See **Counter-Reformation.**

Catholicism. For those who are not Roman Catholics the term "Catholic" has two separate meanings. The more general refers to the whole body of Christians throughout the world, the more specific refers to a particular view of Christianity. In this latter sense the Church of England, the Orthodox Eastern Churches, and others consider themselves "Catholic" meaning that (a) they belong to Christ's Church as organised on an accepted basis of faith and order; (b) they insist on the necessity of "liturgical" worship through its established forms (e.g., baptism, holy communion); (c) they emphasise the continuity of Christian tradition by the use of ancient creeds (e.g., the Apostles' Creed, the Nicene Creed) and regard the ministry as a succession (Apostolic succession) deriving from early practice.

In this sense there is no necessary contradiction between Catholicism and Protestantism regarded as a renewal of the Church in the 16th cent. by an appeal to the Scriptures as interpreted by the early Fathers of the Church.

This definition obviously excludes Quakers, Christian Scientists, and many Nonconformist sects. See also **Roman Catholic Church.**

Characterology, the attempt made over many centuries to classify people into personality types on the basis of physical or psychological characteristics. The first attempt was made by Hippocrates in the 5th cent. B.C. who classified temperaments into the sanguine (or optimistic), the melancholic, the choleric (or aggressive), and the phlegmatic (or placid).

Theophrastus, a pupil of Aristotle, described, with examples, thirty extreme types of personality (e.g. the talkative, the boorish, the miserly, etc.); these were basically literary and imaginative but at same time "physiognomy" arose which attempted to interpret character from the face.

Physiognomy subsequently became of importance again during the Renaissance and there are still those today who believe in it in spite of the fact that, broadly speaking, there is no connection whatever between facial features and personality (i.e. although it may be possible to tell from the features that a man is an idiot or some extreme abnormal type and some idea of character may be obtained from an individual's characteristic facial expressions, it is not possible to tell from the shape of the nose, height of the brow, or dominance of the lower jaw, whether anyone is weak, intellectual or determined). The old contention of the 19th century. Italian criminologist Cesare Lombroso that criminals show typical facial characteristics was convincingly disproved by Karl Pearson when he found that 3,000 criminals showed no major differences of features, carefully measured from a similar number of students at Oxford and Cambridge.

It has, however, been noted that people in general tend to be intellectual or emotional, inward- or outward-looking, and this observation is reflected in the classification of the

Scottish psychologist, Alexander Bain (d. 1903), into intellectual, artistic, and practical; Nietzsche's Apollonian and Dionysian types; William James's "tender" and "toughminded"; and C. G. Jung's introvert and extrovert.

Some connection has been found between temperament and body-build. The German psychiatrist Ernst Kretschmer (1888–1964) showed that manic-depressive patients and normal people who are extroverted and tend to alternate in mood (as do manic-depressives to an exaggerated degree) were usually short and stout or thick-set in build; schizophrenics and normal people, who both show shyness, serious or introverted reactions, were usually tall and slender. The former of "pyknic" body-build are "cyclothyme" in temperament, the latter with "schizothyme" temperament are of two bodily types—tall and thin or "asthenic" and the muscularly well-proportioned or "athletic".

The American Sheldon has confirmed these observations on the whole and gone into further details. According to him the basic body types are: (1) *endomorphic* (rounded build), corresponding to Kretschmer's pyknic, normally associated with the *viscerotonic* temperament (relaxed, sociable); (2) *mesomorphic* (squarish, athletic build), normally associated with the *somatotonic* temperament (energetic, assertive); and (3) *ectomorphic* (linear build) often associated with the *cerebrotonic* temperament (anxious, restless).

Glandular and metabolic factors have considerable effect on human personality and also, to some extent, on physique. It is not too surprising, therefore, to find an association between body build (or "somatotype" as Sheldon termed it) and general mood. Genetic conditions which shape, for example, the face can lead scientists to diagnose inherited disease.

Charismatic, the evangelical, 'New Church' Christian movement that has broken away from the traditional Church. The 'house church' movement is part of this rapidly-growing movement, which started in Britain with the 1987 'March for Jesus'.

Chartism, a socialistic movement in England (1837–55) which attempted to better the conditions of the working classes. Named after "The People's Charter" of Francis Place (1838), its radical programme demanded: (1) universal manhood suffrage; (2) vote by ballot; (3) equal electoral districts; (4) annual parliament; (5) payment of members; (6) abolition of their property qualifications.

Chartism was supported by the Christian socialists (*q.v.*), J. F. D. Maurice (1805–72), and Charles Kingsley (1819– 75) with certain qualifications. The movement, the first mass organisation of the industrial working class, had considerable influence on the evolution of socialism in England.

The movement failed from internal divisions.

Chauvinism, a term applied to any excessive devotion to cause, particularly a patriotic or military one. The word is derived from Nicholas Chauvin whose excessive devotion to Napoleon made him a laughing-stock.

Chirology, the subject concerned with the hand as an indicator of psychological and medical significance. Chirology derives from an Oriental tradition concerning mental and physical healing and spirituality and as such encompasses many associated arts and studies of direct relevance to modern day living. Palmistry in the main is a crude folk art and does not attempt to understand or clarify its own teachings.

The Cheirological Society was founded in 1889 by Katherine St. Hill to promote the systematic study of the hand as a serious subject worthy of scientific attention bereft of superstition and fakery. It still exists today and has members throughout the world.

Chiropractic, the art of manipulation of the joints, in particular the spine, as a means of curing disease. Some qualified doctors employ its principles and, as with its near-neighbour osteopathy, it seems on some occasions to be a useful treatment. It was founded in the 19th cent. by D. D. Palmer. Chiropractors are licensed by law in the UK.

Christadelphians, The Christadelphians (or Brothers of Christ) were founded in 1848 by an English doctor, John Thomas, who, having been saved from a shipwreck on his emigration to America, vowed to devote his life to the service of Christ. In 1849, believing that the Last Days had begun, he published Elpis Israel, 'The Hope of Israel' promising the restitution of the nation. It was not designed however to be a replacement for the Bible which Christadelphians regard as inerrant and the sole source of revelation. Congregationalist in background, Thomas also advocated local ecclesiastical authority, but went further in rejecting the need for a priesthood. Critical of other Christian Churches in their approach to the interpretation of the Bible and the nature of Christ, they are neither Trinitarian nor Unitarian in their dogma.

Christadelphians believe strongly in Christ's atoning work, but regard evil as a human failing rather than as the work of a supernatural power. Moreover, they do not believe in the traditional concepts of heaven, hell or the immortality of the soul, believing rather in a millenialist approach to the resurrection of the faithful upon earth. Although previous predictions have proved inaccurate, Christadelphians still feel strongly that the world is in its latter days.

Christianity, the religion founded by Jesus Christ whose teaching is found in the New Testament's four Gospels. Simple as His creed may seem it soon became complicated by the various ways in which Christians interpreted it, and the differences within the early Church are reflected in the numerous Councils held to define truth from heresy. The Eastern Church of the Byzantine Empire from the 5th cent. onwards had differed in various ways from the See of Rome and by 1054 the breach became permanent. The 16th cent. Reformation was the other great break in the unity of the Church and once Protestantism had given in effect the right to each man to interpret the Scriptures in his own way, the tendency to fragmentation increased so that, by 1650, there were no fewer than 180 sects, mostly dogmatic and intolerant towards each other. Today there are thousands more.

There are signs today that the trend of disunity is being reversed. The modern ecumenical movement, which has its roots in the great missionary movement of the 19th cent., aims to bring about a reunion of Christendom by uniting Christians throughout the world on the simple basis of the acceptance of Jesus Christ as God and Saviour, *i.e.*, on the basis of Christian fellowship. The movement finds expression in the World Council of Churches (*q.v.*). The Christian life is expressed in the words of Christ: "Thou shalt love the Lord thy God with all thy heart and thy neighbour as thyself."

For many it is the humanitarian side of Christianity that has meaning today; to accept responsibility for others, as well as for oneself.

Christians today are faced with persecution in numerous countries such as Pakistan, Nigeria, Iraq *etc*. The countries with the most Christians are the USA (260m), Brazil (185m) and Russia (115m) but eventually China could surpass them all. It has over 70 million Christians at present.

Christian Democracy has its roots in the 1891 papal encyclical *Rerum Novarum* of Pope Leo XIII. This encyclical encouraged Roman Catholics to organise and engage with the nascent democracies of Europe. The Roman church expressed anxiety at the growth of atheistic communism, increased material inequality, and the projection of the state's influence deeper into the fabric of social life. During the early 20th century, Christian democracy became less exclusively Roman Catholic as Christian democratic political parties drew in supporters from many Christian denominations.

Christian democratic parties shared an opposition to the increased jurisdiction of the state, particularly at the service of radical political ideology. This rather conservative attitude to government was also combined with a strong commitment to social justice through welfare reform. Following World War II, Christian democratic parties became powerful and popular as they offered a moderate and sceptical approach to the role of government combined with support of redistribution and welfare provision.

Christian Science. Founded around 1866 by Mary Barker Eddy, Christian Science is noted for its belief in the power of spiritual healing practised and inaugurated by Christ Himself. It uses as its key text along with the Bible, 'Science and Health with Key to the Scriptures,' although this has undergone substantial revisions over time. Literature forms a very important part of the life of Christian Scientists, and compulsory purchase of reading material is an important Church practice. The worship follows the 'Church Manual' laid down by Mrs. Eddy in 1895.

Christian Science uses the term healing to refer to all the 'ills' which befall mankind, and they argue that moral regeneration goes hand in hand with physical restoration. Members make a commitment to refrain from harming their bodies to the extent of avoiding tea and coffee, and abstain from non-marital sexual relationships. Nontrinitarian in nature, Christian Scientists believe that the Christ-spirit has been present in good men and women down the ages.

Christian Socialism, a movement launched in 1848, a year of revolutions throughout the continent, by a group in England designed to commit the church to a programme of social reform.

The leaders, notably J. F. D. Maurice, Charles Kingsley (both Anglican clergymen), and John Ludlow were deeply moved by the wretched conditions of the British working class and the two priests had, indeed, given active support to the Chartist movement (*q.v.*). However, all insisted that socialism in its existing forms ignored the spiritual needs of mankind and must be tempered with Christianity. Tracts were written to expose the sweated industries and the evils following the enclosure system; but, more concretely, Christian socialism fostered co-operative workshops and distributive societies based on those of the Rochdale pioneers, organised a working-man's college, and set up elementary classes for education. The traditions of Christian socialism have been carried on by the Fabian Society and by adherents of Guild Socialism.

Church of England. There is some evidence of possible continuity with the Christianity of Roman Britain, but in the main the Church derives from the fusion of the ancient Celtic church with the missionary church of St. Augustine, who founded the See of Canterbury in A.D. 597. To archbishop Theodore in 673 is ascribed the organisation in dioceses with settled boundaries, and in parishes. St. Augustine's church was in communion with Rome from the first, but the Church of England was not brought within papal jurisdiction until after the Norman conquest, and was never under the total domination of Rome.

It remains (at least in one sense) the Catholic Church of England without break of continuity, but during the Reformation the royal supremacy was accepted and that of the pope repudiated. It is the Established Church (*i.e.*, the official church of the realm), crowns the sovereign, and its archbishops and bishops in the House of Lords can act as a kind of "conscience of the state" at every stage of legislation. Some argue that the Church should now be disestablished. The Church is organised in two ecclesiastical provinces (Canterbury and York) and 43 dioceses. There are 16,000 churches, but this total includes 2,000 with less than 10 weekly parishioners. Around 760,000 people regularly attend (a major decline in the last 30 years). Funerals conducted by the Anglican Church are now at their lowest-ever level.

Its traditional forms of worship are embodied in the Book of Common Prayer, but the Alternative Service Book of 1980 is also widely used. A new service book, *Common Worship*, was introduced in 2000. The 39 articles (*see also* **Tractarianism**) embody its main tenets.

In 1992, the General Synod finally accepted the ordination of women priests. The first 32 women priests were ordained on 12 March 1994 in Bristol Cathedral. The first 42 Anglican women priests in Scotland were ordained in the Scottish Episcopal Church in December 1994. (the first female priest in the Anglican Communion was ordained in 1944).

The first women priests in Wales were ordained in 1997, whilst in 1996 the Movement for the Ordination of Women was reformed to campaign for Anglican women bishops. In 2006 the Synod decided that the ordination of women bishops is theologically justified. A further step forward was taken in July 2010, but the 2012 Synod rejected ordination by a mere six votes. In 2014 women were finally victorious in their struggle to become bishops.

Controversy surrounded the decision in 2002 by the Church of England to relax its ban on divorcees remarrying in Church (although remarriage of divorcees was previously forbidden, in practice all 43 dioceses allowed remarriage in certain circumstances).

The crisis reached a new height in 2003, caused by three events: the nomination (and subsequent withdrawal) of the gay Dr Jeffrey John as Bishop of Reading; the election of the openly gay Canon Gene Robinson as Bishop of New Hampshire by the Episcopal Church of America; and the same-sex blessings authorised in New Westminster, Canada.

An emergency conference of the 38 primates held at Lambeth Palace in October 2003 established a commission to investigate these issues, narrowly avoiding schism. The ensuing Windsor Report urged moderation and restraint. The failure of the 2005 Anglican "summit" in Northern Ireland left the Church still facing great divisions. In 2007 Gordon Brown announced that the Prime Minister would no longer have a part to play in selecting bishops.

Against a background of divisions over the issues of gay priests and women bishops, and with falling congregations, the Anglican Church faces a difficult future. At the same time, the expanding population of ethnic minorities is seeing the rise of 'black majority' churches (*e.g* the Redeemed Christian Church of God).

In October 2009 a controversial Vatican initiative offered disaffected Anglicans "personal ordinariates", allowing them to enter into full communion with the Catholic Church whilst preserving elements of their Anglican identity.

In 2011 the Church gave the go-ahead for celebate gay men in civil partnerships to become bishops. In 2013 Justin Welby, the Bishop of Durham, succeeded Rowan Williams as Archbishop of Canterbury. Also in 2013, a new 'super-diocese' of Leeds was created (the first new diocese since 1927). In 2013 the Church in Wales approved women bishops. In January 2015 Libby Lane, the first woman bishop in England, was consecrated as Soffragan Bishop of Stockport. In March 2015 Rachel Treweek was appointed diocesan Bishop of Gloucester. In January 2017 the Church in Wales consecrated its first woman bishop at St. Davids.

The Anglican Communion comprises *c.* 80 million Christians in 44 self-governing churches (in 34 provinces) spread across 164 countries which are in communion with the Church of England. All the bishops of the Anglican Communion meet every ten years in the Lambeth Conference (first held in 1867), over which the Archbishop of Canterbury by custom presides as *primus inter pares.* At the 1968 Conference observers and laymen were admitted for the first time. The 1998 Lambeth Conference (attended by 798 bishops) strongly supported the traditionalists over homosexuality issues.

The 2008 Lambeth Conference, boycotted by many conservative bishops, managed to avoid open schism by some tortuous agreements to keep the divided parties together. Likewise, in 2016, only the suspension of the liberal Episcopal Church in America prevented a deeper split.

Church of Jesus Christ of Latter Day Saints (Mormons). Better known as the Mormon religion, from its origins in New York State in the 1820s, the Church of Jesus Christ of Latter Day Saints now has more than 11 million members worldwide. Although there is much dispute over the details, the movement was founded by Joseph Smith who at the age of 14 asked God which denomination of Christianity was the true one. In a vision, he was told that all were wrong and that he should wait a few years. In 1823, he had another vision of the angel Moroni who directed him to dig up golden plates buried in a hillside. Smith began to translate the text in 'reformed Egyptian hieroglyphs' using special eye-glasses, dictating it to his wife from behind a curtain. The first edition of the 'Book of Mormon: Another Testament of Jesus Christ' was published in 1830. It focuses on two migrations of mysterious Jewish tribes to America, one of whom, the Nephites were visited by Christ after his resurrection. The last of the tribe were the prophet Mormon and his son Moroni who created the golden tablets.

Although continuous revelation remains an important element of doctrine, it can come only from the Presidents of the Church, who have followed Smith. His own authority and power in the early progress of the movement was questioned, leading to dissension and eventually to Smith's murder in 1844. His successor was Brigham Young, who in 1847 led the breakaway to the Great Salt Lake Valley which is now in Utah. Mormons continued to attract hostile criticism however, largely owing to their belief in polygamy which was abandoned in 1890. Of importance for Mormons is the belief that the new Jerusalem will be built in America. They also have an unorthodox belief in the Trinity which claims that both God the Father and God the Son have bodily forms. A key belief is in the pre-existence of souls which come from God who lives with his family on a planet near the star Kolob.

Although Mormons worship in churches, many of their most important rites take place in Temples, and are said to have links with Masonic practices. Special clothing is worn and admission reserved for certain members in order to ensure sacredness. This relates to the very complex system of hierarchy and government within the Church. Mormons have very strict views about morality and oppose the use of any stimulants.

Members are encouraged to give two years free service to the Church, which is often spent abroad in missionary work. In recent years, Mormons have grown rapidly in the developing world. In Britain, there are around 200,000 Mormons. Many Mormons worldwide are leaving over its opposition to same-sex marriage.

Until 1978, the Mormons taught their followers that black people were cursed and they were barred from becoming priests.

Church of Scotland, the established national church of Scotland, presbyterian in constitution, and governed by a hierarchy of courts—the kirk-sessions, the presbyteries, the synods, and the General Assembly. Its congregations have declined rapidly in recent years (from 1,133,000 in 1971 to below 375,000 today). It has only *c.* 800 ministers for its 1,400 congregations. It has recently authorised the approval of same-sex weddings. A serious split arose in May 2009 when the General Assembly upheld the appointment of a gay minister to Queen's Cross parish church. The ban on openly gay ministers was lifted in May 2013. There are ongoing talks with the Church of England to seek agreement based on the Columba Declaration. *See* **Presbyterianism**.

Clairvoyance. *See* **Telepathy**.

Collectivism. The theory of the collective ownership or control of all the means of production, and especially of the land, by the whole community or state, *i.e.* the people collectively, for the benefit of the people as a whole. The term has also acquired a broader sense, to denote the view that the individual is subordinate to the social collectivity. An influential expression of collectivist ideas can be found in Rousseau's *Du contrat social* (1762). It is an important theme in Hegel and Marx, and has been expressed in such movements as socialism, communism and fascism. Collectivism is to be contrasted with individualism (*q.v.*).

Colonialism. Colonialism refers to the kind of imperialism practised by European countries in for example Africa and S.E. Asia, where the colonised country was allowed to have partially autonomous legal and social institutions, while the mother country retained supreme power, and the colonial community had social and political rights denied to the natives. "Neo-colonialism" means the cultural and economic infiltration of developing countries by manipulation of market forces. *See also* **Imperialism**.

Communism, ideally refers to the type of society in which all property belongs to the community and social life is based on the principle "from each according to his ability, to each according to his needs." There would be public ownership of all enterprises and all goods would be free.

Since no such society as yet exists, the word in practice refers to the attempt to achieve such a society by initially overthrowing the capitalist system and establishing a dictatorship of the proletariat (Marx identified the dictatorship with a democratic constitution). Communists believe that their first task is the establishment of socialism under which there remain class distinctions, private property to some extent, and differences between manual and brain workers. The state is regulated on the basis "from each according to his ability, to each according to his work".

Lenin applied Marx's analysis to the conditions which had arisen in 20th-cent. capitalist society. Marxism–Leninism develops continuously with practice since failure to apply its basic principles to changed circumstances and times would result in errors of dogmatism. Mao Tse-tung worked out the techniques of revolutionary action appropriate to China; Che Guevara the tactics appropriate to the peasants of Latin America.

A fundamental principle of communism is the class struggle between oppressed and oppressing classes and between oppressed and oppressor nations. Maoism, for example, held that it was a mistake to lay one sided stress on peaceful transition towards socialism otherwise the revolutionary will of the proletariat becomes passive as well as unprepared for the tasks ahead.

In Russia the civil war developed *after* the revolution; in China the communists fought their civil war *before* they seized power: the Yugoslav partisans won their own guerrilla war *during* their stand against the fascist powers— differences which had important political consequences. Russia suffered decades of isolationism and totalitarian suppression before the old Soviet Union collapsed. *See* **Maoism, Marxism** and **Trotskyism**.

Confucianism. Confucius (Latinised form of K'ung-Fo-tzu) was born in 551 B.C. in the feudal state of Lu in modern Shantung province. He was thus a contemporary of Buddha, although nobody could have been more dissimilar. Where Buddha was metaphysical in his thought, Confucius was practical; Buddha was original, Confucius had hardly an original idea in his head; Buddha wanted to convert individuals to an other-worldly philosophy. Confucius wanted to reform the feudal governments of his time, believing that in this way their subjects would be made happier. Other religions have in their time, been revolutionary; Confucius was a conservative who wanted to bring back a golden age from the past.

Much of his time was spent in going from the court of one feudal lord to another trying to impress them by his example. For he suffered from the curious belief that the example set by the ruler influences his subjects. He made much of etiquette, trembling and speaking in low tones and behaving with "lofty courtesy" to his inferiors. Promoting the idea of "the golden mean", he was not impressed by heroic deeds or unusual people, and was greatly displeased when he heard that a truthful son had reported that his father had stolen a sheep: "Those who are upright", he said, "are different from this; the father conceals the misconduct of the son, and the son conceals the misconduct of the father." One feels that Confucius would have felt not at all out of place in an English public school. Virtue brings its own reward in this world, ceremonial is important, politeness when universal would reduce jealousy and quarrels; "reverence the spirits but keep them far off." Destiny decides to what class a man shall belong, and as destiny is but another name for Nature prayer is unnecessary, for once having received his destiny, a man can demand and obtain from Nature what he chooses, his own will decides. In Confucian society, women played a lowly role.

Congregationalists, the oldest sect of Nonconformists who hold that each church should be independent of external ecclesiastical authority. They took their origin from the Brownists of Elizabeth's days. Robert Browne (*c.* 1550–*c.* 1633), an Anglican clergyman, who had come to reject bishops, was forced with his followers to seek refuge, first in Holland and then in Scotland where he changed his views and was imprisoned by the Kirk.

Later he changed his views and is disowned by Congregationalists because of his reversion to Anglicanism. His former views were spread by Henry Barrow and John Greenwood who, under an Act passed in 1592, were hanged at Tyburn.

They had preached (*a*) that the only head of the church is Jesus Christ; (*b*) that, contrary to Elizabethan doctrine, the church had no relationship to the state; (*c*) that the only statute-book was the Bible whereas the Articles of Religion and Book of Common Prayer were mere Acts of Parliament; (*d*) that each congregation of believers was independent and had the power of choosing its own ministers. The body fled once more to Holland and were among the Pilgrims who set sail in the *Mayflower* in 1620 whilst those who remained were joined by Puritans fleeing from Charles I.

They became free once more to live in England under the Commonwealth only to be repressed again under Charles II. Finally full liberty of worship was granted under William III. In 1833 the Congregational Union of England and Wales was formed which had no legislative power. It issued a Declaration of Faith by which no minister was bound; he was responsible only to his own church.

The sect is widespread both in Britain and the USA where it is held in special honour because of its connection with the Pilgrim Fathers. In 1972 the Congregational Church in England and Wales and the Presbyterian Church of England united to form the United Reformed Church. Those who did not join comprise the Congregational Federation.

Conservatism, is sceptical of rationalism as the lodestar of politics and social life. Conservatives instead prefer the inherited wisdom of tradition and history, regarding the persistence of values and institutions through time as a good pragmatic reason to justify their authority. Edmund Burke crystallised conservatism in his '*Reflections on the Revolution in France*' which argued that society was an organic unity with a naturally hierarchical relationship between its parts. A similar opposition to rationalism in politics was expressed in the 20th century by Michael Oakeshott. Oakeshott argued that socialism's rational approach to politics ignored the style of human relationships that were ordered more by experience, tradition, wisdom and prudence *etc.*

Contemporary conservative politics has been dominated more by neoliberalism (*q.v.*) than traditional conservative values. Contemporary conservatives share an opposition to social democratic values and bureaucratic state institutions, but favour a view of society as a free market rather than an organic unity.

Consumerism. Traditionally, an individual's identity and role in society was seen as determined by what they produced. Being a miner, a farmer, or an office clerk would contribute greatly to the nature of a person's income, social class, and opportunities. Increased prosperity, wider social and geographical mobility, and more pervasive markets have allowed for consumption to be a more important and dominant feature of the identity of persons and societies.

The proliferation of choice and products, combined with relentless advertising, has allowed consumerism to pervade all areas of life and society: toddlers and children are important consumers in contemporary markets.

Consumerism has also encroached on politics, and not simply in the promotion of political parties as brands and products. Parents and the sick are encouraged to see health and education as products to be consumed in a competitive market place. Successive governments justified this on the grounds that people expect choice in all areas of life, and that competition for consumers improves the quality of products, whether toasters, health, or education.

Cooperativism. A cooperative is an organization owned by and operated for the benefit of its members, who may be either workers or customers. They have been set up all over the world, for farming, purchasing of equipment and raw materials, and in wholesaling, retailing, banking, insurance and housing industries. In most cooperatives the members receive a share of the net earnings. The modern consumer cooperative movement started as the Rochdale Pioneers Society in 1844 and developed rapidly in the second half of the 19th century, mostly in the industrial areas of Northern England and Scotland. It spread quickly through northern Europe. Development in the USA and Latin America came later in the 20th century. The Cooperative Bank was established in the UK in 1872.

Coptic Church, the sect of Egyptian Christians who, holding "Monophysite" opinions (*i.e.,* refusing to grant the two natures, God and Man, of Christ), were declared heretical by the Council of Chalcedon in 451. They practise circumcision and have dietary laws. Their language is a direct descendant of ancient Egyptian. Like the Armenians, they are regarded as an heretical branch of Eastern Christianity. Their religious head is Patriarch Tawadros III. They are the largest Christian minority in the Middle East. They are currently suffering persecution.

Corporate State. State whose economic and political life is based on trade and on professional corporations rather than territorial units. Thus members of parliament would be elected by vocational corporations instead of by geographical con-

stituencies and would regulate industrial production and working conditions. The arguments in favour of such a system are that it would exclude party politics, prevent the state from growing too powerful and correspond to the links which truly bind people (professional ties, fellowship in the workplace and shared economic interest) rather than haphazard territorial association and that it would end class warfare. Believers in the theory have no particular bias to right or left although the societies which have come closest to being corporate states were Italy under Fascism and Portugal under the dictator Salazar (1928–74). The Catholic Church tended to favour the idea and Nazi Germany toyed with plans for it.

Counter-Reformation. A movement in the 16th and 17th centuries in Europe, by which the Roman Catholic church reformed itself, defined its doctrines, strengthened its discipline and halted the advance of Protestantism. The Council of Trent (1545–1563) aimed at removing abuses within the church and defining Catholic thought in the debate with Protestantism. New, more active religious orders were founded, in particular the Jesuits (1534).

The greater control exercised over church doctrine was seen in the setting up of the Inquisition and an Index of Prohibited Books. Some historians now prefer the term Catholic Reformation to Counter-Reformation.

Creationism. The theory which attributes the origin of matter, the different species of plants and animals, *etc.,* to "special creation" by a supreme being or deity. This '"Theory of Intelligent Design" suggests that certain organisms are so complex that they could only be the product of supernatural design rather than natural selection. Creationists thus accept that the Book of Genesis is a literal description of the beginning of the world. It is this doctrine which fundamentalist Christians have opposed to the evolutionary theories of Darwin, which are now accepted by most scientists since the publication of *The Origin of Species* in 1859.

An attempt was made in the 1980s in the USA to have creationism taught alongside evolution, but failed in the US Supreme Court.

A second slightly older meaning of the term is in reference to the theory that God creates a soul for every being born.

Cryonics, the practice of preserving humans using ultra-cold temperatures until medicine is sufficiently advanced to restore good health. In 1964, the publication by Robert Ettinger of *Prospect of Immortality* increased interest in the idea.

Cynics, a school of philosophy founded in the time of Alexander the Great by Diogenes. Choosing to live like a dog by rejecting all conventions of religion, manners, or decency, and allegedly living in a tub. Diogenes unwittingly brought on his school the title "Cynic", meaning not "cynical", as the word is understood today, but "canine".

His teacher, Antisthenes, who had been a disciple of Socrates, decided, after the latter's death, that all philosophy was useless quibbling and man's sole aim should be simple goodness. He believed in a return to nature, despised luxury, wanted no government, no private property, and associated with working men and slaves. Far from being cynics in the modern sense, Diogenes and Antisthenes were virtuous anarchists rather like Tolstoy.

D

Dalai Lama. *See* Lamaism.
Dalits. *See* Untouchables.
Daoism. *See* Taoism.
Dead Sea Scrolls. *See* Essenes (J17).
Deism. *See* God and Man.
Demonism, Demons, and the Devil. Demons are ethereal beings of various degrees of significance and power which are believed to be implicated in men's good, but especially evil, fortune. They are common to most cultures. From the anthropological point of view the demon arose as a widespread concept in the following ways: (1) as a psychological projection into the outer world of man's own good or evil emotions and thoughts; (2) as a survival of primitive animism (*q.v.*), thus spirits are believed to haunt places, trees, stones, and other natural objects; (3)

when by warlike invasion the gods of the vanquished become the devils of the conquerors (as
when the Jews occupied Canaan); (4) as a
primitive belief that spirits of the dead continue after death to hover near their former
habitation, and not always entirely welcome to
the living; (5) the conception of a supreme
source of evil (the Devil or Satan) which took
shape among the Jews during their sojourn in
Babylon under the influence of Zoroastrianism
(q.v.), a religion in which the struggle between
the two spirits, Good and Evil, reached its height
in the imagination of the ancient world.

The Satan of the Old Testament was first
regarded as one of God's servants (in the Book of
Job he goes up and down the earth to see whether
God's commands are obeyed), but when the Jews
returned from their captivity he had become
identified with Ahriman, the spirit of evil, who
was in continual conflict with Ahursa Mazda, the
spirit of good. The primitive mind ascribed both
good and evil to one power alone; the division into
God and the Devil, priest and witch, belongs to a
higher stage of civilisation. The worship of evil
itself, or of its personification in Satan, is a
curious practice which seems to have developed
hand-in-hand with Christianity and has often
received steady support from a small but measurable minority.

Determinism and Free-will. The question of
whether man is, or is not, free to mould his own
destiny is one which has exercised the minds of
philosophers since Greek mythology conceived
of the Fates as weaving a web of destiny from
which no man can free himself. Socrates emphasised that man could through knowledge
influence his destiny whilst ignorance made him
the plaything of fate; Plato went further in
pointing out that man can, and does, defeat the
purposes of the universe and its divine Creator.
It is our duty to live a good life, but we can live
a foolish and wicked one if we chose. Aristotle
wrote "Virtue is a disposition or habit involving
deliberate purpose or choice". If this were not
so morality would be a sham.

The Problem for Theology. The last of the
great philosophers of Antiquity and one of the
great influences in moulding Catholic theology was
Plotinus (c. 204–70). Soul, he taught, is free, but
once enmeshed in the body loses its freedom in the
life of sense. Nevertheless, man is free to turn
away from sensuality and towards God who is perfect freedom; for even when incarnated in matter
the soul does not entirely lose the ability to rescue
itself. This conception was carried over into the
beliefs of the early Christian Apologists because it
appeared to be in line with the teaching of Jesus
that He had come to save man from sin. Sin
implies guilt, and guilt implies the freedom to
act otherwise; furthermore an all-good God
cannot be responsible for the sin in the world
which must be man's responsiblity and this
again implies freedom.

Pelagius (c. 355–c. 425), a Welsh priest, not only
believed in free-will but questioning the doctrine
of original sin, said that when men act righteously
it is through their own moral effort, and God
rewards them for their virtues in heaven. This
belief became fairly widespread and was declared
a heresy by the Church, being attacked notably
by St. Augustine (354–430), a contemporary of
Pelagius, who believed in predestination—that,
since the sin of Adam, God had chosen who in all
future history would be saved and who damned.
This represents one tradition in Christianity: the
determinism which leads to Calvinism (q.v.).

St. Thomas Aquinas (1227–74), the greatest
figure of scholasticism and one of the principal
saints in the Roman Catholic Church, compromised between the two positions in the sense that,
believing man to be free, he yet held that Adam's
sin was transmitted to all mankind and only
divine grace can bring salvation. But even when
God wishes to bestow this salvation, the human
will must cooperate. God foresees that some will
not accept the offer of grace and predestines them
to eternal punishment.

The Problem for Philosophy. With the
Renaissance, thinkers began to free themselves
from the domination of the Church and so study
the world objectively and freely without pre-
conceptions. But the more man turned to
science, the more he discovered that the world

was ruled by apparently inexorable laws and,
since the scientist must believe that every event
has a cause, he was led back to determinism.
Man as part of the universe was subject to law
too and all that existed was a vast machine.
Francis Bacon (1561–1626) separated the fields
of religion and science but left man subject
completely to the will of God. Thomas Hobbes
(1588–1679) was a rigid determinist and
materialist although, having had trouble with
the church in France whence, as a royalist, he
had fled, he took care to announce that the
Christian God is the Prime Mover.

Descartes. Modern philosophy begins with
René Descartes (1596–1650), a Frenchman who
tried to reconcile the mechanical scientific universe
of his time with the spiritual need for freedom.
He did this by separating completely mind and
body; the former, he said, is free, the latter
completely determined. But, by admitting that
the will can produce states of body, he was left
with the problem of how this could happen—a
problem which the so-called Occasionists solved
to their own satisfaction by stating that the will
is free and God so arranges the universe that
what a person wills happens. Baruch Spinoza
(1632–77), a Dutch Jew whose independence
of thought had led to his excommunication
from the Amsterdam Synagogue in 1656, was
a complete determinist. He asserted that God
and Nature are one, everything that happens
is a manifestation of God's inscrutable nature,
and it is logically impossible that things could
be other than they are. Thus both Hobbes and
Spinoza were determinists for entirely opposed
reasons. The former as a materialist, the latter
because he believed in the absolute perfection
and universality of God. Yet the great religious
mystic and mathematician Blaise Pascal (1623–
62) held that, no matter what reason and cold
logic may indicate we *know* from direct religious
experience that we are free. John Calvin
(1509–64) and Martin Luther (1483–1546) were
both determinists. See **Calvinism, Lutheranism.**

Locke and Hume. To the British philosophers,
John Locke (1632–1704) and David Hume
(1711–76), free-will was related to personality.
Locke believed that God had implanted in each
individual certain desires and these determine
the will; the desires are already there, but we
use our will to satisfy them. Hume argued that
a man's behaviour is the necessary result of his
character and if he had a different character he
would act otherwise. Accordingly, when a
man's actions arise from his own nature and
desires he is free. He is not free when external
events compel him to act otherwise (e.g., if he
strikes another because his own nature is such
he is free as he is not if he is compelled to do
so against his desire). Leibnitz (1646–1716),
although as a German metaphysical philosopher
holding very different general views, said much
the same thing—that choice is simply selecting
the desire that is strongest. But most of the
18th cent. thinkers after Voltaire, with the great
exceptions of Rousseau and the later German
philosophers Kant, Fichte, Schopenhauer, and
Hegel, who were initially influenced by him,
accepted determinism. Rousseau (1712–78) began
to stem the tide by his declaration that man is a
free soul striving to remain free and only prevented from being so by society and the cold science which stifles his feeling heart. Once again the
will became important as Kant (1724–1804)
asserted that belief in freedom is a moral necessity
although it cannot be proved by reason; the moral
nature of man shows that there is a "transcendental" world beyond the senses where freedom
applies. Fichte and Schelling found freedom in
the Absolute ego or God, of whom each individual
was part and thus also free. Hegel (1770–1831)
saw the whole universe as evolving towards self-
awareness and freedom in man although this could
only be fully realised in a society that makes
for freedom. Even God himself only attains full
consciousness and self-realisation through the
minds of such individuals as are free. This is the
goal of the dialectical process. (See **Dialectical
Materialism.**)

The Scientist's View. For the scientist the
law of cause and effect is a useful hypothesis
since, by and large, it is necessary for him to
assume that all events are caused. Neverthe-

less the modern tendency is to think in terms of statistical probability rather than relentless mechanistic causality, and, although the free-will problem does not concern the scientist as such, it is clear that freedom and determinism (assuming the terms to have any meaning at all) are not necessarily opposed. In sociology, for example, we *know* that certain actions will produce certain results upon the behaviour of people in general, *e.g.*, that raising interest rates will discourage business expansion. But this does not mean that Mr. Brown who decides in the circumstances not to add a new wing to his factory is not using his free-will. Even in the case of atoms, as Dr. Bronowski has pointed out, the observed results of allowing gas under pressure in a cylinder to rush out occur because most of the atoms are "obeying" the scientific "law" relating to such situations. But this does not mean that some atoms are not busy rushing across the stream or even against it—they are, but the general tendency is outwards and that is what we note. Lastly, the modern philosophical school of Logical Analysis would probably ask, not whether Free-will or Determinism is the true belief, but whether the question has any meaning. For what scientific experiment could we set up to prove one or the other true? The reader will note that some of the philosophers mentioned above are using the words to mean quite different concepts.

Dialectical Materialism, the combination of Hegel's dialectic method with a materialist philosophy produced by Karl Marx (1818–83) and his friend Friedrich Engels (1820–95). It is the philosophical basis of both **Marxism** (*q.v.*) and **Communism** (*q.v.*) "Dialectic" to the ancient Greek philosophers meant a kind of dialogue or conversation, as used particularly by Socrates, in which philosophical disputes were resolved by a series of successive contradictions: a thesis is put forward and the opposing side holds its contradiction or antithesis until in the course of argument a synthesis is reached in which the conflicting ideas are resolved.

From Thesis through Antithesis to Synthesis. Hegel in the 19th cent. put forward the view that this process applies to the course of nature and history as they strive towards the perfect state. But to him, as to the Greeks, the conflict was in the field of ideas. The "universal reason" behind events works through the ideas held by a particular society until they are challenged by those of another which supersedes them and in turn, usually by war, becomes the agent of universal reason until the arrival of a new challenger. Hegel therefore regarded war as an instrument of progress and his identifying their own state as the new agent of progress by universal conquest.

Feuerbach, Lassalle, and other early socialists were impressed by some of Hegel's ideas: *e.g.*, that societies evolved (with the assumption that finally their own ideal society would be achieved) and that truth, morals, and concepts were relative so that a society that was "good" at one time was not necessarily so at another.

However, Marx and Engels in effect turned Hegel upside-down, accepted his dialectic but rejected his belief that ideas were the motive force. On the contrary, they said, ideas are determined by social and economic change as a result of materialistic forces. (*See* **Calvinism,** where it is pointed out that the Marxist view is not that Calvin changed men's economic ideas but rather that a developing capitalism unconsciously changed his.) The historical materialism of Marxism purports to show that the inexorable dialectic determines that feudalism is displaced by capitalism and capitalism by creating a proletariat (its antithesis) inevitably leads to socialism and a classless society. The state, as a tool of the dominant class, withers away. Dialectical materialism is applied in all spheres. As a philosophy there is little to be said for it save that it has shown us the close dependence of man's thoughts upon material and social conditions. But as a battle-cry it wielded immense power over the minds of men. *See also under* **Marxism.**

Dianetics. *See* **Scientology.**

Diggers, one of the many sects which flourished under the Commonwealth (others were the Muggletonians, the Levellers, the Millennarians, and the Fifth Monarchy Men), so-called because they attempted to dig (*i.e.* cultivate) untilled land. Gerrard Winstanley, a profoundly religious man, and leader of the Diggers, believed in the economic and social equality of man and castigated the clergy for upholding the class structure of society. In his book *The True Leveller's Standard Advanced* (1649) he wrote: "Every day poor people are forced to work for fourpence a day, though corn is dear. And yet the tithing priest stops their mouth and tells them that "inward satisfaction of mind' was meant by the declaration "the poor shall inherit the earth'. I tell you, the Scripture is to be really and materially fulfilled. You jeer at the name "Leveller'; I tell you Jesus Christ is the Head Leveller".

Diwali, the annual "festival of lights", celebrated by Hindus, Sikhs and Jains, held between mid-October and mid-November.

Doukhobors, a religious sect of Russian origin, founded by a Prussian sergeant at Kharkov in the middle of the 18th cent., and now mainly settled in Canada. Like many other sects they belong to that type of Christianity which seeks direct communication with God and such bodies tend to have certain traits in common, such as belief in the "inner light", opposition to war and authority in general, and often ecstasies which show themselves in physical ways such as shaking, speaking in strange tongues (glossolalia), and other forms of what to the unbeliever seem mass hysteria. Liturgy, ritual, or ceremony is non-existent.

The Doukhobors were persecuted in Tsarist Russia, but in 1898 Tolstoy used his influence to have them removed to Canada in what is now Saskatchewan.

Dowsing. *See* **Radiesthesia.**

Dreamtime, in Australian aboriginal mythology, the period of time when mystic beings shaped the natural environment. Some of these mystic beings took human form. Human life was created by the great fertility mother. To the aborigines, these mystic beings are spiritually alive today. Alternative names for this period are *World Dawn* or *The Dreaming*.

Druidism, the ancient religion of Celtic Britain and Gaul of which Druids were the priesthood. They were finally wiped out by the Roman general Suetonius Paulinus *c.* A.D. 61 in their last stronghold, the island of Anglesey. There are two sources of our present knowledge of Druidism:

(1) the brief and factual records of the Romans, notably Pliny and Julius Caesar, which tell us that they worshipped in sacred oak groves and presumably practised a religion doing reverence to the powers of nature.

(2) the beliefs put forward by William Stukeley, an amateur antiquarian who from 1718 did valuable work by his studies of the stone circles at Stonehenge and Avebury. However, influenced by the Romantic movement, he later put forward the most extravagant theories. Stonehenge and Avebury were depicted as the temples of the "white-haired Druid bard sublime" and an attempt was made to tie up Druidism with early Christianity, above all with the concept of the Trinity. In fact, these circles have no connection with the Druids. They may have made ceremonial use of them but recent evidence suggests that the megalithic stones at Stonehenge belong to a Bronze Age culture (2100–1600 B.C.). Nor have Druidism and Christianity any relationship.

In 2010 Druidism became the first pagan practice in the UK to be given official recognition as a religion by the Charity Commission.

Druze, an offshoot of Islam, with around 200,000 followers in Lebanon and *c.* 1·5 million globally. Most lived in Syria before the 2011 uprising there.

Dualism, any philosophical or theological theory which implies that the universe has a double nature, notably Plato's distinction between appearance and reality, soul and body, ideas and material objects, reason and the evidence of the senses, which infers that behind the world as we perceive it there lies an "ideal" world which is more "real" than that of mere appearance. In religions such as Zoroastrianism or the Gnostic and Manichaeism heresies, it was believed that the universe was ruled by good and evil "principles"—in effect that there was a good God and a bad one. In psychology, dualism refers to the philosophical theories which believe mind and body to be separate entities. The opposite of dualism is monism which asserts the essential unity of the substance of the universe.

An essential problem in the dualistic view lies in the question as to how and where the two separate and distinct properties of the universe interact. Where, for example, does the "mind" actually mesh with the physical mechanics of the brain and body—where does the ghost sit in his machine? Descartes decided that mind and body must interact somewhere and he selected the pineal gland (an apparently functionless part of the brain) as the spot. But this did nothing to explain how two *totally different* aspects of nature can possibly influence each other, and today most philosophers and psychologists reject dualistic views of life and personality as posing more problems than they solve. *See also* **Psychology, Occam's Razor.**

E

Ecumenism, a world movement which springs from the Christian belief that all men are brothers and that the Christian Church should be re-structured to give reality to the belief. Christ's church exists not to serve its own members, but for the service of the whole world. Some see the answer in a united church of a federal type (unity in diversity), others in an organic structure with one set of rules. The period since the convening of the Second Vatican Council by Pope John has been one of prolonged discussion among Christian theologians with the aim of promoting Christian unity.

Education. Education was no great problem to primitive man, but as societies became more complex people began to ask themselves such questions as: *What* should young people be taught? *How* should they be taught? Should the aim of their education be to bring out their individual qualities or rather to make them good servants of the state?

The first teachers were priests who knew most about the traditions, customs, and lore of their societies and thus the first schools were in religious meeting places. This was notably true of the Jews who learned from the rabbis in the synagogue.

The Greeks. We begin, as always, with the Greeks whose city-states, based on slavery, educated men (not women) for the sort of life described in Plato's *Dialogues*—the leisured life of gentlemen arguing the problems of the universe at their banquets or in the market-place. This made it necessary to learn debate and oratory (or rhetoric) especially for those who proposed to take up politics. The Sophist philosophy taught the need to build up convincing arguments in a persuasive manner, to learn the rules of logic and master the laws and customs of the Athenians, and to know the literature of the past so that illustrations might be drawn from it. These strolling philosophers who taught for a fee were individualists showing the student how to advance himself at all costs.

Socrates had a more ethical approach, believing that education was good in itself, made a man happier and a better citizen, and emphasised his position as a member of a group. His method of teaching, the dialectic or "Socratic" method, involved argument and discussion rather than overwhelming others by rhetoric and is briefly mentioned under **Dialectical Materialism** (*q.v.*). Today this method is increasingly used in adult education where a lecture is followed by a period of discussion in which both lecturer and audience participate; for psychologists have shown that people accept ideas more readily when conviction arises through their own arguments.

Socrates' pupil Plato produced in his book *The Republic* one of the first comprehensive systems of education and vocational selection. Believing that essentially men have very different and unequal abilities he considered that in an idealistic or utopian society they should be put into social classes corresponding to these differences, and suggested the following method:

(1) For the first 18 years of a boy's life he should be taught gymnastics and sports, playing and singing music, reading and writing, a knowledge of literature, and if he passed this course sent on to the next stage; those who failed were to become tradesmen and merchants. (2) From 18–20 those successful in the first course were to be given two years of cadet training, the ones thought incapable of further education being placed in the military class as soldiers. (3) The remainder, who were to become the leaders of society, proceeded with advanced studies in philosophy, mathematics, science, and art. Such education was to be a state concern, state supported and controlled, selecting men and training them for service in the state according to their abilities.

Plato's pupil Aristotle even suggested that the state should determine shortly after birth which children should be allowed to live and destroy the physically or mentally handicapped; that marriage should be state-controlled to ensure desirable offspring. However, in their time the leisured and individualistic Sophists held the field and few accepted the educational views of Plato or his pupil.

Rome. The Romans were not philosophers and most of their culture came from Greece. Administration was their chief aptitude and Quintilian (A.D. *c.* 35–*c.* 95) based his higher education on the earlier classical tuition in public speaking, but he is important for emphasising the training of character and for his humanistic approach to the method of teaching that caused his *Institutio oratoria* to be influential for centuries later—indeed one might almost say up to the time of the great Dr. Arnold of Rugby. Education, he believed, should begin early but one must "take care that the child not old enough to love his studies does not come to hate them" by premature forcing; studies must be made pleasant and interesting and students encouraged by praise rather than discouraged when they sometimes fail; play is to be approved of as a sign of a lively disposition and because gloomy, depressed children are not likely to be good students; corporal punishment should never be used because "it is an insult as you will realise if you imagine it yourself". The world became interested not in *what* he taught but *how* he taught it; he was the pioneer of humanistic education and character-training from Vittorino d. Feltre (1378–1446) of Mantua, through Milton and Pope who commended his works to the modern educationists who have studied their pupils as well as their books.

The Middle Ages: *The Religious View.* With the development of Christianity education once more became a religious concern. The earliest converts had to be taught Christian doctrine and were given instruction in "catechumenal" schools before admission to the group, but as the religion came increasingly into contact with other religions or heresies a more serious training was necessary, and from these newer "catechetical" schools, where the method used was the catechism (*i.e.*, question and answer as known to all Presbyterian children today), the Apologists arose among whom were Clement of Alexandria and the great Origen. From this time education became an instrument of the church and in 529 the Emperor Justinian ordered all pagan schools to be closed.

As typical of the best in medieval education we may mention St. Benedict (*c.* 480–*c.* 547) of Monte Cassino. There, in southern Italy, a rule was established which became a part of monastic life in general. Monastic schools were originally intended for the training of would-be monks, but later others were admitted who simply wanted some education; thus two types of school developed one for the *interni* and the other for *externi* or external pupils. Originally studies were merely reading in order to study the Bible, writing to copy the sacred books, and sufficient calculation to be able to work out the advent of holy days or festivals. But by the end of the 6th cent. the "seven liberal arts" (grammar, rhetoric, dialectic, arithmetic, geometry, music, and astronomy) were added.

The Renaissance. The close of the Middle Ages saw the development of two types of secular school. One came with the rise of the new merchant class and the skilled trader whose "guilds" or early trade unions established schools to train young men for their trades but ultimately gave rise to burgher or town schools; the other was the court school founded and supported by the wealthy rulers of the Italian cities—Vittorio da Feltre (mentioned above) presided over the most famous at Mantua.

These Renaissance developments are parallelled in northern Europe by the Protestant reformers who, having with Martin Luther held that everyone should know how to read his Bible in order to interpret it in his own way, were logically committed to popular education, compulsory and universal. In theory this was intended for biblical study, but writing, arithmetic, and other elementary subjects were taught and Luther said that, even if heaven and hell did not exist, education was important. In this sense, universal education is a Protestant conception.

Hobbes and Locke. From this period onwards people were free to put forward any ideas about education, foolish or otherwise, and to create their own types of school. Of English philosophers who theorised about, but did not practise, education we may mention the rationalist Francis Bacon (1561–1626) who saw learning as the dissipation of all prejudices and the collection of concrete facts; the materialist and totalitarian Hobbes (1588–1679) who, as a royalist, believed that the right to determine the kind of education fit for his subjects is one of the absolute rights of the sovereign power or ruler; the gentlemanly Locke (1632–1704) whose ideal was a sound mind in a sound body to be attained by hard physical exercise, wide experience of the world, and enough knowledge to meet the requirements of the pupil's environment. The end result would be one able to get on with his fellows, pious but wise in the ways of the world, independent and able to look after himself, informed but reticent about his knowledge. Classics and religious study were not to be carried to excess, since Locke held that these subjects had been much overrated in the past.

Jean-Jacques Rousseau (1712–78), a forerunner of the Romantic movement (q.v.), which despised society and its institutions, put emotion at a higher level than reason. His book *Emile* describes the education of a boy which is natural and spontaneous. Society, he holds, warps the growing mind and therefore the child should be protected from its influences until his development in accordance with his own nature is so complete that he cannot be harmed by it. During the first 4 years the body should be developed by physical training; from 5 to 12 the child would live in a state of nature such that he could develop his powers of observation and his senses; from 13 books would be used and intellectual training introduced, although only in line with the child's own interests, and he would be given instruction only as he came to ask for it. Moral training and contact with his fellows to learn the principles of sympathy, kindness, and helpfulness to mankind would be given between 15 and 20. Girls, however, should be educated to serve men in a spirit of modesty and restraint. His own five children he deposited in a foundling hospital.

Summary. Broadly speaking, then, there have been four main attitudes to education: (1) religious, with a view to a life beyond death; (2) state-controlled education, with a view to uniform subservience to authority; (3) "gentlemanly" education, with a view to social graces and easy congress in company; (4) the "child-centred" education, which attempts to follow the pupil's inner nature. It is unnecessary to mention the ordinary method of attempting to instil facts without any considerable degree of co-operation between pupil and teacher in order that the former may, with or without interest, follow some occupation in adult life; for this the philosophers did not consider. Today there remain the two fundamental principles: education for the advantage of the state and its ideology or education for individual development and freedom.

Modern Educationalists. Four educationists of the modern period who have influenced us in the direction of freedom were Johann Pestalozzi of Switzerland (1746–1827) who, by trying to understand children, taught the "natural, progressive, and harmonious development of all the powers and capacities of the human being"; Friedrich Froebel (1782–1852) of Germany, the founder of the Kindergarten who, like Pestalozzi, was influenced by Rousseau but realised the need to combine complete personal development with social adjustment; Maria Montessori (1869–1952) whose free methods have revolutionised infant teaching; John Dewey (1859–1952) who held that the best interests of the group are served when the individual develops his own particular talents.

Egalitarianism. The doctrine that human beings are, in an important sense, equal and that it is desirable to remove inequalities by social and political means. It was part of the famous slogan of the French Revolution: "Liberty, Equality, Fraternity". There has been much debate, however, as to what extent human beings are, in fact, equal. Critics of equality as a political ideal argue that it conflicts with other more valuable ideals or social values, and that the different kinds of equality are not compatible.

Eid, the Muslim festival which celebrates the end of Ramadan (the fasting period). It is the holiest day in the Islamic calendar, marking the willingness of Abraham to sacrifice his son Isaac.

Eleatics, the philosophers of Elea in ancient Greece who, at the time when Heraclitus (c. 535–475 B.C.) was teaching that change is all that exists and nothing is permanent, were asserting that change is an illusion. Of the three leaders of this school, Xenophanes asserted that the universe was a solid immovable mass forever the same; Parmenides explained away change as an inconceivable process, its appearance being due to the fact that what we see is unreal; and Zeno (the best-known today) illustrated the same thesis with his famous argument of the arrow which, at any given moment of its flight, must be where it is since it cannot be where it is not. But if it is where it is, it cannot move, this is based, of course, on the delusion that motion is discontinuous.

Elitism. A political theory, largely drawn from the writings of V. Pareto (1848–1923). Power in a society will always be exercised by a minority (the elite) which takes the major decisions. An elite gains its dominant position through possessing certain resources or qualities valued in that particular society, e.g. priests or soldiers or senior state officials. Elites normally aim to continue their domination, but are not always capable of doing so and become displaced by another elite. If elite rule is inevitable then there can be no hope of an egalitarian, socialist society. This analysis of the importance of elites has been very influential. Some sociologists have extended the theory in recent years to argue that in all developed countries there is a plurality of competing elites within different systems of control. Such systems are politics, trade union organisations, cultural and educational institutions.

Empiricism. While not a single school of philosophy, empiricism is an approach to knowledge which holds that if a man wants to know what the universe is like the only correct way to do so is to go and look for himself, to collect facts which come to him through his senses. It is, in essence, the method of science as contrasted with rationalism (q.v.) which in philosophy implies that thinking or reasoning without necessarily referring to external observations can arrive at truth. Empiricism is typically a British attitude, for among the greatest empirical philosophers were John Locke, George Berkeley, and David Hume. See **Rationalism**.

Encyclopedists. The writers (all men) who contributed to the *Encyclopedie* published in France from 1751 to 1772. The work's full title was *Encyclopedie, ou dictionnaire raisonne des sciences, des arts et des metiers*. It was designed as a synoptic description of all branches of human knowledge, and is perhaps the most characteristic work of the Enlightenment (q.v.). The *Encyclopedie* was inspired by Chambers' *Cyclopedia, or a universal dictionary of arts and sciences* published in London in 1728. The project began in 1745, with Denis Diderot and Jean d'Alembert as editors. The latter resigned in 1758, leaving Diderot to shoulder most of the work. In 1772 the project reached 28 volumes; between 1776 and 1780 7 supplementary volumes were published.

Besides Diderot and d'Alembert and many obscure writers, Voltaire, Rousseau and d'Holbach contributed. The work was a showcase for representatives of new schools of thought in all branches of intellectual activity. The work was tolerant, liberal, and also innovative in giving attention to trades and mechanical arts. In its scepticism, its emphasis on being scientific, and its criticism of superstition and contemporary social institutions, the *Encyclopedie* had immense influence.

Enlightenment. A European intellectual movement of the 18th century. Enlightenment thinkers aimed to bring clarity, order and reason, in a word, *light* to regions where formerly there had been mystery, superstition and blind authority, that is, darkness. Man would become enlightened by knowledge and progress to greater happiness and freedom. The movement affected the arts, the sciences, political and social life.

The Enlightenment was prepared by the rise of science from the 16th century on. In particular, the success of Newton (1642–1727) in encapsulating the laws that govern the motion of the planets gave great hopes in man's capacity to attain extensive understanding. According to the German philosopher Kant (1724–1804) the motto of the Enlightenment was "Have courage to use your own understanding". Scientific knowledge was the ideal. If something was held to be true, it had to be based on dispassionate rational investigation. This overrode any claim to knowledge based on authority. One great source of authority was the Christian church, which was widely criticised by Enlightenment thinkers (*e.g.* in Voltaire's *Candide*); another was the despotism and arbitrary power of many states at the time. Although there is now a tendency to be sceptical about the Enlightenment and the power of reason, the belief in human progress through increased knowledge has been one of the most powerful of all ideas.

Epicureanism. The two great schools of the Hellenistic period (*i.e.* the late Greek period beginning with the empire of Alexander the Great) were the Stoics and Epicureans, the former founded by Zeno of Citium (not to be confused with Zeno the Eleatic) (*q.v.*), the latter by Epicurus, born in Samos in 342 B.C.

Both schools settled in Athens, where Epicurus taught that "pleasure is the beginning and end of a happy life." However, he was no sensualist and emphasised the importance of moderation in all things because excesses would lead to pain instead of pleasure and the best of all pleasures were mental ones. Pleasures could be active or passive but the former contain an element of pain since they are the process of satisfying desire not yet satiated. The latter involving the absence of desire are the more pleasant. In fact, Epicurus in his personal life was more stoical than many Stoics and wrote "when I live on bread and water I spit on luxurious pleasures." He disapproved of sexual enjoyment and thought friendship one of the highest of all joys.

A materialist who accepted the atomic theory of Democritus, he was not a determinist, and if he did not dis-believe in the gods he regarded religion and the fear of death as the two primary sources of unhappiness.

Epiphenomenalism. *See* Mind and Body.

Erastianism, the theory that the state has the right to decide the religion of its members, wrongly attributed to Erastus of Switzerland (1524–83) who was believed to have held this doctrine. The term has usually been made use of in a derogatory sense–*e.g.*, by the Scottish churches which held that the "call" of the congregation was the only way to elect ministers at a time when, about the turn of the 17th and 18th cent., they felt that Episcopalianism was being foisted on them. "Episcopalianism" (*i.e.* Anglicanism) with its state church, ecclesiastical hierarchy, and system of livings presented by patrons was to them "Erastian" in addition to its other "unscriptural practices."

Essenes, a Jewish sect which, during the oppressive rule of Herod (d. 4 B.C.), set up monastic communities in the region of the Dead Sea. They refused to be bound by the scriptural interpretations of the Pharisees and adhered rigorously to the letter of Holy Writ, although with additions of their own which cause them by orthodox Jews today to be regarded as a break-away from Judaism. Among their practices and beliefs were purification through baptism, renunciation of sexual pleasures, scrupulous cleanliness, strict observance of the Mosaic law, communal possession, asceticism.

Akin in spirit, though not necessarily identical with them, were the writers of Apocalyptic literature preaching that the evils of the present would shortly be terminated by a new supernatural order heralded by a Messiah who would reign over a restored Israel. The casting out of demons and spiritual healing formed part of these general beliefs which were in the air at that time. The sect has an importance far beyond its size or what has been known about it in the past since the discovery from 1947 onwards of the Dead Sea Scrolls of the Qumran community occupying a monastery in the same area as the Essenes and holding the same type of belief.

These scrolls with their references to a "Teacher of Righteousness" preceding the Messiah have clear relevance to the sources of early Christianity and have given rise to speculations as to whether Jesus might have been influenced by views which, like His own, were unacceptable to orthodox Jews but in line with those of the Dead Sea communities. Some scholars now think that early Christianity was not a sudden development but a gradual one which had its predecessors. A recent view suggests that the Essenes may not have existed as a sect at all.

Ethical Church, a movement typical of 19th cent. rationalism which attempted to combine atheism (or at any rate the absence of any belief in a God which was inconsistent with reason or based on revelation) with the inculcation of moral principles. Prayers were not used and ordinarily the service consisted in the singing of edifying compositions interspersed with readings from poems or prose of a similar nature by great writers holding appropriate views. It terminated in a talk on an ethical or scientific theme. Conway Hall (built 1929) in Red Lion Square, London, belongs to the South Place Ethical Society, founded by Moncure Conway who preached at their Unitarian chapel in South Place, Finsbury, 1864–97.

Eugenics, a 19th-cent. movement largely instigated by the British scientist and mathematician, Sir Francis Galton. Galton argued that many of the most satisfactory attributes of mankind—intelligence, physical strength, resistance to disease, *etc.*—were genetically determined and thus handed down in the normal process of inheritance. From this he reasoned that selective mating of physical "superior" individuals, and its converse, the controlled limitation on the breeding of criminals or the insane, would lead inevitably to a progressive improvement in the overall standards of the human race. In their simplest form these proposals are incontestable, though they do of course introduce marked restrictions on the choice of the individual for marriage and procreation. Even worse is the way in which the argument can be misapplied as in Nazi Germany to include the sterilisation of alcoholics, criminals and even epileptics.

In 1997 it was revealed that extensive sterilisation of mentally-handicapped people had been carried out until the 1970s in Norway and Switzerland.

Euthanasia (mercy killing), the term applied to the painless killing of those (especially the old) suffering from unbearable pain and an illness for which there is no cure. In Britain, attempts in Parliament to introduce its legalisation have failed but in 1993 Holland voted to tolerate euthanasia governed by tight guidelines. Under these procedures, euthanasia is tolerated when the patient is conscious, suffers an incurable disease paired with intolerable pain and clearly requests a "soft death". The World Right to Die Organisation has thriving branches world-wide.

Legislation permitting voluntary euthanasia was passed in the Northern Territory of Australia in 1995 and the world's first legal euthanasia took place in 1996. In 1997 the Liberal Democrats became the first major party in Britain to debate the issue and there is increasing pressure in the UK for reform of the law to make it legal to assist a terminally ill person if they wish to die (currently euthanasia and assisted suicide are illegal in the UK). In 2009 Debbie Purdy (a multiple sclerosis sufferer) won a landmark case when told she was right to demand a written set of criteria outlining when someone might be prosecuted for helping a loved one die abroad.

In 2001 the Dutch government decriminalised mercy killing by passing new legislation. Belgium followed the Dutch example in May 2002. Luxembourg legalised euthanasia in 2010. Switzerland also allows assisted suicide for the terminally ill. France is following a similar path (and euthanasia is legal in Canada since 2016). India has also ruled (in 2011) that life support may legally be withdrawn from some patients. In 2014 Belgium became the first country to allow terminally-ill children to end their lives.

In Britain the landmark report in 2011 of the Commission on Assisted Dying gave strong support to an assisted death in certain circumstances. However, an Assisted Dying Bill was rejected in the House of Commons in September 2015 by 330 votes to 118.

Euthanasia is the biggest bioethical issue of our time. Reform of the law is now being sought in Parliament by such groups as Dignity in Dying.

Evangelicalism, the belief of those Protestant sects which hold that the essence of the Gospel consists in the doctrine of salvation by faith in the atoning death of Christ and not by good works or the sacraments; that worship should be "free" rather than liturgical through established forms; that ritual is unacceptable and superstitious. Evangelicals are Low Churchmen. Nowadays, a new breed of evangelical Christianity is flourishing as a result of the Alpha course and the conservative Reform group. They have a powerful ally in the hardline Anglican Church in Africa.

Evangelism, the preaching of the Gospel, emphasising the necessity for a new birth or conversion. The evangelistic fervour of John Wesley and George Whitefield (*see* Methodism) aroused the great missionary spirit of the late 18th and 19th cent. George Fox, founder of the Society of Friends (*q.v.*), was also an evangelist. Evangelists can be Low, High, or Middle Churchmen.

Evolutionary Psychology, an approach that aims at understanding the relationship between psychological processes, behaviours and the evolutionary mechanisms that have shaped human physiology. It studies the ways in which the survival value of certain behaviours and cognitive abilities may have resulted in current human psychology.

Existentialism, a highly subjective philosophy which many people connect with such names as Jean-Paul Sartre (1905–80) or Albert Camus (1913–60) and assume to be a post-war movement. However, existentialism stems from Sören Kierkegaard (1813–55), the Danish "religious writer"—his own description of himself—in such works as *Either/Or, Fear and Trembling,* and *Concluding Unscientific Postscript.* Between the two world wars translations of Kierkegaard into German influenced Martin Heidegger's great work *Being and Time* and the other great existentialist Karl Jaspers; it has strongly influenced modern Protestant theology notably in Karl Barth, Reinhold Niebuhr, and Paul Tillich and beyond that field the French philosopher Gabriel Marcel, the Spanish writer Unamuno in his well-known *The Tragic Sense of Life,* and Martin Buber of Israel in his *I and Thou.* We have it on Heidegger's authority that "Sartre is no philosopher" even if it is to his works that modern existentialists often turn.

Existentialism is extremely difficult for the non-metaphysically-minded to understand, it deals, not with the nature of the universe or what are ordinarily thought of as philosophical problems but describes an attitude to life or God held by the individual. Briefly, its main essentials are: (1) it distinguishes between *essence, i.e.,* that aspect of an entity which can be observed and known—and its *existence*—the fact of its having a place in a changing and dangerous world which is what really matters; (2) existence being basic, each self-aware individual can grasp his own

existence on reflection in his own immediate experience of himself and his situation as a free being in the world; what he finds is not merely a knowing self but a self that fears, hopes, believes, wills, and is aware of its need to find a purpose, plan, and destiny in life; (3) but we cannot grasp our existence by thought alone; thus the fact "all men must die" relates to the essence of man but it is necessary to be involved, to draw the conclusion as a person that "I too must die" and experience its impact on our own individual existence; (4) because of the preceding, it is necessary to abandon our attitude of objectivity and theoretical detachment when faced by the problems relating to the ultimate purpose of our own life and the basis of our own conduct; life remains closed to those who take no part in it because it can have no significance; (5) it follows that the existentialist cannot be rationalist in his outlook for this is merely an escape into thought from the serious problems of existence; none of the important aspects of life—failure, evil, sin, folly—nor (in the view of Kierkegaard) even the existence of God or the truth of Christianity—can be proved by reason. "God does not exist; He is eternal," was how he expressed it; (6) life is short and limited in space and time, therefore it is foolish to discuss in a leisurely fashion matters of life and death as if there were all eternity to argue them in. It is necessary to make a leap into the unknown, *e.g.,* accepting Christ (in the case of the Christian existentialist) by faith in the sense of giving and risking the self utterly. This means complete commitment, not a dependence on arguments as to whether certain historical events did, or did not, happen.

To summarise: existentialism of whatever type seems to the outsider to be an attitude to life concerning itself with the individual's ultimate problems (mine, not yours); to be anti-rationalist and anti-idealist (in the sense of being, as it seems to the believer, practical)—in effect it seems to say "life is too short to fool about with argument, you must dive in and become committed" to something. Sartre who called himself an "atheist existentialist" was apparently committed to the belief that "hell is other people," but for most critics the main argument against existentialism is that it often rests on a highly specialised personal experience and, as such, is incommunicable.

Existential Psychology, a rather diffuse movement in modern psychology with no specific founder but with a number of figures who, perhaps against their will, acquired leader status. One of the key figures was the British psychiatrist, R. D. Laing (1927–89), whose radical views on psychotherapy were counted as being heretical by the vast majority of his medical colleagues. Laing held that many so-called neurotic and psychotic conditions are essentially not "abnormal" but represent strategies by which an individual may adjust to environmental and personal stress.

Instead of attempting to suppress or eliminate the psychosis in the traditional manner, one should lead the patient through it thus allowing the individual's "unconscious plan" for his own adjustment to be fulfilled.

Exorcism, the removal or ejection of an evil spirit by a ritual or prayer.

F

Fabian Society. The Fabian Society was founded in 1884 with the conviction that social change could be brought about by gradual parliamentary means. (The name is derived from Quintus Fabius Maximus, the Roman general nicknamed "Cunctator," the delayer, who achieved his successes in defending Rome against Hannibal by refusing to give direct battle.) It was a movement of brilliant intellectuals, chief among whom were Sidney and Beatrice Webb, H. G. Wells, G. B. Shaw, Graham Wallas, Sidney Olivier, and Edward Pease. The Society itself was basically a research body which furnished the intellectual information for social reform and supported all contributing to the gradual attainment by parliamentary means of socialism.

The Webbs's analysis of society emphasised that individualist enterprise in capitalism was a hang-over from early days and was bound to defeat itself since socialism is the inevitable accompaniment of modern industrialism; the necessary result of popular government is control of their economic system by the people themselves. Utopian schemes had been doomed to failure because they were based on the fallacy that society is static and that islands of utopias could be formed in the midst of an unchanging and antagonistic environment. On the contrary, it was pointed out, society develops: "The new becomes old, often before it is consciously regarded as new." Social reorganisation cannot usefully be hastened by violent means but only through methods consonant with this natural historical progression—gradual, peaceful, and democratic. The Fabians were convinced that men are rational enough to accept in their common interest developments which can be demonstrated as necessary; thus public opinion will come to see that socialisation of the land and industries is essential.

The Society collaborated first in the formation of the Independent Labour Party and then with the more moderate Labour Party and the trade unions and Co-operative movement. But in general it disapproved of independent trade union action since change should come from the government and take political form. The class-war of Marx was rejected and so too was the idea of the exclusive role of the working class —reform must come from the enlightened co-operation of all classes.

Faith Healing, the belief and practice of curing physical and mental ills by faith in some supernatural power, either allegedly latent in the individual or drawn in some way from God.

Falangists. The Fascist Party of Spain founded in 1933 by José Antonio Primo de Rivera, son of the man who was dictator of the country from 1923 to 1930. The Falange was the only political party allowed in Spain during the Franco era. *See* **Fascism** (*below*).

Falun Gong (**Falun Dufa**), Chinese mystic healing movement, prosecuted by the Beijing government as an 'evil and dangerous cult'. Led by the US-based Li Hongzhi, it is banned in China. The movement, with *c.* 80 million members, is based on the ancient mystical and healing principles of *qigong*. First introduced to the public in China in 1992. Many Falun Gong supporters are in forced labour camps and have suffered torture.

Fascism flourished in countries where the values and institutions of liberal democracy were weak and ineffective, and where political crisis was inflamed by economic calamity. Following defeat in World War I, Germany was stripped of territory and military capacity, and was subject to hefty financial repayments to the victorious powers for the costs of war. The fragile liberal democracy in Germny after 1918 suffered terrible economic shocks resulting in hyperinflation and mass unemployment; Germany significantly failed to entrench stable democratic government.

Fascist parties organised around a fight against the perceived causes of their national crises and found common enemies in communists, trade unionists, liberal democrats, and Jews. Fascists declared that these were corruptions of the authentic will and purity of their nations, and promoted action, conflict, and violence to eradicate these enemies. Fascist movements were highly organised, and hierarchical with charismatic authoritarian leaders.

Italian Fascism. The corporate state set up by Benito Mussolini in Italy claimed to be neither capitalist nor socialist, and after its inception in 1922 the Fascist Party became the only recognised one. Its members wore black shirts, were organised in military formations, used the Roman greeting of the outstretched arm, and adopted as their slogan "Mussolini is always right". Membership of the Party was not allowed to exceed a number thought to be suited to the optimum size of a governing class and new candidates were drawn, after strict examinations, from the youth organisations. The Blackshirts, a fascist militia, existed separately from the army and were ruled by Fascist Headquarters.

At the head of government was Mussolini, "Il Duce" himself, a cabinet of fourteen ministers selected by him and approved by the King to supervise the various functions of government, and the Grand Council or directorate of the Fascist Party, all the members of which were chosen by the Duce. Parliament, which was not allowed to initiate legislation but only to approve decrees from above, consisted of a Senate with life-membership and a Chamber of Fasci and Corporations composed of nominated members of the Party, the National Council of Corporations, and selected representatives of the employers' and employees' confederations. Private enterprise was encouraged and protected but rigidly controlled; strikes were forbidden, but a Charter of Labour enforced the collaboration of workers and employers whose disputes were settled in labour courts presided over by the Party.

All decisions relating to industry were government-controlled (*e.g.*, wages, prices, conditions of employment and dismissal, the expansion or limitation of production), and some industries such as mining, shipping, *etc.* were state-owned.

Italian fascism served as a model in other countries, notably for the German National Socialist Party and in Spain and Japan.

Fascism in Britain. Most European nations between the wars had their small Fascist parties, the British version led by Sir Oswald Mosley. In 1932 Mosley's earlier New Party changed its name to the British Union of Fascists (BUF), adopting uniforms and mass rallies. The BUF urged a radical economic programme to solve the problem of unemployment. The violence of Mosley's supporters towards their opponents at the Olympia Meeting of June 1934, however, alienated public opinion. A series of provocative marches through Jewish districts in London led to clashes between the police and anti-fascist demonstrators, notably at Cable Street in October 1936, leading to the Public Order Act. In May 1940 Mosley and other leading members were detained under the Emergency Powers Defence Regulations and in July the British Union was banned.

German Fascism (**Nazism**) was led by Adolf Hitler's National Socialist German Workers Party (Nazi Party). Hitler emulated the early successes of Mussolini's Italian fascists, but emphasised the racial nature of the German nation. Hitler's Nazis were distinguished by an aggressive anti-Semitism, and a voracious pursuit of *Lebensraum* – a massive German empire, particularly to the east, that could support a 'purified' racial state. Hitler's Nazis pursued their racial fascist ideology by invading Poland, France, Belgium, Denmark, Holland, Yugoslavia, Greece, and Russia. Each military invasion was followed by a political and racial purge organised by the SS. Jews were forced into ghettos, and the Nazis established a system of concentration camps across Europe. Prisoners of these camps were often forced to labour for the Nazi war effort. The Nazis used these camps to enforce their racial ideology of purification, and systematically murdered over 5 million Jews and members of other groups such as political opponents, homosexuals, gypsies, and disabled people. This murderous legacy is remembered as the Holocaust. The exact number of victims of the Holocaust will never be known.

Spanish Fascism. Fascism in Spain developed through the Falange party that fought in the Spanish Civil War with the material support of the fascist governments of Italy and Germany. The Falangists eventually seized power in 1939, when Francisco Franco Bahamonde (1892–1975) became leader of the Falange and Spain. Franco's fascism shared many of the characteristics of the Italian and German movements but also integrated the support of Roman Catholicism. Franco's fascist government persisted until 1975, after which Spain adopted a constitutional monarchy, and the Falange suffered a heavy defeat in democratic elections in 1977.

Neofascism. Although in a sense fascism ended with the defeat of Germany in 1945 there have been persistent revivals in Italy, France, in

Germany following reunification, and in Russia and the Balkans after the collapse of Communism.

Modern fascist parties, the British National Party in Britain, the Freedom Party in Holland, or the National Front in France (now led by Marine Le Pen), concentrate more on the tensions caused by mass immigration into their countries, the arrival of asylum seekers and the onset of Islamic fanaticism. Russian Fascists attack their minorities (especially Muslims).

Fatalism. *See* **Determinism.**

Federalism, belief in the desirability of a political unit consisting of several smaller units, usually termed states, involving a central government and regional or state governments. The states or provinces devolve certain powers over themselves and their citizens to the larger unit, such powers being embodied in a written constitution which can only be amended with the consent of a fixed percentage of the states. The constitution specifies the powers devolved to the federal or central government and the restrictions placed on its interference in the internal affairs of the states.

Given the possibility of disputes as to the spheres of competence of federal and state governments, machinery such as a 'supreme court' is established to interpret the constitution. Examples of federations are the USA, Canada and India. *See also* **World Federalism.**

Federalists. US party which in the early days of American independence in the late 18th century, favoured a concentration of power in the central government. Their opponents, the anti-federalists (later the Democrats) were supporters of the rights of individual states.

Feminism. Feminism is an expression which emerged in the mid-19th century. It is an international movement (there was, for example, a feminist congress in Paris in 1890), which aimed at ending female inequality in male-dominated societies. In early 20th century Britain feminism sought political advance through a militant campaign for women's suffrage, This, and the part played by women in World War One, made it impossible for a male elite to deny women the right to vote. But in each country it became increasingly clear to women that the political process alone left many of their needs unsatisfied, if not unrecognised. However, in post-World War Two Britain, legislation made a gesture towards outlawing discrimination against women at work with the 1970 Equal Pay Act and the 1975 Sex Discrimination Act.

Women's Liberation Movement. This activist feminism of the 1960s and 1970s (primarily in America and Europe as well as Britain), centred on questions of sexuality and the right of women to make choices, for example, over when (and whether) to become pregnant. The contraceptive pill appeared to open up sexual choice for women and to liberate them from traditional responsibilities for home, family and the welfare of children. In practice, it appeared to many women that the pill (as well as having physical side-effects) merely relieved men from a recognition of their own responsibility. The 1967 Abortion Act in Britain implied an acceptance of a woman's right to control her own reproduction, a right which has been systematically but unsuccessfully challenged since.

As western economies faltered in the late 1970s a recurring problem for the movement was consolidating the small gains that had been made. But the women's movement achievements cannot be measured by tangible results alone. A central aspect of the movement was "consciousness-raising", helping women recognise the social roots of their individual oppression.

Friedan and Greer. In their analysis of sexual stereotyping, late 20th century feminist writings—for example, Betty Friedan's *The Feminine Mystique* (1963) and Germaine Greer's *The Female Eunuch* (1970)—encouraged a change in some women's expectations. These writers, and many like them, enabled a new generation of women to challenge the dominant decision-making role of men and to demand acceptance of the principle of equality between the sexes. Dale Spender's *Man Made Language* (1980) pointed to the ways in which the "sexist" structure of language internalised the perpetuation of male

dominance. A simple, but not superficial, result of this is the acceptance of the abbreviation "Ms" rather than "Mrs" or "Miss" on the grounds that the latter presupposed that a woman's identity depended on her marital status.

Although feminism as a movement was loosely structured—there were, for example, early on, differing emphases between socialists, black women, working class women, and lesbians, based on their own experiences—the movement became increasingly fragmented during the 1980s. Some women, who were now building individual careers, distanced themselves from agitation and thought little more could be achieved by collective action. Single-issue pressure groups evolved, focusing on campaigns for change in particular areas.

The Greenham Common Women's Peace Camp which began in the mid-1980s as a protest against the deployment of Cruise missiles in Britain, was able to develop from this into an exemplary feminist action which reverberated internationally. Self-organisation among miners' wives in the 1984–85 strike proved similarly effective.

The irony of "classical" feminism is that it became a concern of the generation that came to maturity in the late 1960s. Their children—and their younger sisters—had absorbed the earlier failures and successes and moved on. By the 1990s, for what became the older generation, there was a view that the earlier movement had implanted unrealistic expectations in women (particularly those with domestic responsibilities), the "double burden" of maintaining a career and home. This led at a time of growing recession and unemployment to an anti-feminist campaign or "backlash", not only among men (which was to be expected) but also among some women who described themselves as post-feminists. Susan Faludi, speaking for a younger generation in *Backlash: The Undeclared War Against Women* (1991) documents a process which attempted to force women back into the home and a return to "traditional" family life.

However, a significant recognition of the altered balance between the sexes came with the 1991 House of Lords decision that rape within marriage was an offence. The mid-1990s saw a new emphasis placed by political parties on the role of the family and its reputed breakdown as the root of many of the problems confronting Western society. This was interpreted by some as an attempt to reverse the social and economic advances achieved by some women in the past half century. Working mothers, for example, were accused of neglecting their prime duty as homemakers, although the research evidence presented was often contradictory.

The new century has seen feminists trying to come to terms with a multicultural society in which the traditional role of women is unacceptable to them.

Feng Shui, a Chinese philosophy whose basic principles seek to change the environment with colours, objects and placement of furniture to counteract negative energy and aid a flow of positive energy.

Fetichism, originally a practice of the peoples of West Africa and elsewhere of attributing magical properties to an object which was used as an amulet, for putting spells on others, or regarded as possessing dangerous powers. In psychology the term refers to a sexual perversion in which objects arouse sexual excitement.

Feudalism. The feudal system took its origins from Saxon times and broadly speaking lasted until the end of the 13th cent. It was a military and political organisation based on land tenure, for, of course, society throughout this period was based almost entirely on agriculture. The activities of men divided them into three classes or estates. The First Estate was the clergy, responsible for man's spiritual needs; the Second was the nobility, including kings and emperor as well as the lesser nobles; the Third was composed of all those who had to do with the economic and mainly agricultural life of Europe. The praying men, the fighting men and administrators, and the toilers were all held to be mutually dependent on each other.

The theory of feudalism, although it by no means always worked out in practice, was as follows: the earth was God's and therefore no man owned land in the modern sense of the word. God had given the pope spiritual charge of men, and secular power over them to the emperor from whom kings held their kingdoms, and in turn the dukes and counts received the land over which they held sway from the king. Members of the Second Estate held their lands on the condition of fulfilling certain obligations to their overlord and to the people living under them, so when a noble received a fief or piece of land he became the vassal of the man who bestowed it. To him he owed military service for a specified period of the year, attendance at court, and giving his lord counsel. He undertook to ransom his lord when he fell into enemy hands and to contribute to his daughter's dowry and at the knighting of his son. In return the lord offered his vassal protection and justice, received the vassal's sons into his household and educated them for knighthood.

The system was complicated by the fact that large fiefs might be subdivided and abbots often governed church lands held in fief from nobles. The serf or toiling man dwelt on the land of a feudal noble or churchman where he rendered service by tilling the soil or carrying out his craft for his manorial lord in return for protection, justice, and the security of his life and land. He was given a share in the common lands or pastures from which he provided for his own needs. In the modern sense he was not free (although at a later stage he could buy his freedom) since he was attached to the soil and could not leave without the lord's permission. On the other hand he could neither be deprived of his land nor lose his livelihood.

Feudal tenures were finally abolished in England by statute in 1660, although they had long been inoperative.

In Japan a feudal system existed up to 1871, in Russia it lasted until 1917.

Fideism. Religious doctrines which hold that the intellect or reason of man is incapable of attaining knowledge of divine matters and that religious faith is the way to truth.

Flying Saucers. In June 1947 a US private pilot, Kenneth Arnold, reported seeing a series of wingless objects flying through the air at a speed which he estimated at thousands of miles an hour. The UFO phenomenon had been born.

A CIA report in 1997 confirmed that over half of all the UFO sightings were actually American spy planes on secret missions (most UFO sightings happened during the paranoia of the Cold War). The advent of the new century has consigned UFOs to history and in 2009 the Ministry of Defence ended all official investigations into UFOs.

Fourierism *See* Utopianism.

Freegan Movement. Freegans are those who try not to interact with the economy. They may live in squats, forage for food, *etc.* Freeganism inspired the US anti-capitalist group Food Not Bombs.

Freemasonry, a widespread, influential secret organisation of English origin. Although it can be traced back to the Middle Ages when itinerant working masons in England and Scotland were organised in lodges with secret signs for the recognition of fellow-members, modern freemasonry first arose in England in the early decades of the 18th cent. On 24 June 1717 London lodges came together at the Goose and Gridiron Ale House in St Paul's Churchyard to form the first Grand Lodge in the world. Freemasons' Hall opened in 1776.

With its clubs for discussion and social meetings (women were excluded) it met a need and became a well-known feature of English life. The movement quickly spread abroad to places which had direct trade links with England. There are now around 200,000 Freemasons in some 8,000 Lodges in England and Wales. Globally, there are around 6 million members. The graded lodge structure, the prestige conferred on members, the symbolism, ritual and ceremony, and the emphasis on mutual help had a lasting appeal. Many establishment figures were members, such as Churchill, the Duke of Wellington and Lord Kitchener.

Membership used to bring definite business and social advantages, particularly in small communities where the leading middle- class figures were generally members. Recently this advantage has markedly declined and freemason lodges nowadays tend to be little more than worthy charitable organisations. Indeed, hundreds of masonic lodges faced closure because of a drastic membership decline. Very few members are under 30. Fear of secret societies has given freemasonry many opponents; it was condemned by the Roman Catholic Church, banned by Fascist dictators, and denounced by the Comintern. A statement from the Congregation for the Doctrine of the Faith in 1981 reminded Catholics that under Article 2335 of the Code of Canon Law they are forbidden under pain of excommunication from joining masonic or similar associations.

Recently, there have been calls for Freemasons who are members of, for example, the judiciary to declare their membership openly.

Freudian theory. *See* Psychoanalysis.

Friends, The Society of. *See* Quakers.

Fundamentalism originated in 19th century America as an opposition to the liberalising trend in theological practice. Fundamentalists rejected the attempt to interpret ancient scripture to make it more relevant to modern society, and argued for a return to a literal reading of the Bible. In the 1960s, such Christian fundamentalists, repulsed by the breakdown in traditional moral and social practices, began organising politically. Groups such as the Christian Coalition and the Moral Majority became powerful within American politics, and campaigned against abortion and gay rights.

The label has now been attached to many other groups who also oppose modern liberal social and political values, and who appeal to a strict literal reading of religious texts or moral values. Such wide usage is probably unhelpful as it may include fundamentalist Muslims inspired by the ideology of Sayyid Qutb (such as Osama Bin Laden) or the so-called Islamic State.

G

Game Theory, an approach to understanding human and animal behaviour which takes the view that psychological insight is best gained by studying the decisions which all living things make constantly and which govern the course of their lives. It proposes that life is basically a strategic game following complex rules which can probably only be understood by a study of the "decision units" as and when they occur. Because one is dealing with highly variable animals controlled by highly complex brains, and not with simple clockwork or electro-mechanical systems, the study of the rules which operate in the game of life is enormously complicated and thus game theory has quickly taken off into advanced mathematics. Game theory, incidentally, can be used to apply to individual action or to the behaviour of groups.

Gay and Lesbian Movement, term for the campaign to remove legal and other discrimination from gay men and lesbian women and to allow them to lead their lives to the full in our society. Its first large-scale manifestation was in America in the 1970s, paralleled in Britain with organisations such as the Gay Liberation Front.

Although, sadly, much discrimination remains, many people now accept that the sexual orientation of a person should not be a ground for any form of discrimination. Issues such as gay priests, and the onset of AIDS, have continued to ensure that "gay rights" remains a controversial area. In a vote in the Commons in March 1999 on the question of equalising the age of consent (there was then a higher minimum age of consent for male homosexual acts than for heterosexual) a majority of 281 to 82 was in favour, but the House of Lords again rejected the reform in April 1999. Eventually the law was changed in December 2000. Gay people have often received support from the European Court of Human Rights.

New legislation has aimed to remove existing laws against anal intercourse, gross indecency and discrimination at work as well as giving new legal rights to gay couples (so they have the same rights—and responsibilities—as heterosexual couples). Controversy over appointing gay priests as bishops still divides the Anglican Church.

In Holland, the Dutch Senate has legalised same sex marriages and given such couples the right to adopt Dutch children. Other countries (such as Sweden and Belgium) have followed. In

London, the GLA set up a London Partnerships Register in September 2001 for the official registration of same sex relationships. Adoption by gay couples became legal in Britain in 2002. The Civil Partnership Act, effective from December 2005, gay couples can enter into 'civil partnership registrations' at register offices. Parts of America (*e.g.* Texas) remain strongly against any form of gay partnerships and the issue is highly controversial. This was all changed in 2015 when the Supreme Court declared marriage a universal right. In 2009 an Indian court ruled that consensual gay sex is not a crime – overturning an 150-year old ban. However, this was itself overruled in 2013. Argentina became the first South American country to legalise same-sex marriages, now followed by Brazil, Chile, Uruguay and Colombia.

South Africa became the fifth nation in the world to authorise same-sex marriages (behind the Netherlands, Belgium, Spain and Canada). Same-sex marriage are now legal in New Zealand and France. Others (such as Ireland and Vietnam) have followed. It is still unlawful in Northern Ireland because of Democratic Unionist opposition.

In February 2013 the House of Commons voted strongly in favour of The Marriage (Same Sex Couples) Bill. This is now law and the first marriages took place on 29 March 2014. Scotland has followed suit.

In some countries, such as Russia Uganda and Nigeria homophobia is rife and attacks on gays are common. Same-sex activity is illegal in 76 countries (37 of them in Africa) and punishable by death in such countries as Afghanistan, Brunei, Sudan and Yemen.

Gestalt Psychology. In the latter half of the 19th cent. it became evident to psychologists that in principle there was no good reason why "mental" events should not be just as measurable and manageable as "physical" ones. Intensive studies of learning, memory, perception, and so on were therefore undertaken and the begining of an empirical science of psychology were underway.

In the early 20th cent. the experiments of Pavlov (*see* **Behaviourism**) and his co-workers suggested that the behaviour of an animal, or even men, might ultimately be reduced to a descriptive account of the activities of nervous reflex loops—the so-called conditioned reflexes.

With the subsequent publication of Watson's important book on Behaviourism in 1914 it looked as though the transfer of psychological studies from the field of philosophy to that of science could now take place. Actually the picture of cerebral and mental pictures which Behaviourism offered was too simple.

Just as Behaviourism implied that there was a fundamental building block (the conditioned reflex) from which all mental events could be constructed, so Victorian physics assumed that the entire universe could be described in terms of a vast collection of atoms pushing each other around like billiard balls. The development of nuclear physics was to shatter the latter dream and at the same time a challenge to the naïve "reflex psychology" came from the Gestalt experimental school.

The founders of this school were Max Wertheimer, Kurt Koffka and Wolfgang Köhler, three young psychologists who in 1912 were conducting experiments—notably in vision— which seemed to expose the inadequacies of the behaviourist position. The Pavlov–Watson view, as we have said, implied that complex sensory events were no more than a numerical sum of individual nervous impulses. Wertheimer's group proposed that certain facts of perceptual experiences (ruled out of court as subjective and therefore unreliable by Watson) implied that the whole (*Gestalt*) was something more than simply the sum of its parts. For example, the presentation of a number of photographs, each slightly different, in rapid series gives rise to cinematographic motion. In basic terms, the eye has received a number of discrete, "still" photographs, and yet "motion" is perceived. What, they asked, was the sensory input corresponding to this motion? Some processes within the brain clearly *added* something to the total input as defined in behaviourist terms.

An obvious alternative—in a different sense modality—is that of the arrangement of musical notes. A cluster of notes played one way might be called a tune; played backwards they may form another tune, or may be meaningless. Yet in all

cases the constituent parts are the same, and yet their relationship to one another is evidently vital. Once again the whole is more than the sum of the parts.

The implications of all this appeared to be that the brain was equipped with the capacity to organise sensory input in certain well-defined ways, and that far from being misleading and scientifically unjustifiable, human subjective studies of visual experience might reveal the very principles of organisation which the brain employs. Take a field of dots, more or less randomly distributed; inspection of the field will soon reveal certain patterns or clusters standing out—the constellations in the night sky are a good illustration. There are many other examples, and Wertheimer and his colleagues in a famous series of experiments made some effort to catalogue them and reduce them to a finite number of "Laws of Perceptual Organisation" which are still quoted today.

Ghosts, belief in ghosts is one of the most common features of supernatural and mystical philosophy. At its roots it is based on the assumption that Man is essentially an individual created of two separate and distinct substances, mind and body. Most religious systems hold to this dualistic view (*see* **Dualism**). The discarnate spirit is normally assumed to progress to some other realm whereupon it loses contact with the mortal world. Occasionally, however, for one reason or another, the spirits may not progress and may become trapped and unable to escape the material world. Traditionally this is supposed to occur when the death of the individual is precipitated by some great tragedy. Serious scientific interest in ghosts has now waned rapidly.

Globalisation. In modern times the nation state has provided a structure for political, economic, and social relationships. Globalisation describes the collapse of the importance of the nation state in these relationships. The ability to communicate, travel, trade, and organise on a global scale, with ease and speed, allows political institutions, corporations, and social movements to thrive unconstrained by the boundaries of nation states.

As examples of globalisation, proponents point to global capital markets and vast free trade areas which allow multinational companies to produce and sell worldwide, the Internet and international travel which enables social movements to pursue causes on a global basis.

Gnosticism. Among the many heresies of early Christianity, especially during its first two centuries, was a group which came under the heading of Gnosticism. This was a system or set of systems which attempted to combine Christian beliefs with others derived from Oriental and Greek sources, especially those which were of a mystical and metaphysical nature, such as the doctrines of Plato and Pythagoras. There were many Gnostic sects, the most celebrated being the Alexandrian school of Valentius (fl. *c.* 136–*c.* 160). "Gnosis" was understood not as meaning "knowledge" or "understanding" as we understand these words, but "revelation." As in other mystical religions, the ultimate object was individual salvation; sacraments took the most varied forms. Many who professed themselves Christians accepted Gnostic doctrines and even orthodox Christianity contains some elements of Gnostic mysticism.

It was left to the bishops and theologians to decide at what point Gnosticism ceased to be orthodox and a difficult task this proved to be. Two of the greatest, Clement of Alexandria and his pupil Origen, unwittingly slipped into heresy when they tried to show that such men as Socrates and Plato, who were in quest of truth, were Christian in intention, and by their lives and works had prepared the way for Christ. Thus they contradicted Church doctrine which specifically said *Extra ecclesiam nulla salus*—outside the Church there is no salvation.

God and Man. The idea of gods came before the idea of God and even earlier in the evolution of religious thought there existed belief in spirits (*see* **Animism**). It was only as a result of a long period of development that the notion of a universal "God" arose, a development documented in the Old Testament. Here we are concerned with the views of philosophers.

Atheism is the positive disbelief in the existence of a God. **Agnosticism** (a term coined by T. H. Huxley, the 19th cent. biologist and contemporary of Darwin) signifies that one cannot know whether God exists or not. **Secularism** (prominent from the 1850s) pursued "a philosophy of life which ignores theology". **Deism** is the acceptance of the existence of God, not through revelation, but as a hypothesis required by reason. **Theism** also accepts the existence of God, but, unlike Deism, does not reject the evidence of revelation (*e.g.*, in the Bible or in the lives of the saints). **Pantheism** is the identification of God with all that exists (*i.e.*, with the whole universe). **Monotheism** is the belief in one God, **Polytheism** the belief in many.

Early Greek Views. Among the early Greek philosophers, Thales (*c.* 624–565 B.C.) of Miletus, in Asia Minor, Anaximander (611–547 B.C.), his pupil, and Anaximenes (b. *c.* 570 B.C.), another Miletan, were men of scientific curiosity and their speculations about the origin of the universe were untouched by religious thought.

They founded the scientific tradition of critical discussion. Heraclitus of Ephesus (*c.* 540–475 B.C.), was concerned with the problem of change. How does a thing change and yet remain itself? For him all things are flames—processes. "Everything is in flux, and nothing is at rest." Empedocles of Agrigentum in Sicily (*c.* 500–c. 430 B.C.) introduced the idea of opposition and affinity. All matter is composed of the so-called four elements—*earth, water, air,* and *fire*—which are in opposition or alliance with each other. All these were materialist philosophers who sought to explain the working of the universe without recourse to the gods.

Socrates, Plato, and Aristotle. Socrates (470–399 B.C.) was primarily concerned with ethical matters and conduct rather than the nature of the universe. For him goodness and virtue come from knowledge. He obeyed an "inner voice" and suffered death rather than give up his philosophy. He believed in the persistence of life after death and was essentially a monotheist. Plato (427–347 B.C.) was chiefly concerned with the nature of reality and thought in terms of absolute truths which were unchanging, logical, and mathematical. (*See* **Mind and Matter.**) Aristotle (384–322 B.C.) took his views of matter not from Democritus (atomic view) but from Empedocles (doctrine of four elements), a view which came to fit in well with orthodox medieval theology. Matter is conceived of as potentially alive and striving to attain its particular form, being moved by divine spirit or mind (*nous*). (An acorn, for example, is matter which contains the form "oak-tree" towards which it strives.) Thus there is a whole series from the simplest level of matter to the perfect living individual. But there must be a supreme source of all movement upon which the whole of Nature depends, a Being that Aristotle describes as the "Unmoved Mover", the ultimate cause of all becoming in the universe. This Being is pure intelligence, a philosopher's God, not a personal one. Unlike Plato, Aristotle did not believe in survival after death, holding that the divine, that is the immortal element in man, is mind.

Among the later Greek thinkers the Epicureans were polytheists whose gods, however, were denied supernatural powers. The Stoics built up a materialist theory of the universe, based on the Aristotelian model. To them God was an all-pervading force, related to the world as the soul is related to the body, but they conceived of it as material. They developed the mystical side of Plato's idealism and were much attracted by Babylonian astrology. They were pantheists. The Sceptics were agnostics.

From Pagan to Christian Thought. Philo, "the Jew of Alexandria," who was about 20 years older than Jesus, tried to show that the Jewish scriptures were in line with the best in Greek thought. He introduced the *Logos* as a bridge between the two systems. Philo's God is remote from the world, above and beyond all thought and being, and as His perfection does not permit direct contact with matter the divine *Logos* acts as intermediary between God and man. Plotinus (204–70), a Roman, the founder of Neoplatonism, was the last of the great pagan philosophers. Like Philo, he believed that God had created the world indirectly through emanations—beings coming

from Him but not of Him. The world needs God but God does not need the world. Creation is a fall from God, especially the human soul when enmeshed in the body and the world of the senses, yet (*see* **Determinism**) man has the ability to free himself from sense domination and turn towards God. Neoplatonism was the final stage of Greek thought drawing inspiration from the mystical side of Plato's idealism and its ethics from Stoicism.

Christianity: St. Augustine of Hippo. It was mainly through St. Augustine (354–430), Bishop of Hippo in North Africa, that certain of the doctrines of Neoplatonism found their way into Christianity. Augustine also emphasised the concept of God as all good, all wise, all knowing, transcendent, the Creator of the universe out of nothing. But, he added, since God knows everything, everything is determined by Him forever. This is the doctrine of predestination and its subsequent history is discussed under **Determinism.**

In the early centuries of Christianity, as we have seen, some found it difficult to reconcile God's perfection with His creation of the universe and introduced the concept of the *Logos* which many identified with Christ. Further, it came to be held that a power of divine origin permeated the universe, namely the Holy Spirit or Holy Ghost. A theory had to be worked out to explain the relationships of these three entities whence arose the conception of the Trinity. God is One; but He is also Three: Father, Son (the *Logos* or Christ), and Holy Ghost.

This doctrine was argued by the Apologists and the Modalists. The former maintained that the *Logos* and the Holy Spirit were emanations from God and that Jesus was the *Logos* in the form of a man. The Modalists held that all three Persons of the Trinity were God in three forms or modes: the *Logos* is God creating, the Holy Spirit God reasoning, and God is God being. This led to a long discussion as to whether the *Logos* was an emanation from God or God in another form; was the *Logos* of like *nature* with God or of the same *substance*?

This was resolved at the Council of Nicaea (325) when Athanasius formulated the orthodox doctrine against Arius (*q.v.*): that the one God is a Trinity of the same substance, three Persons of the same nature—Father, Son, and Holy Ghost.

St. Thomas Aquinas (1227–74), influenced greatly by Aristotle's doctrines, set the pattern for all subsequent Catholic belief even to the present time. He produced rational arguments for God's existence: *e.g.*, Aristotle's argument that, since movement exists, there must be a prime mover, the Unmoved Mover or God; further, we can see that things in the universe are related in a scale from the less to the more complex, from the less to the more perfect, and this leads us to suppose that at the peak there must be a Being with absolute perfection. God is the first and final cause of the universe, absolutely perfect, the Creator of everything out of nothing. He reveals Himself in his Creation and rules the universe through His perfect will. How Aquinas dealt with the problem of predestination is told under **Determinism.**

Break with Medieval Thought. Renaissance thinkers, free to think for themselves, doubted the validity of the arguments of the Schoolmen but most were unwilling to give up the idea of God (nor would it have been safe to do so). Mystics (*see* **Mysticism**) or near-mystics such as Nicholas of Cusa (*c.* 1401–64) and Jacob Boehme (1575–1624) taught that God was not to be found by reason but was a fact of the immediate intuition of the mystical experience.

Giordano Bruno held that God was immanent in the infinite universe. He is the unity of all opposites, a unity without opposites, which the human mind cannot grasp. Bruno was burned at the stake in 1600 at the instigation of the Inquisition (a body which, so we are told, never caused pain to anyone since it was the civil power, not the Inquisition, that carried out the unpleasant sentences) for his heresy.

Francis Bacon, who died in 1626, separated, as was the tendency of that time, science from religion. The latter he divided into the two categories of natural and revealed theology. The former, through the study of nature, may give convincing proof of the existence of a God but nothing more. Of revealed theology he said: "we must quit the small vessel of human reason . . . as we are obliged to obey the divine law, though our will murmurs against it, so we are obliged to believe in the word of God, though our reason is shocked at it."

Hobbes was a complete materialist and one feels that his obeisance to the notion was politic rather than from conviction. However, he does mention God as starting the universe in motion; infers that God is corporeal but denies that His nature can be known.

From Descartes Onwards. Descartes (1596-1650) separated mind and body as different entities but believed that the existence of God could be deduced by the fact that the idea of him existed in the mind. Whatever God puts into man, including his ideas, must be real. God is self-caused, omniscient, omnipotent, eternal, all goodness and truth. But Descartes neglected to explain how mind separate from body can influence body, or God separate from the world can influence matter.

Spinoza (1632-77) declared that all existence is embraced in one substance—God, the all-in-all. He was a pantheist and as such was rejected by his Jewish brethren. But Spinoza's God has neither personality nor consciousness, intelligence nor purpose, although all things follow in strict law from His nature. All the thoughts of everyone in the world, make up God's thoughts.

Bishop Berkeley (1685-1753) took the view that things exist only when they are perceived, and this naturally implies that a tree, for example, ceases to exist when nobody is looking at it. This problem was solved to his own satisfaction by assuming that God, seeing everything, prevented objects from disappearing when we were not present. The world is a creation of God but it is a spiritual or mental world, not a material one.

Hume (1711-76), who was a sceptic, held that human reason cannot demonstrate the existence of God and all past arguments to show that it could were fallacious. Yet we must believe in God since the basis of all hope, morality, and society is based upon the belief. Kant (1724-1804) held a theory similar to that of Hume. We cannot know by reason that God exists, nor can we prove on the basis of argument anything about God. But we can form an idea of the whole of the universe, the one Absolute Whole, and personify it. We need the idea of God on which to base our moral life, although this idea of God is transcendent, *i.e.*, goes beyond experience.

William James (1842-1910), the American philosopher (*see* **Pragmatism**), held much the same view: God cannot be proved to exist, but we have a will to believe which must be satisfied, and the idea works in practice. Hegel (1770-1831) thought of God as a developing process, beginning with "the Absolute" or First Cause and finding its highest expression in man's mind, or reason. It is in man that God most clearly becomes aware of Himself. Comte (1798-1857), the positivist, held that religion belongs to a more primitive state of society.

Many modern liberal theologians, influenced by the developments in science, psychology, and post-modern philosophy, have sought to develop a non-theistic understanding of God. Non-theists reject the notion of God as a being with an identity and a will. Rather than endorse atheism or agnosticism however, non-theists understand God as the shared basis of humanity, or ground of human being. Critics suggest that such non-theism is in fact humanism.

Good and Evil.

Early Philosophers' Views. The early Greek philosophers were chiefly concerned with the laws of the universe, consequently it was common belief that knowledge of these laws, and living according to them, constituted the supreme good. Heraclitus, for example, who taught that all things carried with them their opposites, held that good and evil were like two notes in a harmony, necessary to each other. "It is the opposite which is good for us". Democritus, like Epicurus (*q.v.*), held that the main goal of life is happiness, but

happiness in moderation. The good man is not merely the one who *does* good but who always *wants* to do so: "You can tell the good man not by his deeds alone but by his desires." Such goodness brings happiness, the ultimate goal. On the other hand, many of the wandering Sophist teachers taught that good was merely social convention, that there are no absolute principles of right and wrong, that each man should live according to his desires; make his own moral code. To Socrates knowledge was the highest good because doing wrong is the result of ignorance: "no man is voluntarily bad."

Plato and Aristotle, although differing in many other respects, drew attention to the fact that man is composed of three parts: his desires and appetites, his will, and his reason. A man whose reason rules his will and appetites is not only a good but a happy man; for happiness is not an aim in itself but a by-product of the good life. Aristotle, however, emphasised the goal of self-realisation, and thought that if the goal of life is (as Plato had said) a rational attitude towards the feelings and desires, it needs to be further defined. Aristotle defined it as the "Golden Mean"—the good man is one who does not go to extremes but balances one extreme against another. Thus courage is a mean between cowardice and foolhardiness. The later philosophers Philo and Plotinus held that evil was in the very nature of the body and its senses. Goodness could only be achieved by giving up the life of the senses and, freed from the domination of the body, turning to God, the source of goodness.

Christian Views. St. Augustine taught that everything in the universe is good. Even those things which appear evil are good in that they fit with the harmony of the universe like shadows in a painting. Man should turn his back on the pleasures of the world and turn to the love of God. Peter Abelard (1079-1142) made the more sophisticated distinction when he suggested that the wrongness of an act lies not in the act itself, but in the intention of the doer: "God considers not what is done but in what spirit is it done; and the merit or praise of the agent lies not in the deed but in the intention." If we do what we believe to be right, we may err, but we do not sin. The only sinful man is he who deliberately sets out to do what he knows to be wrong. St. Thomas Aquinas agreed with Aristotle in that he believed the highest good to be realisation of self as God has ordained, and he also agreed with Abelard that intention is important. Even a good act is not good unless the doer intended it to have good consequences. Intention will not make a bad act good, but it is the only thing that will make a good act genuinely good.

In general, Christianity has had difficulties in solving the problem of the existence of evil; for even when one accepts that the evil men do is somehow tied up with the body, it is still difficult to answer the question: how could an all-good God create evil? This is answered in one of two ways: (*a*) that Adam was given free-will and chose to sin (an answer which still does not explain how sin could exist anywhere in the universe of a God who created everything); (*b*) by denying the reality of evil as some Christians have chosen to do (*e.g.*, Christian Science *q.v.*). The Eastern religions, (*see* **Zoroastrianism**), solved the problem in a more realistic way by a dualism which denied that their gods were the creators of the whole universe and allowed the existence of at least two gods, one good and one evil. In Christianity there is, of course, a Devil, but it is not explained whence his evil nature came.

Later Philosophic Views. Hobbes equated good with pleasure and evil with pain. They are relative to the individual man in the sense that "one man's meat is another man's poison." Descartes believed that the power to distinguish between good and evil given by God to man is not complete, so that man does evil through ignorance. We act with insufficient knowledge and on inadequate evidence. Locke, believing that at birth the mind is a blank slate, held that men get their opinions of right and wrong from their parents. By and large, happiness is good and pain is evil. But men do not always agree over what is pleasurable and what not. Hence laws exist and these fall into three categories: (1) the divine law; (2) civil laws; (3) matters of opinion or reputation which are enforced by the fact that men do not like to incur the disapproval of their friends. We learn by experience that evil brings pain and good acts bring pleasure and, basically, one is good because not to be so would bring discomfort.

Kant (*see* **God and Man**) found moral beliefs to be inherent in man whether or not they can be proved by reason. There is a categorical imperative which makes us realise the validity of two universal laws: (1) "always act in such a way that the maxim determining your conduct might well become a universal law; act so that you can will that everybody shall follow the principle of your action; (2) "always act so as to treat humanity, whether in thine own person or in that of another, in every case as an end and never as a means."

Schopenhauer (1788–1860) was influenced by Buddhism and saw the will as a blind impelling striving, and desire as the cause of all suffering. The remedy is to regard sympathy and pity as the basis of all morality and to deny one's individual will. This is made easier if we realise that everyone is part of the Universal Will and therefore the one against whom we are struggling is part of the same whole as ourselves.

John Stuart Mill and Jeremy Bentham were both representatives of the Utilitarian school, believing that good is the greatest good (happiness) of the greatest number (*see* **Utilitarianism**).

Nietzsche. Understanding of good and evil has been challenged radically by the work of Nietzsche. He rejected morality altogether, and argued that it was a sophisticated means of control and oppression. For Nietzsche, morality was a mask for power, and the role of the philosopher was to tear off the mask, and not to justify and enforce the oppression and exploitation allowed by traditional understandings of good and evil. Nietzsche's ideas influenced Foucault, Heidegger, and Sartre, who each challenged the authenticity of moral vocabulary and rules.

Richard Rorty and Michael Walzer, two well-known moral relativists, challenged the nature of good and evil, and argued that there are no objective grounds from which we can justify morality. Relativists want to retain the vocabulary of good and evil, unlike Nietzsche, but argue that good and evil are informed by the particular values and practices of cultures, and can only be judged from within (relative to) those practices.

Whilst these notions of good and evil have sustained serious challenges, many are encouraged by the increased recognition of international human rights, which are based on a commitment to the universality of the value of human life as good, and a violation of those rights as a recognised and punishable evil.

Lastly, there is the view held mostly by political thinkers that good is what is good for society in general (*see* **State and Man**).

Guild Socialism, a British form of syndicalism (*q.v.*) created in 1906 by an architect, A. J. Penty, who was soon joined by A. R. Orage, S. G. Hobson, and G. D. H. Cole. The guild socialists advocated a restoration of the mediaeval guild system as was being recommended by the French syndicalists whose programme involved a return to direct economic action, a functional industrial structure, return of craftsmanship, and distrust of the state. Guild socialists believed that value was created by society as a whole rather than by individuals singly, and that capitalist economists had recommended the acquisition of wealth without emphasising the social responsibilities which wealth should bring. The trade unions were to be organised to take over and run their own industries after nationalisation.

Thus guild socialists were not only against capitalism but also against state socialism in which the state took over the control of industry. Political authority was held to be uncongenial to human freedom and therefore nothing was to be gained by the substitution of state bureaucracy for capitalist control.

The National Guilds League, formed in 1915, advocated abolition of the wages system, self-government in industry and control by a system of national guilds acting in conjunction with

other functional democratic organisations in the community. This body was dissolved in 1925.

H

Hajj, the pilgrimage to Mecca required of all Muslims, the fifth pillar of Islamic practice. A series of profound rituals are undertaken in Mecca.

Hanukkah (Chanukah). The Jewish festival of light, held in December. It means dedication and commemorates the Jewish struggle for religious freedom.

Hasidism (Chasidism). From the Hebrew *hasid*, pious or faithful one. A Jewish mystical movement which began in Poland in the 18th century, and which spread widely, first through Eastern Europe and then into Western Europe and America. The movement was founded by Israel ben Eliezer (1700–60), who came to be known as the Ba'al Shem Tov ("Master of the Good Name"). It was originally opposed to the authority of the rabbis and traditional Jewish practices. According to Hasidism, true religion comes not from study of the sacred texts but from purity of heart, prayer and observance of the commandments. The movement was also characterized by ecstatic forms of worship. Its present day followers are ultra-conservative orthodox Jews.

Hedonism. From Greek *hedone*, pleasure. The theory of ethics in which pleasure is regarded as the chief good, or proper end, of action. This is sometimes called ethical hedonism and is then distinguished from psychological hedonism, which is the theory that behaviour is primarily motivated by the pursuit of pleasure and the avoidance of pain. Psychological hedonism can of course be employed to support ethical hedonism.

This view, that only pleasure is ultimately good, has been held by many distinguished philosophers, including Epicurus, Locke, Hobbes, Hume, Bentham and Mill. In the case of the last two, it is closely associated with utilitarianism (*q.v.*). Although the term "pleasure" suggests physical enjoyments, hedonists have taken it to include intellectual pleasures also. They also argue that many things beside pleasure, such as virtue and knowledge, are desirable in that they produce pleasure.

Hermeneutics. Originally, the study of the general principles of biblical interpretation. The term came into philosophy in the late 19th century to refer to a more general study of interpretation, namely the interpretation of the significance of human actions, utterances, products *etc.*

Hermeticism (or Hermetism). Philosophies based on the Hermetic writings, also called the Hermetica, works on occult, theological and philosophical subjects ascribed to the Egyptian God Thoth (referred to in Greek as Hermes Trismegistos, Hermes the thrice-greatest). This collection, written in Latin and Greek, dates from 2nd–3rd centuries A.D. It reached Europe, from the Arabs, in the late 15th century, and had some influence during the Renaissance. It continues to fascinate modern devotees of magic and astrology.

The term also has a literary sense. It refers to an Italian poetic movement of the 20th century, characterized by brevity and obscurity.

Hinduism, the religion and social institutions of the great majority of the people of India. Hinduism has no fixed scriptural canon but its doctrines are to be found in certain ancient works, notably the *Veda*, the *Brahmanas*, the *Upanishads*, and the *Bhagavad-gita*.

The dark-skinned Dravidians invaded India between *c.* 3250 and 2750 B.C. and established a civilisation in the Indus valley. They were polytheists who worshipped a number of naturegods; some elements of their beliefs persisted into Hinduism. They were subdued by light-skinned Indo-European speakers who invaded from Asia Minor and Iran about 1500 B.C. The language of these people was Vedic, parent of Sanskrit in which their religious literature (the Vedas) came to be written after many centuries of oral transmission.

The *Veda* or Sacred Lore has come down to us in the form of mantras or hymns of which there are four great collections, the best-known being the *Rig-Veda*. These Vedic Aryans worshipped nature-deities, their favourites being Indra (rain),

Agni (fire), and Surya (the sun). Their religion contained no idolatry but became influenced by the beliefs of the Dravidians, Sacrifice and ritual became predominant in a ceremonial religion.

As a reaction a more philosophic form arose (c. 500 B.C.) with its scriptures in the *Upanishads*. At its highest level known as Brahmanism belief is in a subtle and sophisticated form of monotheism (Brahman is an impersonal, all-embracing spirit), but there is a tolerant acceptance of more primitive beliefs. Thus Vishnu (a conservative principle) and Siva (a destructive principle) grew out of Vedic conceptions. The two great doctrines of Hinduism are *karma* and transmigration. The universal desire to be reunited with the absolute (*atman* or Brahman) can be satisfied by following the path of knowledge. Life is a cycle of lives (*samsara*) in which man's destiny is determined by his deeds (*karma*) from which he may seek release (*moksa*) through ascetic practices or the discipline of Yoga (*q.v.*). Failure to achieve release means reincarnation—migration to a higher or lower form of life after death—until the ultimate goal of absorption in the absolute is reached.

In the great Sanskrit epic poems *Ramayana* and *Mahabharata* the deity takes three forms, represented by the divine personalities of Brahma, Vishnu, and Siva. There are also lower gods, demi-gods, supernatural beings, and members of the trinity may even become incarnate, as Vishnu became identified with Krishna, one of the heroes of the *Mahabharata* and the well-known *Bhagavad-gita*.

The Caste System. The ritual and legalistic side of Brahmanism is the caste system based on the elaborate codes of the *Law of Manu*, according to which God created distinct orders of men as He created distinct species of animals and plants. Men are born to be Brahmans, soldiers, agriculturists, or servants, but since a Brahman may marry a woman from any of these castes, an endless number of sub-castes arise. Caste discrimination was outlawed in 1950.

Hinduism has historically shown great tolerance for varieties of belief and practice. Ideas pleasant and unpleasant have been assimilated: fetishism, demon-cults, animal-worship, sexual cults (such as the rites of *Kali* in Kolkata). Today, as would be expected in a country which is in the throes of vast social change, Hinduism itself is changing. Under the impact of modern conditions new ideas are destroying old beliefs and customs. A militant political Hinduism, fanned by the Bharatiya Janata Group (BJP) extols Hindu fundamentalism. There are nearly one billion Hindus worldwide (816,000 in England and Wales at the 2011 Census). Hinduism is now the world's third largest religion. The Hindu temple in Dudley (opened in 2006) is the largest place of Hindu worship in Europe. *See also* **Jainism** and **Sikhism**.

Homoeopathy, an alternative branch of medicine whose motto *Similia Similibus Curantur* (like cures like) sums up its particular approach to therapy. In essence the homoeopathists claim that a disease can be treated by administering quite minute doses of a substance which produce symptoms (in the healthy person) similar to those induced by the disease itself. The founder and populariser of this novel approach to medicine was the German Samuel Hahnemann who was born in 1775, a friend of the physician Mesmer who propagated hypnotherapy. Hahnemann lived to see his ideas spread across the civilised world (despite the grave theoretical difficulties implicit in the question of how the very minute dosages actually achieve any result at all).

The amount of research being carried out in homoeopathy by doctors *etc.*, is phenomenal; furthermore, two real milestones occurred in the UK when papers on homoeopathy were published in *The Lancet* in 1988 and in the *British Medical Journal* in 1989. Scientists in contrast remain convinced sceptics. Indeed, various trials have found no evidence that homoeopathy works any better than a placebo. It is possible the Government will blacklist it on the NHS.

Homosexuality. *See* **Gay Movement.**

Human Rights. *See* **Universal Declaration of Human Rights, J52.**

Humanism, the term applied to (1) a system of education based on the Greek and Latin classics; and (2) the vigorous attitudes that accompanied the end of the Middle Ages and were represented at different periods by the Renaissance, the Reformation, the Industrial Revolution, and the struggle for democracy. These include: release from ecclesiastical authority, the liberation of the intellect, faith in progress, the belief that man himself can improve his own conditions without supernatural help and, indeed has a duty to do so. "Man is the measure of all things" is the keynote of humanism. The humanist has faith in man's intellectual and spiritual resources not only to bring knowledge and understanding of the world but to solve the moral problems of how to use that knowledge.

That man should show respect to man irrespective of class, race or creed is fundamental to the humanist attitude to life. Among the fundamental moral principles he would count freedom, justice and tolerance.

Around 4,200 humanist weddings take place annually in Scotland (where since 2005 they have been legal without an additional civil ceremony).

Hussites, the followers of John Hus, the most famous pupil of John Wyclif. He was the rector of Prague University and, although it is now by no means certain that his beliefs were heretical, he was condemned to death for heresy and burnt at the stake in 1415 at Constance whither he had come with a safe conduct issued by the Emperor Sigismund of Hungary. The latter based his action on the doctrine that no faith need be kept with heretics, but it is obvious that the main objection to Hus was his contempt for authority of any kind. After their leader's death, the Hussites became a formidable body in Bohemia and Moravia. They took up arms on behalf of their faith, their religion being strongly imbued with political feeling (hostility to Germanism and to the supremacy of the Roman Catholic Church). Their religious struggles for reform led to the Hussite Wars during which the movement splintered into several groups.

Hutterites. *See* **Mennonites.**

Hypnosedation. *See* **Mesmerism.**

Hypnotism. *See* **Mesmerism.**

I

I Ching, the Chinese "Book of Changes" which is supposed to provide a practical demonstration of the truths of ancient Chinese philosophy. The method consists of casting forty-nine sticks into two random heaps, or more simply, of tossing three coins to see if there is a preponderance of heads or tails. The coins are cast six times whereupon the head-tail sequence achieved is referred to a coded series of phrases in the book, which are supposed to relate in some way to the question held in the mind when the sticks or coins are being cast. The phrases are without exception vague, and platitudes such as "Evil people do not further the perseverance of the superior man," *etc.*, abound.

Consequently it is not difficult to read into such amorphous stuff a suitable "interpretation" or answer to one's unspoken question. The I Ching was once a great fad in Europe and America.

Iconoclasm. *See* **Icons, L57.**

Idealism, in philosophy, the belief that there is no matter in the universe, that all that exists is mind or spirit. *See* **Mind and Matter** and **Realism.**

Illuminati, a secret society founded in 1776 by Adam Weishaupt, a Bavarian professor of canon law at Ingolstadt, in an attempt to combat superstition and ignorance by founding an association for rational enlightenment and the regeneration of the world. Under conditions of secrecy it sought to penetrate and control the masonic lodges for subversive purposes. Among its members were Goethe and Schiller. The Order spread to Austria, Italy and Hungary but was condemned by the Catholic Church and dissolved in 1785 by the Bavarian government.

Immortality. The belief in a life after death has been widely held since the earliest times. It has certainly not been universal, nor has it always taken a form which everyone would find satisfying. In the early stages of human history or prehistory everything contained a spirit (*see* **Animism**) and it is obvious from the objects left in early graves that the dead were expected to exist in some form after death.

The experience of dreams, too, seemed to suggest to the unsophisticated that there was a part of man which could leave his body and wander elsewhere during sleep.

It will be helpful to classify the various types of belief which have existed in philosophical thought regarding this problem: (1) There is the idea that, although *something* survives bodily death, it is not necessarily eternal. Thus most primitive peoples were prepared to believe that man's spirit haunted the place around his grave and that food and drink should be set out for it, but that this spirit did not go on forever and gradually faded away. (2) The ancient Greeks and Hebrews believed for the most part that the souls of the dead went to a place of shades there to pine for the world of men. Their whining ghosts spent eternity in a dark, uninviting region in misery and remorse. (3) Other people, and there were many more of these, believed in the transmigration of souls with the former life of the individual determining whether his next life would be at a higher or lower level. Sometimes this process seems to have been thought of as simply going on and on, by others (*e.g.*, in Hinduism and Buddhism) as terminating in either non-sentience or union with God but in any case in annihilation of the self as self.

Believers in this theory were the Greek philosophers Pythagoras, Empedocles, Plato (who believed that soul comes from God and strives to return to God, according to his own rather confused notions of the deity. If it fails to free itself completely from the body it will sink lower and lower from one body to another.) Plotinus held similar views to Plato, and many other religious sects in addition to those mentioned have believed in transmigration. (4) The belief of Plato and Aristotle that if souls continue to exist after death there is no reason why they should not have existed before birth (this in part is covered by (3)), but some have pointed out that eternity does not mean "from now on," but the whole of the time before and after "now"—nobody, however, so far as one knows, held that *individual* souls so exist. (5) The theory that the soul does not exist at all and therefore immortality is meaningless: this was held by Anaximenes in early Greek times; by Leucippus, Democritus, and the other Greek atomists; by the Epicureans from the Greek Epicurus to the Roman Lucretius; by the British Hobbes and Hume; by Comte of France; and William James and John Dewey of America. (6) The thesis, held notably by Locke and Kant, that although we cannot prove the reality of soul and immortality by pure reason, belief in them should be held for moral ends. (For the Christian view *see* **God and Man, Determinism and Free-will**.)

Imperialism, the practice by a country, which has become a nation and embarked upon commercial and industrial expansion, of acquiring and administering territories, inhabited by peoples usually at a lower stage of development, as colonies or dependencies. Thus the "typical" imperialist powers of the mid-19th cent. and earlier were Britain, France, Belgium, Holland, Spain and Portugal, whilst Germany, Italy, and Japan, which either did not have unity during this period or adequate industrial expansion, tried to make good their weakness in this direction by war in the late 19th cent.

Individualism. The doctrine that the single person is the basic unit of political analysis. The term covers all political and social philosophies that place a high value on the freedom of the individual. It is believed that the interests of the individual are best served by allowing him maximum freedom and responsibility. Society is seen as a collection of individuals. So individualism opposes controls over the individual, especially when they are exercised by the state. The most extreme form is anarchism, but all individualists believe that government interference should be kept to a minimum. It is opposed to collectivism (*q.v.*). The term was originally used critically, to refer to egoism as a matter of principle.

Intelligent Design (ID). *See* **Creationism**.

Islam, the religion of which Mohammed (570–632) was the prophet, the word signifying submission to the will of God. It is one of the most widespread of religions. Its adherents are called Muslims. Islam came later than the other great monotheistic religions (Judaism and Christianity) and drew its inspiration mainly from Judaism and Nestorianism. Mohammed accepted the inspiration of the Old Testament and claimed to be a successor to Moses, but recognised Jesus only as a prophet.

The Koran (Quran) is the sacred book of Islam. Its revelations are contained in the 114 *suras* or chapters: all but one begin with the words: "In the name of Allah, the Merciful, the Compassionate." It is written in classical Arabic, and Muslims memorise much or all of it. Its ethical teachings are high. Like orthodox Judaism Islam is a literal-minded religion lived in everyday life. No Muslim is in any doubt as to exactly how he should carry on in the events of his day.

The devout Muslim has five duties: (1) Once in his life he must say with absolute conviction: "There is no God but Allah, and Mohammed is His Prophet". (2) Prayer preceded by ablution must be five times daily—on rising, at noon, in midafternoon, after sunset, and before retiring. The face of the worshipper is turned in the direction of Mecca. (3) The giving of alms generously, including provisions for the poor. (4) The keeping of the fast of Ramadan, the holy month, during which believers in good health may neither eat nor drink nor indulge in wordly pleasures between sunrise and sunset. (5) Once in his life a Muslim, if he can, must make the pilgrimage to Mecca. (*see* **Hajj**)

In addition, drinking, gambling, and the eating of pork are forbidden and circumcision is practised. Polygamy is permitted, although decreasing; sexual relations outside marriage are disapproved of; marriage is only with the wife's consent; and divorce may be initiated by either husband or wife. A great advantage in the spread of Islam has been its lack of race prejudice.

Mohammed's main achievements were the destruction of idolatry, the welding of warring tribes into one community, the progress of a conquest which led after his death to the great and cultured empire which spread throughout the Middle East into north Africa, north India, and ultimately to Spain. That it did not spread all over Europe was due to the Muslim defeat by Charles Martel at Poitiers in 732.

The holiest cities of Islam are Mecca, Medina, Jerusalem and Kairouan.

During the 1980s, militant Islam became a major political force in Iran (under Ayatollah Khomeini). Islamic fundamentalism became, in the 1990s, a growing political force in, for example, Algeria, Egypt, Yemen, Afghanistan, Pakistan and much of central Asia.

The most extreme form of fundamentalism to be implemented then was the Taleban regime in Afghanistan until its overthrow. Currently, parts of Iraq Syria and Libya are also witnessing extremist jihadist rule, whilst Boko Haram in northern Nigeria is also brutal.

The number of Muslims in England and Wales was 2,706,066 at the 2011 Census. One-third of these was under 15. This total could rise to over 7 million by 2050. There are over 1,600 mosques and prayer rooms. Nearly half are controlled by the Deobandi sect. The first was established at Woking in Surrey in 1890. The largest mosque in Britain (the Baitul Futuh mosque in Morden) was completed in 2003. The largest mosque in the western world is in Dearborn, Michigan, USA. Globally, there are today an estimated 1,875,000,000 Muslims. (expected to rise to 2·8 billion by 2050).

The Masjid al-Haram mosque in Mecca is the world's largest mosque.

J

Jainism. The Jains are an Indian sect, largely in commerce and finance. Their movement founded by Vardhamana, called Mahavira (the great hero), in the 6th cent. B.C. arose rather earlier than Buddhism in revolt against the ritualism and impersonality of **Hinduism** (*q.v.*). It rejects the authority of the early Hindu Vedas and does away with many of the Hindu deities whose place is largely taken by Jainism's twenty-four immortal saints; it despises caste distinctions and modifies the two great Hindu doctrines of *karma* and transmigration. Jain philosophy is based on *ahimsa*, the sacredness of all life, regarding even plants as the brethren of mankind, and refusing to kill even the smallest insect. The first Jain temple in the Western world opened in 1988 in Leicester.

Of an estimated 5,300,000 Jains world-wide, 98 % of these are in India. Jainism claims over 30,000 devotees in Britain. The largest number outside India live in Kenya.

Jansenism, the name given by the Roman Catholic Church to the heresy of Cornelius Jansen (1585–1638), a Dutch-born professor of theology at Louvain, derived from his work *Augustinus*, published after his death. He proposed that without special grace from God, the performance of his commandments is impossible, that man has no free will, and that most human beings are condemned to damnation. The movement was very influential in France in the 17th century.

Jehovah's Witnesses. One of the best known offshoots of mainstream Christianity, Jehovah's Witnesses are renowned for their doorstep witness. Founded in the second half of the nineteenth century in Pittsburgh by Charles Taze Russel, and taking their name from a passage in Isaiah 43, they are strongly millenialist, and put much emphasis on the return of Christ and his heavenly rule upon earth. Various attempts to set a specific date since 1874 have proved unsuccessful, however. Russel, rejecting the notion of a Hell, put a focus on the nothingness of death until the Second Coming or Rapture. At this point the 144, 000 or 'little flock' will rule with Christ in Heaven, whilst other Jehovah's Witnesses, the 'great crowd' will be ruled on Earth.

They support their beliefs based on the Bible, in particular their own version, The New World Translation. They emphasise the Judaic name for God, Jehovah, and regard him as God alone. They reject the Trinity, and regard Jesus Christ as God's first creation and therefore inferior, and the Holy Spirit as another way of expressing God's power in action. They believe in upholding what they regard as the universal elements of the Mosaic Law, and are well known for their rejection of blood transfusions as non-biblical.

They regard other religions and denominations as false, rejecting in particular strongly hierarchical church organisation, despite criticisms of authoritarianism themselves. At the heart of the movement lies directed Bible study supported by its huge publishing wing, the Watch Tower Bible and Tract Society. There are *c.* 8 million members.

Jesuits. *See* **E7.**

Jesus People, one of the early revivals of interest in the teaching and personality of Jesus Christ which featured from the 1960s as part of the American "Hippy" scene. The Jesus People were generally white but not necessarily of an orthodox Christian background. The cult developed in California.

Jihad, the Islamic term is best translated 'to struggle to the utmost'. In the West it has become synonymous with a holy war.

Judaism, the relgion of the Jews, the oldest of the great monotheist religions, parent of Christianity and Islam, the development of which is presented in the Old Testament. The creed of Judaism is based on the concept of a transcendent and omnipotent One True God, the revelation of His will in the *Torah*, and the special relation between God and His "Chosen People." The idea of Incarnation is rejected, Jesus is not recognised as the Messiah. The *Torah* is the Hebrew name for the Law of Moses (the Pentateuch) which, Judaism holds, was revealed to Moses on Mount Sinai soon after the exodus of the Israelites from Egypt (1230 B.C.).

Most critics today deny the Mosaic authorship of the first five books of the Bible and believe them to be a compilation from four main sources known as J(Jahvist), E (Elohist), D (Deuteronomist) and P (Priestly Code), distinguished from each other by the name used for God, language, style, and internal evidence. From the historical point of view an important influence on Judaism may have been the monotheism of Akhenaten, the "heretic" Pharaoh (note, for example, the striking resemblance between Psalm 104 and Akhenaten's "Hymn to the Sun"). But some scholars now question how monotheistic early Judaism actually was.

Talmud. The Talmud is a book containing the civil and canonical laws of the Jews and includes the *Mishna*, a compilation from oral tradition written in Hebrew, and the *Gemara*, a collection of comments and criticisms by Jewish rabbis, written in Aramaic. There are in fact two Talmuds: the one made in Palestine (the Jerusalem Talmud), finished at the beginning of the 5th cent B.C., and the other made in

Babylon, completed at the end of the 6th cent B.C. Judaism at the beginning of the Christian era had a number of sects: (1) the Pharisees (whose views include the first clear statement of the resurrection of the just to eternal life and the future punishment of the wicked) who held to the *Torah* and the universality of God; (2) the Sadducees, the upper class of priests and wealthy landowners, to whom God was essentially a national God and who placed the interests of the state before the *Torah*; they rejected ideas of resurrection and eternal life; (3) the Essenes (*q.v.*) who were regarded as a puritanical break-away movement by both parties. The views of the Pharisees prevailed.

Jewish Philosophers. Jewish writing continued through the years and some books were added to the *Torah*, among them the Three Major Prophets and certain books of the Twelve Minor Prophets. There were also the Apocalyptic writers who were unorthodox in their preaching of a divinely planned catastrophic end to the world with a "new Heaven and a new earth," preceded by a divine Messiah, and a future life—all of which beliefs influenced early Christianity. Judah Halevi of Toledo (*c.* 1085–*c.* 1140) and Moses Maimonides of Cordova (1135–1204) were the great Jewish philosophers.

Modern Movements in Judaism stem from the Enlightenment, notably with Moses Mendelssohn in the 18th cent. who accepted, as was the tendency of the period, only that which could be proved by reason. He translated the Pentateuch into German thus encouraging German Jews to give up Yiddish and Hebrew for the language of the land and thereby preparing them for their vast contribution to Western civilisation. One of his disciples, David Friedländer (d. 1834) instituted "reform" Judaism.

He wanted to remove anything that would hamper the relationships of Jews with their neighbours or tend to call in doubt their loyalty to their adopted state. A similar movement in America (1885) called for the rejection of dietary laws, the inauguration of Sunday services, and the repudiation of Jewish nationalism.

Between "reform" and orthodoxy there arose the conservative movement which, in England, includes prayers in English in the service, does not segregate men and woman in the synagogue, and translates the Law in a more liberal way. Judaism is essentially a social and family religion which, more than almost any other concerns itself with the observances of every aspect of daily life. As in Islam (*q.v.*) details are laid down in the most minute way for the behaviour of the orthodox.

The home is the main Jewish institution. Circumcision takes place eight days after birth, and a boy becomes a man for religious purposes at his Bar Mitzvah at the age of thirteen.

There are currently divisions in Judaism over the role women can play in Jewish religious life. The Ultra-Orthodox Jews are known as the *haredim*. Only Orthodox Judaism now rejects same sex marriage.

Among festivals are Passover, recalling the Exodus; Rosh Hashanah (the Jewish New Year), the anniversary of the Creation and the beginning of ten days of penitence ending with Yom Kippur (the Day of Atonement), a day of fasting spent in the synagogue; Purim, celebrating the deliverance of the Jews from Haman; and Hanukkah (*q.v.*), celebrating their victory against the Syrians under their leader Judas Maccabeus. A new and semi-religious festival is the Yom Haatzmaut, the anniversary of the birth of the state of Israel.

Countries with the largest Jewish populations are the USA (5,300,000), Israel (5,250,000) and France (521,000). France has Europe's largest Jewish population. At the 2011 Census there were 263,346 Jews in England and Wales. Islam, Hinduism and Sikhism have all overtaken Judaism in numbers in the UK. The Chief Rabbi is Ephraim Mirvis. There are over 16 million Jews world-wide, close to the pre-war figure of 16·5 million.

K

Kabbala. *See* **Cabala.**

Khalsa, the sacred brotherhood of the Sikhs (*q.v.*).

Koran (Quran). *See* **Islam.**

Ku Klux Klan. After the American Civil War (1861–65) southern conservatives and ex-Confederate leaders began to fear both Black and poor White rule. Taxes were rising owing to radical legislation and the tax-burdened and disenfranchised planters finally took to illegal means to achieve their ends by trying to effect an alliance with the poor White and small farmer through appealing to his anti-Black prejudice.

Hence the Ku Klux Klan was formed in 1866 as a secret society by a small group of Confederate veterans in Tennessee with the intention of frightening Blacks by dressing in ghostly white robes in the guise of the spirits of dead soldiers. But the movement spread like wild-fire throughout the South encouraged by small farmers and planters alike. General Nathan Bedford Forrest was appointed "Grand Wizard" of the Klan "empire" and in every community armed Klansmen riding at night horsewhipped "uppity" Blacks, beat Union soldiers, and threatened carpet-bag politicians (i.e., fortunehunters from the North). Soon several similar organisations arose, many of which did not stop at torture or murder.

The Klan was a vicious and contemptible organisation in which former Southern leaders trying to regain control deliberately set poor and middle-class Whites against the Blacks by appeal to race prejudice. Congress struck back with laws and intervention of Federal troops, and after a large number of convictions in South Carolina much of the violence stopped.

After the 1914–18 war the movement, dormant since 1900, revived as a sadistic anti-Black, anti-Jewish, anti-Catholic society, spreading to the north as well as the south. By 1926, the Klan began to subside once more. While it revived again in the mid-1960s, it soon fell back. It number only a few thousand extremists today in 190 branches, but there are many other racist, white power movements.

L

Lamaism, the religion of Tibet. Its beliefs and worship derive from the Mahayana form of Buddhism which was introduced into Tibet in 749. The emphasis laid by its founder on the necessity for self-discipline and conversion through meditation and the study of philosophy deteriorated into formal monasticism and ritualism.

The Dalai Lama, as the reincarnated Buddha, was both king and high priest, a sort of pope and emperor rolled into one. Under him was a hierarchy of officials in which the lowest order was that of the monks who became as numerous as one man in every six or seven of the population. The main work carried out by this vast church-state was the collection of taxes to maintain the monasteries and other religious offices. Second in power to the Dalai Lama was the Panchen or Tashi Lama believed to be a reincarnation of Amitabha, another Buddha.

The Dalai Lama fled to India back in 1959 when the Chinese entered his country. For a brief period following his departure, the Panchen Lama surprised the Western world by publicly welcoming the Communist invasion, but he later renounced the regime. The current Panchen Lama's whereabouts are not known.

Latter-day Saints. See under **Mormons.**

Levellers, an English military-politico-religious party prominent in the Parliamentary Army about 1647 which stood for the rights of the people. See **Diggers.**

Liberalism is the view that government should protect the freedom and property of individuals. Most liberals accept that individuals have the capacity and the right to live their lives as they wish, free from interference by others. Government is legitimate if it enacts and enforces laws that allow individuals to enjoy the greatest amount of freedom in their lives without affecting the freedom of others. Liberalism has always respected private property as it is seen as integral to allowing individuals the means to express their freedom, and as a bulwark against interference of the state or others. Variations on these basic themes of liberalism are found in the work of Hobbes, Locke, Bentham, and Mill, and these ideas became important politically during the 18th and 19th cents.

As levels of prosperity and education grew in the industrial revolution, greater demand for individual political and property rights promoted the cause of the Liberal Party, the successor to the Whigs (a nickname derive from Whigamore, used in the 17th cent. for Scottish dissenters).

Throughout the 19th century, liberal thinkers and politicians widened their view of how the rights and freedoms of individuals could be protected and promoted, and began to see that laws protecting the freedom of individuals from crimes and interference of other individuals must be combined with policies protecting the freedom of individuals from squalor, hunger, and exploitation. This 'New Liberalism' in the thought of T. H. Green and L. T. Hobhouse influenced the welfare reforms of the great Liberal politicians Lloyd-George and William Beveridge.

This 'New Liberalism' understood that the freedom and rights of individuals could only be secured when combined with commitments to equality and social justice. Whilst New Liberals advocated certain policies similar to the emergent Labour Party, the Liberals retained their commitment to individual property rights, which distinguished them from the socialist commitment to collective ownership and class politics. The strength of working class support for the Labour Party heralded a period of electoral decline for the Liberal Party, interrupted by revivals under the leadership of Jo Grimond (1962), Jeremy Thorpe (1974), David Steel (1979). The 1987 election setback heralded a merger between the Liberals and their SDP Alliance partners. The newly formed Liberal Democrats grew steadily under their leader Paddy Ashdown, rising to become a significant third party. Under Charles Kennedy's leadership they won 62 seats in the 2005 election. After the 2010 election they controversially joined a coalition with the Conservatives. In 2015 they suffered severe losses, retaining only 8 seats. For the 2017 election, see **D23**.

Whilst the Liberal Party struggled politically in the 20th cent, liberal beliefs are now arguably dominant politically, socially, and intellectually. The Labour and Conservative parties now both promote explicitly liberal policies, eschewing collective ownership, and socially conservative attitudes respectively. Liberal political philosophy has flourished since the publication of John Rawls's *Theory of Justice*, and many liberals are now motivated to spread their commitments to individuals' rights, legitimate democratic government, and social justice across the globe.

Libertarianism is the view that the moral and material benefit of individuals is best served by a society devoid of government except for the enforcement of rights to life and property. In this way libertarianism differs from anarchism, which argues for the abolition of all authority and government. Famous contemporary libertarians, such as Hayek and Nozick, argue that the pursuit of social justice by the state endangers individual liberty, and threatens tyranny. They argue for a society which operates much like an ideal market where a natural equilibrium of individuals' interests will provide for each person's needs.

Libertarianism's affection for the market has influenced neoliberalism (q.v.). Libertarians disagree with modern liberals on the importance of social justice. Liberals argue that there is a moral duty to seek greater equality, and they embrace democratic institutions as appropriate structures through which to promote social justice. Libertarians need to explain either why social justice is not important, or how it can be achieved without democratic political institutions.

Literary Theory. Modern literary theory is concerned with ways in which meaning is constructed and with ideological influences. It challenges received notions of imagination and inspiration, moral significance, and the personality of the author. Its origins lie partly in semiology and formalism, which concentrate on the actual words and structure of a literary text.

Marxism is also important in the works of such critics as Georg Lukács and Louis Althusser. Later approaches include structuralism and post-structuralism. Feminism has become an increasingly significant form of criticism. Other theories are New Historicism, which examines social and cultural contexts, and Reader-Response Criticism, which analyses readers' constructions of meaning.

Logical Positivism, a school of philosophy founded in Vienna in the 1920s by a group known as "the Vienna circle": their work was based on that of Ernst Mach, but dates in essentials as far back as Hume. Of the leaders of the group, Schlick was murdered by a student, Wittgenstein came to Britain, and Carnap went to America following the entry of the Nazis. Briefly the philosophy differs from all others in that, while most people have believed that a statement might be (a) true, or (b) false, logical positivists consider there to be a third category; a statement may be meaningless. There are only two types of statement which can be said to have meaning: (1) those which are tautological, i.e., those in which the statement is merely a definition of the subject, such as "a triangle is a three-sided plane figure" ("triangle" and "three-sided plane figure" are the same thing); and (2) those which can be tested by sense experience. This definition of meaningfulness excludes a great deal of what has previously been thought to be the field of philosophy; in particular it excludes the possibility of metaphysics.

Thus the question as to whether there is a God or whether free-will exists is strictly meaningless for it is neither a tautological statement nor can it be tested by sense experience.

Lollards, a body of religious reformers and followers of Wyclif who were reviled and persecuted in the reign of Richard II. The name "Lollard" comes from a Flemish word meaning "mutterer"—a term of contempt used to describe the sect. Under Henry V, determined efforts were made to crush the Lollards. Their leader, Sir John Oldcastle, was burnt at the stake (December 1417).

Low Church, term formerly applied to those Anglicans most sympathetic to Protestant nonconformity (i.e., the opposite of the High Church Anglo-Catholics).

Lutheranism. The Reformation had a long history before it became, under Luther and Calvin, an accepted fact. The mediaeval Church had held (as the Catholic Church holds today) that the sacraments were the indispensable means of salvation. Since these were exclusively administered by the clergy, any movement which attacked clerical abuses was forced by sheer necessity to deny the Church's exclusive control of the means of salvation, before it could become free from dependence on a corrupt priesthood. Hence the Albigenses and the Waldenses (qq.v.), the followers of John Hus and Wycliff (see **Anticlericalism**), were bound to deny the authority of the Church and emphasise that of the Bible. Luther began his movement primarily in order to reform the Church from its gross abuses and the famous ninety-five theses of 1517 were not primarily theological but moral complaints dealing with the actual behaviour of the clergy rather than Church beliefs.

Luther began with the support of the peasants who were genuinely shocked at the abuse of indulgences and other matters, but ended up by being supported by the noblemen who wanted to destroy the power of the pope over the German states and looked forward to confiscating the lands and property of the Church. When the peasants wanted the reform of actual economic abuses relating to the feudal system, Luther took the side of the nobles against them. The contemporary movement in Switzerland led by Ulrich Zwingli had no such secular support, and Zwingli was killed in 1531.

Martin Luther (1483–1546) was the son of a miner in Eisleben in Saxony, entered the order of Augustinian Friars in 1505, and later taught at the newly founded university of Wittenberg. After the publication of the theses the real issue so far as the Church was concerned was whether he was willing or not to submit to the authority of his superiors; Luther refused to compromise with his conscience in the famous words: "Here I stand; I can do no other." In a further statement Luther recommended the formation of a German national church, the abolition of indulgences and other means whereby Rome obtained money from Germany, and an end to the celibacy of the clergy. For this he was naturally excommunicated.

His teaching was based on the German translation of the Bible, but he was by no means a fundamentalist: e.g., he denied that the Book of Hebrews was written by Paul, would have nothing to do with the Apocrypha, and regarded the letter of James as "an epistle of straw." The

Scriptures were open to all and could be interpreted by private judgment enlightened by the Spirit of God. One of Luther's key beliefs was Justification by Faith.

Calvin and Luther. Like Calvin, Luther was a predestinarian and determinist, but he was also a conservative and soon became alarmed about the position taken by many extremists once the Reformation was under way. He had really wanted the Church to reform itself, but when he alienated Rome he had perforce to rely more and more on the secular powers which finally resulted in the state-church form which became pronounced in Prussia and later elsewhere.

Whereas Calvin wished the Church to be at least the equal of the State and in some respects its superior, Luther's rebellion resulted in the reverse, a state-controlled episcopalianism.

In 1999 the Lutheran World Federation and the Vatican agreed a historic "Common Statement" on the doctrine of justification. See also **Calvinism**, **Presbyterianism**.

Lycanthropy, the delusion that men may, by the exercise of magical powers or because of some inherited affliction, occasionally transform into wolves. The so-called werewolf is an important feature of mid-European folklore and much the same can be said of the were-tigers and were-bears of Africa and the Far East. Man's fear of werewolves can be seen in prehistoric rock carvings dating back 30,000 years.

M

McLuhanism. According to Marshall McLuhan (1911–80), a Canadian, and former professor of English at Toronto, the way people communicate is more important than what they communicate: hence his famous slogan, "the medium is the message." There have been two great landmarks in human understanding since we learnt to speak and write: the invention of the printed book and the present digital revolution. The printed word took us step by step along the linear, logical path to understanding; television comes at us from all directions at once and now computers have overthrown the regime of "time' and "space'.

McLuhan's importance lies in alerting us to the present clash between two great technologies, the literate and the electromagnetic, and in his vision, beyond the present chaos, of a world drawn tighter together in a "global village" where identity will merge in collectivity and we shall all be able to co-operate for the common good.

Magic, a form of belief originating in very early days and based on early humans' inability to distinguish between similarity and identity. The simplest example would perhaps be the fertility rites in which it is believed that a ceremony involving sexual relations between men and women will bring about fertility in the harvest. Or the idea that sticking pins in an image of an individual will bring about harm or even death to the real person. Magic is regarded by some as a form of early science in that man in his efforts to control Nature had recourse to magical practices when the only methods he knew had failed to bring the desired results. It filled a gap. By others magic is regarded as an elementary stage in the evolution of religion. It can be said to have served a purpose there too. Yet magic differs from religion: religion depends upon a power outside and beyond human beings, whereas magic depends upon nothing but the casting of a spell or the performance of a ceremony.

The idea that "like produces like" is at the roots of imitative magic. It follows that an event can be compelled by imitating it. One engages in swinging, not for pleasure, but to produce a wind as the swing does; ball games are played to get rainy weather because the black ball represents dark rainclouds; other ball games, in which one attempts to catch the ball in a cup or hit it with a stick, represent the sexual act (as some gentlemen at Lords may be distressed to hear) and bring about fertility; in medicine until a few centuries ago herbs were chosen to cure a disease because in some respects their leaves or other parts looked like the part of the body affected. See **Witchcraft** and **Demonism**.

Malthusianism, the theory about population growth put forward by the Rev. Thomas Malthus (1766–1834) in *An Essay on Population* (1798). His three main propositions were (1) "Population is necessarily limited by means of subsistence." (2) "Population invariably increases where means of subsistence increase unless prevented by some very powerful and obvious checks." (3) "These checks, and the checks which repress the superior power of population, and keep its effects on a level with the means of subsistence, are all resolvable into moral restraint, vice and misery."

In other words, no matter how great the food supply may become, human reproductive power will always adjust itself so that food will always be scarce in relation to population; the only means to deal with this is by "moral restraint" (*i.e.*, chastity or not marrying), "vice" (*i.e.*, birth-control methods), or misery (*i.e.*, starvation).

More specifically, Malthus claimed that while food increases by arithmetical progression, population increases by geometrical progression. It is true that these gloomy predictions did not take place in Malthus's time largely owing to the opening up of new areas of land outside Europe, the development of new techniques in agriculture, the growth of international trade to poorer areas, the increased knowledge of birth-control, and developments in medical science which reduced the misery he had predicted.

Furthermore, we now know that as a society becomes industrialised its birth-rate tends to fall. The world's population has increased from about 465 million in 1650 to reach 7·2 billion today.

Manichaeism, an Asiatic religion which developed from Zoroastrianism (*q.v.*) and shows the influence of Buddhism (*q.v.*) and Gnosticism (*q.v.*), being founded by Mani, a Persian who was born in Babylonia, *c.* 216 A.D. Mani presented himself to Shapur I as the founder of a new religion which was to be to Babylonia what Buddhism was to India or Christianity to the West.

His aspiration was to convert the East and he himself made no attempt to interfere directly with Christianity although he represented himself as the Paraclete (the Holy Ghost or "Comforter") and, like Jesus, had twelve disciples. His success in Persia aroused the fury of the Zoroastrian priests who objected to his reforming zeal towards their religion and in 276 Mani was taken prisoner and crucified.

Of Mani's complicated system little can be said here, save that it is based on the struggle of two eternal conflicting principles, God and matter, or light and darkness. Although its founder had no intention of interfering with the West, after his death his followers soon spread the religion from Persia and Mesopotamia to India and China. It reached as far as Spain and Gaul and influenced many of the bishops in Alexandria and in Carthage where for a time St. Augustine accepted Manichaeism. Soon the toleration accorded it under Constantine ended and it was treated as a heresy and violently suppressed. Yet it later influenced many heresies, and even had some influence on orthodox Catholicism which had a genius for picking up elements in other religions which had been shown to appeal to worshippers provided they did not conflict with fundamental beliefs.

Maoism is the branch of communism in China that was shaped by one of the most remarkable statesmen of modern times, Mao Tse-tung (Mao Zedong) (1893–1976). He set the pattern of revolution for poor peasant societies despite the traumas of the "Great Leap Forward" and the Cultural Revolution. Although Marxist theory guided the Chinese communists in their struggle for liberation from the old, bourgeois and feudal China, it was interpreted in a manner peculiar to China and developed to fit into the Chinese way of life and the "thoughts" of Chairman Mao. As early as 1926 Mao had pointed out that the Chinese proletariat had in the peasantry its staunchest and most numerous ally.

The struggles of 1925–49 (the Long March of the Red Army, the Anti-Japanese War, the Civil War against Chiang Kai-shek) were the foundations on which present-day China has been built. Great efforts were made to remove poverty, ignorance,

corruption *etc.* from China. Mao taught that struggle is necessary for the revolution to endure.

However, disillusion with Maoism intensified during the ultra-leftist Cultural Revolution of 1966 to 1976. The radical chaos was ended only by the death of Mao on 9 September 1976.

The decades since the death of Mao Tse-tung have seen a huge shift towards the modernisation of China and the rapid onset of capitalism but with the Communist hierarchy still in control.

However, the terrible excesses of the regime, in which millions died, have caused historians to cast Mao as another Stalin, a tyrant of his time.

Maronites, Christian sect which appeared in Syria in the 6th Cent. They are the largest Christian group in Lebanon. The Maronite patron saint is the Syrian monk Maron (d. *c* 410). The Maronites retain ancient Eastern rites.

Marxism. The sociological theories founded by Karl Marx and Friedrich Engels on which modern communist thought is based. Marx and Engels lived in a period of unrestrained capitalism when exploitation and misery were the lot of the industrial working classes, and it was their humanitarianism and concern for social justice which inspired their work. Marx wrote his *Communist Manifesto* in Brussels in 1848 and in his *Das Kapital* (1867), he worked out a new theory of society. Marx showed that all social systems are economically motivated and change as a result of technical and economic changes in methods of production.

The driving force of social change Marx found to be in the struggle which the oppressed classes wage to secure a better future.

Thus in his celebrated theory of historical materialism he interpreted history in terms of economics and explained the evolution of society in terms of class struggle. (*See* **Dialectical Materialism.**) "In the social production of their means of existence," he wrote, "men enter into definite and unavoidable relations which are independent of their will. These productive relationships correspond to the particular stage in the development of their material productive forces." Marx's theory of historical materialism implies that history is propelled by class struggle with communism and the classless society as the final stage when man will have emancipated himself from the productive process. Marx was the first to put socialism on a rational and scientific basis, and he foretold that socialism would inevitably replace capitalism.

His prophecy, however, came to realisation not in the advanced industrial countries as he had envisaged but in Russia and China. *See* **Communism.**

Materialism. Any theory that tends to the view that only matter or material objects exist and that everything else, notably minds and mental experiences, can be described in material terms. Materialism is thus opposed to dualism or idealism and, in general, to any belief in God, in disembodied spirits *etc.* There is much contemporary philosophical debate as to whether "consciousness" is not a name for something mysterious, but simply a way of talking about the brain. *See also* **Mind and Matter.**

Mechanism. As a theory, the view that everything happens mechanically, that natural phenomena are to be explained by reference to certain laws of nature applied to the behaviour of matter in motion. Through the influence of science, there is a strong tendency in Western thought to compare the universe or parts of it, even human beings, to machines.

Mennonites, a Christian sect rejecting infant baptism. Named after Menno Simons (1496–1559). Its members reject military service and refuse to hold public office. Hutterites share their beliefs. The Amish community, based from the 1700s in Pennsylvania, split from the Mennonites.

They take the Bible literally and at home speak a German language, Pennsylvania Dutch. There are *c.* 500 colonies in North America. Its last church closed in Britain in 2016, but its work continues online.

Mercantilism. Commercial policy pursued by England. Holland and other European nations in the 16th and 17th centuries, as nations expanded the commercial sectors of their economies and a shift of emphasis towards trade and away from domestic agriculture occurred. The policy was aimed at securing an inflow of precious metals and raw materials in return for an outflow of finsihed goods.

Mesmerism, a rapidly vanishing name to denote the practice of hypnosis, which owes its popularity, though not its discovery, to the Austrian physician, Anton Mesmer (1733–1815). Mesmer's contribution was the realisation that a large number of what we would today call psychosomatic or hysterical conditions could be cured (or at least temporarily alleviated) by one or another form of suggestion. Mesmer himself relied on the idea of what he called "animal magnetism," a supposedly potent therapeutic force emanating from the living body which could be controlled by the trained individual.

Mesmer used wands and impressive gadgetry to dispense the marvellous force and he effected a remarkable number of cures of complaints, hitherto looked upon as incurable or totally mysterious in origin—the most typical of these being hysterical blindness, paralysis or deafness, nervous skin conditions, and so on. Hypnosis, which is a valid if very poorly understood psychological phenomenon even today, would probably have been developed much further had not efficient general anaesthetics such as ether, nitrous oxide, *etc.*, been discovered, thus greatly diminishing its role as a pain reliever in surgery. Mesmer, who was three parts charlatan, never really troubled to think deeply about the cause of his undoubted success.

The first man to treat hysteria as a formal class of illness and who made a scientific attempt to treat it with hypnosis was Ambrose Liébeault (1823–1904). He and his colleague Hippolyte Bernheim (1840–1919) believed: (*a*) that hysteria was produced by suggestion, and particularly by autosuggestion on the part of the patient, and (*b*) that suggestion was a normal trait found in varying degrees in everyone. These conclusions are true, but as Freud showed later are far from being the whole truth.

Research published in 2008 showed that hypnosis can indeed work—by producing measurable changes in areas of the human brain linked to memory. Hypnosedation may, for example, reduce the need for general anaesthetic in patients.

Messianism. Most varieties of religious belief rely on the assumption that the deity is a supernatural being either permeating the universe or dwelling in some other sphere, and normally inaccessible to man. Where divine intervention is necessary, the deity is traditionally believed to nominate a human being—in the case of Christianity, for example, Jesus is believed to be the actual son of God. Messianic cults introduce a novel variant on the traditional theme. In these a human being is held to be God himself. He may either nominate himself for this role, relying on his own personality or native talent to acquire the necessary following, or for one reason or another large numbers of people may alight on one individual and declare him the Messiah. While it might seem that beliefs of this kind would be confined to earlier epochs in man's history, this is not the case.

Metapsychology. Not to be confused with parapsychology (*q.v.*). The branch or off-shoot of psychology which goes beyond empirical and experimental studies to consider such philosophical matters as the nature of mind, the reality of free-will and the mind/body problem. It was originally used by Freud as a blanket descriptive term denoting all mental processes, but this usage is now obsolete.

Methodism, the religious movement founded by John Wesley in 1738, with the aim of spreading "scriptural holiness" throughout the land. Up to that time Wesley had been a High Churchman but on a visit to Georgia in the United States he was much impressed by the group known as Moravians (*q.v.*), and on his return to this country was introduced by his brother Charles, who had already become an adherent, to Peter Böhler, a Moravian minister in England. Passing through a period of spiritual commotion following the meeting, he first saw the light at a small service in Aldersgate in May 1738 "where one was reading Luther's preface to the Epistle to the Romans" and from this time all Wesley's energies were devoted to the single object of saving souls.

Early Methodism. Soon Whitefield, a follower with Calvinist views, was preaching throughout the country and Charles Wesley was composing his well-known hymns; John's abilities at this time were taken up in the movement described as "People called Methodists." They were to be arranged in "societies" which were united into "circuits" under a minister, the circuits into "districts" and all knit together into a single body under a conference of ministers which has met annually since 1744. Local lay preachers were also employed and to maintain interest the ministers were moved from circuit to circuit each year.

These chapel services were not originally meant to conflict with the Church of England of which Wesley still considered himself a member. They were purely supplementary, and it used to be the custom (before the Methodists began to count themselves as Nonconformists) for Methodists to attend Church in the morning and Chapel in the evening.

The class-meeting was the unit of the organisation where members met regularly under a chosen leader to tell their "experiences" upon which they were often subjected to severe cross-examination. At the end of every quarter, provided their attendances were regular, they received a ticket of membership which entitled them to come to monthly sacramental services. If attendance was inadequate the name was removed from the list, without appearance on which nobody was deemed a member. The price of the ticket was "a penny a week and a shilling a quarter" but Wesley was not interested in receiving money from anyone who was not utterly devoted to the cause.

The Work of Wesley. John Wesley introduced four other innovations, some of which were regarded by Churchmen who had previously been willing to commend his efforts in bringing religion to the poorer classes as dangerous: (1) He started the Sunday-school scheme and afterwards enthusiastically supported that of John Raikes, often regarded as the founder of the idea; this was of immense importance in the days before the Education Acts. (2) He reintroduced the Agapae or "love feasts" of the early Church which were fellowship meetings deepening the sense of brotherhood of the society. (3) He began to copy the open-air meetings of the eloquent Whitefield and soon unwittingly produced the most extraordinary results, finding that his sermons led to groans, tears, fainting fits, and all sorts of emotional expression. Even his open-air lay speakers produced like results and these came to be associated with Methodism and gave significance to the proud Anglican claim that *their* services would be "without enthusiasm." (4) After some hesitation he ventured to consecrate Dr. Thomas Coke, who was being sent as a missionary to America, as a bishop of his church. In addition to Wesley's religious work he was a great educator of the common man. Thus he introduced the cheap book and the church magazine, publishing books of any sort which he thought would edify and not harm even when the views expressed were different from his own—*e.g.*, Thomas à Kempis's *Imitation of Christ* and works of history, biography, science, and medicine in some cases written by himself. In this way the movement with its cheap books and reading rooms had an influence far beyond its actual membership. Both the Anglican Church and the Evangelical movement of Wilberforce and others profited from Wesley's work.

Later Schisms. Methodism, especially after Wesley's death in 1791, began, like other movements, to develop schisms. These were the long-standing differences which the Baptist movement (*q.v.*) had shown too between Arminian and Calvinist sections—*i.e.*, between those who did and those who did not accept the doctrine of predestination. In the case of the Methodists, this led to a complete break in 1811. Then there were differences associated with the status of the laity, or the relationship of the movement with the Anglican Church. The "Methodist New Connection" of 1797 differed only in giving the laity equal representation with the ministers but the more important break of the Primitive Methodists in 1810 gave still more power to the laity and reintroduced the "camp-meeting" type of service. In 1815 the Bryanites or "Bible Christians" were formed, and a further schism which was even brought before the law courts was ostensibly over the foundation of a theological college. The real reason, of course, was that the ministers were becoming more Tory, whilst the laity were becoming more Radical. Finally in 1932, the Wesleyan Methodists, the Primitive Methodists, and the United Methodists became one Church, the Methodist Church.

Adult Methodist membership has fallen recently, with numbers down to nearly 200,000 (the lowest since 1819).

During 1998, Methodists began the first formal steps towards talks with Anglicans about reunion. Earlier attempts to unite with the Anglicans in 1969 and 1972 ended in failure. The present initiative has not met with success.

The Methodist Church has separately agreed to bless gay couples "married" under the civil partnership law. The Methodist Church has also issued an "unreserved apology" over the large number of historical child abuse cases that have been uncovered.

The World Methodist Council supports the autonomous Methodist churches in the world.

Millenarianism. The belief in a future "millenium", that is, the thousand year reign of Christ on earth. The idea however has pre-Christian roots and is reflected in Jewish and Islamic thought. It is not part of orthodox Christianity, but many sects in the 19th century, like the Plymouth Brethren and Adventists, espoused millenarianism. The idea has since broadened to mean any theory with an expectation of some transforming change: not only the Kingdom of God, but also the just society, harmony among peoples etc.

Mind and Matter. Early peoples could see that there is a distinction between those things which move and do things by themselves and others, such as stones, which do not. Following the early state of Animism (q.v.), in which spirits were believed to have their abode in everything, they began to differentiate between matter or substance and a force which seems to move it and shape it into objects and things. Thus to the Greek Parmenides (fl. c. 475 B.C.), who was a philosopher of pure reason, thought or mind was the creator of what we observe and in some way not quite clear to himself it seemed that mind was the cause of everything. This is perhaps the first expression of the movement known as Idealism which says, in effect, that the whole universe is mental—a creation either of our own minds or the mind of God. But from Anaxagoras (488–428 B.C.) we have the clearer statement that mind or nous causes all movement but is distinct from the substance it moves. He does not, however, think in terms of individual minds but rather of a kind of generalised mind throughout the universe which can be used as an explanation of anything which cannot be explained otherwise. This is the position known as Dualism (see below) which holds that both mind and matter exist and interact but are separate entities.

Dualism. Most people in practice are dualists since, rightly or wrongly, mind and body are thought of as two different things: it is the "commonsense" (although not necessarily the true) point of view. Plato in a much more complex way was also a dualist although he held that the world of matter we observe is in some sense not the genuine world. The real world is the world of ideas and the tree we see is not real but simply matter upon which mind or soul has imprinted the idea of a tree. Everything that exists has its corresponding form in the world of ideas and imprints its pattern on matter. Mind has always existed and, having become entangled with matter, is constantly seeking to free itself and return to God.

Plato's pupil Aristotle had a much more scientific outlook and held that, although it was mind which gave matter its form, mind is not outside matter, as Plato had thought, but inside it as its formative principle. Therefore there could be no mind without matter and no matter without mind; for even the lowest forms of matter have some degree of mind which increases in quantity and quality as we move up the scale to more complex things.

So far, nobody had explained how two such different substances as matter and mind could influence each other in any way, and this remains, in spite of attempts to be mentioned later, a basic problem in philosophy.

Two later ideas, one of them rather foolish and the other simply refusing to answer the question, are typified by the Stoics and some members of the Sceptic school. The first is that only matter exists and what we call mind is merely matter of a finer texture, a view which as an explanation is unlikely to satisfy anyone; the other, that of some Sceptics, is that we can know nothing except the fleeting images or thoughts that flicker through our consciousness. Of either mind or matter we know nothing.

Renaissance Attitude. Christian doctrines have already been dealt with (see **God and Man, Determinism and Free-will**), and the past and future of the soul is dealt with under **Immortality**. Nor need we mention the Renaissance philosophers who were really much more concerned about how to use mind than about its nature. When they did consider the subject they usually dealt with it, as did Francis Bacon, by separating the sphere of science from that of religion and giving the orthodox view of the latter because there were still good reasons for not wishing to annoy the Church.

Hobbes and Descartes. Thomas Hobbes in the 17th cent. was really one of the first to attempt a modern explanation of mind and matter even if his attempt was crude. As a materialist he held that all that exists is matter and hence our thoughts, ideas, images, and actions are really a form of motion taking place within the brain and nerves. This is the materialist theory which states that mind does not exist.

Thus there are three basic theories of the nature of mind and body: idealism, dualism, and materialism, and we may accept any one of the three. But, if we accept dualism, we shall have to explain precisely the relationship between body and mind. In some of his later writings Hobbes seems to suggest that mental processes are the effects of motion rather than motion itself; i.e., they exist, but only as a result of physical processes just as a flame does on a candle. This theory of the relationship is known as epiphenomenalism.

Descartes, the great French contemporary of Hobbes, was a dualist who believed that mind and matter both exist and are entirely different entities; therefore he had to ask himself how, for example, the desire to walk leads to the physical motion of walking. His unsatisfactory answer was that, although animals are pure automatons, man is different in that he has a soul which resides in the pineal gland (a tiny structure in the brain which today we know to be a relic of evolution with no present function whatever). In this gland the mind comes in contact with the "vital spirits" of the body and thus there is interaction between the two. This theory is known as interactionism, and since we do not accept its basis in the function of the pineal gland, we are simply left with the notion of interaction but without the explanation of how it takes place.

Guelincx. One of Descartes's successors, Arnold Guelincx, produced the even more improbable theory of psychophysical parallelism sometimes known as the theory of the "two clocks". Imagine you have two clocks, each keeping perfect time, then supposing you saw one and heard the other, every time one points to the hour the other will strike, giving the impression that the first event causes the second, although in fact they are quite unrelated. So it is with the body and mind in Guelincx's view, each is "wound up" by God in the beginning in such a way as to keep time with the other so that when I have the desire to walk, purely unrelated physical events in my legs cause them to move at the same time. A variety of this theory is occasionism, which says that when something happens in the physical world, God affects us so that we think we are affected by the happening.

The trouble about all these theories is (a)

that they really explain nothing, and (b) that they give us a very peculiar view of God as a celestial showman treating us as puppets when it would surely have been easier to create a world in which mind and matter simply interacted by their very nature. Spinoza, too, believed in a sort of psychophysical parallelism in that he did not think that mind and body interacted. But since in his theory everything is God, mind and matter are simply two sides of the coin.

John Locke, another contemporary, thought of the mind as a blank slate upon which the world writes in the form of sensations, for we have no innate or inborn ideas and mind and matter do interact although he does not tell us how. All we know are sensations—*i.e.,* sense impressions. Bishop Berkeley carried this idea to its logical conclusion: if we know nothing but sensations, we have no reason to suppose that matter exists at all. He was, therefore, an idealist.

The Views of Hume and Kant. David Hume was to go further still and pointed out that, if all we know are sensations, we cannot prove the existence of matter but we cannot prove the existence of mind either. All we can ever know is that ideas, impressions, thoughts, follow each other. We do not even experience a self or personality because every time we look into our "minds" all we really experience are thoughts and impressions. Hume was quick to point out that this was not the same as saying that the self did not exist; it only proved that we cannot know that it does.

Kant made it clear that, although there is a world outside ourselves, we can never know what it is really like. The mind receives impressions and forms them into patterns which conform not to the thing-in-itself but to the nature of mind. Space and time, for example, are not realities but only the form into which our mind fits its sensations. In other words our mind shapes impressions which are no more like the thing in itself than the map of a battlefield with pins showing the position of various army groups at any given moment is like the battlefield. This, of course, is true. From physics and physiology we know that the sounds we hear are "really" waves in the air, the sights we see "really" electromagnetic waves. What guarantee do we have that the source is "really" like the impression received in our brain? Kant was the leader of the great German Idealist movement of the 18th cent. which in effect said: "why bother about matter when all we can ever know is mental?"

Bradley, Bergson and Strawson. The Englishman Bradley, and the Frenchman Henri Bergson in the 19th and early 20th cent. both held in one form or another the belief that mind in some way creates matter and were, therefore, idealists, whereas Comte, the positivist (*q.v.*), and the Americans William James and John Dewey, held that mind is a form of behaviour. Certain acts (*e.g.,* reflexes) are "mindless" because they are deliberate; others which are intended may be described for the sake of convenience as "minded" (*i.e.,* purposeful). But like the majority of modern psychologists—insofar as they take any interest in the subject—they regarded mind as a process going on in the living body. Is there any reason, many now ask, why we should think of mind as being any different in nature from digestion? Both are processes going on in the body, the one in the brain the other in the stomach and intestines. Why should we therefore regard them as "things"?

Peter Strawson's *Individuals* (1959) refreshed several key Kantian arguments, and combined them with an original analytic vigour that helped make the work important and influential in contemporary discussions of mind and matter. Strawson presented a transcendental argument for the necessity of material bodies as the basic particular to the possibility of existence and experience. Persons are able to think of themselves and each other because of our nature as material individuals, as we can cognise and recognise ourselves and others only because of our material embodiment.

Strawson's arguments are controversial to some who follow a more Humean notion of personal identity, but they have inspired a new generation of philosophers to employ transcendental arguments in an attempt to establish the relationship between mind and matter.

Mithraism, a sun-religion which originated in Persia with the worship of the mythical Mithra, the god of light and of truth. It was for two centuries one of early Christianity's most formidable rivals, particularly in the West since the more philosophical Hellenic Christianity of the East had little to fear from it. (Arnold Toynbee has described Mithraism as "a pre-Zoroastrian Iranian paganism—in a Hellenic dress"; Manichaeism as "Zoroastrianism—in a Christian dress".) Mithraism was a mystery faith with secret rites known only to devotees. It appealed to the soldiers of the Roman Army which explains its spread to the farthest limits of the Roman empire and its decline as the Romans retreated. The religion resembled Zoroastrianism (*q.v.*) in that it laid stress on the constant struggle between good and evil and there are a number of parallels with Christianity. *e.g.,* a miraculous birth, death, and a glorious resurrection, a belief in heaven and hell and the immortality of the soul, a last judgment. Both religions held Sunday as the holy day of the week, celebrated 25 December (date of the pagan winter solstice festival) as the birthday of the founder; both celebrated Easter, and in their ceremonies made use of bell, holy water, and the candle.

Mithraism was to reach its height about 275 A.D. and afterwards declined both for the reason given above and, perhaps, because it excluded women, was emotional rather than philosophical, and had no general organisation to direct its course. Yet even today traces of the religion remain and antiquarians are familiar with the image of the sun-god and the inscription *Deo Soli Mithrae, Invicto, Seculari* (dedicated to the sun-god of Mithra, the unconquered).

Modernism. The term has two main connotations:
1. A movement in the Roman Catholic church, *c.* 1890–1910. The 19th century stress on science and the application of scientific methods in fields like history, psychology and philosophy, raised serious problems for traditional Catholic doctrine. The Modernists sought to reinterpret church teaching in the light of this modern knowledge. The movement was condemned as heresy in 1907.
2. The term is more frequently used to refer to the "modern" movement in all the arts in the period *c.* 1900–30, though defining the period it covers is only one of the problems in describing the movement. It is generally seen as an artistic response to the changes which undermined the securities on which 19th century art and literature were founded. Modernism is marked by a greater ambition for works of art themselves. As well as being novels, or paintings, or music, *etc.,* they were increasingly considered, by artists and critics alike, as representing a theoretical programme, attempts to make the audience see or understand the world in a different way. So modernist characteristics include an increased self-consciousness of the artist, and formal experiment employing a wide variety of technical innovations.

In literature the prime works of modernism are T. S. Eliot's *The Waste Land* and James Joyce's *Ulysses*; the most important painters include Picasso and Matisse; and among composers Schoenberg and Stravinsky stand out.

Mohammedanism. *See* Islam.

Monasticism. When in the 4th cent. A.D. Constantine in effect united state and church there were naturally many who hastened to become Christians for the worldly benefits they expected it to bring in view of the new situation. But there were others who, in their efforts to escape from wordly involvement, went into the deserts of North Africa and Syria to live as hermits.

In these regions there grew up large communities of monks whose lives of renunciation made a considerable impression on the Christian world. They were men of all types but the two main groups were those who preferred to live alone and those who preferred a community life. Among the first must be included St. Anthony, the earliest of the hermits, who was born in Egypt *c.* 250 and who lived alone in a hut near his home for fifteen years and then in the desert for a further twenty. As his fame spread Anthony came forth to teach and advocate a life of extreme austerity, until by the end of his life the Thebaid (the desert around Thebes) was full of hermits following his example. (Not unnaturally, he was constantly assailed by lustful visions which he thoughtfully attributed to Satan.) In the Syrian desert St. Simeon Stylites and others were stimulated to even greater austerities and Simeon himself spent many years on the top of a pillar in a space so small that it was only possible to sit or stand.

The first monastery was founded by Pachomius of Egypt *c.* 315 and here the monks had a common life with communal meals, worship, and work mainly of agricultural type. In the Eastern part of the Empire St. Basil (*c.* 360) tried to check the growth of the extreme and spectacular practices of the hermits by organising monasteries in which the ascetic disciplines of fasting, meditation, and prayer, would be balanced by useful and healthy activities. His monasteries had orphanages and schools for boys—not only those who were intended for a monkish life. But the Eastern Church in general continued to favour the hermit life and ascetic extremes.

Western Monasticism. Monastic life was introduced to the West by St. Athanasius in 339 who obtained its recognition from the Church of Rome and St. Augustine introduced it into North Africa beyond Egypt. The movement was promoted also by St. Jerome, St. Martin of Tours, who introduced it into France, and St. Patrick into Ireland. The monastery of Iona was founded by St. Colomba in 566. But it must be remembered that the Celtic Church had a life of its own which owed more to the Egyptian tradition than to Rome. Unlike the more elaborate monasteries of the Continent those of the early Celtic Church were often little more than a cluster of stone bee-hive huts, an oratory, and a stone cross. It had its own religious cere-monies and its own art (notably its beautifully carved crosses and the illuminated manuscripts such as the Lindisfarne Gospel (*c.* 700) and the Irish Book of Kells dating from about the same time). The Scottish St. Ninian played a major part in introducing Egyptian texts and art to Britain where, mixed with Byzantine influences and the art of the Vikings, it produced a typical culture of its own.

Strangely enough, it was the Celts who played almost as large a part in preserving civilisation in Europe during the Dark Ages as the Italians have since. It was St. Columbanus (*c.* 540–615) who founded the great monasteries of Annegray, Luxeuil, and Fontaine in the Vosges country, St. Gall in Switzerland, and Bobbio in the Apennines. So, too, it was the Anglo-Saxon Alcuin (*c.* 735–804) who was called from York by Charlemagne to set up a system of education throughout his empire; the most famous of the monastic schools he founded was at Tours. Among those influenced by him was the philosopher John Scotus Erigena.

Meanwhile from the south, as the disintegrating Roman empire became increasingly corrupt, St. Benedict of Nursia (*c.* 480–*c.* 543) fled the pleasures of Rome to lead a hermit's life near Subiaco. Here he founded some small monasteries, but *c.* 520 made a new settlement, the great monastery of Monte Cassino in southern Italy, where he established a "Rule" for the government of monks. This included both study and work and emphasised that education was necessary for the continuance of Christianity. As his influence spread his Rule was adopted by other monasteries, and schools became part of monastic life. Outside the Roman Catholic Church, both Eastern Orthodox and Anglican Christians owe much to the monastic movement.

Monasticism, is not peculiar to Christianity and forms a major aspect of Buddhism, especially in the form of Lamaism (*q.v.*) in Tibet.

Monophysitism, a heresy of the 5th cent. which grew out of a reaction against Nestorianism (*q.v.*). The majority of Egyptian Christians were Monophysites (Mono-physite = one nature)—*i.e.* they declared Christ's human and divine nature to be one and the same. This view was condemned at the Council of Chalcedon (A.D. 451) which pronounced that Jesus Christ, true God and true man,

has two natures, at once perfectly distinct and inseparably joined in one person and partaking of the one divine substance. However, many continued to hold Monophysite opinions, including the Coptic Church (*q.v.*), declaring the Council to be unoecumenical (*i.e.* not holding the views of the true and universal Christian Church).

Montanism, a Phrygian form of primitive Puritanism with many peculiar tenets into which the early Christian theologian Tertullian (*c.* 150–*c.* 230) was driven by his extremist views that the Christian should keep himself aloof from the world and hold no social intercourse whatever with pagans. The sect had immediate expectation of Christ's second coming and indulged in prophetic utterance which they held to be inspired by the Holy Ghost but which their enemies put down to the work of the Devil.

Moonies. *See under* **Unification Church, J51–2.**

Moral Re-Armament, a campaign launched in 1938 by an American evangelist of Lutheran background, Frank N. D. Buchman (1878–1961), founder of the Oxford Group Movement, and at first associated with the First Century Church Fellowship, a fundamentalist Protestant revivalist movement. On a visit to England in 1920 Buchman preached "world-changing through life-changing" to undergraduates at Oxford, hence the name Oxford Group.

Two of the Group's most typical practices were group confession of sins openly and the "quiet time" set aside during the day to receive messages from the Almighty as to behaviour and current problems. In the eyes of non-Groupers the confession (often of trivial sins) appeared to be exhibitionist and there was felt to be a certain snobbery about the movement which made it strongly conscious of the social status of its converts.

The Oxford Group gave way to Moral Re-Armament, the third phase of Buchmanism. MRA is open to all. Its starting point is the readiness of each person to make real in their own life the changes they wish to see in society. A commitment to search for God's will in daily life forms the basis for creative initiative and common action. Absolute moral standards of honesty, purity, unselfishness and love help to focus the challenge of personal and global change.

The peak of public interest in MRA was probably reached in the 1950s. The phrase "moral rearmament" was coined by the English scientist W. H. Bragg and appropriated by Buchman.

Moravian Church, a revival of the Church of the "Bohemian Brethren" which originated (1457) among some of the followers of John Hus. It developed a kind of Quakerism that rejected the use of force, refused to take oaths, and had no hierarchy. It appears to have been sympathetic towards Calvinism but made unsuccessful approaches to Luther. As a Protestant sect it was ruthlessly persecuted by Ferdinand II and barely managed to survive. However, in the 18th cent. the body was re-established by Count Zinzendorf who offered it a place of safety in Saxony where a town called Herrnhut (God's protection) was built and this became the centre from which Moravian doctrine was spread by missionaries all over the world. Their chief belief (which had a fundamental influence on John Wesley—*see* **Methodism**) was that faith is a direct illumination from God which assures us beyond all possibility of doubt that we are saved, and that no goodness of behaviour, piety, or orthodoxy is of any use without this "sufficient sovereign, saving grace".

Mormons, or **Latter-day Saints.** *See under* **Church of the Latter Day Saints.**

Muggletonians, one of many sects which arose during the Commonwealth but, unlike most of the others (**Levellers** (*q.v.*), **Diggers** (*q.v.*), Fifth Monarchy Men, and the Millenarians) which tended to have a strongly political aspect, this was purely religious. Founded by two journeymen tailors, Lodowick Muggleton and John Reeve, who interpreted the Book of Revelation in their own peculiar way, it was decided that Reeve represented Moses, and Muggleton, Aaron.

They also believed that the Father, not the Son, had died on the cross (an ancient heresy) but added the strange statement that He left Elijah in control during His period on earth. Rejecting the doctrine of the Trinity, they also asserted that

God has a human body.

Multiculturalism. Liberal democracy concentrates on the rights, obligations, and welfare of individuals. Critics argue that this focus on individuals ignores the special needs and identities of groups. Multiculturalism is the view that the state should acknowledge the importance of identity conferring groups, and create a legal and political order in which the multiplicity of groups in any society are allowed to practice their own distinct cultures within the boundaries of mutual respect. Such groups may be based on ethnicity, gender, sexuality, language, or religion.

Multiculturalists may also support special exemptions or privileges for groups, on the grounds that their identity and interests would otherwise be threatened. Examples include recent debates about the wearing of religious clothing in state schools and positive discrimination in the workplace. Opponents of multiculturalism argue that this destroys the shared unity and values of society. Liberals also regard multiculturalism as a nefarious obstruction on the rights of individuals to choose their own identity, and not have it prescribed by others.

Mystery Religions. *See* Orphism.

Mysticism, a religious attitude which concerns itself with direct relationship with God, "reality" as contrasted with appearance or the "ultimate" in one form or another. All the higher religions have had their mystics who have not always been regarded without suspicion by their more orthodox members, and, as Bertrand Russell points out, there has been a remarkable unity of opinion among mystics which almost transcends their religious differences. Thus, characteristic of the mystical experience in general, have been the following features; (1) a belief in insight as opposed to analytical knowledge which is accompanied in the actual experience by the sense of a mystery unveiled, a hidden wisdom become certain beyond the possibility of doubt; this is often preceded by a period of utter hopelessness and isolation described as "the dark night of the soul"; (2) a belief in unity and a refusal to admit opposition or division anywhere; this sometimes appears in the form of what seem to be contradictory statements: "the way up and the way down is one and the same" (Heraclitus). There is no distinction between subject and object, the act of perception and the thing perceived; (3) a denial of the reality of time, since if all is one the distinction of past and future must be illusory; (4) a denial of the reality of evil.

Among the many great mystics have been Meister Eckhart and Jakob Boehme, the German religious mystics of the 13th and 16th cent. respectively, Acharya Sankara of India, and St. Theresa and St. John of the Cross of Spain. Mystical movements within the great religions have been: the Zen (*q.v.*) movement within Buddhism; Taoism in China; the Cabalists and Hasidim in Judaism; and the Sufis within Islam.

N

Nation of Islam. The origins of the Nation of Islam (NOI) can be traced back to Noble Drew Ali, born Timothy Drew, who set up the Moorish Science Temple of America in 1926 on the principle that the black people of the United States could only be united by Islam. In 1930, Master Fard Muhammed, claiming to be Drew's reincarnation, set up the Lost-Found Nation of Islam preaching freedom, equality and the idea that America's blacks were a lost tribe of Muslims known as the Shabazz.

Upon Fard's disappearance in 1934, the movement was taken over by the Honourable Elijah Muhammad who was responsible for much of the theology of the movement, as well as its opposition to the Second World War, for which he was imprisoned until 1946. They have a distinct mythology which regards black people as the original races, and white people as the creation of an evil scientist named Yakub. Based on an interpretation of Ezekiel's eschatological vision, at the end time the black races will have a final victory over their oppressors.

In the 1950s the well known civil rights activist

Malcolm X became a prominent member but his emphasis on traditional Islam as opposed to radical new Black Islam led to his assassination by NOI members in 1965. This led, within the next decade, to a major examination of the movement, in particular by Wallace D. Muhammad, the son of Elijah Muhammad. He changed the name to the American Muslim Mission, linking it to more mainstream Islam, and dropped many of the racially exclusive policies.

The gap which this left was exploited by Louis Farrakhan, a senior NOI member, who broke with Wallace Muhammad in 1978, and re-founded the Nation of Islam. Farrakhan turned his organisation increasingly militant once more, reinstating a strict dress code, and the personal security force known as the Fruit of Islam. The Million Man March in Washington D.C. in 1995 notably raised the profile of the movement, although subsequently Farrakhan was denied entry to Britain on the grounds that his visit would incite racial tension.

Nationalism. Devotion to one's nation and its interests. Politically, this is translated into the theory that each nationality should be organised in a sovereign state. Nationalism first developed in Western Europe with the consolidation of nation states, and brought about the reorganization of Europe in the 19th and 20th centuries, *e.g.* the unification of Italy, the rise of Germany. At first, nationalism was liberal and democratic in tone, but it has also been associated with national expansion at the expense of other nations, and was an essential element of Fascism. In the 20th century it was important in the political awakening of Asia and Africa against colonialism. In Europe, the collapse of Communist regimes led to a resurgence of nationalism (*e.g.* Serbia).

Natural Law, the philosophical doctrine which states that there is a natural moral law, irrespective of time and place, which man can know through his own reason. Originally a product of early rational philosophy, the Christian form of the doctrine is basically due to St. Thomas Aquinas who defined natural law in relation to eternal law, holding that the eternal law is God's reason which governs the relations of all things in the universe to each other. The natural law is that part of the eternal law which relates to man's behaviour. Catholic natural law assumes that the human reason is capable of deriving ultimate rules for right behaviour, since there are in man and his institutions certain foundations produced by God's reason which man's reason can know to be correct and true. Thus, the basis of marriage, property, the state, and the contents of justice are held to be available to man's natural reason. The rules of positive morality and civil law are held to be valid only insofar as they conform to the natural law, which man is not only capable of knowing but also of obeying.

Protestant theologians criticise this notion. Thus Karl Barth and many others hold that sinful and fallen man cannot have any direct knowledge of God or His reason or will without the aid of revelation. Another theologian Niebuhr points out that the principles of the doctrines are too inflexible and that although they are the product of a particular time and circumstance, they are regarded as if they were absolute and eternal. In fact, as most social scientists would also agree, there is no law which can be regarded as "natural" for all men at all times. Nor does it seem sensible to suppose that all or even many men possess either the reason to discern natural law or the ability to obey it; whether or not we accept man's free-will (and not all Protestant sects do), we know as a fact of science that people are not always fully responsible for their actions and some not at all.

Such basic human rights as freedom of speech and religion, and freedom from fear and want, derive from natural law as developed by Locke.

Naturalism. 1. In general, the view that what is studied by the human sciences is all that there is, and that there is no need to go beyond or outside the universe for any explanation.

2. In ethics, the view that value terms can be defined in terms of neutral statements of fact, or derived from such statements.

Naturism. The world's first nudist club was founded in 1891 by Charles Crawford, a British circuit judge serving in Bombay (Mumbai). *Health and*

Efficiency, the world's first naturist magazine, was founded in 1932.

Nazism, the term commonly used for the political and social ideology of the German National Socialist Party inspired and led by Hitler. The term *Nazi* was an abbreviation of *National-sozialistische Deutsche Arbeiterpartei*. Some key dates in the history of Nazism are:

1923 Hitler attempts armed coup in Munich, but fails. Hitler is subsequently arrested.

1924 Hitler convicted of conspiring to commit treason and sentenced to five years' imprisonment. Hitler dictates *Mein Kampf* (My Struggle).

1930 National Socialists win seats in Reichstag.

1933 Hitler appointed Chancellor.

1936 Hitler invades the Rhineland.

1938 Germany annexes Austria in '*Anschluss*', gains partition of Czechoslovakia at Munich.

1939 'Pact of Steel' signed between Germany and Italy. Germany invades Poland, signs pact with Soviet Union.

1940 Germany invades Denmark, Norway, Belgium, Holland, Luxembourg, and France.

1941 Germany invades Yugoslavia, Greece, and Russia.

1942 Wannsee Conference held on 'Final Solution of the Jewish Question.' Persecution of Jews increases across fascist controlled Europe.

1943 Germany destroys Warsaw ghetto after uprising. Italy deports Jews. German forces defeated by British 8th Army in North Africa. Allies invade Sicily. Mussolini arrested, Italy surrenders to Allies. Mussolini freed by German commandos. New Italian government declares war on Germany, which continues to occupy much of Italy.

1944 Allies invade Normandy on D-Day. Assassination attempt by German generals on Hitler narrowly fails. Allies liberate Paris and Rome.

1945 Mussolini assassinated. Allies invade Germany, Nazi death camps liberated. An estimated 6 million Jews were murdered, along with hundreds of thousands of other groups persecuted by the Nazis, including homosexuals, gypsies, disabled people, and Christians. Hitler commits suicide. Germany surrenders on 8 May.

Neocolonialism. *See* **Colonialism**.

Neoconservatism. Whilst sharing such traditional conservative values as patriotic pride, opposition to bureaucratic welfare states, and belief in free trade, neoconservatives differ from traditional conservatives in their views on foreign policy. Particularly strong in American politics, neoconservatives argue that liberal democracy is inherently vulnerable to threats from extreme political ideologies which seek global domination. In order to protect liberal democracy, such states must pursue a policy of military empowerment and intervention against perceived threats. Consequently, neoconservatism's defining feature is the view that liberal democracy must be promoted and protected aggressively in foreign policy. Traditional conservatism, at least in America, tended towards an isolationist foreign policy. Neoconservatives feared such isolationism would lead to appeasement of totalitarianism and increased vulnerability from militarily strong expansionist ideologies, such as Soviet Communism.

Neoconservatives argue that there is a moral obligation on liberal democracies to spread their freedoms around the globe.

Neo-Fascism. *See* **Fascism, J19**.

Neoliberalism. Traditionally, liberalism has prioritised the freedom of the individual and argued that private property is the greatest bulwark against curtailment of an individual's freedom by others. In the late 20th century, neoliberalism developed in response to a perceived assault on individual freedoms that resulted from the pursuit of social justice by social democratic states.

Neoliberals regarded progressive taxation, redistributive fiscal policies, extensive welfare provision, and state ownership of industry as illegitimate and inefficient uses of state power. They criticised particularly the moral and economic dependency encouraged by extensive welfare provision, and argued that welfare discouraged individuals from work and from taking responsibility for the security and prosperity of themselves and their families. Neoliberals such as Thatcher and Reagan argued that the role of the state should be restricted to protecting the freedoms and private property of individuals. Consequently, neoliberals privatised state owned industries and utilities, reduced taxation and public spending, and withdrew welfare support and other redistributive policies. Neoliberalism has come to dominate western electoral politics, and is now promoted in developing nations by such bodies as the IMF, WTO, and World Bank.

Neoplatonism. Movement begun by Plotinus' interpretation of Plato and carried forward by various philosophers of the next three centuries and which had some influence in the Renaissance. Plotinus (205–270) saw reality as hierarchically ordered in a graded series from the divine to the material; man, who contains some part of the divine, longs for union with the highest level. Subsequent Neoplatonists include Porphyry, Iamblichus and Philoponus. (*See also* **Determinism and Free-will** and **God and Man**).

Nestorian Heresy. The 5th cent. of the Christian Church saw a battle of personalities and opinions waged with fanatical fury between St. Cyril, the patriarch of Alexandria, and Nestorius, patriarch of Constantinople. Nestorius maintained that Mary should not be called the mother of God, as she was only the mother of the human and not of the divine nature of Jesus. This view was contradicted by Cyril (one of the most unpleasant saints who ever lived) who held the orthodox view. In addition to his utter destruction of Nestorius by stealthy and unremitting animosity Cyril was also responsible for the lynching of Hypatia, a distinguished mathematician and saintly woman, head of the Neoplatonist school at Alexandria.

As if this were not enough Cyril took pains to stir up pogroms against the very large Jewish colony of Alexandria. At the Council of Ephesus (A.D. 431) the Western Bishops quickly decided for Cyril. This Council (reinforced by the Council of Chalcedon in 451) clarified orthodox Catholic doctrine (*see* **Monophysitism**).

Nestorius became a heretic, was banished to Antioch where he had a short respite of peace, but later, and in spite of his age, was forced to move from one place to another on the borders of Egypt. Later the Nestorian church flourished in Syria and Persia and missions were sent to India and China.

New Age, a quasi-religious movement, based on a millennarian mysticism, astrology and ecology.

New Labour. *See* **Third Way**.

New Liberalism. *See* **Liberalism**.

Nihilism, the name often given to the earliest Russian form of revolutionary anarchism. It originated in the early years of Tsar Alexander II (1818–81), the liberator of the serfs, who, during his attempts to bring about a constitutional monarchy, was killed by a bomb. The term "nihilist", was first used in 1862 by Turgeniev in his novel *Fathers and Children*. *See* **Anarchism**.

Nominalism. Early medieval thinkers were divided into two schools, those who regarded "universals" or abstract concepts as mere names without any corresponding realities (Nominalists), and those who held the opposite doctrine (**Realism**) that general concepts have an existence independent of individual things. The relation between universals and particulars was long a subject of philosophical dispute.

The first person to hold the nominalist doctrine was probably Roscelin or Roscellinus in the late 11th cent., but very little is known of him and none of his works remains except for a single letter to Peter Abelard who was his pupil. Roscelin was born in France, accused twice of heresy but recanted and fled to England where he attacked the views of Anselm, according to whom Roscelin used the phrase that universals were a *flatus voci* or breath of the voice.

The most important nominalist was the Englishman William of Ockham in the 14th cent. who, once and for all, separated the two schools by saying in effect that science is about things (the nominalist view) whereas logic, philosophy, and religion are about terms or concepts (the Platonic tradition).

Nonconformism, the attitude of all those Christian bodies, which do not conform to the doctrines of the Church of England. Up to the passing of the Act of Uniformity in 1662 they were called "puritans" or "dissenters" and were often persecuted. The oldest bodies of nonconformists are the Baptists, Independents, and (in England) the Presbyterians; the Methodists, although dating from 1738, did not consider themselves nonconformists until some time later.

The Presbyterians are the official Church of Scotland where it is the Anglicans (known as "Episcopalians") who are the nonconformists.

O

Objectivism, a philosophy developed by American novelist, Ayn Rand. The briefest summary of Objectivism given by Miss Rand was simply, *"Follow reason"*, but that is rather too terse. Objectivism begins with reality as objective, absolute and independent of any mind perceiving it. Consciousness is the faculty of perceiving that which exists, and therefore, existence precedes consciousness. Human conceptual, volitional consciousness (reason) is man's unique means of survival. Ayn Rand upheld reason as the only means to knowledge with logic as its method. Man should live solely by the guidance of his reason.

Ockham's Razor, the philosophical maxim by which William of Ockham, the 14th cent. Franciscan has become best-known. This states in the form which is most familiar: "Entities are not to be multiplied without necessity" and as such does not appear in his works. He did, however, say something much to the same effect: "It is vain to do with more what can be done with fewer." In other words, if everything in some science can be interpreted without assuming this or that hypothetical entity, there is no ground for assuming it.

Optimism. Originally the doctrine propounded by Leibniz (1646–1716) that the actual world is the "best of all possible worlds", being chosen by the Creator out of all the possible worlds which were present in his thoughts as that in which the most good could be obtained at the cost of the least evil. This view was mocked by Voltaire.

Opus Dei. This strictly orthodox Roman Catholic movement was founded in 1928 by a Spanish priest, Monsignor Josemaria Escriva de Balaguer y Albas, and has increasingly found media attention in recent years. It has been heavily criticised for its authoritarian attitudes towards its members and is regarded by some as a church within a church, with a significant amount of Vatican power. Critics view it in almost cultic terms emphasizing accounts of self-mortification, gender separation, youth recruitment and the inability to break ties with the movement. It has also been challenged over its zealous desire to canonize its founder. Its strong membership amongst the clergy as well as the support of Pope John Paul II has given it much credibility, and many regard it as a way to live out their Catholic faith through receiving spiritual support and by understanding better the doctrines of the Church.

It considers itself to be in total agreement with Catholic teachings. Unlike the rest of the Church, it has no official geographical boundaries, and is united through membership. Around a third of members are 'numeraries' who live apart in single gender communities and take vows of celibacy. Although their income does not go directly to Opus Dei, they make serious financial commitments to the work of the Catholic Church. Other 'associates' live celibate lives outside residences, although some members may be married and live within the wider community.

Orangemen, members of a society formed in Ulster back in 1795 to uphold Protestantism. Their name is taken from King William III, Prince of Orange, who defeated James II at the Battle of the Boyne (1690), hence the enormous banners depicting "King Billy on the Boyne" carried in procession on 12 July each year. The old Unionist Party of Northern Ireland (the ruling political party from 1921 to 1972) was largely maintained by the Orange Order.

Original Sin, in Christian doctrine, the corruption that is born with us, as a result of Adam's fall.

Orphism. A mystical religious cult centred around the figure of Orpheus, that flourished in ancient Greece. Orphics believed in transmigration of souls and that the soul after death might obtain either eternal bliss or temporary or permanent torment according to its way of life upon earth.They held ceremonies of purification, and abstained from eating meat, except on special occasions when it was eaten ritually.Orphism influenced Greek society through the mysteries of Eleusis that were initiation rites to Orphism, and which became central to Greek public religion.Orphic beliefs and rites are also found in the work and followers of Pythagoras and Plato.

Orthodox Eastern Church. There are two groups of Eastern churches: (1) those forming the Orthodox Church dealt with here which include the ancient Byzantine patriarchates of Constantinople, Alexandria, Antioch, and Jerusalem, and the national churches of Russia, Greece, Serbia, Bulgaria, Romania, *etc.* (although Orthodox communities exist all over the world and are no longer confined to geographical areas); (2) the churches which rejected Byzantine orthodoxy during various controversies from the 5th to the 7th cent., notably the Coptic church (*q.v.*) and the Armenian church. Although all Orthodox churches share the same doctrine and traditions they are arranged as national independent bodies each with its own hierarchy. They do not recognise the pope, and the primacy of the patriarch of Constantinople is largely an honorary one. Although claiming to be the One Holy, Catholic, and Apostolic Church its alleged infallibility rests on universal agreement rather than on any one individual, and agreement over the faith comes from the Scriptures interpreted in the light of the Tradition.

The latter includes dogmas relating to the Trinity, Christology, Mariology, and Holy Icons; the testimony of the Fathers (St. Athanasius, St. Basil, St. John Chrysostom, St. Cyril of Alexandria, *etc.*); the canons or rules as formulated by the Councils and the Fathers.

The Orthodox Church did not take part in the great Western controversies about the Bible, nor, of course, in the Reformation. But it saw the breakaway of the Old Believers in the 1650s in protest at the reforms of Patriarch Nikon. Attempts have been made to improve relations between Rome and Constantinople: the two Churches agreed in 1935 to retract the excommunications cast on each other in A.D. 1054, which formalised the Great Schism. After the fall of communism in Russia, the Orthodox Church has revived.

In England, the first purpose-built Orthodox Cathedral was constructed in west London. In 1999 Pope John Paul II visited Romania, the first papal visit to a mainly Orthodox country in almost 1,000 years.

In February 2016 the Russian Orthodox Patriarch Kirill met Pope Francis I in Havana, the first encounter of its kind since the split of 1054. Patriarch Kirill also became the first head of the Russian Church to visit Britain.

In 2016, many Orthodox leaders held a highly-significant gathering in Crete. Although boycotted by Russia, it was the first such meeting since 1054.

Oxford Group. *See* **Moral Re-Armament.**

Oxford Movement. *See* **Tractarianism.**

P

Pacifism. The belief that, because violence and the taking of life is morally wrong, war and the employment of organized armed forces cannot be justified. The word first came into use to describe movements advocating the settlement of disputes by peaceful means. Since the First World War the word has been used to describe the refusal of individuals to undertake military service. The first pacificists were minority Christian groups like the Quakers and Plymouth Brethren. In the 20th century the movement broadened and many democratic nations allow their citizens to abstain from fighting on grounds of principle, often described as "conscientious objection".

Paganism, a form of worship which has its roots in the ancient nature religions of Europe. Pagans reverence the sanctity of the Earth, its people and other life forms. Paganism is still a living religion, the main forms of which include Wicca (witchcraft), Druidry, Asatru and Shamanism.

The Pagan Federation was founded in 1971 to provide information and to counter misconceptions about Paganism. There are over 100,000 practising pagans in Britain (mainly Druids) – a number which has doubled in the last decade.

Pan-Africanism, the perception by people of African origins and descent that they have interests in common. The fight against economic exploitation and for equality has been an important theme.

Pantheism. See **God and Man.**

Panpsychism. Literally, "all-soul-ism", the view that everything that really exists in the world is a mind or consciousness. To be distinguished from "hylozoism", which claims that everything is alive. Panpsychic views can be found in Leibniz and Schopenhauer, and in the 20th century philosopher A. N. Whitehead (1861–1947).

Papal Infallibility. The basis of papal infallibility is (a) that every question of morals and faith is not dealt with in the Bible so it is necessary that there should be a sure court of appeal in case of doubt, and this was provided by Christ when he established the Church as His Teaching Authority upon earth; (b) ultimately this idea of the teaching function of the Church shapes the idea of papal infallibility which asserts that the Pope, when speaking officially on matters of faith or morals, is protected by God against the possibility of error. The doctrine was proclaimed in July 1870.

Infallibility is a strictly limited gift which does not mean that the Pope has extraordinary intelligence, that God helps him to find the answer to every conceivable question, or that Catholics have to accept the Pope's views on politics. He can make mistakes or fall into sin, his scientific or historical opinions may be quite wrong, he may write books that are full of errors. Only in two limited spheres is he infallible and in these only when he speaks officially as the supreme teacher and lawgiver of the Church.

Historically speaking, the Roman Catholic Church of the early 19th cent. was at its lowest ebb of power. Pope Pius IX, in fear of Italian nationalism, revealed his reactionary attitude by the feverish declaration of new dogmas, the canonisation of new saints, the denunciation of all modern ideals in the Syllabus of Errors, and the unqualified defence of his temporal power against the threat of Garibaldi. It is not too much to say that everything regarded as important by freedom-loving and democratic people was opposed by the papacy at that time. In 1870, after a long and protracted struggle, the Vatican Council, convened by Pius IX, pronounced the definition of his infallibility. Döllinger, a German priest and famous historian of the Church, was excommunicated because, like many others, he refused to accept the new dogma. There was clearly a connection between the pronouncement of the Pope's infallibility and his simultaneous loss of temporal power.

After the humanism of the Second Vatican Council (1962–5) Pope Paul's encyclical *Humanae Vitae* (1968), condemning birth control, came as a great disappointment to the many people (including theologians, priests, and laymen) who had expected there would be a change in the Church's teaching. The Church's moral guidance on this controversial issue, however, does not involve the doctrine of infallibility. (The Roman Catholic Church teaches that papal pronouncements are infallible only when they are specifically defined as such.)

This was made clear in July 1973 when the Vatican Sacred Congregation for the Doctrine of the Faith published a document strongly reaffirming papal infallibility. The document also reminded Catholics of their obligation to accept the Catholic Church's unique claims to authenticity.

Parapsychology, the name given to the study of psychical research (q.v.) as an academic discipline, and chosen to denote the topic's supposed status as a branch of psychology. The impetus behind parapsychology came from the psychologist William MacDougall who persuaded Duke University in North Carolina,

USA, to found a department of parapsychology under J. B. Rhine. Throughout the 1930s and 1940s the work of Rhine and his colleagues, who claimed to have produced scientific evidence for the existence of ESP, attracted world-wide attention. Increasing reservations about the interpretation of Rhine's results and an apparent lack of any readily repeatable experiments gradually eroded scientific confidence in the topic.

Parsees. See **Zoroastrianism.**

Pavlovian Theory. See **Behaviourism.**

Pelagianism. The Christian doctrine that each person has responsibility for ensuring his own salvation, apart from the assistance of divine grace. Its name is derived from Pelagius, a British lay monk who came to Rome about 400 A.D. and attacked Augustine's view that moral goodness is only possible through divine grace. Pelagius argued that if men and women were not held to be responsible for their actions, there would be nothing to restrain them from sin. His emphasis on free will and the essential goodness of human nature suggested an optimism that was at odds with doctrines of original sin. Augustine attacked Pelagius' views as heretical, a judgement that was confirmed by the church in 417, when Pelagius was excommunicated.

Pentecostalism, a religious movement within some Christian churches, holding the belief that an essential feature of true Christianity is a vigorous and profound spiritual or mystical experience which occurs after, and seemingly reinforces the initial conversion.

The origins of modern Pentecostalism lie in the occasion on 1 January 1901 when a member of a Bible College in Topeka, Kansas, one Agnes N. Ozman, spontaneously began to speak in an apparently unknown language at one of the College's religious meetings. This "speaking in tongues" was assumed to be evidence of her conversion and "spirit baptism", and became a feature of most Pentecostal meetings in due course.

The movement spread very rapidly across America, particularly in rural communities, and also was a strong feature of Welsh religious life in the early part of the century. Pentecostal services are enthusiastic and rousing with a strong emphasis on music and participation on the part of the congregation. The controversial "Toronto Blessing" features in some services. Pentecostalism is evangelistic in nature and is gaining in strength at the present time.

Some leading Pentecostal groups in Britain include the Assemblies of God, the Elim Pentecostal Church and the fast-growing Redeemed Christian Church of God. There are also a rapidly growing number of Black Pentecostal churches.

Peronism, a political movement begun in the late 1940s in Argentina. It followed the teaching of Juan Peron and his wife Eva.

Personality Cult. Political phenomenon whereby a leader, usually the head of state, is elevated above his colleagues to a position where he is seen as responsible for all the nation's or party's achievements but none of its failures. Such elevation is achieved by a massive propaganda exercise including posters and statues of the leader, the naming of towns after him, etc. Joseph Stalin (1879–1953) set the pattern as Soviet leader but others have followed, for example Adolf Hitler of Germany, Mao Tse-Tung in China and Kim Il-sung (and his successors) in North Korea. Such cults flourish only in totalitarian régimes.

Pessimism. Philosophically this refers to the doctrine associated with Arthur Schopenhauer (1788–1860), that in this world everything tends to evil, that the amount of pain is greater than the amount of pleasure. Of course, pessimistic ideas have a long history. As the Greeks said: "Call no man happy until he is dead." They are also present in the teachings of eastern and western religions, which emphasize the corruptness of this world and the possibility of happiness only in a hereafter. Schopenhauer's pessimism had a strong influence on Nietzsche, and through him on existentialism (q.v.).

Peyotism. A religious movement among North American Indians centred around the *peyote*, a part of the cactus which produces hallucinogenic effects.

Phrenology, a psychological "school" founded

in 1800 by two Germans, Franz Josef Gall and Johann Gaspar Spurzheim. Gall was an anatomist who believed there to be some correspondence between mental faculties and the shape of the head.

Phrenology became fashionable, and people would go to "have their bumps read" just as later many men and women have gone to be psychoanalysed. Roughly speaking, Gall divided the mind into thirty-seven faculties such as destructiveness, suavity, self-esteem, conscientiousness, and so on, and claimed that each of these was located in a definite area of the brain. He further claimed that the areas in the brain corresponded to "bumps" on the skull which could be read by the expert, thus giving a complete account of the character of the subject. In fact, (a) no such faculties are located in the brain anywhere, for this is simply not the way the brain works; (b) the faculties described by Gall are not pure traits which cannot be further analysed and are based on a long outdated psychology; (c) the shape of the brain bears no specific relationship to the shape of the skull.

Phrenology is a pseudo-science; there is no truth in it whatever. But, even so, like astrology, it still has its practitioners.

Physiocrats. A French school of economic thought during the 18th cent., known at the time as *Les Economistes* but in later years named physiocrats by Du Pont de Nemours, a member of the School. Other members were Quesnay, Mirabeau, and the great financier Turgot. The physiocrats held the view, common to the 18th cent., and deriving ultimately from Rousseau, of the goodness and bounty of nature and the goodness of man "as he came from the bosom of nature". The aim of governments, therefore, should be to conform to nature; and so long as men do not interfere with each other's liberty and do not combine among themselves, governments should leave them free to find their own salvation. Criminals, madmen, and monopolists should be eliminated. Otherwise the duty of government is *laissez-faire, laissez passer.*

From this follows the doctrine of free trade between nations on grounds of both justice and economy; for the greater the competition the more will each one strive to economise the cost of his labour to the general advantage. Adam Smith, although not sharing their confidence in human nature, learned much from the physiocrats, eliminated their errors, and greatly developed their teaching.

Physiognomy. *See* **Characterology.**

Pietism, a movement in the Lutheran Church at the end of the 17th cent.—the reaction, after the sufferings of the thirty years' war, of a pious and humiliated people against learning, pomp and ceremony, and stressing the importance of man's personal relationship with God. The writings of Johann Georg Hamann (1730-88) who came from a Pietist family of Königsberg influenced Kierkegaard. The Pietist movement was one root of the great Romantic movement of the 18th century.

Platonism. Philosophical ideas that are inspired by the writings of Plato, usually embracing his belief in a realm of unchanging and eternal realities (specifically, abstract entities or universals) independent of the world perceived by the senses. Most working mathematicians are Platonists, in the sense that they believe that mathematical objects like numbers exist independently of our thought and hence that mathematical statements are true or false independently of our knowledge of them.

Pluralism. (1). In philosophy, any metaphysical view that the world must consist of more than one or two basic kinds of entity; these latter views would be called Monism or Dualism. Pluralists, such as William James, think of themselves as empiricists, reaffirming plain facts of experience against metaphysical extremists and pointing to the irreducible variety of things.

(2). In political thought, it refers to the autonomy enjoyed by disparate groups or institutions within a society and also to the belief that such an arrangement for the distribution of political power should exist. As such it provides an alternative to collectivist doctrines, which may coerce the individual, and individualistic doctrines, which fail to provide an understanding of

the individual's role in society. Pluralism is widely regarded as an ideal, but there is much argument as to how pluralism is to be interpreted in detail and how it is to be applied effectively within a modern society.

Plymouth Brethren, a religious sect founded by John Nelson Darby, a minister of the Protestant Church of Ireland, and Edward Cronin a former Roman Catholic, in 1827. Both were dissatisfied with the lack of spirituality in their own and other churches and joined together in small meetings in Dublin every Sunday for "the breaking of bread". Soon the movement began to spread through Darby's travels and writings and he finally settled in Plymouth, giving the popular name to the "Brethren". Beginning as a movement open to all who felt the need to "keep the unity of the Spirit", it soon began to exclude all who had unorthodox views and split up into smaller groups.

Among these were the "Exclusives", the Kellyites, the Newtonites, and "Bethesda" whose main differences were over problems of church government or prophetical powers.

Today, the majority of Brethren belong to the "Open Brethren" assemblies and, unlike the "Exclusives" hold that the Lord's Supper (a commemorative act of "breaking the bread" observed once a week) is for all Christians who care to join them. Baptism is required and Brethren believe in the personal premillennial second coming of Christ.

Poltergeist, allegedly a noisy type of spirit which specialises in throwing things about, making loud thumpings and bangings, and occasionally bringing in "apports", *i.e.,* objects from elsewhere. Most so-called poltergeist activities are plain frauds, but the others are almost invariably associated with the presence in the house of someone (often, but not always a child) who is suffering from an adolescent malaise or an epileptic condition. The inference is that those activities which are not simply fraudulent are either due to some unknown influence exuded by such mentally disturbed people, or that they are actually carried out by ordinary physical means by such people when in an hysterical state—*i.e.,* unconsciously. The second hypothesis is much the more probable. *See* **Psychic Research.**

Polygamy, the ancient custom whereby a man took more than one wife. Most polygamy today is to be found in some parts of the Islamic world, sub-Saharan Africa and Burma.

Polytheism. *See* **God and Man.**

Populism. A form of politics which emphasizes the virtues of the common people against politicians and intellectuals, who are distrusted as devious and selfish. "The will of the people" can provide sufficient guidance to the statesman. It is not restricted to any one political view and can manifest itself in left, right or centrist forms. It has become a feature of present-day politics (*e.g.* Donald Trump in America, UKIP in Britain and other protest movements in Europe).

Positivism, also known as the **Religion of Humanity,** was founded by Auguste Comte (1798-1857), a famous mathematician and philosopher born in Montpellier, France. His views up to the end of the century attracted many and it would have been impossible throughout that time to read a book on philosophy or sociology that did not mention them, but today his significance is purely of historical interest. In his *Cours de Philosophie Positive* (1830) he put forward the thesis that mankind had seen three great stages in human thought: (1) the theological, during which man seeks for supernatural causes to explain nature and invents gods and devils; (2) the metaphysical, through which he thinks in terms of philosophical and metaphysical abstractions; (3) the last positive or scientific stage when he will proceed by experimental and objective observation to reach "positive truth".

Broadly speaking, there is little to complain of in this analysis; for there does seem to have been some sort of general direction along these lines. However, Comte was not satisfied with having reached this point and felt that his system demanded a religion and, of course, one that was "scientific". This religion was to be the worship of Humanity in place of the personal Deity of earlier times, and for it he supplied not only a Positive Catechism but a treatise on

Sociology in which he declared himself the High Priest of the cult. Since, as it stood, the religion was likely to appear somewhat abstract to many, Comte drew up a list of historical characters whom he regarded as worthy of the same sort of adoration as Catholics accord to their saints.

The new Church attracted few members, even among those who had a high regard for Comte's scientific work, and its only significant adherents were a small group of Oxford scholars and some in his own country. Frederic Harrison was the best-known English adherent and throughout his life continued to preach Comtist doctrines in London to diminishing audiences.

Post-Colonialism has developed as a literary and academic examination of identity and culture in the wake of colonial rule. Post-colonial history has sought to give voice to the peoples colonized, and their experience of its legacy. Academic history has been followed by literature, where authors such as Derek Walcott and Salman Rushdie have studied the history and effect of colonization. The emphasis on the complex inheritance of colonization on culture has led to a wider view of post-colonialism, where the foundations of individual identity and experience are examined as constructions of multiple and not necessarily compatible traditions.

Post-colonialism studies the how colonial powers exploit not only the natural but cultural resources of their colonies, leaving the language, institutions, and identity greatly transformed. This continued inheritance of effect is interrogated to reveal the subtle contours of oppression, and authors such as Edward Said and Homi Bahbha attempt to unpick this entanglement to liberate distinctive ways of thinking and acting from the colonizers' effect.

Postmodernism. Given that "modernism" (*q.v.*) is a term difficult to define, "postmodernism" is an even more elusive concept, though a very fashionable one for describing contemporary art. The modernist tradition of formal and stylistic experiment, added to our increased knowledge of the history of Western and non-Western arts, has provided a vast range of styles, techniques and technologies for the artist to choose from. This extension of choice has simultaneously created uncertainty about their use. If no one or few styles have any authority, then the artist picks and chooses with little commitment, and so tends towards pastiche, parody, quotation, self-reference and eclecticism. The post-modern style is to have no settled style. But it is always dangerous to try and pin down an artistic movement that is still taking place.

Pragmatism, a typically American school of philosophy which comes under the heading of what Bertrand Russell described as a "practical" as opposed to a "theoretical" philosophy. Whereas the latter, to which most of the great philosophical systems belong, seeks disinterested knowledge for its own sake, the former (*a*) regards action as the supreme good, (*b*) considers happiness an effect and knowledge a mere instrument of successful activity.

The originator of pragmatism is usually considered to have been the psychologist William James (1842–1910) although he himself attributed its basic principles to his life-long friend, the American philosopher, Charles Sanders Peirce (1839–1914). The other famous pragmatist was John Dewey, best-known in Europe for his works on education.

James in his book *The Will to Believe* (1896) pointed out that we are often compelled to take a decision where no adequate theoretical grounds for a decision exist; for even to do nothing is to decide. Thus in religion we have a right to adopt a believing attitude although not intellectually fully convinced. We should believe truth and shun error, but the failing of the sceptical philosopher is that he adheres only to the latter rule and thus fails to believe various truths which a less cautious man will accept. If believing truth and avoiding error are equally important, then it is a good idea when we are presented with an alternative to believe one of the possibilities at will, since we then have an even chance of being right, whereas we have none if we suspend judgment. The function of philosophy, according to James, is to find out what difference it makes to the individual if a particular philosophy or world-system is true: "An idea is 'true' so long as to believe it is profitable to our lives" and, he adds, the truth is only the expedient in our way of thinking . . . in the long run and on the whole of course". Thus "if the hypothesis of God works satisfactorily in the widest sense of the word, it is true".

Bertrand Russell's reply to this assertion is: "I have always found that the hypothesis of Santa Claus 'works satisfactorily in the widest sense of the word'; therefore 'Santa Claus exists' is true, although Santa Claus does not exist."

Russell adds that James's concept of truth simply omits the question whether God really *is* in His heaven; if He is a useful hypothesis that is enough. "God the Architect of the Cosmos is forgotten; all that is remembered is belief in God, and its effects upon the creatures inhabiting our petty planet. No wonder the Pope condemned the pragmatic defence of religion."

Predestination. *See* **Calvinism.**

Presbyterianism, a system of ecclesiastical government of the Protestant churches which look back to John Calvin as their Reformation leader. The ministry consists of presbyters who are all of equal rank. Its doctrinal standards are contained in the *Westminster Confession of Faith* (1647) which is, in general, accepted by English, Scottish, and American Presbyterians as the most thorough and logical statement in existence of the Calvinist creed. The Church of Scotland is the leading Presbyterian church in the British Isles.

The Reformation in Scotland was preceded by the same sort of awareness of the moral corruption of the Roman Church as had happened elsewhere, but for a variety of political and emotional reasons the majority of the Scottish people (unlike the English who had been satisfied with the mere exchange of Crown for Pope) were determined on a fundamental change of doctrine, discipline, and worship, rather than a reform of manners.

John Knox. The Scottish preachers had learned Protestantism not from Luther but from Calvin and their leader John Knox had worked in Geneva with Calvin and was resolved to introduce the system into Scotland. In 1557 the "Lords of the Congregation" signed the Common Band (*i.e.*, a bond or covenant) to maintain "the blessed Word of God and his congregation" against their enemies, and demanded the right to worship as they had chosen. However, the real date of the Scottish Reforma- tion is August 1560 when Mary of Guise (the regent for Mary Queen of Scots who was not yet of age) died and the Estates met to settle their affairs without foreign pressure; the *Scots Confession* was drawn up and signed by Knox and adopted by the Estates.

The ideas on which the Reformed Kirk was based are found in the *Scots Confession*, the *Book of Discipline*, and the *Book of Common Order*, the so-called Knox's liturgy. Knox's liturgy, the same as that used in Geneva but translated into English, was used until Laud's attempt to force an Anglican liturgy on the Kirk led to an abandonment of both in favour of "free prayers."

The Presbyterian Tradition. This includes uncompromising stress on the Word of God contained in the Scriptures of the Old and New Testaments as the supreme rule of faith and life, and on the value of a highly trained ministry, which has given the Church of Scotland, a high reputation for scholarship and has in turn influenced the standard of education in Scotland. The unity of the Church is guaranteed by providing for democratic representation in a hierarchy of courts (unlike the Anglican Church, which is a hierarchy of persons). The local kirk-session consists of the minister and popularly elected elders (laymen). Ministers, elected by their flocks, are ordained by presbyters (ministers already ordained). Above the kirk-session is the court of the presbytery which has jurisdiction over a specified area; above that the court of synod which rules over many presbyteries; and finally the General Assembly which is the Supreme Court of the Church with both judicial and legislative powers, and over which the Moderator of the General Assembly presides. The function of the elders is to help the minister in the work and government of the kirk.

The episcopacy set up by James VI and I, and maintained by Charles I was brought to an end by the Glasgow Assembly (1638), but General Assemblies were abolished by Oliver Cromwell and at the Restoration Charles II re-established episcopacy. The Covenanters who resisted were hunted down, imprisoned, transported, or executed over a period of nearly thirty years before William of Orange came to the throne and Presbyterianism was re-established (1690).

In 1972 the Presbyterian and Congregationalist Churches in England were merged to form the United Reformed Church. See **Church of Scotland, Calvinism.**

Protestant, the name first applied to those who favoured the cause of Martin Luther and who protested against the intolerant decisions of the Catholic majority at the second Diet of Speyer (1529), revoking earlier decisions of the first Diet of Speyer tolerating the Reformers in certain cases (1526).

In general the name "Protestant" is applied to those Churches which severed connection with Rome at the time of the Reformation. The essence of Protestantism is the acceptance by the individual Christian of his direct responsibility to God rather than to the Church. See also **Lutheranism, Presbyterianism, Calvinism.**

Psychiatry, a branch of medicine concerned with the treatment of psychological problems and mental illness. It uses drugs and psychotherapeutic techniques.

Psychic Research is a general term for the various approaches to the scientific investigation of the paranormal, in particular supposed extrasensory powers of the mind, but also manifestations such as ghosts, poltergeists, spiritualistic phenomena, *etc.*

In recent years the word parapsychology has also come into use, particularly for the investigation of ESP (extra-sensory perception) in a laboratory setting.

Psychoanalysis, an approach to the study of human personality involving the rigorous probing, with the assistance of a specially trained practitioner, of an individual's personal problems, motives, goals and attitudes to life in general. Often, and quite understandably, confused with psychology (of which it is merely a part), psychoanalysis has an interesting historical background and has attracted the interest of philosophers, scientists and medical experts since it emerged as a radical and controversial form of mental therapy at the turn of the century. The traditionally accepted founder is the great Austrian Sigmund Freud, but he never failed to acknowledge the impetus that had been given to his own ideas by his talented friend, the physiologist Joseph Breuer, who for most of his working life had been interested in the curious phenomena associated with hypnosis. Breuer had successfully cured the hysterical paralysis of a young woman patient and had noticed that under hypnosis the girl seemed to be recalling emotional experiences, hitherto forgotten, which bore some relationship to the symptoms of her illness.

Developing this with other patients Breuer then found that the mere recalling and discussing of the emotional events under hypnosis seemed to produce a dramatic alleviation of the symptoms—a phenomenon which came to be known as *catharsis.* Breuer also noticed another curious side-effect, that his women patients fell embarrassingly and violently in love with him, and he gradually dropped the practice of "mental catharsis", possibly feeling that it was a bit too dangerous to handle. This left the field clear for Freud, whose brilliant mind began to search beyond the therapeutic aspects of the topic to see what light might be thrown on the nature of human personality and psychological mechanisms in general. The most important question concerned the "forgotten" emotional material which turned up, apparently out of the blue, during the hypnotic session. Freud rightly saw that this posed problems for the current theories of memory, for how could something once forgotten (a) continue to have an effect on the individual without his being aware of it, and (b) ultimately be brought back to conscious memory again. It must be remembered that at this time memory was considered to be a fairly simple process—information was stored in the brain and was gradually eroded or destroyed with the passage of time and the decay of brain cells.

Once lost, it was believed, memories were gone for ever, or at best only partially and inaccurately reproducible. Furthermore, human beings were supposed to be rational (if frequently wilful) creatures who never did anything without thinking about it (if only briefly) beforehand and without being well aware of their reasons for so doing.

The Genius of Freud. It was within this framework that Sigmund Freud had his great insight, one which many people believe to be one of the most important ideas given to mankind. This was simply the realisation that the human mind was not a simple entity controlling the brain and body more or less at will, but a complex system made up of a number of integrated parts with at least two major subdivisions—the conscious and the unconscious. The former concerned itself with the normal round of human behaviour, including the larger part of rational thought, conversation, *etc.*, and large areas of memory. The latter was principally devoted to the automatic control of bodily functions, such as respiration, cardiac activity, various types of emotional behaviour not subject to much conscious modification and a large storehouse of relevant "memories" again not normally accessible to the conscious mind. Occasionally, Freud proposed, an exceedingly unpleasant emotional or otherwise painful event might be so troublesome if held in the conscious mind's store, that it would get shoved down into the unconscious or "repressed" where it would cease to trouble the individual in his normal life. The advantages of this mechanism are obvious, but they also brought with them hazards. With certain kinds of memory, particularly those involving psychological rather than physical pain—as for example a severe sexual conflict or marital problem—repression might be used as a device to save the individual from facing his problem in the "real" world, where he might be able ultimately to solve it, by merely hiding it away in the unconscious and thus pretending it did not exist. Unfortunately, Freud believed, conflicts of this kind were not snuffed out when consigned to the basements of the mind, but rather tended to smoulder on, affecting the individual in various ways which he could not understand. Repressed marital conflicts might give rise to impotence, for example, or perhaps to homosexual behaviour. Guilt at improper social actions similarly repressed might provoke nervous tics, local paralysis, *etc, etc.* Following this line of reasoning, Freud argued that if the unwisely repressed material could be dredged up and the individual forced to face the crisis and not deny it, then rapid alleviations of symptoms and full recovery should follow.

The Achievement of Freud. To the great psychologist and his growing band of followers the stage seemed to be set for a dramatic breakthrough not only in mental therapy but also in a general understanding of the nature of human personality. To his pleasure—for various reasons he was never too happy about hypnosis—Freud discovered that with due patience, skill and guidance an individual could be led to resurrect the material repressed in his unconscious mind in the normal, as opposed to the hypnotic, state. This technique, involving long sessions consisting of intimate discussions between patient and therapist became known as psychoanalysis, and it has steadily evolved from its experimental beginnings in the medical schools and universities of Vienna to being a major system of psychotherapy with a world-wide following and important theoretical connotations. Psychoanalysis, as practised today, consists of a number of meetings between doctor and patient in which the latter is slowly taught to approach and enter the *territory* of his subconscious mind, and examine the strange and "forgotten" material within. A successful analysis, it is claimed, gives the individual greater insight into his own personality and a fuller understanding of the potent unconscious forces which are at work within him.

Freud's initial ideas were of course tentative, and meant to be so. He was however a didactic and forceful personality himself, unwilling to compromise on many points which became controversial as the technique and practice of psychoanalysis developed. The outcome was that some of his early followers, notably the equally brilliant Carl Jung and Alfred Adler, broke away to found their own "schools" or versions of psychoanalysis. Jungian analysis, practised by the followers of C. G. Jung is an important aspect of psycho-analysis.

All psychoanalysts, Freudian and Jungian, must have a lengthy training analysis by a training analyst from a recognised institute. This is not restricted to individuals qualified in medicine or psychology. Today, psychoanalysis is coming under increasing scrutiny, and its claims are being treated with a good deal of reservation. Notable antagonists include the English psychologist Professor H. J. Eysenck. Analysts respond by saying that their system is closer to an art than a craft and not amenable to routine scientific experiment.

The controversy will no doubt continue for some time to come, but whatever its validity as therapy, the basic ideas behind psycho-analysis—notably the reality and power of the unconscious mind—are beyond question and have given human beings definite and major insights into the greatest enigma of all—the workings of the human mind.

Psychology is the study of people: how they think, how they act, react and interact. Psychology is concerned with all aspects of behaviour and the thoughts, feelings and motivation underlying such behaviour. Modern psychology is thus the science of human behaviour and experience. *See* **Adlerian Psychology, Biopsychology, Evolutionary Psychology, Gestalt Psychology** *etc.*

Psychotherapy, a method aimed at alleviating mental and emotional suffering through a specialised relationship between therapist and patient. The whole range of psychotherapies is represented on the National Register, which is compiled by the UK Council for Psychotherapy. This incorporates eight different models, each one of which holds in common a theory about the human mind, a concept of the development of the individual, and a theory of change.

Purim is the celebration of the saving of the Jewish community of Persia, as retold in the Book of Esther, known as the Megillah. It is a day of great feasting and rejoicing, but has its focal point in the reading of a scroll of Esther in the synagogue, once in the morning and once in the evening. It is a time for the whole Jewish community to come together, but women have a special place on account of Esther's courageous acts.

Puritans were a separate sect before the accession of Edward VI, but did not become prominent till the reign of Elizabeth. Afterwards they split up into Independents and Presbyterians, and the influence of Oliver Cromwell made the former supreme. Since the Revolution the word has been replaced by "Nonconformist' or 'Dissenter', but, of course, Roman Catholics in England and Protestant Episcopalians in Scotland are just as much Nonconformists or Dissenters as Baptists or Methodists.

Pyramidology, a curious belief that the dimensions of the Great Pyramid at Giza, if studied carefully, reveal principles of fundamental historical and religious significance. The perpetrator of this was a Victorian publisher, John Taylor, who discovered that if you divide the height of the pyramid into twice the side of its base you get a number very similar to *pi*—a number of considerable mathematical importance. Later discoveries in the same vein include the finding that the base of the pyramid (when divided by the width of a single casing stone) equals exactly 365—number of days in the year. Many books have been written on the interpretation of the dimensions of the pyramid, none of which has any scientific or archaeological validity. Pyramidology is simply a classic example of the well-known fact that hunting through even a random array of numbers will turn up sequences which appear to be "significant"—always provided that one carefully selects the numbers one wants and rejects those that one doesn't!

Pyrrhonism, a sceptical philosophy which doubts everything. (*See* **Scepticism**)

Pythagoreanism. The school of thought initiated by the followers of Pythagoras. It is to be distinguished from Pythagoras himself, whose own doctrines are difficult to determine. The Pythagoreans believed that at its deepest level, reality is mathematical in nature, that is, all things can be ultimately reduced to numerical relationships. Their theory of number was applied to music theory, acoustics, geometry and astronomy. The doctrine of the "harmony of the spheres" seems to have started with them: certain parameters characterizing the planets are related to one another "harmoniously" by a mathematical rule. The revolution of each planet produces a distinct tone, and the whole set corresponds to the notes of a scale.

They also held a doctrine of metempsychosis: the soul transmigrates through successive reincarnations to union with the divine.

Q

Quakers, (**Religious Society of Friends**), a religious body founded in England in the 17th cent. by George Fox (1624–91). The essence of their faith is that every individual person has the power of direct communication with God who will guide him into the ways of truth. This power comes from the "inner light" of his own heart, the light of Christ, Quakers meet for worship avoiding all ritual, without ordained ministers or prepared sermons; often there is silence until someone is moved by the Holy Spirit to utter his message.

In the early days Quakers gave vent to violent outbursts and disturbed church services. Friends had the habit of preaching at anyone who happened to be nearby, their denunciation of "steeple-houses" and references to the "inner light," their addressing everyone as "thee" and "thou," their refusal to go beyond "yea" and "nay" in making an assertion and refusing to go further in taking an oath, must have played some part in bringing about the savage persecutions they were forced to endure.

Many emigrated to Pennsylvania, founded by William Penn in 1682, and missionaries were sent to many parts of the world. The former violence gave way to gentleness. Friends not only refused to take part in war but even refused to resist personal violence. They took the lead in abolishing slavery, worked for prison reform and better education.

Many Quakers are quiet, sincere, undemonstrative people, sometimes given to a somewhat serious turn of mind. The former peculiarities of custom and dress have been dropped and interpretation of the Scriptures is more liberal.

Quakers refuse to take part in warfare, but they are always ready to help the victims of war. Quakers have also played a major part in the struggle for human rights—campaigning against slavery and for equality for women. In 2009 they became Britain's first church to allow marriage between gay couples.

Quietism, a doctrine of extreme asceticism and contemplative devotion, embodied in the works of Michael Molinos, a 17th cent. Spanish priest, and condemned by Rome. It taught that the chief duty of man is to be occupied in the continual contemplation of God, so as to become totally independent of outward circumstances and the influence of the senses. Quietists taught that when this stage of perfection is reached the soul has no further need for prayer and other external devotional practices.

Similar doctrines have been taught in the Muslim and Hindu religions. *See* **Yoga**.

Qigong, ancient Chinese belief that the energy of the body can be channeled using breathing, massage and meditation techniques.

Quran (**Koran**). *See* **Islam**.

R

Racism, the doctrine that one race is inherently superior or inferior to others, one of the bases of racial prejudice. It has no connection whatever with the study of race as a concept, nor with the investigation of racial differences.

Radiesthesia, the detection, either by some "psychic" faculty or with special equipment, of radiations alleged to be given off by all living things and natural substances such as water, oil, metal, etc. The word radiesthesia is in fact a fancy modern name for the ancient practice of "dowsing," whereby an individual is supposed to be able to detect the presence of hidden underground water by following the movements of a hazel twig held in his hands. Dowsers, or water diviners, as they are sometimes called, claim also to be able to detect the presence of minerals and, hard though it may seem to believe, have actually been hired by major oil companies to prospect for desert wells—though without any notable success. Dowsers are still employed today to locate water for farms or to locate underground pipes and cables. Science rejects their claims

Ramadan. The ninth month of the Islamic calendar during which the Prophet received his first revelations from God. Mohammed had traditionally spent this month fasting and praying, but now it is a compulsory duty for Muslims to fast between the hours of sunrise and sunset, known as *Sawm*. This fast extends to food, drink, cigarettes, chewing gum and sexual relations. Its purpose is to concentrate the heart on God without distraction and to develop self-control. It is traditionally broken each day with *iftar*, some dates and water, following the Prophet's example. A later meal will then follow. Whilst it is a duty, certain groups will be excused including the aged and those under twelve years of age. Pregnant or nursing mothers as well as travellers are temporarily excused with the understanding that fast days will be made up at a later date.

Following the lunar calendar, Ramadan moves forward ten or eleven days each year. As such, *Sawm* can be a very testing experience during the height of summer.

Ranters, a fanatical antinomian (holding the doctrine that Christians are not bound to keep the law of God) and pantheistic sect in Commonwealth England. The name was also applied to the Primitive Methodists because of their noisy preaching.

Rastafari (Rastafarianism), a Caribbean religious movement which took root in Jamaica in the 1930s following the teachings of Marcus Garvey who set up the "Black Star Liner" for the repatriation of Africans abroad. Rastafari look to Ethiopia as their spiritual home since that country was the one part of Africa not to be colonised permanently (it was invaded by Mussolini in the 1930s). Reggae is their music. Many Rastafari smoke marijuana as a spiritual act. Coffee, milk and alcohol are usually avoided.

Rationalism is defined as "the treating of reason as the ultimate authority in religion and the rejection of doctrines not consonant with reason." In practice, rationalism had a double significance: (1) the doctrine as defined above, and (2) a 19th cent. movement which was given to what was then known as "free-thought," "secularism," or agnosticism—*i.e.*, it was in the positive sense antireligious and was represented by various bodies such as the Secular Society, the National Secular Society, and the Rationalist Press Association (founded in 1899).

The great rationalists of the 17th century were Descartes, Spinoza and Leibniz.

Realism is a word which has so many meanings, and such contradictory ones, in various spheres, that it is difficult to define. We shall limit ourselves to its significance in philosophy. In philosophy, "realism" has two different meanings, diametrically opposed. (1) The most usual meaning is the one we should least expect from the everyday sense of the word—*i.e.*, it refers to all those philosophies from Plato onwards which maintained that the world of appearance is illusory and that ideas, forms, or universals are the only true realities, belonging to the world beyond matter and appearance—the world of God or mind. In early mediaeval times St. Thomas Aquinas was the chief exponent of this doctrine which was held by the scholastics as opposed to the Nominalists (*q.v.*). (2) In its modern everyday meaning "realism" is the belief that the universe is real and not a creation of mind, that there is a reality that causes the appearance, the "thing-in-itself" as Kant described it. Material things may not really be what they appear to be (*e.g.* a noise is not the "bang" we experience but a series of

shock-waves passing through the atmosphere), yet, for all that, we can be sure that matter exists and it is very possible (some might add) that mind does not.

Reformation, the great religious movement of the 16th cent., which resulted in the establishment of Protestantism. John Wyclif (d. 1384), John Hus (d. 1415) and others had sounded the warning note, and when later on Luther took up the cause in Germany, and Zwingli in Switzerland, adherents soon became numerous. The wholesale vending of indulgences by the papal agents had incensed the people, and when Luther denounced these things he spoke to willing ears. After much controversy, the reformers boldly propounded the principles of the new doctrine, and the struggle for religious supremacy grew bitter. They claimed justification (salvation) by faith, and the use as well as the authority of the Scriptures, rejecting the doctrine of transubstantiation, the adoration of the Virgin and Saints, and the headship of the Pope. Luther was excommunicated. But the Reformation principles spread and ultimately a great part of Germany, as well as Switzerland, the Low Countries, Scandinavia, England, and Scotland were won over to the new faith.

In England Henry VIII readily espoused the Reformation, his own personal quarrel with the Pope acting as an incentive. Under Mary there was a brief and sanguinary reaction, but Elizabeth gave completeness to the work which her father had initiated. *See* **Lutheranism, Calvinism, Presbyterianism, Baptists,** *etc.*

Reiki, a form of spiritual healing which originated in Japan.

Relativism. Theories or doctrines that truth, morality *etc.* are relative to situations and are not absolute. The view that all truth is relative is associated with Scepticism (*q.v.*). In the area of morality, it is the view that there are no absolute or universal criteria for ethical judgements. This view is often a reaction to the differences in moral belief between different societies. It is objected against relativism that there must be standards by which to measure the correctness of judgements or beliefs.

Religious Society of Friends. *See* **Quakers.**

Renaissance, the revival of art and letters, under the influence of classical models, which began in Italy in the 14th century. It is a term which must be used with care for the following reasons: (1) Although it was first used in the form *rinascita* (re-birth) by Vasari in 1550 and people living at that time certainly were aware that something new was happening, the word had no wide currency until used by the Swiss historian Jacob Burchardt in his classic *The Civilization of the Renaissance in Italy* (1860). (2) The term as used today refers not only to art in its widest sense but to a total change in man's outlook on life which extended into philosophical, scientific, economic, and technical fields. (3) Spreading from Italy there were renaissance movements in France, Spain, Germany, and northern Europe, all widely different with varying delays in time.

The real cause of the Renaissance was not the fall of Constantinople, the invention of printing, or the discovery of America, though these were phases in the process; it was, quite simply, money. The birth of a new merchant class gave rise to individualist attitudes in economic affairs which prepared the way for individualism and humanism. The new wealthy class in time became patrons of the arts whereas previously the Church had been the major patron and controller. Thus the artist became more free to express himself, more respected, and being more well-to-do could afford to ignore the Church and even, in time, the views of his patrons.

It is true that art continued to serve to a considerable extent the purposes of faith, but it was judged from the standpoint of art. Medieval art was meant to elevate and teach man: Renaissance art to delight his senses and enrich his life. From this free and questing spirit acquired from economic individualism came the rise of modern science and technology; here Italy learned much from the Arab scholars who had translated and commented upon the philosophical, medical, and mathematical texts of antiquity, while denying themselves any interest in Greek art and literature. Arabic

Latin versions of Aristotle were in use well into the 16th cent. The Byzantine culture, though it had preserved the Greek tradition and gave supremacy to Plato, had made no move forward. But the Greek scholars who fled to Italy after the fall of Constantinople brought with them an immense cargo of classical manuscripts. The recovery of these Greek masterpieces, their translation into the vernaculars, and the invention of printing, made possible a fuller understanding of the Greek spirit.

It was the bringing together of the two heritages, Greek science, and Greek literature, that gave birth to a new vision. But it was not only Aristotle and Plato who were being studied but Ovid, Catullus, Horace, Pliny and Lucretius. What interested Renaissance man was the humanism of the Latin writers, their attitude to science, their scepticism.

Early Renaissance. The period *c.* 1400–1500 is known as the Early Renaissance. During this time such painters as Masaccio, Uccello, Piero della Francesca, Botticelli, and Giovanni Bellini were laying the foundations of drawing and painting for all subsequent periods including our own. They concerned themselves with such problems as anatomy, composition, perspective, and representation of space, creating in effect a grammar or textbook of visual expression.

High Renaissance. The term High Renaissance is reserved for a very brief period when a pure, balanced, classical harmony was achieved and artists were in complete control of the techniques learned earlier. The High Renaissance lasted only from *c.* 1500 to 1527 (the date of the sack of Rome), yet that interval included the earlier works of Michelangelo, most of Leonardo's, and all the Roman works of Raphael.

Ritualism, a tendency which, during the 19th cent., developed in the High Church section of the Church of England to make use of those vestments, candles, incense, *etc.* which are usually regarded as features of the Church of Rome. Since some opposition was aroused, a Ritual Commission was appointed in 1904 to take evidence and try to find some common basis on which High and Low Church could agree with respect to ceremonial. The report of 1906 in effect recommended the giving of greater powers to bishops to suppress objectionable practices.

Although they are often associated together, it is worth while pointing out that there was no special connection between the Oxford Movement or Tractarians (*q.v.*) and Ritualism because Pusey disliked ritual and even Newman, who eventually went over to Rome, held simple services at his church of St. Mary's.

Roman Catholic Church, the Christian organisation which acknowledges the Pope as the lawful successor of St. Peter, the apostle appointed by Christ to be the head of His Church. The reforming impulse at the Second Vatican Council (1962–5), summoned by Pope John, set in train movements towards religious unity and the reform and modernisation of the Church. Pope Paul made changes in the government and liturgy of the Church but refused to allow birth control, the marriage of priests or a greater role for women.

A historic meeting took place in 1982 between Rome and Canterbury when Pope John Paul II made the first papal visit to Britain. The 1993 papal encyclical, *Veritatis Splendor*, forcefully restating the Catholic opposition to artificial birth control, reopened Catholic divisions on this issue. The English text of the Catechism of the Catholic Church, the first complete survey of Roman Catholic teaching since the 16th century, was published in 1994.

In 1995 the Pope's encyclical *Evangelium Vitae* (Gospel of Life) repeated his attacks on abortion, euthanasia, suicide and *in vitro* fertilisation. Many liberal Roman Catholics were unhappy with the more conservative pronouncements of the Pope. During his pontificate, Pope John Paul canonised more saints than any Pope in history.

Some Anglicans (opposed to women priests) have moved to join the Catholic Church. The resignation in September 1996 of the Bishop of Argyll reinforced the growing debate on celibacy in the priesthood (the celibacy rule dates from 1139). In March 2000 the Pope sought a historic pardon for the sins of the Church (the *mea culpa*). With the death of Pope John Paul II in April

2005 the Roman Catholic Church entered a new era. Over recent years, weekly attendance at Sunday Mass in England declined from 1·7 million in 1989 to 1,000,000 today. Entrants to the priesthood are also declining. The number of Roman Catholic priests in the world is around 400,000. The Church has also been severely damaged by revelations of extensive child sexual abuse.

The most important Catholic countries (by numbers) are Brazil (*c.* 123 million), Mexico (94 million), the Philippines (66 million) and the USA (also 66 million). The Basilica of Our Lady of Peace in Yamoussoukro, Ivory Coast, is the world's largest church. There are currently more Muslims in the world than Catholics.

In 2013 Roman Catholics were shocked by the resignation of Pope Benedict XVI–the first in modern times. He was succeeded by Pope Francis I who had emphasised poverty and green issues. In February 2016 Pope Francis met Russian Orthodox Patriarch Kirill in Cuba, the first such meeting since the 1054 split. Also in 2016, the Pope established a commission to consider the ordination of women deacons.

Romantic Movement or **Romanticism** is the name given not so much to an individual way of thinking but to the gradual but radical transformation of basic human values that occurred in the Western world round about the latter part of the 18th cent. It was a great breakthrough in European consciousness and arose through the writings of certain men living during the half-century or more following, say, 1760. It arose when there was a revolution in basic values—in art, morals, politics, religion, *etc.* The new view was of a world transcending the old one, infinitely larger and more varied.

To understand the Romantic movement it is necessary first to take note of the climate of thought preceding the great change; then to account for its beginning in Germany where it did (*see* **Pietism**) during the latter part of the 18th cent., and finally to appraise the writings of those men whose ideas fermented the new awakening. Briefly, the shift was away from French classicism and from belief in the all-pervasive power of human reason (the Enlightenment) towards the unfettered freedom that the new consciousness was able to engender. What mattered was to live a passionate and vigorous life, to dedicate oneself to an ideal, no matter what the cost (*e.g.*, Byron).

The ideas of the Enlightenment (*e.g.*, Fontenelle, Voltaire, Montesquieu) had been attacked by the Germans Hamann and Herder and by the ideas of the English philosopher Hume, but Kant, Schiller, and Fichte, Goethe's novel *Wilhelm Meister*, and the French Revolution all had profound effects on the aesthetic, moral, social, and political thought of the time. Friedrich Schlegel (1772–1829) said: "There is in man a satisfied desire to soar into infinity; a feverish longing to break through the narrow bonds of individuality." Romanticism undermined the notion that in matters of value there are objective criteria which operate between men. Henceforth there was to be a resurgence of the human spirit, deep and profound, that is still going on.

Rosicrucians, a mystical society founded in the 16th cent. by Christian Rosenkreuz which attempted to forge a theoretical link between the great Egyptian religions and the Church of Rome, drawing rituals and philosophy from both camps. The Society did not long survive the death of its founder (he managed to reach the age of 106 incidentally) but has been revived in succeeding centuries by a series of rivalling factions.

Perhaps the most famous of these is the Rosicrucian Order which has become well-known in the Western world as a result of its heavy advertising in the popular press. Founded by the American H. Spencer Lewis, this offers a simple and good-natured doctrine preaching the Brotherhood of Man, the reincarnation of the soul and the immense latent potential of the human mind.

S

Sabbatarianism, the belief held by those Christians who regard the first day of the week as the Sabbath and wish to respect it as a holy day according to the 4th Commandment. Sabbatarianism became a principal characteristic of Presbyterianism (q.v.).

Observance of the Sabbath has declined in recent years along with the general fall in church attendance and the advent of sporting, leisure and now shopping, gaming and more relaxed licensing laws on the Sabbath since 1994.

Salafism, a form of Sunni Islam. The movement has strict, conservative views and its followers are sometimes known as Wahabis (see **J53**).

Salvation Army. The religious movement which in 1878 became known by this name arose from the Christian Mission meetings which the Rev. William Booth and his devoted wife had held in the East End of London for the previous thirteen years. Its primary aim was, and still is, to preach the gospel of Jesus Christ to men and women untouched by ordinary religious efforts. The founder devoted his life to the salvation of the submerged classes whose conditions at that time were unspeakably dreadful. Originally his aim had been to convert people and then send them on to the churches, but he soon found that few religious bodies would accept these "low-class" men and women. So it was that social work became part of their effort. Practical help like the provision of soup-kitchens, accompanied spiritual ministration.

Soon, in the interests of more effective "warfare" against social evils, a military form of organisation, with uniforms, brass bands, and religious songs, was introduced. Its magazine *The War Cry* gave as its aim "to carry the Blood of Christ and the Fire of the Holy Ghost into every part of the world.'

General Booth saw with blinding clarity that conversion must be accompanied by an improvement of external conditions. Various books had earlier described the terrible conditions of the slums, but in 1890 he produced a monumental survey entitled *In Darkest England and the Way Out.* From that time forward the Army was accepted and its facilities made use of by the authorities. Today its spiritual and social activities have spread across the whole world; every one, no matter what class, colour, or creed he may belong to, is a "brother for whom Christ died."

Scepticism. From the Greek, *skepsis,* enquiry or questioning. The philosophical attitude of doubting claims to knowledge. It springs from observations that the senses are unreliable, that the best methods often fall short of reaching the truth, and that experts often disagree. Sceptical attitudes emerge early in ancient Greek philosophy, but were only systemized into a school of thought by Pyrrho (c. 360–c. 270 B.C.). The Greek Sceptics proposed *epoche,* or suspension of belief, and aimed at *ataraxia,* tranquility of mind.

Scepticism is a recurring theme in Western philosophy, for example in Montaigne (1533–92) and Bayle (1647–1706). The most powerful sceptical thinker of the modern age is David Hume (1711–76). His arguments throw doubt upon induction, the notion of causality, the identity of the self and the existence of the external world.

The term is associated with Descartes (1596–1650), though Descartes himself is not a sceptic. It refers to his "method of doubt", which attempted to put knowledge upon a sure foundation by suspending Judgement on any proposition whose truth could be doubted, until one can be found that is absolutely certain. This secure point is the famous "I think therefore I am".

Scholasticism. From the time of Augustine to the middle of the 9th cent. philosophy, like science, was dead or merely a repetition of what had gone before. But about that time there arose a new interest in the subject, although (since by then Western Europe was entirely under the authority of the Catholic Church) the main form it took was an attempt to justify Church teaching in the light of Greek philosophy.

Those who made this attempt to reconcile Christian beliefs with the best in Plato and Aristotle were known as "schoolmen" and the philosophies which they developed were known as "scholasticism." Among the most famous schoolmen must be counted John Scotus Erigena (c. 800–c. 877), born in Ireland and probably the earliest; St. Anselm, archbishop of Canterbury (1033–1109); the great Peter

Abelard whose school was in Paris (1079–1142); Bernard of Chartres, his contemporary; and the best-known of all, St. Thomas Aquinas in Naples (1225–74), who was given the name of the "Angelic Doctor."

The philosophies of these men are discussed under various headings (**God and Man, Determinism and Free-will**), but being severely limited by the Church their doctrines differed from each other much less than those of later philosophical schools. However, one of the great arguments was between the orthodox Realists (q.v.) and the Nominalists (q.v.) and a second was between the Thomists (or followers of St. Thomas Aquinas) and the Scotists (followers of John Duns Scotus—not to be confused with John Scotus Erigena).

The two latter schools were known as the Ancients, whilst the followers of William of Occam, the Nominalist, were known as the Terminalists. All became reconciled in 1482 in face of the increasing threat from humanism of which the great exponent was Erasmus of Rotterdam (1466–1536).

Scientology, an applied religious philosophy dealing with the study of knowledge, which through the application of its technology, claims to bring about desirable changes in the conditions of life. The word Scientology comes from the Latin word *Scio* (knowing in the fullest meaning of the word) and the Greek word *Logos* (study of). Developed and founded by author, philosopher and humanitarian L. Ron Hubbard (1911–86). Scientology purports to explain all of life's difficulties and contradictions in terms of occurrences in past lives. These mental blocks are removed so the individual can return to the deified state from which he came many incarnations ago.

Until the late 1960s the worldwide headquarters was in East Grinstead, Sussex. This is now the UK headquarters. Scientology ® is a registered trademark.

Secularism. *See* **God and Man** and **Rationalism.**

Semiology, Semiotics. These two words are now used almost interchangeably. The original sense of semiotics was the study of signs and sign-using behaviour, and was propounded by the American philosopher Peirce (1839–1914). Semiotics was divided into three branches: syntactics, the study of grammar; semantics, the study of meaning; and pragmatics, the study of the purposes and effects of meaningful utterances. Under the influence of the French linguist de Saussure (1857–1913) the term has broadened to the study of any means by which human beings communicate, not only through language, but also through gestures, clothes, objects, advertisements *etc.*

Societies have a multiplicity of language-like "codes" by which objects like cars and buildings have cultural meanings over and above their functions.

Shakers, members of a revivalist group, styled by themselves "The United Society of Believers in Christ's Second Appearing," who seceded from Quakerism in 1747 though adhering to many of the Quaker tenets. The community was joined in 1758 by Ann Lee, a young convert from Manchester, who had "revelations" that she was the female Christ; "Mother Ann" was accepted as their leader. Under the influence of her prophetic visions she set out with nine followers for "Immanuel's land" in America and the community settled near Albany, capital of New York state.

They were known as the "Shakers" in ridicule because they were given to involuntary movements in moments of religious ecstasy. Central to their faith was the belief in the dual role of God through the male and female Christ: the male principle came to earth in Jesus; the female principle, in "Mother Ann." The sexes were equal and women preached as often as men at their meetings which sometimes included sacred dances—nevertheless the two sexes, even in dancing, kept apart.

Their communistic way of living brought them economic prosperity, the Shakers becoming known as good agriculturists and craftsmen, noted for their furniture and textiles. After 1860, however, the movement began to decline and it is now virtually extinct.

Shamans, the medicine men found in many primitive societies who used their magical arts to work cures, and protect the group from evil influences.

J47

The *shaman* was a man apart and wore special garments to show his authority.

Shiites or Shia, a Muslim sect, opposed by the orthodox Sunnites who see them as heretics. The dispute, which came almost immediately after the death of the Prophet and led to bitter feuding, had little to do with matters of doctrine as such but with the succession. After Mohammed's death, there were three possible claimants: Ali, the husband of his daughter Fatima, and two others, one of whom gave up his claim in favour of the other, Abu Bakr. The orthodox selected Abu Bakr, who was shortly assassinated, and the same happened to his successor as Ali was passed over again. The Shiites maintain that Ali was the true vicar of the Prophet, and that the three orthodox predecessors were usurpers.

In Iraq, the majority Shiites enjoyed a revival of influence after the fall of Saddam Hussein (under whose regime they were oppressed). They are dominant in Iran. Elsewhere Shia now number 60 % of the population in Iraq, 60 % in Bahrein, 40 % in Lebanon, 30 % in Kuwait and 12 % in Saudi Arabia.

Current Shiite-Sunni conflicts in the Middle East are causing major population shifts.

Shintoism, literally means "teaching of the Gods". It is a native Japanese religion, with a strong bias towards ancestor worship and the divine powers of natural forces. Unusual in that it had no recognised founder nor written dogma, Shintoism permeated Japanese life in a most vigorous way until the defeat of the country at the hands of the Allied Powers in 1945. In the 1500 years of its existence the Shinto religion produced tens of thousands of unique and beautiful shrines throughout Japan. Vast numbers of these were destroyed by bombing in the Second World War.

Shintoism was disestablished by the US occupying forces in 1945 and Hirohito "abdicated" his divine powers.

The first written record of Shinto beliefs and customs was completed in A.D. 712.

Shoah or catastrophe is the name often given by Jews to the period of persecution by the Nazis during World War II. Yom Ha-Shoah is a day of remembrance for the near six million Jewish victims of the Holocaust. It is marked simply with special services and the lighting of candles. A special ceremony takes place at Yad Veshem, the permanent Holocaust memorial outside Jerusalem. A law passed by the Israeli Knesset forbids public entertainment on the evening of 27 Nisan.

Sikhism. The Sikh community of the Punjab, which has played a significant part in the history of modern India, came into being during a period of religious revival in India in the 15th and 16th cent. It was originally founded as a religious sect by Guru (teacher) Nanak (1469–1538) who emphasised the fundamental truth of all religions, and whose mission was to put an end to religious conflict. He condemned the formalism both of Hinduism and Islam, preaching the gospel of universal toleration, and the unity of the Godhead, whether He be called Allah, Vishnu, or God. His ideas were welcomed by the great Mogul Emperor Akbar (1542–1605). Thus a succession of Gurus were able to live in peace after Nanak's death; they established the great Sikh centre at Amritsar, compiled the sacred writings (the *Adi Granth*), and improved their organisation as a sect.

But the peace did not last long, for an emperor arose who was a fanatical Muslim, in face of whom the last Guru, Govind Singh (1666–1708), whose father was put to death for refusal to embrace Islam, had to make himself a warrior and instil into the Sikhs a more warlike spirit.

A number of ceremonies were instituted by Govind Singh; admission to the fraternity was by special rite; caste distinctions were abolished; hair was worn long; the word singh, meaning lion, was added to the original name. They were able to organise themselves into 12 *misls* or confederacies but divisions appeared with the disappearance of a common enemy and it was not until the rise of Ranjit Singh (1780–1839) that a single powerful Sikh kingdom was established, its influence only being checked by the English, with whom a treaty of friendship was made. After the death of Ranjit Singh two Anglo-Sikh wars followed, in 1845–46, and 1848–49, which resulted in British annexation of the Punjab and the end of Sikh independence. In the two world wars the Sikhs proved among the most loyal of Britain's Indian subjects.

The partitioning of the subcontinent of India in 1947 into two states, one predominantly Hindu and the other predominantly Muslim, presented a considerable problem in the Punjab, which was divided in such a way as to leave 2 million Sikhs in Pakistan, and a considerable number of Muslims in the Indian Punjab.

Although numbering less than 3 per cent. of the population the Sikhs are a continuing factor in Indian political life. Demands for Sikh independence led to the storming by Indian troops of the Golden Temple at Amritsar on 6 June 1984. In October 1984, Mrs. Gandhi was assassinated by Sikh extremists.

There are now around 423,000 Sikhs in England and Wales. The largest Sikh temple outside India was opened in Southall (which boasts a very large Sikh community) in March 2003. Other large Sikh communities are in Birmingham and Leicester. The first Sikh arrived in Britain in 1854. Worldwide, Sikhism is the fifth largest religion in the world. There are *c* 30 million Sikhs worldwide.

Slavery. *See* **Anti-Slavery International.**

Socialism, is a form of society in which men and women are not divided into opposing economic classes but live together under conditions of approximate social and economic equality, using in common the means that lie to their hands of promoting social welfare. The brotherhood of man inspires the aims of socialism in foreign, colonial, social, and economic policies alike.

The word "socialism" first came into general use in England *c.* 1834 in connection with Robert Owen's "village of cooperation" at New Lanark. About the middle of the 19th cent., Charles Kingsley and others established a form of Christian socialism, and William Morris, John Burns *etc.* founded a Socialist League in 1886.

With the development of trade unions the socialist movement took a more practical trend. Fabianism (*q.v.*) associated in its early days with the names of Beatrice and Sidney Webb and George Bernard Shaw, aimed at the gradual reorganisation of society by creating intelligent public opinion by education and legislation. The British Labour Party believed in peaceful and constitutional change to socialism by democratic methods based upon popular consent. The Labour Government of 1945–51 initiated a major period of social reform and public ownership and remains perhaps the greatest reforming government of the 20th century.

Socialists oppose the liberal view that government should be principally concerned with individuals' rights to property and freedom. Socialists argue that people are integrally social and political animals and seek to live in a society that values cooperation, common ownership, and mutual assistance instead of competition, private property, and self-interest.

Whilst socialism in the 19th century emphasised economic inequalities, throughout the 20th century socialism broadened its old horizons with a concern for the importance of gender, race, sexuality and culture in our social relationships. Consequently, movements such as the New Left in Britain have campaigned for greater justice and equality for women, ethnic minorities, and homosexual people, whilst emphasising that the machinery of exploitation and oppression operates through cultural practices as well as economic.

Soka Gakkai, Japan's largest religious organisation with 10 million followers. Founded in 1930 as the lay arm of a venerable Buddhist sect.

Solipsism. The theory that nothing really exists but oneself and one's mental states. No philosopher has deliberately held this view, but it is often seen to follow from certain views, for example, the belief that all one can know is oneself and one's immediate knowledge. The theory is intrinsically absurd, but it is difficult to refute.

Spiritualism is a religion which requires to be distinguished from psychical research (*q.v.*) which is a scientific attempt carried on by both believers and non-believers to investigate psychic phenomena including those not necessarily connected with "spirits"—*e.g.*, telepathy or clairvoyance and precognition. As a religion (although for that matter the whole of history is filled with attempts to get in touch with the "spirit world") Spiritualism begins with the American Andrew Jackson

Davis who in 1847 published *Nature's Divine Revelations*, a book which is still widely read. In this Davis states that on the death of the physical body, the human spirit remains alive and moves on to one or another of a considerable range of worlds or "spheres" where it commences yet another stage of existence. Since the spirit has not died, but exists with full (and possibly even expanded) consciousness, there should be no reason, Davis argues, why it should not make its presence known to the beings it has temporarily left behind on earth.

The movement today, which still has a large and often articulate following, now concentrates on the less controversial areas of "mental mediumship," clairvoyance and the like, or on the very widespread practice of "spirit healing." Where people are not deliberately deluded by bogus mediums acting for monetary reward, Spiritualism may have an emotional role to play in the life of people whose happiness has been affected by bereavement.

Stalinism. The methods and policies associated with Joseph Stalin (1879–1953), leader of the USSR from 1929 until his death. This form of despotism consisted of the concentration of power in his own hands, and the ruthless suppression of dissent, plus a "cult of personality", which used every means of propaganda to present Stalin as a benevolent ruler. For many historians, Stalin is the greatest mass murderer of modern times (along with Mao and Hitler).

State and Man. Most of the early civilisations such as those of Egypt and Babylonia were theocratic, that is to say, they were arranged in a hierarchy with, at the peak, a king who was also an incarnation of the god. It is with the rise of the city states of ancient Greece that the problem really began to be discussed.

The Greek Approach. The early pre-Socratic philosophers Democritus and the Pythagorean school for example, held that the individual should subordinate himself to the whole; they had no doubt that the citizen's first duty was to the state. The Greeks until the time of Plato were not really thinking in terms of individual rights, nor had they given much thought to what form the state should take—they simply accepted it. The first great attempt to describe the ideal state is to be found in Plato's *The Republic* which is referred to elsewhere (*see* **Education**). His pupil Aristotle did not try to form a utopia but made many comments on the nature of government. Thus, while agreeing that the state was more important than any individual person, he distinguished between good and bad states, and pointed out that to the extent that the state does not enable its citizens to lead virtuous and useful lives it is evil. A good constitution must recognise the inequalities between human beings and confer on them rights according to their abilities: among these inequalities are those of personal ability, property, birth, and status, as freeman or slave. The best forms of rule were monarchy, aristocracy, and democracy; the worst forms—tyranny, oligarchy (or rule of a powerful few), and ochlocracy (or mob-rule). The later Greek thinkers of Hellenistic times held two opposed points of view. The Epicureans (*q.v.*) taught that all social life is based upon self-interest and we become members of a group for our own convenience; therefore there are no absolute rights and laws—what is good is what members decide at that time to be good, and when they change their minds the law must change too. Injustice is not an evil in any god-given sense; we behave justly simply because if injustice became the general rule, we ourselves should suffer. The Stoics (*q.v.*), on the other hand, held that the state must dominate the individual completely and everyone must carry out, first and foremost, his social duties and be willing to sacrifice everything for it; but the state of the Stoics was no narrowly national one, but one that strove to become a universal brotherhood.

The Christian Approach. The orthodox Christian view is expressed in St. Augustine's book *The City of God*. Here it is held that the church, as the worldly incarnation of the City of God, is to be supreme over the state, and the head of the church is to be supreme over secular rulers. In addition it must be recognised that, whilst the secular ruler can make mistakes, the church does not, since it is the representative of God's kingdom on earth.

The Secular State. During the Renaissance (*q.v.*) many rulers, petty and otherwise, were seeking absolute authority. Two notable thinkers at this stage were Niccolo Machiavelli (1469–1527) in Italy and Thomas Hobbes (1588–1679) in England, where, of course, the Renaissance arrived later in history. Both supported absolute monarchy against the former domination of the church. The name of Machiavelli has become a by-word for any behaviour that is cunning and unscrupulous, but he was not really as bad as he is usually painted. It is, indeed, true that in his book *The Prince* he showed in the greatest detail the methods by which a ruler could gain absolute control and destroy civic freedom, but this despotism was intended as merely a necessary intermediate stage towards his real idea which was a free, united Italian nation wholly independent of the church.

Hobbes was a materialist whose thesis was that man is naturally a ferocious animal whose basic impulse is war and pillage and the destruction of whatever stands in his way to gain his desires. But if he allowed himself to behave in this way his life would be "nasty, brutish, and short" so he creates a society in which he voluntarily gives up many of his rights and hands them over to a powerful ruler in his own interest. But having done this he must obey; even when the ruler is unjust, as he has no right to complain because anything is better than a return to his natural state.

The religion of the king must be the religion of the people and the only things no ruler has the right to do is to cause a man to commit suicide or murder or to make him confess to a crime.

Views of Locke: Live and Let Live. John Locke (1632–1704) disagreed with these views. Man is naturally peaceful and co-operative and therefore social life comes readily to him. He sets up an authority in order to preserve the group and that is why laws are made; but the function of the state is strictly limited to maintaining the public good and beyond this men are to be left free. Therefore absolute power and the doctrine of the Divine Right of Kings were wrong because power ultimately rests with the people who have the right to make and break governments. It is also wrong that those who make the laws should be able to execute them. This is the important British doctrine of the separation of powers between the legislature and the executive which is regarded as one of the bases of democracy.

Rousseau's Social Doctrine. The only other views that we need to consider here are those of Jean-Jacques Rousseau (1712–78) and Herbert Spencer (1820–1903), since the views of the two important intervening figures, Hegel and Karl Marx, are dealt with elsewhere (*see* **Dialectical Materialism**) and after Spencer we come to a stage where political philosophy begins to merge with sociology and the social sciences. Rousseau is a puzzling figure. On the one hand he has been hailed as the prophet of freedom and on the other as the father of modern totalitarianism. His book *Social Contract* (1762) begins with the words: "Man is born free, and everywhere he is in chains." He says that he is in favour, not merely of democracy, but of direct democracy in which everyone has to give his assent to all measures as in the Greek city-states and in Geneva, of which city he was a citizen. (This method is still in force in respect of some measures in the Swiss cantons.)

Natural society is based on a "social contract" or mutual agreement and Rousseau speaks of a "return to nature" which would ensure the sovereignty of the people at all times. Thus far, he seems to agree with Locke but soon we find that he is more akin to Hobbes, since (as the twentieth century showed) nothing is more tyrannical than the absolute rule of all the people. (Public opinion is more Hitlerian than Hitler.) As it turns out, then, the "social contract" consists in "the total alienation of each associate, together with all his rights, to the whole community" and "each of us puts his person and all his power in common under the supreme direction of the general will."

Rousseau admired direct democracy in the small city-state, but if his doctrine is applied to large states, then the "general will" becomes absolute. It is in this sense that he is regarded as the forerunner of totalitarianism. Herbert Spencer is quoted only as an example of the inappropriate application of a biological theory to social issues. Influenced by Darwin's thesis of natural selection, he saw in society a struggle in which the fittest survived and the less fit perished. Each individual had the right to preserve himself, but in the case of human beings this depended upon group life in which, to some extent, each individual is limited by the rights of others. But this should not go too far, and he condemned the socialism of J. S. Mill which (a) would give over-much protection to the unfit, and (b) would give the state powers which it has no right to since the best government is the least government. In accordance with Darwinism free competition was essential.

State Capitalism. Lenin's description of the compromise made with financial interests in 1918 to ensure Communist survival, while simultaneously reinforcing central control over the economy. More recently, a pejorative description of Soviet socialism in which a privileged bureaucracy is said collectively to dominate economic life with the same relationship to the working class as employers under private capitalism.

Stoics, the followers of Zeno, a Greek philosopher in the 4th cent. B.C., who received their name from the fact that they were taught in the Stoa Poikile or Painted Porch of Athens. They believed that since the world is the creation of divine wisdom and is governed by divine law, it is man's duty to accept his fate. Zeno conceived virtue to be the highest good and condemned the passions. (*See* **God and Man, State and Man, Determinism and Free-will.**)

Structuralism. 1. Psychology. The name of a school of thought whose influence has not lasted. It sought to investigate the structure of consciousness through the analysis, by introspection, of simple forms of sensation, thought, images, *etc.* and then find out how these components fitted together in complex forms. The school, which is mainly identified with Edward Titchener (1867–1927), discounted the value of analysing the significance of mental experience, and of examining the functions of the mind.

2. Linguistics. The theory that language is best described in terms of its irreducible structural units in morphology (the study of word structure) and phonology (the study of sound systems).

3. Social Sciences. Theories or methods of analysis characterised by a preoccupation, not simply with structures, but with such structures as can be held to underlie and generate the phenomena under observation. To use a distinction of the linguist Noam Chomsky (b. 1928), the concern is with deep structures rather than surface structures. The main influences on the movement have been the theories of the French anthropologist Claude Levi-Strauss (1908–2009). According to him, universal patterns of cultural and social systems are products of the invariant "deep" structure of the human mind. He believed that structural similarities underlie all cultures and that an analysis of the relationships between cultures could provide insight into innate and universal principles of human thought.

Structural analysis has also been applied to literary theory, *e.g.* by the French critic Roland Barthes (1915–80). *See under* **Literary Theory**.

Subjectivism. In moral philosophy, the belief that all moral attitudes are merely a matter of personal taste. According to this an assertion like "Abortion is wrong" does not express an objective truth but means that the speaker or, more broadly, his society, or people in general, disapprove of abortion.

Sufism. A mystical movement within Islam. It started as a reaction against the legalistic approach of early Islam, seeking to establish a more personal relationship with Allah, or God. The objective of Sufism is perfection of the individual and union with God. Sufi orders were first established in the 12th century and some are still thriving today. Sufism has been very important in the history of Islamic faith and had a great influence on Muslim literature, and created a genre of mystical love poetry.

Suicide. *See* **Euthanasia.**

Sukkot, a Jewish holiday, also called the Feast of Tabernacles.

Sunnites, the orthodox sect of Islam (*q.v.*) as contrasted with the Shiites or Shia (*q.v.*).

Surrealism. *See* **Section N.**

Swedenborgianism. The Church of the New Jerusalem, based on the writings of Emanuel Swedenborg (1688–1772), was founded by his followers eleven years after his death. The New Church is essentially a movement bearing the same relationship to Christianity as Christianity does to Judaism. Swedenborg's many works include the 12-volume *Arcana Caelestia* (*Heavenly Secrets*) (1749–56).

Synchronicity, an attempt by the psychologist, Carl Gustav Jung, to explain the apparently significant relationship between certain events in the physical universe which seem to have no obvious "causal" link. This rather involved concept is easily understood if one realises that almost all scientific and philosophical beliefs are based on the notion that the continuous process of change which is taking place in ourselves and in the universe around us is dependent upon a principle known as causality.

We can express this another way by saying an object moves because it has been pushed or pulled by another. We see because light strikes the retina and signals pass up the nervous system to the brain. A stone falls to the ground because the earth's gravity is pulling it towards its centre, *etc.*, *etc.* For all practical purposes every event can be looked upon as being "caused" by some other prior event and this is obviously one of the most important principles of the operation of the universe. Jung, however, felt that there is a sufficiently large body of evidence to suggest that events may be linked in a significant (*i.e.*, nonchance) way without there being any true causal relationship between them.

The classic example he held to be the supposed predictive power of astrology by which there appears to be a relationship between the stellar configurations and the personality and lifepattern of individuals on earth. Jung was scientist enough to realise that there could be no causal connection between the aspect of the stars and the lives of people billions of miles from them, yet felt the evidence for astrology was strong enough to demand an alternative non-causal explanation.

The trouble with synchronicity, which has not made much impact on the world of physics or of psychology, is that it is not really an explanation at all but merely a convenient word to describe some puzzling correspondences. The real question, of course, is whether there really are events occurring which are significantly but not *causally* linked, and most scientists today would hold that there were not.

Syndicalism, a form of socialist doctrine which aims at the ownership and control of all industries by the workers, contrasted with the more conventional type of socialism which advocates ownership and control by the state. Since syndicalists have preferred to improve the conditions of the workers by direct action, *e.g.*, strikes and working to rule, rather than through the usual parliamentary procedures, they have been closely related to anarchists (*q.v.*) and are sometimes described as anarcho-syndicalists.

Under syndicalism there would be no state; for the state would be replaced by a federation of units based on functional economic organisation rather than on geographical representation. The movement had bodies in the United Kingdom, where guild socialism (*q.v.*) was strongly influenced by its doctrines, in France, Germany, Italy, Spain, Argentina, and Mexico, but these gradually declined after the first world war.

Fascism (*q.v.*) was also strongly influenced by the revolutionary syndicalism of Georges Sorel.

T

Talmud. *See* **Judaism.**

Tantra. 1. Tantric Buddhism. Tantra refers to a series of ritual texts said to have been first transmitted by the Buddha himself. The tantras speak of the evocation of various gods, the pursuit of magical powers, the use of chants, and the attainment of enlightenment through meditation and yoga. Tantric theory and practice is a development within the Mahayana Buddhist tradition. It died out in India but moved to Tibet. The most famous tantra is the *Tibetan Book of the Dead*.

2. Tantric Hinduism. Within Hinduism tantra refers to a group of Sanskrit texts not part of the orthodox Veda (*see* **Hinduism**). These are concerned with acquiring spiritual power and liberation in life, through practices aiming at purifying the body and controlling one's mental processes.

Taoism is still one of the great Eastern creeds. Its alleged founder, Lao-tze, is said to have been born in Honan about 604 B.C.; he is also said to be the author of the bible of Taoism, the *Tao-te-ching*, or in English *The Way of Life*, and to have disapproved of Confucius.

This would hardly be surprising; for Taoism is eminently a mystical religion recommending doing nothing and resisting nothing, whereas **Confucianism** (*q.v.*) is eminently a practical code of living and its founder insisted on intervening in everything to do with social life. But the truth as revealed by modern scholarship is rather different. We are told that the poems of the *Tao-te-ching* are anonymous and probably originated among recluses in lonely valleys long before the time of Confucius; they were collected and given form at some time late in the 3rd cent. B.C. and their authorship attributed to Lao-tze. It is entirely possible that no such peson ever existed (unlike Confucius, who certainly did), but if there were such a man he appears to have used a pseudonym since "Lao" is not a surname but an adjective meaning "old" and it was customary to attribute important works to old men on account of their supposed wisdom.

Lao-tze simply means "the old philosopher", and although the *Tao-te-ching* is one of the most remarkable and instructive books ever written it is as anonymous as the Border Ballads.

It is apparent that the religion learned both from the ancient Chinese mystics and from Brahmanism: *Tao*, the Way, is impalpable, invisible, and incapable of being expressed in words. But it can be attained by virtue, by compassion, humility, and non-violence. Out of weakness comes true strength whereas violence is not only wrong but defeats its own ends. There is no personal God and such gods as men imagine are mere emanations of *Tao* which gives life to all things. *Tao* is Being. Works are worthless and internal renunciation is far better than anything that follows from the use of force because passive resistance convinces the other from within that he is in error, whereas violence only compels the external appearance of conviction whilst inwardly the individual is as before. "It is wealth to be content; it is wilful to force one's way on others."

Later Lao-tze became a divinity and indeed one of a Trinity each worshipped in the form of idols (which the founder had hated). Soon there was worship of the forces of nature: the stars, the tides, the sun and moon, and a thousand other deities among whom Confucius was one. The purest mysticism and wisdom had been utterly corrupted by contact with the world.

Taoism is now reviving in China where its membership has tripled in the last 20 years.

Telepathy and Clairvoyance. Telepathy is the alleged communication between one mind and another other than through the ordinary sense channels. Clairvoyance is the supposed faculty of "seeing" objects or events which, by reason of space and time or other causes, are not discernible through the ordinary sense of vision. Such claims have been made from time immemorial but it was not until the 20th century that the phenomena were investigated scientifically. The first studies were undertaken by the Society for Psychical Research, which was founded in 1882 with Professor Henry Sidgwick as its first president.

It would be odd if some scientists were not interested in ESP because of the enormous weight of anecdotal evidence which has built up over centuries to support it. The weakness of the scientific as opposed to the casual evidence is however

exemplified by the failure of ESP researchers to produce a reliable "repeatable" experiment.

Terrorism. A form of political violence used against governments, groups or individuals with the purpose of creating a climate of fear in which the aims of the terrorists may be fulfilled. The term derives from the "Reign of Terror" in the French Revolution. In the 20th century it was closely associated with the violence of small political movements of both the extreme left and right, attempting to overthrow existing political institutions.

It has often been used as part of nationalist movements seeking to remove colonial governments, as in the expulsion of Britain from Kenya and France from Algeria. There is also what is known as "*state terrorism*", as practised by totalitarian regimes such as Hitler's Germany and Stalin's Soviet Union. The 'War on Terror' was launched by the United States following the al-Qaeda attack of 11 September 2001.

Theism. *See* **God and Man.**

Theosophy (Sanskrit *Brahma Vidya* = divine wisdom), a system of thought that draws on the mystical teachings of those who assert the spiritual nature of the universe, and the divine nature of man. It insists that man is capable of intuitive insight into the nature of God. The way to wisdom, or self-knowledge, is through the practice of **Yoga** (*q.v.*). Theosophy has close connections with Indian thought through Vedic, Buddhist, and Brahmanist literature. The modern Theosophical Society was founded by Mme H. P. Blavatsky and others in 1875, and popularised by Mrs. Annie Besant.

Third Way (New Labour). Social democratic political parties suffered successive defeats at the hands of neoliberal conservatives throughout the 1980s and 1990s. New Labour/Third Way politics attempted to apply and adapt traditional social democratic values to this hostile political landscape. Third Way politicians such as Bill Clinton and Tony Blair accepted the policies of privatisation, low taxes, and reduced welfare provision, and in many cases extended neoliberal policies to areas of public services untouched by Thatcher and Reagan. Whilst rejecting increased progressive taxation, Third Way/New Labour politicians attempted to promote social justice by spending the fruits of growing neoliberal economies on health, education, and anti-poverty measures.

This increase in public spending redistributed wealth in some areas of society, for example child poverty in the UK. Increasingly, Third Way/New Labour policies changed the role of the state from owner and direct provider, to regulator and enforcer of central government's targets.

Traditional social democrats argue that Third Way/New Labour politics ignores the value of equality in social justice, and neoliberal conservatives argue that Third Way/New Labour public spending is parasitic on their economic reforms and legacy of growth.

New Labour was finally buried in September 2015 when Jeremy Corbyn became Labour leader.

Toronto Blessing. *See* **Pentecostalism.**

Tory, a name given in 1680 by English Protestants to those who did not wish to exclude a Catholic heir from the succession to the throne of Charles II. It then remained the name of one of the two great political parties (*see* **Whigs**) until 1832, when the Tory Party restyled itself the Conservative Party. The term now denotes a supporter or member of the Conservative Party.

Totalitarianism. Totalitarian government is one which tolerates only one political party, to which all other institutions are subordinated, and which usually demands the complete subservience of the individual to the government. The Italian dictator Mussolini coined the term in the 1920s to describe the new fascist state of Italy, and the word has become synonymous with absolute single-party government, as in Nazi Germany or Soviet Russia.

Totalitarianism is distinguished from authoritarianism, dictatorship, and tyranny as it employs the tools of industrial modernity to enforce its control. It is therefore often regarded as a distinctly 20th century phenomenon, where technology allows authoritarian, dictatorial tyrannies to control and direct society to an unprecedented total extent.

Totemism. A totem is an animal, plant or object with which a social or religious group feels a special affinity and which is often considered to be the mythical ancestor of the group. The totem is worshipped or esteemed by members of the group or clan bearing its name. Totemism is the form of social organization consisting of such clans. Membership of the clan is inherited and life-long; but marriage is usually with a partner outside the totemic clan. Totem poles (as erected by North American Indians) are a way of representing the clan's guardian spirit. Totemism has been important in the religion and society of many less developed peoples.

Tractarianism, a Catholic revival movement, also known as the **Oxford Movement** (not to be confused with the so-called Oxford Group), which had its beginnings at Oxford in 1833. The leaders included the Oxford high churchmen E. B. Pusey, J. Keble and J. H. Newman.

Through the *Tracts for the Times* (1833–41), a series of pamphlets which were sent to every parsonage in England, they sought to expose the dangers which they considered to be threatening the church from secular authority. The immediate cause of the movement was the Reform Act (1832) which meant that the state was no longer in the safe keeping of Tories and Churchmen but that power was falling into the hands of Liberals and Dissenters. They advocated a higher degree of ceremonial in worship nearer the Roman communion. In *Tract 90* (the last) Newman showed how the Thirty-nine Articles themselves, which were regarded as the bulwark of Protestantism, could be made to square with Roman doctrine. It was obvious which direction the movement was taking and the romanizing tendency was widely resented. In 1845 Newman went over to Rome. He was beatified in 2010.

Pusey and Keble persisted in their efforts to secure recognition of Catholic liturgy and doctrine in the Anglican Church. Catholicism of the Anglican type (*i.e.*, Catholic in ritual, ceremony, and everything save submission to the Pope) is termed Anglo-Catholicism (*q.v.*).

Transcendental Meditation, popularised in the West by the Maharishi Mahesh Yogi, who achieved sensational worldwide publicity by his "conversion" of the Beatles. This is a simple meditational system which it is claimed is an aid to relaxation and the reduction of psychological and physical stress. It is a technique which can be taught in a relatively short, concentrated period of time, provided that someone trained by the Maharishi is the teacher. The pupil or would-be meditator is given a *mantra*—letting his thoughts flow freely while sitting in a comfortable position. Very many claims are made on behalf of the system. As with most cults, religious and occult systems, there is an initial psychological benefit to anyone who becomes deeply involved. Nevertheless, apart from this simple "participation-effect", there is some evidence that the body's autonomic functions (heart rate, respiratory cycle, brain waves, *etc.*) can be modified by certain individuals including yogis.

The movement in Britain is based at Mentmore Towers in Buckinghamshire. The movement recruits heavily on campuses in America, but has been the subject of many complaints by parents.

Transcendentalism. 1. A term used to refer to the transcendental idealism of Immanuel Kant (1724–1804). See **Mind and Matter**.

2. A movement established in the United States in the 1830s, much influenced by German idealism and Platonism, which included Ralph Waldo Emerson (1803–82) and Henry Thoreau (1817–62) among its main members. Transcendentalism's characteristic belief was in the supremacy of insight over logic and experience for the revelation of the deepest truths. It tended towards mysticism, pantheism and optimism about the progress of the spirit. Although the movement's followers believed that true reform must come from within the individual, they took part in contemporary reform movements.

Transcendentalism itself faded with the coming of the American Civil War, but it had a strong influence on the writings of Whitman, Emily Dickinson and Hawthorne.

Transubstantiation, the conversion in the Eucharist of the bread and wine into the body and blood of Christ—a doctrine of the Catholic Church.

Trinity. The Christian doctrine that God exists in three persons, all co-equal, and indivisible, of the same substance—God the Father, God the Son (who became incarnate as Jesus), begotten of the Father, and God the Holy Ghost, proceeding from Father and Son. The system denying the Trinity is Unitarianism (*q.v.*).

Trotskyism, a form of communism supporting the views of Leon Trotsky, the assumed name of Lev Bronstein (1879–1940) who, in 1924, was ousted from power by Stalin and later exiled and assassinated in Mexico. Trotsky held that excessive Russian nationalism was incompatible with genuine international communism and that Stalin was concentrating on the economic development of the Soviet Union to an extent which could only lead to a bureaucratic state with a purely nationalist outlook.

After the Hungarian uprising in 1956, which was ruthlessly suppressed by the Soviet Armed Forces, a wave of resignations from Western Communist parties took place, many of the dissidents joining the Trotskyist movement. Trotsky laid emphasis on the idea of 'permanent revolution' and his supporters formed the Fourth International.

Trotskyism in Britain was influenced by Tony Cliff's *State Capitalism in Russia* (1955) and the formation of the Socialist Workers' Party, and the Militant tendency. Both Militant and the SWP sought to agitate for revolution by influencing working class organisations and most notably, in the case of Militant, entering the Labour Party.

Trotskyite Militants developed a particular position of strength in Liverpool, and attempted to implement an ambitious programme of public expenditure whilst freezing income. It is argued that the strategy was to induce a crisis in traditional democratic institutions that Trotskyites believed oppressed workers, and to ferment revolutionary fervour in the midst of such chaos.

Today the Socialist Workers' Party remains the most active Trotskyist group in Britain, but its numerical support is very small. Also active is the Alliance for Workers' Liberty.

In the 2015 general election it fielded candidates standing as Trade Union and Socialist Coalition (TUSC).

U

Ufology. See **Flying Saucers.**

Uniates, a sometimes derogatory term for the Eastern Orthodox Churches which are in full communion with the Roman Catholic Church, recognise the authority of the Pope and in faith and doctrine are totally Catholic. However, they retain their traditional liturgies and separate canon law and permit their priests to marry.

Unification Church (Moonies). Better known to outsiders as the Moonies, the Unification Church is part of a larger organisation now known as the Family Federation for World Peace and Unification. Its founder was the Reverend Sun Myung Moon, who in 1936, at the age of 16, had a vision of Christ who told him to further God's Kingdom on Earth. Following intensive personal prayer and study, he began preaching in 1945. Following release from Communist imprisonment in North Korea, he founded the Unification Church in 1954.

The group continue to be anti-communist and have been linked to several right-wing politicians around the globe. They have significant business interests and own the *Washington Times* amongst other companies. Moon himself was prosecuted for tax evasion and was criticised for the scale of his personal fortune. The Church also has a charity wing, the International Relief Friendship Foundation and sponsors cultural enterprises.

In 1959, the Church expanded abroad, using young people to raise the profile, finances and recruitment by selling flowers and candles on the street. The Church was particularly accused of 'love-bombing' new recruits into full membership. Amongst its main tenets is the authority of Moon's own publication *Discourse on the Principle* or *Divine Principle* as equal to the Bible. One key principle is the understanding of the Fall in which Eve has sex with the fallen angel Lucifer and then with Adam in repentance. It is this abuse of love which caused mankind's separation from God. Jesus was sent to restore the ideal family, the Church's Trinity of God, Man and Woman, by having a family rather than in death and resurrection. His failure required the resending of the Messiah, Moon himself, to establish the perfect marriage, although he has had between two and four wives.

Despite these claims, the Church believes that neither Jesus nor Moon is God, but that they are prophets. Mass arranged marriages with partners selected by Moon have become the hallmark of the movement, although they are not legally binding. Sun Myung Moon himself died in 2012, aged 92.

Unitarianism has no special doctrines, although clearly, as the name indicates, belief is in the single personality of God, *i.e.*, anti-trinitarian. This general statement, however, can be interpreted with varying degrees of subtlety. Thus unitarian belief may range from a sort of Arianism which accepts that, although Christ was not of divine nature, divine powers had been delegated to him by the Father, to the simple belief that Christ was a man like anyone else, and his goodness was of the same nature as that of many other great and good men. Indeed, today many Unitarians deny belief in a personal God and interpret their religion in purely moral terms, putting their faith in the value of love and the brotherhood of man. The Toleration Act (1689) excluded Unitarians but from 1813 they were legally tolerated in England. Nevertheless attempts were made to turn them out of their chapels on the ground that the preachers did not hold the views of the original founders of the endowments. But this ended with the Dissenting Chapels Act of 1845. In America no such difficulties existed, and in the Boston of the 19th century many of the great literary figures were openly unitarian in both belief and name: *e.g.*, Emerson, Longfellow, Lowell.

United Reform Church. *See* **Presbyterianism.**

Universal Declaration of Human Rights. This landmark in the evolution of human rights was adopted in 1948 by the UN General Assembly in Paris. Among other things, it recognised the "inherent dignity" and "inalienable rights of all members of the human family". The Declaration built on the 'Four Freedoms' announced by Franklin D. Roosevelt in 1941 – freedom of speech and expression, of religion, from want and from fear.

Untouchables (Dalits), the lowest caste in Hindu society. There are over 200 million in India. They suffer persecution and are under pressure to revert to Hinduism if they have converted. *See* **Hinduism.**

Utilitarianism, a school of moral philosophy of which the main proponents were J. S. Mill (1806–73) and Jeremy Bentham (1748–1832). Bentham based his ethical theory upon the utilitarian principle that the greatest happiness of the greatest number is the criterion of morality. What is good is pleasure or happiness; what is bad is pain. If we act on this basis of self-interest (pursuing what we believe to be our own happiness), then what we do will automatically be for the general good. The serious failing of this thesis is (1) that it makes no distinction between the quality of one pleasure and another, and (2) that Bentham failed to see that the law might not be framed and administered by men as benevolent as himself. J. S. Mill accepted Bentham's position in general but seeing its failings emphasised (1) that self-interest was an inadequate basis for utilitarianism and suggested that we should take as the real criterion of good the social consequences of the act; (2) that some pleasures rank higher than others and held that those of the intellect are superior to those of the senses. Not only is the social factor emphasised, but emphasis is also placed on the nature of the act.

Utopias. The name 'utopia' is taken from two Greek words meaning 'nowhere' and was first used in 1516 by Sir Thomas More (1478–1535) as the title of his book referring to a mythical island in the south Pacific where he sited his ideal society. Since then it has been used of any ideal or fanciful society. More's *Utopia* and James Harrington's *The Commonwealth of Oceana* (1656) shared a similar concern with the causes of human misery, and presented their imaginary societies as ideals against which the iniquities of their contemporary realities were rendered vividly.

These early modern English utopias described societies where land and property were owned in common, thereby arguing strongly that private property creates conflict and a self-interested striving for advantage that undermines personal and civic virtue. In More's *Utopia* society was guided by the good of the community, and featured compulsory schooling, free health care, and equality between the sexes. Harrington's republican commonwealth allowed all citizens to share in governance through secret ballots, a written constitution, and a separation of powers between legislature and executive. These ideas compared starkly with the attitudes and institutions of their authors' day, and the genre of the utopia allowed for serious moral and political questions to be raised in fictional setting.

Saint-Simon. Claude Henri, Comte de Saint-Simon (1760–1825), writing in his *New Christianity* (1825), developed the previous utopian writers' commitment to a shared ownership of property. Saint-Simon opposed inheritance and promoted an ideal society where each worked for the public good and was rewarded according to merit. Saint-Simon's work is regarded as a foundation of French socialism, and marked the close relationship that utopian and socialist thought would develop throughout the 19th century.

Fourier and Owen. This relationship was further expressed in the work of François Fourier and Robert Owen. Fourier's utopia features people who are integrally good and co-operative. When organised into small productive units, called phalanxes, these idealised people could live without the need for central government. Their lives would be occupied with productive and necessary work, and although they would be allowed private property, this property would be widely dispersed through the sale of shares. Fourier's ideas found popularity with many social reformers in the USA, and were taken up by Thoreau, Hawthorne, and Emerson. An American Fourier colony known as Brook Farm was established and carried on for eight years.

Robert Owen (1771–1858) a wealthy textile manufacturer and philanthropist, established communities founded on a kind of utopian socialism in Lanarkshire, Hampshire, and in America. The workers in Lanark were given better housing and education for their children, and it was administered as a co-operative self-supporting community in Scotland. Whilst the social experiments of followers of Fourier and Owen may not have achieved lasting effect, they showed that not all utopias are entirely fanciful and imaginary.

More Recent Writings. Whilst utopian writing continued into the 20th century, notably in the genres of fantasy and science fiction, many authors have sought to explore imagined societies characterised by catastrophe and failure. George Orwell's *1984* (published in 1949) is an imagined dystopia where democracy and liberty have collapsed into unremitting totalitarianism.

Feminist authors have used dystopic writing to characterise the oppression of women, and Margaret Atwood's *The Handmaid's Tale* (1986) is an important work in this area.

V

Vaisakhi, the most important day in the Sikh calendar. It commemorates the beginning of Sikhism as a collective faith.

Vedanta. An ancient system of Indian thought. It is expressed in commentaries on the *Brahma Sutras.* A key figure is Shankara (788–820 A.D.) who founded what is known as Advaita Vedanta.

Vegans, *see under* **Vegetarianism.**

Vegetarianism, a way of life practised by those who abstain from meat. Strict vegetarians (Vegans) also excude all animal products (*e.g.* butter, eggs milk) from their diet as well as "hidden" animal products such as gelatin and rennet (an enzyme used to make cheese). Around 542,000 people in Britain class themselves as Vegans.

Vitalism, the philosophical doctrine that the behaviour of the living organism is, at least in part, due to a vital principle which cannot possibly be explained wholly in terms of physics and chemistry. This belief was held by the rationalist thinker C. E. M. Joad (1891–1953) and is implicit in Henri Bergson's (1859–1941) theory of creative evolution. It was maintained by Bergson that evolution, like the work of an artist, is creative and therefore unpredictable; that a vague need exists beforehand within the animal or plant before the means of satisfying the need develops. Thus we might assume that sightless animals developed the need to become aware of objects before they were in physical contact with them and that this ultimately led to the origins of organs of sight.

During the 20th century a form of vitalism described as "emergent evolution" was put forward. This theory maintains that when two or more simple entities come together there may arise a new property which none of them previously possessed. Today biologists would say that it is the *arrangement* of atoms that counts, different arrangements exhibiting different properties, and that biological organisation is an essentially dynamic affair.

W

Wahabis, members of an Arabian sect of Islam which originated in the teaching of Muhammad Ibn Abd-al-Wahab, born at the end of the 17th cent. He was deeply resentful of Ottoman rule which, in addition to its tyranny, had brought about innovations in the religion which Muhammad regarded as a perversion of its original form. He proceeded to reform Islam to its earliest conditions and impressed his beliefs on Sheikh Mohammed Ibn Saud.

Under the successors of Ibn Saud the power of the Wahabis spread over much of Arabia where it is dominant today in Saudi Arabia. Its particular characteristic is that it refuses to accept symbolic or mystical interpretations of the words of the Prophet and accepts quite literally the teaching of Islam. It is, in fact, a type of Muslim fundamentalism. Although crushed by the Ottomans in 1811–15, the movement remains an important element in Islam.

Partly in reaction to what it sees as the decadence of the West, and partly as a result of Saudi oil wealth, it now wields increasing influence.

Waldenses (Waldensians), a movement also known as "The Poor Men of Lyons," founded by Peter Waldo of that city about the same time, and in the same part of southern France, as the Albigenses (*q.v.*) with whom, however, they had nothing in common.

Their main belief was a return to Apostolic simplicity, based on reading the Bible in their own language; their doctrines were somewhat similar to those of the Mennonites and the Quakers. However, they did not wish to separate themselves from the Church and were originally protected by several Popes until the Lateran Council of 1215 excluded them mainly for the crime of preaching without ecclesiastical permission. From this time they were subjected to persecution, yet maintained some contact with the Church until the Reformation when they chose to take the side of the Protestants. Situated mainly on the sides of the Alps, half in Piedmont and half in France, they were persecuted or not according to the contemporary political convenience of the Dukes of Savoy, and the major attempt to destroy them called forth Oliver Cromwell's intervention and the famous sonnet of Milton. The sect survived, and still exists, having been granted full equality of rights with his Catholic subjects by Charles Edward of Piedmont in 1848.

Wandjina, the ancestral spirit beings of the Aboriginal people in Western Australia. They can be found depicted on cave walls and rock shelters.

Weathermen. Far left group whose aim was to overthrow the American political system. The group's name was borrowed from the lyrics of songwriter Bob Dylan. Its membership was drawn from the well-educated, and it committed specific and well-planned acts of violence.

Whig. In 1680, a term derisively applied to politicians who sought to exclude Roman Catholics from succession to the throne, it thereafter became the name of the political party opposed to the Tory (*q.v.*) party. At first dominated by the nobility, it represented those forces which hoped to limit the power of the monarch and to increase the power of Parliament. The Whigs (the governing party in 1868 under Gladstone) formed an element in the emerging Victorian Liberal Party.

Witchcraft, the exercise of supposedly supernatural powers for evil purposes (black magic). It has a history dating back to classical times (*e.g.* the en-

chantress Medea in Greek mythology). Accounts of witchcraft were widespread in the medieval period and Draconian opposition to its practices by the Church led to scores of witch trials, ruthless persecution and torture. Between 1400 and 1750 it is estimated over 100,000 people, the vast majority women, were prosecuted for witchcraft .

Many innocent people perished, especially after the promulgation of the bull *Summis desiderantes* by Pope Innocent VIII in 1484. In 1494 the *Malleus Maleficarum* (Hammer of Witches) codified the rules for detecting acts of witchcraft.

Today it is now known that the victims of the famous Salem witch trials in North America were suffering from ergot poisoning, which was mistaken for witchcraft. Three centuries later they have finally been exonerated. In the 1990s, the Catholic Church established a commission in the Czech Republic to review the notorious Sumperk witch trials of 1679 (when 100 people were burnt alive in Moravia). It is a sign of changing attitudes.

Few people realise how deeply the notion of witchcraft is implanted in our minds. For example, the Witchcraft Act was not finally repealed in Britain until the 1950s. In the Australian State of Victoria it was not legalised until 2005!

The last woman to be executed in Europe for witchcraft (the Swiss maid Anna Goeldi in 1782) was finally exonerated in 2008. The last conviction for witchcraft in England was in 1712. In 1736 the Witchcraft Act in England finally ended witch hunts and trials.

Today, *wicca* is the fastest-growing religious group in the United Kingdom. Witchcraft can still be found in parts of Africa and Asia (*e.g.* Tanzania and Assam). Doreen Valiente is hailed as the "mother of modern witchcraft".

Women's Liberation Movement. *See under* Feminism.

World Congress of Faiths, an inter-religious movement which aims to break down barriers between faiths. The first step was taken by the world's parliament of religions held in Chicago in 1893; similar gatherings were held subsequently at intervals in Europe; but the actual organisation was formed in 1936 by Sir Francis Younghusband; and now an annual conference is held.

World Council of Churches, a forum of Christian Churches from all over the world (including the Churches of the Protestant, Anglican, and Orthodox traditions, but excluding the Roman Catholic Church), engaged in extending Christian mission and unity throughout the world. This modern ecumenical movement stems from the great World Missionary Conference held at Edinburgh in 1910. The World Council was founded in 1948 and meets for consultation from time to time.

World Federalism, the extension of the principle of federalism (already an established political system in such countries as Canada, Germany, Switzerland and the USA) to a world, international order, to prevent wars and to tackle *global* issues on a *global* basis. The Association of World Federalists campaigns for this objective.

Y

Yazidis, members of an ancient and secretive faith, a synthesis of Zoroastrianism and Christianity. Found in Iraq, Syria, Georgia and America they have been persecuted by militant Islamists. Back in 1892 they were slaughtered by the forces of the Ottoman Empire.

Yin and Yang, the two basic forces in ancient Chinese thought. Yang is associated with masculinity, heat, light, creation *etc.*, yin with femininity, coldness, dark, passivity *etc. See also* **Confucianism, Taoism.**

Yoga, a Hindu discipline which teaches a technique for freeing the mind from attachment to the senses, so that once freed the soul may become fused with the universal spirit (*atman* or Brahman), which is its natural goal. This is the sole function of the psychological and physical exercises which the Yogi undertakes, although few ever reach the final stage of *Samadhi* or union with Brahman which is said to take place in eight levels of attainment. These are: (1) *Yama*, which involves the extinction of desire and egotism and their replacement by charity and unselfishness; (2) *Niyama*, during which certain rules of conduct must be adopted, such as cleanliness, the pursuit of devotional studies, and the carrying out of rituals of purification; (3) *Asana*, or the attainment of correct posture and the reduction to a minimum of all bodily movement (the usual posture of the concentrating Yogi is the "lotus position" familiar from pictures); (4) *Pranayama*, the tight control of the life-force or breath in which there are two stages at which the practitioner hopes to arrive, the first being complete absorption in the act of breathing which empties the mind of any other thought, the second being the ability almost to cease to breathe which allegedly enables him to achieve marvellous feats of endurance; (5) *Pratyahara* or abstraction which means the mind's complete withdrawal from the world of sense; (6) *Dharana* in which an attempt is made to think of one thing only which finally becomes a repetition of the sacred syllable OM; (7) *dhyana*, meditation, which finally leads to (8) *Samadhi* the trance state which is a sign of the complete unity of soul with reality.

Yoga is very old, and when the sage Patanjali (*c.* 300 B.C.) composed the book containing these instructions, the *Yoga Sutras*, he was probably collecting from many ancient traditions perhaps dating back to *c.*2,500 B.C. Some of the claims made by Yogis seem, to the Western mind, frankly incredible; but in the West Yoga methods have been used at the lower levels in order to gain improved self-control, better posture, and improved health.

Yom Kippur, the Day of Atonement, the final day of repentance begun at Rosh Hashanah, and the holiest day in the Jewish calendar. It is referred to as the Sabbath of Sabbaths and is typified by twenty-five hours of fasting. Prior to this is a feast with festival candles. Each individual must attempt to confess not only their sins to God, but ask forgiveness from others on the eve of Yom Kippur.

An important part of the *teshuvah* or repentance is the general confession in the synagogue. Readings will tell of the ancient atonement involving a scapegoat in Leviticus; Deuteronomy 30, and the prophetic book of Jonah. The message of all is God's infinite capacity to forgive even those who are undeserving. The last service of the day will end with the opening of the Shema, 'Hear O Israel, the Lord is our God. The Lord is One', and the triumphant cry of Elijah, 'The Lord, He is God'. The last act will be the blowing of the *shofar* to bring the fast to a close.

Z

Zen Buddhism, a Buddhist sect which is believed to have arisen in 6th century. China but has flourished chiefly in Japan. The sect places absolute faith in a person's own inner being. Apparently the intention is that, so far from indulging in inward meditations or such practices as the Yogi uses, the student must learn to act spontaneously, without thinking, and without self-consciousness or hesitation.

This is the main purpose of the *koan*, the logically insoluble riddle which the pupil must try to solve. One such is the question put by master to pupil: "A girl is walking down the street, is she the younger or the older sister?" The correct answer, it seems, is to say nothing but put on a mincing gait, to *become* the girl, thus showing that what matters is the experience of being and not its verbal description. Another *koan*: "What is the Buddha?" "Three pounds of flax" is attributed to T'ungshan in the 9th cent. and a later authority's comment is that "none can excel it as regards its irrationality which cuts off all passages to speculation." Zen, in effect, teaches the uselessness of trying to use words to discuss the Absolute.

Zen came to Japan in the 13th cent., more than five centuries after Confucianism or the orthodox forms of Buddhism, and immediately gained acceptance whilst becoming typically Japanese in the process. One of the reasons why it appealed must have been that its spontaneity and insistence on action without thought, its emphasis on the uselessness of mere words, and such categories as logical opposites, had an inevitable attraction for a people given to seriousness, formality, and logic to a degree which was almost stifling. Therefore Zen began to impregnate every aspect of life in Japan, and one of the results of its emphasis on spontaneous action rather than reason was its acceptance by the Samurai, the ferocious warrior class, in such activities as swordsmanship, archery. Japanese wrestling, and later Judo and the Kamikaze dive-bombers. But much of Japanese art, especially landscape gardening and flower-arrangement, was influenced similarly, and Zen is even used in Japanese psychiatry.

The very strict life of the Zen monks is based largely on doing things, learning through experience; the periods of meditation in the Zendo hall are punctuated by sharp slaps on the face administered by the abbot to those who are unsatisfactory pupils. Maybe it is its appearance of nihilism and its appeal to the irrational and spontaneous which attracts the Western world at a time when to many the world seems without meaning and life over-regimented. The three main schools of Zen Buddhism are Soto, Rinzai and Obaku.

However, it has influenced such various aspects of Western life as philosophy (Heidegger), psychiatry (Erich Fromm and Hubert Benoit), writing (Aldous Huxley), and painting (*Die Zen Gruppe* in Germany).

Zionism, a belief in the need to establish an autonomous Jewish home in Palestine which, in its modern form, began with Theodor Herzl (1860–1904), a Hungarian journalist working in Vienna. Although Herzl was a more or less assimilated Jew, he was forced by the Dreyfus case and the pogroms in Eastern Europe to conclude that there was no real safety for the Jewish people until they had their own state.

The Jews, of course, had always in a religious sense thought of Palestine as a spiritual homeland and prayed "next year in Jerusalem," but the religious had thought of this in a philosophical way as affirming old loyalties, not as recommending the formation of an actual state. Thus Herzl was opposed both by many of the religious Jews, and, at the other extreme, by those who felt themselves to be assimilated and in many cases without religious faith.

Even after the Balfour Declaration of 1917, there was not a considerable flow of Jews to Palestine, which at that time was populated mainly by Arabs. But the persecutions of Hitler changed all this and, after bitter struggles, the Jewish state was proclaimed in 1948. Today Zionism is supported by the vast majority of the Jewish communities everywhere. In the 1990s, a major exodus of Jews from Russia to Israel (made possible by the demise of the Soviet Union) introduced a new phase in the history of Zionism.

Zoroastrianism was at one time one of the great world religions. Under the Achaemenidae (*c.* 550–330 B.C.) Zoroastrianism was the state religion of Persia. Alexander's conquest in 331 B.C. brought disruption but the religion flourished again under the Sassanian dynasty (A.D. *c.* 226–640). With the advance of the Muslim Arabs in the 7th cent. Zoroastrianism finally gave way to Islam. A number of devotees fled to India there to become the Parsees (literally meaning "Persians in India"). In Iran itself a few scattered societies remain, perhaps numbering around 30,000 followers. Globally, there are *c.* 145,000 adherents.

The name Zoroaster is the Greek rendering of Zarathustra, the prophet who came to purify the ancient religion of Persia. It is thought that he lived at the beginning of the 6th cent. B.C. He never claimed for himself divine powers but was given them by his followers.

The basis of Zoroastrianism is the age-long war between good and evil, Ahura Mazda heading the good spirits and Ahriman the evil ones. Morality is very important since by doing right the worshipper is supporting Ahura Mazda against Ahriman, and the evil-doers will be punished in the last days when Ahura Mazda wins his inevitable victory.

The sacred book of this religion is the *Avesta*. If Zoroastrianism has little authority today, it had a very considerable influence in the past. Its doctrines penetrated into Judaism (*q.v.*) and, through Gnosticism, Christianity. The worship of Mithra by the Romans was an impure version of Zoroastrianism. Manichaeism (*q.v.*) was a Zoroastrian heresy and the Albigensianism of mediaeval times was the last relic of a belief which had impressed itself deeply in the minds of men.

The best known practice of the faith is probably sky burial.

GAZETTEER OF THE BRITISH ISLES

This concise gazetteer of the British Isles includes not only towns and cities but also a variety of natural features, from lakes and mountains to forests and rivers. Also included are many smaller places with special literary, musical, artistic or military links as well as those associated with our industrial heritage.

GAZETTEER OF THE BRITISH ISLES

ABBREVIATIONS USED IN THE GAZETTEER

a. = area
admin. = administrative
agr. = agriculture
alt. = altitude
anc. = ancient
arch. = archaeological
a.s.l. = above sea-level
ass. = associated
auth. = authority
bdr. = border
bdy. = boundary
bldg. = building
bor. = borough
C. = cape
c. = city; circa, *c.* = about
can. = canton
cap. = capital
cas. = castle
cath. = cathedral
C.B. = county borough
ch. = chief
cm = centimetres
co. = county
col. = colony
colly. = colliery
comm. = commercial
conurb. = conurbation
cst. = coast
ctr. = centre
cty. = country
dep. = department
dist. = district
div. = division
E. = east or easterly
elec. = electrical
engin. = engineering
esp. = especially
exp. = exports

F. = firth
fed. = federal
fish. pt. = fishing port
fortfd. = fortified
gen. = general
G.N.P. = gross national
    product
gr. = great, group
gtr. = greater
ha = hectares
hgst. = highest
I. = island
impt. = important
inc. = including
indep. = independent
inds. = industries
industl. = industrial
Is. = Islands
km = kilometres
km² = square kilometres
L. = lake
l. = length
l. gov. = local government
lge. = large
lgst. = largest
lt. = light
m = metres
machin. = machinery
M.B. = metropolitan borough
met. a. = metropolitan area
met. co. = metropolitan
    county
mftg. = manufacturing
mkg. = making
mkt. = market
mm = millimetres
mnfs. = manufactures
mng. = mining

mtn. = mountain
mun. = municipality
N. = north or northerly
nat. = national
non-met. co = non-metropolitan
    county
nr. = near
p. = population
par. = parish
penin. = peninsula
pref. = prefecture
prin. = principal
prod. = product
prot. = protectorate
prov. = province
pt. = port
R. = river
residtl. = residential
rly. = railway
S. = south or southerly
shipbldg. = shipbuilding
sm. = small
spt. = seaport
st. = state
sta. = station
sub. = suburb
t. = town
terr. = territory
tr. = trade
trib. = tributary
U.D. = urban district
unit. = unitary
univ. = university
v. = village
W. = west or westerly
wkg. = working
wks. = works
wkshps. = workshops

NOTES FOR USERS OF THE GAZETTEER

Industries.

In many countries (not least Britain) old industries have gradually faded away. Because the gazetteer aims to be in part a historical guide, mention of these industries has been retained (even though the factories may have closed).

Population Figures.

Total population figures from a census count are no longer regarded as necessarily more accurate than estimates arrived at by other methods. The usefulness of censuses lies rather in the additional information which they provide. Even so, some countries like the Netherlands have given up censuses altogether.

The gazetteer therefore no longer distinguishes between census figures and estimates but includes reliable figures from whatever source. For smaller towns, population figures below 20,000 are not always given here.

New Cities.

To celebrate the Millennium, three places were granted city status. These were Inverness, Wolverhampton and Brighton & Hove. Five more cities were created to mark the 2002 Golden Jubilee. These were Preston, Newport (in Gwent), Stirling and, in Northern Ireland, Lisburn and Newry. In the previous 40 years, the only cities to be created were Swansea (1969), Derby (1977), Sunderland (1992) and, in 1994, Armagh and St. Davids. For the 2012 Diamond Jubilee, three new cities were named: Chelmsford, Perth and St Asaph.

Census 2011.

The last census took place on 27 March 2011. The results showed a fast-growing population, especially in cities such as Manchester, Leicester and parts of London (*e.g.* Newham, Tower Hamlets). Britain's population also has increasing numbers of over-65s.

'The total population of England and Wales on Census day was 56·1 million. One in six (9·2 million) were aged 65 or over.' Those over 90 had risen from 336,000 to 429,000. Over half the population were women. The next decennial census is due in 2021. It is likely to be the last survey in its present form.

Local Government Reorganisation 1996.

The eight counties of Wales were replaced on 1 April 1996 by 22 unitary authorities and the 12 regions of Scotland by 32 unitary authorities. Thirteen English unitary authorities were also created on that date, with a further 13 being created on 1 April 1997.

Local Government Reorganisation 2009.

On 1 April 2009, extensive reorganisation took place in the old counties of Cornwall, Durham, Northumberland, Shropshire and Wiltshire. In each of these 5 counties a single "super-size" unitary authority replaced the old local government structure. In Bedfordshire and Cheshire, the old structure was replaced by two new unitary authorities in each county. In all 44 old authorities were replaced by 9 new bodies.

A

Abbots Langley, v., Herts., **Eng.**; birthplace of Nicholas Breakspeare (Pope Adrian IV).

Abercarn, t., Caerphilly, **Wales**; tinplate, knitting pins; former colliery t.; p. 15,100.

Aberdare, t., Rhondda, Cynon, Taff, **Wales**; on R. Cynon: wire cables; former coal-mng.; p. 29,040.

Aberdeen, royal burgh, unit.auth. created in 1996, formerly part of Grampian, E. **Scot.**; between mouths of Rs. Dee and Don; impt. fishing pt.; established itself as centre of rapidly growing N. Sea oil ind.; "granite-city"— much granite used in central bldgs.; univs., cath.; p. (2011) 223,000 (unit.auth.).

Aberdeenshire, E. **Scot.**, unit.auth. created in 1996, incorporating historic co. which became part of Grampian in 1974; bordered N. and E. by N. Sea; inc. cstl. ts. of Fraserburgh, Peterhead and Stonehaven; p. (2010) 243,500.

Aberfeldy, burgh, Perth and Kinross, **Scot.**; in Strath Tay, 6 km below Loch Tay; mkt.; salmon and trout fishing resort; p. 1,900.

Abergavenny, sm. t., Monmouthshire, **Wales**; on R. Usk; scene of massacre of Welsh chiefs; light engin.; cas.; p. 26,000.

Aberlour, Charlestown of, burgh, Moray, **Scot.**; on R. Spey, 19 km S. of Elgin; p. 790.

Abernethy, burgh, Perth and Kinross, **Scot.**; on R. Tay, once cap. of Pictish Kings; p. (2002) 945.

Abertillery, sm. t., Blaenau Gwent, **Wales**; formerly collieries, tinplate.

Aberystwyth, t., Ceredigion, **Wales**; on Cardigan Bay at mouth of R. Ystwyth, resort; cas., univ.; Nat. Library of Wales; p. (2006) 12,700. Its pier was the first to be built in Wales.

Abingdon, Vale of White Horse, Oxon., **Eng.**; mkt. t. on R. Thames; leather gds.; mediaeval and Georgian bldgs.; p. 37,250.

Abinger Hammer, v., Surrey, **Eng.**; former centre of Weald iron industry.

Aboyne and Glentanner, par., Aberdeenshire, **Scot.**; on R. Dee nr. Ballater; Highland games; p. 2,250.

Abram, t., Gtr. Manchester, **Eng.**; engin.; p. 12,500.

Accrington, t., Hyndburn, Lancs., **Eng.**; 32 km N. of Manchester; former cotton ctr.; textile machin., more diversified new inds.; p. 36,000.

Acton. *See* Ealing.

Adlington, t., Lancs., **Eng.**; nr. Chorley; former cotton spinning t.

Adwick le Street, t., South Yorks, **Eng.**; coal; home of George Washington's family; p. (2011) 11,000.

Ailsa Craig, rocky I., S. Ayrshire, **Scot.**; alt. 340 m; gannetry; puffins returned to breed after 50 years (2002). Granite in demand for curling.

Airdrie, burgh, N. Lanarkshire, **Scot.**; 19 km E. of Glasgow; iron inds., brick and concrete wks., steel tubes, pharmaceutics; p. 36,900.

Aire, R., West Yorks., **Eng.**; trib. of Ouse; major valley for power production; length 112 km.

Aldeburgh, spt., Suffolk Coastal, Suffolk, **Eng.**; famous for annual music festival; p. 3,100.

Aldermaston, Berkshire, **Eng.**; atomic weapons research ctr.

Alderney, I., dependency of **Guernsey**; horticulture, tourism; a. 794 ha; p. 2,900.

Aldershot, t., Rushmoor, Hants., **Eng.**; bricks; lge. military camp; p.59,950.

Aldridge, t., West Midlands, **Eng.**; plastics, packing cases; expanded t.

Alfreton, t., Amber Valley, Derbys., **Eng.**; mkt. t.; formerly coal mng.; hosiery, knitwear; p. 23,000.

Allen, Bog of, R.o.I.; peat bogs, peat cutting, cultivation; a. 958 km².

Allerdale, l. gov. dist., Cumbria, **Eng.**; cstl. dist. inc. Workington, Maryport, Cockermouth and Keswick; p. (2011) 96,400.

Alloa, sm. burgh, Clackmannan, **Scot.**; on N. bank of R. Forth; tiles, glass, distilling; p. 19,000.

Alnwick, t., former l. gov. dist., Northumberland, **Eng.**; cas.; mkt. t.; p. (2001) 31,029 (dist.), (2001) 7,700 (t.). The castle is known as "the Windsor of the North". Since 2009 part of new unit. auth.

Alrewas, Staffs, home of the National Memorial Arboretum.

Althorp, (Northants), seat of Earl Spencer; burial place of Princess Diana (1997).

Altrincham, mkt. t., Trafford, Gtr. Manchester, **Eng.**; engin.; residtl.; p. 41,000.

Alva, burgh, Clackmannan, **Scot.**; at S. foot of Ochil Hills, 5 km N. of Alloa; woollens, printing, fruit and fish canning; p. 5,250.

Ambleside, tourist ctr., Cumbria, **Eng.**; N. of L. Windermere.

Amersham, t., Bucks., **Eng.**; radio isotopes; lt. inds., 17th cent. mkt. hall; p. 22,500.

Amesbury, site in Wiltshire, the home of Stonehenge.

Amlwch, t., Isle of Anglesey, **Wales**; N. cst. resort; pt.; oil terminal.

Ampthill, Mid Beds., **Eng**; mkt. t.; p. 7,000.

Andover, mkt. t., Test Valley, Hants., **Eng.**; prehistoric earthwks.; expanded t.; p. 39,000.

Anglesey. *See* Isle of Anglesey.

Angus, E.**Scot.**, unit.auth. created in 1996, reinstating most of historic co. which became part of Tayside in 1974; bordered E. by N. Sea; inc. ts. of Arbroath, Forfar and Montrose; p. (2010) 110,300.

Annan, royal burgh, Dumfries and Galloway, **Scot.**; on R. Annan, 3 km from its mouth in Solway F.; Chapelcross reactor sta.; p. 8,500.

Antrim, former co.; l. gov. dist., **N. Ireland**; fertile lowland a., arable agr.; borders L. Neagh in S.W. and A. mtns. in N.E.; p. (2010) 54,100. *See* D11.

Antrim, mkt. t., **N. Ireland**; on Lough Neagh; linen, nylon; p. 21,000.

Appleby, sm.mkt.t., Cumbria. Famous annual horse fair since 18th cent.

Aran Is.; Galway, **R.o.I.**; inc. anc. religious ctr. and l. of Inishmore; fishing; agr.; a. 47 km².

Arbroath, royal burgh, Angus, **Scot.**; engin., textiles, fishing pt.; holiday resort; p. 23,200.

Ardglass, sm. t., Down, **N. Ireland**; one of N.I.'s impt. fishing pts.

Ardnacrusha, Clare, **R.o.I.**; power sta. on R. Shannon, 5 km N. of Limerick; p. 600.

Ardrishaig, sm. spt., Argyll and Bute, **Scot.**; on Loch Gilp, at entrance to Crinan Canal; p. 1,320.

Ardrossan, burgh, N. Ayrshire, S.W. **Scot.**; resort and spt. on Firth of Clyde; oil storage, ship-bldg., road bitumen, engin.; p. 11,100.

Ards, l. gov. dist., **N. Ireland**; formerly part of Down; N. of Strangford L.; main t. Newtownards; p. (2010) 78,250. *See* D11.

Argyll and Bute, W. **Scot.**; unit.auth. created in 1996, incorporating most of historic co. of **Argyllshire** which became part of Strathclyde in 1974; rural a. N.W. of Glasgow conurb.; p. (2010) 90,100.

Arklow, sm. t., spt., Wicklow, **R.o.I.**; fisheries, pottery; fertiliser plant; resort.

Armadale, burgh, W. Lothian, **Scot.**; 16 km S.W. Linlithgow; p. 9,000.

Armagh, former co.; l. gov. dist., **N. Ireland**; lowland in N. rising to over 450 m adjoins **R.o.I.** border; mainly rural; p. 58,950. *See* D11.

Armagh, co., **N.Ireland**; caths.; linen, whiskey; p. 15,000.

Arran, I., N. Ayrshire, **Scot.**; in Firth of Clyde; contains many summer resorts; a. 4,500. The sea around designated Marine Protection Area (2014)

Arthur's Seat, famous hill, Edinburgh, **Scot.**; 251 m.

Arun, l. gov. dist., West Sussex, **Eng.**; W. section of S. Downs and ts. of Arundel, Littlehampton and Bognor Regis; p. (2010) 147,000.

Arundel, t., Arun, West Sussex, **Eng.**; mkt. t. on Arun R.; Arundel Castle, seat of Duke of Norfolk; p. 3,600.

Ascot, v., Berks., **Eng.**; racecourse at Ascot Heath.

Ashbourne, mkt. t., Derbys. Dales, **Eng.**; nr. Dovedale; quarrying, milk processing; antiques p. 7,000.

Ashburton, t., Teignbridge, Devon, **Eng.**; old mkt. t., S. gateway to Dartmoor; anc. stannary t.

Ashby-de-la-Zouch, t., North West Leics., **Eng.**; hosiery; p. (2011) 11,500.

Ashdown Forest, East Sussex, **Eng.**; heath and woodland; site of former iron industry.

Ashfield, l. gov. dist., Notts., **Eng.**; comprises Sutton-in-Ashfield, Hucknall and Kirkby-in-Ashfield; p. (2010) 116,500.

Ashford, t., l. gov. dist., Kent, **Eng.**; mkt. t., rly. works, site of international station at northern end of channel tunnel; high-speed rly. link to London; p. (2010) 114,000. (dist.).

Ashington, t., Wansbeck, Northumberland, **Eng.**; coal mng., p. 27,750.

Ashton-in-Makerfield, t. Gtr. Manchester, **Eng.**; nr. Wigan; former coal mng.; p. 29,500.

Ashton-under-Lyne, t., Tameside, Gtr. Manchester, **Eng.**; textiles, lt. engin., tobacco; p. 44,000.

Aspull, t., Gtr. Manchester, **Eng.**; nr. Wigan; former coal mng.

Athelney, hill, formerly encircled by marsh nr. Taunton, Somerset, **Eng.**; between the Rs. Tone and Parret; King Alfred's hiding-place.

Atherstone, t., North Warwicks., **Eng.**; N. of Coventry; mkt. t., footwear, granite quarrying; p. 11,900.

Athlone, t., Westmeath, **R.o.I.**; on R. Shannon; radio sta.; textiles; p. 15,500.

Atholl, dist., N. Perth and Kinross, **Scot.**; extensive deer forests and grouse moors.

Auchterarder, burgh, Perth and Kinross, **Scot.**; 24 km S.W. of Perth; health resort on S. slopes of Vale of Strathearn; woollen inds.; p. (2011) 4,000.

Auchtermuchty, burgh, Fife, **Scot.**; at S. foot of Lomond Hills, 14 km N.E. of Alloa; distilling (now closed down); p. 2,050.

Audenshaw, t., Gtr. Manchester, **Eng.**; metals, leather, pharmaceuticals.

Aughrim, v., Galway, **R.o.I.**; battle (1691) between William III and James II.

Avebury, v., Wilts,. **Eng.**; mediaeval v. outside Neolithic circle and avenues, nr. Silbury Hill; lgst. prehistoric structure in England.

Aviemore, t., Highland, **Scot.**; on R. Spey, 19 km S.W. of Grantown; winter sports; p. 2,450.

Avon, R., Wiltshire/Bath and N.E. Somerset/ Bristol, **Eng.**; flows from Cotswolds to enter Bristol Channel at Avonmouth; spectacular lime-stone gorge between Bristol and the sea; length 128 km.

Avon, R., Warwicks., **Eng.**; flows past Stratford-on-A., to reach Severn R. at Tewkesbury; fertile agr. valley; string of ts. along course; length 152 km.

Avon, R., Wilts./Hants./Dorset, **Eng.**; flows past Salisbury into English Channel at Christchurch; length 112 km.

Avonmouth, outport of Bristol, at mouth of R. Avon, **Eng.**; docks; seed crushing, petrol refinery, non-ferrous metal and chemical plants.

Awe, Loch, Argyll and Bute, **Scot.**; 13 km W. of Inveraray, bordered by Ben Cruachan; length 40 km; salmon and trout fishing; hydroelec. sta. at Cruachan.

Axholme, Isle of, flat lowland a., N. Lincs., **Eng.**; W. of Trent R.; drained by Vermuyden in 17th cent.

Aylesbury, co. t., Aylesbury Vale, Bucks., **Eng.**; mkt. t.; expanded t.; p. 71,000.

Aylesbury Vale, l. gov. dist., Bucks., **Eng.**; a. in N.W. of co. inc. Aylesbury and Buckingham; p. (2010) 175,000.

Aylesford, mkt. t., Kent, **Eng.**; N.W. Maidstone; p. 25,000.

Ayr, royal burgh, S. Ayrshire, **Scot.**; pt. on F. of Clyde, 48 km S.W. of Glasgow; Burns born nearby; race course (venue for Scottish Grand National); p. 47,500.

Ayrshire, historic co., W. **Scot.**; now divided into E., N., and S. Ayrshire.

Aysgarth, v. Richmondshire, North Yorks., **Eng.**; on R. Ure in Wensleydale; famous for its waterfalls.

B

Bacton, v., Norfolk, **Eng.**; terminal for S. gasfields in N. Sea.

Bacup, t., Rossendale, S.E. Lancs., **Eng.**; 32 km N. of Manchester; textiles, felts, footwear; p. 14,000.

Bagshot, t., Surrey Heath, Surrey, **Eng.**; heath of same name; historically old postal town, 42 km S.W. of London; residtl.; p. 5,900.

Baildon, sm. t., West Yorks., **Eng.**; nr. Bradford; moorland resort.

Bakewell, t., Derbys Dales. **Eng.**; tourist ctr. Peak District; agr., mng.; p. 4,000. Home of the Bakewell tart.

Bala, sm. t., Gwynedd, N. **Wales**; mkt. town; tourism.

Bala, L., Gwynedd, N. **Wales**; drained by the Dee.

Balbriggan, spt., Dublin, **R.o.I.**; p. 7,650.

Balcombe, v. West Sussex, **Eng.** Scene of anti-fracking protests, 2013.

Baldock, sm. t., North Herts., **Eng.**; on N. edge of Chiltern Hills and Gr. N. Road; hosiery, malting, lt. engin.

Ballachulish, v., Highland, **Scot.**; on S. shore of Loch Leven, N.E. of Oban; tourism; ferry across Loch Linnhe, new road bridge; p. 620.

Ballina, t., spt., Mayo, **R.o.I.**; salmon fishing.

Ballinasloe, sm. t., Galway and Roscommon, **R.o.I.**; agr. ctr.; cattle mkt.; terminus of Grand Canal.

Ballybunion, sm. resort, Kerry, **R.o.I.**; at mouth of R. Shannon.

Ballycastle, spt., mkt. t., Moyle, **N. Ireland**; abbey and cas. ruins; seaside resort.

Ballyclare, sm. t., Newtownabbey, **N. Ireland**; paper, linen, dyeing, asbestos-cement prod.

Ballymena, mkt. t., l. gov. dist., **N. Ireland**; on R. Braid; linen and dyeing; major tyre factory (now closed); p. 28,000 (t.) *See* D11.

Ballymoney, mkt. t., l. gov. dist., **N. Ireland**; 64 km N.W. of Belfast; linen; p. (2010) 30,500 (dist.). *See* D11.

Ballyshannon, sm. spt., Donegal, **R.o.I.**; at mouth of R. Erne; salmon fishery; resort; hydro-electric power plant.

Balmoral Cas., Aberdeenshire, **Scot.**; royal residence, on R. Dee, 13 km W. of Ballater.

Bamburgh, t., Northumberland, **Eng.**; former cap. of Bernicia and Northumbria; cas.; birthplace of Grace Darling.

Banagher, v., Offaly, **R.o.I.**; impt. crossing of R. Shannon.

Banbridge, t., l. gov. dist., **N. Ireland**; on Bann R.; linen; p. (2010) 47,500 (dist.). *See* D11.

Banbury, mkt. t., Cherwell, Oxford, **Eng.**; 128 km from London; aluminium ind., furniture, printing, ladies' wear; expanded t.; old livestock market closed (1998); p. 44,500.

Banchory, burgh, Aberdeenshire, **Scot.**; on R. Dee, 27 km S.W. of Aberdeen; p. (2002) 6,034.

Banff, royal burgh, Aberdeenshire, **Scot.**; on Moray F. at mouth of R. Deveron; fisheries; tourism; p. 4,100.

Banffshire, historic co., E. **Scot.** now divided between Aberdeenshire and Moray.

Bangor, sm. t., North Down, **N. Ireland**; spt. on S. shore of Belfast Lough, 16 km N.E. of Belfast; lt. inds.; carpets, hosiery; seaside resort.

Bangor, t., Gwynedd, **Wales**; pt. on S. shore of Menai Strait; cath., univ.; lt. engin.; tourist ctr.; p. 13,900.

Bann, Upper and Lower R., **N. Ireland**; rises in Mtns. of Mourne, and flows through Lough Neagh to Atlantic nr. Coleraine; length 144 km.

Bannockburn, moor, t. nr. Stirling, **Scot.**; Bruce's victory over Edward II on 23–24 June, 1314 established Scotland's independence; p. 7,650.

Banstead, Surrey, **Eng.**; dormitory t.; l. gov. dist. with Reigate; p. (2011) 39,000 (t.) (with Tadworth).

Bantry Bay, Cork, **R.o.I.**; Atlantic inlet; natural harbour utilised mainly by oil-storage depot.

Barbican, dist., City of London, **Eng.**; inc. major housing scheme to attract p. back into c.; cultural amenities.

Barking and Dagenham, outer bor., E. London, **Eng.**; on Rs. Roding and Thames; diversified inds. inc. huge Ford motor wks.; p. (2011) 185,900. Major housing development planned at Barking Riverside.

Barmouth, t., Gwynedd, **Wales**; pt. on Cardigan Bay; chemicals; resort; p. 2,600.

Barnard Castle, Teesdale, Durham, **Eng.**; mkt. t.; woollens, penicillin; cas.; p. 6,600.

Barnet, former U.D., Herts., **Eng.**; now outer bor., Greater London; comprising Finchley, Hendon, Barnet, East Barnet and Friern Barnet; p. (2011) 356,400.

Barnsley, t., met. dist., South Yorks., **Eng.**; machin., plastics; carpets; tourism centred on old industrial heritage; p. (2010) 226,200 (dist.).

Barnstaple, North Devon, **Eng.**; mkt. t., pt. on R. Taw; seaside resort; p. 28,000.

Barra Is., Outer Hebrides, Western Isles, **Scot.**; light-house on Barra Head. Landing strip on beach (since 1936); tourism, p. 1,000.

Barrow-in-Furness, spt., l. gov. dist., Cumbria, **Eng.**; iron and steel ind.; shipbldg., submarines; p. (2011) 69,100 (dist.).

Barry, t., Vale of Glamorgan, **Wales**; rapid growth in 19th cent. as outport of Cardiff; modern light inds., replacing coal and tinplate inds.; p. (2011) 52,000.

Barton-on-Humber, mkt. t., N. Lincs., **Eng.**; anc. bldg. pt.; S. site of Humber Bridge; p. 9,750.

Basildon, t., l. gov. dist., Essex, **Eng.**; new t. 1949; light inds.; old town (Upper Basildon) on the lower R. Thames; p. (2010) 173,000 (dist.), (2010) 101,000. (t.).

Basingstoke, t., part of l. gov. dist. of **Basingstoke and Deane**, N. Hants., **Eng.**; 80 km W. of London; expanded t.; light inds.; p. (2010) 162,000 (dist.).

Bassenthwaite, L., L. Dist., Cumbria, **Eng.**; most N. of lge. Ls.; drained to Solway Firth by R. Derwent; length 6 km, width 1·6 km.

Bassetlaw, l. gov. dist., N. Notts., **Eng.**; based on Worksop and East Retford; p. (2010) 112,000.

Bath, c., Bath and N.E. Somerset, **Eng.**; Roman baths, hot springs, medicinal waters; fine Regency architecture; univs.; elec. engin. p.86,000. Now a World Heritage Site.

Bath and North East Somerset, unit.auth. created in 1996, formerly part of Avon, **Eng.**; bordered by Mendips in S.; p. (2010) 181,000.

Bathgate, burgh, W. Lothian, **Scot.**; coal mng.; automobile ind.; p. 15,500.

Batley, t. West Yorks., **Eng.**; heavy woollens, shoddy; p. 50,500.

Battersea, dist., London, **Eng.**; S. of R. Thames; famous park; lge. power sta., Europe's largest brick building; part of Wandsworth.

Battle, t., Rother, East Sussex, **Eng.**; battle of Hastings 1066; abbey; p. 6,000.

Beachy Head, chalk headland, S.W. of Eastbourne, East Sussex, **Eng.**; 175 m high. Major cliff fall, 1999.

Beaconsfield, t., South Bucks., **Eng.**; residtl; home of Edmund Burke; very expensive housing; p. 13,500.

Bearsden, burgh, E. Dunbartonshire, **Scot.**; residtl.; p. 28,500.

Beaulieu, v., Hants, **Eng.**; on Beaulieu R.; Cistercian abbey; National Motor Museum (founded by Lord Beaumont).

Beauly, t., Highland, **Scot.**; on Beauly R.; ruined priory; p. 1,200.

Bebington, Wirral, Merseyside, **Eng.**; part of pt. of Liverpool; soap, chemicals, engin.; p. 58,000.

Beccles, Waveney, Suffolk, **Eng.**; sm. mkt. t. on R. Waveney S. of Broads; resort, agr. inds.

Beddington and Wallington. *See* **Sutton.**

Bedford, co. t. and now unit. authority, **Eng.**; on R. Ouse, 80 km N. of London; gen. engin., inc. marine and elec., bricks, aero research; Bunyan imprisoned; large Italian community; p. (2010) 156,000 (unit.auth).

Bedfordshire, old non-met. co., **Eng.**; crossed by Chilterns; agr.; mkt. gardening, brickmkg.; cement, vehicles, engin. New structure (2009) of unit.auths.

Bedford Level, once over 162,000 ha. of peat marsh in S. Fenland, **Eng.**; first successful draining initiated by Earl of Bedford 1634.

Bedlington, sm. t., Wansbeck, Northumberland, **Eng.**; nr. Blyth; former coal mng.; electronics.

Bedloe's I., or **Liberty I.**, N.Y. harbour, **USA**; on which the statue of Liberty stands.

Bedworth, t., Warwicks., **Eng.**; l. gov. dist. with Nuneaton; nr. Coventry; coal mng., limestone quarrying, engin., textiles; p. 31,000.

Beeston and Stapleford, Broxtowe, Notts., **Eng.**; sub. of Nottingham; engin., drugs, HQ of Boots; p. 67,500.

Belfast, l. gov. dist., cap. of **N. Ireland**; pt. on Belfast Lough; once Britain's lgst. single shipyard, now all closed; linen mnf., (once known as Linenopolis), rope, tobacco, distilling, aircraft, fertilisers, computers; oil refinery on E. side of harbour; univ.; Stormont Castle; city airport renamed George Best airport; Linen Hall Library (f.1788 as the Belfast Reading Society); Titanic Belfast, major museum attraction; p. (2010) 268,500.

Bell Rock (**Inchcape I.**), rock and lighthouse 19 km S.E. of Arbroath, **Scot.**

Belper, mkt. t., Amber Valley, Derbys., **Eng.**; hosiery, textiles, oil wks., p. (2010) 22,500.

Belvoir (pronounced Beaver), **Vale of**, Melton Leics., **Eng.**; clay vale, cattle, sheep; Stilton cheese; recent development of coalfield.

Bembridge, v., E. cst., I. of Wight, **Eng.**; resort.

Benbecula I., Outer Hebrides, Western Isles, **Scot.**; between Is. of N. and S. Uist; airpt. in N.; fishing; p. 1,800.

Benfleet, t., Castle Point, Essex, **Eng.**; p. 49,000.

Ben Lawers, mtn., Perth and Kinross, **Scot.**; by Loch Tay; arctic and alpine flora; alt. 1,215 m.

Ben Macdhui, mtn., Aberdeenshire, **Scot.**; Cairngorm gr.; second highest peak in Brit. Is.; alt. 1,310 m.

Ben Nevis, mtn., Highland, **Scot.**; volcanic; hgst. peak in Brit. Isles; alt. 1,345 m. Only an average of 736 hours of sunshine annually, the lowest in the UK.

Bentley with Arksey, t., South Yorks., **Eng.**; p. 34,000.

Ben Wyvis, mtn., Highland, **Scot.**; nr. Dingwall; alt.

1,046 m.

Ben-y-Gloe, mtn., Glen Tilt, Perth and Kinross, **Scot.**; alt. 1,120 m.

Bere Regis, mkt. t., Dorset, **Eng.**; Saxon royal residence.

Berkeley, v., Gloucs., **Eng.**; nr. R. Severn, 24 km N. of Bristol; scene of murder of Edward II; nuclear power-sta. decommissioning.

Berkhamsted, Dacorum, Herts., **Eng.**; mkt. t.; cas. ruins, 17th cent. school; the birth-place of William Cowper the poet; p. (2011) 19,950.

Berkshire, former co., **Eng.**; chalk downland inc. Inkpen Beacon, White Horse Hills; drained by Thames and tribs.; residtl.; electronics, biscuits; Windsor Gr. Park; Ascot racecourse.

Berwickshire, historic co., S. **Scot.**, now part of Borders.

Berwick-upon-Tweed, former l. gov. dist., Northumberland, **Eng.**; spt. on mouth of Tweed; border t., changed between England and Scotland 15 times in history; fishing, lt. engin., tweeds, knitwear; cas. ruins; England's most northerly town; p. (2011), 26,250. Now part of new unit.auth.

Bethesda, sm. t., Gwynedd, **Wales**; slate, lt. engin; infamous Penrhyn Slate Quarry strike, 1900–03.

Bethnal Green, dist., London, **Eng.**; in E. End of London; now in Tower Hamlets.

Betws-y-coed, t., Conwy, **Wales**; waterfalls; tourism.

Beverley, mkt. t., E. Riding of Yorks., **Eng.**; famous minster (13th cent.); p. (2011) 30,200 (t.).

Bewdley, Wyre Forest, Worcs., **Eng.**; sm. mkt. t. on R. Severn; birthplace of Stanley Baldwin; residtl.

Bexhill-on-Sea, t., Rother, East Sussex, **Eng.**; resort; p. 40,250. Highest proportion of centenarians in the UK.

Bexley, former bor., W. Kent; now outer bor., Greater London, **Eng.**; inc. Sidcup, Crayford and Erith; p. (2011) 232,000.

Bicester, Cherwell, Oxford, **Eng.**; anc. mkt. t., N.E. of Oxford; priory (1182) now in ruins; p. (2011) 32,000. New town proposed, 2014. Designer shopping centre at Bicester village.

Biddulph, t., Staffs. Moorlands, Staffs., **Eng.**; coal mng., machin., furniture; residtl.; p. 18,000.

Bideford, Torridge, N. Devon, **Eng.**; pt. on estuary R. Torridge; mkt.; resort; p. 15,000.

Biggar, sm. burgh, S. Lanarkshire, **Scot.**; 213 m alt. in Southern Uplands; p. 2,200.

Biggin Hill, London Borough, Bromley, **Eng.**; nr. Orpington; famous airfield in Battle of Britain.

Biggleswade, sm. t., Mid Beds., **Eng.**; in valley of R. Ivel, 14 km S.E. of Bedford; ctr. of fruit-growing and mkt. gardening dist.; hydraulic machin. tools, hosiery, caravans.

Billingham, t., Stockton-on-Tees, **Eng.**; on N. of Tees estuary; petrochemical plant; p. 36,000.

Billingsgate, London, **Eng.**; old river-gate and wharf, formerly ch. fish mkt. of England; now moved to Isle of Dog s.

Bingley, West Yorks., **Eng.**; mkt. t. on R. Aire 26 km N.W. of Leeds; textiles, engin., agr.; p. 20,000.

Birkenhead, Wirral, Merseyside, **Eng.**; spt. on R. Mersey, opposite Liverpool; handles industl. goods; heavy and pt. processing inds.; shipbldg.; p. 84,500.

Birmingham, c., met. dist., West Midlands, **Eng.**; industl. cap. Midlands, second lgst. c. Gt. Britain; industl. inds.; motor vehicles, components and accessories (Longbridge once known as 'car city'); univs., cath.; new Bull Ring (2003); p. (2010) 1,016,700 (dist.); new public library (largest in Europe) opened 2013. Official reopening of New St. railway station (2015).

Birnam, v., Perth and Kinross, **Scot.**; location of Birnam Wood in *Macbeth*; former royal forest; p. 1,100 (with Dunkeld).

Birr, t. Offaly, **R.o.I.**; mkt. t. on Brosna R.; observatory; p. 4,100.

Bishop Auckland, t., Wear Valley, Durham, **Eng.**; palace of Bishop of Durham; iron, lt. engin.; former coal mng.; p. 25,200.

Bishopbriggs, sm. burgh, E. Dunbartonshire, **Scot.**; p. 23,000.

Bishop Rock, isolated rock, lighthouse, Scilly Is., **Eng.**; 58 km S.W. of Land's End, Cornwall; recognised internationally as E. end of trans-Atlantic ocean crossing.

Bishop's Stortford, East Herts., **Eng.**; mkt. t. on Stort R.; light inds.; Norman cas.; p. (2001) 35,325.

Blaby, t. and l. gov. dist., Leics., **Eng.**; sm. a. S.W. of Leicester; p. (2011) 93,500 (dist.), 8,000 (t.).

Blackburn, t., (unit. auth with **Darwen**)., Lancs., **Eng.**; once major cotton weaving ctr.; engin., lt. inds.; p. (2011) 147,500.

Black Country, Midlands, **Eng.**; formerly impt. ironworking and coal-mng. dist. mainly in S. West Midlands; now area of light engineering.

Blackdown Hills, Devon and Somerset, **Eng.**; sandstone hills rising over 305 m.

Blackheath, open common, S.E. London, **Eng.**; mustering place of Wat Tyler's (1381) and Jack Cade's (1450) revolutionary peasants; now main attraction of expensive residtl. a.; a. 108 ha.

Black Mtn., Powys and Carmarthenshire, S. **Wales**; rises to 802 m; sandstone plateau; moorland; valleys used for reservoirs.

Black Mtns., Powys, S. **Wales**; rise to 811 m at Waun Fâch.

Blackpool, t., unit.auth., Lancs., **Eng.**; on cst. of Fylde dist.; one of major Brit. resorts; (16 million visitors annually); p. (2011) 142,100. Blackpool Illuminations began in 1879. Blackpool Tower was built in 1894. Large Polish community.

Blackrod, t., Gtr. Manchester, **Eng.**; nr. Chorley; former cotton weaving; p. 6,000.

Blacksod Bay, cst. of Mayo, **R.o.I.**

Blackwater, R., **N. Ireland**; rising in Dungannon, it forms border with **R.o.I.**; enters L. Neagh; 80 km long.

Blackwater, R., **R.o.I.**; flows from Knockanefune to enter Atl. Oc. at pt. and resort of Youghal; chain of sm. ts. along course; 144 km long.

Blackwood, sm. t., Caerphilly, S.E. **Wales**; N. of Abercarn.

Blaenau Ffestiniog, t., Gwynedd, N. **Wales**; at head of Vale of Ffestiniog, 14 km E. of Porthmadog; consists of Ffestiniog and Blaenau Ffestiniog; slate quarries; pumped-storage hydroelec. sta. (1963); cement; narrow gauge rly.; p. 4,800.

Blaenau Gwent, S. **Wales**, unit.auth. created in 1996 from former l. gov. dist.; inland valley a. inc. Ebbw Vale and Abertillery; p. (2011) 69,800.

Blaenavon, sm. t., Torfaen, **Wales**; former coal mng. a., UNESCO World Heritage Site; also site of National Mining Museum of Wales.

Blair Atholl, v., Perth and Kinross, **Scot.**; tourist resort; cas.; seat of Duke of Atholl.

Blairgowrie and **Rattray**, burgh, Perth and Kinross, **Scot.**; at foot of Scottish Highlands; mkt. t. in Strathmore fruit growing dist.; p. 8,100.

Blakeney, v., N. Norfolk, **Eng.**; nr. sand spit; yachting; wild fowl.

Blandford or **Blandford Forum**, North Dorset, **Eng.**; on R. Stour; sm. pastoral mkt. t. since 13th cent.

Blantyre, v., S. Lanarkshire, **Scot.**; Lower B. birthplace of David Livingstone and also Socialist leader Keir Hardie; p. 17,500.

Blarney, v., 6 km N.W. Cork, **R.o.I.**; cas. and Blarney stone.

Blasket Is., Kerry. **R.o.I.**; rocky Is.; lighthouse.

Blaydon, t. N.E. **Eng.**; former coal mng.; p. 15,510.

Blessington, L., Wicklow, **R.o.I.**; glacial L., now serves as reservoir for Dublin.

Bletchley, Milton Keynes, **Eng.**; expanded t.; p. 48,500.

Bletchley Park, Bucks, **Eng.**; wartime code-breaking centre (cracked Enigma cipher). Now high-tech museum.

Bloomsbury, dist., London, **Eng.**; once fashionable dist. with many squares; famous literary history; inc. Brit. Museum, Univ. of London.

Blyth., spt., Northumberland, **Eng.**; on former coalfield; p. 36,000 (t.).

Bodmin, co. t., North Cornwall, **Eng.**; on S.W. flank of Bodmin moor; china clay, lt. engin.; p. 18,500.

Bodmin Moor, upland, N.E. Cornwall, **Eng.**; lower slopes cultivated, higher slopes used for sheep pastures; average alt. 300 m, highest point, Brown Willy, alt. 419 m; major ctr. of china clay quarrying.

Bognor Regis, t., Arun, West Sussex. **Eng.**; residtl.; seaside resort; popular conference centre; p. 63,000.

Boldon, t., Tyne and Wear, **Eng.**; p. 13,000.

Bolsover, t., l. gov. dist., Derbys., **Eng.**; limestone, textiles; cas.; Hardwick Hall 6 km to S.; p. (2010) 74,500 (dist.).

Bolton, t., met. dist., Gtr. Manchester, **Eng.**; cotton, textiles, engin.; univ.; p. (2011) 276,800 (dist.).

Bolton Abbey, North Yorks. **Eng.**; ruined Augustinian Priory.

Bo'ness, burgh, Falkirk, **Scot.**; spt. on Firth of Forth, 6 km E. of Grangemouth; foundries; timber yards; p. 14,250.

Bonnyrigg and **Lasswade**, burgh, Midlothian, **Scot.**, 11 km S.E. of Edinburgh, p. 14,900.

Bootle, t., Sefton, Merseyside, **Eng.**; on E. side of entrance to Mersey estuary; dockside inds. including tanning, ship-repairing; tin plant; p. (2001) 59,123.

Borders, unit.auth., created in 1996 from former Region, **Scot.**; occupies E. half of Southern Uplands; hilly cty. drained by R. Tweed and tribs.; rural a. interspersed by mkt. and indl ts.; p. (2010) 113,000.

Borehamwood, t., Herts., **Eng.**; lt. engin., computers, film studios; p. 32,500.

Borrowdale, valley, Cumbria, **Eng.**; tourist resort; former graphite mines.

Boscastle, spt., Cornwall, **Eng.**; resort; pilchard fishing; sm. harbour built for slate exp.; devastating flood, 16 Aug. 2004.

Boston, t., l. gov. dist., Lincs., **Eng.**; sm. pt. on Witham R., agr. mkt., fruit and vegetable canning; many migrant workers (esp. E. European); home of Oldrids Department Store; p. (2011) 65,000 (dist.).

Bosworth or **Market Bosworth**, t., Leics., **Eng.**; battle between Richard III and Henry VII, 1485; see **Hinckley**.

Bourne, sm. t., South Kesteven, Lincs., **Eng.**; home of Hereward the Wake; also home of Raymond Mays, racing driver; agr. machin, printing.

Bournemouth, t., Dorset, **Eng.**, unit.auth. created in 1997, formerly part of Hampshire; on S. cst., E. of Poole Harbour; seaside resort; univ; conference ctr.; cosmopolitan community; major digital economy; p. (2010) 164,100 (unit.auth).

Bournville, garden sub. founded by George Cadbury (1897), 6 km S.W. of Birmingham **Eng.**; chocolate and cocoa wks; long-time ban on alcohol.

Bourton-on-the-Water, v., Gloucs. **Eng.**; tourist ctr. The 'Venice of the Cotswolds'.

Bow or **Stratford-de-Bow**, Tower Hamlets, E. London, **Eng.**; 5 km from St. Paul's.

Bow Fell, mtn., Cumbria, **Eng.**; at head of Borrowdale, 6 km N.W. of West Water. 903 m.

Bowland, Forest of, W. offshoot of Pennines, Lancs., **Eng.**; between Rs. Lune and Ribble; area of outstanding natural beauty; reservoirs.

Bowness, v., Cumbria, **Eng.**; Western end of Hadrian's Wall.

Bowness, t., Cumbria, **Eng.**; on L. Windermere; tourist ctr.

Box Hill, nr. Dorking, Surrey, **Eng.**; E. of R. Mole gap through N. Downs; chalk; wooded, fine views; alt. 233 m.

Boyne, R., **R.o.I.**; flows to Irish Sea; Battle of the Boyne (1690) fought at Oldbridge, 5 km W. of Drogheda; salmon fishing; 128 km long.

Brackley, t., South Northants., **Eng.**; flour milling, brewing; former prosperous wool tr.; p. 10,500.

Bracknell, t., part of unit.auth. of **Bracknell Forest**, Berks., **Eng.**; on Thames Valley terrace, 16 km S. of Windsor; new t. designated 1949 to meet overspill needs from London; engin., plastics; major redev. of town centre planned; p. (2010) 115,000 (unit.auth).

Bradford, c., met. dist., West Yorks., **Eng.**; 14 km W. of Leeds; comm. ctr. of wool-textile inds.; impt. for worsted; engin. and chem. inds.; univ.; birthplace of Delius and J. B. Priestley; p. 522,500 (dist.).

Bradford-on-Avon, sm. t., West Wilts., **Eng.**; on the Bristol Avon; former ctr. of wool ind.; major Roman remains currently being excavated.

Braemar, dist. in Grampians, Aberdeenshire, **Scot.**; containing Balmoral estate.

Braeriach, mtn., Aberdeenshire, **Scot.**; alt. 1,296 m.

Braintree, t., l. gov. dist., Essex, **Eng.**; on Blackwater; rayon mftg., metal windows, engin.; p. (2010) 142,000 (dist.).

Brandon, t., Suffolk, **Eng.**; ctr. of Breckland; expanded t.

Brandon and **Byshottles**, ts., former U.D., Durham, **Eng.**; former coal-mng. a.

Bray, t., Wicklow, **R.o.I.**; on Irish Sea cst.; popular resort; p. 27,500.

Brechin, royal burgh, Angus, **Scot.**; on S. Esk; cath.; whisky; p. 7,350.

Breckland, dist., S.W. Norfolk, N.W. Suffolk, **Eng.**; chalk overlain by glacial sands; heathland and coniferous plantations; l. gov. dist., inc. Thetford, Swaffham and East Dereham; p. (2010) 132,100.

Brecknockshire, historic co., S. **Wales**, now part of Powys.

Brecon (Brecknock), sm. t., Powys, **Wales**; on R. Usk.

Brecon Beacons, mtns., S. **Wales**; 8 km S. of Brecon; highest peak 888 m; sandstone moorland; Nat. Park.

Bredbury and **Romiley**, ts., Gtr. Manchester, **Eng.**; paper, engin., dyeing, textiles; p. 29,000.

Brendon Hills, Somerset, **Eng.**; extension of Exmoor, rising to over 400 m.

Brent, outer bor., Greater London, **Eng.**; inc. Wembley and Willesden; p. (2011) 311,000.

Brentford and Chiswick. *See* **Hounslow.**

Brentwood, bor., l.gov.dist., Essex, **Eng.**; residentl.; new R.C. cath. (1991); p. (2010) 73,000. (dist.).

Bressay I., Shetland Is., **Scot**; p. 350.

Bridgend, t., unit.auth. created in 1996 from former l. gov. dist. of Ogwr, S. **Wales**; industl. trading estate; Ford car plant; former coal mng. a.; p. (2011) 139,200 (unit.auth.).

Bridge of Allan, burgh, Stirling, **Scot.**; 3 km N. of Stirling; p. 5,100.

Bridgewater Canal, Worsley–Manchester–Runcorn, Gtr. Manchester and Cheshire, **Eng.**; crosses ship canal by means of Barton swing bridge; 61 km long.

Bridgnorth, sm.t., former l. gov. dist., Shrops., **Eng.**; cas.; aluminium prods; light inds; n. terminus, Severn Valley Rly; now part of unit.auth.

Bridgwater, t., Sedgemoor, Somerset, **Eng.**; on R. Parrett, 16 km from Bristol Channel; engin., wire rope, cellophane; p. 35,250.

Bridlington, t., E. Riding of Yorks., **Eng.**; on Bridlington Bay, S. of Flamborough Head; fishing; seaside resort; priory (12th century); p. 35,000. First mentioned in 1086 Domesday Book.

Bridport, West Dorset, **Eng.**; mkt. t.; seaside resort; p. 12,500.

Brierley Hill, t., West Midlands, **Eng.**; on W. edge of Black Cty.; cut glass, castable metal gds., firebricks, roofing and tiling, iron and steel.

Brigg, mkt. t., N. Lincs., **Eng.**; ctr. of agr. dist. between Lincoln Heights and Wolds; p. 6,000.

Brighouse, t., Calderdale, West Yorks., **Eng.**; on R. Calder, 5 km S.E. of Halifax; textiles and engin.; p. 33,000.

Brightlingsea, t., Tendring, Essex, **Eng.**; on R. Colne; oysters, boatbldg., yachting; p. 7,500.

Brighton, c., unit.auth. created in 1997, formerly part of East Sussex, **Eng.**; 80 km S. of London on S. cst.; seaside resort and residtl. t.; Royal Pavilion (1817); Palace Pier (first opened, 1899); univs.; lt. inds.; Brighton & Hove created Millennium City, 2000; new observation tower (Brighton Eye); Volks railway (world's oldest operating electric rly.); new i360 viewing tower (opened 2016); p. (2010) 257,000 (unit.auth.), (2011) 138,000 (t.).

Bristol, c., unit.auth. created in 1996, formerly part of Avon, **Eng.**; pt. on R. Avon 14 km from Bristol Channel; outport at Avonmouth; cath., univs.; docks; aircraft engin., tobacco, paint, printing and lt. inds.; British Empire & Commonwealth Museum (2002); European Green Capital, 2015; p. (2010) 423,000. (unit.auth.). First smoke-free outdoor public spaces (since 2015). The Bristol Old Vic is Britain's oldest working theatre.

Bristol Channel, arm of Atl. Oc. between S. cst. of Wales and Somerset and Devon, **Eng.**; tidal bores.

British Is., archipelago, N.W. Europe; comprising 2 lge. Is. of Great Britain and Ireland and 5,000 sm. Is.; a. 315,029 km².

Brixham, S. Devon, **Eng.**; incorporated in Torbay; fishing; resort.

Broadstairs, Thanet, Kent, **Eng.**; seaside resort; 5 km N.E. of Ramsgate; p. 23,950. Favourite holiday spot of Charles Dickens.

Broads, The, Norfolk, **Eng.**; series of Ls. formed by mediaeval turf cutting in lower alluvial reaches of Rs. Bure, Waveney, and Yare; yachting, fishing, tourism; lge. part forms **Broadland**, l. gov. dist., p. 116,000.

Bromley, outer bor. of London, **Eng.**; inc. Beckenham, Orpington, Penge, and Chislehurst; p. (2011) 310,000.

Bromsgrove, t. and l. gov. dist., Worcs., **Eng.**; mkt. t., 21 km S.W. Birmingham; wrought ironwk., lt. engin.; p. (2010) 93,000 (dist.), (2011) 30,500 (t.).

Bromyard, Worcs., **Eng.**; sm. mkt. t.; p. 3,500.

Brora, t., Highland, **Scot.**; on E. cst., 19 km N.E. of Dornoch Firth; Harris Tweed ind.; tourism.

Brownhills, t., West Midlands, **Eng.**; former mng. t.; expanded t.; p. 19,000.

Broxbourne, t., l. gov. dist., Herts., **Eng.**; on gravel terrace to W. of R. Lea; ctr. of very intensively cultivated dist.; lt. inds.; world's biggest printing plant; p. (2010) 93,000 (dist.).

Broxtowe, l. gov. dist., Notts., **Eng.**; made up of Beeston and Stapleford and Eastwood; p.

(2010) 111,900.

Buchan Ness, C., nr. Peterhead, E. **Scot**.

Buckfastleigh, sm. t., S. Devon, **Eng.**; wool, quarrying; nearby Benedictine abbey on site of mediaeval Cistercian abbey.

Buckhaven and Methil, burgh, Fife, **Scot.**; on N. side of Firth of Forth, 13 km N.E. of Kirkcaldy; coal; p. 16,900.

Buckie, burgh, Moray, **Scot.**; boat- and yacht-bldg.; fisheries; p. 8,200.

Buckingham, Aylesbury Vale, Bucks., **Eng.**; mkt. t. on R. Ouse, 24 km N.W. of Aylesbury; home of the Independent University.

Buckinghamshire, non-met. co., **Eng.**; crossed by Chilterns and Vale of Aylesbury; rural and wooded, dairy farming; co. t. Aylesbury; mnfs. chiefly in High Wycombe; p. (2009) 404,000.

Buckley, t., Flintshire, **Wales**; p. 18,500.

Bude. *See* **Stratton and Bude.**

Budleigh Salterton, East Devon, **Eng.**; resort; birthplace of Raleigh; p. 3,900.

Builth Wells, t., Powys, **Wales**; on upper course of R. Wye; medicinal springs; p. 2,800.

Buncrana, mkt. t., Donegal, **R.o.I.**; salmon fishing; seaside resort; p. 4,100.

Bungay, Waveney, Suffolk, **Eng.**; mkt. t. on R. Waveney; printing, leather gds.; p. (2011), 3,750.

Bure, R., Norfolk, **Eng.**; lower course forms part of Norfolk Broads; joins Yare at Yarmouth; 93 km.

Burgess Hill, t., Mid Sussex, West Sussex, **Eng.**; bricks, tiles; p. 31,000.

Burghead, burgh, Moray, **Scot.**; fish pt., resort; p. 1,695.

Burnham Beeches, Berks./Bucks., **Eng.**; part of anc. forest acquired 1879 for public use; a. 243 ha.

Burnham-on-Crouch, t., Essex, **Eng.**; pt., yachting, boat-bldg.; p. 7,500.

Burnham-on-Sea, t., Sedgemoor, Somerset, **Eng.**; on Bridgwater Bay; resort; p. 20,500.

Burnley, t., l. gov. dist., Lancs., **Eng.**; textiles, engin., car accessories; p. (2011) 87,500 (dist.).

Burntisland, royal burgh, Fife, **Scot.**; on F. of Forth; p. 5,750.

Burray, one of the Orkney Is., **Scot.**; p. 360.

Burry Port, sm. t., Carmarthenshire, **Wales**.

Burslem. *See* **Stoke-on-Trent.**

Burton-on-Trent, t., East Staffs., **Eng.**; brewing, malting, home of National Brewing Centre; rubber gds.; p. 44,000.

Bury, t., met. dist., Gtr. Manchester, **Eng.**; on R. Irwell to S. of Rossendale Fells; cotton, textiles; birthplace of Robert Peel; p. (2011) 185,100 (dist.).

Bury St. Edmunds, (St. Edmundsbury,) Suffolk, **Eng.**; old mkt. t., on R. Lark, abbey ruins; farm implements, sugar-beet processing; expanded t.; p. 38,500.

Bushey, t., Hertsmere, Herts., **Eng.**; residtl.; p. 19,000.

Bute, I, Argyll and Bute, **Scot**; p. 7,500. The chief town is Rothesay.

Buttermere, L., Cumbria, **Eng.**

Butt of Lewis, promontory with lighthouse; Lewis, Hebrides, **Scot.**

Buxton, t., High Peak, Derbys., **Eng.**; spa; bottling plant; lime-stone quarrying; Opera House; p. 21,500.

C

Caerleon, t., Newport, **Wales**; on R. Usk, 5 km N.E. of Newport; Roman Isca Silurum remains; agr. machin., tools, bricks.

Caernarfon, t., Gwynedd, N. **Wales**; pt. on S. shore of Menai strait; cas.; birthplace of Edward II; bricks, plastics.

Caernarvonshire, historic co., N.W. **Wales**; now part of Gwynedd.

Caerphilly, t., unit.auth. created in 1996 from former l. gov. dists. of Islwyn and Rhymney Valley, S. **Wales**; cas.; lt. inds.; former coal mng. a.; p. (2011) 178,800 (unit. auth.).

Cahir, t., Tipperary, **R.o.I.**; on R. Suir; anc. cas. and abbey; salmon fishing; p. 2,100.

Cairngorm, mtns., Moray, Aberdeenshire and Highland, **Scot.**; rise to 1,310 m (Ben Macdhui); form part of Highlands; nat. nature reserve of arctic flora and fauna; opened in 2003 as Scotland's second National Park, the largest in the UK; winter sports (Britain's largest ski resort).

Cairntoul, mtn., Aberdeenshire, **Scot.**; alt. 1,294 m.

Caistor, sm. t., West Lindsey, Lincs., **Eng.**; site of Roman camp in Lincs. Wolds.

Caithness, historic co., N. **Scot.**, now part of Highland.

Calderdale, met. dist., West Yorks., **Eng.**; chief t. Halifax; also inc. Todmorden, Brighouse, Hebden Royd, Ripponden and Sowerby Bridge; p. (2011) 203,800.

Calder Hall, Cumbria, **Eng.**; first full-scale nuclear power sta. in world (1956); now closed.

Caldey, I., off Pembrokeshire cst., **Wales**; lighthouse; Trappist monastery.

Caledonian Canal, from Inverness to Fort William, **Scot.**, connecting North Sea with Atl. Oc.; 100 km long; opened 1822.

Callander, burgh, Stirling, **Scot.**; mkt. t. on R. Teith, 24 km N.W. of Stirling; "the gate of the Highlands", tourism; p. 2,800.

Calne, North Wilts., **Eng.**; mkt. t. on Marden R.

Cam (Granta), R., Cambridge, **Eng.**; trib. of R. Ouse; flows through the "backs" at Cambridge; 64 km long.

Camberley, t., Surrey, **Eng.**; Royal Military Staff College, Royal Military Academy, Sandhurst; p. 48,500 (with Frimley).

Camborne, t., Cornwall, **Eng.**; 18 km S.W. Truro; old tin and copper mines; engin., radio-television assembly; textiles, chemicals; p. (2011) 37,100 (inc. Redruth).

Cambourne, planned new town near Cambridge.

Cambrian Mtns., **Wales**; collective name for mtns. of N. and Central Wales inc. Snowdonia and Cader Idris.

Cambridge, univ. c., co. t., l. gov. dist., Cambridgeshire, **Eng.**; on Cam R.; famous univ. with residtl. colleges; leading ctr. of high-tech and research-based inds.; new Global Science Centre; world's longest guided busway (opened 2011); new rly.link to Oxford proposed; p. (2010) 123,000 (dist.).

Cambridgeshire, non-met. co., **Eng.**; low-lying, sloping from E. Anglian Heights in S.E. to Fens in N.; crossed by Rs. flowing to Wash; rich soils aid intensive agr. and mkt. gardening; inc. former cos. of Huntingdon, Peterborough and Isle of Ely; ch. t. Cambridge; p. (2010) 607,000.

Camden, inner bor., N. London, **Eng.**; inc. Hampstead, Holborn, and St. Pancras; major redevelopment of formerly depressed Kings Cross area; p. (2011) 220,300.

Campbeltown, royal burgh, spt., Argyll and Bute, **Scot.**; distilling, fishing; ctr. for construction of offshore oil platforms; p. 5,200.

Campsie Fells, range of hills, Stirling/E. Dunbartonshire, **Scot.**; highest point, 578 m.

Cannock Chase, upland a., Staffs., **Eng.**; close to Midlands conurb.; forms l. gov. dist. based on Cannock t.; p. (2010) 95,000 (dist.).

Canterbury, c., l. gov. dist., Kent, **Eng.**; at foot of N. Downs on R. Stour; univs.; cath. founded A.D. 597 by St. Augustine; famous shrine of Thomas Becket; now World Heritage Site; p. (2010) 149,000 (dist.), 45,000 (t.).

Canvey I., Castle Point, Essex, **Eng.**; fronting the Thames; expanded t.; resort; radio components, bookbinding, iron and wire wks., oil refinery; liquid gas terminal; devastating flood, 1953; concrete sea walls; p. (2011) 38,500.

Caradon, former l. gov. dist., Cornwall, **Eng.**; a. between Tamar and S. cst.; inc. Looe, Saltash and Liskeard; now part of new unit.auth.

Cardiff, c., cap. of **Wales**, unit. auth. created in 1996 from former l. gov. dist.; at mouth of R. Taff on Bristol Channel, formerly one of world's gr. coal-shipping pts.; univs, cath., cas.; docks at Barry; iron and steel wks., flour mills; major regeneration of Cardiff Tiger Bay area; Coal Exchange (1883); home of Millennium Stadium; location of Welsh Assembly; new Wales Millenium Centre; massive city expansion plan agreed (2016); p. (2011) 346,100 (unit. auth.).

Cardigan, sm. t., Ceredigion, S. **Wales**; at mouth of Teifi R.; former pt., now mkt. ctr.

Cardiganshire. *See* Ceredigion.

Carlisle, c., l. gov. dist., Cumbria, **Eng.**; on Eden R.; pt. and route ctr.; Norman cas.; cath.; univ. (Cumbria); textiles, plasterboard, flour, bacon, biscuits, metal boxes; p. (2011) 107,500 (dist.).

Carlow, co., S.E. Leinster, **R.o.I.**; arable agr. and livestock; co. t. Carlow; a. 896 km²; p. 54,332.

Carlow, co. t., Carlow co., **R.o.I.**; cath.; mkt., agr. processing; p. 15,000.

Carlton, t., Gedling, Notts., **Eng.**; 3 km N.E. Nottingham; hosiery; p. 49,950.

Carmarthen, t., Carmarthenshire, **Wales**; on Towy R.; impt. agr. ctr.; cas. ruins; p. 15,000.

Carmarthenshire, S.W. **Wales**, unit. auth. created in 1996 from former l. gov. dists. of Carmarthen, Dinefwr and Llanelli, reinstating historic co. split up in 1974; stock rearing and fattening; industl. in S.E.; p. (2011) 183,800.

Carnoustie, burgh, Angus, **Scot.**; on N. Sea; 10 km S.W. of Arbroath; resort; famous golf course; p. 11,200.

Carrantuohill, mtn., Kerry, **R.o.I.**; 1,041 m, loftiest in all Ireland.

Carrick, former l. gov. dist., Cornwall, **Eng.**; stretched across penin. and surrounds Fal estuary; inc. Truro, Penryn and Falmouth.

Carrickfergus, t., l. gov. dist., **N. Ireland**; pt. on N. shore of Belfast Lough; textiles, nylon fibres, tobacco inds.; p. (2010) 40,250 (dist.). *See* D11.

Carrick-on-Shannon, co. t., R. D., Leitrim, **R.o.I.**; on flat land in Upper Shannon valley; p. of t. 2,300.

Carrick-on-Suir, sm. mkt. t., Tipperary, **R.o.I.**; leather prods.; N.W. of Waterford.

Carron, v., Falkirk, **Scot.**; nr. Falkirk; site of first ironwks. in E. Lowlands of Scot; p. 5,600.

Carron, Loch, inlet, W. cst., Highland, **Scot.**; followed by rly. from Dingwall to Kyle of Lochalsh.

Carse of Gowrie, Perth and Kinross, **Scot.**; fertile coastal dist. between Perth and Dundee, S. of Sidlaw Hills; soft fruits, especially raspberries.

Carsington, reservoir opened 1992, S. Derbyshire.

Carter Fell, mtn., a summit of the Cheviot hills, on the Eng./Scot. border, 554 m.

Cashel, mkt. t., Tipperary, **R.o.I.**; anc. seat of kings of Munster; ruins of cath. on Rock of Cashel; p. 2,500.

Casquets, dangerous rocks, 11 km W. of Alderney, Channel Is., **Eng.**; lighthouse.

Castlebar, cap. Mayo, **R.o.I.**; mkt. t.; p. 8,000.

Castlecary, v., N. Lanarkshire, **Scot.**; sta. on Roman wall; silica, fire clay deposits.

Castle Donington, t., Leicestershire, **Eng.**; East Midlands airpt.; power sta. (now demolished). New distribution hub.

Castle Douglas, burgh, Dumfries and Galloway, **Scot.**; nr. R. Dee; nearby cas.; stock mkt.; p. 3,750.

Castleford, t., West Yorks., **Eng.**; 16 km S.E. of Leeds at confluence of Rs. Aire and Calder; coal mng., chemical, glass, and clothing mnfs, flour milling, brick mkg.; p. 38,250.

Castle Morpeth, former l. gov. dist., Northumberland, **Eng.**; based on Morpeth.

Castle Point, l. gov. dist., Essex, **Eng.**; comprises Canvey I. and Benfleet; p. (2010) 90,000.

Castlereagh, l. gov. dist., **N. Ireland**; inc. S.E. outskirts of Belfast; p. (2010) 67,000. *See* D11.

Castleton, v., Derbys., **Eng.**; on Hope R.; tourist ctr. for Peak District; nearby fluorspar mines.

Castletown, t., **Isle of Man**; former cap.; pt., cas. tower.

Caterham and **Warlingham**, ts., former U.D. Tandridge, Surrey, **Eng.**; on N. Downs; residtl.; p. 33,500.

Cavan, inland co., **R.o.I.**; agr. a. with many Ls.; depopulation; borders Ulster; a. 1,932 km²; p. (2011) 72,874.

Cavan, sm. co. t., Cavan **R.o.I.**; 115 km S.W. Belfast; mkt.; cath.

Central Clydeside, conurb., **Scot.**, based on Glasgow and includes other urban areas (Bearsden, Milngavie, Clydebank, Cumbernauld, Kilsyth, East Kilbride, Eastwood, Hamilton, Monklands, Motherwell, Renfrew and Strathkelvin).

Ceredigion, W. **Wales**, unit. auth. created in 1996 from former l. gov. dist., reinstating historic co. of Cardiganshire disbanded in 1974; upland a. drained by the Teifi and Ystwyth Rs.; ch. t. Aberystwyth; p. (2011) 75,900.

Chadderton, t., Gtr. Manchester, **Eng.**; engin., chemicals, textiles; p. 33,950.

Chalfont St. Giles, v., Bucks., **Eng.**; in London commuter belt; home of the poet Milton.

Channel Is., gr. of self-governing Is. belonging to the Brit. Crown off N.W. cst. France, of which the lgst. are Jersey, Guernsey, Alderney, and Sark; part of the old duchy of Normandy; vegetables, flowers, fruit, granite; two famous breeds of dairy cattle; tourist resort; impt. banking and insurance ctr. encouraged by low taxes; retirement ctr.; a. 194 km²; p. 140,000.

Chapelcross, nr. Annan, Dumfries and Galloway, **Scot.**; nuclear power sta., producing electricity for nat. grid.

Chapel-en-le-Frith, mkt. t., High Peak, Derbys., Eng.; brake-linings; p. 9,400.

Chard, sm. mkt. t., Somerset **Eng.**; lace, engin., shirt and cotton mftg.

Charnwood Forest, upland dist., Leics., **Eng.**; to W. of Soar valley, 19 km N.W. of Leicester; composed of anc. rocks; stone-crushing; largely forests; alt. 180–275 m; forms l. gov. dist. of **Charnwood** inc. Loughborough and Shepshed; p. (2010) 166,000.

Chatham, t., Rochester upon Medway, Kent, **Eng.**; on estuary of R. Medway; lt. inds.; famous naval dockyard established by Henry VIII; now planned as heritage site; p. 70,500.

Chatsworth, Derbys., **Eng.**; on R. Derwent; seat of the dukes of Devonshire.

Chatteris, Fenland, Cambridge, **Eng.**; sm. mkt. t.

Cheadle, sm. t., Staffs. Moorland, Staffs., **Eng.**; metal mnfs.; former coal-mng. a.

Cheadle and Gatley, ts., Gtr. Manchester, **Eng.**; textile finishing and bleaching, residtl.; p. 59,000.

Cheddar, v., Somerset, **Eng.**; famous limestone caves and gorge in Mendips; cheese, strawberries.

Chelmsford, co. t., l. gov. dist., Essex, **Eng.**; 48 km N.E. London; cath.; agr. mkt.; p. (2010) 167,250 (dist.), (2001) 99,962 (t.). Created a Jubilee City, 2012.

Chelsea, dist., London, **Eng.**; fashionable residtl. dist. *See* Kensington.

Cheltenham, t., l. gov. dist., Gloucs., **Eng.**; spa; educational ctr.; precision instruments; birthplace of Gustav Holst; location of GCHQ; p. (2010) 112,200 (dist.), 94,000 (t.).

Chepstow, sm. mkt. t., Monmouthshire, **Wales**; on R. Wye, 3 km above confluence with R. Severn; ruined cas.

Chequers, official residence of Brit. prime ministers, 3 km S. of Wendover, Bucks., **Eng.**; gift of Lord Lee of Fareham.

Cheriton, dist. near Folkestone, Kent, **Eng.**; Channel Tunnel, linked to Sangatte, Calais, France opened 1994.

Chertsey, sm. t., Runnymede, Surrey, **Eng.**; on S. bank of R. Thames, 6 km below Staines.

Cherwell, l. gov. dist., Oxon., **Eng.**; stretches from Banbury to Bicester; p. (2010) 137,900.

Cherwell, R., trib. of Thames, nr. Oxford, **Eng.**; length 48 km.

Chesham, t., Bucks., **Eng.**; in heart of Chiltern Hills; printing, lt. engin.; residtl; p. 22,000.

Cheshire, old non-met. co., N.W. **Eng.**; lowland a. drained by Rs. Dee and Mersey, bounded by Pennines in E.; dairying and mkt. gardening; chemical ind. based on salt deposits around Northwich; heavy inds. in and around Warrington; attracting many high technology inds.; much of co. residtl. for Liverpool and Manchester; now organised into two new unit. auths. (**Cheshire East** and **Cheshire West and Chester**).

Cheshunt, t., Herts., **Eng.**; in Lea valley, 11 km S. of Hertford; bricks, mkt. gardening, horticulture; p. 57,000.

Chesil Bank, Dorset, **Eng.**; shingle ridge enclosing the Fleet lagoon running from I. of Portland to Bridport.

Chester, c., former l. gov. dist., Cheshire, **Eng.**; at head of estuary of R. Dee; cath., anc. walls and old timbered houses; Roman c. of Deva site of legionary barracks; remains of largest amphitheatre, dating from A.D. 280, ever found in Britain; engin., metal goods; univ.; p. 82,750 (c.). It has the oldest racecourse in the UK.

Chesterfield, mkt. t., colly. dist., l. gov. dist., Derbys., **Eng.**; on Rother R.; 13 km S. of Sheffield; variety of heavy inds.; 14th cent. church with crooked spire; p. (2010) 101,000 (dist.).

Chester-le-Street, t., former l. gov. dist., Durham, **Eng.**; clothing, confectionery, sand wkg.; p.36,500 (t.). Now part of unit. auth.

Cheviot Hills, range between **Scot.** and **Eng.**; hgst. summit, the Cheviot, 816 m.

Chichester, t., l. gov. dist., West Sussex, **Eng.**; on S. cst. plain, 18 km W. of Arundel; cath.; univ.; p. (2010) 111,000 (dist.), 29,000 (t.).

Chickerell, E. Dorset, **Eng.**; 5 km N.W. of Weymouth; East Fleet, a sea-fed tidal estuary, lies to the west of the village.

Chigwell, sm. t., Epping Forest, Essex, **Eng.**; on borders of Epping Forest; Hainault Estate now incorporated in Redbridge, Greater London.

Chiltern, l. gov. dist., Bucks., **Eng.**; inc. part of C. Hills and Chesham and Amersham; p. (2010) 91,000.

Chiltern Hills, chalk escarpment, Oxon., Bucks., Beds., and Herts., **Eng.**; cut by no. of impt.

gaps used by main communications; sheep and barley; hgst. point 276 m nr. Wendover.

Chippenham, North Wilts., **Eng.**; mkt. t. on R. Avon; rly. signal and brake equipment, bacon curing, tanning; p. 27,000.

Chipping Campden, v., Gloucs., **Eng.**; in Cotswold Hills; formerly impt. for woollens; tourism; p. c. 1,750.

Chipping Norton, mkt. t., Oxford, **Eng.**; nr. Banbury; formerly impt. for woollens; p. 6,000.

Chipping Sodbury, mkt. t., S. Gloucs., **Eng.**; 13 km N.E. of Bristol; p. 34,000.

Chirk, sm. t., Wrexham, **Wales**; on R. Cleriog, S. of Wrexham; slate, former coal mng. a.; cas.

Chislehurst. *See* Bromley.

Chorley, t., l. gov. dist., N. Lancs., **Eng.**; on W. flank of Rossendale Fells, 11 km S.E. of Preston; cotton, engin.; expansion as new t. with Leyland; p. (2011) 107,200. *See* **Central Lancashire.**

Chorleywood, t., Three Rivers, Herts., **Eng.**; nr. Watford; p. 9,500.

Christchurch, t., l. gov. dist., Dorset, **Eng.**; on S. cst. 8 km E. of Bournemouth; holiday resort; 30 % of population aged over 65; p. (2011) 55,000.

Chudleigh, mkt. t., Devon, **Eng.**; on R. Teign; stone quarrying.

Church, Hyndburn, sub. of Accrington, Lancs., **Eng.**; engin.

Church Stretton, mkt. t., Shrops., **Eng.**; tourism; p. 3,950.

Cinderford, t., Gloucs., **Eng.**; former ctr. of coalmng. a. of Forest of Dean; new lt. industl. estate; p. 9,750.

Cinque Ports, confederation of anc. **Eng.** pts. on cst. of Kent and Sussex; original 5: Sandwich, Dover, Hythe, Romney, Hastings; Winchelsea, and Rye added later.

Cirencester, sm. t., Cotswold, Gloucs., **Eng.**; Roman Corineum; former woollen t.; famous church; Royal Agricultural University.

Clackmannan, t., central **Scot.**, unit. auth. created in 1996, reinstating historic co. of **Clackmannanshire** which became part of Central Region in 1974; bordered S.W. by R. Forth; ch. t. Alloa; p. (2009) 3,600 (t.), (2010) 50,600 (unit. auth.).

Clacton-on-Sea, t., Tendring, Essex, **Eng.**; on E. cst. 19 km S.E. of Colchester; seaside resort; lt. inds.; residtl.; p. 52,500.

Clapham, S. London rly. junction; busiest station in Britain.

Clare, co., Munster, **R.o.I.**; cstl. co. bounded in S. and E. by R. Shannon; mainly agr. and tourism; inc. cliffs of Moher; Shannon airpt. and tax-free industl. development scheme; co. t. Ennis; a. 3,351 km²; p. (2011) 116,885.

Clare I., Clew Bay, Mayo, **R.o.I.**; tiny pop.

Clay Cross, t., Derbys., **Eng.**; former ctr. coal mng. (first developed by George Stephenson 1838) iron, engin.; p. 21,500 (with North Wingfield).

Clayton-le-Moors, t., Hyndburn, Lancs., **Eng.**; nr. Blackburn; textile machin., cotton and blanket weaving, bristles, soap; p. 7,200.

Clear C., southernmost point of Ireland, Clear I., **R.o.I.**; off S.W. cst. of Cork.

Cleator Moor, t. Cumbria, **Eng.**; former colly. t.; p. 7,000.

Cleckheaton, t., West Yorks., **Eng.**; nr. Bradford; woollens, blankets, asbestos; p. 27,250.

Cleethorpes, t., N.E. Lincs., **Eng.**; 5 km S. of Grimsby; resort; famous pier (opened in 1873) now restored, p.32,250.

Clerkenwell, industl. dist., London, **Eng.**; immediately N. of the City; once famous for jewellery.

Clevedon, sm. t., N. Somerset, **Eng.**; at mouth of R. Severn; seaside resort; quarrying, bricks.

Cleveland Hills, North Yorks., Redcar and Cleveland, **Eng.**; part of N. York Moors; once mined for iron ore, impt. potash deposit.

Clifton, sub., Bristol, **Eng.**; on R. Avon; mineral springs; famous suspension bridge, opened 1864.

Clitheroe, sm. t., Ribble Valley, Lancs., **Eng.**; in Ribble valley; mkt. t. for rural a.; limestone quarrying nearby.

Clonakilty, sm. t., Cork, **R.o.I.**; nr. Bandon; sm. harbour; agr. prods.

Clones, mkt. t. on Ulster border, Monaghan, **R.o.I.**; rly. ctr.; p. 2,500.

Clonmacnoise, v., Offaly, **R.o.I.**; ecclesiastical ruins.

Clonmel (Cluain Meala), t., Tipperary, **R.o.I.**; on R. Suir; agr. ctr.; fairs; cider, footwear. The name means 'Vale of Honey'.

Clowne, t., Derbys., Eng.; coal mng.; p. 7,750.

Clwyd, R., Denbighshire, N. Wales; flows into Irish Sea at Rhyl; length 48 km.

Clydach, t., Swansea, Wales; on R. Tawe, 8 km N.E. Swansea; steel wks., nickel refineries.

Clyde, R., central Scot.; flows through industl. belt into Firth of C.; Glasgow, Greenock, Clydebank main pts.; hydroelec. stas.; twin-road tunnel under R. in Glasgow (Whiteinch–Linthouse) completed 1963; 170 km long.

Clydebank, t., W. Dunbartonshire, Scot.; on Clyde adjoining Glasgow; tyres; p. 30,500.

Clyde, Firth of, stretches from Dumbarton to Ailsa Craig, Scot.; Bute, Arran, Gr. and Little Cumbrae ch. Is.; 102 km long.

Coalbrookdale, v., Shrops, Eng.; old coal and iron mines; home of iron master Abraham Darby. See Bridges, Section L.

Coalville, t., North West Leics., Eng.; nr. Ashby-de-la-Zouch; former coal mng., engin., elastic webbing; Amazon distrib.ctr.; p. 32,500.

Coatbridge, burgh, N. Lanarkshire, Scot., 16 km E. of Glasgow; coal, iron and steel, prefabricated houses, tubes engin.; p. 42,000.

Cockenzie and Port Seton, small burgh, E. Lothian, Scot.; fishing pts. on F. of Forth; p. 5,650.

Cockermouth, t., Allerdale, Cumbria, Eng.; slate, shoe mftg., plywood, concrete prods.; birthplace of Wordsworth; p. 8,100. Severe flooding in November 2009.

Colchester, t., l. gov. dist., Essex, Eng.; pre-Roman t. of Camulodunum on R. Colne; univ.; lt. inds., engin., oyster fisheries; old garrison town; pt.; p. (2010) 180,000 (dist.). First capital of Roman Britain. Largest Roman arcade in Britain recently unearthed.

Coldstream, t., Borders, Scot.; on Eng. border; agr. machin., knitwear; p. 1,900.

Coleraine, t., l. gov. dist., N. Ireland; pt. on R. Bann, 6 km from sea; univ.inen, acrilan mftg., distilling; p. (2010) 57,000 (dist.). See D11.

Coleshill, t., North Warwickshire, Eng.; lurgi gasification plant; p. 6,500.

Coll, I. off cst. of Mull, Argyll and Bute, Scot.; agr., lobster fishing.

Colne, t., Pendle, E. Lancs., Eng.; p. 20,900.

Colne, R., Eng.; trib. of Thames rising in Chilterns.

Colonsay, I., Inner Hebrides, Argyll and Bute, Scot.; 13 km long; ecclesiastical antiquities; p. 350.

Colwyn Bay, t., Conwy, N. Wales; on cst. 10 km E. of Llandudno; seaside resort; oldest operating cinema (Theatr Colwyn); p. 30,000.

Combe Martin, v., Devon, Eng.; 8 km E. of Ilfracombe; seaside resort.

Congleton, t., former l. gov. dist., E. Cheshire, Eng.; on S.W. margin of Pennines; once impt. for silk; p. 26,000 (t.).

Conisborough, sm. t., South Yorks., Eng.; limestone, bricks, tiles.

Coniston Water, L., Cumbria, Eng.; focus of tourism in L. Dist.; 8-8 km long.

Connacht, prov., R.o.I.; inc. Galway, Mayo, Sligo, Leitrim, Roscommon; mtnous in W.; farming, fishing; a. 17,775 km²; p. (2011) 542,000.

Connah's Quay, sm. t., Flintshire, Wales; lt. engin.

Connemara, mtns., dist., R.o.I.; Co. Galway; many lakes and bogs; tourist resort.

Consett, t., Derwentside, Durham, Eng.; on edge of Pennines, 16 km S.W. Newcastle; iron, steel closed (1980), coal mng.; p. 21,100.

Conwy, spt., N. Wales; mediaeval walled t. at mouth of R. Conwy; sm. seaside resort; cas.; quarrying, lt. engin.; unit. auth. created in 1996 from former l. gov. dists. of Aberconwy and Colwyn; inc. Conwy Valley and coastal resorts of Conwy, Llandudno and Colwyn Bay; p. (2011) 115,200 (unit. auth.).

Cookstown, mkt. t., l. gov. dist., N. Ireland; cement wks.; p. (2010) 36,500 (dist.). See D11.

Copeland, l. gov. dist., Cumbria, Eng.; cstl. a. N. of Barrow and inc. Whitehaven and Millom; p. (2011) 70,600.

Coquet, R., Eng; longest river in Northumberland.

Corbridge, sm. t., Northumberland, Eng.; on R. Tyne, nr. Hexham; 17th cent. bridge; Roman t. nearby.

Corby, t., l. gov. dist., Northants., Eng.; 11 km N. of Kettering; new t.; former steel wks., large Scottish pop.; p. (2010) 56,000 (dist.), (2011) 50,000 (t.).

Cork, co., R.o.I.; lgst. and most S.; mtns.; dairying, brewing, agr., fisheries; cap. Cork; a. 7,485 km²; p. (2011) 399.216.

Cork, spt., Cork, R.o.I.; at mouth of R. Lee; cath., univ.; woollens, butter, cattle, brewing; p. (2011) 118,912.

Cornwall and Isles of Growing calls Scilly, old non-met. co., S.W. Eng.; penin. bordering Atl. Oc. and Eng. Channel; granite moorlands supply kaolin; formerly tin mining; mild maritime climate encourages tourism, dairying, and mkt. gardening; many small fishing vs.; co. t. Bodmin; Now a supersize unit. auth.; p. 533,000 (2010). Known as Kernow in Cornish. Growing calls for a Cornish Assembly.

Corrib, Lough, Galway and Mayo, R.o.I.; drained by Corrib R. into Galway Bay; impt. brown trout fishery; a. 176 km².

Corryvreckan, strait and whirlpool between Jura and Scarba Is., Inner Hebrides, Scot.; whirlpool caused by tidal movement over variable sea bed.

Coryton, t., Essex, Eng.; on Thames, oil refining; oil pipeline to Stanlow refinery.

Cotswold, l. gov. dist., Gloucs., Eng.; lge a. covering C. Hills and inc. Cirencester and Northleach; p. (2010) 83,000.

Cotswold Hills, W. Eng.; limestone escarpment; Gloucs., Oxon.; once famous for woollens; source of Thames and tribs.; highest point Cleeve Cloud, 309 m; tourism.

Coventry, c. met. dist., West Midlands, Eng.; 29 km E.S.E. of Birmingham; former ctr. of cycle, motor cycle, motor car and aircraft engines, engin.; tools; chemicals; projectiles, textiles; cath.; univ.; p. 310,000. Wartime bombing raid on city, 14 Nov. 1940.

Cowbridge, sm. t., Vale of Glamorgan, S. Wales; nr. Cardiff.

Cowdenbeath, burgh, Fife, Scot.; 8 km N.E. of Dunfermline; coal mng.; p. 11,900.

Cowes, resort and pt., I. of Wight, Eng.; on estuary of R. Medina; regattas and yacht bldg.; p. 17,500.

Craigavon, c., l. gov. dist., N. Ireland; new "city in a garden" under construction, 16 km long, merging Portadown and Lurgan, linked by motorway, to provide major base for ind.; p. (2010) 92,500 (dist.). See D11.

Crail, royal burgh, Fife, Scot.; cstl. resort; p. 1,700.

Cramlington, t., Northumberland, Eng.; 13 km N. of Newcastle; new t.; p. 29,000.

Cranborne Chase, Wilts., Eng.; chalk upland of over 275 m; extension of Salisbury Plain.

Cranbrook, sm. mkt. t., Kent, Eng.; hops and grain; former weaving t.

Craven, dist., central Pennines, Eng.; relatively low limestone plateau, alt. mainly below 240 m; drained by R. Ribble to S.W., R. Aire to S.E.; sheep rearing in valleys, cattle for fattening, root and fodder crops; forms l. gov. dist. based on Skipton and Settle; p. (2010) 56,000.

Crawley, t., l. gov. dist., West Sussex, Eng.; on N.W. flank of Weald, 14 km S. of Reigate; new t. (1947); engin., pharmaceuticals, metal, leather, wooden goods; p. (2010) 101,000 (dist.).

Crayford. See Bexley.

Creag Meagaidh, mtn., Highland, Scot.; alt. 1,128 m.

Cree, R., Dumfries and Galloway, Scot.; flows into Wigtown Bay.

Creswell Crags, Derbyshire, Eng.; limestone gorge and world-famous prehistoric cave paintings; home to Ice Age people.

Crewe, t., Cheshire, Eng.; 32 km S.E. of Chester; lge. rly. wks.; impt. rly. junc.; aircraft and refrigerator wks.; clothing, engin., motor vehicles; expanded t.; p. 69,100 (t.).

Crewkerne, mkt. t., Somerset, Eng.; 13 km S.W. of Yeovil; leather; grammar school (1499); p. 7,100.

Crickhowell, mkt.t., Brecon, Wales. Popular tourist centre, on edge of Black Mountains; p. 2,800.

Cricklade, t., N. Wilts., Eng.; on R. Thames, 13 km N.W. of Swindon; fortified Saxon town; p. 3,900.

Crieff, t., Perth and Kinross, Scot.; on R. Earn; summer resort; p.6,750.

Crinan Canal, across peninsula of Argyll and Bute, S.W. Scot.; connects Loch Gilp with Atl. Oc.; 14 km long.

Croaghpatrick, mtns., May, R.o.I.; 766 m.

Cromarty, burgh, Highland, Scot.; N.E. cst. of Black Isle; offshore oil platforms at Nigg, C. Firth; p. 725. Perfect example of 18th century seaport. Birthplace of Hugh Miller.

Cromer, t., North Norfolk, Eng.; on N. cst. of E. Anglia; seaside resort; p. 7,600.

Cromford, v., Derbys., Eng.; Richard Arkwright's first waterpowered mill (1771); cotton; p. 2,600 (with Matlock Bath). Cromford Mills now World Heritage Site.

Crook and Willington, ts., former U.D., Wear Valley, Durham, **Eng.**; varied inds. to replace coal mng.

Crosby, t., Sefton, Merseyside, **Eng.**; on Liverpool Bay 5 km N. of Bootle, Seaforth container pt.; residtl.; seaside resort; p. 52,500.

Cross Fell, mtn., Cumbria, **Eng.**; on E. border of co.; alt. 894 m; highest point of the Pennines.

Crowland, sm. t., Lincs., **Eng.**; mkt. t. in the Fens, on R. Welland; 8th-cent. abbey ruins.

Croydon, residtl. t., **Eng.**; now outer bor., Greater London; inc. Coulsdon and Purley; lt. inds.; major office ctr.; growing tech hub; minster; tramlink network; p. (2011) 363,400.

Crummock Water, L. Dist., Cumbria, **Eng.**; ribbon L.

Cuckmere, R., Sussex, **Eng.**; passes through S. Downs in beautiful gap; length 37 km.

Cudworth, South Yorks., **Eng.**; p. 12,000.

Cuillin Hills, mtns., I. of Skye, **Scot.**; attaining 992 m in Sgurr Alasdair.

Culloden Moor, 10 km E. of Inverness, **Scot.**; defeat of Prince Charles Edward Stuart's high-landers by Duke of Cumberland's forces (1746).

Culross, royal burgh, Fife, **Scot.**; belongs to Nat. Trust; abbey.

Cumberland, historic co., N. **Eng.**; now part of Cumbria non-met. co.

Cumbernauld, new t. (1955), N. Lanarkshire, **Scot.**; to house 50,000 overspill from Glasgow; mnfs. of adding machines rapidly declining with use of computers; p. 51,500.

Cumbrae, Gt. and Little, Is. in F. of Clyde, off cst. of N. Ayrshire, **Scot.**

Cumbria, non-met. co., N.W. **Eng.**; centred on L. Dist. where rugged glaciated scenery encourages tourism, sheep farming, forestry and water storage; Cumberland coalfield on W. cst. and declining heavy inds. being replaced by new lt. inds.; ch. ts. Carlisle and Barrow; p. (2011) 499,900. Severe flooding in 2009 and 2015.

Cumbrian Mtns., L. Dist., Cumbria, **Eng.**

Cumnock, t., E. Ayrshire, **Scot.**, hilly dist. S. of Glasgow; p. 9,900.

Curragh, plain, Kildare, **R.o.I.**; turf; racecourse.

Cwmbran, t., Torfaen, **Wales**; in valley of Afon Lwyd, 8 km N. of Newport; new t. (1949); motor accessories, wire, elec. prods., bricks, tiles, pipes.

D

Dacorum, l. gov. dist., Herts., **Eng.**; a. of Chil-terns inc. Tring, Berkhamsted and Hemel Hempstead; p. (2012) 145,000.

Dagenham, dist. former M.B., **Eng.**; now forms part of Greater London bor. of Barking; on N. bank of R. Thames with river-side Ford motor works.

Dalgety, t., on Fife cst., **Scot.**; p. 10,500.

Dalkeith, burgh, Midlothian, **Scot.**; 10 km S.E. of Edinburgh; mkt. t.; p. 11,950.

Dalton-in Furness, t., Cumbria, **Eng.**; limestone quarrying, textiles; abbey ruins; p. 7,750.

Daresbury, v., Cheshire, **Eng.**; birthplace of C. L. Dodgson (Lewis Carroll).

Darlaston, t., West Midlands, **Eng.**; nuts, bolts, fabricated steel mnfs., drop forgings, car com-ponents; pig iron plant closed.

Darlington, t., unit. auth. created in 1997, formerly part of Durham, **Eng.**; bridge bldg., woollen yarn mnf., engin., rly. wagons, steel wks.; p. (2011) 105,600 (unit.auth).

Dart, R., Devon, **Eng.**; rises in Dartmoor, flows S. into English Channel at Dartmouth; pictur-esque estuary; 74 km long.

Dartford, t., l. gov. dist., Kent, **Eng.**; S. side of Thames estuary; Dartford–Purfleet road tunnel (1963); road bridge (1991); engin., chemi-cals, quarrying, paper; nr. Bluewater shopping complex; p. (2010) 92,000 (dist.), 58,000 (t.).

Dartmoor, high granite plateau, S.W. Devon, **Eng.**; rough moorland; sheep, cattle, and wild ponies; granite tors; Nat. Park; tourism; granite quarries, reservoirs; prison at Prince-town, (closure now planned); china clay (Lee Moor) now extends into Nat. Park; discovery of tungsten, lgst. deposit in W. Europe but conflicts with conservation; a. 583 km²; hgst. point High Willays, 622 m.

Dartmouth, spt., S. Devon, **Eng.**; on W. of estuary of R. Dart; Royal Naval College; pottery; yachting, holiday resort.

Darvel, burgh, E. Ayrshire, **Scot.**; on R. Irvine, 13km E. Kilmarnock; birthplace of Sir Alexander

Fleming, discoverer of penicillin; p. 3,400.

Darwen, t., N.E. Lancs., **Eng.**; on flank of Rossen-dale Fells, 5 km S. of Blackburn; tile and glaze bricks, paint, wallpaper, plastics; with **Blackburn** a unit.auth.

Daventry, t., l. gov. dist., Northampton, **Eng.**; 14 km S.E of Rugby; boot-mkg., lt. engin.; radio-transmission sta.; expanded t.; p. (2010) 80,000 (dist.).

Dawley, t., The Wrekin, Shrops., **Eng.**; on S.E. flank of the Wrekin; ironwks., pipe, cement, roadstone, asphalt and brick wks., engin.; part of Telford new t. (1963).

Dawlish, t., Teignbridge, S. Devon, **Eng.**; on S. cst. between estuaries of Rs. Exe and Teign; seaside resort; flower tr.; p. 9,900.

Deal, anc. pt., E. Kent, **Eng.**; on S.E. cst., 11 km N.E. Dover; opposite Goodwin Sands; seaside resort; p. 30,750.

Dean, Forest of. See **Forest of Dean.**

Dee, R., N. **Wales** and Cheshire, **Eng.**; 144 km long; lge. silted estuary, use for water storage planned.

Dee, R., Aberdeenshire, **Scot.**; picturesque, tourism; 139 km long.

Denbighshire, N. **Wales**, unit. auth. created in 1996 from former l. gov. dists. of Glyndŵr and Rhuddlan, reinstating part of historic co. split up in 1974; inc. cst. t. of Prestatyn and Rhyl and inland rural a.; p. (2011) 93,700.

Denbigh, t., Denbighshire, **Wales**; in Vale of Clwyd, 16 km S. of Rhyl; cas.; tourism; dairy prods.; birthplace of Stanley the explorer; p. 9,000.

Denby Dale, sm. t., West Yorks., **Eng.**; 13 km W. of Barnsley; woollen textiles; p. 2,500.

Denholme, t., West Yorks., **Eng.**; nr. Bradford; dairying, textiles; p. 2,300.

Denny and Dunipace, burgh, Falkirk, **Scot.**; 10 km W. of Falkirk; steel castings, concrete, p. 13,750.

Denton, t., Gtr. Manchester, **Eng.**; nr. Manchester; felt-hat mkg.; p. 27,350.

Deptford. See **Lewisham.**

Derby, c., unit. auth. created in 1997, formerly part of Derbys., **Eng.**; on R. Derwent; general engin., aero-engines, man-made fibres; univ.; Toyota car plant; p. (2010) 240,500. (unit. auth.). Smallest cathedral in England.

Derbyshire, non-met. co., **Eng.**; much of a. occupied by Pennines and Peak Dist. Nat. Park.; coalfield and industl. a. in E.; forms part of Manchester met. a. in N.W.; p. (2010) 763,000.

Derbyshire Dales, l. gov. dist., Derbys., **Eng.**; Pennine a. inc. Matlock, Bakewell and Ashbourne; p. (2010) 75,000.

Derg, Lough, in basin of R. Shannon, **R.o.I.**; separating Galway and Clare from Tipperary.

Derg, L., Donegal, **R.o.I.**, with cave on I. visited by pilgrims; known as "St Patrick's Purgatory".

Derry.; l. gov. dist., N. **Ireland**; borders R.o.I. and L. Foyle; Sperrin Mtns. in S.; p. (2010) 110,000.

Derry. See **Londonderry.**

Derwent, R., Derbys., **Eng.**; trib. of R. Trent; length 96 km.

Derwent, R., North Yorks, **Eng.**; trib. of R. Ouse; length 91 km.

Derwentside, former l. gov. dist., Durham, **Eng.**; inc. Consett, Stanley etc. Now part of unit. auth.

Derwentwater, L., Cumbria, **Eng.**; 5 km long.

Desborough, t., Northants., **Eng.**; boot and shoe mnfs., iron mng.; p. 7,600.

Devizes, t., Kennet, Wilts., **Eng.**; mkt. t., on Kennet and Avon canal at foot of Marlborough Downs; bricks, tiles, bacon-curing; p. 14,500.

Devon, non-met. co., S.W. **Eng.**; between English and Bristol Channels; attractive cstl. scenery, Nat. Parks of Dartmoor and Exmoor encourage tourism; mixed farming; modern lt. inds.; major ctrs. of p. at Plymouth, Torbay, Exeter; p. (2009) 755,000.

Dewsbury, t., West Yorks., **Eng.**; on R. Calder, 13 km from Leeds; heavy woollens, shoddy, coalmng.; dyewks.; large Muslim population, especially in Saville Town; p. 55,200.

Didcot, sm. t., Oxon, **Eng.**; 16 km S. of Oxford; Grand Prix engin.; rly. ctr.; historic cooling tow-ers demolished (2014); p. 26,500.

Dingle B., Kerry, **R.o.I.**; long inlet of sea on Atl. cst.

Dingwall, royal burgh, Highland, **Scot.**; at head of Cromarty F.; rly. junction; cattle mkt.; admin. ctr.; distilling; handloom weaving; p. 5,250.

Diss, North Norfolk, **Eng.**; mkt. t. on R. Waveney, 45 km S.W. of Norwich; p. 7,500.

Ditchling Beacon, 10 km N. of Brighton, East Sussex, **Eng.**; hgst point of South Downs, 248 m.

Docklands, expanding area of former docks, E. London; commercial and office devt; expensive housing; light railway; Canary Wharf, once tallest bldg. in London.

Dodworth, t., South Yorks., **Eng.**; nr. Barnsley.

Dogger Bank, sandbank in N. Sea, between England and Denmark; depth varies from 6 to 37 m; valuable fishing ground.

Doggerland. The vast land bridge to Europe (now long submerged). Britain's Atlantis.

Dolgellau, sm. t., Gwynedd, **N. Wales**; agr., quarrying, timber, p. 2,500.

Dollar, burgh, Clackmannan, **Scot.**; at foot of Ochil Hills; p. 2,950.

Don, R., South Yorks., **Eng.**; trib. of R. Ouse, 112 km long. Formerly heavily-polluted, now transformed.

Don, R., Aberdeen/Aberdeenshire, **Scot.**; flows into N. Sea nr. Aberdeen; salmon; 131 km long.

Doncaster, t., met. dist., South Yorks., **Eng.**; on Don R., 27 km N.E. of Sheffield; now major distribution centre; nylon mftg.; racecourse; new Robin Hood airport, 7 mile S.E. of town; p. (2011) 302,400 (dist.), 69,000 (t.).

Donegal, sm. spt., Co. Donegal, **R.o.I.**; on W. cst. on Donegal Bay; tweeds, carpets.

Donegal (Tirconnail), co., N.W. **R.o.I.**; fishing poor agr.; cloth, hydroelectric power; co. t. Lifford; a. 4,830 km²; p. (2011) 160,927.

Dorchester, co. t., West Dorset, **Eng.**; mkt. t. on R. Frome; lime, agr., engin.; Roman remains; nearby prehistoric Maiden Castle; linked with the name of Thomas Hardy; p. 19,100.

Dorking, t., Mole Valley, Surrey, **Eng.**; on R. Mole to S. of gap through N. Downs; mkt., residtl.; lt. inds.; p. 19,000.

Dorset, non-met. co., S. **Eng.**; borders English Channel along attractive cliffed cst. formed by E.–W. limestone ridges; Portland stone quarried; many tourist resorts; mkt. ts. serve agr. interior; p. (2009) 408,000.

Dorset Heights, hills, extend E. to W. across central Dorset, **Eng.**; chalk; pastoral farming, sheep; some cultivation where soil is deep enough; rise to 250–275 m.

Douglas, t., cap. of **Isle of Man**; 120 km W. of Liverpool, **Eng.**; spt; resort; nearby freeport (1983) gaining from low tax rate; p. 23,000.

Dounreay, Highland, **Scot.**; fast-breeder nuclear reactors. Closure of plant announced (1998).

Dove, R., Derbys. and Staffs., **Eng.**; trib. of Trent; flows through beautiful dales; 77 km long.

Dovedale, valley, Derbys., **Eng.**; steeply sloping limestone ravine of R. Dove; tourism; created National Nature Reserve (2006).

Dover, packet pt., l. gov. dist., Kent, **Eng.**; Cinque pt.; nearest spt. to France, the Strait of D. being only 34 km wide; ch. pt. for Continent; cas.; p. (2010) 107,000 (dist.), 35,000 (t.).

Dovey, R., **Wales**; flows from Cambrian Mtns. and enters Cardigan Bay by a wide estuary.

Down, former co.; l. gov. dist., **N. Ireland**; borders Strangford Lough and Dundrum Bay; agr. and fisheries; p. (2010) 70,500. *See* D11.

Downham Market, sm. t., West Norfolk, **Eng.**; on R. Ouse; flour-milling, malting, sheet-metal wks.

Downpatrick, sm. t., Down, **N. Ireland**; on R. Quoile.

Downs, natural harbour of refuge for shipping between Kent cst. and Goodwin Sands in the English Channel.

Drax, West Yorks., **Eng.**; thermal elec. power sta. linked to Selby coalfield.

Drogheda, spt., Louth, **R.o.I.**; considerable tr. in agr. produce, salmon, etc.; stormed by Cromwell in 1649; p. 24,900.

Droitwich, t., Wychavon, Worcs., **Eng.**; brine baths; lt. inds.; expanded t.; p. 23,100.

Dromore, sm. mkt. t., Banbridge, **N. Ireland**; on Lagan R.; linen.

Dronfield, t., North East Derbys., **Eng.**; between Chesterfield and Sheffield; edged tools, engin. and agr. implements; p. 21,950.

Droylsden, t., Gtr. Manchester, **Eng.**; sub. of Manchester; chemicals; textiles; p. 23,750.

Dublin, co., **R.o.I.**; co. t. Dublin; a. (inc. c. of Dublin) 922 km²; p. (2011) 1,270,603.

Dublin (Irish *Baile Átha Cliath*), C.B., cap. of **R.o.I.**; co. t. Co. Dublin; at mouth of R. Liffey; ctr. of govt., commerce, ind., and culture; cath., univ.; Abbey Theatre; brewing, distilling, food processing; Swift was buried here; p. (2011) 525,383 (city).

Dudley, t., met. dist., West Midlands, **Eng.**; cas.; engin.; cables, chains; p. (2001) 305,155 (dist.), 199,500 (t.).

Dukeries. *See* **Section L.**

Dukinfield, t., Tameside, Gtr. Manchester, **Eng.**; 10 km E. of Manchester; textiles, engin., rope and twine; p. 18,250.

Dulwich, residtl. sub. in bor. of Southwark, Greater London, **Eng.**; village character with lge. park and public school. Dulwich Picture Gallery (opened 1817).

Dumbarton, royal burgh, W. Dunbartonshire, **Scot.**; on N. bank of R. Clyde, 19 km below Glasgow; shipbldg., valve and tube-mkg., iron; p. 21,200.

Dumfries, royal burgh, Dumfries and Galloway, **Scot.**; on R. Nith, 16 km from Solway F.; p. (2011) 31,950.

Dumfries and Galloway, unit. auth. created in 1996 from former Region, S. **Scot.**; occupies W. half of Southern Uplands; drained by R. Nith; sparse rural p.; p. (2010) 148,750.

Dumfriesshire, historic co., S. **Scot.**; now part of Dumfries and Galloway.

Dunbar, royal burgh, E. Lothian, **Scot.**; sm. fishing pt.; Cromwell's victory 1650; p. 6,490.

Dunbartonshire, historic co., central **Scot.**; now divided between Argyll and Bute, W. Dunbartonshire, E. Dunbartonshire and N. Lanarkshire.

Dunblane, mkt. burgh, Stirling, **Scot.**; on Allan Water, 8 km from Stirling; Gothic cath. now used as par. church; scene of horrific school massacre, 1996; p. 8,100.

Dundalk, t., cap. of Co. Louth, **R.o.I.**; harbour.

Dundee, c., spt., royal burgh, unit. auth. created in 1996, formerly part of Tayside, E. **Scot.**; on F. of Tay, 80 km N. Edinburgh; jute mnf. (ended 1999); engin., computers, refrigerators, clocks, watches, preserves, linoleum; publishing., univs; new Dundee V&A Museum of Design; p. (2010) 143,500 (unit. auth.). Famous for "jute, jain and journalism".

Dundonald, t. E. of Belfast, **N. Ireland**; p. 13,500.

Dunfermline, royal burgh, Fife, **Scot.**; 22 km E. of Alloa; linen, rubber prods., synthetic fibre; birthplace of Charles I and Andrew Carnegie; cap. of Scot. 1057–93; p. 40,500.

Dungannon, mkt. t., l. gov. dist., **N. Ireland**; linen, bricks; p. (2010) 56,500 (dist.). *See* D11.

Dungeness, headland of shingle, Kent, **Eng.**; 16 km S.E. of Rye; two Magnox nuclear power stas.; linked by power cable to France 1961.

Dunkeld, t., Perth and Kinross, **Scot.**; on R. Tay at entrance to Strathmore; cath., ecclesiastical ctr. in 9th cent.; tourism; p. 1,100 (with Birnam).

Dun Laoghaire (Kingstown), t., Dublin, **R.o.I.**; spt., fishing; ferry to Eng.; p. 56,000.

Dunoon, burgh, Argyll and Bute, **Scot.**; on N. side of F. of Clyde, anc. cas.; resort; p.9,250.

Duns, burgh, Borders, **Scot.**; agr. and allied inds.; mkt. t.; cas.; p. 2,750.

Dunsinane, hill, Perth and Kinross, **Scot.**; nr. Perth; alt. 309 m; referred to by Shakespeare in *Macbeth*.

Dunstable, t., South Beds., **Eng.**; on N. edge of Chiltern Hills, 6 km W. of Luton; motor vehicles, engin., cement, rubber, and plastic gds.; p. (2011) 51,250.

Dunwich, old t., Suffolk; **Eng;** 'Britain's Atlantis'; collapsed into North Sea in medieval times after coastal erosion.

Durham, c., co. t., old l. gov. dist., Durham, N.E. **Eng.**; sited within a meander of R. Wear; cath. cas., univ.; pipe organ mftg., confectionery; World Heritage Site; p. 44,000 (c.). Now part of new unit. auth.

Durham, old non-met. co., N.E. **Eng.**; between Rs. Tyne and Tees; stretches from attractive Pennine moorland in W. to coalfield and industl. a. with many sm. ts. in E.; borders the N. Sea; Now a new unit. auth; p. 513,200 (2011).

Dursley, sm. t., Gloucs., **Eng.**; 21 km S.W. of Gloucester; agr. machin.; 18th cent. mkt. house.

E

Ealing, outer bor., Greater London, **Eng.**; comprising former bors. of Acton, Ealing, and Southall; univ.; p. (2011) 338,400. In Victorian times dubbed the Queen of the Suburbs.

Earl's Court, residtl. a., London, **Eng.**; Bor. of Kensington and Chelsea, contains E.C. exhibition hall. Huge redevelopment plan announced (2011).

Easington, former l. gov. dist., Durham, **Eng.**; colly. closed 1993; now part of Peterlee; p. (2011) 95,000.

Easington, v., E. Riding of Yorks., **Eng.**; nr. Hull;

natural gas terminal; new gas pipeline to Norway (opened 2006); p. 8,100.

East Anglia, comprises Norfolk and Suffolk, **Eng.**; former Anglo-Saxon kingdom; one of Britain's most productive agr. regions.

East Anglian Heights, hills, extend S.W. to N.E. across N.E. Hertfordshire, N. Essex, and S.W. Suffolk, **Eng.**; chalk overlain by glacial clays and sands; smooth, rolling surface; region of lge. farms and lge. fields, mixed farms mainly grain; rarely exceed 180 m.

East Ayrshire, unit. auth. created in 1996, formerly part of Strathclyde, **W. Scot.**; ch. t. Kilmarnock; p. (2010) 120,500.

East Bergholt, v., Suffolk, **Eng.**; birthplace of Constable.

Eastbourne, t., l. gov. dist., East Sussex, **Eng.**; on S. cst. to E. of Beachy Head; seaside resort; p. (2010) 96,000 (dist.) Pier damaged by fire (2014).

East Cambridgeshire, l. gov. dist., Cambs., **Eng.**; a. N.E. of Cambridge inc. Ely; p. (2010) 82,000.

East Dereham, t., Breckland, Norfolk, **Eng.**; 22 km W. of Norwich; agr. implements; p. 13,500.

East Devon, l. gov. dist., Devon, **Eng.**; Exmouth, Sidmouth and Seaton on cst. and inland ts. Honiton and Ottery St. Mary; p. (2010) 133,000.

East Dorset, l. gov. dist., Dorset, **Eng.**; rural a. based on Wimborne Minster; p. (2010) 86,000.

East Dunbartonshire, unit. auth. created in 1996, formerly part of Strathclyde, central **Scot.**; lies immediately N. of Glasgow; p. (2010) 105,000.

East Grinstead, t., West Sussex, **Eng.**; in ctr. of Weald, 14 km W. of Tunbridge Wells; famous hospital for plastic surgery; p. 27,100.

East Ham. *See* **Newham.**

East Hampshire, l. gov. dist., Hants., **Eng.**; stretches from Alton to Petersfield; p. (2010) 112,000.

East Hertfordshire, l. gov. dist., Herts., **Eng.**; lge a. inc. Ware, Bishop's Stortford, Hertford and Sawbridgeworth; p. (2010) 135,000.

East Kilbride, t., S. Lanarkshire, **Scot.**; 11 km S.S.E. of Glasgow; new t. 1947; lge. agr. machin., aero engines, engin., elec. prods., seawater distillation plant; knitwear, clothing; p. 74,850.

Eastleigh, t., l. gov. dist., Hants., **Eng.**; rly. engin., many new inds.; p. 113,000 (dist.), 53,000 (t.).

East Lindsey, l. gov. dist., Lincs., **Eng.**; lge. a. on E. cst. inc. Louth, Mablethorpe, Horncastle, Skegness and Alford; p. (2010) 141,000.

East Lothian, E. Scot., unit. auth. created in 1996, incorporating most of historic co. which became part of Lothian in 1974; lies E. of Edinburgh, bordered N.E. by N. Sea, S.W. by Lammermuir Hills; p. (2010) 96,950.

East Northamptonshire, l. gov. dist., Northants., **Eng.**; stretches from Oundle to Irthlingborough, Rushden, Raunds and Higham Ferrers; p. (2010) 85,900.

East Renfrewshire, unit. auth. created in 1996, formerly part of Strathclyde, **W. Scot.**; lies immediately S.W. of Glasgow; p. (2010) 89,250.

East Riding of Yorkshire, unit. auth. created in 1996, formerly part of Humberside, **Eng.**; lge. a. N. of the R. Humber inc. Holderness Peninsula and ts. of Beverley and Bridlington; p. (2010) 336,000.

East Staffordshire, l. gov. dist., Staffs., **Eng.**; stretches from Uttoxeter to Burton-on-Trent; p. (2010) 109,000.

East Sussex, non-met. co., S.E. **Eng.**; mainly rural, urban growth on cst., where resorts, retirement and dormitory ts. for London, inc. Hastings and Eastbourne; crossed by S. Downs in S. terminating at Beachy Head, Ashdown Forest in N.; p. (2009) 511,000.

Eastwood, sm. t., Broxtowe, Notts., **Eng.**; birthplace of D. H. Lawrence; coal.

Ebbsfleet, Kent, **Eng.** Designated as a new garden city in 2014.

Ebbw Vale, t., Blaenau Gwent, **Wales**; 27 km N.W. of Newport; coal, iron, tinplate, bricks, pipes, precast concrete; end of steel-making, 2002; p. 22,000.

Eccles, Gtr. Manchester, **Eng.**; 6 km W. of Manchester; chemicals; p. 37,100.

Eday, I., Orkney Is., **Scot.**; the Ocelli of Ptolemy.

Eddystone, rock with lighthouse, Eng. Channel; S.W. of Plymouth.

Eden, Vale of, fertile belt in Cumbria, **Eng.**; between barren hills of Pennines and L. Dist.; occupied by R. Eden; mkt. ts. Appleby and Penrith; forms l. gov. dist. Eden, inc. Penrith, Alston and Appleby; p. (2011) 52,600.

Edgehill, ridge, 24 km S. of Warwick, **Eng.**; scene of first battle of civil war, 1642.

Edinburgh, c., cap. of **Scot.**, unit. auth. created in 1996, formerly part of Lothian; royal burgh on F. of Forth; univs., cas.; palace (Holyrood); caths., printing, publishing, brewing, electronics equipment, rubber prods.; Edinburgh Festival in August; UNESCO's first world City of Literature (2004); Leith, with docks is joined to E.; new tram-link to airport opened, 2014; p. (2010) 478,000.

Egham, t., Runnymede, Surrey, **Eng.**; on R. Thames, nr. Staines; contains field of Runnymede; residtl.; p. (2011) 29,500.

Egremont, sm. mkt. t., Cumbria, **Eng.**; 10 km S. of Whitehaven; limestone; former iron ore mng.; p. 7,200.

Eigg, I., Inner Hebrides, Highland, **Scot.**; 24 km S.W. of Mallaig; basaltic rocks on cst.; no electric power until 2008; rises to 393 m; p. (2017) 105.

Eire. *See* **Ireland, Republic of.**

Elan, R. Powys, **Wales**; rises on S.E. sides of Plynlimon, flows into R. Wye; lower valley contains series of 4 lge. reservoirs, capacity 45,460 million litres; ch. an important source of water for Birmingham.

Elgin, royal burgh, Moray, **Scot.**; pt. Lossiemouth, whisky; ruins anc. cath.; p. 21,150.

Elie and Earlsferry, burgh, Fife, **Scot.**; summer resort.

Elland, t., West Yorks., **Eng.**; on R. Calder, 5 km S.E. of Halifax; textiles; p. 14,750.

Ellesmere, sm. mkt. t., Shrops., **Eng.**; nearby lake; extensive tourism.

Ellesmere Port, t., N.W. Cheshire, **Eng.**; on Manchester Ship Canal and 14 km S.S.E. of Liverpool; metal mfftg., paper, engin., oil refineries; cars; expanded t.; p. 67,100. Known as the home of the Vauxhall Astra.

Ellon, burgh, Aberdeenshire, **Scot.**; on R. Ythan; p. 9,000.

Elmbridge, l. gov. dist., Surrey, **Eng.**; close to Gtr. London; inc. Esher, Walton and Weybridge; p. (2010) 131,000.

Elstow, v., Beds., **Eng.**; birthplace of John Bunyan.

Elstree, t., Hertsmere, Herts., **Eng.**; 6 km W. of Barnet; residtl.; films, lt. engin., silk hosiery.

Ely, c., Cambridge, **Eng.**; on S. fringe of Fens; mkt., cath.; agr. ctr.; p. 11,000.

Ely, I. of. *See* **Cambridgeshire.**

Enfield, outer bor., Greater London, **Eng.**; comprising Edmonton, Enfield, and Southgate; p. (2011) 312,500.

England, southern and lgst. political div. of U.K.; bounded by Wales on W., by Scot. on N. and separated from continent of Europe by English Channel and North Sea; highly industl., circa 80 per cent of p. live in urban areas; major trading nation through main pts. London, Liverpool, Southampton; increasing contrast between prosperous S. and depressed N. and W.; very varied geology and topography produce contrasts in landscape, matched by climatic variability; increasingly attractive as tourist area although urban and agr. pressures on rural countryside cause concern in such a densely populated cty.; excellent road and rail network; rich and varied cultural heritage and historic bldgs.; rising population; cap. London; p. (2015) 54,400,000.

English Channel (La Manche), narrow sea separating England from France; extends from Strait of Dover to Land's End in Cornwall; length 480 km, greatest width 248 km.; now crossed by Channel Tunnel *See* **Cheriton.**

Enham-Alamein, Hants., **Eng.**; rehabilitation ctr. for disabled ex-service men; 4 km N. of Andover; lt. inds.

Ennerdale Water, L., Cumbria, **Eng.**

Enniscorthy, mkt. t., Wexford, **R.o.I.**; cath.; p. 7,600.

Enniskillen, t., Fermanagh, **N. Ireland**; brewing, nylon mftg., meat processing; IRA bomb outrage, 8 Nov. 1987; p. 12,000.

Epping Forest, Essex, **Eng.**; forest a. N.E. of London free to public (opened by Queen Victoria 1882); formerly part of royal hunting forest; also l. gov. dist., inc. Chigwell, Waltham Abbey and Ongar; p. (2010) 123,750.

Epsom and Ewell, ts., l. gov. dist., Surrey, **Eng.**; 29 km S.W. of London; residtl., racecourse; p. (2010) 72,500 (dist.).

Epworth, v., N. Lincs., **Eng.**; birthplace of John Wesley.

Erewash, l. gov. dist., Derbys., **Eng.**; a. close to Nottingham inc. Ilkeston and Long Eaton; p. (2010) 111,400.

Ericht, Loch, Scot.; in central Grampians; 25 km long; hydroelec. scheme.

Erith, former M.B., Kent, **Eng.**; on Thames estuary; plastics, paints, varnishes, timber, concrete; now inc. in London bor. of Bexley.

Erne, R., **N. Ireland/R.o.I.**; links Ls. in Cavan and Fermanagh; 115 km long.

Esher, t., Elmbridge, Surrey, **Eng.**; on R. Mole, residtl.; Sandown Park racecourse; p. 53,000.

Esk, R., Borders, **Scot.**; Cumbria, **Eng.**; attractive agr. valley; flows into Solway F. from confluence of Black and White Esk Rs.; 37 km long.

Essex, non-met. co., **Eng.**; bounded on S. by Thames, on E. by N. Sea; co. t. Chelmsford; on London clay and chalk; agr.; wheat, barley, sugar-beet; mkt. gardens; S.W. of co. forms part of Greater London with mftg. subs.; oil refineries at Shell Haven; civil nuclear power sta. at Bradwell; p. (2010) 1,401,000.

Eston, t., Redcar and Cleveland, **Eng.**; 5 km E. of Middlesbrough; shipbldg. and repairing; p. 34,000 (with South Bank).

Eton, t., Berks., **Eng.**; on N. bank of R. Thames opposite Windsor; public school, founded by Henry VI; p. 2,100.

Etruria, t., Stoke, **Eng.**; part of Stoke-on-Trent; seat of Josiah Wedgwood's potteries (1769).

Evesham, mkt. t., Wychavon, Worcs., **Eng.**; on R. Avon, in Vale of Evesham, 24 km S.E. of Worcester; fruit ctr.; tourism; p. 22,900.

Exe, R., Somerset and Devon, **Eng.**; rises on Exmoor, flows S. via Exeter to English Channel at Exmouth; 86 km long.

Exeter, l. gov. dist., cath. c., co. t., Devon, **Eng.**; former Roman Isca; E. of Dartmoor on R. Exe; mkt. t.; univ.; aircraft components; airport; p. (2010) 123,000 (dist.).

Exmoor, Somerset and Devon, **Eng.**; sandstone moorland, deep wooded valleys; Nat. Park.

Exmouth, mkt. t., East Devon, **Eng.**; on estuary of R. Exe; holiday resort; official gateway to the Jurassic Coast; p. 36,880 (2010).

Eye, mkt. t., Mid Suffolk, **Eng.**; 29 km N. of Ipswich; anc. church.

Eyemouth, burgh, Borders, **Scot.**; on E. cst. 14 km N. of Berwick; fishing; p. 4,000.

F

Failsworth, t. Gtr. Manchester, **Eng.**; N.E. of Manchester; textiles, elec. gds.; p. 20,500.

Fair I., midway between Shetland and Orkney, **Scot.**; bird sanctuary; famous for brightly patterned, hand-knitted jumpers; a shipping area. It is the UK's most remote inhabited island. Acquired by National Trust, 1954.

Falkirk, burgh, unit. auth. created in 1996, formerly part of Central Region, **Scot.**; 16 km S.E. of Stirling, bordered N.E. by F. of Forth; foundries, bricks, chemical, aluminium wks., concrete, timber yards; battles 1298 and 1746; p. (2011) 153,000 (unit. auth.).

Falkland, burgh, Fife, **Scot.**; 5 km S. of Auchtermuchty; mkt.; p. 1,250.

Falmouth, t., Carrick, Cornwall, **Eng.**; on W. side of estuary of R. Fal. 16 km S. of Truro; sheltered harbourage; offshore oil supply base; seaside resort; fisheries, ship repairing, mng., quarrying, lt. engin.; cas.; new Maritime Museum opened, 2002; Univ. Coll. Falmouth, created Cornwall's first full univ., 2012; pt.; p. 22,000.

Fareham, t., l. gov. dist., Hants., **Eng.**; at N.W. corner of Portsmouth Harbour; p. (2010) 110,000 (dist.).

Faringdon, mkt. t., Vale of White Horse, Oxon., **Eng.**; Faringdon Folly; p. 5,500.

Farnborough, t., Rushmoor, Hants., **Eng.**; Aldershot military camp; Royal Aircraft Establishment; p. 58,250.

Farne Is., gr. of islets off Northumberland cst., **Eng.**; bird sanctuary; National Trust. Home to 40,000 pairs of puffins.

Farnham, t., Waverley, Surrey, **Eng.**; at N. foot of N. Downs, 16 km W. of Guildford; p. 37,000.

Farnworth, t., Gtr. Manchester, **Eng.**; nr. Bolton, textiles, engin., paper; p. 26,000.

Fastnet, lighthouse in Atl. Oc., 7·2 km S.W. C. Clare, Irish cst.

Faversham, pt., Swale, N.E. Kent, **Eng.**; at head of F. creek; mkt.; fruit, hops; p. 18,000.

Fawley, t., Hants., **Eng.**; on W. shore Southampton Water; lge. oil refinery with pipeline to Staines and Heathrow Airpt.

Featherstone, sm. t., West Yorks., **Eng.**

Felixstowe, pt., Suffolk Coastal, Suffolk, **Eng.**; container pt.; deepwater terminal opened (2011); seaside resort; p. 32,000.

Felling, Tyne and Wear, **Eng.**; Tyneside mftg. dist.; p. 35,000.

Feltham. See **Hounslow.**

Fenland, l. gov. dist., Cambs., **Eng.**; agr. a. in N. of co. including Wisbech, Chatteris, March, Whittlesey and North Witchford; p. (2010) 92,000.

Fens, The, low-lying dist. around the Wash, **Eng.**; artificial drainage first begun in 17th cent.; impt. agr. dist.; root crops, wheat, fruit, bulbs; a. 3,367 km².

Fermanagh, former co.; l. gov. dist., **N. Ireland**; bisected by R. Erne and lakes; stock raising, dairying; p. (2010) 62,500. See **D11.**

Ferryhill, v., Durham, **Eng.**; 8 km S. of Durham, in gap through limestone ridge which separates Wear valley from Tees valley; commands main N. to S. route along lowland E. of Pennines.

Ffestiniog. See **Blaenau Ffestiniog.**

Fife, E. **Scot.**, unit. auth. created in 1996, reinstating historic co. which became Region in 1974; occupies a. between Tay and Forth estuaries; industl. dist. based originally on coalfields; Longannet colliery remains; p. (2011) 364,000.

Filton, Bristol, **Eng.**; aircraft wks.

Finchley. See **Barnet.**

Findhorn, v., Moray, **Scot.**; resort; 12th cent. abbey; remains of port washed away in 1702 now rediscovered; p. 900.

Fingal's Cave, Staffa I., Inner Hebrides, W. **Scot.**; basaltic columns.

Finsbury. See **Islington.**

Fishguard, spt., Pembrokeshire, **Wales**; on S. of Cardigan Bay; ferry connection to Rosslare (Ireland); p. 3,000.

Flag Fen, nr. Peterborough; major Bronze Age site.

Flamborough Head, promontory of Yorks. cst., **Eng.**; steep chalk cliffs; lighthouse; anc., Brit. earthwork (Danes' dyke).

Fleet, t., Hart, Hants., **Eng.**; 6 km N.W. of Aldershot; p. 33,500.

Fleetwood, spt., Wyre, Lancs., **Eng.**; at mouth of Wyre, Morecambe Bay; deep-sea fish. pt.; fish processing; lge. chemical plant nearby; pier destroyed by fire, 2008; p. 27,500.

Flint, t., Flintshire, **Wales**; viscose textile yarn, cas. ruins; p. 12,500.

Flintshire, N.E. **Wales,** unit. auth. created in 1996 from former l. gov. dists. of Alyn and Deeside and Delyn, reinstating part of historic co. split up in 1974; inc. ts. of Buckley, Connah's Quay, Flint and Mold; p. (2011) 152,500.

Flodden, v. Northumberland, **Eng.**; on R. Till; battle between James IV of Scot. and the English under the Earl of Surrey 1513.

Fochabers, v., Moray, **Scot.**; nr. mouth of Spey; tourist resort; food canning; p. 1,530.

Folkestone, t., Shepway, Kent, **Eng.**; seaside resort; p. 46,500. Last racecourse in Kent (closure now threatened).

Foreland, N. and S., two headlands on E. cst. Kent, **Eng.**; between which are the Goodwin Sands and Pegwell Bay; lighthouses; sea battle between de Ruyter and Monk (1666).

Forest Heath, l. gov. dist., Suffolk, **Eng.**; part of Breckland inc. Mildenhall and Newmarket; p. (2010) 64,400.

Forest of Dean, Gloucs., **Eng.**; between Wye and Severn Rs.; former Royal Forest; Forestry Commission plantations; former coal mng. a.; tourism; new lt. industl. estates; forms l. gov. dist.; p. (2010) 82,000.

Forfar, royal burgh, Angus, **Scot.**; jute, linen; p. 13,500.

Forres, royal burgh, Moray, **Scot.**; on Findhorn R. nr. Moray F.; agr., forestry, engin., distilleries; cas.; p. 9,050.

Forth, R., **Scot.**; formed by two headstreams rising to N. of Ben Lomond which meet nr. Aberfoyle; takes meandering course to Alloa, then it expands into Firth of Forth; 165 km long.

Forth, Firth of, lge. inlet, E. cst. of **Scot.**; submerged estuary of R. Forth; navigable by lge. vessels for 64 km inland to Grange-mouth; other pts., Leith, Rosyth (naval), Bo'ness; l. (to Alloa) 80 km; the Forth rly. bridge (1890) spans the F. at Queensferry; road bridge (1964). Repainting of rly. bridge completed, 2011. Bridge now a World Heritage Site. New Queensferry Crossing (opened 2017), (the UK's tallest bridge). Bass Rock (world's largest colony of gannets).

Forth and Clyde Canal, Scot.; links F. of Forth at Grangemouth and F. of Clyde at Glasgow; not completely navigable; 61 km long.

Fortrose, t., royal burgh, Ross and Cromarty, Scot.; on S. cst. of Black Isle, on Moray F.; p. 1,240.

Fort William, burgh, Highland, Scot.; nr. head of Loch Linnhe, at base of Ben Nevis; aluminium factory; pulp- and paper-mill at Corpach; p. 10,100.

Fotheringhay, v., Northampton, Eng.; on R. Nene; Mary Queen of Scots beheaded (1587) in F. Castle.

Foula. Island near Shetland, with the world's largest colony of great skuas. Smallpox epidemic devastated human population, early 1900s.

Foulness I., S. Essex, Eng.; at mouth of R. Crouch; owned by Min. of Defence; site of projected third London airport of Maplin, now abandoned; projected container and oil pt.

Fountains Abbey, ruined Cistercian abbey, North Yorks., Eng.; founded in 1132, lasting until 1539; nr. Ripon. Now a World Heritage Site.

Fowey, sm. spt., Cornwall, Eng.; nr. mouth of R. Fowey; exp. kaolin; resort; fishing; p. 2,200.

Foyers, Falls of, Highland, Scot.; E. of Loch Ness, nr. Fort Augustus; aluminium wks., the first hydroelectric plant erected in Britain (1896).

Foyle, Lough, inlet, N. Ireland; between Donegal (R.o.I.) and Londonderry; outlet of R. F.; Londonderry t. at head of inlet.

Foynes Is., R.o.I.; oil terminal on N. side, E. of Battery Point.

Framlingham, mkt. t., Suffolk, Eng.; N.E. of Ipswich; cas.

Fraserburgh, spt., burgh, Aberdeenshire, Scot.; the largst shellfish pt. in Europe; p. 12,000.

Freshwater, sm. t., I. of Wight, Eng.; at W. end of I., 13 km W. of Newport; resort; p. 7,700 (with Totland).

Friern Barnet. See Barnet.

Frimley and Camberley, ts., Surrey Heath, Surrey, Eng.; 5 km N. of Farnborough; lt. engin., military training ctr.; p. 47,500.

Frinton and Walton, Tendring, Essex, Eng.; on E. cst., 8 km N.E. of Clacton; seaside resort.

Frome, mkt. t., Mendip, Somerset, Eng.; on R. Frome, 18 km S. of Bath; p. 24,900.

Frome, R., Dorset, Eng.; flows from N. Dorset Downs into Poole Harbour.

Fulham. See Hammersmith.

Furness, dist., Cumbria, Eng.; between Morecambe Bay and the Irish Sea.

Fylde, W. Lancs., Eng.; low plain behind coastal sand dunes; pig- and poultry-rearing dist.; ch. t. Blackpool; l. gov. dist. excluding Blackpool; p. (2011) 75,800.

Fylingdales, ballistic missile early warning sta. on N. Yorks. moors, Eng.

Fyne, Loch, on Argyll and Bute cst., W. Scot.; an arm of F. of Clyde; offshore oil platform construction: 64 km long.

G

Gainsborough, t., West Lindsey, Lincs., Eng.; on R. Trent; agr. implements, milling, packing and wrapping machin.; mkt.; George Eliot's St. Ogg's in *Mill on the Floss*; p. 21,000.

Galashiels, burgh, Borders, Scot.; on Gala Water, 3 km above confluence with R. Tweed; tweeds, woollens; p. 11,500. New Border Railway (opened 2015) links Tweedbank to Edinburgh.

Galloway, anc. dist. S.W. Scot.; now part of Dumfries and Galloway.

Galloway, Mull of, the extremity of the Rinns of G., the most southern pt. of Scot.

Galston, burgh, E. Ayrshire, Scot.; on R. Irvine, nr. Kilmarnock; p. 5,200.

Galway, co., Galway Bay, Connacht, R.o.I.; fishery, cattle, marble quarrying; a. 6,351 km²; p. (2011) 175,000.

Galway, co. t. and cultural ctr. Galway, R.o.I.; univ.; spt., fishing; textiles, printing; p. (2011) 75,414.

Garforth, t., West Yorks., Eng.; new lt. inds.; p. 15,000.

Gateshead, t., met. dist., Tyne and Wear, Eng.; on R. Tyne opposite Newcastle; engin., food processing, pumps, paper; pt.; Millennium Bridge (2000); Baltic Art Gallery (opened 2002); Sage music centre; p. (2011) 200,200 (dist.).

Gatwick, West Sussex, Eng.; 40 km S. London; first airport in world where trunk road, main rly. line and air facilities were all combined in one unit. Now UK's second busiest airport.

Gedling, l. gov. dist., Notts., Eng.; Basford, Carlton and Arnold and N.E. outskirts of Nottingham; p. (2010) 112,000.

Giant's Causeway, basaltic columns on promontory of N. cst. of Moyle, N. Ireland.

Gillingham, t., l. gov. dist., Kent, Eng.; 3 km E. of Chatham; on R. Medway; naval and military establishments; cement, lt. inds.; p. (2011) 102,000 (dist.).

Girvan, burgh, S. Ayrshire, Scot.; on F. of Clyde, 29 km S.W. of Ayr; summer resort; p. 7,150.

Glamis, v., Angus, Scot.; G. cas. childhood home of Queen Elizabeth the Queen Mother, and featured in Shakespeare's *Macbeth*.

Glamorgan, historic co., S. Wales, now divided into 8 unit. auths. inc. Cardiff and Swansea.

Glamorgan, Vale of. See Gwent, Plain of.

Glasgow, c., burgh, unit. auth. created in 1996, formerly part of Strathclyde, W. Scot.; on R. Clyde; leading spt. and 3rd lgst. c. in Gt. Britain; major progress in urban renewal; ctr. of industl. belt; shipbldg., iron and steel, heavy and lt. engin., electronics equipment, printing; univs., cath.; p. (2010) 589,000 (unit. auth.). Hosted 2014 Commonwealth Games.

Glas Maol, mtn., Angus, Scot.; part of the Braes of Angus; alt. 1,068 m.

Glastonbury, sm. t., Somerset, Eng.; on R. Brue, ruins of ancient abbey; nearby prehistoric lake villages; famous music festival (biggest in UK) in fields of Worthy Farm since 1970.

Glen Affric, Highland, Scot.; 48 km S.W. of Inverness; drained E. to Moray F.; hydroelectric scheme.

Glencoe, Highland, Scot.; S.E. of Ballachulish; scene of massacre of MacDonalds 1692.

Glendalough, Wicklow, R.o.I.; scenic valley with Ls. and monastic ruins; tourism.

Glen Garry, Perth and Kinross, Scot.; used by Perth to Inverness rly. on S. approach to Drumochter Pass.

Glen More, Scottish valley traversed by Caledonian Canal from Fort William to Inverness.

Glenrothes, t., Fife, Scot.; new t. (1948); electronics; p. 37,500.

Glen Roy, Highland, Scot.; 24 km N.E. of Fort William; remarkable terraces, remains of series of glacial lakes.

Glossop, t., High Peak, Derbys., Eng.; at foot of Pennines; paper, food-canning, textile finishing; mkt.; p. 34,000.

Gloucester, cath. c., l. gov. dist., Eng.; on R. Severn; the Roman Glevum; cath., on site of Benedictine abbey; aircraft mftg. and repair; engin., nylon; p. (2010) 115,000 (dist.).

Gloucestershire, non-met. co., W. Eng.; situated around lower Severn basin, Cotswolds, Forest of Dean; sheep, dairy and fruit farming; major ctrs. of p. at Gloucester and Cheltenham; p. (2010) 583,500.

Glynde, v., Sussex, Eng.; nearby Tudor manor and opera house of Glyndebourne.

Godalming, t., Waverley, Surrey, Eng.; 6 km S.W. of Guildford; first public supply of elec. 1881; Charterhouse School; p. 22,500.

Gogmagog Hills, Cambs., Eng.; low chalk upland, S. of Breckland; traces of Roman entrenchment.

Golden Vale, dist., Limerick, Tipperary, R.o.I.; drained W. to Shannon and E. to Suir; rich farming a., beef and dairy cattle, pigs.

Goodwin Sands, dangerous sandbanks off E. cst. of Kent, Eng.; shielding the Down roadstead.

Goodwood, v., West Sussex, Eng.; racecourse and motor racing; home of Dukes of Richmond. Modern Rolls Royce car plant.

Goole, t., Eng.; second pt. of Hull on Humber; shipbldg., flour milling, fertilisers, alum and dextrine mftg.; p. 20,500. Now Britain's most inland port.

Goonhilly Downs, Cornwall, Eng.; satellite communications sta. of Post Office.

Goring Gap, Berks./Oxon., Eng.; where R. Thames cuts through Chilterns and Berkshire Downs.

Gorseinon, t., Swansea, S. Wales; nr. Loughour estuary, 6 km N.W. of Swansea; former steelwks., zinc refineries; p. 19,500.

Gosforth, t., sub. to Newcastle upon Tyne, Tyne and Wear, Eng.; p. 24,500.

Gosport, t., l. gov. dist., Hants., Eng.; naval depot W. of Portsmouth to which it is linked by ferry; marine engin.; hovercraft museum; p. (2010) 80,200 (dist.).

Gotham, v., Notts., Eng.; gypsum mng. and plaster wks.; p. 1,650.

Gourock, burgh, Inverclyde, **Scot.**; on F. of Clyde, 3 km W. of Greenock; ferry to Dunoon; resort; p. 12,100.

Gower, peninsula, Swansea, **Wales**; tourism.

Grampians, mtns. of Scot.; forming natural bdy. between Highlands and Lowlands; inc. Ben Nevis, the hgst. peak (1,344 m), the Cairngorms and Schiehallion.

Grange, t., South Lakeland, Cumbria, **Eng.**; on N. cst. of Morecambe Bay; popular summer resort.

Grangemouth, burgh, Falkirk, **Scot.**; on F. of Forth; shipbldg. and repair, marine engin., oil refining, projected new facility to import shale gas; petroleum prods., chemicals, pharmaceutics; electronics and elec. ind.; oil pipeline to Finnart; p. 18,300.

Grantham, t., S. Kesteven, Lincs., **Eng.**; on Witham R.; tanning, agr. machin., engin., brewing, malting, expanded t.; birthplace of Margaret Thatcher; p. 35,500.

Grantown-on-Spey, burgh, Highland, **Scot.**; on R. Spey; resort; p. 2,300.

Grasmere, v., Cumbria, **Eng.**; at head of Grasmere L.; home of Wordsworth.

Gravesend, spt., Gravesham, Kent, **Eng.**; S. bank R. Thames facing Tilbury; pilot sta. for Port of London; paper, cement; oil refinery projected; new Sikh temple; world's oldest surviving castiron pier; p. 54,500.

Gravesham, l. gov. dist., Kent, **Eng.**; based on Gravesend and surrounding dist.; p. (2010) 97,900.

Great Britain. *See* **England, Scotland, Wales, British Isles.**

Great Driffield, t., E. Riding of Yorks, **Eng.**; on Yorks. Wolds 21 km N. of Beverley; p. 9,900.

Great Dunmow, mkt. t., Uttlesford, Essex, **Eng.**; on R. Chelmer; 16 km N.W. of Chelmsford.

Greater Manchester, former met. co., pt., N.W. **Eng.**; lge. urban a. centred on major comm. ctr. of M., with former cotton spinning ts. to N., inc. Bolton, Bury and Rochdale; dormitory ts. to S.; former concentration on textile mftg. now reduced and inds. diversified; major industl. estate at Trafford Park; p. 2,700,000.

Great Fisher Bank, submarine sandbank in N. Sea; 320 km E. of Aberdeen, 160 km S.W. of Stavanger; valuable fishing-ground; depth of water, from 45–75 m.

Great Gable, mtn., Cumbria, **Eng.**; alt. 899 m.

Great Grimsby, spt., N.E. Lincs., **Eng.**; on S. bank of R. Humber; major distant waters fish. pt.; foodprocessing; fish fingers first produced, 1955; p. 88,000.

Great Harwood, t., Hyndburn, Lancs., **Eng.**; 8 km N.E. of Blackburn; textiles, aero-engin.; p. 12,000.

Great Torrington, sm. t., Torridge, Devon, **Eng.**; on R. Torridge; mkt., processing of agr. prod.

Great Yarmouth, spt., l. gov. dist., Norfolk, **Eng.**; at mouth of R. Yare; holiday resort; fish and food processing plants; base for N. Sea gas; support port for offshore oil and gas industries; p. (2010) 94,000 (dist.), 60,000 (t.).

Greenock, spt., burgh, Inverclyde, **Scot.**; on S. shore of F. of Clyde, 40 km W. of Glasgow; container facilities; shipbldg., sugar refining, woollens, chemicals, aluminium casting, tinplate inds.; birthplace of James Watt; p. 46,500.

Greenwich, inner bor., London, **Eng.**; inc. most of former bor. of Woolwich on S. bank of R. Thames; famous for its hospital, observatory (now moved to Cambridge) and R.N. College (now closed); univ.; longitudes conventionally calculated from Greenwich meridian; site of Millennium Exhibition and Village; created Royal Borough for 2012 Diamond Jubilee; maritime Greenwich now World Heritage Site; Britain's first urban cable car system (opened 2012); extensive residential development along the Thames; p. (2011) 255,000.

Gretna (Green), v., Dumfries and Galloway, **Scot.**; on Eng. border; famous as place of runaway marriages until 1940; now major tourist centre (as romantic capital of Scotland); near to Quintinshill (site of 1915 rail disaster); p. 2,800.

Grimsby. *See* **Great Grimsby.**

Guernsey, I., Channel Is., between cst. of France and Eng.; tomatoes, grapes (under glass), flowers, cattle, tourist resort, t. and ch. spt. St. Peter Port; banking; a. 6,335 ha; p. 66,000.

Guildford, co. t., l. gov. dist., Surrey, **Eng.**; 48 km S.W. London; on gap cut by R. Wey through N. Downs, cath., univ.; lt. inds.; residtl., cas.; p. (2010) 136,000 (dist.), 71,000 (t.).

Guisborough, t., Redcar and Cleveland, **Eng.**; at foot of Cleveland Hills; former ctr. of iron mng.; 12th cent. abbey ruins; p. 19,100.

Gwent, Plain of (Vale of Glamorgan), lowland dist., S. **Wales**; lies S. of moorland of S. Wales coalfield, extends E. into Monmouthshire; fertile soils; mixed farming except in industl. areas of Cardiff, Barry.

Gwynedd, N.W. **Wales**, unit. auth. created in 1996 from former l. gov. dists. of Arfon, Dwyfor and Meirionnydd; mtnous. a. except cst.; sparse p. inland where hill farming; inc. Snowdonia Nat. Park, Lleyn Penin., and ts. of Bangor and Caernarfon; p. (2011) 121,900.

H

Hackney, inner bor., N.E. London, **Eng.**; incorporates former bors. of Shoreditch and Stoke Newington; p. (2011) 246,000.

Haddington, burgh, E. Lothian, **Scot.**; on R. Tyne, 26 km E. of Edinburgh; woollen mnf.; grain mkt., corn mills, lt. engin., hosiery; p. 9,350.

Hadleigh, sm. t., Babergh, Suffolk, **Eng.**; mkt.; flourmilling.

Hadrian's Wall, part of frontier barrier, N. **Eng.**; stretching across Tyne–Solway isthmus, 118 km long. *See* **Roman Walls, Section L.**

Hailsham, mkt. t., Wealden, East Sussex, **Eng.**; 8 km N. of Eastbourne; p. 19,000.

Hale, sm. t., Trafford, Gtr. Manchester, **Eng.**; residtl.

Halesowen, t., S.W. of Birmingham, West Midlands, **Eng.**; weldless tubes, elec. gds., stainless steel forgings, engin.; p. 56,500.

Halesworth, t., Suffolk, **Eng.**; on R. Blyth, 14 km S.W. of Beccles; p. 4,950.

Halifax, t., Calderdale, West Yorks., **Eng.**; on E. flanks of Pennines; carpets, textiles, machine tools; cast iron wks.; p. 84,850. The historic Piece Hall (1789) now a shopping centre. First toffee factory in the world built here (1898).

Halstead, t., Essex, **Eng.**; on R. Colne, N.W. of Colchester; rayon weaving; p. 9,850.

Halton, unit. auth. and t., Cheshire, **Eng.**; surrounds Mersey R. and inc. Runcorn and Widnes; p. (2011) 125,800 (unit. auth.).

Haltwhistle, mkt. t., Tynedale, Northumberland, **Eng.**; on R. South Tyne; old coal-mng. dist.; p. 4,000.

Hamble, Hants, **Eng.**; yachting ctr.; p. 3,700.

Hambledon, v. Hants, **Eng.** This was 'the cradle of English cricket' in the 18th century when the local club became the accepted authority on the game.

Hambledon, t. and l. gov. dist., North Yorks., **Eng.**; inc. Northallerton, Bedale and Thirsk; p. (2010) 87,000 (dist.).

Hamilton, burgh, S. Lanarkshire, **Scot.**; in Clyde valley, 16 km S.E. of Glasgow; admin. ctr.; elec. prods., carpet mftg., cottons, woollens, knitwear; Rudolf Hess landed near Duke of Hamilton's estate 1941; p. 49,400.

Hammersmith and Fulham, Thames-side inner bor., London, **Eng.**; inc. former bor. of Fulham; industl., residtl.; p. (2011) 182,500.

Hampshire, non-met. co., S. **Eng.**; inc. Hampshire basin of chalk covered in clay and sand; inc. infertile heath and New Forest; lt. inds.; tourism, seaside resorts; co. t. Winchester; p. (2010) 1,286,500.

Hampstead, inc. in Greater London, **Eng.**; hilltop v. with nearby heathland. *See* **Camden.**

Hampton, Thames-side t., Richmond upon Thames, London, **Eng.**; Hampton Court Palace; Hampton Wick E. of H. Court.

Hanley. *See* **Stoke-on-Trent.**

Harborough, l. gov. dist., S. Leics., **Eng.**; based on Market Harborough and Lutterworth; p. (2010) 83,000.

Haringey, outer bor., Greater London, **Eng.**; comprising former bors. of Hornsey, Tottenham, and Wood Green; p. (2011) 255,000. Areas of high unemployment. Rioting in 2011.

Harlech, t., Gwynedd, **Wales**; on Cardigan Bay 16 km N. of Barmouth; farming; cas.; resort; p. 1,500.

Harlow, t., l. gov. dist., Essex, **Eng.**; in valley of R. Stort, 35 km N.E. of London; new t. (1947); spreads S.W. from nucleus of old mkt. t. of H.; engin., glass, furniture mkg., metallurgy; p. (2010) 79,100.

Harpenden, t., Herts., **Eng.**; in Chiltern Hills, 8 km N. of St. Albans; Rothamsted agr. experimental sta.; residtl.; p. 29,500.

Harris, S. part of Lewis I., Outer Hebrides, Western Isles, **Scot.**; and several sm. Is.

Harrogate, t., l. gov. dist., North Yorks., **Eng.**; in valley of R. Nidd, 22 km N. of Leeds; spa; favoured a. for retirement; p. (2010) 161,000 (dist.).

Harrow, outer bor., Greater London, **Eng.**; public school; camera mftg.; p. (2011) 239,250.

Hart, l. gov. dist., N.E. Hants., **Eng.**; comprises Fleet and Hartley Wintney; p. (2010) 90,100.

Hartlepool, spt., unit. auth. created in 1996, formerly part of Cleveland, **Eng.**; on E. cst., 5 km N. of Tees estuary; shipbldg., lt. inds.; timber, iron and steel inds., pipe making; advanced gas-cooled reactor nuclear power sta; p. (2011) 92,000 (unit. auth.).

Harwell, v. Oxon., **Eng.**; 19 km S. of Oxford; Atomic Energy Authority nuclear power research establishment; p. 2,500.

Harwich, spt., Tendring, Essex, **Eng.**; on S. cst. of estuary of R. Stour; ferry port for Belgium, Neth., Denmark; docks, container facilities, naval base; p. 21,500.

Haslemere, t., Waverley, Surrey, **Eng.**; nr. Hindhead; mkt.; residtl., lt. inds.; p. 13,500.

Haslingden, t., Rossendale, Lancs., **Eng.**; on Rossendale Fells, 5 km S. of Accrington; heavy industl. textiles, waste-spinning; p. 15,500.

Hastings, t., l. gov. dist., East Sussex, **Eng.**; on S. cst., midway between Beachy Head and Dungeness; seaside resort; Cinque Port; cas.; Norman victory over Saxons, 1066; pier destroyed by fire, 2010; restoration began, 2012; p. (2010) 86,000 (dist.).

Hatfield, t., Welwyn and Hatfield, Herts., **Eng.**; 30 km N. of London; new t. (1948) which grew around old t. of Bishops Hatfield; computers; univ.; p.34,000.

Havant, t., l. gov. dist., **Eng.**; at foot Portsdowns Hill, 10 km N.E. of Portsmouth; p. (2010) 117,500 (dist.), 46,000(t.).

Haverfordwest, t., Pembrokeshire, **Wales**; 10 km N.E. of Milford Haven; agr. mkt.; Norman castle; p. 14,000.

Haverhill, t., St. Edmundsbury, Suffolk, **Eng.**; expanded t.; textiles; p. 23,000.

Havering, outer bor., E. London, **Eng.**; inc. Hornchurch and Romford; p. (2011) 237,200.

Hawarden, t., Flintshire, N. **Wales**; steel plant; home of Gladstone.

Hawick, burgh, Borders, **Scot.**; on R. Teviot, 28 km S.W. of Kelso; hosiery, tweed, and woollens; p. 14,980.

Haworth, t., West Yorks., **Eng.**; nr. Keighley; home of the Brontës; p. 5,250.

Hay-on-Wye, sm. t., Powys, **Wales**; on R. Wye; cas.; mkt.; the "second-hand book capital of the world".

Haydock, t., Merseyside, **Eng.**; coal mng.; inc. H. Park racecourse; p. 17,250.

Hayes and Harlington. See Hillingdon.

Hayling Island, resort, Hants., **Eng.**; E. of Portsmouth; p. 14,900.

Haywards Heath, residtl. t. West Sussex, **Eng.**; p. (2011) 30,100.

Hazel Grove and Bramhall, subs. of Stockport, Gtr. Manchester, **Eng.**; p. 39,300.

Headingley, sub., Leeds, West Yorks., **Eng.** mainly residtl.; county cricket ground.

Heanor, t., Amber Valley, Derbys., **Eng.**; 11 km N.E. of Derby; hosiery, pottery, prefabricated timber bldgs. mftg.; p. 23,000.

Heathrow, London airport, **Eng.**; 24 km W. of central London, S. of M4 motorway; on Piccadilly tube line; fast rail link to Paddington; new Terminal 5. See also Section L.

Hebburn, t., Tyne and Wear, **Eng.**; on R. Tyne 6 km below Gateshead; former shipbldg., engin.; p. (2011) 22,000.

Hebrides or **Western Isles**, **Scot.**; grouped as Outer and Inner Hebrides; ch. t. Stornoway, Lewis. Depopulation in Outer Hebrides.

Heckmondwike, t., West Yorks., **Eng.**; wool textiles; p. 9,000.

Hedon, sm. t., E. Riding of Yorks., **Eng.**; former spt.

Helensburgh, t., Argyll and Bute, W. **Scot.**; on the Clyde; resort; p. 14,950.

Helford, R., Cornwall, **Eng.**; oysters, tourism.

Helmsley, mkt. t., Ryedale, North Yorks., **Eng.**; cas.

Helston, sm. mkt. t., Kerrier, Cornwall, **Eng.**; on R. Cober, 13 km W. of Falmouth; tourist ctr.; famous festival of floral dance (8 May); soup- canning.

Helvellyn, mtn., L. Dist., Cumbria, **Eng.**; severely eroded by ice; alt. 951 m; sharp ridge of Striding Edge.

Hemel Hempstead, t., Dacorum, Herts., **Eng.**;

---

new t. (1947), on S. slopes of Chilterns; scientific glass, elec. engin., cars; p. 84,950.

Henley-on-Thames, t., South Oxfordshire, Oxon., **Eng.**; 8 km N.E. of Reading; mkt. gardening, brewing; annual regatta since 1839; Henley Bridge built 1786; p. 10,500.

Hensbarrow, upland a., Cornwall, **Eng.**; granite; kaolin-mng. dist., kaolin exp. by sea from Fowey; rises to over 300 m; a. 70 km².

Hereford and Worcester, non-met. co. (until 1998), **Eng.**; crossed by Wye and Severn valleys, separated by Malvern Hills; mainly agr.; beef, dairy and fruit farming; major ts. Hereford and Worcester; p. (1995) 694,300. Worcs. and Hereford separated in 1998. Herefordshire now a unit.auth., p. 180,000.

Hereford, co. t., l. gov. unit. auth., **Eng.**; on R. Wye; cath.; mkt.; tiles, engin.; timber, cider and preserves; racecourse closed (2012); p. (2001) 57,000 (ct.).

Herne Bay, sm. t., Kent, **Eng.**; on cst., 19 km W. of Margate. Home of the world's first freestanding purpose-built clock tower (built in 1837).

Herstmonceux, v. nr. Hastings, Sussex, **Eng.**; cas.; frmr. site of Royal Greenwich Observatory (now Science Centre).

Hertford, co. t., East Herts., **Eng.**; on R. Lea, 32 km N. of London; pharmaceutics, flour milling, rolling stock, diesels, brewing; p. 25,500.

Hertfordshire, non-met. co., **Eng.**; borders Greater London on S.; ch. ctr. St. Albans; drained by Rs. Thames and Lea; intensive agr., lt. inds.; new ts. Welwyn, Stevenage, Hatfield, Hemel Hempstead; p. (2010) 1,080,000.

Hertsmere, l. gov. dist., Herts., **Eng.**; a. close to London, inc. Bushey, Elstree and Potters Bar; p. (2010) 99,000.

Hetton, t., Tyne and Wear, **Eng.**; 8 km N.E. of Durham; coal-mng. dist.; p. 13,900.

Hexham, sm. mkt. t., Tynedale, Northumberland, **Eng.**; on R. Tyne, 32 km W. of Newcastle; priory.

Heysham. See Morecambe and Heysham.

Heywood, t., Gtr. Manchester, **Eng.**; 5 km E. of Bury; chemicals, engin.; p. 28,900.

Higham Ferrers, sm. mkt. t., East Northants, **Eng.**; 5 km E. of Wellingborough; footwear and leather dressing.

Highland, N. **Scot.**, unit. auth. created in 1996 from former Region and part of Strathclyde; inc. I. of Skye and Inner Hebrides; rugged mtns. inland; p. concentrated around cst.; off- shore oil; stock raising, forestry, tourism; p. (2010) 221,000.

High Peak, l. gov. dist., Derbys., **Eng.**; a. of Pennines inc. New Mills, Glossop, Whaley Bridge and Buxton; p. (2010) 93,000.

High Willhays, hgst. summit, Dartmoor, Devon, **Eng.**; 621 m.

High Wycombe, t., Bucks., **Eng.**; 13 km N. of Maidenhead; furniture, paper-mkg., egg processing; in popular London commuter belt; univ. (Buckinghamshire New University); p. 78,500.

Hillingdon, outer bor. Greater London, **Eng.**; comprising Hayes and Harlington, Ruislip and Northwood Yiewsley, W. Drayton, and Uxbridge; p. (2011) 274,000. Large ethnic minority population.

Hinckley, mkt. t., Leics., **Eng.**; hosiery, cardboard boxes, dye-wks., engin.; with Market Bosworth forms l. gov. dist. of Hinckley and Bosworth; p. (2010) 105,000 (dist.).

Hindhead, sm. t. and hill common, Surrey, nr. Haslemere, **Eng.**

Hindley, t., Gtr. Manchester, **Eng.**; 3 km S.E. of Wigan; paint, rubber; p. 23,975.

Hinkley Point, Somerset, **Eng.**; two nuclear power-sta., one Magnox, one advanced gas-cooled reactor.

Hitchin, t., North Herts., **Eng.**; in gap through Chiltern Hills, 56 km N. of London; lt. engin., tanning, chemicals, distilling; mkt.; p. (2011) 34,000.

Hoddesdon, t., Herts., **Eng.**; in Lea valley, 6 km S. of Ware; food processing; p. 36,400.

Hog's Back, Surrey, **Eng.**; steep chalk ridge; alt. 154 m.

Holbeach, sm. mkt. t., S. Lincs., **Eng.**; in Fens, 11 km E. of Spalding; brewing; ctr. of bulb-growing dist.

Holborn. See Camden.

Holderness, peninsula, E. Riding of Yorks., **Eng.**; between R. Humber and N. Sea; agr.

Holland, Parts of. See Lincolnshire.

Holmesdale, Vale of, Kent, E. Surrey, **Eng.**; extends along foot of N. Downs escarpment; drained by Rs. Mole, Darent, Medway, Len, Stour; heavy clay soils; ch. ts. Dorking, Reigate, Sevenoaks, Maidstone, Ashford, which have grown up in gaps through hills to N. and S. of Vale; length 96 km, average width 2 km.

Holmfirth, t., West Yorks., **Eng.**; 8 km S. of

Huddersfield, textiles, engin.; p. 23,100.
Holt, sm. mkt. t., N. Norfolk, **Eng.**; 8 km S.W. of Sheringham; 16th-cent. school.
Holt, t., Wrexham, **Wales**; on R. Dee, 11 km S. of Chester; cas. ruins.
Holyhead, spt., Isle of Anglesey, **Wales**; on Holyhead I.; lt. engin., woodwkg., clocks; site for aluminium smelter; p. (2012) 13,500. Its Welsh name is Caergybi.
Holy I. (**Lindisfarne**), off cst. of Northumberland, **Eng.**
Holy I., **Scot.**, in F. of Clyde, nr. I. of Arran.
Holy I., off cst. of Isle of Anglesey, **Wales**.
Holywell, sm. mkt. t., Flintshire, N. **Wales**; woollen, rayon and paper inds.
Home Counties, term applied to the geographical counties adjoining London, *i.e.*, Middlesex, Surrey, Essex, and Kent; sometimes Hertfordshire, Buckinghamshire, and Berkshire are included, and occasionally Sussex.
Honiton, t., East Devon, **Eng.**; on R. Otter, 26 km E. of Exeter; mkt.; trout-fishing; formerly lace making; p. 8,300.
Horncastle, mkt. t., E. Lindsey, Lincs., **Eng.**; at confluence of Rs. Bain and Waring at foot of Lincoln Wolds; mkt.; vegetable-processing; p. 5,200.
Hornsea, t., E. Riding of Yorks., **Eng.**; on E. cst., N.E. of Hull; seaside resort; p. 8,000.
Hornsey. *See* **Haringey**.
Horsforth, t., West Yorks., **Eng.**; in Aire valley N.W. of Leeds; cloth, tanning, lt. engin.; p. 19,500.
Horsham, t., l. gov. dist., West Sussex, **Eng.**; on R. Arun at W. end of forested dist. of the High Weald; agr., timber, engin., chemicals; Shelley's birthplace; impt. commuting centre; p. (2010) 131,000 (dist.).
Horwich, t., Gtr. Manchester, **Eng.**; on W. edge of Rossendale Fells, N.W. of Bolton; rly. t.; engin.; rly. workshops closed (1983); p. 20,000.
Houghton-le-Spring, t., Tyne and Wear, **Eng.**; S. of Sunderland; former coal mng.; p. (2011) 37,000.
Hounslow, outer bor., Greater London, **Eng.**; inc. former bors. of Brentford and Chiswick, Heston and Isleworth, Feltham and Hounslow; rubber goods; p. (2011) 254,000.
Hove, t., Brighton and Hove, **Eng.**; on S. cst., contiguous with Brighton; residtl.; resort; p. 74,000.
Hoylake, t., Wirral, Merseyside, **Eng.**; on N. cst. of Wirral peninsula; residtl.; golf course; p. 26,000.
Hucknall, t., Ashfield, Nottingham, **Eng.**; hosiery, coal; p. 29,900.
Huddersfield, t., West Yorks., **Eng.**; on edge of Pennines, 16 km S. of Bradford; wool, textiles, chemicals, engin.; univ.; birthplace of Labour leader, Harold Wilson; p. 150,000.
Hugh Town, cap. of the Scilly Isles, **Eng.**; on St. Mary's I.
Hull or **Kingston upon Hull**, c., unit. auth. of Kingston upon Hull created in 1996, formerly part of Humberside, **Eng.**; major spt. of UK; at influx of R. Hull in estuary of Humber; originally laid out by Edward I; lge. docks; premier distant water fishing pt.; inds. inc. oil-extracting, flour milling, sawmilling, chemicals, engin.; univs.; p. (2010) 259,000 (unit. auth.). The only city in Britain with white telephone boxes. Its historic fish market closed in 2011. Chosen as UK City of Culture for 2017. One of the three most bombed cities in World War II. William Wilberforce was MP here in 18th century. Holy Trinity Church is largest parish church in England. Ferens Art Gallery reopened (2017).
Humber, estuary of Rs. Ouse and Trent, **Eng.**; fine waterway; 2–13 km wide, 61 km long; Humber bridge opened (1981), longest single span suspension bridge in Britain.
Hunstanton, t., West Norfolk, **Eng.**; S.E. shore of Wash; seaside resort; p. 4,500.
Hunterston, N. Ayrshire, **Scot.**; civil nuclear power sta.; integrated iron and steel wks., engin. of oil platforms and oil terminal planned.
Huntingdon, t. located in the historic co. of Huntingdonshire, E. **Eng.**, now l. gov. dist. within Cambs. on R. Ouse; expanded t.; canning, engin., processed rubber, confectionery; birthplace of Cromwell, who was later MP for Huntingdon; home of the poet Cowper; p. (2010) 169,000 (dist.).
Huntly, burgh, Aberdeenshire, **Scot.**; at confluence of Rs. Bogie and Deveron; agr. mkt.; p. 4,500.
Huyton with Roby, Knowsley, Merseyside, **Eng.**; sub. of Liverpool; p. 55,250.
Hyde, t., Tameside, Gtr. Manchester, **Eng.**; on R.

Tame, 11 km S.E. of Manchester; paints, chemicals, food-processing; p. 32,500.
Hyndburn, l. gov. dist., Lancs., **Eng.**; inc. Colne Valley ts. of Accrington, Great Harwood, Rishton, Clayton-le-Moors, Church and Oswaldtwistle; p. (2011) 80,700.
Hythe, sm.t., Shepway, Kent, **Eng.**; on S. cst., 5 km W. of Folkestone; Cinque pt.; military canal passing through t., used for boating.

I

Idle, t., West Yorks., **Eng.**; in Aire valley, 5 km N. of Bradford; woollens.
Ilchester, t., Somerset, **Eng.**; on R. Yeo; N.W. of Yeovil; birthplace of Roger Bacon; p. 1,800.
Ilford. *See* **Redbridge**.
Ilfracombe, sm. t., North Devon, **Eng.**; sm. pt. on cst. of Bristol Channel; resort.
Ilkeston, t., Erewash, Derbys., **Eng.**; W. of Nottingham, iron, engin., plastics; p. 38,000.
Ilkley, t., spa, West Yorks., **Eng.**; on R. Wharfe, N.W. of Leeds; local mkt.; p. 15,350.
Ilminster, sm. t., Somerset, **Eng.**; 16 km S.E. of Taunton; cutstone, concrete, radio valves.
Immingham, pt., N.E. Lincs., **Eng.**; on the Humber, N.W. of Grimsby; lge. docks; new deep-sea oil and coal terminals; chemical engin., refinery nearby at Killingholme; p. 13,000.
Ince-in-Makerfield, sm. t., Gtr. Manchester, **Eng.**; nr. Wigan; engin.
Ingleborough, mtn., near Settle, North Yorks., **Eng.**; underground caves, stalactites; made of limestone and millstone grit; alt. 724 m.
Inishmore, lgst. of Aran gr., Galway, **R.o.I.**; fishing.
Inveraray, burgh, Argyll and Bute, **Scot.**; nr. head of Loch Fyne; herring fishing; p. 500.
Inverbervie, burgh, Aberdeenshire, **Scot.**; on E. cst., 13 km S. of Stonehaven; linen; p. 2,100.
Inverclyde, unit. auth. created in 1996, formerly part of Strathclyde, **W. Scot.**; on F. of Clyde, inc. Gourock and Greenock; p. (2010) 80,400.
Invergordon, burgh, spt., Highland, **Scot.**; on N. side of Cromarty F., 19 km N.E. of Dingwall; former naval pt.; whisky distillery; p. (2012) 3,890.
Inverkeithing, royal burgh, Fife, **Scot.**; on F. of Forth, nr. Dunfermline; shipbreaking, papermkg., quarrying; p. 5,500.
Inverkip, par., v., Inverclyde, **Scot.**; 10 km S.W. of Greenock; par. contains Gourock; resort; p. 1,650.
Inverness, c., royal burgh, Highland, N.E. **Scot.**; on Moray F.; distilling, lt. engin., tweeds; sm. pt.; most northerly city in British Isles; tourism; created a Millennium City, 2000; p. 57,000.
Inverness-shire, historic co., N.W. **Scot.**, now part of Highland.
Inverurie, royal burgh, Aberdeenshire, **Scot.**; on R. Don, 22 km N.W. of Aberdeen; rly. ctr., mkt. t.; tourism; p. 10,950.
Iona, I., off cst. of Mull, Argyll and Bute, **Scot.**; early Scottish Christian ctr.; restored abbey; St. Columba's burial place; ancient burial place of Scottish kings; p. 130.
Ipswich, co. t., l. gov. dist., Suffolk, **Eng.**; pt. on estuary of R. Orwell; increasingly impt. container pt.; exp. timber, grain and malt; birthplace of Cardinal Wolsey; engin.; site of campus of University of Suffolk; p. (2010) 122,000 (dist.).
Ireland, I., W. of Gt. Britain, separated by Irish Sea; divided politically into R.o.I. (Eire) and N. Ireland (Ulster, part of U.K.); ch. physical features, L. Neagh in N.E., Ls. of Killarney in S.W.; Rs. Shannon, Boyne, Blackwater; mtns. of Mourne, Wicklow, and Kerry; mild moist climate; called "emerald isle"; pastoral agr., especially dairying; tourism; a. 83,937 km².
Ireland, Republic of, indep. st., W. Europe; comprises 26 of 32 cos. making up I. of Ireland; member of EU; ring of highlands surround central lowland basin, much of which is peat-covered; economy based on agr., especially dairying; exps. butter, cheese, bacon; new govt.-encouraged inds.; mineral resources; tourism; cap. Dublin; a. 68,894 km²; p. (2011) 4,581,269.
Irish Sea, Brit. Is.; between Gt. Britain and Ireland, connecting N. and S. with Atl. Oc.; 320 km long; 80–224 km wide; greatest depth 840 m; a. 18,130 km².
Ironbridge, t., Shrops., **Eng.**; scene of Darby's iron ind.; derives name from first cast-iron bridge (1779) which here crosses Severn; now

inc. in Telford new t.; p. 2,650.

Irvine, royal burgh, N. Ayrshire, **Scot.**; nr. mouth of R. Irvine; new t. (1966); cas.; hosiery, lt. engin., bottle wks., chemicals; p. 33,750.

Irwell, R., Gtr. Manchester, **Eng.**; flows through Manchester to the Mersey via Manchester Ship Canal; 48 km long.

Islay, I. Inner Hebrides, Argyll and Bute, **Scot.**; farming, dairying; whisky tourism (8 distilleries on island); world's largest tidal power scheme planned; p. (2012) 3,450. Known as the Queen of the Hebrides. Bowmore is the largest town.

Isle of Anglesey, **(Ynys Mon)**, N.W. **Wales**, separated from mainland by Menai Straits; former stronghold of Druids, attacked by Romans A.D. 61; mainly agr. and tourism; unit. auth. created in 1996 from former l. gov. dist., reinstating historic co. disbanded in 1974; p. (2011) 69,700. Known to the Romans as Mona.

Isle of Grain, Kent, **Eng.**; flat promontory at confluence of Thames and Medway, once separated from mainland by a tidal estuary; lge oil refinery; pipelines to Walton-on-Thames and Heathrow Airport.

Isle of Man, Brit. dependency, Irish Sea; high plateau N.E. to S.W.; ch. t. Douglas; old cap. Castletown; admin. according to own laws; tourism; growing Manx identity; reintroduction of Manx Gaelic into schools; a. 572 km², p. (2009) 82,000. Ellan Vannin is its Manx name.

Isles of Scilly, archipelago, unit.auth., 45 km. S.W. of Land's End, Cornwall, **Eng.**; early flowers and vegetables benefit from mild winter climate; tourism; p. (2010) 2,220.

Isle of Wight, unit. auth. created in 1995, **Eng.**; English Channel, separated from Hampshire by Spithead and the Solent; crossed by chalk hills, terminating in the Needles; holiday resort; ch. ts. Newport, Ryde, Cowes; p. (2010) 141,000. Home of Robin Hill Country Park, Quarr Abbey and Culver Down.

Islington, inner bor., London, **Eng.**; N. of City; incorporates Finsbury; univ.; residtl.; clocks, precision engin.; p. (2011) 206,000.

J

Jarrow, t., South Tyneside, Tyne and Wear, **Eng.**; on S. bank of Tyne, 11 km below Gateshead; grew up as shipbldg. ctr.; in depression; hunger march to London 1936; new inds; steel and tube wks., oil storage; die-castings; home of the Venerable Bede; p. 28,000.

Jedburgh, royal burgh, Borders, **Scot.**; on Jed Water, S.W. of Kelso; tweeds, woollens, rayon; abbey ruins; p. 4,250.

Jersey, lgst. of Channel Is., 21 km W. of Fr. cst.; potatoes (famous Jersey royals); tomatoes, cauliflowers, flowers, fruit.cattle; tourist resort; banking; ch. t. St. Helier;a. 117 km²; p. 91,500. The famous cider orchards had vanished by 1810.

John o' Groat's House, place nr. Duncansby Head, Highland, **Scot.**

Johnstone, burgh, Renfrewshire, **Scot.**; on R. Black Cart, nr. Paisley; machine tools, textiles, iron and brass foundry; p. 17,250.

Jura, I., Argyll and Bute, **Scot.**; off W. cst.

Jurassic Coast, England's first natural World Heritage Site. Runs 95 miles from East Devon to Dorset. Part of new national path.

K

Katrine, **Loch**, Stirling, **Scot.**; beautiful woodland and moorland scenery; source of Glasgow water supply; scene of Scott's *Lady of the Lake*; 13 km long, *c.* 1·6 km wide.

Kearsley, sm. t., Gtr. Manchester, **Eng.**; chemicals.

Keighley, t., West Yorks., **Eng.**; in Aire valley, 24 km N.W. of Leeds; woollen and worsteds; p. 50,250.

Keith, burgh, Moray, **Scot.**; mkt. t. in agr. dist.; p. 4,500.

Kells or **Ceannanus Mor**, mkt. t., Co. Meath, **R.o.I.**; notable for monastic remains and illuminated Book of Kells, now in library of Trinity College, Dublin; p. 2,300.

Kelso, burgh, Borders, **Scot.**; at confluence of Rs. Teviot and Tweed; p. 5,250.

Kendal, l. gov. dist., Cumbria, **Eng.**; mkt. ctr.; tourism; p. 29,000. Severe recent flooding.

Kenilworth, t., Warwicks., **Eng.**; 6 km S.W. of

Coventry; mkt.; ruined cas.; p. 23,000.

Kennet, former l. gov. dist., Wiltshire, **Eng.**; stretched from Marlborough to Devizes. Abolished, 2009.

Kennet, R., Wilts. and Berks., **Eng.**; trib. of R. Thames; followed by main rly. London to W. of Eng.; 70 km long.

Kennington, dist., in London bor. of Lambeth, **Eng.**; inc. the Kia Oval cricket ground, home of Surrey C.C.

Kensington and Chelsea, **Royal Borough of**, inner bor., W. London, **Eng.**; mainly residtl.; contains Kensington Palace and Gardens; p. 158,700.

Kent, non-met. co., **Eng.**; intensive agr.; mkt. gardening, orchards, hops; "Garden of England"; crossed by N. Downs and Weald; industl. zone bordering Thames and Medway estuaries; tourist resorts and cross-channel ferry pts. on cst.; London commuter hinterland; co. t. Maidstone; p. (2010) 1,407,000.

Kerrier, former l. gov. dist., Cornwall, **Eng.**; a. inc. Lizard penin. and Helston. Abolished, 2009.

Kerry, coastal co., Munster, **R.o.I.**; deeply indented cst.; cap. Tralee; tourism; a. 4,703 km²; p. (2011) 145,048.

Keswick, Allerdale, Cumbria, **Eng.**; on Greta R.; at N. end of L. Derwentwater; tourist ctr.; mkt. Major floods, 2015.

Kettering, l. gov. dist., mkt. t., Northants., **Eng.**; nr. Wellingborough; footwear; iron mng.; p. (2010) 91,000 (dist.).

Kew, dist., London bor. of Richmond upon Thames, **Eng.**; contains Kew botanical gardens, now World Heritage Site.

Keynsham, sm. t., Bath and N .E. Somerset, **Eng.**; expanded; closure of chocolate factory, 2010.

Kidderminster, t., Wyre Forest, Worcs., **Eng.**; on R. Stour 6 km above its confluence with R. Severn; carpets, engin., sugar-beet refining, textile machin., elec. vehicles, drop forgings; p. 56,500.

Kidsgrove, t., "Potteries," Stoke, **Eng.**; 5 km N.W. of Stoke-on-Trent; chemicals, metal wks., rayon, silk and nylon spinning, ceramics; p. 29,000.

Kidwelly, Carmarthenshire, **Wales**; sm. mkt. t.; sm. harbour; cas.

Kielder, reservoir, Northumberland, **Eng.**; one of lgst. man-made lakes in Europe.

Kildare, inland co., Leinster, **R.o.I.**; dairying, cereals; co. t. Naas; a. 1,694 km²; p. 209,955 (2011).

Kildare, sm. mkt. t., cap. of Kildare, **R.o.I.**; cath.; close by is the famous racecourse, the Curragh.

Kilkenny, inland co., Leinster, **R.o.I.**; cap. Kilkenny; pastoral farming, black marble; a. 2,062 km²; p. 95,360 (2011).

Kilkenny, sm. t., cap. of Kilkenny, **R.o.I.**; on R. Nore; local mkt., caths., cas.

Killaloe, v., Co. Clare, **R.o.I.**; crossing point for R. Shannon; cath.

Killarney, t., Kerry, **R.o.I.**; local mkt.; tourist ctr. for the Ls. of K.; p. 7,500.

Killarney, **Lakes of**, Kerry, **R.o.I.**; Lower, Middle and Upper, celebrated for their beauty; tourist resorts; Muckross on Middle L. site of anc. abbey.

Killiecrankie, **Pass of**, Scot.; on R. Garry; at S. approach to Drumochter Pass; used by main rly. Perth to Inverness; scene of battle 1691.

Killingworth, t., Tyne and Wear, **Eng.**; 6 km N.E. of Newcastle; new t.; proposed p. 20,000.

Kilmarnock, burgh, E. Ayrshire, **Scot.**; on R. Irvine, 17 km N.E. of Ayr.; p. 45,000.

Kilrenny and **Anstruther**, sm. t., Fife, **Scot.**, at entrance to F. of Forth; fishing, hosiery, oilskin mnfs.

Kilrush, sm. spt., U.D., Co. Clare, **R.o.I.**; on R. Shannon.

Kilsyth, burgh, N. Lanarkshire, **Scot.**; at S. foot of Campsie Fells, 16 km W. of Falkirk; p. 9,950.

Kilwinning, burgh, N. Ayrshire, **Scot.**; 8 km E. of Ardrossan; p. 16,100.

Kincardineshire, historic co., E. **Scot.**, now part of Aberdeenshire.

Kinder Scout, plateau; N. Derbys., **Eng.**; hgst. point of the Peak dist.; alt. 637 m; declared National Nature Reserve, 2009; scene of "mass trespass" by walkers, 1932.

Kinghorn, t., Fife, **Scot.**; on F. of Forth, 5 km S. of Kirkcaldy; p. 2,950.

Kingsbridge, t., South Hams, S. Devon, **Eng.**; at head of Kingsbridge estuary, 16 km S.W. of Dartmouth; mkt.; p. 5,500.

King's Lynn, spt., West Norfolk, **Eng.**; at mouth of Gr. Ouse; historic royal charter, 1204; once most important port in England (and old Hanseatic port); docks; fishing base; agr. machin., canning, chemical fertilisers, shoes; expanded t.;

part of l. gov. dist. of **King's Lynn and West Norfolk;** p. (2010) 145,000 (dist.).

Kingston upon Hull. *See* Hull.

Kingston upon Thames, former M.B., Surrey, **Eng.;** now **The Royal Borough of Kingston-upon-Thames,** outer bor. of Greater London; inc. bors. of Malden and Coombe and Surbiton; residtl. with Richmond Park, Hampton Court, Bushey Park nearby; aircraft parts; univ.; p. (2011) 160,200.

Kingswood, t., S. Gloucs., **Eng.;** nr. Bristol; elec. vehicles, motor cycles, boots, brushes, tools; school founded by John Wesley; p.62,000.

Kington, sm. mkt. t., Hereford, **Eng.;** 19 km W. of Leominster.

Kinlochleven, v., Highland, **Scot.;** at head of Loch Leven; hydroelec. power sta.; aluminium smelting; p. 910.

Kinross, burgh, Perth and Kinross, **Scot.;** on Loch Leven, 26 km N.E. of Alloa; textiles; resort; p. (2011) 4,750.

Kinross-shire, historic co., E. **Scot.,** now part of Perth and Kinross.

Kinsale, t., Cork, **R.o.I.;** sm. fish pt. on K. harbour; tourism; natural gas field; p. 1,900.

Kintyre, peninsula, Argyll and Bute, **Scot.;** terminates in Mull of Kintyre; 67 km long, 16 km wide.

Kirkburton, sm. t., West Yorks., **Eng.;** S.E. of Huddersfield; woollens.

Kirkby, t., Knowsley, Merseyside, **Eng.;** p. 40,750.

Kirkby in Ashfield, t., Ashfield, Notts., **Eng.;** 16 km N.W. of Nottingham; p. 28,000.

Kirkbymoorside, t., Ryedale, North Yorks., **Eng.;** nr. Vale of Pickering; mkt.-place; sailplanes, gliders; p. 2,750.

Kirkcaldy, royal burgh, Fife, **Scot.;** spt. on N. side of F. of Forth; linoleum, engin.; birthplace of Adam Smith; p. 47,250.

Kirkcudbright, royal burgh, Dumfries and Galloway, **Scot.;** on R. Dee at influx into K. Bay, S.W. of Dumfries; agr. ctr., cas., abbey; p. 3,500.

Kirkcudbrightshire, historic co., S. **Scot.,** now part of Dumfries and Galloway.

Kirkham, sm. t., Kirklees, Lancs., **Eng.;** textiles.

Kirkintilloch, burgh, E. Dunbartonshire, **Scot.;** on Forth and Clyde Canal; engin.; p. (2002) 20,281.

Kirklees, met. dist., West Yorks., **Eng.;** comprises Huddersfield, Dewsbury, Batley, Spenborough, Colne Valley, Meltham, Holmfirth, Denby Dale, Kirkburton, Heckmondwike and Mirfield; p. (2011) 422,500.

Kirkstone Pass, mtn. pass, Cumbria, **Eng.;** used by main road between Ullswater and Windermere Lakes.

Kirkwall, royal burgh, Mainland I., Orkney Is., **Scot.;** cath.; p. 6,700.

Kirriemuir, burgh, Angus, **Scot.;** on N. margin of Strathmore, 8 km W. of Forfar; jute-weaving; birthplace of J. M. Barrie; p. 5,950.

Knaresborough, t., North Yorks., **Eng.;** 5 km N.E. of Harrogate; mkt.; cas. ruins; p. 14,500.

Knighton, t., Powys, **Wales;** on R. Teme; mkt.; p. 3,100.

Knottingley, v., West Yorks., **Eng.;** on R. Aire, 19 km S.E. of Leeds; engin., glass, tar distilling, chemicals; coal mng; p. 15,200.

Knowsley, met. dist., Merseyside, **Eng.;** comprises Kirkby, Prescot and Huyton with Roby; p. 152,000.

Knutsford, sm. t., N.E. Cheshire, **Eng.;** mkt.; home of Mrs. Gaskell, author of *Cranford.*

Kyle of Lochalsh, v., Highland, **Scot.;** at entrance to Loch Alsh, facing S. end of I. of Skye; terminus of rly. across Highlands from Dingwall; ch. pt. for ferries to N.W. cst., I. of Skye, Outer Hebrides; p. 750.

L

Ladybank, burgh, Fife, **Scot.;** 8 km S.W. of Cupar.

Lake District, almost circular mtnous. a., Cumbria, **Eng.;** 17 major and many smaller Ls. formed by glacial erosion and deposition; nominated in 2014 for consideration as a World Heritage Site. Lake District national park now linked to Yorkshire Dales national park.

Lambeth, inner bor., London, **Eng.;** L. palace, residence of Archbishop of Canterbury; p. (2011) 303,150.

Lampeter, t., Ceredigion, S. **Wales;** on R. Teifi; mkt.; univ; p. 2,100.

Lanark, royal burgh, S. Lanarkshire, **Scot.;** in Clyde valley 35 km S.E. of Glasgow; hosiery; ctr. of mkt. gardening a.; nr. New Lanark model t. built by Robert Owen; p.8,600.

Lanarkshire, historic co., central **Scot.;** now divided between Glasgow, N. and S. Lanarkshire.

Lancashire, non-met. co., N.W. **Eng.;** major growth of p. in 19th cent. based on prod. of cotton and coal; main industl. ctrs. now outside co. in Merseyside and Gtr. Manchester met. cos.; Pennines in E.; extensive lowland in W.; admin. ctr. Preston; p. (2010) 1,171,000.

Lancaster, c., co. t., l. gov. dist., Lancs., **Eng.;** 10 km up R. Lune; cas., univ.; linoleum, vinyl, clothing; Ashton Memorial (the Taj Mahal of the North); p. (2011) 138,400 (dist.).

Land's End, extreme S.W. point of **Eng.** on Cornish cst.

Langdale Pikes, L. Dist., **Eng.;** 2 peaks Harrison Stickle (733 m), Pike o'-Stickel (709 m); very popular rambling and climbing area; 5 km W. of Grasmere.

Largo, v., Fife, **Scot.;** fishing, holiday resort; birthplace of Alexander Selkirk.

Lasswade. *See* Bonnyrigg and Lasswade.

Launceston, t., North Cornwall, **Eng.;** agr. mkt.; quarrying, lt. engin.; p. 6,900.

Laurencekirk, burgh, Aberdeenshire, **Scot.;** agr. ctr. in the Howe of Mearns; p. 1,900.

Lavenham, sm. t., Suffolk, **Eng.;** a ctr. of the wool tr. in 15th cent., still has its medieval character.

Lea or **Lee,** R., **Eng.;** rises in Chiltern Hills nr. Luton, flows S. and E. into R. Thames through industl. zone of N.E. London; valley to become a regional park; mkt. gardening a.; 74 km long.

Leamington (Royal Leamington Spa), t., Warwicks., **Eng.;** on R. Leam, trib. of Avon, 3 km N.E. of Warwick; spa; engin. inds.; p. 62,500.

Leatherhead, t., Mole Valley, Surrey, **Eng.;** on R. Mole to N. of gap through N. Downs; residtl.; p. 43,500.

Ledbury, t., Hereford, **Eng.;** at W. foot of Malvern hills; fruit preserving, tanning; 17th cent. mkt. hall; birthplace of John Masefield; p. 7,000.

Leeds, c., met. dist., West Yorks., **Eng.;** on R. Aire; at E. margin of Pennines; univs.; lge. clothing ind., varied engin. mnfs., paper and printing; with Bradford forms conurb. of W. Yorks., p. (2011) 751,500 (dist.). New Trinity Leeds shopping mall. Major arts centre (*e.g.* Opera North and Northern Ballet). Leeds Library (f. 1768).

Leek, mkt. t., Moorlands, Staffs., **Eng.;** 18 km N.E. of Stoke-on-Trent; silk mnfs., butter; p. 20,000.

Lee-on-the-Solent, t., Hants., **Eng.;** p. 8,000.

Leicester, c., unit. auth. created in 1997, formerly part of Leics., **Eng.;** on R. Soar; univs. (Leicester and De Montfort); footwear, hosiery, knitwear, *etc.* now declined; major out-of-town shopping complex at Fosse Park; modern King Power football stadium; Curve Theatre; National Space Science Centre; Roman remains; Richard III Visitor Centre opened (2014); historic Silver Arcade reopened, 2013; famous 'Golden Mile' (Belgrave Road); p. (2011) 330,000 (unit. auth.). Now largest city in East Midlands and first UK city with majority non-white population.

Leicestershire, non-met. co., **Eng.;** mainly rural, low-lying Midland co., but inc. Charnwood Forest; mixed agr., former coalfield; hosiery and footwear inds.; major shale deposits in n. of county; p. (2010) 646,000.

Leigh, t., Gtr. Manchester, **Eng.;** 8 km S.E. of Wigan; textiles; p. 44,000.

Leighton Buzzard, t., South Beds., **Eng.;** at N.E. end of Vale of Aylesbury; tiles, engin., sand quarrying; p.34,000 (inc. Linslade).

Leinster, S.E. prov., **R.o.I.;** bulk of recent Irish p. increase; a. 19,637 km²; p. 2,501,208 (2011).

Leith, t., Edinburgh, **Scot.;** shipbldg., timber, whisky; outport for Edinburgh.

Lennoxtown, t., E. Dunbartonshire, **Scot.;** aluminium wks.; p. 3,800.

Leominster, sm. mkt. t., Hereford, **Eng.;** 19 km N. of Hereford; once famed for woollen ind.; enormous Saxon rotunda uncovered; p. 42,000.

Lerwick, t., Shetland Is., **Scot.;** on Mainland; fishing; p. 6,950.

Leslie, burgh, Fifeshire, **Scot.;** 11 km N. of Kirkcaldy; paper, bleaching; p. (2002) 2,998.

Letchworth (Garden City), t., North Herts., **Eng.;** at foot of Chiltern Hills, 3 km N.E. of Hitchin; first garden c., founded by Sir Ebenezer Howard 1903; office equipment; expanded t.; p. 34,000.

Letterkenny, t., Co. Donegal, **R.o.I.;** on Lough Swilly; tourist ctr.; p. 6,800.

Leven, burgh, Fife, **Scot.**; on N. side of F. of Forth; resort; p. 8,300.

Leven, Loch, Perth and Kinross, **Scot.**; ass. with escape of Mary Queen of Scots from Castle I. 1568.

Lewes, t., l. gov. dist., East Sussex, **Eng.**; on R. Ouse at N. entrance to gap through S. Downs; mkt., cas., printing, light inds.; famous bonfire night celebrations; site of Battle of Lewes, 14 May 1264; p. (2010) 95,000 (dist.), (2011) 17,750 (t.).

Lewis (Leodhais), I., Outer Hebrides, Western Isles, **Scot.**; fishing, tweeds; proposals for world's biggest on-shore wind farm rejected; first Sunday ferry to mainland (July 2009); seaweed farming industry; ch. t. Stornoway; p. 22,000 (with Harris).

Lewisham, inner bor., London, **Eng.**; inc. Deptford; residtl.; industl.; p. (2011) 276,000.

Leyland, t., Lancs., **Eng.**; 8 km S. of Preston; motor vehicles, rubber; p. (2010) 32,000. See **Central Lancashire.**

Lichfield, c., l. gov. dist., Staffs., **Eng.**; cath.; agr. and lt. inds.; expanded t.; birthplace of Dr. Samuel Johnson; p. (2010) 98,000 (dist.).

Lickey Hills, gr. of hills, Hereford and Worcs., **Eng.**; 6 km S.W. of Birmingham; reveal anc. rocks underlying younger sediments; rise to 292 m, largely wooded.

Liffey, R., **R.o.I.**; rises in Wicklow Mtns. and enters Irish Sea at Dublin.

Limavady, t., l. gov. dist., **N. Ireland**; mkt.; linen; p. (2010) 34,100 (dist.). See **D11.**

Limerick, co., Munster, **R.o.I.**; agr.; livestock, fishing: a. 3,385 km²; p. (2011) 134,527.

Limerick, cap. of Limerick, **R.o.I.**; spt. at head of Shannon estuary; bacon, tanning, shipbldg.; p. (2011) 56,779 (city).

Lincoln, c., co. t., l. gov. dist., Lincs., **Eng.**; on R. Witham in gap through Lincoln Edge; impt. Roman t.; cath., cas.; heavy engin., iron foundries, bricks, lime, seed milling, malting; univ campus; p. (2010) 88,000 (dist.) The cathedral spire was the tallest building in the medieval world.

Lincoln Edge, limestone ridge, Lincs. and N. Lincs., **Eng.**; runs N. from Ancaster through Lincoln to Humber; narrow ridge with steep scarp slope to W., broken by R. Witham at Lincoln; iron-ore deposits worked in N. nr. Scunthorpe; sheep, barley; rarely exceeds 90 m alt.

Lincolnshire, non-met. co., **Eng.**; between the Humber R. and the Wash; fertile soil on low-lying fenland; intensive agr., arable crops, bulbs, market gardening; food processing; formerly divided into 3 admin. parts: Holland, Kesteven, and Lindsey; p. (2010) 701,000.

Lincoln Wolds, low plateau, Lincs. and N. Lincs., **Eng.**; runs N. 72 km from Wash to Humber; chalk covered with glacial deposits; mixed farming, grains, roots, sheep; lge. farm units; scantily populated; rise to approx. 135 m.

Lindisfarne or **Holy I.,** off cst. of Northumberland, **Eng.**; connected to mainland by stretch of sand and causeway at low tide; abbey founded 635 A.D. as first base of Celtic Christianity in **Eng.**; Lindisfarne castle; p. 180.

Lindsey. See **Lincolnshire.**

Linlithgow, burgh, W. Lothian, **Scot.**; distilling, brewing, paper, shoes; birthplace of Mary Queen of Scots; p. 14,000.

Linnhe, Loch, Highland, Argyll and Bute, **Scot.**; 21 miles long; entrance to Caledonian Canal.

Linslade. See **Leighton Buzzard.**

Lisburn, c., l. gov. dist., **N. Ireland**; on R. Lagan, 10 km S.W. of Belfast; p. (2010) 116,000 (dist.). Created a city, 2002. See **D11.**

Liskeard, sm. mkt. t., Caradon, Cornwall, **Eng.**; on R. Looe at S. edge of Bodmin Moor.

Litherland, t., Sefton, Merseyside, **Eng.**; N. sub. of Liverpool; p. 22,750.

Littleborough, t., Gtr. Manchester, **Eng.**; textiles and textile finishing; p. 14,000.

Little Dunmow, v., 3 km E. of Great Dunmow; Uttlesford, Essex, **Eng.**; historic Dunmow Flitch (side of bacon); bacon factory closed (1983).

Littlehampton, t., Arun, West Sussex, **Eng.**; on S. cst. at mouth of R. Arun; holiday resort, sm. spt.; p. 57,000.

Little Lever, t., Gtr. Manchester, **Eng.**; 5 km S.E. of Bolton; residtl. and industl.; p. 11,750.

Liverpool, c., spt., met. dist., Merseyside, **Eng.**; on N. bank at entrance to Mersey estuary; deep-sea container berths at Seaforth; shipping and ship-repairing; elec. mnfs. and engin., flour milling, sugar refining, seed and rubber processing, cars; cath., univs.; second Mersey tunnel opened 1971; birthplace of The Beatles; European City of Culture, 2008; Tate Liverpool (art gallery); World Heritage Centre (waterfront); p. (2001) 439,473 (dist.). New Museum of Liverpool opened in 2011 (largest new museum for over a century in Britain).

Livingston, new t. (1962), W. Lothian, **Scot.**; nick-named 'Silicon Glen'; p. 52,000.

Lizard, The, C., Cornwall, **Eng.**; S. point of Eng.

Llandeilo, sm. mkt. t., Carmarthenshire, **Wales**; in Vale of Towy, E. of Carmarthen; cas.

Llandovery, sm. t., Carmarthenshire, **Wales**; on R. Bran, nr. confluence with Towy; mkt. town.

Llandrindod Wells, sm. t., Powys, **Wales**; medicinal waters; p. 4,500.

Llandudno, t., Conwy, **Wales**; between Gr. Ormes and Little Ormes; site of Britain's largest prehistoric mine; seafront has longest pier in Wales (2,300ft). p. 15,100.

Llanelli, t., Carmarthenshire, **Wales**; pt. on Burry inlet, 18 km N.W. of Swansea; industl. and comm. ctr.; coal mng., steel and tinplate wks., mng. machin.; cas.; p. 47,000.

Llanfairfechan, sm. t., Conwy, **Wales**; at foot of Penmaenmawr mtn.; resort; granite quarrying.

Llangefni, sm. t., Isle of Anglesey, **Wales**; in ctr. of the I.; mkt. and agr. t.; p. 4,900.

Llangollen, t., Denbighshire, **Wales**; on R. Dee; Vale of L., tourist ctr.; annual International Eisteddfod; p. 3,500.

Llanidloes, sm. t., Powys, **Wales**; on R. Severn; surrounded by hills; anc. mkt. house.

Llanrwst, sm. mkt. t., Conwy, **Wales**; on R. Conwy; tourist ctr.

Llanstephan, v., Carmarthenshire, **Wales**; at mouth of R. Towy; ruins of Norman cas.

Llantrisant, new t., Rhondda, Cynon, Taff, S. **Wales**; iron-ore quarrying; Royal Mint; p. 9,500 (with Pontyclun).

Llantwit Major, t. Vale of Glamorgan, **Wales**; famous centre of learning in Celtic times.

Llanwrtyd Wells, t., Powys, **Wales**; Britain's smallest town (p.850).

Lleyn, peninsula, Gwynedd, N. **Wales**; from Snowdonia to Bardsey I.; crystalline rocks form hills in E., otherwise low, undulating; pastoral farming, sheep, cattle; sm. seaside resorts; ch. t. Pwllheli.

Loanhead, burgh, Midlothian, **Scot.**; 8 km S.E. of Edinburgh; coal, engin.; p. 6,450.

Lochalsh. See **Kyle of Lochalsh.**

Lochgelly, burgh, Fife, **Scot.**; nr. Dunfermline; p. 6,800.

Lochgilphead, Argyll and Bute, **Scot.**; at head of Loch Gilp, 3 km N. of Ardrishaig; tourist ctr.; p. 2,400.

Lochmaben, burgh, Dumfries and Galloway, **Scot.**; in Annandale, 11 km N.E. of Dumfries; p. (2010) 2,000.

Lockerbie, burgh, Dumfries and Galloway, **Scot.**; in Annandale, 16 km E. of Dumfries; sheep mkt.; air disaster 1988, caused by terrorist bomb; p. (2011) 4,200.

Lodore Falls, waterfalls, Cumbria, **Eng.**; in Watendlath beck at foot of Derwentwater.

Loftus, sm. t. Redcar and Cleveland, **Eng.**; on N.E.flank of Cleveland Hills.

Lomond, Loch, Stirling, lgst. loch in **Scot.**, studded with 38 Is., surrounded by hills with Ben Lomond on E. side. Centrepiece of Scotland's first National Park.

London, cap. of U.K., **Eng.**; at head of Thames estuary; seat of govt., world ctr. of finance and communication; cultural and artistic ctr.; comprises the City, (12 inner and 20 outer bors.; Port of London; upstream docks now closed; main pt. downstream at Tilbury; losing p. and inds. to outer met. a.; univs. (London, Brunel, City *etc.*), caths., historic bldgs., theatres, museums, galleries, libraries, and parks; new GLA elected, May 2000; hosted 2012 Olympics; p. (2011) 7,400 (City of London), (2015) 8,630,000 (Greater London). The 2015 figure is an all-time record for London (higher than in 1939).

Londonderry (Derry) c., Derry, **N. Ireland**; on R. Foyle, 6 km upstream from Lough Foyle; regional education hub and admin centre; training ctr. for ind.; tourism; the London prefix added to Derry in 1613, when James I granted a royal charter. p. 108,000. See **D11.**

Long Eaton, t. Erewash, Derbys., **Eng.**; on R. Trent, 8 km S.W. of Nottingham; former ctr. for lace mftg., elec. cables, hosiery; p. 47,450.

Longford, co., Leinster, **R.o.I.**; peat bogs; dairy farming; co. t. Longford; a. 1,090 km²; p. 38,970.

Longford, co. t., Longford, **R.o.I.**; cas., cath.; mkt. t.

Long Forties Bank, submarine sandbank, N. Sea; 128 km E. of Aberdeen; valuable fishing-grounds; depth of water, from 45–75 m.

Longridge, t., Ribble Valley, Lancs., **Eng.**; 10 km N.E. of Preston; p. 7,700.

Longstanton, Cambs., **Eng.**; proposed site of new town between Cambridge and Huntingdon.

Looe, t. Caradon, Cornwall, **Eng.**; on Looe estuary; holiday resort; p. 5,000.

Lossiemouth, burgh, Moray, **Scot.**; on Moray F., 8 km N. of Elgin; birthplace of Ramsay MacDonald; fishing; p. 6,950.

Lostwithiel, sm. mkt. t. Cornwall, **Eng.**; on R. Fowey S.E. of Bodmin; anc. Stannary t.

Loughborough, t., Charnwood, Leics., **Eng.**; on R. Soar 16 km N. of Leicester; engin., elec. gds., chemicals, textiles; univ.; former hosiery t.; bell foundry; home of National Cricket Academy; p. 57,500.

Louth, t., East Lindsey, Lincs., **Eng.**; on E. edge of Lincoln Wolds; abbey ruins; cattle mkt., farm implements, corrugated board; p. 15,100.

Louth, maritime co., Leinster, **R.o.I.**; mtns., bog and barren land; salmon fishing; cap. Dundalk; a. 818 km²; p. 122,808 (2011).

Lowestoft, old fish pt., Waveney, Suffolk, **Eng.**; on E. Anglian cst. 14 km S. of Gr. Yarmouth; holiday resort, nr. Broads; food processing plants; base for N. Sea gas; p. 69,000.

Lowther Hills, mtns., between S. Lanarkshire and Dumfries and Galloway **Scot.**; hgst. point 733 m.

Ludlow, t., South Shrops., **Eng.**; agr. mkt.; agr. engin.; cas.; p. 10,000.

Lulworth Cove, sm. inlet, Dorset, **Eng.**; scenic cove.

Lundy I., Bristol Channel, N. Devon, **Eng.**; 19 km N.W. of Hartland Point; wildlife sanctuary; about 5 km long and 1 km wide. Lundy was the UK's first marine nature reserve.

Lune, R., Cumbria, **Eng.**; flows 72 km to Irish Sea; attractive valley.

Lurgan, t., Craigavon, **N. Ireland**; textiles, tobacco mftg.; merging with Portadown to form new c. of Craigavon; p. 22,000.

Luton, t., unit. auth. created in 1997, formerly part of Beds., **Eng.**; in Chiltern Hills nr. source of R. Lea; motor vehicles (last remaining UK centre of van production); engin., hat mkg., aircraft, instruments; expanded t.; univ.; expanding airport (now renamed London Luton Airport); car production ended (2002); p. (2010) 192,000 (unit. auth.).

Lutterworth, t., Leics., **Eng.**; church with relics of John Wyclif, religious reformer; Magna Park nearby, Europe's largest distribution centre; p. 8,500.

Lydd, Shepway, Kent, **Eng.**; anc. t. on Romney marsh, at edge of Dungeness shingle; explosive lyddite mnf.; airport (known as London Ashford), p. 3,500.

Lydney, t., Gloucs., **Eng.**; in Forest of Dean; spt. on Severn estuary; new lt. inds.; p. 8,000.

Lyme Regis, spt., West Dorset, **Eng.**; on bdy. of Devon and Dorset; holiday resort; massive sea defence works; p. 4,000.

Lymington, t., Hants., **Eng.**; on the Solent; ferry to I. of Wight; yacht and sailing clubs; p. 14,900.

Lymm, t., Cheshire, **Eng.**; 8 km W. of Altrincham; mainly residtl.; p. 10,000.

Lyndhurst, v., Hants, **Eng.**; recognised as cap. of New Forest; tourism; p. 2,700.

Lynton, sm. t., North Devon, **Eng.**; 27 km W. of Minehead on Bristol Channel; tourist ctr. for Exmoor; sm. harbour of Lynmouth 130 m below; devastating flood of R. Lyn 1952.

Lytham St. Annes, t., N. Lancs., **Eng.**; on N. cst. of Ribble estuary, 6 km S. of Blackpool holiday ctr.; p. 42,000.

M

Mablethorpe, t., East Lindsey, Lincs., **Eng.**; holiday resort; p. 10,000. Major beach renourishment.

Macclesfield, t., Cheshire, **Eng.**; at foot of Pennines, 16 km S. of Stockport; on R. Bollin; mkt., textiles, clothing, paper prods., engin.; expanded t.; famous old silk capital of England; p. (2011) 51,950. (t.).

Macduff, spt., burgh, Aberdeenshire, **Scot.**; 3 km E. of Banff; fishing; p. 3,800.

Macgillicuddy's Reeks, mtns., Kerry, **R.o.I.**; highest peak, Carantuohil, 1,041 m.

Machynlleth, t., Powys, **Wales**; on R. Dovey; alternative technology research; clothing; tourism; p. 2,300. Known as the ancient capital of Wales, though never officially recognised as such.

Maentwrog, v., Gwynedd, N. **Wales**; in Vale of Ffestiniog, 3 km E. of Ffestiniog; hydro-electric power sta. run by Nuclear Electric.

Maesteg, t., Bridgend, **Wales**; dormitory t. for steel wks. at Pt. Talbot; cosmetics; p. 21,000.

Maidenhead, t., Windsor and Maidenhead, Berks., **Eng.**; on R. Thames, 14 km above Windsor; residtl.; p. (2011) 60,500. Now an affluent commuter centre. See **Windsor**.

Maidens, The, gr. of dangerous rocks off Larne cst., **N. Ireland**.

Maidstone, co. t., l. gov. dist., Kent, **Eng.**; on R. Medway; regional ctr.; brewing, paper, agr. tools, confectionery, timber inds.; p. (2010) 145,000 (dist.).

Mainland, I., lgst. of Shetland Is., **Scot.**; p. 18,000.

Mainland, I., Orkney Is. See **Pomona**.

Maldon, t., l. gov. dist., Essex, **Eng.**; sm. pt. at head of Blackwater estuary; agr. machin., steel window-frames; p. (2010) 63,000 (dist.).

Malham Cove, North Yorks., **Eng.**; in Craven dist. of N. Pennines, 16 km N.W. of Skipton; semi-circular amphitheatre limestone cliffs from base of which emerges R. Aire.

Malin Head, Donegal, **R.o.I.**; most N. point.

Malling, t., Kent, **Eng.**; 5 km W. of Maidstone; fruit, chemicals. See **Tonbridge**.

Mallow, mkt. t., Cork, **R.o.I.**; on R. Blackwater; agr. fishing, flour mills, tanneries, condensed milk, dehydrated foods; p. (2000) 6,500.

Malmesbury, t., North Wilts., **Eng.**; anc. hilltop t. in Cotswolds; mkt.; abbey; elec. engin.; new univ. campus planned; birthplace of Thomas Hobbes; p. 4,750.

Maltby, sm. t., Rotherham, South Yorks., **Eng.**

Malton, sm. mkt. t., North Yorks., **Eng.**; on R. Derwent, in S.W. of Vale of Pickering; brewing.

Malvern, t., Worcs., **Eng.**; at E. foot of Malvern hills; spa; annual dramatic festival; Elgar lived here; p. 32,500.

Malvern Hills, narrow ridge forming bdy. between Worcs. and Hereford, **Eng.**; rises very abruptly from Severn valley to over 300 m between Malvern and Bromsberrow; moorland, woodland on lower slopes; forms l. gov. dist.; p. (2010) 75,000.

Mam Soul, mtn., Highland, **Scot.**; alt. 1,178 m.

Manacle Rocks, dangerous reef off cst. of Cornwall, **Eng.**; 12 km S. of Falmouth.

Manchester, c., Gtr. Manchester, **Eng.**; on R. Irwell; terminus of Manchester Ship Canal; ctr. of cotton and man-made fibre textile inds.; heavy, lt., and elec. engin., machine tools, petro-chemicals, dyestuffs, pharmaceutical prods.; univs; cultural and recreational cap. of N.W. Eng.; city centre rebuilt after IRA bomb, reopened 1999; Museum of Science and Industry (opened 1983); Imperial War Museum (North), opened 2002; p. (2011) 503,000 (met. dist.) Now designated a city region (2011) when Greater Manchester combined authority established.

Manchester Ship Canal, ship canal, Cheshire/ Merseyside/Gtr. Manchester, **Eng.**; joins Manchester to Mersey estuary at Eastham; 57 km long.

Mansfield, t., l. gov. dist., Notts., **Eng.**; on E. flank of Pennines, 19 km N. of Nottingham; 2 remaining coal mines; sand-quarrying, textiles, footwear, metal boxes, machin.; p. (2010) 101,000 (dist.); 70,500 (t.).

Mansfield Woodhouse, t., Notts., **Eng.**; 3 km N. of Mansfield; stone quarries; Roman remains; p. 19,500.

Manston, Kent, **Eng.**; former RAF base, now Kent International Airport.

March, mkt. t., Fenland, Cambs., **Eng.**; on R. Nene in Fens; rly. junc.; farm tools; p. 15,100.

Maree, Loch, Highland, **Scot.**; 21 km long, c. 3 km wide; rocky shores; studded with wooded islets.

Margam, part of Pt. Talbot, Neath Pt. Talbot, S. **Wales**; on cst. of Swansea Bay; lge. steelworks; lgst. steel-rolling mill in Europe.

Margate, t., Kent, **Eng.**; W. of N. Foreland, in the Isle of Thanet; resort; Dreamland amusement park (reopened 2015); Turner Centre; p. 61,500.

Market Drayton, sm. t., North Shrops., **Eng.**; on Tern, 21 km S.W. of Newcastle-under-Lyme; dairy products; processed food.

Market Harborough, t., Harborough, Leics., **Eng.**; on R. Welland, 13 km N.W. of Kettering; elec. engin., foodstuffs, corsetry; p. 21,500.

Market Rasen, t., West Lindsey, Lincs., **Eng.**; agr. ctr.; racecourse; p. 3,400.

Markinch, burgh, Fife, **Scot.**; 13 km N. of Kirkcaldy; paper mftg.; p. 2,300.

Marlborough, t., Wycombe, Wilts., **Eng.**; on R. Kennet in heart of Marlborough Downs; public school; p. 7,000.

Marlborough Downs, hills, Wilts., **Eng.**; chalk; highest point, Milk Hill, 298 m.

Marlow, t., Bucks., **Eng.**; on R. Thames; mkt.; tourist ctr.; home of Shelley; p. 17,500.

Marple, t., Gtr. Manchester, **Eng.**; 5 km. E. of Stockport; engin., residtl.; p. 20,500.

Marske-by-the-Sea, sm. t. Langbaurgh, Cleveland, **Eng.**; seaside resort.

Maryport, t., Allerdale, Cumbria, **Eng.**; former pt.; modern lt. inds.; p. 10,250.

Masham, t., North Yorks., **Eng.**; on R. Ure; mkt.

Mask, L., Mayo and Galway, **R.o.I.**; 19 km long 3–6 km wide.

Matlock, t., Derbys. Dales, **Eng.**; on R. Derwent; 24 km N. of Derby; admin. ctr.; tourist ctr., limestone quarrying; Peak District Mining Museum.

Mauchline, mkt. t., E. Ayrshire, **Scot.**; associated with Robert Burns; p. 4,200.

Maybole, burgh, S. Ayrshire, **Scot.**; 13 km S. of Ayr; commuter centre; cas.; p. (2002) 4,650.

Mayfair, dist., City of Westminster, London, **Eng.**; fashionable residtl. and comm. a., to E. of Hyde Park; clubs and hotels.

Mayo, maritime co., Connacht, **R.o.I.**; broken cst., much barren mtn. land, many lge. lakes; agr.; co. t. Castlebar, a. 5,506 km²; p. (2011) 130,552. New development of natural gas.

Meath, maritime co., Leinster, **R.o.I.**; pastoral; co. t., Trim; a. 2,347 km²; p. 184,034 (2011).

Medway, unit. auth. and R., Kent, **Eng.**; flows N.E. past Tonbridge, Maidstone and Rochester (where it becomes estuarial) to mouth of Thames; 112 km long; Medway Bridge completed 1962. p. (2010) 254,000 (unit auth.).

Melksham, t., West Wilts., **Eng.**; on R. Avon, 8 km N.E. of Bradford-on-Avon; rubber wks., engin., flour mills, creameries; p. 14,300.

Melrose, burgh, Borders, **Scot.**; on R. Tweed; 6 km E. of Galashiels; ruined abbey; p. 1,700.

Melton Mowbray, t., Leics., **Eng.**; on Lincoln Heights, 24 km N.E. of Leicester; mkt., hunting dist.; famous pork pies (name now legally protected); footwear, pet foods, Stilton cheese; with surrounding a. forms l. gov. dist. of **Melton**; p. (2010) 49,250 (dist.), (2010) 26,000 (t.).

Menai Strait, separates Isle of Anglesey from mainland, **Wales**; crossed by Telford's suspension bridge (1825) and Britannia rly. bridge (1850).

Mendip Hills, Somerset, **Eng.**; limestone range containing many karst features inc. Cheddar gorge and Wookey Hole; a. of outstanding natural beauty; quarrying; hgst. point 325 m; forms l. gov. dist. **Mendip**, inc. Frome, Wells, Shepton Mallet, Glastonbury and Street; p. 110,000.

Merionethshire, historic co., N.W. **Wales**, now part of Gwynedd.

Mersea, I., at mouth of R. Colne, Essex, **Eng.**; oysters; holiday resort; 8 km long, 3 km wide.

Merse of Berwick, region, S.E. **Scot.**; lower valleys of Rs. Tweed and Teviot; glacial clays; arable agr. for barley, wheat; dairy cattle; ch. t. Berwick-on-Tweed.

Mersey, R., Cheshire/Gtr. Manchester/Merseyside, **Eng.**; enters Irish Sea by fine estuary at Liverpool; 109 km long.

Merseyside, former met. co., N.W. **Eng.**; a. around lower Mersey estuary inc. N. Wirral penin., pts. of Liverpool, Birkenhead and Bootle; many chem. and pt. processing inds.

Merthyr Tydfil, t., unit. auth. created in 1996 from former l. gov. dist., S. **Wales**; in narrow valley of R. Taff, 35 km N.W. of Cardiff; former coal mng. ctr.; aircraft, bricks, elec. domestic prods.; p. (2011) 58,800 (unit auth.).

Merton, outer bor., Greater London, **Eng.**; inc. former bors. of Mitcham, Wimbledon, and Merton and Morden; p. (2011) 199,750.

Mexborough, t., South Yorks., **Eng.**; on R. Don, 16 km above Doncaster; potteries; p. 16,100.

Mid Bedfordshire, former l. gov. dist., Beds., **Eng.**; a. N. of Luton and inc. Biggleswade, Sandy and Ampthill. Abolished, 2009.

Mid Devon, l. gov. dist., Devon, **Eng.**; based on Tiverton; p. (2010) 77,000.

Middlesbrough, t., unit. auth. created in 1996, formerly part of Cleveland, **Eng.**; expanded t.; pt. on S. side of Tees estuary; impt. iron and steel ind., engin., chemicals; p. (2011) 138,400 (unit. auth.).

Middlesex, historic co., S.E. **Eng.**; N. of R. Thames; largely absorbed in Greater London 1964.

Middleton, t., Gtr. Manchester, **Eng.**; in valley of R. Irk; p. 46,000.

Middlewich, t., Cheshire, **Eng.**; on Rs. Dane, Wheelock and Croco, 8 km N. of Crewe; salt, chemicals, clothing; p. 11,000.

Midhurst, sm. t., West Sussex, **Eng.**; on R. Rother; polo grounds; birthplace of Richard Cobden.

Midlands, region, **Eng.**; comprises cos. of Staffs, Derbys., Notts., Leics., Warwicks., Northants.; includes Birmingham conurbation.

Midlothian, E. **Scot.**, unit. auth. created in 1996, incorporating part of historic co. which was divided between the Borders and Lothian in 1974 and is now divided between Borders, E. Lothian, Edinburgh, Midlothian and W. Lothian; p. (2010) 81,000.

Mid Suffolk, l. gov. dist., Suffolk, **Eng.**; rural a. inc. Eye and Stowmarket; p. (2010) 95,000.

Mid Sussex, l. gov. dist., West Sussex, **Eng.**; a. inc. Cuckfield and Burgess Hill; p. (2010) 131,450.

Mildenhall, t., Forest Heath, Suffolk, **Eng.**; on R. Lark; 13th cent. church; old RAF. sta. nearby; expanded t.; p. 10,750.

Milford Haven, spt., Pembrokeshire, **Wales**; magnificent deepwater harbour; major tanker terminal (250,000 tonnes); 2 refineries; pipeline from Angle Bay to Llandarcy (nr. Swansea); major white fish pt.; huge storage facilities for liquefied natural gas; now largest port in Wales; p. 15,000.

Millom, t., Copeland, Cumbria, **Eng.**; on N.W. cst. of Duddon estuary; ironwks. (closed 1968 after 100 years); hosiery; declining p.; p. 6,900.

Millport, burgh, N. Ayrshire, **Scot.**; on Gr. Cumbrae I., in F. of Clyde; resort; cath.; p. 1,350.

Milngavie, burgh, E. Dunbartonshire, **Scot.**; 8 km N.W. of Glasgow; textiles; p. 13,000.

Milton Keynes, t., unit. auth. created in 1997, formerly part of Bucks., **Eng.**; new c. for London overspill comprising Bletchley, Wolverton and Stony Stratford; Open University; massive pop. increase (to 370,000) planned by 2024; p. (2011) 249,000 (unit. auth.).

Minch, The, channel between the mainland of **Scot.** and the N. portion of Outer Hebrides, 38–64 km wide; very rapid current.

Minch, The Little, channel between I. of Skye, **Scot.**, and the middle portion of Outer Hebrides, 22–32 km wide.

Minchinhampton, sm. t., Gloucs., **Eng.**; in Cotswolds, 6 km S.E. of Stroud.

Minehead, sm. t., West Somerset, **Eng.**; at N. foot of Exmoor, on Bristol Channel cst.; mkt.; resort.

Mingulay, Hebridean island, abandoned in 1912.

Mirfield, t., West Yorks., **Eng.**; on R. Calder, 5 km S.W. of Dewsbury; woollens; p. 19,250.

Moffat, burgh, Dumfries and Galloway, **Scot.**; 24 km N.W. of Lockerbie; resort; p. 2,550.

Mold, sm. t., Flintshire, N. **Wales**; on R. Alyn; chemicals, roadstone; p. 9,000.

Mole R., Surrey, **Eng.**; rises in central Weald, flows N. into R. Thames nr. Molesey; cuts impt. gap through N. Downs between Dorking and Leatherhead; 80 km long.

Mole Valley, l. gov. dist., Surrey, **Eng.**; based on Mole R. ts. of Leatherhead and Dorking; p. (2010) 82,000.

Monadhliath Mtns., Highland, **Scot.**; between Spey R. and Loch Ness; hgst. peak Carn Mairg, 1,216m.

Monaghan, co., **R.o.I.**; mainly pastoral and agr.; a. 1,295km²; p. (2011) 60,495.

Monaghan, co., Monaghan, **R.o.I.**; on the Ulster canal; cath.; p. 6,250.

Monmouth, t., Monmouthshire, **Wales**; at confluence of Rs. Wye and Monnow; mkt. ctr.; timber, crushed limestone; p. 8,000.

Monmouthshire, S.E. **Wales**, unit. auth. created in 1996 from former l. gov. dist., reinstating part of historic co. split up in 1974; drained by the Usk and Wye Rs.; inc. ts. of Abergavenny, Chepstow and Monmouth; p. (2011) 91,300.

Montgomery, t., Powys, central **Wales**; in upper Severn valley, 13 km N.E. of Newtown; cas.

Montgomeryshire, historic co., central Wales, now part of Powys.

Montrose, spt., burgh, Angus, **Scot.**; on E. cst. at mouth of S. Esk R.; chemicals, rope wks., vegetable-canning, boat-bldg., fishing; supply base for N. Sea oil; p. (2011) 11,000.

Moray, E. **Scot.**, unit. auth. created in 1996, incorporating historic co. of **Morayshire** which became part of Grampian in 1974; borders M. Firth; arable agr.; p. (2010) 88,000.

Moray Firth, arm of N. Sea; on Scottish E. cst., between Highland and; plans for lge.-scale industl. expansion; offshore oil platforms at Arderseir; valuable inshore oilfield.

Morecambe and Heysham, ts., N. Lancs., **Eng.**; on S. shore of M. Bay; M. holiday resort; H., pt. for N. Ireland and oil refinery; two advanced gas-cooled nuclear power stas.; p. 50,250.

Morecambe Bay, between Lancs. and Cumbria, **Eng.**; isolates Furness dist. of Lancs.; many proposed barrages across Bay, now project increasingly probable as water shortage in N.W. Eng. grows; discoveries of nat. gas.

Morley, t., West Yorks., **Eng.**; 5 km S.W. of Leeds; woollens, quarrying; p. 55,000.

Morpeth, t., Northumberland, **Eng.**; finely situated in valley of Wansbeck; coal mng., iron-founding; mkt.; Norman cas. remains; p. 15,000.

Mossley, t., Tameside, Gtr. Manchester, **Eng.** 5 km E. of Oldham; mkt. t., textiles; p. 11,000.

Motherwell, burgh, N. Lanarkshire, **Scot.**; in Clyde valley, 24 km S.E. of Glasgow; iron, coal Ravenscraig steelworks, machin., engin., textiles; p. 31,000.

Mountain Ash, t., Rhondda, Cynon, Taff, **Wales**; in narrow valley 5 km S.E. of Aberdare; former coal mng. a.; p. 22,000.

Mount's Bay, inlet, S. cst., Cornwall, **Eng.**; 32 km wide; fishery grounds.

Mousehole, v., Cornwall, **Eng.**; nr. Penzance; former fishing pt.; now reliant on tourism.

Moyle, l. gov. dist., **N. Ireland**; borders N.E. cst.; inc. Rathlin I., Giants Causeway; main t. Ballycastle; p. (2010) 17,000. *See* **D11.**

Mull, I., Argyll and Bute, **Scot.**; included in Hebrides; pastoral farming, fishing, tourism; ch. t. Tobermory; p. 2,850.

Mullet, The, peninsula, W. cst. Mayo, **R.o.I.**

Mullingar, c. t., Westmeath, **R.o.I.**; on Brosna R.; mkt., agr. ctr.; cath.; p. 8,500.

Munster, prov., S.W. **R.o.I.**; includes cos. Waterford, Kerry, Cork, Limerick, Clare, Tipperary; a. 24,540 km², p. 1,243,726 (2011).

Musselburgh, burgh, East Lothian, **Scot.**; on F. of Forth at mouth of R. Esk; wire, cables, nets, twine; paper mkg.; golf course; campus of Queen Margaret University; p. 22,500.

Must Farm, Cambridgeshire, **Eng.** Major archaeological Bronze Age site – the 'British Pompeii'.

N

Naas, co. t., Co. Kildare, **R.o.I.**; former cap. of Leinster prov.; p. 10,000.

Nailsworth, t., Gloucs., **Eng.**; in Cotswold Hills 6 km S. of Stroud; p. 5,500.

Nairn, royal burgh, Highland, **Scot.**; fishing ctr.; cas.; p. 8,500.

Nairnshire, historic co., E. **Scot.**, now part of Highland.

Nantwich, mkt. t., Crewe and N. Cheshire, **Eng.**; on R. Weaver, 5 km S.W. of Crewe; brine baths; clothing, food prods.; annual cheese fair (largest in world); p. 13,000; *see* **Crewe.**

Naseby, v., Northants., **Eng.**; battle where parliamentarians under Fairfax and Cromwell beat royalists under Charles I and Prince Rupert 1645.

Naver, R., Highland, **Scot.**; flows N. to Pentland Firth; valley once densely p., cleared early 19th cent. to make room for sheep.

Naze, The, headland in Essex, 5 m. s. of Harwich.

Neagh, Lough, L., **N. Ireland**; lgst. freshwater L. in Brit. Is.; a. 396 km²; drained by R. Bann.

Neath, t., Neath Pt. Talbot, **Wales**; 10 km up R. Neath from Swansea Bay; coal, aluminium inds., oil refining; cas., abbey; p. 47,000.

Neath Port Talbot, S. **Wales,** unit. auth. created in 1996 from former l. gov. dists. of Neath and Pt. Talbot; p. (2011) 139,800.

Needles, chalk stacks in English Channel, off W. cst. of I. of Wight, **Eng.**

Nelson, t., Pendle, Lancs., **Eng.**; on N. flank of Rossendale 5 km N.E. of Burnley; cotton, iron and brick wks., lt. engin., paper; p. (2001) 28,998.

Nene, R., Northants., **Eng.**; rises nr. Naseby and flows 144 km to the Wash.

Ness, Loch, Highland, **Scot.**; occupies N.E. end of Glen More; forms link in Caledonian Canal; very deep; 36·4 km long.

Neston, t., Cheshire, **Eng.**; on N. side of Dee estuary; residtl.; p. 17,000. *See* **Ellesmere Port.**

Newark, mkt. t., part of l. gov. dist. of **Newark and Sherwood,** Notts., **Eng.**; on R. Trent 27 km N.E. of Nottingham; ball bearings, brewing and malting; cas.; coal mining at Bilsthorpe; p. (2010) 113,150 (dist.), 36,000 (t.).

Newbiggin-by-the-Sea, t., Wansbeck, Northumberland, **Eng.**; sm. seaside resort; p. 7,350.

New Brighton, t., Merseyside, **Eng.**; at entrance to Mersey estuary; residtl. dist. of Wallasey, resort.

Newburgh, burgh, Fife, **Scot.**; on S. side of F. of Tay, 13 km E. of Perth; fish. pt.; former linoleum industry; p. 2,050.

Newburn, t., Tyne and Wear, **Eng.**; on R. Tyne. 5 km W. of Newcastle; pure graphite for nuclear reactors; p. 42,000.

Newbury, t., l. gov. dist., Berks., **Eng.**; on R. Kennet, 27 km S.W. of Reading; engin., furniture, cardboard box making; mkt.; race-course; controversial by-pass opened, 1998; p. 35,000.

Newcastle, spt., on Dundrum Bay; Down, **N. Ireland**; resort; p. 7,500.

Newcastle-under-Lyme, t., l. gov. dist., Staffs., **Eng.**; 3 km W. of Stoke-on-Trent, on Lyme Brook; coal mng.; brick and tile mnfs.; p. (2010) 124,500 (dist.), (2001) 74,427 (t.).

Newcastle upon Tyne, c., met. dist., Tyne and Wear, **Eng.**; spt. on N. bank of Tyne R., 16 km from N. Sea; shipbldg., heavy engin., chemicals; connected by bridges across Tyne to Gateshead; univs., cath., many fine public bldgs., partially preserved in redevelopment of c. ctr.; airport; metro system; new City Library opened (2009); p. (2011) 280,200 (dist.).

Newent, mkt. t., Gloucs., **Eng.**; 13 km S. of Ledbury.

New Forest, forest and heathland, Hants., **Eng.**; relic of Royal Forest; now partly owned by Forestry Commission; proposed as new National Park (1999); pasture, ponies, tourism, residtl.; oil reserves but no drilling yet as conflicts with conservation; ch. t. Lyndhurst; forms l. gov. dist.; p. (2010) 175,000.

New Galloway, burgh, Dumfries and Galloway, **Scot.**; on R. Dee; nearby Clatteringshaws hydroelec. sta.

Newham, inner bor., Greater London, **Eng.**; W. of R. Lea; contained Royal group of London docks (now all closed); p. and industl. decentralisation from a.; proposed Stratford City devel., one of largest in London; Stratford site of 2012 Olympic stadium; Westfield Stratford City opened 2011; p. (2011) 308,010.

Newhaven, t., East Sussex, **Eng.**; on S. cst. at mouth of R. Ouse, 14 km E. of Brighton; pass- seaport pt. for Dieppe; boat-bldg. and lt. indus.; p. 12,500.

New Holland, v., N. Lincs., **Eng.**; rly. terminus, ferry pt. for crossing to Hull.

Newmarket, t., Forest Heath, Suffolk, **Eng.**; at foot of E. Anglian Heights; horse racing centre; p. 17,500.

New Mills, industl. t., High Peak, Derbys., **Eng.**; at W. foot of Pennines; textile printing, bleaching and dyeing; rayon, paper; p. 9,500.

Newmilns and Greenholm, burgh, E. Ayrshire, **Scot.**; on R. Irvine, 19 km E. of Kilmarnock; muslin and lace curtain mnf.; p. (2002) 3,057.

Newport-on-Tay, burgh, Fife, **Scot.**; on S. side of F. of Tay, opposite Dundee; p. (2002) 4,214.

Newport, cap. I. of Wight, **Eng.**; on R. Medina, in gap through central chalk ridge; mkt.; brewing, joinery, bait mnfs.; prison; p. 23,500.

Newport, sm. mkt. t., The Wrekin, Shrops., **Eng.**; 13 km N.E. of Wellington. Harper Adams University.

Newport, c., unit. auth. created in 1996 from former l. gov. dist., S.E. **Wales**; on R. Usk, 8 km from its mouth; timber terminal and deep-water berth; engin., iron and steel, aluminium, paperboard, confectionery, chemicals, plastics; new univ. campus; p. (2011) 145,700 (unit. auth.). Created a city, 2002.

Newport Pagnell, mkt. t., Bucks., **Eng.**; on R. Ouse; mnfs. Aston Martin cars; p. 13,200.

New Quay, t., Ceredigion, **Wales**; on cst. of Cardigan Bay; fishing; resort; p. 8,000.

Newquay, t., Restormel, Cornwall, **Eng.**; on N. Cornish cst.; seaside resort; p. 17,900. The surfing capital of Britain.

New Radnor, t., Powys, **Wales**; on slope of Radnor Forest, 10 km S.W. of Presteign.

New Romney, t., Shepway, Kent, **Eng.**; nr. S. cst. to E. of Dungeness; in rich agr. dist. of Romney Marsh; Cinque pt.; old harbour silted up by shingle, now a mile from sea; p. 8,850.

New Ross, mkt. t., Wexford, **R.o.I.**; brewing and malting; p. 5,600.

Newry, c., Newry and Mourne, **N. Ireland**; pt. at head of Carlingford Lough; machin., rope, brewing; p. 24,000. Created a city, 2002.

Newry and Mourne, l. gov. dist., **N. Ireland**; surrounds t. of N., borders R.o.I., Irish Sea; inc. Mtns. of Mourne. *See* **D11.**

Newton Abbot, mk. t., Teignbridge, Devon, **Eng.**;

at head of Teign estuary; rly. junc.; pottery, lt. engin.; agr. processing; p. 24,650.

Newton Aycliffe, t., Durham, **Eng.**; 10 km N.W. of Darlington; new t. (1947); engin., textiles, plastics, paint; Hitachi high-speed inter-city train factory opened, 2015; p. 25,750.

Newton-le-Willows, t., Merseyside, **Eng.**; engin., printing, sugar-refining; p. 21,500.

Newton-Stewart, burgh, Dumfries and Galloway, **Scot.**; on R. Cree, 8 km N. of Wigtown; mkt.; wool, creameries and agr. inds.; p. 3,600.

Newtown and **Llanllwchaiarn**, mkt. t., Powys, **Wales**; on R. Severn 13 km S.W. of Montgomery; precision instruments, machine tools; p. 10,900.

Newtownabbey, t., l. gov. dist., **N. Ireland**; sub. of Belfast, textiles, lt. inds.; p. (2010) 83,800 (dist.) *See* **D11**.

Newtownards, spt., mkt., Ards, **N. Ireland**; 11 km E. of Belfast; textile and engin. inds.; p. 24,000.

Newtown St Boswells, burgh, Borders, **Scot.**; p. (2010) 1,200.

Neyland, sm. t., Pembrokeshire, **Wales**; on Milford Haven; rly. terminus and sm. pt.

Nidd, R., trib. of R. Ouse, North Yorks., **Eng.**; 80 km long.

Nith, R., S.W. **Scot.**; flows to Solway F., S. of Dumfries; followed by main rly. from Carlisle to Kilmarnock and Glasgow; 114 km long.

Norfolk, non-met. co., E. **Eng.**; low-lying fens in W.; low sandy cst. suffers from erosion; intensive arable agr. on lge. farms; wheat, barley, root crops; inds. based on agr. processing and provision of agr. requisites; tourism on Norfolk Broads; co. t.. Norwich; p. (2010) 852,000.

Normanton, t., West Yorks., **Eng.**; 5 km N.E. of Wakefield; coal mng.; p. 19,100.

Northallerton, mkt. t., Hambleton, North Yorks., admin. ctr., **Eng.**; in broad gap between Cleveland hills and Pennines; in dairy farming and agr. dist.; p. 15,000.

Northampton, co. t., l. gov. dist., Northants., **Eng.**; on R. Nene; footwear, engin., leather prods.; new t. designation; univ.; p. (2010) 205,000 (dist.)

Northamptonshire, non-met. co., **Eng.**; E. Midlands; chiefly agr.; iron mng. and mftg.; footwear, engin., leather; p. (2010) 686,000. Known as the 'Queen of the Shires'.

North Atlantic Drift, drift of surface waters of Atl. Oc. N.E. from Gulf Stream towards Europe; relatively warm; supplies prevailing S.W. winds with warmth and moisture to modify climate of Brit. Is. and N.W. Europe.

North Ayrshire, unit. auth. created in 1996, formerly part of Strathclyde, W. **Scot.**, borders F. of Clyde and inc. I. of Arran; p. (2010) 136,000.

North Berwick, royal burgh, E. Lothian, **Scot.**; on S. of F. of Forth, 32 km E. of Edinburgh; resort; golf course; also fishing pt.; p. (2011) 6,300.

North Channel, gives access from Atl. Oc. to Irish Sea between S.W. Scotland (Dumfries and Galloway) and N.E. Ireland (Larne); length 96 km; narrowest width 24 km.

North Cornwall, former l. gov. dist., **Eng.**; lge. a. on cst. stretching from Bodmin right to Bude; now part of new unit. auth. for Cornwall.

North Devon, l. gov. dist., **Eng.**; inc. Exmoor and ts. of Barnstaple, Ilfracombe and Lynton; p. (2010) 92,000.

North Dorset, l. gov. dist., Dorset, **Eng.**; mainly rural but including ts. of Shaftesbury, Sturminster Newton and Blandford Forum; p. (2010) 68,000.

North Down, l. gov. dist., **N. Ireland**; borders Belfast Lough; main ts. Bangor, Holywood; p. (2010) 79,700. *See* **D11**.

North Downs, Surrey/Kent, **Eng.**; chalk escarpment running E. to W. across S.E. Eng.; form "white cliffs of Dover"; followed in part by Pilgrim's Way; Box Hill 233 m.

North East Derbyshire, l. gov. dist., Derbys., **Eng.**; industl. a. of Clay Cross and Dronfield; p. (2010) 98,100.

North East Lincolnshire, unit. auth. created in 1996, formerly part of Humberside, **Eng.**; inc. t. of Great Grimsby and Humberside resort of Cleethorpes; p. (2010) 158,000.

Northern Ireland, part of **UK.**; occupies N.E. a. of Ireland, now consisting of 11 l. gov. dists.; mild, temperate climate, exploited by dairy farming using excellent grass; arable agr. inc. barley, potatoes; traditional inds. inc. linen, shipbldg., food-processing, tobacco; modern inds. encouraged by extensive government aid inc. artificial fibres, carpets, elec. and aero-engin.; heavily dependent upon Brit. mkt.; serious social disturbance after 1969, based upon longstanding religious differences between Roman Catholic and Protestant as a result of discrimination against minority; Catholics now (2001) 44 % of pop., Protestants 53 %; Stormont Parliament replaced by Assembly (suspended 29 May 1974 and direct rule resumed); new Assembly created (for details, *see* **Section D**); returns 18 members to Westminster (17 prior to May 1997 general election); a. 14,121 km²; p. (mid-2015) 1,830,000.

Northfleet, t., Kent, **Eng.**; on S. bank of R. Thames, adjoining Gravesend; paper, rubber, tyres, cables; p. 24,000.

North Foreland, E. Kent, **Eng.**; chalk headland.

North Hertfordshire, l. gov. dist., Herts., **Eng.**; stretches from Baldock, Letchworth and Hitchin to Royston; p. (2010) 124,000.

North Kesteven, l. gov. dist., Lincs., **Eng.**; rural a. based on Sleaford; p. (2010) 106,000.

North Lanarkshire, unit. auth. created in 1996, formerly part of Strathclyde, central **Scot.**; lies immediately E. of Glasgow; p. (2010) 326,500.

Northleach, t., Cotswold, Gloucs., **Eng.**; once impt. woollen tr.

North Lincolnshire, unit. auth. created in 1996, formerly part of Humberside, **Eng.**; a. S. of the R. Humber inc. lowland a. of I. of Axholme and ts. of Barton-on-Humber, Brigg, Goole and Scunthorpe; p. (2010) 160,250.

North Norfolk, l. gov. dist., Norfolk, **Eng.**; cstl. a. inc. Wells-next-the-Sea, Cromer, Sheringham, Walsingham and North Walsham; p. (2010) 101,350.

North Sea, arm of the Atl., E. of Gr. Brit., W. of Norway, Sweden, and N. Germany, and N. of Holland, Belgium, and France; length 960 km, width 640 km; gd. fisheries; major natural gas, coal and oil deposits.

North Shields, t., frm. Tyne and Wear, **Eng.**; Tyne pt.; fishing pt.; marine engines, chain cables, anchors, rope; mkt.; p. 39,500.

North Shropshire, former l. gov. dist., Shrops., **Eng.**; a. N. of Shrewsbury and inc. Market Drayton.

North Somerset, unit. auth. created in 1996, formerly part of Avon, **Eng.**; inc. ts. of Clevedon and Weston-super-Mare; p. (2010) 207,000.

Northstowe, Cambs. New town planned as largest since creation of Milton Keynes. Old RAF base.

North Tyneside, met. bor., frm. Tyne and Wear, **Eng.**; comprises Tynemouth, Whitley Bay and Wallsend; p. (2011) 200,800.

Northumberland, old non-met. co., N. **Eng.**; on border of Scot. along Cheviots and R. Tweed; drained by Tyne, Blyth, Coquet Rs.; pastoral agr., especially sheep; coal mng., with former impt. exp. to London and S.E. Eng.; isolation and wild landscape attractive to tourists; now a new unit. auth.; p. (2011) 316,000.

Northumbria, Anglo-Saxon kingdom stretching from the Humber to the Forth; conquered by the Danes 9th cent.

North Walsham, mkt. t., North Norfolk, **Eng.**; 22 km N. of Norwich; former wool-weaving ctr.

North Warwickshire, l. gov. dist., Warwicks., **Eng.**; based on Atherstone; p. (2010) 62,250.

North West Leicestershire, l. gov. dist., Leics., **Eng.**; inc. Ashby de la Zouch, Ashby Woulds, Coalville and Castle Donington; p. (2010) 91,000.

Northwich, t., Cheshire, **Eng.**; on R. Weaver; impt. chemical inds. based originally upon local salt deposits, now much subsidence in a. due to salt extraction; p. 40,200.

North Wiltshire, former l. gov. dist., Wilts., **Eng.**; rural a. inc. ts. of Calne, Chippenham and Malmesbury. Now part of new unit. auth.

North York Moors, limestone plateau, North Yorks., **Eng.**; lies S. of estuary of R. Tees, heather moorland; some pastoral farming on lower slopes; alt. varies from 300–450 m; formerly impt. iron-ore quarrying along N. edge. Massive potash mine proposed near Whitby.

North Yorkshire, non-met. co., N. **Eng.**; inc. much of former N. Riding; stretches from Pennines (W.) to Vale of York (central), N. York Moors and Yorks. Wolds (E.); crossed by R. Ouse and tribs.; mainly rural, mixed agr.; ch. ts. cstl. resort of Scarborough and spa of Harrogate; p. (2010) 601,000.

Norton-Radstock, sm. t., Bath and N.E. Somerset, **Eng.**; footwear, sm. coalfield.

Norwich, c., co. t., l. gov. dist., Norfolk, **Eng.**; on

R. Wensum just above confluence with R. Yare; univ.; cath.; 32 medieval churches; cas.; cultural and agr. ctr.; food mnfs., footwear, printing; decentralization of office employment from London; new Forum opened (2001); p. (2010) 136,000 (dist.).

Nottingham, c., co. t., unit. auth. l. gov. dist., Notts., **Eng.**; a bridging point over Trent R.; lace, hosiery, tobacco, pharmaceutical; Raleigh cycles (production ended, 2002); univs., cas.; p. (2011) 305,700 (unit. auth.).

Nottinghamshire, non-met. co., Midlands, **Eng.**; contains part of productive E. Midlands coalfield serving many power stas. along Trent R.; urban growth concentrated mainly on coalfield; engin., hosiery; wheat, barley, cattle, roses; brilliantly characterised in writings of D. H. Lawrence; p. (2010) 778,000.

Nuneaton, t., part of l. gov. dist. of **Nuneaton and Bedworth,** Warwicks., **Eng.**; on Anker R.; old coal mng., textiles, lt. inds.; mkt.; the birthplace of George Eliot; now commuter centre for Coventry and Birmingham; p. (2010) 122,000 (dist.).

O

Oadby, t., Leics., **Eng.**; 5 km S.E. of Leicester; footwear; part of l. gov. dist. of **Oadby and Wigston,** S. of Leicester; p. (2010) 57,500 (dist.).

Oakengates, t., The Wrekin, Shrops., **Eng.**; 24 km N.W. of Wolverhampton; iron and steel, precast concrete, engin.; now part of new t. of Telford; p. 32,000.

Oakham, t., Rutland, **Eng.**; mkt.; hosiery, footwear, p. 9,200. The Cotswolds of the north.

Oban, spt., burgh, Argyll and Bute, **Scot.**; on F. of Lorne; resort; ctr. for local shipping; woollens, tartans; p. 8,250.

Ochil Hills, volcanic hill-range, **Scot.**; stretching 40 km N.E. to S.W. from F. of Tay to nr. Stirling; loftiest Ben Cleugh, 721 m; beautiful glens and valleys.

Offaly, co., Leinster, **R.o.I.**; much marshy land (inc. Bog of Allen), barren uplands (inc. Slieve Bloom); pastoral agr., wheat; p. mainly rural; agr. processing inds. in ts.; co. t. Tullamore; a. 1,999 km², p. 76,806 (2011).

Ogmore Vale, t., Bridgend, **Wales**; in narrow valley, 10 km N. of Bridgend; industl.; cas.; p. 6,950.

Oich, Loch, Gr. Glen, Highland, **Scot.**; forms part of Caledonian Canal.

Okehampton, mt. t., West Devon, **Eng.**; on N. flank of Dartmoor; granite quarries; p. 5,100.

Oldbury. *See* **Warley.**

Oldbury-on-Severn, S. Gloucs., **Eng.**; nuclear power sta.

Oldham, c., met. dist., Gtr. Manchester, **Eng.**; on R. Medlock, 11 km N.E. of Manchester; manmade fibre and cotton textiles, machin.; industl. diversification inc. electro- and aero-engin., leather, paints; major areas of social deprivation; p. (2011) 224,900 (dist.).

Oldmeldrum, burgh, Aberdeenshire, **Scot.**; 6 km N.E. of Inverurie; p. 2,000.

Olney, t., Milton Keynes, **Eng.**; mkt., dairy produce; Shrove Tuesday pancake race; p. 4,600.

Omagh, t., l. gov. dist., **N. Ireland**; tourist ctr.; bomb killed 29 people, Aug. 1998; p (2011) 52,200 (dist.). *See* **D11.**

Ord of Caithness, hill, headland, nr. Helmsdale, **Scot.**; alt. 366 m.

Orford Ness, coastal sandspit, Suffolk, **Eng.**; cas. keep at Orford.

Orkney Islands, l. gov. auth., **Scot.**; gr. of 68 Is. in N. Sea, inc. Pomona, Sanday, Westray; 29 inhabited; important neolithic burial chambers; famous stone circles (World Heritage Site); farming, fishing; North Sea oil; cap. Kirkwall; total a. c. 932 km²; p. (2011) 21,350. Population shares genetic characteristics with Norway.

Ormskirk, t., West Lancs., **Eng.**; 22 km N.E. of Liverpool; in mkt. gardening a.; lt. engin., clothing; univ. (Edge Hill); p. 24,000.

Orpington. *See* **Bromley.**

Ossett, t., West Yorks., **Eng.**; 5 km W. of Wakefield; p. 21,500.

Oswaldtwistle, t., Hyndburn, Lancs., **Eng.**; at N. foot of Rossendale Fells; chemicals, textiles.

Oswestry, t., former l. gov. dist., Shrops., **Eng.**; at foot of Welsh mtns., cas.; engin.; p. (2011) 16,500 (t.).

Otley, sm. t., West Yorks., **Eng.**; on R. Wharfe; printing, machin., wool, paper mkg., leather, furnishings; birthplace of Thomas Chippendale.

Ottery St. Mary, sm. mkt. t., East Devon, **Eng.**; 16 km E. of Exeter; birthplace of Coleridge.

Oulton Broad, L., Suffolk, **Eng.**; nr. Lowestoft. *See* **Broads.**

Oundle, mkt. t., East Northants., **Eng.**; on R. Nene; public school.

Ouse or Great Ouse, R., **Eng.**; rises in S. Northamptonshire and flows N.E. via the Fens to the Wash; 250 km long.

Ouse, R., East Sussex, **Eng.**; flows to English Channel at Newhaven; 48 km long.

Ouse, R., York/North Yorks., **Eng.**; formed by R. Ure at Ouse Gill Beck, flows to Humber estuary; 208 km long.

Outer Hebrides. *See* **Hebrides.**

Oxford, c., l. gov. dist., Oxon., **Eng.**; between R. Thames and R. Cherwell; 13th cent. univ. and residtl. colleges; also Oxford Brookes Univ., printing, cars; p. (2010) 154,000 (dist.). Charles I held his court here after 1642 in the civil war. New direct rly. link to London Marylebone, opened 2015.

Oxfordshire, non-met. co., **Eng.**; formed by Chilterns and Cotswolds, drained by R. Thames and tribs.; mainly agr. with lge. arable farms; p. (2010) 640,000.

P

Paddington. *See* **Westminster, City of.**

Padiham, sm. t., Lancs., **Eng.**; at N. foot of Rossendale Fells, textiles, engin.

Padstow, mkt. t. Camel estuary, Cornwall, **Eng.**; silting has caused pt. decline; lt. inds.; seaside resort; p. 2,600.

Paignton, t., S. Devon, **Eng.**; incorporated in Torbay; resort; p. 46,100.

Paisley, burgh, Renfrewshire, **Scot.**; 8 km W. of Glasgow; anc. abbey; former inds. included shipbldg., chemicals, engin., preserves, car bodies, cotton thread; univ; p. 75,000.

Peak Dist., Pennine hill dist., mid-**Eng.**; extends from Chesterfield to Buxton, and Ashbourne to Glossop; composed of limestone with typical karst features; within P.D. Nat. Park, tourist and recreation a. for cities to E. (Sheffield) and W. (Manchester); limestone quarrying for cement.

Peebles, royal burgh, Borders, **Scot.**; on upper course of R. Tweed; woollen cloth, knitwear; mkt., tourist ctr.; p. 8,100.

Peeblesshire, historic co., S. **Scot.**; now part of Borders.

Peel, t., Isle of Man; resort, fishing pt. midway along W. cst.; cas., cath.; p. 3,950.

Peel Fell, mtn. Northumberland, Eng.; 1,964 ft.

Pembroke, mkt. t., Pembrokeshire, **Wales**; on S. side of Milford Haven; sm. pt.; dock facilities; cas.; ruins of Monkton priory; birth-place of Henry VII; p. 7,000.

Pembroke Dock, Pembrokeshire, **Wales**; site of government dockyard (1814) with consequent growth of a new t.; p. 8,950.

Pembrokeshire, S.W. **Wales**, unit. auth. created in 1996 from former l. gov. dists. of Preseli, Pembrokeshire and South Pembrokeshire, reinstating historic co. split up in 1974; p. (2011) 122,400.

Penarth, t., Vale of Glamorgan, **Wales**; former sm. pt. on Severn estuary, 3 km S. of Cardiff; seaside resort; p. 26,000.

Pendle, l. gov. dist., Lancs., **Eng.**; ts. of Barrowford, Colne and Nelson; p. (2011) 90,000.

Penistone, sm. t., South Yorks., **Eng.**; on R. Don; steel; mkt.

Penmaenmawr, t., Conwy, **Wales**; 6 km. S.W. of Conwy; resort.

Pennine Range, mtn. range, "backbone of England," extends 224 km southwards from Cheviot hills to Derbyshire; limestone, millstone grit; moorland sheep, dairying in valleys, quarrying, tourism; inc. Peak Dist. Nat. Park and Pennine Way long distance route; water supply, forestry; Cross Fell, 895 m.

Penrith, sm. mkt. t., Eden, Cumbria, **Eng.**; at N. foot of Shap Fell, 29 km S.E. of Carlisle; agr. mkt.; tourist ctr.; p. 13,000.

Penryn, t., Carrick, Cornwall, **Eng.**; on R. Fal estuary; sm. pt., boat repairs; once ctr. of granite quarrying; p. 7,500.

Pentonville, dist., London, **Eng.**; prison; birthplace of John Stuart Mill.

Pentland Firth, strait, between Orkney Is. and Highland, **Scot.**, connecting N. Sea and Atl. Oc.;

largest tidal energy scheme in Europe given go-ahead (2013).

Pentland Hills, range, *Scot.*; extend from Lanark to Edinburgh; hgst. Scald Law, 878 m.

Penwith, former l. gov. dist., Cornwall, *Eng.*; S.W. tip of Cornwall inc. Penzance, St. Just and St. Ives. Now part of new Cornish unit. auth.

Penzance, t., Penwith, Cornwall, *Eng.*; on Mount's Bay; tourist ctr.; ferry to Scilly Isles; engin.; birthplace of Sir Humphrey Davy; p. 20,000.

Pershore, t., Wychavon, Worcs., *Eng.*; on R. Avon; ctr. of fruit-growing a.; p. 7,350.

Perth, c., royal burgh, Perth and Kinross, *Scot.*; on R. Tay; rly. junction; cap. of Scot. until assassination of James I, 1437; impt. cattle mkt.; cath; p. (2002) 43,450. Known as the 'Gateway to the Highlands'. Created a Jubilee City, 2012.

Perth and Kinross, unit. auth. created in 1996, formerly part of Tayside, E. *Scot.*; p. (2010) 146,000.

Perthshire, historic co., E. *Scot.*, now divided between Perth and Kinross and Stirling.

Peterborough, c., unit. auth., Cambs., *Eng.*; on R. Nene on margin of Fens; cath.; rly ctr.; ctr. of brick ind. (Oxford clay around Fletton); diesel engines, agr. machin., gen. engin.; t. expanded very much; large Polish migrant population (c. 10,000); p. (2011) 184,000 (unit. auth.).

Peterborough, Soke of. *See* **Cambridgeshire.**

Peterhead, spt., burgh, Aberdeenshire, *Scot.*; on E. cst., 43 km N.E. of Aberdeen; herring fisheries, leading white fish port; fish-processing, granite quarrying; supply base for N. Sea oil; p. 18,100.

Peterlee, new t. (1948), Durham, *Eng.*; old coal-mng. dist.; science-based inds.; p. (2010) 30,000.

Petersfield, sm. t., East Hants., *Eng.*; on R. Rother, N.W. of Chichester; mkt.

Petworth, sm. mkt. t., West Sussex, *Eng.*; in Rother valley, 19 km N.E. of Chichester; associated with Turner.

Pevensey Levels, marshy a., East Sussex, *Eng.*; now largely drained, cattle pastures; a. 62 km².

Pickering, mkt. t., Ryedale, North Yorks., *Eng.*; on N. margin of Vale of P.; church with murals; cas.; gas terminal; p. 6,000.

Pickering, Vale of, North Yorks., *Eng.*, wide, flat-floored vale, once occupied by glacial lake; bounded to N. by N. York Moors, to S. by York Wolds; drained W. by R. Derwent, alluvial soils, marshy in ctr.; crop farming along margins, cattle grazing in damper meadows in ctr., ch. ts. Pickering, Malton, Helmsley.

Pitlochry, burgh, Perth and Kinross, *Scot.*; on R. Tummel, 6 km S. of Pass of Killiecrankie; summer resort; distilleries, hydros; p. (2002) 2,564.

Pittenweem, burgh, Fife, *Scot.*; at entrance to F. of Forth; fisheries; p. (2002) 1,747.

Plymouth, c., spt., unit. auth., S. Devon, *Eng.*; on Plymouth Sound; comprises the "three towns" of Plymouth, Devonport, and Stonehouse; Brit. fleet faced Armada 1588; R.C. cath., guildhall, museum; Naval dockyard; seaside resort; fishing and fish-canning; lt. inds.; univ.; deposit of tungsten thought to be lgst. in W. Europe but lies within Dartmoor Nat. Park; p. (2010) 253,000 (unit. auth.). The airport was closed in 2011.

Plynlimmon, mtn., Powys and Ceredigion, *Wales*; alt. 753 m; source of R. Severn.

Pocklington, sm. mkt. t., East Riding of Yorks., *Eng.*; foot of York Wolds, 19 km E. of York; ctr. of agr. dist.; 16th cent. grammar school.

Pomona (Mainland), lgst of the Orkney Is., *Scot.*; Kirkwall (cap.) and Stromness on I.; p. 15,000.

Pontardawe, t., Neath Pt. Talbot, S. *Wales*; on R. Tawe, N.E. of Swansea; zinc smelting and refining; p. 19,000.

Pontefract, mkt. t., West Yorks., *Eng.*; 11 km E. of Wakefield; coal, furniture, historic liquorice etr., mkt. gardening; cas. ruins; p. 29,000.

Pontypool, t., Torfaen, *Wales*; steel, glass, bricks, tin galvanising, nylon at Manhilad; p. 36,000.

Pontypridd, t., Rhondda, Cynon, Taff, *Wales*; on R. Taff, 19 km N.W. of Cardiff; formerly coal, iron-founding; univ; p. 30,000.

Poole, t., unit. auth. created in 1997, formerly part of Dorset, *Eng.*; spt. on Poole Harbour, 6 km W. of Bournemouth; imports clay for local pottery inds; petroleum production began 1979; tourism, yachting, marine engin., chemicals; p. (2010) 139,000 (unit. auth.).

Portadown, sm. t., Craigavon, *N. Ireland*; on R. Bann, 40 km S.W. of Belfast; linen (no longer manufac-

tured); food processing; merged with Lurgan to form new c. of Craigavon.

Portaferry, spt., Ards, *N. Ireland*; shipping fisheries; p. 3,400.

Portarlington, mkt. t., Offaly, *R.o.I.*; farming; first place to have elec. power-sta. using local peat fuel.

Port Erin, v., *Isle of Man*; on S.E. cst.; seaside resort, fisheries.

Port Glasgow, burgh, spt., Inverclyde, *Scot.*; on S. bank of R. Clyde, 27 km below Glasgow; ship-bldg. and repairing, textiles, rope, canvas mftg.; p. 17,000.

Porthcawl, t., Bridgend, *Wales*; on cst. 16 km S.E. of Pt. Talbot; resort; p. 17,000.

Porthmadog (Portmadoc), t., Gwynedd, *Wales*; pt. on Tremadog Bay; terminus of Festiniog lt. rly.; p. 3,250.

Portishead, pt., N. Somerset, *Eng.*; on Severn estuary 5 km S.W. of Avonmouth; p. 15,000.

Portknockie, burgh, Moray, *Scot.*; on N. Buchan cst., 8 km E. of Buckie; sm. fish. pt.; p. 1,200.

Portland, t., Weymouth and P., Dorset, *Eng.*; 6 km S. of Weymouth on sheltered N.E. side of I. of Portland; lge artificial harbour; former naval base, prison.

Portland, I. of, Dorset, *Eng.*; limestone mass, linked to mainland by shingle spit, Chesil Bank, terminates S. in Portland Bill; former naval base, Borstal institution; limestone quarrying; masonry wks. Jurassica tourist attraction planned.

Portobello, resort, *Scot.*; on F. of Forth, 5 km E. of Edinburgh.

Portree, spt., v., I. of Skye, Highland, *Scot.*; land-locked harbour on P. Bay, Sound of Raasay; fishing; tweed mill; p. 1,950.

Portrush, spt., Coleraine, *N. Ireland*; 8 km N. of Coleraine; tourism; p. 5,900.

Portsdown Hill, chalk ridge, Hants., *Eng.*; extends E. to W. behind Portsmouth from Havant to Fareham.

Portsea I., fortfd. I., between Portsmouth and Langston harbours, Portsmouth, *Eng.*

Portslade-by-Sea, t., Brighton and Hove, *Eng.*; W. of Hove; p. 19,500.

Portsmouth, c., naval pt., unit. auth. created in 1997, Hants., *Eng.*; opposite Isle of Wight; famous naval establishment; Portsmouth is the garrison t.; Portsea has the naval dockyards, Landport is residtl., and Southsea is a popular resort; end of future naval shipbuilding announced, November 2013; across the harbour is Gosport; shipbldg.; univ.; birthplace of Charles Dickens and I. K. Brunel; Spinnaker Tower; first 20 mph city-wide speed limit; New Mary Rose Museum opened, 2013; D-Day Museum (reopening 2019 as International Museum of D-Day); p. (2010) 199,500 (unit. auth.).

Port Sunlight, Merseyside, *Eng.*; garden v. founded 1888 by Lord Leverhulme for the employees of the Port Sunlight factories. Soap production ended (2000).

Port Talbot, t., Neath Port Talbot, S. *Wales*; on E. side of Swansea Bay; impt. iron and steel ind., copper, coal; new deep-water harbour serves as ore terminal; p. 38,000. Steel now in decline.

Potteries, The, dist., Stoke, *Eng.*; ctr. of earthenware ind., comprising ts. Burslem, Hanley, Fenton, Tunstall, Stoke and Longton.

Potters Bar, t., Hertsmere, Herts., *Eng.*; residtl.; in London commuter belt; p. (2001) 22,008.

Poulton-le-Fylde, sm. t., Lancs., *Eng.*; ctr. of mkt. gardening, poultry rearing dist.

Powys, central *Wales*, unit. auth. created in 1996 from former l. gov. dists. of Brecknock, Montgomeryshire and Radnorshire; mtnous a. bordering Eng.; forestry, stockraising and water catchment for Eng.; crossed by Rs. Wye and Severn; sparse p.; p. (2011) 133,000.

Powys, Vale of, Powys, *Wales*; drained by R. Severn; cattle-rearing; ch. t. Welshpool.

Prescot, mftg. t., Knowsley, Merseyside, *Eng.*; 6 km. S.W. of St. Helens; mkt., elec. cable ind.; p. 37,100.

Prestatyn, t., Denbighshire, *Wales*; on N. cst., 5 km E. of Rhyl; seaside resort.

Presteigne, mkt. t., Powys, *Wales*; on R. Lugg, 16 km N.W. of Leominster; p. 1,900.

Preston, c., l. gov. dist., Lancs., *Eng.*; pt. on R. Ribble; textiles, engin., aircraft wks.; p. (2011) 140,200 (dist.).

Prestonpans, burgh, E. Lothian, S.E. *Scot.*; on F. of Forth, 14 km E. of Edinburgh; scene of Jacobite victory 1745; p. 7,500.

Prestwich, t., Gtr. Manchester, **Eng.**; in valley of R. Irwell, 6 km N.W. of Manchester; cotton bleaching and dyeing, soap, furnishings; p. (2001) 31,693.

Prestwick, burgh, S. Ayrshire, **Scot.**; on F. of Clyde, 5 km N. of Ayr; golfing ctr.; major international airpt. and freeport (1984); resort; p. 15,000.

Prudhoe, Northumberland, **Eng.**; former coal mng. t.; chemicals, paper.

Pudsey, t., West Yorks., **Eng.**; between Leeds and Bradford; woollens; p. 34,000.

Purbeck, I. of, sm. penin., Dorset cst., **Eng.**; anc. v. of Corfe Castle in ctr.; limestone ("Purbeck marble") quarries; site of Britain's lgst. onshore oilfield; once a royal deer forest; forms 1. gov. dist. of **Purbeck**, inc. Wareham and Swanage; p. (2010) 46,000.

Putney, sub. of London, **Eng.**; Thameside dist.

Pwllheli, t., Gwynedd, N. **Wales**; sm. pt. on S. cst. Lleyn Peninsula; seaside resort; in-shore fishing, boat-bldg.; p. 4,000. Given its charter by Edward, the Black Prince.

Q

Quantock Hills, Somerset, **Eng.**; S. of Bridgwater Bay; hgst. pt. 385 m.

Queensbury and Shelf, sm. t., West Yorks., **Eng.**; textiles.

Queensferry, royal burgh, Edinburgh, **Scot.**; at S. end of Forth road and rail bridges; p. 9,800.

Quorndon (Quorn), sm. t., Leics., **Eng.**; on R. Soar, 5 km S. of Loughborough; former ctr. of fox-hunting dist.; p. 4,900.

R

Raasay, I., E. of Skye, Highland, **Scot.**; 21 km long, 5·6 km wide.

Radcliffe, t., Gtr. Manchester, **Eng.**; N.W. of Manchester; paper, engin.; p. 34,000.

Radnorshire, historic co., central **Wales**, now part of Powys.

Rainford, sm. t., Merseyside, **Eng.**; nr. St. Helens; former coal-mng. a.

Ramsbottom, t., Lancs., **Eng.**; on R. Irwell, 6 km N. of Bury; engin., paper, textiles; p. 18,500.

Ramsey, sm. mkt. t., Cambs., **Eng.**; on edge of Fens, 11 km N. of St. Ives; engin.; abbey ruins.

Ramsey, t., spt., I. of Man, **Eng.**; on N.E. cst.; holiday resort; p. 6,750.

Ramsgate, t., Kent, **Eng.**; on S. cst. of I. of Thanet; seaside resort; p. 39,000.

Rannoch, Loch, Perth and Kinross, **Scot.**; 14 km long, 1·6 km wide; drained to R. Tay.

Raunds, t., East Northants., **Eng.**; 8 km N.E. of Wellingborough; p. 7,550.

Ravenglass, t., Cumbria, **Eng.**; nr. mouth of R. Esk; old t.; Roman remains.

Rawmarsh, t., South Yorks., **Eng.**; 3 km N.E. of Rotherham; engin.; p. 19,000.

Rawtenstall, t., Rossendale, Lancs., **Eng.**; on R. Irwell in ctr. of Rossendale Fells; felts; footwear, textiles; p. 22,000.

Rayleigh, t., Rochford, Essex, **Eng.**; 8 km N.W. of Southend; dormitory for London; p. 31,000.

Reading, t., unit. auth., Berks., **Eng.**; at confluence of Rs. Thames and Kennet; univ.; biscuits, engin., electronics, mkt. gardening, tin- box mftg., printing; second biggest rly. interchange outside London; p. (2010) 146,000 (unit.auth.).

Redbridge, outer bor., E. London, **Eng.**; incorporates Ilford, Wanstead and Woodford, Chigwell (Hainault Estate), Dagenham (N. Chadwell Heath ward); mainly residtl.; p. (2011) 279,000.

Redcar, t., Redcar and Cleveland, **Eng.**; lge. iron and steel wks. (opened 1917, closed 2015); p. (2011) 135,200.

Redcar and Cleveland, unit. auth. created in 1996, formerly part of Cleveland, **Eng.**; inc. Cleveland Hills and ts. of Guisborough, Redcar and Skelton; p. (2011) 135,200.

Redditch, t., 1. gov. dist., Worcs., **Eng.**; 19 km S. of Birmingham; needles, fishing tackle, cycles, springs, aluminium alloys; new t. (1964); p. (2010) 80,000.

Redruth, t., Cornwall, **Eng.**; once major ctr. of tin mng.; p. 36,750 (inc. Camborne).

Ree, Lough, L., **R.o.I.**; between Roscommon, Longford and Westmeath, an extension of R. Shannon; 27 km long.

Reigate, t., Surrey, **Eng.**; at foot of N. Downs, 8 km E. of Dorking; dormitory for London; part of 1. gov. dist., **Reigate and Banstead**; p. (2010) 135,000 (dist.), (2001) 50,436 (t.) (with Redhill).

Renfrew, royal burgh, Renfrewshire, **Scot.**; nr. R. Clyde, 8 km W. of Glasgow; p. 20,750.

Renfrewshire, W. **Scot.**, unit. auth. created in 1996, incorporating part of historic co. which became part of Strathclyde in 1974 and is now divided between Inverclyde, E. Renfrewshire and Renfrewshire; lies immediately W. of Glasgow; p. 2,600.

Repton, t., South Derbyshire, **Eng.**; famous public school in priory; former Saxon cap. of Mercia; p.2,500.

Restormel, former 1. gov. dist., Cornwall, **Eng.**; inc. N. and S. cst. and ts. of Newquay and St. Austell. Now part of new Cornish unit. auth.

Rheidol, R., Ceredigion, **Wales**; flows from Plynlimmon in deeply incised valley (Devil's Bridge) to Aberystwyth; famous narrow-gauge rly; hydroelec. power; 38 km long.

Rhondda, t., Rhondda, Cynon, Taff, **Wales**; in narrow R. valley; former coal mng. ctr.; lt. inds. introduced since 1930s depression; picturesque a. in upper R. valley; p. 58,000.

Rhondda, Cynon, Taff, S. Wales, unit. auth. created in 1996 from former 1. gov. dists. of Cynon Valley, Rhondda and Taff-Ely; upland in N. dissected by deep R. valleys containing former coal mng. settlements; inc. ts. of Aberdare and Pontypridd; p. (2011) 234,400.

Rhyl, t., Denbighshire, N. **Wales**; at entrance Vale of Clwyd; resort developed from sm. fishing v.; p. 24,000.

Rhymney, t., Caerphilly, **Wales**; on R. Rhymney, E. of Merthyr Tydfil; former colly. and iron founding ctr.; engin.; p. 8,000.

Ribble Valley, 1. gov. dist., N. Lancs., **Eng.**; inc. Forest of Bowland and ts. of Clitheroe and Longridge; p. (2011) 57,100.

Richborough, pt., Kent, **Eng.**; at mouth of R. Stour; Caesar's ch. pt., major Roman remains; pt. has been privately redeveloped; chemicals.

Richmond, t., North Yorks., **Eng.**; at E. foot of Pennines on R. Swale; mkt. t., agr. tr.; 14th cent. grammar school; Norman cas.; forms 1. gov. dist. of **Richmondshire** with surrounding a. of Aysgarth and Leyburn; p. (2010) 51,400 (dist.), 8,000 (t.).

Richmond upon Thames, outer bor., Greater London, **Eng.**; inc. Barnes, Richmond and Twickenham; industl. and residtl.; park and Kew Gardens; St. Mary's univ. (Twickenham); p. (2011) 187,000.

Rickmansworth, t., Three Rivers, Herts., **Eng.**; residtl. sub of London; p. 11,250.

Ripley, mkt. t., Amber Valley, Derbys., **Eng.**; 11 km N.E. of Derby; coal, iron, heavy engin.; bricks, agr. implements; p. 19,000.

Ripon, c., North Yorks., **Eng.**; on R. Ure; cath.; old mkt. square; old custom of wakeman; tourism; p. 14,250.

Robin Hood's Bay, v., North Yorks., **Eng.**; picturesque site in inlet; tourism, fishing.

Rochdale, t., met. dist., Gtr. Manchester, **Eng.**; at S. foot of Rossendale Fells, on R. Roch; textiles, engin., asbestos; co-operative movement started (1844); p. (2011) 211,700 (dist.).

Rochester, t., part of 1. gov. dist. of **Rochester-upon-Medway**, Kent, **Eng.**; on R. Medway, adjoining Chatham; cath., cas.; many associations with Dickens; aeronautical, elec. and mechanical engin., paint, varnish, cement; p. (1995) 144,200 (dist.).

Rochford, t. and 1. gov. dist., Essex, **Eng.**; cstl. a. inc. Rochford and Rayleigh; p. (2010) 83,000 (dist.).

Rockall, sm. I., **Atl. Oc.**; lies 320 km W. of Outer Hebrides; forms hgst. part of submarine bank which forms good fishing-ground; uninhabited; annexed by Britain 1955; formally incorporated into Inverness-shire (1972) to ensure control of oil and natural gas deposits; claimed also by Ireland and Iceland; rock samples aged 1,000 million years place it with some Canadian rocks.

Rockall Deep, submarine trench, N. **Atl. Oc.**; between N.W. Ireland and Rockall I.; suspected oil and natural gas reserves.

Romford. *See* Havering.

Romney Marsh, coastal marsh, Shepway, Kent,

Eng.; formed by blocking of R. Rother by shingle spit of Dungeness which extends from Rye to Hythe; largely drained; pastures for special Romney Marsh breed of sheep; a. 129 km².

Romsey, sm. t., Test Valley, Hants., **Eng.**; on R. Test, 14 km N.W. of Southampton; mkt. ctr.; Norman abbey.

Ronaldshay, North, most N. of Orkney Is., **Scot.**; p. 90.

Ronaldshay, South, most S. of Orkney Is. **Scot.**; p. 940.

Roscommon, co. t., Roscommon, **R.o.I.**; mkt.; cas., priory; p. 1,750.

Roscommon, inland co., Connaught, **R.o.I.**; extensive peat bog and Ls.; pastoral agr., cap. R.; a. 2,458 km²; p. (2011) 63,898.

Ross and Cromarty, historic co., N.W. **Scot.**, now part of Highland.

Rossendale Fells (or Forest), upland, S.E. Lancs./ Gtr. Manchester, **Eng.**; extension of Pennines between Rs. Mersey and Ribble; millstone grit moorland used for reservoirs; alt. mainly above 360 m; forms l. gov. dist. **Rossendale** in Lancs., inc. ts. of Haslingden, Rawtenstall, Bacup and Whitworth; p. (2010) 67,100.

Rosslare, spt., Wexford, **R.o.I.**; on extreme S.E. of Ireland; connections to Fishguard; p. 700.

Ross-on-Wye, t., South Herefordshire, Hereford, **Eng.**; mkt.; tourism; p. 9,750.

Rosyth, t., Fife, **Scot.**; naval dockyard (closed 1995); p. 12,500.

Rothamsted, v., Herts., **Eng.**; in Chiltern Hills, S. of Harpenden; famous agr. research sta.

Rother, l. gov. dist., East Sussex, **Eng.**; rural a. inc. Rye, Bexhill and Battle; p. (2010) 88,000.

Rother, R., Derbys. and South Yorks., **Eng.**; flows to R. Don at Rotherham; 34 km long.

Rother, R., East Sussex and Kent, **Eng.**; rises in the Weald, flows S.E. into English Channel at Rye; 50 km long.

Rotherham, t., met. dist., South Yorks., **Eng.**; on R. Don, 6 km N.E. of Sheffield; coal mining, iron, steel, wire, springs, glass; Magna Science Centre; p. (2011) 257,300 (dist.).

Rothes, burgh, Moray, **Scot.**; on R. Spey 19 km S.E. of Elgin; p. 1,190.

Rothesay, royal burgh, Argyll and Bute., **Scot.**; on E. cst. of I. of Bute in F. of Clyde; tourism; p. 5,100.

Rothwell, West Yorks., **Eng.**; on R. Aire, suburb of Leeds; old coal-mng. ctr., engin.

Roxburghshire, historic co., S. **Scot.**; now part of Borders.

Royston, sm. mkt. t., North Herts., **Eng.**; at N. foot of E. Anglian Heights, 11 km N.E. of Baldock.

Royton, t., Gtr. Manchester, **Eng.**; 13 km N.E. of Manchester; textiles; p. 22,000.

Rugby, mkt. t., l. gov. dist., Warwicks., **Eng.**; on R. Avon, 18 km E. of Coventry; famous public school; elec. and gen. engin., motor and aircraft patterns; p. (2010) 92,000 (dist.).

Rugeley, mkt. t., Staffs, **Eng.**; on R. Trent, 14 km S.E. of Stafford; coal, iron, tanning; expanded t.; new Amazon processing centre; p. 23,000.

Rum (Rhum), I., Inner Hebrides, Highland, **Scot.**; nature reserve, highland ecology. Spelling of the name changed from Rhum to Rum in 1991.

Runcorn, t., Halton, Cheshire, **Eng.**; on S. side of Mersey estuary; new t. (1964); chemicals; pipeline carrying petrochemical feedstock from Teeside; p. 61,500.

Runnymede, site of signing of Magna Carta; l. gov. dist., Surrey, **Eng.**; comprises Egham and Chertsey; p. (2010) 83,500.

Rushcliffe, l. gov. dist., Notts., **Eng.**; a. S.E. of Nottingham inc. West Bridgeford; p. (2010) 110,000.

Rushden, t., East Northants., **Eng.**; 5 km E. of Wellingborough; shoes; p. 26,000.

Rushmoor, l. gov. dist., Hants., **Eng.**; small a. of Farnborough and Aldershot; p. 92,000.

Rutherglen, royal burgh, Glasgow, **Scot.**; on R. Clyde, S.E. of Glasgow; chemicals, tubes, paper.

Ruthin, sm. t., Denbighshire, **Wales**; Vale of Clwyd, 13 km S.E. of Denbigh.

Rutland, Eng., unit. auth. created in 1997, reinstating historic co. based on Oakham which became part of Leicestershire in 1974; p. (2010) 39,400.

Rutland Water, reservoir, Rutland, **Eng**. Largest man-made lake in northern Europe.

Rydal Water, L., nr. Ambleside, Cumbria, **Eng.**;

adjacent v. contains Rydal Mount, home of Wordsworth.

Ryde, t., I. of Wight, **Eng.**; on N.E. cst.; yachting ctr. and seaside resort; boat and yacht bldg.; steamer connection across Spithead to Portsmouth; p. 23,000.

Rye, sm. t., Rother, East Sussex, **Eng.**; at mouth of R. Rother to W. of Dungeness; Cinque pts.; Ypres cas.; tourist ctr.

Ryedale, l. gov. dist., North Yorks., **Eng.**; lge. a. inc. Malton, Pickering, Norton, Kirby Moorside and Helmsley; p. (2010) 53,500.

Ryton, sm. t., Tyne and Wear, **Eng.**; on R. Tyne, W. of Newcastle.

S

Saddleback (Blencathara), mtn., Cumbria, **Eng.**; nr. Keswick; alt. 868 m.

Saddleworth, sm. t., Gtr. Manchester, **Eng.**; in Pennines, 8 km N.E. of Oldham; woollens, paper mkg., engin. Once part of Yorkshire.

Saffron Walden, sm. mkt. t., Uttlesford, Essex, **Eng.**; on E. Anglian heights; cas., abbey ruins; saffron crocus once cultivated.

St. Abb's Head, rocky promontory, lighthouse, Borders, **Scot.**

St. Albans, c., l. gov. dist., Herts., **Eng.**; on N. margin of Vale of St. Albans, 32 km N.W. of London; faces remains of Roman Verulamium across R. Ver; lt. inds., electronics, instrument mkg.; cath.; residtl.; p. (2010) 134,000 (dist.), 85,000 (c.).

St. Andrews, royal burgh, Fife, **Scot.**; seaside resort; univ.; famous golf course; p. (2010) 14,500. Known as the home of golf.

St. Asaph, sm. t., Denbighshire, N. **Wales**; on R. Clwyd. Created a Jubilee City, 2012.

St. Austell, mkt. t., Restormel, Cornwall, **Eng.**; on S. flank of Hensbarrow; ctr. of Cornwall's china clay ind.; p. 22,500. Near to Eden Project, the West Country's biggest tourist attraction.

St. Bees Head, promontory, 4 km N.W. of St. Bees, Cumbria, **Eng.**; freestone quarries, anhydrite.

St. Brides Bay, Pembrokeshire, **Wales**.

St. Davids, c., Pembrokeshire, **Wales**; 24 km S.W. of Fishguard; on site of anc. Minevia; cath., ruins of Bishop Gower's palace (1342); major tourist centre; p. 1,900.

St. David's Head, promontory, Pembrokeshire, **Wales**.

St. Edmundsbury, l. gov. dist., Suffolk, **Eng.**; based on Bury St. Edmunds and inc. Haverhill; p. (2010) 104,000.

St. George's Channel, part of Irish Sea, separating Wales from Ireland.

St. Govan's Head, promontory, Pembrokeshire, **Wales**.

St. Helens, t., met. dist., Merseyside, **Eng.**; 19 km E. of Liverpool; connected by canal with R. Mersey; coal, iron, alkali; copper smelting, glass, fibreglass, plastics; p. (2011) 175,300 (dist.). The Pilkington glass business first established in 1826.

St. Helier, spt., Jersey, Channel Is.; resort; cas.; tr. in early vegetables.

St. Ives, sm. t., Penwith, Cornwall, **Eng.**; at entrance to St. Ives Bay; fishing, holiday resort; Tate St Ives (art gallery).

St. Ives, sm. t., Camb., **Eng.**; on R. Ouse, 6 km E. of Huntingdon; borders the Fens; R. Ouse crossed by 16th cent. bridge containing a chapel.

St. John's Wood, residtl. dist., Westminster London, **Eng.**; contains Lord's Cricket Ground, home of English cricket.

St. Just, sm. t., Penwith, Cornwall, **Eng.**; nr. Lands End, 10 km W. of Penzance; former tin-mng. ctr.

St. Kilda, rocky I., most W. of the Hebrides, **Scot.**; 5 km long; bird sanctuary, famous for its wren; World Heritage Site. Highest sea stacks and cliffs in Britain. Last inhabitants left in 1930.

St. Marylebone. See **Westminster, City of**.

St. Mawes, v., Cornwall, **Eng.**; on E. cst. of estuary of R. Fal; cas.; holiday resort, fishing.

St. Michael's Mt., castled rock, Cornwall, **Eng.**; the anc. Ictis; alt. 70 m.

St. Monans, burgh, Fife, **Scot.**; resort; p. 1,450.

St. Neots, mkt. t., Cambs. **Eng.**; on R. Ouse, 16 km N.E. of Bedford; brewing, milling, papermkg.; expanded t.; p. 30,000.

St. Pancras. See **Camden**.

St. Peter Port, spt., cap. of Guernsey, exp. fruit, flowers, vegetables; resort.

Salcombe, sm. t., South Hams, S. Devon, **Eng.**; mkt.; fishing; resort.

Sale, t., Trafford, Gtr. Manchester, **Eng.**; residtl. sub. of Manchester; p. 56,000.

Salford, c., met. dist., Gtr. Manchester, **Eng.**; on R. Irwell, adjoining Manchester; inc. terminal docks of Manchester Ship Canal; univ.; varied inds.; p. and industl. decentralization; Lowry Arts Centre opened, Apr. 2000; Media City UK development in Salford Quays; location of northern hub of BBC; p. (2011) 233,900 (dist.).

Salisbury (New Sarum), cath. c., historic county town; old l. gov. dist., Wilts., **Eng.**; on S. edge of Salisbury Plain at confluence of Rs. Avon, Ebble, Nadder, Wylye and Bourne; Old Sarum to N. was the Roman Sorbiodunum and present site represents a move (1220) to a more sheltered and better watered a. in valley; cath. pure Early English with tallest spire in Eng. (123 m); ctr. medieval woollen ind.; engin. ind.; p. 41,000; also world's oldest working clock; Now part of new unit. auth.

Salisbury Plain, Wilts., **Eng.**; chalk upland, N. of Salisbury; Stonehenge; army training a.; a. 777 km².

Salop. *See* Shropshire.

Saltaire. *See* E19.

Saltash, sm. mkt. t., Caradon, Cornwall, **Eng.**; on W. side of Tamar estuary; Brunel's rly. bridge (1859) and toll road bridge.

Saltburn-by-the-Sea, t., Redcar and Cleveland, **Eng.**; seaside resort; 16 km E. of Middlesbrough.

Saltcoats, burgh, N. Ayrshire, **Scot.**; on Firth of Clyde 3 km S. of Ardrossan; sm. harbour; hosiery; mainly residtl.; p. 11,800.

Sanday, I., Barra Is., Orkney Is., **Scot.**; flat, many shipwrecks; agr., fishing.

Sandbach, sm. mkt. t., Cheshire, **Eng.**; 8 km N.E. of Crewe; salt, chemicals, comm. vehicles.

Sandhurst, v., Berkshire, **Eng.**; 16 km S.E. of Reading; Royal Military Academy.

Sandlings, The, S.E. Suffolk, **Eng.**; a. of glacial sands, forming heathland, making for difficult agriculture.

Sandown-Shanklin, sm. t., I. of Wight, **Eng.**; on Sandown Bay; resort.

Sandringham, v., Norfolk, **Eng.**; Royal residence since 1861.

Sandwell, met. dist., West Midlands, **Eng.**; comprises Warley and West Bromwich; p. (2010) 285,000.

Sandwich, sm. t., Kent, **Eng.**; Cinque pt. at mouth of Stour R.; harbour silted up 16th cent.; Royal St. George Golf Club; p. 6,800.

Sandy, sm. t., Mid Beds., **Eng.**; 5 km N.W. of Biggleswade; mkt. gardening.

Sanquhar, burgh, Dumfries and Galloway, **Scot.**; coal mng., brick mkg.; p. 2,050.

Sark, I., dependency of **Guernsey**, Channel Is.; 10 km E. of Guernsey; picturesque scenery; old feudal structure only reformed in 2006; tourist ctr.; farming; a. 516 ha; p. (2015) 600.

Sark, R., forms extreme W. bdy. between **Scot.** and **Eng.**

Sawbridgeworth, sm. t., East Herts., **Eng.**; on R. Stort, 6 km S. of Bishops Stortford.

Saxham, t., Suffolk, **Eng.**; agr. machin.

Saxmundham, sm. mkt. t., Suffolk Coastal, Suffolk, **Eng.**; 29 km N.E. of Ipswich.

Scafell Pike, mtn., Cumbria, **Eng.**; in Cumbrian Mtns., Lake Dist.; highest in Eng.; alt. 979 m.

Scalby, sm. t., North Yorks., **Eng.**; 5 km N.W. of Scarborough.

Scalloway, Shetland Is., **Scot.**; on W. cst. of Mainland; the anc. cap.; ruined cas.; fish. pt.; p. 820.

Scalpay, I., off E. cst. of Skye, Highland, **Scot.**

Scalpay, I., Harris, Outer Hebrides, Western Isles, **Scot.**

Scapa Flow, strait, N. **Scot.**; between Pomona and Hoy, Orkney Is.; surrendered German fleet scuttled 1919; Brit. battleship *Royal Oak* sunk at anchor 1939.

Scarba, I., Argyll and Bute, **Scot.**; off N. end of Jura, red deer in woods and moorlands.

Scarborough, t., l. gov. dist., North Yorks., **Eng.**; on E. cst.; seaside resort; cas.; former spa; p. (2010) 109,000 (dist.).

Scilly Is., *See* Isles of Scilly.

Scone, par., Perth and Kinross, **Scot.**; place of residence and also of coronation of early Scottish kings; from here Edward I removed Stone of Destiny to Westminster Abbey 1297; tourism.

Scotland, Brit. Is., N. part of **Gt. Britain**; 32 unit. auths. created in 1996; devolution referendum in 1997 voted for new Scottish Parliament. Independence rejected in September 2014 referendum. Physically divided into 3 parts; (1) the Highlands and Is., an upland a. suffering from depopulation, economically reliant on stock-rearing, tourism, hydroelec. power, whisky and fishing; instrusive impact of N. Sea oil on N.E. cst.; (2) the Central Lowlands, containing most p., based in industl. ts. on sm. coalfields, inc. lgst. c. Glasgow and cap. Edinburgh; (3) the S. Uplands, a stock-rearing a. bordering Eng.; p. (2015) 5,320,000.

Scunthorpe, t., N. Lincs., **Eng.**; on Lincoln Edge, 10 km S. of Humber; iron, limestone mng. and major iron and steel ind.; p. 73,000.

Seaford, t., East Sussex, **Eng.**; 5 km E. of Newhaven; seaside resort; declined as a pt. with shift of Ouse R. channel to Newhaven; p. (2010) 22,500.

Seaforth, Loch, Lewis, Outer Hebrides, **Scot.**; 22 km long.

Seaham, spt., Durham, **Eng.**; Seaham Harbour on E. cst. 6 km S. of Sunderland; colly. workings extend under sea, closed 1993; p. (2010) 21,200.

Seaton, sm. t., East Devon, **Eng.**; on Lyme Bay at mouth of R. Axe, seaside resort; freestone quarries.

Seaton Delaval, sm. t., Blyth Valley, Northumberland, **Eng.**; former coal mng.

Sedbergh, mkt. t., South Lakeland, Cumbria, **Eng.**; woollen ind., public school; p. 2,000. Formerly part of Yorkshire.

Sedgefield, sm. t., former l. gov. dist., S.E. Durham, **Eng.**; in fertile agr. a.; cattle mkt.; racecourse. Now part of new unit. auth.

Sedgemoor, l. gov. dist., Somerset, **Eng.**; based on Bridgwater, Burnham and surrounding a.; p. (2010) 113,000.

Sefton, met. dist., Merseyside, **Eng.**; comprises Crosby, Bootle and Litherland; p. (2011) 285,000.

Selby, mkt. t., l. gov. dist., North Yorks., **Eng.**; on R. Ouse, 20 km. S. of York; anc. abbey church; flour milling, flax, oil-cake; development of major coalfield after 1983 linked to bldg. of power sta. in Aire Valley, but closure of Selby mine in 2004; p. (2010) 82,000. (dist.), 17,000 (t.).

Selkirk, royal burgh, Borders, **Scot.**; on Etterick Water; 6 km S. of Galashiels; mkt. t.; tartans, tweeds; p.5,900.

Selkirkshire, historic co., S. **Scot.**; now part of Borders.

Sellafield, nuclear power plant, Cumbria, **Eng.**; formerly Windscale; reprocesses nuclear waste; demolition of cooling towers began, 2007; site of proposed National Nuclear Laboratory.

Settle, mkt. t., Craven, North Yorks., **Eng.**; on R. Ribble in heart of Craven dist.; tourist ctr. for limestone cty. of N. Pennines.

Sevenoaks, mkt. t., l. gov. dist., Kent, **Eng.**; in Vale of Holmesdale; residtl.; agr., lt. inds.; Knole Park; public school founded in 1432; p. (2010) 115,000. (dist.).

Severn, R., W. of **Eng.** and N. **Wales**; rises in Powys and flows to Bristol Channel; suspension bridge at estuary opened 1966; several proposals for major economic development around shores of estuary; 344 km long.

Severn Tunnel, **Eng.**; under estuary of R. Severn between Pilning (S. Gloucs.) and Severn Tunnel Junction (Monmouthshire); carries main rly. from London to S. **Wales**; longest main-line rly. tunnel in Brit. Is.; 7 km long.

Shaftesbury, sm. mkt. t., North Dorset, **Eng.**; Saxon hilltop t., abbey ruins; ctr. for agr. a.

Shannon Airport, Clare, **R.o.I.**; N.W. of Limerick; on main transatlantic air route; ctr. of customsfree industl. estate built (1958) to compensate for decline in air traffic with larger planes.

Shannon, R., **Ireland**; separates Connaught from provs. of Leinster and Munster, flows to Atl. at Loop Head; hydroelectric power sta. at Ardnacrusha; 358 km long. Longest river in the British Isles.

Shap, mkt. t., Cumbria, **Eng.**; nearby in Shap Fell 279 m, an impt. pass traversed by rly. and by a main road; granite quarries.

Shapinsay, I., Orkney Is., **Scot.**; p. 320.

Sheerness, Kent, **Eng.**; on I. of Sheppey at entrance to estuary of R. Medway; former royal dockyard and garrison; deepwater comm. pt.; electronics, furniture, coach bldg.

Sheffield, c., met. dist., South Yorks., **Eng.**; on cramped site at confluence of Rs. Sheaf and Don; univs.; heavy engin. ctr., famous for high quality steels, cutlery, tools; major devolution of power proposed (2015), p. (2011) 552,700 (dist.), (2010)

442,000 (c.).

Shellhaven, oil refineries, Essex, **Eng.**; on N. side of Thames estuary, nr. Standord-le-Hope.

Sheppey, I. of, Kent, Swale, **Eng.**; in Thames estuary E. of mouth of R. Medway; sheep-raising; steel wks.; ch. t., Sheerness; a. 117 km².

Shepshed, sm. t., Charnwood, Leics., **Eng.**; 5 km W. of Loughborough; hosiery. Old centre of wool trade (once known as Sheepshead).

Shepton Mallet, sm. mkt. t., Mendip, Somerset, **Eng.**; at foot of Mendip Hills, 8 km S.E of Wells; old woollen ctr.; bacon curing, brewing.

Shepway, l. gov. dist., S.E. Kent, **Eng.**; cstl. a. of Folkestone, Hythe, New Romney and Lydd; p. (2010) 115,000.

Sherborne, sm. mkt. t., West Dorset, **Eng.**; 6 km E. of Yeovil; famous abbey and school; Norman cas. ruins; glass fibre.

Sheringham, sm. t., North Norfolk, **Eng.**; on cst. 6 km W. of Cromer; resort; fishing.

Sherwood Forest, anc. royal woodland, Notts., **Eng.**; now restricted to infertile Bunter Sandstone cty.; inc. several estates and parks, notably the Dukeries; National Nature Reserve (2002).

Shetland Is., l. gov. auth., **Scot.**; 80 km N.E. of the Orkneys; about 100 in gr., ch. I., Mainland; lge. number of rainy days, but climate mild and tourists attracted by isolation, scenery and wildlife; Fair Isle famous for knitted clothes; fishing, livestock, agr., potatoes; rapid growth with oil drilling in N. Sea: oil terminal of Sullum Voe; wreck of oil tanker *Braer*, Jan 1992; new deepwater gas fields; ch. t. Lerwick; p. (2009) 22,250.

Shillelagh, v., Wicklow, **R.o.I.**; oak forest, gave its name to oak or blackthorn cudgel.

Shin, Loch, Highland, **Scot.**; 26 km long; drained by R. Shin to R. Oykell.

Shipley, t., West Yorks., **Eng.**; on R. Aire, 13 km N.W. of Leeds; worsted mnfs.; inc. model v. of Saltaire, built by Titus Salt (1851) to house his alpaca mill workers; p. 29,000.

Shoreham-by-Sea, sm. t., Adur, West Sussex, **Eng.**; at mouth of R. Adur, 6 km E. of Worthing; spt. and mkt. t.; oil jetty; boat bldg., chemicals.

Shrewsbury, co. t., Shrops., **Eng.**; on R. Severn 19 km above Ironbridge gorge between the Wrekin and Wenlock Edge; agr. and dairy equipment, machin., elec. prods.; cattle and sheep mkt.; public school; p. 68,000.

Shropshire (**Salop**), old non-met co., **Eng.**; on Welsh border, crossed by R. Severn; fine pastoral cty.; with hills and woodland, agr. and dairying; industl. activity at co. t. Shrewsbury; p. (2010) 293,000. Now a unitary authority.

Sidlaw Hills, low mtn. range, Angus, **Scot.**; max. alt. 455 m.

Sidmouth, sm. mkt. t., East Devon, **Eng.**; on S. cst., 24 km S.E. of Exeter; resort; retirement ctr.

Silchester, par., Hants., **Eng.**; ruins of Roman t., Calleva Atrebatum; impt. ctr. of Roman communications network.

Silsden, t., West Yorks., **Eng.**; wool textiles.

Sittingbourne and Milton, mkt. t., Swale, Kent, **Eng.**; on Milton Creek, 14 km E. of Chatham; paper mills, brick wks.; cement; insecticides; ctr. of fruit-growing dist.; p. 40,500.

Sizewell, Suffolk, **Eng.**; Magnox nuclear power sta.; Britain's 1st pressurised water nuclear reactor sta.

Skara Brae, prehistoric v., Mainland, Orkney Is., **Scot.**; v. excavated from under sand dunes.

Skegness, t., East Lindsey, Lincs., **Eng.**; on E. cst.; resort; lt. engin.; p. 20,500.

Skelmersdale, t., West Lancs., **Eng.**; coal, bricks, drainpipes; new t. (1961); p. (2001) 39,279.

Skelton, sm. t., Redcar and Cleveland, **Eng.**; at N. foot of Cleveland Hills, 16 km E. of Middlesbrough; steel flooring.

Skiddaw, mtn., Cumbria, **Eng.**; E. of Bassenthwaite L.; alt. 931 m.

Skipton, sm. t., Craven, North Yorks., **Eng.**; on R. Aire; cotton and rayon inds.; cas.

Skye, I., lgst. of Inner Hebrides, Highland, **Scot.**; connected by bridge to mainland 1995; mtnous.; sheep-farming and fisheries; tourism; only t. Portree; a. 1,417 km²; p. 9,400. Now officially known by its Gaelic name Eilean a' Cheo ('the misty isle'). Richest dinosaur finds in Scotland.

Sleaford, sm. mkt. t., North Kesteven, Lincs., **Eng.**; 19 km N.E. of Grantham; agr. implements.

Sleat, Sound of, Highland, **Scot.**; separates I. of Skye from the mainland; 11 km wide.

Sligo, co., Connacht, **R.o.I.**; borders Atl. Oc.; rises to Ox Mtns. over 600 m; pastoral agr.; co. t. S.; a. 1,909 km²; p. (2011) 65,270.

Sligo, co. t., Sligo, **R.o.I.**; on S. Bay; pt., exp. agr. prods.; abbey ruins; cath.

Slough, t., l. gov. dist., Berks., **Eng.**; on river terrace N. of R. Thames, 37 km W. of London; many lt. inds.; home of Mars bar production since 1932; p. (2011) 140,000 (unit.auth.).

Smethwick. *See* **Warley**.

Snaefell, highest mtn., **Isle of Man**; alt. 620 m.

Snowdon, mtn., Gwynedd, **Wales**; highest in Eng. and Wales, alt. 1,086 m; Snowdon Mountain Railway (opened 1896 brings visitors from Llanberis; forms part of Snowdonia Nat. Park.

Soar, R., Leics., Notts., **Eng.**; rises S. of Leics., flows N.W. to join R. Trent; 69 km long.

Soho, dist., London, **Eng.**; settled by Fr. Huguenots 16th cent.; high proportion of foreign residents, known as London's "Latin quarter"; bars, clubs, theatres, restaurants, film-company offices. Once the violin-making centre of Britain.

Solent, The, strait separating I. of Wight from Hampshire mainland, **Eng.**;

Solihull, t., met. dist., West Midlands, **Eng.**; 8 km S.W. of Birmingham; residtl.; motor vehicles; p. 203,000 (dist.).

Solway Firth, arm of **Irish Sea**, Dumfries and Galloway, Scot., and Cumbria, Eng.; 6 km long.

Somersby, v., Lincs., **Eng.**; the birthplace of Tennyson.

Somerset, non-met. co., S.W. **Eng.**; inc. part of Exmoor, Mendips, Quantocks and Blackdown Hills; to N. is drained marshland of Somerset levels; severe flooding, 2014; dairying; coastal resorts; co. t. Taunton; p. (2010) 526,000.

Southall. *See* **Ealing**.

Southampton, co., spt., unit. auth. created in 1997, part of Hants., **Eng.**; at head of Southampton Water on the peninsula between estuaries of Rs. Test and Itchen; univs.; decline of passenger liners, now one of Britain's biggest container pts.; ship repairing; oil refining, cable mkg., electronics, synthetic rubber; p. (2010) 235,000 (unit. auth.).

South Ayrshire, unit. auth. created in 1996, formerly part of Strathclyde, S.W. **Scot.**; borders F. of Clyde; ch. t. Ayr; p. (2010) 111,450.

South Bedfordshire, former l. gov. dist., Beds., **Eng.**; close to Luton and inc. Dunstable and Leighton-Linslade.

South Buckinghamshire, l. gov. dist., Bucks., **Eng.**; based on Beaconsfield; p. (2010) 65,000.

South Cambridgeshire, l. gov. dist., Cambs., **Eng.**; rural a. surrounding Cambridge; p. (2010) 140,000.

South Derbyshire, l. gov. dist., Derbys., **Eng.**; a. S. of Derby and inc. Repton and Swadlingcote; p. (2010) 95,000.

South Downs, chalk escarpment, East and West Sussex and Hants., **Eng.**; stretch from Chichester to Eastbourne; rise to over 240 m.; now a new National Park (fully operational, 2011).

Southend-on-Sea, t., unit. auth., Essex, **Eng.**; on N. side of Thames estuary; varied lt. inds.; air ferry terminal; resort; dormitory for London; pier (longest pleasure pier in the world) badly damaged (2005); p. (2010) 164,000 (unit auth.).

Southern Uplands, region, S. **Scot.**; broad belt of hilly cty., N. part bleak moorland, S. part deeply cut by glens; sheep-rearing; dairying in valleys.

South Gloucestershire, unit. auth. created in 1996, formerly part of Avon, **Eng.**; inc. ts. of Chipping Sodbury and Kingswood; p. (2010) 258,000.

South Hams, l. gov. dist., S. Devon, **Eng.**; a. between Torquay and Plymouth inc. Totnes, Kingsbridge and Salcombe; p. (2010) 83,000.

South Herefordshire, l. gov. dist., Hereford., **Eng.**; lge rural a. which inc. Ross-on-Wye.

South Holland, l. gov. dist., Lincs., **Eng.**; fenland a. around Spalding; p. (2011) 88,000.

South Kensington, dist., W. London, **Eng.**; contains Victoria and Albert Museum, Geological and Science Museums, British Museum of Natural History, Commonwealth Institute, Albert Hall.

South Kesteven, l. gov. dist., Lincs., **Eng.**; rural a. and ts. of Grantham and Bourne; p. 131,000.

South Lakeland, l. gov. dist., Cumbria, **Eng.**; lge. a. around Morecambe Bay and inc. Ulverston, Grange, Kendal and Sedbergh; p. (2011) 103,700.

South Lanarkshire, unit. auth. created in 1996, formerly part of Strathclyde, S. **Scot.**; lies S. of central Clydeside conurb.; p. (2010) 311,000.

South Norfolk, l. gov. dist., Norfolk, **Eng.**; lge. a. inc. Diss and Wymondham; p. (2010) 119,000.

South Northamptonshire, l. gov. dist., Northants.,

Eng.; inc. Brackley and Towcester; p. (2010) 91,200.

South Oxfordshire, l. gov. dist., Oxon., **Eng.**; Wallingford, Thame and Henley-on-Thames; p. (2010) 119,000.

Southport, t., Sefton, Merseyside, **Eng.**; on S. side of Ribble estuary; 29 km N. of Liverpool; leisure centre; residtl.; p. 92,000.

South Ribble, l. gov. dist., Lancs., **Eng.**; a. S. of Preston and inc. Walton-le-Dale; p. (2010) 107,250.

South Shields, t., frm. Tyne and Wear, **Eng.**; pt. on S. bank at mouth of R. Tyne; holiday resort; marine engin., new lt. inds.; p. 83,100.

South Shropshire, former l. gov. dist., Shrops., **Eng.**; S. of Shrewsbury and inc. Ludlow. Abolished, 2009.

South Somerset, l. gov. dist. inc. Yeovil; p. (2010) 159,000.

South Staffordshire, l. gov. dist., Staffs., **Eng.**; a. borders W. Midlands conurb.; p. (2010) 106,000.

South Tyneside, met. bor., frm. Tyne and Wear, **Eng.**; comprises Jarrow, Hebburn and South Shields; p. (2011) 148,100.

Southwark, inner bor., London, **Eng.**; S. of R. Thames, incorporating former bors. of Bermondsey and Camberwell; cath.; site of former Globe theatre; p. (2011) 288,500.

Southwick, t., Adur, West Sussex, **Eng.**; on S. cst. 6 km W. of Brighton; p. 11,350.

Southwold, spt., Waveney, Suffolk, **Eng.**; on E. cst. 13 km S. of Lowestoft; fishing; resort; new pier opened (2001).

South Yorkshire, met. co., **Eng.**; mainly industl. a. E. of Pennines; inc. productive coalfield nr. Barnsley and Doncaster and steel producing ts. of Sheffield and Rotherham.

Sowerby Bridge, t., Calderdale, West Yorks., **Eng.**; on R. Calder, 5 km W. of Halifax; woollens.

Spalding, mkt. t., South Holland, Lincs., **Eng.**; in Fens, 16 km up R. Welland from Wash; agr., bulb mkt.; agr. machin., sugar-beet, fruit canning; p. 23,000.

Spelthorne, l. gov. dist., Surrey, **Eng.**; close to Gtr. London; inc. Staines and Sunbury-on-Thames; p. (2010) 91,000.

Spennymoor, sm. t., Durham, **Eng.**; growing industl. t. S. of Durham. Old coal, iron and steel industries developed after railway arrived in 1836.

Sperrin Mtns., Strabane, **N. Ireland**; peat-covered schists; Sawell, 683 m.

Spey, R., Moray, Highland, the most rapid in **Scot.**, flows N.E. to Moray Firth; used for hydroelec. power; 171·2 km long. Whisky tourism on Speyside.

Spitalfields, par., E. London, **Eng.**; formerly noted for silk weaving, introduced by Huguenots in the 17th cent.; name derives from spital or hospital of St. Mary, founded in 12th cent.

Spithead, roadstead, between Portsmouth and I. of Wight, **Eng.**; used by ships of Royal Navy.

Spurn Head, E. Riding of Yorks., **Eng.**; sand spit at mouth of Humber estuary.

Staffa, I. on Inner Hebrides, W. **Scot.**; 10 km N. of Iona, off W. cst. Mull; grand basaltic caverns, inc. Fingal's Cave, 69 m long, 13 m wide, 20 m high.

Stafford, co. t., l. gov. dist., Staffs., **Eng.**; on R. Sow, 24 km N. of Wolverhampton; heavy elec. and other engin.; expanded t.; p. (2010) 125,000 (dist.), 64,500 (t.).

Staffordshire, non-met. co., W. Midlands, **Eng.**; plain drained by R. Trent and tribs.; p. (2010) 830,500.

Staffordshire Moorlands, l. gov. dist., Staffs., **Eng.**; borders S. Pennines and inc. Leek, Biddulph and Cheadle; p. (2010) 95,400.

Staines, mkt. t., Spelthorne, Surrey, **Eng.**; on R. Thames, 6 km S.E. of Windsor; nr. birthplace of Matthew Arnold; p. 52,000. Calls to rename the town Staines-upon-Thames.

Stainmore, pass, North Yorks./Durham, **Eng.**; crosses N. Pennines from Greta valley into upper Eden valley; used by main road; alt. 418 m.

Staithes, v., North Yorks., **Eng.**; potash mng.

Stalybridge, t., Gtr. Manchester, **Eng.**; on R. Tame, 13 km E. of Manchester; cotton and wool engin., plastics, rubber, gds., elec. cables; p. 23,000.

Stamford, mkt. t., Lincs., **Eng.**; old bldgs., one of 5 Danelaw ts.; agr. inds., elec. gds., plastics; p. 18,000.

Stanley, t., Derwentside, Durham, **Eng.**; former colly. dist.; p. 30,500.

Stanlow, Cheshire, **Eng.**; petrol refinery, oil storage, docks, chemicals, linked to Anglesey by major pipeline.

Stansted, site of London's third airport; 55 km N.E. of London. Plans for further major expansion proposed in 2013.

Staveley, t., Derbys., **Eng.**; 5 km N.E. of Chesterfield; iron, chemicals, concrete and iron pipes; p. 25,000.

Stevenage, t., l. gov. dist., Herts., **Eng.**; 6 km S.E. of Hitchin; first new t. to be designated under the New Towns Act 1946; old t. known in Domesday as Stevenach; agr., lt. engin., elec. goods, 2011, aircraft parts; p. (2011) 84,000 (dist.).

Stevenston, burgh, N. Ayrshire, **Scot.**; p. (2002) 9,129.

Steventon, v., Hants., **Eng.**; birthplace of Jane Austen.

Stewarton, burgh, E. Ayrshire, **Scot.**; woollens, carpets; p. (2002) 6,582.

Steyning, v., West Sussex, **Eng.**; on R. Adur, 6 km N. of Shoreham at entrance to gap through S. Downs; residtl.

Stilton, v., Cambs., **Eng.**; 10 km S.W. of Peterborough; famous for cheese.

Stirling, royal burgh, unit. auth. created in 1996, formerly part of Central Region, **Scot.**; stretches from Grampian mtns. to Central Lowlands; c. lies on R. Forth in gap between Campsie Fells and Ochil Hills; cas., univ.; coal mng., engin., concrete, wool, rubber prods.; p. (2009) 34,000 (c.), (2010) 89,000 (unit. auth.). Created a city, 2002.

Stirlingshire, historic co., central **Scot.**, now divided between E. Dunbartonshire, Falkirk, N. Lanarkshire and Stirling.

Stockport, t., met. dist., Gtr. Manchester, **Eng.**; on R. Mersey, S.E. of Manchester; cotton manmade fibres, engin.; p. (2011) 283,300 (dist.).

Stocksbridge, t., South Yorks., **Eng.**; iron and steel.

Stockton-on-Tees, mkt. t. 6 km W. of Middlesbrough, **Eng.**; unit. auth. created in 1996, formerly part of Cleveland; inc. t. of Billingham; impt. iron and steel inds., plywood; first rly. for passenger traffic opened 1825 between Stockton and Darlington; 18th cent. town hall; p. (2011) 191,600 (unit. auth.).

Stoke Newington. *See* **Hackney.**

Stoke-on-Trent, c., unit. auth. of **Stoke** created in 1997, formerly part of Staffs., **Eng.**; at S.W. foot of the Pennines; formed in 1910 by union of the five towns of Arnold Bennett's novels, Hanley, Burslem, Tunstall, Longton, and Fenton (with Stoke-on-Trent); ceramics, iron and steel, engin., brick and tile works, rubber prods.; univ.; p. (2010) 240,000 (unit. auth.).

Stone, sm. mkt. t., Staffs., **Eng.**; on R. Trent, 11 km S. of Stoke-on-Trent; footwear, tiles, porcelain, scientific glassware.

Stonehaven, t., burgh, Aberdeenshire, **Scot.**; fish. pt. on E. cst., 22 km S. of Aberdeen, distilling, net mftg.; p. 9,600.

Stonehenge, prehistoric gr. of monumental stones, on Salisbury Plain, Wilts., **Eng.**; date of erection est. between 2100–1600 B.C.; now UNESCO World Heritage Site. *See* **E20** and **E35.**

Stornoway (**Steornabhagh**), sm. spt., burgh, Western Isles, **Scot.**; on E. cst. of I. of Lewis, Outer Hebrides; ctr. Harris Tweed ind.; fishing ctr.

Stour, R., Kent, **Eng.**; flows past Canterbury to Pegwell Bay; 64 km long.

Stour, R., Somerset, Dorset, **Eng.**; trib. of R. Avon.

Stour, R., Suffolk and Essex, **Eng.**; flows E. to sea at Harwich; 67 km long.

Stour, R., Hereford and Worcs./West Midlands, **Eng.**; trib. of R. Severn; 32 km long.

Stourbridge, t., West Midlands, **Eng.**; on R. Stour; 14 km W. of Birmingham; brick and glass wks.; p. 56,000.

Stourport-on-Severn, sm. mkt. t., Worcs., **Eng.**; at confluence of Rs. Stour and Severn; carpets, iron and steel gds.; old canal and R. pt.

Stowmarket, t., Mid Suffolk, **Eng.**; on R. Gipping, 18 km N.W. of Ipswich; paint factory.

Strabane, t., l. gov. dist., **N. Ireland**; agr. ctr., shirt mkg.; p. (2010) 40,000. *See* **D11.**

Strangford Lough, arm of sea, Down and Ards, **N. Ireland**; 29 km long, 10 km wide at entrance.

Stranraer, royal burgh, Dumfries and Galloway, **Scot.**; at head of Loch Ryan; steamer service to Larne, N. Ireland; creameries, brewing, knitwear; cas.; mkt.; p. 11,100.

Stratford. *See* **Newham.**

Stratford-on-Avon, t., l. gov. dist., Warwicks., **Eng.**; on R. Avon; birthplace of Shakespeare; memorial theatre, library; many bldgs. ass. with Shakespeare; tourist ctr.; lt. inds.; p. (2010)

119,000 (dist.).

Strathmore, lowland belt, central **Scot.**; flanked to N. by Grampians, to S. by Sidlaw and Ochil Hills; drained by Rs. Earn, Tay, Isla, S. Esk; famous for cereals and small fruits; length 96 km, width 11–16 km.

Strathspey, valley of the Spey, **Scot.**; 112 km long.

Stratton and Bude, North Cornwall, **Eng.**; 19 km S. of Hartland Point; resort.

Street, v., Mendip, Somerset, **Eng.**; at foot of Polden Hills, 11 km S.W. of Wells; footwear, leather industries.

Stretford, t., Gtr. Manchester, **Eng.**; borders Manchester Ship Canal; inc. Trafford Park industl. estate; residtl.; Lancashire co. cricket ground, Manchester United football ground at Old Trafford; p. 43,000.

Stromness, burgh, Mainland, Orkney Is., **Scot.**; 21 km W. of Kirkwall; mkt., fish. pt.; p. (2011) 1,625.

Stronsay, I., Orkney Is., **Scot.**; p. 390.

Stroud, mkt. t., l. gov. dist., Gloucs., **Eng.**; on R. Frome, in Cotswolds; former ctr. of impt. cloth ind. in W. Eng.; woollens, dyes, plastics, engin.; p. (2010) 111,000 (dist.), 41,000 (t.).

Sturminster Newton, sm. t., North Dorset, **Eng.**; impt. cattle mkt. on Stour R.; creameries.

Sudbury, t., Babergh, Suffolk, **Eng.**; on R. Stour, 19 km N.W. of Colchester; p. 20,900.

Suffolk, non-met. co., E. Anglia, **Eng.**; bounded on E. by N. Sea, drowned coastline; rises to 90 m in E. Anglian Heights in W.; impt. agr. a., lge. farms, mixed farming; inds. based on agr.; many expanded ts. in S.; co. t. Ipswich; p. (2010) 717,000.

Suffolk Coastal, l. gov. dist., E. Suffolk, **Eng.**; lge. rural a. inc. ts. of Leiston-cum-Sizewell, Saxmundham, Aldeburgh, Woodbridge and Felixstowe; p. (2010) 126,000.

Sullum Voe, Shetland Is., **Scot.**; oil terminal and receiving ctr. for N. Sea oil.

Sunbury-on-Thames, t., Spelthorne, Surrey, **Eng.**; W. of London; residtl., water wks., gravel pits; petrol research establishment; p. 28,000.

Sunderland, c. (1992), spt., met. dist., frmr Tyne and Wear, **Eng.**; at mouth of R. Wear; precision and aero-engin., univ., shipbldg (once the home of 65 shipyards); Nissan car plant (largest car plant in the UK); p. (2011) 275,500 (dist.).

Surbiton, Gtr. London, **Eng.**; on R. Thames, inc. in Royal Borough of Kingston-upon-Thames; residtl.; lt. engin., elec. components.

Surrey, non-met. co., S. **Eng.**; S. of R. Thames inc. part of N. Downs; serves as dormitory a. and recreational dist. for London; mkt. gardening, dairying; co. t. Guildford; p. (2010) 1,110,000.

Surrey Heath, l. gov. dist., Surrey, **Eng.**; based on Bagshot, Frimley and Camberley; p. (2010) 83,500.

Sussex. *See* **East Sussex,** and **West Sussex.**

Sutherland, historic co., N.W. Scot., now part of Highland.

Sutton, outer bor., Greater London, **Eng.**; inc. former bors. of Beddington and Wallington, Sutton and Cheam, and Carshalton; residtl.; p. (2011) 190,250.

Sutton Coldfield, t., West Midlands, **Eng.**; 10 km N.E. of Birmingham; residtl.; hardware, plastics; p. 107,000.

Sutton-in-Ashfield, t., Ashfield, Notts., **Eng.**; 5 km S.W. of Mansfield; lt. engin.; hosiery; former coalmng. dist.; p. 42,500.

Swadlincote, t., South Derbys., **Eng.**; 5 km E. of Burton-on-Trent; potteries; p. 40,100.

Swaffham, sm. mkt. t., Breckland, Norfolk, **Eng.**; fruit canning.

Swale, R., North Yorks., **Eng.**; joins R. Ure; 96 km long.

Swale, l. gov. dist., mid Kent, **Eng.**; nr. Thames estuary inc. Sittingbourne, Faversham and I. of Sheppey; p. (2010) 132,000.

Swanage, sm. mkt. t., Dorset, **Eng.**; on bay, E. cst. I. of Purbeck; seaside resort; restored steam rly. link to nearby Wareham.

Swansea, c., spt., **Wales**; on Swansea Bay; univs.; grew with exp. of coal; now imports minerals; copper and zinc refining; steel, aluminium, wire, plastics; unit. auth. created in 1996 from former l. gov. dists. of Lliw Valley and Swansea; inc. Gower Penin.; world's first tidal lagoon power station planned; The Tower, Meridian Quay (tallest building in Wales). p. (2011) 239,800 (unit. auth.). Once known as 'Copperopolis'.

Swilly, Lough, N.E. Donegal, **R.o.I.**; arm of Atl. Oc.

between Fanad Point and Dunaff Head; extends 40 km inland.

Swindon, t., unit. auth. created in 1997, formerly part of Wilts., **Eng.**; in upper Thames Valley (Vale of White Horse), 43 km S.W. of Oxford; impt. rly. junc.; rly. workshops closed (1986); Railway Village Muesum; mkt. for local dist.; heavy engin., textiles, tobacco; expanded, fast-growing t.; one of largest housing projects in Europe; ctr. for micro-electronics inds.; location of UK Space Agency; also Museum of Computing; p. (2011) 209,000.

Swinton and Pendlebury, ts., Gtr. Manchester, **Eng.**; 8 km W. of Manchester; former cotton spinning, engin.; p. 42,000.

T

Taff, R., S.**Wales**; rises in Brecon Beacons, flows S.E. across coalfield to Bristol Channel at Cardiff; 64 km long. Once heavily polluted, now revitalised.

Tamar, R., Devon and Cornwall, **Eng.**; flows S. to Plymouth Sound; 72 km long.

Tameside, met. dist., Gtr. Manchester, **Eng.**; comprises Dukinfield, Ashton-under-Lyne, Hyde and Mossley; p. (2011) 219,000.

Tamworth, t., l. gov. dist., Staffs., **Eng.**; on R. Tame, 8 km S.E. of Lichfield; anc. cas.; lt. engin.; expanded t.; p. (2010) 76,500 (dist.). The official capital of Mercia under King Offa.

Tandridge, l. gov. dist., Surrey, **Eng.**; inc. Caterham and Godstone; p. (2010) 83,500.

Taunton, co. t., Somerset, **Eng.**; on R. Tone at W. end of Vale of Taunton; old cas.; with Wellington forms l. gov. dist. of **Taunton Deane;** p. (2010) 108,750 (dist.), 58,000 (t.).

Tavistock, mkt. t., West Devon, **Eng.**; on R. Tavy; anc. stannary t.; Drake born nearby.

Taw, R., Devon, **Eng.**; flows from Dartmoor to Barnstaple Bay; 80 km long.

Tawe, R., S. **Wales**; flows into Swansea Bay; 104 km long.

Tay, R., **Scot.**; flows S.E. from Loch Tay in Perth and Kinross, to Firth of Tay; longest R. in Scot., 188 km long; salmon fisheries.

Tay, Firth of, lge. inlet, E. cst. **Scot.**; extends inland almost to Perth.

Tayport, burgh, Fife, **Scot.**; at entrance to Firth of Tay; opposite Broughty Ferry; linen, jute; p. 3,950.

Team Valley, Tyne and Wear, **Eng.**; impt. trading estate.

Tees, R., N. **Eng.**; rises on Cross Fell, Cumbria, flows E. to N. Sea between Hartlepool and Redcar; old heavy inds. in lower section; 112 km long.

Teesdale, former l. gov. dist., Durham, **Eng.**; Pennine a. inc. Barnard Castle.

Teesport, oil refinery, between Redcar and Middlesbrough, Redcar and Cleveland, **Eng.**

Teesside, former admin. dist., N.E. **Eng.**; inc. Middlesbrough, Redcar, Thornaby-on-Tees, Stockton-on-Tees, Billingham, and Eston.

Teifi, R., S. **Wales**; rises in Cambrian mtns., flows S.W. to Cardigan Bay; 150 km long.

Teign, R., Devon, **Eng.**; flows to sea at pt. of Teignmouth from Dartmoor; picturesque estuary; 48 km long.

Teignbridge, l. gov. dist., S. Devon, **Eng.**; lower T. valley and ts. of Dawlish, Teignmouth, Newton Abbot and Ashburton; p. (2010) 127,000.

Teignmouth, sm. t., Teignbridge, Devon, **Eng.**; at mouth of R. Teign, 21 km S. of Exeter; resort; revival of pt. with ball clay exp.

Telford, new t. (1963), Shropshire, **Eng.**; 32 km W. of Wolverhampton; part of **Telford and Wrekin,** unit. auth. p. (2010) 161,900 (unit. auth.); (2011) 41,000 (c.).

Teme, R., on border of Wales and Hereford and Worcs., **Eng.**; tributary of R. Severn; 112 km long.

Tenby, sm. mkt. t., Pembrokeshire, **Wales**; on W. side of Carmarthen Bay, Bristol Channel; seaside resort; walled cas. t.

Tendring, l. gov. dist., E. Essex, **Eng.**; inc. cstl. ts. of Harwich, Frinton, Clacton and Brightlingsea; p. (2010) 147,000.

Tenterden, sm. mkt. t., Kent, **Eng.**; 13 km N. of Rye; grew with wool tr., church with famous tower.

Test Valley, l. gov. dist., W. Hants., **Eng.**; stretches from Andover to Romsey; p. (2010) 115,000.

Tetbury, mkt.t., Glos, **Eng**; site of the National Arboretum.

Teviot, R., Borders, **Scot.**; trib. of R. Tweed; 59 km long.

Tewkesbury, mkt. t., l. gov. dist., Gloucs., **Eng.**; on R. Avon, close to confluence with R. Severn; Norman abbey; p. (2010) 79,000 (dist.), 11,100 (t.).

Thame, sm. mkt. t., South Oxford, **Eng.**; on R. Thame, 11 km S.W. of Aylesbury.

Thames, R., **Eng.**; rises in Cotswold hills and flows past Oxford, Reading, Windsor, and London to the N. Sea; tribs. inc. Windrush, Cherwell, Thame, Kennet, Colne, Lea, and Roding; estuary impt. industl. a. with many oil refineries; flood barrier at Silvertown in Woolwich (1983), 336 km long; major regeneration of Thames Gateway area.

Thameshaven, lge. oil refinery, Essex, **Eng.**; on N. cst. of Thames estuary 13 km below Tilbury.

Thanet, I. of, lge. promontory, N.E. extremity of Kent, **Eng.**; formed by bifurcation of R. Stour; also forms l. gov. dist. of **Thanet,** inc. Margate, Ramsgate, and Broadstairs; p. (2010) 130,000.

Thetford, Breckland, Norfolk, **Eng.**; on Little Ouse; industl. estate for London overspill; fruit and vegetable canning, pulp mftg., engin.; p. (2015) 24,750. Thetford Priory over 800 years old.

Thirsk, mkt. t., Hambleton, North Yorks., **Eng.**; in wide gap between Pennines and Cleveland Hills, 11 km S.E. of Northallerton; racecourse.

Thornaby-on-Tees. See **Teesside.**

Thornbury, mkt. t., S. Gloucs., **Eng.**; 16 km N. of Bristol; aircraft mftg.; expanded t.; Oldbury Magnox nuclear power sta.; p. 15,000.

Thornton Cleveleys, t., Wyre, Lancs., **Eng.**; 6 km N.E. of Blackpool; resort; p. 32,000.

Three Rivers, l. gov. dist., S.W. Herts., **Eng.**; close to London and inc. Rickmansworth and Chorleywood; p. (2010) 88,000.

Thurles, mkt. t., Tipperary, **R.o.I.**; on R. Suir; agr. processing; cath., cas.; p. 7,250.

Thurrock, t., unit. auth. Essex, **Eng.**; on Thames, nr. Tilbury; oil refining, metal refining, cement, paper board; new deepsea container port to open in 2013; p. (2010) 151,750 (unit. auth.).

Thurso, burgh, Highland, **Scot.**; nr. Dounreay; anc. stronghold of Vikings; p. 7,800.

Tideswell, sm. t., Derbys., **Eng.**; tourist ctr.; limestone quarrying in a.; lge. 14th cent. church known as "cath. of the Peak."

Tillicoultry, burgh, Clackmannan, **Scot.**; on Devon R.; woollen and worsted fabrics; p. 5,500.

Tintagel, v., Cornwall, **Eng.**; ruined Norman cas.; reputed birthplace of King Arthur; old Iron Age settlement nearby (with evidence of ancient trading in tin).

Tintern, v., Monmouthshire, **Wales**; Cistercian abbey.

Tipperary, inland co., Munster, **R.o.I.**; drained by Rs. Suir and Shannon; mtnous., Knockmealdown and Galty mtns.; fertile Golden Vale in S.W.; dairying, sugar-beet; divided into N. and S. Ridings; co. t. Clonmel.

Tipperary, t., Tipperary, **R.o.I.**; 46 km S.E. Limerick; dairy processing.

Tiverton, sm. mkt. t., Mid Devon, **Eng.**; 22 km N. Exeter; once famous for lace; textiles, engin.

Tobermory, burgh, Argyll and Bute, **Scot.**; on I. of Mull at N. entrance to Sound of Mull; fish. pt., resort; p. 995.

Todmorden, sm. mkt. t., Calderdale, West Yorks., **Eng.**; nr. source of R. Calder, 10 km S.W. of Rochdale; cottons, machin. Market held since 1801.

Tolpuddle, v., Dorset, **Eng.**; 11 km N.E. of Dorchester; famous for Tolpuddle martyrs, agr. labourers condemned to transportation for trying to form a trade union (1834).

Tonbridge, t., Kent, **Eng.**; on R. Medway; food processing; lt. inds., inc. cricket balls; Norman cas. gatehouse; public school; part of l. gov. dist. of **Tonbridge and Malling;** p. (2010) 117,000 (dist.).

Torbay, unit. auth., S. Devon, **Eng.**; formed by amalgamation of Torquay, Paignton and Brixham; located around Tor Bay; tourism; p. (2010) 133,900 (unit. auth.).

Torfaen, S.E. **Wales,** unit. auth. created in 1996 from former l. gov. dist.; inc. ts. of Cwmbran and Pontypool; p. (2011) 91,100.

Torness, East Lothian, **Scot.**; site of advanced gas cooled nuclear power sta.

Torpoint, t., Cornwall, **Eng.**; on Plymouth Sound.

Torquay, t., S. Devon, **Eng.**; incorporated in Torbay; on N. side of Tor Bay; seaside resort with all-year season; p. 61,000.

Torridge, R., Devon, **Eng.**; flows from Hartland dist. to a confluence with the Taw at Bideford Bay; 85 km long.

Torridge, l. gov. dist., N.W. Devon, **Eng.**; inc. N. cst. ts. of Northam and Bideford and stretches inland to Great Torrington; p. (2010) 66,000.

Totnes, sm. t., South Hams, Devon, **Eng.**; on R. Dart 10 km N.W. of Dartmouth; mediaeval t.; agr. mkt., food processing.

Towcester, sm. mkt. t., South Northants., **Eng.**; 14 km S.W. of Northampton; "Eatanswill" of *Pickwick Papers.*

Tower Hamlets, inner bor., E. London, **Eng.**; inc. former bors. of Bethnal Green, Stepney and Poplar; undergoing rapid economic and social change as p. and inds. are decentralised; site of lge. a. of London Docks now all closed but largely redeveloped; clothing.; p. (2011) 254,000.

Towton, v., North Yorks., **Eng.**; nearby Towton field, scene of bloodiest battle of Wars of the Roses 1461: Lancastrians under Henry VI defeated by Yorkists under Edward IV.

Trafford, met. dist., Gtr. Manchester **Eng.**; comprises Sale, Hale, Altrincham, Urmston and Stretford; p. (2011) 226,600.

Tralee, mkt. t., spt., Kerry, **R.o.I.**; on R. Lee; exp. grain, butter; p. 16,500.

Tredegar, sm. t., Blaenau Gwent, **Wales**; in narrow valley 5 km W. of Ebbw Vale; engin.; home of Aneurin Bevan.

Treforest, t., Rhondda, Cynon, Taff, **Wales**; on R. Taff; lge. trading estate established in 1930s to alleviate unemployment in primary inds. of S. Wales; aircraft accessories, electronics, chemical, pharmaceutical, rayon, metal wks.

Trent, R., **Eng.**; rises in N. Staffs, flows round S. Pennines and joins the Ouse to form estuary of the Humber; many power stas. along its banks; polluted waterway, especially between Humber and Nottingham; 240 km long.

Trim, co. t., Meath, **R.o.I.**; sm. mkt. t. on R. Boyne; anc. seat of Irish Parliament.

Tring, mkt. t., Dacorum, Herts., **Eng.**; in gap through Chiltern hills, 14 km N.W. of Hemel Hempstead; p. 12.,250.

Troon, burgh, S. Ayrshire, **Scot.**; on F. of Clyde, 10 km N. of Ayr; good harbour and graving docks; shipbldg., hosiery; seawater distillation research ctr. project; resort; p. 15,100.

Trossachs, Stirling, **Scot.**; picturesque wooded glen; tourist resort.

Trowbridge, mkt. t. and county admin. ctr., West Wilts., **Eng.**; cloth wks., bacon curing, dairying, engin.; p. 31,000.

Truro, c., Carrick, Cornwall, **Eng.**; at confluence of Rs. Kenwyn and Allen; mkt. t.; admin. ctr. of Cornwall; cath.; p. 21,200.

Tullamore, mkt. t., Offaly, **R.o.I.**; on Grand Canal; farming, distilling, brewing; p. 9,000.

Tunbridge Wells (officially **Royal Tunbridge Wells**), t., l. gov. dist., Kent, **Eng.**; on border of East Sussex; chalybeate waters; attractive 17th cent. promenade known as "The Pantiles"; p. (2010) 107,000 (dist.).

Tweed, R., S.E. **Scot.**; rises in Tweeddale and finally reaches sea at Berwick; salmon fisheries; length 155 km.

Twickenham. See **Richmond-upon-Thames.**

Tyne, R., frmer Tyne and Wear, Durham and Northumberland, **Eng.**; formed by confluence of N. Tyne and S. Tyne at Hexham; flows E. to sea at Tyne-mouth and S. Shields; valley gives easy route across mtns. from Newcastle to Carlisle; lower course forms harbour (with shipbldg. and other wks.) from Newcastle to Tynemouth; road tunnel between Wallsend and Jarrow; 1·28 km long.

Tynedale, former l. gov. dist., W. Northumberland, **Eng.**; lge. inland a. inc. Haltwhistle, Hexham and Prudoe.

Tynemouth, sm. t., North Tyneside, frmly Tyne and Wear, **Eng.**; pt. on N. bank of Tyne R.; ruined priory and cas.; residtl., resort.

Tyne and Wear, former met. co., N.E. **Eng.**; mainly industl. a. around lower T. and W. Rs.; inc. Newcastle-upon-Tyne, Tynemouth, Gateshead, South Shields and Sunderland; traditionally ass. with shipbldg. and coal mng., but inds. increasingly diversified; p. (2011) 1,104,800.

Tyrone, former co., **N. Ireland**; now replaced by Strabane, Omagh, Dungannon and Cookstown l. gov. dists.

Tywyn, mkt. t., Gwynedd, **Wales**; on cst. of Cardigan Bay, 5 km N.W. of Aberdyfi; p. 3,000.

U

Uckfield, sm. mkt. t., East Sussex, **Eng.**; 13 km N.E. of Lewes; the old centre of former Sussex iron ind.

Uist, **N.** and **S.**, Is., Outer Hebrides, Western Isles, **Scot.**; indented csts.; N. Uist boggy in E., hilly in W.; S. Uist smaller but mtnous.; crofting, fishing.

Ullapool, v., Highland, **Scot.**; fish. pt. (herring landings), on L. Broom, 72 km N.W. of Inverness; landed more fish in 1981 than any other British pt.; attractive mtn. and cst. scenery in a.; p. (2010) 1,400.

Ullswater, L., Cumbria, **Eng.**; 13 km long; supplies water to Manchester; attractive tourist a.

Ulster. anc. prov of **Ireland**. consisting of counties of Cavan, Donegal, Monaghan and the six counties now **N. Ireland**. The six counties of Northern Ireland (*q.v.*) are Antrim, Armagh, Down, Fermanagh, Londonderry and Tyrone.

Ulva, I., Argyll and Bute, **Scot.**; off W. cst. of Mull; 8 km long.

Ulverston, sm. mkt. t., South Lakeland, Cumbria, **Eng.**; nr. Morecambe Bay; antibiotics, elec. gds.

United Kingdom, cty., N.W. Europe; separated from continent of Europe by English Channel; consists of Gr. Britain (Eng., Wales, Scot.) and N. Ireland; membership of EU rejected in June 2016 referendum; a. 244,022 km²; p. (2017) 65,400,000 (expected to reach 70 million by 2027). Some estimates project a population of 85 million by 2080.

Unst, I., Shetland Is., **Scot.**; most N. of gr.; length 20 km; p. 1,020. Northernmost inhabited island in UK.

Ure, R., North Yorks., **Eng.**; flows E. and S.E. to join the Swale, then forms the Ouse at Ouse Gill Beck; upper part of valley known as Wensleydale; 80 km long.

Urmston, Trafford, Gtr. Manchester, **Eng.**; residtl. sub. of Manchester; inc. part of Trafford Park industl. estate; p. 41,000.

Usk, mkt. t., Monmouthshire, **Wales**; 13th cent. cas.

Usk, R., Gwent, S. **Wales**; flows S. through Monmouthshire and Newport to Bristol Channel; picturesque, good fishing; 91 km long.

Uttlesford, l. gov. dist., Essex, **Eng.**; inc. Saffron Walden and Dunmow; p. (2011) 79,000.

V

Vale of Glamorgan, The, S. **Wales**, unit. auth. created in 1996 from former l. gov. dist; lowland bordering Bristol Channel; inc. cstl. ts. of Barry and Penarth; p. (2011) 126,300.

Vale of White Horse, l. gov. dist., Oxon., **Eng.**; based on Abingdon, Faringdon and Wantage; p. (2010) 117,000.

Vale Royal, former l. gov. dist., Cheshire, **Eng.**; a. in ctr. of co. and inc. saltfield ts. of Northwich and Winsford. Abolished, 2009.

Ventnor, t., I. of Wight, **Eng.**; on S. cst. 18 km S. of Ryde; mild climate, tourist and health resort.

Vyrnwy, L., reservoir, Powys, **Wales**; with dam 360 m long supplies water for population of Liverpool; a. 454 ha.

W

Wadebridge, sm. spt., Cornwall, **Eng.**; at head of Camel estuary, 10 km N.W. of Bodmin; agr. mkt.

Wakefield, c., met. dist., West Yorks., **Eng.**; on R. Calder; 13 km S. of Leeds; cath.; former ctr. of coal mng. a.; woollen and worsted prods., chemicals, engin.; p. (2011) 325,800 (dist.).

Wales, principality, **Great Britain**; mostly mtnous.; Cambrian mtns. rise to 1,085 m at Snowdon; contrast between N. and Central Wales (pastoral farming, forestry, water supply, tourism, rural depopulation) and S. Wales (former coalfield, metal-based inds., lge. ts.); referendum (1997) paved way for new Welsh Assembly; cap. Cardiff; p. (2015) 3,100,000.

Wallasea, I., Essex, **Eng.** Europe's largest man-made coastal reserve (Wallasea Wetlands). Created 2006. Flooded in 2015.

Wallasey, t., Wirral, adjoining Birkenhead, Merseyside, **Eng.**; residtl., seaside resort (New Brighton); p. 59,750.

Wallingford, t., S. Oxon., **Eng.**; on R. Thames, to N. of its gap between Chilterns and Lambourn Downs.

Wallsend, t., frmly. Tyne and Wear, **Eng.**; on N. bank of Tyne, 6 km below Newcastle; Tyne tunnel links with Jarrow; shipbldg., engin., iron, plywood; at end of Hadrian's Wall; p. 43,000.

Walmer, t., Kent, **Eng.**; 3 km S. of Deal; holiday resort; cas., residence of Warden of Cinque Ports.

Walney, I., off cst. of Cumbria, **Eng.**; opposite Barrow.

Walsall, t., met. dist., West Midlands, **Eng.**; 8 km E. of Wolverhampton; leather and iron prods., engin., steel tubes; p. (2011) 258,000 (dist.).

Walsingham, v., North Norfolk, **Eng.**; many old bldgs., priory ruins, abbey; pilgrimage ctr.

Waltham Abbey, sm. t., Epping Forest, Essex, **Eng.**; 21 km N.E. London, on edge of Epping Forest; Norman nave of abbey part of parish church.

Waltham Forest, outer bor., E. London, **Eng.**; incorporating former bors. of Chingford, Leyton, Walthamstow; industl. and residtl.; p. (2011) 258,000.

Walthamstow. *See* **Waltham Forest**.

Walton and **Weybridge**, ts., Elmbridge, Surrey, **Eng.**; on R. Thames, 27 km S.W. of London; eng., aircraft; p. 54,000.

Wandsworth, inner bor., S.W. London, **Eng.**; inc. Battersea; on R. Wandle at influx into Thames; oil mills, metal wks., paper, formerly brewing; p. (2011) 307,000.

Wansbeck, R., Northumberland, **Eng.**; flows E. from Pennines into N. Sea 5 km N. of Blyth.

Wansbeck, former l. gov. dist., Northumberland, **Eng.**; inc. Newbiggin, Ashington and Bedlington. Abolished, 2009.

Wantage, mkt. t., Oxon., **Eng.**; in Vale of the White Horse; birthplace of King Alfred.

Wapping, Thames-side dist.; ctr. of printing inds. (some now moving); London, **Eng.**

Ware, sm. mkt. t., East Herts., **Eng.**; on R. Lea; 3 km N.E. of Hertford.

Wareham, sm. mkt. t., Purbeck, Dorset, **Eng.**; on R. Frome, on N. of I. of Purbeck, 13 km S.W. of Poole.

Warminster, sm. t., West Wilts., **Eng.**; on Wylye watershed at edge of Salisbury Plain; agr. mkt.

Warrenpoint, sm. spt., Newry and Mourne, **N. Ireland**; at head of Carlingford Lough.

Warrington, t., unit. auth., Cheshire, **Eng.**; on R. Mersey and Manchester Ship Canal; metal inds. (wire-drawing), chemicals, brewing, paper; expanded as new c. (to take people from Manchester); attracting high technology inds.; p. (2011) 202,200 (unit. auth.).

Warsop, sm. t., Notts., **Eng.**; 6 km N.E. of Mansfield; limestone, gravel.

Warwick, co. t., l. gov. dist., Warwicks., **Eng.**; on R. Avon, 13 km S.W. of Coventry; cas.; agr. implements, brewing, malting; p. (2010) 136,000 (dist.); 25,000 (t.).

Warwickshire, non-met. co., W. Midlands, **Eng.**; undulating, drained by tribs. of Rs. Severn and Trent, crossed by Cotswolds to S.; sm. coalfield to N.; potential new coalfield in S.; p. (2010) 531,500.

Wash, The, bay, N. Sea between Lincs. and Norfolk, **Eng.**; 35 km long, 24 km wide; partly reclaimed to form the Fens.

Washington, t., Tyne and Wear, **Eng.**; 8 km S.E. of Gateshead; coal, iron and steel, stone quarrying, chemicals; new t. 1964; p. 54,000.

Wast Water, L. Dist., deepest L. in **Eng.**; 5 km long, 79 m deep.

Watchet, sm. t., West Somerset, **Eng.**; sm. pt. on cst. of Bristol Channel.

Waterford, co., Munster, **R.o.I.**; mtnous. co. in S.E.; mainly agr., dairying, pigs; fishing; co. t. Waterford; a. 1,867 km²; p. (2011) 66,960.

Waterford, co. t., spt., Waterford, **R.o.I.**; on R. Suir; cath.; brewing, fishing, glass mnfs.; p. (2011) 46,747 (t.).

Watford, t., l. gov. dist., Herts., **Eng.**; on R. Colne, 26 km N.W. of London; mkt.; varied inds.; paper, printing; home of Camelot (lottery operator) and Leavesden film studio; p. (2010) 81,000 (dist.).

Waveney, R., Norfolk and Suffolk, **Eng.**; 80 km long.

Waveney, l. gov. dist., Suffolk, **Eng.**; based on Lowestoft, Beccles and Bungay; p. (2010) 118,000.

Waverley, l. gov. dist., Surrey, **Eng.**; inc. Farnham, Godalming and Haslemere; p. (2010) 119,000.

Weald, The, wooded and pastoral tracts S.E. **Eng.**; extending from Folkestone, Kent, through Surrey, Hants., and Sussex to the sea at Beachy Head; former a. of iron working; name derived from German *Wald* = forest.

Wealden, l. gov. dist., East Sussex, **Eng.**; stretches from Uckfield to S. cst.; p. (2010) 143,000.

Wear, R., Durham/Tyne and Wear, **Eng.**; rises in Pennines, flows through Durham to N. Sea at Sunderland; 96 km long.

Wear Valley, former l. gov. dist., Durham, **Eng.**; Pennine a. inc. Bishop Auckland, Crook and Willington. Abolished, 2009.

Weaver, R., Cheshire, **Eng.**; industl. trib. of R. Mersey; 72 km long.

Wednesbury, t, West Midlands, **Eng.**; former metal wkg. t.

Wednesfield, t., West Midlands, **Eng.**; metal tubes, materials handling engin.; expanded t.

Wellingborough, t., l. gov. dist., Northants., **Eng.**; on R. Nene, 14 km N.E. of Northampton; mkt.; footwear; expanded t.; p. (2010) 76,500 (dist.), (2001) 46,959 (t.).

Wellington, sm. mkt. t., Somerset, **Eng.**; 10 km S.W. Taunton, anc. woollen ind. still survives.

Wells, cath. t., Mendip, Somerset, **Eng.**; on S. flank of Mendip hills; cath., bishop's palace; paper mftg.; tourism; p. 10,250.

Welshpool, mkt. t., Powys, **Wales**; on R. Severn; nearby is Powys cas.; p.5,900.

Welwyn Garden City, t., Welwyn-Hatfield, Herts., **Eng.**; 34 km N. of London; founded by Sir Ebenezer Howard (1920) as first satellite t. of London; new t. 1948; pharmaceuticals, plastics, radio, and electronics, lt. inds.; p. (2011) 43,000.

Welwyn Hatfield, l. gov. dist., Herts., **Eng.**; comprises Welwyn Garden City and Hatfield; p. (2010) 108,000.

Wembley, former M.B., Middx., **Eng.**; now inc. in Brent outer bor. Greater London; lt. inds.; home of Wembley Stadium (now redeveloped as 90,000 seat stadium); British Empire Exhibition 1924–5. Wembley Stadium scene of England's 1966 World Cup triumph. Wembley Arena (formerly the Empire Pool, once the world's longest pool).

Wenlock Edge, narrow ridge, Shrops., **Eng.**; extends 29 km S.W. from Much Wenlock to Craven Arms; limestone; moorland, mainly above 290 m.

Wensleydale, North Yorks., **Eng.**; valley in N. Pennines drained E. by R. Ure; cattle reared for fattening on lowland farms; some dairying (cheese); length 56 km.

Wessex, anc. kingdom, S. **Eng.**; inc. Berks., Hants., Wilts., Dorset, Somerset and Devon. It was "the realm of the Western Saxons".

West Berkshire, unit. auth., Berks, **Eng**. p. (2010) 153,900.

West Bridgford, t., Rushcliffe, Notts., **Eng.**; at junc. of Grantham canal with R. Trent; residtl. sub. of Nottingham; p. 44,900.

West Bromwich, t., Sandwell, West Midlands, **Eng.**; on R. Thame, 8 km N.W. of Birmingham; heavy engin. and allied inds., chemicals, springs, oil refining; new Alsop-designed arts centre (2008); p. 139,000.

West Derbyshire. *See* Derbyshire Dales.

West Devon, l. gov. dist., Devon, **Eng.**; rural W. of Dartmoor and ts. of Tavistock and Okehampton; p. (2010) 53,000.

West Dorset, l. gov. dist., Dorset, **Eng.**; inc. Lyme Regis, Bridport, Sherborne and Dorchester; p. (2010) 97,000.

West Dunbartonshire, unit. auth. created in 1996, formerly part of Strathclyde, **W. Scot.**; bordered S. by R. Clyde and N. by Loch Lomond; p. (2010) 91,000.

Western Isles, l. gov. auth., **Scot.**; remote a. of Outer Hebrides; pastoral farming and fishing are the traditional livelihood; p. (2010) 26,200.

West Ham, former C.B., Essex, **Eng.**; sub. to E. of London; bordered by Rs. Thames and Lea; now inc. in Newham bor., Greater London.

West Lancashire, l. gov. dist., Lancs., **Eng.**; N. of Merseyside, inc. Skelmersdale and Ormskirk; p. (2010) 109,000.

West Lindsey, l. gov. dist., Lincs., **Eng.**; lge. a. N. of Lincoln and inc. Market Rasen and Gainsborough; p. (2010) 89,000.

West Lothian, central **Scot.**; unit. auth. created in 1996, incorporating most of historic co. which became part of Lothian in 1974 and is now divided between Edinburgh, Falkirk, and W. Lothian; industl. dist. in Central Lowlands close to Edinburgh; p. (2010) 171,250.

Westmeath, co., Leinster, **R.o.I.**; drained by R. Shannon, many Ls.; dairying; co. to Mullingar; ch. t. Athlone; a. 1,834 km²; p. 85,961.

West Mersea, sm. t., Essex, **Eng.**; on Mersea I.

West Midlands, former met. co., **Eng.**; mainly industl. a. centred around Birmingham and the S. Staffs. coalfield (Black Country) and Coventry; many forms of engin. and light inds. inc. vehicle mftg.; p. (2001) 2,555,592.

Westminster, City of, inner bor., London, **Eng.**; on N. bank of R. Thames; W. of City of London; incorporates former bors. of Paddington and St. Marylebone; contains Houses of Parliament, Westminster Abbey, Government offices, Royal Palaces (Buckingham Palace and St. James's); p. (2011) 219,500.

Westmorland, historic co., **Eng.**; now part of Cumbria.

Weston-super-Mare, t., in N. Somerset loc. govt. dist.; **Eng.**; on Bristol Channel, 32 km S.W. of Bristol; holiday resort; pier destroyed by fire, 2008; renovated (2010); expanded t.; p. 73,500.

West Oxfordshire, l. gov. dist., Oxon., **Eng.**; inc. Cotswolds and ts. of Chipping Norton, Witney and Woodstock; p. (2010) 102,000.

Westport, spt., Mayo, **R.o.I.**; on Clew Bay; fishing; mkt.; p. c. 3,500.

Westray, I., Orkney Is., **Scot.**; 16 km long.

West Somerset, l. gov. dist., Somerset, **Eng.**; inc. Exmoor and cstl. ts. of Watchet and Minehead; p. (2010) 35,400.

West Sussex, non-met. co., S.E. **Eng.**; crossed by E.–W. chalk ridge of S. Downs and forested Weald; diverse agr.; dormitory, retirement and tourist ts. on cst. inc. Bognor Regis and Worthing; Crawley new t. in N.; p. (2010) 782,300.

Westward Ho!, v., N. Devon, **Eng.**; named after Kingsley's novel.

West Wiltshire, former l. gov. dist., Wilts., **Eng.**; stretches from Melksham, Bradford-on-Avon and Trowbridge to Warminster. Abolished, 2009.

West Yorkshire, met. co., **Eng.**; industl. and mainly built-up a. E. of Pennines; traditionally ass. with woollen textile mftg.; inc. major ctrs. of Bradford and Leeds; p. (2001) 2,079,211.

Wetherby, sm. t., West Yorks., **Eng.**; on R. Wharfe mkt., t.; racecourse; p. (2009) 10,560 (t.).

Wexford, coastal co., Leinster, S.E. **R.o.I.**; farming, fishing; cap. Wexford; a. 2,334 km²; p. 145,000.

Wexford, t., cap. of Wexford; Leinster, S.E. **R.o.I.**; on R. Slaney; agr. processing; outport at Rosslare; p. 11,000.

Wey, R., Hants., Surrey, **Eng.**; rises in W. Weald, flows N. into R. Thames nr. Weybridge; cuts inspt. gap through N. Downs at Guildford; length 56 km.

Weybridge. *See* Walton and Weybridge.

Weymouth, t., part of l. gov. dist. of Weymouth and Portland, Dorset, **Eng.**; on Weymouth Bay, 13 km S. of Dorchester; torpedo and boatbldg., bricks, tiles, engin.; popular holiday resort; p. (2010) 65,000 (dist.), 48,000 (t.).

Whaley Bridge, t., High Peak, Derbys., **Eng.**; textile bleaching and finishing; p. 4,750.

Wharfe, R., West and North Yorks., **Eng.**; trib. of R. Ouse; 96 km long.

Whickham, t., Tyne and Wear, **Eng.**; nr. Gateshead; chemicals, paper; p. 18,100.

Whitburn, burgh, W. Lothian, **Scot.**; 32 km S.W. of Edinburgh; limestone; p. (2002) 10,391.

Whitby, sm. t., North Yorks., **Eng.**; at mouth of R. Esk, 27 km N.W. of Scarborough; anc. spt. and fishing t.; now popular coastal resort; abbey; famous for jet ornaments; potash mined nearby.

Whitchurch, t., Shrops., **Eng.**; 21 km S.W. of Crewe; dairy prods; p. 8,150.

Whiteadder, R., Borders, **Scot.**; trib. of R. Tweed; 54 km long.

Whitehaven, spt., Copeland, Cumbria, **Eng.**; on

Solway F. 5 km N. of St. Bees Head; methane gas, cement, chemicals; p. (2011) 25,100.

Whitehead, sm. t., Carrickfergus, **N. Ireland**; at entrance to Belfast Lough; seaside resort.

Whitley Bay, t., North Tyneside, **Eng.**; 5 km N. of Tynemouth; seaside resort; p. (2011) 37,400.

Whitstable, spt., Kent, **Eng.**; on Thames estuary 10 km N. of Canterbury; holiday resort, oysters; p.29,650.

Whittlesey, sm. t., Fenland, Cambs., **Eng.**; in the Fens, 13 km W. of March; bricks, mkt. gardening.

Wick, spt., sm. burgh, Highland, **Scot.**; on E. cst., 22 km S. of John O'Groats; airport to Orkneys and Shetlands; old herring fishing ctr.; p. 7,400.

Wicklow, coastal co., Leinster, **R.o.I.**; crossed by Wicklow mtns.; pastoral agr. and tourism; cap. Wicklow; a. 2,033 km², p. 136,448 (2011).

Wicklow, t., cap. of Wicklow, Leinster, **R.o.I.**; on S.E. cst., 56 km S. of Dublin; mkt.; sm. seaside resort; p. 6,000.

Wicklow, mtns., Wicklow, **R.o.I.**; highest summit Lugnaquillia, 927 m.

Widecombe, v., Devon, **Eng.**; Dartmoor tourist ctr.; famous through ballad "Widecombe Fair."

Widnes, t., Halton, Cheshire, **Eng.**; on R. Mersey 19 km E. of Liverpool; impt. chemical inds.; expanded t.; p. 56,500.

Wigan, t., met. dist., Gtr. Manchester, **Eng.**; 26 km N.E. of Liverpool; engin., chemicals, cement, food processing, paper; former coal mng. ctr.; p. (2011) 317,800 (dist.).

Wigston, t., Leics., **Eng.**; 6 km S. of Leicester; engin., hosiery; p. 34,500. *See* **Oadby.**

Wigtown, sm. burgh, Dumfries and Galloway, **Scot.**; on W. Bay, Solway F.; located in historic co. of **Wigtownshire,** now part of Dumfries and Galloway; p. 987.

Willenhall, t., West Midlands, **Eng.**; locks and keys, drop forgings.

Willesden, former M.B., Middx., **Eng.**; now inc. in Brent outer bor., Greater London impt. rly. junc.; residtl. and industl.

Wilmslow, t., Cheshire, **Eng.**; on R. Bollen, 10 km S.W. of Stockport; residtl.; pharmaceuticals; p. 35,500.

Wilton, sm. t., Wilts., **Eng.**; on R. Wylye, 5 km W. of Salisbury; agr. mkt., carpets, felt; anc. cap. of Wessex; many old bldgs.

Wilton, industl. estate, Redcar and Cleveland, **Eng.**; on S. side of Tees estuary; heavy organic- and petro-chemicals; nylon polymer plant.

Wiltshire, old non-met. co., **Eng.**; crossed by chalk downland and Salisbury Plain; barley, wheat, dairying, pigs; co. t. Salisbury; p. (2010) 455,000. Reorganised as new unit. auth., 2009.

Wimbledon, dist., London, **Eng.**; lge. open common; site of international tennis tournament; part of London Bor. of Merton. Tramlink to Croydon opened in 2000.

Wimborne Minster, sm. mkt. t., Dorset, **Eng.**; on R. Stour; Roman settlement and home of early Saxon kings; Badbury Rings earthworks nearby.

Winchcombe, t., Gloucs., **Eng.**; nr. Cheltenham; old mills; pottery, paper; nearby cas.; p. 4,750.

Winchelsea, anc. t., East Sussex, **Eng.**; 3 km S.W. of Rye; once impt. walled spt. and Cinque port, now 3 km inland.

Winchester, cath. c., l. gov. dist., Hants., **Eng.**; on R. Itchen, 19 km N. of Southampton; anc. Anglo-Saxon cap. of Wessex; meeting place of parliaments until time of Henry VII; cath.; public school; univ.; p. (2010) 113,000 (dist.), 37,500 (t).

Windermere, sm. t. Cumbria, **Eng.** and lgst. English L.; outlet to Morecambe Bay; supplies water to Manchester; 16 km long, 1·6 km wide.

Windrush, R., Oxford, Gloucs., **Eng.**; trib. of Thames.

Windscale. *See* **Sellafield.**

Windsor, t., part of unit. auth. of **Windsor and Maidenhead,** Berks., **Eng.**; on R. Thames, 32 km W. of London; Windsor has famous royal cas. (founded by William the Conqueror) and park, St. George's Chapel and the Royal Mausoleum; p. (2010) 143,000 (unit. auth.), (2011) 35,000 (t.) (with Eton).

Winsford, t., Cheshire, **Eng.**; on R. Weaver; 6 km S. of Northwich; ctr. of salt inds., chemicals; computer peripherals; p. 30,300.

Wirksworth, sm. t., West Derbys., **Eng.**; in Pennines, 8 km S. of Matlock; limestone, fluorspar wks.; ctr. of former lead mng.

Wirral, penin., met. dist., Merseyside, **Eng.**;

between estuaries of Dee and Mersey; residtl.; comprises Wallasey, Birkenhead, Bebington and Hoylake; p. 320,000.

Wisbech, t., Fenland, Cambs., **Eng.**; on R. Nene, 18 km from its mouth in the Wash; mkt. gardening, fruit growing and canning, agr. implements; p. 28,000 (now home to major influx of migrant workers from Eastern Europe).

Witham, sm. t., Essex, **Eng.**; 14 km N.E. of Chelmsford; ctr. of mkt. gardening a.; expanded t.

Witham, R., Leics. and Lincs., **Eng.**; flows into the Wash; cuts impressive gap through Lincoln.

Witney, sm. t., Oxford, **Eng.**; on R. Windrush, 16 km W. of Oxford; woollens, blankets, gloves.

Wivenhoe, sm. t., Essex, **Eng.**; on R. Colne; boatbldg., oysters, lt. inds.

Woburn, t., Beds., **Eng.**; 8 km N.E. of Leighton Buzzard; Woburn Abbey (seat of Dukes of Bedford).

Woking, t., l. gov. dist., Surrey, **Eng.**; 6 km N. of Guildford; residtl.; near to Brookwood Cemetery, the largest in Europe. p. (2011) 99,000 (dist.).

Wokingham, mkt. t., unit auth., Berks., **Eng.**; 8 km S.E. of Reading; agr. tr. and machin.; p. (2010) 159,000 (unit. auth.), 40,000 (t.).

Wolsingham, sm. t., Durham, **Eng.**; on R. Wear.

Wolverhampton, c., met. dist., West Midlands, **Eng.**; heavy and lt. engin., boilers, rayon, elec. engin. and apparatus, iron wks., aircraft and motor components, hollow-ware, tools, *etc.*; p. (2001) 236,582 (dist.). Created a Millennium City, 2000. New Jaguar Land Rover plant to be built.

Wolverton, t., Milton Keynes, **Eng.**; on R. Ouse, 24 km S.W. of Bedford; p. 62,000. Longest continuously opened railway works in the world (since September 1838).

Wombwell, t., South Yorks., **Eng.**; at E. foot of Pennines, 11 km N. of Sheffield; p. 16,000.

Woodbridge, t., Suffolk Coastal, Suffolk, **Eng.**; on R. Deben; boat-building, tourism.

Wood Green, former M.B., Middx., **Eng.**; now inc. in Haringey outer bor., Greater London.

Woodhall Spa, t., East Lindsey, Lincs., **Eng.**; 6 km S.W. of Horncastle; former spa, bromoiodine springs; resort.

Woodstock, t., Oxford, **Eng.**; on Glyme R., 11 km N.W. of Oxford; glove mnfs.; Blenheim Palace.

Wookey Hole, cave, Mendip Hills, Somerset, **Eng.**; at foot of limestone hills, 3 km N.W. of Wells; R. Axe emerges from the cave.

Woolwich, dist. former met. bor., London, **Eng.**; on either side of R. Thames; impt. Tudor dockyard, now closed; now part of Greenwich and Newham bors. Major regeneration project (Woolwich Central) announced in 2011.

Wootton Bassett (Royal Wootton Bassett), mkt. t., N. Wilts., **Eng.**; expanded since the 1960s to provide housing for people wkg. in Swindon; national focus for hailing return of soldiers killed overseas until 2011.

Worcester, c. and l. gov. dist., Worcs., **Eng.**; on R. Severn, 38 km N. of Gloucester; cath.; machin., porcelain, glove mkg.; univ., birthplace of Elgar; p. (2011) 99,000 (dist.).

Worcestershire, historic Midland co., **Eng.**; part of Hereford and Worcs. until 1998; now recreated separate county; p. (2010) 558,500.

Workington, t., Allerdale, Cumbria, **Eng.**; sm. spt. on Solway F. at mouth of Derwent R., first Bessemer steel plant, closed (1981), engin.; industl. diversification on nearby industl. estates, inc. bus wks.; p. 21,500.

Worksop, t., Bassetlaw, Notts., **Eng.**; 24 km S.E. of Sheffield; coal-mng. dist.; brewing, knitwear, glass, flour; p. 39,100.

Worms Head, promontory at W. end of Gower Peninsula, **Wales.**

Worthing, t., l. gov. dist., West Sussex, **Eng.**; on S. cst., 16 km W. of Brighton; resort, popular as retirement ctr.; p. (2011) 104,000 (dist.).

Wrath, C., N.W. Scot. Highest mainland cliffs in Britain.

Wrekin, The, l. gov. dist., Shrops., **Eng.**; inc. Newport, Wellington, Oakengates and Dawley; p. 149,000.

Wrexham, t. 18 km S.W. of Chester, N.E. **Wales,** unit. auth. created in 1996 from former l. gov. dists. of Wrexham Maelor and Glyndŵr; p. (2011) 134,800 (unit. auth.). New 'superjail' opened. The home of Glyndŵr University

Wroxeter, v., Shrops., **Eng.**; on R. Severn, 8 km S.E. Shrewsbury; Roman sta. Uriconium; lost Roman harbour uncovered (2000).

Wychavon, l. gov. dist., Worcs., **Eng.**; inc. Vale of Evesham and Pershore in S. and Droitwich in N.; p. (2011) 117,000.

Wycombe, l. gov. dist., Bucks., **Eng.**; close to Oxon. and inc. High Wycombe and Marlow; p. (2011) 171,500.

Wye, R., Bucks., **Eng.**; rises in Chiltern hills, flows S.E. to R. Thames at Cookham.

Wye, R., **Eng.** and **Wales**; rises in Plynlimmon, flows S.E. into R. Severn at Chepstow; forms deeply incised valley at Symond's Yat; 208 km long.

Wye, t., Kent, **Eng.**; nr. Ashford; impt. agr. college.

Wylfa Head, Anglesey, Isle of, N. **Wales**; Magnox nuclear power sta.

Wymondham, sm. t., South Norfolk, **Eng.**; 14 km S.W. of Norwich; mkt.; Benedictine abbey founded 1107.

Wyre, l. gov. dist., Lancs., **Eng.**; inc. Preesall, Fleetwood and Thornton Cleveleys; p. (2011) 108,000.

Wyre Forest, l. gov. dist., Worcs., **Eng.**; inc. Bewdley, Kidderminster and Stourport; p. (2011) 98,000.

Y

Yare, R., Norfolk, **Eng.**; flows E. to N. Sea at Gorleston; forms part of Norfolk Broads navigable waterways; 80 km long.

Yarmouth. *See* **Great Yarmouth**.

Yeo or **Ivel**, R., Dorset, Somerset, **Eng.**; trib. of R. Parrett; 38 km long.

Yeovil, sm. mkt. t., Somerset, **Eng.**; on R. Yeo; glove mnf., aero-engin., agr. machin., dairy processing.

Ynys Mon. *See* **Isle of Anglesey**.

York, c., unit. auth. created in 1996, formerly part of North Yorks. **Eng.**; on R. Ouse; in central position in Vale of York; anc. part of c. enclosed by walls; minster, cas., univs.; chocolate, confectionery, rly.

museum; Jarvik Viking Centre; renovated Art Gallery (reopened 2015); Yorkshire Eye attraction; p. (2010) 195,000 (unit. auth.), 140,000. (c.). Magnificent York Minster.

York, Vale of, broad lowland, North Yorks/York, **Eng.**; between Pennines and N. Yorks. Moors and Yorks. Wolds; drained to Humber by R. Ouse and tribs.; glacial and alluvial soils have required draining; crop farming, wheat, barley, root-crops, associated with fattening of beef cattle; settlement mainly marginal; ch. t. York; length 96 km, width from 16 km in N. to 48 km in S.

Yorkshire, historic co., N. **Eng.**; formerly divided into 3 separate admin. parts (Ridings); N., E., and W.; now split into the non-met. co. of N. Yorks., the met. cos. of W. Yorks. and S. Yorks., and 8 unit. auths. inc. Kingston upon Hull, Middlesbrough and York. Yorkshire Dales national park now linked to Lake District national park.

Yorkshire Moors, hills, North Yorks. and Redcar and Cleveland, **Eng.**; inc. N. Yorks. Moors, Cleveland Hills and Hambleton Hills; bounded to N. by Tees valley, S. by Vale of Pickering, W. by Swale valley, E. by sea; composed of oolitic limestone; good sheep pastures; impt. iron-ore deposits worked in Cleveland Hills; max. alt. 454 m.

Yorkshire Wolds, hills, E. Riding of Yorks., **Eng.**; extend N.E. from Humber and terminate in Flamborough Head; chalk; good sheep pasture; average alt. 180 m.

Ystwyth, R., Ceredigion, **Wales**; flows 40 km to join R. Rheidol at Aberystwyth.

Z

Zetland. *See* **Shetland**.

GENERAL
INFORMATION

This section contains many hundreds of entries, all arranged alphabetically. Entries range across a wide spectrum of human knowledge, from common garden birds to astrolabes and ziggurats and from religious festivals to life expectancy. There are also entries for many scientific terms, from astrophysics to zodiacal light. Readers may wish to refer to Section E for key historical terms, Section G for the Nobel Prizes and Section N for art and architecture and Section P for music and dance. Cross references direct the reader to fuller information elsewhere in the book.

COMMON WEIGHTS AND MEASURES

Introductory Note

The scientist nowadays mainly uses the SI system of units. SI is short for *"Système International d'Unités"* and it is a system of metric units which has come into international use through the agency of such bodies as the General Conference of the International Bureau of Weights and Measures and the International Organisation for Standardisation (ISO) in whose work Britain participates.

The Base SI Units

The seven main base SI units, namely the **metre**, **kilogram**, the **second**, the **ampère**, the **kelvin**, the **candela** and the **mole** are defined and discussed further on **T58–9**.

The Imperial System of Units

The SI system is not the only system of units in use today, although it is the one most favoured by scientists. The Imperial system is widely used in the UK and other English speaking countries and some Imperial weights and measures are given below:

Length

1 nail	= 2_ in
1 link	= 7·92 in
12 in	= 1 ft
3 ft	= 1 yd
22 yd	= 1 chain
10 chains	= 1 furlong
8 furlongs	= 1 mile = 1760 yd = 5280 ft

Area

1210 yd^2	= 1 rood
4 roods	= 1 acre = 4840 yd^2
640 acres	= 1 mile^2

Volume

$$1728 \text{ in}^3 = 1 \text{ ft}^3$$
$$27 \text{ ft}^3 = 1 \text{ yd}^3$$

Capacity

4 gills	= 1 pint
2 pints	= 1 quart
4 quarts	= 1 gallon
2 gallons	= 1 peck
4 pecks	= 1 bushel
8 bushels	= 1 quarter
36 bushels	= 1 chaldron
1 gal	= 277·274 in^3

Weight (Avoirdupois)

(System used in commerce)

1 dram	= 27·343 75 grains
16 drams	= 1 oz = 437·5 grains
16 oz	= 1 lb = 7000 grains
14 lb	= 1 stone
28 lb	= 1 quarter
4 quarters	= 1 cwt = 112 lb
20 cwt	= ton = 2240 lb

Troy Weight

1 pennyweight	= 24 grains
480 grains	= 1 ounce

The only unit of troy weight which is legal for use in trade in Britain is the ounce Troy, and weighings of precious metal are made in multiples and decimals of this unit.

The term *carat* is not a unit of weight for precious metals, but is used to denote the quality of gold plate, *etc.*, and is a figure indicating the number of 24ths of pure gold in the alloy, *e.g.*, a 9 carat gold ring consists of nine parts of pure gold and fifteen parts of base metals.

Nautical Measures

1 nautical mile = 6080 ft = 1853·18 m
1 knot = 1 nautical mile per hour = 1·151 mile/h

Note.—The international nautical mile of 1852 m is now used.

Some Common Equivalents

Length
		Reciprocal
1 cm	= 0·394 in	2·540
1 m	= 1·094 yd	0·914
1 km	= 0·621 mile	1·609

Area
1 m^2	= 1·196 yd^2	0·836
1 km^2	= 0·386 mile^2	2·590
1 hectare	= 2·471 acres	0·405

Volume
1 m^3	= 1·308 yd^3	0·765
1 litre	= 0·220 gallon	4·546

Mass
1 kg	= 2·205 lb	0·454
1 tonne	= 0·984 ton	1·016

Temperature

$$C = (F - 32) \div 1·8$$
$$F = (1·8 \times C) + 32$$

Some Common Abbreviations

mm	= millimetre
cm	= centimetre
m	= metre
km	= kilometre
km/h	= kilometres per hour
g	= gram
kg	= kilogram
tonne	= metric ton
m^2	= square metre
km^2	= square kilometre
ha	= hectare
m^3	= cubic metre
s	= second
min	= minute
h	= hour

Scientific and Technical Terms

A discussion of many of the more complex scientific and technical terms now in use can be found on **T58–9**.

GENERAL INFORMATION

A

Aardvark (Dutch *aarde* = earth + *vark* = pig), a large nocturnal mammal found only in Africa. It feeds on termites and ants.

Aardwolf, a small insectivore (related to the hyena family). Its acute hearing enables it to locate termites. A single aardwolf can eat 200,000 termites in a night.

Abacus, a device for making arithmetical calculations, consisting of parallel bars on which are strung movable coloured beads. The earliest form of this instrument was used in Mesopotamia about 3000 B.C. An efficient form of the abacus is still used in parts of Asia.

Abalone, shellfish regarded in the Far East as an aphrodisiac. The colourful pearly interior of the shell is used for beads and ornaments.

Aberdevine. Another name for the siskin.

Aberration, in astronomy, is the apparent displacement of a star due to the speed of the observer with the earth (*see* **Parallax**). In optics (i) **Spherical Aberration** is when there is blurring of the image and fringes of colour at its edges, due to failure of lens to bring light to a single focus; (ii) **Chromatic Aberration** is due to the refractive index of glass being different for light of different colours. For instance, violet light is bent more than red.

Abiogenesis, or spontaneous generation; the origination of living from non-living matter. The term is applied to such discredited ideas as that frogs could be generated spontaneously by the action of sunlight on mud, or maggots arise spontaneously in dead meat without any eggs from which the maggots hatch being present. Spallanzani (1729–99) upset the hypothesis; Pasteur dealt it a death-blow.

Abominable Snowman. *See* **Yeti.**

Aborigines, a term for the original inhabitants of a country, in particular the indigenous people of Australia. In contrast to their complex social and religious customs, the material culture of Australian aboriginals was very low and ill adapted to stand up to contact with Europeans.

The passage of the Native Rights Act in 1993 generated heated debate and led to the controversial Native Title Amendment Bill. In 1999 the Australian parliament formally apologised to them for the "hurt and trauma" caused by white settlement. A further apology for the "stolen generations" of children of aborigines was made in 2008. Recent years have seen a new respect for aborigine painting. Alcohol abuse and poor diet still contribute to low life expectancy. The aboriginal population is now ½ million (back to its 18th century level). The first Aborigine was elected to the Australian Parliament in August 2010 and the first Aborigine elected leader of a provincial government in 2013.

Aborigines have lived in Australia for 50,000 years since the Old Stone Age. There is evidence they studied the movements of the Sun 10,000 years ago.

Absolute Temperature, Absolute Zero. This is a refined notion requiring some study of thermodynamics for its full understanding. For setting up an absolute temperature scale one must first assign a numerical value to one fixed temperature. For this, the triple point of water has been chosen, *i.e.*, the temperature at which solid, liquid, and gaseous water are all in equilibrium. The triple point is defined to be 273·16 K where K is read for kelvin (after Lord Kelvin). This temperature is 0·01°C on the Celsius scale (*q.v.*) and is thus very close to the melting point of ice. Suppose the pressure and volume of a mass of gas are measured (i) at the triple point of water, giving (pV)tr as the product of the pressure and volume; and (ii) at any unknown temperature T K, giving (pV) as the product. Then the absolute temperature, T K, is defined by

$$T \text{ K} = 273 \cdot 16 \frac{(pV)}{(pV)\text{tr}}$$

It is to be understood that the gas pressure is very low. The nature of the gas is immaterial.

More subtly, it can be shown that the temperature so defined is identical with that derived in a rather abstract way in the science of thermodynamics. The absolute scale is therefore also called the thermodynamic scale. Absolute temperatures can be obtained from Celsius temperatures by adding 273·15; thus the absolute temperature of melting ice is 273·15 K. Conversely, absolute zero is a temperature 273·15 K below the temperature of melting ice, *i.e.*, −273·15°C. Theory shows that absolute zero is unattainable, but it has been approached to within about 1 millionth of a degree. Within ten or so degrees of absolute zero, matter develops some remarkable properties. *See also* **Kelvin, Cryogenics, Superconductor, Helium.**

Acacia. The thorny tree of Africa.

Acadians. *See* **Cajuns.**

Acetic Acid, an organic acid produced when ordinary (ethyl) alcohol is fermented by the organism called *Acetobacter aceti.* The same oxidation process yields vinegar: this is a weak and crude solution of acetic acid obtained by trickling dilute alcoholic liquor over beechwood shavings at 35°C. The souring of wine is due to the same process. Acetic acid is used as a food preservative and flavouring material, and in the manufacture of cellulose acetate and white lead.

Acetylene (also called ethyne), a compound of carbon and hydrogen prepared from calcium carbide and water. A very reactive gas, it is used industrially on a large scale to prepare acetaldehyde, chlorohydrocarbon solvents, and many intermediates for plastics manufacture. Burns in air with a highly luminous flame, formerly used for lighting purposes, but is now widely used, with oxygen, in welding. For safe storage and transportation it is dissolved in acetone.

Acid Rain is the name given to rain, snow or sleet contaminated with acid substances so that its acidity is greater than the limit expected by normal concentrations of carbon dioxide dissolving in the rain to give carbonic acid (*pH* 5·5–5·6). The *pH* (*q.v.*) of acid rain therefore is less than about 5·5. The increased acidity is caused by larger concentrations of a number of contaminants, principally the strong acids, nitric and sulphuric, which arise from industrial effluents containing oxides of nitrogen and sulphur. In some European and North American areas such contamination can give a rain *pH* as low as 3 (which is 100 times more acid than *pH* 5). The acid rain can mark fruit and leaves, and adversely affect soil but its main effect is on the aquatic ecosystems especially in regions which cannot naturally buffer acidic inputs such as those with thin soils and granite rocks.

Acids, substances having a tendency to lose a positive ion (a proton). This general definition overcomes difficulties of earlier views which merely described their properties and asserted that they are chemically opposite to bases. As a whole acids contain ionisable hydrogen, replaceable by a metal, to form a salt. In-organic acids are compounds of non-metals or metalloids, *e.g.*, sulphuric, phosphoric acid. Carboxylic acids contain the group –COOH.

Actinaria. *See* **Sea Anemones.**

Actinides, the fourteen metallic elements from thorium (no. 90) to lawrencium (no. 103). All known isotopes of these elements are radioactive and those with atomic number greater than 92 (uranium) have been produced only in significant quantities artificially. Plutonium (no. 94) is obtained from uranium during the course of nuclear reactor operation and the higher transuranic elements can be made from it by the successive capture of neutrons or nuclei of light atoms. The availability of only minute quantities of short-lived isotopes makes the determination of the physical and chemical properties of the higher actinides very difficult. Claims for the discovery of new elements can therefore be controversial and since the discoverers can name the elements their naming is also controversial. There were three different reports for Nobelium (no. 102). Lawrencium (no. 103) is called Jolistium by Russian authors. Element no. 104 was reported in 1964 by a Russian group and called Kurchatovium but is called Rutherfordium (Rf) in the West. Element no. 105 is called Hahnium (Hn).

Advent, the period including four Sundays devoted to religious preparation for Christmas.

Advocatus Diaboli ("the devil's advocate"), a Roman Catholic functionary who presents opposing evidence in regard to the life of any deceased person it may be proposed to canonise.

Aerodynamics, the science of gases (especially air) in motion, particularly in relation to aircraft (aeronautics). The idea of imitating the birds by the use of wings is of ancient origin. Leonardo da Vinci first carried out experiments in a scientific manner. The invention of the balloon in 1783 and the researches of scientists and engineers in the 19th cent. ultimately led to the development of the aeroplane.

Aerogel. A material which is the lightest solid yet known to man.

Aerolites, the name given to the class of meteorites composed chiefly of heavy silicates. The other two main classes are *siderolites* (nickel–iron and silicates) and *siderites* (nickel–iron).

Aerosol, a suspension of a liquid in a gas; for example, a fog is very small drops of water suspended in air. Formed by spraying the liquid in air, aerosols are used to disperse liquid over a wide area in crop spraying, air freshening and pest control. *See also* **Fluorocarbons.**

Afrikander, type of cattle bred in South Africa.

Afrikaner, an Afrikaans-speaking South African, usually of Dutch descent.

After-damp occurs in a mine after an explosion, causing suffocation. It is composed mainly of carbon dioxide and nitrogen and contains water vapour and carbon monoxide.

Agaric, large fungi of the family *Agaricaceae,* which includes the mushroom and what are popularly called "toadstools", though the idea that these two lay terms sharply differentiate between edible and poisonous fungi is an incorrect one. Characteristic of the agarics is the presence of a cap or *pileus* (bearing underneath the spore-shedding gills) and a stalk or *stipe.*

Agave, the American aloe or Century Plant which sometimes does not attain to flowering maturity under sixty or seventy years, and then dies. The flower spray may reach a height of 6 m and in its development the rush of sap is so great that the Mexicans collect for brewing the strong spirit called mescal. 1,000 litres of sap can be obtained from a single plant. Some species of agave yield sisal (for making cord and rope).

Agouti. A strange jungle rodent whose teeth can open Brazil nuts.

Air, a mixture of gases in the earth's atmosphere, the main constituents being nitrogen, oxygen and argon. Dry air contains these gases in the following proportions by volume: nitrogen 78·06 %, oxygen 21 %, argon 0·94 %. Other gases are also present in small amounts. Of particular importance are water vapour and carbon dioxide. Water vapour is not only critical for life forms on land but also a major factor in the behaviour of the atmosphere—weather and climate. Carbon dioxide is utilised by green plants in photosynthesis.

Air also contains traces of ammonia, nitrogen oxides, hydrogen, sulphur dioxide, ozone, and of the rare gases, helium, krypton, neon and xenon. Near cities and industrial areas there are also large quantities of dust and smoke particles (up to 100,000 particles per cc), and traces of other gases from industrial processes.

A litre of air at 0°C and 760 mm pressure weighs 1·2932 g. *See also* **Atmosphere, Pollution.**

Air Glow is the general name given to a large number of relatively weak optical emissions from the earth's upper atmosphere in the height range 70 to 400 km (approx.). It is distinct from the aurora polaris (*q.v.*) which is usually much brighter and normally only observable at high latitudes. Air glow is produced by a combination of photochemical reactions in the upper atmosphere, excitation by photoelectrons, or by solar ultra-violet light. In the latter case it is more correctly called "dayglow." These

emissions occur in the ultra-violet and infra-red spectral regions as well as in visible light.

Alabaster, a soft crystalline form of sulphate of lime, or granulated gypsum, easily worked for statuary and other ornamental articles, and capable of being highly polished. Volterra, in Tuscany, yields the finest; that in highest ancient repute came from Alabastron in Egypt.

Alb, white priestly vestment reaching to the feet.

Albatross, a large sea-bird of almost pure white, black and white, or brown plumage. It nests in colonies on remote islands, but at other times rarely approaches land. Of the 22 species, no less than 17 are now facing extinction.

Modern long-line fishing methods are threatening the albatross with extinction (an albatross is killed every five minutes by the fishing industry).

Contrary to popular belief, it has now been discovered that the albatross does *not* wander aimlessly but for purposes of breeding and foraging. One recent survey found that some albatrosses make astonishing round-the-world journeys in as little as 46 days. The albatross has the longest wingspan of any bird. It is the greatest of all the ocean wanderers.

Albert Memorial, a large Gothic monument designed by Sir George Gilbert Scott, and embellished with sculptures by eminent artists. Erected in memory of Prince Albert in Kensington Gardens.

Alcázar. Palace of the Moorish kings at Seville, famed for the beauty of its halls and gardens.

Alcoholics Anonymous, organisation first formed to help alcoholics in the USA in 1935. The first group was formed in Britain in 1948 in London.

Alcohols. A class of organic compounds of general formula R–OH, where R is an aliphatic radical. "Alcohol" is the name used for ethyl alcohol (ethanol); this is produced by distilling fermented liquors, and synthetically from ethylene, a product of petroleum cracking. Industrially ethyl alcohol is used in the manufacture of chloroform, ether, perfumes, *etc.*

Diluted with wood alcohol or other denaturants ethyl alcohol is called "methylated spirits"; the denaturants are varied according to the industrial purposes for which it is required, the methylated spirits then being largely exempt from duty. Wood alcohol (methyl alcohol or methanol) can be obtained by distilling wood or synthetically from water gas.

Alcoholic Strength. In 1980 Great Britain adopted the OIML (International Organisation of Legal Metrology) system of spirit strength measurement in metric units as required by EEC directive. The alcoholic strength of wine is expressed in percentage volume ("% vol") terms, *i.e.,* the number of volumes of pure alcohol in 100 volumes of the product at 20°C. For spirits the quantity for duty is the litre of alcohol at 20°C. For example, a case of 12 bottles of 75 cl each = 9 litres; at 40% volume 9 litres = 9 × 40% = 3.60 litres of alcohol. The alcoholic strength of spirits and liqueurs appearing on bottle labels is increasingly shown in % vol. terms (*e.g.*, "40.5% vol").

The USA continues to use the US proof gallon (1·37 US proof gallons = 1 British proof gallon).

Aldebaran. A giant orange star that has inflated to 45 times the diameter of our Sun.

Aldehyde, the generic term for a class of chemical compounds of general formula R–CHO, where R is an organic radical. Except for formaldehyde, which is a gas, aldehydes are volatile liquids. They are produced by oxidation of primary alcohols. Most important aldehyde is formaldehyde (methanal) used in making the plastics described as formaldehyde resins. Formalin (formaldehyde solution in water) is much used for preserving zoological specimens.

Alder, a river-side tree of the genus *Alnus,* including some 30 species and found in north temperate regions and the Andes. The only species native to Britain is *A. glutinosa,* which has been described as "guardian of river-banks" because of the way its roots bind together the sand and stones, and so slow down erosion. The wood is used for furniture and charcoal.

Aldine Editions are the beautiful books printed in Venice by the Renaissance printer Aldo Pio Manuzio and his family between 1490 and 1597. Italics were first introduced in these books.

Algae, flowerless plants living mostly in water. Seaweeds and the green pond scums are the best known algae. The green powder found on trees is a microscopic alga (*Protococcus*). Microalgae have potential to be a new-energy source.

Algebra, a branch of mathematics in which symbols are used in place of numbers. Sir Isaac Newton styled it the "universal arithmetic". The Chinese were able to solve the quadratic equation before the Christian era but it was Al-Khowarizmi, an Arab mathematician of the early 9th cent., who introduced algebra to Europe.

Alhambra, the ancient palace of the Moorish kings at Granada in Spain, built in the 13th and 14th cent. Though part of the castle was turned into a modern palace under Charles V, the most beautiful parts of the interior are still preserved—the graceful halls and dwelling-rooms grouped round the Court of Alberca and the Court of Lions, with their fountains, arcades, and lovely gardens.

Aliphatic describes derivatives of hydrocarbons having chains of carbon atoms, as distinct from rings of carbon atoms as in benzene (*see* **Aromatic**). The gas butane is aliphatic.

Alkali, the general name given to a number of chemicals which are bases (*q.v.*). The term should be limited to the hydroxides of metals in the first and second group of the periodic table and of ammonia, *e.g.*, NaOH, KOH. They are used commercially in the manufacture of paper, glass, soap, and artificial silk. The word comes from the Arabic *al-kali* meaning calcined wood ashes. Alkalis are very soluble in water and neutralise acids to form salts and water.

Alkaloids, a large group of natural products which contain nitrogen; they are usually basic. Isolated from plants and animals, they include some hormones, vitamins, and drugs. Examples are nicotine, adrenalin, and cocaine. Many alkaloids are made synthetically for medicinal use, *e.g.*, morphine, quinine. Their function in plants is not well understood. *See* **Belladonna**.

Alligator, the crocodile of America, found in the lower Mississippi and adjacent lakes *etc*. There is also a Chinese species. Alligators have broader snouts than other crocodiles. Male alligators emit low frequency growls to attract females.

Allotropy. Depending on the temperature, pressure or method of preparation, an element may exist in one of several forms, each having different physical properties (crystal structure, electrical conductivity, melting point, *etc.*). This is known as allotropy and the different forms of the element are called allotropes. Many elements exhibit allotropy, *e.g.*, sulphur, phosphorus, oxygen, tin and carbon, the most well-known allotropes of carbon being diamond and graphite.

Alloys are combinations of metals made for their valuable special properties, *e.g.*, durability, strength, lightness, magnetism, rust-resistance, *etc*. Some well-known ones are brass (zinc + copper), coinage bronze (copper + zinc + tin), steels (iron + carbon + various other materials), soft solder (tin + lead), dental fillings (mercury + various ingredients).

All Saints' Day (1 Nov) is common to both the Anglican and Roman Catholic Churches, and is in commemoration of the saints generally, or such as have no special day set apart for them. Instituted by Pope Gregory IV in A.D. 835. It was formerly called "All Hallows".

All Souls' Day (2 Nov) is a festival of the Roman Catholic Church, intended for the mitigation by prayer of the sufferings of souls in purgatory. The commemoration was enjoined by Abbot Odilo of Cluny during the 11th cent. upon the monastic order over which he presided, and was afterwards adopted generally in the Roman Communion.

Allspice, a flavouring obtained from a West Indian tree of the myrtle family, *Pimenta officinalis*, likened to the flavour of cinnamon, nutmeg and cloves combined. The berries resemble peppercorns and are used as a spice in mincemeat, *etc*.

Alluvium, river transported deposits of sand, mud and gravel which accumulate to form distinctive features such as levées, flood plains and deltas. The frequent renewal of alluvium by flooding causes riverine lands to be some of the most fertile. In Asia alluvial lands support high densities of population, *e.g.*, The Hwang-ho plains and the Ganges delta.

Almond, the fruit of the *Amygdalus communis*, originally indigenous to Persia, Asia Minor and

N. Africa; now cultivated in Italy, Spain, France, the USA and Australia. It yields both bitter and sweet oil. Bitter almond oil is obtained by macerating and distilling the ripe seeds; it is used for flavouring and scenting purposes, its fragrant odour being due to the presence of benzaldehyde and hydrogen cyanide.

When the seeds are pressed sweet almond oil results: this is used in perfumery, and also as a lubricant for very delicate machinery.

Almuce, a fur stole worn by certain canons.

Aloe, large plants of the lily family, with about 180 species found mainly in the S. African veldt and karroo. The bitter purgative drug (aloes) is prepared by evaporating the plant's sap. *See* **Agave**.

Alpaca, a South American ruminant related to the llama whose long, fine wool is woven into a soft dress fabric known by the same name. Sir Titus Salt first manufactured alpaca cloth (1836).

Until three decades ago, all the world's alpacas were to be found in Peru. Their wool is so soft it was worn by Inca rulers and is still in great demand today.

Alpha Particle, or Alpha-ray, fast-moving helium nucleus ejected by some radioactive atoms, *e.g.*, polonium. It is a combination of 2 neutrons and 2 protons.

Alphabet (so called from the first two letters of the Greek alphabet—alpha, beta) is the term applied to the collection of letters from which the words of a language are made up. It grew out of the knowledge that all words can be expressed by a limited number of sounds arranged in various combinations. The Phoenicians were the first to make use of an alphabetic script derived from an earlier Semitic alphabet (earliest known inscriptions *c*. 1500–950 B.C.) from which all other alphabets have sprung. The stages in the development of the alphabet were mnemonic (memory aids), pictorial (actual pictures), ideographic (symbols), and lastly phonetic. All the ideographic systems died out, with the exception of that of the Chinese.*See also* **Greek Alphabet, G9**.

Altimeter, an instrument used in aircraft to estimate altitude; its usual essential feature is an aneroid barometer which registers the decrease of pressure with height. Roughly 1 millibar corresponds to 9 m. To read an aircraft altimeter correct for its destination, the zero setting must be adjusted for difference of ground height and difference of surface pressure, especially when pressure is falling or when flying towards low pressure.

Altitude, an astronomical term used to signify the angular elevation of a heavenly body; this is measured with a quadrant or sextant. In aeronautics it is the height above sea-level.

Alum is a compound salt used in various industrial processes, especially dyeing, its constituents being the sulphate of one univalent metal or radical (*e.g.*, potassium, sodium, ammonium, rubidium, caesium, silver, thallium) and the sulphate of a tervalent metal (*e.g.*, aluminium, iron, chromium, manganese), and water of crystallisation.

William Pochin (1794–1850) developed the synthetic process which made alum cake (alum does not occur naturally in England).

Alumina is the oxide of aluminium. Very valuable as a refractory material. The ruby is almost 100 per cent. alumina; so also are the emerald, oriental amethyst, etc. An hydrated aluminium oxide is bauxite, chief ore of aluminium from which the metal is extracted electrolytically.

Aluminium, element no. 13, symbol Al, is a light metal which conducts electricity well. Its specific gravity at 20°C is 2·705. Melting point of aluminium is 660·2°C. It is made commercially by electrolysing bauxite dissolved in cryolite (double fluoride of aluminium and sodium). Aluminium alloys are being increasingly used for construction purposes.

Amadavat, a popular cage bird of the weaver family, mainly crimson with spots, so named because the first specimens came from Ahmadabad in India about 1700.

Amalgam is the term applied to any alloy of which mercury forms a part.

Amber, a brittle resinous substance; in origin, fossilised resin. Obtained mostly from the Baltic coasts, and used for ornaments *etc.*

Ambergris is a waxy substance produced in the intestines of the sperm whale, and generally found floating on the sea. It is a valuable perfumery material.

Amblyopsis, a species of fish, practically sightless, and with inoperative organs of hearing and feeling, that inhabit the Mammoth Cave of Kentucky. A remarkable illustration of the failure of senses not brought into use.

Amethyst, the violet variety of quartz, used as a precious stone, containing traces of manganese, titanium and iron. The finest coloured specimens come from Brazil and the Urals.

Amice, a white linen vestment worn by Roman Catholic and many Anglican priests when officiating at Mass or Holy Eucharist.

Amines, organic chemicals composed of carbon, hydrogen and nitrogen. They are derived from ammonia, which they resemble in smell and chemical characteristics. The smell of bad fish is due to the presence of amines. Important industrially as intermediates in a wide variety of products, for example, the synthesis of dye-stuffs and man-made fibres such as nylon.

Amino acids, organic compounds containing an amine group and a carboxylic acid group. They are the "building bricks" of proteins (*q.v.*).

Ammeter, an instrument for measuring the current flowing in an electric circuit. A contraction of ampere-meter. *See* Ampere.

Ammonia, a colourless gaseous compound comprising three atoms of hydrogen to one of nitrogen. Formerly it was made by heating the horns and hoofs of deer, acquiring the name of spirits of hartshorn. The ammonia of commerce is now procured by coal decomposition in the course of gas-making and by direct synthesis. In the very important Haber process of ammonia production by fixation of atmospheric nitrogen, the nitrogen is made to combine with hydrogen and the ammonia so prepared is converted into nitric acid, ammonium nitrate or ammonium sulphate. The Haber process made Germany self-sufficient in nitrates in the first world war. Anhydrous ammonia is ammonia in liquid or gas form – a commonly used fertiliser. Ammonia itself could become the clean fuel of the future.

Ammonites, extinct animals related to the Nautilus. The chambered shell is coiled, usually in a plane spiral. They are confined to Mesozoic rocks. They were once one of the most prolific species on the planet. Named after the Egyptian god Ammon.

Ammonium, the basic radical of ammonium salts, Composed of one atom of nitrogen and four of hydrogen, it behaves chemically like an ion of a monovalent alkali metal. Ammonium chloride is known as "sal ammoniac". "Sal volatile" is ammonium carbonate.

Amnesty, an act of grace by which a ruler or governing power pardons political offenders.

Amnesty International is the world's largest human rights organisation. It seeks to secure the release of prisoners of conscience, works for fair and prompt trials for all political prisoners, and campaigns against torture and the death penalty.
Since 1961, Amnesty has taken on many thousands of cases. There are now well over 4½ million members in local groups spread across almost all the countries of the world. The equivalent US organisation is Human Rights Watch.

Amorphous, a term used to indicate the absence of crystalline form in any body or substance.

Ampere, unit of electric current in the SI system of units; named after André Marie Ampère, who in the 1820s helped to lay the foundations of modern electromagnetism. Defined as that constant current which, if maintained in two parallel rectilinear conductors of infinite length, of negligible circular cross section, and placed at a distance of one metre apart in a vacuum, would produce between these conductors a force equal to 2×10^{-7} newton per metre. *See* **T59.**

Amphioxus *or* **Lancelet,** a primitive chordate (*q.v.*), occurring in sand-banks.

Anabolism. *See* **Catabolism.**

Analysis is one of the major branches of mathematics and includes the theories of differentiation, integration, differential equations etc.

Anchor, an instrument used for keeping ships

stationary. Great improvements have been introduced in recent years, stockless anchors being now chiefly used, consisting of a shank and a loose fluke. Lloyd's rules prescribe the number and weight of anchors which must be carried by merchant ships.

Anchorite is a religious person who retires into solitude to employ himself with holy thoughts. Among the early Christians, anchorites were numerous, but in the Western Church they have been few. Their reputation for wisdom and prescience was high, and kings and rulers in olden days would visit their cells for counsel.
An anchorite or "ankret" was in medieval times a source of fame and often much profit to the monastic house within which he was voluntarily immured.

Anchovy, a fish of the herring family, distinguished by its large mouth and projecting snout, once plentiful in the Mediterranean. Stocks are recovering due to climate change and decline in predators.

Ancient Lights are rights of light enjoyed by a property owner over adjoining land. Such a right is obtained either by uninterrupted enjoyment for twenty years, or by written authority, and once legally established cannot be upset, no building being permissible that would seriously interfere with the privilege.

Anemometer, an instrument for measuring the strength of the wind. In the most widely used pattern the rotation, about a vertical axis, of a group of hemispherical or conical cups gives a measure of the total flow of air past the cups, various registering devices being employed.
The Dines anemograph provides a continuous record of the variation in both velocity and direction; changes of pressure produced in a horizontal tube, kept pointing into the wind by a vane, cause a float, to which a pen is attached, to rise and fall in sympathy with the gusts and lulls.
The hot-wire anemometer, depending upon the change of electrical resistance experienced by a heated wire when cooled, enables very gentle air currents to be investigated.

Aneroid is the kind of barometer which does not depend upon atmospheric support of a mercury (or other liquid) column. It consists of a metallic box, partially exhausted of air, with a corrugated lid which moves with atmospheric changes. A lever system magnifies the lid movements about 200 times and atmospheric pressure is read from a dial. The construction of the vacuum chamber provides automatic compensation for temperature changes. An aneroid barometer is the basic component of an altimeter.

Angelica, an aromatic plant of the Umbelliferae order, *Angelica officinalis,* valuable as a flavouring and possessing medical properties. Once supposed to protect against poison.

Angelus, a church bell rung in Roman Catholic countries, at morn, noon, and sunset, to remind the faithful to say their Angelic Salutation.

Angles, a northern tribe originally settled in Schleswig, who with the Saxons and Jutes invaded Britain in the 5th cent.

Ångström, a unit of length equal to 10^{-10} metres. It is used by astronomers to specify the wavelength of light and ultraviolet radiation. Named after the Swedish physicist A. J. Ångström (1814–74).

Aniline, a simple aromatic compound ($C_6H_5NH_2$) related to benzene and ammonia. It is obtained from coal-tar. The name recalls the fact that it was first prepared by distilling indigo (*anil* is Portuguese for indigo). In 1856 W. H. Perkin (1838–1907) discovered the first aniline or coal-tar dye, mauve, and thus founded the modern dyestuff industry.

Animal Kingdom. *See* **Section T.**

Anise, an umbelliferous plant (*Pimpinella anisum*) found in Egypt and the Levant, and valued for its fruit, aniseed, possessing certain medicinal properties and yielding an aromatic, volatile oil. Also used in cooking. The anise of the Bible is *Anethum graveolens, i.e.,* dill.

Anointing is the pouring of consecrated oil upon the body as a mark of supreme honour. In England it is restricted chiefly to the ceremony of the monarch's coronation, and the spoon with which the oil is applied forms part of the English regalia. In the Roman Catholic Church anointing represents the sacrament of extreme unction.

Ant. There are over 6,000 species of ants, which belong to the same order (Hymenoptera) as the bees, wasps and ichneumon flies. They are social in habit, living in communities of varying size and development. There are three basic castes in ants—the females or *queens*, the *males*, and the *workers* (the last-named being neuter), although specialised forms of workers are sometimes found, *e.g.*, the *soldiers* of the harvesting ants. In the communities of those species of ants which evolved most recently there is a highly complex social life and well-developed division of labour. Some species of these ants make slaves of other species, stealing the cocoons before the adult forms emerge.

Many ants "milk" green-flies, which they protect for their honey-like secretion, and most ants' nests contain many "guests", such as beetles and silver fish. Some ants harvest grains of corn, and others, from S. America, live on fungi which they cultivate in underground "mushroom beds". Ants have lived on the Earth for more than 100 million years.

Antarctic Exploration. In earlier centuries it was thought that a great continent must exist in the southern hemisphere, around the South Pole, to balance the known land masses in the north. Its supposed extent was greatly reduced in the 18th cent., particularly when Capt, Cook sailed for the first time south of the Antarctic Circle, reaching the edge of the ice-pack.

A portion of the ice-covered continent—the coast of Graham Land—was first sighted by Lieut. Edward Bransfield in 1820. The first extensive exploration was made by Capt. James Clarke Ross, who with the *Erebus* and *Terror* penetrated into the Ross Sea in 1841, and discovered the Ross Ice Barrier in 78° South lat.

The Norwegian, C. E. Borchgrevink, in 1898–1900, was the first to winter in the Antarctic and to travel on the ice barrier. The British share in this work was carried out by Capt. R. F. Scott's expedition in the *Discovery*, 1901–4. Scott's party sledged across the barrier to 82° 17′ South, then a record "farthest south". A little later, Ernest Shackleton beat this by travelling to within 160 km of the South Pole. The Scottish polar explorer William Spiers Bruce led the Scottish national Antarctic Expedition of 1902 in the *Scotia* and discovered Coats Land and founded an observatory on the South Orkneys.

In 1910 Captain Scott organised his second expedition in *Terra Nova*, and became engaged against his will in a "race for the Pole" when, after his departure, the Norwegian Arctic explorer, Roald Amundsen, suddenly announced that he was sailing for the Antarctic. Amundsen set up his base at the eastern end of the Barrier, and, relying on dog teams for hauling his sledges, reached the Pole on 14 December 1911.

Meanwhile Scott and his party, their start delayed by adverse weather, were marching southwards, man-hauling their sledges, for Scott was against the use of dogs. After an arduous journey they reached the Pole one month after Amundsen. The return was a struggle against the weather and fatigue, until at last they perished within a few kilometres of their base.

After the first world war the development of the whaling industry greatly stimulated further exploration. Outstanding expeditions included that of Admiral R. E. Byrd, 1929, when he flew over the South Pole; the British Graham Land expedition, 1934, which carried out the first extensive mapping of any part of the Antarctic continent; and the US Navy's Antarctic Expedition of 1940, when the whole continent was circumnavigated.

Some years later, the Antarctic was the scene of much activity during the International Geophysical Year (1957–58). The Commonwealth Trans-Antarctic Expedition set out from opposite sides of the continent and met at the South Pole, the UK party, led by Sir Vivian Fuchs, from the Falklands, and Sir Edmund Hillary and his party from New Zealand. The UK party accomplished the first crossing of the White Continent in 99 days. In 1993, the explorers Sir Ranulph Fiennes and Dr Michael Stroud completed the first unsupported crossing of the Antarctic land mass and the longest unsupported polar journey—both world records. In December 1994, Liv Arnesen (Norway) became the first woman to reach the South Pole alone.

Scientists now working in Antarctica have discovered that around 190,000,000 years ago the frozen waste was once a huge forest roamed by plant-eating dinosaurs. Meanwhile climate warming is now melting the Antarctic ice at a faster rate than at any time in the last 1,000 years (much faster than previously thought). In 2016 scientists discovered an enormous "Grand Canyon" much larger than the American Grand Canyon. Lake Vostok has revealed unknown bacterial life forms. Primitive microbes (*archaea*) have been found in Lake Whillans.

Although Antarctica is home to penguins, whales, seals and numerous birds there are no polar bears. Jellyfish are likely to replace penguins as the dominant species. Thriving ecosystems of clams and bacteria have now been discovered deep below the surface. Since light does not penetrate the organisms do not photosynthesise but use methane to make energy.

The temperature on the polar plateau is −60°C for half the year. The lowest recorded temperature is −93.2°C (in August 2010). Antarctica is the coldest, most isolated and hostile place on earth. Scientists estimate that its vast ice sheets contain *c.* 90% of the world's known fresh water.

Fascination with the wilderness of Antarctica—the last wilderness on the planet—is resulting in a growth of tourism to see the Gentoo penguins *etc.*

Anteaters, a small family (the Myrmecophagidae) of mammals from Central and South America. They feed on ants, termites and other insects which they gather with a long tongue covered with sticky saliva. The anteater is the only mammal without teeth.

Antelope, a variety of hoofed mammal, including gazelles, pronghorns *etc*. They are mainly to be found in Africa. The rare Saiga antelope, found in Mongolia and Russia, is critically endangered. Rarest of all is the hirola of Kenya. The pronghorn is the fastest of all antelopes–it can outrun a cheetah.

Antennae are paired feelers of insects and crustaceans, In radio, the term "antenna" is the equivalent to "aerial".

Anthem, A musical setting of a religious text (biblical or otherwise) in English, for choir with or without instrumental accompaniment. A "full" anthem is choral throughout: a "verse" anthem includes solo voice(s). The genre flourished in the Reformation and early Stuart periods (Tallis, Byrd, Tomkins) and after the Restoration (Locke, Humfrey, Purcell). Later composers of anthems include S.S. Wesley, Stainer, Stanford, Howells and Leighton.

Anthracite is a black coal with a brilliant lustre. It contains 92 per cent. and over of carbon and burns slowly, without smoke or flame. *See* **Coal.**

Anthropocene Epoch. A term which renames the current geological epoch to reflect the impact of humans. The term is particularly used of the atomic age which began in 1945. The Dutch Nobel Laureate Paul Crutzen popularised the term in 2000.

Anthropoid, meaning "resembling man", a sub-order of the primate mammals including man and also the gibbon, chimpanzee, orang-utan, and gorilla.

Anticyclone, a region where barometric pressure is greater than that of its surroundings. Such a system is distinguished on weather charts by a pattern of isobars, usually circular or oval-shaped, enclosing the centre of high pressure where the air is calm. In the remaining areas light or moderately strong winds blow spirally outwards in a clockwise direction in the Northern Hemisphere (and in the reverse direction in the Southern Hemisphere), in accordance with Buys Ballot's law (an observer with back to wind in Northern Hemisphere has lower pressure to left; in Southern to right). Over the British Isles anticyclonic weather is generally quiet and settled, being fair, warm, and sunny in summer and either very cold and often foggy or overcast and gloomy in winter. These systems move slowly and sometimes remain practically stationary for days at a time, that over Siberia being particularly well defined.

Extensive belts of almost permanent anticyclones occur in latitudes 30° N and 30° S. Persistent anticyclonic weather with easterly winds brings our coldest weather.

Antikythera Mechanism. An ancient Greek calculator, rescued from the seabed, which predicted astronomical phenomenon such as solar eclipses (and also dates of the Olympics) with remarkable accuracy. It dates from the 2nd cent. B.C.

Antimony. Metal element, no. 51, symbol Sb. In group 5 of the periodic table. Exists in various forms, the stable form being a grey metal with a layer structure. The other forms are non-conductors. On being burned, it gives off dense fumes of oxide of antimony. By itself it is not of special utility; but as an alloy for hardening other metals, it is much used. As an alloy with lead for type-metal, and with tin and copper or zinc for Britannia-metal, it is of great value. Most important antimony ore is stibnite (antimony sulphide).

Anti-Pope, one elected in opposition to one held to be canonically chosen; applied to the popes Clement VII and Benedict XIII, who resided at Avignon during the Great Schism (1378–1417).

Anti-Proton, the "negative proton", an atomic particle created in high energy collisions of nuclear particles. *See* **Section T.**

Antlers are the branched horns of deer, the branches being called tines. Antlers originate as outgrowths of the frontal bone, and are usually shed once a year. Except in the reindeer and caribou they are restricted to the male.

Antonine Wall. *See* **Roman Walls.**

Aotearoa, meaning "Long White Cloud", the Maori name for New Zealand.

Ape, a term applied to the gorilla, chimpanzee, orang-utan and gibbon—the anthropoid apes.

Aphelion, the point in the orbit of a planet farthest from the sun; the opposite of perihelion. At aphelion the earth is 1.52×10^8 km from the sun.

Aphids, green-flies or plant lice, a numerous species of destructive insects living on young shoots and foliage, some on roots. Reproduction is by *parthenogenesis* (virgin birth). The process means females can become pregnant even before they are born.

Apis, the sacred bull worshipped by the ancient Egyptians; also the scientific name for the bee.

Apogee, that point in the orbit of a heavenly body which is farthest from the earth; used in relation to the sun, moon and artificial satellites. The sun's apogee corresponds to the earth's aphelion. *See* **Perigee.**

Apostasy is a revolt, by an individual or party, from one form of opinions or doctrinate to another. Julian, the Roman Emperor (331–63), brought up as a Christian, became converted to paganism and on coming to the throne (361), proclaimed religious toleration. Hence his name, Julian the Apostate.

Apostles' Creed, the name of the most ancient of the Church's statements of its belief: "I believe in God the Father Almighty; and in Jesus Christ his only Son our Lord, who was born of the Holy Ghost and the Virgin Mary."

A later version is used in the Church of England at morning and evening prayer.

Appian Way, the oldest and finest of the Roman roads originally laid by Appius Claudius (312 B.C.) from Rome to Capua and thence to Brundisium (Brindisi).

Approved Schools were residential schools, subject to Home Office inspection, for the training of young persons under 17 who were guilty of offences or in need of care and protection and had been sent to them by magistrates from juvenile or other courts. The approved school order was abolished by the Children and Young Persons Act 1969. *See* **Young Offenders' Institutions.**

April, the fourth month of the year, from the Roman *Aprilis* derived from *aperire* "to open" —the period when the buds begin to open.

Apse is a semicircular recess, arched or dome-roofed, at the end of the choir, aisles, or nave of a church.

Aquaculture, or fish-farming, is the fastest-growing sector of the world food economy. Half of all fish consumed by humans comes from aqua-culture now.

Aqueducts are conduits in which water flows or is conveyed from its source to the place where it is to be used. Most famous builders were the Romans and the oldest Roman aqueduct was the Aqua Appia, which dates from about 310 B.C. Among modern aqueducts may be mentioned that of Glasgow, which brings water to that city from Loch Katrine; that of Manchester, which taps Thirlmere; that of Liverpool, with Lake Vyrnwy in North Wales as its source, and the

Fron Aqueduct, Powys, which carries water to the Birmingham area. The Pontcysylte aqueduct in Clwyd (the longest and highest in the UK) is now a world heritage site. Massive modern aqueducts have been constructed in China.

Arabian Nights Entertainment or the **Book of a Thousand and One Nights,** a collection of fascinating tales of the Orient, of mixed Indian, Persian, Arabic, and Egyptian origination, and first made known in Europe by Antoine Galland's French translation (1704–17) from Arabian texts. The "master" tale tells how the princess Shahrazad so beguiles the king by telling of the tales over one thousand and one nights that her life was spared.

English translators include E. W. Lane (1840), Sir Richard Burton (1885–8), and John Payne (1882–4).

Arabic Numerals. The modern system of numbering, 0, 1, 2, 3, 4, 5, 6, 7, 8, 9, in which the digits depend on their position for their value is called the Arabic numerical notation. The method is, in fact, of Indian origin. By the 9th cent. Hindu science was available in Arabic, and the Persian mathematician Al-Kwarizimi (*c.* 830) in his *Arithmetic* used the so-called "Arabic" system of numbering. Gradually the method spread to Europe, taking the place of the Roman system which was useless for calculation.

The West is indebted to the Arabs for the zero symbol. It made the invention of decimal fractions possible.

Aragonite, the unstable form of calcium carbonate found as a mineral in some young deposits. It crystallises in the orthorhombic system but tends to revert to calcite.

Archaeopteryx, a fossil bird providing a connecting link between reptiles and birds. It had feathers, jaws with teeth, no bill, reptilian bones and skull, a long tail, and it probably used its fore-limbs for gliding flight. The first specimen, found in 1861, in the Solenhofen limestone of Bavaria, is in London's Natural History Museum. It is *c.* 147 million years old.

Archbishop, the chief of the bishops of an ecclesiastical province in the Orthodox, Roman Catholic, and Anglican churches. In the Church of England there are two archbishops, the Archbishop of Canterbury, called the Primate of *all* England, and the Archbishop of York, styled the Primate of England. *See also* **G11.**

Archimedes' Principle. When a body is weighed in air and then in any fluid, the apparent loss in weight is equal to the weight of fluid displaced. This scientific fact was noted by the Syracusan philosopher Archimedes (287–212 B.C.) and is used as a basis for density measurements.

Arctic Exploration. Modern exploration of the Arctic began in the 16th century when sailors sought to reach the East Indies by passing through the Arctic to the Pacific Ocean.

The North-east Passage, via the shores of northern Asia, was the first attempted. In 1553 and 1554 the English navigators Sir Richard Chancellor and Stephen Burrough sailed into the White Sea, but were prevented by storms and ice from advancing farther eastwards. The project was later revived by the Dutch; Barendts in 1594 discovered Spitsbergen, but failed to get beyond Novaya Zemlya. It was not until 1879 that the Swedish geologist, A. E. Nordenskjöld, in the *Vega*, reached the Pacific.

The attempts to find a North-west Passage were more numerous and determined. In 1585 John Davis penetrated Davis Strait and coasted along Baffin Island. Hopes ran high when Henry Hudson discovered Hudson Bay in 1610, but a practicable passage continued to elude explorers. The problem was to find a navigable route through the maze of channels in the short summer season, and to avoid being frozen in with supplies exhausted. After the Napoleonic Wars the Admiralty sent out many naval expeditions which culminated in Sir John Franklin's expedition with the *Erebus* and *Terror* in 1845. The ships were beset by ice in Victoria Channel and, after Franklin's death, were abandoned by their crews, who perished from scurvy and starvation on their march southwards. To ascertain their fate, several further expeditions were despatched, and the crew of the *Investigator*, commanded by R. J. M'Clure, sailing eastwards from Bering Strait, were the first to make the Passage, though they were obliged to abandon their ship.

It was to be thirty years before the Norwegian, Roald Amundsen, succeeded in sailing the *Gjoa* from the east to west. In the meantime, the North Pole had become the goal of explorers. Nansen, in 1893, put the *Fram* into the ice-pack to drift across the Polar basin, and himself made an unsuccessful attempt on the Pole across the pack. This was eventually achieved by the American explorer Robert E. Peary, who after several expeditions in the North Greenland region, sledged to the Pole with Eskimo companions in 1909.

The next phase was the employment of airships. In 1926 Admiral Byrd made the first flight over the Pole, and in the same year Amundsen and Lincoln Ellsworth flew the airship *Norge* from Spitsbergern to Point Barrow Alaska. Two years later, the *Italia*, commanded by the Italian, Nobile, was wrecked on a return flight from the Pole, and Amundsen lost his life in an attempt to rescue the survivors. Wally Herbert, the explorer who completed the first surface crossing of the Arctic Ocean in 1969 was knighted in 2000. The first voyage under the North Pole was made in 1958 by the American nuclear-powered submarine *Nautilus*.

Scientists are currently reporting that the North Pole icecap itself is today melting faster than previously thought, thus threatening many Arctic species. In time this will allow the economic exploitation of this unexplored region.

Evidence recently uncovered shows that humans inhabited the Arctic 40,000 years ago.

Environmentalists are striving to prevent oil drilling in the Arctic, where a fifth of the word's undiscovered oil and gas is believed to be. They maintain that drilling, even with new technology, will do great damage.

Global warming may even cause the Arctic to vanish by *c.* 2080, with summers seeing the melting of the Arctic ice-cap. The Ward Hunt ice shelf (the largest in the Arctic) is already breaking up. In 2016 the area of the Arctic covered by ice dropped to a record low.

In 2007 Russian explorers planted their national flag on the seabed under the North Pole. Other countries (*e.g.* Denmark and Canada) have claims on the potential of the Arctic. *See also* **North-East Passage** and **North-West Passage**.

Arenaceous Rocks, the rocks composed of grains of sand, chiefly sandstones; quartz is the most abundant mineral in these rocks.

Argali, the Mongolian mountain sheep, the biggest sheep in the world.

Argillaceous Rocks are a sedimentary group, including the shales and clays.

Argon, chemical element no. 18, symbol A. This was the first of the inert gases (*q.v.*) to be isolated from air by Rayleigh and Ramsay in 1894. Argon is used for filling gas-filled metal filament electric lamps. In gas discharge tube it gives a blue glow. *See also* **Rare Gases**.

Arithmetic, the branch of mathematics that deals with numerical calculations as in counting, measuring, weighing. The early civilisations used simple arithmetic for commercial pur-poses, employing symbols and later letters of the alphabet as numerals.

When Hindu-Arabic numerals replaced Roman numerals in the Middle Ages it meant a great step forward and led to many rapid developments—logarithms, slide-rule, calculating machines.

Arithmetic Progression, a sequence of numbers in which the successor of each number is obtained by adding or subtracting a fixed number, for example 2, 5, 8, 11, . . . or 100, 95, 90, 85. . . .

Armadillo, a genus of animals related to the sloths and anteaters, belonging to South America, and carrying a hard bony covering over the back, under which one species (*Tolypeutes*) can completely conceal itself when attacked, rolling itself up like a hedgehog. The Brazilian three-banded armadillo (the mascot for the 2014 World Cup) is under threat. Some armadillos carry the leprosy disease. They can be found as far north as Nebraska and Wisconsin.

Armageddon, according to the Revelation of St. John, the great battle in which the last conflict between good and evil is to be fought.

Armed Forces Day was first held in Britain on 27 June 2009 to honour our armed forces.

Armillary Sphere, an early form of astronomical apparatus with a number of circles representing equator, meridian, ecliptic, *etc.* Used by Hipparchus and Ptolemy and up to the time of Tycho Brahe for determining the position of the stars.

Armistice Day, the day (11 Nov 1918) when the First World War ended is now commemorated each year with a 2-minute silence on Remembrance Sunday.

Aromatic. A term used by chemists, originally to describe compounds like benzene, having a characteristic smell. It is a term which implies a collection of chemical characteristics, the salient features being a flat ring structure and a general similarity to benzene.

Arsenic, a metalloid element, no. 33, symbol As in group 5 of the periodic table usually met with as a constituent of other minerals, sometimes by itself. Its compounds are very poisonous. Lead arsenate is a powerful insecticide used for spraying fruit trees. The more stable allotropic form (grey) has a layer structure, and conducts electricity. Curiously, arsenic trioxide can help fight many cancers.

Artesian Wells take their name from Artois in France, where the first wells of this kind were constructed in 1126. They are to be found only when a water-bearing bed is sandwiched between two impervious beds. When a boring is made to the lower part of the bed, the pressure of water is sufficient to cause the water to overflow at the surface. Artesian wells were known to ancient Egypt and China, and have existed in the Sahara since the earliest times. The fountains in Trafalgar Square were once fed by artesian wells sunk through the London clay into the chalk about 250 m.

Articles. The *Six Articles* are those contained in an Act of Henry VIII, and were of Roman Catholic origin. The *Thirty-nine Articles* were drawn up for the English church at the Reformation. They are printed at the back of the Prayer Book. Candidates for holy orders in the Church of England are required to subscribe to them.

Arum, a genus of plants of the *Araceae* family of which there is but one British species, the wake-robin or cuckoo-pint, sometimes also styled "Lords and Ladies".

Arundel Marbles, a collection of ancient Greek sculptures formed by Thomas Howard, Earl of Arundel in the 17th cent. and presented to Oxford University by his grandson, Henry Howard, who became Duke of Norfolk.

Aryans, nomadic peoples who made their way in successive waves from the Eurasian steppes to the Indus and the Nile during the first half of the 2nd millennium B.C. They crossed the Hindu Kush into N.W. India and settled in the valleys of the Indus and Ganges, where an earlier Indus civilisation had flourished, *c.* 3240–2750 B.C. Their religious ideas are reflected in the Veda (oldest Hindu scriptures, written down many centuries later in Vedic, parent language of Sanskrit). Those who made their way to Syria and Egypt founded the Hyksos empire (*c.* 1720–1550 B.C.).

The Aryans introduced the horse-drawn chariot and spoke a language from which the great Indo-European family of languages is derived, with one group in India and Iran, and another in Europe. Because of the Nazi misuse of the term, Aryan is now referred to as proto-Indo-European. *See also* **Indo-European Languages.**

Asafoetida, an acrid, strong-smelling gum resin exuded from the stem of umbelliferous plant, *Ferula foetida*, found in Iran and Afghanistan. Formerly used medicinally to treat hysteria; still used in cooking in such countries as India.

Ascension Day, or Holy Thursday, is the 40th day after Easter.

Ascot Races are an annual fashionable function dating from 1711 and taking place on Ascot Heath, only 10 km from Windsor, in June. These races have always had royal patronage. The course is *c.* 3 km long.

Ash, a familiar deciduous tree of the genus *Fraxinus*, of over 60 species, native to North temperate regions. The ash held an important place in Norse mythology, as it was supposed to support the heavens with its roots in Hell. The species native to Britain, and also to Europe, is *F. excelsior*, a tall tree with compound leaves, greenish flowers, winged seeds, and black buds in winter. It is a valuable timber tree, tough and elastic, and much used for wheels and handles.

The rowan, or mountain ash, *Sorbus aucuparia*, with similar leaves and orange berries, belongs to a different family. *F. pendula* or weeping ash is a strain which makes an ideal natural summer house. The fungal disease *Chalara fraxinea*, first discovered in Denmark in 2003, spread to Britain in 2012. This ash dieback seems unstoppable. There is currently no known treatment and all across Europe the ash tree could die out completely.

Ashes, The, the symbol which distinguishes the winning cricket team in the Australian Test Matches. In 1882 the Australians won at the Oval by 7 runs. After the match the following epitaph appeared in the *Sporting Times*: "In affectionate remembrance of English Cricket which died at the Oval on 29 Aug. 1882, deeply lamented by a large circle of sorrowing friends and acquaintances. R.I.P. NB. The body will be cremated and the ashes taken to Australia." When the English Eleven went to Australia the same winter it was said that they had come to recover the "ashes". England won two out of three matches, and after the third match the ashes of what was believed to have been a bail were presented in an urn to Ivo Bligh, later Lord Darnley. He bequeathed the urn to the MCC. It is now in the Memorial Gallery at Lord's. However, several historians have doubted the truth of this story. England reclaimed the Ashes in 2015.

Ashmolean Museum, the oldest public museum in the world. Located in Oxford, it was founded in 1683 by Elias Ashmole (1617–92). It reopened in November 2009 after major refurbishment.

Ash Wednesday, first day of Lent.

Asteroids are the tumbling rocks of the solar system. They move in orbits mainly between those of Mars and Jupiter (the asteroid belt). The first to be discovered (by Piazzi in 1801) was Ceres. Many tens of thousands more have since been discovered, of which over 2,000 now have well-determined orbits and have been named. Among the largest are Ceres (800 km), Pallas (500 km) and Vesta (530 km). Then come Hygiea, Davida, Interamnia, Europa, Eunomia, Sylvia and Psyche. Few others have diameters of more than 80 km, while those of the majority are less than 5 or 10 km. Of particular interest are the Trojan group, located at the two stable "Lagrangian" points in Jupiter's orbit round the sun, where their locations make isosceles triangles with the sun and Jupiter. Also, a number of asteroids have orbits like that of Icarus which at perigee (*q.v.*) comes close to the sun.

The first probe designed to study asteroids (NEAR, Near Asteroid Rendezvous), launched in 1996, landed on the Eros 433 asteroid in 2001. This is one of the largest near-Earth asteroids. The Hayabusa probe was the first to land on an asteroid and then return to Earth. The Osiris-Rex probe, launched in 2016, will return to Earth in 2023 with samples from asteroid 1999 RQ36. The Dawn probe launched in 2007 is visiting Ceres (*q.v.*) and Vesta (*q.v.*). Many asteroids are now known to carry ice and water.

The small icy asteroid Chariklo is the smallest known object in the Solar System with its own ring system. The largest asteroid crater on earth has been found in the Australian outback.

NASA has now discovered over 10,000 near-Earth objects.

Astrobiology, a discipline bringing together those searching for extra-terrestrial life in space.

Astrolabe, a medieval scientific instrument for taking altitudes, observing the sun by day and the stars by night, and used for telling the time and finding the latitude. Used by the ancient Greeks, later by the Arabs and Persians, and introduced into Europe in the 14th cent.

Astronomer Royal. *See* **Astronomy** (*below*).

Astronomical Unit, the mean distance between the centres of the sun and earth, or the semi-major axis of the earth's orbit, has a value of about 1·495979 × 10^8 km (149,597,900 km). This value has been constantly improved over the past 300 years, first using observations of the planets, later transits of Venus across the sun's disc, then observations of minor planets such as Eros as they came near the earth, and now by the transit time of a radar beam bounced off the planet Venus. The astronomical unit is

fundamental for astronomers. *See* **Parsec.**

Astronomy. The Pythagoreans believed the stars and planets moved with uniform circular velocity in crystalline spheres, centred round the earth (the "harmony of the spheres"). Hipparchus (190–120 B.C.) made the first star catalogue, discovered the precession of the equinoxes and introduced the idea of epicyclic motion. His planetary system, in the form it was presented by Ptolemy 200 years later, held until the Renaissance when Copernicus revived the heretical view first put forward by Aristarchus of Samos (310–230 B.C.) that the sun and not the earth was at the centre.

Galileo, accurate observer and experimenter, went beyond Copernicus; helped by the contributions of Tycho Brahe, Giordano Bruno, Kepler and others, he was able to overthrow the Ptolemaic system of the heavenly spheres and Aristotelian philosophy and pave the way for Newton and modern astronomy. To Galileo we owe the conception of acceleration; to Newton the theory of universal gravitation; they showed that the same laws govern both celestial and terrestrial physics. Three landmarks in more recent times were the discovery of Uranus by Herschel in 1781 which extended the solar system as then recognised; the estimation by Hubble in 1924 of the distance of Andromeda, which showed that our Galaxy was just one of many; and Einstein's theory of relativity which improved on Newton's theory of the solar system by bringing gravitation into the domain of space-time. Today optical, radio, sub-mm, ultra-violet, gamma ray and X-ray telescopes on the Earth and in space are revolutionising our understanding of astronomy.

The following have held the post of **Astronomer Royal** (period of office in brackets): John Flamsteed (1675–1719), Edmund Halley (1719–42), James Bradley (1742–62), Nathaniel Bliss (1762–65), Nevil Maskelyne (1765–1811), John Pond (1811–35), Sir George Airy (1835–81), Sir William Christie (1881–1910), Sir Frank Dyson (1910–33), Sir Harold Spencer Jones (1933–55), Sir Richard Woolley (1956–72), Sir Martin Ryle (1972–82), Sir Francis Graham Smith (1982–90), Sir Arnold Wolfendale (1991–95) and Sir (now Lord) Martin Rees (1995–). *See also* **Radio Astronomy.**

Astrophysics, the study of the properties, evolution and constitution of objects in the universe. It is concerned with the production and expenditure of energy in such systems as the stars and galaxies and their evolution. It was developed in the 19th century with the application of spectroscopy to the universe at large. Modern advances in particle physics, cosmology, X-ray, gamma-ray, infra-red, ultraviolet and radio astronomy revolutionised this subject. *See* **Astronomy, Cosmology.**

Athanasian Creed, one of the three ancient creeds of the Christian Church, often referred to as the *Quicunque Vult.* It is a statement of the doctrine of the Trinity and the Incarnation, and though named after St. Athanasius, it is thought to be the work of St. Ambrose (339–97).

Atmosphere is the gaseous envelope of the earth, and consists of a mixture of gases (*see* **Air**) and water vapour, the variability of the latter being of great importance meteorologically. The ozone layer, which absorbs solar ultra-violet radiation which would be lethal to plant life if it reached the ground lies between 12 to 50 km above the earth. The lower level of the atmosphere up to a height of about 12 km (10 km at the Poles and 16 km at the Equator) is known as the *troposphere,* and it is here that most weather phenomena occur.

This is the region of most interest to the forecaster studying temperature, humidity, wind-speed, and the movement of air masses. Temperature falls with height by about 1°C per 152 m in this layer. The *tropopause* is the boundary between the troposphere and the *stratosphere.* Temperature varies little in the lower levels of this region: it is mainly cloudless, and has no vertical currents. Strangely enough, the lowest temperatures of the atmosphere are to be found not at the Poles, but at about 18 km above the Equator, where a temperature as low as −80°C has been recorded!

Temperatures begin to rise about 32 km from the earth's surface at about the same rate as they fall in the troposphere owing to the absorption of solar radiation by the concentration of ozone. The stratospheric air is extremely dry. Near the 100 km level a number of important atmospheric phenomena occur. Above this level the oxygen becomes predominantly monatomic in contrast to the normal diatomic form at lower altitudes. This is the *ionosphere* (q.v.). This layer acts as an electrical radio mirror which makes long-distance radio transmission possible. The region of the Van Allen belts (q.v.) above the earth is called the magnetosphere (q.v.).

The auroras are most frequently observed at altitudes between about 100 and 400 km but do extend at times far higher.

Many aspects of the upper air can still only be studied through space-research techniques. These include the composition and temperature of the charged particles in the ionosphere, the location of the electric currents in the ionosphere which produce the regular variations of the compass needle, as well as those which circulate during magnetic storms, the variation of the intensity of different radiation in the air-glow (q.v.) with height, the composition of the air at heights above 32 km, and so on. In addition, the pressures, density, temperatures, and wind distribution of the neutral atmosphere can be studied more directly, in much greater detail, and up to much greater altitudes than is possible if one is confined to the use of equipment on the ground. Instruments outside the atmosphere can make systematic observations on a world-wide basis of the atmospheric circulation, through observation of cloud cover and of the thermal radiation into space from the atmosphere. Such observations are of great importance for meteorology.

The atmospheres of other planets are vastly different to our own. For example, the Venusian atmosphere is considerably denser than the Earth's and is composed primarily of carbon dioxide. Carbon dioxide is also the main constituent of the Martian atmosphere, although this is much thinner than that of the Earth. Titan, the largest satellite of Saturn, has a nitrogen-rich atmosphere. *See also* **Ionosphere.**

Atmospherics are electrical impulses which originate in atmospheric electrical discharges such as lightning. They give rise to crashing background noises in the loudspeakers of radio sets, interfering with reception at distances of up to 6,400 km from the centre of the disturbance. The location of atmospherics with the aid of radio direction-finding methods gives warning of thunderstorms.

Atom. *See* **Section T.**

Atomic Clock. *See* **Clock.**

Atomic Pile, an apparatus containing a fissionable element and a moderator, such as heavy water or graphite, in which a self-sustaining fission process proceeds at a controllable rate. The first atomic pile, constructed on a squash court at Chicago, was operated for the first time on 2 December 1942, under the direction of Enrico Fermi. The pile contained 12,400 lb (5,580 kg) of uranium. *See* **Nuclear Reactors.**

Augsburg Confession, name given to the doctrine of faith of the Lutheran churches, drawn up by Melanchthon and endorsed by Luther for the Diet of Augsburg (1530).

August, named after the Emperor Augustus, because it was his "lucky" month.

Auks, duck-like sea-birds, black and white, with short, narrow wings, compact bodies and legs set well back. Breed in colonies on rocky coasts of N. Europe (incl. British Isles) and spend most time in coastal waters. Migrate south in winter. The Auk family includes the Razorbill, Little Auk, Guillemot and Puffin.

The Great Auk became extinct in 1844 after ruthless hunting for its feathers.

Aurochs were long-horned beasts, an ancestor of domestic cattle. They died out in Britain nearly 3,000 years ago. They stood six feet tall.

Aurora Polaris. This wonderful phenomenon of the night sky is a common sight at high northern and southern latitudes, where it is called the *aurora borealis* and the *aurora australis* respectively. It is visible less often at temperate latitudes, and only rarely in the tropics. The auroral ovals, or zones of maximum frequency of aurora, surround both of the earth's geomagnetic poles, and the northern auroral oval includes the northern parts of Scandinavia, Canada and Alaska. The aurora is the visible manifestation of complex plasma processes

occurring within the earth's magnetosphere (q.v.), whereby streams of high-energy electrons and protons (mainly) are accelerated and dumped via the earth's magnetic field lines into the upper atmosphere. This mechanism produces the light emission of the aurora.

The brightest aurora, which may also extend to lower latitudes, occurs during geomagnetic storms, which are complex and large-scale plasma instabilities within the magnetosphere triggered by fluctuations in the solar wind (q.v.) —usually ascribed to "M" regions on the sun associated with coronal holes, flares and active sunspot groups.

Auroral displays may take several forms—a faint glow, a diffuse ribbon of light crossing the heavens, great folded waving curtains or draperies, or the entire sky may be flooded with a rapidly varying brilliant panoply of light.

The aurora is a kind of light essentially different from that of the rainbow which is a partly subjective phenomenon. Each beholder sees his own rainbow, whose light is sunlight refracted and reflected by many raindrops. The raindrops that produce his rainbow depend on his position as well as on the direction of the sun. The aurora, on the contrary, is a light as objective as that of a candle, though produced differently. It is a self-luminescence of the air in regions of the atmosphere that lie far above the clouds.

Images from NASA's Polar spacecraft have confirmed the theory that auroras in the northern and southern hemispheres are nearly mirror images of each other. Such planets as Jupiter and Saturn have their own aurora.

Auto-da-Fé, or Act of Faith, was the ceremony connected with the sentencing of heretics under the Inquisition of Spain and Portugal, those found guilty being imprisoned or burned alive.

Automation is a technical word used to designate the adoption of methods of automatic control either of manufacturing processes or of any business process involving a large mass of routine work. The word is used in broader and narrower senses. In its broadest sense it covers any form of mechanisation which largely replaces human labour by the work of automatic or semi-automatic machines, such as has been in progress continuously since the Industrial Revolution; but it it better kept to a narrower meaning, in which it is confined to the modern development of electronic or similar devices, involving feedback (automatic detection and correction of malfunction). Human labour is virtually eliminated.

Autumn, the third season of the year, begins with the autumnal equinox, and ends with the winter solstice, but the term is used to cover the period from mid-August to mid-November.

Auxins, "plant hormones", the organic substances produced by plants to regulate growth. Synthetic auxins are now widely used, *e.g.*, for promotion of root formation in cuttings, differential weed control, prevention of premature dropping of fruit, in storage of potatoes *etc.* and to overcome frost damage to fruit buds.

Avalanches occur when layers of snow become unstable. Each of these 'white deaths' can send more than 1 million tons of ice, rock and snow thundering down mountain-sides.

Average is a single number designed to give a typical example of a set of numbers, *e.g.*, a cricketer's batting average for a season gives an idea of his typical score. There are several kinds of average and their uses are studied in the science of statistics (q.v.). A statement that "so and so is the average value" can be misleading if one does not know which average is meant. Three common averages are: the arithmetic average (or mean), the mode, and the median. The arithmetic average of n numbers is found by adding them together and dividing by n; this is a very common method of averaging. The mode of n numbers is the most frequently occurring number. The median is the middle number, *i.e.*, the number which is smaller than just as many of the other numbers as it exceeds. Of the numbers 1, 2, 2, 2, 3, 4, 5, 6, 8, 9, the arithmetic means is 4, the mode is 2, the median is 3.

Avocet, a graceful wading bird related to the stilts, of black-and-white plumage, bluish legs, and slender upturned bill. There are four species.

Avocets nest in colonies. The return of the avocet has been an astonishing success story for the RSPB. It has an elaborate and fascinating courtship ritual.

Avogadro's Hypothesis. This is a fundamental concept of chemistry. Equal volumes of all gases under the same conditions of temperature and pressure contain the same number of molecules. This law was instrumental in assigning the formulae of molecules. The hypothesis was put forward in 1811, but not accepted until 1860.

Aye-Aye, the world's largest nocturnal primate.

Axion, a particle whose existence was first suggested in 1974. It weighs nothing, has no electric charge and exists for less than a nanosecond—but it may be a major component of dark matter.

Aztecs, the name of a powerful people found in Mexico when the Spaniards first discovered that country. At the height of Aztec power, c. 1325, their empire controlled a huge area of central America. There was an intricate system of tributes and blood sacrifice. The Spanish conquest obliterated much of their history and tradition. Centred on the capital Tenochtitlan, the empire stretched as far as Guatemala, Belize and El Salvador. Aztec cities are today acknowledged as design masterpieces.

B

Babiroussa, a ferocious, long-legged wild pig, native of Sulawesi, sometimes called the horned-hog, because of the long upper tusks in the male, which are developments of the canine teeth.

Baboon, monkeys belonging to the African genus *Papio.* They are considered the lowest of the Old World (Catarrhine) monkeys, and walk on all fours. In the main terrestrial, but take to trees after food. The mandrill is closely related. The DNA of baboons is 91 % the same as human.

Babylonian Captivity, the period spent by the Jews in Babylon after Jerusalem fell to Nebuchadnezzar, the Babylonian emperor, in 586 B.C.

The term is also applied to the period 1309–78 when the papacy moved to Avignon.

Baccalaureate, a broadly-based academic diploma widely-used in Europe. It is set by a Swiss-based examination board.

Bacteriophage (Phage), literally "bacteria eater", *i.e.,* a virus which specifically infects bacteria. In common with viruses which attack animal or plant cells, isolated phages are inert, and can only reproduce by making use of the chemical apparatus of a more sophisticated host cell (in this case a bacterium). However phages may be of two types, virulent or temperate. Virulent phages completely disrupt the normal functioning of the infected bacterium and adapt its reproductive mechanism to produce more phage. This eventually kills the bacterium and the newly assembled phages are released. Temperate phages on the other hand may enter into a remarkable symbiotic relationship with the bacterium, known as lysogeny. The phage genetic material is incorporated into that of the bacterium and is reproduced each time the still functioning bacterium subsequently divides. Furthermore the bacterium is immune from attack by potentially virulent phages of the same type. When such lysogenic bacteria die, phage particles may again be released. Phages carried in lysogenic bacteria are in a state known as prophage and it is often difficult to obtain pure, prophage-free strains of bacteria. Phages have been extensively used in research on genetics and molecular biology.

Badger, a carnivorous mammal related to the weasel, of nocturnal and burrowing habits, inoffensive, subsisting chiefly on roots and insects, though sometimes mice, young rabbits and eggs form part of its diet. The badger does little harm and quite a lot of good. In Britain the badger is partly protected, but Ministry officials may destroy the animal in areas where bovine TB exists. Pilot badger culls began in the West Country in 2013 (badgers are blamed for the spread of bovine TB by urinating on the fields where cattle graze). These culls are now being extended. The 1992 Badger Protection Act led to greatly increased numbers.

Bagpipe. Once popular all over Europe, this instrument is still played in Scotland, Ireland,

Brittany and elsewhere. The bag acts as a reservoir of air and, when squeezed by the player's arm, forces air through the pipes. One of these, the Chanter pipe, provides the tune and is played by the fingers as in a flageolet. The remainder, the Drone pipes, give a continuous, unvarying note.

Bailey Bridge, invented by Sir Donald Bailey and first used in the N. African campaign 1942–3. Built up of prefabricated girders, it can be easily transported and erected.

Bailiwick, a feudal term denoting the limits of a bailiff 's jurisdiction. The term has survived in the Channel Islands (e.g. Jersey and Guernsey).

Baldachin (It. *Baldachino*), a canopy usually supported by four pillars over throne, altar *etc.*

Balearic Crane, the crowned crane of the Balearic Islands and the North African mainland, distinguished by its yellowish, black-tipped occipital tuft and by its trumpet note.

Baleen *or* "whalebone" the name given to a series of horny plates growing from the roof of the mouth in those whales classified as Whalebone or Baleen Whales (*Mystacoceti*). There are 300–400 or so plates on each side. Their inner edges are frayed, the whole system constituting a filter for collecting minute organisms used for food.

The Baleen Whales include the Right-Whales, Pacific Grey-Whales and Rorquals. *See* **Whales.**

Ballet is a combination of four arts; dancing, music, painting, and drama, each of which is ideally of equal importance. The movement of the individual dancers and the "orchestration" of the whole group is in the hands of the choreographer. The dancer's training follows certain basic rules but save in classical ballet there is considerable freedom of movement.

Ballet today developed professionally at the Court of King Louis XIV of France, though it owes its origins to Italy and in the earliest times to Greece and Rome. Its movements were made up from the dances of courtiers, country folk and tumblers. Technique grew more complex as costume became modified, the body gaining complete freedom with the invention of tights. A succession of great dancers—French, Italian and latterly Russian left their imprint on the art. Contemporary ballet reflects the aesthetics of the Russian, Sergei Diaghilev. In England Dame Ninette de Valois laid the foundation of a national ballet, at Sadler's Wells and Covent Garden. A Royal Charter was granted in 1957 setting up the Royal Ballet to co-ordinate the work of the Sadler's Wells group. *See* **Section P.**

Ballistics, the science dealing with the motion of projectiles, especially shells, bombs and rockets.

Balloon, the modern balloon consists of a bag of plastic material inflated with a gas lighter than air. The first ascent by man in a hot-air balloon was made on 21 November 1783, and in a hydrogen balloon on 1 December 1783. The most famous of the early scientific flights by manned balloons were those of the Englishmen Coxwell and Glaisher, in 1862, when a height of 11 km was reached. The first aerial crossing of the English Channel by Blanchard and Jeffries was made on 7 January 1785. Piccard's ascent to 16 km, in 1931, marked the conquest of the stratosphere. Four years later the American balloon *Explorer II*, inflated with nearly 112,000 m³ of helium, carried a team of scientists with their floating laboratory to an altitude of 23 km. In 2002 the American Steve Fossett became the first solo balloonist to circle the globe non-stop. In 2016 the fastest around-the-globe record was established by a Russian priest, Father Fedor Konyukhov.

Balsam, a big genus (140 species) of flowering plants. Many species are cultivated for their showy flowers, *e.g., Impatiens noli-me-tangere,* the yellow balsam or "touch-me-not", so called because the fruit explodes when touched, slinging out the seeds. Balsam fir is a conifer (*Abies balsamea*) from which Canada balsam gum is obtained.

Bamboo, a genus of strong grasses, some species growing to over 36m in height; much used in Asia for all kinds of purposes. Half the world's woody bamboo species is under threat of extinction as a result of forest destruction. China producer c. 80 % of the world's bamboo, while around 1 bn people live in houses made of bamboo.

Banana (family *Musaceae*), a large herbaceous plant cultivated in moist regions of the tropics, and one of the most productive plants known. The main areas of commercial cultivation are in tropical America, the Canary Islands and West

Africa. Bananas have overtaken the apple to become the favourite fruit in Britain, but they are threatened with a rapidly-spreading fungal disease (known as Panama disease).

Bandicoots, Australasian marsupial mammals, of the size of a large rat or rabbit. They are burrowing animals living largely on insects. The rabbit-eared bandicoot, restricted to Australia, has shrew-like snout, long ears like a rabbit, long crested tail, and a silky coat. The long-nosed bandicoot has a spiny coat and comes from E. Australia. The pig-footed bandicoot has two functional toes on the foot, like a pig.

Bank of England. Founded by Royal Charter on 27 July 1694. Known as "The Old Lady of Threadneedle Street". It was established to raise funds for William III's; war against France.

Bank Holidays. Public holidays in England and Wales comprise at present six bank holidays (New Year's Day, Easter Monday, May Day, Spring and Late Summer Holidays at the end of May and August respectively, and Boxing Day), with also two common law holidays (Good Friday and Christmas Day); in Scotland (beginning in 1996) seven bank holidays (New Year's Day, Good Friday, Easter Monday, May Day, Spring and Late Summer Holidays at the end of May and August respectively, and Christmas Day); and in Northern Ireland seven bank holidays (New Year's Day, St. Patrick's Day, Easter Monday, May Day, the Spring Late Summer Holidays at the end of May and August respectively, and Boxing Day) plus two other public holidays (Easter Tuesday and the anniversary of the Battle of the Boyne).

There are holidays in lieu of those public holidays which fall at weekends. In Scotland and Northern Ireland a general holiday is not necessarily observed on the same day as a bank holiday.

Bantu (native word = people), term loosely used for large family of black races of Southern Africa.

Baobab, a tropical African tree. The species *Adansonia digitata* is one of the largest trees known, though not the tallest; the trunk can reach 9 m in thickness. The fruit is woody, but its juice provides a cooling beverage (high in vitamin C). Its fruit is a powerhouse of nutrients. The bark yields a fibre used for making rope and cloth.

The baobab is the national symbol of Madagascar.

Barbary Ape, a large monkey belonging to the genus *Macaca*. It is the only monkey living in relative freedom in Europe, a small colony existing on the Rock of Gibraltar. It has no tail.

Barberry, a genus of berry-producing shrubs containing a hundred species. Several species are cultivated for their flowers and bright berries. Has an interesting pollination mechanism; the base of each stamen is sensitive to touch, and insects probing for nectar cause top of stamen to spring inwards, so dusting visitor's head with pollen which can then be carried to the next flower visited. The common barberry (*Berberis communis*) harbours one stage of the fungus that causes rust of wheat.

Barbican, a fortified entrance to a castle or city, with projecting towers. In the London area called Barbican there was formerly a barbican in front of the city gates.

Barbiturates. A group of drugs derived from a parent compound called barbituric acid: phenobarbitone is the best-known example. They induce sleep and are used in the manufacture of sleeping pills, but they can be habit forming.

Barcarolle, a Venetian gondolier's song.

Bard, among the ancient Celts a poet or minstrel whose mission was to sing of heroic deeds. He was supposed to have the gift of prophecy, and was exempt from taxes and military service.

Barilla, soda carbonate or soda ash obtained by burning certain salt-marsh plants (*e.g.*, the saltwort, *Salsola kali*). It used to be in great demand, until the product of the Leblanc and then the Solvay ammonia-soda process was made available by the chemical industry.

Barium, metal element, no. 56, symbol Ba. In group 2 of the periodic table. The metal is soft and easily cut. It occurs as the sulphate and carbonate in nature. It was first prepared by Sir Humphry Davy in 1808, as an amalgam, by electrolysis of barium chloride. The pure metal was not isolated until 1901.

Barnacles constitute a sub-class (*Cirripedia*) of the Crustacea. The barnacle fouling the bottom of ships is the Goose Barnacle, which has a long muscular stalk and a shell composed of five plates. The Acorn Barnacles, which cover rocks, breakwaters, etc., just below high-water mark are similarly constructed, but have no stalk. The manner of feeding of barnacles was vividly described by T. H. Huxley, who said the barnacle is "a crustacean fixed by its head kicking the food into its mouth with its legs". It was a naval surgeon, J. Vaughan Thompson, who discovered in 1830 that barnacles have a free-swimming larva (or nauplius). In the Middle Ages a curious myth grew up to the effect that the Barnacle changed into a sea-bird called, for that reason, the Barnacle Goose.

Barnard's Star. A star discovered by the American astronomer Edward Emerson Barnard in 1916 and which has the largest stellarproper motion known. Barnard's Star is one of the closest stars to us and also one of the intrinsically faintest stars known.

Barometer is an instrument for measuring atmospheric pressure, invented at Florence by Torricelli, pupil of Galileo, in 1643. The standard method consists of balancing the air column against a column of mercury, used on account of its high density. The mercury is contained in a long glass tube, closed at one end, and inverted in a cistern also containing mercury. The height of the mercury column, supporting the air column, is taken as the pressure at the time, and can be read off very accurately by means of a vernier scale. Present-day tendency is to express the readings in units of pressure instead of length, the millibar being adopted (1 mb = 1,000 dynes per sq. cm.; 1,000 mb ≡ 75 cm of mercury approx.). The standard instrument is correct for pressures at 0°C in Lat. 45°, so that corrections have to be applied for temperatures and latitudes other than these. Also a correction has to be made for reducing the pressure to mean sea level. *See* **Aneroid.**

Baron, title given in feudal England to a man who held his land directly from the king by military or other honourable service. The first baron created by letters patent was John Beauchamp de Holt, Baron of Kidderminster, in 1387. A baron is a member of the fifth and last grade of the peerage of the United Kingdom and is addressed as "Lord". Life peers and life peeresses rank with hereditary barons and baronesses according to the date of their creation. In Scotland the term baron is used of the possessor of a feudal fief, or the representative by descent of such a fief. The equivalent of the English baron, as a rank of the Scottish peerage, is Lord of Parliament.

Baronet, the lowest hereditary title, instituted by James I to provide funds for the colonisation of Ulster. The first baronet was Sir Nicholas Bacon. Between 1964 and 1983 no recommendations for hereditary honours were made. In 1990 the Queen bestowed the title on Denis Thatcher.

Barque, a small sailing vessel with three or four masts. A three-masted barque has fore- and mainmasts square-rigged, the mizzenmast fore- and aft-rigged.

Barramundi, a tropical fish much prized in Australia.

Barrow is an ancient artificial mound of earth or stone raised over the site of a burial. In Britain barrows were built from 2500 B.C. until the late Saxon period, but the Egyptian are the earliest barrows known, the great pyramids being a spectacular development of the custom of ceremonial burial. Silbury Hill, south of Avebury, is the biggest artificial mound in Europe, 512 m in circuit at the base, 96 m at top, and 41 m high.

Baryons, the group of heavier subatomic particles which includes the proton, neutron, lambda and omega-minus particles (and their corresponding anti-particles, called anti-baryons). Baryons interact by means of all the known forces of nature (strong, weak, electromagnetic and gravitational). However, in any closed system the total baryon number (*i.e.*, the number of baryons minus the number of anti-baryons) is constant. This means that the proton, being the lightest known baryon, must be stable against spontaneous decay. Unlike the lighter leptons (*q.v.*), baryons are now thought to have internal structure reflecting the fact that they are composed of quarks (*q.v.*) *See also* **Section T.**

Basalt Rocks are fine-grained, dark coloured, of igneous origin and occur either as lava flows as in

Mull and Staffa, or as intrusive sheets, like the Edinburgh Castle Rock and Salisbury Crags. One of the best examples of columnar basalt is the Giant's Causeway in Ireland.

Basanite (Lydian Stone), a smooth black siliceous mineral, or flinty jasper; a crypto-crystalline quartz used as a touchstone for testing the purity of gold, *etc.*, by means of the mark left after rubbing the metal with it.

Base, a substance having a tendency to accept a proton (H⁺). This is a wide definition and covers unconventional types of compounds. In aqueous solution bases dissolve with formation of hydroxyl ions, and will neutralise an acid to form a salt. In non-aqueous solvents, like liquid ammonia or hydrogen fluoride, compounds classically regarded as salts can be bases, *e.g.*, sodium fluoride is a base in hydrogen fluoride solution.

Basilisk, is a lizard of aquatic habits, with an elevated crest (which it can erect or depress at will) down the centre of its back.

Basques, people of N. Spain and S.W. France, oldest surviving racial group in Europe, who have preserved their unique ancient language.

Bastille, a castle or fortress in Paris, built in the 14th cent., and used as a state prison, especially for political offenders. It was stormed and demolished on 14 July 1789, at the start of the Revolution.

Bastinado, a cruel punishment, by beating with a pliable cane on the soles of the feet.

Bats. These mammals fly by means of a membrane stretched between each of the long fingers of the hand and between the fifth finger and the body. Another membrane stretches between the legs and the tail. Most British bats, including the pipistrelle, long-eared bats, noctules, belong to the family *Vespertilionidae* (with the exception of the horseshoe bats which belong to the family *Rhinolophidae*). These all feed on insects which they catch on the wing. Vampire bats (there are 3 species) are found across Latin America. Vampire bats use infra-red sensors on their noses to find blood close to the skin of their victims. A drug derived from vampire bat saliva is being used to help stroke victims.

The problem of how bats can detect their insect prey and avoid obstacles when flying in total darkness was solved with the advent of sensitive ultrasonic recording devices.

Scientists now know that bats can distinguish between two objects the width of a pencil line apart by using their sonar echo. Blindness does not affect this ability but deafness leaves bats comparatively helpless. Bats also adjust their internal compasses to the way light is scattered at sunset. A unique array of wing sensors gives bats the key to their aerial manoeuvrability.

One of the most interesting types of bat is the fishing bat (*Noctilio*) found in central America, which can detect fish by being able to receive echoes from the ripples they make on the water surface. Across the world, there are 1,100 species of bats, but around one in five is now at risk from habitat loss. There are 17 breeding species of bat in Britain, but their numbers have now revived after a long decline. The bamboo bat of China is one of the tiniest mammals in the world. The Australian fruit bat (or flying fox) is the largest in the world. *See* **Ultrasonics.**

Bath, Order of the, Britain's second oldest order of knighthood. Exclusive to men since its institution by Henry IV in 1399, women became eligible for admission to the order in 1971.

Battery, Electric, the common term for an electric cell but really meaning a combination of two or more cells. A cell is a device for converting stored chemical energy into electricity which can then be used for heat, light, traction, or any desired purpose. A *primary* cell will do this until the chemical action is completed and the cell is then useless. In a *secondary* cell, the chemical actions are reversible and the cell can be returned to its initial condition and used again. This is done by passing an electric current through—a process called recharging.

A common primary cell is the Leclanché dry cell; used in torches. This works by the action of sal-ammoniac on electrodes made of zinc and carbon. About a century after it came into common use it is still the chief source of power for portable equipment in armed forces. A common secondary cell is the lead and sulphuric

acid accumulator used in cars. Many other types of cell are known and some are under development because the demands of space travel, medicine, warfare, *etc.*, call for batteries of lighter weight, greater reliability, or special properties. *See* **Fuel Cell, Energy Conversion.**

Bauxite, the chief source of aluminium. Chemically it is aluminium oxide. Aluminium metal is made industrially by electrolysing purified bauxite dissolved in fused cryolite.

Bayeux Tapestry, famous embroidery representing the conquest of England by William the Conqueror. It is embroidered on a band of linen 70 m long and 51 cm wide in blue, green, red and yellow, divided into 72 scenes ranging over the whole story of the conquest. The accepted view is that the tapestry was commissioned for Bayeux Cathedral, but another interpretation is that it is an Anglo-Norman secular work of art, much influenced by the contemporary *chansons de geste* (songs of deeds), executed by English embroiderers for a Norman patron. A representation can be seen in the V&A Museum.

Beagle, a small hound that tracks by scent.

Bears belong to the Ursidae family of the Carnivora. They are plantigrade mammals, walking (like humans) on the soles of their feet. Found in most parts of the world except Australia. The common Brown Bear was once spread over the whole of Europe; it became extinct in England about the 11th cent.; 2–2·5 m in length, and stands 1 m or more at the shoulder.

The Grizzly Bear of N. America is larger, and the coat is shorter and greyer. The Polar Bear is remarkable in having a white coat all the year round; it spends much time in water, and unlike other bears is entirely carnivorous. The polar bear is the most powerful of all predators. Bearbaiting was made illegal in England in 1835. The brown bears of Europe are at last witnessing a revival. The spectacled bear is the most threatened. Sloth bears are indeed true bears, but gain their name from their resemblance to sloths.

It is now known that polar bears are cannibals. Climate change poses a challenge to the future of the Arctic polar bear (there are around 20–30,000 polar bears in the wild, from Russia to Alaska and from Canada to Greenland and Norway's Svalbard archipelago). They are now on the endangered list, but attempts to ban the international trade in their skins, teeth *etc* failed in 2010.

Beaver, a genus of mammals of the Rodentia order, with short, scaly ears, webbed hind feet, and a long broad scaly tail. They grow up to 1·2 m long, and live in communities, constructing complex dams and lodges where they breed. They have now made an impressive comeback to Britain and Europe. The beaver, Europe's largest rodent, weighs nearly 45lbs. Hunted for its pelts. Newborn beavers are known as kits. They are rightly called busy beavers.

Bedlam (a corruption of Bethlehem) was a priory in Bishopsgate, afterwards converted into a hospital for lunatics. The asylum was transferred to St. George's Field, Lambeth, in 1815.

Bedouin, the nomads of the desert. The name comes from the Arabic for desert dweller.

Bee. *See* **Humble-bee L54–5.**

Beech, a deciduous tree belonging to the genus *Fagus* of some eight or nine species found in north temperate regions. The common beech, *F. sylvatica*, is believed to be native to Britain and is one of our finest trees, with massive trunk, long, pointed winter buds, and smooth, grey bark. There is little undergrowth under its dense shade. It is shorter-lived than the oak taking about 200 years to reach full size and then declining. The timber of beech has a variety of uses, *e.g.*, spoons, handles, chairs, *etc.*

Bee-eater, name of a family of brilliantly coloured birds closely related to the rollers and kingfishers inhabiting the tropical and sub-tropical parts of Africa, Asia and Europe. The European species successfully nested in Britain back in the 1950s.

With their long curved beaks they catch insects on the wing, especially bees and butterflies, and lay their eggs in dark tunnels.

Beefeater, *See* **Yeomen of the Guard.**

Beeswax, the secretion of the bee, used for the formation of the cells or honey-comb of the hive; when melted it is what is commercially known as yellow wax, white wax being made by bleaching. Being impervious to water, it acts as a good resistant and is an article of much utility.

Beetles (Coleoptera) constitute one of the biggest orders of insects, numbering over 350,000 species. There are two pairs of wings; the hind pair are used for flight, while the front pair are hardened to form a pair of protective covers (elytra). Some beetles have lost the power of flight and then the elytra are joined together. Beetles are the planet's most enduring species.

Bell, a hollow body of metal used for making sounds. Bells are usually made from bell-metal, an alloy of copper and tin. Small bells used for interior functions are often made of silver, gold or brass. Ordinary hand-bells are of brass. From the 7th cent. large bells were used in England in cathedrals, churches and monasteries. The greatest bell in the world is the "King of Bells" in the Kremlin at Moscow which weighs about 198 tonnes, is 627 cm high and 691 cm in diameter. It was cast in 1733 but cracked in the furnace (the broken part weighed 11 tonnes) and is now preserved as a national treasure.

The Great Bell (Great Paul) at St. Paul's, cast in 1881, weighs nearly 17 tonnes and is the largest in the UK.

Other huge bells are the Great Bell at Beijing (53 tonnes); Nanjing (22 tonnes); Cologne Cathedral (25 tonnes); Big Ben, Westminster (over 13 tonnes); Great Peter, York Minster (10 tonnes). The Curfew Bell is rung in some parts of England to this day, notably at Ripon.

The number of changes that can be rung on a peal of bells is the *factorial* of the number of bells. Thus four bells allow 24 and eight bells 40,320.

Belladonna or **Deadly Nightshade** (*Atropa bella-donna*), a well-known poisonous wild plant found in Southern Europe and Western Asia. The alkaloid atropine it contains is valuable in medicine, although a large dose is poisonous.

Benedicite, the canticle in the Book of Common Prayer, "The Song of the Three Holy Children".

Benedictines are monks and nuns of the Benedictine Order who live under the rule of St. Benedict—the monastic code whose influence on the religious and cultural life of the West has been so powerful. The rule is marked by an absence of extravagant asceticism.

The greatest of the early Benedictines was Pope Gregory I (590–604) who sent St. Augustine of Canterbury to convert Anglo-Saxon England. Gregorian plainsong is named after him. Benedictine (probably the oldest liqueur in the world) was first made by a Benedictine monk.

Benin Bronzes, the name for hundreds of artefacts looted in colonial times from Benin City in southern Nigeria. They were created by the Edo people from the 13th century.

Benzene. An aromatic hydrocarbon obtained from coal tar and some petroleum fractions. It is a volatile inflammable liquid with a characteristic smell. The molecule consists of a flat ring of six carbon atoms, each bound to one hydrogen atom. Benzene is the parent member of many aromatic organic compounds and is widely used in industry to synthesise intermediates for fibres, dyestuffs, explosives *etc.*

Beryl, a mineral, of which the emerald is a grass-green variety. It is composed of beryllium and aluminium silicates. The pure mineral is colourless; the colour of most beryl comes from traces of impurities, notably iron and chromium. Otherwise it is yellowish, greenish-yellow, or blue, and is found in veins which traverse granite or gneiss, or embedded in granite, and sometimes in alluvial soil formed from such rocks.

Beryllium. Metallic element, no. 4, symbol Be. Very similar to aluminium, it is stronger than steel and only one-quarter its weight. It is not very abundant, its main source is the mineral, beryl. Copper containing 2 per cent. beryllium is used for making springs. Because of its special properties the metal is used as a component in spacecraft, missiles and nuclear reactors. This accounts for its recent development on a technical scale. The metal powder is toxic.

Bessemer Process for making steel depends on the forcing of atmospheric air into molten pig iron to burn out the impurities. Ousted by the oxygen converter. *See* **Steel.**

Betel, the leaf of an Indian climbing plant, of pungent, narcotic properties. It is destructive to the teeth, and reddens the gums and lips.

Bhang, the Indian name for the hemp plant *Cannabis sativa,* the leaves and seed-capsules of which are chewed or smoked. The drug which comes from flowers of the female plant is called hashish in Arabia and marihuana in the USA.

Big Bang Theory, a cosmological model in which all the radiation and matter in the universe originated in an explosion at a finite time in the past. It is thought the universe came into existence between 10 and 15 thousand million years ago.

Billion, formerly in English usage a million million; now a thousand million or 10^9.

Binary Notation, for numbers, is a way of representing numbers using only two digits, 0 and 1. Electronic digital computers handle numbers in this form. The ordinary, or decimal numbers, 0, 1, 2, 3, 4, 5, 6, 7, 8, 9, 10 are written in binary notation as follows: 0, 1, 10, 11, 100, 101, 110, 111, 1000, 1001, 1010. The reader might divine the rules from this. The point is you "carry 1", *i.e.*, move the digit 1 a place to the left, when you reach 2. In decimal notation you move 1 a place left when you reach 10. In other words, instead of columns for units, tens, hundreds, thousands, *etc.*, the columns are for units, twos, fours, eights, *etc.* In binary notation: "1 + 1 = 0 with 1 to carry". Since every digit in binary notation is either 0 or 1 it requires one bit of information to specify a binary digit.

Bioethanol, a derivative of ethanol in the form of ethyl-tertio-butyl-ether (ETBE), used as fuel and processed from agricultural crops (*e.g.* rape). The first plant in Britain opened in Norfolk in 2008.

Biofluorescence, the process that enables organisms to absorb light, transform it and reflect it in a different colour.

Biological Clock. All living organisms undergo cyclical changes in activity of some sort. These are linked to the changes in their environment which are produced by the alternation of night and day, the phases of the moon and the tides, and the cycle of the seasons. These cycles of activity frequently persist if the organism is put into a constant environment in which there appear to be no external clues as to what time or what season it is. A squirrel, for example, wakes up at about the same time each evening even when it is put into constant darkness. It is usual to refer to these activity patterns as being driven by a biological clock inside the organism. But very little is known about how these biological clocks work.

Biological Warfare is the use for warlike purposes of bacteria, viruses, fungi, or other biological agents.

Bioluminescence. The spectacular, magical light produced by such living things as glow-worms, fire-flies and plankton.

Biometrics, detailed measurements of human characteristics, such as the iris or fingerprints, now used in high-tech security systems. Airports are starting to use retinal scans to check identities.

Biosensors, micro-electronic or optoelectronic devices used to sense the presence of chemicals. This new technique for diagnosis and analysis has a host of applications in medicine, industry *etc.*

Biosphere, that part of the earth in which life exists—a very thin layer near the surface bounded by regions too hostile for life processes to occur. The upper limit is at about 9,000 m above sea level and the lower limit at about 10,000 m in the deep oceans. Ample supplies of solar energy, liquid water and places where liquid, solid and gas all meet seem to be requirements for a biosphere to exist and for all the biological cycles of water, oxygen, mineral, nitrogen, *etc.*, to function.

Birch, a genus of deciduous trees including about 40 species and found only in northern regions. Birches native to Britain, and to Europe generally, are of two species—the silver birch, *Betula pendula,* with its graceful, drooping branches and triangular leaves, and the white birch, *Betula pubescens,* which has erect branches and soft oval leaves. Birch timber is an important plywood timber, the bark is used for tanning leather, and wintergreen oil comes from the bark of black birch, *Betula lenta,* a North American species. The birch is not long-lived.

Birds, or Aves, are, next to mammals, the highest class of animal life. There are two kinds of modern birds—*Carinatae,* possessing keeled breast-bones and having the power of flight; *Ratitae,* having raft-like breast-bones, and incapable of flight; and a sub-class of fossil birds, Archaeornithes, including *Archaeopteryx.*

Estimates of the number of species breeding in Britain vary, but there are probably *c.* 244. The commonest are wrens, house sparrows, blackbirds, chaffinches, robins and starlings. Many bird species are continuing to decline (in the UK. The cuckoo, nightingale, willow tit, starling and turtle dove are under great pressure). Some, however, are thriving as a result of conservation projects (*e.g.* kingfishers, stone-curlews and buzzards). Birds in Britain are now laying their eggs earlier to combat earlier springs. Light receptors deep in their brains detect the changing day length.

The wheatear is usually the first of the migratory birds to return, often reaching Britain at the end of February and always before the middle of March; the sand martin is the first of the "early swallows" to return, followed by the house martin. The first cuckoo arrives about the middle of April, and the whinchat, garden warbler, and sedge warbler during the last week in April. The nightjar, spotted flycatcher, and red-backed shrike are not seen until the first week in May. The swift is among the last to return from Africa and the earliest to depart. The smallest flying bird in the world is the bee hummingbird.

Bird-nesting is illegal in Britain. With the passing of the Wildlife and Countryside Act in 1980 the trapping and caging of numerous birds was made illegal in Britain.

Some scientists think birds did not evolve from feathered dinosaurs but rather from prehistoric lizards (*archosaurs*). Some birds have reached the age of 80, but until ringing them in the nest began we knew little of their lifespan.

Modern research has shown that birds rival dolphins and chimpanzees in intelligence. Birds can understand each other's intentions and can use tools more efficiently than chimpanzees. Even though some birds only have pea-sized brains, their mental capacities can surpass those of chimps. However, scientists have now proven that birdsong is innate and not learned (and baby birds are known to babble as they learn to sing, just as human infants do). *See also* **Section T.**

Birds of Paradise, over 40 species of tropical birds inhabiting the dense forests of New Guinea and neighbouring islands. The male birds are remarkable for their brilliant plumage, long tail feathers, and ruffs on wings and neck, which are displayed to advantage during courtship. There are 38 species found in New Guinea. Related to the Bower Birds of Australia.

Biretta, a four-cornered head-covering worn by ecclesiastics of the Roman Church and varying in colour according to rank. A cardinal's biretta is red, a bishop's purple, a priest's black.

Bise, a keen dry north wind prevalent in Switzerland and South France.

Bisextile. *See* **Leap Year.**

Bishop is a Christian ecclesiastic, a person consecrated for the spiritual government of an area, a diocese or province, to the spiritual oversight of which he has been appointed (diocesan bishops), or to aid a bishop so appointed (suffragan bishops). In the Church of England, two, Canterbury and York, are archbishops having primacy in the respective provinces.

The archbishops of Canterbury and York and the bishops of London, Durham and Winchester and 21 other diocesan bishops in order of seniority are spiritual peers, and sit in the House of Lords. The (Disestablished) Church of Ireland has two archbishops and twelve bishops; the (Disestablished) Church of Wales an archbishop and five bishops and the Episcopal Church in Scotland seven bishops. *See also* **Cardinal.**

Bismuth, metallic element, no. 83, symbol Bi, in group 5 of the periodic table. Like antimony, the stable form is a grey, brittle, layer structure; electrical conductor. It is readily fusible, melting at 264°C and boiling at about 1420°C. Wood's metal, an alloy with one of the lowest melting points (under 65°C, so that a spoon made of it will melt when placed in a cup of hot tea), contains four parts bismuth, two parts lead, one part tin, one part cadmium.

Bison, a genus of wild cattle, distinguished from the ox by its shorter, wider skull, beard under the chin, high forequarters, and, in winter, a great mane of woolly hair covering head and forequarters. There are two species, the European and the American bison. The European bison, which tends to browse (or munch trees and leaves rather than graze) is now making a comeback in Eastern Europe. Once, up to 60 million bison roamed the great plains west of the Mississippi. They are better known as American buffalo. The largest wild population today is in Yellowstone.

Bit, formerly the word often referred to the metal piece in the mouth of a bridled horse, now more likely to be a technical expression in the mouth of a computer expert. A bit is a unit of information; it is the information that can be conveyed by indicating which of two possibilities obtains. Any object that can be either of two states can therefore store one bit of information. In a technical device, the two states could be the presence or the absence of a magnetic field, or of an electric voltage. Since all numbers can be represented in the binary system (*see* **Binary Notation**) by a row of digits which are *either* 0 *or* 1, it takes one bit of information to specify a binary digit. Bit is short for binary digit.

Bittern, a bird of the heron genus, with long, loose plumage on the front and sides of the neck. It is a solitary bird inhabiting marshes, but rare in Britain where its numbers fell to *c.* 15 breeding pairs in Norfolk, Suffolk and Lancashire. An ambitious scheme was launched in 1995 to save it from extinction underway all across the country.

Bivalves, shell-fish whose shell consists of two hinged valves, lying one on each side of the body, such as mussels, oysters and cockles.

Blackbird, or **Merle,** a member of the Thrush family, a familiar song bird in Britain. Male is all-black with orange bill; female is mottled brown with brown bill; the young are spotted brown. Blackbirds patrol their patches, chasing away rivals. Blackbird numbers are now reviving slightly.

Blackcock and Greyhen (as the female is called) are closely related to the Capercaillies but smaller. They nest on the ground and prefer wooded country to open moors. Found in northern half of northern hemisphere. Polygamous, they perform excited courtship dances; the male is a handsome blue-black bird with white undertail, the female dark brown mottled.

Black Holes. Section T, Part I.

Black-letter, the Old English or Gothic type first used in printing blocks.

Black Woodpecker (*Dryocopus martius*), a black bird about the size of a rook, with slightly crested scarlet crown, found in parts of Europe.

Blenny, a group of marine fishes with spiny rays part of the fin running along the back. Several species are found around the British coast.

Blood Moon, a total lunar eclipse. Once seen as a harbinger of doom.

Bluebird, a migratory bird of North America, deriving its name from its deep blue plumage, it has a pleasant warbling song and is a familiar sight in the woods from early spring to November. In India and Malaysia there is the Fairy Bluebird; the male is black with shiny blue upper parts. Used as the symbol of happiness by Maeterlinck in his play *The Blue Bird.* It is the state bird of New York.

Blue Marlin, the world's ultimate game fish, now threatened with extinction by over-fishing.

Blue Peter, a blue flag with a white square in the centre, is hoisted 24 hours before a ship leaves harbour (the letter P in the alphabet of the International Code of Signals).

Blue Ribbon, a term in general use to denote the highest honour or prize attainable in any field or competition. Thus the Derby is the blue ribbon of the turf. The expression is derived from the highest Order of Knighthood in the gift of the British Crown, the insignia of which is a garter of blue velvet.

Blue Sun, Blue Moon, etc., a phenomenon caused by the differential scattering of sunlight by transparent particles suspended in the atmosphere, the effect being that blue light is transmitted, and red light extinguished to direct vision. The dust from the Krakatoa eruption in 1883 and the drifting smoke from the forest fires in Alberta, Canada, in 1950 gave rise to "blue" moons and suns, phenomena sufficiently rare to be described as occurring "once in a blue moon".

Bluetongue, virulent virus, carried by midges, which mainly affects sheep (but also cattle and goats).

Boa, a term applied to a family of snakes of large size, some attaining a length of 9 m. They are not poisonous, but kill their prey by crushing — constriction—hence the name "boa constric-tor".

They occur both in the Old World and the New, but are more abundant in the latter. Most Boas retain the eggs within the body until young are fully developed, whereas the Pythons almost all lay leather-shelled eggs.

Boar, or **Wild Hog**, an animal largely distributed over the forest regions of Europe, Asia, Africa and South America. It has a longer snout and shorter ears than its descendant the domestic hog, and is provided with tusks. Having to forage for itself, it is a more active and intelligent animal than the pig of the sty.

Boat, an open vessel, propelled by oars or sails, or both. The boats of a ship of war are the launch, barge, pinnace, yawl, cutters, jolly boat and gig; of a merchant vessel, the launch, skiff, jolly boat or yawl, stern boat, quarter-boat and captain's gig.

Bode's Law, a numerical relationship formulated by Bode in 1772 (though pointed out earlier by J. D. Titius of Wittenberg), which states that the relative mean distances of the planets from the sun are found by adding 4 to each of the terms 0, 3, 6, 12, 24, 48, 96, and dividing each number by 10. The gap between Mars and Jupiter caused Bode to predict the existence of a planet there, later confirmed by the discovery of Ceres and other minor planets. The law breaks down for Neptune and Pluto.

Boers, name given to Dutch settlers, largely farmers, in South Africa after the 17th century. Discontented with British rule in the Cape after 1820, they emigrated northwards in 1835–37; after much fighting with the local people, they founded the Orange Free State (1836) and the Transvaal Republic (1848). The Transvaal declared itself independent in 1852. In 1877, after war with the Zulus, it was annexed to the British dominions; in 1879 it was declared a Crown Colony. For the **Boer War**, *see* **E3**.

Boiling-point is the temperature at which a liquid boils. At that point the pressure of the vapour is equal to the pressure of the atmosphere. Under increased pressure the b.p. rises and under less pressure, as on the top of a mountain, it is lower. At standard atmospheric pressure (760 mm of mercury) the b.p. of water is 100°C; alcohol 78·4°C; ether 35·6°C.

Bonobo, or pygmy chimpanzee, is man's closest relative (sharing 98 % of DNA). It lives in forests south of the Congo river. Some of its communication sounds resemble those of human babies. It is at home foraging in water.

Book of Deer, the oldest (10th century) surviving Scottish manuscript with the earliest known examples of written Gaelic.

Book of Hours, the most widespread devotional work of the Middle Ages. Most surviving copies are 15th century, but the earliest (the de Brailes Hours) dates from c. 1240.

Books, Classification of. All libraries are classified to facilitate reference, but the favourite system is the Dewey Decimal System, which divides the whole field of knowledge into ten Main Classes. Each of these Main Classes is again subdivided into ten main divisions. As an example: the main class of Sociology receives the number 300. This range 300 to 400 (the next main class) is graduated into tens, and Economics is 330. The range 330 to 340 is again graduated, and the subject of Labour and Capital is 331. This process is carried on by decimals so that 331·2 deals with Remuneration for Work, 331·22 with Wage Scales *etc.*

Borax (Sodium Pyroborate) is a white, soluble, crystalline salt. It is widely and diversely used, *e.g.*, as a mild antiseptic, in glazing pottery, in soldering, in the making of pyrex glass, as a cleansing agent and sometimes as a food preservative. Borax occurs naturally in the salt lakes of Tibet, where it is called tincal.

Bore. An almost vertical wall of water which passes upstream along certain estuaries. Its formation requires special conditions of river flow, incoming high tide, and shape of river channel. It can be spectacular and dangerous.

In Britain the best known is the Severn bore which can be over a metre high and move at 16–19 km/h. It occurs around 12 times a year. In parts of Britain the bore is called an eagre. There are c. 60 bores in the world.

Boron. A metalloid element, no. 5, symbol B. There are two forms, one crystalline, the other

amorphous. It is not very abundant in nature but occurs in concentrated deposits. It is best known in boric acid, which is used as a mild antiseptic (called boracic acid) and borax (*q.v.*). Boron compounds are essential to some plants, *e.g.*, beans. Used in the preparation of various special-purpose alloys, such as impact resistant steel. Compounds of boron and hydrogen are used as rocket fuels.

Borstal, an institution where young offenders under 21 on conviction were sent for detention and reform. The first was opened in 1902 at Borstal, near Rochester in Kent. Borstals were abolished by the 1982 Criminal Justice Act.

Bourgeoisie, a term used by Marxists to indicate those who do not, like the proletariat, live by the sale of their labour. They include, on the one hand, industrialists and financiers or members of the liberal professions and, on the other, small artisans and shop-keepers.

Bovine Spongiform Encephalopathy (BSE). *See under* **Mad Cow Disease.**

Bow, an instrument for propelling arrows, and, in the days when it was a weapon of war, was usually made of yew or ash, and was about 2 m long, with an arrow c. 1 m long. It was the weapon with which Crécy, Poitiers and Agincourt were won. The cross-bow was Italian and was adopted in France, but did not become popular in Britain.

Bow Bells is the peal of the London church of St. Mary-le-Bow, Cheapside, within sound of which one must be born to be entitled to be called a "cockney". Bow Bells had not been heard since 1939, but they once again rang out over the City of London on 20 December 1961.

Bowdler, to expurgate a book. Derived from Thomas Bowdler (1754–1825), the editor of the Family Shakespeare, in which he edited out some words. His prudery met with ridicule and hence the words "bowdlerism" "bowdlerist", *etc.*

Bower Bird, native to Australia and New Guinea and related to the Bird of Paradise, though often less striking in appearance. In the mating season the male builds a "bower" of sticks and grasses for elaborate courtship displays.

The Gardener Bower Bird of Papua makes a lawn in front of his bower and adorns it with bright coloured pebbles and flowers which are replaced as they wither. The female builds her nest away from the bower. So far, 18 species of bower bird have been identified.

Boxgrove. Site near Halnaker, West Sussex. In 1993 archaeologists found the 500,000 year old left shin bone of "Boxgrove Man", making it the site of the oldest human inhabitant in England.

Boy Scouts. Movement founded by Lord Baden-Powell in 1907, now with over 28 million members. Baden-Powell's book *Scouting for Boys* was published in 2008. The Girl Guides (renamed Girlguiding in 2002) were founded in 1910 by Agnes Baden-Powell. Scouts (and Guides) now offer an oath of allegiance that does not require a pledge of allegiance to God. One in four Scouts in the UK are now girls.

Boycott, a term used in connection with a person that the general body of people, or a party or society, refuse to have dealings with. Originally used when Captain Boycott (1832–97) was made the victim of a conspiracy by the Irish Land League which prevented him making any purchases or holding any social intercourse in his district. He had incurred the League's hostility by a number of evictions.

Bramley Apples actually take their name from a cottage owner in Southwell, Nottinghamshire.The name now has protected status.

Brass, an exceedingly useful alloy of copper and zinc. Much brass is about two-thirds copper but different proportions give different properties. It is harder than copper and easily worked. Brass in the Bible probably refers to bronze.

Breadfruit Tree (*Artocarpus altilis*), a native of the South Sea Islands; the fruits are a brownish green, about the size of a melon, and contain a white pulpy substance which is roasted before being eaten. The tree grows 12 m or more. Captain Bligh's ship *Bounty* was on a voyage to Jamaica carrying a cargo of 1,000 breadfruit trees when the mutiny occurred.

Breeder Reactor, a kind of nuclear reactor (*q.v.*) which besides producing energy by the fission process also produces ("breeds") more nuclear fuel at the same time. A typical reaction is: a neutron induces fission of a U-235 nucleus which breaks up into two medium-sized nuclei and some neutrons; one of the latter then enters a U-238 nucleus turning it into U-239 which then decays radioactively *via* neptunium into plutonium which is useful fuel. There are technical problems in breeder reactors which have delayed their practical use.

Breviary (Lat. *breviarium* = abridgment), the short prayer-book of the Roman Catholic Church which gives the Divine Office, *i.e.*, the services to be said daily. The directions for Mass are in the Missal. The current Roman breviary is a simplified version of the one decreed by the Council of Trent, 1568. *See also* **Matins.**

Bridges are structures for continuing a road, railway, or canal across a river, valley, ravine, or a road or railway at a lower level. From early times bridges were made of timber, stone, or brick, and it was not until the 19th cent. that wrought- and cast-iron were used. Today the materials mostly used are steel and reinforced concrete. Among the most famous of ancient bridges is that of S. Angelo at Rome, built by Hadrian as the Pons Aelius, A.D. 134. The Rialto bridge at Venice dates from 1588. The Ponte Santa Trinita at Florence, one of the finest Renaissance bridges and deemed the most beautiful in the world, was destroyed by German mines in 1944 but has now been reconstructed just as it was before. The first stone bridge across the Thames was begun in 1176. It had 19 arches and was lined with houses and stood until 1831 when it was replaced by the granite bridge designed by Sir John Rennie which stood until 1972. This has been replaced by a three-span concrete bridge with a six-lane carriageway and two footways.

The first cast-iron bridge was built by Abraham Darby at Coalbrookdale, Shropshire, in 1779. Telford's Menai suspension bridge (1825) has since been enlarged, the original design maintained. Robert Stephenson's tubular bridge across the Menai Straits (1850) was the prototype of all modern plate girder railway bridges.

Other bridges are the Niagara (suspension), Forth railway bridge (cantilever), London Tower bridge (suspension), Tay railway bridge, Victoria Jubilee bridge across the St. Lawrence at Montreal (an open steel structure), Sydney Harbour bridge, Lower Zambesi bridge, Storstrom bridge in Denmark, Auckland Harbour bridge, and Verrazano-Narrows bridge spanning New York's harbour from Brooklyn to Staten I., exceeding by 18 m the centre span of San Francisco's Golden Gate bridge.

Work on a suspension bridge 2-miles long, linking Italy and Sicily, should begin in the near future. Europe's longest road and rail bridge (opened in July 2000) is the Öresund Bridge, which links middle Denmark and southern Sweden. The longest suspension bridge in the world links Hong Kong to its new airport. Europe's longest suspension bridge (opened in 1998) links the Danish island of Sjaelland (on which Copenhagen stands) to Funen. In 2007 Egypt and Saudi Arabia planned to build a bridge across the Gulf of Aqaba, linking Africa and Arabia. China now has 9 of the world's 12 longest bridges, (including a 34 mile bridge linking Hong Kong, Macau and Zhuhai)

British bridges include the road suspension bridge across the Firth of Forth, completed 1964, the Severn suspension bridge (from which the design principles for the new bridge across the Bosporus were taken) and the Tay road bridge, both completed 1966, and the Humber suspension bridge, linking Hull and Grimsby, opened in 1981. When completed, it was the longest single- span suspension bridge in the world (1,410 m). The M25 "Dartford" bridge (opened 1991) is the largest cable-stayed bridge in Europe.

The second Severn bridge, which opened in June 1996 is the longest in Britain. The proposed New Wear Crossing (in the Sunderland Strategic Transport Corridor) will be the tallest in England. The new Queensferry Crossing is the tallest bridge in the UK.

Europe's highest road bridge (the Millau viaduct over the River Tarn in the Massif Central) was opened in 2004. It is 343m (1,125ft) tall and 2·4km (1·5 miles) long. The world's highest bridges are now in China. *See also* **Bailey Bridge.**

Bridleway. In English law a highway over which the public have the following, but no other, rights of way: that is to say, a right of way on foot and a right of way on horseback or leading a horse, with or without a right to drive animals of any description along the highway.

Britannia Metal, an alloy of tin, antimony and copper, harder than pure tin, corrosion-resistant, used for teapots, jugs (often electro-plated).

British Association for the Advancement of Science, The, was founded in 1831 by a group of British scientists under Charles Babbage (1792–1871) to stimulate scientific inquiry.

British Commonwealth. The Commonwealth is a free association of independent member nations and their dependencies. The political status of the member nations is clarified and given legal substance in the *Statute of Westminster* drawn up in 1931, before the Commonwealth was founded, by the United Kingdom and the Dominions. The original Dominions were Australia, Canada, Irish Free State, Newfoundland, New Zealand and South Africa. On 1 June 1994, South Africa rejoined the Commonwealth, having left in 1961. In 1995 Cameroon and Mozambique joined the Commonwealth (and Rwanda in 2009). *See* **D24.**

British Legion. *See* **Royal British Legion.**

British Library *See* **Libraries, L66.**

British Museum, was created by an Act of Parliament in 1753, when the Sir Hans Sloane collection, which the British Government had acquired for £20,000, was added to the Cottonian Library and the Harleian Manuscripts. It was opened to the public in 1759 at Montague House Bloomsbury. The acquisition of the library of George III (known as the King's Library) in 1823 led to the construction of the present building with the new wing (1829), quadrangle (1852), domed reading room (1857), and later additions. The books and the reading room are now part of the British Library (*see also under* **Libraries**). The Natural History Department was transferred to South Kensington in the 1880s. As a museum it is perhaps the most famous in the world with its priceless collections. Its treasures include the Elgin Marbles (*q.v.*), the Rosetta Stone (*q.v.*) and the Portland Vase (*q.v.*). The famous domed Reading Room closed in 1997. It is the second most popular cultural institution in the world (after the Louvre in Paris). It attracts around 6·8 million visitors annually.

British Standard Time, The British Standard Time Act of 1968 put Britain an hour ahead of Greenwich Mean Time (GMT) throughout the year for an experimental 3 years. This brought Britain into line with countries in Western Europe where Central European Time is observed. In 1970 Parliament called for the restoration of the previous position—BST in the summer months and GMT in the winter—as from 31 October 1971.

Attempts to change the law once again to give lighter evenings (but darker mornings) have gained much public support in recent years.

Brittle Stars, organisms resembling starfish. They use their arms (instead of tube feet) to move. They hide in coral crevices, emerging at night to feed.

Brocken-spectre or Glory. The series of coloured rings which an observer sees around the shadow of his own head (or an aeroplane in which he is travelling) as cast upon a bank of mist or thin cloud. This effect is produced by reflection and refraction of sunlight in minute water-droplets in the air just as in a rainbow.

Bromine. A non-metal element, no. 35, symbol Br, member of the halogen family (*q.v.*). It is a red, evil-smelling liquid (Greek *bromos*, a stink). It is an abundant element. In the USA bromine is extracted from sea-water on a large scale. It unites readily with many other elements, the products being termed bromides. Its derivatives with organic compounds are used in synthetic chemistry. Bromoform is a liquid resembling chloroform. Bromides were formerly used extensively in medicine to calm excitement.

Bronze is primarily an alloy of copper and tin, and was one of the earliest alloys known. The Bronze Age (began c. 4,000 B.C. in Middle East) in the evolution of tool-using man came before the Iron Age (*c.* 2,000 B.C.) Some modern bronzes contain zinc or lead also, and a trace of phosphorus is present in "Phosphor-bronze". Major Bronze Age (2,700–700 B.C.) sites in Britain are Stonehenge and the Avebury Stone Circle (both in Wiltshire).

BSE. *See* **Mad Cow Disease.**

Bubble Chamber. An instrument used by physicists to reveal the tracks of fast fundamental particles (*e.g.*, those produced in large accelerating machines) in a form suitable for photography; closely related to the Wilson cloud chamber (*q.v.*), but the particles leave trails of small bubbles in a superheated liquid (often liquid hydrogen) instead of droplets of liquid in a supersaturated gas.

Buckingham Palace, London residence of British sovereigns since 1837. Originally built for the Duke of Buckingham (1703); bought by George III in 1762 and remodelled by Nash 1825–36.

Buntings, name of a group of finches, seed-eating birds, usually found in open country. The Yellowhammer, Reed Bunting, Corn Bunting and Cirl Bunting are resident in Britain; the Snow Bunting (which breeds in small numbers in Scotland) and Lapland Bunting are regular winter visitors. The Ortolan is a rare visitor.

Burbot, also known as fresh-water cod or eelpout, is the only freshwater fish to have died out in Britain in the last 100 years.

Burka, the Muslim headscarf or veil.

Bustard, type of bird, related to the crane. The great bustard (the heaviest flying bird in the world) is being reintroduced into Britain after an absence of 200 years. Its first three chicks were hatched in 2009. The great bustard is the county bird of Wiltshire. It had been hunted to extinction in Britain. The last great bustard in the UK was shot in 1832 by a vicar.

Butane, a colourless inflammable gas made of carbon and hydrogen; formula C_4H_{10}. Found in natural gas and made as a by-product of oil refining.

Butane, like propane (*q.v.*), can easily be liquefied and moved safely in cans and tanks. It is thus useful as a "portable gas supply"; also used in internal combustion fuels.

Butterflies, like moths belong to the order *Lepidoptera.* There are *c.* 20,000 species (though many are in decline). There are four stages in the evolution of a butterfly: *egg, caterpillar, pupa* and *adult butterfly.* They are now known to have a geomagnetic compass.

The world's largest sanctuary for butterflies (Butterfly World) has been opened near St. Albans to help stem the decline of Britain's surviving 56 resident species (5 have died out over the last 100 years). Some butterflies are migrating from Europe to Britain because of climate change.

Buzzard, magnificent dark brown birds, three feet long, with an eye as large as a human eye. They need woods to nest in and land to forage over. In the 19th century they were hunted almost to extinction by landowners.

C

Cacao, Theobroma cacao, is an evergreen tree, from 4–6 m high, growing abundantly in tropical America, West Africa, the Caribbean, Sri Lanka, *etc.*, yielding seeds, called cocoa beans from which cocoa and chocolate are manufactured. The fruit is 17–25 cm long, hard and ridged; inside are the beans, covered with a reddish-brown skin, which are first fermented, then dried. The trees mature at five to eight years and produce two crops a year. Chocolate was first introduced to England around 1652. The Englishman, Joseph Fry, created the first chocolate bar in 1847, but *c.* 3,500 years earlier the Mayas of central America drank *cacao.* Ivory Coast is the major producer. There is concern that surging demand in India and China, plus droughts and diseases, will lead to a worldwide shortage.

Cactus, a family of flowering plants numbering about 1,480 species adapted to living in very dry situations. The stem is usually fleshy, being composed of succulent tissue, remarkably retentive of water; commonly equipped with sharp thorns which deter animals from eating them. The roots are generally very long, tapping soil water over a large area; a "prickly pear" cactus may have roots covering a circular area 7 m or more in diameter. The leaves are commonly insignificant or absent, and the stem takes over the photosynthetic leaf function and becomes accordingly flattened to expose greater area to sunlight and air. In some kinds of cactus (*e.g., Echinocactus*) the stem is shaped almost like a sea-urchin. Many species are now threatened with extinction. Some giant cactuses can live up to 200 years.

Cadmium. A metallic element, no. 48, symbol Cd, chemically similar to zinc and mercury. Used in alloys to lower the melting point, as in Wood's metal with bismuth and tin. Alloyed with copper to make electric cables. Like zinc, it is a protective metal and is used in electroplating. The cadmium-vapour lamp gives a characteristic frequency used in measuring wavelength.

Caesium, also spelt **Cesium,** is an alkali metal element, no. 55, symbol Cs, in first group of the periodic table. It resembles rubidium and potassium and was discovered by Bunsen and Kirchoff in 1860. It was the first element whose existence was discovered spectro-scopically. The caesium atom consists of a heavy nucleus surrounded by 55 electrons, 54 of which are arranged in stable orbits, and one of which, known as the valency electron, is in a less stable orbit surrounding them. Used in the construction of photo-electric cells and as an accurate time standard (atomic clock).

Cajuns, corruption of Acadians. French-speaking inhabitants of Louisiana, descended from French Canadians who emigrated from Nova Scotia.

Calcium, a silvery-white metallic element, no. 20, symbol Ca. It melts at 810°C and is very reactive. It was discovered by Sir Humphry Davy in 1808, but not until 1898 was it obtained pure, by Moissan. Does not occur as metal in nature, but calcium compounds make up a large part of the earth's crust. Most important calcium sources are marble, limestone, chalk (all three are, chemically, calcium carbonate); dolomite, which is the double carbonate of calcium and magnesium; gypsum, a hydrated calcium sulphate; calcium phosphate and calcium fluoride. Igneous rocks contain much calcium silicate.

Calcium compounds are essential to plants and are used in fertilisers. Animals require calcium and phosphorus for bone and teeth formation; deficiency is treated by administration of calcium phosphate. Strontium is chemically similar to calcium, and the radioactive strontium 90 from atomic "fall-out" is easily assimilated by the body. Calcium is the most abundant metallic element in the human body.

Calendar, a collection of tables showing the days and months of the year, astronomical recurrences, chronological references, *etc.* The Julian Calendar, with its leap year, introduced by Julius Caesar, fixed the average length of the year at 365¼ days, which was about 11 minutes too long (the earth completes its orbit in 365 days 5 hours 48 minutes 46 seconds of mean solar time). The cumulative error was rectified by the Gregorian Calendar, introduced in Italy in 1582, whereby century years do not count as leap years unless divisible by 400. This is the the rule we now follow. England did not adopt the reformed calendar until 1752, when she found herself 11 days behind the Continent. Until then, New Year's Day in England was on 25 March. Hence, in 1752, after the 11 days had been rectified, the new financial year began on 6 April—as it still does! The Gregorian Calendar did not come into use in Russia until 1918. Old Style and New Style dates are classed as "O.S." "N.S.".

The Chinese Lunar Calendar is based on cycles of the moon (hence Chinese New Year can fall anytime between late January and mid-February). Chinese New Year traditionally lasts for 15 days. *See also* **G25.**

Calends, the first day of the month in Roman times.

Callisto. A moon of Jupiter with a subsurface ocean. Callisto is larger than the planet Mercury.

Calorie. Unit of quantity of heat. The "small" or fundamental calorie is the amount of heat required to raise the temperature of 1 gram of water from 14·5° to 15·5°C and is equal to 4·185 joules. This is the gram-calorie used in physics and chemistry. The large Calorie (written with a capital C), commonly used in nutritional connotations, is equal to 1000 small calories and is called the kilogram-calorie.

Cambridge University had a sufficiently good teaching reputation to attract Oxford students in 1209, when lectures at their own university were suspended. In 1226 it had a Chancellor who was recognised by King and Pope. The first college to be founded was Peterhouse in 1284.

The university was reorganised and granted a Charter of Incorporation by an act of 1571. The colleges with their dates of foundation are Christ's (1505), Churchill (1960), Clare (1326), Clare Hall

(1966), Corpus Christi (1352), Darwin (1964), Downing (1800), Emmanuel (1584), Fitzwilliam (1966), Gonville and Caius (1348), Jesus (1496), King's (1441), Magdalene (1542), Pembroke (1347), Peterhouse (1284), Queens' (1448), Robinson (1977) St. Catharine's (1473), St. Edmund's (1896), St. John's (1511), Selwyn (1882), Sidney Sussex (1596), Trinity (1546), Trinity Hall (1350) and Wolfson (1965). (Wolfson was the first College to admit both men and women as students and Fellows).

The women's colleges to emerge were: Girton (1869), Newnham (1871), New Hall (1954) (now renamed Murray Edwards College) and Hughes Hall (formerly Cambridge T. C.) (1885) (a full member in 2006). Lucy Cavendish College (1965) received full college status in 1997. Homerton (f. 1824) became a full Cambridge college in March 2010.

Women were admitted to degrees (but not allowed to sit for examination) in 1920, and to full membership of the University in 1948. Newnham and New Hall still remain as all-women colleges.

Camel, a large ruminant quadruped, inhabiting Asia and Africa, where it is largely used as a beast of burden. There are two species—the *Arabian* camel or dromedary, with only one hump; and the *Bactrian*, or double-humped camel. There are no wild dromedaries, and the only wild bactrians occur in the Gobi Desert. The camel is able to go for long periods without water, not, as was formerly believed, because it stored water in its hump, but because of the unique mechanism of its physiology which enables it to conserve water at the expense of not sweating until 40°C is reached. Female camels are known as she-camels. In Australia, there are more than 750,000 camels in the vast interior. Millions of years ago, camels lived in the forests deep in the Arctic Circle. There were no camels in Biblical times (despite the assertion of the Bible). Camels can run as fast as thoroughbred horses.

Campanile, or bell-tower, is separate from but usually adjoining its parent church. The most famous are in Italy. Giotto's tower at Florence, adjoining the cathedral of Santa Maria del Fiore, is architecturally the finest in the world. Others are at Cremona, the loftiest in Italy (110 m) and Pisa (the leaning tower). The magnificent pointed campanile of St. Mark's, Venice, which collapsed in 1902 (and since rebuilt in its original form), was begun in 902.

Canal, an artificial watercourse used for navigation which changes its level by means of locks. The completion of the Bridgewater Canal in 1761 to take coal from Worsley to Manchester marked the beginning of canal building in industrial Britain.

There are over 4,000 km of navigable inland waterways in the UK today, c. 3,200 km of which are under the control of the new Canal and River Trust (which replaced British Waterways in 2012). The English network is based on the four great estuaries, Mersey, Humber, Severn and Thames.

Canal building gave rise to the new discipline of civil engineering.

Cancer, Tropic of. *See* Tropics, L110.

Candela unit of luminous intensity, symbol cd. An idea of the value which this unit represents may be gained from the fact that light obtained from a 40 W filament-type electric lamp or bulb is approximately the same as would be given by a point source of luminous intensity 30 cd. *See* **SI units, Section T.**

Candlemas, the halfway point between the winter solstice and the spring equinox.

Candy Floss (known in America as cotton candy). Made entirely from sugar. It was invented in 1897.

Cannabis, a bushy plant found wild in many parts of the world. Cannabis was reclassified from a Class B to a Class C drug in 2004. From January 2009 it reverted to a Class B drug (users caught with it 3 times will be arrested). Using cannabis can lead to future mental health problems (although it has been used medicinally in China and India for a long time). Uruguay has introduced a legal, national market in cannabis and Jamaica has decriminalised its use. Alaska, Oregon, Colorado, Washington State and the District of Columbia now allow possession of small amounts. Synthetic cannabis is known as 'spice' or black mamba. New approaches to legalise use of the drug are being urged.

Canonical Hours, seven in number in the Western Church; Matins and Lauds, before dawn; Prime, early morning service; Terce, 9 a.m.; Sext, noon;

Nones, 3 p.m.; Vespers, 4 p.m.; Compline, bed-time.

Canonisation, the entering of one of the faithful departed on the list of saints of the Roman Catholic Church. The rules governing canonisation were simplified by papal decree in 1969. Beatification, by which a person is called blessed, is usually followed by canonisation.

Canticles, the name given to the scriptural passages from the Bible sung by the congregation in the various Christian liturgies. They are the *Benedicite, Benedictus, Magnificat, Nunc Dimittis.*

Capercaillie, the largest of the grouse family, found in the Scottish highlands and the pine forests and mountainous regions of Northern and Central Europe and Asia. The bird was reintroduced to Scotland by Sir Thomas Buxton in 1830.

Capital Punishment. *See* **Death Penalty, L30.**

Capricorn, Tropic of. *See* **Tropics, L110.**

Capuchins are members of a mendicant order of Franciscans, founded in the 16th cent. with the aim of restoring the primitive and stricter observance of the rule of St. Francis, so called from the capuce (pointed cowl) worn by them.

Capybara, a cousin of the guinea pig, found in South America. It is the largest rodent in the world.

Caracals, the largest of the African small cats.

Carat, a term used in assessing the value of gold and precious stones. In connection with gold, it represents the proportion of pure gold contained in any gold alloy, and for this purpose the metal is divided into 24 parts. Thus 24-carat indicates pure gold, and any lesser number of carats shows the proportion of gold contained in the alloy. The carat as a measure of weight is now obsolete, having been replaced by the *metric carat* of 0·2 grams.

Caravan, a band of travellers or traders who journeyed together for safety across the deserts, sometimes numbering many hundreds. The great caravan routes from Egypt to Babylon and from Palestine to Yemen linked up with the Syrian ports and so with Western sea commerce.

Carbon, a non-metallic chemical element no. 6, symbol C, which occurs in crystalline form as diamonds and graphite; amorphous forms of carbon include charcoal and soot, while coke consists mainly of elementary carbon. The biochemistry of plants and animals largely hinges upon carbon compounds. The study of carbon compounds is called Organic Chemistry.

Carbon 14. A radioactive isotope of carbon, discovered in 1940, with a half-life c. 6,000 years, used in following the path of compounds and their assimilation in the body. Also used in determination of the age of carbon-containing materials such as trees.

Carbon Dioxide. Commonest of the oxides of carbon. It is formed when carbon and its compounds are burnt with abundant supply of air, and when carbon compounds are oxidised in the respiration process of animals. The atmosphere contains carbon dioxide to the extent of about 325 ppm and is increasing by about 1 ppm per year, principally because of the burning of fossil fuels and possibly because of deforestation which not only leaves more oxidisible material but lowers the amount of carbon dioxide removed by photosynthesis.

Carbon Monoxide is a colourless gas with no taste or smell. It is formed when coal and coke are burnt with a restricted supply of air; the blue flame to be seen in a coke brazier, for instance, is the flame of carbon monoxide. This gas is very poisonous, forming with the haemoglobin of the blood a compound which is useless for respiration and cherry red in colour, which gives a visible sympton of poisoning by carbon monoxide. With nickel it forms a volatile compound, called nickel carbonyl, and this reaction is the basis of the Mond process for extracting nickel.

Cardinal, one of the chief dignitaries of the Roman Catholic Church who constitute the Pope's council, or Sacred College, and when the papal chair is vacant elect by secret ballot a Pope from among themselves. There are three orders: cardinal bishops, members of the Roman Curia (the central administration of the Church) and bishops of sees near Rome; cardinal deacons, also members of the Curia, holding titular bishoprics; and cardinal priests who exercise pastoral duties over sees removed from Rome, though some are members of the Curia.

After the surprise resignation in 2013 of Pope Benedict XVI (the first resignation in the modern era), the College of Cardinals comprised 115 members (under 80) eligible to elect the new Pope.

Papal insignia were trimmed of embellishment by

papal decree in 1969 with the abolition, subsequently revoked, of the famous red hat (the *galero*) and the shoes with buckles. Cardinals aged 80 and over may not enter a conclave to elect a pope. There are now around 225 cardinals. For the first time ever, most cardinals now come from outside Europe.

Cardinal Virtues, according to Plato these were justice, prudence, temperance, fortitude—*natural* virtues unlike the *theological* virtues of the Catholic Church, faith, hope, charity.

Caribou, reindeer (*q.v.*) of N. America.

Carmelites, a body of mendicant friars taking their name from Mount Carmel, where the order was first established in the 12th cent. The original rule of the order required absolute poverty, abstinence from meat and a hermit life. The rigidity of the rule of the order was mitigated by Innocent IV. They wear a brown habit with white mantle, hence their name of White Friars. The order of Carmelite nuns was instituted in the 15th cent.

Carmine. *See* **Cochineal**.

Carp, a well-known fresh-water fish, found in plenty in most European and Asiatic still waters; reaches a length of about 60 cm and under favourable conditions lives for about 40 years. Familiar British members of the family are the roach, rudd, dace, chub, gudgeon, tench, minnow, barbel, bream and bleak.

The goldfish, popular in ornamental ponds, is the domesticated variety of Asian origin.

Carthusians, an order of monks founded in 1084 by St. Bruno at the Grande Chartreuse near Grenoble, and introduced into England about a century later. They built the Charterhouse (corruption of Chartreuse) in London in 1371.

The chief characteristics of the order are a separate dwelling-house in the precincts of the charterhouse for each monk, and the general assembly in the Church twice in the day and once at night. They wear a white habit, with white scapular and hood. The liqueur *Chartreuse* was invented by the order and is still their valuable secret.

Casein, the chief protein in milk and cheese. It is coagulated by the action of rennet or acid. An important class of plastics ("casein plastics") are produced from it, and these plastics are converted into buttons, kitting-needles, *etc*. 36,000 litres of milk yield about 1 tonne of casein.

Cassowary, a genus of ostrich-like birds which, together with the emu, forms a separate order found only in Australasia. All three species are black, with brightly coloured necks, and with a horny crest on the head. Noted for fleetness and their ferocious kick.

Castor-oil Plant (*Ricinus communis*), an African shrub now cultivated in most tropical countries. It has broad palmate leaves and bears a spiny fruit containing seeds which when pressed yield the well-known oil.

Cat, general name for all 37 members of the class *Felidae* of the carnivorous order, from the lion down to the domestic cat. The latter is believed to be descended from the European and African wild cats. Egypt first domesticated the cat.

Members of the cat family include tigers, lions, cheetahs, jaguars, pumas, leopards *etc*. The world's rarest big cat is the Amur leopard, whilst there only 200 Arabian leopards left in the wild.

Catabolism, Anabolism, are the terms used to describe the two types of metabolic pathway. Catabolic pathways are routes by which large organic molecules are broken up by enzymes into their simpler constituents *e.g.*, starch into glucose. The anabolic pathways are the routes by which complex molecules are synthesised from simple subunits, *e.g.*, proteins from amino acids.

Catacombs, caves or tunnels used as burial places, especially by early Christians and Jews. The coffins were stacked on shelves in vaults or niches.

Catalyst. A substance which alters the rate of reaction without itself being chemically changed. Various aluminium and titanium compounds are catalysts in the formation of polythene from ethylene. Palladium catalyses the reaction of hydrogen with oxygen (hence its use in gas lighters). Enzymes in the body hasten the breakdown of carbohydrates and proteins by catalytic action. *See also* **Section T**.

Cataracts are huge waterfalls. The most famous are Niagara in North America, the Orinoco in South America, the Victoria Falls on the Zambesi, and the Rhine Falls at Schaffhausen.

Caterpillar, the larva of a butterfly or moth,

worm-like in its segmented body, with 3 pairs of jointed true legs, often curiously marked and coloured, and frequently more or less hairy. The world's first amphibious caterpillars were discovered in Hawaii in 2010.

Cathedral, the chief church of a diocese, so called from its containing a Bishop's seat, or episcopal chair. Some celebrated cathedrals are St. John Lateran of Rome, Notre Dame of Paris, the cathedrals of Cologne and Milan, St. Paul's in London, Canterbury, York Minster, and the cathedrals of Durham, Norwich and Winchester.

Cat's eye, a kind of quartz, much valued as a gem, opalescent, and of various shades. For long used in roads to mark guidelines for motorists, but now replaced by solar-powered studs.

Cave Art. *See* **N5**.

Caves, natural hollow places in the earth, frequently found in Carboniferous limestone areas. The underground caves are formed by the action of rainwater carrying carbon dioxide, a dilute acid which slowly attacks the limestone rocks. Caves still remain the least explored places on earth! The world's largest cave passage was discovered in 2009 in the Vietnamese jungle.

The main caves in the British Isles are in the Mendips, Derbyshire, Yorkshire, South Wales and in County Clare. Many British inland caves are thought to have been formed at the end of the Ice Age when the water table rose. Britain's largest known underground chamber is the Frozen Deep, below Cheddar Gorge in Somerset. The study of caves is known as spelaeology.

Caviar. *See under* **Sturgeon**.

Cedar, a dark-leaved, cone-bearing, horizontal-branched evergreen tree that grows to a considerable height and girth, the best known species in Britain being the Cedar of Lebanon, which was introduced in the 17th cent. The Egyptians used the resin of the Lebanese cedar to mummify their dead, whilst the Phoenicians built their ships from its timber. The Atlas Mountains Cedar is now under serious threat.

Celestial Sphere. The sky seen as an imaginary sphere that surrounds the earth. A fundamental tool in positional astronomy, it provides a surface on which to draw and study planetary movements *etc*.

Celluloid, one of the first synthetic thermoplastic materials, discovered by Alexander Parkes in 1865 when he was attempting to produce synthetic horn. It is made by treating cellulose nitrate with camphor and alcohol.

Photographic film is made of a similar, but less-inflammable material, formed by the use of cellulose acetate instead of the nitrate.

Cellulose, a carbohydrate, and a constituent of nearly all plants. Cellulose occurs in an almost pure state in the fibres of linen (flax), absorbent cotton, jute, and filter-paper.

Celsius was the 18th cent. Swedish scientist after whom the Celsius temperature scale is named. Since 1954, °C stands for "degree Celsius" instead of "degree Centigrade" but this is only a change in name. Both symbols refer to the temperature scale which calls the melting point of ice 0°C and the boiling point of water at one atmosphere pressure 100°C. *See* **Absolute Temperature**.

Celts, an ancient race originating in the third millennium B.C. in the Alps, united by a common language and culture, who spread westward into Spain, northward into Britain, eastward to the Black Sea, reaching Galatia in Asia Minor. More recent research now suggests they spread from West to East. The "La Tène" iron-age Celts invaded Britain *c*. 250 B.C. After Britain was conquered by the Romans and invaded by the Angles and Saxons there remained as areas of Celtic speech only Wales (Brythonic speakers), Ireland, Scotland, the Isle of Man (Gaelic speakers), and Cornwall. The late Celtic period in Britain produced a distinctive Christian art (*e.g.*, the Lindisfarne Gospel *c*, 700, and the Irish Book of Kells).

Surviving Celtic languages are Welsh, Irish, Breton, Scots Gaelic and a tiny Cornish tradition. Manx Gaelic is on the point of extinction. DNA analysis has shown that our indigenous Celts are descended from tribes of Spanish fishermen.

Centrifuge, a machine which produces large accelerations by utilising the radial force caused by rotating a body about a fixed centre. Centrifuges have found extensive application in modern science. They can be used for the separation of one size of particle from another in biochemistry or in the training of astronauts where the accelerations occurring during rocket lift off can be simulated in a centrifuge on the ground.

Ceramics, are substances in which a combination of one or more metals with oxygen confers special and valuable properties. These include hardness, and resistance to heat and chemicals. Ceramic comes from the Greeek word for pottery, and pottery materials of mud and clay were probably the first man-made ceramics. Nowadays the range is enormous and growing; apart from all the pottery materials, there are firebricks, gems, glasses, concretes, nuclear reactor fuel elements, special materials for electronic devices, coloured pigments, electrical insulators, abrasives, and many other things. The scientific study of ceramics is part of materials science (*q.v.*).

Ceres, the largest object in the asteroid belt between Mars and Jupiter. Discovered in 1801. A dwarf planet. Visited in 2011 by the Dawn probe. which is now in orbit around it.

Cerium, a scarce metallic element, no. 58, symbol Ce, discovered by Berzelius in 1803. A mixture of cerium and thorium nitrates is used in the manufacture of gas mantles, which owe their incandescent property to the deposit of cerium and thorium oxide with which they are coated.

CERN, French acronym for the European Laboratory for Particle Physics in Geneva. In 1989, the Large Electron Positron collider (LEP) was opened there. A long-awaited attempt to recreate the swirl of matter just after the "Big Bang" created the universe is now underway. It has resulted in the creation of a 'mini Big Bang' generating temperatures of 10 trillion degrees centigrade – melting even protons and neutrons. An even bigger machine is planned – the International Linear Collider. This will smash electrons into their antimatter eqvalent – positrons. See also **Higgs Boson.**

Chaffinch. See **Finch, L40.**

Chalcedony, a mixture of crystalline silica and amorphous hydrated silica, *i.e.*, of quartz and opal. It has a waxy lustre, and is much used by jewellers for necklaces, bracelets, *etc.* Commonly it is white or creamy. Its bright orange-red variety is called carnelian; its brown variety, sard. Chrysoprase, plasma and bloodstone are varieties which are respectively pale apple-green, dark leek-green and green with red spots.

Chalk, a white limestone, calcium carbonate, found in the Upper Cretaceous deposits (formed from the shells of minute marine organisms). As chalk is porous, few streams form on its surface and consequently it is eroded slowly, although generally speaking it is a soft rock. Its juxtaposition with soft impervious clay in some areas results in its forming steep ridges known as escarpments, *e.g.*, N. and S. Downs and Chilterns. In contrast to the dry upland surfaces of chalk, lower levels are frequently saturated with water which emerges as springs.

Chamberlain, Lord, the senior officer of The Royal Household who is responsible for all ceremonial within the palace, but not the coronation or state opening of parliament. He is also in charge of appointments to The Royal Household. His duty as censor of plays was abolished in 1968.

Chamberlain, Lord Great, one of the great officers of state whose duties are now mainly ceremonial. He attends the monarch at the state opening of parliament and at the coronation and is custodian of the Palace of Westminster (Houses of Parliament). The office is hereditary, dating from Norman times, and is held for one reign in turn by descendants of the De Veres, Earls of Oxford.

Chameleon, a family of lizards with numerous species. Their ability to change colour is well known, but exaggerated, and is due to the movement of pigment cells beneath the skin. They are slow, arboreal, and mainly insectivorous. Found in Africa, India and Arabia.

Chamois, a species of antelope, native of Western Europe and Asia. About the size of a goat, it lives in mountainous regions, and possesses wonderful leaping power, so that it is very difficult to capture. Its flesh is much esteemed, and from its skin chamois leather is made, although today sheep and goat skins are usually substituted. The mating season is October-November and the fawns are born in May or June. Live to be 20–25 years old.

Champagne is made from one of three grape varieties – *pinot noir, pinot meunier* and *chardonnay.* The fizz comes from adding sugar and yeast. It comes from the Champagne district of France (now granted World Heritage status).

Chancellor, Lord, the highest judicial functionary in Britain who also acted until 2006 as Speaker of the House of Lords (There is now a Lord Speaker). The Chancellor is a privy councillor and cabinet minister by virtue of office and was formerly a peer of the realm. Early Lord Chancellors were often ecclesiastics and custodians of the Great Seal. The current Lord Chancellor is Elizabeth Truss, the first-ever woman to hold the post.

Channel Tunnel, a scheme to bore a tunnel through 32–48 km of chalk under the sea between Dover and Calais has been a subject for discussion ever since Albert Mathieu first conceived the idea as a practical possibility in 1802.

The tunnel was officially opened on 6 May 1994, but fare paying passenger services did not start until 14 November 1994.

Chapel Royal, a church dedicated to the use of the Sovereign and Court. They include St. James's Palace, Buckingham Palace, Windsor, Hampton Court, the Tower, and Holyrood.

Charcoal, a term applied to wood that has been subjected to a process of slow smothered combustion. More generally it refers to the carbonaceous remains of vegetable, animal, or combustible mineral substances submitted to a similar process. Charcoal from special woods (in particular buckthorn) is used in making gunpowder. Bone charcoal finds use in sugar refining, as it removes dark colouring matter present in the crude syrup.

Charge-Coupled Device (CCD), a light-sensitive electronic detector, invented in 1970 and now widely used in cameras, hand-held video recorders and in astronomy. CCDs revolutionised astronomy, replacing the photographic plate.

Charon, the largest of Pluto's five known moons, visited by the New Horizons probe in 2015.

Chasuble, a sleeveless vestment worn by ecclesiastics over the alb during Mass.

Cheese, an article of food made from the curd of milk, which is separated from the whey and pressed in moulds and gradually dried. There are about 500 varieties differing with method of preparation and quality of milk. They used to be made in the regions after which they are named but nowadays many of them are mass produced.

Cheeses may be divided into 3 main classes: (1) soft, *e.g.*, Camembert, Cambridge, l'Evêque; (2) blue-veined, *e.g.*, Stilton, Gorgonzola, Roquefort (made from ewe's milk), (3) hard-pressed, *e.g.*, Cheddar, Cheshire, Gruyère, Parmesan, Gouda.

Cheetah or "hunting leopard", the large spotted cat of Africa and Southern Asia, the swiftest four-footed animal alive. The cheetah has now joined the list of endangered species. It became extinct in India in the mid-20th century.

Chelsea Pensioners, the former soldiers (around 440 in all) who live in the Royal Hospital in Chelsea. They wear distinctive red tunics. The first women pensioners moved in during 2009.

Chemical Warfare. This term is usually restricted to mean the use in war of anti-personnel gases, aerosols and smokes, although explosives, napalm, herbicides and defoliants are also chemical agents that are used in war. Poison gas was first used on a large scale in the first world war by Germany in 1915 at the Battle of Ypres. Over 100,000 fatalities resulted from the use of principally chlorine, phosgene and mustard gas.

Worldwide revulsion resulted in the Geneva Protocol of 1925 which prohibited the use of both chemical and bacteriological weapons. It has now been ratified by many nations.

The Protocol has been generally well observed although notable violations have been by the Italians in Abyssinia (1935–36), the Japanese in China during the second world war (when over 100,000 were killed in Zhejiang Province), the Americans in S.E. Asia in the 1960s and Iraq (against the Kurds in the 1980s). Under the 1993 Chemical Weapons Convention (in force since 1997) the signatories are obliged to remove chemical weapons left in other countries. Chemical weapons have been used recently in Syria, Iraq and Sudan.

Chernobyl Disaster Site in the Ukraine of 1986 Soviet nuclear disaster. The scale of the disaster was kept from the Russian people.

Chestnut, the fruit of trees of the genus *Castanea*, members of the family *Fagaceae*. C. *sativa* is the sweet or Spanish chestnut, C. *dentata* the

American chestnut and C. *crenata* the Japanese chestnut. The nut is edible. The wood is used in carpentry and fencing. *See also* **Horse Chestnut.**

Chiltern Hundreds, three hundreds—Stoke, Burnham and Desborough—the stewardship of which is now a nominal office under the Chancellor of the Exchequer. Since about 1750 the nomination to it has been used as a method of enabling a member of Parliament to resign his seat on the plea that he holds an office of honour and profit under the crown. An alternate symbolic post is the stewardship of the Manor of Northstead in Yorkshire.

Chimaera, a type of fish (mostly made up of cartilage) related to sharks and rays. They use their long snouts to search the sea floor for their prey.

Chimpanzee, a large anthropoid ape, a native of tropical Africa, of a dark brown colour, with arms reaching to the knee, and capable of walking upright. Its brain is about a third of the weight of the human brain, but is anatomically similar. The animal has considerable intelligence and powers of learning. Chimpanzees have cultures as distinct as those found in human societies. It is now believed that they pass on new customs and technologies socially rather than genetically. The AIDS virus is believed to have come from chimpanzees. There is a 98·5% match between the DNA of chimpanzees and humans. *See also* **Bonobo.**

China Clay. *See* **Kaolin.**

Chinchilla, a South American burrowing rodent. Grey in colour, and white underneath.

Chivalry an international brotherhood of knights formed primarily during the 13th cent. to fight against the Muslims in the Crusades (**E4**). For the French the major battle was against the Muslims in the Holy Land and North Africa, the Spaniards fought the same enemy in their own country, and the Germans were concerned with the heathen of Baltic lands, but Chaucer's "very perfect gentle knight" had fought in all these areas. One did not easily become a knight who had to be of noble birth and then pass through a period of probation, starting as a boy page in the castle of a great lord, serving his elders while he was taught manners, singing *etc.*

Probably he learned Latin, but he certainly learned French, which was the international language of knights as Latin was of scholars. At fourteen he became a squire and learned to fight with sword, battle-axe and lance, and to endure conditions of hard living while carrying out his duties of waiting on his lord, looking after his horses, and in time accompanying him in battle. Only if he showed himself suitable was he finally knighted by a stroke of the hand or sword on the shoulder from the king or lord.

Knighthood was an international order and had its special code of behaviour; to honour one's sworn word, to protect the weak, to respect women, and defend the Faith.

Chlorine, a gaseous element, no. 17, symbol Cl, of the halogen family, first isolated in 1774 by Scheele by the action of manganese dioxide on hydrochloric acid. It unites easily with many other elements, the compounds resulting being termed chlorides. The gaseous element is greenish-yellow, with a pungent odour. It is a suffocating gas, injuring the lungs at a concentration as low as 1 part in 50,000, and was used during the first world war as a poison gas. It has a powerful bleaching action, being used in form of bleaching powder, made by combining lime and chlorine.

Chloroform, a volatile colourless liquid, compounded of carbon, hydrogen, and chlorine. It is a powerful solvent, not naturally occurring but synthesised on a large scale. When the vapour is inhaled it produces unconsciousness and insensibility to pain. It owes its discovery to Liebig, and its first application for medical purposes to Sir James Young Simpson.

Chlorophyll, the green pigment contained in the leaves of plants, discovered by P. J. Pelletier (1788–1829) and J. B. Caventou (1795–1877) in 1818. Enables the plant to absorb sunlight and so to build up sugar. *See* **Photosynthesis, Section T.**

Chocolate. *See* **Cacao.**

Chough, a member of the crow family, of glossy blue-green-black plumage, whose long curved bill and legs are coral red. It used to be abundant on the cliffs of Cornwall, but its haunts are now restricted to the rocky outcrops of the western coasts and in the mountains near by. It nests in cleft rocks and caves. The Alpine chough with yellow bill inhabits the mountainous districts of Europe and Asia. The chough is the emblem of Cornwall and appears on its coat of arms.

Christmas means "mass of Christ" from the old English *Cristes maesse,* and is celebrated by the Western church on 25 December. The date of 25 December as the day of Nativity was not generally observed until the 5th cent. A.D., though, as the winter solstice, it had long been observed as a pagan festival of *sol invictus* (unconquered sun).

The first Christmas card dates from about 1843 and the Christmas tree, of pagan origin, was introduced into England from Germany. Santa Claus is a corruption of Santa Nikolaus (St. Nicholas) patron saint of children, whose feast day is on 6 December.

Chromium, a very hard, bluish-white metal element, no. 24, symbol Cr, melting at very high temperature (above 1,900°C). Its chief ore is chromite or chrome iron-ore (ferrous chromite). "Ferro-chrome" is produced by heating chromite and anthracite in an electric furnace, and chrome steels are prepared by adding the pre-calculated amount of ferro-chrome to melted steel. Best known chrome steel is stainless steel first made by Brearley in 1912 and then developed enormously at Sheffield. A typical formula is 18 per cent. chromium, 8 per cent. nickel, 74 per cent. iron.

Equally important are Stellite alloys, containing chromium, cobalt, tungsten (or molybdenum), which have made possible modern high-speed cutting tools. Dies used in manufacture of plastics are commonly of chrome steel. The elementary metal finds little use alone except in chromium-plating for motor cars, *etc.*

Chromosomes, the structures contained within the nucleus of every animal and plant cell by which genetic information is transmitted. The chromosome number in somatic (body) cells is constant for each species of plant and animal, *e.g.,* man (46), cat (38), mouse (40) honey bee (16), fruit fly *Drosophila* (8), potato (48).

Chromosomes are long molecules composed of deoxyribonucleoproteins (*i.e.,* proteins and DNA). Human chromosomes have been the subject of much recent research since it has been found that certain disorders are associated with chromosomal aberration, *e.g.,* in Down's Syndrome an extra chromosome is present. In 1997 US scientists created the first artificial human chromosomes *See also* **Section T.**

Chub. *See* **Carp.**

Church Commissioners. The Church Commissioners were established in 1948 by the amalgamation of Queen Anne's Bounty (established 1704) and the Ecclesiastical Commissioners (established 1836) to administer Church revenues and to manage Church property.

Cid, El, a famous Spanish hero of the 11th cent., Don Rodrigo Diaz de Vivar, also called Cid Campeador, whose exploits, against Christians and Moors alike, are widely celebrated.

Cilia, minute hair-like projections on the surface of some cells, which beat together in wavelike movements like the wind over a corn-field.

These movements can be used as a means of locomotion as in the aquatic organism paramecium. Cilia are also found on the outer layers of the human trachea where they waft particles upwards to the throat, thus protecting the lungs. *See also* **Flagella.**

Cinque Ports, a number of seaport towns on the coast of Kent and Sussex, originally five; Hastings, New Romney, Hythe, Dover and Sandwich. Winchelsea and Rye were added later.

These ports were required to furnish a certain number of ships, ready for service, and in return they were granted many privileges. The official residence of the Lord Warden is Walmer Castle, near Dover. The first woman to hold the office was the Queen Mother (from 1979 to 2002).

Cistercians, an order of monks and nuns taking their names from Cîteaux, near Dijon, where their first monastery was established in 1098. The order was noted for the severity of its rule. They were famous agriculturists. The habit is white, with a black cowl or hood.

Civets, creatures with cat-like bodies, but not cats at all. They are related to the mongoose.

Civil List is the estimate of the expenses incurred by the Sovereign in conducting her official business and engagements and those of the members of her family during each year. The amount is granted by Parliament upon the recommendation of a Select Committee and has to be settled afresh in the first six months of a new reign. The Civil List of Queen Victoria was £385,000; Edward VII and George V, £470,000; Edward VIII and George VI, £410,000; Elizabeth II £475,000. In 1990, a fixed 10-year Civil List arrangement was agreed for all the Royal Family. This was changed in 1992. Now only the Queen and Prince Philip receive Civil List (Sovereign Grant) payments.

The Prince of Wales does not receive a Civil List payment but derives his revenue from the Duchy of Cornwall. Other resources available to the Queen include (1) the sums which Parliament votes to government departments each year, e.g., upkeep of palaces (Department of the Environment); (2) privy purse (revenues of the Duchy of Lancaster); (3) personal fortune, the size of which is not disclosed. In 1992 the Queen agreed to pay tax on her private income and meet the working expenses of junior members of the Royal Family.

The system under which annual payments are made by the Government to the Queen was changed by the Civil List Act 1975; payments are now included in the annual estimates in the same way as the expenditure of a government department. In July 2000 the Civil List was frozen for ten years (until the end of 2010). It was frozen again in 2010. The new Sovereign Support Grant replaced the Civil List in 2013. For 2016–17, it rose to £42·8 million.

Cleopatra's Needle on the Thames Embankment is from the time of Tuthmosis III (1500–1450 B.C.). The monolith had nothing to do with Cleopatra, as it only came to Alexandria after her death. It was first erected at the Biblical On (Greek Heliopolis), sacred City of the Sun. It was presented to the British Government by Mehemet Ali in 1819, but not brought to this country until 1878. Weight c. 183 tonnes; height, 20·8 m. Pollution has now changed its former rose-red granite to a grubby grey.

Climate is the total experience of the weather at any place over a specific period of time. Not only averages but extremes of temperature, variation of humidity, duration of sunshine and cloud cover, amount of rainfall and frequency of snow, frost, gales, etc., are amongst the data normally investigated. The interiors of great land masses are characterised by large ranges of temperature and low rainfall (continental climate), while proximity to oceans has an ameliorating effect with increase in rainfall (oceanic climate).

Presence of mountain ranges and lakes and configuration generally produce local modifications of climate, also apparent between the centre and the outlying suburbs of a city. Latitude introduces zones of climate, e.g., tropical rain, subtropical steppe and desert, temperate rain and polar. See also **Section V**.

Clock, a device for measuring the passage of time. The earliest timekeeper was the shadow-clock, a primitive form of sundial, used in Ancient Egypt about 1500 B.C. To find the time at night the water clock or clepsydra was used. The sand-glass dates from the 15th cent.

No one knows when mechanical clocks were first invented, but it is known that a complicated mechanical clock driven by water and controlled by a weighbridge escarpment was built in Peking in 1090. The Dover Clock in the Science Museum is not the earliest surviving clock in England, as was once believed, but early 17th cent. The Salisbury Cathedral clock dates from 1386 and that of Wells Cathedral from 1392. The pendulum clock was invented by the Dutch scientist Christiaan Huygens (1625–95). The first watches were made in Nuremberg shortly after 1500. The marine chronometer is a high-precision timepiece used at sea for giving Greenwich mean time. The quartz-crystal clocks are accurate to one thousandth of a second a day, and the improved atomic clock, developed at the British National Physical Laboratory, which uses the natural vibrations of the caesium atom, is an almost absolute measure of time. Its accuracy of 1 sec. in 300 years has been improved to 1 sec. in 1,000 years.

Cloud Chamber, an apparatus invented by C. T. R. Wilson in which the tracks of atomic particles can be made visible. Just as the vapour trails tell of the track of an invisible aircraft high up in the air,

so the vapour trails of an unseeable particle can tell of its behaviour. The rays under investigation pass through a chamber containing a gas, e.g., air thoroughly cleansed of dust, supersaturated with water, or alcohol- vapour. As the particle passes through it forms a track of tiny water droplets which can be photographed. After a long and honourable history this wonderful instrument is now virtually obsolete. A later ingenious device for tracking fast fundamental particles is the Bubble chamber (q.v.).

Clouds are formed by the cooling of moist air, the type depending on the way the air cools and the height at which condensation occurs.

There are three main classes: (1) high cloud (about 6,100 m)—cirrus (delicate and fibrous), cirrostratus (thin white veil), and cirrocumulus (delicately rippled) consisting of ice crystals; (2) medium cloud (above 2,100 m)—altostratus (dense, greyish veil) and altocumulus (broken flattened cloudlets)—chiefly water particles, often supercooled; (3) low cloud (from near ground to 2,100 m)—cumulus (fair weather, broken, dome-topped), cumulonimbus (heavy, towering to great heights), stratocumulus (layer of globular masses or rolls), stratus (like fog but off the ground), nimbostratus (low, rainy cloud).

The highest clouds of all, and the rarest, are the noctilucent, seen only on summer nights in high latitudes. They form at about 80 km above the earth and consist of ice-coated dust from meteors. The spread of these noctilucent clouds may be due to global warming.

Clouds were first classified by the Quaker, Luke Howard in 1804. The World Meteorological Organisation is the body in charge of cloud naming.

On Venus, clouds are made of sulphuric acid. Those on Jupiter consist of ammonia.

Clover, plants of the Trifolium genus, family Leguminosae, with about 250 species. These are "nitrogen fixing" plants and include red clover, white clover, alsike clover and crimson clover. They are of great importance in agriculture because in a good pasture they supply directly or indirectly most of the protein available to the animals. Seed of "wild white" clover has been accepted since about 1939 as the indispensable plant of good United Kingdom grassland, largely through the efforts of pioneers like D. A. Gilchrist (1859–1927).

Clownfish, a tropical fish very popular as a family pet (it was the star of the film Finding Nemo). Clownfish lose their hearing if they grow up in water with high acidity. They only migrate long distances as larvae.

Coal. Until recently the most important single fuel has been coal. It is a mineral of organic origin, formed from the remains of vegetation which over millions of years has changed to coal by the effects of heat and pressure from overlying rock or water. All coal contains moisture, inflammable volatiles, mineral impurities (some of which remain as coal ash after the coal is burnt), and fixed carbon (the coke that is left after the volatiles have been driven off). The relative proportions vary—from Anthracite, a hard coal containing the highest proportion of fixed carbon, to Lignite or brown coal which is little more than a hard peat.

In the UK, coal long formed the basis of past industrial prosperity. Peak output occurred in 1913 when 290 million tonnes were mined, one third of which was exported. At the end of the second world war production had fallen to 186 million tonnes and was far below demand.

In 1947 the British coal industry was brought under public ownership and all its assets were vested in the National Coal Board. During the next ten years great efforts were made to increase coal output but, quite suddenly in 1956, demand for coal fell as oil became a popular fuel. The fall in demand was accompanied by increasing productivity, both mines and miners having been cut in their numbers by over half. Then as a result of the high cost of oil in 1973 came expansion of the industry. From 1984 the coal industry faced a bitter strike over plans to make large-scale pit closures. The defeat of the miners weakened the NUM and its leader, Arthur Scargill. The Government decision (in 1992) to close many of the remaining collieries and to privatise the industry created a bitter political controversy. By early 1995 the last pits had been privatised and the workforce decimated, the closure of Kellingley colliery in Yorkshire in 2015 ended underground mining in Britain. But around 40% of Britain's electricity is still provided by coal from abroad. These coal-fired power stations will be phased out by 2023. Today there is a huge demand for coal from India (which has huge reserves) and China.

Coat of Arms, in heraldry, a device containing a family's armorial bearings. In medieval times the coat upon which such device was embroidered; knights wore it over their armour.

Coati, a fox-sized creature belonging to the racoon family. Usually found in South America.

Cobalt, element no. 27, symbol Co, a white metal melting at 1490°C. Two main ores are *cobalt glance* (in which the element is combined with arsenic and sulphur) and *smaltite* (cobalt arsenide). The principal sources are Ontario and Congo. Various cobalt alloys are important, *e.g.*, stellite, ferrocobalt and carboloy. Its monoxide is an important colouring medium, and is used for colouring glass and porcelain blue and in mobilephone batteries. Discovered by the Swedist chemist Georg Brandt.

Cobra, hooded and very venomous snakes. The best known species are the Indian Cobra, the Egyptian Cobra, and the Black-necked Cobra. Their food consists chiefly of small rodents, The King Cobra is almost exclusively a snake-eater. The "Spitting" Cobras (or Ringhals) of S. Africa are a related genus, capable of spitting their venom several yards. The King Cobra possesses enough venom to kill 100 people.

Coca, a S. American shrub, *Erythroxylon coca*, also cultivated in Java. The leaves yield cocaine, classified as a dangerous drug. When the local people chew the leaves they are enabled to withstand hunger and fatigue, as cocaine acts both as a mental stimulant and as an anaesthetic on the mucous lining of the stomach. Colombia is a centre of the trade (along with Peru and Bolivia).

Cochineal *or* **Carmine,** a dyestuff consisting of the dried bodies of the female scale insect (*Dactylopius coccus*) which feeds on cacti. Of ancient origin, the dye was well known to the Aztecs, and was used widely in the Middle Ages. The scarlet tunics worn by the English during the Napoleonic wars owed their colour to carmine.

Cockatoo, a member of the parrot family, bearing a crest of feathers on the head, native to Australia and adjacent regions. Predominant colour is white tinged with yellow or scarlet while some species have dark plumage. The cockatoo of New Guinea is slaty black with pale red cheeks and can crack Kanary nuts. Its survival is threatened by the pet trade.

Cockchafer (*Melolontha*), one of the most destructive of beetles, the larvae feeding on roots. It is about 2·5 cm in length, of a brownish colour, and emits a loud whirring sound when flying.

Cockle, the popular name of the bi-valve shellfish of the genus *Cardium*, found in sandy bays.

Cockroach, inaccurately called the "black beetle"; a pest of bakeries and kitchens. In Britain two species are commonly found; the Common Cockroach (*Blatta orientalis*), about 2·5 cm long, with the wing covers long in the male and short in the female; and the German Cockroach (*Blatta germanica*), now the most common, half the size, dark yellow, with both sexes fully winged. All species have long antennae and flattened, leathery, shiny bodies. They are nocturnal and omnivorous. Cockroaches are the nimblest creatures on Earth and survived the extinction of the dinosaurs. They have extremely powerful jaws. There are 4,600 named species.

Cocoa. See Cacao.

Coconut Palm (*Cocos nucifera*), a tropical tree, growing to a height of 30 m, with a slender trunk surmounted by giant feather-like leaves. One of the most important sources of food and raw material for people living in the tropics. The juice of the fruit, or coconut, is drunk; the kernel is eaten fresh or dried to form copra, which yields oil used for feeding stuffs and oil, used in the manufacture of soap, margarine, cosmetics, *etc.*; leaves are used for thatching; leaf stalks for canes, fence posts, *etc.*, and the trunk for houses and bridges.

The main producing areas are: Indonesia, Philippines, Malaysia, Sri Lanka, south India and the Caribbean, but demand outstrips supply.

Codes, a term used to designate a system of laws properly classified. The Code of Hammurabi, king of Babylon, *c.* 1751 B.C., had extensive influence over a long period. The Romans formulated several codes of historic importance including the Theodosian Code which summarised the Roman laws from the time of Constantine to 438 A.D. The final codification was made under order of the Emperor Justinian by his chief minister Tribonian and published in 529 with a new edition in 534. The most important of modern codes is the *Code Napoléon*, compiled between 1803 and 1810, and still in force. It has been used as an example for the codification of the laws of a number of countries from America to Japan. Under Frederick the Great the law of Prussia was codified. English law has never been codified, although the law on some subjects has been gathered up into a single statute. The Law Commission Act, 1965, sought to consolidate and codify the law.

Codex, a collection of written pages, stitched and bound together. The oldest extant Greek codex is the Sinaiaticus of the 4th cent. (*see below*). The Vatican codex (4th cent.) and the Alexandrine codex (5th cent.) are other examples. See Papyri.

Codex Sinaiaticus. The British Museum, in 1933, purchased the *Codex Sinaiticus* from the Soviet Government for £100,000. The Sinaiaticus was written on 347 vellum leaves some fifteen to sixteen hundred years ago and the binding into 2 volumes was completed by Douglas Cockerill and his son in 1936. It was sold in 1981 for $5·2 million. It is one of the world's most important Christian manuscripts. Written in Greek at the time of Constantine, it once contained the whole Old and New Testaments and the Aprocrypha, but the Old Testament has been lost.

Coelacanth, a primitive fish living off the Comoros Islands (and also off Indonesia). The coelacanth represents the period in history when fish began slowly to evolve into four-legged animals. Its survival is now threatened by fishing fleets.

Coffee, a shrub found originally in Arabia and Ethiopia, but now extensively grown in Brazil, Colombia, Ivory Coast, Uganda, Angola and Central America. It yields a seed or berry which after undergoing the necessary preparation, is ground and used in most countries as a breakfast beverage. The best coffee is the Mocha, an Arabian variety. The stimulating effect of coffee is due to the caffeine, which is also present in tea. The beverage was introduced into Europe in the 17th cent., and the first London coffee shop was opened in 1652. It has become the daytime drink of our age. The largest coffee producers are Brazil, followed by Vietnam and Indonesia. Coffee could become a high-profile victim of climate change unless new types of bean can be produced. See also R17.

Coinage. See Currency.

Coke is the solid residue remaining when coal is carbonised and nearly all the volatile constituents have been driven off. Used as fuel, and as an agent for reducing metallic oxides to metals.

Coleoptera. See Beetles.

College of Arms. See Heralds, College of.

Colorado Beetle, a serious pest of potato crops. Both adults and larvae feed on the foliage where the orange eggs are laid. The grub is reddish, with two rows of small black spots on each side. The adults are about 1·2 cm long with yellow and black striped wing cases. The beetle is avoided by birds because of its nasty taste, and is controlled by arsenical sprays.

Colosseum, the name of the Flavian amphitheatre at Rome, begun by Vespasian and finished by Titus A.D. 80. In general outline it still remains one of the most magnificent ruins in the world. In the arena the famous gladiatorial displays and mimic naval battles used to be given, and about 50,000 spectators could be accommodated.

Colossus is the name which the ancients gave to any statue of gigantic size. The Colossus at Rhodes, which was a bronze statue of the sun god, Helios, was the most famous, and reckoned among the seven wonders of the world. It stood over 30 m high at the mouth of the harbour. It fell in an earthquake in 224 B.C.

Colugo, also known as "flying lemur," caguan or kubuk, a remarkable mammal which may be regarded as an aberrant insectivore or an aberrant form of the earliest ancestor of the bats. It has nothing to do with lemurs. There are two genera, one inhabiting the Philippines and one inhabiting Malaysia. They have a parachute-like membrane which covers them from the neck to the tip of the tail, by means of which they can glide from treetop to ground.

Comets are celestial bodies which generally move about the solar system in elongated elliptical or nearly parabolic orbits. Most comets are in the latter category, having extremely long orbital periods, up to millions of years, and have therefore only been seen once in recorded history. They spend most of their lifetimes at extremely large distances from the sun, far outside Pluto's orbit. Those in elliptical orbits appear periodically and a few have been observed regularly.

Halley's comet, named after Edmund Halley, who first correctly predicted that this comet would reappear in 1758, was first observed in Roman times and is one of the brightest of the periodic comets. The nucleus of a comet, which appears as a faint star when the comet is very far from the sun, is no longer believed to be a frozen mixture of dust and materials called "ices".

The core is now thought to be composed of hard material, not dust. Approaching the sun, the comet is heated by sunlight and the surface material is first vaporised and later photo-dissociated and ionised by sunlight. The gases and ions produce the fuzzy look of the coma of the comet. Under the influence of sunlight acting on dust, and the solar wind and interplanetary field acting on the ions, the cometary tail (often multiple) is produced. This may stretch up to 200 million km, pointing away from the sun.

Donati's comet (1858) was possibly the most spectacular of all and was visible even in daylight. Kohoutek's comet (1975) was the first to be observed from space by the American Skylab and Russian Soyuz. Images from the Hubble telescope suggest there are many millions (if not billions) of comets orbiting the Sun in a belt that lies beyond the orbit of Neptune and engulfs that of Pluto. (*see* **Oort Cloud**).

A spectacular comet appearance in 1997 was Hale-Bopp (which was last visible from Earth *c.* 2600 B.C. The Rosetta space mission (from 2004 to 2016) landed a robot on the comet 67P in November 2014. Although it landed awkwardly and soon lost power, it nonetheless revealed that comets contain organic materials. They suggest that comets could be the messengers of life.

The Stardust space probe, launched in 1999, has collected grains of stardust dating from before the Sun was born. The probe has also gathered glycine, an amino acid (a vital building block of life) from a comet tail. In 2005 the Deep Impact probe collided with Tempel 1 to collect data.

The longest comet tail ever recorded (350 million miles) was observed in 2000 (a trail left by the comet Hyakutake).

Commons are the remnants of the medieval open fields round villages in which the villagers had rights in common, *e.g.,* (i) **estover**—the right of taking wood for house building or firewood; (ii) **pasture**—the right of grazing beasts; (iii) **turbary**—the right of digging turf; (iv) **piscary**—the right to fish. Many of these common lands were enclosed during the agrarian revolution which went on steadily in England from the 15th cent. onwards, and with their enclosure common rights vanished. A Royal Commission on Common Land described the commons in 1965 as the "last reservoir of uncommitted land" which provide, as far as the public is concerned, by far the largest part of the accessible open spaces of the country.

Under the Commons Registration Act, 1965, it was the duty of the relevant local council to make a register of all common land and all town and village greens in their areas.

Today there are around 1·3 million acres of common land in England and Wales, held by a variety of bodies. There are *c.* 10,000 village greens, some under threat from developers.

Compass *or* **Mariner's Compass.** It has been known since very early times that an iron needle, suspended freely to hang horizontally when not magnetised, comes to rest roughly along the geographical north–south line when magnetised. Further, it generally does not hang horizontally. This is the essential behaviour of the *compass*, a navigational instrument whose invention is obscure but which seems to have been known to the Chinese 4,500 years ago. That the behaviour of the compass shows the existence of a *magnetic field* associated with the Earth was first fully recognised by William Gilbert in 1600.

Aircraft and ships now largely employ gyrostatic compasses which are not affected by electrical and magnetic disturbances. Sperry, Brown and Anschutz are three important types of gyroscopic compass.

Composite Materials, or more simply composites, are materials which derive useful properties by combining the virtues of two or more components. Combining clay with straw to make tougher bricks is an ancient example in which fibres (straw) are embedded in a matrix or body (the clay). A modern example is fibreglass in which glass fibres are embedded in a plastic matrix. Nature also uses composites as in bamboo in which a lignin matrix binds together the fibres of cellulose to make a light strong structure. Composites may contain flakes or particles embedded in the matrix instead of fibres—it depends on the application. Although the idea is not new composite technology has made rapid strides in the last few decades guided by scientific insight into the nature of solids and the origin of their stengths and weaknesses.

The motivation had been that scientifically designed composites offer materials with exceptional strength/weight ratio, desirable magnetic properties and other technological advantages which meet the extreme demands of a variety of industries. For example, composite aluminium containing boron fibres or resin containing graphite fibres can have strength/ weight ratios over twice that of highstrength solid aluminium.

Conclave, an assembly of Roman Catholic car-dinals met together to elect a pope. The last Conclave was held in the Vatican in March 2013 when the 115 cardinal-electors chose Cardinal Jorge Mario Bergoglio of Argentina as the successor to Benedict XVI. A Jesuit, he was also the first Pope from the Americas. He took the name Francis I.

Concorde, supersonic airliner whose first flight was from Toulouse on 2 March 1969 and the first British flight from Felton in Bristol on 9 April 1969. More than 2¼ million passengers travelled on Concorde between 1976 and its withdrawal from service in 2004. The plane could cruise at 1,350 mph at altitudes up to 60,000 ft. In February 1996 it flew from New York to London in 2 hrs 52 mins.

Condor, a large eagle of brilliant black plumage with a circlet of white feathers round its neck. It is a native of the Andes. There are two types of New World condor, the Andean and the Californian. Both are black, but the Andean condor has a pink head, the Californian a yellow head and red neck. They are among the rarest of birds. The condor acts as the vulture of the Andes.

Coniferae are cone-bearing trees, including firs, pines, cedars, cypresses, junipers, yews, *etc.,* and are widely distributed in temperate regions. Urgent conservation measures are needed to protect some of these trees.

Constellation, a grouping of stars that forms a pattern when seen from Earth. There are a total of 88 constellations in use on modern star charts, some of which are much larger than others. The stars within a particular constellation are not necessarily close to each other in space. In most cases they only appear close together due to their lying in more or less the same line of sight as seen from Earth.

Constitution, the fundamental organic law or principles of government of a nation, state, society, or other organisation, embodied in written documents, or implied in the institutions and customs of the country or society.

Continent, a word used in physical geography to denote the larger continuous land masses in contrast to the great oceans of the earth. They are: Eurasia (conventionally regarded as 2 continents, Europe and Asia), Africa, North America, South America, Australia and Antarctica. (Australasia is Australia, New Zealand and adjacent islands. Oceania is Australasia and the many islands of the S.W. Pacific.)

Continental Drift. The hypothesis of drifting continents is due to F. B. Taylor, an American geologist who published his theory in 1908, and to the Austrian meteorologist Alfred Wegener. The latter was impressed by the matching coasts of South America and Africa, which seemed to him to fit together like the pieces of a jigsaw puzzle. Since then other people have taken up and developed the idea. See **Plate Tectonics, Section V.**

Conurbation, a term used in reference to an extensive and continuous area of urban land-use. Conurbations are frequently formed by the physical coalescence of several formerly free-standing towns. They may themselves coalesce to form an even higher order (a megalopolis).

Convocation, an assembly called together to deliberate ecclesiastical affairs. In the Church of England the provinces of Canterbury and York each have their convocation. The term is also applied to certain academic gatherings.

Coot. A very widely distributed bird of the rail family and a common resident of the British Isles. The adult is black with a conspicuous white bald shield on the forehead and a white bill. The juvenile is brownish grey with whitish breast and throat. The coot flies heavily, but swims well. It dives frequently and can remain submerged for a considerable time. It is pugnacious and in winter gregarious. The food is chiefly vegetable. The large nest is usually built among aquatic vegetation and the young are fed by both parents. The Crested Coot, occurs in S. Europe.

Copernicium. Element No.112, 277 times heavier than hydrogen and produced by nuclear fusion.

Copper, one of the most familiar of metals, element no. 29, symbol Cu, used in ancient times as an alloy with tin in producing bronze, and preceding iron as an industrial material. Copper ores are most abundant in the USA, Chile, Canada, Zambia and Congo. All copper compounds are poisonous. Called the "red metal".

Copyright. Under the old Copyright Act, 1956, copyright subsists in every original literary, dramatic, musical, and artistic work if the author is a British subject or a citizen of the Republic of Ireland or resident in the United Kingdom, or if the work is first published in the UK.

The Act provided that, except in certain special cases, the author of the work shall be the first owner of the copyright, and there are no formalities, such as registration or payment of fees, to be accomplished. Copyright includes the right to reproduce the work in any material form, to perform the work in public, or, if the work is unpublished, to publish the work.

The Act also protected sound recordings, films and television and sound broadcasts. Literary, dramatic, musical and artistic works which enjoy the protection of the Act are automatically protected in those countries which are parties to the Berne Copyright Convention or the Universal Copyright Convention.

In general, copyright in literary, dramatic, musical and artistic works is vested in the author for the period of his or her lifetime and 50 years following after which it passes into the public domain and becomes freely available to any who wish to make use of it. The EU has proposed extending copyright protection to 95 years.

The Copyright Libraries, entitled to receive copies of books published in the United Kingdom are given under **Libraries.** The Berne Copyright Convention and the Universal Copyright Convention were revised at a diplomatic conference held in Paris in 1971. The effect of the revisions allows any national of a developing country to obtain, under certain conditions, a compulsory licence to translate and publish a copyright work for the purpose of teaching, scholarship and research, upon payment of compensation to the copyright owner of the original work.

The Copyright Designs and Patents Act, 1988, updated the old law on copyright (and has itself been amended in the light of recent EU regulations). The first new unified EU patents were issued in 2014. In the USA, the 1998 Digital Millennium Copyright Act was enacted to combat Internet piracy (but was soon obsolete).

Coral, an order of small marine animals closely related to the sea-anemone, but differing from it in their ability to develop a limy skeleton. They multiply sexually and by budding. The structure of the coral secretions assumes a variety of forms, fan-like, tree-like, mushroom shape, and so forth. Red coral (the skeleton of *Corallium rubrum*) is mainly obtained from the Mediterranean.

The coral reefs of the Pacific and Indian Oceans are often many miles in extent. The largest is the Great Barrier Reef, which is 1,400 miles long and 150 miles across at its widest. Living corals occur only in warm seas at about 23°C. Scientists have predicted that most coral reefs will have been destroyed within 30 years by rising sea temperatures caused by global warming. They are also threatened by deep-sea trawling.

Corals adapt their shape and form according to the ratio of magnesium to calcium in the water. They are the rainforests of the seas and maybe the medicine cabinets of the future.

Cordite, a smokeless explosive adopted for small arms and heavy artillery by the UK in the naval and military services in 1889, and composed of 58 parts of nitro-glycerine, 37 of gun-cotton, and 5 of vaseline. It is a jelly or plastic dough, and used in the form of sticks. Invented by Sir Frederick Abel and Sir James Dewar in 1889.

Cork, the bark of a species of oak, *Quercus suber*, grown largely in the South of Europe and North America. The cork tree is said to yield bark every six to ten years for 150 years, and grows to a height of from 6–12 m. Its lightness, impermeability, and elasticity enable it to be used for a variety of commercial purposes, especially for stoppers of bottles.

Cormorant, a large, long-billed water-bird which captures fish by diving. The common cormorant has bronze-black plumage with white cheeks and sides and is found round the sea coasts of most parts of the world, including the British Isles. It nests in colonies on sea cliffs and rocky ledges. The Shag or Green Cormorant is a smaller bird with green-black plumage and a crest.

Corncrake. Once a regular summer visitor to Britain. The harsh and piercing note of this bird was a familiar sound in cornfields. After nearly becoming extinct, its numbers are reviving.

Cornish. *See* **Kernewek.**

Corona or **Solar Corona,** the outer atmosphere of the sun. This glows by virtue of light emitted by the sun and scattered by electrons and dust particles at various heights in the sun's atmosphere and also by light emitted from ionised atoms in the corona itself. Corona light is much fainter than the bright disc of the sun and is invisible against the normal blue of the sky. During total solar eclipses, the corona can be seen by the human eye as a faint glow extending irregularly outwards a few solar diameters from the sun. The sun's atmosphere extends much further than this but is invisible to the eye at large distances from the sun.

The corona gases are thought to be very hot (millions of degrees) and in complex violent motion; the gross structure of the corona is connected with the sunspot cycle.

Corporal Punishment in Britain has seen much recent legislation. Caning in state schools was made illegal in 1986 (in public schools in 1999). Birching as a judicial punishment was abolished in 1948. Flogging was stopped in the Royal Navy in 1957 and in prisons and borstals in 1967. The 'reasonable chastisement' of children allowed under the 1933 Children and Young Persons Act has been challenged (*e.g.* in 1998 in the European Court).

An attempt to ban any form of smacking was defeated in November 2004. The first country to ban smacking was Sweden in 1979.

Cortes, the Parliaments of Spain and Portugal.

Cosmic Rays are a form of radiation coming from outer space, of deep penetrating power and of great scientific interest. The rays consist of extremely energetic atomic particles—protons, electrons and some heavier nucleons—travelling at speeds very close to that of light. A complex series of events result from their collision with the atmosphere, giving rise to showers of secondary high-energy particles.

Low energy cosmic rays can be studied from space satellites and space probes. Intermediate energy cosmic rays are investigated using sensitive detector arrays on mountain tops or space-satellites. High-energy cosmic rays can only be studied indirectly at ground level. The great interest is because we now believe their origin to be in, or associated with, some of the most interesting objects in the universe—supernovae, neutron stars, pulsars and perhaps some gigantic galactic nuclei. *See* **Section T, Part I.**

Cosmology. *See* **Section T.**

Cotton, the name of a plant of several species bearing large yellow flowers with purple centres. These centres expand into pods, which at maturity burst and yield the white fibrous substances known as cotton. The raw cotton contains a large proportion of seeds which are removed by "ginning". Long before the Christian era, cotton had been grown and used with great skill in India to make fabrics. The industry was not introduced into England until the middle of the 17th cent. when Protestant refugees from Flanders came to settle in the wool textile districts of East Anglia and Lancashire. With improvements in machinery and expansion of overseas trade in the 18th and 19th cent., Lancashire became the centre of the world's cotton industry but now man-made fibres have taken the place of cotton. The largest cotton producers in the world are China, the United States and Uzbekistan.

Cotton Gin, invented in 1793 by the American Eli Whitney. By automating the production of cotton fibre from seed pods, it revolutionised cotton-growing.

Coulomb, a unit of electric charge, named after the French naval engineer, Charles Augustin de Coulomb (1736–1806), equal to the quantity of electricity transferred in one second by a current of one ampere.

Council of Trent. See **Trent, Council of.**

County. After the 1972 reorganisation of local government in the UK the distinction between *administrative* counties and *geographical* counties no longer existed. Certain geographical counties disappeared (*e.g.,* Pembroke), new counties appeared (*e.g.,* Gwynedd), See also **Section D.**

Court Leet, a court of record held annually before the steward of any particular manor or lordship; originally there was only one court for a manor, but in the time of Edward I it branched into two, the court baton and the court leet.

Courts. See **Magistrates.**

Coyote, an animal belonging to the dog family. Native to North and Central America, it displays an exceptional capacity for survival. Coywolves have resulted from interbreeding with wolves.

Coypu or **Nutria Rat,** a large beaver-like rodent found naturally in S. America.

Crane, a large, graceful wading-bird with elegant long legs and neck, greyish plumage, superficially resembling the heron and related to the bustard. They migrate in V or W formation and have trumpet-like voices. There are fourteen species, found in all continents except S. America, including the Crowned Crane with golden coronet and the Demoiselle with tuft-like crest of white feathers. The Common Crane nested in East Anglia in medieval times. They mate with their partners for life.

Creed (Latin *credo* = I believe), is a formal statement of belief. The three orthodox Christian creeds are the **Apostles' Creed** (a summary of their teaching), the **Nicene Creed** (drawn up by the Church Council at Nicaea in A.D. 325 to define its theological doctrines), and the **Athanasian Creed** (on the nature and divinity of Christ).

Cremation, ancient custom, revived in Victorian times, of burning the dead. Cremation was first legalised in Great Britain in 1884 and the first crematorium opened at Woking in that year. Earlier Sir Henry Thompson had founded the Cremation Society of England in 1874.

Application for cremation must be accompanied by two medical certificates. Orthodox Jews and Muslims forbid cremation. Nowadays, most Britons choose cremation.

Creutzfeldt-Jakob Disease, See **Mad Cow Disease.**

Cricket, a genus of insects of the grasshopper order which move by leaps. The male produces a chirping noise by rubbing its wing-covers together. Just as the males inherit the nerve machinery for emitting the song of the species, so the females receive and respond to that song and to no other. Our warming climate means the chirping of crickets is now more common.

Crinoids. See **Sea Lily.**

Crocodiles and their allies (alligators, caymans and gavials) are the largest of modern reptiles. They are well equipped for a predatory life in shallow waters, having powerful tails and strong jaws. Their eggs are laid on land, in sand or decomposing vegetation. Their wounds never become infected because of a bacteria-destroying protein in their blood. There are 23 species and they are capable of complex navigation over long distances. The Gharial crocodile of India and Nepal is rapidly declining. However, in Australia

salt water crocodiles are increasing. Crocodiles are responsible for the deaths of around 2,000 people each year.

Crow, a family of birds including many well-known species such as the rook, raven, jackdaw, carrion crow, hooded crow, magpie, nutcrackers, jaw and chough. They are intelligent birds.

Crufts, the most famous dog show, first held in Islington in 1891 with 2,437 entries and 36 breeds.

Crux. See under **Southern Cross.**

Cryogenics (Greek roots: productive of cold) is the science dealing with the production of very low temperatures and the study of their physical and technological consequences. "Very low" is often taken to mean below about −150°C.

The growth of cryogenics (essentially a 20th-cent. science) is connected with the discovery of how to liquefy all gases including even helium which resisted liquefaction until 1908. Scientifically, cryogenics is important partly because special phenomena (*e.g.,* superconductivity (*q.v.*)) appear at lower temperatures and partly because more can be learned about ordinary properties by studying them in the absence of heat.

Technologically, cryogenics is becoming more and more significant, for example, liquefied gases are rocket propellants, superconductors make valuable magnets, tissue-freezing techniques (using very cold liquids) have been introduced into surgery. The low-density ice, known as *glassy water,* may be able to be used to "freeze" human bodies successfully. See **Absolute Temperature.**

Crystal, in everyday usage, a solid chemical substance bounded by plane surfaces which show a regular geometrical arrangement as, *e.g.,* quartz crystals, rock salt, snow flakes. In physics the term means any substances whose atoms are arranged in a regular three-dimensional array. This includes most solids, even those not particularly crystalline in appearance, *e.g.,* a lump of lead. See **Glass** and **Liquid Crystals.**

Cuckoo, a well-known migratory bird which is found in Great Britain from April to July, hawk-like in shape, with a very characteristic note, uttered during the mating season only by the male. The hen has a soft bubbling call. It lays its eggs in the nests of other birds, *e.g.,* the meadow pipit and hedge sparrow, but only one egg in each nest. Feeds mainly on insects, particularly hairy caterpillars. For many years, its numbers have been in serious decline, partly because it still arrives in Britain at its traditional time when insect levels have now peaked. It migrates 4,000 miles to West Africa.

Cucurbitaceae. See **Gourd Family.**

Cuneiform, (Latin = *wedge-shaped*), an ancient method of writing by impressing wedge-like strokes into tablets of damp clay which when dried and hardened formed a permanent script, Cuneiform writing developed from its original pictographic form into a phonetic writing and can be traced back to the non-Semitic Sumerians of ancient Mesopotamia, the earliest civilisation known to us. It passed to the Semitic Accadians of Babylonia in the 3rd millennium B.C. who adapted it to their own language. Decipherment by Sir Henry Rawlinson, 1835. One of the first written scripts in history.

Curfew (Old F. *covre-feu* = cover fire), a regulation common throughout Europe in medieval times by which, at a fixed hour in the evening, the church bell was rung as a signal that fires were to be put out and the people were to go to bed. The custom originated in the fear of fire when buildings were built of timber.

Curia, the central government of the Roman Catholic Church. Its twelve Sacred Congregations or "ministries" were reduced to nine from 1968.

Curie, a measure of the rate at which radio-active material emits radiation. One curie is a disintegration rate of 3.7×10^{10} disintegrations per second.

Curlew, a wading-bird of which there are several species. It frequents marshy places, feeds on worms, insects, molluscs and berries and has a long, down-curved bill. Now in serious decline. It has an evocative call.

Currency is the name given to the types of cash money—metal or paper—in use in an area (*e.g.* pound, sterling, dollar, Euro). It also designates the actual coins or notes issued. Its amount is usually subject to regulation by the Government, or by a Central Bank acting on the Government's behalf. Britain changed over to a £-based decimal currency in February 1971.

On 1 January 1985, ½p coins ceased to be legal tender. The old "halfpenny" first appeared in 1280. The Royal Mint produced a smaller and lighter 50p coin. The old 50p ceased to be legal tender on 28 February 1998. The first two-colour coin (the £2 coin) entered circulation in June 1998. A new design £20 banknote became legal tender in June 1999. It featured new devices to protect against counterfeiting. The most recent £20 note bears the image of Adam Smith, the first Scot on an English banknote. From 2016 plastic £5 bank notes were in wide circulation (they began circulating at Scotland's Clydesdale Bank in 2015). A £10 note followed in 2017 and a £20 note by 2020. A 12-sided £1 coin was introduced in March 2017.

There are plans for Wales to have its own bank notes for the first time.

The first pound coin was minted in 1489 by Henry VII. It was made of gold and became known as the sovereign.

Cybernetics, the science concerned with the automatic control and communication processes in both animals and machines. Thus it is concerned with brain function, information theory, electronic computers, and automation.

Cyclamen. The national flower of Cyprus.

Cyclone, a term usually applied to a tropical revolving storm. Cyclones often occur towards the end of the hot seasons and are mainly confined to tracks in the western areas of the oceans, being known as hurricanes (Caribbean and Pacific), cyclones (Indian Ocean) and typhoons (China Seas). The circulation of air in a cyclone is similar to that in the *depression* of temperate latitudes, but the region of low pressure is much more localised and the pressure gradients steeper. Winds of hurricane strength and torrential rain occur generally, although at the centre of the storm there is a small area, known as the "eye", where fair, calm weather prevails. Hurricane Andrew, which hit Florida in August 1992, left 250,000 people homeless. Hurricane Katrina devastated the New Orleans area in August 2005 leaving an untold number of dead. The USA was hit again in 2012 when Hurricane Sandy left a trail of devastation centred on New York and New Jersey.

Half the cyclones in the world are formed in the Pacific Ocean.

Cyclotron, a machine for accelerating charged particles such as protons to very high energies. Devised by E. O. Lawrence in California in 1930, it uses a magnetic field to make the particles traverse nearly circular paths and an electric field to give them an additional pulse of energy each time round. The accelerated particles impinge on targets, and the resulting events are a basic source of information for nuclear physicists. The cyclotron is obsolescent and has led to the development of other machines, *e.g.*, betatrons, synchrotrons. Britain has two major national high-energy machines: a 7 GeV proton synchroton (to be closed and replaced by a "spallation neutron source"), and a 5 GeV electron synchrotron.

D

Dab, a flatfish species of fish found in the North Sea. A relatively unloved species.

Dactylopterus, a fish of the gurnard family, with wing-like pectoral fins; sometimes known as the flying fish, though that appellation is more generally given to *Exocaetus exiliens*.

Daddy Longlegs, or **Crane-fly**, a slender long-legged fly of the family Tipulidae. The larvae which do damage to lawns and plants are called leather-jackets. The Americans call Harvestmen (*q.v.*) daddy longlegs.

Daguerreotype, the first practical photographic process, invented in Paris by M. Daguerre during the years 1824–39. The light-sensitive plate was prepared by bringing iodine in contact with a plate of silver. After exposure a positive image came by development of the plate in mercury vapour. Even for openair scenes the first daguerreotypes involved exposure of 5–10 minutes. The picture came in one copy and the process was therefore of limited use. The wet collodion process (1851) rendered the technique obsolete.

Dail Eireann, the name of the national parliament of the Irish Republic.

Dalai Lama, the temporal and religious leader of

Tibet. The present Dalai Lama, Tenzin Gyabo (b. 1935), the 14th reincarnation, fled to India in 1959. Awarded the 1989 Nobel Peace Prize. He may well be the last Dalai Lama.

Lamas (meaning 'superior ones') are Tibetan Buddhist monks. The Panchen Lama is held to be the reincarnation of the Buddha of Light. *See* **Lamaism, J29.**

Dances come in a whole variety of types. The waltz originated in the 18th century, but achieved pre-eminence in the 19th century. The music of Johann Strauss the Younger earned him the title of 'Waltz King'. *See* **Special Topic, end Section P.**

Dark Matter. It is thought that dark matter (so-called because it is invisible) makes up about 82 % of space in the universe. We know it exists from its gravitational effect which can bend light. It is dark matter that holds the galaxy together. It appears to be composed of sub-atomic particles that do not interact at all with the visible matter of stars and planets. Dark energy is the mysterious force causing the universe to expand.

Darter 1. Snakebirds are a genus of the pelican family, with long, pointed bill and serpent-like neck and resembling cormorants in appearance. There are 5 species. 2. Numerous species of small freshwater fish belonging to the perch family, found in N. America.

Date Palm. *Phoenix dactylifera*, one of the oldest known food plants widely cultivated in N. Africa and W. Asia. It grows to 30 m and continues to bear for 2 or 3 centuries, its fruit being of great value as a food. From the leaves the Africans make roofs for their huts; ropes are made from the fibrous parts of the stalks; and the sap furnishes a stimulating beverage.

Day is the most natural unit of time and may be defined as the period of rotation of the earth relative to any selected heavenly body. Relative to the sun it is called the *solar day*. Relative to a fixed star it is called the *sidereal day*. Owing to irregularities in the earth's movements, the time taken for the earth to rotate through 360° relative to the sun is variable, and so the *mean solar day* of 24 hours has been introduced, which is the average throughout the year. The *mean solar day* is our standard, used for purposes of the calendar, and astronomers use *sidereal* clocks to check mean solar time. In practice, for convenience, the sidereal day is determined by the earth's rotation relative to the vernal equinox or first point of Aries, and is equal to 23 hours 56 minutes and 4·091 seconds of mean solar time (*i.e.*, about 4 minutes shorter than a solar day). Around 600 million years ago, a day was only 21·9 hours long.

The lengths of day on other planets can differ greatly to that of the Earth. Jupiter spins once every 10 hours or so while the length of a day on Venus is equal to 243·01 Earth days, longer than its year of 224·7 days. *See* **Time.**

DDT (dichloro-dephenyl-trichloroethane). A very powerful insecticide which has had wide success in the control of diseases, such as malaria and typhus which are carried by insects. Mosquito swamps are sprayed with DDT to kill the carriers. Because this toxic chemical breaks down very slowly it builds up in birds and animals and its use is now banned in Britain. Its detection in Antarctic wild life confirmed that DDT pollution was virtually worldwide.

Dead Languages include the ancient Greek and Latin tongues, which are no longer spoken in everyday usage but are preserved in literature.

Deadly Nightshade. *See* **Belladonna.**

Dean, a Church of England dignitary, ranking below a bishop, and the head of the chapter of a cathedral. A Rural Dean supervises a *deanery*.

Death Penalty. The last British executions were in 1964. Capital punishment was abolished for murder in 1969 and for all offences in 1998. In 2010, at least 23 countries around the world held judicial executions, while 139 have abolished the death penalty. In 2013 Maryland became the 18th state in the USA to abolish the death penalty. (only Texas, Georgia and Missouri now regularly use the death penalty.) The number of global executions is at its highest for many years.

Death Watch Beetle (*Xestobium rufovillosum*), a wood-boring beetle, larger than the common furniture beetle, found chiefly in the old oak beams of churches and other historic buildings. The grub bores from 4–12 years. The name "death watch" comes from the superstition that the ticking sound, made by the beetle striking its head against the wood, is a sign of approaching death.

The death watch beetle found in the roof of Westminster Hall was smoked out by means of an insecticide called gamma benzine hexachloride. *See also* **Furniture Beetle, Woodworm.**

December, the last month of the year in our calendar, and the tenth in the old Roman.

Decibel, the name of the unit used to measure the relative loudness of sounds. The unit denotes the ratio between two amounts of electric or acoustic power. Named after Alexander Graham Bell, its symbol is db.

Deciduous Trees are such as shed their leaves at certain seasons as distinguished from evergreens or permanent foliaged trees or shrubs.

Deckchairs. A patent for these adjustable folding chairs was taken out in 1886 by the Englishman John Thomas Moore. Manufacture first began in Macclesfield in Cheshire.

Defender of the Faith (*Defensor Fidei*), the title conferred upon Henry VIII by Pope Leo X in 1521 for entering the debate against Luther with his pamphlet in defence of the Seven Sacraments. After Henry assumed headship of the Church of England the Pope withdrew the title but it was confirmed to him by Parliament in 1544 and has been used ever since by English monarchs.

Dehydrate, to eliminate the water from a substance. The process of dehydration is now widely used in the food industry in making such things as dried egg and packet soups. Most vegetables contain over 90 per cent of water, and much of this can be removed under vacuum at low temperatures without impairing the flavour.

Deliquescence, the process of dissolving by the absorption of moisture from the atmosphere. For instance, chromic acid crystals on exposure to the air quickly deliquesce.

Democratic Party, one of the two great American political parties, originated about 1787, advocating restrictions on the federal governments and in opposition to the federalists. It was in 1825 that a group who were in favour of high tariffs seceded, later to become the Republican Party.

The Democratic Party was split again over slavery before the Civil War (1861–65), and in the main the southern states have been loyal supporters of the Democrats. The economic depression helped the Democrats to power in 1932 (*see* **New Deal**) and they held office until 1953 when Eisenhower became President.

In 1960 Kennedy just won the Presidency and in 1964 Lyndon Johnson swept in with a landslide victory over the Republican candidate. In 1968 and 1972 the Democratic candidates were beaten by Nixon. In 1976 Jimmy Carter won an easy victory, but after that the Democrats lost three successive presidential elections (1980, 1984, 1988) before winning a narrow but convincing victory under Bill Clinton in the 1992 election. It won again in 1996. The bitterly-divided 2000 presidential election resulted in a narrow Republican victory. A further defeat in the 2004 presidential election was finally put behind them when the Democrats won an historic victory in 2008 under Barack Obama. They won a narrow but decisive victory in 2012. Hillary Clinton became the first woman to lead her party into a presidential election. She was defeated by Donald Trump (although she won more of the popular vote).

The symbol of the party is a donkey, invented by the cartoonist Thomas Nast.

Dendrochronology. The science of establishing the age of trees. *See* **Tree Rings.**

Dendrite, a stone or mineral on or in which treelike tracery appears, the result of the action of the hydrous oxide of manganese.

Density, a measure of the mass per unit volume of a material, usually expressed in grams per cubic centimetre. *Specific gravity* is the ratio of the density of a material to that of water at the temperature under consideration to that of water at the temperature of its maximum density ($4°C$). In grams per cubic centimetre the density of gold is 19·3, silver 10·5, lead 11·3, water 0·99997, air 0·00129.

Depression, a region where barometric pressure is lower than that of its surroundings. These areas of low pressure are usually less extensive than anticyclones (*q.v.*) and may vary from hundreds to thousands of kilometres in diameter. The winds, often of gale force where the depression is deep, blow round the system in an anticlockwise direction in the Northern Hemisphere (in the reverse direction in the Southern Hemisphere). Well above the earth's surface the winds blow along rather than down the pressure gradient but near the surface, friction causes the winds to blow slightly (*c.* 15°) across the isobars. The depression exists only as long as more air diverges out of its upper parts than converges into its lower parts.

Most depressions which cross the British Isles travel from the Atlantic, sometimes in series or families at rates from a few kilometres to a thousand kilometres a day, bringing their generally unsettled weather with them.

Derby, The, the most famous flat race for 3-year-old colts. First run at Epsom Downs on 4 May 1780. The most successful Derby jockey is Lester Piggott (9 wins). The largest Derby field was 34 in 1862 (a maximum of 20 was set in 2003). It is Britain's richest horse race. *See* **Section S.**

Desalinisation, the process of It is Britain's richest horse race. Minerals, chiefly salt, from sea or brackish water to pro-vide pure water for drinking or industry. Small-scale desalinisation by distillation has been practised for many years on ships and small islands. By the 1960s, many large-scale distillation plants were in operation, many of them in hot dry countries as in the Middle East. Kuwait, for example, used oil revenues to buy desalination plant and powers the plant with natural gas. As water for large population centres becomes more precious and desalinisation techniques more efficient, the process may be more and more used though it is expensive in capital outlay and in the cost of heating required to distil the water. Worldwide 80 million cubic metres of desalinated water are now produced daily.

Deserts, vast, barren, stone or sandy wastes where there is almost no rainfall and little or no vegetation (although their eco-systems are more complex than once thought).

These regions are found in the interior of the continents Africa, Asia and America between 20° and 30° north and south of the equator. Europe is the only continent without deserts. The most famous are the Sahara, the largest in the world, the Gobi desert of central Asia, the Kalahari desert of south-west Africa and the great Australian desert (the second largest in the world). The Atacama desert in Chile is the driest in the world. The Sahara is larger than either Australia or the United States. The Gobi desert is the most northerly in the world. Some 6,000 years ago the area was still wet.

The growing extension of deserts (desertification) is thought to result from both climatic change and also human interference.

Détente. Diplomatic term signifying the relaxation of strained relations between states. The term is usually applied to the improved relations, beginning in 1969, between the Warsaw Pact countries (led by the USSR), and the West (headed by the USA), which were inaugurated by SALT (the Strategic Arms Limitation Talks). These ended in agreement on arms reductions in May 1973. The continued build-up of Soviet arms and the invasion by the USSR of Afghanistan in 1979 questioned the validity of détente. The tension was finally eased with the fall of Communism.

Deuterium or "heavy hydrogen". The second isotope of hydrogen; the third is called tritium. Deuterium atoms have in their nuclei a neutron as well as a proton; tritium nuclei have two neutrons and one proton. In ordinary hydrogen gas about one out of every 5,000 atoms is a deuterium atom. Deuterium was discovered in 1932 by Professor Harold Urey. The oxide of deuterium corresponding to water is called "heavy water". The nucleus of the deuterium atom is called a deuteron. An anti-deuteron consisting of anti-proton and anti-neutron was produced at Brookhaven in 1965, the first compound anti-nucleus ever to be produced.

Devonian System in geology refers to the strata between the Silurian and the Carboniferous formations. It includes the Old Red Sandstone formation. The fauna of the Devonian include the group of fishes known as the Rhipidistra (on the evolutionary route towards the amphibians), Actinistia (coelacanth), and the Dipnoi or lung fishes.

Dew, moisture deposited by condensation of water vapour on exposed objects especially during calm, cloudless nights. The loss of heat from the ground after sunset, by radiation, causes the layer of atmosphere close to the surface to be chilled below the temperature (the dew-point) at which the air is saturated with vapour. Part of the vapour condensed may be transpired from blades of grass and foliage of plants.

Dew Pond is a shallow artificial pond which is on high ground and rarely dries up, even during prolonged droughts, despite being used by cattle and sheep as a drinking source. The name arose from the belief that dew deposits at night provided the moisture for replenishment. Drainage of rainwater and mist condensed on neighbouring trees and shrubs are probably more important factors.

Diamond, a mineral, one of the two crystalline forms of the element carbon (the other is graphite), the hardest known substance, used as a gem and in industry. India was the first country to mine diamonds (the Koh-i-noor, which means "mountain of light", known since 1304, came from Golconda near Hyderabad and came into British possession when the Punjab was annexed in 1849). The diamond mines of South Africa were discovered in 1869.

Other important diamond producing countries today are Russia, Congo, Botswana, Australia, Namibia, Angola and Tanzania. The world's biggest diamond used to be the Cullinan I (or Great Star of Africa) discovered near Pretoria, South Africa, in 1905. Since 1990 it has been the Golden Jubilee (now set in the King of Thailand's sceptre). Diamonds can be made artificially by subjecting carbon to very high temperatures and pressures; many industrial diamonds are made this way.

Antwerp is the main diamond centre of the world, London the main marketing centre, Amsterdam the main diamond cutting centre.

A planet composed almost entirely of diamond was found in 2011, 4,000 light years away!. And scientists now believe such outer planets as Uranus and Neptune could have diamond in their cores.

Diatoms. One-celled algae, common in fresh and salt water. Distinctive feature is the siliceous wall which is in two halves, one fitting over the other like the lid of a box. These walls are often very finely and beautifully sculptured. The diatoms constitute a class of the plant kingdom known as the Bacillariophyta. *Diatom ooze* is a deep-sea deposit made up of diatom shells. *Diatomite* or *diatomaceous earth* is the mineral form that such diatom oozes assume (sometimes known as kieselguhr which mixed with nitroglycerine yields dynamite).

Diesel Engine, an engine in which the liquid fuel is introduced into a compressed or partially compressed charge of air, and which does not need an extraneous source of ignition. The modern oil engine has been evolved mainly from the principles enunciated by Herbert Akroyd-Stuart in his patent of 1890 and, like the steam and other inventions, represents the improvements achieved by many men, including those by Rudolf Diesel of Germany, in respect of high compression pressures and greater fuel economy.

Diffusion is the process of mixing which occurs when two liquids or gases are in contact. It is most rapid between gases, and, as laid down by Graham's law, "the rates of diffusion of different gases are in the inverse proportion to the square roots of their relative densities". Diffusion arises through the continual movement of molecules. Even in solids diffusion can occur. If a block of gold and a block of silver are welded together, after some time particles of gold are found in the silver, and *vice versa*.

Digital Television. See **Television.**

Dimensions in common speech are the magnitudes of length, breadth and thickness giving, the size of an object, thus a line has only one dimension: length; a plane surface two: length and breadth; and a solid three: length breadth and thickness.

In mathematics, hypothetical objects with any number of dimensions are considered. In physics and mechanics, dimensions are numbers which relate the units in which any quantity is measured to the so-called fundamental units. The latter are usually but not necessarily those of length, mass and time.

Dimorphism, the quality of assuming two distinct forms. For instance, carbon, which is graphite in one form, is the diamond in another.

Dingoes, often considered the native dog of Australia, are in fact a unique species. Their future is in doubt because so many are kept as pets and mate with other breeds. Australia's largest land predator. Also known as the warrigal.

Dinosaur, the name given to a group of extinct rep-

tiles of the Mesozoic period, some of which were of immense size. Modern research suggests that a huge asteroid impact 60 million years ago, rather than volcanic activity ended their 160 million year reign. It is believed that dinosaurs began the evolution into birds. The earliest dinosaur bones date back over 250 million years. Dinosaurs were the most successful animals the world has known (dinosaur remains have even been found under Antarctica). In 2014, a 'super-massive' species of dinosaurs was discovered in Argentina. Tyrannosauros rex, one of the most feared dinosaurs, had serrated teeth that could tear through bone and sinew. Around 50 different dinosaur species have been found in the UK. See **Diplodocus.**

Diplodocus, one of the best known of the extinct mammoth dinosaurs. Fossil remains have been discovered in the Jurassic rocks of the United States. Some reached a length of over 24 m.

Dipnoi or **Lung Fishes.** These have the air bladder adapted to function as a lung, and they can remain alive when the stream or marsh in which they live dries up. Species of lung fish occur in Australia, Africa and S. America.

Dippers are Britain's only aquatic songbird.

Diptera, an order of insects. Their main characteristic is that they are two-winged, and the common house-fly is the best-known example. There are at least 50,000 species of these insects, including gnats, blow-flies, mosquitoes and tsetses.

Diptych was a folding two-leaved tablet of wood, ivory, or metal, with polished inner surfaces, utilised for writing with the style by the ancient Greeks and Romans. The same term was applied to the tablets on which the names of the persons to be commemorated were inscribed in the early Church. See **N6.**

Discus, a circular piece of metal or stone about 30 cm in diameter, used in athletic contests by the ancient Greeks and Romans. Throwing the discus was a very favourite game, which was deemed worthy of celebration in Myron's famous *Discobolus* (*c.* 460 B.C.–450 B.C.).

Disk, an astronomical term for the seemingly flat surface of celestial bodies as seen by the eye.

Distillation, a process used to separate liquids of different boiling points. This is effected by placing the mixture in a distillation apparatus and heating. The liquid with the lower boiling point distils over first, the vapour being condensed and collected, forming the first *fraction.* With continued heating the second liquid reaches its boiling point, distils over and the mixture is said to be *fractionated.* Mixtures of liquids with close very high boiling points require more elaborate apparatus.

Fractional distillation is a common process in the chemical industry (*e.g.* petroleum refining).

DNA (Deoxyribonucleic Acid), a polymer molecule in the form of a double-strand helix containing many thousands of sub-units. Contains the genetic information coded in sequences of sub units called bases. The Nobel Prize for medicine was awarded in 1962 for the discovery of the structure of DNA. See **Human Genome Project, Nucleic Acids.** and **T46–8.**

DNA Database. The world's first police DNA database was established at the Forensic Science Laboratory, Birmingham in April 1995. The database allows police to compare genetic material from crime scenes with DNA profiles of convicted criminals. DNA profiling has been developed from genetic fingerprinting, an earlier technique pioneered in the mid-1980s by Sir Alec Jeffreys of Leicester University.

Docks are enclosed water spaces where ships rest while being loaded or unloaded, repaired, or waiting for cargo. There are three main types: the wet dock in which water is maintained at the level of high tide so that vessels remain afloat while loading and unloading; the tidal dock, with open entrance to permit free ebb and flow of tide (*e.g.,* Glasgow, Southampton (which has double tides)); and the dry dock, or graving dock, for overhauling and repairing vessels, so constructed that, after a ship has been docked, the water can be drawn off (*e.g.,* Southampton, Tilbury). The floating dock is a type of dry dock. Advances in the handling of cargo, *e.g.,* containers, have led to modernisation. Under the 1991 Ports Act many ports were privatised.

Dodo, an extinct flightless bird (more slender than once thought), which lived on the island of Mauritius up until *c.* 300 years ago. Another species, the white dodo, lived on Réunion. By the end of the 17th cent. Mauritius, Rodriguez, and Réunion had all been colonised, and the dodo along with many other birds vanished forever because of their inability to stand up to man and the animals imported by him. In *c.* 150 years 45 species were lost forever.

DNA scientists have found that the Nicobar pigeon of SE Asia is the dodo's nearest relative. Scans of a dodo skull have revealed that the dodo was a relatively wise bird with an unusually enhanced sense of smell.

Dog-days, a period of 40 days (3 July–11 August) when Sirius (the Dog Star) rises and sets with the sun. The ancient superstition found in Greek literature, was that this star affected the canine race.

Dogfish, a large family of small sharks, seldom more than 1 m in length. The flesh is sold as "rock salmon". The eggs are contained in horny cases called "mermaid's purses". The commonest of the British dogfishes are the spurdogs.

Doldrums, a nautical term applied to those areas of the Atlantic and Pacific within a few degrees of the Equator towards which the trade winds blow and where the weather is calm, hot and sultry. Pressure is low and the air often rises to produce heavy tropical rainfall and squalls, rendering navigation difficult.

Dolomite, a limestone containing appreciable magnesium; also the mineral dolomite, a double cabonate of magnesium and calcium.

Dolphin, a mammal of the whale order, from 2–2·4 m long, with a long, sharp snout, and of an active disposition. They abound in most seas and swim in shoals. A few species live in large rivers (Ganges and Amazon). They can cruise for long periods at around 15 knots and produce bursts of speed in the region of 20 knots, the water apparently flowing smoothly past their bodies. Dolphins are some of the most intelligent of mammals and are the subject of scientific experiments in language and communication. They are masters of teamwork when searching for food. Dolphins use echoes (the skill known as echolocation) and also electric sensors to locate food or detect other creatures. Scientists now know that dolphins stun their prey by blasting them with sound. Dolphins are the only animals apart from humans to develop a natural form of Type 2 diabetes. They also call each other using individual signature whistles, in much the same way as human beings use names. Thankfully, the last British dolphinarium closed in 1993.

Dominicans, an order of mendicant preaching friars founded by St. Dominic in Languedoc in 1215 and confirmed by the Pope in 1216. The rule of the order was rigorous. The dress was a white habit and scapular with a long black mantle. This gave them the name of Black Friars. Their official name is Friars Preachers.

Donjon, the keep, or inner tower of a castle, and the strongest and most secure portion of the structure. This was the last refuge of the garrison, and there was usually a prison on the lower floor, hence the name *dungeon*.

Don Juan, the legendary hero of many famous works, supposedly based on the life and character of the unscrupulous gallant Don Juan Tenorio of 14th-cent. Seville. The first dramatisation of the legend and the most famous is Tirso de Molina's *El Burlador de Sevilla.* Don Juan was also the subject of Molière's *Le Festin de Pierre,* Mozart's *Don Giovanni,* Byron's *Don Juan,* and José Zorilla's *Don Juan Tenorio.* The latter is played on All Saints' Day throughout Spanish-speaking countries.

Don Quixote, the "knight of the doleful countenance", the hero and title of Cervantes' classic novel of 16th-cent. Spain. Don Quijote de la Mancha, a gentle country gentleman of lofty but unpractical ideals, having read many chivalric romances, believes he is called upon to redress the wrongs of the world. Mounted on his nag Rosinante and accompanied by his companion Sancho Panza, a hard-headed peasant, he sets out on his journeys of knight-errantry.

Dormouse, a family of small, squirrel-like rodents widely distributed throughout Europe and Asia, and living mainly on fruit and nuts. It is nocturnal and sleeps through the winter. One of nature's most secretive creatures, it is threatened with extinction in parts of Britain. The hazel dormouse is particularly threatened by habitat loss. However,

the edible dormouse is a threat to our countryside.

Dotterel, a handsome bird of the plover family found in northern Europe and Siberia.

Downing St, one of the most famous streets of London, off the west side of Whitehall. The official residence of the Prime Minister is at no. 10; that of the Chancellor of the Exchequer at no. 11. The public is now excluded from the street, named after an MP, George Downing (*c.* 1623–84).

Drachm (or **Drachma**), an ancient Greek silver coin and weight. One drachma was equivalent to six obols. The word has survived as the name of a weight: Avoirdupois, one-sixteenth part of an ounce; Apothecaries' Weight, one-eighth part of an ounce.

Draco. *See* **Flying Lizard.**

Drag. Term used in mechanics for resistance offered by a fluid to the passage of a body moving through it. When speed of sound is reached drag increases abruptly. The lift/drag ratio gives the aeroplane designer his measure of aerodynamic efficiency.

Dragon, a fabulous monster common to folk-lore in most countries; generally represented as a winged reptile with fiery eyes and breath of flame. A dragon guarded the garden of the Hesperides; St. George, England's patron saint, is supposed to have overcome the dragon; in heraldry the dragon has also a conspicuous place; and in China it was the imperial emblem.

Dragonet, the name of the fish of the *Callionymus* genus, beautifully coloured, and about 30 cm in length. They are common on the British coast and in the Mediterranean.

Dragon Fly, the common name of a well-known order of insects having two pairs of membraneous wings, and often of very brilliant colours. They are swift of flight and may be seen hovering over sheets of water in the sunshine all through the summer. Emperor dragonflies are the UK's biggest and fastest insects. They can reach speeds of 20 mph. Today, they are threatened by pollution and invasive species.

Dragon's Blood, a dark-red resinous substance obtained from the fruit of a Malay palm, and possessing medicinal virtues. In a special technique used for making line blocks in printing, dragon's blood is used.

Drawbridge, a bridge that can be lifted up so that no passage can be made across it. It was a usual feature of a fortified castle in the Middle Ages, and was raised or lowered by chains and levers. It spanned the fosse, and on the approach of an attacking party was raised and formed a special barricade to the gate. Modern drawbridges are such as are raised to allow of the passage of boats up and down a river or estuary. The Tower Bridge is a famous London bridge of this type.

Driving Standards Agency, the national body responsible for driving tests for cars, lorries, buses *etc.* It also supervises approved driving instructors.

Driving Test. The cost of a car driving test rose to £62 from April 2009 (£75 for evenings and weekends). The driving test for car drivers now takes around 40 minutes. The first driving test in the UK took place on 1 June 1935. Driving licences were standardised across the EU from 2012. At age 70 drivers face a mandatory renewal each three years (it is planned to raise this to 75). The separate driving test for taxi drivers is to be scrapped.

Drongo. The King Crow or Indian Black Drongo is frequently seen in India perched on branches or telephone wires, darting suddenly to catch insects and to attack crows and hawks. Other members of the family are found in Asia, Africa and Australia. Its plumage is black with steel-blue gloss. It is an exellent mimic.

Drosophila or **Fruit Fly.** More has been learnt by geneticists from breeding experiments with this insect than with any other.

Drought occurs when there has been an absence of rain for a long period or a marked deficiency of precipitation over a much longer period in a climatic zone where precipitation is ordinarily adequate for vegetation or agriculture. river flow and water supplies. It is different from *aridity* which refers to the extreme dryness of desert or arid regions where rainless periods characterise the climate. Hitherto in the British Isles "an absolute drought" was defined as "a period of at least 15 consecutive days without measurable rainfall".

L33

In the British Isles droughts occur from time to time but very long rainless spells at a place are rather rare. The longest recorded spell in the British Isles with no measurable daily rainfall lasted 61 days at Liss (Hants) from 16 March to 15 May 1893. Over the country as a whole the 12-month period beginning 1 May 1975 was the driest such period since records began. The South of England faced water restrictions in 2006 after 2005 was the third driest year on record since 1897. In many places the summer of 1995 was the driest since records began in 1727. Prolonged drought causes long-term changes to woodlands.

Drupe is the scientific term for stone fruit. The stone forms the inner part (*endocarp*) of the fruit, and encloses a seed or kernel which is liberated after the flesh part (*pericarp*) rots.

Dry-rot, the term was first used about 1775 to describe the fungal decay of timber in buildings. Creosote distilled from coal tar is the standard material for preservation of timber, and penta-chlorophenol and copper naphthenate are two compounds now extensively used. Dry wood always escapes dry-rot. Chief fungi causing dry-rot are *Merulius* and *Poria*.

Duck, water bird smaller than the related goose and swan, which together form the family Antidae. Duck refers to the female, drake to the male. The duck family falls into two separate groups: the river or freshwater (surface feeding) ducks, such as the mallard, pintail, wigeon, shoveler, mandarin, teal, garganey; and the sea (diving) ducks, such as the goldeneye, pochard, scoter, eider, and the fish-eating mer-gansers or "sawbills". The ancestor of all domestic breeds, with the exception of the muscovy, is the mallard (now in serious decline).

Duckbill, *Ornithorhynchus anatinus*, also duck-billed platypus, a fur-covered, egg-laying, nest-building mammal native to Australia and Tasmania. It has webbed feet and a muzzle like a duck's bill and is about 50 cm long. Adopted as the mascot for the 2000 Olympic Games in Sydney, but its numbers are declining. DNA evidence has now revealed it really is an amalgam of mammal, reptile and bird.

Duckweed is the world's smallest flowering plant (and one of the fastest growing).

Ductility is a property possessed by most metals which renders them capable of being stretched without breaking. Gold is the most, and lead the least ductile of metals, the order being gold, silver, platinum, iron, copper, palladium, aluminium, zinc, tin, lead. The spider and the silk-worm produce secretions of notable ductility.

Dugong. A marine mammal, belonging to the order Sirenia (sea-cows). Inhabits the Red Sea and Indian Ocean; also found as far East as the Philippines and Australia (where most are to be found). Lives on sea-weed. Related to the Manatee.

Duke, the highest rank in the British peerage. Edward, the Black Prince, eldest son of Edward III, who died before his father, was the first English duke, being created Duke of Cornwall in 1337. Since then all Princes of Wales have held that title.

Dukeries, a stretch of English woodland and park country, mainly in Nottinghamshire, comprising the adjacent demesnes of several English dukes and nobles. The Dukeries include Sherwood Forest and the estates of Welbeck Abbey, Clumber Park, Worksop Manor and Thoresby Hall.

Dunes. Sand dunes are elliptical or crescent-shaped mounds of loose sand produced by wind action. The dune has a gentle slope on wind-ward side; a steep slope on the leeward side.

Dung Beetle, known for feeding on faeces. It can pull more than 1,000 times its own body weight.

Dunlin, very common small wading-bird of the Sandpiper family nesting in Britain. Its range extends to other areas where it also breeds.

Dunmow Flitch, a custom which originated in the parish of Little Dunmow, Essex, in the reign of Henry III, which was that the husband who was prepared to swear before the prior, convent, and townsfolk of Dunmow that he had not re-pented of marriage or quarrelled with his wife for a year and a day, should be rewarded with the gift of a flitch of bacon.

Dunnock (*Prunella modularis*), a small bird of rich brown and dark grey plumage common in gardens and hedgerows. Sings a cheerful song all the year round. Called the hedge-sparrow in southern England. Another member of the same family, the larger Alpine Accentor (*Prunella collaris*), is found on rocky mountain slopes.

Duodecimo, a sheet of paper folded into twelve leaves, written "12mo".

Durian, a pungent fruit, popular in S.E. Asia. Its smell is horrendous and it inhibits the breakdown of alcohol.

Dust, solid particles of matter floating in the atmos-phere, produced chiefly by volcanic eruptions, sand-storms in desert regions, and industrial and domestic smoke. When the island of Krakatoa erupted in 1883, more than 4 km^2 of dust was thrown into the air and carried three times round the earth by the explosive wave. The particles in dust-storms are much finer than those in sand-storms and are swept up to far greater heights. The local whirlwinds which form over loose dry soils are termed dust-devils.

Dutch Elm Disease. *See under* Elm.

Dwarf Planets. *See* T8–9.

Dyke. A wall-like intrusion of igneous rock which cuts across the bedding or other layered structure of the country rock; the word also signifies in alternative usage, a sea-wall and an open drain.

Dynamite, a powerful explosive whose chief ele-ment is nitro-glycerine. It was discovered by Nobel in 1867, who absorbed nitro-glycerine in kieselguhr. It has a disruptive force of about eight times that of gunpowder.

Dynamo. Machine for transforming mechanical energy into electrical energy. Depends on principle of electromagnetic induction whereby a current is produced in a conductor (*e.g.*, copper wire) traversing a magnetic field.

The two essential parts of a dynamo are the conductors or *armature* and the *field magnets*.

E

Eagle, large bird of prey with huge hooked bill, related to the buzzard, kite, hawk, harrier, falcon and vulture, together forming the family *Falconidae*. There are many species to be found throughout the world, the Golden, Imperial, Tawny, Spotted and Lesser Spotted being found in Europe. The Golden Eagle, a magnificent-looking bird, nests in the Scottish Highlands. The White-tailed Sea Eagle, which used to breed in Britain, is now rare here.

The eagle has been the symbol of royal power for over 5,000 years, and the American or Bald Eagle is the emblem of the United States. Bald eagle numbers have now revived.

Eagre. *See* Bore.

Earl, a British title of nobility of the third rank, duke and marquis coming first and second. The title dates from Saxon times, and until 1337 ranked highest in our peerage.

Earl-Marshal, in England ranks as the eighth of the great officers of state, is head of the College of Arms, attends the sovereign in opening and closing the session of Parliament, arranges state processions (especially coronations) and assists in introducing newly created peers in the Lords. The office is hereditary in the Dukes of Norfolk.

Earth, our habitable globe, is the third of the planets of the solar system in order from the sun and on an average throughout the year takes 24 hours to turn completely round relative to the sun, the whole earth revolving round the sun in a slightly elliptical orbit once in a year of 365·2564 days. The mean dis-tance of the earth from the sun is 149,597,900 km.

Modern earth satellite studies have shown that small variations of the surface gravity field (or geoid) occur which are believed to be related more to the structures deep within the earth's mantle than to the location and dimension of crustal features, such as oceans, continents etc.

The crust of the earth consists of a skin, 30 km thick under the continents, but only about 6–8 km thick under the ocean bed, comprised of rocks and sediments or soil. At the base of the crust is a sharp discontinuity (the Mohorovičíc Discon-tinuity) to denser rocks of the mantle. This region, nearly 3,000 km thick, is in a process of slow but inexorable change, one of convection responding to heat sources (due mainly to radioactivity in materials within the earth). This slow convection is responsible for many changes in the surface of the earth—continental drift (*q.v.*), earthquakes and volcanic activity.

The core is a region of very high density and temperature, comprised of heavy elements such as iron and nickel. The crustal rocks are mainly comprised of oxygen, silicon, aluminium, sodium, potassium, iron, calcium and magnesium, with traces of many other elements. The mass of the earth is c. 6,000 million million million tonnes, and it was formed c. 4,567 million years ago (some scientists believe c. 4,467 million years ago).
Earth has only one natural satellite, the moon. *See* **Section V.**

Earthquake, a sudden violent disturbance of the earth's crust; the region of the surface immediately above the "focus", or source where the earthquake originates, is termed the "epicentre". On account of their destructive power earthquakes have attracted attention from the earliest times, but accurate study dates only from the 19th century and the development of a world-wide network of recording stations.

The majority of severe earthquakes result from fractures, usually along existing faults, in underlying rock strata subjected to great strains, the shearing movement sometimes extending to the surface. These dislocations set up vibrations which are propagated as waves throughout the bulk of the earth or round the crust. Often the main shock is followed by smaller aftershocks.

Minor local earthquakes may be attributed to the effects of volcanic activity, but most of the larger ones originate in nonvolcanic regions along well-marked lines of weakness in the earth's crust. Generally the ground is felt to tremble, undergoing oscillations which may gradually or suddenly increase and accompanied by sounds.

When there is movement of the sea-bed a tsunami (*q.v.*) may result. One of the most devastating of modern times (9·3 on the Richter scale) took place on 26 December 2004 under the Indian Ocean. Its epicentre was near northern Sumatra. Over 220,000 people died (and unknown thousands went missing) in its wake. Earthquakes may add to global warming by releasing greenhouse gases from the ocean floor.

Among the notable shocks of the 20th century and after were those of San Francisco (1906), Messina (1908), China (1920), Japan (1923), Napier, New Zealand (1931), Ionian Is. (1953), Chile (1960), Iran (1962), Yugoslavia (1963), China (1976), Mexico (1985) Armenia (1988), N.W. Iran (1990), Los Angeles (1994), Kobe (Japan), 1995, Turkey and Taiwan (1999) and Christchurch, New Zealand, 2011. The most devastating earthquake in recorded history hit Shanxi (China) in 1556, killing 830,000 people. The 1755 Lisbon earthquake was the most powerful to hit Europe.

Research has suggested that the collapse of the walls of Jericho in biblical times was due to an earthquake. In the last 100 years, one million people have died in earthquakes. In 2015, Nepal suffered severe damage. *See* **Richter Scale.**

Earthworm, of which there are 25 native species in the UK, has a cylindrical body, tapering at both ends and segmented into rings. It moves by contraction of its rings, aided by retractive bristles; is eyeless, but has a mouth, gullet and stomach. Earthworms exist in immense numbers, and perform an important part in the scheme of nature by loosening the soil and rendering it more amenable to tillage. They also form a valuable food for birds and many mammals, and are unequalled as bait for certain kinds of fish. The New Zealand flatworm (now spreading in Britain) is devouring native earthworms.

Earwig, a genus of insects possessing two pairs of wings and anal forceps. It is nocturnal, lives on vegetable matter, and hides by day under stones or in flowers, *e.g.*, dahlias.

Easter, the annual Christian festival in commemoration of the resurrection of Christ, the English name being derived from Eostre, goddess of Spring. The date cannot fall earlier than 22 March nor later than 25 April. Many disputes arose among the early Christians as to the proper time to celebrate this day which governs all other movable feasts. It was eventually ruled at the Council of Nicaea in 325 that Easter Day should be the first Sunday after the full moon following the vernal equinox. If this happens to be a Sunday, then Easter Day is the Sunday after. A fixed date for Easter is now under consideration.
For dates of Easter, *see* **G25.**

Eau-de-Cologne, a popular distilled perfume first manufactured at Cologne in the 18th cent. by Johann Maria Farina, an Italian.

Ebony, a name applied to various hard black woods, the best of which are grown in Mauritius and Sri Lanka. There are also Indian and American varieties. Only the inner portions, the heartwood, of the trees are of the necessary hardness and blackness. Ebony is largely used in ornamental cabinet work, for piano keys, *etc.*

E-books are digital editions of books which can be downloaded to your home computer. They can be read on an E-reader device (*e.g.* Kindle from Amazon or iPad or Nook). More recent devices include the iPadmini, Kindle Fire and Surface.

Ecce Homo ("Behold the Man!"), the pictures and sculptures depicting Christ crowned with thorns.

Echidna, the spiny Australian anteater.

E-cigarettes. Around 2·8 million people in Britain use vaping in an attempt to give up smoking. E-cigarettes are 95% safer than tobacco, with no serious side-effects found so far.

Eclipse, the partial or complete obscuring of one heavenly body by another. An eclipse of the sun occurs when the moon, which is 1/400th of the diameter of the sun and about 1/390th as far away, obscures some portion of the sun as seen by an observer on the earth. A total eclipse occurs when the whole of the sun's disc is covered by the moon. Astronomers travel many thousands of miles to observe the outer layers of the sun and its corona, which is only possible when the light from the sun is totally obscured by the moon during the few minutes of an eclipse.

The spectacular solar eclipse of 11 August 1999 and the partial eclipse of 20 March 2015 attracted great attention (being Britain's first major solar eclipses for 70 years). Previous total solar eclipses occurred over parts of the UK in 1424, 1433, 1598, 1652, 1715, 1724, 1927 and 1954 (visible from the Shetland Is.). A similar magnitude solar eclipse to 2015 will not occur until 12 August 2026.

The next total eclipse visible from the UK will not occur until 23 September 2090. An eclipse of the Moon occurs when the Moon moves into the Earth's shadow. When this happens, the sunlight is cut off and the lunar surface becomes quite dark until it emerges from the shadow again. Lunar eclipses can be either partial or total, depending on whether all or part of the Moon moves into the Earth's shadow. They are more common than solar eclipses.

The longest solar eclipse this century (6 mins., 39 seconds) swept across Asia in July 2009. It will not be surpassed until 13 June 2132.

On 6 June 2012 there was a Transit of Venus (when Earth, Venus and the Sun all line up and the planet's disc travels across the face of our star). The next transit is not until 2117.

Ecliptic is the sun's apparent path in the sky: the great circle described by the sun from west to east in the course of a year. The sun is exactly on the equator on approx. 21 March, and 23 September, and the points where the celestial equator and ecliptic intersect on these days are called the *equinoctial points.* On approx. 21 June and 22 December the sun reaches its greatest and least midday elevation and its greatest distance north and south of the equator. The points on the ecliptic on these days are called the *solstices.* These four points are equidistant from each other by 90°. The angle of the ecliptic to the earth's equator is called the obliquity of the ecliptic. Due to the gravitational perturbations of the other planets, both the equinoctial point and the obliquity of the ecliptic change with time. The value of the obliquity is c. 23·5.

Ecology, a term first described by the German biologist Haeckel in the 19th cent., is the study of the inter-relationships between living organisms and their environment. **Autecology** is the study of the environmental relationships of *individual* plants and species. **Synecology** is the study of plant and animal *communities* living together as groups. *See also* **Section T.**

Ecumenical Council, a general council of the Christian Church summoned when important questions of Church doctrine and policy are to be decided. The early councils were predominantly Greek and convoked by the emperor. Those sumoned by the pope when they meet at the Lateran Palace in Rome are called Lateran Councils; others have met at Constance, Florence,

Trent and the Vatican. Their decisions are not binding on the rest of Christendom. Only 21 Ecumenical Councils have been held in the history of Christendom. The first was held at Nicaea in 325 when the mystery of the Trinity was defined.

The 21st (known as the 2nd Vatican Council), convened by Pope John, opened in October 1962 in St. Peter's, Rome, and ended in December 1965.

Edda, the name given to two important collections of early Icelandic literature—*the Elder or Poetic Edda*, poems handed down from the 9th and 10th cent., probably Norwegian in origin, and the *Younger* or *Prose Edda* of Snorri Sturluson compiled about 1230. They treat of legends of an early Scandinavian civilisation.

Eddystone Lighthouse, 21 km south of Plymouth, is one of the most isolated in the world. The tower is 51 m high, and its light can be seen for 28 km. The present structure is the fourth that has occupied this dangerous position. The first was of wood, completed by Winstanley in 1698, but it was destroyed by storm in 1703. In 1708 a second and stronger lighthouse was built by Rudyerd. This lasted until 1755, when it was destroyed by fire. Smeaton built the third lighthouse of granite and this withstood storm and tempest for over a hundred years, 1759–1881. The present lighthouse, also of granite, was built 1879–81 on a nearby rock by Sir James Douglass.

Eden Project, a giant greenhouse in Cornwall. Opened 2001, it recreates climates for over 10,000 species. A series of domes (biomes) creates environments from arid deserts to the world's largest indoor rainforest. It now plans to build a pioneering geothermal plant.

Eels, edible fishes of the order Apodes, with snakelike body covered with minute scales embedded in the skin. The common or fresh-water eel *Anguilla anguilla* is found in the Atlantic coastal areas of N. America and Europe and in the Mediterranean, and breeds S.E. of Bermuda. The electric eel of S. America is able to cause electric shocks. Commercial sand eel fishing in the North Sea and elsewhere is depriving many birds, fish and marine mammals of their food.

Eel numbers are now declining due to loss of habitats, pollution and changes to ocean currents caused by global warming. The European eel, found in British rivers and streams, has declined by 90% since the 1980s. The last eel fisherman in England was forced to stop work in 2016.

Eels can make epic journeys of 4,500 miles to their spawning grounds. The hatched larvae make the return journey floating on ocean currents. The tiny juveniles are known as glass eels.

Egret, a slender, graceful bird of the heron family, of pure white plumage, famed for its beautiful silky plumes (aigrettes), which appear in the breeding season, and for which it was ruthlessly hunted and would have been exterminated had not international action been taken to protect it. The Little Egret with black bill, black legs, and yellow feet breeds in Mediterranean lands.

Eider, a large diving duck, found along the rocky coasts of northern latitudes, well known for the beautifully warm soft down, called "eider down", which the female bird plucks from her breast to line her nest. In Norway and Iceland the haunts of the eider are preserved and the birds protected by law on account of the much prized "eider down", which is collected from the nests just before the breeding season.

Eider down" is so elastic that a kilogram of it will fill an ordinary bed covering.

Eiffel Tower, built by the French engineer Alexandre Gustave Eiffel (1832–1923) for the Paris Exhibition of 1889. The tower which is made of iron is 300 m high and weighs *c.* 7,000 tonnes. Now Europe's most popular tourist site.

Eisteddfod (a sitting) was originally a congress of Welsh bards and minstrels, and dates from before the 12th cent. These assemblies, discontinued for a long period, were resumed in 1819, and have been held yearly since, each lasting three or four days. Their object is to foster the Welsh patriotic spirit; they are devoted to orations and competitions in poetry, singing and harp-playing. Prizes are awarded.

Eland, largest species of antelope, native of Africa; large pointed horns, stands 1·5 m high at the withers, and weighs several hundred kg.

Elder, small trees of the *Sambucus* genus, with pinnate leaves, and clusters of white flowers and,

later, small purplish-black berries. The black elder, the best known, thrives in Britain. A wine is made from its berries. Once regarded as sacred.

El Dorado, a "golden land", was an idea very much favoured in the days of the early Spanish explorers. It was believed that somewhere on the South American continent there was a country abounding in gold and precious stones. Many expeditions were fitted out to discover it. Sir Walter Raleigh also embarked on this quest.

Electret, a piece of solid matter which retains a permanent electric polarisation analogous to the magnetic polarisation of a permanent magnet. There are various recipes for making them; carnauba wax is a common constituent.

Electricity. See **Section T** and **Energy Conversion.**

Electric Telegraph may be said to date from 1836, when Sir Charles Wheatstone and his co-inventor Cooke introduced their Single-Needle instrument, which was soon followed by the Double-Needle apparatus, Morse, in 1837, invented his famous recording instrument. The first electric cable was between Dover and France, and was laid in 1850. The first Atlantic cable was laid in 1858, and the second in 1866.

It was in 1899 that the very first Marconi wireless telegraph messages were sent between England and France.

Electroencephalograph, an instrument which records the minute voltages produced by the electrical activity of the brain by means of electrodes taped to the scalp. The record of brain waves, known as EEG, shows that there is a general cycle of activity in the brain that underlies both sleep and wakefulness.

Electrolysis is the condition established when an electric current passes through a conducting substance, between electrodes, resulting in decomposition and separation into constituents. Water thus becomes decomposed into hydrogen and oxygen.

Electromagnetic Radiation. Radiation consisting of oscillating electronic and magnetic fields travelling together through space. Including visible light, the speed of travel is around 300,000 kms per second. Together with visible light, many different types exist including gamma rays, X-rays, ultraviolet and infrared radiation, microwaves and radio waves.

Electromagnetic Waves. See **Section T**

Electron. See **Section T.**

Electronics. The science which deals with the behaviour and control of free electrons. It started with the discovery of the electron by Sir J. J. Thomson in 1897. The practical applications, constituting electronic engineering, have given us radio, radar, photo-electric cells, cathode-ray oscillographs, electronic microscopes and television. Electronics uses devices like transistors such that the electrons move inside solid matter instead of *in vacuo*. This is sometimes referred to as "solid state electronics". *See also* **Microelectronics.**

Electron Microscope. A microscope in which beams of electrons are focused by magnetic lenses in a manner analogous to the focusing of light beams in the ordinary optical microscope. Modern electron microscopes have very high resolving power and can magnify up to 1,500,000 times, making it possible to explore the cell and the virus. A development of the electron microscope is the scanning electron microscope (stereoscan), developed at Cambridge, which can examine an essentially thick object, giving a very large depth of focus.

Electronvolt, unit of energy used in nuclear physics. It is the amount of energy required to move one electronic charge through a potential difference of one volt. It is very small—$1·6 \times 10^{19}$ joules and therefore suited to atomic physics. 1 MeV = a million electronvolts; 1 GeV = a thousand million electronvolts; these larger units are used in high energy physics.

Elementary Particle, one of the basic constituents of the material universe. The idea that matter consists of tiny particles goes back to classical times but the modern concept of the atom grew out of the chemistry and physics of the 19th cent. With the discovery of the electron in 1897 and the rise of nuclear physics in the 20th cent., the chemical atom was understood to be a structure built of even more fundamental particles—the electron, the proton and the neutron. In the last few decades, many more particles have been discovered, especially in the study of cosmic rays and by the use of large accelerating machines like those at CERN (Geneva) and Brookhaven National Laboratory (Long Island, New York). Among the later discoveries are the neutrino, the positron, the antiproton, the muon, the pion *etc*. These differ in electric charge and mass and other intrinsic properties and many have only a very short lifetime before they change into something else. Whether there is a small number of really elementary particles out of which all the others can be constructed is an unanswered question of contemporary physics. *See* **Section T.**

Elements. In chemistry, substances which cannot be separated into two or more simpler chemical substances. 91 elements are found naturally on the earth, some are observed spectroscopically in the stars and planets, and a further number have been made artificially. Between them these elements can appear in some 1,200 different isotopes, of which 317 occur in Nature. (There are 274 stable isotopes among 81 stable elements.) *See* **Table of Elements, T56.**

Elephant, a proboscidian mammal of which only two species survive—the Asiatic, in India, and the African elephant. No other animals possess a trunk. Both males and females have large ivory tusks.

The Indian elephant is usually *c*. 2·7 m high and weighs about 3 tonnes; African elephants are larger, weighing about 6 tonnes, and are usually much fiercer. Several fossil elephants of still larger bulk have been discovered, including the mammoth and the mastodon. The Indian elephant is domesticated and used as a beast of burden, and may live 70 years. The ivory trade (banned in 1989) was responsible for the mass slaughter of perhaps 700,000 elephants. This evil trade still continues clandestinely. Nowadays less than 50,000 Asian elephants still survive, with perhaps 352,000 African savanna elephants. One hundred years ago there were *c*. 5 million African elephants. Elephants are famed for their memory (they never forget) but they are the only mammal that cannot jump. Their memory (of where to find water or food) is a key to their survival. They also pick up noise through their feet. Despite their size, elephants will turn tail and flee at the sound of a swarm of bees. They have a remarkable sense of smell. They are also excellent swimmers. The rumbling sounds they produce are an important form of communication.

The world's smallest elephant (the Bornean) is strictly a sub-species and much endangered.

Elephant Bird, the largest bird which ever lived. A flightless creature, indigenous to Madagascar, it was more than 10ft tall, weighing over 1,000 lbs.

Elephant Seal. *See* **Sea Elephant.**

Eleusinian Mysteries, festivals common throughout ancient Greece, agricultural in their symbolism.

Elgin Marbles, a collection of ancient Greek sculptures and architectural fragments got together by the 7th Earl of Elgin and brought to England between 1802 and 1812. These celebrated treasures had originally formed part of the Parthenon at Athens, and were probably carved by pupils of the sculptor Phidias. Lord Elgin expended over £70,000 upon them, and they were purchased for £35,000 for the British Museum.

In 1997 the Labour Government ruled out their return. However, one possible compromise would be their return on loan to Greece.

Elk, the largest animal of the deer family, with enormous antlers, and standing, when mature, about 2 m high. The American moose is of the same family.

Elm, a stately, wide-spreading tree having some 20 species spread over north-temperate regions, several of which are native and peculiar to Britain. The grandest of the field elms is the English elm, *Ulmus procera*, which may reach a height of *c*. 42 m and a girth of 8 m. The wych elm, *U. glabra*, or Scots elm, is a valuable hardwood and used in boat-building. The fungus that causes Dutch elm disease is carried from tree to tree by a bark beetle. The fungus came from infected veneer logs from central Europe. Ironically the disease was named after the Dutch workers who discovered its cause! Since re-entering Britain in 1963, Dutch elm disease has caused the death of many million trees. Genetically-modified elms, resistant to the disease, are now being developed.

El Nino, a climate phenomenon that has caused extreme weather, floods and droughts (as well as pushing global temperatures higher). It results from the interaction of the ocean and atmosphere in parts of the Pacific. Some years have been especially badly affected (1982–83, 1997–98).

Elzevir, the name of a celebrated family of Dutch printers, who produced editions of Latin, French and German classics, which were highly valued for their beauty of type and accuracy of printing. They flourished in the 17th cent.

Ember-days are set apart for fasting and prayer in the Western Church, at the periods appointed for ordination, viz., the Wednesday, Friday and Saturday after the first Sunday in Lent, Whit-Sunday, 14 September (Holy Cross Day), and 13 December (St. Lucia's Day).

Emerald. The rich green variety of beryl (beryllium aluminium silicate). The colour is due to the presence of chromium oxide.

Emu, a towering, flightless bird. A protected species which appears on the Australian national coat of arms alongside the kangaroo.

Encaenia, a festival commemorating a dedication; at Oxford University the annual commemoration of benefactors, accompanied by the conferring of honorary degrees, is held in June.

Enceladus, Saturn's sixth largest moon. Its wrinkled landscape and spouting jets suggest underground waters, which could harbour life. These enormous geysers from its south pole blast ice and vapour hundreds of miles into space.

Encryption, the sending of messages written in code. The term is now used in computing.

Encyclical Letters, a term used in reference to letters addressed by the Pope to his bishops upon matters of doctrine or discipline.

Encyclopaedists, a term first applied to the eminent writers who collaborated in the French *Encyclopédie* (1751–65). They included Diderot, D'Alembert, Voltaire and Helvetius; their works had great influence in popularising the social ideas which resulted in the French Revolution.

Energy. One of the most fundamental concepts of science. A body in motion possesses *kinetic energy* as a result of the *work* done by the forces creating the motion. But a force which does work to stretch a spring does not create motion. Instead, the work is stored up in the spring and is one example of *potential energy*. A raised body also possesses potential energy which turns into kinetic when the body falls. The *heat energy* contained in a body is the sum of the kinetic and potential energy of the constituent atoms which are vibrating all the time. Heat and motion are obtainable from electrical, magnetic, chemical, atomic, and other sources, and physicists therefore define corresponding forms of energy.

All forms of energy are transferable into one another *without loss or gain*. This is the Law of Conservation of Energy. It is one of the most fundamental laws of science, and its general validity is the reason why energy is an important idea. Since Einstein, it has been recognised that mass also is interchangeable with energy. *See also* **Nuclear Energy.**

Energy Conversion. For practical purposes it is frequently necessary to change energy from one into another of its many forms; indeed almost every activity does this in one way or another. The primary sources of energy are the sun, uranium and other elements from which nuclear energy can be drawn, and the tides. The sun is not much used *directly* because its heat is intermittent and not very intense, but solar cookers and refrigerators have been invented and solar batteries (*q.v.*) are used in spacecraft. The sun can be used *indirectly* because it has produced, *via* living processes, fossil fuels like coal and oil and still continues to generate winds, rain and rivers and hence hydroelectric and wind power. Commonly both fossil fuels and the energy of river or tidal waters are converted into electricity. Wind-mill type electricity generators are also common.

The bulk of electricity production is a two-stage process: first fossil or nuclear fuel is used to create heat (*see* **Nuclear Reactors**); then the heat is used to raise steam and drive generators. Efforts are being made to convert heat into electricity more directly, *e.g.*, by using thermoelectric or thermionic effects (*q.v.*), but these have not been used for large-scale production. Once electrical energy is available, factories can make chemical batteries in great numbers and these can then be used as portable energy sources, as can petrol and other refined forms of fossil fuel. *See* **Battery, Fuel Cell, Solar Battery.**

Enthalpy, another name for the heat content (H) of a system in thermodynamics. If a system generates heat it is presumed that the heat comes from the enthalpy of the system which by the 1st law of thermodynamics thus falls. It can be combined with the entropy (S) in an equation which defines the important thermodynamic quantity called the Gibbs Free Energy: $G = H - TS$ where T is the thermodynamic temperature. G is important in the prediction of chemical change.

Entropy, one of the most important quantities in thermodynamics, symbol S. According to Clausius' statement of the Second Law the entropy of an isolated system cannot decrease. Although introduced by Clausius it arose from a consideration of Carnot's studies of the limitation of the convertibility of heat into work. It is most easily viewed as disorder in the statistical approach introduced by Boltzmann. This may be illustrated by considering the separate sets of coloured balls in a box. This is an ordered arrangement (of low entropy). The natural tendency is for the balls to mix and for the colours to become disordered (of higher entropy). We do not expect the opposite process for the balls to spontaneously separate, *i.e.*, we do not expect the entropy to decrease. In the context of energy changes, say in heat engines, the entropy change is equal to the heat change divided by the (thermodynamic) temperature.

Enzymes. Organic catalysts which accelerate chemical processes occurring in living organisms. There are a large number present in the cell, and most have a high degree of specificity. Enzyme mechanisms are the key to basic biological processes. *See* **Section T.**

Ephemoptera or **May-flies,** are an order of insects. In the larval condition they exist from two to three years aquatically, but no sooner do they arrive at maturity than their lives are hurried to a close. They swarm up on warm summer nights, take no food, propagate and perish.

Epic of Gilgamesh. The 3,000 year-old Mesopotamian poem which recounts the mythical adventures of King Gilgamesh. It recounts the story of a great flood.

Epigenetics is the study of how gene behaviour changes.

Equator, the imaginary great circle of the earth, every point of which is 90 degrees from the earth's poles, and dividing the northern from the southern hemisphere. It is from this circle that the latitude of places north and south is reckoned. The celestial equator is the circle in which the plane of the earth's equator meets the celestial sphere (the imaginary sphere, in which the observer is at the centre, used for representing the apparent positions of the heavenly bodies).

Equinox, the time when the sun crosses the plane of the earth's equator, making day and night of equal length. These occur on about 21 March and 23 Sept. *See* **Ecliptic.**

Eras are distinctive periods of time associated with some remarkable historical event or personage. *The Christian era* is computed according to a 6th-century. reckoning to begin with Jesus's birth, A.D. 1. Scholars now believe that Jesus was born *c.* 4 B.C. The *Jewish era* dates from 3761 B.C.; the *Julian era* from the alteration of the calendar by Julius Caesar in 45 B.C. The *Muslim era* dates from the *Hejira*, or the flight of Mohammed from Mecca to Medina, which is A.D., 622, 16 July, in the Julian Calendar.

Erbium, a rare-earth metal, discovered by Mosander in 1842. Element no. 68, symbol Er.

Erg, the unit of work and energy in the centimetre-gram-second system; the energy involved when a force of 1 dyne moves its point of application through a distance of 1 cm.

Eris (Xena), now classified as a dwarf planet (*see* **T9**). Eris was the Greek goddess of chaos and strife. It has a moon, Dysnomia and is the largest dwarf planet.

Ernie, the name given to the "electronic random number indicator equipment", the electronic machine which selected the prizewinning numbers in the first Premium Bond draw, June 1957. (The original Ernie is in the Science Museum).
The lowest value Bond to win £1 million was a £3 Bond bought in February 1959 which won the prize in July 2004. The cap on Premium Bond investments was raised to £50,000 in June 2015. Premium Bonds can no longer be bought at Post Offices.

Eros. This asteroid is 24–32 km in diameter. It comes closer to the earth than any other member of the solar system with the exception of the moon and several very small asteroids. Determination of solar parallax based on observations of Eros in 1930–31 yielded until then the most accurate estimate of the distance of the sun from the earth. *See* **Astronomical Unit.**

Erse, a term used by Lowland Scottish, and English writers for the Gaelic language spoken in the Highlands of Scotland. Sometimes erroneously applied to Irish, the Gaelic language as spoken in Ireland and revived as an official language in more recent times. Dr. Johnson, Sir Walter Scott, and other writers used "Erse" to signify Scottish Gaelic. The language of the Scottish Lowlands (that used by Robert Burns) is related to the English language and not to Gaelic and is variously termed Scots, Braid Scots, Doric, Scottish vernacular, and Lallans.

Escurial or **Escorial,** Spanish monastery built in the mountains near Madrid by Philip II to commemorate the victory over the French at Saint-Quentin (1557). A palace was added later.

Eskimo. Popular name for the Inuit peoples of the Arctic, living in Canada, Greenland, Alaska and the northern territories of Russia. Canada has granted self-government to an Arctic Eskimo territory (Nunavut) (effective from 1999). Their lifestyle is now threatened by global warming.

Esperanto, an artificial international language created by Ludwig Zamenhof of Warsaw and first published in 1887. It does not seek to replace national languages but to serve as a second language for international communication. It is based on the internationality of many words in the principal modern languages, and is entirely phonetic in spelling and pronunciation.
There are over 200 artificial languages including Volapuk, Ido, Glosa and Tutonish.

Estates of the Realm in Britain are the Lords Spiritual, the Lords Temporal and the Commons.

Esters. Organic chemicals formed by combining an alcohol with an acid. They have a pleasant smell, and occur naturally in plants as the scent of flowers. Manufactured for use in the perfumery industry, and as flavourings in food. Some esters are used as solvents, notably amylacetate ("pear drops") in quick-drying paints. The polymeric fibre "Terylene" consists of chains of molecules containing many ester groups, formed by reacting an alcohol having two alcoholic (OH) groups with an acid having two acid (COOH) groups.

Ether, in chemistry, is a volatile inflammable liquid composed of carbon, hydrogen and oxygen. It is a valuable anaesthetic obtained by heating alcohol with sulphuric acid. In physics, in the 19th cent., all space was supposed to be filled with a substance called ether, the chief property of which was to carry light waves, *i.e.*, light was supposed to be waves in this all-pervading medium known as the ether. Speculation and experiment concerned with the ether were very fruitful in advancing physics. Ultimately the attempts by Michelson and Morley to detect the motion of the earth through the ether were unsuccessful in this respect but profoundly successful in stimulating the theory of relativity. The ether concept has now been abandoned.

Ethylene (also called ethene). A gas compounded of carbon and hydrogen, it is related to acetylene and ethane. Industrially it is obtained as a by-product in petroleum refining. It has wide uses as a starting material in the industrial manufacture of intermediates, especially alcohol. Its most important application is in the production of polythene (poly-ethylene). *See* **Catalyst.**

Etruscans, people now known to have come from Asia Minor who colonised Italy about 900 B.C., settled in what is now Tuscany and part of Umbria, reached the height of their civilisation about 500 B.C. They built a network of states stretching from the Alps to Naples. They were skilled technicians in bronze, silver and goldwork. Evidence of their advanced civilisation was unearthed in 1998 beneath the ruins of Pompeii. The language of the Etruscans has only partly been deciphered.

Euro, the name for the single European currency launched on 1 January 1999. From 1 January 2002 the new notes and coins replaced old currencies in the 'eurozone'. On 1 January 2011 Estonia became the 17th country to join. Slovenia joined in 2013 and Latvia in 2014. Lithuania

L38

became the 19th eurozone member in January 2015 (the last of the Baltic States to join).

Europa, fourth largest moon of the planet Jupiter, (q.v.) on which scientists believe the preconditions for life could exist. NASA is planning further missions to Europa. Instead of a solid surface, Europa is covered in a 10-mile thick layer of brittle ice, below which liquid salty oceans have been found. Plumes of water vapour erupting from near the South Pole have now been observed. Surface temperature is −145°C. Europa has a system of plate tectonics similar to Earth.

European Space Agency was created in 1975 with headquarters in Paris. Examples of space research which it has undertaken include the Giotto probe to Halley's Comet, involvement with the Cassini mission to Saturn and the space station Spacelab. It has launched a number of satellites including X-ray multi-mirror telescope (XMM) and Cluster II satellites. ESA has also launched a number of satellites in its four 'cornerstone' missions, including solar astronomy (STEP), Far Infrared Space Telescope (FIRST) the Rosetta cometary mission and XMM. In 2016 the ESA published the most complete map ever of the stars.

Europium, element no. 63, symbol Eu, discovered by Demarcay in 1906. A rare-earth metal.

Evaporation is the process by which a solid or liquid is resolved into vapour by heat. The opposite process is condensation. Wherever a liquid or solid surface is exposed, evaporation takes place into the space above. If the vapour is continually removed the solid or liquid vanishes into vapour; the higher the temperature the quicker the process. If the vapour is confined, then it collects, getting more concentrated until as many atoms of vapour are condensing as are evaporating. The vapour is then said to be saturated. Evaporation of water from the sea, soil, plants, skin, etc., is continuously in progress.

Event Horizon. The boundary of a black hole beyond which nothing returns. See **Black Hole.**

Everest Expeditions. For many years after Everest had been shown to be the highest mountain in the world, political conditions in Nepal, lying south of the summit, and in Tibet, to the north, prevented mountaineers from attempting an ascent. At last in 1921 the Tibetan authorities gave permission, and the first expedition, organised by the Royal Geographical Society and the Alpine Club, was sent out. This was primarily a reconnaissance; besides mapping the northern flanks, it found a practicable route up the mountain. By 1939, six further expeditions had climbed on the northern face. Some were baulked by bad weather, others by the effect of high altitudes on the human body.

Nevertheless, some important climbs were accomplished. In 1924, for example, Colonel E. F. Norton reached 8,589 m, and it was on this expedition that George Mallory and Andrew Irvine were seen going well at about the same height. They never returned, however. The body of Mallory was eventually found in 1999.

When the 1953 Expedition led by Col. John Hunt (later Lord Hunt) was being organised, stress was laid on three main points; proper acclimatisation of the climbers; use of oxygen for the final stages; and the establishment of very high altitude camps, so that the final assault parties would set out fresh and unencumbered. Great attention was also paid to recent developments in diet, clothing and equipment.

In all these matters the 1953 expedition was able to draw on the accumulated experience of its predecessors. By the end of April, a base camp had been established below the ice-fall.

The next critical stage was the ascent of the steep head of the cwm, the Lhotse face, with the threat of avalanches always present. By most strenuous efforts, a camp was established on the South Col (7,869 m) on 21 May. From this camp on 26 May, T. D. Bourdillon and R. C. Evans climbed the South Peak of Everest (8,760 m),then the highest altitude ever attained. On 28 May Edmund Hillary and the Sherpa leader, Tenzing Norgay, spent the night at the highest camp (8,510 m) and on the following day, 29 May, climbed to the South Summit, negotiated the difficult final ridge, and reached the summit of Everest. On 17 May 1993 (exactly 40 years later) Rebecca Stephens became the first British woman to conquer Everest (the first-ever woman to climb Everest was the Japanese Junko Tabei on 16 May 1975).

Since 1953, around 283 people have died trying to climb Everest and over 7,400 have climbed it.

The Chinese (whose official name for Everest is Qoomolangma) claim they first mapped the peak in 1717. They say Everest is 8,844 metres high.

Evolution, The theory, as laid down by Darwin, is that all existing species, genera and classes of animals and plants have developed from a few simple forms by processes of change and selection.

Up to the time of Darwin many believed that life had been created suddenly at the beginning of the world which God had created, according to Archbishop Usher, on 22 October 4004 B.C.

The evidence of the rocks, however, has given a proper, scientific theory of creation, and by studying the fossils preserved in the various layers of the earth's crust the past history of the earth has been pieced together. Darwin has been called the Newton of biology. See **Section V.**

Exchequer, which derives its name from the checkered tablecloth on which accounts were calculated in early Norman times, is a term connected with the revenues of the Crown. In former times it had jurisdiction in all revenue matters. The term Exchequer is now applied to the Governmental department which deals with the public revenues.

Exoplanets see **T9.**

Exploration. Modern exploration began in the second half of the 15th cent. with the voyages of the great Portuguese and Spanish discoverers. They were followed by sailors of other European nations, who profited from their developments in navigation and from their charts, and in less than one hundred years the coastlines of much of the Americas, Africa and SW Asia had been revealed and the globe circumnavigated.

The motives of these early explorers were mixed: they were seeking adventure, trade, plunder, national power and conversion of the local people. Few if any were directly interested in advancing scientific knowledge. But from the reports of their voyages, scholars at home compiled descriptions of the new worlds.

One of the earliest English expeditions to be despatched for scientific research was that of William Dampier on the *Roebuck*, which was sent out by the Admiralty in 1699 to examine the coasts of North-west Australia. In the 18th cent. British explorers were at work mainly in the Pacific Ocean, with the object of breaking the Spanish monopoly of trade. Capt. James Cook sailed thither in 1769 to observe first the transit of Venus at Tahiti, and then to search for the alleged great southern continent. On this voyage he discovered and charted much of the coasts of New Zealand and the east coast of Australia. On his second voyage he was the first to sail across the Antarctic Circle, and he showed that the southern continent was much smaller than had been supposed.

By 1800 the outlines of the continents, except for Antarctica were known, and explorers in the 19th cent. were largely engaged in opening up the interiors. In Africa British explorers solved two problems which had puzzled men for centuries: Mungo Park and Richard Lander established the true course of the River Niger, and Sir Richard Burton, J. H. Speke, Sir Samuel Baker and others revealed the true sources of the Nile. The greatest African explorer of that age was undoubtedly David Livingstone, the missionary, who in three great journeys explored the Zambesi and the Great Lakes, spreading Christianity and fighting the slave trade.

In North America Alexander Mackenzie was the first to cross the main breadth of the continent from sea to sea. In Asia famous explorers included Charles Doughty, who explored in Arabia, and Sir Francis Younghusband, who journeyed across the Gobi and the Himalayas.

Explosives, substances which burn violently to produce gases that an explosion is induced. Gunpowder was the first explosive to be used; Roger Bacon's powder, consisting of charcoal, sulphur and saltpetre, was the only effective explosive until the 19th cent., but it was difficult to control. Nitroglycerine (glyceryl trinitrate) was first compounded in 1847 by adding glycerine to a mixture of sulphuric acid and nitric acid. In 1866 Alfred Nobel discovered how to make dynamite by absorbing nitroglycerine in the fine sand kieselguhr. Cordite was the joint invention of Sir Frederick Abel and Sir James Dewar (1889).

It came into general use as a propellant. High explosives, providing bursting charge for shells and bombs, include TNT (trinitrotoluene), picric acid, cyclonite (RDX) and many others. Slurry explosives can be pumped on to the site and therefore offer advantages in transportation and safety; they are also waterproof.

Chemical explosives have now been eclipsed by nuclear explosives.

Expressionism. *See* **Section N.**

F

Fables are fictitious narratives intended to enforce some moral precept, and may be either in prose or verse, and deal with personified animals and objects or with human beings. Aesop in ancient times and Hans Christian Andersen and the Brothers Grimm (in many of their stories) in later days, have given fables. Mention must also be made of La Fontaine and Krylov.

Fairs were established in mediaeval times as a means of bringing traders and customers together at stated periods, and formed the chief means of distribution. The great English fairs of early times were those of Winchester and Stourbridge near Cambridge. Traders from the Netherlands and the Baltic gathered there with the great merchants of London, and goods of every kind, wholesale and retail, were sold.

One of the biggest trade fairs was at Nijni-Novgorod, founded in the 17th cent.; other big continental fairs were those of Leipzig (founded in the 12th cent.), Lyons and Prague.

Fairy Rings are the circles caused in grassland by certain fungi. The circles expand outwards as the fungus spreads, the fruiting bodies being at the periphery. Farther inward where the fungi are decaying the grass grows more strongly, fertilised by the nitrogen released from the rotting fungi. Once these rings were held to be the scene of fairy dances.

Falcon, name given to diurnal birds of prey which belong to the same family, *Falconidae*, as the hawk, eagle, buzzard, kite and harrier. They are swift of wing and feed on birds and small mammals. These birds have long, pointed wings, strong, hooked and notched bill, long, curved claws and an eye of great power. They are found all over the world. Those that breed in Britain are the Kestrel (the most common), Hobby (one of the swiftest of European birds), Merlin and Peregrine, a swift and magnificent bird with slate-grey back, blackish crown, black "moustache" and whitish breast. The peregrine is now in decline because of pesticides getting into its food supply.

Other members of the family are the Gyr Falcon from northern latitudes, Iceland and Greenland, which is a winter visitor to Britain, the Lanner, Saker, Eleonora's falcon, Red-footed falcon and the Lesser Kestrel. The Gyr Falcon and the Peregrine were used in the sport of falconry in olden times. Because of its fearlessness and larger size, the female bird was used.

When the quarry was sighted, the bird was unhooded, set free, and after mounting high into the air would dart swiftly down to strike the prey. The heron was the usual victim.

Research has proved that diving peregrine falcons are the fastest birds in the world and that the Gyr Falcons are secret seabirds.

Fall-out. Radioactive material produced by nuclear explosions which may cause bodily and genetic damage. (1) *Local fall-out*, due to the return to earth of larger particles, occurs locally, and within a few hours after the explosion; (2) *Tropospheric fall-out*, due to particles which remain in the troposphere and come down within a month or so, possibly all over the world, but within the altitude in which the explosion occurred; (3) *Stratospheric fall-out*, which comes from fragments taken up into the stratosphere and then deposited, in the course of many years, uniformly all over the globe.

The two radioactive materials which have given rise to the greatest concern for the health of the individual are strontium-90 and iodine-131. Both these materials are liable to become con-

centrated in certain parts of the human body, strontium-90 in bone and iodine-131 in the thyroid gland. Radiation exposure may produce genetic effects, that is effects which may show up in succeeding generations.

An extensive survey was carried out by scientists of the US Atomic Energy Commission on the islands of Bikini atoll, site of some 23 nuclear tests, 1946–58. Their records, published in 1969, revealed that the intensity of radioactivity underneath the point of explosion was still exceedingly high. Most of the radiation remaining was due to the radioactive isotope caesium-137.

Fantail, a variety of the domestic pigeon; also a genus of Australian birds of the *Muscicapidae* family. A small New Zealand bird is called a fantail.

Fan Tracery. *See* **Section N.**

Fata Morgana, the name given to a curious mirage often observed over the Straits of Messina, attributed to the magic of the fairy Morgana, half-sister of King Arthur, who was fabled to live in Calabria.

Fathers of the Church were early writers who laid the foundations of Christian ritual and doctrine. The earliest were the Apostolic Fathers (*q.v.*).

The Four Fathers of the early Latin Church were St. Ambrose, St. Jerome, St. Augustine and St. Gregory the Great. The Four Fathers of the Greek Church were St. Basil, St. Gregory Nazianzen, St. John Chrysostom and St. Athanasius.

Fathom, a nautical measure, the six-foot stretch (1·8 m) of a man's arms. Replaced by the metre on British Admiralty charts, but continued on yachtsmen's coastal charts.

Fatigue, a condition leading to breakage when a solid component, *e.g.*, an axle, is subjected to a large number of fluctuating repetitive stresses. Fatigue is the cause of most failures in service of metal engineering components though fatigue is not confined to metallic materials alone.

Fatigue failures result from the *repetition*, not simply from the *size* of the stresses; indeed, fatigue breakage can result from stresses much lower than the material could stand if the load were applied steadily. Fatigue causes minute cracks, usually at the surface, which grow and spread. Early detection is difficult and fatigue, discovered by the engineers of the 19th cent., remains a severe engineering problem.

Fats are important foodstuffs. In physiology they constitute a valuable form of reserve food. They contain carbon, hydrogen and oxygen; chemically they are described as esters of glycerol (glycerine). The commonest fats are stearin, palmitin and olein, esters formed by the combination of glycerol with stearic, palmitic and oleic acid respectively. Fats are converted into soap by alkali; this process (saponification) also releases glycerol.

Fatwa, an edict issued by a Muslim religious leader (*e.g.* the death threat to Salman Rushdie issued in 1989 by Ayatollah Khomeini).

Fault, a term designating a breakage coupled with displacement of geological strata.

Fauvism. *See* **Section N.**

February, the second month of the year, contains in ordinary years 28 days, but in leap years 29 days. When first introduced into the Roman calendar by Numa, *c.* 700 B.C. it was made the last month of the year, preceding January, but in 452 B.C. the position of the two months was changed, February following January.

Félibrige, a movement founded in 1854 to revive the ancient glories of Provence, initiated by the French poet Frédéric Mistral.

Felspar, the name given to a group of minerals, silicates of aluminium with some calcium and sodium, or potassium, which make up probably more than half of the earth's crust. It is formed in granite and other rocks, both igneous and metamorphic.

Female Genital Mutilation (FGM), the abhorrent practice of removing the external genitalia of young women for non-medical reasons, usually between the ages of 5 and 8. Documented widely in Africa and the Middle East. Criminalised in the UK in 1985. Around 25 % of all cases of FGM worldwide occur in Nigeria.

Fenestella, the niche set apart on the south side of the altar for the piscina in Roman Catholic churches.

Fermentation, the action of chemical ferments or *enzymes* in bringing about chemical changes in the materials of living animals and plants, *e.g.*, the breaking-down of sugar by yeast into alcohol.

Ferret, a domesticated polecat. It is about half the size of a cat and is bred in captivity to hunt rats and rabbits. It has a long sinuous body and short legs which enable it to enter rabbit and rat holes and chase the quarry out to guns or into nets.

Ferrites are compounds containing iron, oxygen, and one or two of a certain range of other possible metallic elements. Ferrites have become very important technically, because, unlike ordinary magnetic materials, they combine strong magnetism with electrical insulating properties. Ferrite-rod aerials became common in portable radios, and ferrite devices were used in radar.

Fieldfare, the largest member of the thrush family, a regular winter visitor to Britain from Scandinavia. It is brown in colour with a lighter spotted breast and a grey head.

Field-Marshal, the highest ranking title in the British army, and only bestowed on royal personages and generals who have attained great distinction. The first British Field-Marshal was created in 1736, when John, Duke of Argyll, had the title conferred upon him.

Fighting-Fish, small pugnacious Thai fish with long caudal and ventral fins. They are kept in glass globes in Thailand, and when brought into contact will fight to the death.

Filibuster, a name first given to pirates and buccaneers in the 17th cent. who took possession of small islands or lonely coast lands, and there maintained themselves apart from any governing authority. In later times the term was used to specify men taking part in expeditions whose object was to appropriate tracts of country, and settle upon them in disregard of international law. The most notable expeditions of this kind in modern times were those of Narciso Lopez against Cuba in 1850–51, and of William Walker against Nicaragua, between 1855 and 1860. Both leaders were captured and executed. The term is also used to express the right of a minority in the US Senate for unlimited debate, which is used on occasions to delay legislation.

Finches, a large family of small birds belonging to the Passerine or perching order of birds. There are about 200 species, including greenfinch, hawfinch, chaffinch, goldfinch, siskin, bullfinch, crossbill, linnet, twite and bunting. Finch numbers are in decline (greenfinch have suffered a disease of the mouth preventing them from feeding). Around 6 million pairs of chaffinches nest in Britain.

Fir, a cone-bearing tree with small evergreen leaves and of considerable use as timber. There are two types: the Silver Firs and the Douglas Firs numbering about 25 species. All these firs attain to a considerable height, and all yield turpentine or other resinous material.

Fire-damp. *See* Methane.

Fire-Fly, a small winged insect of the *Eleteridae* family, it is able to throw out a strong phosphorescent light in the dark. There are some remarkable specimens in tropical countries. They are not flies at all but beetles.

Fireworks. *See* Explosives.

Firkin, a former measure of capacity, the fourth part of a barrel, now only used in reference to a small cask or tub for butter, lard, *etc.*

Fischer-Tropsch Process. A process for making synthetic petrol from carbon monoxide and hydrogen. The synthesis is accelerated by cobalt-thoria and nickel-thoria catalysts.

Fish Louse. Parasitic crustacea found on marine and fresh-water fishes and whales.

Fission, Nuclear. A nuclear reaction in which the nucleus of an atom (*e.g.*, uranium 235, plutonium) captures a neutron, and the unstable nucleus so produced breaks into two nearly equal fragments and throws out several neutrons as well. In biology the term fission is applied to reproduction by fragmentation of a single-cell organism, as in amoeba.

Flagella, single hair-like projections found on many micro-organisms. Their sole function is, by complicated motion, to move the organism about. They are longer and less versatile than cilia.(*q.v.*).

Flag Officer, a British naval officer who enjoys the right of carrying a flag at the mast-head of his

ship, and is of the rank of Admiral of the Fleet, Admiral, Vice-Admiral or Rear-Admiral.

Flagship, the ship that flies the Admiral's flag, and from which orders proceed.

Flamingo, a strangely beautiful and extremely slender wading bird of white and rose-pink plumage with long, slender legs and neck and a long, down-curved bill with which it rakes the mud and obtains its food of worms and molluscs.

The wings are bright crimson, bordered with black, and a flock in flight is a picture of singular beauty. The lesser flamingo is shorter and darker than its larger cousin. It also has a deep red bill. There is a large and famous colony in the Camargue, S.E. France. Flamingos are pink because they eat carotene-rich brine shrimps. Flamingos eat with their heads upside down.

Flash-Point. This is found by heating an oil in a special cup and taking the temperature at which sufficient vapour is produced to ignite when a small flame is applied. It is an index of the inflammability of oils.

Flavonoids, a group of compounds, found in most fruit and vegetables, with powerful antioxidant properties.

Fleas. Fleas are small parasitic insects belonging to the order *Aphaniptera* (so called because these creatures have no wings). They obtain their food by sucking blood from their host. They are laterally compressed, which immediately distinguishes them from lice. The human flea (*Pulex irritans*) is able to jump vertically a distance of over 18 cm.

Fleet Prison, a noted debtors' prison that stood on the east side of Farringdon Street, London. It was notorious for the cruelties inflicted on prisoners, particularly under the wardenship of Thomas Bainbridge who took charge in 1728. It was pulled down in 1846.

Fleet Street, a famous thoroughfare in London, until 1990 the centre of journalism and the press, though it was long celebrated for its taverns.

It takes its name from the Fleet stream which used to run from Hampstead through Holborn to the Thames at Blackfriars.

Flemings, the Dutch-speaking people of Flanders, whose medieval ancestors excelled in the textile arts: England owes its early eminence as a manufacturing nation to the migration of numbers of Flemings to this country in the 16th and 17th cent. *See also* **Walloons.**

Fleur de Lis, the former national emblem of France, the flower of the lily. It was superseded by the Tricolour in 1789.

Flint, consists of granular chalcedony with some opaline silica, and occurs as nodules and bands in the Chalk. It is hard and has a conchoidal fracture, so enabling it to be used in making cutting implements in prehistoric times. Before the invention of lucifer matches, it was used along with steel for striking lights.

Flint implements are objects found in the younger geological strata, and constituting evidence of the condition and life of the period. They include knives, clubs, arrow-heads, scrapers, *etc.*, used as weapons, tools and possibly as surgical instruments and in religious ceremonies. Ritual weapons and sacrificial knives continued to be made of stone long after the introduction of metals for practical purposes.

Flounder, one of the most familiar of the smaller flat fishes common round the British coasts, and seldom attaining a weight of over 1·3 kg.

Fluoridation, the process of adding the element fluorine, in the form of suitable compounds, to something deficient in it. Commonly met with as a proposal to add fluorides (fluorine compounds) to drinking water to combat dental decay, especially in children. Some toothpastes are fluoridated and fluoride can also be taken as tablets and in other ways. In 1976 a working party of the Royal College of Physicians recommended that water supplies should be fluoridated when the natural fluoride level is below 1 mg/litre. This recommendation drew on many investigations throughout the world giving evidence for the effectiveness of fluoride in the prevention of decay without harmful side-effects. There is, however, a body of opinion unconvinced by this, one argument being that to take or not to take fluoride should be a personal decision.

Fluorine, chemical element, no. 9, member of the halogen family, symbol F, it is found in combination with calcium in fluorspar, and occurs in minute quantities in certain other minerals. Discovered by Scheele in 1771, it was first obtained by Moissan in 1886. A pale yellow gas, it is very reactive and combines with most elements except oxygen. Its acid, hydrogen fluoride, etches glass, the fluorine combining with the silicon to form volatile silicon fluoride. Organic fluorine compounds have found use as very stable polymers which resist a wide variety of chemical actions.

Fluorescent Lamp. *See under* **Electric Light and Ultra-Violet Rays.**

Fluorocarbons are hydrocarbons in which some or all of the hydrogen atoms have been replaced by atoms of chlorine or fluorine. They are non-toxic, non-flammable and chemically inert gases or low boiling point liquids. These properties make them very suitable for use as refrigerants, and propellants in fire-extinguishers and aerosols. The most widely used fluorocarbons are the chlorofluoromethanes (CCl_2F_2, CCl_3F and $CHClF_2$). In 1974 it was first suggested that the vast release of fluorocarbons into the atmosphere due to the greatly increased use of aerosols could cause a significant depletion of the protective ozone (*q.v.*) layer in the upper atmosphere. The mechanism for this involves the decomposition of fluorocarbons at high altitudes as a result of intense solar irradiation. The chlorine atoms so released can then catalyse the conversion of ozone into ordinary molecular oxygen. The degree of ozone depletion that will result is a matter of current controversy. Similarly, opinions differ as to the detrimental effect ozone depletion might have on the incidence of skin cancer and on the climate.

Fluorspar, a mineral; chemically calcium fluoride. Can be colourless, green or yellow, but is most commonly purple. Blue fluorspar under the name of Derbyshire "blue John" has been used for ornamental purposes.

Fly, the popular name for a large number of insects with one pair of wings and a proboscis terminating in a sucker through which fluid substances can be drawn up. The best-known species are the common house-fly, the blue-bottle and the blow-fly. In the larval form flies are maggots, and feed upon decaying substances, animal flesh, *etc.* Flies are able to walk upon ceilings or upright surfaces by having suckers at the soles of their feet. *See* **Diptera.**

Flycatcher, name of a large family of small birds, the Muscicapidae. They are insect feeders, catch their food in the air, and are distributed over most countries of the world. The spotted and the pied nest in Britain, which they visit from April to September.

Flying Fish are frequently to be seen in southern waters, and are capable of gliding considerable distances without touching the water. To build up speed for its "take-off " the fish swims rapidly, to break the surface at 24–32 km/h. Maximum air speed is about 64 km/h.

Flying Fox, the largest member of the bat family. Like other bats, it is nocturnal, but it feeds entirely on fruits.

Flying Lemur. *See* **Colugo.**

Flying Lizard, or *Draco,* an Asiatic lizard, possessing wing-like projections from each side which enable it to make flying leaps through the air, though not sufficient for continuous flight.

Flying Squirrel, rodents of which there are several species in Europe, Asia and America. It possesses a parachute-like fold of skin by means of which it projects itself through the air. In appearance they are much like ordinary squirrels, to which they are related. African flying squirrels belong to a different family.

Fog is caused by the presence of particles of condensed water vapour or smoke in the surface layers of the atmosphere, the term being applied meteorologically when the resulting obscurity is such as to render objects invisible at distances of up to 1 km. Fogs are frequently formed when the air near the ground is cooled below its dew-point temperature by radiation on a still, cloudless night; by flowing over a relatively cold land or water mass; or by mixing with a colder air stream. An accumulation of smoke over a large city may cause a high fog cutting off the daylight and producing gloom. *See* **Pollution, Aerosol.**

Foie Gras, a delicacy made from the liver of a duck or goose fattened by force-feeding. This cruel method of production is outlawed in Britain.

Foliation, a geological term for rocks whose component minerals are arranged in parallel layers as the result of strong metamorphic action.

Folio, a printing term for a sheet of paper folded once, a half sheet constituting a leaf.

Folklore concerns itself with the traditional beliefs, customs, institutions and sayings that have been handed down from generation to generation by word of mouth and with the observation, recording and interpretation of such traditions. (The word *folklore* itself was first suggested and used—as two words *Folk Lore*—by W. J. Thoms in the *Athenaeum* of 22 August 1846, and was at once absorbed into the English language.)

Traditional lore of this kind takes very many forms and ranges from omens of good and bad luck (spilling the salt, breaking a mirror, dropping an umbrella, *etc.*) and the wearing of amulets or the possession of talismans (such as the horseshoe) as protection against misfortune, to elaborate ceremonial dances such as the Abbots Bromley Horn Dance, the Hobby horses of Padstow and Minehead the Northern sword-dances and the Christmas mummers' plays. Especially important are the beliefs and customs associated with birth, marriage, death *etc.*

Another very large section of the subject of folklore deals with the traditional sayings and practices associated with particular days and seasons of the year—calendar customs, as they are called. The eating of pancakes on Shrove Tuesday; Mother Sunday customs and the simnel cake; Good Friday as the right day for planting potatoes, but emphatically the wrong day for washing clothes or cutting one's finger-nails; the necessity of wearing something new on Easter Sunday; the children's maypole dances and May garlands; midsummer fires; All Hallowe'en as the most favourable occasion for divining the future—especially in respect of marriage—and for games and sports such as apple-bobbing; the numerous practices accompanying the harvest. All these are examples of calendar customs; their full story would occupy several volumes.

Folklorists are interested in such oral tradition because they think that to a large extent it is able to assist other historic methods—ethnographical, linguistic, archaeological, *etc.*—in the elucidation of the early story of man.

The Folk-Lore Society was founded in 1878. Song and dance has its own English Folk Dance and Song Society.

Food Standards Agency, an independent watchdog set up in April 2000 by the Government to restore consumer confidence in food safety.

Foot-and-Mouth Disease, a highly contagious infection among cloven-hoofed animals with a devastating impact on farming. The 2001 outbreak devastated such areas as Cumbria. The outbreak was declared over in January 2002.

Footpath. In English law a highway over which the public have a right of way on foot only, other than such a highway at the roadside.

Force, as a term in physics, signifies an influence or exertion which, when made to act upon a body, tends to move it if at rest, or to affect or stop its progress if it be already in motion. In the c.g.s. system, the unit of force is the dyne; in the foot-pound-second system, the poundal; in the SI system, the newton.

Formaldehyde. Chemically it lies between methyl alcohol and formic acid; oxidation of methyl alcohol yields formaldehyde, and oxidation of formaldehyde produces formic acid. It is used as a disinfectant, in silvering mirrors, and in the manufacture of phenolformaldehyde plastics (of which bakelite is the best-known example). Solutions of formaldehyde in water, formalin, are used to preserve biological specimens.

Forme, a body of letterpress type, composed and secured for printing from; or a stereotype or electrotype. The former was used more for newspaper formes and the latter was used in book work.

Formic Acid can be obtained from a colourless fluid secreted by ants and other insects and plants. It is a strong irritant. Commercially it is obtained from sodium formate, which is synthesised by the absorption of carbon monoxide in caustic soda. It is used in the electroplating, tanning and textile industries.

Fossa, a solitary animal, related to mongooses. They are found in Madagascar, where they will eat lemurs.

Fossils. Remains of animals and plants, or direct evidence of their presence, preserved in rocks. They include petrified skeletons and shells, leaf imprints, footprints, *etc.*

Fox, carnivorous animal of the canine family, found in considerable numbers in most parts of the world. The common fox *Vulpes vulpes* of Europe is a burrowing animal of nocturnal habits, living upon birds, rabbits and poultry.

Among other species are the Arctic fox and the red fox of North America, of which the valuable silver fox, coveted for its fur, is a variety. An estimated 15% of foxes are now to be found in our suburbs, scavenging the streets at night (around 10,000 foxes now live in London).

The hunting of foxes with dogs in England and Wales became a criminal offence in February 2005, following successive votes to ban foxhunting by the House of Commons (and the eventual use of the Parliament Act to force legislation through). In Scotland, hunting with hounds became illegal in 2002.

Fox-Shark *or* **Thresher Shark,** a large species of shark common in the Atlantic and in the Mediterranean. It is very destructive to small fish, but although it attains a length of 4·5 m it is not dangerous to humans.

Fracking, the contentious natural gas extraction technology involving deep drilling. Large amounts of water, sand and chemicals are blasted down a well to release the gas in the shale rock below. The word is short for hydraulic fracturing. It is strongly opposed by environmentalists, but licences for fracking are being granted.

Franciscans. *See* **Friars.**

Frankincense is of two kinds, one being used as incense in certain religious services and obtained from olibanum, an Eastern shrub. It provided rich revenue for the ancient Nabatean empire. The other is a resinous exudation derived from firs and pines, and largely used in pharmacy.

Freeport, a port exempt from customs duties and regulations. The north German towns of the Hanseatic League were among the earliest and most famous freeports.

Freira, small grey and white sea bird. Extremely rare, it nests on the island of Madeira. Likely to become the first European species to face extinction since the Great Auk in 1844.

French Horn. *See* **Horn.**

Friars, members of certain mendicant orders of the Catholic Church. The four chief orders are the Franciscans or Grey Friars, the Dominicans or Black Friars, the Carmelites or White Friars and the Augustinians (Austin Friars).

Friday, the 6th day of the week, named after Frigga (Freyja), the wife of Odin. It is the Muslim Sabbath and a general abstinence day of the Roman Catholic Church.

Frigate-Bird, a web-footed bird widely distributed over tropical latitudes, and deriving its name from its great expanse of wing and forked tail, resembling the shape of a swift vessel. It feeds on flying fish mostly, being unable to dive and also steals from other birds. The male is the national bird of Antigua and Barbuda. They have a phenomenal mastery of air currents..

Frog, a familiar amphibian, breathing through gills in the earlier (tadpole) part of its existence and through lungs later. It remains three months in the tadpole stage. The frog hibernates underwater in the mud during the winter.

Britain now has only one species of native frog, the common frog (*Rana temporaria*). Frogs are now threatened by global warming which is leading to outbreaks of *chytrid* (a fungal infection). They are also threatened by ranavirus. Globally, over 170 species have become extinct in the last two decades. A frog with green blood anf turquoise bones was recently discovered in Cambodia. In Ecuador there are 492 different kinds of frogs, while 12 new nocturnal frog species were found in India in 2011. The world's tiniest frog was discovered in New Guinea in 2012. Some frogs can jump 50 times their body length!

Frost occurs when the temperature falls to, or below, 0°C, which is freezing point. Hoar frost is applied to the needles or feather-like crystals of the ice deposited on the ground, in the same manner as dew. Glazed frost is the clear icy coating which may be formed as a result of rain falling on objects whose temperatures are below the freezing point. These layers of ice, often rendering roads impassable for traffic, damaging overhead power and communication systems and endangering aircraft, can also be caused by condensation from warm, damp winds coming into contact with very cold air and freezing surfaces.

Froth-Hopper *or* **Frog-Hopper.** A family of bugs (belonging to the insect order *Hemiptera*) which in the larval stage surround themselves with a protective mass of froth ("cuckoo spit"). These insects, which suck the sap of plants, bear a faint resemblance to frogs, and the adults possess great leaping powers.

Fruit Fly. *See* **Drosophila.**

Fuel Cells were first demonstrated in action when in 1959 Bacon of Cambridge University used his fuel cell to drive a fork-lift truck and a welding machine. The Bacon fuel cell consists of two electrodes of porous nickel dipping into a solution of caustic potash in water. One electrode is supplied with hydrogen gas from an outside cylinder and the other with oxygen. These gases, forming layers on the nickel, are the active chemicals. The oxygen combines with water to make two negatively charged ions, each consisting of an oxygen and a hydrogen atom joined together (a hydroxyl ion). The hydroxyl ions travel through the solution to the hydrogen electrode, where they combine with hydrogen to form neutral water. Their negative charge (one electron per ion involved) has now arrived at the hydrogen electrode and is ready to flow back to the other electrode through any outside circuit that is provided. This flow constitutes the useful electric current, and it has been provided at the expense of creating water out of the original hydrogen and oxygen. The water can be removed as steam.

What is the advantage of all this? In the first place the fuel gases are easy to make and to store in cylinders. Supplying a new gas cylinder is easier and quicker than recharging an ordinary accumulator. Furthermore, a fuel cell is lighter for a given power than an accumulator; satellite designers have found them useful. The fuel cell is not damaged by heavy overloading, and this is valuable for application to vehicle driving. Fuel-cell-driven buses combine the advantage of diesel buses and trolleybuses.

Fulani, a people of Hamitic stock widely distributed in N.W. Africa, chiefly in Nigeria. There are two main branches: the dark-skinned Fulani, settled farmers and city dwellers, Muslim in religion; and the lightcoloured Bororo'en who are semi-nomadic herdsmen. The Fulani are different from any tribe in W. Africa though they resemble in some ways the Masai of E. Africa. The Fulani conquered the Hausa states at the beginning of the 19th cent. which passed under British suzerainty after 1903. Sokoto, built in 1810, was capital of the Fulani empire.

Fuller's Earth, a special kind of clay or marl possessing highly absorbent qualities, originally used in the "fulling"—that is, cleansing and felting—of cloth. Now used in clarifying oils. Deposits in America and also in the south of England.

Function. In mathematics, one quantity y is said to be a function of another quantity x, written $y = f(x)$, if a change in x results in some corresponding change in y. Thus $\sin x$ or $\log x$ are functions of x. If y depends not only on x but on several other quantities as well, y is called a function of many variables.

Fungi, unique class of plants, which reproduce from spores and lack the green colouring matter *chlorophyll*. It includes moulds, rusts, mildews, smuts, mushrooms, *etc.* Potato blight is a fungus disease which caused the failure of the potato crop in Ireland in 1846. Around 200,000 different fungi are known. *See also* **Section T.**

Furniture Beetle (*Anobium punctatum*). The common furniture beetle is responsible for 80 per cent of all woodworm damage and is the great pest of the comparatively modern house, causing damage in the main to softwood roofing and flooring timbers. Adults are 3 mm long. The grub tunnels for about 33 months. *See also* **Woodworm, Death Watch Beetle.**

L43

G

Gabardine, a long, loose, coarse, over-garment, worn by the poor in the Middle Ages, and pre-scribed by law as the distinctive garment of the Jews. The name is now given to a cloth of wool and cotton used to make raincoats.

Gabbro, a kind of igneous rock, often very coarse-grained, containing a good deal of plagioclase felspar, and monoclinic pyroxene; it may occasionally also include biotite, magnetite, ilmenite and hornblende. A gabbro containing nickel at Sudbury in Canada is one of the richest sources known of that metal.

Gadfly, a widely distributed family of flies with only one pair of wings, including the horse fly. The females are very voracious, being able to bite through the skin and suck the blood of animals. The males are harmless.

Gadolinium. An element, no. 64, symbol Gd, be-longing to the rare-earths metals discovered in 1886 by Marignac. It is strongly magnetic.

Gaelic, relating to the Gaels and their language, a term now applied only to the Celtic people inhab-iting the Highlands of Scotland, but formerly also to the Celts of Ireland and the Isle of Man. A cen-tury ago, 200,000 people spoke Scottish Gaelic. Now only 60,000 do (2001 census) and the lan-guage could soon face extinction. The Scottish Parliament has now given Gaelic equal status with English as the official language of Scotland.

Gaitskellites. Members of the Labour Party who supported the moderate and reformist policies of Hugh Gaitskell (1906–63) in the late 1950s and early 1960s.

Galago, "Bush Babies," related to the lemur, native to Africa, large-eyed and nocturnal.

Galaxy (or Milky Way Galaxy), the giant star system to which our Sun belongs. On a clear moon-less night a swathe of light can be seen stretching across the sky from horizon to horizon. This dra-matic sight led the ancient Greeks to describe it as a river of milk flowing from the breast of Hera, wife of Zeus—the word "galaxy" comes from the Greek word for milk. The Romans saw this as Via Lactea, or Milky Way.

The Galaxy contains *c.* 400 billion stars and has a spiral structure that is highly flattened. The stars are organised into a thin disc with an ellip-soidal bulge, or nucleus, at its centre. The system is embedded in a roughly spherical halo of stars and globular clusters. The entire Galaxy is ro-tating about the black hole at its centre. The Sun is situated near the inner edge of one of the spiral arms. At the Sun's distance from the centre, the rotation of the disc stars are 220 km per second. It takes the Sun 230 million years to travel once around the Milky Way. The Milky Way is up to 100 million light years in diameter. At its centre is a super-massive black hole.

The halo of the Galaxy is much less populated than the disc and its full extent is still uncertain. Many astronomers now believe there is a dark halo of unseen matter stretching out to a radius of about 100 thousand parsecs. The presence of such a halo is inferred from the manner in which the Galaxy rotates and the gravitational effect on the more distant globular clusters in the halo and on nearby dwarf galaxies.

In 2010 astronomers reported the most distant galaxy cluster yet discovered, 13·1 billion light years from Earth. In 2012 the oldest galaxy ever discovered was found by Japanese astronomers. The biggest known galaxy is IC 1011. In around 4 billion years astronomers believe the Andromeda Galaxy (twice the size of the Milky Way) will col-lide with the Milky Way – causing total chaos. Andromeda hosts around 1 trillion stars. There are an estimated 200 *billion* galaxies, with some 1,000 times bigger than our Milky Way. The Gaia space telescope will map the Milky Way. It seems our Milky Way has absorbed smaller galaxies dur-ing its life. Nine 'dwarf galaxies' have been identi-fied orbiting the Milky Way.

Gale, a high wind now technically defined as one of at least Beaufort force 8. Between thirty and forty gales a year occur on the north and west coasts of the British Isles and only about half of this number in the south-east. At St. Ann's Head, Dyfed, the anemometer registered a gust of 113 mile/h (182 km/h) on 18 Jan. 1945, which is a record for these islands. Gusts exceeding 113 km/

h are rarely experienced in London. Gale warnings are issued by the Meteorological Office.

Galileo Space Mission. *See under* **Jupiter.**

Gall, abnormal vegetable growths caused by insects, mites, bacteria, or fungi, found on all parts of the plant. Oak-apples, Robin's pin-cushion (on wild rose), "witches' brooms" (on trees) are examples. Some are useful com-mercially, *e.g.*, oak apples yield tannic acid.

Galleon, the name given to the old three-decked Spanish treasure vessels employed in conveying the precious minerals from the American colonies to Spain. The term is often applied to any large, especially stately, sailing vessel.

Galley, an oar-propelled boat used by the ancient Greeks and Romans for transport, manned by slaves. They were also used as warships. When so used the sides were raised to protect the rowers.

Gallic Acid, obtained from gall nuts, sumach, tea, coffee, and the seeds of the mango, is used in the manufacture of inks and as an astringent in medicine. It was discovered by C. W. Scheele (1742–86), a Swedish chemist.

Gallium, metallic element, no. 31, symbol Ga, related to aluminium, but which can be cut with a knife. It was discovered spectroscopically by L. de Boisbaudran in 1875. Long before Mendeleyev had predicted that an element with its properties would be found to fill the then existing gap in the Periodic Table.

Gallup Poll, a system, introduced by Dr. Gallup in the United States, for testing public opinion.

Galvanised Iron is iron coated with zinc. The name comes from the fact that such a coat protective against rust could be deposited electrolytically. Electrodeposition may be used, but the cheaper and more common process depends on dipping the iron in a bath of molten zinc.

Gamboge, a resinous gum obtained from the sap of *Garcinia morella,* a tree native to Thailand, Cambodia and Sri Lanka, and used as a yellow pigment in paints and also as a purgative.

Game is the term applied to wild animals which are protected from indiscriminate slaughter by Game Laws. In the UK game comprehends deer, hares, pheasants, partridges, grouse, black game, moor game, woodcocks, bustards and certain other birds and animals.

Game can only be killed (with few exceptions) by persons holding game licences. Occupiers of land and one other person authorised by them in each case are allowed to kill hares and rabbits on their land without licence.

Game cannot be sold except by a person hold-ing a proper licence. There is a "close time" prescribed for the different classes of game; for in-stance, the selling or exposing for sale of any hare or leveret during March, April, May, June or July is prohibited by law. Grouse cannot be shot be-tween 11 December and 11 August; partridges between 2 February and 31 August; pheasants between 2 February and 30 September; and black game between 11 December and 10 August. The shooting of grouse, pheasants *etc.* is bitterly opposed by many people.

Game reserves are legally protected areas for natural vegetation and wild life.

Gaming, *or* **Gambling**—*i.e.*, staking money on the chances of a game—differs from betting in that it depends upon the result of a trial of skill or a turn of chance. The 1959 Betting and Gaming Act replaced all the old laws on gaming, which went back to an Act of 1541 entitled "An Acte for Mayntenance of Artyllarie and debarringe of unlauful games", under which some games were unlawful if played for money in any cir-cumstances. Roulette and any game of dice were among such games. Under the 1959 Act any game was lawful, subject to certain conditions. Since then the Betting, Gaming and Lotteries Act, 1963, and the Gaming Act, 1968, have been passed, to deal with unlawful gaming and to pre-vent the exploitation of gaming by commercial interests. The playing of bingo is now restricted to clubs licensed for bingo only. Sunday betting on dogs and horses became legal in 1995. Playing of fruit machines in betting shops is now legal.

The 2005 Gambling Bill proposed a major expansion of regional casinos (with unlimited jackpots). A new Gambling Commission was also proposed. Casinos would be open to the public, not operating as 24-hour membership clubs as they do now. The regulation of internet gambling is now of major concern, as in widespread advertising on TV. Addiction to gambling is soaring, particularly misuse of fixed-odds terminals. *See also* **National Lottery.**

Gamma Ray. *See* **Section T.**

Gamma Ray Bursts, intense flashes of gamma rays, detected at energies up to one million electron-volts. Measurements have revealed that the distribution of the bursts is uniformly distributed across the sky and they are thought to originate outside our Galaxy. The physical origin is thought to mark the destruction of a massive star. *See* **Black hole, Neutron star.**

Gammexane, a powerful insecticide, used particularly to kill the tsetse fly and mosquito.

Ganesh, Hindu deity made up of four creatures: man, elephant, serpent and mouse.

Gannet, a fish-eating bird which dives on its prey from a great height, swallowing it under water, is found in large numbers off the coast of Scotland, and has breeding stations in the Hebrides, St. Kilda, Ailsa Craig, the Bass Rock, Grassholme Island and on Ortac and Les Etacs (rocks off Alderney). It is a bird of white plumage, black tips to long narrow wings and wedge-shaped tail, and weighs about 3 kg. The gannet breeds in colonies on ledges of steep, rocky, island cliffs. Related to the cormorants, pelicans and frigate-birds.

Ganymede, a moon of Jupiter. It is the first moon we know which possesses an independent magnetic field. It has a thin atmospheric layer and is believed to have a deep salty ocean beneath its crust, containing more water than all the oceans on Earth. It is the solar system's biggest moon (almost the size of Mars) and a mission to explore it will be launched in 2022.

Garden Cities in England were founded by Ebenezer Howard (1850–1928), and his radical ideas were put forward in his book *Tomorrow—A Peaceful Path to Real Reform* (later re-issued as *Garden Cities of Tomorrow*). New towns should be so placed and planned as to get the best of town and country life, an adaptation of the model villages of certain industrial philanthropists such as Salt, Richardson, Cadbury, Leverhulme *etc.* The Garden City Association (later the Town and Country Planning Association) was formed in 1899, and the first garden city was begun at Letchworth in 1903 and successfully established. Welwyn Garden City (1919) was Howard's foundation. New garden cities at Ebbsfleet in Kent and at Bicester were proposed in 2014.

Gardener-Bird, a bird possessing many of the characteristics of the bower bird, found only in Papua-New Guinea. *See also* **Bower Bird.**

Gargantua, the giant hero of Rabelais' satire, of immense eating and drinking capacity, symbolical of the greed of the Church.

Gargoyle, a projecting spout for carrying off water from the roof gutter of a building. Gargoyles are only found in old structures, modern water-pipe systems having rendered them unnecessary.

In Gothic architecture they were turned to architectural account and made to take all kinds of grotesque forms—grinning goblins, hideous monsters, dragons and so forth.

Garlic, a bulbous plant of the same genus as the onion and the leek, and a favourite condiment in the famed Mediterranean diet. It has a very strong odour and pungent taste. The smaller you chop garlic, the more pungent it becomes. Giant garlic (Aglione) is odourless and also milder than common garlic.

Garnet, a group of minerals; chemically they are orthosilicates of the metals calcium, magnesium, titanium, iron, aluminium. Garnets can be coloured yellow, brown, black, green or red; the blood-red garnet is an important gemstone.

Garrotte, a method of strangulation used as capital punishment in Spain, and consisting of a collar which is compressed by a screw that causes death by piercing the spinal marrow. Garrotting was also applied to a system of highway robbery common in England in 1862–63, the assailants seizing their victims from behind, and by a sudden compression of the windpipe disabling them until the robbery was completed.

Garter. The Most Noble Order of the Garter was founded (*c.* 1348) by King Edward III, and is the premier order of knighthood in Great Britain. The traditional story associating the garter and the motto with the Countess of Salisbury, who it was said dropped her garter while dancing with the King, who said "honi soit qui mal y pense" cannot be accepted.

The Order was originally limited to the Sovereign and 25 knights, but the number has been extended, and it may now be bestowed on royal personages and leading representatives of the British peerage. The insignia of the order are the garter of dark-blue velvet with the motto in letters of gold, the mantle of dark-blue velvet lined with white silk, the surcoat and hood, and the gold-and-enamel collar. The garter is worn on the left leg below the knee and by women as a sash over the left shoulder.

Modern recipients have been the Princess Royal (1994), Sir Edmund Hillary, Baroness Thatcher (1995) and John Major (2005). *See* **Knighthood.**

Gas is an elastic fluid substance, the molecules of which are in constant rapid motion, and exerting pressure. The technique whereby gases are liquefied depends on increasing pressure and diminishing temperature. Each gas has a critical point; unless the temperature is brought down to this point no amount of pressure will bring about liquefaction. The last gas to be liquefied was helium (1908).

Gas from coal was first used as an illuminating agent by William Murdoch towards the end of the 18th cent. in Birmingham, and about 1807 was introduced in London, one side of Pall Mall being lighted with it. It became widely used as an illuminant, and for space heating and cooking. In the UK increasing attention has been paid to the use of a primary fuel—natural gas—instead of producing gas from coal or oil. Shale gas is creating vast new energy supplies.

Gas, Natural, natural mixture of gases often present with deposits of petroleum, found issuing from the ground in many parts of the world—in the oilfields of Venezuela and the Caucasus, in China, Saudi Arabia, but chiefly in North America. Its chief component is methane. Large industrial centres have made use of this gas since the latter part of the 19th cent., but much of this valuable fuel still goes to waste.

Pipelines have been constructed to deliver the gas to where it is wanted. Britain began to ship liquid methane from the Saharan oilfield in 1964. Some of the world's largest natural gas fields have been discovered in the North Sea.

Domestic gas appliances have to be modified if the natural product is substituted for ordinary town gas because the burning characteristics are different. Oil production from the North Sea fields began in 1975 and the main single source of gas in the UK is now natural gas. A new source of energy is shale gas, extracted by fracking (*q.v*). *See also* **Liquefied Natural Gas.**

Gas Turbine. In this kind of engine mechanical movement is produced by a jet of gas impinging on a turbine wheel; used in aeroplanes, locomotives and ships. These engines are mechanically simple compared with internal combustion engines, and require less maintenance.

Gauge, a standard dimension or measurement, applied in various branches of construction. Thus the standard railway gauge is 4 ft 8½ in (143·5 cm) in the UK, USA and most European countries. Russia uses the broader gauge of 5 ft (152 cm). Narrow railway gauges of different standards are in use on very steep inclines in various countries. Other standard gauges are fixed in building and gun-boring.

Gauls were inhabitants of ancient Gaul, what is now France, Belgium and parts of the Netherlands, Switzerland and Germany.

Gault, a stratum of blue clay between the Lower Greensand and the Chalk. A typical section of the Gault can be seen at Folkestone.

Gauss, a unit of magnetic induction in the cgs system, named after the great German mathematician and astronomer, K. F. Gauss.

Gazelles, a group of small, graceful antelopes which live in the drier regions of Africa and Asia. They can run very fast at speeds of over 64 km/h.

GCSE, (General Certificate of Secondary Education), the school-leaving examination, introduced in 1988, which replaced the existing GCE and CSE examinations. In 2013, it was announced that a new syllabus would begin in 2015, with new grades. Some axed GCSEs began to disappear from 2017.

Geckos are nocturnal lizards. The secret of their ability to scuttle along ceilings lies in the millions of microscopic hairs on their feet which harness intermolecular forces to adhere to surfaces. They are the only lizards with a voice.

Gegenschein. A faint oval-shaped glow situated at the point in the sky directly opposite the Sun and caused by the reflection of sunlight from tiny interplanetary dust particles.

Geiger Counter, an electrical device, invented by Geiger, which can detect individual atomic particles, *e.g.*, electrons, protons, *etc.* It often consists of a tube of gas at a few cm Hg pressure, fitted with two electrodes—a cylinder and an axial wire. A high voltage is kept across the electrodes, and the passage of a charged particle through the gas releases ions which permit a momentary discharge between the electrodes.

Electronic circuits register this discharge as a "count". Geiger counters are used to detect and measure radioactivity and cosmic rays both for technical and research purposes.

Geisha, traditional female entertainer of Japan.

Gelatine, a transparent, tasteless, organic substance obtained from animal membranes, bones, tendons, etc., by boiling in water. It is of various kinds, according to the substance used in making it. Isinglass, the purest form of it, is made from air-bladders and other membranes of fish, while the coarser kind—glue—is made from hoofs, skin, hides, *etc.* Its constituents are carbon, hydrogen, oxygen and nitrogen.

Gelatine is applied to an immense variety of purposes, from the making of food jellies to photographic materials.

Geminids. The name of a spectacular meteor shower which appears in mid-December each year.

Gemsbok, a large South African antelope of the open dry plains, sandy coloured with black and white markings on its face, and with long straight horns.

Generation, a time-measure reckoned at about 30 years when children are ready to replace parents; also the body of persons existing at the same time or period.

Generation, Spontaneous. *See* Abiogenesis.

Genes, the elementary units of heredity. They exist as highly differentiated regions arranged along the length of the chromosomes which the nuclei of cells carry. A chromosome may carry hundreds or even thousands of genes, each with its own particular structure and specific properties. The position of a particular gene on a chromosome is called its locus. The material of the gene is DNA (*q.v.*). See **T33.**

Genesis Mission, space probe launched in 2001. Its 3-year mission was to capture and return to Earth *c.* 10–20 micrograms of solar wind.

Genetic Code. The elucidation of the structure of DNA (*q.v.*) for which Crick, Wilkins and Watson were jointly awarded the 1962 Nobel Prize for medicine, revealed the code or chemical dictionary out of which messages serving as blueprints for living structures can be made. *See* **Human Genome Project, L54.**

Genetic Engineering is the name given to the introduction of human choice and design criteria into the construction and combination of genes. This refers not to breeding by selection, a traditional process, but to the biochemical alteration of the actual DNA in cells so as to produce novel self-reproducing organisms. Such manipulations became possible when techniques were discovered for severing and rejoining DNA molecules and inserting sections into them.

As a result, when biologists realised they could create new lifeforms, *e.g.*, bacteria, with novel genes, they appreciated that, as well as medically beneficial strains, new virulent forms might by accident be produced and escape into the world.

Human beings may in time be able to design the genes of higher animals and even of humans themselves and thus consciously influence biological evolution. *See* **T46–8.**

Genetic Fingerprinting. *See* DNA Database.

Genetics. *See* **T30(2)** and **T46–8.**

Genocide is an international crime, defined by the General Assembly of the United Nations in 1948 as "acts committed with intent to destroy, in whole or in part a national, ethnic, racial or religious group as such". The UN Convention came into force in 1951. Some recent conflicts (as in Rwanda) have seen acts of genocide, but the worst example is the Jewish Holocaust (See J19). The term is attributed to the Polish Jewish legal scholar, Raphael Lemkin, in 1943.

Genomes. *See* **T46–8.**

Genus, a term applied in biology to designate a group of similar species. A group of similar genera is called a family.

Geodesy, the science of calculating the configuration and extent of the earth's surface, and determining exact geographical positions and directions, with variations of gravity *etc.* Land-surveying is a branch of geodesy.

Geography, science concerned with the spatial organisation of natural features and life and man-made artifacts upon and immediately above the surface of the earth. It is increasingly concerned with the processes by which such patterns are generated.

Geology, the science which deals with the condition and structure of the earth, and the evidence afforded of ancient forms of life. The geological strata are classified in the following categories: *Primary* or *Palaeozoic* (the oldest fossil-bearing rocks including the Cambrian, Ordovician, Silurian, Devonian, Carboniferous, Permian); *Secondary* or *Mesozoic* (Triassic, Jurassic, Cretaceous); *Tertiary* or *Cainozoic* (Eocene, Oligocene, Miocene, Pliocene, Pleistocene); *Post tertiary* (recent rocks). See **Section V.**

Geometrical Progression, term used to indicate a succession of numbers which increase or decrease at an equal ratio—as 3, 9, 27; or 64, 16, 4.

Geometry is the branch of mathematics which demonstrates the properties of figures, and the distances of points of space from each other by means of deductions. It is a science of reason from fundamental axioms, and was perfected by Euclid about 300 B.C. The books of Euclid contain a full elucidation of the science. The ancient Babylonians used a complex form of geometry to track the movements of Jupiter.

Geophysics, the branches of physics which are concerned with the earth and its atmosphere. Meteorology, geomagnetism, aurora and airglow, ionosphere, solar activity, cosmic rays, glaciology, oceanography, seismology, rockets and satellites—all these are geophysical subjects.

Geothermal Energy. Some of the heavy elements within the earth's crust are radioactive and this gives rise to a temperature rise towards the centre of the earth. The practical exploitation of this geothermal energy comes about when there are hot springs or geysers. It is believed that these are caused by rainwater slowly percolating down to the hot rocks and blowing out as steam. The homes of people living in Reykjavik are heated by geothermal steam and there are a number of small power stations in various parts of the world. Although the costs in the few cases where geothermal power has actually been exploited are remarkably low, the expense of drilling, *etc.*, required when attempting to exploit the heat in the rocks where surface manifestations do not occur, is likely to limit the use of this source of power.

Geothermal Heating. The earth's interior is hot and in certain localities, often adjacent to volcanic or earthquake-prone regions, reservoirs of hot water or steam exist at accessible depths. Natural hot geysers occur in many such places and people, *e.g.*, the ancient Romans and present-day Japanese, use natural hot water for bathing, cooking and laundry. Occasionally the subterranean reserves permit large-scale power generation by drilling for hot steam and passing it into turbines to produce electricity. Pioneering work on this was done at Lardarello in Italy. Other sites are in New Zealand, California, Japan and Iceland.

Germanium. A grey, hard, brittle chemical element, no. 32, symbol Ge, chemically related to silicon and tin. Discovered by Winkler in 1886. Its richest ore is germanite containing 6% of the metal. Coal is also a relatively rich source. Since 1948 it has assumed great importance as a semi-conducting material for making transistors (*q.v.*). Because of this it has been so intensively studied that more is known about its properties than any other element.

Gesta Romanorum (Latin = deeds of the Romans), a medieval collection of Latin stories of unknown authorship which circulated widely in Europe during the Middle Ages. First printed in the

15th cent. The stories were used by Chaucer, Shakespeare and others.

Gestation, the carrying of young in animals during pregnancy, varies considerably in its length. In the case of an elephant, the period is 21 months; a camel, 12 months; a cow, 9 months; a cat, 8 weeks; a horse, 48 weeks; a dog, 9 weeks; and a pig, 16 weeks. Hens "sit" for 21 days; geese, 30; swans, 42; turkeys, 28.

Geysers, hot springs of volcanic origination and action, are remarkable for the fact that they throw out huge streams of boiling water instead of lava as in the case of a volcano.

The most famous geysers are those of Iceland, which number over a hundred, the principal one having an opening of 21 m in diameter and discharging a column of water to a height of 61 m. There are many geysers in the Yellowstone Park (USA) and some in New Zealand.

The word geyser comes from a hot spring called Geysir in Iceland.

Ghetto, confined area of a town in which Jews or some other minority were once forced to live.

Ghost-Moth or **Ghost Swift,** an interesting nocturnal insect (*Hepialus humuli*) common in England, possessing in the male a white collar and known for its habit of hovering with a pendulum-like action in the twilight over a particular spot where the female is concealed.

Gibbon, the name of a long-armed ape mainly inhabiting S.E. Asia. It is without tail, and possesses the power of very rapid movement among the trees of the forests. They communicate with each other using organised sound patterns like early human language.

Gin, a popular spirit distilled from malt or barley and flavoured with the juniper berry. The main varieties are the English and American, known as "Gin" or "Dry Gin", and the Dutch, referred to as "jenever" or "Hollandse jenever". In Germany and Austria it is called "Schnapps". The word "Gin" is an abbreviation of "Geneva", both being primarily derived from the French *genièvre* (juniper). The 'gin craze' in Britain refers to the period around 1710–50.

Ginkgo. *See* **Maidenhair Tree.**

Giraffe, the tallest of existing animals, reaching a height of from 5–6 m when full grown. Its sloping back and elongated neck seem to be the natural evolution of an animal that has to feed on the branches of trees. It is a native of Africa, is of a light fawn colour marked with darker spots and has a prehensile tongue. Its remarkable eyesight can spot a predator two miles away. It needs only two hours' sleep. The latest DNA research has shown that giraffes are in fact four separate species.

Girl Guides. *See* **Boy Scouts.**

Glaciers form in higher mountain ranges, and are immense consolidated masses of snow, which are gradually impelled by their force down the mountain-sides until they reach a point where the temperature causes them to melt, and they run off in streams. From Alpine glaciers the five great rivers, the Rhine, the Po, the Rhône, the Inn and the Adige, have their source. The longest Swiss glacier is the Gross Aletsch, which sometimes extends over 16 km.

Some of the glaciers of the Himalayas are four times as long. The Muir in Alaska is of enormous magnitude, and that of Justedlals Brae in Norway is the largest in Europe. Recent high levels of glacial retreat no doubt reflect global warming but could have disastrous consequences for irrigation, hydroelectric schemes *etc.* They could dilute the Gulf Stream and greatly affect the climate of the UK. It is believed the Great Andean Glacier (and many in Tibet) will soon disappear. There is concern over the glaciers of Greenland and West Antarctica. The emission of soot in the Industrial Revolution melted some Alpine glaciers. Glaciers harbour highly active communities of bacteria, viruses and microscopic plants.

In 2008 glaciers half a mile thick and tens of miles long were discovered on Mars.

Gladiators were professional athletes and combatants in ancient Rome, contesting with each other or with wild beasts. At first they were drawn from the slave and prisoner classes exclusively, but so much were the successful gladiators held in esteem that men came to make a profession of athletics, and gladiatorial training schools were established. When a gladiator

was vanquished without being killed in combat, it was left with the spectators to decide his fate, death being voted by holding the hands out with the thumb turned inward, and life by putting forth the hands with the thumb extended. Gladiatorial shows were the chief public displays in Rome from the 3rd to the 4th cent. A.D.

Glass is an amorphous, man-made substance, fluid when hot, solid, though fragile, when cooled. It is made of sand mixed with an alkaline flux, usually soda or potash. While hot, glass can be formed into almost any shape by moulding, blowing or, since the early 19th cent., by machine pressing. Unrefined glass normally has a greenish tinge, due to the iron content of most sands, but it is transparent or at least translucent. To make truly colourless glass is a difficult and expensive process, and such glass resembling the natural mineral, rock crystal, is given the name crystal. Glass can be tinted by the addition of various metallic oxides, cobalt producing blue, manganese mauve, *etc.* Because it is at once solid and transparent, glass is the perfect material for windows for which it has been used since Roman times. And since it can be made cheaply and is easy to clean, it has been used for containers in homes, shops and pharmacies, again since Roman days. Glass can also be made into things of beauty, by the use of coloured glass and by cutting, engraving, painting and gilding.

The earliest vessels of glass so far found come from Egypt and date back to *c.* 1500 B.C. With the invention of glass-blowing in the 1st cent. A.D., the use of glass spread throughout the Roman empire. Many varieties were made, including superb art glass like the Portland vase. The Arabs were great glassmakers after the 7th cent.

During the Renaissance the Venetians made luxurious art glass, rich in colour and often manipulated into fantastic forms, Bohemia's 17th-cent. glass is wonderfully engraved with pictures and cut into glittering facets.

During the 1670s in England George Ravenscroft invented a new, heavy, water-clear crystal, with an addition of lead as the magic ingredient, and English lead glass is still the basis for all modern crystals.

Glass-Snake, genus, *Ophisaurus*, of legless lizards with long fragile tails capable of re-generation when broken. Six species are known; in S.E. Europe, S.W. Asia, S.E. Asia and N. America. Attains a length of about 60 cm; main colouring, green, with black and yellow markings.

Glauconite. A green mineral, chemically a hydrated silicate of potassium and iron. Often found in marine sands (hence these rocks are known as "greensands") and sandstones.

Glaucus is a curious genus of sea slugs often called the Sea Lizard belonging to the molluscs. It has no shell and has a soft body, with horny mouth and four tentacles. It is a native of the Atlantic, and is not more than 30 cm long.

Glee, an unaccompanied piece for three or more voices. Glee-singing was popular in England during the 18th and early 19th centuries.

Globe Theatre. The original Globe Theatre was built on Bankside, London in 1599 and pulled down in 1644. Its foundations were excavated in 1989. Sam Wanamaker (1919–93), the actor, and Theo Crosby (1925–94), the architect had already conceived and designed a near-replica, which was built near the site of the Elizabethan theatre.

Globigerina, an oceanic unicellular animalcule with a perforated shell, and occurring in certain parts of the Atlantic in such vast numbers as to form a bed of chalk ooze with their empty shells.

Glow-worm, a beetle, possessing the power (much stronger in the female than the male) of emitting phosphorescent light from the hind end of the body. The brighter the light, the more males they attract. The female is wingless.

Glucinium. *See* **Beryllium.**

Glucose, Dextrose or **Grape Sugar** is a carbohydrate (*q.v.*). It is produced by hydrolysis from cane sugar, dextrine, starch, cellulose, *etc.*, by the action of reagents. It also occurs in many plants, fruits and honey. In brewing glucose is prepared by the conversion of starch by sulphuric acid. Malt also converts starch into glucose.

Glutton or **Wolverine,** the biggest animal of the weasel family, inhabits the northernmost parts of Europe and America. In build it resembles the bear, and is rather larger than a badger. Its fur is of a brown-black hue, but coarse.

Glycerine *or* **Glycerol**, occurs in natural fats combined with fatty acids, and is obtained by decomposing those substances with alkalis or by superheated steam. It is colourless and oily and sweet, and put to many uses, being widely utilised for medicaments, for lubricating purposes, and in the manufacture of nitro-glycerine.

Glycols. Organic compounds containing two alcohol groups. Ethylene glycol is the most widely known example; it is used as an anti-freeze in motor-car radiators on account of its property of greatly reducing the freezing point of water. Also used in the manufacture of "Terylene". *See* Esters.

Glyptodont, an extinct species of gigantic armadillo, fossil remains of which have been discovered in S. America. It was some 2·7 m long, carried a huge tortoise-like shell and had fluted teeth.

Gneiss, a metamorphic rock usually containing quartz, felspar and mica. It is banded, the light-coloured minerals being concentrated apart from the dark minerals.

Gnu or **Wildebeest,** a large antelope from Africa south of the Sahara, distinguished by its very short thick neck and large head with a pronounced roman nose. There are two species; the white-tailed gnu is almost extinct, the brindled gnu is still common and migrates in vast herds.

Goat-Moth (*Cossus cossus*), a large moth of the *Cossidae* family, common in Britain, evil-smelling and very destructive in the larval stage to trees of the poplar and willow genus, into the wood of which the caterpillar bores during its three years' period of development.

Goats are horned ruminant quadrupeds, indigenous to the Eastern Hemisphere, but now domesticated in all parts of the world. Though related to the sheep, they are a much hardier and more active animal. The male has a tuft of hair under the chin. Many species, including those of Cashmere and Angora, are valuable for their hair, which is used for fine fabrics.

Goat milk is nutritive, and goat-skins are in demand for leather for gloves, shoes, *etc.* Recent research has shown that the goat pre-dates any other animal as the first to be domesticated by humans. Goat is the world's most popular meat, eaten by 70 % of the world's population.

Gog and **Magog,** two legendary City of London giants who were brought captive to London and made to serve as prisoners at the Palace of Brute, which stood on the site of Guildhall. Effigies of the giants have stood in Guildhall since the time of Henry V. They were destroyed in the Great Fire of 1666, replaced in 1672 and used to be carried through the streets of London in the Lord Mayor's Show. The present figures replaced those carved in 1708 by Richard Saunders, which were destroyed in an air raid during the second world war. In the Bible, Ezekiel also makes reference to Gog and Magog.

Gold. Metallic element, no. 79, symbol Au (Latin *Aurum*) related to silver and copper, the coinage metals. The greatest amount of gold is obtained by treating gold-bearing quartz by the cyanide process. The gold is dissolved out by cyanide solution, which is then run into long boxes filled with zinc shavings when the gold is precipitated as a black slime. This is melted with an oxidising agent to remove the zinc. South Africa has traditionally been the world's largest gold producer, but has now been overtaken by China. India is the biggest market for gold jewellery. The price of gold rises on economic uncertainty (as in the 2011 sovereign debt crisis). Much gold is recycled. The oldest gold artefacts ever found date to around 4,500 B.C.

Gold-Beaters' Skin is the outside membrane of the large intestine of the ox, specially prepared and used by gold-beaters for placing between the leaves of gold while they beat them. Thin membrane is of great tenacity, and gets beaten to such extreme thinness that it is used to put on cuts and bruises.

Gold Standard. Under the gold-standard system which was widely prevalent up to 1941, each gold-standard country fixed the value of its currency in terms of a weight of gold of a certain fineness and was, broadly speaking, ready to exchange its currency freely for gold, which could then be exported without restriction.

This involved keeping a gold reserve big enough to meet all likely demands and also to serve as a backing for the issue of notes. The gold standard had to be given up during the first world war; and though it was in substance restored in Great Britain in 1925 (when Churchill was Chancellor), the restoration was never complete. Sterling had to be devalued in the crisis of 1931 and the UK was forced off the gold standard.

Golden Eagle. *See* Eagle.

Goldeneye, a species of wild duck, widely distributed over Arctic regions. It is a passage-migrant and a winter-visitor to the UK. Distinguished by a large white spot in front of each eye on a dark ground.

Golden Number, the number of any year in the metonic cycle of 19 years, deriving its name from the fact that in the old calendars it was always printed in gold. It is found by adding 1 to the number of the year A.D. and dividing by 19, the remainder being the Golden Number; or, if no remainder, the Golden Number is 19.

Goldfish, or *Carassius auratus* were introduced to Britain in the 18th century. Numbering 125 breeds, their sense of smell is even better than a bloodhound. First recorded in China, A.D. 400.

Goldsmiths Company, one of the richest London City Companies; the official assayers of gold and silver, invested with the power of "hall-marking" the quality of objects made from these metals. First charter granted in 1327.

Gondola, the old regulation black boats so common on the canals of Venice, propelled by a gondolier with one oar who stands at the stern.

Gondwana, the name of the ancient southern land mass linking Antarctica, Australia, India *etc.*

Gonfalon, the pennon affixed to a lance, spear or standard, consisting usually of two or three streamers and made to turn like a weather-cock.

Gonzo Journalism, a highly subjective and personal style of writing in which the writer is an essential part of the story. The leading exponent was Hunter S. Thompson.

Gophers. Rodent mammals. The pocket gophers are stout-bodied burrowers common in the USA. The slender burrowing gophers, also called "ground squirrels", occur in central and western USA. The sisel or suslik is a related European species. They are a great pest.

Gorilla, the largest of the anthropoid apes, found in the forests of Equatorial Africa, and at maturity standing from 1·2–1·5 m high. Eastern mountain gorillas are one of the most endangered species in the world. They are our largest living primates on Earth. Now less than 700 survive in the Congo, Rwanda and Uganda. The Western Lowland gorilla (the world's most common gorilla) is now on the endangered list, also threatened by habitat loss and hunting.

Goshawk (*Accipiter gentilis*), a diurnal bird of prey, fearless and extremely agile; loves wooded country and is very destructive of poultry and game-birds. It resembles the peregrine falcon in appearance, but has shorter, rounded wings. This bird was a great favourite of falconers in medieval times. A few have now been reintroduced from Scandinavia but are believed to be causing decline to the kestrel.

Goths. A Teutonic people who originally came from southern Sweden (Gotland) and by the 3rd cent. were settled in the region north of the Black Sea. They began to encroach on the Roman Empire and early in the 4th cent. split into two divisions: the "wise" Goths or Visigoths between the Danube and the Dniester (referred to as the West Goths), and the "bright" Goths or Ostrogoths in southern Russia on the Dnieper (known as East Goths).

The Ostrogoths were later conquered by the Huns *c.* 370, while the Visigoths under Alaric devastated Greece and sacked Rome in 410. Eventually the Visigoths spread to France and Spain and their last king Roderick fell in battle against the Moors in 711. The Ostrogoths regained their independence on the death of Attila in 453 and under king Theodoric the Great conquered Italy in 493. They lost their identity after Justinian regained Italy, 525–552.

Gourd Family *or* **Cucurbitaceae.** This family of about 650 species of flowering plants includes the gourds, pumpkins, cantaloupes, cucumber, gherkin, water-melon and squashes. Most abundant in the tropics, the cucurbits are mainly climbing annuals with very rapid growth. The bathroom loofah is the skeleton of one cucurbit fruit, *Luffa cylindrica*. The squirting cucumber is another member of the family.

Governor. A device attached to an engine, turbine, compressor, *etc.*, which automatically controls the engine's speed in accordance with power demand. Most governors depend upon the centrifugal action of two or more balls which are thrown outwards as their speed of rotation increases and actuate a throttle valve or cut-off. The centrifugal governor was invented by Thomas Mead, patented by him in 1787. Watt adapted it to the steam engine.

Grail, Legend of the Holy, a tale of Celtic origin which became part of Arthurian legend. According to the Christian version the grail was the cup which Christ used at the Last Supper, brought to England by St. Joseph of Arimathea. Its link to Glastonbury Abbey was invented by medieval monks.

Grand Prix, the "French Derby" was established by Napoleon III, in 1863. It is the chief French race and is for three-year-olds. The term is now also widely used in motor racing.

Granite is a coarsely crystalline igneous rock consisting of quartz and alkali felspars plus mica or hornblende. It is a much used ornamental and building stone; it forms the high ground of Dartmoor and Bodmin Moor.

Graphene, the thinnest material in the world (200,000 times thinner than the line down the centre of this page). Almost completely transparent. It has exceptional electrical qualities and is likely to transform medicine, technology and computing.

Graphite *or* **Plumbago,** commonly called black-lead, is a form of carbon occurring in foliated masses in marble, schist, *etc.* It is soft, will make black marks on paper or other plain surfaces, and is mainly used for lead pencils. It is also a valuable lubricant. Pure graphite has found a use with the construction of atomic piles. China, India and Canada are the main producers.

Graphology, the science which interprets and analyses the way letters are formed and shaped.

Graptolites, fossil animals confined to Cambrian, Ordovician and Silurian strata.

Grasshopper. There are eleven species of these leaping insects which are related to the locusts and crickets. Most are vegetarians; some eat flies and caterpillars also. The chirping sound they make is made by scraping the hind legs against the wings; in some species a noise is produced by rubbing the wings together.

Gravitation. One of the four types of force known to physics. The others are electromagnetic, the weak nuclear and the strong nuclear forces. Gravitational forces are an attraction that one piece of matter has for another; they dominate astronomical phenomena, but inside the atom they are negligible compared with the other types of force. Einstein's General Theory of Relativity is the only theory which attempts to interpret gravitational forces in terms of more fundamental concepts. Scientists have now proved that gravity does indeed travel at the speed of light. They have also detected ripples of gravity from black holes.

Graylag, the ordinary wild grey goose of Europe, the species from which domestic geese are derived; frequents fens and marshes; breeds in Iceland, Scandinavia and Scotland; it has pinkish legs and feet and lack of black markings on bill.

Great Auk. *See under* Auks.

Great Wall of China, enormous system of walls (1,500 miles in length) built to protect China's northern frontier. Completed 204 B.C. It is the longest man-made structure on Earth. The best preserved sections are near Beijing but erosion, tourism *etc.* are causing much damage.

Grebe, a diving bird of beautiful plumage found over a great part of the world on lakes and oceans. The two species familiar in Great Britain are the Dabchick or Little Grebe and the large and handsome Great Crested Grebe, which has a feathery tuft, lost in the autumn, on each side of the head. Grebes have remarkable courtship displays. The breast feathers are of a downy softness and silver lustre.

Greek Fire, a combustible supposed to have been composed of sulphur, nitre, naphtha and asphalt, used with destructive effect by the Greeks of the Byzantine Empire in their wars.

Greek Mysteries. *See* Mysteries, Greek.

Green Plover. *See* Lapwing.

Greenwich Mean Time. The first Nautical Almanac, for the use of navigators and astronomers, was published by the Astronomer Royal in 1767. It was based on the meridian at Greenwich, with longitude measured east and west of 0°. A master clock, which still exists, was built at Greenwich Observatory in 1852 to control the railway station clocks and Greenwich Mean Time, or Railway Time as it was sometimes called, prevailed. In 1884 Greenwich was chosen as the prime meridian of the world and GMT became known as Universal Time. The time-keeping role is now done by the International Bureau of Weights and Measures. GMT has become UCT (Universal Coordinated Time). Recently, the Daylight Extra Now group has campaigned to abolish GMT and have an extra hour of daylight in the evening. There is now a movement to replace GMT in favour of a time defined by a linked collection of 400 atomic clocks. *See also* **British Standard Time** and **T59**.

Gregorian Calendar. *See* Calendar.

Gresham's Law states that if money, *i.e.*, money with the higher intrinsic value, and bad money are in circulation together, the bad money will tend to drive out the good money from circulation. For instance, the good money is more likely to be melted down or demanded in payment by foreign creditors.

Gretna Green, a celebrated village in Annandale and Eskdale, just over the border from England, where runaway marriages were performed from 1754 to 1856 (now a romantic wedding venue).

Griffin, in ancient mythology, a winged creature with an eagle's head and the body of a lion, found in ancient sculptures of Persia and Assyria. Its origin is traced to the Hittites.

Grilse, a salmon that has only been once to the sea.

Grimm's Law, formulated by Jacob Grimm, an eminent German philologist, lays down a principle of consonantal change in the Germanic languages. Thus, Lat. *pater*, Eng. *father*, Ger. *Vater*; Lat. *frater*, Eng. *brother*, Ger. *Bruder*.

Grogram (French = *gros grain*), a kind of rough fabric made of wool and some other fibre, such as silk, mohair or cotton.

Grotto, a natural or artificial cave. Among the most famous are the blue grotto of Capri and the grotto of Antiparos (Cyclades, Aegean).

Ground Wave, that part of the energy emitted by a radio transmitter which travels along the ground; as opposed to the sky wave which is reflected back to earth by the ionosphere.

With the lower radio-frequencies, the ground wave can be picked up over several thousand miles; in the broadcasting band, over a hundred or so miles; it is almost useless at high frequencies.

Groundnut. *See* Peanut.

Grouse, game bird of the northern latitudes where some 20 species occur. They are stout, compact, ground-dwelling birds, protectively plumaged (the willow grouse turns white in winter), the male usually being larger and more brightly coloured than the female. The red grouse of the British moorlands has been introduced into Belgium and Germany. Of the same family are the blackcock, ptarmigan, capercaillie, American prairie-hen and the partridge. The black grouse in Britain is in rapid decline.

Guanaco, a large species of llama, common to South America. Utilised as a beast of burden.

Guano, the excrement of sea-birds, found in large quantities on the rocky islands of the western coasts of South America and the Nauru Islands. It forms a useful fertilising agent, being rich in phosphate and ammonia, and first came into use in 1841, since which time Peruvian guano has been a recognised article of commerce.

Beds of guano from 15–18 m in thickness are not uncommon. Fish guano and bat guano from caves in South America and the Bahamas are also used as fertilisers.

Gudgeon, a small fresh-water fish of the carp family with 2 small barbels on the upper lip. A recent immigrant, *topmouth gudgeon*, poses a major threat.

Guildhall, the place of assembly of the members of a guild, and at one time, when guilds were in full strength, was practically the Town Hall. The London Guildhall is today the hall of meeting for the City of London Corporation.

Guilds for the fostering and protection of various trades have existed in England since Anglo-Saxon times and from the 12th to the 16th cent.

exercised great influence and enjoyed many privileges. There were trades' guilds and craftsmen's guilds, and in all large cities and towns there was a guild hall.

Their successes led to many monopolistic abuses, and in the end it became necessary to free the country from their restrictive power.

The City Guilds (Livery Companies of the City of London) derive their name from the 14th cent. dress assumed by their members.

Guillemot, a genus of sea-birds of the auk family, common in Northern Europe, two species—the Common Guillemot and the Black Guillemot—being natives of our own sea coasts, nesting on the cliffs. Brünnich's Guillemot, an Arctic species, is a rare straggler in Britain. When food is scarce, guillemots will kill the unattended chicks of other pairs.

Guillotine, the method of execution during the French Revolution. Devised by Joseph Guillotin (1738–1814). Last used in France in 1977. It was actually designed to make death as quick and painless as possible!

Guinea, an English gold coin of the value of twenty-one shillings, current from 1663–1817, and deriving its name from the first guinea coinage having been struck from gold obtained on the coast of Guinea.

Guinea-Pig, a rodent of the cavy family about 25 cm in length and with a tail so short that it does not project outside the body. It makes an excellent pet, though easily frightened. Its ancestors were species of the wild cavy of S. America domesticated by the Incas of Peru.

Gules, a heraldic term, denoting a rose of red tincture, indicated by vertical lines drawn or engraved without colour.

Gulf Stream is confined entirely to the western side of the N. Atlantic and is the warm-water current flowing through the Straits of Florida from the Gulf of Mexico parallel to the American coast up as far as Cape Hatteras. From there it continues north-eastwards as a slower, broader, cooler (yet even so, relatively warm) drift of water, merging with the North Atlantic Drift and losing its identity about 40° N. Lat., 60° W. Long. It is a common error to attribute the warmth of the British Isles and Western Europe generally to the Gulf Stream but this has no influence whatever except in so far as it feeds the North Atlantic Drift. The Gulf Stream and North Atlantic Drift owe their movement to the direction of the prevailing winds.

It is the south-westerly airstream coming from warmer regions and passing over the waters of the Atlantic Drift that brings the warmth inland to influence the climate of Western Europe.

Gull. An extremely well-known, long-winged seabird with rather short legs and webbed feet. In almost all adults the body and tail are white whilst the back and most of the wings are grey or black. In the majority of cases the plumage of juveniles is partly or entirely dusky. Gulls are omnivorous, and are very useful as scavengers. They follow ships and quickly seize on any refuse which may be thrown overboard.

There are 44 species, which vary in size from moderately small to large. With certain exceptions, such as the Kittiwake in the North Atlantic, they are normally not found very far from land.

They are sociable and mostly breed in colonies on cliff-ledges, on islands, beaches and sandhills and.among vegetation in swamps, sometimes a long.way from the sea. The nest is usually substantial, and the eggs generally number from two to three. Of the 29 species breeding in the northern hemisphere, 14 occur in the British Isles. The pure white Ivory Gull is the most northerly of birds. Sabine's and the Swallow-tailed Gull have forked tails. Ross's Gull has a black ring round the neck and one species, Franklin's Gull, migrates from the North, where it breeds, to pass the winter in the Southern hemisphere. The breeding population of herring gulls in the UK is now reported to be falling sharply. The population of urban gulls in Britain is rising very fast. Gulls and their nests are protected under the 1981 Wildlife and Countryside Act.

Gums are glutinous compounds obtained from vegetable sources, soluble in cold or hot water, but not in alcohol. There are innumerable varieties. Gum Arabic is exuded from a species of acacia grown in Senegal, the Sudan, Arabia, India *etc.*, and is a valuable commercial product, used in dyeing, ink-making, as a mucilage, and in medicine. Indiarubber is an elastic gum. Gums are also made from starch, potatoes, *etc.* Chewing gum products were first made in the 1860s.

Gun-Cotton, a powerful explosive manufactured by subjecting a prepared cotton to the prolonged action of a mixture of three parts sulphuric acid and one part of nitric acid. It burns without explosion on ignition, but by percussion explodes with a force five times greater than gunpowder does.

Gunpowder, also called "black powder", the oldest of explosive mixtures, consists of saltpetre, sulphur and charcoal, intimately mixed.

Gurkhas, famous regiment of the British Army, first formed by Nepalese fighters in 1815. The Gurkhas have been awarded 13 VCs. Their legal right to stay in Britain was won in 2009.

Gurnard, a sea-fish, with large, bony head and diminutive body, of which there are some forty species. They are plentiful in British waters. Often used for soups and stock.

Gymnasium, originally the name given in ancient Greece to the public places where Greek youth used to exercise and receive instruction. Plato, Aristotle and other great teachers lectured there. The Greek institution was never very popular with the Romans, and it was not until the 18th and 19th cent. that the cult of combining physical with intellectual activity revived. In Germany the name was applied to the classical grammar school.

Gypsies, a race of Indian origin; their language, Romany, is related to the languages of N.W. India. The Roma are nowadays spread over many parts of the world, but are most common in Europe where they appeared at the end of the Middle Ages.

The English name *gypsy* comes from the Byzantine Greek for Egyptian; other European names are *Zigeuner* (Ger.), *zingaro* (It.), *fzigany* (Magyar), all resembling the Persian *singar* = a saddler. Their history has been one of persecution. Hitler treated them like the Jews.

In Britain after 1945 they were kept increasingly on the move, but in 1968 Parliament passed a Bill to make the provision of sites a duty of local authorities. However, the 1994 Criminal Justice and Public Order Act made it much easier to move on unwelcome gypsies. Economic pressure has largely removed their traditional crafts of tinkering, basket-making and peg-making. The majority now deal in scrap-iron. Today there are around 12½ million European Gypsies and in some parts (such as Hungary, Bulgaria, Romania, the Czech Republic and Slovakia) they are again subject to ill-treatment or discrimination.

The Romani language is not yet recognised as a minority language in the UK.

Gypsum, a whitish mineral consisting of hydrated sulphate of calcium. The finest gypsum is alabaster. When heated gypsum is converted into the powder called Plaster of Paris; the water it loses can be taken up when the plaster is wetted, and the reconversion of Plaster of Paris into gypsum accounts for the way in which the former sets hard. The name "Plaster of Paris" came from the location of important gypsum quarries in the Montmartre district of Paris. It was found after the flood disasters of January 1953 that gypsum could undo the effect of sea-water. By spreading it for the rain to wash into the soil, thousands of acres of farmland in Holland and Britain were made productive again.

Gyroscope is a symmetrical rapidly rotating object, typically wheel-like, which because of its mass and rotation possesses a lot of the dynamical property known as angular momentum. Basic dynamical laws tell us that angular momentum is conserved and a consequence of this is that the axis of rotation tends to stay pointing in the same direction. Disturbing influences make a gyroscope's motion complicated but the general effect of the presence of a gyroscope attached to any body is to help to stabilise the body's motion. This is made use of in reducing the rocking of ships and in compasses and control systems in aircraft, torpedoes *etc.*

H

Habeas Corpus, the name given to a writ ordering the body of a person under restraint or imprisonment to be brought into court for full inquiry into the legality of the restraint to be made.

The first Habeas Corpus Act was passed in 1679, though nominally such a right had existed from Magna Carta, but some of the more despotic kings had disregarded it. In times of public peril the privilege of *habeas corpus* is sometimes temporarily suspended.

Haber–Ostveldt Process, the important industrial process for synthesising ammonia from atmospheric nitrogen. Nitrogen and hydrogen are combined at high pressure (*c.* 350 atmospheres) and moderately high temperature (500°C) using a catalyst (made largely of iron). A yield of 30 % is obtained. The majority of the world's ammonia is produced in this way or from methods derived from it.

Haddock, one of the best-known fishes abounding in northern seas and averaging about 1·8 kg in weight. Related to the cod. Largely used for curing, and sold as "finnan haddies". Its spawning grounds are off Norway, Iceland and the Faroe Islands.

Hade of veins, a mining term indicating the particular inclination that any vein, seam or strata may have from the perpendicular; thus, in Weardale the veins mainly "hade" to the north.

Hadrian's Wall. *See* **Roman Walls.**

Haematite, ferric oxide, one of the principal iron ores, containing about 70 % of the metal. It is usually found in kidney-shaped masses, and is specular, red or brown, in thin fragments but greyish in bulk.

Haemocyanin, the respiratory pigment of crustaceans and molluscs. It functions like haemoglobin, from which it differs in containing copper instead of iron and being blue when oxidised instead of red.

Haemoglobin, the pigment containing iron which gives red blood corpuscles their colour. It is a respiratory pigment, having the property of picking up oxygen when the blood passes through the lungs to produce the compound known as oxyhaemoglobin. In other parts of the body the oxyhaemoglobin breaks down, liberating oxygen, which is used in the oxidation process (respiration) that the body tissues carry on.

Hafiz, a title conferred upon any Muslim who has committed the whole of the Koran to memory.

Hafnium, a metallic element, no. 72, symbol Hf, discovered by Coster and Hevesy in 1922 and important in the atomic-energy field. It occurs in most zirconium minerals to the extent of *c.* 5 %. It may replace silicon in new computer chips.

Hagiology, a branch of literature that is wholly given up to the history of the saints, and the setting out of their stories and legends.

Hail, hard, roughly spherical balls of ice, consisting of white cores covered by layers of both transparent and opaque ice, frequently falling during thunderstorms. They usually do not exceed 2·5 cm in size, but hailstones as large as tennis balls have been observed. The general theory of a hailstone is that near the top of a cumulonimbus cloud a raindrop becomes frozen, grows in size by condensation and through collisions with snow particles, and eventually becomes so weighty as to overcome the ascending air currents in the cloud. Falling, it first encounters supercooled water drops, immediately freezing on it, increasing the white core, and then at lower levels ordinary water drops, freezing more slowly, making a layer of clear ice.

Before the hailstone arrives at the ground gusts and lulls may transport it several times up and down both regions, adding alternate coatings of soft white and hard clear ice.

Halcyon, a term associated in olden times with the kingfisher and days of soothing calm, "halcyon days" being a frequently used expression. The legend was that the kingfisher laid its eggs on the surface of the sea at the time of the winter solstice when the sea was unruffled. (Halcyon is the Greek for kingfisher.)

Halibut, one of the largest of the flat fishes,

averaging when full grown from 1·2–1·8 m in length, and highly esteemed for the table. Specimens of still larger size occasionally occur. It is plentifully distributed. Its two eyes are on the right side of the head.

Hallmark. A mark or group of marks, impressed by an assay office on gold or silver articles (and on platinum since 1974) guaranteeing the standard of fineness of the precious metal used in them. These marks, which have been applied to silver made in London since the beginning of the 14th cent. and perhaps earlier, make it possible to establish the year and place of assay and also the name of the maker. English pieces of silver usually have not less than four marks, viz., (1) town mark; (2) maker's mark; (3) date letter; (4) sterling mark.

The town mark is rarely changed; in London a crowned leopard's head was used from the earliest days until 1820 with only minor modifications, except for the period 1697–1720 when a lion's head erased was substituted; since 1820 the crown has been omitted.

Until the late 17th cent. a symbol was often used as a maker's mark, from 1696–1720 the first two letters of the maker's surname, and subsequently the maker's initials. Owing to the destruction of the earlier mark plates at Goldsmiths' Hall no maker's name prior to the late 17th cent. can be identified with certainty.

The London date letter is changed at the end of May each year, so each letter covers seven months of one year and five months of the following. The London date cycle has usually consisted of twenty letters: the alphabet of each cycle is of different style, and the letters are enclosed in shields of different shape.

The sterling mark, the lion passant, was introduced in 1544 and continued in use until 1697, when the higher Britannia standard was introduced in order to discourage the practice current amongst goldsmiths of melting down coin of the realm to make plate. The leopard's head crowned and the lion passant were then replaced by a figure of Britannia and a lion's head erased. Though the regulation imposing a higher standard was withdrawn in 1720, a small amount of Britannia standard silver continued to be made and still is made.

From 1784 until 1890 a plate tax was levied on all silver assayed in Great Britain and an additional duty mark, the sovereign's head, was used during this period. A Jubilee mark bearing the head of George V and of Queen Mary was used between the years 1933 and 1935, and in 1953 a coronation mark with the head of Queen Elizabeth was introduced. A special Millennium hallmark was available in 1999 and 2000.

Under the Hallmarking Act 1973 the hallmarking of platinum is now compulsory; the hallmark symbol is an orb surmounted by a cross and encompassed by a pentagon. There are now assay offices in London, Birmingham, Sheffield and Edinburgh.

Halloween (31 October), the eve of All Saints' Day, a time associated, especially in Scotland, with certain old traditions. It is the night when young men and women are supposed, by observing certain rites, to have their future wives and husbands disclosed to them. In old Gaelic culture it celebrated the end of the harvest season.

Halo, a luminous circle usually of 22° radius, surrounding sun or moon, produced by the refraction and reflection of light by ice crystals of high cirrus cloud. It is a very common occurrence, in the British Isles almost one day in three. The inner side is red and the outer a whitish-yellow colour.

"Mock suns", *i.e.*, patches of light at the same elevation as the sun are much rarer occurrences, sometimes being of great beauty and brilliance. Halo is the Greek for threshing-floor. *See* **Corona.**

Halogens, the group name for the five nonmetallic elements fluorine, chlorine, bromine, iodine and astatine. The term "halogen" means "salt-producer".

Halteres, the modified hind-wings of the twowinged flies or *Diptera* (*e.g.*, the house-fly). The equilibrium in flight of these insects depends on the halteres, commonly called "balancers".

Hand, a measure of 4 in (10 cm), the average size of the palm; used in reckoning height of horses.

Handfasting, an informal marriage custom once

prevalent in Scotland, whereby a man and woman bound themselves to cohabit for a year and a day, and at the end of that period either confirmed their contract by a regular marriage or separated.

Hansard, the title given to the official reports of Parliamentary debates, so named after Luke Hansard who in 1774 became partner in a firm of printers to the House of Commons. His son T. C. Hansard was first the printer and then the publisher of an unofficial series of parliamentary debates inaugurated by William Cobbett in 1803. In 1909 production was taken over by H.M. Stationery Office and today's volumes contain full, substantially verbatim, reports of what is said in both Houses of Parliament.

Hara-kiri, the custom of suicide, as formerly practised in Japan, when in disgrace.

Hare, a rabbit-like animal with longer ears and legs. There are many kinds of hare distributed over the northern hemisphere and in Africa south to the Cape. They do not burrow as do rabbits but rely.on camouflage, speed and mobility for safety. Hares box females to show off their strength. Sightings of hares across Britain have.declined sharply in the last 50 years. Hare-coursing was banned in 2005. *See* **Game.**

Harleian MSS. comprise some thousands of volumes of MSS. and documents, collected by the first Earl of Oxford (1661–1724) and his son Edward. After the death of the latter, his widow handed the MSS. over to the nation for £10,000, and they are now in the British Museum.

Harlequin, the buffoon of ancient Italian comedy. As adapted to the British stage, however, harlequin is a pantomime character only, in love with Columbine, appearing in parti-coloured garments and carrying a wand, by which he exercises a magic influence in thwarting the fantastic tricks of the clown and pantaloon.

Harmattan, a dry wind which may blow between January and May across the Sahara to the Gulf of Guinea. Although affording relief from the tropical heat, vegetation withers because of its extreme dryness and much irritation is caused by the clouds of fine dust which it carries.

Harmonic Motion, regular periodic motion of the kind exemplified by a ball bobbing up and down at the end of a spring, and by the piston in a steam engine. It may be simple (simple harmonic motion) or composed of two or more simple harmonic motions. In simple harmonic motion the acceleration is proportional to the distance of the moving body from its original rest position.

Harp-seal, the ordinary Greenland seal, with a dark harp-shaped marking on its back, hence its name. It abounds in Newfoundland waters and further northward towards the Arctic.

Harpy Eagle, a large bird of prey named from the winged monsters of Greek mythology, inhabiting the forest regions of Central and South America. There are eight species, one with handsome grey plumage and large crest which attacks and kills animals much larger than itself, and was called by the Aztecs "winged wolf ".

Harrier, a bird of prey of the falcon family; of the various species distributed over the world, three breed in Britain: the moorland Hen harrier, the Marsh harrier and Montagu's harrier. They are large birds with long tails, long legs, long wings and gliding flight. They nest on the ground and eat small mammals, frogs, lizards and small birds. Breeding pairs of hen harriers are being introduced to areas of the UK where they are now extinct.

Hartebeest, common African antelope of a grey-brown colour, with ringed and knotted horns bending backward and tapering to sharp points: gregarious, of large size. There are several species.

Harvest Bug, a very small insect, of a dark red colour, which appears in large numbers in the fields in autumn, and is peculiarly irritating to animals and man by the tenacity with which it attaches itself to the skin and burrows underneath. Probably the larvae of spinning mites (Trombidoids). In the USA they are called "chiggers".

Harvest Moon, the full moon that occurs nearest to the autumn equinox, in September. It rises for several nights running about the same time, and yields an unusually brilliant series of moonlight nights.

Harvestmen are, like spiders, members of the arachnid class but belong to the distinctly different order of Phalangida. They are common in the countryside in autumn and have small oval bodies and eight long slender legs which besides being mere organs of locomotion also act as sense organs. Known as "daddy longlegs" in America and Britain.

Hashish, an Arabic word for the narcotic substance prepared from the hemp plant (*Cannabis sativa*). It is known by a variety of names, *e.g.*, bhang in India and marijuana in America.

Hatchment, in heraldry, is a square board, in vertical diagonal position, placed outside a house or on the tomb at the death of a member of a family and so arranged that it indicates the sex and condition of the deceased.

Hawaiian Goose. *See* **Néné.**

Hawfinch, a well-known European bird of the finch family, having a variegated plumage, a sturdy bill and black-and-white tail. In England it is found in the Midland and Eastern counties, and locally in Scotland. Its numbers are now in sharp decline.

Hawk. This name is applied to almost any diurnal bird of prey other than eagle, falcon or vulture, but in its strict sense applies only to the *Accipiter* genus—the small Sparrow Hawk and the larger Goshawk, round-winged, long-tailed birds with barred under-parts. They prey upon small birds captured in flight and small mammals.

Hawkbit. A small bright yellow dandelion.

Hawk-moths, a large species of moths, thick of body and strong of wing, which fly with rapid swooping motion, hence the name. There are numerous handsome species in Britain.

Heat, It was established in the 19th century that heat is a form of energy; it is in fact the combined kinetic and potential energy of the atoms of which a body is composed. Heat can be turned into other forms of energy, *e.g.*, a red hot body loses heat by radiating it in the form of electromagnetic waves ("radiant heat"—chiefly infra-red rays). Heat may also be transferred from one place to another by conduction and, in fluids, by convection. All three processes occur as a glowing fire heats a room.

A unit quantity of heat is the calorie, which is the amount of heat sufficient to raise the temperature of 1 g of water by 1°C. In general, adding heat to a body raises its temperature. The number of calories required per gram of material to raise the temperature 1°C is called the *specific heat* of the material. However, adding heat may not raise the temperature-but may instead cause a change of state, *e.g.*, from solid to liquid (melting) or liquid to gas (evaporation). The amount of heat required to melt 1 gram of a solid is called the latent heat of melting. Similarly, there is a latent heat of evaporation. Strictly speaking, the specific and latent heats of a substance depend on how much its pressure and volume are allowed to vary during the measurements. Water has a high specific heat, and this makes the oceans a vast heat reservoir, a factor of great meteorological significance. The science of heat is called thermodynamics.

Heat Pump, essentially a refrigerator working in reverse, *i.e.*, a device which warms up one place, say, a house by releasing into it heat transferred from another place, say, the air or earth outside the house. The idea is attributed to Lord Kelvin (1852) and later Haldane used a heat pump to heat his house in Scotland. In Summer, a house could be cooled by operating the device in reverse. As in a domestic refrigerator, the heat is transferred by a suitable fluid whose circulation has to be driven by an external supply of energy, *e.g.*, by running a mechanical compressor. With good design and favourable conditions, the energy required to run the heat pump is considerably less than would be required to produce the same warming effect directly.

Heath, flowering plants of the *Ericaceae* family. Heaths are widely distributed over uncultivated spaces of Europe and Africa. In Britain they are represented by heather (of which there are several species) and ling (*Calluna vulgaris*), which cover thousands of acres of moorland.

Some of the African or Cape heaths are very beautiful and much prized by florists. One species of heath (*Erica arborea*) which grows in S. Europe and N. Africa has close-grained woody rootstock used for making briar pipes.

In N. Europe acid heathlands, dominated by heather and ling, form one of the most widespread vegetation areas created by man through the widespread destruction of forests, grazing *etc.*

Heathrow Airport, originally called London Airport (Heathrow) and named after a village where Terminal 3 now stands. It opened on 1 January 1946. The airport handles more than 82 airlines from 85 countries and offers direct flights to more than 180 destinations. In 2010 Beijing international airport overtook Heathrow as the second busiest in the world.

Terminal 5 was finally given approval in 2001. It opened in March 2008 after a £4·3 billion development (the biggest in UK airport history).

A new terminal, dubbed Heathrow East replaces Terminals 1 and 2. Estimates suggest Heathrow handled over 75 million passenger in 2016. Plans for a third runway were approved in January 2009 despite much opposition.

Future airport capacity in the London area was the subject of an inquiry under Sir Howard Davies. It made controversial recommendations to expand Heathrow, which the Government now supports.

Hedgehog. This much-loved nocturnal little creature, with its prickly spines, is fast disappearing in Britain. Since 2003 it has fallen by over 30 % to under a million. In the 1950s, there were over 35 million. There are calls for the hedgehog to be our national animal.

Hegira, an Arab term signifying departure or flight, used in reference to Mohammed's departure from Mecca, A.D. 622, from which date the Muslim era is reckoned.

Helicopter, heavier-than-air aircraft which obtains its lift from blades rotating above the fuselage in windmill-fashion. The first successful helicopters were the Focke-Wulf 61, a German machine (1936), and the VS-300, designed by Igor Sikorsky, flown in 1937. Helicopters can hover, and rise and descend vertically, in addition to being capable of horizontal flight.

Heliosphere, the huge region surrounding the Sun that is permeated by the solar wind. The heliosphere is bounded by the *heliopause*, its outer limit, four times further away than Pluto.

Heliotrope, a favourite sweet-scented flowering plant, common in tropical and sub-tropical countries; the Peruvian heliotrope is the "cherry pie" of our summer garden borders.

Helium, a gaseous element, no. 2, symbol He, first discovered by means of the spectroscope in the sun's atmosphere. This discovery, made in 1868 by the astronomer Sir Norman Lockyer, was followed in 1895 by Sir William Ramsay's proof that the element existed on earth. He found it in the uranium ore, clevite. Later it was established that helium is formed by the radioactive decay of many elements which emit α-particles (nuclei of helium atoms) and is contained in all radioactive minerals. The largest source of helium is natural gas, the richest in helium being the gas from certain wells in Utah, USA. Next to hydrogen, helium is the lightest gas known, has a lifting power equal to 92 % of hydrogen and the advantage that it is inert and non-inflammable. It is used for inflating airships. Ordinary air contains 1 part in 200,000 of helium. It was the last gaseous element to be liquefied, this being achieved by Onnes in 1908 in Leyden. Helium accounts for about 24 % of the mass of the universe.

Liquid helium has remarkable properties not fully understood. It is indispensable in cryogenics (*q.v.*) as a medium for cooling other substances to temperatures near absolute zero. Hydrogen fusion in the "H bomb" produces helium. Helium-3, is a lighter version used in MRI scanners. It could be used for nuclear fusion.

A vast new reserve of helium was found in 2016 beneath the Great Rift Valley in Tanzania.

Hellebore, a plant of the *Ranunculaceae* (buttercup) family. The best-known British examples are the green and stinking varieties. There is also a garden kind which flowers in December called the Christmas Rose. Hellebore yields a bitter substance once much used as a purgative.

Hemiptera, the order of insects to which belong the true bugs. Their wing structure is in most species incomplete, hence the term hemiptera (half-wing). This order includes the familiar water insects, the water boatman and water skater, also the aphids, cicadas, leaf hoppers, scale insects.

Hemlock, a tall, green plant of the *Umbelliferae* family, growing in all parts of Britain, and containing a strong alkaloid poison. Used medicinally, this alkaline substance is of considerable service, being a powerful sedative. According to Pliny, hemlock was the poison used by the Athenians in putting criminals to death. Socrates met his fate this way in 399 B.C..

Hemp (*Cannabis sativa*), name of a plant native to Asia, now cultivated widely for the valuable fibre contained in the stalk or in some species in the leaves. Hemp fibre has been replaced by cotton for textiles and by jute for sacks and is now chiefly used for cordage and twine. It contains a resinous substance from which the narcotic hashish is made. The seed yields a valuable oil. The term hemp is also used for other fibre plants, *e.g.* manila hemp from the Philippines, sunn hemp from India, sisal from W. and E. Africa and phormium from New Zealand.

Henbane, a plant found in Britain and other parts of Europe and Northern Asia. It belongs to the potato family *Solanaceae*, grows mostly on waste ground and bears yellow-brown flowers veined with purple. The leaves yield a poisonous alkaloid substance which is of great use in medicine. Tincture of henbane is often preferred to laudanum.

Hepatics. See **Liverworts.**

Heracleum, a plant of the *Umbelliferae* family, common in southern and central Europe, though only one species, the cow parsnip, grows in England. It has a bitter root, and the juice of the stem yields an intoxicating liquor.

Herald, an officer of state empowered to make formal proclamations and deliver messages from the sovereign or other high personage whom he serves. In the developments which took place in armorial bearings, the herald was charged with the duty of their proper depiction.

Heraldry, the knowledge of armorial bearings, was mainly the outcome of the love of outward distinction which prevailed in mediaeval times, "Heraldry," says Stubbs, "became a handmaid of chivalry, and the marshalling of badges, crests, coat-armour, pennons, helmets and other devices of distinction grew into an important branch of knowledge." The *shield*, or *escutcheon*, is the ground upon which armorial signs are traced, the colour of the shield being called the *tincture*, the signs recorded the *charges*.

There are seven *tinctures—or* (gold), *argent* (silver), *gules* (red), *azure* (blue), *vert* (green), *purpure* (purple) and *sable* (black). The *charges* are classed as "Honourable" and "Subordinate" ordinaries, comprising lines and geometrical forms; and "Common" ordinaries, which latter includes all representations of natural objects.

There is also a system of external signs, such as crowns, mitres *etc.*, each having its distinctive significance. See **Hatchment, Quartering, Rampant.**

Heralds' College or College of Arms, was incorporated by Richard III in 1483. Its head is the Earl Marshal (an office hereditary in the family of the Dukes of Norfolk), and there are three Kings of Arms, six Heralds and four Pursuivants. The business transacted is wholly connected with the tracing of genealogies and the granting of armorial bearings. In Scotland the Heraldic functions are performed by the Lord Lyon King of Arms.

Herbarium, a systematically classified collection of preserved plants. One of the largest in the world is at the Royal Botanic Gardens at Kew.

Heredity is the study of the transmission of physical and mental characteristics from one generation to another. Gregor Mendel (1822–84) established the principle embodied in Mendel's law in his work published in 1866.

The ideas which he put forward were forgotten until the early years of the 20th century, but today they form the basis of the modern study of genetics. Genes are the units of heredity; they are contained in the chromosomes of the cell nucleus. In human cells there are 46 chromosomes—22 pairs of characteristic shape, and a 23rd (the sex chromosomes) similar in women and dissimilar in men, which unite in the process of fertilisation. An individual can only develop, even under the most favourable surroundings, as far as his inherited characteristics, *i.e.,* his genes will allow him to do. It is in the development of personality that the interplay between heredity and environment becomes most apparent.

Hermaphrodite, animals or plants possessing both male and female reproductive organs, *e.g.,* snails, earthworms, most flowering plants.

Hermit Crab, a decapod, with a soft asymmetrical body which it protects by thrusting it into an empty gastropod shell, *e.g.,* whelk, which it carries about, only abandoning it as needed for a larger one. Found in all seas, many live in commensal relationship with sea anemones *etc.*

Heron, a large wading bird with long curved neck and pointed bill, is a member of the *Ardeidae* family, of which there are many species. Egrets and bitterns are included as herons. Herons are to be met with in marsh lands and near rivers and lakes, where they feed on fish and frogs. They nest in trees in large numbers, these colonies being called *heronries.*

The common heron is native to England, and other species from the Continent are also visitors.

Herring (*Clupes harengus*), an important food-fish inhabiting the North Sea which has been subjected to much overfishing. In Britain the once-important herring industry is now based on the Shetlands and some coastal ports of E. Scotland and N.E. England. Marine biologists have reported on its unique structure for hearing which makes it receptive to sound frequencies over a very wide range and able to determine distance, direction and source of sound.

Hibernation, the dormant condition in which many mammals, reptiles, amphibians, insects, plants, *etc.*, pass the winter months. The rate of metabolism slows down, and the body temperature drops to that of the surroundings. Work on these low temperatures and their physiological effect has led to improved surgical techniques. Animals of the torrid regions pass through an analogous period (*aestivation*) during the hot season, when the sources of food are dried up. The only creatures in Britain to hibernate are bats, dormice and hedgehogs. The Alaskan squirrel has the longest hibernation.

Hickory, several species of American tree of the walnut family, remarkable for its very hard, solid, heavy white wood, and bearing an edible, four-lobed nut.

Hieroglyphics are the earliest form of pictured symbolic expressionn, and are supposed to have been introduced by the ancient Egyptians. They consist of varied depictions of animals, plants, signs and objects, and in their later examples express, in abridged form, ideas and records from which significant historical information has been gleaned. The deciphering of Egyptian hieroglyphics long proved elusive, but gradually the key to the riddle was discovered, and most of the ancient records can now be understood. Besides the Egyptian there are also Hittite, Minoan and Mayan hieroglyphic scripts. See **Rosetta Stone.**

Hi-Fi (**High Fidelity**). A term used since the late 1940s to describe domestic sound reproducing equipment and originally implying superlative performance and particularly stereo capability as opposed to mere mono. In this usage it is now somewhat dated. The criteria for hi-fidelity performance were originally difficult to achieve in practise and therefore the appellation was of some consequence, but recent advances in technology, design, component standards and quality assurance procedures have ensured that the criteria can be met by almost every product on the market. Recent usage does not necessarily imply a qualitative judgment but simply describes equipment for home use. A Hi Fi system would probably include a number of sources such as a turntable and a tonearm combination for replaying vinyl discs, a tuner for receiving radio broadcasts or a compact disc (CD) player, in combination with a pre-amplifier/amplifier and loudspeakers or headphones. Quite frequently some sort of recording device such as a cassette deck will also be present.

From the early 1980s the compact disc became the primary distribution medium for prerecorded music, almost completely replacing vinyl discs. It was not until the late 1980s that digital recording systems such as RDAT (Rotary-head Digital Audio Tape) became available. With the more recent developments of DCC (Digital Compact Cassette) and MD (Mini Disc), consumers now have a choice of digital recording systems.

Higgs Boson, nicknamed the 'God particle'. It is a sub-atomic particle that remains the only element of particle physics theory whose existence had not been absolutely confirmed. But scientists at CERN finally found it in 2012.

Hindi, the official language of India.

Hindustani, the spoken form of Hindi (written in Devanagari script) and Urdu (written in Arabic characters).

Hippogriff, a fabulous monster like a horse in body, but with the head, wings and front legs and claws of an eagle.

Hippopotamus (**"River-horse"**) is the largest living representative of the hippopotamidae family, widely distributed over Africa, where it lives in herds. It is of immense bulk, attaining a length of 3·6 m and a weight of 4 tonnes and stands about 1·5 m high. Its skin is hairless and about 5 cm thick, and it has a pair of tusks often weighing as much as 2·7 kg. It leads an amphibious way of life, and lives entirely on vegetation, both aquatic and terrestrial. The pigmy hippopotamus, which occurs in forests and swamps in W. Africa, is only half the size. Only around 3,000 are left in the wild. Hippos are now known to be related to dolphins and whales.

Histology is the study of the structure of plant and animal tissues. These mainly consist of groups of cells with similar functions, *e.g.* brain tissue.

Hobby, a bird of the falcon family, 30–35 cm long. Local breeding visitor to England and Wales, April–September; irregular visitor to Scotland and Ireland. They winter in Africa.

Hog, the common name of animals of the Suidae family, including the wild boar, pig and sow. The wild boar, *Sus scrofa*, is the common ancestor. The skin of the hog is covered with bristles, the snout truncated and each foot has four hoofed toes. Hogs are omnivorous feeders and eat almost anything that is given them.

Hogmanay, the Scottish New Year's Eve festival and a national holiday of the country. The custom of demanding Hogmanay bread is still upheld in many parts of Scotland.

Hogshead, a cask of varying capacity, also a specific measure. In the old English measure a hogshead was 63 old gallons of wine (=52½ imperial gallons = 238·6 litres). Of beer 54 old gallons make a hogshead.

Holly, a hardy evergreen shrub, largely grown in England. Its bright dark green prickly curved leaves and clusters of red berries are familiar in all parts of the country, and used as house decoration between Christmas Eve and Twelfth Night, probably a relic from ancient customs. Its wood is white and hard, valued for carved work, while its bark yields a gummy substance which is converted into birdlime.

Holocaust. See **German Fascism, J19(2), Genocide (L45).**

Holocaust Memorial Day, first marked in Britain on 27 January 2001 (the anniversary of the liberation of Auschwitz-Birkenau in 1945). It is distinct from Yom HaShoah, the Jewish day of remembrance for the Jewish victims of the Nazis. This falls in late April.

Hologram, a photographic record, taken under special optical conditions, of light reflected from a scene or object. The hologram is typically a piece of film. However it is nothing like a photographic negative of the ordinary kind; for one thing it will show an unintelligible pattern of light and dark patches. Nevertheless if it is illuminated (again under special optical conditions) the light coming through it will form a *three dimensional* image of the original object. Another radical difference between a hologram and an ordinary film is that if the hologram is cut up, each fragment can be used to construct the entire image.

Holography, as a method of recording and reproducing photographic information, was conceived by Gabor in 1947 but was only fully realised in practice after the invention of the laser, which made available powerful sources of coherent light.

Holothurians. See **Sea Cucumbers.**

Holy Coat of Trèves, a garment preserved in the Cathedral of Trèves, said to have been worn by Christ. It was brought from Jerusalem by the Empress Helena in the 4th century.

Holy Grail. See **Grail.**

Holy Rood, an annual Roman Catholic festival held on 14 September to celebrate the Elevation of the Cross in commemoration of its re-erection in Jerusalem by the Emperor Heraclius in 628 after retaking it from the Persians. Also included in the Church of England calendar.

Holy Water, water blessed by a priest and kept in small fonts at the entrance to Roman Catholic and some Anglican churches.

Holy Week, the week before Easter Sunday, embracing the days of the Sufferings of Christ. It includes Good Friday and Holy Saturday.

Honey, the sweet syrup formed by bees from the nectar of flower, the sucrose in the nectar being converted into a mixture of the simple sugars, glucose and fructose. Hybla, an ancient town of Sicily, on the southern slope of Mt. Etna, was famous for its honey.

Honey-eater, an Australian bird (of which there are many species) provided with a long curved bill and tufted tongue. It lives by sucking the nectar from the flowers which abound in rural parts of Australia and New Zealand.

Hookah, an Oriental pipe for tobacco smoking, the smoke being drawn through the water of a goblet by means of a long flexible tube.

Hoopoe, a very handsome pink bird with vivid black and white-barred wings and tail and black-tipped crest which opens like a fan. It ranges over Europe, Asia and Africa. It has bred in England and Wales and occurs in the UK in small numbers at all seasons. Other species are confined to Africa, Madagascar and India.
It has now been officially chosen as the national bird of Israel.

Hops, the female "cones" of the hop plant used in brewing; their essential oils give to beer an aromatic flavour, and their tannin and resin act as a preservative as well as accounting for the bitter taste desired. The hop is a perennial climber belonging to the mulberry family. The male and female organs are on separate plants; as only the female flower-heads are commercially useful.
Female plants predominate in a hop gar- den, only a very few male plants being grown so that the female flowers can be fertilised.

Horizon, the limit of vision, the apparent line where sea and sky, or land and sky meet. This is termed the visible horizon. An ordinary person at the height of 1·5 m can see for 4·8 km, at 6 m 9·6 km, at 15 m 14·8 km and at 305 m 67·5 km. The figures are approximate.

Hormone, a chemical substance which is released by one part of the body and produces a response in other parts after having been carried there by the bloodstream or other transport system.
Prolactin, for example, is a hormone produced by the pituitary gland of nursing mothers and serves to stimulate and maintain the milk supply.

Horn or **French Horn,** a brass instrument of the trumpet family (i.e., played by three valves) whose tube is very thin and long (Horn in F = 12 ft). In consequence the tube is curled in a complicated manner. Owing to the sweet tone it is capable of producing, the Horn sometimes plays as part of the wood-wind.

Hornbill, large bird found in Africa and oriental regions. Some species have a casque or a horny growth above the very powerful beak. It feeds on fruits. When the female has laid her eggs in the hollow of a tree, the male bird stops up the entrance, and keeps her imprisoned until the hatching is completed and the young ones are able to fly. There are c. 45 species. They mate for life. They also play a vital role in dispersing seeds in the rainforests.

Hornblende, the commonest member of the amphibole group of minerals, a silicate of calcium, magnesium, iron and aluminium, of a dark green colour. A constituent of numerous rocks.

Horned Viper, any of a number of species of African viper which have scales over each eye resembling horns. Their bite is usually very poisonous. The significance of the horns is not known.

Hornet, a name for many of the bigger wasps. It usually nests in hollow trees, and despite its rather fiercesome appearance does not sting unless unduly provoked. The Asian hornet is bigger and more destructive. Now found in the UK.

Horology, the science of time-measurement, including the construction and management of clocks, watches, etc. Instruments of this kind are not known to have existed before the 12th cent. and until the coming of the pendulum in the 17th cent., clocks were ill-regulated and frequently inaccurate.
The time-recording mechanisms of the present day include (a) the clock, which shows the hours and minutes by hands, and strikes the hours, and sometimes quarters; (b) the timepiece, which is not generally a fixture and shows the time, but does not strike; (c) the watch, which is a pocket timekeeper; (d) the chronometer, which indicates the minutest portions of times; (e) electric timepieces, mains electric clocks; (f) the highly accurate quartz- crystal and atomic clocks used for astronomical purposes. See Clock.

Horse Chestnut, one of the large forest trees, with ample branches, and full foliage, and much esteemed for parks and ornamental grounds. The flowers, which appear in May, are white tinged with red and yellow. The tree is native to mountainous northern Greece. The Bleeding Canker disease is lethal to horse chestnuts. See also under Chestnut.

Horse Guards, the building in Whitehall which until 1872 was the headquarters of the Commander-in-Chief of the British Army. The archway is still sentinelled by mounted guards.

Horse Latitudes, the latitudes of the sub-tropical high pressure systems, between the trade winds and the prevailing westerlies, characterised by light variable winds and low humidity.

Hospitallers, Knights. See E6.

Hottentots, name given to certain African people by Dutch settlers in the 17th cent. They used to occupy much of Cape Colony and though driven out a number still survive in Namibia.

Hounds are dogs that were originally bred and trained for hunting, such as the greyhound, fox-hound, bloodhound, beagle, harrier, etc., but now often kept also as domestic dogs.
The greyhound, deerhound and wolf hound hunt by sight, the others, with the bloodhound first in order, track by scent.

House Flies are world-wide and prolific. Their eggs are hatched within 24 hours of being laid, and full maturity is attained in a month. They feed on decayed animal and vegetable matter.

Hovercraft, or air cushion vehicle, is a craft which is lifted on a pad of air underneath it. This pad or cushion must be at a pressure higher than that of the atmosphere and it is made by sucking in air above the craft and ejecting it in a downward stream all round the lower edge. Hovercraft were devised by Cockerell in the 1950s and a full-scale example appeared in June 1959.
The air pad support means that hovercraft can move over land, water or marsh. Cross-Channel hovercraft were introduced in 1966. The last cross-Channel service was withdrawn in 2000.

Howler Monkey, a genus of South American monkey noted for a laryngeal conformation which enables it to emit a loud reverberant noise something between a yell and a howl.

Huanuco-bark, a medicinal bark, brought from the Peruvian town of that name, and derived from the Cinchona micrantha tree.

Hubble Constant, a mathematical value that assesses the speed at which the universe is expanding.

Hubble Telescope. See Telescope.

Hubble's Law, the law, first proposed by Edwin Hubble in 1929 stating that the velocity of a distant galaxy is directly proportional to its distance. This means that the most distant galaxies are moving fastest away from us.

Human Genome Project, the global scientific effort launched in the 1990s to unravel the human genetic blueprint. The tiny nematode worm became the first creature to have its entire genetic blueprint decoded. In 1999, for the first time, the complete genetic code of a human chromosome (chromosome 22) was deciphered. It revealed the existence of hundreds of genes, previously unknown in humans, but playing a vital role in disease. Scientists finished a preliminary draft of the human genome code in 2000. Scientists finished a complete sequence in April 2003. In 2012 the genetic "control panel" of the human body, which regulates the activity of our 23,000 genes was revealed for the first time.

Humble-bee (Bumble-bee), this is the common name of the insects of the genus bombus, of the Hymenoptera order. They live in small communities comprising males, females and drones, their habitations being underground. They do not have one queen bee only like the hive bee, but several females occupy the same nest, and these alone live through the winter, breeding and forming new colonies in the spring. Their sting does not have a barb like the honey bee's.

Humidity, the state of the atmosphere with respect to the water-vapour it contains. "Absolute humidity" is defined as the density of the vapour present, while "relative humidity" indicates the degree of saturation.

Humming Birds are so called because of the humming noise made by the vibration of their wings in flying (they flap their wings 50 times a second). They are of radiant plumage, and are among the smallest birds. The smallest bird in the world is the Fairy or Princess Helen's humming bird of Cuba, whose body is only 5·7 cm long. There are from four to five hundred species, and they are confined wholly to North and South America, being most numerous in the tropical latitudes. They have long, slender bills and tubular tongues which reach down into flowers to suck up the nectar on which they feed. They are crucial pollinators of flowering plants across the Americas.

Hummum, the original name for what is now called the Turkish Bath in the UK. One of the first of these baths was the Hummum in Covent Garden, London.

Hurdy-Gurdy, a rustic musical stringed instrument of the lute order, the sounds of which are produced by the action of a rosined wheel turned by the right hand, the notes being made by the fingering of the left hand. It dates from at least the 12th century.

Hurricane. *See* **Cyclone, Wind.**

Hydra, an aquatic animal of simple structure, whose body is in the form of a cylindrical tube, with a disc-shaped base by which it attaches itself to any shifting substance. Its mouth is surrounded by tentacles by which it catches its food. The Hydra can reproduce lost parts.

Hydrates are compounds containing water of crystallisation.

Hydraulic Ram, a form of automatic pump, used to raise water to a height by the action of its own falling velocity.

Hydraulics, the science of applied hydrodynamics, or water-machine engineering, ranging from pumps to marine engines.

Hydrocarbons are compounds of carbon and hydrogen. They include the *paraffins*, which are saturated compounds (*e.g.*, methane); the ethylene, acetylene and other series which are unsaturated; compounds with ring structures, *e.g.*, benzene, naphthalene and anthracene. Petroleum is composed almost entirely of hydrocarbons.

Hydrochloric Acid, a solution of hydrogen chloride gas in water, and resulting in considerable quantities as a by-product of the soda-ash or salt-cake manufacture. Its solution forms the common hydrochloric or muriatic acid of commerce. It is present to the extent of nearly half a per cent, in the digestive juice secreted by the stomach.

Hydrocyanic Acid, cyanide of hydrogen or prussic acid; very poisonous, and of the odour of bitter almonds. It is formed by the action of acids on sodium or potassium cyanide. Used to kill wasps (and in the gas chamber in the USA). It is a very important chemical on account of the reactions of its derivatives in many synthetic fields. Discovered by Scheele in 1782.

Hydroelectric Schemes. The sun's energy has been indirectly exploited in the past by harnessing the energy of the winds and rain. The climate is due, essentially, to differential heating of the earth. The resulting convection currents in the air (the motion of which is complicated by the rotation of the earth) give rise to winds. Moisture is collected from the sea and deposited high up on mountains as rain. Some of the gravitational energy may be collected as hydropower. Simple windmills or waterwheels are too undependable to be used.

The modern form of the waterwheel—the hydroelectric generation plant —is extensively used in mountainous countries and about a third of the world's electricity is produced by this means. The essential requirements for a modern hydroelectric scheme are a river with a sufficient flow of water to provide the required power, a large "head" of water so that a cheap, compact turbine can be used and a

dam so that water can be stored until it is required. In some cases a hydroelectric scheme is made economic by being associated with an irrigation or drainage scheme. Such multi-purpose schemes are especially important in India and Pakistan, where most hydro projects are of this type. Other early examples include the Snowy Mountains scheme in Australia and the Aswan High Dam in Egypt. More recent is the massive Three Gorges Dam in China.

Although over 90 per cent of the electricity in certain individual countries, most notably Norway, Sweden, Portugal, Switzerland and Uganda is now produced from hydroelectric schemes, only a relatively small fraction of the total potential has been exploited. This fraction varies from about a third in Western Europe to a quarter in the United States to a very small fraction in Canada, Africa or Asia.

Hydrofluoric Acid is obtained by distillation of fluorspar with sulphuric acid, and is a compound of fluorine and hydrogen. Highly corrosive, it is a valuable agent in etching on glass, and a rapid decomposer of animal matter.

Hydrogen, symbol H, the simplest element, with an atomic number of 1, colourless, and the lightest of all substances. Cavendish in 1766 was the first to recognise that it was an element. It is 14·4 times as light as air, and is found in a free state in volcanic regions. It can be obtained by the action of metals on acids, and forms an explosive mixture with air, burning with oxygen to form water. Commercially it is used to produce the very hot flame of the oxyhydrogen blowpipe for cutting metals; to fill balloons and airships; to harden certain oils and render them suitable for margarine and soap production. In warfare, the hydrogen bomb is potentially hundreds of times more powerful than an atomic bomb.

The gas can be liquefied, and the presence of the isotope deuterium was detected by Urey in 1931 in the residue of the evaporated liquid. The third isotope, tritium, is very rare. Vast quantities of hydrogen gas are thought to exist in the Earth's crust. *See also* **Deuterium, Tritium.**

Hydrogen Sulphide is the toxic, flammable colourless gas (produced by humans and animals as wind).

Hydrography, the science of water measurement, as applied to seas, rivers, lakes, currents, reefs, *etc.*, and embracing the whole art of navigation.

Hydrometer, an instrument for measuring the specific gravity of liquids, especially for ascertaining the strength of spirituous liquors and solutions. It is usually in the form of a glass bulb, to the lower end of which a smaller bulb, containing mercury, is attached which forces the instrument to sink into the liquid which it is to test. The larger bulb has a scale fixed to it, and the indication on this scale of the sinking point shows the specific gravity. There are many varieties: Twaddell's—a pear-shaped bulb containing mercury: Beaumé's, of similar construction, but applicable to liquids both heavier and lighter than water: Sykes', largely employed for deterinining the strength of alcohol: and Nicholson's, used for taking of specific gravities of solids.

Hydropathy, the method of treating disease with water, either by bathing or drinking. Natural springs of special chemical and therapeutic properties, such as sulphur springs, and other mineral sources, have been used since prehistoric times for this purpose. It is probably one of the most ancient methods of cure. The beneficial effects of pure water treatment have long been advocated. Hydropathic establishments have been set up in many health resorts.

Hydropolitics, term for the political struggle for water resources.

Hydroponics, or soilless growth, is the craft and science of growing plants in liquid nutrients instead of soil. Originally a laboratory technique, hydroponics has become since the 1930s a practical method of vegetable, fruit and flower production on both small and large scale. Basically, the growing plants have their roots in troughs of nutrient solution, either in or out of doors. Advantages include: much higher crop yields; the close control of weeds and diseases; quicker growth; and, very important, the possibilities of growing food in places where ordinary agriculture would be impracticable, *e.g.*, deserts and stony land, city roofs, in houses and in remote situations like Antarctic stations.

Hydroponics is widely practised and contributes usefully to agriculture and horticulture in many countries, including the USA, Britain, India and France. Its value in spaceships and planetary colonies has often been pointed out.

Hydrostatics, the science of the pressure and equilibrium of liquids that are non-elastic.

Hydrozoa are a class of water animals of the *Coelenterata* phylum to which hydra (*q.v.*) belongs. In one order of the hydrozoa, free-swimming colonies showing marked division of labour between the individual units occur; this order includes the Portuguese man-of-war.

Hyena, a nocturnal carnivore with powerful jaws. The striped hyenas inhabit N. Africa and S.W. India. The brown hyenas with long shaggy hair are natives of S. Africa. The spotted, or laughing hyena, noted for the cry from which its name is derived, is also confined to Africa. Hyenas are more intelligent than previously believed.

Hygrometer, an instrument for measuring the amount of water vapour in the atmosphere. A simple form of hygrometer, known as the wet-and-dry bulb, consists of two vertical thermometers affixed to a frame. One bulb is exposed to the air, and the other is covered with muslin which dips into a water-bath to keep it moist. If the air is saturated, it takes up no moisture from the wet bulb and the two thermometers read the same. If the air is not saturated, evaporation takes place from the wet bulb, latent heat is absorbed from the air and the temperature of the wet bulb is lower than that of the dry bulb. Relative humidity and dew-point of the air can then be derived from suitable tables. Hygrometers depending upon the expansion of human hair and gold-beater's skin and the deposition of dew on a polished surface, when cooled sufficiently, are also in general use. *See* **Humidity.**

Hymenoptera, the order of insects to which bees, wasps, hornets, ants and sawflies belong. They have a well-defined waist, two pairs of membranous wings coupled together, mouth parts modified for biting or sucking; the females possess an ovipositor used for depositing eggs and is sometimes modified for stinging. There are over 70,000 species in this order and many live in highly organised communities. *See also* **Ichneumon Fly.**

Hyperbola. A curve described by certain comets that go round the sun and never return.

Hypsometer, an instrument formerly used by mountaineers to find the height above sea-level by indirectly measuring the atmospheric pressure by determining the boiling point of water at the particular height. Based on the fact that as pressure decreases with height so the boiling point is lowered. Superseded by the aneroid barometer.

I

Iapetus. The icy moon of Saturn. It has a unique ridge (the Great Wall) running round its equator.

Ibex, wild goats of several species found in the mountain regions of Europe, Asia and Africa. The male has exceedingly large curved ridged horns. The species that lives in the Alps is called the Steinbock or bouquetin. The Pyrenean ibex (or *bucardo*) was hunted to extinction.

Ibis, belongs to a family of birds related to the stork. The sacred ibis of ancient Egypt is now extinct in Egypt but is found in the lakes and swamps of the Sudan near the Upper Nile. It has white and black plumage and a long curved beak. Other species are found elsewhere, the Glossy Ibis (black plumage glossed with purple and green) occasionally visiting England. There are now less than 220 Bald Ibis in the world (all in Morocco).

Ibo (Igbo), a numerous people of S.E. Nigeria. After the end of British rule they were active in their struggle for national independence and under their leader, Ojukwu, embarked upon the secessionist state of Biafra and the unsuccessful civil war against Federal forces. Today there are over 20 million Ibo speakers. The Hausa and the Yoruba are the other main Nigerian groups.

Ice is frozen water. It is a colourless, crystalline and brittle solid. Being only 92 % as dense as

water, it floats on the latter; the expansion which occurs as water changes into ice causes the fracture of water-pipes, though the fracture only becomes obvious when the ice melts and leaks out through the crack. The temperature at which ice forms is 0°C, 32°F. Ice can be melted by pressure, and the ease and smoothness with which one is able to skate on ice depends on this phenomenon.

Ice Ages. Periods during which the continents were partly or largely covered by ice-sheets and glaciers. The present-day ice-sheets of Greenland and Antarctica are relics of the most recent ice age (one of the eight major ones during the past 700,000 years), which began in the Pleistocene and ended about 10,000 years ago. During this last great glaciation ice sheets covered the northern part of Europe, Asia and North America. Carbon dioxide escaping from the depths of the ocean helped end the last Ice Age. There is evidence that periodic changes in the earth's orbit around the sun caused the ice ages. The earth is now in one of its warm periods. During the last Ice Age Britain was home to woolly rhinoceroses, mammoths, reindeer *etc.* A "Little Ice Age" gripped Europe from the mid-1400s until the mid-1800s, and was at its coldest from 1645 to 1715. The worst winter of all was 1683–84.

Icebergs are detached masses of glacier which subside into the sea and float as wind or current may take them. About one-ninth of an iceberg is above sea-level. The North Atlantic is the chief home of icebergs, which reach the ocean from the ice-clad plateaux of Greenland. Some of these floating masses of ice are of enormous proportions, and in the spring and early summer seasons are a great menace to the safety of ships, as was disastrously shown in the *Titanic* catastrophe of 1912. The increasing numbers of icebergs provide evidence of global warming and pose a growing risk to shipping. The largest iceberg ever recorded (half the size of Wales) broke away from the Ross Ice Shelf in Antarctica in 2000.

Ice-breaker, a special heavy bow-plated ship for forcing a way through ice and used especially at ports of the Baltic Sea and the Great Lakes region of Canada which freeze during the winter.

Icelandic Literature, the old Norse literature, centred about Iceland, which includes numerous works of poetry, mythology and history of interest and importance. Much of this literature is in the saga form. *See also* **Edda.**

Iceland Moss, a kind of lichen (*Cetraria islandica*) which grows in great quantities in the mountain regions of Iceland and other Northern countries. It possesses certain nutritive qualities and is of some value in medicine.

Iceland Spar, a colourless form of calcite (calcium carbonate), frequently found in association with metallic ores; it has the power to produce strong double refraction of light so that two images are seen of an object viewed through a piece of Iceland spar. Once used in optical apparatus for producing polarised light.

Iceni, an ancient British people who lived in Norfolk and other parts of Eastern England. Their most famous ruler was Queen Boadicea (Boudicca), who led her people against the Romans in A.D. 61.

Ice Giants, The frozen planets such as Neptune and Uranus.

Ice Man, name given to the frozen corpse of a middle-aged man, 5,300 years old, found in 1991 on a glacier in the Ötztal Alps. It is now thought that Ötzi (as he is known) died from a lesion in an artery in his left shoulder caused by an arrowhead. His full genome was decoded in 2012. He suffered from a very modern problem: tooth decay caused by sugar.

Ice Plant, also called "dew plant" and "diamond plant". A South African mesembryanthemum commonly grown in British gardens. from 1690.

Ice Saints, St. Mamertus, St. Pancras, St. Servatius and St. Boniface, so called because of the legendary cold on these Saints' Days, namely, 11–14 May.

Ichneumon, the Egyptian mongoose, popularly known as "Pharaoh's Rat". It is of great use in checking the multiplication of reptiles. It is frequently domesticated.

Ichneumon Fly, a numerous group of parasitic hymenopterous insects abounding in many lands, and all having the peculiarity of depositing their eggs in the bodies of other insects. It destroys swarms of caterpillars, which become the unwilling hosts of its progeny.

Ichthyology, the natural history of fishes.

Ichthyosaurus was a gigantic marine reptile of the Mesozoic age. The fossils are mostly found in the lias formation. Some were over 9 m.

Icon, an image of a sacred personage used in the home or in churches for devotional purposes. Icons can be painted on wood, perhaps with the figures picked out against a golden background, or they can be cast in bronze, in the form of a crucifix, diptych (*q.v.*) or triptych with details in coloured enamels. Subjects are taken from the life of Christ or of the Saints. In churches several icons are sometimes placed together on a screen (the iconostasis, which divides the altar and sanctuary from the main body of the church). The earliest preserved icons date from the 12th cent.

Icons are much venerated in Russia and remain, still in their archaic stylised form of mediaeval origin, a characteristic feature of the Greek and Russian Orthodox Churches.

The violent destruction of icons (*iconoclasm*) was a feature of the Protestant reformation.

ID Cards. Today *c.* 100 countries have compulsory ID cards, including Germany, Belgium and Spain. The ID cards introduced in Britain during the Second World War were abolished in 1952. ID cards became compulsory for students from outside the EU from November 2008. They are credit-card size plastic strips with the holder's name, photo, reference no. *etc.*

India, with its 1·2 billion people, is planning to introduce cyber-age biometric ID cards.

Ides, in the ancient Roman Calendar, the 15th of March, May, July, October, and the 13th of all other months; always the eighth day after the Nones.

Idiom, an expression characteristic of a country, district, dialect or language, which usually gives strength and force to a phrase or sentence. The idioms of a language are its distinctive marks, and the best writers are the most idiomatic.

Idris, a famous giant belonging to the myths of Wales, commemorated by a chair of rock on the top of the Cader Idris mountain in Gwynedd.

Igneous Rocks are such as have been molten under conditions of great heat at some stage in their history: *e.g.*, granite, basalt.

Ignis Fatuus *or* **"Will-o'-the-wisp",** a phosphorescent light which may often be seen on summer and autumn evenings hovering over marshy ground or graveyards. Its nature is hardly understood, though it is generally believed to be the result of the spontaneous combustion of the gases from decaying organic matter.

In ancient times when marshy grounds were common, this "dancing light" was very frequently visible and was regarded with superstition.

Iguana, large South American lizard, with a long tail, a scaly back and head, a thick fleshy tongue and a prominent dew-lap in the throat. Specimens of the different species average 1·2–1·5 m in length, and they live mostly in trees, though they are equally at home on land or in the water. The flesh of some species is sometimes eaten, as are also the eggs. The tails of iguanas may sometimes be twice as long as their bodies. Marine iguanas graze on the sea flooor.

Iguanodon, a genus of extinct dinosaurs, whose fossils are found in the Jurassic and Cretaceous rocks. Iguanodons were 4·5–7·6 m long, and walked on their hind legs, the front legs being small and adapted for grasping the branches of trees on the leaves of which they fed.

Ilex, mentioned by classical authors, the holm- or holly-oak, which flourishes round the Mediterranean. To botanists Ilex is the genus to which the holly and maté plant belong.

Iliad, the great epic poem of ancient Greece attributed to Homer (*c.* 700 B.C.). It consists of ancient folk tale and saga, welded into an artistic unity, having as plot the abduction of Helen by Paris to Troy and the subsequent siege of Troy.

Ilmenite, a mineral widespread in igneous rocks: chemically it is an oxide of iron and titanium. Rich deposits have recently been found in the Allard Lake area of Quebec: the Travancore sands are also a source of ilmenite.

Immortelles are wreaths, crosses or other designs made from what are called everlasting flowers, which are obtained from certain plants of the Composite order, and retain their colours and compactness for a long time. Immortelles are largely used as mementoes for decorating graves.

Imprimatur, originally an official licence to print and an important formula in the early days of printing.

Incas, an Indian people who inhabited ancient Peru, founded a great empire and civilisation; overthrown by the Spaniards in 1533. It was the largest pre-Columbian empire, embracing 10 million people with an advanced network of roads.

Incense, an aromatic resinous substance which, under combustion, exhales a pungent odour, and is used, mixed with certain fragment perfumes, in the celebration of Mass in Roman Catholic churches. Olibanum or frankincense is ordinarily the leading ingredient.

Incisors, the sharp-edged cutting teeth at the front of mammalian jaws. Rodents have long, sharp incisor teeth. Elephant tusks are modified incisors.

Independence Day, commemorates the adoption of the Declaration of Independence on 4 July 1776. 4 July is celebrated as a holiday in the USA.

Independent Schools. *See under* **Public Schools.**

Index. The name given to a list of books, prepared by papal authority, which are declared to be dangerous to faith and morals, and therefore forbidden to Roman Catholics, called the *Index librorum prohibitorum.* One of the reforms of the Vatican Council was the closing in 1966 of the Curia office which judged writings for the Church's Index of forbidden books, though the Index itself still remains. The Pope ordered that nothing should be placed on the Index until the author had been given a chance of explaining his views. The first Index was issued by Pope Pius IV, in 1559.

Indian Summer, a period of dry, sunny weather extending deep into autumn. The term comes from early settlers in North America.

Indicators, substances which by a marked change in colour are used to indicate the course of a chemical reaction. Litmus paper, for instance, is red with acids and blue with alkalis. In biological work some radioactive substances are used as tracer elements.

Indigo, the substance obtained from the plant *Indigofera tinctoria,* a native of S. Asia, India being the chief producing country. The colouring matter is the result of the decomposition and fermentation of a glucoside contained in the plant. This is afterwards dried and becomes the caked indigo of commerce. Natural indigo has been eclipsed by artificial indigo, a coal-tar dye which came into commercial production at the end of the last century, and which is cheaper and more uniform in quality.

Indium, a scarce lead-coloured metallic element, no. 49, symbol In, found in zinc blende in Saxony and certain other ores. Discovered in 1863 by Reich and Richter. It is an important material in the manufacture of transistors.

Indo-European Languages. Term for a wide spectrum of languages whose common origin has been traced to Anatolia (Turkey), *c.* 9,500 years ago. The languages include English, German, French, Spanish, Russian, Persian, Hindi *etc.*

Indulgence, in the Catholic Church the remission granted by ecclesiastical authority to a repentant sinner of the temporal punishment still due after the guilt of sin has been forgiven by God.

The indiscriminate sale of Indulgences by Tetzel and other Papal agents in the 16th cent. was one of the grievances which led to the Reformation. The Council of Trent made such traffic unlawful. They were associated with some of the worst examples of corruption.

Industrial Archaeology, the study and recording of the buildings, equipment *etc* of past industry.

Industrialisation is simply a name for industrial development. It is customarily used in particular to designate the course of events in a hitherto underdeveloped country which is seeking to increase its wealth and productivity by the introduction of more advanced techniques and by the establishment of industries previously not carried on within it. The word usually covers not only the development of modern industrial production but also the provision of electric power-stations, irrigation works and transport and other developments designed to improve production in any field by methods involving large capital investments. One often-quoted example by historians of rapid industrialisation was the Soviet Union, which, because it was unable to get the capital from abroad, had to carry it through by ruthless restriction of the people's consuming power.

Industrialisation has usually meant a high concentration on the expansion of the basic heavy industries and of power supply, coupled with much slower development of the industries supplying consumer goods and of agricultural production.

Inert Gases. *See* Rare Gases.

Inertia, a term used in mechanics for the property of matter by which it offers resistance to a change in its state of rest or in its state or direction of motion.

Inertial Navigation, an automatic method of dead-reckoning which at present finds its chief application in guided missiles, submarines and aircraft. Navigation by this means is carried out with reference to inertial space (*i.e.*, space which is stationary with respect to the fixed stars) and not to the surface of the earth as in normal navigation (latitude and longitude). This is done by means of high-accuracy gyroscopes combined with highly sensitive accelerometers in an apparatus known as the Ship's Inertial Navigation System. The American nuclear-powered submarine *Nautilus* pioneered the new north-west passage under the polar ice by this method of dead-reckoning in 1958.

Inflorescence, a flowering shoot. Many arrangements of the flowers are possible and there are many kinds of inflorescence; *e.g.*, the spike, catkin, umbel, capitulum (in composites).

Infra-red Radiation, electromagnetic radiation lying between the radio and visible bands of the electromagnetic spectrum. The wavelengths involved are from 0.8 micrometres (0.8×10^{-6}) to 1000 micrometres. Astronomers sub-divide this waveband into near, mid and far infra-red. Radiation above 300 micrometres is now called submillimetre radiation. Infra-red photography uses materials specially sensitized to infra-red radiation; applications include night time photography, haze-penetration and camouflage and forgery detection.

Infra-red Space Observatory (ISO), an orbiting telescope launched in 1995. By peering into the clouds of gas and dust in deep space it astonished astronomers by discovering vast quantities of water in the deserts of space. It ceased functioning in 1998. The Space Infra-Red Telescope Facility, the largest, most sensitive telescope of its type sent into space, was launched in 2003.

Infula, a sacred fillet, of woollen material, worn on the forehead by priests, magistrates and rulers in Roman times, also by persons fleeing for protection to sanctuary. Later, each of the two lappets of a bishop's mitre.

Ingoldsby Legends, a series of whimsical metrical tales written by the Rev. R. H. Barham, and first published in *Bentley's Miscellany* in 1837. The best known is the *Jackdaw of Rheims*.

Initiative. *See* Referendum.

Ink, a liquid pigment ordinarily made from an infusion of nut-galls, copperas and gum arabic. Shumac is substituted for nut-galls for inferior inks. An acid is sometimes added to prevent oxidation, and for the blue-black inks a small quantity of solution of indigo serves for colouring. Copying ink contains glycerine or sugar, which keeps the ink moist. Lampblack used to be the leading ingredient in printer's ink but now new methods of manufacturing have been developed. Marking ink is composed of a solution of nitrate of silver, gum, ammonia and carbonate of soda. For red, blue and other coloured inks, colouring solutions are used, *e.g.* Prussian blue. The earliest examples of ink writing (on wooden tablets) ever found in Britain were recovered from the well of a Roman villa (3rd cent. A.D.) at Chew Stoke, Somerset in 1954.

Ink Sac, a glandular organ found in squids and other cephalopods which contains an inky solution. When roused the animal discharges the contents of the ink sac into the water, to make a cloud through which its enemies cannot see. The pigment, sepia, comes from the ink sac of the cuttlefish.

Inns of Court, the four bodies in London which enjoy the privilege of calling candidates to the bar after they have studied for a certain number of terms and passed certain examinations. The Inns are: the Inner Temple, the Middle Temple,

Lincoln's Inn and Gray's Inn.

Inquisition, a Roman Catholic ecclesiastical court which became a formidable weapon of the Church in the 13th cent. under Pope Innocent III in dealing with charges of heresy. It was effectively set up in the various Catholic countries of the Continent, obtaining its fullest and most sweeping organisation in Spain in the days of Ferdinand and Isabella, when Torquemada was made Grand Inquisitor, and used its powers with terrible severity. (*See* Auto-da-fé). In the 18th century its influence began to wane, and the jurisdiction of the Congregation of the Holy Office at Rome was limited to the suppression of heretical literature (*see* Index).

The attitude of the Catholic Church to the Inquisition is now changing.

Insectivorous Plants, plants which trap insects with special mechanisms. Plant enzymes or bacteria digest the prey, providing the plants with nitrogen usually scarce in the soil in which they grow. The most common British species are the Sun-dew and the Bladderwort.

Insects. This huge class of invertebrate animals (*see* Arthropods, Section T) includes over one million species. Insects are ubiquitous except in the sea, only a very few species being adapted to marine existence. Characteristic features are: the body is divided into three parts, head, thorax and abdomen: the head carries a pair of antennae, the thorax three pairs of legs and usually two pairs of wings. The most primitive insects constituting the sub-class *Apterygota* are wingless.

The other important sub-class, *Pterygota*, is divided into the *Exopterygota* (*Hemimetabola*), which have a simple metamorphosis, *e.g.*, cockroach, and the *Endopterygota* (*Holometabola*), with a complex metamorphosis, *e.g.*, butterfly, bee. Although many are parasitic on man, animals and plants, innumerable animals and some plants use them as food, and many flowering plants are dependent on a variety of insects for pollination. The disappearance of insect species in Britain is now of major concern.

Insignia, marks or badges of office or honour, such as stars, ribbons, *etc.*

Institut de France was formed in 1795, and after various modifications was in 1832 organised on its present basis. Its five academies are—the Académie Française, Académie des Inscriptions et Belles-Lettres, Académie des Sciences, Académie des Beaux-Arts, and the Académie des Sciences morales et politiques. It is restricted to 40 members.

Instruments, Musical. Musical instruments may be classified in a number of ways, but in general they fall into one of the three main classes, String, Wind and Percussion, according to how the sound is produced.

Stringed Instruments are those which produce the sound by the vibration of a string: (*a*) by plucking, as in Harp, Lyre, Psaltery, Zither, Lute, Guitar, Balalaika, Ukelele, Harpsichord; (*b*) by friction (bowed), as in Crwth, Rebec, Viol, Violin, Marine Trumpet, Hurdy-Gurdy; (*c*) by striking (hammered), as in Dulcimer, Pianoforte, Clavichord; (*d*) by wind (blown), as in the Aeolian Harp.

Wind Instruments are those in which the air in the instruments is set in vibration: (*a*) by blowing into a tube (flue-voiced), as in Recorder, Pandean Pipe, Flute, Organ; (*b*) by means of reeds (reed-voiced), as in Oboe, Clarinet, Saxophone, Bagpipe, Cor Anglais, Bassoon, Organ reed-stops; (*c*) those in which the sound is produced by the vibration of the player's lips against the mouthpiece (lip-voiced), as in Bugle, Horn, Trumpet, Tuba, Trombone, Saxhorn, Flügelhorn, Cornet. In the modern orchestra these are the *Brass*: the flute, oboe and clarinet families are the *Woodwinds*.

Percussion Instruments include the Drums, Cymbals, Tambourines, Castenets.

Insulator, a substance that will not conduct electric current. Many solids, liquids and gases are important insulators—rubber, cotton, silk, plastics, porcelain, glass, air, oil. If the applied voltage is too high, all insulators will "break down", *i.e.*, conduct electricity perhaps with resulting breakage, puncture or charring.

Thermal insulators will not conduct heat; they are usually the same kinds of substance as electrical insulators.

Intelligence. Intelligence has been variously defined as the innate potential of a person to learn and understand; to make appropriate judgments; to see the relationships between things; to profit from experience; or to meet adequately new problems and conditions in life. There are many lines of evidence to show that intellectual capacity is closely related to heredity and influenced by environmental factors. The idea of intelligence testing was first devised by the French psychologist Binet at the start of the 20th century. He was asked by the French government to invent a test which would weed out backward children in state schools, and thus save public money and avoid holding back the work of the class by teaching children who were incapable of learning at a given standard.

Briefly, a series of problems are given to a large number of children and it is thus found out which series can be solved by the average child of a given age-group; if a child of 7 can only pass the tests suitable to the average child of 6, then his mental age is 6. The intelligence quotient or IQ is discovered by dividing his mental age by his chronological age and multiplying by 100. A gifted child can usually be spotted at an early age. Although IQ tests are the standard method of estimating intelligence, they are not universally accepted as a criterion; a teacher's general judgment may be the best assessment. High intelligence may be inherited, but fail to develop to the full because facilities for education are not available.

Recent research suggests that the growth of the brain may be permanently affected by undernutrition at the time of its fastest growth (the last weeks before birth, and, to a lesser extent, the first weeks after birth). At this vulnerable period even minor deprivation can affect the rate and final extent of growth of the brain.

Interest is the payment made for the use of borrowed money over time. The rate of interest is the rate per cent per annum charged for such loans. There are many such rates, varying with the length of time for which the loans are made, and with the degree of risk, if any, that the loans will not be duly repaid. Short-term loans are usually cheaper than long-term: the lowest rates are usually for "call money" repayable immediately on demand.

Bank loans, though usually made for fairly short terms, command higher rates. Long-term loans are made chiefly to public authorities, or as bonds or debentures to business concerns.

International Criminal Court (ICC) is the first-ever permanent, treaty-based criminal court. It was established by the UN to prosecute and punish war crimes, genocide and "crimes against humanity". It was established in 2002 at The Hague. In recent years some African countries, as well as Russia, have left.

International Date Line, a line along the 180° meridian marking the difference in time between E. and W. For the westward-bound traveller crossing the line the date would be put forward one day, for the eastward-bound, back one day. To avoid difference of date in adjacent land areas, the line deviates from the 180° meridian where this crosses land.

International Standard Book Numbers (ISBNs), the system used to identify uniquely a title or edition of a book. The old 10-digit figure increased to 13 in January 2007.

Introit, the psalm sung by the choir as the priest approaches the altar to celebrate the Eucharist.

Inuit. See under **Eskimo.**

Invention of the Cross is the Roman Catholic festival held on 3 May, to celebrate the finding of the alleged True Cross at Calvary by the Empress St. Helena in 326. Also included in the Church of England calendar. See **Holy Rood.**

Io, satellite of Jupiter (q.v.). It was discovered by Galileo in 1610. It is the most volcanically active place in our solar system. (just one volcano on Io sends out more heat than all the volcanoes on Earth). Temperatures of 1700°C have been recorded and there are c. 300–500 active volcanoes. Scientists have observed new forms of mountain-building not seen anywhere else. In 2001, scientists discovered a giant 47-mile wide crater (called Tupan Patera) on the surface of Io. Its yellow surface is made up of frozen sulphur.

Iodine, a non-metal element, no. 53, symbol I, member of the halogen family (q.v.), a substance formerly exclusively obtained from the ribbon-wrack seaweeds. These were burnt and the ashes (kelp)

extracted with water. After concentrating the iodides, these were distilled with manganese dioxide and sulphuric acid to yield iodine vapour which was condensed in stoneware bottles. Nearly all iodine now in use is derived from the iodine salt present in Chile saltpetre (natural sodium nitrate). Iodine is used in photography, as an antiseptic solution in alcohol or potassium iodide (tincture of iodine), and in medicine. Doctors are now concerned about rising levels of iodine deficiency (especially in pregnant women).Discovered by Courtois in 1812.

Ionosphere. Although a certain degree of ionisation occurs at all levels of the atmosphere due to cosmic rays and the radioactivity of rocks, etc., the ionosphere is normally denoted as the region above about 70 km where the ultra-violet component of sunlight is able to ionise a significant fraction of the atoms and molecules present. This ionisation causes the reflection of radio waves by which the ionosphere was initially discovered and for many years, explored.

The nomenclature of the ionospheric layers—"D" region up to about 95 km, "E" region 95 km to about 180 km, and "F" region above 180 km—is due to the historical observations of radio wave reflections from these "layers". Satellite and rocket observations have shown that the structure is in fact more continuous.

Solar flares and aurora cause enhancements of the electron density in the ionosphere, which may result in the disturbance of radio communications over very large distances (radio blackouts). See also under **Atmosphere, Aurora, Magnetosphere.**

Ions, electrically charged atoms, or groups of atoms. Atoms of the metals lose electrons to become positively charged ions, e.g., the sodium ion (Na⁺) has one electron less than the atom. The non-metal ions are negatively charged, e.g., the chloride ion (Cl⁻) has one electron more than the atom. Similarly, a group like the sulphate ion (SO_4^{2-}) has more electrons than the constituent atoms. Thus, the hydrogen atom without its electron is a hydrogen ion or *proton* and the helium atom without its two electrons is a helium ion or *alpha-particle*.

When an electric force is applied to certain solutions, the ions into which molecules of the dissolved substance are broken up are attracted to the oppositely charged electrodes, their movements constituting an electric current through the solution. In the same way gases, including air, conduct electricity by virtue of free ions. Combustion, radio-activity and ultra-violet and cosmic radiations produce ionisation.

iPhone, is the latest development of the mobile phone. It offers music, Internet access, e-mail and an advanced digital camera. It also plays videos, shows album artwork and can function as a personal organiser, etc.

Iridium, a white and very hard metallic element, no. 77, symbol Ir, discovered by Tennant in 1804. It occurs naturally as an alloy with platinum or osmium; tips for fountain-pen nibs have been made from the former native alloy. The former standard metre was composed of platinum–iridium alloy (see **Metre**) as are parts of scientific apparatus and surgical tools that must be non-corrodible.

Iris, the typical genus of the botanical order *Iridacae*, with tuberous rhizomes and swordshaped leaves, many of the family having beautiful flowers. About 100 species of Iris are recorded from the northern temperate zone, the most common species wild in Britain being the yellow flag. Orris root, used in perfumery, comes from another iris species.

Iron is a metallic element, no. 26, symbol Fe (Latin *ferrum*), occurring widely in nature in such ores as hæmatite, loadstone (magnetic iron oxide), spathic ore and iron pyrites. It is extracted by a process known as smelting, with coke and limestone in a furnace. Its many uses are familiar, the most important being in the manufacture of cast- and wrought-iron products and of steels, which are alloys mainly of iron with added carbon and various metals. Iron rust is formed by the action of oxygen and water, and is a coating of iron oxide. See **Smelting.**

Ironclads, ships of war cased in iron or steel plates of sufficient thickness to resist projectiles. They were first introduced (1858) in the French Navy, and in 1860 the first British ironclad, the *Warrior*, was launched.

Irrational Number, a number such as the square

root of two, or pi, which cannot be expressed as the ratio of two whole numbers. *See* **Rational Number, and *Pi*.**

Irrigation, an artificial method of providing water for the growth of plants on lands where the natural supply of water is deficient. For many hundreds of years techniques of irrigation have been slow and primitive (*e.g.*, tanks, inundation canals and the Archimedes screw) and consequent inefficiencies include large water losses by evaporation and seepage, and the watering of only a small area. New developments in perennial irrigation, using barrages, large reservoirs and pumping stations, permit vast tracts of land to be irrigated. Yet these are not without their problems as witnessed after the construction of the Aswan High Dam on the Nile where complex problems of delta erosion and dam lake silting ensued. Irrigation also serves the purpose of supplying *warmth* in winter; *e.g.*, in the English water-meadows, and in the more highly developed Italian *marcite* and winter-meadows, where the water is mostly applied in winter when there is plenty of rain. There are several other functions of irrigation; *e.g.*, washing out of excess salts and the renewing of fertility by the addition of alluvium.

Isobars are the lines drawn on charts linking together points of equal barometric pressure.

Isochasms, lines connecting places at which there is an equal probability of seeing an aurora, taking the average over a number of years, based on the auroral catalogue of Fritz.

Isomers are chemical compounds having the same composition but different structural arrangements, and consequently different physical and chemical properties. For example, ethyl alcohol and methyl ether are isomers, since the molecules of both are built up of two atoms of carbon, six of hydrogen and one of oxygen, *viz.*, C_2H_6O; ethyl alcohol, C_2H_5OH; and methyl ether, CH_3OCH_3.

Isotherms are lines drawn on charts through points of equal temperature.

Isotopes. When one talks of an element, say, uranium or lead, the name of the element is a generic name for a collection of uranium species and lead species. The different species are called isotopes. For any particular element, the number and arrangement of electrons around the nucleus are the same in all the isotopes, so all the isotopes have the same chemical properties. Soddy has described isotopes as "elements, the atoms of which have similar outsides but different insides".

For example, in the nucleus of the uranium isotopes, U 235, U 238 and U 239, there are respectively 143, 146 and 147 neutrons, but all have 92 protons. The isotopes have different atomic weights, in this instance respectively 235, 238 and 239. All have the same chemical properties.

Ivory, the dentine substance of which the tusks of the elephant, hippopotamus, walrus, *etc.*, are composed. The tusks of the African elephant sometimes weigh as much as 45 kg, and reach a length of 2·4–2·7 m. A world-wide ban on trading in ivory was imposed in 1990, but pressure has resulted in a partial lifting of this ban.

Ivory Gull, a small, beautifully shaped sea-bird with striking all-white plumage and black legs which breeds on the rocky shores of the Arctic, being found farther north than any other bird; it occasionally wanders south in the winter.

J

Jabiru, the Brazilian name for the giant stork of South America.

Jacamar, from *Jacameri*, the Brazilian name for a smallish bird with long, sharply pointed bill and brilliant plumage which inhabits the tropical regions of South America east of the Andes. These birds are seen sitting motionless on trees, darting off at intervals, like flycatchers, to catch insects on the wing.

Jacanas, small water birds with immensely long toes which enable them to walk on water lily leaves. They are sometimes called "lily-trotters" and are found in tropical Africa and America. They live in swamps and feed on seeds and insects. Sometimes brilliantly coloured.

Jack, a small schooner-rigged vessel, used in the Newfoundland fisheries; a pike; an oscillating lever; a device used in roasting meat.

Jackal, *Canis aureus,* a small wild dog related to the wolf and resembling a fox. The Common Jackal is found in S.E. Europe, India and Sri Lanka; other species inhabit Africa and Egypt. The jackal is a well-known scavenger. It hunts singly or in pairs, unlike the wolf.

Jackdaw, one of the smaller members of the Crow family. This European bird is typically black with grey collar. It is easily tamed and delights in making off with and taking to its nest bright objects, such as silverware.

Jade, an exquisite kind of hardstone, ranging in colour from a whitish green to a deep mauvish brown. It can be translucent or opaque and sometimes it is veined. Jade is the common name for two minerals—the rarer *jadeite* (found in Burma, Tibet and China), a sodium-aluminium-silicate, and *nephrite* (found in New Zealand, China, Turkestan and Siberia), a calcium-magnesium silicate. The presence of small quantities of other chemicals accounts for the wide range of shades. In China jade was for centuries the symbol of imperial authority; spiritual qualities have been ascribed to it, and it has been fashioned into ritual objects, also into miniature sculptures of animals or even whole landscapes, charming to look at and incredibly skilfully made.

The Chinese word for jade is *yü*, used as a symbol for all that is noble, beautiful and pure. The statue at the Jade Buddha Palace in China weighs 260 tons.

Jaguar, a South American carnivorous animal resembling the leopard, but larger and more powerful. It preys on other animals but rarely attacks humans.

January, the first month of the year, named after Janus, the two-faced god of the Romans. It was the *Wolf monath* and *Aefter Yule* of the Saxons.

Japanese knotweed, bamboo-like weed which can grow to 3m.in just 10 weeks. It spreads very quickly and can push through tarmac and concrete.

Jasmine, a graceful climber belonging to the olive family with odoriferous blossom, originally a Persian plant, but now acclimatised in many varieties in almost all parts of the world. Two species (the common jasmine and the Spanish jasmine) yield oils used in perfumery.

Jasper, a precious stone of the chalcedony variety, opaque, and coloured red, brown, yellow and sometimes green. It was greatly esteemed in classical times, the Bible having numerous allusions to it.

Jay, a gaily-coloured bird of the Crow family, of many species—the Blue jay of N. America, the Canada jay, sometimes called "whisky jack", the Siberian jay and the British jay, fawn-coloured with black and whitish crest and bright blue feathers in the wings. It lives in woods and like the magpie, takes the eggs and young of small nesting birds.

Jazz a rhythmical syncopated music characterised by a strong element of improvisation in the performance, *See* **Section P.**

Jean, a stout kind of twilled cotton cloth, resembling fustian. Blue jeans, adopted by American city youngsters from farmworkers, became the fashion elsewhere. Worn not only as overalls by workmen but by both sexes in leisure time.

Jellyfish. The jellyfishes, which have gelatinous, translucent bodies fringed at the margin with delicate tentacles, constitute the coelenterate order *Scyphozoa*. The mouth, with a squarish opening, is seen on the underside, and there are four horseshoe-shaped sex organs. They are 95 per cent water. There are over 2,000 species worldwide (but only *c.*70 are dangerous to humans). They are difficult to study in laboratories The number of jellyfish in UK waters is rising fast.

Jerboa, small jumping mammals of the Rodent order. These mice-like animals have long tufted tails and very long hind legs, the front legs not being used for locomotion. They are found in Africa, Asia *etc.*

Jerusalem Chamber, a room in Westminster Abbey, deriving its name from the circumstance of its having originally been decorated with a view of Jerusalem. Henry IV died in this chamber, and the Committee for the Revision of the Bible met there in 1870 and later.

Jesuits, members of the Roman Catholic religious order founded by Ignatius Loyola in 1540. A long and vigorous course of study is prescribed before they are admitted into the privileges of full membership. They are required to take the vows of voluntary poverty, perfect chastity, perfect obedience and complete submission to the Pope with regard to the Mission of the Order. Pope Paul VI gave them the particular mission of initiating a dialogue with atheists.

Jet, a deep black fossil substance admitting of a high polish and much used for jewellery, ornaments and trimming. It is a form of lignite, the most important British deposit being found near Whitby, where jet manufacture has been an established industry for a long period.

Jet Engine, an aeroplane engine which derives its thrust from the high velocity of the gases it ejects. The essential units in a jet engine are a rotary compressor and a gas turbine, the latter driving the compressor. The first reliable, high-performance jet propulsion engine for aircraft was invented by Sir Frank Whittle.

Jet Stream, a meteorological term coined in 1946 to describe the relatively narrow belt of strong winds (160–320 km/h) at levels in the atmosphere from 5–11 km. These winds are important in forecasting weather, and can be a valuable aid to aircraft.

From the ground, where there may be little wind, it can sometimes be seen as high cirrus cloud moving across the sky at high speed.

Jew's Harp. The name is believed to be a corruption of "jaws harp." This instrument consists of a metal frame with a central tongue of spring steel. The frame is pressed against the teeth, and the tongue of the harp is twanged with the finger, the mouth acting as a resonating chamber. By altering the shape of the mouth the resonant frequency and therefore the note can be varied.

Jockey Club, the governing body that, although possessing no legal status, frames rules and laws by which horse-racing and turf matters are regulated. The club-house is at Newmarket.

John Bull, the typical figure of an Englishman, bluff and burly. Arbuthnot's *History of John Bull* is supposed to have originated the character.

John Dory, a fish found in most temperate seas and common in British waters. It is of a golden-yellow colour (*jaune doré*), has a high dorsal fin with long filaments projecting from the spines, very protractile jaws and is much valued as a table fish. According to legend the dark spot on each side of its body is the thumbprint of St. Peter who took a coin from the fish's mouth.

John o' Groat's House, W. of Duncansby Head, Caithness, popularly named as the northernmost point of Scotland. According to legend the house, which has now disappeared, was built in octagonal form by a Dutchman Jan de Groot who came to live there in the 16th cent. The site is marked and an inn erected near it in 1876.

Jongleurs were minstrels and jesters who wandered from town to town singing songs, playing musical instruments, dancing and giving entertainments in medieval France and Norman England. Jongleurs were low-born in contrast to the Troubadours, who were often of the nobility.

Joule, a unit of energy in the SI system of units, defined as the work done when the point of application of a force of one newton is displaced through a distance of one metre in the direction of the force. Named after J. P. Joule (1818–89). The relationship between mechanical energy and heat energy is called the mechanical equivalent of heat. One British Thermal Unit (Btu) is equivalent to 778 ft.lb or 252 calories or $1 \cdot 054 \times 10^{10}$ ergs or, in SI units, $1054 \cdot 35$ joules. *See* **Section T.**

Julian Calendar, named after Julius Caesar, who in 45 B.C., finding the Roman year 90 days in advance of the real time, was the first to adopt the calculation of time by the solar year, the average length being fixed at $365\frac{1}{4}$ days. There was still an overplus of a few minutes every year, and this was rectified by the Gregorian Calendar, introduced in Italy in 1582 and adopted in England in 1752, from which date what is called the "New Style" begins.

July, the seventh month of the year, named after Julius Caesar. It was the *Maed monath* (Meadmonth) of the Saxons.

June, the sixth month of the year, containing 30 days and deriving its name from Juno. It was the *Sear* (Dry) *monath* of the Saxons.

Juniper, one of only three native English conifers. A distinctive, sprawling evergreen only to be found on rocky soils in remote upland areas. Its berries are a main flavouring ingredient of gin but they are now being attacked by a deadly fungal disease.

Jupiter is the largest of the planets, 11 times the diameter of the earth, 318 times its mass but only one fourth its density. It is the fifth farthest from the sun and is the second brightest. Our knowledge of Jupiter, with its 67 known moons, its ring and its magnetosphere was greatly increased in 1979 by data from the Voyager 1 and 2 space-probes which passed the planet at distances of 349,000 km and 722,000 km on March 5 and July 9 respectively. Jupiter is a gaseous planet composed mainly of hydrogen and helium like the sun, possibly with a small molten core of silicates. The centre is presumed to be at a very high temperature (30,000°C) and enormous pressures—a hundred million earth atmospheres—which make hydrogen not only liquid but metallic. This metallic flux leads to intense magnetic fields. Jupiter's large magnetosphere is distorted by the solar wind and contains trapped high energy particles in radiation belts which would be lethal to man. Its existence was confirmed by Pioneer 11 in 1974.

It is now brown that Jupiter's huge magnetic field extends out to Saturn.

Jupiter's outer gaseous surface is very cold (−120°C) and consists of three layers of crystal clouds (ice ammonium hydrogensulphide and ammonia) interspersed with gaseous hydrogen and helium. It shows massive persistent features like the swirling high pressure Red Spot (larger when first seen in 1664 but which could hold two earths) and the neighbouring white oval formations. All these features are in relative motion, some moving east and others west which account for Jupiter's banded appearance. The persistence of the features arises because Jupiter has no terrain to break them up and because the surface temperature is low. Lightning continuously flashes over the Jovian surface and at the poles there are large auroras caused by an electric current of five million amperes which flows from the poles out to Io, one of the four moons discovered in 1610 by Galileo. The others were Europa, Ganymede and Callisto.

The fourteenth moon was found in 1979 by Voyager 2 at the outer edge of the thin ring of particles discovered by Voyager 1, which also discovered high plumes due to volcanic activity on Io, the first seen beyond earth (although a recent suggestion is that the plumes are caused by the electric current). Io's sulphurous surface shows no meteoric craters and Europa's smooth ice surface shows only a few impacts and is probably young, unlike the older Ganymede and Callisto whose ice-crust surfaces have many. Ganymede's crust has been reworked, however, by extensive tectonic movements. Ganymede is now known to be the largest moon in the solar system, larger than the planet Mercury. A total of 63 moons around Jupiter has now been discovered. In 1994, Jupiter was struck by the Shoemaker-Levy-9 comet whose impact sent seismic waves across the planet.

In 1995, the Hubble telescope found oxygen on Europa. Late in 1995 the Galileo spacecraft successfully entered the atmosphere of Jupiter. First data from Galileo suggested Jupiter's atmosphere was hotter and drier than expected with hurricane winds of 330 mph. Images from Galileo in 1997 appeared to show iceberg-like structures on Europa. The origin of Jupiter's swirling rings was discovered in 1998 to be the detritus thrown up by meteoroids crashing into the moons Amalthea, Thebe etc. Colour images of Io taken in January 2001 show great volcanic activity. The first pictures of Callisto (2001) showed jagged hills of ice and rock. The 14-year mission of Galileo ended in September 2003 when it crashed onto the surface of Jupiter. It had found volcanic activity on Io perhaps 100 times greater than on Earth.

Juno was launched on a 5-year unmanned journey to Jupiter in August 2011, arriving in 2016 after a long $1 \cdot 74$ million mile journey. Successfully flying just 2,500 miles above Jupiter's clouds, its mission was to study the planet's composition and gases and peer into its Great Red Spot. A mission to explore the moons of Jupiter (the Jupiter Icy Moons Explorer) is planned for 2022.

Jurassic Formation, a series of rocks (the evidences of which are most marked in the Jura Mountains) coming between the Cretaceous and Triassic groups and including the Oolite and the Lias. It is a formation rich in fauna, abounding in echinoids, lamellibranchs, ammonites and belemnites; large reptiles, marine and land, are common, as are the plants called cyads. In Britain the Jurassic outcrop extends from the Dorset coast to the Yorkshire moors.

Jury, a body of private citizens chosen and sworn to hear and pass verdict upon evidence brought forward at a trial, inquest or inquiry. The origin of the English jury is obscure but it is thought to have been introduced by the Normans. The jurors are the sole judges of the true facts upon the evidence laid before them.

Under the Criminal Justice Act of 1967 their verdicts in criminal courts in England and Wales no longer had to be unanimous but may be by a majority of 10 to 2. The age limit has been reduced from 21 to 18. The upper age limit has been raised to 75. Since 2004, judges, lawyers and peers have been eligible for jury service.

In Scotland 45 jurors are summoned in criminal cases, of whom 15 are chosen by ballot, and majority verdicts are accepted: not guilty, not proven and guilty. Proposals to limit the right to trial by jury (and scrap the double jeopardy rule) have attracted much criticism.

Justices of the Peace. *See* **Magistrates**.

Jute, the name given to the fibre of a plant grown largely in Bangladesh in the Ganges delta and used for the manufacture of coarse cloths, cordage and sacks. Kolkata (Calcutta) is the biggest jute-manufacturing centre of the world, as Dundee was in the 19th cent.

Jutes, a Low German race who in the 5th cent. invaded SE England, establishing themselves in Kent and making Canterbury their capital.

K

Kakapo, a slow-moving flightless parrot, once extremely common in New Zealand but since the 1950s very threatened. Also called owl parrots. The heaviest parrot species in the world. It is now the subject of an intense conservation project.

Kangaroo, pouched (marsupial) mammals of Australia and adjacent islands. There are over 20 species, the smaller ones being known as "wallabies". Kangaroos leap in a succession of springy bounds 3–6 m long, the forefeet not touching the ground. They can reach a height of over 2 m and a weight of 90 kg. First seen by white men when Capt. Cook's expedition visited Australia in 1770. Related genera include the tree kangaroos, rat kangaroos and the Tasmanian Jerboa kangaroo. There are an estimated 20 million kangaroos in Australia and their numbers are out of control. In New Guinea they have taken to the trees.

Kaolin or China Clay is an essential ingredient in hard-paste porcelain (*q.v.*). It results from the decomposition of felspar, and is widely found in China, Japan and the USA. The richest deposits in Europe are in Cornwall, near Limoges in France, and in the Czech and Slovak Republics. Today the largest use is in making glossy paper.

Kea, the Alpine parrot of New Zealand.

Kelvin. The measure of temperature on the absolute scale. The Kelvin scale is a development of the scale invented by Celsius (*q.v.*) for everyday use, long known as the "centigrade" scale; the degree interval on both scales is the same. The conversion formula for the Kelvin scale is $K = C + 273 \cdot 15$. *See* **Absolute Temperature**.

Kerguelen, the lost continent formed 110 million years ago which sank back beneath the present Indian Ocean 20 million years ago.

Kernewek. The native language of Cornwall which almost died out in 1777 (when the last native speaker died) but is now being revived. In 2002, Cornish was granted protection under the EU charter on "minority languages". A "standard" form of Cornish was agreed in 2008. Cornwall is now getting bilingual road signs. There are over 3,000 speakers worldwide (compared to 200 in 1985). Around 600 people speak Cornish as a main

languge. The Bible was translated into Cornish in 2011. There are now Cornish-language rock bands. There are also calls for a Cornish Assembly.

Kestrel, the most common British falcon, well known for its habit of hovering for minutes at a time with vibrating wings and then swooping down to attack mice and insects. The male has spotted chestnut-brown back, greyish head and tail, with a broad black band near tip. Kestrel numbers are now rapidly declining.

Ketones. A class of organic compounds, related to aldehydes, of general formula R_2CO (where R is an organic radical). The simpler ketones, especially acetone, are widely used as solvents for lacquers, synthetic rubber and polymers, such as cellulose acetate and perspex. More complex ketones occur in nature, and some are used in the perfumery industry. Muscone (from the musk deer (*q.v.*)) is an example.

Kew Gardens, officially known as the Royal Botanic Gardens, are among the most celebrated gardens in the world. They were started in 1759 by Princess Augusta of Saxe-Gotha, widow of Frederick, Prince of Wales, and mother of George III. They remained private property until 1841, when control passed to the Commissioners of Woods and Forests. They now cover 326 acres and are run by an independent body under the 1983 National Heritage Act. Since 1841 the gardens have been open to the public. Now a World Heritage Site. They are home to the Millenium Seed Bank. Kew now publishes an annual "State of the World's Plants."

Keys, House of, is the Manx representative assembly. *See* **Tynwald**.

Khaki, a clay-coloured cloth adopted for uniforms in the British Army in the time of the war with the Boers, and used in the first and second world wars. First used by Indian regiments.

Kibbutz (Hebrew, gathering). Israeli collective farm.

Kilogram, unit of mass, defined as the mass of the international prototype kilogram of platinum-iridium kept at the International Bureau of Weights and Measures at Sèvres. A remeasurement of Avogadro's Number (**T24**) may lead to an atomic standard of mass (the second and the metre are already defined in atomic terms), but this depends on the precision with which atoms can be counted. One kilogram equals 2·205 pounds.

Kilowatt. Unit of power. *See* **Watt**.

Kinetic Energy, the energy (*q.v.*) possessed by a particle or body in virtue of its motion. If the motion is destroyed, *e.g.*, by the impact of the body with an obstacle, the kinetic energy vanishes, being turned into some other form of energy such as heat and sound. If the body has mass m and speed v its kinetic energy (leaving out corrections due to relativity) is $\frac{1}{2}mv^2$.

King Crab, remarkable arthropods now classified separately from both Arachnids and Crustacea which they resemble, inhabiting the sea coasts of America, Japan, India and Malay Peninsula, carrying a spade shaped shell, and having a long pointed spine projecting from the posterior.

The body comprises three separate sections articulated together. These crabs—in America known commonly as the horseshoe crab because of their shape—are from 45–60 cm in length. Fossil king crabs are found as far back as the Silurian. There are about six living species.

Kingfisher, a well-known family of brilliant-plumaged birds, found in all continents, comprising over 250 species and sub-species. The British kingfisher, *Aceldo atthis*, haunts the rivers and streams, and is one of the most beautiful of native birds, having iridescent blue-green, white and rich chestnut in its plumage and bright-red feet. All kingfishers have long, dagger-shaped bills. In the Malayan region, New Guinea, the Moluccas and Australia, the varieties are very numerous. The quaint *Laughing Jackass* of Australia is among the largest of the kingfisher family. The European kingfisher is the bird of the Greek legend of the Halcyon. Cleaner rivers and more sensible management of river banks are encouraging the kingfisher to return, but recently numbers have declined. Kingfishers must eat their own body-weight in fish every day.

King-of-Arms, the name of the chief officials of the Heralds' College. There are several in England —the principal are the Garter, Norroy and Ulster, Clarenceux. *See* **Heralds' College**.

Kirimon (*Kiri no go Mon*) and **Kikumon** (*Kiki no*

go Mon), the two Japanese imperial crests, the first a design of leaves, stems and flowers of the Paulownia plant, and the other representing the sixteen-petalled chrysanthemum.

Kite, name of several birds of prey, widely distributed, related to the hawks and eagles, graceful in flight, and distinguished by their long wings and deeply forked tails. The red kite, light chestnut brown, once the most familiar bird of prey in Britain, seen scavenging the streets of London, became extinct. But since its reintroduction in 1989 it is threatening some songbird species. There are now c.3,000.

The Egyptian kite and the pariah kite of India, notorious for their thefts, are closely related to the black kite, a smaller European species, with less forked tail and blackish-brown plumage.

Kittiwake, a beautiful white and pearl-grey gull with black legs, dark eyes and greenish-yellow bill. Its range is wide, and includes the British Isles, where it is a local resident. The flight of this only truly oceanic gull, which except in the breeding-season is generally found offshore, is graceful, swift and buoyant. A triangular black patch, noticeable on the ends of the wings when open, is characteristic of the species, as is the call kitti-wake, from which the bird derives its name. It nests in colonies on the ledges of caves and steep cliffs. It is now struggling to survive in Britain.

Kiwi, flightless, stoutly-built birds of New Zealand now very rare. They are little larger than a domestic hen, and lay astonishingly large eggs for their size. Incubation and care of chicks fall to the male bird. They have rudimentary wings concealed by the plumage, and the feathers are hair-like. They are nocturnal. They are the only bird to have nostrils at the end of their beaks. They are the national emblem of New Zealand.

Knighthood In Britain the main orders of knighthood are those of the Garter, the Bath, the Thistle and St. Patrick; in addition to which there are several other orders, e.g. the Order of St. Michael and St. George. There are also Knights Bachelors not associated with any special order. The title is not hereditary, and ranks below that of a baronet, though both are entitled to the prefix "Sir".

Knights of Malta. See **Hospitallers, Knights.**

Knot, a nautical measure of speed (1 sea mile per hour), and formerly measured by a log-line, divided by knots at equal distances $\frac{1}{120}$ of a geographical mile. The number of knots travelled by the ship in a half a minute corresponded to the numbers of sea miles it travelled per hour. A sea mile is equal to about $1\frac{1}{8}$ of a statute mile or 1·9 km. Also, a grey and white wading bird, usually a winter visitor to Britain found in flocks on the coast.

Knotweed. See **Japanese knotweed.**

Knout, a whip of many thongs, often fatal in its effects, formerly used in Russia for flogging.

Koala, the Australian arboreal marsupial mammal that looks like a cute teddy-bear, with ashy-grey fur, bushy ears and rudimentary tail. It feeds on the leaves and shoots of certain eucalyptus trees, and is not more than 60 cm in length. Today fewer than 50,000 remain and their habitat is threatened. All the moisture they need comes from eucalyptus leaves. They suffer severely from stress. The new-born "joey" develops in its mother's pouch. Koalas sleep 19 hours a day! They hug trees to stop overheating. In 2012 Australia listed them as a threatened species.

Kohl, a powder prepared from antimony or burnt almond shells, and in common use by Asian women for darkening the eyelids.

Komodo Dragon. See under **Monitor.**

Kookaburra, an Australian bird distinguished by its unusual laughing sound.

Koto, a musical instrument in general use in Japan consisting of a series of 13 silken strings stretched across a curved wooden surface, and played with the fingers. It is a sort of horizontal harp.

Kremlin, the citadel or walled area within a Russian city which during the Middle Ages served as an administrative and religious centre and offered protection. That of Moscow contains the cathedral where the Tsars were crowned, an imperial palace and the "King of Bells" (see **Bells**). Its walls which are topped with towers were built in the 15th cent.

Krill, shrimp-like crustaceans at the heart of the food chain in the oceans. Their decline around Antarctica is threatening the eco-system.

Krypton, one of the rare gas elements, no. 36, symbol Kr, occurring in the air to the extent of 1 part in 20 million. It was discovered in 1898 by Ramsay and Travers. It is used in gas-filled electric lamps.

Kuiper Belt. A disc of many millions of comets that is formed on the plane of the solar system and lies 12–15 billion kms from the Sun. It includes Pluto.

Kumara. See **Sweet Potato.**

Kurds, an Indo-European people who have faced repeated oppression in Iraq and Turkey (and to a lesser extent in Iran and Syria). Kurdistan, the mountainous 'land of the Kurds', which has been their homeland for thousands of years, straddles the four countries just mentioned. Their religion is Sunni Muslim. They number around 34 million, the biggest ethnic group in the world with no state. Iraq's northern Kurdish region has been autonomous since 1991. Kurds are currently battling Islamic extremists in this region, but are again being attacked by Turkey. In 2016 the Kurds of Iran resumed an armed struggle.

Kusti, the sacred cord or girdle of the Parsees, consisting of 72 threads—the number of the chapters of the Yasna—and two branches, each branch containing six knots, together standing for the 12 months of the year.

Kyrie Eleison ("Lord, have mercy"), the name of a common form of prayer in some Christian Churches; also applied to the English Church responses after the recital of the commandments.

L

Labradorite, a felspar rich in calcium and of a pearly lustre on cleavage, found in masses in igneous rocks. The best comes from Labrador.

Labyrinth, or **Maze,** a combination of roads and passages so constructed as to render it difficult for anyone ignorant of the clue to trace the way to the central part. The Egyptian labyrinth near Lake Moeris had 3,000 rooms, half of them below ground and the remainder above.

The labyrinth in Crete, according to Greek myth, was built by Daedalus to house the Minotaur. There was one at Lemnos, renowned for its stalactite columns; and another at Clusium built by Porsenna, King of Etruria, c.520 B.C.

The labyrinth in which Fair Rosamond was concealed was at Woodstock. Hampton Court maze dates from the 16th cent.

Labyrinthodonts, gigantic fossil amphibians which get their name from the curious labyrinthine structure of their teeth, probably an evolutionary link between fishes and reptiles. They occur in the Carboniferous, Permian and Triassic formations, and remains have been found in Britain and other parts of Europe.

Their heads were long, and their footprints closely resemble the prints of the human hand.

Lac, a resinous matter deposited on the branches of a number of tropical trees by the females of the lac insect, the exudation including eggs and a viscous covering. At the gathering time the twigs are broken off and dried in the sun, when the insects die, and the lac that remains is termed stick-lac. From this, by the removal of extraneous accretions and dissolving, seed-lac is produced.

Shell-lac is seed-lac after it has been melted and otherwise prepared, and this is the best known of the lacs, used in printing and making varnishes, sealing-wax etc.

Lace, a delicate fabric of linen, silk or cotton threads, made by hand or machinery, and worked in various ornamental designs. The kinds of lace are many, deriving their distinctive names either from the method employed in production or from the place where any special variety was originally made. The best-known makes are pillow or bobbin-lace, woven and plaited by hand; needle-point lace, worked by the needle over a traced design; and machine lace, which practically dates from Heathcote's invention of the early part of the 19th cent.

Some of the most famed laces are the following: Alençon, a needle-point lace; Brussels, a very fine kind, with needle-point sprigs and flowers;

Chantilly, a silk variety with flowers and open-work; *Cluny*, a netlace with darned stitch; *Honiton*, a delicate kind with dainty sprigs and figures; *Mechlin*, generally made in one piece and very varied in design; and *Valenciennes*, or bobbin lace, of great durability, the pattern and ground of which are made at the same time, being one of the best and most costly of laces, now manufactured mainly in Belgium. Nottingham was famous for its lace.

Lace-Wings, insects with frail, transparent and much-veined wings whose grubs eat large numbers of insect pests such as aphids. The eggs are borne at the ends of threads attached to plants.

Ladino, a hybrid language which mixed Hebrew and Spanish.

Ladybird, the common name of a large family of beetles—the *Coccinellidae*. The insect is usually of a red or yellow colour with small black or coloured spots. Ladybirds are of good service to the gardener because their larvae feed on aphids. The number of spots varies from 2 to 26. There are *c.* 2,000 species (42 found in Britain). There was an explosion in numbers in 1976. Now, they are under threat in Britain from a foreign invader, the Asian harlequin ladybird which arrived in 2004 and eats all our native species.

Lady-Day, the day of the festival of the Annunciation of the Virgin Mary, 25 March. One of the four English quarter days.

Lake Dwelling, the name given to certain prehistoric habitations which were thought to have stood on platforms over lakes, like villages in certain Pacific islands.

Lakes are bodies of water collected in depressions of the earth's surface. The most notable lakes are the Great Lake series of North America, including Superior, Michigan, Huron, Erie and Ontario, all discharging into the St. Lawrence River. Africa has an enormous area of lakes, including Mobutu Sese Soko and Victoria, forming the sources of the White Nile. Smaller lakes are numerous in other countries—Switzerland, Finland, Italy, England, Ireland, Scotland, all having their lake regions, where the scenery is invariably beautiful and romantic.

The Kariba Dam (Zimbabwe–Zambia border) and the Nasser (Egypt) are the largest man-made lakes in the world.

Many of the world's lakes are now diminishing because of global demand for water, but global warming could cause lakes in the Himalayas to burst their banks. Among lakes now in major decline are Lake Chad in Africa, Lake Balkash in central Asia and the Aral Sea.

Lake School, the name given, at first in ridicule, to a distinguished trio of poets—Wordsworth, Coleridge and Southey—who made their homes in the English Lake District.

Lamellibranchs (Pelecypods), the class of aquatic, bi-valve molluscs to which the oysters, cockles, mussels, clams and scallops belong. In these animals the body, which is compressed laterally, is enclosed in two hinged shells held together by muscular action. The gills are thin plates hence the name "lamellibranchs".

Lamination, stratification on a very fine scale, as in shales.

Lammas Day is one of the oldest of the Church festivals, probably derived from the loaf-mass (*hlafmaesse*) of the Anglo-Saxons. It occurs on 1 August. It was formerly the day when loaves were given in place of first-fruit offerings and marked the transition from summer to autumn.

Lammergeyer, the bearded vulture of alpine regions, resembling an eagle in appearance. It has a white head with black tufts at base of the bill, and its general plumage is dark brown, nearly black. It is found in the remote mountain ranges from southern Spain and parts of Africa to China, and is becoming scarce. Its diet is 90 % bone marrow.

Lampblack, a carboniferous pigment obtained from flame-smoke, and now produced in specially constructed furnaces in which bodies rich in carbon, such as tar, resin, petroleum, *etc.*, are burned. The smoke or soot resulting is collected from the sides of the furnace, and forms lampblack. It finds use in making printer's ink, black paint, *etc.* and in making dynamo brushes and arc-lamp carbons.

Lamprey. Eel-like fish having no scales, bones, paired fins or jaws. They attach themselves by their mouths to fish whose blood they suck. Together with the hagfishes, the lampreys are placed in a special class—the Cyclostomes. There are three British lampreys. Lamprey pie was once very popular. They are the world's oldest living vertebrate.

Lancelet. *See* **Amphioxus**.

Land Crab, a family of crabs (*Gecarcinidae*) which live mainly on land, though migrating to the seas to deposit their eggs.

Landrail, old word for Corncrake (*q.v.*).

Landslip, a sudden downward sliding under gravity of large masses of rock, soil, *etc.*; often set off by earthquake shock or saturation of a particular stratum with water. Many serious landslides have occurred from time to time. In 1618, an earthfall happened at Plurs, on Lake Como, involving the destruction of many buildings and the loss of numerous lives. In 1806 a portion of Rossberg mountain in Switzerland slipped from its position, and falling into the valley below buried many villages and hamlets and over 800 people. A chalk cliff 30–45 m high and 1·2 km long fell at Lyme Regis, in Dorset, in 1839, doing great damage. Over 200 people were killed by a landslip in Naini Tal, in India, in 1880; and at Quebec, in 1889, a rocky eminence called Cape Diamond gave way, buildings being destroyed and lives lost.

Notable landslips have occurred at Amalfi (Italy) in 1924, at Murchiston (New Zealand) in 1929, at Aberfan (Wales) in 1966, near St. Gervais (France) in 1970 and at Guinsaugon in the southern Philippines in 2006. *See also* tsunamis (**L110**).

Languages. Around 6,000 languages are spoken in the world today, but many are fast disappearing. The most widely-spoken are Chinese (all varieties), Spanish, English, Arabic and Hindi. *See also under* **Gaelic, Sanskrit, Aryan** *etc.*

Langue d'oc and Langue d'oïl, the two principal mediaeval French dialects, *oc* and *oïl* being their respective words for the affirmative particle (modern French *oui*). *Langue d'oc*, spoken south of the Loire, was the language of the troubadours. Provençal, one of its dialects had a literary revival in the 19th cent. under the influence of the poet Frédéric Mistral. *Langue d'oïl* was spoken in northern France, and it was the dialect of the Paris region, becoming into modern French.

Lantern Fly, bugs belonging to the family *Fulgoridae* in which the head is drawn out to form a lantern-like structure. In no instance is the "lantern" luminous as once thought.

Lanthanides, the fourteen metallic elements following lanthanum in the Periodic Table, *i.e.*, the elements cerium (no. 58) to lutetium (no. 71). They are also known as the rare-earth metals, though they are in fact all more terrestrially abundant than, for instance, mercury or arsenic (with the exception of the unstable radioactive element promethium, no. 61).

The lanthanides are distinguished by having an incomplete inner electron sub-shell (the 4f level), this feature giving them interesting magnetic properties. For instance, gadolinium, holmium and dysprosium are ferromagnetic at low temperatures. Chemically, the lanthanides behave similarly, being highly reactive metals usually forming trivalent salts. *See* **Periodic Table, T57.**

Lapis Lazuli, an azure-blue mineral, being a silicate of aluminium and sodium. The pigment ultramarine is made by grinding it, though artificial ultramarine has largely superseded it. The mineral (also called *lazurite*) has been used as a gemstone from antiquity.

Lapps. *See* **Sami, L96.**

Lapwing or **Green Plover**, familiar British bird on moors and marshlands with iridescent greenish-black plumage, white underparts and black crest. Often called the "peewit" from its cry. Protected since 1967. Once common, now special.

Larboard is the old nautical term indicating the left-hand side of a ship, and changed by Admiralty order to "port" in 1844. Starboard is the right-hand side.

Larch, a familiar coniferous tree in the mountain regions of northern Europe, and though not native to Britain, the Common Larch is successfully cultivated in various parts of the kingdom. It is one of the best of all turpentine-yielding trees, and the bark is valued for tanning. The larch is an unusual conifer in being deciduous.

Lark, a family of song birds (*Alaudidae*) of many

species, some of which—notably the skylark—are famed for their habit of soaring into the air, singing all the while. They build their nests on the ground in the open country and, except for the black lark of Russia, have streaked brown plumage. The skylark and woodlark are the best known British species, while the crested lark and shore lark are among the occasional visitors. Africa has the greatest number of larks; America has only one species, the horned lark.

Larkspur, the common name of the genus *Delphinium*, a favourite flower introduced into British gardens from Switzerland in 1573. The common larkspur is *D. consolida*.

Larva, undeveloped form of any animal which before maturity undergoes metamorphosis, often different from the adult in structure and habits.

Laser. A remarkable kind of light source that was discovered in 1960. With the laser it is possible to probe the behaviour of matter under the influence of enormous energy densities, range and survey vast distances to microscopic accuracy and send millions of telephone and television messages between any two points that can see each other with telescopes. Laser light, in contrast to natural light, is coherent and can be expressed as a regular progression of waves carrying energy along a particular path.

The essential difference is that laser light is an orderly sort of wave motion in contrast to ordinary light which is inherently unsteady and thus an inefficient carrier of information in time.

The name *maser*, which is the microwave parent of the laser, derives from the expression "microwave amplification by the stimulated emission of radiation". Upon application to light wavelengths the microwave part of the name lost its meaning and the term maser became generally descriptive of any device in which stimulated emission dominates.

Laser Fusion is a method by which it has been proposed that thermonuclear reactions may be controlled and exploited as a source of energy (*see* Nuclear Fusion). The idea is to irradiate a millimetre-sized pellet of a mixture of frozen deuterium and tritium with a short ($\sim 10^{-9}$ s) but very intense pulse of energy in the form of laser light. This has the effect of both compressing the pellet by a factor of at least a thousand and heating it to about 10^8 °C. Under these conditions, thermonuclear reactions (principally $^2D + ^3T \rightarrow {}^4He + {}^1n$) proceed sufficiently fast that a net output of energy is obtained before the pellet explosively separates.

Formidable technical problems need solving before laser fusion can become a practical proposition. These include the development of efficient high-powered lasers and the design of a suitable reactor that can withstand up to 100 micro-hydrogen bomb explosions per second. It is still not clear whether this method of controlling nuclear fusion is more practical than the more conventional approach involving the magnetic confinement of plasmas.

Latent Heat is the quantity of heat required to convert 1 gram of a substance from one form into another. For example, when a solid changes into a liquid or a liquid into a gas, the addition of heat to bring about the change produces no rise in temperature, the energy being absorbed in the form of latent heat. An equal amount is released when the process is reversed. The latent heat of fusion of ice is about 79·6 calories per gram, that of the vaporisation of water about 539 calories per gram.

Lateran Councils were the religious conventions held in the Lateran basilica at Rome for deciding important questions of Church doctrine. The most brilliant was that of 1215.

Laterite refers to any tropical soil or soil horizon rich in hydrated ferric and aluminium oxides which harden when exposed to the atmosphere. It is difficult to cultivate and is commonly used for bricks and road metal. Laterite buildings have been known to withstand the weathering for many centuries and some of fine examples are found in India and S.E. Asia.

Latitude of a point on the earth's surface is its angular distance from the equator, measured on the surface of the earth in degrees, minutes and seconds. Thus the equator is 0° Lat. and the poles 90° Lat. (N. or S.). First determined by Hipparchus of Nicaea about 160 B.C. Lati-

tude introduces zones of climate, *e.g.*, tropical rain, subtropical steppe, temperate rain *etc.*

Laughing Gas. *See* Nitrous Oxide.

Launce *or* **Sand Eel**, a family of eel-like sea fishes found in large numbers on the coasts of North America and Europe. There are two species common to British waters. These fishes are of a bright silvery hue, and live much in the sand underneath the water. They are prized as food.

Laurentian Shield refers to the Pre-Cambrian rocks in the region of the Upper Lakes of Canada, nearly 5 million sq km in extent. Of enormous importance to Canada on account of the mineral wealth, forests yielding valuable timber and wood-pulp, and water-power.

Lava, the molten rock which is erupted from a volcanic vent or fissure. Also the same material which has cooled and solidified.

Lawn, very fine sun-bleached linen It used to be called "cloth of Rheims".

Lead, a soft malleable metallic element, no. 82, symbol Pb (Latin *plumbum*), occurring in numerous ores, which are easily smelted. Its most important source is the mineral galena which consists chiefly of lead sulphide; rarely is it found free. Lead is largely used in plumbing on account of its pliability, and in nuclear reactors as a shield against radiation because of its high density.

As an alloy element it combines in the formation of type metal, stereo metal, shot metal, pewter and many other compounds. Oxides of lead are used in some types of glass and in the manufacture of paints (red lead). All lead compounds are poisonous.

Leading producers of lead are the USA (Missouri), Australia (Broken Hill) and Russia. Britain was once a major centre of lead mining.

Leaf Miners, insect larvae which tunnel between the upper and lower skins of leaves. Most leaf miners are caterpillars of tiny moths; some sawfly larvae have the same habit.

Leap Year *or* **Bissextile**, was fixed by Julius Caesar, 45 B.C., the addition of one day in every four years bringing the measure of the calendar year even with the astronomical year with three minutes per year over. The Gregorian Calendar corrected this by dropping leap year at the centuries not divisible by 400. For instance, 1700, 1800 and 1900 were not leap years, but 1600 and 2000 were. The next will be 2400.

Leather was made in ancient Egypt, Greece and Rome, and has through succeeding centuries played an important part in the service of man. It consists of the dressed hides or skins of animals after the process of tanning has been gone through. Untanned skins are known as pelts.

Leather is classed either according to the skins from which it is made or the system of preparation employed. The best-known kinds are morocco, kid, Russian, chamois, Cordovan, grained, patent, russet, tan, calf and Hungarian.

Leech, an aquatic blood-sucking worm, mostly found in fresh-water ponds. Each end of the body is provided with a sucker, but that at the head end has jaws and teeth. There are 650 different species. The medicinal leech has three jaws. Used medicinally since the 6th cent. B.C. Leeches will not let go of their host until they are full, so removal has to be done carefully.

Leedsichthys, an extinct ancient fish, the largest the world has ever seen.

Leeward, a nautical term, meaning the sheltered side of a vessel—that is, the opposite side to that from which the wind is blowing.

Legion of Honour, the French order for distinguished services, military or civil, was instituted by Napoleon I in 1802, and confirmed and modified under later rules. There are five grades—Grands Croix, Grands Officiers, Commandeurs, Officiers and Chevaliers.

Legume, the fruit typical of the pea, bean family.

Lemming, small light-brown rodents with dark spots, now found only in Russia and Canada, about 12 cm long, with a short stump of a tail. The migrations of the lemming are famous, probably caused by overbreeding when food is plentiful. So insistent is the urge to keep moving that these animals will march on into the sea in their thousands and be drowned. Lemmings were around in Britain until *c.*8,000 B.C.

Lemur, almost the most primitive member of the primate order of mammals. They are noted for having strong pliant toes enabling them to use

L66

their feet as hands, and also well-developed thumbs on the hands. They have long squirrel-like tails, fox-shaped heads and large staring eyes. True lemurs are confined to Madagascar, which has c 100 types; closely related are the "bush-babies" of southern Africa. The Indri is the largest – and loudest – of the lemurs. The mouse lemur is the world's smallest primate. The Madagascan lemur is the most threatened primate group on earth as its forest habitat changes. Lemurs operate in a matriarchal society.

Lenses, pieces of transparent material designed to focus an image of an illuminated object. Usually of glass, but plastic lenses are common, and quartz, etc. are used for special purposes. The surfaces of the simplest lenses are parts of spheres. Lenses which are thickest, or thinnest, at the centre are called convex and concave respectively. Lenses of complex shape are often used in microscopes, etc. Electron lenses are arrangements of electric or magnetic fields which focus beams of electrons, e.g., on to TV screens.

Lent, forty days' of fasting before Easter.

Leopard. See Cat.

Lepidoptera, order of insects with scaly wings and bodies, to which the butterflies and moths belong.

Leptons. A group of particles which include electrons, neutrinos and muons. All are much lighter than protons or any baryons (q.v.).

Lepus, the constellation of the Hare, situated under the Orion group, and one of the constellations with which the ancients were familiar.

Lewis, a contrivance for stone-lifting, the principle of which was known to the ancient Romans; it consists of two dovetail tenons of iron or other metal, expanded by an intervening key in a dovetail-shaped mortice in the stone, and shackled by a ringed bolt to the hoisting chain.

Leyden Jar, the earliest form of electrical condenser. Its invention is usually credited to Muschenbroeck of Leyden (1745). It consisted of a jar coated inside and out with tinfoil for about two-thirds of its height and having its inner coating connected with the top by a brass knob and chain. The jar was charged by connecting it to an electrostatic machine.

Lias, a geological term referring to the lower section of the Jurassic group, and mainly comprising shales and limestones.

Libraries, before the invention of printing, were few, and collected together at enormous cost. At Nineveh remains of libraries, consisting of tablets of baked clay, have been discovered. There were two libraries at Alexandria containing a vast collection of rolls or volumes, founded by Ptolemy I Soter (367–382 B.C.) and established by Ptolemy II Philadelphus (309–246 B.C.).

The great libraries of later times included the Vatican Library at Rome, moved to its present premises in 1588; the Royal Library in Paris which later became the Bibliothèque Nationale; The Astor Library, New York; and in England, the Bodleian Library, Oxford, and the British Library (see below). After 1850 public libraries were established in all the chief cities. The first lending library was opened in Edinburgh in 1726.

The British Library in London, the National Library of Scotland, in Edinburgh, that of Wales in Aberystwyth, the Bodleian Library of Oxford, Cambridge University Library and Trinity College Dublin comprise the "copyright" libraries, entitled to receive a copy of each new book and journal published in Britain (as well as every electronic publication). The British Library Act 1972 brought together into a single organisation (a) the former British Museum Library (the books remaining in the Museum) and the Science Reference Library in Holborn and Bayswater, the whole now being known as the British Library, Reference Division; (b) the former National Lending Library for Science and Technology and its arts and humanities counterpart, the National Central Library, together now known as the British Library, Lending Division and located at Boston Spa, Yorkshire. The new British Library has been granted Grade I listed status.

The major Reference Division, near Euston Station, was officially opened on 25 June 1998. Lending Division remains in Yorkshire. The British Library holds 14 million books on 390 miles of shelves.

Great emphasis is being placed on new developments in IT to transform libraries into a fully electronic network. Book borrowing is declining but Internet use of libraries is rising rapidly. On average, libraries now only spend 8·7% of their overall expenditure on books. Current expenditure cuts are threatening many local libraries, but Europe's largest public library opened in Birmingham in 2013.

Libretto (It. booklet), the literary text of an opera or oratorio. Usually the composer and the librettist collaborate in the writing of an opera, but several composers (e.g., Wagner) wrote their own librettos. Boito, librettist to Verdi for Otello and Falstaff, himself composed two operas Mefistofele and Nerone. Most famous of Italian opera librettists was the poet and dramatist Metastasio (1698–1782). His librettos were set to music by many composers.

Licence is a permission given to do some act, which without such permission, it would be unlawful to do. Licences are required for operating TVs (see L106), for driving a motor vehicle, for killing game, for setting up as a bookmaker, for selling beer, wines and spirits, tobacco, etc. and for importing certain items such as arms, ammunition, etc. The dog licence was abolished in 1988.

Lichens. In every lichen, two plants are associated, one being an alga and the other a fungus. The fungus derives its food from the alga; probably the alga gains too from the association, being protected against desiccation by the fungus (an example of symbiosis). Lichens are the first plants to colonise bare rocks.

Lido. Public open-air swimming pool, popular from the 1920s.

Lifeboats were invented by three men, Lionel Lukin who converted a coble into a boat for saving life in 1785; William Wouldhave, who discovered how to make a boat right herself if she capsized; and Henry Greathead, who built a lifeboat, partly from Wouldhave's model, in 1789. This boat was stationed at South Shields, although the earliest recorded reference to a lifeboat station was in 1770 at Formby, Lancs. It was not until 1851 that the first lifeboat able to self-right was built, and a motor was first installed in a lifeboat in 1904. Mersey class lifeboats, introduced in 1988, have twin turbo-charged diesel engines with maximum speed of 17·5 knots. Most coastal lifeboats in this country are maintained by the Royal National Lifeboat Institution founded by Sir William Hillary on 4 March 1824. It is supported entirely by voluntary contributions, and has saved over 137,000 people. Its headquarters are in Poole, Dorset. In 2017, its operating cost exceeded £410,000 each day of the year. There are 230 lifeboat stations around the UK and Ireland. The busiest is on the Thames in London. Since 1824, 778 lifeboat crewmen have died on rescue missions.

Life Expectancy. See Longevity, L68.

Light, a particular kind of electromagnetic disturbance capable of travelling through space, and some kinds of matter, and of affecting our eyes to cause vision. Its finite speed was first demonstrated by O. Römer, using observations of the eclipses of Jupiter's satellites in 1675.

In 1860 Maxwell showed that light waves are electromagnetic. Since Einstein's theory of relativity (1905) it has been generally realised that the speed of light is a fundamental natural constant. Visible light with wavelengths between about 4 and 7×10^{-5} cm is only a small part of the electromagnetic spectrum. The speed of light in vacuum is c. $2 \cdot 997925 \times 10^8$ m/s. Scientists have now succeeded in "freezing" light (for a few hundredths of a millisecond) in an experiment that could help develop super-computers.

Light-Emitting Diodes (LEDs), the replacement for the traditional light bulb. They have no filament to burn out, but are not as popular as the old bulbs.

Light Year, a measure of astronomical distance, equal to the distance light travels in a period of one year. A light year is $9 \cdot 463 \times 10^{12}$ km. The unit parsec is now preferred. (1 pc = 3·2616 l.y.).

Lighthouses, to warn ships of dangerous places and indicate coasts, points, harbours, etc., have existed since the building of the Pharos, a tower of white marble 183 m high, built by Ptolemy II Philadelphus at Alexandria about 283 B.C. In early lighthouses the lights were simple fires. The most famous and one of the earliest UK lighthouses is the Eddystone (q.v.).

The only surviving medieval lighthouse in Britain is St. Catherine's on the Isle of Wight.

The lighthouses of England and Wales, the Channel Islands and Gibraltar are under the control of Trinity House; Commissioners of Northern Lighthouses control those of Scotland; the Commissioners of Irish Lights control the coasts of Ireland. Particulars of lights in all parts of the world were published for the guidance of navigation in the *Admiralty Lists of Lights*. Under the 1987 Pilotage Act, responsibility for pilotage now rests with harbour authorities. All lighthouses are now automatic, the last manned lighthouse in Britain went over to computer control in 1998. Trinity House built its first lighthouse at Lowestoft in 1609. *See also* **Eddystone Lighthouse**.

Lightning, the flash of a discharge of electricity between two clouds, or between a cloud and the earth, when the strength of the electric fields becomes so great as to break down the resistance of the intervening air. With "forked" lightning the actual path, often branched, is visible, while with "sheet" lightning the flash is hidden by the clouds which themselves are illuminated. "Ball" lightning or fireballs is the name given to the luminous balls which have been seen floating in the air during a thunderstorm.

A flash consists of a number of separate strokes, usually four or five, and the discharge of electricity to earth begins with a faintly luminous "leader" moving downwards and branching at intervals. As the ground is approached a much brighter luminosity travels back along the conducting channels, lighting up with several branches. The multiple strokes which follow in fractions of a second have the same "return" nature and are rarely branched.

Lightning flashes to earth damage structures, cause loss of life and endanger overhead power systems, often interrupting electricity supply. Such storms generally affect radio transmissions and present hazards to aircraft. Thunderclouds may develop energy far exceeding that of our largest power generating stations.

Lightning occurs most frequently close to the Equator. It is rarer in cold climates. There are about four million lightning strikes each day across the world.

Megalightning is lightning that strikes from the clouds up into space and is thousands of times more powerful than conventional lightning.

Fear of lightning is called *astraphobia*.

Lightning Conductor, a metal rod, the upper part of which is of copper with a conical point, the lower portion being iron, which extends into the earth. Its effect is to gather to itself the surrounding electricity and discharge it into the earth, thus preventing its falling upon the protected building. In ships, lightning conductors are fixed to the masts and carried down through the ship's keel-sheathing. Benjamin Franklin was the first to realise the possibilities of lightning protection and, in 1752, carried out his famous experiment of drawing electricity from thunder-clouds with the aid of a sharp-pointed conductor fixed to a kite.

Lillibulero, an old marching song arranged by Purcell. With words by Wharton, it is said to have "sung James II out of three kingdoms". Used by the wartime BBC as a station identification signal preceding news bulletins.

Lily Family (Liliaceae), one of the largest families of flowering plants, with 200 genera and 2,500 species. It includes the true lilies (*Lilium*), tulips and hyacinths. Vegetables belonging to the family are the onion and asparagus.

Limes, trees of the genus *Tilia*, including some 30 species spread over north temperate regions. The word is a corruption of "linden". Limes native to Britain are the small-leaved *T. cordata* and the broad-leaved *T. platyphyllos*.

The hybrid *T. vulgaris* was introduced into Britain from the Continent during the 17th cent. and is frequently seen in streets and parks. Lime-wood was used by Grinling Gibbons for his fruit, flower and bird decorations.

Limestones, sedimentary rocks composed wholly or largely of calcium carbonate and formed by two main processes, (1) organic (skeletal remains of organisms), *e.g.*, chalk (*q.v.*) and (2) chemical (precipitation of calcium carbonate), *e.g.*, oolite (*q.v.*). Marble is limestone that will polish after cutting.

Limpet, a primitive snail that lives attached to rocks. Their teeth are made of the strongest biological material we know of.

Lindisfarne Gospels. *See under* **Illuminated MSS (N9)**.

Linear B, the mysterious language found on tablets in Knossos, Crete, in 1900.

Linen, a textile fabric manufactured from flax fibre, known to the ancient Egyptians, and first manufactured in England under Henry III by Flemish weavers. The greatest linen-manufacturing region in the world was Northern Ireland (largely yarns and the lighter types of fabrics); Scotland produced coarse linens and canvas as well as household linens.

Ling, a sea-fish common on the coasts of Britain, and abounding in more northern waters. It averages about 1 m in length, and is a voracious feeder, living chiefly on small fish. Ling is also the name applied to *Calluna vulgaris*, the plant commonly called "heather".

Linnean Society, famous society founded in 1788 to foster the study of natural history. Named after Carl Linnaeus.

Linseed, the seed of the flax plant, containing, apart from its fibrous substance, certain oily and nitrogenous matter of considerable commercial value. This yields linseed oil. Some of the residue is used to make cattle food.

Lion, the most impressive of the Cat family. It is chiefly found in open bush country in Africa. Asiatic lions are now only found in India. Its large square head, its flowing mane (in the males only) and its tufted tail distinguish it. Tip to tip it can reach a length of 3m; a weight of 225 kg. African lion numbers have now fallen to below 30,000, down from 200,000 in 25 years. Many are dying from Lentivirus, the lion form of AIDS.

Lions live in groups known as prides.

Lion and Unicorn, the supporting figures of the royal arms of Great Britain, date from the union of Scotland with England (1603) at the accession of James I (James VI of Scotland), the lion representing England and the unicorn Scotland.

Liquefied Natural Gas (LNG), gas which has been condensed into liquid, which reduces its volume to just 1/600th of its normal form, enabling it to be easily transported. Major storage facilities have been developed at Milford Haven.

Liqueurs are essences combined with alcoholic liquid, and are of many kinds, named according to their flavouring or place of production.

Liquid, the name given to matter in such state that it takes its shape from the containing vessel.

Liquid Crystals form a special class of substance and are true liquids in that they flow easily and can be poured. However, unlike ordinary liquids, liquid crystals have their molecules arranged with geometrical regularity in one or two dimensions, so that they have a certain internal structure similar to that of solid crystals. They are fairly complicated chemicals with somewhat elongated molecules. Liquid crystals are of interest to biologists as well as to chemists and physicists, and not just because they account for the iridescence of beetles. Some body fluids are in fact liquid crystals. There are also technological applications because of their unique electrical and optical properties.

Litanies were first used in church processions in the 5th cent. The first English litany was commanded to be recited by Henry VIII in 1544.

Lithium, a soft metallic element, no. 3, symbol Li, similar to sodium. It is very reactive and is stored under paraffin oil. It is the lightest metal element. The main sources are Bolivia, Chile and Australia. There has been a surge in demand for its use as a component of rechargeable batteries.

Litre, a metric measure, was abolished in 1964 as a scientific unit of volume, but remains as a special name for the cubic decimetre and as an everyday unit, *e.g.*, a litre of petrol.

Liturgy, the name given to the Church ritual, though strictly applying only to the portion used in the celebration of the Eucharist or Lord's Supper. The Anglican liturgy is laid down in the Book of Common Prayer (1662).

The Alternative Service Book dates from 1980. The new book of prayer, *Common Worship*, was introduced on 3 December 2000.

Liverworts (Hepatics), a class of simple green plants related to the mosses. Liverworts are most common in damp situations, such as the banks of ditches. The majority of British species are leafy, only some are thalloid.

Lizard, the name given to a diversified order of reptiles, of which there are *c.* 1,600 species. They include the geckos, chameleons, glass snakes *etc.* A previously unknown species of legless lizards was discovered in 2008 in the grasslands of Brazil. The lizard uses its tail to stabilise its body in mid-air.

Llama, mammals related to the camels, from which

they differ in small size, absence of the humps, and more woolly coat. The domestic llama of S. America is used as a beast of burden, also providing wool, meat and milk. *See also* **Alpaca, Guanaco.**

Loadstone *or* **Lodestone,** an oxide of iron, found chiefly in Sweden and Norway. Its scientific name is magnetite. It has the power of attracting pieces of iron and served as the first magnets used in compasses. One of the class of non-metallic magnetic materials known as "ferrites" (q.v.).

Lobsters are marine crustacean animals existing in large numbers in the northern seas of Europe and America and in fair proportion on some British coasts (e.g. the Channel Islands).

Locust, insects of the grasshopper family, but much more powerful. They are inhabitants of hot countries, and often make their appearance in untold millions, like clouds, devastating all the vegetation that comes within their course.

The locust-tree (*Ceratonia siliqua*) is supposed to have furnished food to St. John the Baptist while in the wilderness, and its "beans" have accordingly been styled "St. John's Bread".

Loess, a deposit of silt or marl laid down by wind action. The biggest loess deposits are in Asia, the source of the dust of which they are composed probably being the deserts of Central Asia. Large deposits in Europe originated from the edge of ice sheets during the Ice Age.

Logarithms, a system of calculation invented by John Napier in 1614, and later developed by Henry Briggs. Thus if a number is expressed as the power of another number, *i.e.*, if $a = b^n$, then n is said to be the logarithm of a to base b, written logba. Common logs are to base 10 and Napierian to base $2.7182818\ldots$, expressed as e.

Lombards, a German people, originating on the Elber, who settled in Italy in the 6th cent., occupying northern and central regions, and establishing a kingdom with Pavia as capital. They were conquered by Charlemagne in 774, but left their name to the region of Lombardy.

Lombard Street, London, takes its name from the Lombard merchants and bankers who came to settle there in the 12th cent.

London Clay, geological stratum which occupies much of the London Basin and part of the Hampshire Basin. It represents the lower stratum of the Eocene. Outside the metropolis, brickfields utilise the clay for brickmaking. Water held down in the Chalk by this impervious stratum is tapped by a number of artesian wells in London. The tunnels of the underground run through the London Clay.

London Eye, the "big wheel" by the Thames, nearly three times as high as Tower Bridge. The wheel can carry 15,000 visitors a day. The world's tallest Ferris wheel is now in Nanchang, China.

London University. Originated in the foundation of a non-sectarian college in Gower Street in 1828. Among the chief colleges are: UCL (University College London), King's College, (inc. former Chelsea College and Queen Elizabeth), Imperial College of Science and Technology, London School of Economics, School of Oriental and African Studies, Queen Mary, Birkbeck (founded in 1823 and specialising in part-time evening study), together with Royal Holloway. London University was the first to open all degrees to women (as from 1878). The London Institute became the University of the Arts in 2004.

London Zoo. *See* **Zoological Gardens, L118.**

Longevity. Life expectancy in Britain today is 78·8 for men and 82·8 for women. This compares to 48 and 51 back in 1906. This trend for a longer life-span is continuing in the United Kingdom. Every hour, life expectancy in Britain rises by another 16 minutes! There are now more pensioners than children in the UK and there are over 3 million people aged over 80. By 2061, around 26% of our population will be over 65 (compared to *c.* 18% in 2017).

Already Britain has the oldest population in the EU. Over 21% of Britons are now over 60 and over 1·5 million are over 85 (compared to 200,000 in 1951). Britain had 14,500 centenarians in 2016 (compared to 2,500 in 1980).

The highest life expectancy in the world for women is currently Japan (86·0). For men, Iceland leads with 80·0. Japan comes second and Sweden third. Over a quarter of Japan's population is aged 65 or over.

The number of centenarians is also rapidly increasing. Living to over 100 will one day be rou-

tine (*e.g.* in Japan which will have 1 million centenarians in 2050). In Britain it is projected that 660,000 women and 541,000 men will be over 100 in 2074. By 2050, the world may have around 400 million people aged 80 or over.

The longest-lived person on record is Jeanne Louise Calment (of France) who died in 1997 aged 122 years and 164 days.

However, in contrast to this increasing longevity in developed countries, there are many low statistics for lifespan in Africa, Asia *etc.*

Longitude of a point on the earth's surface is the angle which the meridian through the poles and that point makes with some standard meridian. The meridian through Greenwich is usually accepted as the standard meridian and the longitude is measured east or west of that line. As the earth revolves through 360° in 24 h, 15° longitude represent 1 hour's difference in apparent time.

Lord Chamberlain. *See* **Chamberlain, Lord.**

Lord Chancellor. *See* **Chancellor, Lord.**

Lord Lieutenant is the Queen's representative in the county, and his office is now largely ceremonial. On his recommendation the magistrates or JPs are appointed by the Lord Chancellor. The office was created in 1549.

Louse, parasitic insect found on the skin of birds and mammals. The two sub-species that parasitise humans are the body louse and the head louse. Typhus can be transmitted by lice.

Louvre, one of the old royal palaces of Paris, was built in its present form partly by Francis I and added to by later monarchs, Louis XIV completing the edifice. Napoleon I turned it into a museum and enriched it with the plunder of many foreign art galleries.

The great extension to the Louvre building begun by Napoleon I was completed under Napoleon III in 1857. Much injury was done to the building during the Commune of 1871. Amongst other famous treasures it houses the Venus de Milo and Leonardo da Vinci's masterpiece, *La Gioconda.*

Lung Fishes. *See* **Dipnoi.**

Lutecium, element (no. 71) of the rare-earth metals discovered in 1907 by Urbain. Symbol Lu.

Lynx, cats of sturdy build, with tufted ears and spotted fur, inhabiting many parts of the world, including Northern and Central Europe. They can ravage sheep and goats.

Lyon King of Arms, the President of the Scottish Lyon Court, and head of the heraldic organisation for Scotland.

Lyre-Bird, a remarkable family of Australian birds, the males of which possess a beautiful lyre-shaped tail. The bird is not more than 38 cm long, but its tail, displayed during its remarkable courtship dance, is 58 cm in length. There are two species: the Superb and Albert's.

M

Macaque. A family of monkeys which includes the Barbary ape (specimens of which live on Gibraltar), the Rhesus macaque (the organ grinder's monkey and the one used for experimental work in the investigation of disease), the Bonnet monkey of southern India and Sri Lanka, the Crab-eating and the Pig-tailed monkeys of south-eastern Asia.

Macaw, a genus of large parrots with brilliant scarlet and sky-blue plumage, with interminglings of green. Native to South and Central America. Many species currently face extinction. They are the largest members of the parrot family.

Mace, originally a weapon of offence, now an ensign of authority borne before officers of state and other dignitaries. In the House of Commons the mace is handed to an official of the Crown by the Sergeant-at-Arms at the close of a session.

Mach Number. Unit of flight speed. The ratio of speed of flight to speed of sound under same conditions of pressure and density. Speed of sound at sea-level is 762 mile/h (1,226 km/h), so flight speed of 381 mile/h (613 km/h) is equivalent to a Mach Number of ½. At supersonic speeds the Mach Number is greater than 1; subsonic speeds, less than 1.

Mackerel, a sea-fish existing in large numbers in the northern Atlantic off America and Europe.

L69

They are beautiful fish with a streamlined body and among the fastest fish in the sea. Caution is needed that they are not over-fished.

Macromolecules are very large molecules about 10,000 times or more as heavy as ordinary small molecules like hydrogen. Most are built up from a large number of simple sub-units, *i.e.*, are polymers (*q.v.*). The term macromolecule is often used in biology, *e.g.*, starch and cellulose are biological macromolecules, both built from glucose sub-units. Other important ones are proteins and nucleic acids. The properties of macromolecules depend on the sub-units of which they are composed.

Mad Cow Disease, the common name for Bovine Spongiform Encephalopathy (BSE), a fatal brain disease in cattle. Concern resurfaced in 1996 over possible links with the brain disorder variant Creutzfeldt-Jakob disease (vCJD) which had begun to claim human lives. The Government admitted that it was possible that mad cow disease might be passed to humans by eating beef. Selective culling of cattle was begun.

Renewed concerns about long-term health risks to humans led the government to impose a ban on the sale of all cuts of beef off the bone in 1997. The EU ban on British beef exports was lifted in 2006. Over 183,000 cases of BSE have been confirmed in the UK since 1986. It has now almost died out amongst the world's cattle but a new case was reported in America in 2012.

Madder, one of the most important of dye-stuffs, largely used in producing Turkey-red dye, but now superseded by synthetic alizarin. Natural madder is the root of the *Rubia tinctorum*.

Maelstrom, a great whirlpool. The most famous is that off the coast of Norway, between the islands of Moskenès and Mosken, of the Lofoten group.

Mafia. A term which is connected with Italo- American organised serious crime. Historically, remoteness from the central government of Italy encouraged the growth in Sicily in the 19th century of *mafiosi*, key men who gained power through fear and violence.

Emigration of vast numbers of southern Italians to the United States led to a new type of urban *mafioso* who became connected with gangsterism and vice.

Sometimes called the *Cosa Nostra*, the organisation has infiltrated city governments and is reputed to be in control of drug smuggling and other illegal operations. Organisations of gangsters similar to the Mafia are thriving.

Magellanic Clouds, two small irregular galaxies that are close neighbours to our own Galaxy, first recorded in 1519 by Ferdinand Magellan. Both clouds are visible, with the naked eye, from the southern hemisphere. The Large Magellanic Cloud is 163,000 light years away and the Small Magellanic Cloud is 195,000 light years.

Magenta, a blue-red aniline dye discovered in 1859 by Sir W. H. Perkin, and named after the battle of that year between the French and Austrians.

Magic. *See* **Section J.**

Magic Circle, the world's most famous magical society. Its motto is *Indocilis Privata Loqui* which means "not apt to disclose secrets". This prestigious institution was established in 1905.

Magistrates *or* **Justices of the Peace** preside over petty sessional and Youth Courts *etc.* and are appointed by the Lord Chancellor on the recommendation of the Lord Lieutenant of the County.

Most JPs are laymen and unpaid. In certain big towns a legally-qualified, paid, full-time magistrate is appointed, known as a stipendiary magistrate. In London stipendiaries are known as Metropolitan Stipendiary Magistrates. JPs are no longer appointed over the age of 60 and they must retire when they reach 70. The judicial office of JP derives from a statute of 1361. Magistrates, though mostly laymen and unpaid, are now subject to compulsory training but they remain overwhelmingly white and middle-aged.

Magma, molten rock material rich in volatile constituents prior to its eruption at the surface. With the loss of volatiles it becomes lava.

Magnesium, a metallic element, no. 12, symbol Mg, first isolated in 1808 by Sir Humphry Davy, who prepared it by electrolysing the chloride. Its chief ores are magnesite and dolomite. Industrially it is obtained by electrolysis. Many important light alloys contain magnesium. The metal burns with a very bright light, and for this reason it is used in photographers' flash bulbs and also in firework manufacture.

Magnetic Navigation. The ability of some creatures as varied as salmon and monarch butterflies, to navigate by means of a protein bundle buried in their cells.

Magnetic Storms. These are the effects of magnetospheric storms observed world-wide at ground level as fluctuations of as much as 5 % in the earth's magnetic field. These are especially prevalent during sunspot maximums – a time when the sun is more active. The largest effects are observed at high latitudes, in the auroral ovals, and are due to electric currents flowing in the ionosphere and between the ionosphere and the magnetosphere. There may be concurrent disruption of radio communications. *See* **Magnetosphere** and **Aurora Polaris.**

Magnetism, originally the name given to the quality of attraction for iron possessed by lodestone (*q.v.*). Now known to be a phenomenon inseparably connected with electricity. Strong magnetic attraction is possessed by a comparatively small class of substances; iron, nickel and cobalt are the most common, but some are less well known, *e.g.*, gadolinium.

Many alloys have valuable magnetic properties which make possible numberless technical devices. New magnetic substances are being developed (*see* **Ferrites**).

The earth itself acts like a huge magnet with its axis inclined at about 11° to the axis of rotation, the magnetic poles being on the Boothia Peninsula (North Canada) and South Victoria Land (Antarctica). The magnetic field at the surface consists of the regular field of a magnetised sphere with an irregular field superimposed upon it. Variation in the magnetic forces occurs from place to place and from time to time, and maps showing the distribution over the globe of points of the same declination (*i.e.*, the angle which the magnetic meridian makes with the geographical one) are of the utmost importance in navigation. Little is known regarding the origin of the main (regular) field of the earth, but it is believed that the irregularities are due to the presence of intense electric currents in the upper atmosphere and local magnetisation of rock strata. It is now known that Earth's magnetic field is *c.* 4 billion years old.

In 1967 the discovery was made of isolated magnetic poles, *i.e.*, north and south magnetic poles existing separately, just as positive and negative electrical charges exist separately.

This discovery ranked as one of the great experimental results of the 20th cent., because of its significance for the theory of electromagnetism and fundamental particles. Magnetic field strengths are measured in gauss (cgs) or tesla (SI) units.

Scientists have now discovered that the magnetic field surrounding the Earth (protecting us from harmful radiation) is fast weakening.

The gradual shifts in the location of the north and south magnetic poles are known as *secular variations*. A complete reversal of the north and south poles may eventually occur.

Magnetohydro-dynamics. A current-carrying wire always experiences a force if it is in a magnetic field. This is the well-known electrodynamic force, and electric motors work because of it. If the current is carried in a fluid, *e.g.*, a liquid metal or a plasma, these forces cause bodily movements to the fluid, which are in general very difficult to calculate. The forces are then called *magnetohydro-dynamic forces*. Now magnetic fields are themselves produced by electric currents; so a current flowing in a fluid produces a magnetic field, which then reacts on the fluid itself by means of the magnetohydrodynamic forces. In the Harwell machine Zeta, which was used to study technical problems of thermonuclear reactions, this effect acted so as to constrict the electric discharge on to the axis of the tube and thus keeps it away from the walls. This action was assisted by an extra magnetic field produced by a separate current flowing in metallic conductors outside the tube. Thus the hot plasma was contained by magnetohydro-dynamic forces and not at all by the material tube wall. In practical devices of the future magnetic forces may have to sustain plasma pressure of 60 atmospheres—a pressure for which a thick steel wall would normally be used! *See also* **Plasma Physics.**

Magnetosphere. The magnetic field of the earth

prevents the plasma of the solar wind from directly impinging on the earth's upper atmosphere and ionosphere. The cavity thus maintained within the solar wind is known as the magnetosphere. The tenuous plasma within this cavity is partly of solar and partly of terrestrial origin, from the solar wind and the ionosphere respectively. These plasmas are subject to large perturbations, known as magnetospheric storms, triggered by fluctuations within the solar wind. These storms generate intense auroral displays, magnetic field fluctuations at ground level, and often major disturbances of the upper atmosphere and ionosphere which may result in disruption of radio communications. The inner parts of the magnetosphere contain the Van Allen radiation belts (q.v.). On the sunward side the magnetosphere extends to between 12 and 20 earth radii.

However, on the side of the earth away from the sun it extends, like a comet tail, for many millions of km. Jupiter's large magnetic field produces a large magnetosphere, one of the largest features in our planetary system being as large as the Sun itself. The magnetic field of Mars vanished about 4 billion years ago.

Magnitude in astronomy is a measure of the apparent brightness of a star, which is inversely proportional to the square of its distance. A low number indicates a bright star, and a high one a faint star. The *absolute magnitude* is a measure of *real* brightness, *i.e.*, the brightness a star would have at a standard distance away of 10 parsecs (32·6 light years). The distance can be calculated if the apparent and absolute magnitudes are known. Another magnitude system used by astronomers is bolometric magnitude, which is a measure of the total radiation emitted by a star at all wavelengths. *See* **Light Year** and **Parsec**.

Magnum, equivalent to 2 bottles of champagne. A jeroboam is four.

Magpie, a well-known bird of the crow family, of glossy black and white plumage, famed for its intelligence and mischievous propensities. Now scientists have found that magpies are wary of shiny objects--contrary to folklore.

Magyars, the Hungarian race who came to eastern Europe from S.W. Asia and settled in Hungary in the 10th cent. Their language belongs to the Finno-Ugrian group.

Maidenhair Tree *or* **Ginkgo**. This tree takes its name from the shape of its leaves, which resemble those of the maidenhair fern. Widely cultivated in China and Japan. It is the only survivor of an order of gymnosperms which flourished in Mesozoic times. Botanically interesting because the male gametes are motile. It is the national tree of China and can survive for 1,000 years. Its DNA was decoded in 2016.

Makar. The national poet of Scotland. The current makar is Jackie Kay. Previous holders are Edwin Morgan and Liz Lochhead.

Mallard. *See under* **Duck**.

Malmaison, château at Rueil-Malmaison, a western suburb of Paris. It derives its name from having been inhabited in the 11th cent. by the Norman brigand Odon, and afterwards, according to the tradition, by evil spirits, exorcised by the monks of St. Denis. It was the residence of Napoleon and of the Empress Josephine after her divorce. She died there in 1814. In 1900 it was given to the nation.

Mammoth, extinct elephants of gigantic size. In 1799 the first perfectly preserved specimen was found in Siberia in a block of ice. It was in prehistoric times found in Britain and other parts of Europe, as well as in Asia and America. The extinction of the mammoth is now known to have been a gradual process, possibly aided by the replacement of nutritious herbs by grass. Scientists have uncovered the complete genome of the woolly mammoth. The age of mammoths can be worked out from their tusks.

Mammoth Cave of Kentucky, one of the largest known limestone caverns in the world, with subterranean passages at different levels, lakes and rivers (the Echo R. flows 110 m below the surface); stalactites and stalagmites abound.

Manatee, an aquatic mammal of the sea cow (Sirenia) order of mammals, averaging when full grown from 3-3·6 m in length, with shovelshaped tail, and forelimbs and nails which almost give the appearance of arms and hands. Gentle and trusting (and

very slow) they are under threat from humans. Protected in Florida. In spite of their ungainly aspect, they are linked to the legend of mermaids.

Mandarin, the name given to a powerful Chinese official, civil or military, under the old régime, whose rank was shown by the wearing of a button on the cap. Mandarin is also the official language of China, spoken by most of the 1·3 billion people.

Manga, term for a wide range of Japanese comics (graphic books).

Manganese, a metallic element, no. 25, symbol Mn, discovered by Scheele, 1774. It is white-grey, not very hard (it forms a hard alloy with carbon), brittle, and tarnishes when exposed to air. Its chief ore is pyrolusite (manganese dioxide). Steels containing manganese are very tough. Manganese added to glass makes it clear or violet-coloured.

Mangosteen, a tropical evergreen tree from Indonesia.

Mangroves provide a natural breakwater. Their tangled roots can live in salt water. Mangrove forests are highly endangered habitats because of warming seas. The largest in the world is found in the Sundarbans in India.

Maniple, eucharistic vestment worn over left arm.

Manna, a tree of the ash genus, *Fraxinus ornus*, growing in the South of Europe and in the East and exuding a sweet substance which is gathered, boiled and eaten.

Manometer, instrument used to measure gas pressure. Usually a 7-tube containing water or mercury, one end open to the atmosphere, the other to the gas whose pressure is to be measured. More sensitive for small pressures than the Bourdon gauge.

Mansion House, the official residence of the Lord Mayor of London, stands opposite to the Bank of England, and was erected in 1739–53 from the designs of George Dance.

Mantis. Large insects belonging to the same order as the locusts and grasshoppers. The manner in which the forelegs are held, as though in suppliance, has gained for these insects the common name of "praying mantis".

Manx, Celtic dialect (Manx Gaelic) of the Isle of Man. The last surviving native speaker died in 1974.

Maoris, the race living in New Zealand at the time it was first visited by Captain Cook in 1769. They are believed to have migrated from Polynesia about 1350. Up to 1871 they were frequently in arms against the European settlers but their high intelligence and stamina enabled them to adapt themselves and the New Zealand laws have encouraged equal citizenship. They now number over 630,000. In 1994 Maoris in the upper North Island were offered land and money in compensation for land seized unjustly in the 19th century.

Maple, trees native to the northern hemisphere. There are over 100 species. The sycamore is the best-known species growing in Britain. The sugar maple abounds in Canada and the eastern parts of the United States. The sugar is tapped by boring holes in the tree in February and March, and the juice that escapes is collected and evaporated. The maple-leaf is the Canadian national emblem.

Mappa Mundi, the world-famous medieval map of the world, now housed in Hereford Cathedral.

Mara. The giant guinea pig of Patagonia which hops like an antelope.

Marathon, first run by Pheidippides from Marathon to Athens in 490 B.C. to announce the Greek victory over the Persians. The modern marathon is 26 miles 385 yards.

Marble is limestone in its hardest and most crystalline form. There are many varieties—33 were used in the building of the Paris Opera House— but white is the purest and rarest. White marble was used by the ancient Greeks for their temples and statues. Among the famous marbles of Italy are the Carrara and Siena marbles. Devonshire and Derbyshire yield some beautiful marbles and Connemara furnishes a serpentine-marble.

March, the third month of the year, and the first of the old Roman Calendar. It was named after the god Mars, and was the *Hlyd* (storm) *monath* of the Anglo-Saxons.

Mardi Gras, the last day of the Carnival in Trinidad, New Orleans, Rio *etc*, (Shrove Tuesday).

Mariner's Compass. *See* **Compass.**

Marionettes are puppets moved by strings. They originated in the *Fantoccini* of the 15th cent. which had such a vogue in Italy. The English *Punch and Judy* is a version of Punchinello.

Marmoset, small monkeys confined to the New World. Very squirrel-like in appearance, with long bushy tails, and thick woolly fur, they are pretty little animals and the smallest of all monkeys. There are claws, not nails, on their digits, the big toe excepted.

Marquess *or* **Marquis,** title next in precedent to that of duke. The first English marquess was Rovery de Vere, Earl of Oxford, so honoured in 1385.

Mars, the fourth nearest planet to the sun. The enormous amount of new information from the pioneer visits to Mars, primarily by the US *Mariner* and *Viking* spacecraft, back in 1971 and 1976 respectively, revolutionised our understanding of the planet. These missions showed that the planet's surface displayed many contrasts—the ancient crated terrains glimpsed previously, enormous volcanos, far larger than any on earth, vast wastelands, particularly near the polar regions, scoured by wind-blown dust over many aeons, and most tantalising, in many regions water had set unmistakable marks.

We see the plains which have been subject to great deluges of rain in, probably, a number of different episodes over hundreds of millions of years. Other regions, extending over hundreds of km, show great gorges and canyons cut by catastrophic floods, when some natural dam has burst, releasing the pent-up waters of a gigantic lake or sea. This pictorial evidence, and more detailed information from the *Viking* spacecraft tell us that its climate was once quite different from that observed today. The atmosphere, if only for brief interludes, must have been much denser, and warmer, and rain must have been able to fall.

Mars today seems too cold and dry for water but there are polar ice caps, and the nature of the meteoric craters suggests that the surface is rock over ice and solid carbon dioxide. Evidence continues to mount that a deep ocean once covered a third of the Martian surface. The search for life carried out by *Viking* produced much new information, but no traces of organic compounds as evidence, or precursors, of life.

Mars has two small moons, Phobos and Deimos, each believed to be captured asteroids. Early findings from the Mars *Pathfinder* mission (which landed on Mars in 1997) suggest there was abundant water in the past and also that Mars may be much more like Earth than previously thought. In 2001 the *Odyssey* probe entered into Martian orbit after a 285-million mile journey from Earth. Its mission was to scour the planet for signs of life. Its evidence of underground ice reservoirs at the South Pole was subsequently confirmed after 2003 by Europe's *Mars Express*. Mars clearly has water. It may even have been the 'Blue Planet' three billion years ago.

The ambitious Mars Science Laboratory (popularly known as Curiosity) was launched in October 2011. After 36 weeks, flying 352 million miles, it landed in August 2012. Curiosity is the largest extraterrestrial rover ever built. It is designed to search for signs of past life and has already found proof of early rivers on Mars. It has also detected burps of methane, maybe produced by bacteria. In 2015, streaks of salty water were detected flowing in the summer seasons. The Maven project, to study the planet's upper atmosphere, went into orbit in 2014.

Several new scientific projects (such as Orion) are planned to further our knowledge of the planet. China plans a mission in 2020. Manned missions in the 2030s are being planned by NASA.

Marseillaise, the French national hymn, written and composed by Rouget de L'Isle, a French engineer officer, who was inspired to write it in 1792 to encourage the Strasburg conscripts. It immediately became popular, and received its name because it was sung by the Marseillaise troops while marching into Paris.

Marshalsea, a former prison in Southwark, London, closed 1849. It existed as early as Edward III's time and was used as a jail for royal servants convicted of offences. In its later days it became a debtors' prison. Dickens described it in *Little Dorrit.*

Marsupials, members of the order of pouched mammals. Except for the opossums of America, all marsupials occur in Australasia, and include kangaroos, wallabies and wombats. Scientists now believe they first originated in China.

Marten, carnivorous animals of the weasel family; one species (the Pine Marten) was once common in Britain. Now it is returning in remoter areas. Most famous for their fur are the Siberian Sable

and the American Marten.

Martial Arts, a term for such forms of combat as jujitsu, judo, kendo, kenjutsu and karate (which uses punches, knees and kicks to take out a foe).

Martin, a well-known bird-visitor to Britain. It belongs to the swallow family, and the two species that spend their summers here are the house-martin, which makes its nest of mud under the eaves of houses, and the sand martin, which builds in sandy banks.

Martinmas *or* **St. Martin's Day,** falls on 11 November, and is one of the Scottish quarter days. St. Martin was a very popular Saint with our ancestors. It was the important date when "Martlemas Beef" was dried in the chimney, and enough bacon and mutton cured to last until the spring. This diet of dried meat without vegetables caused scurvy. A late spell of fine weather at Martinmas is called St. Martin's Summer.

Martyrs. People who suffer death in testimony to their faith. Stephen (Acts 6; 7) was the first Christian martyr in 39. Historical tradition maintains that both St. Peter and St. Paul were martyred in Rome.

Mason-Dixon Line, the boundary line between Pennsylvania and Maryland, for long a source of dispute, drawn up by two English surveyors, Charles Mason and Jeremiah Dixon, between 1763 and 1767. It came to designate the boundary dividing the slave states from the free states of America, and is still used in distinguishing the "North" from the "South".

Masques were light dramatic compositions set to music and performed on special occasions. One famous example is Milton's "Comus", which was given at Ludlow Castle in 1634.

Mass, the service in the Roman Catholic Church defined as the Propitiary Sacrifice of Calvary, reoffered by the Priest acting *in persona Christi.* It was first celebrated in Latin in the 4th cent., and was introduced into England in the 7th cent. The use of a vernacular language was sanctioned by the 2nd Vatican Council (1965).

Mass Spectrograph, an instrument for separating isotopes. It works by sorting electrified particles according to their masses; the particles stream through a magnetic and possibly an electric field, and the lightest particles undergo the greatest deflection. *See* **Spectrograph.**

Mast, a long round piece of timber or tubular steel or iron, standing upright in a vessel, and supporting the yards, sails and rigging in general. The earliest ships had only one mast, carrying a simple sail. The number increased until there were 4 or 5, or even more. Above the lower mast of a sailing-ship comes the topmast, and above that, the topgallantmast and royalmast.

The position of each mast is indicated by a prefix, as foremast, foreroyalmast, mainmast, *etc.* The foremast is in the fore of the ship, the mainmast in the centre and the mizzen nearest the stern. In large vessels nowadays the mast does not extend to the keel, as it formerly did, but is usually stopped at the second deck.

Master of the Revels a former Court official upon whom devolved the arrangement of Court festivities. The office is at least as old as the time of Edward III. By 1737 it seems to have died.

Master of the Rolls, one of the senior English judges, since 1881 a judge of the Court of Appeal only. He has charge of the rolls or records of Chancery and ranks next to the Lord Chancellor and Lord Chief Justice.

Mastodon, an extinct order of quadruped closely resembling the elephant, but larger.

Materials Science is a blend of science and technology; it is the use of scientific research methods to study and improve materials for practical use.

Mathematics is a body of knowledge expressed in a language of symbols. *Pure* mathematics studies the propositions that can be deduced in this language by applying definite rules of reasoning to sets of axioms. In *Applied* mathematics, the mathematical language is used, often with great effect, to discuss problems of the real world, such as mechanics, statistics and science generally.

Matins, the first of the services of the day in the Roman Catholic Church and Morning Prayer in the Anglican Church. The daily service in the Roman breviary (*q.v.*) used to consist of eight offices or "hours", fixed by canon, for prayer and devotion but since the second Vatican Council the structure has been simplified. Formerly, Matins was recited or sung at midnight, Lauds at sunrise,

Prime at 6 a.m., Terce at 9 a.m., Sext at midday, Nones at 3 p.m., Vespers at sunset and Compline before retiring for the night. Lauds are now commonly joined to Matins.

Matrix, a rectangular array of numbers considered as a single mathematical object. There are special rules for multiplying and adding matrices and they are often used in mathematics, physics and elsewhere to simplify calculations and as a notational device.

Maundy Thursday, the day before Good Friday, commemorates the Last Supper. "Maundy" derives from Christ's command (mandatum) to his disciples on that day to love one another. For many centuries the sovereigns of England, through their almoners, have distributed money, food and clothing to "as many old men and as many old women as the Sovereign is years of age". This ceremony is still observed, maundy coins being struck from standard silver.

Mausoleum, a special place of sepulture, generally for the reception of the remains of members of a royal or other family of distinction. The name is derived from the tomb of King Mausolus at Halicarnassus, erected 352 B.C., and forming one of the seven wonders of the ancient world. Another mausoleum is that of Hadrian in Rome.

Mauve, a colouring matter produced from lichens by Dr. Stenhouse in 1848, but in 1856 obtained from aniline by William Perkin (1838–1907), who gave it the name Mauveen. This was the first synthetic organic dyestuff ever to be produced, which led to the building up of the great synthetic dyestuffs industry (which Germany dominated before the first world war).

May, the fifth month of the year, but the third of the ancient Roman calendar. Supposed to be named after Maia, the mother of Mercury, to whom sacrifices were offered on the first day of this month. In England May Day was once the occasion of many festivities, including the crowning of the May Queen.

Maya, a civilisation centred on Guatemala, Belize, Honduras *etc.* which peaked *c.* A.D. 300–900. The Copan Ruins, the birthplace of the great Mayan civilisation, is a UNESCO World Heritage Site. A prolonged drought may have destroyed its empire. Hundreds of ancient Mayan cities have been located. The Mayan Calendar began in 3,114 B.C..

May Fly. *See* Ephemeptera.

Mazarin Bible, an edition of the Latin Vulgate, acknowledged as the masterpiece of the Gutenberg press (1456). It was the first book completely printed from movable types. The first copy to capture the attention of scholars was found in the library of Cardinal Mazarin, in Paris. Also called the Gutenberg or the 42-line Bible.

Maze. *See* Labyrinth.

Mead, a fermented honey drink. Its earliest orgins have been traced to *c.* 7,000 B.C. in China. It features prominently in Norse mythology. Often drunk at weddings, hence the term honeymoon

Mean. In statistics and mathematics generally understood to be the arithmetic mean. The geometric mean between two quantities is the square root of their product. *See* **Average.**

Mechanical Equivalent of Heat. *See* **Joule.**

Medals, as decorations for military service, were first issued in this country by Charles I, who ordered medals for gallantry to be distributed to certain soldiers in 1643. Medals were also issued to officers and men who were victorious against the Dutch fleet in 1653. After Lord Howe's victory in 1794 a naval medal was instituted. Medals were also struck for the victory of Waterloo and for most later wars.

The Victoria Cross, a special reward for personal gallantry, was instituted in 1856. The George Cross for gallantry instituted in 1940 ranks next to the Victoria Cross. The Military Cross was instituted in 1914. The first awards of the new Elizabeth Cross were made in 2009.

Meerkat. The small mongoose of southern Africa. A group is known as a mob.

Megalith, a prehistoric monument, consisting of a large single stone or a group of such stones, in a circle as at Stonehenge or in burial chambers as at New Grange, Ireland.

Meiosis, special type of cell division by which the gametes or sex cells are generated, resulting in the sperm or ovum receiving only half the number of chromosomes found in a somatic cell. *See* **Mitosis.**

Mela, the Sanskrit term for a gathering or community festival. In India the Hindu Maha Kumbh Mela in 2001 drew 70 million pilgrims (the largest human gathering in history). It takes place every 12 years.

Mendicant Friars, certain religious orders which spread over Europe in the 13th cent., and comprised the Franciscans, Dominicans, Augustines and Carmelites. Originally they depended entirely on alms.

Mercator's Projection, a method of indicating meridians and parallels of latitudes on maps, introduced by Mercator in the 16th cent., and still universally used in navigators' charts.

Mercury, the second smallest of the planets (*c.* one-twentieth of the earth's mass) is the closest to the sun at little more than one-third of the earth's average distance. It appears to resemble the earth in its interior and has about the same density but its surface resembles the moon and is heavily cratered. Its dark surface may be the result of carbon-rich material dropped by passing comets.

Mercury was visited by Mariner 10 which passed within a few hundred kilometres back in March 1974 and which relayed pictures on the two following passes in September 1974 and March 1975 before control of its altitude was lost. It nevertheless continued to revisit Mercury every 176 days (two mercurian years). Mariner 10 was guided to Mercury by the gravitational field of Venus before it became a satellite of the smallest planet. The relayed pictures showed that the planet has an approximately 59-day rotation period exactly two thirds of its orbital period of 88 days. This relationship means that unlike on earth the seasonal variations are with longitude not latitude. Surface temperatures vary from 400°C to −200°C and there is virtually no atmosphere except a thin envelope of helium gas. Mercury has a huge iron core, making the planet incredibly dense. Mercury also possesses the wildest swings in temperature in the solar system (from 427°C to −173°C).

Mariner 10 measured a small magnetic field at the surface about 1% of the earth's but much stronger than for Venus or Mars. There are no moons.

The *Messenger* spacecraft, launched in 2004, is now orbiting Mercury following its arrival in 2011 (it achieved its first fly-by in 2008). It went on to take images of the "dark side" of Mercury never before seen in detail. *Messenger* revealed evidence of significant volcanic activity on the planet before crashing into Mercury in 2015.

The BepiColombo mission to Mercury was launched in 2013. It is due to arrive in 2019.

Mercury *or* **Quicksilver,** element no. 80, symbol Hg (Latin *hydrargyrum*) is one of the oldest- known metals, whose chief ore is the sulphide, cinnabar, found in certain parts of Spain, China, Japan and South America. It is liquid at ordinary temperature and is used in the construction of barometers and thermometers. Alloys of mercury are called amalgams. It is also of great value in medicine. The metal is used in the mercury-vapour (or "sunlight") lamp, since the vapour gives a bright yellow-white glow in an electric discharge.

Meridian, an imaginary circle extending through the North and South Poles and any given place. When the sun is at its midday height at any place it is "on the meridian"; hence the terms ante-meridian (a.m.) and post-meridian (p.m.). *See also* **Greenwich Mean Time.**

Merino Sheep were imported into England from Spain in 1788 and had great influence in improving native breeds regarding wool. They produce the finest wool.

Merit, Order of, founded by King Edward VII in 1902 as a special distinction for eminent men and women without conferring a knighthood upon them. The Order has twenty-four British companions in addition to foreign honorary members limited in number, as the choice of members is, by the Sovereign's pleasure. Lord Kelvin was the founder companion. Florence Nightingale (1907), Professor Dorothy Hodgkin (1965), Dame Veronica Wedgwood (1969), Mother Theresa of Calcutta (honorary member, 1983), Margaret Thatcher (1990) and Betty Boothroyd (2005) are among the few women to have received this decoration. Nelson Mandela was made an honorary member in 1995. A recent recipient is David Hockney (2012).

Merk. The silver currency used in 16th and 17th century Scotland.

Mesons (from Greek *meso* = middle). One of the four groups of sub-atomic particle given by the Standard Model: gauge bosons (the most famous of which is the photon), the leptons (very light particles, including the electron), the mesons and the baryons. The latter two groups (together termed hadrons) are not truly fundamental, being made up of different combinations of quarks (three quarks forming a baryon, two a meson). The mesons are characterised by their instability; their life expectancy does not exceed 5×10^{-8} seconds. Examples of the meson group are the pions, the kaons, the charmed D's, the upsilon particle and the bottom B's.

Mesozoic. The geological era, including the Triassic, Jurassic and Cretaceous rocks.

Metamorphic Rocks are such geological deposits as have undergone alterations of structure and mineral reorganisation. The most active agents in producing these metamorphic changes are heat, water and pressure.

Metamorphosis, period of development from egg to adult, during which the animals have different forms, as found, *e.g.*, in the life histories of frogs.

Meteorites are small bodies, asteroids, or fragments of asteroids, which survive their fiery passage through the earth's atmosphere and hit the ground. The present surfaces of the moon, Mars and Mercury tell us that all the planets have been subjected since their formation to bombardment by meteorites. Though some large craters are still to be found on the earth, most have disappeared due to extensive weathering over thousands of millions of years. In some meteorites iron and nickel are the chief metals (siderites), others are like rock (aerolites). The iron meteorites are more common amongst those which have been preserved, but falls of rock-like meteorites occur more frequently. At L'Aigle in France in 1803 from 2000 to 3000 meteorite stones fell; this convinced scientists that meteorites really came from outside our atmosphere.

The largest meteorite stone actually known to have fallen to earth is one which descended in Emmott County, Iowa, in 1870, weighing 197 kg. A meteorite weighing no less than 37 tonnes found in Greenland is now in New York.

On 30 June 1908, an enormous object fell in Siberia in a sparsely-inhabited region. A hot blast destoyed all trees within a radius of about 8–16 km. There is still controversy about the Siberian meteorite, whether it was an asteroid or the nucleus of a small comet. *See* **Asteroid**.

Meteoroid, the collective term for meteoritic material found in the solar system. Meteoroids are normally produced by the decay of short-period comets and the collisional fragmentation of asteroids. When meteoroids fall into the Earth's atmosphere they burn up producing a meteor. *See* **Asteroid**.

Meteorology, the science of the atmosphere considered as a heat engine. Deals with weather, climate, optical phenomena, atmospheric electricity, physical processes such as radiation and precipitation, the dynamics and structure of cyclones, anticyclones, *etc.* Meteorological observing stations are in operation all over the world.

Instruments now carried by earth satellites (*e.g.*, *Tiros*, *Nimbus*) outside the atmosphere can make systematic observations on a worldwide basis of the atmosphere. A new generation of weather satellites (Meteosat Second Generation, MSG) was launched in 2002.

Meteors or more commonly, "shooting stars", are small objects which enter the upper atmosphere to burn up in a bright streak of light. Their origin is mainly in the dust particles ejected in large quantities from comets. Some, particularly the larger and more brilliant ones, called fireballs, are debris of asteroids. Those which reach the earth's surface are called meteorites (*q.v.*).

Methane. The simplest hydrocarbon, compounded of one carbon atom and four hydrogen atoms. This gas occurs over marshes and swamps, where it is liberated in the decay of vegetable matter. It is the main constituent of natural gas, and also occurs in coal-mines, where it is called "fire-damp" because of the explosive character of its mixture with air.

Formerly this natural gas was removed from the coal seams and ran to waste; now in many countries it has commercial uses.

Methane hydrate (or fire ice) has now been extracted from frozen deposits under the sea.

Methylated Spirit, a mixture of 90 parts by volume ethyl alcohol, $9\frac{1}{2}$ parts wood naphtha (methyl alcohol), $\frac{1}{2}$ part crude pyridine, together with small amounts of petroleum oil and methyl violet dye. Industrial methylated spirit consists of a mixture of 95 parts by volume ethyl alcohol and 5 parts wood naphtha. It is used as a solvent and a fuel.

Metre (1), the rhythmical pattern of Verse. (2), unit of length in the metric system; since 1983 has been redefined as "the length of the path travelled by light in vacuum during a time interval of 1/299 792 458 of a second". This definition replaces that adopted in 1960 which used the wavelength of the orange-red line of krypton-86. Before that the "international prototype metre" was the distance between marks on the platinum-iridium bar placed at Sèvres in 1889.

Metric System, the system of weights and measures based on the gram and the metre, smaller and larger units being decimals and multiples of the primary units respectively. A decimal currency was adopted in France in 1795 and the metric system of weights and measures in 1799. (In that year the quadrant of the earth was surveyed and the standard metre adopted.) Since then the metric system has been adopted in most of the continental countries and is used universally in scientific work.

In Britain, it was not until 1965 that the Government encouraged the adoption of the metric system of weights and measures. The changeover to decimal coinage was made in 1971; the system of weights and measures in industry is now mainly metric and "Metrication Day" for the ordinary shopper came on 1 October 1995. The final changeover to the metric system came on 31 December 2009. *See* **T58–60** for **SI** units.

Mica. The mica of commerce is a nearly transparent mineral, which has great heat-resisting power, and can be split into thin plates. The most important micas are muscovite (potassium mica), the commoner variety, phlogopite (magnesium mica) and biotite (the magnesium and iron mica).

Michael, St., and George, St., an order of knighthood originally founded for the Ionian Isles and Malta in 1818, and reorganised in 1869 to admit Crown servants connected with the Colonies.

Michaelmas Day, the festival day of St. Michael and All Angels, 29 September. Goose fairs were held at this time and goose was eaten.

Microbe, a term proposed by Sédillot in 1878 to denote any microscopic organism, vegetable or animal, or found on the borderland between the two great natural kingdoms. The term is commonly used, but not by scientists.

Microelectronics, a rapidly expanding sub-field of electronics. It reduces entire electronic circuits to minute size and embeds them in tiny chips of solid material. These are then called integrated circuits. A circuit consisting of, say, a dozen transistors and fifty resistors can be built into a small piece of semiconductor (*q.v.*) measuring not more than a couple of millimetres in any direction. Hundreds of these circuits can be made simultaneously in penny-size wafers of silicon about one-hundredth of an inch thick. There are great advantages in cheapness, reliability, robustness and speed of electronic performance. The small size is in itself an advantage in space vehicles and medical instruments and computing.

Micrometer, an instrument for measuring minute distances; usually attached to the eye-pieces of a microscope or telescope, and consisting of two very fine hairs or wires stretched across the field of view, one fixed, the other movable. It was invented by William Gascoigne in the 17th cent. and improved by later inventors. Sir Joseph Whitworth made one in 1858 designed to measure the millionth part of an inch.

Micro-organisms, the collective term applied to several types of organism, the most important of which are fungi, viruses, bacteria and protozoa. It is a classification of convenience in biological studies. These organisms are generally simple in their environmental requirements. This makes them very suitable for modern biological research. Much of the information on the nature of the genetic code was obtained from these organisms.

Microphone, device for converting the acoustic energy of sound waves into waves of electrical tiny, used in sound amplifying systems. Developed independently by Edison (1877) and Hughes (1878).

Microscope, invented about 1590 by Janssen, and improved by Galileo, Fontana and others, is an instrument which by a lens system magnifies tiny objects. Microscopes are simple, compound and binocular. *See also* **Electron Microscope.**

Mid-Atlantic Ridge. The world's largest mountain range, stretching 10,000 miles along the ocean floor. It is home to a deep-sea wonderland.

Midge, a biting insect, the scourge of the Scottish Highlands. Mild winters and warm wet summers have seen them spread to the rest of Britain.

Midrash, name given to the homiletical interpretation of some of the Hebrew Scriptures in which allegory and legendary illustration were freely used. Compiled by Jewish rabbis from *c.* A.D. 200.

Midsummer's Day. The halfway point in the calendar year (24 June) and one of the old Quarter Days. Not to be confused with the summer solstice.

Milky Way. *See* **Galaxy.**

Millennium, a period of a thousand years. The term is specifically used of the period of a thousand years during which, according to Rev. xx. 1–5, Christ will reign in person on earth. *See also* **Millennarianism, J33.**

Millipede. Arthropods **(Section T)** allied to the centipedes, from which they differ in having two pairs of legs to each body segment (except the first three) instead of one pair. Worm-like in shape but with a pair of antennae on the head, they can do much harm to garden plants, unlike centipedes which are beneficial. A 420 million-year-old millipede fossil found in Scotland provides evidence it was the earliest creature known to have lived on dry land. Despite their name, they do not have a thousand legs.

Millstone-Grit, a series of grits and sandstones of deltaic origin underlying the coal measures of the Carboniferous system and attaining in England a thickness in parts of 1,525 m. It is from this rock that millstones were made.

Mimicry, protective similarity of an animal to another animal or to inanimate objects. Examples of the former are the hover flies, which mimic wasps and bees; of the latter, leaf insects, stick insects and caterpillars that look like dead twigs.

Minimum Wage. *See* **National Living Wage.**

Mink. Semi-aquatic mammals closely related to polecats. There is one American species and one European. The fur, which varies from light to dark brown, is soft and thick, and is among the most valuable of commercial furs. They are now well-established in the wild in the UK. Mink usually produce a litter of up to 10 kits. They live in holes in riverbanks.

Minnesingers were minstrel poets of Germany who, during the 12th and 13th cent., composed and sang verses of heroism and love. They were of knightly rank, like the French troubadours.

Minnow, a small fresh-water fish of the carp family, abounding in all the waters of Europe; it has a mottled back and silvery belly, and forms a popular bait for trout.

Minstrels were originally specially appointed instrumentalists and singers—pipers, harpers and gleemen—engaged by barons and manorial lords to amuse their tenants. Later, minstrels assumed nomadic habits, made their way into the houses of the great and were generally welcome. By Elizabeth's time, however, they were too numerous, and classed as vagabonds. Minstrels' galleries can be found in some parish churches.

Miracle Plays, medieval verse plays, popular in England in the 15th cent., usually religious.

Mirage, an optical illusion caused by unequal temperatures in different layers of the atmosphere near the earth's surface. These temperature variations alter the refracting power of the air and cause light rays to be curved, making the air act as a huge distorting lens. This can happen at sea, in deserts and elsewhere and various types of mirage are known. A common kind in deserts curves light from the sky so that it appears to come from the ground, deceiving the observer into thinking that the sky is reflected in a lake of water.

Mishna, the first part of the Talmud, setting forth the "Oral Law" of the Jews.

Missal, the name of the mass-book of the Roman Church compiled 492–96 by Pope Gelasius I. The missal used until modern times was sanctioned by the Council of Trent, 1546–63, but the current missal was authorised by Pope Paul VI in 1969 after the Second Vatican Council. In the Anglican Communion the Book of Common Prayer superseded the Missal in 1549.

Mistle Thrush receives its name from its partiality to the mistletoe-berry. Larger than the songthrush, with spotted breast not speckled.

Mistletoe, a parasitic evergreen with white berries used as a decoration at Christmas-time. The familiar mistletoe of Europe is the *Viscum album,* which grows on the boughs of lime, willow, apple, poplar, maple, ash, hawthorn but seldom on oak-trees. It was sacred to the Druids, and in Norse mythology it was a mistletoe dart that killed the god Baldur. Mistletoe is spreading fast in the UK, helped by the blackcap warbler wintering here.

Mistral, a cold, dry, northerly wind peculiar to the French coast of the Mediterranean.

Mitosis, cell division whereby each daughter cell receives the same number of chromosomes as the parent cell. When the gametes (sex cells) are formed a special type of division occurs (meiosis) in which the number of chromosomes is halved.

Mitre, the twofold pointed head-dress of bishops and certain abbots of the Church.

Moa, the name for several species of ostrich-like extinct birds related to the New Zealand kiwi. The largest species, *Diornis maximus,* stood 2·6 m high, while the smallest, *Anomalopteryx parva,* was nearer the size of a turkey. This wingless bird became extinct because of hunting by the Maoris from whom the name comes.

Moderator, a material used to slow down neutrons in an atomic pile. Examples are pure graphite and heavy water. *See* **Nuclear Reactors.**

Mohole Project, a scheme to bore through the earth's crust to take samples of the mantle rocks beneath. The project, however, was cancelled in 1966 on account of the escalating cost.

The boundary between the earth's crustal and mantle rocks is known as the Mohorovičic Discontinuity, or Moho. The technology of deep sea drilling came from this project.

Molasses, sugar-cane juice in its uncrystallised form after boiling. The crystallised part is the raw sugar. Used to make rum.

Mole, a small burrowing animal with long, sensitive nose, about the size of a small rat, with short legs and forefeet armed with strong claws for digging in the earth. Their subterranean dwellings are of curiously ingenious construction, and they do not often leave them except to make raids on mice, frogs, snails, *etc.* The earthworm is the mole's chief item of food.

Not to be confused with the vole which has a blunt nose. Warm, wet weather has caused mole numbers in the UK to increase.

Mole, or gram molecular weight.

Molecular Anthropology, the relatively new science of the study of the DNA of indigenous peoples to throw new light on human evolution.

Molecular Biology, a rapidly expanding branch of science mainly concerned with cell structure and function at a molecular level, in particular with genes and enzymes and the interaction between the two. Research work in Britain led to the unravelling of the structure of DNA, the hereditary substance of the genes and the nature of the genetic code. *See* **Section T.**

Molecule. A group of atoms held together by chemical forces. *See* **Section T,** *also* **Macro-molecule.**

Molybdenum, element no. 42, symbol Mo, a fairly hard white metal with properties resembling those of chromium. Its commonest ore is the sulphide, molybdenite. The chief use of the metals is in the manufacture of alloy steels.

Monazite, a cerium mineral containing some thorium. Occurs as grains, often as sand ("monazite sands"), derived from granites.

Monday, the second day of the week, called by the Anglo-Saxons *Monandaeg* (moon-day).

Mongoose, species of mammals related to the civets, feeding on vermin and reptiles. These animals, which have long tails and short legs, occur in Africa and Asia (especially India). The biggest mongoose is the Egyptian ichneumon, introduced into the West Indies because of its ability to kill large poisonous snakes.

Monitor, family of lizards resembling dragons. There are *c.* 30 species widely distributed over the tropics. The largest is the komodo dragon whose saliva contains deadly bacteria. This carnivorous animal kills its prey with venom, not bacteria-filled bites, as previously thought. The komodo dragon is now an endangered species. Komodo dragons are the largest lizards. They can grow to 3 m (10 ft) and weigh over 90 kg (200 lbs). They have an incredible sense of smell.

Monkey Nut. *See* **Peanut.**

Monsoons, regular persistent winds which blow at certain seasons in middle latitudes, mainly in South and East Asia. Their occurrence is related to the great changes of pressure which take place between summer and winter over the land mass. In India the south-west monsoon (June–October) is moisture-laden from its long passage over the sea and in the higher regions, especially, there is heavy rainfall. Sudden reversal of the wind results in the cold north-east monsoon (October–March) which is dry on account of the shelter afforded by the mountain ranges to the north. Frequently the term "monsoon" is applied to denote the associated rainfall, not the actual winds. The word monsoon comes from the Arabic *mawsim*.

Month, the 12th part of the calendar year. A lunar month is the interval of new moon to new moon or full moon to full moon; mean length, 29 days, 12 hours, 44 minutes, 2·87 seconds. A sidereal month represents the time of the moon's revolution from a given star back to the same again, 27 days, 7 hours, 43 minutes, 11·5 seconds. In English law, since 1926, a month means a calendar month.

Monument of London, a 202 ft (61·6 m) column, overlooking Billingsgate, designed by Wren and erected (1671–77) to mark the starting-point of the Great Fire of London (1666). The original inscription upon it ascribed the fire to "the treachery and malice of the popish faction", which stood until 1831, when the words were erased as objectionable. The black marble staircase has 345 steps (311 to the balcony).

Moon, the earth's satellite, 3,475 km in diameter and 384,400 km distant from the earth. It rotates in the same time as it revolves round the earth (27 days 7 hours 43 minutes), so that the same face is always presented to the earth. The lunar surface is pockmarked with innumerable collisions with solid particles of all sizes.

Unlike the earth, it is unprotected by any atmosphere and for aeons of time it has been exposed to every kind of cosmic influence, including the parching effect of solar radiation. All moonlight derives from the sun but on the whole it is a pretty poor reflector. The exploration of the moon by means of rockets began in 1959 when the Russian *Luna 2* crashed on the plains of the *Mare Imbrium*. 21 July 1969 will be remembered as the date of the *Apollo* triumphs when man first set foot on the moon.

The samples of lunar rock and dust brought back to earth were closely studied by lunar scientists. Samples date back further than any found on Earth as yet. The most famous, known as the Genesis Rock, is 4,100 million years old. Scientists believe ice may exist in a deep crater near the lunar south pole. The existence of water was confirmed by the *Lunar Prospector* probe in 1998, the first moonshot for 25 years and new estimates in 2011 suggest the Moon contains 100 times more water than previously thought. The Hermite crater, near the moon's north pole, is the coldest known place in the solar system (−238°C).

Recently, scientists have calculated the age of the moon as 4·5 billion years (*i.e. c.* 30 million years after Earth's formation). Scientists believe our Moon was spun off from Earth after a giant collision. In 2018 China plans to land a probe on the dark side of the Moon.

Moonbow. A phenomenon that occurs when a full moon shines during rain.

Moorhen, a widely distributed bird of the rail family, a common resident in the British Isles. The adult is blackish with white under tail coverts, a white line on the flanks and a yellowtipped bill. The frontal shield and the base of the bill are vermilion. It bobs its head, flirts its tail and dives well. The nest is usually placed close to the water's edge or on an overhanging branch. In feeding the young the parents are sometimes helped by their offspring of a previous brood of the season. In N. America it is known as the Florida Gallinule.

Moors, the name given to the Muslims who live in N.W. Africa and to those who once lived in Spain. In 711 Moorish Arabs invaded Spain and spread beyond the Pyrenees into France, where they were driven back by the end of the century. Spain, however, remained virtually under Moorish domination until the 11th cent. and during that period was the most civilised and prosperous part of Western Europe.

In the arts and sciences the impact of Moorish culture was profound and lasting. Examples of the brilliant splendour of Moorish architecture are still to be seen in Toledo, Córdoba, Seville and Granada. During the long struggle for the Christian reconquest thousands were killed and expelled, and in 1492 Granada, their last remaining kingdom, was forced to surrender.

They were virtually exterminated by the Inquisition, and the last were expelled in 1609.

Moose, the largest members of the deer family. The N. American Moose stands up to 2·4 m high, and has huge palmate antlers, but it is declining fast. There is another New World species, occurring in Alaska. The European species is known as the elk.

Morse Alphabet, a system of dots and dashes intended to be used in combination with the indicator in telegraphy; but usually read by sound, the receiving operator writing down the words in the system as transmitted. This system of signals was invented by the American inventor and artist Samuel Finley Breese Morse (1791–1872) of Charlestown, Massachusetts. The Morse Code was replaced on 31 December 1997 by more advanced technology.

Mosque, a house or any open space of prayer for Muslims. The mosque has many functions—social and educational as well as religious. Britain now has over 1,600 mosques and about 2,500 imams.

Mosquito, small two-winged flies with long legs and slender body. Their larvae are aquatic. Only females of some species are blood-suckers, and thus come to transmit the blood parasites which cause malaria and dengue fever, for example. There are 32 recorded species. Diseases carried by mosquitos kill 250,000 people a month globally. Global warming is enabling mosquitos to spread into new areas, such as Europe, bringing tropical diseases. Genetically-modified mosquitos are being bred to destroy malaria and new repellents are being used. *See* **DDT** *and* **Gammexane.**

Mosses. With liverworts, mosses comprise an important group of relatively simple non-vascular land plants, the bryophytes (**Section T**). They are usually small plants, the largest between 30–70 cm high, having been recorded in the Southern Hemisphere. Mosses rarely occur singly, but usually form cushions or small colonies on moist soil, bark, wood, rock or walls. The genus *sphagnum* known as "peat" or "bog moss" is of commercial value in horticulture. In Lancashire and Cheshire lowland moors in which sphagnum is common are known as "mosses". Reindeer moss is a lichen and Spanish moss a seed plant.

Moths, of the insect order, *Lepidoptera*, differing from butterflies which have clubbed antennae, in having feathery, sometimes thin, pointed antennae, rarely clubbed. Most are nocturnal, and the pupae are usually brown and enclosed in a cocoon unlike those of the butterfly, which are usually naked. There are over 2,500 species in Britain, but many of these beautiful insects have been in decline in recent years. (*e.g.* the garden tiger). The Atlas moth is the largest in the world with a wing span the size of a dinner plate. In Britain moths are attracting much interest. *See also* **Lepidoptera.**

Motion, Laws of. According to Newton: (1) A body continues in its state of rest or uniform motion in a straight line except in so far as it is compelled by external forces to change that state. (2) Rate of change of momentum is proportional to the applied force, and takes place in the direction in which the force acts. (3) To every action there is an equal and opposite reaction. These laws are the basis of almost all engineering and everyday mechanics. Corrections to them have been made by relativity and the quantum theory. *See* **Section T.**

Mule, a cross between a male ass and a horse mare; a hinny is a cross between an ass mare and a horse stallion. Also the name of the spinning machine invented by Crompton in 1779 which combined the principle of Hargreaves' spinning jenny with the machine invented by Arkwright.

Mummification, (the preservation of dead bodies) was

famously carried out extensively in ancient Egypt and Peru. The custom was also widespread in ancient Britain.

Musk Deer, a small deer of the Himalayas, standing about 51 cm high. It is grey in colour, slightly brindled, and carries a small pouch in the abdominal region, containing what is commercially known as musk. The active constituent of musk, muscone, is now made synthetically.

Mutton Bird, an Australian name of controversial origin for a shearwater or petrel, *e.g.*, the Short-tailed and Sooty Shearwaters and the Great-winged, Kermadec, and White-headed Petrels. The young are taken by hand for human food. Also known as the titi in New Zealand.

Myrrh, a resinous substance obtained from a tree of the natural order *Amyridaceae*, growing plentifully in Ethiopia and Arabia. Its use for embalming, medical and aromatic purposes may be traced back to the most ancient times.

Mysteries, Greek, secret mystic ceremonies of the ancient Greeks, religious drama accompanied by dancing, the most well known being the Eleusinian and Orphic ceremonies.

Mystery Plays were medieval religious dramas performed at great ecclesiastical festivals, particularly in France and Bavaria, staging the Nativity, Passion and Resurrection stories.

N

Nadir, one of the two poles of the horizon, the other being the zenith. The nadir is the pole vertically below the observer's feet.

Nanotechnology. The science of working with tiny things—*e.g.* atoms and molecules. It may well revolutionise electronics, medicine *etc.*

Naphtha, a liquid combustible believed to have been one of the ingredients of "Greek fire". Naphtha is a light, highly inflammable oil obtained by distilling petroleum, shale oil, or coal tar. The petroleum naphtha consists of a mixture of paraffins; that from shale contains olefines as well as paraffins. Coal-tar naphtha contains xylol.

Naphthalene is an aromatic hydrocarbon; it is obtained from coal tar, and its derivatives are much used in the manufactures of colours for dyers and printers. "Moth balls" are made of naphthalene.

Naqba (Catastrophe), the Palestinian term for the expulsion of Arabs from their traditional homeland when the State of Israel was created in 1948.

Nardus, a genus of coarse grasses, growing on bleak upland heaths and hill slopes. *Nardus stricta*, known as "mat-weed", is a British species.

Narghile, an oriental tobacco pipe so constructed that smoke passes through water and up a long flexible tube before reaching lips of the smoker.

NASA, the United States government agency which carries out research into spaceflight and aeronautics. NASA was founded in 1958.

National Anthem. The national anthem of the United Kingdom, "God save the King (Queen)", probably dates from the late-17th cent, to mid-18th cent. It was sung in 1745, the year of the landing of the Young Pretender. It had no one composer and was probably a recasting of folk-tunes and plainsong. Resemblances can be traced in pieces by Purcell and John Bull. There are now calls for a specific English national anthem.

National Archives, formerly the Public Record Office and previously in Chancery Lane, London. It is now an executive agency of the Ministry of Justice. The National Archives are where the Public Records of England are preserved, including Domesday Book. These records are all now in Kew.

Modern records are subject to at least a 30-year restriction on access. Some records may be closed for 100 years. A recent proposal called for the halving from 30 to 15 years of current rules of access. A phased reduction to 20 years is now being implemented.

National Curriculum. The Education Reform Act (1988) originally provided for a national curriculum in state schools in England and Wales with three *core subjects* – maths, English and science – and also seven *foundation subjects* – history, geography, technology, music, art, physical education, and a modern language.

In 1995 the compulsory curriculum was reduced (history and geography were no longer compulsory after 14) and attempts to reduce teachers' workloads were made.

Under reforms in 2013, a new curriculum has been taught in schools since September 2014. Its emphasis is on a more traditional academic curriculum (the old 12-times table is now back in fashion). Primary school children will learn more British history and more science will be taught at secondary level. Computing and foreign language skills will be encouraged.

National Cycle Network, an ambitious project to build traffic-free cycle routes. When completed it will put 20 million people within a 10-minute cycle ride of their nearest route.

National Forest, a new forest given approval by the government in 1991. It covers 194 sq. miles in Derbyshire, Leicestershire and Staffordshire and 8·5 million trees have been planted.

National Gallery, established in 1824 at Pall Mall, London, with the Angerstein Collection of 38 pictures, purchased for £60,000, as a nucleus. The existing building which was opened in 1838 has been enlarged several times. It attracts over 6 million visitors each year. The National Gallery at Millbank, the Tate Gallery, was given to the nation by Sir Henry Tate in 1897. *See* **Tate Britain**.

Nationalisation is the taking over by the State of the ownership and operation of an industry or service—*e.g.*, coal-mining, railways, transport, gas *etc.* The banking crisis of 2008 resulted in widespread part-nationalisation of some banks.

National Living Wage. The former National Minimum Wage became law on 1 April 1999. Workers aged 22 or more had to be paid a minimum £3·60 per hour (18–21 year olds at least £3·00).This rate has gradually been increased. From April 2017 the rate was £7·50 an hour and this is planned to reach £9 an hour by 2020 for those over 25. There are calls for the National Living Wage to be raised significantly, nearer to the real 'living wage'.

National Lottery, proposed in 1992 Budget. The first National Lottery draw was on 19 November 1994. The last previous national lottery in Britain was in 1826. Oflot is the Office of the National Lottery. The mid-week lottery draw began in February 1997. In 2002 the National Lottery was revamped with a new name, Lotto. The new Health Lottery was started in 2011.

National Nature Reserves (NNRs), reserves to safeguard flora, fauna and physical features, managed by English Nature, the Countryside Council for Wales and Scottish Natural Heritage.

National Parks. Under the National Parks Act 1949 a National Parks Commission was set up to create National Parks in England and Wales. Thirteen have now been established: Peak District, Lake District, Snowdonia, Yorkshire Dales, Exmoor, Brecon Beacons, Dartmoor, Pembrokeshire Coast (the only coastal national park), North York Moors, Northumberland, New Forest, South Downs and The Broads.

National Physical Laboratory, situated at Teddington, is one of the world's largest and best-equipped laboratories. It also maintains British primary standards and physical units. First established in 1900 and managed by the Royal Society. Under privatisation it became an Executive Agency in 1990.

National Portrait Gallery, established in 1856, and now located in a building adjoining the National Gallery. Contains portraits of eminent people in British history as well as a valuable collection of medals and autographs.

National Trust, founded in 1895. "A non-profit-making organisation incorporated by Act of Parliament for the purposes of promoting the permanent preservation of lands and buildings of historic interest or natural beauty for the benefit and access of the people." As a consequence of gifts and public-spirited individuals the Trust, now Britain's largest conservation charity, protects 247,000 hectares of countryside, 1,141 kilometres of coastline and 630 properties (including 200 country houses). The Trust also embraces 28 castles and 6 World Heritage Sites. It is now widening its work to include public parks, *etc.*

Since 1946 lands and houses may be given to the National Trust in lieu of inheritance tax.

NATO, the North Atlantic Treaty Organisation, established 4 April 1949. A defence grouping of Western European states, America and Canada.

Britain is a member. The Russian equivalent was the Warsaw Pact (signed 1955, disbanded, 1991). In March 1999 NATO was extended to include Hungary, Poland and the Czech Republic. Seven additional nations were invited to join NATO at the 2002 Prague Summit. These were Latvia, Estonia, Lithuania, Bulgaria, Romania, Slovakia and Slovenia. After the 2001 terrorist attack, NATO invoked Article 5 of its treaty (commiting signatories to come to the aid of another member) for the first time in its history. In early 2003 NATO was faced with an internal crisis over war in Iraq.

The biggest expansion in NATO's history was in 2004 as 7 former communist countries joined. In 2008 Albania and Croatia were admitted. Montenegro will become the 29th member. Other countries hoping to join, such as Georgia and Ukraine, are unlikely to become members within the next few years. In 2009 France returned as a core member after 43 years of semi-detachment.

The Secretary General of NATO (since 2014) has been Jens Stoltenberg (Norway).

Natterjack, a curious warty, prominent-eyed, brown toad (*Bufo calamita*), having a bright yellow line down the middle of its back. It utters a muttering sort of croak, hence its name.

Natural Gas. *See* Gas.

Natural Numbers, the counting numbers 1, 2, 3, 4, 5, ...

"Nautical Almanac", published under the authority of the Admiralty, contains information specially prepared for the use of navigators and astronomers. It first appeared in 1767.

Nautilus, a term now applied only to the pearly-shelled nautilus, the sole surviving example of the four-gilled section of the *Cephalopoda*. Its fossil relatives are called Ammonites. The spiral shell is divided into a number of compartments, the animal living in the last and largest chamber. There are three or four species, all living in tropical seas. The Paper Nautilus is not related to the Pearly Nautilus, belonging to the same order as the octopus.

Nave is the body or main open portion of a church.

Nazca, an ancient civilisation in what is now southern Peru.

Neanderthal, a valley lying between Düsseldorf and Wuppertal, where in a limestone cave a skull of a very early species of prehistoric man was discovered in 1856. *See* **T55.**

Nebra Disc. Bronze Age German artefact, 3,600 years old, used for calculating time

Nebula, a cloud of gas and dust in space. There are three basic types; emission nebulae create their own light, shining through the effects of very hot stars embedded within them; dust particles within reflection nebulae simply reflect the light from accompanying stars; dark nebulae contain no stars and appear as dark patches against a brighter background. They are the cosmic dust clouds where stars are born and die.

Negus, title of the kings of Abyssinia or Ethiopia. The last emperor of Ethiopia, Haile Selassie, was deposed by a military *coup d'état* in 1974.

Nekton, term used to differentiate actively swimming aquatic organisms (*e.g.*, fishes) from the "drifters" or plankton.

Nelson Column, in Trafalgar Square, London, designed by William Railton, was chosen from among a number of designs—temples, obelisks and various sculptural groups—sent in as a result of a competition held in 1839. The erection of the column was begun in 1840. Twenty-six years later the lions designed by Landseer were set up at the foot of the completed column. The statue of Nelson himself was made by E. H. Bailey and the bronze reliefs at the base executed by Carew, Woodington, Ternouth and Watson, representing the Battles of the Nile, St. Vincent, Copenhagen and Trafalgar. Height 52 m, executed in Dartmoor granite from Foggin Tor quarries.

Néné *or* **Hawaiian Goose.** This rare bird was famously saved from extinction at the Severn Wildfowl Trust at Slimbridge by Sir Peter Scott (1909–89).

Neodymium, element no. 60, symbol Nd, belonging to the rare earth metals. Discovered 1885. Named after the Greek word for "new twin', from twin lines in its spectrum.

Neon, inert gas present in air to the extent of about 1 part in 65,000. The crimson glow produced when an electric discharge passes through the gas is familiar in advertising signs. Element no. 10, symbol Ne.

Neptune. This is now classed as the most distant of the *classical* planets, estimated to be about 4,497 × 10^6 km from the sun, and taking 164·79 years to revolve around it. Discovered by the German astronomers Galle and D'Arrest in Sept. 1846, after its existence had been predicted by Leverrier and Adams. The planet was visited by Voyager 2 in 1989, its last planetary stop. This revealed Neptune had eight moons (not just Triton and Nereid as previously thought) and a ring system. By 2017 the number of Neptune's known moons had risen to 14 with Triton the largest. Its diameter is 49,528 km. A huge Earth-sized storm has been observed, which has been named the "Great Dark Spot'. Winds blow at nearly 900 mph around Neptune's equator, making it the windiest corner of the solar system.

The planet is now known to be surrounded by six rings. It has an average temperature of –218°C and 900 times less sunlight than reaches Earth. Its winter lasts 41 years. Beyond Neptune are the *dwarf planets* (*see* **T9**).

Neptunium, element no. 93, symbol Np, one of the four new elements discovered during the progress of the atomic bomb project in the second world war, Neptunium is formed when a neutron enters nucleus of Uranium 238, and it decays radioactively to yield plutonium.

Neutrino, a neutral particle which carries energy and spin and although possessing little or no mass plays an important part in the interaction of other fundamental particles. The discovery that there are in fact two distinct neutrinos, each with its counterpart, was discovered in 1962. Neutrinos barely interact with normal matter, passing through the Earth as if it did not exist.

The neutrino was 'weighed' for the first time in 2002. *See* **Section T.**

Neutron, a neutral particle present in all atomic nuclei except the hydrogen nucleus which is a single proton. In the development of nuclear science and technology the neutron has played a most important role and neutrons produce the radioisotopes now widely used in medicine, agriculture and industry. Neutrons and protons are termed nucleons. *See* **Section T.**

Neutron Bomb, a thermonuclear fusion weapon which produces increased lethal radiation while the destructive blast and fallout are significantly less than for a fission weapon of equivalent yield; it kills organic life while sparing property, except within a small radius.

Neutron Star. An extremely dense compact star that has undergone huge gravitational collapse so that most of its material has been compressed into neutrons. They are the remaining core after a star has undergone a supernova explosion. A typical neutron star may be only about 15km across and has an intense magnetic field.

New Commonwealth, term used to describe the former British colonies which became members of the Commonwealth following their post-World War II independence. The New Commonwealth, mainly black and Asian, was contrasted with the 'old' white Commonwealth dominions.

Newgate Prison was situated at the western end of Newgate Street, opposite the Old Bailey at the site of one of the old London city gates. There is a record of a prison upon this spot in the 13th cent. Later a new one was built by the executors of Richard Whittington, but this was destroyed by the Great Fire in 1666. Still another new prison on this site was erected between 1778 and 1780. In the Gordon Riots it was destroyed by fire and re-erected. Not used as a prison after 1880.

Newspapers. The first news-books to be published at regular intervals in Britain appeared in 1662 with news of what was going on abroad translated from German and Italian news-sheets. Licence to print was obtained from the Star Chamber, which until its aboli-tion in 1641 allowed only the print-ing of foreign news. With the lifting of the ban on domestic news the Press became free.

In the reign of Queen Anne newspapers employed writers of great intellectual power and versatility. Despite the newspaper tax introduced in 1712, the number of newspapers published in London in 1776 had increased to 53, though the standard of writing declined.

The development of the Press was greatly assisted in the 19th cent. by the abolition of the "taxes on knowledge", by the introduction of the cheap postal system and by improvements in printing, distribution, advertising *etc.*

The *London Gazette*, founded in 1665 (and still appearing twice weekly as the official organ of the Government), is the oldest newspaper living. *The Times* began as the *Daily Universal Register* in 1785, and adopted its present title on 1 January 1788.

The *Manchester Guardian* (renamed *Guardian* in 1959), began life as a weekly in 1821, and became a daily in 1855. The *Scotsman*, founded as a weekly in 1817 and established as a daily in 1855, and the *Glasgow Herald*, which began as the *Glasgow Advertiser* in 1783, are the leading Scottish newspapers. The first evening newspaper, the *Star and Evening Advertiser* was published in London in 1788. During 1989, the last national newspapers left Fleet St. The very last journalists left in 2016. In 1993 *The Guardian* acquired *The Observer*. In November 2003 a "compact" version of *The Times* was published. The "Berliner" *Guardian* was launched on 12 September 2005. *The Observer* followed on 8 January 2006.

The *Independent*, founded in 1986, ceased print publication in 2016 (becoming the first digital-only national newspaper). A new paper, *New Day*, began on 29 February 2016 (the first new daily paper for 30 years). It closed after only nine weeks.

Newt, amphibian of lizard shape and mottled markings. There are three British species, the largest being the Great-Crested Newt (*Triturus cristatus*), which attains a length of 15 cm.

Newton, the unit of force in the SI system of units. Under its influence a body with a mass of 1 kilogram will accelerate at a rate of 1 metre per second each second.

Newton's Rings. Concentric circular rings, due to the phenomenon of interference, which are seen around the point of contact of a slightly convex lens with a flat plate of glass.

New Towns. Under the New Town Act 1946 and subsequent Acts some 33 new towns were designated in Britain; 23 are in England and Wales, five in Scotland and four in Northern Ireland. They were: Basildon, Bracknell, Crawley, Harlow, Hatfield, Hemel Hempstead, Milton Keynes, Northampton, Peterborough, Stevenage and Welwyn (to relieve housing problems in Greater London); Newton Aycliffe, Corby, Cwmbran, Peterlee and Washington (to serve the special needs of their areas); Newtown (to help stem rural depopulation in mid-Wales); Runcorn and Skelmersdale (to meet the overspill needs of Liverpool and north Merseyside); Telford and Redditch (to take population from Birmingham); Warrington (expanded to take people from Liverpool and Manchester); Central Lancashire New Town (based on existing towns of Preston, Leyland and Chorley).

The five Scottish new towns comprise Cumbernauld, East Kilbride, Glenrothes, Irvine and Livingston. In Northern Ireland Craigavon was developed as a new city; Antrim and Ballymena were to become centres of economic growth; Londonderry and the surrounding district were designated as an area of special development.

Plans were announced in 2008 for 15 new *eco-towns*, to be built by 2020. They will be carbon-free and pathfinders in terms of areas of sustainability. These plans were subsequently scaled down. Sites approved in 2009 were Rackheath (Norfolk), Whitehill Bordon (East Hampshire), North West Bicester (Oxfordshire) and the China Clay Community (near St. Austell, Cornwall).

New Year's Day, 1 January. The first New Year's festival of which we know is that constituted by Numa 713 B.C., and dedicated to Janus.

Nibelungenlied, the German epic of the early 13th century, comprising numerous mythical poems or sagas. Wagner's *The Ring of the Nibelungs* was based on Norse legends and the Nibelungenlied.

Nicene Creed, a summary of the principles of Christian faith, first issued in 325 by the Council of Nicaea (summoned by the emperor Constantine the Great) for the purpose of thwarting the Arian heresy and asserting the godhead of Christ. Date of Easter fixed at Council of Nicaea.

Nickel, silver-coloured metallic element, no. 28, symbol Ni, fairly soft though harder than iron. Chief source of the metal is the nickel sulphide in iron-copper pyrites deposits in Ontario. Chief uses are: in electroplating, in coins, as an element in alloy steels. A novel method of making pure nickel (by treating the metal with carbon monoxide and heating

the resulting liquid, nickel carbonyl) was developed in 1890 by Mond. This discovery led to many technical advances in industrial chemistry, one of which is the production of catalysts. Discovered by Crondstedt in 1751 as an impurity in copper ore. Substituted for silver in French coinage in about 1882.

Night Heron, a stocky, short-legged heron of black and white plumage, red eyes and yellowish legs, crepuscular except in breeding season, and an occasional visitor to Britain.

Nightingale, a once familiar singing bird which visits the southern counties of England every summer, and is sometimes found as far north as Yorkshire. It is a shy, brown bird, not often seen, but the song of the male, usually heard in the late evening or early morning, is of remarkable sweetness and variety. After its wooing period is over its song ceases. There are now less than 6,000 singing male nightingales left in Britain.

Nightjar, nocturnal, insectivorous bird, owl-like in appearance, with mottled brown plumage of "dead leaf" pattern, and a churring song. It is a common breeding visitor from Africa to the British Isles, April to September, laying its eggs on bare ground. It lies motionless on the ground, giving it a near-perfect camouflage.

Niobium is a metal element, no. 41, symbol Nb, related to vanadium. Technical development has been slow because of its rare occurrence, although niobium is now used in ferrous alloys to increase resistance to corrosion and produce steel which can be used at high temperatures.

Niqab, the face veil worn by some Muslim women. It was banned in France in 2012.

Nitre *or* **Saltpetre**, is now mostly manufactured by the double decomposition of sodium nitrate and potassium chloride. Its chief use is the manufacture of gunpowder and fireworks. It has been manufactured in England since 1625.

Nitrogen, a non-combustible gaseous element, no. 7, symbol N, devoid of taste or smell, and constituting nearly four-fifths of the atmospheric air. Nitrogen compounds are essential to plants and animals, and are used in fertilisers. Nitrogen pollution in the soil is now a major threat.

Nitro-Glycerine, an explosive yellow fluid produced by mixing small quantities of glycerine with a combination of one part of nitric acid and two parts of sulphuric acid. By itself it is a dangerously explosive substance to handle. In 1867, Nobel produced dynamite, a safe explosive made by absorbing nitro-glycerine in kieselguhr.

Nitrous Oxide, a compound of nitrogen and oxygen possessing mild anaesthetic power. Termed "laughing gas" on account of its exhilarating effect. It is still used in dentistry, and for minor operations and has proved useful in a new technique for finding leaks in water mains.

Nobel Prizes. The Nobel Foundation was established to give effect to the wishes expressed by Alfred Nobel (*see* **Section B**) in his Will. *See* **G17–20**.

Nones, dates of the Roman calendar which fell on the 5th of each month, excepting March, May, July and October, when they fell on the 7th.

North-East Passage, from the North Atlantic to Bering Strait was rapidly developed by the former USSR as a northern sea route to render accessible vast areas of northern Siberia. Attempts to find a North-East passage were made by Englishmen and Dutchmen in the 16th cent. but they were always defeated by the ice, for the sea is completely frozen for some 4,800 km for 9 months of the year. A Swede succeeded in sailing from Europe to Japan via the Arctic between 1878 and 1880. In 2009 two German container ships successfully navigated the Russian North-East Passage across Arctic waters from the Pacific for the first time. Other vessels (including Chinese merchant ships) have followed. *See also* **Arctic Exploration.**

North-West Passage, from the Atlantic to the Pacific through the Arctic Seas, has been the dream of navigators for centuries. Attempts to find it were made in the 16th and early 17th cent. by John and Sebastian Cabot, Frobisher, Gilbert, Davis, Hudson and Baffin. Two centuries later Ross, Parry, Franklin and others made the attempt; but it was not until 1903–5 that Amundsen, discoverer of the South Pole, made the complete voyage in the *Gjoa*. The Canadian icebreaker *Labrador* was the first deep-draft vessel to traverse the North-West Passage

(1954) and the US tanker *Manhattan* was the first commercial vessel to do so (1969). Continued global warming has now opened up the prospect of commercial shipping for longer periods each summer, a development that could change the face of world trade. Indeed, before too long, ships could even be sailing over the North Pole.

Canada claims authority over the North-West Passage shipping route whilst the USA insists it is an international waterway.

Notornis. *See* **Takahe.**

Notre Dame, the famous Paris cathedral, was founded in 1163. Famous Gothic architecture.

Notting Hill Carnival. A Caribbean festival, first held in St. Pancras Town Hall in January 1959. Now one of the largest street festivals in Western Europe.

November, the 9th month of the year originally, but from *c.* 700 B.C., when Numa added January and February, it became the 11th month.

Nuclear Energy. Atomic nuclei consist of protons and neutrons joined in various proportions (**T11**). The heaviest naturally occurring nucleus contains 238 particles (92 protons, 146 neutrons) and is uranium 238 (U^{238}); the lightest is hydrogen, which consists of 1 proton. Neutrons and protons attract one another by very strong forces which are not at all well understood; they are called *nuclear forces.* Consequently it requires energy to be supplied if a nucleus is to be pulled apart into its constituent particles. The energy is required to overcome the attractions of the nuclear forces. Conversely, when the particles rush together to form a nucleus energy is released as heat or radiation.

The energy released when protons and neutrons coalesce to form a nucleus is called *Binding Energy.* The binding energy of a nucleus divided by the number of particles involved is called the binding energy per particle, which we will call B. It is very difficult to overestimate the importance of B to the human race. B varies from nucleus to nucleus, and the exact form of its variation is only roughly understood at the present time. But the most significant thing is that B is greatest for elements of medium atomic weight and lowest at the heavy (uranium) and light (hydrogen) ends of the periodic table. This means that if middleweight nuclei can be formed either from heavy ones or from light ones, B increases and energy is released in either case.

Nuclear Fission. *See under* **Fission.**

Nuclear Fusion. If light nuclei are hurled at high speeds into intimate contact they sometimes coalesce and release binding energy (*see* **Nuclear Energy**). This has been studied in laboratories where powerful and energy-consuming machines accelerate small numbers of particles for purely experimental purposes. If useful amounts of energy are to be gained these fusion reactions will have to occur on a bigger scale in an apparatus from which the resulting heat can be extracted in a controlled way.

The one "useful" fusion device so far made is the thermonuclear bomb ("H-bomb"). Thermonuclear is the important word. If a suitable gas can be raised to a very high temperature the nuclei are stripped of their electrons and all particles move with very high speeds. The gas is then called a plasma. High enough temperatures will make speeds great enough for fusion reactions to occur and nuclear energy to be released. This is a thermonuclear reaction. For example, in deuterium gas, at temperatures over a million degrees Centigrade, the deuterium nuclei (*i.e.*, heavy hydrogen nuclei consisting of 1 proton joined to 1 neutron) interact to produce helium nuclei. To obtain a net gain in energy from this process, the temperature must be raised to about 100 million degrees C and maintained long enough; otherwise the energy released is less than that required to heat the fuel and to make up for heat losses.

New attempts to study the staggering technical problems are being made, and fusion research is very active in Britain, the USA, Japan and the Russian Federation. The joint European Torus (JET) fusion research project sited at Culham near Oxford aims to develop a new source of energy for the generation of electricity for the 21st cent. In 1991, the JET project achieved a two minute successful nuclear fusion, bringing nearer the prospect of new energy sources. A new way to use lasers to make atoms fuse together to release vast amounts of fusion energy was reported in 2001. The new technique is known as "fast ignition".

Nuclear Power Stations. In 2017 Britain generated around 21 % of her electricity in nuclear power stations. (compared to 75 % in France) The numerous older nuclear power stations all developed from the classic Calder Hall type, burning natural uranium inserted in a graphite moderator and cooled by carbon dioxide gas.

They were called Magnox stations because the fuel elements of natural uranium rods are encased in magnesium alloy cans (the last Magnox station, Wylfa I, has now closed). A second nuclear power programme based on the advanced gas cooled reactor (AGR) at Windscale included the reactors at Dungeness "B", (1983) and those at Hinkley Point "B", Hunterston "B", Hartlepool (Cleveland) and Heysham (Lancashire). In 1987, after the Layfield Report, the Government gave approval for the Sizewell B project to become Britain's first pressurised water reactor.

In 1994 the Government gave the go-ahead for the controversial Thorp nuclear reprocessing plant at Sellafield. The Sizewell B PWR became the latest nuclear power station in February 1995. After the Government's 1995 Nuclear Review, the industry was substantially restructured in preparation for privatisation in July 1996.

In January 2008 uncertainty over the future of nuclear power seemed to end when the government gave the go-ahead for a new generation of nuclear power stations. No limits were put on their numbers. In 2013 the go-ahead was given to build Hinkley Point C in Somerset but the project remains beset by controversy.

Nuclear Reactors are pieces of apparatus designed to permit nuclear chain reactions to occur under controlled conditions. (Uncontrolled chain reactions are dangerous, *e.g.* atomic bombs.) The success of a reactor depends on the neutrons reaching the U^{235} nuclei to produce more fissions and not being wasted in irrelevant processes or simply escaping through the wall of the apparatus (neutrons are quite difficult to contain). The neutrons leaving the scene of fission are rapidly moving, and they stand more chance of causing another fission if they are slowed down. Consequently a material other than the uranium has to be present to facilitate this, and it is called a moderator. A useful moderator is pure graphite.

Thus a reactor may consist of alternate blocks of uranium and graphite. If the reactor is too small so many neutrons escape that there are not enough to keep the chain reaction going. The reactor must therefore be greater than a certain *critical size.* In order to intensify or damp down the chain reaction it is arranged for pieces of neutron-absorbing material, such as cadmium, to be inserted or withdrawn as required. While the chain reaction is proceeding countless numbers of fissions are occurring, each one liberating energy which turns into heat. The temperature therefore increases, and to prevent a catastrophic rise, cooling has to be provided.

Hence the reactor has cooling pipes through which a fluid coolant is pumped. The coolant carries the heat away and, in a reactor designed to produce electrical power, the heat is taken to steam-raising boilers and the high-pressure steam is led to turbines which drive the electric generators.

What has been described above is the type of reactor first used for power production at Calder Hall (1956). This was a graphitemoderated, gascooled reactor using as fuel natural uranium (*i.e.*, fissile U^{235} greatly diluted with U^{238}). Other thermal types of nuclear reactor are the advanced gas-cooled reactor (AGR), the high temperature reactor (HTR), the steam-generating heavy-water (SGHWR) and the light-water reactor (LWR). It is also possible to make reactors work without slowing the neutrons with a moderator; these are called *fast reactors.* The design of the prototype fast reactor (PFR) at Dounreay was based on experience gained with the Dounreay experimental fast breeder reactor (closed 1977 after 17 years' safe operation) which was the first to produce electricity on a commercial scale (1962) and achieved the highest power output of any of its type in the world. These fast reactors can produce new nuclear fuel in the course of their operation and therefore offer great economies; but they are more difficult to develop than thermal reactors.

The fuel is made from the mixed oxides of plutonium and uranium and the coolant is liquid sodium metal.

Environmental considerations have become of increasing concern. Most of the products of the fission process are of necessity radioactive isotopes: they could be gaseous, like krypton, xenon and tritium or solid like strontium, caesium, zirconium and ruthenium. There are also present the new radioactive elements plutonium, curium, actinium, *etc*.

Furthermore, in both the nuclear reactor and in the plant which is used to chemically treat and reprocess the nuclear fuel, radioactivity will be induced in associated structural materials, to varying degrees. In this latter case, unlike the former, the radioactive waste with which one is left can to a great extent be selected and is largely overshadowed in importance by the waste arising from the fission and breeding processes. Even if the whole of the UK electrical power was produced by nuclear means, the volumes of such wastes would be relatively small and need in principle tens of acres of storage area. Much of the activity would decay in a decade, but that associated with the elements bred from uranium, would be present for thousands of years: Pu^{239} has a half-life of 25,000 years.

Segregation of the various types of activity is feasible; their incorporation into physically and chemically stable form has received a great deal of study so that storage, readily monitored even for many generations, seems entirely possible.

The radioactive properties of these wastes can only be changed by nuclear reactions. Bombardment with neutrons or other highly energetic particles can bring about such reactions so that forms of "nuclear incineration" are feasible but are not yet fully explored.

Nucleic Acids. Living matter is built up of cells each of which has a nucleus surrounded by cytoplasm. Cell nuclei are composed chiefly of substances called nucleoproteins, which consist of a protein attached to a nucleic acid (this original name is still used, although nucleic acids are found in the cytoplasm as well as the nucleus). Nucleic acids are complex organic structures made up of chains of compounds called nucleotides.

Nucleotide molecules have a sugar group attached to a nitrogenous base and a phosphate group. Only two sugar groups are found in the nucleotides, ribose, giving rise to ribonucleic acids (RNAs), found mainly in the cytoplasm) and deoxyribose, which forms deoxyribonucleic acids (DNAs, found mainly in cell nuclei). Seven different nitrogenous bases have been isolated, so that a number of different nucleotides are possible. A repeating, regular pattern of nucleotides is linked by the phosphate groups, forming nucleic acids.

The functions of nucleic acids are of fundamental importance. They are concerned in the process of transmission of inherited qualities in reproduction and in building up body proteins.

Nucleosynthesis, the creation of the elements in the universe. This occurred approximately 100 seconds after the big bang, ceasing *c*. 900 seconds later.

Nuthatch, name of a number of tree-creeping birds, plump, with a short tail, bluish-grey plumage and black stripe under eye. Nest in holes and wedge nuts in bark of trees, hammering them to get a kernel. There are three European species, one, *Sitta europaea*, thriving in England.

Nutria Rat. *See* **Coypu.**

Nylon, a generic term for any long-chain synthetic polymeric amide which has recurring amide groups as an integral part of the main polymer chain, and which is capable of being formed into a filament in which the structural elements are orientated in the direction of the axis. The first nylon of commercial interest was made in 1935, and the world's first nylon factory—in the United States—began production in 1940.

O

Oak, a tree of the genus *Quercus*, including some 300 species distributed over the northern hemisphere and into the tropics. Two species are native to Britain, *Q. petraea*, more common in the west and north on shallower, lighter soils, and *Q. robur*, more common in the south on deeper, heavier soils. Oak timber is much prized for its strength and durability, and from the time of the Spanish Armada to Nelson's day was in great demand for naval construction. It has always been used for

building, flooring, furniture and cabinet work. Oaks support more life than any other British tree. The oak is attacked by many insects, the round nut-like oak galls, or oak-apples, being produced by the sting of certain minute gall wasps.

Recently a new threat (acute oak decline) has been confirmed in England. Caterpillars of the Oak Processionary Moth are a growing threat.

"Oaks", a famous race for three-year-old fillies run at Epsom one day after the "Derby".

Oarfish. *See* **Ribbon Fish.**

Obelisk, a tapering monolithic column, square at the base and pyramidal at the top, regarded by the ancient Egyptians as a sacred stone and usually found at the entrance to the sun temples. Many were transported from Egypt and set up at various times: there is one in the Place de la Concorde in Paris, and one on the Embankment in London—Cleopatra's Needle—first erected at Heliopolis, centre of the sun-cult, by Tuthmosis III *c*. 1500 B.C.

Observatories. *See* **Astronomy** *and* **Telescope.**

Obsidian, a black volcanic glass-like rock. It played a key role in some early Meso-American civilisations.

Occitane, language still spoken in southern France.

Occultation, the passage of one celestial object in front of another, where the closer object has a larger apparent diameter than the more distant one and which, therefore, temporarily hides it from view. An example is the passage of the Moon across the Sun during a total solar eclipse.

Ocean, comprises the great body of water which covers seven-tenths of the surface of the earth, and has an average depth of 3·2 km. The principal oceans are the Pacific, Atlantic, Indian and Arctic. The greatest ocean depth is in the Pacific, in the Mindanao Deep, 37,782 ft (11,524 m). More than 70 % of our planet's surface is covered by water. The oceans are now warming at their fastest rate for 3,000 years and sea levels are rising. Scientists are noting that warming temperatures are bringing subtropical fish species to the seas around Britain.

The current Neptune Project is creating a massive submarine laboratory to examine the almost unknown world on the ocean floor. Many thousands of previously unknown living creatures have been identified in the World Register of Marine Species. The Register now contains the names of more than 227,000 creatures—still only a fraction of marine life. Scientists are now planning to map the ocean floors by 2030. Commercial deep-sea mining of the natural mineral resources of the oceans is also beginning.

Ocean Currents are well-defined streams running over certain portions of the ocean and caused mainly by wind-friction, slope of the sea surface and differences in density of the water, all movements being influenced by the deflective forces due to the earth's rotation. The climatic importance of the great ocean currents is that they constitute one means whereby heat is transferred from lower to higher latitudes.

Oceanography is the scientific study of the world ocean, *i.e.*, the single connected body of water that covers 70·8 per cent of the earth's surface.

Modern oceanography dates from the voyage of HMS *Challenger* (1872–6) during which wide-ranging observations of the ocean were made.

Ocelot, the wild cat of S. America. It is about 1·2 m in length, including tail, and of a grey or tawny colour and spotted. Closely related to the Leopard. Now almost extinct in the Amazon rain forest.

Octane Number, the index of the knock-rating of petrol. It is based on the arbitrary scale in which iso-octane (which does not cause "knocking") has a value of 100, and normal heptane (which is prone to "knocking") has a value of 0. A good fuel for modern cars must have an octane number greater than 80.

October, the 10th month, but the 8th in the old Roman calendar. It was held sacred to Mars.

Octopus, a genus of marine molluscs with eight tentacles that bear suckers. They have three hearts, blue blood, an excellent sense of touch and very good eyesight. Its genome has been decoded. A previously unknown species was found in 2016 in the Pacific.

Odyssey, Homer's epic setting forth the incidents of the wanderings of Odysseus on his way back to Ithaca after the siege of Troy.

Oersted, a unit of magnetic-field intensity in the cgs system.

Ohm's Law, propounded by G. S. Ohm in 1826, is expressed in the equation: electromotive force (in volts) = current (in amperes) × resistance (in ohms). The ohm is the unit of electrical resistance in the metre-kilogram-second system.

Oil. The great expansion in energy demand over recent years has been met to a large extent by petroleum oil. This contains a wide range of hydrocarbon molecules of varying complexity. The various components are separated from each other by making use of their different boiling points. Crude oil is heated in the base of a fractionating tower; the various components condense at different temperatures in trays at different levels of the tower.

The fraction of a given composition can be increased by "cracking" or breaking down the heavier hydrocarbons into lighter ones.

The cutback and the rise in the price of Middle Eastern oil following the 1973 Arab- Israeli war was succeeded for 25 years by a glut of oil and falling prices. Fears over world oil supplies caused the price to rise sharply (it touched $140 in 2008) but the price rapidly fell to below $50 as global recession deepened. It rose again in 2012 but collapsed late in 2014 and was down to below $30 by Spring 2016 before a recovery began.

Development began in 1996 of oil production in the Atlantic (there are huge reserves in the Foinaven field west of the Shetland Islands). This area is known as the "new North Sea". The first British North Sea field (the Argyll) dried up in 1992 having produced 97m barrels. Britain's largest on-shore oilfield is at Wytch Farm (Dorset).

In 2000, output of crude oil and natural gas liquids in the UK averaged 2·7 million barrels a day (making the UK the world's tenth largest producer). UK oil production peaked in 2002.

Major new oilfields continue to be found (*e.g.* offshore Brazil, West Africa, Gulf of Mexico). Some leading oil producers are Russia, Saudi Arabia, the USA, Iran and China. By 2020, the USA is set to be the largest crude oil producer. In 2012 China overtook the USA to become the top oil importer. Venezuela has the largest proven reserves of crude oil, surpassing even Saudi Arabia.

Okapi, nocturnal secretive ruminant mammal, smaller than the giraffe, chestnut brown in colour with zebrastriped legs, native to the Congo, where civil war has devastated its numbers.

Olbers' Comet was discovered in 1815 by Olbers the German astronomer. Olbers also discovered the asteroids Pallas and Vesta (1802–07).

Old Red Sandstone, the continental rocks formed during the Devonian period. *See also* **Geology.**

Olefines, a series of hydrocarbons, in which the hydrogen atoms are double the number of carbon. The first member of the series is ethylene.

Olinguito, a newly-discovered carnivorous mammal. It is a tree-dwelling relative of the raccoon. Found in Colombia and Ecuador.

Olive. This small tree, whose fruit yields olive oil, is a native of the eastern Mediterranean, but has been introduced into cultivation elsewhere. The green unripe fruit is pickled in brine for table olives. Olive oil production can be traced back at least to 2,400 B.C. in Syria.The Ancient Greeks called olive oil liquid gold. Spain is the biggest producer of olive oil. "Olive tree leprosy" is a serious threat in Italy. New sources of olive oil are Morocco, China and Latin America.

Olmec, ancient civilisation of Mesoamerica (Central America), now seen as the "mother culture" of the Maya and Aztec. They developed urban ritual and political centres and may have been the first to formalise structured writing. They worshipped the mythical were-jaguar. They used rubber and built pyramids.

Olympiads were periods of four years which elapsed between each celebration of the Olympic games, held at Olympia in honour of Zeus. These festivals included competitions in literature, art, drama, rhetoric, music and gymnastics, and they were continued, with intervals, from 776 B.C. to A.D. 394. Modern Olympics have taken place at Athens 1896, Paris 1900, St. Louis 1904, London 1908, Stockholm 1912, Antwerp 1920, Paris 1924, Amsterdam 1928, Los Angeles 1932, Berlin 1936, London 1948, Helsinki 1952, Melbourne 1956, Rome 1960, Tokyo 1964, Mexico City 1968, Munich 1972, Montreal 1976, Moscow 1980, Los Angeles 1984, Seoul 1988, Barcelona in 1992, Atlanta, Georgia, 1996 (the Centennial Olympics), Sydney, 2000, Athens, 2004, Beijing in 2008, London 2012 and Rio de Janeiro (2016). Tokyo will host the 2020 Olympics.

The first Winter Olympics were held at Chamonix in 1924. The last were in Sochi in Russia in 2014. The next will be in 2018 in Pyeongchang (S. Korea). Beijing will host the 2022 Winter Olympics (the first city to host both the Summer and Winter games).

Onomasticians are scientists who study the fascinating subject of names—names of places and names of people—to find out their origins. They tell us, for example, that Cambridge is an Anglo-Norman corruption of *Grantabrycg* =bridge over the Granta; that Harrow-on-the-Hill was an early Anglo-Saxon settlement—"heathen temple on the hill"; that we owe the ridings of Yorkshire to the Vikings (Old Norse *thrithungr* = third part); that in Scotland -*ton* and -*toun* indicate not a town but a hamlet or village.

Onyx *or* **Sardonyx,** a variety of chalcedony built up of different-coloured layers, which are parallel and straight (not curved as in agate).

Oolite, a geological term for the Jurassic oolitic limestones existing through a long stretch of country extending from Yorkshire to Dorset. It abounds in fossils of molluscs and reptiles.

The term "oolite" derives from the fact that these rocks are made of egg-shaped particles of calcium carbonate.

Oort Cloud, the hypothetical swarm of billions of comets that surrounds our solar system, *c.* 50,000 times further from the Sun than our Earth. The Oort Cloud represents the outermost limits of the Sun's gravitational influence.

Opal, a mineral consisting of hydrous silica, occurring in numerous varieties and colours. Opals have been prized as gems since at least 400 B.C.

Their unique internal "fire" or opalescence is a result of the diffraction of light by a regular array of tiny silica spheres, about 100 nm in diameter, of which gem opals are now known to be composed. Opal miners are called gougers. Chief source—the Andanooka and Coober Pedy fields of South Australia.

Open University. *See* **Universities.**

Opossum, marsupial mammals found in the more southerly of the United States, South America and Australasia. They are arboreal except for the water-opossum, which eats fish.

Optics, the branch of physics which investigates the nature and properties of light and the phenomena of colour. Burning lenses were known to the ancient Greeks and Ptolemy wrote a treatise on optics A.D. 150. Lenses as visual aids were known in ancient China but eyeglasses were not in use until the 13th cent. Spectacles were in more general use after the invention of printing in the 15th cent. The camera obscura was invented in the 16th cent. and the telescope and microscope early in the 17th cent.

Oracles were in ancient times supposed to be words spoken by the gods, and it was the custom on important occasions to consult them about the future. The Greeks had the Oracles of Zeus at Dodona, and Apollo at Delphi, while the Romans consulted the Oracles of Mars, Fortune *etc.*

Orange, a fruit growing in most sub-tropical climates. It is grown on an evergreen tree that attains a height of about 6 m at maturity.

Orangutan, one of the largest of the anthropoid apes, found only in the swampy forests of Borneo and Sumatra. When full-grown it stands over 1·2 m in height and weighs *c.* 67 kg. Fruit is the mainstay of their diet. The male may live up to 45 years. All of the great apes face a threatened future from deforestation and demands for food ("bushmeat"). Attempts to protect them are underway. They can swim across rivers and are one of the smartest species on the planet. They spend more time walking on the ground than previously thought. Young orangutans have the longest childhood of any nonhuman primate.

Orbit, is the path of one celestial object around another. For example, the path of the Earth around the Sun.

Orca. *See* **Whales.**

Orchestra. The composition of a typical symphony orchestra is as follows: STRINGS: 1st Violin (16), 2nd Violin (16), Viola (12), Violoncello (12), Double Bass (8). WOODWIND: Flute (3–4), Piccolo (1), Oboe (3), Cor Anglais (1), Bass Oboe (1), Clarinet (3), Bass Clarinet (1), Bassoon (3), Contra-bassoon (1). BRASS: Horn (6), Trumpet (5), Trombone (3–4), Tuba (2). PERCUSSION: Timpani (3–6), Side Drum (1), Bass Drum (1), Cymbals (1), Harp (2).

Order of Merit. *See* **Merit, Order of.**

Ordination, the ceremony of installing ministers or clergymen in clerical offices. In the Anglican and Catholic Churches the rites of Ordination are performed by bishops; among Nonconformists it is done by the governing bodies. The first women were ordained Anglican priests in 1994.

Ordnance Survey. Founded initially in 1791 as the Trigonometrical Survey, the Ordnance Survey was established by the 1841 Ordnance Survey Act. The famous maps were first produced on a scale of 1 inch to the mile (but are now available on various scales and constantly revised). In 2016 it released a map of Mars, its first non-Earth map.

Organic Farming, means the production of food or other farm produce without artificial fertilisers or chemical pesticides.

Organic Light Emitting Diode (OLED), a light source based on natural bioluminescence (q.v).

Orimulsion, an emulsified bitumen fuel which comes from Venezuela.

Orioles, brilliantly coloured birds, members of the passerine family *Oriolidae*, found in the tropical regions of Asia, Africa and Australia. The golden oriole, perhaps the most beautiful of them all, with brilliant yellow plumage, black wings and tail, winters in Africa, visits England and is known to have nested here.

Orion, a famous constellation of the heavens, comprising nearly a hundred stars, all visible to the naked eye. It contains three stars of the second magnitude in a line, called "Orion's Belt".

Ormer, a shellfish (*Haliotis tuberculata*) which occurs in the Channel Islands and on parts of the French coast. It is a great delicacy.

Ornithology, the scientific study of birds.

Ornithorhynchus. *See* **Duckbill.**

Orogeny, large-scale earth movements, including faulting and folding and sometimes igneous activity, which produce a linear belt of mountains, *e.g.*, the Alpine orogeny in Europe.

Orphrey, the name of an ornamental strip richly embroidered on ecclesiastical vestments.

Orrery, an instrument used in the 18th and early 19th cent. which showed the motions of the planets round the sun and the satellites round their primaries. The first orrery made was named after Charles Boyle, Earl of Orrery.

Ortolan, small songbird, now a protected species. Almost hunted out of existence as a delicacy for gourmets in France. Illegal hunting still continues.

Oryx, the inspiration behind the myth of the unicorn. An oryx can travel longer without water than a camel.

Osborne House, near Cowes, in the Isle of Wight. Queen Victoria's favourite winter-residence, and where she died.

Osier, a species of willow growing in damp soils and yielding branches utilised in basket-making.

Osmium, a very hard, bluish-white metallic element, no. 76, symbol Os, of the platinum group and one of the heaviest of known metals. It is obtained from certain sands of S. America, California, Australia and Russia. The alloy of osmium and iridium (osmiridium) provides tips for gold fountain-pen nibs. Discovered by Tennant in 1803.

Osmosis, the process by which absorption of liquids through semi-permeable membranes takes place. A solution exerts osmotic pressure (O.P.) or suction in proportion to concentration but also depending on kind of dissolved substance. The roots of the higher plants are covered with fine root-hairs, within the cell-walls of which the sap is normally of a higher concentration than the dissolved matter in the surrounding soil. The root-hairs, therefore, draw into themselves these weaker salt-solutions. (The explanation of water and salt exchanges is complicated by the selective ability of some cells (*e.g.*, roots) to accept or reject particular dissolved substances along with the water. The absorption of salts by a plant is selective, each plant selecting through the semi-permeable membranes of its root-hairs those substances which are most suited to it.)

Osprey (*Pandion haliaëtus*), a large and magnificent bird of prey, dark brown above and nearly white below. The head is whitish with a dark band from eye to nape. To the British Isles it is a rare passage migrant. Back in 1955, thanks to the energy of the Royal Society for the Protection of Birds, a pair nested in a Scots pine in Inverness-shire and reared three young. Since then many more ospreys have fledged. Food consists almost entirely of fish, which the bird seizes with its talons. The so-called osprey plumes in

fact come from the egret. Ospreys are found on all continents except Antarctica.

Ostrich, the largest living bird, related to the rhea, emu and extinct moa, now found only on the sandy plains of Africa and parts of S.W. Asia. The male has beautiful white plumes on wings and tail. The wings are useless in flight, but the birds have a speed exceeding that of the swiftest horse. An ostrich's egg weighs 1·3 kg. The idea that ostriches bury their heads in the sand comes from an optical illusion.

Otary, any seal which has external ears (as opposed to the *true seals* which lack them). The eared seals make up the family *Otariidae,* which includes the Sea-lion and the Fur-seal.

Otter, an aquatic carnivorous mammal widely distributed over Europe, and until the 1950s very common in England and Wales. The otter averages about 60 cm in length, exclusive of tail, has web-feet and is a very expert swimmer. Otters are harmless and their hunting is a cruel and senseless blood sport. Having almost disappeared by 1980, the otter is now protected by the 1981 Wildlife and Countryside Act. By 2011 the otter had returned to every English county. Indeed, it is now more numerous than at any time since the Second World War (much to the dismay of some anglers). The Otter Trust is based at Earsham near Bungay, Suffolk. Otters have the densest fur in the animal world and also have unique throat markings.

There are 13 species of otter, but only the Eurasian *Lutra lutra* is native to Britain. An otter's den is called a holt or pouch.

Ounce or **Snow Leopard,** a very beautiful pale spotted cat from the Himalayas the size of a labrador retriever but with a long furry tail. They are hunted for their pelts. Only c. 3,500 are now left across all of central Asia, with only 300 in Nepal.

Outcrop. Where a bed of rock appears at the surface of the ground, there is an outcrop of the particular rock. The mining of outcrop coal is called open-cast mining.

Oviparous, a term referring to animals which lay eggs to be hatched outside the body of the parent.

Ovipositor, the organ by means of which female insects lay their eggs.

Owls, nocturnal birds of prey, will 240 species found everywhere except Antarctica. Their forward-looking eyes, embedded in rings of feathers, give them a characteristic "owl-like" appearance, and their plumage, usually a mottled blend of browns and greys, is so soft that their flight is almost noiseless. Their unique downy wings allow them to fly silently. Owls live on small mammals, reptiles, birds, insects and fish, and are very valuable birds to the farmer. British owls include the barn owl (screech owl), short-eared owl, long-eared owl, tawny owl and little owl (introduced to Britain in the 19th century by landowners).

Ox, the popular name of the mammals included in the genus *Bos.* They are hollow-horned ruminants and hoofed quadrupeds, there are c. 240 species globally, to be found on every continent except Antaretica and include the various classes of domestic cattle as well as the different wild species. The adult male is called a bull, the female a cow and the young a calf. The best-known breeds of domesticated cattle are the Durham or Shorthorn, the Angus, the Jersey, Ayrshire, Suffolk and Hereford.

Oxalic Acid, an organic acid obtained from numerous plants, such as sorrel and rhubarb, and produced artificially for commercial purposes from sawdust, treated with caustic potash or caustic soda. It combines with metals to form oxalates; used in the manufacture of ink.

Oxford Clay, a geological formation consisting of a bed of blue clay c. 200 m thick, and forming the lower portion of the Upper Jurassic. It makes good bricks.

Oxford University. There was a school at Oxford as early as 1115 and it is known that Robert Pullen, a theologian from Paris, lectured there in 1133. Allusions to Oxford as the most celebrated centre of learning in England occurred in a work of Gerald of Wales in 1184–5. Early foundations were University College (1249), Balliol (about 1263), Merton (1264). In 1571 the university was reorganised and granted a Charter of Incorporation.

Other colleges and halls with their dates of foundation incude: All Souls (1438), Brasenose (1509), Christ Church (1546), Corpus Christi (1517), Exeter (1314), Hertford (1874), Jesus (1571), Keble (1868),

Linacre (1962), Lincoln (1427), Magdalen (1458), New College (1379), Nuffield (1937), Oriel (1326), Pembroke (1624), Queen's (1340), St. Anthony's (1950), St. Catherine's (1962), St. Cross (1965), St. Edmund Hall (1270), St. John's (1555), St. Peter's (1929), St. Stephen's House (1876), Trinity (1554), Wadham (1612), Wolfson (1965), Worcester (1714), Campion Hall (1962), St. Benet's Hall (1964), Mansfield (1886), Regent's Park (1958), Templeton (1984), Harris Manchester College (1990), Kellogg College (1990, formerly Rewley House) and Wycliffe Hall (1996). The most recent foundation is the merged Green Templeton College (2008).

The original women's colleges were:— Lady Margaret Hall (1878), Somerville (1879), St. Hugh's (1886), St. Hilda's (1893) and St. Anne's (1952). Women were not admitted to degrees (though allowed to sit for examination) till 1920.

The last women-only college was St Hilda's (which finally agreed to admit men in 2006). St Benet's had no women undergraduates until 2016.

Oxygen is the most abundant of all terrestrial elements, no. 8, symbol O. In combination, this gaseous element forms about 46% of the earth's crust; one-fifth of the atmosphere; eight-ninths by weight of all water. Discovered independently by Scheele (*c.* 1773) and Priestley (1774). It is colourless, tasteless and odourless, and forms the chief life-supporting element of our world.

Oxyrhynchus Papyri, the famous hoard of 500,000 documentary fragments unearthed over 100 years ago in central Egypt. Many contain writings from famous authors such as Sophocles, Euripides, Hesiod *etc.*, lost for millennia. The fragments are now housed in the Sackler Library in Oxford.

Oyster, a bivalve mollusc, of the genus *Ostrea*, having very numerous species and abounding in nearly all seas. The shell is rough and irregular. They filter up to 50 gallons of sea water daily. Oysters are exceedingly prolific, spawning in May and June. The Whitstable oyster beds have existed since pre-Roman times.

The famous Delaware Bay oysters have been around for at least 450 million years.

Oystercatcher, a wading bird with black and white plumage and long, orange bill, inhabiting estuaries and sea-shores. Feeds on mussels, shell fish, *etc.*, but not oysters. They can be found on the banks of the Thames.

Ozone, a modified form of oxygen, containing three atoms of oxygen per molecule instead of two. It is prepared by passing oxygen through a silent electric discharge. When present in air to the extent of 1 part in 4 million parts of air it kills bacteria, and has been used for this purpose in ventilating systems, *e.g.*, that of underground railways. It is present in extremely small quantities in the lower atmosphere (*q.v.*) but is comparatively plentiful at heights between 12 and 50 km.

As ozone absorbs ultraviolet light of certain wavelengths, spectroscopic methods, involving the analysis of sunlight, are chiefly used in ozone determination.

P

Paca, a genus of large rodents found in Central and South America, and resembling the guinea-pig. It is of nocturnal habits, has streaked and spotted fur and lives on fruits and plants.

Pacific Ocean. The first European to recognise the Pacific as distinct from the Atlantic was the Spanish explorer, Vasco Nuñez de Balboa, who discovered its eastern shore from a peak in Panama in 1513. The first European to sail upon it was Magellan, who entered it by the strait that bears his name in 1520 Drake was the first Englishman to sail upon it in 1577.

The world's greatest known ocean depth is in the Mindanao Trench, off the Philippines, 37,782 ft (11,524 m). A thriving community of microbes was found there in 2013–the deepest living organisms yet discovered.

Pagan, *See* Paganism, Section J.

Pagoda, the name given in China, India *etc.* to a high pyramidal tower, usually, but not necessarily, connected with a temple.

Palaeontology, the science which is devoted to the investigation of fossils: animal (palaeozoology) and plants (palaeobotany). By studying the markings and fossils of living things in the

stratified rocks, palaeontologists have been able to establish with astonishing accuracy a record of the evolution of life through geological time. The geologist at the same time with the evidence of the fossils has been able to work out the order and the age of the rocks. *See also* **Section T.**

Palimpsests are ancient MSS. or parchments which have been partly effaced and used for fresh writings. Many valuable MSS. were thus lost, but sometimes the second writing has been washed out, enabling the original writings to be deciphered. Among such restorations are a dialogue of Cicero's, a part of a book of Livy.

Palladium, a scarce metallic element, no. 46, symbol Pd, similar to platinum, with which it is usually found. It is an expensive metal, with desirable properties as a catalyst in reactions involving hydrogen, since it has a remarkable capacity for absorbing this gas; for example, coal gas and air will inflame in the presence of palladium at room temperature. It forms a silver-white alloy with gold, and this is used in some kinds of jewellery. It is used in expensive watches to make non-magnetic springs but its main use is in catalytic converters. Russia is the world's largest producer.

Pallium, a vestmental ornamentation of white wool presented by the Pope to new archbishops.

Palm, a large straight-trunked plant or tree common to tropical countries, and usually fruit yielding, such as dates, coconuts, *etc.* Many commodities useful to man are obtained from plants of the Palm family (*Palmaceae*). New palm oil plantations are clearing huge swathes of rain forest to make way for this profitable cash crop.

Palm Sunday, the Sunday before Easter, upon which occasion it is customary to carry palms to the churches in some countries, in commemoration of Christ's entry into Jerusalem for the Feast of the Passover, when the people went to greet Him with palm branches.

Panama Canal. In 1903 the United States signed a treaty with Panama (which had previously seceded from Columbia) which gave the United States rights in perpetuity over a 16 km-wide strip of land extending across the isthmus for the purposes of building and running the canal.

The canal connects the Atlantic and Pacific Oceans, is just over 80 kilometres long (with sea approaches) and the depth varies from 12 to 26 m. It is constructed above sea-level, with locks, and has been available for commercial shipping since 3 August 1914. Under the agreement reached in 1978 the USA formally returned the canal to Panama in December 1999. The biggest expansion of the canal since its opening was completed in 2016.

Panda, *or* **Cat-Bear,** is related to the Raccoon. There are two kinds, the Red or True Panda, resembling a large domestic cat, which lives in the eastern Himalayas and S.W. China, and the Giant Panda, which is more like a bear in appearance and inhabits the mountains of western China. Both frequent the dense bamboo forests of those regions. Today around 2,000 giant pandas survive in the wild in China, but numbers are rising. The famous Wolong Panda Reserve is in Sichuan Province in China.

The secretive courtship and mating of pandas has now been filmed—male pandas make loud yelping and barking noises to scare off potential competitors! Female pandas are receptive to mating for only 36 hours a year. Pandas can survive on shoots and leaves by expending very small amounts of energy.

Pangaea. The original vast continent on Earth.

Pangolin, the scientific name of the "scaly anteater", a toothless mammal, found in W. Africa and S.E. Asia. It has a long extensible tongue which it uses in catching ants and termites, its chief food. When attacked the pangolin rolls itself into a ball, and its scales assume the form of sharp spikes.

Pangolins have an Order of their own—the *Pholidota*, the scale-bearers. The animal is now threatened with extinction by hunting not just for meat but for their scales and body parts in Asia.

Pantagruel, the leading character in one of the satires of Rabelais.

Pantheon, the famous temple in Rome, originally consecrated to the gods, built by Agrippa in 27 B.C. and rebuilt in the 2nd cent. by Hadrian. Its splendid dome and portico make it one of the most interesting architectural monuments of ancient days. Since the 7th cent. it has been used as a Christian church. One theory suggests the Pantheon was originally a colossal sun dial.

Panther, another name for the leopard, *Panthera pardus*, related to the lion, carnivorous, active climber, found in India, and other parts of Asia, also in Africa.

Paper has been known in one form or another from very early times. As early as 3,500 B.C., the papyrus reeds of the Nile swamps served the ancient Egyptians for sheets upon which to inscribe their records. Almost all surviving Greek and Roman literature is written on this. The Chinese and Japanese, centuries later, were using something more akin to modern paper in substance, an Asiatic paper-mulberry, yielding a smooth fibrous material, being utilised.

With the spread of learning in Western Europe the necessity of a readier medium made itself felt and paper began to be manufactured from pulped rags and other substances. The first known English paper-mill was Sele mill near Stevenage, built about 1490, which produced the paper for an edition of Chaucer in 1498. Other mills were set up under Elizabeth, using linen and cotton as raw material. Other papermaking staples were later introduced, such as surat, wood-pulp *etc.* Bleaching of paper with chlorine was invented in 1774.

The chief raw material in the paper industry is wood-pulp, the main exporters being Canada, Sweden and Finland. Canada is the world's chief producer of newsprint.

Papyrus, the earliest known paper made in Egypt at a very remote period from a tall species of reed, *Cyperus papyrus.* This plant is to be found all over tropical Africa, especially in the "sudd" region of the White Nile. *See also* **Codex**.

Parachute, the umbrella-shaped safety device used in emergency by the crew and passengers of aircraft. The first parachute descent from a great height was made in 1797 by André Garnerin who dropped 915 m from a balloon. Rate of descent for a parachute jump is *c.* 5 m/s.

Paraffin, a mixture of hydrocarbons of higher boiling point than petrol. Paraffin was first obtained by distillation of coal, the process being discovered about 1830. About 1848, James Young procured it from mineral oil, and Irish peat also yielded it. The main source of paraffin supply today is crude petroleum. Used in the manufacture of candles, for waterproofing and numerous other purposes.

Parakeets, various small parrots of vivid plumage native to Australia, Polynesia, Asia and Africa. One of the loveliest of the parakeets is the budgerigar of Australia. They tend to travel in large flocks in the wild. Their diet consists of fruit, nuts and berries. They were introduced to England in 1840. Their population is now booming, especially in South-East England. The bright green ring-necked parakeet is now Britain's only wild parrot. They are having a significant impact on our native birds.

Parallax, the change in direction of a body caused by a change in position of the observer. If the parallax is measured (in degrees of angle) and the distance between the two observation points is known the distance of the observed body can be calculated. The distance of heavenly bodies has been found this way. The first stellar distances were so obtained in 1838 by Henderson, Struve and Bessel. Stellar distances are so great that even when the two observations are made at opposite points of the earth's orbit round the sun, the parallax is always less than 1·0″ of arc. *See* **Aberration**.

Parameter, a number which is fixed for the application of a theory to one particular situation but may be different for other situations. For example, in a theory of motion near the surface of a planet the acceleration due to gravity may be regarded as a parameter constant for a particular planet but differing from planet to planet.

Parchment, made chiefly from the skins of animals, usually of goats and sheep, was employed in olden times before printing was invented and superseded papyrus as writing material. Vegetable parchment, invented by W. E. Gaine in 1853, though not equal in strength and durability to skin parchment, is about five times stronger than ordinary paper. Vellum is parchment made from the skins of young calves or lambs.

Parquetry, the name of a style of flooring consisting of small rectangular wooden blocks laid down according to geometrical pattern.

Parrot, the popular name of a widely distributed family of tropical birds, including the African grey parrot, the green parrot of South America —both familiar cage pets in this country—and also the various parakeets, cockatoos, macaws, *etc.* Many of these birds possess a remarkable gift of imitating sound, especially human voices. Of the 330 remaining parrot species in the world, conservationists have warned that 89 could disappear, through habitat destruction, hunting for food and the demands of the pet trade.

Parsec, modern unit of astronomical distance, particularly for distances beyond the solar system. One parsec equals 206,265 Astronomical Units (AU), and 3·26 light-years. *See* **Astronomical Unit, Light-year**.

Parthenogenesis. The development of animals from unfertilised eggs. The drones of the honey bee are parthenogenetic, and the phenomenon is also common among aphids.

Parthenon, the famous Temple of Athena on the Acropolis at Athens, was built under the rule of Pericles between 447 B.C. and 432 B.C. It was made wholly of marble without mortar. The famous sculptured friezes, known as the Elgin Marbles, are now in the British Museum. It is now believed the Parthenon was once painted with splashes of colour.

Particulates, microscopic specks of acids and chemicals in the atmosphere. When inhaled into the lungs (*e.g.* from vehicle emissions) they can cause serious health problems.

Partisans. Term originating with the Russians who raided French supply lines on Napoleon's 1812 Moscow campaign; now used generally to refer to armed bands offering resistance behind enemy lines. In World War II it took on a specifically left-wing connotation when Stalin urged partisan activities in German-occupied Russian territory in 1941–42. At the same time communist-led partisan bands were formed in Albania, Slovakia and Greece. In Yugoslavia the communists led by Tito styled themselves 'partisans' in July 1941.

Partridge, a well-known British game-bird. Two species are found in Britain, but numbers are falling rapidly, partly due to pesticides.

Passport is an official document issued to a person by his own government, certifying to his citizenship and permitting him to travel abroad. Passports to British subjects issued by the United Kingdom Passport Agency (under the control of the Home Office) authorise the bearer to leave the country and guarantee him or her the state's protection.

Renewal passports at present cost £72·50—and are issued for a period of 10 years. Children under 16 now require separate passports (costing £46·00). For those making more frequent visits abroad a 94-page passport, first issued in 1973, can be obtained. Fast-track passports (processed in just one week) are more expensive (£103).

Free standard 32-page passports for those born on or before 2 September 1929 began in 2004.

From 1988, British citizens began using a common wine-coloured EU passport. Existing blue passports remained valid until 1999. The old one-year British visitor's passport and the British Excursion Document (used by short-stay visitors to France) were abolished from early 1996. To facilitate obtaining a 10-year passport, an application can now be handed in at any post office (for a small extra charge).

The main passport office is at 2 Marsham Street, London, SWIP 4DF. The Passport Advice Line number is 0300 222 0000.

Over 49 million British citizens hold a passport and 6 million are issued annually. Passports in future will have biometric (*q.v.*) details added. Since 2006 adults applying for a passport for the first time have had to do so in person.

*p*C **Value,** introduced by Dr. C. L. Whittles in 1935 as a measure of salinity of aqueous solutions (soil extract, irrigation water, *etc.*); defined as the negative logarithm of specific electrical conductivity in reciprocal ohms. Alone or joined with *pH* (*q.v.*) is useful as an index of osmotic pressure (*see* **Osmosis**) and related hindrance to plant growth resulting from excess of fertiliser or soil salts. If manuring is balanced, growth is best about *p*C 3·3.

Peacock, a bird of large size and beautiful plumage, its characteristic feature being a tail of brilliant "eyed" feathers, which it can erect and spread out, the males possessing resplendent feathering to a much greater extent than the females. It is related to the pheasant; one species is found wild in the forests of India, and another inhabits Burma and the Malaysian regions. In Africa there is the Congo Peacock.

Peanut, Groundnut or **Monkey Nut.** A member of the pea family native to S. America, but now cultivated in many parts of the world. After pollination, the flower stalk bends down and buries the pod containing the peas ("nuts") in the ground. The oil from these "nuts" can be used for margarine manufacture.

Pearl is produced by certain shelled molluscs, chiefly the oyster. The inner surface of the shells of the pearl oyster yield "mother-ofpearl", and distinct pearls are believed to be morbid secretions, caused by some external irritation. Many fine pearls are found in the actual body of the oyster. The Persian Gulf, Sri Lanka, the northwest coast of Western Australia, many Pacific islands and the Gulf of Mexico are among the most productive pearlfishing grounds. In ancient times Britain was renowned for its pearl fisheries, the pearls being obtained from a species of freshwater mussel. Western Australia has produced a 40-grain pearl, the finest the world has seen.

The largest pearl ever found was the "Beresford-Hope Pearl", which weighed 1,800 grains.

Peat, decayed vegetable matter found mostly in marshy positions, and common in Ireland and Scotland. Peat is coal in its first stage of development; burnt for fuel in many cottages.

Peccary, a pig-like animal native to the Americas. There are two species: the collared peccary and the white-lipped peccary, the latter being in danger of extinction.

Peewit. Another name for the green plover or northern lapwing.

Pelican, a genus of bird with long depressed bill pouched underneath, thus able to hold fish in reserve. It has immense wings and webbed feet. There are eight species.

Pemmican, venison or other meat, sliced, dried, pounded and made into cakes, used by explorers and others when out of reach of fresh meat.

Penguin, a genus of flightless, fish-eating sea-birds of the southern hemisphere. They are stoutbodied, short-necked and of small, moderate or large size. The Emperor and King Penguins make no nest but protect and incubate the single egg by carrying it in the down feathers between the feet and the body. Other species brood in the usual way and may lay up to three eggs. Penguins use their flippers for swimming under water. All 18 species are bluish-grey or blackish above and white below. They are very sociable and breed in colonies. They have more feathers than any other bird. The emperor penguins use a unique vocal 'identity code' to pick out their families.

All penguins live in the southern hemisphere, except for the Galapagos penguin which lives near the equator (the only penguin found in the tropics). Eleven penguin species (including Emperor penguins) are under threat (partly because melting ice is destroying their nest sites). Climate change also means longer foraging trips to feed themselves and their chicks.

It is now known that each penguin has a unique pattern of spots on its chest—as individual as human fingerprints.

The oldest penguin fossils (c. 12 million years old) have been found in South Africa, where penguins can still be found.

Penny Black, the most famous British postage stamp ever. It was the world's first adhesive postage stamp. In use, 6 May 1840 until Jan. 1841. Followed by the 'Twopenny Blue'. The first perforated stamp followed in 1854.

Pentagon, government office in Washington, housing the US Defence Department.

Pentaquark. See **Quark.**

Penumbra, the half shadow of the Earth or Moon during an eclipse. The term is also used to describe the lighter, outer part of a sunspot.

Pepys Diary, by Samuel Pepys, was first published in 1825. It gives a picture of the social life of the period 1 January 1660 to 31 May 1669. He bequeathed the manuscript, together with his library, to Magdalene College, Cambridge.

Perch, a well-known family of fresh-water fish, with dark striped sides. The common perch of British rivers and lakes falls an easy prey to the angler because of its voracity.

Peregrine. See under **Falcon.**

Perfumes are essences or odours obtained from floral and other substances. The chief flower perfumes are those obtained from rose, jasmine, orange flower, violet and acacia. Heliotrope perfume is largely obtained from vanilla and almonds. Among the aromatic herbs which yield attractive perfumes are the rosemary, thyme, geranium, lavender, *etc.*, while orange peel, citron peel, musk, sandalwood, patchouli and other vegetable products are largely drawn upon. Many of the popular perfumes of today are chemically prepared *See* **Musk Deer.**

Perigee, the closest point of the orbit of an object such as a satellite to the earth. The opposite of apogee (*q.v.*).

Perihelion. That point in a planet's orbit when it is nearest to the sun; opposite of aphelion. The earth is at perihelion (1.47×10^8 km) in midwinter, about 3 January.

Peripatus, an animal which stands as a link between the annelid worms and the arthropods. Wormlike with short unjointed legs it breathes by a system of air tubes like those in insects. Certain other points of internal structure point to a relationship with annelid worms.

There are some fifty species, the best known being the S. African *Peripatus capensis.*

Perjury, the offence of giving false evidence. In ancient Romans threw the perjurer from the Tarpeian Rock, and after the Empire was Christianised, those who swore falsely upon the Gospel had their tongues cut out. The usual punishment in England from the 16th to 19th cent. was the pillory, fine and prison.

Permian Formation, a group of rocks lying between the Trias and the Carboniferous strata. It has three subdivisions, Upper, Middle and Lower.

Per Procurationem signature means that the subject of the correspondence has been put into the writer's care by his principal for him to use his personal judgment in the matter, and that he is authorised to sign on behalf of his principal. Normally contracted to *per pro* or *p.p.*

Perseids, a major meteorite shower, maximizing on 12 Aug. The shower has been regularly observed since the 19th century. First recorded in A.D. 36.

Peruke, the name given to the wigs worn by men in the latter half of the 18th cent. Wigs are still worn by the Speaker of the House of Commons, judges and barristers (though now only in criminal courts, not family or civil cases). Wigs are not worn in the Supreme Court.

Petrel, the name given to a member of a large, widely-distributed family of sea-birds of great diversity of size and colouring and distinguished by tube-like external nostrils. They usually skim low over the waves, and some, for this reason, are known as shearwaters. The storm petrel or Mother Carey's chicken occasionally patters along the surface, and is often called Little Peter—a reference to St. Peter walking on the water. Except when breeding, petrels are always at sea. They mostly nest in holes and crevices on islands and lay one egg, which is invariably white. The storm petrel, Leach's petrel, Manx shearwater and the fulmar petrel are resident in the UK. *See also* **Mutton Bird.**

Petroleum. See **Oil.**

Pewter, alloy of tin and lead formerly used for making household utensils and ornaments.

***p*H Value.** Introduced in 1909 by the Danish chemist Sørensen to indicate hydrogen-ion concentration on the basis of electrical conductivity and a view of ionisation since discarded; is now taken as a logarithmic scale of acidity or alkalinity of aqueous solutions: acidity 0–7, neutrality at 7·0, alkalinity 7–14. The *p*H of blood is 7·35°–7·45° (faintly alkaline).

Phage. See **Bacteriophage.**

Phalanger, pouched marsupial mammals. They are arboreal and superficially resemble squirrels. There are two genera of flying phalangers or flying squirrels, which have a remarkable membrane along each side of the body enabling the animals to glide through the air. The members of the phalanger family are confined to the Australasian and Asian regions.

Phalangid, a member of the arachnid family Phalangida: popularly known as "harvesters".

Phalanx, a name applied by the ancient Greeks to

a body of pike-men drawn up in close array, with overlapping shields, and eight, ten or more rows deep. The Macedonians stood 16 rows deep. As many as 500 men could be in the front row.

Pharos, the name of the first lighthouse, built by Ptolemy II *c.* 280 B.C., on the Isle of Pharos, at the entrance to the harbour of Alexandria. It was said to be 180 m high. One of the "seven wonders" of the ancient world.

Pheasant. They are birds related to the partridges, quails, peacocks, chickens and turkeys, males distinguished by their brilliant plumage and long tapering tail. First found by the Greeks in Georgia where the River Phasis flows through to the Black Sea. It has remarkably powerful muscles for take-off, but its flight is cumbersome.

Phillippics, the oration delivered by Demosthenes, 352–341 B.C., against Philip of Macedon— remarkable for their bitter invective. The word was also used for Cicero's speeches against Antony.

Phoebe, the outermost moon of Saturn, thought to have begun life as an icy comet.

Phosphorus is a non-metal element, no. 15, symbol P. Most familiar as a waxy, yellow solid which is spontaneously inflammable in air. It has chemical similarities to arsenic, like which it is very poisonous. It was discovered by Brandt in urine in 1669. It is found in most animal and vegetable tissues. It is an essential element of all plants and of the bones of animals. In combination with various metals it forms different phosphates, which are largely utilised as manures. The chief commercial use of phosphorus is in the preparation of matches.

Photoelectric Cell, a device which gives a useful electrical response to light falling on it. There are several kinds depending on the different effects which light may have on a suitably chosen solid (usually a semiconductor), *viz.*, the emission of electrons from the surface ("photoemissive cell"); change in electrical resistance ("photoconducting cell"); generation of electric current from a specially designed semiconductor structure ("barrier layer" or "photovoltaic cell", "solar battery"). Different cells respond differently to lights of various wavelength and must be chosen for each application. *See also* **Solar Battery.**

Photogrammetry, the science of measurement from photographs taken from an aircraft.

Photon. When light behaves like a stream of discrete particles and not like waves, the particles are called photons. *See* **Section T.**

Photosynthesis. *See* **Section T.**

Phylloxera, a genus of plant-lice related to the aphids, which attacks the grape vine. Many vineyards of France, in common with the rest of Europe, were replanted with native vines grafted on immune stocks from California in 1879 after being ravaged by the insect (which came from America). Curiously enough, the remedy also came from America, the vine stocks there being immune to phylloxera.

Phytoplankton, tiny marine plants that live in the upper layers of the sea.

Pi is the unique number denoted by the Greek letter π and obtained by dividing the length of the circumference of any circle by its diameter. Its value is approximately 3·14159. It remains one of the most fascinating figures in mathematics.

Picts, inhabitants of Scotland in pre-Roman times, are held by some historians to be a branch of the old Celtic race, by others to have been of Scythian origin. They occupied the north-eastern portion of Scotland, and were subdued by the Scots in Argyll in the 9th cent., Kenneth MacAlpin becoming king of a united kingdom of the Picts and Scots—the kingdom of Alban.

Pike, a familiar fresh-water fish abundant in the temperate regions of both hemispheres. It forms good sport for the angler in rivers and lakes, and sometimes attains a weight of from 9–13 kg. It is extremely voracious, is covered with small scales and has a ferocious-looking head.

Pilchard, a fish of the herring family, but with smaller scales and more rounded back. It used to appear off the Cornish coasts in vast shoals, but over-fishing has led to a decline. They are now usually known as Cornish sardines. Climate warming may bring pilchards to the North Sea.

Pilgrimage. The undertaking of a journey to a religious place or shrine. An early recorded pilgrimage is that of the Empress Helena to Jerusalem in 326. In the Middle Ages pilgrimages became common, and were undertaken by monarchs and people of

rank in all Christian countries. Muslims have been making pilgrimages to Mecca (the *Hajj*) since the death of the Prophet, as required by the Koran.

Pillar Boxes (Post Boxes). The first post box in Britain was in Jersey. The first standard red box appeared in London in July 1874 (earlier standard boxes had been green). There are *c.* 115,000 UK pillar boxes.

Pillory, a wooden instrument of punishment in use in England until 1837. It consisted of a pair of movable boards with holes through which the culprit's head and hands were put, and was usually erected on a scaffold. While a person was undergoing this punishment the mob generally pelted him with stones and rubbish, sometimes to his serious injury. People convicted of forgery, perjury or libel were often condemned to the pillory, but from 1816–1837 the only offence for which it could be inflicted was perjury.

Piltdown Man, a fossilised skull and jawbone, apparently found in a Sussex gravel pit in 1912 by Charles Dawson. It was declared a fake in 1953 and is now known to have been the work of Dawson himself.

Pine, a conifer of the genus *Pinus*, which flourishes all over the northern hemisphere and includes 80–90 species, which afford valuable timber and yield turpentine and tar. The Scots Pine, *Pinus silvestris*, with its blue-green, short needles, set in pairs, and its rosy-orange branches, is native to Britain, as it is to the whole of Europe. It provides the red and yellow deal in everyday use.

Pine Marten. *See under* **Marten.**

Pipit. The most southerly songbird in the world.

Piracy, was at its height in the "Golden Age of Piracy" from 1650 to 1720. Among famous pirates is Blackbeard (his real name was Edward Teach) who terrorised the Caribbean from 1716 to 1718. Today piracy is rife off the coasts of West Africa and in the Straits of Malacca.

Pirarucu, the largest fish to be found in the Amazon.

Pitcairn Islanders were originally the mutineers of the *Bounty*. They took possession of the island in 1790, and it was not until 1814 that their whereabouts was ascertained, accidentally, by a passing ship. The mutineers, under their leader, Adams, had settled down to a communal existence, married Tahitian women and increased so in numbers that they were too many for the island to support, and in 1856 they were removed to Norfolk Island. A small number returned to Pitcairn.

Pitchblende *or* **Uraninite,** a relatively scarce mineral. It is nearly all uranium oxide, but lead, thorium, *etc.*, are also present. Pitchblende was the material in which radium was discovered by the Curies. Sources include the Great Lakes region of Canada.

Pitohui, a song-bird found in Papua New Guinea which produces a powerful nerve toxin.

Planemos, term for mini-stars, perhaps 100 times smaller than our own sun.

Planetarium, a complex optical system which projects into the interior of a dome a replica of all the phenomena of the sky that can be seen by the naked eye, *e.g.*, sun, moon, planets, *etc.*

Planets, the name given to such celestial bodies as revolve round the sun in elliptical orbits. The name was first used by the Greeks to indicate their difference from the fixed stars. There are eight *classical* planets, Mercury, Venus, Earth, Mars, Jupiter, Saturn, Uranus and Neptune. The term *inferior planets* refers to those whose orbits are nearer the sun than Earth's orbit.

Saturn, Uranus and Jupiter are ringed. Many important questions can be answered by means of probes sent to the neighbourhood of the planets. These include the measurement of the magnetic field, if any, of the planets, the study of their atmospheres *etc.* With instruments landed gently on the surface it is possible to investigate surface conditions and composition.

The US Mars probe *Mariner IV* pictures of the Martian surface in 1965, the Russian *Venus IV* in 1967 made a soft-landing on Venus, and the US *Pioneer 11* came within 43,000 km of Jupiter in December 1974. Two US *Voyager* spacecraft were launched in 1977 flying by Jupiter (1979), Saturn (1980, 1981) Uranus (1986) and Neptune (1989), sending back important new data. Exciting pictures were received in 1998 from the Hubble telescope of a planet outside our own solar system. By summer 2013 *c.*800 extra-solar planets had been detected by astronomers (some very similar to Earth). In the whole Milky Way there could be 10 billion planets capable of supporting life.

Recent decades have seen numerous exciting space missions, mainly to Mars (NASA's Mars Surveyor missions) and also Saturn (Cassini) and Pluto (New Horizons). The Cassini spacecraft is the biggest interplanetary spacecraft ever launched by NASA. In 2004 it arrived at Saturn and began conducting the most extensive survey to date of any planetary system. Cassini has released the Huygens probe into the atmosphere of Saturn's largest moon, Titan.

A gas-giant planet 3 times older than Earth and 800 times larger (near 37 Gem) was discovered in 2003. The first photograph of a planet (2M1207b) beyond our solar system was made in 2004. The largest known planet which orbits another star (TrES-4 in the constellation of Hercules) was discovered in 2008.

In 2011 a planet which orbits two suns (and has two sunsets) was found and in 2012 a planet-like object was found in the Oort Cloud at the edge of the Solar System.

For the new classification of *dwarf planets* and *plutoids*, see **T8–9**.

Plankton, a word which first came into biological use in 1886 to describe the usually microscopic plants and animals floating, swimming and drifting in the surface waters of the sea. To be distinguished from *nekton* (swimming animals like fishes and squids) and *benthos* (plants and animals living on the sea bottom, like fixed algae, sponges, *etc.*). Of great economic importance, providing food for fish and whales. They number billions of trillions, but are threatened by pesticides and pollution.

Plankton played a major role in the formation of Earth's first breathable air. And without Plankton there would be no fish in the sea.

Plants. *See* **Section T**.

Plasma Physics is the physics of wholly ionised gases, *i.e.*, gases in which the atoms initially present have lost practically the whole of the electrons that usually surround their nuclei, so that the gas consists of a mixture of two components, positively charged ions and negatively charged electrons. The physical properties of a *plasma* are very different from those of an unionised gas. In particular, a plasma has a high electrical conductivity and can carry large currents. *See also* **Nuclear Fusion**.

Plastics, a broad term covering those substances which become plastic when subjected to increased temperatures or pressures. The Plastics Industry is based on synthetic organic examples of this group. There are two classes of plastics: the *thermoplastic*, which become plastic every time they are heated (*e.g.* cellulosic plastics) and *thermosetting*, which undergo chemical change when heated, so that once set they cannot be rendered plastic again (*e.g.*, Bakelite). Plastics are composed of long-chained molecules, *e.g.*, polyethylene. Plastic is nearly indestructible.

Platinum, a metallic element, no. 78, symbol Pt. It is a scarce white metal generally allied with iridium, osmium, ruthenium and palladium. It can only be melted in an oxyhydrogen or electric furnace, but can be rolled out into a film-like sheet, or drawn out to the finest wire; being resistant to acids it is termed a noble metal. Named after the Spanish for "silver-coloured" *–platina*. First found in the sands of the River Pinto in S. America. Used in jewellery and catalytic converters. The world's largest producer is South Africa.

Platonic Solids, five regular solid figures known to the ancient world. They are: the tetrahedron (4 triangular faces), cube (6 square faces), octahedron (8 triangular faces), dodecahedron (12 five-sided faces), icosahedron (20 triangular faces). All the faces and angles of each solid are identical.

Platypus. *See under* **Duckbill**.

Pleiades, famous cluster of stars in the constellation of Taurus. Of the seven principal stars in the group, one is rather faint, and many myths have sprung up about this "lost Pleiad".

Pleistocene, the geological period that succeeded the Pliocene. During the Pleistocene, also known as the *Great Ice Age*, there were four cold periods, when the ice sheets covered northern Europe and N. America, separated by warm periods when the glaciers drew back into the mountains. The transition to Pleistocene took place *c.* 1,850,000 years ago.

Pliocene, the geological period preceding the Pleistocene, and the last major division of the Tertiary strata. It began fifteen million years ago.

Plover, wading birds, widely distributed over marshy places of Europe. Several species occur in Britain, including the Golden-plover, the Ringed plover, Kentish plover and Dotterel. There is now genetic evidence that the Kentish plover is not related to other plovers. Ringed plovers first nested in Britain in 1938.

Pluto, the last "planet" to be discovered was searched for following the 1914 predictions of P. Lowell and duly discovered by C. W. Tombaugh at the Flagstaff Observatory in Arizona in January 1930. Generally the most distant of the planets its orbit is much more elliptical than the other planetary orbits and so it sometimes approaches the sun closer than Neptune. It was thought to be different from the other outer Jovian planets which are gaseous and to consist of rock covered in frozen methane gas. The diameter of Pluto is 2370 km.

Pluto's largest moon, Charon, was detected in 1978 by earth-based telescopes using special photometric measurements. It is composed almost entirely of ice. Four further moons (Nix, Hydra, Kerberos and Styx) have been found. Images of the surface of Pluto reveal ragged icy polar caps and clusters of bright and dark features. Its atmosphere freezes in winters lasting 100 years.

Pluto was long considered the outermost planet of the solar system, but a new object, Sedna, was discovered in 2004, three times further from the earth. It was named Sedna after the Eskimo goddess of the seas. In 2006, Pluto, Sedna and other distant objects were renamed *dwarf planets* (*see* **T8–9**). There are many hundreds of Pluto-sized objects in the outer solar system. An even more distant planet-like object was discovered in the Oort Cloud in 2012.

For recent discoveries, *see* **T9**.

Plutonium, a chemical element, no. 94, symbol Pu, capable of nuclear fission in the same way as Uranium 235. Not until after it had been synthesised in atomic piles during the second world war was it shown to occur in infinitesimally small traces in nature. Its synthesis in the atomic pile depends on the capture by Uranium 238 nuclei of neutrons; immediate product of this reaction is the element neptunium, but this undergoes rapid radioactive disintegration to plutonium.

Pochard. One of Britain's most popular duck species, but now in decline.

Poet Laureate is the poet attached to the royal household, an office officially established in 1668, though its origins go back to the early Middle Ages, when minstrels were employed at the courts of English kings. Chaucer, Skelton and Spenser, though not court poets, were all unofficial poets laureate. Ben Jonson has been called the first "official laureate" (1616), but the office was not officially recognised until 1668, when Dryden was formally granted the office. It is customary for the poet laureate to write verse in celebration of events of national importance. The current Poet Laureate is Dame Carol Ann Duffy, the first woman (and the first Scot) to hold the post. The post (once for life, but now for 10 years) carries an annual stipend of £5,000 and 630 bottles of sherry.

Some famous holders have been John Dryden 1668–1689, Robert Southey 1813–1843, William Wordsworth 1843–1850, Alfred Tennyson 1850–1892, Alfred Austin 1896–1913, John Masefield 1930–1967, Cecil Day-Lewis 1968–1972. Sir John Betjeman 1972–1984, Ted Hughes 1984–1998 and Sir Andrew Motion 1999–2009.

Polar Bear. *See* **Bear**.

Polecat, an animal of a dark-brown colour, about 46 cm in length, exclusive of tail; the ears and face-markings are white or light brown. It is carnivorous and belongs to the weasel family.

Pole-Star is of the second magnitude, and the last in the tail of the Little Bear constellation. Being near the North pole of the heavens—never more than about one degree from due north—it always remains visible in the Northern hemisphere; hence its use as a guide to seamen.

Police, a regular force established for the preservation of law and order and the prevention and detection of crime. The powers they have vary from country to country and with the type of government; the more civilised and democratic the state, the less police intervention. England, compared with countries abroad, was slow to develop a police force, and it was not until 1829 that Sir Robert Peel's Metropolitan Police Act established a regular force for the metropolis, later legislation establishing county and borough forces maintained by local police authorities throughout England and Wales. Up to that time police duties were discharged by individual constables and watchmen appointed by local areas in England and Wales. In Scotland the City of Glasgow Police was formed in 1800.

The current structure in England and Wales is as follows:

1. County forces (currently 43).

2. Combined forces, covering more than one county.

3. The Metropolitan Police Authority (MPA), covering an area within a 15-mile (24-km) radius of Charing Cross, but excluding the City of London (since 2000 under the GLA).

4. The City of London Force under the Court of Common Council.

In Scotland, the 8 former police forces became the single Police Scotland on 1 April 2013.

In Northern Ireland, the Royal Ulster Constabulary (RUC) became the Police Service of Northern Ireland in 2001.

The 2,700 strong Ministry of Defence Police (MDP) guard military sites and the nuclear weapons bases.

Police ranks are: chief constable, assistant chief constable, chief superintendent, superintendent, chief inspector, inspector, sergeant and constable. In the Metropolitan Police area the chief officer is the Commissioner of Police of the Metropolis.

The 1994 Police and Magistrates Court Act changed the relationship between central government, police authorities and chief constables. The National Crime Squad (NCS) to tackle organised crime was launched in April 1998. In 1997 Britain ratified the treaty creating Europol (the first EU country to do so). In 2004 the Independent Police Complaints Commission (IPCC) replaced the Police Complaints Authority. This in turn was renamed in 2016 as the Office for Police Conduct and its powers enhanced.

The problem of racism in the police force is currently of particular concern. Recruitment for the police among ethnic minorities is also now a priority to achieve a balanced force. The police have also been brought within the provisions of the Race Relations Act and civilians will head police complaint inquiries. Britain's first black chief constable was appointed in 2003 (to head the Kent force). In 2016, however all 43 heads of the police forces in England and Wales were white.

The first 41 elections in England and Wales for Police and Crime Commissioners (outside London) were held in 2012. They were marked by considerable apathy. The second elections were in 2016, when turnout rose to 25%. The National Crime Agency replaced the discredited Serious Organised Crime Agency in October 2013.

Poll Tax, common name for the Community Charge. It was replaced by the Council Tax from 1993.

Pollock, a white fish plentiful in seas off north Alaska. It has a similar texture to cod.

Polonium, a radioactive element, no. 84, symbol Po, discovered by Madame Curie in 1898, and named after her native land of Poland.

Polymerisation is the linking together of small molecules to make a large long-chain molecule. The general name for polymers of ethylene is Polythene, a wax-like plastic solid.

Pomegranate. A fleshy fruit whose juice has medicinal properties including management of blood sugar levels. There is evidence it delays the ageing process.

Pomology, the science of fruit-growing.

Pope, The, the head of the Roman Catholic Church, recognised by that Church as the lawful successor of St. Peter. He is elected by the body of Cardinals. After 1870, when the King of Italy deposed the holder from temporal power, no Pope left the Vatican between appointment and death until 1929, when peace was made between the Church and State in Italy. *See also* **G11.**

Population. *See under* **World Population, L117.**

Porphyry, a form of crystalline rock of many varieties that in ancient Egypt was quarried and used for the decorative portions of buildings and vessels. The term is applied generally to the eruptive rocks in which large well-formed crystals of one mineral are set in a matrix of other minerals.

Porpoise, a highly intelligent marine mammal of the dolphin and whale family, and a common inhabitant of northern seas. Porpoises travel in shoals, their progression being marked by constant leapings and plungings. Their average length is from 1.2-1.5 m. There are several species, nearly all confined to northern oceans. Porpoises are threatened by climate change and the illegal trade in their bladders.

Portreeve was an official appointed to superintend a port or harbour, and before the name of mayor was used for the chief magistrate of London.

Positron, the "positive electron", an atomic particle having the same mass but an electric charge equal but opposite to that of an electron. It was discovered in 1932. *See also* **Section T.**

Possum, an Australian mammal. The rare white possum is now threatened by global warming.

Post Office, The. This is now a State-owned Limited Company. Its corporate name was briefly changed to Consignia before becoming Royal Mail. In 2002 it announced over 15,000 job cuts amid a growing financial crisis. Meanwhile, the Post Office lost its monopoly of mail delivery on 1 January 2006. Closure of post offices is an area of public concern (their numbers declined from 25,000 in 1964 to only around 11,500 in 2017). The Coalition Government sold off most of the Royal Mail. The Royal Mail dates back to 1516.

Potassium, off a metal most of the, no. 19, symbol K (German *Kalium*). It is similar to sodium, reacting violently with water. It was discovered by Sir Humphry Davy in 1807, and is now generally obtained by the electrolysis of fused potassium hydroxide or chloride/fluoride mixture. Its principal minerals are caranallite and kainite, and it is relatively common in rocks, accounting for about $2\frac{1}{2}\%$ of the earth's crust. An essential element for healthy plant growth; the ashes of plants are relatively rich in potassium. Potash is the common name for potassium compounds.

Potatoes. First cultivated in Peru *c.* 2,000 B.C. Brought to Europe following the Spanish conquest of the Incas (traditionally Sir Walter Raleigh is credited with introducing them to England). The sequencing of the DNA of the potato was completed in 2011, opening up the prospect of new and improved types.

Prado Gallery, the great public picture collection of Madrid, containing a superb collection of paintings by Velasquez, Murillo, Raphael, Titian, Dürer, Van Dyck, Rubens and Goya.

Prefect, chief magistrates in ancient Rome. The title is now applied to the chiefs of administration of the departments of France.

Premium Bonds. *See* **Ernie, L37.**

Printing by movable types was first used in Europe in 1454 by Johann Gutenberg, a citizen of Mainz (typeset books had been produced in China and Korea very much earlier). The invention is also claimed for Laurens Koster of Haarlem. It was introduced into England by Caxton, who set up a printing press in Westminster in 1476. Gothic characters were first used, being superseded by Roman letters in 1518. In 1798 Earl Stanhope replaced the wood printing press by one of iron.

In 1814 Friedrich Koenig applied the principle of steam power to the press. Mr. John Walter, of *The Times* newspaper, was the first to use the steam press. Improvements were introduced by Applegarth and Cowper in 1828 and great strides were made in 1858 when the Hoe machine was put on the market. Then came the Walter press in 1866 which printed on continuous rolls of paper from curved stereotyped plates. The Monotype machine casts single letters and the Linotype whole lines. The term letterpress is used for all printing methods using plates where the characters stand in *relief.* The other main printing methods are *intaglio* and *planographic.*

The development of computer technology has produced the biggest revolution in since Caxton.

Prion, a tiny micro-organism, one hundred times smaller than a virus.

Privatisation, selling of state-owned industries to private businesses and individuals, encouraged by the government after 1979 as part of its free market policies. Among the industries partly or wholly sold off were British Aerospace and Britoil (1983), British Telecom (1984) and British Gas (1986). Others included British Airways, British Coal and later British Rail. A further aspect of privatisation was the requirement of local authorities to contract out activities to private companies and the introduction of "internal markets" in the NHS.

The privatisation of the Tote was completed during 2011 and Royal Mail during 2015.

Privy Council, The is the Sovereign's own council, consisting of about 300 persons who have reached eminence in some branch of public affairs (Cabinet ministers must be Privy Counsellors), on whose advice and through which the Sovereign exercises his or her statutory and a number of prerogative powers. From it have sprung many organs of the constitution and many of our government departments have grown from committees of the Privy Council.

Thus the Judiciary or courts of justice have grown from the Sovereign's Council sitting as a Court of Justice, and today the Judicial Committee of the Privy Council is a body of distinguished lawyers acting as a Court of Appeal from courts of the Commonwealth.

Probation Officers are attached to particular Courts, sometimes a Magistrates' or a higher court. Sometimes an offender is not sentenced to punishment, but is released "on probation", that is on the condition that he behaves well and follows directions given by the Court or by a probation officer. The probation officer undertakes the "after care" of those released from prison or Young Offenders' Institutions. Parts of the probation service have now been privatised.

Productivity. Physical productivity is the output of products during a time unit, *e.g.*, so many products per man hour, or day, or year. Total productivity is the sum of all the units of product created during the given time.

Labour productivity is the part of the total that is attributed to labour as a factor of production. Productivity of capital is the element attributed to capital as a factor.

Productivity of land is the element attributed to the natural powers of the soil, as distinct from what is contributed by the application to it of capital or labour.

Prokaryotes. The first single-celled primitive life-forms to energe on Earth, c. 3·5 billion years ago.

Propane, a colourless inflammable gas made of carbon and hydrogen; formula C_3H_8. It is easily liquefied and transported liquid in cylinders and tanks. In this form it is familiar as a "portable gas supply" for domestic and industrial uses. It is sometimes mixed with butane for this purpose.

Propane occurs in natural gas and is a by-product of oil refining.

Proteins are the main chemical substances of living matter: they are a part of every living cell and are found in all animals and plants. All proteins are basically constructed of carbon hydrogen, oxygen and nitrogen, and some contain sulphur, phosphorus (nucleoproteins) and iron (haemoglobin). Proteins are built up of very long chains of amino-acids connected by amide linkages (the synthetic polymers such as "nylon" and casein plastics (from milk) are built up of the same linkages). The structure of protein molecules allows a variety of function. Enzymes, which bring about chemical reactions in living cells, are proteins having specific properties. *See also* **Section T.**

Proton, a basic constituent of the atomic nucleus, positively charged, having a mass about 1836 times that of the electron. It is a positive hydrogen ion.

Prout's Hypothesis. The English chemist William Prout (1785–1850) advanced the idea that all atoms are made of hydrogen, and their weights are exact multiples of the weight of a hydrogen atom.

With the modification that neutrons as well as protons occur in the nucleus, Prout's belief has been substantially vindicated.

Provost, a Scottish official similar in rank to an English mayor. The Provosts of Edinburgh, Glasgow, Aberdeen, Perth and Dundee are styled Lords Provost.

Ptarmigan, birds of the grouse family, one species of which inhabits the Scottish Highlands. In the winter the bird assumes a white plumage – the only British bird to turn completely white.

Ptomaines, amino acids produced during the putrefaction of proteins of animal origin. Not a cause of food poisoning, as was once generally supposed, which is almost invariably due to certain specific bacteria.

Publicans, under the Roman Empire, were people who farmed the public taxes. It is this class of officials that we find alluded to in the New Testament.

Public Corporations, statutory bodies which operated major industries and services in the public interest, *e.g.*, UK Atomic Energy Authority, Bank of England, BBC, Electricity Authorities, Gas Council, British Coal Corporation, British Steel Corporation, British Railways Board, the Post Office, British National Oil Corporation, British Nuclear Fuels, British Airports Authority. They were accountable to Parliament but their staffs were not civil servants. *See also* **Privatisation.**

Public Lending Right, a scheme established by Act of Parliament in 1979 which gives authors the legal right to receive remuneration from the government for the use by the public of their work through the public library system. Payments (*c.* £6·6 million each year) are now made to *c.* 22,000 authors, illustrators and other contributors. The scheme is now administered by the British Library.

Public Record Office. *See* **National Archives.**

Public Schools. The Public Schools Act of 1864 named nine "public" schools: Eton, Harrow, Rugby, Winchester, Westminster, Shrewsbury, Charterhouse, St. Paul's and Merchant Taylors'. Today the term embraces many more, and can be applied to all those schools which belong to the Headmasters' Conference as distinct from the Headmasters' Association.

There are very many such schools in Britain, including such famous examples as Eton College (founded 1440), Harrow (1571), Uppingham (1584), Rugby (1567) and Sevenoaks (1418).

Public schools for girls include: Cheltenham Ladies' College (founded by Miss Beale in 1853), North London Collegiate School (founded by Miss Buss in 1850) and Roedean (1885).

Many public schools have become coeducational. Public Schools are now known as Independent Schools. In July 2000 a national code of boarding standards was set out, outlawing old-fashioned punishments and ceremonies.

Puffin, bird of the auk (*q.v.*) family. It has a large deep bill and is found in the N.E. Atlantic. In Britain, the largest colony is found on the archipelago of St Kilda, off the west coast of Scotland. Its young are called pufflings.

Pulsars. A regular pulsing of radiation which almost certainly comes from a swiftly rotating neutron star. The pulse of radiation ranges from around 1·6 milliseconds to 4 seconds. The radiation sweeps past the Earth in an identical manner to the flashes produced by a lighthouse lamp. Originally discovered at radio wavelengths, a few have been discovered in other wavebands.

Puma, mountain-lion or cougar, a large wild cat found throughout the Americas. It looks like a lean greyish lioness. The "lion of the Andes". It is now returning in the Rocky Mountains.

Putsch. A conspiracy to overthrow a regime by force. The term is often used of the abortive Kapp putsch of March 1920 in Germany.

Pyramids of Egypt, on the west bank of the Nile, are vast stone or brick-built structures with inner chambers and subterranean entrances, built by the Pharaohs as royal tombs and dating from about 2700 B.C. The most celebrated are at Gizeh built during the 4th dynasty. The largest, originally 147 m high, is called the Great Pyramid, one of the seven wonders of the world, built by the Pharaoh Khufu, better known as Cheops, and there he was buried, 100,000 men, according to Herodotus, being employed for 20 years upon it. Chephren, successor of Cheops, erected the second pyramid, and the third was built by Mycerinus, a son of Cheops. There is now increasing evidence that slaves did not build them.

The pyramid at Meidum built by King Snefru, founder of the 4th dynasty, is the most imposing of all. The Step Pyramid of King Djoser is believed to be Egypt's oldest pyramid. There are in fact more pyramids located in Sudan than in Egypt (where so far 118 have been found).

Over a dozen civilisations, notably the Mayans, Incas and Aztecs, also built pyramids (indeed the largest by volume is the Great Pyramid of Cholula in Mexico). Peru has more pyramids than Egypt, especially in the Andes Valleys of northern Peru. A pyramid pre-dating those of Egypt has been found in Kazakhstan.

New satellite imaging techniques are discovering previously unknown pyramids in Egypt.

Pythons, large snakes, non-poisonous and destroying their prey by crushing it. Some species may reach 9 m in length, and prey upon deer and other small mammals. Found in Asia, Africa and Australia. They lay eggs.

Q

Quadrant, an astronomical instrument for measuring altitudes, superseded for navigational purposes in modern times by the sextant. It consists of a graduated arc of 90° with a movable radius for measuring angles on it.

Quagga, an extinct African animal, resembling a zebra from the front and a horse from the back.

Quai d'Orsay. An embankment in Paris where the French Foreign Office is situated.

Quail, an edible bird of the partridge family, of which only one species, the Common Quail, is found in England. It is not more than 20 cm long. It is found in most of the warmer regions of the world and is protected in England and Wales.

Quantum Theory. The rapid development of quantum theory has been almost entirely due to the experimental and theoretical study of the interactions between electromagnetic radiation and matter. One of the first steps was taken when it was discovered that the electrons emitted from metals due to the action of ultra-violet radiation have an energy which is not related to the intensity of the incident radiation, but is dependent on its wavelength. Einstein showed in 1905 that this could only be explained on the basis that energy is transferred between radiation and matter in finite amounts, or *quanta*, which are inversely proportional to wavelength. *See also* **Section T.**

Quarantine, the strict control of animals *etc.* to prevent rabies and other diseases entering the country. Dogs, cats and rabbits are eligible to enter under the Pet Travel Scheme from rabies-free countries.

Quarks are hypothetical subnuclear particles which were postulated by theoretical physicists concerned with the so-called elementary particles. There are believed to be six kinds of quarks. Quarks carry electrical charges which are fractions of those carried by familiar particles like electrons and protons. This and other special properties of quarks make them suitable for explaining the existence of the large number of other particles referred to in **Section T.**

In 2015 the *pentaquark* was discovered. It amounts to a new form of matter..

Quartering, in heraldry, is the disposition of various escutcheons or coats of arms in their proper "quarters" of the family shield, in such order as indicates the alliances with other families.

Quartermaster, a military officer charged with the provisioning and superintendence of soldiers in camp or barracks, and holding the equivalent rank to a lieutenant. The Quartermaster-General is an officer who presides over the provisioning department of the whole army.

A Quartermaster in the Navy is a petty officer responsible to the Officer of the Watch; at sea for the correct steering of the ship and in harbour for the running of the ship's routine.

Quarto, a sheet of paper folded twice to make four leaves, or eight pages; abbreviated to "4to".

Quartz is a common and usually colourless mineral, occurring both crystallised and massive. In the first form it is in hexagonal prisms, terminating in pyramids. When pure its specific gravity is 2·66. It is one of the constituents of granite, gneiss, *etc.* Among the quartz varieties are *rock crystal* (colourless), *smoky quartz* (yellow or brown), *amethyst* (purple), *rose quartz* (pink) and *milky quartz* (white).

Quartz veins in metamorphic rocks may yield rich deposits of gold. Mining for gold in the rock is termed *quartz-mining.*

Quasars, or in preferred terminology, quasi-stellar radio-sources, form a new class of astronomical objects, first identified in the period 1960 to 1962. They have enormous energy output, and are at vast distances. Many are strong sources of radio waves and fluctuate in intensity.

We now know that quasars propel out from feeding, super-massive, black holes to be found at the centre of most galaxies. Research on black holes is a key area in astronomy at the present time.

Queen Anne's Bounty, established by Queen Anne in 1704 for the augmentation of the maintenance of the poor clergy.

After 1 April 1948 Queen Anne's Bounty and the Ecclesiastical Commissioners ceased to exist and became embodied in the Church Commissioners for England.

Queen's (or King's) Speech is the speech prepared by the Government in consultation with the Queen and delivered in person or by her deputy, at the opening of a Parliamentary session.

Quetzal, a green bird with iridescent plumage, once revered as a god by the Aztecs.

Quicksilver. *See* **Mercury.**

Quince, a fruit belonging to the apple and pear family.

Quinoa, a grain-like food from the Andes, rich in energy.

Quirinal, one of the seven hills of Rome.

Quoll, a cat-sized animal with a dappled coat and bushy tail. Found in Australia.

Quorum, the number of members of any body or company necessary to be present at any meeting or commission before business can begin.

R

Rabbi, a Jewish term applied to specially ordained officials who pronounce upon questions of legal form and ritual, and also generally accorded to any Jewish scholar of eminence.

Rabbits, herbivorous burrowing mammals. In their wild state they have brownish fur and erect ears. They breed rapidly, having several litters a year. Decimated by the disease myxomatosis, they have been threatened by a deadly new disease RVHD (Rabbit Viral Haemorrhagic Disease), first reported in China in 1984. Rabbits can eat up to one-third of their body weight in a single evening. The 37 million rabbits in Britain are threatened with a return of myxomatosis. Popular breeds of pet rabbits are Flemish giant, dwarf lop and English spot.

Rabies, a virus infection affecting animals (*e.g.* dogs, foxes). Since strict quarantine laws in 1901, Britain has been free of rabies. Proposals for reviewing Britain's anti-rabies laws have recently been put forward.

Raccoon, plantigrade carnivorous mammals common to the American continent. There are several species. The common Raccoon (*Procyon lotor*) is about 60 cm long, with a bush ringed tail and sharp snout.

Race. Traditionally anthropologists have been concerned with the differences between the races of Man. Anthropology dismisses theories of a superior race as unscientific: there is not the slightest evidence that one race differs in any way from another in its psychological potentialities; Jews, Irish, Scots, *etc* do differ: but their differences are due to their situation and not to anything inborn.

Nowadays the term race is generally defined to refer to a group or category of persons connected by a common origin (*i.e.* ethnicity).

Raceme, an inflorescence in which the main stem bears stalked flowers, *e.g.*, lupin, foxglove. The youngest flowers at the tip of this axis.

Radar. The basic principle of radar is very similar to that of sight. We switch on a light in the dark, and we *see* an object because the light waves are reflected from it and return to our eye, which is able to detect them. Similarly, the radar station *sees* an object because the invisible radio waves sent out from the transmitter are reflected from it and return to the receiver, which is able to detect them. Thus radar is the use of radio signals that man broadcasts.

The utilisation of radio waves for the detection of reflecting surfaces began with the classical experiment of the late Sir Edward Appleton in 1925, which he conducted in order to demonstrate the existence of the Heaviside layer in the upper atmosphere. During the course of the last war developments took place which tremendously improved the methods and instruments used. As in the case of so many of the inventions primarily developed for the purpose of waging war, many useful applications have been found for radar in times of peace, and, in particular, it has proved of great service as an aid to aerial and marine navigation, and in meteorology, astronomy and even medicine. Radar astronomy investigates the cosmos with the echoes of signals sent out from the Earth.

Radiation, energy emitted in the form of a beam of rays or waves, *e.g.*, acoustic (sound) radiation from a loudspeaker, radiant heat from a fire, β-radiation from a radioactive substance. The radiation of electromagnetic waves from a body depends on its temperature, the amount of energy radiated per second being proportional to the fourth power of the absolute temperature. The hotter the body, the shorter the wavelengths of the radiation; thus the colour of a glowing body depends on its temperature.

Of paramount importance to us is radiation from the sun. Amongst other radiations, the sun sends ultra-violet, visible and infra-red (heat) waves. The principal gases of the atmosphere are transparent to practically all of the solar and sky radiation and also that which the earth re-transmits to space. Carbon dioxide and water vapour, however, strongly absorb certain types, the latter, as clouds, playing an important rôle in regulating the temperature of the globe. The cooling of the ground on a clear night is a result of the outgoing long-wave radiation exceeding that coming down from the sky; at sunrise cooling ceases as the incoming radiation becomes sufficient to compensate for the loss of heat.

Radiation, Cosmic. *See* **Section T, Part I.**

Radio. The theory of electromagnetic waves—of which the radio wave is one—was originated by the British physicist James Clerk Maxwell. He was able to show that both electrical and optical phenomena in space are essentially similar in character, and that the waves if short in wavelength are those of light, and if of longer wavelength those of radio waves.

Heinrich Hertz made many useful discoveries about the waves themselves, and about their behaviour under differing conditions, and about the apparatus for producing them. Marconi developed the practical use of radio waves. Analogue radio sets will be consigned to history by 2018, overtaken by digital.

Radio methods are vital for the transmission of observed data from space vehicles back to earth, a process known as "telemetering." This is done by converting the observations into electrical pulses which actuate a suitable radio transmitter so that it radiates a signal, in coded form, which can be received at a ground station and decoded. The transmission of such a signal can also be remotely controlled by means of signals from the earth. Photographic and television techniques may also be employed for obtaining the desired information and sending it back to earth, as in the case of the Russian picture of the reverse side of the moon and the American pictures of the lunar surface.

Data may be stored within the spacecraft for a time, and then, upon receipt of a particular radio signal from the earth transmitted by the spacecraft at a time convenient for its reception. Soviet scientists, by a special technique, were able in the case of their *Venus IV* probe (October 1967) to parachute an instrumented canister from the spacecraft so that it could descend slowly to the surface of the planet. Another breathtaking achievement was the transformation of the faintest of signals from a billion miles away into superb pictures of the planet Saturn and its rings *See also* **Radio Astronomy, Telemetry.**

Radioactivity is the spontaneous transformation of atomic nuclei, accompanied by the emission of ionising radiations. It was discovered in 1896 by Becquerel, who noticed that salts containing uranium sent off radiations which, like X-rays, can blacken a photographic plate.

Two years later Marie and Pierre Curie discovered several new chemical elements which possessed the same property, but many times more intense than uranium; the most important of these was radium. Shortly afterwards it was established, mainly by Rutherford, that three types of radiations called α-, β- and γ- rays, are emitted from radioactive substances.

It was also Rutherford who, jointly with Soddy, deduced that the emission of the radiations is associated with the spontaneous disin-tegration of atoms which result in the transfor-mation of one radioactive substance into another. A series of such transformations ends when a stable element is pro-duced. All of the heavy radioactive elements can be arranged in three radioactive series, called, the uranium, thorium and actinium series. Initially, radioactivity was thought to be a property con-fined only to a few elements occurring in nature.

In 1934, however, Irene and Frederick Joliot-Curie discovered that ordinary elements can be transformed into radioactive forms by sub-jecting them to bombardment with α-particles. Following this, it was found that beams of other fast particles produced in accelerators can also render ordinary substances radioac-tive. Nowadays it is known that radioactivity is a general property of matter; any chemical element can be produced in one or more radio-active forms, or isotopes. *See* **Section T.**

Radio Astronomy. The science of radio astronomy makes use of radio apparatus and techniques for the observation of events occur-ring in far distant parts of the universe, and, in so doing, is able to enlarge upon the obser-vational field of optical astronomy in a re-markable way. By means of radio telescopes it is possible to observe parts of the universe so far distant that the radio waves received have taken thousands of millions of years to travel from their source to the earth, and thus to observe happenings which may have occurred near the beginning of the history of the universe. Thus radio astronomy works with signals broadcast by objects in space.

There are two main types of radio telescope. The first, known as the interferometer, uses aerials spaced at large distances to obtain very high angular resolution. Indeed, the so-called very long baseline interferometers (VLBI) use receivers with separations of many thousands of km to obtain higher resolution than any opti-cal telescope. The second, and "steerable", type, is that of the radio telescope at Jodrell Bank, Cheshire, which consists of an enormous concave metal bowl, with the radio aerials at its centre. This, though it has a lower "reso-lution", can be directed or "steered" on to any part of the sky which is above the horizon. The interferometers, particularly the VLBI, have been used to examine the fine structure of many objects, including the nuclei of large and unusual galaxies. The jet-like structures recently found in several galaxies are of particular interest.

As well as exploring the structure of gas clouds and clusters in our galaxy and in more distant ones, several of the large steerable telescopes have been used as radar antennae, for example to explore the surface of the cloud-covered Venus, and to locate suitable landing sites for the *Viking* spacecraft which explored Mars.

Alma (the Atacama Large Millimetre Submillimetre Array) in Chile opened in 2013. The world's largest radio telescope (known as Fast) was completed in China in 2016.

Radiocarbon Dating is a method of dating the origin of organic materials or objects by observ-ing their radioactivity. It is of great import-ance to archaeology because it enables pre-historic dates back to about 50,000 B.C. to be established for animal and vegetable remains. It works because cosmic rays (*q.v.*) entering the atmosphere create neutrons which convert nitrogen in the air to radioactive carbon. This forms radioactive carbon dioxide and gets in-corporated into animals and vegetables through-out the world along with ordinary carbon di-oxide in a definite ratio, approximately 1 radio carbon atom to 0.8×10^{13} ordinary carbon atoms.

When the tissue dies it stops inter-changing its carbon with the atmosphere, *e.g.*, by breathing, and the radioactive carbon in it gradually turns into nitrogen emitting a β-particle (**Section T**). The radiocarbon content decreases by about 1 % in 88 years. By measuring the proportion of radioactive carbon left in, say, dead wood, and comparing it with living wood, the age of the dead sample can be calculated in the laboratory.

It is now believed by scientists that the pro-portion of radioactive carbon in the atmosphere varied from time to time in the past because changes in the earth's magnetic field affected the cosmic rays. This has to be allowed for in calculat-ing the radiocarbon date. One use of radiocarbon dating has been to trace the spread of agriculture through the world from its origin in the Near East *c.* 7000 B.C. *See* **Tree Rings.**

Radiosonde, a weather station in miniature carried aloft by a free balloon to heights normally in the neighbourhood of 16 km. Signals representa-tive of values of atmospheric pressure, tem-perature and humidity are transmitted to ground receiving apparatus. The position of the balloon at any instant can be determined by radar, enabling the speed and direction of the upper winds to be deduced.

Radium, a radioactive metallic element, no. 88, symbol Ra, discovered by Marie and Pierre Curie in 1898. Atomic weight 226. Radiotherapy (use of X-rays from radium) is used to treat cancer.

Radon, a radioactive gaseous element, no. 86, symbol Rn, formed by radioactive decay of radium. Its discovery completed the series of elements known as the inert (or rare) gases. Radon has increasingly been linked to lung cancer.

Railways. In 1948 the railways of Britain were unified as British Railways (British Rail). Under the Transport Act 1962 the British Railways Board was set up to manage railway affairs. The most far-reaching change since 1955 has been the replacement of steam by electric and diesel.

Under Beeching the British Railways Board planned a viable railway system by closing uneconomic branch lines.

Under the Transport Act 1968 some railway passenger services became eligible for grants on social grounds, including urban railways and unprofitable rural services. High-speed inter-city passenger services came into operation in 1976 and in 1985 it was announced that the Advanced Passenger Train would go into production.

Following the 1993 Railways Act, the privatisation of British Rail began on 1 April 1994 when a new company, Railtrack, took over the management of the track, signalling and other infrastructure. In 1994, the government announced its intention to privatise Railtrack, which owned 2,500 stations and 11,000 miles of track. This took place in 1996. The first privatised rail services since 1948 began in February 1996.

In 2001, Railtrack collapsed, to be replaced in 2002 by Network Rail. In 2003, following widespread safety concerns, Network Rail took over maintenance work from private contractors. However, the future of Network Rail (now a state-owned corporation) is under consideration. A new 208 mph UK speed record was established by Eurostar in Kent in July 2003. Eurostar trains began using St. Pancras International from November 2007. Britain's first commuter high-speed train service (from Ashford to London) ran in December 2008. In 2009, plans were announced to electrify the London-Cardiff route and in 2012 plans to electrify the line from St. Pancras to Sheffield by 2023 were put forward. The first phase of the controversial HS2 line is due to be completed by 2026. A possible HS3 route has been proposed to link Liverpool, Manchester, Leeds and Hull. The number of rail journeys reached a record high in 2016, doubling in a decade.

Among railway facts are the following:
(1) the **highest** railway in the world runs from Beijing to Lhasa (in Tibet).
(2) the **straightest** is the 297-mile journey across the Nullabar Plain in Australia.
(3) the **longest** is the 6,346 mile route from Moscow to Pyongyang (in North Korea).
(4) the **fastest** speed achieved (currently c. 602 km/h) is by the Japanese Maglev train.
(5) the **busiest** railway station in the world is Shinjuku in Tokyo.
(6) the **longest railway tunnel** in the world (57·1 km) opened in 2016 in under Switzerland's Gothard Pass.

In 2013 the world's longest high-speed rail line opened in China. It links Guangzhou in the south with Beijing, the capital-a distance of 1,428 miles.

With 1½ million employees, Indian Railways is the largest employer in the world.

Rain. When moist air rises into lower temperatures and becomes saturated, condensation takes place on the numerous hygroscopic particles present in the atmosphere. If the temperature is above freezing a cloud of small droplets is formed. These droplets may then grow larger by coalescing with each other as they pass through the cloud until their weight is great enough to make them fall to the earth as rain. In clouds which extend above freezing level, snow and rain both form from the prefer-ential growth of ice crystals at the expense of liquid water droplets. If the resultant ice particle melts as it falls to earth, it gives rain: if not it gives snow. See also **Acid Rain.**

Rainbow, a beautiful colour effect visible to an observer with back to the sun and facing a rain

shower, caused by the refraction and reflection of sunlight in minute water-droplets in the air. From high in the air it would be possible to see a rainbow as a complete circle, but from the ground the most that can be seen is a semi-circle when the sun is just on the horizon; the higher the sun is, the smaller the arc of the rainbow. When conditions are suitable two bows are seen, the secondary with the colours of the spectrum reversed.

The colours of the rainbow are seven; red, orange, yellow, green, blue, indigo and violet—the colours of the spectrum. See also **Aurora.**

Raingauge, an instrument consisting of a deep metal funnel whose stem dips into a graduated glass jar from which the depth of the rain water collected can be read. Continuous records of rainfall are provided by self-registering instruments.

Ramblers' Association, an organisation formed with 1,200 members in 1935 and which now numbers c. 100,000. It has played a decisive influence on the creation of new long-distance paths. It supports the "Right to Roam" across all uncultivated land and in 1996 launched the 'Free Your Paths' campaign. The Countryside and Rights of Way Act came into force on 19 September 2004, opening up 4,000 sq. miles of mountain, moor and heath.

Rambouillet, a royal French château (14th cent., rebuilt 18th cent.), near Paris, and the official summer residence of the President of the French Republic. Also the name of the literary salon of the Marquise de Rambouillet (1588-1665).

Rampant, in heraldry, is a term applied to the figure of an animal with forelegs elevated, the dexter uppermost. When the animal is shown side-faced it is *rampant displayed*, when full-face, *rampant guardant*; when looking back *rampant reguardant*; and when in sitting position *rampant sejant*.

Rape, a cruciferous plant yielding coleseed or rapeseed, extensively grown in all parts of Europe, India *etc.* Rape oil is made from the seeds and as oilcake is a valuable animal feeding-stuff. Since 1970 UK production has soared.

Rare Gases (also called **Inert Gases**). These are a group of elements which are chemically inert, comprising helium, neon, argon, krypton, xenon and radon. Cavendish in 1785 noticed that there was in air some gas which was not oxygen, nitrogen or carbon dioxide, but it was not until 1894 that the first of the rare gases was found by Rayleigh and Ramsay. This they called argon (inert). After the discovery of helium in 1895 Kayser, Rayleigh and Travers soon isolated the other gases except radon, which was later detected as a radioactive decay product of radium. Some of these inert gases are used to fill electric-light bulbs, and helium is used in balloons, since it is very light and non-imflammable.

Rat, a well-known group of rodent embracing over 60 species. The *brown rat* appeared in Europe early in the 18th cent., coming from the East and entering by way of Russia; now it is widespread. The *black rat*, which was the common rat before the arrival of the brown species, is a smaller animal and now scarce. The largest is the Bosavi woolly rat, found in Papua New Guinea.

Rational Number, a number which can be expressed as a ratio of two whole numbers. Examples are 2, ⅓, 0·3, −8. See **Irrational Number.**

Rattlesnake, venomous snakes which obtain their name from the possession of a rattle in the end of their tail, consisting of horny pieces so arranged that when vibrated they make a rattling sound. They are only found in N. and S. America.

Raven, a black-plumaged bird of the crow family, with raucous voice and massive bill. Occurs in many parts of Europe, Asia and America. Ravens were once a symbol of death and foreboding. Dickens had one, described in *Barnaby Rudge.*

Ray, fish with a very flat body and broad and fleshy pectoral fins, related to the sharks. There are c. 500 species. Also known as *skate.* Manta rays are remarkably beautiful and have the largest brains of all fish. This 'gentle giant' is also a predator of the deep.

Razorbill, a sea-bird of the auk family, having a high, furrowed bill and black-and-white plumage. It inhabits rocky cliffs during the breeding seson, and at other times is mostly out on the open sea.

Rectifier, an electrical device which will allow electric current to flow in one direction only and can therefore be used for turning alternating current into direct current. Since electricity is usually supplied in alternating form and frequently needed in direct form, rectifiers are of very common use in both industry and the home, for example in radio and television and for battery chargers. Rectifying properties are possessed by a number of different devices, one of which is a thermionic diode (*see* **Valve**).

Very large valves filled with mercury vapour are often used for rectifying heavy currents for industrial purposes. Many other rectifiers use semiconductors in close contact with metals or with other semiconductors because such junctions have the property of passing electric current easily only in one direction.

Recusants, people who refused to attend the Anglican Church or to accept the ecclesiastical supremacy of the Crown in the 16th and 17th cent.

Red Rum, the most famouse racehorse of modern times. Winner of three Grand Nationals (1973, 1974, 1977). His trainer was Ginger McCain (1930–2011).

Redbreast. *See* **Robin.**

Redstart, a small bird of the Thrush family of handsome plumage and striking song. Two species visit Great Britain: the Common Redstart, with bright chestnut rump and tail, white forehead and black cheeks, favours wooded country, and the Black Redstart, with black breast and throat, chestnut tail and white wing bars, prefers rocky ground or ruins, and breeds in S. England.

Redwing, a bird of the Thrush family which finds its way to this country for the winter. Resembles the song thrush, but distinguished by smaller size, buffish-white eye-stripe, chestnut flanks and underwings. It has bred in Scotland and on Fair Isle.

Redwood *or* **Sequoia.** This genus of coniferous tree comprises two species of Redwoods occuring in N.W. America. Specimens of one species, the Giant Redwood, reach a height of over 90 m and a thickness of 11 m. The age of the largest, the General Sherman tree, is put at over 3,500 years.

Reeve. *See* **Ruff.**

Referendum and Initiative, two methods by which the wishes of electors may be expressed with regard to proposed legislation. It is developed to the highest extent in Switzerland. In a *Referendum* some specific matter is referred to the electors. The *Initiative* is the means by which electors can compel their representatives to consider a specific issue. The British Labour Government held a referendum in June 1975, on whether to remain in or withdraw from the European Economic Community. The result was for continued membership.

More recently referenda have been held in Scotland and Wales over devolution of power to elected assemblies. In May 1998 Londoners voted in favour of an elected Assembly and Mayor. In 1999 Australia voted against becoming a republic in a referendum. In 2002 Switzerland voted to join the UN. In 2005 both France and the Netherlands rejected the proposed new EU constitution. In June 2008 Ireland rejected the EU Treaty of Lisbon in a referendum but in October 2009 a second referendum reversed this. A referendum in the UK on electoral reform was held in May 2011. The result was a decisive rejection of the AV system by 67·9 % to 32·1 %. A referendum on Independence for Scotland was held on 18 September 2014. The outcome was a 55 % to 45 % vote to stay in the UK.

A referendum on the EU was held in the United Kingdom on 23 June 2016. The outcome was a dramatic vote to leave the EU. *See* **D22.**

Refraction, the change of direction which light rays undergo when passing from one medium to another. The phenomenon is due to the fact that in different media light (and other forms of radiation) has different speeds.

Refractory, a substance capable of standing high temperatures and therefore useful for making furnaces and allied apparatus. Some insulating refractories are fire-clay, alumina, porcelain, carborundum, graphite and silica. Some refractory metals are platinum, molybdenum, tungsten and also the alloys nichrome, chromel and alumel.

Refuge, charity supporting women experiencing domestic violence. Its national crisis line (0990 995 443) is available 24 hours a day.

Reindeer, a genus of deer horned in both sexes, occurring only in northerly regions. It has an average height of 1·3 m, is very fleet of foot and the Laplanders utilise it for draught purposes and for food. All reindeer antlers are a unique shape. Climate change (and the Arctic thaw) is causing a fall in Canadian reindeer numbers. The Svalbard reindeer is the most northerly herbivore in the world.

Relativity. The laws of relativity have been substantially proved and have revolutionised our ideas as to the nature of space, time, matter and energy and forced us to think along new lines. In 1949 a new theory by Einstein was announced which sets forth in a series of equations the laws governing both gravitation and electromagnetism, which is said to bridge the gap that separates the universe of the stars and galaxies and the universe of the atom. At present the one is explained by relativity, the other rests on the quantum theory **Section T.**

Remembrance Sunday. *See* **Armistic Day, L9.**

Republican Party of the United States was born by the fusion in 1854 of the group who called themselves National Republicans, having split from the Democrats over tariffs in 1825, and the northern Democrats, both of them being opposed to slavery. It came to power when Abraham Lincoln was elected President in 1860 and won 14 of the 18 presidential elections held between 1860 and 1932. It was defeated in 1932 largely as a result of the economic depression and reached its lowest ebb in the years of Roosevelt's New Deal (*q.v.*) The Party went on being defeated every four years until Eisenhower's victory in 1952. Nixon narrowly failed to defeat Kennedy in 1960 and Goldwater was decisively beaten by Lyndon Johnson in 1964. In 1968 and again in 1972 Nixon was successful in winning the Presidency. His fall from power in the aftermath of Watergate made 1974 a bad year for the Republican Party. In 1980 and in 1984, Reagan won landslide victories. George Bush completed a trio of Republican victories in 1988.

George Bush was himself defeated by Bill Clinton in 1992. The party was again defeated in the 1996 presidential election but narrowly sec-ured the election of George W. Bush in 2000. In November 2004 Bush secured a more decisive victory for the Republicans, but the 2008 elections saw a heavy defeat. Under Mitt Romney the party was again defeated in the 2012 Presidential election. It made a recovery in the 2014 mid-term elections. The 2016 presidential election was won by the right-wing maverick Republican Donald Trump.

The symbol of the Party is an elephant, the invention of Thomas Nast, a cartoonist, in 1874.

Reredos, the ornamental screen at the back of the altar or communion table. It is often of a highly decorative character and is an architectural feature in many churches in Spain. Other examples are to be found in the following cathedrals in England: Southwark, St. Albans, Winchester, Durham and Liverpool.

Resins, natural resins are vegetable compounds largely employed in the industrial arts. They comprise india-rubber, amber, mastic, copal, *etc.* "Synthetic resins" is a term sometimes used as a synonym for "plastics".

Reuter, an international news agency, founded by Baron J. de Reuter in 1849.

Rhea, a large flightless bird, the "ostrich" of S. America, distinguished from the ostrich proper by smaller size, longer beak, larger wings, no tail and 3 toes instead of 2. There are 2 species. It can run at up to 40 mph.

Rhinoceros, a large almost hairless animal related to the horse. Two kinds in Africa and several others in Asia. They have a horn, sometimes two, over the snout composed of modified hair. Most are leaf eaters but the largest species, the white rhino of South Africa, is a grazer. They have been much hunted for their horns. Their numbers, which fell sharply in the last two decades, now total around 20,000. The Western Black Rhino of Africa was declared extinct in 2011. Almost all white rhinos are found in South Africa, Namibia, Kenya and Zimbabwe.

Rhubarb was known to the Chinese by 2,700 B.C. Cultivated originally for its medicinal properties. Imported into the UK since the 18th century.

Rhodium, a metallic element, no. 45, symbol Rh, discovered by Wollaston in 1804. It is found in platinum ores in small amounts, generally less than 2 per cent. With platinum it gives a hard and durable alloy. It is also used, instead of silver, in putting the reflecting layer on a mirror.

Ribbon Fish *or* **Oarfish,** a deep-sea fish, deriving its name from its ribbon-like shape. Though fairly long, it is only a few centimetres thick. The ribbon fish is rarely met with because of its habitat, and most of what is known about it was first learnt from specimens cast ashore.

Rice, a grain-yielding grass, of which thousands of strains are known today, extensively cultivated in China, India, S.E. Asia and certain parts of America, and forming the main food of the peoples of China, Japan, India and S.E. Asia. Some 95 per cent. of the world's rice is produced and consumed in the Orient. The grain with the husk is known as "paddy". Arrack, an alcoholic liquor, is made from fermented rice seeds. There are over 120,000 varieties of rice with a range of exotic names, *e.g.* Basmati, Jasmine, Texmati. It is hoped new GM strains of rice with a greater yield will help to feed the world.

Richter Scale, a series of numbers used to record the relative magnitude of earthquakes. Devised by F. Richter of the California Institute of Technology. An earthquake is given a number on the scale by measuring the amplitude of earth movements, *i.e.,* the size of the to and fro motion in an earthquake wave, with a special instrument called a seismometer. The reading is corrected by calculation to allow for the distance of the instrument from the earthquake and the corrected results by observers at different places agree quite well. The scale is logarithmic, *i.e.,* earthquakes differing by one unit on the Richter scale are a factor 10 different in amplitude. An earthquake allotted zero on the scale would give a reading of 10^{-6} m on a standard seismometer 100 km from the centre of the earthquake. Smaller disturbances would have negative values on the scale. The largest earthquakes had Richter values between $+8$ and $+9$, *i.e.,* they had 10^{+8} to 10^{+9} bigger amplitudes than earthquakes of magnitude zero.

There is no upper or lower limits to the scale.

Rickshaw. Name derived from Japanese for "human-powered vehicle". Rickshaws reached India in the 1880s but are now banned in Kolkata.

Rime, a crystalline deposit of ice formed on objects exposed to wet fog at the same time as frost.

Rinderpest *or* **Cattle Plague,** is a highly contagious disease affecting cattle, sheep and other ruminants. In Europe the disease has been eradicated, but it was formerly very widespread and caused great loss of life among cattle. The disease is caused by a filtrable virus, and is attended by fever and congestion of the mucous membranes.

Ring Dove *or* **Wood Pigeon,** a blue-grey bird, distinguished from other pigeons by larger size (41 cm), white wing-bar, glossy green-and-purple neck and white half-collar. It is very common in Britain.

RNA (Ribonucleic Acid). *See* **Nucleic Acids, L80.**

Roaring Forties, name applied to the prevailing westerly winds over the oceans in the temperate latitudes of the Southern Hemisphere. Because they are unimpeded by large land areas the winds are more regular and stronger than the westerlies in the Northern Hemisphere.

Robin (or Redbreast). A small bird with olive-brown upper parts and orange-red forehead, throat and breast; both sexes look alike. The young are speckled, lacking the red breast. Its wide European distribution includes the British Isles, where it is the national bird. It also occurs in N. Africa and W. Asia. The nest is placed in a great variety of situations including holes in banks, trees and walls; in sheds, amongst ivy and sometimes in old tins. Nesting-boxes are readily adopted, but care should be taken to ensure that the entrance-hole is small enough to exclude starlings. Robins are pugnacious and defend their territories with vigour (around 10% die defending their territory). Urban robins sing at night to avoid the daytime noise of human society!

Their very attractive appearance, trustful disposition, engaging ways and sweet song make them extremely popular. Robin numbers which were declining because of cold and rain, habitat loss and pollution revived in the late 1990s.

The name robin is also applied to a number of very different birds, one of which, the American Robin, occasionally wanders to Europe.

Robots. Derived from the Czech word *robota,* meaning forced labour or drudgery. The word was first used by the Czech writer Karel Capek in 1920. The development of humanoid robots is currently well advanced. Many fear robots may cause mass unemployment.

Rock Dove, the grey pigeon *Columbia livia* of Europe and Asia. It is the ancestor of the domestic pigeons as Darwin was the first to show.

Rockets were invented by the Chinese as long ago as the 11th cent. The Germans devised the huge V2 rocket, carrying a ton of explosive, which was used near the end of the war to bombard London. Rockets are propelled by the burning of fuel (*e.g.,* hydrogen), the exhaust, ejected at high velocity, thrusts the rocket forward.

The provision of enough launching velocity involves the use of rocket motors with adequate thrust. To launch a satellite into an orbit circulating within a few hundred kilometres of the surface a velocity of 29,000 km/h must be imparted. This may be done by using a multi-stage launching system. When the first-stage motor has burned out it drops off, so that, when the second-stage motor ignites, it does not have to support the weight of the first-stage, and so on. If the launching velocity is increased to 40,000 km/h the vehicle will not return to the neighbourhood of the earth but pass out of the range of the earth's gravitational pull completely.

Unless the launching velocity reaches 161,000 km/h it will not escape from the sun and will become an artificial planet.

Rock Magnetism. The study of naturally occurring magnetism in rocks is a subject which has gained considerable importance in recent years. There are two principal reasons for this. One is that this so-called "fossilised magnetism" may be able to tell us more about the past history of the earth's magnetic field. The other is that after many years of heated dispute between geologists rock magnetism promises to settle once and for all the controversy as to whether or not the continents have changed their relative positions in past times (continental drift theory (*q.v.*)). This branch of geophysical research, in addition to its academic interest, may well have important economic consequences.

Thus, it might, for instance, become possible to locate mineral deposits once accumulated under special conditions at certain latitudes but now drifted to other places. Salt and similar deposits formed by the continuous evaporation of solutions in hot countries are one example; oil may well be another. There has been a steady change in rock magnetisation direction with geological time. It is known with some accuracy that the most recent reversal took place 700,000 years ago. It has been found that the older the rock, the farther removed is its fossil magnetisation from the present field.

Roe, popular name given to organs in fish which produce eggs and sperms. "Hard roe" is that of the female and consists of eggs; that of the male is the soft roe or milt.

Roe Deer (*Capreolus capreolus*) deer native to Europe. Found in England and Scotland but not Ireland. "Roebuck" is the name of the male adult.

Roller, a tropical Old World bird of the *Coraciidae* family, related to the hoopoe, kingfisher and bee-eater, of strikingly brilliant blue, chestnut, greenish-blue plumage. There are fifteen species, one of which breeds in the far north and visits the British Isles on its migrations to and from its winter quarters in Africa.

Roman Numerals. See **G9.**

Roman Roads, long-lasting highways constructed by the Romans. The best known British roads were *Ermine Street* (London, Lincoln, York), *Fosse Way* (Lincoln through Leicester, Cirencester, Bath, Exeter) and *Watling Street* (Channel Ports, London to Shropshire). New lidar techniques are revealing more lost Roman roads.

Roman Towns. *See* **G12.**

Roman Walls were built as frontier barriers under the Emperors Hadrian (76–138) and Antoninus Pius (86–161). Hadrian's works, linking Wall-send-on-Tyne with Bowness-on-Solway, comprised a twenty-foot stone wall, ditches, turrets, "milecastles", fortresses and a double earthen mound, or "Vallum". Impressive ruins are still visible at Chesters and Housesteads.

Antoninus Pius, Hadrian's successor, made a further advance, but the turf wall which he built between Forth and Clyde was soon abandoned. Septimius Severus (146–211) restored Hadrian's wall after the assassination of Commodus and the subsequent civil wars. It was finally abandoned between 380 and 390. It is now a UNESCO World Heritage Site.

Romany. *See* **Gypsies.**

Rood Screen, an ornamental partition, separating the choir from the nave in a church, and supporting a crucifix or rood.

Rook, a member of the crow family, abounding in most parts of the British Isles and found in Europe, Asia and N. Africa. It has been introduced into New Zealand. Rooks usually nest in colonies in tall trees. They are highly intelligent birds, adept at making and using tools.

Rosary, a circular chain of beads, used by Catholics when reciting a particular form of prayer. Each bead represents an entire prayer, and the combined prayers constitute the Rosary.

Rosetta Space Mission. *See under* **Comets.**

Rosetta Stone, discovered in 1799 by the French at Rosetta in Egypt, and deposited in the British Museum. It is a piece of black basalt about 91 cm long, and contains a decree of the Egyptian priests of Ptolemy V Epiphanes (205–181 B.C.) in (1) hieroglyphics, (2) demotic and (3) Greek characters.

It was the three different inscriptions on the same stone that enabled hieroglyphic writing to be deciphered.

Rotary Engine. *See* **Wankel Engine.**

Rotten Row, a corruption of *route de roi* (king's drive), the riding resort in Hyde Park.

Roulette, a gambling game played on a table carrying a revolving wheel divided into 37 compartments. Each compartment bears a number, 0 (zero) and 1 to 36. The numbers are mixed and do not follow any particular order. Of these 37 numbers 18 are black and 18 are red, whereas zero is green. The players stake their money on any compartment, colour or combination of numbers. The wheel is whirled round and a ball is set rolling in the opposite direction, dropping finally into one of the compartments, deciding the winning number and colour.

Royal Academy of Arts was founded in London in 1768, under the patronage of George III. The early exhibitions of the Academy were held first in Pall Mall, and later in Somerset House where the exhibitions continued to be held until 1836, when the National Gallery being built, the Academy moved its quarters to that building. In 1869 the present Royal Academy at Burlington House was opened. List of presidents: Sir Joshua Reynolds (1768), Benjamin West (1792), James Wyatt (1805), B. West (1806), Sir Thomas Lawrence (1820), Sir M. A. Shee (1830), Sir C. Eastlake (1850), Sir F. Grant (1866), Lord Leighton, (1878), Sir J. E. Millais (1896), Sir E. J. Poynter (1896), Sir Aston Webb (1919), Sir F. Dicksee (1924), Sir William Llewellyn (1928), Sir E. Lutyens (1938), Sir A. J. Munnings (1944), Sir Gerald F. Kelly (1949), Sir A. E. Richardson (1954), Sir Charles Wheeler (1956), Sir Thomas Monnington (1966), Sir Hugh Casson (1976), Sir Roger de Grey (1984), Sir Philip Dowson (1993), Professor Sir Phillip King (1999), Sir Nicholas Grimshaw, 2004–11 and the engraver Christopher La Brun, 2011–.

Royal Botanic Gardens. *See* **Kew Gardens.**

Royal British Legion, the ex-servicemen's welfare organization founded by Earl Haig in 1921. A non-political organization, it organizes the sale of poppies on Remembrance Day. It has around 350,000 active members.

Royal Hospital, Chelsea, built by Wren, opened in 1694 as an institution for invalid soldiers.

Royal Institution, established 1799, and incorporated by Royal Charter in 1800 for "the promotion, extension and diffusion of Science and of Useful Knowledge". It was in the building of the Institution that Faraday conducted his experiments. It is now also famous for its Christmas lectures begun by Faraday in 1825.

Royal Mail. *See* **Post Office.**

Royal Society was founded in 1660 and incorporated by Royal Charter in 1662. A leading early figure was Sir Robert Moray. Viscount Brouncker was named the first president. Its *Philosophical Transactions* date from 1665.

Among those who served as president of the Royal Society are Sir Christopher Wren, Pepys, Sir Isaac Newton, Sir Joseph Banks, Sir Humphry Davy, Prof. T. H. Huxley, Lord Rayleigh, Sir Archibald Geikie, Sir J. J. Thomson, Lord Rutherford, Sir William Henry Bragg, Sir Henry Dale, Lord Adrian, Lord Florey, Lord Blackett,

Sir Alan Hodgkin, Lord Todd, Sir Andrew Huxley, Lord Porter, Lord May and Lord Rees. The current (since December 2015) President is Professor Sir Venki Ramakrishnan.

Royal Society for the Protection of Birds (RSPB), one of the foremost conservation societies. With over 1 million members it is the largest wildlife organisation in Western Europe. It formed its 200th nature reserve in 2007 (in Sutton Fen).

Rubber, substance obtained from the milky juice (latex) exuded by certain tropical trees and shrubs after tapping. Demand spread so rapidly in the 19th cent. that plantations were established wherever the tree would grow. Seeds of the Para rubber tree (*Hevea brasiliensis*) native to the Amazon basin were obtained by Kew, the young plants shipped to Ceylon and it was from these cultivated trees that the vast plantations of Malaysia and Indonesia developed (by the 1930s Asia dominated the rubber market). Recent years have seen great advances in the production of synthetic rubber.

Prehispanic peoples (*e.g.* the Olmec) used rubber 3,500 years ago.

Rubicon, a small river falling into the Adriatic, and forming one of the Italian boundaries, the crossing of which anciently involved decisive action and constituted a declaration of war. Thus the phrase "crossing the Rubicon", denoting an act from which there is no withdrawal.

Rubidium, a metallic element, no. 37, symbol Rb, most closely resembling potassium. It is silver-white and very soft, and was discovered in 1861 by Bunsen and Kirchhoff, using the spectroscope. It is rare, occurring in small amounts in the mica called lepidolite and in potash salts of the Stassfurt deposits in Germany.

Rubik's Cube was invented in 1974 by the Hungarian, Ernö Rubik, a professor of architecture and design.

Rubrics are instructions in regard to the ceremonies of the Church, appearing in red in the Prayer Book.

Ruby is a deep red variety of Corundum (aluminium oxide); one of the most valued of precious stones. Burma yields some of the finest, and rubies of inferior colour are found in Thailand, Sri Lanka, South Africa and Brazil.

Rudd, a fresh-water fish of wide distribution, plentiful in the rivers of Britain. It is of a reddish-gold colour, with a greenish-blue beard.

Ruff, a bird related to the common sandpiper, once common in the Fen districts. The males have a ruff of feathers round the neck in the breeding season. The female is the Reeve.

Ruffe *or* **Pope,** a small fresh-water fish common in most parts of central Europe, and similar to the ordinary perch. It is found in British rivers.

"Rule, Britannia!" the national sea-song of England, was written by James Thomson (1700–48), the author of the "Seasons", and set to music by Dr. Arne about 1740. The poet's words were "Britannia, rule the waves!" but it is usually rendered "Britannia rules the waves."

Rum, a ardent spirit distilled from molasses, and containing from 40 to 50 per cent. of alcohol. It is chiefly manufactured in the Caribbean, and derives its special flavour from a volatile oil.

Ruminants, animals that chew the cud, having a compartmented stomach, enabling them to swallow food, and later to bring it back to the mouth for mastication; *e.g.*, sheep, goats.

While in the rumen some digestion of food, especially cellulose, takes place by bacterial action.

Runcible Spoon, a kind of fork used for pickles having three broad prongs. The word was used by Edward Lear about 1870 as a nonsense word and may be derived from *Rouncival* meaning large or huge from the bones said to have been dug up at *Roncesvalles* where Roland fell. Rouncival peas are the large peas called "marrowfats".

Runes, certain characters of an alphabet found in inscriptions in the Germanic languages, found cut into buildings and implements of stone or wood in many parts of northern Europe, including Britain. The runic alphabet originally had 24 letters. Scholars agree that some runes derive from Greek, others from Latin.

Ruskin College, the first residential college for working people, founded at Oxford in 1899 by the American Walter Vrooman.

Russification. To make Russian in culture, language,

customs, *etc.* Both under the Tsar and communist rule, attempts were made at Russifying the national minorities of the empire and the USSR to prevent regionalism and a break-up of the state.

Rusts, parasitic fungi, some common species of which have reddish spores which in a mass have a rusty appearance. A well-known species is the Wheat Rust (*Puccinia graminis*), which has an alternative host in the barberry.

Ruthenium, a greyish-white metallic element, no. 44, symbol Ru, discovered by Claus in 1845. It is harder and more brittle than platinum, in whose ores it occurs.

Rutile, mineral titanium dioxide. It is found in many igneous rocks, and in gneisses and schists, Its commonest colour is reddish-brown.

S

Sabbath and Sunday. Sunday, or the Lord's Day, is the first day of the week in the Christian year. It was substituted for the Jewish Sabbath in the 1st century, A.D. as the Christian day of worship in commemoration of the Resurrection. *See also* **Sabbatarianism, Section J.**

Sabbatical Year was instituted by the Jews in ancient times for the purpose of giving the soil a rest from cultivation. This was every seventh year. In universities a sabbatical year is a year of absence for study and travel.

Sable, a furred mammal of the weasel family mainly inhabiting Siberia. It is bright brown in colour, and has a long, bushy tail. American sable is a marten.

Saccharin, a white crystalline solid manufactured from toluene, 550 times as sweet as cane sugar. It is used as a sweetening agent; as a substitute for sugar when sugar is forbidden, as in certain diseases, or when there is a shortage.

Safety Lamp, as used in coal-mines, was invented by Sir Humphry Davy in 1816. The flame is enclosed in a cage of fine-meshed wire which allows air to enter and promote burning, but conducts away the heat generated in combustion so that no product of combustion escapes at a temperature high enough to ignite explosive gases in the mine.

Saffron, a plant similar to a purple crocus. It is used for orange flavouring and colouring. Nearly all saffron comes from Iran. In Spain saffron gives paella its distinctive flavour and much saffron is grown in La Mancha. It is the world's most expensive spice. It was once an important crop in East Anglia.

Sainfoin, a widely cultivated forage plant, especially adapted for sheep. It is of strong, leafy growth and bears bright red flowers. It belongs to the same family of plants as peas and beans.

St. Elmo's Fire, a glowing brush-like discharge of electricity which takes place from sharp-pointed objects on mountains or the masts of ships exposed to the intense electric fields of thunder-clouds.

St. John's Wort, a shrublike wild plant with bright yellow flowers. It yields hypericum and is used as an effective remedy for depression, but prolonged use can cause diarrhoea.

St. Martin's Summer. In traditional folklore, a time of relatively warm weather in Novemeber.

St. Paul's Cathedral is the third cathedral church to be built on the site. It was preceded by a Norman building which was practically destroyed by the Great Fire in 1666. This followed a Saxon church which was burnt in 1086. The present building was designed by Sir Christopher Wren. The foundation stone was laid in 1675 and the structure was completed in 1710. It cost a little under £748,000. Its central feature is the dome, crowned by its cupola and lantern with the golden ball and cross. It escaped serious damage during the blitz.

Saints' Days. In the liturgy of the Roman Catholic church a saint is commemorated and his intercession sought on a special day (saint's day), usually the anniversary of his death. Pope Paul decreed that from 1 January 1970 many saints were to be dropped from the calendar and others demoted. There are now only 153 saints' days plus those in honour of the Apostles, Saint Joseph and the Virgin Mary. The festival of All Saints is on 1 November.

Saladin Tithe. A tax levied in 1188 in England and France to raise money to wage a crusade against Saladin, the Muslim leader. The tithe, which was levied at a tenth of income and the value of capital, represented the first attempt to tax personal property and was levied on both laity and clergy.

Salamanders are amphibia superficially resembling lizards, from which they differ in having a moist skin and no scales. The axolotl is a salamander famous for its ability to regenerate. The ancestors of giant salamanders once walked on land. They are the world's largest amphibian, but critically endangered.

Salmon, a fish notable for its habit of returning from the sea to spawn in the river where it was itself hatched (guided, it is now known), by the use of magnetic fields). Their origin can be inferred from the chemical composition of certain blood proteins. Salmon from the two sides of the Atlantic migrate to communal feeding grounds off Greenland. The decline of wild salmon in Scottish rivers is now alarming conservationists. Scotland currently has the world's third largest salmon farming industry. Salmon is Scotland's largest food export. Young salmon are known as smolt. The greatest runs of wild salmon are in Alaska.

Saltire. The national flag of Scotland.

Saltpetre. *See* **Nitre.**

Salvarsan, the organic arsenical compound asphenamine, which Ehrlich discovered was able to kill inside the human body the spirochaete germ that causes syphilis. Also known as "606". It was superseded first by neosalvarsan and now by penicillin.

Salvation Army. *See* **Section J.**

Samarium, metallic element, no. 62, symbol Sm, one of the lanthanides (*q.v.*). Discovered in 1879 by Boisbaudran.

Sami (Laplanders), the bedouin of the far north, the last nomadic tribes of Europe. Their way of life is intimately bound up with the reindeer. The reindeer herds feed, clothe and shelter the Sami of Finland, Norway and Sweden.

San Andreas Fault, is the dividing line between the North American plate and the North Pacific Ocean plate where "plate" means one of the rigid sections of the earth's crust as conceived in the theory of plate tectonics (*q.v.*).

The fault runs roughly north-west-south-east in California passing near San Francisco. The Pacific Ocean bed and the North American continent are sliding past each other along this fault at about 5 cm per year. As at all plate-to-plate boundaries—another is the Western Pacific coast—the San Andreas fault is the scene of great earthquake activity. Between 1934 and 1970 there were over 7,000 earthquakes severer than magnitude 4 on the Richter scale (*q.v.*) in and near southern California.

Because of large population centres, the activity of San Andreas region is studied with great care and some apprehension about a repeat of the San Francisco earthquake of 1906 which caused displacements of up to 6·4 m along the San Andreas Fault.

Sand Eel. *See* **Launce.**

Sanderling, small wading bird of sandpiper family; breeds in tundra regions of far north, and is seen on sandy beaches of Britain as a winter visitor. Conspicuous white wing stripe and, like Curlew, Sandpiper, Knot, Dunlin and other members of sandpiper family, has marked change of plumage between winter and summer.

Sandpiper, small- to medium-sized wading birds of several species whose migratory powers are so great that they are found in most parts of the world. They include the Common Sandpiper, a bird about 18 cm long, greenish-brown head and back, white under-parts, beak long and slender; Purple, Wood and Curlew-Sandpipers.

Sanskrit, the language of ancient India, spoken by the Brahmins, and existing in early Oriental literature. It was the language of literature and government until *c.* A.D. 1100. It is now confined to temples and places of learning. It is an Indo-European language, related to Latin and Greek.

Saponin. The term is a generic one applied to a range of organic compounds which produce frothy, soapy solutions. Saponins are extracted from the soapwort root, horse chestnut seeds, *etc.* Saponin is the basis of the "foam" used for fire fighting; it can be used like soap to make insecticides and fungicides adhere to the leaves of plants. Also used as detergents.

Sapphic Verse, a form of verse said to have been invented by Sappho, the lyric poetess of Lesbos.

Sapphire, a valuable deep blue variety of Corundum (aluminium oxide) found mostly in India, Sri Lanka and Northern Italy. Synthetic sapphire is often used for gramophone styli.

Saracen, the name given in classic times to the Arab tribes of Syria and adjacent territories. In the Middle Ages the common designation among Christians for their Muslim enemies.

Sarcophagus, the name given to a stone coffin, such as was used by the ancient Egyptians, Greeks, and Romans, for receiving the remains of their famous dead. These sarcophagi were often decorated with carvings and sculptures.

Sardines. See **Pilchards.**

Sardonyx. See **Onyx.**

Sargassum. Floating brown seaweed, kept buoyant by air sacs. Found in the Caribbean.

Satellite Communication, the system for transmitting telephone and television signals over long distances. The global satellite system Intelsat (International Telecommunications Satellite Organisation) was founded in 1964 to establish a worldwide system on a commercial basis. The first generation of Intelsat satellites to be launched was *Early Bird* in June 1965.

Today, satellites have a vast range of functions. Some astronomical earth satellites study the radiations from space that cannot penetrate the atmosphere: X-ray, gamma-ray, ultraviolet and infra-red astronomy have been revolutionised by satellites. Satellites are crucial for communications, weather forecasting, *etc.*

Satrap, the name given to the governor of a province (satrapy) in the ancient Persian monarchy.

Saturday, the seventh day of the week (the Jewish Sabbath), derived name from planet Saturn.

Saturn, the sixth planet in order from the sun, from which it is distant 1427×10^6 km and around which it makes a revolution in 29·46 years. It is 120,200 km in diameter or 9·42 times as large as the Earth and rotates on its axis in 10h 14 min. Saturn is so light it could float on water.

Saturn is noted for its magnificent ring system which is composed of myriads of ice-covered particles. These rings are denser and lumpier than once thought. Among the planet's 62 moons are Mimas, Enceladus, Tethys, Dione, Titan, Rhea, Hyperion, Iapetus and Phoebe. Saturn itself is named after the Roman god of agriculture.

Titan is the largest (radius 2,575 km), being the second largest satellite in the solar system, about the size of the planet Mercury. Galileo was the first to observe that Saturn was ringed; Christiaan Huygens the first to study the nature of the rings; and Jacques Cassini the first to suggest that they were composed of myriads of particles.

Our knowledge of the planet and its moons and rings was greatly increased by the spacecrafts Pioneer 11 (flyby Sept 1979), Voyager 1 (flyby autumn 1980) and Voyager 2 (flyby Aug 1981).

The Cassini-Huygens space probe, launched in 1997, captured spectacular images of Saturn and its 30 rings in 2004. It has sent back images of Saturn's moon Enceladus which acts like a pressure cooker, shooting jets of ice and water vapour from its south pole. It has also explained why Iapetus gets lighter and darker. Saturn is home to the solar system's longest continuously observed thunderstorm (breaking its own 225-day record in 2009). In 2009 a colossal new outer ring (located 3·7 million miles from the planet) was discovered.

The Great White Spot on the surface of Saturn is caused by lightning 10,000 times stronger than that experienced on Earth. *See* **Voyager 1 and 2.**

Sawfly. These insects are considered to be the most primitive members of the order (*Hymenopetra*) to which the bees and wasps belong. In appearance they resemble somewhat the latter, but there is no waist separating thorax and abdomen. The ovipositor is never used as a sting; usually it is saw-like so that the female can use it to make incisions into tissues of plants where the eggs are laid. The larvae look like caterpillars of butterflies and moths.

Saxons, a Teutonic race originally inhabiting what is now Holstein. By the 7th cent. they had, with the Angles and Jutes, conquered and colonised most of England. The three main Anglo-Saxon kingdoms were Northumbria, Mercia and Wessex. The Saxons first arrived *c.* 449 A.D.

Scallop, marine bivalve molluscs of the genus

Pecten, which is widely distributed. The scalloped edge to the shell results from a pattern of radiating groves. Related to the oyster.

Scandium, a metallic element, no. 21, symbol Sc. It was discovered in 1879 by Nilson, and occurs in small quantities in certain rarer minerals.

Scarabaeidae, a family of beetles (Scarabs) widely distributed through Africa, Asia and Europe. It is to this genus that the "Sacred Beetle" of the Egyptians belongs, and numerous representations of it are found on ancient monuments.

Sceptre, the staff or rod used since ancient times to symbolise supreme authority. The sceptre used for the coronation of Queen Elizabeth II is the one made for Charles II. It is about 90 cm long and tipped with a jewelled cross.

Schism, an ecclesiastical term for division in a church. The East–West Schism was the separation of the Greek Church from the Latin, finally established in 1054. The Great Schism was the division in the Roman Catholic Church from 1378 to 1415, when there were two lines of popes, one at Rome and one at Avignon.

Schist, the geological name of certain metamorphic rocks composed for the most part of mineral with thin plate-like crystals (*e.g.,* mica) so that the layers of a schist are closely parallel. Quartz occurs in schists, and where it preponderates the term "quartz schist" is applied.

Scientific Units. The International Bureau of Weights and Measures at Sèvres near Paris, is the custodian of accurate scientific measurement in terms of internationally agreed units.

Methods of measurement are continually being improved and measurements of new kinds coming into use. In defining units certain principles are essential:

(i) units should be so defined that measurements made in one laboratory should be reproducible in another with as much consistency as possible;

(ii) units of all kinds should, so far as practical, form an interrelated system based on as few fundamental units as possible;

(iii) the fundamental units adopted should have a natural basis, independent of particular man-made objects.

An invariable universal natural standard was achieved for the metre in 1958 when it was defined in terms of the wavelength of a line in the spectrum of krypton-86. This was changed in 1983. *See* **Metre** and **SI Units.**

Scone, Stone of, the ancient symbol of Scottish sovereignty. Known as the 'Stone of Destiny' it was placed in Edinburgh Castle in November 1996 (having been removed from Scotland in 1296 by Edward I, the 'Hammer of the Scots'). On Christmas Day 1950 the stone was stolen by four Scottish students.

Scorpion. The scorpions constitute an order of the arthropods. Distinctive features are the pair of powerful claws at the head and a "sting" at the tail, which curves over the back in attack or defence so that it points forwards. The poison injected by the sting is potent, causing instant death in spiders, centipedes, *etc.*, and acute discomfort to humans. A cornered scorpion cannot sting itself to death; scorpions are immune to their own poison.

Scorpion Fly. The scorpion fly, of which there are less than 500 species, constitute a separate order of insects, the *Mecoptera.* They have 2 pairs of membranous wings, and gain their popular name because in some species the end of the abdomen is turned up, though it does not function as a sting.

Scrabble. Game invented in 1931 by the American architect Alfred Butts.

Scree *or* **Talus,** the mass of loose, angular rock fragments which accumulate towards the bottom of hill-sides and mountain-sides. These fragments have been detached by weathering processes, in particular frost action.

Scythians, nomadic conquerors and skilled horsemen (9th–3rd cent. B.C.) who inhabited much of Southern Europe and Asiatic Russia.

Sea Anemones *or* **Actinaria,** an order of marine animals of the coelenterate class *Antozia.* They form a large and varied group of over 1,100 species and they occur in many beautiful colours, flower-like in form.

Seaborgium, 106th element in the periodic table, named in 1994 after Glenn T. Seaborg (1912–99).

Sea Butterfly, marine molluscs which propel themselves by two "wings", or side expansions of the foot. They constitute the order *Pteropoda*.

Sea Cow. *See* **Manatee** and **Dugong.**

Sea Cucumbers *or* **Holothurians.** These animals constitute the class of echinoderms called *Holothuroidea*. They are elongated and worm-like, with a ring of about twenty tentacles round the mouth. There are *c*. 500 species. Criminals are poaching them for the lucrative Chinese market.

Sea Eagle, a genus of flesh-eating birds related to the true eagles, kites and other birds of prey. Examples are the Bald Eagle, emblem of the USA, White-tailed Eagle (Grey Sea Eagle), and Steller's Sea Eagle of the Pacific coast of Asia. Last known in Britain in 1911, but successfully reintroduced from Norway to the coast of Scotland in 1975 and now breeding well.

Sea Elephant *or* **Elephant Seal,** a curious genus of seal, the males of which possess a proboscis of *c*. 30 cm in length that suggests an elephant's trunk. They are found on the coast of California and in parts of the Southern Ocean. Antarctic elephant seals can dive to 6,000 ft. and stay submerged for up to two hours.

Sea Gravimeter, an instrument to determine the density of the earth's crust beneath the oceans. Designed by Dr. A. Graf of Munich and Dr. J. Lamar Worzel of Columbia University, it can detect changes of one-millionth of the value of gravity at the earth's surface.

Sea Hare, a genus of molluscs (*Aplysia*), so-called because of resemblance to a crouching hare. The shell is thin curved plate largely sunk in the animal's body. They have four tentacles, occur in Britain in the laminaria or ribbon wrack zone, and discharge a purple fluid when molested.

Sea Horse, sea-fish (*Hippocampus*), very numerous in the tropics and comprising some twenty species. Their bodies are ringed and they have prehensile tails. Their heads are horse-shaped, and they swim in a vertical position. The seahorse is unique in that males become pregnant. The females transfer eggs to a pouch in the male where he fertilises them. Seahorses do not mate for life and most are bisexual. The spiny seahorse and short-snouted seahorse live in British coastal waters. The seahorse is now a protected creature. They click to attract a mate.

Seal, a marine mammal of the *Phocidae* family. They are found in the cold seas of the world, including the waters around Britain. There is a ban on the sale of seal products in Europe.

Sea Lily. A class of echinoderms, the sea lilies may be roughly described as "stalked starfishes". There are about 400 living species and several thousand extinct species are known. Otherwise called Crinoids.

Sea Lizard. *See* **Glaucus.**

Sea Mouse, a genus of marine worms called *Aphrodite*, oval in shape, 20–23 cm long, iridescent, covered with fine bristles.

Seasons comprise the four natural divisions of the year, and are due to the inclinations of the earth's axis to the plane of the ecliptic (*q.v.*).

Sea Squirts *or* **Tunicates.** These animals are placed in the sub-phylum called *Urochorda*; found growing in rounded, jelly-like masses on rocks near low-water level. They get their name through the water jets they discharge.

Sea Urchin. Around 700 species forming the class *Echinoidae*. The body is globular and covered with spines which may be used for both defence and locomotion. The main organs of locomotion are the tube feet, as in starfishes.

Secondary Sexual Characters, characters of animals which are distinctive of sex, but have no direct connection with the reproductive process. Examples are: the mane of the lion and the antlers of some deer.

Secretary Bird, so called because of the quill-like plumes about its ears, is a bird of prey related to the eagles and vultures; common in Africa, and of considerable service as an exterminator of snakes. It is a large bird about 1·2 m in height.

Sedimentary Rocks. *See* **T63.**

Sedna. *See* **Pluto.**

Seismology, the branch of geophysics devoted to the study of earthquakes and other earth movements. The instruments registering earth tremors are termed seismographs.

In order to record the displacements completely, at one station, three seismographs are necessary to show the two horizontal and the vertical components of the motion. *See* **Richter Scale** and **Earthquakes.**

Selenium, a non-metallic element, no. 34, symbol Se; related to sulphur it is a dark red colour, and solid, found associated with sulphur, iron, pyrites, *etc.*, though only in small quantities.

It is a semiconductor (*q.v.*) and its special electrical properties have led to its use in photo-electric cells and rectifiers. Selenium is widely used in the chemical industry as a catalyst (*q.v.*) in producing aromatic hydrocarbons from less useful hydrocarbons. Also used in making some types of glass.

Recently, selenium has been seen to be helpful in reducing the risk of prostate cancer.

Selfish Genes. Genes are understood to be relatively small sequences of DNA, which are likely to last for many generations. Selfish Gene Theory proposes that the primary function of genes is self replication. The purpose of the organism in which the genes are carried is to ensure that the genes survive and reproduce whether they are advantageous to the organism or not. *See* Richard Dawkins, *The Selfish Gene* (1976).

Semiconductors, substances with numerous special and useful electrical properties. These include:

(i) they conduct electricity much better than do insulators, but much less well than metals (hence their name);

(ii) their power to conduct depends strongly on their temperatures—making them useful for temperature sensitive devices;

(iii) they are sensitive to light—hence their use in photoelectric cells and solar batteries;

(iv) when in contact with metals, or with other suitable semiconductors, they form a boundary layer which conducts electricity much better one way than the other—this is the basis of many rectifiers some of which, called crystal diodes, are an important component in electronic devices;

(v) their electrical properties can be greatly influenced by putting in minute amounts of impurity, this enables semiconductor devices, especially transistors, to be made with carefully selected properties.

Semiconductors were known to Faraday, but the semiconductor age really arrived with the invention of the transistor (*q.v.*) in 1947. The ubiquitous transistor is only one of very many semiconductor devices which perform a variety of functions in technical apparatus of all kinds.

Semiconductors used in technology are usually small crystals, frequently of germanium or silicon, and their robustness and small power consumption often make them superior to other devices, such as thermionic valves, which they often replace. Other semiconducting materials are cadmium sulphide, selenium lead telluride, indium antimonide.

Senate, the higher governing Assembly of a Legislature. The word, applied primarily to the Roman council, is also used to denote the upper chamber in France, the United States, *etc.*

Sensitive Plant. A species of Mimosa (*Mimosa pudica*), whose leaves are extremely sensitive to touch, shaking and burning.

Sepia, the "ink" of the cuttlefish. *See* **Ink Sac.**

September, the ninth month of the year, and the seventh of the old Roman calendar; hence the name, from Septimus. The designation was several times changed by the Emperors, but none of the new names survived for long.

Septuagesima Sunday, the 3rd Sunday before Lent.

Sequoia. *See under* **Redwood.**

Serpentine, a mineral; chemically a hydrous silicate of magnesium. Green serpentine is used as an ornament stone. Fibrous serpentine is called asbestos.

Serval, a collie-dog-sized cat, long-limbed and spotted, from Africa. Preys on a variety of animals, from lizards to small antelope. Black servals occur mainly in mountainous regions.

Set, both in everyday speech (as in tea set, chess set) and in mathematics, a set is a collection of things. The members of the set can be specified by listing them or by describing the properties necessary for membership of the set, *e.g.*, the set of ginger-haired boxers. Set theory is a very important branch of mathematics founded by a great mathematician, Georg Cantor (1845– 1918).

Its development has influenced many other branches of mathematics.

Seven Deadly Sins. *See* Sins.

Seven Wonders of the World were: 1. The Pyramids of Egypt; 2. the Tomb of Mausolus, King of Caria (hence the word mausoleum); 3. the Temple of Diana at Ephesus; 4. the Walls and Hanging Gardens of Babylon; 5. the Colossus at Rhodes; 6. the Ivory and Gold Statue of Jupiter Olympus; and 7. the Pharos, or lighthouse, built at Alexandria by Ptolemy Philadelphus, King of Egypt (the foundations of this were discovered in 2005 by French archaeologists). There are now plans to reconstruct this. One modern theory suggests the Hanging Gardens of Babylon were built near Nineveh by the Assyrian monarch Sennacherib. Some people class the Terracotta Army (*q.v.*), found in China, as an eighth wonder of the world.

Sexagesima Sunday, the 2nd Sunday before Lent.

Sextant, a reflecting instrument for measuring the angular distances of objects. It is of special importance in navigation and surveying, and contains 60 degrees described on a graduated arc. A small telescope is attached and there are also a couple of mirrors which reflect the distant objects so as to enable them to be accurately observed.

The invention is attributed to John Hadley, and to Thomas Godfrey independently, about 1780. The principle had been foreseen, and its application described, at earlier dates by Newton, Halley and Hooke.

Shad, a marine fish belonging to the same genus as the herring. It is found along the Atlantic Coast of the USA, and ascends rivers to spawn.

Shagreen, shark's skin: also untanned leather of peculiar grain made from skins of wild asses, camels and horses.

Shalloon, a kind of cloth manufactured from wool and worsted, and used chiefly for women's dresses and coat linings. It was first made at Châlons-sur-Marne. It was called "chalouns" by Chaucer and "shalloons" by Swift.

Shamrock, the three-leaved clover-like plant native to Ireland and its national emblem.

Shard. *See under* Skyscrapers.

Shark, a large and powerful ocean fish, comprising *c.* 510 species, very widely distributed, but most numerous in tropical seas. They have formidable teeth and are the most carnivorous of all fishes. They usually attain a large size, the whale-shark being often of a length of 15 m. Commercially the shark yields shagreen from its skin, the fins are made into gelatine, and an oil is obtained from the liver. Many shark species are now threatened with extinction as a result of over-fishing by man (*e.g.* in the Indian Ocean and the NW Atlantic). Female hammerhead sharks can reproduce without having sex. Sharks can only swim forwards. The whale shark is the biggest fish in the sea. It is now known that sharks are colour blind. Despite human fear of shark attacks, more people die from coconuts falling on their heads than from shark attacks!. Asian demand for shark fins causes a cruel slaughter each year, estimated at 90 million sharks. Around half the shark species live in the deep seas.

The Greenland shark can live for over 270 years, making it the longest-living vertebrate.

Sheep, a well-known family of ruminants of great utility as wool-producers, and for food. From the earliest times sheep have been a source of wealth to England. So much were they valued in the 15th and 16th cent., that their exportation was frequently prohibited.

Sheep are classified as (1) longwools; (2) shortwools; and (3) mountain breeds. Most of the long-wools carry Leicester blood in their ancestry and the shortwooled Down breeds carry the blood of the Southdown. The Southdown produced the present Suffolk, one of the most popular breeds. Cheviot is an important mountain breed. Of the foreign breeds the most valued are the Merino sheep (*q.v*) of Spain, which yield a fine long wool. The first successful cloning of an adult sheep (Dolly) was achieved in 1997. *See also* Wool.

Shelduck, a handsome genus of surface-feeding ducks, one of which, the common shelduck, is an inhabitant of Great Britain. It is a beautiful white-and-chestnut plumaged bird with dark-green head and neck and red bill. The ruddy shelduck appears in Britain occasionally.

Shell Shock. Term used in the First World War for the mental disorientation suffered by troops resulting from the constant noise of artillery barrages in the trenches. Troops suffered terrible flashbacks and nightmares.

Shellac. This resin is the secretion of the lac insect (*Coccus lacca*), which occurs in the forests of Assam and Thailand. It is used for making varnish *See also* Lac.

Shelter, the charity for the homeless, founded 1966.

Sherardizing. Process for coating steel or iron parts with zinc to prevent corrosion.

Shilling has been an English coin from Saxon times, but it was not of the value of 12 pence until after the Conquest. It was interchangeable with the 5 new pence decimal piece which came into circulation in 1968. A new, smaller 5p coin was introduced after 1991.

Ships have existed from prehistoric times. There is mention of one that sailed from Egypt to Greece in 1485 B.C., and in 786 B.C. the Tyrians built a double-decked vessel. No double-decked ship was known in England, however, before the *Royal Harry* was built by Henry VII, and it was not until the 17th cent. that shipbuilding was carried on in Great Britain as a prominent industry. For some famous ships in history, see **G23–4.**

Shoddy, the name given to a kind of cloth mainly composed of woollen or worsted rags, torn up and re-fabricated by powerful machinery. It was first made at Batley in Yorkshire *c.* 1813.

Shooting Star, the popular name for a meteor.

Shot, the name given to solid projectiles fired from guns. In the time of Henry V stone shot was used, later leaden shot, then iron, and finally steel, introduced by Sir Joseph Whitworth.

Shrike, a large and varied family of birds of hawk-like behaviour found in all continents except S. America. The Red-backed Shrike, which winters in Africa, is a breeding visitor to England and Wales. It is commonly called the "Butcher Bird" from the way it impales its prey (small birds and insects) on thorn-twigs.

The other species on the British list are the Great Grey Shrike, the Lesser Grey Shrike, the Woodchat Shrike, and the Masked Shrike.

Shrove Tuesday, the day before the first day of Lent, receiving its name from the old custom of shriving, or making confession, on that day. In England the day has always been associated with the making of pancakes.

Silence, Tower of, or *dakhma,* a tower about 8 m high, built by the Parsees for their dead.

Silicon, an important non-metallic element, no. 14, symbol Si, it is related to carbon. Next to oxygen, it is the most abundant constituent of the earth's crust (27 % by weight). It occurs in many rocks, and its oxide occurs in many forms (*e.g.* quartz, sand, flint, agate, chalcedony, opal, *etc.*). Principally used as a semiconducting material for making transistors and similar devices. The circuitry of the computer is etched on a chip of silicon.

Silicones are synthetic organic derivatives of silicon which because of their high resistance to heat and moisture have special uses, *e.g.*, lubricants, heat-resistant resins and lacquers, and water-repellent finishes. Silicones are compounds in which the molecules consist of chains of atoms of silicon and oxygen alternately. Silicones were developed in the United States from discoveries first made by Prof. F. S. Kipping at Nottingham University. Manufacture began in Britain in 1950, and in the form of fluids, resins, rubbers and greases they find wide use in industry.

Silk, the name given to a soft glossy fabric manufactured from the fine thread produced by the silkworm. It was known to, and highly prized in antiquity, being at one time paid for, weight for weight, with gold. The manufacture of silk was carried on in Sicily in the 12th cent., later spreading to Italy, Spain and France, where Lyons has been the great centre of production from 1450 to this day. It was not manufactured in England before 1604; but when certain French refugees established themselves at Spitalfields in 1688, the industry was developed and became of importance. In the 18th cent. the Lombes of Derby achieved great success in this industry.

Japan, China, Italy, and Korea are the chief silk-producing countries. Silk was first produced in ancient China *c.* 2,640 B.C.

Silk Road. A network of great trading routes which linked China to the Mediterranean. A constant flow of goods, wealth and culture (as well as diseases) spread along the route.

Silkworm, the larva of a species of moth, *Bombux mori.* It is native to China, and has been cultivated with success in India, Iran, Turkey and Italy. The silkworm of commerce feeds on mulberry leaves and produces a cocoon of silk varying in colour from white to orange. The cocoon is the silken habitation constructed by the worm for its entrance upon the pupal condition, and to obtain the silk the pupa is killed by immersing in hot water.

Sill, a sheet-like mass of igneous rock which has been intruded parallel with the stratification of the country rock, cf. a dyke.

Silurian. This geological period is one of the major subdivisions of the Palaeozoic era. Its beginning is estimated at 440 million years ago, and the period lasted about 40 million years. Maximum thickness of the Silurian strata in Britain measures 4,575 m.

Silver, a white precious metallic element, no. 47, symbol Ag (Latin *argentum*) found in a free state, also in certain combinations, and in a variety of ores. The chief silver-producing regions are the Andes and Cordilleras. Peru, Bolivia and Mexico have yielded vast supplies of the metal since the 16th century, and Colorado and Nevada in the United States have also been very prolific. Today, Mexico is the world's largest silver producer.

In England standard silver (that used for coinage) formerly contained 92½ per cent. fine silver and 7½ per cent. alloy, but when the price rose to 89½d. per oz and the coins became worth more than the face value, the Coinage Act of 1920 was passed, reducing the fineness to half.

To provide silver bullion for industry and for a fund towards the redemption of our silver debt to America, it was decided in 1946 to replace the United Kingdom silver coinage by one made of cupro-nickel (75 per cent. copper, 25 per cent. nickel). Maundy money, however, is of the original silver standard. Silver chloride and bromide are used in photography.

Simony, the offence of trading in church offices, has been contrary to English law since the time of Edward VI. Elizabeth also promulgated laws against simony. Strict laws still exist.

Sinn Fein (*Irish* = ourselves alone), Irish nationalistic movement founded in 1905 which developed into a mass republican party and triumphed in the establishment of the Irish Free State.

A continuing group survived which represents politically the outlawed I.R.A. In Northern Ireland Sinn Fein was legalized in 1974 and is now a mainstream political party.

Sins, The Seven Deadly or Capital Sins are pride, avarice, lust, anger, gluttony, envy and sloth.

Sirius, the dog-star, so called because of its situation in the mouth of the Dog (Canis Major, so it is the brightest star in the sky, and is also one of the nearest to us.

Sirocco, a warm, southerly, often dust-laden, wind blowing across Mediterranean lands from the Sahara, in advance of an eastward-moving depression over the Mediterranean.

Siskin, a small bird of the finch family, common in Northern regions, nesting in Britain. The common Siskin has a yellow-green colour and is a lively, swift-flying bird with a stout bill.

Sistine Chapel, the chapel of the Pope in the Vatican, renowned for its frescoes by Michelangelo.

SI Units (*Système International d'Unités*) form an internationally recognised system of metric units for scientific and technical quantities. The basic units of length, time, mass, electric current, temperature, amount of substance, and luminous intensity are, respectively the metre, second, kilogram, ampere, kelvin (*see* **Absolute Temperature**), mole (*see* **T24**) and candela.

The SI was agreed for general adoption by a number of international organisations such as the General Conference on Weights and Measures (1960). Most countries have made or are making the SI the only legally recognised set of Units. *See also* **T58–61.**

Skate. *See* **Ray.**

Skink. The skinks constitute a large family of lizards with large smooth scales, under each of which is a bony plate. The largest species, found in Australia, is about 61 cm long. Some skinks have adopted a burrowing habit and degeneration of the limbs is associated with this. The Common Skink is a small species *c.* 12 cm long, living in deserts of N. Africa.

Skua, falcon-like marine birds related to the gulls found throughout the world. Known as "Robber Birds" because they steal not only the young

and eggs of other birds but also their food. The Arctic Skua breeds as far south as Scotland. The Great Skua breeds in both Antarctica and Arctica. Other species are the Pomarine, the Long-tailed, and McCormick's Skua.

Skunk, a North American mammal of the weasel family, with short legs and long bushy tail. All fifteen species are black and white, some being striped and the rest spotted. It secretes and ejects at will a potent foul-smelling fluid.

Sky. The blue colour of the sky on a summer's day is the result of the scattering of light waves by particles of dust and vapour in the earth's atmosphere. Blue light having almost the smallest wavelength in the visible spectrum (0·00004 cm) is scattered laterally about 10 times as much as the red (0·00007 cm).

Skylark. *See* **Lark.**

Skyscraper. Owing to lack of ground space, and increasing cost of land, buildings are being made higher than broader; hence the name. The structures are constructed of steel framework usually clothed in concrete or reinforced concrete.

The first modern skyscraper was the Home Insurance Building in Chicago, designed (1883) by William Le Baron. The New York skyscrapers include the Empire State building (102 stories), Chrysler (77 stories), Rockefeller Center (70 stories), and 60 Wall Tower (67 stories). The World Trade Center building (110 stories) was destroyed in the September 2001 terrorist attack. It will be replaced by the Freedom Tower.

Even taller than any New York skyscraper is the Sears Tower, Chicago (447m). The Petronas Towers in Kuala Lumpur (opened in 1996) reach 450 m (1477ft). Even taller is the Shanghai World Finance Centre, China. Opened in 2008, at 492 m high it is the highest skyscraper in China. The tallest of all is the Burj Khalifa (Dubai) (828m), opened in 2010. All of these will be topped by the planned Kingdom Tower in Jeddah, Saudi Arabia (1 km, 3,280ft high, due to be finished in 2020).

The tallest completed building in the UK used to be the 50-storey Canary Wharf tower (243·7m), visible from 20 miles away in Kent. It overtook Tower 42 (formerly the NatWest Bank tower) (183m) and the BT radio tower (177m). It has now been overtaken by the London Bridge Tower (the 'Shard of Glass'), which on completion in 2012 was the tallest (1,017 ft) in the European Union. Hong Kong boasts over 1220 skyscrapers. The tallest *structure* in Britain is the IBA mast at Belmont, Lincs.

The tallest *residential* building in the world is the Trump World Tower in New York, but Dubai plans a 2,332ft apartment block (Dubai One).

The tallest public viewing tower in the UK is the Spinnaker Tower (360ft) in Portsmouth.

Slate, fine-grained clayey rocks which have undergone metamorphism. They cleave easily, and it is this property of cleavage which makes them a valuable source of roofing material. Important quarries producing mainly green slate are in the Coniston–Ambleside area of the Lake District.

Slavery. In its earlier forms, as in the times of ancient Greece and Rome, in the feudal ages, when vassalage and villeinage existed, and in the serfdom of Russia and other northern nations, slavery was attended by many inhumanities and evils; but perhaps in the slavery system which prevailed in the British colonies for upwards of 200 years and in certain parts of the USA up to 1865, it attained its highest point of inhumanity.

In 1833 the Act of Emancipation was passed, emancipating all slaves in British territories, though slavery continued to be practised in parts of Africa (*e.g.* Mauritania) long after that date.

Concern about widespread forms of slavery has led in Britain to the passing of a landmark Modern Slavery Act and the appointment of the first Independent Anti Slavery Commissioner (currently Kevin Hyland). There are still even today an estimated 36 million people living in servitude in the world (around half of these are in India).

Slide Rule, an instrument which consists of two logarithmic scales sliding alongside each other. By its use multiplication, division, extraction of roots, *etc.*, are speedily carried out.

Sloes are blackthorn berries, a wild autumn fruit. The sloe shrub has savage thorns. Sloe gin remains a popular Christmas beverage.

Sloth, a curious family of nocturnal mammals, only found in Central and South America. They dwell almost entirely in the trees, proceeding from branch to branch with their bodies hanging downwards, their weight being supported by their large hook-like claws. They eat foliage. Their reputation for slothfulness is wildly exaggerated but their body is totally adapted to save energy.

Slow-Worm, a species of lizard found in Britain which lacks legs. Silver with longitudinal brown stripes, it lives almost entirely on slugs.

Smelting. The process of heating an ore with a reducing agent to convert ore into metal, and with a flux to convert rocky impurities into a slag that will float on top of the molten metal. Slag and metal can then be tapped separately. An example is iron smelting; the reducing agent is coke, and limestone is added as the flux; the smelting is carried out in a blast furnace.

Smoking. See **Tobacco.**

Snake. The snakes constitute the important reptilian order *Ophidia*. Snakes have a scaly, cylindrical, limbless body, lidless eyes, forked tongue, and the upper and lower jaws joined at the chin by an elastic ligament. Most (but not all) snakes have teeth used for seizing prey, and the poisonous varieties are furnished with poison fangs in the upper jaw. Snakes use their forked tongue not only to taste but to smell their prey. It is now known that giant snakes' homing instinct is due to the earth's magnetic field.

Over 2,500 species of snakes are known, divided into 13 families. Some, such as the Black Mamba and Egyptian Cobra, are deadly to humans. There are 3 British species—the grass-snake, smooth-snake and adder. The adder is the only venomous snake in the UK. Global stocks of snakebite anti-venom are running low.

Snipe, a wading bird, long-legged, with a long, slender, straight bill, brown plumage, and zig-zag flight. The Common Snipe breeds locally throughout Britain; the Great Snipe and small Jack Snipe are occasional visitors. The close season is 1 February to 11 August.

Snow. When water vapour condenses at high levels at a temperature below freezing (sublimation), a cloud of ice particles is formed. If these frozen droplets are small, they fall slowly and gradually assume a feathery crystalline structure, reaching the earth as snowflakes if the temperature remains below freezing. There are 121 different types of snowflake, but no two snowflakes are identical. Every snowflake that has ever fallen is unique.

Snowdrops, One of our most loved flowers, but not native to Britain (they came from Italy).

Snow Leopard. See **Ounce.**

Snuff, the generic term for fine-ground smokeless tobacco. The habit is now more popular again.

Soda, carbonate of sodium, is now mainly obtained by certain processes of manufacture from common salt. It was formerly obtained from the ashes of plants. Bicarbonate of sodium is the primary product in the Solvay or Ammoniasoda method for commercial manufacture of soda; it is also formed when carbon dioxide is passed into strong soda solution. The bicarbonate is used in medicine and in the preparation of baking powder.

Sodium, a metallic element, no. 11, symbol Na (Latin *Natrium*), first obtained by Sir Humphry Davy in 1807 from caustic soda by means of the electric battery. Its chloride is *common salt*; the deposits of salt (*e.g.*, in Cheshire and at Stassfurt) have come into existence through the drying up of inland seas. Salt occurs in sea-water to the extent of about 3 per cent.; the Dead Sea contains about 22 per cent. The blood of animals is maintained at a level of about 0·6% sodium chloride. Sodium in the sun's atmosphere was confirmed in 1859 by Kirchhoff from his spectroscopic observations.

Liquid sodium metal has properties which make it suitable as a coolant in some nuclear reactors; a technique of handling this very reactive liquid has had to be developed.

Soil Erosion occurs when the soil is removed from an area at a faster rate than soil formation. This situation usually occurs as a result of man's interference with the natural balance of the environment by the removal of natural vegetation, overgrazing or by poor farming techniques. Soil thus exposed is then removed by the wind (as in the Dust Bowl in the 1930s) or by rain in the form of gully or sheet erosion (as in the Tennessee Valley, USA). Methods introduced to stop soil erosion include contour ploughing, afforestation and dry farming techniques.

Solar Battery, one of the innumerable devices made possible by the development of semi-conducting materials, notably germanium and silicon. This device creates an electric current from light falling on it. The current can be put to use or stored in storage batteries. The energy of the current is derived from the sunlight. The solar battery is thus an *energy converting* apparatus. Solar batteries have provided power for the instruments in satellites.

Solar Corona. See **Corona.**

Solar Eclipse. See **Eclipse.**

Solar System, the system dominated by the Sun, containing the major planets and their satellites, the plutoids (dwarf planets), the asteroids, comets, meteoroids, interplanetary gas *etc.* See **T3.**

Solar Wind, a continuous stream of electrically charged particles blowing outwards from the sun, supplemented from time to time by intense outbursts from regions of the sun's surface. These streams of protons and electrons on encountering the earth's magnetic field distort it and cause magnetic storms (*q.v.*) and aurorae.

Soldering is a means of joining together two pieces of material, usually metals, by melting a third metal (the solder) into the joint. The solder solidifies in the pores of the other metals and holds them together. The materials to be joined are not themselves melted so the technique requires less heat than welding. Solders are alloys; there are many kinds depending on the materials to be joined and the strength of joint desired. See **Welding.**

Solstice, the point at which the sun is most distant from the equator.

Solvents. The abuse of solvents such as glue, paints, *etc.* has grown among teenagers. Solvent abuse can lead to brain damage and dependence.

Soundings at sea, to determine depth at any point, have been taken in all seas, and with considerable accuracy. A deep reading was that of the *Challenger* expedition in 1873, near St. Thomas's in the North Atlantic, when 3,875 fathoms (7,091 m) were sounded. In 1851 H.M.S. *Challenger* recorded the then maximum ocean depth in the Marianas Trench (W. Pacific) by echo-sounding as between 5,882 and 5,950 fathoms (10,764 and 10,800 m). Another deep was located in the S. Pacific in 1952–53 of 5,814 fathoms (10,640 m) in the Tonga Trench, 290 km S. of Tonga Tabu. Since then greater depths have been recorded, in the Marianas Trench and the Mindanao Deep. See **Pacific Ocean.**

Southern Cross, popular name of *Crux.* It is the smallest constellation in the entire sky and can be observed from latitudes below +30°. Its four brightest stars form a conspicuous Latin cross. It is now known to have 8 stars. The constellation is a vital guide to seafarers.

Sovereign Support Grant. See **Civil List.**

Soviet Union. See **Union of Soviet Socialist Republics.**

Space Flight. The Soviet Union was the first country to launch a man into space and bring him safely back to earth. This epoch-making event took place on 12 April 1961, when Yuri Gagarin, tragically killed in an air crash in 1968, circled the earth in a spaceship weighing about 4,826 kg. It was launched by rocket in an elliptical orbit with greatest height 300 km and least 175 km. From that time on, both Russians and Americans completed ever longer times in space. Lovell and Aldrin (60 orbits) were among the first to complete successful missions in space. Leonov was the first to perform an extravehicular (EVA) experiment (1965).

Russia was the first to achieve an automatic docking (link-up) between two unmanned spacecraft in orbital flight (October 1967), and of two unmanned spacecraft (January 1969). The American *Apollo* mission was accomplished when Armstrong and Aldrin became the first men to set foot on the moon (July 1969). A joint Soviet-American project culminated in a *Soyuz-Apollo* link-up 225 km up on 17 July 1975. On 11 January 1978 two Soviet spacecraft docked with an orbiting laboratory, the first triple link-up in space.

The first free walk in space was made by two American astronauts on 7 February 1984 from the space shuttle *Challenger.*

The *Challenger* disaster in 1986 disrupted America's space programme. *Challenger* has been succeeded by *Endeavour,* the most technologically advanced shuttle yet developed.

In 1991, Helen Sharman became the first Briton in space, whilst in 1995, Michael Foale became the first Briton to walk in space. The first "official" walk was by Major Tim Peake in 2016. In 1995, the Russian cosmonaut Valeri Poliakov broke the existing record for the longest continuous time spent in space when he completed 438 days aboard the Mir space station. The current world record is held by the Russian Gennady Padalka who has spent 879 days in space spread over five missions. The US astronaut Shannon Lucid spent 188 days and 5 hours in space in 1996, a record for a woman.

The loss of the US space shuttle *Columbia* in February 2003 was a very serious setback. In October 2003 China became the third nation to send a man into space.

Since the Space Age began in 1957 over 6,500 satellites and spacecraft had been launched from over 30 countries by 2012. Over 500 people from 40 nations have gone into space. However, a massive amount of debris is now orbiting Earth from these activities.

Space Research. By space research we mean scientific research work which can only be carried to otherwise inaccessible observing locations by rocket propulsion. Such propulsion does not rely on the presence of an atmosphere to provide oxygen so that it is capable in principle of conveying objects to unlimited distances.

Space research is not a single discipline, but can provide data of great importance for many, such as the physics of the earth, the sun, moon and other bodies of the solar system, astronomy, geodesy and the study of gravitation. The prospect of investigating the biological conditions on different planets such as Mars and Venus is also opened, as well as that of experimental biological studies under conditions of zero gravity.

During recent decades both the American and Russian space programmes have developed the concept of space stations. There have now been successful soft landings on Mars and Venus, and "fly by" visits to Jupiter and Saturn. Voyager 2 (*q.v.*) left Saturn in 1981 visiting the planets Uranus (1986) and Neptune (1989) and continuing beyond.

The launching of the Galileo probe into the atmosphere around Jupiter late in 1995 greatly increased our knowledge of that planet. The Cassini Mission to Saturn was launched in 1997.

NASA probes to search for evidence of past life on Mars successfully landed in January 2004. The Rosetta Space Mission successfully linked up with a comet in 2014. More recently Pluto was visited by the New Horizons spacecraft in 2015.

A host of deep space missions have been recently launched to investigate the nature of our universe including X-ray, UV and Gamma-ray space telescopes (*see* **European Space Agency**) as well as the microwave telescopes launched by NASA (MAP) and ESA (PLANCK) between 2000 and 2007 respectively.

Space Shuttle. The first reusable manned space vehicle, *Columbia*, was launched on 12 April 1981 from Cape Canaveral, Florida. It orbited the earth 36 times and returned on 14 April landing in California after a flight of 34 h 22 min. The 1986 *Challenger* shuttle exploded and in 2003 *Columbia* broke up on re-entry. The space shuttle made its final mission in 2011. *See also* **Space Flight**.

Spacetime, the single physical entity into which the concepts of space and time are unified such that any event can be specified by four coordinates, three giving the position of space and one the time. The concept was used by Einstein in both the special and general theories of relativity.

Sparrow, name given to finch-like birds found in most parts of the world, of which the House Sparrow *Passer domesticus*, is the most familiar of British birds. Also native to Britain is the rural Tree Sparrow, distinguished from the male House Sparrow by its chestnut crown. Other European species are the Italian, Spanish and Rock Sparrows. House sparrows are in decline, in part because houseowners are filling gaps in their eaves through which birds gained access to the roof.

Specific Gravity, the ratio of the mass of a particular volume of a substance to the mass of an equal volume of water at 4°C. *See* **Hydrometer.**

Spectral Classification, the different groups into which all stars such as our Sun may be classified. The majority of stars can be divided into seven spectral types O, B, A, F, G, K, M. O type stars are the hottest and M the coolest. The stellar types are subdivided into 10 subclasses denoted by the digits 0 to 9. Our Sun is a G2 star.

Spectrograph. An instrument used to separate and record spectral components of light or other radiation. They are a crucial astronomical tool for analysing the physical processes and composition of stars and other celestial objects. *See below.*

Spectroscopy. Newton's arrangement with the prism was the first spectroscope; its function was to separate out the colour components of a source of light. Two hundred years elapsed before this apparatus was developed into a precise scientific instrument, capable of measuring both the wavelength and intensity of each colour component. In this form it is called a spectrometer. All atoms and molecules have well defined characteristic spectra which can be used to recognise them. In order to produce emission spectra it is necessary to energise the material under investigation by some means, such as by heating in a flame. The resulting radiation then consists largely of sharp bright lines, characteristic of the material. Absorption spectra are produced by interposing the experimental material between a white light source and the spectrometer. Then dark lines are seen, corresponding to absorptions of energy, in exactly the same places as the bright lines are observed in the emission spectra.

Spectroscopic techniques have now been developed to such an extent that accurate measurements of wavelength and intensity are possible not only in the visible region, but over almost the whole of the electromagnetic spectrum. Two of the most useful types for the chemist are infrared spectroscopy which reveals absorption characteristic of the type of chemical bonds because of their different bond vibration frequencies and nuclear magnetic resonance spectroscopy which operates in the radiofrequency region. It reveals the structure environments of atoms containing particular nuclei.

Not only does spectroscopy play an important rôle in probing the structure of matter, but it can be applied in the field of astronomy. The use of radio wave spectroscopy has led to the discovery of several new types of stellar object.

Spelaeology. *See* **Caves.**

Sphenodon. *See* **Tuatara.**

Spiders. *See* **T36(1)** under arthropods.

Spirituals, Afro-American melodies with religious inspiration and which are still spontaneously created, but have also passed into art-music.

Sponge. *See* **Porifera, Section T.**

Spoonbill, a long-legged, marsh bird, closely related to the ibis and stork, remarkable for its snow-white plumage and broad, flat, spoon-shaped bill. The European species has not bred in England since the beginning of the 17th cent., but is still a regular summer visitor from the Netherlands, where it nests in colonies in reed beds and islets.

Sputniks, the name of the Russian earth satellites first launched in 1957. *Sputnik I*, launched 4 October 1957, became the first man-made earth satellite. *Sputnik II*, launched a month later carried a dog as passenger. *Sputnik III*, launched in May 1958, was the first space laboratory.

Squirrels. The red squirrel is our only native squirrel. Except in Scotland (where there are over 100,000) numbers have plummeted since the introduction of the grey squirrel from North America.

Stalactites are deposits of calcium carbonate formed on the roofs and sides of limestone caves, and in tunnels, under bridges, and other places where the carbonic acid of rain-water percolates through and partly dissolves the limestone, resulting in the growth of icicle-like forms that often assume groupings. The water that drops from these may deposit further calcium carbonate, which accumulates and hardens into sharp mounds or hillocks called *stalagmites*. These can reveal climate history.

Standard Deviation. In statistics it is often desirable to compare the variability or "spread" of different sets of data. For example, two kinds of light bulb could have the same average life but one kind could be more uniform or consistent than the other. The standard deviation is one of the commonest measures of spread.

It is found as follows. If x is one of the data and $\bar{x}$ is the mean of all the x's, then $x - \bar{x}$ is called the deviation. Every deviation is now squared and the average squared deviation calculated. The standard deviation is then the square root of the average squared deviation.

The lifetimes of the more uniform kind of light bulb would have a smaller standard deviation than those of the more erratic one.

Starboard. The right-hand side of a ship.

Starling (*Sturnus vulgaris*), a well-known European bird now common in many parts of the world. It has handsome iridescent blackish plumage and nests in holes and crevices. Flocks of starlings (murmurings) can be seen wheeling in the air; thousands roost on buildings in the heart of London. Other European species are the Spotless and Rose-coloured starlings. The latter sometimes wander to the British Isles. Starling numbers have decreased in recent years.

Statue of Liberty, presented to the USA by the Frenchman Ferdinand de Lesseps in 1884.

Steam Engine, a machine whereby steam becomes the active agent of the working of machinery, and of very wide application. The leading types of steam engine are: (*a*) condensing, or low-pressure engines, where the steam is generated by a boiler; (*b*) non-condensing, in which the cylinder exhausts its steam into the open air. Engines of the latter type are used where portable engines are required.

Steam-Hammer, invented (1839) by the Scottish engineer James Nasmyth. Consists basically of a vertical steam cylinder atop two legs with piston-rod passing through cylinder base and attached to a tup (hammer) of from 100 kg to 15 tonnes which rests on an anvil. The tup slides in V grooves on inside of legs. Length of stroke and therefore weight of blow can be accurately controlled from a light tap to a massive punch.

It made possible the forging in one piece of multi-throw crankshafts for marine engines, *etc.* and the mass production of high-class axles and wheels, con rods and buffers, *etc.* for locomotives and rolling stock.

Stearin is the portion of fatty matters and oils which remains solid at an ordinary temperature, and is a compound of stearic acid with glycerine. It is largely used in the manufacture of candles. With caustic soda stearin forms a soap (sodium stearate), which is present in most commercial soaps which contain sodium palmitate and oleate in addition.

Steel, an alloy of iron and carbon, with varying proportions of other minerals. The famous blades of Damascus and steels of Toledo were made by the cementation and crucible method. The metal produced by the "Bessemer process" (*q.v.*) is of great value for structural purposes, rails, *etc.*

The technique known as continuous casting bypasses some major steps in the conventional process of steel-making.

Stereophonic Broadcasting. A person having normal hearing is able to determine the direction from which a sound reaches him by virtue of the fact that he has two ears, and, therefore, the sound will reach one of them a fraction of a second before it reaches the other. This difference in arrival time allows the brain to calculate direction.

Stereophonic broadcasting restores the listener's ability to locate the position in space of the various sources of sound and to follow movement (just as if he or she were in a concert hall).

To do this it is necessary to use two microphones in the studio—to simulate the two human ears—and to transmit their outputs, through two similar, but separate, chains of equipment, to two radio receivers and their two loudspeakers, which must be placed some distance apart, in the listener's home.

The main work on two-channel stereophony was done by A.D. Blumlein (1903–42), his original patent being dated 1931.

Stereotype, a metal cast taken from movable type which has been set up in the ordinary way. The first to introduce the process in practical form in this country was William Ged of Edinburgh in 1730. An impression of the type matter is first taken by means of a mould of prepared plaster of Paris or moistened sheets of specially prepared paper and when molten stereo metal is poured upon the mould and allowed to cool and harden, the stereo plate is formed, and can be printed from as a solid block for some time.

Steroids. A class of structurally related compounds, based on a system of condensed rings of carbon and hydrogen, which are widely distributed in animals and plants. Included in the steroid family are sterols, found in all animal cells, vitamin D, sex hormones, bile acids and cortisone.

Stickleback, a family of small spiny-finned fish widely distributed in both fresh and salt water. Male constructs roofed nest held together by sticky secretion from glands near kidneys. Several females deposit eggs therein which he guards until after young are hatched.

Stirrup, a loop of metal 7-shaped strap suspended from the sides of the saddle, used for mounting and to support the horseman's foot. They were used as far back as the early Iron Age, and it is believed that they were used in battle in Europe in A.D. 378, when the Gothic cavalry defeated the legionaries of the Emperor Valens at Adrianople. Stirrups relieved the tension of the rider's knees and so enabled him to be armed from top to toe.

Stoat, a slender, carnivorous mammal with short legs, related to the weasels. The stoat is distinguished from the latter by its longer tail, which has a black tip. The black tip is retained even in the winter when the animal turns white, the fur then being known as "ermine". It is found in northern latitudes, and is abundant in Arctic America. A stoat can take on a rabbit twice its size.

Stoma (pl. **Stomata**), microscopic pores on the surfaces of leaves through which gaseous exchanges take place and water is lost. It is estimated that a single maize plant bears 200 million stomata, usually closed at night.

Stone of Scone. *See under* **Scone.**

Stone-Flies, comprise the order of insects called *Plecoptera*, which includes some 700 species, of which about thirty occur in Britain. The wings are membranous, and two long, thread-like feelers protrude at the tail end. The larvae are aquatic.

Stork, a family of heron-like birds with long bills, freely distributed over Europe, Asia, Africa and S. America. The White Stork is an occasional visitor to England, and, more rarely, the Black Stork; these are the only two European storks.

Stratosphere, a layer of the earth's atmosphere which lies between the tropopause (*c.* 12 km above the earth) and the stratopause (*c.* 50 km). The ozone layer lies within the stratosphere and is responsible for the relatively high temperature there. The region is less turbulent than the troposphere, and is usually clear of clouds *etc*, making it attractive for air transport.

Stratum (pl. **Strata**), a bed or layer of rock.

Strontium. This silver-white metallic element, no. 38, was discovered by Hope and Klaproth in 1793, and isolated by Sir Humphry Davy in 1808. The chief strontium minerals are celestite (sulphate) and strontianite (carbonate). Compounds of strontium give a brilliant colour to fireworks and signal flares. Radioactive isotopes of strontium (strontium-90) are formed as fission products in nuclear explosions and tend to collect in bone on account of the chemical similarity of strontium and calcium. *See* **Fall-out.**

Stuart. The Scottish dynasty which provided England with its monarchs from 1603 to 1688 (James I, Charles I, Charles II and James II).

Sturgeon, a large fish found in northern seas and rivers with five rows of bony plates along the back and sides and pointed mouth with four barbels. Caviar (traditionally eaten with an ivory spoon) is prepared from sturgeon ova. The Caspian sturgeon is now a fast-disappearing species (because of over-farming). Pollution threatens the wild Chinese strugeon of the Yangtze River. In 2006 a ban was announced on the international trade in caviar. There are 27 species of sturgeon.

The once common Atlantic sturgeon is now only found in the Garonne in France.

Sublimation, when a solid substance is heated and turns into vapour without passing through the liquid stage and then condenses as a solid on a cold surface, it is said to "sublime" and the process is called "sublimation". Iodine behaves in this way, and sublimation is used as a method of purifying it.

Submarine, the first submarine, the *Nautilus*, was designed by Robert Fulton and tried out in the river Seine and in the sea off Brest in 1801. The idea was too revolutionary to find acceptance and it was not until electricity for under-water propulsion became available that the submarine underwent extensive development. Britain became interested around 1901 and the Germans developed it and made it into an instrument of warfare. The first voyage under the North Pole was made in 1958 by the American nuclearpowered submarine *Nautilus*. The Government in March 1982 decided to replace the Polaris force with a new fleet of

Trident II submarines at a cost of £7,500m. The first Trident submarine, HMS *Vanguard*, was launched in 1992. The fourth (and final) Trident submarine was launched in September 1998. In 2010 the Coalition Government said that Trident would remain in service until 2028. The current Conservative Government plans a £41 billion replacement to be in service c. 2030.

Women have been allowed to serve in Royal Navy submarines since 2013.

Submillimetre Astronomy, the branch of astronomy that deals with the wavelength range 0·3 to 1 millimetre. It is the highest frequency range in which radio astronomy can be carried out and is particularly important because of the large number of molecular emission lines found in this range.

Su Doku. The modern Su Doku puzzle was invented by American architect Howard Garns in 1979. It was taken up by a Japanese publisher in the 1980s. The original puzzle format derives from the "Latin Squares" idea of the famous Swiss mathematician Leonard Euler (1707–83) and was very popular in France after 1895.

Suez Canal, connecting the Mediterranean and the Red Sea, was built by the French engineer Ferdinand de Lesseps and opened in 1869. An Egyptian company, *Canal Maritime de Suez*, was formed in 1866 with a capital of 200 million francs. The British Government acquired 176,602 shares out of a total of 400,000 for £4 million. Under the Convention of 1888 all nations were granted freedom of navigation without discrimination in peace or war. The right was recognised by Egypt in the Anglo-Egyptian Agreement of 1954, under which Britain agreed to give up the Suez base. The Suez Canal Company was nationalised by the Egyptian Government without warning in 1956, since when it has been widened and deepened and the average time of transit reduced. In 2014 work began on a massive new channel to be dug alongside the existing canal. This was opened in 2015, allowing two-way traffic on the waterway.

Suffolk Punch, once one of the most popular draught horses working the land. The UK's oldest native horse, but its future is under threat.

Sugar, to the chemist the term is a generic one covering a group of carbohydrates, including cane sugar (sucrose), glucose, fructose, and maltose. In ordinary parlance sugar means sucrose, which is obtained from the sugar cane, sugar beet or sugar maple. Natural unrefined cane sugar—sometimes called *muscovado*, the Portuguese word for unrefined—is brown.

Sulphur, element no. 16, is a brittle, crystalline solid, symbol S, abounding in the vicinity of volcanoes. It is yellow in colour. It occurs in combination with other elements, as sulphates and sulphides, and allied with oxygen, hydrogen, chlorine, *etc.*, is of great commercial utility. Used in its pure state it constitutes the inflammable element in gunpowder; it is also used for matches and for making sulphuric acid.

Sulphuric Acid, a compound of great commercial importance, used in many manufactures, and composed of sulphur, oxygen and hydrogen. Extremely corrosive, and is present in acid rain *(q.v.)*.

Sumptuary Laws. Medieval attempt to maintain stability by imposing consumer laws on different orders in society. The wives of merchants were forbidden to dress in the style of wives of the nobility, and clergy were not allowed to wear the clothes of the laity.

Sun, the centre of our solar system, is only one of many billions of stars in our galaxy. The earth orbits the sun, which has a diameter of 1·39 million km, at a distance of 149·6 million km. The sun thus has a volume a million times that of the earth. At the surface, the gravitational field is 28 times that at the earth's surface. It rotates on its axis from east to west, though not as a solid, the solar equator turning once in about 25½ days and the poles in about 34 days.

Large spots are observed on the sun which form and disappear at irregular intervals. The area of the disc covered by the spots, however, reaches a maximum roughly every 11 years, when the sun's heat seems rather greater than usual and magnetic storms more frequent (sunspot cycle). Spectrum analysis shows that the sun is composed of many elements found in the earth. Its surface temperature is c. 5,500°C.

The earth is in the outer atmosphere of the sun and subject to its winds and storms. The apparently inexhaustible heat of the sun, which has maintained life on the earth for millions of years, is derived from the destruction of matter, involved in the transmutation of hydrogen nuclei into helium nuclei, in which process about four million tonnes of matter are destroyed every second. At this rate of conversion the sun will go on radiating for 30,000 million years. Eventually, billions of years from now, our Sun will become a death star, having first swollen to 250 times its present size.

Modern research has shown that the Sun blows out bubbles—known as coronal mass ejections (CMEs)—every few days at a speed of 90,000 miles an hour. These can wipe out satellite communications and bring down power systems on Earth. The interior of the Sun is also more strange than suspected. Astronomers have found that, while the Sun's surface is resonating, regions below the surface appear to be smooth and flat. Eventually, in 6 billion years time, the Sun will expand into a red giant and burn up the Earth.

Our knowledge of the Sun has been transformed by the Solar Heliospheric Observatory (SOHO) and Ulysses satellites launched in 1995 and 1990 respectively. SOHO has been studying the Sun's internal structure and processes which form and heat the solar corona that give rise to the solar wind. Ulysses has examined the solar wind especially over the polar regions.

In 2010 the Solar Dynamics Observatory was launched to examine the solar magnetic field during a 5-year mission. A new mission, Solar Orbiter, is planned for 2018. One of the mysteries to solve is why the corona (outer atmosphere) is hotter than the surface. *See* **T8–9**.

Sunday. *See* **Sabbath**.

Superconductor, a metal in a state in which its electrical resistance has entirely vanished so that electric currents can flow indefinitely without generating heat or decreasing in strength.

The superconducting state of metals was first discovered in mercury by Onnes in Leiden in 1911. There are many magnetic and thermal properties associated with superconductivity and the phenomenon as a whole has proved to be of great scientific interest.

Many metals and alloys were found to show the property but only at very low temperatures—below c. −260°C. There is a growing number of practical applications, *e.g.*, coils of superconducting wire (kept very cold by liquid helium) can be made to carry enough electric current to produce strong magnetic fields. Such fields are very constant and do not require the large supply of electrical power that ordinary electromagnets need. By the 1990s, scientists were on the point of developing a revolutionary material that would superconduct (*i.e.* lose all electrical resistance) at *room temperature*.

Supernova. These huge stellar explosions are caused when white dwarves (the collapsed remnants of old stars) either collide or merge. This explosion blows off most or all of the star's outer regions and is the result of an uncontrolled nuclear reaction in the core. The core of the supernova may go on to form a neutron star or black hole.

Observationally, supernova have been divided into two groups, based on the absence (type I) or presence (type II) of hydrogen. Recent observations have revealed a rich diversity of types and so sub-classifications have occurred. Supernova 1987A was the first naked-eye supernova since 1604 and the remnants of the explosion are still being studied. *See* **Neutron Star, Black Hole**.

Supersonic Speed, a speed greater than the speed of sound (in air at sea-level sound waves travel at about 1223 km/h). When a body travels at a speed which is greater than the speed at which disturbances themselves can travel, a mechanism exists for the generation of waves of enhanced intensity. Thus aircraft travelling at supersonic speeds produce shock waves in the air somewhat analogous to the bow waves of fast-moving ships. These shock waves are regions of intensely disturbed air which produce the sonic boom effect so distressing to people living near supersonic routes. *Supersonic* is not to be confused with *ultrasonic (q.v.)*.

Surface Tension. The surfaces of fluids behave in some respects as though they were covered by a stretched elastic membrane. This property is called "surface tension". The action of detergents may be attributed in part to a reduction in the surface tension of water, allowing it to wet the surface of dirty articles.

Swans, large, graceful birds which together with

the ducks and geese form the family Anatidae. There are three European species with white plumage; the Mute Swan distinguished by its orange bill with black knob (less prominent in female), a familiar sight on the rivers and ornamental lakes of Great Britain. Two wild swans are winter visitors here, the Whooper and Bewick's Swan (although Bewick Swan numbers are in decline). The "pen" (female) and "cob" (male) are not as monogamous as once thought. There are around 7,000 pairs of breeding swans. Outside of captivity, swans have an average lifespan of 12 years. The young swans are called "cygnets". The scientific name of a mute swan is *Cygnus olor*.

Swan-upping. The annual census of the Thames swans which takes place during the third week of July. This ancient ceremony dates back to the 12th cent. when all the Thames swans were declared to be Royal birds owned by the Crown.

Two city guilds—the Vintners' and Dyers' Companies—own about a third of the 200 swans now on the Thames. This privilege was granted to them by King Edward IV in return for money.

Sweet Potato. This plant (*Ipomoea batatas*), which is a climbing perennial belonging to the convolvulus family, has thick roots that are rich in starch, and are eaten like potatoes. A native of the W. Indies and Central America, new varieties of sweet potato have been bred which stand cooler climates. The sweet potato of New Zealand is called the Kumara.

Swift, a bird so-called from the extreme speed of its flight, resembling a swallow but related to the humming-bird. It has long, scythe-like wings, sooty-black plumage and greyish-white chin. There are several species inhabiting most parts of the world, particularly the tropics. The British breeding bird is among the latest to return from Africa and the earliest to go. Swifts are the only birds to use saliva for their nests. One oriental species builds its nest entirely from saliva. Swifts are known to fly as high as 10,000ft at night-time. They are in decline because of the growing popularity of home improvements!

Sword, hand weapon of metal used in open combat, characterised by a longish blade. During the Middle Ages the most famous blades were those made by the Arabs at Damascus and in Toledo.

Symbiosis is when two organisms live together and both derive mutual benefit from the association. An example is the symbiosis of an alga and a fungus in lichens; another is the ordinary pea plant and the bacteria which live in the nodules on the pea's roots.

Synapse is the point of association between one nerve cell and another. The nervous impulse travelling along one nerve has to be transmitted to the next across a minute gap. This is the synaptic gap. The mode of transmission is chemical though it was at first thought to be electrical. The impulse arriving at the synapse releases a chemical transmitter which diffuses across the gap and stimulates an impulse in the adjacent nerve cell.

Synod, an assembly of the clergy of a particular church, state, province, or diocese. The Synod of Whitby (664) settled the dispute between the Celtic and the Roman churches over Easter in favour of the Roman system of reckoning.

Synoptic Charts. These are meteorological charts used in forecasting on which weather conditions at a network of stations are recorded.

T

Taj Mahal, the white marble mausoleum built at Agra by Shah Jehan in memory of his favourite wife who died 1629. Over 20,000 men were occupied for over 20 years in its erection. Urgent action is needed to protect the Mausoleum.

Takahe or Notornis, large New Zealand bird of the rail family which for many years was believed to be extinct. The bird is strictly protected.

Tantalum, a scarce bluish metallic element, no. 73, symbol Ta, discovered by Ekeburg in 1802. Chemically related to vanadium and niobium, it is usually associated with the latter in nature. For several purposes it can be used in place of platinum, and it finds application in the making of surgical instruments. Tantalum is very hard, and resistant to acids (other than hydrofluoric). Tantalum is a vital component of mobile phones.

Taoiseach, the name for the Irish Prime Minister.

Tapirs. The tapirs constitute a family close to the horse family and the rhinoceros in the Ungulate order. They have four toes on the front feet and three on the hind. The snout is drawn out into a short trunk. The largest tapir is the Malayan tapir, which stands 1 m at the shoulder. Five species occur in C. and S. America, but the Brazilian tapir is very threatened by habitat destruction. The fifth species (known as a kobomani) was only found in 2015 in the Brazilian Amazon.

Tar is a dark viscid product obtained from the destructive distillation of wood, coal, peat, *etc.* Wood tar is acid owing to the presence of acetic acid ("pyroligneous acid"). The highest proportion of coal tar goes into road making. Distillation of coal tar yields many valuable compounds, including benzene, phenol (carbolic acid), naphthalene and creosote; the final residue after distillation is pitch. Based on the chemical manipulation of compounds from coal tar is the preparation of many perfumes, food essences, drugs, antiseptics and plastics.

Tasmanian Devils. About the size of a dog, these are the world's largest carnivorous marsupials. They are threatened with extinction.

Taste. According to the Ancient Greeks, there were four tastes: sweet, sour, salty and bitter. The ancient Chinese added a fifth, namely spicy. Our human brain has specialist neurons for each of five taste categories.

Tate Britain, named after its founder, Sir Henry Tate, at Millbank, London, was opened in 1897; Sir Henry Tate bore the cost of the building (£80,000) and also gave the nucleus of the present collection. "The Turner Wing", the gift of Sir Joseph Duveen, was added in 1910. The Tate Gallery was renamed Tate Britain in March 2000. It has recenly undergone a £45 million transformation.

Tate Modern, which is along the Thames at Bankside, houses contemporary international art works. It was opened on 12 May 2000. A new wing opened in June 2016.

Tay Bridge spans the Tay at Dundee, opened for rail traffic on 20 June 1887. A previous bridge, completed in 1877, was blown down on 28 December 1879, as a train was passing over it. A new bridge was opened on 18 August 1966 for road traffic, 2,244 m in length, the longest road bridge in Britain when it was first opened.

Tea. *See* R19.

Teal, the smallest of the European ducks and next to the Mallard the commonest British species. It is a handsome swift flier, but not as swift as the Garganey or Summer Teal.

Telecommunications. The sending of messages over a distance. The term is generally applied to the sending of messages by telegraph, telephone, radio, television or radar. The first submarine telegraph cable between England and France was laid in 1850 and, following Hertz's investigations into electric waves, Marconi's invention led to Britain being linked with Europe by wireless telegraphy in 1899. The first permanently successful telegraph cable across the Atlantic was laid in 1866. The first telephone service between London and Paris was opened in 1891.

The electro-magnetic telephone was invented by Alexander Graham Bell, a Scottish-born American, in 1876.

The first submarine telephone cable to span the Atlantic was laid in 1956 connecting Britain with Canada and the United States.

The spectacular advances in space research depended on the new tools of work provided by parallel developments in telecommunications. *See* **Satellite Communication, Radar, Radio, Television.**

Telemetry, measurement at remote distances by means of a radio-link from the object (missile or satellite) to the ground. The third Russian sputnik, for instance, carried apparatus for measuring, among other things, the pressure and composition of the atmosphere, and the intensity of different kinds of radiation from the sun. Its radio transmitter, powered by solar-energy batteries, sent out the information in coded form by means of uninterrupted signals.

Radio telemetry from inside the body is increasingly used in medical and biological research; miniature radio transmitters can be swallowed or implanted in man or animal to detect physiological conditions.

Teleprinter, a telegraph transmitter with a typewriter keyboard, by which characters of a message are transmitted electrically in combinations of 5 units, being recorded similarly by the receiving instrument, which then translates the matter mechanically into printed characters.

Telescope, an optical instrument for viewing objects at a distance, "the astronomer's intelligencer". Lippershey is credited with construction of the first in 1608; Galileo constructed several from 1609 and Newton was the first to construct a reflecting telescope. The ordinary telescope consists of an object-glass and an eye-lens, with two intermediates to bring the object into an erect position. A lens brings it near to us, and the magnifier enlarges it for inspection. A refracting telescope gathers the rays together near the eye-piece and is necessarily limited as to size, but the reflecting telescope collects the rays on a larger mirror. These are thrown back to the eye-piece.

The world's largest optical reflecting telescopes are the 10m Keck telescope at Mauna Kea in Hawaii (USA), the Very Large Telescope (VLT) located at the European Southern Observatory (ESO) sited on Cerro Paranal in Chile, consisting of four 8m telescopes and the 8m Gemini telescopes on Mauna Kea and Chile. The VLT is itself due to be superseded by the ELT (Extremely Large Telescope), also to be based at ESO.

UK Infrared Telescope (UKIRT) is the world's largest infrared telescope. The mirror is 3·8 metres in diameter. The *Hale* 200 in telescope at Mount Palomar revealed objects never before photographed; it is able to probe space and photograph remote galaxies out to a limiting distance of 2,000 million light years. The *Schmidt* telescope at Mount Palomar has been used to make a huge map of the universe.

Today the largest single radio dish in the world is the non-steerable 300 m instrument at Arecibo in Puerto Rico. Another instrument of radio astronomy is the interferometer which consists of spaced aerials. The biggest of these is in New Mexico. In 1990, the project to put the Hubble Space Telescope into space became reality. The Hubble used gravity to magnify distant galaxies and its findings gave scientists new evidence of the age of the universe. It has peered into space to capture light generated 13 billion years ago.

A new type of telescope named COAST (Cambridge Optical Aperture Synthesis Telescope) has been perfected that can take even sharper pictures than the Hubble. The world's biggest radio telescope, the Very Long Baseline Interferometer, (VLBI), a series of linked instruments stretching from the Caribbean to Hawaii, is now operational.

This huge array of detectors is capable of seeing detail equivalent to a postage stamp 7,500 miles away.

In 2015 Jodrell Bank was confirmed as headquarters of the massive Square Kilometre Array (SKA), due to be fully operational by 2025.

Other projects include the European Extremely Large Telescope (E-ELT) which will pick out the pinpricks of light reflected from planets as they orbit stars. It will have a 39·3m (130ft) mirror.

In April 2009 the Kepler space telescope (the biggest camera in space) was launched to search for extra-terrestrial life (it found over 3,500 planets). Its successor in 2018 will be the James Webb telescope, the ultimate cosmos explorer. *See also* **Astronomy, Radio Astronomy, Infra-Red Space Observatory, Space Research** *etc.*

Television, or the transmission of images of moving objects by radio or via the cable and satellite systems. To understand the problems of television it is necessary to consider the action of the human eye. Basically the eye consists of a lens which projects an image of the scene before it upon the retina, a light-sensitive screen at the back of the eye. The retina is made up of several millions of tiny light sensitive elements, each quite separate and distinct from its neighbours, and each separately connected to the brain by an individual fibre in the optic nerve. Thus the eye is a very complex organ, and it is able to pick out numbers of tiny details from a scene and convey each detail separately and simultaneously to the brain. It does not send a blend of different points of light and shade in the same way that the ear sends a blend of different sounds; if it did the brain would receive a completely unintelligible blur.

From this it is clear that a TV system which transmitted a mixture of detail would be useless; it must transmit all the details in a scene separately, yet almost simultaneously, and re-

assemble them at such a speed that the eye cannot observe the building-up process.

A means of doing this was provided by Nipkow in 1884, when he invented his famous scanning disc, and later Weiller invented the mirror drum for the same purpose. Such mechanical devices as these held the field for many years and in 1923 Baird in this country and Jenkins in America were both using them for the experiments which, in 1925, led to the successful transmission of shadows and simple outlines. It was not until 1926, however, that the first practical demonstration of television took place when Baird transmitted by radio moving pictures of living human faces over a short distance.

The BBC began televised broadcasts in 1930; the ITA in 1955. The first television exchange across the Atlantic was made in 1962 by way of the *Telstar* satellite.

A major development underway in the 1990s was the advent of digital television. For the past 75 years, television broadcasting had used the same analogue technology. Over the next few years the move to digital systems was to dramatically increase the number of channels available for broadcast. In 1996 the British government legislated to allow licensing for six groups of digital channels, or multiplexes. The BBC, for example, was granted its own multiplex and a financing deal designed to help with the transition to digital formats. Now, advances in technology allow not only vastly more audio and visual services, but also a degree of interaction; the use of a television can blur with that of a telephone or a computer. For the time being, both industry and consumers face a bewildering array of unstandardised technologies.

In 1998 the BBC began transmissions of BBC1 and BBC2 in digital widescreen format and BSkyB began a 200-channel digital service.

BBC Choice was BBC's first new general television channel for 34 years. In September 2001, the Government approved eight BBC digital services (including BBC4, two TV channels for children and five digital radio stations). The collapse of ITV Digital in 2002 led eventually to the launch of BBC Freeview. The new BBC3 digital service (aimed at 18–35 year olds) was launched in 2003.

TV manufacturers are now competing for the heavy demand for liquid crystal (LCD) televisions. In 2005 the government confirmed that the UK would switch to digital TV by 2012. Border began the initial switchover in 2007 and the last analogue signals ended in the UK on 24 October 2012.

High definition (HD)TV is the biggest change in TV picture quality in decades, with up to 4 times more picture detail than previously. The next big step forward is ultra high-definition television (UHDTV).

Television Licence. The cost of a current colour TV licence rose from £145·50 to £147·00 from April 2017. Free TV licences for all those aged 75 or over (or households with someone of this age) were introduced from October 2000. If you are 74 (and will turn 75 during your next licensed year) you qualify for a reduced fee Short Term Licence. From September 2016 those without a TV who watch BBC iPlayer on a tablet or phone must pay the full licence.

Tellurium, a relatively scarce element, no. 52, symbol Te, discovered in 1782 by von Reichenstein. Chemically it behaves rather like sulphur; its salts are known as tellurides. It occurs chiefly combined with metals in ores of gold, silver, copper and lead. It is a semiconductor, and some of its compounds (also semiconductors) are used in technical devices.

Telomerase. Structures on the tips of chromosomes which slowly get shorter with age.

Temperature. *See* **T58.**

Templars were soldier knights organised in the 12th century for the purpose of protecting pilgrims in their journeyings to and from Jerusalem, and obtained their name from having had granted to them by Baldwin II a temple for their accommodation. At first they were non-military, and wore neither crests nor helmets, but a long wide mantle and a red cross on the left shoulder. They were established in England about 1180. Important in the Crusades.

In the 12th century they founded numerous religious houses in various parts of Europe and became possessed of considerable wealth. It was this that caused their downfall. Kings and Popes alike grew jealous of their influence, and they were subjected to much persecution, and Pope Clement V abolished the Order in 1312. Edward II in 1308 seized all the property of the English Templars. The English possessions of the Order were transferred to the Hospitallers of St. John, afterwards called the Knights of Malta. *See also* **Hospitallers, Knights, Teutonic Order.**

Temple. Of the temples built by the ancient Greeks, Olympia, Athens and Delphi were the most famous. The Temple of Diana at Ephesus was another. The Temple of Solomon at Jerusalem was destroyed and rebuilt several times; Herod's Temple was destroyed by the Romans in A.D. 70.

Temple Bar, an historic gateway (designed by Sir Christopher Wren in 1672) that until 1877 stood at the junction of the Strand and Fleet Street, London, dividing the City from Westminster.

It was re-erected at the entrance to Theobald's Park, near Cheshunt, Herts., in 1888.

Terbium, an element, no. 65, symbol Tb, discovered in 1842 by Mosander and a rare-earth metal.

Teredo, the scientific name of the ship-worm, a peculiar bivalve mollusc, which lodges itself when young on the bottoms of wooden ships and bores its way inwards, causing much damage.

Termites, also known as *White Ants,* though they are not related to the true ants and are placed in an entirely different insect order (*Isoptera*). They abound in the tropics and also occur in temperate countries, though only two species are common in Europe. There is no British species. They live in colonies and their nests take the form of mounds of earth and wood, cemented together with saliva, and up to 6 m in height. Five separate castes are recognised, three of them being capable of reproduction, and the other two are sterile.

Tern. This slender, gull-like bird has long pointed wings, a deeply-forked tail, pale grey and white plumage, black cap, and is a very graceful flier. There are several species. The Arctic tern winters in the Antarctic, returning to find a nesting place in the spring. It holds the record for long-distance migration, flying from the Farne Islands off Northumberland to the Antarctic and back.

Terracotta Army, the thousands of life-sized figures in fired clay of soldiers who were to guard China's Emperor Qiu Shihuangdi after his death in the 3rd century B.C. Discovered at Xian in 1974. So far 8,000 figures have been unearthed. The Xian site covers an area of 56 square miles, with new discoveries continuing to be made.

Terrapin, a kind of fresh-water tortoise. Native to tropical areas of Asia and Central America. Popular as pets, in the wild they prey on frogspawn, dragonfly larvae *etc.*

Tertiary Rocks, in geology the rocks formed during the Caenozoic era comprising the Eocene, Oligocene, Miocene and Pliocene periods.

Teutonic Order, of German military knights, was founded in the Holy Land at the end of the 12th century for succouring the wounded of the Crusader army before Acre. They were dispersed in the 15th century. but the Order continued to exist until 1809, when Napoleon I confiscated its properties. In 1840 the order was resuscitated in Austria as a semi-religious knighthood. *See also* **Hospitallers, Knights, Templars.**

Textured Vegetable Protein, often referred to as TVP, is an edible protein material given a fibrous texture in the course of its manufacture from agricultural products. Nutritionally the material resembles meat and the extent to which it also resembles meat in succulence, flavour, *etc.* depends on the sophistication of the manufacturing technique and on the skill of the cook.

The common starting material is the soya bean which is rich in protein and oil. The latter is removed, also for use in the food industry, and the residue is further processed to concentrate the protein and to remove unwanted flavours.

A paste of suitable consistency is then forced under pressure through small holes and solidified as fibres. Bound together with a suitable binder and appropriately flavoured, these fibres form a lump of protein substance like meat.

Thallium, a blue-grey metallic element, no. 81, symbol Tl, discovered by Crookes in 1861. It is obtained from the flue dust resulting from the burning of pyrites for making sulphuric acid.

Thanksgiving Day, a national holiday in the United States, observed on the fourth Thursday in November: instituted in 1621 to celebrate the occasion of their first successful harvest.

Theia. The name given to the massive Mars-sized object which is believed to have collided with Earth, giving birth to our moon.

Theodolite. The instrument used by surveyors for measuring angles in the horizontal and vertical planes; also used in meteorology for following balloons to measure windspeed *etc.*

Therm. The charges for gas for lighting and heating (formerly reckoned at per cubic foot) are now based on the calorific, or heat, value of the gas, and the unit used is termed a therm. The therm is 100,000 British thermal units.

Thermionic Emission is the departure of charged particles from matter under the influence of heat. The higher the temperature the greater the flow of escaping particles. The most common example is the emission of electrons from red-hot electrodes—this is the basic phenomenon made use of in thermionic valves (*see* **Valve**). If the hot electrode (the cathode) is enclosed in an evacuated or gas-filled bulb, the emitted electrons can be collected at another electrode (the anode) and will flow through an external circuit back to the emitter. Thus an electric current has been generated by heat.

Thermodynamics, a term first applied by Joule to designate that branch of physical science which treats of the relations of heat to work. What is called the first law of thermodynamics is thus stated by Clerk Maxwell: "When work is transformed into heat, or heat into work, the quantity of work is mechanically equivalent to the quantity of heat." In one of its many formulations, the second law asserts that "the heat tends to flow from a body of hotter temperature to one that is colder, and will not naturally flow in any other way." *See* **Heat.**

Thermo-electric Devices. If two wires of different materials are formed into a loop and if the two joins are kept at different temperatures a current flows in the loop. This was discovered by Seebeck in 1822, and the device is called a thermocouple. The electric current could in principle be made to drive some useful machine, and the energy comes from the heat that is absorbed by the thermocouple—if one part of the thermocouple is not hotter than the others it will not work. It has long been realised that this is a device that converts heat directly into electricity without raising steam and driving dynamos as in a power-station. However, until recently nobody has used thermocouples for much besides temperature measurement, for which they are exceedingly useful. The new development is the manufacture of semiconductors (*q.v.*); for the thermo-electric effects of these new materials are much greater than those of metals. A material much studied in this connection is a compound of bismuth and tellurium, bismuth telluride. It is now practicable to generate useful electricity from suitably designed thermocouples. For example, Russia produces a thermo-electric device which uses the heat from the chimney of a domestic oil-lamp to produce enough electricity to work a radio. Presumably this is very useful in remote parts with no electricity supply. However, the possibilities do not stop there. Indeed, thermocouples can produce electricity direct from the warmth of sunlight on a scale and at a cost comparable with older fuel-burning power-stations.

Thermometer, an instrument by which the temperature of bodies is ascertained. The most familiar kind of thermometer consists of a glass tube with a very small bore, containing, in general, mercury or alcohol. This expands or contracts with variation in the temperature, and the length of the thread of mercury or alcohol gives the temperature reading on a scale graduated in degrees. *See also* end **Section T58–60.**

Thermonuclear Reactions. *See* **Nuclear Fusion.**

Thirty-nine Articles. *See* **Articles.**

Thistle, Order of. *See* **Knighthood.**

Thorium, a scarce, silvery white, metal element, no. 90, symbol Th, discovered by Berzelius in 1828. All substances containing thorium are radioactive. Chief source of thorium is monazite sand, big deposits of which occur in Travancore (India), Brazil and the USA. Important as a potential source of atomic energy since the discovery that it can be transmuted into U^{233}, which is capable of fission like U^{235}. Named after the Norse God Thor.

Thrush, a large family of song-birds of the *Passeriform* order, distributed all over the world. The British species include the robin, redstart, nightingale, song-thrush (or mavis), blackbird, mistle-thrush and ring-ouzel of the mountains. Large numbers of migrant fieldfares and redwings from northern Europe are winter visitors.

Thunder, the sound heard after the occurrence of a lightning flash. It is due to vibrations of the air along the path of the flash, which are set up by the sudden heating (and expansion) followed by the rapid cooling (and contraction) to which the air is subjected.

It is unusual for thunder to be heard more than 16 km away, the distance being estimated roughly by allowing 1 km for every 3 seconds which elapse between seeing the flash and hearing the thunder. Continued rolling of thunder results from the zig-zag nature of the flash and the multiple strokes of which it is composed, variations in the energy developed along the path, and echo effects. Thunder-storms are caused by powerful rising currents of air within towering cumulonimbus clouds. New evidence suggests thunderstorms can trigger asthma attacks. *Thundersnow* is the spectacle of thunder and lightning erupting during heavy snowfall.

Thursday, the 5th day of the week, named after Thor, the Scandinavian deity. To the Romans Thursday was *dies Jovis*, or Jupiter's day.

Tidal Power. The principle of exploiting the energy of the tides is similar to hydro-power since it involves the harnessing of falling water. A barrage across a bay or estuary is filled during flow tide and closed during ebb tide creating a difference in level. When the water is allowed to fall towards the lower side of the barrage it operates a turbine which drives a generator. *See also* **Hydroelectric Schemes.**

Tides, the periodical rise and fall of the waters of the ocean and its arms, are due to the gravitational effect of the moon and sun. Newton was the first to give a general explanation of the phenomenon of the tides. He supposed the ocean to cover the whole earth and to assume at each instant a figure of equilibrium, under the combined gravitational influence of earth, sun and moon, thus making and controlling the tides. At most places there are two tides a day, and the times of high- and low-water vary according to the positions of the sun and moon relative to the earth.

When earth, moon and sun are in line (at full moon and new moon) the gravitational pull is greatest and we get "spring" tides. When sun and moon are at right angles (first and third quarters of the moon's phases) we get smaller "neap" tides.

Tiger, a powerful carnivorous animal of the cat family, which occurs in India and certain other parts of Asia. Its skin is of a tawny yellow, relieved by black stripings of great beauty of formation. Some tigers attain a length of from 3 to 3·6 m. There are now only an estimated 3,900 adult tigers in the wild, whereas in 1900 there were 40,000 tigers in India alone. The tiger is proving remarkably resilient but fears that it will face extinction still remain, particularly in India. Only in 13 countries do tigers still roam free. Tigers are still kept in captivity to perform or for medicinal purposes. The Siberian tiger is the world's largest cat. The tiger was listed as an endangered species in 1972. The only remaining island tiger is the Sumatran. (*c.* 500 remain).

Time. The measurement of time has become of increasing importance to man with the advance of civilisation. It was at first almost inevitably based on the succession of night and day, the waxing and the waning of the moon, and on the changing seasons of the year, and the astronomical observation of these three periodic effects has served as the basis of time measurement until recent years. The precision of the observations has continually increased, and clocks have been developed for dividing the day into smaller units. The clocks were adjusted so as to keep in step with the rotation of the earth on its axis, but now an atomic standard of time has been developed. *See* **Clock, Greenwich Mean Time, British Standard Time.**

Tin is a white, metal element, no. 50, symbol Sn (Latin *Stannum*), whose commonest ore is cassiterite (tin oxide), which occurs in Malaysia, Indonesia, Bolivia, Congo, Nigeria and Cornwall. It protects iron from rusting, and the tin coating on tinplate is applied by dipping the thin steel sheet in molten tin or by electrolysis. Tin alloys of importance include solder, bronze, pewter and Britannia metal. South Crofty, the last tin mine in Europe, was closed in March 1998 (but Hemerdon mine reopened in 2007). The tin mine landscape of Cornwall and West Devon was declared a World Heritage Site in 2006.

Tincal. *See* **Borax.**

Tit *or* **Titmouse,** a small insectivorous bird of the woodlands and forests, bright of plumage and very active and agile, often seen hanging upside down searching for food. There are over fifty species, eight of which occur in Britain: the Great and Blue Tits, the Cole Tit, Marsh Tit, Willow Tit, Bearded Tit, Long-tailed or "Bottle" Tit and the Scottish Crested Tit. The Willow Tit is in serious decline in Britain.

Titan, the largest moon of Saturn (*q.v.*). It is the only moon in the solar system with a thick atmosphere. The Cassini Mission beamed back the first images of Titan in 2004. Its Huygens probe confirmed that Titan contains water and vital organic chemicals and its dark equatorial regions have deserts, lakes and rivers. Vast lakes of liquid methane have been discovered on the surface and scientists are eager to explore these further. Its surface temperature drops to −183°C. Titan is the second largest moon in the solar system. Its largest sea is named Kraken Mare.

Titanium, a scarce metallic element, no. 22, symbol Ti, difficult to extract from ores, found in association with oxygen in rutile, anatase and brookite, as well as with certain magnetic iron ores. It combines with nitrogen at a high temperature. Discovered by the Rev. William Gregor in 1791.

Titanium alloys, being very resistant to stress and corrosion, and combining strength with lightness, find wide application. They are popular as wedding rings. Titanium dioxide is now used in making paints.

Titanosaur. The name of the largest dinosaur yet found. Found by an Argentinian shepherd in 2014. It lived more than 100 million years ago and weighed 70 tonnes.

Tithes, an ecclesiastical tax consisting of a tenth part of the annual produce. After the Tithes' Commutation Act of 1836, tithes were gradually converted into rent charges.

TNT (**Trinitrotoluene**). A high explosive formed by the action of a mixture of nitric and sulphuric acids on toluene. Not highly sensitive to shock, it can be used in shells without danger.

Toad, an amphibian, differing from the frog in having a dry, warty skin, a heavier, squat build and shorter limbs. It has a similar metamorphosis, is largely nocturnal, and will wander far from water after the breeding season. Two toads occur in Britain, the Common Toad and the Natterjack. The latter have a narrow light stripe running down the middle of the back. Numbers in Britain are in dramatic decline. The cane toad is Australia's most notorious pest, having been introduced from Hawaii in 1935. Mild winters have harmed toad numbers in Britain.

Tobacco is made from the leaves of various narcotic plants of the *Nicotiana* family, which contain a volatile oil and an alkaloid called nicotine. Tobacco is grown in countries with a warm climate. The leaves are first dried, then cut into small pieces, moistened and compressed, and in this form it is known as cut or "shag" tobacco; when moistened with syrup or treacle and pressed into cakes, it is Cavendish; when twisted into string form, it is "twist" or "pig-tail". For cigars the midribs of the dry leaves are removed, and what is left is moistened and rolled into cylindrical shape. For snuff, the tobacco leaves are moistened and allowed to ferment, then dried, powdered and scented.

Smoking in public places was outlawed in Scotland from March 2006 (it is also banned in Ireland, New Zealand, Norway, *etc*). France has banned smoking in cafés and bars and the world's biggest smoking ban is planned for India. Increasingly tough anti-smoking laws are now a global phenomenon.

A wide-ranging ban on smoking in indoor public places was introduced into England in 2007. The minimum age for buying tobacco in England was raised from 16 to 18 in October 2007 (and tobacco now has to be sold "under the counter" in shops). Smoking has been banned in cars where children are passengers from December 2016 in England. Scotland has similar laws.

In 2000, 5,500 *billion* cigarettes were consumed world-wide, compared with 600 billion in 1930. The world's biggest tobacco markets are China, Russia, the USA and Japan. Tobacco today kills more people than narcotics, alcohol, HIV, suicide, homicide and car crashes combined – around 5·7 million annually. Britain now has fewer smokers than any major developed country.

Tolls. Payments for privileges of passage were first exacted in respect of ships passing up rivers, tolls being demanded on the Elbe in 1109. Tolls for land passage are said to have originated in England in 1269, toll-bars being erected at certain distances on the high-roads in the 17th cent., where toll had to be paid for all vehicles passing to and fro. After about 1825 they began to disappear, but still linger on some country roads and bridges. Today, tolls are a feature of motorways and major bridges.

Tonic Sol-Fa, a system of musical notation in which monosyllables are substituted for notes. Thus the major diatonic scale is represented by Doh, Ray, Me, Fah, Soh, La, Te, Doh.

Topaz, a transparent mineral gem, being a silicate and fluoride of aluminium and generally found in granite rocks. Its colour is yellow, but it also occurs in pink and blue shades. The best kinds come from Brazil.

Topiary, the art of clipping and trimming trees, shrubs, *etc.*, into highly ornamental shapes. In Britain this art goes back before Elizabethan times when gardens were formal and the shapes simple and symmetrical. By the end of Queen Anne's reign topiary had become much more elaborate, and all kinds of fanciful shapes were produced. Pliny in his *Letters* tells how box hedges were clipped even in Roman times.

Topology is a branch of mathematics which studies geometrical objects from the point of view of their general shape rather than their precise measurements. For example, from the point of view of topology a ring doughnut and a picture frame have the same shape because they both have one single hole through them.

Topology is used to deduce geometrical facts about an irregularly shaped object such as the Earth from the geometry of a regular object such as a perfect sphere of the same general shape.

Tornado, a violent whirlwind, characterised by a black, funnel-shaped cloud hanging from heavy cumulonimbus and travelling at speeds up to 60 km/h. Tornadoes vary in diameter from less than a metre to a kilometre and occur frequently in the Mid-West region of the USA (known as tornado alley), where it has been estimated that the circling winds of the vortex may reach a velocity of 600 km/h. A severe tornado in Britain struck old Portsmouth and Southsea in 1810. Tornadoes are measured on a scale of 1 to 5. In West Africa the term is applied to thundery squalls. The world's deadliest tornado struck Bangladesh on 26 April 1989.

Tortoises and Turtles, are cold-blooded reptiles, four-footed and encased in a strong shell protection, the shells of some species being of beautifully horny substance and design, once in much demand for combs, spectacle frames and ornamental work. It is the custom to designate the land species as tortoises and the aquatic kinds as turtles. The green turtle, so called because its fat has a green tinge, is sadly in great demand for soup. Together the tortoises and turtles make up the reptilian order called *Chelonia,* the biggest representatives of which are the giant land tortoises of the Galapagos Islands, reaching a weight of 225 kg and living a century. Some of these giant tortoises are said to have lived 200 or 300 years.

The market for food and medicines is driving tortoises and turtles towards extinction. Rising temperatures now threaten male green turtles. The world's smallest tortoise is the South African speckled padloper. Tortoises first appear in the fossil record *c.* 225 million years ago. Turtles can make epic voyages – from Africa to South America. The leatherback turtle has survived for more than 100 million years and probably uses a magnetic or solar compass to navigate.

Toucan, a South and Central American family of brilliantly coloured birds, noted for their huge bills. Toucans live on fruit, are of arboreal habits, and nest in holes. There are *c.* 37 species.

Touchstone, a kind of jasper called by the ancients "Lydian stone", of economic value in testing the quality of metal alloys, especially gold alloys. The testing process is very simple. The alloy is drawn across the broken surface of the Touchstone, and from the nature of the mark or streak it makes the quality of the alloy can be ascertained.

Tourmaline, a mineral occurring in different colours in prismatic crystals. It is a well-known example of a pyro-electric crystal, *i.e.,* one that has a permanent electric polarisation. A double silicate of aluminium and boron.

Tournaments were equestrian contests between military knights and others armed with lances. The Normans introduced them to England.

Trademark, a mark used in relation to goods for the purpose of indicating a connection in the course of trade between the goods and some person having the right, either as a proprietor or registered user, to use the mark. Trade marks can be registered, the registration holding good for 7 years and being renewable thereafter indefinitely for periods of 14 years. Infringement of a registered trademark renders the infringer liable to damages. In 1994, a new law was brought in to harmonise British trademark law with the EU. Owners of registered trademarks will now also be able to have their sign protected in international law.

Trade Winds form part of the circulation of air round the great permanent anticyclones of the tropics and blow inwards from north-east (Northern Hemisphere) and south-east (Southern Hemisphere) towards the equatorial region of low pressure. Atlantic trades are more regular than those of the Pacific. The belts may extend over 2,400 km of latitude and, with the Doldrums, move north and south in sympathy with the seasonal changes in the sun's declination, the average annual range being about 5 degrees of latitude.

Trafalgar Square. The site has often been referred to as the finest in Europe. It was conceived originally as a square by John Nash (1752–1835) when the project was considered of linking Whitehall with Bloomsbury and the British Museum. It was to be named after the new monarch as King William the Fourth's Square but on the suggestion of George Ledwell Taylor (a property owner near the site) alteration to the more popular name Trafalgar Square was agreed to by the King. On the north side the National Gallery was planned by Nash and erected by William Wilkins on the place of the Royal Mews— a work of William Kent a century before. The lay- out was the idea of Charles Barry but he did not approve the erection of the Nelson column.

His idea was for the square to have a grand flight of steps from the north side with sculptural figures of Wellington and Nelson but the Commons decided otherwise and the column as designed by William Railton was begun in 1840. Now the newly-reconstructed Trafalgar Square more closely resembles the original grand Piazza plan.

The two fountains by Barry were supplanted in 1948 by ones designed (1938) by Sir Edwin Lutyens. Executed in Portland stone they are flanked by some bronze sculptures. In the same year memorial busts of Lords Jellicoe and Beatty were placed by the north wall.

The traditional Norwegian Christmas tree has been given by the people of Oslo since 1947.

Transactinides. See **T56**.

Transept. The cross aisles of a church, projecting at right angles from the nave or choir.

Transistor. An electronic device consisting of a small piece of semiconducting solid (usually germanium or silicon) to which contact is made at appropriate places by three wires. The three parts resemble in function (not construction or behaviour) the cathode, anode, and grid of a thermionic valve, and transistors can perform many of the operations that valves had originally been used for in radio, television, *etc.* They possess several advantages over valves since there is no need for evacuated glass bulbs nor for a heated emitter to give off electrons. This lead to much greater compactness and economy as well as to a much longer life. Just as the valve was superseded by the transistor, the transistor was replaced with the integrated circuit. The transistor was invented by the Americans Bardeen, Brattain and Shockley in 1948.

T-ray. Terahertz radiation, electromagnetic waves that can pass through objects, sniff out explosives *etc.* On the radiation spectrum they lie between radio waves and infra-red light.

Treasure-Trove, a legal term applying to treasure

(coin, bullion, gold or silver articles) found hidden in the earth or other place, for which no owner can be discovered. The treasure legally belongs to the Crown, but it is the practice to return to the finder all articles not required for national museums and to reward him, jointly with the landowner, with the full market value of such as may be retained.

It is the duty of the finder to report to the Coroner for the district in which the find is made. People are obliged to report items more than 300 years old under the 1996 Treasure Act.

Tree Frog, occurs most commonly in America and Australasia. The common European tree frog is a brilliant green animal, the adhesive discs at the tips of its fingers and toes enabling it to cling to trees, etc., with ease.

Tree Rings as Natural Calendar. The approximate relationship between radiocarbon dating (q.v.) and true calendar age for the past 7,000 years has been established from measurements on tree-rings. Because one tree-ring is formed annually and its thickness is characteristic of the climatic conditions during its growth, it is possible, by comparing distinctive groups of rings, to date a series of trees. By using the long-lived Bristle Cone pines, tree-rings dating back to 500 B.C. have been obtained. Some corrections and adjustments are needed for very old dates.

These corrections are far less than those proved necessary after the publication of the first radiocarbon dates. Tree-rings (based on the measurement of deuterium in wood) can also show the pattern of temperature fluctuations and thus make it possible to trace climatic changes before written records began. The term for tree-ring dating is *dendrochronology*.

Tree Shrew, an arboreal insectivorous mammal of Asia belonging to the family *Tupaiidae*. Tree shrews are related to the shrews, though in appearance they resemble squirrels except for their sharply pointed snout.

Trees. *See under* **Ash, Elm, Oak** etc.

Trent, Council of, the longest and one of the most important in the history of the Roman Catholic Church, was convened to combat the doctrines of Martin Luther. It first sat in 1545, the last sitting being in 1563. At this Council the general policy, principles and dogmas of the Roman Catholic Church were settled.

Triassic *or* **Trias,** the earliest geological period in the Mesozoic era, which began some 225 million years ago. Triassic formations 7,600 m thick occur in the Alps. Modern insects were appearing, and also small reptile-like mammals. Other important Triassic animals were: dinosaurs, ichthyosaurs (marine reptiles), and pterosaurs (flying reptiles). *See* **Section T.**

Tribunes, name assigned to officers of different descriptions in ancient Rome. The original tribunes were the commanders of contingents of cavalry and infantry. The most important tribunes were the tribunes of the plebs, first elected in 494 B.C. as the outcome of the struggle between the patrician and the plebeian orders. They held the power of veto and their persons were sacred.

Trichoptera. This is the insect order comprising the Caddis-flies. These are moth-like insects having hairs on the wings. They are usually found fluttering weakly near water. The larvae are aquatic and are remarkable for the cases (caddis cases) which they build out of sticks, small stones, sand grains, and shells.

Tricolour, the flag of the French Republic since 1789, consisting of three nearly equal vertical bands of blue, white and red (ratio 90 : 99 : 111).

Trident. *See* **Submarine, L103.**

Trilobites, extinct marine arthropods, most abundant in the Cambrian and Ordovician systems. Their appearance may be roughly described as resembling that of a woodlouse, and like that animal the trilobites were capable of rolling their bodies up into a ball.

Trinity House, on Tower Hill, London, was incorporated in 1514 as an association for piloting ships, and has ever since been entrusted with various matters connected with the regulation of British navigation. Since 1854 the lighthouses of the country have been under its supervision. The acting Elder Brethren act as Nautical Assessors in Marine cases which are tried by the High Court of Justice. Under the 1987 Pilotage Act, Trinity House lost its responsibility as the principal pilotage authority to local harbour authorities.

Trireme, an ancient vessel with three rows of oars of great effectuality in early naval warfare. Mentioned by Thucydides. It was a long, narrow vessel propelled by 170 rowers. The Romans copied it from the Greeks.

Tritium, a radioactive isotope of hydrogen which has three times the weight of the ordinary hydrogen atom. It is produced by bombarding an isotope of lithium with neutrons and has a half-life of 12½ years, decaying with the emission of β-particles (electrons).

Triton, the largest of Neptune's moons, possibly a "captured" dwarf planet.

Tropic-Bird, a long-tailed sea bird, of which there are 3 species (the Red-billed, the White-tailed, and the Red-tailed), frequenting the tropical regions of the Atlantic, Pacific and Indian oceans. They are often called Bo'sun Birds.

Tropics, the term generally refers to the limits of the area of Earth's surface in which the sun can be directly overhead. The Tropic of Cancer is 23° 30′ N, the Tropic of Capricorn 23° 30′ S of the Equator. Climatologists and geographers have less rigid definitions. Global warming is moving the tropics nearer the poles.

Troposphere. The atmospheric layer which extends from the earth's surface to the stratosphere. As a general rule temperature falls as altitude increases. *See* **Atmosphere.**

Troubadours, lyric poets who flourished from the 12th to the end of the 13th cent., chiefly in Provence and the north of Italy. They were often knightly amateurs, and cultivated a lyrical poetry intricate in metre and rhyme and usually of a romantic amatory strain, written in the *langue d'oc. See also* **Jongleurs.**

Trouvère *or* **Trouveur,** medieval poet of northern France, whose compositions were of a more elaborate character—epics, romances, fables, and chansons de geste—than those of the troubadour of the south. The poetry was written in the *langue d'oïl.* Flourished c. 12th–13th cent.

Truffles are subterranean edible fungi much esteemed for seasoning purposes. There are many species, and they are found in considerable quantities in France and Italy, less commonly in Britain, because of the decline of our ancient woodland. They are often met with under beech or oak trees, and prefer calcareous soils, but there are no positive indications on the surface to show where they are, and they are not to be cultivated. Hogs, and also trained dogs, are used to scent them out. Truffles are called the 'diamonds of the culinary world' in the USA.

Tsetse, an African dipterous fly belonging to the same family as the house-fly. It is a serious economic pest as it transmits the protozoon causing African sleeping sickness when it pierces human skin in order to suck blood.

Tsunami, a seismic sea wave originating from any one of several submarine geological phenomena such as volcanic explosions, landslides or earth movements. Tsunamis are extremely long waves which travel in the open ocean at speeds up to 640 km/h. In deep water their height is only barely perceptible, but on reaching shallow coastal water they may attain heights of up to 30 m and can cause devastation to low-lying areas (as in 2004 around the Indian Ocean). The Pacific Ocean, whose rim is a seismically active area, is particularly susceptible to tsunamis. Tsunamis are often incorrectly referred to as tidal waves.

The devastation and loss of life caused by the 26 December 2004 Indian Ocean tsunami was without equal in modern times (c. 230,000 died). A further devastating tsunami hit Japan in 2011.

Tuatara *or* **Sphenodon,** a reptile of great antiquity, the sole surviving species of the *Rhynchocephalia,* found in New Zealand. It has a rudimentary third eye on the top of the head; this is called the pineal eye and corresponds to tissue which in mammals forms the pineal gland.

Tube Foot, the characteristic organ of locomotion of starfishes and kindred animals. They are arranged in pairs along the underside of the arms, and their sucker-like ends can grip a surface very tightly. The action of the suckers depends on hydraulic pressure.

Tuesday, the third day of the week, named from the Saxon deity Tuisto, Tiw or Tuesco. To the Romans it was the day of Mars.

Tuileries, a French royal and imperial palace dating from 1564. It was attacked by insurgents in 1792,

1830 and 1848, and was burned down during the Commune of Paris in 1871.

Tumulus, a mound of earth raised over the bodies of the dead. The mound of Marathon, enclosing the bodies of the Athenians who were killed in the famous battle with the Persians, is a celebrated tumulus. Such mounds were commonly raised over the tombs of the distinguished dead in ancient times, and sometimes enclosed heavy structures of masonry. The Roman "barrows" were tumuli. Evidence of such mounds are frequent in prehistoric remains.

Tuna *or* **Tunny,** a large marine fish belonging to the mackerel family, frequenting the warm waters of the Atlantic, Pacific and Mediterranean. Tuna fisheries are a major industry. The Japanese appetite for raw tuna (served as *sushi*) is leading to the extinction of the southern bluefin tuna.

Tundra, the vast treeless plains lying in northern N. America and northern Russia where long severe winters and permanently frozen subsoils (permafrost) have resulted in specially adapted plant communities. The summer thaw and impervious permafrost cause waterlogging of lowland areas and marsh plants occur on these sites. In summer the ground cover of lichens and mosses with some flowering plants is distinctive. Stunted willows and birches may occur.

Tungsten, a hard, brittle metallic element, no. 74, symbol W (it was formerly called wolfram), silver to grey in colour. Its chief ores are wolframite (iron and manganese tungstate) and scheelite (calcium tungstate). Tungsten is alloyed in steel for the manufacture of cutting tools; also in the non-ferrous alloy stellite. Electric lamp filaments are made from tungsten. Tungsten carbide is one of the hardest substances known and is used for tipping tools.

Tunicates. *See* **Sea Squirts.**

Turbines propelled by steam provide power for the propulsion of many ships, and on land steam turbines became a principal source of power, being used in large central electricity stations, for instance, to convert heat energy into electrical energy. The first gas-turbine ship had its trials in 1947.

Turbot, a large flat fish, highly valued as food. It often attains from 13 to 18 kg in weight. Its flesh is white and firm. It is confined to European waters, and is caught by line or trawl.

Turkey, a fowl of American origin, brought to Europe from America soon after the discovery of that country. It was a domesticated bird in England in the first half of the 16th cent.

Turmeric, spice used to flavour curries which is now believed to have anti-cancer properties.

Turpentine, an oily substance obtained from coniferous trees, mostly pines and firs. It is widely used especially in making paints and varnishes, and also has medicinal properties.

Turquoise, formerly called Turkey-Stone, is a blue or greenish-blue precious stone, the earliest and best specimens of which came from Persia. It is composed of a phosphate of aluminium, with small proportions of copper and iron. India, Tibet, and Silesia yield turquoises, and a variety is found in New Mexico and Nevada. The first specimens were imported through Turkey. Turquoise has been mined since at least 6,000 B.C.

Turtle. *See under* **Tortoises.**

Turtle Dove, a summer visitor from Africa to southern England. It is a small, slender bird with reddish-brown upper parts, pinkish throat, black tail with white edges, and a repeated purring note. Turtle doves are a symbol of love and fertility.

Tweed. A rough-surfaced fabric of the twilled type, usually all-wool, though cheaper kinds may include cotton. Of a soft, open, flexible texture, it may have a check, twill or herring-bone pattern. Harris, Lewis, Bannockburn and Donegal tweeds are well known.

Twelfth Night is properly the eve of the feast of the Epiphany. It was once the most popular festival next to Christmas. Some people wrongly believe Twelfth Night falls at the end of the 12th day after Christmas.

Twilight. There are several different classifications of twilight, each of which is based on the angular distance of the Sun below the observer's horizon. Civil twilight begins or ends when the centre of the solar disc is 6° below the horizon, nautical twilight beginning and ending when the centre is 12° below. The brightest stars are visible during nautical twilight. The third is astronomical twilight, at which time stars of 6th magnitude are visible provided the sky is clear. Astronomical twilight starts and finishes when the centre of the Sun is 18° below the horizon.

Tyburn, a former small tributary of the Thames, which gave its name to the district where Marble Arch and Hyde Park now stand. Here public executions formerly took place.

Tycoon, the title by which the commander-in-chief of the Japanese army (virtually the ruler of Japan) was formerly described by foreigners. (In Japanese *taikun* means great lord or prince.) The term is now applied, usually in a derogatory sense, to an influential business magnate.

Tynwald, the title given to the Parliament of the Isle of Man, which includes the Governor and Council (the Upper House), and the House of Keys, the representative assembly. This practically constitutes Home Rule, the Acts passed by the Tynwald simply requiring the assent of the Sovereign.

Typhoon. *See* **Cyclone.**

U

Ultramarine, a sky-blue pigment obtained from *Lapis lazuli,* a stone found in Tibet, Iran, Siberia and some other countries. A cheaper ultramarine is now produced by grinding and heating a mixture of clay, sulphur, carbonate of soda and resin.

Ultrasonics, sound waves of frequency so high as to be inaudible to humans, *i.e.,* above 15,000 Hz (Hz is SI unit for cycle per sec.). Ultrasonic waves are commonly produced by causing a solid object to vibrate with a suitable high frequency and to impart its vibrations to the air or other fluid. The object may be a quartz or othercrystal in which vibrations are excited electrically, or a nickel component which is magnetically energised. There are numerous technical applications, *e.g.* submarine echo soundings, flaw detection in castings, drilling glass and ceramics, ultrasound investigations in medicine *etc.* Ultrasonic waves are an important tool of research in physics. Bats produce very loud sounds when they are flying, but at ultrasonic frequencies (20,000 to 150,000 Hz)

Ultra-Violet Rays. These are invisible electromagnetic rays whose wavelengths are less than 3900 Å. (Angstrom = one hundred-millionth of a centimetre.) The sun's radiation is rich in ultra-violet light, but much of it never reaches the earth, being absorbed by molecules of atmospheric gases (in particular, ozone) as well as by soot and smoke particles. One beneficial effect of ultra-violet light on human beings is that it brings about synthesis of vitamin-D from certain fatty substances (called sterols) in the skin. The wavelengths which effect this vitamin synthesis also cause sun tan and sun burn. Ultra-violet lamps (which are mercury-vapour discharge lamps) are also used for sterilising the air inside buildings, their rays being lethal to bacteria. Many substances fluoresce under ultra-violet light; for instance, zinc silicate glows green, while cadmium borate throws out red light. This phenomenon is applied in fluorescent lamps, the light of requisite hue being secured by judicious mixture of the fluorescent materials which coat the lamp.

Umbra, the full shadow of the earth or moon during an eclipse. The term is also used to describe the darker, cooler central region of a sunspot.

Unciae. The Romans took over the Egyptian cubit and divided it into 16 digits as well as into 12 parts called *unciae,* the *uncia* being the origin of the inch.

Unicorn, a fabulous single-horned animal. In fact the "Siberian unicorn" lived alongside early humans in Kazakhstan 29,000 years ago. Creatures like this were described by the Greek physician Ctesias *c.* 400 B.C. In heraldry its form is horse-like, with the tail of a lion and pointed single horn growing out of the forehead. In the Middle Ages the unicorn was a symbol of virginity.

Union Jack, the common name for the official 'Union Flag' of the United Kingdom since 1801 (the Union with Ireland). Jack derives from the nautical term for flag. Commissioned by James I in 1606 to represent the union of England and Scotland (updated in 1801 when Ireland was added).

Union of Great Britain and Ireland was proposed in the Irish Parliament in January 1799 after the 1798 Rebellion and came into force on 1 January 1801.

The troubled history of Ireland, associated with the question of self-government, nationalism, land and religion, culminated in the Easter revolution of 1916. A treaty giving the 26 southern counties independence in 1921, as the Irish Free State, was followed by a period of internal dissension. In 1937 a new constitution was enacted in Ireland in which no reference was made to the Crown. This, however, left in force the External Relations Act of 1936 and with its repeal in 1948, Ireland separated itself from the British Crown and thus severed the last constitutional link with the Commonwealth, and became an independent Republic.

Union of Soviet Socialist Republics (USSR). The Union of Soviet Socialist Republics was formally constituted on 6 July 1923, covering most of the old Russian Empire overthrown in the Communist revolution of 1917, minus the territories which formed Finland, Poland, the Baltic Republics and East Prussia. With the fall of communism, it collapsed in 1991.

Universal Credit. A new single payment for those unemployed or on low incomes, replacing tax credit, housing benefit, JSA, income support etc. Pilot schemes are now being introduced, but have encountered problems.

Universe, See Section T, Part I.

Universities are institutions of higher education whose principal objects are the increase of knowledge over a wide field through original thought and research and the teaching of students. Such societies existed in ancient Greece and India, but the origin of the University as we know it today lies in medieval Europe.

The first bodies to become recognised under this description were at Bologna and Paris in the first half of the 12th cent.; Oxford was founded by an early migration of scholars from Paris, and Cambridge began with a migration from Oxford.

Other Universities began to emerge all over Europe, including three in Scotland—St. Andrews (1411), Glasgow (1451) and Aberdeen (1494)—which were followed by Edinburgh in 1582. These six bodies remained the only Universities in Great Britain until the foundation in 1826–29 of University and King's Colleges in London (resulting in the establishment of the University of London in 1836) and of the University of Durham in 1832.

The 35 old-established universities in England were: Aston, Bath, Birmingham, Bradford, Bristol, Brunel, Buckingham, Cambridge, The City, Durham, East Anglia, Essex, Exeter, Hull, Keele, Kent, Lancaster, Leeds, Leicester, Liverpool, London, Loughborough, Manchester, Newcastle, Nottingham, Open, Oxford, Reading, Salford, Sheffield, Southampton, Surrey, Sussex, Warwick and York. Other old institutions of university standard were the University of Manchester Institute of Science and Technology; the Manchester Business School; the London Graduate School of Business Studies; Cranfield Institute of Technology; and the Royal College of Art.

Wales used to have one University (The University of Wales with colleges at Aberystwyth, Bangor, Cardiff and Swansea) in addition to the Welsh National School of Medicine, the Institute of Science and T7echnology, and St. David's, Lampeter. Scotland had eight: Aberdeen, Dundee (1967), Edinburgh, Glasgow, Heriot-Watt (1966), St. Andrews, Stirling (1967), and Strathclyde (1964), Britain's first technological University. Northern Ireland has two: Queen's University, Belfast and the New University of Ulster at Coleraine.

The Open University (OU) received its charter in 1969; it provides degrees and other courses and began its broadcasts in January 1971. More students register with the OU each year than with any other English university.

The Republic of Ireland has the University of Dublin (Trinity College, Dublin), the National University of Ireland, Dublin City University and the University of Limerick among its most famous seats of learning.

In the United States the best known are Harvard (1636), Yale (1701), Princeton (1746), Columbia (1754), Cornell (1865), California (Berkeley), Massachusetts Institute of Technology. In 1972 the European University Institute was established with headquarters in Florence.

In Britain, many universities receive aid from the State in the form of grants from the Higher Education Funding Council which oversees the distribution of state finance. But they are selfgoverning institutions free from State control. In 1992, the distinction between the former polytechnics and the older universities ended. In 2013 a new generation of University Technical Colleges was inaugurated (e.g. at Greenwich). The University of the Creative Arts dates from 2008. The College of Law is now the University of Law, having the largest law school in the country.

The ending of free tuition for students (from September 1998) and the other implications of the 1997 Dearing Report, heralded a revolution in higher education. The debate on "top-up" fees has aroused much passion. In addition, new two-year 'foundation degrees' were planned which began in September 2001. Some smaller colleges and specialist institutions became universities after changes announced in 2012. (e.g. Harper Adams University in Shropshire). Some prominent private for profit universities are the University of Law and BPP University College of Professional Studies.

A very different type of organisation is the University of the Third Age (U3A), which is essentially a collective of older people who meet to participate in an exchange of information and ideas. Since its arrival in 1981, it has grown enormously. Now it has 985 study groups with nearly 400,000 persons enrolled. Its website is www.u3a.org.uk.

See also entries for **Cambridge University, Oxford University** and **London University.**

Unknown Warrior, the tomb of the Unknown Warrior is in Westminster Abbey. In the United States, it is in Arlington National Cemetery. Such tombs serve as a memorial to all the war dead.

Uraninite. See **Pitchblende.**

Uranium, a metallic element, no. 92, symbol U, discovered by Klaproth in 1789 in pitchblende. It is a white metal which tarnishes readily in air. Great developments have followed the discovery that the nucleus of the uranium isotope U^{235} undergoes fission, and uranium minerals have become very important since it was found that atomic energy could be released controllably by taking advantage of fission. Before atomic energy work began to take the major part of the world's output of uranium minerals, the chief users of uranium compounds were the ceramics and textile industries. Britain imports its uranium from Australia and Canada. See **Nuclear Reactors, Nuclear Fission.**

Uranus. This planet was discovered by Herschel in March 1781. Its diameter is 51,118 km and its mean distance from the Sun is $2,871 \times 10^6$ km. When Voyager 2 visited Uranus in January 1986, it raised the number of known moons orbiting the planet from five to 15 (this total has now grown to 27). Puck is the largest inner moon. The number of known rings surrounding Uranus was also increased to 11. Uranus has a large axial tilt which means that it rotates on its side. Each pole faces the Sun every half-revolution around the Sun, i.e. every 42 years. The dark rings of Uranus have now been seen end-on for the first time. See **Section T, Part I and Voyager.**

Urea, the final product in mammals of the breakdown of nitrogenous waste, e.g., excess amino-acids. It is very soluble in water and is ex-creted in urine. In 1828 Wohler synthesised urea from inorganic matter. This was the first laboratory synthesis of an organic substance and refuted the idea that living creatures or life force are needed to create such substances.

Ursa Major and **Ursa Minor** ("Greater Bear" and "Lesser Bear"), two celebrated constellations, each of seven stars, in the northern celestial hemisphere, familiar since ancient times. Ursa Major has also been called "the Plough", "Charles's (Charlemagne's) Wain" or "the Wagon". The "Pointers" in this group of bright stars point to the brightest star in Ursa Minor, the Pole Star. Called the Big Dipper and the Little Dipper in the USA.

V

Valency. A term used by chemists to describe the combining ability of an element with respect to hydrogen. Thus oxygen, which forms water, H_2O, with hydrogen is said to have a valency of two, nitrogen (forms ammonia, NH_3) three, and carbon (forms methane, CH_4) four. Chlorine forms hydrogen chloride, HCl, and is said to be monovalent. This empirical approach cannot account for valency in such compounds as carbon monoxide, CO, which appears to require both elements to have the same valency.

With the discovery of the electron it was realised that the concept of valency and chemical bonds is intimately concerned with the electronic structure of atoms, and theories have been advanced to explain why the same element can have different valencies in different compounds. Iron, for example, can have a valency of two ($FeCl_2$, ferrous chloride) or three ($FeCl_3$, ferric chloride). See **Section T, Part II and Table of Elements (T56)**.

Valentine's Day (14 February), is a festival in celebration of St. Valentine, one of the Christian martyrs of the 3rd cent. A sweetheart or Valentine is chosen on that day and letters or cards sent secretly to the loved one. The first printed Valentine cards in England date from the late 18th century.

Valkyries, See **I33**.

Valve, an electronic device consisting of two or more metal plates (electrodes) usually enclosed in an evacuated glass bulb. One of the electrodes is heated causing electrons to be emitted. If a positive voltage is applied to the other electrode, the electrons will move towards it and the valve must conduct electricity. The current will only flow in one direction as the electrons are emitted only from one direction. A valve with two electrodes is called a diode, but by putting in one or more intermediate electrodes the flow of current can be sensitively controlled and the valves are then called triodes, pentodes, *etc.*, according to the total number of electrodes in them.

Valves originally found extensive applications in amplifiers, rectifiers, oscillators and many electronic devices, but have now been superseded by transistors, which in turn have been replaced by the integrated circuit and the micro-chip.

Vanadium, a scarce metallic element, no. 23, symbol V, whose chief ores are carnotite and patronite. Some iron ores contain it. Most of the vanadium commercially produced finds its way into vanadium steels, which are used for tools and parts of vehicles, being hard, tough and very resistant to shocks. The oxide is used as a catalyst in making sulphuric aicd. Named after the old Norse name for the Scandinavian goddess Freyja.

Van Allen Belts. One of the most remarkable discoveries of the International Geophysical Year (1957–58), was that the earth is surrounded by a great belt of radiation.

Evidence came from *Sputnik II* (which carried the dog Laika) and from the American satellites, *Explorers I* and *III*. The American scientist, J. A. van Allen, was able to explain the puzzling data collected from these satellites. Subsequent observations with deep space-probes showed that there are in fact two zones of high intensity particle radiation surrounding the earth, one concentrated at a distance of about 1,600 km, the other at about 24,000 km. A close relation exists between the shapes of the zones and the earth's magnetic field. Jupiter is surrounded by a dense belt of trapped high-energy particles.

Vatican, the Papal residence at Rome, a famous palace on the hill adjacent to St. Peter's. Works of Michelangelo glorify the Sistine Chapel.

Vauxhall Gardens, a famous London pleasure resort from the early part of the 18th to the middle of the 19th cent. It was here that many great singers appeared and where the earliest balloon ascents were made.

Venus, the brightest of all the planets, whose orbit lies between the orbits of Mercury and Earth. It is second in order from the sun (*q.v.*). It approaches the earth to within 40 million km. It moves around the sun in the same direction as Earth and the other planets but rotates in the opposite sense. It has been visited by a number of American and Russian probes, some flybys, some soft-landings, others atmospheric probes.

It has 90 times the atmospheric pressure of the earth and temperatures of 450°C. It is covered in a very thick cloud mainly of carbon dioxide which some scientists believe acts like a greenhouse trapping the heat from the sun. Complex reactions occur in the atmosphere and the rain consists mainly of sulphuric and hydrochloric acid. The cloud rotates about six times faster than Venus rotates and swirls into the polar regions like giant whirlpools.

The *Venus Express*, which went into orbit in 2006, was flawlessly collecting vital information about the hot, turbulent atmosphere of the planet until 2015. The atmosphere is now known to be very fickle, changing its structure daily. *Venus Express* revealed images of 225mph winds bearing across the planet (the superrotation of Venus).

Much information has come from both the Pioneer Venus orbiter and the Magellan probe, which between them have mapped nearly the entire Venusian surface. There are two major continents, Aphrodite Terra, is about the size of Africa, and the smaller Ishtar Terra, about the size of Australia, which consists of a very high plateau (c. 3,300 m) and a mountain range dominated by Maxwell Montes at 10,600 m higher than Everest). Aphrodite Terra has a deep trench 2,900 m below "sea level". Most of the planet (60 per cent) is relatively flat. There are no moons.

The Magellan probe (1990) revealed a carbon dioxide atmosphere, 100 times thicker than Earth's, with sulphur escaped from volcanoes as well as the longest channel (4,200 miles) in the solar system. It found that there are no asteroid impact craters bigger than 5 miles across.

Venus has an ozone layer hundreds of times less dense than Earth's and there is tantalising evidence of active valcanoes.

Venus Fly-trap, a well-known insectivorous plant (*Dionaea muscipula*) occurring in Carolina in damp mossy places. It is related to the Sundew. The leaf is the organ that catches the insects. The leaf blade is in two halves, hinged along the centre line. Each half bears three sensitive hairs called "trigger hairs". When an insect touches a trigger, the two halves of the leaf clap together, trapping the insect between them, when it is digested by a secretion (digestive enzymes) from the leaf.

Vernalization. Seeds which, after being exposed to a low temperature, produce plants that flower earlier than usual are said to have been "vernalized". This technique of seed treatment devised by Lysenko is called vernalization.

Vesta, second largest object in the asteroid belt (523 km in diameter). It has more in common with a planet than an asteroid. The Dawn probe visits it in 2015. Also a Roman goddess (*See* **I29**).

Victoria and Albert Museum, in Kensington, London, was begun in 1852 as the Museum of Ornamental Art at Marlborough House. The present building was completed in 1909. It is one of the great museums of the world for the fine arts. The new British Galleries were opened in 2001. A new V&A East is planned for 2021.

The V&A now also administers Ham House (Richmond) and Osterley Park House. The Museum of Childhood (Bethnal Green) is a branch of the V&A. Its enchanting exhibits include c. 8,000 dolls. Apsley House (home of the 1st Duke of Wellington) is also part of the V&A. For further details, see www.vam.ac.uk.

Victoria Cross, an order of merit for conspicuous valour, awarded to members of the Army, Navy and Air Force. The first investiture was in June 1857. The VC has been awarded only 1,354 times (the two youngest VCs were aged only 15).

Videotape Recording (VTR), technique for recording television programmes on to magnetic tape. The original means of storing programmes for broadcast or library purposes was by filming productions from high-quality monitors, an expensive and slow process, since the film had to be chemically developed and edited in the conventional way. The difficulty in establishing an instant play-back system along the lines of the sound tape recording system lay in the high speed and large amount of tape needed to accommodate the picture signal. The BBC experimented with a machine called VERA, but it was an American machine, the Ampex VR100, which provided the breakthrough. This recorded the picture across a wider tape rather than along it, and moving at a slower speed. The modern domestic recorder is usually of the VHS standard, while broadcasters use the higher quality systems, such as Betacam. DVDs have now replaced the older VCRs (the last was produced in 2016). The new generation of high-definition DVDs store up to six times as much data on disc.

Vikings. Scandinavian warriors who from the 8th to the 10th cent. were the terror of northern waters. Sometimes the Viking raids reached south to the Mediterranean and east to the White Sea. Their leader Rurik founded the first Russian kingdom of Novgorod in A.D. 862. The Icelandic Vikings under Eric the Red discovered Greenland in A.D. 982 and a warm period in world climate allowed many to settle there. Their expeditions took them to Labrador and Newfoundland (which they named Vinland). The final extent of their settlement remains disputed). They excelled in shipbuilding, were fine sailors and craftsmen. They were also traders with cities as far away as Constantinople. They established Dublin as a major slaving centre. The name may derive from *vik*, a sheltered deep-water bay now called a *fjord*. The first Viking raid on England was at Lindisfarne in 789 A.D.

The old belief that Vikings floated their dead leaders out to sea in burning boats is a myth.

It is now believed many Viking women accompanied their menfolk in their longboats. Apart from Orkney, there is little genetic signature in Britain from the Vikings.

Village Green. See **Commons.**

Vinyl Plastics are polymers made from derivatives of ethylene, examples are polyvinyl chloride (PVC), which is used in making plastic pipes and kitchen utensils, among other things; polyvinyl acetate used in the paint industry and in bonding laminated articles like plywood; and polystyrene (polyvinyl benzene) used in making electrical fittings and for lenses.

Viper, a family of poisonous snakes in which the venom-conducting fangs hinge forward when the snake bites. One species is found in Britain, the common viper or adder.

Visibility is defined by the distance at which the farthest of a series of objects, specially selected to show against the skyline or in good contrast with their background, can be distinguished. Visibility depends chiefly upon the concentration of water or dust particles suspended in the air. Instruments are available to measure the obscurity of the atmosphere more directly, including that at night. A large lapse rate of temperature and a strong wind are favourable to good visibility; a small lapse rate, calm or light wind favourable to bad visibility. Fog is when the visibility is less than 1,000 m; mist or haze when it is between 1,000 and 2,000 m. See **Pollution.**

Viscount, a title of rank coming between that of Earl and Baron. The title originally stood for deputy-earl. The first English Viscount was Viscount Beaumont, created in 1440.

Vitamins, name of a group of organic substances found in relatively minute amounts in certain foodstuffs, essential for growth and the maintenance of normal bodily function. See **Z40.**

Volcanoes are vents through which magma reaches the surface as lava flows, or as the solid products, *e.g.*, ashes and bombs, of explosive eruption. The vent may be cylindrical or it may be a long fissure.

The former type usually builds up cones, *e.g.*, Vesuvius. Notable active volcanoes are Etna, Vesuvius and Stromboli, in Italy (known as the lighthouse of the Mediterranean). Soufrière on Montserrat; and Mont Pelée on Martinique. The last-named was in violent eruption in 1902, when the chief town of St. Pierre was destroyed. The world's most active volcano is Kilauea on Hawaii. Europe's most active volcano is Mt. Etna. The highest volcano in the world is Kilimanjaro, in Africa.

Volcanic eruptions are sometimes linked with brilliant sunset phenomena, *e.g.*, the Indonesian island of Krakatoa (1883), whose atmospheric and tidal effects were recorded all over the world, and Agung on the island of Bali (1963), which had been dormant for 120 years. In 1991, the eruption of Mt Pinatubo in the Philippines killed 300 people, while in 1997 Montserrat was threatened by the Soufrière eruption.

The famous eruption at Vesuvius took place on 24 August 79 A.D. whilst the huge eruption on the Greek island of Santorini occurred in *c.* 1450 B.C.

The huge eruption at Tambora (Indonesia) in 1815 killed an estimated 90,000 people. The ash clouds which followed the Eyjafjallajökull volcanic eruption in April 2010 caused massive disruption to air travel. There are towering volcanoes on Mars far higher than any on Earth. Venus has over 50,000 volcanoes. The discovery of volcanoes on Io, a moon of Jupiter, was a major scientific advance.

The deepest undersea volcanoes on Earth were found in 2010, three miles beneath the surface of the Caribbean. The largest volcano yet discovered lies below the Pacific Ocean. Indeed major underwater volcanoes can produce new volcanic islands.

Vole, a small rodent with blunt nose, round face and short tail. Three kinds occur in Britain: the field, the bank and the water vole. The water vole is now our fastest declining mammal, due to loss of habitat and mink predators. It kicks up clouds of mud in water when threatened. Known as a water rat, its numbers have fallen 90 % since 1990.

Volt, the electromotive force unit, named after Alessandro Volta (1745–1827), and defined in terms of the coulomb, the second and the joule.

Voyagers 1 and 2. These spacecraft were launched from Earth on 5 Sept. 1977 and 20 Aug. 1977 respectively as a follow-on mission to the earlier and successful Pioneer 10 and 11 spacecraft.

Both probes were launched towards the planets of the outer solar system. Voyager 1 reached Jupiter in 1979 and flew by the moons Callisto, Ganymede, Europa and Io. It was then set on a course for Saturn, examining the rings and the satellite Titan, before heading out of the solar system with no further planetary encounters. Voyager 2 also flew to Jupiter and then to Saturn.

The flyby of Saturn by Voyager 2 in Aug. 1981 was carefully planned to obtain the maximum of new information to complement that obtained from Voyager 1 to help understand some of the perplexing new phenomena, and revealed even more new features of this beautiful and still enigmatic planet. Even after its Saturn flyby, the work of Voyager 2 was far from complete: its swing by Saturn redirected it toward Uranus, on which it provided our first close-up data in Jan. 1986, and from there it continued to Neptune in 1989, taking advantage of a unique arrangement of all four of the outer planets, Jupiter, Saturn, Uranus and Neptune, which only occurs once every 200 years.

Voyager 1, which would not pass particularly close to any planet after Saturn, carries a multilingual goodwill message as well as musical selections to far outside our solar system. It will not reach its nearest star, Sirius, for 360,000 years.

In March 1990, Voyager I beamed back its last colour photographs. By then it was 3,500 million miles from Earth, travelling at 37,000 mph. In 2012 it left the confines of our solar system, to become the most distance human made object.

Voyager 2 has now also headed out of the solar system and gone on to make and transmit observations of the solar heliosphere.

Vraic, a name for seaweed in the Channel Islands, where it is extensively used as a manure.

Vulture, a famous bird of prey of two distinctive groups; that of the Old World, whose nostrils are separated by a bony partition, and the New World vulture, which has no such division. There are 23 species worldwide.

Vultures feed on carrion and are the great scavengers of tropical regions. The European species are the Egyptian vulture, Griffon vulture, Black vulture and Bearded vulture. Vultures have no feathers on the head and neck. Vultures in India and across Africa are in critical decline, killed off by feeding on carcasses of livestock which have been given anti-inflammatory drugs or poisoned by poachers.

W

Wading Birds, *Charadriiformes,* an order of migratory, long-legged, long-billed birds, frequenting marshes and shallow waters. They include the plovers, avocets, stilts, oystercatchers, curlews, godwits, dunlins, sandpipers, redshanks, greenshanks, snipe, woodcocks, the pratincole of the Mediterranean and the sun bittern of tropical America. Many species breed in Britain.

Wagtails, familar long-tailed small birds, the most common British species being the Pied or Water (with sub-species White) Grey and the Yellow (sub-species Blue). Wagtails nest in holes.

Walloons, name given to the French-speaking population of the southern provinces of Belgium, in contrast to the Flemings or Dutch-speaking population of the northern provinces. The Walloon areas contain much heavy industry.

Walpurgis Night, the night before 1 May, when witches were supposed to have liberty to roam. Named after St Walpurgis, an English nun,

Walrus, a very large marine mammal, related to the seals having in the upper jaw two large curved tusks, which average in length from 38 to 60 cm. It lives on bi-valve molluscs, and inhabits the Arctic seas. An adult walrus can exceed 4 m in length and weigh over a tonne. The mammal is now threatened by melting sea ice and there are calls for it to become a protected species.

Wankel Engine *or* **Rotary Engine,** is an internal combustion engine invented by Felix Wankel in the 1930s and greatly developed since. The ordinary internal combustion engine has to convert reciprocating motion of the pistons into rotary motion. In the Wankel engine the explosion of the fuel and air mixture drives a moving part (the rotor) directly into rotatory motion, and the rotor itself opens and closes the fuel inlet and exhaust ports. The three spaces between the triangular rotor and its specially shaped housing act successively as intake, compression, explosion and exhaust chambers as the rotor revolves. There are no valves and far fewer moving parts than in an ordinary piston engine. The Wankel engine is claimed to have many advantages in that it is smaller and lighter for a given horse-power, relatively simple, quieter and freer from vibration, and could contribute to pollution control.

Warblers, a family of small, lively song-birds closely related to the flycatchers and thrushes. Represented in Britain by about 36 species, including the chiffchaff, one of the earliest of our spring visitors, willow-warbler, wood-warbler, garden-warbler, whitethroat, sedge and grasshopper-warbler. The blackpoll warbler migrates from Canada to South America, one of the longest overwater flights recorded for a song bird.

Warrigal. *See* **Dingo.**

Wasps. *See* **Hornets.**

Water is the simplest compound of hydrogen and oxygen. It is formed when an electric spark is passed through a mixture of the gases, and is a product of combustion of all hydrogen-containing compounds, *e.g.*, petrol, coal, coal gas and wood.

Water is essential to living matter, and is the medium which carries food to animals and plants. Salts in hard water may be removed by distillation of the water or by a process known as ion-exchange (water softening). Pure water freezes at 0°C and boils at 100°C and is used as a standard of temperature on this scale. It has a maximum density at 4°C. Heating water above 100°C converts it into steam, which is used under pressure to convert heat energy into useful work, as in electrical power stations and steam engines.

Water gas is a mixture mainly of carbon monoxide and hydrogen formed by blowing steam and oxygen through red-hot coke: it is used as a fuel. Water is one of the very few compounds which freezes from the surface down rather than from the bulk of the liquid up. This property has important consequences on the preservation of life in rivers and lakes when they are frozen.

The Drinking Water Inspectorate set up in January 1990 has responsibility for checking that water supplied by the water companies is wholesome and fit to drink when it reaches your home.

The growing pressure for available water world-wide means that water has become the oil of the 21st century. At present 11 % of the world's population do not have access to safe drinking water. Around 1,400 children die each day because of dirty water and poor sanitation.

Waterfalls, the world's highest (in ft) are the Angel Falls in Venezuela (3,212), the Tugela Falls in South Africa (3,110) and the Utigord in Norway at 2,625.

Water Hyacinth (*Eichhornia crassipes*), a beautiful aquatic plant native to Brazil which has spread to other favourable equatorial regions of the world causing havoc on account of its abnormal rate of reproduction away from its natural environment. In recent years it has invaded the Nile and the Congo, forming vast floating carpets which block the channels, clog the paddles of river craft and deoxygenate the water, killing the fish. It is being held in check by spraying with herbicides.

Water Rat. *See* **Vole.**

Waterloo Bridge, crossing the Thames, was built by Rennie, and opened in 1817. It had nine arches, each 120 ft (36 m) span, was built of granite, and had a length (with approaches) of 2,456 ft (749 m).

The present bridge, completed in 1942, and formally opened 10 December 1945, is a fine example of reinforced concrete construction. (Architect, Sir Giles Gilbert-Scott.)

Watling Street, the name of the old Roman road which ran from the Channel ports by way of London to Shropshire. *See* **Roman Roads** (**L94**).

Watt. A unit of electrical power equivalent to 1 joule of work per second, named after James Watt (1736–1819). A kilowatt is 1,000 watts.

Wattle. The national flower of Australia.

Waxbill, a small Oriental and African bird of the *Estrildidae* family, with wax-like bill and beautifully variegated plumage. The Java sparrow, and the Blue-breasted waxbill are attractive, but sadly still find their way into cages.

Weasel. A carnivore mammal found in Britain, smallest member of the group including the Stoat, Polecat, and Pine-marten, about 20 cm long. Its fur is reddish on the upper side of the animal, white on the under side; it may all turn white in winter with the exception of the tail.

Weather is generally accepted as being the current state of the atmosphere, particularly as regards its pressure and temperature, wind, cloud and precipitation. Many other features such as fog, sunshine duration, humidity, pressure tendency, may be added to the list, all items of which are routinely observed by specially instrumented stations usually sponsored by the national meteorological services. Day-to-day changes in the weather as experienced by the individual are due to the passage of circulation systems, many of which bring clearly recognisable areas of "good" (*i.e.*, calm and sunny) weather as frequently occurs in anticyclones and "bad" (*i.e.*, cold, windy, cloudy and rainy) weather.

Clearly, the weather in any place at any time is primarily determined by the frequency and intensity of synoptic-scale weather circulation systems (*c.* 3,000 km across). Local weather (over areas of *c.* 100 km) may be heavily influenced by topography, *e.g.*, valley fogs, frost hollows.

Weather Lore. Before instruments were invented to measure atmospheric conditions, man relied on his own observation of wind and sky, behaviour of birds and animals, and came to associate certain phenomena with types of weather. Many popular weather rhymes have survived the centuries, and as long as forecasting is confined to the next few days there is something to be said for them, particularly those dealing with the winds.

Weaver Bird, the popular name for a large group of finch-like birds belonging to the family *Ploceidae*, found principally in Africa but also in Southern Asia, Australia, and Europe and remarkable for their habit of building nests formed of blades of grass dexterously interwoven and suspended from the boughs of trees.

Weaving. *See* **Section N.**

Wedding Anniversaries are: first, Paper; second, Cotton; third, Leather; fourth, Fruit and Flowers; fifth, Wooden; sixth, Sugar; seventh, Woollen; eighth, Bronze; ninth, Pottery; tenth, Tin; twelfth, Silk and Fine Linen; fifteenth, Crystal; twentieth, China; twenty-fifth, Silver; thirtieth, Pearl; thirty-fifth, Coral; fortieth, Ruby; forty-fifth, Sapphire; fiftieth, Golden; fifty-fifth, Emerald; sixtieth, Diamond; sixty-fifth, Platinum or Blue Sapphire; seventieth, Platinum; seventy-fifth, Diamond or Gold; Oak (for eightieth).

Wednesday, the 4th day of the week, derived its name from Woden or Odin, the Norse god of war.

Weights and Measures. *See* **L2** and **T58–60.**

Welding is a means of joining together two pieces of material, often metals, by heating the joint until the substances melt locally, run together, and then solidify. The heating can be by burning gas (*e.g.*, oxy-acetylene welding) or electric current (electric arc welding). Techniques exist for welding anything from hair-like wires to massive steel plates. *See* **Soldering.**

Werewolf, a man or woman, who according to mediaeval belief, could be turned by witchcraft or magic into a wolf, eat human flesh or drink human blood and turn into himself again. This belief was widely held in Europe, and similar superstitions prevail among most primitive peoples, *e.g.*, the "leopard man" of some African tribes. Lycanthropy (from Gr. = wolfman) is when the patient imagines himself a beast.

Westminster Abbey. *See* **E21.**

Westminster Cathedral, seat of the Roman Catholic Archbishop of Westminster. It was designed by J. F. Bentley and built betwen 1895 and 1910. It is of red brick, in early Christian Byzantine style with a domed campanile, 283 ft (86 m) high.

Westminster Hall, adjoining the House of Parliament, was built as a Banqueting Hall by William Rufus, and many courtly festivals were held there in succeeding centuries. King John then established the Law Courts there. It now forms a gigantic hallway, leading to the Houses of Parliament. Charles I, Sir Thomas More, and Warren Hastings were tried there.

Whale, a completely aquatic mammal; the fore- limbs are modified to form fin-like paddles and there is little external trace of the hindlimbs.

There are two major groups of whales—the *Toothed Whales,* including the Sperm-whale (Cachalot), Dolphin, Killer-whales and Porpoises; and the *Whalebone Whales.* In the latter a series of whalebone plates grow down from the roof of the mouth, and, being frayed at their edges into a hairy fringe, together constitute a filtering mechanism. The animal takes in sea water containing minute organisms on which it feeds; the mouth is then closed and the tongue raised when the water is forced out through the filter, on which is left the food. As the tongue is lowered, the whalebone plates straighten up, flicking the food on to the tongue, which transfers it to the gut. Most whale oil is obtained from the thick layer of fat under the skin (blubber), but in the Sperm-whale there is a large reserve of oil in the head. One of the major users of sperm oil is the leather industry. Ambergris used in perfumery comes from the intestine of whales.

The number of whales that may be killed in a season is limited by International Convention. Today the main whaling nations are Japan, Iceland and Norway. South Georgia was once home to the world's largest whaling station.

It is estimated that 2 million whales were killed by humans during the 20th century. In 1994 a whale sanctuary around Antarctica was established by the International Whaling Commission. The sanctuary banned commercial whaling in the Southern Ocean for at least 10 years. Sadly, blue whales, the the largest and heaviest inhabitants of the ocean, have seen their population decimated. The humpback whale has now revived in numbers to over 40,000 mature individuals. Sperm whale numbers have now plummeted.

Scientists have found that Beluga whales travel thousands of miles to feast on stocks of cod and halibut after navigating by the stars or Earth's magnetic field. Today the northern right whale is threatened by busy Atlantic shipping lanes. The sperm whale is the world's loudest animal. Orca is the name for the killer whale. The *narval* is the unicorn of the Arctic. The blue whale can weigh 200 tons, making it the biggest creature that ever lived.

Whimbrels. Somewhat similar birds to curlews, with long legs and a long down-curved beak.

Whinchats, summer visitors to Britain. These lively, orange-breasted birds properly belong to the flycatcher family (not the thrush).

Whiskers in physics and materials science *(q.v.)* are tiny rods of crystal, thinner than human hair and perhaps 1 cm long. Their importance lies in the fact that such crystals are free from the defects described on **T21.** They are also free from surface cracks and steps. This means they are immensely strong because failures of strength in ordinary solids are due to imperfections and cracks of one kind or another. Large numbers of whiskers of strong solids like graphite or silicon carbide embedded in a matrix of softer matter such as plastic make a very strong new material.

White Ants. *See* Termites.

White Elephant, a gift that causes the recipient more trouble or cost than it is worth; derived from an old-time custom of the Kings of Thailand who presented a white elephant to a courtier whom it was desired to ruin.

Whitehall Palace, built within sight of Westminster by Hubert de Burgh, Earl of Kent, round about 1240, was the residence of the Archbishops of York until Wolsey presented it to Henry VIII in 1530. From then until 1697, when it was burned down, it continued to be the favourite town residence of royalty, and to the Stuarts especially it was a great centre of court festivities. In those days, with its grounds, it extended from the Strand to the river. The only portion of Whitehall Palace now standing is the Banqueting Hall built by Inigo Jones, on a scaffold projected from the front of which Charles I was beheaded. A block of government buildings has been built on part of the site of the old Palace.

White House, the official residence at Washington of the President of the United States. It was built in 1792, having been designed by an Irishman, James Hoban. In 1814 British troops captured Washington and set fire to the White House.

Whitsuntide, the festival celebrating the descent of the Holy Ghost. It occurs seven weeks after Easter.

Widow Bird, certain species of African weaver birds with predominantly black plumage. In the breeding season the male birds are strikingly beautiful, with scarlet and buff markings and long tail feathers. They are social parasites and trick other birds into rearing their young.

Wig. *See* Peruke.

Wigeon, a surface-feeding duck of northern Europe, known in Britain more as a winter visitor than a nesting bird. It feeds in flocks in the muddy estuaries and has a characteristic "whee-oo" call.

Wildebeest. *See* Gnu.

Willow, a water-side-loving tree of the genus *Salix,* to which the osiers belong. The best cricket-bat blades are made from a white willow, *S. alba* var. *caerulea,* a fine tree with bluish-green leaves, mostly found in Essex. Willow is also used for polo balls. Weeping willow, *S. baby-lonica,* is native to China and is the willow seen on Old China willow-pattern plates.

Wind, air set in motion by special atmospheric conditions, is of various degrees, from a slight rustling breeze to a hurricane. Winds are *constant,* as in trade winds or anti-trade winds; *periodic,* in monsoons and other wind visitations occurring according to influences of season; *cyclonic* and *anti-cyclonic,* when their motion is spiral: *whirlwinds, hurricanes,* and *tornados,* when high temperature and great density induce extreme agitation.

Ordinarily, a wind is named from the point of the compass from which it blows, or it may be expressed in degrees from due north. The *sirocco,* the *mistral,* and the *simoom* are local forms of winds of great velocity. A *blizzard* is a biting blast of icy temperature. The winds of Antarctica are the most ferocious on the planet. Wind speeds are measured by the Beaufort Scale, devised by Francis Beaufort in 1805. The first UK storm to be named was Abigail in November 2015.

Wind Farms. Britain is the windiest country in Europe and has more offshore wind farms than anywhere else in Europe. The biggest offshore windfarm in the world was inaugurated in the North Sea in September 2009. Horns Rev 2 is 30km off the coast of Jutland. The huge Walney offshore windfarm (off the coast of Cumbria) is due to open in 2018. Huge projects are planned for Dogger Bank Teesside and the Hornsea project, 75 miles off Grimsby. The earliest windfarm in Britain opened in 1991 near Delabole in Cornwall.

Windmills were in use in Persia by A.D. 644. However, they were not much seen in Europe before the 13th cent. Wind sawmills were invented by a Dutchman in the 17th cent., and one was erected near the Strand in London in 1633. Great improvements have been made in these mills, especially in the USA, where, by the application of the windshaft principle, much space is saved and the mills can be used for pumping, grinding *etc.*

Among fine examples of working-mill restorations are Stainsby watermill in Derbyshire, Sacrewell in Peterborough and Gelli Groes in Gwent.

Windows (Old Norse *vindauga* = wind-eye), an opening in a wall of a building to admit light and air, and to afford a view of what is outside. In northern Europe windows, as the derivation of the word implies, were first used for ventilation and glass was not used in private houses before the end of the 12th cent. In early Gothic (12th cent.) windows were still small and narrow, with rounded heads. In Early English (13th cent.) they became longer and the heads pointed. In the Decorated period (14th cent.) windows were mullioned (divided by slender bars into panes) and the pointed heads often traceried.

In Tudor times windows were larger and the bay-window (projecting from the wall) and the oriel window *(q.v.)* were much in vogue; in the late 18th cent. curved bays (called bowwindows) became fashionable. Sash windows (invented by the English) with wooden frames and divided into equal rectangular panes were used in Queen Anne and Georgian houses. Their design was influenced by a passion for symmetry; they were very efficient ventilators. The French window reaches to the floor and has double casements opening as doors. A Dormer window is a vertical window set on the sloping side of a roof.

Woad, a plant (*Isastis tinctoria*) largely used by ancient Britons for the blue dye obtained from the leaves. It is a biennial plant belonging to the same family (*Cruciferae*) as the wallflower. It is now being considered as a potential source of ink for computer printers and as an anti-tumour agent in the battle against cancer.

Wolverine. See **Glutton.**

Wolves, well-known carnivorous animals still found in many parts of Europe, but not existing in Britain since the middle of the 17th cent. The last wolf in Scotland was killed in 1680. They usually hunt in packs and live in family groups. In parts of Europe, careful conservation has seen their numbers increase, as in north-west Spain. Grey wolves (Europe's second largest predator after the brown bear) have now returned to Germany. They howl to proclaim territory.

Women's Institutes (WI) were originally founded in Canada in 1897. The movement spread to Britain, with the first branch opening in Wales in 1915. It has around 215,000 members in the UK.

Woodcock, a wading bird, valued for its flesh. It is a member of the snipe family, and breeds in Britain. The parent bird is able to carry its young between its thigh and body when flying to and from the feeding spots. It is one of the birds protected by the Game Laws.

Woodhenge, popular name for the traces of an elaborate wooden temple, dating back 5,000 years, found at Stanton Drew in Somerset in 1997.

Woodpecker, a familiar tree-climbing, insectivorous bird of conspicuous plumage, of which three species are found in Britain, the green woodpecker or yaffle (because of its harsh cry), the great spotted, and the lesser spotted.

They build in the hollows of trees. Yaffle has a long sticky tongue for licking up ground insects, especially ants. The great and lesser woodpeckers obtain insects by digging into tree trunks with strong, chisel-like bills, spearing the insects with a sharp tongue. The metallic drumming sound made by the birds in spring is thought to be caused by their beaks hammering away at some hard resounding substance. Their numbers have declined markedly in recent years.

Wood Pigeon. See **Ring Dove.**

Wood's Metal, an alloy with a very low melting point (65°C, which is under 150°F) so that a spoon made of it will melt when used to stir a cup of tea. Contains bismuth 4 parts, lead 2 parts, tin 1 part, cadmium 1 part. Its use as a heat exchanger has now been superseded by silicone oils, which have a wider temperature range.

Woodworm. Four beetles are mainly responsible for woodworm damage: common furniture beetle (*Anobium punctatum*), powder post beetle (*Lyctus brunneus*), death watch beetle (*Xestobium rufovillosum*), and house longhorn beetle (*Hylotrupes bajulus*). Particular attention should be paid to wood in damp, dark and out-of-the-way places, and the backs and underneaths of furniture. The most frequent cause of woodworm damage is the common furniture beetle (*q.v.*).

Wool is a fibre, made up of very long protein molecules. It has been largely grown and used in the manufacture of cloth in England since before the Roman invasion. It is grown on the backs of sheep, and is of various kinds, according to the breed of sheep from which it is derived. Wool differs from hair in that it has a wavy, serrated fibre, its curl being a notable characteristic, whereas hair has a smooth surface comparatively free from serratures. Long wools were mostly used for the manufacture of worsted goods, and short wools for woollen cloths.

The finest wools are obtained from the fleece of the Spanish merino sheep. Australia, New Zealand, Argentina and South Africa are among the greatest wool-producing countries. China is the world's largest consumer of wool.

Woolsack, the name given to the seat formerly occupied by the Lord Chancellor in the House of Lords. It is a large square bag of wool, without back or arms, covered with red cloth. At the time when it was first used, in the reign of Edward III, wool was the great staple commodity of the country and, it is said, chosen for the seat of judges as a constant reminder of the main source of the national wealth. The Lord Chancellor was "appointed to the woolsack". Since 2006 the Woolsack has been occupied by the Lord Speaker.

Wombat, small Australian marsupial mammal whose survival is now threatened, by a mysterious skin disease. It resembles a small bear.

Workers' Educational Association (WEA), the largest

voluntary sector provider of adult education courses in the UK. Founded in 1903 to support the educational needs of working people.

World Heritage Sites, established under the World Heritage Convention to secure lasting protection for sites of outstanding universal value. In Britain the sites include Canterbury Cathedral; Durham Cathedral and Castle; Studley Royal Gardens and Fountains Abbey; Ironbridge Gorge; the prehistoric stone circles of Stonehenge and Avebury; Blenheim Palace; the city of Bath; Hadrian's Wall; the Tower of London; the Palace of Westminster; the islands of St Kilda; Edinburgh Old and New Towns; the North Wales castles and town walls of Edward I, the Giants' Causeway, in Northern Ireland and maritime Greenwich. England's first natural World Heritage Site is the 95-mile 'Jurassic Coast', in Dorset and Devon. The UK now has 29 World Heritage sites (the Forth Bridge attained this status in 2015). There are now around 1,017 sites worldwide.

Around the world, UNESCO's sites include the Great Wall of China; the Pyramids and Grand Canyon; the Taj Mahal; Persepolis, the capital of ancient Persia; Australia's Great Barrier Reef and the Inca town on Machu Picchu in Peru. Recently designated sites include Robben Island, the Darjeeling Himalayan railway, the Red Fort in Delhi, the Shia holy city of Samarra and the old town of Corfu.

World Population. According to United Nations sources world population has now reached around 7·25 billion. Over half live in Asia, where the population of India will overtake China by 2022.

Different countries are at different stages in a demographic transition from the stability provided by a combination of high birth rate and high death rate to that provided by a combination of low birth rate and low death rate. Their recent population history and current trend of growth, the age-structure of their population, and consequently their population potential for the near future are all widely different. Most rapid growth is in Africa with rates of over 3 per cent in some countries. (Africa could have 4·2 billion people by 2099).

It is estimated that about one in 25 of all human beings who have ever lived are alive today. It took 115 years for the world's population to rise from one to two thousand million; in a further 35 years it rose from two thousand million to three; in only 15 more years from four to five thousand million. It is estimated to reach over 9·7 billion by 2050 and perhaps 11·2 billion by 2099.

In 1970, only two cities had a population of over 10 million. Today there are 21 such conurbations, spread from China and Japan to Mexico.

The countries with the largest populations are China (1·39 bn) and India (1·27 bn), followed by the USA, Indonesia, Brazil and Pakistan. See also **Longevity (L68)** for facts on life expectancy.

Wrasse, a large reef fish. Threatened with extinction because it is a luxury food in Asia. Recent film footage has shown a tuskfish (a type of wrasse) using tools.

Wren, a family of small passerine birds possessing upturned tails, most abundant in South America. The British species is an interesting singing bird with a surprising loud note for its size.

X

Xenoliths, the term for those bits of rock trapped when lava hardens.

Xenon a rare gaseous element, no.54, symbol Xe, occurring in minute quantities in the atmosphere, discovered by Sir William Ramsay and M. W. Travers in 1898. See **Rare Gases.**

X-Rays were discovered in 1895 by Professor Röntgen, of Wurzburg. X-rays are produced when heavy metal atoms (*e.g.* tungsten) are struck by electrons of sufficient energy. X-rays are now commonly used to examine the internal structure of many opaque objects. In medicine, industry and for security, examination may be conducted without physical invasion. X-rays may also be used to probe the structure of matter, for example the atomic structure of crystals. The discovery in the 1960s that cosmic objects emitted intense X-rays has led to many important discoveries.

Xylem, the woody tissue of higher plants whose function is to conduct water and mineral salts upwards, and to provide mechanical support.

Y

Yacht, a light vessel now much used for pleasure trips and racing. The first yachting club was the Cork Harbour Club, started about 1720; and in 1812 the Royal Yacht Squadron was founded at Cowes. The Royal Thames Yacht Club dates from 1823.

Yak, a long-haired ox, found in Tibet. Used as a beast of burden, and also kept for milk and meat.

Yard, a standard measure of 36 in, the word being derived from the Saxon gryd, or rod. The yard and pound are now defined by reference to the metre and the kilogram: yard = 0·9144 of a metre; pound = 0·45359237 of a kilogram. By international agreement the metre is defined by reference to the wavelength of krypton-86 light.

Yellowhammer, a common British bird of the bunting family, of lemon-yellow and brown plumage. Nests on or near the ground. Recent years have seen its numbers decline. Its nickname is the Scottish canary.

Yeomen of the Guard are a body of Foot Guards established in the reign of Henry VII for the protection of the Royal Person. Yeomen are now about 100 in number, and their duties consist in being present on ceremonial State occasions, the yearly distribution of Maundy Money, and the searching of the vaults of the Houses of Parliament on Guy Fawkes' day.

"Beefeater" is the nickname of both Yeomen of the Guard and Yeomen Warders of the Tower, and they both wear the Tudor style of dress, but with one distinction, the Yeomen of the Guard wear a cross belt, the Warders do not. The first female Beefeater began work in 2007.

Yeti, opinions differ as to whether this is a mythical inhabitant of the Himalayas, a primitive primate or bear. Evidence produced in 2013 suggested the yeti is an animal descended from an ancient hybrid species of polar bear. In North America, the creature is known as *bigfoot* or *sasquatch*, but no hard evidence of its existence has been found.

Yiddish, language whose basic grammar and vocabulary are Germanic (but it is a complete language in itself). It was the language of most Jews of Eastern Europe before the Second World War.

Young Offenders' Institutions. The Criminal Justice Act 1988 replaced youth custody and detention centre training with the sentence of detention in a young offender institution for all young people aged 15 to 20 whom the courts decided needed custodial treatment. More recently the Crime and Disorder Act 1998 modified this sentence with the creation of the detention and training order, combining custody and community supervision, for young offenders under the age of 18. A government review in 2016 called for the abandonment of the present system.

Ytterbium, a chemical, no.70, symbol Yb, element discovered by Urbain in 1907; one of the group of rare earth metals.

Yttrium, a chemical element, no.39, symbol Y, discovered by Mosander in 1842. It is found in a few rare minerals such as gadolinite, xenotine, fergusonite and euxenite. One of the group of rare earth metals.

Yurt. A Mongolian tent, circular in shape and made of skins. Used by nomads.

Z

Zamboni Pile, a dry galvanic battery, which can provide small amounts of high-voltage current over a very long time. At Oxford a couple of Zamboni piles have kept a bell ringing for over a hundred years. These piles in the second world war were perfected and produced in quantity, being the most convenient source of current for infra-red signalling devices.

Zebra, an African quadruped of whitish-grey colour, with regular black stripings, perhaps the most beautiful member of the Equine family. Rather larger than an ass and smaller than the horse, it has a tufted tail, is of light build, wild and fleet of foot. The Zebra may be threatened with extinction—already the fate of the Quagga species—because of its slaughter by man for its beautiful skin. Each year in Africa, zebra go on a spectacular migration to their breeding grounds, making

the longest land migration in Africa. The name derives from *zevra,* an old Portuguese word for wild ass. Theories that their stripes kept away flies or lions have been disproved.

Zebra Crossings, the familiar road crossings for pedestrians were first introduced in 1949. Originally blue and yellow before becoming black and white.

Zenith, the highest point in the heavens above an observer's head, the opposite pole to the nadir.

Zeppelin, name of the airships developed in the First World War by Germany, kept aloft by hydrogen. There were 52 zeppelin raids on Britain killing 600 civilians.The loss of the *Hindenburg,* which burst into flames in 1937 trying to land at Lakehurst, New Jersey, put an end to their popularity.

Zero, the cypher signifying nothing originally came from China. The West is indebted to the Arabs for it, who themselves obtained it from India and passed it to European mathematicians towards the end of the Middle Ages. The zero has also been found in Babylonian cuneiform. The Greeks had no such symbol, which hindered the development of their mathematics. The use of zero led to the invention of decimal fractions and to the later developments in astronomy, physics and chemistry. For absolute zero on the temperature scale *see* **Absolute Temperature.**

Ziggurats, famous Babylonian religious centres, among the finest monuments of the ancient world. They had a distinctive terraced structure.

Zinc, a familiar metallic element, no.30, symbol Zn, known to the ancients, and used by them in the making of brass. It occurs as the sulphide, carbonate, *etc.* The ores of zinc are crushed, roasted and reduced with coal. In combination with copper it constitutes the familiar alloy called brass, and zinc itself is much used for roofing *etc.*

Zirconium, metallic element, no.40, symbol Zr, was discovered by Klaproth in the sand of the rivers of Sri Lanka in 1789. The crystalline metal is white, soft and ductile; in its amorphous condition it is a blue-black powder. Zirconium is used in atomic reactors as containers for fuel elements.

Zodiac, an imaginary zone or belt of the sky enclosing the circuit over which the principal planets travel. It is divided into 12 equal spaces of 30 degrees each, comprising respectively the 12 signs of the zodiac—Aries, Taurus, Gemini, Cancer, Leo, Virgo, Libra, Scorpio, Sagittarius, Capricornus, Aquarius and Pisces. The idea of the zodiac originated with the Babylonians about 2000 B.C. and passed by way of the Greeks to the Western world.

The traditional 12 signs of the zodiac were thrown into turmoil when a 13th sign – Ophiucus – was added by astrologers. *See also* **G25.**

Zodiacal Band, a very faint band of light sometimes seen stretching along the ecliptic joining the Zodiacal Light to the Gegenschein and, like them, caused by the reflection of sunlight from interplanetary dust particles.

Zodiacal Light, a faint cone of light occasionally seen stretching along the zodiac from the western horizon after evening twilight or the eastern horizon before morning twilight. It is believed to be due to the scattering of the sun's light by dust particles in orbit round the sun and extending beyond the earth. Recent observations at the high altitudes station at Chacaltaya in the Andes suggest that the dust is travelling round the sun in regular planetary orbits.

Zonda, a warm moist wind in Argentina of great velocity blowing from the north or northwest, and, like the Sirocco in Southern Europe, causing much discomfort. It happens when a depression is moving across the pampas, bringing with it a mass of air from the humid tropics. It is followed by a refreshing wind from the south east.

Zoological Gardens of London were opened in 1828, and belong to the Zoological Society of London. They contain one of the largest collections of living animals in the world (*c.* 18,000 animals).

The Society maintains an open-air zoo at Whipsnade, on the edge of Dunstable Downs.

Zoology, the branch of science concerned with animal life, anatomy and behaviour.

Zulus, one of the peoples of South Africa. Prior to white rule, the Zulus were ruled by a succession of paramount chiefs, reaching the zenith of their powers under King Shaka in the 1820s. Their power was crushed by the British at Ulundi in 1879 (after the Zulus had earlier routed the British at Isandlwana).

LITERARY
COMPANION

This section provides a concise outline of English Literature from the
earliest times to the first decades of
the present century. Arranged as a
chronological survey, it covers such
great poets and writers as Chaucer,
Shakespeare, Milton and Dickens
as well as the major figures of more
recent times. Also included are surveys of twentieth century poetry and
drama.

TABLE OF CONTENTS

LITERARY COMPANION

SURVEY OF ENGLISH LITERATURE

OLD ENGLISH LITERATURE

The origins of English Literature go back before the Norman Conquest, when a rich literary and cultural tradition, centred in the monasteries that were the repositories of early English Christianity, was developed. While much of the writing that emerged from the monasteries was written in Latin, Old English (or Anglo-Saxon), the language of the Germanic peoples who had first invaded England in the fifth century, emerged as one of the most prestigious early vernacular languages.

Beowulf and Old English Poetry

Old English poetry was mainly written in alliterative verse. It boasts one undisputed masterpiece, Beowulf, a heroic epic probably composed in the eighth century and preserved in a single tenth century manuscript (the Nowell Codex in the British Library). In the first part, the Scandinavian protagonist, Beowulf, successfully defends his uncle's kingdom by killing the monster Grendel and, on the following night, Grendel's mother. In the second part, set fifty years later, Beowulf has himself become king. He once again saves his people, this time by slaying a dragon, but is fatally wounded in the process. Beowulf is considered a great poem, because of its assured epic tone, its moving alliterative verse and its powerful heroic narrative, which involves complex parallels between episodes. It also provides a detailed picture of a pagan Germanic culture, centred on an aristocratic mead hall and kinship loyalties. However, this culture is observed at a time of transition and numerous passages contain a strong vein of Christian morality.

Other notable Anglo-Saxon poems also bring Germanic and Christian elements together. They include the elegies, The Wanderer and The Seafarer, The Battle of Maldon, which takes the heroic defeat of an English army by the Danes in 991 as its subject and more generally seems to be a celebration of fighting for a lost cause, poems on Old Testament themes such as Judith and Genesis A and Genesis B and visionary Christian works such as The Dream of the Rood.

Old English Prose

The best-known Old English prose work is the Anglo-Saxon Chronicle, a collection of texts that provides an invaluable historical record of events in the period, narrated in a circumstantial style that lacks the literary merit of the classics of Old English verse. The Chronicle originated in the reign of Alfred the Great, King of Wessex (871–99), a major patron of learning who was responsible for the translation of several important Latin works into English. These include Boethius's Consolation of Philosophy, St. Augustine's Soliloquies and the Ecclesiastical History of the English People by the Venerable Bede, an English monk who lived his life in Northumbria. Bede's History (c. 771) is widely regarded as the most important English work of its kind written before the Renaissance. The prose literature of the Anglo-Saxon period is also notable for homilies and translations of Classical, as well as Christian, texts.

After 1066, as a consequence of Norman rule, Old English lost ground to French and Latin as a literary language, particularly since it existed in numerous regional and local dialects. The records in the Anglo-Saxon Chronicle continue into the twelfth century, but the post-Norman Conquest entries are characterized by linguistic variations.

MIDDLE ENGLISH LITERATURE

The twelfth and thirteenth centuries were a comparatively quiet era in the annals of English literature. In contrast, the fourteenth century saw an efflorescence of writing in the various dialects of English. Foremost among the authors of this period was Geoffrey Chaucer, who wrote in the East Midland dialect of English, which gradually became accepted as the standard form of the language, although orthography and pronunciation continued to be extremely varied. Other major writers of the period included William Langland, the so-called Gawain poet and John Gower, who wrote in English, Latin and French. Towards the end of the medieval period, literature moved into a new phase with the invention of the printing press and one of the books published by the pioneer English printer, William Caxton, was Sir Thomas Malory's masterpiece the Morte D'Arthur, which crystallized many of the concerns of the Age of Chivalry.

Morality Plays and Mystery Plays

Other significant literature of the period includes a broad range of anonymous oral ballads and equally anonymous religious and secular lyrics. The period also saw the beginnings of significant English drama in the shape of morality plays and the cycles of mystery plays, which were popular from the thirteenth to the sixteenth century. Although much of the literature of the medieval era is religious in outlook, reflecting the extent to which social life was shaped by Christian belief, the emergence of a writer such as Chaucer signals a more secular approach that looks forward to the Humanist spirit of the Renaissance. Elsewhere spiritual and secular concerns are not so sharply divided as the modern reader may initially suppose: the mystery plays were performed by trade guilds and included episodes that deviated from their ostensibly devotional purpose. Similarly medieval religious lyrics frequently employ the language of profane love in sacred contexts.

William Langland

Langland's allegorical masterpiece, Piers Plowman, exists in three versions, dating from around 1360 to 1387. Little is known about the poet himself, though he wrote in the West Midlands dialect and his work demonstrates a familiarity with parts of modern Worcestershire. The main form of Piers Plowman is a dream vision, but it does not employ this mode consistently. It moves between abstract personification and specific representation of aspects of late fourteenth-century social life. Its dreamer protagonist experiences considerable difficulties as he wrestles with personifications of his moral weaknesses and the poem ends with his realization that his quest for spiritual regeneration must commence all over again. At the same time, through a series of interlocking allegories, it represents the corrupt state of secular society and the Church. The figure of Piers Plowman appears intermittently as an embodiment of the ideal Christian life, as incarnated in a distinctively West Midlands rural form.

The Gawain Poet

Sir Gawain and the Green Knight is the best-known work of a poet who is also believed to have composed three religious allegories, Pearl, Patience and Cleanness, which have survived in the same manuscript. The poems were written in the West Midlands dialect of English in the second half of the fourteenth century. There is no external evidence to corroborate the assumption that all four are the work of a single author, but internal evidence and their common source suggest this. Gawain and the Green Knight is an Arthurian romance written in alliterative verse. Its intricate narrative tells how a mysterious outsider, the green knight, comes to King Arthur's court one New Year's Eve and challenges any of the knights to deal him a single axe-blow, to be returned by the green knight a year later. Sir Gawain accepts the challenge and delivers an apparently mortal blow when he decapitates the green knight. However, the knight picks up his head and leaves, reminding Gawain of his promise. The following year Gawain journeys to the knight's home at the Green Chapel and experiences a series of events in which his integrity is tested and finally found partly wanting. He is punished accordingly, when the third of three feints the knight delivers lightly nicks his neck. The main events of the poem have been interpreted as an allegory of seasonal renewal, in which chivalric values are thrown into conflict with an older set of English values associated with pagan traditions of ritual regeneration.

Pearl, *Patience* and *Cleanness* are also moral homilies, but are more obviously Christian. *Pearl* is a dream allegory about death containing a vision of the New Jerusalem from the *Book of Revelation*. *Patience* takes its didactic lesson from the story of Jonah. *Cleanness* (also known as *Purity*) employs a broad range of Old and New Testament references.

Geoffrey Chaucer (c. 1343–1400)

In addition to being the foremost English writer of his era, Chaucer held a number of prominent public offices, initially under the patronage of John of Gaunt and his *Book of the Duchess* (c. 1369) is generally considered to be an elegy for Gaunt's wife, Blanche of Lancaster. The son of a London vintner, Chaucer studied at the Inner Temple and saw military service in France during Edward III's campaigns in the Hundred Years War. He held a number of positions at court and travelled abroad on diplomatic missions to France and Italy, which was to be a particularly important influence on his development as a writer and where he may have met Boccaccio and Petrarch. In 1374 he became a customs controller in the port of London. During the last two decades of his life, when he was composing his *magnum opus*, *The Canterbury Tales*, he held appointments as knight of the shire for Kent, Clerk of the King's Works and a deputy forester in Somerset. On his death, he was buried in Westminster Abbey.

When Edmund Spenser was laid to rest beside him in 1599, their tombs became the basis of Poets' Corner, though Chaucer's burial in the Abbey was not in recognition of his poetic achievement, but because he had been Clerk of Works in the building of Westminster Palace.

Chaucer's Masterpiece

Chaucer's masterpiece, *The Canterbury Tales* (begun c. 1387) comprises the General Prologue, which describes the coming together of a group of travellers about to embark on a pilgrimage to Thomas à Becket's shrine in Canterbury, at the Tabard Inn in Southwark, and twenty-four tales told on the pilgrimage itself: two by the figure of Chaucer himself; the remainder by members of the company. It is often believed to have been inspired by Boccaccio's *Decameron*, in which a hundred tales are told during the course of ten days by ten fugitives from plague-ridden Florence. However, Chaucer does not acknowledge a direct debt to Boccaccio and there are other precedents for linked series of stories in the medieval period. The pilgrims' tavern host, Harry Bailly, proposes that each of them should tell four stories, two on the road to Canterbury and two on the return journey; and he promises the teller of the best tale a free supper. This scheme is never completed and the prize is not awarded, but *The Canterbury Tales* remains the outstanding literary achievement of the fourteenth century, offering a panoramic view of the various orders of society, lay and clerical, with each of the pilgrims being subject to scrutiny by Chaucer's discerning and judicious eye. Incomplete though it is, the series' linking of characters and tales and its exchanges of dialogue between the various pilgrims lend it a degree of dramatic unity rare in such sequences.

The General Prologue provides thumbnail sketches of twenty-one of the pilgrims, each of whom is realized as a rounded figure through a deft and economic choice of characterizing physical and moral qualities. Chaucer's tone varies and while some of the characters are viewed as exemplars of virtue, he characteristically draws attention to their failings through the medium of a laconic irony, which moves between gentle mockery and more savage condemnation and establishes him as the first great English satirist. Similarly, some of the characters, such as "the "verray parfit gentil knight", are rendered as idealized types, but more generally the portraiture of the Prologue is highly individualized and moves away from the allegorical characteriza-

tion typical of much medieval literature. Its characters provide a vivid cross-section of the society of the period and collectively can be seen as a social microcosm. They include: representatives of chivalric society, such as the knight and his squire; clerical figures, including a monk, a friar and a prioress; and people engaged in a wide variety of secular occupations, among them a lawyer, a miller, a merchant, a cook and a physician.

Though the majority of the pilgrims are men and the few female travellers are mainly members of religious orders, Chaucer's ensemble is notable for the presence of one of the most vividly realized female characters in early English writing, the Wife of Bath.

Variety in Chaucer's Tales

The tales themselves demonstrate a remarkable variety of range, tone and subject-matter. Taken together, they offer an encyclopaedic overview of many of the literary and cultural concerns of the period. They move between tragic romances such as *The Knight's Tale*, narratives that probe complex moral issues, such as *The Franklin's Tale*, parodies such as Chaucer's *Tale of Sir Thopas* and ribald and bawdy comic works, such as *The Miller's Tale*. The predominant metre of the work is rhyming couplets, but again Chaucer's approach is exceptionally diverse: he employs a wide range of verse forms as well as occasionally, as in the *Tale of Melibee*, writing in prose. The tales draw on an extensive range of medieval literary forms, including saints' lives, verse romance, *fabliau* (a fable form, often centred on a battle of wits and containing scatological and other forms of broad comic humour) and homily.

Use of Ambiguity

In *The Nun's Priest's Tale*, widely regarded as a work that typifies the ambiguity of Chaucer's tone, an apparently mock-heroic animal fable, which moves between witty playfulness and complex philosophical commentary, ends with a directive to take its pious moral seriously, leaving readers to decide whether to follow this instruction or to view it as an example of Chaucer's sly irony. *The Wife of Bath's Tale* is preceded by a lengthy prologue in which the wife provides an autobiographical account of her life, including details of her five marriages. This draws on anti-feminist literary conventions of the period, but again Chaucer's complexity of tone opens up the possibility of reading the Wife as a prototype feminist. In contrast, her tale, which is taken from the popular medieval story of "the loathly lady", is uncharacteristically serious. It does, however, demonstrate continuity with its prologue, since it is also about women's "maistrie" (or sovereignty) over men, suggesting that Chaucer may be more concerned with thematic links than consistent characterization.

Other Works by Chaucer

After *The Canterbury Tales*, *Troilus and Criseyde* (c. 1385) is generally considered to be Chaucer's finest achievement. Written in rhyme royal, it is a narrative poem of over 8,000 lines, which has been called the first English novel. Set inside Troy during the Trojan War, it describes how the warrior Troilus falls in love with Criseyde, how they are brought together by her uncle and guardian Pandare, how Criseyde subsequently betrays Troilus after they have been separated and how a grief-stricken Troilus is killed in battle. Chaucer appears to have taken the story from Boccaccio's *Il Filostrato*, but he develops his source-material into a highly complex moral fable, notable for the sophisticated rendition of its protagonists' psychologies. Typically Chaucerian in its ambiguity of tone, the poem mainly suggests a lofty, tragic vision of experience, which emphasizes the vanity of human life.

However, it also includes comedy, mainly in the characterization of Pandare, and its closing sections contain a series of Christian and other moralizing reflections, which partly negate the tragic view.

Chaucer also wrote numerous other poems, several of which adapted French and Italian models into the English vernacular tradition, which he played a central part in developing. The *Book of the Duchess* and *The Parliament of Fowls* (c. 1380) were inspired by the French tradition of the allegorical dream poem. In the latter, a group of birds engage in a debate about marriage, which contrasts the ideal of courtly love with a more pragmatic approach. In the unfinished *House of Fame* (c. 1379), Chaucer parodied aspects of Dante's *Divine Comedy* in a cryptic dream vision, whose purpose remains uncertain. His other works include translations of Boethius's *De Consolatione (On the Consolation of Philosophy)* and part of one of the great classics of medieval romance literature, the French *Roman de la Rose*; and the prose work, *Treatise on the Astrolabe*, which is believed to have been written for his son, "little Lewis".

The Ballad

Ballads are short narrative poems of anonymous composition, originally intended to be sung. They customarily express and enforce aspects of the folk imagination and as a consequence of oral transmission, usually exist in several versions. The most popular stanza form employed in ballads involves alternating four-beat and three-beat lines and a similarly alternating rhyme scheme (abab), but ballads also employ numerous other forms. The ballad particularly flourished in Northern England and Scotland from around 1200 to 1700. Popular ballads of the period include "Lord Randal", "Sir Patrick Spens", "Edward", "The Unquiet Grave" and "Thomas Rhymer". Ballads treat a broad range of subjects, but prominent types deal with tragic family themes, romantic love, the supernatural and the exploits of outlaws such as Robin Hood.

Morality and Mystery Plays

Often grouped together, morality and mystery plays represent two distinct forms of medieval drama. Morality plays were dramatized allegories of virtues and vices fighting for a human soul. The first morality plays date from the early fifteenth century, but the form continued to be popular in the Elizabethan period at the time of the upheavals brought about by the Reformation. *The Castle of Perseverance* (c. 1420), *Mankind* (c. 1465) and *Everyman* (c. 1510) are the best-known examples of the form. In John Skelton's *Magnyfycence* (c. 1515), a late example of the genre, an excessively magnanimous prince is ruined by his generosity, before being educated into more prudent behaviour by qualities such as Good Hope and Perseverance.

In England mystery plays, sometimes also known as "miracle plays", were based on Biblical subjects. (In other parts of Europe the term "miracle plays" was reserved for stories of saints' lives.) Initially mystery plays were staged in churches on religious holidays such as Corpus Christi and Whitsuntide. Later they became more secular and were staged in market places by trade guilds. Hence the use of the name "mystery", which derives from the Middle English word for a skilled trade. Increasingly, the plays were performed as sequences.

Cycles of English mystery plays from York, Chester, Coventry and Wakefield have come down to posterity almost intact. They are notable for their blend of simple homiletic instruction and interludes of broad comic portraiture.

Sir Thomas Malory (died c. 1471)

One of the earliest books printed in England, Malory's *Morte D'Arthur* (1485; written c. 1469) is the greatest English contribution to "the matter of Britain", the widely circulating corpus of stories about the Arthurian legend. Written in prose, the *Morte D'Arthur* is divided into eight tales and twenty-one books. The tales begin with the story of Arthur's birth and early life and the establishment of the Round Table and conclude with a narrative of the collapse of his court, when he discovers his wife Guinevere's adultery with Sir Lancelot, and his subsequent death in battle. The fifth tale, which tells the story of Tristram and Isolde (Tristan and Iseult), occupies almost half the work.

RENAISSANCE LITERATURE

Renaissance Poetry and Prose

During the Renaissance period, writers and thinkers turned to the Greek and Roman classics for cultural inspiration, replacing medieval literature's absorption in Christian and chivalric concerns with a Humanist spirit that encouraged scientific inquiry, a more eclectic approach to learning and an expansionist vigour that was as keen to develop new literary forms as it was to discover new worlds.

Characteristically, Renaissance men, such as Sir Walter Raleigh (c. 1554–1618), the famous courtier and adventurer, moved between active involvement in the public life of the day and literary and cultural pursuits, without becoming dilettantes. Raleigh not only wrote accounts of his travels in the New World, such as *A Discovery of the Empire of Guiana* (1596), and *The History of the World* (1614), but also a significant body of poetry, notable for its melancholy reflections on the transitory nature of existence. Conversely, John Donne (*see below*), who is best known as a poet, accompanied the Earl of Essex and Raleigh on expeditions against the Spanish. Henry VIII's Lord Chancellor, Sir Thomas More (1478–1535), who was executed for his unbending allegiance to papal authority, produced *Utopia* (1515) which gave a name to the genre of writing about ideal fictional states founded nearly two millennia earlier by Plato's *Republic*.

Wyatt, Howard and Sidney

Sir Thomas Wyatt (c. 1503–42) and Henry Howard, Earl of Surrey (c. 1517–47) pioneered several of the metres and conventions that became staples of English verse during the next three centuries. They introduced the Petrarchan form of the sonnet and *terza rima*, the three-line stanza used by Dante in the *Divine Comedy*, into English; and Surrey's translation of parts of Virgil's *Aeneid* established blank verse (unrhymed iambic pentameters) as the standard metre of much subsequent English poetry, including Elizabethan dramatic verse and narrative long poems, varying from Milton's *Paradise Lost* to Wordsworth's *Prelude*. Neither Wyatt nor Surrey saw their poems published in their own lifetime. Both were better known for their public activities. So too was another Renaissance man, Sir Philip Sidney (1554–86), whose major works were also published posthumously. His *Astrophel and Stella* (1591) is the most famous of the pre-Shakespearean sonnet sequences. Sidney's *Arcadia* (1590) blends prose romance with verse eclogue to create an idealized, pastoral world, inspired by Virgil and other classical poets.

Edmund Spenser (c. 1552–99)

Spenser's masterpiece, *The Faerie Queene* (1590-96) is both a definitive work of the Elizabethan age, drawing on the heroic traditions of classical epic, and the last great English example of a medieval romance. The "queene" of the title is Gloriana, or Elizabeth I, and the poet celebrates her reign and authority in a series of adventures set in the courtly past, in each of which one of her knights exemplifies a particular virtue in action. Spenser invented his own unique nine-line stanza (with the rhyme-scheme ababbcbcc). This became known as the Spenserian stanza and was subsequently used by Romantic poets such as Byron and Keats in an endeavour to recapture the spirit of the medieval world, in a manner not dissimilar from Spenser's attempt to invest his own period with medieval values. Spenser's other works include a pastoral sequence expressing nostalgia for a past golden age, *The Shephearde's Calender* (1579), a collection of love sonnets, *Amoretti* (1595) and the marriage song *Epithalamion* (1595).

Christopher Marlowe (1564–93)

Marlowe preceded Shakespeare as the first great tragic dramatist of the Elizabethan age. He also established the blank verse line as the dominant metre of the drama of the period, refining its use beyond that of its earlier exponents. His plays mostly deal with megalomaniac protagonists, whose obsession with an extreme form of power or knowledge leads to their downfall. *Tamburlaine the Great* (Parts I and II, 1587) narrates the rise and fall of a military overreacher in characteristically hyperbolic language. In *The Jew of Malta* (c. 1590) the protagonist, Barabas, is a Machiavellian hero-villain, whose revenge on the Christian society that confiscates his wealth attracts a good deal of sympathy.

More complex in characterization than Marlowe's earlier tragedies, but less extravagant in its versification, *Edward II* (1592) did much to establish the genre of the Elizabethan historical play. It anticipates Shakespeare's *Richard II* as a tragedy of a weak king betrayed by favourites and a tendency towards histrionic behaviour, though Marlowe places more emphasis on shifting fortune as a cause of tragedy.

Dr Faustus (1594) is a tragedy of damnation, which also anticipates Shakespeare, in this case *Macbeth*, in certain respects. It is, however, more explicitly theological, demonstrating a debt to the medieval morality play (*see above*). It tells the story of the necromancer Faust, who sells his soul to the Devil in return for twenty-four years during which he will enjoy infinite power and knowledge. Though parts of the text are disputed, it contains some of Marlowe's finest verse, including the protagonist's famous response to a vision of Helen of Troy, whom he summons up as an ideal of womanhood: "Was this the face that launched a thousand ships?"; and his poignant monologue as he awaits his tragic fate: "See, see, where Christ's blood streams in the firmament!"

Marlowe's work as a poet includes *Hero and Leander* (1598) and the song "The Passionate Shepherd to His Love" (1599). His outspoken views and notorious private life led to his being accused of atheism, blasphemy and homosexuality. He was allegedly involved in criminal activities on more than one occasion and eventually murdered in a Deptford tavern, possibly as a result of his involvement in espionage, but more probably as a consequence of a dispute over the bill.

The University Wits

"The University Wits" is the name given to the group of writers particularly responsible for the rapid rise of Elizabethan drama as the pre-eminent cultural form of the day during the last two decades of the sixteenth century, but also notable for their achievements in prose. Their plays includes Robert Greene's *Friar Bacon and Friar Bungay* (1589) and George Peele's *The Old Wives' Tale* (1595). Their prose works include John Lyly's romances *Euphues: The Anatomy of Wit* (1578) and *Euphues and His England* (1580) and Thomas Nashe's picaresque *The Unfortunate Traveller* (1594). *The Spanish Tragedy* (1592) by Thomas Kyd, another highly popular play of the late sixteenth century, anticipates Jacobean tragedy in its extensive use of violence and themes of madness and revenge.

Francis Bacon (1551–1626)

One of the leading public figures of the day, Bacon held the offices of Solicitor-General, Attorney-General, Lord Keeper of the Seal and Lord Chancellor of England, before falling from office in disgrace in 1621. He was the central English figure in the movement away from the Scholasticism of the medieval clerics, the dominant intellectual tradition at the beginning of his life, towards the Humanism that came to be seen as the embodiment of the Renaissance spirit. In *The Advancement of Learning* (1605) and *Novum Organum* (1620), he argued for a new spirit of empirical scientific inquiry that would be the scholarly equivalent of the great Elizabethan voyages of discovery.

His other works include the unfinished utopian fiction *The New Atlantis* (1627), in which a group of English sailors discover a Pacific island, where a college of sciences that can be seen as a blueprint for the Royal Society (subsequently founded in England in 1660) flourishes. Some commentators who have cast doubts on Shakespeare's authorship of his plays have asserted the claims of Bacon as a more likely author of "Shakespeare".

William Shakespeare (1564–1616)

Shakespeare's Life

Comparatively little is known about the life of England's greatest dramatist. He was born in Stratford-upon-Avon in 1564, probably educated at the local grammar school and in 1582 married Anne Hathaway, who bore him three children: a daughter, Susanna, and the twins Judith and Hamnet, who died at the age of eleven. Some time between the years 1585 and 1592, Shakespeare left Stratford and pursued a career as an actor and dramatist in London. After initially struggling to establish himself, he became a founder member of one of the leading theatrical companies of the day, the Lord Chamberlain's Men, in 1594 and by the mid-1590s his reputation as the period's leading playwright was assured. His greatest works belong to the latter part of this decade and the first years of the seventeenth century. Many were first performed at the Globe Theatre, built on the south bank of the Thames in 1599, in which Shakespeare was a shareholder. Somewhere around 1613, when the Globe burned down, he appears to have left London and spent the last years of his life in Stratford, where he died and was buried in 1616. The posthumous collection of his plays in the First Folio of 1623 ensured their preservation for posterity, though many also exist in earlier quarto editions. The evidence for precise dating of his plays is often slim. Here they are grouped by period or genre.

Early Plays: 1590–95

Shakespeare's first plays offer glimpses of his later genius, but are frequently indistinguishable from the work of his dramatic contemporaries. The first of the three parts of *Henry VI* is of uncertain authorship, but the plays are among Shakespeare's earliest dramatic work. *Richard III*, a more accomplished history play with a memorable hero-villain, is often grouped with them.

Shakespeare's early comedies frequently take their subjects from classical drama and are heavily reliant on farce and situational humour, often built around disguise, mistakes and trickery. They include *The Comedy of Errors*, *The Taming of the Shrew* and *The Two Gentlemen of Verona*. *Love's Labour's Lost* is a virtuoso satire of inflated language, such as that used in Lyly's *Euphues*, though Shakespeare displays an obvious relish for the wordplay and linguistic excess that are the ostensible objects of his irony.

He also wrote two tragedies during this period. Popular in its own day, *Titus Andronicus*, which has much in common with a play such as Kyd's *Spanish Tragedy* in its use of violence, madness and revenge, is probably Shakespeare's earliest tragedy. *Romeo and Juliet*, the legendary story of the "star-cross'd lovers" who become victims of their feuding Verona families' enmity towards one another, is a more carefully plotted and moving work, which has retained its popularity across the centuries.

History Plays and Roman Plays: 1595–1608

While they ostensibly deal with subject-matter from England's past, Shakespeare's history plays often have an allegorical relevance to Tudor debates about the Constitution and good government. So too do his Roman plays. After the three parts of *Henry VI* and *Richard III*, Shakespeare wrote a second tetralogy of history plays (1595–99). This begins with *Richard II*, a tragic study of a monarch who, like Marlow's *Edward II*, proves unsuited to kingship. The poetic dreamer, Richard, loses his throne to his more pragmatic cousin, Bolingbroke, who becomes Henry IV in the next two plays of the tetralogy. *Henry IV*, Parts I and II are, however, as much concerned with the coming of age of Henry's son, Prince Hal, the future Henry V, as with his own struggles to put down rebellions.

The two plays are also notable for one of Shakespeare's richest comic creations, Falstaff, a larger-than-life character who has affinities with the medieval Lord of Misrule figure, but whose complexity frustrates easy labels. Initially, Prince Hal enjoys Falstaff's convivial company, but when he becomes king at the end of the second part, he disowns him, in a scene which some commentators feel demonstrates his hard-heartedness, in order to assume the duties of his role. In *Henry V*, he takes on the mantle of England's military leader in battles against the French and the play has remained popular as a celebration of nationalism. Falstaff reappears in the comedy *The Merry Wives of Windsor* (*c.* 1600), allegedly revived at Queen Elizabeth's request.

Shakespeare's histories also include the less highly regarded *King John* (*c.* 1596) and parts of *Henry VIII* (*c.* 1612), which was probably a collaboration with John Fletcher.

The Roman plays, *Julius Caesar, Antony and Cleopatra* and *Coriolanus*, belong to the years 1599–1608. Like the history plays, *Julius Caesar* has obvious relevance to contemporary debates about government. When Caesar is assassinated, the motivation of his killers is complex. The integrity of their leader Brutus, "the noblest Roman of them all", is never seriously questioned, though the actions taken to avenge Caesar by Mark Anthony, whose oration over his dead body is an outstanding example of persuasive political rhetoric, are also presented sympathetically. In *Antony and Cleopatra*, Antony is torn between the Roman values of reason and political calculation and Cleopatra's Egyptian world of obsessive passion. His love for Cleopatra leads to his neglect of duty, with tragic consequences for both protagonists. *Cymbeline* depicts the tragedy of a Roman hero destroyed by his pride and haughty aloofness from the people.

Comedies: 1595–1600

Shakespeare's most famous comedies, *Much Ado About Nothing, As You Like It* and *Twelfth Night*, belong to his middle period (1598–1600). They were preceded by *A Midsummer Night's Dream* (1595–6), a comic fantasy in which a group of rustics stage their version of a tragic love story, with hilarious consequences. The rustics' play is, however, located in a world where serious romantic values have been turned upside down for a single night by fairies. The middle comedies use idealized settings and romantic plots and move between broad humour and a more serious examination of male-female relationships and social attitudes. *Much Ado About Nothing* includes one of Shakespeare's most memorable couples, Beatrice and Benedick, whose verbal sparring makes their relationship much more dramatically animated than that of the play's more conventional romantic lovers, Claudio and Hero. *Twelfth Night* contrasts the values of "cakes and ale" with a more Puritanical approach to social conduct that had come to characterize areas of Elizabethan life. The middle comedies make extensive use of disguise, pretence and mistaken identity. These elements are both a source of humour and a basis for a probing investigation of issues of identity.

The Great Tragedies: 1600–06

Shakespeare's most famous tragedies, *Hamlet, Othello, King Lear* and *Macbeth*, were written in the early years of the seventeenth century. They are generally regarded as his greatest achievement, containing some of his finest dramatic verse and exploring the ambiguities of human behaviour through a focus on the forces that lead to the downfall of their essentially noble male protagonists. The plays have generally, though not always, been viewed as tragedies of character rather than fate and each of the heroes has weaknesses that cause his tragedy. Thus the undoing of Othello, a Moorish general in the service of the Venetian Republic, has frequently been attributed to his jealousy and his malleability in the hands of the villain, Iago. However, from another point of view his tragedy can be seen as that of a racial outsider in a European society, which respects his professional abilities but is less generous towards him when he marries a senator's daughter. In a play that can be seen as a companion-piece to this aspect of *Othello*, the tragic-comic *Merchant of Venice* (1596–7), the Jewish moneylender Shylock is also denied the same basic human rights as other Venetians, though he is less sympathetically portrayed than Othello. Hamlet's tragedy has been ascribed to numerous causes, among them his inability to move from introspection to action and his Oedipal love for his mother. Macbeth, a killer-poet who becomes king after murdering those who stand in his way, can be seen as a later version of Richard III. Egged on by his wife, Shakespeare's most compelling female villain, he becomes a personification of the dictum that power corrupts. Shakespeare's most wide-ranging tragedy, *King Lear*, focuses on an ageing protagonist whose lack of self-knowledge prevents him from distinguishing between the hypocrisy of his two elder daughters and the sincerity and love of his youngest. Towards the end

of the play, in a movement which anticipates the mood of Shakespeare's late romances, he learns the truth, but only when he is dying as a "foolish fond old man". *Lear* is, however, more than simply a tragedy of character; it also depicts human beings as the "sport" of the gods, powerless to resist the forces of fate.

Problem Plays: 1601–05

All's Well That Ends Well, Measure for Measure and *Troilus and Cressida* have generally been referred to as Shakespeare's "problem plays". They were written around the same time as the great tragedies and have also been called "bitter comedies". The three plays are problematic, not only because of the difficulty of classifying them as a particular form of drama, such as tragedy or comedy, but also because of their complex treatment of moral questions, which are frequently left unresolved. The troubling treatment of sexuality and politics in *Measure for Measure* has increased its popularity in recent decades and it has been seen to have considerable contemporary relevance. *Two Noble Kinsmen* (c. 1613), to which Shakespeare probably contributed, in which case it was his last dramatic work, has also been classified as a problem play.

The Late Romances: 1609–11

In his three late plays, *Cymbeline, The Winter's Tale* and *The Tempest*, Shakespeare subsumes tragedy in a larger vision of reconciliation and regeneration, a mood anticipated by a play such as *King Lear*, where the tragic consequences of actions still prove inescapable. Sometimes styled "tragic-comedies", the late romances create a form of drama that is uniquely their own, flouting many of the conventions of both classical and contemporary theatre in the process.

In each of the plays, the protagonist has to come to terms with a sin or omission and manages to do so through the agency of his daughter. *The Tempest*, usually seen as Shakespeare's final dramatic statement, is a particularly enigmatic play, which contains some of his finest poetry. It has been variously interpreted as an allegory of New World colonialism, in which Shakespeare was clearly interested, as a fable about the artistic neglect of worldly responsibilities and as a dramatic treatment of the pastoral contrast between primitive innocence and cultivated experience, which moves beyond a simple opposition between utopian nature and corrupt nurture. The play ends with the magician, Prospero, relinquishing his right to conjure up spirits and declaring "Now my charms are all o'erthrown,/ And what strength I have's mine own", an utterance which has been related to Shakespeare himself, who also appears to be forsaking *his* "art to enchant".

Shakespeare's Poetry

In addition to the plays, Shakespeare also produced a considerable body of non-dramatic verse, including two poems inspired by Ovid: the mythological erotic poem, *Venus and Adonis* (1593), which was his most popular work in his own life-time; and *The Rape of Lucrece* (1594), a narrative poem notable for its portrayal of the protagonist's psychological conflict. Shorter verse ascribed to Shakespeare includes contributions to *The Passionate Pilgrim* (1599), a collection published under his name, the metaphysical poem, "The Phoenix and the Turtle" (1601) and "A Lover's Complaint" (1609).

Shakespeare's *Sonnets* (1609) are his finest achievement in non-dramatic verse. They comprise 154 love poems, probably written between 1592 and 1598, in the fourteen-line verse-form that had been imported into England from Italy. Shakespeare reinvented the form, using the rhyme-scheme ababcdcdefefgg and thus establishing what has become known as the Shakespearean sonnet. The *Sonnets* fall into three main sequences: poems addressed to a young man, a "dark lady" and a rival poet. Sonnets 18 ("Shall I compare thee to a summer's day?") and 130 ("My mistress' eyes are nothing like the sun") are among the most quoted.

SEVENTEENTH-CENTURY LITERATURE

Jacobean Drama

Strictly speaking, "Jacobean drama" refers to plays produced during the reign of James I (1603–25), but the term is used more broadly to describe the theatre of the early seventeenth century, in which the expansionist mood of the Elizabethan age gave way to a more sombre and pessimistic vision, characteristic of the new era.

James came to the throne with the reputation of being a believer in witchcraft, which he had written about in his *Daemonologie* (1597); Robert Burton's *Anatomy of Melancholy* (c. 1621) provided a quasi-scientific classification of various forms of depression; tragedies, full of violence, cynicism and intrigue, captured the mood of Jacobean gloom; and John Marston's tragic-comedy, *The Malcontent* (1604), written in collaboration with John Webster, created the quintessential stage figure of the age, that of the malcontent or cynical outsider. The malcontent also appeared in the character of Bosola in Webster's *Duchess of Malfi* (1623) and even Hamlet can be seen as an early version of the type.

John Webster (c.1580–c.1632) and John Ford (1586–c. 1640)

Despite their reputation for unrelieved cynicism and gloom, vigorous language lends the best Jacobean tragedies as much dramatic energy as their more optimistic Elizabethan forerunners. The most famous tragic playwrights of the period were John Webster and John Ford. Webster's *The White Devil* (1612) and *The Duchess of Malfi* are revenge plays based on historical events with Italian settings. Centred on the political and personal intrigue popularly associated with Renaissance Italy, they achieve their effect through dramatically powerful individual scenes and set-pieces, in which murders, sensational violence, madness and destructive passion loom large.

Ford's best-known plays, *The Broken Heart* (1633) and *'Tis Pity She's a Whore* (1633) place as much emphasis on pathos as tragedy. In *'Tis Pity*, the plot centres on the tragic love of a brother and sister, but the play goes beyond the sensationalism of the incest theme through its use of moving verse and imagery. Other outstanding tragedies of the period include Cyril Tourneur's *Revenger's Tragedy* (1607) and Thomas Middleton and William Rowley's masterpiece *The Changeling* (c. 1622).

Ben Jonson (1572–1637)

Jonson was the leading comic dramatist of the period. His plays *Every Man in his Humour* (1598) and *Every Man out of his Humour* (1599) were first performed in the Elizabethan era, but his best-known work belongs to the Jacobean age, during which he enjoyed royal patronage and wrote a number of court masques with scenery designed by the famous architect Inigo Jones. He is noted for his *Comedy of Humours*, in which particular characters represent an aspect, or Humour, of humanity. Based on early medical beliefs about the forces that determine character (blood, phlegm, melancholy and choler), this approach can be seen as the basis for the type-characters of Restoration Comedy and of later novelists such as Henry Fielding and Charles Dickens.

Jonson's major plays are *Volpone or the Fox* (1605–6), which despite its Venetian setting is generally viewed as a satire on the emergent London merchant classes; and *Epicene, or, The Silent Woman* (1609), *The Alchemist* (1610) and *Bartholomew Fair* (1614), in each of which trickery is an impetus for the action. Jonson also wrote a body of non-dramatic verse, which includes *Epigrams* (1616), *The Forest* (1616) and *The Underwood* (1640), and the tragedy *Sejanus* (1603). The circle of poets who wrote under his influence were known as "the tribe of Ben". They include Robert Herrick, Richard Lovelace and Sir John Suckling.

Francis Beaumont's *The Knight of the Burning Pestle* (1607) is a satire of aspects of contemporary taste, which employs the form of a play-within-a-play. A grocer interrupts the frame-play, "The London Merchant", to insist that his apprentice be given a part. This wish is granted and the apprentice's subsequent appearance as a grocer-errant pokes fun at both middle-class cultural aspirations and chivalric conventions.

The Metaphysical Poets

"Metaphysical" is the term generally used to classify a number of seventeenth-century poets, including John Donne, George Herbert, Andrew Marvell, Thomas Carew, Thomas Traherne, Richard Crashaw, Henry Vaughan and Abraham Cowley. These poets have been called "metaphysical", because of their use of elaborate conceits (metaphors, similes and other forms of imagery) and paradoxes. However, this is only one aspect of their primarily lyric verse technique and there are as many differences between them as there are similarities.

Recent attempts to replace the "metaphysical" label have included calling the poets "the School of Donne" and "the Fantasticks", but these are only marginally more useful terms, particularly since the poets had little sense of themselves as a group. The most famous of all metaphysical conceits is John Donne's comparison, in his poem "A Valediction Forbidding Mourning", of two lovers to the twin points of a compass: the suggestion is that however far they may stray from one another, the lovers remained linked. Other metaphysical images are drawn from cartography, science, Scripture and medicine.

The term "metaphysical" originated in the early seventeenth century with William Drummond, who used it in a censorious way to attack those of his poetic contemporaries who used metaphysical ideas. Towards the end of the century, John Dryden criticized Donne by saying "He affects the metaphysics in his amorous verses . . . where nature only should reign".

In the eighteenth century, writing from a neo-classical point of view, founded on a belief in the commonality of human experience, Samuel Johnson attacked the poets' use of extravagant and highly specialized imagery as "a kind of *discordia concors*", in which "the most heterogeneous ideas are yoked by violence together". Johnson's attack contributed to the decline of the poets' reputation. This lasted until an influential 1921 review by T.S. Eliot helped rehabilitate the poets and reclaim "metaphysical" from being a term of abuse. Eliot praised the "metaphysicals" for their "direct sensuous apprehension of thought" and "recreation of thought into feeling", qualities that had been denied them by commentators such as Johnson.

John Donne (1572–1631)

Donne's work can be divided into two main categories: the secular love poetry of his "Songs and Sonnets"; and a body of devotional writing, which includes his "Holy Sonnets" and sermons, that was mainly written in the later part of his life, after he was ordained into the Anglican Church in 1615. He became Dean of St. Paul's in 1621 and was famed as one of the finest preachers of his age. It is, however, mistaken to draw a sharp distinction between the secular and spiritual aspects of Donne's writing. An attempt to spiritualise the carnal side of his nature characterizes much of his amorous verse and his work is surprisingly modern in the openness and psychological complexity of its treatment of sexual passion. His divine poetry moves in the opposite direction, frequently using physically direct language in spiritual contexts, as when he asks God to ravish his soul. It often expresses doubt, not about Christian doctrine, but about whether the poet himself, as a particular sinner, will be saved from damnation.

Donne's complex metaphysical imagery is tempered by a conversational directness rare among his poetic predecessors and, since the rehabilitation of the metaphysical poets in the early twentieth century, his poetry has been viewed as particularly modern. His most famous love poems include "The Ecstasy", "The Canonization", "The Sun Rising", "The Good Morrow", "The Flea", "A Valediction Forbidding Mourning" and "Go and Catch a Falling Star". His religious writing includes his sonnet to death ("Death be not proud"), his "Hymn to God the Father" and his Meditation 12, from which the phrases "No man is an island" and "Do not ask for whom the bell tolls, it tolls for thee" have passed into the language. Donne also produced numerous epigrams, elegies and some early satirical verse.

George Herbert (1593–1633)

Like Donne's, Herbert's poetry demonstrates metrical variety, conversational directness and a highly imaginative use of conceits. It is, however, more consistently devotional than Donne's. Most of Herbert's work appeared in *The Temple* (1633), a poetic testament in which the various parts are intricately arranged to provide a moving and multi-faceted expression of his Christian faith. It deals with the immature soul's progression towards salvation through immersion in central aspects of Christian belief, including the resurrection, the importance of the sacraments and the need for communal worship.

Herbert is particularly remembered for his two pattern-poems, "The Altar" and "Easter Wings", where the shape of the poem as it appears on the page mirrors its subject, but these are his only poems of this kind. "The Collar" and "Jordan", I and II, are among his other best-known poems. His elder brother, Edward, Lord Herbert of Cherbury, was also a notable metaphysical poet.

Andrew Marvell (1621–78)

Marvell lived through the turbulent years of England's Civil War, occupying a number of political offices, including that of MP for Hull for nearly twenty years. His poetry exhibits a range of styles that both reflect the political vicissitudes of the period and his remarkable personal capacity to capture different moods. Although he excelled as a writer of witty metaphysical verse, his most lasting achievement is his lyric poetry, which includes one of the greatest English love poems, "To His Coy Mistress". His long poem, "Upon Appleton House", which was dedicated to the parliamentarian general, Sir Thomas Fairfax, celebrates the virtues of the rural country house as a retreat from the schisms of seventeenth-century life.

Marvell's capacity to balance opposed perspectives with a judiciousness rare in the period is seen at its best in his "Horatian Ode upon Cromwell's Return from Ireland", which carefully distributes its sympathies between Charles I and the avowed subject of the ode, Cromwell. Marvell was John Milton's assistant during the last years of the Commonwealth period (1657–60) and is credited with having intervened to save Milton from imprisonment and possible execution at the time of the Restoration. In his later years, he deserted the lyric for panegyrics and satires concerned with public issues.

Women Writers of the Seventeenth Century

While seventeenth-century public life was largely the preserve of men and few women writers were published in their own lifetime, recent research has directed attention to the very significant literary achievements of the female authors of the period. Lady Mary Wroth's prose romance *Urania* (1621) achieved a degree of contemporary notoriety through its treatment of court scandals. Today it is more interesting as an early feminist classic. It tells the stories of several women in unhappy marriages or relationships and in search of identities that are independent of men. Margaret Cavendish, Duchess of Newcastle, apologised for her "audacity in writing at all, being a woman", but nevertheless produced twenty-two works in a range of genres, including *Poems and Fancies* (1653) and *The Description of a New World called the Blazing World* (1666), an early science-fiction romance. Dorothy Osborne is noted for a volume of just seventy-seven letters, written to her future husband, Sir William Temple, Jonathan Swift's patron, between 1652 and 1654. Collectively, the letters form a miniature masterpiece that provides a vivid insight into upper-class seventeenth-century domestic life and the writer's own introspective psyche. The prolific Aphra Behn wrote the short novel *Oroonoko, or The Royal Slave* (1688), about an African-born prince, who leads an unsuccessful slave rebellion in Surinam, and numerous dramatic comedies (*see later*).

Restoration Drama

In 1642, when Cromwell and his Puritan supporters, who believed that acting was an immoral pursuit, gained control of Parliament, the London theatres were closed. They did not reopen until the accession of Charles II in 1660. The drama of the next forty years is generally called "Restoration Drama", though there are considerable differences between plays produced in the early part of the period and those staged in the closing decades of the seventeenth century. Comedy was the dominant form of the era, though heroic plays such as Dryden's *Aureng-Zebe* (1676) and his retelling of the Antony and Cleopatra story, *All for Love* (1678), and Thomas Otway's *Venice Preserved* (1682) also made a distinctive contribution to the development of the English theatre of the period.

Restoration Comedy is notable for its use of type-characters, in the tradition of Ben Jonson's *Comedy of Humours* (*see* **M9**). Such types include foppish noblemen, witty young women, rakes, cuckolds, promiscuous wives, country gentlemen and scheming servants. The early comedies of the period reacted against Puritan prudery by depicting cynically amoral upper-class relationships, employing plots centred on sexual and financial intrigues and making extensive use of wit, bawdy and innuendo.

Their attitude to gender relations has sometimes been seen as a reflection of the debauchery of the aristocratic society of Charles II's court. William Wycherley's *The Country Wife* (1675), in which a countrywoman newly arrived in London quickly becomes adept in the licentious ways of the capital, is one of the finest examples of this phase of Restoration Comedy. Wycherley's other plays include *The Plain Dealer* (1676).

Wit continues to be a staple of the later plays, but a subtler Comedy of Manners replaces the broad humour of the earlier drama. In William Congreve's *The Way of the World* (1700), the culminating achievement of Restoration comedy, courtship and marriage remain central concerns, but they are explored through a more questioning and sensitive use of witty repartee. Congreve's other comedies include *The Double Dealer* (1693) and *Love for Love* (1695). *The Way of the World* was written in the wake of the Anglican clergyman, Jeremy Collier's *Short View of the Immorality and the Profaneness of the English Stage* (1698), which played a significant part in changing attitudes towards theatrical propriety and decency. Early eighteenth-century comedy was to desert the broad humour of the Restoration play for more sentimental comedy.

Other Restoration Dramatists

Other notable Restoration dramatists include George Etherege, author of *The Man of Mode* (1676), the famous architect Sir John Vanbrugh, who wrote *The Relapse* (1696) and Thomas Southerne, author of *The Wives' Excuse* (1691), which exposes the effects of the sexual hypocrisy of the period on women. In Shakespeare's plays, female roles had been played by boys; in Restoration comedy women's parts were now taken by actresses, one of whom was Charles II's mistress, Nell Gwyn.

The period also saw the emergence of a professional woman dramatist, Aphra Behn, whose plays, which include *The Rover* (1677), *The City Heiress* (1682) and *The Lucky Chance* (1686), offer a more serious investigation of gender relations than can be found in most, if not all, of her male contemporaries. Behn's novel *Oroonoko* (*see above*) was dramatized by Southerne in a version first performed in 1695.

John Bunyan (1628–88)

Best-known for *The Pilgrim's Progress*, which remained the most widely read book in the English language, after the Authorized Version of the Bible, until the twentieth century, Bunyan wrote in a plain prose style that anticipates the novel. His first major work, *Grace Abounding to the Chief of Sinners* (1666), describes its author's conversion from a wicked early life and his subsequent call to the ministry. Typical of the Puritan spiritual autobiography of the period, it is a homiletic work, providing an example for others to follow, and has little in common with autobiographies which stress the subject's individuality.

Bunyan spent two periods in Bedford jail (1660–72 and 1675) for unlicensed preaching at a time when divine services could only be conducted according to the forms of the Church of England. He is believed to have written most of the first part of *Pilgrim's Progress* (1678) during his second period of imprisonment. It is a dream allegory which tells the story of an Everyman figure, Christian's journey from the City of Destruction to the Celestial City through such landscapes as the Slough of Despond, the Valley of the Shadow of Death, Doubting Castle and the country of Beulah. This is a "progress" which enacts the individual soul's journey to salvation. Travelling through these varied and difficult surroundings, Christian meets allegorical figures such as Worldly Wiseman, Hopeful and Giant Despair, who represent aspects of both his own character and of contemporary seventeenth-century life. Bunyan's simple, realistic prose has a Biblical quality. Though Christian moves through allegorical terrain, commentators have commented on Bunyan's realism and noted that the contours of his spiritual landscapes resemble those of his native Bedfordshire.

In the second part of *Pilgrim's Progress* (1684), Christian's wife, Christiana, follows in his footsteps, but her journey to heaven is less arduous than his, particularly since she receives more support along the way. This shift in emphasis may reflect Bunyan's desire to focus on the importance of community in the Christian struggle. His other major works, *The Life and Death of Mr Badman* (1680) and *The Holy War* (1682), are also religious allegories.

John Milton (1608–74)

England's greatest epic poet and one of its literature's most extraordinary polymaths, Milton was a Puritan who initially seems to have been drawn to a clerical career, but instead pursued his Christian beliefs and political convictions through the medium of literary works that linked Classical and Christian learning. He suffered from failing eyesight during the 1640s and was completely blind from 1652. The date of his famous "Sonnet on His Blindness" is uncertain, but it probably belongs to the mid-1650s. During the interregnum period he held office as Latin Secretary to the Council of State. In 1660 he published a revised edition of his *Ready and Easy Way to Establish a Free Commonwealth* (1659), a principled if imprudent argument for republicanism at a time when the monarchy was being restored. He was briefly jailed, but escaped a longer period of imprisonment, or possible execution. His masterpiece, the epic *Paradise Lost* (1667), which was probably begun before the Restoration, its sequel, *Paradise Regained* (1671) and his "Greek" tragedy, *Samson Agonistes* (1671), were products of his later years.

Milton's Early Works

Milton's early works include: "Ode upon the Morning of Christ's Nativity" (1629), the masque *Comus* (1637) and "L'Allegro" and "Il Penseroso" (1645; written *c.* 1631), a complementary pair of poems in octosyllabic couplets, which respectively illustrate the qualities of the happy, outgoing man and the melancholy, contemplative man. "Lycidas" (1637), a response to the drowning of Milton's Cambridge contemporary, Edward King, is one of the great English elegies. It expands from being a meditation on a premature individual death into a moving reflection on the transience of human life and the poet's own uncertainties about his personal future, before concluding with an expression of faith in the immortality of the soul. In the 1640s, Milton produced numerous prose pamphlets, including *The Doctrine and Discipline of Divorce* (1643), written shortly after his first wife, Mary, had left him a few weeks after their marriage, and *Areopagitica* (1644), a famous, early defence of the freedom of the press.

Milton's Masterpiece

Paradise Lost is written in blank verse and employs many of the conventions of the Greek and Latin epics, including elevated language, a heroic theme, breadth of scope, the Invocation to the Muse (in this case the Greek muse of astronomy, Urania, now transformed into a Christian) and epic

similes. The poem's declared purpose is "to justify the ways of God to men", but many critics have seen Milton's Satan as the greatest creation of the poem and taken the view that his use of classical heroic models is at odds with the avowed Christian message of the poem. The most famous expression of this viewpoint is the Romantic poet William Blake's contention that Milton was "a true poet and of the Devil's party without knowing it". If one agrees with such a reading, it lends support to the view that Milton's republican response to the political situation of his day led him, consciously or unconsciously, to adopt a revolutionary attitude to authority, as represented by God in the poem.

However, although the first two books of *Paradise Lost* depict Satan in heroic terms, its later sections are more centrally concerned with its avowed subject, "man's first disobedience, and the fruit/ of that forbidden tree". They tell the story of Adam and Eve's expulsion from the garden of Eden in a lofty and dignified style which expands outwards from its ostensible subject to provide an encyclopaedic view of human history from a Christian point of view.

Two Diarists: Pepys and Evelyn

The Restoration period is also notable for the work of the two most famous English diarists. The diaries of the naval administrator Samuel Pepys (1633–1703) provide a vivid picture of London life from 1660 to 1669, including accounts of events such as the Coronation of Charles II, the Plague and the Fire of London, as well as demonstrating Pepys's own idiosyncrasies and vanity. His fascination with details and flair for chronicling them makes his writing one of the most illuminating records of the age. The memoirs of his friend, John Evelyn (1620-1706), are less spontaneous, but only slightly less colourful. Beginning rather earlier, they span a longer period, detailing Evelyn's more considered impressions of events from 1657, when Cromwell was offered the Crown, to the Glorious Revolution of 1688.

John Dryden (1631–1700)

Dryden is the quintessential writer of the late seventeenth century, a man who managed to retain royal favour through many of the political changes of the period, as well as producing major work in most of the dominant literary forms of the age. He became Poet Laureate in 1668 and kept this position after converting to Catholicism, when James II succeeded to the throne in 1685. It was only on the accession of William and Mary that he lost the patronage he had enjoyed for more than twenty years. Beginning with *Astraea Redux* (1660), a panegyric celebrating the restoration of the Stuart monarchy, he responded to many of the major public events of the next three decades. *Annus Mirabilis* (1667) demonstrates a similar royalist vision in its treatment of the Dutch War of 1665–6 and the Fire of London. Because of his ability to adapt to different regimes, he has variously been seen as an opportunist and as a man who had the mental flexibility to avoid being compromised by taking up intransigent positions.

The Achievements of Dryden

Dryden was the first great English master of the heroic couplet (rhymed iambic pentameters) and he anticipated Alexander Pope's perfection of this verse form as a vehicle for satire. As a poet, he is best known for his satires. These include *Absalom and Achitophel* (1681; Part II, mainly by Nahum Tate, 1682), an allegory which uses an Old Testament parallel to attack the attempt by the Earl of Shaftesbury and the Duke of Monmouth to replace James, Duke of York as Charles II's heir; and his richest comic work *MacFlecknoe* (1682), a mock heroic poem, lambasting the dramatist Thomas Shadwell and bad art more generally. Dryden also wrote a number of fine Pindaric odes, including "A Song for St Cecilia's Day" (1687) and "Alexander's Feast; or, The Power of Music" (1697), and the didactic religious allegories, *Religio Laici* (1682) and *The Hind and the Panther* (1687). The former defended Anglicanism; the latter Catholicism. His work as a dramatist includes the blank verse heroic plays *All for Love* (*see above*) and *The Conquest of Granada* (1670), which was famously parodied in Buckingham's burlesque play *The Rehearsal* (1671), and a number of tragic-comedies, among them *Marriage à la Mode* (1672).

Dryden is often considered the first major English literary theorist. His *Essay of Dramatick Poesie* (1668) discusses the merits of various forms of drama and justifies his own practice as a dramatist; his *Discourse concerning the Original and Progress of Satire* (1693) examines the appropriateness of the methods of Horace and Juvenal for English satirists and in so doing established the groundwork for one of the key debates of the next century, when Pope produced imitations of Horace and Johnson preferred the model of Juvenal. Dryden was also one of the leading translators of his age, producing an especially fine translation of Virgil's *Aeneid* (1697).

His final work, *Fables, Ancient and Modern* (1700), included translations of Homer, Boccaccio and Chaucer.

John Wilmot, Earl of Rochester (1647–80)

Rochester's dissolute aristocratic life-style has led to his being seen as a representative figure of the Restoration period. He was famed as a libertine, drinker and poseur. His verse was noted for its sexual explicitness and poems such as " A Ramble in St. James's Park" enjoyed an underground reputation as pornographic classics. However, Rochester's poetry also has a serious and reflective side and he is one of the first masters of Augustan satirical verse. His most famous poem, "A Satire against Reason and Mankind" (1675), explores tensions between rationalism and sensuality. Rochester also wrote some fine lyric poetry and introduced the form of the classical "imitation" into English verse.

THE EIGHTEENTH-CENTURY NOVEL

Daniel Defoe (1660–1731)

Defoe is generally considered the first great English novelist, since his work is written with a degree of circumstantial realism unprecedented in earlier English prose fiction. He was nearing sixty years of age when his first novel *Robinson Crusoe* (1719) was published. Prior to this he had led an eventful life as a journalist, businessman and political writer, whose publications had included *The True-Born Englishman* (1701), a satirical work praising William III and defending religious minorities, and *The Shortest Way with the Dissenters* (1702), which mocked Anglican intolerance of nonconformists.

The Original Desert Island Novel

The original desert island novel, *Robinson Crusoe* has been interpreted in numerous ways: as a romantic adventure story; as a spiritual autobiography, a secular equivalent of Bunyan's *Grace Abounding*; as an economic success-story that offers a blueprint for capitalism; as one of the modern world's first great do-it-yourself manuals, an account of survival without the usual props of civilization; and, since it is set in the Caribbean, as a narrative of New World utopianism. It was followed by sequels detailing Crusoe's *Farther Adventures* (1719) and *Serious Reflections* (1720) and six other novels, of which *Moll Flanders* (1722) is the best known. Like *Robinson Crusoe*, the novel, which charts Moll's rogue's progress through English society, has also been viewed as both a spiritual autobiography and an economic success-story, though its setting within society makes it superficially very different and finally it is difficult to take the putative religious elements seriously. Nevertheless it offers a striking portrait of the exploits of a woman who has to live by her wits in order to make her way in society and whose situation justifies her resorting to picaroon cunning in the eyes of many readers.

Roxana (1724) tells a similar story of wickedness and repentance, though the penitence is more perfunctory. Defoe's other novels were *Captain Singleton* (1720), *Memoirs of a Cavalier* (1720), *Colonel Jack* (1722) and *A Journal of the Plague Year* (1722), which made extensive use of documentary records of the 1665 London Plague. In his later years he published the three-volume *A Tour through the Whole Island of Great Britain* (1724–6) and *The Complete English Tradesman* (1725–7).

Samuel Richardson (1689–1761)

Richardson was a middle-aged printer, who became an overnight celebrity when his epistolary novel *Pamela, or Virtue Rewarded* appeared in 1740. Originally conceived as "a series of familiar letters" for "country readers ... unable to indite for themselves", it tells the story of a servant girl who defends her virginity against the advances of her aristocratic master and eventually wins his hand in marriage. The novel established a plot pattern that would become one of the staples of English romantic fiction: the vicissitudes in the relationship between a woman and a man who is her social superior. The first section of *Pamela* is notable for skilful use of the epistolary form for dramatic effect. However, when the letters give way to a journal, much of this immediacy is lost. The second part (1741) depicts Pamela's adaptation to her new social rank and the ways in which she handles her husband's transgressions.

Richardson's Masterpiece

Richardson's masterpiece *Clarissa* (1747–8), originally published in seven volumes and one of the longest novels in the English language, also focuses on the figure of a threatened heroine, this time a woman of higher social rank. Its use of the epistolary form is altogether more complex than that of *Pamela*, with the letters being shared between four main correspondents; and the representation of moral issues and sexual conflict is also more probing and disturbing than in the earlier novel. Clarissa is another personification of virtue, but she is secretly fascinated by the rakish male protagonist, Lovelace, who eventually rapes her. Lovelace, in turn, is one of the most powerfully drawn characters in early English fiction: his struggle to balance his sexual urges with his respect for the virtuous Clarissa demonstrates a psychological complexity that is at variance with the ostensible simplism of Richardson's avowed morality and the tragic outcome can be seen as an indictment of eighteenth-century gender roles.

Richardson also published *Sir Charles Grandison* (1753–4), in which he switched his main focus to the portrayal of male virtue.

Henry Fielding (1707–54)

Fielding was a leading comic dramatist until 1737, when the Licensing Act, generally considered to have been introduced in response to his attacks on the Whig government of the day, imposed censorship on stage performances and put an end to his career as a playwright. He became a reforming magistrate and, along with his brother John, founded Britain's first police force, the Bow Street Runners.

His First Novels

Fielding's career as a novelist began as a response to what he viewed as the hypocrisy and prurience of Richardson's *Pamela*. In his anonymously published parody, *Shamela* (1741), the unprincipled heroine is a whore and trickster, who schemes to entrap her master into marriage. Fielding's first major novel, *Joseph Andrews* (1742), also took its initial inspiration from *Pamela*. In the opening sections, he reversed gender roles to show male virtue, personified by Pamela's brother Joseph, under attack from predatory females. However, parody is discarded in the main part of the novel, where Joseph undertakes a picaresque journey through the countryside with the book's most memorable figure, the Quixotic clergyman Parson Adams. The episodic format of the journey affords Fielding numerous opportunities to engineer comic situations. At the same time, particularly through the character of Adams, he dramatizes a very different kind of morality from Richardson's Puritanism: that of latitudinarian Anglicanism, which placed its emphasis on salvation through good deeds rather than professions of faith.

Fielding's Masterpiece

The same morality informs Fielding's masterpiece *Tom Jones* (1749), which he termed "a comic epic in prose". More generally, the novel is a brilliantly plotted comic picaresque, which provides a panoramic overview of English life in the middle of the eighteenth century. In the central section, a journey through the countryside at the time of the Jacobite rebellion includes a wide-ranging portrait gallery of social types and a series of farcical encounters that shows the influence of Fielding's experience as a comic dramatist. This is framed by sections set in the West Country and London, which suggest that the values of the rural squirearchy are preferable to those of the genteel society of London.

The novel also propounds a sexual ethic which is in marked contrast to Richardson's conception of "virtue"; the hero Tom is excused for being unfaithful to his beloved Sophie on three occasions on the grounds that he is essentially goodhearted. In the conclusion, the revelation that the "foundling" Tom is really a gentleman secures his promotion in the social hierarchy, just as marriage elevates Pamela, though there is a significant difference in that in Fielding's world nobility remains a matter of birth, not social advancement. *Tom Jones* is also notable for the introductory chapters to its eighteen books, which discourse on a range of subjects, including the novel itself, and in so doing anticipate the self-reflexive style of Sterne's *Tristram Shandy*.

Fielding's other works include: *Jonathan Wild* (1743), an ironic novel which followed Gay's *Beggar's Opera* in attacking prominent public figures, notably the prime minister Robert Walpole, through the guise of a eulogistic account of the "greatness" of a notorious contemporary criminal; *A Journey from this World to the Next* (1743); his last novel, *Amelia* (1751), in which he deserted his customary comic mode of writing for a more Richardsonian consideration of morality in domestic life; and the posthumously published *Journal of a Voyage to Lisbon* (1755).

Tobias Smollett (1721–71)

While Defoe and Fielding had used elements from the Spanish picaresque novel in their fiction, it was the Scottish-born Smollett who became the most significant early English exponent of the genre, which he employed for satirical purposes and social comment. Prior to the publication of his first novel, *Roderick Random* (1748), he had been a surgeon's mate and the novel is particularly notable for its scenes of nautical life. *Peregrine Pickle* (1751), in which the rogue hero moves in a higher social sphere and travels in mainland Europe is often more savage in its satirical attacks and uncompromisingly graphic in its representation of physical characteristics. It was followed by *Ferdinand Count Fathom* (1753), a novel employing mock-heroic and Gothic elements to recount the adventures of its bogus "count", and *Sir Launcelot Greaves* (1760–1), chiefly remembered as an imitation of Cervantes' *Don Quixote*, which Smollett had translated into English, and as the first work by a major novelist to be serialized in a magazine.

His Finest Novel

In his last novel, *Humphry Clinker* (1771), which has generally been viewed as his finest, Smollett uses the epistolary technique to chronicle the picaresque story of a travelling expedition. His characteristically savage representation of the unsavoury and brutal aspects of eighteenth-century life gives way to a more reflective style, though the novel's delineation of a cross-section of British life still includes harsh caricatures. The story is told by a number of letter-writers, with the figure of the elderly squire, Matthew Bramble, who combines misanthropic and sentimental qualities and has sometimes been seen as a mouthpiece for Smollett's own opinions, at the centre. Smollett also published *Complete History of England* (1757–8) and *Travels through France and Italy* (1766).

Laurence Sterne (1713–68)

Like Defoe and Richardson, Sterne came to the novel comparatively late in life. A Yorkshire parson, involved in the ecclesiastical politics of the diocese of York, he, too, achieved overnight fame with the publication of his first major fiction: Volumes One and Two of his novel, *The Life and Opinions of Tristram Shandy* (1760–67), after which he found himself lionized in literary London. *Tristram Shandy* is often regarded as one of the great eccentricities of English literature. Critics such as Dr Johnson, who said, "Nothing odd will do. *Tristram Shandy* did not last long ", have been proved wrong, but Sterne's work does flout most of the conventions that had already come to be associated with the fledgling genre of the novel. An apparently uncompleted nine-volume novel, it is a fictional autobiography in which Tristram sets out to reveal everything about his life and opinions, beginning with the night of his botched conception.

He does not arrive at the moment of his birth until the third volume and the novel provides a catalogue of false starts, digressions, accidents and comic misfortunes. Despite Tristram's avowed intention to tell his story from beginning to end, it lacks linear progression (it concludes more than four years before it begins), has missing chapters and a blank page and includes very little narrative action.

As such it becomes a kind of parody of the type of fictional autobiography that Defoe writes, in which events, objects and characters are exhaustively described. Yet it succeeds brilliantly as a novel of a completely different kind—a novel about novel-writing—and the Russian formalist critic, Victor Shklovsky, who takes the view that fiction is finally about its own processes, has commented that its self-parody makes it "the most typical novel of world literature".

Sterne is also known for another whimsical, uncompleted novel, *A Sentimental Journey* (1768), which traces the sentimental adventures of its hero, Parson Yorick, in France, poking fun at the accounts of travellers such as Smollett, called Smelfungus here, as it does so. The book owed much of its contemporary appeal to its sentimentality, viewed by Yorick as a form of spontaneous benevolence that spreads outwards from particular individuals to affect all those with whom they come into contact. However, for the modern reader, it is difficult not to view Yorick's sentimental effusions ironically, particularly when they occur in the context of his prurient encounters with women. Sterne's other writing includes his sermons, published as *The Sermons of Mr Yorick* (1760–69), and the *Journal to Eliza* (written 1767; published 1904).

The Gothic Novel

As a reaction against the neo-classical beliefs that had dominated culture early in the century, the later eighteenth century revived Gothic forms in literature and architecture, preferring to draw its inspiration from a tradition associated with the medieval rather than the classical period. Horace Walpole built his Gothic castle, Strawberry Hill, at Twickenham and wrote a pioneering Gothic novel, *The Castle of Otranto* (1764). William Beckford's *Vathek* (1786) introduced Gothic elements into another fashionable and exotic romantic form, the Oriental tale, and he built a massive Gothic folly, Fonthill Abbey in Wiltshire, which collapsed less than thirty years later. Other prominent Gothic novels of the period include Anne Radcliffe's *The Mysteries of Udolpho* (1794) and Matthew Lewis's *The Monk* (1796).

The staples of the form, on which its individual exponents worked variations, were quickly established: sensation, mystery, suspense, horror, supernatural happenings, Italian settings, Gothic architecture and persecuted heroines. William Godwin expanded its possibilities by introducing a degree of psychological subtlety that had not hitherto been characteristic of the genre into his more realistic *Caleb Williams* (1794), a novel which is also noteworthy for protesting against the mistreatment of the socially disadvantaged and as an early example of the novel of crime and detection.

The First Gothic Masterpiece

The Gothic novel produced its first undisputed masterpiece in Godwin's daughter, Mary Shelley's *Frankenstein, or the Modern Prometheus* (1818), a novel which dramatizes ethical issues concerning the right to create life with great imaginative power. While there is horror a-plenty in *Frankenstein*, its main appeal lies in the psychology of its protagonists and it is as much concerned with the mental torments of the scientist, Victor Frankenstein, who gives life to the monster for which the numerous popular spin-offs of the book are best known, as with the sufferings of the creature himself.

Other Novelists

Until comparatively recently, the achievements of eighteenth-century women novelists received much less recognition than those of their male contemporaries or their nineteenth-century female successors. Fanny Burney's novels were a notable exception: *Evelina* (1778) followed Richardson in using the epistolary form, taking a young woman's introduction into society as its main theme; *Cecilia* (1782) describes the fortunes of an heiress who is exploited by her guardians. Other important novels by women writers include Fielding's sister Sarah's *David Simple* (1744–53), which challenged the gender norms of the period, Charlotte Lennox's *The Female Quixote* (1752), whose heroine's beliefs about life are modelled on the conventions of French heroic romances, and Elizabeth Inchbald's *A Simple Story* (1791) and *Nature and Art* (1796).

Apart from the fiction of Richardson and Sterne, sentimental novels of the period include Oliver Goldsmith's *The Vicar of Wakefield* (1766), in which the eponymous Dr Primrose has to learn to temper his instinctive magnanimity with worldly wisdom and Robert Mackenzie's *Man of Feeling* (1771), another novel which, while seizing every opportunity to evoke pathos, also cautions against the dangers of ingenuous good-heartedness.

Towards the end of the century, along with Godwin, novelists such as Robert Bage and Thomas Holcroft began to challenge the class assumptions of most earlier fiction. Holcroft's *Anna St. Ives* (1792) offers a variation on the basic plot of *Clarissa* by adding a third main character, a gardener who provides the heroine with an alternative to the aristocratic rake, and in so doing introduced the first proletarian hero into the English novel.

THE ENGLISH AUGUSTANS

Introduction

Writers of the late seventeenth and early eighteenth century who took their inspiration from the classics have frequently been referred to as "The English Augustans". The term derives from an essay by Goldsmith, who used it to suggest a parallel between the Rome of the Emperor Augustus (27 B.C.–14 A.D.) and Queen Anne's England (1702–14). It has been applied more generally to the Restoration era and most of the eighteenth century. Augustan writing is characterized by its emphasis on order, reason and decorum, its admiration for the classics and a belief in the commonality of human experience. In Johnson's words, "Great thoughts are always general and consist in positions not limited by exceptions". The major writers of England's Augustan Age were Dryden, Swift, Pope and Johnson. Gibbon's *Decline and Fall of the Roman Empire* (1776–88), which, in addition to chronicling its historical subject, can be seen as an elegy for the loss of the classical world, is often regarded as the last great Augustan classic.

Jonathan Swift (1667–1745)

Swift was born and brought up in Dublin, but spent his early adulthood moving between England and Ireland, where he served as an Anglican priest from 1694 and was later appointed as Dean of St Patrick's Cathedral in Dublin in 1713. He became increasingly committed to Irish political causes and his pamphlets protesting against English colonial exploitation made him a national hero in Ireland. They include *The Drapier's Letters* (1724), in which he assumed the persona of a Dublin draper to successfully oppose the introduction of a new form of coinage into Ireland, and the savagely ironic "A Modest Proposal" (1729), in which a supposedly moderate speaker exhorts the poor of Ireland to fatten their own children to provide food for the rich, since, after all, they have been metaphorically eaten by their English landlords already. Swift's health failed as he grew older and the ferocity of his satire led to claims that he had gone mad. It seems

more likely that the symptoms of his Menière's syndrome, from which he had long suffered, had grown worse with age.

His Two Masterpieces

Perhaps the greatest of all British ironists, Swift's first masterpiece was *The Tale of a Tub* volume (1704), which comprises the title-work, "The Battle of the Books" and "The Mechanical Operation of the Spirit". "The Tale of a Tub" is an elaborate satire on aberrations in modern learning. It includes Swift's famous "Digression on Madness", in which a crazed speaker argues the case for the social and moral usefulness of insanity. While the work's digressions are central, the tale itself is an allegory of three brothers, who represent the Catholic, Anglican and dissenting branches of Christianity, with Swift demonstrating a preference for the Anglican middle way. "The Battle of the Books" stages a mock-heroic battle between ancient and modern volumes in the King's library as a device for debating the relative merits of classical and modern learning. The outcome is left undecided, but at the moment when the work breaks off, the ancients appear to be winning the day.

Swift's second masterpiece, *Gulliver's Travels* (1726), is superficially much more straightforward and its opening part, in which the hero finds himself a giant among the six-inch high people of Lilliput, has had an enduring appeal for children. However, Gulliver's Lilliputian experience also works on a more complex, allegorical level: it offers a satirical critique of contemporary British and European society. This is typical of the work as a whole and, as it continues, the tone of the *Travels* gradually darkens. In Part II, Gulliver visits the land of Brobdingnag, where the formula of Lilliput is reversed, as he finds himself a pigmy among giants. This perspective provides Swift with opportunities to illustrate the grossness of the human body, an aspect of his writing which has led to his being charged with misanthropy. The third part, in which Gulliver visits several places, satirizes what Swift saw as the excesses of modern scientific inquiry, particularly the experiments of the Royal Society.

The darkening vision reaches a climax in Part IV, in which Gulliver travels to the land of the Houyhnhnms, a species of super-rational horses, who stand in marked opposition to the other beings that inhabit their country, the bestial and filthy Yahoos. The Yahoos are identified with humankind and by the time Gulliver finally returns home his faith in human nature has collapsed to a point where he prefers the company of his horses to his family.

His Other Works

Swift's other works include the early *Bickerstaff Papers* (1708), in which he parodied the contemporary astrologer, Isaac Partridge by predicting his death and then subsequently, falsely, claiming he was really dead, and *The Journal to Stella* (1710–13), a collection of letters written to Esther Johnson, one of the two women in his life. Swift also produced a considerable body of poetry, mainly written in quatrains, which is generally less assured than his prose. His best known poems include "Baucis and Philemon", "Cadenus and Vanessa" and "Verses on the Death of Dr Swift".

Alexander Pope (1688–1744)

The greatest satirist of his age, Pope is generally regarded as Dryden's heir. Like Dryden he was a neo-classicist who used the heroic couplet to write scathing indictments of what he saw as failings in social and personal morality. In his own day his most popular works were his translations of Homer's *Iliad* (1720) and *Odyssey* (1725–6). Posterity has seen his witty satires as his greatest achievement. As a Catholic in the early eighteenth century, Pope was prevented from attending university and had private tutors. This and his physical make-up—he was approximately four feet six inches high and suffered from poor health throughout his life—led his critics to see Pope's satire as vindictive and personally motivated. In his own view, he was a compulsive moralist, who adhered to Dryden's view that "the true end of satire is the amendment of vices by correction".

Pope's first major poem, *An Essay on Criticism*

(1711), is both his artistic manifesto and an exploration of the state of literature at the time. It outlines his classical humanist creed and his belief that "True wit is Nature to advantage dressed/ What oft was thought but ne'er so well expressed". *Windsor Forest* (1713) is a pastoral celebrating the Peace of Utrecht, which ended the War of the Spanish Succession. In *The Rape of the Lock* (1712; enlarged 1714), Pope used the mock heroic form to poke gentle fun at a prank in Catholic high society and in so doing pointed up the distance between contemporary polite society and the world of classical epic, for example by modelling an account of the heroine's putting on her make-up on Homer's account of the arming of Achilles.

His Debt to Horace

The classical writer to whom Pope was most indebted was Horace and he imitated him in life as well as literature, seeing his own villa on the banks of the Thames at Twickenham as his equivalent of Horace's Sabine farm. His *Essay on Criticism* was modelled on Horace's *Ars Poetica* and he later wrote a series of poems, which imitated Horace's epistles and satires. While each of these poems has a particular addressee and specific satirical targets, collectively they demonstrate a preference for the values of the rural gentry over the newly emergent mercantilist classes. However, their abiding interest owes more to their comic portraiture and mastery of versification than their moral attitudes. The *Essay on Man* (1733–4), a philosophical poem on humanity's place in the universe, which was widely admired in its own day, remains notable for its aphorisms, but its didacticism leads to an unevenness of tone, as conversational passages give way to over-solemn moralizing.

In one sense, Pope's second major mock-epic poem, *The Dunciad* (first version 1728; final enlarged version 1743), is his equivalent of Dryden's *MacFlecknoe*, since, like the earlier poem, it mocks dullness through the use of elevation, and in so doing deflates its subjects, the literary poetasters of the period. However, *The Dunciad* is a work that rises above its mock-heroic origins and ribald comedy to assume the status of serious epic. Its wide-ranging allusions provide a catalogue of contemporary literary and social vices; and its fourth book, added towards the end of Pope's life, is especially notable for references to Milton's *Paradise Lost*, which link the poem's literary dunces to a broader vision of creeping moral chaos and disorder. The poem ends with a lament for the loss of classical humanist values, as the influence of dullness spreads outwards to engulf the whole of society.

Samuel Johnson (1707–84)

Born in Lichfield, Johnson went to London in 1737, along with his pupil David Garrick, who became the leading actor of his age, just as Johnson became its most famous writer. He was far from successful during his first years in the capital and his poem *London* (1738), a Juvenalian satire contrasting the values of the country and the city, expresses his early feelings of disillusionment. He struggled to establish himself as a writer, a predicament which probably led him to identify with his friend Richard Savage, an account of whose life he published in 1744. *The Life of Savage* is both the most immediate and the most polemical of Johnson's biographies: his personal involvement with his subject, whose controversial claim to be the repudiated illegitimate son of the Countess of Macclesfield Johnson fully supported, lend it a vivid first-hand quality lacking in his later *Lives of the English Poets* (1781). Johnson gradually established himself through his work in a range of genres and when George III granted him a royal pension in 1762, his financial position was secure. In later life he became a focal point for London literary life and his influence extended far beyond his own writings.

In 1764, along with the artist Sir Joshua Reynolds, he founded the Literary Club, whose members included Garrick, Oliver Goldsmith and Edmund Burke.

His Extraordinary Versatility

Johnson produced significant work in virtually every eighteenth-century literary form. His tragedy *Irene* was staged by Garrick in 1749. As a periodical essayist, he wrote two essays a week for *The Rambler* from 1750 to 1752 and weekly essays for *The Idler* from 1758 to 1760. As a lexicographer, he compiled his *Dictionary of the English Language* (1755) in eight years, while the French Academy's similar project is said to have taken forty men forty years. It was the first English dictionary to provide etymologies and literary examples of the usage of words as well as definitions, and is particularly remembered for the humour of Johnson's sometimes individualistic definitions. He referred to a lexicographer as "a harmless drudge" and defined oats as "A grain which in England is generally given to horses, but in Scotland supports the people". His alleged prejudice against Scotland lent a particular edge to his relationship with his Scottish biographer, James Boswell, whom he first met in 1763. However, his attitude changed after a journey to Scotland with Boswell, which resulted in Johnson's *Journey to the Western Islands of Scotland* (1775) and Boswell's *Journal of a Tour to the Hebrides* (1785).

Poet, Novelist, Editor and Critic

As a poet, Johnson followed *London* with another Juvenalian satire, *The Vanity of Human Wishes* (1749), his most important poem, in which he takes a lofty, ironic view of human aspirations. His only novel *Rasselas* (1759) is similar in theme. It employs the form of the Eastern Tale to investigate possibilities for human happiness, with the eponymous hero, a prince of Abyssinia, being schooled by the worldly wise philosopher, Imlac, who tells him "Human life is everywhere a state in which much is to be endured, and little to be enjoyed". As an editor, Johnson produced an edition of *Shakespeare's Plays* (1765), more notable for its literary criticism than its elucidation of Shakespeare's texts.

His abilities as a critic also informed his *Lives of the English Poets*, the most comprehensive biographical collection of the century, which combines biography with criticism and a "character" of the poet. The *Lives* vary considerably in direction and quality and while none is as tendentious as the earlier *Life of Savage*, several, such as "The Life of Cowley", in which Johnson attacked the Metaphysical Poets, are openly polemical in their advocacy of a particular attitude or approach. Along with Cowley, the lives of Milton and Pope are among the finest.

Finally, Johnson's reputation owes at least as much to his being the subject of one of the greatest biographies in the English language, Boswell's *Life of Johnson* (1791), which records his witty conversation and personal eccentricities, along with a circumstantial account of his personal and public life that makes him the most fully documented subject in eighteenth-century literature.

Personal Writings

Biography and autobiography came of age in the late eighteenth century. Johnson's *Lives of the English Poets* are often opinionated, but demonstrate an attention to individual detail that had been rare in earlier personal writings. Boswell's *Life of Johnson* is widely regarded as the first modern biography, since it demonstrates an unprecedented attention to researched detail, a commitment to accuracy and an endeavour to treat its subject's life exhaustively. Boswell brings Johnson alive by including details of his mannerisms and records of his *bon mots*, in dramatic scenes, some of which he consciously engineers. He also kept intimate journals of his own life, which remained unpublished until the twentieth century. Best known among these is his *London Journal, 1762–63*, a fascinating companion-piece to the section of the *Life of Johnson* in which he first becomes acquainted with his subject, since it records his private emotions and amorous encounters from the same period.

Gibbon's *Autobiography* (originally entitled *Memoirs of My Life and Writings*, 1796) is an account of the forces that shaped the character of the historian of *The Decline and Fall of the Roman Empire*, written in a detached, ironic style. Other notable personal writings of the age include the diary of Fanny Burney and the letters of Horace Walpole and Lord Chesterfield, whose missives to his natural son collectively come to form a conduct book instructing a young gentleman in matters of breeding, morality and intrigue.

The Periodical Essay

Joseph Addison and Richard Steele's *The Spectator* (1711–14) established the essay as an important genre in its own right. Its essays are notable for their observations on the manners of the period and for their creation of a club, whose members include representatives of various aspects of early eighteenth-century life, with the country gentleman, Sir Roger de Coverley, being the most memorable. The periodical essay flourished throughout the century and important later sequences include Johnson's *Rambler* essays, which range over a broad sweep of subjects, often offering moral instruction, and Oliver Goldsmith's *Citizen of the World* (1760–62), a collection of letters supposedly written by and to a Chinese visitor to London, which provides apparently ingenuous comments on English manners and customs

Poetry of Landscape and Reflection

As the century progressed, classical models for poetry were gradually replaced by approaches that anticipated the Romantic Movement in their concern with Nature, individual emotions, the sublime, rural life and melancholy thoughts. Thomson's *Seasons* (1726–30) looks back to classical pastoral and forwards to the Romantic emphasis on Nature's influence on human sensibilities. Edward Young's *Night Thoughts* (1742–6) is the most famous longer work of the "graveyard poets", whose melancholy meditations on mortality took their inspiration from graveyard settings. The greatest of such poems is Thomas Gray's "Elegy Written in a Country Churchyard" (1751), where the slow, measured verse provides a vehicle for an elegiac meditation on the transience of human life and the particular fate of the humble villagers who are buried in the churchyard.

Village life is also the subject of Goldsmith's *The Deserted Village* (1770), an elegy for rural life which laments the depopulation of the countryside occasioned by the agrarian revolution and the enclosure of common land, and George Crabbe's *The Village* (1783), which took issue with Goldsmith's idealized view of the rural past. William Cowper's finest achievement, *The Task* (1785) is an introspective poem on the pleasures of country life. Other notable eighteenth-century poets whose meditative response to landscape anticipates the Romantics include William Collins, Mark Akenside and Christopher Smart.

Eighteenth-Century Drama

The beginning of the eighteenth century saw a reaction against the licentiousness of Restoration Comedy in favour of a drama that placed its main emphasis on sentimentalism and the cultivation of fine feelings. The cult of sentimentalism continued to exert an important influence on English drama for more than half a century; and representative plays in this genre include Colley Cibber's *The Careless Husband* (1702), Steele's *The Conscious Lovers* (1722) and Richard Cumberland's *The West Indian* (1771).

The early part of the century also saw the growth of a very different kind of drama, the burlesque play. The popularity of the burlesque can be dated back to George Villiers's parody of Restoration heroic drama, *The Rehearsal* (1671), but it assumed new dimensions with the success of John Gay's masterpiece, *The Beggar's Opera* (1728). Ostensibly a satire on the contemporary vogue for Italian opera, Gay's play broadens out into a wide-ranging critique of the social life of the period, in which aristocrats are replaced by highwaymen and merchants by fences. Much of its appeal arose from its lively music, which replaced operatic arias with popular ballads. Other notable burlesques include Gay's *The What d'ye Call It* (1715), Fielding's *Tom Thumb* (1730) and Henry Carey's *Chrononhotonthologos* (1734).

Oliver Goldsmith (1728–74)

Oliver Goldsmith initiated a movement away from sentimental comedy in his essay, "Comparison between Laughing and Sentimental Comedy" (1773), which attacked the vogue for sentimentalism and argued that humour should return to the English stage. His play, *The Good Natur'd Man*

(1768) is a particularly interesting dramatization of the debate about the form that comedy should take, as its hero is both satirized for his foolish magnanimity and genuinely benevolent. Goldsmith's most famous play, *She Stoops to Conquer* (1773), in which a young gentleman mistakes his prospective father-in-law's house for an inn, has had a much more enduring appeal, based as it is on a series of comic misunderstandings that rise above its period and setting.

Richard Brinsley Sheridan (1751–1816)

Goldsmith's contemporary, Richard Brinsley Sheridan, also transcended the conventions of sentimental comedy. His plays employ a broad range of comic effects that derive their humour from situation, character and verbal wit. *The Rivals* (1775), a comedy of manners set in fashionable Bath society, is best remembered for its broad comic characters, particularly Mrs Malaprop, whose habit of confusing similar sounding words (*e.g.* her reference to "an allegory on the banks of the Nile") was responsible for the introduction of the term "malapropism" into the language. Sheridan's *The School for Scandal* (1777), a play which redeploys character types from Restoration comedy and makes brilliant use of comic situations, is the finest achievement of late eighteenth-century comedy.

THE ENGLISH ROMANTICS

Introduction

The end of the eighteenth century saw a major shift in literary and cultural taste with the emergence of the Romantic Movement. Its most important characteristics included a belief in the shaping power of the imagination (defined in a range of ways by the various Romantics) rather than reason, a stress on individual experience and a desertion of neo-classical norms in favour of a more emotive and spontaneous approach to life. However, no two major Romantic poets held the same beliefs and Byron's poetic practice was markedly different from those of his contemporaries.

The beginnings of English Romanticism are usually associated with the Lake Poets, Wordsworth, Coleridge and Southey, but it had evolved gradually and Romantic elements can be found in such diverse forms as earlier eighteenth-century poetry of landscape and reflection, the Gothic novel, a growth of interest in the classical notion of the sublime, late eighteenth-century sentimentalism and a fascination with the pictorial, particularly as mediated by Italian landscape painting.

William Blake (1757–1827)

Blake was a writer and artist whose genius developed outside the dominant cultural conventions of his day. Educated at home, he was apprenticed to an engraver at the age of fourteen. He developed a new method of "illuminated printing", in which he blended the text of his poems with colour engravings, and a distinctive symbolism which expressed his highly personal visionary philosophy. His artistic individuality was complemented by his nonconformist views. The son of a dissenter, he was influenced by the beliefs of the Swedish mystic, Emmanuel Swedenborg and the egalitarian political philosophy of his friends and contemporaries, William Godwin and Thomas Paine.

An early volume of *Poetical Sketches* (1783) was followed by his most popular work, the collection of lyrics *Songs of Innocence* (1789), which was expanded to become *Songs of Innocence and Experience* (1795). The latter volume's sub-title indicates its intention to depict "the two contrary states of the human soul" and it includes paired poems, such as "The Lamb" and "The Tyger", which illustrate the dialectical opposition between the Edenic innocence of childhood and the corrupted experience of adulthood. Other poems in the collection include "The Little Black Boy" and "The Chimney Sweeper".

His Mystical Vision

Blake's mystical vision receives extended expression in his numerous prophetic books, where the style is in marked contrast to the apparent simplism of his *Songs*, though profundity and naivety often co-exist. The prophetic books, which he wrote, engraved and published himself, include: *Visions of the Daughters of Albion* (1793), *America: A Prophecy* (1793), *The Book of Urizen* (1794), *The Book of Ahania* (1795), *The Book of Los* and *The Song of Los* (1795), *Jerusalem: The Emanation of the Giant Albion* (1804–20) and *The Ghost of Abel* (1822). Blake was fascinated by *Paradise Lost*, taking the view that "Milton was a true poet and of the devil's party without knowing it". He attacked Milton in his "Los" sequence, which inverts aspects of *Paradise Lost*, and in *Milton: A Poem in Two Books* (1804–8). The latter contains his short poem, "Jerusalem", from which the popular hymn was later taken. Blake's most important prose work, *The Marriage of Heaven and Hell* (1790–93), is a collection of aphorisms, which again demonstrates his belief that "without contraries is no progression".

William Wordsworth (1770–1850)

Wordsworth was university-educated, but the key formative influence on his artistic development, which he describes in his poetic autobiography *The Prelude*, was his early love of Nature, developed during his boyhood in the English Lake District. A walking tour in France, the Alps and Italy and a further visit to France during the first phase of the French Revolution also contributed significantly to the shaping of his poetic sensibility.

His Earliest Verse

The diction of Wordsworth's earliest verse is barely distinguishable from that of most of his contemporaries, but his first major work, *Lyrical Ballads* (1798), to which Coleridge also contributed, signalled one of the most radical changes in English poetry. Unfavourably received on its first appearance, the volume focuses on humble countryfolk, children and dispossessed mothers, describing their lives in a style of cultivated simplicity based on "the language of conversation in the middle and lower classes of society". Among its best-known poems are "We Are Seven", "The Thorn", "Simon Lee" and "The Idiot Boy". It also contains one of Wordsworth's most famous poems, "Lines written a few miles above Tintern Abbey", a meditation on the effect this landscape has had on his "moral being".

In the Preface to the second edition (1800), in which the poem "Michael" was added, Wordsworth provides a manifesto for his kind of Romantic verse, stressing that the principle object of the poems has been "to choose incidents and situations from common life, and to relate or describe them, throughout, in a selection of language really used by men". He explains that "Humble and rustic life was generally chosen, because, in that condition, the essential passions of the heart find a better soil in which they can attain their maturity, are less under restraint, and speak a plainer and more emphatic language". He also adumbrates his belief that "all good poetry is the spontaneous overflow of powerful feeling", another facet of his work which represents a marked departure from neo-classical poetic practice.

His Finest Long Poem

Wordsworth's finest long poem *The Prelude* exists in two versions (1805 and 1850), neither of which was published in his own life-time. Although it is an autobiography, it places its emphasis on "the growth of a poet's mind" (its sub-title) and Wordsworth dramatizes his own experience as representative of the poetic life. Written in blank verse, it describes his upbringing in the Lake District, his disenchantment with conventional forms of learning, town life and the political philosophy of William Godwin and the French Jacobins, who had been early inspirations to him. Against these, he sets the power of the poetic imagination, acting in communion with a Pantheistic Nature. The poem was intended as an introduction to a long philosophical poem to be called *The Recluse*, but only the second part of this, *The Excursion* (1814), which suffers in comparison with *The Prelude*, was ever completed.

Wordsworth's last major collection of shorter pieces, *Poems in Two Volumes*, was published in 1807. It includes some of his best-loved poems, among them "Daffodils" ("I wandered lonely as a cloud"), his sonnet "Composed Upon Westminster Bridge" ("Earth has not any thing to show more fair") and one of his finest tributes to rural simplicity, "Resolution and Independence", also known as "The Leech-Gatherer". His ode, "Intimations of Immortality from Recollections of Early Childhood", also published in this volume, is both a celebration of childhood innocence and a lament for the loss of the "visionary gleam" that has provided his early poetic inspiration. He published numerous further volumes, including *The White Doe of Rylstone* (1815), *Peter Bell* (1819) and *Sonnets* (1838). He became Poet Laureate in 1843, but virtually all his important poetry had been written in the first half of his life.

Samuel Taylor Coleridge (1772–1834)

Wordsworth's collaborator on the *Lyrical Ballads*, Coleridge had developed a distinctive range of republican and millenarian beliefs, again associated with the optimism of the first phase of the French Revolution, prior to meeting Wordsworth in 1797. Wordsworth's belief in the power of Nature probably influenced his conversation poem "Frost at Midnight" (1798) and during the first year of their friendship he wrote three of his most important poems, "The Rime of the Ancient Mariner", "Christabel" and "Kubla Khan". "The Ancient Mariner" appeared in the *Lyrical Ballads* (1798). Written in ballad metre, it is a tale of crime and absolution, told to a wedding guest, whom the mariner detains to listen to his story. The mariner shoots an albatross, a supposed good omen, during a voyage in the southern seas. When his ship subsequently suffers misfortunes, he is blamed by his crewmates for their sufferings and in the conclusion is absolved by a hermit. The ostensibly simple Christian morality of the ending is undermined by the existential arbitrariness inherent in the poem's depiction of sin and redemption and the mariner's intrusion into the festive occasion of the wedding leaves his auditor "a sadder and a wiser man".

"Kubla Khan" and "Christabel" were published in *Christabel and Other Poems* (1816). The former is a symbolically powerful, but obscure fragment, reputedly produced after a laudanum-induced dream. Its use of luxuriant, oriental imagery creates an evocative Romantic ambience that overshadows any clear meaning, but suggests an allegory about creativity. The equally enigmatic and unfinished "Christabel" is more obviously an allegory, about innocence, which draws on Gothic motifs. "Dejection: An Ode" (1802) begins by expressing sentiments reminiscent of Wordsworth's comments on his waning creative powers in the Immortality Ode and continues by looking for solace in the power of the imagination rather than external Nature. Coleridge's poetic gifts fell away in later life, a decline which has variously been attributed to the ending of his friendship with Wordsworth and his addiction to opium.

His Other Writings

Along with his comparatively small corpus of poems, Coleridge's most important contribution to the development of English Romanticism was his *Biographia Literaria* (1817), an extended prose work which blends autobiography and philosophical deliberations in a haphazard structure that allows him free rein to express his thoughts on life and literature. It is most notable for Coleridge's reflections on the psychology of the creative process, particularly his belief in the imagination's capacity to unify opposing aspects in the human psyche and contemporary society. Its numerous other subjects include a critique of Wordsworth, discussion of the philosophy of Kant and his contemporaries, essays on Shakespeare and advice to aspiring writers.

Table Talk (1836) is a record of Coleridge's conversations, for which he became famous in later life.

George Gordon Byron, Lord (1786–1824)

From one point of view, Byron was the archetypal English Romantic poet: his public persona perfectly fitted the nineteenth-century's conception of what such a poet should be and his fame throughout Europe was unrivalled. However, his poetry demonstrates little affinity with the more introspective aspects of the Romantic imagination and it is formally the most classical work produced by any of the major English Romantics. An admirer of Pope, Byron wrote much of his early verse in heroic couplets and throughout his work "Romantic" themes are tempered by a witty epigrammatic style that is more characteristic of Augustan verse.

His Early Life

Byron's inheritance of an aristocratic title, a club-foot, sexual abuse by his nurse and an incestuous relationship with his half-sister, Augusta Leigh, all contributed to making his early years markedly different from those of the other English Romantics. After a strict Scottish Calvinist upbringing, he became the sixth Baron Byron and inherited the family estate at Newstead Abbey in Nottingham-shire when he was ten. His reputation as a libertine, atheist and radical idealist began during his time at Cambridge. His first important work was Cantos I and II of *Childe Harold's Pilgrimage* (1812; Cantos III and IV, 1816 and 1818), a poem in Spenserian stanzas about the European wanderings of a young man disillusioned with his hedonistic life-style. It was followed by a series of hastily written verse tales—*The Bride of Abydos* (1813), *The Giaour* (1813), *The Corsair* (1814) and *Lara* (1814)—most notable for their development of the figure of "the Byronic hero", a romantic adventurer with a mysterious past. Along with Shelley and Mary Wollstonecraft Godwin, Byron left England in 1816 and after a stay in Switzerland settled in Italy. He died in Greece of fever, having gone there to fight in the Greek struggle for Independence from Turkey.

His Later Period

Most of Byron's best work belongs to his later period. It includes one of his finest shorter poems, *The Prisoner of Chillon* (1816), the dramatic poem, *Manfred* (1817), in which the hero is an outcast haunted by past crimes, and the "Venetian tale", *Beppo* (1818), written in ottava rima, a form which ideally suited his witty imagination. He also employed ottava rima in two of his finest poems, *The Vision of Judgement* (1822) and *Don Juan* (1819–24). The *Vision* is a wickedly funny parody of the Poet Laureate Robert Southey's similarly named poem (1821) about George III's arrival in heaven.

Don Juan, the unfinished thirteen-canto poem for which Byron is best known to posterity, is an epic account of the exploits of the legendary Spanish philanderer. Its use of ottava rima provides Byron with a perfect vehicle for a witty picaresque consideration of a range of contemporary philosophical and social issues, as well as ample opportunity to project himself into the complex figure of his protagonist. His play *Cain* (1821), in which the archetypal murderer of the Book of Genesis becomes a sympathetic rebel learning about the universe under the instruction of Lucifer, is his most extreme treatment of the figure of the exiled expatriate.

Percy Bysshe Shelley (1792–1822)

Expelled from Oxford, after writing a pamphlet advocating atheism, Shelley was the most reviled of the Romantic poets in his own day. He was also the most intellectually intense of the younger generation of Romantics and his poetry is suffused with a philosophical seriousness not to be found in Byron's work and a seemingly artless spontaneity not to be found in Keats's more direct and controlled imagery. His most famous statement on the imagination comes in his *Defence of Poetry* (written 1821; published 1840), which sees poets as the "unacknowledged legislators of the world" and champions the power of inspiration, which he associates with a Platonic view of life. Shelley was an ardent admirer of the Pantheism of "Tintern Abbey", but like Byron he felt that Wordsworth had betrayed his early radicalism. His first important poem, *Queen Mab* (1813) is a radical attack on a broad range of social targets, including marriage and institutionalized Christianity, in which the fairy queen of the title looks forward to a future in which society's ills will be cured. *Alastor, or the Spirit of Solitude* (1816) is a more introspective poem, which depicts an idealist's failure to find an external correlative for his dreams. The Odes, "Hymn to Intellectual Beauty" and "Mont Blanc", also belong to this phase of Shelley's career.

Shelley and Revolutionary Causes

At a time when absolutist governments were being reinstated in several parts of Europe in the wake of the Battle of Waterloo, Shelley wrote various poems and plays supporting revolutionary political causes. *The Revolt of Islam* (1818), a long poem in Spenserian stanzas, combines a radical political impulse with his idealized belief in human perfectibility. *The Cenci* (1819) is a verse tragedy based on a Renaissance legend, in which Shelley found a perfect subject for one of his most powerful allegories about resistance to tyranny. His masterpiece, *Prometheus Unbound* (1820), is a passionate lyrical drama, which takes the Greek Titan who rebelled against Jupiter, the king of the gods, as its hero. Rooted in Shelley's Platonic beliefs, the play operates on a number of levels, but is most obviously a socio-political allegory, protesting against all forms of tyranny. Like Byron, Shelley supported the Greek struggle against Turkish rule, and his last completed work, *Hellas* (1822), was a lyrical drama inspired by this cause.

Epipsychidion (1821) is an autobiographical poem about a Dantean quest for ideal beauty, which also deals with the creative process. Shelley's famous elegy on Keats's death, *Adonais* (1821), both laments his younger contemporary's passing and pays tribute to his poetic genius, which Shelley believed had not been sufficiently recognized. The poem also reflects Keats's own belief in the immortality conferred by beauty. Shelley's satires include "England in 1819", a vitriolic sonnet on the state of the nation at the end of George III's reign and *The Mask of Anarchy* (written 1819; published 1832), his most ambitious work of this kind, which responded to the news of the "Peterloo Massacre" of 1819, by equating the government's behaviour in ordering soldiers to shoot peaceful demonstrators for political reform with anarchy.

His shorter poems, which mainly take political freedom and love as their themes, include "Ode to Liberty", "Ode to Naples", "The Cloud", "The Indian Serenade", "Ozymandias", "Ode to the West Wind" and "To a Skylark".

Shelley drowned when his boat capsized in a storm off the coast of Italy, where he had been living since 1818. At the time of his death he was working on another Dantean poem, *The Triumph of Life* (1824), a dream allegory about the human condition, which breaks off at a point where it appears to be suggesting not the triumph, but the meaninglessness, of life.

John Keats (1795–1821)

The son of a livery-stable manager, Keats became a certificated apothecary in 1816 and subsequently trained as a surgeon, but abandoned this profession to pursue a literary career. His first collection, *Poems* (1817), which received a hostile critical reception, included "Sleep and Poetry" and the sonnet "On First Looking into Chapman's Homer". It was followed by *Endymion* (1818), a romance in four books, based on the Greek legend of a shepherd who falls in love with the moon goddess and is spirited away to live with her eternally. Best remembered for its opening line, "A thing of beauty is a joy for ever", *Endymion* is an uneven allegory about the poet-dreamer's quest for perfection.

His Finest Poetry

Keats's finest poetry appeared a year before his early death in *Poems of 1820*. This includes three narrative poems dramatizing a conflict between romantic enchantment and a world of colder actuality. In "Lamia", a young man's love for a serpent that has taken human shape ends when a philosopher calls her by her real name and she reverts to her original identity. In "Isabella or the Pot of Basil", Keats took his story from Boccaccio, using the appropriately Italianate stanza form of ottava rima for his medieval Italian subject. Romantic love is once again destroyed, when the Florentine heroine's beloved is murdered by her proud brothers.

In "The Eve of St Agnes", his most assured longer poem, Keats employed the Spenserian stanza for another medieval subject. Breathing life into the legend that a virgin may see a vision of her lover on St Agnes's Eve, he produced some of his most perfectly realized physical description to depict a vivid contrast between the wintry cold of external nature and the sensuous warmth of the lovers' interior, in this case allowing the romantic dream world to evade the constraints of everyday reality.

Poems of 1820 also contains Keats's unfinished epic poem, "Hyperion", and the five odes which secured his reputation as one of the greatest of English poets. The richly luxuriant language of the odes embodies Keats's belief in the power of beauty, while also lamenting its transience. "Beauty that must die" is the central theme of "To Autumn" and "To Melancholy". "On a Grecian Urn" suggests the ambiguity of the immortality conferred by art, by reflecting on the paradoxical spring-like situation of two lovers, who transcend death through being depicted on the urn, but whose love remains unconsummated in the frozen stasis of such representation. It culminates with the famous utterance, "Beauty is truth, truth beauty,—that is all/Ye know on earth, and all ye need to know". "To a Nightingale" sees the bird as a symbol of artistic immortality that offers release from "the weariness, the fever, and the fret" of the everyday world. "To Psyche" addresses a neglected pagan goddess who symbolises the human soul made immortal through love.

Seriously ill with tuberculosis, Keats travelled to Italy in late 1820 and died there the following year. He had composed his own epitaph: "Here lies one whose name was writ in water".

Other Romantic Poets

Although he died before the Romantic period, Thomas Chatterton, who committed suicide in 1770 at the age of seventeen, came to be seen as the epitome of Romantic genius, unable to survive in a hostile world. Keats dedicated *Endymion* to him and Wordsworth, referred to him as the "marvellous boy", whose early "gladness" descended into "despondency and madness" ("Resolution and Independence"). Henry Wallis's 1856 Pre-Raphaelite painting further contributed to the growth of the Chatterton myth.

Scotland's most famous poet, Robert Burns, was another important precursor of the Romantic movement, both in his use of ordinary speech in *Poems Chiefly in the Scottish Dialect* (1786), which Wordsworth and Coleridge greatly admired, and for his treatment of rustic and Gothic themes in works such as his finest narrative poem, *Tam o'Shanter* (1791).

Leigh Hunt, who was influential in promoting the reputations of Keats and Shelley, is best remembered for *The Story of Rimini* (1816) and his *Autobiography* (1850). Coleridge's associate, Robert Southey, was held in considerable esteem in his own day and became Poet Laureate in 1813, but his reputation declined after his death. Sir Walter Scott first established his reputation as a writer of historical verse romances and his work in this genre includes *The Lay of the Last Minstrel* (1805) and *Marmion* (1808). John Clare, the "Northamptonshire peasant poet", was acclaimed for his *Poems Descriptive of Rural Life and Scenery* (1820) and subsequently published *The Village Minstrel* (1821) and *The Shepherd's Calendar* (1827), but spent most of his later life in a lunatic asylum, where he continued to write.

Notable Romantic women poets include Hannah More, Charlotte Smith, Ann Yearsley, Mary Robinson, Helen Maria Williams and Felicia Dorothea Hemans, several of whom wrote poems that contributed to the campaign for the abolition of the slave trade. Byron's former lover, Lady Caroline Lamb, wrote *A New Canto* (1819), in which she adopted the persona of Byron and appropriated the style of *Don Juan* in order to mock him, along with a range of targets from contemporary society.

Romantic Prose

In addition to the Preface to the *Lyrical Ballads*, Coleridge's *Biographia Literaria* and Shelley's *Defence of Poetry*, other important non-fictional prose of the Romantic period includes Mary Wollstonecraft's pioneering feminist work, *A Vindication of the Rights of Women* (1792), which makes a powerful case for gender equality and among other things sees "female" characteristics such as submissiveness as the product of nurture rather than nature. William Godwin's *Enquiry Concerning Political Justice* (1793), which set out a

philosophy of human perfectibility, was the most influential political treatise of the early Romantic period, but its fame was comparatively short-lived.

Edmund Burke's prose masterpiece, *Reflections on the Revolution in France* (1790), took a conservative stand against the changes effected by the Jacobin revolutionaries and more generally lamented, "The age of chivalry is gone. That of sophisters, economists, and calculators, has succeeded; and the glory of Europe is extinguished forever."

Thomas Paine's *The Rights of Man* (1791–2) responded to Burke by justifying the revolutionaries and arguing the case for natural rights shared by all men; and, in its second part, compared the new French and American constitutions with that of Britain, to the detriment of the latter.

Important collections of essays include William Hazlitt's *English Comic Writers* (1819) and *The Spirit of the Age* (1825), a collection of portraits of his contemporaries, and Charles Lamb's *Essays of Elia* (Vol. I, 1823; Vol. II, 1833). Thomas De Quincey's autobiographical *Confessions of an English Opium Eater* (1822; enlarged 1856) describes the effects of his addiction to laudanum and his gradual success in moderating his habit. Keats's letters are notable for his comments on "beauty", "truth" and the Romantic imagination.

EARLY NINETEENTH-CENTURY FICTION

Sir Walter Scott (1771–1832)

The most highly regarded Romantic novelist of the nineteenth century, Scott began his writing career as a poet, achieving critical and popular success with *The Lay of the Last Minstrel* (1805), a six-canto poem in ballad verse based on a traditional story about a sixteenth-century feud in the Scottish Borders. Several further long narrative poems in a similar vein, including *Marmion* (1808) and *The Lady of the Lake* (1810), followed. Scott's first novel *Waverley* (1814) propelled his reputation to new heights and he followed this with several more "Waverley novels", which also offered vivid portraits of various aspects of recent Scottish history: *Guy Mannering* (1815), *The Antiquary* (1816), *The Black Dwarf* (1816), *Old Mortality* (1816), *Rob Roy* (1817), *The Heart of Midlothian* (1818), *The Bride of Lammermoor* (1819) and *A Legend of Montrose* (1819).

Beginning with *Ivanhoe* (1820), a romance set in the England of Richard I's time, Scott extended his prolific talents to fiction that recreated a broader range of historical eras and locations. Novels from this phase of his career include *The Abbot* (1820), *Kenilworth* (1821), *The Fortunes of Nigel* (1822), *Peveril of the Peak* (1822) *Quentin Durward* (1823), *Redgauntlet* (1824) and *The Talisman* (1825). *St Ronan's Well* (1824), a novel of manners set in a Scottish spa, was a rare departure into the nineteenth century.

He was knighted in 1820 and continued to be held in high esteem, but suffered financial ruin in 1825 and his novels written after this, which include *Woodstock* (1826) and *The Fair Maid of Perth* (1828), show a falling off in his talent.

The Strength of Scott's Writing

Scott's fiction drew on his reading of ballads and medieval romances and his various other antiquarian interests. Its strengths lie in its atmospheric descriptions of landscape, its vivid depiction of minor characters, its skill in evoking past periods—albeit in a romanticized manner—and its capacity for chronicling historical processes. During his lifetime he was frequently compared with Shakespeare and his reputation remained high throughout the nineteenth century, nowhere more so than in his native Scotland, where he became a cultural icon and a model for Victorian codes of genteel behaviour. Changes in taste, particularly a reaction against the kind of melodramatic romanticism his fiction embodies, subsequently led to a decline in his popularity, though he continues to be respected as a major regional novelist and as the author of memorable shorter poems (originally in his longer works), *e.g.* "Lochinvar" and "Breathes There the Man".

Jane Austen (1775-1817)

The daughter of a Hampshire rector, Jane Austen has been described as the first major modern novelist. Her superficially restrained and psychologically subtle fiction is a world away from the expansiveness and magniloquence of Scott, but it has stood the test of time better and today she is the most widely read novelist of her era. Her first piece of extended fiction, *Love and Friendship* (1790), was a burlesque of Richardson and in one sense her work belongs to the counter-tradition of Fielding, since it employs irony to satirize deviations from social norms. However, its range is narrower than Fielding's—it usually deals with "three or four families in a country village", with occasional forays into fashionable town society—and her characterization is more complex.

Her first full-length novel *Northanger Abbey* (posthumously published in 1818) involves a satire on Gothic fiction such as *The Mysteries of Udolpho*, as the heroine Catherine Moreland wrongly imagines that that the house of the title conceals dark secrets. It also engages with the themes that dominate Austen's subsequent fiction: the witty observation of social manners and the moral education of the heroine. The ironic first sentence of *Pride and Prejudice* (1813), "It is a truth universally acknowledged, that a single man in possession of a good fortune, must be in want of a wife", introduces the principal subject of Austen's most famous comedy of manners. The "universally acknowledged" truth in question represents the perspective of Mrs Bennet, the mother of five daughters whom she is anxious to marry off, and courtship and marriage are the pivot on which the plot turns. The central figure is Mrs Bennet's second daughter, Elizabeth, who initially rejects the advances of the seemingly arrogant Fitzwilliam D'Arcy, believing him to be the author of her family's misfortunes, but comes to learn that her prejudice, which has caused her to misinterpret his character, surpasses his pride.

The Success of *Emma*

The heroine of *Emma* (1816) is generally viewed as Austen's most lively creation; she is certainly her most meddlesome. Her efforts to broker a marriage for the illegitimate Harriet Smith, whom she adopts as a protegée, prove disastrous. Her blindness to her own feelings involves a level of self-delusion that outstrips that of either Catherine Moreland or Elizabeth Bennet, but once again the novel charts her moral education and she is finally united with the discerning Mr. Knightley. The heroine of *Mansfield Park* (1814), Fanny Price, is more passive. She is the virtuous poor relative in the house of the well-to-do Bertram family and her integrity offers a sharp contrast to the moral laxity that invades the country house of the title while its patriarch, Sir Thomas Bertram is away in Antigua. The house represents a stable upper middle class English social world, which is contrasted with disorder in the urban worlds of London and Portsmouth. Order is finally restored and Fanny's story has a Cinderella-like happy ending, when her love for Sir Thomas's son, Edmund, results in marriage.

Austen's other major novels, written at the opposite ends of her writing career, *Sense and Sensibility* (1811) and *Persuasion* (1818), both deal with conflicts between love and family obligations and include sections set in fashionable town society.

Thomas Love Peacock (1785-1866)

A close friend of Shelley, whom he often advised on literary and philosophical matters, Peacock is best remembered as a satirical novelist, whose fiction debates and ridicules many of the fashionable social and political attitudes of his day. Several of his novels employ a country house setting, in which a group of guests discuss contemporary intellectual controversies, while the novels themselves incorporate a miscellany of farcical elements, songs and improbable love stories that culminate in incongruously perfunctory happy endings. Novels of this kind include *Headlong Hall* (1816), where the characters represent opposed political and social views and the action ends in four hastily contrived marriages, *Nightmare Abbey* (1818), in which the attitudes of Coleridge, Byron and Shelley are all mocked, *Crotchet Castle* (1831), in which a Coleridge figure is once again included among the satirical portraits, and the later *Gryll Grange* (1860-1), in which a satirical view of mid-Victorian England is juxtaposed with a nostalgic vision of the recent past. His other novels include *Maid Marian* (1822) and *The Misfortunes of Elphin* (1829).

THE VICTORIAN NOVEL

Charles Dickens (1812-70)

Dickens's extraordinary popularity began with the publication of *The Pickwick Papers* (1836-7), which grew from a commission to write a series of sporting sketches and which contains the first of his many memorable characters that have become part of the English popular imagination, Mr Pickwick and his manservant Sam Weller. Prior to this, he had published *Sketches by Boz* (1835-6). *Oliver Twist* (1838) was his first popular masterpiece to combine vivid action and characterization with a critique of the divisions of the class-ridden society of his day, which he felt had been intensified by measures such as the Poor Law of 1834. It was followed by: *Nicholas Nickleby* (1839), which in its scenes set at Dotheboys Hall attacked the harsh regime of contemporary Yorkshire boarding schools; the hugely popular, albeit sentimental *The Old Curiosity Shop* (1841); *Barnaby Rudge* (1841); and *Martin Chuzzlewit* (1843).

The 1840s also saw the publication of the first and best-loved of his Christmas books, *A Christmas Carol* (1843), in which he created the memorable figure of the miser, Ebenezer Scrooge.

His Finest Novels

In the years that followed Dickens produced many of his finest novels: *Dombey and Son* (1848); *David Copperfield* (1850), his most autobiographical work as well as his own favourite novel; *Bleak House* (1853); *Hard Times* (1854), an attack on Utilitarianism set in the fictional northern city of Coketown; *Little Dorrit* (1857); *A Tale of Two Cities* (1859), a novel set during the French Revolution; *Great Expectations* (1861); and *Our Mutual Friend* (1865). All of these novels blend serious social criticism and entertainment, albeit in varying degrees.

Great Expectations, with its rich gallery of characters (the betrayed spinster Miss Havisham, the blacksmith Joe Gargery, the convict Magwitch, the lawyer Jaggers and his clerk Wemmick's Aged Parent among them), keeps these two aspects of his work in perfect balance, as the hero Pip slowly comes to recognize the class snobbery that has made him ashamed of his early origins.

Bleak House, where the interminable case of Jarndyce and Jarndyce serves as a metaphor for the British legal system and *Little Dorrit*, where the bureaucracy of the Circumlocution Office becomes a central symbol of the paralysis at the heart of government, are longer and more complex novels that also show Dickens's talent at its finest.

Dickens and Social Injustice

Dickens's concern with social injustices has often been seen to stem from his early experience of life. His father, on whom he based aspects of Mr Micawber in *David Copperfield*, was jailed for debt in London's Marshalsea prison, which becomes a central setting in *Little Dorrit*. As a consequence of the family's misfortunes, Dickens himself had to work in a blacking factory, where he became aware of the seamier side of London life at an early age.

Dickens has been criticized for his sentimentality, the disorderliness of some of his plots and his tendency to replace character with caricature. He remains one of the greatest storytellers in English literature, a social critic whose reforming fervour played a part in eradicating some of the social ills he dramatized, a writer with a unique flair for bringing the many facets of London life alive in an almost tactile way and the creator of many of the most memorable characters in the English novel.

Arguably the most prodigious genius among Victorian writers, he gave highly popular public readings of his work throughout his career. He collapsed during his final reading tour (1869-70) and died soon afterwards, leaving his last novel, *The Mystery of Edwin Drood* (1870) incomplete.

William Makepeace Thackeray (1811–63)

In the middle of the nineteenth century, when his most successful novel *Vanity Fair* (1847-8) was serialized at the same time as *David Copperfield*, Thackeray's work was frequently compared with that of Dickens, though his popularity with the general public never reached quite the same heights. A satirist of class snobbery, he did not share Dickens's sympathy for the criminalized poor. Thus the picaresque hero of his novel *The Luck of Barry Lyndon* (1844), set in the eighteenth century, is a figure who has more affinities with Fielding's Jonathan Wild than the characters of *Oliver Twist*.

His first major success came with *The Book of Snobs* (1846-7), a collection of portraits originally published in the magazine *Punch*, which casts a critical eye on Victorian class-consciousness.

Vanity Fair and Henry Esmond

Vanity Fair, one of the masterpieces of nineteenth-century "realism", offers a satirical critique of upper middle-class society at the beginning of the nineteenth century. Sub-titled a "novel without a hero", its declared purpose is "to indicate, in cheerful terms, that we are for the most part an abominably foolish and selfish people 'desperately wicked' and all eager after vanities". The machinations of its most memorable character, the scheming Becky Sharp, as she makes her way up the social ladder, attract the sympathy of many readers, in much the same way as Defoe's Moll Flanders' predicament has been seen to vindicate *her* behaviour.

Thackeray admired *The English Humorists of the Eighteenth Century* (the title of a lectures series he published in 1853) and like *Barry Lyndon*, his novel *Henry Esmond* (1852) and its sequel *The Virginians* (1857) were set in this century. *Henry Esmond*, his finest achievement after *Vanity Fair*, deserts the romantic heroism characteristic of much historical fiction in favour of psychological complexity and an ambiguous representation of social forces. At the end of the novel, Henry moves to Virginia and *The Virginians*, which includes scenes set against the backdrop of the American War of Independence, follows the fortunes of later generations of his family.

Other Novels

Thackeray's other novels include *Catherine* (1839–40), the semi-autobiographical *Pendennis* (1850) and *The Newcomes* (1853-5). His fiction frequently employs direct addresses to his readers, *e.g.* "If Miss Rebecca Sharp had determined in her heart upon making the conquest of this big beau, I don't think, ladies, we have any right to blame her." This intrusiveness has seemed dated to some modern readers, but admiration for his comic realism and his satirical exposure of Victorian hypocrisy have helped to re-establish Thackeray's reputation as a major novelist in recent years.

The Brontës

Although *Jane Eyre* (1847) and *Wuthering Heights* (1847) are universally accepted as classics of English fiction, in their own day they were controversial works that challenged the conventions of early Victorian fiction and the social values of the era, particularly with regard to their representation of male-female relationships. Their respective authors, Charlotte (1816-55) and Emily (1818–48) Brontë published their work under names that concealed their gender identity, Currer and Ellis Bell, while their sister Anne (1820–49) wrote under the name of Acton Bell.

Early Life

The sisters grew up in a parsonage in the then-remote village of Haworth on the edge of the Yorkshire moors. As children, they invented their own private fictional worlds, which particularly in the case of Emily seem to prefigure the alternative worlds of their adult writing. They were strongly influenced by the Romantics (particularly Byron)

and their novels introduced a new Romantic dimension into prose fiction, particularly in their emphasis on the interconnectedness of external nature and human character and their use of patterns of unifying organic imagery.

The central situation of Charlotte's masterpiece *Jane Eyre* is a sophisticated version of the plot of Richardson's *Pamela*: Jane is a governess, who finds herself torn between the conflicting claims of passion and restraint, when her employer Rochester, whose "mad" wife, Bertha, is immured in the attic of his house, tries to persuade her into an extra-marital liaison. Circumstances finally allow Jane, who takes the view that "Women are supposed to be very calm generally: but women feel just as men feel", to reconcile the forces that threaten to tear her apart and marry Rochester on equal terms, having inherited money of her own. She becomes her "own mistress" and escapes from the position of social inferiority that characterizes the situation of many earlier heroines of English novels.

Wuthering Heights

No such resolution is possible in the story of the love of Cathy and Heathcliff, which dominates Emily Brontë's only published novel, *Wuthering Heights*. Its plot dramatizes a disparity in social background and world-views that drives the lovers apart and the novel reaches a tragic conclusion midway when Cathy dies. Nevertheless the commitment to passion is more total than in *Jane Eyre*: love transcends the grave when, after her death, Cathy's ghost haunts Heathcliff. At the same time, *Wuthering Heights* encompasses several other stories, centred on relationships between the contrasted Linton and Earnshaw families across two generations and reconciliations are achieved at the end. The novel's narrative technique is one of the most complex to be found in English fiction prior to the work of Joseph Conrad and Henry James. Its intricately plotted time-scheme and its two narrators, the outsider Lockwood and the old family servant Nelly Dean, lend credence to what might otherwise seem a far-fetched sequence of events. Charlotte's other novels were *Shirley* (1849), *Villette* (1853) and *The Professor* (1857).

Anne Brontë

Anne Brontë is remembered as the author of *Agnes Grey* (1847), which like *Jane Eyre* deals with the life of a governess, and the darker, more complex *Tenant of Wildfell Hall* (1848). The latter's account of a woman's suffering at the hands of a drunken husband seems remarkably modern, but on its first appearance represented another aspect of the Brontës' fiction that challenged contemporary expectations. Prior to the success of their novels, the three sisters had published *Poems by Currer, Ellis, and Acton Bell* (1846). Emily, who wrote a number of powerful short lyrics on death, is generally considered the finest poet of the three.

Anthony Trollope (1815–82)

Trollope is best remembered for his Barsetshire and Palliser series of novels, but together they constitute less than a quarter of his prolific fictional output. He first became famous with his fourth novel, *The Warden* (1855), which inaugurated the sequence set in the fictional West Country county of Barsetshire. It was followed by *Barchester Towers* (1857), a perceptive study of the impact of social changes on the community, which further augmented Trollope's reputation with the reading public. The other volumes in the series, which benefit from being read as part of the evolving sequence, are *Doctor Thorne* (1858), *Framley Parsonage* (1860–1), *The Small House at Allington* (1862–4) and *The Last Chronicle of Barsetshire* (1866–7). The Barsetshire novels offer a microcosm of English rural society in transition in the mid-Victorian period with a particular insight into ecclesiastical politics. Their particular strength lies in their realistic rendition of "ordinary" events.

Trollope's later fiction, including his Palliser novels, is more concerned with urban society and parliamentary political life. The Palliser novels are *Can You Forgive Her?* (1864–5), *Phineas Finn: The Irish Member* (1867–8), *The Eustace Diamonds* (1871–3), *Phineas Redux* (1873–4), *The Prime Minister* (1875–6) and *The Duke's Children*

(1879–80). Other later novels include *The Claverings* (1866–7), *He Knew He Was Right* (1868–9), *The American Senator* (1876-7) and *Dr Wortle's School* (1880). His longest novel, *The Way We Live Now* (1874–5), a satire on speculative commercialism, is now sometimes regarded as his finest work. Its depiction of stock exchange gambling has given it a particular relevance for contemporary society.

Trollope travelled widely, recording his impressions of other societies in such works as *The West Indies and the Spanish Main* (1859) and *Australia and New Zealand* (1873–4). For most of his life he worked for the post office and, literature apart, has a claim to fame as the man responsible for the installation of the first post box: on Guernsey in 1852.

The Condition of England Novel

Towards the middle of the nineteenth century a sense of the widening gaps between different segments of English society was expressed in a group of novels primarily concerned with what later became known as "the Condition of England". Such novels included Benjamin Disraeli's *Coningsby* (1844) and *Sybil* (1845), Elizabeth Gaskell's *Mary Barton* (1848) and *North and South* (1855), Charles Kingsley's *Alton Locke* (1850) and Dickens's *Hard Times*. Partly inspired by Carlyle's warning that the class divisions created by the Industrial Revolution were a recipe for revolution, Condition of England novels drew attention to disparities between the industrialized north and the more affluent south, the human consequences of mechanization, the need for a more egalitarian educational system and abuses of power occasioned by the new manufacturing industries.

George Eliot (1819–80)

George Eliot (the pen name of Mary Ann Evans) grew up in the English Midlands and her early fiction deals with the lives and loves of ordinary people from the region. It includes the three stories that make up *Scenes of Clerical Life* (1858) and the novels, *Adam Bede* (1859), *The Mill on the Floss* (1860) and *Silas Marner* (1861). *Adam Bede* tells the tragic story of Hetty Sorrel, who murders her illegitimate child. *The Mill on the Floss* is a more autobiographical work, in which the imaginative heroine Maggie Tulliver struggles to find love and self-fulfilment. The shorter *Silas Marner* is a moral fable about a miserly weaver, who is brought back into the human fold by the advent of a small child into his solitary life.

George Eliot's Masterpiece

If Eliot's career had ended here, she would be remembered as a fine regional novelist, with a talent for exploring the intricacies of human motivation, but her subsequent fiction is more ambitious in scope and more penetrating in its analysis of social issues. After broadening her fictional horizons with *Romola* (1862–3), a historical novel set in Renaissance Florence, she subsequently published three novels that were markedly more complex than her early work. *Felix Holt: The Radical* (1866), in which she attempts to emulate the form of a Greek tragic trilogy, is about rural electioneering at the time of the First Reform Bill (1832), a defining moment in British social history. Her masterpiece, *Middlemarch* (1871–2), a novel of epic proportions, is set in the same period. It interweaves four complex stories, to provide an intellectually probing study of "provincial life" during a time of rapid change. Its more memorable characters include Dorothea Brooke, a later more developed version of Maggie Tulliver, her academically sterile husband Casaubon, who is trying to write a "key to all mythologies" and the progressive young doctor, Tertius Lydgate, whose passion for medicine parallels Dorothea's for scholarship. However, its overall effect depends less upon the success of its individual characters than its skill in demonstrating their interaction in the novel's social microcosm.

A similar tone of high seriousness informs *Daniel Deronda* (1874–6), in which two plots gradually converge, with the initially self-centred Gwendolen Harleth finding sustenance in the moral and emotional values of Judaism, a corpus that offers an alternative to her laissez-faire English upbringing.

Robert Louis Stevenson (1850–94)

The Edinburgh-born Stevenson was one of the most prodigious and eclectic talents of nineteenth-century writing, though he is best remembered as the author of classic children's books and one of the great horror stories of English literature, *The Strange Case of Dr Jekyll and Mr Hyde* (1886). *Treasure Island* (1883) with its boy-narrator Jim Hawkins's story of buried treasure and pirates is both a brilliant piece of children's fiction and a novel that suggests the complexities of "evil", one of Stevenson's recurrent themes, in its representation of the figure of Long John Silver. Earlier R.M. Ballantyne's *The Coral Island* (1871) had made a similar use of an island setting for an adventure story that derives much of its appeal from taking a group of boys into unknown territory.

Stevenson's *Kidnapped* (1886) is a darker tale of dispossession, in which the hero David Balfour suffers at the hands of his cruel Uncle Ebenezer. *Dr Jekyll and Mr Hyde* is a study of a split personality, which among other things reflects Victorian unease about the impact of Darwinian theory on beliefs about identity. Other important novels by Stevenson include the sequel to *Kidnapped, Catriona* (1893), *The Black Arrow* (1888) and *The Master of Ballantrae* (1889). Suffering from ill health, he left Britain in 1888 and settled in Samoa, enjoying a new lease of literary life. His writing during his Samoan years, which includes the novellas, *The Beach of Fales* (1893) and *The Ebb-Tide* (1894), protests against the colonial exploitation of the South Seas.

Schoolboy Fiction, Adventure Stories and the Literature of Empire

Unlike Stevenson, the majority of other Victorian writers of adventure stories can be seen as contributing, intentionally or otherwise, to the late Victorian literature of Empire, often developing links between the values instilled in the English public school and subsequent service in the Empire. Classic schoolboy novels that suggest such connections include Thomas Hughes's *Tom Brown's Schooldays* (1857) and Rudyard Kipling's *Stalky & Co* (1899), which closes with its former schoolboys in India. Such writing was also a staple of popular magazines such as the *Boys Own Paper*, where writers like Talbot Baines Reed, later famed for the classic public school novel, *The Fifth Form at St Dominic's* (serialized in the *Boys Own Paper* in 1907), linked team games and a sporting ethic of fair play with Christian morality and charitable work in the Empire.

Haggard and Henty

Rider Haggard's *King Solomon's Mines* (1885), the story of an expedition to find diamonds in southern Africa and its sequels *Allan Quatermain* (1887) and *She* (1887) are notable among the many adventure novels of the period. The heroic thrust of Haggard's work was sometimes seen as a counterforce to naturalism's more pessimistic view of people's capacity to influence their situation. G.A. Henty's numerous tales of heroic virtue, such as *With Clive in India* (1884) and *With Wolfe in Canada* (1887), characteristically link derring-do, Christianity and Empire. Other romances of the period with "exotic" locations include Anthony Hope Hawkins's *The Prisoner of Zenda* (1894), in which Hope created the mythical European country of Ruritania, and W.H. Hudson's *Green Mansions* (1904), a tale set in the South American rain forest.

Earlier Captain Frederick Marryat's stories of sea adventurers had included *Peter Simple* (1834) and *Mr Midshipman Easy* (1836). John Buchan continued the tradition of adventure writing in the early twentieth century with novels such as *Prester John* (1910) and *The Thirty-Nine Steps* (1915).

Novels of Sensation and Mystery

The Victorian vogue for melodrama, sensation and mystery reached its apogee in the novels of Wilkie Collins, whose *The Woman in White* (1860) demonstrates considerable skill in creating suspense. Collins's *The Moonstone* (1868) laid the groundwork for the modern detective novel, though the American Edgar Allan Poe, had pioneered detective fiction in his short stories about August

Dupin, particularly "Murders in the Rue Morgue" and "The Purloined Letter". Dupin was a forerunner of the most famous detective of the nineteenth century, Sir Arthur Conan Doyle Sherlock Holmes, whose use of deductive reasoning demonstrated a similar fascination with what Poe termed "ratiocination". At the beginning of the twentieth century, the Catholic convert G.K. Chesterton took the figure in a new direction by relating his detective, Father Brown's skill in solving crimes to his capacity to understand evil.

Sir Arthur Conan Doyle (1859–1930)

Holmes and his omnipresent assistant, Dr Watson first appeared in the novels *A Study in Scarlet* (1887) and *The Sign of Four* (1890), but it was the short stories that Conan Doyle wrote for *The Strand Magazine* in the 1890s that secured his popularity. They were collected in *The Adventures of Sherlock Holmes* (1892) and *The Memoirs of Sherlock Holmes* (1894). Doyle killed Holmes off, when he had him plunge to his death at the Reichenbach Falls in Switzerland in a struggle with his arch-enemy Professor Moriarty, but he was forced to resurrect him in response to public demand. The detective reappeared in several subsequent volumes, including Doyle's best-known work, *The Hound of the Baskervilles* (1902) and the short story collections, *The Return of Sherlock Holmes* (1905) and *The Case-Book of Sherlock Holmes* (1927).

The Gothic Novel

At the end of the nineteenth century, the Gothic novel reached new heights in Bram Stoker's classic vampire novel, *Dracula* (1897). Written as a series of first-person narratives that partly help to authenticate its sensational subject-matter, Stoker's novel drew on pre-existing vampire literature to create the figure of the Transylvanian Count who has become the archetypal vampire of the popular imagination. Contemporary reviewers appear to have been blind to the sexual implications of vampirism, which were to become a major part of the Dracula myth in the film treatments of the twentieth century.

Thomas Hardy (1840–1928)

Often described as England's one major tragic novelist, Hardy set his work in the fictional West Country region of Wessex, based on his native Dorset. It provided him with an environment that was both very specifically localized and a stage for archetypal human dramas. In all his novels, the human action is played out against a vividly realized rural landscape, which can become a character in its own right. *The Return of the Native* (1878) is set against the landscape of Egdon Heath, described at the outset as having "a lonely face, suggesting tragic possibilities". The setting of *The Woodlanders* (1887), Hintock Woods, is similarly crucial to the action, while the experiences of the heroine of *Tess of the D'Urbervilles* (1891) in a number of different landscapes reflect her situation and state of mind at each particular juncture.

The causes of Hardy's tragic protagonists' downfalls vary. Sometimes, as in *The Mayor of Casterbridge* (1886), where he quotes the dictum, "character is fate", they can be attributed to character flaws: Henchard, the mayor of the novel's title, sells his wife, while drunk. Elsewhere, as in *Tess of the D'Urbervilles*, where Hardy writes in the final paragraph "The President of the Immortals, in Aeschylean phrase, had ended his sport with Tess", fate seems the dominant force. At the same time Tess, like several other Hardy characters, is a victim of the moral conventions of her day and throughout his work, Hardy demonstrates an acute sense of the impact of social forces, particularly moral codes and mechanization, on individuals and agrarian communities. His other major novels include *Under the Greenwood Tree* (1872), *Far from the Madding Crowd* (1874), *The Trumpet-Major* (1880) and *Jude the Obscure* (1896).

Later Novels and Poetry

The later novels, *Tess* and *Jude*, are not without melodrama, but the tragic fates of their protagonists suggest the influence of Naturalism and a belief in social determinism. The sub-title of *Tess*, "a pure woman", attracted criticism, since in conventional terms its heroine was a "fallen woman"; and the sympathetic representation of extramarital sexual relations in *Jude the Obscure* evoked a similar response. When a copy of *Jude* was burned by a bishop on the grounds of the novel's supposed obscenity, Hardy forsook fiction and turned to poetry, commenting ruefully, "Nobody will be hurt by my poetry, because nobody will read it".

He wrote verse throughout the remainder of his life. His poetry ranges between simple ballads of folk experience that drew on local Dorset traditions, particularly the work of the Dorset poet, William Barnes, and more personal lyrics, notable among which is a series of elegiac poems written after the death of his wife, Emma, in 1912. These were published in *Satires of Circumstance, Lyrics and Reveries* (1914). His other poetry includes *Wessex Poems and Other Verses* (1898), *Poems of the Past and Present* (1902) and the epic drama, *The Dynasts* (1903–08).

Naturalism in English Fiction

In the latter part of the nineteenth century, the collapse of traditional belief-systems, the influence of Darwinism and a growing awareness of the effect of environment on character led to the rise of the heightened form of social realism known as "Naturalism". Its major theorist was the French novelist Émile Zola and it was never as important a movement in England as in France and the USA, where its practitioners included Stephen Crane, Frank Norris and Theodore Dreiser. Notable English naturalistic novels of the *fin de siècle* years include George Gissing's *New Grub Street* (1891) and George Moore's *Esther Waters* (1894) and its influence is also apparent in the determinism of Hardy's *Tess* and *Jude*.

The continuing, albeit limited, popularity of Naturalism in the early twentieth century can be seen in Arnold Bennett's novels, such as *The Old Wives' Tale* (1908) and *Riceyman Steps* (1923), which provide meticulously detailed, warts-and-all accounts of the lives of ordinary people. However, for Modernist writers such as Virginia Woolf and D.H. Lawrence, Naturalism was a form of fiction that, despite its care in rendering such details, failed to engage with all that was most vital in human experience. Woolf distanced herself from Bennett in her essay "Mr Bennett and Mrs Brown", in which she argued he completely failed to capture the character of people, such as "Mrs Brown", an ordinary woman in a railway carriage. Lawrence referred to Bennett as "an old imitator", commenting scathingly, "Tell Arnold Bennett that all rules of construction hold good only for novels which are copies of other novels".

VICTORIAN LITERATURE

Elizabeth Barrett Browning (1806–61)

Born in England into a plantation-owning Jamaican Creole family, Elizabeth Barrett became a vehement critic of slavery and other social injustices. Sometimes remembered as the wife of Robert Browning, particularly as represented in the film versions of Rudolf Besier's play *The Barretts of Wimpole Street* (1930), she was a major poet in her own right. She was considered a strong candidate for the post of Poet Laureate when Wordsworth died in 1850 and had a greater reputation as a poet than her husband-to-be when they met in 1845.

Her first volume to attract critical favour was *The Seraphim and Other Poems* (1838). A lung condition she first developed as a child, a spinal injury and grief at her brother's death from drowning in 1838 rendered her an invalid and recluse in the house of her domineering father. *Poems* (1844), which included "The Cry of the Children", secured her reputation and led to the beginnings of her correspondence with Browning. After their elopement and marriage, they moved to Florence, where her health improved and she lived for the remainder of her life.

Her *Sonnets from the Portuguese*, which appeared in *Poems* (1850), is a sequence of forty-four love poems written to Browning, which has no connection with any Portuguese originals. It contains her most famous poem, "How do I love thee,/ Let me count the ways". *Aurora Leigh* (1857) is a verse novel, in which she explores a broad range of social issues, including the "Woman Question", the predicament of the poor, child labour and the role of poetry. Her support for Italian unification informs *Casa Guidi Windows* (1851) and *Poems before Congress* (1860). Her *Last Poems* were published posthumously in 1862. Her popularity declined after her death, but the feminist dimension of her work and its engagement with other social and political issues have occasioned a revival of interest in recent decades.

Alfred, Lord Tennyson (1809–92)

Raised in a Lincolnshire rectory, Tennyson attended Cambridge, where he developed a close friendship with Arthur Hugh Hallam, with whom he subsequently travelled in continental Europe. His *Poems, Chiefly Lyrical* (1830), written under the influence of the Romantics, met with little success, but includes a number of poems for which he is remembered, among them "Mariana", "The Palace of Art" and "The Lady of Shalott", his first important poem on an Arthurian subject. *Poems* (1833) includes "The Two Voices" and "The Lotos-Eaters". Hallam had become engaged to Tennyson's sister, Emily, but died suddenly at the age of twenty-two, and the grief-stricken Tennyson commenced the sequence of 131 elegiac poems that would eventually be published as *In Memoriam: A.H.H.* (1850) in 1833. *English Idyls and Other Poems* (1842) contains some of his finest short poems: "Morte d'Arthur", "Ulysses", "Break, break, break" and "Locksley Hall", a disappointed lover's trochaic monologue, which engages with the state of contemporary society.

His Best-Known Lyrics

The Princess (1847) is a long blank verse poem, containing some of Tennyson's best-known lyrics, including "Tears, Idle Tears". Later satirized by Gilbert and Sullivan in their comic-opera *Princess Ida*, it is an incipiently feminist poem: the eponymous heroine rejects her betrothed and founds a university for women. The lovers *are* eventually united, but the romantic resolution is tempered by a passage which looks forward to their married future in which "man be more of woman, she of man". *In Memoriam* begins as a moving expression of personal loss, but expands outwards to encompass a wide range of philosophical and social issues, progressing from a deep sense of doubt to an affirmative conclusion in which new scientific knowledge is reconciled with Biblical teachings. It was published in the year of Wordsworth's death and its immediate popularity was a factor in Tennyson's succeeding him as Poet Laureate.

Tennyson and Queen Victoria

His work was greatly admired by Prince Albert, Queen Victoria's consort, and he became the favourite poet of the Queen herself, who is said to have held his poems second only to the Bible. He eventually accepted a baronetcy from her in 1884. Tennyson's Laureateship led to the writing of poems on such subjects as the death of Wellington (1852), the opening of the International Exhibition of 1862 and, most famously, "The Charge of the Light Brigade" (1854). *Maud* (1855) is a mono-drama about a luckless young man, which inveighs against the materialism of the age and contains a number of popular lyrics.

The *Idylls of the King* (1859–85) is a series of twelve poems on the Arthurian legend, which have the encyclopaedic range of epic poetry and include several self-contained narratives, such as that of Geraint and Enid. They were enormously popular in Tennyson's own day, but have been less well regarded by subsequent critics and the consensus of later opinion has been that his greatest gift was as a lyric poet. However, read as an allegory in which the fortunes of Camelot relate to contemporary society, the *Idylls* offer a fascinating exploration of the changing spirit of the age. *Tiresias and Other Poems* (1885) includes "Locksley Hall Sixty Years After", another expression of personal loss that offers a conservative commentary on the state of the nation, as the speaker attacks the dominance of scientific values and the social consequences of industrialization.

Other work from the period of Tennyson's

Laureateship includes the highly popular narrative poem, *Enoch Arden* (1864), *Ballads and Other Poems* (1880) and the plays, *Queen Mary* (1875), *The Cup* (1884) and *Becket* (1884). By the time of his death Tennyson was a public institution, but his reputation had dwindled among his younger contemporaries.

Robert Browning (1812–89)

Browning was born into a nonconformist family in South London and was mainly privately educated. His early work was written under the influence of Shelley, and in poems such as *Paracelsus* (1835), a study of the Swiss alchemist, and *Sordello* (1840), in which he took one of Dante's contemporaries as his subject, he combined metaphysical and poetic inquiry with a talent for dramatizing individual psychologies that was to become one of the main characteristics of his subsequent verse.

His greatest achievements were in the form of the dramatic monologue, a genre he made uniquely his own, creating personae with a psychological complexity more normally associated with the novel and rendering them in a range of colloquial and unconventional registers. Most of his finest work in this mode was published in the various parts of *Bells and Pomegranates* (1841–6) and *Men and Women* (1855). It includes "My Last Duchess", "The Bishop Orders His Tomb at St Praxed's Church", "Fra Lippo Lippi", "Bishop Blougram's Apology" and "Andrea del Sarto". His skill as a writer of narrative poems can be seen in "The Pied Piper of Hamelin", "How They Brought the Good News from Ghent to Aix" and "Childe Roland to the Dark Tower Came".

Browning's plays mainly belong to his early period. They include *Pippa Passes* (1841), *A Blot in the 'Scutcheon* (1843) and *Colombe's Birthday* (1844). Some were never intended for performance and generally they show a surer touch in the handling of character than action.

Marriage and Italy

Browning's admiration for Elizabeth Barrett's poetry led him to write to her and they eventually eloped and married in 1846. They settled in Italy, a country which he had first visited in 1838 and which provided the inspiration for many of his most famous works, and lived there until her death in 1861. His "Home Thoughts from Abroad", particularly remembered for its opening "Oh, to be in England/ Now that April's there", was written in Tuscany. The serialized publication of *The Ring and the Book* (1868–9), a poem of more than 20,000 lines, in monthly instalments, secured Browning's reputation with a wider reading public. It tells the story of a seventeenth-century Roman murder from several different viewpoints, once again demonstrating his virtuosity in handling dramatized figures, while also covering an encyclopaedic range of subjects.

During his later years Browning's poetic output continued unabated. Notable works from his last two decades include *Red-Cotton Nightcap Country* (1873), *The Inn Album* (1875), *Dramatic Idyls* (1879–80) and *Asolando* (1889). The foundation of the Browning Society in 1881 reflects the adulation in which he was held by a section of the late Victorian reading public. Along with Tennyson, he was regarded as one of the two pre-eminent poets of the period.

Matthew Arnold (1822–88)

The son of Thomas Arnold, the famous headmaster who made Rugby School a model for nineteenth-century middle-class education, Matthew Arnold was a polymath who took a leading role in many of the cultural debates of the Victorian era and became Professor of Poetry at Oxford in 1858. Today he is best known for his literary criticism and writings on the state of English culture. However, his poetry includes some of the finest nineteenth-century lyrics, among them his "Marguerite" poems and his best-known short poem, "Dover Beach" (1867), a powerful expression of the uncertainties of the age, written in melancholy slow-moving verse. Three longer narrative poems, "Tristram and Iseult" (1852), "Sohrab and Rustum" (1853) and "Balder Dead" (1855) respectively turned to medieval, eastern and Norse mythology for heroic subjects, while treating them in an unconventionally sombre vein. Arnold's elegiac poems include "The Scholar-Gipsy" (1853), which laments the impossibility of a simple pastoral response to landscape in the troubled climate of Victorian doubt, and "Thyrsis" (1867), a monody on the death of his friend, Arthur Hugh Clough. *Empedocles on Etna* (1852) is a verse drama.

Arnold's Literary Criticism

Arnold's literary criticism laid the foundations for the development of the subject along detached and "disinterested" lines and was influential in the construction of English literature as an object of academic study in the late nineteenth and early twentieth century. *Culture and Anarchy* (1869) advanced an idealistic view of culture as a kind of secular religion, seeing it as "the best that has been thought and said in the world", a definition that remained popular until the middle of the twentieth century. Written under the influence of Cardinal Newman, his later writings on the religious controversies of the day, which include *Literature and Dogma* (1873), were an attempt to reconcile rationalism and faith. Arnold saw his work as a response to the main movements of Victorian thought that combined the emotion of Tennyson with the intellect of Browning. In his poem "To a Friend", he said of Sophocles that he "saw life steadily, and saw it whole" and his own response to what he viewed as the "sick disease" of contemporary life can be seen as similarly balanced and harmonious.

The Rossettis and the Pre-Raphaelites

Founded in 1848, the Pre-Raphaelite Brotherhood was a movement in art and literature that rejected the prevalent cultural fashions of the day in favour of a return to what it saw as the simplicity of the medieval era. Its members included Holman Hunt, John Everett Millais and Dante Gabriel Rossetti. While its most significant achievements were in painting, its poetry included noteworthy work by Rossetti, which employed archaic language and mystical symbolism and, with the exception of "Jenny" (1870), a ballad about a London prostitute, found its subjects in medieval, particularly Arthurian, legends.

His best-known poem, "The Blessed Damozel" (1850), reflects an idealized Platonic conception of love and was followed by his later painting of the same theme. Rossetti's sister, Christina, is best known for her collection *Goblin Market and Other Poems* (1862). Contemporary critics have found homoerotic tendencies and a tension between sensuality and renunciation in its title-poem, a gnomic allegory about two sisters who exemplify different aspects of nineteenth-century womanhood. Such a tension is typical of much of her poetry, in which a mystical spiritualism, born out of her high Anglican faith, co-exists with eroticism. Her verse demonstrates considerable technical virtuosity and she was a particularly accomplished writer of sonnets.

Her later collections include *The Prince's Progress and Other Poems* (1866) and *A Pageant and Other Poems* (1881). Several other poets were associated with the Pre-Raphaelites, though they were not members of the original Brotherhood. These included Algernon Charles Swinburne, George Meredith and William Morris.

Gerard Manley Hopkins (1844–89)

Hopkins was a Catholic convert, who was ordained as a Jesuit priest in 1877. An important poetic innovator, he developed his "sprung rhythm" technique, which attempts to reflect speech rhythms by using a prosody based on number of stresses (not the feet) in a line, with unaccented syllables being discounted. He combines this distinctive approach to metre with extensive use of alliteration and assonance. His formal innovation was complemented by his ideas on "inscape", the term he coined to describe the distinctive spiritual essence formed by the parts that make up the organic integrity of a thing, and "instress", the energy which secures this coherence and which radiates from the inscape into the mind of its beholder.

"The Wreck of the Deutschland" (written 1876) responds to a shipping disaster, in which five Franciscan nuns were drowned, with a meditation on Christ's passion and an expression of his own faith in God, which links Hopkins's poetic and spiritual beliefs: "His mystery must be instressed, stressed; / For I greet him the days I meet him, and bless when I understand." It was followed by "The Windhover" and "Pied Beauty" (written 1877). His poetry was unknown during his own life-time, but became influential after his friend Robert Bridges's posthumous edition, *Poems* (1918).

Among his other best-known poems are the early "Heaven-Haven" and the late "Carrion Comfort" (one of his "terrible" sonnets) and "That Nature is a Heraclitean Fire", a powerful poetic statement of Christ's immanence in humanity.

Victorian Prose

The rapid social changes caused by the Industrial Revolution and the challenge to traditional beliefs brought about by Darwin's theory of evolution, the Higher Criticism of the Bible and a range of other scientific and intellectual developments led to the emergence of some of English literature's most extraordinary prose writers, whose works combined artistic and cultural concerns with broader social and religious commentary.

Thomas Carlyle (1795–1881)

One of the most influential thinkers of the nineteenth century, Carlyle came from a Scottish Presbyterian background and was strongly influenced by the German philosophical tradition. *Sartor Resartus* (1833–4), an eccentric work, starting from the proposition that clothes represent the provisional nature of the human condition, introduced his mannered prose style, full of neologisms, exclamations and archaisms, which later came to be known as "Carlylese". His fame as a historian was assured with the publication of his *History of the French Revolution* (1837). *On Heroes, Hero-Worship and the Heroic in History* (1841) discusses the characteristics of representative heroes, such as Odin, Muhammad, Dante and Rousseau. *Past and Present* (1843), which looks back to medieval times to comment on the situation of the new urban poor, provided an inspiration for certain sections of the working men's movement. However, although his writing is informed by a strong sense of social conscience, Carlyle's anti-democratic identification with heroic leader figures led to a decline in his reputation in the twentieth century.

John Ruskin (1819–1900)

Ruskin's work brings together a broad range of artistic, philosophical and social concerns. He first achieved fame as an art critic with *Modern Painters* (Vol. I, 1843; later volumes, 1846–60). This was followed by *The Seven Lamps of Architecture* (1849) and *The Stones of Venice* (1851–3), the work that best demonstrates his extraordinary capacity for blending specialist art criticism with commentary on the social implications of cultural production. It broadens out from an attack on the romantic sentimentalization of Venetian architecture to contrast the degradation of industrial society's working practices with the labour conditions that existed in feudal times. His work as an art critic championed the Gothic and the paintings of the Pre-Raphaelite Brotherhood.

He became a major campaigner for social reform and was active in a wide range of causes. Like William Morris, he was an advocate of craftsmanship and an opponent of what he saw as the deleterious human consequences of mass production. During his later years he started an unfinished autobiography, *Praeterita* (1885–9).

William Morris (1834–96)

The main founder of the Arts and Crafts Movement, Morris pioneered new standards in architecture, interior furnishings, printing, bookbinding, textiles and glasswork. He was associated with the Pre-Raphaelites and like them and like Ruskin, he attempted to counter what he saw as the vulgarity of contemporary taste by returning to medieval practices. Morris's ideas about design were accompanied by strong socialist convictions and he also produced numerous literary works. His poetic sequence, *The Earthly Paradise* (1868–70) is a late Romantic work which draws on Norse and other mythologies. The prose work, *A Dream of John Ball* (1888) looks back to the fourteenth-century Peasants' Revolt to find alternatives to the values of contemporary England; the utopian fantasy, *News from Nowhere* (1890) looks forwards to a socialist future in which craftsmanship has replaced factory production.

The Aesthetic Movement

Another strain in later nineteenth-century thinking came to the fore in the *fin de siècle* aesthetic movement, which rejected the utilitarianism that marked much Victorian intellectual inquiry in favour of a belief in "art for art's sake". This phrase was coined by Walter Pater, in the conclusion to his *Studies in the History of the Renaissance* (1873), but Pater subsequently distanced himself from it.

Pater's best-known work, *Marius the Epicurean* (1885), is a philosophical romance set in ancient Rome, written in his characteristically polished prose. Other prominent figures in the movement included Max Beerbohm, Oscar Wilde and the illustrator Aubrey Beardsley, art editor of the periodical *The Yellow Book* (1894–7), which shocked many of its late Victorian readers with what they saw as its decadence.

Victorian Drama

The nineteenth century was not one of the great ages of the English theatre, but during the Victorian era, plays such as Dion Boucicault's *London Assurance* (1841) and Leopold Lewis's *The Bells* (1871), the story of a man haunted to his death by a murder he has committed, were highly regarded for their melodramatic appeal. Towards the end of the century melodrama became the object of parodies such as Gilbert and Sullivan's *Ruddigore* (1887), while A.W. Pinero's The *Second Mrs Tanqueray* (1893), an attack on the sexual double standards of the day, achieved fame as a more serious treatment of Victorian hypocrisy.

Oscar Wilde (1854–1900)

The hypocrisy of the period is also a prime target of the plays of Oscar Wilde, whose comedy of manners *The Importance of Being Earnest* (1895), in which brilliant epigrams combine with comedy based on mistaken or false identities, is one of the wittiest plays in the English language. Wilde's other comedies, *Lady Windermere's Fan* (1892), *A Woman of No Importance* (1893) and *An Ideal Husband* (1895), are also memorable for their aphorisms and their ingenious manipulation of situation.

Wilde also produced notable work in other genres, including *The Picture of Dorian Gray* (1890), a novel in which the Faustian protagonist sells his soul for eternal youth and which suggests the decadence underlying the genteel facade of polite society, and *Lord Arthur Savile's Crime and Other Stories* (1891). The poem *The Ballad of Reading Gaol* (1898) was a product of his experience serving a two-year sentence in the jail after a conviction for homosexuality.

George Bernard Shaw (1856–1950)

By the end of the nineteenth century, the influence of the Norwegian playwright Henrik Ibsen's naturalistic drama began to be felt in Britain and the early plays of the Irish-born George Bernard Shaw, such as *Arms and the Man* (1894), *The Devil's Disciple* (1897) and *You Never Can Tell* (1899), show the influence of his revolt against the artificiality of nineteenth-century stage conventions.

Shaw was a Fabian socialist, whose dramas of ideas were enlivened by memorable characterization and witty dialogue. His finest plays belong to the first part of the twentieth century. They include *Man and Superman* (1903), *Major Barbara* (1907) and *Pygmalion* (1913), the story of the metamorphosis of a Cockney flower-girl into a lady, from which the musical *My Fair Lady* (1956) was adapted. In *Heartbreak House* (1920), the house of the title suggests the condition of England at the outbreak of World War I and the play's characters are riddled with uncertainties. *Saint Joan* (1923) presents Joan of Arc as a woman born ahead of her time. Shaw's other plays include *Candida* (1897), *Caesar and Cleopatra* (1899), *Captain Brassbound's Conversion* (1900), *The Doctor's Dilemma* (1906),

Back to Methuselah (1922), *The Apple Cart* (1929) and *The Millionairess* (1936). He was awarded the Nobel Prize for Literature in 1925.

W.B. Yeats (1865–1939) and the Irish Literary Renaissance

One of Ireland's greatest poets, Yeats's early work was inspired by traditional Celtic mythology and the beginnings of what was to be a life-long interest in magic and the occult. He was the leading figure in the Irish literary renaissance of the late nineteenth and early twentieth centuries, a movement which endeavoured to counteract the predominantly negative view of the country's culture that was prevalent in his youth and which can be seen as an artistic equivalent of Irish political nationalism. His anthology *The Celtic Twilight* (1893) gave a name to a pre-existing vogue for Gaelic legend and played a significant role in its dissemination.

Yeats's early verse was primarily lyrical. It includes poems such as "The Lake Isle of Innisfree" and "When You Are Old", along with treatments of mythical subjects such as "Fergus and the Druid" and "Cuchulain's Fight with the Sea". In the late 1890s, along with Lady Augusta Gregory and others, he helped found the Irish Literary Theatre, a group dedicated to establishing a national drama, and his play *The Countess Cathleen* (1899) was its first production. The group's efforts resulted in the founding of Ireland's most famous theatrical venue, the Abbey Theatre, which opened in Dublin in 1904. His other plays include his best-known dramatic work, the one-act *Cathleen Ni Houlihan* (1902), which again took its subject from traditional Irish legend, *Deirdre* (1907), *At the Hawk's Well* (1915) and *Purgatory* (1938).

The Later Period

Yeats's later poems blend the lyricism of his early work with a more mature and reflective approach, in which the sometimes gratuitous obscurity of his use of symbols is replaced by a more sustained system of symbolism, based on the Italian philosopher Giambattista Vico's view of history and explained in his prose work, *A Vision* (1937). Many of his major poems appear in the collections, *The Wild Swans at Coole* (1919), *Michael Robartes and the Dancer* (1921) and *The Tower* (1928). Other volumes include *The Wanderings of Oisin* (1889), *The Rose* (1893), *The Wind Among the Reeds* (1899), *The Green Helmet* (1910), *Responsibilities* (1914), *The Winding Stair* (1933) and *Last Poems* (1939). Yeats's finest poems include "Easter 1916", an elegiac response to the political uprising of that year, the powerfully cryptic "Second Coming", in which artistic and political concerns are fused, and two of the greatest poetic meditations on ageing in the English language: "Sailing to Byzantium" and "Among School Children". Yeats became a member of the Irish Senate in the 1920s and was awarded the Nobel Prize for Literature in 1923.

J.M. Synge (1871–1909) and Later Irish Dramatists

Along with Yeats and Lady Gregory, Synge was the other key figure in the movement that led to the opening of the Abbey Theatre. His contribution to the Irish literary renaissance differs from Yeats's in that it lacks obvious political commitment. His plays were inspired by a series of visits to the remote Aran Islands between 1898 and 1902 and are lyrical homages to the individualism and humour of the peasantry of the West of Ireland. They include the one-act *In the Shadow of the Glen* (1903) and *Riders to the Sea* (1904), his masterpiece *The Playboy of the Western World* (1907), in which he achieved his finest representation of the speech of the region, albeit while incurring the wrath of Irish patriots who objected to his debunking of idealized views of the West, and *Deirdre of the Sorrows* (1910), in which he took his subject from Irish mythology.

Subsequent landmarks in Irish theatre include Sean O'Casey *Juno and the Paycock* (1924), *The Plough and the Stars* (1926) and *The Silver Tassie* (1928), Brendan Behan's *The Quare Fellow* (1954) and *The Hostage* (1958), Brian Friels's *Translations* (1980) and *Dancing at Lughnasa* (1990) and Billy Roche's *Amphibians* (1992).

MODERN FICTION

Henry James (1843–1916)

Along with Joseph Conrad, who was also born in the mid-nineteenth century, James was one of the founding figures of the modern novel in English. The fiction of James and Conrad is modern in its emphasis on the subjectivity of perceptions and the relativism of beliefs and its employment of narrative strategies that reflect this shift in focus. James was also the first great theorist of the modern novel, producing a body of critical work that argued for a movement away from the "loose and baggy monsters" of nineteenth-century fiction towards a more serious "art of fiction" of the kind developed by Flaubert and Turgenev in France. He was a particular pioneer of what he variously called "the point of view", "centres of consciousness" and "scenic reflectors", *i.e.* the angle of vision from which a narrative is seen and told.

His Early Work

James was born in the United States and his early novels *Roderick Hudson* (1875), *The American* (1877) and *The Europeans* (1878) introduce the subject that dominates much of his fiction, the "international theme": the contrast between English and American manners. *Roderick Hudson* and *The American* both describe the experiences of American innocents abroad in Europe, though ultimately their protagonists suffer very different fates. *The Europeans* reverses the formula by taking "European" American expatriates to Massachusetts and dramatizing the differences between their lifestyles and those of their New England cousins. In the novella, *Daisy Miller* (1878), James's first notable popular success, another American innocent becomes a victim of European experience, when she flouts social conventions and dies after contracting malaria in the symbolic arena of the Coliseum. The masterpiece of the first phase of James's career, *The Portrait of a Lady* (1881), is the subtlest and most fully developed of his early explorations of the ironies surrounding the encounter between American and European culture and its characters, including the heroine Isabel Archer, and situations are among his most finely drawn.

His Later Work

Innocence and experience also lie at the heart of James novels which desert the international theme, such as *What Maisie Knew* (1897), *The Spoils of Poynton* (1897) and *The Awkward Age* (1899), and his classic "ghost story", *The Turn of the Screw* (1898). *The Turn* uses point of view in a highly complex way, leaving its readers unsure as to whether its narrator-protagonist, a governess figure in the tradition of Jane Eyre, is reliable or unreliable and having to choose between various possible explanations of the apparitions she has "seen", including whether she is really looking at ghosts or hallucinating, possibly because of sexual repression. In the 1890s James aspired to become a successful dramatist, but after the failure of his play *Guy Domville* (1895) on the London stage, he returned to fiction. In the same decade he wrote most of his best-known short stories, publishing the collections *The Lesson of the Master* (1892), *The Real Thing* (1893), *Terminations* (1895) and *Embarrassments* (1896), which includes "The Figure in the Carpet".

Three Late Masterpieces

In his three late masterpieces, *The Wings of the Dove* (1902), *The Ambassadors* (1903) and *The Golden Bowl* (1904), James returned to variations on the international theme. Written in an often-labyrinthine prose style, they become detective-stories of consciousness, in which the characters struggle to come to terms with hidden forces of betrayal *and* their own capacity for self-deception. His other novels include *Washington Square* (1880), *The Bostonians* (1886) and *The Princess Casamassima* (1886). His volumes of critical prose include *French Poets and Novelists* (1878), *The Art of Fiction* (1885) and *Notes on Novelists* (1914).

H.G. Wells (1866–1946)

Wells's writing blends invention with socialist commentary on the present and future state of society and after World War I he mainly produced novels of ideas that took an increasingly pessimistic view of the direction in which civilization was moving. His beliefs about literature represent an opposite extreme from those of Henry James, with whom he engaged in a debate about the nature and function of fiction. Wells took the view that novels should serve a melioristic function and maintained that their form should reflect the disorderliness of experience; James argued for "selection" rather than "saturation" and for the need for art to shape "reality".

Wells's most significant novels appeared in the early years of his career and fall into two groups: science-fiction romances, mainly written in the 1890s, and social comedies, mainly written in first years of the twentieth century. His science fiction includes *The Time Machine* (1895), *The Island of Dr Moreau* (1896), *The Invisible Man* (1897) and *The War of the Worlds* (1898). Unlike the slightly earlier science-fiction writing of Jules Verne, where the main interest is in science itself, Wells's work in the genre usually offers allegories of contemporary social situations rather than prophecies of the future or adventure-stories. Thus the story of a Martian invasion of London in *The War of the Worlds* hints at the dangers of imperial complacency.

Wells's social comedies are novels in the tradition of Dickens, which characteristically blend comedy and pathos in their accounts of lower middle-class "little men" struggling to achieve a better life, often through self-education. They include *Love and Mr Lewisham* (1900), *Kipps* (1905), *Tono-Bungay* (1909) and *The History of Mr Polly* (1910).

Joseph Conrad (1857–1924)

Although, like Henry James, Conrad is generally regarded as an English novelist, he was born into a Polish family in a part of the Ukraine that had been annexed by Russia. This and his subsequent twenty-year career as a merchant sailor who travelled to all the world's continents gave him first-hand insight into many forms of imperialism, which would become a central subject in his fiction. His first novel *Almayer's Folly* (1895) did not appear until he was thirty-eight, a year after he had completed his final voyage as a sailor. He was subsequently permanently resident in England, but most of his fiction was set in countries he had visited during his years at sea.

Conrad's Complex Structures

Conrad's fiction creates a relativistic atmosphere by employing complex and unchronological time-structures, multiple points of view and narrators whose reliability is open to question. It reveals an ironic scepticism about human motivation, particularly as manifest in the colonizing enterprises of European nations in the late nineteenth-century phase of imperialist expansion. In his most famous work, the novella *Heart of Darkness* (1902), the narrator Marlow journeys upriver in an unnamed Central African country, clearly based on the Congo, in search of Kurtz, an ivory-trader and supposed emissary of European light, whom it appears has become devilishly corrupt and insane. The story provides an indictment of the economic exploitation involved in colonialism, but has itself been attacked as "racist", particularly by African commentators such as the novelist Chinua Achebe, on the grounds that its Africans are shadowy beings, denied any life of their own. Marlow is also the narrator of another of Conrad's finest works, the novel *Lord Jim* (1900), a tale of lost honour mainly set in the Arabian Sea and Sumatra, and of the short story "Youth" (1902) and the novel *Chance* (1913–14), his first popular success.

Conrad's Masterpiece

Conrad's masterpiece *Nostromo* (1904) is a study of the corrosive power of materialism, set in the fictional South American republic of Costaguana. Again the novel moves between several characters and viewpoints to demonstrate its thesis that "There was something inherent in the necessities of successful action which carried with it the moral degradation of the idea". In *The Secret Agent* (1907), Conrad explores similar issues in a story set in Britain. Its detached, ironic account of an anarchist cell's attempt to blow up the Greenwich Observatory suggests the relationship between corruption in personal and public spheres. Conrad's other novels include *An Outcast of the Islands* (1896), *Under Western Eyes* (1911), *Victory* (1915), *The Rescue* (1920) and *The Rover* (1923).

Much of his best work is in the form of shorter fiction. In addition to "Youth" and *Heart of Darkness*, his novellas and stories include "The *Nigger* of the 'Narcissus'" (1897), "Typhoon" (1902), "Amy Foster" (1903), "The Secret Sharer" (1912) and *The Shadow-Line* (1917). *The Mirror of the Sea* (1906) and *A Personal Record* (1912) are volumes of his reminiscences.

Rudyard Kipling (1865–1936)

Born in Bombay (now Mumbai), Kipling enjoyed an unparalleled reputation as the poet of the British Empire and most of his work expresses supposed virtues of the imperialist ethic, such as self-reliance and courage in adversity. *Plain Tales from the Hills* (1888) and *Soldiers Three* (1888) are collections of his early short stories about Anglo-Indian life; his poems of the same period are collected in *Barrack-Room Ballads* (1892) and other volumes. His masterpiece *Kim* (1901) is a novel of espionage, which transcends the "boy's own" adventure mould in which it is cast to provide an encyclopaedic view of aspects of Indian life, especially during its account of the orphan protagonist's picaresque journey along the Great Trunk Road.

His Children's Books

Kipling was also a highly popular author of children's books and his writing in this genre includes *The Jungle Book* (1894), *The Second Jungle Book* (1895), *Just So Stories* (1902) and *Puck of Pook's Hill* (1906). His other works include the novel, *The Light That Failed* (1890), *Stalky and Co.* (1899) and also a posthumously published volume of autobiography, *Something of Myself* (1937). He became the first English winner of the Nobel Prize for Literature in 1907.

His reputation declined after his death, but with the passage of time it has enjoyed a partial rehabilitation, as more measured assessments have seen beyond the stereotypical view of him as a jingoistic imperialist. Although his writing *is* frequently chauvinistic, it demonstrates an insider's sensitivity to aspects of Indian life that was rare among his Anglo-Indian contemporaries.

His most famous poems include "Mandalay," "The White Man's Burden", "Gunga Din", "Recessional" and "If" ("If you can meet with Triumph and Disaster/ And treat those two impostors just the same;/ ... you'll be a Man, my son!").

E.M. Forster (1879–1970)

On the surface the five novels E.M. Forster published during his life-time are social comedies in the tradition of Fielding and Jane Austen. Liberal humanist in outlook, they characteristically compare different sets of social mores, both within and outside England. *Where Angels Fear to Tread* (1905) and *A Room with a View* (1908) contrast the intolerance of certain sectors of English middle-class society with the more open-minded attitudes of Italy. In *The Longest Journey* (1907), the Cambridge-educated hero Rickie's experience of marriage and family life ends in tragedy. Forster's most accomplished "English" novel, *Howards End* (1910), is a late Edwardian Condition of England novel, in which ownership of the rural house of the title becomes the central tearing-point of the plot. In a contrast reminiscent of that between city and country values in Jane Austen's *Mansfield Park*, the stability represented by the house is imperilled by a world of "telegrams and anger" that threatens to overtake the more cultured values initially associated with it.

A Passage to India

Howards End's epigraph, "Only connect", typifies Forster's insistence on the need for cultural dialogue and this theme is central to his finest novel, *A Passage to India* (1924), in which symbolic patterns that sometimes suggest mystical connections belie the view that he was simply a writer of social comedies. The novel grew out of his experience in India as secretary and companion to a maharajah, which he wrote about in *The Hill of Devi* (1953). It deals with three aspects of Indian life: the côterie society of an Anglo-Indian Club, whose exclusivity Forster satirizes; the abortive attempt by a liberal Englishman and a Muslim doctor to develop and sustain a friendship; and a more spiritual "Hindu" India, which offers a possibility for "connections" across cultures, where the other areas of contact have failed.

Maurice

After Forster's death, a sixth novel, *Maurice* (1971), written around 1914 but previously suppressed because of its overtly homosexual theme, was published. It partly reshaped views of Forster's earlier fiction, in which marriage and heterosexual love are treated in a manner that is at best conventional and at worst uncomfortable, by suggesting an alternative way of viewing the male friendships in these novels.

Forster also wrote numerous short stories, collected in *The Life to Come* (1972), and an influential study of the novel, *Aspects of the Novel* (1927), notable for its emphasis on "rhythm", the use of recurrent images as a structuring device for fiction and for the distinctions he drew between "flat" and "round" characters and between "story" and "plot". As an example of the latter distinction, he maintained that "The king died and then the queen died" is a story, while "The king died, and then the queen died of grief" is a plot. His numerous essays are collected in *Abinger Harvest* (1936) and *Two Cheers for Democracy* (1951).

James Joyce (1882–1941)

Joyce was born into an Irish Catholic family, but like Stephen Dedalus, the protagonist of his first novel, *A Portrait of the Artist as a Young Man* (1916), he became increasingly disillusioned with the shaping forces of his upbringing, Catholicism, Irish nationalism and family allegiances, and replaced early thoughts of entering the priesthood with a quasi-religious devotion to art. He left Dublin in 1904 and lived in mainland Europe for the remainder of his life. However, all his work is about Dublin and he once said, "if I can get to the heart of Dublin, I can get to the heart of all the cities in the world".

Early Writings

Written in a sparse and unembellished prose style, *Dubliners* (1914) is a collection of short stories about aspects of the city's life. Joyce's declared aim was "to write a chapter of the moral history of my country" and the volume offers an indictment of what he saw as the "paralysis" stifling individual growth in Ireland. The stories generally end with an "epiphany", a sudden moment of revelation, in which characters achieve an awareness hitherto lacking to them.

The main emphasis of *A Portrait of the Artist as a Young Man* is on the growth of the artist, Stephen Dedalus's consciousness. The novel describes his struggle against the forces that threaten to hinder his development and his rejection of the priesthood and is notable for its use of the stream-of-consciousness technique. Beginning with a form of monologue that attempts to convey the thought-processes of a young child, it moves through a range of increasingly complex styles and culminates with Stephen's commitment to an art based on "silence, exile and cunning". By the conclusion, the novel has become an artistic manifesto that prepares the way for the task Joyce was to undertake in his masterpiece, the comic epic *Ulysses* (1922).

His Masterpiece

In the first three sections of *Ulysses*, Stephen Dedalus is once again central and the emphasis is on the problems facing the Joycean artist figure. Subsequently, the main protagonist is the Irish-Jewish advertisement canvasser, Leopold Bloom, an "ordinary man" who is Joyce's modern-day Ulyssses. Bloom provides a focus for representing a broader cross-section of Dublin life and the main part of the novel gives an account of his wanderings through the streets of the city on a single day in 1904, Joyce's equivalent of Homer's narrative of Ulyssses' ten-years of travelling in the Eastern Mediterranean.

Ulysses is divided into eighteen sections, each of which is written in a different style, chosen for its relevance to the material it portrays. Joyce also takes the stream-of-consciousness technique further, employing variations suited to the thought-processes of the particular character being portrayed. It concludes with a monologue by its third major character, Bloom's wife, Molly, one of the most fully realized characters in Modernist fiction. Written in an unpunctuated prose that endeavours to mirror the flow of her emotions, Molly's monologue is Joyce's most brilliant *tour de force* in the use of the stream-of-consciousness technique.

Joyce's final novel, *Finnegans Wake* (1939), was his most ambitious. It describes the dreams of H.C. Earwicker, his wife Anna Livia Plurabelle and their children, during the course of a single Dublin night. From this limited vantage point, Joyce expands outwards to encompass an encyclopaedic range of human experience. The novel's dream-like method is indebted to contemporary psychoanalytic theory. It is written in a style full of portmanteau words and neologisms, presenting its readers with a level of difficulty besides which *Ulysses* seems comparatively straightforward.

Virginia Woolf (1882–1941)

Along with Joyce, his exact contemporary, Virginia Woolf pioneered the use of the stream-of-consciousness monologue as a technique for representing the flow of subjective mental processes, which is central to the view of character embodied in her novels. In her essay "Modern Fiction" (1925), she wrote, "Examine for a moment an ordinary mind on an ordinary day. The mind receives a myriad impressions—trivial, fantastic, evanescent, or engraved with the sharpness of steel. From all sides they come, an incessant shower of innumerable atoms; and as they fall ... the accent falls differently from of old."

The technique can be seen at its best in her three finest novels, *Mrs Dalloway* (1925), *To the Lighthouse* (1927) and *The Waves* (1931). As with Joyce's *Ulysses*, the action of *Mrs Dalloway* takes place on a single day, but the focus on the protagonist's consciousness sketches in her previous life through her memories, as well as providing access to her innermost feelings. The intensely subjective action of *To the Lighthouse* takes place on two days ten years apart. These are separated by a short central section, in which catastrophic external events that have taken place in the intervening years are recorded in a shockingly perfunctory way. The novel's characters live in solipsistic mental worlds and loneliness and the difficulty of communication are among its major themes, as is a quest for stability amid the flux of experience.

The most experimental of Woolf's novels, *The Waves* follows the lives of six characters from infancy to old age through their own interior monologues, which are punctuated by passages that describe natural phenomena and seasonal changes.

Her most extravagant novel, *Orlando* (1928), is a mock-biography of its androgynous protagonist, which ranges across four centuries. Her other novels include *Night and Day* (1919), *Jacob's Room* (1922) and *The Years* (1937).

Woolf and First-Wave Feminism

Woolf's fiction interrogates the gender norms of her day and her non-fiction writing, such as *A Room of One's Own* (1929), in which she specifically discusses the problems facing the female artist, made an important contribution to the first wave of twentieth-century feminism. Its lesser-known sequel, *Three Guineas* (1938), analyses the social and economic exclusion of women, particularly in higher education, and suggests that they could provide a challenge to authoritarianism and the rise of fascism. Her collections of essays include *The Common Reader* (1925), *The Second Common Reader* (1933) and *The Death of the Moth* (1942). Her final novel *Between the Acts* (1941) was published posthumously, after she had committed suicide by drowning herself.

Woolf was a leading figure in the Bloomsbury Group, a circle of writers and artists committed to moving culture beyond what they saw as the narrowness of Victorian artistic and moral standards. Other members included the artist Roger Fry, the economist John Maynard Keynes, the biographer Lytton Strachey and the writers E.M. Forster, Vita Sackville-West and Woolf's husband, Leonard, founder of the innovative Hogarth Press and author of the novel *The Village in the Jungle* (1913).

D.H. Lawrence (1885–1930)

Lawrence shared the Modernist interest in inner mental states, rejecting what he referred to as "the old stable ego of the character" for a view of consciousness founded on the ebb and flow of emotions. Though his fiction is less abstract than that of his Modernist contemporaries, Joyce and Woolf, he also challenged the conventions of earlier fiction. He saw the novel as a genre that "can inform and lead into new places the flow of our sympathetic consciousness" and developed a theory of organic form, in which novels create their own spontaneously developed shape, to embody this.

Sons and Lovers

His semi-autobiographical novel, *Sons and Lovers* (1913), set in the Nottinghamshire mining area where he grew up, is Lawrence's *Portrait of the Artist as a Young Man*, though his artistic technique is very different from Joyce's. It describes the early life and loves of its hero, Paul Morel, particularly his Oedipal feelings for his mother and his relationships with two contrasted women, the puritanical Miriam and the more sensuous Clara. It was followed by two of Lawrence's finest novels, *The Rainbow* (1915) and *Women in Love* (1920). *The Rainbow* deals with the quest of three generations of the Brangwen family to achieve the harmony between flesh and spirit suggested by the image of the rainbow itself. It represents Lawrence's first major development of his ideas on sexual "otherness". *Women in Love* was originally conceived as a sequel to *The Rainbow*, but in its finished form is markedly different in focus and approach, though the two novels share a common character, Ursula Brangwen.

In *Women in Love* Lawrence sets the relationships of a central quartet of characters against the backcloth of an England in transition, which he views more pessimistically than in *The Rainbow*.

Lawrence left England in 1919 and subsequently lived in Italy, Ceylon, Australia, Mexico and New Mexico, writing novels set in three of these countries: *Aaron's Rod* (1922) in Italy, *Kangaroo* (1923) in Australia and *The Plumed Serpent* (1926) in Mexico. At their worst, these more hastily composed novels—*Kangaroo* is said to have been written in six weeks—are verbose and art is replaced by overwritten polemic. They share a common concern with "leadership", turning towards "dark gods" and an anti-democratic view of society.

Lady Chatterley's Lover

The sexually explicit accounts of lovemaking and the use of four-letter words in Lawrence's final and most controversial novel, *Lady Chatterley's Lover* (1928), led to its full text being banned in Britain and the United States for thirty years. Then, in 1960, a landmark court case, which had an important effect on English censorship laws, found in favour of an unexpurgated Penguin edition. The novel's graphic account of the titular heroine's turning away from her impotent husband for a passionate relationship with the gamekeeper on his estate marked a return to Lawrence's best work. *The First Lady Chatterley* (1944) and *John Thomas and Lady Jane* (1972) are earlier versions.

His Shorter Fiction

Lawrence's shorter fiction contains some of his finest writing. His short story collections include *The Prussian Officer* (1914), *England, My England* (1922), *The Woman Who Rode Away* (1928) and *Love among the Haystacks* (1930); his novellas include *The Fox* (1922), *The Ladybird* and *The Captain's Doll* (1923), *St Mawr* and *The Princess* (1925) and *The Virgin and the Gipsy* (1930). His travel-writing includes three books about Italy, *Twilight in Italy* (1916), *Sea and Sardinia* (1921) and *Etruscan Places* (1932), and *Mornings in Mexico* (1927). He also published the novels, *The White Peacock* (1911), *The Trespasser* (1912), *The Lost Girl* (1920) and (with M.L. Skinner) *The Boy in the Bush* (1924).

The Novel in the 1930s and 1940s: Huxley and Orwell

Influenced by the Depression, the rise of Fascism and events such as the Spanish Civil War, novelists of the 1930s turned away from the artistic experimentalism and interest in inner mental states that had characterized the fiction of their Modernist predecessors towards more realistic modes of writing and a more direct engagement with social issues.

Aldous Huxley's novel, *Brave New World* (1932) typifies the period's sense of the threat posed by totalitarianism. George Orwell's *Keep the Aspidistra Flying* (1936) and *Coming Up for Air* (1939) reflect his concern with an England in transition. Huxley's other novels include *Antic Hay* (1923), *Point Counter Point* (1928) and *Eyeless in Gaza* (1936); Orwell also wrote *Burmese Days* (1934) and *A Clergyman's Daughter* (1935).

Subsequently Orwell's critique of society turned to more pessimistic allegorical modes: *Animal Farm* (1945) uses the form of the animal fable for a satirical attack on Stalinist Communism ("All animals are equal, but some animals are more equal than others"), while *Nineteen Eighty-Four* (1949) is a science-fiction novel in the tradition of *Brave New World*, in which a future dystopia offers a thinly-veiled picture of the present.

Christopher Isherwood and Evelyn Waugh

Christopher Isherwood's novels set in the Berlin of the early 1930s, *Mr Norris Changes Trains* (1935) and *Goodbye to Berlin* (1939), a sequence of six diaries and sketches, are witty portraits of "lost" people living in a society moving towards fascism. The opening diary in the latter work contains the famous passage in which Isherwood outlines his quasi-objective narrative method: "I am a camera with its shutter open, quite passive, recording, not thinking". This provided the title for John van Druten's 1951 stage dramatization, which took Isherwood's most memorable character, the cabaret performer Sally Bowles, as its central figure and which provided the basis for the musical *Cabaret* (1966), a work that also drew on Bertolt Brecht and Kurt Weill's *Threepenny Opera* (1928).

Evelyn Waugh's witty portraits of the upper echelons of English society in his novels of the 1930s—*Vile Bodies* (1930), *Black Mischief* (1932), *A Handful of Dust* (1934) and *Scoop* (1938)—established him as the finest satirist of his generation. In his later work, which includes his most popular novel, *Brideshead Revisited* (1945) and his World War II "Sword of Honour" trilogy, *Men at Arms* (1952), *Officers and Gentlemen* (1955) and *Unconditional Surrender* (1961), his characteristic wit is combined with a more elegiac perspective.

Other novelists at the height of their powers during the lean publishing years of the 1940s include Joyce Cary, L.P. Hartley, Elizabeth Bowen, Henry Green and Elizabeth Taylor.

Graham Greene (1904–91)

Beginning with *The Man Within* (1929), Greene's career spanned six decades. In his early "trilogy", *Brighton Rock* (1938), *The Power and the Glory* (1940) and *The Heart of the Matter* (1948), characters wrestle with dilemmas posed by Catholic consciences in varied settings: an English seaside resort, Mexico and West Africa respectively. Many Greene novels achieve their effect through placing their characters in unromantic expatriate situations, including Vietnam in *The Quiet American* (1955), a Congo leper colony in *A Burnt-Out Case* (1961), which takes an Albert Schweitzer-like figure for its protagonist, and Argentina in *The Honorary Consul* (1973). In these novels set in "faraway" places, the plot frequently turns upon an incident in which the central character grapples with a difficult moral choice. *The End of the Affair* (1951) employs a similar pattern for a novel in which the action takes place in London during and just after World War II.

The "Entertainments"

Greene made a distinction between his novels and his "entertainments", several of which were developed as film-scripts. The "entertainments", which draw on the conventions of the thriller, include *Stamboul Train* (1932), *The Confidential Agent* (1939), *The Third Man* (1950), a work set in post-war Vienna and adapted from Greene's screenplay for Carol Reed's highly acclaimed 1949 film, *Loser Takes All* (1955) and *Our Man in Havana* (1958). His numerous other novels include *It's a Battlefield* (1934), *England Made Me* (1935), *The Comedians* (1966), *Travels with My Aunt* (1969), *The Human Factor* (1978) and *Doctor Fischer of Geneva* (1980).

Greene also wrote a number of plays, the travel books *Journey without Maps* (1936) and *The Lawless Roads* (1939) and the autobiographical volumes *A Sort of Life* (1972) and *Ways of Escape* (1980).

Samuel Beckett (1906–89)

Beckett is best known for his absurdist play, *Waiting for Godot* (*En attendant Godot* 1952; English translation 1953), a work devoid of conventional action in which two tramps spend their time in seemingly idle chatter, while they wait for the eponymous Godot, who never arrives. He was a major novelist in the tradition of his Irish compatriot, James Joyce, whom he followed into exile in Paris. He wrote the majority of his plays and novels in French, subsequently translating them into English.

The protagonists of his finest achievement in fiction, the trilogy of novels, *Molloy* (1951), *Malone Dies* (1951) and *The Unnamable* (1953), probe the limits of language in a struggle to understand their selfhood. The minimalist action of the three novels is pared down to a point where it is virtually non-existent and fiction's ability to encapsulate external reality is called into question. Beckett also wrote the novels *Murphy* (1938) and *Watt* (1953) and the short story collection *More Pricks than Kicks* (1934). His other plays include *Endgame* (1957), *Krapp's Last Tape* (1958), *Happy Days* (1961) and *Play* (1964). He was awarded the Nobel Prize for Literature in 1969.

Flann O'Brien's whimsical masterpiece *At Swim-Two-Birds* (1939) is a comic novel in the tradition of Joyce and Beckett. It combines realistic scenes from student life with fantasy and folklore in a highly inventive and self-reflexive fictional farrago. O'Brien's other novels were *The Dalkey Archive* (1964) and *The Third Policeman* (1967).

Novelists of the 1950s and 1960s

The changing face of English society in the post-World War II period had a major impact on the novel in the 1950s and early 1960s, when a number of important works dealing with regional, particularly northern, working-class culture appeared. Prior to this, comic novels such as John Wain's *Hurry On Down* (1953) and Sir Kingsley Amis's *Lucky Jim* (1954) had expressed a new generation's cynicism about the pretensions of their elders, albeit from a more privileged social standpoint.

George Orwell's account of his encounter with northern working-class society in *The Road to Wigan Pier* (1937) was a work which, despite its socialist inclinations, had something of the travel-writer's perspective about it, in that it was written from the viewpoint of a visitor to a "depressed" area hitherto unknown to him. In contrast, the post-war generation of working-class novelists wrote from inside the experiences they depicted.

Screen Adaptations

Several of their most important works were adapted for the screen and became major British films in the 1960s. These include John Braine's *Room at the Top* (1957; film 1959), Alan Sillitoe's *Saturday Night and Sunday Morning* (1958; film 1960), Stan Barstow's *A Kind of Loving* (1960; film 1962) and David Storey's *This Sporting Life* (1962; film 1963). The Londoner B.S. Johnson's work, which is currently enjoying a revival, is working-class fiction of a rather different kind. It combines socialist commitment with formal experimentation and metafictive self-consciousness in a manner rare among his contemporaries. In his box-novel *The Unfortunates* (1969), Johnson invites his readers to shuffle the loose-leaf sections before reading. In *Christie Malry's Own Double-Entry* (1973), he playfully parodies classic techniques of English realism.

Other Novelists of the Period

The most ambitious fictional sequence of the period, Lawrence Durrell's *The Alexandria Quartet* (1957–60), a work made up of a triptych of novels that view the same events from different perspectives and a fourth which is a genuine sequel narrating later occurrences, offers a conscious "challenge to the serial form of the conventional novel". Other novelists who produced important work during this period include Muriel Spark, Angus Wilson, Anthony Powell, whose wide-ranging sequence, *A Dance to the Music of Time*, appeared between 1951 and 1975, and Doris Lessing, whose multi-stranded metafictive novel about "free women", *The Golden Notebook* (1962), is an early classic of the second wave of twentieth-century feminism. Doris Lessing was awarded the Nobel Prize for Literature in 2007. She died in 2013.

Margaret Drabble began her career with *A Summer Birdcage* (1963), *The Garrick Year* (1964) and *Jerusalem the Golden* (1967). Anthony Burgess's virtuoso talent ranged over a broad range of subjects, including a trilogy of novels about Malaya (1956-9), futuristic "ultraviolence" in the verbally innovative *A Clockwork Orange* (1962), which achieved cult notoriety after the banning of Stanley Kubrick's 1971 film version, and Shakespeare's life in *Nothing Like the Sun* (1964). Jean Rhys, whose early work about the lives of single women in Paris and London appeared in the inter-war years, published her masterpiece *Wide Sargasso Sea*, the story of the "mad" first wife of Mr Rochester in *Jane Eyre* in 1966.

Sir William Golding (1911–93)

Golding's first novel *Lord of the Flies* (1954) is a pessimistic twentieth-century reworking of R.M. Ballantyne's *The Coral Island*, in which a group of boys marooned on a desert island gradually revert to savagery. Like all Golding's novels, it is a moral allegory, which probes below the surface of existence to disclose elemental forces in human nature, which are often evil. *Pincher Martin* (1956) is an even bleaker parable of the predicament of a spiritual castaway, while *The Spire* (1964) is a symbolic fable about the building of Salisbury Cathedral. *Rites of Passage* (1980), which won the Booker Prize, is the first part of a maritime trilogy that concludes with *Close Quarters* (1987) and *Fire Down Below* (1989).

His other novels include *The Inheritors* (1955), *Free Fall* (1959), *The Pyramid* (1967), *The Scorpion God* (1971) and *Darkness Visible* (1979). Golding was awarded the Nobel Prize for Literature in 1983 and knighted in 1988.

Dame Iris Murdoch (1919–99)

Murdoch was a professional philosopher, who produced significant work on existentialism and other philosophical systems concerned with free will and ethics. This is reflected in the central conflicts of her novels, which frequently suggest the limits of human freedom. Set in a remote Celtic landscape, suggestive of the west of Ireland, *The Unicorn* (1963) explores issues of altruism and supposed self-sacrifice, reversing conventional notions of guilt and innocence. *A Severed Head* (1961) is a comedy of sexual manners, in which the multiple and often-unexpected comings together among the limited cast of characters border on farce, but also involve a searching investigation of the ethics of personal relationships.

Other Murdoch novels that have received particular praise include *The Bell* (1958), a novel set in a religious community, and the Booker Prize-winning *The Sea, The Sea* (1978). She was a prolific writer, who had a particular talent for observing both "sacred" and "profane" love with an ironist's eye. Her other novels include *Under the Net* (1954), *An*

Unofficial Rose (1962), *The Italian Girl* (1964), *The Nice and the Good* (1968), *Bruno's Dream* (1969), *An Accidental Man* (1971) and *The Black Prince* (1973).

John Fowles (1926–2005)

Fowles's reputation mainly rests on *The Magus* (1966; revised version 1977), a powerful and ultimately open-ended *Bildungsroman*, in which reality and illusion are blurred, as the young protagonist is subjected to a seemingly endless series of initiations on a Greek island, and *The French Lieutenant's Woman* (1969), which blends a nineteenth-century story, partly written as a pastiche of a Victorian novel, with self-reflexive commentary on its own processes and the values of the Victorian age. *Daniel Martin* (1977) is a more realistic Condition of England novel, which particularly concerns itself with liberal humanist values. Fowles's other fiction includes the novels *The Collector* (1963), *Mantissa* (1983) and *A Maggot* (1985) and the short-story collection, *The Ebony Tower* (1974). *The Aristos* (1964) is a study in existentialist ethics, which as in Iris Murdoch's novels, are an important area of debate in Fowles's fiction, though he is more positive in his assessment of the individual's capacity for choice.

Sir V.S. Naipaul (1932–)

Born in Trinidad, Naipaul came to Britain in 1950 and has lived in the UK ever since, albeit while travelling extensively to research his often acerbic travel-books about "third-world" societies. These include *The Middle Passage* (1962), *An Area of Darkness* (1964) and *Among the Believers* (1981). His best novels include *A House for Mr Biswas* (1961), a tragic-comic novel of epic sweep about its Trinidadian protagonist's attempt to acquire his own house and with it a sense of self-worth, *The Mimic Men* (1967), *A Bend in the River* (1979) and *The Enigma of Arrival* (1987), a novel that blends thinly-veiled autobiography and reflections on the making of the Wiltshire landscape where the protagonist is now living. Beginning with *In a Free State* (1971), which won the Booker Prize, his work has increasingly broken down the distinction between fiction and non-fiction. Naipaul was knighted in 1990, became the first winner of the David Cohen Prize for "lifetime achievement by a living British writer" in 1993 and was awarded the Nobel Prize for Literature in 2001.

Others novelists of the post-World War II generation of Caribbean migrants to Britain included George Lamming, author of *In the Castle of My Skin* (1953), *Water with Berries* (1971) and *Natives of My Person* (1972), and Sam Selvon, whose memorable novels of Caribbean immigrants' lives in London include *The Lonely Londoners* (1956), *The Housing Lark* (1965) and *Moses Ascending* (1975). The British writer, Colin MacInnes chronicles similar experiences in *City of Spades* (1957).

Angela Carter (1940-92)

Carter's fiction, which combines a materialist critique of society with extravagant fantasies, has often been described as magic realist. It draws on a range of non-realist narrative forms, including fairy tale, science fiction allegory, Hollywood wish-fulfilment fantasy, circus performance and the Gothic. Through these Carter expresses a feminist desire to elude definition by the norms of patriarchal rationalism, providing a variety of alternative representations of gender and sexuality. Her concern with female desire is to the fore in her early novels, *The Magic Toyshop* (1967), *Heroes and Villains* (1969) and *The Infernal Desire Machines of Dr Hoffman* (1972). The short stories of *The Bloody Chamber* (1979) rework fairy tales by Charles Perrault—such as Bluebeard, Beauty and the Beast and Red Riding Hood—as fables of the unconscious that are frequently concerned with sexuality.

Her other major novels are *The Passion of New Eve* (1977), *Nights at the Circus* (1984) and *Wise Children* (1991). Her most significant non-fiction work is the cultural history *The Sadeian Woman* (1979).

Two Campus Novelists

Sir Malcolm Bradbury and David Lodge both combined successful careers as academics and novelists, developing the genre of the campus novel that had been pioneered in England by Amis's *Lucky Jim*. Bradbury's *The History Man* (1975) satirizes the fashionable, but self-serving side of 1960's culture through the figure of a university lecturer in the newly emergent discipline of sociology. His other academic satires include *Eating People is Wrong* (1959), *Stepping Westward* (1965), *Rates of Exchange* (1982) and *Dr Criminale* (1992).

Lodge's *Changing Places* (1975) and its sequel *Small World* (1984) are more formally innovative satires of academic life. His other novels include *The British Museum is Falling Down* (1965), *Nice Work* (1988), a cleverly plotted latter-day Condition of England novel, based around the relationship between the managing director of an engineering firm and a lecturer in English literature, and *Paradise News* (1992).

Two Writers of Fantasy

J.R.R. Tolkien was an academic who made a very different contribution to twentieth-century fiction. His professional expertise in Anglo-Saxon culture informs the mythological landscape of Middle Earth he created for his *Lord of the Rings* trilogy (1954-55). This followed his earlier work *The Hobbit* (1937), in which he introduced the popular characters of the gnome Bilbo Baggins and the wizard Gandalf. Like Mervyn Peake's Gothic *Gormenghast* trilogy—*Titus Groan* (1946), *Gormenghast* (1950) and *Titus Alone* (1959)—*The Lord of the Rings* invents a self-contained fantastic world. Its popularity with readers has increased since Tolkien's death in 1973, making the trilogy a *contemporary* classic.

TWENTIETH-CENTURY POETRY

Poets of World War I

The poetry of the "Great War" gave a new sharpness of perspective to early twentieth-century English verse, which in the preceding years had generally been traditional in both form and theme, as it were celebrating the stability of a seemingly changeless England that was in fact about to disappear forever. Rupert Brooke's question (in his poem "The Old Vicarage, Grantchester"), "And is there honey still for tea?", expresses a mood of Edwardian and Georgian nostalgia that was to be shattered by the advent of the war. Brooke died early in the war, in 1915, and his best-known poem, "The Soldier" ("If I should die think only this of me ..."), conveys an idealistic view of warfare, from which poets who experienced its traumas would soon depart.

Siegfried Sassoon debunked the romantic attitude to war in poems such as "Counter-Attack", "Does It Matter?" and "Suicide in the Trenches". "Dulce et Decorum Est" by Wilfred Owen, who was killed in November 1918, a week before the Armistice was signed, is only marginally less savage in its ironic indictment of the patriotic ethic that sanctioned the atrocities of the war. Several of Owen's major poems, such as "Anthem for Doomed Youth" and "Strange Meeting", conjure up a nightmarish world, which both reflects the horror of the war and expresses a sense of a more general existential futility. Other important poets of World War I include Isaac Rosenberg and Edward Thomas. World War I poetry by women includes work by Rose Macauley and Edith Sitwell.

T.S. Eliot (1888–1965)

Often regarded as the finest and most influential poet of the early twentieth century, Eliot was also a dramatist and a major critic. He studied philosophy at Harvard, where he first developed his ideas on poetry and the literary tradition. Rejecting the Romantic view of the power of the individual imagination, he favoured a classical model of literary influence and drew on a wide range of sources, including the French symbolist poets, the metaphysicals, Dante and Eastern verse and philosophy. The symbolists were an important influence on *Prufrock and Other Poems* (1917), a volume that takes its title from his *vers libre* study of a little man figure, grappling with the realities of daily routine and ageing.

A Growing Reputation

Eliot settled in England in 1915, where, encouraged by his similarly minded compatriot, Ezra Pound, his poetic talent blossomed. *Poems* (1919), which included "Gerontion", a vivid exploration of the psychology of old age, was followed by his masterpiece, *The Wasteland* (1922), a compressed epic dedicated to Pound, who played a crucial role in editing the poem, cutting it down to half its original length. One of the most influential poems of the twentieth century, it draws on a range of literatures and mythologies, particularly the Grail quest, to suggest the aridity of post-World War I urban life and posits the message of the *Bhagavad Gita* as an alternative to Western materialism. The poem's ellipses, sharp juxtapositions and dense allusiveness were highly innovatory when it appeared.

At the same time as Eliot's reputation as a poet was being secured, his essay-collections, *The Sacred Wood* (1920), *Homage to John Dryden* (1924) and *For Lancelot Andrewes: Essays on Style and Order* (1928), established his reputation as a critic. In these he developed his beliefs on the importance of impersonality in art, stressing the need to find an "objective correlative" for the evocation of emotion and, in the highly influential "Tradition and the Individual Talent", arguing that "the most individual parts of [a poet's] work may be those in which the dead poets, his ancestors, assert their immortality most vigorously". In the 1930s Eliot's criticism increasingly turned its attention to broad social issues, deserting the strictly literary for cultural commentary in the tradition of Matthew Arnold.

His later collections include *The Use of Poetry and the Use of Criticism* (1933), *After Strange Gods* (1934), *Notes Towards a Definition of Culture* (1948), *Poetry and Poets* (1957) and *To Criticize the Critic* (1965).

Beginning with *Poems 1909–25* (1925), which includes "The Hollow Men", his poetry became increasingly religious in orientation and in 1927 he became an Anglo-Catholic. His religious ideas were developed in "The Journey of the Magi" (1927) and "Ash Wednesday" (1930) and the major achievement of his later career *Four Quartets* (1943), which brought together "Burnt Norton" (1935), "East Coker" (1940), "The Dry Salvages" (1941) and "Little Gidding" (1942). His children's collection, *Old Possum's Book of Practical Cats* (1939), provided the inspiration for the Andrew Lloyd Webber musical *Cats* (1981).

In the 1930s, Eliot began to write verse drama in an attempt to revive this neglected genre. His most famous play was *Murder in the Cathedral* (1935), a poetic account of the death of Thomas Beckett. His other plays include *The Family Reunion* (1939), *The Cocktail Party* (1950) and *The Elder Statesman* (1959). Along with the verse drama of Christopher Fry, author of *A Phoenix Too Frequent* (1946) and *The Lady's Not for Burning* (1948), his plays made a significant contribution to English theatre during a fairly barren period.

In 1948, Eliot was awarded both the Nobel Prize for Literature and the Order of Merit. His writing apart, he exercised considerable influence on the course of English poetry as a director of the publishers Faber and Faber, though what was perceived as the conservative tendency of his thinking led some of his younger contemporaries to resist the potent influence of poems such as *The Wasteland*.

Ezra Pound (1885–1972)

Like Eliot, Pound was an American expatriate, who settled in Europe, where in the years immediately before World War I he became a leading figure among the Imagists, a movement which advocated experimentation with verse forms, freedom of expression and the use of concise, concrete imagery. He also played an important role in furthering the careers of a number of major Modernist writers, including those of Joyce and Eliot.

Estimates of his own poetry, which can be recondite and obscure, vary. It includes *Personae* (1910), *Homage to Sextus Propertius* (1919) and his most accessible work, *Hugh Selwyn Mauberley* (1920). In 1925, he published the first volume of his *Cantos*, a project on which he would continue to work throughout the remainder of his career. The *Cantos* form a sequence of epic scope, which, like Eliot's work, draws on an eclectic mélange of cultural traditions in an attempt to evolve an aesthetic practice suitable for the modern age. Pound was also a notable translator, producing free, creative translations from the many literatures and cultures that inform the *Cantos*. These include Anglo-Saxon, Chinese, classical Greek, medieval Provençal and Japanese Noh theatre.

He became disillusioned with what he saw as the decadence of post-World War I Europe and, in the 1930s, his artistic elitism drew him towards Italian fascism. During World War II he broadcast propaganda for the Axis. At the end of the war he was indicted for treason and confined to an American hospital after being declared mentally unfit to answer the charges brought against him. On his release in 1958, he returned to Italy, where he lived for the remainder of his life.

W.H. Auden (1907–73) and the Poets of the 1930s

Auden was the leading figure among a group of writers who attended Oxford in the late 1920s and one of the finest English poets of the twentieth century. His verse is remarkably varied in its subjects, but his early collections, *Poems* (1930), *The Orators* (1932) and *Look Stranger!* (1936), display a recurrent concern with left-wing political causes such as the republican struggle in Spain, which was shared by many of his contemporaries, and post-Freudian psychology. He analyses social issues and sexual repression with a quasi-clinical detachment, using everyday language in an innovative manner, while making encoded references to homosexuality.

Auden moved to the USA in 1939 and deserted the socialist commitment of his 1930's poetry for a more elusive and abstract verse, which partly reflects his return to the Christian beliefs of his early upbringing, but more generally displays a reluctance to being categorized. Subsequent collections include *New Year Letter* (1941; US title *The Double Man*), *For the Time Being: A Christmas Oratorio* (1944), *The Age of Anxiety* (1947), *Nones* (1951), *The Shield of Achilles* (1955), *Homage to Clio* (1960), *About the House* (1965) and *Epistle to a Godson* (1972). With his companion Chester Kallman, he wrote the libretto for Stravinsky's *The Rake's Progress* (1951). Earlier he had collaborated with Christopher Isherwood on the plays, *The Dog beneath the Skin* (1935), *The Ascent of F6* (1936) and *On the Frontier* (1938).

Several of Auden's Oxford contemporaries, including Stephen Spender, C. Day-Lewis, Louis MacNeice, Rex Warner and John Betjeman, went on to become leading poets of their generation. The most important British poet to emerge during the 1940s was the Welsh writer, Dylan Thomas, whose "play for voices" *Under Milk Wood* (1954) was completed shortly before his early death in 1953.

Stevie Smith (1902–71)

Smith's verse is remarkable for its capacity to make poetry out of the everyday, giving voice to the concerns of suburban women and ordinary people more generally with a distinctive and idiosyncratic voice. Her best-known poem, the title-piece of her collection *Not Waving, But Drowning* (1957), in which a dying man says "I was much too far out all my life/ And not waving but drowning", typifies her ability to evoke existential concerns in a casual, seemingly off-hand manner. Smith published her first collection of verse, *A Good Time was Had by All* in 1937 and was also the author of a number of novels, but her reputation grew considerably during her later years, when her public readings of her work, for which she adopted a

seemingly naïve girlish persona, attracted a cult following.

Philip Larkin (1922–85) and The Movement

The Movement was the name given to a group of British poets that emerged in the 1950s about the same time as the Angry Young Men of the English stage. They brought a freshness of diction to English poetry, expressing everyday concerns in plain language and traditional verse forms. However, as with the Angry Young Men, their break with earlier literary language was often accompanied by a conservative response to British society. The Movement's poets included Philip Larkin, who was both the finest and the most representative poet of the group, Kingsley Amis, Donald Davie and Thom Gunn. Other notable poets of their generation include R.S. Thomas and D.J. Enright.

Larkin's collections include *The Whitsun Weddings* (1964), and *High Windows* (1974); and the title-poem of the former, "This Be the Verse" and "Church Windows" are among his best-known individual poems. The cool restraint of his verse has been associated with the bleak social climate of post-war England, but it is also expressive of a reticent temperament that was averse to ostentatious displays of emotion.

Ted Hughes (1930–98)

Hughes's work, which introduced a new vitality and urgency into English poetry, has been seen as a reaction against the Movement's devotion to the commonplace. Following in the tradition of D.H. Lawrence's nature poetry, it often uses animals, such as the trickster figure Crow, as anthropomorphic expressions of elemental human instincts operating outside customary social constraints. The poetic intensity of Hughes's verse evokes the raw power of nature and primeval landscapes wounded by the scars of industrialization. His collections include *The Hawk in the Rain* (1957), *Lupercal* (1960), *Wodwo* (1967), *Crow* (1970), *Remains of Elmet* (1979), *Moortown* (1979) and *Wolfwatching* (1989). He became Poet Laureate in 1984. He was preceded in this office by Sir John Betjeman, and succeeded by Sir Andrew Motion.

Marriage to Sylvia Plath

Hughes was married to the American poet Sylvia Plath from 1956 to 1963, when she committed suicide, and his controversial relationship with her has been the subject of several books, including his own poetic sequence, *Birthday Letters* (1998), which has been hailed as one of his finest works. He also produced a number of acclaimed children's books and versions of classical works, including *Tales from Ovid* (1997) and *The Oresteia* (1999).

LATER TWENTIETH-CENTURY DRAMA

Angry Young Men and Kitchen Sink Drama

The 1950s saw the emergence of a drama that turned away from the middle-class social worlds that had dominated the English stage in the middle of the twentieth century, in such plays as Sir Terence Rattigan's *The Browning Version* (1948) and *Separate Tables* (1954), towards work that offered a broader range of perspectives. Jimmy Porter, the hero of the first major salvo in this theatrical revolution, John Osborne's *Look Back in Anger* (1956), emerged as an archetypal "angry young man", challenging what he sees as the smug values of an earlier generation. However, Osborne's subsequent plays, which include a nostalgic study of an ageing music hall performer, *The Entertainer* (1957), *Luther* (1961) and *Inadmissible Evidence* (1964), failed to sustain the challenge. Osborne subsequently returned to the character of Jimmy Porter in *Déjà Vu* (1992).

Unlike Osborne, who had received a public school education, Arnold Wesker was born and brought up in a working-class milieu, in London's East End.

This provides the subject-matter for his more obviously proletarian trilogy, *Chicken Soup with Barley* (1958), *Roots* (1959) and *I'm Talking about Jerusalem* (1960) and plays such as *The Kitchen* (1959), while *Chips with Everything* (1962) drew on his experience in the RAF.

Set in working-class Salford, Shelagh Delaney's *A Taste of Honey* (1958), a play about a teenage single mother's relationships with her own irresponsible mother, the black sailor who fathers her child, and a gay art student who helps her with her baby, also brought new material onto the English stage. Written while its author was still herself a teenager, the play was first staged by Joan Littlewood's Theatre Workshop, a socialist company committed to broadening the repertory of English theatre and bringing drama to audiences that would not previously have frequented the theatre.

Other notable Theatre Workshop productions included *Oh What a Lovely War* (1963), a musical about World War I devised by Littlewood, which reflected changing attitudes to English society in the post-World War II period and remained popular during the years of protest against the Vietnam War.

Harold Pinter (1930–2008)

Harold Pinter's technically innovative plays also took British theatre into new territory. They are typically set in claustrophobic environments and, like such plays as Samuel Beckett's *Waiting for Godot* and Jean-Paul Sartre's *In Camera*, deal with bare, existential situations, in which characters appear to be grappling with undefined threats. Their enigmatic, laconic dialogue creates considerable dramatic tension, even as it obscures the possibility of narrative resolution.

His Rise to Prominence

Pinter first came to prominence as the author of *The Room* (1957), *The Birthday Party* (1957), *The Dumb Waiter* (1960) and *The Caretaker* (1960) established him as one of the most important figures among the new wave of British dramatists. His reputation was further consolidated by his screenplays for Joseph Losey's films *The Servant* (1963), *Accident* (1967) and *The Go-Between* (1970). Other major Pinter plays include *The Lover* (1963), *The Homecoming* (1965), *Old Times* (1971), *No Man's Land* (1975), *Betrayal* (1978) and *Mountain Language* (1988). His other film scripts include those for notable film versions of *The Caretaker* (1963), *The Birthday Party* (1967) and *The Homecoming* (1973) and the screenplays for several adaptations of novels including *The Quiller Memorandum* (1966), *The French Lieutenant's Woman* (1981) and *The Handmaid's Tale* (1990).

Sir Tom Stoppard (1937–)

Born in Assam of Czech parents, Stoppard is a dramatist, whose highly popular absurdist play *Rosencrantz and Guildenstern are Dead* (1966), in which minor characters from *Hamlet* await their call to action in a manner reminiscent of Beckett's *Waiting for Godot*, immediately established his reputation as one of the cleverest playwrights of his generation. Like his subsequent works, *The Real Inspector Hound* (1968) and *After Magritte* (1970), the play investigates different levels of theatrical reality. *Jumpers* (1972), in which a murder mystery, song and dance and philosophical discussion are brought together, and *Travesties* (1974), in which famous historical figures collaborate on a 1917 production of Oscar Wilde's *The Importance of Being Earnest*, are among his finest work.

Subsequent plays such as *Night and Day* (1978) and the one-act *Doggs Hamlet* and *Cahoot's Macbeth* (both 1979) move beyond the existential absurdism of his early work to demonstrate a greater concern with social issues. Stoppard's other plays include *Dirty Linen* (1976), *The Real Thing* (1982), *Hapgood* (1988), *Arcadia* (1993), *Indian Ink* (1995), *The Invention of Love* (1997), and *The Coast of Utopia*, (2002), a trilogy about nineteenth-century Russian revolutionaries.

His work for the cinema includes the screenplays for *Brazil* (1985), *Empire of the Sun* (1987), *The*

Russia House (1990) and *Shakespeare in Love* (1998), for which he won an Oscar. He was knighted in 1997.

Other Dramatists of the 1960s and 1970s

Joe Orton became something of an icon for the Gay Liberation movement, after his early death in 1967 at the age of thirty-three. His plays, *Entertaining Mr. Sloan* (1964), *Loot* (1966) and *What the Butler Saw* (1969), are black comedies that blend Pinteresque menace with the traditions of more conventional farce to produce a unique postmodern mixture of the bizarre and the outrageous. Orton was murdered by his partner, the playwright Kenneth Halliwell, author of *Little Malcolm and His Struggle against the Eunuchs* (1965), who then took his own life.

Generally considered the most radical dramatist to come to the fore in the 1960s, Edward Bond achieved notoriety when his play *Saved* (1965) was banned, because of a scene in which a baby is stoned. Subsequently, his historical fantasy *Early Morning* (1968) suffered a similar fate. However, the seemingly sensational cruelty of Bond's early work can be seen as a Marxist critique of the deprivation of certain sectors of British society; and it expresses a viewpoint that became more prominent in the ensuing decades. His subsequent plays turn their attention to representing aspects of the literary heritage in equally controversial ways: *Lear* (1971) is a revisionist version of Shakespeare's *King Lear*, which shows the influence of the Theatre of Cruelty that had become popular in the 1960s and Bond returned to Shakespeare for *Bingo* (1973), a play about the Bard's last days. *The Fool* (1975) is a dramatization of the madness of the nineteenth-century poet, John Clare. Bond's other plays include *The Sea* (1973), *The Woman* (1978), *Restoration* (1981), *The Company of Men* (1992) and the television drama *Olly's Prison* (1993).

Dennis Potter (1935–94)

Dennis Potter established his reputation as one of the leading television dramatists with a play about a miner's son who becomes a parliamentary candidate, *Vote, Vote, Vote for Nigel Barton* (1965), and its sequel, *Stand Up, Nigel Barton* (1965). Beginning with *Pennies from Heaven* (1978), which follows the fortunes of a sheet-music salesman in the 1930s, he subsequently became better known for multi-part series that make highly effective use of popular music to express their protagonists' inner feelings, along with the spirit of the decades in which they are set. Like his subsequent series, *The Singing Detective* (1986), which is generally regarded as his most significant achievement, and *Lipstick on Your Collar* (1993), *Pennies from Heaven* uses its musical sequences as surreal counterpoint to the realism of the main action.

Potter's other work includes *Blue Remembered Hills* (1979), a nostalgic play about childhood set in the Forest of Dean where he grew up, and two further series that were screened after his death in 1994: *Karaoke* (1996) and *Cold Lazarus* (1996).

Sir Alan Ayckbourn (1939–)

Ayckbourn's reputation has been two-fold: as a major proponent of English regional theatre, who has been the guiding force behind the success of the Stephen Joseph Theatre in Scarborough; and as a prolific playwright, whose ostensibly light farces have received considerable acclaim through televised productions and on the West End stage. His fame as a chronicler of contemporary middle-class angst has grown steadily, to a point where it is possible to regard him as a major social commentator, though his theatrical milieu is a world away from that of the more obviously political dramatists of his generation. His plays include *Absurd Person Singular* (1972), the trilogy grouped under the title *The Norman Conquests* (1973), *Bedroom Farce* (1975), *A Chorus of Disapproval* (1984), *A Small Family Business* (1987), *Man of the Moment* (1988) and the two-part *House and Garden* (1999). He was knighted in 1997.

INTRODUCTION TO ART AND ARCHITECTURE

This popular section offers a concise introduction to some of the key terms, movements and styles in the history of art and architecture from ancient Greece to our own time. Terms included here range from Abstract Expressionism to Pop Art and from Neoclassicism to Socialist Realism. Readers may wish to refer to Section B for brief biographical details of major painters, artists, sculptors and architects.

PART I. THE WORLD OF ART

References to famous artists (indicated by *q.v.*) are to be found in **Section B, Prominent People**.

A

Aboriginal rock painting, colourful visual representations and engravings on rocks, ranging from hand or boomerang stencils to images of almost microscopic detail. It is often seen as the most original form of Indigenous Australian art. Made from water and spittle mixed with ochre and other rock pigments, this form of specific Australian art complemented the versions performed on other people's bodies or bark. It was used to mark territory, record history and tell stories recorded in the Dreamtime (*see* **J14**).

Abstract art designates paintings, prints or sculptures in which the subject-matter is simplified or schematised to a point that its representational qualities are subordinate to its form and colour. Examples include Cubism and Futurism (*q.v.*). The term is sometimes used loosely to indicate non-objective (*q.v.*) painting.

Abstract Expressionism, a term embracing a diverse group of artists (including Jackson Pollock and Willem de Kooning) working in New York during the 1940s. Their work emphasised the precedence of the creative process over the finished product, giving rise to the name Action Painting (*q.v.*). Although not an organised movement, Abstract Expressionism was influential in Europe and America. It changed the face of art for ever.

Academy, an official institution concerned with the training of artists and/or the promotion of art. Academies were initially a means of raising the social status of the artist, and they were often under aristocratic or royal patronage. The first art academies in Florence (founded 1563) and Rome (founded 1593) influenced the foundation of other academies throughout Europe in the seventeenth and eighteenth centuries, including France (1648) and England (1768), and in America in the nineteenth century. Academies were increasingly governed by a rigid set of hierarchies and a stultifying training programme, but they nevertheless exerted great influence in Europe and America until the mid-nineteenth century, when excluded artists (such as the Impressionists, *q.v.*) actively rebelled against their authority.

Action Painting is often used synonymously with Abstract Expressionism (*q.v.*), but it refers primarily to a method employed by artists such as Jackson Pollock. It involves applying paint to a canvas in a spontaneous manner, by allowing it to drip or splash. The term suggests that the process of painting itself is the primary concern of the artist.

Aerial perspective, or atmospheric perspective, refers to a sense of depth created by gradations of colour, rather than by the strictly mathematical formulas of perspective (*q.v.*). From the seventeenth century, much landscape painting, including that of Claude (*q.v.*) and Turner (*q.v.*) relies on this method.

Aesthetic Movement does not refer to an organised group of artists. It classifies a general cultural tendency in art, literature and interior design in late nineteenth-century England and, to a lesser extent, America, which encompassed a fascination for morbidity, decadence and sexuality. This cultivation of amorality included the idea of "art for art's sake", which allowed art to exist apart from any moral or didactic purpose. Oscar Wilde (*q.v.*) was the movement's most famous exponent, and the artists James MacNeill Whistler (*q.v.*) and Aubrey Beardsley (*q.v.*) were also considered "Aesthetes".

Aesthetics is a branch of philosophy concerned with concepts of art and beauty. The term was coined in the eighteenth century when the questions of how people perceive art and why they respond to it were considered by theorists such as Johann Joachim Winckelmann, Gotthold Ephraim Lessing (*q.v.*) and Immanuel Kant (*q.v.*).

Agitprop, agitational propaganda art, used to disseminate communist ideas and manipulate ideological beliefs, particularly by the Communist Party in Bolshevist Russia (later the Soviet Union) following the 1917 Revolution. Based on a combination of rational and emotional appeal and initially focused on the re-enactment of representative moments leading to the establishment of the "dictatorship of the proletariat", agitprop had a variety of manifestations. It ranged from conventional artistic forms to "agit-trains" and "agit-boats"—educational and publicity vehicles meant to take the Revolution to the remotest corners of Russia through showing films of Lenin and Trotsky, very explicit theatrical performances, manifestoes and pamphlets. Later in the western world the term acquired negative connotations associated with extreme left-wing political orientations that recalled those of communist Russia.

Alla prima, Italian for "at first", is a method of oil painting which involves applying paint in one session. By avoiding the contrivance of preliminary underdrawing or underpainting, the artist can achieve by this method a sense of spontaneity. This technique was favoured by the Impressionists (*q.v.*).

Altarpiece, an object placed on or behind an altar, usually in a church. Altarpieces generally contain painting or sculpture and devotional or Biblical scenes, which are intended to enhance the spiritual experience of the worshipper. The subject-matter of altarpieces usually consists of images of the Madonna and Child with saints and/or donors (**N6**), or scenes from the life of the Virgin or Christ.

Alto-Relievo (high-relief), a term applied to sculptured designs which are depicted in prominent relief on a flat surface, technically signifying that the projections exceeds one-half the true proportions of the objects represented. **Basso-relievo** (low-relief) is carving kept lower than one-half such projection.

American Scene Painting, the realist, anti-modernist style of painting that spread in United States mainstream art during the Great Depression and aimed at defining an American art style in reaction to modernism, which was seen as a European import. The term is believed to derive from Henry James's 1907 book of essays and impressions *The American Scene* and encompasses two main schools within the movement: Regionalism (depicting rural scenes from an idealised nationalist perspective) and Social Realism (focusing on urban scenes). The main representatives are Charles Burchfield and Edward Hopper.

Antipodeans, a group of Australian painters (including Arthur Boyd and John Perceval) consecrated by an exhibition in Melbourne in 1959, with a manifesto written by the art historian Bernard Smith that stated the aesthetic superiority of figurative art over abstraction. The *Antipodean Manifesto* was to a great extent a reaction against the exhibition *The New American Painting* that toured Europe in 1958–59, championing abstraction.

Aquatint is a process of engraving which produces tonal effects similar to those of watercolour. It was especially common in England from the late eighteenth century for topographical views, and it has since been used to different effect by such artists as Goya (*q.v.*) and Picasso (*q.v.*).

Armory Show, an exhibition held in a Regimental Armory in New York in 1913. The presentation of over 1000 works included Impressionism (*q.v.*), Post-Impressionism (*q.v.*) and contemporary European and American painting. It had a radical impact on the development of American modern art.

Art Brut was the name given by Jean Dubuffet to the art of schizophrenics, prisoners and other individuals producing art outside the official and formal institutions and training traditions of the art establishment. Dubuffet believed that such "unsweetened" or untrained art was superior to the contrived and socially controlled productions of "fine artists". In English it is often referred to as "Outsider Art", the title of a 1972 book by Roger Cardinal.

Art Deco, the name given by modern collectors to the decorative style of the 1920s and 1930s; it is derived from the long official name of the Paris Exhibition of 1925, which was almost exclusively devoted to "les Arts Décoratifs". Art Deco runs parallel in time with Functionalism (q.v.) but unlike that austere and philosophical style, Art Deco is gay, elegant and even frivolous, being a creation of fashionable Paris. It is related superficially to Cubism, using squares, circles and triangles in interesting combinations for ornament. Another popular motif is the modern girl with her shingled head dancing the tango or drinking cocktails. The style is brash and worldly, but in its best expressions full of charm and vitality. Famous names within the style are the glassmaker Rene Lalique (1860–1945), the fashion designers Gabrielle Chanel and Elsa Schiaparelli, and the decorator and illustrator Erte (Roman de Tirtoff, b. 1829).

There was a revival of Art Deco, in films like "Bonny and Clyde" (1967) or "The Great Gatsby" (1974).

Art Nouveau (German *Jugend Stil*) was prevalent in architecture and decoration in Europe and the USA c, 1885–1910. It was rooted in the thoughts of Ruskin and William Morris and Pre-Raphaelite and Symbolist art. In reaction against the impersonal uniformity of industrial products which were flooding the market, artists turned to Nature for their inspiration, choosing organically growing forms, flowers or animals, as motifs for decoration or even for shaping whole objects. Another favourite motif was Romantic Woman with long robes and flowing hair, as interpreted so beautifully by Aubrey Beardsley. The sharply undulating line with a whiplash rhythm is a recurring theme. Famous names are the glass-makers Emile Gallé in France and Louis Comfort Tiffany in New York, the English goldsmith Charles Robert Ashbee (1863–1942), Henry Van de Velde (1863–1957) in Belgium and Charles Rennie Mackintosh (1868–1928) in Scotland, both architects and interior decorators, and in pure architecture Antonio Gaudi of Barcelona (1852–1926) and Victor Horta of Brussels (1861–1947).

Arte Povera literally translates "impoverished art", and it was a term invented by the Italian art critic Germano Celant in the 1960s. It refers to disposable and Minimal (q.v.) art composed of perishable and easily accessible items such as sand and newspaper. Its premise was to detach art from market forces by stripping it of its consumer value, although ironically *Arte Povera* now fetches high prices. Its adherents include Michelangelo Pistoletto and Mario Ceroli.

Arts and Crafts Movement, the English revival of decorative art encouraging individual skill and the proletarian work ethic which began about 1875 as a revolt against the existing vulgarity of internal decoration and furnishings and the pettiness of academic art. Inspired by William Morris and Burne-Jones together with Rossetti, it was strongly influenced by the former's mediaevalism, his hatred of industrialism, and his own version of socialism which included the regeneration of man by handicrafts. His firm of Morris & Co. produced wallpapers, tapestries, furniture, stained-glass windows, carpets and fabrics in a style totally different from that of contemporary Victorian decoration. Morris's Kelmscott Press did much to raise the standards of book design and printing. *See* **Art Nouveau** (above).

Ashcan School, a name given retrospectively to a group of American artists who explored similar themes of city life between c. 1908 and the First World War. The original group was dominated by Henri Bellows, but it was later extended to include artists such as Edward Hopper. The name "ashcan" referred to the city dust-bins and thus evocatively defined the group's interest in the supposedly ugly side of city life.

Assemblage is a term, coined by Jean Dubuffet in 1953, often used to define a work of art which has been constructed from a variety of found (q.v.) materials. It is the three-dimensional equivalent of collage (q.v.).

Atelier is the French word for studio, but it refers more specifically to nineteenth-century studios in which a nude model was provided for artists to paint. This type of informal setting was also called an *atelier libre* (free studio), because unlike official art schools, it was open to all. Somewhat confusingly, *ateliers* were also known as academies (q.v.), the most notable of which was the Académie Julian, where Matisse (q.v.) studied. Although professional artists usually provided tuition, *ateliers* often worked without instructors.

Attribution, a claim that a work is by a specific artist, based on stylistic and documentary evidence.

Automatism is the process of producing a work of art or literature "automatically", or without the intervention of conscious thinking. It was favoured by Surrealist (q.v.) artists, who felt that they could use it to tap important subconscious thoughts. Joan Miró and André Masson used this technique most effectively, but only as a starting point for a work of art. The Abstract Expressionists (q.v.) embraced automatism more wholeheartedly, especially through Action Painting (q.v.).

Avant-garde is generally used in reference to art of the late nineteenth and early twentieth centuries, although it is employed loosely for other innovative periods of art history as well. It indicates art which is perceived as "progressive" or which challenges conventions or traditions. The concept helped perpetuate the Romantic notion of the elite artist as an individual working in opposition to inherited tradition.

B

Baldacchino (baldachin), a canopy placed over a throne, an altar or a holy place, such as the location of a saint's relics. Although it could sometimes be a moveable object in holy processions, it was usually a fixed part of a church, as in Bernini's elaborate *baldacchino* in St. Peters, Rome.

Barbizon School, a school of mid-19th-cent. land-scape painters whose main tenet was a return to nature with an exact rendering of peasant life and country scenery painted on the spot. It was named after the village of that name in the Forest of Fontainebleau, where its chief members—Millet, Theodore Rousseau, Daubigny and Diaz—made their home. Their practice of painting direct from nature, made them the precursors of Impressionism (q.v.).

Baroque, a term used for the art style of the period c. 1600–1720 which was the artistic accompaniment of the Jesuit counter-Reformation. Its most obvious characteristics are: (a) its emotional appeal and dramatic intensity both related to its deliberate intention as propaganda ("a good picture makes better religious propaganda than a sermon" said one of its exponents); (b) in architecture, a style which is heavily and sometimes almost grotesquely ornate, plentifully covered with voluptuous sculpture on which draperies float rather than hang, with twisted and spiral instead of plain or fluted columns, and unnecessary windows or recesses added for ornament rather than use; (c) its emphasis on the whole at the expense of the parts such that a building's sculpture merges into its architecture and both into its painting (Baroque paintings are as closely knit as a jig-saw puzzle so that one cannot isolate individual figures as would be possible in a Renaissance one).

Baroque architecture owing to its origin is found mainly in the Catholic countries; Italy, France, Austria, Bavaria, e.g., the Barberini Palace, Rome, designed by its greatest exponent Bernini and others; the Church of the Invalides, Paris. Baroque artists include Caravaggio, Guido Reni, Murillo and Rubens, the greatest Northern Baroque painter. The Baroque style merges gradually into Rococo (q.v.).

Bas-Relief. ("low relief"), a class of sculptures the figures of which are only slightly raised from the surface of the stone or clay on which the design is wrought.

Benin Bronzes, a collection of more than 1,000 brass plaques from the royal palace of the Kingdom of Benin, They were seized by a British force in the "punitive expedition" of 1897 and given to the British Foreign Office. Currently 200 of them are in the British Museum; others are in different collections and 50 were claimed by Nigeria, who bought them from the British Museum in the period from the 1950s to 1980s. The bronzes date back to the thirteenth to sixteenth centuries and depict animal scenes and scenes of court life. They were cast in matching pairs and served as mural decorations in the palace.

Biedermeier refers to German, Austrian and Scandinavian art produced between the time of Napoleon's defeat (1815) and the period of European revolutions (1848). Its name derives from a conflation of two characters in a satirical Munich magazine, and it is therefore meant to be slightly mocking or pejorative. It signifies a sentimental Realist (*q.v.*) style favoured by the increasingly prosperous middle classes, and practised by such artists as Ferdinand Waldmüller and Carl Spitzweg, especially in landscape and genre (*q.v.*) scenes.

Biomorphic forms are abstract shapes based on organic sources such as plants. In painting and sculpture, biomorphism became popular with Surrealist (*q.v.*) artists such as Yves Tanguy and Jean Arp, who exploited its sexually suggestive nature.

Bitumen is a brown pigment commonly used by English artists in the eighteenth and early nineteenth centuries. It contributes to the richness of a painting's tone, but it darkens and becomes opaque over time and causes chemical reactions which ultimately damage the paint surface. *See* **Craquelure.**

Black Mountain College, leading progressive American art school, active in North Carolina between 1933 and 1957, which encouraged an interdisciplinary, experimental, informal, collaborative approach to the arts and a tight connection between education and experience. Founded by former faculty of Rollins College led by John Andrew Rice, Black Mountain pushed the principles of Bauhaus further and emphasised the need to turn students' attention away from an idealisation of the cultures of Europe to their own immediate perceptions and skills. Many important American artists of the 1960s (such as John Cage, Merce Cunningham, Willem and Elaine de Kooning, Walter Gropius, Robert Motherwell, Robert Rauschenberg, Joel Oppenheimer *etc.*) taught at or were influenced by Black Mountain.

Blaue Reiter, Der (the Blue Rider) was a group of artists based in Munich who banded together in 1911 to challenge the academic conventions of contemporary art. Among their membership were Wassily Kandinsky and Franz Marc, who invented the name to signify their belief in the spiritual significance of horses and the colour blue. An interest in the "Geist", or the inner nature of man, governed their paintings and the themes of their only publications, the *Blaue Reiter Almanac* (1912). They sponsored two travelling exhibitions in 1912 and 1913 which brought together progressive tendencies in European art. Their interest in the spiritual qualities of line and colour made their work an important contribution to Expressionism (*q.v.*).

Bloomsbury Group, a group of British writers and artists most influential between *c.* 1910 and *c.* 1940. One of the members, Roger Fry (*q.v.*), organised the so-called "Post-Impressionist" exhibitions in 1910 and 1912 in which many works by Cézanne (*q.v.*), Manet, Van Gogh (*q.v.*) and Gauguin received their first English showing. Fry's insistence on the importance of colour and "significant form" influenced the work of Duncan Grant and Vanessa Bell and fostered an interest in decorative art best seen today in Grant's former Sussex home, Charleston.

Bodegón is Spanish for "tavern". In art, it refers to a type of genre painting (*q.v.*) set in a kitchen and including still-life detail. Velásquez (*q.v.*) produced several *bodegones* early in his career.

Body Art, art that uses the artist's body, rather than other materials, as its medium. Most often it consists of tattoos, body-piercing and body-painting. Most extreme forms, present in socially engaged art, include mutilation, self-inflicted pain and ritualistic acts of endurance in order to make strong anti-establishment statements. French artist Orlan in the 1990s is famous for using plastic surgery to produce body features based on Renaissance masterpieces and to protest against current standards of beauty.

Body art is closely related to conceptual art and performance art and was promoted by their

flourishing in the 1960s and 1970s. Body art is not an exclusively western form: an influential source is eastern theatre, such as the kathakali dance-drama of Kerala, which uses exquisite make-up based on a complex colour code that contributes to the communication of meaning in the performance.

Bozzetto, Italian for "sketch", but, more precisely, a small-scale model for sculpture made in clay or wax, rather than a sketch for painting.

Brücke, Die (the Bridge), a German Expressionist group formed in Dresden in *c.* 1905. The four original members, Ernst Ludwig Kirchner, Erich Heckel, Karl Schmidt-Rottluff and Fritz Bleyl, were architecture students rather than trained artists, and they cultivated a crude, untutored style as a means of perpetuating their interest in non-European art. They had a strong social consciousness and hoped to foster changes in society through their art, although these ideas were never clearly articulated. Their most notable contribution was a revival of the woodcut (*q.v.*) technique. In *c.* 1911 several members of the group moved to Berlin, and Kirchner began painting scenes of city life which stressed claustrophobia and corruption. Internal dissension led to the dissolution of the group in 1913.

Brutalism, the term for the concrete edges and urban grey buildings of the 1950s and 1960s.

Burin, a hand-held steel tool used in engraving to cut into a metal plate. It is also called a graver. As it must cut directly into the plate, more forceful pressure is applied than is needed with an etching needle, which scratches into a resinous ground.

Burr. In engraving, a metal shaving remaining after a plate has been cut by a burin (*q.v.*). In line engravings (*q.v.*) the burr is scraped away, but in drypoint (*q.v.*) it is often left to create furry tonal effects in the print.

Byzantine Art developed in the eastern part of the Roman empire after Constantine founded the city of Constantinople (A.D. 330). It has many sources—Greek, Syrian, Egyptian and Islamic — and reached its zenith in the reign of Justinian (527–65). The major art form was ecclesiastical architecture, the basic plan of which was Roman—either basilican (symmetrical about an axis) or centralised (symmetrical about a point). Arched construction was developed, and the dome became the most typical feature, although, unlike the Roman dome which was placed on a round apartment, the Byzantine dome was placed on a square one on independent pendentives. Frequently small domes were clustered round a large one as in the case of the great church of Santa Sophia (537), the climax of Byzantine architecture. Usually the churches were small and include those of SS. Sergius and Bacchus, Sta. Irene (in Constantinople), S. Vitale in Ravenna, and the much later and larger St. Mark's in Venice.

Byzantine art also took the form of miniatures, enamels, jewels, and textiles, but mosaics, frescos, and icons (*q.v.*) are its greatest treasures.

C

Cabaret Voltaire was the night club in Zürich in which the European Dadaism (*q.v.*) movement began. During the First World War, artists and intellectuals who were pacifists or dissenters gathered in neutral Switzerland. Among this group, Tristan Tzara, Jean Arp and Hugo Ball staged a series of events at the Cabaret Voltaire in 1916 which were intended to express their outrage at the futility of modern life and the chaos of war.

Cabinet pictures, small paintings originally intended to be hung in the limited confines of seventeenth-century Dutch bourgeois interiors. These paintings consisted primarily of still-life, landscape or genre (*q.v.*), and their emergence in seventeenth-century northern Europe signalled the new importance of a wealthy art-buying middle-class.

Camden Town Group, an organisation of English artists who broke from the New English Art Club (*q.v.*) in *c.* 1911. Following the example of Sickert's (*q.v.*) works, Harold Gilman, Charles Ginner and Spencer Gore concentrated on painting the ordinary or even ugly aspects of London life. The group was characterised by a common enthusiasm for Post-Impressionism (*q.v.*), which they helped to popularise in England.

Camera obscura, Latin for "dark chamber", is a dark box in which an image is projected through a lens to allow artists to copy it easily. A precursor of photography, the camera obscura was used by such artists as Vermeer (q.v.) and Canaletto (q.v.) to facilitate a sense of spatial illusion and accuracy in their works.

Caricature, a portrait in which characteristic features are exaggerated or distorted to produce a comic effect. The first are thought to have been made in seventeenth-century Italy by Annibale Carracci. Caricature was popular in eighteenth- and nineteenth-century England, where it became a vehicle for political satire in the hands of James Gillray (q.v.) and George Cruikshank (q.v.).

German artists such as George Grosz and Otto Dix produced a more vicious form of political and social caricature during the 1920s.

Cartoon today signifies a comic strip or children's animation, but in the sixteenth century, it referred to a preparatory drawing which was the same size as the finished work and which was used to plan out the work itself. Raphael's cartoons for tapestry (now at the V&A Museum, London) are the most famous extant example.

Cassone, Italian for "coffer" or "chest". In fifteenth- and sixteenth-century Italy, cassoni were used for marriage chests, and they were richly, if sometimes crudely, painted, usually with a mythological scene containing a theme of love or marriage.

Cave Paintings are the oldest forms of art to survive. Among the most famous are those at Lascaux in the Dordogne in France. The 17,000 year-old paintings (known as the "Sistine Chapel of Prehistory") feature deer, lions, horses and other animals. These paintings are now threatened by bacterial and fungal infection. Other paintings in the Dordogne, found in 2007, date back 37,000 years. Cave art found in NW Spain dates back 40,800 years. Exciting new cave art was discovered in 2016, in the Basque town of Lekeitio. Women played an important part in these early paintings. Cave paintings in Indonesia are as old as any found in Europe.

Chiaroscuro (Italian "clear-dark"), a term used in painting to denote the disposition of light and shade. Rembrandt is unrivalled as a painter for his contrasts of light and shadows.

Chinoiserie, European decorative designs based on Chinese ornamentation. Chinoiserie was fashionable during the Rococo (q.v.) period, especially prevalent in decorative arts, landscape gardening and architecture.

Chromolithography, a type of colour lithography (q.v.) in which a separate plate is used to print each colour.

Classicism, like its derivatives "classic" and "classical", is a term often used loosely and inaccurately to refer to the best example of a period or style. In its strictest sense, it signifies an emulation of ancient Greek or Roman art, or the conscious attempt to recall the order and harmony associated with ancient sculpture and architecture. See **Neo-classical style**.

Cloisonnism is used to describe the style adopted by Gauguin in the 1880s. It refers to the use of large patches of colour surrounded by outlines, which recall the effects of stained glass windows. The term originally referred to enamel painting.

Collage (from French "coller", to stick) objects such as newspaper, string or cloth which are pasted onto paper or canvas. Although it had long been an amateur pastime, this technique was first employed seriously by Picasso (q.v.) in Still Life with Chair Caning (1912), which signalled a move away from his Analytical Cubist works, towards the creation of Synthetic Cubism.

Collage was also later used satirically or humorously in the works of the German Dada (q.v.) artists, such as George Grosz and Kurt Schwitters, and for its startling juxtapositions in the works of Surrealists (q.v.) such as Max Ernst.

Colour Field Painting was a style of abstract painting prevalent in America during the 1950s and involving artists such as Barnett Newman, Mark Rothko and Clifford Still. Although included under the umbrella of Abstract Expressionism (q.v.), these artists were concerned more with large expanses of pure colour than with the Action Painting (q.v.) technique of other Abstract Expressionists such as Jackson Pollock.

Column, in architecture, is an upright solid body serving as a support or decoration to a building.

Columns consist of a pedestal, a shaft, and a capital, over which the supported entablature rises. They are named according to the styles of architecture of which they form part, e.g. Doric, Tuscan, Ionic, Corinthian or Composite .

Complementary colours are green, orange and violet. They are produced when two primary colours (q.v.) are mixed together. Green is the complementary of red as it is produced by mixing blue and yellow; blue is the complementary of orange, and violet is the complementary of yellow.

Conceptual Art is a product of the late 1960s. Artists rejected traditional methods of producing and displaying art, and relied instead on photographs, videos and language to take the place of easel painting. In Conceptual Art, the idea is more important than the finished product.

Concrete Art, an autonomous form of abstraction that avoids all figurative reference and symbolical associations with reality and argues that lines and colours are concrete in themselves. It evolved from De Stijl, futurism and Kandinsky's abstract use of colour and geometrical shapes. The term was coined by Theo van Doesburg, whose Abstraction-Creation group in Paris was dedicated to the establishment of this art form in the 1930s.

The Swiss painter Max Bill continued it beyond World War II. Concrete Art led to Minimal Art and Op Art.

Constructivism, a Russian art movement initiated by Vladimir Tatlin in c. 1913. After visiting Picasso (q.v.) in Paris, Tatlin returned to Russia with the idea that a "culture of materials" could result in an art which had social purpose. However, subsequent Constructivists were divided between the concept of art as utilitarian and the idea that art should be pure form. The Russian Revolution in 1917 gave the movement new impetus, but it was condemned by the Soviets in 1922 and then spread exclusively in Western Europe.

Contrapposto is usually used in relation to Italian Renaissance painting and sculpture, although it has been applied more widely. It refers to a twisted torso posture which creates an elegant S-curve. Used most effectively by Michelangelo (q.v.) in his David, contrapposto became more elaborate and virtuosic in the hands of Mannerist (q.v.) artists such as Giambologna.

Conversation piece, an informal group portrait, usually of a family or friends. Its precedents are in Dutch seventeenth-century group portraiture, but it became more popular in eighteenth-century England through the work of such artists as William Hogarth (q.v.) and Johan Zoffany. Conversation pieces usually showed a family or friends in a domestic interior or standing before a country seat, and they gave the effect of cultivated informality.

Craquelure, the pattern of cracks on the surface of a canvas when the paint deteriorates.

Cubism, the name of a revolutionary movement in art created by the two painters Picasso and Braque and prominent in France between 1907 and 1914. Rejecting purely visual effects, they approached nature from an intellectual point of view, reducing it to mathematical orderliness. Its respectable grandparent was Cézanne who had once written: "you must see in nature the cylinder, the sphere, and the cone"—a concept which, together with the contemporary interest in Black sculpture, moved the two founders of the movement to experiment with the reduction of natural forms to their basic geometrical shapes. In practice, this meant combining several views of the object all more or less superimposed in order to express the idea of the object rather than any one view of it. The name Cubism was derisive and the movement aroused the same opposition as Impressionism, Fauvism and the later Futurism. Picasso's Les Demoiselles d'Avignon (1907; Museum of Modern Art, New York) was his first painting that announced the emergence of Cubism. Three phases are recognised: (1) Cubism under the influence of Cézanne; (2) high or analytical Cubism (c. 1909–12) concentrating on the breaking-down of form to the exclusion of interest in colour; (3) synthetic Cubism (c. 1913) making use of collage in which pieces of pasted-on paper (illustrations, wallpaper, newspaper) and other materials were used in addition to paint.

Amongst other early Cubists were such figures as Metzinger, Gleizes, Gris and Léger.

D

Dadaism (French *Dada* = hobby-horse) was an eccentric and nihilistic precursor of **Surrealism** (*q.v.*) resulting from the shock produced by the first world war. Beginning in Cabaret Voltaire (*q.v.*) Zurich about 1915, it spread to other continental cities, such as Berlin and Paris, dying out in 1922. The movement was deliberately anti-art, destructive, and without meaning; it intended to scandalise by such tricks as "compositions" made out of anything that came to hand—buttons, bus tickets, pieces of wire, bits of tin, *etc.* Other excesses included randomly ordered poetry, Dada night-clubs, plays, and short-lived newspapers. Many Dadaist painters became Surrealists at a later stage, but where Surrealism is a deliberate attempt to present dreamlike images, Dadaism was sheer anarchism and randomness. Leading Dadaists were Hans Arp, Marcel Duchamp, André Breton, Kurt Schwitters and Max Ernst.

Damaskeening, the art of inlaying one metal upon another, largely practised in the East in mediaeval times, in the decoration of sword blades.

Dau al Set (Catalan *The Seven-Spotted Dice*), an avant-garde association of Catalan artists (Joan Brossa, Arnau Puig, Modest Cuixart, Joan Ponç, Antoni Tàpies and Joan Josep Tharrats), upholding Surrealist, existentialist and Marxist views, founded in Barcelona in 1948. The association published a periodical of the same name, which suggested pushing artistic experimentation beyond expected limits (since six is the maximum number of spots on the side of a dice). The periodical continued until 1956 with some changes in format. It played an important part in rejecting the political establishment and promoting avant-garde artistic thinking in Spain.

Decalcomania (French *décalcomanie*, from *décalquer*, "to transfer" and *manie*, "mania"), a decorative technique of transferring images (engravings and prints) from one surface to another, which is believed to have been invented by the Spanish Surrealist Oscar Dominguez in Paris in 1935. The technique consisted of covering a sheet of paper with splashes of paint that were then covered with another sheet and rubbed gently, producing fantastic shapes and effects free from the prejudice of any subject or form. Decalcomania was widely used by Max Ernst in painting and by Richard Genovese in photography.

Degenerate Art (**Entartete Kunst**), the name given by Adolf Hitler (*q.v.*) to art which he felt was produced by Marxists or Jews and/or which had a negative subject-matter that did not glorify the German people. He contrasted "Degenerate Art" with his favoured brand of Nazi realism, which idealised German Aryan character and culture.

The contrast between these two forms was highlighted in 1937, when a "Degenerate Art" exhibition and a "German Art Exhibition" were held simultaneously in Munich. After these exhibitions, the "degenerate" paintings were either sold to raise money for Germany or destroyed. This label encompassed the art of most modern movements, particularly Expressionism (*q.v.*).

Diorama, a type of large painting invented by Daguerre in 1822. Like the panorama (*q.v.*), the diorama contained effects of atmosphere which were achieved by using translucent canvas, movement and special lighting. Three-dimensional elements, such as real plants or animals were also employed to make the effects of dioramas more convincing. Dioramas were an accessible form of public entertainment in the early nineteenth century.

Diptych can refer to a type of altarpiece created when two panels are hinged together. Unlike triptychs (*q.v.*) and other polyptychs (*q.v.*), diptychs were often small and used for private devotional purposes in the Middle Ages.

Divisionism, the name given to the theory developed by Seurat and others, which suggests that colour placed on a canvas in unmixed dots will give the optical effect of being mixed. The technique of Divisionism has also been called pointillism (*q.v.*) or Neo-Impressionism (*q.v.*). Divisionism also refers to an Italian art movement of the late nineteenth and early twentieth centuries in which such an application of colour is employed.

Donor, a person who has given an altarpiece (*q.v.*) or other devotional image to a church as a means of securing God's grace. The term is most appropriately applied to late Medieval and early Renaissance art in Italy and the North. Artists such as Jan van Eyck and Hugo van der Goes included portraits of donors in their altar-pieces.

Drip painting, a technique used by Jackson Pollock and other Abstract Expressionists (*q.v.*) which involves applying paint not with a brush but through other methods (*e.g.* dripping or splashing).

Drypoint, an engraving (*q.v.*) technique used from the late fifteenth century which is similar to etching in its method. To make a drypoint, a copper plate is cut directly, producing a burr (*q.v.*), which softens the tonal effect. This technique is often used in combination with others, but it has the disadvantage of producing only a limited number of impressions, before the burr is worn away.

E

Earthwork (**Land Art**), a dispersed tendency in art of the late 1960s, which involved using large expanses of natural spaces. Earth art employs the landscape for artistic purposes and thus opposes the sophisticated industrialisation of city culture. Examples of this genre, such as Robert Smithson's *Spiral Jetty* (1970), need to be seen from aircraft or by means of photography.

Embossing, the art of stamping in relief, letters or designs upon pliant substances.

Empire, the style created in France during the reign of Napoleon in architecture and all the arts. It is austerely classical, making much use of columns, pediments and the like in buildings as well as furniture, with eagles and sphinxes, reminiscent of Napoleon's campaigns, as ornaments. The style is heavy, grandiose and with a strong element of the heroic. A typical monument is the *Arc de Triomphe* in Paris (begun 1806), almost a repetition of a Roman model. In painting Jacques Louis David interpreted the style with heroic subjects taken from mythology or from Napoleon's career. The style was transmitted to the rest of Europe.

Encaustic, an ancient technique of painting in which pigments are submerged in soft hot wax. Examples of the encaustic process can be seen on Egyptian mummy cases. Despite the allure of the technique, there have been very few successful attempts to revive it through the centuries.

Engraving is the art of cutting, incising or otherwise forming designs of pictures on wood, stone, or metal surfaces for reproduction by some method of printing. Wood-engraving was the earliest in the field, dating from the 15th cent. Later, engraving on steel and copper plates was introduced, and mezzotint (*q.v.*), lithography (*q.v.*), stipple, aquatint, *etc.* Most modern methods of reproduction are based on photography.

Entablature, that portion of a building which surmounts the columns and extends to the roof of the tympana of the pediments; it comprises the architrave, the frieze and the cornice.

Environmental Art, art form based on the creation of a three-dimensional space in which the spectator can be completely enclosed and subject to a set of multiple sensorial (visual, kinetic, tactile and even olfactory) stimuli. It is characteristic of some of the surrealist experimentation of the 1920s and 1930s, but developed as a movement in the 1950s and 1960s in close connection with "happenings". More recently the term has also been used to refer to art concerned with ecological issues or which aims to protect the environment

Etching, a print technique in which an acid resistant ground is cut by a thin metal pencil. Parts of the plate are then "stopped out" or covered with a protective material, and the plate is dipped into acid which eats away at the exposed areas. The technique is simpler and more spontaneous than engraving (*q.v.*) and produces more convincing tonal gradations.

Euston Road School, a group of artists who studied together in the late 1930s at the School of Drawing and Painting on Euston Road in London. The group included William Coldstream, Lawrence Gowing, Claude Rogers and Victor Pasmore, and they rejected Modernist abstraction and Surrealism (*q.v.*) in favour of a return to an impressionistic rendering of everyday life.

Expressionism, a modern art movement confined primarily to the non-Latin countries of Europe which sought to give expression to strong intimate and personal emotions by means of distortions of line and colour and simplified style which carried a greater impact in terms of feeling. Broadly speaking, this has been characteristic of northern art in general. (*See* **Gothic**) .

The term is usually used of the modern movement which influenced the Post-impressionists and subsequent movements in France. Tired of the naturalism of the Impressionists, such artists as van Gogh, Gauguin, Matisse and Rouault, together with the Fauvists (*q.v.*) made use of simple outlines and strong colours.

Apart from Toulouse-Lautrec, the principal Expressionists were Norwegian, like Munch, or German, like the painters of *Die Brücke* and *Der Blaue Reiter* groups. Individual artists were Ensor, Kokoschka, Nolde, Rouault and Soutine. *See also* **Blaue Reiter, Der** and **Brücke, Die**.

Exquisite corpse (French *cadavre exquis*), a game consisting of the collective making of a sentence or an image by a group of people and folding the paper on which it has been written to cover what has been done so far so that no member of the group is aware of what the others have contributed. In the case of drawing, the end of each part was left visible so that the next player could start from it, without being aware of its original meaning. It was favoured by Surrealists (André Breton, Yves Tanguy *etc.*) as a way of exploring the depths of the unconscious or the role of chance in creation.

F

Fan Tracery, a complicated style of roof-vaulting, elaborately moulded, in which the lines of the curves in the masonry or other material employed diverge equally in every direction. It is characteristic of the late Perpendicular period of Gothic architecture, and may be seen in St. George's Chapel at Windsor and the Chapel of Henry VII at Westminster Abbey.

Fancy picture is a vague term, usually used to define late eighteenth-century English paintings with fanciful subject matter. Gainsborough's (*q.v.*) idyllic evocations of rural life and portraits of winsome "peasant" children were given this name by his critics. Fancy pictures, unlike genre (*q.v.*) paintings, are not concerned with the mundane aspects of daily life.

Fauvism (French *Fauve* = wild beast), a term used, at first contemptuously, to describe the work of a group of French painters who first exhibited at the Salon d'Automne in Paris in 1905. The most prominent among them was Henri Matisse. Forms are freely distorted and colours are selected and applied for their emotive power with no necessary reference to the "real" colour of the object in question. Other famous *Fauves* were Derain, Vlaminck and Rouault. By 1907 the group was fading and by 1908 its members went their separate ways.

Federal Art Project (**FAP**), a project designed to employ and promote artists through the Depression years in the United States, which ran between 1935 and 1943 as part of President Franklin D. Roosevelt's New Deal. Directed by Holger Cahill, a museum administrator and expert in American folk art, the project employed artists to decorate public buildings, produce posters, prints, murals and various other craft works and set up community arts centres and galleries in parts of the country where there was virtually no artistic activity. The project aimed at stimulating artistic production, instruction and research and is famous for having produced more than 200,000 separate art works.

Feminist art history, a movement in art-historical scholarship since the late 1960s, prompted by the Women's Liberation Movement, which involves a reassessment of both women artists and of how women were and are perceived in art. Feminist art history challenges the canon of male "genius" artists by questioning the male dominance of art academies and art criticism. Such dominance has caused both the exclusion of women from professional art training and the relegation of women to the subject-matter of painting, or merely the object of male desire. Feminist art history has also been concerned with conflicting problems of gender and class, and with sexual theories, including those of Freud.

Fête galante, or "courtship party", was a name given to the paintings of the French artist Watteau (*q.v.*) in the early eighteenth century. It refers to a number of courtly paintings by him which show groups of men, women and characters from Italian theatre.

Fontainebleau, School of indicates two "schools" of sixteenth-century European art. The first of these originated in the 1530s, when the French king, Francis I, hired Italian artists to decorate his new palace at Fontainebleau. Artists such as Rosso Fiorentino and Niccolo dell'Abbate produced an elegant, mannered style which was much imitated in painting, sculpture and the decorative arts. The second school of Fontainebleau was a later development of the first.

Foreshortening, a use of perspective to create an illusion of depth related to individual figures or objects, rather than space. Foreshortening was used during the Renaissance by artists such as Mantegna to show their command of illusionism.

Formalism, an approach to art in which the formal qualities of art work (line, shape and colour) are seen as instruments of meaning-production and prevail over representational, ethical and social considerations. Formalism has been central to the development of all forms of abstraction since the beginning of the twentieth century. Art critics such as Clive Bell and Roger Fry in Britain and Clement Greenberg in the United States were among the main promoters of such "pure" views in art criticism. They have been strongly opposed by supporters of the idea that form and content must go together and that that art must always provide some kind of representation of reality.

Found object (**objet trouvé**) refers to a natural or man-made object which is displayed as a work of art. Found objects are not made by artists, but artists sometimes use them as a starting point for a creative idea. They were particularly used by the Surrealists.

Fresco, a painting executed upon plaster walls or ceilings, a technique which has remained unchanged since it was practised by the great Renaissance artists.

Frottage, a technique employed by Surrealist (*q.v.*) artists such as Max Ernst, which involves placing a piece of paper over an object and rubbing the paper with chalk or charcoal. The impression left on the paper was used as a starting point for a work of art.

Functionalism, in architecture, a movement originated by Le Corbusier, Swiss-born French architect and town-planner, who applied the austere principles of the Purist movement in painting to his own art. From about 1924 he designed in concrete, steel and glass, buildings in which every part had a significance in terms of function on the theory that objects created to carry out their particular function to perfection cannot help being beautiful. "A house is a machine for living in." The style was in vogue between the two wars and is still very much used.

Futurism, an Italian school of art and literature initiated by Marinetti, an Italian writer and mountebank friend of Mussolini at a later period. Its origin took the form of a manifesto published in Paris in 1909 in which Marinetti glorified violence, war and the machine age. In its aggression it favoured the growth of fascism. One of the distinctive features of Futurist art was the use of the principle of "simultaneity" in which the same figure (*e.g.*, a woman descending a flight of stairs) is represented in successive positions like film "stills" superimposed on each other. In spite of two further manifestoes it was not until 1911 that the first examples of Futurist painting and sculpture appeared by the artists Severini, Balla and Boccioni. Apart from the principle of simultaneity, Futurism derived from Cubist and Post-impressionist techniques. The movement faded out in the first world war.

G

Genre means literally "type" or "kind", and it signifies the painting of ordinary people or everyday life. Various genre details began appearing regularly in fifteenth and sixteenth-century Netherlandish painting, the most notable examples of which are Pieter Bruegel's peasant subjects. Genre painting became a distinctive class of painting in seventeenth-century Holland, when a prosperous middle-class preferred such accessible images to abstruse historical subjects.

Gesso (Italian "chalk"), an absorbant ground (q.v.) used in Medieval and also Renaissance panel painting. Several layers of gesso were laid onto a surface before the paint was applied. Its brilliant white colour added to the luminosity of these paintings.

Giralda, a beautiful and remarkable surviving example of Arabian art, erected in the late twelfth century at Seville.

Glasgow School refers both to the "Glasgow Boys" and to the followers of Charles Rennie Mackintosh's art nouveau (q.v.) style. The former was a group of Scottish painters influenced by Whistler (q.v.) and the French Impressionists (q.v.) and flourishing in the 1880s and 1890s.

Glaze, a thin transparent layer of paint put over the canvas surface to create a luminous effect. Because the glaze is transparent, it allows layers underneath to shine through.

Gouache, a type of watercolour in which the paint is dense and opaque, rather than transparent. It was used commonly in medieval manuscript illumination (q.v.), but was less popular for topographical watercolours produced in the eighteenth and nineteenth centuries. It is also known as body colour.

Graffiti Art derives from the vandalistic urban practice of applying images or letters with a spray-can on walls without permission and is hence also called Spraycan or Subway art. It is particularly related to a trend in New York in the 1980s, consecrated artistically by the opening of the Museum of American Graffiti in 1989. Representatives were Jean-Michel Basquiat, who took street art into the mainstream, and Keith Haring, who painted graffiti-inspired cartoon-like images. Graffiti is an expression of dissident art.

Grand Manner refers to the elevated style associated with history painting (q.v.). It was discussed by Joshua Reynolds (q.v.) in his Royal Academy discourses of the late eighteenth century. Reynolds described the Grand Manner as an art which stressed general concepts as opposed to particular details.

Greek Art. *See* **Hellenic Art**.

Grisaille paintings are executed in grey or monochrome. They were often meant to imitate sculpture and were commonly used on the closed panels of altarpieces (q.v.) to create an austere image appropriate for Lent or fast days.

Ground, the substance placed on the surface of a canvas or panel on which the colours are painted. The ground comes between the canvas itself and the paint, and serves both to preserve the painting and create a more satisfactory visual effect.

Group of Seven, a group of Canadian landscape painters who exhibited together in the early 1920s and 1930s. It included Lawren Harris and A. Y. Jackson. Their aim was to create a specifically Canadian brand of modern painting, using familiar Ontario landscapes and an Expressionist (q.v.) colourism.

H

Happening, a seemingly spontaneous event, which takes on qualities of both art and theatre, although it is more ephemeral than art and less coherent than theatre. Coined by Alan Kaprow in the late 1950s the term is applied to art of the 1960s which involved performance and required the presence of an audience.

Harlem Renaissance, major African-American cultural movement based in Harlem, New York, whose main focus was literary, but which also included important artistic manifestations, as shown and encouraged by Alain Locke in his books *Negro Art: Past and Present* (1936) and *The Negro in Art* (1941). Harlem Renaissance artists, such as Aaron Douglas and Palmer Hayden, explored the ancestral heritage of black people in the US, tracing it back to its African sources.

Hatching, the use of parallel lines drawn or painted close together to create tonal effects. Cross-hatch-

ing refers to the use of crossed lines for the same purpose.

Hellenic Art. The art of ancient Greece may be roughly divided into three periods: the prehistoric period (c. 1600–1000 B.C.) of the bronze age Mycenaeans; the archaic period (c. 700–500 B.C.); and the classical period (c. 500–300 B.C.). Of the first period centred on Mycenae in Peloponnesus but extending to the coasts of Asia and the city of Troy we can mention only the massive stone gateways and the shaft graves of Mycenae, where the archaeologist Schliemann discovered painted vases, gold cups, bronze swords and ornaments of what had once been a great, if primitive, civilisation. During the archaic period sculpture was the principal form of art expression. The magnificent male and female figures are reminiscent of Egyptian art, but are distinctive in liveliness of facial expression. The vase-paintings of this period became more elaborate, depicting scenes from mythology or ceremonial events.

Typical of classical Greek art is the representation of the beautiful and healthy human body deliberately posed and often carrying out heroic or athletic acts. The vast majority of these statues are known to us only through Roman copies. The *Hermes* of Praxiteles (born c. 385 B.C.) is possibly the only existing statue which can be assigned fairly certainly to an individual artist.

Almost the whole of the Greek genius in architecture was expended on temples which are all basically similar in design—a rectangle with a low-pitched gabled roof resting on side walls. The three orders Doric, Corinthian and Ionic mainly referred to the type of column used, but naturally the whole building was influenced thereby. Some of the main buildings are on the Acropolis, a hill outside Athens, on which stand the Parthenon (from the outer frieze of which the Elgin marbles (q.v.), now mostly in the British Museum, were taken), the Erechtheum, famous for its Porch of Maidens, and the gateway known as the Propylaea with its broad flight of marble steps.

Apart from that on vases, no Greek painting has come down to us, although Greek painters existed and were noted in their time. All we have are copies in mosaic and fresco made by the Romans, at Naples and Pompeii.

Of Greek literature for the early period (i.e., the archaic age) belong Homer's *Iliad* and *Odyssey*. Hesiod's long poem *Work and Days* and Sappho's love poems, and Pindar's Odes. The period of Pericles in the 5th cent. B.C. produced more great literature than any comparable period in history: the philosophical writings of Plato and Aristotle, the tragedies of Aeschylus, Euripides and Sophocles, the comedies of Aristophanes—all these are still part of the European tradition, and together with Greek architecture played a major part in the Renaissance.

Hellenistic Art, the age of the period of Greek civilisation which began with the conquests of Alexander the Great (356–323 B.C.) and lasted until his former empire (which encompassed most of the Middle East and part of North Africa) was conquered by the Romans in 146 B.C. Culturally it was an important period because it spread Greek culture far beyond its original boundaries—even as far as the north of India, and its centres spread from Athens to the cities of Alexandria in Egypt, Antioch in Syria and Pergamum in Asia Minor. But equally Eastern culture spread to the West: democracy was replaced by absolute monarchy, cosmopolitanism took the place of the Greek tendency to believe that all who were not Greeks were barbarians, and mystical philosophies took the place of Greek rationalism.

This was a sensuous, secular, pleasure-loving, rootless society, and these tendencies were reflected in its art.

Hellenistic sculpture was sensual, effeminate, excessive and violently emotional, depicting individuals and not always noble or beautiful ones. (Classical Greek sculpture was idealistic, showed types rather than individuals and appealed to the intellect rather than the emotions.) Some of the best examples came from the school at Pergamum and later from the island of Rhodes, and the titles themselves speak of their nature: *The Dying Gaul*, *Gaul Slaying his Wife and Himself* and the famous

Laocoön (representing Laocoön and his two sons being crushed by two enormous serpents). All these date from about 240 to 50 B.C.—for the culture did not immediately end with the Roman conquest.

The great frieze of the altar of the temple in Pergamum depicts a battle between gods and giants with tremendous realism and brutal violence far removed from the serene art of classical times. Portrait sculpture is typical of Hellenistic art, where it may almost be said to have been invented, since such ventures in the past had been idealistic rather than realistic.

The great Hellenistic cities were geometrically planned and fine public buildings made their appearance in which the slender and graceful Ionic of the ornate Corinthian columns took the place of the more austere and heavy classical ones. Alexandria was celebrated for its vast libraries and was the centre of a brilliant intellectual life (the Septuagint or Greek translation of the Bible was prepared here). Here too worked the mathematicians Euclid and Archimedes, the physicians Erasistratus and Herophilus, and the geographer Pytheas.

But Hellenistic literature was a pale reflection of the glories of the past and we mention only the comedies of Menander and the pastoral verse of Theocritus of Syracuse.

Hieratic Art, a type of art (typified by the major part of the art of ancient Egypt) which is (*a*) exclusively religious and (*b*) conventionally based on earlier forms and traditions.

History painting represents scenes from the Bible, mythology, ancient history or classical literature which have an elevated or moralising theme. The idea that history painting was the highest form of art was cultivated by the French Academy in the seventeenth century and the Royal Academy of England in the eighteenth.

Hudson River School, a loosely linked group of American artists, including Thomas Cole and F. E. Church, who practised in the middle of the nineteenth century. They painted mostly landscapes, concentrating on the more remote parts of the north-eastern United States, and they were influenced by the Sublime (*q.v.*) paintings of the English artists Turner (*q.v.*) and John Martin.

Their emphasis on a specifically American landscape, especially the Hudson River Valley which gave the group its name, had a distinctly nationalist flavour.

ing. It gained its name, at first contemptuously, in 1874 from a picture painted by Claude Monet and named by the artist *Impression: soleil levant* ("Impression: sunrise"), which showed the play of light on water with the observer looking straight into the rising sun. Although intended to be the ultimate form of naturalism the inspiration of the school had been the scientific study of light with an attempt to render the play of light on the surface of objects.

Feeling that putting a line around a form was bound to cause it to look unnatural, the Impressionists used bright colours corresponding to the spectrum and unmixed on the palette, and noted that an object of any given colour casts a shadow tinged with the complementary one (*e.g.*, red-green, yellow-blue). Hence bright sunlight was represented in clear yellows and orange with violet shadows. The first Impressionist exhibition held in Paris in 1874 aroused derision with its paintings by Monet, Renoir, Sisley, Pissaro, Cézanne and Degas among others. Impressionism subsequently led to the entirely artistic and anti-naturalist movement of Post-impressionism. Cézanne, who felt that he wanted to produce "something solid and durable, like the art of the museums" was only dubiously impressionist, as were also Degas and Renoir. Of course, in the wider sense of the word (*i.e.*, the recording of an ephemeral impression of a scene), Whistler, Turner and even Rembrandt used the technique.

Intaglio, a term used to describe types of printing such as etching and engraving in which the design on the plate is incised. This is opposed to relief printing, such as woodcuts (*q.v.*), in which the raised portion creates the design.

International Gothic, a style of art that existed throughout Europe in the late fourteenth and early fifteenth centuries. The style was characterized by an aristocratic elegance and a combination of Gothic (*q.v.*) mannerism with a new interest in realistic depiction. The style was spread by itinerant artists, and is best typified by Gentile da Fabriano and Jacopo Bellini in Italy and the Limbourg brothers in France.

Intimisme refers to the scenes of domestic interiors painted by Edouard Vuillard and Pierre Bonnard in the late 19th and early 20th centuries.

Intonaco, the final layer of plaster onto which frescos are painted. It serves as a protective ground between the other layers of plaster and the paint itself.

I

Icon, in Byzantine culture, a sacred image of Christ or saints. The reverence for such images was often connected to idolatry and led to the Iconoclastic Controversy of the eighth century. Icons are common in Greek and Russian orthodox churches, and the image itself was interpreted as an intercessor between the worshipper and the holy person depicted.

Iconography, the study of signs and symbols in art, or the interpretation of subject-matter. This practice often involves a strict set of rules, and it requires a detailed knowledge of diverse religious, literary and classical sources.

Illuminated MSS. of great value and beauty of decoration exist in most public museums and in many private collections, some of them being of great antiquity, especially those of ancient Egypt executed on papyri. Greek and Latin specimens are also numerous, and the British Museum contains fine examples of all these kinds and also an extensive collection of medieval English MSS.

The 1,300-year-old Lindisfarne Gospels are believed to have been written and painted by just one person, Bishop Eadfrith of Lindisfarne, working around 715–720 in honour of St Cuthbert.

Impasto, oil or acrylic paint applied thickly to the surface of the canvas so that the brush strokes themselves are noticeable. This technique was commonly used by artists from the nineteenth century such as Vincent van Gogh as a means of emphasising the paint surface and thus drawing attention away from the illusionistic qualities of painting.

Impressionism, the most important and influential movement in 19th cent. European paint-

J

Junk Art, or trash art, particularly referring to sculptures, was popular in the late 1950s, when artists began using rubbish and other rejected items of consumer culture to create works of art. Generally, Junk Art refers to assemblages *e.g.* those produced by Robert Rauschenberg (1925–2008), a pivotal figure in a great age of American painting.

K

Kinetic Art denotes works of art which actually move or give the illusion of so doing. An early exponent of kinetic art was the American sculptor Alexander Calder (1898–1976) when he launched his famous "mobiles" in the early 1950s. Since then, constructions which rotate, jump, blink with lights, *etc.* have been made by many artists and the genre is being further elaborated upon today. Kinetic painters give a visual illusion of movement to their pictures by the use of particular colour contrasts or by a skilful play with spirals, squares, *etc.* in black and white, sometimes with colours blended in.

Kit-Cat in the early eighteenth century was a name given to a club of Whigs who met in a tavern overseen by Christopher Catling. In artistic terms, the name refers to a series of portraits painted by Godfrey Kneller (*q.v.*) which represented the Kit-Cat Club members. Kneller's innovatory works were larger than half-length portraits but smaller than whole-lengths, and through the inclusion of at least one-hand, they allowed a greater variety of posing than previous small portraits. Kit-Cat later came to refer to a portrait of this size (136″ × 28″). Kit-Kat chocolate bars are thought to have taken their name from the club.

Kitchen Sink School was a group of artists, including John Bratby, who produced Social Realist (*q.v.*) paintings after the Second World War. The name "kitchen sink" referred originally to the concerns of the "Angry Young Man" movement initiated by the playwright John Osborne in 1956. This cultural tendency embraced a strong working-class consciousness as well as post-war disillusionment.

Kitsch (German "vulgar trash") describes art defined from an elitist perspective as being of inferior, even degenerate taste, a vulgar, sentimental, inferior copy of an existing style. In the 1930s Kitsch was theorised by Theodor Adorno as an outcome of what he calls the "culture industry" and by Clement Greenberg as the product of a bourgeois world dominated by money and desire, targeting an audience incapable of genuine aesthetic enjoyment due to their lack of education and interested only in consumption. For Milan Kundera, Kitsch was one of the instruments through which totalitarian systems controlled the masses and levelled their cultural standard by imposing a sanitised view of the world in which all answers are given. The term was at least partly rehabilitated by Pop art (*q.v.*) and further by Postmodernism, whose ironic, pastichising outlook is predicated on the blurring of the boundaries between "high" and "low" art.

In the United States, the term "schlock" (from Yiddish "cheap", "defective goods") is sometimes used as equivalent to Kitsch.

L

Land Art *See* **Earthwork.**

Lay figure, a jointed doll or dummy used by portrait painters especially in the eighteenth century. Lay figures could be manipulated to provide a diversity of poses, and they could be dressed to allow a more detailed study of costume. Their use reflected the general artificiality of portrait painting in eighteenth-century England and the need for short cuts to produce speedy results.

Linocut, a woodcut (*q.v.*) in which the plate is made from linoleum rather than wood. The soft flexibility of the linoleum allows for an easier process of cutting and larger, bolder effects. It was invented by the artists of Die Brücke (*q.v.*) and used by Kandinsky.

Lithography, the art of drawing on stone and printing therefrom, was discovered by Alois Senefelder about 1796, and was introduced into England a few years later. Many improvements in the art have been made, especially in chrome-lithography and photo-lithography.

Luminism is not a movement as such, but a name given to works produced by American landscape painters that capitalised on the importance of light effects in the nineteenth century. Artists such as George Caleb Bingham and the painters of the Hudson River School (*q.v.*) produced panoramic views dominated by sky. Luminism is also characterised by smooth canvases in which no obvious brush strokes or paint surface could be detected. These qualities distinguished it from the visible brush strokes of the impressionists (*q.v.*).

M

Macchiaioli, I, a group of Italian artists working mainly in Florence between 1855 and 1865. The name refers to the *macchia* or patches of colour that they used in their paintings. They were influenced by the Barbizon School (*q.v.*), and their technique in many ways prefigured that of the Impressionists (*q.v.*).

Magic Realism refers generally to a type of painting which combines a realistic technique with fanciful or dream-like subject matter, as in the paintings of René Magritte and other Surrealists (*q.v.*). In its strictest sense, Magic Realism was a type of German realist art produced in the 1920s; it is contrasted with Verism (*q.v.*), and both are considered aspects of *Neue Sachlichkeit* (*q.v.*). The

term was coined by the German critic Franz Roh.

Mannerism, a sixteenth-century art movement, chronologically positioned between the High Renaissance (*q.v.*) and the later Baroque (*q.v.*). Unlike these movements, the characteristics of Mannerism are less defined. Generally, Mannerist paintings are distinguished by their sophistication, artificiality and anatomical distortion. They include unusual or brash colours and sometimes their treatment of subject-matter is disturbing. Parmigianino and Giulio Romano (*q.v.*) produced works considered Mannerist, but the term is also applied to artists such as Tintoretto (*q.v.*) and El Greco. It has been used equally to refer to sixteenth-century architecture in which playful satires on classical forms are apparent.

Maquette, a clay or wax model for sculpture.

Marxist art history was a development in art-historical scholarship which sought to align art with the economic and political conditions behind its production. Although Marx himself did not tackle the subject of aesthetics, art historians have applied Marx's ideas of class struggle and bourgeois/proletarian conflict to pictures. With the collapse of communism following the fall of the Soviet Union the term is no longer in common usage.

Medium, strictly speaking, is the liquid, whether oil or egg yolk, used with colour pigments to make paint. In a more general sense, it refers to painting, sculpture, charcoal drawing or any other method used by an artist.

Metaphysical Painting (Pittura Metafisica), a name given to the work of Giorgio de Chirico (*q.v.*) and Carlo Carrà. These two artists met in a military hospital in Ferrara in 1917, where they gave this name to paintings which avoided the mechanical nature of modernist movements such as Cubism (*q.v.*) in favour of a dream-like evocation of more spiritual concerns. Their works contained unusual combinations of images which were painted in a realistic style, and they employed methods such as perspective (*q.v.*) drawn from Italian Renaissance painting. The dream imagery of de Chirico was very influential on the Surrealists (*q.v.*), particularly those who practised Magic Realism (*q.v.*).

Mezzotint, a technical method for producing graphic work and works of art. A copper plate is made rough by close cross-hatching, so that a print from it produces an even black. When parts of the cross-hatching are scraped away, these areas will come out white when printed. By skilful use of his tools, the artist or technician can produce pictures finely graded from black to white and with a velvety black as background. The principles of the method were known and practised, for instance, by Rembrandt, but mezzotint became most popular for the reproduction of famous paintings from the end of the 18th cent.

Miniature, a small painting, usually a portrait. The term originally referred to medieval manuscript illumination (*q.v.*), but by the sixteenth century, it was used to signify small pictures painted on card. Miniatures became especially popular for keepsake portraits in the eighteenth century, and they often parroted the currently fashionable styles of oil painting.

Minimal Art was a movement which began in the United States in the 1960s. As its name implies it involves art, usually sculpture, which is reduced to its most essential form. Examples tend to be assemblages (*q.v.*) composed largely of limited abstract shapes. It has been seen as a reaction against Expressionism.

Mobile, a type of sculpture popularised by Alexander Calder in the 1930s. Mobiles are composed of flat geometric shapes hung on string and wire and allowed to move, or are moved by mechanical means. If mechanical means are used, mobiles can be considered Kinetic Art (*q.v.*).

Modello, a small preliminary painting used as a "try out" for a larger painting. Unlike sketches, which are often unfinished or merely summary, modelli prefigure the final painting in great detail. In the Renaissance (*see* **Section J**) they were used as a sort of advertisement by artists trying to convince patrons of the worth of their work.

Monotype, as the name suggests, refers to a printing process whereby only one impression can be made from each prepared plate. Monotypes are created by painting in oils directly onto a copper plate and then pressing the plate onto a piece of paper. This process was popular with twentieth-century artists such as Chagall (q.v.).

Montage, like collage (q.v.) involves the arrangement of diverse images together on a sheet of paper. But montage refers specifically to components which are complete in themselves (see photomontage), rather than abstract forms.

Mosaic, art of arranging small pieces of coloured glass, marble, or other materials in such a fashion as to produce a decorative pattern. Some of the best examples of Byzantine mosaics are to be seen at Ravenna, Rome, Venice and Sicily.

N

Nabis, the (the "Prophets"), the group of French painters who followed the Symbolist (q.v.) concerns of Gauguin. Between 1889 and 1899, Pierre Bonnard (q.v.), Edouard Vuillard and Maurice Denis explored the symbolic possibilities of colour first examined by Gauguin in 1888. They were particularly interested in the use of large patches of colour to convey spiritual intensity. See Cloisonnism.

Naive Art results from either a real or seeming lack of technical skill. This produces child-like images which offer a very literal form of Realism (q.v.). Paradoxically, naive art became popular in the late nineteenth and twentieth centuries, with the work of artists such as Le Douanier Rousseau (q.v.). A revival of interest in the simple expression of children's art which characterised modern movements such as German Expressionism (q.v.) may be partly responsible for this.

Narrative Art, a type of art popular during the late 19th cent. based on the principle: "every picture tells a story". The term, although often applied derisively, suitably describes many works of considerable artistic merit: e.g., Hogarth's Marriage à la Mode, the Bayeux Tapestry, etc.

Naturalism in painting has been defined as "a direct and spontaneous approach to nature" —to landscape primarily. Constable, Turner and Boudin were among the great naturalist painters of the 19th cent.

Nazarenes, a group of German Romantic artists who worked in Rome in the early nineteenth century. In 1809 Friedrich Overbeck and Franz Pforr formed an artistic organisation called the Brotherhood of St. Luke in Vienna. They carried their interest in the revival of religious art to Rome in 1810, where they moved into an abandoned monastery and were joined by other artists. They hoped to capture the spirit of the Middle Ages through historical and religious subjects, and they were instrumental in the revival of fresco (q.v.) technique.

Their large-scale murals and historical scenes for the German ruling class led them to be associated with the intensification of German nationalism in the nineteenth century.

Neo-Classical Style, term applied to the revival of classical logic and order after the extravagances of Rococo (q.v.), beginning in France in the mid-18th cent. and finding expression in architecture and the decorative arts. The style retains some of the daintiness of Rococo, furniture is on a small scale, often gilt, and silks and porcelain favour pastel shades. Straight lines take the place of the wild curvatures of Rococo and classical details like festoons and urn forms are used in many contexts and materials. Its English version is closely associated with the name of the architect Robert Adam whose light and graceful adaptations of Greek and Roman forms were introduced into English country houses. In France the style is sometimes called Style Louis XVI. Eventually the Neo-Classical style merges into Empire (q.v.).

Neo-Expressionism, or Bad Art, refers to an international art movement of the late 1970s and 1980s involving the revival of Expressionism (q.v.) concerns. The prominent artists include George Baselitz and Francesco Clemente.

Neo-Impressionism, a development of Impressionism (q.v.) by Seurat and Signac during the 1880s who devised the method of painting known as pointillism (the application of pure colours in minute touches or spots to form a composite whole, based on a knowledge of the laws of colour and optics).

One of the best-known examples of this technique is Seurat's Sunday Afternoon on the Grand Jatte.

Neo-Plasticism was a name used by Mondrian for a type of art which avoids representation in favour of abstraction. Mondrian's principles resulted in canvases which consisted solely of primary colours, black and white, and horizontal and vertical lines. His intention was to create an art which could have meaning for everyone, but paradoxically, his works usually puzzle the uninitiated. Neo-Plasticism was promoted by the journal, De Stijl (q.v.).

Neo-Romanticism is a British art movement which began before the Second World War. Artists such as John Piper and Graham Sutherland (q.v.) initiated a revival of interest in the Romantic landscape painting of William Blake (q.v.) and Samuel Palmer (q.v.). This concern for evocative native landscapes was a manifestation of pre-war nationalism.

Neue Sachlichkeit, Die (The New Objectivity), a name given by the art dealer G. F. Hartlaub to describe a diverse group of German artists who rejected abstraction during the 1920s. These artists all attempted to represent reality, either through a precise, detailed Magic Realism (q.v.) or a satirical and scathing Verism (q.v.). The first Neue Sachlichkeit exhibition was in 1923. The movement ended with the rise of the Nazis in the 1930s.

New English Art Club, an organisation formed in 1886 in reaction against the stale practices and politics of the Royal Academy. The members of this group, including Walter Sickert (q.v.) and Philip Wilson Steer (q.v.) were trained in France, and they preferred the informal atelier (q.v.) system of education to the rigid strictures of the Royal Academy Schools. Their work was influenced by Whistler (q.v.) and Jules Bastien-Lepage.

Newlyn School, the name given to a group of artists who congregated in Newlyn, Cornwall during the 1880s and 1890s. The group included Laura Knight and Stanhope Forbes, and they were particularly concerned with plein air (q.v.) painting.

Non-Objective Art is the correct name for what is usually called Abstract Art (q.v.). Its name suggests that the representational object has been obliterated, whereas "abstract" implies that the work of art is a simplification or modification of some real object.

Novecento Italiano, an Italian art movement of the 1920s which encouraged a return to the principles of Italian Renaissance (see Section J) art. The interest in the Italian past was more than simply a stylistic phenomenon, as it was strongly connected with the nationalist spirit of Fascism. The artists of the group included Mario Sironi and Achille Funi, and they held their first exhibition in the Pesaro Gallery, Milan, in 1922.

Novembergruppe, a group of left-wing Berlin artists formed in 1918. The members, including Max Pechstein, were committed to socialist principles and wanted an art capable of appealing to the masses. The name of the group came from the November Communist uprising in Berlin of 1918.

O

Objet trouvé. See Found object.

Omega Workshops, a cooperative founded by Roger Fry (q.v.) in 1913 aimed at producing quality decorative art. The artists of the Bloomsbury Group (q.v.), such as Duncan Grant and Vanessa Bell, were involved, and they decorated furniture for a small number of patrons. The impracticalities of their enterprise led to the organisation's demise in 1920, after sales had declined during World War I.

Op Art, an art based solely on perceptual or optical effects, which was particularly popular in the 1960s. Its practitioners included Bridget Riley.

Orphism (Orphic Cubism). In response to the monochromatic coldness of Cubism (q.v.), the artists Robert and Sonia Delaunay began producing paintings in which colour was fragmented in the same way that the Cubists broke up form. This prismatic treatment of colour was called Orphism by the poet Apollinaire in 1912. Orphism differs further from Cubism in its emphasis on movement and city life, qualities more obviously characteristic of Futurism. Orphist paintings eventually became totally abstract, but the movement did not last beyond the First World War.

P

Panorama, a circular painting placed inside a large cylinder, in which people can sit or stand. Panoramas could be walked around, or they were moved mechanically to create a sense of total environment. They were invented in Scotland by Robert Barker, who painted panoramic views of Edinburgh in the late eighteenth century, and they quickly became a popular form of entertainment. Their subjects included exotic scenes and Picturesque (*q.v.*) landscapes, but they also depicted recent military campaigns during the Napoleonic wars. This latter quality gave panoramas the value of reportage and enhanced their accessibility to a wider public.

Papier collé. French for "pasted paper", a type of collage (*q.v.*) popularised by Braque from 1913. This involved gluing bits of wallpaper or newspaper to a canvas. This process became a major aspect of Synthetic Cubism (*q.v.*), and it was used by Matisse (*q.v.*) for his paper cutouts.

Pastel, a chalk composed of powdered pigments which produces delicate but fragile images. The soft quality of pastel became especially popular in eighteenth-century European portraits.

Pentimento, bits of painting which become visible when the top layer of paint wears away. Often pentimenti signal an artist's earlier rejected experiments, and they are therefore used both as authentication and as a means of studying the processes of work stages of an artist.

Performance Art is a general term referring to a quasi-theatrical event which is considered art. The agitational demonstrations of the Futurists (*q.v.*), the nonsense recitations of the Dadaists (*q.v.*) and the Happenings (*q.v.*) of the 1960s are all examples of this type of art.

Perspective, a space-creating device used most frequently by Italian Renaissance (*see* **Section J**) artists. Linear or one-point perspective involves mathematically calculating a vanishing point where a series of parallel lines converge. In Renaissance painting, these lines are often created by floor patterns or carefully placed bodies, which lead the eye back into the picture to give a sense of depth. The creation of three-dimensional effects on a two-dimensional surface was particularly important for the Renaissance idea of optical illusionism, although the effect produced by perspective is only approximate to true visual experience. One-point perspective was used less frequently after the fifteenth century, but aerial perspective (*q.v.*) was commonly employed for several centuries afterwards.

Photomontage, a type of montage (*q.v.*) consisting wholly or partly of photographs. This technique was common among the Berlin Dada artists (*q.v.*), who used photographs from fashion magazines and other forms of popular culture to make satirical attacks on the superficiality of Weimar society.

Picturesque, with a capital "p", is an aesthetic term related to the "sublime" (*q.v.*) coined by William Gilpin in the eighteenth century to describe landscapes which looked "like a picture". Like the Sublime, the Picturesque was said to instill emotions in the observer, who associated the sight of rough beauty, ruins or irregular landscapes with various sentimental or melancholy moods. In the 1790s the term became the focus of a heated aesthetic debate which included such participants as Richard Payne Knight and Uvedale Price. The growing popularity of Picturesque ideas inspired artists and amateurs to take Picturesque tours, as in the Lake District and Wales, in order to discover the possibilities in rugged and unusual landscapes.

Pietà (Italian for "pity"), a devotional image of the Virgin Mary with the dead Christ on her lap. Michelangelo's Pietà, now in St. Peter's, Rome, is the most famous example.

Plein air (French for "open air"), refers to painting out of doors. Before the nineteenth century, landscape painters commonly produced their works in a studio from sketches or studies. The French Barbizon (*q.v.*) painters cultivated the opposing practice of painting outside—a method

that was wholeheartedly adopted by the Impressionists (*q.v.*).

Polyptych, an altarpiece (*q.v.*) with more than one panel, such as a diptych (*q.v.*) or triptych (*q.v.*).

Pop Art, a phenomenon of the 1960s and 1970s which involved transforming objects of popular culture into works of art. The movement started in Britain, when a group of artists at the Institute of Contemporary Arts began using images from comic books and advertising in their art. Pop art either attacks modern consumer culture or it glorifies it nostalgically. Its main practitioners were Peter Blake and Richard Hamilton in England and Andy Warhol and Roy Lichtenstein in America. Lichtenstein's Whaam! and Crying Girl paintings defined the 1960s movement. Their female counterparts included Pauline Boty, Rosalyn Drexler and Marisol.

Portland Vase, one of the most renowned specimens of ancient art, long in the possession of the Portland family. In 1810 it was loaned to the British Museum. Here it was shattered in 1845 by a stone from a maniac's hand, but has been skilfully restored. It is said to have been found in the 17th cent. in an ancient tomb near Rome. It was purchased from the Barberini family in 1770 by Sir Wm. Hamilton, subsequently sold to the Duchess of Portland. The vase, which is actually a two-handled urn, stands about 25 cm high, is of transparent dark blue glass, ornamented with figures cut in relief in overlaid white opaque glass. It was purchased by the British Museum in 1945. *See* Glass, Section L.

Post-Impressionism, a term introduced by Roger Fry to describe the exhibition of paintings sponsored by himself in London (1910–11) officially entitled "Manet and the Post-Impressionists". The exhibition included paintings by Manet, Cézanne, Gauguin, Van Gogh, Seurat, Signac, works by Matisse, Rouault and the *Fauves* (*q.v.*), and sculpture by Maillol. In a second exhibition, held in 1912, Picasso and the Cubists were also represented.

The term therefore refers to the movement in modern art which reacted against the transient naturalism of the Impressionists by concerning itself primarily with colour, form and solidity. Most artists include Cézanne, Van Gogh and Gauguin as the main Post-Impressionists and maintain that it prepared the way for Fauvism, Cubism and Expressionism.

Post-Modernism is a cultural phenomenon. From the end of the Second World War, the failure of Modernism in all of its manifestations was evident, and artists, architects and writers began seeking other solutions to the problems of contemporary life. Post-Modernism is not one style but many styles, and it is often self-referential, playful or parodic. The exact meaning of the term which came into general use in the 1970s, and those works of art which fall within its parameters, are a subject of continual debate, but a number of post-war developments, such as Happenings (*q.v.*) could be seen to be in its sphere.

Post-Painterly Abstraction was a term invented by the critic Clement Greenberg in 1964 to refer to non-objective (*q.v.*) artists who were not members of the Abstract Expressionist (*q.v.*) movement. The paintings of Kenneth Noland, Frank Stella and others were considered to fall within this definition, as they painted canvases with large patches of colour and which were carefully planned, rather than spontaneous, as in Action Painting (*q.v.*).

Predella, the panel or panels running along the bottom of an Italian Renaissance (*see* **Section J**) painting, and usually containing a series of narrative scenes to complement the main devotional subject of the altarpiece itself.

Pre-Raphaelite Brotherhood was the name given to their school of thought by three British artists, Dante Gabriel Rossetti, J. E. Millais and W. Holman Hunt, who in 1848 revolted against the academic art of their time and advocated a return to the style of the Italian painters prior to Raphael—the simple naturalism of the Primitives, such as Botticelli, Fra Angelico and Filippo Lippi. Thus they avoided the use of heavy shadows and painted on a white ground in bright colours—a technique which aroused the ire of those used to the dark and murky canvases of the contemporary romantic artists. Although they held these principles in common the three members of the "P.R.B.", as it was popularly called, were really quite different in other respects. Thus Rossetti (who for some reason is always thought of as the typical Pre-Raphaelite) produced works of a highly romanticised mediaevalism which, apart from certain aspects of technique, bear not the slightest resemblance to the sentimental naturalism of Millais or the much more dramatic realism of Holman Hunt (*e.g.*, in *The Scapegoat*). The Brotherhood was later joined by a number of lesser artists, but its works are not commonly accepted with enthusiasm today when the general feeling is that they are sentimental and religiose rather than the product of deeply-felt emotions. Ruskin in his writings had defended their work but the movement ended in 1853.

Primitive Art. The word "primitive" has a number of different meanings: (1) the art of prehistoric communities (*e.g.*, the famous animal cave-drawings of the Aurignacians, *c.* 25,000 B.C., at Altamira in Spain); (2) the art of modern primitive communities (*e.g.*, Bushman rock-paintings); (3) child art; (4) peasant art which springs from a spontaneous desire to impart beauty to objects of daily use and shows a tendency towards abstraction. Peasant art has many features in common the world over, the woodcarving of the Norsemen being almost indistinguishable from that of the Maoris; (5) the modern school of primitive painting in which naïveté of presentation is either the aim of a highly sophisticated mind (*e.g.*, the self-taught French painter Le Douanier Rousseau (d. 1910), or arises naturally from a simple one (the American "grandma" Moses (d. 1961) who began to paint in her seventies). *See also* **Cave Paintings, N5.**

Provenance records the whole history of the ownership of a painting, from its first commission or sale to its present location. A confident provenance is often used to authenticate a work of art, but it can be equally revealing about patterns of taste and art purchase through the centuries.

Purism was a reaction against Cubism (*q.v.*) advocating machine-like clarity and observation which drew upon some of Cubism's methods. The term was coined in 1918 when Amédée Ozenfant's book *Après le Cubisme* rejected the "decorative" qualities of Cubist painting, which he felt did not respond properly to the needs of modern industrial society. Purist painters such as Charles-Edouard Jeanneret (Le Corbusier, *q.v.*) and Ferdinand Léger embraced this "machine aesthetic", but it was most influential on architecture.

Putto, a fat naked boy used as a decorative addition to painting and sculpture, especially in the Baroque (*q.v.*) period.

R

Rayonism was a short-lived Russian art movement including the work of Mikhail Larianov and Natalia Goncharova. The ideas behind it were consolidated in the 1913 Moscow Target exhibition. In the exhibition catalogue, Larianov described Rayonism as a combination of Cubism (*q.v.*), Futurism (*q.v.*) and Orphism (*q.v.*). It involved the use of intersecting rays of light, and partial or total abstraction.

Ready-made was a word used by the twentieth-century artist Marcel Duchamp to signify an object selected by an artist to be displayed as a work of art. The artist does not actually produce the work but merely presents it, thus changing the significance of an otherwise ordinary object. A ready-made is similar to a found object (*q.v.*), but it is less concerned with aesthetic values. The presentation of a ready-made in some ways undermines the whole process of production and display of art and should be considered as a somewhat cynical statement.

Realism is a vague term. As a movement in art it can be said to have started with Gustave Courbet in the mid-19th cent. in his revolt against the classicism of Ingres and the romanticism of Delacroix. He was a man of strong radical views, and like Zola, Balzac and Flaubert in literature, turned to the actuality of everyday life, recording it with frankness and vigour. Some young English painters, notably Bratby, of the "kitchen sink"

school, practise what some describe as social realism. In another sense, realism is an attitude concerned with interpreting the essential nature of the subject, revealing truths hidden by the accidentals of ordinary visual appearance. Thus form becomes more significant than content. Beginning with Cézanne and Van Gogh this trend passes on to Cubist and Abstract painting. *See also* **Section J** (philosophy).

Regency Style is the English version of the French Empire (*q.v.*) and approximately covers the period of the regency of Prince George, later George IV, from 1811 to 1820. It is somewhat less austere than the French style, and contains elements of the fantastic and exotic absent from Empire. The most famous monument of Regency style is the Royal Pavilion at Brighton, built for the Prince Regent by John Nash. (Regency style should not be confused with the *Régence* style in France, fashionable during the regency period between the death of Louis XIV in 1715 and the ascent to the throne of Louis XV in 1723. Here the English equivalent is Queen Anne style.)

Relief in sculpture is of three kinds—high relief (*alto-relievo*), in which the figures stand out to the extent of one-half of their natural proportions, low-relief (*basso-relievo*) when the figures project but slightly; and middle-relief (*mezzo-relievo*), when the projection is intermediate.

Renaissance. *See* **Section J.**

Repoussoir is French for "to push back". It signifies an object, usually a tree, which borders the foreground of a picture and draws the eye deeper into the space of a painting. It is especially used in landscape paintings by artists such as Claude (*q.v.*), where it serves a primarily compositional purpose.

Rococo, an architectural style which was, in effect, the final stage of **Baroque** (*q.v.*). The name first came into use about 1830 to describe the period 1720–70 and means "shell-shaped" (French *Rocaille*), since the shell was a favourite motif in Rococo ornamentation. At about the beginning of the 18th cent. the heavy older type of Baroque began to show even less restraint than had characterised it in the past; it became still less utilitarian, and showed a kind of playful light-hearted vitality which manifested itself in a wealth of ornamental invention. Baroque was flamboyant and robust, Rococo dainty, graceful and smiling. Its ornaments are frequently asymmetrical, and in this Rococo is unique among the historical styles of Europe. In architecture Rococo is naturally found in those areas where the Baroque flourished, *i.e.*, Munich, Prague, Vienna and Dresden. In painting, the best expressions of Rococo are to be seen in the works of the French painters Watteau (d. 1721), Boucher (d. 1770), and Fragonard (d. 1806).

Romanticism. *See* **Section J.**

S

Sacra conversazione, a type of altarpiece (*q.v.*) which originated in fifteenth-century Italy. It consists of the Madonna and Child with a group of saints standing around her. It departs from the Gothic (*q.v.*) tradition of separating the Madonna from saints in polyptychs (*q.v.*), and it also allows a greater apparent ease of association among holy figures.

St. Ives painters, a group of artists who congregated in St. Ives, Cornwall, in 1939. The group included Adrian Stokes, Barbara Hepworth and Ben Nicholson (*q.v.*). Unlike other such artistic colonies, this group was diverse in both style and subject-matter, though it tended to favour avant-garde work.

Salon, a French royally-sanctioned art institution. In 1667 the first salon was the exhibition of works by artists of the Académie Royale, shown in the Salon d'Apollon of the Louvre. There academic artists exhibited occasionally until 1737, when exhibitions became a biennial event. Art exhibitions were consolidated into the academic structure in the eighteenth century through the introduction of juries, who rejected paintings they did not feel appropriate for the Salon. After the French Revolution, the Salon was held every year and became increasingly important in the French art world until the 1860s, when it was challenged by alternative salons (*see* **Salon des Refusés, Salon d'Automne** and **Salon des Indépendants**).

Salon d'Automne, one of the salons formed in competition to the official academy Salon (*q.v.*). It began holding exhibitions from 1903, the most famous of which was the 1905 exhibition. This included works by Matisse, Dérain and Vlaminck which started the "Fauvist" movement.

Salon des Indépendants, one of the salons formed in competition to the official academy Salon (*q.v.*). It began in 1884 on the initiative of the *Société des Artistes Indépendants*, which included among its membership Seurat and Signac. This Salon rejected the jury system of the official Salon and became a major showplace for Post-Impressionist (*q.v.*) painting.

Salon des Refusés, an alternative salon set up in 1863 to house all the paintings rejected by the official Salon (*q.v.*). It resulted from an intensification of the anger and discouragement of French artists whose works had been consistently rejected by the Salon. To appease them, Napoleon III allowed all rejected works to be exhibited separately. The exhibition induced much derision and distaste in a conservative public, but it became the starting point for a more considered reaction against the French Academy and the hegemony of the official Salon. Manet's (*q.v.*) *Déjeuner sur l'herbe* was one of the works shown here.

Scumbling, when an opaque colour is applied over an already existing colour but allows the other colour to show through. Scumbling creates a textured or broken effect on the canvas surface.

Secession (Sezession), the name given to a series of rebellions against the academic system in Germany and Austria during the 1890s. Throughout Europe at this time, the limitations of academies were becoming apparent to artists who wanted to experiment with new methods, ideas and techniques. The Munich Secession was the first to express this sense of rebellion by turning away from academic classicism towards an art nouveau (*q.v.*) style. Closely following this were the Vienna Secession (beginning 1897), which was also sympathetic to art nouveau, and the Berlin Secession (from 1899) which encouraged an Impressionist (*q.v.*) style.

Secco, Italian for "dry", a term applied to fresco painting. Usually in a fresco, the plaster is painted while wet, but the *secco* method involves waiting for the plaster to dry before painting it. In the Middle Ages and the Renaissance (*see* **Section J**), this technique was usually used for touching up a finished fresco. If it was used exclusively, it caused more rapid deterioration in the painting.

Serial Art, a term used mainly in the United States to identify two forms of avant-garde which have in common a mathematical structuring principle. One refers to works conceived as part of a series or a larger group in which the meaning of individual parts is related to the meaning of the whole on a repetitive basis. The intention is to free the work of art from the tyranny of traditional concepts such as originality and uniqueness. The other, more specific understanding of the term is related to a type of minimal art in which simple, uniform, mass-produced component parts are put together in a regular pattern. Artists who have produced serial art include Tony Smith and Carl Andre.

Seriography. *See* **Silk screen printing.** (*below*).

Shunga The erotic art of Japan. It flourished first in painted scrolls.

Sfumato, Italian for "smoke", is a term used in the sixteenth century to signify gradations of colour and tone which avoided stark outlines and created a sense of depth. It was applied especially to the soft tonal effects of Leonardo da Vinci's (*q.v.*) paintings.

Silk screen printing is also called seriography. It is a Japanese technique imported into Europe in the nineteenth century, which involves masking a silk screen with pieces of paper or cardboard and then pressing colour through the screen onto a piece of paper beneath it. Although a skilled designer is necessary for a successful silk screen print, the actual process of making the print can be carried out by anyone.

Sinopia, an earthy red-brown colour used to make a preliminary drawing for a fresco in the Middle Ages and also the Renaissance. The sinopia was applied first, then covered with intonaco (*q.v.*), which was then painted. It served as a prepara-tory sketch over which the final painting could be constructed.

Sistine Chapel. *See* **Section L.**

Social Realism, a type of Realism (*q.v.*) concerned not just with style but with subject-matter. The term is applied to paintings of the nineteenth and twentieth centuries which have social or political subtexts, especially of a Leftist variety. Social Realism possibly began with Courbet, whose unapologetic, even heroic, paintings of peasants were especially subversive during a period of political unrest in Europe (*c.* 1848–9). The term has also been used to describe the work of the American Ashcan School (*q.v.*) and the British Kitchen Sink School (*q.v.*).

Socialist Realism, as opposed to Social Realism (*q.v.*), had a very specific propagandist purpose. In its strictest sense, it signified the official art of the Communist USSR developed under Stalin's dictatorship. Its structures were laid down by the 1934 Soviet Congress. It used a Realist (*q.v.*) style with proletariat subject-matter as a form of instruction to the people. From 1934 until *glasnost*, it was the only official art of the Soviet Union.

Stijl, De (Dutch, "The Style"), a Dutch art magazine which perpetuated the Neo-Plasticism (*q.v.*) of Piet Mondrian and Theo van Doesburg. The magazine began in 1917, and its articles stressed pure abstract or non-objective (*q.v.*) form in painting, sculpture and architecture. Its subsequent influence was primarily in the realm of architecture, and the ideas of *De Stijl* were particularly influential in reforming the Bauhaus (*q.v.*) when Doesburg visited it in 1923.

Still-life, a type of painting which precludes the depiction of human beings and concentrates on everyday objects such as fruit or flowers. It was popularised in Holland during the seventeenth century, when its immediate appeal was appreciated by the art-buying middle-class, and it continued to be popular throughout the eighteenth and nineteenth centuries, when its most notable practitioners were Chardin (*q.v.*) and Cézanne (*q.v.*). Still-lifes (the accepted plural form) often took on emblematic or moralistic meanings, reflecting the vanity or transience of human existence, but despite their potential depth of meaning, they were considered the lowest category of painting by European art academies (*q.v.*).

This relegation of still-lifes also accentuated the repression of women artists, as they were excluded from official training institutions and often painted solely still-lifes.

Sublime, a term which has an ancient origin but was brought into the realm of aesthetics during the eighteenth century. Edmund Burke's (*q.v.*) *Enquiry Into the Origins of Our Idea of the Sublime and the Beautiful* (1757) postulated an aesthetic category which engaged the emotions. The sublime involved a feeling of awe or terror inspired by overwhelming natural forces. Burke's writings were influential on the growth of Gothic novels, and they were later used to good effect in landscape painting by artists such as Turner (*q.v.*) and John Martin.

Subway Art. *See* **Graffiti Art.**

Superrealism (Hyperrealism, Photorealism) describes paintings of the 1970s onwards which attempted to evoke a photographic illusion of reality. In some cases, the artist actually copies a photograph.

Suprematism, a term invented by the Russian artist Kasimir Malevich to describe his non-objective (*q.v.*) paintings, such as *White on White*. The theory behind Suprematism is complicated and involves an attempt to articulate in visual terms a "fourth dimension". Malevich's first exercises in Suprematism occurred in 1913, and he officially christened the movement in 1915.

Surrealism. The aim of the Surrealist school of painting and sculpture is to overcome the barriers between conscious and unconscious mind, the real and unreal worlds of waking and dreaming. As such it has a long and respectable ancestry, although the term was not in use until 1922 when it was picked by André Breton from Guillaume Apollinaire who had used it in connection with certain works by Chagall.

However, Bosch in the 15th cent., Fuseli and Goya in the 18th, and many other purveyors of the weird and fantastic were the forerunners of modern Surrealism. The modern movement has broadly speaking taken two different directions: the first was towards complete fantasy and absurdity which took the form of "found objects"—*e.g.* a bird-cage filled with sugarcubes and a thermometer, a bottle-dryer, a bicycle wheel, or abstract works with strange and apparently irrelevant titles such as Paul Klee's *Twittering Machine*; the second towards highly detailed and realistic paintings of objects placed in strange juxtapositions—*e.g.*, Salvador Dali's trees with limp watches drooping over their branches.

Symbolism began as a literary term referring to French poetry of the 1850s, but in the 1880s and 1890s it was applied to painting. Symbolist artists rejected the tenets of Impressionism (*q.v.*), which they saw as too involved with perceptual response. Instead they concentrated on the representation of spiritual and subjective feelings, which often manifested themselves in religious or erotic subject-matter. Its French exponents included Puvis de Chavannes, Odilon Redon and Gustav Moreau, but the ideas of Symbolism soon spread throughout Europe.

Synchromism, an abstract movement founded in 1912 by two American artists living in Paris, Stanton MacDonald-Wright and Morgan Russell. Synchromism aims to unite music and painting by orchestrating colours like notes in the process of composing a symphony. The results are usually abstract dynamic shapes with a central vortex that explodes in complex colour harmonies.

Synthetism refers to the work of Gauguin's followers who, in the 1890s, produced paintings which included large patches of concentrated colour surrounded by black lines, as in Gauguin's *cloisonnism*. The root word "synthesis" refers to Gauguin's idea that painting should represent a concentrated synthesis of the artist's emotions. Synthetist artists painted from memory, rather than copied the world before them as the Impressionists (*q.v.*) had done.

T

Tachisme is sometimes used synonymously with Abstract Expressionism (*q.v.*), but it strictly refers to a French movement of the 1950s which consisted of paintings composed of large blobs or *taches* of colour. It derives its name from the French for stain or splash.

Tapestry, a fabric largely used in earlier ages for wall decoration and hangings. It was known to the ancient Greeks, but in its modern form came into prominence in the 15th and 16th cent., when it was manufactured in a marked degree of excellence by the weavers of Flanders, especially those of Arras. The manufacture was introduced into England early in the 17th cent. Nowadays the term is applied to worsted cloths for furniture coverings, and there are also various kinds of tapestry carpets now made. The most famous tapestries of old times were the Aubusson Tapestry and the Savonnerie. The Gobelin Tapestry factory, originated in Paris in the reign of Francis I, is still a national establishment. *See also* Bayeux Tapestry, Section L.

Tempera, a painting technique used commonly by medieval artists before it was superseded by oil painting in the fifteenth century. It is made by mixing powdered colour with egg yolk, egg white or the whole egg to create an opaque paint.

Tonalism, a term coined by the painter Samuel Isham (1855–1914) in his book *The History of American Painting* (1905) to refer to a trend in American painting in which idealised, intimate romanticised landscapes predominate and resemble Impressionism and Pictorial photography, popular at the same time. Tonalism was practised by painters such as George Innes and Dwyght Tryon and by James Abbott McNeill Whistler, even though he did not technically belong to the American trend as he was mostly based in Europe.

Tondo, Italian for "round", is a circular painting or sculpture, popular in fifteenth-century Italy.

Triptych, an altarpiece composed of three panels hinged together. This is one of the most common types of altarpieces, as the two outer panels can fold together over the inner panel. The outer panels were thus usually painted on the inside and the outside to allow two different visual effects.

Trompe l'oeil literally means to "fool the eye". It refers to a considered attempt at illusionism that makes it difficult to tell whether or not a painted surface is real. *Trompe l'oeil* devices were commonly used in ceiling painting, and they were employed by the Cubists (*q.v.*) to create an amusing dissonance between optical space and the perspective distortions of Cubist space.

V

Varnish is a transparent hard, protective film, usually painted or sprayed over a finished painting in order to preserve it. Although varnish will help the paint to remain stable, it often darkens over time and paradoxically can cause extreme damage to a painting's surface.

Verism was a name given to the German *Neue Sachlichkeit* (*q.v.*) artists such as George Grosz and Otto Dix, who produced scathing, and often disturbing, satires on Weimar society in the 1920s.

Vienna School of Fantastic Realism. Founded by Ernst Fuchs (1930–2015), it emphasised clarity and detail.

Vorticism, a term coined by Ezra Pound to name a British art movement which began in 1913 on the initiative of Wyndham Lewis, Ezra Pound (*q.v.*) and Edward Wadsworth. The movement brought both Cubism (*q.v.*) and Futurism (*q.v.*) into England, as its practitioners were concerned with modern life as well as with the abrogation of the stale stability of established art. From 1914 the artists produced a magazine called *BLAST*, and they held their only exhibition in 1915. The First World War dissipated their momentum.

W

Wanderers, The, a group of nineteenth-century Russian artists who attempted to carry their ideas to the country peasantry. Reacting against the elitism of the Imperial Academy of Arts in St. Petersburg, artists such as Ilya Repin established itinerant exhibitions to show their Social Realist (*q.v.*) paintings of Russian peasant life and Russian history. Founded in 1870, the Wanderers continued to exist until the early twentieth century.

Watercolour, a technique of painting involving water soluble colours. Watercolour creates a transparent effect, as opposed to the opaque effect of gouache, (*q.v.*), which is particularly useful for landscape painting. It was used by Dürer (*q.v.*) in the early sixteenth century for landscape sketches, but it only became popular at the end of the eighteenth century with the growth of Picturesque (*q.v.*) tourism. The ease of using watercolour made it a particularly appropriate technique for amateurs.

Weaving. The interlacing of two or more threads at right angles to form a fabric is a craft that has been practised since ancient times. The main principle of the weaving loom is the same today as it was thousands of years ago; a warp extends lengthwise through the loom, the threads being held in separate regular order by being passed through a reed or "slay", while the weft is crossed through alternating threads of the warp by means of a shuttle which holds the weft. Thus the fabric is built up. Weaving was done by hand up to the early part of the 19th cent., when Cartwright's steam-power loom was introduced. The Jacquard loom for weaving figured designs dates from 1801.

Woodcut, a print technique which involves cutting into a block of wood, inking the block and then pressing it onto a piece of paper. The raised portions of the wood create the design, and the cut portions read as white spaces on the final print. It is one of the oldest printing techniques, and it was used from the fifteenth century. It was superseded by engraving (*q.v.*), but it was revived in the early twentieth century by the German Expressionists.

World of Art (Mir Iskusstva), influential Russian art magazine and art movement which began in St. Petersburg in 1899. It was directed against the seeming parochialism of Russian art.

PART II. AN INTRODUCTION TO ARCHITECTURE

This basic introduction to British architecture deals with the chronological development of building styles and types from classical times to the present day. Leading architects are discussed with reference to their outstanding surviving creations. Although the study focuses deliberately on Britain, the important influences from overseas are discussed as are the classical Greek and Roman models on which much of the country's building was indirectly or directly based. A glossary of some terms is also included.

GREEK ARCHITECTURE

Although the Greeks never settled in Britain, their buildings are important here not so much in themselves but as a source and inspiration for later architects. The Greeks were responsible for devising the three basic orders in classical architecture: Doric, Ionic and most latterly Corinthian.

These orders with their particular base, shaft, capital and entablatures formed the basic vocabulary of Greek and Roman building and in their turn lay at the basis of Western European architecture from the Renaissance until the dawn of the Modern movement. The Greeks also made important discoveries about proportion and tricks of perspective, giving their columns and beams a slight curve (entasis, *q.v*) to make them appear straight when viewed from a distance. These fundamental rules together with the Greek building system represent the very basic sources of architecture.

The Greek Temple.

The typical Greek temple structure consists of an outer row of Doric columns arranged in a rectangular plan. These surround the central enclosed place of worship and support the low-pitched gabled roof with its decorated pediment. With a much revised interior construction, this basic plan was subsequently adopted by European architects in the early 19th cent as a suitable framework for town halls or important public buildings. Greek architecture rose to prominence at the end of the 18th cent. in Britain when discoveries of archaeological remains by travellers and antiquarians on the Grand Tour stimulated its revival. Greek temples and their decorative devices became the models for churches, country houses and government buildings. However, the enthusiasm was relatively short-lived and Roman models took the place of Greek.

Famous Surviving Examples.

Some of the finest examples of surviving Greek temple buildings include: the Temple of Poseidon, Paestum (*c.* 460 B.C.), the Theseion, Athens (449–444 B.C.) and the Parthenon, Athens (447–432 B.C.), while the Theatre at Epidauros (*c.* 350 B.C.) and the restored Stadium at Athens (*c.* 160 A.D.) provide instances of other building types.

ROMAN ARCHITECTURE

As well as designing a wide range of building types, the Romans, like the Greeks before them, were responsible for devising an important set of architectural rules and orders. From the Greeks they adopted the three orders of pillar and beam construction (Doric, Ionic and Corinthian) which they modified to suit themselves and added a further two of their own—Tuscan Doric and Composite. Corinthian and Ionic capitals combined.

In practice, their most popular liking was for the Tuscan Doric (a slim, unfluted shaft with a simple capital and base) and the Corinthian (a richly adorned capital decorated with acanthus leaf motifs and often supported by a fluted shaft). But in a manner unknown in Greece, the Romans frequently applied their orders to what was in essence a pier and arch structure—superimposing orders on top of one another to form the outer walls of a two- or three-storey building. Engineering techniques advanced further under the Romans, principally the introduction of the arch, which allowed them to extend the structural possibilities available to architects. Temples, villas, public buildings and forts are characteristic of the Roman occupation of Britain and it is a tribute to their sound construction that many survive at a variety of sites throughout the country.

Examples of Roman Architecture.

Villas have been preserved at Verulamium (St. Albans), Chedworth in Gloucester, Bignor in Sussex, and at Lullingstone, while the Aquae Sulis at Bath is a splendid public bath and spa. Military garrisons and forts include Corstopitum (Corbridge, Northumberland), Burgh Castle, Great Yarmouth, while a fort on Hadrian's Wall survives at Borcovicium (Housesteads, Northumberland). There is a splendid Roman palace at Fishbourne, near Chichester, discovered in 1960.

As in the case of Greek architecture, Roman buildings, their orders and rules were studied, reproduced and used as the basis for Western architecture from the Renaissance onwards. Their importance lies for British architecture, therefore, not so much in themselves but as an inspiration for others at a time when engineering and building techniques were more advanced, allowing architects to develop classical principles to lengths undreamed of in ancient Greece and Rome.

ROMANESQUE ARCHITECTURE

Romanesque architecture in Britain corresponds with the rule of the Anglo-Saxon and early Norman kings, the period from the departure of the Romans in the 4th cent. A.D. until the dawn of Gothic building in the latter part of the 12th. Because of its very age and the fact that most buildings were constructed from timber, Anglo-Saxon architecture has few representatives in England today. The soundest—their small solid stone churches—have proved the most durable. Towers at Earls Barton and at Sompting and churches at Bradford-on-Avon, Wiltshire, Boarhunt, Hampshire and Worth, Sussex are among the few surviving examples of Saxon building. Characteristic features include rows of plain round-arched windows, pilaster strips forming simple decorative patterns, thick ragstone or rubble walls, small openings and plain arches.

Norman Castles and Cathedrals.

Under the Normans, a particularly warlike race, architectural building extended to embrace castles, though a number of fine cathedrals and churches were also built. All are typified by the plain roundarch. Columns, circular in cross-section, and decoration generally were simply executed with no apparent reference to classical architecture. These were solid, soundly engineered structures with little pretension to style. Because of the tendency to rebuild or enlarge castles and cathedrals not many examples have survived: there are, however, a few which are outstanding: the White Tower at the Tower of London (1086–97), Castle Hedingham, Essex (*c.* 1140) and Orford Castle, Suffolk (1166–72) all of which consist of a central keep set on an artificial mound and surrounded by earthworks.

In the ecclesiastical field, the nave of Durham Cathedral (1110–33) has splendid dog-tooth decorated columns and arches; other predominantly Norman cathedrals include Norwich and Chichester, while the naves at Rochester, St. Albans, Chichester, Hereford, Peterborough and Ely all include Norman building. As with the castles, they are massively constructed from stone.

GOTHIC ARCHITECTURE

The architecture of the Middle Ages, whose most characteristic feature was the pointed arch, is said to have spanned the 13th to the 15th cents. Gothic building is essentially a structural system based on arches, piers, vaults and buttresses arranged and decorated to an overall plan. In the absence of great Gothic castles or private houses, the system was most fully developed and seen to best effect in cathedrals and monasteries in mediaeval Britain.

The Three Main Periods.

Following a transitional phase from *c.* 1150 to 1190 when, for example, pointed arches were introduced into structures otherwise Romanesque in character, Gothic architecture has traditionally been divided into three periods: Early English, 1190–1310, occasionally known as the lancet style from the typical shape of the long narrow windows, Decorated, 1310–1380, where the degree of decoration is heightened, window tracery being symmetrical in form or "Geometrical", followed by a period of increasingly complex and more flowing patterns called "Curvilinear", and finally the Perpendicular phase, 1380–1485, when the term "Rectilinear" is used to describe larger windows divided by horizontal tracery members or transoms.

While good examples of each of these three phases and their intermediate transitional phases survive in Britain, it is often possible when visiting a large cathedral to distinguish them all exhibited in various parts of the same building. Cathedral construction took many generations and as architects and masons were succeeded so new ideas of design became incorporated in the overall plan. The progressive expansion and re-building of Canterbury Cathedral throughout the mediaeval period has meant that it is possible to see here most styles of building from Norman through to Perpendicular; the same may also be said of York and Worcester.

However, Salisbury Cathedral (1220–65) was almost wholly constructed in the Early English period and remains one of Britain's most complete and coherent designs. Lincoln too is mostly Early English with Decorated additions.

Improvements in Structural Techniques.

In general it is possible to say that as structural techniques improved in the Middle Ages, the massive character of the Early English period gradually gave way to thinner walls, more complicated and loftier vaulting supported by splendid buttresses, increasingly ornate collections of columns and capitals, more elaborate tracery in larger windows filled with vivid stained glass pictures and a greater concern with surface ornament. Towers are late Gothic features and they, in common with the building below, assumed the decorative characteristics of the Perpendicular phase, replacing the spires which had dominated the Early English and Decorated churches and cathedrals.

The Castles of Wales.

Generally speaking castles became less buildings of war and more country houses as the Middle Ages passed. The Early English period corresponded under Edward I with a great castle building era in Wales and produced possibly the finest defensive garrisons of the time. Harlech (1283–90) and Beaumaris (1283–1323) both have solidly built rings of battlemented and turreted wall, allowing the defenders to retreat into progressively more solid and awesome towers for a last-ditch defence. Bodiam Castle (1385), built in the following cent., only boasts an outer wall though it is surrounded by a moat; the living conditions are more spacious and less care is taken to see that they are protected. Finally Oxburgh Hall (1482), a 15th-cent. manor house, has virtually given up all pretence of being a castle, retaining only the square plan and central courtyard in its design. Although the outer walls are solidly built, there are no proper battlements or turrets, the living quarters forming the square plan. Still not quite a country house, Oxburgh Hall indicates that the day of the castle, though not the garrison, had largely passed.

TUDOR ARCHITECTURE

The architecture of the Tudor monarchs (from Henry VII's accession in 1485 until Elizabeth I's death in 1603) witnessed for the moment the penultimate phase of Gothic building and the flowering of the country house. While European architects

and particularly those in Italy were re-discovering classical antiquity, Britain, which had recently left the Papal fold, was pursuing a severely national or vernacular line (*q.v.*) Tudor architecture was essentially Perpendicular Gothic modified in places by a few graftings from the Renaissance in Italy.

A strong accent was placed on local building styles and materials. Where stone was unavailable patterned bricks became common, featuring as finely decorated chimney stacks, which contrasted pleasantly with drip-mould windows and doorways. Leaded lozenge windows emitted light into linenfold panelled rooms.

Houses increased in size with the addition of summer and winter parlours, studies, bedrooms and for the first time, state rooms, like the great chamber and the dining chamber. Hampton Court Palace (*c.* 1520) provides an excellent example of Tudor building on a grand scale constructed from red brick with stone dressings, oriel windows over the gateways and finely carved chimneys. Barrington Court (1518) is a smaller country house with individual Gothic features treated in a very English fashion: square-headed windows with mullions and transoms, sharply pitched roofs and gables and a symmetrical plan with a central porch

Elizabethan Country Houses.

In the Elizabethan period houses were generally constructed on the E plan with the central porch forming the third bar between the two wings. However, fine stone country houses, square in plan built around a central courtyard, include Longleat House, Wiltshire (1567–80) and Wollaton Hall, Nottingham (1580–88) designed by Robert Smithson (*c.* 1536–1614), while Montacute House, Somerset (1580–99), and Pitchford, Shropshire (1560–70) are based on the E plan. In this later period elevations showed a greater unity and symmetry then before and were lit by much broader areas of window.

The central feature of the façade was often a two-or three-storey porch or pavilion decorated with strapwork ornamentation and topped by a pediment containing a Gothic coat of arms. The porch at Kirby Hall. Northampton (1575) shows French inspiration, that at Cobham Hall, (1594) Flemish.

JACOBEAN AND STUART ARCHITECTURE

The Jacobean period (1603–25) witnessed the final phase of Gothic building in England before it was revived in the late 18th cent. Designs tended to be simpler and more restrained than under Elizabeth and exhibited a growing tendency to employ Italianate ornament rather then Gothic. Symmetrically arranged in traditional fashion, the following houses are representative of the Jacobean period: Hatfield House, Hertfordshire (1607–11) designed by Robert Lyminge, Bramshill, Hampshire (1605–12), Audley End, Essex (1603–16) and Charlton House, London (1607–12). In a sense this was a transitional phase between the English vernacular Gothic of the Tudor period and the influence of the Italian Renaissance under Jones and Wren. In their restraint, the great Jacobean houses have a classical feeling but in the retention of many late mediaeval features, such as mullioned windows and turrets they justify the contemporary appelation "King Jamie's Gothic".

The Work of Inigo Jones.

By contrast the Stuart period (1625–1702) by admitting the influence of European architecture, produced one of the richest periods in English building. Its first leader was Inigo Jones (1573–1652) designer of the Queen's House, Greenwich (1616–35) and the Banqueting Hall, Whitehall (1619–22) together with a large number of country houses.

Jones began life as a designer of scenery and costumes for court masques but having made two visits to Italy to study the work of Palladio, he brought back to England a pure Italian Renaissance style which was then of a wholly new character. Putting his knowledge and ideas to work as Surveyor-General of Works to the Crown in his two seminal designs, the Queen's House and the Banqueting Hall, Jones's work through the influence of Palladio marked a return to classical models so long ignored in Britain. However, because of the original and startling nature of these two designs, his influence was not immediate and most early 17th-cent. country houses are Jacobean rather than classical in style.

Sir Christopher Wren.

Sir Christopher Wren (1632–1723), who focused his attentions on church builing, followed in Jones' footsteps as the architectural leader of the latter part of the cent. St. Paul's Cathedral (1675–1710) forms the centrepiece of his work in rebuilding London's churches after the Great Fire of 1666, while St. Martin Ludgate (1677–84), St. Clement Danes, Strand (1680–82) and St. Mary-le-Bow, Cheapside (1670–73) should not be forgotten. He also designed the additions to Hampton Court Palace (1689–94), Chelsea Hospital (1682–91) and Tom Tower, Christ Church College Oxford (1682).

With the exception of the latter, these buildings clearly derived their influence from the Italian Renaissance, obeying its rules of construction as well as using its orders. Unlike Jones, Wren succeeded in developing the style in such a way—by drawing on French and Dutch examples as well and by inclining it towards the Baroque—that he produced a distinctly English version of classicism. His structural skills were remarkable as demonstrated by his masterly use of traditional materials and by the Portland stone which he introduced to London where it became so popular.

English Baroque.

Towards the end of the cent and in the early years of the 18th cent. there developed a new and more vigorous form of classicism—the so-called English Baroque. Rules and conventions were ignored or bent to achieve arresting affects of grandeur, richness and movement. The leaders of this movement were Wren's pupil Nicholas Hawksmoor (1661–1736) and Sir John Vanbrugh (1664–1726), men who no longer felt constrained by the self-imposed discipline of their predecessors. Plan and details were handled with great confidence, featuring twisted and rusticated columns, elaborate curved entablatures and pediments accompanied by a great display of ornament and sculpture of abounding vitality.

These buildings were constructed on a grand scale such as Vanburgh's Blenheim Palace, Oxford (1704–20) and Castle Howard, Yorkshire (1699–1712), while Hawksmoor designed parts of All Souls (1715–40) and Queen's College, Oxford (1709–38).

PALLADIAN ARCHITECTURE

Following the vigorous and expansive Continental treatment of buildings in the Baroque period, English architects moved towards a more restrained approach. For their guide they selected Colen Campbell's *Vitruvius Britannicus*, a folio of engravings of classical buildings in Britain, first appearing in 1715. This represented not only a return to British examples, but also a return to a rational system of architecture, where restraint, order and symmetry were paramount. Andrea Palladio's (1508–80) classical villas formed a second major source for English architects. For example, Lord Burlington's villa. Chiswick House (begun 1725), was a scaled-down version of Palladio's Villa Rotunda at Vicenza (1550–53), while Campbell's design for Mereworth Castle, Kent (1723–25) was a slightly enlarged interpretation. The Palladian movement, taking its name from Palladio, represented a fresh devotion to antiquity, not necessarily antiquity as it really had been, but as Englishmen now viewed it.

Palladian Country Houses.

The Palladian movement probably found its finest expression in the country house. Its characteristic features include: a strictly formal three-part grouping, comprising a central block with pedimented porch or portico and two widely spaced symmetrical wings connected to it by single-storey passages, screens or colonnades. The basement floor is usually rusticated and forms a plinth to the Giant Order which extends through the two principal stories of the façade to a decorative entablature. Restraint in the use of ornament, with stress on order and proportion, characterise these cleanly

executed stone houses. It was a patriotic movement drawing on the designs of Inigo Jones, who in the early 17th cent. had first been responsible for the introduction of this interpretation of Italian Renaissance architecture.

The Typical Town House.

The Palladian schema was also readily applied to the town house. Usually three storeys high, these restrained brick buildings were despised by the Victorians for their simplicity and lack of stylistic variety and ornament. The ground and second floor windows were usually of roughly the same size (the former being slightly larger), while the first floor had the largest, demonstrating its importance—here were the dining and reception rooms. The top floor had the smallest, partly as they lit the servants' quarters, but also to bring the upward movement of the eye to a halt beneath the entablature, above which there might be an attic. There was normally a minimum of adornment, being limited to the columns placed at the entrance or the cast-iron railings around the steps and pavement.

THE GREEK REVIVAL

Although the Palladian movement was classical in origin, it largely confined itself to Roman models. The development of the study of archaeology and a rising interest in Greek civilisation, made available a growing volume of material for architects interested in classical buildings. Although Greek archaeological discoveries were being made in the mid-18th cent. Greek architecture did not become fashionable until the 1790s and experienced a fairly short-lived popularity, falling from favour in the 1830s, though certain architects, such as Alexander "Greek" Thomson (1817–75) in Glasgow, did revive its use in the latter part of the 19th cent.

Like the Palladian movement, the Greek Revival stressed symmetry, order and proportion, but was responsible for introducing a new range of architectural features. The Greek Doric and Ionic orders were adopted, while their entrances and window surrounds superseded the Roman arch. Greek details were used for decoration, including echinus moulding, key and disc string courses *etc*.

The Work of John Nash.

One of its greatest exponents, though not a purist, was John Nash (1752–1835) who was responsible for re-building the main thoroughfares between Regent's and St. James's Park. His London Park Crescent (begun 1812) features a splendid sweep of coupled Greek Ionic columns, while Cumberland Terrace (1827) has a central Ionic portico and pilasters arranged in the Giant Order. Sir Robert Smirke (1780–1867) similarly resorted to the Greek style for his Covent Garden Theatre (1808–09, burnt down 1856), and General Post Office (1824–29, demolished 1913), while W. and H. W. Inwood's St. Pancras Church (1819–22) exhibits a full range of Greek features including a low-pitched Ionic portico and classical statues supporting the aisles.

THE GOTHIC REVIVAL

The Gothic Revival, like the Greek Revival, had its origins in the awakening interest in archaeology and British history. Unlike Palladian buildings, Gothic was founded in the philosophy of the "Picturesque". In a sense its principles were the very opposite of those encompassed by notions of classical beauty. The picturesque derived its appeal from an asymmetrical arrangement of differing forms and it was this sense of variety and surprise which gave it interest. Its features, which were supposedly selected from England's medieval past, included the pointed arch, tracery, buttresses, towers, turrets and battlements, *etc*.

Although Gothic gained a certain acceptance in the latter part of the 18th cent. (Horace Walpole's (1717–97) house. Strawberry Hill, Twickenham was built from 1748 onwards), it did not gain wide popularity until the decline of the Greek Revival when Romantic thought had triumphed over Enlightened opinion, and rules had been replaced by passions.

The Contribution of Pugin.

Before the 1830s most Gothic buildings, though dressed in 14th-century clothes, had conformed to symmetrical classical plans and were scarcely truthful representations of their mediaeval counterparts. The move towards a more genuinely picturesque interpretation was publicised by A. W. N. Pugin (1812–52). A practising architect himself, Pugin wrote a series of studies extolling the virtues of Christian architecture. Although mostly concerned with churches, his principles were taken up and developed to cover other building types. Essentially, he argued that function should dictate design not pre-conceived classical rules, and that buildings should be constructed in a moral style (for him, English Gothic) which alone had the ability to elevate the population. By publicising Gothic (Pugin together with Charles Barry was responsible for the design of the Houses of Parliament, from 1837). Pugin paved the way for the "battle of the styles" that was to break out in the mid-19th cent.

NEO-CLASSICAL ARCHITECTURE

Having seen that the Greek Revival was based on a re-discovery of antiquity, the same is also true of the Neo-Classical movement. Following the Palladian tradition, there arose a fresh interest in Italian Renaissance building, though no longer treated in a rigid and severely ordered fashion. Romanticism had supplanted the Enlightenment and men felt that the free flow of the passions had more to offer than pure reason. The Greek Revival was followed in the 1840s and '50s by a Graeco-Roman phase of great magnificence used for public buildings such as the St. George's Hall, Liverpool (1840–54) by H. Lonsdale Elmes (1814–1847), and the Fitzwilliam Museum, Cambridge (1837–47) by George Basevi (1794–1845), although both were actually completed by C. R. Cockerell (1788–1845). Although most of these buildings were Roman in inspiration, in some later examples architects no longer felt bound to distinguish between Greek and Roman models and used forms of decoration for each civilisation, no longer rigorous in their obedience to tradition.

The Genius of Soane.

The leaders of the Neo-Classical movement were Sir Charles Barry (1795–1860) and C. R. Cockerell, though it would be wrong to omit the original genius of Sir John Soane (1753–1831) from any consideration of British architecture. Not strictly speaking a Neo-Classicist, Soane's very originality makes him difficult to categorise, but he probably occupies a transitional position between the rigid Palladian schema and the greater freedom and adventurousness of the Neo-Classicists. He evolved a personal style that blended Baroque grandeur of composition with a Grecian severity of detail. Although not prolific in output, his austerity, crisp lines, simplicity of surface and feeling for cubic relations and space, were all manifested in his own house, No. 13 Lincoln's Inn Fields (1812–13), now the Soane Museum. Unfortunately his finest work at the Bank of England, the Bank Stock Office (1792–93) and the Dividend Office (1818–23) were both demolished in 1927.

Barry and Cockerell.

But to return to Barry and Cockerell, the former is perhaps best known for his design of London clubs: the Travellers (1829–31) and its neighbour the Reform (1837–41) are his finest. Barry used Italian Renaissance palaces (adapted from originals in Florence and Venice) for his designs and this resulted in the use of the term "palazzo" style. In contrast with the earlier Palladian movement (and offering certain similarities to the work of Inigo Jones), Barry's designs were not as tightly restrained by classical rules of proportion and construction but influenced by Romanticism and hence were more vigorous, lively and plastic than 18th-cent, palace designs. Other good examples of Neo-Classical architecture include the Free Trade Hall, Manchester (1853–54), by Edward Walters (1808–72), Barry's Athenaeum, Manchester (1837–39), the Bristol branch of the Bank of England (1844–46) and the Liverpool branch (1845–58) both by C. R. Cockerell.

THE HIGH VICTORIAN MOVEMENT

In many ways the High Victorian movement represented an extension of Pugin's principles, a romantic development of his views. Its leaders were John Ruskin (1819–1900), who never designed a single building and William Butterfield (1814–1900), who never wrote a single treatise. As writer and architect respectively, they publicised and practised the art of High Victorian building. Ruskin argued in the *Seven Lamps of Architecture* (1849) and the *Stones of Venice* (1853) that the finest examples of Mediaeval Gothic architecture were to be seen in the great Italian cities of Venice and Florence. Their aristocratic and mercantile palaces, together with the splendid churches and eathedrals, provided the models for Ruskin's theories. He believed in vigorous and powerful designs—on balance, he suggested, Pugin's many churches lacked mass and power—and in a sense he succeeded in synthesising Burke's views on the sublime with those of Uvedale Price and Pugin on the picturesque. Ruskin applied the sublime notions of scale, mass and awe to the Venetian Gothic of mediaeval Italy, while Pugin preferred Early English as a morally purer style; Ruskin and the later Victorians were more eclectic and went abroad for their inspiration.

Ruskin and his supporters also believed that buildings should be constructed from polychrome materials, and executed by the most skilled of craftsmen. Multi-coloured stones, the use of different coloured bricks and terra-cotta, providing that they were not machine-made or moulded, were the hall-marks of their buildings. The skills of the Christian craftsmen eulogised in Ruskin's writing were later to be selected and used as the basis for the Arts and Crafts movement by William Morris and his followers.

High Victorian Churches.

One of the first High Victorian churches was Butterfield's All Saints, Margaret Street, London (1850–59), whose richness and powerful design was later surpassed by his designs for Keble College, Oxford, where the magnificent chapel (1867–83) formed the centrepiece. Although originally applied to churches, High Victorian Gothic was felt to be almost universally applicable to all building types—a style for the period, again in contrast to Pugin's Gothic. Indeed some of the most successful buildings of the time were its public buildings—clear expressions of Victorian society—such as town halls, museums, public libraries, universities, mechanics' institutes, workhouses and prisons. Councils who commissioned them saw these structures as permanent expressions of their pride and status, sparing no expense on their construction and adornment. Alfred Waterhouse (1830–1905) designed Manchester Town Hall (1868–77), the Albert Memorial, London (1863–72) and the Prudential Assurance Building, Holborn (1878–85): Sir George Gilbert Scott (1811–78), another great exponent of High Gothic, designed St. Pancras station and hotel (1868–74) and Glasgow University (1868–71).

The Battle of the Styles.

These examples are, of course, all Gothic but it ought to be remembered that the High Victorian period corresponded with the so-called "battle of the styles". This resulted from the continued popularity of Italianate architecture producing a division in popular taste. As Gothic became more elaborate in ornament, open to foreign influence, and richly executed, so Italianate buildings received similar treatment. Scott's Foreign Office buildings, Whitehall (1860–75), and Cuthbert Broderick's (1822–1905) Town Hall, Leeds (1853–59), a grandiose example of High Victorian classicism, are instances of the continued popularity of Italianate or Roman models, while the National Westminster Bank, Bishopsgate, London (1865) by John Gibson is classical rather than Gothic in inspiration.

EDWARDIAN ARCHITECTURE

In some senses Edwardian architecture may be viewed as a reaction to the highly ornate and richly executed Gothic of the Victorian period. As before, no one style came to the fore and the period was characterised by a number of revivals often executed in a more simple if equally exuberant and confident manner. For house building, small office blocks and flats, the Queen Anne style was judged to be appropriate, while for public buildings, city offices, department stores and important monuments, the Renaissance and Baroque styles of the 17th cent. were adapted to suit modern conditions.

Examples of Baroque include Selfridges Store, Oxford Street (1907–09) whose façade was designed by the American architect Francis Swales, and Colchester Town Hall (1897–1902) by John Belcher (1841–1913), while Renaissance designs include Ralph Knott's London County Hall, on the South Bank (1912–22) and Sir Edwin Lutyen's (1869–1944) Britannic House, Finsbury Square (1926).

Although these buildings were technically quite advanced—they were constructed using the new steel framework, the first English building of this type being the Ritz Hotel, Piccadilly (1905–06) by Mewes and Davis—their façades, unlike contemporary American buildings, did not reflect their modern internal structure but concealed it beneath styles adapted from former ages. One of the few buildings to reflect its internal framework in a modified classical façade was Kodak House, Kingsway, London (1910–11) designed by Sir John Burnet (1857–1938).

New Sources of Inspiration.

Those architects who did not necessarily draw on the past for their inspiration found two other developments of interest: Art Nouveau and the Arts and Crafts movement (see **N3**). The former was a style of decoration and building chiefly founded on the Continent, coming to the fore between 1890 and 1910 when it was adopted in Britain by Arthur Mackmurdo (1851–1942), the Scottish architect, and Charles Rennie Mackintosh (1868–1928), designer of the Glasgow School of Art (1897–1909). These architects not only designed the outward form of their buildings but also took responsibility for their interiors, fixtures and fittings. Characteristic art nouveau shapes included hearts, lilies and other stylised flowers linked together with flowing materials and stems.

The Arts and Crafts Movement.

The Arts and Crafts movement, which was closely related to the more European art nouveau, led by William Morris (1834–96) and Philip Webb (1831–1915) was in part a development of Ruskin's views. They passionately believed in the traditional skills of the craftsman and attempted to use his abilities and designs as the basis for their house and church building together with their contents. One of the movement's most successful exponents was C. F. A. Voysey (1857–1941), a disciple of Norman Shaw and Morris. As a house designer he went some way towards breaking with the past by discarding definite period styles, such as Queen Anne then so popular among other English architects, for a "free traditionalism" based on old English cottage and farm house vernacular. Working with traditional materials—timber, tiles, bricks, leaded windows and stone—he introduced a fresh note of simplicity and naturalism, a personal style that was plagiarised in the inter-war period when vast sweeps of suburban Britain were constructed.

Norman Shaw.

The Edwardian era was a particularly eclectic period when architects felt free to design buildings in a number of styles derived from a variety of sources. No one illustrates this trend better than Norman Shaw (1831–1912). New Scotland Yard, London (1887–88), typically constructed in red brick and white Portland stone has fenestration which follows a regular Queen Anne pattern, enlivened by the addition of Scottish baronial corner turrets, with Baroque finishes to the gables and entrances. His last major work, the Piccadilly Hotel, London (1905–08) is a splendid expression of Neo-Baroque featuring a central open Ionic colonnade supported by a vigorously rusticated arcade flanked by flowing gabled wings.

THE MODERN MOVEMENT

In sharp contrast to the Arts and Crafts movement and indeed to almost all that had gone before, modern architecture as it developed in the early years of the 20th cent., was based on a break with historical tradition and founded on a functional approach to the fullest use of new building materials and engineering techniques. Not since Joseph Paxton's (1803–65) use of iron and glass in prefabricated sections in the design of the Crystal Palace (1850–51), had such an original course been pursued.

The First Advances.

The first real advances in modern architecture, however, did not occur in Britain but in America, France and Germany. The French had pioneered the use of reinforced concrete. The Americans, particularly Louis Sullivan, in Chicago and New York designed towering sky-scraper blocks made possible by the use of the steel skeleton, while in Germany Peter Behrens (who designed the Turbine Factory, Berlin, 1909) and his pupil Walter Gropius (designer of the Fagus Factory, Alfeld-an-der-Leine, 1911–14) when commissioned to build prestigious factories, were among the first to use these materials as originally as they could by concentrating on forms and the devastating effects they could achieve by exploiting their technical strengths.

The Inter-War Years.

Britain was slow to follow in their footsteps and there are not many fine examples of modern architecture to be seen dating from the inter-war period. The exceptions include Sir Owen Williams's Chemical Factory for Boots at Beeston, Notts (1930–32) which made startling use of reinforced concrete and glass based on a cantilevered structure. The Shakespeare Memorial Theatre at Stratford-upon-Avon (1928–34) was constructed from brick with very little reference to any historical styles, while Peter Jones's Store in Sloane Square, London (1935–36) exhibited the original use of glass in an articulated façade, the use of a steel frame construction allowing maximum floor space and free circulation. The Finsbury Health Centre, London (1938–39) has a concrete frame and façades faced with glazed tiles, the windows of the two-storey wing blocks, that frame the central entrance building, being linked vertically with opaque glass panels.

THE POSTWAR ERA

The plan of a modern building is not preconceived in the way that a Palladian country house would, for example, have symmetrical wings and central entrance portico, but good modern architecture evolves from a study of the proposed function of a building and the needs of the occupants. Its shape should emerge, therefore, as the architect discovers more about its role. Elevations develop organically from the plan and reflect the inner plan externally. There has been an emphasis on economy, not only on utilitarian grounds, but because the trend has been against applied decoration, in part simply a reaction to what had come before—the Edwardian period had already witnessed a refinement and reduction in the degree of ornamentation. An important development was the increased use of prefabricated materials in modular designs. Reinforced concrete or steel columns and beams form the strong framework to which are attached pre-cast wall and window units to form standard-sized cubes and rectangles.

Post-War Failings.

However, much that was built in Britain in the 1960s and 1970s, when the economy was expanding and there were political pressures on architects and planners, even failed to live up to the criteria laid down by the earlier thinkers on modern design.

Many of these buildings did not take proper account of their occupants' needs; tower blocks though often successful as offices or hotels proved unsuitable for families as homes and created more problems than they solved.

Unfortunately insufficient research was undertaken into the long-term performance of new building techniques and materials. The Ronan Point disaster in 1968, when part of a tower block collapsed like a pack of cards, revealed the inadequacy of some types of system building, while other buildings subject to ten years' weathering soon became blackened, lost parts of their tile façade or did not stand up to the test of continuous use. Often bland, repetitive and unimaginative in their exteriors, many cost-effective modern buidlings are far from aesthetically satisfying. Too many examples of modern architecture are inherently brutal, dull and unsatisfying. However, there are some buildings which certainly deserve attention and judged against the best from the past would be of comparable merit. Coventry Cathedral (1951–1962), the Festival Theatre, Chichester (1962) and the Playhouse, Nottingham (1964) are good examples.

High Tech and Deconstructivism.

The term Late Modernism is used of the architecture of the period from 1945 to c. 1970 (in Britain the term Contemporary Style refers to the years 1945 to 1956 in particular). For the more recent period the terms Corporate Modernism and High-Tech Architecture obviously reflect the luxury office blocks of the great multi-national companies.

Deconstructivism (used of the period after 1980) emphasises the bending of traditional building frames and the distorting of the old rectilineal concepts of building.

Other features of recent architecture are the vastly increased use of computer-aided design and an increasingly international desire to strip buildings of much of their ornamentation.

Some notable architectural developments include the Tate Modern, Norman Foster's Jubilee Line station at Canary Wharf and the National Botanical Gardens in Wales. Foster's other work includes the Great Court in the British Museum and Chep Lap Kok airport in Hong Kong. The new century is continuing this era of innovation. There is also an urge to build higher and higher skyscrapers (see **L100**), such as The Shard in London (completed in 2012). This was conceived by Renzo Piano whilst Cesar Pelli designed One Canada Square in Canary Wharf. The Lloyds Building and the Cheesegrater were designed by Richard Rogers.

Mention must also be made of the national showpieces designed by Zaha Hadid–China's Guangzhou Opera House, Spain's Bridge Pavilion in Zaragoza etc.

GLOSSARY OF ARCHITECTURAL TERMS

Abacus. The thin slab forming the upper member of a capital (see illustration of orders).

Acanthus. A form of curved ornament based on the leaves of the acanthus plant, native of southeastern Europe. The leaves were stylised by Greek sculptors of antiquity to form the characteristic ornament of Corinthian and Composite capitals and on mouldings generally.

Acroterion. A block of stone resting on the top or at the end of a pediment to support a figure or carved ornament.

Aisle. An open space in a church running parallel with the nave.

Alcove. A recessed space in a wall, usually vaulted and originally the place for a bed.

Anthemion. A characteristic Greek form of ornament based on the honeysuckle flower and leaves.

Apron. A raised panel, sometimes shaped and decorated immediately below the sill of a window.

Apse. A semi-circular extension at the eastern end of a church.

Arabesque. A flowing interlaced type of ornament based on complex geometrical patterns, originally devised by Arabian artists.

Arcade. A row of arches supported by columns, either part of a building or free standing.

Arch. An arrangement of wedge-shaped masonry or bricks arranged in a semi-circle and usually supporting the weight above.

Architecture. The art and science of building. The provision of shelter for mankind by the orderly arrangement of materials in a manner which expresses man's attitude to living. Until the last 150 years structural methods were limited to timber frames, columns, lintels, load-bearing walls, arches, vaults, and domes in brick or stone.

From these few basic elements have evolved the great variety of historic styles of building to be found throughout the world. To give but one example, the Greeks created those systems of decorated columns and beams, known as the Orders, which were adapted by the Romans, revived decoratively rather than structurally during the Renaissance and are still used in debased form on the more presumptuous type of modern building.

This, and the development of new structural techniques and materials (steel, aluminium, sheet glass, reinforced concrete, plastics and plywoods, to name a few), have made the interest in historic styles of less importance.

Modern architecture is the creation of buildings with the highest possible standards of functional performance in terms of efficient planning and structure, good lighting, adequate heating etc.

Architrave. The lowest division of an entablature, a moulded lintel between two columns (see illustration of orders).

Arrow Loop. A vertical slot formed in the walls or battlements of a castle or fortification through which archers could fire their arrows.

Bailey. A court in a fortified mediaeval castle, lying between the outer walls and the keep.

Balustrade. A railing consisting of a series of balusters, an individual column, supporting a continuous horizontal member.

Barbican. A small tower or fort built outside a castle to form the first line of defence.

Bargeboard. Carved woodwork covering the joint between a gable end and the roofing material forming an overhanging verge.

Barrel Vault. A continuous arched roof or ceiling of semi-circular form.

Bastion. A tower-like structure projecting from the angles of the outer wall or along its length.

Bauhaus. A German institution for the training of architects, artists and industrial designers founded in 1919 at Weimar by Walter Gropius, (d. 1969). It was closed by Hitler in 1933 and reopened at Chicago. The Bauhaus doctrine held that there should be no separation between architecture and the fine and applied arts; that art, science and technology should co-operate to create "the compositely inseparable work of art, the great building". The original institution, at the instigation of Gropius, included on its teaching staff not only architects and technicians but also such noted artists as Paul Klee and Wassily Kandinsky.

Belvedere. A look-out place such as a turret or high platform on the roof of a house to provide a view of the surrounding countryside.

Blind Arcade. A row of arched recesses in a wall.

Boss. An ornament covering the intersection point of the ribs in a roof.

Buttress. A support against and joined to a wall to strengthen it.

Campanile. A bell tower often detached from the main building.

Cantilever. A beam or slab supported at one end only and counterbalanced.

Cap. The topmost member of the pedestal in a classical order.

Capital. The moulded or sculptured head of a column (see illustration of orders).

Coffer (also known as a **caisson**). A recessed panel, usually ornamented in the under-surface of a ceiling, barrel-vault or balcony.

Composite order. A Roman order of architecture which combines the characteristics of the Ionic and Corinthian orders.

Corbel. A strong supporting member, of stone or timber, projecting from a wall to support a beam or other feature.

Cornice. The top division of an entablature.

Cupola. A small dome-like roof or lantern. An ornate turret attached to a roof to give light to an interior or to contain a bell.

Dentil. A small square block used in series for ornamentation in Ionic and Corinthian cornices.

Dormer. A window that projects from a sloping roof having vertical sides and front.

Dressings. Blocks of stone cut to true plane faces or shaped for use as quoins or keystones.

Dripmould or Dripshone. A Gothic moulding shaped to throw water clear of the door or window below following the curve of an arch.

Eaves. The lowest part of a roof, overhanging the top of a wall.

Egg and Dart. Patterns carved on an ovolo moulding based on the design of eggs and arrow-heads arranged alternately.

Engaged Column. A column apparently partly embedded in a wall, also known as attached columns.

Entablature. The upper part of an order, consisting of the architrave, frieze and cornice.

Entasis. The slightly convex curve to the side of a column, formed in order to counteract the optical illusion of the outline being concave should the sides be straight.

Finial. A carved or moulded ornament which crowns a pinnacle, gable or spire.

Fluting. Shallow, rounded grooves applied to any surface but often to the shaft of a column.

Frieze. The member of an entablature between the cornice and the architrave, frequently ornamented in all orders except the Tuscan.

Functionalism. *See N7.*

Gable. The triangular wall surface formed by the meeting of two sloping wall lines at the end of a ridged roof.

Hipped Roof. A pitched roof, the end of which is also sloped back, meeting the sides in a pair of hips.

Keep. The great tower or innermost stronghold of a medieval castle.

Key. The central voussoir (*q.v.*) of an arch. sometimes ornamented with carving, situated at the crown of the arch.

Lancet. A tall narrow, sharply pointed Gothic window, a feature of the Early English style.

Lantern. A small ornamental open or glazed turret on a roof or dome to light or ventilate the interior.

Linen-fold Panelling. A decorative device of folded linen used on panelling and furniture in the Tudor period.

Lintel. The horizontal member, supported at each end, which spans two columns.

Lunette. A semi-circular (or circular) window.

Machicolation. The holes between the corbels of a projecting parapet through which missiles were dropped in a mediaeval castle. Later the design was used for purely decorative purposes.

Mansard Roof. A form of pitched roof with two slopes on each side to increase the space inside, the upper slope being steeper than the lower.

Mullions. The vertical bars dividing the lights in a window, forming a highly decorative feature in the Tudor period of English Gothic architecture. The cross-beam or horizontal bar of wood or stone in a mullioned window is styled a transom. *See* **Windows, Section L.**

Nave. That part of a church between the choir and the western entrance, separated from the aisles.

Obelisk. A tall stone pillar with four tapering sides and a pointed pyramidal top.

Ogee. An "S"-shaped curve featured in an arch.

Order of Architecture. A column with a base, shaft and entablature. The orders evolved by the Greeks were Doric, Ionic and Corinthian. The Romans added the Tuscan and the Composite.

Oriel Window. This is a window projected from the front of a building, rectangular, triangular, or pentagonal. The ordinary bay window and bow window are varieties of Oriel. When an Oriel window does not reach to the ground it usually

rests upon moulded sills supported by corbels.

Ovolo. A small convex moulding.

Palmette. A stylised leaf ornament, said to resemble a palm leaf.

Parapet. A low wall at the edge of a roof, generally formed by an upward extension of the wall below, often enlivened by sections of balustrade (*q.v.*).

Pargetting, Parging. The plastering of a wall or ceiling and often patterned or decorated by scratching or modelling in low relief in the plaster coating.

Pediment. The triangular low-pitched gable end of a Greek or Roman temple. Pediments are often also used for decorative purposes over windows or doors when they may be either angled, curved or broken, the latter when the apex of the triangle is omitted and replaced by ogee curves ending in scrolls with an ornamental feature inbetween.

Pilaster. A rectangular column, projecting slightly from the wall and conforming to the design of the orders.

Porch. A roof structure forming a small room to shelter the entrance of a house.

Porte-Cochère. An entrance porch for carriages to a house from the street allowing people to alight from the vehicle and enter under cover.

Portico. An imposing kind of porch in the Classical manner consisting of a low-pitched roof supported by columns, finish with a triangular pediment and often approached by a flight of steps.

Quoin. The emphasised bricks or stones at the angle of a building.

Relieving Arch. An arch constructed above a square-headed opening in a wall, relieving the lintel or beam over it from some of the weight above.

Rotunda. An isolated building, circular in plan, often with a domed roof.

Rusticated. When the joints between stone or brick are emphasised by deep grooves or channels to impart the impression of strength or massiveness.

Segmental Arch. An arch in which the contour is a segment of a circle.

Soffit. The under surface of an architectural feature, *e.g.* an arch, cornice, window or door head.

Spandrel. The triangular space enclosed by the curve of an arch.

Strapwork. An Elizabethan form of decoration consisting of enriched interlacing bands, generally used on ceilings and occasionally on panels.

String Course. A continuous horizontal band, either plain or moulded, projecting from the face of a structure.

Stucco. External plastering, often moulded and painted to appear like stone.

Terra-Cotta. A hard unglazed pottery ware of fine texture, made from fine brick earth, burnt in moulds and used for decoration or as facing material.

Transom. A horizontal member dividing a window into two rows of lights.

Tympanum. This is, in architectural phraseology, the triangular space at the back of a pediment, or, indeed, any space in a similar position, as over a window or between the lintel and the arch of a doorway. In ecclesiastical edifices the tympanum is often adorned with sculpture.

Venetian Window. A window consisting of three lights, one arched large centre one, and two narrow square-headed side lights.

Vermiculated. A form of rusticated (*q.v.*) masonry where the face of each block is carved with short, irregular wavy channels and hollows.

Vernacular Style. The native way of building, unaffected by classical rules. The Tudor style in Britain was truly vernacular.

Voussoir. A wedge-shaped brick or block of stone forming the components of an arch.

Weather-boarding. Horizontal, overlapping planks of timber, fixed to an internal framework, forming the outside wall of a building.

THE
WORLD OF
MUSIC

The story of music as it has evolved
in the Western world, with an outline historical narrative, a glossary
of musical terms and an index to
composers. The period covered runs
from early secular music through the
Renaissance and Baroque, and the
glory of Bach and Handel to the
vibrant music forms of more recent
times. The Section also provides an
introduction to some of the most
popular dances in Britain, Europe
and America.

TABLE OF CONTENTS

THE WORLD OF MUSIC

In writing this section no special knowledge on the part of the reader is assumed; it is for those who want to know about the history of music, how different styles evolved, and how one composer influenced another. It is a background to music as the science section is a background to science, and just as the latter cannot show the reader the colours of the spectrum but only tell of Newton's experiments and of the relationship between colour and wavelength, so in this section we can only describe human achievements in the world of sound. But knowing something about composers, their work, and when they lived can help to bring fuller understanding and enjoyment when listening to their music.

The section is in four parts:

I. Historical Narrative and Discussion
II. Glossary of Musical Terms
III. Index to Composers
IV. Special Topic

I. HISTORICAL NARRATIVE AND DISCUSSION

The history of music, like that of any people or art, is not one of uninterrupted progress towards some ideal perfection. For five centuries or more music in the West has achieved peaks of accomplishment in one style or another before society has dictated or composers have felt the need for something new and different. Thus Wagner's music-drama *Parsifal*, lasting five hours, is not necessarily a more rewarding work than what Monteverdi achieved in *Orfeo* 250 years earlier. More complex yes, more rewarding—well, that is for the listener to judge.

We must keep this in mind when considering the development of music from a starting point of, say, early plainchant down to the complicated structures of a Schoenberg in our own day. In this development there is no true dividing line between one period and another, nor must simplifying terms such as "classical" or "romantic" be taken too literally.

Introduction.

In the recent past, general histories of music usually started from around 1600 with the implication that earlier music was primitive, and not worth serious consideration. This view has changed, largely as a result of the number of excellent performances and recordings available of medieval music by groups such as Gothic Voices, and the Hilliard Ensemble. These performances show that the music of the 14th and 15th centuries is just as complex and beautiful as anything written afterwards. There are clear parallels between the highly structured works of Machaut and Dufay, and the music of the mid to late 20th century.

Defining Medieval Music.

The term 'medieval' in music usually means the period from approximately AD 900–1500, beginning with the earliest examples of music notation, and ending with the transition to the Renaissance. In the medieval period, most performed music was monophonic (made up from a single line), improvised, and secular, probably with some form of drone. Most church music of the period was also monophonic, in the form of plainchant, with the more elaborate polyphonic settings of the mass reserved for special occasions.

Plainchant.

Plainchant is the fundamental basis of all Western music, and consists of a monodic song setting of the Christian liturgy in free rhythm. In monasteries today it is heard either with equal notes or a long-short rhythmic pattern, as there is no consensus. The pitches used are based on one of the 7 church modes such as the dorian (d, e, f, g, a, b, c, d). All medieval music is modal, the difference with tonal music being that there is much less of a pull to a key centre—it is less 'goal oriented'.

The Evolution of Organum.

In around 900 the first medieval treatise on music was written entitled *Musica Enchiriadis*. This contained some of the first examples of notated polyphonic music (music made up of more than one line), which is called *organum*. This genre evolved as an elaboration of plainchant, increasing the majesty of the liturgy. The first examples of what is termed '*florid organum*' occurred in the 12th century in Santiago de Compostela in Spain, and in St. Martial at Limoges in France. Florid organum consists of sustained notes of the plainchant, with florid quicker moving lines over this base. The technique evolved into a highly structured method of composition, which can be seen in the music of the 12th century Notre Dame School in Paris.

Leonin and Perotin.

The two names associated with this school are Leonin (*fl.* 1175) and Perotin (*fl.* 1183), although very little is known about their lives. Leonin composed a cycle of two part graduals, alleluias, and responsories for the church year called the *Magnus Liber Organi* (or great book of organi). Perotin expanded this work by composing new substitute sections called *clausulae*, which use the melismatic or florid part of a plainchant as its structural basis or tenor. There are usually 2 or 3 upper voices placed above the tenor, and all the parts move at the same pace. The term 'Tenor' is not the voice type, but the term for the main structural voice, usually the lowest.

The Motet.

The development of the clausula is significant because it creates a greater compositional freedom for the composers of the time, allowing them to display their artistry. The motet evolved from the clausula, and flourished in the 13th and 14th centuries. It consisted of the setting of a new text to an existing clausula, and the name came from the French for word: '*mot*'. With the development of the motet, the music became separated from the liturgy, and the words could now be based on love, and politics, as well as spiritual themes.

The Use of Isorhythm.

The main structural feature of the medieval

motet is the use of isorhythm. This technique consists of a repeated rhythmic pattern, known as a talea, in the tenor, which is projected onto a repeating pattern of pitches, usually derived from a plainchant known as the color. The other parts created free polyphony around the slower moving tenor, using bare sounding perfect fifths and unisons as the basic harmonic consonance of the music.

The Notation of Rhythm.

The next main musical development in the later 13th century was in the notation of rhythm. Until Franco of Cologne's treatise of 1260 *Ars Cantus Mensurabilis* or 'Art of Measured Song', rhythms had been restricted to a small number of 'modal' patterns. Franco codified a new way of notation which allowed each note to have a number of different durations, creating far more rhythmic flexibility, and establishing the basis of a system that has not fundamentally changed upto the present day.

Ars Nova.

Philippe de Vitry (1291–1361), a French composer and theorist, built upon this in his treatise *Ars Nova* or 'New Technique/Craft' written in 1316, and also in his rhythmically complex motets. Once the term 'Ars Nova' gained currency as a description of the music of the 14th century, the previous period of the Notre Dame School, became described as 'Ars Antique', or 'Old Technique/Craft'. The music of the 14th century became much richer and more varied as a direct result of this innovation of notational practice.

Probably the most significant and versatile composer of this time was the Frenchman Guillaume de Machaut (1300–77). Machaut was a canon, a poet, and secretary to several kings, and his compositional output included secular chansons such as lais, ballades and rondeaux, as well as motets and the seminal *Notre Dame* Mass. The latter, probably a mature work, is very signicant because it was the first time a composer had written a complete mass cycle—a complete setting of the ordinary of the mass. It is an austere but very beautiful work and uses both isorhythmic and discant styles. Discant style is used for the longer texts such as the Gloria, and consists of one note per syllable of text. The isorhythmic movements such as the Kyrie are melismatic, and therefore they have many notes for each syllable.

The Cantus Firmus.

It was not until the following century that the composition of complete mass cycles became the norm. The main innovation in the composition of masses in the 15th century was probably first used in Britain, and is the use of a Cantus Firmus to unify the mass cycle. A Cantus Firmus is a pre-existing melody which is used as the structural basis of the mass, and is usually in the Tenor although it can be found in the other voices. The melody could be plainchant or a well known secular song, such as the French *L'Homme Armé*, which was particularly popular. Another significant shift is the development of more 'tonal' sounding harmonies and cadences.

The Work of Dunstable.

The British composer John Dunstable (1385–1453) was significant in the development of a more consonant and richer harmonic language on the mainland of Europe, particular the use of 3rds and 6ths. The evolution of style can be heard in the music of 15th century composers such as Guillaume Dufay (1400–74), and Josquin des Préz (1440–1521) which paved the way for the rich harmony and polyphony of the Renaissance. The medieval period showed an extraordinary evolution of style and technique, and produced music which is as beautiful and subtle as any work produced in later eras.

Josquin and his Successors.

Josquin des Prez was the outstanding composer of his generation, recognised as such by his contemporaries. His works combine technical mastery with imagination and attention to the text. The handling of the cantus firmus in his masses shows a variety of approaches, from the strict planning of the *Missa L'homme armé super voces musicales* to the freedom of his late masterpiece the *Missa Pange lingua*. His contemporaries include Isaac (*c.* 1450–1517) and de la Rue (*c.* 1460–1518), both of whom, like Josquin, explored the possibilities of canon as a structural basis for compositions. Josquin's music is noted for clarity and balance of texture and structure. Composers of the post-Josquin period, notably Willaert (*c.* 1490–1562), Gombert (*c.* 1500–56) and Clemens non Papa (*c.* 1510–58) developed instead a style pervaded by the technique of imitation, with full textures and a sense of seamless continuity.

An important advance in the early 16th cent. was the development of music printing, associated particularly with Petrucci in Venice and Attaignant in Paris; this made music much more widely available, and contributed to the spread of domestic music-making.

Reformation and Counter-Reformation.

The religious upheavals of the 16th and 17th cents. had their effect on music. Martin Luther was a keen musician, and allowed music a significant role in the liturgy of the new Lutheran churches; the chorale, or congregational hymn, sung in German, was the main new genre, to which Luther himself contributed many examples. A fine tradition of Lutheran church music developed over two centuries, represented by such composers as Praetorius, Schütz, Buxtehude and the Bach family. The more radical, Reformed Protestantism, however, under the leadership of Calvin in Geneva, gave music a much less important place, distrusting any kind of elaborate musical effects in worship. Organs were removed from churches and singing was restricted to metrical psalms. In England, the distinctive national church established under Elizabeth I—Protestant in doctrine, but Catholic in aspects of organisation and liturgy—provided plentiful opportunities for a strong musical culture; anthems and settings of the service attracted some of the most gifted musicians of the later Tudor and early Stuart period. The Catholic Counter-Reformation also turned its attention to music: the Council of Trent recommended a simplified musical style suitable for the clear enunciation of the text.

The Late Renaissance: Palestrina, Victoria, Lassus and Byrd.

The final flowering of Renaissance music is represented at its best by four composers. Palestrina (*c.* 1525–94), working for his whole career in or near Rome, is noted for the purity of his style, which for centuries to come would be taken as a model of "strict" counterpoint. Victoria (*c.* 1548–1611) studied in Rome, but spent his last three decades in his native Spain, where he continued the tradition of Spanish sacred music of Morales (*c.* 1500–53) and Guerrero (*c.* 1528–99). Victoria's output is notable for religious intensity and sensitivity to the text. Lassus (1532–94), Franco-Flemish by origin, spent virtually all his career in the Bavarian court at Munich, but was renowned throughout Europe. He produced a prodigious amount of sacred music with a wide expressive range from the exuberant to the penitential, and also composed many secular vocal works in French, German and Italian. In England, Byrd (*c.* 1540–1623) was a Catholic, but was so highly regarded by Elizabeth I that in 1575 she granted him and his colleague and co-religionist Tallis (*c.* 1505–85) an exclusive licence to print music. He was equally at home setting Latin texts and writing music for the new English liturgy; his music is full of expansive, rich polyphony infused with rhythmic life.

The Venetian Tradition.

Venice had a distinctive musical tradition, with music playing a major role in state occasions. Willaert, working at St. Mark's Basilica, established the polychoral style, in which music is shared between two (or more) choirs, spatially separated. This technique was extended by Andrea and Giovanni Gabrieli (uncle and nephew), incorporating solo voices and instruments in ever-varying textures—a fine example is Giovanni Gabrieli's *In ecclesiis*. Concerted instrumental music, especially for brass, was another important part of the Venetian repertoire.

Instrumental Music.

The 16th cent. saw instrumental (especially keyboard) music emerge as a significant genre in its own right. The Spaniard Cabezón (*c.* 1510–66) was a pioneer, and his example was followed by a whole group of English composers, notably Byrd, Bull, Gibbons and Farnaby; in turn, this English school had its influence on the Dutchman Sweelinck (1562–1621) and thereby, indirectly, on composers in Germany; Frescobaldi (1583–1643) was the out-standing figure in Italy. A variety of music was composed: pieces based on polyphonic vocal styles (ricercars, canzonas, fantasias); improvisatory types (preludes, toccatas); dances; and variations based on dances and popular songs.

The Madrigal.

The main form of secular vocal music in the Renaissance period was the madrigal, an Italian form (though some of its practitioners were Flemish). Whereas sacred vocal polyphony, even at its most expressive, tended to adhere to rules of harmony and part-writing, the passionate, thinly disguised eroticism of madrigal poetry led composers such as de Rore, de Wert, Marenzio, Monteverdi and Gesualdo to extremes of experimentation in which musical coherence and balance took second place to conveying every last detail of the text. The English madrigal, influenced by Italian models, in particular Marenzio, had a relatively short-lived life, flourishing in the work of composers such as Wilbye and Weelkes.

The Early Baroque and the Beginnings of Opera.

The name "Baroque" is commonly given to the period starting around 1600. Various elements came together at this time to change radically the direction of music. Emphasis on the solo voice (or instrument) with chordal accompaniment, and a sense of directed harmonic movement built upon the bass line, are crucial developments; equally significant is the new sense of drama, evident in all the arts of the period, and exemplified strikingly by the birth of opera. Towards the end of the 16th cent. a group of artistic intellectuals (the *Camerata*) met in Florence and conceived the idea of reviving the original performance style of Greek tragedy. They cast Greek mythological subjects in dramatic form and set them to music of a new declamatory type, recitative. The earliest examples were Péri's *Dafne* (1597), now lost, and his *Euridice* (1600).

Monteverdi's Operas.

It was *Orfeo* (1607) by Monteverdi (1567–1643) that showed the full potential of musical drama; it features not only highly expressive recitative, but arias, dances and madrigalesque choruses, and contains colourful instrumentation. Of Monteverdi's later stage works, his final opera, *L'Incoronazione di Poppea* (1642), is based not on mythology but on an episode in Roman history; it is remarkably "modern" in its focus on the psychology and emotions of its characters, unerringly delineated in musical terms. Monteverdi's successors were Cavalli (1602–76) and Cesti (1623–69), in whose works the distinction between aria and recitative became more fixed and there was increasing emphasis on vocal display.

Seventeenth-Century Sacred Music in Italy: Monteverdi and Carissimi.

New soloistic styles also affected sacred music, but without completely replacing the old polyphonic methods. Monteverdi's great *Vespers* of 1610 were a compendium of current choral, solo and instrumental techniques, and his later collections of sacred music were both varied and up-to-date.

The main new genre of sacred music in the earlier 17th cent. was the oratorio, particularly cultivated in Rome by Carissimi (1605–74); his oratorios are sacred dramas—biblical stories (in Latin) set to music for soloists and chorus, but performed unstaged. *Jephte* is perhaps Carissimi's masterpiece, and it influenced Handel's own setting of the Jephtha story a century later.

German Music from Schütz to Buxtehude.

Italian influences came to Germany especially through the music of Heinrich Schütz (1585–1672), who studied with Giovanni Gabrieli in 1609–12; he visited Venice again in 1628–9, becoming acquainted with the latest developments pioneered by Monteverdi. He composed the first German opera, *Daphne* (1627), now lost; apart from this and a set of Italian madrigals, his output consists of sacred music for the Lutheran church. Schütz's ability to match his music to the text, and his dramatic and pictorial sense, are remarkable, whether in the spacious polychoral writing of the *Psalmen Davids*, the atmospheric depiction of St. Paul's conversion (in *Saul, Saul*), the colourful instrumentation of the *Christmas Story*, or the austere Passion settings (Matthew, Luke and John). Johann Herman Schein (1586–1630) is also a significant figure in church music; unlike Schütz, he made considerable use of Lutheran chorales. Samuel Scheidt (1587–1654) is important chiefly for his instrumental music.

The Danish-born Dietrich Buxtehude (1637–1707) was the outstanding figure in North German music of his generation. His church cantatas and organ music influenced J. S. Bach. The devotional spirit in the Catholic South is represented by Heinrich Biber (1644–1704), whose "Mystery" (or "Rosary") Sonatas for violin (of which he was a virtuoso exponent) are notable for their experimental use of *scordatura* (non-standard tunings of the strings).

Seventeenth-Century Music in France and England.

French opera was from the beginning associated with the court ballet. The Italian-born Jean-Baptiste Lully (*c.* 1632–87) created the characteristic form of the *tragédie lyrique*, which dominated the French musical stage until the mid-18th cent. In Lully's operas the libretto plays a vital role, the text being set in a flexible, naturalistic way, with a less clear distinction between recitative and aria than in Italian opera. The orchestration, chorus and dances assume greater importance than in the contemporary Italian form. In his lifetime, Lully's musical monopoly under Louis XIV limited the outlets for other opera composers. An outstanding opera composed and performed after Lully's death is *Médée* (1693) by Marc-Antoine Charpentier (1643–1704). Charpentier is best known, however, for his church music, of which the *Te Deum* (*c.* 1691) is a colourful example.

In the instrumental field, the lute music of Denis Gaultier (1603–72) stimulated the development of an idiomatic harpsichord style in the dance suites of J.C. de Chambonnières (1602–72), Louis Couperin (1626–61) and J.-H. d'Anglebert (1635–91).

In England, opera developed from the Masque, an entertainment consisting of dances, songs and poetry, with elaborate stage effects, often incorporated into a drama. Examples are Henry Lawes's (1596–1662) setting of Milton's *Comus* (1634), and *Cupid and Death* (1653) by Matthew Locke (1622–77) and Christophper Gibbons (1615–76). John Blow's (1649–1708) *Venus and Adonis* (*c.* 1684) is called a masque but is in effect an opera, with the whole text being sung.

Henry Purcell.

It was Henry Purcell (1659–95), Blow's pupil, who in *Dido and Aeneas* really exploited the new medium by his power of subtle musical characterisation. Dido's lament "When I am laid in earth" uses typically bold harmonic effects to achieve a remarkable expressive power. These works by Blow and Purcell, however, are exceptions. The favoured form was the semi-opera – essentially a play with a substantial amount of music – to which Purcell contributed some fine examples, such as *The Fairy Queen* (1692).

Purcell's sacred music is also of a high order, representing the culmination of the Restoration style forged from earlier English and newly fashionable Italian and French influences by such composers as Matthew Locke and Pelham Humfrey (1647–74). Purcell's instrumental music includes work in older genres (the Fantasias for viols, which are imaginative, even eccentric, in their approach to harmony and counterpoint); he also adopted the new Italian violinistic style in his Sonatas of Three and Four Parts.

The Concerto Grosso.

The idea of groups of instruments set off against each other goes back to the early 17th cent. (e.g. Giovanni Gabrieli's Sonata pian'e forte). With Arcangelo Corelli (1653–1713) the concerto grosso took a more definite shape, alternating a solo group of instruments with the main body of strings in three or more contrasting movements. Guiseppe Torelli (1658–1709), Francesco Geminiani (1687–1762) and Tommaso Albinoni (1671–1750) were other notable contributors to the form, but none of the composers so far mentioned has today achieved the popularity of the priest Antonio Vivaldi (c. 1678–1741), himself a violinist, who had at his disposal the orchestra at the Ospedale della Pieta in Venice. The young women at this music school also contributed the vocal side of the concerts there of which there are many descriptions. One says: "They sing like angels, play the violin, flute, organ, oboe, cello, bassoon—in short no instrument is large enough to frighten them . . . I swear nothing is so charming than to see a young and pretty nun, dressed in white, a sprig of pomegranate blossom behind one ear, leading the orchestra, and beating time with all the grace and precision imaginable." For this body, Vivaldi wrote about 500 concertos which maintain a remarkably even quality, but "The Four Seasons" are perhaps the most felicitous.

Chamber Music.

In the field of chamber music the trio sonata became the predominant genre by the late 17th cent., and again Corelli was a major figure in its evolution. Trio sonatas were composed for two treble instruments (most commonly violins) and continuo, and fell into two main types: the Sonata da chiesa (Church sonata, generally with a slow-fast-slow-fast pattern of movements), and the Sonata da camera (Chamber sonata, a dance suite).

Meanwhile the tradition of French harpsichord music culminated in the work of Jean-Philippe Rameau (1683-1764) and François Couperin (1668-1733). Masters of keyboard style and harmonic invention, they wrote many pieces of subtle charm and exquisite craftsmanship, often with descriptive, and sometimes enigmatic, titles.

Bach and Handel.

The contrasting figures of J. S. Bach (1685 – 1750) and Handel (1685 – 1759) dominate the first half of the 18th cent. Bach was essentially a provincial musician, from an extended family of musicians, working for the court (at Weimar, 1708-17, and Anhalt-Cöthen, 1717-23) and the Lutheran church (in Leipzig from 1723). Handel, on the other hand, was widely travelled beyond his native Germany, spending some time in Italy before settling in England and eventually becoming a naturalised English subject; although he had noble patrons and composed music for state occasions (notably the four anthems for the coronation of George II), he was mainly a freelance composer – indeed a businessman – writing for and dependent upon the public. Both composers, however, show an extraordinary breadth of achievement, expressive range and depth, and strong musical personalities.

The Music of Bach.

Bach composed in all the main genres of his time except opera. He absorbed and transcended the "national" styles (Italian, French, German) of his day. As a master of contrapuntal writing he was

second to none, but he rose above technical brilliance to achieve intense emotional and expressive power. He systematically explored the possibilities of musical forms (in e.g. the Well-tempered Clavier – generally known as the "48" – two sets of preludes and fugues in all the major and minor keys), structural devices (e.g. both variation and canon in the "Goldberg" Variations for harpsichord and the late canonic variations for organ on the chorale Von Himmel Hoch) and themes (in the Musical Offering and Art of Fugue, his last, incomplete work).

Central to Bach's achievement is his Lutheran church music – notably the more than two hundred cantatas (mostly from his Leipzig years, but some composed in Weimar) and the St. John (1724) and St. Matthew Passions (1729). The Passions combine highly dramatic setting of the New Testament story of Christ's death with expressive commentary; soloists and choir take part in the narrative (as the various characters, the crowd etc.) and reflect on it in extended and often elaborate arias and choruses, while the inclusion of chorales (Lutheran hymns), as in the cantatas, enables the congregation itself to participate. In contrast to these works intended for use in the church service, is the so-called B minor Mass (the title is not Bach's), a large-scale setting of the Roman Catholic Mass, which Bach compiled in the 1740s, mainly adapting music from his earlier compositions. This hugely impressive work could hardly have been meant for performance in Lutheran Leipzig; perhaps Bach put it together for his own satisfaction.

Bach made important contributions to the various instrumental forms of his time, both solo and concerted. His organ music – preludes and fugues, chorale preludes, trio sonatas – is central to the repertoire of the instrument. The sonatas and partitas for unaccompanied violin and suites for unaccompanied cello combine meditative depth and rhythmic life. The violin concertos build upon the three-movement model developed by Vivaldi, while the six Brandenburg Concertos, each for a different combination of instruments, are a culmination of the tradition of the concerto grosso.

Handel's Operas.

The first part of Handel's career in London, from 1711, was dominated by the composition of Italian operas, the second part from the late 1730s, by oratorios. While the latter have never fallen out of favour, the former were largely neglected for more than two centuries (except for occasional arias which remained popular as recital pieces or in various adaptations – most famously "Ombra mai fù" from Serse, better known as "Handel's Largo"). The tradition within which Handel was composing, with its succession of recitatives and arias, provided little opportunity in musical terms for dramatic development or interaction between the characters; by comparison with Mozartian opera, or with many operas of the 19th and 20th cents., the form is static, and it could easily become little more than a vehicle for vocal display. Handel's masterpieces in the genre, however, are much more than this, and reassessment of his operas in recent decades has led to a renewed appreciation of their musical qualities – memorable melody, daring harmony, imaginative instrumentation – and of the vivid characterisation they contain. Most important, the modern productions have shown that they can be made to work in the theatre, and a number of them are now regularly found in the repertoire of opera-houses.

Handel's Oratorios.

As the vogue for Italian opera waned Handel turned to oratorio as a new form of large-scale vocal music for public consumption – indeed, he virtually invented the English oratorio. Operatic in conception, the Handelian oratorio is an unstaged musical drama on a biblical subject (usually from the Old Testament), with a libretto in English. Crucial is the important role of the chorus, taking part in and commenting on the action (whereas choruses feature scarcely at all in Handel's Italian operas.) The great sequence of Handel's oratorios started with Saul in 1738, running through to Jephtha in 1751. Handel's most popular oratorio Messiah (1741), is an exception to the general type being based around the figure of Christ and using exclusively biblical words. Handel's dramatic and pictorial sense and his ability to create striking effects are demonstrated time and again in his oratorios.

In his instrumental and orchestral works Handel was less systematic in approach than Bach; for example, his keyboard suites vary considerably in their format, unlike the suites and partitas of Bach with their regular, standard succession of dance movements. The Concerti Grossi Op.3 and Op.6 show a colourful use of instrumental resources, as do occasional works such as the *Water Music* and the *Royal Fireworks Music*. The organ concertos call for some virtuosity; Handel would often play them between the acts of his oratorios.

Developing New Styles.

Even while Bach and Handel were creating the corwning achievements of baroque polyphony, new styles were emerging which were eventually to result in the high classical style of the later 18th cent. Among the contributing features were: a preference for accompaniment rather than polyphonic textures; relative simplicity of harmony; symmetry and regularity of phrase structure; and a general elegance of style. These tendencies can be found in the earlier part of the 18th cent. in *e.g.* the keyboard sonatas of Domencio Scarlatti (1685-1737), in the Italian opera overture (or *sinfonia*, the foundation of the classical symphony), and in comic opera, *e.g.* *La serva padrona* by Pergolesi (1710-36), and continued through the middle years of the century. One of the most important later representatives of this "gallant" or "rococo" manner was J.C. Bach (1735-82), whose sonata and concertos had a strong influence on Mozart.

Music in the "pre-classical" period was, however, by no means always light-hearted or simple. Intensity of expression by means of minor keys, chromatic harmony, urgent, incisive rhythm and dramatic contrast is found in *e.g.* some of the keyboard music of the 1740s and later of C.P.E. Bach (1714-88); the term *empfindsamer Stil* ("expressive style") is often applied to this music. Various works of the late 1760s and early 1770s, notably some of Haydn's symphonies (*e.g.* No.49 in F minor, iLa Passionei of 1768) display similar emotionalism, and have been compared with the contemporary *Sturm und Drang* ("Storm and stress") movement in literature. Aspects of this more serious approach were absorbed into the emerging classical style.

The invention and rapid development of the fortepiano from the 1730s was to have far-reaching consequences. With its capacity for a range of dynamics it eventually replaced the harpsichord and clavichord as the preferred stringed key board instrument for public and domestic music-making. The beginnings of the modern orchestra also date from this period; the court of Mannheim's orchestra was of a standard unheard hitherto, and the Mannheim composers, notably Johann Stamitz (1717-57), played an important part in the development of the symphony, although this is overshadowed by the achievements of Haydn in the service of Prince Esterházy.

Haydn and Mozart.

These two figures dominate the second half of the 18th cent. as Bach and Handel do the first. In a brief space only a general picture can be presented of their huge output and influence. Of Haydn's 104 symphonies (there may even be others) nearly all are worthy of study and hearing. The craftsmanship is always remarkable, the invention ever new. Indeed without Haydn's harmonic daring or his melodic ingenuity, the even greater symphonic thought of Beethoven would have been impossible: Haydn laid the groundwork on which his successor built towering edifices. A work such as the 93rd symphony in D is typical of his mature style with its searching introduction, powerfully wrought, earnestly argued first movement, beautiful *Largo* and resourceful bustling finale. Haydn did not fight shy of contrapuntal writing: the development section of this symphony's first movement and the finale are evidence of that, but it was only as an integral part of a predominantly homophonic technique.

Mozart's symphonies are not so different in form from Haydn's but—and this must be a subjective judgment—he put more emotional feeling into his. Nobody could listen to the heartsearching first movement of his 40th symphony without being deeply moved. It was in his final three works in the medium that Mozart brought his symphonic art to perfection, and these obviously had an effect on Haydn's later symphonies written after them. For passion and tenderness contained within a classical form these late symphonies, and many other of Mozart's works, have yet to be surpassed.

Haydn, who has been rightly termed "the Father of the Symphony", was also the founder of the string quartet—perhaps the most perfect, because the most exactly balanced, form of musical expression. The four instruments—two violins, viola, and cello—discuss, argue, commune with each other over the whole gamut of feeling. In his quartets Haydn's mastery of structure is even more amazing than in his symphonies. Mozart's quartets (especially the six devoted to Haydn) and even more his quintets achieve miracles of beauty in sound, nowhere more so than in the first movement of the G minor (his most personal key) quintet. The two late piano quartets show how the piano *can* be combined with strings. His clarinet quintet is also a masterly work.

Mozart's Concertos.

Haydn did not leave any concertos of consequence. Mozart's, especially those for piano, are among his greatest works. As a brilliant clavier player himself, he showed a consummate skill in writing for the keyboard. Although the instrument he knew was slightly less advanced than the piano today, his concertos call for virtuosity in execution, yet they are as searching in emotional content as the late symphonies and quartets. Indeed the C major concerto (K. 467) and the C minor (K. 491) may be said to hold the quintessential Mozart. As well as twenty (mature) piano concertos, Mozart wrote six for the violin, four for the horn, and eighteen others, but none of these can be placed in quite the same class.

Of their church music, Haydn's sixteen masses and his oratorios—*The Creation* and *The Seasons* (both late works)—are perhaps more worthy of attention than Mozart's various masses, but we must not forget Mozart's final work—the Requiem or the serene late Motet *Ave Verum Corpus*.

Eighteenth-Century Opera.

Mozart—for many the first great opera composer—did not, of course, create his masterpieces out of nothing. In France, Lully was followed by Rameau (1683-1764), who carried on his tradition of using classical themes but developed a more flexible style of recitative and greatly increased vividness of expression. But it was Gluck (1714-87) who more than anyone broke out of the straitjacket of the now ossified Italian form of opera—dominated by the singer—and showed just what could be achieved in moving human terms.

Drama in music really came of age with his *Orfeo e Euridice* (1762), *Alceste* (1767) and *Iphigénie en Tauride* (1779). His simplicity and poignancy of expression were not lost on Mozart.

Meanwhile in Germany a kind of opera called *Singspiel* appeared during the 18th cent. Breaking away from classical themes, mundane stories were told in dialogue and music.

Until quite recently Haydn's operas were dismissed as unworthy representations of his genius but, chiefly through the enlightening efforts of the Haydn scholar, H. C. Robbins Landon, some of his fifteen surviving works in the medium have been successfully revived. They have proved to be perfectly viable for the stage and, especially in the ensembles, full of that delightful invention to be found in the rest of his opus, if on a less fully developed scale. Still as musical drama they inevitably fall far short of Mozart's achievements, for the younger composer seems to have had an instinctive feeling for the stage. Into his operas he poured his most intense, personal music. He vividly portrays the foibles, desires, loves, and aspirations of mankind.

The earlier, immature stage pieces of his youth led to such works as *Lucio Silla* (1772) and *La Finta Giardiniera* (1775) with their first glimpses of the glories to come. His first indubitably great opera is *Idomeneo* (1781). Despite its unpromisingly static plot, *Idomeneo* reveals Mozart's stature through its ability to breathe new life into a conventional *opera seria* form. Though influenced by Gluck it is yet more human and touching in its musical expression. To succeed this Mozart wrote a much more frivolous piece *Die Entführung aus dem Serail*. Stemming from the *Singspiel* tradition, it none the less creates real-life characters who have much charming music to sing.

Mozart's Masterpieces.

After three lesser pieces Mozart embarked on his four masterpieces—*Le Nozze di Figaro* (1786), *Don Giovanni* (1787), *Così fan tutte* (1790), and *Die Zauberflöte* (1791).

Figaro, as well as being a delightful comedy, explores more fully than any previous opera situation and character, which find expression in beautiful arias and in two finales of symphonic proportion. In *Don Giovanni*, less satisfactory as a dramatic structure, the range of musical characterisation and insight into human motives is widened still further. *Così* lyrically but humorously expresses the follies of love. Mozart could not help but love his characters and his music for them is at one and the same time amusing and heartfelt, *Die Zauberflöte*—The Magic Flute—displays Mozart's deep-felt concern for his fellow men and for truth in an opera of great spiritual strength. Nor has opera any more loveable personality than the birdcatcher Papageno. Mozart's final opera *La Clemenza di Tito*, extolling imperial magnanimity, has never achieved the success or popularity of his other maturer stage works, though it contains much excellent music, and has recently been revived with honour in several opera houses.

Beethoven.

Mozart was the last major composer to depend, to any large extent, on private patronage for his living, and even he left the service of the Archbishop of Salzburg because he could not stand the restrictions imposed on his freedom. Henceforth composers would have to stand on their own two feet with all the advantages (liberty) and disadvantages (lack of security) that implied. Beethoven (1770–1827) was the first such composer of importance.

Although his work is usually divided into three periods, that division is somewhat too arbitrary, for no other composer in history, with the possible exception of Wagner, has shown such a continual development of his genius. Coming at just the right moment in musical history, he crowned the achievements of Haydn and Mozart with music of the utmost profundity of thought and feeling that looks back to its classical heritage and forward to the romantic movement of the 19th cent. His influence on musical thinking and writing is incalculable.

His first period shows his strong melodic gifts and the beginning of his individuality in developing form and structure to suit his own ends and match his particular genius. Unusual keys are explored, unusual harmonic procedures employed.

With the "Eroica" (his third symphony) he established his position as a great composer. The unity of purpose he here achieved within a long and diverse structure is truly staggering, even today. In the first movement alone the formal invention and cogency went far beyond what even Mozart had achieved in his "Jupiter" symphony, and the second movement—a vast funeral March—has an overwhelmingly tragic emotional content. But the "Eroica" was followed by six equally great symphonies, each one as varied, as inventive, as unified as the others. The ninth symphony is significant both for its length and its finale. Here Beethoven crowns three superb instrumental movements with a choral movement that, as well as summing up all that has gone

before, expresses in music the joy in existence more ecstatically than any other work.

The burning intensity of Beethoven's genius is just as evident in his chamber music. His quartets are the product of a revolutionary age in which the social graces and formal restraint of the 18th cent. were thrown off in a search for a more personal mode of expression. The early op. 18 set, and the Razoumovsky quartets, op. 59, go even beyond the range of Haydn's and Mozart's works in the medium but it was in his late quartets, his final musical testament, that Beethoven refined and distilled his art for posterity. No words can possibly describe their unique quality, but any and every chance should be taken to make their acquaintance; the effort required will be more than amply rewarded.

The early piano concertos do not reach quite that level of attainment, but the last three, together with the violin concerto, are on a par with the finest of the symphonies and quartets, as well as being considerable tests of the performers' technique. The Triple Concerto for piano, violin, and cello is an unusual and rewarding work.

His Choral Work.

Beethoven's grandest choral work—and one of the most noble in existence—is the Mass in D (*Missa Solemnis*). Its vast scale and sublime utterance often defeat performers, but when it is successfully done there is no more spiritually uplifting experience for the listener, except perhaps Beethoven's only opera, *Fidelio*. This simple escape story was transformed by Beethoven's creative fire into a universal symbol of liberty, the composer identifying himself with the struggle for freedom from tyranny and release from darkness.

Beethoven lived in a period of war and revolution. A passionate believer in the brotherhood of man and in liberty, he was shocked to find his ideals thrown over by revolutionaries-turned-dictators. His own tragedy of deafness, which came upon him at the moment of his triumph, nearly submerged him, but in the end he won through and produced the string of masterpieces from the "Eroica" onwards. Hope springing from despair, love from hatred, victory over defeat, these are the unquenchable legacies left by Beethoven.

The Romantic Movement.

Inevitably, the Romantic movement in literature that burst forth about 1800 was bound to have its counterpart in music. And so it was. Breaking the classical bonds, composers such as Schubert, Schumann, Liszt, and Berlioz sought a new freedom in musical expression. Form became of less importance than content; and that content often had literary connections. For their purposes a larger orchestra was needed and supplied, but the miniature, the song especially, because of its very personal connotation, was also a favourite form.

Schubert.

Schubert (1797–1828)—described by Liszt as "the most poetic of musicians"—is perhaps the greatest lyrical genius in musical history. In him the Viennese tradition and influence of Haydn, Mozart, and Beethoven reached its zenith. The song was always Schubert's starting point, so it is hardly surprising that his reputation as a song writer has never been impaired but in his symphonic and instrumental works too it is always his inexhaustible fund of melody that first calls for attention. Nobody could listen to his "Trout" quintet, for piano and strings, his octet, his fifth symphony, or his song cycle *Die Schöne Müllerin* without being enchanted and invigorated by the sheer tunefulness of the music. But there is much more to Schubert than this: his understanding of the possibilities of harmonic change, his grasp of orchestral coloration (in the great C major symphony, for instance), his free use of sonata structure.

Although Mozart, Haydn, and Beethoven had

all contributed to the song as an art form, it was with Schubert that it achieved its first full flowering. If he had written nothing but his songs, his place in the musical firmament would be assured. With his *Erlkönig* in 1815 the German *Lied* came of age and from then until the end of his life he wrote more than six hundred songs, hardly a dud among them. Whether it is the charm of *Heidenröslein*, the drama of *Der Doppelgänger* or the numbed intensity of the *Winterreise* cycle, Schubert unerringly went to the heart of a poet's meaning; indeed he often raised poor verses to an inspired level by his settings.

There is only room to mention one or two other composers, some of them wrongly neglected, who were roughly contemporaries of Beethoven and Schubert: the Czech Dussek (1760–1812), who like Beethoven bridges the classical-romantic gulf, Boccherini (1743–1805), the two Italian opera composers Cimarosa (1749–1801) and Paisiello (1740–1816), the Frenchman Méhul (1763–1817) and the German Hummel (1778–1837).

Weber (1786–1826) lacked Beethoven's energy and constructive powers and Schubert's sheer lyrical profundity, but he is an important figure, especially in the field of opera, where his *Der Freischütz* and *Oberon* led the way to a more flexible, dramatically realistic form of opera. His vivid imagination exactly fitted the new romantic mood abroad. The sheer beauty in the melodic shape of his music is undeniable. His instrumental works are attractive but insubstantial.

Mendelssohn.

Mendelssohn (1809–47) was the civilised craftsman among the Romantic composers. A boy genius—many of his finest works were written before he was twenty—he maintained the importance of classical form while imbuing it with his own affectionate brand of poetic sensibility.

His third and fourth symphonies—the "Scottish" and "The Italian"—(and possibly the fifth "The Reformation"), his string quartets (some of which go deeper than the rest of his music), octet, violin concerto, first piano concerto, and of course, the incidental music to "A Midsummer Night's Dream" represent his tidy yet effervescent style at its most winning.

Schumann.

Schumann (1810–56) is less easy to categorise. His early romantic flame was burnt out by some flaw in his intellectual and/or emotional make-up, and his inspiration seems to have declined in later years. No matter, by then he had given us the marvellous song cycles of 1840, an ever fresh piano concerto, many fine piano solos, including the mercurial, popular *Carnaval* and four symphonies, which, if not structurally perfect, contain much lovely music.

The joys and sorrows of love and the feeling for natural beauty are all mirrored in these charming, lyrical works, and in the piano quintet.

Berlioz.

Berlioz (1803–69) and Liszt (1811–86) are the two most typical representative composers of the Romantic era. Both have always been controversial figures, with ardent advocates and opponents either unduly enthusiastic or unfairly derogatory. Berlioz might be termed the perfect painter in music. With an uncanny mastery of orchestral sound he could conjure up the countryside, the supernatural and the historical with the utmost ease. He based his music on the "direct reaction to feeling" and a desire to illustrate literature by musical means. That his technical expertise was not always the equal of his undoubted genius, can be heard in many of his larger works such as the dramatic cantata *The Damnation of Faust* and the dramatic symphony *Romeo and Juliet*, yet most people are willing to overlook the occasional vulgarity for the ineffable beauty of his many fine pages, but brutal cuts in his music, such as are often made in, for instance, his epic opera *The Trojans* only have the effect of reducing the stature of his works. We must accept him, warts and all. Anyone who has seen the two parts of

The Trojans, presented complete in one evening at Covent Garden, will realise that Berlioz knew what he was about.

His output is not quantitatively large but includes several monumental works, as well as *The Trojans*, The *Requiem* ("Grand Messe des Morts") requires a tenor solo, huge chorus and orchestra, and brass bands, although Berlioz uses these forces fastidiously. The *Symphonie funèbre et triomphale* calls in its original form, for choir brass, and strings. But Berlioz was just as happy writing on a smaller scale as his exquisite song cycle, to words of Théophile Gautier, *Nuits d'Eté*, shows. Gautier perhaps summed up better than anyone Berlioz's singular talent: "In that renaissance of the 1830s Berlioz represents the romantic musical idea, the breaking up of old moulds, the substitution of new forms for unvaried square rhythms, a complex and competent richness of orchestration, truth of local colour, unexpected effects in sound, tumultuous and Shakespearian depth of passion, amorous or melancholy dreaminess, longings and questionings of the soul, infinite and mysterious sentiments not to be rendered in words, and that something more than all which escapes language but may be divined in music."

Liszt.

During his lifetime Liszt was fêted and honoured not only by his musical colleagues but by the world at large, which idolised him and his piano. Then his reputation took a plunge from which it has only recently recovered. To be sure much of his early music is glitter and gloss, but his symphonies and tone poems—especially the Faust Symphony, the Dante Symphony (both, of course, inspired by literature), and *Orpheus* and *Prometheus*—and his late piano works show that he was an extraordinary harmonic innovator. The piano sonata in B minor brings his romantic, wilful temperament within a reasonably stable, pianistic form, and as such is a landmark in the repertory of the instrument. Liszt's output was prodigious, but the inquiring listener should explore the more original of his compositions already mentioned to appreciate his fertile genius.

Chopin.

Chopin (1810–49) was the master of the keyboard, par excellence. His development of the technical and expressive capabilities of the piano is unique in musical history. His inventive powers were poured out with nervous passionate energy and in a highly individual style through twenty astonishing, possibly agonised years of creative activity before his early death. A Chopin melody, limpid, transparent, singing, can be recognised easily by anyone, but his style gradually developed into something more subtle, more satisfying than pure melody. He took the greatest care of every detail so that any alteration, however small, upsets the perfect balance of his work. His poetic sensibility can be found in any of his works; for his constructive ability we must turn to the Ballades, the B minor Sonata, and the Barcarolle, while the Preludes and Studies blend technical powers and emotional expressiveness in ideal proportions.

Nineteenth-Century Opera.

After Mozart's operas and Beethoven's *Fidelio* the medium might have been expected to decline. Instead it took on a new, if different, lease of life that culminated in Verdi's extraordinary output.

Rossini (1792–1868) created a world of exuberant high spirits in his operatic works that are as cheerful and heart-warming today as they were when they were first performed.

He always worked in and around the lyric theatres of Italy and between 1810 and 1830 poured out a stream of works, not all of which can be expected to be masterpieces. However, *Il Barbiere di Siviglia*, *L'Italiana in Algieri*, *La Cenerentola* and *Le Comte Ory* will always delight audiences as long as opera houses exist. Although these works are difficult to sing really well, their vitality and charm can never be submerged even by poor voices or indifferent staging.

His German contemporaries were critical of his confidence and frivolity, but his works show a consistency of invention and an irresistible tunefulness that anyone might envy. In recent years, there has also been a renewed interest in his more serious operas—*Otello* (1816), *La Gazza Ladra* (1817), *Semiramide* (1823), *La Siège de Corinthe* (1820), and *Guillaume Tell* (1829)—which were certainly surpassed in dramatic power by his successors but which nevertheless are not to be despised or neglected.

William Tell, to give it its most popular title, was his last work for the stage although he lived on for nearly forty years in retirement in Paris, scene of many of his greatest successes. There he enjoyed good living, dispensing *bons mots*, and occasionally composing trifles. An exception is the unpretentious *Petite Messe Solennelle*, written originally for soloists, chorus, a harmonium, and two pianos. Rossini later orchestrated it, but he would not allow it to be performed during his lifetime. The first public performance was on 28 February 1869, as near as possible to the 78th anniversary of the composer's birth on Leap Year Day 1792.

Bellini.

In contrast to the mercurial Rossini, Vincenzo Bellini (1801–85) was an exquisite, romantic figure dealing with exquisite, romantic stories, an operatic equivalent to Chopin, who much admired him. His delicate, sinuous vocal line (in the arias) and brilliant acrobatics in the final sections (cabalettas) require singers of the utmost accomplishment to do them justice, although his music is never as florid as Rossini's. His most typical and popular works are probably *La Sonnambula* (1831), *Norma* (1831) and *I Puritani* (1835). The first is a tender, homely country story, the second an almost heroic lyrical drama of sacrifice, and the third a rather unsatisfactory historical story redeemed by its appealing music.

Donizetti.

Gaetano Donizetti (1797–1848) was an even more prolific operatic composer than Rossini. He wrote at least 75 works, mostly for the Italian stage, several of which, such as *Alfredo il Grande* or *Emilia di Liverpool*, are never likely to be revived, but during the past few years, with the renewed interest in what are called the *Ottocento* operas, many of his serious operas have been resuscitated and found as enjoyable in performance as his more frequently heard comedies.

He was a well-grounded musician and although his invention is often criticised for being too tied to the conventions of his day performances often belie this reputation, his dramatic instinct proving sure. *Lucia di Lammermoor*, because of the chances it offers to a coloratura soprano with tragic pretensions, has always held the stage and of late, *Lucrezia Borgia*, *Anna Bolena*, *La Favorita*, and *Poliuto* have all been successfully revived. Of his lighter works, the comedies *L'Elixir d'Amore* and *Don Pasquale* have never declined in popularity. One of his last works was *Linda di Chamounix* (1842) which he wrote for Vienna where it aroused such enthusiasm that the Emperor appointed him Court Composer and Master of the Imperial Chapel.

French Opera.

The taste in Paris was for more and more lavish productions. Following Spontini (1774–1851), whose works were comparatively austere, came Halévy (1799–1862) and Giacomo Meyerbeer (1791–1864) whose operas contain all the ingredients that came to be expected of "Grand Opera"— spectacle, huge ensembles, showpieces for the soloists, and extended, if superfluous ballet. Drawing from Italian, German, and French traditions Meyerbeer's works contained everything the public wanted, yet today they are seldom revived, perhaps because his creative powers were essentially derivative, yet when they *are* given, operas like *Les Huguenots*, *Le Prophète*, and *L'Africaine* still have the power to fascinate and his influence on his successors, notably Wagner, was considerable.

Verdi.

Italian opera in the 19th cent. culminated in the works of Giuseppe Verdi (1813–1901), who rose from a peasant background to become his country's most noted composer, as well as something of a natural hero during the period of the Risorgimento. His earliest works, indeed, often roused his hearers to patriotic fervour. For instance, *Nabucco* (1841), with its theme of an oppressed people seeking deliverance, was treated as a symbol of the Italians' fight for freedom.

Musically, Verdi developed out of all recognition during the course of his long career. The continuously flowing structure of his last two operas *Otello* and *Falstaff* is very far removed from the start-stop formulas, inherited from his predecessors, of his first works, yet even they are touched, in harmonic subtleties, orchestral felicities, and a sense of drama, by a spark of genius, a burning inspiration that sets him apart from all other operatic composers. *Ernani* (1844), *I due Foscari* (1844), and *Luisa Miller* (1849) all have foretastes of glories to come even if as a whole they are flawed dramas, and these "galley years", as Verdi himself later described them, gave him the essential know-how to produce his later, greater operas, as well as establishing him incontrovertibly as the most popular Italian composer of the time.

Verdi's Masterpieces.

However, it was with *Rigoletto* (1851), *Il Trovatore* (1853), and *La Traviata* (1853) that Verdi first really staked his claim to immortality. In these pieces his increasing dramatic mastery is married to a wonderful flow of lyrical melody, at the same time controlled by a fine musical sensibility. They were followed by four operas— *Simon Boccanegra* (1857), *Un Ballo in Maschera* (1858), *La Forza del Destino* (1862), and *Macbeth* (revised version, 1865)—in which Verdi overcame complexities of story line by his continually developing musical powers. This period is crowned by *Don Carlos* (written for the Paris Opéra, 1867) a masterly exercise in combining private and public situations in a single, grand, and characterful work. In some respects Verdi never surpassed the subtlety of his writing in this opera. *Aïda* (1871) carried on the process but the characterisation in this ever-popular piece is less refined than in *Don Carlos*, if the grandeur of the design is more spectacular.

The success of *Otello* (1887) owes nearly as much to the skill of Boito whose literary ability combined with musical knowledge (he was himself a composer) presented Verdi with an ideal libretto for his seamless music in which the drama moves inevitably to its tragic end. Recitative, aria, ensemble are fused in a single, swiftly moving music-drama, which in its very different way equals that of Wagner. *Falstaff* (1893) achieves the same success in the field of comic opera, a brilliant, mercurial ending to a distinguished career.

If Verdi had written only these two final masterpieces his place in musical history would still have been assured.

Brahms.

Brahms (1833–97) has justly been described as "a romantic spirit controlled by a classical intellect," for while complying with most of the formal regulations of sonata form he imbued them with an emotional content that accorded with his time. Indeed Schumann declared that he was the "one man who would be singled out to make articulate in an ideal way the highest expression of our time."

Perhaps in his chamber music will be found the quintessence of his art. The piano and clarinet quintets, the two string sextets, the horn trio, and the violin sonatas all are designed on a large scale yet the expression remains intimate, the design and structure clear.

The symphonies and concertos, though, remain his most popular works; they are part of the solid repertory of every orchestra and most piano and violin players in the world. Their high seriousness, constant lyrical beauty, and control of form are deeply satisfying. They do not provide the extremes of passion and excitement provided by his contemporaries, but their study provides continuous absorption and delight. The double concerto for violin and cello deserves a mention as a unique work in music.

Brahms wrote more than two hundred songs in which the desire for melodic beauty takes precedence over the words and meaning. Many are set to poor poetry, but hidden away are still some unexplored treasures, and the Four Serious Songs, at least, are tragic masterpieces. In a lighter vein the two sets of *Liebeslieder Walzer* for four voices are irresistible. The choral Requiem, too, is a fine work.

Bruckner.

In recent years Bruckner's reputation *vis-à-vis* his great contemporary Brahms has been enhanced in England. The old conception of him as a naïve Austrian unable to grasp the fundamentals of symphonic architecture has died hard, and the prevailing popularity of his grandest works is at last gaining him his rightful place in the 19thcent. firmament. The nine symphonies and the masses are his chief claim to immortality. They contain melodies of unforgettable beauty, symphonic paragraphs of unparalleled grandeur, and an appreciation of formal development that, though different, is equally as valid as that of Brahms.

The movements of his symphonies are long and he often pauses, as if for breath and to admire the scenery, before he reaches the climactic peak of his musical journey. His idiom is best approached by a newcomer to his work through the fourth and seventh symphonies as they are perhaps the easiest to understand, but the fifth, sixth, eighth, and ninth (unfinished) are just as beautiful—and cogently argued—once one has acquired the knack, so to speak, of listening to his music. Most of these works are now to be heard in their original form, stripped of the veneer of "improvements" suggested to the diffident composer by his friends.

The masses, which translate Bruckner's symphonic ideas to the choral plain, and Bruckner's delightful string quintet are worth study.

Wagner.

Praised only this side of idolatry by his admirers, unmercifully criticised by his detractors, Richard Wagner (1813–83) is perhaps the most controversial composer in musical history. And so it was bound to be with such a revolutionary figure, whose writings, other than his music, contain, to say the least, dubious theories and whose operas, composed to his own libretti, broke the bonds of the form as known until his time. He regarded music-drama as a fusion of all the arts—music, literature, painting—in one unity. With *The Ring of the Nibelungs* he achieved his purpose; no other work of art has ever tried to encompass the whole of existence. Today, and surely forever, musicians, philosophers, and writers will argue over its meaning, and each age will reinterpret it according to its own lights.

His Transformation of Opera.

But before he reached this pinnacle of achievement, Wagner gradually transformed opera—through *Rienzi*, *The Flying Dutchman*, *Tannhäuser*, and *Lohengrin*—so that a new mould was fashioned to take what he wanted to pour into it. He introduced the *Leitmotiv*, a musical theme that could be associated with a particular person, situation, or idea, each time it occurred. Slowly he developed the musical form so that the drama could unfold continuously without breaks for arias. By the time he began to write *Tristan and Isolde* and *Die Meistersinger*, he had perfected his methods and had he never undertaken *The Ring* that tragedy and that comedy would have assured him his place in the musical firmament. Indeed,

Die Meistersinger is considered a masterpiece even by those who are not willing or prepared to accept the rest of the Wagnerian ethos.

The length and complexity of these operas, and of *Parsifal*, a work of unique beauty in spite of certain *longueurs*, means that it is almost essential to prepare oneself by homework, with libretti and records, before attempting to assimilate them in the opera house. The added effort is well worth while for the ultimate musical satisfaction they bring because Wagner was more than an operatic reformer; he opened up a new harmonic language (especially in the use of chromaticism) that was logically to develop into the atonality of the 20th cent.

Wolf.

As Wagner was the culmination of the 19th cent. symphonic and operatic tradition, so Hugo Wolf (1860–1903) summed up, if he did not surpass, the achievements in song-writing of Schubert, Schumann, and Loewe (1796–1869).

Wolf was a lonely, pathetic man. He lived much of his life in poverty, and eventually lost his reason and died of an incurable disease. These circumstances account perhaps for his almost feverish bursts of creative activity, which were also the outward sign of his burning genius.

His greatest contributions to the art of *Lieder* were his extraordinary insight into the poet's meaning and the harmonic means by which he heightened the expression of the words. He raised the importance of the piano part even higher than had Schumann, and in some of his songs the vocal part takes the form of a free declamation over a repeated idea in the piano. However, in the main the vocal and piano parts are interweaved with great subtlety, and he unerringly matched the very varied moods of the poems he chose to set.

His greatest creative period was between early 1888 and early 1890 when songs poured from his pen daily—more than 50 settings of the German poet Mörike, 20 of Eichendorff, more than 50 of Goethe, and more than 40 of Heyse and Geibel (the Spanish Song-book). Later he composed songs from Heyse's Italian Song-book and the three Michelangelo sonnets. And the range of his creative understanding was wide, taking in the almost wild passion of the Spanish songs, the humanity and humour of the Italian love-songs, the titanic power of *Prometheus* (Goethe), the varying moods of the Mörike book, and the intangible power of the Michelangelo sonnets. There are almost inexhaustible riches here for the inquiring mind to discover. Outside *Lieder*, Wolf 's output is small, but it includes a sadly neglected opera, *Der Corregidor*, the Italian Serenade for string quartet (alternatively for small orchestra) and a tone poem *Penthesilea*.

National Movements.

During the course of the 19th cent., alongside the emergence of national political identity, came the rise of nationalism in music, fertilising traditional Western—that is basically German—musical forms with folk material. Of these groups the Russian is certainly the most important, if not the most vital.

Glinka.

Glinka (1804–57) was the first important Russian composer of the national school and, although his two operas *A Life for the Tsar* (sometimes called *Ivan Susanin*) and *Russlan and Ludmilla* are strongly influenced by Italian models, they do introduce Russian song and harmony into the texture. He undoubtedly influenced Borodin (1833–87), Cui (1835–1918), Balakirev (1837–1910), Mussorgsky (1839–81) and Rimsky-Korsakov (1844–1908)—the so-called "Five" of 19th-cent. Russian music.

Each was very much an individualist too. Borodin was a lecturer in chemistry who wrote in his spare time. His two symphonies, two string quartets led up to his most notable work, the opera *Prince Igor*, left incomplete at his death. Balakirev, a friend and adviser to the rest of the group, wrote little himself, but his orchestral works and the piano fantasia, *Islamey*, are worthy of investigation.

Mussorgsky.

Modest Mussorgsky (1839–81) is today seen as the most important and inspired of "The Five." More than the others he used Russian song and Russian speech as the basis of his operas in which he portrayed the lives and destinies of his own people. Although his capacities were seriously impaired by an uncongenial job, poverty, and drinking, he produced two great operas, *Boris Godunov* and *Khovanshchina*, and another *Sorochintsy Fair* that is immensely enjoyable. *Boris* should be given in its original, with spare orchestration, but more often than not it is heard in Rimsky-Korsakov's more elaborate revision. In any case the opera exists in various versions, none of them necessarily the right one; what is important is to hear it in one or the other because of its great portrayal of Boris's personality set against the background of the Russian people, unforgettably presented in choral outbursts. *Khovanshchina* was completed by Rimsky-Korsakov, *Sorochintsy Fair* by Tcherepnin (although other versions also exist). Mussorgsky's songs explore a new vein of naturalistic vocal declamation. Each of the four *Songs and Dances of Death* is a miniature drama worthy of Wolf, although of course in a quite other idiom. The *Nursery* songs miraculously conjure up a child's world as seen from a child's point of view. Many of the individual songs, the *Sunless* cycle too, should be investigated.

Rimsky-Korsakov.

Rimsky-Korsakov (1844–1908) is perhaps a less attractive figure because so much of his music seems heartless or merely decorative, but this judgment is probably made on the strength of hearing *Shéhérazade* and the *Capriccio Espagnol* a few too many times. Such of his 15 operas as are played evince a (literally) fantastic mind and lyrical vein, and it is a pity that *Sadko*, *The Snow Maiden*, and *The Tsar's Bride*, at least, are not heard more often.

Tchaikovsky.

Peter Ilyich Tchaikovsky (1840–93) is a more universally admired figure than any of "The Five" and his music is indubitably closer to the mainstream than theirs in that it adheres more nearly to Western European forms. His popularity is due to his unhesitating appeal to the emotions and to his tender, often pathetic melodic expression. His lyrical gift is stronger than his sense of architecture, as he himself admitted. Yet his later symphonies—the fourth, fifth, and sixth (the *Pathétique*)—are all cogently enough argued and invigorating, as can be heard in the hands of a conductor willing to emphasise their formal power rather than their tendency towards sentimentality; the orchestral craftsmanship is also superb.

The three piano concertos and the violin concerto offer rare opportunities for virtuoso display within a reasonably dramatic structure and his various overtures are always exciting to hear.

The three ballets—*The Sleeping Beauty*, *Swan Lake*, and *Nutcracker* show Tchaikovsky's skill on a smaller and perhaps more congenial scale, but only two of his operas—*Eugene Onegin* and *The Queen of Spades*—survive in regular performance. They demonstrate his ability to delineate character and his always eloquent melodic invention.

Smetana.

The Czech national school is dominated by two composers—Smetana (1824–84) and Dvořák (1841–1904). In his own country Smetana holds a unique position as the father of his country's music—which is remarkable when you consider

that he lived in a country that was then under Austrian rule and never spoke the Czech language perfectly. Yet his music is filled with the spirit of Czech history and national life, and many of his operas, his most important contribution, deal purely with national subjects. The reawakening of interest in things national, after Austria's defeat by Italy in 1859, led to the establishment of a Provisional Theatre in 1862 and Smetana's first opera *The Brandenburgers in Bohemia* was produced there in 1866, but its success was eclipsed by the enormous popularity of *The Bartered Bride*, which appeared the same year. Its melodic charm, lively characterisation and cosy humour have carried it round the world and it is the one Smetana opera to be in the repertory of most opera houses. However, his next opera *Dalibor* (1868) is considered by some authorities as his masterpiece. It is conceived on a heroic scale, and frequently rises to great dramatic heights.

His later operas include *Libuse* (1872) a solemn festival tableau, *The Two Widows* (1874), a delightful comedy, *The Kiss* (1876), *The Secret* (1878), and *The Devil's Wall* (1882).

His Orchestral Work.

His main orchestral work *Má Vlast* (My Country), written between 1874 and 1879, is a cycle of six symphonic poems nobly depicting the life and legends of his country. He composed only three mature chamber works—an elegiac piano trio, written in 1855 in memory of the death of his eldest daughter, and two string quartets, both autobiographical. The first in E minor (1876)—"From My Life"—tells of his youth and aspirations until a terrible, screeching E in *altissimo* describes the onset of deafness; the second in D minor, sadly neglected, was described by the composer as an attempt to explain the "whirlwind of music in the head of one, who has lost his hearing," and was probably influenced by Beethoven's later music.

Dvořák.

Dvořák combined a fecund melodic gift with an intelligent grasp of structure. His symphonies and chamber music are mostly written in classical form, yet the works are imbued with a spontaneity and freshness that have not lost one whit of their charm over the years.

He wrote nine symphonies and, although only the last three or four are regularly performed, they are mostly mature works, several of which, for instance No. 7 in D minor (formerly known as No. 2) reach a tragic grandeur at times. They are all orchestrated in a masterly way and are full of delightful detail. Dvořák wanted to show that a Brahms could come out of Bohemia—and he succeeded in doing so while maintaining a definitely individual flavour, strongly influenced by natural rhythms.

He wrote three concertos, one each for piano, violin, and cello. The earlier ones are interesting without being quite in the first flight of the composer's output, but the cello concerto of 1895 is perhaps the composer's crowning achievement—warm, mellifluous, romantic.

He wrote chamber music throughout his long creative life. Some of the early works are weak and derivative, but the later string quartets, the "Dumky" trio, and the piano quartet and quintet are expressive and full of unforced invention. Dvořák felt himself somewhat hampered when setting words, nevertheless his *Stabat Mater* and *Te Deum* are both deeply felt choral works and he wrote songs throughout his career, many of them very fine indeed. He wrote ten operas, but only *Rusalka* (1901) is internationally known.

Janáček.

The Moravian composer Leos Janáček (1858–1928) spent most of his life in Brno as a working musician. His music has recently come to be recognised as some of the most original written in the past hundred years. His operas, in which he closely followed the inflection of the speech of his native land, are his finest works. Over the score of his last opera, *From the House of the Dead*, he wrote the words "In every human being there is a divine spark", and it is this deep love of humanity that permeates all his works. Of his operas *Kátya Kabanová* (1921) and *The Cunning Little Vixen* (1924), the *Makropoulos Affair* (1926), and *From the House of the Dead* (adapted from a Dostoyevsky novel, 1928) are the most important and they have all been produced in Britain in recent years.

His original genius is very clearly evident in all of them.

Among his orchestral works *Taras Bulba* and *Sinfonietta* should be noted, and his two string quartets, very difficult to play, should be better known. The song cycle, *Diary of one who has disappeared*, for tenor, contralto, and three female voices with piano, and the Glagolithic Mass contain music of much expressive beauty.

Hungary: Bartók and Kodály.

The Hungarian musical outburst came somewhat later than that of other countries. Its great figure is Bela Bartók (1881–1945) who, as well as being a national figure, has proved an influential composer in the whole of 20th-cent. music. His mind was full of folk music, but it was transmuted by his strongly personal style and powerful intellect into something highly original. His music is tense and volatile but this restlessness is sometimes relieved by a kind of other-wordly, ethereal lyricism, as in the lovely slow movements of his quartets.

Bartók was affected as much by the musical innovations of Debussy and Stravinsky (*see below*) as by East European, notably Magyar, folk music. Many of his works are an attempt to meld the two together.

The most important part of his output is undoubtedly his string quartets which cover most of his creative life. To this intimate form he confided his personal innermost thoughts and in it conducted his most far-reaching musical experiments, thereby extending its boundaries beyond anything previously known. As with Beethoven's late quartets many of Bartók's rely on organic or cyclic development while remaining just within the laws of classical form. As Mosco Carner puts it, "For profundity of thought, imaginative power, logic of structure, diversity of formal details, and enlargement of the technical scope, they stand unrivalled in the field of modern chamber music."

The most important of his orchestral works are the three piano concertos, of which the first two are harsh and uncompromising, and fiendishly difficult to play, while the third, written in 1945, is mellower and more diatonic. The second violin concerto (1937–8) shows the various elements of Bartók's style in full flower, by turns exuberant, passionate, and brilliant. The *Music for Strings, Percussion and Celesta* (1937) is remarkable for its strange sonorities and its fascinating texture. The *Concerto for Orchestra* (1944) is more immediately appealing and again shows the composer in complete command of a large canvas. Of the piano works *Mikrokosmos* (1935) and the sonata for two pianos and percussion (1937) are worth investigating.

His chief stage pieces are *The Miraculous Mandarin* (1919), a harsh, cruel ballet which drew appropriately dramatic music from the composer, and the opera *Duke Bluebeard's Castle* (1911), a luscious, original score that makes one regret that he wrote no more operas later in his career for our pleasure.

Kodály (1882–1967) was from early years closely associated with Bartók and with him collected Hungarian folk melodies using many of them in his music. He worked in many forms and the more important of his works are the *Peacock Variations* for orchestra, the choral *Psalmus Hungaricus* and *Te Deum*, The *Dances of Galánta*, and the opera *Háry János*, and the sonatas for cello and for unaccompanied cello.

Sibelius, Nielsen and Grieg.

Among Scandinavian composers the Finn Jean Sibelius (1865–1957) and the Dane Carl Nielsen (1865–1931) are outstanding. Sibelius is a lone northern figure ploughing his own furrow oblivious or, at any rate, ignoring the unusual developments that were taking place in Central Europe, yet his seven symphonies are strong as granite, honest, rugged works that will undoubtedly stand the test of time. They are not by any means all similar in mood, or even form. The first is very much influenced by Tchaikovsky and Borodin, the second and third show a more personal style developing, the fourth is terse and tragic, the fifth lyrical, bright, and lucid; the sixth is perhaps most typically Sibelian in its evocation of primeval nature, and the seventh—in one continuous movement—is a more purely abstract piece, notable for its structural logic and the grandness of its themes. The violin concerto is the most easily understood of the composer's main works and has a grateful part for the soloist.

The tone poems *The Swan of Tuonela*, *Pohjola's Daughter*, *En Saga*, *Night Ride and Sunrise*, *The Bard*, and *Tapiola* uncannily evoke the icy words of the legends of the far north, and the primeval forces of nature. Sibelius's one string quartet *Voces Intimae* and many of his songs are worth hearing too. His music, reviled in some quarters during the 1950s, has since been restored to favour, and seems to be enjoyed again by critics and the general public alike.

Carl Nielsen (1865–1931) is another individualist. His six symphonies, like Sibelius's seven, are the most important part of his output, but whereas Sibelius was dealing with a huge, uninhabited northern landscape, Nielsen is more friendly and serene in his music, which is seldom forbidding, always inventive, throwing a new light, through unusual ideas about harmony, structure and tonality, on traditional forms. He also wrote highly individual concertos for the flute and clarinet, four string quartets and two operas— the dramatic, rather Brahmsian *Saul and David* (1902) and a delightful comedy, *Maskarade* (1906), full of lyrical music.

Edward Grieg (1843–1907), the Norwegian composer, was essentially a miniaturist whose range of feeling was not wide but whose music is always gentle and appealing. His most notable works are the romantic piano concerto, the atmospheric incidental music to Ibsen's play *Peer Gynt*, the charming *Lyric Suite*, and the small piano pieces.

Elgar and the English Revival.

After the death of Purcell there is hardly a name in English music worth speaking of until the 19th cent. when Hubert Parry (1848–1918) and Charles Villiers Stanford (1852–1924), actually an Irishman, led a revival. Their music is seldom heard today, but their pioneer work paved the way for Edward Elgar (1857–1934). Although all were influenced by Brahms they nevertheless managed to establish a new English tradition that has been carried on in our own day. Elgar's symphonies are laid out on a grand, leisurely scale and they are both eloquent and exhilarating. His violin concerto has an elegiac slow movement as has the glorious cello concerto and both contain many fine opportunities for the soloist. The cello concerto is as appealing a work as any by Elgar expressing his innermost thoughts. His *Enigma Variations* are a series of portraits in sound of his friends, but there is another overall theme to go with them that has never been identified. This has not prevented the work from becoming Elgar's most popular, not surprisingly when one considers its charm and melodiousness.

Three other orchestral pieces that should not be neglected are his symphonic study *Falstaff*, a many-sided musical picture of the Fat Knight, and the overtures *Cockaigne*, a happy evocation of London, and *In the South*, inspired by a visit to Italy. His three late chamber works, written when he was 61, are reticent, economic pieces that remove any misconception of Elgar as a bombastic composer. His songs are mostly feeble, but the oratorios, notably *The Dream of Gerontius*, show the composer's ability to control a large canvas.

French Music.

The Belgian César Franck (1822–90) was the main figure in mid-19th-cent. France. His influence spread even wider than his music of which only the D minor Symphony, the Symphonic Variations for piano and orchestra, the piano quintet, and the violin sonata are likely to be encountered today. The leading French opera composers of that time were Gounod (1818–93), Bizet (1838–75) and Massenet (1842–1912). Gounod's *Faust*, Bizet's *Carmen* (composed just before his untimely death when he caught cold after a swim) and Massenet's *Manon* all retain a deserved place in the repertory; each is a well-judged mini-drama unafraid of romantic ardour and forceful, histrionic strokes. Some of Massenet's other numerous operas, such as *Werther* and *Don Quichotte*, have enjoyed a revival in recent years.

Debussy.

Concurrently with similar movements in French painting and poetry came the French Impressionist composers at the end of the 19th cent. Their leader—and one of the great seminal forces of modern music—was Claude Debussy (1862–1918). His aim was to capture a mood or sensation, and he did that by more or less inventing a fresh system of harmony using a whole-tone scale, unusual chords, and by creating in the orchestra new, highly personal textures—there is no mistaking the Debussy idiom once you have heard at least one piece by him. His impressionistic style did not lead him, however, to abandon form as some have suggested, and his main works are just as closely organised as those by classical German composers. His music is sensuous and poetic yet nearly always structurally satisfying as well.

His reputation, at least with the general musical public, rests largely on his orchestral music, a few piano pieces and his only opera *Pelléas et Mélisande*. *La Mer* is a scintillating evocation of the sea in all its moods; *Nocturnes*, *Images*, and *Prélude à l'Après-midi d'un Faune* exactly suggest different places, times, moods—the "Iberia" and "Gigues" sections of *Images*, calling to mind respectively the spirit of Spain and the flickering light of a rainy English night. *Pelléas*, based on a Symbolist drama by Maeterlinck, tells a story of love, jealousy, and murder in predominantly restrained yet emotionally loaded terms. It is an elusive original work that has no predecessor or successor. Intensely atmospheric, rivetingly beautiful, it weaves an irresistible spell over the listener.

Debussy's chamber music is unjustly neglected. His string quartet (1893) was one of the first works in which he displayed his new and strange world of sound, and the three late sonatas, one for violin, one for cello, and the third for flute, viola, and harp are elliptical, compressed pieces which seem to be questing disjointedly into new regions of sound. His songs too, are worthy of investigation, and his piano music, especially the twenty-four Preludes and some of the shorter pieces, contain some of his most imaginative and original ideas and thoughts.

Gabriel Fauré (1845–1924) is a difficult figure to place. He lived through all kinds of musical revolutions yet they seemed to affect the character of his work very little. He has never been, and is never likely to be, a widely known or popular composer, yet his music has a reticence and delicacy that is very appealing. Despite his dreamy, retiring art he was not a recluse, but a very sociable man.

He was content with forms as he found them, but he imbued them with a very personal, human style. Perhaps his art is best heard in his songs. They are not overtly passionate or dramatic but the long, sinuous melodies and subtle harmonies are exquisitely wrought. Of the song-cycles, *La Bonne Chanson*, *Cinq Mélodies* (Verlaine), *Le Chanson d'Eve*, and *L'Horizon Chimérique* are best known. The last written in 1922, when the composer was seventy-seven, is a beautiful setting of words by a soldier killed in the first World War. There are also many remarkable single songs, many of them settings of poems by Verlaine. His opera *Pénélope*, based on the classical heroine, is unjustly neglected.

He wrote few orchestral pieces, but the *Ballade* for piano and orchestra and the *Pavane* are among his most typical, delicate compositions, and his outstanding piano music, modelled on Chopin's, includes Nocturnes, Impromptus, and Barcarolles. His chamber music covers more than half a century from the violin sonata of 1876 to the string quartet written the year he died. In that period he composed two piano quartets, two piano quintets, another violin sonata and two cello sonatas, the later works failing to show quite the unforced lyrical grace of the earlier ones. Perhaps Fauré is best approached with the first piano quartet, a charming, easily assimilated work, and the beautiful choral *Requiem*.

Saint-Saëns (1835–1921), an accomplished, cultivated musician, has had a "bad press" but his craftsmanship, as displayed in his symphonies, concertos, and *Samson et Dalila* (one among his 12 operas) is not to be despised.

Henri Duparc (1844–1933), despite a very long life, is known today only for a group of songs he wrote before he was forty. They are among the most emotionally direct yet tasteful melodies ever written. Paul Dukas (1865–1935) is another figure off the beaten track, as it were. He, too, is known only for a handful of compositions. He was strongly influenced by Vincent d'Indy (1851–1931) and the school who strongly opposed Debussy's new ideas, yet he could not help but come under Debussy's spell. Dukas's one great work is his opera *Ariane et Barbe-Bleue*, the text adapted from a Maeterlinck play written with the composer in mind.

Maurice Ravel (1875–1937), a pupil of Fauré, followed in Debussy's footsteps, although his later pieces were more ascetic. Indeed, he was one of the most fastidious of composers, always seeking, and often finding, artistic perfection. The works he wrote before 1918 are definitely of the Impressionist School and it would be difficult to imagine more beautiful sounds than are to be found in the ballet *Daphnis et Chloé*, in the song-cycle *Shéhérazade*, and the piano fantasy *Gaspard de la Nuit*. His first style was summed up in the A minor piano trio (1915). In his later music Ravel was struggling, not always successfully, to keep up with new developments such as jazz and atonality. The piano concerto, for instance, shows very strongly the influence of jazz.

Outstanding orchestral works of his, other than *Daphnis* are *Rapsodie espagnole* (1907), *La Valse* (1920), a sumptuous evocation of the Vienna waltz, and the ever-popular *Boléro*. Two chamber works, besides the trio, are masterpieces—the string quartet (1902–3) and the Introduction and Allegro for Harp, String Quartet, Flute, and Clarinet. This Septet composed in 1906, ravishes the senses with magical sound.

Ravel's piano pieces are perhaps his most notable contribution to music, combining an extraordinary feeling for the instrument's technical possibilities with the sensibility of a Chopin, and in this field *Jeux d'eau*, *Miroirs*, and *Ma Mère l'Oye*, all written just after the turn of the century, come very close to the perfection of *Gaspard de la Nuit*. His songs show his unusual appreciation of the need to fuse poetic and musical values, and he set exotic poems for preference.

His work in this field includes the cycle *Histoires naturelles* (1906), acutely observed settings of five poems about birds and animals; *Cinq Mélodies populaires grecques* (1907), charming settings of Greek folk songs; *Trois Poèmes de Mallarmé* (1913); and *Chansons madécasses* (1926), suitably exotic settings of three poems by an 18th-cent. Creole poet called Parny. Finally in 1932 came *Don Quichotte à Dulcinée*, three poems by Paul Morand, Ravel's last composition.

Ravel wrote two operas—the slight but moderately amusing *L'Heure espagnole* (1907), nicely orchestrated in a faintly and appropriately Spanish style and *L'Enfant et les Sortilèges* (1925) to a story by Colette, a delicious fantasy about a naughty child who gets his due punishment for tormenting animals and destroying furniture.

French music after Debussy and Ravel was dominated by the slighter composers known as *Les Six*, the most important of whom were Arthur Honegger (1892–1955, Swiss born), Darius Milhaud (1892–1974) and Francis Poulenc (1890–1963). Each has contributed music of some wit and charm to the repertory. They were influenced by Erik Satie (1866–1925), an eccentric but interesting figure who wrote works with odd titles such as *Three Pear Shaped Pieces*. His music is entirely unsentimental, often ironic.

Spain.

Felipe Pedrell (1841–1922) has been aptly described as the midwife of Spanish nationalist music. As a musicologist and teacher he strongly influenced the two main composers of the school, Manuel de Falla (1876–1946) and Enrique Granados (1867–1916). Falla's output was not large and most of it was written around the years of the first world war. The pre-war years were spent in Paris where Falla came under the influence of Debussy. However his style is individual and evokes all the passion and gaiety of his native land. Perhaps his most typical works are in two ballets *Love the Magician* (1915) and *The Three-Cornered Hat* (1919). The opera *La Vida Breve* (1905) despite its weak libretto also has much appeal. The vivacity and smouldering passion at the heart of the country's character is conjured up by the *Seven Popular Songs* (1914) and the *Nights in the Gardens of Spain* (1916) for piano and orchestra. His later works, especially the harpsichord concerto of 1926, show Falla tending towards a less ebullient, more restrained style. The second opera, *Master Peter's Puppet Show* (1923) is a miniaturist work, refined and intense. His third opera *Atlantida*, left unfinished at his death, was completed by his pupil Ernesto Halffter and first staged in 1962.

Granados was perhaps a more restrictedly Spanish composer than Falla, but his music is unfailingly attractive and deserves to be better known. The opera *Goyescas* (1916) is most famous for the second interlude and opening of Act III—*La Maja y el Ruiseñor* (The Lover and the Nightingale), a haunting, sinuous melody for soprano, generally heard in its original form as a piano solo.

The chief claim to fame of Albéniz (1860–1909) is *Ibéria*, masterly descriptive pieces for piano. Many of his other piano works are now more well known in the form of very effective guitar arrangements.

Turina (1882–1949), attempted a more cosmopolitan style, but his most often heard music is typically Spanish.

The Late German Romantics.

While composers such as Debussy, Sibelius, Stravinsky and Schoenberg (see below for the latter pair) were striking out along new paths, Richard Strauss (1864–1949) continued in the trend of 19th-cent. German composers; he was the tradition's last great figure. At least two of his operas—*Salome* and *Elektra*—were considered shocking at the time, but today we can hear that they are essentially big-scale, romantic works—natural successors to Wagner's—however startling the harmonies may once have seemed.

If Strauss did not achieve the granite intellectual greatness of Beethoven or Wagner, there is no denying his melodic genius and powers of fertile invention which overlaid the streak of vulgarity and inflation in his musical make-up. His first outstanding achievement was in the field of the symphonic poem, where he carried the work of composers such as Liszt and Berlioz to its logical conclusion. Starting with *Don Juan* in 1888 and ending with *Sinfonia Domestica* in 1903 he wrote a series of kaleidoscopic works, full of enormous vitality, endless melody, and fascinating orchestration. The most easily assimiliated—and the most popular—are *Don Juan* and *Till Eulenspiegel* but some of the longer works, notably *Also Sprach Zarathustra* (based on Nietzsche's prose poem) and *Don Quixote* (based, of course, on Cervantes's great work) will reward the persistent, inquiring mind with long hours of enthralled listening. Other works sound somewhat dated in their bombastic over-confidence, though Strauss's skill in composition seldom flagged at this stage of his long creative career.

The symphonic poems all tell something of a story usually based on a literary source, but it is not essential to the enjoyment of the music to know what this is, although it may be helpful.

The Reputation of Strauss.

Strauss's reputation is even more solidly based on his fifteen operas, the earliest of which *Guntram* was first performed in 1894, the last, *Capriccio*, in 1942. During these years the essentials of Strauss's style changed little, though it became very much more refined as the years passed. His first operatic period ended with the violent, sensual tragedies *Salome* (1905) and *Elektra* (1909), the latter being his first collaboration with his chief librettist, Hugo von Hofmannsthal. Then came their unique *Der Rosenkavalier* (1911), which filters the charm and the decadence of 18th-cent. Vienna through early 20th-cent. eyes. This was followed by *Ariadne auf Naxos* (1912). Originally intended to be given after Molière's *Le Bourgeois Gentilhomme*, it was later presented (1916) without the play but with an amusing Prologue, written by von Hofmannsthal. *Die Frau ohne Schatten* is the most grandiose result of the Strauss–Hofmannsthal partnership. It is a complex psychological allegory, but Strauss's contribution is not on as consistently lofty a level as is his librettist's. *Intermezzo* (1924), which has a libretto by Strauss himself, is a largely autobiographical domestic comedy, which has lately gained in reputation as a compact, charming piece.

With *Die Aegyptische Helena* (1928), an opera on a mythical theme, and *Arabella* (1933), another sensuous Viennese comedy, the Strauss–Hofmannsthal collaboration ended on account of the librettist's death.

Strauss then wrote *Die Schweigsame Frau* (1935) to a libretto by Stefan Zweig, based on a play by Ben Jonson, and *Friedenstag* (1938), *Daphne* (1938)—a beautiful opera—and *Die Liebe der Danae* (written 1938–40) with Josef Gregor as librettist. His swan-song was *Capriccio*, a dramatisation of the old argument about the relative importance of words and music in opera. The libretto is by the conductor Clemens Krauss and the opera, a serene, melodious work, was a fit end to a great operatic career.

However, Strauss went on composing till nearly the end of his life, adding a group of late orchestral pieces to his already large catalogue of works. The *Metamorphosen*, for 23 solo string instruments, is probably the best of these. During his long creative career he wrote numerous songs, many of them, such as *Morgen*, *Wiegenlied* and *Ruhe, meine Seele* of surpassing beauty.

Reger and Pfitzner.

Other notable figures in German music at this time were Max Reger (1873–1916), a somewhat ponderous but highly accomplished composer who, in a quarter of a century of creative life, wrote more than 150 works, of which his sets of variations, his piano concerto, and chamber music are probably the most impressive. Hans Pfitzner (1869–1949), another German traditionalist, is chiefly remembered today for his opera *Palestrina*, about events, now known to be spurious, in the life of the 16th-cent. Italian composer.

Gustav Mahler.

Gustav Mahler (1860–1911), the Austrian Jewish composer, is one of the most important figures in 20th-cent. music. In a sense he bridges the gulf between the late Romantics, who were tending more and more towards chromaticism and away from established key relationships, and the atonalists, who abandoned the key system entirely. His detractors maintain that his inflation of allegedly banal Viennese beer-house music to unheard-of lengths rules him out of court as a serious writer. His admirers would claim that his music encompasses the whole of life in enormous, valid structures. The truth, if truth there be, perhaps lies somewhere in between: if his material does not always justify the length of his symphonies, and if there are occasional imperfections and *longueurs*, these shortcomings are worth enduring for the sake of the depth of utterance, the humanity and the poetry of the great pages.

His music is undoubtedly best approached through his songs, where the words force him to discipline his wide-ranging vision. *Lieder eines fahrenden Gesellen* (1884), to his own words, *Kindertotenlieder* (1901–4), to poems by Rückert, and some individual songs perfectly relate words to music, and are all of a poignant loveliness. Similarly *Das Lied von der Erde* (1908), especially the last of the six songs, is a touching farewell to the world, nobly expressed.

Mahler's Symphonies.

The ten symphonies, however, are Mahler's most impressive legacy to posterity. They are almost impossible to characterise briefly so vast are they in terms of both length and variety. The first, fourth and ninth are probably the easiest to grasp but the fifth, sixth and seventh, despite flaws, contain some of his most awe-inspiring conceptions. The second and third, both of which use soloists and chorus, are revolutionary in orchestration and structure; they both try, inevitably without complete success, to carry out the composer's dictum, "a symphony should be like the world—it must contain everything." The eighth is even more gargantuan, but as in all Mahler's work size does not mean loss of clarity or an overloading of the structure. Part one—a mighty choral invocation—is a visionary setting of the mediaeval hymn *Veni Creator Spiritus*. Part two, which incorporates adagio, scherzo, and finale in one, is a setting of the final scene of Goethe's *Faust*. Until recently all of Mahler's unfinished tenth symphony that was ever performed was the Adagio, but the musicologist and Mahler scholar, the late Deryck Cooke, provided a performing version of the symphony to critical and popular acclaim during the 1960s and thus added a noble, and also optimistic epilogue to the Mahler opus. The debate over the quality of Mahler's music is not likely to continue; one fact, however, that cannot be gain-said is his popularity with an ever-increasing audience, largely made up of young people. There must be something in his uncertainty and intense self-inquiry that appeals.

Schoenberg and the Second Viennese School.

Arnold Schoenberg (1874–1951) revolutionised Western music by his twelve-note method—a system which uses all the notes of the chromatic scale "and denies the supremacy of a tonal centre," as Schoenberg himself puts it. This serial technique of composition, as it is commonly called, naturally sounds strange to an ear acclimatised to music written, as it were, with a home base, but Schoenberg and his disciples Berg and Webern showed that the system could produce works that were something more than mere intellectual exercises. None of the recent advances in music would have been possible without Schoenberg.

Schoenberg always considered himself as much as a composer as a theorist or teacher, and his works are supposed to appeal as much to the emotions as to the intellect, although to be understood they do, of course, require the listener's concentrated attention. To appreciate how his ideas developed it is necessary to hear first his pre-atonal music, such as the *Gurrelieder* (1900–1) and *Verklärte Nacht* (1899), in which he carried Wagnerian chromaticism to extreme lengths. The *Gurrelieder*, in particular, is a luxuriant, overblown work that shows the Wagnerian idiom in an advanced stage of decay, in spite of many beautiful pages of music. In his succeeding works the feeling of tonality began to disappear until in the Three Piano Pieces (opus 11), of 1909, he finally

rejected tonality, although the new 12-note scheme is not yet evident; traces of the old order can still be heard. The succeeding works were mostly short, highly compressed, and very expressive. Schoenberg was reaching out for a new system, which would "justify the dissonant character of these harmonies and determine their successions." By 1923 he had formulated his 12-note system and the Five Piano Pieces (opus 23), and the Serenade (opus 24) of that year, can thus be considered the first works that used a note-row as the fundamental basis of their composition. Between 1910 and 1915, however, the Russian composer Alexander Skryabin (1872–1915) had attempted to define a new method of composition of his own employing the "mystic chord" of ascending fourths, but his scheme proved comparatively abortive when compared with Schoenberg's. Josef Hauer (1883–1959) also developed a 12-note system which he propounded in 1919 and he always considered himself, rather than Schoenberg, as the true founder of the system. He later worked out a system of tropes (*i.e.*, half-series of six notes).

Schoenberg's Later Work.

To return to Schoenberg, in later works he shows much more freedom and assurance in the use of his system. The wind quintet (1924), the Variations for Orchestra, opus 31 (1927–8), the third (1926), and fourth (1936) string quartets, and the string trio (1946) are modern classics of their kind; they require concentrated listening and a degree of understanding of the unfamiliar style of composition. The set of songs with piano *Das Buch der hängenden Gärten* (opus 15), written in 1908, *Pierrot Lunaire*, opus 21 (1912) and the Four Songs, opus 22 (1913–14) provide a kind of bridge between tonality and atonality that the adventurous mind should cross. The monodrama *Erwartung* (1909) is another fascinating work, but perhaps the unfinished *Moses and Aaron* (1932) is Schoenberg's masterpiece as its production at Covent Garden in 1965 showed. Here, for certain, the composer matched his obvious intellectual capacities with an evident emotional content and managed to combine *Sprechgesang* (speech-song) and singing with a real degree of success.

It is only in recent years that Schoenberg's music has had a real chance to make its mark through the essential prerequisite of frequent performance. If his idiom now seems approachable, and a reasonably natural outcome of late 19th-cent. developments, it is perhaps because other, more recent composers have extended the boundaries of sound much further.

Disciples of Schoenberg.

Schoenberg's two most respected disciples were Anton Webern (1883–1945) and Alban Berg (1885–1935). Webern's output is small, reaching only to opus 31, and many of his works are very brief. They are exquisitely precise, and delicate almost to a fault. He was trying to distil the essence of each note and in so doing carried the 12-note system to its most extreme and cerebral limit. His music has often been described as pointillist in the sense that one note is entirely separated from the next, there being little discernible melody. Beyond Webern's music, there is indeed the sound of nothingness, and he was rightly described during his lifetime as the "composer of the *pianissimo espressivo*". In his later works, Webern tended towards a strict, and often ingenious use of form and the Variations for Orchestra of 1940 are a good example of this and of his delicacy of orchestration. Webern's influence has perhaps been greater than the impact of his own music, even though he has had no direct successor.

Berg's music is much more accessible. Like Webern his total output was not large, but nearly all his works are substantial additions to the repertory. He is also the directest link between Mahler and the second Viennese School, as Mahler's music influenced him strongly. He studied with Schoenberg from 1904 to 1910. His music is more intense, more lyrical, and less attenuated in sound than Schoenberg's or Webern's. His humanity and abiding compassion can be heard most strongly in his finest opera *Wozzeck* (1925) and his violin concerto (1935), written as an elegy on the death of Manon Gropius, a beautiful 18-year-old girl. Both works are very carefully designed yet formal considerations are never allowed to submerge feeling, and the note-row is fully integrated into the structure.

Both *Wozzeck* and the unfinished but rewarding *Lulu* are concerned with society's outcasts who are treated with great tenderness in both operas. The later work is entirely dodecaphonic, all the opera's episodes being based on a theme associated with Lulu. Between these operas Berg wrote the highly complex Chamber Concerto for piano, violin, and thirteen wind instruments (1925) and the expressive Lyric Suite (1926). Among his other works the Seven Early Songs (1908–9) and the concert aria *Der Wein* (1929) are notable.

Stravinsky.

Igor Stravinsky (1882–1971) was another vital figure in 20th-cent. music. If his influence has been in quite another and perhaps less drastic direction than Schoenberg's it is hardly less important. Indeed, future musical historians may consider his achievement the more significant. He has been compared with the painter Picasso in his almost hectic desire to keep up with the times, yet, although he wrote in a number of very different styles over a period of fifty years, every work of his is stamped with his own definitive musical personality. His most revolutionary and seminal work is undoubtedly *The Rite of Spring* (written for the ballet impresario Diaghilev), which caused a furore when it first appeared in 1913, and although it no longer shocks, the rhythmical energy, the fierce angular thematic material, and the sheer virtuosity of the orchestration will always have the power to excite new audiences. Before *The Rite* Stravinsky had written two ballets for Diaghilev—*The Firebird* and *Petrushka*—that are no less filled with vitality and new, albeit not so violent, sounds. During the next thirty years Stravinsky wrote a series of ballet works, gradually becoming more austere and refined in composition. *Apollo* (1928) and *Orpheus* (1947) belong among his best scores.

The Versatility of Stravinsky.

Stravinsky did not confine himself in stage works to the ballet. *The Nightingale* (1914) is a charming, early opera; *The Soldiers Tale* (1918) is a witty combination of narration, mime, and dance; *Les Noces* (1923) is a concise, original choreographic cantata for soloists and chorus; *Oedipus Rex* (1927) is a dignified version of the Sophocles play, which can be staged or given on the concert platform; either way it is a moving experience. *Perséphone* (1934), a melodrama for reciter, chorus, and orchestra is an appealling, lucid score. After the war his most important stage work by far was *The Rake's Progress* (1951), with a libretto by W. H. Auden and Chester Kallman. This fascinating opera is deliberately based on 18th-cent. forms and the music itself is neo-classical, always attractive, often haunting.

Stravinsky was no laggard in writing for the concert-platform either. The finest of his orchestral pieces are probably the fervent choral *Symphony of Psalms* (1930), the violin concerto (1931) and the aggressive compact Symphony in Three Movements (1945). Of his chamber music the octet (1923), a duo concertant (1932), and septet (1952) are probably the most important, but no piece, even the dryest and most pedantic, is without redeeming features.

Stravinsky is often thought of as an aloof, detached figure. He has been castigated for his lack of lyrical warmth. But in spite of his own professed desire to drain his music of specific emotion, craftsmanship and originality, often with a strange other-worldly beauty added, are unmistakably there throughout his many scores.

Busoni.

Italian music in the early part of the century

was dominated by two very different composers—Ferruccio Busoni (1866–1924) and Giacomo Puccini (1858–1924). Busoni is a difficult figure to place. His austere, intellectual power is never called in question, but he seldom, if ever, succeeded in translating his technical prowess into altogether successful compositions. We can admire the strength, honesty, and often beauty of such works as his huge piano concerto (1903–4), *Fantasia Contrappuntistica* (1912)—for piano solo—and his unfinished opera *Doktor Faust* without ever capitulating to them entirely. None the less, it has to be admitted that those who have studied his music closely have always fallen completely under his spell. In style his music is anti-Romantic and often neo-Classical yet he was an ardent admirer of Liszt and more especially of Liszt's realisation of the possibilities of the pianoforte. Busoni, himself a great pianist, carried on where Liszt had left off in his own piano music, in which form and expression often find their perfect balance. *Doktor Faust* is undoubtedly his most important opera but *Die Brautwahl* (1908–10) and *Turandot* (1917) have many points of interest too.

Puccini.

Puccini's *Turandot*—his last opera—is a much grander version of the same Gozzi fable and the culmination of this great opera composer's work. His achievement is at an almost directly opposite pole to Busoni's. Not for him the severity or intellectuality of his contemporary. He sought and found an almost ideal fusion of straight-forward lyricism and dramatic truth. His music unerringly follows the pathos and passion of the stories he sets and all his characters "live" as human beings. That, and his abundant flow of easy, soaring melody, are the reasons for his immense popular success, unequalled by any other 20th-cent. composer. Whether it is the pathetic Mimi (*La Bohème*—1896) and Cio-Cio-San, (*Madam Butterfly*—1904), the evil Scarpia (*Tosca* —1900), the cunning Schicchi (*Gianni Schicchi*— 1918), the ardent Rodolfo (*La Bohème*) and Cavaradossi (*Tosca*), or the ice-cold Turandot (*Turandot*—1926). Puccini's musical characterisation is unfailing. And he backs his *verismo* vocal writing with an orchestral tissue that faithfully reflects the milieu of each opera, for instance, Japanese for *Butterfly*, Chinese for *Turandot*, while never losing his particular brand of Italian warmth. His orchestration is always subtle and luminous. Other Italian composers who wrote operas in the *versimo* style of Puccini were Leoncavallo (1858–1919), Mascagni (1865–1945), and Giordano (1867–1948). Mascagni's *Cavalleria Rusticana* and Leoncavallo's *Pagliacci* are both widely performed.

Prokofiev.

Sergey Prokofiev (1891–1953) spent part of his creative life in his native Russia, the rest (1918–34) abroad, mostly in Paris. His early music, apart from the popular Classical Symphony (1916–17) tended to be acid and harsh, but on his return to Russia his style, though still frequently satirical, became warmer, more Romantic. The third piano concerto (1917) and the second symphony (1924) are good examples of the former period, the ballets *Romeo and Juliet* (1935) and *Cinderella* (1941–4) and the fifth (1944) and sixth (1946) symphonies of the latter. His music gives the impression of immense rhythmical energy, as in the outer movements of several of his nine piano sonatas, but this fierce drive is often leavened by the soft, wistful lights of his slow movements. His second string quartet (1941), perhaps, presents all the elements of his music in the kindest light.

His strong leaning towards fantasy and mordant parody is felt in his earlier operas *The Love of the Three Oranges* (1921) and *The Fiery Angel* (1922–5). Towards the end of his life much of Prokofiev's music fell into official disfavour.

Shostakovich.

Dmitri Shostakovich (1906–75) also suffered from attacks on his style. He had to conform to Stalin's requirements for writing music, but he survived and continued to produce music of universal significance, for example, his later string quartets. Like Prokofiev, his music falls into two very distinct styles: one humorous and spiky, the other intense, very personal and often large-scale in its implications. Not all his symphonies reach the expressive depths of numbers one, five, six, eight, ten and fourteen, but they all have rewarding passages, and his violin and cello concertos are of high quality. He also wrote fifteen string quartets, a piano quintet (an attractive piece) and two operas: the satirical *The Nose* (1930) and *Katrina Ismailova* (1934, revised 1959), originally known as "Lady Macbeth of Mtsensk."

Rachmaninov.

Although Sergey Rachmaninov (1873–1943) was born in Russia, he left his home country in 1918, fearing the Soviet régime, and lived mostly in Switzerland and the United States (where he died). His music is chiefly notable for its Romanticism, nostalgic melody, nervous energy and, in the piano works, its opportunities for displays of virtuosity. The first three piano concertos, the third symphony, the piano preludes, and the Rhapsody on a theme of Paganini, are his most typical and attractive works, and many of his songs are touching and beautiful. He wrote three operas.

Weill and Hindemith.

Kurt Weill (1900–50) is chiefly known for his sociopolitically pointed operas, such as *Die Dreigroschenoper* (1929), *Mahagonny* (1929), *Der Jasager* (1930) and *Happy End* (1929), all effective works on the stage, and for his particular brand of brittle, yet fundamentally romantic music. His influence on later composers has been considerable.

Paul Hindemith (1895–1963) in his later years wrote in a strictly tonal, often neo-classical idiom, after being one of the most advanced intellectuals of his time. As well as many chamber and orchestral works, he wrote three formidable operas: *Die Harmonie der Welt*, *Cardillac* and *Mathis der Maler*.

Ives and Copland.

Charles Ives (1874–1954) is generally recognised as the first American composer of major stature. Most of his works were composed before about 1920, while he was pursuing a successful career in insurance. Ives' music is noted for his thorough-going eclecticism and his refusal to be bound by rules and conventions. His work anticipates many 20th century techniques, such as polytonality and polyrhythm, which he seems to have arrived at independently of others. Folk song, hymn tunes, dance music and the sound of the brass band all appear in his compositions, many of which are evocative of his New England background (*e.g. Three Places in New England*, the *Holidays Symphony*, the *Concord* Sonata). It was not until the 1930s that Ives began to achieve recognition, but his influence on later American composers can hardly be exaggerated.

Aaron Copland (1900–90) was a composer who had absorbed a variety of influences—from his Jewish background, contemporary Europe, American folk music and jazz, Latin American music—while writing music which is instantly recognisable as his own in its clean textures and taut rhythms. Early works such as the Piano Concerto (1927) show the use of jazz styles, while the Piano Variations (1930) combine inventiveness and technical discipline in a tough, concentrated and highly dissonant piece. A move towards a simpler, more immediately appealing idiom is evident in pieces like *El Salón México* (1936), and the ballets *Billy the Kid* (1938), *Rodeo* (1938) and *Appalachian Spring* (1944) and the Third Symphony (1946). These works remain Copland's most popular and frequently performed pieces. A number of works from the 1950s and 1960s experiment with serial techniques, while retaining his individual voice. Also popular is his Fanfare for the Common Man.

Vaughan Williams, Holst and Delius.

The twentieth century revival of music in England owes much to Ralph Vaughan Williams (1872–1958) and Gustav Holst (1874–1934). The English folk song revival, associated with Cecil Sharp, was in full swing during their formative years, and both composers produced arrangements of folk songs as well as assimilating the folk idiom into their own styles. The influence of 16th century polyphony is also strong in Vaughan Williams' music, the most obvious example being the *Fantasia on a Theme by Thomas Tallis* (1909). Vaughan Williams' strongest works (*e.g.* the first, fourth, fifth and sixth symphonies, the ballet *Job*, the choral *Dona Nobis Pacem*) show his characteristic alternation of the forceful and the contemplative.

Holst was a more enigmatic figure. Only his suite *The Planets* and the choral work *The Hymn of Jesus* have established themselves in the regular repertory, but his bold harmonic experiments and the austerity, even mysticism, of his style as heard in the opera *Savitri* and the orchestral piece *Egdon Heath* are perhaps more typical of this composer.

Frederick Delius (1862–1934) was the major English composer to fall under the sway of French impressionism, though his English (north country) background, his friendship with Grieg, and the time he spent in America all contributed to the formation of his musical style. He lived in France from 1888 onwards. His most important works are the atmospheric tone-poems for orchestra, such as *Brigg Fair*, the vocal and orchestral *A Mass of Life*, *Sea Drift* and *Appalachia*, and the opera *A Village Romeo and Juliet*.

Sir William Walton.

Sir William Walton (1902–83) became known as an *enfant terrible* with the witty and irreverent *Façade* (1923) for speaker and chamber orchestra (with words by Edith Sitwell). The poetic Viola Concerto (1929) shows another side of his musical character. His First Symphony (1934–5) is an arresting, dramatic score and the colourful oratorio *Belshazzar's Feast* (1931) is a landmark in choral music. Walton's rhythms show the influence of jazz and of Stravinsky but he is generally felt to be a quintessentially English composer. An Elgarian element is clear in such occasional pieces as the coronation marches *Crown Imperial* (1937) and *Orb and Sceptre* (1953).

Benjamin Britten.

Benjamin Britten (1913–76) did as much as anyone to establish English music on the forefront of the international stage. Much of his music seems to have an immediate appeal to large audiences and certainly his many stage works earned him quite exceptional prestige both at home and abroad. *Peter Grimes* (1945), *Billy Budd* (1951), *Gloriana* (1953), *A Midsummer Night's Dream* (1960) all show his mastery of stage technique and the first two are also moving human documents. On a smaller scale he has achieved as much with his chamber operas—*The Rape of Lucretia* (1946), *Albert Herring* (1947), *The Turn of the Screw* (1954)—and the three Parables for Church Performance—*Curlew River* (1964), *The Burning Fiery Furnace* (1966) and *The Prodigal Son* (1968). His operatic output was crowned by *Death in Venice* (1973). If he had written nothing else, these dramatic works would have marked him out as a composer of outstanding imaginative gifts. In addition to these, however, the choral works culminating in the *War Requiem* (1962), the various song cycles written, like so much else, for his friend Peter Pears, the *Serenade* for tenor, horn and strings, *Nocturne* for tenor and orchestra, the three *Canticles*, and the *Spring Symphony* are further evidence of both his intense emotional commitment and his technical skill. Despite the strong influence of such composers as Purcell, Schubert, Verdi, Mahler and Berg, his style is entirely his own; his musical personality combines, it has been said, "a deep nostalgia for the innocence of childhood, a mercurial sense of humour and a passionate sympathy with the victims of prejudice and misunderstanding."

Sir Michael Tippett.

This last quality was also evident in the emotional

make up of Sir Michael Tippett (1905–98), as expressed in such works as the oratorio *A Child of our Time* (1941) one of his earliest successes, which shows both his compassion and his ability to write on a large scale. This and the Concerto for Double String Orchestra (1939) remain his most popular works. Tippett was open to a wide range of influences, both musical (from English Madrigals, Monteverdi and Beethoven to Negro spirituals and jazz) and non-musical (*e.g.* the ideas of Jung). His early style—often richly lyrical and affirmative of the continued power of tonality—reached its culmination in his allegorical opera *The Midsummer Marriage* (1952), the Piano Concerto (1955) and the Second Symphony (1957). A new style, spare and incisive, with structure arising from the juxtaposition of contrasting ideas rather than from a process of development, was evident in his second opera, *King Priam* (1961) and its offshoots, the Second Piano Sonata (1962) and Concerto for Orchestra (1963).

The mystical, ecstatic *The Vision of St. Augustine* (1965), a complex, difficult but rewarding work, is one of his finest from this period. The opera *The Knot Garden* (1970) exemplifies again Tippett's concern with human relationships and the need for self-knowledge. Tippett never ceased to explore and experiment; his inspiration still seems as fresh as ever. His most recent works, *The Mask of Time*— a huge choral piece—and the Fourth Piano Sonata (1984) have something of the quality of summarising statements about the musical and non-musical concerns of a lifetime.

Olivier Messiaen.

Amongst the many schools and groups of composers in the twentieth century, two major figures stand apart, Olivier Messiaen (1908–92) and Elliott Carter. Both born in 1908, each is an individualist of great influence and stature who has pursued his own path to a personal style of composition.

A devout Catholic, Messiaen viewed himself as a theological composer and music as a medium for a profound communication, celebration and contemplation of the love and mystery of God. Few of his works are liturgical but most have religious and doctrinal themes, for example *La Nativité du Seigneur* (1935) for organ and *Vingt Regards sur l'Enfant-Jésus* (1944) for piano. Messiaen was inspired to compose by hearing the music of Debussy. This influence can be particularly seen in Messiaen's flexible rhythms, sensitive scoring and use of timbre. Indeed, he identifies sounds with colours and views composition as painting. The other major early influence was that of the East, particularly India.

Elements of Messiaen's Music.

Messiaen often uses Hindu rhythmic patterns alongside Greek poetic metres, plainsong and other medieval techniques and Stravinskian devices. The sum of these can be seen in *Quatuor pour la fin du temps* for violin, clarinet, cello and piano which he composed in a prisoner of war camp in 1940. A very complex work, it reflects the primacy Messiaen gives to rhythmic control. Its overwhelming impression however is of lush and exotic sounds and textures. Similarly, the vibrant colours and rhythms of the massive *Turangalila-symphonie* (1946–8) for orchestra effectively realise the ideas of life and vitality embodied in the Sanskrit title.

After *Turangalila*, Messiaen adopted a less luxurious style. It was works such as the *Livre d'orgue* (1951) which profoundly influenced many young composers of post-war years in the use of systematic transformations of rhythm and dynamics using a system of modes in a quasi-serial fashion. For Messiaen it is the seven harmonic modes, inspired by Debussy, Liszt and the Russian "Five", which are perhaps more important because they give his music its unique sound quality.

The 1950s saw the integration of the final element crucial to Messiaen's music; birdsong. A keen ornithologist, he collected and accurately notated the songs of many birds for incorporation into compositions. *Catalogue d'oiseaux* (1951–8) is a collection of thirteen piano pieces featuring French bird songs.

Messiaen after 1960.

Since 1960, his style has become less complex to the ear. To encounter the many elements of his

music one can do little better than to listen to *La Transfiguration de Notre Seigneur Jésus-Christ* (1963–9) for one hundred voices, seven instrumental soloists and a large orchestra. Its subject is the mystery of God, his relationship with man and nature as a revelation of God. Messiaen draws upon all his compositional techniques in a spellbinding and overwhelming work that is a profound affirmation of faith. It is fitting that his opera (1973–83), *St François d'Assise* is about the saint who is best known for his great spirituality and for gaining inspiration and insight from nature. *Éclairs sur l'Au-delà* (1988–92) was Messiaen's final completed work and successfully explores much of his earlier musical elements.

Elliott Carter.

Elliott Carter (1908–2012) concentrated on problems of language and structure in a dramatic context unlike Messiaen's preoccupations with colour and the communication of religious truths. Carter's early works reflect a variety of influences: Stravinsky, Hindemith and the English Virginalists. He consciously aimed at a simple, lyrical, accessible style, for example, in the ballet, *Pocahontas* (1938–9) and *Holiday Overture* (1944). During those war years however there occurred a change of direction. The Piano Sonata (1945–6) saw the start of a compositional style where instruments were endowed with personalities who act as protagonists in a drama. His ideas crystallised in the *String Quartet No. 1* (1950– 1) after an absorbing study of the music of Ives, Cowell and African and Oriental music. It led to the use of very complex rhythmic relationships and a very tightly-knit pitch structure that could be traced back to a simple and small source, in this case a four-note chord. After this Carter refined his portrayal of his dramatis personae such that in *String Quartet No. 2* (1959) his players each have a separate personality defined by melodic material, gestures and rhythms. They converse, argue and enact that work's dramatic programme. *String Quartet No. 3* (1971) marked a shift in approach. Although the players were still "personalities", the work relied heavily on the use of contrast between strict and flexible writing between members of two duos. The *Symphony of Three Orchestras* (1975–7) and *Triple Duo* (1983) continue to explore the possibilities of simultaneous presentation of independent and sometimes unrelated processes.

The works of Carter's very productive final years, such as *Interventions* for piano and orchestra (2007), the song-cycle *A Sunbeam's Architecture* (2010) and *String Trio* (2011), demonstrate his continued compositional mastery and invention.

The Avant Garde since 1945.

The early post-war years saw a renewed interest in "twelve-note techniques" otherwise known as "serialism". Composers like Stravinsky and Dallapiccola (1904–75), who had shunned serialism in earlier years, began to experiment and absorb serial techniques into their musical style. Stravinsky, for example, in works such as *Threni* (1957–8) explored ideas of varied repetition both of small ideas and large sections, in a serial context. A clear example to listen to is the fifteen-minute *Requiem Canticles* (1964–6). During the progression from its Prelude to Postlude, one can hear the piece subtly develop. The succeeding movements, and phrases within movements, slightly alter that which has gone before, evolving into something fresh.

Serialism.

This period also saw the emergence of a new generation of composers, keen to jettison the past and begin anew. Serialism was a favoured tool, its revival stemming from Paris, where Webern's pupil René Leibowitz was teaching, and the USA where Schoenberg had fled from Nazi Germany. The American Milton Babbitt (1916–2011) was much concerned with codifying serial techniques. His younger European counterparts Pierre Boulez (1925–2016) and Karlheinz Stockhausen (1928–2007) sought to increase the number of musical elements that could be controlled by a predetermined method. They sought to emulate the rigorous methods of Webern, hoping to control not only pitch, but also rhythm, timbre *etc.* In doing so they hoped to create an impersonal, emotionally restrained music.

Attention went first to controlling rhythm. Forerunners of this control can be seen in movement three of Berg's *Lyric Suite* and in Webern's Op.30 Variations. However, the catalyst came from Messiaen. He inspired his pupil Boulez to explore the possibilities of rhythmic and dynamic serialism in his Second Piano Sonata (1951). The performance of Messiaen's *Modes de valeurs et d'intensités* (1949) at the Darmstadt Summer School proved decisive for Stockhausen. Although not serial, the piece established scales of pitch, length of note (duration), loudness and attack. The 1950s were to see this potential for serialism taken to extremes. Boulez reached "total serialism" in *Structures 1a* for piano. However, having attained it he soon became frustrated with its restrictions. Some of the more fantastic and exotic elements of earlier works were allowed to reappear. *Le Marteau sans Maître* (1952–4) for mezzo-soprano and six instruments is a masterly setting of three surreal poems by René Char, with instrumental interludes. It is the contrasts of timbres, of flexible and regular pulsing rhythms, of sound and silence that are spellbinding. The virtuosic serial workings are hidden.

The Achievement of Total Serialism.

Stockhausen reached total serialism in *Kreuzspiel* (1951) for oboe, bass clarinet, piano and percussion. Each note's pitch, length, dynamic and timbre are part of a predetermined plan. All are concerned with "Kreuzspiel" or "crossplay". Its various processes reverse or change over throughout so that at the end we have returned full circle. The effect is of clearcut lines where each note is weighted. However, despite the intention of the composer, the effect is not unemotional, especially with the insistent throbbing of the percussion, and the piece builds to a series of climaxes before dying away. *Punkte* (points) (1952) for orchestra finds each note being treated as an isolated point of sound. It illustrates some of the problems of total serialism; often very difficult to play, it can be monotonous or lack focal points, appearing to be random rather than rigorously controlled. Stockhausen therefore transferred his attention to using not points but bursts of sound and moved towards possibly his most significant contribution to music, "moment form". There, different aspects of a note, chord or sound are suspended in eternity for contemplation and re-examination. Works became longer, slower and had a greater emphasis on colour and the effects of spatial separation, both between sounds and between their sources. *Carré* (1959–60) uses four orchestras between which chords move and evolve.

Although unifying principles in pitch content *etc.* might be present, "strict" serialism had been gently left behind, until *Mantra* (1970). This work for two pianos, percussion and two electronic ring modulators is totally based on a thirteen-note row, the mantra, with a different duration, mode of attack and dynamic for each note. These permeate the whole piece. For example, each of the thirteen sections is dominated by one of the thirteen types of attack. The work's climax is the coda where the 156 versions of the mantra used are rushed through in a few minutes. The work is important, not only as marking a return to serialism and notated music, but also in its rediscovery of melody.

Later Serialism.

Since the 1960s serialism and integral serialism have had less of an influence in Europe, although they continued to hold a fascination for American composers such as Milton Babbit (1916–2011). Composers have used the underlying concept of serialism (*i.e.* using a systematic approach to detailed structuring) without using the technique in any strict sense. Examples of this include Maxwell Davies's use of magic number squares (*see below*), and Harrison Birtwistle's use of random numbers to generate rhythmic and melodic elements. The Hungarian composer György Ligeti (1923–2006) used very tightly controlled canonic music which he described as 'micropolyphony' which, though not serial, has a similarly organised and systematic approach. One of the reasons for the use of systems is to take some of the decision-making out of the compositional process. Birtwistle has said that he

would seize up if he had to make all the decisions!

Mathematics and Music.

The younger generation of composers often used mathematical systems in composing which were not necessarily serial. A good example was Sir Peter Maxwell Davies (1934–2016). The use of durational ratios, ciphers and magic squares features prominently in his work, partly reflecting his interest in medieval music. A magic square is a number square where the sum of any line is the same. This becomes the basis for a composition by assigning notes to the numbers—a technique that Davies often used after the mid-1970s. For example, in *Ave Maris Stella* (1975), each of the nine movements uses a different transformation of the square and follows a characteristic route through the square. The work is governed by the square at all levels: it even determines the precise length of each movement. Far from being a mathematical exercise however the piece shows masterly control which is particularly revealed in its drama and the beauty of its colours.

Mathematical processes of a different type were taken up by the Greek, Xenakis (1922–2001), possibly because of his original training as an engineer and architect in France. His rejection of serialism led to the use of "stochastic" principles, derived from the mathematical laws governing probability. He also applied mathematical set theory to composition. The use of these ideas however is not audible. In *Nomos Alpha* (1965) for solo cello, for example, it is the use of contrasts, texture *etc.*, which give shape and form for the listener.

Eastern Influences.

Although for many serialism represented the way of reviving music after the excesses of romanticism, some looked beyond Europe to the East. John Cage (1912–92) found inspiration there, studying Zen Buddhism in the early 1950s. By using the "chance operations" of the Chinese *I Ching* (Book of Changes) Cage brought a new radical approach to Western music. *Music of Changes* (1951) for piano is fully notated but its content is the result of operations where chance has a role. The use of "indeterminacy" or "chance" gave the performer an active role in determining the course of a piece. This might come about by providing "graphic notation"—an artist's impression of what the piece might sound like. Thus Earle Brown's *December 1952* is a visual design to be realised on any instrument as the performer sees fit. Alternatively the composer could give the performer control over the order of sections or their content. *Twenty-five pages* (1953) by Brown is for one to twenty-five pianos. Each person has twenty-five pages and may arrange them in any order before commencing. Thus music was no longer to be necessarily a progression of fixed and immutable steps to an endpoint. This and other traditional assumptions about music were challenged in Cage's most well-known outrage, *4' 33"*. The performer does not play any notes at all. The music consists of the sounds in the environment that occur during a period of four minutes and thirty-three seconds.

Chance and Indeterminacy.

In 1957, both Stockhausen and Boulez took to chance having realised that total control was an impossibility. The more rigorous the control of musical elements, the more impossible it became to realise it accurately. Stockhausen's first experiment with chance techniques was Piano Piece XI which is a single page with nineteen fragments of music. They may be played in any order but the tempo, dynamic and attack must be that shown at the end of the previous fragment. After one fragment has been played three times the work ends. Boulez's Third Piano Sonata was less free. There the choices are in the nature of varying routes through the piece. Boulez saw his music as using a form of control that is not random but akin to throwing a dice. Limited choices in the combination of instruments and their choice of lines form the basis of *Pli selon pli* (1957–65) for soprano and orchestra, offering Boulez a way "to fix the infinite".

For Stockhausen, chance has been a way to encourage performer participation and the development of "intuitive music-making". In *Prozession* (1967) for example, performers react to what is going on guided by plus or minus signs in the score which denote whether the response should be positive or negative. It has worked well in combination with the ideas behind moment form. *Stimmung* (1968) is a 45 minute meditation on one chord whose parts and overtones emerge and merge into the whole, punctuated by erotic poems, magic numbers and words which are delivered in response to chance operations. The climax of these ideas may be seen in *Aus den Sieben Tagen* (1968) where the score for each of the seven movements is a short poem.

Witold Lutoslawski.

Use of indeterminacy does not necessarily have to be so extreme. For Witold Lutoslawski (1913–93) use of controlled chance techniques has provided a way for composing atonal music without embracing serialism. During 1955–60 Lutoslawski evolved a harmonic language which used twelve-note chords for expression and colour. In 1960 he heard a performance of Cage's Piano Concerto and realised that he could use chance techniques to add a rhythmic freedom and new types of texture to his music. The exact combination of sounds at any given moment is often a matter of chance but the overall effect is planned. Textures are created by the constant repetition of small melodic ideas and simple rhythms in different parts, creating a kaleidoscope of sound, and by lines of counterpoint set off against each other, often sliding from one note to another blurring the transition between chords. The music of Lutoslawski is a fine example of the use of chance as a tool in compositions which still have strong links to tradition. The direction and drama of works such as *Mi-Parti* (1976) and his Third Symphony (1983) are firmly in the composer's hands, relying heavily on his skilful sense of harmonic movement, use of colour and proportion. Only small rhythmic details are left to chance.

The Music of Ligeti.

Ligeti's music often sounds as if it were chance-like but in fact his massive textural structures of the 1960s are controlled by highly organised arhythmic canons. Each instrument or voice follows the same line of notes but with different rhythmic values. The listener hears a kaleidoscopic and ever-changing background cluster. Works from this period include: *Atmosphères* for orchestra (1961), *Requiem* (1963–5), and *Lux Aeterna* for voices (1966). Ligeti's music was made famous when the above works were used (without the composer's permission) by Stanley Kubrick in his film *2001: a Space Odyssey*. Ligeti's music since the 1970s shows a rediscovery of elements that he had previously shunned such as melody, harmony and even tonality/modality. Typical examples include Horn Trio (1982), Piano Concerto (1988) and Violin Concerto (1992) which show influences from African music, fractal geometry and the piano music of the American Conlon Nancarrow (1912–97). The rediscovery of previously rejected elements can also be seen in the music of the Polish composer Krzysztof Penderecki (b. 1933) and Luciano Berio (1925–2003), and can be seen as a symptom of the existence of Post-Modernism in music.

The Advent of Electronic Music.

An important part of the post-war struggle with musical language has been the development of electronic means to generate, manipulate and record sounds. Its pioneer was the Frenchman Edgard Varèse (1883–1965). Before the war he had been an independent and radical composer much concerned with the exploration of new sounds. This had led to an emphasis on the exploitation of percussion effects in works such as *Intégrales* (1924–5) and *Ionisation* (1933). The following work *Ecuatorial* (1934) explored further, using primitive electrically generated sounds produced by two Ondes Martenot. However the catalyst for further development was the invention of the tape recorder which provided an easy means to store sounds that could then be rearranged by cutting and rejoining the tape in different ways. Varèse explored these possibilities in *Déserts* (1949–54) which alternated recorded and instrumental sounds in an atmospheric work which really seems to conjure up the aridity and emptiness of the desert. Recorded sound offered the possibility

of creating illusions of aural space by technical manipulation and by judicious positioning and control of loudspeakers. This is a fundamental part of Varèse's great masterpiece, *Poème Electronique* (1958) which used soprano, chorus, bells, organs and artificial sounds. Its spatial effects were achieved by using many loudspeakers positioned around a specially designed pavilion at the 1958 Brussels Exhibition.

Generally, electronic music-making required a studio and the 1950s saw the setting up of important studios in Paris and Cologne. In Paris Pierre Schaeffer (1910–95) pioneered *"musique concrète"* which used altered and rearranged natural sounds, for example, the sound of a steam train, to create a musical piece. At Cologne where Stockhausen worked, the emphasis was on new synthetic sounds.

The Potential of Electronic Music.

Electronic music had the potential to generate complex, accurate serial structures through precise electronic operations. Boulez's studies in this however did not satisfy him and he neglected the medium until 1970 when he became Director of IRCAM (*Institut de Recherche et de Coordination Acoustique/Musique*). Stockhausen however found electronic music an ideal medium to create a musical unity far beyond that of serialism; pitch, timbre, rhythm and form could be seen as different aspects of the same thing—vibration. He did not restrict himself to pure synthetic sounds and in 1955–6 created perhaps his most well-known electronic work, *Gesang der Jünglinge*.

With *Kontakte* (1958–60) for piano, percussion and tape, Stockhausen began an exploration of the interplay between live performers and electronic sound which still preoccupies him today. The work explores "contact" between real and artificial sounds and between the elements of music. Compared to pure electronic music, the presence of the live performers made it easier to listen to, providing a visual focus and making each performance unique. The next step was to create "live" electronic music where performers created their electronic sounds on stage. Cage had already begun this in 1960 with *Cartridge Music*. Unlike Stockhausen's first attempt, *Mikrophonie I* (1964–5), *Cartridge Music* gives much freedom to the performer in creating the electronic effects. A desire to create a world music led to one of the most vast electronic works to date, *Hymnen* (1966–7), a two-hour work for quadraphonic tape or tapes, soloists and optional symphony orchestra. Stockhausen constructed it out of national anthems from all over the world. Inspired by the occult *Urantia Book*, he became more ambitious still, seeking a galactic music. *Sirius* (1977) for four soloists and electronic music deals with the arrival on earth of four visitors from the star Sirius.

Electronic Music in America.

In America, developments have followed a different course. There, the use of computer synthesised sounds has been the main interest because of the computer's superior control and accuracy. It has allowed the continuation of abstract composition where complicated operations are achieved simply and effectively.

Minimalism.

The transformation of existing material on tape has been a crucial part of an American movement dating from the 1960s known as "Minimalism'. Its chief exponents are Steve Reich (b. 1936), Philip Glass (b. 1937), Terry Riley (b. 1935), La Monte Young (b. 1935) and John Adams (b. 1947). Minimal music uses material which is limited in pitch, rhythm and timbres; the elements are subjected to simple transformations relying heavily on repetition. Of great importance are the subtle evolution from one idea to another as repetitions are modified, and the use of "phasing" techniques. Phasing is the effect of altering the rate of repetition between parts repeating the same material so that it is no longer synchronised. The effect of works such as *Drumming* (1971) by Reich may appear long and non-dramatic. However, the listener is not expected to concentrate all the time but to become aware of a piece's various elements and processes. The music's patterns will change as the listener's attention shifts from one aspect to another. As in moment form, minimalist works owe much to Indian concepts of time as a circular rather than linear phenomenon. In recent years, the minimalists have developed their style and there are greater differences between the four. Glass has written several operas including *Einstein on the Beach* (1975), *Satyagraha* (1980), *Akhenaten* (1983), *The Voyage* (1992) and *Galileo Galilei* (2001).

Reich's other works include *The Four Sections* (1987) for orchestra, *The Cave* (1993), a multimedia extravaganza, and *WTC 9/11* (2011), commissioned by the Kronos Quartet for the 10th anniversary of the attacks on the World Trade Center.

Music Theatre.

During the early post-war years many composers were grappling with the tools of composition. Only more "traditional" writers such as Britten, Tippett and Hans Werner Henze (1926–2012) were engaged in writing opera. By 1970 however, most composers were including elements of theatre in their work.

One of the major composers of "traditional" opera was Henze. His first three operas draw heavily on the past. For example, *Boulevard Solitude* (1952) updates the story of Manon, a nineteenth-century favourite. After moving to Italy in 1953, Henze's stance appeared more traditional still as lyrical elements became more dominant in contrast to the abstract athematic style of contemporaries such as Stockhausen. Increasingly Henze's operas began to reflect his preoccupation with socialism. The *Bassarids* (1966), for example, examines through a mythological guise the precipitation of social upheaval and disruption. The oratorio *Das Floss der "Medusa"* (1968) is dedicated to Che Guevara and provoked such struggles between police and left-wing students at its premiere that Henze went to Cuba for a year. There he was inspired to write *El Cimarrón* (1969–70), a vocal monologue portraying a Cuban runaway slave accompanied by flute, guitar and percussion. For a while, Henze continued to reject the traditional opera format because of its bourgeois overtones, preferring a more intimate, chamber style. But in 1976 Henze returned to opera with *We come to the River*. It reflected a renewal of Italianate lyricism, the exploitation of opera's full potential and a less overt political message.

Exponents of Music Theatre.

Luigi Nono (1924–90) also exploited theatre for political ends, beginning with *Intolleranza* (1960). However he found greater resource than Henze in contemporary developments, taking full advantage of the opportunities offered by electronics. *Contrappunto dialettico della mente* (1967–8) includes the sounds of political demonstrations. Like Henze, Nono also returned to the opera house after a long break from large-scale opera with *Al gran sole carico d'amore* (1972–4), which consolidated the techniques he had developed in the previous decade.

"Theatre" was a dominant characteristic in the works of Luciano Berio (1925–2003). One of his most famous works is *Circles* (1960) for female voice, harp and percussion. The virtuosic technique used there and in other works was inspired by the phenomenal vocal elasticity of his then wife, Cathy Berberian. 'Circles' are depicted at many different levels in the work's structure and content. More importantly, these are underlined by the singer moving about the stage during the performance.

Berio's next few works became overtly political, culminating in *Laborintus II* (1965) which was intended as an attack on capitalism via a musical collage and extracts from Dante's *Inferno*. Many of Berio's larger scale works since *Laborintus II* have been theatrical in their virtuosity and instrumental technique. For example, *Sequenza IV* (1965) demands a pianist with very agile feet. This type of dramatic gesture is much seen in Stockhausen's work, particularly those written for his own music ensemble, for example, *Solo* (1966). Since *Alphabet für Liege* (1972) his work became increasingly theatrical and from 1978 Stockhausen spent the latter part of his life writing *Licht* (1977–2003), the opera cycle based on the seven days of the week.

Influences on Other Composers.

The small-scale synthesis of text, music and gesture characteristic of Berio greatly influenced

British work in music theatre, notably the work of Sir Peter Maxwell Davies and Sir Harrison Birtwistle. Davies' work was very powerful particularly through its use of parody and wild use of outrageous gesture. *Vesalii Icones* (1969) used a naked male dancer portraying parts of the Stations of the Cross and scenes from the anatomy text by Vesalius. It is a good example of parody, particularly of what Davies saw as nineteenth-century grossness—it includes a vile distortion of a Victorian hymn tune which turns into a foxtrot, both played on a honky-tonk piano. Many of his works feature a single vocal soloist, with instrumental back-up, who plays the part of a crazed, obsessive individual. For example, *Eight Songs for a Mad King* (1969) features the instrumentalists in giant bird cages who must suffer the mad ravings of George III played by the singer.

Davies wrote three full-scale operas: *Taverner* (1962–8), *The Martyrdom of St. Magnus* (1976) and *Resurrection* (1987). *Taverner* deals with two fundamental preoccupations of Davies—the nature of faith and betrayal—and uses both musical and dramatic parody to convey its message. *St. Magnus* was written after Davies moved to Orkney. It reflects a change in style, uses only a small orchestra and is for production "in the round". Latterly Maxwell Davies explored the traditional orchestral sound world, through the composition of 10 symphonies which were strongly influenced by Sibelius. From 2004 to 2014 he was Master of the Queen's Musick. Created Companion of Honour (2014). He died in 2016.

Birtwistle's first major dramatic work was a chamber opera, *Punch and Judy* (1966) which uses grotesque and violent gestures. However, while Davies' roots may lie with early Schoenberg, Birtwistle has found inspiration in the clear-cut lines and ritualism of Stravinsky. Possibly his most significant work to date is *The Mask of Orpheus* (1973–5 and 1981–3). He has written a further four operas: *Gawain* (1981–91); *The Second Mrs. Kong* (1994), *The Last Supper* (2000) and *The Minotaur* (2008). He was made a Companion of Honour in 2001.

Music of the Late Twentieth Century.

Brian Ferneyhough (b. 1943) is continuing to expand the chamber music repertoire using traditional structures as a framework for music in which micro-tones play an increasingly important part. A significant part of his output before 1990 is the group of seven compositions, *Carceri d'invenzione* (1981–6), 'dungeons of invention' referring to the etchings of Piranesi. He has become the focus of a style of composition named 'the New Complexity' which pushes the techniques of players to their limits and creates extremely complex textures. His recent work includes his 6th String Quartet (2010).

Robin Holloway (b. 1943) has written a number of works taking music by earlier composers as a starting-point, *e.g. Scenes from Schumann* (1970) for orchestra, *Gilded Goldbergs* (1992–7, after Bach) for two pianos. Nigel Osborne (b. 1948) has used electronic and non-Western music in his work, gravitating recently towards vocal works. 1986 saw the premiere of his theatre piece, *Hells Angels*. Other recent operas are *Where the Wild Things Are* (1984) and *Higglety, Pigglety Pop!* (1985) by Oliver Knussen (b. 1952) which attracted acclaim for a young composer already noted for his symphonies, vocal and chamber work. Tim Souster (1943–94) was active in composing and promoting electronic music of all types, some influenced by rock music. A good example is his *Quartet with Tape* (1985).

George Benjamin (b. 1960) won fame early with *Ringed by the Flat Horizon* (1980); a recent work is the opera *Written on Skin* (2012).

Diversity of Approach.

The British composers who emerged in the 1980s and 1990s were diverse in their compositional approaches and interests. One feature they do have in common is an eclecticism drawing from a wide range of sources such as football chants (Turnage), jazz (Butler) and Celtic culture (MacMillan and Weir). There has also been a trend towards greater approachability in the style and language of their music. There has been a realisation that audiences have been alienated in the past, and composers have attempted to make their music more communicative. One manifestation of this is the apparent 'rediscovery' of tonality or modality.

Some Late Twentieth Century British Composers.

Mark-Anthony Turnage (b. 1960) is one of the most characteristic and popular composers of his generation. He uses material from popular culture in his music (like Martland and MacMillan) including rhythmic and melodic elements, which can be most clearly seen in his controversial opera *Greek* (1990), a setting of Steven Berkoff's play. His rich and colourful orchestration can be heard in his orchestral works such as *Three Screaming Popes* (1989), *Momentum* (1990–1), *Drowned Out* (1993) and his highly successful opera *The Silver Tassie* (1997–9). Recent major works are the opera *Anna Nicole* (2011) and the orchestral *Frieze* (2013), composed as a response to Beethoven's 9th Symphony. Awarded CBE in 2015.

James MacMillan (b. 1959) is a part of the general rebirth of the arts in Scotland and shows something of his Celtic heritage in such works as *The Confessions of Isobel Gowrie* (1990) which explores a wide range of Scottish traditional music. His music since *Litanies of Iron and Stone* (1987) shows an increase in rhythmic drive, perhaps influenced by his interest in rock music, and also an increasing approachability. His major compositions since *Litanies* have mostly used external political or religious subjects as inspiration, for example *The Exorcism of Rio Sumpul* (1989) which is based on a helicopter raid on a village in El Salvador. His musical language is characterised by colourful instrumentation, a powerful rhythmic drive and an eloquent lyricism, which can be seen clearly in his popular *Veni Veni Emmanuel* (1993) written for the percussionist Evelyn Glennie. His first full-scale opera was *Ines de Castro* (1995). His Catholic faith has inspired works such as the *St John Passion* (2007) and *Credo* (2012). He became involved in setting up a music festival in Cumnock, Ayrshire.

Judith Weir (b. 1954) also makes reference to her Celtic heritage in her music. Her main compositional output is in the area of opera and music drama. *A Night at the Chinese Opera* (1987) is perhaps her best known work to date and is evidence of her interest in Chinese Yuan dramas. Her two later operas use magical stories: *The Vanishing Bridegroom* (1990) is based on 3 linked Scottish folktales, and *Blond Eckbert* (1994, for the English National Opera) on a fairytale by the German Romantic writer Ludwig Tieck. Her musical language shows influences from folk music, tonality and composers such as Stravinsky, Janáček and Peter Maxwell Davies. Her latest large-scale works are *Concrete* (2007), written for the BBC Symphony Orchestra and Chorus, a kind of musical history of London, and the opera *Miss Fortune* (2011). She was appointed Master of the Queen's Musick in 2014.

Martin Butler (b. 1960) like MacMillan has shown a shift in his musical language from a Modernist approach to one which is more eclectic and expressive. As he states: "Recent pieces of mine have drawn, more or less directly, on Irish and bluegrass fiddle music, Latin salsa and dance music, and various types of jazz." Examples showing these influences include *Jazz Machines* (1990) for chamber ensemble, *Bluegrass Variations* (1988) for violin, and *Tin Pan Ballet* (1986) for ensemble and DX7 synthesiser. One of his most distinctive works is his opera *Craig's Progress* (1994) which uses the "twin inheritances of opera and comic books". *Préludes Inégales* for piano (2013) combines improvised and fully composed elements. Other recent works include *Rondes d'automne* (2011) for wind and strings.

Steve Martland (1959–2013) was a key figure of radical minimalism and owed much of his musical development to his studies with Louis Andriessen at the Royal Conservatory in The Hague. His music, like that of MacMillan, was strongly shaped by his socialist politics and was characterised by uncompromising aggression and bold sonorities. Like Andriessen he explored hocketing techniques in works like *Drill* (1987) and *Birthday Hocket* (1989), both for 2 pianos. His larger scale works include *Babi Yar* (1983) for large orchestra in 3 groups and *Crossing the Border* (1990–91) for String Orchestra. Later

works are *Darwin* (2009) for choir, brass quintet and organ, setting extracts from Darwin's *Origin of Species* alongside a letter from Darwin's wife Emma; *Sea Songs* (2011) for choir; and *Beat the Retreat* (2012) for 11 players.

Thomas Adès (b. 1971) is one of the most distinctive and accomplished British composers of a younger generation. He made a swift rise to prominence through his beautifully crafted works such as *Asyla* (1997), the Chamber Symphony (1990) and his first chamber opera: *Powder Her Face* (1995), based on the life of the notorious Duchess of Argyll. His works show traces of the textural music of Ligeti but also reference jazz and popular music to create an approachable but highly wrought musical language. His largest and most ambitious work to date is his opera *The Tempest* (2003–4) based on Shakespeare's play which was commissioned by the Royal Opera House.

Recent works include *Polaris* (2010) for orchestra (plus moving images on 5 video screens), *Totentanz* (2013) for mezzo-soprano, baritone and orchestra and *The Exterminating Angel* (2016).

Prospect and Retrospect.

The major shift in contemporary music over the last 30 years has been towards a more tonal/modal music with a parallel shift towards greater comprehensibility. It is likely that successful composers in the future will be those who communicate directly with their audience. Some of the British composers discussed earlier, such as Weir and Turnage, show this characteristic, although this is not to suggest that their music is without depth or richness.

There has also been a continued interest of composers into popular idioms and an exploration of the grey areas in between genres. Minimalism and Post-Minimalism, which explore the interesting area of contemporary music, popular music and world music, continue to thrive and evolve into more sophisticated and varied forms. It would be wrong to suggest that the tougher, more modernist style of music will disappear over the coming years, diversity of style and pluralism will continue to be a defining characteristic of New Music. Some of the most innovative current composers and stylistic groupings are outlined below.

Popular Minimalism: Michael Nyman.

The British composer Michael Nyman (b. 1944) is an example of a composer who writes music which cannot be easily categorised, as it consists of an amalgam of Minimalism, Baroque Ground Bass and Popular rhythms. Nyman's most characteristic works have been those written for Peter Greenaway's films such as *The Draughtsman's Contract* (1982), *A Zed and Two Noughts* (1985) and *The Cook, The Thief, His Wife, and Her Lover* (1989) which show a powerful and distinctive style. Nyman's music for *The Piano* (1992), directed by Jane Campion, is less hard-edged and original than his earlier works, but it does suit the film and has brought him much popularity. Non-film music includes; the chamber opera *The Man Who Mistook His Wife for a Hat* (1987) based on the case-study by psychiatrist Oliver Sacks and the music of Schumann; a Piano Concerto (1993) based on music from *The Piano*; five string quartets (1985, 1988, 1990, 1995 & 2011); and *I Sonetti Lussuriosi* (2007) for soprano and orchestra on erotic texts by the Renaissance poet Pietro Aretino. A recent substantial work is *Through the Only Window* (2012) for string quartet and piano. In 2014, he wrote a memorial to the Hillsborough victims, he wrote *Symphony No. 11: Memorial*.

Post-Minimalism: John Adams.

The American composer John Adams is considered to be a significant innovator in the Minimalist genre. His recent style could be better classified as Post-Modernist or perhaps Post-Minimalist as he avoids the austere Minimalism of Steve Reich or Philip Glass, in favour of a richer and more backward looking style. *Grand Pianola Music* (1981) for chamber orchestra, 3 sopranos and 2 solo pianos is an example of this more eclectic approach using jazz-like harmony and a banal tune at the end which is very reminiscent of Beethoven's *Ode to Joy*.

Adams, like Glass, has latterly explored the larger canvas of opera using relatively recent historical events for the plots. Examples include: *Nixon in China* (1987) which outlines the historic meeting between President Nixon and Chairman Mao; and *The Death of Klinghoffer* (1991) which highlights the eternal clash of the Arabs and the Jews. What Adams's music shows above all is the increasing pluralism in the styles of contemporary music which include popular idioms and also the raiding of past musical genres to create a fascinating blend of disparate materials. His range is evident in the recent oratorio *The Gospel According to the Other Mary* (2012) and the Saxophone Concerto (2013).

The Modernists: Birtwistle, Stockhausen, Boulez.

Modernist composers, who reject the notion that there are 'easy answers' in art, will continue to have a significant role in contemporary music. The leading 'Modernists' include Stockhausen, Boulez, Birtwistle, Xenakis, Ligeti, and Ferneyhough. Their music is very diverse in style but they have a common commitment to atonal music, the use of systems in their music and an avoidance of the approachability of the Post-Modernists such as Holloway or the American David Del Tredici (b. 1937), or the Mystics such as Pärt, Tavener or Górecki.

Harrison Birtwistle is a British composer who has continued to use an uncompromising, non-tonal and often very aggressive musical language. He is also a figure who is seen as the most original and distinctive voice of his generation. His musical development can be seen as the gradual evolution of one basic approach which shows increasing refinement of technique, but without changing his main focus on the issue of the structuring of time. In addition to the operas mentioned above, significant works include: *Earth Dances* for large orchestra (1985–6), which shows a complex layering of strata, like the earth's crust; *Pulse Shadows* for soprano and string quartet (1989–96), including settings of poems by Paul Celan; *The Shadow of Night* for orchestra (2001); and a Violin Concerto (2009–10). A more recent choral work is *The Moth Requiem*.

In the 1995 last night of the Proms, John Drummond, the controller of Radio 3, had the audacity to commission Birtwistle to write *Panic* for John Harle, the saxophonist. The result was a wild and virtuoso work which sounds almost like free jazz. It caused uproar as it brought an example of modernist violence into what is usually a cosy, musically mediocre and blatant jingoistic event.

Other Modernists have perhaps fared less well in recent decades. Boulez, the archetypal Modernist, appeared to be rewriting old works such as the orchestral *Notations* (1977–) or continuations of existing works.

Stockhausen continued with his seven opera project *Licht* which he began in 1977 and completed in 2003, but he became increasingly isolated, working with a very close-knit group of players, including several of his family members. All his compositional work was focused on *Licht* which has much in common with Wagner's *The Ring* – however *Licht* seems to lack the unity and perhaps the consistency of *The Ring*. It seemed that Stockhausen was no longer the innovator of earlier years, and had perhaps lost his direction.

Mystics and the New Simplicity: Arvo Pärt.

As part of the shift towards a greater comprehensibility in music, a number of composers have written music imbued with mysticism, usually allied to an increased religious devotion. Arvo Pärt (b. 1935), the Estonian, is an example of a composer whose earlier works are in the Modernist serial tradition but who had a change of heart in the late 1960s. At this time he made an intensive study of Gregorian Chant, 13th century Notre Dame Organum, and Renaissance Polyphony.

He managed to incur the wrath of the old communist authorities throughout his career, firstly as a serial composer, then as a composer using religious texts, and finally, when Western Serialism was becoming accepted in the 1970s, he shifted to a new simplicity in his music. His most significant works in the later style include: *Tabula Rasa*, a double concerto for two violins (1977); *Passio* for voices and instruments (1982); *Stabat Mater* for soprano, alto and strings (1985); *Litany* for soloists,

choir and orchestra (1994); and Symphony No.4 (2008).

Some Other Composers.

Other composers who have embraced a mystical and simple approach in their music include: Sir John Tavener the British composer of Eastern Orthodox faith; Henryk Górecki (1933–2010), the Polish composer whose Symphony No. 3 (1976) was a chart hit; and the Georgian symphonic composer Giya Kancheli (b. 1935). A forerunner of this approach was the prolific Armenian-American composer Alan Hovhaness (1911–2000).

Popular Music and Jazz.

The evolution of popular music and jazz is arguably the most far-reaching musical development of recent times. Many of the world's population have heard of Michael Jackson, or The Beatles, but few will have heard of such significant musical figures as Arnold Schönberg or Pierre Boulez. The audience for contemporary classical or 'art' music is an ever-shrinking one, and only styles which have links with popular music, such as minimalism, or look to the past, such as post-Modernist/neo-Romantic music, have any significant audience. Therefore popular music could be considered by future musicologists as the most significant musical genre of the twentieth century.

The term 'popular music' is problematic as not all popular music is actually that popular or commercial, but it has come to mean music which has its roots in the blues. Popular music is aimed at the whole spectrum of the population, whereas classical or 'art' music has always had a following among the educated middle classes, and therefore could be considered elitist.

The roots of present day popular music include folk song, African music, ballads, blues, jazz, and ragtime as well as elements of Western classical music. The development of blues, jazz and popular music will be outlined below.

The Blues: Origins.

The origins of the blues are a mixture of African influences brought by the slaves to North America, work songs used on the plantations, and Western musical elements. The work songs were sung by the slaves as they worked and had a call and response pattern. One man would sing the verse and the rest of the workers would reply with a chorus. The style of singing was different from the Western approach as it included growls, cries, and falsetto avoiding a pure tone. Rhythm is also a more developed feature in African music and the blues and jazz reflect this.

The field holler was a variety of work song which was sung by a lone worker and consisted of a long, tremulous one or two line call, often in falsetto, and comparatively free in form. This type of call has been recorded in the savannah parts of West Africa.

Other elements contributing to the origins of the blues include reels, dances, and jigs of Anglo-Scottish-Irish origin with African rhythmic elements and tuning, played on banjos (a descendant of the African *bania*) and fiddles. European-influenced song forms were also adopted by the Black Americans in the nineteenth century.

The Structure of the Blues.

The structure of the blues may have been heavily influenced by ballads such as *Railroad Bill* which was popular among black vocalists of the nineteenth century. This had the form of a couplet with a rhyming third line as a chorus. In blues the couplet was replaced with a repeated line:

See, see rider, see what you have done,
See, see rider, see what you have done,
You've made me love you, now my man done come.

The basic blues structure consisted of three lines within a 12 bar stanza and the rhyme schemes included *aaa*, *abb*, *abc* but *aab* predominated. The chord sequence, which was usually played by the guitar, can be described as follows (one chord per bar in the key of C major):

I (CEG), I, I, I, IV (FAC), IV, I, I, V⁷ (GBDF),
IV, I, V⁷ (last line I).

This is the most simple form and there are many variants.

The scale used by blues vocalists and instrumentalists is called the blues scale, because of the flattened or 'blue' notes. In the key of C major, the simplest scale consists of C E♭ F G B♭ which is also a pentatonic scale found in much folk music. The 'blue' notes are the E♭ and B♭ although a vocalist may not bend the notes exactly to these pitches.

The rhythmic language of the blues is also significant and includes syncopation; a displacement of the beat, and 'swung' quavers, consisting of the first quaver of a pair being longer and heavier than the second, rather than being equal as in classical music. Many of the above technical features, such as the 12 bar blues sequence, the blues scale, and the rhythmic style, can be observed in jazz and popular music.

Early Blues Singers.

The term 'blues' relating to song probably did not emerge until after 1900, but the original sixteenth century meaning was 'a condition of melancholy or depression' which describes the nature of many blues lyrics. The early blues singers, based in the South of the United States, worked in 'medicine shows' to attract buyers for dubious patent medicines. Wandering blues singers, rather like the French medieval troubadours, sang and played for their living, and helped to disseminate the blues in the early years of the present century. By 1910 white folk song collectors had noted the existence of the blues and in 1912 *Dallas Blues* by Hart Wand and Lloyd Garret was published – the first published example.

It is unlikely that the large number of published blues songs had a major effect on blues singers as few could read music. Probably the blues were passed on orally, and later, through recordings. The blues originated in the South, known as the Delta Blues, but in the 1920s blues singers moved North to record, along with the jazz musicians.

Classic Blues.

Mamie Smith (1883–1946) was the first black singer whose records were sold to the black public. *Crazy Blues*, which was recorded in 1920 and sold 75,000 copies in one month, made her a fortune and encouraged other black singers to follow her example, recording specifically for black listeners on what were dubbed 'race records'.

The term 'Classic Blues' refers to the songs of women singers based in New York and Chicago, particularly the larger-voiced contraltos who focused on blues and were backed by jazz musicians. Gertrude 'Ma' Rainey (1886–1939) was a significant example who was closest to the folk tradition. She was known as the 'Mother of the Blues', worked with Louis Armstrong on *Jelly Bean Blues* (1924), and made over 100 records in five years.

Bessie Smith (1894–1937) is probably the best known blues singer and her recording of *Down Hearted Blues* (1923) established her as the most successful black artist of the time. Her singing showed a powerful, emotional involvement, particularly noticeable in her slow blues songs.

The Influence of the Great Depression.

The poor conditions of the Depression may have partly triggered a more aggressive and powerful blues sound in the 1930s, with larger bands and the introduction of drummers and electrical amplification. This style of blues has been described as 'Urban Blues' and the guitarist Big Bill Broonzy (1893–1958) was an important exponent. In the early 1930s he added a trumpet, clarinet, a second guitar and a bass to make his Memphis Five Band, later adding a drummer. This created a music which had the drive needed for dancing. Other pioneers of Urban Blues include Tampa Red with his Chicago Five.

The evolution of blues into an ensemble-based genre continued after the war with singers like Muddy Waters (1915–83) and B.B. King (1925–2015). King, while remaining true to the blues form, explored aspects of jazz, gospel, and soul, with an innovative and expressive guitar technique.

The blues have continued to have a significant role in music, but the genre has been largely absorbed into popular music.

The Origins of Jazz.

It is difficult to give a comprehensive definition of jazz because of the variety of different styles within the genre. Generally, jazz shows a heightened preoccupation with rhythm, an emphasis on free improvisation, and usually a tonal/modal basis. Jazz emerged around the same time as the blues, and shares some of the latter's origins. Jazz has also had a significant influence on 'classical' composers, examples including Milhaud's *Le Creation du Monde* and Stravinsky's *Ragtime*.

Jazz originated in New Orleans around 1900, although the precise nature of the music played at that time is unclear because the earliest recording was made in 1917 by the white Original Dixieland Jazz Band. New Orleans jazz consisted of dense counterpoint from the front line wind instruments: saxophone, cornet, clarinet, and trombone, using material from the blues, marches or ragtime. The melody was usually embellished on the cornet with a higher counter-melody on the clarinet or saxophone. The rhythm section consisted of a piano, guitar or banjo playing the harmony, the drummer playing syncopated march rhythms, and a tuba or bass saxophone playing the bass line. There were short breaks for improvised solos from the wind players.

In the 1920s and 1930s the most innovative jazz musicians worked in Chicago and New York, and there was a musical shift towards more complex harmony, with a more subtle approach to improvisation. This can be seen in Bix Beiderbecke's (1903–31) cornet playing, for example *Davenport Blues* (1925) which shows a more expanded and imaginative approach to the improvised solo. Louis Armstrong (1901–71) with his Hot Five and Hot Seven had a more aggressive and rhythmically adventurous approach, which had a greater impact on the style.

Other significant bands that moved to Chicago in the 1920s include King Oliver's Creole Jazz Band and Jelly Roll Morton's band.

The 1920s.

In the 1920s another strand emerged known as orchestral jazz which can be seen in Fletcher Henderson's (1897–1952) band, partly due to the work of his arranger Don Redman. His approach to arranging was to use the sections: saxophones, brass (trumpets and trombones), and a rhythm section of banjo, tuba, piano and drums. Henderson created a combination of arranged big band sound with swinging jazz solos by such players as Louis Armstrong.

The term 'swing' describes the bands of the 1930s onwards, and also refers to the rhythmic approach where all quavers were 'swung' in a triplet rhythm. The difference between the 'swing' bands and their precursors is that the former had a greater control of the arrangement, and a tighter and more unified rhythm.

Duke Ellington.

Duke Ellington (1899–1974) and his Orchestra had a major impact on the development of big band composition, exploring a new range of expression. His compositions include miniature tone-poems such as *Daybreak Express* (1933), recompositions such as *Ebony Rhapsody* (1934) based on Liszt's *Hungarian Rhapsody No. 2* and solo concertos like *Clarinet Lament* (1936).

Benny Goodman (1909–86) was the significant white band leader of the period and succeeded in transforming Fletcher Henderson's approach with a more classically-based accuracy. He kept the swing element but removed the more adventurous approach to expression and note bending of the black bands.

Bebop.

In the 1940s a new style appeared called 'Bebop' or 'Bop' which consisted of complex, jagged, and stabbing harmonies, combined with free flowing scalic improvisation. The finest exponent of bebop was the alto saxophonist Charlie Parker (1920–55). He generally worked in small ensembles and played breathtaking improvisations of chromatic and irregular melodies, using rhythms which contradicted the underlaying pulse. Other important bebop players include the trumpeters Dizzy Gillespie and Miles Davis, and the pianist Thelonious Monk, all of whom played with Parker. Bebop marked a radical shift in the development of jazz as it allowed a much freer mode of expression, comparable with contemporary 'art' music.

Cool, Free Jazz and Fusion.

Miles Davis (1926–91) was unusual among jazz musicians as he successfully transformed his style several times, including swing, bebop, cool, modal jazz, fusion and funk. *The Birth of the Cool* (1949–50) with his own 9-piece band created a new sound which eschewed the frenetic activity of bebop for a drier, mellower, and 'cooler' sound. Other musicians working in this almost classical chamber of music style included Lennie Tristano and Gill Evans. In *A Kind of Blue* (1959) Davis continued his development into modal jazz where long stretches of music are based on one chord, with the improvised solos on a compatible mode.

The next step entailed removing the chord progressions completely, which Ornette Coleman (b. 1930) did in his 'free jazz' by removing harmony instruments from his groups. In addition, tempo and the time signature are variable in his work, giving his music a very fluid rhythmic flow. *Free Jazz* (1960) is Coleman's seminal recording, and his work was continued by the pianist Cecil Taylor and the trumpeter Don Cherry.

In the 1960s 'pop music' dominated the musical scene and in this period the use of electronics and musical elements from rock 'n' roll can be observed. Miles Davis' *Bitches Brew* (1969) is a good example of the fusion of jazz and rock. From 1970 to the present day the jazz scene has similar characteristics to that of contemporary 'art' music in the multiplicity of coexisting styles. This makes it difficult to identify a clear direction of development.

The most innovative current jazz performers include the pianist Keith Jarrett, George Russell, Anthony Braxton and Evan Parker.

Popular Music: Origins.

Popular Music can be defined as music which is aimed at the populace rather than an elite. Its abbreviated form 'pop', has been used since the 1950s, although one early use of this word was for a popular concert – first recorded in 1862. Popular music of the eighteenth and nineteenth centuries was briefer, simpler, and lighter than contemporaneous classical music.

In the early twentieth century, song writers such as Jerome Kern, Irving Berlin, George Gershwin, and Cole Porter, continued to develop the popular song often using 32 bar ballad form. This consisted of an introductory verse of 16 or 32 bars followed by a more memorable and lyrical chorus of 32 bars constructed of 4×8 bar sections: AABA. The songs were more imaginative than the above formula suggests and used sophisticated harmony influenced by both jazz and classical music. Tin Pan Alley was the area in New York City where many popular songs from the 1920s to 1950s were composed and published. 'Popular music' is now generally used for music since the 1950s with roots in rock 'n' roll, covering music as diverse as 'The Sex Pistols' and Cliff Richard.

Rock 'n' Roll and Rock.

Rock'n'roll is a form of rhythmicised blues, evolving from rhythm and blues, and was meant for dancing. Its tempo was fast and furious, the words were largely sexually based, the dynamic was loud, and the vocal style was both aggressive and semi-shouted.

The instrumentation was dominated by electric guitars, saxophones, and a powerful rhythm section of drums, piano and bass, with a strong emphasis on the first beat of each bar. Major US performers include Bill Haley and his Comets, Jerry Lee Lewis, Elvis Presley, Chuck Berry and Little Richard.

The 1960s: The Beatles.

In the early 1960s rock 'n' roll was revitalised by the rise of new bands including the Beach Boys in the US and British groups such as the Beatles (*see* **B6**), the Rolling Stones, and the Who. These groups helped transform the genre into a varied and sophisticated form which became 'rock'. Also very important was the iconic music of David Bowie (*see* **B9**) and the works of Bob Dylan (*see* **B21**).

The main features of 'rock' were developed in California by the Byrds and other bands in San Francisco. Rock had the flexibility and potential to create more varied and complex structures. The Beatles illustrated this greater sophistication in albums such as *Revolver* (1966) and *Sgt. Pepper's Lonely Hearts Club Band* (1967). Their contribution to the development of popular music was immense through the unfolding of a varied and distinctive musical language, and also their evolution of studio techniques, including multi-tracking and sound processing. They disengaged their music from the 'live performance' which would have been impossible for many of their best recorded songs. Many rate the Beatles as the greatest rock 'n' roll artists of all time.

The basic characteristics of rock are an instrumentation of electric guitars, bass guitar, keyboard and drums; a fast, pounding rhythm from the bass and drums; and rather egocentric performances.

Michael Jackson: The 'King of Pop'.

Michael Jackson (1958–2009), the 'King of Pop' as he was widely acclaimed, was one of the most successful popular music entertainers of all time. His album *Thriller* (released in 1982) became an all-time bestseller. His performances were brilliant, but his personal life was troubled.

Born in Gary, Indiana, the seventh of nine children, he began performing at the age of 5. He subsequently became lead singer of the Jackson 5, but it was as a soloist that he found the greatest fame. His album *Thriller* (for which he will always be remembered) was followed by *Bad* (1987) and *Dangerous* (1991). A great dancer as well as a singer, his appeal was phenomenal - going beyond age, race or class. Michael Jackson also wrote and composed many of his greatest hits.

Heavy Metal.

Heavy metal was developed from the blues progressions of the late 1960s by 'power trios' like Cream and the Jimi Hendrix Experience. It consisted of guitar-based rock with highly amplified and virtuosic guitar and bass, creating a 'wall of sound'. In the 1970s heavy metal bands included Deep Purple, Steppenwolf and Black Sabbath who were followed by the new wave of British bands such as Def Leppard and Iron Maiden. Live performance is very important for heavy metal, as fans enjoy interacting with the performers.

Punk.

Punk was a term originally given to garage-based US rock of the 1960s, but was more famously used for music in 1976 played by the British bands, Sex Pistols, Clash, and Buzzcocks, who had been influenced by Richard Hell, and Patti Smith playing in New York City. Punk attempted to make rock 'dangerous' again, consisting of aggressive, anti-establishment lyrics, very basic guitar-based rock played at great speed. Punk evolved into New Wave which has similar energy but with more finesse and musical technique. Examples include Blondie and Talking Heads.

Reggae.

Reggae also emerged in the 1970s consisting of a

Jamaican pop style developed from Ska (a shuffling hybrid of rhythm and blues) and Mento. The music is much slower and more sensuous than other popular genres and has a hypnotic, bass-dominated sound, a 'chopped off' beat, and often a lyrical and expressive vocal line. Bob Marley was the most impressive performer, along with Desmond Dekker and Jimmy Cliff.

Disco, House and Techno.

In the last 40 years music for dancing has become prevalent through the Discotheque and latterly the 'Rave'. Disco consists of a thumping bass drum on each beat of the music and is considered a debased form of pop music. It was promoted by the film *Saturday Night Fever* (1977) and is a relatively simple style, making use of drum machines and synthesisers which give it an anonymous quality.

House is based on Disco and consists of the warm, feel-good music of the late 1980s. The term comes from the use of warehouses for performance, and it originated in Chicago with Frankie Knuckles. The 'godfather of house music' died in 2014. His biggest 'hit' was *The Whistle Song* in 1991.

Techno, originating in Detroit, was also a development of the 1980s. It is a percussion-based electronic dance music, with stripped-down drum beats and bass lines. UK labels include Rising High and Warp and successful groups are Prodigy, Orbital, and L.F.O.. Most techno uses a 'groove' or movement by repetition, which builds up an evolving musical texture like minimalist music.

Grunge.

Originating in Seattle during the mid-1980s, the grunge movement has largely usurped traditional heavy metal to become one of the most influential rock sounds of the 1990s. Essentially a mixture of blues-based chord progressions, punk-like energy levels and nihilistic lyrical content, the typical grunge song contrasts quieter, contemplative verses against raging, aggressive choruses. To achieve the deep and sinister sound at the heart of the music, grunge performers often de-tune their guitars and basses from standard concert pitch by up to two whole tones.

Since the movement came to world-wide prominence in 1992, grunge's most commercially successful acts have included Pearl Jam, Soundgarden and Alice In Chains. But by far the most important band to emerge from the genre was Seattle-based group Nirvana, whose second album, *Nevermind*, encapsulated much of grunge's intrinsic appeal. Unfortunately, Nirvana's singer/songwriter Kurt Cobain reacted badly to the demands of fame and subsequently took his own life in 1994. He has since become a cultural icon to disaffected teenagers everywhere. Though its forward momentum was temporarily checked by Cobain's death, grunge continues to grow with newer groups such as Live, Bush, Ash and Korn all expanding on the form's more dominant musical themes.

Brit-Pop.

After a particularly uneventful period in the history of British pop, a slew of similarlly themed bands emerged in 1993 and commercially re-invigorated the domestic music scene. Taking their blueprint from the sounds and styles of the 1960s—with the music of The Beatles and The Kinks a clear reference point—groups such as Manchester's Oasis, London's Blur and Sheffield's Pulp all but dominated the UK charts in the 1990s. In direct opposition to America's grunge movement, the lyrical content of much of Brit-Pop is optimistic in nature, with images of casual hedonism and wry social commentary well to the fore.

Conversely, as the genre continues to evolve, emergent acts such as Radiohead and The Verve are directly challenging the more formulaic aspects of the Brit-Pop sound. More 'rock' than 'pop', these groups employ odd time signatures, thicker orchestral textures and lyrical themes of paranoia and rigorous self-examination to inform their music. The result of such experimentation has meant that original Brit-Pop acts have been forced

to re-evaluate their position and explore wider musical themes in an effort to compete.

Boy Bands/Girl Bands.

One of the more interesting developments to come out of the popular music scene was the increasing proliferation of boy/girl bands. Unlike most pop acts that hone their musical craft in rehearsal rooms and concert halls over a period of years, the majority of boy/girl bands are 'manufactured', with group members brought together by prospective managers through the process of audition.

As record producers and professional song-writers often provide these acts with their material, the skills required of the average boy/girl band member differ greatly from more traditional groups. In place of instrumental prowess, they must be youthful in appearance, able dancers and reasonably proficient singers. When marketed properly, these acts have achieved huge chart success, finding a dedicated fanbase consisting not only of teenagers, but also children very much younger.

A sterling example of a successful boy band was Take That, who enjoyed an almost Beatles-like public profile until their break-up at the start of 1996. (After his departure from Take That, Robbie Williams went on to achieve great acclaim as a soloist, reaching new pinnacles in his career).

Within months, Take That had been replaced in the public's affections by two more boy bands, Boyzone and the Backstreet Boys. They were followed later by One Direction.

By far the most commercially profitable of the all girl groups has been the Spice Girls, who dominated both the UK and US charts with their blend of soulful melodies and appealing dance routines. Their simple mantra of 'Girl Power' has also become a catchphrase for many teenagers.

Though boy and girl bands offer little in developmental terms to the course of popular music, their success indicated a trend towards a more generalised form of entertainment within the pop scene, where the ability to dance well was as highly prized as a fine singing voice.

Jungle.

Jungle is a loose term used to describe a frenetically paced form of dance music that originated in the UK 'rave/club' scene in the early 1990s. Like Techno music, jungle is percussion based and reliant on the use of drum machines and synthesisers to provide its centralised core. Yet, where it differs from techno and house music is in the profound absence of mid-range frequencies, with virtually no vocals or guitar used to enhance melody. Instead, both bass and treble frequencies are heavily compressed, creating a thunderous, filtered sound. To add to the sense of musical drama, jungle moves at a pace of approximately 156–180 BPM (beats per minute), almost double the speed of the average pop song.

Some of jungle music's more notable performers include Tricky and Goldie.

Drum and Bass.

Drum and bass is similar to jungle music in that it relies heavily on rhythm to enforce its point. However, in stark contrast to jungle's more repetitive approach, drum and bass often manipulates time signatures, speeding the beat up and down at irregular intervals to create a jarring musical effect. Because it compresses and stretches four bar progressions, drum and bass is often compared to jazz/ bebop in terms of musical sensibility and performance. Roni Size is considered to be Great Britain's leading exponent of the drum and bass style.

Ambient.

Ambient is one of the most recent musical genres to emerge from the UK club scene. Effectively, it is a music of texture, where minimalist drum machine patterns and pulsating synthesisers are employed to invoke a sense of atmosphere and general relaxation. Less frenetic than either jungle or drum and bass, ambient is often played in smaller rooms within clubs.

II. GLOSSARY OF MUSICAL TERMS

A. Note of scale, commonly used for tuning instruments.

Absolute Music. Music without any literary descriptive or other kind of reference.

A Capella. Literally means "in the church style." Unaccompanied.

Accelerando. Quickening of the pace.

Accidental. The sign which alters the pitch of a note; ♯ (sharp) raises and a ♭ (flat) lowers note by one semitone, ✗ (double sharp) and ♭♭ (double flat) alter by two semitones.

Accompaniment. Instrumental or piano part forming background to a solo voice or instrument.

Ad lib. (L. *ad libitum*). Direction on music that strict time need not be observed.

Adagio. At a slow pace.

Aeolian mode. One of the scales in mediaeval music, represented by the white keys of the piano from A to A.

Air (Ayre). A simple tune for voice or instrument.

Alberti Bass. Characteristic 18th century keyboard figuration derived by splitting chord(s) of an accompanying part. Tradition credits Alberti as its inventor.

Allegretto. Not quite so fast as *Allegro*.

Allegro. Fast, but not too fast.

Alto. An unusually high type of male voice; also the vocal part sung by women and boys with a low range.

Ambrosian Chant. Plainsong introduced into church music by St. Ambrose, bishop of Milan (d. 397), and differing from Gregorian chant.

Andante. At a walking pace, not so slow as *Adagio* nor as fast as *Allegretto*.

Andantino. A little faster than *Andante*.

Animato. Lively.

Answer. Entry in a fugue or invention which imitates or "answers" the theme at a different pitch.

Anthem. Composition for use in church during a service by a choir with or without soloists.

Antiphonal. Using groups of instruments or singers placed apart.

Appoggiatura. An ornament consisting of a note just above or below a note of a chord, and resolving onto that note.

Arabesque. Usually a short piece, highly decorated.

Arco. Direction for string instruments to play with bow.

Aria. Vocal solo, usually in opera or oratorio, often in three sections with the third part being a repeat of the first. An *Arietta* is a shorter, lighter kind of aria.

Arioso. In the style of an aria; halfway between aria and recitative.

Arpeggio. Notes of a chord played in a broken, spread-out manner, as on a harp.

Ars antiqua. The old medieval music, based on organum and plainsong, before the introduction of *Ars nova* in 14th cent.

Ars Nova. New style of composition in 14th century France and Italy. It has greater variety in rhythm and independence in part-writing.

Atonal. Not in any key; hence *Atonality*.

Aubade. Morning song.

Augmentation. The enlargement of a melody by lengthening the time value of its notes.

Augmented. Enlarged verrsion of a perfect or major interval, *e.g.* semitone greater than a perfect fourth is an augmented fourth.

B. Note of scale, represented in Germany by *H*.

Bagatelle. A short, generally light piece of music. Beethoven wrote 26 Bagatelles.

Ballad. Either a narrative song or an 18th-cent. drawing-room song.

Ballade. A substantial and dramatic work, often for piano. Notable examples are by Chopin and Brahms.

Ballet. See **P38**.

Banjolele. A cross between a banjo and a ukelele.

Bar. A metrical division of music; the perpendicular line in musical notation to indicate this.

Barcarolle. A boating-song, in particular one associated with Venetian gondoliers.

Baritone. A male voice, between tenor and bass.

Baroque. A term applied, loosely, to music written in the 17th and 18th cent., roughly corresponding to baroque in architecture.

Bass. The lowest male voice; lowest part of a composition.

Bass Drum. Largest of the drum family, placed upright and struck on the side.

Bassoon. The lowest of the woodwind instruments, uses double reed.

Beat. Music's rhythmic pulse.

Bel canto. Literally "beautiful singing"—in the old Italian style with pure tone and exact phrasing.

Berceuse. Cradle song.

Binary. A piece in two sections is said to be binary in form. The balance is obtained by a second phrase (or section) answering the first.

Bitonality. Use of two keys at once.

Bow. Stick with horsehair stretched across it for playing string instruments.

Brass. Used as a collective noun for all brass or metal instruments.

Breve. Note, rarely used nowadays, with time value of two semibreves.

Bridge. Wood support over which strings are stretched on a violin, cello, *etc.*

Buffo(a). Comic, as in *buffo bass* or *opera buffa*.

C. Note of scale.

Cabaletta. Final, quick section of an aria or duet.

Cadence. A progression of two or three chords at the end of a phrase, section or piece.

Cadenza. Solo vocal or instrumental passage, either written or improvised, giving soloist chance to display technical skill to audience.

Calando. Becoming quieter and slower.

Canon. A piece or section of music resulting from one line of music being repeated in exact imitation in the other part(s) which enter in succession.

Cantabile. Song-like, flowing and expressive.

Cantata. Vocal work for soloist(s) and/or choir.

Cantilena. Sustained, smooth melodic line.

Cantus firmus. Literally "fixed song." Basic melody from 14th to 17th cent., around which other voices wove contrapuntal parts.

Canzonet. Light songs written in England *c.* 1600.

Carillon. A set of bells in tower of church, played from a keyboard below.

Carol. Christmas (or, less commonly, Easter) song.

Castrato. Artificially-created male soprano and alto, fashionable in 17th and 18th cent. (The castration of vocally gifted boys prevailed in Italy until the 19th cent.)

Catch. A part-song like a round, in vogue in England from 16th to 19th cent.

Cavatina. An operatic song in one section, or a slow song-like instrumental movement.

Celesta. Keyboard instrument with metal bars struck by hammers.

Cello (abbr. of *violoncello*). Four-stringed instrument, played with bow, with a bass range. Comes between viola and double bass in string family.

Cembalo. Originally the Italian name for the dulcimer, but also applied to the harpsichord.

Chaconne. Vocal or instrumental piece with repeated bass.

Chamber Music. Music for a relatively small number of performers (generally between two and ten).

Chanson. Type of part-song current in France from 14th to 16th cent.

Chant. Term used for various types of singing (generally in religious context), often of a rhythmically free nature.

Choir. Body of singers, used either in church or at concerts.

Chorales. German Lutheran hymns, often made use of by Bach.

Chord. Any combination of notes heard together. *See also* **Triad**.

Chording. Spacing of intervals in a chord.

Chorus. Substantial body of singers, usually singing in four parts.

Chromatic. Using a scale of nothing but semitones.

Clarinet. Woodwind instrument with single reed in use since mid-18th cent.

Clavichord. Keyboard instrument having strings struck by metal tangents, much in use during 17th and 18th cent. as solo instrument.

Clavier. Keyboard. Used in German (*Klavier*) for piano.

Clef. Sign in stave that fixes place of each note.

Coda. Closing section of a composition.

Coloratura. Term to denote florid singing.

Common chord. *See* Triad.

Common Time. Four crotchets to the bar, 4/4 time.

Compass. Range of notes covered by voice or instruments.

Composition. Piece of music, originated by a composer's own imagination; act of writing such a piece.

Compound Time. Metre where beats are subdivided into threes rather than twos. *See* Simple time.

Con Brio. With dash.

Concert. Public performance of any music.

Concertato. Writing for several solo instruments to be played together.

Concerto. Work for one or more solo instruments and orchestra.

Concerto grosso. Orchestral work common in 17th and 18th cent. with prominent parts for small groups of instruments.

Concord. Opposite of discord, *i.e.*, notes that when sounded together satisfy the ear. (Conventional term in that its application varies according to the predominant musical style of the period.)

Consecutive. Progression of harmonic intervals of like kind.

Consonance. Like Concord.

Continuo. Bass line in 17th and 18th century music. Played by a bass instrument and keyboard, the latter improvising on the indicated harmonies.

Contralto. A woman's voice with a low range.

Counterpoint. Simultaneous combination of two or more melodies to create a satisfying musical texture. Where one melody is added to another, one is called the other's counterpoint. The adjective of counterpoint is contrapuntal.

Counter-tenor. Another name for male alto.

Courante. A dance in triple time.

Crescendo. Getting louder.

Crook. Detachable section of tubing on brass instruments that change the tuning.

Crotchet. Note that equals two quavers in time value.

Cycle. Set of works, especially songs, intended to be sung as group.

Cyclic form. Form of work in two or more movements in which the same musical themes recur.

Cymbal. Percussion instrument in the form of a metal plate; often two are struck against each other.

D. Note of scale.

Da Capo (abbr. D.C.). From the beginning. A *Da Capo* aria is one in which the whole first section is repeated after a contrasting middle section.

Descant. Additional part (sometimes improvised) sung against a melody.

Development. Working-out section of movement in sonata form. *See* Sonata.

Diatonic. Opposite of chromatic; using proper notes of a major or minor scale.

Diminished. Lessened version of perfect or minor interval, *e.g.*, semitone less than a perfect fifth is a diminished fifth.

Diminuendo. Becoming quieter.

Diminution. Reducing a phrase of melody by shortening time value of notes.

Discord. Opposite of concord, *i.e.*, notes that sounded together produce a clash of harmonies.

Dissonance. Like discord.

Divertimento. A piece, usually orchestral, in several movements; like a suite.

Dodecaphonic. Pertaining to 12-note method of composition.

Dominant. Fifth note of major or minor scale above tonic (key) note.

Dorian Mode. One of the scales in medieval music, represented by the white keys on the piano from D to D.

Dot. Placed over note indicates staccato; placed after note indicates time value to be increased by half.

Double bar. Two upright lines marking the end of a composition or a section of it.

Double bass. Largest and lowest instrument of violin family; played with bow or plucked.

Drone. Unvarying sustained note, often in the bass, for example, the permanent bass note of a bagpipe.

Drum. Variety of percussion instruments on which sound is produced by hitting a skin stretched tightly over a hollow cylinder or hemisphere.

Duet. Combination of two performers; composition for such a combination.

Duple Time. Metre in which there are two beats to a bar.

Dynamics. Gradations of loudness or softness in music.

E. Note of scale.

Encore. Request from audience for repeat of work, or extra item in a programme.

English horn (*Cor anglais*). Woodwind instrument with double reed of oboe family with lower range than oboe.

Enharmonic. Refers to use of different letter names for the same note, *e.g.* F and E♯. Often exploited to achieve modulation between distantly related keys.

Ensemble. Teamwork in performance; item in opera for several singers with or without chorus; a group of performers of no fixed number.

Episode. Section in composition occurring between appearances of main musical material.

Exposition. Setting out of thematic material in a sonata-form composition.

Expression marks. Indication by composer of how he wants his music performed.

F. Note of scale.

False relation. A clash of harmony produced when two notes of the same letter-name but differently inflected (*e.g.* A natural and A flat) are played simultaneously or straight after one another.

Falsetto. The kind of singing by male voices

above normal register and sounding like an unbroken voice.

Fanfare. Flourish of trumpets.

Fantasy. A piece suggesting free play of composer's imagination, or a piece based on known tunes (folk, operatic, etc.).

Fermata. Pause indicated by sign ⌒ prolonging note beyond its normal length.

Fifth. Interval taking five steps in the scale. A perfect fifth (say, C to G) includes three whole tones and a semitone; a diminished fifth is a semitone less, an augmented fifth a semitone more.

Figure. A short phrase, especially one that is repeated.

Fingering. Use of fingers to play instrument, or the indication above notes to show what fingers should be used.

Flat. Term indicating a lowering of pitch by a semitone, or to describe a performer playing under the note.

Florid. Term used to describe decorative passages.

Flute. Woodwind instrument, blown sideways. It is played through a hole, not a reed. Nowadays, sometimes made of metal.

Folksong. Traditional tune, often in different versions, handed down aurally from generation to generation.

Form. Course or layout of a composition, especially when in various sections.

Fortissimo. Very loud.

Fourth. Interval taking four steps in scale. A perfect fourth (say, C to F) contains two whole tones and a semitone. A diminished fourth is a semitone less, and an augmented fourth a semitone more.

Fugato. In the manner of a fugue.

Fugue. Contrapuntal composition for various parts based on one or more subjects treated imitatively.

G. Note of scale.

Galant. Used to designate elegant style of 18th-cent. music.

Galliard. Lively dance dating back to 15th cent. or before.

Gamelan. A percussion orchestra from Indonesia.

Gavotte. Dance in 4/4 time, beginning on third beat in bar.

Giusto. Strict, proper.

Glee. An unaccompanied part-song. See **Section L**.

Glissando. Rapid sliding scales up and down piano or other instruments.

Glockenspiel. Percussion instrument consisting of tuned steel bars and played with two hammers or keyboard.

Grave. In slow tempo.

Grazioso. Gracefully.

Gregorian Chant. Plainsong collected and supervised mainly by Pope Gregory (d. 604).

Ground Bass. A bass part that is repeated throughout a piece with varying material on top.

Guitar. Plucked string instrument of Spanish origin, with six strings of three-octave compass.

H. German note-symbol for B.

Harmony. Simultaneous sounding of notes so as to make musical sense.

Harp. Plucked string instrument of ancient origin, the strings stretched parallel across its frame. On the modern concert harp, the basic scale of C flat major is altered by a set of pedals.

Harpsichord. Keyboard stringed instrument played by means of keyboard similar to a piano but producing its notes by a plucking, rather than a striking action.

Homophonic. Opposite of polyphonic, i.e., indicated parts move together in a composition, a single melody being accompanied by block chords, as distinct from the contrapuntal movement of different melodies.

Horn. Brass instrument with coiled tubes. Valves introduced in the 19th cent. made full chromatic use of instrument possible.

Imitation. Repetition, exactly, or at least recognisably, of a previously heard figure.

Impromptu. A short, seemingly improvised piece of music, especially by Schubert or Chopin.

Improvise. To perform according to fancy or imagination, sometimes on a given theme.

In alt. The octave above the treble clef; in altissimo, octave above that.

Instrumentation. Writing music for particular instruments, using the composer's knowledge of what sounds well on different instruments.

Interlude. Piece played between two sections of a composition.

Intermezzo. Formerly meant interlude, now often used for pieces played between acts of operas.

Interval. Distance in pitch between two notes.

Ionian mode. One of the scales in mediaeval music, represented on piano by white keys between C and C, identical therefore to modern C major scale.

Isorhythm. Medieval technique using repetitions of a rhythm but with different notes. Much used in 14th and 15th century motets. See **P3–4**.

Jig. Old dance usually in 6/8 or 12/8 time.

Kettledrum (It. pl. Timpani). Drum with skin drawn over a cauldron-shaped receptacle, can be tuned to definite pitch by turning handles on rim, thus tightening or relaxing skin.

Key. Lever by means of which piano, organ, etc., produces note; classification, in relatively modern times, of notes of a scale. Any piece of music in major or minor is in the key of its tonic or keynote.

Keyboard. Term used to describe instruments with a continuous row of keys.

Key-signature. Indication on written music, usually at the beginning of each line, of the number of flats or sharps in the key of a composition.

Kitchen Department. Humorous term for percussion section of an orchestra.

Lament. Musical piece of sad or deathly significance.

Largamente. Spaciously.

Largo. Slow.

Leading-motive (Ger. Leitmotiv). Short theme, suggesting person, idea, or image, quoted throughout composition to indicate that person, etc.

Legato. In a smooth style (of performance, etc.).

Lento. Slow.

Libretto. Text of an opera. See **Section L**.

Lied (pl. Lieder). German word for song, particularly used of the songs with piano accompaniment of Schubert, Schumann, Brahms, and Wolf.

Lute. String instrument plucked with fingers, used in 16th- and 17th-cent. music especially.

Lydian mode. One of the scales in mediaeval music, represented by white keys of piano between F and F.

Lyre. Ancient Greek plucked string instrument.

Madrigal. Composition for several voices, setting secular text; especially prominent in Italy and England in 16th and early 17th cent. See **P5**.

Maestoso. Stately.

Major. One of the two main scales of the tonal system with semitones between the third and fourth, and the seventh and eighth notes. Identical with Ionian mode.

Mandolin(e). Plucked string instrument of Italian origin.

Manual. A keyboard for the hands, used mostly in connection with the organ.

Master of the King's (or Queen's) Musick. Title of British court appointment, with no precise duties.

Melisma. Group of notes sung to a single syllable.

Mélodie. Literally a melody or tune; has come to mean a French song (*cf.* German *Lied*).

Metronome. Small machine in use since the beginning of the 19th cent., to determine the pace of any composition by the beats of the music, *e.g.*, ♩ = 60 at the head of the music indicates sixty crotchets to the minute.

Mezzo, Mezza. (It. = "half ") *Mezza voce* means using the half voice (a tone between normal singing and whispering). *Mezzo-soprano*, voice between soprano and contralto.

Minim. Note that equals two crotchets in time value.

Minor. One of the two main scales of the tonal system (cf. major), identical with Aeolian mode. It has two forms—the harmonic and melodic, the former having a sharpened seventh note, the latter having the sixth and seventh notes sharpened in its ascending version.

Minuet. Originally French 18th-cent. dance in triple time, then the usual third movement in symphonic form (with a contrasting trio section) until succeeded by scherzo.

Mixolydian mode. One of the medieval scales represented by the white keys on the piano from G to G.

Modes. Scales prevalent in the Middle Ages. *See* Aeolian, Dorian, Ionian, Lydian, Mixolydian, Phrygian.

Modulate. Changing from key to key in a composition, not directly but according to musical "grammar".

Molto. Much, very; thus *allegro molto.*

Motet. Sacred, polyphonic vocal composition. More loosely, any choral composition for use in church but not set to words of the liturgy. *See* **P3**.

Motive, motif. Short, easily recognised melodic figure.

Motto. Well-defined theme recurring throughout a composition, *cf. Idée fixe* in Berlioz's *Symphonie Fantastique.*

Movement. A piece which is complete in itself but forms part of a larger composition.

Music drama. Term used to describe Wagner's, and sometimes other large-scale operas.

Mutes. Devices used to damp the sound of various instruments.

Natural (of a note or key). Not sharp or flat.

Neoclassical. Clear-cut style, originating during 1920s, that uses 17th and 18th century forms and styles. It constituted a reaction to the excesses of romanticism.

Ninth. Interval taking nine steps, *e.g.*, from C upwards an octave and a whole tone to D.

Nocturne. Literally a "night-piece" hence usually of lyrical character.

Nonet. Composition for nine instruments.

Notation. System of writing down music.

Note. Single sound of specified pitch and duration; symbol to represent this.

Obbligato. Instrumental part having a special or essential rôle in a piece.

Oboe. Woodwind instrument with double reed, descended from hautboy; as such, in use since 16th cent., in modern form since 18th cent.

Octave. Interval taking eight steps of scale, with top and bottom notes having same "name"; C to C is an octave.

Octet. Composition for eight instruments or voices.

Ondes Martenol. Belongs to a class of melodic instruments in which the tone is produced by electrical vibrations controlled by the movement of the hands not touching the instrument.

Opera. Musical work for the stage with singing characters, originated *c.* 1600 in Italy.

Opera buffa (It.), **Opéra bouffe** (Fr.). Comic opera (in the English sense), *not* to be confused with *Opéra comique* (Fr.) which is opera with spoken dialogue and need not be humorous.

Opera seria. Chief operatic form of 17th and 18th cent., usually set to very formal librettos, concerning gods or heroes of ancient history.

Operetta. Lighter type of opera.

Opus (abbr. *Op.*). With number following *opus* indicates order of a composer's composition.

Oratorio. Vocal work, usually for soloists and choir with instrumental accompaniment, generally with setting of a religious text.

Orchestra. Term to designate large, or largish, body of instrumentalists; originated in 17th cent.

Orchestration. Art of setting out work for instruments of an orchestra. To be distinguished from *Instrumentation* (*q.v.*).

Organ. Elaborate keyboard instrument in which air is blown through pipes by bellows to sound notes. Tone is altered by selection of various stops and, since the 16th cent., a pedal keyboard has also been incorporated.

Organum. In medieval music a part sung as an accompaniment below or above the melody of plainsong, usually at the interval of a fourth or fifth; also, loosely, this method of singing in parts.

Ornament. Notes that are added to a given melody by composer or performer as an embellishment.

Overture. Instrumental introduction or prelude to larger work, usually opera. A concert overture is an independent orchestral piece, not part of an opera but often having a descriptive character.

Part. Music of one performer in an ensemble; single strand in a composition.

Part-song. Vocal composition in several parts.

Passacaglia. Composition in which a tune is constantly repeated, usually in the bass.

Passage. Section of a composition.

Passion. Musical setting of the New Testament story of Christ's trial and crucifixion.

Pastiche. Piece deliberately written in another composer's style.

Pavan(e). Moderately paced dance dating from 16th cent. or earlier.

Pedal point. Held note, usually in bass, against which other parts move.

Pentatonic. Scale of five notes, *e.g.*, the black keys of the piano.

Percussion. Collective title for instruments of the orchestra that are sounded by being struck by hand or stick.

Phrygian Mode. One of the scales of medieval music, represented by the white keys on piano from E to E.

Piano. Soft, abbr. *p*; *pp=pianissimo*, very soft; instrument, invented in 18th cent., having strings struck by hammer, as opposed to the earlier harpsichord where they are plucked. The modern piano has 88 keys and can be either "upright" (vertical) or "grand" (horizontal).

Pianoforte. Almost obsolete full Italian name for the piano.

Pitch. Exact height or depth of a particular musical sound or note.

Pizzicato. Direction for stringed instruments, that the strings should be plucked instead of bowed.

Plainchant, Plainsong. Medieval church music consisting of single line of melody without harmony or definite rhythm. *See* **P3**.

Polka. Dance in 2/4 time originating in 19th cent. Bohemia.

Polonaise. Polish dance generally in 3/4 time.

Polyphony. Combination of two or more musical lines as in *counterpoint*.

Polytonality. Simultaneous use of several keys.

Postlude. Closing piece or section.

Prelude. Introductory piece.

Presto. Very fast. *Prestissimo.* Still faster.

Progression. Movement from one chord to next to make musical sense.

Quartet. Work written for four instruments or voices; group to play or sing such a work.

Quaver. Note that equals two semiquavers or half a crotchet.

Quintet. Work written for five instruments or voices; group to play or sing such a work.

Rallentando. Slowing down.

Recapitulation. Section of composition that repeats original material in something like its original form.

Recitative. Term used for declamation in singing written in ordinary notation but allowing rhythmical licence.

Recorder. Woodwind instrument, forerunner of flute.

Reed. Vibrating tongue of woodwind instruments.

Register. Set of organ pipes controlled by a particular stop; used in reference to different ranges of instrument or voice (*e.g.*, chest register).

Relative. Term used with major and minor keys with a common key-signature (*e.g.* G major and E minor).

Répétiteur. Member of opera house's musical staff who coaches singers in their parts.

Requiem. Properly a mass for the dead, the term is extended to cover musical settings by Palestrina, Mozart, Verdi and others.

Rest. Notation of silence in composition, having a definite length like a note.

Retrograde. Term used to describe a melody played backwards.

Rhapsody. Work having a free form with a degree of romantic content.

Rhythm. Everything concerned with the time of music (*i.e.*, beats, accent, metre, *etc.*) as opposed to the pitch side.

Ritardando. Slowing down.

Ritenuto. Held back (referring to tempo).

Ritornello. Passage, usually instrumental, that recurs in a piece.

Romance, Romanza. Title for piece of vague song-like character.

Romantic. Term used vaguely to describe music of 19th cent. that often has other than purely musical source of inspiration.

Rondo. Form in which one section keeps on recurring between other passages.

Rubato. Manner of performing a piece without keeping strictly to time.

Sackbut. Early form of trombone.

Saxophone. Wind instrument made of brass, but using a reed like a woodwind instrument.

Scale. Progression of adjoining notes upwards or downwards.

Scherzo. Literally "a joke". Often used as a light movement in the middle of a sonata type work.

Score. Copy of any music written in several parts.

Second. Interval taking two steps in scale, *e.g.*, C to D flat, or to D.

Semibreve. Note that equals two minims or half a breve.

Semiquaver. Note that equals half a quaver.

Semitone. Smallest interval commonly used in Western music.

Septet. Composition for seven instruments or voices.

Sequence. Repetition of phrase at a higher or lower pitch.

Serenade. Usually an evening song or instrumental work.

Seventh. Interval taking seven steps in the scale.

Sextet. Composition for six instruments or voices.

Sharp. Term indicating a raising of pitch by a semitone.

Shawm. Early woodwind instrument, forerunner of oboe.

Simple time. Metre in which beats are subdivided into two. *See* Compound time.

Sinfonietta. Small symphony.

Sixth. Interval taking six steps in the scale.

Solo. Piece or part of a piece for one performer playing or singing alone.

Sonata. Work for one or two players (occasionally more), generally in three or four movements. **Sonata form** is the form usually found in the first movement (and often in subsequent movements) many sonatas and symphonies, consisting of exposition, development and recapitulation.

Song. Any short vocal composition.

Soprano. Highest female voice.

Sostenuto. Sustained, broadly.

Sotto voce. Whispered, scarcely audible, applied to vocal as well as instrumental music.

Spinet. A small keyboard instrument belonging to the harpsichord (*q.v.*) family.

Spirituals. Afro-American melodies with religious inspiration and which are still spontaneously created, but have also passed into art-music.

Sprechgesang. (Ger. Speech-song.) Vocal utterance somewhere between speech and song.

Staccato. Perform music in short, detached manner.

Staff. Horizontal lines on which music is usually written.

Stop. Lever by which organ registration can be altered.

String(s). Strands of gut or metal set in vibration to produce musical sounds on string or keyboard instruments. Plural refers to violins, violas, cellos, and basses of orchestra.

Study. Instrumental piece, usually one used for technical exercise or to display technical skills, but often having artistic merits as well (*e.g.*, Chopin's).

Subject(s). Theme or group of notes that forms principal idea or ideas in composition.

Suite. Work in several movements. The dance suite was a favourite instrumental form in the early 18th century.

Symphony. Orchestral work of serious purpose usually in four movements, occasionally given name (*e.g.*, Beethoven's "Choral" symphony).

Syncopation. Displacement of musical accent.

Tempo. Pace, speed of music.

Tenor. Highest normal male voice.

Ternary. A piece in three sections is said to be in ternary form. The balance is obtained by repeating the first phrase or section (though it need not be exact or complete) after a second of equal importance.

Tessitura. Compass into which voice or instrument comfortably falls.

Theme. Same as *subject* but can also be used for a whole musical statement as in "theme and variations."

Third. Interval taking three steps in scale.

Time. Rhythmical division of music.

Timpani. *See* **Kettledrum.**

Toccata. Instrumental piece usually needing rapid, brilliant execution.

Tonality. Key, or feeling for a definite key.

Tone. Quality of musical sound; interval of two semitones.

Tonic Sol-fa. System of musical notation to simplify sight-reading.

Transcribe. Arrange piece for different medium from that originally intended; transfer piece from one style of notation to another; notate an originally unnotated piece.

Transition. Passage that joins two themes or sections of a composition.

Transpose. To move a musical idea, theme or piece to a different key from its original.

Treble. Highest part in vocal composition; high boy's voice.

Triad. Three note chord. Usually consists of a note and those a third and fifth above.

Trio. Work written for three instruments or voices; group to play or sing such a work.

Trombone. Brass instrument with slide adjusting length of tube.

Trumpet. Brass instrument of considerable antiquity; modern version has three valves to make it into a chromatic instrument.

Tuba. Deepest-toned brass instrument with three or four valves.

Twelve-note. 20th-cent. technique of composition using full chromatic scale with each note having equal importance. Notes are placed in particular order as the basis of works.

Unison. Two parts sung or played together at same pitch.

Valve. Mechanism, invented in early 19th cent. to add to brass instruments allowing them to play full chromatic scale.

Variation. Altered version of theme or passage. Such variations may be closely allied to or depart widely from the original.

Verismo. Term to describe Italian operas written in "realist" style at the turn of the 20th century.

Vibrato. Rapid fluctuation in pitch of voice or instrument. Exaggerated it is referred to as a "wobble" (of singers).

Viol. String instrument of various sizes in vogue until end of 17th cent.

Viola. Tenor instrument of violin family.

Violin. Musical four-string instrument, played with bow, which superseded viol at beginning of 18th cent.

Virginals. English keyboard instrument, similar to harpsichord of 17th and 18th cent.

Vivace. Lively.

Voluntary. Organ piece for church use, but not during service.

Waltz. Dance in triple time, fashionable in 19th cent. *See* **P36.**

Whole-tone scale. Scale progressing by whole tones. Only two are possible, one beginning on C, the other on C sharp.

Xylophone. Percussion instrument with series of wood bars tuned in a chromatic scale and played with sticks.

Zarzuela. A traditional Spanish form of operetta.

Zither. String instrument laid on knees and plucked. Common in Central-European folk music.

III. INDEX TO COMPOSERS

IV. SPECIAL TOPIC

DANCE IN THE WEST.

SOCIAL DANCES.

In earliest times, dances performed solely for the enjoyment of the participants were what we would now term folk dances. In these, the dancers formed a pattern such as a circle or a line, and all performed the same steps. Such dances still exist but are now more likely to be performed as an entertainment rather than as a purely social activity. A different type of social dancing developed in Europe from medieval times, with couples dancing together. The *pavane*, a majestic, processional dance in a four-in-a-measure (occasionally two) rhythm, and the contrasting *galliard*, with rapid and complex steps to three-in-a-measure, both originating from Italy, were popular in the sixteenth century. In the seventeenth century, the *minuet* and the *gavotte* were popular dances at the court of Louis XIV of France. Both were slow, stately dances but in different rhythms, the minuet in a measure of three and the gavotte in four. These dances were imported into England by Charles II and kept their popularity for many years, the minuet especially, which was the most favoured dance of the eighteenth century until about 1790.

The style of social dance in the Europe and America of the nineteenth and twentieth centuries was, however, overwhelmingly ballroom dance, performed by couples and including such dances as the waltz, fox-trot and polka as well as Latin-American inspired dances such as the tango, rumba and samba, and this was dominant until the more individualistic discotheque styles of the 1960s onwards.

The following are in very approximate order of appearance.

Tarantella.

A folk dance of Italy in accelerating 3/8 or 6/8 time, usually danced by couples. Its name is derived from the city of Taranto where in the fourteenth century, according to legend, people bitten by the tarantula spider danced to sweat the poison out of their systems.

Mazurka.

A Polish national dance for a circle of couples, first recorded in the sixteenth century. Danced in triple time with the accent on the second or third beat, it is characterised by foot stamping and clicking of heels. It became popular as a ballroom dance in Europe and the United States in the late nineteenth century.

Square Dance.

The best-known and most popular folk dance in the United States. Danced by four couples standing in a square, whose movements, based on a smooth 'shuffling' walk, are prompted by the singing and patter of a 'caller'. Its origins can be traced to earlier dances in square formation such as the *cotillon*, a stately French dance popular at the court of Louis XV later supplanted by the *quadrille*, and to the intermingling of the various dances brought to the New World from Europe by the first settlers. After being eclipsed in the cities by new medieval dances in the nineteenth and early twentieth centuries, it enjoyed a revival in the 1930s and 40s which has maintained its popularity.

Line Dancing.

Essentially any dance where groups of dancers standing in a line (or lines) perform the same moves, but usually referring to country and western style line dances whose origins probably go back to the first American settlers. This style of dancing enjoyed a renaissance in America during the 1970s. It arrived in the UK in the 1990s, where it is still popular.

Waltz.

The first of the modern ballroom dances, the waltz originated in central Europe in the eighteenth century and was derived from the *Ländler*, a traditional couple dance of Bavaria and Austria. Danced to music in 3/4 time, it consists of a step-slide-step pattern performed by couples rotating around each other as they circle the dance floor – rapidly in the original Viennese waltz, more slowly in its later American version. It was initially seen as degenerate but became the most popular ballroom dance of the nineteenth century.

Polka.

A vigorous Bohemian dance to music in 2/4 time, the polka consists of three quick steps and a hop (the Czech *pulka*, 'half step'). Introduced in Paris in 1843, it became a serious rival in popularity to the waltz.

Quadrille.

An early nineteenth-century ballroom dance for couples in a square formation. Popular in France at the court of Napoleon I, it was brought to England in 1815.

Lancers.

A nineteenth-century variant of the *quadrille*. From *Quadrille des lanciers*, a dance invented in Dublin in 1818 by a French dancing teacher.

Barn Dance.

A rural American dance introduced into Britain in the late nineteenth century. Derived from the *Schottische*, a German couple dance, it was originally called the Military Schottische. The origin of its current name is uncertain as it may refer to dancing in a barn or it may refer to its being first danced to a song with the title *Dancing in the Barn*.

Cakewalk.

A dance of Afro-American origin in the nineteenth century, modelled on walking competitions in the southern states. It is named from the cake given as a prize for the most imaginative steps. Performed by a couple strutting arm-in-arm, it became a ballroom dance towards the end of the century after gaining popularity through stage shows.

Tango.

Originated as a rather disreputable dance in Buenos Aires, Argentina, about 1880. After becoming socially acceptable in the early 1900s it became highly popular in Europe by 1915. It is characterised by rapid long steps and sudden turns of the head and feet.

Fox-trot.

Introduced around 1914, it was named from the trotting step in the comedian Harry Fox's act. It consists of a series of walking steps and quarter turns, two slow steps forward then two quick steps to the side, to music in syncopated 4/4 rhythm.

Charleston.

Popular dance craze of the mid-1920s, originally an Afro-American solo dance and named after Charleston, South Carolina, where it was first performed in 1903. It is a fast-tempo dance to a syncopated 4/4 rhythm and the basic step is side-kicking from the knee.

Black Bottom.

Popular dance of the 1920s of Afro-American origin in New York, incorporating shuffling, stomping steps and swaying knees to a rhythm based on the Charleston.

Quickstep.

A dance in duple time, originating in the 1920s, which is basically a faster version of the fox-trot.

Rumba.

A Cuban dance of two quick side steps and one slow forward step to syncopated 4/4 time music, it is best known for the dancers' swinging side to side hip movements. It became internationally popular in the early twentieth century.

Paso Doble.

A moderately fast two-step South American dance of the 20th century. (Spanish for 'double step').

Conga.

Afro-Cuban dance which became popular in America and Paris during the 1930s. It consists of three steps forward followed by a kick. Although it can be danced solo or by a couple, it is best known as performed by a single-file column of people zig-zagging around the room, each person holding on to the hips of the person in front.

Mambo

Cuban dance invented in the late 1930s by the double-bass player, Israel 'Cachao' López, by speeding up and syncopating older Cuban dance styles.

Salsa.

A comprehensive term for dances of shared Cuban and Afro-American origins.

Samba.

Of Brazilian origin, it became popular in western Europe and the United States in the 1940s. It has simple forward and backward steps and rocking body movements and is danced to syncopated 4/4 time music.

Swing.

A generic term for American dances emanating from the North American swing jazz movement, such as the lindy hop, jitterbug and jive. (*See below*).

Lindy Hop.

The first and most athletic form of swing dancing, performed by black dancers in the United States and believed to be named after Lindbergh's flight across the Atlantic in 1927. Born in 1928 during a dance marathon of the Depression when one of the contestants broke away from his partner to improvise solo steps, it was the first dance in which couples began to 'do their own thing'. In the dance halls of Harlem it became increasingly flamboyant, with spinning, jumping, and throwing partners around.

The style died out with the advent of the Twist but there was a revival in Britain and America in the 1980s and 1990s, led by companies such as the Jiving Lindy Hoppers of London.

Jitterbug.

A form of swing dancing. Basically the lindy hop which had become popular with white dancers in America during the 'swing era' of the 1930s, producing a slightly less acrobatic, more refined variation. The jitterbug was popular in Europe during and immediately after the Second World War, having been brought over by American servicemen.

Boogie-woogie.

An Afro-American dance in which the dancer moves forward with knees together and hips swaying from side to side. It developed in the 1940s with the rise of boogie-woogie music, and was basically a modified version of the lindy hop to suit faster music.

Jive.

Based on the swing dancing brought to Europe in the 1940s, jive was its most popular form at the start of the rock and roll era. Today it is the form of competitive swing dancing internationally recognised. A simpler form, Modern Jive, arose in the 1980s. This has also been known as Ceroc, LeRoc or French Jive.

Rock'n'Roll.

Originally the dance performed to the rock and roll music of the 1950s, and evolved from the lindy hop and boogie-woogie into an even more athletic dance. It was popularised by the American band leader Bill Haley (1925–81), in particular with his number *Rock Around the Clock* in 1953. It is now a choreographed acrobatic dance designed for stage or competition performance by couples or groups.

Cha-Cha-Cha.

A variant of the mambo which was popular in the 1950s. The basic movement is three steps followed by a shuffle. Created by the Cuban composer Enrique Jorrin.

Bossa Nova.

A lively Brazilian dance of the late 1950s in syncopated 2/4 time, similar to the samba. Bossa nova music was a fusion of the samba and jazz. The name is from the Portuguese *bossa*, trend, and *nova*, new.

Merengue.

Originating in the Dominican Republic and Haiti, it became popular as a ballroom dance in the United States in the 1950s and 1970s. A couple dance to music in 4/4 time, it is danced with a 'limp' step, the weight being always on the same foot.

Twist.

A lively non-touching dance of the early 1960s which is performed on the spot by rocking with bent knees from side to side and up and down while twisting the body. It was made famous by the Chubby Checker song of the same name in 1960, and was deemed socially acceptable for all, coming as it did after the more outrageous rock'n'roll dances performed by teenagers.

Reggae.

Strongly accentuated off-beat dance, originating in Jamaica in the mid-1960s. The name probably comes from the Jamaican/English *rege-rege*, ragged clothing. *See also* **P26**.

Disco Dancing.

Freestyle modern dance with exaggerated hand and arm movements, popularised by the film *Saturday Night Fever* (1977).

Hip-hop.

Originating in New York during the late 1960s as part of a generalised Hispanic and Afro-American hip-hop culture, which included rap, hip-hop dance styles mainly comprise breakdance and body-popping. The latter consists of robotic move-and-freeze actions of the joints in quick succession giving the dancer a mechanical appearance.

Breakdancing.

A street dance style from the hip-hop culture of the South Bronx, New York City, in the 1970s. Acrobatic and energetic, it is characterised by fast footwork and body spins ending in a 'freeze' position. The name relates to the original music for the dance, which consisted of repetitions of a percussion 'break' extracted from a musical number and strung together by the DJ.

DANCE AS SHOW BUSINESS.

In almost all its guises dance is meant to be watched as well as performed. Even religious dance often assumes a spectator. The explosion in the entertainment industry in America and Europe from the later nineteenth century onwards inevitably extended to dance, and one of its most obvious and popular manifestations is tap dance.

Tap Dance.

In tap dancing the dancer wears shoes fitted with small metal plates under the toe and heel in order to produce audible beats from the foot rhythmically striking the floor. This style of dance evolved during the nineteenth century in the United States, principally from an amalgamation of the Irish jig, the Lancashire clog dance and African tribal dances. Initially the shoes for the resulting dance style (known as 'soft shoe') did not have metal taps; these were introduced later when the style evolved through various stages into modern rhythm tap, which became the most popular form of stage dancing during the first thirty years of the twentieth century. Among its well-known exponents were Fred Astaire, Ginger Rogers and Gene Kelly.

In the twenty-first century, it is exerting growing attraction on amateur dancers.

Ballet.

Dance as high art in the western world, however, is represented by the highly disciplined and sophisticated art of ballet. Ballet combines dance with the arts of music and painting to tell a story or create an atmosphere. The music must be closely linked with the dance in tempo and spirit, and the art of the painter is employed in creating the decorative background and the costumes.

(i) Origins.

Ballet is a comparatively young art, with its origins in the revival in fifteenth-century Italy of the art of pantomime, which had been popular in Roman times. This was an entertainment where a story was mimed while a chorus sang or declaimed the action of the scene. The earliest recorded entertainment of this kind was in 1489, to celebrate the marriage of the Duke of Milan. A century later Catherine de Medici, the widow of the king of France, introduced this style of entertainment to the French court, where in 1581 the first recorded instance of dance and music arranged in a coherent dramatic form was composed, the *Ballet Comique de la Reyne*. The male and female characters were all played by men and the ladies of the court supplied the chorus, the *corps de ballet*. For many years ballet remained popular with succeeding French kings, who often took part in them themselves, culminating in the founding of *L'Académie Royale de Musique et de Danse* in 1661 by Louis XIV. Towards the end of the seventeenth century ballet moved from the court to the stage and women were no longer confined to the *corps de ballet*, although they were still the ladies of the court until the first appearance of a professional dancer in 1721. When Marie Taglioni appeared in *La Sylphide* at the Paris Opéra in 1832 it heralded the era of Romantic ballet and the adulation of the ballerina at the expense of the other aspects of ballet. The only true surviving ballet from this period is *Giselle*.

(ii) Ballet in Russia.

The first academy of dancing had been founded in 1735 and an Imperial Ballet School established in St Petersburg in 1775. At first the influence of Paris was strong, with a succession of ballet masters from there coming to Russia, until one, arriving in St Petersburg in 1801, encouraged the development of a Russian ballet tradition by incorporating their own national dances.

It was in St Petersburg after 1862 that the revival of ballet as an artistic unity occurred, where Marius Petipa worked closely with composers of the music. The great classical ballets with music by Tchaikovsky were produced at this time. The next stage in the development of ballet was due to the great impresario Diaghilev, who gathered around him some of the greatest dancers, musicians and artists of the time – including notably, at various times, Stravinsky as composer and Picasso as designer of backdrops – to create exciting new ballets which he brought to Paris in 1909 and London in 1911. Their success revolutionised ballet everywhere except in Russia, which continued with the classical tradition.

(iii) Ballet in England.

The foundations of ballet in England were laid by two women who had both worked in Diaghilev's company: Marie Rambert as a teacher and Ninette de Valois as a dancer. They created the Ballet Rambert company and the Vic-Wells Company respectively, the forerunners of the modern ballet companies, notably the Royal Ballet.

THE CINEMA

This section provides a brief but wide-ranging introduction to the world of the cinema. It includes sections on how the cinema has evolved, entries on many famous directors, actors and actresses as well as a wide-ranging glossary of key film terms (from cult movie to Hollywood Ten and Ealing comedy). There is also a list of major Oscar Winners.

TABLE OF CONTENTS

THE CINEMA

1. THE EVOLUTION OF THE CINEMA

THE HISTORICAL BACKGROUND

The Lumière Brothers

It was in December 1895 that the Lumière brothers, Louis and Auguste, organised what is generally regarded as the first exhibition of "moving pictures" for admission money. The event was really the culmination of numerous photographic developments that had taken place over the preceeding decades. These included Eadweard Muybridge's famous photographs of horses in motion in 1871; Etienne Julius Marey's development of a so-called "photographic rifle" with which he could take ten pictures a second (the term "shooting" for a film is commonly thought to derive from this); George Eastman's launch in 1888 of the Kodak camera and his development of the celluloid roll film; and Thomas Edison's production in 1891 of the 35mm film and, with his brilliant assistant W.K.L. Dickson, the later development of the Kinetoscope which showed photographic moving pictures in a peepshow.

Georges Méliès

The Lumière brothers owned a factory that manufactured cameras and photographic equipment and envisaged the motion picture primarily as an extension and promotion of this. Their work, mostly documentary with a number of comic or light dramatic set-pieces, is seen as a major precursor of realism in the cinema. Roughly contemporary with them was the stage magician, Georges Méliès who made the first trick films, using a variety of artificial devices and special effects to tell entertaining science and pseudo-historic tales. In some ways, the Lumières and Méliès exemplify the two major tendencies to which the cinema has been drawn throughout its history: film as magic carpet (the Méliès tradition) or film as window on the world (the Lumière tradition), film as dream or film as document.

The Coming of Sound

Despite many innovations (such as three-dimensional cinema, which has made a recent comeback, the technical battery of cinema has remained in many respects remarkably moderate. Special effects, the development of sophisticated animation techniques, quadrophonic sound in certain large city-centre cinemas, and an increasingly sophisticated range of colour techniques are all quantitative rather than qualitative modifications, and plans to enlarge the sensory battery of cinema through pumping appropriate scents in the cinema (and even providing spectators with suitable tactile stimuli) have never developed in any sustained way. The major date in the history of the medium remains 1927, the year of the first sound film (*The Jazz Singer*, with Al Jolson).

Sound was fiercely resisted (by Charlie Chaplin among others), but its possibilities were so rapidly recognised, not least by Rene Clair and Alfred Hitchcock who both made early innovatory use of it, that its survival was never long in jeopardy.

Introduction of Colour

As well as sound, another major technical development was in colour photography. Film prints had been tinted from the earliest days (a fact worth bearing in mind when it is sometimes assumed that all silent films were monochrome) but colour of a high technical standard did not become widely used until after the Second World War. Colour first tended to be used for fantasy or adventure genres or spectaculars such as *Gone With the Wind* (1939), and it was not until the mid 1960s that sales of film to television more or less demanded that every film be made in colour. Nevertheless, there are a number of films that continue to be filmed in black and white, not out of a hostility to colour, but for purposes of, for example, nostalgia (as in Woody Allen's *Manhattan*, 1979 or *Purple Rose of Cairo*, 1985), brutal realism (Scorsese's *Raging Bull*, 1980), pastiche and homage (Tim Burton's *Ed Wood*, 1994) and of dramatic newsreel evocation (as in Spielberg's *Schindler's List* of 1993, with its momentary bursts of colour). A recent example is George Clooney's film about the McCarthyist era, *Good Night and Good Luck* (2005). Colour has also often been used expressively: for example, to evoke a mood (as in Antonioni's *Red Desert* of 1964) or as dramatic motif (the menacing use of red in Nicolas Roeg's *Don't Look Now* of 1973) or to suggest a process of ironic distancing from a set of stylistic conventions (as with the deliberately lurid colours in Douglas Sirk's melodramas).

Although its use has sometimes been unimaginative and blandly naturalistic, colour has become a rich and important part of cinematic language and it has been shown that it can co-exist with black and white, sometimes even in the same film.

The Coming of the Big Screen

Another technical development was that of the big screen—in processes such as Cinerama, Cinemascope, Todd-AO—particularly associated with the fifties and sixties, when Hollywood's response to the threat of television was not necessarily to make movies better but at least to make them wider. Many directors hated this development, feeling that the new screen shape was only suitable for filming duck-shoots or dachshunds and not permitting the kind of concentrated detail a director had formerly required. "You can't get a close-up of a finger nail," commented Alfred Hitchcock disdainfully. Nevertheless, a director like Nicholas Ray (who had noted that every technical advance of the cinema had generally been greeted with dismay) demonstrated in a film like *Rebel Without a Cause* (1955) that it was possible to use colour and widescreen for eloquently expressive purposes. A film like Kenneth Branagh's *Hamlet* (1997) was made in 70mm in an attempt to emulate the visual splendour of epics of three decades earlier, such as *Lawrence of Arabia* (1962).

Computer Animation

In recent years, video technology had made it more possible for new film-makers to engage in comparatively inexpensive, independent and experimental work: experienced directors such as Antonioni, Godard and Chris Marker have also made use of this. But the major advances in the last two decades have been in the area of special effects as generated by new technologies of computer animation. These have brought new virtuosity into the realm of the Disney cartoon; new visual wonders into spectaculars such as *Jurassic Park* (1993), *Men in Black* (1997) and *Gladiator* (2000); and fresh tricks of illusion in their capacity seamlessly to blend live-action and animation or computer re-touching, as seen in the films of Robert Zemeckis such as *Who Framed Roger Rabbit* (1988) and *Forrest Gump* (1994).

The downside of this is the danger that technology for its own sake might come to overwhelm narrative, characterisation, artistic creativity: precisely those qualities which made cinema not simply one of the technological wonders of the twentieth century but its major new art form.

MAJOR DATES AND THEIR SIGNIFICANCE

1895

On 28 December, the Lumière brothers gave the first paying show of films, at the Grand Café in Paris—a programme of documentary and comedy shorts.

1896

2 February—the Lumière programme screened at the Regent Street Polytechnic in London, the first film-show in Britain. Later that year, the British film pioneer, R. W. Paul made a celebrated film of the Derby.

1903

Edwin S. Porter made the most famous of all early silent films, *The Great Train Robbery*, credited as being the first Western and the first film to tell a story. Porter was later to direct a film called *Rescued From an Eagle's Nest* (1907), the leading role being taken by a young actor called Lawrence Griffith who was later to change his initials to DW and his profession to director.

1909

The theatrical producers Klaw and Erlanger forbade their contracted actors to appear in films—a sign both of the way theatre looked down on the movies but also feared their competition.

1910

D. W. Griffith made a film in California, partly to avoid the prohibitive actions against independents by the New York based Motion Pictures Patent Company and partly because of the more favourable climate for filming. It marked the beginning of what was to become Hollywood.

1911

The first fan magazines, *Motion Picture Story Magazine* and *Photoplay* began publication in the USA. The era of the star was about to emerge, particularly when, in an elaborate publicity stunt, the independent producer Carl Laemmle revealed the identity of the 'Biograph girl' as Florence Lawrence.

1912

Adolph Zukor established the Famous Plays Film Company and had a big success with the distribution of *Queen Elizabeth* starring the legendary Sarah Bernhardt. "Mister Zukor," she told him, "you have put the best of me in pickle for all time."

1913

Mack Sennett made his first films from Keystone studios.

1914

The release of the first Chaplin film, *Making a Living*. His first appearance as the Tramp occurred shortly after in *Kid Auto Races at Venice*.

1916

The release of D. W. Griffith's *Intolerance*, whose narrative and technique baffled early audiences but which was to prove an enormous influence on future film makers, such as Eisenstein and Pudovkin.

1917

Chaplin signed a million dollar contract making him the highest paid screen star up to this point.

1919

United Artists formed, with Chaplin, Mary Pickford, Douglas Fairbanks and D. W. Griffiths as partners.

1921

Roscoe "Fatty" Arbuckle was charged with the rape and murder of Virginia Rappe. Although later acquitted on all charges, his career never recovered and it was one of several scandals to rock Hollywood in the early 1920s—*e.g.* the unsolved murder of the director William Desmond Taylor in 1922, the death through morphine addiction of the actor Wallace Reid in 1923. The Arbuckle scandal "drew the lightning on us all," said Gloria Swanson: it reflected the sometimes morbid fascination of the public and the press with film stars that was later to become recognised as part of the price of fame and to have an impact on the development of some film careers (*e.g.* Chaplin, Ingrid Bergman, Marilyn Monroe).

1922

Lenin told the People's Commissar for Education: "Of all the arts, to us cinema is the most important." Robert Flaherty makes *Nanook of the North*, often seen as the first great documentary film.

1925

Director Mauritz Stiller and actress Greta Garbo left Sweden for Hollywood. The year of Eisenstein's film, *The Battleship Potemkin*, revolutionary in both theme and technique.

1927

The dawn of sound. Al Jolson's "You ain't heard nothing yet" in *The Jazz Singer*, were the first words spoken on a film soundtrack.

1928

Mickey Mouse made his first appearance in *Plane Crazy*.

1929

The Great Depression hit the American stock market, but cinema proved resilient.

1933

Following Adolf Hitler's rise to power, Joseph Goebbels became Minister for Information in Germany and assumed total control over the national cinema. Acclaimed director of *Metropolis* (1926) and *M* (1931), Fritz Lang was invited to become head of the national film industry: instead he emigrated to America.

1936

Hollywood's Anti-Nazi League was founded, foremost amongst its members being Dorothy Parker, Fritz Lang and Fredric March. (A decade later the League will be denounced by the newly constituted House UnAmerican Activities Committee as a Communist front.)

1938

Former child star Jackie Coogan (immortalised in Chaplin's *The Kid* of 1921) sued his mother and stepfather for the recovery of earnings in his period of popularity. He won the case but the money was swallowed up in legal costs. (Fifty years on, star of *Home Alone* Macaulay Culkin would experience not dissimilar problems).

1939

The outbreak of the Second World War was marked by the banning of Renoir's *La Règle du Jeu* in France and the departure of many European directors for Hollywood. Fritz Lang had already left; Renoir left France in 1940. A golden year for Hollywood cinema, culminating in the huge success of *Gone with the Wind*.

1940

Tom and Jerry appeared in their first movie, *Puss gets the Boot* and Bugs Bunny asked "What's up, Doc?" in *A Wild Hare*. Meanwhile the British Ministry of Information took over the GPO Film Unit and proceeded to sponsor a major series of wartime documentaries.

1941

Germany invaded Russia, and the entire Soviet industry turned itself over to the war effort. In Hollywood there were two remarkable directing debuts: Orson Welles's *Citizen Kane* and John Huston's *The Maltese Falcon*.

1942

First use of the term "neo-realism" by the Italian critic Umberto Barbaro. Marcel Carné began work on *Les Enfants du Paradis* which took three years to make. One of the reasons for this was that it kept cast and production-team away from the fighting.

1946

The opening of the first Cannes Film Festival—originally planned for 1939 but postponed on account of the war. The peak year for box-office attendance in America (4,500 million entries)..

1947

The US House UnAmerican Activities Committee (HUAC) began hearings in Los Angeles to root out "Communists" (*i.e.* liberals) in the industry. The investigation, begun on 18 October, wreaked enormous personal, financial, and artistic havoc. Cheryl Crawford, Elia Kazan and Lee Strasberg opened the Actors' Studio (home of 'The Method') in New York.

1948

French critic Alexandre Astruc predicted that the cinema would become "a means of writing just as flexible and subtle as written language", in an article that would have a tremendous impact on the French *Nouvelle Vague* directors.

1949

The release of Henry Cornelius's *Passport to Pimlico*, Alexander Mackendrick's *Whisky Galore* and Robert Hamer's *Kind Hearts and Coronets* highlighted a series of distinctive films emanating from Michael Balcon's Ealing Studios, whose humour and superb cast of character-actors ensured their success until the last of the great comedies (*The Ladykillers*) six years later.

1951

Akira Kurosawa's *Rashomon* won the Golden Lion at the Venice Film Festival, introducing the West to Japanese cinema.

1952

Charlie Chaplin, in England for his film *Limelight*, learned his re-entry permit to America had been rescinded, beginning a twenty year period of exile from that country. Twentieth Century Fox announced the imminent launching of their new wide screen system, Cinemascope. 3-D was invented, one of its successes being *House of Wax*, directed by the one-eyed André De Toth.

1956

Satyajit Ray's *Pather Panchali* won a major award at the Cannes Festival, although a young French critic walked out of the screening declaring he was not interested in a film about Indian peasants: his name was Francois Truffaut.

1959

Francois Truffaut's *Les Quatre Cents Coups* and

Godard's *Breathless* inaugurated what came to be known as the French *Nouvelle Vague*.

1960

Kirk Douglas (with *Spartacus*) and Otto Preminger (with *Exodus*) effectively ended the "anti-communist" blacklist when they employed as screenwriter the formerly blacklisted Dalton Trumbo. Antonioni's *L'Avventura* was noisily barracked at the Cannes Film Festival: within eighteen months, he was to be the most fashionable and esteemed director in Europe.

1961

Luis Buñuel invited to return to Spain; he did so with *Viridiana*, infuriating the Franco régime.

1968

Cannes Film Festival ended abruptly when there were demonstrations in support of student protests. In America, the youth rebellion movie of the fifties took on a new lease of life, culminating in the success of Dennis Hopper's *Easy Rider* (1969).

1975

Steven Spielberg had a huge box-office success with *Jaws*, to be topped two years later by his friend and fellow "movie brat" George Lucas, with *Star Wars*.

1987

Bernardo Bertolucci's *The Last Emperor* is the first Western film to be shot in Beijing. It coincided with a new Western interest in Chinese film.

1988

Krzysztof Kieslowski's *A Short Film About Killing* (U.S. title: *Thou Shalt Not Kill*) was voted best film at the first European Film Awards.

1996

Mike Leigh's *Secrets and Lies* won the Golden Palm at the Cannes Film Festival and the director celebrated his victory as a comeback for the modestly priced film that deals with human values. By way of contrast, a Hollywood epic about alien invasion, *Independence Day*—a B-picture in all but inflated cost and special effects grandeur—became the box-office blockbuster of the summer. The death of Krzysztof Kieslowski.

1998

The death of director Akira Kurosawa, one of the giants of post-war cinema. The success of Spielberg's *Saving Private Ryan* sparks a new interest in films about World War Two.

1999

Box office success of *Shakespeare in Love* which goes on to win 7 Oscars. Death of Japanese filmmaker Keisuke Kinoshita.

2000

British theatre director Sam Mendes wins an Oscar for his first film, *American Beauty*. Meanwhile two of the major European talents of the 1990s, Spain's Pedro Almodovar and Denmark's Lars von Trier are also rewarded. Almodovar's *All About My Mother* wins the best foreign film Oscar; Von Trier's *Dancer in the Dark* controversially wins the Golden Palm at Cannes.

2001

Death of American film producer/director Stanley Kramer whose films as producer included *The Wild One* and *High Noon*. Ang Lee makes a huge crossover success, an arthouse martial arts movie,

Crouching Tiger, Hidden Dragon, that wins four Oscars. Steven Spielberg completes *A.I.*

2004

Lord of the Rings: Return of the King triumphs at Oscars. Mel Gibson's *The Passion of the Christ* is a huge success.

2007

Dame Helen Mirren wins Best Actress Oscar for her role in *The Queen*. (First British actress to win this award since Emma Thompson in 1992). Deaths of two towering giants of European cinema, Michelangelo Antonioni and Ingmar Bergman.

2008

Deaths of Oscar-winning directors Anthony Minghella and Sydney Pollack.

2009

Triumph for *Slumdog Millionaire* (taking 8 Oscars); Kate Winslet finally wins coveted Best Actress award.

2010

Death of French New Wave director Eric Rohmer, best-known for *My Night at Maud's* and *Claire's Knee*. *Avatar* becomes the biggest grossing film of all time (surpassing James Cameron's other huge hit, *Titanic*). Death of Chabrol.

2011

Triumph for *The King's Speech* at the Oscars in

February 2011. Death of screen legend Elizabeth Taylor. Other deaths in 2011 included Ken Russell, Susannah York and Bollywood legend Dev Anand.

2012

Deaths of film producers Richard Zanuck and Tony Scott (whose films included *Top Gun*).

2013

Bollywood celebrates its centenary. Daniel Day-Lewis wins record third Best Actor at Oscars. Deaths of Bryan Forbes and Peter O'Toole.

2014

Death of Shirley Temple, Hollywood's favourite child actress. Deaths of Mickey Rooney, Robin Williams and Lauren Bacall.

2015

Death of Mike Nichols, Oscar-winning director of *The Graduate* (1967) *Frozen* becomes the highest grossing animated film of all time. *Volte face* by Sony Pictures over *The Interview*. Deaths of Omar Sharif, Anita Ekberg (famous for *La Dolce Vita*), Sam Goldwyn Jr. and Maureen O'Hara

2016

Deaths of Robert Vaughn, Gene Wilder, Zsa Zsa Gabor (better known for her nine marriages) and Debbie Reynolds.

2017

Fiasco over best picture. Mahershala Ali becomes first Muslim actor to win an Oscar.

2.   THE LEADING CINEMA DIRECTORS

Allen, Woody (b. 1935)

Woody Allen first achieved star status as an actor in movies he himself directed, playing a walking worry-bead who wore his urban anxiety like a red badge of courage. Films like *Take the Money and Run* (1969), *Bananas* (1971) and *Love and Death* (1975) seemed to align him with prior film farceurs like his favourite, Bob Hope. He became more ambitious and intellectual, with films such as *Annie Hall* (1977) and *Stardust Memories* (1980) being anguished as well as amusing self-portraits, and *Interiors* (1978) being a study of family breakdown closer to Chekhov than Chaplin. Films such as *Zelig* (1983) and *The Purple Rose of Cairo* (1985) have shown him to be the technical equal of any contemporary American director, whilst *Hannah and her Sisters* (1986) and *Crimes and Misdemeanours* (1989) have the philosophical density of a Russian novel.

However, after *Husbands and Wives* (1992) and a bitter and much publicised split with his partner Mia Farrow, he has returned to comedy, spicing the humour with considerable formal adventurousness for a dwindling but loyal following. A film made in Britain, *Match Point* (2005) was his most acclaimed in years, unlike *Cassandra's Dream* (2007).

Almodovar, Pedro (b. 1951)

Almodovar came to international attention with *Women on the Verge of a Nervous Breakdown* (1988), which won numerous awards and was a typical example of what has since been called "Almodrama"—emotionally extravagant and sexually outrageous stories that revel in passionate extremes and narrative quirkiness. A film-maker of the post-Franco era whose work has tended to ignore or reject his country's political past, Almodovar's recent films have shown a new depth and compassion in their exploration of the hidden by-ways of love. *Talk to Her* (2002) won him a best screenwriting Oscar. Other key films: *Matador*

(1986), *Tie Me Up! Tie Me Down!* (1990), *High Heels* (1991), *Live Flesh* (1998), *All About My Mother* (1999), *Bad Education* (2004), *Volver* (2006), *The Skin I live in* (2011) and, most recently, *Live Flesh* (2015).

Altman, Robert (1925–2006)

Innovative, iconoclastic director who shot to prominence with the military comedy *M:A:S:H* (1970), and then proceeded to subvert some of America's major film genres, notably in his western *McCabe and Mrs. Miller* (1971), which was more about the rise of capitalism than the growth of civilisation, and in his private-eye movie, *The Long Goodbye* (1973), where he debunked Raymond Chandler's knight-errant hero, Philip Marlowe. His epic and ironic fresco on the American Dream, *Nashville* (1975) was a highpoint when after that he became ever more esoteric and experimental. Nevertheless, in films like his imaginative realisation of the play, *Come Back to the Five and Dime, Jimmy Dean, Jimmy Dean* (1982), and the made-for-TV biopic of Van Gogh, *Vincent and Theo* (1990), he showed he could still spring some surprises.

His Hollywood satire, *The Player* (1992) was his most acclaimed film for a decade; his ambitious adaptation of Raymond Carver short stories, *Short Cuts* (1994) was no less impressive; and his country house satire *Gosford Park* (2001) was both a critical and commercial success. He was awarded an honorary Oscar in 2006.

Antonioni, Michelangelo (1912–2007)

Antonioni was the director who made alienation fashionable in the early 1960s with his trilogy *L'Avventura* (1960), *La Notte* (1961) and *The Eclipse* (1962), which explored the gap between his characters' material affluence and their spiritual impoverishment. He also gave alienation a palpable visual form, each shot an eloquent comment on the tension between protagonist and environment.

These films remain his greatest achievement, and in Monica Vitti he found a leading lady whose haunted performances greatly enhanced the emotional impact of his work. His other major films include *Le Amiche—The Girl Friends* (1955), *The Red Desert* (1964), *Blow-Up* (1966) and *The Passenger* (1975).

Bergman, Ingmar (1918–2007)

The definitive example of the film artist, by virtue of the maturity and complexity of his themes and of the control he had over all aspects of his films—writing, casting *etc*. Since he established his international reputation with a trio of masterly works in the 1950s—*Smiles of a Summer Night* (1955), *The Seventh Seal* (1956) and *Wild Strawberries* (1957)—he enjoyed almost complete creative freedom. Films like *The Seventh Seal*, *Through a Glass Darkly* (1960) and *Winter Light* (1962) test the validity of an individual's religious faith in a world of fearful cruelty, whilst a masterpiece like *Persona* (1966) is a revelatory study of character and creativity, superbly acted by Bibi Andersson and Liv Ullmann. There are those who criticise Bergman for the narrowness of his social range, his limited political vision, his spiritual masochism. But to Bergman the camera eye was the window of the soul and few have probed more deeply to the roots of human personality. And it is not all Scandinavian gloom. In *Fanny and Alexander* (1983), he created a wonderful reminder of his story-telling gifts, his rich visual sense, and his capacity to embrace life with all its pain, perils, and pleasures.

Bergman's autobiography, *The Magic Lantern* was published in 1988; and his screenplay about the early life of his parents, *Best Intentions* (1992) was memorably filmed by Bille August. Another screenplay, *Faithless* (2000) has been directed by Liv Ullmann and he himself returned to direction with *Sarabande* (2005).

Bertolucci, Bernardo (b. 1940)

The Italian Communist Party evolved in the seventies the conception of the "historic compromise"—a tactical alliance on the part of a self-styled revolutionary party with progressive reformist forces. Bertolucci's aesthetic strategy can be seen as an (unconscious?) embodiment of this—a "message" of revolution often clothed in the glossy, star-studded forms of bourgeois Hollywood cinema, as in the two-part *1900* of 1976. Likewise, in *Last Tango in Paris* (1972), the brutal sexual frankness for which the film rapidly became notorious is cushioned by the reassuring Hollywood deep-orange glow in which the scenes are shot and the presence of attested Hollywood rebel Marlon Brando. He won an Oscar for the opulent epic, *The Last Emperor* (1987), and *The Dreamers* (2003) was a return to form, but his best films are his early works—*Before the Revolution* (1964), *The Spider's Stratagem* (1970), *The Conformist* (1970)—which combine an incisive political and psychological analysis with a poetic and lyrical style.

Brooks, Richard (1912–92)

Leading writer-director of the postwar American cinema. Author of the novel on which the film *Crossfire* (1947) was based and co-writer on Huston's powerful allegory *Key Largo* (1948), Brooks made his directing debut in 1950 and became a specialist in accessible, highly charged adaptations of literary classics. His best film is *Elmer Gantry* (1960), an incisive dissection of American evangelism that won Oscars for Brooks (as screenwriter) and its star, Burt Lancaster and features the characteristic Brooks protagonist: a dynamic, divided individualist treading a tightrope between redemption and damnation. Key films: *Blackboard Jungle* (1955), *Cat on a Hot Tin Roof* (1958), *Sweet Bird of Youth* (1962), *Lord Jim* (1965), *The Professionals* (1966), *In Cold Blood* (1967).

Buñuel, Luis (1900–83)

Buñuel began his career by collaborating with

Salvador Dali on a surrealist short, *Un Chien Andalou* (1928) and then scandalised audiences with *L'Age d'Or* (1930), which attacked the Church ("Thank God I'm an atheist", Buñuel declared) and bourgeois morality (which Buñuel always found deeply immoral). A powerful, hallucinatory film about violence and poverty in the slums, *Los Olvidados* (1950) launched a second phase of his career, and his religious assaults were continued in *El* (1953), which equated religious orthodoxy with emotional repression, and *Nazarin* (1958) and *Viridiana* (1961), which showed the impossibility of a modern Christ surviving in today's society. In his final years, he took pleasure not so much in savaging the bourgeoisie as in, metaphorically speaking, poisoning their food, serving them a dainty cultural dish with a sinister undertaste. *Belle de Jour* (1967), *Tristana* (1970) and *The Discreet Charm of the Bourgeoisie* (1972) are all slyly subversive, surreal works, dealing with the split between appearance and reality, decorum and desire. He believed man was unconsciously a slave to custom and to social orthodoxy and, with his enthusiasm for symbols and the world of dreams, which reveal the hidden fears and desires of modern man, Buñuel did everything in his power to shock man out of his complacency. His impish spirit was also revealed in his appropriately liberating autobiography, *My Last Breath*, published in 1983.

Capra, Frank (1897–1991)

The films of Sicilian-born Frank Capra embodied the American Dream. His major works were comedies with a strong moral lesson, and their message of optimism over adversity cheered up audiences during the Depression. His films were essentially variations on David and Goliath, with the common man victorious over seemingly insurmountable odds. His main characters, such as Gary Cooper's Mr. Deeds in *Mr. Deeds Goes To Town* (1936) or James Stewart's Mr. Smith in *Mr Smith Goes to Washington* (1939) were innocent idealists who vanquished the cynical, the crooked and the corrupt. After winning three directing Oscars in the 1930s, Capra never recovered his popularity after World War Two and retired after *A Pocketful of Miracles* in 1961. His testament is the aptly entitled *It's A Wonderful Life* (1946), a beautiful fantasy, with dark undertones.

Carné, Marcel (1909–96)

Carné occupied a role in the immediately pre-war cinema in many ways similar to that of Antonioni in the early sixties—the poet of an age's style of despair, whose fatalism receives tangible support and embodiment from the skilful use of decor and architecture. In Carné's case these were entirely studio-bound (his mature masterpieces eschewed location filming entirely), which may be one reason why his output has dated compared with, say, Renoir's. But *Quai des Brumes* (1938) and *Le Jour Se Leve* (1939) provide atmospheric frameworks for the acting of Jean Gabin, and *Les Enfants du Paradis* (1945), the three-and-a-half-hour tale of lost love and cynicism in the theatrical world of nineteenth-century Paris, remains exciting through its amalgam of "period" style and a tortured consciousness evocative of the time at which it was made. With Rene Clement (director of *Jeux Interdits*, 1952) and Henri-Georges Clouzot (maker of *Wages of Fear*, 1952 and *Les Diaboliques*, 1955) Carné fell out of fashion at the time of the less studio-and-script-bound films of the *Nouvelle Vague*, but in 1979, French critics voted *Les Enfants du Paradis* as the best French film ever made.

Cassavetes, John (1929–89)

Actor-director who, with associates such as his actress-wife Gena Rowlands and actor-friends such as Peter Falk and Ben Gazzara, made offbeat films that focused more on intimate relationships than exciting narrative. Improvisational and unashamedly indulgent, the films have been an inspiration to independent film-makers wishing to eschew the mainstream. Films include: *Shadows* (1960), *Faces* (1968), *Husbands* (1970), *A Woman Under the Influence* (1974), *Killing of a Chinese Bookie* (1976), *Love Streams* (1982).

Chabrol, Claude (1930–2010)

Like Godard and Truffaut, Chabrol first distinguished himself as an abrasive and articulate critic on the magazine *Cahiers du Cinema* before branching into direction. With Eric Rohmer (later also to become a director), he also wrote an influential book at this time on the films of Alfred Hitchcock. Hitchcock has been a strong influence on Chabrol's films, which are often cynical detective stories or psychological suspense thrillers set against carefully observed French provincial settings. He is a cool anatomist of the discreet charms and deadly passions of the bourgeoisie. His key films include *Les Cousins* (1958), *Les Bonnes Femmes* (1960), *Les Biches* (1968), *La Femme Infidele* (1969), *Killer!— Que la Bete meure* (1969), *Les Noces Rouges* (1973) and his best film, *Le Boucher* (1970). More recent work, such as *Judgment in Stone* (1994), adapted from a novel by Ruth Rendell, and *Merci Pour Le Chocolat* (2000) shows he has lost none of his animosity to the bourgeois nor his capacity to disturb.

Chen, Kaige (b. 1952)

With Zhang Yimou, the leading director of the so-called 'fifth generation' of film makers who graduated from the Beijing Film Academy in 1982, following its re-opening after Mao Tse-Tung's Cultural Revolution. His first film, *Yellow Earth* (1984) made an impact in the West comparable to that of *Rashomon* and *Pather Panchali* in its revelation of a new national cinema, and his reputation was consolidated by *Farewell My Concubine* (1993), which shared the top prize at Cannes with *The Piano* and was nominated for an Oscar. However, his first Hollywood film, *Killing Me Softly* (2002) was widely deemed a soft-porn disaster. Other films: *The Big Parade* (1985), *King of the Children* (1987), *Life on a string* (1991), *Temptress Moon* (1997), *The Emperor and the Assassin* (2000).

Clair, Rene (1898–1981)

The first great European musical director. His early interest in asynchronous sound (*i.e.* that which does not always correspond to what we see going on on the screen) led him to attach equal importance to natural noise and music and to dialogue in his early sound films (such as *Sous les Toits de Paris* of 1930). A delight in dance—the choreographed quality of fights, chases and crowd scenes—permeates his two most successful works, *Le Million* and the simplistic but vivacious satire on industrialisation, *A Nous la Liberté* (both 1931) which greatly influenced Chaplin's *Modern Times*.

Cocteau, Jean (1889–1963)

Cocteau was a poet who expressed himself variously in fiction, drama, painting and drawing as well as through the cinema. *Beauty and the Beast* (1946) was an imaginative telling of the familiar tale, with Jean Marais both frightening and poignant as the Beast. In *Orphée* of 1950 he produced one of the cinema's unquestioned fantastic masterpieces, using mirrors as links between the world of the living and that of the dead to great effect, and playing upon the connection between love and death in a way that must have influenced the makers of *Last Year in Marienbad* (Resnais and Robbe-Grillet) eleven years later.

Coen, Joel (b. 1958)

With his brother Ethan (who co-writes and produces), Joel Coen has fashioned some of the most original modern American films, darkly comic, densely plotted dramas that blend passion with pastiche. Their acclaimed film, *No Country for Old Men* (2007) won the Oscar for best film. Key films: *Blood Simple* (1983), *Raising Arizona* (1987), *Miller's Crossing* (1990), *Barton Fink* (1991), *Fargo* (1996), *O Brother, Where Art Thou* (2000), *The Man Who Wasn't There* (2001).

Coppola, Francis Ford (b. 1939)

The Godfather of modern American cinema, confidante and father-figure to the new generation of directors (such as George Lucas and Steven Spielberg) who emerged from film school to storm Hollywood in the early 1970s. Coppola's *The Godfather* (1972) and *The Godfather, Part II* (1974) combined the sweep of a dynastic family melodrama with a mature political analysis of corporate America. The former restored Marlon Brando to superstardom; the latter made stars of Al Pacino and Robert De Niro. Two other major films of the decade were *The Conversation* (1974), a tale of treacherous tapes and an atmosphere of paranoia that evoked Watergate; and *Apocalypse Now* (1979), in which America's incursion into Vietnam was interpreted as a mad, metaphysical journey into the heart of darkness. Since then Coppola has seemed something of a lost soul, searching for inspiration, marking time and, with *Godfather III* (1990) and a revised, extended version of *Apocalypse Now* (premiered at Cannes in 2001) revisiting old haunts. His daughter Sofia is a talented director

Costa Gavras, Constantin (b. 1933)

The cinema's specialist director of the political thriller, throwing up large social issues of corruption and responsibility under the guise of suspense melodrama. He achieved international prominence with *Z* (1969), an indictment of the repressive regime in Greece, and he has had equal success in the mainstream commercial cinema, particularly with *Missing* (1982) and *Music Box* (1989). His film *Amen* (2002), was a typically controversial critique of the Catholic church's failure to attack the Holocaust.

Cronenberg, David (b. 1943)

Canada's most controversial film export, whose early reputation was made with stomach-churning, mind-exploding horror films. Critical respectability came with *The Fly* (1986) and *Dead Ringers* (1988), which married the gore with intellect and compassion, but controversy flared again over his adaptation of J. G. Ballard's notorious novel about eroticism and the automobile, *Crash* (1996). *Spider* (2002) was shown to great acclaim at the Cannes Film Festival. He has had some success with more mainstream films, such as *A History of Violence* (2005) and *Eastern Promises* (2007).

Cukor, George (1899–1983)

Cukor came to Hollywood from directing on the New York stage, and this theatrical background was an important clue to his work. His films were often adaptations of plays, like *Gaslight* (1944); he was always intrigued by theatrical people indulging a flair for the dramatic, either on stage, like Ronald Colman in *A Double Life* (1947), or in a courtroom, like Spencer Tracy and Katherine Hepburn in *Adam's Rib* (1949); and his films are particularly remembered for their performances, *e.g.* Greta Garbo's in *Camille* (1937) or Judy Garland's in *A Star is Born* (1954). Cukor was one of the most civilised of Hollywood directors, versatile and visually stylish, but particularly revelling in the sex-war comedies of Tracy and Hepburn, such as *Adam's Rib* and *Pat and Mike* (1952).

Curtiz, Michael (1888–1962)

Hungarian-born super-professional of Hollywood's heyday. He began his association with Warner Brothers in 1926, making over a hundred films there of every conceivable genre and with stars such as Errol Flynn, James Cagney and Humphrey Bogart. His famous films include *Angels With Dirty Faces* (1938), *Yankee Doodle Dandy* (1942), *Mildred Pierce* (1945) and the immortal *Casablanca* (1943).

De Mille, Cecil B. (1881–1959)

An innovative director in the silent era, Cecil B. De Mille became indelibly associated in his later career with bigness in the movies. His gigantic epics include *The Sign of the Cross* with Charles Laughton in 1932, and two spectacularly tasteless versions of *The Ten Commandments* (1923 and 1956). The films themselves matter less nowadays than the reputation for scale and the consistently successful box-office returns. Joseph L. Mankiewicz observed: "He had his finger up the pulse of America."

De Sica, Vittorio (1902–74)

Although he began his screen career as an actor, Vittorio De Sica is remembered principally for a remarkable group of films he made immediately after World War II, collaborating with writer Cesare Zavattini on works which are regarded as key examples of Italian neo-realism; *Shoeshine* (1946), *Bicycle Thieves* (1948) and *Umberto D* (1952). These sympathetic studies of the poor were heavily criticised in their own country (for political simplemindedness by the Left and for unflattering and unpatriotic portraiture of Italy by the Right) but were widely acclaimed abroad. With the decline of neo-realism in the early 1950s, De Sica was never to scale the same heights, though he did direct Sophia Loren to an Oscar winning performance in *Two Women* (1961), and experienced critical acclaim for two of his final films, *The Garden of the Finzi Continis* (1971) and *A Brief Vacation* (1973).

Dreyer, Carl Theodor (1889–1968)

Dreyer is still regarded as the greatest artist in the history of Danish cinema, though it was in France that he directed his first masterpiece, *The Passion of Joan of Arc* (1928), with its remarkable leading performance by Renee Falconetti in her only screen role. The austerity and apparent Protestant guilt that pervade his work compare interestingly with Robert Bresson's Catholic severity. Dreyer's last film, *Gertrud* (1964) was derided at its premiere, but it is now regarded as one of his finest works, both for its steady satire of the bourgeoisie and its sympathy with women and hatred of their oppression. The slowness of his work still causes difficulty, but the fantastical quality of *Vampyr* (1932), and the undercutting of fanaticism in *Days of Wrath* (1943) and *Ordet/The Word* (1955) are nowadays widely appreciated.

Eisenstein, Sergei (1898–1948)

A prominent theorist as well as practitioner, Eisenstein's Marxist awareness of society as founded upon conflict rather than harmony led him to develop a theory of *montage*, or meaning built up by collision and clash of images. This theory found illustration in what are at the same time highly effective Socialist propaganda films: *The Battleship Potemkin* of 1925, whose massacre-sequence on the steps of the port of Odessa is among the most famous in cinematic history; *October* of 1927 (in which the Menshevik or moderate leader Kerensky is denigrated when his image is followed by that of a peacock—an example of the *montage* technique); and the more contorted and baroque *Ivan the Terrible* (Part one, 1942; Part two, 1945). This last caused Eisenstein to fall into disfavour with Stalin (who may have taken the portrait of the tyrant Ivan to be a reflection upon himself), and the financial difficulties and persecution because of his homosexuality led to his premature death of a heart attack. "Of all the arts", said Lenin, "for us the cinema is the most important." In Soviet Russia its most important voice was Eisenstein who, in finding filmic forms to express collectivism and brotherhood, gave substance to a national ideology.

Fassbinder, Rainer Werner (1946–82)

Phenomenally prolific director of the German cinema of the 1970s, Fassbinder's films at their best combined the political commitment of a Godard with the heady melodrama of a Hollywood director he much admired, Douglas Sirk. His best film is probably *The Marriage of Maria Braun* (1979), an extraordinary allegory of the history of post-war Germany. His best melodramatic films are *The Merchant of Four Seasons* (1972), *The Bitter Tears of Petra von Kant* (1972), *Fear Eats the Soul* (1974) and *Veronika Voss* (1981).

Fellini, Federico (1920–93)

Fellini was an example of the director as star, delighting in treading a thin line between self-expression and self-indulgence. The films recall his early experience in the circus and as a cartoonist, being populated by grotesques and having a unique mixture of risk and spectacle, fantasy and fact. *I Vitelloni* (1953), a semi-autobiographical account of his wastrel adolescent days, established Fellini's reputation; it was enhanced by the international success of his next film, *La Strada* (1954), a parable of body and spirit, love and salvation. With *La Dolce Vita* (1960), a sensational view of contemporary Roman society, Fellini entered his decadent

phase, which was to be continued in such films as *Fellini Satyricon* (1969) and *Fellini's Casanova* (1976). His most highly regarded films are his most autobiographical, *8½* (1963), in which a film director encounters a creative crisis and ransacks his past for inspiration, and *Amarcord* (1973) which is a remembrance of his childhood.

Flaherty, Robert (1884–1951)

Often referred to as the "father of film documentary", Flaherty was actually as much a Romantic as a realist. He has been criticised for the political absences in his movies but he was not a polemicist but a poet, making films that were either hymns to a vanishing way of life or recorded elemental struggles between Man and Nature. His best films were his first, and last: respectively, *Nanook of the North* (1922) and *Louisiana Story* (1948).

Ford, John (1895–1973)

"My name's John Ford," he said. "I make Westerns." He not only made them: he transformed them into poetic statements of the American spirit. Particularly celebrated are those he made starring John Wayne: *Stagecoach* (1939), an odyssey of Western outcasts across hostile territory; *The Searchers* (1956), in which Wayne's bitter racialism is eventually tamed; and *The Man Who Shot Liberty Valance* (1962) which pits Wayne against James Stewart. But he also excelled with Henry Fonda (*Drums Along the Mohawk* of 1939, and in non-Western films (*The Grapes of Wrath*, 1940). His greatest limitation is that he is pre-eminently a man's director, whose bourbon-soaked camaraderie and stress on tough, determined action in some of his less successful films palls rapidly. His greatest strengths are as the unsurpassed chronicler of pioneering America and as the sympathetic observer of the endurance of the common people; and his insights into prejudice, injustice and the tragedy of destroyed families. "This is the West, sir", says the newspaper editor of *Liberty Valance*. "When the legend becomes fact, print the legend". Ford printed the legend better than anyone. Other key films: *The Informer* (1935), *The Prisoner of Shark Island* (1936), *How Green Was My Valley* (1941), *My Darling Clementine* (1946), *Fort Apache* (1948) and *The Quiet Man* (1952).

Forman, Milos (b. 1932)

Forman was one of a group of directors of the so-called Czech New Wave of the 1960s, whose comedies such as *A Blonde in Love* (1965) and *The Fireman's Ball* (1967) audaciously satirised authority, both parental and political. In Paris in 1968 when the Soviet tanks rolled into Prague and there was a clampdown on artistic expression, Forman eventually emigrated to America, where he continued to score notable successes with offbeat films, most famously with *One Flew Over the Cuckoo's Nest* (1975) and *Amadeus* (1984).

Fuller, Samuel (1912–97)

A ferocious action director, castigated as neo-Fascist by his adversaries and lauded by his advocates for the tough, unsparing economy and desperate honesty of his work. Fuller worked across different genres, including the spy-thriller (*Pickup on South Street*, 1953) and the Western (*Run of the Arrow*, 1957). In *Shock Corridor* of 1963, his finest and most revelatory work, he combined the investigative-journalist picture with the drama of psychological horror to create an unnerving dissection of American prejudices and fears. His later films were few and far between, though *White Dog* (1983) showed that, given the opportunity, Fuller had lost none of his bite. His was tabloid cinema, done with tremendous verve, admired by modern directors.

Gance, Abel (1889–1981)

"The day of the Image has arrived", proclaimed Abel Gance at the triumphant premiere of his five-and-a-half-hour epic, *Napoleon* (1927), which deployed superimposition, slow-motion, split-screen, colour, and a triple-screen process, Polyvision, that anticipated Cinerama by nearly thirty years. Alas, Gance was mistaken: sound was round the corner and the visual innovations of *Napoleon* were rendered virtually obsolete before they had begun. Not until the film's restoration in 1980 was Gance's achievement appreciated and his own reputation restored as a great innovator of the silent screen.

Godard, Jean-Luc (b. 1930)

"We are the children of Marx and Coca-Cola", claimed Godard in the 1960s, when he seemed the most radical, innovative and controversial director in world cinema. The turning-point was *Weekend* (1967), an apocalyptic black-comedy of chaos and cannibalism, of social and cultural breakdown. From his early films, which were often love letters to the Hollywood cinema, he had moved to an alternative political cinema that seemed to demand not audiences but disciples. His influence on all spheres of alternative, independent, avant-garde film theory and practice continues to be immense. Other key films: *Breathless* (1959), *Vivre sa Vie* (1962), *Le Mepris-Contempt* (1963), *Une Femme Mariee* (1964), *Pierrot le Fou* (1965), *Tout Va Bien* (1972) and *Bridges of Sarajevo* (2014).

Griffith, D. W. (1875–1948)

Griffith more than any other individual was responsible for the cinema moving from short one and two-reelers to the grand epic scale. *The Birth of a Nation* (1915), despite overt racism, was the most exciting attempt the cinema had hitherto made to capture and reconstruct the course of historical events, and broke all box-office records as well as profoundly influencing Eisenstein. Its successor, *Intolerance* (1916), was even more grandiose and cost unimaginable sums by the standards of those days. Apart from *Broken Blossoms* (1919) and *Way Down East* (1920), Griffith's later films were undistinguished and his career ended in a prolonged, drink-sodden decline. Although sometimes criticised for his Victorian melodrama, Griffith is more properly remembered for his popularisation of feature-length narrative; his revelation of the creative possibilities of montage; and his encouragement of a new subtlety and realism in screen performance. He was the first figure to give this new mass medium intellectual respectability.

Hamer, Robert (1911–63)

The problem child of Ealing studios, whose career was to decline due to alcoholism and what producer Michael Balcon was to call Hamer's "self-destructive streak", but who was responsible for at least three classics of British film: "The Haunted Mirror" episode from *Dead of Night* (1945); the neo-realist melodrama about the London underworld, *It Always Rains on Sunday* (1947); and, above all, the black comedy, *Kind Hearts and Coronets* (1949) in which Dennis Price purrs through some of the most suavely literate dialogue in British cinema as he attempts to kill off eight Alec Guinnesses on his way to a dukedom.

Hawks, Howard (1896–1977)

One of the most versatile and consistent operators within the Hollywood studio system. Whatever genre he worked in, it was transmuted and made more ambiguous. Thus the Western *Rio Bravo* (1959) contains a minimum of big-scale outdoor action and a maximum of charged conversation; private-eye classic *The Big Sleep* (1946) is concerned with Bogart's process of ironic self-discovery rather than with who-dunnit (a question to which Hawks himself never worked out the answer); and the action in the civil-aviation drama *Only Angels Have Wings* (1939) takes place predominantly on the ground. His comedies, notably those with Cary Grant, hilariously subvert sex stereotypes, as in *Bringing Up Baby* (1938), *His Girl Friday* (1940) and *I Was a Male War Bride* (1949).

Herzog, Werner (b. 1942)

One of the most exciting of the new German directors in the 1970s, his treatment of madness is particularly penetrating. This is normally undertaken within the context of a part-historical, part-fictional society, as with the paranoia of the sixteenth-century Amazon conquistador in *Aguirre, Wrath of God* (1972), the scandalous insights of the supposed "savage" in *The Enigma of Kaspar Hauser*

(1974), and the odd symbiosis between predator and victim in his Murnau remake *Nosferatu the Vampyre* (1978). "Dreams move mountains", says Herzog: it is his philosophy of cinema. Other films: *Grizzly Man* (2005) and *The Bad Lieutenant* (2010).

Hitchcock, Sir Alfred (1899–1980)

For half a century Hitchcock was the acknowledged master of mystery and suspense, whose coldly planned delight in playing on his audience's nerves has occasioned violent disagreement between those who see him as the medium's leading exponent of predestination and those for whom he is but a limited practical joker in bad taste. *Psycho* (1960) remains the most notorious film, less now perhaps for the murder of Janet Leigh in her shower than for the *coup de grace* when the murderer's "real identity" is revealed near the end. *North by North-West* of the previous year is among his most accomplished works, a comic spy-thriller based (like so much that is funniest in Hollywood cinema) on a mistake involving the identity of Cary Grant.

Sexually perverse or tabooed areas which the conventional narrative cinema perforce ignored or treated as marginal assume central (though often implicit) places in his work, *cf.* the latent homosexuality in *Strangers on a Train* (1951), the Grand Guignol parody of an Oedipus complex in *Psycho* and the treatment of repression and the traumatic return of what has been "forgotten" (*i.e.* repressed) in *Marnie* (1964). In recent years his early English films have been revalued and upgraded, and the sexual politics of his films have been analysed. His earliest surviving film, *The White Shadow* (1924) was rediscovered in 2011.

He continues to fascinate because of the multi-sided personality of his work, which reveals at once the mask of a joker of genius, a nihilist, a Catholic moralist, a Freudian sexual psychologist and, in his greatest work, *Vertigo* (1958) an anguished romantic. In 2012, indeed, *Vertigo* was voted the greatest film of all time – a fitting tribute.

Other key films include: *Blackmail* (1929), *The Thirty-Nine Steps* (1935), *Sabotage* (1937), *The Lady Vanishes* (1938), *Rebecca* (1940), *Shadow of a Doubt* (1943), *Notorious* (1946), *Rope* (1948), *Rear Window* (1954) and *The Birds* (1963). For a recent biography, see Peter Ackroyd, *Alfred Hitchcock* (2015).

Huston, John (1906–87)

1941 marked two of the most sensationally successful debuts in directorial history—Orson Welles with *Citizen Kane* and Huston's *The Maltese Falcon*, an elegantly perverse private-eye tale in which double-crosses occur at a bewildering rate, thereby setting the mould for the *film noir* that was so prominent later in the decade. Huston's career intermittently maintained this initial impetus, though public and critical reception of his works was not always judicious: *Freud: The Secret Passion* (1962), a remarkable drama ahead of its time, was ill received, whereas *The African Queen*, for which Bogart won an Oscar in 1952, is an overrated, though entertaining, film. Huston was intrigued by over-reachers, people who pursue their dreams to the point of obsession. Even when their obsessions blow up in their faces, as they do in two of his best films, *The Treasure of the Sierra Madre* (1948) and *The Man who would be King* (1975), Huston is still impressed by the grandeur of human aspiration, by the ironies of courage and cowardice, by the stirring way humanity challenges its fate. His work was uneven but his career ended on a high note: a typically literate adaptation of a literary classic, *Under the Volcano* (1984); an impish Mafia black comedy, *Prizzi's Honor* (1985); and a serene rendering of James Joyce's elegiac short story, *The Dead* (1987).His direction also helped win Oscars for his family: for father Walter in *Sierra Madre*, and for daughter Anjelica in *Prizzi's Honor*. Other films: *Key Largo* (1948), *Moby Dick* (1956), *The Misfits* (1961), *Reflections in a Golden Eye* (1967), *Fat City* (1972), *Wise Blood* (1979).

Kazan, Elia (1909–2003)

Dynamic director who founded the Actor's Studio with Lee Strasberg and is responsible for bringing the Method style of acting into the American cinema. His association on three films with Marlon Brando—*A Streetcar named Desire* (1951), *Viva*

Zapata (1952) and *On the Waterfront* (1954)—was significant for its establishment of the prototype Kazan hero: a rebel, anguished and ambivalent about his personal situation and social responsibilities but with a tremendous drive to solve his problems. *On the Waterfront* was particularly controversial for its so-called "glorification of the informer" (an ex-Communist, Kazan had named names to the House UnAmerican Activities Committee in 1952). He also directed James Dean in *East of Eden* (1955), Montgomery Clift in *Wild River* (1960) and Robert De Niro in *The Last Tycoon* (1976), though in his later years he occupied himself mainly in writing novels and a revelatory autobiography, *A Life*. Amid much controversy, he was awarded an honorary Oscar in 1999.

Kiarostami, Abbas (b.1940)

A leading figure of the new Iranian cinema. *Close-Up* (1989), an ironic and technically adroit story (based on fact) of a movie fanatic who impersonates a film director, first brought him to the attention of critics in the West. Since then, his films have been widely praised for their humanistic observation (often compared with that of directors such as Renoir, De Sica and Satyajit Ray) and their sympathetic insights into modern Iranian society. Key films include: *The Traveller* (1974), *Where is My Friend's House?* (1987), *Homework* (1989), *And Life Goes On* (1992), *A Taste of Cherry* (1997), *The Wind Will Carry Us* (1999), *Ten* (2002).

Kieslowski, Krzysztof (1941–96)

The greatest Polish directors, like Andrzej Wajda and Krzysztof Zanussi, see cinema as the nation's social conscience, the art-form that most courageously interrogates the country's moral and political values. Kieslowski was in that tradition and is best known abroad for his contemporary TV films on the theme of the Ten Commandments, two of which were expanded to feature-film length: *A Short Film About Killing* (1988) and *A Short Film About Love* (1989); and for his *Three Colours* trilogy, *Blue* (1993), *White* (1993) and *Red* (1994), which for some critics represents the finest achievement of European cinema in the 1990s. Other key films include: *Camera Buff* (1979), *No End* (1984), *The Double Life of Veronique* (1991).

Kubrick, Stanley (1928–99)

For Kubrick, the cinema was a laboratory for observation and experiment and his findings provoked more critical debate than any American director since Orson Welles. Two films in the 1960s particularly confirmed his extraordinary gifts: the nuclear comedy, *Dr. Strangelove* (1964), which showed the tension between man and the machine; and his sci-fi epic, *2001: A Space Odyssey* (1968), a vast enigmatic meditation on evolution and the degree to which man has been mastered by the technology he has created. His following two films, *A Clockwork Orange* (1971) and *Barry Lyndon* (1975) were amongst the most controversial of the next decade, the former for its violence in depicting the issue of free-will, the latter for its sumptuousness in anatomising high society at the end of the eighteenth-century. Some were disappointed with his labyrinthine horror film, *The Shining* (1980) and his Vietnam movie *Full Metal Jacket* (1987), but until his death he remained a key figure in modern film, analysing the tensions between the individual and history, man and science, language and social conditioning with a disturbingly clinical detachment. Other key films: *Paths of Glory* (1957), *Lolita* (1962) and *Eyes Wide Shut* (1999).

Kurosawa, Akira (1910–98)

Kurosawa was the first Japanese director to make a major impact on Western audiences with *Rashomon*, the recounting of a rape and murder from four separate perspectives, which was the great success of the Venice Film Festival in 1951. Compared to such as Mizoguchi and Ozu his work looks Westernised, but this can be of positive benefit, as in the Samurai "Westerns" he made with the actor Toshiro Mifune, where classic Western plot-schemes are translated into stylised Japanese settings (*The Seven Samurai*, 1954; *Sanjuro*, 1962). He also made highly praised adaptations of

Shakespeare, *Throne of Blood* (1957), a version of *Macbeth*, and *Ran* (1985), an interpretation of *King Lear*. Psychological extremes always excited Kurosawa, and his pulsating visual style can be understood in terms of finding a powerful visual pattern to reflect the feverish inner intensity of his characters. But one should not overlook the strong humanist vein in Kurosawa, expressed most movingly in *Living* (1952). Other key films: *Drunken Angel* (1948), *The Idiot* (1951), *I Live in Fear* (1955), *The Lower Depths* (1957) and *Kagemusha* (1980).

Lang, Fritz (1890–1976)

Lang began as a leading exponent of German Expressionism, with the psychodrama *M* (1931), starring Peter Lorre as the self-hating child murderer, and *Metropolis* (1926), a science-fiction evocation of a nightmarish industrial city of the future. Goebbels was very taken with the latter film, and offered Lang the job of film-propaganda director to the Third Reich. Instead, he fled to America, and proceeded to provide auteurist critics with one of their juiciest test-cases by adapting his preoccupations with fate, revenge, and the social outcast to the turbulent American society of the pre-war and wartime years (*Fury*, 1936), and to genres such as the Western (*Rancho Notorious* in 1952) and the gangster film (*The Big Heat* in 1953). Two Edward G. Robinson performances—as a Professor implicated in murder in *The Woman in the Window* (1944) and as an artist infatuated with a prostitute in *Scarlet Street* (1945)—embody to perfection the typical Lang hero, trapped by personality, circumstance and environment. He is still arguably the most formidable pessimist in film history, and his presentation of fear and alienation in the modern metropolis profoundly influenced Godard, Hitchcock, Kubrick *etc*.

Lean, Sir David (1908–91)

The popular cinema's master story-teller. In *Brief Encounter* (1945), he made the British cinema's greatest love story; his Dickens' adaptations, *Great Expectations* (1946) and *Oliver Twist* (1948) have never been surpassed; and with *The Bridge on the River Kwai* (1957), *Lawrence of Arabia* (1962) and *Doctor Zhivago* (1965), he managed to align epic perspectives with intimate and intense characterisation. After the failure of *Ryan's Daughter* in 1970, his reputation slumped: "bourgeois impersonality" was the label given to his films. But the success of *A Passage to India* (1984) helped to force a re-evaluation of his work and recognise its individual qualities: the emotional repression of his heroines; the visionary madness of his heroes; the spirit of place that pulses in his films; and his sensitivity to the erratic, exotic emotions that lurk beneath the surface of English propriety. Other key films include: *The Sound Barrier* (1952), *Hobson's Choice* (1954) and *Summer Madness* (1955).

Lee, Ang (b.1954)

Emigrating from his native Taiwan to America in 1978 and learning his film craft at New York's University Film School, Ang Lee has amassed the most varied body of work of any director of the last decade. It ranges from domestic drama to a western; from martial arts to Jane Austen; from low-key comedy of observation, like the delightful *Pushing Hands* (1992), to high-tech comic-strip fantasy such as *Hulk* (2003) ; and from the visual splendour of *Crouching Tiger, Hidden Dragon* (2000) to the psychological depth of *The Ice Storm* (1997) and *Brokeback Mountain* (2005). Other key films: *The Wedding Banquet* (1993), *Eat Drink Man Woman* (1994), *Sense and Sensibility* (1995), *Ride with the Devil* (1999), *Lust, Caution* (2007), *Taking Woodstock* (2009) and *Life of Pi* (2012).

Leigh, Mike (b. 1943)

English director of international reputation after his success with *Secrets and Lies* (1996), a tragi-comic study of family relationships that is Leigh's forte. He had made his first film as far back as 1971, but only in the last two decades has he really developed some cinematic continuity. Cineastes cherish his quirky insight into character and his sharp, astringent, satire of middle-class mores. Key films: *Bleak Moments* (1971), *High Hopes* (1988), *Life is Sweet*

(1990), *Naked* (1993), *Career Girls* (1997), *Topsy Turvy* (1999), *All or Nothing* (2002), *Vera Drake* (2004), *Happy Go Lucky* (2008) and *Another Year* (2010).

Leone, Sergio (1921–89)

Leone will always be remembered as the director who re-invigorated the western genre in the 1960s and made a star of Clint Eastwood. His spaghetti westerns—*A Fistful of Dollars* (1964), *For a Few Dollars More* (1965), *The Good, the Bad and the Ugly* (1966)—were an iconoclastic blend of parody and anti-heroism that appealed to a distrustful, anarchic age. His later films, *Once Upon a Time in the West* (1968) and *Once Upon a Time in America* (1984) were operatic meditations on the western and the gangster film respectively.

Loach, Ken (b. 1936)

Untamed radical film-maker who cut his teeth on social realist TV dramas, notably the massively influential *Cathy Come Home*, and then brought the same intensity to his feature films, most memorably in *Kes* (1969), a work much admired for its social critique and documentary-style technique by directors such as Kieslowski. Like Mike Leigh, Loach experienced a new lease of life in the 1990s, twice winning the European Film of the Year Award—for *Riff-Raff* (1990) and *Land and Freedom* (1995)—without compromising his vision, integrity or socialism. His film, *The Wind that Shakes the Barley* (2006) won the Golden Palm at Cannes. In 2016 he won a second Golden Palm for *I, Daniel Blake*.

Losey, Joseph (1909–84)

There were several Joseph Loseys: the American Losey renowned for cogent moral fables such as *The Prowler* (1951) before the McCarthyist blacklist forced him out of America; the British Losey in which, with collaborators like actors Stanley Baker and Dirk Bogarde and writer Harold Pinter, he analysed the sexual mores and class corruption of English society, as in *The Servant* (1963), *Accident* (1967) and *The Go-Between* (1971); and the European Losey of the final phase of his career, when he adapted classics such as *A Doll's House* (1973) or Mozart's *Don Giovanni* (1980) or offered trenchant insights into recent political history, as in *The Assassination of Trotsky* (1972) and *Mr. Klein* (1976). With a style often verging on the baroque, Losey tackled a variety of subject matter, but the themes were consistent: the hypocrisy and deceit of dominant social and sexual attitudes. He had one of the most lucid intellects in movies. Other key films include: *The Boy with Green Hair* (1948), *Blind Date* (1959), *The Criminal* (1960), *King and Country* (1964) and *Secret Ceremony* (1968).

Lubitsch, Ernst (1892–1947)

The master of sophisticated sex comedy who, in Billy Wilder's phrase, "could do more with a closed door than most modern directors can do with an entire bedroom". Born in Berlin, Lubitsch brought a European flavour to Hollywood farce, satirising the pretension and insensitivity that sometimes go with wealth and position. His best remembered films are *Ninotchka* (1939), in which Garbo laughs, and *To Be or Not to Be* (1942), in which Jack Benny plays Hamlet. They are not only comedies: they are fervent anti-Nazi satires made at a time when Lubitsch must have known that the Europe of his youth, so lovingly evoked on screen, was being destroyed forever. Other key films: *Trouble in Paradise* (1932) and *The Shop Around the Corner* (1940).

Lumet, Sidney (1924–2011)

The most enduring of the generation of directors (including John Frankenheimer, Martin Ritt and Franklin Schaffner) who graduated to the cinema in the 1950s after learning their craft on television. Lumet's first film, the jury-room drama, *12 Angry Men* (1957) was an instant classic, and his best films have often returned to the themes of justice, law and order, civic corruption and abuse of police power. A child actor on stage, he has developed a powerful rapport with actors and some of his films rival Kazan's in the skill and intensity of the performances. Arguably over-prolific, undeniably humourless, Lumet has nevertheless amassed a powerful body of work that testifies to his talent, professionalism and liberal values. Key films include: *Long Day's Journey into Night* (1962), *Fail Safe* (1964), *The Hill* (1965), *Dog Day Afternoon* (1975), *Network* (1976), *Prince of the City* (1981), *The Verdict* (1982), *Running on Empty* (1987) and *Before the Devil Knows You're Dead* (2007).

Lynch, David (b. 1946)

One of the modern cinema's most unnerving directors. He achieved instant notoriety with the gruesome *Eraserhead* (1976); had a deserved success with the compassionate *The Elephant Man* (1980); but has since polarised critical opinion with such films as *Wild at Heart* (1990) and *Lost Highway* (1997), psychologically challenging or pretentiously incoherent, according to taste. His most fully achieved works to date are *Blue Velvet* (1987), a nightmarish investigation of the dark sexual secrets of 'typical' small-town America; and *Mulholland Drive* (2001), a mysterious mesmerising look at the American Dream.

Mackendrick, Alexander (1912–93)

The most consistently brilliant of the Ealing directors, making four of its most successful and enduring comedies: *Whisky Galore* (1949), *The Man in the White Suit* (1951), *The Maggie* (1954) and *The Lady-Killers* (1955). His American debut—an exposé of yellow journalism—*Sweet Smell of Success* (1957) was also remarkable, but after a series of abortive projects in the 1960s, Mackendrick retired from directing to become Dean of the film department of the California Institute of the Arts. He left behind a fine body of work, notable for its extraordinary insights into the world of children, its fascination with the dangers of innocence, and its mordant observation of the intricate yet inevitable ways in which humans fail to communicate. Other key films: *Mandy* (1952), *Sammy Going South* (1963) and *A High Wind in Jamaica* (1965).

Malle, Louis (1932–95)

Formerly an assistant to Robert Bresson and Jacques Cousteau, Louis Malle developed into one of the most esteemed of international directors. He made films as dashing as *Zazie dans le Metro* (1960), as disturbing as *Lacombe Lucien* (1973), as atmospheric as *Atlantic City* (1980), and as moving as *Au Revoir les Enfants* (1987). Malle often challenged the norms of society and the boundaries of cinema, exploring such risky subjects as eroticism (in *Les Amants* in 1958), incest (in *Murmur of the Heart* in 1971) and child prostitution (in *Pretty Baby* in 1979) and yet still achieving popular success and critical acclaim. Isolation and social alienation were recurrent themes, fittingly so perhaps for one of the least predictable and most individualistic filmmakers of modern times. Other key films include: *Lift to the Scaffold* (1957), *Le Feu Follet* (1963), *My Dinner With Andre* (1982) and *Damage* (1992).

Mankiewicz, Joseph L. (1909–93)

To those who find Mankiewicz's films too wordy, he replied: "There can never be an excess of *good* talk". Mankiewicz was one of the most eloquent of Hollywood's writer directors, who began by writing dialogue for W. C. Fields and, he claims, Rin-Rin-Tin (an unused screen-play about a dog that hates its master, a familiar Mankiewicz theme). His greatest period was during the ten years after the War, in which he won the writing and directing Oscars for two consecutive years (for *A Letter to Three Wives* in 1949 and *All About Eve* in 1950) and also made Hollywood's best Shakespearian film (*Julius Caesar* in 1952). His career never really picked up momentum after his labours on the mammothly expensive *Cleopatra* (1963), though he was proud to claim that his last film *Sleuth* (1972) is the only film ever to have its entire cast—*i.e.* Laurence Olivier and Michael Caine—nominated for Oscars. There are a lot of interesting recurrent motifs in Mankiewicz—generation conflict, ghosts from the past that will not stay dead—and nobody has made more haunting use of the flashback. Other key films: *The Ghost and Mrs. Muir* (1947), *Five Fingers* (1952), *The Barefoot Contessa* (1954) and *Suddenly Last Summer* (1959).

Mann, Anthony (1909–67)

Anthony Mann is best remembered for a series of Westerns he made with actor James Stewart, which were striking for their dramatic use of landscape and the psychological instability of their heroes. In *Winchester 73* (1950), *Bend of the River* (1952), *The Naked Spur* (1953), and *The Far Country* (1955), Stewart plays an ostensibly noble but actually neurotic hero who, whilst undertaking a perilous journey across a treacherous landscape, must also root out the evil in himself. Mann also made fine thrillers, a classic epic (*El Cid* in 1961) and even a stylish musical (*The Glenn Miller Story* in 1954) but it was the Mann of the Western that really showed his quality as a director. Other key films: *The Man from Laramie* (1955), *Man of the West* (1958) and *The Fall of the Roman Empire* (1964).

Melville, Jean-Pierre (1917–73)

Melville was something of a father figure of the *Nouvelle Vague* because of his economical and independent production methods. He made an exemplary adaptation of Jean Cocteau's novel *Les Enfants Terribles* (1950). However, he is most celebrated for a series of poetic, stylised existential gangster films. among them *Second Breath* (1966), *The Samurai* (1967), and *The Red Circle* (1970), which particularly took their inspiration from Melville's favourite director, John Huston. (Melville had chosen his pseudonym after his favourite author, Herman Melville: his actual surname was Grumbach). Perhaps his masterpiece, though, and certainly his most personal film, is *Army of the Shadows* (1969), a film about the French Resistance that drew on his own personal experience in the war.

Minnelli, Vincente (1910–86)

The name Vincente Minnelli is synonymous with the MGM musical—*Meet Me in St. Louis* (1944), *An American in Paris* (1951), *The Band Wagon* (1953), *Gigi* (1958) and others. Yet he was also adept at comedy, and did some remarkably intense melodramas, of which *Lust for Life* (1955), his bio-pic of Van Gogh, and *The Bad and the Beautiful* (1952), his glittering dissection of Hollywood ruthlessness, are particularly notable. He was interested in the plight of the artist in society, and the superiority of the world of imagination to that of reality. Hollywood's Dream Factory proved a most congenial environment for this most elegant of stylists. Other key films: *The Pirate* (1948), *Madame Bovary* (1949), *Father of the Bride* (1950). *Brigadoon* (1953), *The Cobweb* (1955) and *Some Came Running* (1958).

Mizoguchi, Kenji (1898–1956)

For many, Mizoguchi is the greatest of all Japanese directors, but his films are still not that well known in the West. The most famous is *Ugetsu Monogatari* (1953), a ravishingly beautiful tale of ghosts and greed. Its articulation of history and fantasy, its lyrical style and its commitment to the treatment of women as equals are characteristic of the director. Other masterpieces include: *The Story of the Last Chrysanthemums* (1939), *The Life of Oharu* (1952), *Sansho the Bailiff* (1954).

Murnau, F. W. (1889–1931)

Murnau is renowned for three classics of silent film: *Nosferatu* (1922), the cinema's first version of the *Dracula* story and still the most frightening; *The Last Laugh* (1924), credited as being one of the few silent films to dispense with titles and remarkable for its fluid camera movement; and *Sunrise* (1927), his first American film. Tragically he was killed in a car crash in 1931.

Olmi, Ermanno (b. 1931)

An Italian director whose work is characterised by a sympathy for the working man and by a concern for human dignity. In films such as *Il Posto* (1961) and *The Tree of Wooden Clogs* (1979), he kept the spirit of neo-realism alive.

Ophuls, Max (1902–57)

For a long time regarded as a talented minor director of exquisite trifles, Ophuls has been reinstated by modern criticism to his rightful place as one of the greatest of forties and fifties directors. *Lola Montes* (1955) was his last film, about the beautiful "adventuress" who allows herself to be put on display in a circus ring at the end of her career. The swooping camera-movements and awareness of how feminine sexuality necessarily connotes being an object to be looked at are in evidence too in *Madame de . . .* (1953), as well as in the films he made in Austria, Germany and France before setting out to pursue his career in Hollywood. His best American film was the beautiful tragic romance, *Letter from an Unknown Woman* (1948); whilst both *Caught* (1949) and *The Reckless Moment* (1949) took conventional women's magazine material and, through intense visual style, transformed them into tense and subversive comments on romantic obsession and domestic imprisonment.

Oshima, Nagisa (b. 1932)

His name became familiar to most filmgoers only with *Ai No Corrida* (otherwise *Empire of the Senses*) in 1975. An innkeeper and his ex-servant make untiring love until she, at his behest, strangles him in the moment of orgasm. The much-touted erotic frankness–certainly far less surrogate than that in *Last Tango in Paris*—assumes its importance only when seen in conjunction with the film's critique of the situation of women in Japanese society. In his first international film, *Merry Christmas, Mr. Lawrence* (1983), he explored the strange bond which grows between a Japanese captain and a British prisoner of war: a variation of his typical themes of forbidden passion, and his preoccupation with society's "enemies" whose psychology he seeks to understand. He completed a documentary for the BBC, *Kyoto, My Mother's Place* (1991), which gives a fascinating account of his background. Other key films: *Diary of A Shinjuku Thief* (1968), *Boy* (1969), *The Ceremony* (1971) and *Empire of Passion* (1978).

Ozu, Yasujiro (1903–63)

Like Mizoguchi, Ozu is a director long known to the Western public through only one work—*Tokyo Story* of 1953, about a visit paid by an elderly couple to their children in the capital. Ozu's style is slow, his narrative-lines not exactly eventful, his photography from a low level (the seated position traditional for social intercourse in Japan) perhaps difficult for Westerners to adjust to. But now he is accepted as one of the most important innovators in film language, for the way in which his small-scale stories distil much that is important in Japanese life and history, and for the separating out of individual actions and gestures so that spectators have time fully to appreciate their implications. Key films include: *I Was Born But . . .* (1932), *There was a Father* (1942), *Late Spring* (1949), *Early Summer* (1951), *Good Morning* (1959) and *An Autumn Afternoon* (1962).

Pasolini, Pier Paolo (1922–76)

Pasolini's notorious death—murdered by a homosexual pick-up—could almost have been engineered as a publicity stunt to launch his final film, *Salo or the 120 Days of Sodom* (1976), in which the combination of intense and complex visual lucidity with a recoiling from the tyrannies of the twentieth century already evident in *Pigsty* (1969) reaches its zenith. Ideological revulsion from the present and an interest in the possibilities of film language motivate Pasolini's curious "Marxist-Freudian-Catholic" rewritings of classics for the screen—*Medea* (1969) and *The Decameron* (1971). His complex artistry is seen at its best in his first film, *Accatone!* (1961) and *The Gospel According to St. Matthew* (1964), an austere rendering of the Biblical story far removed from the Hollywood epic, and movingly attempting to reconcile Pasolini's Marxist political outlook with his religious mysticism.

Peckinpah, Sam (1925–84)

Peckinpah was a Hollywood maverick, associated with scenes of graphic violence photographed in loving slow motion. In fact, he had something of the visual lyricism and raucous male humour of John Ford, though whereas Ford disclosed the poetry behind America's pioneering past, Peckinpah explored its passions and perversions as well. He will always be remembered for *The Wild Bunch* (1969), his radical, revisionist Western that majestically dragged the genre, kicking and screaming, into the 20th century. Other key films: *Guns in the Afternoon* (1962), *Major Dundee* (1965), *Straw Dogs* (1971), *Pat Garrett and Billy the Kid* (1973) and *Cross of Iron* (1977).

Penn, Arthur (b. 1922)

An abrasive stylist, notable for his subversive way with popular film genres, his investigation of the reality behind legendary figures, and his insertion of counter-culture attitudes into mainstream movie-making. Key films: *The Left-Handed Gun* (1958), *The Miracle Worker* (1962), *Bonnie and Clyde* (1967), *Alice's Restaurant* (1969) and *Night Moves* (1975).

Polanski, Roman (b. 1933)

From early Surrealist shorts, Polanski moved into feature-length dramas of sexual tension with *Knife in the Water* (1962) and *Repulsion* (shot in England in 1965). The reputation for kinkiness he thereby gained was tragically highlighted when his wife, the actress Sharon Tate, was butchered by crazed followers of Charles Manson in 1969. His major box- office success has been the private-eye drama *Chinatown* (1974), in which Polanski himself slits open the nose of the character played by Jack Nicholson. He also breathed flesh and blood into the horror film with *Rosemary's Baby* (1968) and fresh life into the filmed literary classic with *Tess* (1979). His traumatic life has been recounted in his autobiography, *Roman*. His film, *The Pianist* (2002) was a major return to form and won him an unexpected Oscar as best director. Other key films: *Cul-de-Sac* (1966), *Macbeth* (1971), *The Tenant* (1976), *Oliver Twist* (2005), *The Ghost* (2010) and *Carnage* (2011).

Powell, Michael (1905–90) and Pressburger, Emeric (1902–88)

British cinema's most full-blooded fantasists, who peaked in the 1940s with such passionate and visually imaginative films as *The Life and Death of Colonel Blimp* (1943), *I Know Where I'm Going* (1945), *A Matter of Life and Death* (1946), *Black Narcissus* (1947) and their greatest success, *The Red Shoes* (1948). From the late 1950s, Powell went solo and created an enormous furore with *Peeping Tom* (1960), which was critically reviled at the time but has since attained classic status and is deeply admired by cineastes and fellow directors such as Martin Scorsese.

Preminger, Otto (1906–86)

Talented tyrant who thrived on controversy, whether it involved the use of "naughty" words in *The Moon is Blue* (1953) or the depiction of the world of the drug addict in *The Man with the Golden Arm* (1955). His best films are the detective thriller, *Laura* (1945), one of a number of Preminger's features about mysterious, irresistible women who lure men to their doom; and the courtroom drama *Anatomy of a Murder* (1959), a masterpiece of objectivity and ambiguity. Other films: *Angel Face* (1953), *Carmen Jones* (1954), *Bonjour Tristesse* (1957), *Advise and Consent* (1962), *The Cardinal* (1963).

Ray, Nicholas (1911–78)

Ray was one of the most inventive and consistent of Hollywood action directors, whose rhetorical question summed up his philosophy of cinema: "If it were all in the script, why make the film?" *Rebel Without A Cause* (1955) blazed the trail for a host of movies about rebellious youth, but the dignity of James Dean's performance and the symbolic richness of Ray's *mise-en-scene* have caused it to survive longer than most of its imitators. He enjoyed success also with Bogart, in *In a Lonely Place* (1950) and Robert Mitchum, *The Lusty Men* (1952). The critics of *Cahiers du Cinema* particularly championed Ray's more extreme stylistic exercises, such as the feminist Western, *Johnny Guitar* (1954) and the baroque gangster film, *Party Girl* (1958). Alienated youth, the rebel, the outsider: these were the figures with whom Ray identified, sometimes

melodramatically, often poetically. Other key films: *They Live By Night* (1948), *Knock on Any Door* (1949), *On Dangerous Ground* (1952), *Bigger Than Life* (1956) and *Bitter Victory* (1957).

Ray, Satyajit (1921–92)

Pather Panchali of 1955 introduced Indian cinema to a wider audience, and launched a highly successful trilogy, completed by *Aparajito* of 1957 and *The World of Apu* of 1959. The withdrawn, analytical style of Ray's output expanded with some of his work in the seventies (see *Company Limited*, 1972) to a greater awareness of the problems of Westernised India. His films were rooted in the tradition of the humanist documentary, influenced by the social concern of Italian neo-realists, and inspired by the natural lyricism of a director like Jean Renoir. Other key films: *The Music Room* (1958), *Charulata* (1964), *Days and Nights in the Forest* (1970), *The Middle Man* (1976), *The Chess Players* (1977) and *The Home and the World* (1984).

Reed, Sir Carol (1906–76)

Reed's reputation as one of the key directors of post-war British cinema rests on a small number of films: the Expressionist, *Odd Man Out* (1947), the last day-in-the-life of an IRA man on the run, and two adaptations of Graham Greene stories, *The Fallen Idol* (1948) and *The Third Man* (1949). Overall his films are notable for a self-effacing craftsmanship, a sympathy with the world of children, and a fascination with confrontations between innocence and experience. He won an Oscar for *Oliver!* (1968). Other key films include *Outcast of the Islands* (1951), one of the cinema's best adaptations of Conrad; and *The Man Between* (1953), using its post-war Berlin setting less evocatively than post-war Vienna in *The Third Man* but a gripping human drama nonetheless.

Renoir, Jean (1899–1979)

A career spanning nearly fifty years included one of the first great dramas to be shot entirely on location, *Toni*, made with a largely non-professional cast in the South of France in 1935; two magnificent performances from Michel Simon, in *La Chienne* (1931) and *Boudu Sauve Des Eaux* (1932); a period funded by the Left-wing Popular Front that produced the film about a workers' cooperative, *Le Crime de Monsieur Lange* (1935); and a forties and fifties output as an exile in Hollywood of considerable merit, including *The Southerner* of 1945. These would be enough to mark Renoir out as a significant director even were it not for his two pre- Second-World-War masterpieces, *La Grande Illusion* (1937),a drama set in a POW camp, and the matchless *La Regle du Jeu* of 1939. This savage and frequently hilarious drama of love, class-antagonism, and the ambiguous corruption of aristocratic style so quickly achieved recognition as a masterpiece that it requires an effort now to remind ourselves that it was banned on first release.

Resnais, Alain (1922–2014)

Resnais began as a documentarist, and made his first feature film in 1959—*Hiroshima Mon Amour*, from a screenplay by the novelist Marguerite Duras. *Hiroshima*'s concern with the interaction of time, place and memory was taken up and amplified in *Last Year in Marienbad* (1961), where there is no reassuring continuity of character or coherence of time or space other than that imposed ambiguously, from moment to moment by the "eternal present" of the screen. Speculation about *Marienbad* reached quasi-metaphysical heights that frequently tended to obscure the dazzling frozen eroticism of its *mise-en-scene*, its masterful exploitation of the dreamlike aspect of film-watching, and the performances of Georgio Albertazzi and Delphine Seyrig. Memory and imagination continued to be important preoccupations in his work, and he long remained one of the great "modernist" innovators of contemporary cinema, continually exploring new areas of expression. Key films: *Night and Fog* (1956), *Muriel* (1963), *Providence* (1977), *L'Amour à Mort* (1984), *Private Fears in Public Places* (2006), *Wild Grass* (2009).

Rosi, Francesco (b. 1922)

Rosi began as an assistant to Luchino Visconti and is perhaps best known as the maker of the Placido Domingo film of *Carmen* (1984). But his natural home is the world of political corruption and paranoia, and no modern film-maker can match him for his trenchant critique of the institutions of power. His key films in this vein are *Salvatore Giuliano* (1961), *Hands Over the City* (1963), *The Mattei Affair* (1972), *Illustrious Corpses* (1976), *Christ Stopped at Eboli* (1979) and *Three Brothers* (1981).

Rossellini, Roberto (1906–77)

A key figure in the Italian neo-realist movement, whose early films were made on shoestring budgets and in often difficult conditions (*e.g. Rome, Open City*, 1945, about the anti-Fascist Resistance, shot when Mussolini's troops were still occupying Rome). *Voyage in Italy* (1953), in its open-endedness and preoccupation with George Sanders' and Ingrid Bergman's fluctuating senses of cultural alienation, foreshadowed the psychological explorations of Antonioni. Other key films: *Germany Year Zero* (1948), *Stromboli* (1949) and *The Rise of Louis XIV* (1966).

Rossen, Robert (1908–66)

One of the most socially aware of Hollywood directors who made his mark in the late 1940s with a hard-hitting boxing saga *Body and Soul* (1947), which was actually an allegory of capitalist corruption, and the Oscar-winning *All the King's Men* (1949), an indictment of creeping political Fascism. But then, hounded by the House UnAmerican Activities Committee for his Communist affiliations, he finally recanted and named names. He was able to work again but became, according to friends, a haunted, withdrawn individual. But his last two films were remarkable returns to form: a study of character and courage around the pool table, *The Hustler* (1961), and a study of madness, *Lilith* (1964), which was condemned on its first release but has gained an underground reputation as one of the most lyrical films of the American cinema.

Sautet, Claude (1924–2000)

Highly regarded French director who began as a screenwriter and who belatedly secured recognition as a subtle anatomist of human behaviour through the international success of *Un Coeur en Hiver—A Heart in Winter* (1993) and *Nelly and M. Arnaud* (1995). Other key films: *Les Choses de la Vie—The Things of Life* (1970), *Cesar et Rosalie* (1972), *Une Histoire Simple—A Simple Story* (1978).

Scorsese, Martin (b. 1942)

Arguably the most exciting of modern American film-makers. His movies are notable for their restless camera movement which reflects the inner tension of the characters. He has collaborated particularly closely with actor Robert De Niro, forging the most important actor-director partnership in American film since Brando and Kazan in the 1950s. Together they have made emotionally lacerating films about troubled masculinity and with a religious sense of redemption. Sometimes criticised for misogyny, his films are among the most disturbing and challenging of mainstream cinema. Key films: *Mean Streets* (1973), *Taxi Driver* (1976), *Raging Bull* (1980), *The King of Comedy* (1983), *Goodfellas* (1990) *Cape Fear* (1991), *The Age of Innocence* (1993), *Casino* (1995), *Kundun* (1997), *Bringing Out the Dead* (1999), *The Gangs of New York* (2002), *The Aviator* (2004), *The Departed* (2006) (which won him an Oscar for Best Director), *Shutter Island* (2010), *The Wolf of Wall Street* (2013) and *Silence* (2016), set in 17th century Japan.

Siegel, Don (1912–91)

Siegel learnt his craft as head of montage at Warners before gaining a reputation on low budget thrillers such as *Riot in Cell Block 11* (1954), *Baby Face Nelson* (1957) and *The Line Up* (1958), that combined sharp observation of the social outsider with a real flair for staging violent action. The sci-fi classic *Invasion of the Body Snatchers* (1956) and a brilliant re-make of *The Killers* (1964) cemented his cult status, and his career achieved a decisive upturn through his association on five films with Clint Eastwood, notably on *Dirty Harry* (1971), where they created arguably the most controversial anti-hero of postwar cinema. Other key films: *Hell is for Heroes* (1962), *Madigan* (1968), *The Beguiled* (1971), *The Shootist* (1976) and *Escape from Alcatraz* (1979).

Siodmak, Robert (1900–73)

Siodmak made his directing debut on the low budget German film, *Menschen am Sonntag- People on Sunday* (1929), a work that has become famous for also launching the careers of directors Billy Wilder and Fred Zinnemann and cameraman Eugene Schufftan. Like them, Siodmak moved to Hollywood, and he did his best work during the 1940s, making a number of fatalistic, visually gloomy dramas that are acknowledged as classics of film noir or Grand Guignol suspense: *Phantom Lady* (1944), *The Spiral Staircase* (1945), *The Killers* (1946), *Cry of the City* (1948), *Criss Cross* (1949).

Sirk, Douglas (1900–87)

Long regarded as a curiosity, Sirk was a Danish expatriate whose melodramas, richly shot and distinguished by narrative flamboyance, were at first treated with mild condescension. *Written on the Wind* (1956) was among the first to gain serious acceptance, with its dramatisation of the conflicts within a wealthy oil family whose problems (alcoholism, instability, sexual promiscuity) were sympathetically presented in a highly-coloured style.

His other works, notably *All That Heaven Allows* (1955) and *Imitation of Life* (1959), also began to receive more serious and sympathetic treatment as ironic and subversive critiques of middle-class America: they had a profound influence on the work of Fassbinder and inspired the recent film, *Far from Heaven* (2002). Other key films: *There's Always Tomorrow* (1956), *Tarnished Angels* (1957) and *A Time to Love and A Time to Die* (1958).

Spielberg, Steven (b. 1947)

The most successful director in the history of cinema, notably for four films: *Jaws* (1975), *Close Encounters of the Third Kind* (1977), *E.T.—the Extra-Terrestrial* (1982) and *Jurassic Park* (1993). His films are basically about ordinary people in extraordinary situations, and he directs these with a witty eye for the mores of American suburbia and a tremendous flair for suspense. A new maturity came into his work with *The Color Purple* (1985), *Empire of the Sun* (1987) and *Schindler's List* (1993), his unexpected powerful film of the holocaust. Often attacked for sentimentality, his work has been defended by the novelist J.G. Ballard, who has described Spielberg as the "Puccini of cinema – too sweet for some tastes, but what melodies, what orchestrations, what cathedrals of emotion ..." Other key films: *Duel* (1971), *The Sugarland Express* (1974), *Raiders of the Lost Ark* (1981), *Amistad* (1997), *Saving Private Ryan* (1998), *Minority Report* (2002), *The War of the Worlds* (2005), *War Horse* (2011) and *Lincoln* (2013). His *Bridge of Spies* and *Ready Player One* are his most recent works. Awarded Honorary Knighthood, 2001.

Stevens, George (1904–75)

Beginning as a camerman on Laurel and Hardy shorts, Stevens' early reputation as a director was in comedy: *Woman of the Year* (1942) and *The More the Merrier* (1943). But his war experience, which included being part of the American force that liberated Dachau, changed his sensibility: comedy receded and his films became full of a feeling of tragic sacrifice. *The Diary of Anne Frank* (1959) is his memorial to the war dead. His own movie monument is probably a trio of films that encapsulates his sympathy for the outsider and constitutes his epic reassessment of the American Dream: *A Place in the Sun* (1951), *Shane* (1953), and *Giant* (1956). Other key films: *Alice Adams* (1935), *Gunga Din* (1939), *Talk of the Town* (1942), *I Remember Mama* (1948) and *The Greatest Story Ever Told* (1965).

Stone, Oliver (b. 1946)

Vietnam vet turned polemicist director. He turned his Army experience into compelling cinema in *Platoon* (1986) and *Born on the Fourth of July*

(1989), for which he won directing Oscars, and his bio-pics of *JFK* (1991), *Nixon* (1995) and *George W. Bush, 'W'* (2008) were powerfully paranoid assaults on the American political system. Often derided for the extreme views and excessive violence of his films, Stone has been nonetheless a provocative influence. Other key films: *Salvador* (1985), *Wall Street* (1987), *Natural Born Killers* (1995).

Sturges, John (1911–92)

One of the finest directors of westerns. His masterpiece is *Bad Day at Black Rock* (1955), which is both modern western and suspense thriller, and his other contributions to the genre include: *Escape from Fort Bravo* (1954), *Gunfight at the O.K. Corral* (1957), *The Law and Jake Wade* (1958), *Last Train from Gun Hill* (1959), and *The Magnificent Seven* (1960). Also of note is the classic war film, *The Great Escape* (1963).

Sturges, Preston (1898–1959)

One of the first great writer-directors of the sound era in Hollywood, Sturges sold his screenplay *The Great McGinty* (1940) to Paramount for ten dollars on the condition he was allowed to direct. It was the first of eight comedies he wrote and directed within four years, each of which was interesting, some of which—*The Lady Eve* (1941), *Sullivan's Travels* (1942), *Palm Beach Story* (1942)—are classics. His comedies are distinguished by a frantic pace, tremendous ingenuity of dialogue and situation, and an air of shrill desperation. His characters comprise hapless millionaires, seductive gold-diggers and frustrated inventors, all whipped together in a sustained assault on American sacred cows.

Tarantino, Quentin (b.1963)

Former video store clerk and movie fanatic who became the most copied and discussed cult director of the 1990s. His first film, *Reservoir Dogs* (1991), about a heist that goes wrong, showed his gift for sharp dialogue and ingenious story-telling, but it was his second, *Pulp Fiction* (1994) that really caught the popular, post-modernist imagination. This underworld tale, with its outrageous violence, narrative surprises and subversively playful tone amidst the pervasive amorality, has since been much imitated but never equalled—not even, to date, by Tarantino himself. His *Inglourious Basterds* was released in 2009 and *Django Unchained* in 2013. His most recent film is *The Hateful Eight* (2015).

Tarkovsky, Andrey (1932–86)

The greatest Soviet film-maker since Eisenstein—and the resemblance ends there. Tarkovsky found his inspiration not in the spirit of the Russian Revolution but in the spirituality of the classic Russian novel, and the questions his films posed were not about the nature of political power but about the possibilities of personal salvation. This inevitably brought him into conflict with the Soviet authorities, who disliked the unsocialist, surreal, avant-garde qualities in films such as *Andrei Rublev* (1966) and *Mirror* (1974). They also took exception to Tarkovsky's thinly concealed allegory of the struggles of the artist in a repressive society. His last films were made in exile, and his final film, *The Sacrifice* (1985), a typically hallucinatory drama about a dream of nuclear holocaust averted, was one of his most movingly accessible and affirmative. A dreamer, a poet, a prophet, Tarkovsky's provocative and challenging thoughts on cinema were published in his book, *Sculpting in Time* (1987). Other key films: *Ivan's Childhood* (1962), *Solaris* (1971), *Stalker* (1979) and *Nostalgia* (1982).

Trier, Lars von (b.1956)

A signatory to the Dogme 95 manifesto which rejected cinema artifice and extravagance, von Trier has nevertheless made films of prodigious imagination and experimentation that have provoked extreme critical reaction, both for and against. Few would deny his claim to be the most important Danish film-maker since Carl Dreyer, although many would query his self-description as the world's greatest director. Key films: *The Element of Crime* (1984), *Europa* (1991), *The Kingdom* (1994), *Breaking the Waves* (1996), *The Idiots* (1998), *Dancer in the Dark* (2000), *Dogville*

(2003) and *Antichrist* (2009).

Truffaut, François (1932–84)

With Godard, one of the outstanding early names of the so-called French "New Wave". Truffaut's early work reveals a delight in the possibilities of the cinematic medium (notably in evoking situations of emotional fluidity and ambiguity) that is often exhilarating, as in *Shoot the Pianist* (with Charles Aznavour, 1960) and his masterpiece, *Jules et Jim* (1961). This deals with a menage a trois in the France of the beginning of the century, portrayed with tragic irony and a light yet serious treatment of historical and cultural influences on the relationship between Catherine (Jeanne Moreau) and her two lovers, the German Jules and the Frenchman Jim. His first feature film, *The 400 Blows* (1959) drew on his own difficult childhood and delinquent adolescence, and later films like *L'Enfant Sauvage* (1970) also deal sensitively with the world of childhood. He also made films like *Fahrenheit 451* (1965) and *The Bride Wore Black* (1968) in homage to Hitchcock. In the 1970s he made two of his most haunting films on his favourite theme of romantic obsession, *The Story of Adele H* (1975), and *The Green Room* (1978), but he also made one of the most affectionate of all films about film-making, *Day for Night* (1973). Truffaut loved movies and his death left cineastes feeling that they had lost a member of the family.

Vertov, Dziga (1896–1934)

Often seen as the great documentary director, as Eisenstein was the great feature director, of the early Bolshevik Russian days. His principal work is *The Man with a Movie Camera* (1929), an exhilarating exploration of the relationship between the camera, the person holding it, and the subject-matter being filmed.

Vidor, King (1894–1982)

A pioneer of the cinema, responsible for two of the masterpieces of American silent film, the World War One drama, *The Big Parade* (1925), and the urban realist classic, *The Crowd* (1928). His films of the sound era were less distinguished, curiously at their most impressive when he foresook realism in favour of melodrama. Key films include: *Hallelujah* (1929), *Our Daily Bread* (1934), *Stella Dallas* (1937), *The Citadel* (1938), *Duel in the Sun* (1947), *Ruby Gentry* (1952), *War and Peace* (1956).

Vigo, Jean (1905–34)

A great Surrealist director, whose early death from tuberculosis meant that he produced only two feature films, both masterpieces: *Zero de Conduite* (1933), an account of a rebellion in a repressive boys' school whose fragmentary, night-marish quality (partly a result of the tight conditions under which it was shot) is exceptional, and *L'Atalante* (1934), about a honeymoon on a barge, a haunting blend of lyricism and realism.

Visconti, Luchino (1906–77)

The most inventive and extravagant of the Italian neo-realists. Visconti came to attention with *La Terra Trema* (1948), about Sicilian fishermen; a mixture of tragic fatalism and concern for social change characteristic of Visconti pervades this, as it does the operatic *Rocco and his Brothers* of 1960 and his adaptation of the novel by Lampedusa, *The Leopard* (1963). Aristocrat yet communist, arthouse director who loved working with stars (like Dirk Bogarde and Burt Lancaster), Visconti was a strange mixture of extremes. His films dealt with forbidden passions; tormented heroes imprisoned by the standards of a society they despise; and superficially cultured ways of life in their death-throes. Nobody recreated the past more sumptuously on the screen than Visconti nor photographed doom more voluptuously. Other key films: *Ossessione* (1942), *Senso* (1954), *The Damned* (1969), *Death in Venice* (1971), *Ludwig* (1972) and *Conversation Piece* (1974).

Von Sternberg, Josef (1894–1969)

The supreme exponent of cinema as icon, of the image whose lavish and elaborate composition is its most immediately apparent justification. Yet his films are astounding essays on the infinite varieties of love, in which the love object (invariably Marlene Dietrich) is alternately the exploited victim or the tyrannical temptress. He never created real worlds: his films are stylised sound stages of dream and desire. Key films: *The Blue Angel* (1930), *Morocco* (1930), *Shanghai Express* (1932), *The Scarlet Empress* (1934) and *The Devil is a Woman* (1935).

Von Stroheim, Erich (1885–1957)

"By God I told them the truth" said Stroheim of his classic film *Greed* (1923). Unfortunately for MGM, he told it at excessive length, and the film was cut from 42 to 10 reels in length. Stroheim's career as director never recovered from this. But John Grierson was to call him "the director of directors", for his unflinching realism and fanatical attention to detail. Billy Wilder thought he was ten years ahead of his time, though Stroheim contradicted him: "No—twenty". Key films: *Foolish Wives* (1922), *Merry-Go-Round* (1923) and *Queen Kelly* (1928).

Wajda, Andrzej (1926–2016)

Perhaps the most important film-maker Poland has ever produced. Wajda grew up in Poland during the Nazi occupation and his famous trilogy—*A Generation* (1955), *Kanal* (1956) and *Ashes and Diamonds* (1958)—records the wartime suffering and courage and the scramble for political power that followed the liberation. *Ashes and Diamonds*, in particular, with its charismatic performance by Zbigniew Cybulski, exemplified Wajda's fascination with heroes who refuse to follow the tide of history and attempt to shape their own destinies through extreme action. For a time, history took second place to psychology and symbolism in his work. But in the mid 1970s, he returned head-on to contemporary issues, tackling the theme of censorship, political blackmail and the film-maker's responsibilities in *Man of Marble* (1976), and celebrating the rise of Solidarity in *Man of Iron* (1980) in a tone of prophetically precarious optimism. Wajda's films were often set in transitional periods where one era has died and another is struggling to be born. His own career was also subject to the turbulent tides of history, facing censorship, exile and rejection, but his achievements stand as an inspiring example of artistic talent surviving against difficult odds. Other key films: *Innocent Sorcerers* (1961), *Everything for Sale* (1968), *The Wedding* (1973), *The Conductor* (1980), *Korczak* (1988) and *Katyn* (2007).

Welles, Orson (1915–85)

Welles made his debut with *Citizen Kane* in 1941; over seventy years later, it is still a popular choice as the best film ever. Innovatory in film language (in its bold and extensive use of "deep-focus"—the camera plunging into the imaginary "depth" of the screen), suggestive in its plot (about a tycoon, modelled on William Randolph Hearst, whose public success is seen as a remedy for private unhappiness), electric in the quality of its camerawork and ensemble acting, and with its finale (the "secret" of Kane's life—the name of his confiscated childhood sledge, Rosebud) the most ironically well-kept secret in cinema history, the film succeeded on so many levels that hindsight almost suggests that Welles's subsequent career had to be an anti-climax. He filmed Shakespeare (*Macbeth*, 1948, *Othello*, 1952, *Chimes at Midnight*, 1966), Kafka (*The Trial*, 1963) and a "documentary" about forgeries (*F. for Fake*, 1975), none to the effect of *Kane*. Nevertheless the qualities of his other films should not be overlooked: the tenderness of *The Magnificent Ambersons* (1942), the *film noir* virtuosity of *Lady from Shanghai* (1948), the magisterial study of police corruption in *Touch of Evil* (1958).

It is tempting to see *Kane* as a prophetic study of a promise unfulfilled, and Welles's career certainly had more than its share of disappointments and frustrations. But he still remains a giant of the cinema, probing themes of power and corruption with that virtuoso camera style that he said "describes that sense of vertigo, uncertainty, lack of stability, that melange of movement and tension that is our universe".

Wenders, Wim (b. 1945)

One of the major figures of the "New German Cinema" of the 1970s, cooler and less didactic than Fassbinder, more streetwise and less anti-American than Herzog. His ambivalent response to America's "Coca-colonisation" of Europe was explored in *The American Friend* (1977), which had guest roles for Nicholas Ray and Samuel Fuller; and films such as *The Goalkeeper's Fear of the Penalty* (1972) and *Kings of the Road* (1976) elaborated his interest in the alienation of the modern environment and the rootlessness of modern man. His biggest international successes to date are *Paris Texas* (1984), a film as remarkable for its disorienting landscape as its characters or story; and *Wings of Desire* (1987) which won the top prize at the Cannes Film Festival.

Wilder, Billy (1906–2002)

"It's not important that a director knows how to write," said Billy Wilder, "but it is important that he knows how to read." Fleeing from Nazi Europe and becoming a Hollywood screenwriter for, among others, Ernst Lubitsch, Wilder became a director in order to protect his own scripts. *Double Indemnity* (1944), *The Lost Weekend* (1945) and *Sunset Boulevard* (1950) were wonderfully macabre demonstrations of his talents, and films like *Ace in the Hole* (1951), *Some Like it Hot* (1959) and *The Apartment* (1960) consolidated his reputation as the sharpest satirist in Hollywood, with an unusually mordant view of human nature that did not, however, preclude the possibility of redemption. *Sabrina* (1954) and *Avanti!* (1972) showed the melting of American materialism by European romanticism. His care for structure, his unceasing verbal wit and the intelligence of his character development made Wilder's overall achievement the equal of any Hollywood director's of the sound era. Other key films: *Stalag 17* (1953), *Witness for the Prosecution* (1957), *One, Two, Three* (1961), *The Fortune Cookie* (1966), *The Private Life of Sherlock Holmes* (1970) and *Fedora* (1978).

Wong, Kar-Wei (b.1958)

Major figure of Hong Kong cinema, a director who specialises in visually exquisite, emotionally delicate stories of unrequited, unconsummated or understated love. This is seen to particularly exhilarating effect in *Chungking Express* (1994), his most famous film to date and one of the best films of the 1990s. Other key films: *As Tears Go By* (1988), *Fallen Angels* (1995), *Happy Together* (1997), *In the Mood for Love* (2000) and *2046* (2004).

Wyler, William (1902–81)

One of the master craftsmen of Hollywood film. As well as winning three Oscars for himself (for *Mrs. Miniver*, 1942; *The Best Years of Our Lives*, 1946; and *Ben-Hur*, 1959), Wyler elicited more than a dozen Oscar-winning performances from his casts. Although he could handle the epic canvas as well as anyone, his forte was for drama in a confined setting and struggles for territorial advantage in a marriage or family. *The Little Foxes*, (1941), *The Heiress* (1949) and *Carrie* (1952) are all masterpieces of domestic claustrophobia. Whilst his heroes tended to be withdrawn figures, needing to be convinced of the necessity for action (like the pacifist hero of *The Big Country*, (1958)), his heroines are more often dynamic creatures, kicking against the constraints of a masculine world. No wonder he was Bette Davis's favourite director and directed her in some of her best films: *Jezebel* (1938), *The Letter* (1940) and *The Little Foxes*. Although recurrent patterns and themes are discernible in his films (unrequited love, class confrontations between the complacent and the envious), he tended, like Huston, to subordinate his personality to the requirements of the story. For this reason, he has often been underestimated by *auteurist* critics. But if a great director is simply someone who has made a number of great films, Wyler was a great director. Other key films: *Dodsworth* (1936), *Wuthering Heights* (1939), *Roman Holiday* (1952) and *The Children's Hour* (1961).

Yimou, Zhang (b. 1950)

One of the key figures of modern Chinese cinema,

an actor and cameraman (on Chen Kaige's *Yellow Earth* and *The Big Parade*) before turning to direction. Behind the sumptuous visual surfaces of his films lurk some telling observations on politics and patriarchy that have sometimes antagonised the Chinese authorities. His films also made a major star of his then leading actress Gong Li, whose characterisations often and excitingly subvert the stereotype of female submissiveness. The epic adventures *Hero* (2003) and *House of Flying Daggers* (2004) both proved an unexpected crossover success. Key films: *Red Sorghum* (1988), *Ju Dou* (1990), *Raise the Red Lantern* (1991), *The Story of Qui Ju* (1992), *Shanghai Triad* (1995), *Not One Less* (2000) and *The Great Wall* (2017).

Zinnemann, Fred (1907–97)

Born in Vienna, Zinnemann came to America in 1929, but his career did not really take off until *The Search* in 1948, a story of European children orphaned by the war and which presaged a number of his films about the impact and aftermath of war. But it was the western *High Noon* (1952) that established both Zinnemann's reputation and his fundamental theme: that of individual conscience. At considerable personal risk but on a point of principle, a character takes a stand against a community or institution that wishes him to compromise and conform: it is the theme also of *From Here to Eternity* (1953), *The Nun's Story* (1959) and *A Man for All Seasons* (1966). Unusually for Hollywood, these were dramas of reaction, not action, and with melancholy rather than happy endings. Their critical and commercial success testified to Zinnemann's skill at popularising complex themes without compromising his vision. Other key films: *The Seventh Cross* (1944), *Act of Violence* (1949), *Member of the Wedding* (1952), *Day of the Jackal* (1973) and *Julia* (1977).

3.   FAMOUS SCREEN ACTORS AND ACTRESSES

Andrews, Dame Julie (b. 1935)

The archetype of screen virtue who reached her peak of popularity in the mid-1960s with *Mary Poppins* (1964) and *The Sound of Music* (1965), in both of which her "English rose" image and pure singing voice enchanted audiences. She later made a number of films for her second husband, director Blake Edwards, but without the same success.

Arbuckle, "Fatty" (1887–1933)

Superb silent comedian whose career was ruined when accused of the rape and murder of a starlet Virginia Rappe at a wild Hollywood party in 1921. Although completely cleared of all charges, Arbuckle was never allowed to appear on the screen again (the whole story is told in David Yallop's book, *The Day the Laughter Stopped*). Buster Keaton, who owed his start in movies to Arbuckle, said he learnt everything about film from him.

Astaire, Fred (1899–1987)

"Can't act, slightly bald, can dance a little", was the verdict of the screen test of Astaire, who, in partnership with Ginger Rogers, was to become the most stylish screen dancer in Hollywood history. He starred in such classic musicals as *Top Hat* (1935), *Swing Time* (1936), *Easter Parade* (1948) and *Funny Face* (1956). Turned to straight acting in his later career with such effect that Spencer Tracy felt threatened and sent the following wire to his friend: "You stop acting or I'll start dancing!"

Bacall, Lauren (1924–2014)

Bacall was one of the first examples of Hollywood's skill at playing on-and-off screen personas off against each other. Opposite Humphrey Bogart in *To Have and Have Not* (1944), she enchanted him on the screen as she did in real life while the film was being shot. (They were later to be married.) Her performance there is a remarkably knowing and ironic one (particularly in the famous scene where she tells Bogart how to whistle for her if he wants anything), and she was to play similar roles opposite him in *The Big Sleep* (1946), *Dark Passage* (Delmer Daves, 1947) and *Key Largo* (John Huston, 1948). Although she was never really able to repeat her success with Bogart, her persona in these films is interesting as a contrast to the submissive view of women often purveyed by Hollywood. She was a great survivor and was nominated for an Oscar for her role in Barbra Streisand's *A Mirror has Two Faces* (1996). The last of the Hollywood greats.

Bardot, Brigitte (b. 1934)

"Created" by her then-husband Roger Vadim in *And God Created Woman* (1956), Bardot epitomised a certain popular view of French female sexuality—poutingly sensual, sporting a St. Tropez suntan and little else besides, as ardent and capricious in her off-screen romances as in those for the cameras. In Julien Duvivier's *La Femme et le Pantin* (1958) and Vadim's *Warrior's Rest* (1962) she exploited this role to perfection; but she did show that she had some acting ability in *Le Mepris*, made for Jean-Luc Godard in 1963, in *Viva Maria* (1965) for Louis Malle, and in *La Verité* (1960) for Henri-Georges Clouzot. Retired from the screen to devote herself to ecological issues.

Beatty, Warren (b. 1937)

Many people think of Beatty's career as beginning with *Bonnie and Clyde* (Arthur Penn, 1967), in which his performance as the debonair yet sexually insecure bandit Clyde steals the show. But he sprang to prominence as early as 1961 (Elia Kazan's *Splendour in the Grass*), and has appeared infrequently, but always to great effect, ever since, his best post-Bonnie performance perhaps being the gambler McCabe in Altman's *McCabe and Mrs. Miller* (1971). Directorial ambitions then preoccupied him more than acting, and he won an Oscar for the direction of *Reds* (1981). He appeared as a controversially honest politician in *Bulworth* (1998)—a role he has sometimes threatened to play in real life.

Belmondo, Jean-Paul (b. 1933)

Belmondo sprang to fame with his performance as the confusedly amoral Michel Poiccard in Godard's *Breathless* (1959). This earned him recognition as one of the first "anti-heroes" of the European cinema, concerned with discovering himself through action and, in his second masterpiece for Godard, *Pierrot le Fou* (1965), contemplation as well. Both films featured Belmondo "betrayed", ostensibly by the women he chose (Jean Seberg and Anna Karina respectively), but as much by his own insecure openness. His later work (including *Borsalino* for Deray in 1970, and *Stavisky* for Resnais in 1974) tended to be glossier and more spectacular, to the detriment of the "anti-hero" persona, though he scored a big personal success in Claude Lelouch's updating of *Les Miserables* (1994).

Bergman, Ingrid (1915–82)

Enticed, like Greta Garbo, from Sweden to Hollywood at the end of the thirties, Bergman became one of Hollywood's star actresses, particularly in exotic "European" roles like that of Humphrey Bogart's lost *grand amour* in Michael Curtiz's *Casablanca* (1943) and in three films for Hitchcock, *Spellbound* (1945), *Notorious* (1946) and *Under Capricorn* (1949). She went on to freelance in Europe in the fifties, notably for Roberto Rosselini (whom she married), in neo-realist classics such as *Stromboli* (1950) and *Voyage in Italy* (1953). Made a triumphant comeback to Hollywood in *Anastasia* (1956), and in her later years had great success in *The Murder on the Orient Express* (1974), for which she won her third Oscar, and in Ingmar Bergman's *Autumn Sonata* (1978).

Binoche, Juliette (b. 1964)

Born in Paris, Juliette Binoche has become one of the star actresses of modern European cinema, whose screen aura of wounded sensuality has been deployed to powerful effect by major directors such as Louis Malle in *Damage* (1992), Krzysztof Kieslowski in *Three Colours: Blue* (1993) and Michael Haneke in *Code Unknown* (1999) and *Caché* (2005).

She enhanced her international profile with an Oscar-winning performance as the nurse in *The English Patient* (1996) and also scored a personal success in the popular romance, *Chocolat* (2000).

Bogarde, Sir Dirk (1921–99)

It takes an effort to remind ourselves that the Bogarde destroyed by his death-wish passion for a young boy in Visconti's *Death in Venice* (1971) began his acting career in British comedy and melo-drama and acquired real prominence as the accident-prone medical student in the "Doctor" films of the late fifties. His fine performance as a homosexual barrister in *Victim* (1960) marked a turning point and Joseph Losey exploited his dramatic acting talent in *The Servant* (1963), which played off his British reserve against a highly-charged situation as Losey was also to do in *Accident* (1967). The association with Visconti confirmed him as one of the screen's subtlest and most accomplished actors.

Bogart, Humphrey (1899–1957)

One of the all-time superstars. Bogart began as a stage actor and graduated to screen stardom with one of his theatre roles, the psychopathic gangster in *The Petrified Forest* (1936). He became famous in the forties as an "outsider" figure, caught up in cor-rupt or devious situations from which he tried to stay aloof through a basic decency masquerading as hard-bitten cynicism. *Casablanca* (1943) revealed the persona to have a soft heart, in the scenes where he drinks to forget his love for Ingrid Bergman—or rather to remember it—and where he sacrifices it in the airport scene at the end with the immortal: "Here's looking at you, kid". For Howard Hawks he made *To Have and Have Not* in 1944 and *The Big Sleep* in 1946, both with Lauren Bacall and both exploiting the same persona. Small wonder that fifties anti-hero Belmondo elevated him to a god in *Breathless* (Godard, 1959), as did Woody Allen in a different way in *Play it Again, Sam* (1972). Closely associated with director John Huston, for whom he made six films, including *The Maltese Falcon* (1941), *The Treasure of the Sierra Madre* (1948) and the film which won his Oscar, *The African Queen* (1951).

Bow, Clara (1905–65)

Known as the "It" girl because of her enormously popular personal success in the film *It* (1927). Epitomised the "Roaring 20s" during the silent era but her career then foundered because of sound, scandals and mental illness. She was the Monroe of her time: a sad fate.

Brando, Marlon (1924–2004)

Brando came to the cinema from the stage, a leading proponent of the "Method" school of acting which relied upon naturalistic empathy with the part rather than careful professional stylisation. Laconic violence, often tending to the inarticulate, was his early stock-in-trade, exemplified in *A Streetcar Named Desire* (1951) and *On The Water-front* (1954), both directed by Elia Kazan. Other rebels vied with Brando in the late fifties and sixties, and his career went into an eclipse from which it was rescued by two very different, but remarkable, performances as men aware that they have passed their personal peak—the *Mafioso* Don Corleone in Coppola's *The Godfather* (1972), and the self-loathing American in Bertolucci's *Last Tango in Paris* (1973). He later tended to confine himself to expensive guest performances in movies like *Superman* (1980), though he gave a superb character performance as a Scottish liberal lawyer in the anti-apartheid drama, *A Dry White Season* (1989). Published a much publicised autobiography in 1994.

Brooks, Louise (1906–85)

Magnetic star whose film fame rests mainly on one charismatic performance: as Lulu in G. W. Pabst's *Pandora's Box* (1929). She retired from the screen in the early 1930s and led a reclusive life, though briefly surfaced to write a marvellous book of memoirs, *Lulu in Hollywood*.

Burton, Richard (1925–84)

Burton was initially a leading stage Shakespearian, but better-known to the cinema public for his flam-boyant romance with Elizabeth Taylor. His perfor-mance as the verbally aggressive college professor in Mike Nichols's *Who's Afraid of Virginia Woolf ?* (1966) marked him out as a great screen actor, as did his performance in *The Spy who came in from the Cold* (1965).

He was nominated seven times for the coveted Oscar without winning: his last performance was as the sinister interrogator O'Brien in the 1984 screen adaptation of George Orwell's *1984*.

Cagney, James (1899–1986)

Pugnacious leading man who started out as a dancer but whose energy and vitality made him ideal for the dynamic gangster movies of the 1930s, such as *Public Enemy* (1931), *Angels with Dirty Faces* (1938) and *The Roaring Twenties* (1939). Won an Oscar for *Yankee Doodle Dandy* (1942) but his most memorable characterisation was probably as the psychopathic, mother-fixated Cody Jarrett in Raoul Walsh's *White Heat* (1949).

Caine, Sir Michael (b. 1933)

Durable, dependable British star who, rather like Robert Mitchum, conceals his range and profession-alism beneath a deceptively languid style. Came to the fore in the 1960s, particularly for his perfor-mance in the title role of *Alfie* (1966): thereafter he has remained in demand through a skilful balance of the commercial with the more challenging. Won supporting actor Oscars for *Hannah and Her Sisters* (1986) and *The Cider House Rules* (1999).

Other films include *Zulu* (1964), *Get Carter* (1971), *The Man Who Would be King* (1975), *Educating Rita* (1983), *Little Voice* (1998), *The Quiet American* (2002) and *Harry Brown* (2009).

Chaplin, Sir Charles (1889–1977)

Still the most famous film star and director in the history of movies. His creation of the "little man"— the wistful tramp figure who fantasises his way out of the hardships of life—achieved success on an unprecedented scale and effectively made the transition from silent shorts to feature-length films, the most famous being *The Gold Rush* (1925). He fought hard against the coming of sound, refusing to use any apart from music and sound effects in *City Lights* (1931), where the blend of slapstick and suspense was particularly well achieved. His later films, like *Modern Times* (1936), *The Great Dictator* (1940) and *Monsieur Verdoux* (1947) were infused with his socialist political sympathies which set him at odds with the American authorities and led to his exile in 1952.

He remains the most significant and creative film comic of the twentieth century.

Christie, Julie (b. 1941)

Beautiful British actress who shot to international stardom with her performance in *Darling* (1965) and *Doctor Zhivago* (1965). Her best films include *Petulia* (1968), *The Go-Between* (1971), *McCabe and Mrs. Miller* (1971) and *Don't Look Now* (1973). In recent years, she has developed into a character actress of stature, particularly with her perfor-mances in *Hamlet* (1997), *Afterglow* (1997) and *Away from Her* (2007).

Clift, Montgomery (1920–66)

Clift now enjoys a vogue as one of the great Hollywood victims, destroyed by drink, pills and inability to come to terms with his homosexuality. This litany should not obscure the fact that he was a tremendously gifted screen actor, as a tormented priest in *I Confess* (Hitchcock, 1952), as a cowboy opposite John Wayne in Hawk's *Red River* (1948), or with Clark Gable and Marilyn Monroe in that most macabre of pictures (it marked the end of virtually all its stars' careers), John Huston's *The Misfits* of 1961. Other key performances include *A Place in the Sun* (Stevens, 1951), *From Here to Eternity* (Zinnemann, 1953) and *Freud* (Huston, 1962). Speaking of his tormented personality, Marilyn Monroe once commented: "He's the only person I know who's in worse shape than I am."

Connery, Sir Sean (b. 1930)

Connery achieved early fame as the first of the screen James Bonds, but has been recognised as one of the best character-actor stars of modern cinema. Won an Oscar for *The Untouchables* (1987) and has also given fine performances in such films as Hitchcock's *Marnie* (1964), *The Hill* (1965), *The Man Who Would be King* (1975), *Robin and Marian* (1976), *Cuba* (1979) and *The Name of the Rose* (1987). Knighted in New Year Honours, 2000.

Cooper, Gary (1901–61)

Cooper embodied quintessential American decency—not blustering like Wayne nor cynical like Bogart. His most famous roles are as the decent lad up from the country putting sophisticates to shame in *Mr. Deeds Goes to Town* (Frank Capra, 1936), the pacifist soldier in Hawks's *Sergeant York* (1941), and the lone sheriff in Zinnemann's *High Noon* (1952) confronting four gunmen out for revenge.

Crawford, Joan (1906–77)

The leading unhappy-in-love female star of the thirties and early forties (as in Cukor's *The Women* of 1939), Crawford won an Oscar for *Mildred Pierce* (Michael Curtiz, 1945). In later life a successful and immensely wealthy businesswoman, she was better known perhaps as a star than for any individual performances, and as the subject of her daughter's sensational memoir, *Mommie Dearest*, filmed in 1981 with Faye Dunaway as Crawford. Played masochist to Bette Davis's sadist in *Whatever Happened to Baby Jane?* (1962).

Crowe, Russell (b. 1964)

Like Mel Gibson before him, Crowe established a successful film career in Australia before moving to Hollywood. Such roles as the policeman in *L.A. Confidential* (1997) and the Roman hero of *Gladiator* (2000) seemed to type him as a virile leading man of the old school, but he has also shown himself adept at character roles, such as the mentally unstable mathematician in *A Beautiful Mind* (2001) and, particularly, as the whistle-blower in Michael Mann's critique of the tobacco industry, *The Insider* (1999).

Cruise, Tom (b. 1962)

Of the group of young American actors who shot to fame in the 1980s and were known collectively as the "brat pack", Cruise has proved to be the most durable, combining good looks with career shrewdness. He has had his glossy hits like *Top Gun* (1986) and *Mission Impossible* (1995) but he has also, as learning experience, played unselfish supporting roles to two Oscar-winning performances—Paul Newman's in *The Color of Money* (1986) and Dustin Hoffman's in *Rain Man* (1988). The benefit of such experience can be seen in his performances in *Born on the Fourth of July* (1989), *Jerry Maguire* (1996), *Magnolia* (1999) and his work with Stanley Kubrick on that director's final film, *Eyes Wide Shut* (1999).

Davis, Bette (1908–89)

"Nobody's as good as Bette when she's bad" was the slogan coined for Bette Davis, who excelled at playing dynamic or queen-bitch heroines. Among her major screen performances were three for William Wyler, *Jezebel* (1938), *The Letter* (1940) and *The Little Foxes* (1941), and when her career seemed destined for oblivion in the late 1940s, she returned with one of the classic characterisations of the screen, as the dominating actress Margot Channing in *All About Eve* (1950). Her autobiography *The Lonely Life* (1962) is one of the frankest and most intelligent of any screen star.

Day, Doris (b. 1924)

Pure, wholesome singing star who achieved her peak of popularity in the 1950s and early 1960s, particularly in a series of romantic comedies she made with Rock Hudson, including *Pillow Talk* (1959), *Lover Come Back* (1962) and *Send Me No Flowers* (1964). Appropriated by the feminists, who admire her screen persona for its career-woman independence and its healthy suspicion of male seductive strategies. Certainly someone who can upstage performers such as James Cagney (in *Love Me or Leave Me*, 1954), James Stewart (in *The Man Who Knew Too Much*, 1956) and Clark Gable (in *Teacher's Pet*, 1958) was no mean actress.

Day-Lewis, Daniel. See B19.

Dean, James (1931–55)

Dean made three starring feature roles before his death in a car crash in 1955. But those three, and particularly *Rebel Without a Cause* for Nicholas Ray in 1955, were enough to establish him as Hollywood's leading rebel (along with Brando—and how fascinating subsequent rivalry between their careers would have been). In *Rebel* Dean showed himself as a gentler, more idealistic figure than Brando, particularly in his "adoption" of the young runaway Sal Mineo. In *East of Eden* (Kazan, 1955), it is again his idealism that leads him to look out his mother, now running a whore-house, with disastrous results. In *Giant* (Stevens, 1956) he is an independent cowboy whose discovery of oil on his land will transform him into an isolated tycoon.

De Niro, Robert (b. 1943)

Perhaps the finest American screen actor since Brando, noted for the dedication with which he immerses himself in his roles (*e.g.*, his gaining sixty pounds in weight to play the role of Jake LaMotta in decline in *Raging Bull*). He has had a particularly important collaboration with director Martin Scorsese, for whom he has turned in some of his finest studies of violent yet tortured masculinity: *Mean Streets* (1973), *Taxi Driver* (1976), *Raging Bull* (1980), *Cape Fear* (1991), *Casino* (1995). Other important films include: *The Godfather Part II* (1974), *The Deer Hunter* (1978).

Dietrich, Marlene (1902–92)

Overnight fame came Dietrich's way when Joseph von Sternberg cast her as the sensuous and manipulative night-club singer Lola in *The Blue Angel* (1930). She manipulates Emil Jannings's school teacher there as Sternberg's camera manipulates her (and us, the spectators), through a sequence of lushly masochistic masterpieces including *The Scarlet Empress* (1934). Her post-Sternberg career diversified into cabaret performance, and her subsequent movies, including *The Flame of New Orleans* for Rene Clair in 1941 and *Rancho Notorious* for Fritz Lang in 1952, did not attain the same heights as her work for Sternberg, though she gave striking performances in two Billy Wilder films, *A Foreign Affair* (1948) and *Witness for the Prosecution* (1957), and a memorable cameo in Welles's *Touch of Evil* (1958).

Douglas, Kirk (b. 1916)

Dimpled-chin he-man of the American screen, who excelled in roles of unscrupulous, ambitious anti-heroes, such as those in *Champion* (1949), *Ace in the Hole* (1951) and *The Bad and the Beautiful* (1952), though a more sensitive and tormented side to his persona is also seen in such films as *Lust for Life* (1955), in which he plays Van Gogh, and *Paths of Glory* (1957). The father of actor Michael Douglas.

Eastwood, Clint (b. 1930)

Eastwood is in the great tradition of stars like John Wayne and Gary Cooper who projects pure Americanism and rectifies wrongs, though in a more ferocious manner than his predecessors. Became a star for his "Man With No Name" characterisation in Sergio Leone's violent, stylised "Dollars" westerns; and became a superstar after playing the tough cop in *Dirty Harry* (1971). Sometimes attacked for their Fascist overtones, Eastwood's films have also been praised for their strong female roles, Eastwood's willingness to examine his own screen persona, and their engagement with contemporary issues. Eastwood is also a prolific director, sometimes starring in his own films (*e.g. The Outlaw Josey Wales*, 1976) and sometimes not (*Bird*, 1988), *Mystic River*, (2003). His revisionist Western *Unforgiven* (1992) was widely acclaimed as a classic and won him a directing "Oscar", as did the sensitive drama, *Million Dollar Baby* (2004). His war films, *Flags of Our Fathers* (2006) and *Letters from Iwo Jima* (2007) have also been widely acclaimed.

Fairbanks, Douglas (1883–1939)

The supreme action man of silent cinema, excelling in such features as *The Three Musketeers* (1921), *Robin Hood* (1922) and *The Thief of Bagdad* (1924). Age and sound took their toll of his popularity as did his divorce from Mary Pickford in 1936, after a marriage of sixteen years. But during the silent era, nobody epitomised screen heroism more exuberantly.

Fields, W. C. (1879–1946)

Fields is the polar opposite of Chaplin as a screen comedian, in that, while the "little fellow" courts audience affection, Fields does everything in his drunken, misogynistic, mean, cynical, ill-tempered power to repel it. Through such titles as *Mrs. Wiggs of the Cabbage Patch* (Norman Taurog, 1934) and *Never Give a Sucker an Even Break* (Edward Cline, 1941), he paraded preposterous situations (usually of his own invention), and a battery of dislikes that included wives, children, domestic animals and authority figures. His best films were *It's A Gift* (1935) and *The Bank Dick* (1940). When he was discovered on his death-bed reading the Bible, he explained that he was "looking for loopholes".

Finch, Peter (1916–77)

Rugged yet subtle screen performer, who won the British Academy Award four times for his performances in *A Town Like Alice* (1956), *The Trials of Oscar Wilde* (1960), *No Love for Johnnie* (1961) and *Sunday, Bloody Sunday* (1971). He won a posthumous Oscar for his role in *Network* (1976).

Finney, Albert (b. 1936)

Finney made a big impression with his first screen performances in such films as *Saturday Night and Sunday Morning* (1961) and *Tom Jones* (1963), and was hailed as "a second Olivier". But, unlike Richard Burton, he preferred to eschew screen stardom in favour of theatrical work. The most powerful of his later film performances has been as the drunken Consul in Huston's adaptation of Malcolm Lowry's novel, *Under the Volcano* (1984). Co-starred with Julia Roberts to fine effect in *Erin Brockovich* (2000).

Flynn, Errol (1909–59)

The swashbuckling leading man of a host of popular films. Born in Hobart, Tasmania he became an American citizen in 1942. Between 1935 and 1942 he acted in some of the most enduringly popular films of all time. These included *Captain Blood; The Charge of the Light Brigade; The Adventures of Robin Hood; The Dawn Patrol; Dodge City; The Sea Hawk; They Died With Their Boots On;* and *Gentleman Jim*. His private life ensured he was rarely out of the news. He was married three times and died aged only 50 when hard living finally caught up with him (he famously spent much of his time in bars, bed and the headlines).

He was the father of the actor and journalist Sean Flynn.

Fonda, Henry (1905–82)

One of the major Hollywood leading men of the late thirties and forties, with distinguished starring roles for Fritz Lang (as the runaway in *You Only Live Once*, 1937) and John Ford (in *Young Mr. Lincoln* and *Drums Along the Mohawk*, both 1939, and *The Grapes of Wrath* (1940). His honest and conscientious stance was just right for the immediate

pre- and post-war years. After a lull in his screen career, he made a successful comeback in such films as *Mister Roberts* (1955), *Twelve Angry Men* (1957) and *The Best Man* (1964), and won a long-awaited Oscar for his last film, *On Golden Pond* (1981), co-starring with his daughter Jane.

Fonda, Jane (b. 1937)

Began her career in "sex-symbol" roles—in Hollywood and for her then husband Roger Vadim—that now appear incongruous in the light of her progressive political position (Edward Dmytryk's *Walk on the Wild Side*, 1962; Vadim's *Barbarella*, 1968). Her involvement with the women's movement and anti-Vietnam campaigns took her into such films as *Klute* (Pakula, 1971), where she plays a prostitute who regards herself as "the only truly liberated woman". She won an Oscar for *Klute* and won again later in the decade for *Coming Home* (1978).

Ford, Harrison (b. 1942)

Recently voted the world's most popular film star, a well-earned reward for an actor whose career had begun with discouraging slowness. The turning point came with his role as Han Solo in *Star Wars* (1977) and his stardom was augmented when he became Steven Spielberg's Indiana Jones, a characterisation much admired for its difficult combination of athleticism and wit. An accomplished actor in both romantic comedy and complex character roles (*e.g. in Witness* and *The Mosquito Coast*), he is liked best by the public as a taciturn action man of the old school, even when, as in the film *Air Force One* (1997), he also happens to be President of the USA.

Foster, Jodie (b. 1962)

Child star who has developed into one of the foremost feminist talents of the cinema. Played a precocious moll in the child gangster spoof, *Bugsy Malone* (1976) and then created a furore with her role as an under-age prostitute in *Taxi Driver* (1976), fanned even further when an attempted assassination of President Reagan was said to have been inspired by the gunman's infatuation with Foster's role in that movie. She survived the attendant notoriety to develop into one of the modern screen's most adventurous actresses, winning Oscars for her performances as a rape victim in *The Accused* (1988) and a feisty female investigator in *Silence of the Lambs* (1991). She can direct too.

Gable, Clark (1901–60)

Gable was Hollywood's number one heartthrob in the years immediately preceding the war. His open-handed cheerfulness and easy-going Americanism now might appear dated, but they bowled over a long list of leading ladies, including Claudette Colbert (in Frank Capra's *It Happened One Night*, 1934) and Vivien Leigh (in the Fleming/Cukor/Wood success *Gone with the Wind*, 1939). He is proof that Hollywood male chauvinism did not need the bullying qualities of a John Wayne to make its mark. He gave perhaps his greatest performance in his last film, *The Misfits* (1961).

Garbo, Greta (1905–90)

A career that lasted only seventeen years and a reclusive retirement combined to create the "Garbo myth" of world-weary, capricious and lonesome sensuality, which must be one of the most potent in cinema history. She moved from Sweden to Hollywood under the aegis of the director Mauritz Stiller in 1926, to become MGM's major star, whose every move was heralded by a barrage of studio publicity (thus, "Garbo talks!" before Clarence Brown's *Anna Christie* in 1930, and "Garbo laughs!" before *Ninotchka*, made for Ernst Lubitsch in 1939). Unlike her romantic co-star in the silent period, John Gilbert, Garbo triumphantly made the transition to talkies, her greatest successes being in *Queen Christina* (1934) and *Camille* (1937). But after the disaster of *Two-Faced Woman* (1941) she retired.

Garland, Judy (1922–69)

A prominent teenage star who became famous

through her performance in *The Wizard of Oz* (Victor Fleming, 1939), where she first performed the song whose soaring yearning was to become her hallmark—"Over the Rainbow". She starred in musicals for her then-husband, Vincente Minnelli (including *Meet Me in St. Louis*, 1944), but the pattern of breakdown, emotional turmoil, and abuse of barbiturates had set in by the beginning of the fifties. Stage appearances and nervous breakdowns between them crowded out her mature film career, though her performance in *A Star is Born* (1954) was a tour-de-force.

Gibson, Mel (b. 1956)

'The most interesting young actor of his period,' said Franco Zeffirelli when casting Mel Gibson as Hamlet. An odd role ostensibly for the star of action extravaganzas like *Mad Max* (1979) and *Lethal Weapon* (1987) but then again, perhaps not: all are heroes unhinged by violent destruction of their family lives and who affect an antic disposition to cope with their torment. Gibson is good at character extremes, as well as being a competent director and a glamour film star of a kind rarely seen since the 1930s. Though actually born in New York, his first film successes were in Australia, but like director Peter Weir, for whom he starred in *Gallipoli* (1981) and *The Year of Living Dangerously* (1983), he moved to Hollywood in the early 1980s and has not looked back. Won a directing Oscar for *Braveheart* (1995) and created enormous controversy with a personal project inspired by his religious beliefs, *The Passion of the Christ* (2004).

Gish, Lillian (1896–1993)

The longest career of movie actors—from D. W. Griffith's *An Unseen Enemy* (1912) through to Lindsay Anderson's *The Whales of August* (1987). She radiated innocence for Griffith in *The Birth of a Nation* (1915) and *Intolerance* (1916), before leaving his Biograph company to make more money, first for Inspiration and then for MGM. During the sound era, her screen appearances were intermittent, though she was particularly effective as the brave schoolma'am facing up to Robert Mitchum's demonic preacher in *The Night of the Hunter* (1955). Her performances in Griffith's *Broken Blossoms* (1919) and Victor Seastrom's *The Wind* (1928) are among the greatest of the silent film era.

Grant, Cary (1904–86)

His British origin shows in his debonair style and curious "mid-Atlantic" accent (imitated by Tony Curtis in Billy Wilder's *Some Like it Hot*, 1959). Beneath his gentlemanly urbanity, frenzy, even insanity, never seem far away, which accounts for the matchless ambiguity of his greatest performances—as the suspected wife-murderer in Hitchcock's *Suspicion* (1941), as baiting foil to Mae West in Wesley Ruggles's *I'm No Angel* (1933), as advertising man pursued across America by spies in *North by North-West* (Hitchcock, 1959), and above all the victim of the insecurity that stems from sex-stereotyping in the comedies he made opposite various leading ladies for Howard Hawks—*Bringing Up Baby* (with Katharine Hepburn, 1938), *His Girl Friday* (with Rosalind Russell, 1940), and *I Was a Male War Bride* (with Ann Sheridan, 1949). Small wonder that he won an Oscar in 1970 for "sheer brilliance".

Guinness, Sir Alec (1914–2000)

Guinness came to prominence as a screen actor in the great Ealing comedies, notably *Kind Hearts and Coronets* (1949), *The Man in the White Suit* (1951), *The Lavender Hill Mob* (1952), and *The Ladykillers* (1955). He also developed a close working relationship with David Lean, and won an Oscar for his superb performance in Lean's *The Bridge on the River Kwai* (1957). An actor of unobtrusive subtlety and infinite resource, he achieved his biggest popular success in *Star Wars* (1977) but more representative of his skills were his masterly characterisations in such films as *Tunes of Glory* (1960) and *Little Dorritt* (1987).

Hackman, Gene (b. 1931)

One of the most durable and dependable charac-

ter stars of modern American cinema., at home in comedy but at his best when giving subtle emotional colouring to 'average' men with a darker side to their natures. His most famous role is still probably that of the rebellious rule-breaking cop, 'Popeye' Doyle in *The French Connection* (1971), for which he won an Oscar, as he did also for his performance as the sadistic sheriff in Clint Eastwood's *Unforgiven* (1992). But his great performances are legion: *The Conversation* (1974), *Night Moves* (1975), *Eureka* (1982), *Under Fire* (1983), *Target* (1985), *Mississippi Burning* (1988), *Class Action* (1991).

Hanks, Tom (b. 1956)

Popular leading man of the last decade in both comedy and dramatic roles, who became the first actor since Spencer Tracy to win the Best Actor Oscar in consecutive years: for *Philadelphia* (1993) and *Forrest Gump* (1994). His acceptance speeches have become something to be feared, however: in one, he inadvertently 'outed' a former drama teacher. Other key films: *Big* (1988), *Sleepless in Seattle* (1993), *Apollo 13* (1995), *Saving Private Ryan* (1998) and *Road to Perdition* (2002).

Hepburn, Audrey (1929–93)

Enchanting elfin actress who won an Oscar in her first starring role, *Roman Holiday* (Wyler, 1953). She then proceeded to bewitch some of Hollywood's most eminent senior citizens—Humphrey Bogart in *Sabrina* (1954), Gary Cooper in *Love in the Afternoon* (1957), Cary Grant in *Charade* (1963), Rex Harrison in *My Fair Lady* (1964). An adept comedienne, she also proved herself a formidable dramatic actress in *The Nun's Story* (1959), *The Children's Hour* (1961) and *Robin and Marian* (1976). She then virtually retired though Spielberg cast her appropriately as an angel in *Always* (1989).

Hepburn, Katharine (1909–2003)

The most intelligent and astringent of all screen comediennes—if not all screen actresses. She remained resolutely outside the mould of female stardom, regarded for years as box-office poison and relying on her mind rather than her body for impact. Her most celebrated films are those made with her long-time off-screen lover, Spencer Tracy—notably *Adam's Rib* and *Pat and Mike* for George Cukor (1949 and 1952 respectively), and *State of the Union* for Frank Capra in 1948. But her warm sharpness was equally in evidence with Cary Grant (*Bringing Up Baby* for Hawks in 1938) and Humphrey Bogart (*The African Queen* for John Huston in 1951). Winner of four best actress Oscars (more than any other recipient), she published a set of autobiographical memoirs, *Me* (1991). Her greatest screen performances include *Alice Adams* (1935), *Summer Madness* (1955), *Suddenly Last Summer* (1959) and *Long Day's Journey into Night* (1962).

Heston, Charlton (1923–2008)

Heston's first starring role was in C. B. DeMille's circus epic, *The Greatest Show on Earth* (1952). He later specialised in epic roles, bringing dignity and integrity to the genre, particularly in his title performances in *Ben Hur* (1959) and *El Cid* (1961). His historical roles ranged from Cardinal Richelieu to General Gordon, from Moses to Michelangelo: his best modern film role was probably in Welles's *Touch of Evil* (1958). He also excelled in westerns, in *The Big Country* (1958) and *Will Penny* (1968).

Hoffman, Dustin (b. 1937)

Earnest, intense method actor whose perfectionism has sometimes driven co-stars to distraction (Olivier: "Dustin is very talented—but why doesn't he just act?") but has certainly produced the goods—Oscars for his performances in *Kramer vs. Kramer* (1979) and *The Rain Man* (1988). Other important roles: *The Graduate* (1967), *Lenny* (1974), *All the President's Men* (1976), and *Tootsie* (1982). Now a film director (*e.g. Quartet*).

Holden, William (1918–81)

Handsome leading man of the 1940s rescued from bland B-picture roles by Billy Wilder, who cast him as a screen writing gigolo in *Sunset Boulevard* (1950) and as a captive capitalist in *Stalag 17* (1953), for which Holden won an Oscar. After a lean spell in the 1960s, his career revived with his splendid leading performance in *The Wild Bunch* (1969), and before his death, he gave further thoughtful characterisations in *Network* (1976) and *Fedora* (1978). Other key roles: *Golden Boy* (1939), *Sabrina* (1954), *Picnic* (1955) and *The Bridge on the River Kwai* (1957).

Hopkins, Sir Anthony (b. 1937)

Theatrically trained, Hopkins is sometimes seen as the natural successor to Richard Burton and Sir Laurence Olivier: indeed, he dubbed Olivier's voice when *Spartacus* was re-released in an extended version. For all his versatility and skill, however, he seems likely to be remembered most for his performance as a monster, the cannibalistic Hannibal Lecter in *The Silence of the Lambs* (1991). Other key performances: *The Lion in Winter* (1968), *Juggernaut* (1974), *The Elephant Man* (1980), *The Bounty* (1984), *Howards End* (1992), *The Remains of the Day* (1993), *Nixon* (1995), *Amistad* (1997).

Howard, Trevor (1916–87)

Leathery character actor of the British cinema, reputedly Graham Greene's favourite. Capable of acting just about anyone off the screen, which might be the reason that he only rarely got the parts (and therefore the recognition) that he deserved. Important films include: *Brief Encounter* (1945), *The Third Man* (1949), *Outcast of The Islands* (1951), *The Key* (1958), *Sons and Lovers* (1960), *Mutiny on the Bounty* (1962) and *Ludwig* (1972).

Hudson, Rock (1925–85)

Solid Hollywood leading man who sprang back into the public eye in the 1980s because of his death from AIDS. This rather contradicted his screen image as the all-American romantic hero. An effective screen actor in dramas such as *Giant* (1956) or comedies such as *Send Me No Flowers* (1964), he had, in retrospect, his most resonant role in John Frankenheimer's sci-fi horror film, *Seconds* (1966), where a dissatisfied middle-aged man fakes his own death and, through plastic surgery, starts a new life looking like Rock Hudson—and finds that soul-destroying also.

Huppert, Isabelle (b. 1955)

She came to prominence with a beautiful performance in *The Lacemaker* (1977), playing an unaffected girl whose emotional vulnerability leads to a complete mental breakdown after an unhappy love affair. The fragility seemed so natural and believable that one has since been often taken aback by her range and resource, particularly in some of her films for Claude Chabrol, where she has revealed surprising ferocity behind the freckle-faced exterior. Her performance in Michael Haneke's *The Piano Teacher* (2001), where she plays a music teacher with secret sado-masochistic tendencies, is a *tour-de-force*.

Jannings, Emil (1884–1950)

A king of the German silent cinema, but ruined by the coming of sound (which showed up his thick accent) and also his collaboration with the Nazis. His massive self-sentimentalisation and Prussian obsession with lost status were triumphant in Murnau's *The Last Laugh* (1924), and even more so in his role as the puritanical schoolteacher Professor Rath, destroyed by his passion for Marlene Dietrich's Lola in Sternberg's *The Blue Angel* (1930). This performance remains the greatest monument of male sexual humiliation in cinema history. He epitomised silent film acting at its most Expressionist and expressive, though Luis Buñuel said he preferred Buster Keaton.

Karloff, Boris (1887–1969)

Here again on- and off-screen personas interacted intriguingly. Mild mannered English cricket-loving gentleman William Henry Pratt became the best-known horror star in Hollywood history with his performance as the blundering yet tender-hearted monster in James Whale's *Frankenstein* in 1931.

Thenceforth his legendary status was secure, and augmented by his work for Karl Freund (*The Mummy* of 1932) and Charles Vidor (*The Mask of Fu Manchu*, 1932). As moving as his performance in *Frankenstein* in many ways is his valedictory appearance in Peter Bogdanovich's *Targets* (shot in the year of his death) where he plays a retired Hollywood horror star whose essential kindness is appalled by the horror of American society.

Keaton, Buster (1895–1966)

Arguably the greatest director and the greatest actor of the American silent era. As an actor, Keaton's deadpan appearance, often almost suicidal insistence on choreographing and carrying out all his own stunts, and awareness of the element of fantasy identification in cinema have ensured that his performances remain consistently exciting and do not date. As a director, he masterfully exploited the relationship between man and machine—driver/train and actor/camera—in *The General* of 1926, and that between cinema and dream in *Sherlock Junior* of 1924. His career was undermined as much by the classic Hollywood afflictions—marital problems and drinking—as by the coming of sound.

But his reputation has soared since his death, and works such as *Our Hospitality* (1923), *Seven Chances* (1925), *The Navigator* (1927) and *Steamboat Bill Jr.* (1928), along with his aforementioned films, are now regarded as comedy classics. Appeared alongside Chaplin in an unforgettable routine in the latter's *Limelight* (1952).

Kelly, Gene (1912–96)

The most inventive and adventurous actor-choreographer of the American screen. Rival to Fred Astaire as Hollywood's dancing master, Kelly was even more creative in furthering the boundaries of the film musical, particularly in a trio of magnificent musicals he co-directed with Stanley Donen: *On the Town* (1949), *Singin' in the Rain* (1952) and *It's Always Fair Weather* (1955).

Kelly, Grace (1928–82)

Aloof but elegant leading lady who made her first major impression as Gary Cooper's Quaker wife in *High Noon* (1952) and then as the archetypal Hitchcockian ice-cool blonde in *Dial M for Murder* (1954), *Rear Window* (1954) and *To Catch a Thief* (1955). Her dramatic prowess was revealed in her Oscar-winning role in *The Country Girl* (1954) but she gave up stardom for royalty when she married Prince Rainier of Monaco in 1956.

Kerr, Deborah (1921–2007)

One of the most versatile and sensitive of British screen actresses, whose persona of "English rose" was changed when she played the nymphomaniac wife of an Army Captain in *From Here to Eternity* (1953). She seemed at her finest either when playing nuns with a hint of neurosis—*Black Narcissus* (1947), *Heaven Knows, Mr. Allison* (1957)—or prim teachers or governesses wrestling privately with emotional repression—*The King and I* (1955), *Tea and Sympathy* (1956), *The Innocents* (1961).

Kidman, Nicole (b. 1968)

Formerly married to Tom Cruise, she seems to share Cruise's ability to choose her roles with some shrewdness. As a consequence, she has matured into a screen actress of considerable subtlety and force. She won an Oscar for her portrayal of Virginia Woolf in *The Hours* (2002). Other important films: *Dead Calm* (1989), *Malice* (1993), *To Die For* (1995), *Portrait of a Lady* (1996), *Eyes Wide Shut* (1999), *Moulin Rouge* (2001), *The Others* (2001) and *Dogville* (2003).

Lancaster, Burt (1913–94)

Acrobat turned actor, who revealed a sensitive interior behind his action-man mask. He won an Oscar for his role as a religious charlatan in *Elmer Gantry* (1960), and a Venice Festival award for a more introvert performance in *Bird Man of Alcatraz* (1962). "A deeply mysterious man" was the verdict on him of Luchino Visconti, who directed him to great effect in *The Leopard* (1963) and *Conversation*

Piece (1974), and he triumphed also under Louis Malle in *Atlantic City* (1980). He had a career of fascinating contrasts, between swashbuckling and sensitive roles. Other key films include: *The Killers* (1946), *The Crimson Pirate* (1952), *From Here to Eternity* (1953), *Sweet Smell of Success* (1957), *1900* (1976) and *Twilight's Last Gleaming* (1977).

Laughton, Charles (1899–1962)

Bulky actor of phenomenal power and range, with the occasional tendency to ham but also capable of producing magical effects with a sympathetic director. It is sometimes thought that his heyday was in the thirties, when he excelled in *The Private Life of Henry VIII* (1933), *Ruggles of Red Gap* (1935), *Mutiny on the Bounty* (1935) and *The Hunchback of Notre Dame* (1939). But he was no less remarkable in later films such as *Hobson's Choice* (1953), *Witness for the Prosecution* (1957), *Spartacus* (1960) and *Advise and Consent* (1962). There is a sense of relish about his greatest acting, whether playing saint or sadist. One should not forget also his one and only film as director, an altogether remarkable, poetic thriller *The Night of the Hunter* (1955) that constitutes one of the most extraordinary directing debuts in cinema history.

Laurel (1890–1965) and Hardy (1892–1957)

The first great comedy partnership in films, and never surpassed. Their films usually involve frantic attempts to gain social acceptance (*e.g.* as pianomovers or salesmen), that lead to the disasters ruefully described by Hardy as "another nice mess". Their features, including *Pack Up Your Troubles* (Marshall and Raymond McCarey, 1932) and *A Chump at Oxford* (Alfred Goulding, 1940), retain the personas—sly and skinny Stan and overweight Ollie trying to cling on to his dignity—almost intact. The comedy of failure in its purest, most unpretentious form. Key films include: *Big Business* (1929), *The Music Box* (1932), *Sons of the Desert* (1934), *Way Out West* (1937).

Leigh, Vivien (1913–67)

Fragile and exquisite English actress who remarkably scored her greatest film triumphs in two quintessentially American roles: as Scarlett O'Hara in *Gone With the Wind* (1939) and as Blanche DuBois in *A Streetcar Named Desire* (1951). Married to Laurence Olivier in 1940, her later career was blighted by physical and mental illness. She was divorced from Olivier in 1960, and her last major film roles were in *The Roman Spring of Mrs. Stone* (1961) and *Ship of Fools* (1965).

Lemmon, Jack (1925–2001)

Consummate film actor who is probably most associated in the public mind with a series of sublime comedy characterisations in films of Billy Wilder, such as *Some Like it Hot* (1959), *The Apartment* (1960), *The Fortune Cookie* (1966), and *Avanti!* (1972). But he was an equally forceful straight actor, as films such as *Days of Wine and Roses* (1962), *The China Syndrome* (1979), *Missing* (1982) and *Glengarry Glen Ross* (1992) demonstrate. The screen's best tragi-comedian since Chaplin.

Loren, Sophia (b. 1934)

Epitomises the stereotype of Latin female sexuality for the moviegoer, much as Marcello Mastroianni did for the male. She began for Hollywood in ripely sensual roles (e.g. *Desire under the Elms* for Delbert Mann in 1958), before moving on to more demanding dramatic parts, such as Vittorio de Sica's *Two Women* for which she won an Oscar in 1961.

Lorre, Peter (1904–64)

Among his best-known films there is only one in which he actually starred: *M* for Fritz Lang in 1931, where he portrayed a demented child-murderer, contorting his features as much as Lang's direction contorted the screen images. But he became one of Hollywood's most memorable supporting actors, as the crazed hitman in Huston's *The Maltese Falcon* (1941), and for Michael Curtiz (in *Casablanca* of 1943 and *Passage to Marseilles* of 1944) and Frank Capra (*Arsenic and Old Lace*, 1944). Like Karloff

but in a very different way, he excelled at suggesting sensitivity beneath the contortions of horror and malice.

Maclaine, Shirley (b. 1934)

Prodigiously talented dancer-cum-comedienne-cum dramatic actress. Won an Oscar for *Terms of Endearment* (1983), but her best films are the early ones: *The Trouble With Harry* (1955), *Some Came Running* (1958), *The Apartment* (1960), *The Children's Hour* (1961) and *Sweet Charity* (1969).

March, Fredric (1897–1975)

One of Hollywood's finest character actors, particularly when portraying ostensibly decent men with darker sides to their personalities. This was shown to particular effect in *Dr. Jekyll and Mr. Hyde* (1932) but was also a feature of some other of his major roles: *Les Miserables* (1935), *The Best Years of our Lives* (1946), *Death of a Salesman* (1952), *Executive Suite* (1954), *The Desperate Hours* (1955) and *Inherit the Wind* (1960).

Marx Brothers: Chico (1887–1961), Harpo (1888–1964), Groucho (1890–1978)

Hollywood's undisputed great comic family. Groucho's undammable flow of insult and wisecrack, Chico's illogicalities and prevarications (delivered in a heavy mock-Italian accent), and Harpo's mute mime form an unbeatable trio, whether in the early Paramount features (such as *Duck Soup* for Leo McCarey in 1933) or in their later work for MGM, where musical and romantic interludes irksomely break up the stream of comedy (as in *A Day at the Races*—Sam Wood, 1937). Their most popular film, and Groucho's favourite, was *A Night at the Opera* (1935). (Another brother Zeppo appeared in some of their earlier films, either as an improbable romantic lead or even, in *Horse Feathers* of 1932, as Groucho's son.)

Mason, James (1909–84)

Mason's style migrated successfully from the British industry (as in *Odd Man Out*—Carol Reed, 1947) to Hollywood and the international circuit. He was an urbane villain for Hitchcock in *North by North-West* (1959), and a suitable articulate and obsessed lover for *Lolita* (Stanley Kubrick, 1962), somewhat removed from the persona of the romantic sadist with which he had first shot to fame (in *The Man in Grey*, 1943 and *The Wicked Lady*, 1945). One of those screen actors like Trevor Howard or David Niven who seemed incapable of giving a bad performance, however bad the film was around him. When the film was good—like, say, *Five Fingers* (1952), *A Star is Born* (1954), *The Pumpkin Eater* (1964), *The Verdict* (1982)—he could be quite exceptional.

Mastroianni, Marcello (1924–96)

The ultimate listless Latin lover, who seems wearied by the very thought of all the women to whom he is supposed to appeal. This quality in fact enables his screen persona to work quite subversively against the macho ideal of Hollywood, as in Fellini's *La Dolce Vita* (1960), where he plays a disillusioned journalist, or Antonioni's *La Notte* (1961), as the exhausted husband of Jeanne Moreau. His finest performance remains that in Fellini's 8½ (1963), as the film director (an obvious alter ego to Fellini), whose very prostration and inability to organise his neuroses into cinematic form at the end provide the mainspring that enables him to do so. The films with Fellini and Antonioni remain his best-known work. His later successes included *Macaroni* (1985), opposite Jack Lemmon; *Ginger and Fred* (1986), for Fellini; and a particularly intense performance in *The Beekeeper* (1986) for Greece's major contemporary director, Theo Angelopoulous.

McQueen, Steve (1930–80)

Supercool but smouldering anti-hero and loner, McQueen became a star after his POW antics on a motorbike in John Sturges' *The Great Escape* (1963). Best remembered for action roles like *The Magnificent Seven* (1960) or *Bullitt* (1968), McQueen was showing signs of greater artistic ambition towards the end of his life, producing as well as starring in an adaptation of Ibsen's *An Enemy of the People* (1979) and contributing a finely shaded, poignant performance in the elegiac Western, *Tom Horn* (1980).

Mifune, Toshiro (1920–97)

Japanese actor whose robust style, ironic as well as dramatic, was indelibly associated with the films he made for Kurosawa, including *Rashomon* (1951), *Seven Samurai* (1954), *Throne of Blood* (1957) and *Yojimbo* (1961). He also appeared in the occasional Hollywood film, most notably opposite Lee Marvin in *Hell in the Pacific* (1969).

Mitchum, Robert (1917–97)

A deceptively outstanding film actor whose lazy style concealed enormous range and prodigious depth. Directors as exacting as John Huston (*Heaven Knows Mr. Allison*, 1957) and Fred Zinnemann (*The Sundowners*, 1960) testified to Mitchum's exceptional abilities. Only once nominated for an Oscar (for *The Story of G.I. Joe*, 1945), his memorable performances include *Pursued* (1947), *Build My Gallows High* (1947), *The Lusty Men* (1952), *The Night of the Hunter* (1955), *Cape Fear* (1962), *Ryan's Daughter* (1970), *The Friends of Eddie Coyle* (1973), *The Last Tycoon* (1976).

Monroe, Marilyn (1926–62)

Not the original cinematic sex symbol—that distinction belongs to Mary Pickford or Rudolph Valentino—but Monroe is certainly the best-known. Nowhere else have the on-and-off screen persona interacted to such devastating, and finally destructive, effect. She began as a "dumb blonde" in the early fifties before producers and directors recognised in her vulnerability and ambivalent attitude towards her own sexuality—pride tempered by the desire to be appreciated for something more—outstanding qualities. Her best films remain comedies in which her ambivalence was played upon to enrich the texture of the movies: *Bus Stop* for Joshua Logan in 1956, and for Billy Wilder, *The Seven-Year Itch* of 1955, and *Some Like It Hot* in 1959. She gave an extraordinary dramatic performance in Huston's *The Misfits* (1961), but was dismissed from her final project (Cukor's *Something's Got to Give*) for unreliability in 1962, and not long afterwards committed suicide. Revelations of her off-screen loneliness and the mysterious circumstances of her death went to fuel what is still Hollywood's most potent and macabre legend.

Moreau, Jeanne (b. 1928)

Described as the "thinking man's actress', and whose name was synonymous with some of the greatest and most controversial European art movies of the late fifties and early sixties: Malle's *The Lovers* (1958), Truffaut's *Jules et Jim* (1961), Antonioni's *La Notte* (1962) and Buñuel's *Diary of a Chambermaid* (1964).

Newman, Paul (1925–2008)

Blue-eyed boy of modern American film, exceptionally good looking and a considerable actor to boot. Early Oscar-nominated performances in *Cat on a Hot Tin Roof* (1958), *The Hustler* (1961), *Hud* (1963) and *Cool Hand Luke* (1967) testified to Newman's great skill in revealing an attractive, adventurous side to roles which, in other hands, could have seemed unsympathetic and morbid. He finally won his Oscar for *The Color of Money* (1986), Scorsese's sequel to *The Hustler*. He also proved himself a sympathetic director, particularly of his actress-wife Joanne Woodward, in films such as *Rachel, Rachel* (1968) and *The Glass Menagerie* (1987).

Nicholson, Jack (b. 1937)

Nicholson broke into public prominence with his performance as the alcoholic ne'er-do-well in Hopper's *Easy Rider* (1969), and has remained at the top ever since with sardonic yet often tender performances. The versatility that often goes with understatement has enabled him to give outstand-

ing performances as a drop-out classical musician (Bob Rafelson's *Five Easy Pieces* in 1970), a private eye (Polanski's *Chinatown* in 1974), a rebel in a mental hospital (Milos Forman's *One Flew Over The Cuckoo's Nest*, 1975), a cynical writer (James L. Brooks' *As Good as it Gets*, 1997) a retired cop (*The Pledge*, 2001), and a widower reappraising his life (*About Schmidt*, 2002).

Olivier, Sir Laurence (1907–89)

Perhaps the most exciting and respected actor of his generation, Olivier will first be remembered and revered for his achievement as actor and director in bringing Shakespeare to vivid life on screen with *Henry V* (1944), *Hamlet* (1948) and *Richard III* (1955). But his most subtle screen acting was to be found in two films he made for Wyler, *Wuthering Heights* (1939) and *Carrie* (1952), and one for Hitchcock, *Rebecca* (1940). His last major film role was in Mankiewicz's *Sleuth* (1972).

Pacino, Al (b. 1940)

Born in New York of Sicilian descent and an apostle of the great acting teacher Lee Strasberg, Pacino shot to prominence with his performance as Michael Corleone in *The Godfather* (1972), a role he was to repeat and refine in two sequels. An actor of great resource and range, he rivals DeNiro as the most admired American screen actor since Marlon Brando. Key films include: *Godfather II* (1974), *Dog Day Afternoon* (1975), *Scarface* (1983), *Glengarry Glen Ross* (1992), *Heat* (1996), *Looking for Richard* (1996), *The Insider* (1999) and *Insomnia* (2002).

Peck, Gregory (1916–2003)

Archetypal screen symbol of liberal integrity, particularly embodied in his performance as the lawyer defending an unjustly accused Negro in *To Kill a Mockingbird* (1962), for which he justly won an Oscar. Other important films: *Gentleman's Agreement* (1947), *The Gunfighter* (1950), *Roman Holiday* (1953), *Moby Dick* (1956), *The Big Country* (1958), *The Stalking Moon* (1968) and *I Walk the Line* (1970).

Pickford, Mary (1893–1979)

The sentimentality of Pickford's early performances for D. W. Griffith between 1909 and 1912, and her peak period as "America's Sweetheart" when married to Douglas Fairbanks (*Daddy Long Legs* for Marshall Neilan in 1919, *Pollyanna* for Paul Powell in 1920) are considerably less interesting today than her ideological role as what Basil Wright has dubbed the "hearth goddess" of domesticity and her early status as one of the first multi-millionaire film stars.

Poitier, Sidney (b. 1924)

Ground-breaking black actor, one of the first to attain Hollywood star status. Poitier won an Oscar for a now virtually forgotten movie, *Lilies of the Field* (1963), and is better remembered for such films as *The Defiant Ones* (1958), *In The Heat of the Night* (1967) and *Guess Who's Coming to Dinner* (1967). Also an accomplished director, though definitely in the commercial mainstream rather than in the radical alternative lane chosen by the new generation of black American directors such as Spike Lee and John Singleton.

Rains, Claude (1889–1967)

Soft-spoken, diminutive actor whose first screen triumph was in a part in which his face was only shown in the very last shot: namely, the eponymous hero of *The Invisible Man* (1932). A favourite co-star of Bette Davis, he was incomparable at portraying suave villainy, notably in *The Adventures of Robin Hood* (1938) and, of course, *Casablanca* (1943), but, for all his seeming dryness, he could also give uncommon intensity to the feelings of scorned love: his performances as the humiliated husbands in Hitchcock's *Notorious* (1946) and Lean's *The Passionate Friends* (1949) throb with a poignant romantic anguish.

Redford, Robert (b. 1937)

Redford is distinguished from his "peer-group" stars such as Beatty and Nicholson by a resolute rejection of the trappings of stardom. Athletically handsome (like John Wayne he went to university on a sports scholarship), he struck gold with *Butch Cassidy and the Sundance Kid* (George Roy Hill, 1969), and created perhaps his most successful dramatic role in the Scott Fitzgerald adaptation, *The Great Gatsby* for Jack Clayton in 1974. His directing debut, *Ordinary People* (1980) won him an Oscar.

His most lasting monument might well be the Sundance Institute, which he founded in 1980 and which has since become a training ground and launching pad for some of America's finest young independent film makers.

Roberts, Julia (b. 1967)

Former model who has developed into one of the star actresses of modern cinema, culminating in her critically acclaimed, Oscar winning performance in *Erin Brockovich* (2000). Other key films: *Pretty Woman* (1990), *Sleeping with the Enemy* (1990) and *Everyone Says I Love You* (1996).

Robinson, Edward G. (1893–1973)

Robinson made his name in gangster film roles such as *Little Ceasar* (1931) and as Johnny Rocco in Huston's *Key Largo* (1948). But he was actually a highly skilled actor in a variety of parts, at his best perhaps in two psychological dramas for Fritz Lang, *Woman in the Window* (1944) and *Scarlet Street* (1945); as the insurance investigator in Wilder's *Double Indemnity* (1944); and as a roguish diamond smuggler in Mackendrick's *Sammy Going South* (1963).

Schwarzenegger, Arnold (b. 1947)

Born in Graz, Austria, Schwarzenegger was a champion body-builder before he turned to acting in roles that exploited both his physique and his robotic histrionics. His persona has essentially been that of a slow-witted, thickly accented superhero whose muscle power far exceeds his intellect, and he has maintained a mass following not only through his screen heroics but also a genial willingness to poke fun at his own image. Married to the niece of President of John F. Kennedy, he was elected Republican Governor of California.

Other major films: *Stay Hungry* (1976), *Conan the Barbarian* (1982), *The Terminator* (1984) and *Total Recall* (1990).

Scott, George C. (1926–99)

On his day, one of the screen's most powerful and exciting actors. His first important role was as a razor-sharp prosecutor in Preminger's *Anatomy of a Murder* (1959), putting James Stewart on his mettle, and he followed it with an equally incisive characterisation as the sinister, Mephistophelian gambler in *The Hustler* (1961) who covets Paul Newman's soul. A dazzling comic turn as a war-mongering General in Kubrick's *Dr Strangelove* (1964), contemplating global annihilation with a sort of maniacal glee, revealed his acting range, as did his subtle, moving performance in Richard Lester's *Petulia* (1968) as a doctor experiencing a mid-life crisis in a late 1960s America that is itself about to implode. As forthright off the screen as on, he turned down his Oscar for *Patton* (1970) out of distaste for what he called the demeaning "meat parade" of the Awards ceremony.

Sharif, Omar (1932–2015)

The smouldering Egyptian actor forever famous for his roles in *Lawrence of Arabia* and *Doctor Zhivago*, where he played the title role. He was born in Alexandria. His image was of the gambling bridge-playing playboy.

Signoret, Simone (1921–85)

Classy French actress who excelled at playing lovelorn women, most memorably in Jacques Becker's *Casque d'Or* (1952) and Jack Clayton's *Room at the Top* (1959). Among her other important films are *La Ronde* (1950), *Les Diaboliques* (1955), *The Army of the Shadows* (1969) and *Madame Rosa* (1977).

Stanwyck, Barbara (1907–90)

Vibrant, strong actress, much appreciated by directors such as Capra, DeMille, Lang, Sirk for her utter professionalism. Her stock-in-trade was as a hard-as-nails heroine who knew her own mind and was sometimes not to be trusted. Nominated for an Oscar four times without winning (for *Stella Dallas*, 1937; *Ball of Fire*, 1942; *Double Indemnity*, 1944; and *Sorry, Wrong Number*, 1948), she was finally given an honorary Oscar in 1982. Other key films: *The Bitter Tea of General Yen* (1933), *Annie Oakley* (1935), *The Lady Eve* (1941), *The Furies* (1950), *There's Always Tomorrow* (1956).

Stewart, James (1908–97)

Directors found complex uses for the slow drawl and shy demeanour of this adroit screen actor: all-American integrity, in his films for Capra (*Mr. Smith goes to Washington*, 1939; *It's A Wonderful Life*, 1946); seething inner intensity in his Anthony Mann westerns; and romantic vulnerability in his Alfred Hitchcock movies, most disturbingly and tragically so in *Vertigo* (1958). A versatile performer, who combined exceptional dramatic power, seen at its best in Preminger's *Anatomy of a Murder* (1959), with a flair for comedy: his performance in Cukor's *Philadelphia Story* (1940) won him an Oscar.

Streep, Meryl (b. 1951)

One of the leading ladies of the modern screen, who at one stage seemed to snatch all the big parts, whether they were English, Danish, Polish, or Australian, let alone American. She might not always move the heart, but the acting intelligence and technique are formidable. Her key films include: *The Deer Hunter* (1978), *Kramer Vs. Kramer* (1979), *The French Lieutenant's Woman* (1981), *Sophie's Choice* (1982), *Out of Africa* (1985), *The Bridges of Madison County* (1995), *The Hours* (2002), *Mamma Mia!* (2008) and *The Iron Lady* (for which she won a Best Actress Oscar).

Swanson, Gloria (1897–1983)

Perhaps the most glamorous of silent screen stars, particularly in her films for Cecil B. DeMille, like *Male and Female* (1919). She lost much of her wealth when producing *Queen Kelly* (1928), a film she stopped in mid-production owing to director Erich von Stroheim's extravagance: and talkies proved a problem. However, she made a triumphant return to the screen as Norma Desmond in Billy Wilder's *Sunset Boulevard* (1950), as the former silent star dreaming of a comeback. When the brash screenwriter says she used to be big, she snaps back: "I *am* big. It's the pictures that got small."

Tati, Jacques (1908–82)

Like Keaton, Tati's claim to fame is based on his direction as much as on his acting. Indeed it could be said that the two in a sense came into conflict in his later career, his directorial skill and concern with elaborate mechanised set-pieces causing his output to be irregular and often working against his lanky, absent-minded quality as a clown. *Mr. Hulot's Holiday* (1953) remains one of the greatest silent comedies in cinema history (sound was actually added after shooting, but its contribution to the comic impact is minimal), and Tati's greatest achievement in that film is perhaps the way in which he manages to render a specifically French social stereotype—the would-be sporting bourgeois on a seaside holiday—appealing to a much wider audience. Later films like *Mon Oncle* (1958), *Playtime* (1968) and *Traffic* (1971) have an almost mathematical precision in their comedy lay-out and a serious underlying theme: the decline of individuality in an age of mechanisation.

Taylor, Dame Elizabeth (1932–2011)

Taylor started out as a child-star in Clarence Brown's *National Velvet* (1944) before becoming one of the major Hollywood sex symbols of the fifties, dark and sultry in Richard Brooks's *Cat on a Hot Tin Roof* (1958) and Mankiewicz's *Suddenly Last Summer* (1959). After her marriage to Richard Burton their off-and-on screen persona were profitably played off against each other, this culminating in her Oscar-winning performance in Mike Nichols's *Who's Afraid of Virginia Woolf!* (1966). Directors like George Stevens and Joseph Losey spoke glowingly of her skill as a screen actress, but it was as a star that she excelled, and nobody symbolised celluloid glamour more seductively. From being its loveliest child star, Elizabeth Taylor came to be fairly regarded as Hollywood's Queen Mother.

Other important films: *Father of the Bride* (1950), *A Place in the Sun* (1951), *Butterfield 8* (1960), *Cleopatra* (1963), *Reflections in a Golden Eye* (1967) and *Secret Ceremony* (1968).

Temple, Shirley (1928–2014)

The most famous of all child stars, precociously talented at singing, dancing and emoting. The top box-office attraction of 1938, she was a has-been by 1940, and spent her adult life engaged not in movies but in Republican politics. Main films include: *Little Miss Marker* (1934), *Wee Willie Winkie* (1937) and *Rebecca of Sunnybrook Farm* (1938).

Tracy, Spencer (1900–67)

Tracy successfully embodied in the thirties and forties certain "all-American" qualities—bluff decency, perceptive kind-heartedness, the "Honest Joe" syndrome—marked in such movies as Fritz Lang's *Fury* (1936) and Frank Borzage's *Big City* (1937). With Katharine Hepburn, he formed one of the archetypal American-movie couples. They strike sparks off each other in *Adam's Rib* and *Pat and Mike* for George Cukor (1949 and 1952 respectively), and in work for such directors as George Stevens and Frank Capra. An actor's actor, so natural that he seemed not to be acting at all, he was greatly admired by his peers, not least by Laurence Olivier, who commented: "I've learned more about acting from watching Tracy than in any other way. He has great truth in everything he does."

His key films included: *San Francisco* (1936), *Captains Courageous* (1937), *Boys' Town* (1938), *Woman of the Year* (1942), *Father of the Bride* (1950), *The Actress* (1953), *Bad Day at Black Rock* (1955), *Inherit the Wind* (1960) and *Judgment at Nuremberg* (1961).

Valentino, Rudolph (1895–1926)

Valentino was one of the first major Hollywood sex symbols whose funeral after a premature death

from peritonitis was followed by thousands of sobbing fans. This now seems ironic due not only to changes in film fashions and sexual coding that make his savagely passionate oriental in *The Sheik* (George Melford, 1921) appear passé, but also to subsequent revelations about his unconsummated first marriage, homosexual tendencies and domination by his second wife, who took charge of his career and mismanaged it abominably. To women he symbolised exotic eroticism; to men, to quote an infamous *Chicago Tribune* editorial, a "painted pansy".

His premature death (which is often a smart career move, as one cynical journalist remarked) only fanned the legend and the controversy. Other important films: *The Four Horsemen of the Apocalypse* (1921), *Blood and Sand* (1922) and *Son of the Sheik* (1926).

Wayne, John (1907–79)

Wayne remains perhaps Hollywood's greatest, most loved and most hated star. Loved, by Western fans the world over for performances that set the mould for the horseback hero—big physically and spiritually, charismatically dominating with men, awkward and latently sentimental with women, always coming out on top in a crisis. Hated, for his uncompromising right-wing political stance which led him to endorse the McCarthyite persecutions of the fifties and to give active support to the American invasion of Vietnam, even making a film—*The Green Berets* (1968)— in support of it. As an actor, Wayne revealed in his best parts more sensitivity than he often cared to off-screen—as the outlaw Ringo in Ford's *Stagecoach* (1939) who ends up with the prostitute Dallas, as the tamed Comanche-hater Ethan Edwards in Ford's *The Searchers* (1956), who walks off into the barren landscape at the end, and as the sheriff in Hawks's *Rio Bravo* (1959), holding a motley posse together by force of personality. He won an Oscar for *True Grit* (1969). Other important films: *Fort Apache* (1948), *Red River* (1949), *She Wore a Yellow Ribbon* (1949), *Sands of Iwo Jima* (1950), *The Quiet Man* (1952), *The Man Who Shot Liberty Valance* (1962) and *The Shootist* (1976).

West, Mae (1892–1980)

"I was Snow White—but I drifted." So said Mae West, whose raunchy style was seen at its best on film in *She Done Him Wrong* (1933) and *I'm No Angel* (1933). This blousy buxom blonde appealed to men because of her sex-appeal, and to women because of the way she seized the sexual initiative from the male and sent up his desires. Unfortunately the production code of 1934, which laid down strict guidelines on the treatment of sex on film, inhibited Miss West's screen career. Other key films include: *Belle of the Nineties* (1934) and *My Little Chickadee* (1940).

4. GLOSSARY OF FILM TERMS

Art director, technician responsible for the designing of the sets

Art-house film, a film commonly thought by critics to have artistic merit and often shown at specialist rather than mainstream cinemas.

Auteur, literally French for 'author', but generally a complimentary term bestowed by critics on a director whose films are deemed to exhibit stylistic and thematic distinctiveness and distinction. The so-called 'auteur theory', popularised in France in the 1950s, ascribed overall responsibility for the creation and quality of a film to its director, thereby renewing critical analysis of much previously neglected Hollywood work. The *'politique des auteurs'* (policy of authors) was first stated by François Truffaut in the January 1954 issue of *Cahiers du Cinema*; the main exponent of the auteur theory in America was the critic Andrew Sarris.

Back lighting, lighting directed at the camera from

behind the subject, which is therefore silhouetted.

Back projection, background scene projected onto a screen behind the action to give the impression the actors are on a real location. A convention of classic Hollywood cinema that can now look dated, it became a source of keen critical debate in Hitchcock's *Marnie* (1964), where its perceptible use was both attacked for technical sloppiness and defended as expressively appropriate and meaningful.

Best boy, the main assistant to a film's chief electrician.

Bio-pic, a film about the life of a real person. It was a kind of film particularly popularised by Warner Brothers in the 1930s *e.g. The Story of Louis Pasteur* (1936) and *The Life of Emile Zola* (1937). Writers, sportsmen, composers, scientists, painters have all come under the spotlight: recent real-life subjects whose life and work have inspired successful films range from Virginia Woolf and

Truman Capote to Mohammed Ali.

B-picture, generally a modest, low-budget production that, during the cinema's peak of popularity between 1930 and 1960, preceded the main feature. Often of low quality (one remembers the mortifying comment in the 1957 British comedy, *The Smallest Show on Earth*: 'She was as pretty as a picture- a B-picture, mind you'), B-pictures could sometimes prove to be useful training grounds for directors (*e.g.* Fred Zinnemann) who were to move on to bigger things, and some of the films were to become cult classics.

Camera angle, looking up, looking down, tilted (the latter used particularly strikingly in Carol Reed's 1949 classic, *The Third Man* to suggest a world out of joint).

Cannes Film Festival, the most glamorous of the annual international film festivals, generally taking place in May and whose top prize, the 'Golden Palm' gives its recipient valuable prestige and publicity.

CGI, or computer generated images, as seen to spectacular effect in such films as *Jurassic Park* (1993), *Toy Story* (1995), and *Gladiator* (2000). As George Lucas told Martin Scorsese during the shooting of his lavishly expensive *Gangs of New York* (2002): 'Sets like that can be done with computers now.'

Chiaroscuro, a striking or stylised use of light and shadow.

Cinemascope, a wide-screen process developed by Twentieth Century Fox and first used for their religious epic, *The Robe* (1953).

Cinema verité, literally 'cinema truth': it signified a kind of documentary cinema that used lightweight, hand-held equipment, minimal crews and interview techniques on real locations.

Crane shot, a shot where the camera is mounted on a crane and rises above the ground to offer an aerial perspective on the action. A famous example is the shot in Fred Zinnemann's *High Noon* (1952), where the crane shot of the Marshal in the empty street prior to his confrontation with the four outlaws emphasises his isolation, rejection and vulnerability.

Crosscutting, cutting back and forth from one action to another, giving the impression of parallel action and the events happening simultaneously or one event commenting on the other. Famous examples include the finale of D W Griffith's *Intolerance* (1916), where the chase to save the pardoned hero from execution in the modern story is crosscut with Christ's procession to Calvary; and the scene in Francis Ford Coppola's *The Godfather* (1972), where the baptism of Michael Corleone's godson is crosscut with the violent elimination of Corleone's Mafia rivals.

Cult movie, a film which gathers an underground reputation as a classic because of its appreciation by a specialist audience of followers, often in defiance of mainstream taste.

Cut, change from one shot to another. *See also* **Crosscutting** and **Match cut.**

Day for night, a technique used for shooting night sequences during daytime with the use of special lens filters. Alluded to in François Truffaut's film about film-making, *La Nuit Americaine—Day for Night* (1973)

Deep focus, a photographic technique in which objects far away from the camera as well as those in the foreground of the frame are in focus at the same time. It was particularly associated with the cameraman Gregg Toland and his work on the 1940s films of Orson Welles (*Citizen Kane*) and William Wyler (*The Little Foxes*, *The Best Years of our Lives*). It was considered to be an enhancement of film realism by the influential French film theorist, André Bazin.

Director's cut, a re-edited version of a classic film that supposedly restores, or more closely represents, the director's original intentions. Examples include David Lean's *Lawrence of Arabia*, Sam Peckinpah's *Pat Garrett and Billy the Kid* and Ridley Scott's *Blade Runner*.

Dissolve, a visible transition where one shot fades out as another fades in. A powerful example occurs in Hitchcock's *The Wrong Man* (1957), where Hitchcock slowly dissolves from a shot of unjustly accused Henry Fonda as he prays for help to that of the actual criminal about to attempt a robbery that will clear Fonda's name.

Documentary, a term first coined by John Grierson when describing Robert Flaherty's film about the daily life of a Polynesian youth, *Moana* (1926). It derived from the French word *documentaire*, which the French used to describe travelogues, but it has come to be applied to all non-fiction films that show real events and people, albeit covering a wide variety of styles.

Dogme 95, a manifesto by key Danish film-makers such as Lars von Trier and Thomas Vinterberg, which eschewed the cinema of spectacle and special effects and lauded the 'inspiration of limitation' (natural sound, location shooting, hand-held camerawork *etc.*) An antithesis to the *Titanic* kind of cinema, its practice was short-lived—seen at its best in Vinterberg's *Festen* (1995) and its most controversial in von Trier's *The Idiots* (1998)—but, as the British director Michael Winterbottom commented, 'it was attractive as a polemic or provocation.'

Ealing comedy, a series of British comedies made at Ealing studios in West London that poked fun at bureaucracy, officialdom and the quaintness of British character. Its heyday was between 1949 and 1955, framed by the two darkest and most subversive achievements of the genre, Robert Hamer's *Kind Hearts and Coronets* and Alexander Mackendrick's *The Ladykillers*.

Establishing shot, opening shot of a scene that establishes the location or setting.

Fade in/Fade out, an optical device whereby the image appears/disappears gradually.

Film noir, films with a grim urban setting that deal mainly with dark and violent passions (often triggered by a seductive *femme fatale*) in a downbeat way. The term was applied by French critics to American thrillers of the 1940s, particularly those directed by European émigrés like Billy Wilder (*Double Indemnity*), Robert Siodmak (*The Killers*) and Fritz Lang (*Woman in the Window, Scarlet Street*), who intensified their themes with distorted imagery and stylised use of lighting and shadow that also owed something to German Expressionism (*see below*).

Fish-eye lens, a lens with such a wide angle that it distorts the image: used particularly effectively by cameraman James Wong Howe in John Frankenheimer's *Seconds* (1966) to enhance the horror of Rock Hudson's final journey to the operating table.

Flashback, scene or shot that disrupts the chronological narrative of a film to show events that happened in the past or before the main story began.

Flashforward, scene or shot that interrupts the chronological flow of a narrative to show future events.

Free cinema, a documentary movement in England in the 1950s that was a precursor of the British New Wave films of the early 1960s and was a springboard for the careers in film of directors such as Lindsay Anderson, Karel Reisz and Tony Richardson, who wished to bring a grittier honesty and realism to their portrait of English society.

Freeze frame, a shot where the action is 'frozen' into stillness, as in the famous endings of François Truffaut's *Les Quatre Cents Coups* (1959), George Roy Hill's *Butch Cassidy and the Sundance Kid* (1969), and Ridley Scott's *Thelma and Louise* (1992).

Gaffer, the chief electrician on a production.

Genre, a type or class of film (*e.g.* the musical, the western).

German expressionism, a style of film common in Germany in the twenties, typified by dramatic lighting, distorted sets, symbolic action and characterisation, as in, for example, Robert Wiene's *The Cabinet of Dr Caligari* (1919).

Hammer horror, English horror films from Hammer studios which made stars of regulars such as Peter Cushing and Sir Christopher Lee and cult figures of directors such as Terence Fisher.

Hays Office, essentially the body that regulated what constituted good taste and acceptable behaviour on screen during the heyday of Hollywood. It was run by a former lawyer and conservative politician, Will Hays, and was the creation of the studio moguls in 1930, designed to improve the image of Hollywood after a series of highly publicised scandals about 'immoral' behaviour. The so-called Hays Code had an enormous influence on the content of Hollywood films until its termination in 1966.

Hollywood Ten, the ten artists who were imprisoned for contempt of Congress in 1948 when they refused to disclose their political affiliations to the

House UnAmerican Activities Committee (HUAC) during its infamous investigation into so-called 'Communist infiltration into the Hollywood motion picture industry'. The investigation provoked a climate of fear and period of blacklisting that permanently scarred the film community.

The ten individuals were producer-director Herbert Biberman, director Edward Dmytryk, producer-writer Adrian Scott, and writers Alvah Bessie, Lester Cole, Ring Lardner Jr., John Howard Lawson, Albert Maltz, Samuel Ornitz and Dalton Trumbo.

Kuleshov experiment, a montage experiment by the early Soviet director, Lev Kuleshov, which juxtaposed shots of the actor, Ivan Mozhukin with different objects to generate different meanings—*i.e.* the same expression of the actor juxtaposed with a shot of a child, a plate of soup, a coffin, was read by audiences to express tenderness, hunger and grief, respectively. In other words, the meaning was not in the shot itself but in the combination of images, showing the power of editing to alter perception. Subsequent film theorists have cast doubt on the claims and even existence of this experiment, but it did influence attitudes to the cinema and montage. Hitchcock's *Rear Window* (1954) could be said to derive its whole editing style from this 'experiment'.

MacGuffin, a term associated with Alfred Hitchcock and applied to a plot device that is of little interest in itself but is there simply to generate the action (like the microfilm that James Mason is trying to smuggle out of the country in *North by Northwest*).

Match cut, two shots linked by some aural or visual connection, like the moment in Stanley Kubrick's *2001:A Space Odyssey* (1968), where a bone tossed in the air by a primordial ape is visually displaced by the shot of a spinning spacecraft; or the moment in Nicolas Roeg's *Don't Look Now* (1973), where the director cuts from the wife's scream on seeing her dead daughter to the drill her husband is using in his reconstruction work on the church in Venice, a sound match and cut that, as Roeg said, fires the viewer like a bullet into the future.

Method acting, a style of acting influenced by the teachings of Konstantine Stanislavsky (1863–1938), which aimed to increase the realism of a performance by encouraging the actor to draw on his or her personal experiences to 'become' the character. Closely associated with the Actors' Studio in New York, it came to public attention in the 1950s through the striking and influential performances of actors such as Marlon Brando, James Dean and Paul Newman.

Mise-en-scene, literally, 'staging'—the way in which the elements and components in a film are arranged and encompassed by the camera, or the term normally used to denote that part of the cinematic process that takes place on the set, as opposed to montage, which takes place afterwards.

Montage, the juxtaposition of material (successive shots, or items within a shot) to suggest meaning—as when Eisenstein in *Battleship Potemkin* (1925) evokes anger at the massacre on the Odessa Steps by showing three successive shots of stone lions in various positions, shot to look as though they are one lion rising to its feet and roaring its fury. Or simply another word for a film's editing.

Movie brats, a new generation of Hollywood directors, many of them from film school, who exploded onto the scene in the early 1970s—(*e.g.* George Lucas, Brian DePalma, Martin Scorsese, Steven Spielberg).

Narration, the various means by which the events of the plot can be placed before the viewer. Also used of voice-over narration, a technique particularly associated with the fatalism of film noir, like that of the mortally wounded hero in *Double Indemnity* (1944) as he confesses his crime into a dictaphone, or that of the writer in *Sunset Boulevard* (1950), who, lying dead at the bottom of a movie star's swimming pool, reflects on how he got there.

Narrative, structured series of events, linked by cause and effect, that provides the film's plot.

Nickelodeon, a makeshift movie theatre in the early days of cinema, so called because the admission price was only a nickel.

Neo-realism, connected with movement out of the studio, shooting on real locations, absence of a script and/or non-professional casts, all designed simultaneously to cut costs and increase the impression of spontaneity and real life. Inaugurated by Renoir but particularly associated with Italian directors of the immediate post-war period (Rossellini, Visconti, DeSica), who rejected the escapism of the national cinema to make films that reflected contemporary social conditions.

Nouvelle Vague, a term for a loose heterogeneous group of young French film critics (including Chabrol, Godard and Truffaut), who went into direction in the late 1950s and early 1960s and created an enormous impact with their experimental style and their laconic sense of existential amorality.

Pan, a shot where the camera looks around from a stationary position. It can be used for dramatic effect, as in John Ford's *Stagecoach* (1939), when a brief panning shot reveals the presence of an Indian war party just when the stagecoach seems to be heading for safety; or, more elaborately, in John Frankenheimer's *The Manchurian Candidate* (1962), where a 360-degree panning shot introduces the film's famous brainwashing sequence.

Point of view shot, a shot where the action is seen through the eyes of a particular character, the shot generally preceded or followed by the shot of the character looking. Used with particular effectiveness by Hitchcock in films such as *Rear Window* and *Vertigo* (1958). Robert Montgomery's *Lady in the Lake* (1948) also experimented with a subjective camera by showing us only what the leading character saw and only showing the character himself in mirror shots.

Romcom. Romantic comedy.

Screwball comedy, a type of comedy particularly popularised by directors like Howard Hawks and Preston Sturges in the 1930s and early 1940s and characterised by frantic action, rapier wit, and a couple in a bizarre situation. Fine examples would include: Capra's *It Happened One Night* (1934), Hawks's *Bringing Up Baby* (1938) and Sturges' *Palm Beach Story* (1942).

Silent period, roughly that period of film history between the Lumières in 1895 and *The Jazz Singer* in 1927, when most films were shot without sound, although, when exhibited, were often supported by sound effects and live piano accompaniment.

Sleeper, a term used of a film which initially escapes attention but gradually acquires a following, either cult or commercial.

Sneak preview, a tryout of a film to gauge audience reaction. In some notorious cases, such as Orson Welles's *The Magnificent Ambersons* (1942) and John Huston's *The Red Badge of Courage* (1951), the disastrous preview response caused the studios to panic and butcher the films through desperate re-editing.

Spaghetti western, a western made in Italy by Italian film-makers, which commonly stylises the action and often parodies genre conventions. The genre became particularly popular in the 1960s because of the successful association on the 'Dollars' films of actor Clint Eastwood and director Sergio Leone.

Storyboard, series of sketches of the shots that comprise a scene and a useful reference for a director when shooting particularly complicated pieces of action.

Ten-minute take, a ten-minute sequence filmed in a single take without cuts. Particularly associated with Alfred Hitchcock and his deployment of the technique in *Rope* (1948) and *Under Capricorn* (1949).

Tracking shot, camera moves forward or backwards in order to follow subject, a technique taken to an extreme in the elaborate three-minute continuous shot that opens Orson Welles's *Touch of Evil* (1958) and to which Robert Altman pays homage in *The Player* (1992).

Zoom shot, a shot during which the focal length of the lens is adjusted and gives the impression of optical motion without moving the camera backwards or forwards. The zoom lens has been used to particularly expressive effect by directors such as Robert Altman and Stanley Kubrick.

5. THE OSCAR WINNERS

Introduction

The film industry's most glittering prize remains the Hollywood Academy Award, or "Oscar". The "Oscar" came about as a result of the formation of the Academy of Motion Picture Arts and Sciences in 1927. The Academy thought it would gain additional prestige and publicity if it gave out annual awards for artistic and technical merit. The first awards ceremony was in May 1929 and was a modest affair.

The Statuette

The Oscar itself is a gold-plated statuette of a knight holding a crusader's sword and standing on a reel of film whose five spokes symbolise the original branches of the Academy (actors, directors, producers, technicians and writers). Legend has it that the name comes from a secretary Margaret Herrick, later an executive director of the Academy, who commented one day that the statuette "reminds me of my uncle Oscar". The first documented use of the nickname Oscar was in 1934.

Oscar Records

Ben-Hur (1959), *Titanic* (1997) and *Lord of the Rings: Return of the King* (2003) hold the record number of Oscars—11. *West Side Story* (1961) won 10; *Gone With the Wind* (1939), *Gigi* (1958), *The Last Emperor* (1987) and *The English Patient* (1996) each won nine.

Katharine Hepburn has won more major acting Oscars than any other star (4). Bette Davis, Luise Rainer, Olivia de Havilland, Ingrid Bergman, Glenda Jackson, Jane Fonda, Sally Field, Elizabeth Taylor, Jodie Foster and Hilary Swank have won Best Actress twice; Sir Daniel Day-Lewis has won Best Actor a record three times. Other actors to have won twice are Spencer Tracy, Fredric March, Gary Cooper, Marlon Brando, Dustin Hoffman, Jack Nicholson, Tom Hanks, and Sean Penn.

Best Actor

1927–28	Emil Jannings, *The Way of All Flesh*
1928–29	Warner Baxter, *In Old Arizona*
1929–30	George Arliss, *Disraeli*
1930–31	Lionel Barrymore, *A Free Soul*
1931–32	Fredric March, *Dr Jekyll and Mr Hyde*; Wallace Beery, *The Champ* (tie)
1932–33	Charles Laughton, *Private Life of Henry VIII*
1934	Clark Gable, *It Happened One Night*
1935	Victor McLaglen, *The Informer*
1936	Paul Muni, *Story of Louis Pasteur*
1937	Spencer Tracy, *Captains Courageous*
1938	Spencer Tracy, *Boys Town*
1939	Robert Donat, *Goodbye Mr Chips*
1940	James Stewart, *The Philadelphia Story*
1941	Gary Cooper, *Sergeant York*
1942	James Cagney, *Yankee Doodle Dandy*
1943	Paul Lukas, *Watch on the Rhine*
1944	Bing Crosby, *Going My Way*
1945	Ray Milland, *The Lost Weekend*
1946	Fredric March, *The Best Years of Our Lives*
1947	Ronald Colman, *A Double Life*
1948	Laurence Olivier, *Hamlet*
1949	Broderick Crawford, *All the King's Men*
1950	José Ferrer, *Cyrano de Bergerac*
1951	Humphrey Bogart, *The African Queen*
1952	Gary Cooper, *High Noon*
1953	William Holden, *Stalag 17*
1954	Marlon Brando, *On the Waterfront*
1955	Ernest Borgnine, *Marty*
1956	Yul Brynner, *The King and I*
1957	Alec Guinness, *The Bridge on the River Kwai*
1958	David Niven, *Separate Tables*
1959	Charlton Heston, *Ben-Hur*
1960	Burt Lancaster, *Elmer Gantry*
1961	Maximilian Schell, *Judgment at Nuremberg*
1962	Gregory Peck, *To Kill a Mockingbird*
1963	Sidney Poitier, *Lilies of the Field*
1964	Rex Harrison, *My Fair Lady*
1965	Lee Marvin, *Cat Ballou*
1966	Paul Scofield, *A Man for All Seasons*
1967	Rod Steiger, *In the Heat of the Night*
1968	Cliff Robertson, *Charly*
1969	John Wayne, *True Grit*
1970	George C. Scott, *Patton* (refused)
1971	Gene Hackman, *The French Connection*
1972	Marlon Brando, *The Godfather* (refused)
1973	Jack Lemmon, *Save the Tiger*
1974	Art Carney, *Harry and Tonto*
1975	Jack Nicholson, *One Flew Over the Cuckoo's Nest*
1976	Peter Finch, *Network*
1977	Richard Dreyfuss, *The Goodbye Girl*
1978	Jon Voight, *Coming Home*
1979	Dustin Hoffman, *Kramer vs. Kramer*
1980	Robert DeNiro, *Raging Bull*
1981	Henry Fonda, *On Golden Pond*
1982	Ben Kingsley, *Gandhi*
1983	Robert Duvall, *Tender Mercies*
1984	F. Murray Abraham, *Amadeus*
1985	William Hurt, *Kiss of the Spider Woman*
1986	Paul Newman, *The Color of Money*
1987	Michael Douglas, *Wall Street*
1988	Dustin Hoffman, *Rain Man*
1989	Daniel Day-Lewis, *My Left Foot*
1990	Jeremy Irons, *Reversal of Fortune*
1991	Anthony Hopkins, *The Silence of the Lambs*
1992	Al Pacino, *Scent of a Woman*
1993	Tom Hanks, *Philadelphia*
1994	Tom Hanks, *Forrest Gump*
1995	Nicolas Cage, *Leaving Las Vegas*
1996	Geoffrey Rush, *Shine*
1997	Jack Nicholson, *As Good As It Gets*
1998	Roberto Benigni, *Life is Beautiful*
1999	Kevin Spacey, *American Beauty*
2000	Russell Crowe, *Gladiator*
2001	Denzel Washington, *Training Day*
2002	Adrien Brody, *The Pianist*
2003	Sean Penn, *Mystic River*
2004	Jamie Foxx, *Ray*
2005	Philip Seymour Hoffman, *Capote*
2006	Forest Whitaker, *The Last King of Scotland*
2007	Daniel Day-Lewis, *There Will Be Blood*
2008	Sean Penn, *Milk*
2009	Jeff Bridges, *Crazy Heart*
2010	Colin Firth, *The King's Speech*
2011	Jean Dujardin, *The Artist*
2012	Daniel Day-Lewis, *Lincoln*
2013	Matthew McConaughey, *Dallas Buyers Club*
2014	Eddie Redmayne, *The Theory of Everything*
2015	Leonardo DiCaprio, *The Revenant*
2016	Casey Affleck, *Manchester by the Sea*

Best Actress

1927–28	Janet Gaynor, *Seventh Heaven*
1928–29	Mary Pickford, *Coquette*
1929–30	Norma Shearer, *The Divorcee*
1930–31	Marie Dressler, *Min and Bill*
1931–32	Helen Hayes, *Sin of Madelon Claudet*
1932–33	Katharine Hepburn, *Morning Glory*
1934	Claudette Colbert, *It Happened One Night*
1935	Bette Davis, *Dangerous*
1936	Luise Rainer, *The Great Ziegfeld*
1937	Luise Rainer, *The Good Earth*
1938	Bette Davis, *Jezebel*
1939	Vivien Leigh, *Gone With the Wind*
1940	Ginger Rogers, *Kitty Foyle*
1941	Joan Fontaine, *Suspicion*
1942	Greer Garson, *Mrs Miniver*
1943	Jennifer Jones, *The Song of Bernadette*
1944	Ingrid Bergman, *Gaslight*
1945	Joan Crawford, *Mildred Pierce*
1946	Olivia de Havilland, *To Each His Own*
1947	Loretta Young, *The Farmer's Daughter*
1948	Jane Wyman, *Johnny Belinda*
1949	Olivia de Havilland, *The Heiress*
1950	Judy Holliday, *Born Yesterday*
1951	Vivien Leigh, *A Streetcar Named Desire*
1952	Shirley Booth, *Come Back, Little Sheba*
1953	Audrey Hepburn, *Roman Holiday*
1954	Grace Kelly, *Country Girl*
1955	Anna Magnani, *The Rose Tattoo*
1956	Ingrid Bergman, *Anastasia*
1957	Joanne Woodward, *The Three Faces of Eve*
1958	Susan Hayward, *I Want to Live*

1959	Simone Signoret, *Room at the Top*
1960	Elizabeth Taylor, *Butterfield 8*
1961	Sophia Loren, *Two Women*
1962	Anne Bancroft, *The Miracle Worker*
1963	Patricia Neal, *Hud*
1964	Julie Andrews, *Mary Poppins*
1965	Julie Christie, *Darling*
1966	Elizabeth Taylor, *Who's Afraid of Virginia Woolf?*
1967	Katharine Hepburn, *Guess Who's Coming to Dinner*
1968	Katharine Hepburn, *The Lion in Winter*; Barbra Streisand, *Funny Girl* (tie)
1969	Maggie Smith, *The Prime of Miss Jean Brodie*
1970	Glenda Jackson, *Women in Love*
1971	Jane Fonda, *Klute*
1972	Liza Minnelli, *Cabaret*
1973	Glenda Jackson, *A Touch of Class*
1974	Ellen Burstyn, *Alice Doesn't Live Here Anymore*
1975	Louise Fletcher, *One Flew Over the Cuckoo's Nest*
1976	Faye Dunaway, *Network*
1977	Diane Keaton, *Annie Hall*
1978	Jane Fonda, *Coming Home*
1979	Sally Field, *Norma Rae*
1980	Sissy Spacek, *Coal Miner's Daughter*
1981	Katharine Hepburn, *On Golden Pond*
1982	Meryl Streep, *Sophie's Choice*
1983	Shirley MacLaine, *Terms of Endearment*
1984	Sally Field, *Places in the Heart*
1985	Geraldine Page, *The Trip to Bountiful*
1986	Marlee Matlin, *Children of a Lesser God*
1987	Cher, *Moonstruck*
1988	Jodie Foster, *The Accused*
1989	Jessica Tandy, *Driving Miss Daisy*
1990	Kathy Bates, *Misery*
1991	Jodie Foster, *The Silence of the Lambs*
1992	Emma Thompson, *Howards End*
1993	Holly Hunter, *The Piano*
1994	Jessica Lange, *Blue Sky*
1995	Susan Sarandon, *Dead Man Walking*
1996	Frances McDormand, *Fargo*
1997	Helen Hunt, *As Good As It Gets*
1998	Gwyneth Paltrow, *Shakespeare in Love*
1999	Hilary Swank, *Boys Don't Cry*
2000	Julia Roberts, *Erin Brockovich*
2001	Halle Berry, *Monster's Ball*
2002	Nicole Kidman, *The Hours*
2003	Charlize Theron, *Monster*
2004	Hilary Swank, *Million Dollar Baby*
2005	Reese Witherspoon, *Walk the Line*
2006	Helen Mirren, *The Queen*
2007	Marion Cotillard, *La Vie en Rose*
2008	Kate Winslet, *The Reader*
2009	Sandra Bullock, *The Blind Side*
2010	Natalie Portman, *Black Swan*
2011	Meryl Streep, *The Iron Lady*
2012	Jennifer Lawrence, *Silver Linings Playbook*
2013	Cate Blanchett, *Blue Jasmine*
2014	Julianne Moore, *Still Alice*
2015	Brie Larson *Room*
2016	Emma Stone *La La Land*

1952	*Greatest Show on Earth*
1953	*From Here to Eternity*
1954	*On the Waterfront*
1955	*Marty*
1956	*Around the World in 80 Days*
1957	*The Bridge on the River Kwai*
1958	*Gigi*
1959	*Ben-Hur*
1960	*The Apartment*
1961	*West Side Story*
1962	*Lawrence of Arabia*
1963	*Tom Jones*
1964	*My Fair Lady*
1965	*The Sound of Music*
1966	*A Man for All Seasons*
1967	*In the Heat of the Night*
1968	*Oliver*
1969	*Midnight Cowboy*
1970	*Patton*
1971	*The French Connection*
1972	*The Godfather*
1973	*The Sting*
1974	*The Godfather, Part II*
1975	*One Flew Over the Cuckoo's Nest*
1976	*Rocky*
1977	*Annie Hall*
1978	*The Deer Hunter*
1979	*Kramer vs. Kramer*
1980	*Ordinary People*
1981	*Chariots of Fire*
1982	*Gandhi*
1983	*Terms of Endearment*
1984	*Amadeus*
1985	*Out of Africa*
1986	*Platoon*
1987	*The Last Emperor*
1988	*Rain Man*
1989	*Driving Miss Daisy*
1990	*Dances with Wolves*
1991	*The Silence of the Lambs*
1992	*Unforgiven*
1993	*Schindler's List*
1994	*Forrest Gump*
1995	*Braveheart*
1996	*The English Patient*
1997	*Titanic*
1998	*Shakespeare in Love*
1999	*American Beauty*
2000	*Gladiator*
2001	*A Beautiful Mind*
2002	*Chicago*
2003	*Lord of the Rings: Return of the King*
2004	*Million Dollar Baby*
2005	*Crash*
2006	*The Departed*
2007	*No Country For Old Men*
2008	*Slumdog Millionaire*
2009	*The Hurt Locker*
2010	*The King's Speech*
2011	*The Artist*
2012	*Argo*
2013	*12 Years a Slave*
2014	*Birdman*
2015	*Spotlight*
2016	*Moonlight*

Best Film

1927–28	*Wings*
1928–29	*Broadway Melody*
1929–30	*All Quiet on the Western Front*
1930–31	*Cimarron*
1931–32	*Grand Hotel*
	Special: *Mickey Mouse*
1932–33	*Cavalcade*
1934	*It Happened One Night*
1935	*Mutiny on the Bounty*
1936	*The Great Ziegfeld*
1937	*Life of Emile Zola*
1938	*You Can't Take It With You*
1939	*Gone With the Wind*
1940	*Rebecca*
1941	*How Green Was My Valley*
1942	*Mrs Miniver*
1943	*Casablanca*
1944	*Going My Way*
1945	*The Lost Weekend*
1946	*The Best Years of Our Lives*
1947	*Gentleman's Agreement*
1948	*Hamlet*
1949	*All the King's Men*
1950	*All About Eve*
1951	*An American in Paris*

Best Director

1927–28	Frank Borzage, *Seventh Heaven*
	Lewis Milestone, *Two Arabian Knights*
1928–29	Frank Lloyd, *The Divine Lady*
1929–30	Lewis Milestone, *All Quiet on the Western Front*
1930–31	Norman Taurog, *Skippy*
1931–32	Frank Borzage, *Bad Girl*
1932–33	Frank Lloyd, *Cavalcade*
1934	Frank Capra, *It Happened One Night*
1935	John Ford, *The Informer*
1936	Frank Capra, *Mr Deeds Goes to Town*
1937	Leo McCarey, *The Awful Truth*
1938	Frank Capra, *You Can't Take It With You*
1939	Victor Fleming, *Gone with the Wind*
1940	John Ford, *The Grapes of Wrath*
1941	John Ford, *How Green Was My Valley*
1942	William Wyler, *Mrs Miniver*
1943	Michael Curtiz, *Casablanca*
1944	Leo McCarey, *Going My Way*
1945	Billy Wilder, *The Lost Weekend*
1946	William Wyler, *The Best Years of Our Lives*
1947	Elia Kazan, *Gentleman's Agreement*
1948	John Huston, *Treasure of the Sierra Madre*
1949	Joseph L. Mankiewicz, *A Letter to Three Wives*

1950	Joseph L. Mankiewicz, *All About Eve*
1951	George Stevens, *A Place in the Sun*
1952	John Ford, *The Quiet Man*
1953	Fred Zinnemann, *From Here to Eternity*
1954	Elia Kazan, *On the Waterfront*
1955	Delbert Mann, *Marty*
1956	George Stevens, *Giant*
1957	David Lean, *The Bridge on the River Kwai*
1958	Vincente Minnelli, *Gigi*
1959	William Wyler, *Ben-Hur*
1960	Billy Wilder, *The Apartment*
1961	Jerome Robbins, Robert Wise, *West Side Story*
1962	David Lean, *Lawrence of Arabia*
1963	Tony Richardson, *Tom Jones*
1964	George Cukor, *My Fair Lady*
1965	Robert Wise, *The Sound of Music*
1966	Fred Zinnemann, *A Man for All Seasons*
1967	Mike Nichols, *The Graduate*
1968	Sir Carol Reed, *Oliver*
1969	John Schlesinger, *Midnight Cowboy*
1970	Franklin J. Schaffner, *Patton*
1971	William Friedkin, *The French Connection*
1972	Bob Fosse, *Cabaret*
1973	George Roy Hill, *The Sting*
1974	Francis Ford Coppola, *The Godfather, Part II*
1975	Milos Forman, *One Flew Over the Cuckoo's Nest*
1976	John Avildsen, *Rocky*
1977	Woody Allen, *Annie Hall*
1978	Michael Cimino, *The Deer Hunter*
1979	Robert Benton, *Kramer vs. Kramer*
1980	Robert Redford, *Ordinary People*
1981	Warren Beatty, *Reds*
1982	Richard Attenborough, *Gandhi*
1983	James L. Brooks, *Terms of Endearment*
1984	Milos Forman, *Amadeus*
1985	Sydney Pollack, *Out of Africa*
1986	Oliver Stone, *Platoon*
1987	Bernardo Bertolucci, *The Last Emperor*
1988	Barry Levinson, *Rain Man*
1989	Oliver Stone, *Born on the Fourth of July*
1990	Kevin Costner, *Dances with Wolves*
1991	Jonathan Demme, *The Silence of the Lambs*
1992	Clint Eastwood, *Unforgiven*
1993	Steven Spielberg, *Schindler's List*
1994	Robert Zemeckis, *Forrest Gump*
1995	Mel Gibson, *Braveheart*
1996	Anthony Minghella, *The English Patient*
1997	James Cameron, *Titanic*
1998	Steven Spielberg, *Saving Private Ryan*
1999	Sam Mendes, *American Beauty*
2000	Steven Soderbergh, *Traffic*
2001	Ron Howard, *A Beautiful Mind*
2002	Roman Polanski, *The Pianist*
2003	Peter Jackson, *Lord of the Rings: Return of the King*
2004	Clint Eastwood, *Million Dollar Baby*
2005	Ang Lee, *Brokeback Mountain*
2006	Martin Scorsese, *The Departed*
2007	Joel and Ethan Coen, *No Country for Old Men*
2008	Danny Boyle, *Slumdog Millionaire*
2009	Kathryn Bigelow, *The Hurt Locker*
2010	Tom Hooper, *The King's Speech*
2011	Michel Hazanavicius, *The Artist*
2012	Ang Lee, *Life of Pi*
2013	Alfonso Cuarón, *Gravity*
2014	Alejandro G Iñárritu, *Birdman*
2015	Alejandro G Iñárritu, *The Revenant*
2016	Damien Chazelle, *La La Land*

FOOD AND DRINK

This new sections examines the world of food and drink, from the famous wines of Europe to a glossary of spirits and liqueurs and background articles on our favourite beverages, tea and coffee. There is also a glossary of food, including such exotic items as sushi, paneer, satay, couscous and biryani.

TABLE OF CONTENTS

FOOD AND DRINK

I. THE WORLD OF WINE

INTRODUCTION.

Wine is simply an alcoholic beverage made by fermenting the sugars in grape juice, making alcohol. This simple definition belies the multifarious variables, both natural and man-made which affect the final taste. Different soils, grape varieties and climates, the decisions made by the grape farmer and the wine maker, and the vagaries of the weather mean that there is infinite variety in wine. This choice is what makes wine so fascinating. It is, however, too easy to forget that wine is, for many, one of the staples of life; as much part of the daily routine as bread. As such it is a simple and healthy beverage, something to be talked over, not talked about.

Most of the world's wine is produced in Europe. Italy and France are the biggest producers, followed by Spain. Wine consumption is similarly concentrated in the producing countries, with France, for example consuming over 60 litres per capita, compared with a quarter of this in the UK. Consumption is declining in the major producing countries, but increasing in many countries like the United Kingdom where production is limited. Meanwhile China is now the world's second-largest grower by area under cultivation (after Spain).

History.

It is probable that the first wine was accidental. Perhaps wild grapes were left too long in a pot after being gathered. The weight of the grapes would cause those at the bottom to split, releasing juice which will ferment spontaneously as the necessary yeasts exist naturally on the grapes. The first recorded vineyard in the Judaic and Christian world appears in Genesis. Once the Ark landed after the great flood, Noah planted a vineyard, presumably on the slopes of Mount Ararat. Archaeological evidence too points to south-eastern Europe or the Middle East being wine's original home. Some of today's grape varieties bear witness to the middle eastern connection – the Syrah or Shiraz grape, originally from Syria, and the Muscat.

Wine was certainly known in ancient Egypt and Greece but it was Rome that spread viticulture far and wide. The histories of many of Europe's vineyard regions, from the Rhône to England start with "the vine was originally brought by the Romans". In only a few areas, such as Jerez in Southern Spain, were the Phoenicians responsible. Beyond Europe and the Mediterranean, the wine grape travelled with the European discoverers. Portuguese navigators and Spanish conquistadors were Catholics; they needed wine for the sacrament. Vineyards were established in South America in the 16th century, later spreading into California and the rest of North America. The Cape of Good Hope, established as a victualling station for the Dutch East India Company, was planted with fruit including vines, and the first grapes were pressed in 1652. Australasian vineyards were first planted with cuttings from the Cape.

The Taste of Wine.

A number of different factors influence the taste of wine. Climate, weather and soil are natural. Man can only make minor adjustments to this. The decision as to which grape variety to plant is that of the grower, but it is influenced heavily by the climate. Some grapes, such as Riesling, excel in cold areas, others can resist drought and excessive heat. Human influence is most important in grape growing (viticulture) and wine making (vinification) as at each stage of these processes decisions have to be made which will influence its character and quality.

Climate.

Since wine is made from grapes, it follows that it can be made anywhere that grapes can be made to ripen, from as far north as Britain to as far south as New Zealand. In practice there are two bands, one each side of the equator, within which the wine vine, *Vitis vinifera* produces well, situated approximately within the latitudes of 30° to 50° north and south of the equator. Within these zones the climate is suitable for vine cultivation. Other areas are either too cold for the grapes to ripen, or too warm, so the vine turns its energies to vegetative growth rather than fruit production. These bands cover large climatic variations. In the northern hemisphere the band stretches from Germany and southern Britain to North Africa. In the cooler climates, those nearer to the poles, the grapes are only just ripe and produce lighter wines, often with crisp, refreshing acidity. Most of these are white wines. The warmer climatic zones produce riper grapes with higher sugar content and lower acidity. This translates into higher alcohol and lower acidity in the wines, and the wines tend to have more body. The black grapes needed for red wine need more sun, so these areas produce more red wine.

Climate is affected by other geographical features such as proximity to or distance from large bodies of water, ocean currents, altitude and topography. Neighbouring vineyards can produce very different wines, particularly in the more marginal areas. In the Mosel in Germany the best wines are planted on steep south-facing slopes overlooking the river. The next plot of land, perhaps just around the next bend in the river, might be more shaded, to the detriment of the wines.

Weather.

A region's climate is separate and distinct from its weather. The climate is a function of the geography. The topography and latitude do not vary, whereas weather patterns can alter from one year to the next. This is why one hears about good or bad vintages; a cold night in spring, or rain at the wrong time can adversely affect the crop. Annual weather conditions, sometimes philosophically referred to as the luck of the year, have more influence on wines from the traditional areas of western Europe, where the weather is variable, than "newer" areas such as Australia where the weather is more stable.

Soil.

Soil can have a profound influence on the taste of a wine, as can be seen from the subtle difference between wines from neighbouring vineyards. Vines assimilate trace elements through their roots which alter the chemical composition of the wine. The role of the soil is, however, generally more prosaic. Vines need good drainage, so chalk in Champagne and gravel in the Médoc are ideal. Other hotter areas, like the Sherry region in Spain, rely on the absorbent subsoil to retain water for the vine in the dry summers. Many vineyards are planted in soil which could not support any other agriculture because vines can stand poor soil.

Grape Variety.

As with most fruit, different grape varieties have different flavours, which show in the finished wine. Thousands of different grape varieties are used in wine production. Most are undistinguished, found only in certain areas where they make indifferent wine. However, other varieties have distinctive, recognizable flavours. These more noble grapes are often used unblended, sold under the varietal name. Grapes like Cabernet Sauvignon, Pinot Noir and Chardonnay have become popular internationally. They often flourish in their new homes to the extent that they have become better known there than in the original regions. New Zealand has adopted Sauvignon Blanc, and Australia Shiraz, developing their own particular and highly successful styles.

Grape Growing (Viticulture).

The vine needs careful tending if viticulture is to be profitable. Vines grow prolifically during the spring and summer, so in the winter they are severely pruned. A hedge of vines six or seven feet tall will be reduced to a series of small canes, or short spurs, as the pruners remove the dormant wood. Pruning not only allows access for other vineyard operations, it can also be used to control the quantity and quality of the fruit. Received wisdom is that these are inversely related, so a grower aiming for a high quality wine will prune even more severely to reduce the yield, whereas a bulk producer will maximize it. The main task for the viticulturalist during the rest of the year is controlling the pests and diseases that can attack the vine. Control of fungal and viral infection, and protection from birds and small animals and insect pests is vital. The most serious vineyard pest is *Phylloxera vastarix*, the vine louse accidentally imported to Europe from America during the 19th century. It devastated European vineyards, almost wiping out production until it was discovered that vines grafted onto rootstocks of American native vines were tolerant to it. Since then virtually all European vines have had to be grafted.

Once ripe, the grapes will be harvested, either by hand or machine, and taken to the winery to be made into wine.

Wine Making (Vinification).

Ripe grapes contain all the components required to make wine. The grape consists of a soft pulp gorged with sugar, water and acids, contained in a thin skin which contains colouring, additional flavouring matter and tannins. Tannins are an important preservative in red wines. On the surface of the grape there is a waxy bloom of yeast, required for fermentation. Wine making is thus a natural process; the wine maker's job is to control this.

White Wine Production.

White wine can be made from black or white grapes as all the colouring matter in black grapes is in the skins. The grapes will be pressed and the resulting clear juice (called *must*) transferred to a fermenting vessel where yeasts, either natural or added, convert the sugar into alcohol. For white wine the fermenters are usually kept cool to maintain the aromatic characters. After fermentation the young wine will be clarified and allowed to mature. Most white wines are matured for a short time only, some spending time in oak barrels to add flavour and complexity.

Many white wines are dry, *i.e.* with no detectable sweetness, but there are a number of medium-dry and sweet white wines. To make inexpensive medium-dry wines a quantity of unfermented sterile grape juice is added to the wine just before bottling. High quality classic dessert wines, Sauternes, Tokaji *etc.*, are made with grapes in which the sugars have been concentrated by the action of a fungus called *Botrytis cinerea*. This shrivels the grapes so they look like mouldy raisins. They may look unappealing, but the wines are stunning. It is also possible to make a sweet wine by removing the yeasts physically by using a filter. This method is used in the production of wines such as Asti.

Red and Rosé Wine Production.

Black grapes are needed here. They are crushed, to break the skins and release the must, then fermented in contact with skins. As the alcohol is formed it extracts some of the colour and tannin, aided by stirring the wines up with pumps or paddles. For rosé wine the still fermenting must will be drained off after a day or two, when it has acquired some, but not much, colour. Red wines spend between five and fourteen days in contact with the skins, depending on the style required. Maturation will follow. For wines like Beaujolais this might only be a few weeks in large inert vats.

Other wines, such as fine Claret or Rioja might spend many months in oak barrels, followed by years, or even decades, in bottle, before reaching their peak.

Reading the Label.

A wine label is an advertisement, but also an identity card, giving all manner of information about the contents. It is a passport, permitting the wine to leave the producer's cellar and even reflects the character of the wine maker. Within the European Union (EU) wine legislation has codified regional, national and supranational regulations. Labels, like the wines themselves, must adhere to a host of rules, most of which consumers can ignore. Outside the EU the rules are less strict, but producers hoping to export must prove the integrity of their labels.

Wine Quality Grades.

All wine produced in the EU is officially categorised as either "Table Wine" or "Quality Wine". Table wine is required to reach certain minimum standards only, whereas quality wine must come from a stated region and should be typical of the area in which the grapes were grown. The use of the word "Quality" is potentially confusing. Quality wine must exhibit particular qualities, rather than necessarily being of intrinsically high quality. Quality wines are subject to controls on the area of production, type of grape varieties, minimum alcohol levels and methods of viticulture and vinification. Terms indicating Quality Wine include: *Vin Délimité de Qualité Supérieure* (VDQS) and *Appellation d'Origine Contrôlée* (AC) (France); *Qualitätswein bestimmte Anbaugebiete* (QbA) and *Qualitätswein mit Prädikat* (QmP) (Germany); *Denominazione di Origine Controllata* and *Denominazione di Origine Controllata e Garantita* (DOC and DOCG) (Italy); *Denominación de Origen* and *Denominación de Origen Calificada* (DO and DOC) (Spain) and *Denominação de Origem Controlada* in Portugal.

Category Changes.

Following revised labels, designed to make French wine more competitive globally, all French wines are now classed in one of three categories: *Vignobles de France* (Wines of France); *IGP* (*Indication Geographique Protegée* or Protected Geographical Region), which corresponds to existing *Vin de Pays*; and *AOP* (*Appellation d'Origine Protegée*) which tallies with the old AOC (*Appellation d'Origine Controlée*).

The labels now have the name of the grape and the year it was produced. Other changes mean any type of vine can be planted anywhere in France.

Table wines are usually labelled simply as table wine, but in the language of the producing country; *Vin de Table*, *Deutscher Tafelwein*, *Vinho de Mesa etc.* There is a higher grade of table wine which is usually well worth looking out for. These are the Country Wines, *Vins de Pays* in France, which often represent excellent value for money. Outside the EU, in particular in the New World, such rules do not apply. Here the producer's name is paramount and terms such as "Reserve", "Estate Wine", "Limited Release" *etc.* are used to denote the wines with the greatest character.

Other information on the label will include the country of origin, perhaps the region and maybe the grape variety. Each of these give some clue as to the taste of the wine. The year of vintage, when the grapes were picked and wine made, may also appear. This only indicates that all the wine in the bottle comes from the stated year. With the exception of Port and Champagne there is nothing inherently better about vintage wines; non-vintage wines can be as good.

WINES OF EUROPE.

FRANCE.

France has long been the United Kingdom's most important supplier of wines. We have been buying her wines since long before Eleanor of Aquitaine married Henri d'Anjou, thus bringing Bordeaux and England under the same crown.

Although the totals vary from year to year, around forty per cent of all wine consumed in the UK comes from France; nearly five bottles out of every case (12 bottles) sold. The range of prices and qualities from France is probably greater than anywhere else in the world, from the basic *Vin Rouge* to the finest Bordeaux and Burgundies selling for thousands of pounds a case in the auction rooms of London and New York.

The main wine producing regions are:

* *Bordeaux
* *Burgundy
* *Alsace
* *Loire Valley
* *Rhône Valley
* *Languedoc-Roussillon

Bordeaux.

For 300 years, after 1154, Bordeaux and England shared a monarch. Trade was further aided by the accessibility of the city of Bordeaux, on the Garonne, for ships from London and Bristol. In spite of subsequent political upheavals and Anglo-French wars, claret, the red wine of Bordeaux, remained a popular wine, keeping the smugglers busy when trade with France was proscribed.

Bordeaux is the largest fine wine producing region of France, accounting for about ten per cent of France's total wine production. The range includes some of the finest red and sweet white wines produced anywhere in the world, but the majority of wines called "Bordeaux" are simply everyday wines, best drunk young. The city that gives the region its name lies on the river Garonne. This large river joins the Dordogne to form the Gironde, a wide navigable estuary which eventually flows into the Bay of Biscay. The rivers, the Gironde and the proximity of the Atlantic Ocean give Bordeaux a maritime climate; mild and free of extremes, but humid which can be a problem for the viticulturalist.

This is an area of blended wines; only few varietal wines are sold. The red wines are made principally from Cabernet Sauvignon and Cabernet Franc, related varieties which give high tannin and acidity to the wine with Merlot, which produces higher alcohol, having a softer taste and less tannin. Generally the higher the Cabernet content, the longer the ageing required because of the tannin. Basic Bordeaux Rouge will have a high Merlot content so as to be easy to drink when young.

The two Bordeaux districts that use the highest proportion of Cabernet are the Médoc and Graves. The best wines need time to mature and soften, both in cask and bottle. The best known Merlot-dominated areas are St Emilion and Pomerol. The white wines are made predominantly from a blend of Sauvignon Blanc, an aromatic grape giving high acidity, and Sémillon, a thin skinned grape, easily attacked by noble rot, the basis of the sweet wines such as Sauternes.

Bordeaux is divided into several districts, those with the highest reputation are covered below.

Médoc A C.

The Médoc, the most famous of the Bordeaux districts, is divided into two. The Haut-Médoc, the southern part, being the better. Within the Haut Médoc are the famous communes, or parishes, of St Estèphe, Pauillac, St Julien and Margaux. The wines, which are all red, are usually sold under the names of the châteaux, or estate, where the grapes were grown. In 1855, to coincide with an exhibition in Paris, the best wines of Bordeaux were classified. All but one of the red wines come from the Haut-Médoc. The exception, Château Haut Brion, is from Graves. Hundreds of châteaux were eligible, yet a mere 62 were classified as *Cru classé* ("classed growths"), or vineyard. Five levels were identified, first to fifth growth. Originally only four châteaux, the greatest of all, were given the designation *premier cru* or first growth. Apart from the changes of ownership and occasional renaming of vineyards,

the only change to the classification since its inception has been the promotion of Château Mouton Rothschild to First Growth in 1973.

Cru classé wines are thus inevitably expensive. *Cru Bourgeois*, a later classification, indicates above average, more affordable Bordeaux. Recent improvements have resulted in many of these having reached comparable quality to some *Cru Classé*.

Graves A C.

Graves is named for its gravel soil. Here red and white wines are produced, the latter in dry or off-dry styles. The northern part, around the city of Bordeaux, produces the best quality. Acknowledging this, the area was granted the AC Pessac-Léognan in 1987. Château Haut Brion is included in this appellation.

Sauternes A C.

Sauternes lies 30 miles south-east of Bordeaux, surrounded by Graves. Sauternes is always white and sweet, ideally made from grapes affected by *Botrytis cinerea*. The shrivelled grapes yield very concentrated juice which results in fine sweet wines. Like the Médoc, Sauternes was classified in 1855. Château d'Yquem became the only *Premier Grand Cru Classé*. There are also *Premier* and *Deuxième Cru Châteaux*.

Barsac is a commune within Sauternes. Its wines may be labelled Barsac or Sauternes, so all Barsac is Sauternes, but not all Sauternes is Barsac.

St Emilion A C.

On the right bank the soil is heavier, and the terrain hillier. The Merlot grown here gives wines rich in flavour, but which mature earlier than the wines of the Médoc. St Emilion is an Appellation for red wines only. Classification came later here, in 1955. In contrast to the Médoc it is revised every decade, so there is a variable number of classified Châteaux. The two most famous are Châteaux Ausone and Cheval Blanc.

Pomerol.

Pomerol is a small commune adjoining St Emilion making red wine only, again from the Merlot. No classification exists here but the two top wines, Châteaux Pétrus and Le Pin, regularly command prices higher than the first growths of the Médoc.

Burgundy.

Burgundy was probably the first of the French regions to establish a reputation beyond its frontiers, largely because of the interest taken by the Dukes of Burgundy. The first recorded edict to control wine quality was issued by Philip the Bold in 1395. Realising that the Gamay grape did not make good wine in northern Burgundy, he banished it from that area. Demand for fine Burgundy outstrips supply, largely because Burgundian production, excluding Beaujolais, is about 20% that of Bordeaux. Fine Burgundy is never cheap. Burgundy is in central France, between Dijon and Lyon. It also includes Chablis, 60 miles to the north-west of Dijon, and Beaujolais. The climate here is more continental, characterised by extremes of temperature.

Only four grapes are important; in contrast to Bordeaux, they are largely used unblended. The red wines are made from Gamay in Beaujolais, giving soft, quaffable wines. More serious wines are made further north from Pinot Noir. From the best vineyards very fine wines result, medium in colour relying on high acidity rather than tannin to survive long ageing. Chardonnay makes all classic white Burgundy. Often fermented and aged in wood to add complexity and depth of flavour, Burgundy is the traditional home of that most international of jet-set grape varieties. Perhaps surprisingly, given the grape's international repute, Chardonnay almost never appears on Burgundian labels. Some wine is also made from Aligoté, a lesser white grape, usually sold under a varietal label, *e.g.* Bourgogne Aligoté.

The Appellations of Burgundy.

Most Burgundy is sold under a generic appellation, Bourgogne Rouge and Bourgogne Blanc. A higher appellation is the district one, such as Côte de Beaune or Haute Côte de Nuits. But it is the commune and vineyard appellations on which Burgundy's reputation rests. As in Bordeaux, the districts are divided into communes. Wines produced entirely from grapes grown in a particular commune take its name, e.g. Meursault. In the nineteenth century, at a time of poor sales in the area, communes added their name to that of their most famous vineyard, so the commune of Gevrey added the name of the vineyard of Chambertin becoming Gevrey-Chambertin. Nuits-St George and Puligny-Montrachet are other examples.

The best vineyards are classified as *Premier Cru* or *Grand Cru*. In the past one has had to know the long list of these to recognise them from the label. Nowadays most producers are more explicit, clearly boasting of the higher grading.

There are five main districts in Burgundy. From the north the first is Chablis, producing white wine only from Chardonnay. Bone dry and almost flinty in character, Chablis rarely sees oak, so this is unadorned Chardonnay. The Côte d'Or, the golden slope between Dijon and Santenay is the heart of Burgundy. Here some of the most sought after red and white wines in the world are produced. It comprises the Côte de Nuits in the north, largely a red wine area, and the Côte de Beaune, where both Pinot Noir and Chardonnay are grown. Côte de Nuits includes such famous names as Gevrey-Chambertin, Nuits-St Georges and Chambolle-Musigny; the stars of the Côte de Beaune include Meursault and Puligny-Montrachet, Volnay and Pommard. Further south are the districts of Chalonnaise and Maconnais. Here more affordable Burgundies, both red and white are produced, an ideal introduction to the region. In red wine Macon forms the transition between the Côte d'Or and Beaujolais, being a blend of Pinot Noir and Gamay.

Beaujolais.

Beaujolais produces light fruity red wines from Gamay. Most are best drunk young, indeed most Beaujolais is drunk in the year of vintage, as Beaujolais Nouveau, released in November when the wine is two months old. The north of the district produces fuller wines, under the appellations of Beaujolais Villages or, better still, one of the ten communes, the best known being St Amour, Fleurie and Moulin-à-Vent.

Alsace.

Alsace, in north-eastern France, borders Germany. The border has moved at various times in history so Alsace has been German, and the Germanic influence is still visible in the architecture and vineyards of the area. Unusually for French wines, Alsace wines are usually varietally labelled, the most important being: Riesling, Gewurztraminer, Sylvaner, Pinot Gris and Pinot Blanc. A little red wine from Pinot Noir is also produced. Although made from Germanic grapes, and bottled in tall green flutes like Mosel bottles, Alsace wines are distinctly French, made to accompany the rich and diverse cuisine of the region. Unlike most German wine exported, the wines from here are generally dry with strong varietal character. They include the spicy, exotic Gewurztraminer, oily Pinot Gris and steely Riesling. Wines labelled "Reserve" or "Selection" or something similar, are blended from better vats, the pick of the crop. Vendange Tardive and Selection de Grains Nobles are rare and exquisite late picked wines, off-dry to sweet in taste.

Loire Valley.

The Loire is the longest river in France, rising in the Massif Central. Viticulturally only the lower half is considered "the Loire". Each of the four subregions – Nantais, Anjou-Saumur, Touraine and Central vineyards – has its own climate and wines. Most wines are made from one varietal, but here the name of the village or region is paramount. In this northerly part of France the climate is generally cool so white and rosé wines dominate.

Nantais is the home of Muscadet, one of the largest selling quality wines in the UK. Muscadet is the name of the grape as well as the wine, a dry, fairly neutral white wine usually drunk young and fresh to accompany lightly flavoured seafood.

Anjou-Saumur produces mostly dry white wines,

from the Chenin Blanc under the Saumur appellation, and red, white and rosé as Anjou. The medium sweet Rosé d'Anjou has been the introductory wine for a generation of British wine lovers. The enclave of Côteaux du Layon produces sweet and medium sweet wine from the Chenin Blanc. This sheltered area, influenced by the river Layon, benefits from noble rot.

Farther up river in *Touraine* Chenin Blanc is joined by Sauvignon Blanc. Sauvignon is often used for the Touraine appellation, but Chenin makes the area's most famous appellation, Vouvray. From one grape a wide variety of styles are produced; dry, medium or sweet, still or sparkling. Confusingly the label does not always reveal the style of wine in the bottle, you need to trust your wine merchant.

The *Central Vineyards* are so-called because they are close to the centre of France. Here Sauvignon produces the famous Pouilly Fumé and Sancerre; appellations for what until recently was universally considered the world's best Sauvignon.

Some red wines are made in the Loire. As well as Anjou Rouge there are Chinon and Bourgueil, made from the Cabernet Franc, and red Sancerre from Pinot Noir.

Rhône Valley.

The Rhône Valley is one of the oldest wine producing regions of France. It is certain that wine existed there by c. 600 BC, and it is believed that the steep terraced vineyards of the northern Rhône were the earliest French vine plantations.

Historically Rhône wines were blended with lighter wines, including claret. Recently though their quality has begun to be appreciated, and finally the best are achieving prices comparable with Bordeaux and Burgundy. The region starts south of Lyons at Vienne and extends south to Avignon. It divides neatly in two with a gap around Montélimar, more famous for nougat. The northern and southern districts produce quite different styles of wine, a result of different topography, soils, grapes and climates. Basic Côtes du Rhône can be produced anywhere in the region, but in practice it is nearly always a southern Rhône wine. As with Beaujolais, there is a higher grade, labelled Côtes du Rhône Villages. This is more concentrated and fuller bodied.

The Northern Rhône.

The Northern Rhône comprises a steep hillside, facing east. Here the cliffs are so steep that terraces are required, and all the vineyard functions have to be done by hand. The grape here is Syrah, perhaps now better known by the Australian name Shiraz. Big, full flavoured wines with the structure to age result, sold under the names of the communes such as Côte Rôtie, Cornas and Hermitage. In the middle of the Northern Rhône lie two small, but very prestigious white wine vineyards, Condrieu and Chateau Grillet, producing the epitome of an unusual, flavoursome variety called Viognier.

The Southern Rhône.

The Southern Rhône is less uniform. The valley broadens out to a wide plain, the climate becomes very Mediterranean, with olives and oranges a frequent sight. The range of grapes here also broadens out. Over a dozen different varieties are permitted, but the Grenache is the most widely employed. Relatively pale coloured wines, with high alcohol and little staying power can result, but the majority of producers use judicious amounts of other grapes as improvers to their blends. In contrast to the north, this is the home of large volume average wines plus a few greats, including Châteauneuf-du-Pape, Gigondas and the dry rosé Tavel.

From 1309 to 1378, the Popes lived at Avignon. Pope John XXII built a new palace in the southern Rhône, hence Châteauneuf-du-Pape.

Languedoc-Roussillon.

This great swathe of vineyard extends from the Spanish border to the Rhône estuary and produces one third of all French wines. Once derided, the "Midi" is now a hotbed of innovation in viticulture and vinification. Once the source of much of the EU wine lake, today the emphasis is on quality.

A mix of local grapes goes into the area's appellations, which include Fitou, Côtes du Roussillon,

Corbières and Minervois, but it is the international varieties used in the increasingly successful Vin de Pays which are changing the area's reputation.

Famous grapes, handled well, and marketed by variety offer the consumer a reliable and understandable product, at prices which offer excellent value.

GERMANY.

Germany maintains its ranking as one of the chief UK wine suppliers. For many, Germany is the introduction to wine drinking, but there is far more to Germany than Liebfraumilch. Germany's vineyards are in the south of the country, on the limit of vine cultivation. The climate is cool and damp, so the quality of the vintage depends heavily on the weather. The best vineyards are planted on steep south-facing hillsides, suntraps to collect every available solar ray. In such a marginal climate ripe grapes are at a premium, German wine legislation reflects this.

Deutscher Tafelwein and *Deutscher Landwein* are the two grades of table wine. Little is produced and even less exported. About 95% of Germany's wine is quality wine, of which there are two grades. *Qualitätswein bestimmte Anbaugebiete* (QbA, or simply *Qualitätswein*) is the basic category. The wine will come from one of the thirteen *Anbaugebiete* (regions) which is stated on the label.

Each region is divided into districts, *Bereiche*, such as Bereich Bernkastel in the Mosel. Most individual wines come from single vineyards, *Einzellage*. For commercial reasons a group of vineyards producing similar wines may be grouped together into a *Grosslage*; examples include Niersteiner Gutes Domtal and Piesporter Michelsberg. Riper grapes than QbA can go to make *Qualitätswein mit Prädikat* (QmP). Again the wine must come only from the *Anbaugebiet* stated, but it is the level of ripeness, rather than the provenance which gains the wine its esteem. The categories, in ascending order of natural grape sugar at time of harvesting, are as follows:

Kabinett, from grapes harvested at the normal time but with higher natural grape sugar. These are amongst the lightest and most delicate of all wines.

Spätlese indicates late harvest; a more intense and concentrated style.

Auslese, where only extra ripe bunches are selected.

Beerenauslese wines are made from individually selected berries, a labour of love. These overripe individual grapes, normally affected by noble rot, produce wines with considerable residual sweetness.

Eiswein grapes have their sugar concentrated by freezing, on the vine. Frosts of -8 to $-10°C$ are needed, for a minimum of about eight hours. This freezes the water in the grapes which are pressed when frozen. The resulting juice makes rare wines of great richness.

Trockenbeerenauslese is the highest grade, made from individually selected, heavily botrytised grapes which have shrivelled like raisins.

It is the sugar level of the grape, not the wine, which determines the quality level. *Kabinett*, *Spätlese*, and even occasionally *Auslese* wine are available in dry (trocken) styles, although medium sweet is more normal.

Germany has many grape varieties but three are particularly important. Riesling is the finest German grape. Late ripening, but with fine flavours and acidity, it allows wine to mature almost indefinitely. Silvaner ripens earlier than Riesling, giving firm spicy wines. The productive Müller-Thurgau variety was developed because of the climate. It yields generously and is precocious, an insurance against the inclement autumns. Müller-Thurgau accounts for more vineyard area than any other variety.

There are thirteen vineyard regions in Germany, six are important for exports. All follow the routes of Germany's great rivers.

The Mosel.

Mosel-Saar-Ruwer produces pale, light in body yet intensely elegant wines. The steep, south facing slopes of the Mosel and its tributaries, with their slate soil, collect the warmth of the sun to ripen the grapes.

Rheinhessen and Pfalz.

These are the country's two largest regions. Their wines are fuller in style than Mosel. Generically these wines are referred to as "hock", from the village of Hocheim. Most Rheinhessen and Pfalz wines seen in export markets are Müller Thurgau based blends, sold as Liebfraumilch or Niersteiner Gutes Domtal. The vineyards around Nierstein, however, are capable of producing some stunning wines.

Rheingau.

Only here does the Rhine (in German, Rhein) flow east to west, giving the northern bank, the Rheingau, a perfect southerly exposure. Its aspect and topography make this the ideal area for Riesling, representing four-fifths of the regions' vineyards. Rheingau is home to some of Germany's greatest wine estates such as Vollrads, and Johannisberg, and famous villages such as Rüdesheim and Geisenheim.

Nahe.

This area marks the transition between the fuller Rhine styles and the delicate Mosel wines, in addition to producing some Liebfraumilch.

Baden.

Baden, opposite Alsace in the far south of Germany, is becoming important in export markets. The warmer climate permits fuller bodied wines, both red and white. They are mostly dry, and often appear more French, being bottled in shorter, wider bottles, like those used for Burgundy.

Liebfraumilch.

Liebfraumilch is not a region but a style of blended wine. The name originated from a vineyard at Worms in the Rheinhessen, but the wine can come from any one of the four Rhine regions, Rheinhessen, Pfalz, Rheingau or Nahe. The law requires it to be soft, fruity and easy to drink. It must be of QbA status.

ITALY.

So successful is the vine in Italy that the Greeks called the country Oenotria, the land of the vine. Fittingly, Italy is still the world's largest wine producer. Wine is integrally linked to the culture of the country. Wine is a staple part of the diet. A meal is not a meal without wine. As such the wines must match the local food, as diverse and individualistic as the Italian people.

Italy is made up of twenty regions, each individual and each intent on protecting its own identity. It is a long country, covering ten degrees of latitude; the climate, the people and the culture are very different from Piedmont to Sicily.

DOC (*Denominazione di Origine Controllata*) was introduced in 1963 with the rules designed along the same lines as *Appellation Controllée*. Very soon there were hundreds of DOC wines. To differentiate themselves, certain highly reputed areas were granted a higher grading, DOCG (*Denominazione di Origine Controllata e Garantita*). DOCG imposes stricter controls, including mandatory regional bottling and organoleptic analysis. There are currently over a dozen DOCGs, a number which is growing steadily.

Table wine (*Vino da Tavola*) is normally simple, everyday, cheap wine, often sold in two litre bottles. Some producers, however, deliberately break the DOC rules by, for example, growing the "wrong" grape variety. The resulting wine is *Vino da Tavola*, but often more expensive than DOC.

An enormous number of grape varieties are cultivated in Italy. Some, like Nebbiolo, Lambrusco, Sangiovese and Verdiccio are natives, rarely grown elsewhere. There are also historical imports, now naturalised Italians. Pinot Grigio and Merlot, introduced at the time of Napoleon, are widely used in northern Italian wines. Additionally there are the inevitable internationals, Chardonnay and Cabernet Sauvignon.

DOC and DOCG wines always state the area of origin *e.g.* Barolo, Frascati. In some cases the region is prefixed with the grape as well: examples being Barbera d'Alba and Merlot di Pramaggiore.

Principal Wines.

Although Italy produces a vast range of wines, many are not exported in large volumes. The principal export wines are:

*Barolo DOCG – a Nebbilo based red wine from the village of Barolo in Piedmont, the foothills of the Alps. It must be at least three years old before sale, but then has great additional ageing potential. Barolo is a very full bodied wine with high alcohol, tannin and acidity.

*Barbaresco DOCG – is a red wine from the Nebbiolo grape grown in Piedmont. Similar to Barolo in style, though Barbaresco generally is a touch lighter.

*Valpolicella DOC – is normally a lighter red wine made from a mixture of grapes grown in vineyards near Verona, in the north east. Most Valpolicella should be drunk young.

*Soave DOC – a very dry but fruity white wine named after the commune of Soave near Verona.

*Lambrusco – a lightly sparkling and usually medium sweet Central Italian wine from the grape of the same name. Lambrusco is a black grape, so red, white and rosé wines can be made. Most is sold as table wine, but DOC Lambruscos are much finer.

*Pinot Grigio – dry white wine made from the Pinot Grigio grape in many parts of Italy, but particularly in the north east. It is a fresh, fresh wine with a crisp acidity.

*Chianti DOCG – a red wine produced in Tuscany and made from Sangiovese, and other grapes. It can vary in style from light red wines made for early drinking to well-aged wines with great depth of flavour. Chianti Classico, the centre of the area, produces some of the best Chiantis.

*Orvieto DOC – a white wine made in Umbria. Traditionally Orvieto was *abboccato*, or semi sweet, but today most Orvieto is made dry.

*Frascati DOC – is a white wine usually dry, although sweeter styles are permitted under the DOC. It is made just south of Rome. Like many Italian whites, it tends to be light in flavour.

*Prosecco DOCG – made from the glera grape. Only allowed to be called "prosecco" if the grapes are grown in the Veneto or Friuli regions of NE Italy.

SPAIN.

Spain has more land under vines than any other country (though China is a close second), but because of the dry climate, ranks only third in production terms.

Spain's top quality black grape is Tempranillo. Found in both Spain and Portugal, under a whole host of synonyms, this gives the flavour, backbone and structure to all of Spain's top reds. Garnacha is also important, but more for volume. It is widely planted throughout Spain. For white wine the volume grape is Airén, the world's most widely planted variety, all in Spain. It produces refreshing neutral wines if well handled, but is not a high quality grape. Viura is the top white grape.

Spain too has both quality and table wines. Like Italy, there are two categories of Quality Wine, Denominacion de Origen (DO) and Denominacion de Origen Calificada (DOC). There are over fifty DOs, and one DOC, Rioja. Little Spanish table wine, *vino de mesa*, is exported as many DO wines represent better value. The most important exports are:

Rioja.

Rioja is in northern Spain, along the banks of the river Ebro, and its tributary the Rio Oja, which gives the region its name. Divided into three (Alta Alavesa and Baja) the main centres are Logroño and Haro. Most Riojas are blended from the different districts and shipped by merchant houses in these

two towns. Oak maturation, in American oak casks, gives the distinctive flavour to Reserva and Gran Reserva wines, both red and white. Many Riojas are made without wood.

Navarra.

Navarra is north of Rioja. It enjoys a cool, temperate climate, enabling elegant red and white wines to be produced.

La Mancha.

This area is a vast arid plateau south of Madrid. The climate is extreme, scorching in the summer and very cold during the winter. The largest area of production in Spain, much of the wine goes to brandy production. The light wines, both red and white, are steadily improving.

Penedés DO.

Most Cava, Spain's quality sparkling wine, is produced here, west-south-west of Barcelona. This is also an area of innovation, with modern winemakers using blends of traditional local varieties with international ones.

Other areas becoming more important through recent investment and improvement include Somontano, in the foothills of the Pyrenees and Ribera del Duero on the Duero river.

PORTUGAL.

Northern Portugal comprises a coastal littoral, rising steeply to mountainous inland regions. Further south the plains continue further inland. Atlantic winds bring rain during the winter months and the summers are hot.

Portuguese quality wine is categorised as Denominação de Origem Controlada or Indicação de Proveniencia Regulamentada. Often the label will simply give the catch-all initials of VQPRD. The regional wines, and some of the newer DOC wines from the south, Borba, Palmela, Arruda and Arrabida are gradually becoming more important than some of the classic DOC areas.

Portugal's most popular light wine export, selling in large quantities, is the medium dry rosé Mateus and a similar wine, Lancers. These are examples of excellent wine marketing; having no tradition or history, they were invented for export, and have been amongst the biggest selling brands of wine ever since.

Apart from Port, Vinho Verde and Mateus Rosé few other Portuguese light wines have had much export success until recently. The Salazar regime which came to an end in the early 1970s had imposed restrictive practices on the industry, limiting progress. Following the return of democracy and after joining the EU, Portugal has caught up. Traditional areas are improving, while new areas are now getting more international recognition. The main regions are listed below.

Vinho Verde.

"Vinho Verde" means "green wine" a reference to its youthful character. Fresh in acidity and moderate in alcohol, it is best consumed when young (or green). Vinho Verde is produced in northern Portugal. High trained vines give barely ripe grapes, while enabling other agriculture on the same land. More red wine than white wine is produced, but the red is only consumed in Portugal.

Dão.

Dão is south of the Douro valley in northern central Portugal, a wild and beautiful country with terraced vineyards on granite slopes. Until recently the wines tended to be dried out, aged for too long before sale. Investment since 1986 has now rectified this.

Bairrada.

South of Oporto, between Dão and the Atlantic, Bairrada makes some excellent red wines, sometimes matured successfully for several years.

II. GLOSSARY OF FOOD

Abalone An edible mollusc used in Chinese cooking.

Ackee The fruit of a tree originating in Africa and introduced to Jamaica by Captain Bligh. The creamy flesh of the fruit resembles scrambled egg when cooked and is generally accompanied by salted cod fish.

Aïoli A sauce from Provence made by pounding garlic then adding egg yolks and olive oil to make a garlic mayonnaise. Served separately with an assortment of raw and cooked vegetables and fish or cold meat.

Anchoïade A purée of anchovies, garlic and olive oil served on bread or as a dip with raw vegetables. The word comes from the Provence region of France and is sometimes spelt anchoyade.

Angels on Horseback A hot savoury made with oysters wrapped in bacon, grilled and served on toast. (*See also* Devils on Horseback).

Antipasto Italian starter, from the words for "before meal", consisting of cold meats, olives, marinated vegetables. *etc.*

Avgolémono Popular Greek sauce and also soup, based on eggs beaten with lemon juice. For the sauce, stock from the dish it accompanies is added; for the soup, the eggs are added to chicken stock in which some rice has been cooked.

Bacalao The Spanish word for cod which has been salted and dried. Thus preserved it was for centuries an important winter food in many Mediterranean countries.

Baked Alaska A "surprise" dessert of ice cream baked in the oven which was invented by an American physicist in the nineteenth century. The ice cream and a sponge base are enclosed in meringue, cooked quickly to set the meringue, and served hot. The ice cream remains firm and cold due to the low conductivity of the meringue mixture.

Baklava A pastry dessert from Greece and the Middle East made from thin layers of pastry, chopped nuts and honey syrup, and flavoured with cinnamon. Its origins reputedly go back to the eighth century B.C. in Assyria.

Ballottine Boned meat or poultry dish which is stuffed, rolled and tied up in a cloth, then braised or poached. The word derives from the French for "bale". This was traditionally a Romany method of preparing food.

Balti A slow cooked curry sauce to which meat, poultry, fish or vegetables marinated with spices are added. The balti is the large metal bowl in which the dish is cooked and served and derives from the Urdu for "bucket". The dish was introduced to Britain from Pakistan by the Kashmiri community.

Bamia The Arabic word for okra, a popular vegetable in Middle Eastern cooking. Also known as "ladies' fingers" and in Indian cookery as *bhindi*.

Béarnaise sauce A warm egg yolk and butter sauce similar to Hollandaise (*q.v.*) but with the addition of shallots and tarragon.

Beef stroganoff A Russian dish of sautéed strips of lean beef in a sour-cream sauce with onions and, generally, mushrooms, which became popular in England and the US in the 1930s. Named in the nineteenth century from its association with Count Stroganoff, a Russian diplomat.

Bento Popular Japanese lunch box, consisting of salad, rice, dumpling, pickled vegetables and choice of one meat or fish, all served with miso soup.

Bigos A stew of layers of meat and sauerkraut, the Polish national dish.

Bird's nest soup A Chinese soup made from the lining of birds nests.

Biryani An elaborate Indian dish based on rice cooked with meat or chicken, saffron, raisins and nuts.

Blini Russian pancakes made from a twice-risen batter of flour (wheat, buckwheat or rye), milk, eggs, butter, sugar, salt and yeast. Served with a variety of fillings including sour cream, smoked salmon and caviar.

Bolognaise A traditional Italian meat sauce made with minced meat, onions, garlic, tomatoes and mushrooms served with spaghetti.

Bombay duck A dried fish eaten as a savoury with Indian dishes. Known for its pungent smell, the name comes from the Marathi, "bombilla".

Borscht A traditional Russian soup made from beetroot and cabbage which can be served hot or chilled in warm weather.

Bouillabaisse A Mediterranean fish stew, a speciality of Marseilles. The word is the French interpretation of the Provençal for "boil and settle".

Bresaola Dried salt beef cut in thin slices and served with oil, lemon juice and parsley as an *hors d'oeuvre*. A speciality of Lombardy, northern Italy.

Bruschetta Slices of white bread oven-toasted then rubbed with garlic and moistened with olive oil.

Bubble and squeak An English dish which uses leftover cooked potato and cabbage. The name comes from the distinctive sound the ingredients make when fried together.

Bunny Chow Traditional South African dish of hollowed out loaf filled with curried meats.

Burrito Mexican pancake filled with refried beans and cheese. In Spanish its name means little donkey.

Caesar salad Popular American green salad. The ingredients include lettuce and garlic croutons with a dressing of olive oil, lemon juice, raw eggs, parmesan cheese and Worcester sauce.

Callaloo Caribbean soup made from the fleshy leaves of a tropical root vegetable called Taro. Crab meat is usually added to the soup.

Canelloni The term means 'little tubes'. An Italian dish of pasta squares rolled around a stuffing, usually meat-based, and baked in the oven with butter and cheese.

Carbonara An Italian pasta dish where beaten egg and pieces of ham or bacon are stirred into the cooked pasta. The heat of the pasta lightly cooks the egg, then grated Parmesan cheese is added.

Cassata A block of two differently flavoured ice creams with a filling of cream and crystallised fruits soaked in brandy.

Ceviche Seafood marinated in lime juice, onion and coriander. The national dish of Panama.

Chapati Flat Indian bread made with wholemeal flour, salt and water, fried without fat.

Chicken Kiev Chicken breast folded around chilled garlic butter, then coated in egg and breadcrumbs and deep fried. Not, in fact, from Kiev in Ukraine, it was invented by a Frenchman and given its name later in New York to please Russian immigrants.

Chilli con carne A Texan meat stew meaning 'chilli with meat'. Made with cubed or minced beef, onions, tomatoes and chilli peppers with red kidney beans.

Chop suey A bastardised form of Chinese cooking introduced into the United States to cater for American tastes. It consists of small pieces of meat or chicken cooked with vegetables including bean sprouts and bamboo shoots served with rice.

Chorizo A spicy coarse pork sausage with a distinctive red colour from the addition of paprika, popular in Spanish and Mexican cooking. It can be fresh, as is more usual in Mexico, or cured and air-dried for either eating cold or cooking, as is usual in Spain.

Chowder A thick fish soup originating in Newfoundland, popular in the United States. The most popular version is made with clams. The word comes from the French *chaudière* meaning "stewpot".

Chow mein Stir-fried noodles served with a thick sauce containing meat, fish or vegetables popularised by Chinese cooks in the United States in the 1920s.

Ciabatta An Italian long, wide and flat bread loaf with a soft interior and a crisp thin crust. The word is the Italian for slipper which its shape is thought to resemble.

Cicchetti The Venetian equivalent of tapas (small snacks and side dishes).

Club sandwich Sandwich originating in America made with three slices of bread and two layers of filling.

Coq au vin Classic French dish of chicken simmered in red wine with bacon, onions and mushrooms. Chicken joints are browned then flamed in brandy before adding the wine – a whole bottle of Burgundy is usually specified. The sauce is thickened at the end of cooking.

Corn pone Baked or fried bread made from maize flour and buttermilk, popular in the southern states of America. Pone is a Native American word for bread.

Couscous From the Arabic *kuskus* meaning to grind small. North African ground wheat or semolina which is steamed and served with a sauce or stew of meat or vegetables.

Crème brûlée A dessert of rich custard, made from egg yolks, sugar and cream, topped with caramelised sugar and served cold. French for "burnt cream".

Croquette Small deep fried ball or roll of savoury ingredients coated in breadcrumbs.

Croque-madame A croque-monsieur sandwich *(see below)* topped with a fried or poached egg.

Croque-monsieur French toasted cheese and ham sandwich.

Crudités *Hors d'oeuvre* of pieces of raw vegetables dipped into a cold sauce such as vinaigrette or mayonnaise.

Devils on Horseback A variation on Angels on Horseback (q.v.) substituting plums or prunes for oysters which are wrapped in bacon, grilled and served on toast.

Dhal An Indian dish made of stewed dried peas, onion and spices. Lentils are popular but many varieties of dried peas are used, for example chick peas and mung beans.

Dim sum Small steamed Chinese dumplings usually eaten as a snack. A variety of ingredients are used as fillings in combination or on their own. They include meat, fish, chicken and vegetables. The words mean 'little heart'.

Dolmades Greek dish of vine leaves stuffed with rice, meat and herbs.

Döner kebab The term means 'turning roast meat'. Slices of marinated lamb are packed on an upright spit and the meat is grilled as it turns. The outside layers of cooked meat are sliced as the spit turns.

Dopiaza An Indian curry dish characterised by a large amount of onion, of which part is used in the cooking and the remainder is fried and added at the end. The name is Bengali for "twice onions".

Egg fu yong A Chinese dish traditionally made of egg, white crab meat, spring onions and various seasonings. The name comes from the pink and white Hibiscus flower which the finished dish resembles.

Enchilada Fried Mexican tortilla. These can be filled with meat, cheese or vegetables or any combination of these ingredients flavoured with chilli peppers.

Ertwensoep A thick pea soup from Holland made with pork stock, pig's knuckle, onions and thyme.

Fajitas Mexican freshly-cooked flour tortillas to which diners add their own choice of hot and cold fillings then fold to form a pocket around the filling. They are always eaten with the fingers.

Falafel Seasoned vegetarian patties from the Middle East. Made from chickpeas in Israel and from broad beans in Egypt, where they are called fellafel.

Focaccia Flat Italian bread topped with olive oil, spices and other ingredients such as tomato, making it an early prototype of pizza. Its name evolved from the *panis focacius*, bread cooked in the ashes, of ancient Rome.

Fondue Swiss dish of melted cheese cooked with wine and flavoured with garlic. The dish is eaten as it cooks over a low heat by dipping cubes of bread into the fondue. The word comes from the French and means 'melt'.

Frittata An Italian omelette made from lightly beaten eggs to which a variety of ingredients have been added, usually grated cheese or a chopped cooked vegetable such as onion, spinach or artichoke hearts. It is not stirred in the pan but cooked on both sides like a pancake.

Fritto misto An Italian dish of small pieces of meat and vegetable coated in batter and fried in deep oil. The ingredients are very variable, and in the Milanese version egg and breadcrumbs replace the batter and the frying is in butter. Sometimes short for *fritto misto di mare*, which uses small fish and shellfish.

Galangal Popular flavouring ingredient in SE Asia. Member of the ginger family.

Gazpacho An uncooked Spanish vegetable soup served chilled. Chopped onions, tomatoes, sweet peppers and cucumber are blended with vinegar, oil, garlic and breadcrumbs and ice is added to produce the liquid.

Gnocchi Small Italian dumplings boiled and served with melted butter and grated cheese or with a sauce. Made from either flour, potatoes or semolina, plus eggs. Other ingredients can be cheese, Parmesan cheese and spinach.

Goulash Hungarian meat stew with onions and potatoes seasoned with paprika.

Granita Italian water-ice made by freezing a mix of sugar syrup and either fruit juice or black coffee.

Grissini Italian thin crispy breadsticks, a speciality of Turin where it was invented in the seventeenth

century. Considered a more digestible alternative to bread to accompany the *hors d'oeuvre*.

Guacamole A blend of avocado, onion, garlic, lime and coriander, sometimes including tomatoes and chillies. A popular sauce in Mexico, where it is served as a dip with tortilla chips and is an essential accompaniment to *fajitas*.

Gumbo A thick soup from the southern states of America, Gumbo is a name for okra, a vegetable which is one of the main ingredients and gives the dish its smooth, silky texture.

Haggis Sheeps heart, liver, lungs, chopped onions, oatmeal and suet stuffed into the stomach of a sheep to form a large sausage shape and boiled. Usually served with mashed swedes. It is banned in America because it contains lungs.

Halloumi A chewy, squeaky cheese made from a mixture of goat's and sheep's milk.

Halva A Middle Eastern sweetmeat made from ground sesame seeds and honey or sugar. Chopped nuts or dried fruit are sometimes added.

Harissa A fiery condiment of Morocco, Tunisia and Algeria, served with soups and stews. It consists of a purée of red chilli peppers, garlic, cumin and coriander seeds, and olive oil.

Hash The word comes from the French for 'chop up'. Chopped cooked meat (generally corned beef) is mixed with potato and fried or baked.

Hollandaise sauce A warm, slightly frothy, sauce of egg yolks, butter and wine vinegar, served with fish, asparagus or globe artichokes. Although originating in France, its name is from its similarity to earlier Dutch sauces.

Hot-pot A type of baked stew associated with Lancashire consisting of layers of lamb and vegetables topped with thinly sliced potatoes.

Humus A popular Turkish *hors d'oeuvre* made of puréed chickpeas, sesame paste, garlic, olive oil and lemon juice.

Jalfrezi A pungently spicy Indian curry in which marinated pieces of meat or vegetables are stir-fried with green chillies, red peppers, onion, tomatoes and spices to give a dry, thick sauce. Originally an Anglo-Indian dish for using up leftover meat.

Jambalaya A Cajun rice dish which includes beans, shellfish and meat from Louisiana in the USA.

Kebab Small pieces of meat, seasoned, threaded on skewers and cooked over hot embers. This method of cooking meat has been known in the eastern Mediterranean for over 3,000 years. The name may derive from a word meaning "to char".

Kedgeree English breakfast dish of pieces of haddock or kipper cooked with boiled rice and curry paste. The original Hindi recipe consisted of boiled rice and lentils and was called *khichri*.

Korma A rich North-Indian dish of chicken or lamb braised slowly in a marinade of yoghourt and spices. The sauce is often thickened with ground almonds, and sometimes cream is added. Its origin was the Mughal dish of meat braised in oil called *qaurama*.

Lardy cake A sweet sticky English cake made from a white dough mixed with lard, sugar, mixed fruit peel and spices.

Lasagne Italian dish of alternating layers of pasta sheets, Bolognese sauce (q.v.) and béchamel sauce, topped with grated Parmesan cheese. Oven baked.

Lassi An Indian yoghurt drink served cold with the addition either of salt or sweeteners such as honey and often flavoured with rose water.

Latke A Jewish pancake made from grated potato with onions and seasoning.

Lobster Newberg A method of cooking lobster originating at the famous Delmonico's restaurant in New York during the nineteenth century. The lobster is cooked in a cream sauce flavoured with wine and paprika.

Loukanika Smoked wine sausages (a Greek dish).

Madras A hot Anglo-Indian curry sauce for beef made from onions, curry powder and tomatoes, with lemon juice added after cooking the meat.

Marinade Process for tenderising and moisturising meat or fish by soaking in a preparation of acid and oily ingredients, for example, wine, olive oil, lemon juice, vinegar, onion, spices and herbs.

Masala The Indian term for a pre-prepared mix of spices for adding to a dish after cooking. In India such mixes are not used for the cooking process itself. The mix we know as curry powder was invented in England in the nineteenth century, when Indian food became popular.

Meze Greek *hors d'oeuvre*, which may include olives, nuts, rice-stuffed vine leaves and tomatoes, tiny onions in a tomato sauce and feta cheese.

Minestrone An Italian soup of various kinds of vegetables with rice or pasta, served with grated Parmesan cheese. The traditional midday soup of agricultural and manual workers in northern Italy.

Mississippi mud pie An American dessert made of a rich smooth caramel fudge and chocolate mousse on a crisp biscuit base. The name comes from its resemblance to the coffee-coloured clay which forms the banks of the Mississippi river.

Moussaka Greece and Turkey both lay claim to being the originators of this dish and it is eaten throughout the Middle East. It consists of layers of minced lamb, fried aubergine, onion and tomato and cheese covered in a white sauce and baked.

Muesli A Swiss breakfast food made of a mixture of oat flakes, nuts and fruit eaten with milk or yoghurt.

Mulligatawny An Anglo-Indian spicy meat soup. There were no soups in Indian cookery and this was invented in Madras for the English there by adapting a medicinal broth known as "pepper water", in Tamil *molo tunny*.

Naan Flat Indian bread cooked in a *tandoor*, a clay oven. The dough is made from flour, salt and yeast moistened with yoghourt. It is served hot brushed with clarified butter called *ghee*, and is the usual accompaniment to a balti curry.

Nachos A Tex-Mex dish of crisp, hot tortilla corn chips covered in melted cheese and sprinkled with chopped, pickled jalapeño chilli. Reputedly created at a Mexican restaurant in 1943 by Ignacio (Nacho) Anaya, as a quick snack for the wives of airmen stationed just over the border in New Mexico.

Nasi Goreng Originally an Indonesian dish very popular in the Netherlands made of cooked rice fried with finely diced meat, chicken and seafood covered with sliced omelette.

Osso buco Italian dish of veal shin which is sawn in pieces, cooked in white wine, stock and chopped tomatoes, and sprinkled with *gremolata*, a mix of parsley, garlic and lemon peel, before serving. The pieces must remain upright while cooking to retain the marrow: the words mean "marrow-bone".

Paella A Spanish rice dish cooked with saffron which gets its name from the pan in which it is cooked and served. The ingredients are chicken, meat, shellfish and vegetables.

Pancetta Italian dry cured pork belly. It can be eaten cold, or cooked and used in a variety of dishes.

Paneer Indian cottage cheese.

Panettone An Italian cake made from a dough of flour, eggs, butter, sugar and yeast mixed with sultanas and spices. A speciality of Milan and a traditional Christmas gift.

Panforte A rich Italian cake from Siena with nuts, citrus peel and spices, especially cloves.

Panini Italian sandwich made from a bread roll, typically a small ciabatta, filled with salami, ham, cheese, *etc.* Sometimes pressed in a grill and served hot. *Panino* is the Italian for small bread roll.

Paratha Indian bread fried on a griddle. The dough is made from wheat flour called *atta* to form a rich, flaky dough which is spread with clarified butter called *ghee*.

Parfait An iced dessert made by freezing in a mould a light, frothy mixture of sugar syrup, egg yolks and whipped cream, flavoured with liqueur or fruit purée.

Pâté Originally this was the French word which described a baked pastry case filled with finely minced meat, fish, poultry or their livers. The modern version is generally served without the pastry.

Pepperpot Caribbean stew consisting of oxtail, calf's foot, salt beef and chicken, vegetables and chilli peppers. The characteristic flavour comes from cassareep, the juice of the cassava root. This flavouring is poisonous unless it is well cooked in the stew.

Pesto An amalgamation of pounded basil, pine nuts, garlic, Sardo or Parmesan cheese, and olive oil, used as a sauce for pasta and fish and as a flavouring for soups. Originally from Genoa, Italy.

Phaal Invented in the UK by Indian restaurants to be the hottest curry known, due to the high quantity of fresh and dried chilli peppers in its thick tomato-based sauce. The name is borrowed from a very hot dish of southern India which it in no way resembles.

Pitta Flat oval bread from Greece and the Middle East. Pitta is served warm, split in half and filled with meat and salad or dipped in humus or taramasalata.

Pizzaiola An Italian sauce of tomatoes, garlic, and

oregano or basil, originally from Naples. Traditionally served spread on steak.

Polenta A staple food of northern Italy made by boiling yellow maize flour. Although it can be eaten plain boiled it is usually left to cool then cut up and fried.

Poppadom Round, crisp wafers made from lentil flour eaten to accompany Indian meals.

Profiteroles A dessert made from small balls of a pastry made with eggs and sugar which are filled with whipped cream and covered with chocolate sauce. In fact the French term refers only to the pastry balls, which can also have a savoury filling.

Pumpernickel A German rye bread from Westphalia which, sliced and in sealed packs, can be preserved almost indefinitely. The loaves are baked in a tin very slowly and turn dark brown from the smoke of the beech logs fuelling the oven.

Quiche French cream and egg custard with smoked bacon cooked in an open pastry case. Also known as quiche lorraine it is a speciality of the Alsace-Lorraine region.

Ragù An Italian sauce which is the original, and more elaborate version of, Bolognese sauce. Made from minced beef, chicken livers, bacon, carrot, onion, celery, tomato purée, white wine, butter and nutmeg. In Bologna, milk or cream is sometimes added. Served with many kinds of pasta, especially lasagne.

Raita The Indian term for yoghourt with added ingredients – chopped crunchy vegetables or fruit, most commonly cucumber. Served as a cooling side dish with hot, spicy food.

Rambutan A fruit with pink, hairy berries, related to the lychee.

Ratatouille A Provençal dish of vegetables simmered in olive oil. Typical ingredients are aubergines, tomatoes, red peppers, courgettes and garlic.

Ravioli Small packets of thin pasta filled with a meat or cheese stuffing and poached. Served traditionally either in broth or with butter and cheese. Originally so named only in the Piedmont region of Italy.

Rillettes A French cold *hors d'oeuvre* of potted meat, where the meat is shredded rather than minced. Usually pork, but goose and rabbit are also used. Strips of the meat and pork fat are cooked in a little water then the meat is shredded, put in pots and the fat poured over to seal.

Risotto An Italian dish of Piedmontese rice cooked slowly with butter, onion and the gradual addition of just enough liquid, either water, stock or wine, to give a creamy consistency. This method of cooking rice is unique to Italy.

Rogan Josh A medium-hot dish from Kashmir made from cubes of lamb simmered in a rich red spicy sauce. The Hindus flavour it with fennel seeds, asafoetida and red chillies, whereas the Moslems use garlic, onion and the dried flower of the cockscomb plant, which gives it its red colouring *(rogan* is red in Kashmiri).

Rösti A Swiss dish made by grating cooked potato, pressing it into a cake then frying until one side is brown and crusty.

Salade niçoise A popular French salad based on lettuce hearts, hard-boiled eggs, anchovy fillets, black olives and tomatoes with an oil, vinegar and garlic dressing. Other ingredients, such as cooked green beans, potatoes and tunny fish, may be added. Served as an *hors d'oeuvre* or a lunch dish.

Salami A highly seasoned sausage made from chopped lean pork, or pork plus beef or veal, and fat pork, cured with salt then air-dried. The process originated in Italy to preserve meat for the winter. The word is derived from *sal*, the Latin for salt.

Salsa A type of sauce originating in Mexico in which fresh or cooked vegetables or fruit are coarsely cut up and flavoured with herbs and spices. It can be served as a relish or poured over food. The term is the Spanish for sauce.

Saltimbocca An Italian dish of thin slices of veal and ham topped with a sage leaf, rolled together and cooked in butter and Marsala. The word means "jump into the mouth".

Samosas Triangular shaped pastries, deep fried, and filled with potato, vegetables or *keema* (minced lamb). Often flavoured with coriander. A popular Indian dish.

Sandwich Savoury filling between two pieces of bread made popular by the Earl of Sandwich in the eighteenth century. He was unwilling to stop playing cards and asked for a piece of cold beef between two slices of toast.

Sashimi Japanese dish of thin slices of raw fish served with soy or horseradish sauce.

Satay A dish originally from Indonesia and Malaysia, where it is called *sate*. Little skewers of meat, chicken or fish, are marinated with spices then barbecued. The characteristic yellow colour is due to the turmeric used in the marinade. Often served with a spicy peanut sauce.

Sauerkraut Traditional German dish of pickled cabbage. Cabbage is packed with salt and ferments to give it a sour taste. This is also a method of preserving the cabbage.

Shashlik The type of kebab (*q.v.*) popular in the countries of the former Soviet Union and in Mongolia. Meat is marinated overnight before the cubes are threaded on skewers and grilled. Vegetables such as onion and tomato are often interspersed on the skewers.

Shish kebab The term used in the Middle East for the same type of kebab as shashlik (*q.v.*) although the meat is not normally marinated. The words mean "skewered roast meat".

Simnel cake A fruit cake with a layer of almond paste in the centre and topped with almond icing. The traditional gift on Mothering Sunday from daughters away in domestic service.

Skordaliá Greek *hors d'oeuvre* consisting of an amalgamation of garlic mayonnaise, ground almonds, breadcrumbs, lemon juice and parsley.

Smörgåsbord A Swedish buffet meal consisting of a variety of dishes from which a complete meal may be chosen. Smoked or pickled fish, cheese, butter and bread are basic items, others are hot and cold meats, salads, eggs and fruit. The name is from *smörgås* (open sandwich) and *bord* (table).

Spam A processed meat product. Originally from the USA the name comes from spiced ham. It was popular in Britain during the Second World War as a substitute for meat.

Stir-fry A traditional Chinese method of preparing small uniformly sized pieces of food quickly in a wide, deep, pan with a curved bottom made from thin metal called a wok. Its shape ensures that only the bottom of the pan gets hot.

Stollen A German loaf-shaped Advent cake containing dried fruit, candied peel and spices, and sprinkled with icing sugar. A speciality of Dresden. The word means "tunnel", possibly referring to its shape. Stollen dates from the middle ages.

Strudel A traditional pastry of Austria and Hungary, made by spreading a filling on very thin pastry then rolling it up and baking in the oven. The most popular filling in Austria is apple with raisins and cinnamon; in Hungary, poppy seeds and sour cherry. *Strudel* is the German for swirl.

Sukiyaki A Japanese dish of thinly sliced beef, vegetables, beancurd, soy sauce, rice wine (*sake*) and sugar. The dish is cooked at the table. It is said to have been introduced as a means of getting the Japanese to eat more meat.

Summer pudding An English dessert of lightly cooked raspberries and redcurrants encased in soft white bread and chilled overnight so that the juices flavour and colour the bread.

Sushi Japanese snacks consisting of small squares or balls of cold boiled rice mixed with seaweed, vinegar, salt and sugar. These are covered with a variety of food such as mushrooms, fish or omelette.

Tabbouleh Middle Eastern salad made with cracked wheat, herbs, onions and tomatoes.

Taco Filled Mexican pancakes made of wheat or maize flour which are shaped and fried. The traditional filling consists of a mixture of minced beef, beans and a rich tomato sauce flavoured with onions and chilli peppers.

Tagliatelle The most common form of home-made pasta in Italy. A paste of flour and eggs, rolled out and cut into strips, then boiled and served with either butter and Parmesan cheese or with a sauce.

Tajine North-African slow-cooked stew of meat, poultry or game with vegetables, spices and such fruit as olives, apricots and preserved lemons. The name is from the pot it is cooked in, a heavy clay pot with a circular shallow base and a large cone-shaped cover.

Tandoori A *landoor* is the Urdu term for a clay oven. A variety of Indian dishes cooked in this way are given the name tandoori, chicken being the most well known.

Tapas Savoury snacks served in Spanish bars.

Tapénade A Provençal sauce of pounded black olives, anchovy fillets and capers blended with olive oil and lemon juice. Traditionally served with hard-boiled eggs as an *hors d'oeuvre*. The word comes from *tapéno*, the Provençal for capers.

Taquitos Mexican miniature tacos (*q.v.*).

Taramasalata Greek *hors d'oeuvre* of pink cod's roe, garlic, lemon juice, olive oil and breadcrumbs mixed to a paste.

Tempura Japanese method of deep frying seafood and small pieces of vegetables coated in a light batter.

Teriyaki Japanese method of cooking fish or, more rarely, meat, from *teri* (glaze) and *yaki* (to broil). The food is sliced and broiled or grilled with a marinade of soy sauce, *mirin* (Japanese sweet cooking wine), and sugar or honey. The sweetness gives it a characteristic shiny appearance.

Terrine Originally this was the French word for a round or oval earthenware cooking pot, fairly deep and without handles. It came to mean the food cooked in it, and the meaning is now essentially the same as pâté.

Textured vegetable protein A type of meat substitute made from soya beans first marketed in the USA. A paste of soya beans is spun into fibres and formed to resemble meat.

Thali A complete Indian meal of several dishes on a single platter – the traditional family way of eating in the Indian sub-continent.

Tikka Indian dish of grilled marinated chicken pieces on skewers.

Tiramisu An Italian cake made from sponge biscuits soaked in espresso coffee, layered with a mix of cream cheese, egg yolk, sugar and, optionally, Marsala wine, and topped with cocoa. The word means "pick me up".

Toad-in-the hole Fried sausages baked in batter.

Tofu The Japanese name for a kind of cheese made from soya bean milk. It is also popular with vegetarians as a source of protein.

Tortellini Little coils of pasta filled with a rich stuffing and served either in broth or with cheese and butter. A speciality of Bologna, Italy, where it was the traditional dish on Christmas Eve.

Tortilla Flat Mexican pancakes made from corn-meal flour, water and salt, filled with a variety of ingredients such as meat, chicken, refried beans, cheese and salad.

Tournedos Rossini Sautéed medallions of beef fillet topped with foie gras and truffles and served on croûtons with a Madeira sauce. Reputedly created for the composer Rossini.

Tzatziki Greek dip made from cucumber, garlic and yoghurt.

Vinaigrette A salad dressing made from oil and vinegar.

Vindaloo Very hot Indian meat or chicken curry. The addition of vinegar gives this dish its characteristic flavour.

Vol-au-vent French pastry cases filled with meat, fish or other savoury fillings in a creamy sauce. Usually eaten as snacks with drinks.

Waffle American batter cakes cooked in a waffle iron which gives them their distinctive honey-comb appearance. Served warm with maple syrup and butter.

Wasabi A fiery green vegetable used in Japanese cookery. The grated root is similar to horseradish and is often served with sushi.

Waterzooi A Flemish freshwater fish stew. The word is from the Flemish for "water" and "lot".

Wun tun Savoury Chinese dumplings usually made from wheat and filled with meat, fish or vegetables in a seasoned sauce. They are either fried or boiled in a thin soup.

Yoghurt Milk curdled by the action of heat and bacteria to produce a thick liquid with a creamy texture and sharp flavour. It is known to have been eaten in the Middle East at least 8000 years ago. Sales of frozen yoghurt are now rising fast.

Yorkshire pudding English savoury batter pudding made of eggs, flour and salt, baked in the oven and eaten traditionally as an accompaniment to roast beef, potatoes and vegetables, with gravy.

Zaalouk A popular Moroccan dish of roasted aubergine, with various spices added. Often served cold with pitta bread.

Zabaglione Italian name for a frothy custard type pudding served warm and made from Marsala, Madeira or other sweet wine, egg yolks and caster sugar.

Zuppa Inglese Italian trifle made with macaroons soaked in alcohol and covered with cream cheese.

III. BEER AND LAGER

ABV: alcohol by volume.

ale: although the terms `ale' and `beer' are sometimes used as virtual synonyms, the description `beer' was first introduced in the late Middle Ages to designate ale to which hops *(q.v.)* had been added.

Ale had been drunk for at least 4,000 years and was known to the ancient Near East, the Celts and the Anglo-Saxons. Modern ale is fermented at higher temperatures (15–23°C) than lager *(q.v.)* beer and is preferably brewed from winter barley, which gives the ale a robust quality, and in Britain uses fertilised female hops which add an earthy and peppery aroma and flavour to the ale, together with considerable bitterness. Traditionally brewed in hard-water areas rich in minerals. The main styles of ale are old ale, barley wine *(q.v.)*, Dubbel and Trippel *(q.v.)* brown ale, pale ale, porter including stout *(q.v.)* and wheat beer.

barley: recognised for centuries as the best grain for brewing and comprises 30–50% of the grain used, even in `wheat beers'. Characterised as two-row or six-row depending on the number of rows of grain within each ear, the two-row variety has traditionally been preferred for brewing. Czech and German lager brewers have normally insisted on the two-row variety. The best two-row barley, known as `maritime barley', grows on the rich, dark soils near the sea in East Anglia, the Scottish lowlands and Belgium.

The tannins in the husk of the six-row variety, which is the norm in the Mediterranean countries and in the United States, can give rise to a `haze' in the beer which has to be dispelled by additives, such as corn or rice.

barley wine: a style of strong ale originating in nineteenth-century England, but now brewed worldwide. The name derives from its strength of 8–12% ABV which is comparable with that of wine.

bitter: a beer which exploits the bitterness inherent in fertilised hops. The Admiral and Golding varieties of hop are particularly suitable.

brown ale: a description dating from the late seventeenth century, but which has tended to change its meaning over the years. Modern brown ale is dark in colour with the flavours of caramel and chocolate.

Dubbel/Double: The Flemish and French names for the medium-strength (6–7.5% ABV) dark abbey beers, not brewed by monks but in the monastic style.

Guinness: The world's most famous creamy stout, now brewed in more than 150 countries worldwide. Since 2005, however, all the draught Guinness sold in British pubs has been brewed in Dublin, where Arthur Guinness signed a lease on the St James's Gate brewery in 1759.

hops: contrary to much popular belief, hops are not an essential ingredient of beer but are an adjunct to counter both the sweetness of the malt and its susceptibility to bacterial infection. They only appeared in England in the late fifteenth century and their use was banned initially by, amongst others, Henry VIII for the royal breweries, and the city of Norwich. Hops had, however, been used in brewing in central Europe since the eighth century A.D.

Modern English hop-growing is concentrated in Kent and Worcestershire and Britain remains distinctive in allowing the male hop to mate and in exploiting the bitterness and earthiness associated with the fertilised plant.

The citric quality given to beer by the addition of hops is, however, at its most marked with the US varieties, with the Chinook bestowing a strong taste of grapefruit.

hops, noble: the hops grown in such celebrated central European regions as the Hallertau in Bavaria and Zatec in the Czech Republic, and which are renowned both for their aroma and their limited bitterness.

kriek: Belgian fruit beer. The name is from the Flemish word for black cherry, but other soft fruits, particularly raspberries, are often used. The use of fruit to flavour the beer is thought to pre-date the use of hops. *Oude kriek* (old black cherry) is an earlier cherry-steeped lambic beer *(q.v.)* which is now rarely found.

lager: a generic name for the lighter, smoother and softer beers traditionally associated with the German-speaking regions of central Europe, *Lagerbier* literally meaning `beer for keeping'. It is now, however, produced all over Europe and elsewhere. Lager is typically fermented at 7–12°C.

Lager only became popular in Britain in the years following the Second World War, and many of the most famous continental brands, though by no means all, are now brewed in Britain under licence.

Lager brewing is traditionally associated with soft-water areas and prefers to use spring barley which gives the beer its lighter and softer qualities. It also relies on unfertilised hops to avoid astringency and any significant bitterness.

lambic: a style of Belgian beer, produced by spontaneous fermentation in open vessels in brewery attics as a result of the yeast in the air. It is the style of beer most similar to wine produced anywhere in the world, with a refined but acquired taste. `Faro' is a variety of lambic sweetened with sugar.

malt: the modified barley created by the processes in the maltings *(q.v.)* which has a natural biscuity sweetness.

– `dark malt': malt which has been heated to the highest temperature and is used for the brewing of darker beers such as English mild.

– `green malt': malt heated to about 60°C so as to dry it and thereby halt the germination process while preserving the enzymes which will convert the starch into sugar in a later stage in the brewing process.

– `pale malt': malt heated to a higher temperature than `white malt' and traditionally used for ale brewing.

– `smoked malt': malt dried over the traditional variable wood fires which acquires a distinctive smoky taste. Still used for the production of some German beers *(Rauchbier)*.

– `white malt': malt heated to a temperature slightly above 60°C which is maintained over 24 hours. Suited to the brewing of lager beers.

maltings, the: the part of the brewery where the grain is `steeped' or soaked to remove impurities and to allow germination to start. In a traditional brewery, the grain was spread over a floor as a `couch', but it is more normal now to rely on large revolving drums. The resulting `modified' barley is known as `green malt' *(q.v.)*.

mild (ale): dates back to early seventeenth-century Britain, if not earlier, and originally meant young as distinct from aged ale, but now implies `mildly hopped'. It has been largely superseded by bitter and lager, particularly in the south of England, and now only around 10% of the beer sold in British pubs is mild.

minerals: a feature of hard waters which helps to give pale ales their distinctive character. Amongst the more significant is calcium sulphate, or gypsum, which prompts enzymes to turn starch into sugar during `mashing', stabilises the unfermented beer, and activates the yeast. The waters of Burton-on-Trent are rich in gypsum.

oast house: an integral part of the traditional Kentish landscape, the cowl of the oast house ensured a steady draught of warm air over the hops to prevent them from going mouldy. Largely superseded by more industrialised methods, most oast houses have now been converted to domestic use.

oats: used to a limited extent in the brewing of some stouts, but they result in too creamy a flavour for general use.

pale ale: first meant a lightly hopped ale, much less bitter than its modern descendants, but is now a comprehensive term for a wide range of beers derived from predominantly pale malts. It covers English bitter, India pale ale, and strong pale ale of which the ABV can reach 12%, although as much as 29% has been recorded.

Pedigree: a popular, highly-rated beer brewed by Marstons since 1952. Its strength is 4·5 abv.

Pils: short for Pilsener, from the German form of the town of Plzeň, a great brewing centre of the Czech Republic. Most modern lagers are based on the original Pilsner style. Colloquially used as an alternative to `lager' *(q.v.)*.

porter: a dark beer, which took its name in the eighteenth century from London's street porters. A strong porter was a 'stout porter', subsequently shortened to stout *(q.v.)*.

Reinheitsgebot (purity law): the German law dating from the sixteenth century which stipulates that only malted barley or wheat, together with hops, water and yeast, may be used in the production of beer. The law can be seen as setting a 'gold standard', but its proscription of the sugars and unmalted cereals which give such famous beers as English pale ales and Irish stouts their distinctive colours and flavours renders them technically 'impure'.

rice: often used for brewing in the Far East where barley is usually difficult to cultivate.

sorghum: a cereal often used for brewing in Africa where barley is usually difficult to cultivate.

Stella Artois: one of the world's best-selling beers and originally from Leuven, Belgium, but now additionally brewed elsewhere under licence. It is the top-selling beer in Britain and, at 5.1% ABV, marginally stronger than most other lagers.

stout: beer with marked 'body' or density. Guinness *(q.v.)* is probably the most famous such stout.

Trappist beers: the strong, dark beers brewed in Belgium and France by the monks of the reformed Trappist branch of the Cistercian order. The reformed rule was first established at the abbey of La Trappe in Normandy, but the six approved monastery breweries are at Achel, Chimay, Orval, Rochefort, Westmalle and Westvletern. *See also Dubbell/Double* and *Trippell/Triple*.

Trippell/Triple: The Flemish and French names for the strong (7.5–9.5%) amber-coloured abbey beers.

water: an easily overlooked but vital element of beer, constituting 90% of even the strongest. The essential distinction is between hard and soft waters, with the former being needed for pale ales and the latter for lagers. The water of Burton-on-Trent, the home of English pale ales, is notably hard and also rich in salts, whilst that of such famous lager-brewing centres as České Budějovice and Plzeň in the Czech Republic and Munich, Germany, is very soft with minimal mineral content.

wheat beers (white beers): brewed from wheat rather than exclusively from barley, although barley still constitutes 30–50% of the total grain. Despite the great increase in the popularity of wheat beers in recent years, wheat still constitutes only 1% of all the grain used for brewing across the world.

yeast: added to ferment the beer, and the variety chosen has an effect on the aroma and taste of the final beer.

IV. SPIRITS AND LIQUEURS

SPIRITS

Spirits are liquids of high alcoholic strength made by distilling lower strength liquids which have been obtained from the fermentation of a base substance. This base is most commonly either grape juice, a "mash" of grain, or a sugar solution, but other fruit juices and even certain vegetables are also used. For a grain base, the starch is first converted to sugar by a process known as "malting".

The distillation process consists of heating the alcoholic liquid from the fermented base until it vaporises then cooling the vapour until it condenses. The resulting liquid (the distillate) contains alcohol plus some water vapour carrying the flavour of the base. Successive distillations, known as "rectification", increase the alcoholic strength and refine the flavour, sometimes until it disappears altogether, as in many vodkas.

The distilling apparatus is either a pot still or a continuous still. The pot still, shaped like an onion with a spout coming from the top, is not ideal for commercial use as the still must be refilled for each distillation. It does, however, retain more of the flavour of the base and is therefore used for cognac, Scotch and Irish malt whiskies and most rums. The continuous still allows an uninterrupted flow of liquid through rectifying columns. This produces a high strength, colourless and sometimes odourless and tasteless spirit, and is used for grain whisky, gin and vodka.

Aguardente de Caña: A Brazilian spirit distilled from sugar cane sap, literally "cane liquor", it is similar to unmatured white rum. Known as *Cachaça*.

Akvavit or Aquavit: A Scandinavian grain or potato spirit flavoured with spices, made in a similar way to flavoured vodkas. Also called *schnapps*, from old Nordic *snappen* to snatch, from being snatched down the throat in a single gulp.

Arak (or Raki): Perhaps the first spirit ever distilled, allegedly from 800 B.C. in India. Its name is from the Arabic for juice or sap. As Raki, the national spirit of Turkey.

Barack Pálinka: A Hungarian spirit distilled from apricots.

Bitters: The term for any spirit flavoured with bitter herbs or roots. The best known is *Angostura Bitters* which uses gentian on a rum base and is named from the town in Venezuela where it was created by Simon Bolivar's doctor for his troops. Now made in Trinidad, it is principally used for making "pink gin". Other bitters include: *Amer Picon* from France, with a brandy base with gentian, quinine and orange peel; *Campari* and *Fernet Brance* from Italy, both with bitter orange peel; and *Underberg* from Germany.

Brandy: Any spirit distilled from wine. The name is from the German *Gebranntwein*, "burnt wine", via Dutch *brandewijn*. Brandy in some form is made in all wine-producing countries, but the most famous are Cognac and Armagnac from France.

Types of Brandy

Armagnac: Brandy distilled from white wine produced in the Armagnac region in Gascony, France, where it has been made since the 15th century. The wine must be from specified vines within a limited area which is divided into three sectors: *Haut Armagnac*, *Ténarèze*, and *Bas Armagnac*. The finest are from a single area, with the best from *Bas Armagnac*. A blend from more than one sector is described simply as *Armagnac* and labelled according to how long it has been aged in cask: VS/Three Star for 3 years, VO/VSOP/Réserve for 5 years, Extra/XO/Napoléon/V.A.Réserve for 6 years.

Unlike cognac, armagnac comes from a blend of several varieties of grape, is usually distilled in a continous still, and is matured in barrels of local black oak.

Asbach Uralt: a German brandy matured in the same way as cognac and aged for 18 months.

Cognac: Brandy distilled in a pot still from white wine produced from vines grown around the towns of Cognac and Jarnac in France, and aged in Limousin oak casks. Only a single variety of grape, Ugni Blanc, is normally used. The best cognacs are defined by the area of Cognac the grapes come from: Grande Champagne produces the finest cognac, Petite Champagne the next in quality; Fine Champagne is a blend of the two. Blended cognac is defined according to the minimum time it must be aged: VS for 3 years, VSOP for 4 years, and Napoléon, XO and Vieille Réserve for 6 years.

Cognac has been made since the 17th century and is thus a newer brandy than armagnac. The vast majority of cognac is sold to China.

Metaxa: A blend of Greek brandy and sweet Muscat wine from the Greek islands of Samos and Limnos, invented by Spyros Metaxas in 1888.

Pisco: A fine quality clear brandy distilled from Muscat grapes in Peru and Chile. Aged but always colourless as the barrels are so old they have no colour left to impart.

Spanish brandy: Distilled around Jerez using grapes from La Mancha and matured in a solera system in the same way as sherry. Spain is the most significant producer of brandy after France, for both quality and quantity.

Brandy (fruit): Although strictly speaking brandy is a spirit distilled from wine, in practice the term is applied both to some liqueurs (*see* Apricot and Peach Brandy in *Liqueurs*) and to the fruit spirits distilled from fruits other than grapes and made principally in France, especially in Alsace, where they are known as *eaux de vie* or *alcools blancs*. They are also found in Switzerland and Germany. Such spirits are not sweetened and are appreciably stronger than the corresponding liqueurs. They are colourless because not aged, and have a clear pure scent and flavour of the fruit.

Varieties of fruit brandy include: *Framboise* (raspberry), *Mirabelle* and *Quetsch* (types of plum), *Poire Williams* (pear), *Mûre* (blackberry), *Fraise* (strawberry), and *Myrtille* (bilberry). *Kirsch* and *slivovica* (q.v.) are also fruit brandies.

Calvados: Produced in the Calvados region of Normandy, France, by distilling cider. The resulting spirit is aged in oak barrels for at least two years and can be for up to 40 years, which gives it its colour and subtle flavours. Similar labelling to that of cognac is used to indicate its age. The best calvados is from the Pays d'Auge, where the pot still must be used. Other areas use both methods of distilling. The first mention of the spirit was in 1553 and a guild for its distillers was formed in 1600.

A spirit made from apples is made also in New Jersey, USA, known as Applejack.

Gin: Originally a Dutch medicinal concoction of the late sixteenth century which flavoured a neutral grain spirit with juniper berries. Known in Britain as Geneva or Genever from the French *genièvre* (juniper) or as Hollands from its Dutch distillers. Its effect on the then British soldier was dubbed "Dutch courage". It became increasingly popular after William III raised the duty on French wines and brandies, resulting in such widespread drunkenness that in 1736 a tax was imposed which had the effect of prohibiting it to all but the rich. The result was serious riots in London, and the tax law was repealed in 1743. Consumption continued apace, graphically shown in Hogarth's picture of 1750, Gin Lane, but it eventually changed its image from the curse of the urban poor (it was known as "mothers' ruin") to respectability via the cocktails of the 1920s. Gin today is distilled from grain or molasses and must by law be flavoured with juniper berries, but other 'botanicals'" such as coriander seeds, orange and lemon peels, and angelica are used to give a distinct flavour to different products. Modern "boutique" gins are now experimenting with diversified flavours and colours, as in the deep orange Saffron Gin.

Types of gin

Genever: A highly aromatic gin from its use of malt wine, a strong grain spirit made from malted barley. There are two versions: *oude* (old) and *jonge* (young), of which *oude* has a higher proportion of malt wine and so more aromatic than *jonge*, which is drier. Also known as *"hollands"*.

London Dry Gin: An unsweetened gin from unmalted grain, originally made only in London. Now describes this particular style which may be produced anywhere.

Old Tom Gin: A sweetened gin which is now rare. The name is said to be derived from a container once used for dispensing the gin, which was in the shape of a tom-cat—payment was put into the cat's mouth and the gin was served through the cat's paw!

Plymouth Gin: Made only in Plymouth and the original gin used with Angostura bitters to make "pink gin". Originally more aromatic than London gin, but now drier.

Grappa: Italian spirit from the grape residue after making wine. (*See* **Marc**).

Kirsch: A fruit brandy distilled from the juice and ground up stones of Morello cherries. Often used in desserts. A true fruit spirit, unsweetened and not to be confused with cherry brandy. Made in eastern France, the Black Forest region of Germany, Switzerland and Austria.

Marc de (**Bourgogne, Champagne etc.**): Spirit made by distilling the grape residue left after extracting the juice to make wine. Made in the French regions of Burgundy, Champagne, Alsace, Provence and Jura. Also made in Italy where it is called *grappa* and Germany where it is called *Trester Schnapps*.

Mescal/Mezcal: The generic name for spirit distilled in Mexico from the fermented juice of the blue agave plant, after the art of distilling was introduced into Mexico by the Spaniards in the 16th century. The juice is extracted from the *piña*, the huge (50kg) fruit resembling a pineapple at the heart of the plant. One type of mescal has a *maguey* worm (actually a moth larva) in the bottle, originally placed there to show by its preservation the strength of the spirit. Tequila is a refined version of mescal.

Rum: A spirit distilled from sugar cane products, first produced in the 17th century in the West Indies which is still its main source. Puerto Rico is the world's biggest producer. It is usually made from molasses, the by-product of sugar production, but the finest rum is made from pure cane juice. Both methods of distillation are used but the best rums are double-distilled in a pot still. The name is probably an abbreviation of the Latin for sugar, *saccharum*.

In the 18th cent. ratings in the Navy were given a daily ration of half a pint of rum as it could withstand heat better than beer. This practice remained (albeit reduced to a third of a pint!) until 1970.

Types of rum

Dark Rum: Full-bodied rum matured usually for five years in old bourbon whiskey barrels. Then its colour is sometimes enhanced by caramel before bottling. Made in Jamaica and Guyana (where it is called Demerara after the river) from molasses, in Haiti it is made from cane juice.

White Rum: Clear, dry, light-bodied rum from Cuba and Puerto Rico, made from molasses distilled in a continuous still then either bottled immediately or matured for just one year.

Golden Rum: White rum which is matured for three years in charred barrels, which produces a mellow flavour and golden colour.

Slivovica: A spirit distilled from the juice and stones of small black plums. Made primarily in the former Yugoslavia but also in other eastern European countries.

Tequila: A clear or golden spirit from a double distillation of mescal (*See* **Mescal**), named from the town in Mexico where it was first made. Some tequilas are blended with cane spirit, but by law must contain at least 51% agave spirit. Tequila can be matured in wooden casks, which produces the different types: *joven* or *blanco*, less than 60 days; *reposada*, 2–6 months; *anejo*, a year or more. *Curados* is *joven* tequila which has been flavoured. Sales of tequila are soaring with the growing popularity of Mexican new-wave restaurants.

Vodka: Vodka, "little water", is an almost neutral spirit which has been made in Russia and Poland from at least the twelth century but is now produced in many other countries. The base is grain or molasses, or even potatoes though this is rare. The fermented base is twice distilled then filtered through charcoal to remove any unwanted flavours. Like most spirits it was originally medicinal. In Russia it is drunk as part of a meal but in the west, since it is almost tasteless, it is mainly prized as a mixer.

Straight vodkas are not aged but there are some traditional flavoured vodkas which often are: *Wisniowka* is a Polish vodka flavoured with cherries; *Zubrovka* is a Polish rye-based spirit with a blade of bison grass, zubrowka, steeped in it; Gold Vodka, or *starka*, is a Polish vodka aged in wooden casks for 5–10 years and *winiak* has a dark gold colour from aging in old wine casks; Pepper Vodka, or *pertsovska*, is infused with hot and mild red peppers, allegedly from a recipe by Peter the Great.

Nowadays there is a great variety of flavourings, such as lemon, berries, and pepper, found in vodkas produced outside eastern Europe particularly in Sweden, which has also introduced a sparkling vodka. There is even a marmalade vodka produced in Herefordshire by redistilling a potato-based vodka with marmalade and Seville orange peel!

Whisk(e)y: A golden brown spirit distilled from grain, originating in Ireland from an unknown but early date and in Scotland from at least the 15th century. Its name is from the translation of the Latin "*aqua vitae*" into Scots Gaelic as *uisge eatha* and into Irish Gaelic as *usquebaugh*, which by the mid-18th century had become anglicised to whisky in Scotland and whiskey in Ireland. For some time little known outside their home countries, the prime cause of its rise in popularity elsewhere was the phylloxera epidemic of 1870–1900 which largely destroyed the vineyards of Europe. With popularity came imitation and whiskies are now produced all over the world, the best being from Scotland, Ireland, the USA and Canada. The name is "whisky" in Scotland and Canada and "whiskey" in Ireland and the USA.

Scotch Whisky

There are two distinct types made in Scotland: malt whisky and grain whisky. These can be blended to form a third type.

Malt whisky: The most highly prized Scotch whisky. Made from malted barley which has been dried over a peat fire, giving the whisky a distinctive smoky flavour. It is double-distilled in a traditional pot still and matured for 3–20 years. *Single Malt* whiskies are from a single distillery, the most renowned being on Speyside (*e.g.* Glenfiddich and Glenlivet). The rarer *Vatted Malt* whiskies are a blend of single malts.

Grain whisky: Made from both maize and malted barley, distilled in a continuous still and matured for 3 years. A light whisky, quick to mature.

Blended whisky: A blend of malt and grain whisky, lighter than a pure malt. Could not legally be called whisky until 1909.

Irish Whiskey

Made mainly from barley but only a small amount is malted and some oats are added. The process is similar to that for Scotch malt whisky, using a pot still, but the barley is dried in a kiln rather than over a peat fire. It is matured for 5–12 years.

American Whiskey

There are several types. The best are *Bourbon* and *Tennessee*. All are made using the continous still.

Bourbon: A lighter whisky than Scotch, made from at least 51% corn plus malted barley and a little rye then aged for at least one year in single-use charred oak casks. It can only be produced in Kentucky, where it originated in the 18th century.

Corn Whiskey: Made from a minimum 80% corn and aged in uncharred casks.

Light Whiskey: Made from mixed grains and is similar to, but stronger than, *corn whiskey*.

Rye Whiskey: Made in the eastern states from 51% rye and aged in uncharred casks. Also made in Canada.

Tennessee Whiskey: Must be made from 51% of any grain, but usually corn or rye, and is filtered through charcoal. Can only be made in Tennessee.

Canadian Whisky

Smooth, light whiskies made using a similar process to *bourbon*, traditionally with a rye base but often with a higher proportion of corn than rye. Other cereals are added for flavour.

LIQUEURS

Liqueurs are spirits which are blended with a flavouring and then sweetened, and sometimes artificially coloured. The most common flavourings are herbs and fruits, but roots, barks, seeds, spices and flowers are also used. The first known liqueurs were made by monks from their local herbs and were primarily for medicinal use. As enjoyable drinks, liqueurs are now found all over the world, from Japan to Mexico and even in the UK, notably at Lurgashall in Sussex.

The best liqueurs are made by steeping the flavourings in the spirit which is then redistilled, but other methods of extracting the flavours which do not involve distillation are also used, such as maceration.

The following list is not exhaustive but is intended to include most of those which may be encountered with an indication of their flavour.

Advocaat: A Dutch low-strength liqueur made from egg yolks, sugar and brandy. Thick, yellow and creamy, it is a version of egg nog but without milk. Mixed with lemonade it makes a "snowball".

Amaretto: Made from almonds and apricot kernels steeped in brandy. Allegedly first made in Saronno, near Lake Como, Italy, in 1525.

Anisette: An aniseed-flavoured liqueur from France. The recipe is said to have been inherited by Marie Brizard from a West Indian in the 18th century.

Apricot Brandy: An infusion of apricots in brandy, usually from France or Holland.

Aurum: Named from the Latin for gold (allegedly by D'Annunzio), this may refer to its colour or it may have originally contained gold flakes. Made by distilling brandy infused with orange peel and whole oranges then blending this with 4-year-old brandy, adding saffron to enhance the golden colour then maturing in wood. From the Abruzzi mountains in Italy.

Bailey's: A blend of double cream, Irish whiskey, neutral spirits and chocolate, made in Dublin, Ireland. This was the original cream liqueur which has inspired others flavoured with coffee or chocolate.

Bénédictine D.O.M.: A brandy based liqueur flavoured with 27 herbs and spices, originally made by Benedictine monks from Fécamp, Normandy, France, in 1510. The monks considered this liqueur to be one of God's greater glories (D.O.M. stands for *Deo Optimo Maximo*, to God most good, most great). The secret ingredients were lost after the Revolution in 1789 but were rediscovered in the 1860s when production restarted. Still made in Fécamp.

B&B: A blend of Bénédictine and Brandy. Drier than Bénédictine.

Calisay: A herb liqueur with a brandy base from Catalonia, with a slightly bitter after taste from its cinchona bark (quinine) flavouring.

Chambord: A black raspberry liqueur from the Loire Valley, France. Extracts of black raspberries and blackcurrants blended with a blackberry and raspberry infusion are added to cognac, together with vanilla extract and herbs.

Chartreuse: Made by distilling brandy with over 130 herbs and spices, this liqueur was created by the Carthusian monks of the Grande Chartreuse monastery near Grenoble in the 16th century. It is still made by the monks at nearby Voiron despite their having been expelled twice from France, firstly with the Revolution, returning after the defeat of Napoleon, then again in 1903 when they started production in Tarragona, Spain. It was re-established in France in 1932 when they finally returned but continued in Tarragona also until 1991. Aged in cask for up to five years before bottling. There are two varieties: Green Chartreuse, naturally coloured by the chlorophyll in the herbs, is the stronger; Yellow Chartreuse, coloured with saffron, is weaker and sweeter.

Cherry Brandy: An infusion of cherries, with some of their kernels, in brandy. Invented by Thomas Grant of Kent in 1774, using black morello cherries. Most is now made in Holland.

Cointreau: A colourless orange-flavoured liqueur of the Curaçao family, produced in Angers, France, since 1849. (*See* Curaçao).

Crème de . . . : A group of liqueurs named after their flavouring agent, which is usually fruit. They are made by macerating the flavouring in neutral-tasting unaged brandy which is then filtered, sweetened, and sometimes has colouring added. The resulting liquid is not aged and generally has a lower alcoholic strength than the more traditional liqueurs. Popular in cocktails.

Mostly French, some Dutch, the most common are: *Amande* (almond); *Ananas* (pineapple); *Banane* (banana); *Cacao* (from cocoa beans and vanilla, can be brown or colourless); *Cassis* (blackcurrant, originally from Dijon, France); *Fraise/Fraise des Bois* (strawberry, wild strawberry); *Framboise* (raspberry); *Mandarine* (tangerine); *Menthe* (peppermint, green or colourless); *Mûre* (blackberry); *Myrtille* (bilberry); *Noix* (walnut, from Gascony); *Noyau* ('fruit stone', from peach and apricot stones); *Pêche* (peach); *Prunelle* (sloe); *Rose* (rose petals); *Violette* (violets).

Curaçao: Invented by the Dutch using white rum, now made from brandy. This is infused with the dried peel of bitter green oranges from the island of Curaçao in the West Indies. Distillation produces the colourless *triple sec*; this can then be coloured and sweetened to make *Blue Curaçao*, to which Valencia orange peel is added, and *Orange Curaçao*, with added bitters.

Cuarenta y Tres: Made in Cartagena, Spain, since 1924, from a brandy base infused with herbs. The name, forty three, refers to the number of ingredients.

Drambuie: A sweet, golden liqueur made from a mix of Scotch malt and grain whiskies flavoured with herbs and heather honey. Its name is from the Gaelic *An Dram buidheach*, the drink that satisfies. Said to have been a restorative for Bonnie Prince Charlie but not made commercially until 1906. Now made near Edinburgh.

Elixir d'Anvers: A yellow bitter-sweet liqueur from herbs and seeds, made in Antwerp. Invented in 1863.

Forbidden Fruit Liqueur: An American liqueur made from grapefruit with honey and orange in a cognac base.

Frangelico: From Piedmont, Italy, this straw-coloured liqueur is made from hazelnuts, berries and herbs. Its name, from Fra Angelico, shows its monastic origins.

Galliano: A golden coloured liqueur flavoured with liquorice, aniseed, herbs and vanilla, produced in Milan, Italy. Named after a Major in the Italian-Abyssinian war in 1896.

Glayva: A Scotch whisky liqueur flavoured with herbs, honey and orange peel invented mid-19th century. Made near Edinburgh.

Goldwasser: Named from the edible gold flakes in the bottle, this caraway and aniseed flavour liqueur was created in Danzig (Gdansk) in 1598, based on *Kümmel*. Now produced in Berlin.

Grand Marnier: Similar to curaçao but with a base of the highest quality cognac, then aged. French, invented in 1880. (*See* **Curaçao**)

Izarra: A herb liqueur with an armagnac base made in Bayonne. A Basque version of chartreuse, it also comes in a stronger green and a yellow version. The name is Basque for "the star".

Jägermeister: Made in Wolfenbüttel, Germany, from 56 herbs and spices and aged for one year in oak barrels. The name, "master hunter", refers to Saint Hubertus, the patron saint of hunters.

Kahlua: Mexican rich brown liqueur made from sugar cane molasses and coffee beans with vanilla and caramel. Now also made in Europe.

Kümmel: A highly digestive colourless liqueur made by distilling grain spirit with caraway seeds, fennel, cumin, orris root and other herbs. Originating in Holland in 1575, it was taken to Russia by Peter the Great and its chief centre of production in the 19th century was Riga, Latvia. Some was also made in Danzig and was the origin of *Goldwasser*. It is now made in many European countries and the USA.

Limoncello: Made from the zest of lemons and bright yellow, traditionally served ice-cold. Originally from southern Italy but now universal.

Malibu: A Caribbean liqueur made from white rum and coconut.

Mandarine: A French liqueur made by macerating mandarin oranges (tangerines) in cognac. Carotene is added to give a vivid yellowy orange colour then it is aged for several months. Invented by a Belgian in 1892.

Maraschino: A colourless liqueur from Italy made from sour cherries and their crushed stones.

Noix de coco: A coconut-flavoured rum liqueur.

Parfait Amour: Violet coloured and very sweet, from citrus fruits and spices, and subtly scented with violets. Dutch in origin, now also made in France.

Peach Brandy: An infusion of peaches in brandy, usually from France or Holland.

Poire William: Crushed pears infused in brandy, sometimes with a whole pear, achieved by attaching the bottle to the tree for the pear to grow into it. Not to be confused with the fruit brandy, Poire Williams.

Royal Mint Chocolate Liqueur: Created in 1966, this sweet and creamy liqueur has the flavour of an after dinner mint.

Sambuca: An Italian aniseed liqueur flavoured also with elderberries, from which it derives its name (*sambucus nigra*).

Sloe Gin: Made by infusing sloe berries in gin, the deep red liqueur is then matured in wood for several years.

Strega: A yellow liqueur of complex flavours from its use of over 70 herbs including mint and fennel, made in Benevento, Italy, since 1860. The name means "witch".

Tia Maria: A deep brown liqueur of 5-year-old Jamaican rum flavoured with Blue Mountain coffee and spices.

Triple Sec: A colourless curaçao. *See* **Curaçao**.

Van Der Hum: A pale gold South African liqueur, similar to curaçao, from cape brandy and and the *naartje* tangerine. Named Van der Hum ("What's his name") by the Dutch settlers who could not remember who had invented it.

Vieille Cure: A golden liqueur from 50 herbs this is similar to Bénédictine but with a base of both cognac and armagnac. It was made by monks at Cenon in Bordeaux, France, until 1986. The name means "the old vicarage".

ANISEED BASED DRINKS

There is also a family of aniseed based drinks which does not fall readily into the classification of either liqueur or spirit. Most are drunk diluted with water. They include the French *Absinthe* (declared illegal there in 1915), *Pastis* and *Pernod*, the Greek *Ouzo* and the Turkish *Raki*.

V. SPECIAL TOPIC: COFFEE AND TEA

THE HISTORY OF COFFEE

Coffee is currently drunk by about one third of the world's people in quantities larger than those of any other drink. The name may be derived from the Arabic *qahwah*, but more plausibly perhaps from Kefa, a province of south-western Ethiopia from where the wild coffee plant was taken to southern Arabia for cultivation in the fifteenth century. The actual discovery of coffee is shrouded in legend, of which one is that it was revealed to the prophet Mohammed by the Archangel Gabriel. The most popular is that an Arab goatherd, Kaldi, who had been bemused by the unusual behaviour of his flock after the goats had eaten the berries of a particular wild evergreen bush, sampled them for himself in about A.D. 850 and was so stimulated by the experience that he told everybody about his discovery! Although the detail is obviously legendary, the broad outline may not be far from the truth.

Coffee was grown almost exclusively in Yemen until the end of the seventeenth century, and coffee has always been prized, and sometimes condemned, for its stimulating properties which are attributable to the alkaloid, caffeine, found in the green coffee bean.

The Spread of Coffee Drinking

There were attempts by the orthodox in the Islamic world to ban the drinking of coffee particularly during long religious ceremonies because of its stimulating qualities, but they were to no avail and the habit spread rapidly amongst the Arabs and on to their neighbours. It was in the Middle East of the sixteenth century that the coffee house first appeared as a focus for commerce and gossip. Coffee was introduced to Europe in the sixteenth and seventeenth centuries, where again there were some unsuccessful attempts to suppress it. When Pope Clement VIII was asked by Vatican officials at the beginning of the seventeenth century to ban coffee as the notorious drink of the Ottoman Empire, he countered the request by finding it delicious and declaring: "We shall fool Satan by baptising it". His approval was generally shared and its use spread rapidly from one country to another, with the first London coffee house being opened in about 1652.

They became similarly popular in continental Europe and in such American cities as Boston, New York and Philadelphia. The French philosophers, Voltaire and Rousseau, were habitués of *Le Procope*, one of the first coffee houses in Paris, in the eighteenth century, and Johann Sebastian Bach maintained in his *Kaffeekantate* of 1732 that "coffee was lovelier than a thousand kisses". Nevertheless not all coffee house activities were so innocuous—some had rooms set aside for duelling. It was the London coffee houses, however, which became the most famous as centres in which to exchange literary, philosophical and political ideas and in due course to conduct business.

The Café

The first recorded use of the word "café" in English to mean a "coffee house" was in 1816, but coffee lost some of its fashionable allure in the nineteenth century, although it was not until the 1880s that tea became the favoured drink of the majority in Britain and some other parts of northern Europe. The tea shop replaced the coffee house although coffee continued to be drunk in considerable quantities in some circles. Nevertheless, for many Britons the only known form of coffee was "camp coffee"—a black liquid bought in a bottle and then diluted with hot water. In the twentieth century, coffee was missed intensely during the Second World War and its aftermath. Germany tried to cope by substituting acorns for coffee beans—the notorious *Ersatz* coffee. A less extreme approach which is still favoured by some, and actually dates from 1769, is to mix powdered wild chicory root in with the coffee. Even in the western Europe of the late 1940s and early 1950s, coffee smuggling was a highly lucrative and highly dangerous activity.

As is discussed later, such coffee houses have returned to Britain but in the form of the international chain, which stands in marked contrast both to the earlier neighbourhood coffee house and to the combined house and cake shop which remains common in continental Europe and for which Vienna is probably the uncrowned capital.

It must also be remembered that coffee is used not only as a drink but as a flavouring for many desserts and ice creams, and also as the basis for several popular liqueurs including Kahlua and Tia Maria.

The Cultivation of Coffee

The demand for coffee soon led to the plant's cultivation spreading from the Yemen to Indonesia, then the Dutch East Indies, in the seventeenth century, and to the Americas in the eighteenth. The largest focus of production by the late nineteenth century was Brazil. There are some 25 species of the coffee plant but only two are normally cultivated, *coffea arabica* and *coffea canephora*, the latter usually being of the robusta variety. The *arabica* was the first species to be identified and cultivated and is deemed the more aromatic and flavourful. It is grown principally nowadays in Central and South America, the Caribbean and Indonesia.

Most coffees are in practice blends but mild coffees must be made from the quality varieties of *arabica* grown in Central and South America excluding Brazil. The many types of Brazilian *arabica* coffee are considered less refined in taste and aroma. Coffees from Cameroon, Ethiopia, Kenya and Tanzania are varieties related to the mild variety of *arabica*. The robusta variety of *coffea canephora*, which is grown mainly in Africa and Vietnam, is cheaper and has traditionally been less esteemed, but it is stronger and more resistant to disease, more fruit-bearing and more adaptable to warm, humid conditions than any of the *arabica* varieties. It is much used to make instant coffee, a process which was only perfected in the 1950s. The concentration of caffeine in *arabica* varieties ranges from 0·8–1·5 % and in robusta from 1·6–2·5 %.

The Processing of Coffee

The wild coffee plant is an evergreen bush, some 8–10 metres high, bearing a fruit 15–18mm long known as a cherry and red when ripe. The cherry comprises a fleshy pulp and two seeds.

With cultivated coffee, those seeds are separated from the pulp and dried to reduce the water content from 65–70 % by weight to 12–13 %. In the case of most *arabica* coffees, this is achieved by a wet process involving fermentation of the unwanted pulp, and in the case of Brazilians and robustas by a dry process using sunlight or hot air driers. The resulting beans are then graded in accordance with national practice in the absence of any internationally recognised grading standards. Beans produced in humid regions must be exported rapidly to avoid the danger of mould or parasite infection.

The beans are subsequently roasted at a temperature rising to about 220°–230°C (430°–440°F) which reduces their weight by between 14 % and 23 % but expands their size by between 30 % and 100 %. It is at this stage that the characteristic aroma of coffee appears.

The final grinding may be performed by the consumer at home or by the manufacturer industrially followed by the essential packaging of the coffee in hermetically sealed containers to prevent oxidation.

Styles of Coffee

The French diplomat, Talleyrand, maintained that the perfect cup of coffee should be "black as the devil, hot as hell, pure as an angel and sweet as love". Not all would agree and a remarkable range of styles of coffee and coffee-making has evolved to meet changing tastes and circumstances. Some of the more commonly encountered are:

Americano: strong black coffee produced in a coffee machine.

decaffeinated: The beans have been steamed and the increased moisture content has brought the caffeine to their surface. They have then been washed with an organic solvent which is itself steamed off prior to final drying of the bean. Particularly suitable for coffees served late when the stimulus of the caffeine could prevent sleep.

espresso: the famous Italian style created by forcing pressurised boiled water through finely ground coffee in a machine. The resulting drink is highly flavoured with little bitterness because the water has had little contact with the grounds. The following are variations on *espresso*:

cappuccino: an *espresso* coffee with hot milk topped with frothed milk and usually dusted with chocolate powder. Named after the white cowl of the Capuchin friars. It first originated as "*kapuziner*" in the 1700s in Viennese coffee houses.

corretto: a shot of *espresso* "corrected" with a shot of brandy, sambuca or grappa.

latte: a shot of *espresso* topped with hot steamed milk, sometimes covered with steamed froth but with less than for a *cappuccino*.

macchiato: "stained" or "marked" with a little milk.

marocchino: made with a dash of milk and cocoa powder.

(ri)stretto: made with less water and thus stronger.

filter: the hot water is filtered through the coffee using a filter (paper) and drips into a jug below. It is never recirculated.

instant (or soluble): a liquid concentration of coffee has been prepared with hot water and then dehydrated either by spray drying in hot air, by drying under vacuum or by freeze-drying. Hot water is added by the consumer to the soluble granules or powder to create reconstituted instant coffee.

Irish: after-dinner coffee to which Irish whiskey has been added.

percolator: the water is boiled in the percolator and led up to the internal coffee holder by means of a tube whereafter it drips back into the percolator. The process is repeated until the desired strength is reached.

Turkish (known in some countries as Arab or Greek): Finely ground coffee from Mocha (Al-Mukha) in the Yemen and sugar are thrice-boiled in a small metal coffee maker. Traditionally served in very small cups with a large glass of water.

The Renaissance of the Coffee House

As noted earlier, the British coffee house was eclipsed during the nineteenth century by the more fashionable tea shop. Its return to favour can perhaps be dated to the "swinging sixties" when young people and specially students flocked to a new kind of themed coffee shop, of which *Le Macabre* in London's Soho was a particularly well-known example. The coffee was increasingly Italian in style. Most of these independent shops or coffee bars did not last, however, and the real change came with the arrival of the mass-market coffee-shop chain of which *Starbucks* is the exemplar. Founded as a single shop in Seattle, USA, in 1971, it had expanded to 1300 shops by 1997 and to 9000 worldwide by 2005. That expansion did, however, underline the very real differences between the new style of coffee shop chain, which includes such familiar names as *Costa* (now the UK's largest), *Caffè Nero* and *Coffee Republic* as well as *Starbucks*, and the earlier neighbourhood shop. Its ownership, operations and financing are international and the chain has the volatility and vulnerability of modern big business as a whole. *Starbucks* virtually collapsed in 2007 before a rebound which raised profits to their highest ever level in the third quarter of 2010. The coffee shop market as a whole was worth £5 billion in 2010, but the cost of the actual coffee in the cup is barely 5 % of the shop price. Advertising and image are all-important.

There are other significant differences between the contemporary chain shop, of which there are more in the UK than anywhere in Europe, and the earlier coffee shop. They are places of quick refreshment and of general socialising but rarely of business or of philosophical or political discussion. The wheel though may come full circle. Booksellers such as *Foyles* and *Waterstones* regularly include what are primarily coffee houses on their premises. Perhaps the proximity of books will regenerate the fashion for literary discussion also.

THE STORY OF TEA

Tea is now a commonplace drink in most of the world but for many centuries it was unknown outside China. It was first discovered, according to legend, by the emperor Shen Nung in the third millennium B.C., when a leaf from the wild tea tree he was sitting under fell into water being boiled for him to drink and he found the resulting infusion to be pleasantly reviving. Although its true origin is necessarily uncertain, there are early accounts in China of its use as a medicine or a stimulant, and in the first centuries A.D. as a beverage. At that time the leaves were compressed into cakes which were baked then pounded into pieces before boiling water was added. The first account of methods of tea cultivation, processing, and drinking dates from the 3rd century A.D. and tea has been found in tombs of the Han Dynasty (206 B.C.–A.D. 220), one container being clearly labelled with the Chinese character for tea, *ch'a*. By the time of the Tang Dynasty (A.D. 618–906) tea had become the national drink of China.

By the 9th century tea drinking had spread from China to Japan, where it became an important social ritual. In the Japanese tea ceremony, boiling water was poured on to powdered tea and then whisked. It had also spread into Tibet, where it was mixed with butter. It was not until 1606, however, that Dutch traders imported it to Europe, and the earliest record of it in Britain is from an advertisement of 1658 for "Tay alias Tee" in a London coffee house. Then in 1662 came the trigger for its rising popularity: when Catherine of Braganza came from Portugal to marry Charles II her dowry included a chest of tea. It started a fashion at court which spread to the middle classes. The East India Company, which held the monopoly of British trade with the "Indies", brought in the first 100 lbs of China tea from Java in 1664.

The Tea Garden

In the 17th century, tea was drunk in coffee houses, largely by men and invariably with sugar. With the opening of "tea gardens" in the 18th century, of which the most famous was Vauxhall, in London, it became popular with women also. Thomas Twining set up "Tom's Coffee House" in 1706, soon specialising in tea and given the Royal Warrant for it in 1711, which the company still holds. The rise in demand for tea was phenomenal and it was more popular in Britain than any other European country. Initially it was sold by apothecaries and milliners. Consumption increased over the century from 100,000 lbs to 23 million lbs. Tea was, however, costly and highly taxed and smuggling was rife until in 1784 William Pitt the Younger reduced the tax from 119 % to 12½ %, which virtually stopped smuggling.

Tea Production in India

Although by 1830 there were 30 million lbs imported from China, there were doubts over the reliability of Chinese exports and when the East India Company's

monopoly of trade with China ended in 1834 it started its own plantations in India, specifically in Assam, using native labour and, initially, seeds from China. Production there was so successful that by 1888 the amount of tea imported to Britain from India had overtaken that from China. From 1867 it was grown also in Ceylon, where 15 % of the estates were bought by Sir Thomas Lipton in 1890. By 1900 Ceylon was exporting 150 million lbs of tea, mainly to Britain, and India was producing almost 200 million lbs, 85 % of which was exported to Britain. After India and Ceylon became independent in the 1940s, production spread to Kenya.

The demand for fresh tea led to the development of the rapid tea clippers, of which the most famous was the *Cutty Sark*, launched in 1869.

Today, India is the world's largest producer, followed by China, but due to domestic consumption, Sri Lanka (Ceylon) and then Kenya are the largest exporters. In Britain, most tea is sold in teabags, an accidental invention in America in 1908, when tea samples were sent out in silk bags.

The Rise of the Teashop

Despite tea's immense popularity it did not displace coffee as the preferred non-alcoholic drink before the advent of the tearoom in the 1880s, of which the first, allegedly, was at the ABC (Aerated Bread Company) bakery shop at London Bridge station. This was so successful that ABC had opened over 50 more by 1890, soon to be followed by, among others, Lyons on Piccadilly in 1894. By 1900 there were 250 Lyons Tea Shops with their distinctive white and gold decor, fulfilling a need for inexpensive, clean and respectable places for ladies and their children to eat and drink tea. Grander tearooms were found in expensive hotels, with palm courts and tea dances. In Glasgow Charles Rennie Mackintosh designed the elegant Willow Tea Rooms in 1903, and in 1919 the first of today's popular Bettys Café Tea Rooms opened in Harrogate.

Tea and Politics

Unlikely as it may seem for such an innocuous drink, tea has at times played a significant role in world politics, particularly those of the British Empire. Anger at Britain's duty on imported tea led to the "Boston Tea Party" of 1773 when a cargo was tipped overboard in protest, and contributed to the American War of Independence. The ultra-Republicans of today are the "Tea Party". The Opium War of 1840–42 between Britain and China, which made Hong Kong British, occurred when China tried to ban the imports of opium from British India which were paying for Britain's tea. The terrible conditions of workers on the tea plantations of Assam contributed to the rejection of British rule which culminated in Indian independence in 1947. In Ceylon the workers were mainly Tamil immigrants from south India, of whom there were 300,000 by 1900. The tensions between the native Sinhalese and the Tamils ultimately led to the civil war, 1983–2009. British governments treated tea as an "essential" for public morale in both World Wars.

The Cultivation of Tea

Tea is made from the dried leaves of an evergreen tree which is a species of camellia, *Camellia sinensis*, and of which there are two main varieties: *sinensis*, native to China, and *assamica*, native to Assam in India and South-East Asia. Although the tree can grow to over 40 feet, for tea production it must be pruned to a small bush. It grows best in hot, humid conditions with some 100 inches of rain a year, and as a cooler temperature at night produces a better flavoured tea, most is grown on high land in the tropics.

Leaves are harvested from tender new shoots only, plucking no more than two leaves and a bud. The leaves are dried then roasted, after which they are formed into balls and rolled to expel moisture and curl the leaves before a final roasting. Dust is removed by sieving and the leaf is sorted into grades ready for packing in airtight containers.

Green, Black, and White

Initially all tea in China was green, black tea not being produced until the Ming dynasty (1368–1644).

It was green teas which first found their way to the west but black soon followed. It was wrongly thought until 1843 that green and black came from different varieties of tea plant.

To produce green tea, the natural fermentation of the leaves, which starts as soon as they have been picked, must be halted as soon as possible, by either steaming or mild roasting. For black tea, fermentation is encouraged: the leaves are left for several hours then beaten by hand to release the enzymes which brown the leaves. The final roasting is then done at a higher heat to totally blacken the leaves. Teas such as *oolong* and *pouchong* are half-way between green and black, having been allowed to only half ferment before being roasted. White tea, named from the silvery white hairs on the buds which alone constitute the best quality, is the least processed – not rolled and only slightly oxidised.

Initially most tea drunk in Britain was green but by the end of the 18th century black tea had become more popular. This increased the use of milk, which had not previously been common. This change was no doubt in part due to concern at the then use of poisonous copper dyes to augment the colour of green teas. Eventually black teas dominated western taste, but more recently there has been a resurgence of interest in green teas which are seen as having more health benefits.

White teas, with more nutrients and less caffeine, are an even more recent import to interest the health-conscious.

Classification and Types of Tea

Teas are classified first by degree of fermentation, second by geographical region, and third, now only for loose teas, by description of the leaf: *Orange Pekoe* (long and thin), *Pekoe* (shorter and thin) and *Souchong* (broad); these are all prefixed by *Broken* for broken leaves and by *Flowery* if a high proportion of buds.

In addition to these general classifications, there are names for special types of tea. These include:

Earl Grey: A black, traditionally China, tea flavoured with oil of bergamot. Allegedly copied from a blend given to the 2nd Earl Grey, prime minister at the time of the abolition of slavery in the British Empire. Normally drunk without milk.

Gunpowder: A superior tightly rolled small leaf green tea. An original category of China tea named from its resemblance to lead shot.

Jasmine: Green China tea scented with jasmine flowers.

Lapsang Souchong: A smoky black tea from leaves smoked over pine wood. *Souchong* relates to an original category of China tea, denoting a superior quality black tea. Drunk weak without milk.

Russian Caravan: Strong black China tea with a smoky aroma.

Twankay: An old grade of green China tea from wild or semi-wild bushes. Popular in London mid-19th century, it gave rise to the name of the dame in the panto Aladdin, Widow Twankey.

SPORTING ALMANAC

This section provides a wide-ranging variety of tables giving numerous recent winners of major popular sporting competitions, both domestic and international. The results included here range from cricket to football and from the University Boat Race to the Epsom Derby and the Grand National.

TABLE OF CONTENTS

SPORTING ALMANAC

AMERICAN FOOTBALL

WORLD CHAMPIONSHIP SUPERBOWL WINNERS

The first Superbowl was won in 1967 by the Green Bay Packers. Winners since 1997 have been:

XXXI (1997)	Green Bay Packers	XLII (2008)	New York Giants
XXXII (1998)	Denver Broncos	XLIII (2009)	Pittsburgh Steelers
XXXIII (1999)	Denver Broncos	XLIV (2010)	New Orleans Saints
XXXIV (2000)	St Louis Rams	XLV (2011)	Green Bay Packers
XXXV (2001)	Baltimore Ravens	XLVI (2012)	New York Giants
XXXVI (2002)	New England Patriots	XLVII (2013)	Baltimore Ravens
XXXVII (2003)	Tampa Bay Buccaneers	XLVIII (2014)	Seattle Seahawks
XXXVIII (2004)	New England Patriots	XLVIX (2015)	New England Patriots
XXXIX (2005)	New England Patriots	L (2016)	Denver Broncos
XL (2006)	Pittsburgh Steelers	LI (2017)	New England Patriots
XLI (2007)	Indianapolis Colts		

ASSOCIATION FOOTBALL

WORLD CUP WINNERS

1930	Uruguay	1966	England	1994	Brazil
1934	Italy	1970	Brazil	1998	France
1938	Italy	1974	West Germany	2002	Brazil
1950	Uruguay	1978	Argentina	2006	Italy
1954	West Germany	1982	Italy	2010	Spain
1958	Brazil	1986	Argentina	2014	Germany
1962	Brazil	1990	West Germany	2016	Portugal

The 2014 World Cup was hosted by Brazil. The hosts in 2018 are Russia (the Final is on 15 July in Moscow). Countries with 2 or more World Cup wins are Brazil (5), Italy and Germany (4), Argentina and Uruguay (2). England's only win was in 1966.

EUROPEAN CHAMPIONS

1960	USSR	1980	West Germany	2000	France
1964	Spain	1984	France	2004	Greece
1968	Italy	1988	Holland	2008	Spain
1972	West Germany	1992	Denmark	2012	Spain
1976	Czechoslovakia	1996	Germany	2016	Portugal

EUROPEAN CHAMPIONS CUP WINNERS

1955–6	Real Madrid	1976–7	Liverpool	1997–8	Real Madrid
1956–7	Real Madrid	1977–8	Liverpool	1998–9	Manchester United
1957–8	Real Madrid	1978–9	Nottingham Forest	1999–00	Real Madrid
1958–9	Real Madrid	1979–80	Nottingham Forest	2000–01	Bayern Munich
1959–60	Real Madrid	1980–1	Liverpool	2001–02	Real Madrid
1960–1	Benfica	1981–2	Aston Villa	2002–03	AC Milan
1961–2	Benfica	1982–3	SV Hamburg	2003–04	FC Porto
1962–3	AC Milan	1983–4	Liverpool	2004–05	Liverpool
1963–4	Inter Milan	1984–5	Juventus	2005–06	Barcelona
1964–5	Inter Milan	1985–6	Steaua Bucharest	2006–07	AC Milan
1965–6	Real Madrid	1986–7	FC Porto	2007–08	Manchester United
1966–7	Glasgow Celtic	1987–8	PSV Eindhoven	2008–09	Barcelona
1967–8	Manchester United	1988–9	AC Milan	2009–10	Inter Milan
1968–9	AC Milan	1989–90	AC Milan	2010–11	Barcelona
1969–70	Feyenoord	1990–1	Red Star Belgrade	2011–12	Chelsea
1970–1	Ajax Amsterdam	1991–2	Barcelona	2012–13	Bayern Munich
1971–2	Ajax Amsterdam	1992–3	Marseille	2013–14	Real Madrid
1972–3	Ajax Amsterdam	1993–4	AC Milan	2014–15	Barcelona
1973–4	Bayern Munich	1994–5	Ajax Amsterdam	2015–16	Real Madrid
1974–5	Bayern Munich	1995–6	Juventus	2016-17	Real Madrid
1975–6	Bayern Munich	1996–7	Borussia Dortmund		

EUROPEAN CUP–WINNERS' CUP WINNERS (until 1999)

1960–1	Fiorentina	1973–4	FC Magdeburg	1986–7	Ajax Amsterdam
1961–2	Atletico Madrid	1974–5	Dynamo Kiev	1987–8	Mechelen
1962–3	Tottenham Hotspur	1975–6	Anderlecht	1988–9	Barcelona
1963–4	Sporting Lisbon	1976–7	Hamburg SV	1989–90	Sampdoria
1964–5	West Ham United	1977–8	Anderlecht	1990–1	Manchester United
1965–6	Borussia Dortmund	1978–9	Barcelona	1991–2	Werder Bremen
1966–7	Bayern Munich	1979–80	Valencia	1992–3	Parma
1967–8	AC Milan	1980–1	Dynamo Tbilisi	1993–4	Arsenal
1968–9	Slovan Bratislava	1981–2	Barcelona	1994–5	Real Zaragoza
1969–70	Manchester City	1982–3	Aberdeen	1995–6	Paris St Germain
1970–1	Chelsea	1983–4	Juventus	1996–7	Barcelona
1971–2	Glasgow Rangers	1984–5	Everton	1997–8	Chelsea
1972–3	AC Milan	1985–6	Dynamo Kiev	1998–9	Lazio

UEFA EUROPA LEAGUE (formerly UEFA CUP) WINNERS

1957–8	Barcelona	1978–9	Borussia	1997–8	Inter Milan
1959–60	Barcelona		Moenchengladbach	1998–9	Parma
1960–1	AS Roma	1979–80	Eintracht Frankfurt	1999–00	Galatasaray
1961–2	Valencia	1980–1	Ipswich Town	2000–01	Liverpool
1962–3	Valencia	1981–2	IFK Gothenburg	2001–02	Feyenoord
1963–4	Real Zaragoza	1982–3	Anderlecht	2002–03	FC Porto
1964–5	Ferencvaros	1983–4	Tottenham Hotspur	2003–04	Valencia
1965–6	Barcelona	1984–5	Real Madrid	2004–05	CSKA Moscow
1966–7	Dynamo Zagreb	1985–6	Real Madrid	2005–06	Seville
1967–8	Leeds United	1986–7	IFK Gothenbug	2006–07	Seville
1968–9	Newcastle United	1987–8	Bayer Leverkusen	2007–08	Zenit St Petersburg
1969–70	Arsenal	1988–9	Napoli	2008–09	Shakhtar Donetsk
1970–1	Leeds United	1989–90	Juventus	2009–10	Atletico Madrid
1971–2	Tottenham Hotspur	1990–1	Inter Milan	2010–11	FC Porto
1972–3	Liverpool	1991–2	Ajax Amsterdam	2011–12	Atletico Madrid
1973–4	Feyenoord	1992–3	Juventus	2012–13	Chelsea
1974–5	Borussia	1993–4	Inter Milan	2013–14	Seville
	Moenchengladbach	1994–5	Parma	2014–15	Seville
1975–6	Liverpool	1995–6	Bayern Munich	2015–16	Seville
1976–7	Juventus	1996–7	Schalke	2016–17	Manchester United
1977–8	PSV Eindhoven				

ENGLISH FOOTBALL LEAGUE CHAMPIONS (since 1973) (Premier League since 1992)

1972–3	Liverpool	1995–6	Manchester United
1973–4	Leeds United	1996–7	Manchester United
1974–5	Derby County	1997–8	Arsenal
1975–6	Liverpool	1998–9	Manchester United
1976–7	Liverpool	1999–00	Manchester United
1977–8	Nottingham Forest	2000–01	Manchester United
1978–9	Liverpool	2001–02	Arsenal
1979–80	Liverpool	2002–03	Manchester United
1980–1	Aston Villa	2003–04	Arsenal
1981–2	Liverpool	2004–05	Chelsea
1982–3	Liverpool	2005–06	Chelsea
1983–4	Liverpool	2006–07	Manchester United
1984–5	Everton	2007–08	Manchester United
1985–6	Liverpool	2008–09	Manchester United
1986–7	Everton	2009–10	Chelsea
1987–8	Liverpool	2010–11	Manchester United
1988–9	Arsenal	2011–12	Manchester City
1989–90	Liverpool	2012–13	Manchester United
1990–1	Arsenal	2013–14	Manchester City
1991–2	Leeds United	2014–15	Chelsea
1992–3	Manchester United	2015–16	Leicester City
1993–4	Manchester United	2016–17	Chelsea
1994–5	Blackburn Rovers		

Titles won since Football League began in 1888

20	Manchester United		Leeds United
18	Liverpool		Wolverhampton Wanderers
13	Arsenal	2	Burnley, Derby County,
9	Everton		Tottenham Hotspur, Portsmouth,
7	Aston Villa		Preston North End
6	Chelsea, Sunderland	1	Ipswich Town, Leicester City, Nottingham
4	Newcastle United, Sheffield Wednesday,		Forest, Sheffield United,
	Manchester City		West Bromwich Albion
3	Blackburn Rovers, Huddersfield Town,		

ENGLISH FOOTBALL ASSOCIATION CUP WINNERS (since 1966)

1965–6	Everton		1992–3	Arsenal
1966–7	Tottenham Hotspur		1993–4	Manchester United
1967–8	West Bromwich Albion		1994–5	Everton
1968–9	Manchester City		1995–6	Manchester United
1969–70	Chelsea		1996–7	Chelsea
1970–1	Arsenal		1997–8	Arsenal
1971–2	Leeds United		1998–9	Manchester United
1972–3	Sunderland		1999–00	Chelsea
1973–4	Liverpool		2000–01	Liverpool
1974–5	West Ham United		2001–02	Arsenal
1975–6	Southampton		2002–03	Arsenal
1976–7	Manchester United		2003–04	Manchester United
1977–8	Ipswich Town		2004–05	Arsenal
1978–9	Arsenal		2005–06	Liverpool
1979–80	West Ham United		2006–07	Chelsea
1980–1	Tottenham Hotspur		2007–08	Portsmouth
1981–2	Tottenham Hotspur		2008–09	Chelsea
1982–3	Manchester United		2009–10	Chelsea
1983–4	Everton		2010–11	Manchester City
1984–5	Manchester United		2011–12	Chelsea
1985–6	Liverpool		2012–13	Wigan Athletic
1986–7	Coventry City		2013–14	Arsenal
1987–8	Wimbledon		2014–15	Arsenal
1988–9	Liverpool		2015–16	Manchester United
1989–90	Manchester United		2016-17	Arsenal
1990–1	Tottenham Hotspur			
1991–2	Liverpool			

Wins since FA Cup began in 1872

13 Arsenal
12 Manchester United
 8 Tottenham Hotspur
 7 Aston Villa, Chelsea, Liverpool
 6 Blackburn Rovers, Newcastle United
 5 Everton, The Wanderers, West Bromwich
　 Albion, Manchester City
 4 Bolton Wanderers, Sheffield United,
　 Wolverhampton Wanderers
 3 Sheffield Wednesday, West Ham United

 2 Bury, Nottingham Forest, Old Etonians,
　 Portsmouth, Preston North End,
　 Sunderland
 1 Barnsley, Blackburn Olympic, Blackpool,
　 Bradford City, Burnley, Cardiff City, Charlton
　 Athletic, Clapham Rovers, Coventry City,
　 Derby County, Huddersfield Town, Ipswich
　 Town, Leeds United, Notts County,
　 Old Carthusians, Oxford University, Royal
　 Engineers, Southampton, Wigan Athletic,
　 Wimbledon

FOOTBALL LEAGUE & FA CUP 'DOUBLE' WINNERS

1888–9	Preston North End		1993–4	Manchester United	(and also European Champions
1896–7	Aston Villa		1995–6	Manchester United	Cup)
1960–1	Tottenham Hotspur		1997–8	Arsenal	2001–02 Arsenal
1970–1	Arsenal		1998–9	Manchester United	2009–10 Chelsea
1985–6	Liverpool				

ENGLISH FOOTBALL LEAGUE (EFL) CUP WINNERS (since 1964)

1963–4	Leicester City			
1964–5	Chelsea		1990–1	Sheffield Wednesday
1965–6	West Bromwich Albion		1991–2	Manchester United
1966–7	Queen's Park Rangers		1992–3	Arsenal
1967–8	Leeds United		1993–4	Aston Villa
1968–9	Swindon Town		1994–5	Liverpool
1969–70	Manchester City		1995–6	Aston Villa
1970–1	Tottenham Hotspur		1996–7	Leicester City
1971–2	Stoke City		1997–8	Chelsea
1972–3	Tottenham Hotspur		1998–9	Tottenham Hotspur
1973–4	Wolverhampton Wanderers		1999–00	Leicester City
1974–5	Aston Villa		2000–01	Liverpool
1975–6	Manchester City		2001–02	Blackburn Rovers
1976–7	Aston Villa		2002–03	Liverpool
1977–8	Nottingham Forest		2003–04	Middlesbrough
1978–9	Nottingham Forest		2004–05	Chelsea
1979–80	Wolverhampton Wanderers		2005–06	Manchester United
1980–1	Liverpool		2006–07	Chelsea
1981–2	Liverpool		2007–08	Tottenham Hotspur
1982–3	Liverpool		2008–09	Manchester United
1983–4	Liverpool		2010–11	Birmingham
1984–5	Norwich City		2011–12	Liverpool
1985–6	Oxford United		2012–13	Swansea
1986–7	Arsenal		2013–14	Manchester City
1987–8	Luton Town		2014–15	Chelsea
1988–9	Nottingham Forest		2015–16	Manchester City
1989–90	Nottingham Forest		2016–17	Manchester United

SCOTTISH FOOTBALL LEAGUE CHAMPIONS (since 1971)

1971–2	Celtic				
1972–3	Celtic	1987–8	Celtic	2002–03	Rangers
1973–4	Celtic	1988–9	Rangers	2003–04	Celtic
1974–5	Rangers	1989–90	Rangers	2004–05	Rangers
1975–6	Rangers	1990–1	Rangers	2005–06	Celtic
1976–7	Celtic	1991–2	Rangers	2006–07	Celtic
1977–8	Rangers	1992–3	Rangers	2007–08	Celtic
1978–9	Celtic	1993–4	Rangers	2008–09	Rangers
1979–80	Aberdeen	1994–5	Rangers	2009–10	Rangers
1980–1	Celtic	1995–6	Rangers	2010–11	Rangers
1981–2	Celtic	1996–7	Rangers	2011–12	Celtic
1982–3	Dundee United	1997–8	Celtic	2012–13	Celtic
1983–4	Aberdeen	1998–9	Rangers	2013–14	Celtic
1984–5	Aberdeen	1999–00	Rangers	2014–15	Celtic
1985–6	Celtic	2000–01	Celtic	2015–16	Celtic
1986–7	Rangers	2001–02	Celtic	2016-17	Celtic

Titles won since League began in 1890

54	Rangers	4	Aberdeen, Hearts, Hibernian	1	Dundee, Dundee United, Kilmarnock, Motherwell, Third Lanark
48	Celtic	2	Dumbarton		

SCOTTISH CUP WINNERS (since 1971)

1971–2	Celtic	1987–8	Celtic	2003–04	Celtic
1972–3	Rangers	1988–9	Celtic	2004–05	Celtic
1973–4	Celtic	1989–90	Aberdeen	2005–06	Hearts
1974–5	Celtic	1990–1	Motherwell	2006–07	Celtic
1975–6	Rangers	1991–2	Rangers	2007–08	Rangers
1976–7	Celtic	1992–3	Rangers	2008–09	Rangers
1977–8	Rangers	1993–4	Dundee United	2009–10	Dundee United
1978–9	Rangers	1994–5	Celtic	2010–11	Celtic
1979–80	Celtic	1995–6	Rangers	2011–12	Hearts
1980–1	Rangers	1996–7	Kilmarnock	2012–13	Celtic
1981–2	Aberdeen	1997–8	Hearts	2013–14	St Johnstone
1982–3	Aberdeen	1998–9	Rangers	2014–15	Inverness CT
1983–4	Aberdeen	1999–00	Rangers	2015–16	Hibernian
1984–5	Celtic	2000–01	Celtic	2016–17	Celtic
1985–6	Aberdeen	2001–02	Rangers		
1986–7	St Mirren	2002–03	Rangers		

Wins since Scottish Cup began in 1873

37	Celtic	Falkirk, Hibernian, Motherwell, Renton, Third Lanark
33	Rangers	
10	Queen's Park	1 Airdrieonians, Dumbarton, Dundee, East Fife, Hibernian, Inverness CT, Morton, Partick Thistle, St Bernard's, St Johnstone
8	Hearts	
7	Aberdeen	
3	Clyde, Kilmarnock, St Mirren, Vale of Leven	
2	Dunfermline Athletic, Dundee United,	

SCOTTISH LEAGUE CUP WINNERS (CIS INSURANCE CUP) (since 1950)

1950–1	Motherwell	1973–4	Dundee	1995–6	Aberdeen
1951–2	Dundee	1974–5	Celtic	1996–7	Rangers
1952–3	Dundee	1975–6	Rangers	1997–8	Rangers
1953–4	East Fife	1976–7	Aberdeen	1998–9	Rangers
1954–5	Hearts	1977–8	Rangers	1999–00	Celtic
1955–6	Aberdeen	1978–9	Rangers	2000–01	Celtic
1956–7	Celtic	1979–80	Dundee United	2001–02	Rangers
1957–8	Celtic	1980–1	Dundee United	2002–03	Rangers
1958–9	Hearts	1981–2	Rangers	2003–04	Livingston
1959–60	Hearts	1982–3	Celtic	2004–05	Rangers
1960–1	Rangers	1983–4	Rangers	2005–06	Celtic
1961–2	Rangers	1984–5	Rangers	2006–07	Hibernian
1962–3	Hearts	1985–6	Aberdeen	2007–08	Rangers
1963–4	Rangers	1986–7	Rangers	2008–09	Celtic
1964–5	Rangers	1987–8	Rangers	2009–10	Rangers
1965–6	Celtic	1988–9	Rangers	2010–11	Rangers
1966–7	Celtic	1989–90	Aberdeen	2011–12	Kilmarnock
1967–8	Celtic	1990–1	Rangers	2012–13	St Mirren
1968–9	Celtic	1991–2	Hibernian	2013–14	Aberdeen
1969–70	Celtic	1992–3	Rangers	2014–15	Celtic
1970–1	Rangers	1993–4	Rangers	2015–16	Ross County
1971–2	Partick Thistle	1994–5	Raith Rovers	2016–17	Dundee United
1972–3	Hibernian				

SCOTTISH LEAGUE, SCOTTISH CUP AND LEAGUE CUP "TREBLE' WINNERS

1948–9	Rangers	1975–6	Rangers	2000–01	Celtic
1963–4	Rangers	1977–8	Rangers	2002–03	Rangers
1966–7	Celtic	1992–3	Rangers		
1968–9	Celtic	1998–9	Rangers		

BASEBALL

WORLD SERIES WINNERS (since 1970)

1970	Baltimore Orioles	1986	New York Mets	2002	Anaheim Angels
1971	Pittsburgh Pirates	1987	Minnesota Twins	2003	Florida Marlins
1972	Oakland Athletics	1988	Los Angeles Dodgers	2004	Boston Red Sox
1973	Oakland Athletics	1989	Oakland Athletics	2005	Chicago White Sox
1974	Oakland Athletics	1990	Cincinnati Reds	2006	St Louis Cardinals
1975	Cincinnati Reds	1991	Minnesota Twins	2007	Boston Red Sox
1976	Cincinnati Reds	1992	Toronto Blue Jays	2008	Philadelphia Phillies
1977	New York Yankees	1993	Toronto Blue Jays	2009	New York Yankees
1978	New York Yankees	1994	No Competition	2010	San Francisco Giants
1979	Pittsburgh Pirates	1995	Atlanta Braves	2011	St Louis Cardinals
1980	Philadelphia Phillies	1996	New York Yankees	2012	San Francisco Giants
1981	Los Angeles Dodgers	1997	Florida Marlins	2013	Boston Red Sox
1982	St Louis Cardinals	1998	New York Yankees	2014	San Francisco Giants
1983	Baltimore Orioles	1999	New York Yankees	2015	Kansas City Royals
1984	Detroit Tigers	2000	New York Yankees	2016	Chicago Cubs
1985	Kansas City Royals	2001	Arizona Diamondbacks		

Wins since World Series began in 1903

27 New York Yankees
11 St Louis Cardinals
8 Boston Red Sox
5 Cincinnati Reds, Los Angeles Dodgers, New York Giants, Philadelphia Athletics, Pittsburgh Pirates
4 Detroit Tigers, Oakland Athletics
3 Baltimore Orioles, Chicago Cubs, Chicago White Sox, San Francisco Giants

2 Atlanta Braves, Cleveland Indians, Florida Marlins, Kansas City Royals, Minnesota Twins, New York Mets, Philadelphia Phillies, Toronto Blue Jays
1 Anaheim Angels, Arizona Diamondbacks, Brooklyn Dodgers, Milwaukee Braves, Washington Senators

COMMONWEALTH GAMES

	2010 Gold	Silver	Bronze	Total		2014 Gold	Silver	Bronze	Total
1 Australia	74	56	50	180	1 England	58	59	57	174
2 India	39	26	36	101	2 Australia	49	42	46	137
3 England	37	59	44	140	3 Canada	32	16	34	82
4 Canada	26	17	33	76	4 Scotland	19	15	19	53
5 Kenya	12	11	10	33	5 India	15	30	19	64
5 South Africa	12	11	10	33	6 New Zealand	14	14	17	45
7 Malaysia	12	10	14	36	7 South Africa	13	10	17	40
8 Nigeria	11	8	14	33	8 Nigeria	11	11	14	36
9 Singapore	10	12	8	30	9 Kenya	10	10	5	25
10 Scotland	9	10	7	26	10 Jamaica	10	4	8	22

CRICKET

WORLD CUP

1975	West Indies	1992	Pakistan	2007	Australia
1979	West Indies	1996	Sri Lanka	2011	India
1983	India	1999	Australia	2015	Australia
1987	Australia	2003	Australia		

COUNTY CHAMPIONSHIP (since 1952)

1952	Surrey	1974	Worcestershire	1995	Warwickshire
1953	Surrey	1975	Leicestershire	1996	Leicestershire
1954	Surrey	1976	Middlesex	1997	Glamorgan
1955	Surrey	1977	Kent	1998	Leicestershire
1956	Surrey		Middlesex	1999	Surrey
1957	Surrey	1978	Kent	2000	Surrey
1958	Surrey	1979	Essex	2001	Yorkshire
1959	Yorkshire	1980	Middlesex	2002	Surrey
1960	Yorkshire	1981	Nottinghamshire	2003	Sussex
1961	Hampshire	1982	Middlesex	2004	Warwickshire
1962	Yorkshire	1983	Essex	2005	Nottinghamshire
1963	Yorkshire	1984	Essex	2006	Sussex
1964	Worcestershire	1985	Middlesex	2007	Sussex
1965	Worcestershire	1986	Essex	2008	Durham
1966	Yorkshire	1987	Nottinghamshire	2009	Durham
1967	Yorkshire	1988	Worcestershire	2010	Nottinghamshire
1968	Yorkshire	1989	Worcestershire	2011	Lancashire
1969	Glamorgan	1990	Middlesex	2012	Warwickshire
1970	Kent	1991	Essex	2013	Durham
1971	Surrey	1992	Essex	2014	Yorkshire
1972	Warwickshire	1993	Middlesex	2015	Yorkshire
1973	Hampshire	1994	Warwickshire	2016	Middlesex

Wins and shared wins since Championship began in 1864

36	Yorkshire	5	Worcestershire
22	Surrey	4	Gloucestershire
21	Nottinghamshire	3	Durham, Glamorgan, Leicestershire, Sussex
14	Middlesex		
13	Lancashire	2	Hampshire
7	Kent, Warwickshire	1	Derbyshire
6	Essex		

FRIENDS PROVIDENT TROPHY (formerly C & G CUP)

1963	Sussex	1979	Somerset	1995	Warwickshire
1964	Sussex	1980	Middlesex	1996	Lancashire
1965	Yorkshire	1981	Derbyshire	1997	Essex
1966	Warwickshire	1982	Surrey	1998	Lancashire
1967	Kent	1983	Somerset	1999	Gloucestershire
1968	Warwickshire	1984	Middlesex	2000	Gloucestershire
1969	Yorkshire	1985	Essex	2001	Somerset
1970	Lancashire	1986	Sussex	2002	Yorkshire
1971	Lancashire	1987	Nottinghamshire	2003	Gloucestershire
1972	Lancashire	1988	Middlesex	2004	Gloucestershire
1973	Gloucestershire	1989	Warwickshire	2005	Hampshire
1974	Kent	1990	Lancashire	2006	Sussex
1975	Lancashire	1991	Hampshire	2007	Durham
1976	Northamptonshire	1992	Northamptonshire	2008	Essex
1977	Middlesex	1993	Warwickshire	2009	Hampshire
1978	Sussex	1994	Worcestershire		

ROYAL LONDON CUP (old SUNDAY LEAGUE)

1969	Lancashire	1985	Essex	2001	Kent
1970	Lancashire	1986	Hampshire	2002	Glamorgan
1971	Worcestershire	1987	Worcestershire	2003	Surrey
1972	Kent	1988	Worcestershire	2004	Glamorgan
1973	Kent	1989	Lancashire	2005	Essex
1974	Leicestershire	1990	Lancashire	2006	Essex
1975	Hampshire	1991	Nottinghamshire	2007	Worcestershire
1976	Kent	1992	Middlesex	2008	Sussex
1977	Leicestershire	1993	Glamorgan	2009	Sussex
1978	Hampshire	1994	Warwickshire	2010	Warwickshire
1979	Somerset	1995	Kent	2011	Surrey
1980	Warwickshire	1996	Surrey	2012	Hampshire
1981	Essex	1997	Warwickshire	2013	Nottinghamshire
1982	Sussex	1998	Lancashire	2014	Durham
1983	Yorkshire	1999	Lancashire	2015	Gloucestershire
1984	Essex	2000	Gloucestershire	2016	Warwickshire

BENSON & HEDGES CUP WINNERS (ended in 2002)

1972	Leicestershire	1983	Middlesex	1993	Derbyshire
1973	Kent	1984	Lancashire	1994	Warwickshire
1974	Surrey	1985	Leicestershire	1995	Lancashire
1975	Leicestershire	1986	Middlesex	1996	Lancashire
1976	Kent	1987	Yorkshire	1997	Surrey
1977	Gloucestershire	1988	Hampshire	1998	Essex
1978	Kent	1989	Nottinghamshire	1999	Gloucestershire
1979	Essex	1990	Lancashire	2000	Gloucestershire
1980	Northamptonshire	1991	Worcestershire	2001	Surrey
1981	Somerset	1992	Hampshire	2002	Warwickshire
1982	Somerset				

T20 BLAST (TWENTY/20 CUP)

English Counties Winners

2003	Surrey Lions	2010	Hampshire
2004	Leicestershire Foxes	2011	Leicestershire
2005	Somerset	2012	Hampshire
2006	Leicestershire Foxes	2013	Northamptonshire
2007	Kent Spitfires	2014	Warwickshire
2008	Middlesex	2015	Lancashire
2009	Sussex	2016	Northamptonshire

International Winners*

The first **International Twenty/20 World Cup** was held in 2007 in South Africa. The winners were India. In the 2009 Final Pakistan beat Sri Lanka. The winners in 2010 were England, who beat Australia. The winners in 2012 were the West Indies, who beat Sri Lanka. In April 2014 Sri Lanka beat India in the Final. In 2016, in an exciting finish, the West Indies beat England.

2007	India	2012	West Indies
2009	Pakistan	2014	Sri Lanka
2010	England	2016	West Indies

* In 2016 discussions began on holding the event at regular two-year intervals – 2018, 2020, 2022 *etc.*

CYCLING

TOUR DE FRANCE

1988	Pedro Delgado (Spa)
1989	Greg Lemond (USA)
1990	Greg Lemond (USA)
1991	Miguel Indurain (Spa)
1992	Miguel Indurain (Spa)
1993	Miguel Indurain (Spa)
1994	Miguel Indurain (Spa)
1995	Miguel Indurain (Spa)
1996	Bjarne Riis (Den)
1997	Jan Ullrich (Ger)
1998	Marco Pantani (Ita)
1999	Lance Armstrong (USA)**
2000	Lance Armstrong (USA)**
2001	Lance Armstrong (USA)**
2002	Lance Armstrong (USA)**
2003	Lance Armstrong (USA)**
2004	Lance Armstrong (USA)**
2005	Lance Armstrong (USA)**
2006	Oscar Pereiro (Spa)
2007	Alberto Contador (Spa)
2008	Carlos Sastre (Spa)
2009	Alberto Contador (Spa)
2010	Alberto Contador (Spa)
2011	Cadel Evans (Aus)
2012	Bradley Wiggins (UK)*
2013	Chris Froome (UK)
2014	Vincenzo Nibali (Ita)
2015	Chris Froome (UK)
2016	Chris Froome (UK)***

*   The first British cyclist ever to win the Tour de France.
**   Subsequently stripped of the title.
*** The first British cyclist to win the Tour de France three times and the first to successfully defend his title.

GOLF

MAJOR TOURNAMENT WINNERS (since 1953)

	The Open	US Open	The Masters	US PGA
1953	B Hogan (USA)	B Hogan (USA)	B Hogan (USA)	W Burkemo (USA)
1954	P Thomson (Aus)	E Furgol (USA)	S Snead (USA)	C Harbert (USA)
1955	P Thomson (Aus)	J Fleck (USA)	C Middlecoff (USA)	D Ford (USA)
1956	P Thomson (Aus)	C Middlecoff (USA)	J Burke (USA)	J Burke (USA)
1957	B Locke (SAf)	D Mayer (USA)	D Ford (USA)	L Herbert (USA)
1958	P Thomson (Aus)	T Bolt (USA)	A Palmer (USA)	D Finsterwald (USA)
1959	G Player (SAf)	B Caspar (USA)	A Wall (USA)	B Roseburg (USA)
1960	K Nagle (Aus)	A Palmer (USA)	A Palmer (USA)	J Hebert (USA)
1961	A Palmer (USA)	G Littler (USA)	G Player (SAf)	J Barber (USA)
1962	A Palmer (USA)	J Nicklaus (USA)	A Palmer (USA)	G Player (SAf)
1963	B Charles (NZL)	J Boros (USA)	J Nicklaus (USA)	J Nicklaus (USA)
1964	T Lema (USA)	K Venturi (USA)	A Palmer (USA)	B Nichols (USA)
1965	P Thomson (Aus)	G Player (SAf)	J Nicklaus (USA)	D Marr (USA)
1966	J Nicklaus (USA)	B Casper (USA)	J Nicklaus (USA)	A Geiberger (USA)
1967	R De Vicenzo (Arg)	J Nicklaus (USA)	G Brewer (USA)	D January (USA)
1968	G Player (SAf)	L Trevino (USA)	B Goalby (USA)	J Boros (USA)
1969	T Jacklin (GBR)	O Moody (USA)	G Archer (USA)	R Floyd (USA)
1970	J Nicklaus (USA)	T Jacklin (GBR)	B Casper (USA)	D Stockton (USA)
1971	L Trevino (USA)	L Trevino (USA)	C Coody (USA)	J Nicklaus (USA)
1972	L Trevino (USA)	J Nicklaus (USA)	J Nicklaus (USA)	G Player (SAf)
1973	T Weiskopf (USA)	J Miller (USA)	T Aaron (USA)	J Nicklaus (USA)
1974	G Player (SAf)	H Irwin (USA)	G Player (SAf)	L Trevino (USA)
1975	T Watson (USA)	L Graham (USA)	J Nicklaus (USA)	J Nicklaus (USA)
1976	J Miller (USA)	J Pate (USA)	R Floyd (USA)	D Stockton (USA)
1977	T Watson (USA)	H Green (USA)	T Watson (USA)	L Wadkins (USA)
1978	J Nicklaus (USA)	A North (USA)	G Player (SAf)	J Mahaffey (USA)
1979	S Ballesteros (Spa)	H Irwin (USA)	F Zoeller (USA)	D Graham (Aus)
1980	T Watson (USA)	J Nicklaus (USA)	S Ballesteros (Spa)	J Nicklaus (USA)
1981	B Rogers (USA)	D Graham (Aus)	T Watson (USA)	L Nelson (USA)
1982	T Watson (USA)	T Watson (USA)	C Stadler (USA)	R Floyd (USA)
1983	T Watson (USA)	L Nelson (USA)	S Ballesteros (Spa)	H Sutton (USA)
1984	S Ballesteros (Spa)	F Zoeller (USA)	B Crenshaw (USA)	L Trevino (USA)
1985	S Lyle (GBR)	A North (USA)	B Langer (WGR)	H Green (USA)
1986	G Norman (Aus)	R Floyd (USA)	J Nicklaus (USA)	B Tway (USA)
1987	N Faldo (GBR)	S Simpson (USA)	L Mize (USA)	L Nelson (USA)
1988	S Ballesteros (Spa)	C Strange (USA)	S Lyle (GBR)	J Sluman (USA)
1989	M Calcavecchia (USA)	C Strange (USA)	N Faldo (GBR)	P Stewart (USA)
1990	N Faldo (GBR)	H Irwin (USA)	N Faldo (GBR)	W Grady (Aus)
1991	I Baker-Finch (Aus)	P Stewart (USA)	I Woosnam (GBR)	J Daly (USA)

	The Open	US Open	The Masters	US PGA
1992	N Faldo (GBR)	T Kite (USA)	F Couples (USA)	N Price (Zim)
1993	G Norman (Aus)	L Janzen (USA)	B Langer (GER)	P Azinger (USA)
1994	N Price (Zim)	E Els (SAf)	J M Olazabal (Spa)	N Price (Zim)
1995	J Daly (USA)	C Pavin (USA)	B Crenshaw (USA)	S Elkington (Aus)
1996	T Lehman (USA)	S Jones (USA)	N Faldo (GBR)	M Brooks (USA)
1997	J Leonard (USA)	E Els (SAf)	T Woods (USA)	D Love (USA)
1998	M O'Meara (USA)	L Janzen (USA)	M O'Meara (USA)	V Singh (Fij)
1999	P Lawrie (GBR)	P Stewart (USA)	J M Olazabal (Spa)	T Woods (USA)
2000	T Woods (USA)	T Woods (USA)	V Singh (Fij)	T Woods (USA)
2001	D Duval (USA)	R Goosen (SAf)	T Woods (USA)	D Toms (USA)
2002	E Els (SAf)	T Woods (USA)	T Woods (USA)	R Beem (USA)
2003	B Curtis (USA)	J Furyk (USA)	M Weir (Can)	S Micheel (USA)
2004	T Hamilton (USA)	R Goosen (SAf)	P Mickelson (USA)	V Singh (Fij)
2005	T Woods (USA)	M Campbell (NZ)	T Woods (USA)	A Cabrera (Arg)
2006	T Woods (USA)	G Ogilvy (Aus)	P Mickelson (USA)	T Woods (USA)
2007	P Harrington (Ire)	A Cabrera (Arg)	Z Johnson (USA)	T Woods (USA)
2008	P Harrington (Ire)	T Woods (USA)	T Immelman (SAf)	P Harrington (Ire)
2009	S Cink (USA)	L Glover (USA)	A Cabrera (Arg)	Y-E Yang (S Kor)
2010	L Oosthuizen (SAf)	G McDowell (N Ire)	P Mickelson (USA)	M Kaymer (Ger)
2011	D Clarke (N Ire)	R McIlroy (N Ire)	C Schwartzel (SAf)	K Bradley (USA)
2012	E Els (SAf)	W Simpson (USA)	B Watson (USA)	R McIlroy (N Ire)
2013	P Mickelson (USA)	J Rose (GBR)	A Scott (Aus)	J Dufner (USA)
2014	R McIlroy (N Ire)	M Kaymer (Ger)	B Watson (USA)	R McIlroy (N Ire)
2015	Z Johnson (USA)	J Spieth (USA)	J Spieth (USA)	J Day (Aus)
2016	H Stenson (Swe)	D Johnson (USA)	D Willett (Eng)	J Walker (USA)

RYDER CUP WINNERS (POST WAR)

USA v Great Britain

1947	Portland, Oregon	USA	1963	Atlanta, Georgia	USA
1949	Ganton, England	USA	1965	Southport, England	USA
1951	Pinehurst, North Carolina	USA	1967	Houston, Texas	USA
1953	Wentworth, England	USA	1969	Southport, England	Tied
1955	Thunderbird, California	USA	1971	St Louis, Missouri	USA
1957	Lindrick, England	Great Britain	1973	Muirfield, Scotland	USA
1959	Elorado, California	USA	1975	Laurel Valley, Pennsylvania	USA
1961	Royal Lytham, England	USA	1977	Royal Lytham, England	USA

USA v Europe

1979	Greenbrier, West Virginia	USA	2002	The Belfry, England	Europe
1981	Walton Heath, England	USA	2004	Oakland Hills, Detroit, USA	Europe
1983	PGA Course, Florida	USA	2006	K Club, Dublin, Ireland	Europe
1985	The Belfry, England	Europe	2008	Valhalla, nr Louisville, Kentucky	USA
1987	Columbus, Ohio	Europe	2010	Celtic Manor Resort, Newport, Wales	Europe
1989	The Belfry, England	Tied			
1991	Kiawah Island, South Carolina	USA	2012	Medinah Country Club, Chicago, Illinois	Europe
1993	The Belfry, England	USA			
1995	Oak Hill, New York	Europe	2014	Gleneagles, Perthshire, Scotland	Europe
1997	Valderrama, Spain	Europe	2016	Hazeltine National Golf Club, Minnesota	USA
1999	Brookline Country Club, Boston	USA			

Wins since competition began in 1927: USA 26; GB/Europe 13; Tied 2.

HORSE RACING

MAJOR RACE WINNERS (since 2000)

GRAND NATIONAL WINNERS		DERBY WINNERS
2000	Papillon	Sinndar
2001	Red Marauder	Galileo
2002	Bindaree	High Chaparral
2003	Monty's Pass	Kris Kin
2004	Amberleigh House	North Light
2005	Hedgehunter	Motivator
2006	Numbersixvalverde	Sir Percy
2007	Silver Birch	Authorized
2008	Comply or Die	New Approach
2009	Mon Mome	Sea The Stars
2010	Don't Push It	Workforce
2011	Ballabriggs	Pour Moi
2012	Neptune Collonges	Camelot
2013	Auroras Encore	Ruler of the World
2014	Pineau De Re	Australia
2015	Many Clouds	Golden Horn
2016	Rule The World	Harzand
2017	One for Arthur	Wings of Eagles

LAWN TENNIS

GRAND SLAM CHAMPIONSHIP WINNERS – MEN (since 1956)

	Wimbledon	US Open	French Open	Australian Open
1956	L Hoad (Aus)	K Rosewall (Aus)	L Hoad (Aus)	L Hoad (Aus)
1957	L Hoad (Aus)	M Anderson (Aus)	S Davidson (Swe)	A Cooper (Aus)
1958	A Cooper (Aus)	A Cooper (Aus)	M Rose (Aus)	A Cooper (Aus)
1959	A Olmedo (USA)	N Fraser (Aus)	N Pietrangeli (Ita)	A Olmedo (USA)
1960	N Fraser (Aus)	N Fraser (Aus)	N Pietrangeli (Ita)	R Laver (Aus)
1961	R Laver (Aus)	R Emerson (Aus)	M Santana (Spa)	R Emerson (Aus)
1962	R Laver (Aus)	R Laver (Aus)	R Laver (Aus)	R Laver (Aus)
1963	C McKinley (USA)	R Osuna (Mex)	R Emerson (Aus)	R Emerson (Aus)
1964	R Emerson (Aus)	R Emerson (Aus)	M Santana (Spa)	R Emerson (Aus)
1965	R Emerson (Aus)	M Santana (Spa)	F Stolle (Aus)	R Emerson (Aus)
1966	M Santana (Spa)	F Stolle (Aus)	T Roche (Aus)	R Emerson (Aus)
1967	J Newcombe (Aus)	J Newcombe (Aus)	R Emerson (Aus)	R Emerson (Aus)
1968	R Laver (Aus)	A Ashe (USA)	K Rosewall (Aus)	B Bowrey (Aus)
1969	R Laver (Aus)	R Laver (Aus)	R Laver (Aus)	R Laver (Aus)
1970	J Newcombe (Aus)	K Rosewall (Aus)	J Kodes (Cze)	A Ashe (USA)
1971	J Newcombe (Aus)	S Smith (USA)	J Kodes (Cze)	K Rosewall (Aus)
1972	S Smith (USA)	I Nastase (Rom)	A Gimeno (Spa)	K Rosewall (Aus)
1973	J Kodes (Cze)	J Newcombe (Aus)	I Nastase (Rom)	J Newcombe (Aus)
1974	J Connors (USA)	J Connors (USA)	B Borg (Swe)	J Connors (USA)
1975	A Ashe (USA)	M Orantes (Spa)	B Borg (Swe)	J Newcombe (USA)
1976	B Borg (Swe)	J Connors (USA)	A Panatta (Ita)	M Edmondson (Aus)
1977	B Borg (Swe)	G Vilas (Arg)	G Vilas (Arg)	R Tanner (USA)
1978	B Borg (Swe)	J Connors (USA)	B Borg (Swe)	G Vilas (Arg)
1979	B Borg (Swe)	J McEnroe (USA)	B Borg (Swe)	G Vilas (Arg)
1980	B Borg (Swe)	J McEnroe (USA)	B Borg (Swe)	B Teacher (USA)
1981	J McEnroe (USA)	J McEnroe (USA)	B Borg (Swe)	J Kriek (SAf)
1982	J Connors (USA)	J Connors (USA)	M Wilander (Swe)	J Kriek (SAf)
1983	J McEnroe (USA)	J Connors (USA)	Y Noah (Fra)	M Wilander (Swe)
1984	J McEnroe (USA)	J McEnroe (USA)	I Lendl (Cze)	M Wilander (Swe)
1985	B Becker (WGR)	I Lendl (Cze)	M Wilander (Swe)	S Edberg (Swe)
1986	B Becker (WGR)	I Lendl (Cze)	I Lendl (Cze)	—
1987	P Cash (Aus)	I Lendl (Cze)	I Lendl (Cze)	S Edberg (Swe)
1988	S Edberg (Swe)	M Wilander (Swe)	M Wilander (Swe)	M Wilander (Swe)
1989	B Becker (WGR)	B Becker (WGR)	M Chang (USA)	I Lendl (Cze)
1990	S Edberg (Swe)	P Sampras (USA)	A Gomez (Ecu)	I Lendl (Cze)
1991	M Stich (Ger)	S Edberg (Swe)	J Courier (USA)	B Becker (Ger)
1992	A Agassi (USA)	S Edberg (Swe)	J Courier (USA)	J Courier (USA)
1993	P Sampras (USA)	P Sampras (USA)	S Bruguera (Spa)	J Courier (USA)
1994	P Sampras (USA)	A Agassi (USA)	S Bruguera (Spa)	P Sampras (USA)
1995	P Sampras (USA)	P Sampras (USA)	T Muster (Aut)	A Agassi (USA)
1996	R Krajicek (Hol)	P Sampras (USA)	Y Kafelnikov (Rus)	B Becker (Ger)
1997	P Sampras (USA)	P Rafter (Aus)	G Kuerten (Bra)	P Sampras (USA)
1998	P Sampras (USA)	P Rafter (Aus)	C Moya (Spa)	P Korda (Cze)
1999	P Sampras (USA)	A Agassi (USA)	A Agassi (USA)	Y Kafelnikov (Rus)
2000	P Sampras (USA)	M Safin (Rus)	G Kuerten (Bra)	A Agassi (USA)
2001	G Ivanisevic (Cro)	L Hewitt (Aus)	G Kuerten (Bra)	A Agassi (USA)
2002	L Hewitt (Aus)	P Sampras (USA)	A Costa (Spa)	T Johansson (Swe)
2003	R Federer (Swi)	A Roddick (USA)	JC Ferrero (Sp)	A Agassi (USA)
2004	R Federer (Swi)	R Federer (Swi)	G Gaudio (Arg)	R Federer (Swi)
2005	R Federer (Swi)	R Federer (Swi)	R Nadal (Sp)	M Safin (Rus)
2006	R Federer (Swi)	R Federer (Swi)	R Nadal (Sp)	R Federer (Swi)
2007	R Federer (Swi)	R Federer (Swi)	R Nadal (Sp)	R Federer (Swi)
2008	R Nadal (Sp)	R Federer (Swi)	R Nadal (Sp)	N Djokovic (Ser)
2009	R Federer (Swi)	J M del Potro (Arg)	R Federer (Swi)	R Nadal (Sp)
2010	R Nadal (Sp)	R Nadal (Sp)	R Nadal (Sp)	R Federer (Swi)
2011	N Djokovic (Ser)	N Djokovic (Ser)	R Nadal (Sp)	N Djokovic (Ser)
2012	R Federer (Swi)	A Murray (Sco)	R Nadal (Sp)	N Djokovic (Ser)
2013	A Murray (GB)	R Nadal (Sp)	R Nadal (Sp)	N Djokovic (Ser)
2014	N Djokovic (Ser)	M Cilic (Cro)	R Nadal (Sp)	S Wawrinka (Swi)
2015	N Djokovic (Ser)	N Djokovic (Ser)	S Wawrinka (Swi)	N Djokovic (Ser)
2016	A Murray (GB)	S Wawrinka (Swi)	N Djokovic (Ser)	N Djokovic (Ser)

The 2017 season began with Roger Federer (Swi) taking the Australian Open.

GRAND SLAM CHAMPIONSHIP WINNERS – WOMEN (since 1954)

	Wimbledon	US Open	French Open	Australian Open
1954	M Connolly (USA)	D Hart (USA)	M Connolly (USA)	T Long (USA)
1955	L Brough (USA)	D Hart (USA)	A Mortimer (GBR)	B Penrose (Aus)
1956	S Fry (USA)	S Fry (USA)	A Gibson (USA)	M Carter (Aus)
1957	A Gibson (USA)	A Gibson (USA)	S Bloomer (GBR)	S Fry (USA)
1958	A Gibson (USA)	A Gibson (USA)	Z Kormoczy (Hun)	A Mortimer (GBR)
1959	M Bueno (Bra)	M Bueno (Bra)	C Truman (GBR)	M Reitano (Aus)
1960	M Bueno (Bra)	D Hard (USA)	D Hard (USA)	M Smith (Aus)
1961	A Mortimer (GBR)	D Hard (USA)	A Haydon (GBR)	M Smith (Aus)
1962	K Susman (USA)	M Smith (Aus)	M Smith (Aus)	M Smith (Aus)
1963	M Smith (Aus)	M Bueno (Bra)	L Turner (Aus)	M Smith (Aus)
1964	M Bueno (Bra)	M Bueno (Bra)	M Smith (Aus)	M Smith (Aus)
1965	M Smith (Aus)	M Smith (Aus)	L Turner (Aus)	M Smith (Aus)

	Wimbledon	US Open	French Open	Australian Open
1966	B-J King (USA)	M Bueno (Bra)	A Jones (GBR)*	M Smith (Aus)
1967	B-J King (USA)	B-J King (USA)	F Durr (Fra)	N Richey (USA)
1968	B-J King (USA)	V Wade (GBR)	N Richey (USA)	B-J King (USA)
1969	A Jones (GBR)*	M Court (Aus)*	M Court (Aus)*	M Court (Aus)*
1970	M Court (Aus)*	M Court (Aus)*	M Court (Aus)*	M Court (Aus)*
1971	E Goolagong (Aus)	B-J King (USA)	E Goolagong (Aus)	E Goolagong (Aus)
1972	B-J King (USA)	B-J King (USA)	M Court (Aus)*	V Wade (GBR)
1973	B-J King (USA)	M Court (Aus)*	B-J King (USA)	M Court (Aus)*
1974	C Evert (USA)	B-J King (USA)	M Court (Aus)*	E Goolagong (Aus)
1975	B-J King (USA)	C Evert (USA)	C Evert (USA)	E Goolagong (Aus)
1976	C Evert (USA)	C Evert (USA)	S Barker (GBR)	E Cawley (Aus)*
1977	V Wade (GBR)	C Evert (USA)	M Jauseovec (Yug)	K Reid (Aus)
1978	M Navratilova (Cze)	C Evert (USA)	V Ruzici (Rom)	C O'Neill (Aus)
1979	M Navratilova (Cze)	T Austin (USA)	C Evert (USA)	B Jordan (USA)
1980	E Cawley (Aus)*	C Evert (USA)	C Evert (USA)	H Mandlikova (Cze)
1981	C Evert (USA)	T Austin (USA)	H Mandlikova (Cze)	M Navratilova (USA)
1982	M Navratilova (USA)	C Evert (USA)	M Navratilova (USA)	C Evert (USA)
1983	M Navratilova (USA)	M Navratilova (USA)	C Evert (USA)	M Navratilova (USA)
1984	M Navratilova (USA)	M Navratilova (USA)	M Navratilova (USA)	C Evert (USA)
1985	M Navratilova (USA)	H Mandlikova (Cze)	C Evert (USA)	M Navratilova (USA)
1986	M Navratilova (USA)	M Navratilova (USA)	C Evert (USA)	—
1987	M Navratilova (USA)	M Navratilova (USA)	S Graf (WGR)	H Mandlikova (Cze)
1988	S Graf (WGR)	S Graf (WGR)	S Graf (WGR)	S Graf (WGR)
1989	S Graf (WGR)	S Graf (WGR)	A Sanchez (Spa)	S Graf (WGR)
1990	M Navratilova (USA)	G Sabatini (Arg)	M Seles (Yug)	S Graf (WGR)
1991	S Graf (Ger)	M Seles (Yug)	M Seles (Yug)	M Seles (Yug)
1992	S Graf (Ger)	M Seles (Yug)	M Seles (Yug)	M Seles (Yug)
1993	S Graf (Ger)	S Graf (Ger)	S Graf (Ger)	M Seles (Yug)
1994	C Martinez (Spa)	A Sanchez (Spa)	A Sanchez (Spa)	S Graf (Ger)
1995	S Graf (Ger)	S Graf (Ger)	S Graf (Ger)	M Pierce (Fra)
1996	S Graf (Ger)	S Graf (Ger)	S Graf (Ger)	M Seles (USA)
1997	M Hingis (Swi)	M Hingis (Swi)	I Majoli (Cro)	M Hingis (Swi)
1998	J Novotna (Cze)	L Davenport (USA)	A Sanchez (Spa)	M Hingis (Swi)
1999	L Davenport (USA)	S Williams (USA)	S Graf (Ger)	M Hingis (Swi)
2000	V Williams (USA)	V Williams (USA)	M Pierce (Fra)	L Davenport (USA)
2001	V Williams (USA)	V Williams (USA)	J Capriati (USA)	J Capriati (USA)
2002	S Williams (USA)	S Williams (USA)	S Williams (USA)	J Capriati (USA)
2003	S Williams (USA)	J Henin-Hardenne (Bel)	J Henin-Hardenne (Bel)	S Williams (USA)
2004	M Sharapova (Rus)	S Kuznetsova (Rus)	A Myskina (Rus)	J Henin-Hardenne (Bel)
2005	V Williams (USA)	K Clijsters (Bel)	J Henin-Hardenne (Bel)	S Williams (USA)
2006	A Mauresmo (Fra)	M Sharapova (Rus)	J Henin-Hardenne (Bel)	A Mauresmo (Fra)
2007	V Williams (USA)	J Henin-Hardenne (Bel)	J Henin-Hardenne (Bel)	S Williams (USA)
2008	V Williams (USA)	S Williams (USA)	A Ivanovic (Ser)	M Sharapova (Rus)
2009	S Williams (USA)	K Clijsters (Bel)	S Kuznetsova (Rus)	S Williams (USA)
2010	S Williams (USA)	K Clijsters (Bel)	F Schiavone (Ita)	S Williams (USA)
2011	P Kvitova (Cze)	S Stosur (Aus)	Li Na (Chi)	K Clijsters (Bel)
2012	S Williams (USA)	S Williams (USA)	M Sharapova (Rus)	V Azarenka (Belarus)
2013	M Bartoli (Fr)	S Williams (USA)	S Williams (USA)	V Azarenka (Belarus)
2014	P Kvitova (Cze)	S Williams (USA)	M Sharapova (Rus)	Li Na (China)
2015	S Williams (USA)	F Pennetta (Ita)	S Williams (USA)	S Williams (USA)
2016	S Williams (USA)	A Kerber (Ger)	G Muguruza (Sp)	A Kerber (Ger)

The 2017 season opened with Serena Williams (USA) winning the Australian Open.

* Players who have won before under maiden names: A Jones as A Haydon, M Court as M Smith, E Cawley as E Goolagong.

DAVIS CUP WINNERS (since 1960)

1960	Australia	1979	USA	1998	Sweden
1961	Australia	1980	Czechoslovakia	1999	Australia
1962	Australia	1981	USA	2000	Spain
1963	USA	1982	USA	2001	France
1964	Australia	1983	Australia	2002	Russia
1965	Australia	1984	Sweden	2003	Australia
1966	Australia	1985	Sweden	2004	Spain
1967	Australia	1986	Australia	2005	Croatia
1968	USA	1987	Sweden	2006	Russia
1969	USA	1988	West Germany	2007	USA
1970	USA	1989	West Germany	2008	Spain
1971	USA	1990	USA	2009	Spain
1972	USA	1991	France	2010	Serbia
1973	Australia	1992	USA	2011	Spain
1974	South Africa	1993	Germany	2012	Czech Republic
1975	Sweden	1994	Sweden	2013	Czech Republic
1976	Italy	1995	USA	2014	Switzerland
1977	Australia	1996	France	2015	Great Britain*
1978	USA	1997	Sweden	2016	Argentina**

* The first victory for Great Britain since 1936.

** The first-ever victory for Argentina.

Wins since competition began in 1900

32	USA	4	Spain
28	Australia or Australasia	3	Germany or West Germany
10	Great Britain (or British Isles)	2	Russia, Czech Republic
9	France	1	Argentina, Croatia, Czechoslovakia,
7	Sweden		Italy, Serbia, South Africa, Switzerland

MOTOR RACING

FORMULA ONE WORLD CAR CHAMPIONSHIP (since 1969)

	Driver		Car	Constructors Cup
1969	Jackie Stewart	Great Britain	Matra-Ford	Matra-Ford
1970	Jochen Rindt	Austria	Lotus-Ford	Lotus-Ford
1971	Jackie Stewart	Great Britain	Tyrell-Ford	Tyrell-Ford
1972	Emerson Fittipaldi	Brazil	Lotus-Ford	Lotus-Ford
1973	Jackie Stewart	Great Britain	Tyrell-Ford	Lotus-Ford
1974	Emerson Fittipaldi	Brazil	McLaren-Ford	McLaren-Ford
1975	Niki Lauda	Austria	Ferrari	Ferrari
1976	James Hunt	Great Britain	McLaren-Ford	Ferrari
1977	Niki Lauda	Austria	Ferrari	Ferrari
1978	Mario Andretti	USA	Lotus-Ford	Lotus-Ford
1979	Jody Scheckter	South Africa	Ferrari	Ferrari
1980	Alan Jones	Australia	Williams-Ford	Williams-Ford
1981	Nelson Piquet	Brazil	Brabham-Ford	Williams-Ford
1982	Keke Rosberg	Finland	Williams-Ford	Ferrari
1983	Nelson Piquet	Brazil	Brabham-BMW	Ferrari
1984	Niki Lauda	Austria	McLaren-TAG	McLaren-Porsche
1985	Alain Prost	France	McLaren-TAG	McLaren-TAG
1986	Alain Prost	France	McLaren-TAG	Williams-Honda
1987	Nelson Piquet	Brazil	Williams-Honda	Williams-Honda
1988	Ayrton Senna	Brazil	McLaren-Honda	McLaren-Honda
1989	Alain Prost	France	McLaren-Honda	McLaren-Honda
1990	Ayrton Senna	Brazil	McLaren-Honda	McLaren-Honda
1991	Ayrton Senna	Brazil	McLaren-Honda	McLaren-Honda
1992	Nigel Mansell	Great Britain	Williams-Renault	Williams-Renault
1993	Alain Prost	France	Williams-Renault	Williams-Renault
1994	Michael Schumacher	Germany	Benneton-Ford	Williams-Renault
1995	Michael Schumacher	Germany	Benneton-Renault	Benneton-Renault
1996	Damon Hill	Great Britain	Williams-Renault	Williams-Renault
1997	Jacques Villeneuve	Canada	Williams-Renault	Williams-Renault
1998	Mika Hakkinen	Finland	McLaren-Mercedes	McLaren-Mercedes
1999	Mika Hakkinen	Finland	McLaren-Mercedes	Ferrari
2000	Michael Schumacher	Germany	Ferrari	Ferrari
2001	Michael Schumacher	Germany	Ferrari	Ferrari
2002	Michael Schumacher	Germany	Ferrari	Ferrari
2003	Michael Schumacher	Germany	Ferrari	Ferrari
2004	Michael Schumacher	Germany	Ferrari	Ferrari
2005	Fernando Alonso	Spain	Renault	Renault
2006	Fernando Alonso	Spain	Renault	Renault
2007	Kimi Raikkonen	Finland	Ferrari	Ferrari
2008	Lewis Hamilton	Great Britain	McLaren-Mercedes	Ferrari
2009	Jenson Button	Great Britain	Brawn GP	Brawn GP
2010	Sebastian Vettel	Germany	RBR Renault	Red Bull
2011	Sebastian Vettel	Germany	RBR Renault	Red Bull
2012	Sebastian Vettel	Germany	RBR Renault	Red Bull
2013	Sebastian Vettel	Germany	RBR Renault	Red Bull
2014	Lewis Hamilton	Great Britain	Mercedes	Mercedes
2015	Lewis Hamilton*	Great Britain	Mercedes	Mercedes
2016	Nico Rosberg	Germany	Mercedes	Mercedes

* Lewis Hamilton became the first British driver in history to successfully defend his Formula One crown.

Note: In the May 2016 Spanish Grand Prix, the Dutchman Max Verstappen made history by becoming the youngest-ever driver to win a F1 race (aged 18 years and 228 days).

ROWING

THE UNIVERSITY BOAT RACE

The Boat Race is run over 4 miles 374 yards. The record time is held by Cambridge (16 min., 19 secs in 1998). The first race was rowed in 1829 and was won by Oxford at Henley-on-Thames. In 2015, the women's race, which began in 1927, was run for the first time over the same course as the men. Oxford were the winners.

1946	Oxford		2000	Oxford
1947–51	Cambridge		2001	Cambridge
1952	Oxford		2002	Oxford
1953	Cambridge		2003	Oxford
1954	Oxford		2004	Cambridge
1955–8	Cambridge		2005	Oxford
1959–60	Oxford		2006	Oxford
1961–2	Cambridge		2007	Cambridge
1963	Oxford		2008	Oxford
1964	Cambridge		2009	Oxford
1965–7	Oxford		2010	Cambridge
1968–73	Cambridge		2011	Oxford
1974	Oxford		2012	Cambridge
1975	Cambridge		2013	Oxford
1976–85	Oxford		2014	Oxford
1986	Cambridge		2015	Oxford
1987–92	Oxford		2016	Cambridge
1993–9	Cambridge		2017	Oxford

Overall results since race began in 1829

Cambridge   82   Oxford 80   Dead Heat 1 (in 1877)

RUGBY LEAGUE

WORLD CUP

The 2008 World Cup was won by New Zealand, ending a run of Australian victories dating back to 1975. In 2013 Australia regained the trophy, beating New Zealand 34–2. Great Britain has won in 1954, 1960 and 1972.

LEAGUE CHAMPIONS (after 1976)

1976–7	Featherstone Rovers	1986–7	Wigan
1977–8	Widnes	1987–8	Widnes
1978–9	Hull Kingston Rovers	1988–9	Widnes
1979–80	Bradford Northern	1989–90	Wigan
1980–1	Bradford Northern	1990–1	Wigan
1981–2	Leigh	1991–2	Wigan
1982–3	Hull	1992–3	Wigan
1983–4	Hull Kingston Rovers	1993–4	Wigan
1984–5	Hull Kingston Rovers	1994–5	Wigan
1985–6	Halifax	1995–6	Wigan

Wins since competition began in 1906

17	Wigan	4	Swinton
7	Huddersfield, St Helens	3	Halifax, Leeds, Oldham, Warrington, Widnes
6	Hull, Salford	2	Bradford Northern, Hunslet, Leigh, Wakefield Trinity
5	Hull Kingston Rovers	1	Batley, Dewsbury, Featherstone Rovers, Workington Town

SUPER LEAGUE

1996	St Helens Saints		
1997	Bradford Bulls	2007	Leeds Rhinos
1998	Wigan Warriors	2008	Leeds Rhinos
1999	St Helens Saints	2009	Leeds Rhinos
2000	St Helens Saints	2010	Wigan Warriors
2001	Bradford Bulls	2011	Leeds Rhinos
2002	St Helens Saints	2012	Leeds Rhinos
2003	Bradford Bulls	2013	Wigan Warriors
2004	Leeds Rhinos	2014	St Helens Saints
2005	Bradford Bulls	2015	Leeds Rhinos
2006	St Helens Saints	2016	Wigan Warriors

CHALLENGE CUP WINNERS (since 1970)

1970	Castleford		
1971	Leigh	1994	Wigan
1972	St Helens	1995	Wigan
1973	Featherstone Rovers	1996	St Helens Saints
1974	Warrington	1997	St Helens Saints
1975	Widnes	1998	Sheffield Eagles
1976	St Helens	1999	Leeds Rhinos
1977	Leeds	2000	Bradford Bulls
1978	Leeds	2001	St Helens Saints
1979	Widnes	2002	Wigan
1980	Hull Kingston Rovers	2003	Bradford Bulls
1981	Widnes	2004	St Helens Saints
1982	Hull	2005	Hull
1983	Featherstone Rovers	2006	St Helens Saints
1984	Widnes	2007	St Helens Saints
1985	Wigan	2008	St Helens Saints
1986	Castleford	2009	Warrington Wolves
1987	Halifax	2010	Warrington Wolves
1988	Wigan	2011	Wigan
1989	Wigan	2012	Warrington Wolves
1990	Wigan	2013	Wigan
1991	Wigan	2014	Leeds Rhinos
1992	Wigan	2015	Leeds Rhinos
1993	Wigan	2016	Hull FC

Wins since competition began in 1897

19	Wigan		
13	Leeds		
12	St Helens	3	Batley, Featherstone Rovers, Hull, Oldham,
8	Warrington		Swinton
7	Widnes	2	Bradford Bulls, Broughton Rangers,
6	Huddersfield		Dewsbury, Hunslet, Leigh
5	Halifax, Wakefield Trinity	1	Barrow, Hull FC, Hull Kingston Rovers, Rochdale
4	Bradford Northern, Castleford		Hornets, Salford, Sheffield Eagles,
			Workington Town

RUGBY UNION

WORLD CUP WINNERS

1987	New Zealand		2003	England
1991	Australia		2007	South Africa
1995	South Africa		2011	New Zealand
1999	Australia		2015	New Zealand*

* In 2015, New Zealand became the first defending champions to retain their title. Their next defence will be in 2019 in Japan.

SIX NATIONS CHAMPIONSHIP WINNERS (POST WAR)*

1947	England	1970	France	1990	Scotland
1948	Ireland		Wales	1991	England
1949	Ireland	1971	Wales	1992	England
1950	Wales	1972	No competition	1993	France
1951	Ireland	1973	England	1994	Wales
1952	Wales		France	1995	England
1953	England		Ireland	1996	England
1954	England		Scotland	1997	France
	France		Wales	1998	France
	Wales	1974	Ireland	1999	Scotland
1955	France	1975	Wales	2000	England
	Wales	1976	Wales	2001	England
1956	Wales	1977	France	2002	France
1957	England	1978	Wales	2003	England
1958	England	1979	Wales	2004	France
1959	France	1980	England	2005	Wales
1960	England	1981	France	2006	France
	France	1982	Ireland	2007	France
1961	France	1983	France	2008	Wales
1962	France		Ireland	2009	Ireland
1963	England	1984	Scotland	2010	France
1964	Scotland	1985	Ireland	2011	England
	Wales	1986	France	2012	Wales
1965	Wales		Scotland	2013	Wales
1966	Wales	1987	France	2014	Ireland
1967	France	1988	France	2015	Ireland
1968	France		Wales	2016	England
1969	Wales	1989	France	2017	England

* The competition was the Five Nations Championship prior to 2000. A bonus points system was introduced in 2017.

Wins and shared wins since Championship began in 1883:

England 38   Wales 37   France 25   Scotland 22   Ireland 21

Grand Slam Winners:

England	13	Scotland	3
Wales	11	Ireland	2
France	9		

Triple Crown Winners:

England	25	Scotland	10
Wales	22	Ireland	10

HEINEKEN CUP*

1996	Toulouse	2003	Toulouse	2010	Toulouse
1997	Brive	2004	Wasps	2011	Leinster
1998	Bath	2005	Toulouse	2012	Leinster
1999	Ulster	2006	Munster	2013	Toulon
2000	Northampton	2007	Wasps	2014	Toulon
2001	Leicester	2008	Munster		
2002	Leicester	2009	Leinster		

* The Heineken Cup was replaced by the Champions Cup in 2015. This was won by Toulon. In the Challenge Cup Final, between Gloucester and Edinburgh, the victors were Gloucester. In 2016 the Challenge Cup was won by Montpellier and Saracens won the Champions Cup. In 2017 the Champions Cup was won by the defending champions, Saracens.

AVIVA (formerly GUINNESS) ENGLISH LEAGUE CHAMPIONS

1987–8	Leicester	1998–9	Leicester	2008–09	Leicester
1988–9	Bath	1999–00	Leicester	2009–10	Leicester
1989–90	Wasps	2000–01	Leicester	2010–11	Saracens
1990–1	Bath	2001–02	Leicester	2011–12	Harlequins
1991–2	Bath	2002–03	Wasps	2012–13	Leicester
1992–3	Bath	2003–04	Wasps	2013–14	Northampton
1993–4	Bath	2004–05	Wasps	2013–14	Northampton
1994–5	Leicester	2004–05	Wasps	2014–15	Saracens
1995–6	Bath	2005–06	Sale Sharks	2015–16	Saracens
1996–7	Wasps	2006–07	Leicester	2016–17	Exeter
1997–8	Newcastle	2007–08	Wasps		

SNOOKER

WORLD PROFESSIONAL CHAMPIONS

1976	Ray Reardon (Wales)		1997	Ken Doherty (Ireland)
1977	John Spencer (England)		1998	John Higgins (Scotland)
1978	Ray Reardon (Wales)		1999	Stephen Hendry (Scotland)
1979	Terry Griffiths (Wales)		2000	Mark Williams (Wales)
1980	Cliff Thorburn (Canada)		2001	Ronnie O'Sullivan (England)
1981	Steve Davis (England)		2002	Peter Ebdon (England)
1982	Alex Higgins (Northern Ireland)		2003	Mark Williams (Wales)
1983	Steve Davis (England)		2004	Ronnie O'Sullivan (England)
1984	Steve Davis (England)		2005	Shaun Murphy (England)
1985	Dennis Taylor (Northern Ireland)		2006	Graeme Dott (Scotland)
1986	Joe Johnson (England)		2007	John Higgins (Scotland)
1987	Steve Davis (England)		2008	Ronnie O'Sullivan (England)
1988	Steve Davis (England)		2009	John Higgins (Scotland)
1989	Steve Davis (England)		2010	Neil Robertson (Aus)
1990	Stephen Hendry (Scotland)		2011	John Higgins (Scotland)
1991	John Parrott (England)		2012	Ronnie O'Sullivan (England)
1992	Stephen Hendry (Scotland)		2013	Ronnie O'Sullivan (England)
1993	Stephen Hendry (Scotland)		2014	Mark Selby (England)
1994	Stephen Hendry (Scotland)		2015	Stuart Bingham (England)
1995	Stephen Hendry (Scotland)		2016	Mark Selby (England)
1996	Stephen Hendry (Scotland)		2017	Mark Selby (England)

THE 2012 OLYMPICS

MEDALS TABLE
(The Top 12 Countries)

		Gold	Silver	Bronze	Total
1	United States	46	29	29	104
2	China	38	27	23	88
3	Great Britain	29	17	19	65
4	Russia	24	26	32	82
5	South Korea	13	8	7	28
6	Germany	11	19	14	44
7	France	11	11	12	34
8	Italy	8	9	11	28
9	Hungary	8	4	5	17
10	Australia	7	16	12	35
11	Japan	7	14	17	38
12	Kazakhstan	7	1	5	13

THE 2016 OLYMPICS

MEDALS TABLE
(The Top 20 Countries)

		Gold	Silver	Bronze	Total
1	United States	46	37	38	121
2	Great Britain	27	23	17	67
3	China	26	18	26	70
4	Russia	19	18	19	56
5	Germany	17	10	15	42
6	Japan	12	8	21	41
7	France	10	18	14	42
8	South Korea	9	3	9	21
9	Italy	8	12	8	28
10	Australia	8	11	10	29
11	Netherlands	8	7	4	19
12	Hungary	8	3	4	15
13	Brazil	7	6	6	19
14	Spain	7	4	6	17
15	Kenya	6	6	1	13
16	Jamaica	6	3	2	11
17	Croatia	5	3	2	10
18	Cuba	5	2	4	11
19	New Zealand	4	9	5	18
20	Canada	4	3	15	22

THE WORLD OF SCIENCE

A wide-ranging picture of scientific discovery, designed to explain some of the most important concepts in cosmology, physics, chemistry, biology, genetics and the story of human evolution. It also aims to give some account of major developments in astronomy, from extra-solar planets to massive black holes and major space missions. Also included is a variety of useful scientific tables. Readers will find many definitions of scientific terms in the General Information section. For the history and geology of our planet, see Section V.

TABLE OF CONTENTS

THE WORLD OF SCIENCE

In Parts I, II, and III the inanimate universe is described. This is the world of astronomy, space research, physics, and chemistry. There are already many interesting links which join this realm to that of the living and make it difficult to say where the boundary lies. Nevertheless it is still convenient to accord biological science and human evolution two separate chapters, IV and V. Part VI provides some useful scientific tables.

I. ASTRONOMY—UNDERSTANDING THE COSMOS

LOOKING AT THE UNIVERSE

Introduction

We can observe the universe in many different ways. First, there are waves of visible light together with invisible rays of somewhat longer (infra-red) and somewhat shorter (ultra-violet) wavelengths. These waves show us the bright astronomical objects and, to make use of them, astronomers have constructed telescopes of great power and precision backed up with cameras, spectroscopes, and numerous auxiliaries. The biggest telescope in the world is the 10 m reflector based at Mauna Kea in the United States. The earth's atmosphere acts as a distorting and only partially transparent curtain and the erection of telescopes on satellites is beginning to extend optical telescope performance significantly. Indeed, the Hubble Space Telescope, launched back in 1990, has dramatically expanded our knowledge of the universe.

Secondly, there are radio waves of much longer wavelength than light. Radio telescopes are sensitive radio receivers with specialised aerial systems. The scientific stature of modern radio astronomy was first emphasised by the award back in 1974 of the Nobel Physics Prize to two Cambridge radio astronomers, Ryle and Hewish.

Other types of radiation reach the earth from outer space but do not necessarily penetrate the atmosphere. With the advent of satellite-borne detectors, mountain-top telescopes of increasing sophistication and apparatus buried in deep mines, new facets of X-ray, gamma-ray, optical UV and infrared astronomy are now rapidly deepening our knowledge of the nature of the universe and of the violent processes by which galaxies as well as individual stars and planetary systems evolve.

Gravitational Wave Astronomy

Currently, a new area of astronomy called gravitational wave astronomy is being researched. It is predicted by Einstein's general theory of relativity and measures the wobble in space-time caused as massive bodies are accelerated or disturbed.

Vast Distances and Large Numbers

To visualise the huge scale of the universe is almost as much a problem for the scientist as for the layman. The conventional shorthand is to express 1,000 as 10^3; 1,000,000 as 10^6. On this scale the earth is 1.496×10^8 km away from the sun.

These distances are minute by comparison with the distance even to the nearest star, Proxima Centauri, some 4×10^{13} km away. This distance is more conveniently expressed in terms of the travel time of light itself. With a velocity of nearly 300,000 km per second, in a year light travels about 9.46×10^{12} km. The distance to Proxima Centauri is therefore 4.2 light years.

Even this distance, enormous on our terrestrial scale, is a small cosmic distance. The diameter of our Galaxy is about 10^5 light years, while the most distant objects yet observed lie over 1.3×10^{10} light years away. In 2015 scientists found a protogalaxy that is 13.42 billion light years away. Some astronomical distances are shown on **T8**.

PLANETS, STARS AND GALAXIES

The Solar System

The earth is the third, counting outward, of the planets revolving in nearly circular orbits round the sun. Some of their particulars are given in the Table (**T8**). The sun and its planets are the main bodies of the solar system. Mainly between the orbits of Mars and Jupiter revolve numerous small bodies—the dwarf planets and asteroids, the largest of which, Ceres, is only 947 km in diameter.

Apart from these, the solar system is tenuously populated with particles varying in size from about a micron (10^{-6} m) to hundreds of metres in diameter. Some of these objects collide with the earth's atmosphere. The smaller particles (micrometeoroids) are too small to be visible. Larger particles (meteoroids) cause the phenomenon known as meteors (commonly referred to as 'shooting stars') when they burn up at around 100 km altitude. The particle collides with air molecules. This causes frictional heating which usually results in complete vapourization of the particle. Even larger chunks, of rocky or iron composition, cause the rare and brilliant fireballs, some of which survive their high-speed flight through the earth's atmosphere and may later be recovered. Such objects (meteorites) are very important, providing examples of extraterrestrial rocks, and thus giving the composition of some of the most primitive material left in the solar system. Collisions with very large meteorites are now very rare.

The large meteorite crater in Arizona is one recent reminder that such collisions still occur, although much less frequently now. The surfaces of Mercury, the Moon, Mars, and Venus together with those of many other planetary satellites still show the scars from collisions with a multitude of objects of up to tens of km in diameter.

Comets

Comets are fascinating objects which, from time to time, provide a spectacular sight. Many thousands of comets have been observed so far, and scores of new ones are discovered each year. At the heart of every comet is a small nucleus. In 1986 the Giotto space probe revealed that Halley's comet has a potato-shaped nucleus measuring 15 km by 10 km. This nucleus consists of ices of various gases, chiefly water, interspersed with dust particles. In their highly elliptical orbits comets spend most of their life at great distances from the sun, where the temperature is very low because of the feeble solar radiation, so that all the "icy" materials are solid. Periodically, when each comet returns to the inner parts of the solar system, the increasing solar radiation heats the surface layers, evaporating the volatile ices, which carry the surface dust away from the comet nucleus. Solar-radiation pressure, acting on the dust constituents, and the solar wind acting on the ionised constituents, form the gigantic cometary tails which may reach 2×10^8 km in length—larger than the radius of the earth's orbit.

The dramatic impact of the fragments of Comet Shoemaker-Levy 9 on the dark side of Jupiter in 1994 created spots on the planet's surface that were as big as the earth's diameter and that lasted for seven weeks.

Scientists are increasingly convinced comets aided the creation of life on earth.

The Sun

The sun itself is a dense, roughly spherical mass of glowing matter, 1,392,000 km across. Its heat is so intense that the atoms are split into separated electrons and nuclei and matter in such a state is called plasma. At the sun's centre the temperature has the unimaginable value of about 15 million degrees Centigrade (a coal fire is about 800°C). Under such conditions the atomic nuclei frequently collide with one another at great speeds and reactions occur between them. The sun consists largely of hydrogen and, in the very hot plasma, the nuclei of hydrogen atoms interact by a series of reactions whose net result is to turn hydrogen into helium. This is a process which releases energy just as burning does, only these nuclear processes are incomparably more energetic than ordinary burning. In fact, the energy released is great enough to be the source of all the light and heat which the sun has been pouring into space for thousands of millions of years.

The Solar Wind

Emerging from the sun and streaming past the earth is a "solar wind" of fast-moving electrons and protons (**T11**) whose motion is closely linked with the behaviour of an extensive magnetic field based on the sun. In fact, the region round the sun and extending far into space past the earth is full of complex, fluctuating particle streams and magnetic fields which interact with planetary atmospheres causing, among other things, auroras and magnetic storms.

Stars

In colour, brightness, age, and size the sun is typical of many billions of other stars. Only from the human point of view is there anything special about the sun—it is near enough to give us life. Even the possession of a system of revolving planets is now routinely observed in other stars.

No star can radiate energy at the rate the sun does without undergoing internal changes in the course of time. Consequently stars evolve and old processes in them give rise to new. The exact nature of stellar evolution—so far as it is at present understood—would be too complex to describe here in any detail. It involves expansion and contraction, changes of temperature, changes of colour, and changes in chemical compositon as the nuclear processes gradually generate new chemical elements by reactions such as the conversion of hydrogen to helium, helium to neon, neon to magnesium *etc.*

The speed of evolution changes from time to time, but is in any case very slow compared with the pace of terrestrial life; nothing very dramatic may occur for hundreds of millions of years. Evidence for the various phases of evolution is therefore obtained by studying many stars, each at a different stage of its life. Thus astronomers recognise many types with charmingly descriptive names, such as supergiants, blue giants, sub-giants, red, white and brown dwarfs. Hypervelocity stars, first discovered in 2005, can travel at 2 million miles per hour.

Stellar Evolution

The path of stellar evolution may be marked by various explosive events. One of these, which occurs in sufficiently large stars, is an enormous explosion in which a substantial amount of the star is blown away into space in the form of highspeed streams of gas. For about a fortnight, such an exploding star will radiate energy 200 million times as fast as the sun. Japanese and Chinese (but not Western) astronomers recorded such an occurrence in A.D. 1054, and the exploding gases, now called the Crab nebula, can still be seen in powerful telescopes and form a cloud six or seven light-years across. While it lasts, the explosion shows up as an abnormally bright star and is called a *supernova*. In late February 1987 a spectacular supernova was observed in our nearby galaxy the Large Magellanic Cloud. At a distance of only 1.7×10^5 light years this supernova was the closest to the Earth for over 400 years. Many theories have been confirmed by the findings.

Groups of Stars

It is not surprising that ancient peoples saw pictures in the sky. The constellations, however, are not physically connected groups of stars but just happen to be patterns visible from earth. A conspicuous exception to this is the Milky Way, which a telescope resolves into many millions of separate stars. If we could view the Milky Way from a vast distance and see it as a whole we should observe a rather flat wheel of stars with spiral arms something like the sparks of a rotating Catherine wheel. This system of stars is physically connected by gravitational forces and moves through space as a whole; it is called a *galaxy*.

The galaxy is about 10^5 light-years across and contains roughly 10^{11} stars. An inconspicuous one of these stars near the edge of the wheel is our sun; the prominent stars in our night sky are members of the galaxy that happen to be rather near us. Sirius, the brightest, is only 8·6 light-years away.

The galaxy does not contain stars only, there are also clouds of gas and dust, particularly in the plane of the galaxy. Much of the gas is hydrogen, and its detection is difficult. However, gaseous hydrogen gives out radio waves with a wavelength of 21 cm. Radio telescopes are just the instruments to receive these, and workers in Holland, America, and Australia detected the gas clouds by this means. Back in 1952 they found that the hydrogen clouds lie in the spiral arms of the galaxy, and this was some of the strongest early evidence for the spiral form.

Another important feature of the galactic scene is the weak but enormously extensive magnetic field. This is believed to have an intimate connection with the spiral structure.

Globular Clusters

Around the spiral arms, and forming part of the galaxy, are numerous globular clusters of stars. These are roughly spherical, abnormally densely packed, collections of stars with many thousands of members. Because of its form and density, a globular cluster may be assumed to have been formed in one process, not star by star. Thus all its stars are the same age. This is of great interest to astronomers, because they can study differences between stars of similar age but different sizes.

The 21cm radio waves that are given out by hydrogen also gave a startling and wholly unexpected finding. The outer reaches of our galaxy (and others) were seen to be rotating at a constant velocity. This implies that the mass is not concentrated in the centre, as might be expected, but is distributed in a large dark halo extending up to five times the radius of the visible part of the galaxy. The total mass of the Galactic halo is unknown but it is thought to contain at least ten times as much matter than the visible material in the galaxy.

Currently, astronomers are left with the rather fundamental question: what is the majority of the galaxy made of? There are presently a number of competing theories. It may be composed of compact sub-stellar material (such as brown dwarfs or neutron stars) known collectively as MACHOs or some kind of weakly interactive massive particle.

Galaxies

One might be forgiven for assuming that such a vast system as the galaxy is in fact the universe; but this is not so. In the constellation of Andromeda is a famous object which, on close examination, turns out to be another galaxy of size and structure similar to our own. Its distance is given in the table (**T8**). The Andromeda galaxy is the same basic structure as our own, but roughly half as big again. The Milky Way, the Andromeda nebula, and about two dozen other galaxies form a cluster of galaxies called the Local Group. It is indeed a fact that the universe is populated with *groups*, *clusters* and *superclusters*, of *galaxies*. A cluster may contain two or three galaxies, but some contain thousands.

By about 1920 it was known that there were at least half a million galaxies, and with the advent of the 2·54 m. Mt. Wilson telescope this number rose to 10^8. We now know that there are countless billions of galaxies, perhaps even two trillion.

Through the powerful telescopes the nearer galaxies reveal their inner structures. Photographs of galaxies are among the most beautiful and fascinating photographs ever taken.

Most galaxies have a spiral or elliptical structure but about 2 per cent have peculiar wisps and appendages. Some galaxies are strong emitters of radio waves. Another type of galaxy is the starburst galaxy. This is an otherwise normal galaxy in which huge numbers of stars are forming in a small volume at its centre. It is now known that there are super-massive black holes at the centre of galaxies which play a vital part in their evolution.

Rather alarmingly there is an increasingly large amount of information from observations of groups and superclusters of galaxies that they contain significant amounts of dark matter. In a similar way that the mass of the Sun can be calculated by the orbits of the planets, the mass of a galactic group can be found by observing the orbits of galactic members. By observing the galaxies and applying well understood Newtonian mechanics the mass of many clusters has been found.

There seems to be an even larger proportion of dark matter than that found in lone galaxies. This implies that the entire universe is mostly composed of dark matter interacting with ordinary matter only though the force of gravity. Currently there are a large number of major international dark matter experiments trying, quite simply, to discover what the universe is made of. In 2016 scientists discovered the galaxy Dragonfly 44,330 million light years away, which is 99.99 % dark matter.

The Expanding Universe

Two discoveries about galaxies are of the utmost importance. One is that, by and large, clusters of galaxies are uniformly distributed through the universe. The other is that the distant galaxies are receding from us.

How is this known? Many readers may be familiar with the Doppler effect first discovered in 1842. Suppose a stationary body emits waves of any kind and we measure their wavelength, finding it to be L cm. Now suppose the body approaches us; the waves are thereby crowded together in the intervening space and the wavelength appears less than L; if the body recedes the wavelength appears greater than L. The Austrian physicist, J. Doppler (1803–53), discovered the well-known change of pitch of a train whistle as it approaches and passes us. The same principle applies to the light. Every atom emits light of definite wavelengths which appear in a spectroscope as a series of coloured lines—a different series for each atom. If the atom is in a receding body all the lines have slightly longer wavelengths than usual, and the amount of the change depends uniquely on the speed. Longer wavelengths mean that the light is redder than usual, so that a light from a receding body shows a "red shift." The speed of recession can be calculated from the amount of red shift.

Hubble's Law

It was the American astronomer, V. M. Slipher, who first showed (in 1914) that some galaxies emitted light with a red shift. In the 1920s and 1930s the famous astronomer E. Hubble (1889–1953) measured both the distances and red shift of many galaxies and proved what is now known as Hubble's Law about which there is now some controversy. This states that the speed of recession of galaxies is proportional to their distance from us. This does not apply to our neighbours in the Local Group, we and they are keeping together. Hubble's Law has been tested and found to hold for the farthest detectable galaxies; they are about 7×10^9 light-years away and are receding with a speed approaching that of light.

The expansion of the universe does not imply that the Local Group is the centre of the universe —from any other viewpoint in the universe Hubble's Law would also be valid, and the distant galaxies would, similarly, all appear to be rapidly receding.

The Big Bang Theory and the Cosmic Dawn

One possible implication of this most exciting scientific discovery is that, if the galaxies have always been receding, at an early time they must have been closer together. We can calculate that about 10^{10} years ago all the matter of the universe could have been densely packed.

This is called the big bang theory (*See* **L15**). The first 100 million years after the Big Bang, when there was a vast black fog of widely spaced hydrogen atoms, is called the Cosmic Dawn. The central questions of cosmology now concern the ultimate fate of the universe, its size, age and composition. Telescopes of ever increasing sophistication on the Earth and in space are beginning to address these fundamental questions.

Quasars and Pulsars

In November 1962 Australian radio astronomers located a strong radio emitter with sufficient precision for the Mt. Palomar optical astronomers to identify it on photographs and examine the nature of its light. The red shift was so great that the object must be exceedingly distant; on the other hand it looked star-like, much smaller than a galaxy. By the beginning of 1967 over a hundred of these objects had been discovered and other characteristics established, such as strong ultraviolet radiation and inconstancy, in some cases, of the rate at which radiation is emitted. Not all of these so-called quasars are strong radio emitters; some show all the other characteristics except radio emission. It has been estimated that the "quiet" kind are about a hundred times more numerous than the radio kind. One great problem here is: how can such relatively small objects generate such inconceivably great amounts of energy that they appear bright at such huge distances? Recent observations suggest that quasars are only the central visible part of an otherwise undetected galaxy. There may also be a massive black hole near the quasar centre.

Late in 1967, while investigating quasars, Cambridge radio astronomers discovered pulsars, a new type of heavenly body. Their characteristic is the emission of regular pulses of radio waves every second or so. A pulsar in the Crab nebula has a repetition rate even faster—about 1/30 sec— and it follows that pulsars must be very small bodies little if at all bigger than the Earth.

White Dwarfs and Neutron Stars

The existence of such small bodies raises again the problem of the ultimate fate of evolving stars. Much depends on their mass because this determines how strong the inward pull of gravity is. For a star to be at least temporarily stable the inward pull must be balanced by an outward pressure. In the sun this is the pressure of the burning hydrogen and the resulting average density is about 1·4 times that of water (**Table, T8**). In some stars the inward pressure is so great that collapse proceeds until it is balanced by a different type of outward pressure that sets in when electrons and atomic nuclei are forced into proximity.

Stars so formed are the "white dwarfs". They are millions of times denser than the sun—"a matchbox of their matter would weigh a ton"— and they are very small though not small enough to be pulsars. The latter are now generally thought to be a million times denser even than white dwarfs and to consist largely of tightly packed neutrons. They are called *neutron stars*.

Black Holes and Event Horizons

Could the tendency of a massive star to fall inwards ever be so great that no outward pressure known to physics would suffice to balance it? Apparently it could! Astrophysicists know that such a gravitational collapse creates a high density object whose gravitational field is too strong to allow anything—including light waves—ever to leave the body. Such objects are called "black holes" because, light and other signals being unable to emerge from them, their matter has literally disappeared from view.

Black holes could be detected by the disturbance their gravitational attraction causes to neighbouring visible stars and also because atoms attracted by the black hole should emit intense X-rays before falling so far in that they too disappear into the black hole. Both of these detection methods led astronomers to realise there are super massive black holes at the centre of galaxies (including our Milky Way). They are caused by hypernovae. The edge of the black hole is the *event horizon*. The theory of gravitational collapse raises profound and unresolved problems about our physical concepts.

In 2013 scientists discovered compelling evidence of the existence of the biggest black hole ever found, with a mass equivalent to 17 billion of our suns. Even larger black holes may reside elsewhere.

THE ORIGIN, EVOLUTION AND ULTIMATE FATE OF THE UNIVERSE

Scientists can only attempt to explain the universe by relating its observable structure to the features predicted by alternative theories of its origin and development. The time span of all our observations of the Cosmos is very small by comparison with the lifetime of the universe (more than 10^{10} years). Also, contrary to many other scientific disciplines, it is impossible to repeat the "experiment", under controlled conditions. We must, therefore, explore the evolution of the universe by using the fact that light from the most distant galaxies has taken about 10^{10} years to reach us, thus providing us with a crucial view of the universe at a much earlier epoch.

Models of the Universe

Several models of the universe have been based on Einstein's theory of General Relativity (**T17**). Einstein's equations may be solved to predict the evolution of the universe. However, there is a spectrum of solutions which vary from a continuous and indefinite expansion at the present rate to an eventual slowing and subsequent contraction to a dense state, again in the distant future, which hints at a "pulsating" universe.

The Formation of Galaxies and Stars

On any theory of the universe, some explanation has to be found for the existence of clusters of galaxies. In all theories galaxies condense out from dispersed masses of gas, principally hydrogen.

It is believed on theoretical grounds each galaxy could not condense into one enormous star but must form many fragments which shrink separately into clusters of stars. In these clusters many stars, perhaps hundreds or thousands or even millions, are born. A small cluster, visible to the naked eye, is the Pleiades. The Orion nebula, visible as a hazy blob of glowing gas in the sword of Orion, is the scene of much star-forming activity at present. However, the earliest evidence for witnessing the birth of a star came from observations by the Infrared Astronomical Satellite (IRAS). Deep within a gas and dust cloud called the Ophiuchus dark nebula, matter fell inward in a manner predicted by the theories of star formation. At the centre of this collapsing cloud there was an embryonic star perhaps only 30,000 years old.

The Evolutionary Theory

According to the Evolutionary theory the "initial dense state" consisted of very hot plasma in a state of overall expansion. The expanding plasma was both cooling and swirling about. The random swirling produces irregularities in the distribution of the hot gas—here it would be rather denser, there rather less dense. If a sufficiently large mass of denser gas happened to occur, then the gravitational attraction between its own particles would hold it together and maintain its permanent identity, even though the rest of the gas continued to swirl and expand. Such a large mass would gradually condense into fragments to become a cluster of galaxies.

Revolutionary Discoveries

The 1960s witnessed revolutionary developments in both observational and theoretical astronomy. For example, scientists now agree that remote sources of radio waves are more abundant the weaker their intensity. This strongly suggests that they are more abundant at greater distances. Thus the universe is not *uniform* as the original steady-state theory prescribed. Since greater distances correspond to earlier times, any extra abundance of objects observed at the greater distance means that the universe was denser in its younger days than now. This favours an evolutionary theory of the universe.

The same theory requires that the initial dense state of the universe—aptly christened "the primaeval fireball"—should contain intense electromagnetic radiation with a distribution of wavelengths characteristic of the high temperature. As the fireball, *i.e.*, the universe, expanded over a period of about 10^{10} years it cooled, and one feature of this process is that the wavelengths of the radiation increase and their distribution becomes characteristic of a much lower temperature. In fact, the wavelengths should now be concentrated round about 1 mm to 1 cm (corresponding to about $-270°C$) and the radiation should approach the earth uniformly from all directions. Radiation just like this was detected in the 1960s by extremely sensitive instruments both at ground-based observatories and flown from balloon payloads high in the earth's atmosphere— above most of the water vapour and other constituents which interfere with such delicate observations. This "microwave background" radiation strongly supported the evolutionary or "Big Bang" theory as opposed to the "Steady-State" theory, which cannot rationally explain the radiation.

In 1992 data from the Cosmic Background Explorer (COBE) satellite strengthened the Big Bang theory still further. Minute variations in the temperature of the background radiation across the sky help to show that the distribution of matter in the early universe could act as a blueprint for the future large-scale structures we observe today. Back in 2003 a satellite called MAP began to re-measure the cosmic background radiation in exquisite detail.

The Formation of the Chemical Elements

A stable nucleus is one that lasts indefinitely because it is not radioactive. There are 274 known kinds of stable atomic nuclei. These nuclei are the isotopes (*q.v.*) of 81 different chemical elements; the other elements, including, for example, uranium and radium are always radioactive. Some elements are rare, others abundant. The most common ones on earth are oxygen, silicon, aluminium, and iron.

However, the earth is rather atypical. It is especially deficient in hydrogen, because the gravitational attraction of our small planet was not strong enough to prevent this very light gas from escaping into space.

It is possible to examine the chemical constituents of meteorites and to infer the composition of the sun and other stars from the spectrum of the light they emit. By such means, the conclusion has been reached that 93 % of the atoms in our galaxy are hydrogen, 7 % are helium; all the other elements together account for about one in a thousand atoms. A glance at the Table of Elements (*see* **T56**) will show that hydrogen and helium are two of the lightest elements: they are in fact the two simplest. The problem is to explain how the heavier chemical elements appear in the universe at all. It is here that a combination of astronomy and nuclear physics is required.

Energy

We have already referred to the fact that the energy radiated from the sun originates in nuclear reactions which turn hydrogen into helium. Why is energy given out? To answer this question we note that nuclei are made up of *protons* and *neutrons* (*q.v.*). These particles attract one another strongly—that is why a nucleus holds together. To separate the particles, energy would have to be supplied to overcome the attractive forces. This amount of energy is called *binding energy* and is a definite quantity for every kind of nucleus. Conversely, when the particles are brought together to form a nucleus the binding energy is *released* in the form of radiations and heat. Different nuclei consist of different numbers of particles, therefore the relevant quantity to consider is the *binding energy per particle*. Let us call this B. Then if elements of *high* B are formed out of those of *low* B there is a *release* of energy.

Now B is small (relatively) for light elements like lithium, helium, and carbon; it rises to a maximum for elements of middling atomic weight like iron; it falls again for really heavy elements like lead, bismuth, and uranium. Consequently, energy is released by forming middleweight elements either by the splitting up of heavy nuclei ("nuclear fission") or by the joining up of light ones ("nuclear fusion").

The Study of Fusion Processes

It is fusion that is going on in stars. The fusion processes can be studied in laboratories by using large accelerating machines to hurl nuclei at one another to make them coalesce. In stars the necessary high velocity of impact occurs because the plasma is so hot. Gradually the hydrogen is turned into helium, and helium into heavier and heavier elements. This supplies the energy that the stars radiate and simultaneously generates the chemical elements.

The Heaviest Elements

The very heavy elements present a problem. To form them from middleweight elements, energy has to be *supplied*. Since there is plenty of energy inside a star, a certain small number of heavy nuclei will indeed form, but they will continually undergo fission again under the prevailing intense conditions. How do they ever get away to form cool ordinary elements, like lead and bismuth, in the earth? One view links them with the highly explosive supernovae, to which we have already referred earlier. If the heavy elements occur in these stars the force of the explosion disperses them into cool outer space before they have time to undergo the fission that would otherwise have been their fate. The heavy elements are thus seen as the dust and debris of stellar catastrophes. The view is in line with the steady-state theory, because supernovae are always occurring and keeping up the supply of heavy elements. In the evolutionary theory some of the generation of elements is supposed to go on in the very early stages of the initial dense state and to continue in the stars that evolve in the fullness of time. It cannot be claimed that the origin of the chemical elements is completely known, but we have said enough to show that there are plausible theories. Time and more facts will choose between them.

The Formation of the Planets

Precisely how the planetary system was formed is still not understood in detail. From extremely precise observations of the movements of some nearby stars, it seems certain that other planetary systems occur among our stellar neighbours. By inference, it is thus probable that among certain classes of stars, planetary systems are very common throughout the universe.

Two other facts are crucial for any theory of planetary system formation. First, all the planetary orbits lie nearly in the plane perpendicular to the axis of rotation of the sun. The planets' rotations about the sun are all in the same direction and their axes of rotation, with two exceptions (Venus and Uranus), are close to the polar axis of their orbit planes, and in the same sense as their orbital rotation about the sun. Secondly, there is a very strong inverse correlation between planetary distance from the sun and the planet's mean density, particularly if the correct allowance is made for the effects of gravitional compression in the deep interiors of planets (greater in large than in small planets).

Rather than theories which would place planetary formation as either the random collection of pre-formed planets by the sun in its path through the galaxy or as the consequence of a very near encounter between our sun and another star, it is now generally believed that the origin of the planetary system (and most of the satellites, etc.) was a direct consequence of the process which originally formed the sun.

As the primaeval solar nebula contracted, to conserve angular momentum, its rotation rate increased, and a diffuse equatorial disk of dust and gas formed. In the cold outer region (10–20° K) of this disk, all materials except helium and possibly hydrogen could readily condense on dust particles. Near the centre the temperature was higher, increasingly so as the proto-sun heated up, initially by the energy released by its gravitational contraction and, later, by the thermonuclear processes.

The Process of Accretion

Within this rotating and swirling disk of gas and dust, the process of accretion proceeded. Low-velocity collision between dust particles from time to time allowed larger particles to be created, composed of a mixture of the heavier elements and also the "icy" materials, particularly so in the colder outer regions where more of the "ices" were in a frozen state. Virtually our only information on the composition of such particles comes from detailed study of meteorites and from spectroscopic observation of comets. Eventually rocks of the size of centimetres, metres, and even kilometres were built up in this way. The build-up, controlled by low-velocity collisions, particularly of "sticky" materials, and also by electrostatic charges, was, at all times, however, moderated by occasional destructive high-velocity collisions. The relatively high viscosity of the dust and gas mixture throughout the disk must have been very important in producing a relatively uniform, rotational motion throughout the disk.

When "rocks" a few kilometres in size had been created new factors became important. Gravitational forces firstly increased the capacity of the larger "rocks" to accrete additional dust and smaller particles and, secondly, allowed some retention of material after even high-velocity collisions which would have destroyed smaller pieces.

The Giant Planets

The next stage is possibly the most difficult to model. Within a relatively uniform disk containing large numbers of rocks up to a few kilometres in diameter mixed within the residual dust and a large amount of gas, and extending to well outside Pluto's orbit, a small number of massive planets were formed. Some debris now remains as the comets and asteroids; however this debris and all the major planets, including the massive Jupiter, represent in total only a very small percentage of the original material of the solar nebula which was not condensed to form the sun.

It would appear that relatively quickly, during a period of 10^7 or 10^8 years, the large numbers of kilometre-sized objects, by collision and mutual gravitational attraction, formed the nuclei of the present planets and probably, in most cases, their major satellites also, in orbits relatively similar to their present ones. The planet-building process was most efficient at distances from the sun corresponding to the present orbits of Jupiter or Saturn, a compromise between temperature decreasing with distance from the sun, allowing a greater percentage of the total material to be solid and thus available for accretion, and density of material being greater closer to the sun. Most of the exo-planets so far discovered are gas giants.

The Jovian Planets

The outer or "Jovian" planets must have grown quickly, sweeping up hydrogen and helium gas as well as solid particles. Closer to the sun, the "icy" materials, still mainly in gaseous form, could not contribute very significantly to the

THE SOLAR SYSTEM

	Mean distance from Sun (millions of km)	Diameter km	Period of Revolution**	Average density (water = 1)	Number of Satellites
Sun	—	1,392,000	27·30 d		—*
Mercury	57·9	4,878	87·97 d	5·4	0
Venus	108·2	12,104	224·70 d	5·2	0
Earth	149·6	12,756	365·26 d	5·5	1
Mars	227·9	6,795	686·98 d	3·9	2
Jupiter	778·3	142,985	11·86 y	1·3	67*
Saturn	1,427	120,537	29·46 y	0·7	60*
Uranus	2,869·6	51,119	84·01 y	1·3	27*
Neptune	4,496·6	50,538	164·79 y	1·8	14*
Pluto***	5,900	2,370	248·59 y	1·1	5

*These planets also have planetary rings. **d = days y = years. ***Scientists have reclassified Pluto (and the other bodies at the edge of the solar system in the Kuiper belt) (see below).

initial accretion process, so that only smaller planets could form. Owing to their smaller mass, gravitational field and thus lower "escape velocity," they were only able to accrete a small proportion of the heavier gas present within the inner part of the solar system. Thus, at present, these "terrestrial" planets are much denser than the outer "Jovian" planets, much smaller in size, and contain very little hydrogen or helium. The planet-building process was probably ended by two factors: the gravitational disruptive effect of the planets already formed and the enhanced "solar wind" of the young sun, which swept much residual dust and gas out of the solar system.

Before the process was complete, however, the gravitational energy released by the material falling onto the proto-planets plus the radioactive heating of short-lived isotopes present at the time of planetary formation were responsible for melting most of the bodies of the planets and probably all the larger satellites and asteroids.

A Continuing Process

This process allowed gravitational segregation of denser and lighter materials within the planets, and the production of the core, mantle and crustal regions of each of the terrestrial planets. Long after the dust and gas were driven from the solar system and the planet surfaces cooled and solidified, the residual larger rocks and asteroids, of which enormous numbers were originally still present, continued to be swept up by each of the planets. The record of this violent stage of the solar system's development can still be seen in the saturation cratering seen on the Moon, Mercury, and Mars.

Recent Explorations and Debates

In the past six decades, direct space exploration, using automated space probes (and manned spacecraft in the case of the Moon) has enormously increased our knowledge of the solar system. Notable have been the Viking, Pioneer and Voyager projects. The five space probes to Halley's comet in 1986 were also a huge success. Important discoveries have continued to be made by ground-based telescopes that are now comparable in some wavebands to the Hubble Space Telescope thanks

to increasing sophisticated techniques such as the adaptive optics system that accounts for atmospheric ripples. More recently a large number of scientific missions have been launched including the X-ray multimirror telescope (XMM) to observe the universe, the Cluster II satellites observing the Earth's plasma environment, the Cassini mission to Saturn which also carried the Huygens probe to be dropped into Titan's atmosphere, the Mars Pathfinder mission, the Galileo trip to Jupiter, the Ulysses probe investigation of the Sun and the Rosetta mission to land on an asteroid in 2014. The Juno mission to Jupiter arrived in 2016. All have generated great quantities of exciting new scientific data. See also T9(2).

New Solar System Discoveries

Until recently there were thought to be only nine planets in the solar system. But in 2003 a 10th planet was discovered. This planet, which was given the snappy name 2003UB313, is about three times as far from the Sun as Pluto and about as massive.

This discovery, along with the discovery of an orbiting object called Sedna some years later, opened a fierce debate: are they planets at all? What do we mean by a planet? Like 'life' the term 'planet 'has caused much debate.

The Reclassification of Planets

Many astronomers contested that 2003UB313 and Sedna were not planets, which led others to assert that Pluto was not a planet either. This controversy arose because of a large belt of icy objects beyond Neptune, known as the Kuiper belt. These objects are the result of incomplete planet formation in the outer Solar System. They are the remains of the original protoplanetary material.

Some astronomers suggested that Pluto itself was an object just like those in the Kuiper belt, and did not qualify as a planet. Others felt that the word 'planet' should be restricted to objects orbiting stars. Again, opinions as to the validity of this classification were offered and debated in newspapers. It became clear that the International Astronomical Union (the only body empowered to settle both matters) had no formal definition of

SOME ASTRONOMICAL DISTANCES

(1 light-year = 9·46 × 10¹² km).

Object	Distance from Earth (light-years)	Velocity of recession (km per second)	Object	Distance from Earth (light-years)	Velocity of recession (km per second)
Sun	$1·6 \times 10^{-5}$	—	Andromeda Galaxy	$2·2 \times 10^6$	−299
Nearest star (Proxima			Galaxy in Virgo	$7·5 \times 10^7$	1,200
Centauri) .	4·2	—	Galaxy in Gt. Bear	10^9	14,900
Brightest star (Sirius) .	8·6	—	Galaxy in Corona		
Pleiades . . .	410	—	Borealis	$1·3 \times 10^9$	21,600
Centre of Milky Way .	$3·0 \times 10^4$	—	Galaxy in Bootes	$4·5 \times 10^9$	39,300
Magellanic clouds (the			Very remote quasi		
nearest galaxies) .	$1·6 \times 10^5$	—	stellar object	$\sim 1·2 \times 10^{10}$	~280,000

"planet", and an authoritative decision on classification was needed.

Problems of Definition

So why is 'planet' hard to define? Part of the problem is that there are three areas in which the definition could be constructed: first, the *physical properties* of the body itself; second, its *orbital properties* and finally its *formation mechanisms* and *histories*. It is argued that any definition of a planet will be some mix of these characteristics. However, the principal reason for the controversy is that there is no good scientific way to keep Pluto a planet without doing serious disservice to the remainder of the solar system.

Dwarf Planets / Plutoids / Planet Nine

The problem was resolved in August 2006 when a new class of dwarf planets was officially designated. Pluto was removed from the list of *classical planets* (as the other 8 planets were now called) and was joined with Charon, Ceres, Eris (2003 UB313) and the tiny 2012 VP113 to form a new group of *dwarf planets*. The status of Pluto was soon changed yet again, however, in 2008 to become a *plutoid* (*see below*). Eris (the largest dwarf planet) even has its own moon, Dysnomia.

A new category (*plutoid*) was proposed for those dwarf planets beyond Neptune which take more than 200 years to orbit the Sun. Eris (formerly known as Xena), Charon, Haumea, Makemake, Sedna and 2012 VP113 are in this plutoid group.

To add to the problem, early in 2016 it was announced that a new, small planet (10 times the size of Earth) could exist way out nearer the edge of the solar system. It was provisionally named Planet Nine, taking 20,000 years to orbit the Sun.

Extrasolar Planets

Over the last 25 years, scientists have discovered planets orbiting other stars, called *extrasolar planets*. The planets themselves have not been seen – we can only see stars at such large distances because they emit light so powerfully – but they were detected because astronomers observed some stars 'wobbling', from which it was deduced that invisible objects nearby were exerting a gravitational pull.

Not surprisingly, the first such planets to be discovered were very large, Jupiter-sized gas giants. That in itself is not surprising as the technique being used to observe these planets is biased towards finding objects that are big enough and close enough to exert a noticeable gravitational effect on the visible star. Indeed, if alien astronomers performed the same experiments on our own Sun, they might discover Jupiter and possibly Saturn, but they would not be able to detect any other planets.

However, the fact that these planets are so close to the stars they are orbiting is strange. The classical theory of planet formation suggests that big planets like Jupiter and Saturn are formed at much greater distances from the primary star, since the heat of the star during the formation of the stellar system would have otherwise prevented materials from accumulating to form such a big planet. New theories have been devised to explain these strange planets and their odd locations. None are yet satisfactory. In recent years, with improved telescopes and more advanced detection techniques, the number of exoplanets (both large and small) has risen rapidly (and thousands more await confirmation). Billions more almost certainly exist. The Kepler Mission alone detected hundreds of such planets. Entire planetary systems have now been found. These exoplanets also provide proof that planets *do* migrate. One exoplanet has been found with a massive ring system, over 200 times larger than the famous ring systems of Saturn. Planets far older than Earth have been discovered.

An Earth-like planet was found in 2016 which orbits Proxima Centauri, our nearest stellar neighbour, only 4 light years away.

Significant Planetary Missions

(i) Mercury

A space mission to Mercury is quite a challenge. Being closest to the Sun, it is difficult to reach which is why Mercury has only been visited by one spacecraft, Mariner 10 in 1974 and 1975. Much about Mercury remains mysterious. Two new spacecraft will visit Mercury in the next decade. The first called *Messenger* was launched by NASA in 2004 and began to orbit Mercury in 2011 after several flybys. The second spacecraft called BepiColombo set off in 2013 on a journey due to last over four years. These missions will bring us new images and data about this least explored planet.

(ii) Venus

Until fairly recently Venus had been a low priority for planetary probe programs, but ESA committed itself to a Venus orbiter mission named 'Venus Express' which was a follow on from the Mars Express mission. Many of the instruments on the mission were simply upgraded versions of those on the Mars Express platform. After a 153 day cruise the spacecraft arrived at Venus in 2006 and it went on to map the surface and atmosphere of the planet.

(iii) Mars

Mars has been known for thousands of years. It has been extensively studied from ground-based observatories. However, little can be understood from the Earth even with very large telescopes. In 2004 the Mars Expedition Rovers 'Spirit' and 'Opportunity' successfully landed on Mars, their mission to send back geological data. They were still operating after more than four years on Mars, and they have sent back many astonishing pictures.

There are also the Mars orbiters (Mars Global Surveyor, Mars Odyssey, and Mars Express) currently traveling around Mars, carefully mapping the surface and composition and Martian environment.

The exploration of Mars continues. In late 2005 NASA's Mars Reconnaissance Orbiter set sail for Mars. It arrived in 2006 to begin collecting data. The plan was to find safe and scientifically worthy landing sites for future exploration, so it was fitted with cameras to zoom in for extreme close-up photography of the Martian surface and a sounder to find subsurface water.

(iv) Saturn

The only mission dedicated to exploring Saturn was the NASA Cassini space probe, which entered Saturn's orbit in June 2004. Cassini carried the Huygens probe, the first planetary lander built by ESA. Cassini was the biggest and most expensive interplanetary probe ever built and is the first to explore the Saturn system of rings and moons from orbit. Cassini immediately began sending back intriguing images and data. In January 2005 the Huygens Probe fell into the thick atmosphere around Titan, one of Saturn's moons. Titan contains nitrogen, methane and other organic (carbon-based) molecules. Indeed, conditions on Titan are believed to resemble those on Earth 4·6 billion years ago.

(v) Pluto

In July 2015 the New Horizons spacecraft having travelled 4·5 billion kilometres and having been launched back in 2006 passed by Pluto, sending back a welter of tantalising data. It appeared to show a white heart of nitrogen ice (now named the Tombaugh Region), evidence that Pluto is still geographically active, and also an absence of impact craters. On Pluto, frozen flakes of nitrogen fall as snow. Both Pluto and its moon Charon revealed high mountains (some two miles high), deep canyons, ragged cliffs and a youthful crust.

II. PHYSICS—THE FUNDAMENTAL SCIENCE
OF MATTER

WHAT PHYSICS IS ABOUT

Introduction

Anyone compelled by curiosity or professional interest to look into contemporary journals of pure physics research is soon struck by the fact that the traditional division of physics into "heat, light, sound, electricity, and magnetism" has become very blurred.

Current Divisions of Physics

Two different, though complementary, sections can be distinguished. First, there is the physics concerned with the properties of matter in bulk, with solids, liquids, and gases, and with those odd but very important substances, such as paints, plastic solutions, and jelly-like material, which are neither properly solid nor liquid. In this vast domain of physics questions like this are asked: Why is iron magnetic, copper not? What happens when solids melt? Why do some liquids flow more easily than others? Why do some things conduct electricity well, others badly, some not at all? During the last century, particularly the last few decades, it has become clear that such questions can be answered only by raising and solving others first. In particular, we must ask: (i) Of what nature are the invisible particles of which matter is composed? and (ii) How are those particles arranged in bulk matter?

The first of these two questions has generated the second major category of modern physics: this is the physics of particles and of the forces that particles exert on each other. In this field which represents science at its most fundamental questions like this are asked: If matter is composed of small units or particles, what are they like? How many kinds of particle are there? Do the particles possess mass? electric charge? magnetism? How do the particles influence each other? How can their motion be described and predicted?

The discussion which follows has been divided into two main parts (1) **Particles and Forces**, and (2) **The Properties of Matter in Bulk**, with part (1) describing the microscopic structure of matter and part (2) its macroscopic properties.

PARTICLES AND FORCES

Aristotle to Newton

The inference that matter should be composed of small particles or atoms originated, it is true, in classical times. The atomic idea was an attempt to solve the age-old problem of matter and its peculiar properties. The ancients had provided themselves with two solutions to the problem of matter:

(i) **The theory of the four elements** (earth, water, fire, air), from which all different forms of matter were composed by selecting different ratios of the four ingredients. This approach had been used by traditional philosophy and was adopted by Aristotle.

(ii) **The theory of atomism** which postulated the existence of atoms and empty space.

Atomism remained very much in the background in the development of Western Science and persisted even longer in the Arab world. The idea that matter is composed of "small units" was in reality forced into the mental development of mankind by the repeated application of the process of dimension halving. By the time of Newton atomism had come to the fore and Newton con-

sidered that God had made the Universe from "small indivisible grains" of matter. Nevertheless, the search for the "philosopher's stone" was still, in the seventeenth century, the main pursuit of many scientists, but the new chemistry of the seventeenth century made use of atomistic concepts. Newton's physics was a mechanics concerning particles in a vacuum and when Boyle described his gas law (*i.e.*, Pressure × Volume is constant at a fixed temperature) he visualised matter as composed of particles with specific qualitative properties. It was, of course, the advance of experimental techniques which enabled scientists to test theories on the nature of matter.

Dalton and Atomic Theory

The modern view of atomism need be traced no farther than the beginning of the nineteenth century when Dalton and his contemporaries were studying the laws of chemical combination using precise weighing techniques. By that time the distinctions between elements, compounds, and mixtures were already made. Compounds and mixtures are substances which can be separated into smaller amounts of chemically distinguishable constituents.

Elements (*see* **T56**) cannot be so divided. In a mixture the components may be mixed in any proportion and sorted out again by non-chemical means. In a compound the elements are combined in fixed proportions by weight. This last fact gives the clue to atomic theory.

Dalton pointed out that the fixed combining weights of elements could easily be explained if the elements consisted of atoms which combined in simple numerical ratios, *e.g.*, 1 atom of element A with one of B, or one of B with two of C, and so on. For instance, 35·5 g of chlorine combine with 23·0 g of sodium to make 58·5 g of ordinary salt. If we assume one atom of chlorine links with one of sodium, then the atoms themselves must have weights in the ratio 35·5 to 23·0.

This turns out to be consistent with the combining weights of chlorine and sodium in all other compounds in which they both take part. Sometimes two elements combine in several different proportions by weight. But this is easily explained by assuming that the atoms link up in a variety of ways *e.g.*, one iron atom with one oxygen, or two irons with three oxygens, or three irons with four oxygens. Then the three different combining proportions arise from the three different numbers of atoms, *using in each case the same ratio of oxygen atom weight to iron atom weight.*

Atomic Weight

Over the century and a half since Dalton, these ideas have been repeatedly tested by chemical experiments. Nobody now doubts that every chemical element has atoms of characteristic weight. The atomic weight or more properly the relative atomic mass, of an element is by international agreement expressed relative to one isotope (*see* below) of carbon, namely carbon-12 which is given the relative mass of twelve. These numbers are only ratios; the real weight of one single oxygen atom is 2.7×10^{-23} g.

Valency

That the combinations of atoms in definite proportions was necessary to produce compounds, or more correctly molecules, was known from 1808. The reason why only one atom of sodium and one of chlorine was required to produce one molecule of salt was unknown. Further the seemingly odd combinations of two atoms of hydrogen (H) with one of oxygen (O) to give water (H_2O), while only one atom of hydrogen could combine with chlorine to give hydrogen chloride (HCl) could not be explained. This situation was not resolved until around 1860, when the chemical formulae of many molecules were known. It was then discovered that homologies existed in the elements, for example the series Na, K, Rb, Cs, or Fl, Cl, Br, I, and this culminated in the Periodic Table of the elements (*see* **T56**).

Determining Valency

The valency of an atom was determined by its position in the periodic table and determined by the number of electrons which the atom has orbiting its nucleus. Atoms combined to form molecules in a manner which maintained the number of "valence" electrons in a stable grouping of 2, 8, or 18 (*see later*). For example, sodium has one valence electron and chlorine seven, therefore the combination NaCl gives the stable grouping of eight; hydrogen has one and oxygen six, hence it requires two atoms of hydrogen and one of oxygen to give one stable molecule, H_2O. Other more complicated molecular structures and types of bonding between atoms are dealt with in the chemistry section. This discovery of particles smaller than the atom itself was necessary to fully comprehend the nature of valency in atomic combinations.

J. J. Thomson and the Electron

Matter is electrically uncharged in its normal state, but there exist many well-known ways of producing electric charges and currents—rubbing amber, or rotating dynamos, for example. It is therefore necessary to have some theory of electricity linked to the theory of matter. The fundamental experiment in this field was made by J. J. Thomson when, in 1897, he discovered the electron.

If you take two metal electrodes sealed inside a glass vessel and if the pressure of the air is reduced from atmospheric pressure, 76 cm of mercury, to 1 mm of mercury by mechanical pumping and then a high voltage, several kilo-volts, is applied to the electrodes, the negative electrode emits a "radiation" which causes the walls of the tube to glow. The rays are called *cathode rays*. The discovery of the electron was essentially a clarification of the nature of cathode rays. Thomson showed that they were streams of particles with mass and negative electric charge and a general behaviour unlike any other atomic particle known at that time. The importance of this discovery for the world of science cannot be overestimated, and its technical progeny are in every home and factory in X-ray machines, television tubes, and all electronic devices.

Rutherford–Bohr Atom

Since the electrons emerge from matter, they are presumably parts of atoms. The relation between the negative electrons and the positively charged constituents of matter was elucidated by the great experimenter Rutherford and the great theoretician Bohr. Their work, just before the First World War, showed that the positive charge, together with almost all the mass, is concentrated in the central core or nucleus of the atom about which the very light-weight electrons revolve. The diameter of an atom is about 10^{-8} cm, roughly one three-hundred-millionth part of an inch. The central nucleus has a diameter about 10,000 times smaller still. The nucleus and the electrons hold together because of the electric attraction between them.

The positive charge of the nucleus is responsible for holding the electron in the region of space around the nucleus. The electrostatic Coulomb force, if left on its own would quickly attract the electrons into the nucleus but since the electrons move in orbits, circular and elliptical, they experience an outward centrifugal force which balances the inward electrostatic force. The mechanism is similar to that which holds the earth in orbit around the sun, only here a gravitational force replaces the effect of the Coulomb force. Modern theories of the electronic structure of atoms are quantum mechanical (*see below*).

At this stage work could, and did, go on separately along several different lines:

(i) Electrons could be studied on their own. Nowadays the handling of beams of electrons of all sizes and intensities has become a major branch of technology.

(ii) The nucleus could be treated as a special problem, and this led to the mid-20th century flowering of nuclear physics, to the atomic bomb, and to nuclear power.

(iii) The behaviour of electrons in the atom could be analysed; this is the great domain of atomic physics which spreads into many other sciences as well.

Volumes have been written about these three fields, such is their crucial importance.

The Electron

Electrons are expelled from solids by light, heat, electric fields, and other influences. It has therefore been possible to study beams of electrons on their own *in vacuo*. Electrons inside matter, either as constituents, or temporarily in transit, can also be observed by their innumerable effects. These observations all show the particles to be indistinguishable one from another; all electrons are the same wherever they come from. They have a definite mass (9.11×10^{-28} g), a negative electric charge, a magnetic moment, and a "spin" (intrinsic rotatory motion). Only recently have scientists been able to sub-divide electrons into three component parts.

The electronic charge has long been used as a basic unit of charge in atomic physics. The electron has come to be the best known of all the "fundamental particles." It is now used in research as probe for studying the structure of matter, for which it is ideally suited, since it is very much smaller than an atom. A whole field of electron-scattering research which studies the nature and structure of solids, liquids, and gases is being actively conducted in many laboratories.

The Nucleus

The early research programmes in nuclear physics were greatly facilitated by the occurrence in nature of certain unstable (radioactive) nuclei which emit fast-moving fragments. The latter can be used as projectiles to aim at other nuclei as targets; the resulting impacts yield much valuable information. This technique still dominates nuclear physics, though nowadays the projectiles are artificially accelerated by one or other of the large costly machines designed for the purpose.

Protons and Neutrons

The most important early discovery was that the nucleus consists of two types of fundamental particle—the positively charged *proton* and the electrically neutral *neutron*. These two are of nearly equal mass (about 1,800 times that of the electron), and, like electrons, have a magnetic moment and spin. The proton charge is equal to the electron charge, though opposite in sign. Consider a moderately complex nucleus like that of iron. This usually has 30 neutrons and 26 protons. Its atomic weight therefore depends on the total number of neutrons plus protons, but the total charge depends only on the number of protons—called the *atomic number*. The latter is denoted by Z while the total number of neutrons plus protons is called the *mass number* and denoted by M. A species of nucleus with given values of Z and M is called a *nuclide*. Z is also the number of electrons in the atom, since the atom as a whole is electrically neutral. The atomic number determines the chemical nature of the atom (*see below*), so that by altering the number of *neutrons* in a nucleus we do not change the chemical species.

It is thus possible to find—and nowadays to make—nuclei of the same element which nevertheless differ slightly in weight because they have different numbers of neutrons. These are called *isotopes*. Iron isotopes are known with anything from 25 to 36 neutrons, but all have 26 protons. Thus a set of isotopes consists of the various nuclides that have the same Z but different M's.

When the atomic properties of isotopes are measured it is found that small, hyperfine differences in the motions of the electrons around the respective nuclei exist. These result from the different total spin of the isotopes and its effect on the orbiting electrons. This influence of atomic properties by nuclear effects is important in that it provides a link between different fields of research.

Stable Nuclides

The protons and neutrons in a nucleus are bound together by strong forces called *nuclear forces*. In many cases, the forces are so strong that no particles ever escape and the nucleus preserves its identity. There are two hundred and seventy-four different combinations of neutrons and protons of this kind, and they are called the *stable nuclides*. The earth is largely composed of such stable nuclides, because any unstable ones have, in the course of time, spontaneously broken up into stable residues.

Nevertheless, there are some unstable nuclei left on earth. They give rise to the phenomenon of radioactivity which was discovered by Becquerel in 1893.

Unstable Nuclides: Radioactivity

Becquerel found that certain chemicals containing uranium gave off rays capable of blackening a photographic plate, and shortly afterwards Marie and Pierre Curie discovered more substances, including radium, which produce similar but stronger effects. By now, about fifty chemical elements having radioactive properties are known to exist on earth, some, like radium, being strongly radioactive, others, like potassium, being so weak that the radiations are difficult to detect. These are called the *natural radioactive nuclides*.

The main facts about radioactivity are as follows: it is a *nuclear* phenomenon and (with minor exceptions) proceeds quite independently of whatever the electrons in the atom may be doing. Thus, the radioactivity of an atom is not affected by the chemical combination of the atom with other atoms, nor by ordinary physical influences like temperature and pressure. The radioactivity consists of the emission by the substance of certain kinds of rays. The early workers, Rutherford being the giant among them, distinguished three kinds of rays labelled α, β, and γ. These are described below. Whatever kind of ray is examined, it is found that the radiation from a given sample decreases gradually with time according to a definite law which states that the intensity of radiation decreases by half every T seconds. The number T, called the half-life, is constant for each radioactive material, but varies enormously from substance to substance. For instance, radium decreases its activity by a half every 1,602 years, whereas the half-life of one of the astatine isotopes is about $0 \cdot 1 \times 10^{-6}$ sec.

Radioactive Emissions

The three most well-known types of radioactive emission are quite distinct from one another.

(i) **α-rays** or α-particles consist of two protons and two neutrons bound together. They are ejected from the radioactive nucleus with one of several well-defined speeds. These speeds are high, often of the order 10^9 cm per sec. Two protons and two neutrons are the constituents of the nucleus of helium, and α-particles are thus fast-moving helium nuclei.

(ii) **β-rays** are moving electrons. They may emerge from their parent nucleus with any speed from zero to a definite maximum. The maximum speed often approaches that of light, and is different for each isotope. The electron has a positively charged counterpart, the positron (see below), and β-rays are sometimes positrons. To distinguish the two cases, the symbols β^- and β^+ are used. The naturally occurring β-radiations are almost all β^-.

(iii) **γ-rays** travel with the speed of light because they are in fact electromagnetic waves differing from light only in the extreme shortness of their wavelength. They have no electric charge.

It is unusual, though not unheard of, for the same radioactive substance to emit both α- and β-rays. On the other hand, γ-rays frequently accompany either α- or β-rays.

γ-rays pass through matter easily; in fact, they are extra penetrating X-rays. α-rays can be stopped by thin sheets of tissue paper. α-rays brought to rest pick up a pair of electrons from the surrounding matter and become neutral helium atoms, and helium gas from this source is consequently found imprisoned in certain radioactive rocks. β-rays are intermediate in penetrating power between α- and γ-rays.

We must now try to interpret these observations.

Radioactive Disintegration

A nucleus is a collection of neutrons and protons interacting with each other and possessing collectively a certain amount of energy. Just as some human organisations lose their coherence if they accept too many members, so nuclei can remain stable only if (i) the total number of particles is not too great, and (ii) neutrons and protons are there in suitable proportions. Radioactive nuclei are the ones for which either or both these conditions do not hold. Sooner or later such nuclei eject a fragment, thus getting rid of some energy they cannot contain. This is called a *radioactive disintegration*, and the fragments are the α-, β-, and γ-rays. α-emission relieves a nucleus of two neutrons and two protons and some energy; γ-emission simply carries off excess energy without altering the number or kind of particles left behind. β-emission is more complicated. There are no electrons normally present in a nucleus, but they are suddenly created and explosively emitted if a neutron changes into a proton; positive electrons are similarly generated if a proton changes into a neutron. β-emission is therefore a mechanism for changing the ratio of protons to neutrons without altering the total number of particles.

Both α- and β-emission change the Z of a nucleus, and the product, or daughter nucleus, is a different chemical element. α-emission also changes the M. It might happen that the daughter nucleus is unstable, in which case it too will disintegrate. Successive generations are produced until a stable one is reached. Part of such a family tree is shown below. The symbols above the arrows show the kind of rays emitted at each stage, the figures are the mass numbers, M, and the names and symbols of chemical elements can be found on **T56–7**.

$$U^{238} \xrightarrow{\alpha} Th^{234} \xrightarrow{\beta} Pa^{234} \xrightarrow{\beta} U^{234} \xrightarrow{\alpha} Th^{230} \xrightarrow{\alpha}$$

$$Ra^{226} \xrightarrow{\alpha} Rn^{222} \xrightarrow{\alpha} Po^{218} \xrightarrow{\alpha} Pb^{214} \xrightarrow{\beta} Bi^{214} \xrightarrow{\beta}$$

$$Po^{214} \xrightarrow{\alpha} Pb^{210} \xrightarrow{\beta} Bi^{210} \xrightarrow{\beta} Po^{210} \xrightarrow{\alpha} Pb^{206}$$
(Pb^{206} is stable lead).

This family exists naturally on earth, because the head of the family, U^{238}, has so long a half-life ($4 \cdot 5 \times 10^9$ years) that there has not yet been time enough since its formation for it to have disappeared.

Artificial Radioactivity

Many new radioactive isotopes have long been man-made. All that is required is to alter the M or Z (or both) of a stable isotope to a value which is incompatible with stability. The means for doing this is *bombardment*, i.e., stable nuclei are exposed to the impacts of atomic particles such as streams of protons from an accelerator, the neutrons in an atomic reactor, or simply the α-particles from another radioactive substance.

The new material is called an *artificially radio-active isotope*. Artificial radioactivity is not different in kind from that of the naturally radio-active substances, but the half-lives are usually on the short side. Indeed, the isotopes in question would exist in nature but for the fact that their short half-lives ensured their disappearance from the earth long ago.

Suppose a piece of copper is exposed to the intense neutron radiation in an atomic reactor. The more abundant of the two stable isotopes of ordinary copper has thirty-four neutrons and twenty-nine protons (*i.e.*, $Z = 29$, $M = 63$). In the reactor many (not all) of these nuclei absorb a neutron, giving an unstable copper nucleus with $Z = 29$, $M = 64$. When removed from the reactor the specimen is observed to be radioactive with a half-life of 12·8 hours. It is somewhat unusual in that it gives out both β⁻ kind β⁺ rays.

Some nuclei emit electrons, leaving a daughter nucleus with one more positive charge than copper, *i.e.*, a zinc nucleus ($Z = 30$, $M = 64$). One neutron has become a proton, and the resulting zinc nucleus is stable. The others emit positrons, leaving behind a nucleus in which a proton has been turned into a neutron ($Z = 28$, $M = 64$); this is a stable nickel nucleus.

The overall process is one example of the artificial transmutation of the chemical elements which is now a commonplace of nuclear physics. It was first discovered by Irene and Frederick Joliot-Curie in 1934.

Lack of a Complete Theory

Consider now a collection of, say, one million radioactive nuclei of the same kind. It is impossible to tell exactly when any one of them will disintegrate; it is a matter of chance which ones break up first. All we know is that, after a time equal to the half-life, only a half a million will survive unchanged. In general, the more excess energy a nucleus has, the more likely it is to break up, and therefore the shorter the half-life of that particular nuclear species. In principle, to calculate the half-life theoretically, one would have to have a reliable theory of nuclear forces and energies. This is still being sought after, so it is probably fair to say that while the laws of behaviour of radioactive isotopes are well and accurately known, the *explanation* of this behaviour in terms of the properties of protons and neutrons is by no means complete.

Nuclear Fission—Chain Reaction

A discovery important not just for nuclear physics but for the whole of mankind was made by Hahn and Strassman in 1939. This was the discovery of nuclear fission in uranium. One of the natural isotopes of uranium is an unstable one, U^{235}, with 143 neutrons and 92 protons. It normally shows its instability by emitting α- and γ-rays. If uranium is bombarded with neutrons, some U^{235} nuclei temporarily gain an extra neutron, which makes them even less stable. This they show by splitting into two roughly equal parts, called fission fragments, together with two or three neutrons.

There are two highly important things about this disintegration. One is that the two or three neutrons can promote further disintegrations in other uranium nuclei, and the process can therefore be self-propagating: it is then called a *chain reaction*. The other is that the total mass of the fission products is less than that of the original nucleus. This mass difference does not disappear without trace; it turns into energy according to a formula discussed later.

Nuclear Fusion

The ability of two light nuclei to combine and form a heavier nucleus is called fusion. A reaction of this nature does not form a chain process but proceeds in singly induced reactions. A typical fusion reaction is the formation of a helium nucleus (mass 3) from two deuterium nuclei which are made to collide at an energy of 60 keV (speed of $2·4 \times 10^6$ m/s)

i.e., $^2D_1 + {}^2D_1 \rightarrow {}^3He_2$ (0·82 meV) + n(2·45 meV)

where the $^3He_2$ particle has kinetic energy of 0·82 meV and the free neutron has free kinetic energy of 2·45 meV. This type of reaction is exo-energetic, the additional kinetic energy coming from the tighter binding of the nucleus in ^3He than in the two separate deuterium nuclei. The energy released in this form of nuclear reaction is much more than that in a fission process and is responsible for the emitted energy of the sun which burns hydrogen to form helium.

Applications of Nuclear Reactions

The world has two uses for the energy released in nuclear reactions:

(1) nuclear weapons;
(2) nuclear power plants.

The only nuclear bombs to be used in anger employed the fission chain reaction proceeding at a rapid rate which quickly becomes uncontrollable and produces a tremendous explosion. The second generation of nuclear warhead uses the fusion reaction, which is initiated by a fission-reacting detonator to produce an even more destructive blast. The third generation of nuclear warhead uses the large flux of very energetic neutrons to kill biological material, but the blast effect is essentially zero, hence attacks with neutron bombs leave most non-biological material and structures intact.

In the second application the nuclear fission process is controlled to provide a constant source of energy to drive turbines which produce electricity.

Both uses represent epoch-making technical achievements, but mankind has yet to show itself capable of bearing sanely the burden of responsibility which nuclear physicists have laid upon it. One thing is certain: the discoveries will not cease. Already, other fissionable elements have been made and used; new chemical elements have been created; nuclear plants ("atomic piles") have stimulated great demands for new materials that will stand the heat and radiation inside the reactor, and this promotes research in other fields of science; irradiation inside an atomic pile gives new, and potentially useful properties to old materials; nuclear power drives ships and submarines. It is difficult to write even briefly about contemporary nuclear physics without feeling keenly the ambiguity of its powerful promises.

Atoms

A nucleus surrounded by its full complement of electrons is an electrically neutral system called an atom. Neither the atom as a whole, nor its nucleus, counts as a "fundamental particle" because either can be subdivided into more elementary parts, thus:

atom → electrons + nucleus → electrons + neutrons + protons

The chemical identity of the atoms of a given element, which was Dalton's key idea, depends entirely on the number and motion of the electrons. For example, the simplest element, hydrogen, has one proton for a nucleus, and one electron. The latter is comparatively easily detached or disturbed by the electric forces exerted by neighbouring atoms, consequently hydrogen is reactive chemically, *i.e.*, it readily lends its electron to build chemical structures with other equally co-operative elements. The second element, helium, has a nucleus of two protons and two neutrons; outside are two electrons in a particularly stable arrangement.

Both electrons orbit the nucleus in the same spacial orbit, but with their spin directions opposite and at 90° to the plane through the nucleus and the electrons. This pair of electrons is so difficult to disarrange that the special name of closed shells has been coined to cover such cases.

The fact that two electrons can be present in the same orbit is only possible if their spins are anti-parallel (Pauli Exclusion Principle). In the case of a stable group of eight electrons they arrange themselves in groups of two and their spins anti-parallel. Helium with its closed shell will not react chemically, whereas hydrogen, which has an open shell of only one electron, will react very quickly with other atoms.

As the nuclear charge increases, different electron arrangements of greater or lesser stability succeed one another, with every so often a closed shell corresponding to one of the chemically inert gases neon, argon, xenon, krypton.

Such considerations, pursued in sufficient detail, enable atomic physics to account for all the differences and similarities among the chemical elements and, in principle at least, for all other facts of chemistry as well.

Ions

Changes in the atomic properties of an atom are accomplished by altering the position of any electron from one orbit to another. In the limit when an electron is completely removed from the atom, leaving it positively charged, the atom is said to be ionised and is called a positive ion. An atom can be singly or multiply ionised up to a level equal to the number of electrons existing in the neutral atom. In addition, atoms can, through distortion of the existing electrons, accept an additional electron and become negative ions. These can be formed in a resonance scattering process and exist only for life-times of only 10^{-14}s or be formed by chemical reactions. The roles played by negative and positive ions in the upper atmosphere of the earth and stellar atmospheres have been of special interest to atomic physicists since the 1930s.

Maxwell and Electromagnetic Waves

Atoms are held together by the electric attraction of the nucleus for the electrons. Finer details of atomic behaviour depend on the magnetic moments of the particles. Any moving charged particle gives rise to magnetic effects, and in the dynamo a coil moving in a magnet produces an electric current. It can be seen therefore that electric and magnetic phenomena are intimately linked. Any region of space subject to electric and magnetic influences is called an *electromagnetic field*.

In 1862, before the discovery of the electron, Maxwell, while still in his twenties, had perfected a general theory of the electro-magnetic field. This theory today still describes correctly almost all electro-magnetic phenomena. The elegance of this theory is difficult to appreciate, but it alone was the only theory of pre-twentieth century physics which satisfied the prerequisites of Einstein's relativity theory (1905), i.e., inherent in its structure was the concept of relativistic invariance. *Inter alia*, he proved that disturbances in the electric and magnetic conditions at one place could be propagated to another place through empty space, with a definite velocity, just as sound waves are propagated through air. Such electromagnetic disturbances in transit are called *electromagnetic waves*, and their velocity turned out experimentally to be the same as that of light and radio waves—which was a decisive argument to show that both of these phenomena are themselves electro-magnetic waves.

Einstein and Photons

In the years between about 1900 and 1920 this view was upset by Planck, Einstein, Millikan, and others, who focused attention on phenomena (radiant heat, photoelectricity) in which light behaves like a stream of particles and not at all like waves. A wave and a particle are two quite different things, as anyone will admit after a moment's contemplation of, say, the ripples on a pond and a floating tennis ball. The acute question was: is light like waves or particles?

Theoretical physicists have devised means of having it both ways. To say that light behaves as particles means that the waves of the electromagnetic field cannot have their energy subdivided indefinitely. For waves of a given frequency, there is a certain irreducible quantity of energy that must be involved whenever light interacts with anything. This quantity is the product hv where v is the frequency and h is a constant named after Planck. Each such unit is called a *quantum of the electromagnetic field* or a *photon* and is counted as one of the fundamental particles. Frequencies and wavelengths vary widely. Typical wavelengths are: radio—hundreds or thousands of metres; radar—a few centimetres; visible light—5×10^{-5} cm; X-rays—10^{-8} cm.

De Broglie and Particles

Since it seemed possible to attribute particle properties to electro-magnetic waves, then why not associate wave properties with particles. If an electron (mass m) is travelling with a velocity of v cm/s, then De Broglie (1923) suggested that its characteristic wavelength would be given by the relation $mv \lambda = h$; for example if $v = 10^3$ m/s, $m = 9 \times 10^{-31}$ kg, $h = 6.626 \times 10^{-34}$ joules-seconds, then $\lambda = 7.36 \times 10^{-7}$ m, which is the same wavelength as red light. This proposal was confirmed in 1927 by Davisson and Germer when they showed that electrons could produce diffraction, a property until then only associated with light. These wave-like properties are now known to exist for all particles, and we now consider a particle with momentum mv to behave like a wave of wavelength $\lambda = h/mv$.

De Broglie made his revolutionary assertion in his doctoral thesis, and his examiners were so uneasy about the validity of the hypothesis that they were prepared to fail the young man in his examination. Happily for De Broglie, Einstein was visiting that particular university and he was asked his opinion of the idea; his reply ensured success for De Broglie and saved the examiners from future embarrassment.

Molecules

Electrical attractions and interactions of various kinds can cause atoms to combine with each other or themselves to form molecules. Two similar atoms, say hydrogen, combining to form the homonuclear diatomic molecule H_2, while two different atoms, hydrogen and chlorine, will form a heteronuclear diatomic molecule HCl. Molecules have a wide range of complexity, from simple pairs of atoms to highly intricate spirals and chains composed of thousands of atoms. The biological basis of all life is, of course, molecular in both origin and function.

Excited Atoms

Like nuclei, atoms, when given excess energy (insufficient to ionise them), will absorb the energy in one of the electrons, which is then displaced from its equilibrium state to a state (or orbit) of higher energy. It will remain there for typically 10^{-8} seconds before returning to its equilibrium position with the excess energy being emitted as light. The time an atom remains in its excited state can exceed 10^{-8} seconds; lifetimes of 0.1 second are known, and these metastable states are prevented by the atomic properties of the atom from decaying quickly to their equilibrium states. The colour of the light emitted is characteristic of the atom involved, with the more energetic transitions giving blue light while the less energetic transitions give red light. Hence the emitted colour (or wavelength) of the light can be used for chemical identification and study of the various transition probabilities in atoms.

Herein lies the explanation of innumerable natural and technical phenomena, such as the colours of glowing gases whether they exist in the sun and stars, in aurora, or in street-lamps and neon signs. Herein also lies the reason for the importance of spectroscopy, which is the study of the characteristic radiation from excited states for spectroscopy is not only a useful tool for the chemical identification of substances ("spectroscopic analysis") but was one of the main routes along which twentieth-century physicists broke through to a knowledge of the inner nature of the atom.

Forces in Nature

Nature uses four, at high energies three, different forces to make one particle interact with another. The weakest force is **gravity** which although present at all particle interactions, is insignificant in atomic and nuclear interactions. Gravity controls the mass distribution in the universe and the force has an infinite range of interaction.

The **electric force** which also has an infinite range of interaction is much stronger than the gravitational force and is responsible for the binding forces inside atoms by the attraction of nuclei for electrons.

Inside the nucleus two types of interaction take place which require different forces for their existence:

(1) the forces which hold neutrons and protons together in the nucleus and this is the **strong force**, and

(2) the **weak force** which controls the changes in charge state of nucleons, *e.g.*, the β-decay process when a neutron in a nucleus changes into a proton with the ejection of an electron is controlled by the weak force.

Both these nuclear forces are short-range with their radius of influence approximately 10^{-13} cm, with the weak force acting on all matter and the strong force acting on quarks only. In today's parlance, gravity will act on any particle with mass, the electric force on any particle with charge, the strong nuclear on quarks and the weak nuclear on quarks and leptons (*see below*).

Quarks appear to experience short-range freedom of movement combined with a long-range binding. The proton, *i.e.*, the nucleus of atomic hydrogen, is composed of three quarks which move about freely within the shell of the proton; only when one quark tries to escape across the boundary of the proton does it experience a force which rebinds into the proton. Before we discuss further the interactions of these forces we must describe the range of particles which exist in physics.

Elementary Particles

When considering the word elementary in this context the reader should be wary of thinking that it implies some degree of absoluteness. The elementary mass of any particular particle is always highly qualified and subject to change. When a particle is discovered physicists measure its properties, *i.e.*, mass, electric charge, and spin, and determine which of the four forces to which it is subject. In addition, its life-time must be determined to see if the particle is stable or only a transient particle which will break up into other particles. The life-times of unstable particles are extremely short, ranging from 10^{-17}s to 10^{-21}s, and it is debatable if a particle which lasts only for 10^{-21}s should be called a particle. Generally now such short-lived particles are called resonances which are produced in an interaction which is only a step to the final product.

Classification of Particles

The rudimentary classification of particles is into four groups:

(1) **Gauge bosons**
(2) **Leptons**
(3) **Mesons**
(4) **Baryons**

All particles have an anti-particle which has the same mass but opposite charge as the real particle, the only exception being the photon, which is its own anti-particle and forms a group on its own. The leptons (electron, muon, and neutrino) form a stable group of particles and do not react to the strong nuclear force. This group of particles, and the photon, are perhaps the most fundamental of all particles. The mesons are unstable particles and (as will be seen later) exist only to act as a means which enables nucleons to interact with each other. They are subjected to the strong nuclear force. All particles heavier than the proton are called baryons, every one of them, except the proton, is unstable in some degree, and a vast number of them are known. Only a few are listed

in the Table on the next page.

Mesons and baryons are collectively called hadrons. All of these unstable particles have been detected either in the cosmic flux falling on the earth or produced in the very high energy accelerating machines in Europe, the USA *etc.*

Strangeness

Some particles have long life-times $\sim 10^{-9}$ s, which is much larger than that encountered normally. Particles which possessed these long life-times were called "strange". Strangeness describes not a new property of matter but a different quality of matter which persists long enough to enable that particle to engage in strong nuclear-force interactions. Hence strangeness does not persist indefinitely. The decay of a strange particle into other particles with the abolition of strangeness proceeds via the weak nuclear force. The strange (and doubly strange) particles form highly symmetrised shapes when combined with non-strange particles. The pattern itself does not explain anything, but the underlying theory, known as Group Theory, does indicate by symmetry arguments which particle should be necessary to form a complete group. This mathematical procedure had a resounding success when it predicted the existence of a triply strange particle known as "omega minus". The organisation of particles according to properties of mass, spin, and strangeness in groups is now only an organisation exercise, and it will not tell us anything about the composition of nucleons.

Interactions of Particles

The method by which atomic, nuclear, and subnuclear particles interact is via the exchange of energy which can be considered as a particle exchange. The interaction between electric charges proceeds by the exchange of photons. For example, two charges feel each other by one charge emitting a photon which interacts with the second charge. Since the electric force has infinite range, its force-carrying particle has zero mass. The same criteria apply in the gravitational force, where the graviton is the particle which carries the force effect between particles of matter. Since the weak and strong forces are short-range, then their force-carrying particles have finite masses. The weak force is transmitted by W and Z particles and the strong force can be considered as transmitted by mesons. The quarks also interact via the strong force, here carried by gluons (mass at present unknown), which also feel the force themselves. Strangeness is conserved in strong nuclear reactions but not in weak ones.

A theory which combines the electric and weak forces into a single interaction has predicted the masses of the W and Z particles to be around 82 and 93 GeV respectively. Back in 1983 experimental evidence was found by international groups at CERN for the existence of the W particle with the predicted mass thereby giving considerable support to this theory. A long term aim is to unify all the known forces of nature into a single interaction.

Quarks

The stability of the leptons contrasts sharply with the instability of the hadrons (excepting the proton), and this as well as other things had led physicists to consider that all hadrons were composed from different combinations of yet undiscovered particles. Gell-Mann first postulated the existence of three particles from which the nucleons, mesons, and hence all hadrons are composed. These "new" particles are attributed with fractional electric charges of $+\frac{2}{3}$, $-\frac{1}{3}$, and $-\frac{1}{3}$ of the electron charge. The particles were called quarks. The name quark was taken from the novel *Finnegans Wake* by James Joyce, the meaning of which is obscure, which is perhaps appropriate, but as students of Joyce will know, quark means "non sense", and other interpretations as to its meaning, such as the "sound of seagulls" or "quarts" are wrong. The three quarks were called up, down, and strange and

SOME MEMBERS OF THE ATOMIC FAMILY

The numbers in brackets after the name denote first the electric charge and second, the mass. The charge on an electron is counted as -1 unit and the electron mass as $+1$ unit. Thus $(+1,207)$ means the particle has a positive charge of 1 unit and a mass 207 times that of the electron.

The mass energy of an electron is 0·51 MeV, hence conversion to mass energies can be made by multiplying the given mass by 0·51. Thus the muon has a mass energy of 106 MeV. Note: the letter M is used to denote quantities of millions and the letter G to denote quantities of thousand of millions.

Photon (0, 0)	A quantum of electromagnetic radiation, *e.g.*, light, X-rays, γ-rays. The concept was introduced by M. Planck in 1900 when he described the emission of light as taking place in "packets" rather than in a steady stream. The energy of a photon is proportional to the frequency of the radiation and inversely proportional to the wavelength.
	Leptons
Electron (−1, 1)	Discovered by J. J. Thomson in 1897. The number of orbital electrons in an atom determines its chemical properties. Actual rest mass = $9\cdot1 \times 10^{-28}$ g. Emitted as β-rays by some radioactive nuclei. A stable particle.
Positron (+1, 1)	Positive counterpart or, "anti-particle", to the electron. Predicted theoretically by P. A. M. Dirac in 1928 and first discovered in cosmic rays by C. D. Anderson in 1932. Emitted as β-rays by some radioactive nuclei. When positrons and electrons collide they usually annihilate each other and turn into γ-rays; consequently, positrons only last about 10^{-10} sec. within ordinary matter, but are stable in isolation.
Neutrino (0, 0) and **Anti-neutrino** (0, 0)	These particles travel with the speed of light and are distinguished from one another by the relation of their spin to their direction of motion. A neutrino is emitted with the positron during positive β-decay; and an anti-neutrino with the electron during negative β-decay. Their interaction with matter is extremely slight. First postulated by Pauli in 1933 and detected in 1956. π-meson decay also produces neutrinos and anti-neutrinos but in 1962 it was proved experimentally that these are a different species. Thus there are two kinds of neutrino each with an anti-neutrino. All these particles are distinguished from photons by having different spin.
Muon (±1, 207)	Similar to, but heavier than, the electron and positron; disintegrates into electron (or positron if positive) + neutrino + anti-neutrino.
	Mesons
Pion (±1, 273) or (0, 264)	The π-meson. Charged pions decay either into muons and neutrinos or into electrons and neutrinos. Neutral pions decay into γ-rays, into "positron-electron pairs", or both. Pions are intimately connected with nuclear forces, *i.e.*, with the "strong" interaction.
Kaon (±1, 966) or (0, 974)	The K-mesons. These decay in many different ways producing other mesons, electrons, and neutrinos.
	Baryons
Proton (+1, 1836·1)	The positively-charged constituent of nuclei; the hydrogen nucleus is one proton. Fast-moving protons occur in cosmic rays. Does not spontaneously disintegrate.
Anti-proton (−1, 1836·1)	Negative anti-particle of the proton. Its existence was long suspected. Artificially produced and detected for the first time in 1955. Will react with the proton to produce pions or kaons.
Neutron (0, 1838·6)	Discovered by J. Chadwick in 1932. The neutral constituent of nuclei. When free it spontaneously disintegrates into a proton, an electron, and an anti-neutrino, after an average lifetime of about 18 minutes. Passes through matter much more easily than charged particles.
Anti-neutron (0, 1838·6)	The anti-particle of the neutron from which it is distinguished by properties connected with its magnetic moment and spin. Will react with neutron to produce pions or kaons.
Lambda Particle (0, 2183)	Discovered in 1947. Decays into proton plus pion.
Sigma Particle (0 or ±1; about 2330)	Various modes of disintegration, producing neutrons, protons, mesons and lambda particles.
Omega Particle (±1, 3272)	Predicted by scientists and duly discovered at Brookhaven, New York, in 1964.
Psi Particle (0, about 6100)	Discovered independently by two laboratories in the USA 1974.

have the properties given in the Table below:

Name	charge	spin	mass-energy (MeV)
up	$+\frac{2}{3}$	$\frac{1}{2}$	336
down	$-\frac{1}{3}$	$\frac{1}{2}$	338
strange	$-\frac{1}{3}$	$\frac{1}{2}$	540

These particles interact with each other via the strong force. Hence it can be seen that by taking different combinations of quarks, different hadrons can be built up. For example, the proton is two up quarks and one down, the neutron is two down and one up. The simplicity of this system can be appreciated, but the only experimental evidence to support the existence of quarks is indirect.

No one has yet isolated a single quark! Many scientists are seeking ways to produce and detect them, but as of now no claims have stood the test of scrutiny. Further theoretical and experimental evidence has proved the existence of three more quarks, known as top, bottom and charmed (*see below*). These six elementary particles are complimented by six equivalent anti-matter particles, each with the opposite charge of its mate.

The K-mesons, for example, are composed of a quark and an anti-quark either with the spins of the two quarks aligned parallel to give a net spin of one, or aligned antiparallel to give a net spin of zero. The charges +1, −1, and 0 are simply determined by selecting the correct combination of up and down quarks.

Charm

In the quest to unite the weak and electric forces, theoreticians were forced to introduce yet another new particle into the quark family. This was a charmed quark with charge $+\frac{2}{3}$. The four members of the quark family had seemed then to be symmetrical with the four members of the lepton group (electron, muon, and two neutrinos). Since the charmed quark had charge $+\frac{2}{3}$ and mass of 1,500 MeV, it could simply replace the up quark as a building brick in nucleons to produce charmed matter. For example, by replacing the up quark in a proton and a meson by a charmed quark we get a charmed proton and a charmed meson. The first experimental evidence of the existence of charm was obtained by the high-energy physics group at University College, London, working at CERN laboratory, when they established the existence of "a neutral current interaction" in neutrino scattering experiments. Although "naked" charm has never been detected, charmed mesons (masses of 1,865 and 2,020) have been detected by the SPEAR laboratory in USA and charmed anti-protons have also been detected with masses of 2,260 MeV. The experimentally determined masses are in sufficient agreement with theory to confirm the existence of the charmed quark. Theoretical proof for the existence of two more quarks, top and bottom, soon followed and by 1995 both had been discovered by experimentalists.

As a whole, this theory of elementary particles is called the standard model and has become generally accepted. Scientists are not happy to rest with this, however, because the number of unspecified parameters involved (the standard model has about 20 of these) seems too many for a fundamental theory. The search is on for deeper patterns and symmetries to explain matter.

The Higgs Particle

Since the discovery of the top quark, physicists have concentrated their efforts on tracking down an even rarer particle called the Higgs. Finding it would not only continue to validate the standard model, but would also help theorists explain the existence of mass. Since the US government decided to stop funding its expensive Superconducting Supercollider project, the search is wholly in the hands of the Europeans at CERN.

In July 2012 CERN finally confirmed the existence of the Higgs.

QUANTUM THEORY AND RELATIVITY

In our discussion of the nature of the various particles in physics we have alluded to them as being classified with well-defined sizes and weights. Of course, once we consider the physics of matter on a scale which is smaller than that of our everyday comprehension, then the classical physics of Newton is insufficient and we must use quantum physics. In the atomic region of reality we are again faced with the problem of indivisibility where the Greeks stopped their thinking and called the smallest particles of the universe atoms.

Today we know that each separate particle is composed of a definite amount of energy, and the larger the particle, *i.e.*, the more energy it is composed of, the easier it is to detect. We also know that the exchange of force between nucleons is carried by particles and that this inchangeability between mass and energy is a reality of quantum theory. To see this more fully we must realise that quantum theory rests on the theory of measurement! If a particle, of any type or structure, is composed of an amount of energy ΔE, then it is necessary to make measurements on it for a certain minimum time before it is detected. This minimum time Δt is given by the equation $\Delta E \times \Delta t \approx \hbar$, where $\hbar$ is Planck's constant divided by 2π; hence it can be seen that the smaller ΔE, then the longer a measurement must be made to detect the particle.

Correspondingly, the time of measurement itself introduces an uncertainty, ΔE, in the energy of the particle. As well as the parameters ΔE and Δt, a particular physical event can be expressed in terms of its momentum p and position q, and these can also be expressed in a relationship as $\Delta p \times \Delta q \geq \hbar$. Hence one can ask at what position in space, q, is a particular particle with momentum p? Or what exactly is the wavelength of a wave? It may be thought that the first question cannot reasonably be asked of a wave nor the second of a particle, but bearing in mind the dual roles of particles and waves discussed earlier, then these questions can be interchanged.

The Heisenberg Uncertainty Principle

We know that electrons behave both as particles and waves. Since electrons have something in common with both, one question cannot be answered precisely for electrons without ignoring the other; alternatively, both questions can be given an imprecise answer. As the wavelength of electrons is intimately connected with their speed, one has to accept an accurate knowledge of the speed (wavelength) and ignorance of position, or the converse, or *inaccurate* knowledge of both. This is the famous Heisenberg Uncertainty Principle.

Quantum theory is a set of mathematical rules for calculating the behaviour of fundamental particles in accordance with the Uncertainty Principle. In spite of its equivocal-sounding name, the principle has led to an enormous increase in the accuracy with which physical phenomena can be described and predicted. Quantum theory includes all that previous theories did and more.

Quantum theory grew up in the same epoch as the Theory of Relativity. Heroic attempts have been made to combine the two, but with only partial success so far. Relativity is concerned with all motion and all physical laws, but its characteristic manifestations occur only when something is moving with nearly the velocity of light. Quantum theory is likewise all-embracing, but its typical phenomena almost always occur when something on the minute atomic scale is in question. Consequently, the vast majority of everyday mechanics needs no more than the classical theory laid down by Newton, which is neither relativistic nor quantum.

Relativity

Historically, relativity grew out of attempts to measure the speed with which the earth moved through that hypothetical medium called the ether, which was supposed at that time to be the bearer of light waves. To take a simple analogy: sound waves travel through still air with a certain definite speed, v. If you move through the air with speed v' towards oncoming sound waves, they will pass you at the speed $v + v'$. Michelson and Morley, in their celebrated experiment of 1887, failed to find the corresponding behaviour on the part of light. This is so important an experiment that it has been repeated, and repeatedly discussed ever since. In October 1958 the latest and most accurate confirmation of the Michelson–Morley result was announced. It seems as if light always travels with the same speed relative to an observer, however fast he moves relative to anything else. Einstein put it this way: two observers moving with any constant velocity relative to each other will always agree that light travels past them at the same speed; this speed is denoted by c, and is approximately 186,000 miles per second.

It should be remembered that the limiting value of the velocity of light in relativity is a postulate introduced by Einstein not a conclusion which the theory provides. There may exist forms of matter which can travel faster than light!

Nevertheless, the postulate that the maximum velocity encountered in the universe is c, logically developed, leads to remarkable conclusions. For instance: if you walk from tail to nose of an aircraft at 4 mph and the plane is receding from me at 300 mph, then you recede from me at 304 mph "Common sense", Newton, and Einstein would all agree on this. But if you could walk at $0.25c$ and the plane moved at $0.5c$, the Newtonian mechanics would give your recession speed as $0.75c$, whereas Einsteinian relativity would give about $0.67c$.

Although at the everyday speed of 300 mph, the disagreement, though present in principle, is absolutely negligible, at speeds near that of light it is very pronounced. Many experiments show that the relativity answer is right.

Equivalence of Mass and Energy

The most famous consequence of relativity theory from which we derive benefit is the knowledge that mass can be converted into energy. The amount of energy, E, which can be derived from a given mass, m, of any type of material is given by the celebrated equation $E = mc^2$. If we take one gram of ash and convert it into the free energy of which it is composed we would get 10^8 kilowatts of power, sufficient to heat 15 houses for a year. The heat provided by the material which produced the ash is equivalent to that obtained from burning a single match. The massive energy released by $E = mc^2$ has been demonstrated in the power of nuclear weapons, but this energy has also been put to peaceful uses in nuclear-powered electricity generating stations.

In fundamental particle physics the masses of particles were always expressed in units of mass energy using $E = mc^2$ as the conversion equation. This is a matter of convenience from the realisation that mass is simply a condensed form of energy. The mesons which are the force-exchanging particles in the strong interaction have a mass energy of approximately 130 MeV, which is equivalent to a real mass of only 210^{-26} grams. The energy of the sun is provided by the conversion of real mass into light energy through thermonuclear fusion processes.

Mass and Rest Mass

The concept of mass is not a simple idea to grasp, for as we have seen, the mass of a body which is at rest is equivalent to its inherent latent energy. Further complications and interpretations arise when the body starts moving and its mass is no longer necessarily a constant quantity.

A stationary body can be observed to have a mass called its *rest mass*. If the body moves, it has energy of motion and therefore, according to Einstein's mass–energy equation, it increases its mass.

Mass thus depends on speed, but in such a way that there is very little change unless the speed approaches that of light. Many experiments on atomic particles demonstrate this. The interesting question now arises: do all fundamental particles have rest mass? or do some have mass derived solely from their energy? The answer appears to be that photons and neutrinos have no rest mass; all other particles have. The Table on **T16** gives their rest masses.

Special Theory of Relativity

The mathematical development of Einstein's ideas, leading to the conclusions just referred to, constitutes the Special Theory of Relativity. Stated more generally, the theory raises the question whether two observers in uniform relative motion could ever detect, as a result of their relative speed, any difference in the physical laws governing matter, motion, and light. To this, Special Relativity answers: No. The detailed theory involves special consideration of the results the two observers would obtain when measuring (i) the spatial distance, and (ii) the time interval, between the same two events. It turns out that they would not agree on these two points. They would agree, however, on the value of a certain quantity made up jointly of the spatial distance and the time interval in a somewhat complex combination. The intimate mixture of space and time in this quantity has led to the treatment of the three space dimensions and time on an equivalent footing. Hence the frequent references to time as the "fourth dimension". Scientists have devised an extremely elegant presentation of relativity theory by using an extension of ordinary geometry to four dimensions. A line drawn in his four-dimensional space represents the path of a particle in space and time, *i.e.*, the whole history of the particle. Thus the movement of particles in the ordinary world is turned into the geometry of lines in Minkowski's four-dimensional world of "space–time".

General Relativity and Gravitation

In 1915, 10 years after the publication of the Special Theory of Relativity, Einstein published his theory of General Relativity. This apparently innocuous extension of the ideas of special relativity to include accelerated relative motion opened up new and difficult fields of mathematical complexity which, when solved, enabled Einstein to include gravitation in the theory. In discussing the physics of atomic, nuclear, and sub-nuclear particles, we did not include the effect of the gravitational force, since in relation to the Electric, Weak and Strong forces it is extremely small and can be neglected in the discussion of the structure of matter but not in the discussion of astronomical problems and the movements of large-scale electrically uncharged bodies.

It has been usual, ever since Newton, to say that two bodies of mass m_1 and m_2, separated by a distance r attract one another with a force proportional to $m_1 m_2 / r^2$. This is Newton's inverse square law of gravitation which explains the movements of planets and comets and the falling to earth of an apple from a tree.

A Uniform Gravitational Field

The apple's fall is accelerated, and we observe this by noting its position relative to certain marks fixed with respect to us, and by timing it with some sort of clock. This system of location in space and time may be called our "frame of reference". We therefore assert that, in our frame of reference, the apple falls down with an acceleration which Newton saw no alternative but to attribute to a thing called gravitational attraction. Galileo had shown that *all* bodies fall with the same acceleration at all points, and we can now rephrase this by saying that in our frame of reference there is a constant gravitational attraction or *uniform gravitational field*.

Now suppose a collection of falling bodies is observed by us and an intelligent creature, designated C, inhabits one of them. C has his own frame of reference fixed relative to him and we have ours fixed relative to us. In C's frame neither his own body, nor any of the others, is accelerated, and therefore he has no reason to suppose a gravitational force is acting on them. We have, therefore, the following situation:

(i) in our frame, fixed relative to us, we find all the bodies falling subject to a gravitational pull;

(ii) in C's frame, undergoing accelerated fall relative to us, no gravitational field is apparent to C.

It looks, therefore, as if one has only to choose the correct frame of reference for the measurements in order to remove the need for any assumptions about the existence of gravitational fields. This is a simple illustration of the connection between gravitation and frames of reference for the measurement of space and time. Einstein's General Theory of Relativity extends this to cover non-uniform gravitational fields and shows that what Newton taught us to call the gravitational field of material bodies is better thought of as a peculiarity of the space and time in the neighbourhood of such bodies. Since space–time, as we mentioned above, can be expressed in geometrical terms, Einstein has transformed the theory of gravitation into an exercise in the geometry of space–time. Other physicists, in Einstein's tradition, are trying to turn *all* physics into geometry, but no one knows whether this is feasible.

All this abstruse work is much more than a demonstration of mathematical power and elegance. Observable phenomena which fall outside the scope of Newton's theory of gravitation are accounted for by relativity. One is the small but definite discrepancy between the actual orbit of the planet Mercury and the predictions of Newton's theory. Another is the effect of a gravitational field on the wavelength of light emitted by atoms. Similar atoms in different places in a gravitational field emit radiations with slightly different wavelengths. For example, the light from an atom in the intense field of a star should have slightly longer wavelength than the corresponding light from an atom on earth. This effect has always proved very difficult to detect with certainty. However, Einstein's prediction was verified back in 1960.

Quantum Theory and Relativity Combined

The atomic family table refers to "antiparticles". The theory which first introduced such things in 1934 is due to the Cambridge physicist Dirac and was epoch-making. Dirac conceived an equation to describe the motion of electrons subject to the laws of both quantum theory and relativity. His achievement was thus to synthesise these two great ideas. The spin of the electron was originally a supposition that helped to make sense of spectroscopic observations of light emitted from atoms. Dirac's equation made spin a logical consequence of the union of relativity and quantum theory. Perhaps even more important was the brilliant inference that the equation for the electron implied the existence of another particle having the same mass and spin but with a positive instead of a negative electric charge. This object is called the electron's antiparticle and is now well known as a positron. Every particle is now believed to imply an antiparticle, so it is conceivable that the universe could have been (but isn't) an anti-universe, *i.e.*, all the electrons and protons might have been positrons and antiprotons and so on. The laws of physics would still have been applicable, however.

The gravitational force has an infinite range and therefore its force-carrying particles must travel at the speed of light. The graviton is the name of the particle which transmits the gravitational force between bodies with mass. No experiment has yet found the existence of gravitons which are the postulated quanta of gravitational waves. There is an exact analogy between photons, the quanta of electro-magnetic radiation, and gravitons.

Conservation Laws

If charged particles interact, then it is found that the amount of electric charge existing after the reaction is the same as that which existed before the event. This is called the law of the conservation of charge. Many other conservation laws exist in physics, *e.g.*, conservation of mass, energy, angular momentum, linear momentum, and other more abstruse conservation laws exist in particle physics, *e.g.*, conservation of baryons,

leptons, strangeness, isotopic spin, and parity. The last three conservation laws listed have been found to have a limited jurisdiction, and the violation of parity in the weak interaction was a great surprise to physicists.

Any reader who looks in a mirror knows that the left- and right-hand sides of his face are interchanged in the image. Fortunately mirrors do not also turn the image upside down, but, if they did, the face would then have undergone what is called "a parity transformation". A screwdriver driving a right-handed screw downwards becomes, on parity transformation, a screwdriver driving a left-handed screw upwards. The law of conservation of parity is a way of asserting that any physical process that goes on in the world could equally well go on—obeying the same laws—in a parity transformed world. There is nothing left-handed that does not in principle have a right-handed counterpart.

Conservation and Parity

It came as something of a shock when, in 1957, after theoretical proposals by Lee and Yang in America, Wu and co-workers proved that parity was not always conserved. To understand Wu's experiment, we must recall that nuclei can have intrinsic spin. Suppose the axis of spin were downwards into the page and the rotation were suitable for driving an ordinary screw into the page. Then Wu showed that beta-rays from such a nucleus are emitted *preferentially upwards*, *i.e.*, against the direction of travel of the screw. The parity transformed version of this would have the beta-rays preferentially emitted in the same direction as the travel of the screw and, if parity is conserved, this process would happen too. But it does not. If the beta-rays in the experiment had been emitted in equal numbers up and down, then the parity transformed version would have had this feature too (thus conserving parity).

A reprieve for the standard model came when P symmetry was combined with a transformation of charge. But when this new CP symmetry was also found to break down, scientists were forced back to their accelerators to search for either another patch to, or an alternative for, the standard model.

Conclusion

Over a century's development of the atomic ideas has brought a progressive, if jerky, increase in the mathematical precision of the theories. In some fields of particle physics, observations to one part in a million, or even better, can be explained, to that level of accuracy, by the existing theories. At the same time, however, the theories have lost visual definition. An atom was easy enough; so was a light wave conceived like a sound wave in air. Even after Rutherford, an atom consisting of a miniature solar system merely exchanged the solid billiard ball for a system of revolving billiard balls and was no great obstacle to visualisation. But since quantum theory and the Uncertainty Principle, every unambiguous visualisation of fundamental wave-particles leaves out half the picture, and although the electrons are in the atom, we can no longer represent them in definite orbits. The moral seems to be that visualisation is unnecessary, or at best a partial aid to thought.

THE PROPERTIES OF MATTER IN BULK

One of the most obvious and at the same time most wonderful things about the properties of matter is their great variety. Think of air, diamond, mercury, rubber, snow, gold, pitch, asbestos *etc.* Even the differences of state of the same chemical substance are remarkable enough, ice, water, and steam, for example. One of the aims of physics is to reach an understanding of all these different properties by explaining them in terms of the behaviour of the particles discussed in the previous section.

The great success with which this imposing

programme has been carried out indicates the maturity of physics. It is difficult to think of any major property of matter in bulk for which there is not some attempted theoretical explanation, though future physicists will no doubt regard some present-day theories as rudimentary or incorrect.

Physics, Statistics, and Thermodynamics

Take a number equal to the population of London, multiply it by itself, and multiply the product by another million. The answer is about the number of molecules in 1 cubic centimetre of ordinary air. They are constantly moving about and colliding with one another. Even if the nature of the molecules and their laws of motion were perfectly understood, it would clearly be impracticable to calculate the exact paths described by each particle of so vast an assembly. This difficulty brought into being a whole branch of physics concerned with calculating the overall or average properties of large numbers of particles.

Just as statisticians will provide the average height, income, expectation of life, and so on, of the population of London, without knowing everything about every individual, so statistical physicists can work out average properties of molecules or atoms in large groups. This important branch of physics is called *Statistical Mechanics*. It was founded in the nineteenth century by Maxwell, Boltzmann, and Gibbs and is still being actively developed.

Consider now all the molecules in 1 cubic centimetre of air contained in a small box. They are continually bombarding the walls of the box and bouncing off. This hail of impacts (it is actually about 10^{23} impacts per square centimetre per second) is the cause of the pressure which the gas exerts against the walls of the box. Now suppose we pump air in until there is twice as much as before, though the box is still the same size and at the same temperature. This means that the density of the gas (*i.e.*, the mass of 1 unit of volume) has doubled. We should now expect twice as many impacts per second on the walls as before, and consequently twice the pressure. We therefore arrive at a conclusion that, if the volume and temperature are constant, the pressure of a gas is proportional to its density.

This is one of the simplest statistical arguments that can be checked against observation; in fact, it stands the test very well.

Heat, Temperature, and Energy

The proviso about the temperature remaining the same is an important one for the following reason. In the nineteenth century there was much discussion about the nature of heat. To Joule we owe the now well-established view that heat is equivalent to mechanical work. In one of his experiments, in the 1840s, the work necessary to rotate paddle wheels against the resistance of water in a tank generated heat that caused a slight rise in the temperature of the water. Joule found out exactly how much work was equivalent to a given quantity of heat.

However, one can do other things with work besides generating heat; in particular, work creates motion, as when one pushes a car. Bodies in motion possess a special form of energy, called kinetic energy, which is equal to the work done in accelerating them from a state of rest. We have, then, three closely connected ideas: work, heat, and kinetic energy. Now according to the views of the nineteenth century, which are still accepted, any heat given to a gas simply increases the kinetic energy of its molecules; the hotter the gas, the faster its molecules are moving. If, therefore, the gas in our box is allowed to get hotter, there is an increase in molecular speed, and the impacts on the walls become correspondingly more violent. But this means the pressure increases, so we have another law: if the density remains the same, the pressure increases if the temperature does.

Laws of Thermodynamics

Such considerations as these have been pursued with great elaboration and subtlety. The notions

of heat, temperature, energy, and work—familiar but vague in everyday life—have been given precise definitions, and the relations between them have been enshrined in the Laws of Thermodynamics. Enshrined is perhaps a suitable word, because these laws are so soundly and widely based on experimental results that they have greater prestige than any others in physics. If any proposed physical law comes in conflict with thermodynamics then so much the worse for that law—it has to be revised.

It is sometimes asserted that no one is properly educated who does not understand the Second Law of thermodynamics. We cannot, therefore, leave this section without at least stating the two best known thermodynamic laws:

First Law: *If any physical system is given a quantity of heat, and if the system performs some work, then the energy of the system increases by an amount equal to the excess of heat given over work done.* This law asserts that heat, energy, and work are convertible one into the other, and that all such transactions balance exactly. This is one form of a principle accepted as fundamental in all science, *viz.*, the Principle of the Conservation of Energy, according to which energy can never be created or destroyed, but only changed from one form to another.

Second Law: *It is impossible to make an engine which will continuously take heat from a heat source and, by itself, turn it all into an equivalent amount of mechanical work.* In fact, all engines which produce work from heat—steam engines for example—always use only a fraction of the heat they take in and give up the rest to some relatively cool part of the machine. The Second Law makes this obligatory on all work-from-heat devices. This statement of the Second Law has an engineering ring about and, indeed, it arose from the work of the nineteenth-century French engineer Carnot. Nevertheless, it can be rephrased in terms of the concept of *entropy*, and has been applied with unbroken success to all fields of science involving the transfer of heat and allied matters. It sets a definite limit to the kinds of physical and chemical process that can be conceived to take place. Nothing has been known to contravene it.

The States of Matter

The molecular motion in gases has been referred to in the previous section. Tacitly it was assumed that each molecule acted independently of all others, except that collisions occurred between them. In reality, molecules exert attractive forces on one another and, if a gas is cooled so that molecular movements become relatively sluggish, a time comes when the attractive forces succeed in drawing the molecules close together to form a liquid. This process is called condensation.

The molecules in a liquid are packed tightly together and they impede each other's movements. On the other hand, movement still persists, and the molecules struggle about like people in a milling crowd. Besides wandering about, the molecules vibrate. These motions represent the energy contained in the liquid.

The fact that the molecules, though irregularly packed, can still slip past one another and move from place to place, explains the essential property of liquids that distinguishes them from solids—ability to flow. As a matter of fact, although the rather vague assertion that in a liquid molecules are irregularly packed would be generally accepted, there is no agreed opinion on what the irregularity is actually like. Indeed, not only the precise structure of liquids, but the theory of liquids in general, is fraught with such considerable mathematical difficulties that the liquid state is much less well understood than the solid or gaseous.

Most solids are crystals. The popular idea of a crystal is of something which has a more or less regular geometrical form with faces that shut in the light—like snowflakes or gems. However, crystallinity really depends on a regular inner pattern of the atoms, and may or may not show itself on the visible surface. A lump of lead, for example, is crystalline, despite its appearance.

The actual arrangement of the atoms in a crystal can be extremely complex. Some are quite simple, however. The largest model of a crystal structure must surely be the 400-ft. "Atomium" building in the 1958 Brussels Exhibition. This consisted of eight balls, representing atoms, situated at the corners of a cube, and one more ball exactly in the middle. Imagine this repeated in all directions so that every ball is the centre of a cube whose corners are the eight neighbouring balls. This is known to crystallographers and physicists as the "body-centred cubic structure"; it is the actual arrangement of atoms in iron, sodium, chromium, and some other metals. If every ball, instead of being the centre of a cube, were the centre of a regular tetrahedron (a solid figure with four equal triangular faces), and had its four neighbours at the corners of the tetrahedron, then we should have the "diamond structure". This is how the carbon atoms are arranged in diamonds.

In crystals the atoms are locked into a regular ordered structure by attractive forces which give the solid its rigidity and prevent it from flowing. The atoms are so close together that any attempt to press them closer involves crushing or distorting the atoms—a process they resist strongly. This explains why solids (and liquids too) are so difficult to compress. Gases can easily be compressed because there is so much space between the molecules.

Distinction of Solid and Liquid

The distinction between solid and liquid is not so sharp as is commonly supposed. A lump of dough will not bounce, but is plastic; a steel ball-bearing is very elastic and bounces excellently, but one cannot mould it in the fingers. Neither dough nor steel qualifies for description as a liquid. There are, however, substances which can be moulded like plasticine into a ball that will then bounce very well on the floor like an elastic solid, and finally, if left on a flat table, will spread into a pool and drip off the edge like a liquid. There is no point in trying to force such things into rigid categories. One may say instead that for short, sharp impacts the material behaves like an elastic solid, but under long-sustained forces it flows like a liquid. The properties of these, and many other anomalous materials, are increasingly engaging the attention of those who study the science of flow—*rheology*.

It is interesting to see how many familiar and important materials exhibit peculiar rheological behaviour—paint, dough, ball-pen ink, cheese *etc.*

Inside a Crystalline Solid

We now return to our wallpaper analogy. Suppose we have walls papered with a regular pattern of, say, roses, fuchsias, and green leaves. These represent the different kinds of atoms in the solid. Careful observation shows that the whole pattern is shimmering. The flowers and leaves are not stationary, but are undergoing slight random oscillations about their proper positions. In a crystal these movements are called thermal vibrations, and are never absent. The hotter the crystal, the more the vibration, and at a high enough temperature the vibrations become so great that the atoms get right out of position and the pattern disappears altogether, *i.e.*, the crystal melts. Thermal vibrations are essential to the theory of solids, and are responsible for numerous physical properties.

Next we note something extraordinary about some of the papered walls. On these the paper has been hung in irregular patches fitted together like a not very well-made jig-saw puzzle. Lines of roses which should be vertical are horizontal in some patches, oblique in others. This represents the situation in most ordinary solids, for they consist of many small pieces of crystal irregularly packed together.

Such material is called *polycrystalline*, and the small pieces are *crystal grains*. Crystal grains may be almost any size, sometimes visible to the naked eye, as often on galvanised iron.

However, on one wall, we see excellent regularity and no obvious patches at all. The physicist would call this a *single crystal*, and several techniques exist for preparing them. Natural single crystals can be found, and there are some

beautiful large single crystals of rock salt. But on examining the single crystal wall closely, we find a number of places where the paperhanger has failed to make adjacent pieces register perfectly—there is a slight disjointedness. This occurs in real single crystals, and the line along which the structure fails to register is called a *dislocation*. These are much studied by physicists because of their bearing on the mechanical properties of solids, on the yielding of metals under strong stress, for instance.

Types of Impurity

This by no means exhausts the possibilities of the wallpaper analogy; several other phenomena can be found. For example, in a place where there should be a fuchsia there is actually a daffodil—something completely foreign to the pattern. Or perhaps a small wrongly shaped leaf is jammed between the proper leaves in a place that should really be blank. These represent chemical impurity atoms. The first is called *substitutional*, because it occupies the position of an atom that should be there, the second is called *interstitial*, because it does not. Substitutional impurities of indium metal, deliberately added to the semi-conductor silicon, make possible the manufacture of transistors (*see* **Section L**). Some steels derive their valuable properties from interstitial carbon atoms within the iron pattern.

What physicists call a vacancy would occur if a flower or leaf were simply missing. Remembering that all the atoms are vibrating, we should not be surprised if occasionally an atom jumps into a neighbouring vacancy if there happens to be one, *i.e.*, the atom and the vacancy change places. Later this may occur again. In the course of time, a rose which was near the ceiling may make its way to the floor by jumping into vacant rose positions when they occur near enough. This process, which the physicist calls *diffusion*, is also analogous to the game in which numbers or letters can be moved about in a flat box because there is one vacant space to permit adjustment. The more vacancies there are in a crystal, the faster diffusion occurs. It is very slow in solids, but is nevertheless evidence that apparently quiescent materials are really internally active.

Metals, Electricity, and Heat

There is ample evidence that inside metals there are large numbers of free electrons. To illuminate this statement let us take sodium metal as an example. One single sodium atom has a nucleus with eleven protons; there are therefore eleven electrons in the atom. The outermost one is easily detached, leaving a positively charged sodium ion behind. We may think of these ions arranged in the three-dimensional pattern characteristic of sodium crystals. It is the same as the iron structure previously described. The detached electrons, one per atom, occupy the spaces in between. The usual metaphor is that the structure of ions is permeated by a "gas" of electrons. Like all visualisations of fundamental particles, this must be taken as a rough approximation. The important point is that the electrons in the gas are not bound to individual atoms but may wander freely about the crystal, hindered only by the collisions they make with the vibrating ions.

This is the picture as it appeared to physicists of the first decade of the 20th century, and we can explain many properties of metals with it. Naturally the theory has developed greatly since then, thanks to the great work of Lorentz, Sommerfeld, and Bloch; it now relies heavily on quantum theory, but it is surprising how little violence is done to modern ideas by the simple picture we are using.

The free electrons move randomly in all directions at thousands of miles per hour. If the metal is connected across a battery it experiences an electric field. Electrons are negatively charged particles, and are therefore attracted to the electrically positive end of the metal. They can move through the metal because they are free; this flow is not possible to those electrons which remain bound to the ions. The function of the battery is to keep the flow going and, for as long as it is going, it is the electric current.

The flow of electrons is not unimpeded. They constantly collide with the ions and are deflected from the path of flow. This hindrance is what the electrician calls *electrical resistance*. The electric force, due to the battery or a dynamo, accelerates the electrons, thus giving them extra energy; but they lose this to the ions at collisions because the ions recoil and vibrate more than before. The net effect of innumerable collisions is to increase the thermal vibrations of the ions, *i.e.*, to make the metal hotter. This is the explanation of the fact well known to every user of electric irons; that electric current heats the conductor. If a strong current is passed through a wire, the heating is so great the wire glows, as in light bulbs, or melts and breaks, as in blown fuses.

If one end of a metal rod is heated we soon feel the heat at the other end; metals are excellent thermal conductors. This is because the mobile free electrons carry the heat energy down the rod, passing it on to the ions by colliding with them. Substances without free electrons cannot do this, nor can they conduct electricity well; we have, in the free electrons, an explanation of the fact that the good electrical conductors are the good heat conductors. For technical purposes, it would be useful to have electrical insulators that would conduct heat well, and *vice versa*; but this is almost a contradiction in terms, and one can only compromise.

Non-Conductors and Semi-Conductors

There are some elements, and numerous compounds in which all the electrons are so tightly bound to their parent atoms that free electron flow is impossible. These materials are electrical and thermal insulators.

Let us return to our sodium atom. It readily loses its outer electron, forming a positive ion. The ion is very stable; indeed, its electron arrangement resembles the "closed shell" belonging to the inert gas neon. The chlorine atom, on the other hand, would have a very stable structure, resembling the inert gas argon, if only it could be given one extra electron to complete the closed shell. If the outer sodium electron were given to a chlorine atom we should have two stable ions, one positive and one negative. These would then attract each other and form a compound. This is just how common salt, sodium chloride, is formed, and its crystals consist of a regular network of alternate sodium and chlorine ions. As all the electrons are bound to ions, it is not surprising that salt will not conduct electricity or heat to any appreciable extent. Not all insulating compounds are built on this pattern, but all have structures which bind the electrons tightly.

We saw earlier that Nature does not permit a hard-and-fast distinction between solids and liquids; nor does she between conductors and insulators. Back in the 19th century, Faraday knew of substances which would conduct electricity, but rather badly. A common one is the graphite in pencils. Others are the elements selenium, germanium, and silicon, and a considerable number of compounds. These are called semi- conductors.

The Properties of Semi-Conductors

Semi-conductors conduct badly because they have so few free electrons, many thousands of times fewer than metals. In very cold germanium—say, 200 degrees below freezing—all the electrons are tightly bound to atoms and the substance is an insulator. It differs from normal insulators in that, on warming it, the gradually increasing thermal vibration of the crystal detaches some of the electrons, for they are only moderately tightly bound. The warmer the crystal becomes, the more of its electrons become detached and the better it conducts electricity.

By about the temperature of boiling water, there are so many freed electrons that conduction is moderately good, though less good than in metals. This is basic semi-conductor behaviour. As transistors were made of germanium, and as they were of such great technical importance, more knowledge has accumulated about germanium than about any other material.

Magnetism

The most important thing about magnetism is that it is inseparably connected with electricity. Oersted showed this in July 1820, when he deflected a magnetic compass needle by passing an electric current through a wire near it. Since then, many experiments have shown that wherever a current flows there will certainly be a magnetic field in the surrounding space. The laws of this are very well known now—they are the Maxwell equations previously referred to.

Most people first meet magnetism when they pick up pins with a magnet. Where is the electricity here? What is a magnet?

The explanation of magnetism exemplifies beautifully the technique of explaining the bulk properties of matter in terms of fundamental particles. In the atoms the electrons are moving, and a moving electric charge constitutes an electric current. Therefore each moving electron is a tiny source of magnetism. It does not immediately follow that every atom is a source of magnetism because it might—and often does—happen that the magnetic effect of different electrons in the atom cancel out. In helium atoms, for example, the two electrons have equal but opposed magnetic effects. Nevertheless, some atoms and ions have a net effect called their *magnetic moment*. This simply means they behave like tiny magnets. Crystals containing such atoms will be magnetic, though the magnetism is much weaker than in ordinary magnets because the different atoms largely annul one another's effects. In a very limited number of crystals, however, the magnetic ions act on one another in a special way which forces all the atomic magnets to point in the same direction.

Ferromagnetism

The total effect of many co-operating atoms is very strong and the crystal becomes what we normally call a magnet. Iron acts like this, so do cobalt and nickel, the rarer elements gadolinium and dysprosium, and a fair number of alloys. On the whole, this behaviour, which is called *ferromagnetism*, is very rare. The reason for the co-operation of all the atomic magnets is not explained to everyone's satisfaction yet, though the key idea was given by Heisenberg in 1928.

In the section dealing with the electron it was pointed out that every electron has an *intrinsic* magnetic moment. This is in addition to any effect simply due to the electron's motion round a nucleus. The net effects of ions are therefore partly due to the intrinsic magnetism of electrons. In the ferromagnetic metals the latter is by far the most important contribution. Thus we pick up pins, and benefit from magnets in other ways, because innumerable fundamental particles act in co-operation for reasons that are still somewhat obscure. It is interesting to ask whether the electrons responsible for magnetism are the same free electrons that allow the metals to conduct electricity. It is thought not.

We are accustomed to think of magnets as metallic. Nowadays a number of non-metallic magnets are made. They are called *ferrites*, and some are insulators and some are semi-conductors. The combination of magnetism and insulation is technically very valuable in radio, radar, and other applications. The explanation of ferrite behaviour is related to that of metallic ferromagnetism, but is not the same.

Conclusion

The aim of the second part of this account of physics is to show how our conception of fundamental particles allows us to build theories of the properties of matter. This very aim shows that the two "major divisions" of physics referred to at the beginning are divided only in the way that labour is divided by co-operating workers to lighten the task. For the task of physics is a very great one—no less than to explain the behaviour of matter; and since the universe, living and inanimate, is made of matter, physics must necessarily underlie all the other sciences.

III. THE WORLD OF THE CHEMISTS

WHAT CHEMISTRY IS ABOUT

Chemistry is the scientific study of the preparation, composition and architecture of chemical compounds, and of the modes and mechanisms of their transformations or reactions. Natural (and other) processes can be classified as *physical*, in which no chemical reactions occur, for example water running down a hill, and *chemical* if changes occur in the chemical compounds involved. Common examples are the burning of fuel, whether in a biological cell, an internal combustion engine, or a lowly domestic grate. Biological changes at the molecular level in plants and animals generally consist of many chemical reactions, as do some geological changes in rocks and deposits. Chemistry therefore is rooted in physics and interpenetrates biology (biochemistry) and geology (geochemistry). Some of the main sub-divisions of chemistry are delineated in the Table. Chemists not only aim to discover new reactions by trial and error, but by seeking to understand chemical change aspire to design new compounds and reactions. New reactions can be used to produce useful physical *effects* in new ways—like light from the cold chemical candle (chemiluminescence) as the firefly does, and electricity from more efficient batteries and from fuel cells—or to produce new *synthetic products*. These can be faithful copies of compounds like penicillin which have been discovered first in nature, or completely new, invented, compounds like sulphonamide drugs.

This research activity, which is mainly centred in the Universities, is the basis of a large chemical industry, one of the major manufacturing industries. Other branches which deal with more restrictive topics or use combinations of the above for specific goals have names which are self-explanatory, for example:—analytical chemistry, colloid chemistry, pharmaceutical chemistry, chemistry of dyes, petroleum chemistry, polymer chemistry, environmental and medicinal chemistry.

ELEMENTS AND COMPOUNDS

Elements

The reader will find a description of the formation of chemical elements in Part I. They are listed alphabetically in the **Table of Elements** (with their chemical symbols) and in order of atomic number in the **Periodic Table**. Other details may be found in **Section L**. They vary widely in natural abundance terrestrially.

In the earth's crust the most abundant elements are oxygen (O), silicon (Si), aluminium (Al), and iron (Fe). Our familiarity with them varies too, not only because of the rarity of some (thulium, Tm, and radium, Ra) and the artificiality of a few (plutonium, Pu) but because we meet some only in combination with other elements and not in their elemental state, for example, fluorine (F) in fluorides. The most familiar non-metallic elements besides oxygen and nitrogen in their gaseous molecular states (O_2 and N_2) are probably carbon (C), as graphite (or diamond!) and sulphur (S). Among the metallic elements most people know aluminium (Al), tin (Sn) and lead (Pb) from the main groups of the Periodic Table, and the transition metals: iron (Fe), chromium (Cr), nickel (Ni) as well as copper (Cu) and the precious metals silver (Ag), gold (Au) and platinum (Pt). Increasingly familiar because of their use in semi-conductors are the metalloids silicon (Si) and germanium (Ge).

Compounds

Most terrestrial matter as we know it can be classified in terms of the chemical compounds it contains, *i.e.*, is a mixture of compounds. Each compound consists of chemical elements in combination, the relative amount of each being characteristic and definite (Law of Constant Composition). Compounds vary not only in the number of elements combined but also in their proportions: carbon dioxide has twice as much oxygen per carbon as carbon monoxide (*see* atoms and molecules).

The properties of a compound can be, and normally are, very different from the properties of the elements it contains, a fact not commonly recognised in the popular imagination, witness phrases like—"it's good for you, it's got iron in it". This does not mean that elemental metallic iron is present but rather that some seemingly beneficial compound of iron is present. The ambiguity is that although iron is essential to human life in the form of haemoglobin in the blood, it also can form highly poisonous compounds. Similarly arsenic (As), although notoriously poisonous as the element and in some of its compounds, was nevertheless contained in one of the first chemotherapeutic drugs ever produced, salvarsan. The point can be further illustrated with sodium chloride, a water-soluble white crystalline solid, which is a compound of the very reactive metal sodium (capable of reacting violently with water), and of chlorine (known as a poisonous green gas). Similarly diamond (a particular elemental form, or allotrope, of carbon) is one of the hardest known substances but may be combined with hydrogen (the highly inflammable gas which can combine with oxygen gas to give water), to give thousands of different derivatives which include benzene (a liquid), methane (a gas) and various hydrocarbon waxes and polishes.

ATOMS AND MOLECULES

Atoms vary in weight, structure and size from one element to the next, as discussed earlier. Molecules are made from whole numbers of atoms in combination. A particular molecule is characterised by the number of atoms of each of its constituent elements. It has a characteristic weight

MAIN DIVISIONS OF CHEMISTRY		
	Elements, Compounds and reactions involved	*Examples*
Organic Chemistry	Carbon in combination mainly with H, O, N.	Natural products Carbohydrates Steroids Proteins
Inorganic Chemistry	All elements and compounds not covered in organic chemistry. Minerals and salts.	Inorganic polymers (*e.g.*, silicones) Transition metal complexes Organometallic compounds
Physical Chemistry	Mathematical and physical descriptions of organic and inorganic compounds and reactions.	Electrochemistry Chemical thermodynamics Molecular spectroscopy Photochemistry
Biochemistry	The chemistry of biological systems	Enzymes Biosynthesis.

called its *molecular weight* (the sum of the weights of the atoms in it), and a characteristic three dimensional structure (*see below*).

An aggregate of molecules of the same type is a chemical compound, so that the molecule is to a compound as the atom is to an element.

The Mole

It is frequently very useful to know when the amounts of two compounds are the same, not in terms of their masses but in terms of the number of molecules each contains, since chemical reactions occur at the molecular level and involve small integral numbers of molecules of the reacting species at each step. Avogadro first suggested that equal volumes of gases under identical conditions contained equal molecular numbers and it followed that if the weights of two substances were in the ratio of their relative molecular masses (molecular weights) then they too contained equal numbers of molecules. The approximate molecular weights of water (H_2O) and ethanol or ethylalcohol (C_2H_5OH) are 18 and 46 respectively and so 18 g of water for example contain the same number of molecules as 46 g of ethanol.

The amount of substance referred to in each case is called 1 mole. For any compound the weight of 1 mole is equal to the gramme molecular weight. Molecular weights (or relative molecular masses) are now referred to the carbon-12 atomic scale. The modern definition of the mole therefore is that it is the amount of substance which contains the same number of elementary particles as there are atoms in twelve grammes of carbon-12. This number, called Avogadro's number, is $6.022\,169 \times 10^{23}$.

Molecular Structure and Isomers

Modern spectroscopic and diffraction methods have enabled the details of molecular structures to be accurately determined not only with respect to the distances between atoms (normally in the range 1–5 Å", *i.e.*, 100–150 pm for adjacent atoms) and the angles which define the structure, but also with respect to the various internal motions (vibrations and rotations).

Sometimes two (or more) different compounds have the same molecular weight (and are called, therefore, *isomers*) but have different molecular structures in which the same atoms are arranged in different relative positions, and hence have different properties. If two isomeric structures are related as left and right hands are related, the isomers are stereoisomers of a particular class called enantiomers. An example is glucose. Even such subtle variation as this produces differences in properties which can be crucial in biological function or drug metabolism.

A familiar simple example of *structural* isomers are ethylalcohol (or ethanol) and dimethyl ether of formula C_2H_6O. They each can be represented by the structural formulae

$$CH_3-CH_2-OH \text{ and } \begin{matrix} CH_3 \\ O \\ CH_3 \end{matrix}$$

in which the lines represent some of the *covalent chemical bonds* (*see below*). It is these interatomic forces which hold the atoms in specific spatial arrangements. Some examples are shown on **T25**.

CHEMICAL BONDING

The number of possible arrangements of a given set of atoms is limited since each type of atom (each element) is capable of forming only a limited number of bonds, equal to its *valency*. The valency varies from element to element; hydrogen has a valency of one (exceptionally two); oxygen, two; nitrogen, three; and carbon four (hence the molecular formulae H_2, H_2O, NH_3 and CH_4 for hydrogen, water, ammonia and methane respectively).

In some compounds two atoms may be joined by a *multiple bond* so that the valency number may be reached. Examples are the double and triple bonds in ethylene (ethene) and acetylene (ethyne respectively:

$$CH_2 = CH_2 \text{ and } CH \equiv CH$$

The modern theory of chemical bonding is electronic. Bonds are formed:

(i) by the sharing of electrons in pairs between two bonded atoms (*covalent* bonding); or

(ii) by the transfer of an electron from one atom to another to form oppositely charged ions (*ionic* bonding).

The ionic situation is electrically *polar* whereas pure covalent bonds have no polarity. If, however, the shared electrons are not shared equally between the bound atoms some effective electron transfer occurs and the bond has some polar character. Covalent bonds between *dissimilar* atoms are generally polar. If one of the two atoms provides *both* the shared electrons, the polarity is particularly high and the bond is called *dative covalent*.

VALENCIES OF THE ELEMENTS

Electronic Theory of Valency

These ideas of the chemical bond lead to a ready explanation of the valencies of the elements (which are periodic if the elements are arranged in order of atomic number) when combined with knowledge of the electronic structure of atoms.

In the original Bohr theory the electrons of atoms move in well defined orbits arranged in shells. The known elements use seven shells, and each element has its unique number of electrons equal to the atomic number, Z ranging from 1 in hydrogen to 103 in lawrencium. Each element also has its unique arrangement of its electrons in these shells. The build-up of electrons in the above sequence follows well-defined rules. The resulting electron configuration of the elements is an important starting point for a discussion of valency. The shells each have a limited capacity and the numbers of electrons that can be accommodated in the first four labelled 1, 2, 3, 4 (or sometimes K, L, M, N) are 2, 8, 18, 32 respectively. Each of these shells has sub-shells of which there are four main types designated s, p, d and f which can contain 2, 6, 10 and 14 electrons respectively. If all the orbits in a shell have electrons actually present in them the shell is filled or closed and this confers on the shell an unusual stability or inertness. Conversely, unfilled shells lead to activity and the electrons in the incompletely filled shells largely determine the chemical and physical properties of the element and are responsible for the combination of atoms to form molecules. These electrons are referred to as *valence electrons*. The inner shell, *i.e.*, the one nearest the nucleus, can accommodate only two electrons (the element helium has just that number) and the next two shells can hold eight each.

Electropositive Elements

Large atoms, *e.g.*, lead, radium, have many filled shells and, subject to special rules, the general rule is that the inner shells are the filled ones and the outer shell may be incomplete. Elements which have equal numbers of electrons in their outer shell resemble each other and come in the same Group of the Periodic Table. Thus the elements with complete electronic shells are chemically unreactive gases, *e.g.*, argon and neon (minor constituents of the atmosphere). Elements with just one electron in the outer shell are highly reactive metals, *e.g.*, sodium and potassium which lose this electron readily to give monopositive ions, *e.g.*, Na^+. These elements are called electropositive. Contrariwise elements with just one electron too few are electronegative and readily gain one electron either by sharing, or by capture (to form anions, *e.g.*, Cl^-).

More generally, at least for the light elements of Periods 2 and 3 of the Periodic Table, the valence of an element is given by the Group Number, N, *i.e.*, the number of valence electrons which must be lost by the electropositive metals, or by $8-N$, the number of electrons which electronegative elements need to gain.

VALENCE ELECTRONS (N) AND VALENCY (V)

N = 1	2	3	4	5	6	7	8
V = 1	2	3	4	3	2	1	0
Hydrogen							Helium
Sodium	Magnesium	Aluminium	Carbon	Nitrogen	Oxygen	Fluorine	Neon
Potassium	Calcium	Gallium	Silicon	Phosphorus	Sulphur	Chlorine	Argon
			Germanium	Arsenic		Bromine	
			Tin			Iodine	
	Barium		Lead				

←————————— Metals —————————→ ←————————————→ Non-metals:
　　　　　Positive ions　　　　　　　　　　　Covalent　　　Negative ions
　　　　　　　　　　　　　　　　　　　　　　compounds　　or covalent compounds

The covalence of an electronegative element is increased by one if it loses one electron to form a positive ion, and decreased by one if it gains an electron. Thus nitrogen with a covalence 3 can give either N^- which can form 4 covalent bonds (in the ammonium ion, NH_4^-) or the N^- ion with a covalency of 2 (e.g., NH_2^-). Similarly oxygen can give H_3O^+, the hydroxonium ion (the acid principle in water), H_2O (water itself), and OH^- (the hydroxyl ion).

IONIC BONDS, SALTS AND ACIDS

These bonds are normally formed between electropositive elements (at the left of the Periodic Table, e.g., sodium and potassium) and electronegative elements (at the right of the Periodic Table, e.g., oxygen, fluorine, chlorine). The ionic charge may be determined from the valency: Na^+, Mg^{++}, Al^{+++}; $O^=$, Cl^-.

Ions may contain a number of atoms, as shown by many of the common anions: hydroxyl, OH^-; nitrate, NO_3^-; sulphate, SO_4^{2-}; carbonate $CO_3^=$. Ionic solids formed from a metal ion and one of these anions are called *salts* and are derived from the parent *acid* in which the anion is bound to a *hydrogen ion* (or ions): HNO_3, nitric acid; H_2SO_4, sulphuric acid. Sulphuric acid can form two series of salts, one called *normal* based upon the SO_4^{--} ion and a second (called acid salts since they contain a hydrogen) based upon the HSO_4^- ion. Phosphoric acid, H_3PO_4, has three series of salts. A substance which reacts with an acid to form a salt and water as the only products is called a *base*. An example is sodium hydroxide, NaOH (caustic soda).

The ionic forces are less directional in character than covalent bonds are, but in solids the ions are in regular fixed arrangements (see Part II). Each anion is surrounded by cations and is attracted to them by electrostatic Coulomb forces. These are of long range and so the anion is attracted not only to the closest cations. Additionally each cation is surrounded by anions so that the bonding is not localised. The whole solid therefore is like a giant molecule and is not easily broken down by melting. This contrasts with covalent compounds in which the forces between molecules are small, the main attractions being within the molecule.

The structures adopted depend upon the relative numbers of the anions and cations (which are determined by ionic charges) and by the relative ionic sizes, which have been deduced from X-ray diffraction measurements.

COVALENT BONDS

In the simple theory the shared electron pairs are localised between two atoms. Multiple bonds result when there are more pairs shared. The multiplicity (or *bond order*) is then integral. The theory may be extended by admitting that an electron pair may be shared between more than two atoms in *delocalised bonding* which can then give rise to fractional bond orders. The best example is benzene (and graphite) where nine pairs of electrons are shared between six carbon-carbon bonds giving a bond order of 1·5.

Theories of Valency

Modern theories of valency make use of the concepts of quantum mechanics (see T17) in which each of the well-defined electron orbits of the s, p, d and f electrons in the Bohr theory is replaced by the idea of the electron cloud with a spatial electron density and distribution. Each of these electron clouds (now called an orbital) has a definite shape depending upon the type of electrons. The orbitals of s electrons are of spherical shape with a density that falls off with the distance from the nucleus. The peak density occurs at the old Bohr radius. Electrons of the p type have orbitals with double lobes giving the figure of eight or dumbell shape. There are three such orbitals in every shell except the first and they are arranged mutually at right angles. Each one can contain two electrons giving a total of six. The d orbitals are five in number. Each again can contain two electrons giving a total of ten. Four of these d orbitals have shapes like four-leaf clovers, whereas the fifth has two lobes, rather like the p orbitals but with the addition of a torus or doughnut. The shapes of the f orbitals are even more complicated. It is the shape of these orbitals and their relative spatial arrangement which gives the covalent bond its directional character.

Molecular Orbital

The idea of electron sharing between two atoms becomes the notion of overlap of an orbital on one atom with an orbital on another to give a bonding *molecular orbital* which can contain the pair of shared electrons. The bond energy is a maximum when this overlap is optimum and this occurs when the atoms are in certain definite positions thus giving the molecule its own characteristic shape.

Molecular Shape

For elements from the second row of the Periodic Table the number of electrons in the valence shell can be eight arranged in four pairs of orbitals (one 2s and three 2p orbitals). These orbitals can be combined or *hybridised* to give the basic tetrahedral shape (see Fig. 1). Each of these can overlap with say an orbital of a hydrogen atom (the 1s) to give a bonding orbital which can accommodate two electrons. Alternatively each orbital can, if the atom has enough electrons, contain two non-bonding electrons called a *lone pair*. The basic molecular shapes of methane (CH_4), ammonia (NH_3), and water (H_2O) may then be rationalised as in Fig. 1.

The bond angle in methane is the tetrahedral angle (109° 28'). The angles in ammonia (107° 18') and water (104° 30') are smaller probably because the lone pair orbital is slightly more repulsive than the bonding orbital is. This closes down the angles between the bonds.

The lone pairs may be used to bind the hydrogen ions from acids to give tetrahedral NH_4^- and pyramidal H_3O^-. It is the lone pairs therefore which give ammonia and water their basicity. In the modern concept of acids and bases due to Lewis, a base is an electron donor and an acid becomes an electron acceptor. This definition of an acid includes the older idea of it as a hydrogen ion

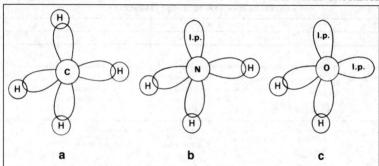

a   **b**   **c**

Fig. 1. The spatial arrangements of the atoms and orbitals in (a) methane (CH_4), (b) ammonia (NH_3) and (c) water (H_2O). The basic shape is tetrahedral and the hybridised orbitals are lone pair orbitals (l.p.) and bonding orbitals.

producer in that the hydrogen ion is an electron acceptor but it is more general—a Lewis acid need not be a protic acid.

Bond Lengths

Many covalent bond distances have been measured and each may be apportioned between the bound atoms to give a self-consistent set of covalent bond-radii for each element which can be used in predictions of molecular structures. These radii vary inversely with the bond order involved. Thus the carbon-carbon bond length varies from 154 pm (*i.e.*, 10^{12}m) for C–C to 135 pm for C=C.

Bond Energies

Bonds differ in their strength depending upon the atoms and the bond order. A double bond between two given atoms is stronger than a single bond but generally not as strong as two single bonds. Thus "unsaturated" compounds, which contain multiple bonds, will tend to form "saturated" compounds containing only single bonds since the energetics are favourable.

Functional Groups

Compounds may be further classified according to certain persistent groups of atoms which have a residual valency and can combine with other groups. Thus the methyl group (CH_3) related to methane (CH_4) by the removal of a hydrogen atom can combine with other atoms or groups of valency one: methyl chloride (chloromathane), CH_3Cl; methyl alcohol (methanol), CH_3OH; dimethyl ether, CH_3OCH_3. Common functional groups are shown in the table.

CHEMICAL ENERGETICS

Chemical reactions are accompanied by energy changes which can be utilised as heat (in fires) or mechanical work (in explosions or rockets), or to produce electric current in batteries. Chemical compounds can therefore be said to store energy and to possess "internal energy". The energy can be thought of as being stored in the chemical bonds. The energy change (at constant volume) in a reaction is then a result of changes (denoted ΔU) in the nett internal energy of the reactants and products by the law of the conservation of energy. If the conditions are those of constant pressure, the energy change is due to overall changes in a closely related properly called enthalpy (ΔH).

It was at one time thought that reactions would proceed only if energy was given out (*exothermic* processes). Although this is now known to be

SOME CLASSES OF SIMPLE ORGANIC COMPOUNDS		
Name	**General Description and Formula**	**Examples**
Alkanes (or paraffins)	"Saturated" hydrocarbons of the general formula C_nH_{2n+2} Contain single bonds only	methane (CH_4) butane (C_4H_{10})
Alkenes (olefins)	"Unsaturated" hydrocarbons of general formula C_nH_{2n} Contain double bonds	ethylene (C_2H_4) styrene ($C_6H_5.C_2H_3$)
Alkynes (acetylenes)	"Unsaturated" hydrocarbon of general formula C_nH_{2n-2} Contain triple bonds	acetylene (C_2H_2)
Alcohols	Contain the OH group, bound for example to an alkyl group $C_nH_{2n+1}OH$	methylalcohol (CH_3OH) ethylalcohol (C_2H_5OH)
Ketones	Contain the C=O group $C_nH_{2n+1}C=O$	acetone ($CH_3)_2CO$
Aldehydes	Contain the CHO group	formaldehyde (HCHO) acetaldehyde (CH_3CHO)
Aromatic hydrocarbons	Ring compounds with reactions similiar to the proto type, benzene (C_6H_6)	napthalene ($C_{10}H_8$) anthracene ($C_{14}H_{10}$)
Phenyl compounds	Derivatives of the phenyl group, C_6H_5	phenol (C_6H_5OH) aniline ($C_6H_5NH_2$)
Heterocyclic compounds	Ring compounds containing mainly carbon atoms and one or more other atoms, *e.g.*, nitrogen	pyridine (C_5H_5N) thiophene (C_4H_4S)

true at the lowest temperature, in other cases a second consideration, the entropy term, needs to be considered, as the existence of *endothermic* changes confirms. A new "energy" term defined to contain the entropy consideration and called the Gibbs Free Energy, *G*, may then be used. Natural or "spontaneous" processes are accompanied by a decrease in the nett value of *G*, and systems tend to assume whichever state has the lowest value of *G*.

Chemical Equilibrium

Certain chemical changes, like physical changes such as raising and lowering weights, or freezing and melting water, may be easily reversed. The forward and backward reactions which are proceeding continuously can then be made to balance out, given enough time, and the system is said to be in equilibrium.

Suppose that *X* and *Y* when mixed are partially converted to *Z* and an equilibrium mixture is obtained under certain defined conditions. The relative amounts $[X]$, $[Y]$, *etc.*, are then definite and governed by the equilibrium constant defined as

$$K = \frac{[Z]}{[X][Y]}$$

Putting it in another way, if we know *K* we can predict the relative amounts of products and reactants, *i.e.*, the extent to which the reaction proceeds. *K* in turn depends upon the change in Gibbs Free Energy for the reaction:

$$\Delta G = -RT \ln K$$

where *R* is the gas constant, and *T* the absolute temperature, and ln denotes the natural logarithm.

Chemical Thermodynamics

The efficiency of a reaction therefore can be predicted theoretically since values for ΔG can frequently be calculated from tabulated values of ΔH and ΔS. Such studies constitute *chemical thermodynamics*, the branch of thermodynamics applied to chemical reactions. It is an essential consideration in industrial processes.

Bond Enthalpies

The enthalpy (*q.v.*) of a molecule can be thought of as the sum of the enthalpies associated with each covalent bond, for each of which there is a characteristic value. Determination and tabulation of these bond energies helps in the prediction of enthalpy changes in new reactions involving covalent molecules. Similarly for ionic solids.

THE SPEED OF REACTIONS—CATALYSIS

A good analogy to illustrate the difference between chemical thermodynamics and kinetics is the downhill flow of water. The water will seek the lowest point where it has the lowest potential energy, and in an analogous way a reaction will try to proceed to the state with the lowest Gibbs Free Energy. However, the speed of both water flow and reaction will depend upon a large number of factors, particularly the available *pathway* (or reaction mechanism). Indeed water at the top of a mountain or in a domestic bath may not flow down at all if a suitable path is blocked say by a hillock (or bath plug). The unblocking may involve the expenditure of energy, for example to lift the water over the dam (or pull out the plug).

Activation Energy

In reactions this type of energy is called the *activation energy*. It can be supplied in a number of ways (*see below*) such as heating. Sometimes it is small and (thankfully) at other times it is large enough that thermodynamically feasible reactions do not occur at all quickly. Each of us is, in fact, *thermodynamically* unstable with respect to our combustion products, mainly CO_2 and H_2O, *i.e.*, we should burn (!), but fortunately we are *kinetically stable*.

Catalysts

A *catalyst* is a substance which will provide an alternative reaction pathway of low activation energy, *i.e.*, it can speed up a reaction, without itself being consumed in the process. The analogy for the water flow would be a tunnel through the hillock.

Catalysts are very important industrially, for example, in the manufacture of sulphuric acid (using platinised asbestos or vanadium pentoxide), in the Haber process for ammonia used for fertilisers (iron derivatives), and in the "cracking" of crude oil to give lighter oils (aluminium oxide). Natural catalysts are called *enzymes* (*q.v.*).

CLASSIFICATION OF REACTIONS

Chemical change can be brought about by a variety of techniques used separately or together:

mixing of single substances

heating single substances or mixtures

electrolysing solutions

exposure to light or radiation

addition of catalysts.

The changes can be classified according to the results produced:

Dissociation—breakdown into simpler substances or ions

Addition—in which one type of molecule or ion is added to another

Polymerisation—reaction of a substance (monomer) with itself to produce larger molecules of the same composition (polymer)

Substitution—in which one particular group in a molecule is replaced by another

Elimination—in which one particular group in a molecule is lost

Exchange—in which two groups are mutually substituted one by the other

Oxidation—removal of electrons (increase of oxidation number), *e.g.*, Fe^{++} ferrous ion is oxidised to ferric, Fe^{+++}

Reduction—the converse of oxidation

Classification by Molecular Mechanism

More significantly modern classifications are based upon the precise *molecular mechanism* employed. Examples are

Nucleophilic attack—where an electron-rich reagent attacks a position of low electron density in a molecule

Electrophilic attack—where an electron-depleted reagent—an electrophile (for example, a positive ion)—attacks a position of high electron density

Bimolecular reaction—one which involves two molecules unlike a monomolecular reaction which involves only one in each step

Precise descriptions can be built up: substitution, nucleophilic, bimolecular.

ELECTROLYTES, ELECTROLYSIS AND ELECTROCHEMICAL CELLS

Electrolytic Solutions

Ionic solids can dissolve in some solvents especially if each has a high dielectric constant to cut down the force of attraction between oppositely charged ions. The process can be assisted by solvation of the ions and also by the entropy changes which favour the less ordered state of affairs—the liquid rather than the ordered solid.

Electrolysis

The oppositely charged ions are capable of independent movement and the application of an electric potential from an external battery or source of direct current to electrodes in the solution will cause the ions to move. The positive ions (cations) will move to the negatively charged electrode (the cathode) and the negatively charged ions (anions) to the positively charged anode. At the electrodes chemical changes occur and ions may be converted to uncharged species and deposited: for example, sodium ions (Na^+) to sodium metal, Na. This process is referred to as electrolysis. Faraday discovered two laws of electrolysis: (i) the amount of any substance deposited (or dissolved) is proportional to the amount of electricity used; (ii) the relative amounts of substances deposited by the same quantity of electricity are in the ratio of their *equivalent weights*.

For any ion discharged below a certain value of the applied voltage the *discharge voltage* is small. In an electrolyte containing many different ionic species therefore, each ionic discharge will occur only as the appropriate potential is reached. For solutions of acids, hydrogen (formed from H^+ ions) is discharged at the cathode, and oxygen (formed from OH^- ions) at the anode. Electrolysis is important commercially for the refining of metals, electroplating, and in the production of many basic chemicals.

Electrochemical Cells

Ever since 1800 when Volta produced an electric battery consisting of alternate plates of silver and zinc separated by cloth impregnated with salt, the search for new batteries has been continuous. In each new battery a different chemical process is harnessed to produce electrical energy. The battery must not only be feasible according to the laws of thermodynamics, but must be practicable and cheap for widespread consumer use.

The voltages developed in any battery can be predicted from a knowledge of the two processes occurring: one at the cathode and the other at the anode. Voltages can be ascribed to each of these "half cells" according to the chemical reaction which occurs and the condition used, for example concentrations of the reactants (the so-called "standard electrode potentials"). The voltage of any combination of two half cells is the sum of the half-cell voltages. Furthermore each of these voltages is related to the change in the Gibbs Free Energy for its reaction and can, in theory, therefore be predicted thermodynamically.

CHEMISTRY IN MODERN LIFE

Chemistry plays a crucial role in modern life, not least in the third world, as well as in the more developed nations. In the UK chemistry has been studied, developed and put to practical use as well as anywhere in the world in modern times. It is no accident that the largest specialised scientific society in the UK is the Royal Society of Chemistry (RSC) and that its forerunner, The Chemical Society, lays claim to being the oldest in the world. The high quality of chemical science at the crucial level of basic research is indicated by the remarkable frequency with which the Nobel Prize in Chemistry has come to the UK The success is not confined to academic activity but, surely as a consequence, it extends to the economic life of the nation.

The UK Chemical Industry

The UK chemical industry is among the largest in the world and one of the most successful. It employs around 200,000 people in over 3,000 companies. In national statistics it is included in the manufacturing sector alongside other sectors which have a high chemical component such as petroleum and petroleum products. Its output covers a very wide range. Firstly there are the so called "basic chemicals", such as sulphuric acid, which are utilised in the manufacturing processes of other sectors.

Chemicals in Agriculture

In agriculture chemicals are not only important in the form of bulk products such as fertilizer, without which modern agriculture could not operate efficiently, but also for the 'finer' chemicals such as herbicides and insecticides. Manufactured synthetic polymers and plastics are omnipresent in modern life, for example in architecture and building as well as in many familiar household products and uses. The list here is long and includes moulded casings for televisions and other electronic and electrical products, kitchen utensils, all forms of coverings from paints and varnishes to fabrics. Then there are the "fine" chemicals: cosmetics and pharmaceuticals, ranging from vanity products to the birth control pill and life-saving synthetic drugs. Petroleum products from oil cover an extremely wide range. Petroleum is a most valuable "feed stock" for other products and in this use it is arguably more unique and precious than as a fuel or energy source.

IV. BIOLOGY—THE SCIENCE OF LIFE

WHAT BIOLOGY IS ABOUT

Biology embraces the study of all living things which exist on earth at the present time and also the recognisable remains of those that are extinct. Living things or organisms range from the apparently simple micro-organisms such as viruses and bacteria to the largest animals and plants.

Living Processes

The enormous variation and complexity of living processes make the task of understanding and defining life a very difficult one. Every living organism undergoes continual physical and chemical changes which, in spite of their diversity, are referred to as the metabolism of the organism. Metabolism involves the processing of food materials, the production of waste products, and all the intermediate stages between these whereby energy and matter are provided for the operation, maintenance, and growth of the organism. These reactions are under very exact chemical or nervous control at every stage and can be slowed down or speeded up as the need arises. Thus the organism can react to changes in the environment in which it lives, adjusting its activities in relation to the external changes. Finally, organisms can reproduce either in an identical or very slightly modified form. In this process new individuals are produced and the species continues to survive.

Differences between offspring and parents can, under certain circumstances, act cumulatively over many generations and so form the basis of evolutionary change in which new species of organism are ultimately formed. Viruses occupy a middle ground between biology and chemistry, as do the more recently discovered transposons, which are organisms in the genetic sense of undergoing replication but are so simple that they are amenable to chemical analysis. However, since these are intimately dependent on cellular organisms, they are included in the study of biology rather than chemistry.

Molecular Biology

It has been evident for many years that the most fundamental aspects of these living processes occur in basic structural units known as cells. The study of living processes at the molecular and cell level has been given a tremendous impetus in recent years by the advent of new techniques which enable microscopic and submicroscopic parts of cells to be examined. Physicists, chemists, and mathematicians have found themselves working alongside biologists in this field and several of the very notable advances have been made by physical scientists.

Molecular biology is a term frequently used in describing this rapidly expanding and fascinating field of research. A guide to some of the key terms in this field can be found on **T46–8**.

EVOLUTION

Introduction.—The idea that species of living organisms could change over long periods of time was considered by some Greek writers and, much later, by the Frenchmen Buffon and Lamarck at the end of the 18th cent. Further, the work of the 18th cent. geologists such as James Hutton and William Smith provided a basis without which the major contribution of Darwin, the great 19th cent. naturalist, would have been impossible. Hutton showed that the earth's surface had undergone prolonged upheavals and volcanic eruptions with consequent changes in sea level. This implied that the earth was much older than had previously been supposed. Smith developed a method of dating the geological strata by means of the fossils found in them and demon-

strated that widely different types of animals and plants existed at different periods of the earth's history. Later in this section (**T63–6**) a more detailed picture is presented of the geological record of evolution.

These discoveries conflicted with the Biblical account in the book of Genesis and, although various attempts were made to explain them away or discredit them, it became abundantly clear that through milllions of years life has been continually changing, with new species constantly arising and many dying out.

The Evidence for Evolution

1. The Geological Record.—It has already been pointed out that successively younger rocks contain fossil remains of different and relatively more complex organisms. The spore-bearing plants preceded the gymnosperms and the angiosperms arose much later. Similarly in the vertebrate series the fish appeared before the amphibia which were followed by the reptiles and later by the air breathing, warm-blooded birds and mammals.

On a more restricted level the evolution of the horse has been worked out in great detail from the small *Eohippus* which was about a foot high and had four digits on the forefeet and three on the hind-feet to the large one-toed animal living today.

However, such complete series are rare and the geological record is very incomplete. There are a number of gaps, particularly between the major groups of organisms. No satisfactory fossil evidence is known of the ancestors of the angiosperms so perhaps they did not grow in conditions which favoured their preservation as fossils. On the other hand, *Archæopteryx* provides an indisputable link between the reptiles and the birds. For more discussion of these topics, *see* **T64–6**.

Although we talk about the age of fishes, the age of reptiles and so on it must be emphasised that these are the periods during which particular groups were abundant or even dominant. Each group probably originated many millions of years before it became widespread. Further, some groups, such as the giant reptiles and the seed-ferns, died out completely whereas others, the fishes and true ferns for example, are still common today although many fishes and ferns that exist today are very different from those of the Devonian and Carboniferous periods. On the other hand some species, *e.g.* the maidenhair tree, have remained unaltered for many millions of years.

2. Geographical Distribution.—Nearly all the marsupials or pouched mammals are found in the Australian continent which was cut off from the mainland about 60 million years ago. All the fossil evidence indicates that at that time the eutherian or placental mammals did not yet exist. The marsupials are the only naturally occurring mammals in Australia but since the isolation of the continent has given rise to a large number of species very similar in appearance to those which evolved elsewhere in the world among the eutherian mammals. There are marsupials which look like wolves, dogs, cats and squirrels; yet they have no close biological relationships to these animals. Further, some marsupials such as the kangaroos have evolved which are unlike any other creatures in the rest of the world. Quite clearly the isolation of Australia so long ago has resulted in the evolution of these distinct types, just as Darwin found in the Galapagos islands where each has its own distinct flora and fauna which differ also from those of the S. American mainland.

3. Anatomy.—The comparative study of the development and mature structure of the mammalian body provides much evidence that all the species have evolved from a single ancestral stock.

Although the arm of an ape, the leg of a dog, the flipper of a whale and the wing of a a bat appear very different externally they are all built on the same skeletal plan. It would be difficult to explain such similarities unless they had all evolved from a common type. There is also evidence that the early development of an animal recapitulates its biological history to a certain extent. For example, the gill slits found in fish are formed during the early stages in the development of a mammal although later they disappear. Finally, apparently useless vestigial structures sometimes occur which would be inexplicable unless regarded in the light of an evolutionary history. In man a small appendix and vestiges of a third eyelid occur but these are functionless although in other animals such structures are well developed and functional, *e.g.*, the appendix in the rabbit.

4. Human Selection.—During his brief history on earth modern man has continually selected and bred animals and plants for his own use. We have only to look at the various breeds of dogs which have been developed from a single wild type to see that under certain circumstances great structural divergence can occur in a species even in a relatively short time. The advent of genetic engineering may represent a qualitatively new form of evolution: many can now bypass the slow process of natural selection for small beneficial alterations in a species by rapid laboratory screening for dramatic changes selected to his advantage.

The Darwinian Theory of Evolution.—Darwin amassed a great deal of information such as that outlined above which convinced him that evolution of life had taken place over millions of years. His was the first real attempt to collect all the evidence scientifically and no other satisfactory alternative explanation of all the facts he presented has been proposed. Perhaps even more important was his attempt to explain *how* evolution had actually occurred. He published his theory after many years of work in his book *The Origin of Species by Means of Natural Selection* in 1859. Some of his ideas have since been modified owing to our increased knowledge of genetics but they are so important that it is worth-while recounting his theory.

1. The Struggle for Existence.—It is clear that in nature there is a severe struggle for existence in all animals and plants. Over a period of time the number of individuals of a species in a given community does not vary greatly. This implies that the number of progeny which survive to become mature breeding individuals more or less replaces the number of mature ones that die. Generally speaking the reproductive output of a species is much greater than this. For example, a single large foxglove plant may produce half a million seeds each one of which is potentially capable of giving rise to a new individual. Obviously nearly all the progeny die before reaching maturity and the chance of any single one surviving is very remote.

2. Variation.—The individuals of any generation of human beings obviously differ from one another and such differences are found in other organisms. It is clear that they vary considerably in structure, colour, activity and so on. Darwin also pointed out that generally these variations were passed on from one generation to the next, for example, the children of tall parents tend to grow tall.

3. Survival of the Fittest.—If there is an intense struggle for existence in their natural environment among individuals of a species having different characteristics, those which are best "fitted" to a given set of conditions are most likely to survive to maturity. These will reproduce and the features which enabled them to survive will be passed on to their offspring. This process is liable to continue and a species will become better adapted to its environment.

4. Natural Selection.—Over a long period of time the environment of a given species is never stable but will change in various ways. As it does so

the characters which best fit the individuals to the changed environment will be selected. If an environmental change affects only part of the range occupied by a species, the populations living in different parts may adapt and come to differ so much that they are no longer able to interbreed, with the result that the original species has now become two distinct species.

Darwin and Lamarck.—Darwin pictured evolution as a slow continuous process with natural selection operating on the small inheritable variations found between the individuals of a species which were undergoing intense competition. This neglects the important effect of the environment on the growth and structure of the individual. It is obvious that external conditions will affect the development of an organism, for example the effect of various soil conditions on the growth of a plant or the amount of food material available to an animal. Lamarck maintained that the characters acquired by an individual owing to the effect of its environment could be passed on to its offspring. Undoubtedly characters are acquired by the individual during its growth but in spite of many attempts to prove otherwise no experiments have been done which prove conclusively that these are inherited by the offspring. Thus Lamarck's theory that evolution has occurred by the inheritance of acquired characters is not widely acceptable today.

Neodarwinism and the "Selfish Gene"

Darwinism received something of a setback during the early years of modern genetics. There did not seem to be much in common between the large mutations studied by geneticists and the small continuous variations which Darwin thought were the basic material upon which selection acted. With time, it became evident that not all mutations are large in their effects and that much of the continuous variation which occurs does indeed have a genetic basis. Mathematicians showed that even small selective advantages would cause genes to spread throughout populations as the generations passed by. Further development of this idea has led to the 'selfish gene' model, in which the struggle for existence, variation and survival of the fittest operate at the level of genes rather than whole animals, which are relegated to the role of mere vehicles allowing the expression of genes and, thus, the struggle between them. Experiments and observations on natural populations showed that evolution—seen as progressive, adaptive genetic change—does indeed occur today. For example, the proportion of dark-coloured moths has greatly increased in many areas where smoke pollution occurs, as a result of predation by birds on the now more obvious light forms. Again, many pest insects have evolved genetic resistance to the insecticides used to attack them.

Increases in the available fossil information suggest that evolution occurs in fits and starts, with long periods of stability alternating with short periods of rapid change. This is called the punctuated equilibrium model, and the 'punctuations' may be associated with sudden changes in climatic conditions.

GENETICS

Mendelism

Genetics is the study of the mechanisms of the hereditary process. Modern genetics began with the experiments of Gregor Mendel, an Austrian monk in 1865. He studied the inheritance of different factors in peas by crossing different strains and counting the numbers of plants with different characters in the succeeding generations.

In one experiment Mendel crossed peas with round seeds with peas having wrinkled seeds. All of the offspring (known as the "first filial" or F1 generation) had round seeds. Mendel allowed these plants to pollinate themselves, and then measured the characteristics of their offspring (the F2 generation). There were 5,474 round-seeded plants and 1,850 wrinkled-seeded plants in the F2 generation, a ratio of very nearly three to one. The character of roundness can be described as being "dominant" over the "recessive" character of wrinkledness.

In order to explain his results Mendel suggested that the characters of roundness and wrinkledness were determined by particulate factors (now called *genes*), and that each plant possessed two genes for each feature. Suppose the gene for roundness is *A* and that for wrinkledness is *a*. Then the parental plants in Mendel's experiment will be represented by *AA* (round seeds) and *aa* (wrinkled seeds). The gametes (the ovules and the sperm nuclei of the pollen grains) will be *A* and *a* respectively. When these combine to form the F1 generation they will produce plants with the genetic constitution *Aa*. Both male and female gametes of the F1 generation are then of the two types *A* and *a*, and these can combine, on self-pollination, in four different ways:

F1	male gamete	female gamete	F2
	A	*A*	*AA*
Aa	*A*	*a*	*Aa*
	a	*A*	*Aa*
	a	*a*	*aa*

The individuals of the F2 generation will thus have genetic constitutions of *AA*, *Aa* and *aa* in the approximate proportions 1 : 2 : 1. Since both *AA* and *Aa* individuals have round seeds, the ratio of round-seeded plants to wrinkled-seeded plants will be about three to one, which indeed it is.

Mendel's results were ignored for many years until their rediscovery at the start of the 20th century. Mendelian ratios were then found to govern inheritance in a large number of other cases, such as coat colour in rabbits and cattle, and white eyes and other characteristics in the fruit fly *Drosophila*. In other cases characteristics are governed by more than one set of genes so the simple mathematical relationships are obscured. This occurs in quantitative features, such as yield in crop plants and weight in animals.

Application of modern statistical methods to Mendel's results suggest that they were subjected to certain 'massaging'—they are in fact simply too good to be true. However, many repeats of his experiments have shown that his conclusions are indeed statistically valid.

Early Chromosome Theory

The chromosomes are dark-staining filaments which, as we shall see later, can be observed in the nucleus at cell division. Their behaviour was described in the nineteenth century, but it was not clear what their function was. After the rediscovery of Mendel's work, Sutton suggested that the genes are carried on chromosomes, since the observed behaviour of the chromosomes corresponded very well with the theoretical behaviour of Mendel's factors.

Further evidence for the chromosome theory of inheritance came from study of the phenomenon known as sex-linkage, in which the expression of a gene depends upon the sex of the individual in which it is found. Haemophilia in man, for example, is a hereditary disease which is normally found only in males, although it is clear that females can act as carriers (Queen Victoria was one, since one of her sons, three of her grandsons and seven of her greatgrandsons were haemophiliacs).

Cytological study shows that there is one pair of chromosomes which differ in the two sexes. In the female (in man and most animals) the two chromosomes of this pair are similar and are known as the X chromosomes. In the male one of these is replaced by a much smaller Y chromosome. Hence recessive genes which are found on only one X chromosome are expressed in the male, since there is no other dominant gene present. A female haemophiliac would have haemophilia genes on both X chromosomes; this could only arise from a carrier mother and a haemophiliac father, a very rare occurrence.

The Composition of Chromosomes

In recent years it has become clear that chromosomes are composed largely of the DNA molecules of the cell nucleus (*q.v.*), to be discussed later. And

since it has become evident that genes are DNA molecules, we now have a firm chemical basis for the assumption that genes are carried on chromosomes. Genetics has thus to some extent become a branch of molecular biology.

Mutations

Sometimes a DNA molecule may not replicate itself exactly during the process of cell division. When this happens the gene which it constitutes has changed its character so as to produce a difference effect when expressed in the individual organism. Such a change is known as a gene mutation. It seems likely, for example, that Queen Victoria's haemophilia gene arose as a mutation in herself or in her mother. Mutations, as we shall see, are of vital importance in providing the genetic variation upon which evolutionary selection can act.

The frequency with which mutations occur is increased by certain chemicals and by ionising radiation. Hence the need for caution in exposing the body to X-rays and to radioactive materials, and the concern over the possible genetic effects of radioactive waste from power stations and from military testing programmes.

THE CELL

Cells were first seen in 1665 by Robert Hooke when he looked at a piece of cork under his primitive microscope. It was not until 1839, however, that Schlieden and Schwann produced the cell doctrine which visualised the cell as both the structural and functional unit of living organisation. Viruses constitute a difficulty since in many ways they are intermediate between living and dead matter. They are absolutely dependent on cells of other organisms for their continued existence. Outside living cells they are inert molecules which may take a crystalline form. Inside a host cell, however, they become disease-producing parasites which multiply and show many of the other properties of living organisms. They are minute and lack the complex organisation usually associated with cells. Notwithstanding their somewhat ambiguous position, the viruses are often treated as though they were single cells or parts of cells and their extreme simplicity has made them ideal material for many types of research at this level.

Structure and Function of Cells

Though the constituent cells of a multicellular organism are usually specialised to perform particular functions, they have a great many features in common. The cell is often said to be made up of a substance called protoplasm, a term for the fundamental material of life which dates from the 19th cent. Protoplasm has two main constituents, the cytoplasm and the nucleus, and is bounded on the outside by a cell or plasma membrane. Plant cells generally have an additional wall composed primarily of cellulose and used for support. The nucleus is the controlling centre of the cell and has rather limited metabolic capabilities. The cytoplasm contains various organelles which operate to produce energy and new cell structure during the normal metabolism of the cell.

Cells take up the raw materials for metabolism through the cell membrane from extracellular fluid which surrounds them. The nutrients include carbohydrates, fats, proteins, minerals, vitamins, and water. Fats and carbohydrates are important principally as sources of energy, though both types of compound are found in permanent cell structure. Proteins are complex substances of high molecular weight which contain nitrogen in addition to the carbon, hydrogen, and oxygen found in the other compounds. They are of fundamental importance in the structure and function of the cell and are built up of a number of simple nitrogen-containing organic molecules called amino acids. There are twenty amino acids occurring commonly in nature so that the number of possible combinations in large protein molecules is quite clearly enormous. A group of proteins whose significance is well established are the enzymes which are the catalysts of chemical reactions in living cells. Each enzyme will control and speed up a specific reaction even though it is present in very small amounts and is usually unchanged at the end of the process. A large number of inorganic mineral salts are essential for cells to function normally. Some, such as sodium, potassium, and calcium salts, are needed in considerable quantity; others are required only in trace amounts and these include iron, copper, and manganese. The trace elements are usually important constituents of enzyme systems. Vitamins are also necessary in very small amounts and many may act as 'co-enzymes', i.e. molecules which must bind to an enzyme before the enzyme is able to catalyse its specific reaction.

I. CYTOPLASM

For a long time cytoplasm was thought to be a homogeneous and structureless substrate in which enzymes occurred as part of a general colloidal system. With the refinement of techniques such as electron microscopy and ultracentrifugation, more and more identifiable components have been found within the cytoplasm. It now seems certain that the material other than these recognisable particles is not a structureless matrix but a highly organised and variable complex, organised around a network of protein filaments called the cyto-skeleton, which is responsible for maintaining the internal distribution of organelles and also for cell movements, as in amoebae.

Mitochondria and Oxidation

Mitochondria vary in shape from cylindrical rods to spheres and in size from 0·2 to 3·0 μm. When seen in the living cell they are in constant motion. The whole structure is enclosed within a thin double membrane, the inner layer of which is thrown into folds extending across the central cavity of the mitochondrion and dividing it into small chambers. The function of mitochondria is to provide energy for the reactions of the rest of the cell. Almost the whole machinery for the oxidation of foodstuffs is to be found in the mitochondria. Slight damage to the mitochondrion will render it unable to carry out a complete cycle of oxidative processes. Destruction of parts of the double membrane system prevents the production of energy-rich phosphate bonds in adenosine triphosphate (ATP) in which energy is stored and transported about the cell.

Chloroplasts

Chloroplasts are particles found in cells in the green parts of plants, in fact they contain the green pigment called chlorophyll. They are involved in the process known as photosynthesis in which energy absorbed from light is used to synthesise carbohydrates from carbon dioxide and water, oxygen being formed as a byproduct.

Chloroplasts are disc-shaped or flat ellipsoids from 2 to 20 μm across, possessing a complex structure which in many ways is reminiscent of that found in mitochondria. A typical double membrane surrounds the structure and the inside is made up very largely of a stack of discs consisting of paired membranes connected at their ends to form closed systems. This seems to be a further development of the type of lamellated structure seen dividing the central cavity of a mitochondrion. The chlorophylls and other pigments, such as the orange yellow carotenoids, seem to be arranged in layers a single molecule thick in the chloroplast discs so that they are maximally exposed to light.

Photosynthesis

Photosynthesis is probably the most important of all biological reactions, and can be regarded as the basis of all higher life, and is responsible for producing the oxygen required for efficient metabolism. The whole animal population of the world, includ-

ing man, is dependent on plants for food since even the meat-eating carnivores prey upon herbivores.

Although scientists continue to make efforts to produce adequate food materials from simple compounds, there is still no better machinery known for doing this than the plant cell. Man is dependent on photosynthesis for his supplies of food and also for much of his fuel, since much of the combustible material removed from the earth is of plant origin.

Ribosomes

Ribosomes, which are tiny granules composed of protein and RNA, are found in the cytoplasm, both free and attached to the surface of a system of membrane tubules called the endoplasmic reticulum, which permeates most of the cell. Ribosomes are responsible for the synthesis of proteins, which are bound to the endoplasmic reticulum and inject their proteins into the system of tubules as they are synthesised. The proteins can then be folded into the correct three-dimensional structure, modified by addition of sugar units, and transported to other parts of the cell. Some proteins accumulate in a special part of the endoplasmic reticulum, the Golgi apparatus, which lacks attached ribosomes and from which small vesicles bud off and later fuse with the plasma membrane to release their contents to the outside of the cell.

Nucleic Acids

The term nucleic acid covers a class of substances, usually of great complexity, built up from smaller units called nucleotides. Each nucleotide consists of a base, united to a sugar, in turn united to phosphoric acid. Nucleotides are joined together in a linear fashion by means of the phosphoric acid residues to form a chain from which the bases project at right angles into the centre of the double helix formed by two DNA molecules. Two types of sugar are found in naturally occurring nucleic acids and these are the ribose of RNA and the deoxyribose of deoxyribonucleic acids (DNA). We shall return to the latter when the nucleus is considered. Four nitrogen-containing bases occur in nucleic acids and in RNA—adenine, cytosine, guanine, and uracil. In DNA the uracil is replaced by thymine.

Protein Synthesis

RNA is predominantly manufactured in the nucleus and subsequently moves out into the cytoplasm. There are three major types of RNA, and all are involved in synthesising proteins. Ribosomal RNA, or rRNA, combines with a number of proteins to form the ribosomes, which act as the assembly line for proteins. Messenger RNA, or mRNA, carries a copy of the structural information encoded by a particular gene and, once in the cytoplasm, associates temporarily with ribosomes to have this information 'translated' into the structure of the protein. Transfer RNA, or tRNA, has a characteristic 'clover-leaf' structure, and picks up amino acids from the cytoplasm and carries them to the ribosome for addition to a growing protein chain. The information in genes and hence in the mRNA molecule is encoded as sequences of three of the nucleotide bases; each such *codon* tells the ribosome to add a particular amino acid to the protein it is making. Thus, as the ribosomes slide along the mRNA molecule, it stops at each codon, waits for the correct tRNA to arrive with the required amino acid, transfers the amino acid from the tRNA molecule to the growing protein, releases the used tRNA, and moves along to the next codon. mRNA molecules contain a number of special 'signal sequences' to tell the ribosome where to start and stop reading its instructions.

Nucleic acids are composed of four different nucleotide bases, while proteins are made using 20 different amino acids; mRNA molecules also need at least one codon as a 'start here' sign and another as a 'stop' sign. Clearly, a code of one base per amino acid would only be able to make proteins with four amino acids; a code of two bases per amino acid would be able to encode 16 amino acids, which is still insufficient. A code using three bases per amino acid can encode 64 amino acids, which is far more than enough, but is nonetheless the minimum that can be used. The genetic code is thus 'redundant', and most amino acids can be specified by more than one codon. Examination of the genetic code showed that redundancy is organised in such a way as to minimise the effects of changes in DNA nucleotides (mutation): thus, the amino acid valine has four codons, GUA, GUU, GUC and GUG, and changes in the last base will have no effect on the protein synthesised. Changes in the first position also have relatively minor effects, because all codons with U in the second position code for amino acids with only slightly different physical and chemical properties. Thus, evolution has taken great care to develop and maintain an optimal system for its own operating.

Cell Membrane

Though the cell membrane plays a most vital part in regulating what can enter and leave the cell, it remains rather poorly understood. It consists of two layers of lipid molecules with protein and other large molecules embedded within it. These protein molecules have many functions, including attachment of cells to each other, signalling the occurrence of extracellular events to the inside of the cell, and transport of water and other molecules into and out of cells. The first of these depends on the proteins and other molecules of different cells recognising each other and having the ability to join together; other adhesion molecules fix cells to various surfaces. Changes in cell recognition proteins are thought to be important in the spread of cancer cells through the body. Signalling functions involve proteins that pass right through the cell membrane and have, on the part exposed outside the cell, the ability to bind specific chemical compounds, such as hormones and neurotransmitters. When this occurs, the physical structure of the transmembrane protein changes, and this change is recognised by other proteins attached to the inner surface of the membrane.

This then induces an alteration in catalytic activity, for example increasing the production of cyclic adenosine mononucleotide (cAMP), which then diffuses to other parts of the cell to initiate changes in the activity of the cell. Such changes include increases in membrane permeability for sodium or potassium (as in nerve cells), increases in corticosteroid synthesis (as in adrenal cells) *etc.*

Second Messengers

The intermediate molecules such as cAMP in the example above are termed 'second messengers'. Transport of many substances, particularly metal ions (sodium, potassium, calcium) and sugars is mediated by membrane proteins which form pores through the membrane. These pores are of different sizes and chemical properties, which allows each pore type to be specific for a given chemical compound; this allows cells to regulate the composition of their contents very precisely. In many cases, regulation is by processes more complex than simple diffusion through a pore that can open and close; some pore proteins can actively pump ions across membranes, to give higher or lower concentrations inside the cell than outside. Such processes can be monitored by impaling cells with microscopic glass electrodes and measuring the voltages across their membranes; manipulation of the external conditions (*e.g.* removing calcium ions and adding substances known to open or close particular types of pore) can be used to determine which pores are active in a given type of cell and see how pore activity changes during biochemical and physiological processes such as conduction of nerve impulses.

II. NUCLEUS

The main regions of the nucleus are the surrounding nuclear membrane, a mass of material known as chromatin, and a small sphere called the nucleolus. The nuclear membrane is a double structure very much like the membranes of the cell surface and endoplasmic reticulum. Suggestions have been made that these membranes are continuous at some regions within the cell.

The status of chromatin was in doubt for many years. Light microscope studies reveal very little structure in the nucleus until the time when the cell is preparing for, and undergoing, division or mitosis. At this time a number of discrete double strands, the chromosomes, are revealed by virtue of their chromatin content—the material stains heavily with basic dyes.

The nucleolus is a specialised region containing copies of the genes encoding ribosomal RNA, and are sites of intensive production of the latter. Thus, cells engaged in high levels of protein synthesis have a more developed nucleolar apparatus.

Mitosis

During division of body cells (mitosis) the chromosomes behave in regular and recognisable sequence. In the first stage called *prophase* they appear and at the same time the nuclear membrane breaks down. Next, in *metaphase*, the chromosomes become arranged across the equator of a spindle-shaped collection of fibrils which appears in the area formerly outlined by the nucleus. Then follows *anaphase* in which the two threads of each chromosome, the chromatids, move to opposite poles of the spindle. Finally in the last stage, *telophase*, nuclear membranes are formed round the two separate collections of chromosome material and the cytoplasm itself divides into two.

Thus two cells are formed each containing the same number of chromosomes as the parent and the cells enter a period of rest, or interphase, between divisions. During interphase the chromatin material disappears as the DNA spreads through the nucleus, the high level of organisation observed during cell division no longer being needed.

Meiosis

Division of germ cells (oocytes, sperm cells) is more complex, and occurs by the process of meiosis. This will not be described in detail here, but the essential point is that the parent cell has two sets of chromosomes, one inherited from the mother and one from the father. During meiosis, these are cut and rejoined to each other to produce 'mosaic' chromosomes, and one set is distributed to each of the two daughter cells. A new organism is formed when a sperm cell delivers its one set of chromosomes to complement the one set present in an egg cell to produce a new cell with two sets, from which the new organism develops.

Genes

These are the elements which contain all hereditary information and the medium whereby hereditary features are transmitted from one cell to the next, either in the same organism or from parents to offspring via the fertilised egg. Experiments indicated that the same genes always occupy the same position on chromosomes and this really demands a structural continuity through the life of the cell.

Thus, the DNA which is loosely packed during interphase, is 'condensed' into chromosomes for cell division by attachment of the necessary proteins; after division, the chromosomes are decondensed to allow the DNA to return to its normal function of specifying the metabolic activity of the cell.

One of the most fundamental problems in biology since the discovery of inheritance by means of genes has been the chemical nature of the genes and how genes are passed from generation to generation in such a way as to explain Mendelian inheritance. Genes have been shown to consist, at the chemical level, of DNA, and the structure of the DNA molecule was established by Watson and Crick.

DNA molecules are usually double-stranded, *i.e.* composed of two linear molecules arranged side by side. This is the explanation for a number of studies which showed that the proportions of the four nucleotide bases in DNA molecules from most sources follow a certain ratio, which results from pairing of A bases in one strand with T bases in the other and vice versa, and C bases in one strand pairing with G bases in the other and, again, vice versa.

The contribution of Watson and Crick, along with their under-known colleague Rosalind Franklin, to show that two linear DNA molecules joined together to form a double helix (*see below*) illustrates the complementary nature of the DNA molecule; the A-T and G-C pairs have different 'lock-and-key' structures which are responsible for the specificity of base pairing.

Molecular Theory of Genetics

The importance of these discoveries is that they provided the structural basis for our understanding of the mechanisms by which a long molecule, about 1 m of DNA in every human cell, can carry out its functions of transcription, replication and repair. These are all copying operations, involving the transmission of genetic information: organisms are the expression of information and DNA is the store of that information.

The information is copied to make RNA (transcription, for making proteins and thus bodies), to make DNA (replication, to make offspring), and to correct errors in one of the two strands (repair, to protect against mutation).

This molecular theory of genetics soon received extensive support, much of it in the form of complex and often subtle laboratory investigations. More dramatic support was provided by Khorana and his group when they started from simple chemicals bought in bottles and used a limited number of enzymes to assemble a bacterial tRNA gene; the artificial gene was found able to carry out many of the functions of the natural gene. Similar studies have resulted in the construction and manipulation of synthetic genes encoding a number of other molecules, particularly hormones. Building on these foundations, molecular genetics has now made vast advances.

FIG. 1. A portion of a DNA molecule showing how it is made up of two strands of nucleotides. Each nucleotide consists of a base, which may be Adenine (A), Thymine (T), Guanine (G), or Cytosine (C), united to the Pentose Sugar, Deoxyribose (S), in turn joined to Phosphoric Acid (P). The nucleotides are linked through the phosphoric acid groups. The two strands are held together by hydrogen bonds between bases, adenine linking only with thymine, and guanine only with cytosine. They are twisted round each other so that the molecule is in the form of a double helix.

Note: Readers may wish to refer to the glossary of terms on **T**46–8 which may provide help for those new to this important area of modern biology.

MULTICELLULAR ORGANISATION

It is axiomatic, if evolutionary theory is accepted, that in the course of very long periods of time there has been a general change in multicellular organisation from the simple aggregation of cells with little individual differentiation, to the highly specialised and differentiated cells and tissues seen in complex animals and plants.

Furthermore the complex organisation must be built up in the lifetime of each animal or plant from the single-celled stage of the fertilised egg. The essential problems in development are: (1) how is the smooth succession of shape changes produced during cell division so that an appropriate and recognisable end product is reached?; (2) how do the cells *differentiate* during this temporal sequence so that those which form part of the eye, say, are different from those of liver?

Differences in Development

There are some important differences in the method of development in animals and plants. In animals there tends to be a relatively short period during which the basic structure is produced and after which growth, repair, and replacement may cause adjustment rather than major change. In higher plants, on the other hand, the apical regions of both roots and shoots remain in a permanently embryonic state and add material, which then differentiates, in a continuous process throughout the life of the plant. In spite of these differences—and in any case there are many exceptions—the two main problems in development are similar in both animals and plants.

Work on Animal Development

A great deal of work has been done on animal development since this takes place in a fairly stereotyped way during a short period of time. The fertilised egg of an animal divides in such a way as to form a hollow ball of cells, the blastula, which folds in on itself to produce a two-layered sac, the gastrula. A third layer, the mesoderm, is now added between the two layers, known as ectoderm on the outside, and endoderm on the inside. At this stage much of the animal's basic structure is established. Many aspects of this orderly sequence can be explained in terms of specific adhesive properties of cells, so that a cell will stick to others of the same type but not to unrelated types. Other mechanical properties such as elasticity, particularly in surface layers, are important in maintaining shape and producing appropriate changes during processes when one layer is folded in on another. Why cells should have the different physical properties necessary to produce an integrated whole embryo is not known, but certainly it cannot be thought that every cell has an absolutely fixed constitution and therefore a predetermined role in development. Large parts of developing embryos can be removed in early stages and their places taken by remaining cells so that intact organisms are still produced.

Formation of Specialised Tissues

This is essentially a problem in the regulation of gene activity since each cell division generally produces daughter cells which are genetically identical. It seems likely therefore that instructions are carried on the chromosomes to cope with all requirements of the organism, but that in specialised cells only a small fraction of this full potential is realised. For a long time embryologists have known that egg cytoplasm shows regional differences which make identical nuclei behave differently, and it is thought that regional cytoplasm can in some way control gene activity. Techniques for the transplantation of nuclei in developing frog embryos have been perfected and it has been possible to put a nucleus from an intestinal cell of a tadpole into an enucleate egg. The egg will go on to develop normally even though its nucleus came from a fully specialised cell derived from endoderm. The embryo will form blood and muscle from the mesodermal layer and all the other components of an organism,

under the influence of a nucleus which normally would have produced none of these things. One can conclude that all the genes are present, even in the nuclei of specialised cells, but that they have to be placed in a suitable cytoplasmic environment in order to be activated. Similar nuclear transplantation experiments indicate that genes can be "turned off" as well as "turned on" by an appropriate cytoplasmic environment, even though the nuclei come from cells which are so specialised as to stop dividing. Chemical signals secreted by cells in particular parts of the embryo are known to play a major role in directing the differentiation of nearby cells to form a variety of body structures. The cells receiving these signals respond differently to the local concentrations of these chemicals.

A study of cell differentiation and the development of multicellular organisation leads us to the view that, important though the nucleus and its genes are in controlling cell activity, an integrated organism is the result of complex interactions between its constituent cells and between the cytoplasm of those cells and their nuclei.

THE CLASSIFICATION OF ORGANISMS

Ray and Linnaeus It was clear to the biologists of the 17th cent. that animals and plants could be fitted into different groups or species. John Ray, a leading biologist of the day, defined a species as a group of individuals capable of interbreeding within the group. This criterion, with its corollary that a species is reproductively isolated from organisms outside the group, has survived more or less unchanged to the present day. The early workers also saw that some species were very similar to one another while others were obviously dissimilar. Systems of classification based on the similarities and differences were drawn up so that all organisms could be fitted into an orderly scheme and species could be given names in accordance with the scheme. The most famous collector and classifier was the Swede, Linnaeus. A very large number of animals and plants are known by the names given to them by Linnaeus.

Systematics, as this type of study is called, acquired a new significance after Darwin and the theory of evolution. The most satisfactory classification became one which reflected the evolution of the organisms classified, a so-called natural classification. It is not always easy to produce because ancestral types tend to become extinct and the problem then becomes one of reconstructing a whole branching system when only the ends of the branches are known. A great deal of the work on systematics has, of necessity, to be done on museum specimens which may be fossils or material preserved in some way by the collectors. The biological criterion of reproductive isolation cannot be used to define a species when the only available representatives are in a preserved state. In this case the scientist must resort to an assessment of structural differences in an attempt to decide whether two organisms are of different species. Other fossil evidence found at the same site as the fossil being classified is often important, in that it can provide evidence of biological and behavioural characteristics such as the type of food consumed and nest-building activity. In recent years computer techniques have been used to compare large numbers of structural differences between groups of animals or plants, as well as physiological and biochemical characteristics. All these techniques have led to the realisation that even the species cannot be regarded as a static point in an evolutionary pattern. Some species die out and others arise as the environment changes.

When the systematist shifts his attention to the higher levels of classification the problems are just as great as at the species level. Different species having features in common can be grouped together into genera, genera into families, families into orders, orders into classes, and classes into phyla. The dividing lines between different groups at all levels is always difficult and in the final analysis somewhat arbitrary since at these levels we do not have any biological criterion such as exists for the species. The evolutionary status of the larger groups is also poorly defined. Many are now recognised to be polyphyletic, which is to say that there are several main evolutionary lines running right through the group.

THE ANIMAL KINGDOM

The animal kingdom is divided into about 24 large groups or *phyla* though the number varies between different classifications. Ten of the more important *phyla* are listed below.

1. Protozoa.—Microscopic, unicellular forms of great variety. Some may have more than one nucleus and others form colonies. Many are able to swim by waving hair-like flagella or cilia. Others move by putting out extensions of the body or pseudopodia into which the rest of the body then flows. Protozoa are found in the sea, in fresh water and in the soil. Some are parasitic and cause important diseases in both animals and humans such as sleeping sickness and malaria.

2. Porifera.—Sponges. Very primitive, multicellular animals whose cells display considerable independence of one another. Largely marine. The body which may become branched and plantlike is supported by a framework of spicules and fibres. The bath sponge is the fibrous skeleton of certain species.

3. Coelenterates.—Hydra, jellyfish, sea anemones, corals. Simple animals which have a body only two cells thick surrounding a gut cavity with a single opening to the outside. Largely marine. Many are colonial. Coral reefs are formed from the calcareous skeletons of these animals.

4. Platyhelminths.—Flatworms, which are free living in water, and liver flukes and tapeworms, which are parasitic. A third, solid block of cells, the mesoderm, has been developed between the two layers of cells seen in the coelenterates. A simple gut may be developed and the reproductive system is complex especially in the parasitic forms.

5. Nematodes.—Roundworms. The body is smooth and pointed at each end. Some of the most numerous and widespread of all animals. Free living in all environments and parasitic in practically all groups of plants and animals. The same level of complexity as the Platyhelminths.

6. Annelids.—Segmented worms such as earthworms, marine worms and leeches. A system of spaces, the body cavity, is developed in the mesoderm so that movements of the main body of the animal and movements of the gut become more or less independent. Digestive, excretory, circulatory, nervous and reproductive systems are all well developed.

7. Arthropods.—A very large, diverse and important group of animals which includes crustaceans such as crabs, shrimps and water fleas; myriapods, such as centipedes and millepedes; insects, and arachnids, such as spiders and scorpions. The arthropods show many of the developments seen in annelids and in addition they possess a jointed, hard *exoskeleton*. Paired appendages grow out from the segments of the body and form antennae, mouth parts, walking legs, *etc.* The muscles within the skeleton are able to exert a fine control over the movement of the appendage. In order to grow these animals have to shed the exoskeleton periodically.
Around 80 per cent of all animal species alive today are arthropods. There are around 350,000 types of beatles alone!

8. Molluscs.—Mussels, clams, oysters, squids, octopods and snails. Complex body form but somewhat different from annelid-arthropod type.

Unsegmented body protected by shell which is variously developed in different types. It forms two valves in mussels and oysters, a spiral structure in snails, is reduced and internal in squids and completely lost in octopods. There are over 70,000 known species of molluscs. The giant clams of the Pacific coral reefs are the largest in the world.

9. Echinoderms.—Starfish, brittle stars, sea cucumbers, sea urchins, and sea lilies. All marine and all radially symmetrical, usually with five radii. Completely unlike the other advanced, major groups. Circulatory, excretory and nervous systems differently developed. Locomotion and feeding by means of hundreds of tube feet projecting from under surface.

10. Chordates.—Sea squirts, Amphioxus, fish, amphibia, reptiles, birds and mammals. Segmented animals which at some stage in their life have gill slits leading from pharynx to the outside and a supporting notochord from which, in all chordates except sea squirts and Amphioxus, is developed a vertebral column or backbone.
Those animals with a backbone are commonly referred to as vertebrates, *all* those without as invertebrates. These are obviously names of convenience having no phylogenetic significance since they lump together totally unrelated phyla in one case and align these with a part of a single phylum in the other. The vertebrates have been investigated more completely than any other animals because of their direct structural and functional relationship with man himself. There are five well defined classes which are listed below.
The first vertebrates were the fish and from them came the amphibia. The amphibia gave rise to the reptiles and both birds and mammals evolved from different reptilian stock.

(a) Fish

Cold blooded, aquatic animals breathing by means of gills. Sharks, rays and dogfish belong to a group known as the elasmobranchs characterised by a skeleton made of cartilage. Bony fish, most of them in a group called the teleosts, include almost all the fresh water fish and the marine fish such as cod, plaice, herring, *etc.*

(b) Amphibia

Cold blooded, more or less terrestrial animals which have to return to water to breed. Five-fingered limbs are developed in place of the fins of fish. The egg hatches into a tadpole larva which is aquatic and breathes by gills. At metamorphosis the larva changes into the terrestrial adult which possesses lungs. Some amphibia such as the axolotl may become sexually mature as a larva and so never metamorphose into the adult. The class includes newts, salamanders, frogs *etc.*

(c) Reptiles

Cold blooded and terrestrial. These animals do not return to water to breed because they have an egg with a relatively impermeable shell containing the food and water requirements of the developing embryo. There is no larval stage.
Present day reptiles such as lizards, snakes and crocodiles are all that remains of a tremendous radiation of dinosaur-like creatures which occurred in the Mesozoic period.

(d) Birds

Warm blooded and adapted for aerial life. The characteristic feathers are both to insulate the body against heat loss and to provide the airfoil surfaces necessary for flight. The birds are an astonishingly uniform group and show less diversity of structure than much lower classification categories (*e.g.*, the teleosts) in other classes. The relationships of the 8,000 or more species of bird are difficult to establish because of this uniformity. It is clear that the flightless forms such as the ostrich are primitive and that the penguins are also in a separate category but the typical modern birds are classified in a large number of rather arbitrary orders. About half of all the known species are placed in one enormous order called the Passeriformes or perching birds.

(e) Mammals

Warm blooded animals which have been successful in a tremendous variety of habitats. Mammals are insulated from the environment by the characteristically hairy and waterproofed skin. They are, with two exceptions, viviparous which means that their young are born alive and in typical mammals at an advanced stage of development. In the marsupials of Australia the young are born at an early stage and transferred to a pouch where they develop further. The two exceptions referred to are primitive monotreme mammals known as the duck-billed platypus and spiny ant-eater and these animals lay eggs. The young of mammals are suckled by means of the milk-producing mammary glands. The mammals include aquatic whales and dolphins, hoofed ungulates, flesh eating carnivores, rodents and insectivores, the aerial bats, and the tree-climbing primates to which man himself belongs.

There are over 5,000 species of mammals on the planet today (and c. 2,000 of them are rodents).

Modern geneticists now put all the placental mammals into four great groups—*Afrotheria, Laurasiatheria, Xenarthra* and *Glires-Euarchonta.* The surprising bedfellows brought about by this new grouping may cause biologists to redraw traditional classifications.

THE PHYSIOLOGY OF ANIMALS

In multicellular animals cells are of various types, constituting distinct tissues and organs which perform special functions in the body. Although each cell has its own complex metabolism there must be coordination between cells forming special tissues and between the tissues which form the whole organism in order for the body to function efficiently. The study of these functional interrelationships at the tissue and organism level of organisation is the province of the physiologist.

1. Movement, Fibrils and Skeletons

(a) **Muscles.**—The prime movers in almost all animal movement are large protein molecules in the form of microscopic fibrillar threads. These fibrils convert the chemical energy stored in the high energy phosphate bonds of ATP into mechanical energy. In the long, thin cells forming the muscles of animals, it has been discovered that there are two sets of fibrils, one formed of a protein called myosin, the other of actin, arranged in a regular, interdigitating fashion. When the muscle contracts the fibrils slide past one another so that, although the fibrils themselves do not change in length, the muscle as a whole develops tension and shortens. Fine bridges extend from the myosin fibrils to attach on to the actin and it is here that the conversion of chemical to mechanical energy goes on.

(b) **Skeletons.**—In order for muscles to work effectively it is necessary for them to operate in some sort of skeletal system. Contraction but not relaxation is an active process; muscles are usually arranged in antagonistic pairs so that one muscle can extend the other. A skeleton also provides a system of levers so that the muscles can do work against the environment in an efficient manner. A simple type of skeleton found in fairly primitive animals is the hydrostatic system of coelenterates and worms. Here the animal can be thought of as a fluid-filled bag or tube which can change shape but whose volume remains constant. By contraction of circular muscles the tube will become long and thin and conversely the contraction of longitudinal

muscles makes the tube short and fat. Examination of an earthworm will demonstrate how alternating waves of activity of this type passing from head to tail can move the animal over the ground. The earthworm shows an advance over the simplest systems because the hydrostatic tube is broken up into small units by the segmentation of the body. This makes local responses possible. The next advance to be seen is the development in animals such as arthropods and vertebrates of a firm skeleton to which muscles are directly attached. The skeleton can then be used to support the body and to engage the environment. It seems to matter little whether an endoskeleton (vertebrates) or exoskeleton (arthropods) is developed since in both cases a tremendous radiation of fins for swimming, legs for walking and wings for flying can be seen. However in other respects these two types of skeleton show significant differences. The exoskeleton for example offers more protection than the endoskeleton while apparently setting an upper size limit. All the really big animals have endoskeletons.

(c) **Cilia.**—Fibrillar systems are also seen in the hair-like cilia which project from the surface of some cells. Cilia are important in a number of ways. They are the organelles of movement in many protozoa, they are used to produce water currents past the bodies of some aquatic animals, and they are of great importance in moving fluid within the body of almost all animals. They beat in a regular fashion, the effective stroke being accomplished with the cilium held straight out from the surface and the recovery stroke with the cilium flexed at the base.

2. Feeding

All animals require complex organic substances, proteins, fats and carbohydrates, together with small amounts of salts and vitamins. These materials are obtained by eating the dead bodies of plants and other animals. They are taken into the alimentary canal and there broken down or digested by enzymes into simpler, soluble amino acids, sugars and fatty acids. These substances are absorbed and distributed to various parts of the body where they are used in cell metabolism (q.v.) or stored for future use.

Macrophagous Feeders. Many animals, called macrophagous feeders, take in relatively large masses of food. Some such as frogs and snakes swallow their food whole, but many break it up first. Arthropods have modified appendages arranged round the mouth for cutting, some molluscs have a rasp-like radula with which to scrape off particles, and many mammals break up their food with jaws and teeth. The teeth are usually well adapted to the type of food. Carnivores have large, sharp canines, premolars and molars with which to tear the flesh of the prey, fish-eating seals have small peg-like teeth to grip the fish and herbivorous ungulates have flat grinding teeth with which they break up hard plant material.

Microphagous Feeders. In contrast, microphagous feeders collect small particles of food material from the environment by continuous filtration. In bivalve molluscs and many marine worms water currents are produced by beating cilia. Food is trapped within the confined space through which the water flows by means of a plentiful supply of sticky mucus in the filtering region. Some crustacea use fine hairs to sieve off food material, often from water currents created by the swimming movements. The most startling of filter feeders is the whalebone whale. As the whale swims forward a stream of water flows in at the front of the mouth and out at the sides via sheets of whalebone which filter off the organisms on which the animal feeds. Though macrophagy seems to favour the attainment of larger size there are exceptions! Another type of particulate feeding is seen in those animals which eat deposits of detritus as do many worms. Finally some animals take in only soluble food materials. These fluid feeders include internal parasites like the tapeworm which absorb substances over the surface of the body, and insects such as the aphid with sucking mouth parts.

3. Respiration. Gills, Lungs and Tracheae

All living cells respire and remain alive only if supplied with oxygen. In a multicellular body, however, many cells are remote from the oxygen of the environment and the need arises for an efficient respiratory system by which oxygen can be taken up and carbon dioxide released. In addition a circulatory system is necessary to transport the oxygen to and from the respiring cells.

(a) Simple Gas Exchange Systems

Animals such as protozoa do not need special structure for gas exchange. Diffusion over the whole body surface ensures an adequate supply of oxygen. Much larger animals such as earthworms also find it possible to rely on diffusion alone, partly because their consumption of oxygen is fairly low, and partly because their bodies are permeable all over. For various reasons most animals restrict the permeability of the outer layers of the body and under these conditions special respiratory areas have to be developed.

(b) Gas Exchange in Water

Aquatic animals, except those such as whales breathing at the surface, have to obtain their oxygen from the supplies which are dissolved in the water. This presents several problems because water is a dense medium, there is not a lot of oxygen in solution, and its diffusion rate is low. For these reasons there is a surprising functional uniformity in gill systems and they are very different from lungs. Gills are fine, finger-like processes with a good blood supply which are held out in a water stream. The water current is brought very close to the gill filaments so that the length of diffusion pathway for oxygen is minimal. There is a "counter current" flow of water and blood so that the water containing most oxygen comes into contact with the blood just leaving the gill. This ensures that most of the oxygen can be transferred from water to blood through the thin gill cells. The efficiency of "counter current" systems is well known to the engineer but they were invented by aquatic animals long before they were by man. These features can be seen in the gills of molluscs, crustacea and fish.

The pumping devices maintaining the water currents also operate economically. Flow is maintained in crustacea by appendages modified to form beating paddles, in many molluscs by ciliary movement, and in fish by the operation of a double pump in mouth and opercular cavities. In almost all cases there is a continuous current over the gills, the water coming in one way and going out another. Thus the animal avoids reversing the flow with the consequent waste of energy in accelerating and decelerating a large mass of water. Fish, for example, take water in at the mouth and force it out through the gill slits (sharks) or operculum (teleosts).

(c) Gas Exchange in Air

Air breathing animals do not encounter these problems since the medium is less dense, contains a great deal (21%) of oxygen and diffusion rates are high. Lungs are therefore in the form of sacs whose walls are well supplied with blood. The area of the walls may be increased by folding so that the lung becomes spongy and full of minute air spaces called alveoli where the gas exchange goes on. Only the main airways receive fresh air as the lung expands; oxygen is renewed in the alveoli by diffusion. Ventilation of the lung is accomplished by a tidal flow of air in and out of the same tubular opening known as the trachea. The actual ventilating mechanism varies in different animals. In the amphibia for example air is forced into the lungs when the floor of the mouth is raised with the mouth and nostrils shut. The lungs are emptied by elastic recoil and by lowering the floor of the mouth. Higher vertebrates use a costal pump which changes the volume of chest and lungs by movements of the ribs. This change in volume is further assisted in mammals by the diaphragm, a sheet of muscle which lies beneath the lungs and separates thorax and abdomen. In many animals sound producing organs are associated with the lungs and trachea. The larynx is a vocal organ in frogs, some lizards, and most notably mammals. In birds voice production takes place in the syrinx situated further down at the base of the trachea.

A completely different gas exchanging system is seen in insects. Branching tubes, known as tracheae, run throughout the body and carry oxygen directly to the cells without the intervention of a blood system. The tracheae communicate with the outside world via a series of holes called spiracles. Although the main tubes may be actively ventilated, diffusion in the system accounts for a large part of the movement of oxygen between the outside world and cells.

4. Circulation

In the larger animals a transport system is necessary to convey materials about the body and in many it is in the form of a blood system. Blood systems are of two types, closed and open.

(a) Open Systems

In an open circulatory system blood is pumped from the heart into a few major arteries but these very quickly give way to large tissue spaces or sinuses so that the tissues and organs of the body are directly bathed in blood. Blood flows slowly from the sinuses back to the heart. Both mollusc and arthropods possess an open system.

(b) Closed Systems

In a closed system blood is pumped round the body in a branching network of arteries and comes into contact with tissues and cells via very thin walled vessels called capillaries. Substances diffuse into and out of the blood through capillary walls. From capillaries, blood enters the veins and so returns to the heart. Blood flow in the tubes of a closed system is much more brisk and blood pressures tend to be higher than in an open system. In annelids the closed system is fairly simple with a vessel above the gut in which blood moves forward connecting to one below in which blood moves backwards. The blood is pumped by peristaltic contraction of the vessels and this system is the precursor of a localised pump. Simple hearts are in fact seen in some annelids.

In vertebrates a well defined heart is always present, situated ventrally at the level of the forelimbs. In fish there is a single auricle and ventricle and the latter pumps blood directly to the gills. From the gills the blood is collected into a dorsal aorta which then branches to serve the rest of the body. Associated with the development of lungs and loss of gills in the tetrapods, we see a progressive modification of this simple pattern. The most posterior gill vessel is taken over as the lung or pulmonary artery and slowly a completely separate circuit evolves. This involves the division of the single heart into right and left sides, the former pumping blood to the lungs and the latter to the body. In the birds and mammals where the division is complete the system can be seen to be functionally satisfactory. Blood flows along the following route: left auricle to left ventricle, to body, to right auricle, to right ventricle, to lungs, to left auricle, and so on. Thus blood charged with oxygen in the lungs returns to the heart before being pumped to the body.

(c) Function of the Blood

Most of the materials transported by the blood such as nutrients, waste materials and hormones are carried in solution in the plasma. The respiratory gases, oxygen and carbon dioxide, are present in greater quantity than would be possible if they were in simple solution. Carbon dioxide is carried in the form of bicarbonate and oxygen combines with blood pigment. The best known blood pigment is haemoglobin which is found in a variety of animals and gives the red colour to blood. When oxygen is present in high concentration, as it is in the lungs, combination occurs to give oxyhaemoglobin. If the concentration of oxygen is low, as it is in the tissues, dissociation occurs and oxygen is given off leaving reduced haemoglobin. Carbon monoxide will combine more readily than oxygen with haemoglobin so that in carbon monoxide poisoning the blood cannot transport oxygen. The haemoglobin of vertebrates is contained in high concentration in red blood corpuscles. The amount of haemoglobin and, hence, oxygen carried is greater than if the pigment is not in corpuscles. In mammals the oxygen carrying capacity of blood is thirty times that of a similar quantity of water. Other blood pigments are the blue haemocyanin found in crustacea and molluscs, and the violet haemerythrin found in some worms. Also present in the blood are various types of white corpuscle which are part of the defence mechanism of the body and ingest invading bacteria. Special blood proteins such as fibrinogen, causing clot formation, and antibodies effective against foreign substances occur in the plasma.

5. Excretion, Ionic Regulation and Kidney Tubules

As the chemical reactions included under the term metabolism proceed, so numerous waste products accumulate. The most important of these are compounds containing nitrogen, such as ammonia, urea and uric acid, arising from the use of protein as an energy source. In terrestrial animals they are removed from the blood by the kidney. The basic unit of a kidney is the tubule; in worms these tubules are not concentrated into a solid kidney but occur, a pair in every segment, right down the body. The kidney tubule begins with an end sac, corpuscle or funnel which is closely associated with the body cavity or the blood system. Fluid is filtered from the body cavity or blood into the corpuscle whence it passes to the tubule proper. During passage down the tubule, useful materials are reabsorbed through the tubule cells into the blood. Unwanted materials remain and pass to the outside world.

Although it is usual to think of kidney function being primarily one of nitrogenous excretion, it is quite common to find that in aquatic animals the kidneys are hardly used for this purpose. In these animals the tubules are primarily concerned in regulating the salt and water levels in the body, nitrogenous wastes being eliminated by diffusion through any permeable surface. In fresh water for example all animals have osmotic problems since the body fluids have a much greater osmotic pressure than the environment. Water tends to enter the body and salts tend to leave. Fresh water animals produce large quantities of very dilute urine, filtering off a lot of blood plasma into the tubules but reabsorbing all wanted materials including the invaluable salts. Fresh water crustacea, molluscs and fish all possess tubules of different morphology which show very similar functional properties.

Different environmental conditions impose different demands on the osmotic and ionic regulating machinery. In very dry conditions, such as in deserts, it is obviously of advantage to reabsorb as much water from the tubule as possible. All animals do this but it is interesting that only birds and mammals have discovered the secret of so concentrating the urine that its salt concentration is higher than that in the blood. This is done by means of a hairpin-like loop in the tubule called the Loop of Henle, another counter current device.

6. Co-ordinating Systems

Overall co-ordination of the animal's body, so that it functions as a whole and reacts appropriately to environmental changes, is largely the province of two systems, one chemical or hormonal, the other nervous. In one respect these are systems for homeostasis, that is for preserving the *status quo*, in spite of considerable environmental fluctuation. Paradoxically they can also initiate change as, for example, one can see in the daily repertoire of complicated behaviour patterns produced by almost any animal.

(a) Nervous Systems

(i) Sensory Information

Before appropriate reactions can be produced to any stimulus it is necessary to measure its intensity, position, duration and, most important, character. This is done by sense organs which are usually specialised to receive stimuli of a single modality or character. Thus photoreceptors detect light, mechanoreceptors detect mechanical disturbance and chemoreceptors detect specific chemicals. In all cases the sense organs produce a message about the stimulus in the form of nerve impulses which travel up the nerve from the sense organ to the rest of the nervous system. Change of stimulus intensity is usually signalled as a change in frequency of nerve impulses. The position of the sense organ which is active indicates the position of the stimulus within or without the body. The duration of the repeated discharge of nerve impulses indicates the duration of the stimulus.

(ii) Simple Networks

The simplest type of nervous system is the network of interconnected nerve cells (neurones) found in the coelenterates. Branching processes of the nerve cells communicate with neighbouring processes at special regions called synapses. Quite complicated behaviour is possible even with this relatively simple system. If a sea anemone is prodded violently it will close up equally violently, showing that activity has spread throughout the network. If it is tickled gently it will respond with local contractions around the site of stimulation. The movements of feeding and locomotion are very delicately performed at appropriate times.

(iii) Central Nervous Systems

In the majority of animals all the nerve cells tend to become collected into a solid mass of tissue referred to as a central nervous system (CNS). Within the mass the nerve cells are interconnected via synapses in the same way as in a nerve net. The connexions with sense organs and muscles are made via long processes called axons. Numbers of axons are usually bound together with connective tissue to form a nerve trunk. In annelids and arthropods the CNS is seen as a ventral cord lying beneath the gut with a swelling or ganglion in each segment of the body. In molluscs, the ganglia are usually more closely grouped around the oesophagus, with the possible provision of a pair of ganglia further back in the viscera. Vertebrates possess a dorsal nerve cord which is uniform in diameter and not ganglionated, though nerves emerge from it in a segmental fashion. The segmental nerves arise in two separate bundles or roots. The **dorsal root** is made up entirely of sensory nerves conveying information to the CNS. The **ventral root** consists of motor nerves which convey nerve impulses to the muscles of limbs and alimentary canal together with other effector organs such as glands.

(iv) Reflexes

A reflex, in which stimulation of a sense organ or sensory nerve results in the almost immediate contraction of a muscle, is the simplest type of CNS activity. Reflexes have been studied in all animals but the best known ones can be seen in frogs, cats, dogs, and sometimes humans. The very simplest is the stretch reflex, in which a stretched muscle is made to contract by activity coming into the CNS from stretch receptors in the muscle. The activity is relayed directly to the motor neurones of the muscle concerned, making them active and thus causing the muscle to contract. This reflex is monosynaptic, *i.e.* there is only the single synaptic connexion between sensory nerve and motor neurone. The knee jerk in humans is a stretch reflex, the stretch being caused by hitting the muscle tendon as it passes over the knee. Much of the recent work on reflexes has been done on this simple system, notably by Eccles. The flexor reflex, which is seen as the sudden withdrawal of a limb from any painful stimulus, is more complicated. Although the stimuli may vary, the withdrawal response is always accomplished by contraction of flexor muscles which bring the limb in towards the body. The reflex is polysynaptic, *i.e.* several intermediate neurones connect the sensory nerves through to the motor neurones.

More complicated still is the scratch reflex in which an animal is made to scratch its flank in response to an irritation or tickling in that region. This reflex demonstrates some of the more involved properties of the CNS For example a dog will continue to scratch for a time after the tickling has stopped, so that the CNS must continue to be active in the absence of sensory stimulation. This has been called after- discharge.

(v) The Brain

The CNS functions in a more complicated way than is suggested by study of the reflexes and most of these higher activities are co-ordinated by the brain. A greater condensation of neurones is seen at the front end of the CNS of all animals because of the larger numbers of sense organs in that region. Brains, which become the dominant part of the CNS, can be seen in arthropods, molluscs and vertebrates. The close association with sense organs is illustrated by the vertebrate brain which is divided into three regions: (*a*) forebrain (nose), (*b*) midbrain (eye) and (*c*) hindbrain (ear and taste).

However, the brain is very much more than a relay station for these stimulus modalities and it receives information from other parts of the body via the spinal cord. All this information is correlated and activity patterns initiated and transmitted to appropriate regions. In lower vertebrates, the roof of the midbrain (the optic tectum) is the important correlation centre and its effectiveness has been well established in studies on instinct and learning in fish. Another region of the brain of importance in all vertebrates is a dorsal upgrowth of the hindbrain called the cerebellum. This is a motor co-ordinating centre which ensures that all activities are performed in a smooth and well balanced way by the muscles and limbs of the body. In reptiles, the forebrain begins to take over the correlation role and in mammals this development reaches its peak in the cerebral cortex. In man the cortex overshadows the rest of the brain and contains over 1,000,000,000 neurones. It is easy to see the magnitude of the problem of understanding a system of this complexity. The bee's brain with far, far fewer cells can initiate complicated behaviour such as the hive dances. The possibilities offered by the human cortex seem vastly greater, though they are often realised in ways which give cause for concern.

At the moment it is still not possible to build a computer with the properties of the human brain, though the first steps have been taken with the development of 'neural networks' of computers, which display a limited amount of learning and integration skills.

(b) Hormonal Regulation

Many aspects of an animal's metabolism are regulated, not by the nervous system, but by specific chemical signals known as hormones which are circulated in the blood stream. Growth, carbohydrate metabolism, salt balance, activity of ovaries and testes and their associated structures, and colour change are all regulated in some way by hormones. The substances are secreted by endocrine glands or ductless glands as they are often called. The important endocrine glands in vertebrates are the thyroid, parathyroid, adrenal, pancreas, the sex glands, and the pituitary.

In the past the endocrine and nervous systems were regarded as exerting an independent control in slightly different functional areas of the body. It is clear now that the integration of the two systems is much greater than was formerly envisaged and in vertebrates is accomplished through the pituitary gland. Secretions of this gland regulate almost all other endocrine glands and the secretions of the pituitary are either produced in the CNS with which it is directly connected or are controlled by CNS secretions. An astonishing, parallel development of other neurosecretory systems, such as those of the pituitary, has been found in a variety of animals and in all types the neurosecretory organ complex is the dominant endocrine gland of the body. In crustacea the so-called X organ complex found within the eyestalk, and in insects neurosecretory cells connecting to the corpora cardiaca glands, occupy the functional position of the vertebrate pituitary. They all regulate growth, metabolism and reproductive physiology, either directly or through the medication of other endocrine glands.

7. Animal Behaviour

In discussing the nervous system we have already dealt with simple mechanisms such as the reflex. Very much more complicated are the instinctive and learned patterns of behaviour studied by animal psychologists and ethologists.

(a) Instinct

Instinct is inborn behaviour which does not have to be learnt and is usually performed in a stereotyped way. For example a gull will retrieve an egg taken out of its nest by shovelling it back with the underside of its beak. The gull will never replace an egg in its nest in any other way, for example by using a wing or leg, and once it has begun a retrieval it will usually continue the movements back to the nest even though the egg is taken away. An instinctive behaviour pattern is triggered off by a particular stimulus or "releaser" which may be a very small part of the total environment. A male stickleback will attack a very crude model with a red belly but will not attack an exact model without it. The red underside appears to be a much more important stimulus than general shape. A particular instinctive pattern cannot always be elicited and the reaction of an animal very largely depends on when the behaviour was last produced. The longer the time that elapses, the easier it is to trigger off the instinctive pattern until eventually it may appear in the absence of an appropriate set of environmental circumstances.

(b) Learning

Learning is that behaviour acquired during the organism's lifetime as a result of experience. Evidence of learning has been seen in many animals from worms upwards though, as might be expected, the more complicated types of learning are found only in those animals with elaborate nervous systems. A simple type of learning is seen when an animal, upon repeated exposure to a stimulus, gradually decreases the normal response which is usually one of flight, until eventually the response may disappear completely. This process is called habituation. More complex are the *conditioned reflexes*, which were first discovered by Pavlov.

In these an animal can in some way connect a conditioned stimulus such as a bell, with an unconditioned stimulus such as meat, so that eventually it salivates when the bell is rung. Trial and error learning of the type needed to be successful in running a maze is more complicated still. In this there is a retrospective element because the reward at the end of the maze comes after all the responses. Many animals can run mazes and the white rat has been extensively used in experiments of this nature. A final category of learning can be called insight learning; in this an animal shows evidence of resolving a new problem without trial and error.

This type of learning involves the perception of relations between different parts of the environment and though there may be examples in arthropods and molluscs the clearest evidence of it is seen in the behaviour of birds and mammals.

8. Reproduction

A single animal may live for a short or long time, but eventually it dies, and the continuance of the species is dependent upon reproduction. Some protozoa, such as *Amoeba*, reproduce asexually by the simple division of the cell to produce two new individuals. Asexual reproduction also occurs in some coelenterates, such as jelly-fish, in which there is an alternation of sexual and asexual generations. However, the vast majority of animals only reproduce sexually.

This involves the fusion of two cells, the gametes, produced by adult individuals, and each zygote thus formed develops into an individual of the next generation. The gametes are of two kinds, the large, spherical, immobile ova produced by the female gonad or ovary and the much smaller motile sperms produced by the male gonad or testis. The motility of the sperms helps them to reach the passive ovum, which contains food reserves to support the early development of the embryo.

Worms.—The flat worms, particularly parasitic forms, have complicated life cycles, and many are hermaphrodite, i.e., each individual has both male and female organs. Cross-fertilisation usually occurs, the sperms from one worm being introduced into the female duct of another. The round worms are unisexual, and internal fertilisation also occurs. Of the annelids the polychaete worms are unisexual, but the ova and sperms are shed into the sea, where fertilisation takes place. However, Lumbricus and the leeches are hermaphrodite, cross-fertilisation takes place and the eggs are laid in cocoons.

Arthropods.—Many crustacea are unisexual, though the sedentary barnacles are hermaphrodite. Internal fertilisation may occur, but in the crabs and crayfish pairing takes place and the sperms are deposited on the tail of the female. When the eggs are shed they become fertilised and remain attached to the abdominal appendages.

Most crustacea have motile larval stages into which the eggs first develop. In Daphnia, the water-flea, parthenogenesis sometimes occurs, i.e., the eggs develop without being fertilised. The sexes are separate in the arachnida and there are usually no larval stages except in the primitive king-crabs. The insects are also unisexual, and the fertilised eggs are laid after copulation. In some, e.g., dragon-flies, an immature nymph similar to the adult is formed, but in flies, beetles, moths, and many others the egg hatches into a larval form. This then develops into a pupa, from which the final adult or imago is produced. In the social ant's nest the workers are sterile females with large heads, reduced eyes, and no wings. The males and queens are winged, and insemination of the latter occurs during the "nuptial" flight.

Molluscs and Echinoderms.—Most lamellibranchs are unisexual, although some species of scallops and oysters are hermaphrodite. There are motile larval forms, and in the swan mussel, Anodonta, the larvae develop in the mantle cavity of the parent and when liberated become attached to the gills or fins of fish, where they remain parasitic for some time. Some gastropods are unisexual, but the slugs and snails are hermaphrodite. In the latter cross-fertilisation occurs, the two approaching snails being stimulated to copulate by firing small sharp darts of calcium carbonate into each other. The echinoderms are unisexual, and fertilisation takes place in the sea. The egg first develops into a ciliated larval form.

Vertebrates.—The sexes are always separate in the vertebrates. In some cartilaginous fish, e.g., dogfish, internal fertilisation occurs and the eggs are laid in protective sacs. In contrast, the bony fish shed ova and sperms into the water, where fertilisation takes place. Although pairing may take place in amphibia, fertilisation occurs in water, and there is usually an aquatic larval stage. The reptiles, birds, and mammals are independent of water for fertilisation, as copulation takes place and the sperms from the male are introduced directly into the female. Most reptiles and all birds lay eggs with hard shells. Development of the embryo in marsupial mammals begins in the female uterus, but is continued in a ventral pouch which surrounds the teat of the mammary gland. In the two lowly species of monotreme mammals the eggs are incubated in a similar pouch.

Finally, in the eutherian mammals the embryo develops in the female uterus and is born at an advanced stage.

Diversity of Sexual Reproduction.—This brief survey will give some idea of the diversity of sexual reproduction in animals. External fertilisation is very much a matter of chance, and large numbers of gametes are produced which offset the great losses of gametes and embryos that this method involves. Internal fertilisation is more certain, and is also independent of external water—an important factor in land animals. In vertebrates particularly there is increase in the care of the young by the parents, involving the development of characters of behaviour as well as those of structure. Some fish lay their eggs in holes or nests which are protected by the male. Similarly, a few frogs build nests, while others carry the eggs about.

Eggs of birds require a constant high temperature for their development, and they are usually incubated by the parents. After hatching the young are fed and guarded by the parents until they can leave the nest and fend for themselves. In the eutherian mammals the embryos are attached to the uterus wall by the placenta, via which food materials pass from the mother. The period of gestation is long, and after birth the young are supplied with milk from the mother until they are weaned and can feed themselves.

Another feature in mammals is the period of "childhood" during which they play and learn and are protected and fed by their parents. The internal fertilisation, internal development, and care and protection of the young after birth which is so conspicuous in the higher vertebrates results in the reduction of losses during the vulnerable embryonic and young stages, and in consequence relatively few progeny are produced by a pair of individuals.

THE PLANT KINGDOM

There are various ways in which the main classes of the plant kingdom can be grouped, but a simple, up-to-date arrangement is given in the chart. Vascular plants are often known as the Tracheophyta because they all possess woody conducting elements. These are absent in non-vascular plants, and the, fungi and algæ are often called Thallophyta, i.e., they have a relatively simple plant body or thallus. Many of the bryophytes also possess a thallus, but in some there is a stem bearing leaves, although a true vascular system is absent. Many thallophytes are aquatic, whereas the tracheophytes are mostly land plants in which the development of woody tissues can be related to the attainment of the land habit as the plant kingdom evolved. However, the chart should not be taken as indicating the evolutionary relationships of the various groups. It is more a convenient arrangement which reflects the relative complexity of the plant body.

1. Bryophyta.—These are the liverworts (Hepaticae) and the mosses (Muscineae). They are all small plants characterised by a sharply defined life-cycle. This consists of an alternation of generations, the "plant" being a gametophyte bearing sex organs. The latter are multicellular, the female archegonium containing a single stationary ovum and the male antheridium producing many motile sperms. The latter are released and swim in water to the archegonium, where fertilisation takes place. After this a sporophyte is formed which is always dependent on the gametophyte and never becomes free living. The sporophyte usually consists of an absorbing foot buried in the tissue of the gametophyte and a stalk or seta bearing at the top a single sporangium. In many mosses this is a complex structure with hygroscopic teeth which move apart only when dry, thus releasing the minute spores only when conditions are suitable for their dissemination in the air. The bryophytes may be looked upon as an evolutionary side-line. However, they occupy suitable "niches" in many plant communities, and species of the bog-moss Sphagnum cover large areas where rainfall is high.

2. Psilopsida.—This is a small group of primitive, vascular, spore-bearing plants. Its only living representatives are two rare genera of the southern hemisphere. However, a number of fossil forms are known from the Devonian period. The best known are those found in the chert at Rhynie in Scotland. The plants are excellently preserved, and their internal structure can be easily seen.

They were probably marsh plants with prostrate and erect leafless stems, although *Asteroxylon* had simple leaves.

3. Sphenopsida.—The only living members of this group are about twenty-five species of horse-tails (*Equisetum*). In the Carboniferous period many tree forms existed (*e.g.*, *Calamites*), the remains of which are very common in coal deposits.

4. Lycopsida.—In the Carboniferous period the tree clubmosses were also prominent members of the forests (*e.g.*, *Lepidodendron*). They often reached 30m in height, were branched or un-branched, and had large simple leaves. They also had extensive root systems. The only living members belong to a few genera of small her-baceous clubmosses, such as *Lycopodium* and *Selaginella*. Like the true mosses, they have an alternation of generations, but the elaborate plant with stem, leaves, and roots is the sporophyte, and the gametophyte is very small. In *Lyco-podium* only one kind of spore is produced, and the resultant gametophyte is bisexual. *Sela-ginella* produces numerous small microspores which give rise to the very reduced male game-tophytes and motile sperms and the few large megaspores which produce the female game-tophytes. The latter are formed within the megaspore wall, which splits to allow the sperms to reach the small archegonia.

5. Filicinae.—These are the true ferns, which in some classifications are put with the horsetails and clubmosses in the Pteridophyta or vascular cryptogams (*i.e.*, vascular plants without seeds). The ferns have a long fossil history, and remains very similar to the living Royal ferns (*Osmunda*) are known from the Carboniferous. The ferns are widespread and particularly abundant in tropical forests. The majority are herbaceous perennial plants, but a few are aquatic, and there are some tree ferns, which may reach 6 m in height. Most ferns possess a stem bearing roots and large leaves or fronds. The plant is the sporophyte and produces numerous spores in sporangia borne on the fronds. Each spore gives rise to a minute green free-living gametophyte known as the prothallus, which bears the archegonia and antheridia. After fertilisation a young sporo-phyte develops, which at first draws nourishment from the prothallus. Thus, as in the Bryophyta, external water is essential for the motile sperms to swim in, and there is a clearly defined alternation of generations, but the sporophyte is a complex independent plant, and the gametophyte is reduced though free-living.

6. Gymnospermae.—These were the dominant land plants in the Mesozoic era, although fossil re-mains are found as far back as the Devonian. The living members still form large forests in the north temperate regions. They are mostly tall evergreen trees with roots, stems, and small leaves. The conifers include the pines (*Pinus*), larches (*Larix*), and yews (*Taxus*). The cycads are a relic group of tropical plants with thick, unbranched trunks and large fern-like leaves. The maiden-hair tree of Japan (*Ginkgo biloba*) has also had a long geological history. Another in-teresting gymnosperm is *Metasequoia*, a genus well known to palaeobotanists. In 1948 a few living specimens were found in a remote area of China. Seeds were collected and plants are now being grown in botanical gardens all over the

world. The gymnosperms are characterised by the production of "naked" seeds, which are usually born on cones. The male pollen grains, which are equivalent to the microspores of *Selaginella*, are carried by wind to the ovule of the female cone. The pollen germinates and the pollen tube carries the male gametes to the reduced archegonia borne on the female pro-thallus, which, unlike those of the ferns, is re-tained within the ovule on the parent plant. After fertilisation an embryo is formed, the pro-thallus becomes the food store or endosperm, and the outer part of the ovule becomes the seed coat. The cycads and *Ginkgo* retain a primitive feature in that the male gametes are motile and they swim to the archegonia from the pollen tube.

7. Angiospermae.—The apparent sudden rise of the angiosperms in the Cretaceous period is still the "abominable mystery" it was to Darwin. Various suggestions have been put forward, but nothing definite is known about the origin of the group. The angiosperms or flowering plants are now the dominant group over most of the land surface of the earth, and at least 250,000 species are known. Apart from the natural vegetation, the majority of our crop and garden plants are angiosperms. They occur in every type of habitat and range in form from gigantic trees to minute plants, such as the duck-weeds. Some are climbers, others succulents, and a number have reverted to the aquatic habit. Although most possess chlorophyll, a few are partial (*e.g.*, mistle-toe) or complete parasites (*e.g.*, dodder).

Flower, Fruit and Seeds.—The diagnostic feature of the group is the production of seeds, which are completely enclosed within the female part of the flower, the ovary. Basically a flower is a short re-productive shoot which bears several whorls of lateral organs. At the base are several, often green, protective sepals forming the calyx, and above this are the often brightly coloured petals of the corolla. Within this are the stamens of the androecium or male part of the flower. Centrally is the female gynoecium of one or more carpels con-taining the ovules. The parts of the flower may be free, as in the buttercup, or fused together. In many species the petals are fused (sympetalous), the stamens are borne on the corolla (epipetalous), and the carpels are fused to form a compound gynoecium (syncarpous). The stamens possess anthers, which produce pollen grains. These are shed and carried by insects or wind to the receptive stigmas of the carpels. Each produces a tube which grows down the style to the ovary and enters an ovule. The ovule is a complex struc-ture containing an ovum and a primary endo-sperm nucleus. Two male nuclei are discharged from the pollen tube, one fuses with the ovum and the other fuses with the primary endosperm nucleus. After this "double fertilisation" an embryo is formed which is embedded in the nutritive endosperm and the outer tissues of the ovule form the seed coat or testa. The ovary of the carpel develops into the fruit containing the seeds.

Fruits are of various kinds, being either *dehiscent* and opening when mature to release the seeds or *indehiscent*, with a succulent or dry wall. The inde-hiscent fruits are shed as a whole, and often contain only a single seed. Seeds and fruits show great variation in structure, and often have adaptations assisting dispersal. Some have hairs or wings which aid wind dispersal, whereas others have hooks or are sticky and are transported by animals. Some have flotation devices and may be carried a great distance from the parent plant by water. Seeds vary in size from the microscopic seeds of orchids to those of the double coconut, which may weigh 18 kg. Only about 10 % of the weight of a seed is water, and the embryo, although alive, is dormant. The bulk of a seed consists of stored food material, commonly fats or starch and proteins, which may be contained in the endosperm surrounding the embryo, although in some species the endosperm is absorbed during seed development and the food is stored in the one or two swollen seed leaves or cotyledons of the embryo.

Classification of Flowering Plants.—John Ray (1627–1705) was the first botanist to recognise the two great divisions of the angiosperms—the dicotyledons with two seed leaves and the monocotyledons with only one. This primary division of the flowering plants is still recognised. Other differences are also found between the two groups. The dicotyledons usually have net-veined leaves and the floral parts are in fours or fives, whereas the monocotyledons usually have leaves with parallel veins and the floral parts are in threes.

Reclassification of Plants

The world's flowering plants were reclassified in 1998 on the basis of their genetic similarity. Previously, the classification of plants had been largely based on their morphology (physical characteristics). New DNA techniques enabled the study of genetic similarity to be incorporated into plant classification. The more similar the patterns within genes, the more recently two species have diverged.

The New System

The addition of sophisticated genetic analysis has allowed relationships to be clarified and evolutionary patterns to be more clearly understood. The new classification, which draws together several lines of evidence, arranges plants that have evolved from the same ancestor in supra-familial groups, or *clades*. A total of 462 Families and 40 Orders of flowering plants are now recognised.

As a result, it is known, for example, that the lotus flower is more closely related to the plane tree than the water-lily, to which it bears a striking resemblance. Orchids are not related to lilies but to the Hypoxidaceae, or yellow stargrasses. The papaya is related to the cabbage. Roses are related to nettles, blackthorns and figs.

For the first time, there is a true scientific basis for classification; a dataset visible to all researchers.

In 2014 botanists were at last allowed to describe plant species in English instead of Latin.

THE PHYSIOLOGY OF PLANTS

Some of the fundamental differences between animals and plants can be ascribed to the ways in which the two groups of living organisms satisfy their requirements for food material. In a simple way at least, an animal can be thought of as a mobile gastro-intestinal tract which is highly specialised to search out and receive food in convenient, concentrated packets. In typical land plants, however, a quite different organisation exists because the organic nutrition is based on the process of photosynthesis in which carbon dioxide from the air is combined with water from the soil to form simple carbohydrates. An expanded foliage system is necessary to absorb carbon dioxide and to expose the photosynthetic pigment, chlorophyll, to sunlight. Similarly, an expanded root system is needed to absorb the other ingredients of nutrition, water and mineral salts, from the soil. The work of the plant physiologist is to understand the relationships between these two expanded systems of root and shoot.

The Spread of Roots

In addition, the physiologist is concerned with the progressive elaboration of root and shoot as the plant grows. Plants show much less specialisation of their cells into discrete tissues and organs than do animals and they also retain special areas,

at root and shoot tips for example, where new cells are added to the structure throughout the life of the plant. In some cases whole plants can be regenerated from very few cells taken almost anywhere from a growing plant body. The orderly regulation of growth and differentiation is thus a basic property of much plant tissue.

1. Movement of Solutes and Water

The movement of water and inorganic solutes in a plant is primarily upwards from the roots where they are absorbed, to the leaves or growing regions where evaporation of water or the use of both water and salts occurs. Water and inorganic ions permeate freely through the cell walls and air spaces of the more peripheral cells of the roots. Equilibrium is established between the insides of cells in this region and the water and salts outside, water tending to enter by osmosis and the salts by diffusion or active transport. Increase in cell volume which would be caused by continual influx of materials is, of course, restricted by the inextensible cell wall. In the centre of the root is a region packed with the specialised conducting tissues called xylem and phloem. These form continuous channels through the root and into the shoot and clearly serve for the conduction of water and substances in solution. In the root this central region is separated from the more peripheral tissue by a single layer of cells, the endodermis. The endodermal layer can actively pump water and salts from the outer regions through into the longitudinal conducting strands of, in this case, the xylem. Evidence for this pumping activity can be seen in the exudation of liquid from the base of a plant stem cut close to ground level. In some cases pressures of 8 to 10 atmospheres have been generated in roots as a result of the pumping action of the endodermal cells.

Transpiration

Water is also moved up a plant by forces generated in the leaves. Constant evaporation from the walls of leaf cells, both on the surface and within the substance of the leaf, causes loss of water from the plant. The process is called transpiration and, within limits, the plant can control transpiration rate by regulating the ease with which water-saturated air passes to the exterior through perforations in the leaf surface called stomata. The diameter of these apertures can be regulated by movements of guard cells surrounding the stomatal openings. Loss of water from the leaf cells is made good by withdrawing more water from the xylem elements within the leaves and stem of the plant. Cohesive forces between water molecules prevent the continuous water columns within the xylem from breaking. The net result is that water is drawn up the stem as transpiration occurs in the leaves. Considerable suction pressures have been measured by suitable manometer systems attached to the cut stems of actively transpiring plants. In addition materials such as dyes or radioactive isotopes have been followed as they move up the conducting xylem vessels at rates which can be related to the rate of transpiration.

2. Movement of Organic Substances

The organic substances, whose site of manufacture is primarily in the leaves, have to be distributed to the rest of the plant body. It is thought that a second conducting tissue, the phloem, is mainly responsible for the distribution of these materials in solution. Ploem is found as a layer of tissue to the outside of the xylem vessels in a plant stem. It consists of conducting cells which are rather different from those of xylem, which serve, as we have seen, mainly in the transport of water and salts. Whereas xylem tissues are composed of dead cells whose cell walls form effective longitudinal conducting channels, phloem is made up mainly of living cells. Elements called sieve tubes are the most important conducting cells in phloem and, during the initial stages of differentiation, a sieve tube has a full complement of cytoplasm and cell organelles. Later differentiation sees the protoplasmic structures break down, but even in mature sieve tubes protoplasmic strands join through the perforated ends of adjacent cells and may extend longitudinally through the conducting elements.

Ringing experiments in which a complete ring of phloem is cut from the outside of a plant, provide evidence of the tissue's function in longitudinal conduction of carbohydrates. Sugars accumulate above such a ring but not below it. Samples of fluid taken from sieve tubes have also revealed high concentrations of carbohydrates in the sap. The method used to obtain such samples is very ingenious. Several aphids are known which parasitise the phloem translocation channels of plants. The aphid is allowed to insert its stylet tip into the phloem vessels and is then anaesthetised and cut off the inserted stylet. Sap exudes from the stylet stump and can be collected and analysed.

3. Growth

Growth is usually, but not always, thought of as involving increase of size as measured by length, volume, or weight. In these terms any unit in a plant, whether root, shoot or fruit would follow a sigmoid growth curve with growth starting slowly, then speeding up, before finally slowing down at maturity leading on to death. Growth may also be considered as an increase in the number of cells, an increase in substances such as water, protein or DNA in the growing system, or an increase in complexity of organisation.

(a) The **organisation of growth**, no matter how it is measured, presents a number of interesting problems. In the first divisions of a fertilised egg, all cells divide. Very soon this property becomes localised, polarity is established, and the young embryo develops a shoot tip and a root tip. These have then become discrete regions of cell division. The cells behind them cease active division, enlarge by developing large vacuoles and form mature plant tissue.
A circular strand of dividing tissue, called the cambium, is left in the stem between differentiated xylem and phloem. The cambium is responsible for growth in girth. The acquisition of polarity has far-reaching consequences, for the behaviour of a shoot tip is very different from that of a root. The shoot tip, for example, gives rise to leaf cells with photosynthesising chloroplasts and it grows upwards away from gravity and towards light. The root tip gives rise to cells which absorb salt and water, and it grows towards gravity and away from light.

(b) Quite a lot is known about the **mechanisms which regulate growth** by cell enlargement in the regions behind the actively dividing tips. Cell enlargement is achieved by the secretion of water and solutes to form a substantial vacuole within the cell, thus causing an overall increase of volume and expansion of the cell wall. The degree of enlargement is affected by external stimuli such as light and gravity, producing the differential growth patterns seen when plants orientate to these stimuli. Substances, called plant hormones or auxins, are now known to be produced at the growing apex and to move back causing vacuole formation in the actively elongating region. The distribution of auxin is affected by light or gravity so that the plant will turn towards or away from the stimulus. Indoleacetic acid is the active growth substance occurring naturally in many plants. Several man-made substances are also effective and are widely used as weedkillers. A group of substances exists in plants to control cell division, just as auxins regulate cell enlargement.

Monera, Protista and Fungi

Monera

Monera are simple single-celled organisms lacking a clearly defined nucleus and membrane-bound subcellular organelles such as mitochondria and chloroplasts; they constitute the prokaryotes, or bacteria, archebacteria and blue-green algae. Many authors believe that the archebacteria should be placed in a kingdom of their own. This is a vast group of minute organisms of very simple structure. They are spherical or rod shaped and may exist as separate cells, some species being motile, or as long chains or irregular masses. There is a wall of complex composition, and cytoplasm which contains glycogen and fat. Electron-microscope studies have revealed the presence of structures which appear to consist of nuclear material. Multiplication is by simple division, which may take place very rapidly.

For example, *Bacillus subtilis* can divide every 20 minutes, so that in 8 hours a single cell may give rise to 16 millions. Limited sexual processes also occur. Bacteria can survive unfavourable conditions by producing a resistant spore within the cell. They do not possess chlorophyll, though a few are pigmented. Most obtain their food already formed, and are thus either saprophytes or parasites.

The saprophytic bacteria occupy a vital position in the living world. They are responsible for most of the decay of dead organic matter, and it has been truly said that without them the surface of the earth would soon become completely covered with the dead bodies of animals and plants.

The Role of Bacteria. Bacteria also play a vital part in the circulation of nitrogen in nature. By breaking down organic material, ammonia is released and ammonium carbonate is formed in the soil. This is oxidised by other bacteria to form nitrates, which can be absorbed by plants again. Yet other bacteria can "fix" atmospheric nitrogen, and one species, *Rhizobium leguminosum*, occurs in the root nodules of the pea plant. Such plants are often grown on poor soils and ploughed in, thus improving the fertility of the soil. The parasitic bacteria are also of great importance, as they are responsible for many diseases of plants, animals, and man. Bacteria themselves are the most abundant form of life on our planet and the first to evolve. No other organism is so adaptable.

Protista

This kingdom consists of algae other than the blue-gree algae, along with protozoa and slime moulds. They are mostly unicellular, microscopic, non-vascular organisms; many are motile by virtue of flagella, cilia and pseudopodia.

These are essentially aquatic organisms which contain chlorophyll. They range from microscopic forms to the large seaweeds. The green algae (Chlorophyceae) live mostly in fresh water and may be unicellular, motile or non-motile, or filamentous, though a few found in tropical seas are more complex. The brown algae (Phaeophyceae) are mostly seaweeds which possess a brown pigment, fucoxanthin, which masks the green chlorophyll. They include the bladder-wracks (*Fucus*) and kelps (*Laminaria*) of our coasts and the seaweeds which form dense floating masses over hundreds of square miles of the Sargasso Sea. Another group is the red algae (Rhodophyceae), mostly seaweeds of delicate form, the unicellular motile diatoms (Bacillariophyceae). All algae possess unicellular reproductive organs. Various types of life cycle occur, the most complex is found in the red algae.

Fungi

These are multicellular non-vascular organisms, (forming mycelia with low levels of differentiation into tissues, and more highly differentiated replicative bodies (*e.g.* mushrooms). None contains chlorophyll. Hence, like the bacteria, they are either parasites on other living plants and animals or saprophytes which live on dead organic matter. Some are unicellular aquatic plants, but many have a body called a mycelium composed of many branched threads or hyphæ. In the higher fungi (*e.g.*, toadstools, bracket fungi, and puff-balls) complex reproductive structures are formed which produce spores. In the aquatic species these may be motile, but the majority form minute, airborne spores. The spore output is often very great, and a single mushroom may produce 1,800 million spores. Some fungi are serious diseases of crop plants, such as potato blight and wheat rust. There are an enormous number of species of fungi.

ECOLOGY

Ecosystems

The important branch of biology which deals with the relationship between living organisms and their environment must now be considered. Living organisms and the physical environment in which they exist form what is termed an ecosystem. Obviously it would be possible to regard the whole world as a giant ecosystem, though for purposes of study it would be extremely unrewarding and impractical. A pond, a rocky or sandy shore, a forest, and a peat bog are examples of ecosystems on a somewhat smaller scale, possessing different properties and containing populations of animals and plants that are different both in number of individuals and in species represented.

The ecologist seeks to understand why a particular species is present in certain numbers in an ecosystem in terms of that species' interaction with all other living organisms (biotic) and with the physical (abiotic) factors of the ecosystem.

1. Abiotic Factors

All living organisms will show ranges of tolerance for abiotic factors such as temperature, humidity, salinity, oxygen levels, amount of light, etc. Clearly, if any factor in the environment moves outside the range of tolerance of a species, it becomes limiting for that particular species which is then excluded from the environment. Within the range of tolerance there will be an optimum value for each abiotic factor at which a species will survive best.

There is not a firm line separating suitable and unsuitable environments, but rather a steady shift from optimum values into conditions in which an organism finds it more and more difficult to survive. One of the most important abiotic factors in an environment is the nature of the substrate upon or within which an organism moves and settles.

(a) **The Terrestrial Environment.**—Soil is the commonest substrate for terrestrial organisms. Particle sizes, ranging from the coarsest gravel soils, through sands and silts to the finely textured clays, have extensive effects on the flora and fauna of any area. Coarsely textured soils are obviously penetrated most easily both by roots and by soil animals. Soils of this type also allow the rapid movement of water and soil gases, but they have the serious disadvantage of poor water retention. The level at which water saturation occurs is known as the water table and is an important abiotic factor. The terrestrial environment tends on the whole to dehydrate organisms and there is always a marked dependence on water supplies.

Soil characteristics also vary with depth. A vertical section through any soil is referred to as its profile and has considerable bearing on the ecosystems in which the soil is involved. The layers, or horizons, of a soil profile vary enormously from one soil to another. Below a surface layer of organic debris one can, in general terms, distinguish a layer of soil from which substances have been leached (A horizon), soil containing the leached-out substances from the layer above (B horizon), the weathered parent material (C horizon), and finally the parent rock or some other stratum beneath the soil (D horizon).

Humus, which is formed from animal and plant remains is of great importance in providing food for soil organisms and chemical elements such as nitrogen, phosphorus, and calcium for plant growth. It is also important in maintaining good soil structure and, though inorganic fertilisers can supply chemical elements, they have little or no effect on structure. Soil requires careful cultivation, and structure is easily disturbed by such things as heavy farm machinery, which can lead to the creation of impermeable layers with the disastrous exclusion of oxygen and oxygen-consuming organisms.

(b) **The Aquatic Environments.**—Marine and freshwater environments together cover more than 75 per cent of the earth's surface and, since they can be occupied throughout their entire depth, offer a much greater volume of living space than does the land. There is only a slight difference between the density of water and of living tissues, so that the bodies of aquatic organisms are very largely supported by the environment and do not need strong woody stems or powerfully muscled limbs to hold them up. Water has a high specific heat, which means that large amounts of heat are needed to raise its temperature. The result is that aquatic environments tend to show much smaller fluctuations in temperature than the terrestrial ones. In general, the larger the volume of water the smaller are the fluctuations in temperature, and so the fauna and flora of the oceans will not show wide temperature tolerance, whereas that of small pools will, but in neither case will the tolerance be so great as that shown by many terrestrial forms. Oxygen and carbon dioxide concentrations are very different in water and in air and are also variable from one aquatic environment to another, making them suitable for the support of different fauna and flora.

Salt Concentration

An important difference between the sea and freshwater is seen when their salt concentrations are determined. Organisms in fresh or in sea water face quite dissimilar problems in osmotic and ionic regulation. Life evolved originally in the sea and the salt concentration in the blood of marine molluscs, crustaceans, and echinoderms, for example, is about the same as in sea water itself. Marine organisms have, on several occasions in the course of their evolution, moved into freshwater. Representatives of the worms, crustaceans, molluscs, and vertebrates have all independently invaded this very dilute habitat. What is more, all these animals show approximately the same types of modification to cope with the change. Their outer layers, in the main, become impermeable and the salt concentration of their blood is reduced considerably and to a spectacularly low level in the freshwater mussel. The kidneys become enlarged and produce a large volume of dilute urine. By these means freshwater animals can cut down loss of their salts. It is interesting that all terrestrial vertebrates, including the mammals have retained a salt concentration in their blood of about half the seawater level and this is partly attributable to their freshwater ancestry. The ultimate development of salinity tolerance is seen in such animals as the salmon and eel which move from fresh to salt water and back again during their life cycle.

2. Biotic Factors

(a) **Associations between Organisms.**—No organism can be considered to be independent of any other organism in an ecosystem but in some cases close associations of various types can be developed between different species or different members of the same species.

Commensalism is an association which benefits one member but has little effect on the other. Small organisms can live within the protective covering offered by a larger individual, as, for example, commensal crabs living within the shell of some species of oyster.

Symbiosis is a somewhat closer association in which both members benefit, as do certain species of green algae and the coelenterates in whose body tissues they live. The algae are protected and the coelenterates benefit from the food produced by the photosynthetic plant. Some symbiotic organisms are unable to survive outside the association. The lichens which are associations of algae and fungi, are examples of this type of symbiosis, as are some of the food-processing micro-organisms together with the animals in whose intestinal tracts they live.

Social Animals. In some cases animals of the same species form social groups in which co-operative effort and division of labour makes them more successful in exploiting a particular environment. Social development is most obvious among certain insects such as termites, ants, wasps, and bees, and among the vertebrates. Social organisation in these groups may lead to the development of different behaviour patterns and ultimately, as in ants and bees, for example, to the evolution of a variety of structural modifications so that different castes are recognisable.

Parasitism. Not all associations are of mutual benefit and when one organism becomes sufficiently specialised so that it can live successfully on materials extracted from another, the latter is always adversely affected. Parasites, by causing disease in, and sometimes the death of, the host, can influence population growth and size. Important groups are bacteria, protozoa, fungi, nematodes (roundworms), and platyhelminths (tapeworms and liver flukes). Viruses are also important disease-producing agents which are incapable of an independent existence outside the cells of the host and utilise the host cell's metabolic pathways directly to synthesise new virus material.

Control of Parasites. Many parasites (and other pests which may disturb the comfort and health of man) can now be controlled to some extent, and, for a variety of reasons, such control procedures have extensive effects on the ecosystems involved. The regulation of some bacterial parasites by means of antibiotics, and control of the insect vectors of organisms such as the malaria parasite by means of insecticides, have both been important factors in the increase in human population. Though the beneficial effects of pest control of all types are clear, the process is not without its difficulties and dangers. Indiscriminate use of many chemical agents has led to the development of resistant strains. In any group of organisms, some will naturally be more resistant to a pesticide or antibiotic than others and these will be the survivors of any treatment that is less than totally effective. They will form the breeding stock for subsequent generations and so progressively more and more resistant types will evolve. Thus, there are now many strains of bacteria resistant to penicillin and other antibiotics.

Parasite Resistance. Even more alarming is the recent discovery that this resistance can be transferred in an infective way between bacteria of different species. Another complication associated with chemical control is that the agent concerned frequently affects a wide spectrum of organisms, including those that are in no sense injurious to man or his crops. Thus DDT kills bees and other pollinating insects unless its application to a crop is very precisely timed. In addition, the accumulation of quantities of chlorinated hydrocarbons such as DDT in the environment is known to have an injurious effect on organisms other than insects. Because these chemicals are broken down very slowly they now form a serious problem in environmental pollution.

Specific Pesticides. Agents such as DDT are now being replaced with much more specific pesticides which inhibit particular stages of development of particular species of pests, *i.e.* growth regulators. Biological control is also becoming much more widely used, and is based on introduction of species which are specific predators of local pest populations.

(*b*) **The Food Factor.**—Plants are the ultimate source of organic food for all animals. The most important food plants are those capable of *photosynthesis* in which organic material is synthesised from carbon dioxide and water, using radiant energy from the sun to drive the reaction. Plants are eaten by herbivores which in turn are eaten by carnivores. It is possible to see many such sequences, called food chains, in all ecosystems.

MOLECULAR BIOLOGY
GLOSSARY OF KEY TERMS

Biotechnology A set of methods for using living organisms to make a variety of products, including alcoholic drinks, bread and medical drugs.

Blotting A method of detecting specific nucleic acid sequences. A mixture of molecules is separated by size on a gel made of agarose, and a filter made of nylon or nitrocellulose is then placed on the gel, so that the nucleic acid molecules bind irreversibly to the filter. A nucleic acid of known sequence, which has been radioactively labelled, is then incubated with the filter so that the labelled nucleic acid sticks ("hybridises") with molecules of complementary sequence attached to the filter, so that the latter can be detected and the size can be measured. When DNA is attached to the filter, the procedure is called Southern blotting after its inventor; when RNA is attached to the filter, it is called Northern blotting. A similar method exists for proteins, using antibodies to detect specific proteins, which is called Western blotting.

cDNA An abbreviation for complementary DNA, which is a DNA "copy" of an mRNA molecule extracted from a cell; this is often the first step in cloning a gene, and is carried out using reverse transcriptase.

Chromosomes Chromosomes are structures found in the nuclei of plant and animal cells and consist of the cell's DNA, along with a number of specialised proteins. The functions of the chromosome are to minimise the space occupied by the DNA—in mammalian cells, up to 2 m of DNA has to be packed into a nucleus only 4–10 μm in diameter—and to distribute newly synthesised DNA to the daughter cells after cell division. Somatic cells (*i.e.* cells not specialising in reproduction) of different species contain different numbers of chromosomes, *e.g.* man (46), cat (38), mouse (40), honey bee (16), *Drosophila* fruit fly (8), and potato (8). The chromosomes in each case consist of 2 sets of paired chromosomes; reproductive cells contain only 1 set of chromosomes, and are thus described as haploid. Bacteria contain a single chromosome, which is much simpler than the chromosomes of higher organisms, and is circular.

Cloning The production of genetically identical copies of a biological material, for example starting from a single cell. In recombinant DNA technology, cloning consists of joining a DNA molecule to a vector (*q.v.*) and putting the resulting recombinant molecule into a bacterium, where the vector then allows large quantities of the DNA molecule of interest to be made.

Cytoplasm *See* **T32.**

Denaturation In general, the breakup of the higher structure of a biological polymer. For example, egg white becomes opaque on cooking because of denaturation of the protein albumin, caused by heat. In nucleic acids, denaturation refers to the breakage of the hydrogen bonds between the nucleotide bases that hold the two strands of a double-stranded DNA molecule together; heating a double-stranded molecule causes the two strands to separate (this is also called "melting"). If a solution of denatured DNA molecules is allowed to cool slowly enough for the separated strands to bump into each other, the double helix re-forms; this is called renaturation, and only occurs when the base sequences of two DNA molecules are complementary to each other (*see* **Nucleic Acids**). Double-stranded molecules consisting of one DNA strand and one RNA strand ("heteroduplexes") can also be formed by this method.

Deoxyribonucleic Acid (DNA) *See* **Nucleic Acid, T47.**

DNA Fingerprinting DNA fingerprinting consists of examining repetitive DNA in the genome for variations in the lengths of restriction fragments. The DNA from the genome is cut with a restriction enzyme known to cut repetitive sequences into short pieces and is then used in blotting experiments using probes that hybridise to the repetitive sequences. Every individual has his own pattern, so that fingerprinting can match blood to a particular person, and patterns are inherited from parent to child, allowing the method to identify relationships between individuals.

Exon *See* **Intron, T47.**

Gene A unit of genetic information, *i.e.* the DNA

sequence encoding one protein or RNA gene product.

Gene Expression The process of making a product (protein or RNA) from a gene. Regardless of the gene product, the first step consists of transcribing the DNA to make an RNA copy; this can be the final product, or it can be translated to make a protein molecule.

Gene Product When the information in a gene is copied, the final product is either a protein or an RNA molecule. The term gene product includes both of these. It does not usually include messenger RNA (mRNA), which is an intermediate between the DNA of the gene and the final protein.

Genetic Code Sequence information in genes is used to specify amino acid sequences in proteins. There are four bases in nucleic acids and 20 amino acids in proteins, so a direct one-to-one correspondence is not possible. Groups of two bases could only store information about eight amino acids. Three bases (a "codon") can store information about 64 amino acids; this is the code that is used. Since there are only 20 amino acids in proteins, the code is quite redundant, most amino acids being represented by 2, 3 or 4 different codons, though these codons are generally related, e.g. GGA, GGT, GGC, and GGG all encode the amino acid glycine. Three of the 64 codons have the special function of telling ribosomes that the protein it is making has come to an end; these are called "stop codons".

Genetic Disease A disease caused by a defect in a gene (i.e. a mutation) or in a chromosome. A well known example of a genetic disease caused by a point mutation is cystic fibrosis. Some types of leukaemia are associated with a chromosomal defect, where the long arms of chromosome 21 are shorter than normal (this is called the Philadelphia chromosome).

Genetic Diversity The number of different alleles in a population. An allele is an individual's version of a particular gene, so the larger and more varied a population, the more different versions of a given gene it will contain, and the greater will be its genetic diversity. The importance of genetic diversity is that a larger allele pool makes a species better able to adapt to changing conditions.

Genome The total set of genetic information in an organism. Physically, the genome corresponds to the sum of all the chromosomes in a cell, i.e. all the DNA that the cell contains. The genome thus consists of all the genes encoding proteins and RNA molecules, as well as large amounts of non-coding or silent DNA. Much of this is made of repeated DNA sequences, which can be classified into a number of families.

Haploid Most animal cells contain two pairs of chromosomes—one from the father and one from the mother, and are called diploid. Reproductive cells (spermatozoa and oocytes) contain only one set of chromosomes and are called haploid. When a spermatozoon and an oocyte fuse, the resulting cell becomes diploid and develops into a new animal. A similar process occurs in plants.

Human Genome Project See **Section L**.

In vitro Used of an experiment that is not carried out in a living body.

In vivo Used of an experiment carried out in a living body.

Intron The nucleic acid sequence of a gene is often much longer than needed to encode the protein or RNA product of that gene. The part of the gene containing protein-encoding information is found to be split up into sometimes numerous small pieces called exons, which are separated by non-coding pieces called introns. Transcription produces an RNA copy (a pre-mRNA) containing both exon and intron sequences. Before the mRNA migrates out of the nucleus, the parts of the pre-mRNA corresponding to the introns are removed, a process called splicing.

Ligase An enzyme that is used in recombinant DNA technology for joining the ends of two DNA molecules together, usually after renaturation of sticky ends. Ligase is involved in the replication and repair of DNA.

mRNA An RNA molecule that is a copy of the base sequence of a gene, and carries that sequence from the nucleus to the cytoplasm to instruct the ribosomes to make a protein of the correct amino acid sequence.

Mutation A change in the sequence of bases in a gene. This can be a change from one base to another (point mutation), or loss or addition of one or more bases from or to a gene sequence (deletions and insertions respectively). Changes which do not alter the structure of the gene product, e.g. mutations in exons and mutations in codons that do not alter the amino acid encoded by those codons, are called silent mutations.

Nucleic Acids Biological polymers consisting of a chain of sugars joined by phosphate groups, where each sugar carries a nucleotide base. There are two important nucleic acids, deoxyribonucleic acid (DNA), which is the chemical of which genes are made in most organisms, and ribonucleic acid (RNA), of which three types (mRNA, rRNA and tRNA) are involved in protein synthesis; some viruses carry their genes in the form of RNA. Nucleic acids store information in the sequence of chemical bases attached to the sugars; the bases in DNA are adenine (A), thymine (T), cytosine (C) and guanine (G), while those in RNA are the same except that uracil (U) replaces thymine. The two ends of a nucleic acid molecule are different; one is called the 5'-end and the other is called the 3'-end. DNA is usually double-stranded; that is, two DNA molecules are linked together side by side and pointing in opposite directions as a double helix, joined by hydrogen bonds between the bases, which point towards the centre of the helix. Because of the chemical structures of the bases, C can only form hydrogen bonds with G and vice versa, T and U can only form bonds with A, while A forms hydrogen bonds with T in DNA and with U in RNA. Thus, if the sequence of bases in one of the two strands in a double-stranded DNA molecule is 5'-CATTG-3', the "complementary" sequence in the other strand will be 3'-GTAAC-5'. The RNA sequence complementary to this DNA sequence will be 3'-GUAAC-5'. Two molecules that have similar sequences are said to be homologous.

Nucleolus A structure within the nucleus, consisting of copies of the cell's ribosomal RNA genes, which are sometimes needed in larger numbers than can be provided within the chromosomes, i.e. when cells have to synthesise large quantities of protein and thus need large numbers of ribosomes.

Nucleotides Nitrogen-containing bases attached to a sugar phosphate. See **Nucleic Acids.**

Oligonucleotides Very short nucleic acid molecules. Oligonucleotides are often used as the probes in blotting studies and other recombinant DNA techniques because oligonucleotides of known sequences can easily be made in the laboratory.

Oncogenes A number of cancers have been found to be caused by viruses. The ability of a virus to cause cancer is conferred upon it by special genes, which are called oncogenes. Oncogenes are usually related to normal cellular genes involved in regulation of cell growth, and cancer due to oncogenes can be thought of as resulting from the abnormal expression of a normal gene.

Peptides Very short proteins.

Plasmid A small circular DNA molecule containing a replication origin (it is thus a replicon) commonly found in bacteria. Plasmids are widely used in recombinant DNA technology as vectors for cloning DNA fragments because of their small size. In nature, plasmids are responsible for a considerable proportion of bacterial antibiotic resistance—moving from cell to cell, they carry antibiotic resistance genes with them.

Polymerase Chain Reaction (PCR) A method for synthesizing relatively large amounts of a nucleic acid of known sequence, using polymerase enzymes and oligonucleotides.

Proteins Biological polymers made of amino acids, of which 20 are used in living organisms. The properties of a particular protein depend on the sequence of amino acids of which it is made, and this sequence is determined by the sequence of nucleotide bases in the gene corresponding to the protein. Proteins can be structural (*e.g.* collagen) or they can be enzymes, which catalyse chemical reactions. Some proteins, such as haemoglobin, have the special function of transporting other chemicals around the body.

Recombinant DNA Technology A more precise term for genetic engineering.

Repetitive Sequences Much of the DNA in the genome of a higher organism does not contain genes, but consists of apparently functionless sequences, some of which are repeated head-to-tail. Genomes contain a number of families of related repeats, and up to 20% of the genome can consist of sequences present at up to 1,000,000 repeated copies.

Replicon A DNA molecule that is able to replicate in a cell. In order to do this, the molecule needs to carry a special sequence called a replication origin, which is the point at which synthesis of new copies of the DNA begins.

Restriction Endonucleases Enzymes found in bacteria that cut DNA molecules; their function is to protect bacteria against infection from viruses. Class II restriction enzymes, the group which is important in recombinant DNA techniques, bind to a short (usually 4 or 6 bases) sequence and cut the DNA in or close to the recognition sequence. Bacteria protect themselves against their own restriction enzymes by chemically modifying their DNA. Restriction enzymes allow DNA molecules whose sequences are known to be cut at predetermined positions. Many enzymes cut the two strands

of a DNA molecule in slightly different places, to leave single-stranded overhangs ("sticky ends"); these can be renatured to join pieces of DNA together in a specific way.

Retrovirus A virus which stores its genetic information in the form of RNA instead of DNA; several are tumour-inducing viruses, and the viruses associated with AIDS are retroviruses. Replication of these viruses starts with making a DNA copy of the RNA genome, using the enzyme reverse transcriptase.

Reverse Transcriptase A viral enzyme found in some viruses that use RNA instead of DNA for their genomes. This enzyme is an RNA-dependent DNA polymerase, and makes a DNA copy of the viral RNA, which is the first step in the replication of such viruses.

Ribonucleic Acid (RNA) *See* Nucleic Acids.

Splicing *See* Intron.

Transcription The process of copying a DNA molecule to make a complementary RNA copy of a gene. Transcription occurs in the nucleus of higher organism cells, and is carried out by enzymes called DNA-dependent RNA polymerases.

Transgene A foreign gene inserted into a higher organism (animal or plant). This is done by inserting the gene into the organism at an early stage of embryonic development; since all the cells of the adult come from these early embryo cells, all adult cells will contain the inserted gene. Such organisms are called transgenic animals or plants.

Translation The process of converting a gene sequence in the form of mRNA into a protein sequence. Translation is carried out by ribosomes.

Vector In recombinant DNA technology, a replicon that is used for cloning DNA sequences. Vectors are usually small and simple replicons, *i.e.* plasmids and bacteriophages.

V.　HUMAN EVOLUTION

Introduction

Although the broad pattern of human evolution is the subject of agreement amongst scientists, almost all the details are contentious. The exact relationship to one another of successive species, for example, is very uncertain and the family tree of modern man is constantly being revised as new evidence and new dating techniques become available.

As just one example, scientists long argued over the fate of 'Neanderthal Man'. Did he evolve with exceptional speed into a modern human, was he conquered and eliminated by modern man, or did he interbreed and lose his distinctive characteristics in the process?

International research into the genetic code of 'Neanderthal Man', the results of which were published in 2010, has, however now established that between 1 and 4 per cent of the DNA of modern non-African humans is Neanderthal in origin. In other words, the first humans to migrate out of their African homeland interbred with the Neanderthals they met, probably in the Middle East some 100,000–50,000 years ago, and in due course carried that genetic material on to Europe, Asia and Australasia.

The story of human evolution is complex as well as contentious and readers may find the following chronology helpful as a brief introduction.

A Note on Terms

Neither scientific nor popular literature is consistent in the use of such words as 'hominid' and 'human'. 'Hominid' can be used as a comprehensive description for the biological family of two-legged primates as a whole, but is more normally restricted to the human lineage only, and that practice has been followed here. Some authorities, however, prefer the term 'hominin' to describe the earliest members of the human family such as the Australopithecines.

The description 'human' is particularly fluid, but is most conveniently applied to hominids who had evolved towards making tools and enjoying some form of social life.

CHRONOLOGICAL TABLE

Years BCE

70 million	The emergence of the primates, the order of mammal to which all humans, apes and monkeys belong.
25 million	The emergence of the biological family which currently comprises the four genera of chimpanzee, gorilla, orangutan, and human (genus homo). The earliest representative, identified in the Fayum, Egypt, known scientifically as *Aegyptopithecus zeuxis* and colloquially as the 'dawn ape', lived in trees and was the size of the modern domestic cat.
25–8 million	The evolution of more than 50 species who were descended from *Aegyptopithecus*, of which one, *Proconsul africanus*, is believed to be the ancestor of modern apes and humans.
20 million	The evolutionary line of the ape diverges from that of the monkey.
18 million	*Proconsul africanus*, the size of the modern baboon and living in trees, speads over East Africa.
5 million	The likely divergence of the human from the chimpanzee evolutionary line.

3·7–1·6 million	The earliest identified hominids (*i.e.* members of the genus *homo*), the Australopithecines, comprising four distinct species. One, the lightly built *australopithecus africanus*, or *gracile* australopithecine, is likely to be the ancestor of modern man. Their remains have been found in Ethiopia, Kenya and South Africa.
	The 'Laetoli footprints' (*see* **T53(2)**) established that the australopithecine was fully bipedal (*i.e.* walking on two legs). This had enabled its forelimbs to develop into arms and hands, permitting the carrying of food over distances, the making of tools and weapons, and the nurturing of children.
2·1–1·7 million	The emergence of *homo habilis*, the first hominid known to have used tools. The distribution of remains parallels that of the australopithecines.
1·6 million	The emergence of *homo erectus*, generally, but not universally, accepted as the ancestor of modern man. Remains have been found in north and east Africa, Europe, Indonesia and China. It survived, at least in China, until as late as 300,000 years ago. Java Man and Peking Man are popular names for the remains found in those places.
1·2–1·1 million	Pioneer man (*homo antecessor*) is active in Spain. Although he used tools, he is not thought to be a direct ancestor of modern man (*homo sapiens*).
990–780,000	The first evidence of man in Britain (Happisburgh, Norfolk). Probably of *homo antecessor*.
560,000	A tooth dating back this far discovered at the Tautavel prehistoric site in France.
500,000	The earliest human remains found in Britain (Boxgrove, West Sussex). Probably of 'Heidelberg Man', an archaic human, who is likely to have been the direct ancestor of modern man, *homo sapiens*, and of whom remains are widespread.
440–270,000	Modern man (*homo sapiens*) and 'Neanderthal Man' start to evolve as separate species from a common ancestor, believed to be 'Heidelberg Man'.
200–150,000	Final evolution, in sub-Saharan Africa, of modern man, *homo sapiens*.
70,000	Modern man migrates out of sub-Saharan Africa (perhaps very much earlier). Human teeth over 80,000 years old have been found in China.
50,000	The migration of modern man extends as far as Australia. The skeleton of Mungo Man (*c.* 42,000 years old). World's oldest axe, dating back 49,000 years, found in Western Australia. The primitive *Homo floresiensis* is wiped out.
35,000	The earliest known figurative art (a 'pornographic' female figurine – the Venus of Höhle Fels – found in Germany). Earliest cave paintings date to this time.
30,000	'Neanderthal Man' very probably becomes extinct as a species.
13,200	The earliest evidence yet found of modern man in the Americas (footprints in British Columbia, Canada). As glaciers retreated early humans followed the bison herds.

THE EMERGENCE OF MAN

New discoveries are constantly causing our views on the fascinating story of human evolution to be revised. The recent find of Sahel Man in Chad, a 'missing link' provisionally dated to *c.* 7,000,000 B.C. could suggest that the very first hominids did not develop in the Rift Valley of Kenya and Ethiopia (often called the Cradle of Civilisation) but in fact 1,500 miles west. Even more exciting and problematic were the discoveries made in caves in South Africa (*see* **Postscript T55(2)**).

Likewise the discovery in 2006 in Ethiopia of the remains of the earliest known child (nicknamed Selam and 'Little Lucy') has begun to unearth new evidence of the link between apes and humans.

Similarly, the widely-reported discovery of the 'Hobbit', the skeleton of a new and completely unexpected species of tiny humans on the remote Indonesian island of Flores, suggests that this very small metre-tall human shared the planet with other humans around 18,000 years ago – not long before the dawn of recorded history.

Systematics

The study of systematics (*q.v.*) shows us that the relationships which form the basic structure of zoological classification set every species in the context of a greater whole—genus, family, order, and so on. *Homo sapiens* is no exception. Man is not the end-product of the entire evolutionary process, as is commonly supposed. On the contrary, man's place in nature is at the end of a relatively short line radiating from among the millions which have evolved since life on Earth began.

The Origin of the Primates

The primates are essentially tropical animals. With the exception of humans, virtually all living species are arboreal, and 80 per cent of them are found in the tropical rain forests. Their most distinctive characteristic is the very general and unspecialised nature of their anatomical structure, and the highly specialised and adaptable nature of their behaviour. While other mammals evolved specialised physical characteristics (the giraffe's long neck, for example), the primates have retained the basic structure of the ancestral mammalian form and have instead adapted their behaviour to suit prevailing circumstances. The human hand is a case in point—it has the same number of bones operated by the same arrangement of muscles as the arboreal primates possessed 45 million years ago, yet the human hand serves a much greater variety of uses.

Early Fossil Evidence

The fossil evidence indicates that primates have existed for at least 70 million years. They were one of the groups of placental mammals which survived the mass-extinction event which closed the Cretaceous period of geological time, about 65 million years ago. The dinosaurs were among those which disappeared with that event, and their passing marks the end of the epoch known as the age of the reptiles. Some reptiles survived, of course, but with the declining prominence of the dinosaurs the mammals flourished, heralding the age of the mammals with a burst of adaptive radiation which eventually took them into every ecological niche which the dinosaurs had previously occupied.

The Early Mammals

The early mammals had lived in the shadow of the dinosaurs for more than 100 million years before the Age of the Reptiles came to a close. They were small (typically about 10 cm long), and occupied parts of the environment that the large reptiles could not reach—the nocturnal world, for instance, (a temporal dimension in which the cold-blooded reptiles could not function), and rocky crags, holes and forest undergrowth. Here they evolved a high degree of sensory perception. Sight, sound, touch and smell assisted their capture of the invertebrate prey upon which they largely subsisted; integration of cerebral and physical equipment was crucial, and while the later evolution of the dinosaurs was concerned primarily with physical structure, that of the early mammals was concerned with the development of brain and behaviour. This equipped them well for the radiation which followed.

Of the various habitats available to the mammals as the age of the reptiles drew to a close, the ancestors of the primates took to the trees. Here they found a rich and varied diet—leaves, buds, fruit, insects, birds' eggs and nestlings—but also a suite of new demands. Life in the trees called for a shift in the emphasis of the mammals' environmental awareness. While the nose had probably been the most important organ of ground-dwelling mammals, the eyes were more crucial in the trees.

The Development of Arboreal Mammals

Because a tree is a spatially restricted environment, an arboreal animal needs to be particularly aware of its whereabouts. It must know if a potential predator is in the same tree, and if a fruit is at the end of a safe branch. It must be able to see clearly and judge distances accurately as it moves through the branches. These requirements favoured the evolution of stereoscopic vision, which was further enhanced by the advent of colour vision.

Life in the branches also called for greater agility. An ability to flex the paws and grasp things was advantageous; digits evolved into fingers, claws into fingernails. Front limbs became principally a means of holding on, while the rear limbs served as a means of propulsion and also of static support. Thus the animals could leap safely about the trees, and also could sit with the spine erect, the head turning with a perceptive eye, the ears twitching.

It can be supposed that the attributes favouring an arboreal existence also promoted yet more cerebral development. A large brain relative to body size evolved; accommodating a larger brain required some restructuring of the skull, which in turn was affected by the masticatory demands of the foods which the animals ate—fruit, leaves, insects, meat.

Such an omnivorous diet calls for neither the specialised canines and slicing teeth of the carnivores, nor the grinding molars of the herbivores. The ancestral set of general all-purpose teeth was retained. The jaws broadened and shortened, the face flattened, the eyes looked forward and the expanding brain took up more and more room at the back of the skull. These interactive and interdependent features evolved over millions of years, a mosaic of cause and effect from which evolved the order of mammals known as the primates.

In basic zoological terms, the primates which evolved from the early arboreal mammals were distinguished from all other placental mammals by the fact that they have retained the four kinds of teeth found in ancestral mammals (incisors, canines, premolars and molars); they can hold things between finger and thumb, they have frontally directed eyes and have a large brain, relative to body size. They are represented today by 193 living species, all but one of which are covered with hair.

Hominid Ancestry

The broadest categories of the primate order were also the earliest to have existed in evolutionary time, and the divisions were created principally by the geographic isolation resulting from the breakup of Gondwanaland, the supercontinent on which the primates had originated. Thus, the tarsier suborder became confined to the islands of Indonesia and the Philippines, and the prosimian suborder is best represented today by the lemurs of Madagascar, where the infraorder has been isolated for close on 60 million years. Another infraorder of prosimian, represented by the pottos, lorises and bushbabies, remained on continental Africa and Asia, and has found isolation in a nocturnal way of life as other primates adopted a diurnal lifestyle.

Isolation similarly split the anthropoid suborder when the landmass of South America broke away from Gondwanaland about 40 million years ago,

carrying with it the primate stock which evolved into the platyrrhines—the New World monkeys. Subsequently, the catarrhine stock left on Gondwanaland split into its two main groups, probably along the lines of diverging dietary preferences. One group adopted a mainly herbivorous diet and gave rise to the Old World monkeys or cercopithecoids (represented today by the baboons and the colobines), while the other retained a more omnivorous diet and produced the hominoids (gibbons, apes and humans).

Dating the Hominid Line

The precise dates at which these splits occurred are uncertain, but the fossil evidence suggests that the hominid line is at least 25 million years old. A putative ancestor from that time has been found in the Fayum, south west of Cairo. The land is arid desert now, but 25 million years ago it was tropical rain forest and swampland, laced with broad meandering rivers. Scientists excavating fossil beds in the region have recovered the remains of a creature which is described formally as *Aegyptopithecus zeuxis*, though it is more colloquially known as the "dawn ape". Jaws and teeth, a skull and the skeletal parts of several individuals suggest that *Aegyptopithecus* was diverse and very generalised in its physical form. Experts have reconstructed from the fossil evidence a picture of a small arboreal primate, about the size of a domestic cat, with a sinuous back, long limbs, and all four feet capable of both grasping branches and conveying food to the mouth. The eyes looked forward, indicating stereoscopic vision, and the brain was larger in proportion to bodyweight than any other mammal.

Early Species

The descendants of *Aegyptopithecus* and its kind appear to have been very successful in evolutionary terms. More than 50 species are known from the fossil record, and hence palaeoanthropologists are inclined to refer to the Miocene (the geological period extending from 26 million to 8 million years ago) as the age of the ape. One of these species, *Proconsul africanus*, is believed to represent the line which led to the modern apes and humans.

First described from a nearly complete face and partial skull discovered by Mary Leakey on Kenya's Rusinga Island, Lake Victoria, in 1948, *Proconsul* was a tree-dwelling animal about the size of a baboon which roamed East Africa about 18 million years ago, sometime after the monkey and ape lines had diverged. More remains were recovered during the 1970s, enabling scientists to reconstruct a skeleton that was essentially 75 percent complete. The result showed an unexpected mixture of characteristics. *Proconsul* had a backbone resembling that of the gibbon, shoulder and elbow joints like those of the chimpanzee, and the wrists of a monkey. Overall, *Proconsul* is quite unlike any living ape, but could be ancestral.

Migration from Africa

Around 17 million years ago, the African continental plate butted up against Europe, raising high mountains and creating a landbridge across which many African animals migrated into Eurasia for the first time. Among them were apes whose fossil remains have also been proposed as candidates for the ancestry of the ape and human lines. *Dryopithecus* was found in Greece, *Ramapithecus* and *Sivapithecus* in the Siwalik Hills of northern Pakistan. The fossil evidence was fragmentary, but for many years *Ramapithecus*, dating from 14 million to 7 million years ago, was almost universally accepted as the earliest known ancestor of the human line. During the early 1980s, however, the discovery of more complete ramapithecine remains showed that it and the sivapithecines are more likely to represent ancestors of the orang-utan on their evolutionary and migratory journey to the south-east Asian islands where they are found today. Consensus opinion now rates the dryopithecines as close cousins headed for extinction, and regards Africa as the cradle of mankind.

The Emergence of Mankind

The question of human origins has intrigued every generation. Charles Darwin himself added a biological dimension with the publication of *The origin of species* in 1859. The controversy aroused by Darwin centred very largely around the mistaken idea that the theory of evolution implied that humans were descendants of the apes. This mistake is still encountered with surprising frequency, even though Darwin's original work and the many studies conducted since then all make the evolutionary proposition quite clear: humans are not descended from the apes, the two branches evolved simultaneously from a common ancestor which existed sometime in the past.

Among evolutionists, the question of human origins is basically a question of when the divergence of the ape and human lines occurred, and what the common ancestor looked like. For the greater part of the time since Darwin's day it has been assumed that the answers to these questions would be supplied by the fossil remains of the ancestral forms which might be recovered from geological deposits of ever-greater antiquity—if only those fossils could be found. Thus began the search for the missing link, as it became popularly known. By the 1960s the results of these fossil hunts had provided the basis for a widely-accepted scenario in which humans had evolved from *Ramapithecus* on a line which had split from the apes some 30 million years ago. Since the 1960s, however, this fossil-based scenario has been displaced by one based on biochemistry which puts the human/ape split at just 5 million years ago.

Modern DNA Evidence

Instead of studying fossil bones, biochemists have used the genetic material (DNA—deoxyribonucleic acid) of related living species to measure the amount of time which has passed since they diverged from a common ancestor. This work is based on three findings: first, DNA accumulates random mutations and changes over time which are evident in the protein structure of all individuals of a species. Second, as two lineages diverge from a common ancestor, each lineage accumulates changes in its DNA which are different from those of the other. Third, the accumulation of changes tends to occur at a regular, almost clocklike rate through time. Clearly, the greater the differences, the longer the divergence, and biochemists have thus been able to put a timescale on the divergence of the apes and humans. The orang-utan split away from the African hominoid stock about 12 million years ago, and the gorilla lineage diverged from the common ancestor of apes and humans about 8 million years ago. The chimpanzee and human lineages were the most recent to diverge from the common ancestor, their split having occurred about 5 million years ago.

Origin of the Hominid Lineage

In one sense the facts of human origins can be reduced to a series of dates at which humans and related species diverged from their common ancestors. But an intriguing question remains even then: what caused the splits; why did the species diverge from their common ancestor?

A species is the result of reproductive isolation. If the individual members of a viable breeding population reproduce only among themselves for any length of time, the genetic changes which accumulate with each generation will eventually produce a closely-related population which is significantly different from both its ancestral stock and the other descendants of that stock. If the process continues long enough a discrete species will have evolved, one which can only produce fertile offspring among its own kind. It can be supposed with some certainty that the reasons for the isolation which provoked speciation lay in the prevailing ecological circumstances of the time. Food supply would have been a primary factor, and this would have been susceptible to other factors such as climatic variation, the incursion of competing animals, climatic changes, or simply the pressures of a growing population.

Divergence of Gorillas and Chimpanzees

Any one or a combination of these ecological factors could have moved a viable breeding population of individuals into reproduction isolation where they might evolve into a discrete species. Migration is the most obvious course by which such isolation could have been achieved—but not the only one. Exploiting an alternative food resource, or adopting different social strategies could have achieved a similar degree of isolation even in close proximity with the ancestral population.

Precisely why the gorilla, chimpanzee and human lineages diverged between 8 million and 5 million years ago is not known. It may have been a consequence of the major climatic fluctuations which occurred during that time, when the overall pattern ranged from hot and dry to wet and very cold. The tropical forests retreated to the equatorial region, woodlands became dominant and grasslands proliferated. And with the changes in vegetation the composition of resident animal populations changed too. Many species became extinct, particularly among the browsers, while the grazers became more numerous. Doubtless the common ancestor of apes and humans was also affected by these developments, but the only certainties are that divergence and speciation occurred during that time, and that the distinctive characteristics of the living species can be considered as adaptations which proved advantageous to a reproductively isolated population.

Distinctive Human Characteristics

The distinctive characteristics of humans are the adaptation to a terrestrial way of life and bipedal locomotion; the much reduced face and jaws, and the greatly enlarged brain. In evolutionary terms, bipedalism was the crucial development, and it has been suggested that this was a consequence of the climatic changes which reduced the forest area and thereby increased competition for its resources. Under pressure from other arboreal primates, the human ancestor found a niche on the savannah. Whatever the case, bipedalism offered extensive evolutionary advantages. This was not because bipedalism itself is a particularly effective means of locomotion but rather because it freed forelimbs from locomotor functions and made them available for other purposes. One of the most important of these was the use of tools, and subsequently toolmaking. When the ancestral hominids first colonised the terrestrial habitat they had few inbuilt defence mechanisms and the ability to use stones, sticks and bones to ward off predators must have been of considerable survival value (as has been observed among present-day chimpanzees when they take to the ground). Initially used for defence, tools eventually were used in attack, heralding the adoption of a hunting mode of life. Toolmaking is also thought to have been one of the practices which favoured the development of language, and, since toolmaking called for fine manipulative skills, hand and brain evolved together; particularly those parts of the brain concerned with precise motor control and tactile sensation.

Advantages of Bipedalism

Another consequence of freeing the forelimbs through bipedalism was that carrying became so much easier. Thus food and other items could be carried over considerable distances and this facilitated the establishment of a home base. Perhaps even more important, the human infant could be carried in its mother's arms and held close to her body, allowing a much closer and more intimate relationship between mother and child than is possible in other animals. In terms of its physical development, the human infant is born in a very immature state; in part because of the limitations to the size of the birth canal imposed by the demands of bipedalism, but especially because of the large brain size of adult humans. It is therefore long dependent on parental care. This raises problems in a society where pregnant women and nursing mothers become dependent upon the group for food. Social bonds were forged in response, and it has been argued that the evolution of the particular form of reproductive cycle found in humans, in which the female is receptive to the male throughout most of her menstrual cycle should be seen as a means of ensuring that a male will be willing to assume responsibility for females and offspring.

FOSSIL EVIDENCE OF HUMAN EVOLUTION

A fundamental premise of palaeoanthropology (the study of man in times past) rests on the contention that unequivocal evidence of human evolution would be found in fossils of known antiquity linking modern man to extinct ancestor. Ideally, the fossils should comprise a series of complete skeletons from a precisely dated sequence of time: this would enable scientists to trace the evolutionary development of humans with complete certainty. But the arbitrary nature of the fossilization process virtually eliminates all chance that such an ideal could ever be achieved or even approached. Far from ideal, palaeoanthropology has had to work with a slowly accumulating collection of diverse and often very fragmentary specimens ever since it became an established discipline in the mid-19th century. In the first fifty years only five specimens were discovered; another twenty-five years passed before a dozen were known, and even today the significant specimens could all be accommodated on a billiard table.

The fossils have come from Europe, the Far East and Africa; they span over 3 million years, but as clues to the process of human evolution during that time they represent a minute fraction of mankind's potential ancestry. It has been calculated that ten skulls from East Turkana in Kenya (an exceptional collection covering 1 million years, for example, represent only one individual in every 100 million.

Problems of Evidence

The shortage of evidence is compounded by other problems. Uncertainties concerning age, for instance, mean that differing features which may represent evolutionary change over time cannot be placed in chronological order. And many fossils are so broken, distorted or incomplete that unequivocal interpretation of their significance is rarely possible. In such cases, different authorities may emphasize the importance of different features with equal validity, and the points distinguishing their interpretations may be so slight that each depends as much upon the proponent's beliefs about the course of human evolution as upon the evidence presented.

Discoveries, including fossils and a trail of fossilized footprints, have, however, shown that hominids were fully bipedal more than 3·6 million years ago, though the configuration of skull and jaw remained distinctly apelike for some time thereafter, while brainsize did not begin to approach modern proportions until 1·5 million years ago.

Finding the Fossils

Fossils (from the latin *fossilis*, meaning dug up) are the end products of a process in which organisms are buried and infiltrated by minerals which replace them, molecule by molecule, until, where organic material existed before, stone remains, exactly preserving the form of the original. Fossils have been the source of virtually all that is known about the evolution of life—from the oldest known forms (microscopic fossil algae dating back to 3·5 billion years) to modern times.

For an organism to become fossilized it must first of all be entrapped in a suitable material, away from the attention of scavengers and decomposers. Aquatic organisms comprise by far the greatest number of fossils, not only because they have been more numerous throughout the history of life, but also because the seabed or lake bottom favours fossilization. Terrestrial organisms are less commonly found as fossils (most are consumed or decomposed by other creatures soon after death), and hominid fossils are among the rarest of all.

Palaeoanthropologists wishing to find the fossil remains of early humans are limited by two major factors. First, humans evolved in the comparatively recent past and were not numerous until recent times—which means that the total number available for fossilization must always have been relatively small. Second, their way of life and the terrain they occupied were unlikely to favour the fossilization of their remains, and there are few places in the world where fossil beds of a suitable age and composition are exposed.

Early European Sites

In scouring the world for potential fossil deposits, palaeoanthropologists have found ancient caves to be a most productive source of fossils (and not only of hominids). Whether originally used as shelters, or as dens to which predators such as leopards or hyenas may have retreated with their victims, bones left in the cave did not decay, but were fossilized as debris and rockfalls filled the caves. The first hominid fossils ever known to science were discovered at cave sites in Europe—Cannstadt in Germany (c.1700); Koestritz, Upper Saxony (1820); Kent's Cavern, Devon (1829); Engis in Belgium (1833), Gibraltar (before 1848), Neanderthal in Germany (1857). Several of the discoveries made before Darwin published his theory of evolution in 1859 received little notice at the time of discovery; some were lost. Investigations moved to the Far East at the end of the 19th century, where *Homo erectus* was recovered from riverbed deposits in Java (1891), and again in cave deposits near Peking (Beijing) during the 1920s.

Fossil Discoveries in Africa: The Olduvai Gorge

Cave sites in South Africa have also proved to be a good source of hominid fossils. Alerted in the 1920s by quarrymen exploiting the lime-rich infills of ancient cave systems in the dolomitic hills, palaeoanthropologists have since recovered a number of important fossils from these sites.

The famed fossil sites of East Africa are predominantly volcanic in origin; the ash settling from eruptions associated with the formation of the Rift Valley having created conditions that were particularly suitable for the fossilization of bone. At Olduvai Gorge in Tanzania, where an ancient lake basin was inundated by successive eruptions of ash and subsequently drained by geological faulting, a river has sliced through the deposits to reveal much evidence of the hominids who frequented the area from at least 2 million years ago. Volcanic eruptions similarly preserved the 3·6 million year old footprint trail at Laetoli, near Olduvai.

As at Olduvai, volcanic activity and a lakeside environment were also responsible for the preservation of hominid fossils dating from 3·1 million years ago which have been found in the Afar depression of Ethiopia, and those dating from 1·8 million years ago found in the Koobi Fora region of the Lake Turkana basin, northern Kenya. *See also* **T**53(2)

Assessing the Age of Hominid Fossils

The age of a fossil is of paramount importance to the palaeoanthropologist in the assessment of its evolutionary significance. Until the late 1950s scientists could do no more than assess the age of their finds in *relative* terms, that is according to the kinds of other fossil animals found in the same deposit or sequence of deposits. The fossil record as a whole gives a broad picture of the order in which various animal forms have evolved and become extinct through the course of geological time. Hominid fossils are not found among the remains of dinosaurs, for instance, so must be younger; on the other hand, they must be older than any extinct animals (such as hyenas and pigs) which may be found in deposits overlaying the hominid beds.

Relative dating was always of limited use to palaeoanthropologists since human evolution occurred in a recent and extremely brief period of geological time (if the whole of Earth history was condensed into 24 hours, man would have existed for little more than one minute). Estimates of the fossils' age in years were made from time to time, but they were rough estimates based on guesses of how fast evolution proceeds, and of the rate at which sedimentary deposits accumulate. Most underestimated the actual ages which were given when developments during the 1950s, enabled geochronologists to give an *absolute* date for hominid fossil deposits.

Methods of Dating

Several methods of absolute dating have been applied to the study of fossil man:

Radiometric Dating is based on the principle that a radioactive "parent" element decays into a stable "daughter" element at a constant rate. Once the rate of decay is known, the age of a sample can be calculated from the ratio of parent to daughter elements which it contains. It should be noted that it is not the fossils themselves that are dated, but the deposits in which they are found. The cave sites of South Africa and elsewhere are devoid of materials suitable for radiometric dating, but the volcanic beds of East Africa have proved especially informative in this respect because they contain the minerals necessary for the *potassium-argon* dating method, which measures the ratio of the radioactive isotope of potassium, K-40, to its decay product, the gas argon 40. Potassium-argon is used for the absolute dating of deposits between 230,000 and 26 million years old, which makes it particularly suited to the needs of palaeoanthropologists.

Fission-Track Dating: a method in which the age of a specimen is assessed from the tracks made by the fission of uranium atoms within them. The density and number of tracks already present in the specimen are compared with those produced when the specimen is exposed to neutron radiation in the laboratory. This comparison provides the basis for an estimate of age.

Radiocarbon Dating: the radioisotope carbon-14 accumulates in living tissue, but begins to decay after death. The rate of decay is known, and so the proportion of carbon-14 remaining in a specimen is a measure of the time which has passed since the organism ceased to live. After about 50,000 years, however, so little carbon-14 remains that dating becomes impossible. This limited timespan makes the methods of little use to palaeoanthropologists, but it has proved immensely useful to archaeologists in the dating of wood and other organic materials.

Thermoluminescence: with the passage of time, certain substances accumulate energy in the form of electrons trapped at defects in the crystal lattice of their constituent minerals. When the materials are heated this energy is given off as a "puff" of light (thermoluminescence, or TL); the intensity of that light is a measure of how long the energy had been accumulating in the material, and this can be set against a known timescale to give an estimate of the material's age. The method has been particularly useful in dating archaeological finds such as pottery, where it is certain that the firing process reset the material's TL clock to zero when the pot was made, but it has also been used to date flints that were dropped in early man's campfires. These go back to 100,000 years ago.

Geomagnetic Dating (also known as **palaeomagnetic dating**): makes use of the fact that the Earth's magnetic field has changed direction many times in its history. When metals are deposited in sediments they align with the prevailing magnetic field, which is then effectively "fossilized" as the sediments harden. The record of these directional changes through geological time establishes a sequence of broad time-segments which can be used for dating deposits directly, or as a check of other methods.

THE FOSSIL LINEAGE

From the earliest days of palaeoanthropological research, investigators have tended to consider the fossils in chronological order (on either the relative or the absolute timescale), from oldest to youngest, and to describe the differences between them as progressive evolutionary changes which have led, ultimately, to modern man. So long as the number of hominid fossils remained small, and the temporal distance between them large, this attractively simple scheme remained valid, inculcating a general readiness to believe that human evolution had been a straightforward single-line affair, unwaveringly directed towards its ultimate expression: *Homo sapiens sapiens* and contentious only in the matter of which human attributes were acquired first—restructuring of the jaw, the bipedal gait, or the large brain?

A Single-Line Sequence?

Straightforward and attractive, yes, but contradicting the evidence of evolution in many other mammalian lineages. The fossil remains of pigs, horses, and antelopes, for example, display a tremendous amount of variation, not only through the geological sequence, but also at any given point on it, indicating that their evolution had been more of a radiation than a single line, with extinctions and proliferations of species occurring at many points in their evolutionary histories. Indeed, the frequency of extinction and speciation found in the fossil record of most organisms whose remains have been found suggests that such patterns are the rule. Why should humans be the exception?

The answer emerging from the tremendous advances made in palaeoanthropological research over the past half century is that they are not. Though the total number of fossil hominids is small (as was the total number of hominids available to be fossilized, especially when compared with the size of living pig, antelope and horse populations), it shows that there have been extinctions and speciations during the course of human evolution too.

The fossil hominids discovered so far date from over 5·5 million years ago to less than 30,000.

The Australopithecines: The Oldest Hominids

Discoveries in Ethiopia and Kenya have suggested that earlier theories may have underestimated the age of our earliest ancestors by as much as two million years. The lineages of these new specimens are, however, not universally accepted. Notwithstanding this, the group called the *Australopithecines* represent the oldest group of hominids, dating from 3·7 to 1·6 million years ago. Most authorities now accept four species—*Australopithecus afarensis*, *A. africanus* (or *gracile*), *A. boisei* and *A. robustus*.

The Work of the Leakey Family

In 1959 Louis Leakey (1903–72) and his wife, Mary (1913–96), recovered an almost complete skull, lacking the mandible, from deposits at Olduvai Gorge in Tanzania subsequently dated at 1·7 million years by the potassium-argon method.

After 1969 teams under the direction of National Museums of Kenya Director, Richard Leakey (1944–), recovered numerous australopithecine fossils with both gracile and robust affinities from 1·4 to 1·8 million year old deposits at East Turkana, northern Kenya. In 1985, the same team recovered a robust australopithecine skull from 2·5 million year old deposits on the west shore of Lake Turkana.

Between 1973 and 1977 joint French and American expeditions recovered large numbers of gracile australopithecine fossils from deposits dated at 2·6 to 3·3 million years ago in the Afar depression region of north-eastern Ethiopia. The fossils proved to be remarkably similar to others found at Laetoli, near Olduvai Gorge, by Mary Leakey in 1974–5 which were dated at 3·6 million years.

The fossil hominids discovered at Laetoli came from the same age deposit as a trail of fossilised footprints, and this circumstantial evidence invites the inference that the trail was made by those same hominids—*A. afarensis*. Evidence has been adduced for and against, but the issue remains contentious.

HOMO HABILIS

The taxon was created by Louis Leakey and his co-authors in their 1964 *Nature* paper describing hominid remains excavated at Olduvai Gorge in 1961 from deposits dated at 1·7 million years by the potassium-argon method. The fossils comprised a lower mandible, skull fragments, and a group of handbones. They were found in association with stone tools, and this was a persuasive factor in the authors' decision to assign the fossils to the genus *Homo*, since no tools had ever been found incontrovertibly associated with the australopithecines and it was generally considered that man by definition was a toolmaker. Hence the name, *Homo habilis*, colloquially translated as "handy man".

More Discoveries at Olduvai

Further remains of *Homo habilis* were found at Olduvai in succeeding years, including teeth, limb bones and a badly crushed and distorted skull. Richard Leakey's team at East Turkana discovered the skull known as 1470 (from its museum accession number KNM-ER 1470), which is informally described as *Homo habilis*, as are sundry other finds from East Turkana. Remains assigned to *Homo habilis* have also been recovered from excavations at the Swartkrans and Sterkfontein cave sites in South Africa, and at deposits in the Omo river basin in southern Ethiopia. In 1986, a new survey of the Olduvai Gorge deposits (led by Donald Johanson), recovered numerous fragments of skull, jaw and limb representing a single individual, which was subsequently assigned to *Homo habilis*.

The fossil evidence of *Homo habilis* recovered to date gives the species wide distribution through Africa, and a timespan dating from 2·1 to 1·8 million years ago. The species' mean brainsize is estimated to have been 750 cc.

The Status of Homo Habilis

The status of *Homo habilis* itself has not been very much clarified in the decades since it was first described. Two main issues have arisen: First, the discovery of *Homo erectus* fossils from 1·6 million year deposits at East Turkana indicates that *Homo habilis* was one of at least three hominid species alive at that time (the other was *A. robustus*), which questions its status as an ancestor of *H. erectus*. Second, the *Homo habilis* fossils discovered at Olduvai in 1986 by Johanson and his team show a considerable degree of affinity with the *Australopithecus afarensis* material dating from more than 3·5 million years ago, which suggests that the ancestral form remained unchanged for a very long time, and that the *Homo* characteristics evident in later specimens of *H. habilis* must have evolved very quickly.

HOMO ERECTUS

The most widespread and longest-surviving of the fossil hominids. Remains have been found in north and east Africa, Europe, Indonesia and China. The fossils date from 1·6 million years ago (West Turkana) to less than 300,000 years (China). Mean brain size ranges from 900 cc in early specimens to 1100 cc in late specimens.

Java Man

The first known specimens were described by Eugene Dubois (1858–1940) in 1894 and included a calotte (the cranial vault) and a complete femur (thighbone) excavated from sedimentary deposits comprising freshwater sandstones, conglomerates and volcanic material at a bend of the Solo river in Central Java, Indonesia. The cranial capacity was relatively small (900 cc) while the femur was entirely human, and this combination led Dubois to assign the fossils to a new species: *Pithecanthropus erectus*, meaning erect ape-man, while the specimen became popularly known as Java Man. When fossils of similar configuration were found in China (Peking Man) both the Java and Peking material was assigned to the taxon *Homo* with sub-specific distinctions made for the Java (*Homo erectus javensis*) and Peking material (*Homo erectus pekinensis*). Subsequently, sub-specific distinctions were dropped and the taxon became known as *Homo*

erectus.

Remains displaying *Homo erectus* characteristics have been recovered in Europe from sites in Germany, Hungary, Greece, and France, and in 1960 a skull found at Olduvai Gorge extended the range of the species to Africa. Subsequently, further remains were found in Morocco and Algeria, in the Omo river basin of Ethiopia, and the Lake Turkana basin, northern Kenya.

The Turkana Boy

In 1985 a virtually complete *Homo erectus* skeleton was found in deposits on the western side of Lake Turkana dated at 1.6 million years old. The remarkable preservation of the specimen is thought to be the result of the body having sunk quickly into lake silts after death. The skeleton is immature, its development matching that of a modern 12 year old. Estimates based on its limb size and modern growth rates suggest that the individual would have stood 1·68 m tall as an adult. Cranial capacity is as yet undetermined, but clearly relatively low. The forehead is low and recedes, as does the chin.

The Affinities of Homo Erectus

Though *Homo erectus* is well positioned in time to be both a descendent of earlier hominid forms and an ancestor of modern humans, several questions arise from its distribution and physical characteristics. Some authorities argue that the Asian and African forms are so distinct that the latter should not be assigned to *Homo erectus*. Others have suggested that the species represents a side branch of human evolution which became extinct, and its co-existence with *Homo habilis* at East Turkana indeed could be seen as reason for dismissing it from the human line.

There is also continuing debate on whether the relatively incomplete material from Europe represents the "true" *Homo erectus* or a group that should be more closely aligned to modern humans. This in turn raises the question of the *Homo erectus/Homo sapiens* transition: was this a gradual change, as some authorities see demonstrated in the Omo material? Or was there a long period of stasis followed by abrupt change?

HOMO ANTECESSOR (PIONEER MAN)

A species identified from a jaw bone and teeth found in the Atapuerca hills near Burgos in Spain and dating back to between 1·2 and 1·1 million years ago.

'East Anglia Man', whose settlements at Pakefield, Suffolk, and Happisburgh, Norfolk, are the oldest ancient human sites yet found in Britain, was probably identical to, or closely related to, *homo antecessor*. The Pakefield site dates back some 700,000 years, but Happisburgh, uncovered in 2010, dates back between 780,000 and 990,000 years and is the earliest human settlement yet found in Northern Europe. More than 70 flint tools and chips have been recovered from Happisburgh, but no human remains, so the identification of 'East Anglia Man' with *homo antecessor*, although highly likely, cannot be proved. He would have arrived in Britain over the land bridge which then linked it with mainland Europe, across what are now the Straits of Dover, to settle in Happisburgh at the mouth of the large river which later shifted its course southwards to become the modern Thames. The rigours of the subsequent Ice Ages would have forced 'East Anglia Man' to migrate back southwards or die out. *Homo antecessor* is not thought to have been a direct ancestor of modern man, *homo sapiens*.

HEIDELBERG MAN

An archaic human whose remains were found in 1907 and who is likely to have been the ancestor of both modern man, *homo sapiens*, and also of 'Neanderthal Man'. 'Heidelberg Man' was characterised by large brow ridges, sloping forehead, and a heavy chinless jaw, and lived between 524,000 and 478,000 years ago.

'Boxgrove Man', whose remains were found at

Boxgrove, near Chichester, West Sussex, in the 1990s, and at some 500,000 years old are the earliest actual human remains yet found in Britain, appears to have been related to 'Heidelberg Man'.

ARCHAIC HOMO SAPIENS

A term applied to specimens which might be said to exemplify the *Homo erectus/Homo sapiens* transition mentioned above, and also integral to the proposition that modern man evolved in Africa in the relatively recent past. The definitive specimen (Rhodesia Man) was discovered in the course of mining operations at Kabwe, Zambia in 1921, and comprises a complete cranium, teeth and skeletal fragments. Recent appraisal of the site and associated finds has suggested that the remains date from at least 125,000 years ago. Cranial capacity is 1280 cc, indicating an enlarged brain.

Numerous specimens assigned to the group have come from more than 30 sites spanning Africa from north to south and covering a timespan ranging from 500,000 to 30,000 years ago. Some display features characteristic of the ancestral hominids, others are entirely modern. An age of about 100,000 years has been given to comparable forms known from Qafzeh in Israel, but all other evidence of anatomically modern man known from outside Africa is significantly younger.

This is seen as indicating that modern man originated in Africa and migrated from there to populate the rest of the world not more than 200,000 years ago.

NEANDERTHAL MAN

The first specimen was discovered by quarrymen clearing a cave in the Neander valley, near Dusseldorf in 1857. Following its classification as a distinct species in 1864, *Homo neanderthalensis* soon became symbolic of a misguided view of early man as an inferior and degenerate version of modern man. Based at first on a shortage of evidence and a determination to believe in the purity of the human line, this misconception was later reinforced by the distinguished palaeontologist Marcellin Boule (1861–1942) in a series of reports on Neanderthal remains found in cave sites at La Chapelle-aux-Saints and La Ferrassie between 1908–1912. Boule interpreted skeletal deformities as indicative of an habitual slouching gait and concluded that Neanderthal Man was every bit as degenerate as had been popularly supposed. Subsequent studies have shown that the deformities were the result of arthritis and that the Neanderthals were a sturdy and successful race, well-adapted to the environmental conditions of their time.

Features of Neanderthal Man

Discoveries of Neanderthal fossils at Engis in Belgium (1832), and Gibraltar (before 1848) predated the original find, and many more remains have been found in Europe, Iraq and Israel. Bone structure and stout muscular attachments indicate that the Neanderthals were generally short and thick-set, with large feet and hands and a body form similar to that of modern cold-adapted people.

Average brain size was over 1400 cc (some 10 percent larger than modern human, relative to body size) and exceeded 1700 cc in some large males. Dating of the fossil sites indicates that the Neanderthals lived from about 130,000 to 35,000 years ago.

Thus they appear to have been a well-adapted and successful group of hunters and gatherers who ranged across Europe with the advance and retreat of the Ice Age.

Indeed it is now thought 'Neanderthal Man' was a positive evolutionary response to the need imposed on man by the Ice Ages to hunt at close quarters, which put a premium on strength rather than on agility. Our old perceptions are changing.

The Affinities of Homo Neanderthalensis

Anatomical characteristics evident in both the Neanderthals and *Homo erectus* indicate that the two shared a common ancestry and possibly even a direct line of descent, but their relationship to modern man is far less clear. There are common characteristics, but much more that is different between the two forms. Moreover, it is generally felt that the proximity of the dates at which the Neanderthals disappeared and the modern humans became prevalent leave little time for evolution to have effected the change from one to the other (but all humans today have some Neanderthal DNA).

After 100,000 years of unchallenged existence, Neanderthals disappeared around 35,000 years ago. Only the remains of people anatomically indistinguishable from modern humans have been recovered from more recent sites. They probably became extinct in Western Europe, possibly Belgium, having lived alongside Homo sapiens for *c.* 20,000 years.

'Neanderthal Man' walked as upright as modern man. He could use fire in a controlled manner and he buried his dead and cared for the sick and elderly. He developed the production of jewellery, possibly, under the influence of modern humans. He etched primitive cave art. Feathers were used as body adornment. Recent evidence suggests they may have used an early form of language.

HOMO SAPIENS SAPIENS

Fossil remains of anatomically modern humans are known from sites in Europe, Africa, the Near East, Asia and Australia. The first and most famous to be found was Cro-Magnon Man, unearthed in the Dordogne region of France in 1868 and dating from about 40,000 years ago. Fragmentary fossils of a wholly modern form recovered from a cave at the Klasie's river mouth in South Africa date back to more than 100,000 years ago, while those from the Mungo site in Australia are from 32,000 years ago. On present knowledge, these two finds represent the greatest time-depth and geographic dispersal of early modern humans.

The dispersal of modern humans appears to have been rapid between 30,000 and 20,000 and became especially so with the domestication of animals and crop plants from about 10,000 years ago. Migration into the Americas was delayed until a landbridge across the Bering Straits opened through glacial ice *c.* 18,000 years ago, but excavations have shown that modern humans were well-established in north America soon thereafter and had spread as far south as the Chilean Andes by 12,000 years ago.

The spread and proliferation of anatomically modern humans is inextricably linked with the development of technological skills, art, and circumstantial evidence of social interaction. While the Neanderthals employed a stone tool technology little improved from earlier forms, the anatomically modern humans introduced the flint-flaking techniques by which a greater variety of tools were made. Personal adornment and careful burial of the dead were features of their lifestyle not so evident among the Neanderthals, and cave paintings speak eloquently of their perceptive talents.

More recent studies of mitochondrial DNA, which is inherited strictly through the maternal line because the sperm does not contribute mitochondria to the fertilised egg cell, show that modern humans can trace their ancestry to a single female, commonly referred to as Eve, a member of a population living in Africa some 150,000 years ago.

POSTSCRIPT: HOMO NALEDI

New members of the human family tree continue to be discovered. A new species *Homo naledi* was discovered in 2013. It had been found in a barely-accessible cave in South Africa near Johannesburg. Around 2,000 specimens have been found, from 12 bodies, of a species that lived *c.* 2 million years ago. It was uniquely adapted both to walk and also climb trees.

VI.　SCIENTIFIC TABLES
TABLE OF ELEMENTS†

Element (Symbol)	Atomic Number	Atomic Weight	Valency	Element (Symbol)	Atomic Number	Atomic Weight	Valency
actinium (Ac)* . . .	89	227		molybdenum (Mo)	42	95.94	
aluminium (Al) . .	13	26·9815	3				
americium (Am)* .	95	243	3, 4, 5, 6	neodymium (Nd)	60	144·24	3
antimony (Sb) . .	51	121·75	3, 5	neon (Ne)	10	20·17	0
argon (Ar).	18	39·944	0	neptunium (Np)*	93	237	4, 5, 6
arsenic (As)	33	74·9216	3, 5	nickel (Ni).	28	58·71	2, 3
astatine (At)* . . .	85	210	1, 3, 5, 7	niobium (Nb). . . .	41	92·906	3, 5
				nitrogen (N)	7	14·0067	3, 5
barium (Ba)	56	137·34	2	nobelium (No)* . .	102	254	
berkelium (Bk)* . .	97	247	3, 4				
beryllium (Be) . . .	4	9·0122	2	osmium (Os)	76	190·2	2, 3, 4, 8
bismuth (Bi)	83	208·980	3, 5	oxygen (O)	8	15·9994	2
boron (B)	5	10·811	3				
bromine (Br)	35	79·904		palladium (Pd). . .	46	106·4	2, 4, 6
				phosphorus (P). . .	15	30·9378	3,5
cadmium (Cd) . . .	48	112·40		platinum (Pt) . . .	78	195·09	2, 4
				plutonium (Pu)* . .	94	244	3, 4, 5, 6
calcium (Ca)	20	40·08	2	polonium (Po)* . .	84	210	
californium (Cf)* .	98	251		potassium (K) . . .	19	39.102	1
carbon (C).	6	12·0111	2, 4	praseodymium			
cerium (Ce)	58	140·12	3, 4	(Pr)	59	140·907	3
caesium (Cs)	55	132·905	1	promethium			
chlorine (Cl).	17	35·453	1, 3, 5, 7	(Pm)*	61	145	3
chromium (Cr) . . .	24	51·996	2, 3, 6	protactinium			
cobalt (Co)	27	58·9332	2, 3	(Pa)*	91	231	
copper (Cu)	29	63·546	1, 2				
curium (Cm)*. . . .	96	247	3	radium (Ra)*. . . .	88	226	2
				radon (Rn)*.	86	222	0
dysprosium (Dy) . .	66	162·50	3	rhenium (Re). . . .	75	186·2	
				rhodium (Rh)	45	102·905	3
einsteinium (Es)* .	99	254		rubidium (Rb) . . .	37	85·47	1
erbium (Er).	68	167·26	3	ruthenium (Ru) . .	44	101·07	3, 4, 6, 8
europium (Eu) . . .	63	151·96	2, 3				
				samarium (Sm) . .	62	150·35	2, 3
fermium (Fm)*. . .	100	253		scandium (Sc) . . .	21	44·956	3
fluorine (F)	9	18·9984	1	selenium (Se)	34	78·96	2, 4, 6
francium (Fr)*. . .	87	223	1	silicon (Si).	14	28·086	4
				silver (Ag).	47	107·870	1
gadolinium (Gd). .	64	157·25	3	sodium (Na)	11	22·9898	1
gallium (Ga)	31	69·72	2, 3	strontium (Sr) . . .	38	87·62	2
germanium (Ge). .	32	72·59	4	sulphur (S)	16	32·064	2, 4, 6
gold (Au)	79	196·967	1, 3				
				tantalum (Ta) . . .	73	180·947	5
hafnium (Hf)	72	178·49	4	technetium (Tc)* .	43	99	6, 7
helium (He).	2	4·0026	0	tellurium (Te) . . .	52	127·60	2, 4, 6
holmium (Ho) . . .	67	164·930	3	terbium (Tb)	65	158·925	3
hydrogen (H). . . .	1	1·00797	1	thallium (Tl)	81	204·37	1, 3
				thorium (Th)	90	232·038	4
indium (In)	49	114·82	3	thulium (Tm). . . .	69	168·934	3
iodine (I)	53	126·904	1, 3, 5, 7	tin (Sn).	50	118·69	2, 4
iridium (Ir)	77	192·2	3, 4	titanium (Ti)	22	47·90	3, 4
iron (Fe).	26	55·847	2, 3	tungsten (see wolfram)			
krypton (Kr)	36	83·8	0	uranium (U)	92	238·03	4, 6
lanthanum (La) . .	57	138·01	3				
lawrencium (Lr)* .	103	257		vanadium (V) . . .	23	50·942	3, 5
lead (Pb).	82	207·19	2, 4				
lithium (Li)	3	6·941	1	wolfram (W)	74	183·85	6
lutetium (Lu). . . .	71	174·97	3				
				xenon (Xe)	54	131·30	0
magnesium (Mg). .	12	24·305	2	ytterbium (Yb) . .	70	173·04	2, 3
manganese (Mn). .	25	54·9380	2,3,4,6,7	yttrium (Y).	39	88·905	3
mendeleevium							
(Md)*	101	256		zinc (Zn).	30	65·37	2
mercury (Hg). . . .	80	200·59	1, 2	zirconium (Zr) . . .	40	91·22	4

* In the cases of these elements, which have been artificially prepared, atomic weight in the chemical sense is meaningless; the integral mass of the most stable isotope known is given

Note: In 1961 the isotope of carbon-12 replaced oxygen as a standard, the weight of its atom being taken as 12. This change has meant a slight adjustment in atomic weights from the old chemical scale

† Those elements with atomic numbers above 103 are called **transactinides**. Although the table below lists those transactinides whose existence is confirmed, their names (and some of their properties) are sometimes only provisional. All elements with an atomic number greater than uranium are termed **transuranics**.

No	Element	No	Element	No	Element
104	unnilquadium (rutherfordium)	110	ununnilium	115	ununpentium (moscovium)
105	unnilpentium (hahnium)		(darmstadtium)	116	ununhexium (tennessine)
106	unnilhexium (seaborgium)	111	unununium (roentgenium)	117	ununseptium (oganesson)
107	unnilseptium (bohrium)	112	ununbium (copernicium)	118	ununoctium
108	unniloctium (hassium)	113	ununtrium (nihonium)		
109	unnilennium (meitnerium)	114	ununquadium		

PERIODIC TABLE

PERIODIC TABLE OF THE ELEMENTS
Key to Chart

Atomic Number → 1
Symbol → B
Atomic Weight → 10.811

GROUP	1A	2A	3B	4B	5B	6B	7B	8			1B	2B	3A	4A	5A	6A	7A	0
Period	Alkali metals	Alkaline earth metals	←—— Transition metals ——→								Noble metals							Inert gases
1	1 H 1·00797																	2 He 4·0026
2	3 Li 6·941	4 Be 9·0122											5 B 10·811	6 C 12·0111	7 N 14·0067	8 O 15·9994	9 F 18·9984	10 Ne 20·179
3	11 Na 22·9898	12 Mg 24·305											13 Al 26·9815	14 Si 28·086	15 P 30·9738	16 S 32·064	17 Cl 35·453	18 Ar 39·948
4	19 K 39·103	20 Ca 40·08	21 Sc 44·9559	22 Ti 47·90	23 V 50·942	24 Cr 51·996	25 Mn 54·938	26 Fe 55·847	27 Co 58·933	28 Ni 58·71	29 Cu 63·546	30 Zn 65·37	31 Ga 69·72	32 Ge 72·59	33 As 74·9216	34 Se 78·96	35 Br 79·904	36 Kr 83·80
5	37 Rb 85·4678	38 Sr 87·62	39 Y 88·9059	40 Zr 91·22	41 Nb 92·9064	42 Mo 95·94	43 Tc 99	44 Ru 101·07	45 Rh 102·905	46 Pd 106·4	47 Ag 107·870	48 Cd 112·40	49 In 114·82	50 Sn 118·69	51 Sb 121·75	52 Te 127·60	53 I 126·904	54 Xe 131·30
6	55 Cs 132·905	56 Ba 137·34	57 La* 138·91	72 Hf 178·49	73 Ta 180·947	74 W 183·85	75 Re 186·2	76 Os 190·09	77 Ir 192·2	78 Pt 195·09	79 Au 196·967	80 Hg 200·59	81 Tl 204·37	82 Pb 207·19	83 Bi 208·980	84 Po 210	85 At 210	86 Rn 222
7	87 Fr 223	88 Ra 226	89 Ac† 227															

* Lanthanides (see L64)

58 Ce 140·12	59 Pr 140·907	60 Nd 144·24	61 Pm 145	62 Sm 150·96	63 Eu 151·96	64 Gd 157·25	65 Tb 158·925	66 Dy 162·50	67 Ho 164·930	68 Er 167·26	69 Tm 168·934	70 Yb 173·04	71 Lu 174·97

† Actinides (see L3)

90 Th 232·038	91 Pa 231	92 U 238·03	93 Np 237	94 Pu 244	95 Am 243	96 Cm 247	97 Bk 247	98 Cf 251	99 Es 254	100 Fm 253	101 Md 256	102 No 254	103 Lr 257

Roman type—metals
Italic type—semiconductors
Bold type—non-metals

These designations refer to the normal materials usually at room temperature. Processes like heating or compressing can turn metals into insulators and vice versa.

Note: It is possible by artificial methods such as bombardment by other nuclei to produce elements with atomic numbers greater than 103. However the very heavy elements tend to be unstable and decay spontaneously into lighter elements. Because the lifetime of such elements is short no element with an atomic number greater than Uranium (92) occurs naturally on earth. *See footnote,* **T56**. In 2016, elements 113, 115, 117 and 118 were officially added to the periodic table by the International Union of Pure and Applied Chemistry.

MEASURES, UNITS AND METROLOGY

Introduction

Before any quantity can be measured one must decide on the *units* used for measurement. For example, a 2 lb loaf of bread when weighed in ounces will give 32, *i.e.* 2 × 16. This is because there are 16 oz in a pound. It would be incorrect to say the weight of the loaf is 2 or 32. We say it is 2 lb or 32 oz and we can convert from one unit to another by knowing the ratio of their sizes.

If a standard pound is kept somewhere this can be used to calibrate other standard weights using accurate scales. These in turn can be used to calibrate other weights which in turn can be compared with the loaf with scales in order to weigh the bread.

The International Prototype Kilogram

Nowadays, for scientific purposes, weights are compared with that of the *international prototype kilogram*, kept at Sèvres in France. For a long time the length of an object was obtained by making a comparison, direct or indirect, with the standard metre if using the metric system or the standard yard if using the Imperial system. The standard metre was the length between two notches on a metal rod, kept at a controlled temperature, at Sèvres. Time is measured in seconds, which at one time was defined as a certain fraction of the tropical year.

The Problem of Definition

Definitions of this kind are unsatisfactory for two reasons. First, the tropical year is not constant and even the most carefully kept metal rods are liable to change their dimensions over a long period of time. Secondly, it is not always convenient to do a comparison with an object kept in France. Nowadays every effort is made to define units in terms of some fundamental property of matter which is reproducible everywhere and does not require comparison with one particular object. The second is now defined using an atomic clock and can be measured to an accuracy of 1 part in 10^{12}. Variations in the rotation of the earth are far greater than this. The metre is nowadays defined in terms of the distance light travels in one second. Although the kilogram could likewise be defined in terms of some fundamental quantity of matter, such as insisting the mass of an electron is 9.1083×10^{-31} kilogram, this quantity is only known to about 2 parts in 10^5. Comparisons with the standard kilogram can lead to an accuracy of the order 10^{-9}, so at present this definition of the kilogram stands.

The SI System

The scientist nowadays mainly uses the SI system of units. SI is short for "Système International d'Unités" and it is a system of metric units which has come into international use through the agency of such bodies as the General Conference of the International Bureau of Weights and Measures and the International Organisation for Standardisation (ISO) in whose work Britain participates.

Definitions of the Base Units

The system uses the *base quantities* listed below:

Quantity	Name of unit	Symbol of unit
Length	metre	m
Mass	kilogram	kg
Time	second	s
Electric current	ampere	A
Thermodynamic temperature	kelvin	K
Luminous intensity	candela	cd
Amount of substance	mole	mol

The seven SI base units are defined as follows:

The **metre** is the length travelled by light in a vacuum in 1/299 792 458 sec. (*See* **Metre, Section L**).

The **kilogram** is the mass of the international prototype of the kilogram (*q.v.*). Scientists use the word 'mass' where the layman would say "weight". Strictly speaking, weight is not a base quantity and is a measure of *force*.

The **second** is the duration of 9 192 631 770 periods of the radiation corresponding to the transition between the two hyperfine levels of the ground state of the caesium-133 atom (*See* **Clock, Section L**).

TABLE I

Quantity	Name of SI unit	Symbol	SI unit in terms of base units or derived units
frequency	hertz	Hz	$1 \text{ Hz} = 1 \text{ s}^{-1}$
volume	stere	st	$1 \text{ st} = 1 \text{ m}^3$
density	kilogram per cubic metre		kg m^{-3}
velocity	metre per second		m s^{-1}
force	newton	N	$1 \text{ N} = 1 \text{ kg m s}^{-2}$
pressure, stress	pascal	Pa	$1 \text{ Pa} = 1 \text{ N m}^{-2}$
viscosity (dynamic)	pascal second		Pa s
work, energy, quantity of heat	joule	J	$1 \text{ J} = 1 \text{ N m}$
power	watt	W	$1 \text{ W} = 1 \text{ J s}^{-1}$
quantity of electricity	coulomb	C	$1 \text{ C} = 1 \text{ A s}$
electric potential, EMF	volt	V	$1 \text{ V} = 1 \text{ W A}^{-1}$
electric field	volt per metre		V m^{-1}
electric capacitance	farad	F	$1 \text{ F} = 1 \text{ C V}^{-1}$
electric resistance	ohm	Ω	$1 \ \Omega = 1 \text{ V A}^{-1}$
electric conductance	siemens	S	$1 \text{ S} = 1 \ \Omega^{-1}$
magnetic flux	weber	Wb	$1 \text{ Wb} = 1 \text{ V s}$
magnetic flux density	tesla	T	$1 \text{ T} = 1 \text{ Wb m}^{-2}$
inductance	henry	H	$1 \text{ H} = 1 \text{ V s A}^{-1}$
magnetic field	ampere per metre		A m^{-1}
luminous flux	lumen	lm	$1 \text{ lm} = 1 \text{ cd sr}$
luminance	candela per square metre		cd m^{-2}
illuminance	lux	lx	$1 \text{ lx} = 1 \text{ lm m}^{-2}$
heat flux density, irradiance	watt per square metre		W m^{-2}
heat capacity	joule per kelvin		J K^{-1}
specific heat capacity	joule per kelvin per kilogram		$\text{J kg}^{-1} \text{ K}^{-1}$
thermal conductivity	watt per metre per kelvin		$\text{W m}^{-1} \text{ K}^{-1}$

The **ampère** is that constant current which, if maintained in two straight parallel conductors of infinite length, of negligible circular cross-section, and placed 1 metre apart in vacuum, would produce between these conductors a force equal to 2×10^{-7} newton per metre of length.

The **kelvin**, unit of thermodynamic temperature, is 1/273·16 of the thermodynamic temperature of the triple point of water (*See* **Absolute Temperature, Section L**).

The **candela** is the luminous intensity, in the perpendicular direction, of a surface of 1/600 000 square metre of a black body at the temperature of freezing plantinum under a pressure of 101 325 newtons per square metre. Luminous intensity is a property of a *source* and is the amount of luminous flux (light) it throws out per steradian.

The **mole** is the amount of substance of a system which contains as many elementary entities as there are atoms in 0·012 kilogram of carbon 12. Since this number is approximately 6·022 17 $\times 10^{23}$ a mole of hydrogen molecules, for example, is approximately this number of hydrogen molecules.

In addition to the base units, two SI *supplementary* units are listed below:

Quantity	Name of unit	Symbol of unit
Plane angle	radian	rad
Solid angle	steradian	sr

They are defined as follows:

The **radian** is the plane angle between two radii of a circle which cut off on the circumference an arc equal in length to the radius.

The **steradian** is the solid angle which, having its vertex at the centre of a sphere, cuts off an area of the surface of the sphere equal to that of a square with sides of length equal to the radius of the sphere.

Derived Units

Most quantities that occur in nature are *derived quantities* and are measured in *derived units*. Speed is a derived quantity which can be measured in metres/sec, so that the units of speed involve the definition of two base units, *i.e.* metres and seconds.

It is said that speed has the dimensions of [length]/[time], also written [L][T]$^{-1}$, since the metre is a measure of length and the second is a measure of time. In any equation in science the dimensions of both sides must always be the same and this is often a useful check of whether the equation is correct. If a mile = 1609·3 metre and an hour = 3600 sec, one mile/hr = 1609·3/3600 m s^{-1}. Conversions between any unit and any other unit which measures the same quantity can be similarly obtained.

Table I (**T58**) gives a list of some important derived quantities that occur in nature and in the fourth column the SI unit that is used to measure it. Some of these derived units have a name (usually that of a famous scientist) and a symbol which are given in the second and third columns. Thus for example, the SI unit of force is a kilogram metre sec^{-2}, but this unit is also given the name of newton. A force of 5 kg m s^{-2} is 5 newton, which can be written "5N".

Multiples and Fractions of Units

Within the SI system there are special prefixes for forming multiples and sub-multiples of its units.

Factor by which the unit is multiplied	Prefix	Symbol
10^{24}	yotta	Y
10^{21}	zeta	Z
10^{18}	exa	E
10^{15}	peta	P
10^{12}	tera	T
10^{9}	giga	G
10^{6}	mega	M
10^{3}	kilo	k
10^{2}	hecto	h
10	deca	da
10^{-1}	deci	d
10^{-2}	centi	c
10^{-3}	milli	m
10^{-6}	micro	m
10^{-9}	nano	n
10^{-12}	pico	p
10^{-15}	femto	f
10^{-18}	atto	a
10^{-21}	zepto	z
10^{-24}	yocto	y

Examples

Examples: one thousandth of a metre is one millimetre (1 mm); one million volts is one megavolt

Time

	second	minute	hour	solar day	year
1 second	= 1	$1·667 \times 10^{-2}$	$2·778 \times 10^{-4}$	$1·157 \times 10^{-5}$	$3·169 \times 10^{-8}$
1 minute	= 60	1	$1·667 \times 10^{-2}$	$6·944 \times 10^{-4}$	$1·901 \times 10^{-6}$
1 hour	= 3600	60	1	$4·167 \times 10^{-2}$	$1·141 \times 10^{-4}$
1 solar day	= 86400	1440	24	1	$2·738 \times 10^{-3}$
1 year	= $3·156 \times 10^{7}$	525,900	8766	365·24	1

Force

	newton	dyne	poundal	kg force	pound force
1 newton	= 1	10^{5}	7·233	0·1020	0·2248
1 dyne	= 10^{-5}	1	$7·233 \times 10^{-5}$	$1·020 \times 10^{-6}$	$2·248 \times 10^{-6}$
1 poundal	= 0·1383	13830	1	0·01410	0·03108
1 kg force	= 9·807	980700	70·93	1	2·205
1lb force	= 4·448	$4·448 \times 10^{5}$	32·17	0·4536	1

Energy, Work, Heat

	joule	kW. hr	ft lb	calory	B.t.u
1 joule	= 1	$2·778 \times 10^{-7}$	0·7376	0·2389	$9·478 \times 10^{-4}$
1 kW. hr	= $3·600 \times 10^{6}$	1	$2·655 \times 10^{6}$	$8·598 \times 10^{5}$	3412
1ft lb	= 1·356	$3·766 \times 10^{-7}$	1	0·3238	$1·285 \times 10^{-3}$
1 calory	= 4·187	$1·163 \times 10^{-6}$	3·088	1	$3·968 \times 10^{-3}$
1 B.t.u.	= 1055	$2·931 \times 10^{-4}$	778·2	252	1

1 kW. hr (kilowatt hour) is 1 unit as measured by the electricity meter.
1 B.t.u. is a British thermal unit and is the amount of heat required to raise the temperature of 1 lb of water by 1° Fahrenheit.
1 Therm is 100 000 B.t.u. and is equivalent to the heat generated by 29·3 units of electricity.
1 calorie is the heat required to raise the temperature of 1 gm of water by 1° C. The calorie as used by weightwatchers is actually 1000 calories as defined above.
1 erg is 10^{-7} joule.
1 electron volt (eV) is $1·6 \times 10^{-19}$ joule.

Angle

	degree	minute	second	radian	revolution
1 degree	= 1	60	3600	$1{\cdot}745 \times 10^{-2}$	$2{\cdot}778 \times 10^{-3}$
1 minute	= $1{\cdot}667 \times 10^{-2}$	1	60	$2{\cdot}909 \times 10^{-4}$	$4{\cdot}630 \times 10^{-5}$
1 second	= $2{\cdot}778 \times 10^{-4}$	$1{\cdot}667 \times 10^{-2}$	1	$4{\cdot}848 \times 10^{-6}$	$7{\cdot}716 \times 10^{-7}$
1 radian	= 57·30	3438	$2{\cdot}063 \times 10^{5}$	1	0·1592
1 revolution	= 360	$2{\cdot}16 \times 10^{4}$	$1{\cdot}296 \times 10^{6}$	6·283	1

1 rt angle = 90°   1 grade = 0·01 rt angle

Pressure

	pascal	millibar	atmosphere	torr	lb/sq in
1 pascal	= 1	0·01	$9{\cdot}869 \times 10^{-6}$	$7{\cdot}501 \times 10^{-3}$	$1{\cdot}450 \times 10^{-4}$
1 millibar	= 100	1	$9{\cdot}869 \times 10^{-4}$	0·7501	0·01450
1 atmosphere	= 101 300	1013	1	760	14·7
1 torr	= 133·3	1·333	$1{\cdot}316 \times 10^{-3}$	1	0·01934
1 lb/sq in	= 6895	68·95	0·06805	51·72	1

1 pascal = 1 newton/sq metre = 10 dyne/sq cm
1 torr is the pressure due to 1 mm of mercury.
By atmosphere is meant "standard atmosphere" which is 760 mm or 29·92 inches of mercury.

(1 MV). These prefixes are *recommended* but other multiples and sub-multiples will be used when convenient, *e.g.*, the centimetre (cm), the cubic decimetre (dm³).

The following is a selection of points to note:

(i) The name litre now means 1 cubic decimetre or 10^{-3}m³ and is a measure of volume.
(ii) Days, hours, and minutes are still used to measure time, though some scientists may prefer to use kiloseconds, *etc.*
(iii) The SI unit of plane angle is the radian (rad), but degrees, minutes and seconds are still used as well. $1° = \dfrac{\pi}{180}$ rad.; 1 rad = 57·295 78° = 57° 7′ 44·81″
(iv) A Celsius temperature, say 15 degrees, is written 15°C; note that 15C would mean 15 coulombs.

The Imperial System of Units (*see* L2)

Temperature

The Celsius scale is the same as the Centigrade scale. To convert from degrees Fahrenheit (°F) to degrees Celsius (°C), subtract 32 from the temperature in Fahrenheit and multiply by 5/9. To convert from Celsius to Fahrenheit multiply the temperature in Celsius by 9/5 and add 32. Applying this rule we obtain:

0° C = 32° F	20° C = 68° F
5° C = 41° F	25° C = 77° F
10° C = 50° F	30° C = 86° F
15° C = 59° F	35° C = 95° F

37° C (normal body temperature) is 98·6 ° F.

The absolute zero temperature (lowest possible temperature) is −273·15° C.

To convert from ° C to degrees Kelvin (° K) add 273·15 to the temperature in Celsius so that the absolute zero is 0° K.

To obtain the temperature according to the Rankine scale add 459·69 to the temperature in Fahrenheit. 0° Rankine is the absolute zero.

PLANET EARTH

This section examines the complex structure of the Earth as well as its early history and the origin and development of life. A Special Topic looks at the challenge of global climate change and progress at the 2015 Paris Conference. For further information on other planets of the Solar System and beyond, see Section T.

TABLE OF CONTENTS

PLANET EARTH

THE EARTH'S STRUCTURE

The Earth is the third of the planets in the Solar System, orbiting the Sun at a distance of approximately 150 million kilometers. The Earth has the shape of a slightly flattened sphere, with an equatorial radius of 6378 km and a polar radius of 6357. It has a mass of 5.97×10^{24} kilograms, a density of about 5.5 grams per cubic centimeter, and an average surface gravitational acceleration of 9.8 meters per second per second.

The Earth is an almost spherical body with an equatorial radius of 6378km, and slightly less along its polar axis (due to the flattening of the poles). Seismic investigations have shown that the Earth is made up of three layers which are distinguished one from another by their composition and density. The central *core* of the planet is the densest of the three; the surrounding *mantle* is a thick shell of less dense rocky material, and above the mantle lies the thinnest, least dense and outermost layer, the *crust*.

The Core

At the centre of the Earth lies the core, a dense mass of iron and nickel with a radius of 3486 km. As there is no way to sample the core, its composition and properties are inferred from seismic studies, astronomical data (the way the Earth interacts with other bodies is affected by the density structure of the planet), and meteorites. (Iron meteorites, which are composed of a mixture of iron and nickel, are thought to come from the cores of asteroids that were smashed apart in collisions with other asteroids.)

The core is divided into two layers. The outer core, which extends to a depth of 5144 km, is liquid. It is thought that the convection of this metallic liquid creates the Earth's magnetic field. Although the inner core is hotter than the outer core, it is under more pressure and is therefore solid. It is a distinct region and the structure of the iron nickel alloy crystals there is different.

Scientists have now discovered that the Earth's inner core is rotating faster than the rest of the planet. No one is certain of the temperature at the centre of the Earth. It may be 4000°C–5000°C, or could be as high as 8000°C.

The Mantle

The thick shell of rocky material which surrounds the core. No one has sampled the mantle directly. Knowledge of its composition and structure comes from a number of sources. Volcanoes occasionally erupt pieces of mantle known as mantle xenoliths, which are primarily composed of dense iron and magnesium-rich (*mafic*) minerals such as olivine and pyroxene. Experiments that simulate the high pressures and temperatures in the mantle have given us a better idea of what minerals can exist there. Geochemical studies of igneous rocks such as basalt, which are thought to be derived directly from the mantle, are also of use in calculating its composition. Seismic studies have given us a view into the physical properties. The velocity of energy waves (seismic waves) traveling through the Earth after an earthquake or explosion depends on the properties of the rock (*e.g.*, density) they are traveling through. Using an array of seismometers recording seismic waves arriving at many different points on the surface, geophysicists can "image" the structure of the crust, mantle, and core.

The mantle is believed to be ultramafic in composition throughout, although the exact mineral assemblage changes with depth as pressure and temperature increase. In addition, there are probably slight differences in composition between the upper and lower sections of the mantle. In places (*e.g.*, below some volcanoes), the mantle is partially molten, but in general, although it is extremely hot, it is solid.

The Crust

The rocky outer shell of the Earth on which all known organisms live and the oceans lie is known as the crust. There are two fundamentally different types of crust: *continental crust*, which makes up the continents; and *oceanic crust*, which underlies the oceans. Continental crust is composed of a wide array of rock types, and has an average composition of that of a granitic rock, with an overall density of about 2.5 g/cc. Continental crust is on average 35 km thick, but is quite thin under some low plains and valleys, and as thick as 70 km under high mountain ranges. Oceanic crust, on the other hand, is composed primarily of the volcanic rock basalt overlain by sediments, and has an average density of about 3 g/cc. It covers 60% of the Earth's surface, but is much thinner than continental crust, on average 7 km. Overall, the crust is relatively cool and brittle, but its properties change with depth. Pressure increases by 300 atmospheres per km, and temperature increases by 25°C/km near the surface.

Plate Tectonics

Perhaps the most fascinating long-term change the surface of the Earth undergoes is that of *plate tectonics*. Plate tectonics is the theory that ascribes the large-scale structures of the Earth's crust (*e.g.*, mountain ranges, rift valleys, continents, and ocean basins) to the interaction of brittle pieces, or *plates*, of crust and upper mantle as they move about on ductile mantle below.

Most evidence of plate tectonics can be found at plate boundaries (or former plate boundaries), where plates are moving against one another. There are three kinds of active plate boundaries: *divergent margins*, where plates are moving apart; *convergent margins*, where plates are moving towards one another; and *transform margins*, where plates are sliding past each other. Each kind of margin is characterized by distinct topography and a particular type of seismic and volcanic activity.

The Mechanism of Plate Tectonics

The mechanism that drives plate tectonics has been a problem since continental drift was first expounded by Alfred Wegener in 1912. The prevailing theory is that the plates are riding around on convection currents in the mantle. Although the mantle is solid, it is extremely hot and under enormous pressures. Over long periods of time, it acts as a fluid. Its behaviour is somewhat analogous to pitch, which shatters when hit quickly with a hammer, but will flow under the force of gravity if left to sit for a while. The convection of the mantle is driven by temperature differences. Hot, buoyant material near the core rises, while cooler, denser material near the surface descends. It is thought that there are a number of large-scale convection cells in the mantle, which drive the plates in different directions above. The heat that drives convection comes from the decay of radioactive elements, and from the heat left over from the Earth's accretion 4.56 billion years ago. There are still many unanswered questions as to the precise nature of mantle convection and exactly how it translates into plate movement.

The Composition of the Earth's Crust

The many different kinds of *rock* found in the Earth's crust are each an assemblage of one or more minerals. A mineral, in its turn, is a discrete solid substance consisting of chemical elements, with a specific chemical composition and a characteristic crystal structure. Iron, for instance, is an element (Fe); iron oxide is a mineral (Fe_2O_4); iron ore is a rock composed of iron and other minerals.

Over 3700 minerals have been identified, but of these about 20 make up more than 95 per cent of the Earth's crust. And of the elements, 12 comprise 99.23 per cent of the total crust mass. Thus the crust consists of a limited number of minerals in which one or more of the 12 abundant elements is an ingredient. Oxygen is the most abundant element, comprising 45.20 per cent by weight of the crust, followed by silicon (27.20 per cent), aluminium (8.00 per cent) and iron (5.80 per cent).

The Rocks

The rocks of which the Earth's crust is composed, though numerous in their different mineral composition, can be grouped in just three families, distinguished one from the other by the manner in which they were formed.

(i) Igneous rocks

(i) **Igneous rocks** (from the Latin *ignis*, fire). Igneous rocks are those which were formed from the cooling and solidification of *lava*, the molten rock which erupts from volcanoes. Basalt is the most common igneous rock, comprising about 80 per cent of all lava erupted by volcanoes.

(ii) Sedimentary rocks

(ii) **Sedimentary rocks**. Those rocks which are formed by the settling and consolidation of materials that had previously existed in some other form. Most originated as loose particles that were eroded from their parent material and transported in suspension by wind, water or ice to some other location, where they were deposited and subsequently consolidated into sedimentary rock – sandstone is a typical example, shale is another. Others were originally organic material, which as it died and decomposed formed beds of sedimentary rock.

Limestone, for example, was originally the shells and remains of marine animals; coal is a combustible sedimentary rock, more than 50 per cent of which is decomposed plant matter.

(iii) Metamorphic rocks

(iii) **Metamorphic rocks**. From the Greek *meta* (meaning change, and *morphe*, meaning form: thus, change of form) are those rocks which have been changed from their original form (either igneous or sedimentary) into something else by the effects of temperature, pressure, or both. The process is analogous to that which occurs when a clay pot is fired in the kiln. The high temperatures trigger a series of chemical reactions in the tiny mineral grains that make up the clay. New compounds form, and the soft malleable clay becomes hard and rigid. Marble is a metamorphic rock, transformed by heat and pressure from the irregularities of sedimentary limestone into a glistening mass of uniformly sized, interlocking grains of soft calcite.

The Rock Cycle

Geologists often refer to the *rock cycle*, the continuous alterations of rocks from one type to another. An igneous rock is broken down by weather and gravity; its pieces accumulate elsewhere as a sediment, the sediment is buried and lithified to form a sedimentary rock; the sedimentary rock is buried further and subject to tremendous heat and pressure; new minerals grow and a metamorphic rock forms; part of the metamorphic rock melts; the molten rock solidifies to form a new igneous rock.

The importance of rocks to earth science is not simply that they give us an indication of the composition of the Earth, but that they are windows into the past. Each type of rock forms in a particular environment. For instance, limestone forms in warm shallow seas, salt in hot deserts, and granite deep underground. Thus the presence of limestone indicates that the area was once a shallow sea, salt that it was once a desert, and granite that thousands of meters of rocks have eroded away to expose the rock below. James Hutton, the founder of modern geology, refered to rocks as "God's books," which tell the story of the Earth.

Minerals

Rocks are solid, naturally-occurring pieces of a planet. Most rocks are composed of one or more minerals (coal is composed of organic material, but it is still considered to be a rock). A mineral is a naturally-occurring, generally inorganic material with a specific chemical composition and a definite crystalline structure (its molecules are arranged in an orderly, repeating pattern). Although water is natural and has a specific composition, it is not a mineral because it is liquid and therefore not crystalline; water-ice, however, is a mineral because it has a crystalline structure.

Groups of Minerals

More than 3500 minerals have been discovered so far, but only about 100 are common in the crust. There are a number of groups of minerals, including carbonates, sulfides, phosphates, and native elements, but the largest group by far is the silicates. Silicates are all composed of silicon-oxygen mole-cules combined with other elements. In fact, there is much more oxygen in the Earth's crust than there is in the atmosphere.

Continents and Oceans

If the surface of the Earth were level, the sea would cover the entire planet. So why are there continents and oceans? One reason is buoyancy. The continental crust and oceanic crust are fundamentally different. The continental crust is thick and relatively light, while the oceanic crust is thin and dense. As a result, the continental crust floats high on the mantle in the same way that a huge, empty ocean liner floats high in the water, whereas the oceanic crust acts more like an overloaded barge.

The state of gravitational equilibrium of the crust is known as *isostasy*, and the flexing of the crust in response to loads imposed or removed from it is known as *isostatic adjustment*. Just as ships and icebergs have a submarine keel that keeps them in balance, so does thick continental crust. The Himalayas, for example, rise almost 9 km above sea level, but *descend* more than 60 km below sea level. It is also this isostatic adjustment that allows rocks that form at depths of many kilometres to buoy up as the rocks above them erode away.

EARTH HISTORY

Age and Origin of the Earth

The current theory of planet formation states that the Sun and planets accreted from a rotating cloud of dust and gas that contracted under the force of gravity about 4·56 billion years ago. Most of the material went in to making the Sun, while the remaining dust and gas accumulated to form rocks, then small bodies known as *planetesimals*, and finally planets. Because of the reworking of rocks on Earth, there are most likely no pieces left of the primitive Earth. The oldest rock dated so far is a 3·96 billion-year-old gneiss from Canada, while the oldest mineral grain is a 4·2 billion-year-old zircon grain from Australia. The 4·56 billion-year-old age of the earth is inferred from the ages of primitive meteorites, which are thought to be relics of the early solar system.

The Timescale

Earth's history is thus long, at least 4,560 million years. This stretch of time is virtually impossible to visualise but an analogy may make it more comprehensible. Imagine that Earth time has been but a single 24 hour day. If the Earth came into being at time zero, 0:00:00, then bombardment by meteorites would have lasted until 3am; there would not have been enough stability for the origin of life until 4am: 5:36am would see the first fossils and traces of bacteria. It would be well past noon before single celled algae appeared and seaweeds not until 20:28pm: 20 minutes later there were jelly fish; trilobites dominated the sea floor by 21:04pm. Plants reached the land by 21:52pm and coal swamps flourished by 22:24pm. Then, 32 minutes later the dinosaurs dominated, to be replaced by mammals at 23:39pm. Not until a minute to midnight did Humans come on the scene.

How Palaeontologists Date Fossils

How can Palaeontologists (geologists that study past life) have any idea about relative dates? Each layer of sedimentary rock contains vital clues to the environment in which that sediment was laid down. This is based on one of the fundamental principles of Geology, that the present is the key to the past, that by studying the sediments in today's environment, one can conclude that the same sediments lithified (cemented into rock) and would have been deposited under similar conditions in the past.

Sedimentary rocks also hold clues to the life forms of the time through the fossils that they contain; some rocks such as a coral limestone will be rich in fossils since coral reefs support a wide variety of creatures; the harsh conditions of a hot desert are not conducive to life. Rocks can be dated by radioactive isotopes so, putting all this evidence together, it is possible to reconstruct the *palaeoenvironment* (past environment) and the community (assemblage) of species that was then living in it. Molecular biology has made dating proteins another possibility.

However, the fossil record does not contain all creatures that have ever lived for, to be preserved as a fossil, an organism must have hard parts such as bone or shell. Only in rare circumstances can jellyfish or bacteria be preserved if the sediments were fine and burial very quick, perhaps by a sub-marine mudslide, so that currents or waves had no chance to stir up the delicate remains.

Main Geological Eras

The table set out later is a history of life on Earth, a time chart summarising the main stages in Earth's history. There are four major chunks of time called Eras, based on the differences in animal groups present in each one: Azoic (no life), Palaeozoic (ancient animals), Mesozoic (middle animals) and Caenozoic (recent animals). The earliest times are conventionally shown at the bottom, in line with another fundamental principle, the Law of Superposition which states that in an undisturbed sequence, a layer of rock will be younger than the ones below it and older than those above it.

Hand in hand with this law is the Law of Fossil Succession, that plants and animals that have parts hard enough to survive burial and compaction change through time and that where there are the same kinds of fossils and assemblages (groups of species together) in rocks of different locations, then they are of the same age. As exploration and technology, such as the scanning electron microscope, advance so the scope for reading the rocks increases, interpretations change and what is written here becomes out of date.

THE DEVELOPMENT OF LIFE

The development of life on Earth has been neither smooth nor gradual. There have been times of abundance balanced by times of major extinctions, of which there have been at least five. Long periods of gradual evolution are punctuated by brief periods of rapid change, either in proliferation, as the explosion of life forms in the Cambrian seas, or in extinction, as the virtual disappearance of the dinosaurs some 70 million years ago whch has so captured the popular imagination and occupied many palaeontologists in debate as to its cause. Changes in palaeogeography, as the continents have shifted positions relative to each other, have prompted radiation or extinction, migration and mixing.

The Origin of Life

How did life originate? The answer can probably only ever be conjectural. It is commonly thought that complex organic molecules, amino acids, synthesized naturally in Precambrian oceans. These basic ingredients of proteins would have had favourable environments of high energy from both the sun (no ozone layer to screen out UV rays) and warm water from volcanic hydrothermal vents. The earliest known fossils are those of prokaryotic cells (small with no nuclei) in the anaerobic (without oxygen) oceans. By 1000 million years ago (mya) eukaryote cells (large, membrane bounded nuclei containing chromosomes) were well established. Here was an opportunity for evolution, since these cells reproduced sexually allowing genetic material to mix and mutate.

To have life means having the ability to reproduce; reproduction requires the passing on of genetic information. This is done on Earth today by the very complex protein substance, DNA (deoxyribonucleic acid). (*see* **Nucleic acid, T47**)

Gradually microbes became more complex and colonial, by 3000 mya creating layered structures called *stromatolites*; these still form today at places such as Hamlyn Pool in Western Australia.

Proterozoic Era Discoveries

The late Proterozoic has been an empty mystery but modern finds are constantly filling in this gap. For example, Ediacara chert from Australia has revealed flat bodied creatures only 0.1mm in size,

610 to 510 million years old. Alongside these are fossils that look like feathery fronds up to a metre long. Others are pouchlike with no recognisable circulatory or nervous system; it is thought that their air-mattress appearance was due to fluid-filled hydraulic support. These have now been discovered in rocks world wide, but were they a life form that failed or the ancestors of modern species? Amongst these fossils have been found trails and holes left by metazoans; it seems that these had been burrowing in sediments since 1000 mya.

What seems certain is that early bacteria developed in the absence of oxygen; the blue-green algae (cyanobacteria) released this vital gas into the oceans and atmosphere, setting the stage for Biology's Big Bang.

The Early Cambrian Period

In the early Cambrian period the world recovered from a severe glaciation (nicknamed Snowball Earth) and shallow seas flooded the continents. (There was an extraordinary radiation of life forms; almost every major group of animals appeared then, 540–500 mya. Indeed, so rapid was this radiation, current research puts it at only 10–20 million years, that it suggests another kind of evolution in very short time periods in addition to the more steady Darwinian one.

The cause of this dramatic explosion is a matter of geological conjecture. Had the cyanobacteria established so much oxygen that more complex life was possible? Was it that so many new species created more diverse food chains such that there was increasing competition in the predator and prey relationship so adaptation was necessary for survival?

The Cambrian Explosion

The Cambrian explosion of life produced important marine creatures such as brachiopods (bivalved marine animals whose valves are not identical) and trilobites (rather like woodlice in appearance, bodies in three sections), with eyes as well developed as any modern insect, in abundance.

Significantly, these creatures had made an advance by developing shells. These gave support for muscles and protection against new predators, something that pre-Cambrian Ediacara species would not have needed.

Astonishingly, every design for a body plan that has ever existed (there are eight main ones) came into being then, and no new ones have appeared since though many minor ones became extinct in the first major extinction recorded in the rocks at the end of the Cambrian Period.

This extinction after such diversity indicates that maybe extinctions do not need a major external cause such as Ice Ages or asteroids after all; perhaps a small evolutionary step creates an advantage to one species that upsets the balance of a whole ecosystem.

The Appearance of Fish

Fish first appear in the fossil record in the Ordovician. Their soft bodies were armoured by external skeletons. By Silurian times, a group of fish emerged with internal skeletons and body armour reduced to scales. By late Devonian times, 370 mya, there were lobe finned fishes that had stout bony supporting appendages, unlike the ray finned fishes (such as trout or salmon of today) that have much thinner bone structures arranged as a fan in their fins. Some of these lobe fins had one upper and two lower bones similar to those of tetrapods (four jointed legged, land living vertebrates); indeed, the first tetrapods evolved in the Devonian, about 360 mya and were the forerunners of amphibians.

The Evolution of Plants

If animals were to occupy the land surface, then plants must have got there first or else there would have been no food source to sustain them. Early plants evolved in water, using currents for reproduction, but in the Silurian, or even earlier than that, there was greening of the land with a skin of cyanobacteria. Once plants developed the capacity to live on land, with spores with walls and stems and leaves with cuticles that would prevent drying out, stomata to control gas exchange, vascular system to circulate water and tough polymers such

TABLE: GEOLOGICAL TIME SCALE

ERA		AGE (MYA, million years ago)	CHARACTERISTICS
CAINOZOIC	QUATERNARY		Modern humans
		2	
	TERTIARY		Mammals & flowering plants diversify. Earliest hominids.
		65	
MESOZOIC	CRETACEOUS		Dinosaurs included in major extinction. Flowering plants common.
		145	
	JURASSIC		Early birds & mammals. Dinosaurs abundant.
		205	
	TRIASSIC		First dinosaurs & mammals. Coniferous trees common.
		250	
PALAEOZOIC	PERMIAN		Mass extinction of many marine species, including trilobites.
		290	
	CARBONIFEROUS		First winged insects. Large primitive trees. First reptiles.
		360	
	DEVONIAN		First seed-bearing plants (ammonoids). Early tetrapods. First amphibians and insects.
		410	
	SILURIAN		First jawed fish, first upright plant.
		440	
	ORDOVICIAN		First land plants and early fish. First jawless vertebrates.
		500	
	CAMBRIAN		Trilobites dominant. First molluscs.
		570	
PRECAMBRIAN	PROTEROZOIC		First invertebrates & multi-celled/ soft-bodied organisms.
		2,500	
	ARCHÆAN		Bacteria/single celled organisms.
		3,800	Oldest known fossils.
	ORIGIN OF EARTH	4,560?	

as lignin to prevent collapse, then invasion was possible. Mosses and liverworts were probably the first: these have different combinations of land requirements, but not all of them.

Developments in the Devonian Era

The oldest known vascular land plant is Cooksonia found in Silurian rocks in Wales and Ireland, only a few millimetres long; by the Devonian they were several centimetres. Other Devonian plants reached 8 metres in height; Carboniferous ones were even taller, the clubmoss Lepidodendron was 50 metres or more and the horsetail, Calamites, was 20 metres. These forests decayed into the coal deposits found today from Pennsylvania to Poland. They contain fossils of insects with 50cm wing spans rather like giant dragonflies. Gymnosperms, seed bearing plants, first arose in the Devonian; they include seed ferns and the most successful conifers that first carried their cones in the Carboniferous forests.

Early Cretaceous was brightened by the first Angiosperms, flowering plants where the ovule is protected, not naked as in the gymnosperms. They have been successful; their almost identical descendants dominate today's plant life.

The Development of Amphibians

The development of amphibians had marked a significant step towards animal life colonising land. They appeared in two major groups, frogs and toads in the Triassic and newts and salamanders in the Jurassic. To move out from water, amphibians had to solve several problems, impermeable skin, air breathing lungs instead of gills, and skeletal support, especially a rib cage to hold up the internal organs—bodies are not weightless on land as they are in water. However, they could not spread far onto land, needing swampy conditions for their eggs. The first recorded reptile was found in Carboniferous tree trunks where it had gone in quest of insects. Reptilian success stems from laying eggs that could keep themselves wet, with amniotic fluid enclosed in a shell. By the Permian, when hot, dry conditions did not favour amphibians, reptiles on land spread wide and grew ever larger.

The Mesozoic Era: Age of the Dinosaur

The next era, the Mesozoic, is most distinguished in the popular imagination by the dinosaurs. There are two important branches in the structure of these reptiles, the Saurischians (lizard-hipped) and the Ornischians (bird-hipped). The saurischians had a pelvis with a pubic bone pointing forward and downwards; the group included the giant vegetarians such as Diplodocus and Brachiosaurus and the carnivorous (meat eating) hunters like Tyrannosaurus Rex and Allosaurus.

It has been accepted for more than a century now that birds are descendants of dinosaurs. The first specimen of the link between them, the famous Archaeopteryx, was discovered in Germany in 1861. The creature had a mouthful of teeth, claws on its wings, long bony tail but also something new in the fossil record, feathers. Archaeopteryx is very similar to dinosaurs of the bird-hipped group that includes the equally famous Velociraptors. There are constantly new fossil finds that help to "flesh out" the evolution of the birds. As tall plants produced layers of vegetation, gliding and then flight became a major way of life (a successful one; 70% of all animal species alive today are insects).

The First Reptiles

Contemporary with the dinosaurs, and poised to assume their dominant role, were warm blooded mammals. The first reptiles with mammal-like features appeared in the Upper Carboniferous, but by Late Triassic, 210 mya, the first true mammals are found. Mammals have dispensed with the need to lay eggs outside of their bodies. There are two ways of doing this; the marsupials give birth to tiny, helpless young that must spend months in a pouch suckling milk. Today the marsupials have reached their greatest variety in Australia, isolated by the separation of continents and free from disturbance by placentals, until invasion by humans.

Placental mammals retain young in the womb for longer, nourished by blood through the placenta. The earliest placentals are Cretaceous but they could not diversify until dinosaurs were no longer competition. Then they rapidly radiated to reach twenty orders in the Palaeocene, the ancestors of all modern groups and others now extinct. These include carnivores, insectivores, rodents, ungulates (like pigs, camels, hippo and cattle) and primates. From these primates, first seen in the Cretaceous, emerged hominids. But that is a different story! (*see* Human Evolution T48–55).

THE MINERAL WORLD

Types of Minerals

Minerals are naturally occurring solid elements or combination of elements; very few elements occur simply on their own (copper, silver and gold are good examples of ones that do) so most minerals are compounds of ions bonded together with an atomic structure. For example, copper is frequently found bonded together with carbonate, $CuCO_3$, as the pretty green mineral malachite or in a brassy one called chalcopyrite where iron is included in the copper carbonate. The presence of some hydroxide in the chemical bonding will result in the glorious blues of azurite.

Chemical Composition of Common Minerals

Each specific chemical composition does not vary, no matter how small the fragments into which a piece may be broken, because that composition is a fixed ratio. Take quartz, one of the most common of all minerals; its chemical formula is SiO_2, which means that for every one silica atom there are two of oxygen. This one:two ratio is constant for all quartz. Each mineral, to a greater or lesser degree, forms crystals that have a distinctive geometry, such as cubes or prisms, whose faces follow the atomic structure of the molecules making up that mineral. A surprising example of how atomic structure affects a mineral's characteristics comes by comparison of graphite with diamond. Both are composed of carbon but in diamond, the carbon atoms are arranged in a cubic lattice, internally so strong that diamond is the hardest known mineral. In graphite, on the other hand, the carbon atoms are weakly bonded together in flat sheets so that it is soft with a greasy feel. The difference is a result of the position in which the carbon grew. Diamond's strength is a result of greater depth; it forms at the equivalent of 150 km or more deep in the Crust.

Constant Characteristics

Since the chemistry of each mineral does not vary, there is a distinctive set of constant characteristics by which each can be identified, such as colour, hardness, lustre, streak on an unglazed tile, form, cleavage (the preferred direction in which a mineral breaks) and density. A good textbook on minerals will describe fully these features but three common examples will illustrate the point. Calcite, quartz and halite are three common, normally colourless minerals which have a non-metallic lustre. Lustre is the way in which a mineral reflects light; it might be metallic, vitreous like glass, pearly, resinous or greasy, looking as if it were coated with oil. One of the first tests to do to tell them apart is hardness, the ability to withstand scratching, which is assessed using Moh's Scale of Hardness.

Hardness: The Moh Scale

Moh was an Austrian geologist who listed ten minerals from the softest, Talc, to the hardest known, Diamond, and assigned them values of 1 to 10 (1 is Talc, 2 Gypsum, 3 Calcite, 4 Fluorite, 5 Apatite, 6 Orthoclase, 7 Quartz, 8 Topaz, 9 Corundum, 10 Diamond). A finger nail is hardness

2·5 so anything that it can scratch will be softer than that; likewise, a steel blade is hardness 6·5 so anything that it will scratch is softer than it and anything that will scratch it is harder than steel. Calcite will scratch halite which has a hardness of 2.

In terms of crystal form all three are different, quartz having well formed six-sided prism shaped ones, calcite has rhombohedral and halite has perfect cubic ones. If the crystals are broken, then both halite and calcite will have perfect cleavage, meaning that they split in planes parallel to the crystal faces; quartz does not have any cleavage and broken faces will be rough or look like the curves of a shell. Streak is not a significant test for these three, unlike haematite which, though it may look grey or brown, leaves a red streak on a tile. However, there are individual clues which readily distinguish the halite from the calcite (the crystal form and hardness leaves us in no doubt about quartz). In a clear and well formed piece of rhomboidal calcite, any image put under it will be double refracted (two images will be seen slightly overlapping). Also, all forms of calcite will fizz with dilute hydrochloric acid. Halite has one unique characteristic, its taste of salt.

Colours

Quartz has been described above and is the only one of the six that is not a whole family of minerals although it has several varieties, distinguished by colour, such as rose quartz which is pink and amethyst, purple. These beautiful colours are the result of trace impurities of atoms such as iron or titanium. In large masses, it can be milk white. Where quartz has precipitated from water, it is fine grained with chalcedony an important variety, called agate when it is decoratively colour banded and flint when it is grey and breaks with a conchoidal fracture resembling the growth rings of a shell.

Olivines are pale yellow-green magnesium iron silicates, with vitreous lustre and hardness of 6·5 to 7. The *Pyroxenes* are a diverse family ranging from dark green to black. *Amphiboles* are ferromagnesian silicates of which hornblende is the most common.

Feldspar, Mica and Calcite

Feldspars are a group of aluminium silicate minerals that account for 60% of all minerals in the Earth's crust, common in oceanic crust and, with quartz, comprising 75% by volume of the continents. The strange name is Swedish and means "field mineral", a reference to the frequency with which it needed clearing from farmland. Feldspar family minerals are not glassy like quartz but appear porcelainic and dull. There are two common types, either orthoclase which is red, pink or whitish, or plagioclase, green, dark grey or white in colour but *striated* (scratched in parallel grooves). When feldspars break, they do so along flat, rectangular faces.

Mica has black/shiny (biotite) and white/pearly (muscovite) forms. Both are distinctive because they can be peeled into thin, flat, transparent sheets.

Calcite is a carbonate, not a silicate, but, though of little significance in terms of the whole crust, it is common in sedimentary rocks at the surface.

Igneous Rock Granite

Igneous rock granite is a very good example to show how minerals form the building blocks of rocks since all the crystals, whether well- or partly-formed, are clearly visible to the naked eye. There are interlocking crystals of feldspar, mica and quartz; usually the feldspar has the best developed crystals because it was the first mineral to begin to crystallise out from the molten magma. Quartz forms at the lowest temperature and so it "fills in" between the pre-existing solids. Often minerals grow in restricted spaces and so perfect faces cannot form. Much more important to a geologist is the angle between the faces which will be constant, in the case of quartz, 60 degrees, no matter what the size of those faces.

Ore minerals have economic importance. Iron as an oxide, either Fe2O3 Haematite or Fe2O4 Magnetite, the only mineral that will swing a compass needle, and with sulphur as pyrite. Others include Bauxite (aluminium) *etc.*

SPECIAL TOPIC

GLOBAL CLIMATE CHANGE

Introduction.

For whatever reasons, there is little doubt that the weather in the UK is becoming more volatile and more extreme. The last few years have seen hotter summer spells, heavier winter snowstorms, massive floods and even tornadoes. Globally, 2016 was officially named the hottest since comparable records began in 1880. In the UK, the mildest and wettest December on record was accompanied by severe floods in Cumbia as well as Scotland. Our weather continues to become increasingly volatile and unpredictable.

It may be thought incongruous to describe climate change as a current environmental controversy. It is after all nothing new. The last Ice Age finally retreated from Britain perhaps only some 12,000 years ago, and the North African coastal plains, much of which are now desert, were the granary of the Roman Empire. What, though, is new is the speed of change and the risk it poses that eco-systems will be unable to adapt at the same rate. The fears of some members of the UN Intergovernmental Panel on Climate Change that southern Africa could face a 100-year drought, convey the scale of that risk.

Even if there is overall adaptation, localised impacts could still be severe. For example, any diversion of the Gulf Stream could give the United Kingdom a climate akin to that of Labrador.

The Impact of Climate Change.

Climatologists have long predicted that global warming would be accompanied by a marked increase in the frequency of extreme weather conditions, and that prediction was borne out in 2010 to a remarkable degree. At the end of July, a temperature of 37·7°C (100°F) was recorded in Moscow, the highest since records began 130 years previously. Even Siberia reached 37°C. The heat was accompanied by the worst drought in more than a century causing catastrophic forest fires across twelve of the country's regions. At the other extreme, southern Asia had its heaviest monsoons in years with 2·5 million people being made homeless by Pakistan's worst floods in 80 years, while temperatures in Buenos Aires, the capital of Argentina, fell to -1·5°C, the lowest ever recorded there.

Figures released by Munich Re, one of the world's largest reinsurance companies in August 2010, showed that the number of floods and landslides across the globe had trebled since 1980 and that the number of storms had doubled. The annual average number of disasters had increased from 339 in the 1980s to 693 between 2000 and 2009.

As one direct consequence, large tracts of low-lying land across the globe are rapidly becoming uninsurable with highly adverse consequences for countries, notably those in the Caribbean, parts of Asia and the Pacific, dependent on inward investment for tourism and other forms of economic development.

The Onset of High Temperatures.

The hottest years globally since records began in the 1860s have now occurred since 1990. The World Meteorological Organisation reported in December 2009 that the ten years from 2000 to 2009 were 0·44°C warmer than the annual average of 14°C between 1961 and 1990. Up to 2017, the ten warmest years in the UK since records began in 1910 have all been since 2000. Meanwhile, Europe and Asia both suffered from extreme temperatures in 2003, with southern France recording temperatures of over 40°C (104°F), some 5–7°C above average. Switzerland had its hottest June for 250 years.

Ironically, the River Elbe, the scene of catastrophic flooding in 2002, experienced such low water levels that navigation had to be suspended. In Britain in August, the London area broke the 100°F (37·9°C) barrier for the very first time.

In India, the pre-monsoon heatwave produced peak temperatures of 45°C, some 2–5°C above average. On the other hand, the USA suffered from 562 tornadoes in May, beating the previous monthly record of 392 in June 1992.

Although the temperature variations involved may appear modest in themselves, they need to be set against the estimate that the last Ice Age was provoked by average temperatures only 4–5°C lower than those with which we are familiar. The sensitivity of the human body to very small fluctuations in blood temperature may be a useful parallel.

The Phenomenon of Global Warming.

Climate change is a comprehensive term for the changes arising from the phenomenon of global warming generated by the build up of what are known as "greenhouse gases" in the atmosphere. The best known of those "greenhouse gases" is carbon dioxide (CO_2), and the first area of controversy, which is essentially scientific, is the actual rate of change and the extent to which it is man-made. The Intergovernmental Panel on Climate Change currently estimates that warming is occurring at a speed of between 1·4°C and 6·4°C every century, rates which may sound modest but which at the higher end of the scale could raise sea levels by up to one metre in the same period. Some scientists believe, however, in the light of the accelerated melting of the Antarctic ice sheet, that the sea level rise could be as much as 1·4 metres. The rate of ice loss from the Antarctic Peninsula rose from an estimated 25 billion to an estimated 60 billion tons a year between 1996 and 2006, which statistic may be compared with the 4 billion tons of drinking water supplied to British households every year.

Similarly, there is now almost unanimous acceptance that global warming is being accelerated by greenhouse gas emissions from the burning of fossil fuels, particularly coal and oil, with natural gas as a lesser but still major contributor.

Although most greenhouse gas emissions are produced by domestic households, industry, commerce and agriculture, road transport is responsible for 21% and that proportion is increasing. Improvements in the domestic and industrial sectors are steadily being outweighed by the increasing levels of use of cars and lorries. Even the substantial gains of 50% or more in fuel efficiency over the last 20 years have been outweighed by longer journeys and the preference for more powerful models. The net result has been that CO_2 emissions from road vehicles have increased by 70%–80% throughout the European Union alone in the last 20 years. The explosion in air transport is adding to the problem significantly.

The UK's Committee on Climate Change recommended back in 2009 that the contribution of road traffic to greenhouse gas emissions be reduced by the introduction of road pricing as an additional tax, with no reduction in fuel duty, and by rigorously enforcing a 60mph limit on motorways, which latter would save 2·9 million tonnes of CO_2 a year.

Rising Sea Levels and Flooding.

Rising sea levels are a daunting threat not only to countries like Bangladesh, where more than 100 million people live on land barely above sea level, but also to those extensive areas of north western Europe like East Anglia, the Netherlands and the German coastal plain where the land drainage of centuries past has caused the soil to dry out and shrink, putting much land significantly below the present sea level. A study published in November 2005 showed that global sea levels were rising twice as fast as they had been 150 years previously.

A particularly severe example of flooding was that of the catchment areas of the Danube and the Elbe back in 2002, which caused incalculable damage in Austria, the Czech Republic and eastern Germany. The historic cultural cities of Salzburg, Prague and Dresden were amongst the areas hardest hit.

The 1992 Rio Conference.

Such anxieties had been aired at the United Nations Conference on Environment and Development held in

Rio in 1992, and led to the drafting of the Convention on Climate Change. The European Union for its part had earlier agreed after much argument to stabilise CO_2 emissions at 1990 levels by the year 2000. The results of these initiatives, in themselves fairly undemanding, remain modest. The EU target was only narrowly met despite the substantial contribution made in some countries, notably the UK, by the substitution of natural gas for coal to generate electricity.

Carbon Taxation and Trading.

Greenhouse gas emissions are unlikely to be stabilised let alone reduced unless fuel use becomes more expensive, which in practice means taxation of energy generated from fossil fuel sources. Although such taxation has the potential to be popular as one facet of a movement away from taxing incomes and employment towards taxing resource consumption, which would help to reduce unemployment, it will be seen as a regressive additional burden unless it forms part of a comprehensive redistributive package. Moreover, it is feared by many in industry, particularly in fields such as chemicals where energy use is high, by governments such as those of Japan and the US which are apprehensive of the impact on their competitiveness, by developing countries who fear their development might be stifled, and by the oil producing countries who do not wish to see a reduction in the sales of what may be their sole significant export.

Taxation in some form is, however, almost certain to come because the challenge of climate change will not go away. Indeed, modest initiatives have been taken in the UK with the introduction of the Climate Change Levy (CCL) and in Germany.

Nevertheless, the currently preferred approach is "carbon trading" whereby every qualifying industrial installation is allocated an emissions allowance. Any installation which emits more than its allocated allowance must buy credits accordingly from one which has emitted less, thus establishing a market price for carbon emissions.

The European Union's own emissions trading scheme became operative on 1 January 2005, but it is widely agreed that the initial allocations were too high and that the resulting emissions trading price has been too low to affect behaviour significantly. The European Commission hopes that stricter allocations in the second phase of the scheme running from 2008 will remedy any such problems. The numerous compromises approved by the EU following the European Council of December 2008 must, however, put that hope in question.

The Kyoto Conference.

It is not surprising against this overall background that the third conference of the 150 parties to the Convention on Climate Change, held in Kyoto, Japan, in December 1997, was politically charged. The European Union, strongly supported by the Association of Small Island States, urged a target of a 15 per cent reduction in emissions of three key greenhouse gases by the year 2010 with Britain being ready to reduce its emissions by 20 per cent in any event. America and Canada were initially unwilling to envisage any reduction at all, although America expected China and India to commit themselves to future reductions. China and the G7 group of developing nations, on the other hand, called for reductions of 35 per cent by the wealthier countries by the year 2020.

A Limited Agreement.

It is perhaps remarkable in these circumstances that any agreement was reached at all, even if it was dubbed second-rate. A Protocol was nevertheless adopted stipulating a binding target of a 5·2 per cent average reduction by the major industrialised countries on 1990 levels of emissions of a "basket" of six greenhouse gases by the years 2008–12. The different regions would, however, receive differential treatment. The EU would make a reduction of 8 per cent as would most of the countries of central and eastern Europe, the United States one of 7 per cent, and Japan and Canada 6 per cent. New Zealand, Russia and the Ukraine would stabilise emissions at 1990 levels but Australia would be allowed an increase of 8 per cent. No emission reductions were required of the developing countries, but America did, however, gain acceptance of the controversial concept of "carbon trading" between developed and developing countries, which is on the one hand a politically realistic approach but on the other a disincentive to real domestic change—a case of do as I say, rather than do as I do. In 2001, however, President Bush took America's opposition to its logical conclusion by withdrawing from the whole Kyoto agreement.

The Failure of the Copenhagen Conference.

The UN had hoped that its long-planned international conference in Copenhagen in December 2009 would be able to negotiate a global agreement to succeed the Kyoto Protocol on its expiry in 2012. The European Union had already committed itself to a reducton of 20 % in greenhouse gas emissions by 2020, compared with 1990 levels, in the belief that cuts of that magnitude by the world's major emitters would be sufficient to keep the rise in global temperatures to no more than 2°C above pre-industrial levels, the maximum increase with which the world is likely to be able to cope without the risk of serious damage. Adherence to the 2°C limit would then require a reduction by 50 % on 1990 levels by 2050.

The hopes of the UN, the EU, and the world's environmentalists were, however, dashed when Brazil, China, India and the African states united to oppose the agreement of any binding international treaty. It is hard to beat the terse judgement of Jonathan Porritt, a former chairman of the UK Sustainable Development Commission: "To bill the Copenhagen accord as anything other than a failure is simply dishonest." Its essential content can be expressed very briefly. Most of the participating nations committed themselves to the general ambition of preventing global temperatures from rising by more than 2°C, but no nation or group of nations was required to make any specific cuts.

Furthermore, poorer nations were promised up to $30 billion to cope with climate change and a goal of $100 billion annually was set for 2020 for helping them to adapt to global warming and adopt clean technology. The source of all this funding was, however, not specified.

Not only was there no treaty, but the accord was not even endorsed by the countries participating, merely noted. Although the Copenhagen Conference was in itself a failure, there were differing views as to whether the outcome should be seen as merely a temporary setback or whether it should be interpreted rather as final notice that the concept of a meaningful international climate treaty was a mirage for the foreseeable future. For the optimists, the important thing was that a global deal was finally struck: for the pessimists the important thing was the emptiness of that deal and in particular the absence of any binding targets.

Doha and Lima.

At the UN Climate Change talks at Doha (in Qatar) in 2012 the poor countries at last received a pledge that they would receive funds from the richer nations for 'loss and damage' they had incurred. Although this was an important advance, the details were obscure and the pledge fell short of legal liability.

In December 2014, the 194 countries represented at the Lima Call for Climate Action made some progress (albeit painfully slow) to commit each country to draw up a national pledge to cut greenhouse gas emissions. It was hoped the 2015 UN summit in Paris would make further progress.

Commitments under Kyoto.

All EU nations were committed under the Kyoto Protocol to reducing their greenhouse gas emissions, which precludes a switch back to coal unless carbon storage can be made a practical proposition or emissions are reduced disproportionately in some other sector, most obviously transport. The UK,Germany and Poland are in any event the only EU member states which still generate a significant proportion of their electricity from coal. Natural gas has been consumed at a rate which can only be described as imprudent, and the EU now envisages that it will have to import 70 % of its needs by 2020.

The demand for gas and oil by China continues to

grow at an extraordinary rate, confirming forecasts by the International Energy Agency that the global demand for oil would increase by almost half over the next 25 years. China's own demand has doubled over the last 10 years, and it is now the world's second largest importer.

The Paris Summit.

Nearly 120 world leaders, and a total of around 40,000 delegates attended the Paris Summit from 30 November to 11 December 2015. Contrary to the expectations of sceptics the agreements reached exceeded expectations. The agreement commits all 195 signatories to a limit of below 2°C on global warming above pre-industrial levels. Countries will meet in 2018 to check on progress. However, the great minus factor of Paris was that so much remains voluntary–there is no real enforcement; nothing is binding and after four years countries can opt out. Whether, as President Hollande of France declared, it is a "major leap for mankind" must remain open to debate.

Subsequent developments have left that debate wide open. On the positive side, the UK succeeded in reducing its emissions by a further 6% in 2016, having done slightly better than the EU average between 1990 and 2014. On the negative side, it has been estimated by government that much of the reduction of 42% on 1990 levels is attributable to the movement of production overseas and that once imports are included the UK's carbon footprint has fallen by only 6% since 1997, whereas emissions associated with imports from China have more than doubled over the same period.

Such considerations have been, however, overshadowed by President Trump's repeal in 2017 of US regulations to restrain carbon emissions. It set a malign precedent.

MEDICAL
MATTERS

Here we give a brief summary of
modern medical knowledge for a
wide variety of the most common
illnesses. The section also looks at
many medical problems of contemporary society, from bowel cancer
to the obesity epidemic and from
the dementia timebomb to shingles
and meningitis. Also included are
such health threats as dengue fever
and the return of rickets. However,
it must not be allowed to replace
your doctor, who should be consulted
if you are at all worried. The main
index at the end of *Pears* provides an
easy reference guide.

TABLE OF CONTENTS

MEDICAL MATTERS

PART I. INTRODUCTION.

TWENTY-FIRST CENTURY MEDICINE

The Medical Revolution.

Much in medicine which is now taken for granted (that for the majority of diseases caused by identifiable organisms there is a specific drug treatment, for example) was undreamed of even as recently as 60 years ago. Progress in diagnosis, in preventive medicine and in treatment, both medical and surgical, has been so rapid as to be almost breathtaking. A doctor retiring from active practice this year has seen smallpox completely eradicated, poliomyelitis practically banished globally, tuberculosis become curable, coronary artery disease relievable surgically and he or she will have witnessed the dramatic progress in the field of molecular biology and in the research by immunologists and geneticists into their efforts to control parasitic diseases like bilharzia, malaria and river blindness that affect millions of people in the Third World. One aspect of medicine and medical thinking still resistant to progress in understanding in spite of continued research is the effect of mind on body.

The Effect of Mind on Body.

Many of us still like to think that our bodies are just something we have got into, like cars, that ill-health is simply something that has "gone wrong" in one system or another and that therefore provided we find the appropriate expert (a chest physician, a gastro-enterologist or an ophthalmic surgeon, for example) to correct the fault, we will recover. Whereas that idea holds good for a broken leg, for instance, with many diseases the idea that mind can be totally separated from the "defective" part just isn't good enough. You cannot simply divorce your stomach, your bowels, your liver or your heart from your "self". They are all part of you and react, as you yourself react, to all the stresses and anxieties, fears and worries that are part and parcel of modern living.

Stress and Anxiety.

Mens sana in corpore sano—a sound mind in a sound body. Your body and its many parts may be helped to normal function by modern medicines and surgery but, in general, it will only stay that way if you can rid yourself of all those emotional blemishes—anger, frustration, fear, worry and anxiety—which trouble you. Easier said than done, of course, but a good physician can help with good advice, with medicines if necessary—or simply with his ear. Emotional stress can not only inhibit healing of such things as duodenal or gastric ulcers but may even *cause* them.

There are many diseases now recognised which are known to be associated with excess stress factors if not actually caused by them. Mainly these are diseases of the digestive tract or of the heart and blood vessels and you will find some of them discussed in the appropriate sections. However, some stress in moderation is probably good for us.

The state of the mind has more influence on bodily functions than you might think and recovery from many serious conditions can be slowed or hastened, depending on your state of mind. Every doctor has had experience of the patient who "loses the will to live", a situation which is unfortunately commoner than the reverse.

Preventive Medicine.

A word about preventive medicine—or helping yourself to health. A great deal of nonsense has been talked about the healthy life; at one time we were told to take eighteen chews to each bite, to do deep breathing, to take plenty of exercise, to get lots of fresh air, to eat regularly (or to indulge in peculiar diets). But more recently eminent doctors have cast doubt on some of these fancies. Moderate exercise is indeed necessary to health, but athletes who indulge in violent exercise have not always been noted for longevity. Fresh air is pleasant and stimulating, but, where actual breathing is concerned, it is no better than the air in most rooms, though secondary smoking is now rightly considered extremely harmful. Certainly, one of the problems of our time is air pollution, but at present we are considering ordinary fresh air in comparison with the air indoors, and, in this case, the experts say there is little difference so far as health is concerned.

Diet.

A balanced diet containing correct amounts of the basic food substances is essential, but there is no evidence that when, or at what intervals, you eat makes the slightest difference—unless you are a sufferer from stomach ulcer, in which case it is necessary that the intervals between meals should not be too long. The whole business of having meals at fixed intervals is nothing but a social convention, and in modern life obviously a matter of convenience. However, there is evidence that it is unwise to eat a heavy meal near bedtime. The biggest challenge for many today is not to eat too much. As discussed later, obesity is becoming one of the great challenges of our time.

Sleep.

Sleep is certainly a necessity. But different people require different amounts of sleep. Some manage on as little as three hours, others need ten or more.

In a number of studies of men and women who lived to a ripe old age it was found that the only factors in common between them were that they had a good balanced diet of healthy food, that they had contented minds, and that they were interested in something which gave them an aim in life. They also came of long-lived families—for living a long and healthy life depends partly upon heredity. This factor we cannot alter!

Key Rules of Health.

(1) Don't abuse your body—*i.e.*, exercise it, feed it sensibly and in moderation and don't poison it with cigarette smoke (yours or anyone else's), with excess alcohol or with harmful drugs

(2) Think positively about health—make it a purpose for living

(3) Turn your thoughts away from those bodily functions (digestion, circulation, breathing and so on) which can look after themselves. Introspection leads to hypochondriasis (unnecessary and excessive worrying about our health).

THE DEVELOPMENT OF MEDICINES.

A great surgeon, the first of the moderns, was Ambrose Paré, who died in 1590, and one of his best known sayings was: "I apply the dressing, but God heals the wound." He was quite right; for until about one hundred years ago, or even less, all the physician could do in most cases was to put the patient in as favourable a state as possible to enable his body to cure itself. There were hardly any specific drugs—drugs that had a direct effect on the disease.

There was quinine, discovered by the Spaniards in America, which was specific for malaria, and there were iron (specific for anaemia) and digitalis (specific for certain types of heart disease), but otherwise nothing until the nineteenth century, when Paul Ehrlich discovered salvarsan, which is specific for syphilis. Ehrlich died in 1914, having conceived the brilliant idea of drugs, which he described as "magic bullets"—*i.e.*, drugs which, like bullets, would be aimed at the real cause of the disease. They would, that is to say, be specific.

Antibiotics (and Antibiotic Resistance).

Since then a multitude of such drugs have been discovered. For example, there were antibiotics, such as penicillin, discovered in 1928 by Fleming at St. Mary's Hospital, Paddington. Later, Florey and Chain in Oxford, helped in the 1939–45 war years by the vast resources of the American pharmaceutical industry, were able to produce penicillin available to the public in sufficient quantities by new techniques of production.

Penicillin is practically non-poisonous (although it is possible to become allergic to it, sometimes with serious results). It can kill some germs in a dilution of one part of penicillin to one million parts of water; it is effective against streptococci, the cause of blood-poisoning, sepsis in wounds, and many other diseases; and also against the germs of gonorrhoea, meningitis of certain types, and syphilis—penicillin is typically active at 1–10 ug/ml *i.e.* 1–10 parts per million. Blood-poisoning, whether from wounds or childbirth, used to be almost incurable—now the rate of cure is around 90 per cent.; gonorrhoea has an almost 100 per cent. rate of cure. In pneumonia the rate is 90 per cent., and early syphilis can be cured in a week, instead of the previous two to three years.

Unfortunately, one of the looming medical crises at the moment is antibiotic resistance. Decades have elapsed since new antibiotics have been found (but a promising discovery was made in 2015). Now in 2017, resistance to antibiotics is a global problem.

Other Types of New Drugs.

But that was only the beginning. Other antibiotics—streptomycin, tetracycline, erythromycin, and many others—have greatly reduced the terrible scourges of the human race, in particular, in the case of streptomycin, tuberculosis. The sulpha group of drugs—sulphadiazine, sulphadimidine, *etc.*—have also proved a great boon. Then there are the newer drugs which have created a revolution in psychiatry—the tranquillisers which relieve anxiety, the drugs which clear up certain types of depression, and substances such as chlorpromazine which make it possible to nurse formerly violent patients in the wards of a general hospital. The antihistamine drugs help in allergies, anticoagulants are of value after heart attacks and levodopa mitigates some of the distressing features of Parkinson's Disease.

The Safety of Drugs.

No drug, old or new, is completely safe—if we define "safe" as meaning having absolutely no potential for harm. The household aspirin, widely used in a variety of conditions for its analgesic (pain-relieving) and antipyretic (fever-reducing) qualities, can cause bleeding from the stomach and small intestine. Phenacetin, at one time a component of compound codeine tablets but now withdrawn, can—with prolonged use—damage the kidney. Chloramphenicol, a powerful antibiotic effective in typhoid fever, typhus and whooping cough, can damage the blood-forming cells of the bone marrow producing an agranulocytosis which can be fatal.

Clearly, in any one case, the doctor must weigh up the advantages and disadvantages of this or that drug before prescribing. Minor, self-limiting illnesses do not require potent, potentially toxic remedies. Chloramphenicol is rarely justified in whooping cough, but would never be withheld from a patient with typhoid fever.

Humans make up a unique species. A new chemical compound promising in animal experiments, for example, as an anti-inflammatory agent, apparently safe when given, say, to mice in a dose 100 times that required to produce that anti-inflammatory effect may, over a long period of time in us, not only have no effect but make his hair fall out or perhaps cause retention of urine.

Nevertheless, some animal species do react like humans, or vice versa, and it is possible to make reasonably accurate extrapolations from animals to man in terms of drug effect. It is also possible to estimate the toxicity of a drug on humans from its toxicity in certain animal species, but the ultimate test comes only when it is given to us.

The 1950s Thalidomide Tragedy.

Thalidomide was unique. In every animal test used throughout the drug industry at that time—it was introduced in the late 1950s—it had a clean bill of health. It was chemically related to other drugs which had been in use for a long time. Overdosage with other sedatives such as the barbiturates was common at that time, although less so now. Overdosage with thalidomide was unlikely to prove fatal. It was marketed in Europe and in Britain as a "safe sedative".

The tragic results that followed its ingestion by women in the early weeks of pregnancy are well known. Over 10,000 babies across 46 countries were born with severe deformities of limbs, internal organs or both. That effect could not have been foretold from any animal tests then in use. Since that date new drugs have been subjected to rigorous testing in various animal species to check the effect on foetal development as a statutory requirement, along with the older tests for toxicity which had always been undertaken by reputable drug companies.

The Control of New Drugs.

Briefly, no new drug or modification of an old one can be sold, whether or not on prescription, unless it has been granted a product licence by the Department of Health and Social Security (DHSS).

Many stages have to be passed to acquire that licence, from the granting of certificates to allow the drug to be tested initially in a limited way in patients in a strictly controlled manner by investigators, to permission for extension of those trials at a later date to include larger numbers of patients or more investigators, to perhaps a "monitored release"—that is, to enable its use in, say, hospitals only—to the final release on the granting of a full product licence.

Furthermore, all the stages are dependent on production of evidence relating to the safety and efficacy of the drug, evidence which may take the drug company months, sometimes years, to produce and which, of course, must be acceptable to the regulatory authority, the London-based European Medicines Agency. Trials may be stopped at any time, for example, if evidence of side effects of an undesirable nature come to light during clinical testing, or when evidence from some other similar compound indicates a likely risk in the use of the drug in question. Of course, "acceptable" means that the strict criteria which have been laid down by the specialist committees appointed to deal with all the various aspects of drug development, such as toxicology, adverse reactions and so forth, have been met.

Surveillance of Side Effects.

As well as all these rigid controls on development and testing in the early stages, there is also a scheme of surveillance for untoward side effects. These are the action, or actions, of a drug apart from its main one. Take the well-known side effect of drowsiness which occurs with certain antihistamine drugs: the main action, the one for which the drug is prescribed, is the mitigation of the effects of allergy, such as urticaria. Drowsiness would be an unwanted effect if the patient is not incapacitated and is able to do his usual job. On the other hand, some antihistamines have an appetite-stimulating effect which could, of course, be a useful attribute in certain situations or even allow the drug to be used solely for that purpose, the anti-allergic effect then being incidental.

New Surgical Advances.

Mention must of course be made of the surgical advances and progress in anaesthesia. Hardly a week goes by without operations being undertaken which seemed inconceivable even as short a time as 50 years ago. Transplantation and re-plantation (the re-attachment of severed limbs) are routine operations; haemodialysis (the 'cleansing' of blood in patients with irreversible kidney disease) is now often undertaken in the patient's own home where, with appropriate adaptation and the modern kidney machine, he or she can run the procedure—single-handed in many instances—and still keep his or her job; and the laser beam is used to deal with detached retinas or to obliterate tiny, microscopic blood vessel 'bubbles' (aneurysms) in the back of the eye while the patient is conscious and cooperative. Keyhole surgery is often the norm (see **Z60**). The list grows daily.

The Conquest of Disease.

As mentioned earlier, doctors and scientists have achieved notable triumphs in curing or preventing once devastating and widespread illnesses such as smallpox and polio. It is hard to realise now that polio was once so widespread and so crippling. Only three decades ago, in 1988, around 350,000 people spread across 125 countries contracted polio. Now in 2017, it is almost eradicated across the globe. The first polio vaccine was created sixty years ago. In the UK the last case was in 1982. Across the world the global eradication campaign has immunised a vast number of children (around 2·5 billion). Only in a very few places (such as Nigeria) are cases now reported. It is one of the great success stories of modern medicine.

LANDMARKS IN PUBLIC HEALTH.

1831–32	First major cholera epidemic stimulated sanitary improvements.
1840	Select Committee on the Health of Towns exposed slum conditions.
1842	Chadwick's Report on the Sanitary Condition of the Labouring Poor.
1847	First Medical Officer of Health in Liverpool. James Simpson discovered chloroform anaesthetic.
1848	Health of Towns Act established central Board of Health and local boards. Further cholera epidemic.
1853	Further cholera epidemic.
1854	Value of efficient nursing demonstrated by Florence Nightingale and Mary Seacole.
1860	First professional training school for nurses at St Thomas' Hospital.
1865–66	Further cholera outbreak.
1867	Lister developed antiseptic techniques.
1868	Invention of thermometer.
1871	Local Government Board set up to supervise poor law and public health.
1872	Public Health Act. Appointment of medical officers of health made compulsory and sanitary authorities set up.
1875	Public Health Act. Local sanitary authorities given power to enforce sanitary regulations including drainage, sanitation and water supplies.
1907	School medical examinations made compulsory and school medical services established.
1911	National Insurance Act. The Act provided insurance against sickness and unemployment to be paid for by contributions from the state, the employer and the employee. It covered those between 16 and 70 years of age, but was limited to industries where unemployment was recurrent. Maternity grants introduced.

1918	Ministry of Health established.
1929	Public Health committees set up by county and county borough councils.
1930	Mental Treatment Act made voluntary treatment possible for mental illness.
1934	Local authorities allowed to provide subsidized or free milk at schools.
1944	Government White Papers *A National Health Service*, *Employment Policy*, and *Social Insurance* accept the principles of a national health service, full employment and a comprehensive system of social welfare (following the 1942 Beveridge Report).
1946	National Health Service Act provided a free medical service for everyone, including free hospital treatment, dental care and opticians' services. The Act came into force in 1948. Doctors and dentists now worked within the National Health Service though they continued to be able to treat private patients as well. Free milk for all school-children introduced.
1954	First kidney transplant.
1967	Abortion Act provides for the legal termination of pregnancy under certain circumstances. Family Planning Act allows local health authorities to provide a family planning service for all who seek it, either directly or through a voluntary body. Advice provided free with graduated charges for contraceptive devices according to the means of the patient.
1971	Abolition of free milk for schoolchildren.
1973	National Health Service Reorganization Act creates area health authorities to coordinate health services within the new local government boundaries set up in 1972.
1978	Health Services Act provides for the withdrawal of private medicine from National Health Service hospitals.
1983	First combined heart and lung transplant.
1990	National Health Service and Community Care Act provides for hospitals to opt out and become self-governing trusts; allows general practitioners to control own budgets; reorganizes system of local community care giving local authorities responsibility for care of elderly people in the community.
1992	Introduction of the Patient's Charter. Some nurses given power to prescribe drugs.
1995	Completion of "internal market" in the National Health Service; all hospital and community care other than in Scottish islands provided by Trusts.
1997	Incoming Labour government in White Paper *The New NHS* proposed abolition of "internal market", reductions in bureaucracy and more spending in specialist areas.
2000	Labour government announces massive increase in spending on the NHS with large increase in numbers of nurses, doctors and consultants, as well as firm commitments to maximum waiting times for treatment.
2008	Publication of the Darzi Report (*Our NHS, Our Future*). Debate over proposed creation of polyclinics.
2009	First-ever constitution for the NHS published, setting out the rights and responsibilities of patients and those who treat them.
2010	Coalition proposes major shift of power over NHS to GPs.
2012	Coalition Health Reform Bill becomes law.
2013	All nurses to be required to have degrees.
2014	Mounting concerns over future NHS funding.
2015	Pioneer devolution of NHS powers to Manchester region. Warnings of excess use of antibiotics.
2016	First robotic kidney transplants in UK.

THE NATIONAL HEALTH SERVICE (NHS).

If you need to find out more about NHS services, www.nhs.uk is the official NHS website that can help you. It provides free, basic information such as addresses, maps and contacts for NHS organisations. In addition, www.nhs.uk holds information about what the NHS has to offer and how you can get access to these services.

Through this easy-to-remember website you can:

* get the latest news about the NHS and current health campaigns;

* find out how to have your say about NHS services;

* learn about the history and structure of the NHS; and;

* look up performance facts and figures.

Prescription Charges.

Currently (May 2017) a charge of £8·60 is payable in England for prescriptions (except for contraceptives which are not charged). Prescription charges have been abolished in Wales and Northern Ireland. In Scotland, their abolition took effect from April 2011.

There are, however, important categories of people exempt from charges. These include children under 16, full-time students under 19 as well as men and women aged 60 or over. Pregnant women who hold an exemption certificate are also included. Diabetics are exempt as are those with such illnesses as fistula, myasthenia gravis, cancer *etc*. Certain people on income support and other benefits are also exempt. Check booklet HC11 available from Post Offices.

The General Medical Council (GMC).

The General Medical Council regulates the medical profession in the United Kingdom. It sets the qualifications and standards required to be registered as a doctor. If found unsafe or unfit it can restrict a doctor's medical practice.

Patients may complain directly to the General Medical Council.

British Medical Association (BMA).

The British Medical Association has over 130,000 members including about 80% of the UK's practising doctors. It represents their interests, and its roles include publishing the *British Medical Journal*.

This respected medical journal is available free on the Internet (*www.bmj.com*) together with an accompanying electronic discussion forum.

Primary Care/Clinical Commissioning Groups.

Primary care describes the service you receive from the NHS staff who look after your health needs in the community. This includes your family doctor, health visitor, community nurse, community pharmacist, optician, dentist, physiotherapist *etc*.

A Primary Care Trust (or PCT for short) is a local NHS organisation, which receives money from the Government to plan and provide health services for local people. The PCT's main aim is to improve the health of local people and deliver the best quality healthcare for the population. They were replaced by Clinical Commissioning Groups in 2013.

The Health Service Ombudsman.

The Health Service Ombudsman looks into complaints made by or on behalf of people who have suffered because of unsatisfactory treatment or service by the NHS. He is completely independent. His services are free.

The Ombudsman also looks into complaints against private health providers, but only if the treatment was funded by the NHS. He can also investigate complaints about other services provided on behalf of the NHS.

Anybody wishing to complain to the Ombudsman must first have put their complaint to the NHS organisation or practitioner concerned, such as the hospital trust, Health Authority, the GP or the dentist. They will give you full details of the NHS complaints procedure and will try to resolve your complaint.

If you are still dissatisfied once you have exhausted the NHS complaints procedure you can complain to the Ombudsman.

To find out more about the NHS complaints procedure, pick up a leaflet from any NHS organisation, the NHS website or your GP or dentist's surgery.

The European Health Insurance Card (EHIC).

The free E111 form which entitled you to free or reduced-cost state healthcare if you fell ill or had an accident while travelling in a European Union (EU) country was replaced with the European Health Insurance Card from 1 January 2006. The card is free and can be applied for on 0845 606 2030 or online at www.ehic.org.uk. Check for any changes to this.

Organ and Tissue Donation.

One of the most useful things we can all consider doing is to donate our own organs. Organ donation is the gift of an organ to help someone who needs a transplant. The generosity of donors and their families enables over 3,000 people in the UK every year to take on a new lease of life. Over 80,000 patients have now received transplants.

One donor can save the life of several people, restore the sight of two others and improve the quality of life of many more. The more people who pledge to donate their organs and tissue after their death, the more people stand to benefit. By choosing to join the NHS Organ Donor Register you could help to make sure life goes on for many others. No less than 22 million people are now (2017) on the Organ Donor Register.

Organs that can be transplanted include kidneys, livers, lungs, pancreas and the small bowel. Tissue donation is the gift of tissue such as corneas, skin, bone, tendons, cartilage and heart valves to help others.

To decide whether or not you wish to become a donor after you have died is something very personal and it is important that everyone makes their own decision.

Wales has now introduced organ donor presumption. Since 2015 people have needed to opt out if they do not wish their organs to be used.

For more information you can phone 0845 606 0400 or contact www.uktransplant.org.uk.

PART II. DISEASES ARRANGED BY CAUSE OR BODY SYSTEM AFFECTED

THE INFECTIOUS DISEASES.

Introduction.

Infectious diseases are those which are caused by an invasion of the human body by organisms from outside (the word "organism" simply means living things, and we are using this word because, as will be seen later, it is not only what are known as "germs" which can cause infection). We know, too, that what is generally typical about this group is: (*a*) that the disease can be passed on from one person to another, and (*b*) that it is usually accompanied by a raised temperature or fever. Now (*a*), of course, is always true, because

the definition of an infectious disease is one that can be passed on to others, but (*b*) is not always true, because a few infections produce little or no temperature, and also because it is possible to have a raised temperature (again in only a few cases) without any infection. For example, certain types of brain injury, tumour, or haemorrhage can produce a raised—or lowered—temperature, and so can the injection of some foreign substance such as milk into the muscles. This is known as "protein shock," and was at one time used in the treatment of certain illnesses.

Finally, solutions of dead germs, such as the antityphoid vaccine given to protect troops in wartime, may lead when injected to very high temperatures. But, by and large, we are entitled to suppose that the patient with a raised temperature is probably suffering from an infection.

Types of Infection.

As we have seen, it is not only germs which cause infections—so from now on we shall give germs their proper name of "bacteria." Here is a list of the chief offenders which are liable to attack our bodies: bacteria, viruses, fungi, amoebae, worms and other parasites.

Bacteria are tiny living things which can be seen only under a fairly powerful microscope. Some are grouped like bunches of grapes (*staphylococci*) or in strings or chains (*streptococci*). They are given these names because "staphylos" is the Greek word for a bunch of grapes, and "streptos" means a chain. Yet others are comma-shaped (such as the cholera vibrio), or shaped like a drumstick—a rod with a small knob at the end (the tetanus bacillus, which causes lockjaw).

Types of Bacteria. It would be a mistake to think that all bacteria are harmful; for without some species we could not survive for long. Indeed, a human being carries around ten times as many bacterial cells as human cells. Our guts team with them. Bacteriologists divide them according to their behaviour in the human body into three groups: saprophytic, parasitic or pathogenic, and symbiotic. The *saprophytic* organisms are the bacteria normally found in the skin, mouth, and intestines; they do us neither harm nor good. The *parasitic*, or as they are more usually called, pathogenic (*i.e.*, disease-producing) organisms, are the harmful ones with which we are naturally more concerned. Lastly, there are the *symbiotic* organisms, which, whilst taking something from the body, give something in return. For example, cattle would not be able to digest the cellulose of the grass they eat were it not for helpful bacteria in the lower parts of the intestines, and there are certain bacteria in the large intestine of man which produce vitamins.

Characteristics of Bacteria. Bacteria have two peculiar characteristics: each reproduces by splitting into two separate individuals as often as every twenty minutes in favourable circumstances like an open wound. If no bacterium were destroyed, one individual could produce a mass of bacteria larger than the whole world in a matter of a few weeks (since each of the offspring also divides into two, which in turn divide again— the progression goes: one gives birth to two, these two to four, the four to eight, eight to sixteen, sixteen to thirty-two, and so on—you will see, if you work it out, that in a short period the figure becomes astronomical). Fortunately, most bacteria do not find themselves in ideal conditions, so for the present the world is safe! The other curious thing about bacteria is that, barring accidents, they are potentially immortal. Under ideal conditions in which no bacteria were killed, none would die; for a bacterium there is no death from old age, no corpse except when it is actively destroyed. It simply goes on dividing, dividing, and subdividing for ever.

How, then, can bacteria be destroyed? Briefly, the answer is that most are destroyed by the natural defences of the body of whatever host they are preying on; others are destroyed by antiseptics and the new drugs; and many are destroyed when they are excreted from the body in the sputum or through the bowels and land in places where they are dried up and cannot survive —although some bacteria in such circumstances can form what are called "spores," rather like the seeds of plants, so making it possible for them to survive in a state of suspended animation for months on end until picked up accidentally by another unfortunate host. Finally, bacteria, in addition to all these possibilities, face another danger: they may themselves develop disease.

Bacteriophages. This disease is caused by even more minute organisms known as bacteriophages (viruses which affect bacteria), discovered by F. W. Twort in 1915. Attack by bacteriophage causes whole groups of bacteria (known as "colonies") to disintegrate and become harmless.

Although bacteriophage have been used in the treatment of some diseases in human beings, this method has now been largely given up, since the new drugs are infinitely more effective.

Other Spirochaetes, like bacteria, are minute organisms, but differ in being shaped somewhat like a corkscrew and in being able to move. Their progress is produced by a sideways wriggling motion. The two main diseases caused by spirochaetes are syphilis and leptospirosis.

Leptospirosis is carried by rats, and is common in those who work in mines. It is now rare in Britain, but still occurs in Egypt, and Malaysia; the infection is passed through the skin where the excreta of infected rats mingle with water on damp ground in the mine where miners kneel. Infection may also occur through eating infected food.

Viruses. Unlike bacteria, viruses are too small to be seen under an ordinary microscope. They can, however, be photographed in some cases under an electron microscope, which uses a magnetic field instead of a glass lens and a stream of electrons in place of a beam of light. Viruses cause such diseases as measles, mumps, poliomyelitis, smallpox, and chickenpox—not to mention such plant and animal diseases as tobacco mosaic disease and foot-and-mouth disease, which often have serious economic consequences. Other virus diseases are swine fever in pigs, influenza in Man, and myxomatosis in rabbits. They also cause the common cold.

Characteristics of Viruses. The main characteristics of viruses are, first, that they can only grow in living cells—unlike bacteria, which readily grow in the laboratory on plates containing a jelly made from meat, broth, gelatin, milk, and other delicacies. The scientist, therefore, must keep them in portions of living tissue kept alive outside the body. Secondly, many are so small that they pass through the pores of the finest filter. Thirdly, a first attack usually produces immunity for life. Second attacks of the common virus diseases mentioned above are very rare; but unfortunately, this rule does not apply to influenza or the common cold. Fourthly, there is reason to believe that viruses represent an extraordinary intermediate stage between the living and non-living; they can, for instance, be produced in crystalline form and yet are just as dangerous when "thawed out." Lastly, the virus diseases have proved for the most part to be little affected by the new antibiotics and other drugs, although vaccination in smallpox and the injection of sera from infected patients in other infections may give immunity for longer or shorter periods, and progress has been made in developing drugs to combat some viruses, such as herpes viruses and the AIDS virus.

Practical Virus Problems. The two great practical problems that doctors face with viruses are: (i) many viruses are unknown because of the difficulty of growing them outside the body in suitable tissue culture. They cannot therefore be conveniently identified in specimens from the patient, as bacteria can; and (ii) most are unaffected by antibiotics like penicillin. It has been a great step forward to grow viruses artificially in tissue culture, in which they are identified indirectly by the effects they have on the cultured *cells*. But since we do not know exactly how to grow some viruses (like those of infective hepatitis) many have still not been seen.

When we recover from a viral illness like chickenpox, we probably do so by producing virus-killing substances such as interferon inside our own cells. Scientists are currently searching for these substances in case they can be used, like penicillin, to cure viral disease.

Fungi. Some infections are caused by fungi— that is to say organisms belonging to the same group as moulds, mushrooms, and toadstools. Penicillin and some other antibiotics are produced from moulds, so, as in the case of bacteria, some fungi are helpful; they even help to destroy each other, as bacteria do. For example actinomyces, which can cause infection of the jaw and other tissues, is destroyed by penicillin.

Most fungal infections are trivial and limited to the skin. But, although trivial, they can be unsightly and uncomfortable. Ringworm of the scalp, dhobie itch—an infection of the groin spread by infected underclothing—and so-called "athlete's foot" are caused by a fungus.

Amoebae. Amoebae are small, single-cell organisms, the largest of which (a harmless type found in stagnant ponds in Britain and elsewhere) is just visible to the naked eye. It is about the size of the head of a pin. Amoebae move, in the species which are capable of moving, by pushing forward a part of the cell in the appropriate direction and causing the rest to flow into the advancing portion. Like bacteria, they reproduce by dividing into halves, each of which becomes a new amoeba.

The main human disease caused by amoebae is amoebic dysentery (not to be confused with bacillary dysentery).

Parasites. These may live on the skin like lice (which can carry typhus) or fleas (carriers of plague) or the parasites of scabies which burrow into the skin, or they may live part of their time in the blood or other tissues, like malaria. They often have complicated life-cycles involving other hosts (like mosquitoes) at certain stages of development.

Worms. Worms are intestinal parasites, but the only common types found in Britain are threadworms, the tiny thread-like worms which cause irritability and itching in the skin of children, less often in adults; round-worms, somewhat resembling the ordinary garden earth-worm, which seldom lead to symptoms; and tape-worms, which may reach a length of 3 or even 6 m. Many parasitic worms (like parasites elsewhere) lead a double life—they spend part of their life in the human intestine and the other part in the muscles of another animal. The tape-worm, for example, whilst in the human intestine, lays eggs which pass out of the body in the excreta, and are then swallowed by pigs, especially in those parts of the world where human excreta are used as manure in the fields. In the pig, the eggs form cysts in the muscles—meat infected in this way is known as "measly pork"—and when, in turn, the meat is eaten by man, the process in the intestine begins all over again.

For a further discussion of diseases spread by parasitic worms, *see* **Z17–18**.

Russian Tape-worm. Less common types include the Russian tape-worm; this type is spread by caviare or undercooked infected fish. The small, leaf-shaped liver fluke lays eggs which are passed into canals or pools in tropical countries in the urine of infected people, hatch out and enter a water snail, and finally leave the snail in the form of small parasites which pierce the skin of bathers, whence they pass to the liver and subsequently the bladder and rectum. This is a serious condition, as is also *filariasis* (another tropical disease), for which, unlike bilharzia—caused by the liver fluke—no cure is known. The tropical disease known as *loa-loa* is caused by a variety of filaria.

How the Infection is Spread.

Infection is spread in many ways, some of which have already been mentioned. In the common fevers found in Europe and elsewhere one of the most frequent ways is by *droplet infection*—that is to say, by minute drops carrying the germs which are coughed or sneezed into the air by someone already suffering from the disease. Such droplets can be projected into the air for 3m or more, and when breathed in by someone within range infection may result. Next commonest mode of spread is perhaps by *infected food, water*, and the dirty hands of those who prepare food: cholera, dysentery, food-poisoning, and typhoid are spread in this way. Spread by *direct contact* is found in the venereal diseases (usually, but not always, spread by sexual intercourse with someone

who already has the disease), and, of course, lice, fleas, and other parasites, including the scabies mite, are spread by contact with the infested individual—or sometimes with his clothes or bed linen. Spread through an *intermediary host*, whether it be lice, fleas, or mosquitoes carrying infection, or the various means adopted by worms, has already been described above, so no more need be said. Lastly, the infection may result from *bacteria already within the body*; for example, Escherichia coli, which lives in the large intestine is harmless there, but if it gets into the bladder or the ureters (the tubes leading from kidney to bladder) a quite unpleasant result may follow in the form of cystitis or pyelonephritis.

How the Body Deals with Infection.

The body has many mechanisms of defence against intruders; these can generally be divided into two types. First, non-specific defence substances such as lysozyme, an enzyme that digests bacterial cell walls, are present in many body fluids, and a system of blood proteins known as the complement cascade punches holes in bacteria to kill them. Interferons and other so-called cytokines are produced when the body's cells are damaged by infection and help other cells to resist infection. A class of blood cell, known as macrophages, responds to infection and other damage by migrating to the affected part of the body and swallows bacteria and cell debris for destruction by the powerful enzymes that they contain. Secondly, specific defences are stimulated by infection: one class of lymphocytes produces antibodies, which recognise particular parts of bacteria and viruses, neutralising them and marking them out for destruction. Another class of lymphocytes hunts for foreign cells and kills them by a variety of methods, bursting them open and leaving debris for the macrophages to clear away.

Immunisation.

Immunity can be induced by immunisation, which can be active or passive. In active immunisation, a vaccine is injected into the body to simulate the first time the body is infected with a disease-causing agent. Vaccines are made either from dead bacteria or viruses or from specially adapted strains which have lost their ability to cause disease. Passive immunisation is used when a person has already been exposed to a disease or when an effective vaccine is not available, and consists of injections of specific gamma-globulin obtained from the blood of a patient who has recently recovered from the disease concerned.

Immunology is one of the fastest-growing areas of medical research, as there are still many infectious diseases which are difficult to treat with antibodies, and manipulation of the immune system has great potential in the fight against cancer.

Antiseptics.

The earliest antiseptic was carbolic acid, used by Lister in his operating-theatre in the form of a fine spray directed throughout the operation on the wound, or sometimes in the form of steam from a kettle containing a solution of carbolic. But carbolic is dangerous, and since Lister's time many more useful antiseptics have been discovered. Acriflavine, thymol, and other old favourites have been discarded too. The various forms of carbolic are still used to disinfect drains, but, to tell the truth, the use of antiseptics nowadays is very limited. In surgery the *antiseptic* method has given way to the *aseptic* method—instead of fighting sepsis we see to it that no possibility of sepsis is present before operating; all instruments, the surgeons' and nurses' hands, the skin, are sterilised—the instruments by boiling, the dressings by dry heat, the hands by soap and water, and almost the only antiseptic used is to clean the patient's skin in the area to be operated on.

Antiseptics are used as first-aid treatment for cuts and wounds, but should be applied only once as a general rule—that is, when the wound is first received. The trouble with antiseptics is that as well as killing germs they also kill the surrounding tissues, which antibiotics never do.

Antibiotics.

Some antibiotics—penicillin, streptomycin, erythromycin and so on—have already long been used by doctors. In recent years many others have been introduced—ampicillin, gentamicin, cephalexin. Indiscriminate use of these drugs (*e.g.* for trivial complaints) has led to problems, the most important being the development of resistance by previously sensitive organisms. This is now reaching crisis proportions. It is not always convenient or possible to be able to identify the particular germ responsible for an infection and determine to which drug it is sensitive, but if there is an initial clinical response, it can be assumed that the "right" drug has been used. It is important to have a full course of treatment— which usually means ten days minimum.

Other problems are hypersensitivity (allergic) reactions which can take many forms. Once hypersensitivity to one of the antibiotics has been identified (penicillin hypersensitivity is not rare) the patient must be made aware of this, and so protect himself from unwitting prescribing by another doctor. Hospital and GP records are clearly marked in such instances but it is very important that the patient himself knows.

Antibiotics are only available on prescription, at least in the UK, but medicine cupboards are full of them, accumulated from unfinished courses. Self-prescribing is tempting but ill-advised; antibiotics must always be given under medical supervision. Side effects are common and some are dangerous. Repeated use may lead to rapid overgrowth of fungi *e.g.* thrush (Candida albicans) normally present in harmless numbers in the alimentary tract with serious, sometimes fatal results.

Nowadays, the growth of drug-resistant infections is becoming a major problem. However, in 2015 the first new class of antibiotics was developed. If approved, they will combat pathogens resistant to today's antibiotics.

General Treatment of Fevers.

Fevers, a rise in body temperature above normal, may be noticeable either by a flushed face or by alternate sensations of heat and cold. A patient with a high temperature may have shivering attacks known as "rigors." Tell the doctor.

A high temperature does not necessarily (especially in a child) mean that the trouble is serious but the lay person should always treat it as such and certainly call a doctor if the patient is a child or an elderly person. The majority of fevers are of a viral origin and usually self limiting. The patient tends to improve rapidly once the temperature is controlled.

Even the trained physician finds it difficult to tell one fever from another in the early days; for most of the common fevers begin in more or less the same way. It is only when a rash or some other more definite sign becomes evident that a certain diagnosis can be made, and these may not show themselves until the patient has been feeling "run-down" and fevered for some days. A clinical thermometer is a useful tool and inexpensive to buy. Control of temperature is important, especially in young children, where a high fever may produce a convulsion. A febrile convulsion is a frightening experience for any parent, particularly as their child may have seemed quite well a few minutes previously. High temperature, twitching, and increased irritation may herald the onset.

Emergency management involves keeping the child on its side to avoid inhalation of vomit, clearing debris around the mouth, removing the clothes and sponging with lukewarm water. Get someone to summon medical help, but never leave an unconscious child alone. Above all, do not panic as the initial episode will usually soon pass.

Briefly, then, the way to treat a fever in the early stages before the doctor comes is as follows:
(1) Put the patient to bed. The child is probably better on the living room sofa where he or she will feel less isolated and is more easily observed.
(2) Give plenty of clear fluids; water, water and fruit

juice, weak tea or lemonade.
(3) Give small amounts of easily digested food but only if the patient requires it.

Aspirin is no longer recommended for the treatment of feverish children, and should not be given to children under 12 years of age. This is because it has been linked to the development of "Reye's Syndrome", an acute encephalopathy or inflammation of the brain with delirium, convulsions and coma. Although very rare, "Reye's Syndrome" carries a high mortality.

Paracetamol and Aspirin. Adults with a history of peptic ulcer or chronic indigestion should also avoid aspirin because of the possible risk of a gastrointestinal bleed. Paracetamol is now the treatment of choice to reduce temperature and relieve headache and elixir preparations are available for children. The dose may be repeated 4/6 hourly and there are no gastro-intestinal side effects.

Medicines containing Paracetamol should be stored in a safe place as overdosage, accidental or otherwise, may cause liver damage without initial drowsiness or loss of consciousness. Symptoms may not be apparent for a number of days.

Other methods of cooling a feverish patient involve removing excess clothing, administering tepid baths or sponging with lukewarm water. Simply standing at an open door and allowing the cool outside air to waft around the feverish child, or the use of fans, can have an immediate effect.

THE INFECTIOUS FEVERS.

The remarks made above apply to the management of *any* fever, and we are now going to discuss particular infectious diseases, beginning with the common childhood fevers, then passing on to less common ones, tropical diseases, and worm and parasitic infestations.

The common infectious fevers are caused by bacteria or viruses, and it is useful to know the meaning of the following terms: *incubation period* is the time which elapses between being infected and developing symptoms; *prodromal period* is the time which elapses between the end of the incubation period and the appearance of a rash; *quarantine period*, the maximum time during which a person who has been in contact with the infection may develop the disease—it is usually two days more than the incubation period; *isolation period* is the time a patient is supposed to be isolated.

Virus Diseases.

First, we shall take the common virus diseases, measles, chickenpox, and rubella or German measles, then the other virus diseases, mumps, infective hepatitis, viral pneumonia, and some other conditions which do not always produce a typical rash as in the case of the first three.

In most of these fevers there is a long incubation period, and one infection gives immunity for life.

Measles. The incubation period is 10–11 days. The first sign is the appearance of symptoms rather like a severe cold. The eyes become red, and exposure to light is unpleasant, the nose runs, the throat becomes inflamed, and a dry, harsh cough develops. There may be headache and the temperature rises to 39°C or more. Usually the patient is a child, and especially typical is the development of so-called Koplik's spots, which are small, bluish-white, raised spots seen on the inside of the cheek at the back of the mouth. The rash begins on the fourth day of the prodromal period, *i.e.*, 14 days after the initial infection. It shows on the forehead and behind the ears, spreading within a day downwards over the whole body; in another two days it starts to disappear, but often leaves behind a sort of brownish staining which may last for one to two weeks.

Measles can be serious, especially in very young children because of its complications, such as bronchopneumonia and infection of the ear, which can now be treated with antibiotics. These drugs have no effect on the measles virus, but only on the secondarily invading bacteria which have invaded the lungs and ear during the illness. The illness can be attenuated or lessened by injection of antibodies (gamma globulin) from an immune adult, and this is often worth while in the very young. After the MMR vaccine was introduced in 1988, measles almost disappeared in Britain but is now reappearing. This was very apparent in the serious Swansea outbreak in 2013. Immunisation rates in Britain had fallen after the unfounded scare over the MMR vaccine, leaving many children vulnerable. Globally, also, measles is making a comeback (around 145,000 people died from measles in 2013 alone). It is known as the silent killer.

Rubella or German Measles. Incubation period 14–19 days. A mild fever, similar to measles except that the rash is usually the first sign that anything is wrong, and the temperature is rarely above 38°C. The eyes may be pink, and there are enlarged glands at the back of the neck. The rash disappears completely in thirty-six hours. There are no complications.

German measles, in itself, is harmless, but if a woman gets the disease in the early months of pregnancy malformations in the child may appear at birth. Vaccination is advised if a girl has not contracted the disease by the time she reaches puberty. There is no special treatment.

Since April 2016 pregnant women have no longer been screened for rubella.

Chickenpox. Incubation period 14–15 days, but may be more variable. In children chickenpox is a mild fever which begins with the appearance of tiny blisters on the chest and back. These later spread outwards to the legs, arms and face, and cause itching. Treatment is the general one for fevers already described. Calamine lotion or dusting powder will be helpful for the irritation, and the child's nails should be cut short to prevent scratching and infection of the spots. Whereas children are usually little bothered by chickenpox, young adults may be much more drastically affected—a temperature of 40°C is not uncommon, and then there may be severe headache.

Shingles is a disease that sometimes follows chickenpox – usually by many years, and results from reactivation of the chicken pox virus, which 'hides' in the spinal cord after a childhood infection. *See also* **Z**49(1).

Mumps. Incubation period 17–18 days. The typical appearance of mumps is a swelling in the salivary glands in front of the ears which makes the face look full. This causes pain later on, and it may be difficult to open the mouth. Temperature is not usually high (about 38°C). Although uncomfortable, mumps is rarely dangerous, but orchitis—swelling of the testicles—is sometimes a complication, especially if the infection occurs beyond childhood. Fluid diet should be given if eating is painful, with mouth-washes, and rest in bed. Mumps is an acute viral illness. It is very often spread by coughs and sneezes.

Infective Hepatitis. "Hepatitis" means inflammation of the liver, and infective hepatitis, which is much the commonest cause of jaundice in young adults, is a viral infection of the liver. The main symptoms are fever, followed by jaundice, which is first noticed in the whites of the eyes as yellow staining, then in the skin. The urine becomes coloured also, and this is most easily noticed if, on shaking in a bottle, the froth shows coloration. If the froth remains white, no jaundice is present. Treatment is a matter for the doctor, but great care should be taken, both by the patient and those in contact with him, to wash the hands thoroughly after urinating or defaecating, after handling utensils from the sickroom *etc.*, for the disease is very infectious.

Hepatitis A is spread in faeces (*i.e.* by poor hygiene), while Hepatitis B and C are spread in blood or saliva (*e.g.* needle sharing). There is a vaccine available for Hepatitis A and B, and people at risk of exposure to infected people should consider it. Perhaps 220,000 people in Britain have Hepatitis C, but only one in ten know they are infected. Cases are rising. A new form of treatment with Pegasys

and Ribavirin will now give optimum results in less than 24 weeks. Hepatitis C was identified in 1988.

Today there are estimated to be *c.* 135 million people in the world with Hepatitis C and *c.* 350–400 million with Hepatitis B (that is *c.* 500 million people, 1 in every 13 on the planet).

Hepatitis A is one of a set of viral diseases of the liver, of which seven – Hepatitis A to G – have now been identified. More may follow.

Viral Pneumonia. Pneumonia is usually caused by bacteria, and when we speak of pneumonia, that is the type we ordinarily refer to. Viral pneumonia can be caused by a variety of viruses. There is no specific treatment so far, and since diagnosis is a specialist matter little more need be said except that the symptoms in general resemble those of ordinary pneumonia. Although there is no specific treatment for virus infections of the lungs, it is always worth while trying antibiotics in view of the possibility that the lung condition may be caused by a secondary invasion of bacteria.

Influenza. While serious epidemics of influenza take the form of a very dramatic and often fatal disease—for example, the epidemic of "Spanish 'flu" which followed the First World War killed more people than the actual fighting—the milder type more usually seen is difficult to distinguish from the common cold. In fact, many people who complain of "a dose of the 'flu" are suffering from simple colds.

However, a sudden onset, aching in the muscles of the back and legs, and redness of the eyes, would suggest influenza, and especially typical is the depression and weakness which follow influenza but not a cold. The measures suggested above for the general treatment of fever should be applied; but the depression and weakness which follow influenza may need special treatment by the doctor. Effective vaccines are now available, and are particularly recommended for the elderly, though immunisation must be carried out each year to overcome the propensity of influenza viruses to change the proteins in their "coats." The search is progressing for a one-shot 'holy grail' vaccine to protect against all types of influenza. A universal flu-jab is now very close.

Colds and Sinusitis. Although we all think we know what a "cold" is, the issue is not so simple; for the symptoms of fever, running nose, and a run- down, "headachy" feeling are to be found in many illnesses. They may be observed, as we have seen, in the early stages of measles before the arrival of the rash, or in a number of other fevers, such as whooping cough. Mild attacks of influenza (*see above*) may resemble the common cold, and blocking of the nose with discharge and fever may be due to *sinusitis*—although here there is usually pain above, between, or below the eyes.

Colds can be caused by any one of more than 100 different viruses known as "rhinoviruses" This is why a single cold does not confer immunity on the sufferer. It is probable that you will not catch a cold from the same virus, at least for the rest of the year, but there are all those others wanting to infect you. We may get over 100 colds in our lifetime, but we never get the same one twice!

Polio, or **Infantile Paralysis** as it used to be known, is caused by a virus which has a particular affinity for the nerve cells of the spinal cord and which results in paralysis of those muscles under the control of the particular group of cells infected. Rarely, the infection is widespread in the nerve tissue causing paralysis of muscles of swallowing and respiration as well as those of the trunk and limbs. The usual pattern is for a single muscle group to be affected, for example, the muscles controlling the movements of the arm at the shoulder. Such paralysis may be transient with complete recovery, partial with some residual weakness, or total, leaving a wasted "flail limb".

At one time in this country epidemics of poliomyelitis were common, mainly affecting children and young adults. There is no doubt that mild forms of the disease were always occurring in very young children, forms never diagnosed as such but conferring a natural immunity in later life.

In common with other infections, poliomyelitis begins with a mild or moderate fever, with a sore throat, headache, nausea and perhaps actual vomiting, some five to 10 days after contact with the virus. There may be rigidity of the neck muscles. Paralysis, if it occurs, will become apparent about the second or third day of illness. This stage may last two or three weeks, by which time the temperature will have subsided and the paralysis started to improve. There is no specific treatment and medical care is confined to symptomatic relief. Difficulty with swallowing and breathing calls for special nursing measures. In severe cases, artificial means of maintaining respiration may have to be continued for months, or for the rest of the patient's life. Many severely paralysed polio victims of the post-war epidemics —the self-styled "responauts"—depend for their lives on artificial respirators ("iron lungs").

With the development of the oral vaccine early in the 1960s, the disease has now virtually disappeared from Great Britain. It is still found in such countries as Afghanistan and Pakistan.

Smallpox. Once a terrible scourge, now eradicated in the UK. The less serious form of the disease, *variola minor*, is still found in some parts of Africa, but all the signs are that it, too, has finally been eradicated. The last case of *variola major* occurred in Bangladesh in 1975, except for at least one accidental infection in England in the 1980s. With the disappearance of the disease vaccination will become unnecessary; however, the WHO plans to store vaccine (which can be done almost indefinitely at a temperature of $-20°C$) in sufficient quantities to vaccinate many millions of people should the need ever arise again.

Glandular Fever. Sometimes called infectious mononucleosis, since one of its features is an increase in a certain type of white cell—the monocyte—and a change in its microscopic characteristics. It is caused by a virus (the Epstein-Barr), predominantly affects young children and adults and although often taking a protracted course, it is not in itself a serious infection. The main symptoms are fever, enlargement of lymph glands in the neck and a sore throat. A transient body rash may be seen occasionally, particularly during or after the treatment of the sore throat with penicillin or one of its synthetic cousins such as ampicillin. Diagnosis without laboratory tests on the blood (the Paul-Bunnel test) may not be easy although the combination of sore throat, swollen neck glands and a rash is highly suspicious. The disease is self-limiting and rest is normally the only treatment.

Rabies. Finally, we shall deal very briefly with a number of less common virus diseases, beginning, as is appropriate, with *hydrophobia* or *rabies*, since it was in this infection that the great French scientist Louis Pasteur (1822–95) showed the possibility of prevention by vaccination.

Rabies is spread by the bite of infected animals, usually dogs, cats, or wolves, who are driven mad by the disease; in Trinidad, however, it has been spread by vampire bats. It is thus a classic *zoonosis*, an illness transmitted from animals to people. Those who are bitten usually show no symptoms for six weeks or more, but sooner or later convulsions and delirium arise, which within four to five days are fatal. In essence, rabies is a form of brain inflammation. Around 60,000 people a year die of the disease, 40,000 in India.

There is no cure once the symptoms have developed, but antirabies serum, followed by anti-rabies inoculation as soon as possible, prevents illness in the majority of cases. Dogs should be muzzled in areas where the disease is common, but quarantining imported dogs has made the infection almost unknown here. Effective immunisation is now available.

Leishmaniasis, or Sandfly Fever, **Dengue,** or break-bone fever, and **Trench Fever** are all somewhat similar conditions in that they resemble influenza and are rarely fatal. Leishmaniasis is found in every continent except Australia. They are all due to viruses, spread in the first case by sandflies in tropical climates; in the second by mosquitoes in tropical climates; and in the third by lice in temperate climates. Urban sprawl in the developing world is also blamed for the spread of dengue. Cases in the UK are rising from travellers in S.E. Asia and the Far East. Around 390 million people worldwide become infected with dengue fever annually, causing around 25,000 deaths. Dengue is the world's most common insect-borne virus. It is also spreading. Symptoms include fever, headache, muscle and joint pains and a skin rash. An experimental dengue fever vaccine was launched in 2016 in the Philippines.

Yellow Fever. Yellow fever is carried by a mosquito known as Aedes, common in South and Central America and in parts of Africa (a massive outbreak occurred in Angola in 2016). For its spread, it therefore needs: a hot climate, the Aedes mosquito, and an infected person.

In yellow fever there is a sudden high temperature, aching of limbs and head, jaundice, and black vomit; the pulse-rate falls as the fever rises. Previous vaccination seems to be preventive if undertaken in time.

Zika Virus. *See* **Z61.**

Ebola Haemorrhagic Fever. *See* **Z62.**

AIDS. AIDS stands for acquired immunodeficiency syndrome, and is caused by the human immunodeficiency virus (HIV). AIDS has become a terrible affliction for the human race, and was first described in 1981. In some areas of the world, AIDS is becoming the scourge of the 21st century.

The statistics are frightening. Since 1981, over 30 million people have died from AIDS. Around 36 million are now infected. There are 15 million children worldwide who have lost one or both parents to AIDS. Over 5 million people have AIDS in South Africa, while Nigeria has around 4 million. AIDS is also a scourge in India. The number of new cases in the UK is rising. A record number of people—103,000, with *c* 6,000 new cases each year—are living with HIV in Britain.

Infection occurs by intercourse, the anal variety apparently being the more dangerous, by direct transmission through infected blood, and congenital transmission from mother to baby.

Thus, the major risk factors for AIDS are male homosexuality, needle sharing by intravenous drug abusers, haemophilia, and having an infected mother. Heterosexual intercourse is also an important mode of spread, especially among prostitutes, who are the most promiscuous members of communities. AIDS can be avoided by restricting sexual relations to the one you trust, and by avoiding *any* contact with other people's blood.

HIV damages the T-lymphocytes that are responsible for protecting the body against infection. with the result that the sufferer becomes prey to a variety of otherwise rare infections such as *Pneumocystis carinii* pneumonia, as well as some rare tumours, particularly Kaposi's sarcoma and lymphomas. The incubation period can be very long, and the first signs are often lethargy, weight loss and swelling of the lymph glands.

There is as yet no effective vaccine (although hopes of victory over AIDS are now rising). Treatment currently consists of taking a number of different anti-viral and enzyme inhibiting drugs. These have numerous side-effects.

Conclusion.

There is no specific cure for most viral diseases, though several can be prevented by immunisation or by social control of the creatures carrying the virus and by the use of common day-to-day hygiene, and drugs are beginning to be introduced against a few viruses. Incubation periods are generally of the order of days, though in the case of the AIDS virus can be measured in years. Where active immunisation is not available, passive protection with gamma globulin is an effective alternative.

Bacterial Diseases.

Bacterial diseases differ from virus infections in a number of respects; their incubation period tends to be shorter: having the disease once does not often confer lifelong protection; and unlike virus diseases, most bacterial diseases respond to one of the antibiotics or sulphonamides. In some cases it is possible to inoculate against the disease to prevent it occurring, as is possible with some of the virus diseases.

Scarlet Fever and Other Streptococcal Infections.

In the days before the arrival of chemotherapy (sulphonamides and antibiotics), streptococci were very much feared and even caused a high mortality, particularly in such susceptible groups as children, and mothers and babies in maternity hospitals. They are still taken very seriously in the latter and rightly so. All signs of infection, such as fever, during the puerperium (the period following childbirth) must be promptly dealt with by a doctor, and only occasionally now is there real cause for anxiety provided treatment is prompt.

Scarlet fever is much less common and very much less serious an illness than it used to be, partly because of the effective treatments available today, but also because of a definite but unexplained reduction in its severity. Perhaps the streptococcus has changed, and certainly the improved physical condition of people who are now much better fed and housed than they were, has helped to ward off the terrors of this disease as of so many other infections.

The disease, which is more common in children, begins with a sore throat and rash. Nowadays treatment with antibiotic drugs usually produces fast recovery in the patient. However, the number of new cases in the UK is now rising fast and there are occasional serious outbreaks. In 2015 scarlet fever cases in the UK reached a 50-year high, particularly among children.

The importance of streptococcal infections has shifted from the initial infection, such as a sore throat, to some serious conditions which occasionally arise as a result of some form of delayed sensitivity to the bacteria. Acute rheumatism or rheumatic fever (not to be confused with rheumatoid arthritis) occasionally arise in people who have had a sore throat a few weeks before. Since the streptococcus is not the direct cause of the damage which may consequently occur in the heart or kidney, the antibiotics are no answer except sometimes to keep off further streptococcal invasions.

Diphtheria.

This used to be an extremely serious disease, but immunisation has made it almost unknown; it is important, therefore, that all children should be immunised. Many modern doctors have never seen a case because it has become so rare, and in spite of the propaganda of certain ill-informed people, this saving of children's lives is entirely the result of nationwide inoculation.

The following description is of historic interest only, and will remain so if a high level of inoculation is kept up by parents.

In a typical case of diphtheria the incubation period is about three days; the patient is a child who becomes ill and pale-looking (i.e., the onset is not sudden, as in many fevers, but insidious); the temperature is only slightly raised to, perhaps, 37° or 38°C, and although there may be no complaint of sore throat, examination will reveal inflammation with—and this is typical of diphtheria —a grey membrane spread over the tonsils, the palate, and the back of the mouth generally. The diphtheria germ does not spread within the body. It stays at the place where it entered (in this case the throat) and sends its toxins throughout the body.

Even after the acute phase is over the patient must not be allowed to walk, because the diphtheria toxin is particularly poisonous to the heart. The ordinary rule is several weeks in bed.

Diphtheria also occurs in the larynx—in pre-inoculation days many children choked to death with this form of the infection; in the nose; and, although this is not generally known, wounds can be infected.

Diphtheria may lead to paralysis of the throat, with difficulty in speaking or swallowing, and paralysis of the eyes or limbs; these are due to neuritis caused by the influence of the toxin on the nerves.

Whooping Cough (Pertussis).

For many years whooping cough was regarded merely as a bother to the patient and a nuisance to others, as, in fact, a trivial disease. Unfortunately, this is not so; because statistics show that it caused more deaths than polio, diphtheria, scarlet fever, and measles put together.

Whooping cough begins in a child as an ordinary cold with cough and slight fever, and this stage lasts for a week or ten days. Then the "paroxysmal stage" begins as a series of coughs following in rapid succession, during which time the patient is unable to breathe. The "whoop" is caused by the noisy indrawing of breath when the fit stops. The face may become blue and congested. Bronchitis is usually present, and bronchopneumonia may result as a complication, so inoculation of all children before the disease has a chance to strike them is most important.

Once whooping cough has begun, there is no specific treatment, although modern drugs can reduce the frequency of the fits of coughing. The antibiotic chloramphenicol has been used for this disease, but the general opinion is that it is ordinarily of little benefit. The cough may last for at least a hundred days. There is an effective vaccine. Cases of whooping cough are now on the increase as the germ is fast-evolving.

Typhus.

This disease used to be known as "jail fever," because it was frequent in prisons; but overcrowding, poverty, and bad hygienic surroundings anywhere are suitable conditions for epidemics of typhus. Improved conditions in industrialised countries have made it unusual, since typhus is carried from one person to another by infected body lice. It is due to the organism *Rickettsia prowazekii*, a very small type of bacterium.

Typhus comes on suddenly with a rise in temperature to about 39°C, but within four days it may be as high as 42°C. There may, or may not, be a rash at this time, and in the second week, when the temperature is at its highest, there is delirium, weakness, and a feeble pulse. The typical typhus rash appears about the fifth day as reddish blotches on the chest, abdomen, and wrists.

Typhus is, needless to say, very serious but responds to modern antibiotics. Preventive measures are directed towards eradicating lice.

Psittacosis.

This disease which is of interest mainly in that it is spread by birds of the parrot group, such as parrots, lovebirds, macaws, and the rest is caused by chlamyclia, which are similar to bacteria. It occasionally occurs here in people who have been in contact with birds of this type, and is serious both to the bird and to its owner. Quarantine regulations greatly reduced the risk of infection in Britain. Concern over renewed outbreaks, not only of psittacosis but a number of economically important diseases such as fowl pest, led to their reintroduction in 1976.

The symptoms of psittacosis are fever, cough, and bronchitis. The disease is especially dangerous to old people, but it responds to the same antibiotics as typhus.

Tuberculosis (Consumption).

No disease is more difficult to describe than tuberculosis; for, like Streptococcus or Staphylococcus, the tubercle germ can attack many parts of the body and manifest itself in many ways. Furthermore, it is a widely spread disease, infecting not only humans but also cattle, birds and reptiles. In Britain, even now, around 9,000 people are still diagnosed with TB each year. Many of these come from South Asia and sub-Saharan Africa. The number of cases is rising. Worldwide, annually, around 1½ million die of TB (i.e. 5,000 every single day). Many millions more carry dormant TB which can become active at anytime. Here were we shall be concerned with those types common to man—the human and bovine (*i.e.*, the type found in cattle which can be spread to man by infected milk).

The tubercle bacillus is particularly hardy, so that when coughed or spat out on the ground it continues to be infectious for a long time. Infection is therefore caused by: (*a*) drinking infected milk; (*b*) droplet infection from aerosols produced by coughing; (*c*) breathing in infected dust. In other words, tuberculosis is caused by absorption through either the lungs or the intestines; the former is common in adults, the latter in children.

The question arises: what conditions predispose to TB—why do some people get over the early infection and others not? There are two answers to this question: one is certain—that those who are impoverished and do not get enough food are liable to TB; the second is not so certain—that mental stress plays some part. Stress causes a general reduction in immunity, predisposing the body to several infections including TB.

In children, lung tuberculosis is not common, but tuberculosis of the bones and glands is, as is also infection in the abdomen, the kidney or spine, and, worst of all, tuberculous meningitis. These are often of the bovine type from infected milk. Ordinarily, TB in children is less serious than adult infections; but tuberculous meningitis used to be almost invariably fatal until streptomycin was discovered.

Adult Tuberculosis usually occurs in the lungs or the pleura—the thin membrane surrounding the lungs. In younger people miliary tuberculosis, which is a form of TB blood-poisoning or septicaemia, is a very serious condition, and the infection spreads quickly throughout the body.

Lung infection begins gradually in someone who has previously felt unwell. There may be cough, and later blood-stained sputum (although blood which is coughed up does not necessarily prove that TB is present). Whatever means of treatment is used, the struggle between disease and patient is likely to be fairly long, but the outlook is now good. The closure of the Swiss sanatoria is due partly to modern disbelief that air in one place is better than that in another, but mainly to improved treatment.

Prevention depends on legal action ensuring tuberculosis-free herds of cattle; on control of spread of the disease by those "open" cases who carry germs in their sputum; on the use of vaccination in childhood with BCG vaccine (which you can ask your doctor about).

Many methods are used in treatment. TB is now a fairly rare disease in developed countries, but there are worries that the emergence of antibiotic resistant strains will lead to an upsurge in its frequency. In Britain, for example, TB can be found in some London boroughs at quite worrying levels. A quick, cheap and accurate blood test for diagnosing TB is now being tested.

Septicaemia. This is more usually known as "blood-poisoning." This occurs generally by spread from some septic area such as a wound (or even a small prick), after childbirth, or any place where certain germs have got admission to the body.

The most usual germ is the Streptococcus, though the pneumococcus—which ordinarily causes pneumonia—and the Staphylococcus may also cause septicaemia.

In septicaemia, the bacteria damage the blood vessels, allowing blood to leak out under the skin. This leaking causes marks on the skin – a rash of red or brown pin prick spots, purple bruises or blood blisters – and reduces the amount of blood reaching vital organs such as the heart and brain.

Fever comes on suddenly and rises rapidly with headaches, sweating, and shivering. The patient is obviously very ill, and later there is wasting and delirium. The white blood cells increase in number. Septicaemia sometimes occurs without any apparent local infection in those who are weak and debilitated. A simple bedside test for blood poisoning is now nearly ready.

Pyaemia is a type of septicaemia which leads to the formation of numerous abscesses throughout the body. Its symptoms are the same as described above, except that the causative germ is usually

the Staphylococcus, and abscesses are found which may need surgical treatment.

The treatment, in both conditions the state of affairs has been revolutionised by the use of antibiotics; cure is now the rule rather than the exception.

Septicaemia should be suspected when any small wound or cut is followed by high temperature and the symptoms described above.

"**Toxaemia**" is the word used when the germs stay in their original position and go on to produce symptoms by spreading their toxins throughout the body. Tetanus, diphtheria, and some kinds of childbirth infection come into this category; the symptoms may vary from mild disturbance to severe illness.

Meningitis means inflammation of the meninges, the covering which, like a layer of plastic, lies over the brain and spinal cord, just as the pleura covers the lungs and the peritoneum covers internal organs in the abdomen. (Hence inflammation of the pleura is known as pleurisy, and inflammation of the peritoneum as peritonitis.)

Various germs may cause meningitis, for example, some viruses, the bacillus of tuberculosis, the pneumococcus, which ordinarily causes pneumonia, and the Streptococcus or Staphylococcus, but often the word refers to *meningococcal meningitis* (caused by the Meningococcus bacteria) occurring at times as an epidemic.

It is commonest in a person's years from infancy to the early twenties, and begins suddenly with headache, vomiting, and fever. The temperature rises quickly, and pain develops in the back and legs; on the second or third day a rash appears on the body, and particularly on the inside of the thighs. Later there is stiffness of the neck, the head may be drawn back, vomiting persists, and the headache can be so severe as to cause the patient to scream with pain.

Fortunately, this type of meningitis (and most of the others) respond to treatment with antibiotics, so the risks are now very much less.

New vaccines are being introduced, but these do not protect against all types of meningococcal meningitis. One new vaccine now available protects against group C meningitis and septicaemia. Also being developed is a blood test that can diagnose meningitis within hours.

In 2013 a vaccine against meningitis B was licensed in the UK and Europe. Since 2015, all babies in England and Wales have been offered a meningitis B jab. A new aggressive strain of meningitis W is now being found in Britain. University students are at particular risk.

Pneumococcal Meningitis is an unusual complication of pneumonia, and the septic types (*streptococcal* or *staphylococcal*) arise either following an infected fracture of the skull or from infection of the ear or mastoid.

Tuberculous Meningitis was originally always fatal, it is now treatable with streptomycin.

All these diseases are very much a matter for specialist and hospital treatment, but it is worth while mentioning viral meningitis, in which, although all the symptoms of meningitis are present, recovery without specific treatment is invariable.

Tetanus is usually known as "lockjaw" because there may be difficulty in opening the mouth, although this is simply part of a spasm of all the muscles of the body. The tetanus bacillus is found in rich soil—hence the disease is less common in desert areas—and tetanus resembles rabies in that: (*a*) it enters at a wound; (*b*) it affects the nervous system; (*c*) it results in fits and ultimately death.

However, active immunisation with TT (tetanus toxoid) has resulted in the disease becoming uncommon, and even when developed, treatment with antitoxin, sedatives, muscle relaxants, and antibiotics may lead to cure.

The bacillus is anaerobic (*i.e.*, does not use oxygen) and is most likely to occur in such situations as when a man digging manure or working in his garden sticks a fork through his foot.

Brucellosis falls into two types: melitensis, which infects goats, and abortus, cattle and pigs. Man gets the disease by close contact with or drinking the milk of infected animals.

In the past, brucellosis was sometimes known as undulant fever, as the fever goes up and down for two to three weeks; it may then go down and rise again, persisting for many months. The disease may occur in Britain, but modern drugs are on the whole successful. A striking feature of the disease is the combination of a high temperature with an appearance of relative well-being.

Glanders (Farcy) is another disease spread by mammals (in this case horses). In glanders there is discharge from the nose and sometimes pneumonia. Occasionally the disease is fatal. In farcy abscesses form, usually along the lymph vessels. Both conditions are very contagious, and treatment is a matter for a specialist; infected horses should be destroyed.

Cholera. Cholera could be classified under the head of food-poisoning, because it is mainly spread by infected water (however, like typhoid, it can also be spread by flies, infected food, and carriers); it could also be classified as a tropical disease, since, although it used to be found in Europe, it is now mainly rife in India where it is indigenous.

Cholera is caused by a vibrio, which is a spiral bacterium, and can be prevented by early inoculation and care over food supplies—boiling water and milk, washing uncooked foods in chlorinated water etc. The highest cholera rate in the world is in Haiti.

The fever begins in the usual way with a short incubation period, followed by abdominal pain, severe vomiting, and diarrhoea. Later with the loss of fluid from the body there may be cramps in the muscles, diarrhoea increases, and the motions become of the typical "rice-water" type —i.e., there is no solid matter, and the appearance is that of water to which a little milk has been added. This stage is followed by collapse, with low pulse and cold hands and feet. Death, if adequate treatment is not available, results in about 70 per cent. of cases.

Cholera can generally be survived simply by replacing the water and salts lost in the diarrhoea, along with antibiotic therapy.

Anthrax. The bacillus of anthrax, like that of tuberculosis, can exist outside the body for long periods, and, like that of tetanus, then takes the form of spores or seed-like bodies. It is spread by infected cattle and horses, which get the disease from eating grass containing spores.

In human beings the form the disease takes depends on where the germ alights. Cutaneous (or skin) anthrax arises from cuts or fly bites, which may cause a large sore like a boil. It is usually curable with antibiotics. Inhalation anthrax sometimes develops in those who inhale the dust from infected hides or wool (hence the name 'wool-sorters' disease," which is a form of bronchitis with blood-stained sputum); it may arise through eating infected meat, causing intestinal anthrax.

Both intestinal and inhalation anthrax are often fatal, but now the genetic code of anthrax has been cracked there is new hope for a cure.

In Russia the disease is known as the Siberian plague. Anthrax spores have survived in the frozen carcasses of animals in Siberia for hundreds of years.

Food Poisoning Diseases.

Strictly speaking there is no such thing as "food poisoning" if one is thinking of "poisoning" in terms of anything apart from germs. All food poisoning is caused by infection of food with bacteria and by no other cause—unless of course, we are thinking of the kind of poisoning which is the concern of the lawyer rather than the doctor!

Here we are considering those diseases which are commonly spread by contaminated food or drink. First, we shall deal with typhoid, paratyphoid, and dysentery—uncommon here in Britain, although Sonné dysentery is fairly frequent. Then there is gastro-enteritis (which means irritation of the stomach and intestines), which is caused by staphylococci and the germs of the salmonella group, and lastly botulism, which is rare.

Typhoid and Paratyphoid. These diseases are spread by infected water, food, or hands—especially uncooked food, such as milk, salads, oysters, and shellfish. Flies, too, play some part in spreading the disease. Some people are "carriers" and carry and excrete the germs without being themselves affected; for example, "Typhoid Mary," a carrier in the USA in the early years of the 20th century.

Deaths from typhoid, still 332 per 1,000,000 in 1870, fell to 198 per 1,000,000 by 1900. In the 1920s the death-rate was only 25 per 1,000,000, and now it is even less in the UK (although it is rising again, probably due to exotic foreign holidays).

Typhoid fever begins like most fevers with headache, raised temperature, and general feeling of unwellness. This stage lasts about a week, and then the rash appears in the form of rose-red spots on the front of the chest and abdomen and on the back. In the second week there is great weakness, sometimes diarrhoea, flatulence, and mental dullness, together with dry and cracked lips and tongue. The third week is the week, in hopeful cases, of gradual decrease in temperature and other symptoms, and the fourth week is the week of convalescence. Complications are perforation of the intestine (which needs surgical treatment), delirium, and bronchitis. Treatment is with chloramphenicol.

Dysentery. Dysentery may be caused either by a bacterium or an amoeba; the first type is known as *bacillary dysentery*, the latter as *amoebic dysentery* (which is dealt with under tropical diseases). Infection is spread in much the same way as in typhoid. There is high fever, abdominal pain, and diarrhoea, at first consisting of faecal matter, then blood and mucus. In severe cases the death-rate used to be over 20 per cent.

Dysentery is caused by several species of bacteria of the genus *Shigella*.

However, in all these infections sulphaguanidine, ampicillin or tetracycline bring rapid relief, but care must be taken to avoid infection of other people.

Diarrhoea and Vomiting. Leaving out typhoid and paratyphoid fevers and dysentery, there is a common group of infections known as "D&V"— diarrhoea and vomiting. In Britain D&V is mostly due to:

(1) Salmonella infection.
(2) Staphylococcal infections.
(3) Other bacteria, ordinarily harmless, such as Escherichia coli, when present in sufficient numbers.
(4) Various viral infections, *e.g.* rotavirus.

Scientists have now developed a vaccine patch that can reduce the risk of traveller's diarrhoea ("Delhi belly"). Diarrhoea still claims the lives of 600,000 people annually in India.

Salmonella Infections are the most serious of this group; they affect the small intestine and produce vomiting, severe abdominal pain, and diarrhoea. These symptoms occur about one day after eating infected food and usually clear up within about two weeks, but occasionally death results. Salmonella bacteria are most likely to be found in meat, egg powder, vegetables, and ducks' eggs. About 100,000 cases are now reported annually.

Staphylococcal Food Poisoning has greatly increased in recent years, so it is important to know what circumstances are likely to cause it. Staphylococci are liable to grow in milk products, such as ice-cream and cream buns. Food poisoning from staphylococci is seldom severe, and recovery takes place in about a week. Nevertheless, it is extremely infectious, and causes a great deal of lost time in industry and temporary illness in institutions; for it is in such situations that it is most likely to occur. The reason for the increase in staphylococcal food poisoning has nothing to do, as many people suppose, with greater use of canned foods, but it has much to do with the greater use of communal feeding and canteen meals. It is *possible* for bacterial toxins in infected food to bring about illness even when the canning process has killed the bacteria, but it is certainly extremely rare. Canned foods, in fact, are much safer than so-called "fresh" foods in this respect—except when they have been opened, left about, and then re-heated. The same applies to the re-heating of any kind of food.

The real enemy is the canteen worker with a boil, a discharging nose, dirty hands, or a septic finger. Occasionally food may be infected in the larder by rats or mice, but the sort of canteen or restaurant where this can happen has little to commend it. Frankly, these infections are caused by dirty or stupid people who do not realise that their sore finger or boil can become someone else's diarrhoea and vomiting. Where children are concerned, the outlook is potentially more serious. Infection is much more common in artificially fed babies or in older children who eat infected ice-cream. However trivial the condition may seem, diarrhoea and vomiting with fever in a child should never be ignored. Those in charge of canteens or restaurants must ensure that staff is supervised, that anyone with a septic infection is put off duty, and that all know about washing after visiting the lavatory and absolute cleanliness. Bacilli normally present in the intestine, such as Escherichia coli, can cause infections if absorbed in large amounts, or if of a different strain from those in the patient's intestine. They are not usually serious.

Botulism. Now uncommon, botulism is caused by a germ, clostridium botulinum, which is peculiar in that, like tetanus, its poison attacks the nervous system rather than the intestines, resulting in fits, double vision, paralysis beginning in the face and spreading downwards, and difficulty in swallowing.

It is found in tinned fruits or vegetables containing the toxin even when the germ has been killed, but, as we have already seen, the toxin comes from the bacilli, not from decomposition of food as such (in fact, food does not decompose in the absence of germs). Death is common in botulism, but an antitoxin is now available which, if used in time, can cure the disease.

The botulinum toxin, which paralyses muscles, has found some medical uses. "Botox" is being used as a cosmetic treatment injected into the fore-head to reduce obvious wrinkles. It may have a more valuable role in overcoming muscle rigidity accompanying a number of medical conditions.

Diseases Caused by Fungi.

Numerous fungi are pathogenic (i.e. cause disease), and fungal diseases may be primary or secondary to other diseases; allergies to fungi are also important. The most common fungal disease is candidiasis, which is infection with the imperfect yeast-like fungus Candida albicans; this frequently infects the feet (athlete's foot), the mouth and the vagina, producing local itching as the main symptom. Athlete's foot affects one in six people.

Ringworm or **Tinea,** despite its name, is not caused by worms but fungi which cause ring-shaped pig-mented patches on the skin, sometimes covered with vesicles or scales.

Actinomycosis, a disease caused by bacteria which superficially resemble fungi, is a serious but treatable condition with inflamed lymph glands around the jaw or ulcerating sores on the skin; it can also affect the lungs, intestines and brain.

The Venereal Diseases.

Sexually transmitted disease (Venereal Disease) is spread by sexual intercourse with an infected person (or with intimate acts associated with it—e.g., "oral sex"). In the last few years in the UK, sexu-ally-transmitted infections have more than dou-bled, with syphilis and gonorrhoea showing alarm-ing increases.

Promiscuity therefore increases the risk. Not all lesions in, on or around the genitals are necessarily venereal disease. If in doubt consult your own doctor or attend one of the many special clinics which can be found in most cities. Their location is usually widely advertised. Always act promptly.

Gonorrhoea is the result of an infection by the gonococcus (Neisseria gonorrhoeae) and ordinarily comes on after an incubation period of three to seven days. However, babies can get an infection of the eyes, known as ophthalmia neonatorum, from their mother if she is infected, and gonor-rhoea in young children is often the result of being in contact with infected towels or clothes. The disease in adults is evident when there is a thick, creamy discharge from the sexual organs and sometimes pain on passing water; in infants ophthalmia is prevented by the use of silver nitrate eye-drops at birth. Gonorrhoea is fairly easily cured by the use of sulpha drugs or penicillin; but unfortunately venereal disease is increasing and drug-resistant forms are becoming more common. These strains may soon prove impossible to treat effectively with current drugs. Cases of gon-orrhoea doubled in England between 2009 and 2015. A large rise is reported in gay and bisexual men. A new drug-resistant strain appeared in 2015, giving doctors great cause for concern about this "supergonorrhoea".

Syphilis is a serious venereal disease caused by a spirochaete (Treponema pallidum). Stories about lavatory seats are simply stories, although it is occasionally possible to get syphilis by other than sexual means. But this is very unusual, although kissing can spread the disease. Child-ren, too, can be born with syphilis (the so-called congenital syphilis).

Adult syphilis begins with a sore, known as a hard chancre, at the point where the spirochete of syphilis has entered; this may be on the lips, through kissing; on the sexual organs, through intercourse; and very rarely, as explained above, elsewhere. In a short time the chancre disappears and all may seem to be well, but this primary stage is followed by a secondary stage with sore throat, a rash, headache, and enlargement of glands. This, if left alone, also clears up, but is followed by the tertiary stage, in which a chronic infection develops in some part of the body which, presumably, is most susceptible in the particular individual. Thus there may be chronic syphilis of the skin, the bones, the heart, liver, or nervous system.

Syphilis, in common with other sexually-transmitted diseases, is growing fast in Britain. There was a 15-fold rise in syphilis in the UK between 1998 and 2003 and it has continued to rise over the last decade, particularly among gay and bisexual men.

Tabes Dorsalis. In the nervous system, the com-monest forms are the two diseases of tabes dorsalis, in which the spinal cord is infected, and GPI (gen-eral paralysis of the insane), in which the brain and mind are affected.

In congenital syphilis the pregnant mother gives her child syphilis. Such infants are often still-born or premature, they look wizened, like little old men, and amongst other symptoms are eye disease, "snuffles," a flattened nose, and when the adult teeth appear the front ones may be notched at the biting surface.

It was for syphilis that Ehrlich produced his "magic bullet"—an arsenical drug, known as sal-varsan, which could attack the organism selectively without harming the body and was the first of the modern specific drugs. Present-day treatment is with penicillin. GPI was once treated with malarial therapy with some success. Penicillin alone is not adequate.

Chancroid produces small septic ulcers around the sex organs, with swelling of the local glands in the groin, which may suppurate. It is caused by a bacillus, and can usually be cleared up by anti-biotics within a week. Scabies and lice often pass from one body to another during sexual intercourse, but are not usually thought of as venereal in origin, although in many cases they are.

Herpes virus infections may be oral ("Cold sores") or genital. These recurrent sores appear particularly at times of physical or emotional stress. They are not curable, but medicines may shorten episodes. Using latex condoms or spermicide may help protect your partner.

HIV/AIDS (see **Z11**) may be spread by sexual intercourse, or by blood. The use of condoms reduces the risk of sexual transmission.

Tropical Diseases.

Nothing is more difficult than to define the term "tropical diseases." One might define them as the diseases which occur in tropical climates—but then measles occurs there too; and if they are defined as those diseases which are found *only* in the tropics, the solution is no easier, since leprosy, cholera, smallpox, and typhus are usually listed as tropical diseases, yet were found here until fairly recently—and the odd case still is.

But what a story could be told about the conquest of those infections which were—and many still are—the scourge of humanity! One day when generals and dictators are forgotten we shall remember that great international army of physicians and bacteriologists who have saved millions of lives and infinitely reduced human suffering: Koch and Ehrlich of Germany, Pasteur and Roux of France, Ross and Jenner of Britain, Reed of America, Noguchi of Japan, and many others.

Relapsing Fever, common in India and Africa, may be louse- or tick-borne; the germ is a spirochaete, similar to that of syphilis, but the disease is non-venereal. Relapsing fever gets its name from the fact that the temperature remains high (39°–41°C) for about a week, returns to normal for a week, and rises again. There may be three to five relapses of this sort. Penicillin is effective; lice or ticks must be eradicated.

Leptospirosis (Weil's disease), is also caused by a spirochaete, and spread by rats. Now it is rarely found in Europe, although it occurred in the trenches during the First World War, in men working in sewers *etc.*

It is rarely fatal, but leads to high fever and jaundice. Penicillin in high dosage or tetracycline at an early stage is essential.

Yaws is also a spirochaetal disease, common in the tropics and particularly in children. It is unpleasant, but not serious, and tends to clear up in a year or so. There are raspberry-like growths on the skin, which disappear with the drugs used in syphilis (although the condition is non-venereal). The Wassermann reaction, positive to syphilis, is also positive in yaws.

Leprosy. Whereas syphilis, relapsing fever, epidemic jaundice, and yaws are caused by spirochaetes, leprosy is caused by a bacillus resembling the bacillus of tuberculosis. Apart from the difficulty of classification, many popular beliefs about the disease are untrue. It is *not* the oldest disease afflicting man; *not* a disease confined to tropical countries; it is *not* very catching; *not* hereditary, *not* incurable; and the fingers and toes do *not* drop off.

Leprosy is a serious disease not because of disfiguring light-coloured skin patches and lumps, but because it destroys peripheral nerves. Leprosy may disappear spontaneously, or it may progress until the face is lion-like and the hands and feet wasted and ulcerated. The disease rarely kills, but it is the world's greatest crippler. Romania is home to the last leper colony in Europe. Leprosy was once fairly common in colder

Western countries, though its extent was exaggerated. The great majority of the people who suffer from leprosy live in tropical countries. There are around 230,000 new cases annually—60% are in India. Prolonged and intimate contact with an "open" case is said to be the main mode of infection, but only one infected husband in twenty passes leprosy to his wife.

The cheap synthetic drug dapsone is highly effective in leprosy, but problems in delivery to third-world settings has resulted in the emergence of resistant strains, so that much more expensive drugs now have to be used. The WHO has launched an ambitious "multi-drug therapy" programme in an attempt to bring this disease under control.

Established deformity (such as claw hand, drop foot, paralysed eyelids) can be mitigated by reconstructive surgery, although lost sensation cannot be restored.

In 2016 India began testing the world's first leprosy vaccine in its leper colonies across the country.

In the past, some Christian missions were concerned with the plight of the leprosy sufferer. Now, non-sectarian voluntary agencies, Governments and the World Health Organisation have joined in the fight against the disease. Enough is known to control the disease and great efforts are now being made to eradicate it.

Plague is another disease caused by bacteria, common in Europe at one time, but now largely restricted to Asia. Nevertheless, it caused millions of deaths in Europe during the years 1348–49 and 1665 and was the "Black Death," which, indeed, changed the course of history. The full DNA of this was uncovered in 2011.

Plague is carried by the bite of the rat or gerbil flea, but, once people become infected, spread may occur from one to the other by droplet infection—*i.e.*, by coughing and sneezing. After an incubation period of two to ten days, fever develops, rather like severe influenza, and in a day or two the glands in the groin begin to swell, followed perhaps by swelling of the glands elsewhere.

Of this usual glandular type (bubonic plague) half of untreated patients die, but if rapidly treated cure is usual. It is also possible to get disease of the lungs from droplet infection and blood-poisoning from infection of the blood-stream. Both the latter types are almost invariably fatal.

Short courses of antibiotics protect contacts. Vaccination is available but usually not used.

Protozoal Diseases.

Nearly all the diseases caused by protozoa are tropical diseases, although one of the best-known protozoans is the harmless amoeba found in British ponds. Protozoal diseases are caused by these organisms, large in comparison with bacteria, which should really be thought of as one-celled animals. Viruses are neither animals nor plants, are much smaller than the other two groups, and have some distinctive characteristics described elsewhere.

Among the diseases caused by protozoa are sleeping sickness or trypanosomiasis, malaria, and amoebic dysentery (as contrasted with bacillary dysentery), another disease, leishmaniasis—also known by the numerous names of kala-azar, dumdum fever, and, in milder form, Delhi boil, Oriental sore, or Baghdad sore—will also be mentioned briefly. More recently, humans have been affected by *cryptosporidosis*. This is an intestinal infection usually passed to humans from farm animals (*e.g.* by infected milk). Symptoms include severe diarrhoea. These infections are few, but important in their influence on man; until recently malaria was responsible for one-fifth of all human sickness, sleeping sickness not so long ago caused a large part of Central Africa to be uninhabitable, and in some areas of the tropics there are probably more people with, than without, amoebic dysentery.

Malaria. The word, of course, means "bad air." When it was formerly found in Britain it was known as *ague*. Yet, although malaria and "bad air" may often go together, and influenza and cold, it does not follow that bad air (whatever that may be) causes malaria nor that cold causes influenza. In fact, the Anopheles mosquito carries the amoeba of malaria, and the mosquito prefers climates which some people might describe as "bad," but it is the amoeba, not the air, which causes the disease. Anyhow, the unfortunate mosquito might well use the phrase honoured by many generations of schoolmasters: "It hurts me more than it hurts you!" For the mosquito, too, is sick, and passes on its sickness to the person it bites.

There are several types of plasmodium—which is the scientific name for this amoeba—producing attacks of fever varying in severity and frequency: benign tertian, quartan, and malignant quartan. Entering the body from the mosquito bite, the parasites penetrate the blood cells, multiply there, and finally burst into the blood stream. When this happens the temperature rises, and then they return to the cells to carry out once more the same procedure. Depending on the type, the attacks of fever may be at intervals of two or three days, severe or milder. When someone with malaria is bitten by a mosquito the infection can be transmitted to the next person it meets, but malaria is not infectious from one person to another directly.

Treatment of Malaria. Quinine, of course, is the time-honoured remedy, but many other drugs are now available: mepacrine, primaquine, chloroquine and some sulpha drugs. The drug must be taken long enough for the infection to die out, otherwise relapses can occur even after leaving a malarial country. Trials of a ground-breaking new vaccine during 2013 have been very exciting. It marks a milestone in the fight against a disease affecting 250 million people each year (90 per cent in Africa). Six hundred thousand people (mainly in Africa) die annually from malaria, mainly children under 5 (it is estimated that one child dies every 45 seconds from the disease). Malaria has killed more people than any other disease in history.

The disease now accounts for around 40% of public health spending in sub-Saharan Africa. New drug-resistant strains of malaria are emerging in South-East Asia. And mosquitoes are breeding in increasing numbers in the UK. Important as are the drugs used in the treatment of malaria, even more so is the control of the parasite-bearing mosquito. The eggs of mosquitoes hatch in water, and there the young or larval forms can be attacked by pouring oil on the surface of pools so that they are unable to breathe, or by introducing small fish which have a partiality for them. Adult mosquitoes can be killed by insecticides or kept away by repellent creams or nets over beds. Prophylaxis with anti-malaria before entering and while living in known malarial zones is important.

Today, many British holidaymakers are now contracting malaria, partly as the result of the emergence of drug-resistant strains of the disease. Over 2,000 British travellers a year contract malaria and ten die. Do contact your doctor and take precautions. There are a variety of antimalarials available, so your GP can advise you.

Blackwater Fever is a sequel to malaria in tropical Africa and some parts of India. Rather illogically, it is described as "Blackwater," although the urine is red and the skin is yellow but the result is due to breaking down of the red blood cells by some malarial toxin. Possibly too much quinine may help in producing the illness. Treatment is to give plenty of fluids and no quinine or any other anti-malarial drugs in the early stages. The death-rate is about 25 per cent.

Trypanosomiasis (Sleeping Sickness) is essentially an African disease (although also found in tropical America) spread by the tsetse fly. Its cause is the type of protozoan known as a trypanosome, almond-shaped with vibrating membranes at the sides which enable it to move through the blood-stream, rather like a flat fish in the water.

There are three stages of the disease: first, the stage of fever with enlarged glands and a rapid pulse; which may continue off and on for three years; secondly, the stage of trembling hands, legs, and tongue, vacant expression, and slow and stumbling speech; thirdly, and lastly, the stage of low temperature, apathy (a zombie-like state), wasting of the muscles, and possibly death.

Treatment is with pentamidine, suramin or melarsoprol—which give good results in early cases. Preventive measures in infected areas include the destruction of tsetse flies by insecticide, the cutting down of forests near rivers which are inhabited by tsetse flies, and some authorities have suggested the shooting of big game which may form a "reservoir" of the parasites, whence tsetse flies can carry them to human beings. For similar reasons infected people should not be allowed to move to noninfected areas. Around 6,000 people die of this disease in sub-Saharan Africa each year.

Amoebic Dysentery, also known as *Amoebiasis,* is caused by the *Entamoeba histolytica,* an amoeba whose cysts are found in food and water, or spread by infected fingers or flies. There is mild fever and diarrhoea which contains blood. The disease may become chronic, and can cause abscesses, usually in the liver but sometimes in the lungs. Amoebiasis is treated with chloroquine or nitroimidazoles.

Leishmaniasis, Kala-azar, or **Dum-Dum Fever,** is another amoebic disease, usually spread in this instance by the bite of sandflies. It is also known as tropical splenomegaly—enlargement of the spleen in ordinary language—since infection results in enlargement of the spleen and liver, low, irregular fever, and death within a year or so. A milder form, affecting the skin, does not lead to kala-azar, and is fairly readily cured. The cure for both conditions is to give injections of antimony.compounds which reduce the death-rate from kala-azar from 80 per cent, to 5 per cent (but left untreated, the disease is fatal).

Diseases Caused by Parasitic Worms.

Many types of worms infest human beings and other animals. They are interesting for such reasons as their size (which may range from the almost invisible to 9 m or more), their life histories, and their serious or trivial consequences on their hosts. We shall mention only a few groups here, and mainly the ones likely to be met with in Europe—the tapeworms, the roundworms, and the threadworms—although some tropical types will be described briefly.

Tapeworms, as we have seen earlier, like many other types of intestinal worm, lead a double life. What usually happens is that the worm breeds in the human intestine, the eggs pass out in the faeces, and are then swallowed by animals eating contaminated material. In the animal the eggs hatch out into larvae—primitive forms which penetrate the muscle, forming cysts—and man is infected in turn by eating its meat. Thus *Taenia solium* gets into the flesh of pigs, which, if imperfectly cooked (measly pork), causes infestation of the intestine in man. It reaches a length of about 3 m. *Taenia saginata,* which reaches a length of about 6 m, is spread in imperfectly cooked beef, and in Baltic countries *Dibothriocephalus latus* gets into the human intestine from caviar or undercooked fish. It reaches the awesome length of 9 m.

Now all the worms we have mentioned so far are found in the human intestine, and the cysts, which are much more dangerous and unpleasant, in the animal's muscles. But in some worms the reverse happens, with the adult in the animal's intestines and the cysts in man. In Australia the dog tapeworm (*Taenia echinococcus*) produces cysts in both sheep and man. This is known as *hydatid disease,* and may remain unsuspected until cysts in the lungs, liver, or else-where become infected or rupture. *Trichinella spiralis* is similar in action, being found in the intestines of pigs and getting into the muscles or other organs of man. The main difference is that this worm migrates from the pig's intestines into its muscles, whence it reaches man in under-cooked pork meat or sausages. The muscular cysts cause swellings and sometimes pain. There are changes in the blood, swelling of the face and leg in the early stages, and fever. *Taenia echinococcus* and *Trichinella spiralis* are small—not more than 0·5 cm in length—but are more serious in their consequences than the large worms. Treatment is very difficult, and ordinarily all that can be done is to deal with individual cysts when they make themselves apparent.

The large tapeworms, *Taenia solium* and *saginata* and *Dibothriocephalus latus*, produce varying symptoms or none at all. Usually they are not discovered until some segments of the worm are excreted, but there may be mild indigestion, excessive hunger, and occasionally anaemia. However, when the worm is discovered the patient, not unnaturally, is likely to become anxious and uncomfortable at the thought of "having" a tapeworm; these symptoms are caused by the worry rather than the worm.

Treatment is, of course, a matter for a doctor, who now has a number of very effective drugs to choose from. One has to make sure that the head of the worm has been removed, otherwise it will continue to grow.

Roundworms are similar both in appearance and size to ordinary earth-worms and the eggs reach man, not from an animal, but from the con-taminated fingers of someone else who handles food. They usually give rise to no symptoms, and are noticed only when discharged in the faeces or occasionally vomited up. Piperazine is an effective treatment. It is now known that King Richard III suffered from roundworms.

Threadworms, as the name suggests, are like small 0·5–1 cm long pieces of white thread. They are very common in children, and live mainly in the caecum—*i.e.*, the part of the large intestine near the appendix. The males, which are the smaller ones, remain there, but the females pass down towards the rectum at night-time and lay their eggs in the area around the anus. Infection is by contaminated hands handling food—especially uncooked food—and water. Thread-worms are not serious, and cause few symptoms other than itching around the anus and between the legs, but heavily infected children may show symptoms of anaemia. The nervousness often shown by such children is usually the result of the irritation produced by the worms in the anal region. Infection is not common in adults, and in children tends to disappear at puberty.

Treatment is, in theory, simple; for the worms are easily destroyed by a number of drugs, such as piperazine and other, more modern drugs. Ointment is applied to the itching area, and the child should be prevented from scratching. How-ever, since the eggs may lie about the house for some time, reinfection often happens, especially if there are several small children in the home who may pass the disease from one to another.

The idea that intestinal worms in general are likely to cause loss of weight by absorbing food eaten by the patient is largely mistaken; for although it is true that they do live on this food, the amount taken is not enough to be significant.

Tropical Worms. *Bilharzia* has been men-tioned before in connection with its frequency in Egypt, although it is also found in other parts of Africa and the Middle East. Overall, around 90 % of cases are found in Africa. There are two main types: one infecting the bladder (*Schistosoma haematobium*), the other the rectum (*Schistosoma mansoni*). *Bilharzia* is more correctly known as *schistosomiasis* and seems to affect children most.

The parasite's fantastic life-history begins when people bathe in infected water, and the small swimming forms known as cercariae pierce and enter the skin—or they may enter the body by drinking infected water. From the skin they pass to the portal vein below the liver, remain there six weeks until they become adult and then swim against the blood-stream down to the pelvis, where the female lays eggs which have a sharp spine.

The parasitic eggs penetrate into the bladder or rectum—depending on the type of fluke—and pass out in the faeces or urine. If they enter water they hatch out into small moving forms which seek out a water-snail, develop further in its body, and leave it in the form of cercariae ready to find a new human victim. The female fluke is slender and round, about 2·5 cm in length, the male, flat and leaf-shaped, is about 2 cm long, and, as we have seen, their grisly courting takes place in the portal vein, whence the impregnated female passes to the bladder (*haemato-bium*) or rectum (*mansoni*) to lay her eggs.

Infection results in raised temperature and, in the urinary type, blood in the urine; in the intestinal type blood is found in the faeces, and there are symptoms resembling dysentery—*e.g.*, diarrhoea. Treatment in both cases is with drugs. Needless to say, attempts should be made at prevention by telling people to avoid infected canals (usually easier said than done), and by peri-odically cutting off the water supply to the canals to kill the snails.

Hookworm Disease, or ankylostomiasis, is found in many parts of the world, especially in miners who work on damp ground. The tiny worm enters the body usually through the feet, passes through the blood-stream to the lungs, eats through into one of the bronchial tubes, climbs the windpipe, and passes down the oesophagus into the stomach to end up in the duodenum. It causes anaemia, can be fairly readily cured, but is occasionally fatal.

Elephantiasis. Some types of parasitic worm are spread by insects. Thus in *Filiariasis* mos-quitoes inject by their bites the infantile forms of a tiny worm which enters the lymphatic channels; there the blockade they cause leads to the swelling of the legs and the lower part of the body with fluid (known as elephantiasis). An animal pill is to be given out in India, where 40 mil-lion people suffer this debilitating illness.

PHYSICAL INJURIES AND FIRST AID.

This section which lists emergencies in alpha-betical order is designed for rapid reference. Yet it would be wise to make sure now of knowing very thoroughly the parts dealing with bleeding, burns, resuscitation, shock and unconsciousness, situ-ations which are immediately life threatening.

Nothing can teach first aid as effectively as attending one of the many courses organised by the three main organisations:

St. John Ambulance Association, 1, 63, York Street, London WIH IPS. *See also* **Z23**.

British Red Cross Society, UK Office, 44 Moorfields, London EC2Y 9AL (www.redcross.org.uk).

St. Andrew's Ambulance Association, Milton Street, Glasgow, C4.

Their local addresses are available on the Internet or in the telephone directory; enquiry will get details of classes held at various hours of the day.

Purpose of First Aid.

First aid is not treatment proper (which is "Second Aid"). It aims to save life, to prevent further harm or suffering and to keep the victim in the best condition until taken over by a doctor or a nurse.

Under ordinary circumstances attempts to do more can be detrimental. If you limit your help to what is outlined here you cannot go wrong.

General Principles.

There are two priorities:

1. That the patient must breathe.
(—*see* **Choking, Resuscitation, Unconsciousness**)
2. That severe bleeding is controlled.
(—*see* **Bleeding**)

In any accident scene try to judge quickly which person most needs immediate attention. Treat a victim where he or she is; do not move him or her unless the surroundings suggest immediate danger (*e.g.*, fire, fumes, collapsing building).

Handle the patient with gentleness and sympathy yet achieve an atmosphere of reassurance and confidence by firm instructions and methodical actions.

Clear away a crowd (always demoralising to the victim) and use likely bystanders to telephone for an ambulance when necessary. Let your message be clear and written if possible. Let it clearly state the exact locality, the number of patients and the nature of their troubles. Always guard against shock (*q.v.*).

Asthma Attacks.

Breathing becomes very difficult, harsh and wheezing, fighting against air passages narrowed in spasm. Fear aggravates and relaxation relieves spasm. Show calm confidence.

1. Allow fresh air ventilation. Loosen tight clothes.
2. Help the mechanics of breathing by telling the patient
to sit upright with a straight back but all the rest of the body relaxed;
to direct breathing movements from the lower part of the chest.
3. Give the patient medicines already prescribed for the emergency but avoid overdose.

Bleeding.

Treat mild bleeding as for wounds (*q.v.*).
For severe bleeding aim to let the blood clot by stopping or slowing the flow.

1. Immediately firmly press the edges of the wound together between fingers and thumb or press the palm of the hand hard down on it. (Maintain this at least ten minutes.)
2. Lie the patient down: elevate a bleeding limb (unless you suspect it to be fractured).
3. Slip a thick pad (handkerchief, gauze, wool) under your hand. Replace the hand pressure with a firmly bound bandage (stocking, belt, scarf).
4. If blood still leaks out add another pad and bandage.
5. Protect against shock (*q.v.*).

Nose Bleeding.

1. Have the patient sit up.
2. Get him or her to pinch between finger and thumb the whole lower half of the nose and maintain this for at least ten minutes. Repeat another ten minutes if necessary.
3. Tell him or her not to sniff or blow his nose.

Ear Bleeding.

1. Bandage or tape a loosely covering dressing (gauze, handkerchief) over the ear.
2. Lie the patient down towards the injured side.—*Nose or ear bleeding which follows a blow to the head may signify a fractured skull which needs immediate medical attention.*

Tooth Socket Bleeding.

This may follow after a dental extraction. Get the patient to bite hard on to a big pad (gauze, bunched-up handkerchief) placed over the bleeding area. He or she maintains pressure at least ten minutes sitting with a hand under the chin and the elbow on a table.

Blood Vomited.

This could appear black due to the effect of stomach acids.

1. Lie the patient down, on his or her side, with the head low.
2. Give him or her nothing to eat or drink.
3. Get a doctor or ambulance.
4. Guard against shock (*q.v.*).

Blood Coughed Up (*see also* Chest Injury).
Blood from the Back Passage.
Blood in the Urine.

However slight and brief the loss, always seek a doctor's opinion.

Blisters.

Leave them intact and protect them with a simple dressing. But if they are so big as to be in the way and need flattening:—

1. Boil a needle for ten minutes: leave it in the water until needed.
2. Wash the blister area with soap and water.
3. Holding the needle by one end pierce the blister at two opposite points. Press down with clean cloth to squeeze the fluid out.
4. Dress it like a wound (*q.v.*).

Burns (*see also* Chemical Burns).

1. Put out flames the quickest way: a douche of water; smothering with cloth (rug, coat, blanket).
2. Remove burnt clothes, but leave on what is adherent to the skin.
3. Cool the burnt part with cold water for at least ten minutes, longer if pain persists. Plunge a limb in a bucket or sink. Cover other parts with a thick cloth soaked in water; renew it if it dries.
4. Lie the patient down; keep a burnt limb elevated; remove possibly constricting things (rings, bracelets) from a burnt region before it swells.
5. Dress the burn as a wound (*q.v.*).
6. Guard against shock (*q.v.*)—in severe burns give to drink half a cupful of tepid water with a pinch of salt and sugar every ten or fifteen minutes.

Car Accidents.

1. Urgently stop severe bleeding (*q.v.*) or give resuscitation (*q.v.*) where this is needed; treat choking (*q.v.*). Unless they are at risk from fire or fumes leave the injured where they are. Look for victims thrown into ditches or over walls and hedges.
2. Minimise risks by forbidding smoking (petrol leak), by switching off the ignition and applying the brakes.
3. Set your own car off the road if possible; at night have its light shining on the scene.
4. Detail bystanders (wearing or carrying white objects at night) to stop approaching traffic on either side.
5. Send a message for help, detailing the exact place, the number injured and the injuries.
6. Give other first aid to those in the cars without trying to move them: attempts to pull them out, especially from a distorted car, can do great harm. Leave to the rescue services.

Chemical Burns.

Rapidly wash away the chemical with copious free-flowing water. Remove any contaminated clothing.
The contaminated eye, closed in painful spasm, may need gently forcing open; let the water flow on it without force and bend the patient towards the affected side so that the washings flow off at once.

Chest Injury.

Where there has been a severe blow or deep wound to the chest, possibly followed by blood being coughed up:

1. Clear the mouth of any obstruction (blood, vomit, dentures).
2. If there is an open wound at once close it with the palm of your hand firmly applied. While you keep it there, improvise a thick pad

(towel, cloth, handkerchief, sock) to replace your hand. Tape or bandage it securely to make an air-tight seal.

3. Loosen tight clothing.

4. Lie the patient down *towards* the injured side. If he or she has difficulty in breathing have him or her half propped up with head and shoulders raised.

5. Cover the patient loosely.

6. Get ambulance urgently.

Choking.

1. With your fingers try to clear any obstruction (food, toy, dentures) from the back of the throat.

2. If this fails tell the patient to relax, to bend well forward; give a hard slap between the shoulder blades. This may loosen the obstruction so that the patient can cough it out. A small child you place head down over your arm or your bent knee. Try up to four separate slaps.

If back slapping fails try to force the matter out by pressure:

1. Patient standing: stand behind him; put both your arms round his waist. Patient lying: turn him on his back; kneel astride him.

2. Place your fist (thumb side first) on his abdomen *between his navel and the lower end of his breast bone*; cover your fist with your other hand.

3. Make firm thrust inwards and upwards. This may propel the obstruction out of his windpipe. Try up to four separate thrusts. If these fail continue alternating four slaps and four thrusts. After each of these be ready to remove immediately any matter propelled into the mouth.

After receiving thrusts the patient must be checked by a doctor lest internal damage has occured.

If an obstruction is not cleared and the patient ceases breathing and collapses begin resuscitation.

Always remember that in the unconscious the tongue may fall back and be an obstruction. *See* **Unconsciousness.**

Cold Effects. *See* Exposure and Hypothermia.

Cramp.

Cramps may follow severe loss of body fluid and minerals—as with severe repeated diarrhoea, vomiting or sweating. Slowly give tepid drinks containing a small pinch of table salt to each cupful or with diluted meat or yeast extracts.

Sudden cramp in a single muscle can be stopped by having the patient strongly stretch the muscle. In the front of the arm: straighten the elbow and swing the arm back. In the front of the thigh bend the knee and swing the leg back. In the back of the thigh: straighten the knee and swing the leg forward. In the calf: bend the foot up at the ankle while straightening the leg.

Diabetes.

Under certain circumstances a diabetic treated with insulin may suddenly collapse through sugar deficiency. Passing through phases of weakness, vagueness, sweating, tremor, uncoordinated actions and slurred speech he or she may go into a coma.

If he or she is conscious give him two teaspoonfuls (or lumps) of glucose or sugar in water. Failing this, give anything sweet; jam, honey, chocolate. This should clear him rapidly but repeat the dose after ten minutes.

If he or she is unconscious send for medical help urgently. Give nothing by mouth and put the patient in the recovery position (*q.v.*).

Ear—object in.

Do not try to poke it out.

A small object (*e.g.*, insect) can sometimes be floated up and out by lying the patient down with the ear uppermost and pouring in a little water or olive oil. But do not try this if the ear drum is possibly damaged or the ear is painful.

Electric Shock.

At once disconnect the current (at the switch or by pulling a plug out). If you cannot do this do not touch the patient but knock him away from his contact with dry non-conducting material; wooden stick, light furniture, folded thick garment.

He may need resuscitation (*q.v.*). He may have sustained a fracture (*q.v.*) or a burn. He may recover, only to collapse later; keep watch and send him to hospital.

Beware of very high voltage currents, as from wires of electric pylons: keep at least 20 feet away and do not try to rescue until the electricity authority has cut the current.

Epileptic Attack.

The patient may suddenly become unconscious, fall and soon begin convulsive jerkings, and sometimes frothing at the mouth.

1. Do not try to stop the jerking, but protect him from banging against furniture. Move the furniture or push cloth in position as buffer.

2. Clear froth from the mouth.

3. Once the convulsions stop put him in the recovery position (*q.v.*)—but beware lest he sustained a fracture (*q.v.*) in falling.

A succession of closely following attacks is dangerous: get medical aid at once.

Exposure.

A hill climber or a worker inadequately dressed against cold weather becomes slow, inefficient, clumsy, drowsy. Eventually he or she collapses and if not properly treated may die.

1. Put the casualty to rest.

2. If you can, get him or her into a warm shelter. Otherwise protect him with screens of clothes or blankets and poles.

3. If he or she is conscious give warm drinks (cocoa, chocolate, tea). On no account give alcohol.

4. Get wet cold clothes off if possible and put casualty in warm dry covers (sleeping bag, blankets). A plastic sheet over those helps to retain heat. Include the head, leaving only the face free. Well-prepared walkers will equip themselves with a special survival bag, now widely available.

Gradual rewarming is given when the patient has become cold gradually. When exposure has been sudden, as with falling in extremely cold water, you can warm up the patient fast in a bath at about 40° C. (103° F.).

Eye Injury.

Fix a loosely covering pad over the eye and get medical aid.—Do *not* use drops or ointments.—If the wound is severe and painful keep the patient on his back and cover both eyes (since movement of the good eye entails that of the injured one).

Eye—Object In.

Have the patient seated in a good light and stand behind him or her. If you can see the object on the white of the eye try to lift it off gently with the rolled-up and moistened twist of a handkerchief. If it does not come easily it may be embedded; leave it alone.

If it is within the coloured part of the eye leave it for a doctor to treat.

If you cannot see it look under the lids. The lower lid you pull down as he or she looks upwards. The upper lid you must evert as he or she looks down; lay a matchstick along the "hinge" of the lid; firmly grasp the edge of the lid and roll it up over the matchstick.

Fainting.

Lie the patient down with his legs higher than his head (if this is not possible, get him seated with his head bent low between his knees); loosen any tight clothes: tell him to breathe deeply and slowly. He should soon recover. A drink of water (provided he is conscious) will help. If he has fainted fully treat as for unconsciousness (*q.v.*).

Fractures.

Always suspect a broken bone where a blow or crush near a bone is followed by pain, swelling, deformity, weakened or restricted movement. Not all these features are always present: sometimes relatively slight pain is the only one.

Your task is to prevent movement which could worsen the condition by shifting a broken edge of bone into an important organ, or by making it pierce hitherto unbroken skin (with a risk of infection). No one will blame you for undue caution—but all will hold you responsible if you allow a fractured bone to do more damage by movement which could have been avoided.

When a fracture is suspected:—

1. Warn the patient not to move and bystanders not to try to lift him or her.

2. At once control any severe bleeding (q.v.). Dress any wound (q.v.) temporarily.

3. Now immobilise the fractured area including the joint at either end. The best splint is the patient's own body; e.g., injured arm secured against chest, injured leg against good leg (move the good leg up to the injured one). Or a thin board or rolled-up newspaper, well buffered with cloths and towels tied round it can be slipped under a fore-arm and wrist. Between the injured part and the splinting surface fill any hollows with firm padding of wool, or bunched-up cloth, socks, handkerchiefs. Tie the whole firmly with bandages (or stocking, thin towels) making the knots over the splint (not the hurt part) and avoiding bandage directly over the level at which you suspect the fracture. Work gently; do not lift or move the injured part.

4. Help to reduce shock (q.v.).

If you expect expert help (doctor, nurse, ambulance) to arrive soon, then omit step 3 above.

The fractured spine. When a blow or fall gives a painful back or neck, the vertebral column may be fractured. Inexpert moving may possibly drive a bone fragment into the spinal cord of nerves, causing paralysis or loss of feeling. It is most important to let the patient lie still until experienced first aiders take over. Keep the patient warm.

Frostbite.

Do not heat the area directly or put it in hot water. Do not rub it.

1. Remove any wet cover (e.g., glove).
2. Remove any tight object (garter, ring, etc.).
3. Cover the area loosely with dry material and let it warm up slowly. Fingers can be tucked under clothes into the opposite armpit. Nose, chin or ear can be covered with a dry hand.

Hanging.

Support the victim by the legs. Get the cord cut and be prepared to receive his or her weight as the person falls. Loosen the cord round the neck. Act fast. Get medical help.
See also **Choking** *and* **Resuscitation.**

Head Injuries.

Blows to the head can cause fracture of the skull and also brain damage.

Fracture of the skull is not always obvious. Skin may swell over the site. Sometimes a fracture of the base of the skull (the body platform within the head at eye and ear level which supports the brain) may show up by bruising round an eye or by blood loss from ear or nose (*see* **Bleeding**).

Brain Damage may be of two kinds:—

Concussion, a temporary "shaking up" of brain tissue causing immediate "knock-out" unconsciousness. Recovery is in anything from a few seconds to several hours.

Compression of the brain develops from bleeding within the skull, from displacement of a fractured bone or from general swelling of the damaged brain tissues within the hard unyielding skull. The patient gradually (minutes or hours) becomes comatose and perhaps unconscious. This condition is dangerous.
The patient is unconscious—see unconsciousness.

The patient is dazed: put him in the recovery position (q.v.) and watch him closely until help comes.

The patient recovers after a knock-out (concussion). He may yet develop features of compression as well. However much he wants to carry on, keep him at rest, under observation and get medical advice.

In all cases remember that head injuries are often accompanied by injuries to other parts of the body.

Heart Attack.

Sudden heart attacks may produce:—

severe gripping pain in the centre of the chest, sometimes spreading to the neck, shoulder or arm; fast weak pulse; breathlessness; pallor and blueness; sweating.

or sudden painless breathlessness with slight cough and very wet bubbly breathing.

In either case send urgently for medical help. Get the patient to rest (in bed if possible). If he or she is very breathless it will be easier for him or her to be in a sitting position, against banked-up pillows. Otherwise have the patient laying down.

Loosen tight clothes. Keep the patient warmly but loosely covered. Mop any sweat from the face.

Heat Effects.

Heat Exhaustion. Anyone working in an unusually hot atmosphere is helped to remain cool by copious sweating which extracts heat from the body as it evaporates off the skin. But this loss of fluid also carries with it essential minerals from the body. The patient may collapse with his temperature normal or just a little raised; his skin is pale, moist and sunken, his pulse fast and weak. Muscles depleted of minerals go into cramp.

Let him rest in a cool place and give him (slowly) fruit juices or water with half a teaspoonful of salt added to each pint.

Heat Stroke happens in unusually hot and moist areas in rare industrial circumstances and in some tropical zones. Evaporation of sweat cannot take place in an atmosphere already saturated with water vapour. The patient becomes burning hot with a red dry skin and a fast forceful pulse. He may suddenly collapse and go into coma.

He must rest, have his clothes removed and be fanned or sponged down with cold (but not iced) water. The condition is dangerous and needs medical help.

Hypothermia.

Small babies and the elderly are specially susceptible to cold, e.g., overnight in a poorly heated bedroom. They become lethargic, comatose and then unconscious. Extremely cold to touch, even under bedclothes, the skin is white (though in babies it may be deceptively pink). Death may follow.

Cover the patient well including the head, leaving the face free. Then put in the recovery position (q.v.). Warm him GRADUALLY by warming the whole room and by giving slowly warm (not hot) drinks. Do NOT give alcohol. Do NOT use electric blankets or hot- water bottles.

Hyperthermia is the opposite of hypothermia.

Insect Bites.

Cool with water or (better) smooth in antihistamine cream.

If a bee sting has been left in the skin pull it out with fine tweezers: apply these well down near the skin so that they do not squeeze in any venom left at the free top of the sting.

Lightning.

As for electric shock (q.v.) except that the patient can be touched at once as he bears no electric charge. Put a dry dressing over any skin burns.

Nose Bleed. See Bleeding.

Nose—Object in.

Do not try to probe it. Unless GENTLE nose blowing gets it out consult a doctor.

Poisoning.

Do not try to administer antidotes. Do not give salt solutions.

If the patient is unconscious.

Treat as for unconsciousness (q.v.).

If he is conscious.

Give, slowly, soothing drinks to dilute the poison (water, barley water, milk and water).

Put him or her in the recovery position (q.v.) while awaiting the ambulance. He or she may lose consciousness.

In all cases.

Get the patient urgently to hospital.

Send with him or her any remaining poison or empty container and a sample of any vomit.

Keep a close watch all the time you are with the patient.

Poisoning by pesticides (weed or insect killers).

The patient must be at complete rest. If the clothes and skin are contaminated with the poison (splashes, spray droplets) remove clothes and wash the skin copiously with water (avoid contaminating yourself). If he or she is conscious give sweetened drinks.

Poisoning by gases.

Get the victim rapidly out of the contaminated atmosphere, but do not venture within this unless you have a lifeline and respirator, with others to safeguard you.

Recovery Position.

This safeguards the patient's comfort and breathing if he is unconscious, or comatose, or likely to lose consciousness. It consists in having him or her—
  laying on his or her side;
  with lower arm and leg stretched out straight behind;
  upper leg and arm bent forward at right angles at hip, knee, shoulder, elbow;
  face tilted slightly downwards and head bent backwards (NO pillow).

This ensures a clear airway and lets any fluid in the mouth (saliva, blood, vomit) flow out and not choke the patient.

To get him or her in position:

1. Empty the pockets; remove items like bracelet or wrist watch. Put the belongings away safely. Loosen tight clothing.
2. Kneel alongside him or her.
3. Straighten the arms alongside the body; tuck the nearer hand below the hip.
4. Put one of your hands under the face to protect it as your other hand pulls them at the hip over towards you, on his or her side.
5. Adjust the limbs.
6. Cover with a blanket or coat.

However, do not move the patient if circumstances suggest he or she received a heavy blow to the backbone. In that case ensure free breathing by keeping the head bent well back (never sideways). Be ready to clear immediately any vomit from his mouth.

Resuscitation.

This is the attempt to restore life to someone who has stopped breathing. NEVER try it unless this really is the case; you will do no harm if the patient has collapsed but is still breathing. Do not try it if the problem is that of fighting against choking (q.v.).

In cases of drowning do not try to tip the patient up to drain out water; this wastes valuable time.

(It is best to have learnt the technique in organised first aid classes, practising only on a manikin.)

Artificial Respiration.

Act very quickly:—

1. Get the patient on his back.
2. Bend his head fully backwards and keep it thus all the time.

3. With fingers rapidly clear out any obstructing matter from mouth and throat.
4. Hold the mouth open (keep your fingers clear of the lips) and pinch the nose shut.
5. Take a deep breath in: open your mouth wide and seal your lips round his or her mouth: breathe firmly into his or her mouth. The air going in should make the chest rise. Do not blow more forcibly than is needed to achieve this.
6. Lift your mouth off. The chest will now sink as air comes out. Meantime you take another breath in.
7. Continue by repeating the breathing processes of steps 5 and 6.

The first four breaths you give quickly. Thereafter time yourself by the rise and the natural fall of the patient's chest.

With small children you need not pinch the nose, but let your mouth seal over both the nose and mouth of the patient. Much gentler blowing is needed, and quite small puffs are right for babies.

Keep on until medical authority takes over.

If patient vomits turn his head to one side and clear out the mouth. Then resume artificial respiration, with the first four breaths quick ones.

Successful artificial respiration should soon improve the patient's colour, and later you may find he begins to breathe for himself, even if only weakly. Watch this closely, for he may cease again.

Heart Compression.

If there is no improvement it may be necessary to add heart compression to artificial respiration. This, however, cannot be safely learnt except from first aid class teaching and demonstration. (See the Introduction to this section.)

Shock.

Failure of the heart and of the circulation of the blood may follow any serious injury (bleeding, wounds, burns, fractures). This can happen in minutes or hours according to the severity of the lesion.

In first aid terms this dangerous physical condition is called Shock. The patient is pale, cold, sweating, faint or comatose, with weak and fast pulse and breathing.

Try to prevent or to minimise the development of shock before it appears by applying the following simple but valuable measures to every badly hurt patient.

1. At once stop severe bleeding (q.v.).
2. Treat the patient where he or she is (unless you both are in an area of danger).
3. Lie the patient down: keep the head low and legs raised (but avoid movement where a fracture is suspected).
4. Loosen tight clothing.
5. Keep the patient warm by covering below and loosely above him or her —but do not use hotwater bottles.
6. Gently dress any wounds—with the minimum of disturbance.
7. Guard the patient's mental state. Be sympathetic but as optimistically reassuring as possible. Never whisper to others. Never assume that because the patient appears unconscious he or she cannot hear and understand what is said.

Do not give the badly injured patient anything to drink. This could worsen his condition and risk vomiting and choking, especially if he becomes unconscious or needs an anaesthetic. If he is very thirsty let him refresh himself by sucking a moistened handkerchief.

Snake Bite.

The adder is the only dangerous snake in Britain. Its bite can cause collapse and great pain, but only very rarely is it fatal.

1. Lie the patient down.
2. Wipe or wash the bite area. Put on a dry dressing.
3. Cover the area with a thick pad and bandage it in position so that it presses down very firmly.

4. Immobilise the bitten part as if it were a fracture (q.v.).
5. Get the patient rapidly to hospital.
6. Reassure him about his recovery. Give aspirin or paracetamol to minimise pain.

You NEVER cut or suck the bite, or apply chemicals. You NEVER use a tourniquet.

Sprains.

These are stretched and torn ligaments at a joint. Immediately after it happens you can reduce the swelling and pain which will follow by applying a cold compress—a cloth soaked in cold water and then wrung out to be just moist. Keep it in position half an hour, and renew it if it gets dry.

Otherwise support the joint firmly with layers of cotton wool interleaved between turns of crepe bandaging. Beware of making it so tight that it interferes with circulation in the limb.

A severe sprain may be difficult to distinguish from a fracture. If in doubt treat as for the latter.

Strains.

A strain is an overstretching of muscle fibres, and is very like a sprain except that it does not necessarily happen at a joint. Treat it as a sprain.

Strokes.

Some part of the brain has sudden damage of its blood supply. The results are as variable as are the functions of the brain: e.g., poor feeling or power in hand, arm or leg, altered speech, loss of bladder control, paralysis of one side, or unconsciousness.

A temporary stroke-like effect (a "*transient ischaemic attack*") may be the forerunner of more serious damage. Get the patient to bed, if necessary in the recovery position, and keep under observation until the doctor arrives.

Unconsciousness.

In first aid finding the cause of unconsciousness is less important than protecting the patient's breathing. The unconscious patient lying on his back and with head straight or bent towards the chest is at risk of choking from his lax tongue, flopping against and obstructing his throat. Correct positioning prevents this. Act methodically:—

1. Has the patient stopped breathing? He or she will urgently need resuscitation (q.v.).
2. Is the airway blocked making breathing difficult? Clear any material from the mouth. Bend the head straight back at the neck (but do not twist or turn it), and keep it there (see Choking).
3. Arrest any severe bleeding (q.v.).
4. Dress any wounds (q.v.).
5. Consider the possibilities of fractures (q.v.). If you suspect they might be present do not move him (specially important if he might have injured the backbone); stay by his head to ensure its proper position and to clear out immediately any fluid (saliva, blood, vomit) which threatens to choke.

If the patient can be moved:—

6. Turn into the recovery position (q.v.)

Two other important points are that you NEVER try to give anything by mouth to the unconscious or comatose, and that you realise how much you must guard your speech, since these patients may overhear what is spoken near them.

Wounds.

The general treatment is simple, and should avoid the use of antiseptics or ointments.

1. At once control any severe bleeding (q.v.).
2. Sit or lay the patient down.
3. Put a clean temporary dressing on the wound.
4. Wash your hands. Prepare dressings and bandages.
5. Wash *around* the wound (but not the open wound itself) with swabs or clean material moistened with soap and water. Use a fresh swab or material area for each stroke.
6. Cover the wound with a large dry dressing. Over this place a thick soft pad. Bandage firmly.
7. Put the injured part at rest.
8. Take measures against shock (q.v.).

Dressings. Gauze from freshly opened pack. Or improvise from clean handkerchief or small towel, held by corners, allowed to fall open and then refolded so that inside surface comes to outside. A leg or arm can be slipped inside a pillowcase.

Padding. Cotton wool. Or improvise from bunched clean handkerchief, sock.

Bandages can be improvised from stockings, necktie, belt.

Object embedded in wound. Do not try to remove it. Cover it with a clean dressing and over this place a "frame" of padding to surround the side of the object and protect above it. You can now apply further padding and bandages without pressing on the object.

Tetanus (lockjaw) is a risk in wounds contaminated with soil or from animals or thorns. Get medical advice.

St. John Ambulance Brigade.

From its origins in 1887, the organisation now boasts many thousand volunteers who deal with over 300,000 casualties each year. These casualties can range from minor upsets such as nose bleeds to victims of heart attacks and broken limbs. The work of the St. John Ambulance is divided into two aspects: the Brigade, which provides volunteers to give first-aid at public meetings *etc.*, and the Association, which is engaged in the task of spreading first-aid education.

THE BLOOD.

Doctors who have made a special study of the blood are known as haematologists. Haematology itself is a complex subject because blood itself is complex and its many functions are not easy to describe and only a brief account is given here. *see also* **Blood groups (Z61)** and **Rhesus factor (Z61)**.

Blood consists of a fluid, called plasma, in which are suspended red and white blood cells and platelets and in which are dissolved many substances from the simple ones like glucose to the complex like hormones, proteins and fats. Total blood volume amounts to about five litres; the blood donor gives about half a litre at a session and feels no ill effects. Loss of a litre or more induces surgical shock (*see* **Physical Injuries and First Aid**). Red cells are red because they carry a protein called haemoglobin which is capable of carrying oxygen. There are about five million red cells for each cubic millimetre of blood (that is an average sized drop), a total of 25 million million circulating in the body at any one time. The life of a red cell is about 120 days; new ones are constantly replacing old ones which are "buried" by the spleen.

The haemoglobin from dead cells is recycled; new cells are generated in the marrow of bones, including the breast bone, from which samples of marrow can be taken by a technique known as sternal puncture. Such samples are studied with a microscope to establish diagnoses of various blood disorders. White cells are of five basic types, the names of which need not concern us here. Each type has a specific function—some act as bacterial scavengers, some are concerned with antibodies (*q.v.*) and some with the general defence system of the body which is concerned with the development and maintenance of immunity to various diseases both bacterial and viral. There are also non-cell particles derived from large cells which the marrow produces. These are platelets, which are concerned with blood clotting. They have the capacity to "stick" to any gaps in blood vessels (such as may be caused by injury or, in the minutest of blood vessels, "wear and tear") and initiate blood clotting. All these types of cells can be studied in the test tube after taking a sample from the patient. This is known as venipuncture, a simple and virtually painless procedure, carried out by doctor or nurse or trained "phlebotomist", by inserting a needle on the end of a syringe into a dilated vein in the crook of the arm. Marrow samples can also be taken, as we have said, from the breast bone—but that is a very different procedure, requiring local anaesthetic and much more skill. For the patient it is not a comfortable procedure either.

Plasma, the fluid part of the blood, is more the province of the biochemist than the haematologist. The immunologist is also interested in plasma and all three disciplines tend to overlap to some degree. Plasma can be studied in the same way as whole blood. A venipuncture is carried out, a chemical added to stop clotting and the cells can then be removed in a centrifuge. If blood is allowed to clot in the test tube, the cells are all caught up in the clot and the plasma remains liquid and can be poured off. It is then known as serum. Plasma contains substances which are either dissolved, that is, in solution, or are held "in suspension". By this is meant that the plasma forms an emulsion because fat particles and some proteins are not soluble and can only form suspensions in this way. The protein and fat particles are in suspension in a like manner. The substances both in solution and in suspension are much too numerous to be dealt with here.

The functions of blood are manifold, but essentially blood is a transport medium, concerned with moving gases (oxygen and carbon dioxide), moving food (protein, carbohydrate, fat, minerals and vitamins), eliminating waste products and protecting and repairing the body.

Red Cell Diseases.

These are of two main groups leading to a shortage of red cells (anaemia), or an excess (polycythaemia). Anaemia is much the more common and there are many different kinds. In all of them the shortage of red cells results in a depletion of the capacity of the blood to carry oxygen. This means that the heart must work harder to send more blood than usual to the tissues, and even so the tissues will often go short. The patient will be persistently tired and listless, and if the anaemia is severe the action of the brain and heart will be seriously impeded, even leading to fainting, cardiac pain, and breathlessness on exertion. All these symptoms, however, can be caused by many other conditions. The only way to be sure they are due to anaemia is by a proper examination of the blood, and even this will not lead to the truth if the picture has been spoilt by the patient taking iron tonics and other remedies of his own accord. Therefore do not dose yourself with tonics, in case you really have anaemia.

Haemorrhagic Anaemia. Anaemia, a shortage of red cells, may be due to a variety of causes, singly or in combination. One very obvious cause is loss of blood or haemorrhage. Following the sudden loss of a half-litre of blood or more, the red-cell-producing bone marrow "factory" will step up its production; but even if it is adequately supplied with all the raw materials such as iron, it may well take many weeks to build up the numbers to normal. A very severe degree of haemorrhagic anaemia is usually treated by blood transfusion. Milder degrees can be treated by taking extra iron, often over a long period of time.

The supply of iron for making new red-cell pigment is nearly always the bottle-neck which limits production. Haemorrhagic anaemia can commonly occur, however, without a sudden severe haemorrhage. From what has been said about the constant replacement of red cells as they wear out, it must be obvious that even if there is only a slight failure to keep pace with the numbers lost, several months of such a failure can eventually deplete the numbers to the level of very severe anaemia.

This situation is common when small amounts of blood are being continuously or repeatedly lost, and here again it is a shortage of dietary iron which is the usual cause of the failure to replace the lost red cells.

Menstrual Loss and Pregnancy.

Normal menstrual loss in women and girls whose diet is on the border-line of iron deficiency is a common cause of progressive tiredness and lack of energy. Where the menstrual flow is heavier than usual, or where it is frankly excessive in older women due to the various common gynaecological disorders, serious anaemia is surprisingly common. During pregnancy a great deal of iron is lost by the mother to the baby, and this, together with the inevitable blood loss at delivery, often makes for a very tired mother indeed, just at the time when there is an enormous amount of work to be done to manufacture milk and attend to all the extra household tasks of baby care. For these reasons it is almost routinely advisable to build up stocks of iron throughout the pregnancy by remembering to take the pills provided. Men as well as women can lose small amounts of blood continuously in later life from gastro-intestinal conditions such as piles, ulcers, and tropical infestations such as hookworm; and here again the anaemia may be just as severe in the long run as that which inevitably follows a sudden, massive haemorrhage.

One extra word of warning. Do not assume because you are pale that you are anaemic. Pallor is a very poor guide, because it is dependent on so many other things, like the blood vessels in your skin, and its thickness and translucency. Nothing but a blood test (which is so easy for your doctor to do) can really tell you if you are anaemic. And if your anaemia is due to a blood-losing condition, then that too must be treated.

Haemolytic Anaemia occurs when for any reason, there are more blood cells than usual being destroyed in the body. This may be because the cells are abnormally fragile, or because normal cells have been attacked by something to which you are allergic, or rarely because you have become sensitive to your own red cells. Sometimes unborn babies have severe haemolytic anaemia, due to an incompatability of blood group (Rh factor) between the mother and the baby, and the same sort of thing happens if incompatible blood is given by mistake in blood transfusion. Up to a point, in mild haemolytic anaemia, the bone marrow can keep pace with the increased loss of cells, but beyond this point anaemia develops.

After incompatible blood transfusions a very dangerous situation results from the effects of the destruction of red cells and the liberation of their products into the blood. One form of jaundice is often produced in haemolytic anaemia, the patient becoming yellow because of the breakdown products of red cells circulating in excess as bile pigments. These latter are normally always present to a small extent due to the normal, comparatively small, rate of destruction of effete red cells.

Aplastic Anaemia is the term given to anaemia due to a virtually total failure of the bone marrow red-cell factory. Sometimes this occurs for no obvious reason. It is sometimes due to a heavy dose of radioactivity or X-rays knocking out the cells of the "factory." It may even be due to cancer cells growing in the bone marrow cavity and not leaving sufficient room for the red marrow cells. It is fortunate that aplastic anaemia is very rare, because it can only be treated by blood transfusions every few weeks for the rest of the patient's life. Very occasionally there have been exceptions to this rule, when the patient's marrow has re-awakened for no apparent reason and suddenly begins to make red cells again. Rapid progress has been made in the treatment of marrow disease with bone marrow grafts.

Pernicious Anaemia. The processes by which red cells are manufactured are complex, and depend, like so many other bodily activities, on the supply of a vitamin containing cobalt, called vitamin B_{12}. This is nearly always present in more than adequate quantities in the diet, but in order for it to be absorbed from the intestine, there must also be a substance called "intrinsic factor" which is normally made by the lining of the stomach. People with pernicious anaemia have suffered a degeneration of the lining of their stomachs, probably because, for some reason, they have become "sensitive" to this part of their own tissue. This kind of civil war within the body is known as an "auto-immune" disease, and is comparable in type with some forms of haemolytic anaemia. In other words they destroy their own stomach lining, fail to produce "intrinsic factor," and as a result fail to absorb vitamin B_{12} into the body. Faced with a failure in the supply of this essential substance, the bone marrow produces too few red cells, and the few that are produced are deformed, much too large, and very fragile. In addition to its role in blood formation, vitamin B_{12} is essential to the normal functioning of the spinal cord, and in long-standing cases of untreated pernicious anaemia, there is often a neurological disability.

Nowadays pernicious anaemia is treated by small occasional injections of the vitamin, whose other name is cyanocobalamin.

Polycythaemia. Too many red cells per cubic millimetre of blood can be found without there being an increase of the total number of red cells in the body. This occurs in dehydration, when there is a loss of plasma without a comparable loss of cells, and is called haemo-concentration. Alternatively, the bone marrow can manufacture more cells than usual as a response to living for long periods at high altitudes. The beneficial result can be that the blood can carry normal amounts of oxygen, even though the supply (in the rarefied air) is reduced.

Finally there is a red cell disease in which the bone marrow factory gets out of control and produces too many cells with no beneficial results. The number in the blood can be double the normal and the blood becomes so thick that the heart has difficulty pumping it round the body.

This disease (*polycythaemia rubra vera*) can be treated by repeatedly bleeding the patient to reduce the numbers of cells. It is now treated very successfully with carefully judged amounts of radioactive phosphorus or certain other "antimitotic" chemicals which reduce the rate of multiplication of bone marrow cells.

White Cell Diseases.

Diseases of the white cells are very much less common but are inevitably serious.

Agranulocytosis. In this condition the number of those white cells which are responsible for phagocytosis of bacteria falls precipitously. The result is that one of the main bodily defences against infection fails, and the patient may die from an overwhelming invasion of germs and the accompanying high fever. The usual cause is abnormal sensitivity to a variety of drugs, often those which are in widespread use and only give trouble in the occasional case. One example among hundreds is the antibiotic chloramphenicol which specifically kills typhoid bacteria and is used for that purpose. It is believed that about one patient in 60,000 becomes sensitive to it and agranulocytosis often fatally follows, though appropriate treat- ment of infections has greatly reduced the likelihood of death. The fact

that almost any drug *can* do this to some people and yet be quite safe for the majority, is one good reason not to dose yourself with over-the-counter medicines.

Leukaemia comprises a range of diseases which involve the abnormal production of white blood cells. Immature or blast cells are produced at an increased rate and tend to infiltrate various areas of the body, for example, bone marrow, lymph nodes and spleen. They are also found in the peripheral blood and cerebrospinal fluid. In spite of their large numbers these cells, because of their abnormality, are unable to deal effectively with infection and anaemia, sepsis and fever can result.

The cause of this cancer is open to speculation but we know there is an increased incidence in those with Down's Syndrome and other chromosomal abnormalities. Viral infections may also be implicated and there is almost certainly an association with ionising radiation.

This latter fact was proved by the increased incidence of leukaemia in those who survived the atomic bombs in Japan at the end of the Second World War. Pregnant women should not be subject to X-Rays as this may cause an increased incidence of leukaemia in their children.

Further research has suggested that workers exposed to small amounts of radioactive material may suffer abnormal spermatic development so that the tendency to leukaemia may be passed on to their unborn children who may be prone to the disease later in life.

The outcome of the illness largely depends on the specific type. Chronic lymphatic leukaemia for example, which tends to affect older people, may have no clinical signs or symptoms. In fact, it can run a very indolent course, require no treatment and be compatible with a normal lifespan. On the other hand, acute myeloid leukaemia which tends to affect younger adults is a very serious disease with an acute onset and which if not treated can prove to be rapidly fatal.

A new treatment which triggers the immune system to attack cancer cells has increased survival rates.

Chronic Myelogenous Leukaemia (CML) results from a particular "translocation" of cellular DNA. The DNA is swapped to an unusual place and instead of working normally, produces an abnormal protein. A new treatment, Glivec, that blocks the abnormal protein, has demonstrated some dramatic improvements in patients.

Childhood Leukaemia is the most common form of childhood cancer, but nevertheless it is quite rare with an incidence of approximately 25 per 1,000,000 children. Over 85 % of all cases involve the type known as acute lymphoblastic leukaemia. With modern treatment, a remission (that is to say, a disease free period) can be induced in over 90 % of children and cure rates are very high. Presenting features of acute leukaemia are tiredness, lethargy, abnormal susceptibility to infection, excessive bruising and occasionally bone or joint pain. A blood count usually helps in the diagnosis but this needs to be confirmed by examination of the bone marrow. Treatment involves repeated courses of cytotoxic drugs, sometimes combined with radiotherapy. For those with more resistant forms of the illness, bone marrow transplantation can often provide a cure. Treatment is best performed in specialist centres where the expertise is available to deal with the complicated drug regimes. With modern treatment the outlook for all forms of leukaemia has much improved. For children, in particular, the outlook has been dramatically transformed and in a great many cases a cure can be successfully achieved. Further information can be obtained from the Leukaemia and Lymphoma Society.

Hodgkin's Disease is a disease in some ways akin to *leukaemia*. Abnormal cells are found in the reticuloedothelial system and proliferate in a disorganised manner, causing enlargement of lymph nodes (glands), spleen and sometimes the liver. Hodgkin's disease, named after a 19th cent. Guy's physician, has been the subject of much research and therapeutic trial. The improvement in outlook for patients with Hodgkin's disease was one of the major success stories of the 1990s. In cases where the disease is caught early, it can be eradicated in over 95 per cent of sufferers (although prognosis has been less marked with non-Hodgkin's lymphoma).

Hæmorrhagic or Bleeding Diseases.

Whenever blood vessels are damaged by injury, there is a remarkable series of mechanisms which automatically come into operation to stem the flow of blood. There is a constriction of all the smaller vessels in the locality. Platelets stick together and release substances which help the vessels to stay constricted as well as others necessary to blood clotting, and yet others which help to bind the clot tightly together. Later, materials appear to prevent too much clotting, and eventually the clot is removed altogether as healing proceeds.

There are some very complicated diseases of this blood-conserving mechanism which can lead to abnormal bleeding, sometimes beneath the skin to produce bruising or even smaller leaks; sometimes leading to a greater loss of blood, particularly following a wound. In some kinds of *purpura* (bleeding tendency) the blood vessels are the cause of the trouble, having become fragile and leaky for a number of reasons. This happens in old age (*senile purpura*), in scurvy, or vitamin C deficiency, as an occasional accompaniment to infective diseases, or as an immunological effect on the lining of blood vessels when the patient becomes sensitised to certain substances (*Schönlein Henoch* or *anaphylactoid purpura*). The latter often follows a streptococcal sore throat, just as rheumatic fever and acute nephritis do; and as well as the purpura there may be joint pains and nephritis. Just as almost any drug or chemical will cause agranulocytosis in some people, so it can also cause anaphylactoid purpura.

Purpura may also be due to a lack of platelets, known as thrombocytopenia (a shortage of thrombocytes or platelets). This can happen if the bone marrow factory is depressed, since this is where platelets too are made. It is therefore a common accompaniment of leukaemia or aplastic anaemia. Or there can be increased destruction of platelets in some diseases of the spleen. Platelets normally last eight to ten days, but their lifespan can be shortened in heart failure, and following massive transfusions, or often for no apparent reason ("idiopathic" thrombocytopenia), when the removal of the spleen can sometimes help.

Clotting Mechanism Defects. Defects of the *clotting mechanism* will lead to a bleeding tendency, and since the mechanism itself is very complex, so is the variety of things which can upset it. The liver provides the blood with many of the substances required for clotting, so it is not surprising that a clotting defect commonly accompanies liver disease. One necessary substance for blood clotting is called "antihaemophilic factor" and is missing from people who have inherited the disease *haemophilia*. These people may die of haemorrhage from quite small cuts or minor surgical procedures.

THE HEART AND BLOOD VESSELS.

The heart consists of about 350g of muscle which makes up the walls of its four chambers. Anatomically the human heart closely resembles the sheeps' hearts to be found in a butcher's shop. Indeed it would be an instructive exercise to dissect one of these in the order described below, since there is no other way of properly appreciating what the chambers, valves, *etc.*, are really like.

There are two quite separate pumps in the heart—one on the owner's right (or on your *left* if you are looking at the front of someone else), and one on his left. The right heart collects spent, deoxygenated, "venous" blood which returns there from the whole of the body, and gives it the comparatively small push required to drive it through the

adjacent lungs. The left heart collects the revitalised, oxygenated "arterial" blood as it leaves the lungs, and gives it the enormous push required to build up the arterial blood pressure, so that it can be forced through all the tissues of the body. As may be expected, the right heart chambers have much thinner walls than the left, since their muscle has less work to do. This will help you get your bearings with the sheep's heart. The tip, or apex, is the lowest part. The thick-feeling side is the left, the thin the right; and the great vessels are at the top.

The Right Atrium.

The upper chamber on the right, or right atrium, has two large openings into it through which all the spent blood arrives from the upper and lower great veins (the superior and inferior venae cavae). Cut open the thin wall of the right atrium with scissors between these two holes to lay open the interior of the chamber, noting the "auricle" or "dog's ear" that forms a small cul-de-sac. The whole chamber is sometimes, inaccurately, called the auricle. You should be able to push a finger downwards into the lower chamber—the right ventricle—through a communicating hole guarded by the three thin cusps of the *tricuspid valve*. These will not obstruct your finger, since they are designed to permit blood flow in the same direction.

The Pulmonary Valve.

When the atrium is full of blood, it squeezes its contents through the tricuspid valve into the right ventricle; and when, a split second later, the ventricle is full and contracts, the three cusps come together to prevent the blood from flowing backwards into the atrium again. Instead the spent blood is driven onwards through the *pulmonary valve* (in the upper part of the right ventricle), through the pulmonary artery, to be delivered to the lungs. The pulmonary valve has three very well-defined cusps which prevent blood from coming back into the ventricle as it relaxes to receive more blood from the atrium before the next contraction or beat.

It is possible to pass a blade of the scissors from the opened-out right atrium, through the tricuspid valve towards the tip of the heart, and cut along the right border of the heart through the thickness of the ventricular muscle. Then cut upwards again, passing the scissors blade through the pulmonary valve and open up the *pulmonary artery*. If you have done this successfully you will have followed the path taken by the spent blood through the right heart to the lungs. Notice the thick round bands of muscle lining the ventricle, and notice too that you have not entered the left heart, which has no connection with the right except in some congenital malformations (*see later*).

The same dissection can now be made of the left heart. Open up the *left atrium*, noting its "dog's ear" or "auricle," pass the scissors down into the *left ventricle* through the two rather flimsy cusps of the *mitral valve*. Notice how much thicker is the muscle of the left ventricle, and cut upwards through the three well-formed cusps of the *aortic valve* into the main artery of the body—the *aorta*.

The Coronary Arteries.

The aorta as it leaves the left heart is distinguishable from the pulmonary artery as it leaves the right, partly by the extreme toughness of the aortic wall (it has to withstand so much more blood-pressure); and partly by the entrances or orifices of the two small branches given off by the aorta, just beyond the valve cusps, which go to supply the heart muscle itself with blood. These are the *coronary arteries* which are so necessary for the heart's own survival.

Cardiac Output.

The amount of blood pumped in unit time, or the *cardiac output*, can be varied a great deal, according to the needs of the moment. This is accomplished by altering both the heart rate and the stroke volume, the amount expelled per beat. Every minute, the healthy adult man at rest shifts about 5 litres of blood through the heart—an amount equivalent to all the blood he possesses. When exercise is taken, or in response to anxiety or fear, this is stepped up many times, so that the muscles can receive a greatly augmented supply of the materials required for action. The controlling mechanisms which allow these changes to be made automatically are partly organised in the brain by the so-called *cardiac centre*; and partly by local mechanical and chemical stimuli to the heart muscle itself. The cardiac centre is continuously receiving information through nerves about the physical and chemical state of the circulation, and also from the mind; which is partly how certain emotions make the heart beat faster. All the information is integrated, and a cardiac output continuously arranged which is appropriate for current demands.

Cardiac Neurosis. In ordinary circumstances at rest, most healthy people are not conscious of their heart-beat. However, there are many perfectly healthy people whose hearts slip in an extra beat occasionally. Sometimes their owners are aware of this and become unnecessarily alarmed. Their fear causes palpitations (a pounding of the heart) and the tension mounts. An undue anxiety about the tricks played by a healthy heart sometimes leads people to interpret minor pains in the chest, or even indigestion, as grave symptoms of heart disease, and the consequent anxiety leads to still worse symptoms. If you are one of these worried people, take your worries to your doctor, and let him decide for you whether there is anything wrong. A hundred to one there isn't.

Many people secretly worry about heart disease and high blood-pressure for years, when very often they are worrying unnecessarily. Even if there is cause for worry, so much can be done for these conditions (as it can for cancer) provided medical advice is taken early in the course of the disease. Remember, too, that the slight feeling of giddiness when you get up suddenly from having been lying down, is often experienced by most normal people; but if you get frightened by it you will begin to breathe more quickly and deeply; and this in itself will make you feel even more faint—and so on.

Heart Failure. When the cardiac output of blood is too little for the requirements of the body, a state of *circulatory failure* has arisen, and when this is due primarily to the heart itself being at fault, it is more properly called *heart failure*. As will be seen, heart failure is not a disease, but the common result of a large number of different diseases. The signs and symptoms produced are caused by two sorts of process: (a) tissues of the body have too little blood flow through them and are therefore undersupplied; (b) blood accumulates and stagnates in tissues, causing congestion, since the failing heart cannot move forward the amount of blood presented to it in the great veins.

Often the left or right side of the heart fails disproportionately. In *left heart failure* the lungs are congested because they are the territory from which the left heart is failing to move blood. The patient has great difficulty with his breathing, and in advanced cases may not be able to breathe when he lies down, because the lungs become so congested and waterlogged. In *right heart failure* the main veins are congested and the other parts of the body become swollen with excess tissue fluid, mainly in the lower parts such as the legs and ankles.

This swelling with fluid is called *oedema*, and in heart failure is only partly due to the mechanics of the failing heart. It is mainly due to the retention of sodium in the body, a situation in which excess water is also retained.

Whatever the actual type of heart failure it is always likely to be a changing condition, since the amount of failure will depend as much on the demands being made as on the state of the heart. For instance, in mild cases at rest when the required cardiac output is small, there may be no signs or symptoms. These may only appear on exertion. Heart failure will be referred to again under the various conditions which cause it.

Treatment of Heart Failure is quite logical. It is aimed at correcting the imbalance between supply and demand of blood, and at the removal of the accumulated excess fluid. We can therefore (a) reduce the body's demand for blood; (b) increase the supply or cardiac output; and (c) promote the excretion of sodium and fluid. Demand for blood is reduced by rest, both physical and mental, and by reduction of weight, since obesity (being overweight) is an additional demand on the cardiovascular system. The cardiac output can be increased by administering a "tonic" to the heart muscle in the form of *digitalis*, which is a powerful heart stimulant derived from foxglove leaf. Fluid (and hence salt) accumulation can be helped by restricting the intake of salt and by giving drugs which promote its excretion by the kidneys (diuretics). Very occasionally, very large accumulations of fluid in the legs, abdomen, or thorax, are tapped and drained physically, with needles. These remarks are of course very general and must not encourage anyone to treat himself for such a potentially serious condition as heart failure. Even such a simple measure as doing without salt can be practised quite unnecessarily by many people for years, simply as a result of reading a paragraph like the above. If you need to reduce salt intake you should be in your doctor's care, and so please let him or her decide.

Congenital Heart Disease. It has been estimated that of all the babies born who survive at least one month, there will be about one in every two hundred with some form of congenital heart disease; that is to say that the heart will have failed to develop properly in embryonic life. In some cases this is associated with a virus disease of the mother (commonly rubella, or German measles) or with certain drugs taken by the mother (*e.g.* thalidomide) at a time, very early in pregnancy, when organs are assuming their adult shape. Parents should see to it that their daughters get German measles vaccine before they grow up; and drugs of all kinds should be avoided where possible during early pregnancy. In most cases of congenital heart disease, however, there is no known cause, and it seems that the manner of formation of the embryonic heart is so delicate that it can be thrown out of gear very easily, perhaps even by chance. Scores of different types of defect occur, singly and in combination.

Any of the valves may be anatomically defective—either failing to close properly (*incompetence*) or being too tight (*stenosis*); the great vessels (pulmonary artery and aorta) may be switched round, or *transposed*, so that they emerge from the wrong ventricle; there may be defects in the wall (*septum*) which separates the atria or the ventricles on each side (*septal defect*, or "hole in the heart"); or there may be a persistence of the vessel which in the foetus normally by-passes the lungs by joining the pulmonary artery to the aorta (*patent ductus arteriosus*). This vessel normally closes at the time of birth when the first breaths are taken, and subsequently disappears, so that the whole output of the heart is then sent round the lungs. Detecting congenital heart disease early is one of the purposes of routine post-natal check-up examinations of the baby. Exact diagnosis requires very complicated techniques, and sometimes the structural defect can be corrected by surgery, with almost miraculous results.

Rheumatic Heart Disease. Acute rheumatic fever is not to be confused with other forms of rheumatism. Many tissues of the body (particularly the heart) are attacked, as well as the joints, and the trouble is due to a sensitivity which has developed to certain bacteria (*haemolytic streptococci*) which have probably caused a sore throat about three weeks before the onset of the disease. Why acute rheumatism only rarely follows streptococcal sore throat is poorly understood, but this is no consolation to the one per cent or so of the population whose hearts bear its scars. During the acute phase of the illness which usually occurs before the age of fifteen, inflammatory damage occurs to the valves, the heart muscle, and the sac in which the heart lives, the *peri-cardium*. So there is a *valvulitis* or *endocarditis*, a *myocarditis* and a *pericarditis*. There may be acute heart failure at this stage if the heart is severely affected. The better-known results of rheumatic heart disease, however, are caused in the ensuing years by scarring of the healed valves. The valves are thickened and deformed. They may have lost their elasticity and stretch, so that they do not close properly (*incompetence*); or they may contract and tighten (*stenosis*). In both cases the heart chamber situated next to the affected valve has to work progressively harder, either because it gets no rest in between beats (in *incompetence*); or it has to force the blood through too narrow a hole (in *stenosis*). The end result is some variety of heart failure (*q.v.*).

Mitral Stenosis. The most commonly affected valve is the mitral, usually causing *mitral stenosis*, in which the opening between the left atrium and the left ventricle will sometimes only admit one finger-tip instead of three fingers as it should. In time the left atrium becomes much enlarged as it overworks to force blood through this narrow orifice. Later still a back pressure develops in the lungs causing congestion and breathlessness; and even later the right ventricle is strained as it tries to force blood into the already congested lung. This is a classic example of the march of trouble backwards from the site of the damaged valve involving first the chamber "behind" it (the left atrium), then the territory "behind" that (the lungs), then the pul-monary arteries taking blood to the lungs, and finally the right ventricle trying to send blood to the pulmonary artery. This steady march of events is usually very slow, and can commonly take twenty years or longer from the initial attack of acute rheumatism to the severer symptoms of advanced mitral stenosis. Treatment is both medical and surgical. The heart failure is treated medically as already described. These days surgical reopening of the valve is almost commonplace, either by inserting a finger through the left auricle and break-ing down the constriction, or by opening up the heart and re-shaping the valve under direct vision. The latter involves the additional problem of by-passing the heart by the use of some sort of external pump and poses additional problems, even though from other points of view it is obviously more convenient.

As always with major surgical procedures much of the problem is in selecting the patients who will benefit from the operation and in whom it is feasible. Quite often there are other valves involved, mainly the aortic or tricuspid or both, and the hydrostatic or "plumbing" problems can be extremely complex. With luck, however, combined with good judgement and good surgery, the lives of incapacitated patients can be trans-formed by mitral, and other valvular, surgery.

Aortic Valve. The *aortic valve* is stenosed or nar-rowed by other degenerative processes besides rheumatism. *Tricuspid stenosis* is nearly always rheumatic in origin.

Coronary Heart Disease. This is the term used whenever the blood supply to the heart muscle (through the coronary arteries) is reduced to such an extent that the heart muscle suffers from a lack of supplies. It has a number of causes, but the only really common one is partial obstruction of the coronary arteries by a condition known as *atheroma* or *atherosclerosis*, and sometimes inaccur-ately called *arteriosclerosis*. This arterial disease is described later (**Z29**). It takes the form of swellings or lumps on the lining of the artery which, if they become large enough to interfere seriously with the flow of blood, produce a blood starvation or *ischaemia* of the tissue being sup-plied. Obviously, the smaller the artery, the more easily will a lump of given size impede the flow. Equally obviously the greater the demand

for blood, as in exercise, the more blood "starva-tion" there will be. There are two degrees of coronary artery disease: one in which the blood flow is reduced to the point where the increased demands of hard work cannot be met, and this results in *angina pectoris* due to *coronary insuffi-ciency*; the other is when the coronary artery becomes completely blocked, preventing the flow of blood, usually by a *thrombus* or clot of blood, and this is *coronary thrombosis*, or heart attack.

Angina Pectoris. Whenever activity is in-creased in any muscle, the demands for oxygen and nutriments from the blood-stream increase, and as these are used up there is an increased production of waste products known as meta-bolites. To meet the demands for a greater supply and a more efficient waste-disposal, the blood flow through the exercising muscle must always be increased. If sufficient increase does not occur, not only will there be a shortage of supplies, but there will also be a pile-up of meta-bolites in the muscle which cannot be carried away. It is mainly because of these latter that pain is caused in ischaemic, or blood-starved muscle, and pain is one of the chief symptoms when heart muscle becomes ischaemic. One important mechanism for increasing blood flow normally to exercising muscle is by automatically dilating the vessels concerned. Diseased vessels, such as coronary arteries when they are affected by athe-roma, are not so easily dilated, although certain drugs which are powerful dilators of arterioles can accomplish a great deal, albeit temporarily. The measures taken to relieve the pain and blood-starvation of angina are two-fold. The patient can reduce the demands of the heart by a rest, and a drug (usually nitroglycerin) can be taken to dilate the coronary vessels of supply.

Another obvious long-term way to reduce demands is for the overweight patient to eat less, and reduce the load of extra body weight on his circulation. It is very frustrating, to say the least, that such an incapacitating and often lethal condition should be caused by the narrowing or blockage of only 5 or 8 cm of narrow piping about 3·5 mm wide. Coronary bypass operations in which the blocked segment is replaced with a piece of blood vessel taken from another part of the body, are now fairly routine.

Angioplasty is where a small balloon, on a wire, is guided into the narrowed arteries of the heart. The balloon is then inflated, opening up the obstructed vessel and allowing adequate blood to reach the heart beyond the narrowing.

Heart Attack (Myocardial Infarction) or Coronary Thrombosis. It should readily be understood from the above description that heart attacks will vary in their severity according to the amount of heart muscle deprived of blood; and this in turn will depend on where in the coronary artery the obstruc-tion occurs. Most usually it is the left ventricular muscle which is cut off from supplies and dies, either in part or in all of its thickness. Since it is the left ventricle which does most of the work of pump-ing blood, serious heart failure is to be expected.

If too much muscle is killed, the heart will simply stop, and the patient will suddenly die. It is much more usual, however, for enough muscle to be left for survival, albeit with a greatly reduced cardiac efficiency. A heart attack is usually accompanied by severe pain, similar to the pain of angina but more severe, and unrelieved by rest or by the pa-tient's usual drugs. Very occasionally the event occurs apparently without pain, or with so little that it is ignored. These so-called "silent" coro-nary attacks can make diagnosis extremely diffi-cult. Since the doctor depends very considerably with heart attacks on an exact, spontaneous description of symptoms for his diagnosis, no description will be given here. There are many over-anxious people who will read these words and could be misled into an unspontaneous de-scription of their own symptoms, and this could make the task of treating them such a problem that they could even be mis-diagnosed as a result. If you have the smallest worry that your chest pain is due to your heart, take your anxiety to your doctor without delay. He will almost certainly be able to reassure you; and if it happens to be your heart after all, you will have taken the first sensible step towards proper treatment. Dangerous as heart attacks are, they are by no means the death warrant that many lay people think, any more than cancer is. The treatment for a true heart attack is urgent and prolonged. Patients must be at complete rest and their pain relieved quickly. The area of heart muscle they have lost must be allowed to heal. Nowadays patients are encouraged to mobilise early, and progressively increase activities over a few days to weeks.

You can help to avoid a heart attack by not smoking, avoiding obesity and living a physically active life. Avoid sudden exercise, however.

Blood Pressure (Hypertension). The blood is under great pressure in the arterial system, since it is this which forces it into all the tissues of the body. It is therefore no more meaningful to say you have "blood pressure" than to say you have a temperature. You would be very badly off without. Blood pressure which is too high (hypertension) can give rise to problems, though not always. It is another of those conditions like angina and cancer, which engender much anxiety among people even when they do not suffer from them.

It is not being suggested here that high blood pressure is a trivial condition, but that it is for doctors to worry about rather than patients! If you ever find out your own blood pressure, never try to work out for yourself what the figures mean. It is much too complicated. Finally, it should be mentioned that high blood pressure may occasionally be associated with, or "secondary to," certain kidney diseases (*nephritis*) including a strange condition known as *toxaemia of pregnancy*, which lasts only as long as the pregnancy, provided great care is taken. Most high blood pressure is "primary", and without any known association or cause. A radical new method of tackling hypertension could involve severing nerves that carry signals from the kidneys to the brain.

In 2010, there were an estimated 1,000 *million* people globally with high blood pressure (a reading of over 140/90 mm of mercury). This number is expected to more than double by 2025.

Low Blood Pressure. Some people seem normally to have surprisingly low blood pressure all the time. There is nothing whatever wrong with this; indeed it may even be beneficial. At least they are unlikely ever to suffer the effects of high blood pressure. The sudden low blood pressure of circulatory failure or shock (**Z27**) is another matter and must be urgently treated.

Irregularities of the Heart Beat. How quickly or how slowly the heart beats is largely under the control of the cardiac centre in the brain and the level of certain hormones in the blood. The *regularity* of the beat, however, is controlled by the so-called pace-maker in the wall of the right atrium, and by the way impulses from the pace-maker travel through specialised conducting heart cells (the bundle of His and its branches) to the ventricles. When any part of this elaborate mechanism is upset, either by altering the bio-chemical or electrical conditions of these specialised tissues, or by killing some of them off by deprivation of blood supply in the course of a heart attack, disordered rhythm can result. Increase (*tachycardia*) or decrease (*bradycardia*) in rate is nearly always a normal response to exercise, or anxiety. Very occasional irregularity, such as the mis-timing of an occasional beat is also quite normal in some people, although many are alarmed by it. Persistent irregularity, however, is abnormal. Its true nature can usually be elucidated by making an electrical record of the heart beat—an electrocardiogram.

The commonest causes are varieties of coronary artery diseases or rheumatic heart disease.

Pericarditis. The heart beats inside a bag or sac. At every beat its outer surface slides against the lining of the sac, lubricated by a small amount of fluid. This is the pericardial sac, the *pericardium* being strictly the lubricated membrane which lines the sac and which also covers the outer surface of the heart. Sometimes inflammation occurs—*pericarditis*—and the sliding surfaces become roughened and even separated by a fluid effusion. Very occasionally, so much fluid accumulates that the heart's action is seriously impeded. Pericarditis may be due to infection or to rheumatic fever, and it usually overlies the area of damaged muscle after a heart attack. This illustrates something which people rarely appreciate—that inflammation is not by any means always due to infection by bacteria. The last two varieties of pericarditis are quite free from germs (sterile).

Myocarditis. A term loosely applied to disorders affecting the heart muscle. There are lots of very rare causes. The really common ones are due to acute or chronic rheumatic causes or to coronary artery disease.

Endocarditis or inflammation of the lining of the heart is a term loosely applied to any disorder of the valves or heart lining. All varieties of rheumatic valvular disease (**Z27**) are included. Bacterial endocarditis in its several forms usually involves valves already damaged by rheumatic disease. It is a complication which is still much to be feared, though somewhat less so now that antibiotic drugs are available.

Atheroma or Atherosclerosis. This is the condition referred to above in which lumps arise on the lining of arterial blood-vessels. Although it is therefore a disease of the arteries, its importance lies in the way blood flow is held up, either by the lumps themselves, or by thrombosis ultimately blocking the narrowed portion of the pipework. The effects on the body are therefore those of depriving the tissues of blood.

It is an astonishing fact that in England and America, more people die of the consequences of atheroma than of any other single disease, including all forms of cancer put together.

Intermittent Claudication. If narrowing of the artery is going to do major harm it is easy to see that it will be of more consequence in those parts of the body where small-bore vessels are supplying tissues whose functions are necessary for life. Exactly such a situation exists in the heart and in the brain. An additional factor is that the arrangement of the blood supply in these tissues is such that any particular area has only one vessel leading to it. This is unusual among the tissues generally, where several alternative, or "collateral" vessels usually supply an area, and where others can take over if one becomes obstructed. We have, therefore, a situation in which perhaps the most important tissues—the heart and the brain—run the greatest risk of deprivation, and this leads to angina and coronary thrombosis on the one hand, and cerebral thrombosis and haemorrhage ("stroke illness") on the other, accounting jointly for about one death in every five. In addition, the effects of atheromatous narrowing are often felt in the legs, where the blood supply to the muscles is inadequate for exercise, leading to intermittent pain comparable with that in the heart in similar circumstances. This is called *intermittent claudication*, or intermittent closing of the leg arteries. In its most severe forms, it leads to the need for amputation, although in most cases early treatment can avoid this. There is intensive research into the causes of atheroma.

Raised Cholesterol. A lot of attention has been given to the amounts of certain fats in the circulating blood, particularly cholesterol. This fat is found in larger amounts in the blood of sufferers from atheroma, and is also found in the arterial lumps themselves. Efforts have therefore been made to reduce blood cholesterol by modifications of the diet, but it has been extremely difficult to prove that this has done any good. Many other factors are known to contribute to atheroma, and hence to heart attacks and strokes, some of which can be reduced and others not. Such factors are age, obesity, high blood pressure, and smoking cigarettes.

People who lead an active life seem to have less trouble than others who are less active. Sudden severe exercise, however, is bad if you are not used to it. It is better, and life saving, to take regular, moderate exercise. Women have less atheroma than men, until the menopause when they begin to catch up, so that hormones have something to do with it.

Aortic Disease. The aorta, the main artery of the body, running from the left ventricle down through the chest and abdomen, also suffers from atheroma, but is too wide (about 2·5 cm across) to become obstructed. However, weaknesses occur in the thickness of its wall, sometimes due to syphilis but nowadays much more usually due to atheroma, which results in a ballooning out of a part of the vessel, rather like you sometimes see in an old bicycle inner tube. In days gone by these *aneurysms*, as the dilations are called, reached an enormous size, and would wear away the breastbone and ribs, to appear as large pulsating masses on the chest. Now that advanced syphilis is less common, atheromatous aneurysm, with a predilection for the abdominal aorta, is the one most commonly seen; and these days it is treated by replacement of the diseased portion of vessel. *Dissecting aneurysms* of the aorta are another variety in which the blood, under high pressure, somehow finds its way in between the layers of the aortic wall and then suddenly rips up and down the whole length of the vessel, separating (or dissecting) one layer from another in its path. Sometimes it tracks back towards the heart and suddenly fills the pericardium with blood to stop the heart's action altogether.

Embolism. This term refers to any object travelling in the circulation and becoming impacted when it reaches a vessel too small for it to pass through. It may be a thrombus (**Z30**), a collection of cancer cells, a group of bacteria, a chunk of infected pus from an abscess, a collection of fat droplets or even a bubble of air. If it originates in a vein it travels to the right heart and to the lungs. If it comes from the left heart or an artery, it will impact in any part of the arterial tree. Reasonably enough an arterial embolus will commonly end up in those parts of the body with the richest blood supply, like the brain, the kidneys, the liver or the bone marrow. A thrombotic embolus will cause death of the tissue in the area previously supplied by the blocked vessel, a condition known as *infarction*. Perhaps the commonest source of thrombotic embolism is the lining of the heart chambers where a thrombus has occurred at the site of muscle damaged by a heart attack.

Pulmonary Embolism. Cases of massive *pulmonary (lung) embolism* are usually the result of the thrombosis of the leg veins in people kept immobile following surgery or childbirth. That is why postoperative patients are got out of bed for a while as soon as the first day after the operation. The cells of a cancer embolus usually die; but if they survive, a new cancer deposit begins to grow where the embolus impacts, and this is one of the ways cancer may spread. An infected embolus may infect the vessel wall when it impacts, producing a weakness which may give way. Air embolism, if enough insoluble gas enters the circulation, can kill by making so much froth in the heart chambers as to impede the normal pumping action. If bubbles pass the lungs and enter the brain, all sorts of neurological disorders like scores of tiny strokes arise. The same sort of thing happens all over the body in the "*bends*" or "*caisson*" *disease*, in which nitrogen dissolved in the blood at high pressure, usually in deep-sea diving, bubbles out of solution if decompression is too rapid. Fat embolism sometimes occurs after fractures, due to marrow fat entering damaged veins and being carried away to the lungs.

Thrombosis. This is not quite the same as clotting. It is the mass which arises when platelets adhere to the lining of blood-vessels or heart chambers. Blood clot accumulates among layers of deposited platelets and the thrombus therefore has structure, unlike pure blood clot. Thrombosis usually occurs when the lining of the vessel or chamber is damaged by atheroma or inflammation, or when the circulation becomes very stagnant. One danger is that it will become dislodged and travel as an embolus during the first week or ten days of its existence. After this time it is usually firmly incorporated into the vessel walls by cells which migrate into it from the surrounding tissue. The other danger is, of course, that the tissue previously supplied by the blocked vessel will die before a collateral circulation can be established. As previously explained, this is called infarction. All the technical terms in this section are used elsewhere and can be looked up.

Varicose Veins. When veins become swollen they also often become tortuous (wriggly), and particularly on the surface of the leg look very unsightly. They are, however, a sign of a sluggish circulation, and are often due to disease in small valves within the veins which normally prevent the blood from pooling backwards, down towards the feet. They are often a normal maternal accompaniment of pregnancy and disappear after the child is born. If allowed to persist, the sluggish circulation allows the formation of unpleasant ulcers, mainly in elderly people. Treatment is according to severity. In the early stages they are helped by supportive stockings. Later, often as an out-patient, the sufferer may have to have them removed. Modern treatment includes microwave or laser therapy.

Raynaud's Disease. This is a strange condition in which the finger tips and in severe cases all the fingers or the whole hand respond in an exaggerated way to cold. The vessels supplying the hand are constricted and the fingers go white as the blood drains from them. Then the capillaries dilate and become distended and filled with blood. But owing to stagnation it is venous and blue, and the fingers are therefore blue. Now we have all experienced this in very cold weather, but sufferers from Raynaud's disease, nearly always women, respond even to very slight cold, like putting their hands into cold water. Even emotional stress will start the process off. In very severe cases the fingers will be so deprived of blood for so long, that sores will develop and fingers can even be lost, but this is very rare, and can be avoided by an operation to cut the nerves which supply the circular muscle of the vessels concerned. In most cases it is sufficient to avoid getting the hands cold. Medicine such as nifedipine can help.

Frostbite. Strictly speaking, this is literally a freezing of the tissues and usually only occurs at temperatures below −13° C. The patient may feel a pricking feeling at first, and feel an area of firmer, pale skin on the cheeks, nose, ears, fingers, or toes. If these parts are numb with cold, the onset of frostbite may not be felt, and will often only be noticed by others. It is important not to rub the affected part nor to apply direct heat in any form. Rapid warming can be harmful; but re-warming by close application of body temperature is good treatment, *e.g.*, fingers can be firmly held in the armpit or a warm hand closely applied to an ear or a nose.

THE RESPIRATORY SYSTEM.

When air is drawn in during the process of breathing, it is brought into very close contact with the blood passing through the lungs. In this way the air we breathe in, which contains 21 per cent oxygen, is confronted with "spent" blood returning from the tissues which contains much less, and oxygen therefore diffuses into the blood from the air. At the same time, the waste gas, carbon dioxide, passes by diffusion in the reverse direction from the blood into the air, because there is much more carbon dioxide in the returning "spent" blood than the tiny amount in the air we breathe. The blood is therefore continually circulating through the lungs and exchanging carbon dioxide for oxygen from the air we breathe in. When we breathe out, we disperse the carbon dioxide into the atmosphere.

The Trachea (Windpipe). When the air enters the nose or mouth, it passes into the windpipe or *trachea*, through the vocal cords in the larynx. The trachea is held open all the time by rings of cartilage and is lined by a mucus-secreting membrane covered by millions of tiny "hairs" or cilia. These continuously waft a sheet of sticky mucus upwards, which traps any dust or other small particles we may have inhaled, until a collection of this material in the pharynx stimulates us to cough and expel the phlegm, usually to be swallowed.

At its lower end, the trachea or windpipe divides into two, the right and left main *bronchus*. Each main bronchial tube enters a lung, one on each side, and proceeds to divide repeatedly within the lung until the air is being carried by more and more smaller and ever smaller tubes called *bronchioles*. There are many millions on each side, and each one ends in a collection of very small balloon-like structures—the air sacs or *alveoli*. If you were to cut across a lung and examine the cut surface in a good light, you would see that it is a spongy tissue, with many millions of tiny holes, each one just visible to the naked eye. These are the air sacs. In their walls run the blood capillaries, each one of which is a branch of the vessels carrying "spent" blood from the right side of the heart. At this stage, the blood is only separated from the air in the sacs by the walls of the capillaries and of the air sacs themselves. Both structures are extremely thin, making for easy diffusion of the gases between blood and air.

The Breathing Mechanism. This is achieved by two muscular mechanisms. One is by the muscles which move the ribs, and the other by the diaphragm, a sheet of muscle which runs across the body, separating the chest cavity from the abdominal cavity. These muscles are all actuated by nerves, just as all other muscles are. Those running to the muscles of breathing are organised by a mechanism in the brain known as the *respiratory centre*. It is this centre—one of the so-called vital centres of the brain—which receives information from many different sources, and translates it into instructions for the breathing mechanism.

Thus, when you run for a bus, you will automatically breathe more deeply and more quickly because the respiratory centre has been informed about all the extra carbon dioxide in your blood which has been produced by the exercising leg muscles. Even the conscious instructions involved when you blow a trumpet or inflate a balloon, all pass first to the respiratory centre. It is the death of the cells of this and other vital centres of the brain that is the ultimate cause of death.

Bronchitis may be acute or chronic. It is an inflammation of the lining mucous membrane of the larger air passages or bronchi, and results in much more secretion than the amount normally produced, mixed with some pus. The acute form is often caused by viruses, with "secondary" infection from bacteria. It may sometimes be caused by irritant gases, like the sulphur dioxide in smog. The chronic, or long-standing form of bronchitis is often associated with *emphysema*, in which the small air sacs of the lung architecture are destroyed or distorted, leaving larger spaces than normal, often surrounded by fibrous scar tissue. Such an arrangement makes the normal gaseous exchange difficult between air and blood.

Smoking causes chronic bronchitis and emphysema, as well as lung cancer (see **Z33**). These illnesses can cause even more trouble than lung cancer since these patients live for many years in chronic sickness.

Each year in the UK 6,000 people die of bronchitis. It certainly is *not* smart to smoke. Patients cough, and produce varying amounts of sputum, or phlegm. They often wheeze like asthmatics. This may go on for many years before the right side of the heart begins to fail. Gradually, during this time, the chest tends to become barrel-shaped. Treatment consists of getting the patient to stop smoking or otherwise contaminating his lungs, preventing infection, particularly during winter months, with germ-killing antibiotics, and breathing exercises.

Smoking. Giving up smoking is a good idea at any stage. Using nicotine replacement gum, patches, or inhalers doubles the chance of successfully quitting. A nicotine-free drug, Zyban, is also available on prescription from your GP. There are also e-cigarettes. Set a day to stop smoking and reinforce your resolve by telling your family and friends, or getting someone to give up with you. The NHS has a Smoking helpline 0800 169 0 169.

Bronchial Asthma is a condition in which the finer air passages become constricted due to an allergic response. In addition, an increased secretion tends to obstruct them and the patient wheezes. In many cases it can be shown that he is allergic to a particular component of dust, or, less commonly, a foodstuff. This is the same sort of thing as occurs in the upper respiratory passages in hay fever, but the effect is on a different, lower part of the respiratory system. Many other cases are due to respiratory infection of some sort, probably combined with an allergy to the bacteria causing it. A predisposition to asthma is often inherited in faulty genes.

Once a patient has become asthmatic, attacks will be triggered off by such additional things as emotional stress, changes in temperature (particularly sudden cold), irritating fumes or smoke, and physical exertion. These are secondary factors, and although much of the treatment is concerned with them, it is unlikely that any of them is a sole cause of the condition. Treatment is directed at the relief of the breathing difficulty and of the wheezing, as well as the control of the causative factors. Many useful drugs are available to dilate the contracted air passages and reduce the obstructing secretions.

Asthma in children often improves as the patient grows up. Asthma is another condition made much worse by smoking, e.g. by parents who smoke in the house). In 2008 an asthma jab (of the drug Xolair) received approval for NHS use for treatment of severe persistent allergic asthma. A new technique, *bronchial thermoplasty*, is also producing good results. It feeds hot air into the lungs. The outlook for new drugs and treatment received a major boost when scientists discovered that an *overactive calcium sensing receptor* causes much of the problem. In 2016 researchers developed an asthma pill hailed as a game changer.

A tiny living mite about 0·3 millimetres long exists in large numbers in nearly all mattresses and floor dust. This is the cause of much asthma.

The National Asthma Campaign has found that Britain has more asthma sufferers than any European country (and asthma is now our biggest childhood disease). The statistics are alarming. Over 5·4 million receive treatment (including around a million children) and 1,250 die each year in the UK.

Bronchiectasis. In this condition the bronchial air passages are abnormally and permanently dilated, and the normal structure of the walls destroyed. It is caused by obstructions of the tubes which lead to dilatation of the parts beyond. Secretions accumulate, and since they cannot easily drain away, they become infected. The infection helps to complete the process of destruction of structures in the bronchial wall. The patient has a chronic cough which often produces large quantities of purulent sputum, and there are often recurrent episodes of pneumonia. Diagnoses of bronchiectasis have risen over the last decade, especially among well-off women.

In some cases, where the disease is localised to one part of the lung, it is often a good idea to cut out that portion, and this is particularly true in young people. Vigorous physiotherapy, involving drainage of the lungs by placing the patient in a suitable posture, together with antibiotic drugs for the infection, are other forms of treatment.

Cystic Fibrosis is an inborn disease which affects chiefly the lungs and the digestive system. It is sometimes called *Fibrocystic disease of the Pancreas*, and sometimes "mucoviscidosis".

Today, cystic fibrosis is known to be the commonest genetically determined disorder affecting children in Britain. One child in 2,000 receives one of the abnormal genes from each parent. Such a child therefore has a double dose of the harmful gene, and will have the disease from birth. One person in 25 of the general population carries only one of these abnormal genes, and such an individual will not have the disease, but will be a carrier of the abnormal gene. If such a seemingly normal carrier marries another carrier, there is a one in four chance of each of their children being affected. The children, therefore, who actually develop cystic fibrosis have inherited the disease *equally* from both parents, who are carriers, but are themselves unaffected by the disease.

The disease is inherited recessively and involves a defect in pumping salt across cell membranes, particularly in glands. The prospects for survival into reasonably healthy adult life are steadily improving, but they depend upon early diagnosis and careful management through childhood. In cystic fibrosis most of the damage is caused by the excessive viscidity, or stickiness, of the mucus which is produced in the breathing tubes as a lubricant, and also in the ducts of the pancreatic gland which provides enzymes to help digestion. Being thick and sticky, instead of thin and slimy as in the normal, this mucus tends to block the passages instead of keeping them clear. The pancreatic cells are permanently destroyed. The gland cannot secrete pancreatic enzymes, and the food, especially protein and fat, is not properly absorbed. This deficiency can be compensated fairly well by giving pancreatic extract by mouth with every meal, and by dietary care.

The major clinical problem is in the lungs. The lung passages normally have a thin coating of mucus which is propelled steadily upwards, and is completely renewed in less than one hour. It moves more suddenly on coughing. In cystic fibrosis this upward movement is slowed down and interrupted. There is difficulty in keeping the passages clear, especially when infection with bacteria or viruses greatly increases the amount of mucus. This results in intermittent blocking of the air passages, difficulty in breathing, incomplete use of the lungs, and persistent local pockets of infection. If such infectious processes are not controlled, areas of lung will be destroyed, chronic infection will persist, and multiple lung cavities will develop. These predispose to further infection, interfering with the natural development of the lung—a process not normally complete until halfway through childhood—thus adding to the respiratory problems the child will face later.

Unless a correct diagnosis is made and proper treatment instituted before the first serious lung infection has occurred, the resulting lung damage may well be permanent. Compared to 20 years ago, the outlook for cystic fibrosis sufferers is continuing to improve. Gene therapy may open exciting possibilities. Life expectancy is increasing. Further information is available from the Cystic Fibrosis Trust, which provides help for the sufferers in the UK, who now number over 10,000.

Lung Transplantation can be done, using lungs from a donor who has died, or part of the lungs from each of two living donors. Half of lung transplant recipients are alive five years after surgery.

Pneumonia. This is an infection of the lung tissue, rather than of the air passages. The lung is the only internal organ which is directly exposed to the air, and since there are germs of all kinds in the air, it is a source of surprise that pneumonia is not a much more common event in all of us. The answer lies, as with all infections, in the fact that it is not simply bacteria which cause disease, but our own lack of resistance to them.

If we allow germs to thrive and multiply by being unhealthy or run down or undernourished, infective disease will occur. If we are fit, the entry of those same harmful germs into the body causes us no inconvenience, unless we are very young, or very old, or unless the invasion of germs is abnormally overwhelming. This helps to explain why pneumonia is so often quoted as a cause of death. In most cases it is merely a terminal event occurring in the elderly sick, whose normal resistance is so far reduced by their illness that they succumb to an invasion which they would normally not notice.

There are two main kinds of pneumonia, and in both the air sacs become filled with inflammatory secretions, making the normally porous lung tissue as solid as liver.

Types of Pneumonia. In *lobar pneumonia*, a whole segment (or lobe) of the lung becomes solid. In *bronchopneumonia*, areas of lung tissue surrounding the smaller bronchioles become consolidated, leaving normal porous lung tissue in between. Bronchopneumonia is the one which occurs in the rather stagnant lungs of people who are already ill or bedridden. Both forms respond to treatment with the appropriate antibiotics, provided any underlying debility does not interfere with the patient's own resistance. In the terminal bronchopneumonia of fatal illness, it is sometimes considered kinder not to treat the additional pneumonia. *Pleurisy* is a natural complication, and before the days of antibiotic drugs *lung abscess* was very much feared. For another form—*viral pneumonia—see* **Z**10(2).

Pneumoconiosis. This is a term which refers to a large group of different diseases, all of which are caused by breathing in some form of dust over a very long period of time. It is therefore an occupational hazard of certain trades. We have already mentioned the mechanisms of mucus secretion in the air passages which normally trap small particles from the air, and prevent them reaching the lung. However, in some occupations there is so much dust breathed in over the months and years that these normal barriers are defeated. About a quarter of the earth's crust consists of silicon, in quartz, flint, or sand.

Silicosis occurs in people who have worked for many years in trades like mining, stone crushing, sandblasting, or metal grinding, who are often breathing silicon dust in high concentration. When the particles arrive in the air sacs, they set up an irritant chemical reaction which produces nodules of scar tissue. Silicosis for some reason predisposes to tuberculosis. Emphysema also occurs and there is a general impairment of respiratory function. Coalminer's pneumoconiosis is somewhat similar to silicosis.

Asbestosis. Asbestos is a complex silicate of magnesium, calcium, and iron. *Asbestosis* is caused by inhaling its fine fibres, and often leads to the appearance of a type of lung cancer called mesothelioma. *Berylliosis* is caused by compounds of beryllium, used in the manufacture of fluorescent lamps. *Farmer's lung* is a pneumoconiosis caused by inhaling hay and grain dust, and is similar to *bagassosis* and *byssinosis* caused by sugar cane and cotton dust respectively. *Mushroom worker's lung* is caused by something in the compost in which mushrooms are commercially grown.

Pulmonary Embolism. This very dangerous, yet quite common condition has already been briefly referred to (**Z**30(1)). It is a cause of tragic, sudden death in people who have had operations or have given birth to babies some days previously, or who have been bedridden for any other cause. The first event is that the blood in the veins of the legs becomes stagnant, due to the lack of exercise; and together with the tendency to clot which often follows surgery or childbirth, the whole length of a leg vein may be obstructed for twelve inches or more by an elongated clot of blood. This does little harm to the circulation of the leg, since there are plenty of other veins for returning blood to the heart. The danger is that the clot will become dislodged and be swept upwards towards the heart by the flow of returning blood. When this happens it is carried by way of the right atrium and ventricle into the pulmonary vessels which normally carry spent blood to the lungs. Here, for the first time, it enters vessels which are getting smaller as they divide, and it then impacts in the main pulmonary artery. The patient, who may have been recovering very well, suddenly collapses and not unusually dies there and then. At autopsy a long coiled-up mass of clot is found obstructing the pulmonary vessels. It often can be seen to form a cast of the leg vein and even bears the marks of the small venous valves which are present at its site of origin. With the dramatic advances being made in chest surgery, it is now sometimes possible in selected cases to operate to remove the clot. Thrombolysis, that is using injected drugs to dissolve clots, may also be used rather than pulmonary embolectomy. Three quarters of all cases of pulmonary embolism die within two hours, and therefore the best hope would be to prevent the occurrence altogether. This is not at present possible, but clotting in leg veins can be discouraged by early exercise following surgery and childbirth.

Patients often resent having to get up the next day because it is so uncomfortable. But it helps avoid pulmonary embolism.

Haemoptysis. This means coughing up blood or blood-stained material. It must be distinguished from *haematemesis*, in which the blood is vomited from the stomach. It must always be taken seriously because of the underlying lung disease which may be present. No one who coughs up blood, in however small a quantity, should neglect to inform their doctor so that its source can be determined. Haemoptysis occurs in a variety of lung disease, some of which is not serious but much of which must be treated immediately if it is not to become so. This is a suitable place to repeat our general rule that you should see your doctor without delay if you have any unexplained bleeding from any part of the body, however well you feel. And this includes haemoptysis.

Fat Embolism. Liquid fat sometimes enters the bloodstream following extensive crush injuries to soft tissue and bone. It splits up into millions of small globules which are carried to the lungs, and impact in small blood vessels there, producing obstruction of the lung circulation and consequent difficulties in breathing.

Lung Cancer. This is one of the commonest and at present most incurable forms of cancer which can occur. It is also probably the easiest to prevent. Each year many thousand people die of lung cancer in Great Britain. Although most are men, the toll among women has been rising fast. Scotland has one of the highest rates of the disease in the world.

There has been no reasonable doubt for very many years now that it is associated with cigarette smoking, and the evidence is overwhelming. However, in spite of this certain knowledge, smoking continues to increase, and every year there are more and more people dying unnecessarily of lung cancer (although it should be stressed not *all* lung cancer originates from smoking).

However, some recent encouraging evidence is emerging that the 50-year epidemic of lung cancer among women in Britain may be coming to an end. At the moment, however, women smokers are nearly 10 times more likely to die of lung cancer than in the 1960s.

Lung cancer grows in the wall of a main bronchial air passage. If it grows inwards it can obstruct the airway, choking that part of the lung it is supplying with air. This causes collapse and infection of the lung and may lead to *lung abscess*. The patient will then cough up blood-stained infected and purulent material. Such a case is comparatively lucky, since the disease declares itself early by producing symptoms. In others, the lump may grow outwards into the surrounding lung and produce no symptoms at all in the early stages. Indeed, it may spread to other parts of the body, like brain or bone or liver before causing any trouble to the patient. If

this happens he may go to his doctor because of fits, changes of personality, or fracture, only to find that the origin of the trouble is in the lung. A gene that can lead to lung cancer in people who have never smoked was found in 2010. A blood test to detect early signs of lung cancer is being developed.

Cure rates are low, although much can be done to relieve the pain and suffering of the last stages of the illness. Survival rates vary from 16–53% at 5 years, depending on the type and severity of disease. Surgery, by removing the lung, and irradiation of the growth are the standard palliative treatment. A new test is now being used to identify lung cancer by detecting unique chemicals in the breath of those suffering from it.

It is not the practice of this Medical Section to alarm the reader unnecessarily, but if only a few are induced to stop giving themselves such a horrible disease, then writing in this way will have been justified. Readers may wish to see the note on **Z31** on giving up smoking. The dangers of e-cigarettes are not yet fully known.

Secondary Cancer of the Lung. In nearly all forms of cancer, the big problem is that it spreads to other parts of the body. If this were not so it could be eradicated by surgical removal more often than it is. One common way in which it spreads from any part of the body is by entering the bloodstream and being carried as clumps of living cancer cells to distant parts. When these come to rest in smaller blood vessels, they begin to grow and colonise the new environment. Such new colonies are called *secondary deposits* or *metastases*. It so happens that all veins (except portal veins of the liver) lead to the right heart and thence directly to the lungs, and for this reason the lungs are a very common site of *secondary* cancer, which may have begun in the bowel, or breast, or indeed anywhere else in the body.

Other common sites of secondary, blood-borne cancer are the brain, liver, bone marrow, and kidney, since all of them have an abundant blood supply, and there is therefore a high chance of the travelling cells arriving there. Secondary cancer of the lung usually consists of several lumps scattered throughout the lung. Lung cancer itself is usually only one growth. One of the main reasons for the success of early diagnosis is that treatment may be possible before blood-borne and other means of spread have occurred. Unfortunately, in the case of primary cancer of the lung, even early diagnosis is of little avail, but in many other common cancers permanent cure is possible if treatment is begun early enough.

Pleurisy. The chest is lined by one layer of a thin membrane called the *pleura*. The lungs are covered and enclosed by a second, continuous layer of this same membrane. When the lungs move during respiration, the pleura covering the lungs rubs against the pleura lining the chest, lubricated by a very thin layer of pleural fluid separating the two pleura. Whenever the pleural surface becomes inflamed, this is known as *pleurisy*. It is nearly always due to inflammatory disease of the adjoining lung, and is therefore not strictly a disease in its own right.

For example, pneumonia, tuberculosis, lung cancer, or a lung infarct will produce a pleurisy if the area of diseased lung adjoins the lung surface. Some-times the area of inflamed inner pleura will tend to stick to its outer layer or rub painfully against it, producing a sharp pain when the patient breathes.

Sometimes a large effusion of fluid is produced which separates the two layers and collapses the lung by occupying space in the chest which the lung should be occupying. This latter is more usual in tuberculosis or cancer.

The lung can be collapsed by the entry of anything between the normally adjacent layers of pleura, for example by accidental rupture of the lung with emphysema (*q.v.*). This condition is called *pneumothorax* or "air in the chest." Bleeding into the cavity between the pleura is called *haemothorax*.

THE DIGESTIVE TRACT AND LARGE INTESTINE.

Introduction.

The digestive tract consists of the mouth, pharynx, oesophagus (or gullet), stomach, small intestine, large intestine (or colon), rectum, and anus. The small intestine is very long, and is subdivided into the duodenum, jejunum, and ileum. It ends at the junction of the ileum with the caecum, where there is a small blind side-tube, the appendix. The caecum leads into the colon. The whole tract has two main mechanical functions and two main biochemical ones. Mechanically, food has to be chewed in the mouth and further minced up by muscular squeezing, mainly by the stomach. It has also to be propelled along by an orderly series of squeezing movements known as *peristalsis*. While it is still in the digestive tract, food has to be digested. That is to say, it has to be broken down chemically into suitable materials for absorption into the system, and secondly, it has to be absorbed across the wall of the intestine into the blood stream, itself a highly complex biochemical process. The blood stream it now enters is a special part of the circulation, the "portal" system, which travels directly to the liver without first passing to the heart. In the liver the broken-down foods are processed and issued in their new form into the general, or "systemic" circulation, by which they are finally carried to all the tissues of the body.

Alimentary Canal. As the food passes along the digestive tract (or alimentary canal), it is mixed with various secretions which are either made in the wall of the tract, or by organs outside the wall connected to the main pathway by small tubes. Examples of the latter are bile, manufactured by the liver and sent into the duodenum through the bile ducts; and pancreatic juice, which comes from the pancreas down the pancreatic ducts, also into the duodenum. These secretions are either digestive juices concerned with splitting up the foodstuffs so that they can be absorbed, or they have a lubricant so that the gut contents slide along easily under the influence of peristalsis. Roughly speaking, it may be said that digestive juices give place to lubricant secretions at the junction between the small and large intestine.

The Digestive Process.

The constituents of the diet are dealt with in a later section. The principal classes with whose digestion we are now concerned are carbohydrates, proteins, and fats.

(i) **Carbohydrates** are sugars and starches. There are many sugars, which may exist alone, in pairs, or with lots of them stuck together. Alone they are such things as glucose or fructose. Common table sugar is a substance called sucrose, formed by sticking one glucose molecule to one fructose molecule. Starch is lots of glucose molecules all stuck together. Digestion of carbohydrates consists of splitting up sugars and starch into single sugars like glucose, since only single sugars can be absorbed into the system. The splitting is done by digestive *enzymes* which are found in the juices secreted into the digestive tract. Sugar-splitters are found in the saliva of the mouth, in the pancreatic juice of the duodenum, and in the duodenum's own juice from its own wall. On the face of it, you might think it would be better to eat glucose which needs no digestion and can be absorbed in this form, than to eat starch which has first to be split; and so a lot of money has been made out of a gullible public by the sale of glucose drinks and powder. In fact digesting starch is no problem whatever, even for the sick, who can obtain their carbohydrate energy just as easily (and much more cheaply) from potatoes as from expensive glucose. The end result of eating both is the same. The starch-splitting enzyme in saliva is mixed with the food as it is chewed, and it is there-fore probably a good idea to chew it well. However, even if the food is bolted it does not seem to matter very much. People without teeth (neither their own nor dentures) seem to digest their carbohydrate quite well, presumably by means of their pancreatic juice at a later stage.

(ii) **Proteins**, which are found in meat, cheese, and eggs, are very large molecules consisting of lots of small ones strung together. Unlike starch, in which all the component glucose molecules are identical, the amino acids of which proteins are composed come in many different types. They all contain nitrogen, and there are about twenty-seven varieties. One protein differs from another in the proportions of the mixture and the order in which they are stuck together. Only single amino acids can be absorbed from the food, and so protein digestion again consists of splitting the material down into its building bricks. There is a strong protein-splitting enzyme in the gastric (or stomach) juice called pepsin, whose job it is to split the long amino-acid chains into shorter chains. Several other protein-splitters in the duodenal and pancreatic juice contrive to break the smaller chains into individual amino acids which are then absorbed and sent to the liver for processing.

(iii) **Fats** mainly consist of glycerol to which are attached three fatty acid molecules for each molecule of glycerol. An enzyme in pancreatic juice splits the fatty acids off the glycerol, but would have some difficulty penetrating the globules of fat without the help of bile. One of the constituents of bile (bile salts) has detergent properties like washing-up powder and breaks the fat globules up into a very fine emulsion so that the enzyme can get at the fat. Some fat particles of this size can even be absorbed as such, without preliminary splitting.

The processes by which all these enzymic secretions are produced are very finely controlled. They are very expensive to make in terms of energy and raw materials, and so it would be very wasteful to produce them all the time, even when there was no food to digest. And so the body has some very well designed automatic arrangements for sampling the foods as they are eaten and passed on, which ensure that exactly the right kind of juice is waiting in every part of the digestive tract for whatever food arrives. As soon as the food is digested the supply of enzymes is automatically switched off, so that there is very little waste of precious materials. It is, of course, beyond the scope of this account to describe the control mechanisms. Suffice it to say that they are operated partly by nerve reflexes which signal the imminent arrival of food, and partly by special hormones produced in various parts of the gut wall.

The best secretion is affected even by psychological factors, so that pleasant company and surroundings, attractive appearance of the food, and an eager anticipation of it all make for good digestion and good health. These psychological factors are all capable of proper scientific investigation and proof. The poor health of those who habitually and irregularly bolt unpalatable food is probably due to such factors as these. So is the failure of appetite in the depressed, the anxious adult, or the scolded child.

Nearly all the digestion which has been described occurs in the stomach and upper part of the small intestine (the duodenum, jejunum, and upper ileum). Almost all absorption of the products of digestion occurs in the small intestine which is long and intricately folded to give it a large surface area for this purpose. The colon, or large intestine, is adapted for conserving water, by removing it from the residual waste material. This has then to be eliminated, and being rather dry its passage has to be lubricated by suitable secretions of mucus.

Constipation. For some people it is entirely normal only to pass motions about once or twice a week. For others the normal frequency is once or twice a day. What is abnormal? The answer is that the only thing worth worrying about is pronounced change of bowel habit, particularly in middle-aged and older people. By a change is meant a change from that individual person's normal routine. Such a pronounced change—either in the direction of constipation or diarrhoea—is worth consulting your doctor about if it persists for more than a week or two.

Constipation should be treated first by diet containing plenty of roughage—bran and oatmeal are excellent—plenty of stewed and fresh fruits, and at least 1½ litres of fluid should be taken daily. Failing that take a proprietary product prepared from senna pods. Never to be taken regularly are liquid paraffin, castor oil *etc.*

Oesophagus.

The oesophagus, or gullet, is more than a simple tube for taking the food from the mouth to the stomach. It is normally closed except when swallowing, and the act of swallowing is very complicated. When the material to be swallowed arrives in the back of the throat there is an automatic mechanism which opens the top end of the oesophagus to receive it, and from then onwards everything happens automatically. The next portion of the tube opens and the top closes strongly, so that the food (or drink) is propelled forcibly down the next segment. Then the part below this relaxes and the material is squeezed further downwards and so on until it arrives in the stomach.

This squeezing (or milking) action is similar to the action known as peristalsis which propels contents in other parts of the gut. Thus when you see someone swallowing a glass of beer very quickly in warm weather, it is not going "down the hatch" under the influence of gravity, however much it may look like it. It is perfectly possible to swallow the same, or any other liquid, standing on your head. Getting into that position is the only difficult part. Sometimes this complicated swallowing mechanism gets out of order, leading to difficulties of swallowing, or *dysphagia*.

Hiatus Hernia. Another disorder known as *hiatus hernia* occurs at the lower end of the oesophagus as it meets the stomach. At this point the oesophagus has to pass through the diaphragm, the sheet of muscle which separates the chest from the abdomen. The muscular fibres of the diaphragm are normally arranged in a ring around the oesophagus. These help to keep the lower end shut, so that the acid contents of the stomach do not regurgitate upwards, causing inflammation (*oesophagitis*) or heartburn. A hiatus hernia is when muscle fibres get slack, and the upper end of the stomach can even slide upwards into the chest. People with hiatus hernia get heartburn after meals, and particularly when they bend down or lie down. Except for very severe forms, which need surgical repair, the treatment is to eat less at a time, reduce the acidity with a suitable antacid and reduce weight so that the weight of the abdomen does not press upwards so much.

Cancer of the Oesophagus.

The other disease of the oesophagus, quite unrelated to the above, is *cancer of the oesophagus*, the cause of which is still unknown in most cases. When cancer occurs in the wall of any tube, it will often encircle the tube and gradually narrow the way through. This is what happens in the oesophagus, leading to difficulty in swallowing, particularly solids. It is a condition usually, of rather elderly men, although it is sometimes associated with a special form of severe anaemia in women.

Treatment is to keep the passage open, either by transplanting a new tube, or more usually, by removing the constricted piece and joining up the remainder.

Britain has the highest levels of this cancer in Europe and there may well be a link to rising obesity levels. Cases of this cancer in men more than doubled in Britain between 1985 and 2015. The toll is still rising with *c.* 8,500 new cases each year.

A fluorescent "throat spray" highlighting abnormal cells can help doctors detect the disease earlier.

The Stomach and Duodenum.

By far the commonest diseases of the stomach and duodenum are *gastric ulcer* and *duodenal ulcer*. They are actually the same condition in two different sites and are often classed together as *peptic ulcer* or *acid-peptic disease*. The ulcers, which are rather like sores on the lining of the stomach or duodenum, may be "acute" or "chronic." Acute ulcers tend to be small and there are often several of them. Chronic ulcers are usually single. They may be small, or they may be several centimetres across. Chronic ulcers smoulder for months and even years, like a sore which will not heal, and a great deal of scar tissue forms in their depths. Thus they may in time erode their way right through the wall of the stomach, destroying all its layers, and begin to eat into surrounding structures like the pancreas or liver. The fact that they do not perforate more frequently is due to all the fibrous scar tissue which is formed during the slow eroding process. Healing of such a destructive ulcer is nevertheless common, and the great problem is how to help the natural healing process to win against the ulcer's tendency to erode.

Treatment of Ulcers.

Ulcers are very commonly associated with the bacterium Helicobacter pylori, which may be the cause of ulcers. Appropriate treatment to eradicate this organism is an important part of ulcer therapy. This extremely common affliction is confined to the human species and has been known since the earliest times. It does not vary very much with diet or with social class. Although occurring at all ages, it usually begins between the ages of twenty and forty, and is most commonly found in men between forty-five and fifty-five. Gastric ulcer is four times, and duodenal ulcer ten times more common in men than in women. It is always due to an inability of the lining to stand up to the normal digestive activity of the stomach contents. These are normally acid and contain a powerful enzyme for digesting proteins. Again it is perhaps more surprising that we all do not digest our own stomachs, rather than that some unfortunate people do digest small areas slowly. In certain abnormal conditions when the stomach stops making acid, ulcers always heal. However, some ulcers occur without excessive secretion of acid and many heal without the acid being neutralised with antacids.

Symptoms of Peptic Ulcers.

All this points to the main trouble being in the response of the lining to acid rather than to the acid itself. Nevertheless, the most effective treatment at present known involves regulating gastric secretion, and particularly its acidity. It is also known that peptic ulcers are more common in people whose occupations involve administrative and professional responsibility, competitive effort and nervous tension, long periods of anxiety or frustration. Presumably the higher nervous system influences these events by the same nerves, which normally help to control secretion.

The main symptom of peptic ulcer is pain, and this usually responds well to proper doses of antacids. Many different varieties are available and a lot of money is made from selling them. When indigestion persists for longer than a few days it is always better to see your doctor so that a proper diagnosis can be made and the best remedies begun. Many other causes exist for similar pains, and you should not try to make the diagnosis yourself. It may be necessary to analyse your gastric secretions in the hospital laboratory. Almost certainly you will have a special X-ray examination, and since the stomach cannot easily be seen on a normal X-ray, they will have to show it up by making you drink a white material containing barium. This will be seen as a silhouette of the stomach and duodenal contents. Searching for an ulcer this way is a highly skilled matter and is performed by doctors specially trained in radiology.

Until recently, no drugs capable of influencing the course of peptic ulcer in any significant manner were available and the physician had to rely on general measures, such as rest, diet and the administration of antacids to relieve pain and discomfort: episodes of acute haemorrhage were not uncommon and required surgical intervention.

Endoscopic Investigation. Most ulceration in the stomach and all in the duodenum is due to bacterial infection, *Helicobacter Pylori*. This damages the intestinal wall and makes damage from the stomach's own acid inevitable. Eradication cures the disease, although re-infection may occur. The gastroenterologist can now pass a *flexible* instrument, the *gastroduodenal endoscope* (the gastroscope is a *rigid* tube), under mild sedation through the patient's gullet and into the stomach and duodenum and view the lesions directly. Once an ulcer is diagnosed, the time has come to stop treating yourself with antacids from the chemist's counter, and to take the ones your doctor decides are best. Smoking should be stopped by ulcer patients because it inhibits healing.

Alcohol tends to increase acid secretion and should be avoided. It is also *extremely important* to avoid taking any form of aspirin, even in quite small amounts, since this can lead to very serious bleeding from the ulcer. The ulcer patient should be warned that hundreds of proprietary preparations contain aspirin and all of them are dangerous for him. Search for the formula in small print on the label before taking any remedy, looking particularly for acetylsalicylic acid—the systematic name for aspirin. Some of the patients with "upset stomach" are, of course, ulcer patients, and some even die of haemorrhage following the ingestion of aspirin.

Complications of Peptic Ulcers.

The main complications of peptic ulcer are bleeding, perforation, and a narrowing of the pylorus, or lower part of the stomach (*pyloric stenosis*). Bleeding is caused by the eroding ulcer eating away at one of the many blood vessels in the stomach or duodenal wall. It leads to the passing of "altered" blood in the stool (*melaena*), or to the vomiting of blood (*haematemesis*). When the initial bleeding occurs, the patient may feel suddenly faint, and a little later will notice the black, tarry colour of his stool. This is sometimes confused with a similiar colour when the patient is taking iron. Peptic ulcer is not the only cause of this very serious haemorrhage, which constitutes a hospital emergency whatever its cause. The treatment, like that of every large haemorrhage, is blood transfusion which must be continued until the bleeding stops, or until the patient is sufficiently fit for surgery, should that be needed.

Perforation is perhaps the most serious complication of peptic ulcer, leading to the spilling of stomach contents within the abdominal cavity. Treatment is invariably surgical, either the closure of the perforation or the partial removal of the stomach.

Surgical removal of part of the stomach is often the only way to treat a peptic ulcer which has had its chance to heal in other ways. It is tempting for the patient to "have it out and done with," but the time for surgery is a matter of fine judgment. So many ulcers heal by medical means if given a chance, and operations are for those which persistently refuse, or are complicated.

Stomach Cancer. The stomach is a fairly common site for primary cancer. There is no known reason for this, and it is particularly important to stress that we know of no connection whatever between the peptic ulcers which have just been discussed and cancer. Stomach cancer used to be the commonest cancer of men, but the current rise of lung cancer has pushed it into second place. There are some strange geographical differences in its distribution. For example, it is much commoner in Japan and Scandinavia than

in England or the USA. It is difficult to see any reason for this in dietary habits. In Wales it causes three times as many deaths as in South-East England. All this is very puzzling, as is so much of our information about cancer generally. One of the main problems with stomach cancer is that it often causes the patient no inconvenience and thus produces no symptoms of note until the disease is far advanced and is difficult to treat.

Treatment is by the surgical removal of the growth, and even in the most advanced cases a great deal can often be done to make the patient more comfortable.

Recently doctors have reported evidence of a link between alcohol, eating processed meat and being overweight and suffering from stomach cancer. The risk of stomach cancer is 1 in 64 for men and 1 in 92 for women in the UK.

The Small Intestine.

The small intestine runs from the stomach to the caecum and comprises the duodenum, jejunum, and ileum in that order. On a more cheerful note it may be remarked that it is very rarely the site of cancer. Its main problems arise in connection with defects in absorption mechanisms, with obstructions, and with a strange inflammatory condition known as *regional enteritis*. Most obstructions are due not to blockages of the tube, but to failures of peristaltic propulsion, the process which is briefly described above under "oesophagus." Such a failure is called *ileus*. When peristalsis stops for any reason, the result is severe dehydration and loss of important chemicals like sodium and chloride from the body. This is because about 9 litres of fluid enter the small intestine each day in the form of digestive juices, and all of this has to be pushed onwards to be reabsorbed into the system at lower levels. If peristalsis fails, this bulk of fluid remains in the small intestine, or is vomited. In both cases it is lost to the body itself, leading to serious dehydration and illness. Treatment is by very careful replacement by transfusion of the fluid and the chemicals lost, and by removal of the trapped fluid within the intestine through a tube threaded down through the mouth.

Regional Enteritis or **Ileitis** is very often known as **Crohn's Disease.** It is a very debilitating condition in which the normally supple wall of the small intestine becomes inflamed and gradually replaced by thick fibrous scar tissue, so that it looks and feels like a thick garden hose. Loops of inflamed gut stick together, and channels open between them, and if the disease progresses a mass of adherent, thickened intestine results to which everything in the neighbourhood also adheres.

However, for some unknown reason some cases do not progress downhill in this way and get better spontaneously. Surgical treatment is necessary for the majority, however, particularly those with advanced disease leading to complications such as obstruction or perforation. Sometimes an early case can be resolved by cutting out the length of affected gut, although recurrences are unfortunately common. A genetic link between Crohn's disease and childhood asthma has now been found. A move is underway to provide special hospital meals for Crohn's disease patients.

Recently a link has been suggested between the upsurge of cases in the USA among women and the explosion in the use of oral contraceptives.

Appendicitis. This must be one of the best-known surgical diseases of the intestinal tract. The appendix is a narrow, blind-ended side tube attached to the caecum near the end of the small intestine. Appendicitis is when it becomes obstructed, or infected, or both. From its position it is almost predictable that it will get obstructed sooner or later by pieces of faecal matter which pass its entrance and which are normally infected. The surprising thing is that it does not happen more often. Once this has occurred, however, a closed abscess forms, and as the abscess distends the appendix, it first weakens its wall, making it gangrenous, and then bursts into the abdominal cavity causing *peritonitis* (*see later*). It would be useless and misleading to describe the symptoms of acute appendicitis in detail, since it is difficult even for experienced doctors to distinguish them from those of several other conditions. Suffice it to say that any severe, persisting pain in the abdomen, whether continuous or intermittent, whether associated with diarrhoea or not, should lead the sufferer to a doctor for a quick diagnosis. Germ-killing antibiotics are useless against appendicitis, and any laxative is extremely dangerous as it may cause an acutely inflamed appendix to perforate.

The Large Intestine or Colon.

The two main serious diseases of the colon are ulcerative colitis and cancer in its various forms.

Ulcerative Colitis is yet another mysterious disease in which severe ulceration of the lining of the colon gives rise most frequently to diarrhoea with the passage of blood and mucus. In fact it can be like dysentery, and it has often been considered to be due to some form of infection. Unfortunately no particular germ can routinely be found in these cases, and the situation is endlessly confused by the presence in the normal bowel of lots of different germs anyway. Nevertheless the ulcerated lining of the bowel certainly does get infected by the germs normally present, and this makes the disease worse. Therefore germ-killing antibiotics are often helpful in alleviating symptoms and can lead to an earlier settling down of the condition, although not to a cure. It has long been known that certain kinds of psychological upset are often associated, but here again the disease is so unpleasant for the sufferer that he is to be forgiven some despondency as a result of, rather than as a cause of, his troubles. It is also suspected that ulcerative colitis may be an auto-immune disease; that is it may represent rejection by the patient of his own colonic lining in a manner somewhat comparable to the tissue rejection which often follows organ transplantation.

Some of the more awkward complications are perforation through the wall of the ulcerated bowel, and sometimes massive haemorrhage occurs. Treatment is with sulphasalazine or drugs derived from it, together with diet and the occasional use of other drugs to minimise symptoms. Surgery may be required to relieve obstruction, deal with perforation, remove affected parts of the bowel, *etc.*

Bowel Cancer (Cancer of the Colon and Rectum). This is another very common form of cancer, which can often be completely cured by surgical removal of the growth provided it is caught in the early stages before it has spread. The commonest symptom is a change in bowel habit, either towards constipation or, more often, towards diarrhoea, in the second half of life. There may be rectal bleeding, or the passage of mucus, and there may be abdominal pain. We cannot too often repeat that any such change of bowel habit, or any unexplained bleeding, should lead the patient promptly to his or her doctor.

Bowel cancer is the fourth most common cause of cancer death in the UK (most deaths occur when cancer spreads to the liver). A landmark study published in 2016 revealed more genetic links to bowel cancer. Cases are also rising. Today a major NHS Bowel Cancer Screening Programme is underway. In 2009 a new technique to identify aggressive bowel cancers was developed.

Diverticulitis. Some people have small pockets or sacs in the wall of the colon known as diverticula. A minority of these sometimes get inflamed, and this is *diverticulitis.* Occasionally perforation occurs. When diverticula are present in the colon but not inflamed, the condition is known as *diverticulosis.*

Hernia or Rupture. This is a condition in which abdominal contents, usually a loop of intestine, protrude forwards through the muscular wall of the abdomen. The wall consists of a sheet of muscle fibres running in several directions.

They normally become tense when we cough, or strain, or in getting up from a recumbent position. There are places in the groin on each side where there is a way through the muscle for the spermatic cord in the male. In many men a weakness can arise at this point, and if it persists, the way through may enlarge and allow loops of bowel to emerge from behind the muscle sheet to appear as a lump under the skin of the groin. On relaxation the lump can be made to disappear by pushing the contents back the way they came; and they will re-emerge when the patient strains. This is an extremely common complaint in men, and it should be treated by an operation in which the muscle wall is repaired.

Strangulated Hernia is the term used when the muscle tightens around the neck of the protruding loop of bowel, cutting off its blood supply. From then onwards the loop becomes gangrenous and the intestine is obstructed by having a part of itself nipped outside the abdominal wall. The patient is in severe pain, vomits continuously, and quickly is liable to get into such a poor condition that surgical relief is difficult. It is therefore a surgical emergency, and it would have been better to have had the relatively simple repair operation earlier and at leisure. Hernia in the region of the groin is of two types: *inguinal hernia* and *femoral hernia,* the difference between them being technical and of no consequence to the patient. They nearly always occur in men.

Incisional Hernia is when the muscle wall has been weakened at the site of an old abdominal operation and has failed to heal properly.

Umbilical Hernia occurs owing to the natural weakness of the abdominal wall at the navel, and is so common in babies as to be almost normal. When a baby cries and thereby puts a strain on his abdominal wall, a lump often appears in the region of the navel, and this can be very alarming for the parents. They should of course show it to their doctor who will nearly always be able to reassure them. It is self-healing without operation in the majority of cases.

Peritonitis. The cavity of the abdomen in which the intestines and other organs lie is called the peritoneal cavity, and it is lined by a thin membrane called the peritoneum. When this becomes inflamed the condition is a serious one and is called *peritonitis.* Inflammation may be bacterial, as occurs following a burst appendix and the spillage of bacteria and pus in the cavity. It may be a sterile peritonitis as often follows perforation of a peptic ulcer, when the inflammation is caused by the acid contents of the stomach. It is always very dangerous, probably because of the large surface area afforded by the peritoneum for the absorption of inflammatory toxins.

Haemorrhoids are simply varicose veins in the rectal and anal regions. They are very common, and are caused probably in about equal degrees by inherited weakness of the veins, strain such as heavy lifting, and constipation (this is one of the very few conditions in which constipation may do some damage, due to the mechanical pressure of hardened faeces in the rectum on the veins).

Pregnant women may develop haemorrhoids or "*piles,*" as they are commonly called, owing to the pressure of the baby's head in the pelvis.

Haemorrhoids may be external or internal, the former being in the anal region below the sphincter, the latter in the rectum; the two usually go together. There may be no symptoms, but the veins are liable to bleed, to get thrombosed (*i.e.,* a clot forms within) or to become infected. When clotting or infection occurs the piles enlarge and tend to be pushed out through the anus during defaecation, when they form extremely painful external swellings. Treatment in simple cases may be by the use of suppositories—cones of a firm grease containing suitable medicaments which are inserted in the rectum—in other cases the veins may be injected, as with varicose veins of the leg, in order to close them, but when there is bleeding, thrombosis, infection, or interference with the bowels they should be removed surgically.

THE LIVER.

The liver is a very large organ and has such a wide variety of known functions (to say nothing of the unknown) that it is also one of the most complicated. Nearly all of its functions are biochemical, and it is often called the laboratory of the body. Thus the liver makes proteins from the amino-acids absorbed from the gut, and breaks down amino-acids and manufactures a waste product (urea) from them.

The liver stores carbohydrates as glycogen, and conducts many of the processes necessary to turn carbohydrates into energy. It manufactures prothrombin with the help of vitamin K, and this is essential for blood clotting. It makes bile and secretes it into the gall bladder and bile ducts (see *later*). The three main constituents of bile (cholesterol, bile pigment or bilirubin, and bile acids) all have to be processed, or metabolised, in the liver during the production of bile. Vitamin B$_{12}$ and iron are also stored and dealt with there, and these are involved in preventing various forms of anæmia.

In addition to all these things the liver is the place where harmful substances, both from within the body and from outside it, are dealt with and rendered harmless. This last function of "detoxication" is often accomplished by making the offending molecules suitable for rapid excretion by the kidneys, or by altering their chemical shape to make them harmless.

For further information readers may wish to consult www.britishlivertrust.org.uk

Liver Cells. Nearly all of these very different things are done by one single type of cell: the liver cell, and it is one of the remarkable features of the design that this cell can be so versatile. There also have to be some very efficient transport systems in the liver, in addition to the usual blood supply and venous drainage possessed by all other tissues.

Fully functioning liver cells have now been produced from artificially created stem cells, offering new hope for people with liver disease.

The Portal Venous System.

One of these is the "portal venous system." Whenever a substance is absorbed across the gut wall from any part of the intestine into the interior of the body it enters the special draining blood vessels of the portal system, which are arranged throughout the length of the digestive tract. All these veins eventually unite in the main portal vein which enters the liver. Everything absorbed from the gut is therefore taken first to the liver to be processed. After this the products are carried away from the liver in the ordinary veins to the heart, and are distributed to the rest of the body by the arterial system. The liver has arteries of its own by which it receives oxygen and nutriment like any other tissue. The fourth transport system collects the bile as it is formed within the liver and delivers it to the gall bladder and bile ducts, which eventually drain it into the duodenum.

Portal Hypertension means high blood pressure in the portal venous system, and is the usual accompaniment to *cirrhosis* (see *later*). When the terminations of the portal veins in the liver are strangled and obstructed by cirrhotic disease, this tends to blow them up, or dilate them with blood. There is a natural escape route for the portal blood where the lower end of the oesophagus or gullet joins the upper end of the stomach. At this place some of the portal veins draining the stomach are connected with the ordinary veins draining the oesophagus so that when pressure rises in the portal system, blood tends to be diverted into these connecting veins, and they in turn become dilated, or varicose.

Trouble begins when these dilated connecting veins, which bulge inwards into the oesophagus, are damaged by food particles passing across them and bleed severely into the stomach. The patient vomits large quantities of blood (*haematemesis*) or passes tarry altered blood in the stool (*melaena*). The other main cause of these is the bleeding which may accompany peptic ulcer (*q.v.*).

Ascites is a second complication of portal hypertension (and hence of cirrhosis). Large amounts of a lymph-like fluid accumulate in the abdominal cavity. The fluid contains a great deal of precious protein and salt which is lost to the body economy. Ascites also sometimes accompanies cancerous deposits in the abdomen.

Jaundice means being yellow because there is too much yellow bile pigment circulating in the blood, and there are three main possible causes for this.

Bile pigment comes from broken-down red blood cells, which normally come to the end of their time after existing for about 120 days. The breakdown products of red cells can always be found in the blood of normal people, but there is normally insufficient colour to show. Abnormal amounts of colour build up quite logically in any of the following three circumstances:

(1) **Haemolytic Jaundice.** If too many red cells are being destroyed and even the normal liver cannot deal with the amount of bile pigment produced, it piles up in the blood, and haemolytic jaundice is the result. The expression simply means jaundice due to (abnormally large) red-cell destruction.

(2) **Hepatocellular Jaundice.** If the liver cells are themselves sick and unable to cope even with the normal amounts of pigment from normal red-cell destruction. Here too the pigment will pile up and cause hepatocellular jaundice, or liver-cell jaundice.

(3) **Obstructive Jaundice.** If the bile ducts carrying bile away from the liver are blocked, then bile will pile up behind the blockage and re-enter the blood stream, causing obstructive jaundice. In this case the rate of red-cell breakdown is normal, and the liver cells are normal: at least for a time.

It is enormously important for the treatment of jaundice for the doctor to diagnose its type correctly, since the treatment varies from surgical relief of obstruction to the medical treatment of viral infection or of excess red-cell destruction. The so-called differential diagnosis of jaundice is often exceptionally difficult, and sometimes requires some very sophisticated laboratory tests and X-rays. At other times it is extremely easy and is obvious from a cursory glance at the urine and the stool. All jaundice is a highly technical matter.

Neonatal Jaundice. There is a special jaundice of newborn babies which resembles haemolytic jaundice and can occasionally have serious consequences for the developing brain (*kernicterus*) if it is allowed to become too severe. When this is threatened, steps are taken to reduce the level of circulating bile pigment by replacement of the baby's blood *etc.*

The commonest cause of hepatocellular jaundice is infective or viral hepatitis. Obstructive jaundice is usually due either to blockage by gallstones (*q.v.*) or by a lump pressing on the bile ducts from an adjacent cancer. This can often be quite satisfactorily relieved by surgery.

Infective Hepatitis. *See* **Z10(1)**.

Cirrhosis. There are many different kinds of cirrhosis, the commonest of which has already been mentioned under *portal hypertension* above. In all cases, liver cells are slowly poisoned and are killed off over a long period of time. In response to this, the surviving liver cells undergo cell division, trying to make good the numbers lost, and at the same time fibrous scar tissue replaces the damaged tissue throughout the organ. The result is a hard, knobbly liver. The many "knobs" are spherical areas of regenerated new cells, and they are separated by thickened bands of scar tissue. All of this destroys the normal architecture and leads to the portal hypertension and ascites mentioned above. In some countries (*e.g.*, France and the United States) excessive alcohol is the main cause of the original liver damage which starts it all off. In others (*e.g.*, South Africa) it seems to be nutritional starvation of the liver. In England much less than half the cases are due to alcohol, and many are thought to be due to a previous episode of infective hepatitis (*q.v.*), but this is not certain. The number of cases of cirrhosis in the UK more than doubled in the ten years to 2010 and alcohol is being blamed. The term "fatty liver" is used when the liver is showing signs of excess alcohol or other problems.

Infective hepatitis is quite common but cirrhosis was comparatively rare. However, excessive alcohol consumption caused deaths from cirrhosis to rise 7-fold from the 1960s to the 1990s (and they are still rising). The worst affected area is the north of England. One treatment for advanced cirrhosis is to replace the liver by transplantation. Live liver transplants began in the UK in 2006.

Cancer of the Liver. Cancer of the liver is quite common, but it is nearly always cancer which has spread in the blood stream from other parts of the body. The liver is a favourite site for such secondary deposits, since it has a large blood supply and will receive a generous helping of anything being carried. It is also a very "fertile soil" for the cancer seedlings to grow in. Primary cancer of the liver, linked to obesity and alcohol, trebled in the 30 years to 2009. Rates for liver cancer in women rose 60% in the last decade.

Gallstones. These are "stones" formed by some of the major constituents of bile coming out of solution and forming solid bodies. They are very common, and often cause no trouble at all. When they do, it is usually a colicky intermittent severe pain. This is due to the muscular walls of the bile passages contracting in an effort to expel an obstructing stone into the duodenum. The second common trouble arising from gallstones is obstructive jaundice, described above. It is small consolation to gallstone sufferers that the stones are often very pretty. If they contain calcium they will be visible on an X-ray. Otherwise they are not seen. Stones often occur in conjunction with inflammation of the gall bladder, known as *cholecystitis*. The treatment for gallstones is to remove them surgically together with the gall bladder if they are causing persistent symptoms. Also, a flexible endoscope can be passed into the intestine and a tiny wire basket passed from it into the bile system to remove stones. Operations are done by keyhole surgery.

The Pancreas is a soft, elongated gland lying behind the stomach; it is *c.* 12·5 cm long and 5 cm wide. Within its tissues lies the duct, which, when it leaves the pancreas, passes into the duodenum near the point of entry of the bile-duct. This duct transmits the juices containing enzymes which aid in the digestion in the small intestine. The pancreas, however, has two main functions: not only does it manufacture these important digestive juices, but in certain specialised areas, the islets of Langerhans, it makes insulin, the hormone which makes it possible for the body to utilise sugar.

Diabetes Mellitus (or ordinary diabetes) is a chronic disorder usually caused by a deficient secretion of insulin. The unused sugar accumulates in the blood and acts as a poison, which, in extreme cases, sends the patient into coma and may—indeed, in former times, usually did—result in death. The treatment of diabetes was revolutionised by the discovery of the hormone insulin by Banting and Best in 1921. On the whole, diabetes is more severe in young people than in the elderly, but with correct treatment it is possible for all cases to lead a

perfectly normal life except for dietary restrictions and insulin injections. Not to be confused with *Diabetes insipidus* (*q.v.*). The main problem with diabetes mellitus now is that the wrong (albeit slightly) blood sugar levels that are found even with good therapy eventually damage small blood vessels, leading to problems with the eyes, peripheral nerves and kidneys. Everyone should ask their GP to test their blood sugar levels regularly.

Globally, cases of diabetes have grown from 153 million in 1980 to over 370 million today. In Britain there are 3·8 million diagnosed cases (expected to rise to 5 million by 2025). It is much more common among ethnic minorities. Diabetes is now one of the great health challenges of our age and urgent research is looking for a cure (or at least a reversal of the condition).

Hypoglycaemia, or low blood sugar (glucose), is something that can be a daily fear for many people living with diabetes. It is most commonly experienced by people with Type 1 diabetes who are unable to produce any insulin. It can also occur in people with Type 2 diabetes who are taking certain diabetes tablets and/or insulin. Hypoglycaemia (or 'hypo') occurs when glucose levels fall too low.

Pancreatitis is a condition where the pancreatic enzymes start digesting the pancreas itself. It may be caused by stones blocking the duct these secretions normally leave the pancreas by, but alcohol may be a cause. It can be a very serious illness. Pancreatic cancer is the 11th most common cancer in the UK (with 7,000 diagnosed annually).

Pancreatic cancer can easily be overlooked and survival rates are poor. Check out www.Pancreatic CancerAction.org.

DIET AND OBESITY.

The basic constituents of any diet are protein, fats, carbohydrates, water, vitamins, minerals, salts, and indigestible roughage (fibre). All are chemicals whose structure and function are reasonably well understood.

In general terms, however, requirements can be described in terms of how many calories there are in the total intake of proteins, fats, and carbohydrates per day, and how these are distributed between the three classes of food. The other substances mentioned above are only required in trace or small amounts except for water; and roughage is only required to aid bowel movement stimulus.

The Process of Digestion.

During the process of digestion (described earlier) all proteins are split into their constituent amino acids; all carbohydrates are split into their constituent simple sugars and most fats are converted into fatty acids and glycerol. At this stage, and not until this stage, all these simpler building bricks derived from the three classes of food are absorbed into the body proper, and taken to the liver and other tissues. Here they are "metabolised." That is to say they are either burned as fuel for the various processes of the body; or they are built up again into proteins, fats, and carbohydrates of the special kinds the body needs. They will either be used to rebuild structures suffering ordinary wear and tear or they will be stored. Many of them will be converted into a different class from the one they came from when they entered the body. For example, excess carbohydrate is converted into fat; or if there is a shortage of carbohydrate, some will be made out of the protein amino-acids which would normally have been used for tissue growth and repair. Thus it is only a generalisation to say that dietary carbohydrates are fuel and proteins are for building bodily structure. The body can convert one into the other, and spoil the calculation.

Diet and Energy.

There is a great deal of confusion in people's minds about *energy*, and that is why the word *fuel* has been used above in connection with carbohydrates. The lay person uses energy as a term meaning something which allows us to leap about, running and jumping and skipping and dancing, and which keeps us from getting tired and run down. Thus, the food industry tells us, we need potatoes or breakfast cereals for these activities or for a hard day's work. This is a deliberate commercial confidence trick, and the scientist is largely to blame. He originally handed out the word energy to an eager food industry and an unsuspecting public, forgetting to explain that he meant it in the strictly scientific sense of fuel for bodily processes. It simply is not true that more potatoes, or more cornflakes will make you more active.

Indeed the reverse is the case, and after a certain point they will only be converted into fat and reduce your activity. The nutritionist measures energy as calories, which are units of heat. You must eat enough of these each day if you wish to remain alive, let alone active.

The Well-Balanced Diet.

All the three main classes of food provide calories, and in an ordinary well-balanced diet about 15 % are provided by protein. Carbohydrates produce most of the remainder. Each gram of fat contains about twice the calories of a similar quantity of carbohydrate. We simply eat less fat than carbohydrate, because fat has a "high satiety value." It takes away the appetite for more. Proteins are mostly found in meat, fish, eggs, cheese, and milk. However, there is quite a lot of protein in many predominantly starchy foods like bread, and such grains as wheat, rice, and corn. Carbohydrates are mainly found in bread, potatoes, sugar, pastry, sweets, and so forth. That is one of the words which fortunately seems to be used by both scientists and laymen in much the same sense.

Some substances are absolutely essential to the body if life is to continue, even if they are only needed in trace amounts. These are substances which the body's own factories (like the liver) cannot make for themselves, even if they are provided with the correct ingredients.

Vitamins.

One group of such substances are the *vitamins*. Some of these are found in predominantly fatty foods (milk, butter, cheese and so on) and are known as the fat-soluble vitamins—Vitamins A, D, E and K; the others are water-soluble—the Vitamin B group and Vitamin C. All have now been chemically identified, are manufactured and can be bought over a pharmacist's counter. The myth has grown up that if a little is good for one then a lot more will be better and there are still many vitamin enthusiasts who consume vast quantities of such manufactured products in the belief that by doing so they will induce extra vitality and energy. Unless your diet is unbalanced in some way (a vegetarian diet may be grossly deficient in Vitamin B_{12}) you will not need extra vitamins.

Fortunately, most people buy food because they like it, not because it does them good; and provided they have normal dietary tastes they will usually get a perfectly adequate selection of the things we have spoken of as necessary for good health. The main danger in Britain is to have a surfeit and become overweight. In addition there are certain times of life when attention should be paid to what is necessary. For example babies and nursing mothers have special dietary needs. *See also* **Z42** for Vitamin A deficiency.

Popular Attitudes and Knowledge.

Recent surveys have revealed some interesting facts about people's attitude to food and their knowledge of it. For example, half the people asked knew that meat was a source of protein, a third mentioned eggs and a fifth cheese, fish, and milk. But practically no one knew there was protein in bread. Yet in England about a fifth of our daily protein intake comes from bread, and nearly a third from cereals as a whole. Fish

is well known as a source of protein, but did you know that on average we only obtain 4 % of our daily protein from fish—less than we get from potatoes (5 %)? No one seems to know that potatoes are an important source of vitamin C, although fruit and vegetables are well-known sources. Calcium is recognised in milk, but most people forget its presence in cheese. Most people are very confused about iron. Why does everyone think it is mainly in green vegetables, when these are really such a poor source? For our daily requirement of iron we would each have to eat 1 kg. of spring greens or peas; or 2 kg. of sprouts! In fact meat provides one of our best sources; onefifth of our daily needs is contained in bread.

Obesity.

Nowadays, obesity has become one of the greatest threats to global health even more so than hunger. Nearly 1·7 *billion* people on our planet are overweight. Being fat is dangerous to health and carries a high mortality. Ask any life insurance company how they view your chances if you are overweight and you will find they are as worried about it as if you had high blood pressure, or smoke heavily. It is a particularly important cause of heart disease. However, it is very important to know exactly what we mean by fatness.

The term *Body Mass Index* (*BMI*) is now a common measure of a person's weight relative to their height (above 25 is overweight, above 30 obese). The ideal ratio is between 18·5 and 25. The average *BMI* of women in the UK is higher than in many EU countries.

If you are overweight according to the tables below you need to slim, and the question is how? Answer: by will-power. There is no other satisfactory method than to decide to eat less. For the time being eat as much fruit, and green vegetables, as

DESIRABLE WEIGHTS FOR MEN AND WOMEN, AGES 25 AND OVER

Men Height (in shoes 2·5 cm heels)	Weight in kilograms (in indoor clothing)		
	Small frame	Medium frame	Large frame
157	51–54·5	53·5–59	57–64
160	52–56	55–60·5	59–65·5
162	53·5–57	56–62	60–67
165	55–59	58–63	61–69
167	56–60·5	59–65	63–71
170	58–62	61–67	64·5–73
172	60–64	63–69	67–75·5
175	62–66	64·5–71	68·5–77
177	63·5–68	66–72·5	70·5–79
180	65·5–70	68–75	72–81
183	67–72	70–77	74–83·5
185	69–73·5	72–79·5	76–86
188	71–76	73·5–82	78·5–88
190	72·5–77·5	76–84	81–90·5
193	74·5–79·5	78–86	82·5–93

Women Height (in shoes 5 cm heels)	Weight in kilograms (in indoor clothing)		
	Small frame	Medium frame	Large frame
147	42–44·5	43·5–48·5	47–54
150	43–46	44·5–50	48–55·5
152	43·5–47	46–51	49·5–57
155	45–48·5	47–53	51–58
157	46–50	48·5–54	52–59·5
160	48–51	50–55·5	53·5–61
162	49–53	51–57	55–63
165	50·5–54	53–59	57–64·5
167	52–56	54·5–61	59–66
170	53·5–58	56–63	60·5–68
172	55·5–59·5	58–65	62–70
175	57–61	60–67	64–72
177	59–63·5	62–68·5	66–74
180	61–65·5	63·5–70·5	68–76
183	63–67	65·5–72	69·5–78·5

you like, but no sugar, starch, sweets, cakes, pastry, or biscuits, and no eating between meals. And cut down on beer and other alcoholic drinks.

At the same time take more exercise. Walk to work. If you make a real and genuine effort for three months without success, you should ask your doctor for advice. Almost certainly you will have to admit you have not really tried. Good luck!

Nowadays, scientists blame genes not poor diet for childhood obesity—but exercise and careful diet remain vital. Remember, the number of under-18s on anti-obesity medicines has risen 15-fold since 1999. Obesity (particularly childhood obesity) is becoming a medical time-bomb and Britain is among the worst offenders.

NUTRITIONAL DISORDERS.

Nutritional Deficiency and Malnutrition.—Until quite recently a consideration of malnutrition would have merely led to an account of how too little food, or a deficiency of certain articles in the diet, produced deficiency diseases at the time of the restriction. For example lack of vitamins of various kinds gives rise to such diseases as rickets, scurvy, beri-beri, and pellagra; and an overall shortage of food to general starvation. These may be considered the immediate or concurrent effects of a poor diet. Modern nutritionists, however, are beginning to be concerned with two more kinds of nutritional disorders; and although the study of both kinds is in its infancy, both will be introduced in this account.

The first deals with the effects of comparatively small amounts of harmful constituents in our diet, introduced either voluntarily or involuntarily, and consumed for a long period of time; and the second with the lasting effects on our adult well-being of nutritional deficiencies in early life even though they have long since been corrected.

When viewed in this light, one or other of these three kinds of nutritional disorder may at this moment be affecting almost every individual in every part of the world, "privileged" or "under-privileged." Let us first define some terms.

Undernutrition, strictly speaking, means a state of affairs in which the quality of the diet is perfectly good. There is the correct balance of the various dietary constituents and all the necessary components are present: but there is simply too little of it. Many hundreds of millions of people throughout the underprivileged world are suffering and dying from this kind of undernutrition, and the simplicity of the problem must be appreciated: they simply need more food of the kind they are at present getting, and which can often be produced locally.

Malnutrition means an imbalance of the various constituents: a relative lack or excess of one or more of them. It usually leads to conditions which are, from the point of view of medical treatment, much more difficult to deal with. And so doctors often class them as "more serious."

The diseases of malnutrition range from the widespread protein deficiencies in other parts of the underprivileged world to *obesity* in our own better-off industrial countries, which is usually due to excess carbohydrate. Make no mistake: obesity (or being overweight) is a widespread disease of nutritional imbalance, and it kills.

Obesity is the commonest form of malnutrition in (for example) England and America today, and is a consequence of the sophistication of our diet in modern times. Recent figures for the UK show that the proportion of obese men rose from 13·2% in 1993 to 22·1% in 2005. The total is still rising. Over 22% of women are now classed as obese. If it is any comfort, obesity is a *global* problem. More people in the world are now fat than are undernourished. In the USA over 32% are now obese—the highest level in the world.

There are high authorities in the world of nutritional science who attribute all this overfed malnutrition to the consumption of refined sugar, or sucrose. They say it is not only the amount of

refined sugar we put in our tea or on our breakfast cereals, but also the amount in sweet cakes, biscuits, drinks, chocolates and sweets, and so forth. For some people it adds up to a phenomenal quantity each day.

This school of thought says we are not so much suffering from a surfeit of carbohydrates or starches, but from this single sugar, sucrose. It is interesting to reflect on the recent banning of the artificial sweetener, cyclamate, by many governments. This substance, having been used extensively throughout the world as an apparently harmless non-fattening substitute for sugar, was suddenly banned in America because in very large doses (equivalent to the amount taken in hundreds of cups of coffee per day for a long time) it was found to produce cancer in rats. It has never been shown to do humans any harm, whereas the effects of sugar in producing an overweight population, thereby indirectly kill tens of thousands of British people each year. This is a fascinating example of the difficulties confronting our legislators in making balanced judgments when deciding to ban a foodstuff, a drug, or an artificial fertiliser.

Childhood Malnutrition.

Protein-Calorie Deficiency is much the most widespread form of malnutrition. In very large underprivileged areas of the world, the childhood population receives such an inadequate diet that children live continuously on the brink of nutritional disaster. It only requires a small extra restriction or stress to topple them over into one of the clinical conditions to be described. At this stage they cease to be merely hungry. They become nutritionally ill. Sometimes the force which produces the disaster is a community catastrophe like a famine, an earthquake, or a war. Sometimes it is a family catastrophe like the loss of a lactating mother or a parental delinquency. Parents abandon young children as often in Africa as anywhere else. Sometimes the clinical nutritional disease is unmasked by a common childhood illness like measles, or gastro-enteritis which the well-fed child would have overcome. The starved child reveals his malnutrition instead and frequently dies.

Kwashiorkor. Protein-Calorie Deficiency is a collection of different kinds of childhood malnutrition. Some are due predominantly to deficiency of protein and are collectively called kwashiorkor, a West African word meaning "red-haired boy" (*see below*). Others are mainly due to a severe deficiency of overall foodstuffs and are called *marasmus*. But in any real-life situation the severe *mal*nutrition of kwashiorkor exists side-by-side with all gradations between itself and the severe *under*nutrition of marasmus, so that many intermediate forms of "marasmic kwashiorkor" are described.

In kwashiorkor the child is typically listless, apathetic, whining, with a reddish discoloration of the hair, a peeling, scaly skin, and with much extra fluid in his tissues causing oedema. He is so listless as not even to be hungry. In marasmus the child is ravenously hungry. He is extremely thin and "starved" looking and is quite a different picture.

There is good reason to believe that even when protein-calorie deficiency is successfully treated, there will always be some lasting restriction of mental function, particularly if the malnutrition occurred as early as the first year of life. This is especially true in situations of appalling poverty in towns, where thousands of babies are not breastfed because their mothers are at work. Many of them die. Some of them are no heavier than their birth weight at one year of age. Breast feeding in an underprivileged community is an essential insurance for childhood health and survival.

Problems of Additives.

Two new avenues of nutritional inquiry were mentioned at the beginning of this section. The impact of very long continued intake of refined sugar over many years on our bodily health is an example of one of them. Scientists and others are also becoming alarmed at the effects of modern food additives when taken, even in small amounts, over a long period. These additives include colouring matter, decolorising chemicals, taste "enhancers," and so forth, which are present in everyone's diet in a "civilised community." We are as unable to avoid a constant dosage with them as if they had been added to our water supply. It is, however, difficult to strike a balanced attitude. It is one thing to suspect that these additives are harmful and quite another to prove it.

Naturally if any of them are shown to produce harm in animals given reasonable quantities they are invariably withdrawn. But in practice it is extremely difficult for animal experiments to mimic the conditions of human intake, especially as the human life span involves eating the substance concerned in small quantities for several decades.

New Views on Nutrition.

The other new topic in nutrition is more soundly based on animal experiment. It has been repeatedly found that if animals do not grow quickly enough at certain early periods of life they not only become small, but they remain smaller than they should be even when they are subsequently given as much as they like to eat. This is true of all animals and birds so far studied. At the moment it is difficult to know whether the same is true of humans and, if so, when is our period of vulnerability. There is some suggestion that the corresponding critical period in humans is during the last part of gestation in the uterus, and the first year or so of postnatal life. This new idea may turn out to be very important for world nutrition. Since there will not be enough food for all the children all the time, it may become important to concentrate our aid to underprivileged countries on certain sections of the population only.

It may be a good idea to see that pregnant mothers and small babies are specially fed. In this way we may be able to put off the periods of inevitable malnutrition until a time of life when it is recoverable. Such a plan would also go a long way to safeguarding the development of the brain which also occurs mostly at the same early time of life.

Even in Britain, we need to be aware of this problem. Vitamin deficiency can still occur, however, in elderly people living alone and not having a well-balanced diet. It also occurs for similar reasons in alcoholics, vagrants, *etc.*

Beri-beri is a group of diseases usually confined to the Far East where a diet of polished rice results in a poor intake of vitamin B_1 (thiamine). In one form there is oedema (*q.v.*); in another the peripheral nerves are affected leading to tingling and numbness. A similar condition is occasionally seen in alcoholics and diabetics. Treatment is with thiamine, and other vitamins too, since most sufferers are going short of more than one.

Pellagra is sometimes found among maize-eating populations and is due to a deficiency of several vitamins including niacin, another member of the B group of vitamins. There is dermatitis on exposed skin, and soreness of the mouth and tongue, with gastro-enteritis.

Scurvy is caused by vitamin C deficiency. It was at one time the scourge of sailors. In children bone growth is affected. At all ages there is bleeding into the skin (bruising), impaired wound healing, mental depression, and anaemia. Most fresh fruit and vegetables contain vitamin C and a diet containing these prevents the disease.

Vitamin A Deficiency is commonly found in children in some underprivileged countries. It causes permanent blindness, with thickening opacity and dryness of the whites of the eyes leading to ulceration of the eye. Beyond a certain stage, therefore, a child's sight cannot be saved. The only real hope is prevention, with an adequate diet.

Rickets, another disease of early childhood, is caused by deficiency of vitamin D. Bones are not properly calcified, and their softness leads to deformities of the legs and many other bones. Vitamin D can either be eaten in the diet or produced under the skin under the influence of sunlight. Therefore rickets commonly occurs when both the diet and the sunlight are inadequate. It was once very common in Victorian England but was almost wiped out after 1945 when margarine was fortified with Vitamin D. It is now making a return in the UK where Vitamin D deficiency levels are running high.

Doctors are reporting a sharp increase in rickets caused by children glued to TV, computers and video games and not going outdoors in the sunshine enough!

THE ENDOCRINE GLANDS.

Glands are structures or organs which manufacture secretions (except for *lymph glands* which are not glands at all and should be called *lymph nodes*). The secretions are of two main kinds. The first are passed down tubes, or ducts, or are secreted directly into the hollow organs, and act locally. Good examples are the salivary glands which make saliva and pass it down ducts into the mouth for digestion of its contents and lubrication. These are *exocrine glands*. The second kind have no ducts, and secrete their product straight into the blood stream. This secretion is called a *hormone* and it is carried to all parts of the body by the blood where it acts at a distance on some remote part. These are the *endocrine glands* or *ductless glands*, and a number of them will be discussed in this section.

The first hormone, or "chemical messenger," was discovered by the British physiologist Starling in 1904, but the effects of removing some of the endocrine glands were known centuries before.

Anterior Pituitary.—Many of the endocrine glands do not act as separate autonomous organs in spite of their great differences. They are organised into a well-disciplined band by a "master-gland" called the anterior pituitary. Somebody once called it the "conductor of the endocrine orchestra" and the phrase is still repeated *ad nauseam* in students' examination papers. The pituitary, consisting of its two parts, anterior and posterior, is not much bigger than a pea and it sits right in the middle of the skull, centrally beneath the brain and joined to the brain by a short stalk. This astonishing tiny nodule of tissue produces at least eight important hormones.

Growth Hormone, which is one of these is necessary for normal growth, and also has an influence on insulin. An excess causes *gigantism* and *acromegaly*, often coinciding with diabetes, and too little results in a form of dwarfism. Three others, known as *gonadotrophic hormones* regulate the cyclical and other activities of the reproductive organs and lactating breast. Another, *thyrotrophic hormone*, regulates thyroid activity.

Adrenocorticotrophic Hormone, or ACTH, as its name implies, looks after the activities of another important endocrine gland, the adrenal cortex. And there are several others.

Hypopituitarism, including *Simmonds' disease* and *Sheehan's disease*, results from destruction of the anterior pituitary. It is extremely rare, and is usually associated with difficult childbirth involving very severe bleeding. There are disturbances of all the functions mentioned above, particularly thyroid and adrenal failure (q.v.) with upset sexual function. Treatment is by replacing the lost hormones.

Hyperpituitarism, including *gigantism* and *acromegaly*, results from over-activity of the anterior pituitary, and is usually due to a tumour or overgrowth of the gland. In acromegaly the growth hormone is produced in excess over a long period of time in an adult. This results in overgrowth of all the organs except the brain, and it is characteristic to find enlarged extremities—feet, hands, and jaw. In gigantism the same has occurred during childhood and the result is a person who may be 2 m tall or more.

Posterior Pituitary. The posterior part of the gland is really a quite separate gland. The main hormone it produces is concerned with the excretion of urine by the kidney (antidiuretic hormone). Deficiency of the hormone results in *diabetes insipidus*, not to be confused with *diabetes mellitus* or "sugar diabetes." In diabetes insipidus, the patient produces enormous quantities of dilute urine. He consequently has a prodigious thirst and consumes astonishing quantities of fluids. Treatment is by replacing the hormone.

Thyroid. The thyroid gland in the neck secretes an iodine containing hormone called thyroxine. Excess of it causes *hyperthyroidism*, *thyrotoxicosis*, or *Graves' disease*. Lack of it produces *cretinism* in the growing child or *myxodoema* in the adult. Thyroxine is concerned with the metabolic rate of cells throughout the body, or the rate at which they work, as well as with the proper growth of developing tissues, especially the brain. Too much thyroxine as in thyrotoxicosis leads to over-activity, warm sweatiness in an over-excitable patient whose pulse is rapid and who is eating ravenously to try to replace the wasted energy. In spite of this the patient is very thin, and often has bulging eyes for a reason not yet understood. Treatment is by drugs which neutralise the thyroxine or by cutting out some of the gland. A *cretin* is a child usually born with insufficient thyroid. He or she is destined to grow poorly, and to mental subnormality of a permanent and distressing kind. If the condition is diagnosed soon after birth (and routine testing is now done) treatment with thyroxine can avert most of the trouble. In myxoedema, thyroxine is deficient in an adult. They become slow in all their bodily processes, the hair thins and their flesh is puffy with a dry, wrinkled skin. Treatment is by thyroid replacement. Rates of thyroid cancer have doubled over the last 25 years.

Goitre means enlargement of the thyroid gland. It may be accompanied by overactivity or underactivity, or with little functional change. One variety (Derbyshire neck) occurs in areas short of iodine in the soil and drinking water.

Adrenal Cortex. The adrenal or suprarenal glands sit, as the name implies, one on top of each kidney. There are two distinct parts: the cortex or outside which secretes steroid hormones, and the *adrenal medulla*, or core, which secretes adrenalin. There are many different steroid hormones in the adrenale cortical secretion, which look after such diverse matters as sodium and potassium balance, sexual function, reaction of the body to stress, and the regulation of sugar levels.

Addison's Disease results from adrenal cortical insufficiency, and is often due to destruction of the gland by tuberculosis. There is weariness, malaise, pigmentation of skin creases and mucous membranes. They are short of sodium and have excess potassium. Treatment is with cortisone or synthetic steroids to replace the missing hormone, and by extra salt by mouth for the lack of sodium.

Cushing's Disease is due to excessive adrenal cortical function, and sometimes also occurs in patients treated with steroids for other purposes. They have a striking redistribution of fat in the face, neck, and trunk, with stretch marks similar to those acquired by most women during pregnancy. The facial obesity makes them "moon-faced," and female patients may suffer masculinisation with deepening of the voice and hirsutism.

Testis. The male testes, as well as producing sperm are also endocrine glands producing steroid hormones known as *androgens*. They are mainly concerned with maintaining secondary sex characteristics. At the time of puberty the controlling secretions from the anterior pituitary begin to appear and androgens are produced. There is a whole range of rare disorders, resulting in everything from precocious puberty to delayed puberty. It should be borne in mind that the normal time of puberty can vary by several years from one boy to another. In passing, it should be noted that any lump or severe pain in a testicle requires urgent medical advice. These may be signs of cancer or twisting of the blood supply, respectively.

Testicular cancer, though rare, is the most common cancer in men aged 15–45. The risk of *testicular cancer* doubles with the use of cannabis. Any problem a man encounters in this area should be discussed urgently with a doctor. The good news is that nearly all men recover from testicular cancer. Men with an abnormally low sperm count are at greater risk.

Ovary. The human ovary has two functions: to produce ova or eggs; and to produce two hormones, oestrogen and progesterone. These functions begin at puberty, one of whose features in the female is the onset of menstruation, or menarche. Just as in boys, the timing of normal puberty is very variable, but on the average, girls achieve puberty before boys. As social conditions improve, the age of menarche is getting younger generation by generation. All the secondary sex characteristics are under the control of the ovarian hormones which are released in response to the appropriate anterior pituitary hormones. The changes which occur in the womb and elsewhere in the intervals between menstrual periods and the periods themselves are controlled by a cyclical or rhythmic secretion, first of oestrogen and then of progesterone, by the ovary. This cycle is upset by pregnancy to allow the development of the embryo.

The cycle can also be upset by taking certain combinations of the two hormones by mouth. These can prevent the formation of ova, and are a popular form of contraception. In late middle age, the ovaries lose their function, the menstrual cycles cease to occur, and reproductive life is at an end. This is called the *menopause* or "change of life," and is sometimes accompanied for a time by distressing symptoms due to a temporary imbalance between oestrogen and progesterone. But many sexual functions continue long after the menopause.

Parathyroid. Four tiny parathyroid glands are buried behind the thyroid gland and are responsible for regulating the body calcium and phosphate. They are therefore particularly important for the building and maintenance of bones and teeth. Since a proper calcium level in the blood is necessary for muscle (including heart muscle) contraction, and for correct functioning of nerves, disorders of the parathyroids can give rise to muscular spasms as well as loss of bone calcium. The latter can result in fragility and fractures. Overactivity of the glands leads to too much calcium and the formation of stones.

Pineal. We end this section with a mystery gland. Like the pituitary it is small—about the size of a pea—and sits well back at the base of the brain. It was endowed in ancient times with metaphysical properties all of which remain speculative. In fish and lizards and certain lower vertebrates it is a kind of third eye, and receives light. In higher mammals, like ourselves, it is so far from any source of light that it could scarcely do so. It can be removed without harm. Indeed it normally becomes calcified and inactive about the time of puberty, and its position seen on X-rays of the skull can be a good guide to whether the brain is being pushed to one side by an abnormal mass.

THE URINARY SYSTEM.

Everyone knows what kidneys look like—in fact, the term "kidney-shaped" is used to describe other objects. Within the kidneys the blood-vessels carrying waste materials subdivide and finally end up in little coils or glomeruli through which waste products are filtered into the other system, the system of tubes which, beginning as tiny cups around the glomeruli, become larger and larger until they join the ureter passing out at the foot of the kidney, the hilum, a point at which both the veins and tubes enter and leave. The kidneys, of course, lie one on each side in the loins, so that if one puts one's hands on the hips and then slides them farther back they will cover the area over the left and right kidney. The ureters pass down on each side to the bladder, which is the storage tank of the products excreted by the kidneys, and lies in the mid-line down low in the abdomen; it is somewhat pear-shaped, and at its base in men there lies the *prostate gland*—a gland which apparently has few functions but can be a nuisance. Its only known function is that it adds something to the semen from the testes without which the semen would be sterile. Then, from the base of the bladder a single tube, the urethra, passes to the outside.

One can visualise the urinary system as a capital Y, in which the two upper limbs are the ureters, the place where they meet is the bladder, and the single limb at the foot is the urethra. Clearly, then, there may be diseases of the kidneys, of the ureters, of the bladder, of the prostate gland, or of the urethra.

Urine: Polyuria and Oliguria.

The amount of urine may be increased or diminished. It is *increased* in the following conditions: after drinking excess of fluids; after taking drugs (known as *diuretics*) which are given to increase the flow; in diabetes of both types—mellitus and insipidus; in some types of chronic kidney disease; and finally, in emotional states of excitement. It is *decreased* in the following conditions: acute nephritis; any disease in which fluid is being lost in other ways, such as diarrhoea or sweating in fevers; when the fluid intake is small; and when both ureters are blocked by stones.

Passing a great deal of urine is known as *polyuria*, passing very little as *oliguria*, passing frequent small amounts is simply called *frequency*. Normally, the urine is acid, but in infections of the bladder it may become alkaline owing to decomposition by bacteria. Abnormal substances, or normal substances in abnormal quantities, may occur in the urine and give the doctor an indication of what is wrong. In fact, urine analysis is a very important part of medical diagnosis. Thus urea is a normal component of urine which is increased in fevers, wasting diseases, or diabetes; the amount of urea is to some extent a measure of the degree of tissue breakdown. Uric acid is found in small quantities in normal urine, but the amount is increased in fevers and after an attack of gout (uric acid is important in the causation of gout).

Oxalates are not ordinarily found in urine, but, since they occur in such foods as rhubarb and strawberries, and some people are unable to deal with them, such individuals may develop problems.

Albumin and Sugar.

Two very important substances which ought not to be in normal urine are albumin and sugar. Albumin is a protein, and its presence in the urine indicates that the filters of the kidney are leaking—they are allowing protein to pass out which ought to remain in the body. Albumin is easily tested for, and its presence may indicate kidney disease or nephritis as it is usually called by doctors. On the other hand, small amounts of albumin occur in fevers and in nervous conditions—*functional albuminuria*. Sugar, too, should not be present, but its presence does not necessarily indicate diabetes; for small amounts may occur in nervous conditions or in some people after taking large quantities of carbohydrate.

Blood in the urine may give it an appearance which varies from bright red to a dark, smoky colour. It is found in many diseases: acute nephritis, stone, tumours, poisoning by certain drugs, infections such as bilharzia or malaria, papilloma (i.e., non-malignant tumour of the bladder), after injury,

in high blood-pressure, scurvy, and blood diseases. Sometimes it occurs for no known reason at all.

Nephritis. It will be remembered that streptococcal infection of the throat may cause in some people disease of the valves in the heart or endocarditis. In such cases, although the germ is found in the throat, it is not found in the heart or anywhere else in the body.

Acute Nephritis occurs in the same circumstances, with the sole difference that it is the kidneys not the heart which are affected.

The disease appears to be an allergic reaction to the toxins of the Streptococcus. The patient, often a child, has a sore throat (and even this may be absent or fail to be noticed) or sometimes the infection may arise in other sites: after scarlet fever, erysipelas, burns, and disease of the ear. A few days later there is headache, vomiting, pain in the loins, slight rise in temperature, and especially typical is *dropsy* or oedema. This begins in the face, first around the eyelids, and then affects the ankles; later it may become more general and affect the rest of the body. Blood and albumin are found in the urine, and the blood pressure is slightly raised. The outlook is usually good if the kidneys are rested by reducing the amount of protein taken in and also the amounts of salt and water. When this is done, the inflammation soon goes and no permanent harm results. In other cases, however, if treatment is inadequate or the condition severe, the symptoms may go, but the albumin found in the urine persists. This means that permanent damage has been done, and although there may be nothing else to show for many years, *chronic nephritis* develops.

Chronic Nephritis. With this disease, the blood pressure continues to rise, and since the filters of the kidneys no longer work efficiently, urea, the principal waste product of the body to be excreted in the urine, is retained in the blood and only small amounts escape from the system. Hence chronic nephritis sooner or later leads to heart failure or haemorrhage in the brain from the rising blood pressure, or to the form of poisoning known as *uraemia* which results from the retention of urea in the blood. Uraemia may come on suddenly or gradually, but ends in progressive coma, drowsiness, and unconsciousness. There may be convulsions and difficulty in breathing to complicate the picture.

Nephrosis is another type of nephritis which seems to have nothing at all to do with streptococcal infections, and the cause of which is completely unknown. Developing in early adult life, its onset is insidious, and the patient first shows signs of oedema in his white and puffy face and the swelling of his legs. (It should be said here that if you have swelling of the ankles or elsewhere, you would be foolish to jump to conclusions; for such swelling is common in many diseases—in heart disease, in allergic conditions, even hot weather.

When the urine is examined in a case of nephrosis it is found to be full of albumin and, as in chronic nephritis, the blood urea starts to rise. The end results of nephrosis are the same as those of chronic nephritis and depend upon the original damage.

The modern diuretics of the thiazide group help to control the oedema and, provided enough healthy tissue remains, remove both the fluid and the waste-products.

Artificial Kidneys or **Dialysers** as they are known, are widely used in patients' own homes, thus obviating in some cases long journeys to hospital twice a week for treatment. Dialysis is a relatively temporary measure; renal transplants now offer real hope to many sufferers although there are far more suitable recipients than potential donors. Currently 2,000 transplants a year come from deceased donors, 1,000 from living donors.

Pyelitis (Pyelonephritis), infection of the pelvis of the kidney, that is to say, of the part where the ureter leaves the kidney. Usually caused by Escherichia coli, which is normally present in the body, or by the Streptococcus. These germs may reach the ureter through the blood-stream or may pass upwards from the bladder. Obstruction anywhere in the urinary tract which causes the urine to stagnate is liable to cause pyelitis. Symptoms come on suddenly, with high fever, pain in the loin (the infection is usually on one side only, and is commoner in women), and pain in the abdomen. When urine is passed there is a burning sensation, and it is passed frequently and in small amounts, On examination, the urine is found to be highly acid and full of Escherichia coli or whatever the causative germ may be.

Pyelitis is fairly readily treated by the antibiotics or sulpha drugs. Plenty of fluids should be given and the urine made alkaline.

Cystitis means inflammation of the bladder, either acute or chronic, and its causes are much the same as in the case of pyelitis. There is pain over the lower abdomen, frequency, and sometimes slight fever. The treatment is as for pyelitis.

Urethritis is an inflammation of the urethra, with burning pain on passing water and frequency. The most serious cause (although it can usually be easily dealt with now) is gonorrhoea. But nonspecific urethritis is common, especially in the newly wed and in this case various germs or none may bring about pain and frequency; there is often a large neurotic element.

Urethritis should be regarded as probably due to gonorrhoea when there is a thick, creamy discharge from the penis or discharge in women following sexual intercourse with an infected person.

Kidney Stones *or* **Renal Calculi** sometimes form, and, as in the case of gall-stones, what causes them is not certain. They may be caused by disorders of metabolism—that is, in the inability of the body to deal with calcium, proteins, uric acid, and other products; or by vitamin deficiency, obstruction in the urinary tract, and urinary infections. But when a stone or stones are formed various events may occur: thus it may remain in the kidney and cause no symptoms; or it may cause repeated attacks of pain, infection, and blood in the urine (haematuria); or it may completely block the passage of urine from the kidney to such a degree that it degenerates and becomes useless; or, lastly, it may pass into the ureter, and when this occurs very severe pain, known as *renal colic*, will occur. A stone passing down the ureter into the bladder may become stuck in the urethra, although this is uncommon, since a stone small enough to get down the ureters is likely to be capable of manoeuvring through the rest of the tract. In fact, about 80–90 per cent. of stones are passed spontaneously.

Stones not passed spontaneously must have to be removed by operation, but whether this is undertaken or not depends on various factors, such as the health of the patient, the amount of trouble caused by the stone, and the health of the other kidney—for it is dangerous to operate on one kidney unless one is sure that the other is functioning efficiently. Lithotripters are also used to fragment stones without needing invasive surgery. Emergency hospital admissions for kidney stones have doubled in the last decade.

Hydronephrosis. If a stone blocks the passage of urine on one side for any length of time *hydronephrosis* may result, in which the part where the ureter enters the kidney swells with the retained urine. Ultimately much of the kidney may be destroyed by the back-pressure. The same effect may be produced by kinking of the ureter or anything else which causes obstruction. Sometimes children are born with hydronephrosis, and when the dilation is due to kinking of the tube the condition may be intermittent, with attacks of renal colic during which only small amounts of urine are passed; this is followed with relief and the passage of large quantities.

Cancer of the Kidney. The kidney may also be the site of tumours and cysts which produce pain in the loins, sometimes a lump over the kidney which can be felt, and blood in the urine. Cases of kidney cancer have risen by a third in the last 15 years.

Cancer of the Bladder is a serious condition in which the bladder may have to be removed, so the urinary flow has then to be directed elsewhere. Either the ureters are brought out on to the skin surface, a procedure known as *cutaneous ureterostomy*, or they

are implanted in the large bowel, so that the urine flows out with the faeces. This is described as *uretero-colostomy*. Men infected with gonorrhoea are twice as likely to develop cancer of the bladder.

There may also be benign tumours of the bladder or *papillomas*, which are soft and bleed easily; a great deal of blood is passed, but there is usually little or no pain. In this, and similar, diseases of the bladder examination of the inside of the organ is carried out by means of a cystoscope, a thin tube which is passed up the urethra with fibre-optic light guides which enable the surgeon to see what is going on. Instruments may also be passed through the tube, and simple papillomas can be cauterised. Similar instruments are used to examine the stomach (gastroscope) and the bronchial tubes (bronchoscope).

When some obstruction in the outlet of the bladder or in the urethra occurs the bladder, of course, fills with urine, which cannot be passed, and very painful dilation occurs. In this case an attempt may be made to pass a catheter, a thin rubber tube, into the bladder to relieve the tension, or if this fails a *suprapubic cystotomy* is performed—an incision is made in the abdomen over the bladder and a tube inserted into it, through which the urine escapes.

This is ordinarily a temporary expedient, and when the patient's health has improved an attempt will be made to remove the cause of obstruction.

Prostate Gland. The common cause of such obstruction is *enlargement of the prostate gland* at the base of the bladder, which surrounds this area and the beginning of the ureter. About 40% of men over sixty have some degree of obstruction due to this cause, and *c.* 20% of these require an operation. More information is available at www.ProstateUK.org

The gland is the size of a walnut, and, as we have seen, its function is to supply part of the fluid which makes up the semen, the male sex secretion. Enlargement of the prostate may be benign or malignant, and, although nobody knows just why, such benign enlargement tends to occur in most men in later life. There may be no symptoms, but characteristically there is frequency during the day and the need to get up at night to pass water. The flow of urine being impeded by constriction of the urethra, the passage is less forceful than normal, and there is a tendency for dribbling to occur. If the obstruction is severe and not relieved the backpressure may be transmitted to the ureters and kidneys, resulting finally in kidney failure and uraemia. The prostate, except in cases of very mild enlargement, has to be removed either through the abdomen or through the perineum (the part of the body lying between the sex organs and the anus). Sometimes, in less serious cases, it is possible without an incision to cut away the obstructing part by an electrocautery inserted, as is a cystoscope, through the urethra.

Prostatectomy was once a serious operation, all the more so because the patient was usually elderly and not in good condition, but new techniques and the use of antibiotics have transformed the outlook.

Cancer of the Prostate is a potentially serious disease, but if diagnosed early and is localised, may be cured by surgery or radiotherapy. If the disease spreads, or has spread at the time of diagnosis, it can often be controlled. It can often be diagnosed early by a PSA blood test (all men should consult their GP from time to time over this). It is the second commonest male cancer in the UK (killing 11,000 men a year). Each year around 42,000 men are diagnosed with this cancer. African-Caribbean men are three times more likely to develop prostate cancer. Asian males are less likely. A new genetic test for the disease is now available. And new blood tests are being developed. Readers may wish to refer to www.prostate-cancer.org.

THE NERVOUS SYSTEM.

The nervous system consists of the central nervous system and the peripheral nervous system. The brain and spinal cord make up the former. The latter consists of the nerve fibres by which the central nervous system is connected to all parts of the body. Human beings have a more complicated brain than any other animal species, but it is only its complexity which makes it different from the brains of other mammals like rats and pigs and cows. We do not have the largest brains, since whales, for example, have much larger ones. Ours is not even the largest for the size of the body.

Before describing some of the diseases of the nervous system it will be helpful to say a little about how it is made and how it works. Each human brain probably contains about ten thousand million (10,000,000,000) nerve cells and perhaps four or five times this number of supporting "glial" cells. Each nerve cell has many long thin branching projections, called dendrites, rather like the branches of a tree, leading to many thousands of "twigs" for each single nerve cell.

At the end of each "twig" there is a special structure called a *synapse* by which contact is made with other nerve cells. It is through these connections that very large numbers of nerve cells give information (or send impulses) to each other so that they can be co-ordinated. As well as these dendritic branches, each nerve cell gives off one large trunk called the *axon*, down which final messages are sent as the result of all the information it receives from its dendrites. Some axons are many feet long. Some end in another synapse, by which the outgoing message is passed to yet another nerve cell. Some axons, those of the peripheral nerves, end directly on organs like muscles or glands, instructing them and making them work.

Transmission of Messages. Messages are passed along dendrites and axons as electrical impulses. These are generated in the nerve cell "body." They are modified according to information received from other nerve cells and propagated down the axon. It is this superficial resemblance to a series of electrical cables which has given rise to comparisons of the brain with a telephone system or a computer, and the comparison is not a bad one. However, the brain generates its own electric power from the fuel brought in its own blood supply; and no spare parts or spare cables are available if the originals should get damaged, except in peripheral nerves. Furthermore the contact of one nerve cell with another through a synapse is not an electrical contact, and neither is the contact between a nerve and the muscle or other organ it is controlling. In both cases the connection is chemical. Thus when an electrical impulse arrives at the end of the nerve fibre, a chemical is released into the gap between it and the next nerve or organ, and it is this chemical which carries the stimulus forward. There is also an arrangement to neutralise the chemical transmitter when the impulse has been transmitted. So the resemblance to a telephone exchange or computer can sometimes be misleading.

Myelin Sheaths.

Many of the nerve axons which transmit electrical impulses are clothed in fatty *myelin sheaths*, a little like the plastic insulation around an electric wire. Here again the resemblance is only partial, since the myelin sheaths are interrupted at regular intervals and these gaps in the insulation play an important role in transmitting the impulse. One of the important functions of the non-nervous *glial* cells of the brain is to manufacture and maintain the myelin sheaths.

The Functions of the Brain.

Many of the functions of the brain are little known, and even the ones we know about are very poorly understood. It is the organ of higher mental function, of the mind and intellect, but much remains to be done on linking the different functions of the brain with the structures found within it. The brain is known to control all bodily functions by means of *motor* and other nerves which carry impulses from the brain outwards to all parts of the body. Sometimes these are under our voluntary control; mostly they are involuntary, reflex or automatic. Reflex actions are the result of impulses passed inwards from the body towards the brain by means of sensory nerves. Information arriving in the brain about the various sensations like heat, pain, touch, position, the need for saliva or gastric juice or even the thought or smell of food, are acted on in the various "centres" in the brain. These send out instructions down the "motor" or "secretary" nerves which instruct the muscles or glands to take appropriate action. Thus a *reflex* has a "sensory ending" which appreciates some sort of sensation. This is converted into an electrical impulse which is sent towards the brain or spinal cord along a sensory or "afferent" nerve. The impulse arrives at a "centre" in the central nervous system which co-ordinates all the relevant information and issues instructions. These travel as impulses outwards, along "efferent" nerves towards "effector" organs like muscles or glands, and an appropriate action occurs automatically.

The pathway from sensory ending to effector organ is called a *reflex arc*. Many reflex activities are partly under voluntary control, although mainly automatic. If you touch something hot you will automatically withdraw your hand. But if it is a hot china cup which has cost you a lot of money, you are capable of overriding the tendency to drop it, at least for a time. Breathing is automatic, but it can also be controlled, again at least for a time.

Clearly the brain is a very delicately organised piece of machinery, and its cells are extremely specialised for their job. Achieving this kind of specialised perfection brings many difficulties, however, and the brain cells have become highly dependent on the proper functioning of the other body systems, especially the blood circulation, the respiratory system, and the systems regulating the detailed nutrient composition of the blood. Failure of these systems, even for a very short time, can damage the nerve cells. Nearly all death is produced this way, by an ultimate interference with nerve cell function.

Recently, scientists have shown that the brains of men and women are wired completely differently.

Vulnerability of the Brain.

We have already mentioned that the brain and spinal cord are unable to repair or replace any components which get damaged. The vulnerability of the brain is even more obvious when it is realised how easily damage and destruction can occur. For example, unless a rich supply of oxygen and glucose is continuously arriving in the blood stream, brain cells will cease to function in a few seconds and will die in a few minutes, and they can never be replaced. This is in marked contrast to other tissues of the body. The leg, for example, may carry on for over half an hour without any blood at all because the muscle and other cells can find other ways of surviving. Thus the brain can be permanently damaged if the blood contains insufficient oxygen (through asphyxia), insufficient glucose, or if the blood pressure falls.

All these are likely to happen to any of us at any time, and so there are elaborate mechanisms trying to prevent them occurring. Much of the subject of physiology is concerned with the mechanisms designed to protect the brain, and most of us ultimately die because they eventually fail. One of the clever features of the body design is that all the mechanisms which protect the brain from a supply failure are controlled by the brain itself. Thus the brain has itself been made to control the heart beat and the breathing and the many other systems which are needed for its own survival.

Diagnostic Techniques in Neurology. The doctor has many ways of testing the nervous system, most of which test its various functions as outlined in the introduction. Thus tests of sensation, muscular movement and reflexes of all kinds as well as the special functions of taste, smell, vision, hearing, speech and intellect play a part.

A great deal can be learned about the brain by *arteriography*. In this test a radio-opaque substance is put into the arteries supplying the brain, and an X-ray picture taken immediately afterwards shows up all the blood vessels. *Myelography* is an X-ray of the spinal cord after a radio-opaque substance has been injected into the space between the spinal cord and the bony vertebral canal housing it.

Computerised tomography (CT) scanning and Magnetic Resonance Imaging (MRI) have now made "invasive" diagnostic tests less necessary.

In another development, *radioactive isotopes* can

be put into the blood stream and carried into the brain where they can be detected from outside the skull by counters. *Electroencephalography* measures the electrical waves generated by the brain by placing electrodes on the scalp. *Electromyography* does the same for muscles.

Consciousness and Unconsciousness (Coma). Everyone knows what consciousness is until he tries to define it. Full consciousness is generally taken to imply not only wakefulness but the total complement of human mental faculties. In clinical medicine, however, something less than this is usually meant. For example a demented person, or one whose memory is lost (*amnesia*), or one whose powers of speech are lost (*aphasia*) may still be "conscious."

There is really a continuous gradation between full consciousness and coma, passing through drowsiness and even "stupor" in which condition a patient can be aroused from coma but sinks back into it when left alone.

Many different things can cause coma ranging from swelling of the brain, compressing it in its rigid box of bone, to disorders in other body systems resulting in a failure to provide for the brain's needs. Examples of the first are bleeding within the brain or *brain tumours*, both of which occupy space and can only do so by producing compression. In the second category are asphyxia preventing oxygen from reaching the brain, lack of glucose in the blood, circulatory failure in which there is insufficient blood, or insufficient blood pressure. Fainting is a comparatively minor example.

Sleep and Insomnia. The real reason for sleep is to produce myelin, to replenish the brain cells. Sleep is quite different from coma or even stupor, since as much oxygen and glucose is necessary asleep as awake. Insomnia is experienced by everyone at some time, and for some reason can be very distressing if it persists. There are three forms: failing to get to sleep, intermittent wakefulness, and awaking early. Nearly all insomniacs sleep more than they think. They should eat light evening meals and avoid stimulants like tea and coffee after mid-day. Elderly people should realise they need less sleep. Being cold or having a full bladder can be a cause. Or simply not being tired. Sedative drugs are a last resort, but they can be useful in "breaking the habit" of wakefulness. Obviously there may be psychological factors such as anxiety and excitement.

Narcolepsy, a true inability to keep awake is rare. The name was coined by Jean Baptiste Édouard Gélineau in 1880.

Headache. We must distinguish between the very common varieties of comparatively trivial significance and the rare ones due to serious causes. Some headaches are due to continuous tightness in muscles of the scalp, and are often "nervous" or psychological in origin. Others result from nose blockage and congestion, sinus problems, eye strain, toothache, *etc.* Migraine is a special kind and will be described below. Very occasionally indeed headache is due to serious disease like brain tumour. Most headache results from "living it up" or being "run down," or both.

The headache of alcoholic hangover is probably due to dehydration. It can often be avoided by consuming a great quantity of water (a half litre or so, before going to bed), but few people are prepared to do this in the circumstances. Be careful when using aspirin, which is a useful remedy for headache, since it is very dangerous for people with stomach complaints. Occasionally aspirin makes the stomach bleed, and this can be so severe as to kill. Paracetamol is much safer.

Migraine. This is a very special variety of "sick headache" and requires special treatment under medical supervision. It has many different forms, but usually there is a definite sequence of events. An attack often starts with some alteration of vision. The patient has shimmering blind spots or other visual disorders. This is followed by a localised severe headache. The whole thing is caused by a poorly understood disorder of the blood vessels. There are special drugs, which are effective, especially if used when the first signs of an attack appear. Handheld devices to "zap" the brain with magnetic pulses have been introduced. A gene

linked to migraine was identified in 2011. Migraine affects more women (18%) than men (8%). It has been linked to brain lesions.

Although there is a direct physical cause for an attack, it is also certain that some of the trouble is psychological tenseness. People with migraine are often rather anxious, striving and perfectionist people. Also it has been noticed that attacks are much less frequent when the necessary pills are being carried available for use. However, as with all other conditions which are partly "psychological" in origin they are none the less distressing for the patient. It simply means that the treatment is also partly psychological. Readers may wish to go to www.migrainetrust.org for further information.

Menière's Disease is one of the conditions in which the organ of balance in the middle ear is affected, giving rise to *vertigo*, a form of giddiness. It usually begins in middle life in the same sort of person who sometimes has migraine. There is buzzing in the ears and some intermittent loss of hearing as well as vertigo. During an attack the patient may be unable to walk because of his loss of balance, and nausea and vomiting are common. Treatment is by special drugs, and occasionally an operation on the ear is necessary.

Epilepsy is a symptom, not a disease, which is common at all ages but especially in children. It is the most common brain disorder in every country. In the UK alone there are 450,000 sufferers. Epilepsy Research UK has a helpful website (www.eruk.uk).

Many varieties of attack occur often in the same patient, the commonest and best known being the *grand mal* or major seizure. In this the patient falls down unconscious and rigid and the jaw is clenched, so that there is danger of the tongue being bitten. This so-called *tonic phase* is followed, within a minute or so, by a *clonic phase* in which the limbs contract rhythmically. The attack ends with the patient going limp and gradually recovering consciousness, a process which may take up to an hour. Occasionally the patient has a brief warning, most often an indescribable feeling in the stomach.

Dravet Syndrome is a severe form of epilepsy.

Minor Seizures. There are two common forms of minor seizure, one occurring mainly in children and the other more often in adults. The common minor attacks in children are often called *petit mal* or *absence*, which well describes the instantaneous and brief loss of consciousness often unaccompanied by any change in posture. Recovery is equally instantaneous. On the other hand, in the other forms of epilepsy which arise from various parts of the brain, but especially from the lobe under the temporal region, there is often a warning similar to that which may precede a major seizure. In these cases the patient shows only confusion, no definite loss of posture, but automatic activity such as fumbling with buttons, muttering, and grimacing. After these attacks there may be a period of confusion in which the patient may wander away and even be violent.

Convulsions. Many people have had one or two fits in their lives, maybe at times of physical or psychological stress. "Fever" or "Febrile" convulsions (often called teething fits in the past) are extremely common in young children and are often thought of as something different from epilepsy since the attacks rarely continue in later years. This form of epilepsy and some cases of *petit mal* are the only forms in which hereditary factors are important in the causation, and these are the least serious forms of epilepsy. They are very rarely associated with serious physical or psychological disturbances. Most other forms of epilepsy are due to a scar or other area of brain damage. It is a proportion of these cases which develop the psychological disturbances that are occasionally very serious.

Not every patient who has had one or two fits need necessarily take regular anticonvulsant drugs; that is drugs which damp down the abnormal excessive activity of the brain that leads to the attacks. Many new drugs can now be used.

Patients, however, often find it difficult to get work because of the reluctance of employers to take on someone who may be more prone to accidents and whose fits may distress other workers. Obviously there are some jobs which epilepsy sufferers should not do because of the danger involved (from for example, moving machinery), and they should not drive a car. A few cases are so severe that work is almost impossible, but employers have a duty whenever possible to employ these people whose mental health may suffer greatly if they are made to feel outcasts and who ordinarily are as efficient, or even more so, as the next person.

Congenital Malformations. The proper shape of the brain and spinal cord is achieved quite early in development by about the thirteenth week after conception. During this time very slight changes in the foetal environment can produce disastrous malformations. The drug thalidomide, for example, operated on other body systems while they were passing through this phase of construction. Some viruses can do the same thing. Most malformations are without known cause, but it is certain that something went wrong at this very early stage, and it only needs a very minor interference with the normal process to do the permanent damage. At about this time the bones of the spine are beginning to enclose, or form a roof over the developing spinal cord. Sometimes they fail to complete the process, resulting in *spina bifida*. If the coverings of the cord protrude through the defect, this is a *meningocoele*, and if the cord itself protrudes it is a *meningomyelocoele*. The whole protrusion may be covered with skin, but if it is not, the cord soon becomes infected. The effect on the patient is variable, according to the amount of damage to the nerve fibres in the cord, and there are varying degrees of paralysis and loss of sensation below the area involved and loss of bowel and bladder control. Much help can often be obtained from surgical repair, but many cases remain in a distressing condition always, and the only really useful attack on the problem is research to find the cause and prevent it happening. The same is true of the *malformations of the brain*. In one of these, hydrocephaly, the narrow channel is blocked which transmits the cerebrospinal fluid from the chambers within the brain where it is secreted to the outer coverings to be taken back into the blood stream. Blockage of the channel (or aqueduct) results in distension of the brain by fluid, enlargement of the head, and mental retardation. Sometimes a by-pass valve can be inserted to restore normal fluid circulation.

Cerebral Palsy is a physically disabling condition of impaired muscle co-ordination caused before, during or shortly after birth by damage to or maldevelopment in the portion of the brain which controls movement. There are 3 main types: *spasticity*, *athetosis*, and *ataxia* depending on what area of the brain has been affected. Inherited defects do not play a large part in cerebral palsy. The general incidence of the disorder is thought to be 2·5 per 1,000 births. For further information and advice contact: SCOPE, 12 Park Crescent, London W1N 4EQ.

Motor Neurone Disease. This is a group of related diseases usually occurring in people over 40, in whom the parts of the brain and spinal cord which look after muscular movement degenerate. The group includes *amyotrophic lateral sclerosis*, *progressive muscular atrophy*, *progressive bulbar palsy*, and *primary lateral sclerosis*.

The results are paralysis or weakness with wasting of the muscles of the body, including those concerned with arms, legs, breathing, speaking, *etc.* At present, it is a fatal, progressive disease. Around half of those diagnosed die within two years. The Motor Neurone Disease Association provides help and advice. *See* www.mndassociation.org

Parkinson's Disease, formerly known as the shaking palsy, derives its present name from the London physician James Parkinson (1755–1824). It is one of the commonest illnesses to affect the human brain with more than one in 500 of the population as a whole (though one in 100 of those above 60 years of age) suffering from it. The average age of onset is about 55 though one in seven contract it before they reach 50. It has three classical features: shaking (or tremor), muscular rigidity and poverty of movement. A stooping, shuffling gait and a mask-like loss of facial expression are common. It is a progressive disease affecting patients in variable degrees of severity and different degrees of progression. A good deal can now be done to help these patients with drugs and since the condition results

from a malfunctioning of brain cells which produce a chemical 'messenger' known as dopamine replacement of this substance by the drug L-Dopa (often accompanied by an additive in a combined preparation) is often the first line of treatment. Occasionally younger patients have benefited from surgical destruction of small areas of diseased brain.

In rare cases the disease is hereditary, but normally the cause is unknown (although a gene responsible for some cases of Parkinson's has been found). A link with depression has also been found. Sometimes people with Parkinson's may also develop dementia–a doubly cruel blow. Scientists are now considering the possibility of using cloned embryonic stem cells.

It is important to remember that many old people have some tremor of the head or hands called *senile tremor* and this is *not* Parkinson's Disease. It is merely one of the features of achieving advanced seniority as a citizen. The Parkinson's Disease Society sponsors medical research and patient welfare.

Chorea. This is a group of diseases in which there is involuntary muscle movement, weakness, and emotional instability. There will be clumsiness, awkward gait, twitching of limbs, face, hands, trunk, or tongue. They include *acute chorea* or *St. Vitus' dance* occurring in children from 5 to 15, *hereditary or Huntington's chorea* occurring in a well-defined genetic pattern and beginning later, between 35 and 50. *Tics* or habit spasms are not part of these diseases but are often of psychological origin. They are usually eye blinking or head shaking.

Stroke Illness *or* Cerebrovascular Diseases. Strokes are due to diseases of the brain's blood vessels which either burst or get blocked. The same blood vessel disorders cause heart attacks by blocking the coronary arteries supplying the heart. Strokes and heart attacks together kill more people than any other single cause including cancer. They account for one death in every five. Perhaps less is known of the cause of this disease than is known about cancer, and much more research is needed to find out if it is to be prevented.

Massive advances in the care and treatment of stroke victims have been made. Treatments such as *thrombolysis* restores the flow of blood to the brain. Improvements in *rehabilitation* have taken giant strides towards limiting long-term effects.

Infarction. If any artery supplying blood to any part of the brain is blocked, the territory supplied will die; and the bodily functions for which that part of the brain is responsible will cease. The process is called *infarction* of the brain, the dead area being an *infarct*. The blockage is usually due to thrombosis of the blood within a vessel, a *thrombus* being a rather complicated clot with a structure of its own. The underlying cause is the arterial disease, *atheroma*, together with stagnation of the circulation. About one blockage in ten is due to a small piece of a much larger thrombus in the heart chambers being flung into the blood stream and impacting in the distant vessel in the brain. This is *cerebral embolism*.

If the area of dead or infarcted brain is not too large the patient will recover from his unconsciousness, but will be left with permanent loss of function (paralysis, *etc.*) related to that part of the brain.

When a blood vessel supplying the brain bursts, this causes *cerebral haemorrhage* or apoplexy. The vessel may be on the surface (*subarachnoid haemorrhage*) or in the depths of the tissue (*intracerebral haemorrhage*). Strokes tend to occur in older people, because the associated arterial disease is a product of age and high blood pressure.

Occasionally a subarachnoid haemorrhage occurs in a younger person with an unsuspected malformation of the arteries of the base of the brain known as a *berry aneurysm*. This is a small berry-sized blown-out balloon due to a defect in the wall of the vessel. Berry aneurysms can often be treated surgically. Intracerebral haemorrhage carries a very poor outlook, however, since much brain tissue is often destroyed by the escaping blood, especially the deep tissues responsible for the vital functions.

Haemorrhage within the brain cavity can also be caused by injury.

Inflammatory Diseases of the Nervous System. The membranes covering the brain are called the meninges. Inflammation of these, nearly always by blood-borne infection or infection following injury, is called *meningitis* (*see* **Z13(2)**). Cerebrospinal or spotted fever was only one variety caused by a germ called "meningococcus."

Almost any other germ may cause meningitis, and when the germ is susceptible to one of the antibiotics it is usually treatable. It will usually be necessary to identify the germ by taking a sample of cerebrospinal fluid from a convenient space around the spinal cord in the lower back. When the disease is caused by the tubercle bacillus (*tuberculous meningitis*) the problem is more difficult because the patient is often not so obviously ill until the later, less treatable stages.

Cerebral Abscess, or abscess of the brain is very serious because it occupies space in the closed box of the skull and compresses the brain, as well as being a destructive process. It may arise due to an infected piece of tissue or pus being carried to the brain in the blood stream from a distant site in the lungs or heart.

Encephalitis. When the brain or cord tissue is itself inflamed it is called *encephalitis* (brain) or *myelitis* (cord) or *encephalo-myelitis* (both).

Herpes Zoster (Shingles) is a common viral infection of the nervous system which affects sensory nerve roots where they enter the spinal cord. The initial symptoms are of pain in the area supplied by the affected nerves—commonly one side of the trunk, the buttock or the face—followed by the appearance of blisters. Treatment nowadays is usually with a course of the drug Zovirax. Soothing lotions may be applied to the blisters and analgesics given for the pain. The disease is fairly short-lived, but neuralgia may persist for weeks after the blisters have healed.

Shingles is interesting in that it is not a *primary* viral infection, but the result of reactivation of the varicella-zoster virus (so called because it causes *either* chicken pox or shingles) which has lain dormant in nerve root cells, probably since childhood. Primary infection with the virus at whatever age causes chicken pox, not shingles; if an adult who has never had chicken pox or shingles comes into contact with a child with chicken pox or an adult with shingles, he is likely to contract the former but not the latter.

Shingles is infectious from the time the blisters appear until they have crusted over and healed. However, it is not as infectious as chicken pox. The NHS offers shingles vaccine for the over-70s.

Multiple Sclerosis (MS) is the most important of the *demyelinating diseases* in which the myelin or "fatty" sheaths which insulate nerve fibres appear to disintegrate. This occurs patchily and seemingly randomly throughout the central nervous system (*i.e.* the brain and spinal cord) and results in interference with the passage of impulses through the affected nerves. Changes in sensation, balance or muscular co-ordination occur at varying intervals of time and spaced out over months or years in such a way as to appear unconnected. There is at present no reliable, objective diagnostic test for multiple sclerosis and diagnosis has to be made from the history of such episodic symptoms.

The cause is unknown, but one theory is that MS is the result of a recrudescence of a dormant viral infection which may be picked up during the teenage years.

Others hold it to be an auto-immune disease. It is commonly held that once diagnosis of MS is made it means a sentence of years of increasingly severe disablement which will progress relentlessly and inexorably. That may be the case, but in fact such a gloomy picture is very uncommon. New treatments (such as injecting patients with their own bone marrow stem cells) continue to give hope for sufferers. A new drug, alemtuzumab, offers promise of reversing the disease in its early stages. Two new treatments, using fingolimod and cladribine, are the first MS treatments in tablet form. Benztropine, a drug used to treat Parkinson's disease, has been found to repair nerve fibres damaged by MS. Recent studies suggest vitamin D plays a major role as well as lack of exposure to strong sunlight. Stem cell treatment may offer exciting future possibilities.

Much research has gone into the natural history of MS and it is clear that there are various distinct patterns of the disease. These cover a wide range of symptom patterns from that characterised by a sudden onset of symptoms with relatively few relapses after the first year, to that manifested by sudden onset followed by unremitting relapses causing progressively greater degrees of physical impairment which may indeed lead to much distressing disability and relatively early death. But between these two extremes, of which the first is far the commonest form for the disease to take and the latter relatively infrequent, there lies a whole range of disease patterns and prediction is difficult.

In 2011 researchers found what they called the "missing link" in treating MS - a new molecule that could lead to drugs to repair damage caused by MS. Also, it appears a 'salt overload' in the brain may be a major factor. There is also evidence linking MS to low levels of Vitamin D. More than 100,000 people in the UK suffer from MS and it is the most common neurological condition affecting young adults.

The Multiple Sclerosis Society exists to sponsor research, to care for patients and to give advice and support to friends and relatives. The web address is www.mssociety.org.uk.

Brain Tumours. The brain is no exception to the rule that any cell in any tissue of the body can suddenly begin to disobey the body's rules regarding its growth and multiplication. A largely unknown mechanism governs how many cells of a certain type there ought to be and calls a halt to cell multiplication when this number is reached. Every now and then one of them turns a blind eye and goes on dividing, and the result is a tumour, or lump, of anarchic cells which obey no rules. Tumours are commonest in cells which normally go on dividing throughout life, in order to replace those lost by wear and tear. Examples are the cells lining the air passages in the lung, or the alimentary tract in the stomach or large bowel. Fortunately for the brain there is little cell division once it has grown. Nerve cells cannot divide at all in adult life, and the supporting glial cells only do so in response to injury.

Primary brain tumours are therefore much less common than those elsewhere. Also many brain tumours like many of those elsewhere, are benign or "innocent" tumours. They are not cancerous, and need only be removed for the patient to be completely cured. The brain, however, is at two major disadvantages compared with other tissues when it comes to tumours. One is that all tumours as they grow take up space, and space in the skull is already fully occupied. Thus even an innocent tumour can compress the brain within its rigid box of bone and become most dangerous until it is removed. The second disadvantage is due to the very large blood supply of the brain. Cancer in other parts of the body spreads partly by sending small pieces of itself to other tissues by way of the blood stream, and those tissues like liver, lung, kidney, and brain which have a big blood supply naturally receive more than their share of other tissues' tumour. These secondary deposits, or *metastases*, cause compression and other trouble in the brain much more frequently than the brain's own primary tumours. Indeed convulsions or other signs of brain disorder may be the first indication that there is a primary tumour in the lung or breast or elsewhere.

Diseases of Peripheral Nerves. Compared with the nerves of the central nervous system (brain and spinal cord), the peripheral nerves are comparatively rarely affected by disease. They have some similarities of structure with central nerve fibres in that their fibres are often covered with myelin sheaths and are arranged in bundles. A special feature, however, is that they are enclosed by connective tissue sheaths and it is probably these which allow a peripheral nerve to grow again, or regenerate, after it has been cut or damaged. Central nerve fibres are unable to do this. After *injury of a peripheral nerve* the part away from the centre is cut off from its parent cell body and it dies. All function, whether motor or sensory, is lost. But in the course of many months the central surviving part grows into the connective tissue sheaths which act like tubes to guide the new nerve to its destination. Provided the cut ends are close enough together and correctly aligned, and provided enough fibres reach their correct destination, good functional recovery is possible.

Neuropathy. A disorder of a peripheral nerve is called a *neuropathy*. There are many kinds. One of the most distressing is *trigeminal neuralgia*, again fortunately rare. The trigeminal or fifth cranial nerve has a motor and sensory territory on the face. In this condition there are paroxysmal episodes of extremely severe pain which may resist all treatment except destruction of the nerve itself with consequent facial paralysis and loss of sensation.

Bell's Palsy is the sudden loss of function of the seventh cranial nerve and there is again paralysis on one side of the face which usually recovers in time. Some bacterial diseases, especially leprosy, invade the nerves themselves. Chronic alcoholism may affect the nerves, as may diabetes, probably by interfering with the nutrition of the nerve cell. So may exposure to arsenic or lead or an unpleasant nerve poison which may contaminate cooking oil known as TOCP, or triorthocresylphosphate.

Muscular Dystrophies. These are a series of diseases of muscle in which there is progressive wasting and weakness of muscle, the causes of which are entirely unknown. They are divided up according to the age of onset and the muscles involved. *Duchenne's muscular dystrophy* occurs in the first decade of life. It affects most of the muscles eventually, including the heart muscle and those concerned with breathing, and so the outlook is not good. It is caused by mutations in DNA that block the body from producing a key muscle protein. Weakness in legs and hips spreads to the rest of the body.

The Muscular Dystrophy Group (Nattrass House, 35 Macaulay Rd. London SW4 0QP) gives great assistance to sufferers.

Myasthenia Gravis. This is a strange disorder of the mechanism which transmits instructions from nerve to muscle at the "neuromuscular junction," leading to extreme weakness.

Creutzfeldt-Jakob Disease causes fatal degeneration of the central nervous system. It may be sporadic, genetic or transmitted, and results from the accumulation of abnormally folded proteins in the brain. It is now clear that some cases resulted from eating animals infected with Bovine Spongiform Encephalopathy, BSE or "mad cow disease".

MENTAL ILLNESS

Conventionally mental illness is divided into two categories, **psychosis** (madness), and **neurosis** (exaggerated symptoms of commonly experienced states). Psychoses are themselves divided into: *organic*, implying that we can identify a physical cause, and *functional*, where the brain structure appears to be intact but its performance is abnormal. This division is now seen to be very blurred since there are physical diseases and drugs which can lower the threshold for response, or alter a person's perceptions so that he appears to be mad, albeit temporarily. The more research is done, the more organic causes are found for this behaviour.

Organic Psychoses: Dementia.

The organic psychoses result from actual damage to the brain. This damage can be caused by disease, as in syphilis; by tumours; by dietary deficiencies, as in inadequate vitamin B12 absorption; by poisons such as alcohol and lead; by drugs such as LSD or amphetamine; by problems of blood circulation such as heart failure or atheroma; and by genetic inheritance. The onset of illness can be either an acute confusional state or a chronic reaction known as *dementia*. The acute episode is characterised by an impairment of consciousness which may vary from difficulty in holding on to the point of a story, to actual coma. The chronic reaction, on the other hand, does not affect consciousness but intellect, memory and personality.

Memory for recent events is lost, while that for remote ones is preserved. About one in ten men and women over the age of 65 is likely to be affected. All GPs have now to be trained to detect the early signs of dementia. *See also* **Z59**.

Alcohol-Related Problems.

Since it is the most commonly and voluntarily ingested poison, it is worth giving a special mention to alcohol. Alcohol-related disabilities can be classed as social, psychological and physical. Social problems are often noticed first, and include failure to perform an expected role as parent or spouse or at work. Psychological difficulties include increased depression and personality deterioration. *Delerium tremens*, (DTs), is an acute confusional state involving intense fear and restlessness with hallucinations.

Most alcoholics experience blackouts ranging from momentary lapses to memory loss involving several hours. Intellectual impairment can occur and may be permanent. Physical problems associated with alcoholism include a doubled death rate, liver damage, gastritis, anaemia, increased rates of cancer, and infections such as TB. Sexual impotence is common. The children of alcoholic mothers are at increased risk of problems.

The Alcoholics Anonymous national helpline number is 0845 769 7555. Drinkline is a free and confidential service (the number is 0800 917 8282).

Schizophrenia.

Functional psychoses broadly fall into two categories: *schizophrenia* and *manic depressive psychosis*. Schizophrenia was a term introduced by Eugene Bleuler in 1911 to describe a group of illnesses in which there was a splitting of the psychic functioning so that the association between two ideas was bizarre, and mood seemed inappropriate to the circumstances. Nowadays schizophrenia is diagnosed on the presence of certain accepted symptoms such as a lack of insight, auditory hallucinations, unreasonable suspicions, a flatness of response *etc*.

Schizophrenia occurs in all societies. About one person in a hundred will develop the condition, and there is an increased risk where close relations are affected. Certainly, DNA mutations play a major role. Vitamin D deficiency also plays a part.

There are many theories of causation though an inheritance factor is clear, but there is argument about what this factor might be, and the extent to which its influence is affected by life events. Theories invoking abnormalities in the substances responsible for the transmission of signals within the brain itself are supported by the fact that some symptoms of schizophrenia can be induced experimentally. But as yet the physical theories are not wholly proven. Genes undoubtedly play a part and a genetic fault linked to the condition was identified in 2013. Over 100 genes play some kind of role in the development of the illness.

The 'double bind' hypothesis of Bateson, that an emotionally disturbed parent, who says one thing to a child but at the same time suggests a deeper, contradictory, message will cause the child to withdraw into a fantasy world, is another explanation. Whatever the role of early experience in causing schizophrenia, current stress brings on an attack.

Schizophrenia affects over 220,000 people in England at any given time. Many people are concerned that schizophrenia remains a 'forgotten illness'.

Treatment of Schizophrenia. This was revolutionised by the use back in the 1950s of phenothiazine drugs which not only tranquillise but also have specific anti-psychotic effects. The fact that schizophrenic patients are increasingly returned to their community, able to function, is due in large part to these pharmacological advances, and to the concept of 'milieu therapy' involving group activities, recreation and occupational therapies. Now, most people who have schizophrenia do not need continuous treatment in hospital.

Bipolar Disorder (BPD) (once known as **Manic Depression**) is characterised by swings of mood between depression and elation without apparent cause, and in this form is called the *bipolar* state.

More frequently, the disease is *unipolar*, showing only periods of depression interspersed with periods of normality. The difficulty in defining depression as an illness is firstly to distinguish it from a symptom, and secondly to make a distinction between normal and morbid depression which is depression of greater severity and duration than would be expected in a given population from the apparent cause. This last is a very subjective rating and this makes depression a difficult subject for research. The expectancy that one will suffer a depressive illness in one's lifetime is about one to three per cent, with females more likely than males. Generally it is accepted as a phenomenon of later life, but can occur at any age. In depression the major symptom is of a persisting sad, despairing mood, especially severe on waking up. Agitation or marked slowing down may be present, and hallucinations are not uncommon. Ideas of unworthiness, guilt *etc.* are frequent, loss of appetite, loss of weight, loss of sexual drive and loss of menstruation are also common. It is now thought that bipolar disorder and schizophrenia may be two versions of the same disease.

Causation of Depression. The cause is another area where authorities are in dispute, and theories abound. Early research pointed to learned helplessness as a cause. In experiments animals exposed to repeated stresses beyond their control, exhibited apathy, difficulty in accepting that they could do anything to help themselves, loss of appetite, and reduced sociability. The idea that depression is the result of aggressive feelings which cannot be channelled out and so are turned in on oneself, is a simplified view of what Freud said. Some support is lent to this idea by the fact that depressive illness is less common in time of war. Certain biochemical changes have been found in the brains of depressed patients, and the anti-depressant drugs work in ways to correct these imbalances, but whether these intra-cellular changes are cause or effect, and how this comes about, is still not entirely clear. Treatment is by specific anti-depressant drugs of which there are now many, by psychotherapy of various kinds, and much more rarely now by ECT.

Mania is a state of elation, hurried speech, and physical overactivity. Irritability is common if the patient is frustrated. Grandiose plans are made and money can be lavishly spent. Gradually as the illness progresses the sufferer becomes confused, angry *etc.* Treatment is usually by lithium.

Neurosis as we now understand it is a concept we owe to Freud, and to him, too, we owe the distinction between the neurotic disorders of *hysteria*, *anxiety* and *obsessionality*, and the disorders of *personality*. Those in the latter category, while having no detectable disease, are treated by psychiatrists as if they had, and this is a decision of society as a whole since the alternative is to refer such people to the legal or social services. Because the category of neurosis is so vague, it is hard to put a figure on how many people may be affected, but researchers in general practice consultations estimate about one in ten women, and half that many men are at risk. The reason for this disparity is not clear, but may be due to factors such as the greater freedom for expression of frustration enjoyed by men in our society than women. The majority of neurotic illnesses clear up, and may do so spontaneously, although obsessional and hypochondriacal symptoms are more persistent.

Anxiety Neurosis as a pathological state is where anxiety is either unrelated to a recognisable threat, or the degree of anxiety is out of proportion to the threat. The mechanism of our response to a threat appears to depend on the level at which the threat is perceived, if at a conscious level, the response is fear, if at an unconscious level, the response is anxiety. Symptoms include weakness, dizziness, sweating and tiredness. The physical symptoms are themselves unpleasant and increase the feelings of being threatened. Treatment may be by reassurance and explanation, by psychotherapy aimed at bringing the threat into conscious appraisal, or by drugs which are now widely, and often inappropriately, prescribed. *Phobic anxiety* occurs when unreasonable fear is focused on a particular object or situation, and leads to avoidance, Claustrophobia, fear of enclosed spaces, and animal phobias are well recognised. Social phobias, such as fear of eating in public or fear of vomiting are often harder for the sufferer to acknowledge. Phobic states are often associated with a traumatic event in the past, and avoidance through fear leads to a form of conditioning which reinforces the fear. Gradually the sufferer extends the range of feared and avoided stimuli. Behavioural therapy offers the chance to reverse this process.

Much is made of the manipulative nature of neurotics, and the idea of secondary gain, where the neurotic is perceived as getting the better of those around him by organising his, and other people's, lives to fit in with his symptoms. Certainly neurotic people can be very irritating in their demands, but their experience is one of personal suffering.

Suicide as a completed act has been on the rise in the UK in males since 2001, with the highest rates to be found in deprived areas. Every day 2 people under 25 die from suicide in the UK. Suicide is the biggest single killer of men between the ages of 20 and 45 in the UK. Lithuania has the highest suicide rate in the world. Worldwide one million people commit suicide annually, a 60% increase in 45 years.

Mental Illness in Childhood can refer to illness specific to children such as autism (*see below*), to emotional disorders, and to disorders of conduct. Because children are dependent on their families, much interest has centred on relationships within the family and on maternal deprivation as factors in the creation of childhood difficulties. The work of Bowlby highlighted problems consequent on the infant's need for attachment being denied, and he expressed the view that poor early experiences led to failures in later life to develop social relationships. Autism is a state where the child displays abnormalities of language, indifference to people, and ritual behaviour. Autistic children do not grow into schizophrenics, they grow up into autistic adults, and most remain severely handicapped. Phobias and obsessional behaviour are common in children and usually appear and disappear rapidly, especially with prompt intervention.

Depressive illness is rare before puberty and where depressive features are seen it is usually in response to environment.

Conduct disorders include persistent lying, stealing, disobeying, truanting, fighting or setting fires. The distinction from delinquency is important since the latter implies breaking the law which is quite common in adolescence. There is a high correlation between these behaviours and difficulty in reading. Treatment is by assessment of the family situation, and by social and educational intervention.

Anorexia Nervosa is usually a disorder of adolescent girls in which food avoidance, weight loss, failure of menstruation and overactivity predominate. Anorexics often display a distorted view of their own bodies, being unable to see how thin they have become. The underlying difficulty may be a need to control something in their life at a time of actual dependence on parents, or an attempt to avoid the challenge of puberty and the demands, particularly of sexuality, that adulthood makes. Treatment is by behaviour modification, supervised weight gain, and psychotherapy. Anorexia has an appreciable death rate (it carries the highest death rate of any psychiatric disorder). A gene linked to the disorder has now been found. There are also suggestions that bacteria which confuse the immune system may play a part. Other patients may be permanently damaged. Today, anorexia is spreading among the very young. And anorexia among males is rising.

Bulimia Nervosa is a variant in which meals, often very large meals, are eaten and then vomiting is induced to get rid of them. It is 5-times more common in an urban environment.

Autism is a profound handicap which is now believed to be caused by brain malfunction linked to foetal hormone levels, often occurring with other disorders, including mental retardation, which affects three times as many boys as girls. It is almost entirely genetic in origin. The spectrum of the autistic condition encompasses dramatically different degrees of severity, varying from profound handicap through to subtle problems of social understanding in people of apparently normal or even superior intelligence. With the right therapy at an early age, continuing through to special education, autistic people can become less indifferent to others and can develop social responsiveness at a simple level. The disease is not irreversible.

There is no present cure for autism; and it is essential that people with autism are cared for in a special community by dedicated staff. It is thought that around 300,000 adults in the UK are autistic.

Asperger Syndrome (AS) is a form of autism. It is more common in boys. The National Autistic Society is a useful source for further information. Common inherited genetic variations that can contribute to autism were discovered in 2009, and a simple brain scan is now being developed to test for autism.

THE SKIN

The skin in the course of development before birth is particularly closely associated with the nervous system. It is therefore not surprising that so many skin diseases are influenced by emotional states. Other causes of skin disease are infectious, glandular disorders, vitamin deficiencies, and the numerous conditions for which no cause has been discovered, but which presumably are due to metabolic disorders.

Itching (or **Pruritus**) is one of the commonest skin symptoms. It may accompany many different general diseases, for example diabetes and jaundice. It may also be troublesome during the menopause (the change of life in women), in old age, or in nervous conditions. Sedatives and sex hormones sometimes help the itching during the menopause. Ointments may be useful.

Itching in the region of the anus and genital organs is relatively common. It may be caused by worms, by irritating vaginal discharge, or by sugar in the urine, as in diabetes. The alteration in the normal bacteria of the bowel which follows treatment with various antibiotics also often causes anal pruritus and soreness. In many cases however the itching has some psychological cause.

In treatment it is important to avoid ointments and creams which contain a local anaesthetic, because these substances can cause severe allergic reactions if used for longer than a few days, and may thus make the condition much worse.

Treatment with a local corticosteroid application is more effective and safer.

Scabies. Parasites such as the *scabies* mite or *lice* can cause severe and persistent itching. The scabies mite is very small, and since it burrows under the skin surface, is unlikely to be seen; it is the cause of itching most commonly between the fingers and on the front of the wrists. The itching is worst when the body becomes heated, as in bed. Treatment consists of painting the body from head to foot with benzyl benzoate application, followed the next day by a hot bath. Since scabies is contracted through close personal contact with an infested person it is desirable for all members of a family to be treated at the same time, even though only one of them is affected.

Lice are also specialists, one type of which affects the scalp, another the body, and a third the genital area. Head lice are destroyed by washing with shampoos containing organophosphorus insecticides such as malathion, body lice by insecticides and genital (pubic) lice by shaving off hair and washing. Obviously, the clothes, especially in the case of body lice, should be disinfested, by using a hot iron particularly over the seams, which lice (for some inexplicable reason) seem to favour. Apart from the discomfort they cause, lice are dangerous as potential carriers of typhus fever. Persistent lice need a prescription-only treatment to eradicate the problem.

Baldness, or Alopecia, is a very common and often distressing condition. Baldness is common in men and often hereditary. In the past, men have been sold a large number of ineffective treatments, but there are now some genuine treatments available. These include a lotion applied to scalp, minoxidil, or tablets, finasteride. For most men, no treatment remains the best option (although surgical hair restoration procedures are rising).

In 2011 the source of signals which trigger hair growth was discovered. These are stem cells within the skin's fatty layer. The discovery raises hopes of growing new hair follicles from these skin cells.

In women the hair often thins out soon after a pregnancy, but a few months later it usually returns to normal. Alopecia is a common side effect of drugs used in treating cancer, because these drugs affect rapidly-growing cells, such as hair follicles.

Seborrhoea is a condition in which there is over-activity of the sebaceous glands. The most usual form it takes is *dandruff*. However, it takes other forms, and those who have dandruff may also have rashes on the face, shoulders, and chest.

In these areas there is a patchy, greasy, and often itchy, rash which does not clear up until the primary condition in the scalp is dealt with. The scalp should be washed with one of the modern sulphur-containing shampoos at least twice a week, and the affected parts on the face and chest can be dealt with by the use of a sulphur lotion (*not* on any account by greasy ointments).

Seborrhoea is not in itself difficult to treat, but since the condition depends on over-secretion of sebum, the skin lubricant, treatment may have to be persisted in during the years of early adulthood, when it is most active.

Scientists have decoded the DNA of dandruff.

Erythema Intertrigo is, quite simply, the sort of irritation which occurs usually from excessive sweating under the armpits, between the legs, and under the breasts in women. All that need be done is to wash frequently and to dust the affected areas after washing with powder. This is the condition which, in the tropics, is known as "prickly heat" and elsewhere as a "sweat rash."

Hyperhidrosis or **excessive sweating** is a problem in some people, especially when the sweating is accompanied with body odour. There is little need for anyone in these days to suffer in this way: for the cosmetic firms have produced many highly efficient deodorants which not only control odour but also control the amount of sweating.

Erysipelas is an infection of the skin caused by the haemolytic streptococcus. It begins as a red, raised area anywhere on the body where the germs have been able to enter through a small crack or cut in the skin. The red area advances and spreads over the body until the disease is got under control. Erysipelas is very infectious, and those who look after the patient should wash their hands thoroughly after contact. At one time the disease used to spread as an epidemic throughout the hospital wards, but this is very rare nowadays. Treatment is, of course, a matter for the doctor.

Chilblains used to be common in cold weather, especially in those with poor circulation. Ordinarily they occur in the toes and fingers, but may appear on the nose and ears. The part affected becomes swollen, dusky, and there is pain and itching, sometimes leading to ulceration. Protection of the body, especially the hands and feet, from cold is the best and the only really effective way of preventing chilblains. Warm lined gloves and footwear, and arm stockings or trousers should be worn outdoors. Adequate heating of rooms is essential: a temperature between 18° and 21°C is recommended. Most tablets, medicines, ointment, or creams for chilblains are useless. A skin affection caused by heat is rather grandiosely described as *crythema ab igne*, and used to be seen on the legs of ladies addicted to roasting their legs before the fire. It takes the form of red patches on the front of the legs.

Dermatitis (Eczema) means "inflammation of the skin," and therefore the word could be, strictly speaking, applied to any skin disease. In fact the term is used almost interchangeably with the term *eczema*. There are three main types of dermatitis or eczema. The first, *primary irritant dermatitis* results from injury of the skin by some powerful chemical, such as strong alkali or turpentine. The second, *contact dermatitis* is due to sensitisation of the skin to some substance which is normally liable to cause this type of allergic sensitivity; examples are nickel (in jewellery and suspender buckles), epoxy resins, rubber additives, primulas and chrysanthemums, and even ingredients of cosmetics. Contact dermatitis may continue for a long time, even after the patient is no longer in contact with the offending material. The third type is often called *constitutional eczema*. Although the skin is apt to react adversely to various irritants and sensitisers the major part is played by the personality, and there is often a history of eczema, hay fever or asthma in the family. Treatment is more difficult, but local corticosteroids and tar, sedatives and psychological treatment can be of great help. A one-off job for eczema sufferers is being developed. Infantile eczema also belongs in this category, but in most patients it disappears as the child grows up. The National Eczema Society is based in London.

Remember, eczema is the itch you must not scratch!

Impetigo is an infectious skin disease caused primarily by the Streptococcus, but later often infected with staphylococci. It usually occurs on the face, and takes the form of blisters filled with pus on a red base; when the blisters burst their place is taken by yellow crusts. Impetigo is very infectious and easily spread by the fingers, dirty towels, or cloths; therefore, one of the first necessities is to prevent infection of others or reinfection of oneself by avoiding scratching and using a different towel each day, which must on no account be used by anyone else. Treatment is simple with an antibacterial ointment, so the main issue is prevention of contamination.

Urticaria or **Nettlerash** is a familiar skin disease in which itching weals appear on the skin, usually for no obvious reason. It is not infectious, and can be caused by nervous stress, certain drugs, allergy to some foods, or even exposure of the skin to cold. In some people it is possible to write on the skin with a fingernail: the "writing" appears in the form of weals. This is known as *dermographism*; it occurs in many normal persons as well as in many patients with urticaria. The antihistamine drugs are the most useful in the treatment of urticaria. Urticarial swelling of the tongue or throat requires urgent medical attention.

Acne, or "**Blackheads**," is a condition found on the face and shoulders; its appearance is so familiar that no description is necessary. Acne is one of those conditions which is the end result of many factors. There is, first, a greasy skin, the result of glandular upset (which is why the disease usually occurs in adolescence); secondly, there is infection of the skin; and thirdly, there is blockage of the sebaceous ducts, which ordinarily allow the grease from the skin to pass out on to the surface. Since the condition starts with excess secretion of grease, ointments should never be used, and probably the best applications are drying lotions containing some sulphur preparation which inhibits secretion of grease. The face should be frequently washed, and it is possible now to obtain detergent solutions which are both antiseptic and prevent grease formation. In severe cases ultraviolet ray treatment may be necessary. Advances are presently being made in the case of vitamin A in treating acne. Acne is now known to be linked to our genes. A new treatment is now being developed with a pill that rapidly dries out greasy skin.

Rosacea is when the nose and cheeks become red and greasy and the skin coarsened, occurs alike to chronic alcoholics and elderly ladies with no vices other than a preference for strong tea. Both cases are associated with indigestion, since, regrettable as it may seem, strong tea and alcohol are about equally liable to cause the gastritis which may be at the root of this complaint. However, in many patients the chronic flushing is caused in other ways and psychological factors are important. Sometimes in men enlargement of the nose may occur. Treatment is with oral tetracyclines.

Lichen Planus is one of the numerous skin diseases which seem to be due to nervous states of tension. It may occur on any part of the body, but is most common on the front of the forearms and legs. The rash takes the form of nodules which are lilac in colour and have a dent on the top; when these disappear a stain is left behind. There is severe itching. Treatment is a matter for a doctor, as it also is in the case of *psoriasis*, a very common disease of largely unknown origin, which is extremely resistant to treatment. It tends to run in families. It takes the form of slightly raised papules, usually on the elbows and knees; typically the papules are covered with dry, silvery-looking scales. Apart from the rash, the patient is usually in perfectly good health and there is no itching. Many drugs have been used in psoriasis, notably chrysarobin, and while it is not difficult to cause the rash (which may occur anywhere on the body) to disappear in one area or even in all areas for a time, it often returns.

Psoriasis. A skin disease which results in patches of inflamed, red skin often covered by silvery scales. It is at present a long-term condition.

Warts, or **Verrucae** are both familiar enough. They are caused by a virus, and are, theoretically at least, contagious. Usually they are found on the hands, but may occur elsewhere. Treatment is best carried out by a doctor, who will use a cautery, a caustic carbon dioxide frozen into "snow." A curious feature of the common wart is that it can sometimes be caused to disappear by suggestion.

Different altogether from the common wart is the *plantar wart*, which occurs on the soles of the feet and causes a good deal of discomfort. It is best dealt with by a chiropodist or in bad cases by a skin specialist since it is highly infectious.

Ichthyosis is a disorder of skin formation with which some unfortunate people are born. The oil and sweat-producing glands do not function well and the skin is dry and scaly like the skin of a fish. It is, however, possible to help the condition, which does not affect the general health, by frequent alkaline baths to wash off the scales, and the subsequent use of lanolin to replace the lacking oil. Large doses of vitamin A often seem to help.

Skin Cancer. Squamous cell skin cancers occur mostly in old people. They are most common on the face or hands, and usually appear as a nodule which breaks down and produces an ulcer. The glands may later be affected, but such cancers can almost invariably be cured unless a considerable time has elapsed during which they have been neglected. They are much more common in persons over-exposed to the ultraviolet in sunlight, and there is great worry that their frequency will increase as the ozone layer of the atmosphere becomes more depleted. Great care should be taken in direct sunlight, especially when sunbathing.

Cases of skin cancer have recently proliferated, probably as a result of global warming which may make time spent in the sunshine more dangerous. Package holidays have also played their part. The risk of developing skin cancer from using sun lamps has trebled in the last 15 years.

A pill to target a faulty gene in malignant melanoma (the deadliest form of skin cancer) has heralded a major breakthrough. Scans can now also be used. Nowadays, 80 per cent of skin cancer sufferers survive. Mortality rates are higher in men than women. A combination of immunotherapy drugs has also proved highly effective.

Basal Cell Skin Cancers were also known as "rodent ulcers", because untreated they act by eating into the tissues in the area where it has started. X-ray therapy or operation is necessary, but the outlook is good. *Cysts* on the skin are due to blockage of the sebaceous glands. They may become very large, and are best removed, as they may become infected. They do not turn into cancer, and there is no such thing as "male" and "female" cysts. It does sometimes happen that *moles*, especially of the bluish-black type, may become malignant, forming a cancer called a *malignant melanoma*. This is a fast growing and extremely dangerous cancer. Any change in size or shape of any mole must be shown to your doctor immediately.

Skin Grafts.

These are a complex subject. They are used basically for a number of conditions in which large areas of skin have been removed from the body, as in burns or serious accidents. In other cases, as in plastic surgery, grafts may be used to make a new nose, eyelids, and so on. The following are the main types:

Split-thickness Grafts are grafts removed from another part of the body by an instrument known as a dermatome, which cuts sections c 10 by 20 cm. containing part of the deep layers of the skin.

Full-thickness Grafts are when the whole thickness of the skin is removed from elsewhere and applied to an area which has to bear friction or heavy weights (*e.g.* hand or foot).

Pedicle Grafts are rather difficult to describe. Briefly, if for example, one wants to make a new nose, one cuts an area of skin and underlying fat about 5 cm wide and 12·5–15 cm long in the abdomen. One end, however, remains attached so that it gets adequate blood supply. The problem is how to get this tissue to the nose, and this is done by a complicated process of leap-frog. First, the free end of the graft is attached to the forearm, whilst its "root" remains in the original site, and when it begins to grow and get its blood supply from the arm, the original "root" is cut. So we now have a "sausage" of tissue attached to the arm. The arm is then lifted to the face and kept firmly in position there until the new free part becomes attached. It is then detached from the arm, modelled to the correct shape, and grows where the nose was.

THE JOINTS.

Rheumatism is a word most doctors wish did not exist. This is partly because it is used for a hotch-potch of diseases, in all of which there is pain and stiffness of what is called the musculo-skeletal system, *i.e.*, the muscles and the joints. It may mainly involve the joints, in which case it should be called arthritis; or it may involve other structures near the joints like tendons, muscles and fibrous tissue. Joints may either suffer from inflammation or degeneration or both, and the trouble may be acute or chronic or both; so it is easy to see what a mix-up the subject becomes, especially when we must include the joints of the spine as well as the limbs, feet and hands.

A good deal of arthritis used to be due to various germs, but these types are much less common now that the infections causing them have become rarer or better treated. They used to include gonorrhoea, tuberculosis, septic joints, syphilis, brucellosis, typhoid fever, dysentery and so on.

The importance of *rheumatic fever*, which is a re-action to an infection (streptococcal sore throat) rather than being actually caused by the Strepto-coccus, is not because it involves the joints. This arthritis quickly clears up, but there may also be disease of the heart (*see* **Z27**).

Rheumatoid Arthritis is a completely different condition in which there is non-infective inflammation of connective tissues throughout the body. In the joints, the normally smooth, lubricated synovial membrane lining the joint cavity becomes scarred, leading to distortion, especially of smaller joints like those of the hand. Another characteristic feature is its capacity to vary in severity from time to time, with a strong tendency to unexplainable periods when it gets better or worse. This makes it extremely difficult to know whether any form of treatment is being useful, since any response may have occurred in any case. As in all diseases which behave like this, especially those in which medical men are also baffled, there are almost as many theories and treatments as there are doctors. It has never been satisfactorily shown to be caused by infection, faulty nutrition, "glands," emotions or personality disturbance, nor is it convincingly inherited. The best current theory links it with an increased sensitivity reaction, perhaps to the body's own tissues, known as "autoimmunity." From the patient's point of view there is swelling and deformity of the joints with tenderness on pressure and pain on movement. Treatment involves a lengthy and complicated regime of rest, relief of pain with anti-inflammatory drugs such as aspirin, exercises and the application of heat, with attention to general physical and mental health. At some stage adrenal corticosteroids (cortisone and its derivatives) are often tried, but although these can give great relief they have to be very carefully used to avoid very unpleasant side-effects. Today, around 400,000 adults (and children) in the UK have this agonising condition.

Osteoarthritis is another completely different condition closely related to the normal processes of ageing. Therefore it occurs in older people and tends to be in larger, weight-bearing joints of the spine, hips and knees rather than in the hand; although the end joint of the fingers is commonly affected. Hard wear and tear, especially that caused by over-weight, or injury may be the beginning of it. It is

not due to diet, and dieting has no part in treatment except in those who need to slim. Physiotherapy, including heat, is helpful. It is not such a relentless condition as rheumatoid arthritis and patients should be reassured about this. It is partly inherited and is the most common form of arthritis.

Around six million people in the UK suffer this pain in one or both knees (often from wear and tear on the cartilage). Readers may also wish to refer to www.arthritiscare.org.uk

Osteoporosis is a reduction in bone density with-out change in the chemical composition of bone, and has many causes including hormone imbalance, poor diet, age and long use of corticosteroid medicines. Hormone replacement therapy after the meno-pause is partly to prevent osteoporosis. Around 3 million people in the UK suffer from osteoporosis, with a heavy annual toll of hip fractures, wrist fractures *etc*. A new treatment is with bisphosphonate medication.

Fibrositis (now more usually called **Fibromyalgia**) and other painful forms of "rheumatism" are very often manifestations of psychological problems.

Backache. A symptom which may be caused by many different diseases—sometimes disease of the vertebrae themselves, sometimes strain of the ligaments, and sometimes inflammation or spasm of the surrounding muscles. "Lumbago" is usually due to inflammation of the muscles in the small of the back. Backache from purely local causes may be treated temporarily by applying heat in the form of a kaolin poultice or a rubber hot-water bottle and taking painkillers. On the other hand, many cases of backache are due to disease elsewhere, so a doctor should be consulted. BackCare is the name of the National Back Pain Association.

Gout. An excruciatingly painful arthritic inflammation of the joints (especially the toe) caused by crystals formed by uric acid. Chronic gout can be avoided by such medication as allopurinol. Gout can lead to kidney stones. Cases of gout, which are most common in men, are rising very rapidly. It is increasing common in people in their 20s and 30s. Obesity is blamed, although gout is known to run in families.

EYES AND THROAT.

Eye Diseases. These are very specialised and only very general information can be given here. The most common is inflammation of the conjunctiva causing redness and usually due to infection or some irritant substance or dust. If it persists and leads to hard crusts of yellow pus on waking in the morning, get it seen by a doctor for treatment probably with antibiotics. First-aiders are usually instructed how to remove small particles of grit from under the lids. (*see* **Z20**).

Remember the eyes are part of the brain: the only visible part. Perhaps this is why people's eyes are so revealing. (*See* **Special Topic Z57**).

Sore Throats are a nuisance we all have to put up with from time to time. If they last more than a few days they should be treated professionally. Never prescribe antibiotics for yourself, especially in lozenge form, and only expect your doctor to give them if other measures fail.

Tonsils and their inflammation may be a problem. It is comparatively rarely that they should be removed. Of course there are many children who benefit so much from having tonsils out that the operation (which has real dangers) is worth doing. But please allow your doctor to decide.

DISEASES OF WOMEN.

Internal Sexual Organs. These, as with the urinary system, can best be described as shaped like a capital Y. At the tips of the arms of the Y are the female sex glands, the ovaries: the two arms running downwards are the Fallopian tubes: the point where the arms meet is the womb or uterus: the single leg of the Y is the vagina. These are the *primary sexual organs* of a woman and they undergo regular cyclical changes in response to the control exercised over them by the pituitary gland, situated in the base of the skull. This control is mediated by chemical messengers (hormones) secreted into the circulation. The ovaries also secrete hormones, oestrogen, and progesterone, and a delicate hormonal balance is maintained between the pituitary gland and the ovaries. Each month an egg cell (ovum) matures and is released from the ovary, usually midway between two menstrual periods: the ovum is wafted along the Fallopian tubes by waves of contraction and if fertilised embeds in the lining of the uterus which has been conditioned to nourish it by the ovarian hormones.

If it is not fertilised the ovum escapes from the uterus, altered hormone levels then cause the lining of the uterus to be shed (this is menstruation), usually about 14 days after ovulation. After menstruation a new cycle begins; another ovum matures and a fresh lining grows in the uterus. These changes recur from puberty to the menopause.

Menstruation does not occur during pregnancy, of which a missed period is often the first sign. However, women do miss periods even though they are not pregnant, and this usually means that some minor and temporary change has occurred in the hormone balance. If three consecutive periods are missed it is wise to consult a doctor.

The Breasts are called *secondary sexual organs* and are also under the influence of the ovarian hormones. Two conditions which need treatment are *mastitis* and *cancer of the breast*, both of which are characterised by lumps within the breast tissue.

Mastitis may be uncomfortable but is not dangerous and can be treated medically, whereas cancer is more serious. The distinction between mastitis and cancer can only be made by a doctor and any woman who discovers a lump in her breast must seek medical aid *at once*. Although death rates from breast cancer fell in the 1990s (partly due to use of the drug tamoxifen) breast cancer has now overtaken lung cancer as the commonest cancer. The lifetime risk of breast cancer has now increased from one in 9 to one in 8.

Lifestyle factors, such as alcohol and obesity, are partly to blame. All women may soon be offered a genetic test (possibly a simple mouth swab) which would tell them if they were likely or unlikely to contract breast cancer. One in three women who get breast cancer are over 70. The drugs tamoxifen and raloxifene are now available for women with a family history of cancer.

Abscesses also occur in the breast, nearly always when the mother is feeding her child. Here again, a lump appears, the breast becomes red and very tender, and the woman may be feverish. Treatment with antibiotics is sometimes successful, especially if the mother consults her doctor quickly, otherwise treatment is by a small operation.

The Ovaries. The two commonest diseases of the ovaries are cysts and disorders arising from hormonal imbalance. The symptoms of ovarian disease are usually abdominal or low back pains, and heavy and painful loss during the periods, which may become irregular. These signs should be taken as a warning to consult a doctor. *Ovarian cancer* is also a very real danger (each year 6,500 women in the UK die from this disease). A gene which raises the risk of ovarian cancer has now been identified.

The Fallopian Tubes. Infection of the Fallopian tubes is called salpingitis. The membrane lining the tubes is continuous with the lining of the uterus, hence an infection is rarely confined to a circumscribed area in either the tubes or the uterus, and pelvic inflammatory disease is a better name for this condition. Pelvic inflammatory disease often follows an abortion, or childbirth where part of the afterbirth (placenta) has been retained, or can spread from an infection in a nearby organ, for example the appendix. Infection is sometimes conveyed by the blood from another septic source in the body. The gonococcus is another cause of infection. The disease is characterised by pain and tenderness in the lower part of the abdomen, accompanied by fever, general malaise and frequently (but not invariably) a vaginal discharge. The treatment of pelvic inflammatory disease is usually medical and is the same irrespective of the primary site of infection. Before the era of antibiotics the disease often became chronic and the Fallopian tubes were frequently blocked by a cicatrising scar, a cause of subsequent sterility.

The Uterus. This is a hollow muscular organ and both its musculature and its lining membrane can be the site of disease. *Fibroids* are non-malignant muscular tumours which develop in many women. The main symptom is a heavy menstrual loss and surgical removal of the uterus (hysterectomy) is often necessary. This can be a major operation, but trans-vaginal hysterectomy, which does not involve opening the abdomen, has made this operation much less daunting. Hysterectomy does not impair sexual pleasure, but no more babies can be conceived. Infection of the lining of the uterus is usually part of a generalised pelvic inflammatory disease (*see* Fallopian tubes).

For those women who lack a viable womb to bear children, medical science is on the verge of providing uterine transplants.

There has been a massive jump in cases of womb cancer, fuelled by a rise in obesity. Around 9,000 women in the UK are now diagnosed annually, up from 4,800 20 years ago.

Cancer of the Uterus (Cervical Cancer). The uterus is pear-shaped and consists of a body and neck. The wide end is uppermost (the body) and the narrow neck (cervix) projects into the top of the vagina. Cancer of the cervix is commonest in middle-aged women who have married young and have had a large family; cancer of the body of the uterus usually occurs after the menopause and is more common in nulliparous women. The symptoms are variable and it is sufficient to emphasise that any woman who has unexpected bleeding, especially after intercourse, whether her periods have stopped or not, *must* see her doctor at once. Cervical cancer is the second commonest cancer in women. A simple urine test may soon be used to screen for cervical cancer.

Cancer Screening. All the treatment depends on individual circumstances, but is usually by operation. It is now possible to detect cancer of the cervix long before symptoms develop and at a stage when the disease can be eradicated by a relatively small operation. This early detection has been made possible by the development of exfoliative cytology. Cells taken from the cervix (without discomfort to the woman) are examined under a microscope. This test is popularly known as the "cancer test" or "cervical smear." A cervical smear is often taken as part of the routine gynaecological examination by consultants, general practitioners, and family planning doctors, and a nationwide screening programme is now in force. It is a big step forward in preventive medicine and may ultimately solve the problem of cancer of the cervix. Every woman between the ages of 25 and 60 should have the test done at least once every 5 years.

A vaccine for cervical cancer was approved for use in the UK in 2006. In 2008, it was decided the HPV vaccination should be offered to all girls aged 12–13 in the UK. The programme has now been extended to those aged up to 18.

Prolapse means a sagging down of the uterus into the vagina and the cervix may even appear at the outside. It is a result of frequent childbirth and laxness of the ligaments which support the uterus: weakness of the vaginal walls often occurs at the same time. The symptoms of uterine prolapse are low back pain and a heavy dragging feeling in the lower abdomen: these are often overshadowed by the distressingly embarrassing incontinence which results from lax vaginal walls. The stress of only a sneeze, a cough, or a giggle often causes the involuntary escape of urine. The cure is operative and very rewarding.

Dysmenorrhoea or pain with the periods, is very common and most women experience this symptom at some time or another. Very often a girl's first periods are troublesome, but dysmenorrhoea develops after a year or two: this suggests that a psychological element is involved. The sensible thing to do, if pain is troublesome, is to see a doctor.

Amenorrhoea means stopping of the periods in a young woman. It may signify pregnancy or glandular disease or it can be purely psychological.

Menopause occurs when the ovaries no longer have any egg cells to release, causing the cessation of the normal menstrual cycle (*see below*). The hormones oestrogen and progesterone are no longer produced, and this change is often accompanied by "hot flushes". Over time women also experience a loss of bone strength (osteoporosis). It was hoped that giving these missing hormones by mouth would improve women's health. However a recent study of 27,000 women showed "**hormone replacement therapy**" caused a small increase in heart attacks, stroke, pulmonary embolus and breast cancers (with one extra such "event" occurring per hundred women treated for five years).

Abortion means the death and expulsion of a foetus before the 24th week of pregnancy. Abortion may happen spontaneously (*i.e.* naturally) or be deliberately induced. If deliberate, it may be legal or illegal (although a woman who aborts herself commits no offence) and the Abortion Act 1967 defines those conditions in which abortion is legal. The two main symptoms of abortion are bleeding and abdominal pain. Any bleeding occurring during pregnancy ought to be reported at once. Pain starts in the back and lower abdomen and is usually spasmodic in character, and like colic it works up to a peak and then temporarily passes off. Any pregnant woman with pain and bleeding should go to bed at once and send for her doctor. When doctors are convinced that a pregnancy should be terminated then an abortion may be performed in hospital.

CONTRACEPTION AND FAMILY PLANNING

In today's world, advice and help on all aspects of contraception and family planning are readily available. Many people will start with their local GP.

In addition, there are helpful websites of such organisations as the Family Planning Association (www.fpa.org.uk) and Marie Stopes International (www.mariestopes.org.uk).

DRUG DEPENDENCE

Dangers of Drug Use.

1. **Toxic Effects.** The drugs which act upon the nervous system, like any others, have characteristic toxic or unwanted effects of their own (incidentally, these may become apparent rapidly; even, on rare occasions, after only a single dose). Such effects may have little or nothing to do with the desired effects for which they are being prescribed and taken. For example, aspirin is liable to cause bleeding, which is occasionally serious, from the lining of the stomach in a large proportion of people who take aspirin regularly. Some drugs may cause rashes and other allergic reactions in susceptible subjects; and jaundice, fainting, tremors, *etc.* are known to occur in some patients taking a variety of other drugs.

2. **"Rebound."** The human body works in such a way, over a variety of its activities, that it tends to return to a "neutral" position after it has departed from this for any reason. For example, over-eating tends to be followed by a lessening of appetite, at least for a time; the runner makes up for his air-deficit during the race by breathing more deeply thereafter; and if, at rest, you breathe for a time more rapidly and deeply than you need, this period will be followed by one in which you breathe *less* often than usual until the balance is restored. These illustrations—and there are others—have nothing to do with drugs; but in a similar way, it seems that if a continued pain, or an unpleasant emotional state such as anxiety or depression is changed into its opposite, or removed altogether by the use of a drug, the prior state may return with increased force when the drug is no longer taken. The "rebound" phenomenon, naturally, encourages the patient to take another dose, and so on.

3. **Habit Formation.** This alternation of mood-changed-by-drug with the disturbed mood itself leads to the habit of taking the drug. The patient comes to rely upon it and to take it anyway, even before the unpleasant state has returned. At this stage he is said to be "habituated"; he has a psychological need for the drug, and later may become disturbed at the possibility that it will not be available when he needs it. This might not matter so greatly, if it were not that continued use of drugs in this way has physical consequences.

4. **Tolerance and Habituation.** The body also tends to restore its own balance when drugs are given, too. It "learns" surprisingly quickly how to deal with substances with which it has never before been confronted, so that it eliminates subsequent doses more and more quickly and completely. Thus the effect of each successive dose is smaller and lasts for progressively shorter periods of time. To counter this, the patient tends to increase the dose: and the vicious circle continues. At this point he has become physically dependent upon the drug: and he may suffer physically—sometimes so severely that he dies—if supplies are not continued.

5. **Lethal Dosages.** As he increases the dose in this way, so his tolerance of its effects increases, to such an extent that after prolonged use he may be taking doses of a drug that are five or ten times greater than those which will kill somebody not dependent upon them in this way. It sometimes happens that a patient develops a renewed craving at some point after a course of treatment, in which the dose of drug has been reduced without removing the underlying cause of his dependence. He may then obtain and use the dose he habitually took before treatment, not knowing that his body will have lost its tolerance of such doses. That dose is now as high for him as for any other person and so may be lethal. There has been a number of deaths for this reason.

Factors in the Causation of Dependence.

The risk of becoming dependent upon a drug is governed by three main factors; the drug itself, the personality of the individual who takes it, and the circumstances in which it is taken.

Most adults have taken alcohol at one time or another, yet *relatively* few are dependent on it (relatively few, but many too many; more than a million in the United Kingdom alone).

Many of us have had morphine or some other strong analgesic for medical reasons, without becoming dependent upon it. However, if we start to take such a drug "for kicks"—as more and more people, particularly teenagers and young adults are doing—it is extremely probable that we shall become dependent upon it.

It is also probable that each one of us would become dependent, were he or she obliged to take it regularly, for long enough, and in sufficient dosage. Thus, although there are personalities—psychopathic, immature, or unstable—that are more prone than others to become dependent if they are exposed to the drug, there are also drugs that are more likely than others to cause such dependence no matter to whom they are given. The extent of the dependence will vary; with some, it is never physiological but remains psychological (but not the less real or disturbing for that). Also, the rate at which dependence develops may vary; and the picture presented by the dependent subject—the extent to which his normal life is impaired, or to which he becomes dangerous to himself or others—varies as well. In a very much oversimplified way, some of these relationships will now be summarised for certain substances.

Types of Dependence.

Heroin, morphine and cocaine are usually injected (with all the risk this implies). Amphetamines ("Benzedrine") are tablets or capsules, and marijuana ("reefer," hashish) is smoked in cigarettes. Heroin and cocaine are now usually taken together. Combinations of drugs often act differently from their individual constituents and patients dependent upon them are even more difficult to treat. The most used drugs in Britain today are ecstasy, cocaine, cannabis and skunk, poppers, speed, meths *etc*, but "legal highs" (which mimic the effects of banned drugs) have surged. These "legal highs" such as meow meow, Spice and Black Mamba have now been banned, but others such as AMT are still legal. They are known as New Psychoactive Substances (NPS).

Psychological Dependence is considerable with heroin, morphine, cocaine, and amphetamine, but much less with marijuana.

Physiological Dependence is great with heroin and morphine, less with barbiturates, alcohol, and amphetamine in that order, and virtually nil with cocaine and marijuana. Personality plays a greater part in initiating dependence on alcohol, marijuana, and barbiturates than with the others. Heroin, cocaine, and morphine are the cause of more antisocial tendencies in dependent people than alcohol, barbiturates, and amphetamine.

One danger of marijuana is that the search for it will lead the searcher into localities where his risk of exposure to even more dangerous influences is greatly increased. It is thus sometimes argued that if it were legal to consume marijuana, the number of young people who yearly become dependent upon the other more dangerous drugs would in fact decrease. There is as yet no evidence for or against this proposition. The number of drug dependent people in the UK is rising fast for heroin, crack and cocaine. and the number of drug deaths in Britain is now among the highest in the world relative to our population.

This number is very large for alcohol (many doctors believe we are in the midst of an alcohol crisis, with all its implications for the NHS) The number of alcohol-related admissions to hospital in England topped a million a year for the first time in 2010 (double the 2002 number). By 2015, alcohol abuse by older women was a serious cause for concern. Very few people are dependent on morphine.

Treatment.

Exhortations, imprisonment, and other moralistic or legalistic approaches are useless. Treatment of any person dependent upon a drug is a matter for a qualified psychotherapist. It is liable to be time-consuming and frustrating for patient and doctor, and it is sometimes unsuccessful. At present, there are too few specialists or centres where treatment can be obtained, although it is to be hoped that this situation will change as the problem is increasingly seen by our society to be of exceptional gravity.

When there is little or no chance of cure, prevention is certainly the best treatment. Drugs should only be taken on the prescription of a doctor: and the patient should remind him from time to time, if this be necessary, that he would like to dispense with his drugs as soon as the doctor thinks it possible.

PART III. SPECIAL TOPICS

THE HUMAN EYE

Light enters the eye through the *cornea*, which coarsely focuses light onto the *retina* at the back of the eye. The light is finely focused by the *lens*, the shape and focussing power of which is controlled by the *ciliary muscles*. To see distant objects these muscles relax and the lens flattens. With age, the lens loses elasticity and it becomes more difficult to focus. The amount of light entering the lens is controlled by the *iris*, which closes the *pupil* in bright light or to improve image quality for close objects. We can see finer detail when the pupil is small. This is contrary to, say, a camera because of imperfections in the cornea curvature. This makes it more difficult to see distant objects at night.

The Retina

The retina contains three types of light-responsive cells, of which *cones* and *rods* are used for vision. The cones are responsible for our perception of colour and come in three types, respectively most sensitive to blue, green and yellow light. In combination, we can see the full range of colour from violet to red, although the precise endpoints of this range vary from person to person. (Other animals see very different colours, for example bees see the spectrum from ultraviolet to orange.) The cones are most sensitive in bright light, whereas the rods allow vision in dim light. Because the rods cannot distinguish between colours, faint coloured objects, such as stars in the night sky, appear black and white. Perceived colours depend on both the cones activated and on contrast, background colour and psychological factors. Pilots can perceive a blue sky to be grey as there is no edge to the colour.

The rods and cones are not evenly distributed. The cones are largely in the *macula*, the middle of the retina, with the rods being entirely absent in the one-third millimetre sized *fovea* at its centre. As a consequence, stars that are too faint to activate the cones are only visible when off-centre in our field of vision. There are far fewer blue cones – and none in the fovea – so very small objects can appear colourless.

The Absorbtion of Light

In the rods and cones, light is absorbed by a chemical called *rhodopsin* (part of which is vitamin A) and generates an electrical signal. Further cells in the retina combine the signals from adjacent rods and cones in order to identify contrast and orientation. These processing cells are unfortunately located in a layer in front of the rods and cones, which degrades the image before it reaches the light-responsive cells. The exception is at the fovea, where the processing cells are shifted to the side and the eye consequently has its greatest *acuity* (ability to resolve small objects). We therefore move our eyes, along a line of print for example, when we need high acuity.

The Optic Nerve

The processing cells produce signals that are transferred to the *visual cortex* in the brain along the *optic nerve*, which exits the retina at the *blind spot* and where there are no light-responsive cells. In the visual cortex, the information from the two eyes is combined and different neurons are activated according to the orientation, depth, motion and colour, for example, of the object that the eye is seeing. We have two eyes with overlapping fields of vision so that we can perceive how far away an object is located, in combination with object familiarity, texture, motion *etc*. Many other animals have a 360 degree visual field but with no (or less) overlap between them.

Other Eye Structures

While vertebrates (animals with skeletons) have broadly the same type of eye as us, invertebrates have different structures with one exception: the octopus. Remarkably, the octopus eye evolved completely independently and yet developed an eye with all the same features and one major improvement: the retina is "inside out". This means that the light reaches the light-responsive cells without having to first pass through the other processing cells in the retina.

The third light-responsive cell type, only discovered in the last few years, forms a web-like structure on the retina and is not involved in vision. The electrical signal from the active chemical in these cells, *melanopsin*, controls the body's circadian rhythms, such as the sleeping and waking cycle, and is thus important in recovering from jet lag. In some other animals, these rhythms are derived from light entering the brain directly, bypassing the eye.

Spectacles and Contact Lenses

In normal vision, light from an object is focused to a point on the retina. For people with *myopia* (short-sightedness) or *hyperopia* (long-sightedness) however, light focuses to a point respectively in front of or behind the retina. With *astigmatism*, light is focused to a line instead of a point, due to asymmetry in the lens. These problems may be corrected by appropriate lenses, either spectacles or contact lenses.

More complex spectacles – described as bifocals, trifocals and varifocals – focus at two or more different distances, suited to common tasks such as reading, in separate regions of the lens. These regions are usually located such that distant objects are viewed through the top part of the lens, but alternative arrangements may be more appropriate for plumbers, for example, who need to see overhead. Some lenses have their near focus set for computer usage, where the distance between the eye and the screen is typically 70 centimetres, rather than reading (40 centimetres). Glasses are also available with photochromic lenses, which darken when they absorb ultraviolet light from the sun. Antireflection coatings on the glass may be used, particularly to provide eye protection from ultraviolet light following corneal replacement.

Advantages of Contact Lens

Contact lenses, in addition to their cosmetic benefit, have several optical advantages over spectacles. A contact lens traps a tear layer between it and the cornea, correcting for irregularities in the corneal surface. In addition, correcting extreme short- or long-sightedness with spectacles uses their optically inferior periphery, a problem which is avoided by contact lenses. Contact lenses come in hard and soft versions and are made from material which allows oxygen to pass through. Although bifocal contact lenses are available, they are difficult for the eye to adapt to and hence separate lenses in each eye for near and distant sight are generally used instead.

Common Vision Defects

Nearly a tenth of males have some *colour blindness* because one of the three cone types is either missing or is sensitive to a slightly different colour from normal. A very small number of people see only in black and white because they have no cones at all. Less commonly, colour blindness is due to damage within the optic nerve or brain.

People with *ambylopia*, or lazy eye, have one strong eye and one weak eye because their vision did not develop normally during childhood. The brain will rely on only one of the two eyes if there is a significant difference between them through damage, unequal focusing or *squint*, leaving the other to become lazy. Ambylopia can often be corrected while the eye is still developing, sometimes simply by the child wearing a patch over the good eye to force the other to strengthen. With squint, the two eyes look in different directions causing double vision and a loss of depth perception. It can often be corrected by surgery to the muscles controlling eyeball movement.

Floaters are the spots and strings superimposed on our vision and which drift around as the eyeball moves. They are strings of the protein collagen in the vitreous, the fluid filling the eyeball, and cannot be safely treated without risking sight.

Myopia is the term for short-sightedness and it is becoming an epidemic, perhaps due to lack of sunlight.

Age-Related Vision Problems

While population longevity continues to increase, the eye is not keeping pace and age-related vision impairment is therefore becoming more widespread. Generally, during childhood, the eye becomes increasingly myopic; later in life, there is a tendency towards long-sightedness. The lens thickens and allows less light through: the infant lens transmits more than 25 times more violet light than a 70-year-old lens. It loses its elasticity and so the eye

becomes unable to change focus, a process called *presbyopia*. In any case, the eye becomes unable to see fine detail or realise that a light is flickering. There is a loss of contrast due to increased scatter within the eye. In particular, this causes increased glare when the eye sees a high variation in brightness, for example when driving at night. The visual system becomes less sensitive, both at the retina and in the brain, leading to a reduction in colour discrimination, depth perception and the size of the visual field. However, changes in light transmission and relative cone sensitivity can be compensated for by the brain.

There are a number of sources of partial and total blindness that are principally age-related:

Macular Degeneration(MD), as the term suggests, is retinal damage in the centre of the field of vision and may appear in sudden or gradual forms, causing difficulty in seeing fine detail such as print. The rarer, sudden degeneration can be impeded by laser photocoagulation, a process which seals the local blood vessels. Macular degeneration cannot be reversed but its effects may be mitigated by retraining the eye to treat the macula as a second blind spot. In the UK around 250,000 people are registered visually impaired because of MD.

MD occurs when the layer of the retina responsible for nourishing the macula's light sesitive rod and cone cells, and for carrying away waste products, starts to function less effectively.

Cells in the macula break down, causing loss of sight in the central part of the field of vision but leaving the side vision, known as peripheral vision, unaffected. A new class of bionic eye implant may soon aid this problem.

Diabetic Retinopathy is where the blood vessels feeding the retina are weakened and consequently cause retinal damage, such as detachment. Again, photocoagulation is used for treatment. If the retina has detached or blood has entered the eye, it may be necessary to replace the vitreous. It is vital for diabetics to be monitored for this condition.

Cataracts. A *cataract* is a loss of lens transparency, causing blindness. The lens in a young person strongly absorbs ultra-violet light, usefully preventing it from reaching the retina. With age, however, the lens yellows. It increasingly absorbs visible light as well and eventually causes cataracts. Diabetes and trauma can also cause cataracts. It is a particular problem in developing countries, where it tends to occur earlier in life – around fifteen years earlier in India than in the USA. Today, it is a routine operation to remove the lens and insert a fixed-focus lens implant to restore sight. While implants with multiple fixed foci are available, patients experience reduced contrast as in-focus and out-of-focus images are always superimposed on the retina.

Now, eyedrops that may cure cataracts are being developed, so avoiding surgery (an estimated 300,000 cataract operations take place annually in the UK).

Glaucoma is damage to the optic nerve. The nerve cells die, usually because the pressure within the eye is too high. The condition is irreversible so early detection is vital. It is controlled using drugs or surgery to reduce the pressure.

Glaucoma is the second largest cause of blindness in the UK, affecting up to 500,000 people (many of whom do not realise they have it).

Eye Tests

The optometrist uses a variety of tests both to measure the eye's error in focusing and to look for evidence of the diseases and defects described above. Test charts and instruments such as the retinoscope are used to measure the eye's focusing ability and determine the appropriate spectacle strength for a patient. A photograph of the retina is used to look for visual signs of damage, including the blood vessels feeding it and the optic nerve at the blind spot. Measurement of the pressure within the eyeball, to test for glaucoma, is done by observing how well a jet of air directed at it is reflected back. The size of the visual field, and the location of any blind spots within it, is tested by flashing a series of separated bright lights and the patient indicating which they can see.

Laser Surgery

The most common use of lasers in medicine is in eye surgery. To remove cataracts or reshape the cornea, light from a laser is used to cut the tissue more precisely than a knife is able to by either breaking the chemical bonds or ionising the structure. Reshaping may be performed either on the cornea's surface or, by cutting open a flap, its interior. It cannot be used to restore the eye's ability to change focus.

FOCUS ON DEMENTIA

Literally 'out of one's mind', dementia is an umbrella term for a set of symptoms which occur when the structure of the brain is damaged in some way, leading to a progressive decline in brain function. There are more than 100 different types of dementia and the symptoms can vary not only with the type but also with the individual person. The most common symptoms are loss of memory, particularly short-term memory, problems with speech and understanding, confusion and mood changes.

Numbers Affected

Dementia is an increasingly common condition which now (2016) affects around 850,000 people in the UK and this is expected to double over the next 30 years. Globally numbers are predicted to have trebled by 2050 to 115 million. Although it can affect younger people – currently over 40,000 in the UK – it is found mainly in those over the age of 65 and the likelihood of developing it becomes greater with advancing age. One in three people over 65 today will die with dementia – more than half with Alzheimers'. A significant factor in the growth in numbers, therefore, is the steady increase in life expectancy. However, increasing numbers of cases of early onset dementia are being identified.

Types of Dementia

Alzheimer's Disease is the most common form of dementia, affecting some 490,000 people in the UK, slightly more women than men. In fact, dementia is now the leading cause of death for women. It is caused by brain cells dying due to small deposits of protein, known as 'plaques', developing between the cells and twisted strands of protein, 'tangles', developing within the cells. Its name is from the German neurologist who first identified them in 1906, Alois Alzheimer (1864–1915). No single cause of the disease has been found. In the 1960s it was suggested that ingestion of aluminium was an important factor but there has been no definitive proof of this and it is now thought more likely to arise from a combination of factors including lifestyle and general health. Even lack of sleep may play a role. A specific part of the brain where Alzheimers' develops has now been located. Low levels of Vitamin D can double the risk.
The disease may be present for up to 20 years before any symptoms appear and the first sign is likely to be memory problems, identified at this stage as mild cognitive impairment (MCI), although it is important to note that not all cases of MCI develop Alzheimer's. Other symptoms which gradually appear and become more severe over a period of seven to ten years include: language difficulties when speaking, problems carrying out everyday activities, confusion and mood swings. There can also be problems in recognizing familiar places and therefore getting lost close to home.
Although there is no cure for the disease, its progress can be slowed temporarily by drug treatment, in particular by drugs which maintain the supply of the chemical acetylcholine, of which there is a shortage in those with Alzheimer's. A blood test to identify Alzheimers' before the worst symptoms develop is very close.

Vascular Dementia is the second most common form of dementia and affects more men than women. It is caused by damage to the vascular system (blood vessels) within the brain, resulting in an insufficient supply of blood to the cells, which are therefore deprived of oxygen and eventually die. There are two main types: one arising from single or multiple strokes, the other from damage to small blood vessels deep within the brain. A third type,

mixed dementia, is when Alzheimer's disease is also present. Many symptoms are similar to those for Alzheimer's, but can also include epileptic seizures and a 'stepped' deterioration. The conditions which can lead to vascular damage include high blood pressure, heart problems, high cholesterol and diabetes, and although the damage cannot be reversed, treatment of any underlying conditions may prevent further damage and thereby slow the progression of the disease.

Dementia with Lewy Bodies (*LBD*) account for 15 % of dementia cases in older people and affects men and women equally. Lewy bodies are tiny spherical protein deposits that develop inside nerve cells in the brain, disrupting the brain's chemical messengers and leading to the degeneration and eventual death of the nerve cells. They are named after Frederic Lewy (1885–1950) who first discovered them in 1912. Why these bodies occur is not yet fully understood. Symptoms specific to LBD include hallucinations, a tendency to fall asleep during the day but have disturbed nights, fainting, falling, and a rapid fluctuation in abilities. It is closely associated with Parkinson's disease, whose sufferers often develop this form of dementia; conversely, at least half of those affected by LBD develop Parkinson's symptoms — slowness, trembling of the limbs, a shuffling walk, loss of facial expression, and changes in the voice. In the later stages of the disease the symptoms are similar to those of Alzheimer's disease. There is no cure but symptoms may be alleviated by certain drugs.

Fronto-Temporal Dementia is a rare type of dementia that usually develops in people under the age of 65 and is caused by damage to the frontal lobe and/or the temporal parts of the brain, the areas responsible for behaviour, emotion and language. The damage may be due to degeneration of the frontal lobe, to motor neurone disease or to Pick's disease, a disease caused by a particular type of protein deposit, a 'Pick body' as discovered by Arnold Pick (1851–1924) in 1892. In up to a half of cases the disease has been inherited, due to defective genes, but where it is not inherited the cause is unknown. The initial symptoms are changes in personality and behaviour, which may show as loss of inhibitions, lack of empathy with others and aggression. There may also be language difficulties and changes in eating habits but memory is initially unaffected. In the later stages, which can occur rapidly or after up to ten years, the symptoms are similar to those for Alzheimer's disease. There is no cure nor can its progress be slowed, and drugs used for Alzheimer's may make the symptoms worse.

Other Causes of Dementia

There are many other rarer diseases that may lead to dementia. *Korsakoff's syndrome* is caused by a lack of thiamine (vitamin B1) in the brain, usually due to heavy alcohol consumption over a long period, and its main symptom is loss of memory. It is named after a Russian psychiatrist specialising in alcohol-related disorders, Sergei Korsakoff (1853–1900), who first recognised its cause.
Treatment is total abstinence from alcohol, a healthy diet and vitamin supplements, which will halt the disease's progress and in some cases effect a complete recovery. *Dementia pugilistica*, commonly known as punch-drunk syndrome, is a decline in mental and physical abilities due to injury to the brain from multiple blows to the head. *Creutzfeldt-Jakob disease (CJD)* and its variant, *BSE (mad cow disease)*, causes dementia by the accumulation in the brain of abnormal prion proteins.

Reducing the Risk

There is no course of action that can guarantee that a person will not develop some form of dementia, particularly once over the age of 80 when one in five people are affected. However by following the general recommendations for a healthy life the risk of developing the most common types can be greatly reduced. The main risk factors for dementia are: smoking, high blood pressure, high cholesterol, obesity, and excessive alcohol consumption. So the risk can be reduced by not smoking, following a

Mediterranean-style diet, taking regular physical exercise and drinking, if at all, in moderation (in fact it is thought that a glass of red wine a day may help to protect against dementia). Continuing to use the brain in new ways, such as learning a language or learning to play a musical instrument, is also helpful, but it is thought that physical exercise, which improves the circulation of blood to the brain, and an active social life are even more important. In this respect, activities such as dancing or singing in a choir may be the ideal activities to combat dementia.

EAR PROBLEMS

The Ear.

This is not merely the outer portion which is visible to all of us—this part of the ear performs the sole function of collecting the sounds and leading them into a tube which consists of three parts: the outer part (which is the part in which the main troubles are collection of wax, small boils, and sometimes skin irritation); the middle ear, which is separated from the outer ear by a membrane, the ear-drum, and the main disorder of which is otitis media, due to infection; lastly, the inner ear, where the sound impulses, transmitted by a chain of tiny bones through the middle ear, reach the nerve which passes them to the brain.

Wax, or Cerumen, is naturally secreted in the ear, but in most cases will dry up and fall out. Some unfortunate people, however, tend to accumulate it, so that after varying periods of time the ear is completely blocked and deafness occurs. Then they have to go to the doctor to have it syringed. There is no cure for this tendency except periodic syringing, although there is an oil on the market which usually softens the wax and makes it come away of itself. *Boils* in this part of the ear are small but rather painful; they should be entrusted to the doctor, who will give something to relieve the pain. However, once the boil has started, it is unlikely to regress, and will probably come to a head and burst, with consequent relief to the patient. Whilst we are dealing with the outer ear it should be said that, like the eyes, it should not be interfered with except by someone who knows something about it. Mothers should not poke the corners of towels into the ear in an attempt to clean it, nor if, as frequently happens, a child puts a bead or a pea into the ear should they try to dig it out. This should be left to the doctor.

Otitis Media, or infection of the middle ear, is another cause of earache, and, since the middle ear is shut off by the ear-drum from contact with the outside world, the ordinary source of infection is from the throat by way of the Eustachian tube, a narrow tube which passes between the back of the throat and the middle ear. Its normal function is to equalise pressure between the middle ear and the atmosphere—that is why, for example, when a large gun is being fired, soldiers are told to keep their mouths open, otherwise their ear-drums might be burst. But not only air but germs can pass up the tube, and when infection exists in the throat (such as adenoids or tonsillitis) it may move up the middle ear and start disease. When this happens, pus begins to form and accumulates until it presses against the ear-drum, which causes severe pain. Without treatment one of two things may then happen: either the ear-drum bursts or the infection may spread backwards into the mastoid area, an area of spongy bone immediately behind the ear. This is known as *mastoiditis*, and together with otitis media, can be dealt with only by a skilled doctor. Sometimes antibiotics are adequate, but in other cases operation is necessary.

Tinnitus is the medical term for noises in the ears, which is one of the commonest conditions met with in the doctor's surgery. There are numerous physical causes, but there can be little doubt that very many of the cases seen are neurotic and show no physical disorder at all. Some of these unfortunate people, who undoubtedly suffer a great deal, go around from one doctor to another seeking relief and failing to find it, because the trouble is so often in their minds rather than their ears. One of the physical causes of tinnitus is *olosclerosis*, a disease of the inner ear in which the tissues become hardened and increasing deafness results. It is now known that tinnitus arises when hairs in the inner ear are damaged and the brain responds by trying to amplify sounds. One treatment is the operation of fenestration or its more recent modifications such as stapedectomy which give good results. Researchers are now working on the possibility of drug treatment by 2020. At present, one in ten people in the UK is affected by everyday tinnitus.

KEYHOLE SURGERY

One of the most fundamental of medical ethics is not to harm the patient. In the field of surgery this can be loosely translated as "do not make holes any bigger than necessary." Although surgeons have always tried to follow this, they have only been able to do so to any great extent since the 1980s and improvements in keyhold surgery have followed the development of fibre-optics. Methods for examining the inside of the body using rigid tubes with mirrors to guide light have been available for many years, but were applicable only to parts of the body which can be reached from the surface in a straight line. Fibre-optic systems allow light to be passed down a flexible bundle of fibres, and this has enormously widened the range of body parts that can be examined for diagnostic purposes. The surgeon can, for example, pass an endoscope down past the vocal cords into the lungs; by bending the flexible tip of the endoscope, he can guide the instrument into even very small bronchial branches, to look for cancers and other lesions.

Endoscopes were taken another step forward with the development of tiny surgical instruments— scissors, diathermy probes and the like—with which small samples of tissue (biopsies) could be removed and brought back out of the body for more detailed examination.

The Advantages of Keyhole Surgery

One major advantage of keyhole surgery is that the reduction in the level of invasiveness needed to treat a condition is dramatically reduced, so that patients have to stay in hospital for only a fraction of the time that would be needed using earlier methods. Keyhole surgery forms an important part of the treatment of coronary sclerosis, where the arteries providing blood to the heart become blocked by the build-up of atheroma. Coronary bypass surgery used to be the "standard" treatment for this condition, and represented major surgery. The keyhole method consists of passing a catheter from the surface of the body into an artery and guiding it into the blockage under the control of X-ray monitoring. A small balloon at the tip of the catheter is then inflated, which opens up the narrowed artery and restores the flow of blood through it, reducing the severity of angina pectoris.

Uses of Keyhole Surgery

Investigation of gastro-intestinal diseases often used to need a major operation, laparotomy. In many cases it is now standard practice to put an endoscope through a tiny incision in the abdominal wall and guide it to the damage for examination and sample collection and, in some cases, repair. Endoscopes can also be passed into the intestines for examination and treatment without any incision at all.

Hysterectomy, another procedure that in the past required laparotomy, is now routinely performed using miniaturised instruments passed into the uterus through the vagina, which reduces hospital in-patient from 10 nights often to only one night. Prostate hypertrophy, in which the prostate gland in men swell ups and blocks the passage of urine, is now treated by tiny instruments passed through the penis, in a procedure known as transurethral prostatectomy. Joint diseases and traumas are often examined and treated by similar methods. Many sportsmen with knee injuries will be familiar with the arthroscope.

Alternative Non-Invasive Surgery

These examples show that keyhole surgery is a form of non-invasive surgery. Other ways of achieving the same effect include the use of focused ultrasonic sound waves to break up kidney stones (lithotrypsy) instead of major abdominal surgery; breast lumps can often be removed by minor procedures guided by extremely accurate X-ray equipment in place of the older lumpectomy and mastectomy approaches. As the application of engineering to surgery spreads, so does keyhole surgery.

MEDICAL NEWS AND NOTES

PET Scans

Positron emission tomography (PET) scans are a recent refinement of the technique of injecting a radioactive marker to study disease. New markers have been developed to measure processes such as glucose metabolism. This makes them particularly useful for examining a range of different cancers, and they may show the spread of cancer much earlier than other tests. They can also help accurately target treatments such as radiation therapy. In future, they may give an idea of response to treatments like chemotherapy, long before the results would otherwise be known.

These tests are not only more sensitive and accurate but often also easier on patients.

Blood Groups

Human blood plasma contains factors which clump, or agglutinate, the red cells of some other people's blood. The main blood groups are called A, B, AB, and O. The plasma of group A blood contains an anti-B factor and *vice versa*, so that people of groups A and B cannot accept each other's blood. Group AB contains neither anti-A nor anti-B factor and people with this group can therefore receive transfusions from both but can give to neither. Group O contains both anti-A and anti-B, and can therefore receive blood only from group O but can donate blood to all groups. It is important that transfused cells should not be agglutinated by the factors in the recipient's plasma. Apart from the so-called ABO system, there are several other blood groupings, one of which is mentioned under **Rhesus Factor.**

Rhesus Factor

Apart from the ABO blood group system (*see above*) there is another blood group system (designated the Rh- system or Rhesus system). Everybody is either Rh-positive or Rh-negative. Three positive factors (denoted C, D, E) and three negative factors (denoted c, d, e) are involved. This system of blood factors is inherited separately from the ABO group, so that one may be A Rh+ or A Rh−, *etc*. Both the positive and the negative factors are antigenic, *i.e.*, if introduced into other blood they will stimulate the production of substances which act in some way against the cells introduced.

Blood Donors

The need for people to give blood has probably never been greater. It is one of the most useful tasks people can do—it only takes about an hour of your time (and the donor hardly feels a thing!) Hospitals need the equivalent of 10,000 blood donations every day. Blood is used not just in accidents and emergencies but in the treatment of cancer and burns, in childbirth, heart surgery and organ transplantation.

Although most people can give blood, only 5% of those who can actually do. Anyone who is not yet a blood donor could start today as long as they are aged between 17 and 59, generally in good health and weigh at least 7st 12lbs (50kg). Existing donors can give blood until they reach 70—ideally three times a year.

For more information readers can contact 0845 7711711 or visit www.blood.co.uk.

Mouth Cancer (Oral Cancer)

A new awareness programme to highlight the spread of mouth cancer was launched back in 2005. With around 8,000 new cases annually in the UK, and over 1,700 deaths, cancer of the lips, tongue, cheek, vocal chords and throat has now become more frequent. The mouth should be examined regularly to check for warning signs such as ulcers that do not heal or red and white patches.

Once considered mainly a disease of men over 50, it now affects more younger men (and the number of women with the disease has risen by a third since 1995). Excess alcohol intake, as well as smoking, are being blamed. Those carrying the HPV virus are also at risk.

Survival rates are very good if the disease is caught early.

Frozen Shoulder

An extremely painful and stiff condition of the shoulder in which movement is very much restricted, even "frozen" altogether. Despite the use of painkillers, in severe cases the condition may last 2 or even 3 years. Pain is worse at night, with sleep often badly disrupted. It is thought to be caused by scar-like tissue forming. For reasons not yet understood, diabetics are more liable to this condition.

Abdominal Aortic Aneurysm (AAA) Screening

AAA screening is a simple ultrasound test which the NHS is offering free of charge to all men in the year they turn 65. The aorta is the main blood vessel that supplies blood to your body. Large aneurysms are rare but can be very serious. As the wall of the aorta stretches it becomes weaker and could give way. If this happens, the person usually dies.

An aorta which is only slightly larger than normal is not dangerous. However, it is still important to know about it so that doctors can monitor the aneurysm to see if it gets bigger. The easist way to find out if you have an aneurysm is to have an ultrasound scan of your abdomen.

Men are six times more likely to have this type of aneurysm than women. The chance of having an aneurysm increases with age.

The Zika Epidemic

The Zika virus was first isolated back in 1947 from a rhesus macaque in the Zika forest of Uganda. The virus is spread by a mosquito, the *Aedes aegypti*, which also carries such other viruses as dengue and yellow fever (*see* **Z11**) and also chikungunya (*see* **Z62**). In May 2015, an outbreak of the disease was reported in Brazil. By early 2016, more than 1·5 million Brazilians had become infected and it had spread to the other countries in South America and the Caribbean. It was set to become a global emergency.

In many cases, symptoms (where they appear) resemble those of the flu and are rarely life threatening. Crucially, however, the Zika virus is linked to birth defects in pregnant women. A child may be born with a smaller head (*microcephaly*) and underdeveloped brain. Hence the Zika virus has become an urgent medical emergency.

If you have to travel in an area where the *Aedes aegypti* mosquito is found, take every precaution to avoid being bitten. Wear long sleeves, long trousers tucked into socks and at night use insect screens, air conditioning *etc*. Also, take up-to-date medical advice.

PART IV. GLOSSARY

Abdominal aortic aneurysms, name for the insidious ballooning of the main blood vessel in the abdomen. Around 10,000 people die annually in the UK when rupturing occurs. Screening can reveal those at risk (*See* **Z61**).

Acoustic Neuromas, benign tumours of the acoustic nerve. They can cause deafness. A link has been noted suggesting they are more common in mobile phone users.

Adenoids, the overgrowth of glandular tissue in the back of the throat. Often caused by infection they usually disappear by the age of 10 .

ADHD (Attention Deficit Hyperactivity Disorder) is a condition affecting some youngsters. Its symptoms of restlessness, forgetfulness and lack of attention (once blamed on bad behaviour) may be linked to the brain chemical dopamine. Sometimes just called ADD (Attention Deficit Disorder). Around half of sufferers find symptoms continue into adult life. A tiny genetic fault is responsible.

Alternative Medicine. *See* **J3**.

AMD. Age-related macular degeneration.

Amniocentesis, a pre-natal test in which a needle is used to extract amniotic fluid.

Anabolic Steroids. Synthetic hormones which stimulate growth, muscle development and sex drive.

Anaesthetic. Any drug used to abolish pain during an operation.

Androgens. The hormones (*e.g.* testosterone) responsible for male characteristics.

Ankylosing Spondylitis (AS). A painful progressive rheumatic disease, mainly but not always of the spine. There is a gradual onset of back pain and stiffness.

Ankylosis. Partial or complete fixation of a joint as after some types of arthritis. In other cases deliberately produced by surgery.

Antibiotics, a collective name for any substance derived from micro-organisms or fungi which is capable of destroying infections. *See* **Z4**.

Antihistamines. Medicines used to treat allergies such as hay fever and rhinitis.

Aphasia. A form of brain damage affecting language.

Arrythmia. Irregular pulse rhythms of the heart.

Avian Flu. *See* **Bird Flu** (*below*).

Barium meal. Barium sulphate is opaque to X-rays and before X-ray pictures of the alimentary canal radiologists give a "barium meal" to the patient so that the alimentary canal shows up more clearly. Barium X-rays can reveal bowel diseases.

Bird Flu (Avian Flu), typical flu-like symptoms, eye infections, pneumonia and respiratory disease contracted from birds, chickens *etc.* in Asia. In 2011 a vaccine-resistant strain appeared in Asia. In 2013 the H7N9 virus emerged in China.

Blood Groups. *See* **Z61**.

Cachexia. Extreme wasting due to disease.

Caesarean operation. When the abdomen has to be opened to remove the child.

Carbohydrates. The scientific name for sugars, starches and cellulose, *See* **Z34**(1), **Z39–40**.

Carcinogen. Any substance which causes cancer.

Cellulitis, inflammation of body tissue, most often below the surface of the skin. It is treated with antibiotics.

Chikungunya, a virus found in the Caribbean. Spread by mosquitoes, it causes fever, rashes and severe joint pain.

Chlamydia, the most common sexually-transmitted infection in Britain. It can lead to pelvic inflammatory disease and infertility. In the UK, one in eight teenage girls has chlamydia. Around 200,000 people test positive each year in the UK. The condition threatens not only female fertility but can make men infertile by damaging their sperm quality. A vaccine is now being developed in America. The signs and symptoms are invisible. Check out www.chlamydiascreening.nhs.uk

Chronic. A chronic disease is one which is prolonged and relatively mild, as opposed to an acute one which is short and severe.

Chronic Fatigue Syndrome. An alternative name for ME (Myalgic Encephalomyelitis). *See* **Z63**.

Claustrophobia. A physical symptom, which causes the individual to be afraid of enclosed spaces.

See under **Obsessional neurosis, Z51**(1).

Clostridium difficile (abbreviated to **C.diff**), a hospital bug causing a severe form of infectious diarrhoea. The number of hospital deaths from this bacterial infection has recently soared. The disease first originated in Montreal, Canada.

Coccyx. The end of the spinal column.

Coeliac Disease. A flattening of the inside of the intestine caused by gluten, the protein found in wheat, rye and barley. Symptoms include abdominal pain, weight loss and poor absorption of nutrients. It is more common in women than men, and is becoming more frequently found in children. More gluten-free foods are now being promoted.

Cortisone. A hormone produced by the adrenal glands. *See* **Z43**(1).

Cot Deaths (properly **Sudden Infant Death Syndrome**). The primary cause of death in babies more than one month old. This very distressing and inexplicable loss of life could be due to defective genes – involving lung function, the immune system *etc.* However, recent research suggests an imbalance of the brain-signalling chemical serotonin could be a factor.

Cryoblation, the freezing of tissue. An increasingly common treatment for corns, warts and also cancer of the kidney, prostate and skin.

Cryosurgery, a pioneering treatment for cancer which destroys tumours by freezing them.

Down's Syndrome, a genetic condition caused by the presence of an extra chromosome—47 instead of 46. Those affected have learning disabilities and difficulties in sitting, crawling and walking. Babies born to older mothers have a higher chance of having Down's syndrome. The NIPT test can detect Down's syndrome from the blood of pregnant women and has raised the prospect of routine screening for the condition for every expectant mother who wants it. About 1 in every 1,000 babies in Britain is born with Down's Syndrome, around 750 each year. Average life expectancy has risen from only 12 in the 1940s, to around 60 today. The new non-invasive pre-natal test (NIPT) could be a second-step in detecting Down's syndrome.

DRE. Digital Rectal Examination.

Dyslexia, a specific learning disability that can affect reading, writing, memory *etc.* It is hereditary and scientists have now discovered the gene responsible for it. New flashing light treatment is having positive results for many sufferers. There are 375,000 children in the UK with dyslexia. Readers may wish to contact www.dyslexiaaction.org.uk

Dysphagia is the term for difficulty in swallowing.

Dyspraxia, a developmental disorder in which the organisation and sequencing of movement is impaired. Boys are four times more likely to be affected than girls. The Dyspraxia Foundation helpline is 01462 454986.

Dystonia A condition in which there is abnormal muscle rigidity, fixed postures and painful spasms.

Ebola Virus Disease (EVD) is a severe and frequently fatal disease, easily spread through contact with the bodily fluids of a person. There is intense weakness, cold, vomiting and diarrhoea, sometimes with internal and external bleeding. It first appeared in Africa in 1976. The worst outbreak yet started in West Africa in 2014. An effective vaccine is now very close.

Economy Class Syndrome is deep vein thrombosis (*see* **Z30**)—a clot in the veins deep in the leg ("deep vein thrombosis") which travels via the bloodstream to the lungs ("pulmonary embolism"). Periods of immobility, such as during long flights, predispose to its development.

Ecstasy ("e" or MDMA) is an illicit drug that stops brain cells from reclaiming a chemical used to signal between cells (*see* **Z46**). This leaves the signal from these cells switched on resulting in an emotional high and a feeling of closeness to others. Users often take it before all night dancing. It occasionally causes an uncontrolled rise in body temperature (hyperthermia) which may be fatal, and may cause depression.

ECG. Electrocardiagram.

ECT. The abbreviated form of the name for a modern type of treatment for certain psychiatric disorders—electro-convulsive-therapy. *See under* **Psychosis, Z50**(1).

Empyema. A collection of pus in the lung (usually a complication of other diseases).

Endemic. Referring to a disease, means prevalent in a particular area.

Endocarditis. Disease of the valves of the heart, *See* **Z29**(2).

Endometriosis, a condition producing pelvic pain in which the endometrial cells lining the uterus start to flourish elsewhere in the body. Diagnosis often takes far too long. It affects 2 million women in the UK, but some doctors are reluctant to provide medication.

Epidermolysis Bullosa (EB). A painful genetic skin blistering condition which makes skin excessively fragile.

Erysipelas. A skin rash infection also called St. Anthony's Fire.

Fibroids. Non-cancerous tumours that grow slowly within the muscular wall of the uterus. *See* **Z55**(2).

Foetal Alcohol Spectrum Disorder (FASD), the umbrella term for a variety of disorders caused by a mother drinking alcohol while pregnant.

Ganglion. A small cystic swelling, usually on the wrist, dealt with by simple surgical treatment.

Gastritis. Inflammation of the stomach.

Gastroscopy. A test to look at the lining of your oesophagus (gullet), stomach and duodenum. The examination is carried out using a thin, flexible telescope called an endoscope or gastroscope. The telescope is about the diameter of a pen.

Genetic Targeting. Prescribing drugs according to a person's genetic profile.

Geriatrics. The medical study of old age.

Gliomas. The most common form of brain tumour.

Gingivitis. Inflammation of the gums due to infection and requiring treatment by a dentist. The classic sign is red, swollen gums which bleed on brushing.

Haemoglobin. The red pigment in the blood.

Halitosis, the correct term for bad breath. Often caused by a problem in the mouth (*e.g.* gum disease or bacteria).

Hallucinogen, a drug which acts upon the brain to create sensory illusions or hallucinations with a variety of emotional effects. One of the most widely studied is LSD (*q.v.*) which will produce symptoms very similar to those found in some mental disorders.

Heller's Syndrome, condition similar to autism (**Z51**).

Heterochromia, the condition in which a person has different coloured eyes (around 1% of people are affected).

HPV (Human Papilloma Virus), a virus now known to be present in cases of cervical cancer. Girls aged 12–17 should be vaccinated to protect them. Boys also are at risk.

Huntington's Chorea, a neurological disease which manifests itself between the ages of 35 and 55. This degenerative condition damages nerve cells in the brain, affecting movement, thinking and behaviour. Far more prevalent than once thought, it is genetically inherited. A drug to reverse the effects is undergoing trials.

Hyperemesis gravidarum. A severe form of morning sickness in pregnancy. Medical treatment involves the use of prochlorperazine, an anti-sickness drug.

Hypno-Anaesthesia, the use of medical hypnosis to overcome pain in place of anaesthetic drugs.

Hypochondriasis, the unfounded belief that one is suffering from a serious disease.

IBD. Inflammatory bowel disorder.

IBS. Irritable Bowel Disease. This includes Ulcerative Colitis and Crohn's Disease. Symptoms may include bloating, constipation and abdominal discomfort. The condition can sometimes be relieved by antibiotics.

Insulin is a hormone which controls the supply of sugar from the blood to muscles. The breakdown of sugar provides energy. In diabetes there is a lack of insulin, causing a build-up of blood sugar which can be released by the injection of insulin. It is secreted by the islet tissue of the pancreas, from which it was isolated in 1922 by Banting and Best. In 1980 insulin became the first product of genetic engineering techniques to reach clinical trials.

Interferon, identified in 1957 as a defence protein produced in animal cells, is also produced in human immune systems. Its use as a possible anti-cancer agent as well as for other complaints has been limited by extraction problems. Modern production is likely to be by genetic engineering.

In 1980 the amino acid sequence was determined for the 150 residues in human interferon.

Laryngitis. Inflammation of the vocal chords, causing hoarseness, loss of voice and sore throat. The singer's nightmare!

LDL (Low-Density Lipoproteins), term for the "bad" type of cholesterol.

Legionnaire's Disease, caused by the Legionella bacterium. Very serious outbreaks (as at Stafford hospital in 1985 when 28 people died) can occur. Sometimes the bacterium is found in recirculating and hot-water systems. A recent outbreak was in Edinburgh in 2012.

Lipoedema. The abnormal build-up of fat cells in the lower half of the body.

LSD (d-lysergic acid diethylamide). An hallucinogenic drug which has provoked much debate. It is active in extremely small quantities and a dose as small as a fifty-millionth part of a gram can cause marked disturbances of the mental function in man. LSD has been used in the study of mental disease because it produces symptoms very similar to mental disorders such as schizophrenia.

Lupus. Disease more prevalent in black people (especially women) which causes the patient's immune system to attack his or her own body tissues. *Lupus: A Guide for Patients* by Graham R V Hughes, £3 including postage is available from Lupus UK, St. James House, Eastern Road, Romford, Essex, RM1 3NH.

Lyme Disease. A virus, spread by ticks, which attacks the nervous system.

Magnetic Resonance Imaging (MRI), a technique for diagnosis based on the emission from the body of electro-magnetic waves. The patient is exposed to radiofrequency radiation. The technique avoids using X-rays.

ME (Myalgic Encephalomyelitis), chronic fatigue syndrome with symptoms of extreme physical or mental exhaustion and muscular pain. Now called Chronic Fatigue Syndrome (CFS). Severe sufferers have to rely on bed rest, but anti-depressants, nutritional guidance and alternative therapies may be beneficial. The cause may be psychological but there is increasing evidence of a biological factor. Once called neurasthenia.

MERS (Middle East Respiratory Syndrome). A similar virus to SARS (*q.v.*). MERS emerged in Saudi Arabia in 2012. Isolated cases have been found as far away as South Korea.

Mesothelioma, an untreatable cancer of the membrane that lines the chest and abdomen. Exposure to asbestos has led to thousands of cases.

Minamata Disease. A neurological disease caused by mercury poisoning.

MMR, a vaccination which immunises against measles, mumps and rubella (German measles). An unfounded scare that the jab increased the risk of autism has led to major outbreaks of measles in recent years.

MRSA (Methicillin Resistant Staphylococcus Aureus), a bacteria resistant to almost all antibiotics. An alarming increase in annual cases of MRSA is now recorded. Hospital-acquired infections (nearly half drug resistant) are a cause of serious concern. A new drug to attack MRSA was announced in May 2008.

Myeloma. A cancer of the bone marrow in which large amounts of paraprotein are produced. The outlook for patients is poor.

Narcotic, is a drug that produces stupor; complete insensibility or sleep. In terms of drug addiction, it has been defined as altering the user's perception of himself and of the external world, being taken primarily for that purpose.

Olfactory. To do with the sense of smell.

Oncology. The study of tumours.

Opium was known in the ancient world, and used by them as a medicine. It is obtained from the poppy flower (*Papaver somniferum*), the unripe "head" or seed capsule of that flower yielding a juice which when dried becomes the opium of commerce. The poppy is cultivated for the sake of this juice, which yields various alkaloids, such as morphine, narcotine, codeine, *etc.* These days the drug is rarely used medicinally.

Ostectomy. The surgical removal of a bone (or part of).

Paediatrics. The study of the diseases of children.

Paget's Disease, a severe bone disease. Symptoms may include curvature of the spine, bowing of the legs *etc.*

Painter's Colic. Intense intestinal pain caused by lead poisoning.

Penicillin. An antibiotic drug produced by the mould *Penicillium notatum*, and discovered by Sir Alexander Fleming in 1928. It is one of the most effective chemotherapeutic agents known. The mould produces a number of penicillins, all of which are effective antibiotics.

Peridontal Disease, inflammation of the tissues which support teeth and attach them to the jaw. **Gingivitis** (*q.v.*) is the term used when inflammation only involves the soft gum. **Periodontitis** is where inflammation reaches the underlying bone.

Pharmaco-genetics. The new science of diagnosing diseases with reference to a person's genetic profile.

Pharmacopoeia, an official publication containing information on the recognised drugs used in medicine. Each country has its own pharmacopoeia. The British Pharmacopoeia (BP) is published under the direction of the General Medical Council. The Pharmaceutical Society issues the British Pharmaceutical Codex (BPC); there is also an International Pharmacopoeia (2 vols.), issued by the World Health Organisation.

Phlebotomy. The letting or taking of blood in the diagnosis and treatment of a disease.

Placebo, medical treatment that the therapist uses deliberately although he knows it is without any specific effect on the condition being treated. There may be various medical reasons for using placebos, *e.g.*, for the beneficial psychological effect on people who like to feel something is being done for them; for differentiating during clinical trials of a new treatment between those persons given the real thing and those given a placebo or inactive imitation.

Plantar fasciitis, a painful inflammation of the tissues of the foot. Sometimes called 'Jogger's Heel'.

Plaque. In dentistry, the film of bacteria which constantly forms on all teeth, leading to tooth decay (dental caries) and peridontal disease (*see above*).

Pneumococcal disease, is the term used to describe a range of illnesses such as pneumonia, septicaemia (blood poisoning) and meningitis (inflammation around the brain), when these are caused by the bacterium *Streptococcus pneumoniae*.

Post-Natal Depression, (now often referred to as "PND") means becoming depressed after having a baby. Sometimes this is easy to explain – the baby is unwanted or abnormal. Mostly, though, the depression makes no obvious sense; but it is one of the most common complications of childbirth.

Postpartum Psychosis. A severe mental illness triggered by childbirth found in one in every 500 mothers. Symptoms include extreme high or low moods, delusions and paranoia. It is classified as a psychiatric emergency.

Pre-eclampsia, a disorder causing high blood pressure among pregnant women. It affects one in 25 pregnant women. In some cases it can be life-threatening to both mother and baby. A new test detects changes in the blood that can mean the placenta is not developing properly.

Progressive Supranuclear Palsy (PSP), a neuro-degenerative disease which affects the brain stem. It was identified as a separate disease in the 1960s. The cause is not yet known and there is at present no cure.

Prostate Specific Antigen (PSA), the chemical 'signature' of an abnormal prostate gland.

Proton beam therapy, a type of radiotherapy which uses a precision high-energy beam of particles to destroy cancer cells. It has certain advantages because it can be controlled by a measure of millimetres.

Psychosomatic diseases. Psychosomatic diseases are those physical ailments due to emotional causes. They include such complaints as high blood-pressure, gastric ulcer *etc*.

Pyorrhoea. An infection of the gums which causes the edges of the tooth sockets to bleed easily when the teeth are being brushed.

Quinine, a vegetable alkaloid obtained from the bark of several trees of the *Cinchona* genus. It is colourless and extremely bitter. The drug, sulphate of quinine, is one of the most valuable medicines, forming a powerful tonic. It is antiperiodic, antipyretic and antineuralgic. In cases of malaria it is the most efficacious remedy of natural origin known.

Radical prostatectomy. An operation to remove the whole prostate gland. Used to treat prostate cancer that is contained within the prostate gland.

Radiotherapy. Any treatment using radioactive particles or high energy rays to destroy tumours or other cancerous cells.

Rhesus Factor. *See* Z61.

Rods and Cones are cells in the retina of the eye which convert light into nervous impulses which can be interpreted by the brain.

RSI (Repetitive Strain Injury), an injury most prevalent among computer users and factory workers. It may begin with a minor ache before eventually becoming a persistent pain. Symptoms include pain in the hands, elbow, wrist or shoulder. Around 450,000 British workers now suffer these upper limb problems.

Salpingitis, infection of the Fallopian tubes. *See* Z55(1).

SARS (Severe Acute Respiratory Syndrome), a deadly flu-like virus which spread rapidly from south China and Hong Kong in 2003. Its main symptoms include fever above 38°C, breathing difficulties, low blood oxygen and a dry cough. A new type of coronavirus (MERS) was detected in 2012. Both SARS and MERS are believed to have originated in wild animals.

Sciatica, painful affliction radiating along the sciatic nerve, extending from the buttocks down the back of the leg to the foot.

Screening is looking for a disease in the absence of symptoms. It may be extremely effective such as for cervical cancer, which can be detected and treated many years before it would otherwise be found. Screening for prostate cancer is controversial, because some men may have treatment for an illness that might not otherwise harm them.

Sickle-cell disease, a hereditary blood disease characterised by the production of an abnormal type of haemaglobin. This painful disease mainly affects people of African descent (but can be found also in the Middle East and India).

Sudden Infant Death Syndrome. *See* Cot Deaths.

Swine Flu. A human variant of swine fever, a respiratory disease affecting pigs. Symptoms are flu-like, including fever, aching body, nausea, sore throat, vomiting and/or diarrhoea. It is spread by coughing, sneezing and touching. H1N1 penetrates deeper into the lungs and can inflict more damage than common seasonal flu. Around 275,000 people (15 times the number first estimated) may have died.

Temperature. The body temperature is regulated by a small area at the base of the brain. Normally it should be about 37°C. *See* Z9(1).

Thalassaemia. A little known but potentially fatal hereditary blood disorder. Around 75% of babies with this disease are born to Asian parents. New scanning techniques are reducing mortality rates.

TIA (Transient Ischaemic Attack). A mini-stroke.

Tourette's Syndrome, a neurological disorder that causes involuntary facial, vocal and muscular tics. The genetic mutation that causes it has now been identified. Named after the French neurologist George Gilles de la Tourette. It is three times more common in men than women.

Trachoma, the world's most common cause of preventable blindness. There are *c.* 320 million people at risk worldwide. It is excruciatingly painful, causing the eyelids to turn inwards.

Viagra, a drug (in the form of a little blue tablet) which counters impotence in men. Demand for sildenafil (which is sold as Viagra) and other erectile dysfunction drugs is rising. A "female Viagra" (flibanserin) has now been developed.

Virotherapy. A new way to tackle cancer cells by the use of viral infections (which are known to eliminate cancer cells). Clinical trials are now underway.

Vitiligo, a common skin condition (affecting 1 in every hundred children and adults) which causes white patches where the skin has lost its pigmentation).

West Nile Disease. A disease spread by mosquitoes which have fed on infected birds. It can be fatal, causing inflammation of the brain and spinal cord. Many people only experience much milder symptoms. There is no vaccine and the disease has now spread to nearly all parts of the world.

Zoonoses, diseases that originate in animals but spread to humans. Their numbers are increasing as animals are driven closer to populated areas.

SUBJECT INDEX

Each section has a letter and, where appropriate, the column is given in brackets after the page number, *e.g.*, T8(1), C20(1). Some of the sections are alphabetically arranged and index themselves. In addition "The World of Music" has a separate index of composers and also a glossary. For historical terms, *see* Section E and for biographical entries *see* Section B.

D

E

I

J

Q

R

THE STORY OF PEARS

1897-2017

The origins of *Pears Cyclopaedia* are no less fascinating than its phenomenal success – a success which produced sales of 3 million copies by the 1930s and at least as many again since. That success dates to 1865, when a young man of 24 joined the business of A&F Pears Ltd, soap makers to Queen Victoria. At a well-known Academy of Dancing and Deportment in the West End, Thomas J Barratt made the acquaintance of the eldest daughter of Mr Francis Pears. Miss Pears became Mrs Barratt and Mr Barratt became the London Manager of Pears!

Thomas Barratt was an advertising genius. He declared that he would advertise as no soapmaker had ever advertised before. In the then relatively new profession of advertising, he made Pears Soap a world-wide name. Such advertisements as "Bubbles" and "Two years ago I used your soap, since when I have used no other" achieved lasting fame.

But perhaps the most original advertisement of all for Pears Soap was the little red *Pears Shilling Cyclopaedia*, first printed for A&F Pears by David Bryce and Son of Glasgow. It was published in December 1897, the year of Queen Victoria's Diamond Jubilee. This first edition contained an English dictionary, a medical dictionary, a gazetteer and atlas, desk information and a compendium of general knowledge entitled "A Mass of Curious and Useful Information about Things that everyone Ought to know in Commerce, History, Science, Religion, Literature and other Topics of Ordinary Conversation".

The idea was to keep the general public informed on the issues of the day, to equip them for social discourse, satisfy their curiosity and widen their learning. Topics ranged from hard facts to questions of etiquette, from why the Russians needed a port on the Mediterranean to the longevity of the clergy!

Although *Pears Cyclopaedia* slipped its connections with soap back in 1960 when the publishing rights were acquired by Pelham Books (and in turn passed to Penguin Books), there has been astonishing editorial continuity (only two editors since 1946, only three in the first 50 years). Now the price is rather more than the original shilling, but *Pears* still represents remarkable value.

Many of the popular features of the early editions were retained. The medical section, the gazetteer, the sections on Science, Literature, Ideas and Beliefs. Historical Events and General Information all remained there. Also there were topics of current social and political interest, specially commissioned for each edition. There are newer, equally popular favourites in the present edition, including Classical Mythology, Sporting Records, the Biblical Glossary, Music and the World of Art. It is this blend of innovation and tradition – the tried and tested facts and figures alongside authoritative new articles in every edition that made *Pears* so popular with generation after generation.

The single most important factor in the *Pears* success story, and the key to its truly unique publishing phenomenon, is that *it is the only book of its kind to be fully revised and updated by a team of experts every year.*

Schools and colleges, offices and libraries, students and researchers, newspapers, radio and TV stations – for all these, and many more, for whom readily accessible, reliable facts at their fingertips are needed. *Pears Cyclopaedia* remained an invaluable companion. Now, the ready availability of electronic information has made the printed reference book no longer commercially competitive. That is progress. But many will miss the passing of a famous book, that in its heyday, had become not only a national institution but also the reliable pathway for successive generations of working-class families to a better education.

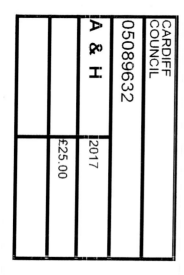

CARDIFF
COUNCIL

05089632

A & H

2017

£25.00

5478179

EUROPE